Spanish
Dictionary
Plus Grammar

D0109125

HarperResource
An Imprint of HarperCollins*Publishers*

second edition 2000

©HarperCollins Publishers 1997, 2000

latest reprint 2001

HarperCollins Publishers
Westerhill Road, Bishopbriggs, Glasgow G64 2QT, Great Britain

www.collins.co.uk

Collins® and Bank of English® are registered trademarks of
HarperCollins Publishers Limited

Collins is an imprint of HarperCollins Publishers

ISBN 0-00-470787-7

HarperCollins Publishers, Inc.
10 East 53rd Street, New York, NY 10022

ISBN 0-06-095692-5

Library of Congress Catalog Card Number: 99-76599*
*Published in the U.S. as *HarperCollins Spanish Concise Dictionary*

www.harpercollins.com

First HarperCollins edition published 1998

01 02 03 04 05 OB 10 9 8 7 6 5 4

HarperCollins books may be purchased for educational, business, or sales
promotional use. For information, please write to: Special Markets Department,
HarperCollins Publishers Inc., 10 East 53rd Street, New York, NY 10022

Dictionary text typeset by Morton Word Processing Ltd, Scarborough
Grammar text typeset by Wordcraft, Glasgow

A catalogue record for this book is available from the British Library

Printed and bound in Great Britain by
Omnia Books Ltd, Glasgow, G64

ÍNDICE DE MATERIAS		CONTENTS	

Jeremy Butterfield, Mike Gonzalez, Gerry Breslin
Teresa Alvarez García, Brian Steel
Ana Cristina Llompart, José Miguel Galván Déniz

editorial staff
Megan Thomson, Val McNulty, Irene Lakhani, Sharon Hunter
Tracy Lomas, Claire Evans, Jane Horwood, Linda Chestnutt
Enrique González Sandinero, Caitlin McMahon

series editor
Lorna Sinclair

editorial management
Vivian Marr

INTRODUCTION

You may be starting Spanish for the first time, or you may wish to extend your knowledge of the language. Perhaps you want to read and study Spanish books, newspapers and magazines, or perhaps simply have a conversation with Spanish speakers. Whatever the reason, whether you're a student, a tourist or want to use Spanish for business, this is the ideal book to help you understand and communicate. This modern, user-friendly dictionary gives priority to everyday vocabulary and the language of current affairs, business, computing and tourism, and, as in all Collins dictionaries, the emphasis is firmly placed on contemporary language and expressions.

HOW TO USE THE DICTIONARY

Below you will find an outline of how information is presented in your dictionary. Our aim is to give you the maximum amount of detail in the clearest and most helpful way.

Entries

A typical entry in your dictionary will be made up of the following elements:

Phonetic transcription

Phonetics appear in square brackets immediately after the headword. They are shown using the International Phonetic Alphabet (IPA), and a complete list of the symbols used in this system can be found on page xiv. The pronunciation given is for Castilian Spanish except where a word is solely used in Latin America, when we give the Latin American pronunciation. A further guide to the differences in types of Spanish pronunciation is given on page xiv.

Grammatical information

All words belong to one of the following parts of speech: noun, verb, adjective, adverb, pronoun, article, conjunction, preposition, abbreviation. Nouns can be singular or plural and, in Spanish, masculine or feminine. Verbs can be transitive, intransitive, reflexive or impersonal. Parts of speech appear in *italics* immediately after the phonetic spelling of the headword. The gender of the translation also appears in *italics* immediately following the key element of the translation, except where this is a regular masculine singular noun ending in "o", or a regular feminine singular noun ending in "a".

Often a word can have more than one part of speech. Just as the English word **chemical** can be an adjective or a noun, the Spanish word **conocido** can be an adjective ("(well-)known") or a noun ("acquaintance"). In the same way the verb **to walk** is sometimes transitive, ie it takes an object ("to walk the dog") and sometimes intransitive, ie it doesn't take an object ("to walk to school"). To help you find the meaning you are looking for quickly and for clarity of presentation, the different part of speech categories are separated by a black lozenge ◆.

Meaning divisions

Most words have more than one meaning. Take, for example, **punch** which can be, amongst other things, a blow with the fist or an object used for making holes. Other words are translated differently depending on the context in which they are used. The transitive verb **to put on**, for example, can be translated by "ponerse", "encender" etc depending on *what* it is you are putting on. To help you select the most appropriate translation in every context, entries are divided according to meaning. Each different meaning is introduced by an "indicator" in *italics* and in brackets. Thus, the examples given above will be shown as follows:

> **punch** n (*blow*) golpe m, puñetazo; (*tool*) punzón m

> **put on** vt (*clothes, lipstick etc*) ponerse; (*light etc*) encender

Likewise, some words can have a different meaning when used to talk about a specific subject area or field. For example **bishop**, which in a religious context means a high-ranking clergyman, is also the name of a chess piece. To show English speakers which translation to use, we have added "subject field labels" in capitals and in brackets, in this case (*CHESS*):

> **bishop** n obispo; (*CHESS*) alfil m

Field labels are often shortened to save space. You will find a complete list of abbreviations used in the dictionary on page xii.

Translations

Most English words have a direct translation in Spanish and vice versa, as shown in the examples given above. Sometimes, however, no exact equivalent exists in the target language. In such cases we have given an approximate equivalent, indicated by the sign ≈. An example is **British Rail**, the Spanish equivalent of which is "RENFE". There is no exact equivalent since the bodies in the two countries are quite different:

> **British Rail (BR)** n ≈ RENFE f (*SP*)

On occasion it is impossible to find even an approximate equivalent. This may be the case, for example, with the names of types of food:

> **fabada** nf bean and sausage stew

Here the translation (which doesn't exist) is replaced by an explanation. For increased clarity the explanation, or "gloss", is shown in *italics*.

It is often the case that a word, or a particular meaning of a word, cannot be translated in isolation. The translation of **Dutch**, for example, is "holandés/esa". However, the phrase **to go Dutch** is rendered by "pagar cada uno lo suyo". Even an expression as simple as **washing powder** needs a separate translation since it translates as "detergente (en polvo)", not "polvo para lavar". This is where your dictionary will prove to be particularly informative and useful since it contains an abundance of compounds, phrases and idiomatic expressions.

Levels of formality and familiarity

In English you instinctively know when to say **I'm broke** or **I'm a bit short of cash** and when to say **I don't have any money**. When you are trying to understand someone who is speaking Spanish, however, or when you yourself try to speak Spanish, it is important to know what is polite and what is less so, and what you can say in a relaxed situation but not in a formal context. To help you with this, on the Spanish-English side we have added the label (*fam*) to show that a Spanish meaning or expression is colloquial, while those meanings or expressions which are vulgar are given an exclamation mark (*fam!*), warning you they can cause serious offence. Note also that on the English-Spanish side, translations which are vulgar are followed by an exclamation mark in brackets.

Keywords

Words labelled in the text as *KEYWORD*s, such as **have** and **do** or their Spanish equivalents **tener** and **hacer**, have been given special treatment because they form the basic elements of the language. This extra help will ensure that you know how to use these complex words with confidence.

Cultural information

Entries which appear separated from the main text by a line above and below them explain aspects of culture in Spanish and English-speaking countries. Subject areas covered include politics, education, media and national festivals.

Spanish alphabetical order

In 1994 the **Real Academia Española** and the Spanish American language academies jointly decided to stop treating CH and LL as separate letters in Spanish, thereby bringing it into line with European spelling norms. This means that **chapa** and **lluvia** will be filed in letters C and L respectively. Of course, it should also be remembered that words like **cancha** and **callar**, with **ch** and **ll** in the middle of the words, will also have changed places alphabetically, now being found after **cáncer** and **cáliz** respectively. Spanish however still has one more letter than English with Ñ treated separately, between N and O.

ABREVIATURAS

ABBREVIATIONS

abreviatura	**ab(b)r**	abbreviation
adjetivo, locución adjetiva	**adj**	adjective, adjectival phrase
administración, lengua administrativa	**ADMIN**	administration
adverbio, locución adverbial	**adv**	adverb, adverbial phrase
agricultura	**AGR**	agriculture
alguien	**algn**	
América Latina	**AM**	Latin America
anatomía	**ANAT**	anatomy
arquitectura	**ARQ, ARCH**	architecture
astrología, astronomía	**ASTRO**	astrology, astronomy
el automóvil	**AUT(O)**	the motor car and motoring
aviación, viajes aéreos	**AVIAT**	flying, air travel
biología	**BIO(L)**	biology
botánica, flores	**BOT**	botany
inglés británico	**BRIT**	British English
química	**CHEM**	chemistry
	CINE	cinema
lengua familiar (! vulgar)	**col (!)**	colloquial usage (! particularly offensive)
comercio, finanzas, banca	**COM(M)**	commerce, finance, banking
informática	**COMPUT**	computing
conjunción	**conj**	conjunction
construcción	**CONSTR**	building
compuesto	**cpd**	compound element
cocina	**CULIN**	cookery
economía	**ECON**	economics
electricidad, electrónica	**ELEC**	electricity, electronics
enseñanza, sistema escolar	**ESCOL**	schooling, schools
España	**ESP**	Spain
especialmente	**esp**	especially
exclamación, interjección	**excl**	exclamation, interjection
femenino	**f**	feminine
lengua familiar (! vulgar)	**fam (!)**	colloquial usage (! particularly offensive)
ferrocarril	**FERRO**	railways
uso figurado	**fig**	figurative use
fotografía	**FOTO**	photography
(verbo inglés) del cual la partícula es inseparable	**fus**	(phrasal verb) where the particle is inseparable
generalmente	**gen**	generally
geografía, geología	**GEO**	geography, geology
geometría	**GEOM**	geometry
informática	**INFORM**	computing
invariable	**inv**	invariable
irregular	**irreg**	irregular
lo jurídico	**JUR**	law
América Latina	**LAM**	Latin America
gramática, lingüística	**LING**	grammar, linguistics
literatura	**LIT**	literature
masculino	**m**	masculine
matemáticas	**MAT(H)**	mathematics
medicina	**MED**	medical term, medicine
masculino/femenino	**m/f**	masculine/feminine

ABREVIATURAS

ABBREVIATIONS

lo militar, ejército	*MIL*	military matters
música	*MUS*	music
sustantivo, nombre	*n*	noun
navegación, náutica	*NAUT*	sailing, navigation
sustantivo no empleado en el plural	*no pl*	collective (uncountable) noun, not used in plural
sustantivo numérico	*num*	numeral noun
complemento	*obj*	(grammatical) object
	o.s.	oneself
peyorativo	*pey, pej*	derogatory, pejorative
fotografía	*PHOT*	photography
fisiología	*PHYSIOL*	physiology
plural	*pl*	plural
política	*POL*	politics
participio de pasado	*pp*	past participle
prefijo	*pref*	prefix
preposición	*prep*	preposition
pronombre	*pron*	pronoun
psicología, psiquiatría	*PSICO, PSYCH*	psychology, psychiatry
tiempo pasado	*pt*	past tense
ferrocarril	*RAIL*	railways
religión, lo eclesiástico	*REL*	religion, church service
	sb	somebody
enseñanza, sistema escolar	*SCOL*	schooling, schools
singular	*sg*	singular
España	*SP*	Spain
	sth	something
subjuntivo	*subjun*	subjunctive
sujeto	*su(b)j*	(grammatical) subject
sufijo	*suff*	suffix
tauromaquia	*TAUR*	bullfighting
también	*tb*	also
teatro	*TEAT*	
técnica, tecnología	*TEC(H)*	technical term, technology
telecomunicaciones	*TELEC, TEL*	telecommunications
	THEAT	theatre
imprenta, tipografía	*TIP, TYP*	typography, printing
televisión	*TV*	television
sistema universitario	*UNIV*	universities
inglés norteamericano	*US*	American English
verbo	*vb*	verb
verbo intransitivo	*vi*	intransitive verb
verbo pronominal	*vr*	reflexive verb
verbo transitivo	*vt*	transitive verb
zoología, animales	*ZOOL*	zoology
marca registrada	®	registered trademark
indica un equivalente cultural	≈	introduces a cultural equivalent

SPANISH PRONUNCIATION

Consonants

b	[b]	<u>b</u>om<u>b</u>a	see notes on *v* below
	[ß]	la<u>b</u>or	
c	[k]	<u>c</u>aja	*c* before *a, o* or *u* is pronounced as in *c*at
ce, ci	[θe, θi]	<u>c</u>ero	*c* before *e* or *i* is pronounced as in *thin*
		<u>c</u>ielo	and as *s* in *s*in in Latin America and parts
	[se, si][1]	vo<u>c</u>ero	of Spain
		noti<u>c</u>iero	
ch	[tʃ]	<u>ch</u>iste	*ch* is pronounced as *ch* in *ch*air
d	[d]	<u>d</u>anés	at the beginning of a word or after *l* or *n*,
	[ð]	ciu<u>d</u>a<u>d</u>	*d* is pronounced as in English. In any other position it is like *th* in *the*
g	[g]	<u>g</u>afas	*g* before *a, o* or *u* is pronounced as in *g*ap,
		<u>g</u>uerra	if at the beginning of a word or after *n*. In
	[ɣ]	pa<u>g</u>a	other positions the sound is softened
ge, gi	[xe, xi]	<u>g</u>ente	*g* before *e* or *i* is pronounced similar to *ch*
		<u>g</u>irar	in Scottish lo*ch*
h		<u>h</u>aber	*h* is always silent in Spanish
j	[x]	<u>j</u>ugar	*j* is pronounced like *ch* in Scottish lo*ch*
ll	[ʎ]	ta<u>ll</u>e	*ll* is pronounced like the *lli* in mi*lli*on
ñ	[ɲ]	ni<u>ñ</u>o	*ñ* is pronounced like the *ni* in o*ni*on
q	[k]	<u>q</u>ue	*q* is pronounced as *k* in *k*ing
r, rr	[r]	quita<u>r</u>	*r* is always pronounced in Spanish, unlike
	[rr]	ga<u>rr</u>a	the silent *r* in dancer. *rr* and *r* at the beginning of a word are trilled, like a Scottish *r*
s	[s]	quizá<u>s</u>	*s* is usually pronounced as in pa*s*s, but
		i<u>s</u>la	before *b, d, g, l, m* or *n* it is pronounced as in ro*s*e
v	[b]	<u>v</u>ía	*v* is pronounced something like *b*. At the
	[ß]	di<u>v</u>idir	beginning of a word or after *m* or *n* it is pronounced as *b* in *b*oy. In any other position it is pronounce with the lips in position to pronounce *b* of *b*oy, but not meeting
w	[b]	<u>w</u>áter	pronounced either like Spanish *b*, or like
	[w]	<u>w</u>hiskey	English *w*
z	[θ]	tena<u>z</u>	*z* is pronounced as *thin thin* and as *s* in
	[s][1]	i<u>z</u>ada	*s*in in Latin America and parts of Spain
	[ks]	tó<u>x</u>ico	*x* is pronounced as in to*x*in except in
	[s]	<u>x</u>enofobia	informal Spanish or at the beginning of a word

f, k, l, m, n, p and t are pronounced as in English.

[1]Only shown in Latin American entries.

Vowels

a	[a]	p<u>a</u>ta	not as long as *a* in f*a*r. When followed by a consonant in the same syllable (i.e. in a closed syllable), as in am*a*nte, the *a* is short, as in b*a*t
e	[e]	m<u>e</u>	like *e* in th*ey*. In a closed syllable, as in g*e*nte, the *e* is short as in p*e*t
i	[i]	p<u>i</u>no	as in m*ea*n or mach*i*ne
o	[o]	l<u>o</u>	as in l*o*cal. In a closed syllable, as in c*o*ntrol, the *o* is short as in c*o*t
u	[u]	l<u>u</u>nes	as in r*u*le. It is silent after *q*, and in *gue*, *gui*, unless marked *güe*, *güi* e.g. antig*ü*edad, when it is pronounced like *w* in *w*olf

Semivowels

i, y	[j]	b<u>i</u>en h<u>i</u>elo <u>y</u>unta	pronounced like *y* in *y*es
u	[w]	h<u>u</u>evo f<u>u</u>ente antig<u>ü</u>edad	unstressed *u* between consonant and vowel is pronounced like *w* in *w*ell. See also notes on *u* above

Dipthongs

ai, ay	[ai]	b<u>ai</u>le	as *i* in r*i*de
au	[au]	<u>au</u>to	as *ou* in sh*ou*t
ei, ey	[ei]	bu<u>ey</u>	as *ey* in gr*ey*
eu	[eu]	d<u>eu</u>da	both elements pronounced independently [e] + [u]
oi, oy	[oi]	h<u>oy</u>	as *oy* in t*oy*

Stress

The rules of stress in Spanish are as follows:

(a) when a word ends in a vowel or in *n* or *s*, the second last syllable is stressed: pat*a*ta, pat*a*tas, c*o*me, c*o*men

(b) when a word ends in a consonant other than *n* or *s*, the stress falls on the last syllable: par*e*d, habl*a*r

(c) when the rules set out in a and b are not applied, an acute accent appears over the stressed vowel: com*ú*n, geograf*í*a, ingl*é*s

In the phonetic transcription, the symbol ['] precedes the syllable on which the stress falls.

In general, we give the pronunciation of each entry in square brackets after the word in question.

SPANISH VERB FORMS

1 Gerund *2* Imperative *3* Present *4* Preterite *5* Future *6* Present subjunctive *7* Imperfect subjunctive *8* Past participle *9* Imperfect

acertar *2* acierta *3* acierto, aciertas, acierta, aciertan *6* acierte, aciertes, acierte, acierten

acordar *2* acuerda *3* acuerdo, acuerdas, acuerda, acuerdan *6* acuerde, acuerdes, acuerde, acuerden

advertir *1* advirtiendo *2* advierte *3* advierto, adviertes, advierte, advierten *4* advirtió, advirtieron *6* advierta, adviertas, advierta, advirtamos, advirtáis, adviertan *7* advirtiera *etc*

agradecer *3* agradezco *6* agradezca *etc*

aparecer *3* aparezco *6* aparezca *etc*

aprobar *2* aprueba *3* apruebo, apruebas, aprueba, aprueban *6* apruebe, apruebes, apruebe, aprueben

atravesar *2* atraviesa *3* atravieso, atraviesas, atraviesa, atraviesan *6* atraviese, atravieses, atraviese, atraviesen

caber *3* quepo *4* cupe, cupiste, cupo, cupimos, cupisteis, cupieron *5* cabré *etc* *6* quepa *etc* *7* cupiera *etc*

caer *1* cayendo *3* caigo *4* cayó, cayeron *6* caiga *etc* *7* cayera *etc*

calentar *2* calienta *3* caliento, calientas, calienta, calientan *6* caliente, calientes, caliente, calienten

cerrar *2* cierra *3* cierro, cierras, cierra, cierran *6* cierre, cierres, cierre, cierren

COMER *1* comiendo *2* come, comed *3* como, comes, come, comemos, coméis, comen *4* comí, comiste, comió, comimos, comisteis, comieron *5* comeré, comerás, comerá, comeremos, comeréis, comerán *6* coma, comas, coma, comamos, comáis, coman *7* comiera, comieras, comiera, comiéramos, comierais, comieran *8* comido *9* comía, comías, comía, comíamos comíais, comían

conocer *3* conozco *6* conozca *etc*

contar *2* cuenta *3* cuento, cuentas, cuenta, cuentan *6* cuente, cuentes, cuente, cuenten

costar *2* cuesta *3* cuesto, cuestas, cuesta, cuestan *6* cueste, cuestes, cueste, cuesten

dar *3* doy *4* di, diste, dio, dimos, disteis, dieron *7* diera *etc*

decir *2* di *3* digo *4* dije, dijiste, dijo, dijimos, dijisteis, dijeron *5* diré *etc* *6* diga *etc* *7* dijera *etc* *8* dicho

despertar *2* despierta *3* despierto, despiertas, despierta, despiertan *6* despierte, despiertes, despierte, despierten

divertir *1* divirtiendo *2* divierte *3* divierto, diviertes, divierte, divierten *4* divirtió, divirtieron *6* divierta, diviertas, divierta, divirtamos, divirtáis, diviertan *7* divirtiera *etc*

dormir *1* durmiendo *2* duerme *3* duermo, duermes, duerme, duermen *4* durmió, durmieron *6* duerma, duermas, duerma, durmamos, durmáis, duerman *7* durmiera *etc*

empezar *2* empieza *3* empiezo, empiezas, empieza, empiezan *4* empecé *6* empiece, empieces, empiece, empecemos, empecéis, empiecen

entender *2* entiende *3* entiendo, entiendes, entiende, entienden *6* entienda, entiendas, entienda, entiendan

ESTAR *2* está *3* estoy, estás, está, están *4* estuve, estuviste, estuvo, estuvimos, estuvisteis, estuvieron *6* esté, estés, esté, estén *7* estuviera *etc*

HABER *3* he, has, ha, hemos, han *4* hube, hubiste, hubo, hubimos, hubisteis, hubieron *5* habré *etc* *6* haya *etc* *7* hubiera *etc*

HABLAR *1* hablando *2* habla, hablad *3* hablo, hablas, habla, hablamos, habláis, hablan *4* hablé, hablaste, habló, hablamos, hablasteis, hablaron *5* hablaré, hablarás, hablará, hablaremos, hablaréis, hablarán *6* hable, hables, hable, hablemos, habléis, hablen *7* hablara, hablaras, hablara, habláramos, hablarais, hablaran *8* hablado *9* hablaba, hablabas, hablaba, hablábamos, hablabais, hablaban

hacer *2* haz *3* hago *4* hice, hiciste, hizo, hicimos, hicisteis, hicieron *5* haré *etc* *6* haga *etc* *7* hiciera *etc* *8* hecho

instruir *1* instruyendo *2* instruye *3* instruyo, instruyes, instruye, instruyen *4* instruyó, instruyeron *6* instruya *etc* *7* instruyera *etc*

ir *1* yendo *2* ve *3* voy, vas, va, vamos, vais, van *4* fui, fuiste, fue, fuimos, fuisteis, fueron *6* vaya, vayas, vaya, vayamos,

vayáis, vayan 7 fuera etc 8 iba, ibas, iba,
íbamos, ibais, iban
jugar 2 juega 3 juego, juegas, juega,
juegan 4 jugué 6 juegue etc
leer 1 leyendo 4 leyó, leyeron 7 leyera etc
morir 1 muriendo 2 muere 3 muero,
mueres, muere, mueren 4 murió,
murieron 6 muera, mueras, muera,
muramos, muráis, mueran 7 muriera etc
8 muerto
mostrar 2 muestra 3 muestro, muestras,
muestra, muestran 6 muestre, muestres,
muestre, muestren
mover 2 mueve 3 muevo, mueves, mueve,
mueven 6 mueva, muevas, mueva,
muevan
negar 2 niega 3 niego, niegas, niega,
niegan 4 negué 6 niegue, niegues,
niegue, neguemos, neguéis, nieguen
ofrecer 3 ofrezco 6 ofrezca etc
oír 1 oyendo 2 oye 3 oigo, oyes, oye, oyen
4 oyó, oyeron 6 oiga etc 7 oyera etc
oler 2 huele 3 huelo, hueles, huele, huelen
6 huela, huelas, huela, huelan
parecer 3 parezco 6 parezca etc
pedir 1 pidiendo 2 pide 3 pido, pides, pide,
piden 4 pidió, pidieron 6 pida etc
7 pidiera etc
pensar 2 piensa 3 pienso, piensas, piensa,
piensan 6 piense, pienses, piense,
piensen
perder 2 pierde 3 pierdo, pierdes, pierde,
pierden 6 pierda, pierdas, pierda,
pierdan
poder 1 pudiendo 2 puede 3 puedo,
puedes, puede, pueden 4 pude, pudiste,
pudo, pudimos, pudisteis, pudieron
5 podré etc 6 pueda, puedas, pueda,
puedan 7 pudiera etc
poner 2 pon 3 pongo 4 puse, pusiste, puso,
pusimos, pusisteis, pusieron 5 pondré
etc 6 ponga etc 7 pusiera etc 8 puesto
preferir 1 prefiriendo 2 prefiere 3 prefiero,
prefieres, prefiere, prefieren 4 prefirió,
prefirieron 6 prefiera, prefieras, prefiera,
prefiramos, prefiráis, prefieran
7 prefiriera etc
querer 2 quiere 3 quiero, quieres, quiere,
quieren 4 quise, quisiste, quiso,
quisimos, quisisteis, quisieron 5 querré
etc 6 quiera, quieras, quiera, quieran
7 quisiera etc
reír 2 ríe 3 río, ríes, ríe, ríen 4 rio, rieron
6 ría, rías, ría, riamos, riáis, rían 7 riera
etc
repetir 1 repitiendo 2 repite 3 repito,

repites, repite, repiten 4 repitió,
repitieron 6 repita etc 7 repitiera etc
rogar 2 ruega 3 ruego, ruegas, ruega,
ruegan 4 rogué 6 ruegue, ruegues,
ruegue, roguemos, roguéis, rueguen
saber 3 sé 4 supe, supiste, supo, supimos,
supisteis, supieron 5 sabré etc 6 sepa etc
7 supiera etc
salir 2 sal 3 salgo 5 saldré etc 6 salga etc
seguir 1 siguiendo 2 sigue 3 sigo, sigues,
sigue, siguen 4 siguió, siguieron 6 siga
etc 7 siguiera etc
sentar 2 sienta 3 siento, sientas, sienta,
sientan 6 siente, sientes, siente, sienten
sentir 1 sintiendo 2 siente 3 siento,
sientes, siente, sienten 4 sintió, sintieron
6 sienta, sientas, sienta, sintamos,
sintáis, sientan 7 sintiera etc
SER 2 sé 3 soy, eres, es, somos, sois, son
4 fui, fuiste, fue, fuimos, fuisteis, fueron
6 sea etc 7 fuera etc 9 era, eras, era,
éramos, erais, eran
servir 1 sirviendo 2 sirve 3 sirvo, sirves,
sirve, sirven 4 sirvió, sirvieron 6 sirva
etc 7 sirviera etc
soñar 2 sueña 3 sueño, sueñas, sueña,
sueñan 6 sueñe, sueñes, sueñe, sueñen
tener 2 ten 3 tengo, tienes, tiene, tienen
4 tuve, tuviste, tuvo, tuvimos, tuvisteis,
tuvieron 5 tendré etc 6 tenga etc
7 tuviera etc
traer 1 trayendo 3 traigo 4 traje, trajiste,
trajo, trajimos, trajisteis, trajeron
6 traiga etc 7 trajera etc
valer 2 val 3 valgo 5 valdré etc 6 valga etc
venir 2 ven 3 vengo, vienes, viene, vienen
4 vine, viniste, vino, vinimos, vinisteis,
vinieron 5 vendré etc 6 venga etc
7 viniera etc
ver 3 veo 6 vea etc 8 visto 9 veía etc
vestir 1 vistiendo 2 viste 3 visto, vistes,
viste, visten 4 vistió, vistieron 6 vista etc
7 vistiera etc
VIVIR 1 viviendo 2 vive, vivid 3 vivo,
vives, vive, vivimos, vivís, viven 4 viví,
viviste, vivió, vivimos, vivisteis,
vivieron 5 viviré, vivirás, vivirá,
viviremos, viviréis, vivirán 6 viva,
vivas, viva, vivamos, viváis, vivan
7 viviera, vivieras, viviera, viviéramos,
vivierais, vivieran 8 vivido 9 vivía,
vivías, vivía, vivíamos, vivías, vivían
volver 2 vuelve 3 vuelvo, vuelves, vuelve,
vuelven 6 vuelva, vuelvas, vuelva,
vuelvan 8 vuelto

For additional information on Spanish verb formation, see pp 6-162 of Grammar section

NÚMEROS

NUMBERS

Spanish	Number	English
uno (un, una)*	1	one
dos	2	two
tres	3	three
cuatro	4	four
cinco	5	five
seis	6	six
siete	7	seven
ocho	8	eight
nueve	9	nine
diez	10	ten
once	11	eleven
doce	12	twelve
trece	13	thirteen
catorce	14	fourteen
quince	15	fifteen
dieciséis	16	sixteen
diecisiete	17	seventeen
dieciocho	18	eighteen
diecinueve	19	nineteen
veinte	20	twenty
veintiuno(-un, -una)*	21	twenty-one
veintidós	22	twenty-two
treinta	30	thirty
treinta y uno(un, una)*	31	thirty-one
treinta y dos	32	thirty-two
cuarenta	40	forty
cincuenta	50	fifty
sesenta	60	sixty
setenta	70	seventy
ochenta	80	eighty
noventa	90	ninety
cien(ciento)**	100	a hundred, one hundred
ciento uno(un, una)*	101	a hundred and one
ciento dos	102	a hundred and two
ciento cincuenta y seis	156	a hundred and fifty-six
doscientos(as)	200	two hundred
trescientos(as)	300	three hundred
quinientos(as)	500	five hundred
mil	1,000	a thousand
mil tres	1,003	a thousand and three
dos mil	2,000	two thousand
un millón	1,000,000	a million

* 'uno' (+ 'veintiuno' etc) agrees in gender (but not number) with its noun: treinta y una personas; the masculine form is shortened to 'un' unless it stands alone: veintiún caballos, veintiuno.

** 'ciento' is used in compound numbers, except when it multiplies: ciento diez, but cien mil. 'Cien' is used before nouns: cien hombres, cien casas.

NÚMEROS

NUMBERS

primero(primer, primera), 1º, 1ᵉʳ/1ª, 1ᵉʳᵃ	first, 1st
segundo(a), 2º/2ª	second, 2nd
tercero(tercer, tercera), 3º, 3ᵉʳ/3ª, 3ᵉʳᵃ	third, 3rd
cuarto(a), 4º/4ª	fourth, 4th
quinto(a)	fifth, 5th
sexto(a)	sixth, 6th
séptimo(a)	seventh
octavo(a)	eighth
noveno(a); nono(a)	ninth
décimo(a)	tenth
undécimo(a)	eleventh
duodécimo(a)	twelfth
decimotercio(a)	thirteenth
decimocuarto(a)	fourteenth
decimoquinto(a)	fifteenth
decimosexto(a)	sixteenth
decimoséptimo(a)	seventeenth
decimoctavo(a)	eighteenth
decimonono(a)	nineteenth
vigésimo(a)	twentieth
vigésimo primero(a)	twenty-first
vigésimo segundo(a)	twenty-second
trigésimo(a)	thirtieth
trigésimo primero(a)	thirty-first
trigésimo segundo(a)	thirty-second
cuadragésimo(a)	fortieth
quincuagésimo(a)	fiftieth
sexagésimo(a)	sixtieth
septuagésimo(a)	seventieth
octogésimo(a)	eightieth
nonagésimo(a)	ninetieth
centésimo(a)	hundredth
centésimo primero(a)	hundred-and-first
milésimo(a)	thousandth

LA HORA

THE TIME

¿qué hora es?

what time is it?

es la una
son las cuatro
medianoche, las doce de la noche
la una (de la madrugada)

it's one o'clock
it's four o'clock
midnight
one o'clock (in the morning), one
    (a.m.)

la una y cinco
la una y diez
la una y cuarto *or* quince
la una y veinticinco

five past one
ten past one
a quarter past one, one fifteen
twenty-five past one, one twenty-
    five

la una y media *or* treinta
las dos menos veinticinco, la una
    treinta y cinco
las dos menos veinte, la una
    cuarenta
las dos menos cuarto, la una
    cuarenta y cinco
las dos menos diez, la una
    cincuenta
mediodía, las doce (de la mañana)
las dos (de la tarde)

half-past one, one thirty
twenty-five to two, one thirty-five

twenty to two, one forty

a quarter to two, one forty-five

ten to two, one fifty

twelve o'clock, midday, noon
two o'clock (in the afternoon), two
    (p.m.)

las siete (de la tarde)

seven o'clock (in the evening),
    seven (p.m.)

¿a qué hora?

at what time?

a medianoche
a las siete
a las una

at midnight
at seven o'clock
at one o'clock

en veinte minutos
hace diez minutos

in twenty minutes
ten minutes ago

LA FECHA

THE DATE

hoy
mañana
pasado mañana
ayer
antes de ayer, anteayer
la víspera
el día siguiente

today
tomorrow
the day after tomorrow
yesterday
the day before yesterday
the day before, the previous day
the next *or* following day

la mañana	morning
la tarde	evening
esta mañana	this morning
esta tarde	this evening
esta tarde	this afternoon
ayer por la mañana	yesterday morning
ayer por la tarde	yesterday evening
mañana por la mañana	tomorrow morning
mañana por la tarde	tomorrow evening
en la noche del sábado al domingo	during Saturday night, during the night of Saturday to Sunday
vendrá el sábado	he's coming on Saturday
los sábados	on Saturdays
todos los sábados	every Saturday
el sábado pasado	last Saturday
el sábado que viene, el próximo sábado	next Saturday
del sábado en ocho días	a week on Saturday
del sábado en quince días	a fortnight or two weeks on Saturday
de lunes a sábado	from Monday to Saturday
todos los días	every day
una vez a la semana	once a week
una vez al mes	once a month
dos veces a la semana	twice a week
hace una semana o ocho días	a week ago
hace quince días	a fortnight or two weeks ago
el año pasado	last year
dentro de dos días	in two days
dentro de ocho días o una semana	in a week
dentro de quince días	in a fortnight or two weeks
el mes que viene, el próximo mes	next month
el año que viene, el próximo año	next year
¿a qué o a cuántos estamos?	*what day is it?*
el 1/24 octubre de 1996	the 1st/24th of October 1996, October 1st/24th 1996
en 1996	in 1996
mil novecientos noventa y cinco	nineteen ninety-five
44 a. de J.C.	44 BC
14 d. de J.C.	14 AD
en el (siglo) XIX	in the nineteenth century
en los años treinta	in the thirties
érase una vez ...	once upon a time ...

Español-Inglés
Spanish-English

Aa

A, a [a] *nf* (*letra*) A, a; **A de Antonio** A for Andrew (*BRIT*) *o* Able (*US*).

═══════════════ *PALABRA CLAVE*

a [a] (*a+el = al*) *prep* **1** (*dirección*) to; **fueron ~ Madrid/Grecia** they went to Madrid/Greece; **me voy ~ casa** I'm going home
2 (*distancia*): **está ~ 15 km de aquí** it's 15 kms from here
3 (*posición*): **estar ~ la mesa** to be at table; **al lado de** next to, beside; **~ la derecha/izquierda** on the right/left; *V tb* **puerta**
4 (*tiempo*): **~ las 10/~ medianoche** at 10/midnight; **¿~ qué hora?** (at) what time?; **~ la mañana siguiente** the following morning; **~ los pocos días** after a few days; **estamos ~ 9 de julio** it's the 9th of July; **~ los 24 años** at the age of 24; **ocho horas al día** eight hours a day; **al año/~ la semana** (*AM*) a year/week later
5 (*manera*): **~ la francesa** the French way; **~ caballo** on horseback; **~ oscuras** in the dark; **~ rayas** striped; **le echaron ~ patadas** they kicked him out
6 (*medio, instrumento*): **~ lápiz** in pencil; **~ mano** by hand; **cocina ~ gas** gas stove
7 (*razón*): **~ 30 ptas el kilo** at 30 pesetas a kilo; **~ más de 50 kms por hora** at more than 50 kms per hour; **poco ~ poco** little by little
8 (*dativo*): **se lo di ~ él** I gave it to him; **se lo compré ~ él** I bought it from him
9 (*complemento directo*): **vi al policía** I saw the policeman
10 (*tras ciertos verbos*): **voy ~ verle** I'm going to see him; **empezó ~ trabajar** he

started working *o* to work; **sabe ~ queso** it tastes of cheese
11 (*+infin*): **al verle, le reconocí inmediatamente** when I saw him I recognized him at once; **el camino ~ recorrer** the distance we (*etc*) have to travel; **¡~ callar!** keep quiet!; **¡~ comer!** let's eat!
12 (*a+que*): **¡~ que llueve!** I bet it's going to rain!; **¿~ qué viene eso?** what's the meaning of this?; **¿~ que sí va a venir?** he IS coming, isn't he?; **¿~ que no lo haces?** – **¡~ que sí!** bet you don't do it! – yes, I WILL!

A. *abr* (*ESCOL*: = *aprobado*) pass.
AA *nfpl abr* = *Aerolíneas Argentinas*.
AA EE *abr* (= *Asuntos Exteriores*): **Min. de AA EE** ≈ FO (*BRIT*).
ab. *abr* (= *abril*) Apr.
abad, esa [a'ßað, 'ðesa] *nm/f* abbot/abbess.
abadía [aßa'ðia] *nf* abbey.
abajo [a'ßaxo] *adv* (*situación*) (down) below, underneath; (*en edificio*) downstairs; (*dirección*) down, downwards; **~ de** *prep* below, under; **el piso de ~** the downstairs flat; **la parte de ~** the lower part; **¡~ el gobierno!** down with the government!; **cuesta/río ~** downhill/downstream; **de arriba ~** from top to bottom; **el ~ firmante** the undersigned; **más ~** lower *o* further down.
abalance [aßa'lanθe] *etc vb V* **abalanzarse**.
abalanzarse [aßalan'θarse] *vr*: **~ sobre** *o* **contra** to throw o.s. at.
abalear [aßale'ar] *vt* (*AM fam*) to shoot.
abalorios [aßa'lorjos] *nmpl* (*chucherías*)

trinkets.

abanderado [aßande'raðo] *nm* standard bearer.

abandonado, a [aßando'naðo, a] *adj* derelict; (*desatendido*) abandoned; (*desierto*) deserted; (*descuidado*) neglected.

abandonar [aßando'nar] *vt* to leave; (*persona*) to abandon, desert; (*cosa*) to abandon, leave behind; (*descuidar*) to neglect; (*renunciar a*) to give up; (*INFORM*) to quit; ~**se** *vr*: ~**se a** to abandon o.s. to; ~**se al alcohol** to take to drink.

abandono [aßan'dono] *nm* (*acto*) desertion, abandonment; (*estado*) abandon, neglect; (*renuncia*) withdrawal, retirement; **ganar por** ~ to win by default.

abanicar [aßani'kar] *vt* to fan.

abanico [aßa'niko] *nm* fan; (*NAUT*) derrick; **en** ~ fan-shaped.

abanique [aßa'nike] *etc vb V* **abanicar**.

abaratar [aßara'tar] *vt* to lower the price of ♦ *vi*, ~**se** *vr* to go *o* come down in price.

abarcar [aßar'kar] *vt* to include, embrace; (*contener*) to comprise; (*AM*) to monopolize; **quien mucho abarca poco aprieta** don't bite off more than you can chew.

abarque [a'ßarke] *etc vb V* **abarcar**.

abarrotado, a [aßarro'taðo, a] *adj* packed; ~ **de** packed *o* bursting with.

abarrote [aßa'rrote] *nm* packing; ~**s** *nmpl* (*AM*) groceries, provisions.

abarrotería [aßarrote'ria] *nf* (*AM*) grocery store.

abarrotero, a [aßarro'tero, a] *nm/f* (*AM*) grocer.

abastecedor, a [aßasteθe'ðor, a] *adj* supplying ♦ *nm/f* supplier.

abastecer [aßaste'θer] *vt*: ~ **(de)** to supply (with).

abastecimiento [aßasteθi'mjento] *nm* supply.

abastezca [aßas'teθka] *etc vb V* **abastecer**.

abasto [a'ßasto] *nm* supply; (*abundancia*) abundance; **no dar** ~ **a algo** not to be able to cope with sth.

abatible [aßa'tißle] *adj*: **asiento** ~ tip-up seat.

abatido, a [aßa'tiðo, a] *adj* dejected, downcast; **estar muy** ~ to be very depressed.

abatimiento [aßati'mjento] *nm* (*depresión*) dejection, depression.

abatir [aßa'tir] *vt* (*muro*) to demolish; (*pájaro*) to shoot *o* bring down; (*fig*) to

depress; ~**se** *vr* to get depressed; ~**se sobre** to swoop *o* pounce on.

abdicación [aßðika'θjon] *nf* abdication.

abdicar [aßði'kar] *vi* to abdicate; ~ **en algn** to abdicate in favour of sb.

abdique [aß'ðike] *etc vb V* **abdicar**.

abdomen [aß'ðomen] *nm* abdomen.

abdominal [aßðomi'nal] *adj* abdominal ♦ *nm*: ~**es** (*DEPORTE*) abdominals; (*ANAT*) abdominals, stomach muscles.

abecedario [aßeθe'ðarjo] *nm* alphabet.

abedul [aße'ðul] *nm* birch.

abeja [a'ßexa] *nf* bee; (*fig: hormiguita*) hard worker.

abejorro [aße'xorro] *nm* bumblebee.

aberración [aßerra'θjon] *nf* aberration.

aberrante [aße'rrante] *adj* (*disparatado*) ridiculous.

abertura [aßer'tura] *nf* = **apertura**.

abertzale [aßer'tʃale] *adj, nm/f* Basque nationalist.

abeto [a'ßeto] *nm* fir.

abierto, a [a'ßjerto, a] *pp de* **abrir** ♦ *adj* open; (*fig: carácter*) frank.

abigarrado, a [aßiɣa'rraðo, a] *adj* multicoloured; (*fig*) motley.

abismal [aßis'mal] *adj* (*fig*) vast, enormous.

abismar [aßis'mar] *vt* to humble, cast down; ~**se** *vr* to sink; (*AM*) to be amazed; ~**se en** (*fig*) to be plunged into.

abismo [a'ßismo] *nm* abyss; **de sus ideas a las mías hay un** ~ our views are worlds apart.

abjurar [aßxu'rar] *vt* to abjure, forswear ♦ *vi*: ~ **de** to abjure, forswear.

ablandar [aßlan'dar] *vt* to soften up; (*conmover*) to touch; (*CULIN*) to tenderize ♦ *vi*, ~**se** *vr* to get softer.

abnegación [aßneɣa'θjon] *nf* self-denial.

abnegado, a [aßne'ɣaðo, a] *adj* self-sacrificing.

abobado, a [aßo'ßaðo, a] *adj* silly.

abobamiento [aßoßa'mjento] *nm* (*asombro*) bewilderment.

abocado, a [aßo'kaðo, a] *adj*: **verse** ~ **al desastre** to be heading for disaster.

abochornar [aßotʃor'nar] *vt* to embarrass; ~**se** *vr* to get flustered; (*BOT*) to wilt; ~**se de** to get embarrassed about.

abofetear [aßofete'ar] *vt* to slap (in the face).

abogacía [aßoɣa'θia] *nf* legal profession; (*ejercicio*) practice of the law.

abogado, a [aßo'ɣaðo, a] *nm/f* lawyer; (*notario*) solicitor; (*asesor*) counsel; (*en tribunal*) barrister, advocate, attorney (*US*); ~ **defensor** defence lawyer *o* attorney (*US*); ~ **del diablo** devil's advocate.

abogar [aβo'ɣar] vi: ~ **por** to plead for; (fig) to advocate.

abogue [a'βoɣe] etc vb V **abogar**.

abolengo [aβo'lengo] nm ancestry, lineage.

abolición [aβoli'θjon] nf abolition.

abolir [aβo'lir] vt to abolish; (cancelar) to cancel.

abolladura [aβoʎa'ðura] nf dent.

abollar [aβo'ʎar] vt to dent.

abominable [aβomi'naβle] adj abominable.

abominación [aβomina'θjon] nf abomination.

abonado, a [aβo'naðo, a] adj (deuda) paid(-up) ♦ nm/f subscriber.

abonar [aβo'nar] vt to pay;(deuda) to settle; (terreno) to fertilize; (Idea) to endorse; ~**se** vr to subscribe; ~ **dinero en una cuenta** to pay money into an account, credit money to an account.

abono [a'βono] nm payment; fertilizer; subscription.

abordable [aβor'ðaβle] adj (persona) approachable.

abordar [aβor'ðar] vt (barco) to board; (asunto) to broach; (individuo) to approach.

aborigen [aβo'rixen] nm/f aborigine.

aborrecer [aβorre'θer] vt to hate, loathe.

aborrezca [nβo'rreθka] etc vb V **aborrecer**.

abortar [aβor'tar] vi (malparir) to have a miscarriage; (deliberadamente) to have an abortion.

aborto [a'βorto] nm miscarriage; abortion.

abotagado, a [aβota'ɣaðo, a] adj swollen.

abotonar [aβoto'nar] vt to button (up), do up.

abovedado, a [aβoβe'ðaðo, a] adj vaulted, domed.

abr. abr (= abril) Apr.

abrace [a'βraθe] etc vb V **abrazar**.

abrasar [aβra'sar] vt to burn (up); (AGR) to dry up, parch.

abrazadera [aβraθa'ðera] nf bracket.

abrazar [aβra'θar] vt to embrace, hug; ~**se** vr to embrace, hug each other.

abrazo [a'βraθo] nm embrace, hug; **un ~** (en carta) with best wishes.

abrebotellas [aβreβo'teʎas] nm inv bottle opener.

abrecartas [aβre'kartas] nm inv letter opener.

abrelatas [aβre'latas] nm inv tin (BRIT) o can (US) opener.

abrevadero [aβreβa'ðero] nm watering place.

abreviar [aβre'βjar] vt to abbreviate;

(texto) to abridge; (plazo) to reduce ♦ vi: **bueno, para** ~ well, to cut a long story short.

abreviatura [aβreβja'tura] nf abbreviation.

abridor [aβri'ðor] nm (de botellas) bottle opener; (de latas) tin (BRIT) o can (US) opener.

abrigar [aβri'ɣar] vt (proteger) to shelter; (suf: ropa) to keep warm; (fig) to cherish; ~**se** vr to take shelter, protect o.s (de from); (con ropa) to cover (o.s.) up; **¡abrígate bien!** wrap up well!

abrigo [a'βriɣo] nm (prenda) coat, overcoat; (lugar protegido) shelter; **al ~ de** in the shelter of.

abrigue [a'βriɣe] etc vb V **abrigar**.

abril [a'βril] nm April.

abrillantar [aβriʎan'tar] vt (pulir) to polish; (fig) to enhance.

abrir [a'βrir] vt to open (up); (camino etc) to open up; (apetito) to whet; (lista) to head ♦ vi to open; ~**se** vr to open (up); (extenderse) to open out; (cielo) to clear; ~ **un negocio** to start up a business; **en un ~ y cerrar de ojos** in the twinkling of an eye; ~**se paso** to find o force a way through.

abrochar [aβro't ʃar] vt (con botones) to button (up); (zapato, con broche) to do up; ~**se** vr: ~ **los zapatos** to tie one's shoelaces.

abrogación [aβroxa'θjon] nf repeal.

abrogar [aβro'ɣar] vt to repeal.

abrumador, a [aβruma'ðor, a] adj (mayoría) overwhelming.

abrumar [aβru'mar] vt to overwhelm; (sobrecargar) to weigh down.

abrupto, a [a'βrupto, a] adj abrupt; (empinado) steep.

absceso [aβs'θeso] nm abscess.

absentismo [aβsen'tismo] nm (de obreros) absenteeism.

absolución [aβsolu'θjon] nf (REL) absolution; (JUR) acquittal.

absoluto, a [aβso'luto, a] adj absolute; (total) utter, complete; **en ~** adv not at all.

absolver [aβsol'βer] vt to absolve; (JUR) to pardon; (: acusado) to acquit.

absorbente [aβsor'βente] adj absorbent; (interesante) absorbing, interesting; (exigente) demanding.

absorber [aβsor'βer] vt to absorb; (embeber) to soak up; ~**se** vr to become absorbed.

absorción [aβsor'θjon] nf absorption; (COM) takeover.

absorto, a [aβ'sorto, a] pp de **absorber** ♦ adj

absorbed, engrossed.

abstemio, a [aßs'temjo, a] *adj* teetotal.

abstención [aßsten'θjon] *nf* abstention.

abstendré [aßsten'dre] *etc vb* V **abstenerse**.

abstenerse [aßste'nerse] *vr*: ~ **(de)** to abstain *o* refrain (from).

abstenga [aßs'tenga] *etc vb* V **abstenerse**.

abstinencia [aßsti'nenθja] *nf* abstinence; (*ayuno*) fasting.

abstracción [aßstrak'θjon] *nf* abstraction.

abstracto, a [aß'strakto, a] *adj* abstract; **en** ~ in the abstract.

abstraer [aßstra'er] *vt* to abstract; ~**se** *vr* to be *o* become absorbed.

abstraído, a [aßstra'iðo, a] *adj* absent-minded.

abstraiga [aßs'traixa] *etc*, **abstraje** [aßs'traxe] *etc*, **abstrayendo** [aßstra'jendo] *etc vb* V **abstraer**.

abstuve [aßs'tuße] *etc vb* V **abstenerse**.

absuelto [aß'swelto] *pp de* **absolver**.

absurdo, a [aß'surðo, a] *adj* absurd; **lo** ~ **es que ...** the ridiculous thing is that ... ♦ *nm* absurdity.

abuchear [aßutʃe'ar] *vt* to boo.

abucheo [aßu'tʃeo] *nm* booing; **ganarse un** ~ (*TEAT*) to be booed.

abuela [a'ßwela] *nf* grandmother; **¡cuéntaselo a tu** ~! (*fam!*) do you think I was born yesterday? (*fam*); **no tener/ necesitar** ~ (*fam*) to be full of o.s./blow one's own trumpet.

abuelita [aßwe'lita] *nf* granny.

abuelo [a'ßwelo] *nm* grandfather; (*antepasado*) ancestor; ~**s** *nmpl* grandparents.

abulense [aßu'lense] *adj o* Ávila ♦ *nm/f* native *o* inhabitant of Ávila.

abulia [a'ßulja] *nf* lethargy.

abúlico, a [a'ßuliko, a] *adj* lethargic.

abultado, a [aßul'taðo, a] *adj* bulky.

abultar [aßul'tar] *vt* to enlarge; (*aumentar*) to increase; (*fig*) to exaggerate ♦ *vi* to be bulky.

abundancia [aßun'danθja] *nf*: **una** ~ **de** plenty of; **en** ~ in abundance.

abundante [aßun'dante] *adj* abundant, plentiful.

abundar [aßun'dar] *vi* to abound, be plentiful; ~ **en una opinión** to share an opinion.

aburguesarse [aßurxe'sarse] *vr* to become middle-class.

aburrido, a [aßu'rriðo, a] *adj* (*hastiado*) bored; (*que aburre*) boring.

aburrimiento [aßurri'mjento] *nm* boredom, tedium.

aburrir [aßu'rrir] *vt* to bore; ~**se** *vr* to be

bored, get bored; ~**se como una almeja** *u* **ostra** to be bored stiff.

abusar [aßu'sar] *vi* to go too far; ~ **de** to abuse.

abusivo, a [aßu'sißo, a] *adj* (*precio*) exorbitant.

abuso [a'ßuso] *nm* abuse; ~ **de confianza** betrayal of trust.

abyecto, a [aß'jekto, a] *adj* wretched, abject.

A.C. *abr* (= *Año de Cristo*) A.D.

a/c *abr* (= *al cuidado de*) c/o; (= *a cuenta*) on account.

acá [a'ka] *adv* (*lugar*) here; **pasearse de** ~ **para allá** to walk up and down; **¡vente para** ~! come over here!; **¿de cuándo** ~? since when?

acabado, a [aka'ßaðo, a] *adj* finished, complete; (*perfecto*) perfect; (*agotado*) worn out; (*fig*) masterly ♦ *nm* finish.

acabar [aka'ßar] *vt* (*llevar a su fin*) to finish, complete; (*consumir*) to use up; (*rematar*) to finish off ♦ *vi* to finish, end; (*morir*) to die; ~**se** *vr* to finish, stop; (*terminarse*) to be over; (*agotarse*) to run out; ~ **con** to put an end to; ~ **mal** to come to a sticky end; **esto acabará conmigo** this will be the end of me; ~ **de llegar** to have just arrived; **acababa de hacerlo** I had just done it; ~ **haciendo** *o* **por hacer algo** to end up (by) doing sth; **¡se acabó!** (*¡basta!*) that's enough!; (*se terminó*) it's all over!; **se me acabó el tabaco** I ran out of cigarettes.

acabóse [aka'ßose] *nm*: **esto es el** ~ this is the limit.

acacia [a'kaθja] *nf* acacia.

academia [aka'ðemja] *nf* academy; (*ESCOL*) private school; V *tb* **colegio**.

académico, a [aka'ðemiko, a] *adj* academic.

acaecer [akae'θer] *vi* to happen, occur.

acaezca [aka'eθka] *etc vb* V **acaecer**.

acallar [aka'ʎar] *vt* (*silenciar*) to silence; (*calmar*) to pacify.

acalorado, a [akalo'raðo, a] *adj* (*discusión*) heated.

acalorarse [akalo'rarse] *vr* (*fig*) to get heated.

acampada [akam'paða] *nf*: **ir de** ~ to go camping.

acampanado, a [akampa'naðo, a] *adj* flared.

acampar [akam'par] *vi* to camp.

acanalado, a [akana'laðo, a] *adj* (*hierro*) corrugated.

acanalar [akana'lar] *vt* to groove; (*ondular*) to corrugate.

acantilado [akanti'laðo] nm cliff.
acaparador, a [akapara'ðor, a] nm/f monopolizer.
acaparar [akapa'rar] vt to monopolize; (acumular) to hoard.
acápite [a'kapite] nm (AM) paragraph; **punto ~** full stop, new paragraph.
acaramelado, a [akarame'laðo, a] adj (CULIN) toffee-coated; (fig) sugary.
acariciar [akari'θjar] vt to caress; (esperanza) to cherish.
acarrear [akarre'ar] vt to transport; (fig) to cause, result in; **le acarreó muchos disgustos** it brought him lots of problems.
acaso [a'kaso] adv perhaps, maybe ♦ nm chance; **¿~ es mi culpa?** (AM fam) what makes you think it's my fault?; **(por) si ~** (just) in case.
acatamiento [akata'mjento] nm respect; (de la ley) observance.
acatar [aka'tar] vt to respect; (ley) to obey, observe.
acatarrarse [akata'rrarse] vr to catch a cold.
acaudalado, a [akauða'laðo, a] adj well-off.
acaudillar [akauði'ʎar] vt to lead, command.
acceder [akθe'ðer] vi to accede, agree; **~ a** (INFORM) to access.
accesible [akθe'siβle] adj accessible; **~ a** open to.
accésit, pl **accésits** [ak'θesit, ak'θesits] nm consolation prize.
acceso [ak'θeso] nm access, entry; (camino) access road; (MED) attack, fit; (de cólera) fit; (POL) accession; (INFORM) access; **~ aleatorio/directo/secuencial o en serie** (INFORM) random/direct/sequential o serial access; **de ~ múltiple** multi-access.
accesorio, a [akθe'sorjo, a] adj accessory ♦ nm accessory; **~s** nmpl (AUTO) accessories, extras; (TEAT) props.
accidentado, a [akθiðen'taðo, a] adj uneven; (montañoso) hilly; (azaroso) eventful ♦ nm/f accident victim.
accidental [akθiðen'tal] adj accidental; (empleo) temporary.
accidentarse [akθiðen'tarse] vr to have an accident.
accidente [akθi'ðente] nm accident; **por ~** by chance; **~s** nmpl unevenness sg, roughness sg.
acción [ak'θjon] nf action; (acto) action, act; (TEAT) plot; (COM) share; (JUR) action, lawsuit; **capital en acciones** share

capital; **~ liberada/ordinaria/preferente** fully-paid/ordinary/preference share.
accionamiento [akθjona'mjento] nm (de máquina) operation.
accionar [akθjo'nar] vt to work, operate; (INFORM) to drive.
accionista [akθjo'nista] nm/f shareholder.
acebo [a'θeβo] nm holly; (árbol) holly tree.
acechanza [aθe'tʃanθa] nf = **acecho**.
acechar [aθe'tʃar] vt to spy on; (aguardar) to lie in wait for.
acecho [a'θetʃo] nm: **estar al ~ (de)** to lie in wait (for).
acedera [aθe'ðera] nf sorrel.
aceitar [aθei'tar] vt to oil, lubricate.
aceite [a'θeite] nm oil; (de oliva) olive oil; **~ de hígado de bacalao** cod-liver oil.
aceitera [aθei'tera] nf oilcan.
aceitoso, a [aθei'toso, a] adj oily.
aceituna [aθei'tuna] nf olive.
aceitunado, a [aθeitu'naðo, a] adj olive cpd; **de tez aceitunada** olive-skinned.
acelerador [aθelera'ðor] nm accelerator.
acelerar [aθele'rar] vt to accelerate; **~se** vr to hurry.
acelga [a'θelɣa] nf chard, beet.
acendrado, a [aθen'draðo, a] adj: **de ~ carácter español** typically Spanish.
acendrar [aθen'drar] vt to purify.
acento [a'θento] nm accent; (acentuación) stress; **~ cerrado** strong o thick accent.
acentuar [aθen'twar] vt to accent; to stress; (fig) to accentuate; (INFORM) to highlight.
acepción [aθep'θjon] nf meaning.
aceptación [aθepta'θjon] nf acceptance; (aprobación) approval.
aceptar [aθep'tar] vt to accept; to approve.
acequia [a'θekja] nf irrigation ditch.
acera [a'θera] nf pavement (BRIT), sidewalk (US).
acerado, a [aθe'raðo, a] adj steel; (afilado) sharp; (fig: duro) steely; (: mordaz) biting.
acerbo, a [a'θerβo, a] adj bitter; (fig) harsh.
acerca [a'θerka]: **~ de** prep about, concerning.
acercar [aθer'kar] vt to bring o move nearer; **~se** vr to approach, come near.
acerico [aθe'riko] nm pincushion.
acero [a'θero] nm steel; **~ inoxidable** stainless steel.
acerque [a'θerke] etc vb V **acercar**.
acérrimo, a [a'θerrimo, a] adj (partidario) staunch; (enemigo) bitter.
acertado, a [aθer'taðo, a] adj correct; (apropiado) apt; (sensato) sensible.
acertar [aθer'tar] vt (blanco) to hit; (solución) to get right; (adivinar) to guess

♦ *vi* to get it right, be right; ~ **a** to manage to; ~ **con** to happen *o* hit on.

acertijo [aθer'tixo] *nm* riddle, puzzle.

acervo [a'θerßo] *nm* heap; ~ **común** undivided estate.

achacar [atʃa'kar] *vt* to attribute.

achacoso, a [atʃa'koso, a] *adj* sickly.

achantar [atʃan'tar] *vt* (*fam*) to scare, frighten; ~**se** *vr* to back down.

achaque [a'tʃake] *etc vb V* **achacar** ♦ *nm* ailment.

achatar [atʃa'tar] *vt* to flatten.

achicar [atʃi'kar] *vt* to reduce; (*humillar*) to humiliate; (*NAUT*) to bale out; ~**se** (*ropa*) to shrink; (*fig*) to humble o.s.

achicharrar [atʃitʃa'rrar] *vt* to scorch, burn.

achicoria [atʃi'korja] *nf* chicory.

achinado, a [atʃi'naðo, a] *adj* (*ojos*) slanting; (*AM*) half-caste.

achique [a'tʃike] *etc vb V* **achicar**.

acholado, a [atʃo'laðo, a] *adj* (*AM*) half-caste.

achuchar [atʃu'tʃar] *vt* to crush.

achuchón [atʃu'tʃon] *nm* shove; **tener un** ~ (*MED*) to be poorly.

achuras [a'tʃuras] *nf* (*AM CULIN*) offal.

aciago, a [a'θjaʏo, a] *adj* ill-fated, fateful.

acicalar [aθika'lar] *vt* to polish; (*adornar*) to bedeck; ~**se** *vr* to get dressed up.

acicate [aθi'kate] *nm* spur; (*fig*) incentive.

acidez [aθi'ðeθ] *nf* acidity.

ácido, a ['aθiðo, a] *adj* sour, acid ♦ *nm* acid; (*fam: droga*) LSD.

acierto [a'θjerto] *etc vb V* **acertar** ♦ *nm* success; (*buen paso*) wise move; (*solución*) solution; (*habilidad*) skill, ability; (*al adivinar*) good guess; **fue un** ~ **suyo** it was a sensible choice on his part.

aclamación [aklama'θjon] *nf* acclamation; (*aplausos*) applause.

aclamar [akla'mar] *vt* to acclaim; to applaud.

aclaración [aklara'θjon] *nf* clarification, explanation.

aclarar [akla'rar] *vt* to clarify, explain; (*ropa*) to rinse ♦ *vi* to clear up; ~**se** *vr* (*suj: persona: explicarse*) to understand; (*fig: asunto*) to become clear; ~**se la garganta** to clear one's throat.

aclaratorio, a [aklara'torjo, a] *adj* explanatory.

aclimatación [aklimata'θjon] *nf* acclimatization.

aclimatar [aklima'tar] *vt* to acclimatize; ~**se** *vr* to become *o* get acclimatized; ~**se a algo** to get used to sth.

acné [ak'ne] *nm* acne.

acobardar [akoßar'ðar] *vt* to daunt, intimidate; ~**se** *vr* (*atemorizarse*) to be intimidated; (*echarse atrás*): ~**se (ante)** to shrink back (from).

acodarse [ako'ðarse] *vr*: ~ **en** to lean on.

acogedor, a [akoxe'ðor, a] *adj* welcoming; (*hospitalario*) hospitable.

acoger [ako'xer] *vt* to welcome; (*abrigar*) to shelter; ~**se** *vr* to take refuge; ~**se a** (*pretexto*) to take refuge in; (*ley*) to resort to.

acogida [ako'xiða] *nf* reception; refuge.

acoja [a'koxa] *etc vb V* **acoger**.

acojonante [akoxo'nante] *adj* (*ESP fam*) tremendous.

acolchar [akol'tʃar] *vt* to pad; (*fig*) to cushion.

acólito [a'kolito] *nm* (*REL*) acolyte; (*fig*) minion.

acometer [akome'ter] *vt* to attack; (*emprender*) to undertake.

acometida [akome'tiða] *nf* attack, assault.

acomodado, a [akomo'ðaðo, a] *adj* (*persona*) well-to-do.

acomodador, a [akomoða'ðor, a] *nm/f* usher(ette).

acomodar [akomo'ðar] *vt* to adjust; (*alojar*) to accommodate; ~**se** *vr* to conform; (*instalarse*) to install o.s.; (*adaptarse*) to adapt o.s.; **¡acomódese a su gusto!** make yourself comfortable!

acomodaticio, a [akomoða'tiθjo, a] *adj* (*pey*) accommodating, obliging; (*manejable*) pliable.

acompañamiento [akompaɲa'mjento] *nm* (*MUS*) accompaniment.

acompañante, a [akompa'ɲante, a] *nm/f* companion.

acompañar [akompa'ɲar] *vt* to accompany, go with; (*documentos*) to enclose; **¿quieres que te acompañe?** do you want me to come with you?; ~ **a algn a la puerta** to see sb to the door *o* out; **le acompaño en el sentimiento** please accept my condolences.

acompasar [akompa'sar] *vt* (*MUS*) to mark the rhythm of.

acomplejado, a [akomple'xaðo, a] *adj* neurotic.

acomplejar [akomple'xar] *vt* to give a complex to; ~**se** *vr*: ~**se (con)** to get a complex (about).

acondicionado, a [akondiθjo'naðo, a] *adj* (*TEC*) in good condition.

acondicionador [akondiθjona'ðor] *nm* conditioner.

acondicionar [akondiθjo'nar] *vt* to get

ready, prepare; (*pelo*) to condition.

acongojar [akongo'xar] *vt* to distress, grieve.

aconsejable [akonse'xaßle] *adj* advisable.

aconsejar [akonse'xar] *vt* to advise, counsel; ~**se** *vr*: ~**se con** *o* **de** to consult.

acontecer [akonte'θer] *vi* to happen, occur.

acontecimiento [akonteθi'mjento] *nm* event.

acontezca [akon'teθka] *etc vb* V **acontecer**.

acopiar [ako'pjar] *vt* (*recoger*) to gather; (*COM*) to buy up.

acopio [a'kopjo] *nm* store, stock.

acoplador [akopla'ðor] *nm*: ~ **acústico** (*INFORM*) acoustic coupler.

acoplamiento [akopla'mjento] *nm* coupling, joint.

acoplar [ako'plar] *vt* to fit; (*ELEC*) to connect; (*vagones*) to couple.

acoquinar [akoki'nar] *vt* to scare; ~**se** *vr* to get scared.

acorazado, a [akora'θaðo, a] *adj* armour-plated, armoured ♦ *nm* battleship.

acordar [akor'ðar] *vt* (*resolver*) to agree, resolve; (*recordar*) to remind; ~**se** *vr* to agree; ~**se** (**de algo**) to remember (sth).

acorde [a'korðe] *adj* (*MUS*) harmonious; ~ **con** (*medidas etc*) in keeping with ♦ *nm* chord.

acordeón [akorðe'on] *nm* accordion.

acordonado, a [akorðo'naðo, a] *adj* (*calle*) cordoned-off.

acorralar [akorra'lar] *vt* to round up, corral; (*fig*) to intimidate.

acortar [akor'tar] *vt* to shorten; (*duración*) to cut short; (*cantidad*) to reduce; ~**se** *vr* to become shorter.

acosar [ako'sar] *vt* to pursue relentlessly; (*fig*) to hound, pester; ~ **a algn a preguntas** to pester sb with questions.

acoso [a'koso] *nm* relentless pursuit; (*fig*) hounding; ~ **sexual** sexual harassment.

acostar [akos'tar] *vt* (*en cama*) to put to bed; (*en suelo*) to lay down; (*barco*) to bring alongside; ~**se** *vr* to go to bed; to lie down.

acostumbrado, a [akostum'braðo, a] *adj* (*habitual*) usual; **estar** ~ **a (hacer) algo** to be used to (doing) sth.

acostumbrar [akostum'brar] *vt*: ~ **a algn a algo** to get sb used to sth ♦ *vi*: ~ **(a hacer algo)** to be in the habit of (doing sth); ~**se** *vr*: ~**se a** to get used to.

acotación [akota'θjon] *nf* (*apunte*) marginal note; (*GEO*) elevation mark; (*de límite*) boundary mark; (*TEAT*) stage direction.

acotar [ako'tar] *vt* (*terreno*) to mark out; (*fig*) to limit; (*caza*) to protect.

acotejar [akote'xar] *vt* (*AM*) to put in order, arrange.

ácrata ['akrata] *adj*, *nm/f* anarchist.

acre ['akre] *adj* (*sabor*) sharp, bitter; (*olor*) acrid; (*fig*) biting ♦ *nm* acre.

acrecentar [akreθen'tar] *vt* to increase, augment.

acreciente [akre'θjente] *etc vb* V **acrecentar**.

acreditado, a [akreði'taðo, a] *adj* (*POL*) accredited; (*COM*): **una casa acreditada** a reputable firm.

acreditar [akreði'tar] *vt* (*garantizar*) to vouch for, guarantee; (*autorizar*) to authorize; (*dar prueba de*) to prove; (*COM*: *abonar*) to credit; (*embajador*) to accredit; ~**se** *vr* to become famous; (*demostrar valía*) to prove one's worth; ~**se de** to get a reputation for.

acreedor, a [akree'ðor, a] *adj*: ~ **a** a worthy of ♦ *nm/f* creditor; ~ **común/diferido/con garantía** (*COM*) unsecured/deferred/secured creditor.

acribillar [akrißi'ʎar] *vt*: ~ **a balazos** to riddle with bullets.

acrimonia [akri'monja], **acritud** [akri'tuð] *nf* acrimony.

acrobacia [akro'ßaθja] *nf* acrobatics; ~ **aérea** aerobatics.

acróbata [a'kroßata] *nm/f* acrobat.

acta ['akta] *nf* certificate; (*de comisión*) minutes *pl*, record; ~ **de nacimiento/de matrimonio** birth/marriage certificate; ~ **notarial** affidavit; **levantar** ~ (*JUR*) to make a formal statement *o* deposition.

actitud [akti'tuð] *nf* attitude; (*postura*) posture; **adoptar una** ~ **firme** to take a firm stand.

activar [akti'ßar] *vt* to activate; (*acelerar*) to speed up.

actividad [aktißi'ðað] *nf* activity; **estar en plena** ~ to be in full swing.

activo, a [ak'tißo, a] *adj* active; (*vivo*) lively ♦ *nm* (*COM*) assets *pl*; ~ **y pasivo** assets and liabilities; ~ **circulante/fijo/inmaterial/invisible** (*COM*) current/fixed/intangible/invisible assets; ~ **realizable** liquid assets; ~**s congelados** *o* **bloqueados** frozen assets; **estar en** ~ (*MIL*) to be on active service.

acto ['akto] *nm* act, action; (*ceremonia*) ceremony; (*TEAT*) act; **en el** ~ immediately; **hacer** ~ **de presencia** (*asistir*) to attend (formally).

actor [ak'tor] *nm* actor; (*JUR*) plaintiff.

actora [ak'tora] *adj*: **parte** ~ prosecution;

(*demandante*) plaintiff.

actriz [ak'triθ] *nf* actress.

actuación [aktwa'θjon] *nf* action; (*comportamiento*) conduct, behaviour; (*JUR*) proceedings *pl*; (*desempeño*) performance.

actual [ak'twal] *adj* present(-day), current; **el 6 del** ~ the 6th of this month.

actualice [aktwa'liθe] *etc vb V* **actualizar**.

actualidad [aktwali'ðað] *nf* present; ~**es** *nfpl* news *sg*; **en la** ~ nowadays, at present; **ser de gran** ~ to be current.

actualización [aktwaliθa'θjon] *nf* updating, modernization.

actualizar [aktwali'θar] *vt* to update, modernize.

actualmente [aktwal'mente] *adv* at present; (*hoy día*) nowadays.

actuar [ak'twar] *vi* (*obrar*) to work, operate; (*actor*) to act, perform ♦ *vt* to work, operate; ~ **de** to act as.

actuario, a [ak'twarjo] *nm/f* clerk; (*COM*) actuary.

acuarela [akwa'rela] *nf* watercolour.

acuario [a'kwarjo] *nm* aquarium; **A**~ (*ASTRO*) Aquarius.

acuartelar [akwarte'lar] *vt* (*MIL: alojar*) to quarter.

acuático, a [a'kwatiko, a] *adj* aquatic.

acuchillar [akutʃi'ʎar] *vt* (*TEC*) to plane (down), smooth.

acuciar [aku'θjar] *vt* to urge on.

acuclillarse [akukli'ʎarse] *vr* to crouch down.

ACUDE [a'kuðe] *nf abr* = *Asociación de Consumidores y Usuarios de España*.

acudir [aku'ðir] *vi* to attend, turn up; ~ **a** to turn to; ~ **en ayuda de** to go to the aid of; ~ **a una cita** to keep an appointment; ~ **a una llamada** to answer a call; **no tener a quién** ~ to have nobody to turn to.

acuerdo [a'kwerðo] *etc vb V* **acordar** ♦ *nm* agreement; (*POL*) resolution; ~ **de pago respectivo** (*COM*) knock-for-knock agreement; **A**~ **general sobre aranceles aduaneros y comercio** (*COM*) General Agreement on Tariffs and Trade; **tomar un** ~ to pass a resolution; **¡de** ~**!** agreed!; **de** ~ **con** (*persona*) in agreement with; (*acción, documento*) in accordance with; **de común** ~ by common consent; **estar de** ~ (*persona*) to agree; **llegar a un** ~ to come to an understanding.

acueste [a'kweste] *etc vb V* **acostar**.

acullá [aku'ʎa] *adv* over there.

acumular [akumu'lar] *vt* to accumulate,

collect.

acunar [aku'nar] *vt* to rock (to sleep).

acuñar [aku'ɲar] *vt* (*moneda*) to mint; (*frase*) to coin.

acuoso, a [a'kwoso, a] *adj* watery.

acupuntura [akupun'tura] *nf* acupuncture.

acurrucarse [akurru'karse] *vr* to crouch; (*ovillarse*) to curl up.

acurruque [aku'rruke] *etc vb V* **acurrucarse**.

acusación [akusa'θjon] *nf* accusation.

acusado, a [aku'saðo, a] *adj* (*JUR*) accused; (*marcado*) marked; (*acento*) strong.

acusar [aku'sar] *vt* to accuse; (*revelar*) to reveal; (*denunciar*) to denounce; (*emoción*) to show; ~ **recibo** to acknowledge receipt; **su rostro acusó extrañeza** his face registered surprise; ~**se** *vr*: ~**se (de)** to confess (to).

acuse [a'kuse] *nm*: ~ **de recibo** acknowledgement of receipt.

acústico, a [a'kustiko, a] *adj* acoustic ♦ *nf* (*de una sala etc*) acoustics *pl*; (*ciencia*) acoustics *sg*.

ADA ['aða] *nf abr* (*ESP*: = *Ayuda del Automovilista*) ≈ AA, RAC (*BRIT*), AAA (*US*).

adagio [a'ðaxjo] *nm* adage; (*MUS*) adagio.

adalid [aða'lið] *nm* leader, champion.

adaptación [aðapta'θjon] *nf* adaptation.

adaptador [aðapta'ðor] *nm* (*ELEC*) adapter.

adaptar [aðap'tar] *vt* to adapt; (*acomodar*) to fit; (*convertir*): ~ **(para)** to convert (to).

adecentar [aðeθen'tar] *vt* to tidy up.

adecuado, a [aðe'kwaðo, a] *adj* (*apto*) suitable; (*oportuno*) appropriate; **el hombre** ~ **para el puesto** the right man for the job.

adecuar [aðe'kwar] *vt* (*adaptar*) to adapt; (*hacer apto*) to make suitable.

adefesio [aðe'fesjo] *nm* (*fam*): **estaba hecha un** ~ she looked a sight.

a. de J.C. *abr* (= *antes de Jesucristo*) B.C.

adelantado, a [aðelan'taðo, a] *adj* advanced; (*reloj*) fast; **pagar por** ~ to pay in advance.

adelantamiento [aðelanta'mjento] *nm* advance, advancement; (*AUTO*) overtaking.

adelantar [aðelan'tar] *vt* to move forward; (*avanzar*) to advance; (*acelerar*) to speed up; (*AUTO*) to overtake ♦ *vi* (*ir delante*) to go ahead; (*progresar*) to improve; (*tb*: ~**se** *vr*: *tomar la delantera*) to go forward, advance; ~**se a algn** to get ahead of sb; ~**se a los deseos de algn** to anticipate sb's wishes.

adelante [aðe'lante] *adv* forward(s),

onward(s), ahead ♦ *excl* come in!; **de hoy en** ~ from now on; **más** ~ later on; (*más allá*) further on.

adelanto [aðe'lanto] *nm* advance; (*mejora*) improvement; (*progreso*) progress; (*dinero*) advance; **los ~s de la ciencia** the advances of science.

adelgace [aðel'ɣaθe] *etc vb V* **adelgazar**.

adelgazar [aðelɣa'θar] *vt* to thin (down); (*afilar*) to taper ♦ *vi* to get thin; (*con régimen*) to slim down, lose weight.

ademán [aðe'man] *nm* gesture; **ademanes** *nmpl* manners; **en** ~ **de** as if to.

además [aðe'mas] *adv* besides; (*por otra parte*) moreover; (*también*) also; ~ **de** besides, in addition to.

ADENA [a'ðena] *nf abr* (*ESP* = *Asociación para la Defensa de la Naturaleza*) organization for nature conservation.

adentrarse [aðen'trarse] *vr*: ~ **en** to go into, get inside; (*penetrar*) to penetrate (into).

adentro [a'ðentro] *adv* inside, in; **mar** ~ out at sea; **tierra** ~ inland ♦ *nm*: **dijo para sus ~s** he said to himself.

adepto, a [a'ðepto, a] *nm/f* supporter.

aderece [aðe'reθe] *etc vb V* **aderezar**.

aderezar [aðere'θar] *vt* (*ensalada*) to dress; (*comida*) to season.

aderezo [aðe'reθo] *nm* dressing; seasoning.

adeudar [aðeu'ðar] *vt* to owe; ~**se** *vr* to run into debt; ~ **una suma en una cuenta** to debit an account with a sum.

a.D.g. *abr* (= *a Dios gracias*) D.G. (= *Deo gratias*: thanks be to God).

adherirse [aðe'rirse] *vr*: ~ **a** to adhere to; (*fig*) to follow.

adhesión [aðe'sjon] *nf* adhesion; (*fig*) adherence.

adhesivo, a [aðe'sißo, a] *adj* adhesive ♦ *nm* sticker.

adhiera [a'ðjera] *etc*, **adhiriendo** [aði'rjendo] *etc vb V* **adherirse**.

adicción [aðik'θjon] *nf* addiction.

adición [aði'θjon] *nf* addition.

adicional [aðiθjo'nal] *adj* additional; (*INFORM*) add-on.

adicionar [aðiθjo'nar] *vt* to add.

adicto, a [a'ðikto, a] *adj*: ~ **a** (*droga etc*) addicted to; (*dedicado*) devoted to ♦ *nm/f* supporter, follower; (*toxicómano etc*) addict.

adiestrar [aðjes'trar] *vt* to train, teach; (*conducir*) to guide, lead; ~**se** *vr* to practise; (*enseñarse*) to train o.s.

adinerado, a [aðine'raðo, a] *adj* wealthy.

adiós [a'ðjos] *excl* (*para despedirse*)

goodbye!, cheerio!; (*al pasar*) hello!

aditivo [aði'tißo] *nm* additive.

adivinanza [aðißi'nanθa] *nf* riddle.

adivinar [aðißi'nar] *vt* (*profetizar*) to prophesy; (*conjeturar*) to guess.

adivino, a [aði'ßino, a] *nm/f* fortune-teller.

adj *abr* (= *adjunto*) encl.

adjetivo [aðxe'tißo] *nm* adjective.

adjudicación [aðxuðika'θjon] *nf* award; (*COM*) adjudication.

adjudicar [aðxuði'kar] *vt* to award; ~**se algo** to appropriate sth.

adjudique [aðxu'ðike] *etc vb V* **adjudicar**.

adjuntar [aðxun'tar] *vt* to attach, enclose.

adjunto, a [að'xunto, a] *adj* attached, enclosed ♦ *nm/f* assistant.

adminículo [aðmi'nikulo] *nm* gadget.

administración [aðministra'θjon] *nf* administration; (*dirección*) management; ~ **pública** civil service; **A~ de Correos** General Post Office.

administrador, a [aðministra'ðor, a] *nm/f* administrator; manager(ess).

administrar [aðminis'trar] *vt* to administer.

administrativo, a [aðministra'tißo, a] *adj* administrative.

admirable [aðmi'raßle] *adj* admirable.

admiración [aðmira'θjon] *nf* admiration; (*asombro*) wonder; (*LING*) exclamation mark.

admirar [aðmi'rar] *vt* to admire; (*extrañar*) to surprise; ~**se** *vr* to be surprised; **se admiró de saberlo** he was amazed to hear it; **no es de** ~ **que ...** it's not surprising that ...

admisible [aðmi'sißle] *adj* admissible.

admisión [aðmi'sjon] *nf* admission; (*reconocimiento*) acceptance.

admitir [aðmi'tir] *vt* to admit; (*aceptar*) to accept; (*dudas*) to leave room for; **esto no admite demora** this must be dealt with immediately.

admón. *abr* (= *administración*) admin.

admonición [aðmoni'θjon] *nf* warning.

ADN *nm abr* (= *ácido desoxirribonucleico*) DNA.

adobar [aðo'ßar] *vt* (*preparar*) to prepare; (*cocinar*) to season.

adobe [a'ðoße] *nm* adobe, sun-dried brick.

adocenado, a [aðoθe'naðo, a] *adj* (*fam*) mediocre.

adoctrinar [aðoktri'nar] *vt* to indoctrinate.

adolecer [aðole'θer] *vi*: ~ **de** to suffer from.

adolescente [aðoles'θente] *nm/f* adolescent, teenager ♦ *adj* adolescent, teenage.

adolezca [aðo'leθka] *etc vb V* **adolecer.**
adonde [a'ðonde] *adv* (to) where.
adónde [a'ðonde] *adv* = **dónde.**
adondequiera [aðonde'kjera] *adv* wherever.
adopción [aðop'θjon] *nf* adoption.
adoptar [aðop'tar] *vt* to adopt.
adoptivo, a [aðop'tiβo, a] *adj* (*padres*) adoptive; (*hijo*) adopted.
adoquín [aðo'kin] *nm* paving stone.
adorar [aðo'rar] *vt* to adore.
adormecer [aðorme'θer] *vt* to put to sleep; ~**se** *vr* to become sleepy; (*dormirse*) to fall asleep.
adormezca [aðor'meθka] *etc vb V* **adormecer.**
adormilarse [aðormi'larse] *vr* to doze.
adornar [aðor'nar] *vt* to adorn.
adorno [a'ðorno] *nm* adornment; (*decoración*) decoration.
adosado, a [aðo'saðo, a] *adj* (*casa*) semidetached.
adquiera [að'kjera] *etc vb V* **adquirir.**
adquirir [aðki'rir] *vt* to acquire, obtain.
adquisición [aðkisi'θjon] *nf* acquisition; (*compra*) purchase.
adrede [a'ðreðe] *adv* on purpose.
Adriático [að'rjatiko] *nm*: **el (Mar)** ~ the Adriatic (Sea).
adscribir [aðskri'βir] *vt* to appoint; **estuvo adscrito al servicio de ...** he was attached to ...
adscrito [að'skrito] *pp de* **adscribir.**
aduana [a'ðwana] *nf* customs *pl*; (*impuesto*) (customs) duty.
aduanero, a [aðwa'nero, a] *adj* customs *cpd* ♦ *nm/f* customs officer.
aducir [aðu'θir] *vt* to adduce; (*dar como prueba*) to offer as proof.
adueñarse [aðwe'ɲarse] *vr*: ~ **de** to take possession of.
adulación [aðula'θjon] *nf* flattery.
adular [aðu'lar] *vt* to flatter.
adulterar [aðulte'rar] *vt* to adulterate ♦ *vi* to commit adultery.
adulterio [aðul'terjo] *nm* adultery.
adúltero, a [a'ðultero, a] *adj* adulterous ♦ *nm/f* adulterer/adulteress.
adulto, a [a'ðulto, a] *adj, nm/f* adult.
adusto, a [a'ðusto, a] *adj* stern; (*austero*) austere.
aduzca [a'ðuθka] *etc vb V* **aducir.**
advenedizo, a [aðβene'ðiθo, a] *nm/f* upstart.
advenimiento [aðβeni'mjento] *nm* arrival; (*al trono*) accession.
adverbio [að'βerβjo] *nm* adverb.
adversario, a [aðβer'sarjo, a] *nm/f* adversary.

adversidad [aðβersi'ðað] *nf* adversity; (*contratiempo*) setback.
adverso, a [að'βerso, a] *adj* adverse; (*suerte*) bad.
advertencia [aðβer'tenθja] *nf* warning; (*prefacio*) preface, foreword.
advertir [aðβer'tir] *vt* (*observar*) to notice; (*avisar*): ~ **a algn de** to warn sb about *o* of.
Adviento [að'βjento] *nm* Advent.
advierta [að'βjerta] *etc*, **advirtiendo** [aðβir'tjendo] *etc vb V* **advertir.**
adyacente [aðja'θente] *adj* adjacent.
aéreo, a [a'ereo, a] *adj* aerial; (*tráfico*) air *cpd*.
aerobic [ae'roβik] *nm* aerobics *sg*.
aerodeslizador [aeroðesliθa'ðor] *nm* hovercraft.
aerodinámico, a [aeroði'namiko, a] *adj* aerodynamic.
aeródromo [ae'roðromo] *nm* aerodrome.
aerograma [aero'ɤrama] *nm* airmail letter.
aeromodelismo [aeromoðe'lismo] *nm* model aircraft making, aeromodelling.
aeromozo, a [aero'moso, a] *nm/f* (AM) flight attendant, air steward(ess).
aeronáutico, a [aero'nautiko, a] *adj* aeronautical.
aeronave [aero'naβe] *nm* spaceship.
aeroplano [aero'plano] *nm* aeroplane.
aeropuerto [aero'pwerto] *nm* airport.
aerosol [aero'sol] *nm* aerosol, spray.
a/f *abr* (= *a favor*) in favour.
afabilidad [afaβili'ðað] *nf* affability, pleasantness.
afable [a'faβle] *adj* affable, pleasant.
afamado, a [afa'maðo, a] *adj* famous.
afán [a'fan] *nm* hard work; (*deseo*) desire; **con** ~ keenly.
afanar [afa'nar] *vt* to harass; (*fam*) to pinch; ~**se** *vr*: ~**se por** to strive to.
afanoso, a [afa'noso, a] *adj* (*trabajo*) hard; (*trabajador*) industrious.
AFE ['afe] *nf abr* (= *Asociación de Futbolistas Españoles*) ≈ F.A.
afear [afe'ar] *vt* to disfigure.
afección [afek'θjon] *nf* affection; (MED) disease.
afectación [afekta'θjon] *nf* affectation.
afectado, a [afek'taðo, a] *adj* affected.
afectar [afek'tar] *vt* to affect, have an effect on; (AM: *dañar*) to hurt; **por lo que afecta a esto** as far as this is concerned.
afectísimo, a [afek'tisimo, a] *adj* affectionate; **suyo** ~ yours truly.
afectivo, a [afek'tiβo, a] *adj* affective.
afecto, a [a'fekto, a] *adj*: ~ **a** fond of; (JUR)

subject to ♦ *nm* affection; **tenerle ~ a
algn** to be fond of sb.
afectuoso, a [afek'twoso, a] *adj*
affectionate.
afeitar [afei'tar] *vt* to shave; **~se** *vr* to
shave.
afeminado, a [afemi'naðo, a] *adj*
effeminate.
aferrar [afe'rrar] *vt* to moor; (*fig*) to grasp
♦ *vi* to moor; **~se** *vr* (*agarrarse*) to cling on;
~se a un principio to stick to a principle;
~se a una esperanza to cling to a hope.
affmo., a. *abr* (= *afectísimo, a*) Yours.
Afganistán [afɣanis'tan] *nm* Afghanistan.
afgano, a [af'ɣano, a] *adj, nm/f* Afghan.
afiance [a'fjanθe] *etc vb* V **afianzar.**
afianzamiento [afjanθa'mjento] *nm*
strengthening; security.
afianzar [afjan'θar] *vt* to strengthen,
secure; **~se** *vr* to steady o.s.;
(*establecerse*) to become established.
afiche [a'fitʃe] *nm* (*AM*) poster.
afición [afi'θjon] *nf*: **~ a** fondness o liking
for; **la ~** the fans *pl*; **pinto por ~** I paint
as a hobby.
aficionado, a [afiθjo'naðo, a] *adj* keen,
enthusiastic; (*no profesional*) amateur
♦ *nm/f* enthusiast, fan; amateur.
aficionar [afiθjo'nar] *vt*: **~ a algn a algo** to
make sb like sth; **~se** *vr*: **~se a algo** to
grow fond of sth.
afilado, a [afi'laðo, a] *adj* sharp.
afilador [afila'ðor] *nm* (*persona*) knife
grinder.
afilalápices [afila'lapiθes] *nm inv* pencil
sharpener.
afilar [afi'lar] *vt* to sharpen; **~se** *vr* (*cara*) to
grow thin.
afiliación [afilja'θjon] *nf* (*de sindicatos*)
membership.
afiliado, a [afi'ljaðo, a] *adj* subsidiary
♦ *nm/f* affiliate.
afiliarse [afi'ljarse] *vr* to affiliate.
afín [a'fin] *adj* (*parecido*) similar; (*conexo*)
related.
afinar [afi'nar] *vt* (*TEC*) to refine; (*MUS*) to
tune ♦ *vi* to play/sing in tune.
afincarse [afin'karse] *vr* to settle.
afinidad [afini'ðað] *nf* affinity; (*parentesco*)
relationship; **por ~** by marriage.
afirmación [afirma'θjon] *nf* affirmation.
afirmar [afir'mar] *vt* to affirm, state;
(*sostener*) to strengthen; **~se** *vr* (*recuperar
el equilibrio*) to steady o.s.; **~se en lo
dicho** to stand by what one has said.
afirmativo, a [afirma'tiβo, a] *adj*
affirmative.
aflicción [aflik'θjon] *nf* affliction; (*dolor*)

grief.
afligir [afli'xir] *vt* to afflict; (*apenar*) to
distress; **~se** *vr*: **~se (por o con o de)** to
grieve (about o at); **no te aflijas tanto**
you must not let it affect you like this.
aflija [a'flixa] *etc vb* V **afligir.**
aflojar [aflo'xar] *vt* to slacken; (*desatar*) to
loosen, undo; (*relajar*) to relax ♦ *vi*
(*amainar*) to drop; (*bajar*) to go down; **~se**
vr to relax.
aflorar [aflo'rar] *vi* (*GEO, fig*) to come to the
surface, emerge.
afluencia [aflu'enθja] *nf* flow.
afluente [aflu'ente] *adj* flowing ♦ *nm* (*GEO*)
tributary.
afluir [aflu'ir] *vi* to flow.
afluya [a'fluja] *etc*, **afluyendo** [aflu'jendo]
etc vb V **afluir.**
afmo., a. *abr* (= *afectísimo, a suyo, a*)
Yours.
afónico, a [a'foniko, a] *adj*: **estar ~** to have
a sore throat; to have lost one's voice.
aforar [afo'rar] *vt* (*TEC*) to gauge; (*fig*) to
value.
aforo [a'foro] *nm* (*TEC*) gauging; (*de teatro
etc*) capacity; **el teatro tiene un ~ de
2,000** the theatre can seat 2,000.
afortunado, a [afortu'naðo, a] *adj*
fortunate, lucky.
afrancesado, a [afranθe'saðo, a] *adj*
francophile; (*pey*) Frenchified.
afrenta [a'frenta] *nf* affront, insult;
(*deshonra*) dishonour (*BRIT*), dishonor
(*US*), shame.
afrentoso, a [afren'toso, a] *adj* insulting;
shameful.
África ['afrika] *nf* Africa; **~ del Sur** South
Africa.
africano, a [afri'kano, a] *adj, nm/f* African.
afrontar [afron'tar] *vt* to confront; (*poner
cara a cara*) to bring face to face.
afuera [a'fwera] *adv* out, outside; **por ~** on
the outside; **~s** *nfpl* outskirts.
ag. *abr* (= *agosto*) Aug.
agachar [aɣa'tʃar] *vt* to bend, bow; **~se** *vr*
to stoop, bend.
agalla [a'ɣaʎa] *nf* (*ZOOL*) gill; **~s** *nfpl* (*MED*)
tonsillitis *sg*; (*ANAT*) tonsils; **tener ~s**
(*fam*) to have guts.
agarradera [aɣarra'ðera] *nf* (*AM*),
agarradero [aɣarra'ðero] *nm* handle; **~s**
nfpl pull *sg*, influence *sg*.
agarrado, a [aɣa'rraðo, a] *adj* mean,
stingy.
agarrar [aɣa'rrar] *vt* to grasp, grab; (*AM*) to
take, catch ♦ *vi* (*planta*) to take root; **~se**
vr to hold on (tightly); (*meterse uno con
otro*) to grapple (with each other);

agarrársela con algn (*AM*) to pick on sb; **agarró y se fue** (*esp AM fam*) he upped and went.

agarrotar [aɣarro'tar] *vt* (*lío*) to tie tightly; (*persona*) to squeeze tightly; (*reo*) to garrotte; ~**se** *vr* (*motor*) to seize up; (*MED*) to stiffen.

agasajar [aɣasa'xar] *vt* to treat well, fête.

agave [a'ɣaβe] *nf* agave.

agazapar [aɣaθa'par] *vt* (*coger*) to grab hold of; ~**se** *vr* (*agacharse*) to crouch down.

agencia [a'xenθja] *nf* agency; ~ **de créditos/publicidad/viajes** credit/ advertising/travel agency; ~ **inmobiliaria** estate agent's (office) (*BRIT*), real estate office (*US*); ~ **matrimonial** marriage bureau.

agenciar [axen'θjar] *vt* to bring about; ~**se** *vr* to look after o.s.; ~**se algo** to get hold of sth.

agenda [a'xenda] *nf* diary; ~ **telefónica** telephone directory.

agente [a'xente] *nm* agent; (*de policía*) policeman; ~ **femenino** policewoman; ~ **acreditado** (*COM*) accredited agent; ~ **de bolsa** stockbroker; ~ **inmobiliario** estate agent (*BRIT*), realtor (*US*); ~ **de negocios** (*COM*) business agent; ~ **de seguros** insurance broker; ~ **de viajes** travel agent; ~**s sociales** social partners.

ágil ['axil] *adj* agile, nimble.

agilidad [axili'ðað] *nf* agility, nimbleness.

agilizar [axili'θar] *vt* to speed up.

agitación [axita'θjon] *nf* (*de mano etc*) shaking, waving; (*de líquido etc*) stirring; agitation.

agitar [axi'tar] *vt* to wave, shake; (*líquido*) to stir; (*fig*) to stir up, excite; ~**se** *vr* to get excited; (*inquietarse*) to get worried *o* upset.

aglomeración [aɣlomera'θjon] *nf*: ~ **de tráfico/gente** traffic jam/mass of people.

aglomerar [aɣlome'rar] *vt*, ~**se** *vr* to crowd together.

agnóstico, a [aɣ'nostiko, a] *adj, nm/f* agnostic.

ag.º *abr* = ag.

agobiante [aɣo'βjante] *adj* (*calor*) oppressive.

agobiar [aɣo'βjar] *vt* to weigh down; (*oprimir*) to oppress; (*cargar*) to burden; **sentirse agobiado por** to be overwhelmed by.

agobio [a'ɣoβjo] *nm* (*peso*) burden; (*fig*) oppressiveness.

agolpamiento [aɣolpa'mjento] *nm* crush.

agolparse [aɣol'parse] *vr* to crowd together.

agonía [aɣo'nia] *nf* death throes *pl*; (*fig*) agony, anguish.

agonice [aɣo'niθe] *etc vb* V **agonizar**.

agonizante [aɣoni'θante] *adj* dying.

agonizar [aɣoni'θar] *vi* (*tb*: **estar agonizando**) to be dying.

agorero, a [aɣo'rero, a] *adj* ominous ♦ *nm/f* soothsayer; **ave agorera** bird of ill omen.

agostar [aɣo'star] *vt* (*quemar*) to parch; (*fig*) to wither.

agosto [a'ɣosto] *nm* August; (*fig*) harvest; **hacer su** ~ to make one's pile.

agotado, a [aɣo'taðo, a] *adj* (*persona*) exhausted; (*acabado*) finished; (*COM*) sold out; (: *libros*) out of print; (*pila*) flat.

agotador, a [aɣota'ðor, a] *adj* exhausting.

agotamiento [aɣota'mjento] *nm* exhaustion.

agotar [aɣo'tar] *vt* to exhaust; (*consumir*) to drain; (*recursos*) to use up, deplete; ~**se** *vr* to be exhausted; (*acabarse*) to run out; (*libro*) to go out of print.

agraciado, a [aɣra'θjaðo, a] *adj* (*atractivo*) attractive; (*en sorteo etc*) lucky.

agraciar [aɣra'θjar] *vt* (*JUR*) to pardon; (*con premio*) to reward; (*hacer más atractivo*) to make more attractive.

agradable [aɣra'ðaβle] *adj* pleasant, nice.

agradar [aɣra'ðar] *vt, vi* to please; ~**se** *vr* to like each other.

agradecer [aɣraðe'θer] *vt* to thank; (*favor etc*) to be grateful for; **le agradecería me enviara ...** I would be grateful if you would send me ...; ~**se** *vr*: **¡se agradece!** much obliged!

agradecido, a [aɣraðe'θiðo, a] *adj* grateful; **¡muy** ~**!** thanks a lot!

agradecimiento [aɣraðeθi'mjento] *nm* thanks *pl*; gratitude.

agradezca [aɣra'ðeθka] *etc vb* V **agradecer**.

agrado [a'ɣraðo] *nm*: **ser de tu** *etc* ~ to be to your *etc* liking.

agrandar [aɣran'dar] *vt* to enlarge; (*fig*) to exaggerate; ~**se** *vr* to get bigger.

agrario, a [a'ɣrarjo, a] *adj* agrarian, land *cpd*; (*política*) agricultural, farming *cpd*.

agravante [aɣra'βante] *adj* aggravating ♦ *nf* complication; **con la** ~ **de que ...** with the further difficulty that ...

agravar [aɣra'βar] *vt* (*pesar sobre*) to make heavier; (*irritar*) to aggravate; ~**se** *vr* to worsen, get worse.

agraviar [aɣra'βjar] *vt* to offend; (*ser injusto con*) to wrong; ~**se** *vr* to take offence.

agravio [a'ɣraβjo] *nm* offence; wrong;

(*JUR*) grievance.

agraz [a'ɤraθ] *nm* (*uva*) sour grape; **en ~** (*fig*) immature.

agredir [aɤre'ðir] *vt* to attack.

agregado [aɤre'ɤaðo] *nm* aggregate; (*persona*) attaché; (*profesor*) assistant professor.

agregar [aɤre'ɤar] *vt* to gather; (*añadir*) to add; (*persona*) to appoint.

agregue [a'ɤreɤe] *etc vb V* agregar.

agresión [aɤre'sjon] *nf* aggression; (*ataque*) attack.

agresivo, a [aɤre'siβo, a] *adj* aggressive.

agreste [a'ɤreste] *adj* (*rural*) rural; (*fig*) rough.

agriar [a'ɤrjar] *vt* (*fig*) to (turn) sour; **~se** *vr* to turn sour.

agrícola [a'ɤrikola] *adj* farming *cpd*, agricultural.

agricultor, a [aɤrikul'tor, a] *nm/f* farmer.

agricultura [aɤrikul'tura] *nf* agriculture, farming.

agridulce [aɤri'ðulθe] *adj* bittersweet; (*CULIN*) sweet and sour.

agrietarse [aɤrje'tarse] *vr* to crack; (*la piel*) to chap.

agrimensor, a [aɤrimen'sor, a] *nm/f* surveyor.

agringado, a [aɤrin'gaðo, a] *adj* gringolike.

agrio, a [a'ɤrjo, a] *adj* bitter.

agronomía [aɤrono'mia] *nf* agronomy, agriculture.

agrónomo, a [a'ɤronomo, a] *nm/f* agronomist, agricultural expert.

agropecuario, a [aɤrope'kwarjo, a] *adj* farming *cpd*, agricultural.

agrupación [aɤrupa'θjon] *nf* group; (*acto*) grouping.

agrupar [aɤru'par] *vt* to group; (*INFORM*) to block; **~se** *vr* (*POL*) to form a group; (*juntarse*) to gather.

agua ['aɤwa] *nf* water; (*NAUT*) wake; (*ARQ*) slope of a roof; **~s** *nfpl* (*de joya*) water *sg*, sparkle *sg*; (*MED*) water *sg*, urine *sg*; (*NAUT*) waters; **~s abajo/arriba** downstream/upstream; **~ bendita/ destilada/potable** holy/distilled/drinking water; **~ caliente** hot water; **~ corriente** running water; **~ de colonia** eau de cologne; **~ mineral (con/sin gas)** (fizzy/ non-fizzy) mineral water; **~s jurisdiccionales** territorial waters; **~s mayores** excrement *sg*; **~ pasada no mueve molino** it's no use crying over spilt milk; **estar con el ~ al cuello** to be up to one's neck; **venir como ~ de mayo** to be a godsend.

aguacate [aɤwa'kate] *nm* avocado (pear).

aguacero [aɤwa'θero] *nm* (heavy) shower, downpour.

aguachirle [aɤwa'tʃirle] *nm* (*bebida*) slops *pl*.

aguado, a [a'ɤwaðo, a] *adj* watery, watered down ♦ *nf* (*AGR*) watering place; (*NAUT*) water supply; (*ARTE*) watercolour.

aguafiestas [aɤwa'fjestas] *nm/f inv* spoilsport.

aguafuerte [aɤwa'fwerte] *nf* etching.

aguaitar [aɤwai'tar] *vt* (*AM*) to watch.

aguanieve [aɤwa'njeβe] *nf* sleet.

aguantable [aɤwan'taβle] *adj* bearable, tolerable.

aguantar [aɤwan'tar] *vt* to bear, put up with; (*sostener*) to hold up ♦ *vi* to last; **~se** *vr* to restrain o.s.; **no sé cómo aguanta** I don't know how he can take it.

aguante [a'ɤwante] *nm* (*paciencia*) patience; (*resistencia*) endurance; (*DEPORTE*) stamina.

aguar [a'ɤwar] *vt* to water down; (*fig*): **~ la fiesta a algn** to spoil sb's fun.

aguardar [aɤwar'ðar] *vt* to wait for.

aguardentoso, a [aɤwarðen'toso, a] *adj* (*pey: voz*) husky, gruff.

aguardiente [aɤwar'ðjente] *nm* brandy, liquor.

aguarrás [aɤwa'rras] *nm* turpentine.

aguce [a'ɤuθe] *etc vb V* aguzar.

agudeza [aɤu'ðeθa] *nf* sharpness; (*ingenio*) wit.

agudice [aɤu'ðiθe] *etc vb V* agudizar.

agudizar [aɤuði'θar] *vt* to sharpen; (*crisis*) to make worse; **~se** *vr* to worsen, deteriorate.

agudo, a [a'ɤuðo, a] *adj* sharp; (*voz*) high-pitched; (*dolor, enfermedad*) acute.

agüe ['aɤwe] *etc vb V* aguar.

agüero [a'ɤwero] *nm*: **buen/mal ~** good/ bad omen; **ser de buen ~** to augur well; **pájaro de mal ~** bird of ill omen.

aguerrido, a [aɤe'rriðo, a] *adj* hardened; (*fig*) experienced.

aguijar [aɤi'xar] *vt* to goad; (*incitar*) to urge on ♦ *vi* to hurry along.

aguijón [aɤi'xon] *nm* sting; (*fig*) spur.

aguijonear [aɤixone'ar] *vt* = aguijar.

águila ['aɤila] *nf* eagle; (*fig*) genius.

aguileño, a [aɤi'leɲo, a] *adj* (*nariz*) aquiline; (*rostro*) sharp-featured.

aguinaldo [aɤi'naldo] *nm* Christmas box.

aguja [a'ɤuxa] *nf* needle; (*de reloj*) hand; (*ARQ*) spire; (*TEC*) firing-pin; **~s** *nfpl* (*ZOOL*) ribs; (*FERRO*) points.

agujerear [aɣuxere'ar] *vt* to make holes in; (*penetrar*) to pierce.

agujero [aɣu'xero] *nm* hole; (*COM*) deficit.

agujetas [aɣu'xetas] *nfpl* stitch *sg*; (*rigidez*) stiffness *sg*.

aguzar [aɣu'θar] *vt* to sharpen; (*fig*) to incite; ~ **el oído** to prick up one's ears.

aherrumbrarse [aerrum'brarse] *vr* to get rusty.

ahí [a'i] *adv* there; (*allá*) over there; **de** ~ **que** so that, with the result that; ~ **llega** here he comes; **por** ~ (*dirección*) that way; **¡hasta** ~ **hemos llegado!** so it has come to this!; **¡**~ **va!** (*objeto*) here it comes!; (*individuo*) there he goes!; ~ **donde le ve** as sure as he's standing there.

ahijado, a [ai'xaðo, a] *nm/f* godson/daughter.

ahijar [ai'xar] *vt*: ~ **algo a algn** (*fig*) to attribute sth to sb.

ahínco [a'inko] *nm* earnestness; **con** ~ eagerly.

ahíto, a [a'ito, a] *adj*: **estoy** ~ I'm full up.

ahogado, a [ao'ɣaðo, a] *adj* (*en agua*) drowned; (*emoción*) pent-up; (*grito*) muffled.

ahogar [ao'ɣar] *vt* (*en agua*) to drown; (*asfixiar*) to suffocate, smother; (*fuego*) to put out; ~**se** *vr* (*en agua*) to drown; (*por asfixia*) to suffocate.

ahogo [a'oɣo] *nm* (*MED*) breathlessness; (*fig*) distress; (*problema económico*) financial difficulty.

ahogue [a'oɣe] *etc vb V* **ahogar**.

ahondar [aon'dar] *vt* to deepen, make deeper; (*fig*) to go deeply into ♦ *vi*: ~ **en** to go deeply into.

ahora [a'ora] *adv* now; (*hace poco*) a moment ago, just now; (*dentro de poco*) in a moment; ~ **voy** I'm coming; ~ **mismo** right now; ~ **bien** now then; **por** ~ for the present.

ahorcado, a [aor'kaðo, a] *nm/f* hanged person.

ahorcar [aor'kar] *vt* to hang; ~**se** *vr* to hang o.s.

ahorita [ao'rita], **ahoritita** [aori'tita] *adv* (*esp AM*: *fam*) right now.

ahorque [a'orke] *etc vb V* **ahorcar**.

ahorrar [ao'rrar] *vt* (*dinero*) to save; (*esfuerzos*) to save, avoid; ~**se** *vr*: ~**se molestias** to save o.s. trouble.

ahorrativo, a [aorra'tiβo, a] *adj* thrifty.

ahorro [a'orro] *nm* (*acto*) saving; (*frugalidad*) thrift; ~**s** *nmpl* savings.

ahuecar [awe'kar] *vt* to hollow (out); (*voz*) to deepen ♦ *vi*: **¡ahueca!** (*fam*) beat it!

(*fam*); ~**se** *vr* to give o.s. airs.

ahueque [a'weke] *etc vb V* **ahuecar**.

ahumar [au'mar] *vt* to smoke, cure; (*llenar de humo*) to fill with smoke ♦ *vi* to smoke; ~**se** *vr* to fill with smoke.

ahuyentar [aujen'tar] *vt* to drive off, frighten off; (*fig*) to dispel.

AI *nf abr* (= *Amnistía Internacional*) AI.

aimara [ai'mara], **aimará** [aima'ra] *adj, nm/f* Aymara.

aindiado, a [aindi'aðo, a] *adj* (*AM*) Indian-like.

airado, a [ai'raðo, a] *adj* angry.

airar [ai'rar] *vt* to anger; ~**se** *vr* to get angry.

aire ['aire] *nm* air; (*viento*) wind; (*corriente*) draught; (*MUS*) tune; ~**s** *nmpl*: **darse** ~**s** to give o.s. airs; **al** ~ **libre** in the open air; ~ **acondicionado** air conditioning; **tener** ~ **de** to look like; **estar de buen/mal** ~ to be in a good/bad mood; **estar en el** ~ (*RADIO*) to be on the air; (*fig*) to be up in the air.

airear [aire'ar] *vt* to ventilate; (*fig*: *asunto*) to air; ~**se** *vr* to take the air.

airoso, a [ai'roso, a] *adj* windy; draughty; (*fig*) graceful.

aislado, a [ais'laðo, a] *adj* (*remoto*) isolated; (*incomunicado*) cut off; (*ELEC*) insulated.

aislante [ais'lante] *nm* (*ELEC*) insulator.

aislar [ais'lar] *vt* to isolate; (*ELEC*) to insulate; ~**se** *vr* to cut o.s. off.

ajar [a'xar] *vt* to spoil; (*fig*) to abuse; ~**se** *vr* to get crumpled; (*fig*: *piel*) to get wrinkled.

ajardinado, a [axarði'naðo, a] *adj* landscaped.

ajedrez [axe'ðreθ] *nm* chess.

ajenjo [a'xenxo] *nm* (*bebida*) absinth(e).

ajeno, a [a'xeno, a] *adj* (*que pertenece a otro*) somebody else's; ~ **a** foreign to; ~ **de** free from, devoid of; **por razones ajenas a nuestra voluntad** for reasons beyond our control.

ajetreado, a [axetre'aðo, a] *adj* busy.

ajetrearse [axetre'arse] *vr* (*atarearse*) to bustle about; (*fatigarse*) to tire o.s. out.

ajetreo [axe'treo] *nm* bustle.

ají [a'xi] *nm* chil(l)i, red pepper; (*salsa*) chil(l)i sauce.

ajiaco [axi'ako] *nm* (*AM*) potato and chil(l)i stew.

ajilimoje [axili'moxe] *nm* sauce of garlic and pepper; ~**s** *nmpl* (*fam*) odds and ends.

ajo ['axo] *nm* garlic; ~ **porro** *o* **puerro** leek; **(tieso) como un** ~ (*fam*) snobbish; **estar**

en el ~ to be mixed up in it.

ajorca [a'xorka] *nf* bracelet.

ajuar [a'xwar] *nm* household furnishings *pl*; (*de novia*) trousseau; (*de niño*) layette.

ajustado, a [axus'taðo, a] *adj* (*tornillo*) tight; (*cálculo*) right; (*ropa*) tight(-fitting); (*DEPORTE*: *resultado*) close.

ajustar [axus'tar] *vt* (*adaptar*) to adjust; (*encajar*) to fit; (*TEC*) to engage; (*TIP*) to make up; (*apretar*) to tighten; (*concertar*) to agree (on); (*reconciliar*) to reconcile; (*cuenta*) to settle ♦ *vi* to fit.

ajuste [a'xuste] *nm* adjustment; (*COSTURA*) fitting; (*acuerdo*) compromise; (*de cuenta*) settlement; (*INFORM*) patch.

al [al] = **a + el**; *V* **a**.

ala ['ala] *nf* wing; (*de sombrero*) brim; (*futbolista*) winger; ~ **delta** hang-glider; **andar con el** ~ **caída** to be downcast; **cortar las** ~**s a algn** to clip sb's wings; **dar** ~**s a algn** to encourage sb.

alabanza [ala'ßanθa] *nf* praise.

alabar [ala'ßar] *vt* to praise.

alacena [ala'θena] *nf* cupboard (*BRIT*), closet (*US*).

alacrán [ala'kran] *nm* scorpion.

ALADI [a'laði] *nf abr* = **Asociación Latinoamericana de Integración**.

alado, a [a'laðo, a] *adj* winged.

ALALC [n'lnlk] *nf abr* (= **Asociación Latinoamericana de Libre Comercio**) LAFTA.

alambicado, a [alambi'kaðo, a] *adj* distilled; (*fig*) affected.

alambicar [alambi'kar] *vt* to distil.

alambique [alam'bike] *etc vb V* **alambicar** ♦ *nm* still.

alambrada [alam'braða] *nf*, **alambrado** [alam'braðo] *nm* wire fence; (*red*) wire netting.

alambre [a'lambre] *nm* wire; ~ **de púas** barbed wire.

alambrista [alam'brista] *nm/f* tightrope walker.

alameda [ala'meða] *nf* (*plantío*) poplar grove; (*lugar de paseo*) avenue, boulevard.

álamo ['alamo] *nm* poplar; ~ **temblón** aspen.

alano [a'lano] *nm* mastiff.

alarde [a'larðe] *nm* show, display; **hacer** ~ **de** to boast of.

alardear [alarðe'ar] *vi* to boast.

alargador [alarxa'ðor] *nm* extension cable *o* lead.

alargar [alar'xar] *vt* to lengthen, extend; (*paso*) to hasten; (*brazo*) to stretch out; (*cuerda*) to pay out; (*conversación*) to spin

out; ~**se** *vr* to get longer.

alargue [a'larxe] *etc vb V* **alargar**.

alarido [ala'riðo] *nm* shriek.

alarma [a'larma] *nf* alarm; **voz de** ~ warning note; **dar la** ~ to raise the alarm.

alarmante [alar'mante] *adj* alarming.

alarmar [alar'mar] *vt* to alarm; ~**se** *vr* to get alarmed.

alavés, esa [ala'ßes, esa] *adj* of Álava ♦ *nm/f* native *o* inhabitant of Álava.

alazán [ala'θan] *nm* sorrel.

alba ['alßa] *nf* dawn.

albacea [alßa'θea] *nm/f* executor/executrix.

albaceteño, a [alßaθe'teɲo, a] *adj* of Albacete ♦ *nm/f* native *o* inhabitant of Albacete.

albahaca [al'ßaka] *nf* (*BOT*) basil.

Albania [al'ßanja] *nf* Albania.

albañal [alßa'ɲal] *nm* drain, sewer.

albañil [alßa'ɲil] *nm* bricklayer; (*cantero*) mason.

albarán [alßa'ran] *nm* (*COM*) invoice.

albarda [al'ßarða] *nf* packsaddle.

albaricoque [alßari'koke] *nm* apricot.

albedrío [alße'ðrio] *nm*: **libre** ~ free will.

alberca [al'ßerka] *nf* reservoir; (*AM*) swimming pool.

albergar [alßer'xar] *vt* to shelter; (*esperanza*) to cherish; ~**se** *vr* (*refugiarse*) to shelter; (*alojarse*) to lodge.

albergue [al'ßerxe] *etc vb V* **albergar** ♦ *nm* shelter, refuge; ~ **de juventud** youth hostel.

albis ['alßis] *adv*: **quedarse en** ~ not to have a clue.

albóndiga [al'ßondixa] *nf* meatball.

albor [al'ßor] *nm* whiteness; (*amanecer*) dawn.

alborada [alßo'raða] *nf* dawn; (*diana*) reveille.

alborear [alßore'ar] *vi* to dawn.

albornoz [alßor'noθ] *nm* (*de los árabes*) burnous; (*para el baño*) bathrobe.

alboroce [alßo'roθe] *etc vb V* **alborozar**.

alborotar [alßoro'tar] *vi* to make a row ♦ *vt* to agitate, stir up; ~**se** *vr* to get excited; (*mar*) to get rough.

alboroto [alßo'roto] *nm* row, uproar.

alborozar [alßoro'θar] *vt* to gladden; ~**se** *vr* to rejoice, be overjoyed.

alborozo [alßo'roθo] *nm* joy.

albricias [al'ßriθjas] *nfpl*: ¡~! good news!

álbum, *pl* **álbums** *o* **álbumes** ['alßum] *nm* album.

albumen [al'ßumen] *nm* egg white, albumen.

alcabala [alka'ßala] *nf* (*AM*) roadblock.

alcachofa [alka't∫ofa] *nf* (globe) artichoke; (*TIP*) golf ball; (*de ducha*) shower head.
alcahueta [alka'weta] *nf* procuress.
alcahuete [alka'wete] *nm* pimp.
alcalde, esa [al'kalde, alkal'desa] *nm/f* mayor(ess).
alcaldía [alkal'dia] *nf* mayoralty; (*lugar*) mayor's office.
álcali ['alkali] *nm* (*QUÍMICA*) alkali.
alcance [al'kanθe] *etc vb V* **alcanzar ♦** *nm* (*MIL, RADIO*) range; (*fig*) scope; (*COM*) adverse balance, deficit; **estar al/fuera del ~ de algn** to be within/beyond one's reach; (*fig*) to be within one's powers/ over one's head; **de gran ~** (*MIL*) long-range; (*fig*) far-reaching.
alcancía [alkan'θia] *nf* money box.
alcanfor [alkan'for] *nm* camphor.
alcantarilla [alkanta'riʎa] *nf* (*de aguas cloacales*) sewer; (*en la calle*) gutter.
alcanzar [alkan'θar] *vt* (*algo: con la mano, el pie*) to reach; (*alguien: en el camino etc*) to catch up (with); (*autobús*) to catch; (*suj: bala*) to hit, strike ♦ *vi* (*ser suficiente*) to be enough; **~ algo a algn** to hand sth to sb; **alcánzame la sal, por favor** pass the salt please; **~ a hacer** to manage to do.
alcaparra [alka'parra] *nf* (*BOT*) caper.
alcatraz [alka'traθ] *nm* gannet.
alcayata [alka'jata] *nf* hook.
alcázar [al'kaθar] *nm* fortress; (*NAUT*) quarter-deck.
alce ['alθe] *etc vb V* **alzar**.
alcista [al'θista] *adj* (*COM, ECON*): **mercado ~** bull market; **la tendencia ~** the upward trend ♦ *nm* speculator.
alcoba [al'koβa] *nf* bedroom.
alcohol [al'kol] *nm* alcohol; **no bebe ~** he doesn't drink (alcohol).
alcoholemia [alkoo'lemia] *nf* blood alcohol level; **prueba de la ~** breath test.
alcoholice [alko'liθe] *etc vb V* **alcoholizarse**.
alcohólico, a [al'koliko, a] *adj, nm/f* alcoholic.
alcoholímetro [alko'limetro] *nm* Breathalyser ®, drunkometer (*US*).
alcoholismo [alko'lismo] *nm* alcoholism.
alcoholizarse [alkoli'θarse] *vr* to become an alcoholic.
alcornoque [alkor'noke] *nm* cork tree; (*fam*) idiot.
alcotana [alko'tana] *nf* pickaxe; (*DEPORTE*) ice-axe.
alcurnia [al'kurnja] *nf* lineage.
alcuza [al'kusa] *nf* (*AM*) cruet.
aldaba [al'daβa] *nf* (door) knocker.
aldea [al'dea] *nf* village.

aldeano, a [alde'ano, a] *adj* village *cpd* ♦ *nm/f* villager.
ale ['ale] *excl* come on!, let's go!
aleación [alea'θjon] *nf* alloy.
aleatorio, a [alea'torjo, a] *adj* random, contingent; **acceso ~** (*INFORM*) random access.
aleccionador, a [alekθjona'ðor, a] *adj* instructive.
aleccionar [alekθjo'nar] *vt* to instruct; (*adiestrar*) to train.
aledaño, a [ale'ðaɲo, a] *adj*: **~ a** bordering on ♦ *nmpl*: **~s** outskirts.
alegación [aleɣa'θjon] *nf* allegation.
alegar [ale'ɣar] *vt* (*dificultad etc*) to plead; (*JUR*) to allege ♦ *vi* (*AM*) to argue; **~ que** ... to give as an excuse that ...
alegato [ale'ɣato] *nm* (*JUR*) allegation; (*escrito*) indictment; (*declaración*) statement; (*AM*) argument.
alegoría [aleɣo'ria] *nf* allegory.
alegrar [ale'ɣrar] *vt* (*causar alegría*) to cheer (up); (*fuego*) to poke; (*fiesta*) to liven up; **~se** *vr* (*fam*) to get merry *o* tight; **~se de** to be glad about.
alegre [a'leɣre] *adj* happy, cheerful; (*fam*) merry, tight; (*licencioso*) risqué, blue.
alegría [ale'ɣria] *nf* happiness; merriment; **~ vital** joie de vivre.
alegrón [ale'ɣron] *nm* (*fig*) sudden joy.
alegue [a'leɣe] *etc vb V* **alegar**.
alejamiento [alexa'mjento] *nm* removal; (*distancia*) remoteness.
alejar [ale'xar] *vt* to move away, remove; (*fig*) to estrange; **~se** *vr* to move away.
alelado, a [ale'laðo, a] *adj* (*bobo*) foolish.
alelar [ale'lar] *vt* to bewilder.
aleluya [ale'luja] *nm* (*canto*) hallelujah.
alemán, ana [ale'man, ana] *adj, nm/f* German ♦ *nm* (*lengua*) German.
Alemania [ale'manja] *nf* Germany; **~ Occidental/Oriental** West/East Germany.
alentador, a [alenta'ðor, a] *adj* encouraging.
alentar [alen'tar] *vt* to encourage.
alergia [a'lerxja] *nf* allergy.
alero [a'lero] *nm* (*de tejado*) eaves *pl*; (*de foca, DEPORTE*) flipper; (*AUTO*) mudguard.
alerta [a'lerta] *adj inv, nm* alert.
aleta [a'leta] *nf* (*de pez*) fin; (*de ave*) wing; (*de coche*) mudguard.
aletargar [aletar'ɣar] *vt* to make drowsy; (*entumecer*) to make numb; **~se** *vr* to grow drowsy; to become numb.
aletargue [ale'tarɣe] *etc vb V* **aletargar**.
aletear [alete'ar] *vi* to flutter; (*ave*) to flap its wings; (*individuo*) to wave one's arms.

alevín [ale'ßin] nm fry, young fish.

alevosía [aleßo'sia] nf treachery.

alfabetización [alfaßetiθa'θjon] nf: campaña de ~ literacy campaign.

alfabeto [alfa'ßeto] nm alphabet.

alfajor [alfa'xor] nm (ESP: polvorón) cake eaten at Christmas time.

alfalfa [al'falfa] nf alfalfa, lucerne.

alfaque [al'fake] nm (NAUT) bar, sandbank.

alfar [al'far] nm (taller) potter's workshop; (arcilla) clay.

alfarería [alfare'ria] nf pottery; (tienda) pottery shop.

alfarero [alfa'rero] nm potter.

alféizar [al'feiθar] nm window-sill.

alférez [al'fereθ] nm (MIL) second lieutenant, (NAUT) ensign.

alfil [al'fil] nm (AJEDREZ) bishop.

alfiler [alfi'ler] nm pin; (broche) clip; (pinza) clothes peg (BRIT) o pin (US); ~ de gancho (AM) safety pin; **prendido con** ~**es** shaky.

alfiletero [alfile'tero] nm needle case.

alfombra [al'fombra] nf carpet; (más pequeña) rug.

alfombrar [alfom'brar] vt to carpet.

alfombrilla [alfom'briʎa] nf rug, mat; (INFORM) mouse mat o pad.

alforja [al'forxa] nf saddlebag.

alforza [al'forθa] nf pleat.

algarabía [alɣara'ßia] nf (fam) gibberish; (griterío) hullabaloo.

algarada [alɣa'raða] nf outcry; **hacer** o **levantar una** ~ to kick up a tremendous fuss.

Algarbe [al'ɣarße] nm: **el** ~ the Algarve.

algarroba [alɣa'rroßa] nf carob.

algarrobo [alɣa'rroßo] nm carob tree.

algas ['alɣas] nfpl seaweed sg.

algazara [alɣa'θara] nf din, uproar.

álgebra ['alxeßra] nf algebra.

álgido, a ['alxiðo, a] adj icy; (momento etc) crucial, decisive.

algo ['alɣo] pron something; (en frases interrogativas) anything ♦ adv somewhat, rather; **por** ~ **será** there must be some reason for it; **es** ~ **difícil** it's a bit awkward.

algodón [alɣo'ðon] nm cotton; (planta) cotton plant; ~ **de azúcar** candy floss (BRIT), cotton candy (US); ~ **hidrófilo** cotton wool (BRIT), absorbent cotton (US).

algodonero, a [alɣoðo'nero, a] adj cotton cpd ♦ nm/f cotton grower ♦ nm cotton plant.

algoritmo [alɣo'ritmo] nm algorithm.

alguacil [alɣwa'θil] nm bailiff; (TAUR) mounted official.

alguien ['alɣjen] pron someone, somebody; (en frases interrogativas) anybody.

alguno, a [al'ɣuno, a] adj (delante de nm: **algún**) some; (después de n): **no tiene talento alguno** he has no talent, he hasn't any talent ♦ pron (alguien) someone, somebody; **algún que otro libro** some book or other; **algún día iré** I'll go one o some day; **sin interés alguno** without the slightest interest; **alguno que otro** an occasional one; **algunos piensan** some (people) think; **alguno de ellos** one of them.

alhaja [a'laxa] nf jewel; (tesoro) precious object, treasure.

alhelí [ale'li] nm wallflower, stock.

aliado, a [a'ljaðo, a] adj allied.

alianza [a'ljanθa] nf (POL etc) alliance; (anillo) wedding ring.

aliar [a'ljar] vt to ally; ~**se** vr to form an alliance.

alias ['aljas] adv alias.

alicaído, a [alika'iðo, a] adj (MED) weak; (fig) depressed.

alicantino, a [alikan'tino, a] adj of Alicante ♦ nm/f native o inhabitant of Alicante.

alicatar [alika'tar] vt to tile.

alicate(s) [ali'kate(s)] nm(pl) pliers pl; ~ **de uñas** nail clippers.

aliciente [ali'θjente] nm incentive; (atracción) attraction.

alienación [aljena'θjon] nf alienation.

aliento [a'ljento] etc vb V **alentar** ♦ nm breath; (respiración) breathing; **sin** ~ breathless; **de un** ~ in one breath; (fig) in one go.

aligerar [alixe'rar] vt to lighten; (reducir) to shorten; (aliviar) to alleviate; (mitigar) to ease.

alijo [a'lixo] nm (NAUT) unloading; (contrabando) smuggled goods.

alimaña [ali'maɲa] nf pest.

alimentación [alimenta'θjon] nf (comida) food; (acción) feeding; (tienda) grocer's (shop); ~ **continua** (en fotocopiadora etc) stream feed.

alimentador [alimenta'ðor] nm: ~ **de papel** sheet-feeder.

alimentar [alimen'tar] vt to feed; (nutrir) to nourish; ~**se** vr: ~**se (de)** to feed (on).

alimenticio, a [alimen'tiθjo, a] adj food cpd; (nutritivo) nourishing, nutritious.

alimento [ali'mento] nm food; (nutrición) nourishment; ~**s** nmpl (JUR) alimony sg.

alimón [ali'mon]: **al** ~ adv jointly, together.

alineación [alinea'θjon] nf alignment; (DEPORTE) line-up.

alineado, a [aline'aðo, a] *adj* (*TIP*): **(no) ~** (un)justified; **~ a la izquierda/derecha** ranged left/right.

alinear [aline'ar] *vt* to align; (*TIP*) to justify; **~se** *vr* to line up; **~se en** to fall in with.

aliñar [ali'ɲar] *vt* (*CULIN*) to dress.

aliño [a'liɲo] *nm* (*CULIN*) dressing.

alisar [ali'sar] *vt* to smooth.

aliso [a'liso] *nm* alder.

alistamiento [alista'mjento] *nm* recruitment.

alistar [alis'tar] *vt* to recruit; **~se** *vr* to enlist; (*inscribirse*) to enrol; (*AM: prepararse*) to get ready.

aliviar [ali'βjar] *vt* (*carga*) to lighten; (*persona*) to relieve; (*dolor*) to relieve, alleviate.

alivio [a'liβjo] *nm* alleviation, relief; **~ de luto** half-mourning.

aljibe [al'xiβe] *nm* cistern.

allá [a'ʎa] *adv* (*lugar*) there; (*por ahí*) over there; (*tiempo*) then; **~ abajo** down there; **más ~** further on; **más ~ de** beyond; **¡~ tú!** that's your problem!

allanamiento [aʎana'mjento] *nm* (*AM POLICÍA*) raid, search; **~ de morada** housebreaking.

allanar [aʎa'nar] *vt* to flatten, level (out); (*igualar*) to smooth (out); (*fig*) to subdue; (*JUR*) to burgle, break into; (*AM POLICÍA*) to raid, search; **~se** *vr* to fall down; **~se a** to submit to, accept.

allegado, a [aʎe'ɣaðo, a] *adj* near, close ♦ *nm/f* relation.

allende [a'ʎende] *adv* on the other side ♦ *prep*: **~ los mares** beyond the seas.

allí [a'ʎi] *adv* there; **~ mismo** right there; **por ~** over there; (*por ese camino*) that way.

alma ['alma] *nf* soul; (*persona*) person; (*TEC*) core; **se le cayó el ~ a los pies** he became very disheartened; **entregar el ~** to pass away; **estar con el ~ en la boca** to be scared to death; **lo siento en el ~** I am truly sorry; **tener el ~ en un hilo** to have one's heart in one's mouth; **estar como ~ en pena** to suffer; **ir como ~ que lleva el diablo** to go at breakneck speed.

almacén [alma'θen] *nm* (*depósito*) warehouse, store; (*MIL*) magazine; (*AM*) grocer's shop, foodstore, grocery store (*US*); **(grandes) almacenes** *nmpl* department store *sg*; **~ depositario** (*COM*) depository.

almacenaje [almaθe'naxe] *nm* storage; **~ secundario** (*INFORM*) backing storage.

almacenamiento [almaθena'mjento] *nm* (*INFORM*) storage; **~ temporal en disco** disk spooling.

almacenar [almaθe'nar] *vt* to store, put in storage; (*INFORM*) to store; (*proveerse*) to stock up with.

almacenero [almaθe'nero] *nm* warehouseman; (*AM*) grocer, shopkeeper.

almanaque [alma'nake] *nm* almanac.

almeja [al'mexa] *nf* clam.

almenas [al'menas] *nfpl* battlements.

almendra [al'mendra] *nf* almond.

almendro [al'mendro] *nm* almond tree.

almeriense [alme'rjense] *adj* of Almería ♦ *nm/f* native *o* inhabitant of Almería.

almiar [al'mjar] *nm* haystack.

almíbar [al'miβar] *nm* syrup.

almidón [almi'ðon] *nm* starch.

almidonado, a [almiðo'naðo, a] *adj* starched.

almidonar [almiðo'nar] *vt* to starch.

almirantazgo [almiran'taɣo] *nm* admiralty.

almirante [almi'rante] *nm* admiral.

almirez [almi'reθ] *nm* mortar.

almizcle [al'miθkle] *nm* musk.

almizclero [almiθ'klero] *nm* musk deer.

almohada [almo'aða] *nf* pillow; (*funda*) pillowcase.

almohadilla [almoa'ðiʎa] *nf* cushion; (*TEC*) pad; (*AM*) pincushion.

almohadillado, a [almoaði'ʎaðo, a] *adj* (*acolchado*) padded.

almohadón [almoa'ðon] *nm* large pillow.

almorcé [almor'θe], **almorcemos** [almor'θemos] *etc vb V* **almorzar**.

almorranas [almo'rranas] *nfpl* piles, haemorrhoids (*BRIT*), hemorrhoids (*US*).

almorzar [almor'θar] *vt*: **~ una tortilla** to have an omelette for lunch ♦ *vi* to (have) lunch.

almuerce [al'mwerθe] *etc vb V* **almorzar**.

almuerzo [al'mwerθo] *etc vb V* **almorzar** ♦ *nm* lunch.

aló [a'lo] *excl* (*esp AM TELEC*) hello!

alocado, a [alo'kaðo, a] *adj* crazy.

alojamiento [aloxa'mjento] *nf* lodging(s) (*pl*); (*viviendas*) housing.

alojar [alo'xar] *vt* to lodge; **~se en** to stay at; (*bala*) to lodge in.

alondra [a'londra] *nf* lark, skylark.

alpaca [al'paka] *nf* alpaca.

alpargata [alpar'ɣata] *nf* espadrille.

Alpes ['alpes] *nmpl*: **los ~** the Alps.

alpinismo [alpi'nismo] *nm* mountaineering, climbing.

alpinista [alpi'nista] *nm/f* mountaineer, climber.

alpino, a [al'pino, a] *adj* alpine.
alpiste [al'piste] *nm* (*semillas*) birdseed; (*AM fam*: *dinero*) dough; (*fam*: *alcohol*) booze.
alquería [alke'ria] *nf* farmhouse.
alquilar [alki'lar] *vt* (*suj*: *propietario*: *inmuebles*) to let, rent (out); (: *coche*) to hire out; (: *TV*) to rent (out); (*suj*: *alquilador*: *inmuebles*, *TV*) to rent; (: *coche*) to hire; "**se alquila casa**" "house to let (*BRIT*) o to rent (*US*)"
alquiler [alki'ler] *nm* renting, letting; hiring; (*arriendo*) rent; hire charge; **de ~** for hire; **~ de automóviles** car hire.
alquimia [al'kimja] *nf* alchemy.
alquitrán [alki'tran] *nm* tar.
alrededor [alreðe'ðor] *adv* around, about; **~es** *nmpl* surroundings; **~ de** *prep* around, about; **mirar a su ~** to look (round) about one.
Alsacia [al'saθja] *nf* Alsace.
alta ['alta] *nf* (*certificate of*) discharge; **dar a algn de ~** to discharge sb; **darse de ~** (*MIL*) to join, enrol; (*DEPORTE*) to declare o.s. fit.
altanería [altane'ria] *nf* haughtiness, arrogance.
altanero, a [alta'nero, a] *adj* haughty, arrogant.
altar [al'tar] *nm* altar.
altavoz [alta'βoθ] *nm* loudspeaker; (*amplificador*) amplifier.
alteración [altera'θjon] *nf* alteration; (*alboroto*) disturbance; **~ del orden público** breach of the peace.
alterar [alte'rar] *vt* to alter; to disturb; **~se** *vr* (*persona*) to get upset.
altercado [alter'kaðo] *nm* argument.
alternar [alter'nar] *vt* to alternate ♦ *vi*, **~se** *vr* to alternate; (*turnar*) to take turns; **~ con** to mix with.
alternativo, a [alterna'tiβo, a] *adj* alternative; (*alterno*) alternating ♦ *nf* alternative; (*elección*) choice; **alternativas** *nfpl* ups and downs; **tomar la alternativa** (*TAUR*) to become a fully-qualified bullfighter.
alterno, a [al'terno, a] *adj* (*BOT, MAT*) alternate; (*ELEC*) alternating.
alteza [al'teθa] *nf* (*tratamiento*) highness.
altibajos [alti'βaxos] *nmpl* ups and downs.
altillo [al'tiʎo] *nm* (*GEO*) small hill; (*AM*) attic.
altiplanicie [altipla'niθje] *nf*, **altiplano** [alti'plano] *nm* high plateau.
altisonante [altiso'nante] *adj* high-flown, high-sounding.
altitud [alti'tuð] *nf* altitude, height; **a una**

~ de at a height of.
altivez [alti'βeθ] *nf* haughtiness, arrogance.
altivo, a [al'tiβo, a] *adj* haughty, arrogant.
alto, a ['alto, a] *adj* high; (*persona*) tall; (*sonido*) high, sharp; (*noble*) high, lofty; (*GEO, clase*) upper ♦ *nm* halt; (*MUS*) alto; (*GEO*) hill; (*AM*) pile ♦ *adv* (*estar*) high; (*hablar*) loud, loudly ♦ *excl* halt!; **la pared tiene 2 metros de ~** the wall is 2 metres high; **en alta mar** on the high seas; **en voz alta** in a loud voice; **las altas horas de la noche** the small (*BRIT*) o wee (*US*) hours; **en lo ~ de** at the top of; **pasar por ~** to overlook; **~s y bajos** ups and downs; **poner la radio más ~** to turn the radio up; **¡más ~, por favor!** louder, please!
altoparlante [altopar'lante] *nm* (*AM*) loudspeaker.
altramuz [altra'muθ] *nm* lupin.
altruismo [al'truismo] *nm* altruism.
altura [al'tura] *nf* height; (*NAUT*) depth; (*GEO*) latitude; **la pared tiene 1.80 de ~** the wall is 1 metre 80 (cm) high; **a esta ~ del año** at this time of the year; **estar a la ~ de las circunstancias** to rise to the occasion; **ha sido un partido de gran ~** it has been a terrific match.
alubia [a'luβja] *nf* French bean, kidney bean.
alucinación [aluθina'θjon] *nf* hallucination.
alucinante [aluθi'nante] *adj* (*fam*: *estupendo*) great, super.
alucinar [aluθi'nar] *vi* to hallucinate ♦ *vt* to deceive; (*fascinar*) to fascinate.
alud [a'luð] *nm* avalanche; (*fig*) flood.
aludir [alu'ðir] *vi*: **~ a** to allude to; **darse por aludido** to take the hint; **no te des por aludido** don't take it personally.
alumbrado [alum'braðo] *nm* lighting.
alumbramiento [alumbra'mjento] *nm* lighting; (*MED*) childbirth, delivery.
alumbrar [alum'brar] *vt* to light (up) ♦ *vi* (*iluminar*) to give light; (*MED*) to give birth.
aluminio [alu'minjo] *nm* aluminium (*BRIT*), aluminum (*US*).
alumnado [alum'naðo] *nm* (*UNIV*) student body; (*ESCOL*) pupils *pl*.
alumno, a [a'lumno, a] *nm/f* pupil, student.
alunice [alu'niθe] *etc vb V* **alunizar**.
alunizar [aluni'θar] *vi* to land on the moon.
alusión [alu'sjon] *nf* allusion.
alusivo, a [alu'siβo, a] *adj* allusive.
aluvión [alu'βjon] *nm* (*GEO*) alluvium; (*fig*) flood; **~ de improperios** torrent of abuse.
alvéolo [al'βeolo] *nm* (*ANAT*) alveolus; (*fig*)

network.

alza ['alθa] *nf* rise; (*MIL*) sight; ~**s fijas/ graduables** fixed/adjustable sights; **al** *o* **en** ~ (*precio*) rising; **jugar al** ~ **to** speculate on a rising *o* bull market; **cotizarse** *o* **estar en** ~ to be rising.

alzado, a [al'θaðo, a] *adj* (*gen*) raised; (*COM*: *precio*) fixed; (: *quiebra*) fradulent; **por un tanto** ~ for a lump sum ♦ *nf* (*de caballos*) height; (*JUR*) appeal.

alzamiento [alθa'mjento] *nm* (*aumento*) rise, increase; (*acción*) lifting, raising; (*mejor postura*) higher bid; (*rebelión*) rising; (*COM*) fraudulent bankruptcy.

alzar [al'θar] *vt* to lift (up); (*precio, muro*) to raise; (*cuello de abrigo*) to turn up; (*AGR*) to gather in; (*TIP*) to gather; ~**se** *vr* to get up, rise; (*rebelarse*) to revolt; (*COM*) to go fraudulently bankrupt; (*JUR*) to appeal; ~**se con el premio** to carry off the prize.

a.m. *abr* (*AM*: = *ante meridiem*) a.m.

ama ['ama] *nf* lady of the house; (*dueña*) owner; (*institutriz*) governess; (*madre adoptiva*) foster mother; ~ **de casa** housewife; ~ **de cría** *o* **de leche** wet-nurse; ~ **de llaves** housekeeper.

amabilidad [amaβili'ðað] *nf* kindness; (*simpatía*) niceness.

amabilísimo, a [amaβi'lisimo, a] *adj* *superlativo de* **amable**.

amable [a'maβle] *adj* kind; nice.

amaestrado, a [amaes'traðo, a] *adj* (*animal*) trained; (: *en circo etc*) performing.

amaestrar [amaes'trar] *vt* to train.

amagar [ama'ɣar] *vt, vi* to threaten.

amago [a'maɣo] *nm* threat; (*gesto*) threatening gesture; (*MED*) symptom.

amague [a'maɣe] *etc vb V* **amagar**.

amainar [amai'nar] *vt* (*NAUT*) to lower, take in; (*fig*) to calm ♦ *vi*, ~**se** *vr* to drop, die down; **el viento amaina** the wind is dropping.

amalgama [amal'ɣama] *nf* amalgam.

amalgamar [amalɣa'mar] *vt* to amalgamate; (*combinar*) to combine, mix.

amamantar [amaman'tar] *vt* to suckle, nurse.

amancebarse [amanθe'βarse] *vr* (*pareja*) to live together.

amanecer [amane'θer] *vi* to dawn; (*fig*) to appear, begin to show ♦ *nm* dawn; **el niño amaneció afiebrado** the child woke up with a fever.

amanerado, a [amane'raðo, a] *adj* affected.

amanezca [ama'neθka] *etc vb V* **amanecer**.

amansar [aman'sar] *vt* to tame; (*persona*) to subdue; ~**se** *vr* (*persona*) to calm down.

amante [a'mante] *adj*: ~ **de** fond of ♦ *nm/f* lover.

amanuense [ama'nwense] *nm* (*escribiente*) scribe; (*copista*) copyist; (*POL*) secretary.

amañar [ama'ɲar] *vt* (*gen*) to do skilfully; (*pey: resultado*) to alter.

amaño [a'maɲo] *nm* (*habilidad*) skill; ~**s** *nmpl* (*TEC*) tools; (*fig*) tricks.

amapola [ama'pola] *nf* poppy.

amar [a'mar] *vt* to love.

amargado, a [amar'ɣaðo, a] *adj* bitter; embittered.

amargar [amar'ɣar] *vt* to make bitter; (*fig*) to embitter; ~**se** *vr* to become embittered.

amargo, a [a'marɣo, a] *adj* bitter.

amargor [amar'ɣor] *nm* (*sabor*) bitterness; (*fig*) grief.

amargue [a'marɣe] *etc vb V* **amargar**.

amargura [amar'ɣura] *nf* = **amargor**.

amarillento, a [amari'ʎento, a] *adj* yellowish; (*tez*) sallow.

amarillismo [amari'ʎismo] *nm* (*de prensa*) sensationalist journalism.

amarillo, a [ama'riʎo, a] *adj*, *nm* yellow.

amarra [a'marra] *nf* (*NAUT*) mooring line; ~**s** *nfpl* (*fig*) protection *sg*; **tener buenas** ~**s** to have good connections; **soltar** ~**s** to set off.

amarrar [ama'rrar] *vt* to moor; (*sujetar*) to tie up.

amartillar [amarti'ʎar] *vt* (*fusil*) to cock.

amasar [ama'sar] *vt* to knead; (*mezclar*) to mix, prepare; (*confeccionar*) to concoct.

amasijo [ama'sixo] *nm* kneading; mixing; (*fig*) hotchpotch.

amateur ['amatur] *nm/f* amateur.

amatista [ama'tista] *nf* amethyst.

amazacotado, a [amaθako'taðo, a] *adj* (*terreno, arroz etc*) lumpy.

amazona [ama'θona] *nf* horsewoman.

Amazonas [ama'θonas] *nm*: **el (Río)** ~ the Amazon.

ambages [am'baxes] *nmpl*: **sin** ~ in plain language.

ámbar ['ambar] *nm* amber.

Amberes [am'beres] *nm* Antwerp.

ambición [ambi'θjon] *nf* ambition.

ambicionar [ambiθjo'nar] *vt* to aspire to.

ambicioso, a [ambi'θjoso, a] *adj* ambitious.

ambidextro, a [ambi'ðekstro, a] *adj* ambidextrous.

ambientación [ambjenta'θjon] *nf* (*CINE, LIT etc*) setting; (*RADIO etc*) sound effects *pl*.

ambientador [ambjenta'ðor] *nm* air freshener.

ambientar [ambjen'tar] *vt* (*gen*) to give an atmosphere to; (*LIT etc*) to set.

ambiente [am'bjente] *nm* (*tb fig*) atmosphere; (*medio*) environment; (*AM*) room.

ambigüedad [ambiɣwe'ðað] *nf* ambiguity.

ambiguo, a [am'biɣwo, a] *adj* ambiguous.

ámbito ['ambito] *nm* (*campo*) field; (*fig*) scope.

ambos, as ['ambos, as] *adj pl, pron pl* both.

ambulancia [ambu'lanθja] *nf* ambulance.

ambulante [ambu'lante] *adj* travelling, itinerant; (*biblioteca*) mobile.

ambulatorio [ambula'torio] *nm* state health-service clinic.

ameba [a'meßa] *nf* amoeba.

amedrentar [ameðren'tar] *vt* to scare.

amén [a'men] *excl* amen; ~ **de** *prep* besides, in addition to; **en un decir** ~ in the twinkling of an eye; **decir** ~ **a todo** to have no mind of one's own.

amenace [ame'naθe] *etc vb V* **amenazar**.

amenaza [ame'naθa] *nf* threat.

amenazar [amena'θar] *vt* to threaten ♦ *vi*: ~ **con hacer** to threaten to do.

amenidad [ameni'ðað] *nf* pleasantness.

ameno, a [a'meno, a] *adj* pleasant.

América [a'merika] *nf* (*continente*) America, the Americas; (*EEUU*) America; (*Hispanoa~*) Latin *o* South America; ~ **del Norte/del Sur** North/South America; ~ **Central/Latina** Central/Latin America.

americanismo [amerika'nismo] *nm* Americanism.

americano, a [ameri'kano, a] *adj, nm/f* (*V* **América**) American; Latin *o* South American ♦ *nf* coat, jacket.

americe [ame'riθe] *etc vb V* **amerizar**.

amerindio, a [ame'rindjo, a] *adj, nm/f* Amerindian, American Indian

amerizaje [ameri'θaxe] *nm* (*AVIAT*) landing (on the sea).

amerizar [ameri'θar] *vi* (*AVIAT*) to land (on the sea).

ametralladora [ametraʎa'ðora] *nf* machine gun.

amianto [a'mjanto] *nm* asbestos.

amigable [ami'ɣaßle] *adj* friendly.

amígdala [a'miɣðala] *nf* tonsil.

amigdalitis [amiɣða'litis] *nf* tonsillitis.

amigo, a [a'miɣo, a] *adj* friendly ♦ *nm/f* friend; (*amante*) lover; ~ **de lo ajeno** thief; ~ **corresponsal** penfriend; **hacerse** ~**s** to become friends; **ser** ~ **de** to like, be fond of; **ser muy** ~**s** to be close friends.

amigote [ami'ɣote] *nm* mate (*BRIT*), buddy.

amilanar [amila'nar] *vt* to scare; ~**se** *vr* to get scared.

aminorar [amino'rar] *vt* to diminish; (*reducir*) to reduce; ~ **la marcha** to slow down.

amistad [amis'tað] *nf* friendship; ~**es** *nfpl* friends.

amistoso, a [ami'stoso, a] *adj* friendly.

amnesia [am'nesja] *nf* amnesia.

amnistía [amnis'tia] *nf* amnesty.

amnistiar [amnis'tjar] *vt* to amnesty, grant an amnesty to.

amo ['amo] *nm* owner; (*jefe*) boss.

amodorrarse [amoðo'rrarse] *vr* to get sleepy.

amolar [amo'lar] *vt* to annoy.

amoldar [amol'dar] *vt* to mould; (*adaptar*) to adapt.

amonestación [amonesta'θjon] *nf* warning; **amonestaciones** *nfpl* marriage banns.

amonestar [amone'star] *vt* to warn; to publish the banns of.

amoniaco [amo'njako] *nm* ammonia.

amontonar [amonto'nar] *vt* to collect, pile up; ~**se** *vr* (*gente*) to crowd together; (*acumularse*) to pile up; (*datos*) to accumulate; (*desastres*) to come one on top of another.

amor [a'mor] *nm* love; (*amante*) lover; **hacer el** ~ to make love; ~ **interesado** cupboard love; ~ **propio** self-respect; **por (el)** ~ **de Dios** for God's sake; **estar al** ~ **de la lumbre** to be close to the fire.

amoratado, a [amora'taðo, a] *adj* purple, blue with cold; (*con cardenales*) bruised.

amordace [amor'ðaθe] *etc vb V* **amordazar**.

amordazar [amorða'θar] *vt* to muzzle; (*fig*) to gag.

amorfo, a [a'morfo, a] *adj* amorphous, shapeless.

amorío [amo'rio] *nm* (*fam*) love affair.

amoroso, a [amo'roso, a] *adj* affectionate, loving.

amortajar [amorta'xar] *vt* (*fig*) to shroud.

amortice [amor'tiθe] *etc vb V* **amortizar**.

amortiguador [amortiɣwa'ðor] *nm* shock absorber; (*parachoques*) bumper; (*silenciador*) silencer; ~**es** *nmpl* (*AUTO*) suspension *sg*.

amortiguar [amorti'ɣwar] *vt* to deaden; (*ruido*) to muffle; (*color*) to soften.

amortigüe [amor'tiɣwe] *etc vb V* **amortiguar**.

amortización [amortiθa'θjon] *nf* redemption; repayment; (*COM*) capital allowance.

amortizar [amorti'θar] *vt* (*ECON: bono*) to redeem; (: *capital*) to write off; (: *préstamo*) to pay off.

amoscarse [amos'karse] *vr* to get cross.

amosque [a'moske] *etc vb* V **amoscarse**.

amotinar [amoti'nar] *vt* to stir up, incite (to riot); ~**se** *vr* to mutiny.

amparar [ampa'rar] *vt* to protect; ~**se** *vr* to seek protection; (*de la lluvia etc*) to shelter.

amparo [am'paro] *nm* help, protection; **al ~ de** under the protection of.

amperímetro [ampe'rimetro] *nm* ammeter.

amperio [am'perjo] *nm* ampère, amp.

ampliable [am'pljaßle] *adj* (*INFORM*) expandable.

ampliación [amplja'θjon] *nf* enlargement; (*extensión*) extension.

ampliar [am'pljar] *vt* to enlarge; to extend.

amplificación [amplifika'θjon] *nf* enlargement.

amplificador [amplifika'ðor] *nm* amplifier.

amplificar [amplifi'kar] *vt* to amplify.

amplifique [ampli'fike] *etc vb* V **amplificar**.

amplio, a ['ampljo, a] *adj* spacious; (*falda etc*) full; (*extenso*) extensive; (*ancho*) wide.

amplitud [ampli'tuð] *nf* spaciousness; extent; (*fig*) amplitude; ~ **de miras** broadmindedness; **de gran ~** far-reaching.

ampolla [am'poʎa] *nf* blister; (*MED*) ampoule.

ampolleta [ampo'ʎeta] *nf* (*AM*) (light) bulb.

ampuloso, a [ampu'loso, a] *adj* bombastic, pompous.

amputar [ampu'tar] *vt* to cut off, amputate.

amueblar [amwe'ßlar] *vt* to furnish.

amuleto [amu'leto] *nm* (lucky) charm.

amurallar [amura'ʎar] *vt* to wall up *o* in.

anacarado, a [anaka'raðo, a] *adj* mother-of-pearl *cpd*.

anacardo [ana'karðo] *nm* cashew (nut).

anaconda [ana'konda] *nf* anaconda.

anacronismo [anakro'nismo] *nm* anachronism.

ánade ['anaðe] *nm* duck.

anagrama [ana'ɣrama] *nm* anagram.

anales [a'nales] *nmpl* annals.

analfabetismo [analfaße'tismo] *nm* illiteracy.

analfabeto, a [analfa'ßeto, a] *adj, nm/f* illiterate.

analgésico [anal'xesiko] *nm* painkiller, analgesic.

analice [ana'liθe] *etc vb* V **analizar**.

análisis [a'nalisis] *nm inv* analysis; ~ **de costos-beneficios** cost-benefit analysis; ~ **de mercados** market research; ~ **de sangre** blood test.

analista [ana'lista] *nm/f* (*gen*) analyst; (*POL, HISTORIA*) chronicler; ~ **de sistemas** (*INFORM*) systems analyst.

analizar [anali'θar] *vt* to analyse.

analogía [analo'xia] *nf* analogy; **por ~ con** on the analogy of.

analógico, a [ana'loxiko, a] *adj* analogue.

análogo, a [a'naloxo, a] *adj* analogous, similar.

ananá(s) [ana'na(s)] *nm* pineapple.

anaquel [ana'kel] *nm* shelf.

anaranjado, a [anaran'xaðo, a] *adj* orange (-coloured).

anarquía [anar'kia] *nf* anarchy.

anarquismo [anar'kismo] *nm* anarchism.

anarquista [anar'kista] *nm/f* anarchist.

anatematizar [anatemati'θar] *vt* (*REL*) to anathematize; (*fig*) to curse.

anatemice [anate'miθe] *etc vb* V **anatemizar**.

anatomía [anato'mia] *nf* anatomy.

anca ['anka] *nf* rump, haunch; ~**s** *nfpl* (*fam*) behind *sg*; **llevar a algn en** ~**s** to carry sb behind one.

ancestral [anθes'tral] *adj* (*costumbre*) age-old.

ancho, a ['antʃo, a] *adj* wide; (*falda*) full; (*fig*) liberal ♦ *nm* width; (*FERRO*) gauge; **le viene muy ~ el cargo** (*fig*) the job is too much for him; **ponerse ~** to get conceited; **quedarse tan ~** to go on as if nothing had happened; **estar a sus anchas** to be at one's ease.

anchoa [an'tʃoa] *nf* anchovy.

anchura [an'tʃura] *nf* width; (*extensión*) wideness.

anchuroso, a [antʃu'roso, a] *adj* wide.

anciano, a [an'θjano, a] *adj* old, aged ♦ *nm/f* old man/woman ♦ *nm* elder.

ancla ['ankla] *nf* anchor; **levar** ~**s** to weigh anchor.

ancladero [ankla'ðero] *nm* anchorage.

anclar [an'klar] *vi* to (drop) anchor.

andadas [an'daðas] *nfpl* (*aventuras*) adventures; **volver a las** ~ to backslide.

andaderas [anda'ðeras] *nfpl* baby-walker *sg*.

andadura [anda'ðura] *nf* gait; (*de caballo*) pace.

Andalucía [andalu'θia] *nf* Andalusia.

andaluz, a [anda'luθ, a] *adj, nm/f* Andalusian.

andamio [an'damjo] *nm*, **andamiaje** [anda'mjaxe] *nm* scaffold(ing).

andanada [anda'naða] *nf* (*fig*) reprimand;
soltarle a algn una ~ to give sb a rocket.

andante [an'dante] *adj*: **caballero ~** knight
errant.

andar [an'dar] *vt* to go, cover, travel ♦ *vi* to
go, walk, travel; (*funcionar*) to go, work;
(*estar*) to be ♦ *nm* walk, gait, pace; **~se** *vr*
(*irse*) to go away *o* off; **~ a pie/a
caballo/en bicicleta** to go on foot/on
horseback/by bicycle; ¡**anda**! (*sorpresa*)
go on!; **anda en** *o* **por los 40** he's about
40; ¿**en qué andas**? what are you up to?;
andamos mal de dinero/tiempo we're
badly off for money/we're short of time;
~se por las ramas to beat about the
bush; **no ~se con rodeos** to call a spade
a spade (*fam*); **todo se andará** all in good
time; **anda por aquí** it's round here
somewhere; **~ haciendo algo** to be doing
sth.

andariego, a [anda'rjeɣo, a] *adj* fond of
travelling.

andas ['andas] *nfpl* stretcher *sg*.

andén [an'den] *nm* (*FERRO*) platform;
(*NAUT*) quayside; (*AM*: *acera*) pavement
(*BRIT*), sidewalk (*US*).

Andes ['andes] *nmpl*: **los ~** the Andes.

andinismo [andin'ismo] *nm* (*AM*)
mountaineering, climbing.

andino, a [an'dino, a] *adj* Andean, of the
Andes.

Andorra [an'dorra] *nf* Andorra.

andrajo [an'draxo] *nm* rag.

andrajoso, a [andra'xoso, a] *adj* ragged.

andurriales [andu'rrjales] *nmpl* out-of-the-
way place *sg*, the sticks; **en esos ~** in
that godforsaken spot.

anduve [an'duβe], **anduviera** [andu'βjera]
etc vb V **andar**.

anécdota [a'nekðota] *nf* anecdote, story.

anegar [ane'xar] *vt* to flood; (*ahogar*) to
drown; **~se** *vr* to drown; (*hundirse*) to
sink.

anegue [a'neɣe] *etc vb V* **anegar**.

anejo, a [a'nexo, a] *adj* attached ♦ *nm* (*ARQ*)
annexe.

anemia [a'nemja] *nf* anaemia.

anestesia [anes'tesja] *nf* anaesthetic; **~
general/local** general/local anaesthetic.

anestesiar [aneste'sjar] *vt* to anaesthetize
(*BRIT*) anesthetize (*US*).

anestésico [anes'tesiko] *nm* anaesthetic.

anexar [anek'sar] *vt* to annex; (*documento*)
to attach; (*INFORM*) to append.

anexión [anek'sjon] *nf*, **anexionamiento**
[aneksjona'mjento] *nm* annexation.

anexionar [aneksjo'nar] *vt* to annex; **~se**
vr: **~ un país** to annex a country.

anexo, a [a'nekso, a] *adj* attached ♦ *nm*
annexe.

anfetamina [anfeta'mina] *nf*
amphetamine.

anfibio, a [an'fiβjo, a] *adj* amphibious ♦ *nm*
amphibian.

anfiteatro [anfite'atro] *nm* amphitheatre;
(*TEAT*) dress circle.

anfitrión, ona [anfi'trjon, ona] *nm/f*
host(ess).

ángel ['anxel] *nm* angel; **~ de la guarda**
guardian angel; **tener ~** to have charm.

Ángeles ['anxeles] *nmpl*: **los ~** Los
Angeles.

angélico, a [an'xeliko, a], **angelical**
[anxeli'kal] *adj* angelic(al).

angina [an'xina] *nf* (*MED*): **~ de pecho**
angina; **tener ~s** to have a sore throat *o*
throat infection.

anglicano, a [angli'kano, a] *adj, nm/f*
Anglican.

anglicismo [angli'θismo] *nm* anglicism.

anglosajón, ona [anglosa'xon, 'xona] *adj,
nm/f* Anglo-Saxon.

Angola [an'gola] *nf* Angola.

angoleño, a [ango'leɲo, a] *adj, nm/f*
Angolan.

angosto, a [an'gosto, a] *adj* narrow.

anguila [an'gila] *nf* eel; **~s** *nfpl* slipway *sg*.

angula [an'gula] *nf* elver, baby eel.

ángulo ['angulo] *nm* angle; (*esquina*)
corner; (*curva*) bend.

angustia [an'gustja] *nf* anguish.

angustiar [angus'tjar] *vt* to distress,
grieve; **~se** *vr* to be distressed (*por* at, on
account of).

anhelante [ane'lante] *adj* eager; (*deseoso*)
longing.

anhelar [ane'lar] *vt* to be eager for; to long
for, desire ♦ *vi* to pant, gasp.

anhelo [a'nelo] *nm* eagerness; desire.

anhídrido [a'niðriðo] *nm*: **~ carbónico**
carbon dioxide.

anidar [ani'ðar] *vt* (*acoger*) to take in,
shelter ♦ *vi* to nest; (*fig*) to make one's
home.

anilina [ani'lina] *nf* aniline.

anilla [a'niʎa] *nf* ring; (**las**) **~s** (*DEPORTE*)
the rings.

anillo [a'niʎo] *nm* ring; **~ de boda** wedding
ring; **~ de compromiso** engagement
ring; **venir como ~ al dedo** to suit to a
tee.

ánima ['anima] *nf* soul; **las ~s** the Angelus
(bell) *sg*.

animación [anima'θjon] *nf* liveliness;
(*vitalidad*) life; (*actividad*) bustle.

animado, a [ani'maðo, a] *adj* (*vivo*) lively;

(*vivaz*) animated; (*concurrido*) bustling; (*alegre*) in high spirits; **dibujos** ~**s** cartoon *sg*.

animador, a [anima'ðor, a] *nm/f* (*TV*) host(ess) ♦ *nf* (*DEPORTE*) cheerleader.

animadversión [animaðßer'sjon] *nf* ill-will, antagonism.

animal [ani'mal] *adj* animal; (*fig*) stupid ♦ *nm* animal; (*fig*) fool; (*bestia*) brute.

animalada [anima'laða] *nf* (*gen*) silly thing (to do *o* say); (*ultraje*) disgrace.

animar [ani'mar] *vt* (*BIO*) to animate, give life to; (*fig*) to liven up, brighten up, cheer up; (*estimular*) to stimulate; ~**se** *vr* to cheer up, feel encouraged; (*decidirse*) to make up one's mind.

ánimo ['animo] *nm* soul, mind; (*valentía*) courage ♦ *excl* cheer up!; **cobrar** ~ to take heart; **dar** ~**(s) a** to encourage.

animoso, a [ani'moso, a] *adj* brave; (*vivo*) lively.

aniñado, a [ani'ɲaðo, a] *adj* (*facción*) childlike; (*carácter*) childish.

aniquilar [aniki'lar] *vt* to annihilate, destroy.

anís [a'nis] *nm* (*grano*) aniseed; (*licor*) anisette.

aniversario [anißer'sarjo] *nm* anniversary.

Ankara [an'kara] *nf* Ankara.

ano ['ano] *nm* anus.

anoche [a'notʃe] *adv* last night; **antes de** ~ the night before last.

anochecer [anotʃe'θer] *vi* to get dark ♦ *nm* nightfall, dark; **al** ~ at nightfall.

anochezca [ano'tʃeθka] *etc vb V* **anochecer**.

anodino, a [ano'ðino, a] *adj* dull, anodyne.

anomalía [anoma'lia] *nf* anomaly.

anonadado, a [anona'ðaðo, a] *adj* stunned.

anonimato [anoni'mato] *nm* anonymity.

anónimo, a [a'nonimo, a] *adj* anonymous; (*COM*) limited ♦ *nm* (*carta*) anonymous letter; (: *maliciosa*) poison-pen letter.

anorak [ano'rak], *pl* **anoraks** *nm* anorak.

anorexia [ano'reksja] *nf* anorexia.

anormal [anor'mal] *adj* abnormal.

anotación [anota'θjon] *nf* note; annotation.

anotar [ano'tar] *vt* to note down; (*comentar*) to annotate.

anquilosado, a [ankilo'saðo, a] *adj* (*fig*) stale, out of date.

anquilosamiento [ankilosa'mjento] *nm* (*fig*) paralysis, stagnation.

ansia ['ansja] *nf* anxiety; (*añoranza*) yearning.

ansiar [an'sjar] *vt* to long for.

ansiedad [ansje'ðað] *nf* anxiety.

ansioso, a [an'sjoso, a] *adj* anxious;

(*anhelante*) eager; ~ **de** *o* **por algo** greedy for sth.

antagónico, a [anta'ɤoniko, a] *adj* antagonistic; (*opuesto*) contrasting.

antagonista [antaɤo'nista] *nm/f* antagonist.

antaño [an'taɲo] *adv* long ago.

Antártico [an'tartiko] *nm*: **el (océano)** ~ the Antarctic (Ocean).

Antártida [an'tartiða] *nf* Antarctica.

ante ['ante] *prep* before, in the presence of; (*encarado con*) faced with ♦ *nm* suede; ~ **todo** above all.

anteanoche [antea'notʃe] *adv* the night before last.

anteayer [antea'jer] *adv* the day before yesterday.

antebrazo [ante'ßraθo] *nm* forearm.

antecámara [ante'kamara] *nf* (*ARQ*) anteroom; (*antesala*) waiting room; (*POL*) lobby.

antecedente [anteθe'ðente] *adj* previous ♦ *nm*: ~**s** *nmpl* (*profesionales*) background *sg*; ~**s penales** criminal record; **no tener** ~**s** to have a clean record; **estar en** ~**s** to be well-informed; **poner a algn en** ~**s** to put sb in the picture.

anteceder [anteθe'ðer] *vt* to precede, go before.

antecesor, a [anteθe'sor, a] *nm/f* predecessor.

antedicho, a [ante'ðitʃo, a] *adj* aforementioned.

antelación [antela'θjon] *nf*: **con** ~ in advance.

antemano [ante'mano]: **de** ~ *adv* beforehand, in advance.

antena [an'tena] *nf* antenna; (*de televisión etc*) aerial.

anteojeras [anteo'xeras] *nfpl* blinkers (*BRIT*), blinders (*US*).

anteojo [ante'oxo] *nm* eyeglass; ~**s** *nmpl* (*esp AM*) glasses, spectacles.

antepasados [antepa'saðos] *nmpl* ancestors.

antepecho [ante'petʃo] *nm* guardrail, parapet; (*repisa*) ledge, sill.

antepondré [antepon'dre] *etc vb V* **anteponer**.

anteponer [antepo'ner] *vt* to place in front; (*fig*) to prefer.

anteponga [ante'ponɤa] *etc vb V* **anteponer**.

anteproyecto [antepro'jekto] *nm* preliminary sketch; (*fig*) blueprint; (*POL*): ~ **de ley** draft bill.

antepuesto, a [ante'pwesto, a] *pp de* **anteponer**.

antepuse [ante'puse] *etc vb V* **anteponer**.

anterior [ante'rjor] *adj* preceding, previous.

anterioridad [anterjori'ðað] *nf*: **con ~ a** prior to, before.

anteriormente [anterjor'mente] *adv* previously, before.

antes ['antes] *adv* sooner; (*primero*) first; (*con prioridad*) before; (*hace tiempo*) previously, once; (*más bien*) rather ♦ *prep*: ~ **de** before ♦ *conj*: ~ **(de) que** before; ~ **bien** (but) rather; **dos días** ~ two days before *o* previously; **mucho/poco** ~ long/shortly before; ~ **muerto que esclavo** better dead than enslaved; **tomo el avión** ~ **que el barco** I take the plane rather than the boat; **cuanto** ~, **lo** ~ **posible** as soon as possible; **cuanto** ~ **mejor** the sooner the better.

antesala [ante'sala] *nf* anteroom.

antiadherente [antiaðe'rente] *adj* nonstick.

antiaéreo, a [antia'ereo, a] *adj* antiaircraft.

antialcohólico, a [antial'koliko, a] *adj*: **centro** ~ (*MED*) detoxification unit.

antibalas [anti'ßalas] *adj inv*: **chaleco** ~ bulletproof jacket.

antibiótico [anti'ßjotiko] *nm* antibiotic.

anticiclón [antiθi'klon] *nm* (*METEOROLOGÍA*) anti-cyclone.

anticipación [antiθipa'θjon] *nf* anticipation; **con 10 minutos de** ~ 10 minutes early.

anticipado, a [antiθi'paðo, a] *adj* (in) advance; **por** ~ in advance.

anticipar [antiθi'par] *vt* to anticipate; (*adelantar*) to bring forward; (*COM*) to advance; **~se** *vr*: **~se a su época** to be ahead of one's time.

anticipo [anti'θipo] *nm* (*COM*) advance; *V tb* **anticipación**.

anticonceptivo, a [antikonθep'tißo, a] *adj*, *nm* contraceptive; **métodos ~s** contraceptive devices.

anticongelante [antikonxe'lante] *nm* antifreeze.

anticonstitucional [antikonstituθjo'nal] *adj* unconstitutional.

anticuado, a [anti'kwaðo, a] *adj* out-ofdate, old-fashioned; (*desusado*) obsolete.

anticuario [anti'kwarjo] *nm* antique dealer.

anticuerpo [anti'kwerpo] *nm* (*MED*) antibody.

antidemocrático, a [antiðemo'kratiko, a] *adj* undemocratic.

antideportivo, a [antiðepor'tißo, a] *adj* unsporting.

antidepresivo [antiðepre'sißo] *nm* antidepressant.

antideslumbrante [antiðeslum'brante] *adj* (*INFORM*) anti-dazzle.

antidoping [anti'ðopin] *adj inv* anti-drug.

antídoto [an'tiðoto] *nm* antidote.

antidroga [anti'ðroɤa] *adj inv* anti-drug; **brigada** ~ drug squad.

antiestético, a [anties'tetiko, a] *adj* unsightly.

antifaz [anti'faθ] *nm* mask; (*velo*) veil.

antigás [anti'gas] *adj inv*: **careta** ~ gasmask.

antigualla [anti'ɣwaʎa] *nf* antique; (*reliquia*) relic; **~s** *nfpl* old things.

antiguamente [antiɣwa'mente] *adv* formerly; (*hace mucho tiempo*) long ago.

antigüedad [antiɣwe'ðað] *nf* antiquity; (*artículo*) antique; (*rango*) seniority.

antiguo, a [an'tiɣwo, a] *adj* old, ancient; (*que fue*) former; **a la antigua** in the oldfashioned way.

antihigiénico, a [anti'xjeniko, a] *adj* unhygienic.

antihistamínico, a [antista'miniko, a] *adj*, *nm* antihistamine.

antiinflacionista [antinflaθjo'nista] *adj* anti-inflationary, counter-inflationary.

antillano, a [anti'ʎano, a] *adj*, *nm/f* West Indian.

Antillas [an'tiʎas] *nfpl*: **las** ~ the West Indies, the Antilles; **el mar de las** ~ the Caribbean Sea.

antílope [an'tilope] *nm* antelope.

antimonopolios [antimono'poljos] *adj inv*: **ley** ~ anti-trust law.

antinatural [antinatu'ral] *adj* unnatural.

antiparras [anti'parras] *nfpl* (*fam*) specs.

antipatía [antipa'tia] *nf* antipathy, dislike.

antipático, a [anti'patiko, a] *adj* disagreeable, unpleasant.

Antípodas [an'tipoðas] *nfpl*: **las** ~ the Antipodes.

antiquísimo, a [anti'kisimo, a] *adj* ancient.

antirreglamentario, a [antirreɣlamen 'tarjo, a] *adj* (*gen*) unlawful; (*POL etc*) unconstitutional.

antirrobo [anti'rroßo] *adj inv*: (*dispositivo*) ~ (*para casas etc*) burglar alarm; (*para coches*) car alarm.

antisemita [antise'mita] *adj* anti-Semitic ♦ *nm/f* anti-Semite.

antiséptico, a [anti'septiko, a] *adj*, *nm* antiseptic.

antiterrorista [antiterro'rista] *adj* antiterrorist; **la lucha** ~ the fight against terrorism.

antítesis [an'titesis] *nf inv* antithesis.

antojadizo, a [antoxa'ðiθo, a] *adj*

capricious.

antojarse [anto'xarse] _vr (desear)_: **se me antoja comprarlo** I have a mind to buy it; _(pensar)_: **se me antoja que** I have a feeling that.

antojo [an'toxo] _nm_ caprice, whim; _(rosa)_ birthmark; _(lunar)_ mole; **hacer a su ~ to** do as one pleases.

antología [antolo'xia] _nf_ anthology.

antonomasia [antono'masja] _nf_: **por ~ par** excellence.

antorcha [an'tortʃa] _nf_ torch.

antro ['antro] _nm_ cavern; **~ de corrupción** _(fig)_ den of iniquity.

antropófago, a [antro'pofaɣo, a] _adj, nm/f_ cannibal.

antropología [antropolo'xia] _nf_ anthropology.

antropólogo, a [antro'poloɣo, a] _nm/f_ anthropologist.

anual [a'nwal] _adj_ annual.

anualidad [anwali'ðað] _nf_ annuity, annual payment; **~ vitalicia** life annuity.

anuario [a'nwarjo] _nm_ yearbook.

anudar [anu'ðar] _vt_ to knot, tie; _(unir)_ to join; **~se** _vr_ to get tied up; **se me anudó la voz** I got a lump in my throat.

anulación [anula'θjon] _nf_ annulment; cancellation; repeal.

anular [anu'lar] _vt_ to annul, cancel; _(suscripción)_ to cancel; _(ley)_ to repeal ♦ _nm_ ring finger.

anunciación [anunθja'θjon] _nf_ announcement; **A~** _(REL)_ Annunciation.

anunciante [anun'θjante] _nm/f (COM)_ advertiser.

anunciar [anun'θjar] _vt_ to announce; _(proclamar)_ to proclaim; _(COM)_ to advertise.

anuncio [a'nunθjo] _nm_ announcement; _(señal)_ sign; _(COM)_ advertisement; _(cartel)_ poster; _(TEAT)_ bill; **~s por palabras** classified ads.

anverso [am'berso] _nm_ obverse.

anzuelo [an'θwelo] _nm_ hook; _(para pescar)_ fish hook; **tragar el ~ to** swallow the bait.

añadido [aɲa'ðiðo] _nm_ addition.

añadidura [aɲaði'ðura] _nf_ addition, extra; **por ~** besides, in addition.

añadir [aɲa'ðir] _vt_ to add.

añejo, a [a'ɲexo, a] _adj_ old; _(vino)_ vintage; _(jamón)_ well-cured.

añicos [a'ɲikos] _nmpl_: **hacer ~ to** smash, shatter; **hacerse ~ to** smash, shatter.

añil [a'ɲil] _nm (BOT, color)_ indigo.

año ['aɲo] _nm_ year; **¡Feliz A~ Nuevo!** Happy New Year!; **tener 15 ~s** to be 15

(years old); **los ~s 80** the eighties; **~ bisiesto/escolar** leap/school year; **~ fiscal** fiscal _o_ tax year; **estar de buen ~** to be in good shape; **en el ~ de la nana** in the year dot; **el ~ que viene** next year.

añoranza [aɲo'ranθa] _nf_ nostalgia; _(anhelo)_ longing.

añorar [aɲo'rar] _vt_ to long for.

añoso, a [a'ɲoso, a] _adj_ ancient, old.

aovado, a [ao'βaðo, a] _adj_ oval.

aovar [ao'βar] _vi_ to lay eggs.

apabullar [apaβu'ʎar] _vt (lit, fig)_ to crush.

apacentar [apaθen'tar] _vt_ to pasture, graze.

apacible [apa'θiβle] _adj_ gentle, mild.

apaciente [apa'θjente] _etc vb_ V **apacentar**.

apaciguar [apaθi'ɣwar] _vt_ to pacify, calm (down).

apacigüe [apa'θiɣwe] _etc vb_ V **apaciguar**.

apadrinar [apaðri'nar] _vt_ to sponsor, support; _(REL)_ to act as godfather to.

apagado, a [apa'ɣaðo, a] _adj (volcán)_ extinct; _(color)_ dull; _(voz)_ quiet; _(sonido)_ muted, muffled; _(persona: apático)_ listless; **estar ~** _(fuego, luz)_ to be out; _(radio, TV etc)_ to be off.

apagar [apa'ɣar] _vt_ to put out; _(color)_ to tone down; _(sonido)_ to silence, muffle; _(sed)_ to quench; _(INFORM)_ to toggle off; **~se** _vr (luz, fuego)_ to go out; _(sonido)_ to die away; _(pasión)_ to wither; **~ el sistema** _(INFORM)_ to close _o_ shut down.

apagón [apa'ɣon] _nm_ blackout, power cut.

apague [a'paɣe] _etc vb_ V **apagar**.

apaisado, a [apai'saðo, a] _adj (papel)_ landscape _cpd_.

apalabrar [apala'βrar] _vt_ to agree to; _(obrero)_ to engage.

Apalaches [apa'latʃes] _nmpl_: **(Montes) ~** Appalachians.

apalear [apale'ar] _vt_ to beat, thrash; _(AGR)_ to winnow.

apañado, a [apa'ɲaðo, a] _adj (mañoso)_ resourceful; _(arreglado)_ tidy; _(útil)_ handy.

apañar [apa'ɲar] _vt_ to pick up; _(asir)_ to take hold of, grasp; _(reparar)_ to mend, patch up; **~se** _vr_ to manage, get along; **apañárselas por su cuenta** to look after number one _(fam)_.

apaño [a'paɲo] _nm (COSTURA)_ patch; _(maña)_ skill; **esto no tiene ~** there's no answer to this one.

aparador [apara'ðor] _nm_ sideboard; _(escaparate)_ shop window.

aparato [apa'rato] _nm_ apparatus; _(máquina)_ machine; _(doméstico)_ appliance; _(boato)_ ostentation; _(INFORM)_

device; ~ **de facsímil** facsimile
(machine), fax; ~ **respiratorio**
respiratory system; ~**s de mando** (*AVIAT
etc*) controls.
aparatoso, a [apara'toso, a] *adj* showy,
ostentatious.
aparcamiento [aparka'mjento] *nm* car
park (*BRIT*), parking lot (*US*).
aparcar [apar'kar] *vt, vi* to park.
aparear [apare'ar] *vt* (*objetos*) to pair,
match; (*animales*) to mate; ~**se** *vr* to form
a pair; to mate.
aparecer [apare'θer] *vi*, ~**se** *vr* to appear;
apareció borracho he turned up drunk.
aparejado, a [apare'xaðo, a] *adj* fit,
suitable; **ir** ~ **con** to go hand in hand
with; **llevar** *o* **traer** ~ to involve.
aparejador, a [aparexa'ðor, a] *nm/f* (*ARQ*)
quantity surveyor.
aparejar [apare'xar] *vt* to prepare; (*caballo*)
to saddle, harness; (*NAUT*) to fit out, rig
out.
aparejo [apa'rexo] *nm* preparation; (*de
caballo*) harness; (*NAUT*) rigging; (*de
poleas*) block and tackle.
aparentar [aparen'tar] *vt* (*edad*) to look;
(*fingir*): ~ **tristeza** to pretend to be sad.
aparente [apa'rente] *adj* apparent;
(*adecuado*) suitable.
aparezca [apa'reθka] *etc vb V* **aparecer**.
aparición [apari'θjon] *nf* appearance; (*de
libro*) publication; (*fantasma*) spectre.
apariencia [apa'rjenθja] *nf* (outward)
appearance; **en** ~ outwardly, seemingly.
aparque [a'parke] *etc vb V* **aparcar**.
apartado, a [apar'taðo, a] *adj* separate;
(*lejano*) remote ♦ *nm* (*tipográfico*) paragraph; ~ **(de correos)** post office box.
apartamento [aparta'mento] *nm*
apartment, flat (*BRIT*).
apartamiento [aparta'mjento] *nm*
separation; (*aislamiento*) remoteness;
(*AM*) apartment, flat (*BRIT*).
apartar [apar'tar] *vt* to separate; (*quitar*) to
remove; (*MINERALOGÍA*) to extract; ~**se** *vr*
(*separarse*) to separate, part; (*irse*) to move
away; (*mantenerse aparte*) to keep away.
aparte [a'parte] *adv* (*separadamente*)
separately; (*además*) besides ♦ *prep*: ~ **de**
apart from ♦ *nm* (*TEAT*) aside;
(*tipográfico*) new paragraph; **"punto y ~"**
"new paragraph".
apasionado, a [apasjo'naðo, a] *adj*
passionate; (*pey*) biassed, prejudiced
♦ *nm/f* admirer.
apasionante [apasjo'nante] *adj* exciting.
apasionar [apasjo'nar] *vt* to arouse passion in; ~**se** *vr* to get excited; **le apasiona**

el fútbol she's crazy about football.
apatía [apa'tia] *nf* apathy.
apático, a [a'patiko, a] *adj* apathetic.
apátrida [a'patriða] *adj* stateless.
Apdo. *nm abr* (= *Apartado (de Correos)*)
P.O. Box.
apeadero [apea'ðero] *nm* halt, stopping
place.
apearse [ape'arse] *vr* (*jinete*) to dismount;
(*bajarse*) to get down *o* out; (*de coche*) to
get out, alight; **no** ~ **del burro** to refuse
to climb down.
apechugar [apetʃu'xar] *vi*: ~ **con algo** to
face up to sth.
apechugue [ape'tʃuxe] *etc vb V* **apechugar**.
apedrear [apeðre'ar] *vt* to stone.
apegarse [ape'sarse] *vr*: ~ **a** to become
attached to.
apego [a'peɣo] *nm* attachment, devotion.
apegue [a'peɣe] *etc vb V* **apegarse**.
apelación [apela'θjon] *nf* appeal.
apelar [ape'lar] *vi* to appeal; ~ **a** (*fig*) to
resort to.
apelativo [apela'tiβo] *nm* (*LING*)
appellative; (*AM*) surname.
apellidar [apeʎi'ðar] *vt* to call, name; ~**se**
vr: **se apellida Pérez** her (sur)name's
Pérez.
apellido [ape'ʎiðo] *nm* surname; *see boxed
note.*

APELLIDO

*In the Spanish-speaking world most
people use two surnames, or* **apellidos**;
*the first is their father's first family name,
and the second their mother's first family
name. For example, if Juan García López
married Carmen Pérez Rodríguez, their
children's surname would be García Pérez.
Married women retain their own
surname(s) and sometimes add their
husband's first surname to theirs: Carmen
Pérez de García. This woman could also be
referred to as (la) Señora de García. In
Latin America the second surname is
usually shortened to an initial in
correspondence: Juan García L.*

---

apelmazado, a [apelma'θaðo, a] *adj*
compact, solid.
apelotonar [apeloto'nar] *vt* to roll into a
ball; ~**se** *vr* (*gente*) to crowd together.
apenar [ape'nar] *vt* to grieve, trouble; (*AM:
avergonzar*) to embarrass; ~**se** *vr* to
grieve; (*AM*) to be embarrassed.
apenas [a'penas] *adv* scarcely, hardly
♦ *conj* as soon as, no sooner.

apéndice [a'pendiθe] *nm* appendix.
apendicitis [apendi'θitis] *nf* appendicitis.
Apeninos [ape'ninos] *nmpl* Apennines.
apercibimiento [aperθißi'mjento] *nm*
(*aviso*) warning.
apercibir [aperθi'ßir] *vt* to prepare; (*avisar*)
to warn; (*JUR*) to summon; (*AM*) to
notice, see; ~**se** *vr* to get ready; ~**se de**
to notice.
aperitivo [aperi'tißo] *nm* (*bebida*) aperitif;
(*comida*) appetizer.
apero [a'pero] *nm* (*AGR*) implement; ~**s**
nmpl farm equipment *sg*.
apertura [aper'tura] *nf* (*gen*) opening; (*POL*)
openness, liberalization; (*TEAT etc*)
beginning; ~ **de un juicio hipotecario**
(*COM*) foreclosure.
aperturismo [apertu'rismo] *nm* (*POL*)
(policy of) liberalization.
apesadumbrar [apesaðum'brar] *vt* to
grieve, sadden; ~**se** *vr* to distress o.s.
apestar [apes'tar] *vt* to infect ♦ *vi*: ~ (**a**) to
stink (of).
apestoso, a [apes'toso, a] *adj* (*hediondo*)
stinking; (*asqueroso*) sickening.
apetecer [apete'θer] *vt*: **¿te apetece una
tortilla?** do you fancy an omelette?
apetecible [apete'θißle] *adj* desirable;
(*comida*) tempting.
apetezca [ape'teθka] *etc vb V* **apetecer.**
apetito [ape'tito] *nm* appetite.
apetitoso, a [apeti'toso, a] *adj* (*gustoso*)
appetizing; (*fig*) tempting.
apiadarse [apja'ðarse] *vr*: ~ **de** to take pity
on.
ápice ['apiθe] *nm* apex; (*fig*) whit, iota; **ni
un** ~ not a whit; **no ceder un** ~ not to
budge an inch.
apicultor, a [apikul'tor, a] *nm/f* beekeeper,
apiarist.
apicultura [apikul'tura] *nf* beekeeping.
apiladora [apila'ðora] *nf* (*para máquina
impresora*) stacker.
apilar [api'lar] *vt* to pile o heap up; ~**se** *vr*
to pile up.
apiñado, a [api'ɲaðo, a] *adj* (*apretado*)
packed.
apiñar [api'ɲar] *vt* to crowd; ~**se** *vr* to
crowd o press together.
apio ['apjo] *nm* celery.
apisonadora [apisona'ðora] *nf* (*máquina*)
steamroller.
aplacar [apla'kar] *vt* to placate; ~**se** *vr* to
calm down.
aplace [a'plaθe] *etc vb V* **aplazar.**
aplanamiento [aplana'mjento] *nm*
smoothing, levelling.
aplanar [apla'nar] *vt* to smooth, level;

(*allanar*) to roll flat, flatten; ~**se** *vr*
(*edificio*) to collapse; (*persona*) to get
discouraged.
aplaque [a'plake] *etc vb V* **aplacar.**
aplastar [aplas'tar] *vt* to squash (flat); (*fig*)
to crush.
aplatanarse [aplata'narse] *vr* to get
lethargic.
aplaudir [aplau'ðir] *vt* to applaud.
aplauso [a'plauso] *nm* applause; (*fig*)
approval, acclaim.
aplazamiento [aplaθa'mjento] *nm*
postponement.
aplazar [apla'θar] *vt* to postpone, defer.
aplicación [aplika'θjon] *nf* application;
(*esfuerzo*) effort; **aplicaciones de gestión**
business applications.
aplicado, a [apli'kaðo, a] *adj* diligent,
hard-working.
aplicar [apli'kar] *vt* (*gen*) to apply; (*poner
en vigor*) to put into effect; (*esfuerzos*) to
devote; ~**se** *vr* to apply o.s.
aplique [a'plike] *etc vb V* **aplicar** ♦ *nm* wall
light o lamp.
aplomo [a'plomo] *nm* aplomb, self-
assurance.
apocado, a [apo'kaðo, a] *adj* timid.
apocamiento [apoka'mjento] *nm* timidity;
(*depresión*) depression.
apocarse [apo'karse] *vr* to feel small o
humiliated.
apocopar [apoko'par] *vt* (*LING*) to shorten.
apócope [a'pokope] *nf* apocopation; **gran
es** ~ **de grande** "gran" is the shortened
form of "grande".
apócrifo, a [a'pokrifo, a] *adj* apocryphal.
apodar [apo'ðar] *vt* to nickname.
apoderado [apoðe'raðo] *nm* agent,
representative.
apoderar [apoðe'rar] *vt* to authorize,
empower; (*JUR*) to grant (a) power of
attorney to; ~**se** *vr*: ~**se de** to take
possession of.
apodo [a'poðo] *nm* nickname.
apogeo [apo'xeo] *nm* peak, summit.
apolillado, a [apoli'ʎaðo, a] *adj* moth-
eaten.
apolillarse [apoli'ʎarse] *vr* to get moth-
eaten.
apología [apolo'xia] *nf* eulogy; (*defensa*)
defence.
apoltronarse [apoltro'narse] *vr* to get lazy.
apoplejía [apople'xia] *nf* apoplexy, stroke.
apoque [a'poke] *etc vb V* **apocar.**
apoquinar [apoki'nar] *vt* (*fam*) to cough
up, fork out.
aporrear [aporre'ar] *vt* to beat (up).
aportación [aporta'θjon] *nf* contribution.

aportar [apor'tar] vt to contribute ♦ vi to reach port.

aposentar [aposen'tar] vt to lodge, put up.

aposento [apo'sento] nm lodging; (habitación) room.

apósito [a'posito] nm (MED) dressing.

apostar [apos'tar] vt to bet, stake; (tropas etc) to station, post ♦ vi to bet.

aposta(s) [a'posta(s)] adv on purpose.

apostatar [aposta'tar] vi (REL) to apostatize; (fig) to change sides.

a posteriori [aposte'rjori] adv at a later date o stage; (LÓGICA) a posteriori.

apostilla [apos'tiʎa] nf note, comment.

apóstol [a'postol] nm apostle.

apóstrofo [a'postrofo] nm apostrophe.

apostura [apos'tura] nf neatness, elegance.

apoteósico, a [apote'osiko, a] adj tremendous.

apoyar [apo'jar] vt to lean, rest; (fig) to support, back; ~**se** vr: ~**se en** to lean on.

apoyo [a'pojo] nm support, backing.

apreciable [apre'θjaßle] adj considerable; (fig) esteemed.

apreciación [apreθja'θjon] nf appreciation; (COM) valuation.

apreciar [apre'θjar] vt to evaluate, assess; (COM) to appreciate, value ♦ vi (ECON) to appreciate.

aprecio [a'preθjo] nm valuation, estimate; (fig) appreciation.

aprehender [apreen'der] vt to apprehend, detain; (ver) to see, observe.

aprehensión [apreen'sjon] nf detention, capture.

apremiante [apre'mjante] adj urgent, pressing.

apremiar [apre'mjar] vt to compel, force ♦ vi to be urgent, press.

apremio [a'premjo] nm urgency; ~ **de pago** demand note.

aprender [apren'der] vt, vi to learn; ~ **a conducir** to learn to drive; ~**se** vr: ~**se algo** to learn sth (off) by heart.

aprendiz, a [apren'diθ, a] nm/f apprentice; (principiante) learner, trainee; ~ **de comercio** business trainee.

aprendizaje [aprendi'θaxe] nm apprenticeship.

aprensión [apren'sjon] nm apprehension, fear.

aprensivo, a [apren'sißo, a] adj apprehensive.

apresar [apre'sar] vt to seize; (capturar) to capture.

aprestar [apres'tar] vt to prepare, get ready; (TEC) to prime, size; ~**se** vr to get ready.

apresto [a'presto] nm (gen) preparation; (sustancia) size.

apresurado, a [apresu'raðo, a] adj hurried, hasty.

apresuramiento [apresura'mjento] nm hurry, haste.

apresurar [apresu'rar] vt to hurry, accelerate; ~**se** vr to hurry, make haste; **me apresuré a sugerir que ...** I hastily suggested that ...

apretado, a [apre'taðo, a] adj tight; (escritura) cramped.

apretar [apre'tar] vt to squeeze, press; (mano) to clasp; (dientes) to grit; (TEC) to tighten; (presionar) to press together, pack ♦ vi to be too tight; ~**se** vr to crowd together; ~ **la mano a algn** to shake sb's hand; ~ **el paso** to quicken one's step.

apretón [apre'ton] nm squeeze; ~ **de manos** handshake.

aprieto [a'prjeto] etc vb V **apretar** ♦ nm squeeze; (dificultad) difficulty, jam; **estar en un** ~ to be in a jam; **ayudar a algn a salir de un** ~ to help sb out of trouble.

a priori [apri'ori] adv beforehand; (LÓGICA) a priori.

aprisa [a'prisa] adv quickly, hurriedly.

aprisionar [aprisjo'nar] vt to imprison.

aprobación [aproßa'θjon] nf approval.

aprobado [apro'ßaðo] nm (nota) pass mark.

aprobar [apro'ßar] vt to approve (of); (examen, materia) to pass ♦ vi to pass.

apropiación [apropja'θjon] nf appropriation.

apropiado, a [apro'pjaðo, a] adj appropriate.

apropiarse [apro'pjarse] vr: ~ **de** to appropriate.

aprovechado, a [aproße'tʃaðo, a] adj industrious, hardworking; (económico) thrifty; (pey) unscrupulous.

aprovechamiento [aproßetʃa'mjento] nm use, exploitation.

aprovechar [aproße'tʃar] vt to use; (explotar) to exploit; (experiencia) to profit from; (oferta, oportunidad) to take advantage of ♦ vi to progress, improve; ~**se** vr: ~**se de** to make use of; (pey) to take advantage of; ¡**que aproveche!** enjoy your meal!

aprovisionar [aproßisjo'nar] vt to supply.

aproximación [aproksima'θjon] nf approximation; (de lotería) consolation prize.

aproximadamente [aproksimaða'mente] adv approximately.

aproximado, a [aproksi'maðo, a] *adj* approximate.

aproximar [aproksi'mar] *vt* to bring nearer; ~**se** *vr* to come near, approach.

apruebe [a'prweße] *etc vb* V **aprobar**.

aptitud [apti'tuð] *nf* aptitude; (*capacidad*) ability; ~ **para los negocios** business sense.

apto, a ['apto, a] *adj* (*apropiado*) fit, suitable (*para* for, to); (*hábil*) capable; ~/**no** ~ **para menores** (*CINE*) suitable/ unsuitable for children.

apuesto, a [a'pwesto, a] *etc vb* V **apostar** ♦ *adj* neat, elegant ♦ *nf* bet, wager.

apuntador [apunta'ðor] *nm* prompter.

apuntalar [apunta'lar] *vt* to prop up.

apuntar [apun'tar] *vt* (*con arma*) to aim at; (*con dedo*) to point at *o* to; (*anotar*) to note (down); (*datos*) to record; (*TEAT*) to prompt; ~**se** *vr* (*DEPORTE: tanto, victoria*) to score; (*ESCOL*) to enrol; ~ **una cantidad en la cuenta de algn** to charge a sum to sb's account; ~**se en un curso** to enrol on a course; **¡yo me apunto!** count me in!

apunte [a'punte] *nm* note; (*TEAT: voz*) prompt; (: *texto*) prompt book.

apuñalar [apuɲa'lar] *vt* to stab.

apurado, a [apu'raðo, a] *adj* needy; (*difícil*) difficult; (*peligroso*) dangerous; (*AM*) hurried, rushed; **estar en una situación apurada** to be in a tight spot; **estar** ~ **to be in a hurry.

apurar [apu'rar] *vt* (*agotar*) to drain; (*recursos*) to use up; (*molestar*) to annoy; ~**se** *vr* (*preocuparse*) to worry; (*esp AM: darse prisa*) to hurry.

apuro [a'puro] *nm* (*aprieto*) fix, jam; (*escasez*) want, hardship; (*vergüenza*) embarrassment; (*AM*) haste, urgency.

aquejado, a [ake'xaðo, a] *adj:* ~ **de** (*MED*) afflicted by.

aquejar [ake'xar] *vt* (*afligir*) to distress; **le aqueja una grave enfermedad** he suffers from a serious disease.

aquel, aquella, aquellos, as [a'kel, a'keʎa, a'keʎos, as] *adj* that; (*pl*) those.

aquél, aquélla, aquéllos, as [a'kel, a'keʎa, a'keʎos, as] *pron* that (one); (*pl*) those (ones).

aquello [a'keʎo] *pron* that, that business.

aquí [a'ki] *adv* (*lugar*) here; (*tiempo*) now; ~ **arriba** up here; ~ **mismo** right here; ~ **yace** here lies; **de** ~ **a siete días** a week from now.

aquietar [akje'tar] *vt* to quieten (down), calm (down).

Aquisgrán [akis'ɤran] *nm* Aachen, Aix-la-Chapelle.

A.R. *abr* (= *Alteza Real*) R.H.

ara ['ara] *nf* (*altar*) altar; **en** ~**s de** for the sake of.

árabe ['araße] *adj* Arab, Arabian, Arabic ♦ *nm/f* Arab ♦ *nm* (*LING*) Arabic.

Arabia [a'raßja] *nf* Arabia; ~ **Saudí** *o* **Saudita** Saudi Arabia.

arábigo, a [a'raßiɤo, a] *adj* Arab, Arabian, Arabic.

arácnido [a'rakniðo] *nm* arachnid.

arado [a'raðo] *nm* plough.

aragonés, esa [araɤo'nes, esa] *adj, nm/f* Aragonese ♦ *nm* (*LING*) Aragonese

arancel [aran'θel] *nm* tariff, duty; ~ **de aduanas** (customs) duty.

arandela [aran'dela] *nf* (*TEC*) washer; (*chorrera*) frill.

araña [a'raɲa] *nf* (*ZOOL*) spider; (*lámpara*) chandelier.

arañar [ara'ɲar] *vt* to scratch.

arañazo [ara'ɲaθo] *nm* scratch.

arar [a'rar] *vt* to plough, till.

araucano, a [arau'kano, a] *adj, nm/f* Araucanian.

arbitraje [arßi'traxe] *nm* arbitration.

arbitrar [arßi'trar] *vt* to arbitrate in; (*recursos*) to bring together; (*DEPORTE*) to referee ♦ *vi* to arbitrate.

arbitrariedad [arßitrarje'ðað] *nf* arbitrariness; (*acto*) arbitrary act.

arbitrario, a [arßi'trarjo] *adj* arbitrary.

arbitrio [ar'ßitrjo] *nm* free will; (*JUR*) adjudication, decision; **dejar al** ~ **de algn** to leave to sb's discretion.

árbitro ['arßitro] *nm* arbitrator; (*DEPORTE*) referee; (*TENIS*) umpire.

árbol ['arßol] *nm* (*BOT*) tree; (*NAUT*) mast; (*TEC*) axle, shaft.

arbolado, a [arßo'laðo, a] *adj* wooded; (*camino*) tree-lined ♦ *nm* woodland.

arboladura [arßola'ðura] *nf* rigging.

arbolar [arßo'lar] *vt* to hoist, raise.

arboleda [arßo'leða] *nf* grove, plantation.

arbusto [ar'ßusto] *nm* bush, shrub.

arca ['arka] *nf* (*hest*, box; **A**~ **de la Alianza** Ark of the Covenant; **A**~ **de Noé** Noah's Ark.

arcada [ar'kaða] *nf* arcade; (*de puente*) arch, span; ~**s** *nfpl* retching *sg*.

arcaico, a [ar'kaiko, a] *adj* archaic.

arce ['arθe] *nm* maple tree.

arcén [ar'θen] *nm* (*de autopista*) hard shoulder; (*de carretera*) verge.

archiconocido, a [artʃikono'θiðo, a] *adj* extremely well-known.

archipiélago [artʃi'pjelaɤo] *nm*

archipelago.

archisabido, a [artʃisaˈβiðo, a] *adj* extremely well-known.

archivador [artʃiβaˈðor] *nm* filing cabinet; ~ **colgante** suspension file.

archivar [artʃiˈβar] *vt* to file (away); (*INFORM*) to archive.

archivo [arˈtʃiβo] *nm* archive(s) (*pl*); (*INFORM*) file, archive; **A~ Nacional** Public Record Office; **~s policíacos** police files; **nombre de** ~ (*INFORM*) filename; ~ **maestro** (*INFORM*) master file; ~ **de transacciones** (*INFORM*) transactions file.

arcilla [arˈθiʎa] *nf* clay.

arco [ˈarko] *nm* arch; (*MAT*) arc; (*MIL, MUS*) bow; (*AM DEPORTE*) goal; · **iris** rainbow.

arcón [arˈkon] *nm* large chest.

arder [arˈðer] *vi* to burn; ~ **sin llama** to smoulder; **estar que arde** (*persona*) to fume.

ardid [arˈðið] *nm* ruse.

ardiente [arˈðjente] *adj* ardent.

ardilla [arˈðiʎa] *nf* squirrel.

ardor [arˈðor] *nm* (*calor*) heat, warmth; (*fig*) ardour; ~ **de estómago** heartburn.

ardoroso, a [arðoˈroso, a] *adj* passionate.

arduo, a [ˈarðwo, a] *adj* arduous.

área [ˈarea] *nf* area; (*DEPORTE*) penalty area; ~ **de oxcedontos** (*INFORM*) overflow area.

ARENA [aˈrena] *nf abr* (*El Salvador: POL*) = *Alianza Republicana Nacionalista*.

arena [aˈrena] *nf* sand; (*de una lucha*) arena.

arenal [areˈnal] *nm* (*arena movediza*) quicksand.

arenga [aˈrenga] *nf* (*fam*) sermon.

arengar [arenˈgar] *vt* to harangue.

arengue [aˈrenge] *etc vb V* **arengar**.

arenillas [areˈniʎas] *nfpl* (*MED*) stones.

arenisca [areˈniska] *nf* sandstone; (*cascajo*) grit.

arenoso, a [areˈnoso, a] *adj* sandy.

arenque [aˈrenke] *nm* herring.

arepa [aˈrepa] *nf* (*AM*) corn pancake.

arete [aˈrete] *nm* earring.

argamasa [arɣaˈmasa] *nf* mortar, plaster.

Argel [arˈxel] *n* Algiers.

Argelia [arˈxelja] *nf* Algeria.

argelino, a [arxeˈlino, a] *adj, nm/f* Algerian.

Argentina [arxenˈtina] *nf:* **(la)** ~ the Argentine, Argentina.

argentino, a [arxenˈtino, a] *adj* Argentinian; (*de plata*) silvery ♦ *nm/f* Argentinian.

argolla [arˈɣoʎa] *nf* (*large*) ring; (*AM: de matrimonio*) wedding ring.

argot [arˈɣo] *nm, pl* **argots** [arˈɣo, arˈɣos] slang.

argucia [arˈɣuθja] *nf* subtlety, sophistry.

argüir [arˈɣwir] *vt* to deduce; (*discutir*) to argue; (*indicar*) to indicate, imply; (*censurar*) to reproach ♦ *vi* to argue.

argumentación [arɣumentaˈθjon] *nf* (line of) argument.

argumentar [arɣumenˈtar] *vt, vi* to argue.

argumento [arɣuˈmento] *nm* argument; (*razonamiento*) reasoning; (*de novela etc*) plot; (*CINE, TV*) storyline.

arguyendo [arɣuˈjendo] *etc vb V* **argüir**.

aria [ˈarja] *nf* aria.

aridez [ariˈðeθ] *nf* aridity, dryness.

árido, a [ˈariðo, a] *adj* arid, dry; **~s** *nmpl* dry goods.

Aries [ˈarjes] *nm* Aries.

ariete [aˈrjete] *nm* battering ram.

ario, a [ˈarjo, a] *adj* Aryan.

arisco, a [aˈrisko, a] *adj* surly; (*insociable*) unsociable.

aristocracia [aristoˈkraθja] *nf* aristocracy.

aristócrata [arisˈtokrata] *nm/f* aristocrat.

aristocrático, a [aristoˈkratiko, a] *adj* aristocratic.

aritmética [aritˈmetika] *nf* arithmetic.

aritmético, a [aritˈmetiko, a] *adj* arithmetic(al) ♦ *nm/f* arithmetician.

arma [ˈarma] *nf* arm; **~s** *nfpl* arms; ~ **blanca** blade, knife; (*espada*) sword, · **de fuego** firearm; **~s cortas** small arms; **rendir las ~s** to lay down one's arms; **ser de ~s tomar** to be somebody to be reckoned with.

armada [arˈmaða] *nf* armada; (*flota*) fleet; *V tb* **armado**.

armadillo [armaˈðiʎo] *nm* armadillo.

armado, a [arˈmaðo, a] *adj* armed; (*TEC*) reinforced.

armador [armaˈðor] *nm* (*NAUT*) shipowner.

armadura [armaˈðura] *nf* (*MIL*) armour; (*TEC*) framework; (*ZOOL*) skeleton; (*FÍSICA*) armature.

armamentista [armamenˈtista], **armamentístico, a** [armamenˈtistiko, a] *adj* arms *cpd*.

armamento [armaˈmento] *nm* armament; (*NAUT*) fitting-out.

armar [arˈmar] *vt* (*soldado*) to arm; (*máquina*) to assemble; (*navío*) to fit out; **~la**, ~ **un lío** to start a row; **~se** *vr:* **~se de valor** to summon up one's courage.

armario [arˈmarjo] *nm* wardrobe.

armatoste [armaˈtoste] *nm* (*mueble*) monstrosity; (*máquina*) contraption.

armazón [armaˈθon] *nf o m* body, chassis; (*de mueble etc*) frame; (*ARQ*) skeleton.

Armenia [arˈmenja] *nf* Armenia.

armería [arme'ria] *nf* (*museo*) military museum; (*tienda*) gunsmith's.

armiño [ar'miɲo] *nm* stoat; (*piel*) ermine.

armisticio [armis'tiθjo] *nm* armistice.

armonía [armo'nia] *nf* harmony.

armónica [ar'monika] *nf* harmonica; *V tb* **armónico**.

armonice [armo'niθe] *etc vb V* **armonizar**.

armónico, a [ar'moniko, a] *adj* harmonic.

armonioso, a [armo'njoso, a] *adj* harmonious.

armonizar [armoni'θar] *vt* to harmonize; (*diferencias*) to reconcile ♦ *vi* to harmonize; ~ **con** (*fig*) to be in keeping with; (*colores*) to tone in with.

arnés [ar'nes] *nm* armour; **arneses** *nmpl* harness *sg*.

aro ['aro] *nm* ring; (*tejo*) quoit; (*AM*: *pendiente*) earring; **entrar por el** ~ to give in.

aroma [a'roma] *nm* aroma.

aromático, a [aro'matiko, a] *adj* aromatic.

arpa ['arpa] *nf* harp.

arpegio [ar'pexjo] *nm* (*MUS*) arpeggio.

arpía [ar'pia] *nf* (*fig*) shrew.

arpillera [arpi'ʎera] *nf* sacking, sackcloth.

arpón [ar'pon] *nm* harpoon.

arquear [arke'ar] *vt* to arch, bend; ~**se** *vr* to arch, bend.

arqueo [ar'keo] *nm* (*gen*) arching; (*NAUT*) tonnage.

arqueología [arkeolo'xia] *nf* archaeology.

arqueológico, a [arkeo'loxiko, a] *adj* archaeological.

arqueólogo, a [arke'oloɣo, a] *nm/f* archaeologist.

arquero [ar'kero] *nm* archer, bowman; (*AM DEPORTE*) goalkeeper.

arquetipo [arke'tipo] *nm* archetype.

arquitecto, a [arki'tekto, a] *nm/f* architect; ~ **paisajista** *o* **de jardines** landscape gardener.

arquitectónico, a [arkitek'toniko, a] *adj* architectural.

arquitectura [arkitek'tura] *nf* architecture.

arrabal [arra'ßal] *nm* suburb; ~**es** *nmpl* outskirts.

arrabalero, a [arraßa'lero, a] *adj* (*fig*) common, coarse.

arracimarse [arraθi'marse] *vr* to cluster together.

arraigado, a [arrai'ɣaðo, a] *adj* deep-rooted; (*fig*) established.

arraigar [arrai'ɣar] *vt* to establish ♦ *vi*, ~**se** *vr* to take root; (*persona*) to settle.

arraigo [a'rraiɣo] *nm* (*raíces*) roots *pl*; (*bienes*) property; (*influencia*) hold; **hombre de** ~ man of property.

arraigue [a'rraiɣe] *etc vb V* **arraigar**.

arrancada [arran'kaða] *nf* (*arranque*) sudden start.

arrancar [arran'kar] *vt* (*sacar*) to extract, pull out; (*arrebatar*) to snatch (away); (*pedazo*) to tear off; (*página*) to rip out; (*suspiro*) to heave; (*AUTO*) to start; (*INFORM*) to boot; (*fig*) to extract ♦ *vi* (*AUTO*, *máquina*) to start; (*ponerse en marcha*) to get going; ~ **información a algn** to extract information from sb; ~ **de** to stem from.

arranque [a'rranke] *etc vb V* **arrancar** ♦ *nm* sudden start; (*AUTO*) start; (*fig*) fit, outburst.

arras ['arras] *nfpl* pledge *sg*, security *sg*.

arrasar [arra'sar] *vt* (*aplanar*) to level, flatten; (*destruir*) to demolish.

arrastrado, a [arras'traðo, a] *adj* poor, wretched.

arrastrador [arrastra'ðor] *nm* (*en máquina impresora*) tractor.

arrastrar [arras'trar] *vt* to drag (along); (*fig*) to drag down, degrade; (*suj: agua, viento*) to carry away ♦ *vi* to drag, trail on the ground; ~**se** *vr* to crawl; (*fig*) to grovel; **llevar algo arrastrado** to drag sth along.

arrastre [a'rrastre] *nm* drag, dragging; (*DEPORTE*) crawl; **estar para el** ~ (*fig*) to have had it; ~ **de papel por fricción/por tracción** (*en máquina impresora*) friction/tractor feed.

array [a'rrai] *nm* (*INFORM*) array; ~ **empaquetado** (*INFORM*) packed array.

arrayán [arra'jan] *nm* myrtle.

arre ['arre] *excl* gee up!

arrear [arre'ar] *vt* to drive on, urge on ♦ *vi* to hurry along.

arrebañar [arreßa'ɲar] *vt* (*juntar*) to scrape together.

arrebatado, a [arreßa'taðo, a] *adj* rash, impetuous; (*repentino*) sudden, hasty.

arrebatar [arreßa'tar] *vt* to snatch (away), seize; (*fig*) to captivate; ~**se** *vr* to get carried away, get excited.

arrebato [arre'ßato] *nm* fit of rage, fury; (*éxtasis*) rapture; **en un** ~ **de cólera** in an outburst of anger.

arrebolar [arreßo'lar] *vt* to redden; ~**se** *vr* (*enrojecer*) to blush.

arrebujar [arreßu'xar] *vt* (*objetos*) to jumble together; ~**se** *vr* to wrap o.s. up.

arrechar [arre't∫ar] (*AM*) *vt* to arouse, excite; ~**se** *vr* to become aroused.

arrechucho [arre't∫ut∫o] *nm* (*MED*) turn.

arreciar [arre'θjar] *vi* to get worse; (*viento*) to get stronger.

arrecife [arre'θife] nm reef.
arredrar [arre'ðrar] vt (hacer retirarse) to drive back; ~se vr (apartarse) to draw back; ~se ante algo to shrink away from sth.
arreglado, a [arre'ɣlaðo, a] adj (ordenado) neat, orderly; (moderado) moderate, reasonable.
arreglar [arre'ɣlar] vt (poner orden) to tidy up; (algo roto) to fix, repair; (problema) to solve; ~se vr to reach an understanding; arreglárselas (fam) to get by, manage.
arreglo [a'rreɣlo] nm settlement; (orden) order; (acuerdo) agreement; (MUS) arrangement, setting; (INFORM) array; con ~ a in accordance with; llegar a un ‧ to reach a compromise.
arrellanarse [arreʎa'narse] vr to sprawl; ~ en el asiento to lie back in one's chair.
arremangar [arreman'gar] vt to roll up, turn up; ~se vr to roll up one's sleeves.
arremangue [arre'mange] etc vb V arremangar.
arremeter [arreme'ter] vt to attack, assault; ~ contra algn to attack sb.
arremetida [arreme'tiða] nf assault.
arremolinarse [arremoli'narse] vr to crowd around, mill around; (corriente) to swirl, eddy.
arrendador, a [arrenda'ðor, a] nm/f landlord/lady.
arrendamiento [arrenda'mjento] nm letting; (el alquilar) hiring; (contrato) lease; (alquiler) rent.
arrendar [arren'dar] vt to let; to hire; to lease; to rent.
arrendatario, a [arrenda'tarjo, a] nm/f tenant.
arreos [a'rreos] nmpl harness sg, trappings.
arrepentido, a [arrepen'tiðo, a] nm/f (POL) reformed terrorist.
arrepentimiento [arrepenti'mjento] nm regret, repentance.
arrepentirse [arrepen'tirse] vr to repent; ~ de (haber hecho) algo to regret (doing) sth.
arrepienta [arre'pjenta] etc,
arrepintiendo [arrepin'tjendo] etc vb V arrepentirse.
arrestar [arres'tar] vt to arrest; (encarcelar) to imprison.
arresto [a'rresto] nm arrest; (MIL) detention; (audacia) boldness, daring; ~ domiciliario house arrest.
arriar [a'rrjar] vt (velas) to haul down; (bandera) to lower, strike; (un cable) to pay out.
arriate [a'rrjate] nm (BOT) bed; (camino) road.

═══════════ **PALABRA CLAVE**

arriba [a'rrißa] adv **1** (posición) above; desde ~ from above; ~ del todo at the very top, right on top; Juan está ~ Juan is upstairs; lo ~ mencionado the aforementioned; aquí/allí ~ up here/ there; está hasta ~ de trabajo (fam) he's up to his eyes in work (fam)
2 (dirección) up, upwards; más ~ higher o further up; calle ~ up the street
3: de ~ abajo from top to bottom; mirar a algn de ~ abajo to look sb up and down
4: para ~: de 5000 pesetas para ~ from 5,000 pesetas up(wards); de la cintura (para) ~ from the waist up
♦ adj: de ~: el piso de ~ the upstairs flat (BRIT) o apartment; la parte de ~ the top o upper part
♦ prep: ~ de (AM) above; ~ de 200 dólares more than 200 dollars
♦ excl: ¡~! up!; ¡manos ~! hands up!; ¡~ España! long live Spain!

arribar [arri'ßar] vi to put into port; (esp AM: llegar) to arrive.
arribista [arri'ßista] nm/f parvenu(e), upstart.
arribo [a'rrißo] nm (esp AM) arrival.
arriendo [a'rrjendo] etc vb V arrendar ♦ nm = arrendamiento.
arriero [a'rrjero] nm muleteer.
arriesgado, a [arrjes'xaðo, a] adj (peligroso) risky; (audaz) bold, daring.
arriesgar [arrjes'xar] vt to risk; (poner en peligro) to endanger; ~se vr to take a risk.
arriesgue [a'rrjesxe] etc vb V arriesgar.
arrimar [arri'mar] vt (acercar) to bring close; (poner de lado) to set aside; ~se vr to come close o closer; ~se a to lean on; (fig) to keep company with; (buscar ayuda) to seek the protection of; arrímate a mí cuddle up to me.
arrinconado, a [arrinko'naðo, a] adj forgotten, neglected.
arrinconar [arrinko'nar] vt to put in a corner; (fig) to put on one side; (abandonar) to push aside.
arriscado, a [arris'kaðo, a] adj (GEO) craggy; (fig) bold, resolute.
arroba [a'rroßa] nf (peso) 25 pounds; (INFORM: en dirección electrónica) at; tiene talento por ~s he has loads o bags of talent.
arrobado, a [arro'ßaðo, a] adj entranced, enchanted.

arrobamiento [arro'ßa'mjento] *nm* ecstasy.
arrobar [arro'ßar] *vt* to enchant; ~**se** *vr* to be enraptured; (*místico*) to go into a trance.
arrodillarse [arroði'ʎarse] *vr* to kneel (down).
arrogancia [arro'ɣanθja] *nf* arrogance.
arrogante [arro'ɣante] *adj* arrogant.
arrojar [arro'xar] *vt* to throw, hurl; (*humo*) to emit, give out; (*COM*) to yield, produce; ~**se** *vr* to throw *o* hurl o.s.
arrojo [a'rroxo] *nm* daring.
arrollador, a [arroʎa'ðor, a] *adj* crushing, overwhelming.
arrollar [arro'ʎar] *vt* (*enrollar*) to roll up; (*suj: inundación*) to wash away; (*AUTO*) to run over; (*DEPORTE*) to crush.
arropar [arro'par] *vt* to cover (up), wrap up; ~**se** *vr* to wrap o.s. up.
arrostrar [arros'trar] *vt* to face (up to); ~**se** *vr*: ~**se con algn** to face up to sb.
arroyo [a'rrojo] *nm* stream; (*de la calle*) gutter; **poner a algn en el** ~ to turn sb onto the streets.
arroz [a'rroθ] *nm* rice; ~ **con leche** rice pudding.
arrozal [arro'θal] *nm* paddy field.
arruga [a'rruɣa] *nf* fold; (*de cara*) wrinkle; (*de vestido*) crease.
arrugar [arru'ɣar] *vt* to fold; to wrinkle; to crease; ~**se** *vr* to get wrinkled; to get creased.
arrugue [a'rruɣe] *etc vb* V **arrugar**.
arruinar [arrwi'nar] *vt* to ruin, wreck; ~**se** *vr* to be ruined.
arrullar [arru'ʎar] *vi* to coo ♦ *vt* to lull to sleep.
arrumaco [arru'mako] *nm* (*caricia*) caress; (*halago*) piece of flattery.
arrumbar [arrum'bar] *vt* (*objeto*) to discard; (*individuo*) to silence.
arrurruz [arru'rruθ] *nm* arrowroot.
arsenal [arse'nal] *nm* naval dockyard; (*MIL*) arsenal.
arsénico [ar'seniko] *nm* arsenic.
arte ['arte] *nm* (*gen m en sg y siempre f en pl*) art; (*maña*) skill, guile; **por** ~ **de magia** (as if) by magic; **no tener** ~ **ni parte en algo** to have nothing whatsoever to do with sth; ~**s** *nfpl* arts; **Bellas A**~**s** Fine Art *sg*; ~**s y oficios** arts and crafts.
artefacto [arte'fakto] *nm* appliance; (*ARQUEOLOGÍA*) artefact.
arteria [ar'terja] *nf* artery.
arterial [arte'rjal] *adj* arterial; (*presión*) blood *cpd*.
arterio(e)sclerosis [arterjo(e)skle'rosis] *nf inv* hardening of the arteries,

arteriosclerosis.
artesa [ar'tesa] *nf* trough.
artesanía [artesa'nia] *nf* craftsmanship; (*artículos*) handicrafts *pl*.
artesano, a [arte'sano, a] *nm/f* artisan, craftsman/woman.
ártico, a ['artiko, a] *adj* Arctic ♦ *nm*: **el** (**océano**) **Á**~ the Arctic (Ocean).
articulación [artikula'θjon] *nf* articulation; (*MED, TEC*) joint.
articulado, a [artiku'laðo, a] *adj* articulated; jointed.
articular [artiku'lar] *vt* to articulate; to join together.
articulista [artiku'lista] *nm/f* columnist, contributor (to a newspaper).
artículo [ar'tikulo] *nm* article; (*cosa*) thing, article; (*TV*) feature, report; ~ **de fondo** leader, editorial; ~**s** *nmpl* goods; ~**s de marca** (*COM*) proprietary goods.
artífice [ar'tifiθe] *nm* artist, craftsman; (*fig*) architect.
artificial [artifi'θjal] *adj* artificial.
artificio [arti'fiθjo] *nm* art, skill; (*artesanía*) craftsmanship; (*astucia*) cunning.
artillería [artiʎe'ria] *nf* artillery.
artillero [arti'ʎero] *nm* artilleryman, gunner.
artilugio [arti'luxjo] *nm* gadget.
artimaña [arti'maɲa] *nf* trap, snare; (*astucia*) cunning.
artista [ar'tista] *nm/f* (*pintor*) artist, painter; (*TEAT*) artist, artiste.
artístico, a [ar'tistiko, a] *adj* artistic.
artritis [ar'tritis] *nf* arthritis.
arveja [ar'ßexa] *nf* (*AM*) pea.
Arz. *abr* (= *Arzobispo*) Abp.
arzobispo [arθo'ßispo] *nm* archbishop.
as [as] *nm* ace; ~ **del fútbol** star player.
asa ['asa] *nf* handle; (*fig*) lever.
asado [a'saðo] *nm* roast (meat); (*AM: barbacoa*) barbecue.
asador [asa'ðor] *nm* (*varilla*) spit; (*aparato*) spit roaster.
asadura(s) [asa'ðura(s)] *nf(pl)* entrails *pl*, offal *sg*; (*CULIN*) chitterlings *pl*.
asaetear [asaete'ar] *vt* (*fig*) to bother.
asalariado, a [asala'rjaðo, a] *adj* paid, wage-earning, salaried ♦ *nm/f* wage earner.
asaltador, a [asalta'ðor, a], **asaltante** [asal'tante] *nm/f* assailant.
asaltar [asal'tar] *vt* to attack, assault; (*fig*) to assail.
asalto [a'salto] *nm* attack, assault; (*DEPORTE*) round.
asamblea [asam'blea] *nf* assembly; (*reunión*) meeting.

asar [a'sar] *vt* to roast; ~ **al horno/a la parrilla** to bake/grill; **~se** *vr* (*fig*): **me aso de calor** I'm roasting; **aquí se asa uno vivo** it's boiling hot here.

asbesto [as'βesto] *nm* asbestos.

ascendencia [asθen'denθja] *nf* ancestry; **de ~ francesa** of French origin.

ascender [asθen'der] *vi* (*subir*) to ascend, rise; (*ser promovido*) to gain promotion ♦ *vt* to promote; **~ a** to amount to.

ascendiente [asθen'djente] *nm* influence ♦ *nm/f* ancestor.

ascensión [asθen'sjon] *nf* ascent; **la A~** the Ascension.

ascenso [as'θenso] *nm* ascent; (*promoción*) promotion.

ascensor [asθen'sor] *nm* lift (*BRIT*), elevator (*US*).

ascético, a [as'θetiko, a] *adj* ascetic.

ascienda [as'θjenda] *etc vb V* **ascender.**

asco ['asko] *nm*: **el ajo me da ~** I hate *o* loathe garlic; **hacer ~s de algo** to turn up one's nose at sth; **estar hecho un ~** to be filthy; **poner a algn de ~** to call sb all sorts of names *o* every name under the sun; **¡qué ~!** how revolting *o* disgusting!

ascua ['askwa] *nf* ember; **arrimar el ~ a su sardina** to look after number one; **estar en ~s** to be on tenterhooks.

aseado, a [ase'aðo, a] *adj* clean; (*arreglado*) tidy; (*pulcro*) smart.

asear [ase'ar] *vt* (*lavar*) to wash; (*ordenar*) to tidy (up).

asechanza [ase't ʃanθa] *nf* trap, snare.

asediar [ase'ðjar] *vt* (*MIL*) to besiege, lay siege to; (*fig*) to chase, pester.

asedio [a'seðjo] *nm* siege; (*COM*) run.

asegurado, a [aseɣu'raðo, a] *adj* insured.

asegurador, a [aseɣura'ðor, a] *nm/f* insurer.

asegurar [aseɣu'rar] *vt* (*consolidar*) to secure, fasten; (*dar garantía de*) to guarantee; (*preservar*) to safeguard; (*afirmar, dar por cierto*) to assure, affirm; (*tranquilizar*) to reassure; (*tomar un seguro*) to insure; **~se** *vr* to assure o.s., make sure.

asemejarse [aseme'xarse] *vr* to be alike; **~ a** to be like, resemble.

asentado, a [asen'taðo, a] *adj* established, settled.

asentar [asen'tar] *vt* (*sentar*) to seat, sit down; (*poner*) to place, establish; (*alisar*) to level, smooth down *o* out; (*anotar*) to note down ♦ *vi* to be suitable, suit.

asentimiento [asenti'mjento] *nm* assent, agreement.

asentir [asen'tir] *vi* to assent, agree.

aseo [a'seo] *nm* cleanliness; **~s** *nmpl* toilet *sg* (*BRIT*), restroom *sg* (*US*), cloakroom *sg*.

aséptico, a [a'septiko, a] *adj* germ-free, free from infection.

asequible [ase'kiβle] *adj* (*precio*) reasonable; (*meta*) attainable; (*persona*) approachable.

aserradero [aserra'ðero] *nm* sawmill.

aserrar [ase'rrar] *vt* to saw.

asesinar [asesi'nar] *vt* to murder; (*POL*) to assassinate.

asesinato [asesi'nato] *nm* murder; assassination.

asesino, a [ase'sino, a] *nm/f* murderer, killer; (*POL*) assassin.

asesor, a [ase'sor, a] *nm/f* adviser, consultant; (*COM*) assessor, consultant; **~ administrativo** management consultant.

asesorar [aseso'rar] *vt* (*JUR*) to advise, give legal advice to; (*COM*) to act as consultant to; **~se** *vr*: **~se con *o* de** to take advice from, consult.

asesoría [aseso'ria] *nf* (*cargo*) consultancy; (*oficina*) consultant's office.

asestar [ases'tar] *vt* (*golpe*) to deal; (*arma*) to aim; (*tiro*) to fire.

aseverar [aseβe'rar] *vt* to assert.

asfaltado, a [asfal'taðo, a] *adj* asphalted ♦ *nm* (*pavimiento*) asphalt.

asfalto [as'falto] *nm* asphalt.

asfixia [as'fiksja] *nf* asphyxia, suffocation.

asfixiar [asfik'sjar] *vt* to asphyxiate, suffocate.

asga ['asɣa] *etc vb V* **asir.**

así [a'si] *adv* (*de esta manera*) in this way, like this, thus; (*aunque*) although; (*tan pronto como*) as soon as; **~ que** so; **~ como** as well as; **~ y todo** even so; **¿no es ~?** isn't it?, didn't you? *etc*; **~ de grande** this big; **¡~ sea!** so be it!; **~ es la vida** such is life, that's life.

Asia ['asja] *nf* Asia.

asiático, a [a'sjatiko, a] *adj, nm/f* Asian, Asiatic.

asidero [asi'ðero] *nm* handle.

asiduidad [asiðwi'ðað] *nf* assiduousness.

asiduo, a [a'siðwo, a] *adj* assiduous; (*frecuente*) frequent ♦ *nm/f* regular (customer).

asiento [a'sjento] *etc vb V* **asentar, asentir** ♦ *nm* (*mueble*) seat, chair; (*de coche, en tribunal etc*) seat; (*localidad*) seat, place; (*fundamento*) site; **~ delantero/trasero** front/back seat.

asierre [a'sjerre] *etc vb V* **aserrar.**

asignación [asiɣna'θjon] *nf* (*atribución*)

assignment; (*reparto*) allocation; (*COM*) allowance; ~ **(semanal)** pocket money; ~ **de presupuesto** budget appropriation.

asignar [asiɣ'nar] *vt* to assign, allocate.

asignatura [asiɣna'tura] *nf* subject; (*curso*) course; ~ **pendiente** (*fig*) matter pending.

asilado, a [asi'laðo, a] *nm/f* refugee.

asilo [a'silo] *nm* (*refugio*) asylum, refuge; (*establecimiento*) home, institution; ~ **político** political asylum.

asimilación [asimila'θjon] *nf* assimilation.

asimilar [asimi'lar] *vt* to assimilate.

asimismo [asi'mismo] *adv* in the same way, likewise.

asintiendo [asin'tjendo] *etc vb* V **asentir**.

asir [a'sir] *vt* to seize, grasp; ~**se** *vr* to take hold; ~**se a** *o* **de** to seize.

asistencia [asis'tenθja] *nf* presence; (*TEAT*) audience; (*MED*) attendance; (*ayuda*) assistance; ~ **social** social *o* welfare work.

asistente, a [asis'tente, a] *nm/f* assistant ♦ *nm* (*MIL*) orderly ♦ *nf* daily help; **los** ~**s** those present; ~ **social** social worker.

asistido, a [asis'tiðo, a] *adj* (*AUTO*: *dirección*) power-assisted; ~ **por ordenador** computer-assisted.

asistir [asis'tir] *vt* to assist, help ♦ *vi*: ~ **a** to attend, be present at.

asma ['asma] *nf* asthma.

asno ['asno] *nm* donkey; (*fig*) ass.

asociación [asoθja'θjon] *nf* association; (*COM*) partnership.

asociado, a [aso'θjaðo, a] *adj* associate ♦ *nm/f* associate; (*COM*) partner.

asociar [aso'θjar] *vt* to associate; ~**se** *vr* to become partners.

asolar [aso'lar] *vt* to destroy.

asolear [asole'ar] *vt* to put in the sun; ~**se** *vr* to sunbathe.

asomar [aso'mar] *vt* to show, stick out ♦ *vi* to appear; ~**se** *vr* to appear, show up; ~ **la cabeza por la ventana** to put one's head out of the window.

asombrar [asom'brar] *vt* to amaze, astonish; ~**se** *vr*: ~**se (de)** (*sorprenderse*) to be amazed (at); (*asustarse*) to be frightened (at).

asombro [a'sombro] *nm* amazement, astonishment.

asombroso, a [asom'broso, a] *adj* amazing, astonishing.

asomo [a'somo] *nm* hint, sign; **ni por** ~ by no means.

asonancia [aso'nanθja] *nf* (*LIT*) assonance; (*fig*) connection; **no tener** ~ **con** to bear no relation to.

asorocharse [asoro'tʃarse] *vr* (*AM*) to get mountain sickness.

aspa ['aspa] *nf* (*cruz*) cross; (*de molino*) sail; **en** ~ X-shaped.

aspaviento [aspa'βjento] *nm* exaggerated display of feeling; (*fam*) fuss.

aspecto [as'pekto] *nm* (*apariencia*) look, appearance; (*fig*) aspect; **bajo ese** ~ from that point of view.

aspereza [aspe'reθa] *nf* roughness; (*de fruta*) sharpness; (*de carácter*) surliness.

áspero, a ['aspero, a] *adj* rough; sharp; harsh.

aspersión [asper'sjon] *nf* sprinkling; (*AGR*) spraying.

aspersor [asper'sor] *nm* sprinkler.

aspiración [aspira'θjon] *nf* breath, inhalation; (*MUS*) short pause; **aspiraciones** *nfpl* aspirations.

aspiradora [aspira'ðora] *nf* vacuum cleaner, Hoover ®.

aspirante [aspi'rante] *nm/f* (*candidato*) candidate; (*DEPORTE*) contender.

aspirar [aspi'rar] *vt* to breathe in ♦ *vi*: ~ **a** to aspire to.

aspirina [aspi'rina] *nf* aspirin.

asquear [aske'ar] *vt* to sicken ♦ *vi* to be sickening; ~**se** *vr* to feel disgusted.

asquerosidad [askerosi'ðað] *nf* (*suciedad*) filth; (*dicho*) obscenity; (*truco*) dirty trick.

asqueroso, a [aske'roso, a] *adj* disgusting, sickening.

asta ['asta] *nf* lance; (*arpón*) spear; (*mango*) shaft, handle; (*ZOOL*) horn; **a media** ~ at half mast.

astado, a [as'taðo, a] *adj* horned ♦ *nm* bull.

asterisco [aste'risko] *nm* asterisk.

asteroide [aste'roiðe] *nm* asteroid.

astigmatismo [astiɣma'tismo] *nm* astigmatism.

astilla [as'tiʎa] *nf* splinter; (*pedacito*) chip; ~**s** *nfpl* firewood *sg*.

astillarse [asti'ʎarse] *vr* to splinter; (*fig*) to shatter.

astillero [asti'ʎero] *nm* shipyard.

astringente [astrin'xente] *adj, nm* astringent.

astro ['astro] *nm* star.

astrología [astrolo'xia] *nf* astrology.

astrólogo, a [as'troloɣo, a] *nm/f* astrologer.

astronauta [astro'nauta] *nm/f* astronaut.

astronave [astro'naβe] *nm* spaceship.

astronomía [astrono'mia] *nf* astronomy.

astronómico, a [astro'nomiko, a] *adj* (*tb fig*) astronomical.

astrónomo, a [as'tronomo, a] *nm/f*

astronomer.

astroso, a [as'troso, a] adj (desaliñado) untidy; (vil) contemptible.

astucia [as'tuθja] nf astuteness; (destreza) clever trick.

asturiano, a [astu'rjano, a] adj, nm/f Asturian.

Asturias [as'turjas] nfpl Asturias; **Príncipe de ~** crown prince.

astuto, a [as'tuto, a] adj astute; (taimado) cunning.

asueto [a'sweto] nm holiday; (tiempo libre) time off; **día de ~** day off; **tarde de ~** (trabajo) afternoon off; (ESCOL) half-holiday.

asumir [asu'mir] vt to assume.

asunción [asun'θjon] nf assumption.

asunto [a'sunto] nm (tema) matter, subject; (negocio) business; **¡eso es ~ mio!** that's my business!; **~s exteriores** foreign affairs; **~s a tratar** agenda sg.

asustadizo, a [asusta'ðiθo, a] adj easily frightened.

asustar [asus'tar] vt to frighten; **~se** vr to be/become frightened.

atacante [ata'kante] nm/f attacker.

atacar [ata'kar] vt to attack.

atadura [ata'ðura] nf bond, tie.

atajar [ata'xar] vt (gen) to stop; (ruta de fuga) to cut off; (discurso) to interrupt ♦ vi to take a short cut.

atajo [a'taxo] nm short cut; (DEPORTE) tackle.

atalaya [ata'laja] nf watchtower.

atañer [ata'ɲer] vi: **~ a** to concern; **en lo que atañe a eso** with regard to that.

ataque [a'take] etc vb V **atacar** ♦ nm attack; **~ cardíaco** heart attack.

atar [a'tar] vt to tie, tie up; **~ la lengua a algn** (fig) to silence sb.

atardecer [atarðe'θer] vi to get dark ♦ nm evening; (crepúsculo) dusk.

atardezca [atar'ðeθka] etc vb V **atardecer**.

atareado, a [atare'aðo, a] adj busy.

atascar [atas'kar] vt to clog up; (obstruir) to jam; (fig) to hinder; **~se** vr to stall; (cañería) to get blocked up; (fig) to get bogged down; (en discurso) to dry up.

atasco [a'tasko] nm obstruction; (AUTO) traffic jam.

atasque [a'taske] etc vb V **atascar**.

ataúd [ata'uð] nm coffin.

ataviar [ata'ßjar] vt to deck, array; **~se** vr to dress up.

atavío [ata'ßio] nm attire, dress; **~s** nmpl finery sg.

ateísmo [ate'ismo] nm atheism.

atemorice [atemo'riθe] etc vb V

atemorizar.

atemorizar [atemori'θar] vt to frighten, scare; **~se** vr to get frightened o scared.

Atenas [a'tenas] nf Athens.

atención [aten'θjon] nf attention; (bondad) kindness ♦ excl (be) careful!, look out!; **en ~ a esto** in view of this.

atender [aten'der] vt to attend to, look after; (TEC) to service; (enfermo) to care for; (ruego) to comply with ♦ vi to pay attention; **~ a** to attend to; (detalles) to take care of.

atendré [aten'dre] etc vb V **atenerse.**

atenerse [ate'nerse] vr: **~ a** to abide by, adhere to.

atenga [a'tenga] etc vb V **atenerse.**

ateniense [ate'njense] adj, nm/f Athenian.

atentado [aten'taðo] nm crime, illegal act; (asalto) assault; (terrorista) attack; **~ contra la vida de algn** attempt on sb's life; **~ golpista** (POL) attempted coup.

atentamente [atenta'mente] adv: **le saluda ~** Yours faithfully.

atentar [aten'tar] vi: **~ a o contra** to commit an outrage against.

atento, a [a'tento, a] adj attentive, observant; (cortés) polite, thoughtful; **su atenta (carta)** (COM) your letter.

atenuante [ate'nwante] adj: **circunstancias ~s** extenuating o mitigating circumstances ♦ nfpl: **~s** extenuating o mitigating circumstances.

atenuar [ate'nwar] vt to attenuate; (disminuir) to lessen, minimize.

ateo, a [a'teo, a] adj atheistic ♦ nm/f atheist.

aterciopelado, a [aterθjope'laðo, a] adj velvety.

aterido, a [ate'riðo, a] adj: **~ de frío** frozen stiff.

aterrador, a [aterra'ðor, a] adj frightening.

aterrar [ate'rrar] vt to frighten; (aterrorizar) to terrify; **~se** vr to be frightened; to be terrified.

aterrice [ate'rriθe] etc vb V **aterrizar.**

aterrizaje [aterri'θaxe] nm landing; **~ forzoso** forced landing.

aterrizar [aterri'θar] vi to land.

aterrorice [aterro'riθe] etc vb V **aterrorizar.**

aterrorizar [aterrori'θar] vt to terrify.

atesorar [ateso'rar] vt to hoard, store up.

atestado, a [ates'taðo, a] adj packed ♦ nm (JUR) affidavit.

atestar [ates'tar] vt to pack, stuff; (JUR) to attest, testify to.

atestiguar [atesti'ɣwar] vt to testify to, bear witness to.

atestigüe [ates'tiɣwe] etc vb V **atestiguar.**

atiborrar [atiβo'rrar] *vt* to fill, stuff; ~**se** *vr* to stuff o.s.

atice [a'tiθe] *etc vb V* **atizar.**

ático ['atiko] *nm* attic; ~ **de lujo** penthouse flat.

atienda [a'tjenda] *etc vb V* **atender.**

atildar [atil'dar] *vt* to criticize; (*TIP*) to put a tilde over; ~**se** *vr* to spruce o.s. up.

atinado, a [ati'naðo, a] *adj* correct; (*sensato*) sensible.

atinar [ati'nar] *vi* (*acertar*) to be right; ~ **con** *o* **en** (*solución*) to hit upon; ~ **a hacer** to manage to do.

atípico, a [a'tipiko, a] *adj* atypical.

atiplado, a [ati'plaðo, a] *adj* (*voz*) high-pitched.

atisbar [atis'βar] *vt* to spy on; (*echar ojeada*) to peep at.

atizar [ati'θar] *vt* to poke; (*horno etc*) to stoke; (*fig*) to stir up, rouse.

atlántico, a [at'lantiko, a] *adj* Atlantic ♦ *nm*: **el** (**océano**) **A**~ the Atlantic (Ocean).

atlas ['atlas] *nm* atlas.

atleta [at'leta] *nm/f* athlete.

atlético, a [at'letiko, a] *adj* athletic.

atletismo [atle'tismo] *nm* athletics *sg.*

atmósfera [at'mosfera] *nf* atmosphere.

atmosférico, a [atmos'feriko, a] *adj* atmospheric.

atol(e) [a'tol(e)] *nm* (*AM*) cornflour drink.

atolladero [atoλa'ðero] *nm*: **estar en un** ~ to be in a jam.

atollarse [ato'λarse] *vr* to get stuck; (*fig*) to get into a jam.

atolondrado, a [atolon'draðo, a] *adj* scatterbrained.

atolondramiento [atolondra'mjento] *nm* bewilderment; (*insensatez*) silliness.

atómico, a [a'tomiko, a] *adj* atomic.

atomizador [atomiθa'ðor] *nm* atomizer.

átomo ['atomo] *nm* atom.

atónito, a [a'tonito, a] *adj* astonished, amazed.

atontado, a [aton'taðo, a] *adj* stunned; (*bobo*) silly, daft.

atontar [aton'tar] *vt* to stun; ~**se** *vr* to become confused.

atorar [ato'rar] *vt* to obstruct; ~**se** *vr* (*atragantarse*) to choke.

atormentar [atormen'tar] *vt* to torture; (*molestar*) to torment; (*acosar*) to plague, harass.

atornillar [atorni'λar] *vt* to screw on *o* down.

atorón [ato'ron] *nm* (*AM*) traffic jam.

atosigar [atosi'γar] *vt* to harass.

atosigue [ato'siγe] *etc vb V* **atosigar.**

atrabiliario, a [atraβi'ljarjo, a] *adj* bad-tempered.

atracadero [atraka'ðero] *nm* pier.

atracador, a [atraka'ðor, a] *nm/f* robber.

atracar [atra'kar] *vt* (*NAUT*) to moor; (*robar*) to hold up, rob ♦ *vi* to moor; ~**se** *vr* (*hartarse*) to stuff o.s.

atracción [atrak'θjon] *nf* attraction.

atraco [a'trako] *nm* holdup, robbery.

atracón [atra'kon] *nm*: **darse** *o* **pegarse un** ~ (**de**) (*fam*) to pig out (on).

atractivo, a [atrak'tiβo, a] *adj* attractive ♦ *nm* attraction; (*belleza*) attractiveness.

atraer [atra'er] *vt* to attract; **dejarse** ~ **por** to be tempted by.

atragantarse [atraγan'tarse] *vr*: ~ (**con algo**) to choke (on sth); **se me ha atragantado el chico ese/el inglés** I don't take to that boy/English.

atraiga [a'traiγa] *etc*, **atraje** [a'traxe] *etc vb V* **atraer.**

atrancar [atran'kar] *vt* (*con tranca, barra*) to bar, bolt.

atranque [a'tranke] *etc vb V* **atrancar.**

atrapar [atra'par] *vt* to trap; (*resfriado etc*) to catch.

atraque [a'trake] *etc vb V* **atracar.**

atrás [a'tras] *adv* (*movimiento*) back(wards); (*lugar*) behind; (*tiempo*) previously; **ir hacia** ~ to go back(wards); to go to the rear; **estar** ~ to be behind *o* at the back.

atrasado, a [atra'saðo, a] *adj* slow; (*pago*) overdue, late; (*país*) backward.

atrasar [atra'sar] *vi* to be slow; ~**se** *vr* to remain behind; (*llegar tarde*) to arrive late.

atraso [a'traso] *nm* slowness; lateness, delay; (*de país*) backwardness; ~**s** *nmpl* arrears.

atravesado, a [atraβe'saðo, a] *adj*: **un tronco** ~ **en la carretera** a tree trunk lying across the road.

atravesar [atraβe'sar] *vt* (*cruzar*) to cross (over); (*traspasar*) to pierce; (*período*) to go through; (*poner al través*) to lay *o* put across; ~**se** *vr* to come in between; (*intervenir*) to interfere.

atraviese [atra'βjese] *etc vb V* **atravesar.**

atrayendo [atra'jendo] *vb V* **atraer.**

atrayente [atra'jente] *adj* attractive.

atreverse [atre'βerse] *vr* to dare; (*insolentarse*) to be insolent.

atrevido, a [atre'βiðo, a] *adj* daring; insolent.

atrevimiento [atreβi'mjento] *nm* daring; insolence.

atribución [atriβu'θjon] *nf* (*LIT*) attribution; **atribuciones** *nfpl* (*POL*) functions; (*ADMIN*) responsibilities.

atribuir [atriβu'ir] vt to attribute; (funciones) to confer.

atribular [atriβu'lar] vt to afflict, distress.

atributo [atri'βuto] nm attribute.

atribuya [atri'βuja] etc, **atribuyendo** [atriβu'jendo] etc vb V **atribuir**.

atril [a'tril] nm lectern; (MUS) music stand.

atrincherarse [atrintʃe'rarse] vr (MIL) to dig (o.s.) in; ~ **en** (fig) to hide behind.

atrio ['atrjo] nm (REL) porch.

atrocidad [atroθi'ðað] nf atrocity, outrage.

atrofiado, a [atro'fjaðo, a] adj (extremidad) withered.

atrofiarse [atro'fjarse] vr (tb fig) to atrophy.

atronador, a [atrona'ðor, a] adj deafening.

atropellar [atrope'ʎar] vt (derribar) to knock over o down; (empujar) to push (aside); (AUTO) to run over o down; (agraviar) to insult; ~**se** vr to act hastily.

atropello [atro'peʎo] nm (AUTO) accident; (empujón) push; (agravio) wrong; (atrocidad) outrage.

atroz [a'troθ] adj atrocious, awful.

A.T.S. nm/f abr (= Ayudante Técnico Sanitario) nurse.

atto., a. abr (= atento, a) Yours faithfully.

attrezzo [a'treθo] nm props pl.

atuendo [a'twendo] nm attire.

atufar [atu'far] vt (suj: olor) to overcome; (molestar) to irritate; ~**se** vr (fig) to get cross.

atún [a'tun] nm tuna, tunny.

aturdir [atur'ðir] vt to stun; (suj: ruido) to deafen; (fig) to dumbfound, bewilder.

atur(r)ullar [atur(r)u'ʎar] vt to bewilder.

atusar [atu'sar] vt (cortar) to trim; (alisar) to smooth (down).

atuve [a'tuβe] etc vb V **atenerse**.

audacia [au'ðaθja] nf boldness, audacity.

audaz [au'ðaθ] adj bold, audacious.

audible [au'ðiβle] adj audible.

audición [auði'θjon] nf hearing; (TEAT) audition; ~ **radiofónica** radio concert.

audiencia [au'ðjenθja] nf audience; (JUR) high court; (POL): ~ **pública** public inquiry.

audífono [au'ðifono] nm hearing aid.

audiovisual [auðjoβi'swal] adj audio-visual.

auditivo, a [auði'tiβo, a] adj hearing cpd; (conducto, nervio) auditory.

auditor [auði'tor] nm (JUR) judge-advocate; (COM) auditor.

auditoría [auðito'ria] nf audit; (profesión) auditing.

auditorio [auði'torjo] nm audience; (sala) auditorium.

auge ['auxe] nm boom; (clímax) climax; (ECON) expansion; **estar en** ~ to thrive.

augurar [auxu'rar] vt to predict; (presagiar) to portend.

augurio [au'xurjo] nm omen.

aula ['aula] nf classroom.

aullar [au'ʎar] vi to howl, yell.

aullido [au'ʎiðo] nm howl, yell.

aumentar [aumen'tar] vt to increase; (precios) to put up; (producción) to step up; (con microscopio, anteojos) to magnify ♦ vi, ~**se** vr to increase, be on the increase.

aumento [au'mento] nm increase; rise.

aún [a'un] adv still, yet.

aun [a'un] adv even.

aunque [a'unke] conj though, although, even though.

aúpa [a'upa] excl up!, come on!; (fam): **una función de** ~ a slap-up do; **una paliza de** ~ a good hiding.

aupar [au'par] vt (levantar) to help up; (fig) to praise.

aura ['aura] nf (atmósfera) aura.

aureola [aure'ola] nf halo.

auricular [auriku'lar] nm earpiece; receiver; ~**es** nmpl headphones.

aurora [au'rora] nf dawn; ~ **boreal(is)** northern lights pl.

auscultar [auskul'tar] vt (MED: pecho) to listen to, sound.

ausencia [au'senθja] nf absence.

ausentarse [ausen'tarse] vr to go away; (por poco tiempo) to go out.

ausente [au'sente] adj absent ♦ nm/f (ESCOL) absentee; (JUR) missing person.

auspiciar [auspi'sjar] vt (AM) to back, sponsor.

auspicios [aus'piθjos] nmpl auspices; (protección) protection sg.

austeridad [austeri'ðað] nf austerity.

austero, a [aus'tero, a] adj austere.

austral [aus'tral] adj southern ♦ nm monetary unit of Argentina (1985-1991).

Australia [aus'tralja] nf Australia.

australiano, a [austra'ljano, a] adj, nm/f Australian.

Austria ['austrja] nf Austria.

austriaco, a [aus'trjako, a], **austríaco, a** [aus'triako, a] adj, nm/f Austrian.

autenticar [autenti'kar] vt to authenticate.

auténtico, a [au'tentiko, a] adj authentic.

autentificar [autentifi'kar] vt to authenticate.

autentique [auten'tike] etc vb V **autentiar**.

auto ['auto] nm (coche) car; (JUR) edict, decree; (: orden) writ; ~**s** nmpl (JUR) proceedings; (: *acta*) court record *sg*; ~ **de comparecencia** summons, subpoena; ~ **de ejecución** writ of execution.

autoadhesivo, a [autoaðe'siβo, a] *adj* self-adhesive; (*sobre*) self-sealing.

autoalimentación [autoalimenta'θjon] *nf* (*INFORM*): ~ **de hojas** automatic paper feed.

autobiografía [autoβjoɣra'fia] *nf* autobiography.

autobronceador [autoβronθea'ðor] *adj* self-tanning.

autobús [auto'βus] *nm* bus (*BRIT*), (passenger) bus (*US*).

autocar [auto'kar] *nm* coach; ~ **de línea** intercity coach.

autocomprobación [autokomproβa'θjon] *nf* (*INFORM*) self-test.

autóctono, a [au'toktono, a] *adj* native, indigenous.

autodefensa [autoðe'fensa] *nf* self-defence.

autodeterminación [autoðetermina'θjon] *nf* self-determination.

autodidacta [autoði'ðakta] *adj* self-taught ♦ *nm/f*: **ser un(a)** ~ to be self-taught.

autoescuela [autoes'kwela] *nf* driving school.

autofinanciado, a [autofinan'θjaðo, a] *adj* self-financing.

autogestión [autoxes'tjon] *nf* self-management.

autógrafo [au'toɣrafo] *nm* autograph.

automación [automa'θjon] *nf* = **automatización**.

autómata [au'tomata] *nm* automaton.

automáticamente [auto'matikamente] *adv* automatically.

automatice [automa'tiθe] *etc vb V* **automatizar**.

automático, a [auto'matiko, a] *adj* automatic ♦ *nm* press stud.

automatización [automatiθa'θjon] *nf*: ~ **de fábricas** factory automation; ~ **de oficinas** office automation.

automatizar [automati'θar] *vt* to automate.

automotor, triz [automo'tor, 'triz] *adj* self-propelled ♦ *nm* diesel train.

automóvil [auto'moβil] *nm* (motor) car (*BRIT*), automobile (*US*).

automovilismo [automoβi'lismo] *nm* (*DEPORTE*) (sports) car racing.

automovilista [automoβi'lista] *nm/f* motorist, driver.

automovilístico, a [automoβi'listiko, a] *adj* (*industria*) car *cpd*.

autonomía [autono'mia] *nf* autonomy; (*ESP POL*) autonomy, self-government;

(: *comunidad*) autonomous region.

autonómico, a [auto'nomiko, a] *adj* (*ESP POL*) relating to autonomy, autonomous; **gobierno** ~ autonomous government.

autónomo, a [au'tonomo, a] *adj* autonomous; (*INFORM*) stand-alone, offline.

autopista [auto'pista] *nf* motorway (*BRIT*), freeway (*US*).

autopsia [au'topsja] *nf* autopsy.

autor, a [au'tor, a] *nm/f* author; **los** ~**es del atentado** those responsible for the attack.

autorice [auto'riθe] *etc vb V* **autorizar**.

autoridad [autori'ðað] *nf* authority; ~ **local** local authority.

autoritario, a [autori'tarjo, a] *adj* authoritarian.

autorización [autoriθa'θjon] *nf* authorization.

autorizado, a [autori'θaðo, a] *adj* authorized; (*aprobado*) approved.

autorizar [autori'θar] *vt* to authorize; to approve.

autorretrato [autorre'trato] *nm* self-portrait.

autoservicio [autoser'βiθjo] *nm* self-service shop *o* store; (*restaurante*) self-service restaurant.

autostop [auto'stop] *nm* hitch-hiking; **hacer** ~ to hitch-hike.

autostopista [autosto'pista] *nm/f* hitch-hiker.

autosuficiencia [autosufi'θjenθja] *nf* self-sufficiency.

autosuficiente [autosufi'θjente] *adj* self-sufficient; (*pey*) smug.

autosugestión [autosuxes'tjon] *nf* autosuggestion.

autovía [auto'βia] *nf* ≈ dual carriageway (*BRIT*), separated highway (*US*).

auxiliar [auksi'ljar] *vt* to help ♦ *nm/f* assistant.

auxilio [auk'siljo] *nm* assistance, help; **primeros** ~**s** first aid *sg*.

Av *abr* (= *Avenida*) Av(e).

a/v *abr* (*COM*: = *a vista*) at sight.

aval [a'βal] *nm* guarantee; (*persona*) guarantor.

avalancha [aβa'lantʃa] *nf* avalanche.

avalar [aβa'lar] *vt* (*COM etc*) to underwrite; (*fig*) to endorse.

avalista [aβa'lista] *nm* (*COM*) endorser.

avance [a'βanθe] *etc vb V* **avanzar** ♦ *nm* advance; (*pago*) advance payment; (*CINE*) trailer.

avanzado, a [aβan'θaðo, a] *adj* advanced; **de edad avanzada**, **de edad** ~ elderly.

avanzar [aβan'θar] *vt, vi* to advance.

avaricia [aβa'riθja] *nf* avarice, greed.

avaricioso, a [aβari'θjoso, a] *adj* avaricious, greedy.

avaro, a [a'βaro, a] *adj* miserly, mean ♦ *nm/f* miser.

avasallar [aβasa'ʎar] *vt* to subdue, subjugate.

avatar [aβa'tar] *nm* change; **-es** ups and downs.

Avda *abr* (= *Avenida*) Av(e).

AVE ['aβe] *nm abr* (= *Alta Velocidad Española*) ≈ Bullet train.

ave ['aβe] *nf* bird; ~ **de rapiña** bird of prey.

avecinarse [aβeθi'narse] *vr* (*tormenta, fig*) to approach, be on the way.

avejentar [aβexen'tar] *vt, vi*, ~**se** *vr* to age.

avellana [aβe'ʎana] *nf* hazelnut.

avellano [aβe'ʎano] *nm* hazel tree.

avemaría [aβema'ria] *nm* Hail Mary, Ave Maria.

avena [a'βena] *nf* oats *pl*.

avendré [aβen'dre] *etc*, **avenga** [a'βenga] *etc vb V* **avenir**.

avenida [aβe'niða] *nf* (*calle*) avenue.

avenir [aβe'nir] *vt* to reconcile; ~**se** *vr* to come to an agreement, reach a compromise.

aventado, a [aβen'taðo, a] *adj* (*AM*) daring.

aventajado, a [aβenta'xaðo, a] *adj* outstanding.

aventajar [aβenta'xar] *vt* (*sobrepasar*) to surpass, outstrip.

aventar [aβen'tar] *vt* to fan, blow; (*grano*) to winnow; (*AM fam: echar*) to chuck out.

aventón [aβen'ton] *nm* (*AM*) push; **pedir** ~ to hitch a lift.

aventura [aβen'tura] *nf* adventure; ~ **sentimental** love affair.

aventurado, a [aβentu'raðo, a] *adj* risky.

aventurar [aβentu'rar] *vt* to risk; ~**se** *vr* to dare; ~**se a hacer algo** to venture to do sth.

aventurero, a [aβentu'rero, a] *adj* adventurous.

avergoncé [aβerɣon'θe], **avergoncemos** [aβerɣon'θemos] *etc vb V* **avergonzar**.

avergonzar [aβerɣon'θar] *vt* to shame; (*desconcertar*) to embarrass; ~**se** *vr* to be ashamed; to be embarrassed.

avergüence [aβer'ɣwenθe] *etc vb V* **avergonzar**.

avería [aβe'ria] *nf* (*TEC*) breakdown, fault.

averiado, a [aβe'rjaðo, a] *adj* broken-down.

averiar [aβe'rjar] *vt* to break; ~**se** *vr* to break down.

averiguación [aβeriɣwa'θjon] *nf* investigation; (*determinación*) ascertainment.

averiguar [aβeri'ɣwar] *vt* to investigate; (*descubrir*) to find out, ascertain.

averigüe [aβe'riɣwe] *etc vb V* **averiguar**.

aversión [aβer'sjon] *nf* aversion, dislike; **cobrar** ~ **a** to take a strong dislike to.

avestruz [aβes'truθ] *nm* ostrich.

aviación [aβja'θjon] *nf* aviation; (*fuerzas aéreas*) air force.

aviado, a [a'βjaðo, a] *adj*: **estar** ~ to be in a mess.

aviador, a [aβja'ðor, a] *nm/f* aviator, airman/woman.

aviar [a'βjar] *vt* to prepare, get ready.

avícola [a'βikola] *adj* poultry *cpd*.

avicultura [aβikul'tura] *nf* poultry farming.

avidez [aβi'ðeθ] *nf* avidity, eagerness.

ávido, a ['aβiðo, a] *adj* avid, eager.

aviente [a'βjente] *etc vb V* **aventar**.

avieso, a [a'βjeso, a] *adj* (*torcido*) distorted; (*perverso*) wicked.

avinagrado, a [aβina'ɣraðo, a] *adj* sour, acid.

avinagrarse [aβina'ɣrarse] *vr* to go *o* turn sour.

avine [a'βine] *etc vb V* **avenir**.

Aviñón [aβi'ɲon] *nm* Avignon.

avío [a'βio] *nm* preparation; ~**s** *nmpl* gear *sg*, kit *sg*.

avión [a'βjon] *nm* aeroplane; (*ave*) martin; ~ **de reacción** jet (plane); **por** ~ (*CORREOS*) by air mail.

avioneta [aβjo'neta] *nf* light aircraft.

avisar [aβi'sar] *vt* (*advertir*) to warn, notify; (*informar*) to tell; (*aconsejar*) to advise, counsel.

aviso [a'βiso] *nm* warning; (*noticia*) notice; (*COM*) demand note; (*INFORM*) prompt; ~ **escrito** notice in writing; **sin previo** ~ without warning; **estar sobre** ~ to be on the look-out.

avispa [a'βispa] *nf* wasp.

avispado, a [aβis'paðo, a] *adj* sharp, clever.

avispero [aβis'pero] *nm* wasp's nest.

avispón [aβis'pon] *nm* hornet.

avistar [aβis'tar] *vt* to sight, spot.

avitaminosis [aβitami'nosis] *nf inv* vitamin deficiency.

avituallar [aβitwa'ʎar] *vt* to supply with food.

avivar [aβi'βar] *vt* to strengthen, intensify; ~**se** *vr* to revive, acquire new life.

avizor [aβi'θor] *adj*: **estar ojo** ~ to be on the alert.

avizorar [aβiθo'rar] *vt* to spy on.

axila [ak'sila] *nf* armpit.

axioma [ak'sjoma] *nm* axiom.

ay [ai] *excl* (*dolor*) ow!, ouch!; (*aflicción*)

oh!, oh dear!; ¡~ de mi! poor me!

aya ['aja] *nf* governess; (*niñera*) nanny.

ayer [a'jer] *adv, nm* yesterday; **antes de ~** the day before yesterday; **~ por la tarde** yesterday afternoon/evening.

aymara, aymará [ai'mara, aima'ra] *adj, nm/f* Aymara.

ayo ['ajo] *nm* tutor.

ayote [a'jote] *nm* (*AM*) pumpkin.

Ayto. *abr* = **Ayuntamiento.**

ayuda [a'juða] *nf* help, assistance; (*MED*) enema ♦ *nm* page; **~ humanitaria** humanitarian aid.

ayudante, a [aju'ðante, a] *nm/f* assistant, helper; (*ESCOL*) assistant; (*MIL*) adjutant.

ayudar [aju'ðar] *vt* to help, assist.

ayunar [aju'nar] *vi* to fast.

ayunas [a'junas] *nfpl*: **estar en ~** (*no haber comido*) to be fasting; (*ignorar*) to be in the dark.

ayuno [a'juno] *nm* fasting.

ayuntamiento [ajunta'mjento] *nm* (*consejo*) town/city council; (*edificio*) town/city hall; (*cópula*) sexual intercourse.

azabache [aθa'ßatʃe] *nm* jet.

azada [a'θaða] *nf* hoe.

azafata [aθa'fata] *nf* air hostess (*BRIT*) o stewardess.

azafate [asa'fate] *nm* (*AM*) tray.

azafrán [aθa'fran] *nm* saffron.

azahar [aθa'ar] *nm* orange/lemon blossom.

azalea [aθa'lea] *nf* azalea.

azar [a'θar] *nm* (*casualidad*) chance, fate; (*desgracia*) misfortune, accident; **por ~** by chance; **al ~** at random.

azaroso, a [aθa'roso, a] *adj* (*arriesgado*) risky; (*vida*) eventful.

Azerbaiyán [aθerba'jan] *nm* Azerbaijan.

azerbaiyano, a [aθerba'jano, a], **azerí** [aθe'ri] *adj, nm/f* Azerbaijani, Azeri.

azogue [a'θoɣe] *nm* mercury.

azor [a'θor] *nm* goshawk.

azoramiento [aθora'mjento] *nm* alarm; (*confusión*) confusion.

azorar [aθo'rar] *vt* to alarm; **~se** *vr* to get alarmed.

Azores [a'θores] *nfpl*: **las (Islas) ~** the Azores.

azotaina [aθo'taina] *nf* beating.

azotar [aθo'tar] *vt* to whip, beat; (*pegar*) to spank.

azote [a'θote] *nm* (*látigo*) whip; (*latigazo*) lash, stroke; (*en las nalgas*) spank; (*calamidad*) calamity.

azotea [aθo'tea] *nf* (flat) roof.

azteca [aθ'teka] *adj, nm/f* Aztec.

azúcar [a'θukar] *nm* sugar.

azucarado, a [aθuka'raðo, a] *adj* sugary, sweet.

azucarero, a [aθuka'rero, a] *adj* sugar *cpd* ♦ *nm* sugar bowl.

azuce [a'θuθe] *etc vb V* **azuzar.**

azucena [aθu'θena] *nf* white lily.

azufre [a'θufre] *nm* sulphur.

azul [a'θul] *adj, nm* blue; **~ celeste/marino** sky/navy blue.

azulejo [aθu'lexo] *nm* tile.

azulgrana [aθul'ɣrana] *adj inv* of Barcelona Football Club ♦ *nm*: **los A~** the Barcelona F.C. players o team.

azuzar [aθu'θar] *vt* to incite, egg on.

B b

B, b [(*ESP*) be, (*AM*) be'larɣa] *nf* (*letra*) B, b; **B de Barcelona** B for Benjamin (*BRIT*) o Baker (*US*).

baba ['baßa] *nf* spittle, saliva; **se le caía la ~** (*fig*) he was thrilled to bits.

babear [baße'ar] *vi* (*echar saliva*) to slobber; (*niño*) to dribble; (*fig*) to drool, slaver.

babel [ba'ßel] *nm o f* bedlam.

babero [ba'ßero] *nm* bib.

Babia ['baßja] *nf*: **estar en ~** to be daydreaming.

bable ['baßle] *nm* Asturian (dialect).

babor [ba'ßor] *nm* port (side); **a ~** to port.

babosada [baßo'saða] *nf*: **decir ~s** (*AM fam*) to talk rubbish.

baboso, a [ba'ßoso, a] *adj* slobbering; (*ZOOL*) slimy; (*AM*) silly ♦ *nm/f* (*AM*) fool.

babucha [ba'ßutʃa] *nf* slipper.

baca ['baka] *nf* (*AUTO*) luggage o roof rack.

bacalao [baka'lao] *nm* cod(fish).

bacanal [baka'nal] *nf* orgy.

bache ['batʃe] *nm* pothole, rut; (*fig*) bad patch.

bachillerato [batʃiʎe'rato] *nm* 2 *year secondary school course*; *V tb* **sistema educativo.**

bacilo [ba'θilo] *nm* bacillus, germ.

bacinica [baθi'nika] *nf*, **bacinilla** [baθi'niʎa] *nf* chamber pot.

bacteria [bak'terja] *nf* bacterium, germ.

bacteriológico, a [bakterjo'loxico, a] *adj* bacteriological; **guerra ~a** germ warfare.

báculo ['bakulo] *nm* stick, staff; (*fig*)
support.
badajo [ba'ðaxo] *nm* clapper (*of a bell*).
bádminton ['baðminton] *nm* badminton.
baf(f)le ['baf(f)le] *nm* (*ELEC*) speaker.
bagaje [ba'ɣaxe] *nm* baggage; (*fig*)
background.
bagatela [baɣa'tela] *nf* trinket, trifle.
Bahama [ba'ama]: **las (Islas)** ~, **las** ~**s** *nfpl*
the Bahamas.
bahía [ba'ia] *nf* bay.
bailar [bai'lar] *vt, vi* to dance.
bailarín, ina [baila'rin, ina] *nm/f* dancer; (*de
ballet*) ballet dancer.
baile ['baile] *nm* dance; (*formal*) ball.
baja ['baxa] *nf* drop, fall; (*ECON*) slump;
(*MIL*) casualty; (*paro*) redundancy; **dar de**
~ (*soldado*) to discharge; (*empleado*) to
dismiss, sack; **darse de** ~ (*retirarse*) to
drop out; (*MED*) to go sick; (*dimitir*) to
resign; **estar de** ~ (*enfermo*) to be off
sick; (*BOLSA*) to be dropping *o* falling;
jugar a la ~ (*ECON*) to speculate on a fall
in prices; *V tb* **bajo**.
bajada [ba'xaða] *nf* descent; (*camino*)
slope; (*de aguas*) ebb.
bajamar [baxa'mar] *nf* low tide.
bajar [ba'xar] *vi* to go *o* come down;
(*temperatura, precios*) to drop, fall ♦ *vt*
(*cabeza*) to bow; (*escalera*) to go *o* come
down; (*radio etc*) to turn down; (*precio,
voz*) to lower; (*llevar abajo*) to take down;
~**se** *vr* (*de vehículo*) to get out; (*de
autobús*) to get off; ~ **de** (*coche*) to get
out of; (*autobús*) to get off; ~**le los
humos a algn** (*fig*) to cut sb down to size.
bajeza [ba'xeθa] *nf* baseness; (*una* ~) vile
deed.
bajío [ba'xio] *nm* shoal, sandbank; (*AM*)
lowlands *pl.*
bajista [ba'xista] *nm/f* (*MUS*) bassist ♦ *adj*
(*BOLSA*) bear *cpd.*
bajo, a ['baxo, a] *adj* (*terreno*) low(-lying);
(*mueble, número, precio*) low; (*piso*)
ground *cpd*; (*de estatura*) small, short;
(*color*) pale; (*sonido*) faint, soft, low; (*voz,
tono*) deep; (*metal*) base ♦ *adv* (*hablar*)
softly, quietly; (*volar*) low ♦ *prep* under,
below, underneath ♦ *nm* (*MUS*) bass;
hablar en voz baja to whisper; ~ **la lluvia**
in the rain.
bajón [ba'xon] *nm* fall, drop.
bajura [ba'xura] *nf*: **pesca de** ~ coastal
fishing.
bakalao [baka'lao] *nm* (*MUS*) rave music.
bala ['bala] *nf* bullet; ~ **de goma** plastic
bullet.
balacera [bala'sera] *nf* (*AM*) shoot-out.

balada [ba'laða] *nf* ballad.
baladí [bala'ði] *adj* trivial.
baladronada [balaðro'naða] *nf* (*dicho*)
boast, brag; (*hecho*) piece of bravado.
balance [ba'lanθe] *nm* (*COM*) balance;
(: *libro*) balance sheet; (: *cuenta general*)
stocktaking; ~ **de comprobación** trial
balance; ~ **consolidado** consolidated
balance sheet; **hacer** ~ to take stock.
balancear [balanθe'ar] *vt* to balance ♦ *vi*,
~**se** *vr* to swing (to and fro); (*vacilar*) to
hesitate.
balanceo [balan'θeo] *nm* swinging.
balandro [ba'landro] *nm* yacht.
balanza [ba'lanθa] *nf* scales *pl*, balance; ~
comercial balance of trade; ~ **de pagos/
de poder(es)** balance of payments/of
power; (*ASTRO*): **B**~ Libra.
balar [ba'lar] *vi* to bleat.
balaustrada [balaus'traða] *nf* balustrade;
(*pasamanos*) banister.
balazo [ba'laθo] *nm* (*tiro*) shot; (*herida*)
bullet wound.
balboa [bal'ßoa] *nf* Panamanian currency
unit.
balbucear [balßuθe'ar] *vi, vt* to stammer,
stutter.
balbuceo [balßu'θeo] *nm* stammering,
stuttering.
balbucir [balßu'θir] *vi, vt* to stammer,
stutter.
balbuzca [bal'ßuθka] *etc vb V* **balbucir**.
Balcanes [bal'kanes] *nmpl*: **los (Montes)** ~
the Balkans, the Balkan Mountains; **la
Península de los** ~ the Balkan
Peninsula.
balcánico, a [bal'kaniko, a] *adj* Balkan.
balcón [bal'kon] *nm* balcony.
balda ['balda] *nf* (*estante*) shelf.
baldar [bal'dar] *vt* to cripple; (*agotar*) to
exhaust.
balde ['balde] *nm* (*esp AM*) bucket, pail; **de**
~ *adv* (for) free, for nothing; **en** ~ *adv* in
vain.
baldío, a [bal'dio, a] *adj* uncultivated;
(*terreno*) waste; (*inútil*) vain ♦ *nm*
wasteland.
baldosa [bal'dosa] *nf* (*azulejo*) floor tile;
(*grande*) flagstone.
baldosín [baldo'sin] *nm* wall tile.
balear [bale'ar] *adj* Balearic, of the
Balearic Islands ♦ *nm/f* native *o*
inhabitant of the Balearic Islands ♦ *vt*
(*AM*) to shoot (at).
Baleares [bale'ares] *nfpl*: **las (Islas)** ~ the
Balearics, the Balearic Islands.
balido [ba'liðo] *nm* bleat, bleating.
balín [ba'lin] *nm* pellet; **balines** *nmpl*

buckshot *sg*.

balística [ba'listika] *nf* ballistics *pl*.

baliza [ba'liθa] *nf* (*AVIAT*) beacon; (*NAUT*) buoy.

ballena [ba'ʎena] *nf* whale.

ballenero, a [baʎe'nero, a] *adj*: **industria ballenera** whaling industry ♦ *nm* (*pescador*) whaler; (*barco*) whaling ship.

ballesta [ba'ʎesta] *nf* crossbow; (*AUTO*) spring.

ballet, *pl* **ballets** [ba'le, ba'les] *nm* ballet.

balneario, a [balne'arjo, a] *adj*: **estación balnearia** (bathing) resort ♦ *nm* spa, health resort.

balompié [balom'pje] *nm* football.

balón [ba'lon] *nm* ball.

baloncesto [balon'θesto] *nm* basketball.

balonmano [balon'mano] *nm* handball.

balonvolea [balombo'lea] *nm* volleyball.

balsa ['balsa] *nf* raft; (*BOT*) balsa wood.

bálsamo ['balsamo] *nm* balsam, balm.

balsón [bal'son] *nm* (*AM*) swamp, bog.

báltico, a ['baltiko, a] *adj* Baltic; **el (Mar) B~** the Baltic (Sea).

baluarte [ba'lwarte] *nm* bastion, bulwark.

bambolearse [bambole'arse] *vr* to swing, sway; (*silla*) to wobble.

bamboleo [bambo'leo] *nm* swinging, swaying; wobbling.

bambú [bam'bu] *nm* bamboo.

banal [ba'nal] *adj* banal, trivial.

banana [ba'nana] *nf* (*AM*) banana.

bananal [bana'nal] *nm* (*AM*) banana plantation.

banano [ba'nano] *nm* (*AM*) banana tree.

banasta [ba'nasta] *nf* large basket, hamper.

banca ['banka] *nf* (*asiento*) bench; (*COM*) banking.

bancario, a [ban'karjo, a] *adj* banking *cpd*, bank *cpd*; **giro ~** bank draft.

bancarrota [banka'rrota] *nf* bankruptcy; **declararse en *o* hacer ~** to go bankrupt.

banco ['banko] *nm* bench; (*ESCOL*) desk; (*COM*) bank; (*GEO*) stratum; **~ comercial *o* mercantil** commercial bank; **~ por acciones** joint-stock bank; **~ de crédito/ de ahorros** credit/savings bank; **~ de arena** sandbank; **~ de datos** (*INFORM*) data bank; **~ de hielo** iceberg.

banda ['banda] *nf* band; (*cinta*) ribbon; (*pandilla*) gang; (*MUS*) brass band; (*NAUT*) side, edge; **la B~ Oriental** Uruguay; **~ sonora** soundtrack; **~ transportadora** conveyor belt.

bandada [ban'daða] *nf* (*de pájaros*) flock;

(*de peces*) shoal.

bandazo [ban'daθo] *nm*: **dar ~s** (*coche*) to veer from side to side.

bandeja [ban'dexa] *nf* tray; **~ de entrada/ salida** in-tray/out-tray.

bandera [ban'dera] *nf* (*de tela*) flag; (*estandarte*) banner; (*INFORM*) marker, flag; **izar la ~** to hoist the flag.

banderilla [bande'riʎa] *nf* banderilla; (*tapa*) *savoury appetizer* (*served on a cocktail stick*).

banderín [bande'rin] *nm* pennant, small flag.

banderola [bande'rola] *nf* (*MIL*) pennant.

bandido [ban'diðo] *nm* bandit.

bando ['bando] *nm* (*edicto*) edict, proclamation; (*facción*) faction; **pasar al otro ~** to change sides; **los ~s** (*REL*) the banns.

bandolera [bando'lera] *nf*: **bolsa de ~** shoulder bag.

bandolero [bando'lero] *nm* bandit, brigand.

bandoneón [bandone'on] *nm* (*AM*) large accordion.

BANESTO [ba'nesto] *nm abr* = *Banco Español de Crédito*.

banquero [ban'kero] *nm* banker.

banqueta [ban'keta] *nf* stool; (*AM*: *acera*) pavement (*BRIT*), sidewalk (*US*).

banquete [ban'kete] *nm* banquet; (*para convidados*) formal dinner; **~ de boda** wedding breakfast.

banquillo [ban'kiʎo] *nm* (*JUR*) dock, prisoner's bench; (*banco*) bench; (*para los pies*) footstool.

bañadera [baɲa'ðera] *nf* (*AM*) bath(tub).

bañado [ba'ɲaðo] *nm* (*AM*) swamp.

bañador [baɲa'ðor] *nm* swimming costume (*BRIT*), bathing suit (*US*).

bañar [ba'ɲar] *vt* (*niño*) to bath, bathe; (*objeto*) to dip; (*de barniz*) to coat; **~se** *vr* (*en el mar*) to bathe, swim; (*en la bañera*) to have a bath.

bañero, a [ba'ɲero, a] *nmf* lifeguard ♦ *nf* bath(tub).

bañista [ba'ɲista] *nm/f* bather.

baño ['baɲo] *nm* (*en bañera*) bath; (*en río, mar*) dip, swim; (*cuarto*) bathroom; (*bañera*) bath(tub); (*capa*) coating; **ir a tomar los ~s** to take the waters.

baptista [bap'tista] *nm/f* Baptist.

baqueano, a, baquiano, a [bake'ano, a, baki'ano, a] *nm/f* (*AM*) guide.

baqueta [ba'keta] *nf* (*MUS*) drumstick.

bar [bar] *nm* bar.

barahúnda [bara'unda] *nf* uproar, hubbub.

baraja [ba'raxa] *nf* pack (of cards); *see boxed note*.

BARAJA ESPAÑOLA

The **baraja española** is the traditional Spanish deck of cards, which differs from a standard poker deck. The four "palos" (suits) are "oros" (golden coins), "copas" (goblets), "espadas" (swords) and "bastos" ("clubs", but not the same as the ones in a poker pack). Every suit has nine numbered cards (although for certain games only seven are used), and three face cards: "sota" (jack), "caballo" (≈ queen) and "rey" (king).

---

barajar [bara'xar] vt (naipes) to shuffle; (fig) to jumble up.

baranda [ba'randa], **barandilla** [baran'diʎa] nf rail, railing.

baratija [bara'tixa] nf trinket; (fig) trifle; **~s** nfpl (COM) cheap goods.

baratillo [bara'tiʎo] nm (tienda) junkshop; (subasta) bargain sale; (conjunto de cosas) second-hand goods pl.

barato, a [ba'rato, a] adj cheap ♦ adv cheap, cheaply.

baratura [bara'tura] nf cheapness.

baraúnda [bara'unda] nf = **barahúnda**.

barba ['barßa] nf (mentón) chin; (pelo) beard; **tener ~** to be unshaven; **hacer algo en las ~s de algn** to do sth under sb's very nose; **reírse en las ~s de algn** to laugh in sb's face.

barbacoa [barßa'koa] nf (parrilla) barbecue; (carne) barbecued meat.

barbaridad [barßari'ðað] nf barbarity; (acto) barbarism; (atrocidad) outrage; **una ~ de** (fam) loads of; **¡qué ~!** (fam) how awful!; **cuesta una ~** (fam) it costs a fortune.

barbarie [bar'ßarje] nf, **barbarismo** [barßa'rismo] nm barbarism; (crueldad) barbarity.

bárbaro, a ['barßaro, a] adj barbarous, cruel; (grosero) rough, uncouth ♦ nm/f barbarian ♦ adv: **lo pasamos ~** (fam) we had a great time; **¡qué ~!** (fam) how marvellous!; **un éxito ~** (fam) a terrific success; **es un tipo ~** (fam) he's a great bloke.

barbecho [bar'ßetʃo] nm fallow land.

barbero [bar'ßero] nm barber, hairdresser.

barbilampiño [barßilam'piɲo] adj smooth-faced; (fig) inexperienced.

barbilla [bar'ßiʎa] nf chin, tip of the chin.

barbitúrico [barßi'turiko] nm barbiturate.

barbo ['barßo] nm: **~ de mar** red mullet.

barbotar [barßo'tar], **barbotear** [barßote'ar] vt, vi to mutter, mumble.

barbudo, a [bar'ßuðo, a] adj bearded.

barbullar [barßu'ʎar] vi to jabber away.

barca ['barka] nf (small) boat; **~ pesquera** fishing boat; **~ de pasaje** ferry.

barcaza [bar'kaθa] nf barge; **~ de desembarco** landing craft.

Barcelona [barθe'lona] nf Barcelona.

barcelonés, esa [barθelo'nes, esa] adj of o from Barcelona ♦ nm/f native o inhabitant of Barcelona.

barco ['barko] nm boat; (buque) ship; (COM etc) vessel; **~ de carga** cargo boat; **~ de guerra** warship; **~ de vela** sailing ship; **ir en ~** to go by boat.

baremo [ba'remo] nm scale; (tabla de cuentas) ready reckoner.

barítono [ba'ritono] nm baritone.

barman ['barman] nm barman.

Barna. abr = **Barcelona**.

barnice [bar'niθe] etc vb V **barnizar**.

barniz [bar'niθ] nm varnish; (en la loza) glaze; (fig) veneer.

barnizar [barni'θar] vt to varnish; (loza) to glaze.

barómetro [ba'rometro] nm barometer.

barón [ba'ron] nm baron.

baronesa [baro'nesa] nf baroness.

barquero [bar'kero] nm boatman.

barquilla [bar'kiʎa] nf (NAUT) log.

barquillo [bar'kiʎo] nm cone, cornet.

barra ['barra] nf bar, rod; (JUR) rail; (: banquillo) dock; (de un bar, café) bar; (de pan) French loaf; (palanca) lever; **~ de carmín** o **de labios** lipstick; **~ espaciadora** (INFORM) space bar; **~ inversa** backslash; **~ libre** free bar; **no pararse en ~s** to stick o stop at nothing.

barrabasada [barraßa'saða] nf (piece of) mischief.

barraca [ba'rraka] nf hut, cabin; (en Valencia) thatched farmhouse; (en feria) booth.

barracón [barra'kon] nm (caseta) big hut.

barragana [barra'yana] nf concubine.

barranca [ba'rranka] nf ravine, gully.

barranco [ba'rranko] nm ravine; (fig) difficulty.

barrena [ba'rrena] nf drill.

barrenar [barre'nar] vt to drill (through).

barrendero, a [barren'dero, a] nm/f street-sweeper.

barreno [ba'rreno] nm large drill.

barreño [ba'rreɲo] nm washing-up bowl.

barrer [ba'rrer] vt to sweep; (quitar) to sweep away; (MIL, NAUT) to sweep, rake (with gunfire) ♦ vi to sweep up.

barrera [ba'rrera] nf barrier; (MIL) barricade; (FERRO) crossing gate; **poner ~s a** to hinder; **~ arancelaria** (COM) tariff barrier; ~ **comercial** (*COM*) trade barrier.

barriada [ba'rrjaða] *nf* quarter, district.

barricada [barri'kaða] *nf* barricade.

barrida [ba'rriða] *nf*, **barrido** [ba'rriðo] *nm* sweep, sweeping.

barriga [ba'rriɣa] *nf* belly; (*panza*) paunch; (*vientre*) guts *pl*; **echar** ~ to get middle-age spread.

barrigón, ona [barri'ɣon, ona], **barrigudo, a** [barri'ɣuðo, a] *adj* potbellied.

barril [ba'rril] *nm* barrel, cask; **cerveza de** ~ draught beer.

barrio ['barrjo] *nm* (*vecindad*) area, neighborhood (*US*); (*en las afueras*) suburb; ~**s bajos** poor quarter *sg*; ~ **chino** red-light district.

barriobajero, a [barrjoßßa'xero, a] *adj* (*vulgar*) common.

barro ['barro] *nm* (*lodo*) mud; (*objetos*) earthenware; (*MED*) pimple.

barroco, a [ba'rroko, a] *adj* Baroque; (*fig*) elaborate ♦ *nm* Baroque.

barrote [ba'rrote] *nm* (*de ventana etc*) bar.

barruntar [barrun'tar] *vt* (*conjeturar*) to guess; (*presentir*) to suspect.

barrunto [ba'rrunto] *nm* guess; suspicion.

bartola [bar'tola]: **a la** ~ *adv*: **tirarse a la** ~ to take it easy, be lazy.

bártulos ['bartulos] *nmpl* things, belongings.

barullo [ba'ruʎo] *nm* row, uproar.

basa ['basa] *nf* (*ARQ*) base.

basamento [basa'mento] *nm* base, plinth.

basar [ba'sar] *vt* to base; ~**se** *vr*: ~**se en** to be based on.

basca ['baska] *nf* nausea.

báscula ['baskula] *nf* (*platform*) scales *pl*; ~ **biestable** (*INFORM*) flip-flop, toggle.

bascular [basku'lar] *vt* (*INFORM*) to toggle.

base ['base] *nf* base; **a** ~ **de** on the basis of, based on; (*mediante*) by means of; **a** ~ **de bien** in abundance; ~ **de conocimiento** knowledge base; ~ **de datos** database.

básico, a ['basiko, a] *adj* basic.

Basilea [basi'lea] *nf* Basle.

basílica [ba'silika] *nf* basilica.

basilisco [basi'lisko] *nm* (*AM*) iguana; **estar hecho un** ~ to be hopping mad.

basket, básquet ['basket] *nm* basketball.

══════════════ *PALABRA CLAVE*

bastante [bas'tante] *adj* **1** (*suficiente*) enough; ~ **dinero** enough *o* sufficient money; ~**s libros** enough books
2 (*valor intensivo*): ~ **gente** quite a lot of people; **tener** ~ **calor** to be rather hot;

hace ~ **tiempo que ocurrió** it happened quite *o* rather a long time ago
♦ *adv*: ~ **bueno/malo** quite good/rather bad; ~ **rico** pretty rich; **(lo)** ~ **inteligente (como) para hacer algo** clever enough *o* sufficiently clever to do sth; **voy a tardar** ~ I'm going to be a while *o* quite some time.

bastar [bas'tar] *vi* to be enough *o* sufficient; ~**se** *vr* to be self-sufficient; ~ **para** to be enough to; **¡basta!** (that's) enough!

bastardilla [bastar'ðiʎa] *nf* italics *pl*.

bastardo, a [bas'tarðo, a] *adj*, *nm/f* bastard.

bastidor [basti'ðor] *nm* frame; (*de coche*) chassis; (*ARTE*) stretcher; (*TEAT*) wing; **entre** ~**es** behind the scenes.

basto, a ['basto, a] *adj* coarse, rough ♦ *nmpl*: ~**s** (*NAIPES*) *one of the suits in the Spanish card deck*; V *tb* **Baraja Española**.

bastón [bas'ton] *nm* stick, staff; (*para pasear*) walking stick; ~ **de mando** baton.

bastonazo [basto'naθo] *nm* blow with a stick.

bastoncillo [baston'θiʎo] *nm* (*tb*: ~ **de algodón**) cotton bud.

basura [ba'sura] *nf* rubbish, refuse (*BRIT*), garbage (*US*).

basurero [basu'rero] *nm* (*hombre*) dustman (*BRIT*), garbage collector *o* man (*US*); (*lugar*) rubbish dump; (*cubo*) (rubbish) bin (*BRIT*), trash can (*US*).

bata ['bata] *nf* (*gen*) dressing gown; (*cubretodo*) smock, overall; (*MED, TEC etc*) lab(oratory) coat.

batacazo [bata'kaθo] *nm* bump.

batalla [ba'taʎa] *nf* battle; **de** ~ for everyday use.

batallar [bata'ʎar] *vi* to fight.

batallón [bata'ʎon] *nm* battalion.

batata [ba'tata] *nf* (*AM*: *CULIN*) sweet potato.

bate ['bate] *nm* (*DEPORTE*) bat.

batea [ba'tea] *nf* (*AM*) washing trough.

bateador [batea'ðor] *nm* (*DEPORTE*) batter, batsman.

batería [bate'ria] *nf* battery; (*MUS*) drums *pl*; (*TEAT*) footlights *pl*; ~ **de cocina** kitchen utensils *pl*.

batiburrillo [batißu'rriʎo] *nm* hotchpotch.

batido, a [ba'tiðo, a] *adj* (*camino*) beaten, well-trodden ♦ *nm* (*CULIN*) batter; ~ (**de leche**) milk shake ♦ *nf* (*AM*) (police) raid.

batidora [bati'ðora] *nf* beater, mixer; ~ **eléctrica** food mixer, blender.

batir [ba'tir] vt to beat, strike; (vencer) to beat, defeat; (revolver) to beat, mix; (pelo) to back-comb; ~**se** vr to fight; ~ **palmas** to clap, applaud.

baturro, a [ba'turro, a] nm/f Aragonese peasant.

batuta [ba'tuta] nf baton; **llevar la** ~ (fig) to be the boss.

baudio ['bauðjo] nm (INFORM) baud.

baúl [ba'ul] nm trunk; (AM AUTO) boot (BRIT), trunk (US).

bautice [bau'tiθe] etc vb V **bautizar**.

bautismo [bau'tismo] nm baptism, christening.

bautista [bau'tista] adj, nm/f Baptist.

bautizar [bauti'θar] vt to baptize, christen; (fam: diluir) to water down; (dar apodo) to dub.

bautizo [bau'tiθo] nm baptism, christening.

bávaro, a ['baßaro, a] adj, nm/f Bavarian.

Baviera [ba'ßjera] nf Bavaria.

baya ['baja] nf berry; V tb **bayo**.

bayeta [ba'jeta] nf (trapo) floorcloth; (AM: pañal) nappy (BRIT), diaper (US).

bayo, a ['bajo, a] adj bay.

bayoneta [bajo'neta] nf bayonet.

baza ['baθa] nf trick; **meter** ~ to butt in.

bazar [ba'θar] nm bazaar.

bazo ['baθo] nm spleen.

bazofia [ba'θofja] nf pigswill (BRIT), hogwash (US); (libro etc) trash.

BCE nm abr (= Banco Central Europeo) ECB.

beatificar [beatifi'kar] vt to beatify.

beato, a [be'ato, a] adj blessed; (piadoso) pious.

bebe (AM), pl **bebes, bebé**, pl **bebés** ['beße, 'beßes, be'ße, be'ßes] nm baby.

bebedero, a [beße'ðero, a] nm (para animales) drinking trough.

bebedizo, a [beße'ðiθo, a] adj drinkable ♦ nm potion.

bebedor, a [beße'ðor, a] adj hard-drinking.

bebé-probeta [be'ße-pro'ßeta], pl **bebés-probeta** nm/f test-tube baby.

beber [be'ßer] vt, vi to drink; ~ **a sorbos/tragos** to sip/gulp; **se lo bebió todo** he drank it all up.

bebido, a [be'ßiðo, a] adj drunk ♦ nf drink.

beca ['beka] nf grant, scholarship.

becado, a [be'kaðo, a] nm/f, **becario, a** [be'karjo, a] nm/f scholarship holder.

becerro [be'θerro] nm yearling calf.

bechamel [betʃa'mel] nf = **besamel**.

becuadro [be'kwaðro] nm (MUS) natural sign.

bedel [be'ðel] nm porter, janitor.

beduino, a [be'ðwino, a] adj, nm/f Bedouin.

befarse [be'farse] vr: ~ **de algo** to scoff at sth.

beige ['beix], **beis** ['beis] adj, nm beige.

béisbol ['beisßol] nm baseball.

bejuco [be'xuko] nm (AM) reed, liana.

beldad [bel'dað] nf beauty.

Belén [be'len] nm Bethlehem; **b**~ (de Navidad) nativity scene, crib.

belga ['belxa] adj, nm/f Belgian.

Bélgica ['belxika] nf Belgium.

Belgrado [bel'xraðo] nm Belgrade.

Belice [be'liθe] nm Belize.

bélico, a ['beliko, a] adj (actitud) warlike.

belicoso, a [beli'koso, a] adj (guerrero) warlike; (agresivo) aggressive, bellicose.

beligerante [belixe'rante] adj belligerent.

bellaco, a [be'ʎako, a] adj sly, cunning ♦ nm villain, rogue.

belladona [beʎa'ðona] nf deadly nightshade.

bellaquería [beʎake'ria] nf (acción) dirty trick; (calidad) wickedness.

belleza [be'ʎeθa] nf beauty.

bello, a ['beʎo, a] adj beautiful, lovely; **Bellas Artes** Fine Art sg.

bellota [be'ʎota] nf acorn.

bemol [be'mol] nm (MUS) flat; **esto tiene** ~**es** (fam) this is a tough one.

bencina [ben'sina] nf (AM) petrol (BRIT), gas (US).

bendecir [bende'θir] vt to bless; ~ **la mesa** to say grace.

bendición [bendi'θjon] nf blessing.

bendiga [ben'dixa] etc, **bendije** [ben'dixe] etc vb V **bendecir**.

bendito, a [ben'dito, a] pp de **bendecir** ♦ adj (santo) blessed; (agua) holy; (afortunado) lucky; (feliz) happy; (sencillo) simple ♦ nm/f simple soul; ¡~ **sea Dios!** thank goodness!; **es un** ~ he's sweet; **dormir como un** ~ to sleep like a log.

benedictino, a [beneðik'tino, a] adj, nm Benedictine.

benefactor, a [benefak'tor, a] nm/f benefactor/benefactress.

beneficencia [benefi'θenθja] nf charity.

beneficiar [benefi'θjar] vt to benefit, be of benefit to; ~**se** vr to benefit, profit.

beneficiario, a [benefi'θjarjo, a] nm/f beneficiary; (de cheque) payee.

beneficio [bene'fiθjo] nm (bien) benefit, advantage; (COM) profit, gain; **a** ~ **de** for the benefit of; **en** ~ **propio** to one's own advantage; ~ **bruto/neto** gross/net profit; ~ **por acción** earnings pl per share.

beneficioso, a [benefi'θjoso, a] adj beneficial.

benéfico, a [be'nefiko, a] adj charitable;

sociedad ~a charity (organization).

benemérito, a [bene'merito, a] *adj* meritorious ♦ *nf*: **la Benemérita** (*ESP*) the Civil Guard; *V tb* **Guardia Civil**.

beneplácito [bene'plaθito] *nm* approval, consent.

benevolencia [beneßo'lenθja] *nf* benevolence, kindness.

benévolo, a [be'neßolo, a] *adj* benevolent, kind.

Bengala [ben'gala] *nf* Bengal; **el Golfo de** ~ the Bay of Bengal.

bengala [ben'gala] *nf* (*MIL*) flare; (*fuego*) Bengal light; (*materia*) rattan.

bengalí [benga'li] *adj, nm/f* Bengali.

benignidad [benixni'ðað] *nf* (*afabilidad*) kindness; (*suavidad*) mildness.

benigno, a [be'nixno, a] *adj* kind; (*suave*) mild; (*MED: tumor*) benign, non-malignant.

benjamín [benxa'min] *nm* youngest child.

beodo, a [be'oðo, a] *adj* drunk ♦ *nm/f* drunkard.

berberecho [berße'retʃo] *nm* cockle.

berenjena [beren'xena] *nf* aubergine (*BRIT*), eggplant (*US*).

berenjenal [berenxe'nal] *nm* (*AGR*) aubergine bed; (*fig*) mess; **en buen** ~ **nos hemos metido** we've got ourselves into a fine mess.

bergantín [berɣan'tin] *nm* brig(antine).

Berlín [ber'lin] *nm* Berlin.

berlinés, esa [berli'nes, esa] *adj* of o from Berlin ♦ *nm/f* Berliner.

bermejo, a [ber'mexo, a] *adj* red.

bermellón [berme'ʎon] *nm* vermilion.

bermudas [ber'muðas] *nfpl* Bermuda shorts.

berrear [berre'ar] *vi* to bellow, low.

berrido [be'rriðo] *nm* bellow(ing).

berrinche [be'rrintʃe] *nm* (*fam*) temper, tantrum.

berro ['berro] *nm* watercress.

berza ['berθa] *nf* cabbage; ~ **lombarda** red cabbage.

besamel [besa'mel], **besamela** [besa'mela] *nf* (*CULIN*) white sauce, bechamel sauce.

besar [be'sar] *vt* to kiss; (*fig: tocar*) to graze; ~**se** *vr* to kiss (one another).

beso ['beso] *nm* kiss.

bestia ['bestja] *nf* beast, animal; (*fig*) idiot; ~ **de carga** beast of burden; ¡~! you idiot!; **¡no seas** ~! (*bruto*) don't be such a brute!; (*idiota*) don't be such an idiot!

bestial [bes'tjal] *adj* bestial; (*fam*) terrific.

bestialidad [bestjali'ðað] *nf* bestiality; (*fam*) stupidity.

besugo [be'suɣo] *nm* sea bream; (*fam*) idiot.

besuguera [besu'ɣera] *nf* (*CULIN*) fish pan.

besuquear [besuke'ar] *vt* to cover with kisses; ~**se** *vr* to kiss and cuddle.

bético, a ['betiko, a] *adj* Andalusian.

betún [be'tun] *nm* shoe polish; (*QUÍMICA*) bitumen, asphalt.

Bib. *abr* = **Biblioteca**.

biberón [biße'ron] *nm* feeding bottle.

Biblia ['bißlja] *nf* Bible.

bíblico, a ['bißliko, a] *adj* biblical.

bibliografía [bißljoɣra'fia] *nf* bibliography.

biblioteca [bißljo'teka] *nf* library; (*estantes*) bookcase, bookshelves *pl*; ~ **de consulta** reference library.

bibliotecario, a [bißljote'karjo, a] *nm/f* librarian.

B.I.C. [bik] *nf abr* (= *Brigada de Investigación Criminal*) ≈ CID (*BRIT*), FBI (*US*).

bicarbonato [bikarßo'nato] *nm* bicarbonate.

biceps ['biθeps] *nm inv* biceps.

bicho ['bitʃo] *nm* (*animal*) small animal; (*sabandija*) bug, insect; (*TAUR*) bull; ~ **raro** (*fam*) queer fish.

bici ['biθi] *nf* (*fam*) bike.

bicicleta [biθi'kleta] *nf* bicycle, cycle; ~ **estática/de montaña** exercise/mountain bike.

bicoca [bi'koka] *nf* (*ESP fam*) cushy job.

BID *n abbr* (= *Banco Interamericano de Desarrollo*) IDB.

bidé [bi'ðe] *nm* bidet.

bidireccional [biðirekθjo'nal] *adj* bidirectional.

bidón [bi'ðon] *nm* (*grande*) drum; (*pequeño*) can.

Bielorrusia [bjelo'rrusja] *nf* Belarus, Byelorussia.

bielorruso, a [bjelo'rruso, a] *adj, nm/f* Belarussian, Belorussian ♦ *nm* (*LING*) Belarussian, Belorussian.

=================== *PALABRA CLAVE*

bien [bjen] *nm* **1** (*bienestar*) good; **te lo digo por tu** ~ I'm telling you for your own good; **el** ~ **y el mal** good and evil
2 (*posesión*): ~**es** goods; ~**es de consumo/equipo** consumer/capital goods; ~**es inmuebles** *o* **raíces**/~**es muebles** real estate *sg*/personal property *sg*
♦ *adv* **1** (*de manera satisfactoria, correcta etc*) well; **trabaja/come** ~ she works/eats well; **contestó** ~ he answered correctly; **oler** ~ to smell nice *o* good; **me siento** ~ I feel fine; **no me siento** ~ I don't feel

very well; **se está** ~ **aquí** it's nice here
2 (*frases*): **hiciste** ~ **en llamarme** you
were right to call me
3 (*valor intensivo*) very; **un cuarto** ~
caliente a nice warm room; ~ **de veces**
lots of times; ~ **se ve que** ... it's quite
clear that ...
4: **estar** ~: **estoy muy** ~ **aquí** I feel very
happy here; **¿te encuentras** ~**?** are you
all right?; **te está** ~ **la falda** (*ser la talla*)
the skirt fits you; (*sentar*) the skirt suits
you; **el libro está muy** ~ the book is
really good; **está** ~ **que vengan** it's all
right for them to come; **¡está** ~**!** **lo haré**
oh all right, I'll do it; **ya está** ~ **de quejas**
that's quite enough complaining
5 (*de buena gana*): **yo** ~ **que iría pero** ...
I'd gladly go but ...
♦ *excl*: **¡**~**!** (*aprobación*) O.K!; **¡muy** ~**!**
well done!; **¡qué** ~**!** great!; ~**, gracias, ¿y**
usted? fine thanks, and you?
♦ *adj inv*: **niño** ~ rich kid; **gente** ~ posh
people
♦ *conj* **1**: ~ ... ~: ~ **en coche** ~ **en tren**
either by car or by train
2: **no** ~ (*esp AM*): **no** ~ **llegue te llamaré**
as soon as I arrive I'll call you
3: **si** ~ even though; *V tb* **más.**

bienal [bje'nal] *adj* biennial.
bienaventurado, a [bjenaßentu'raðo, a]
adj (*feliz*) happy; (*afortunado*) fortunate;
(*REL*) blessed.
bienestar [bjenes'tar] *nm* well-being;
estado de ~ welfare state.
bienhechor, a [bjene't∫or, a] *adj* benefi-
cent ♦ *nm/f* benefactor/benefactress.
bienio ['bjenjo] *nm* two-year period.
bienvenido, a [bjembe'niðo, a] *adj*
welcome ♦ *excl* welcome! ♦ ~ welcome;
dar la bienvenida a algn to welcome sb.
bies ['bjes] *nm*: **falda al** ~ bias-cut skirt;
cortar al ~ to cut on the bias.
bifásico, a [bi'fasiko, a] *adj* (*ELEC*) two-
phase.
bife ['bife] *nm* (*AM*) steak.
bifocal [bifo'kal] *adj* bifocal.
bifurcación [bifurka'θjon] *nf* fork; (*FERRO,
INFORM*) branch.
bifurcarse [bifur'karse] *vr* to fork.
bigamia [bi'ɣamja] *nf* bigamy.
bígamo, a ['biɣamo, a] *adj* bigamous ♦ *nm/f*
bigamist.
bígaro ['biɣaro] *nm* winkle.
bigote [bi'ɣote] *nm* (*tb*: ~**s**) moustache.
bigotudo, a [biɣo'tuðo, a] *adj* with a big
moustache.
bigudí [biɣu'ði] *nm* (hair-)curler.

bikini [bi'kini] *nm* bikini; (*CULIN*) toasted
cheese and ham sandwich.
bilateral [bilate'ral] *adj* bilateral.
bilbaíno, a [bilßa'ino, a] *adj* of *o* from
Bilbao ♦ *nm/f* native *o* inhabitant of
Bilbao.
bilingüe [bi'lingwe] *adj* bilingual.
bilis ['bilis] *nf inv* bile.
billar [bi'ʎar] *nm* billiards *sg*; (*lugar*)
billiard hall; (*galería de atracciones*)
amusement arcade; ~ **americano** pool.
billete [bi'ʎete] *nm* ticket; (*de banco*)
banknote (*BRIT*), bill (*US*); (*carta*) note; ~
sencillo, ~ de ida solamente/~ de ida y
vuelta single (*BRIT*) *o* one-way (*US*)
ticket/return (*BRIT*) *o* round-trip (*US*)
ticket, **sacar (un)** ~ to get a ticket; **un** ~
de 5 libras a five-pound note.
billetera [biʎe'tera] *nf*, **billetero** [biʎe'tero]
nm wallet.
billón [bi'ʎon] *nm* billion.
bimensual [bimen'swal] *adj* twice
monthly.
bimestral [bimes'tral] *adj* bimonthly.
bimestre [bi'mestre] *nm* two-month
period.
bimotor [bimo'tor] *adj* twin-engined ♦ *nm*
twin-engined plane.
binario, a [bi'narjo, a] *adj* (*INFORM*) binary.
bingo ['bingo] *nm* (*juego*) bingo; (*sala*)
bingo hall.
binóculo [bi'nokulo] *nm* pince-nez.
binomio [bi'nomjo] *nm* (*MAT*) binomial.
biodegradable [bioðeɣra'ðaßle] *adj*
biodegradable.
biodiversidad [bioðißersi'ðað] *nf*
biodiversity.
biografía [bjoɣra'fia] *nf* biography.
biográfico, a [bio'ɣrafiko, a] *adj*
biographical.
biógrafo, a [bi'oɣrafo, a] *nm/f* biographer.
biología [biolo'xia] *nf* biology.
biológico, a [bio'loxiko, a] *adj* biological;
(*cultivo, producto*) organic; **guerra**
biológica biological warfare.
biólogo, a [bi'oloxo, a] *nm/f* biologist.
biombo ['bjombo] *nm* (folding) screen.
biopsia [bi'opsja] *nf* biopsy.
bioquímico, a [bio'kimiko, a] *adj*
biochemical ♦ *nm/f* biochemist ♦ *nf*
biochemistry.
biosfera [bios'fera] *nf* biosphere.
bióxido [bi'oksiðo] *nm* dioxide.
bipartidismo [biparti'ðismo] *nm* (*POL*)
two-party system.
biquini [bi'kini] *nm* = **bikini.**
birlar [bir'lar] *vt* (*fam*) to pinch.
birlibirloque [birlißir'loke] *nm*: **por arte de**

~ (as if) by magic.

Birmania [bir'manja] *nf* Burma.

birmano, a [bir'mano, a] *adj nm/f* Burmese.

birrete [bi'rrete] *nm* (*JUR*) judge's cap.

birria ['birrja] *nf* (*fam*): **ser una** ~ to be rubbish; **ir hecho una** ~ to be *o* look a sight.

bis [bis] *excl* encore! ♦ *nm* encore ♦ *adv* (*dos veces*) twice; **viven en el 27** ~ they live at 27a.

bisabuelo, a [bisa'ßwelo, a] *nm/f* great-grandfather/mother; ~**s** *nmpl* great-grandparents.

bisagra [bi'saɣra] *nf* hinge.

bisbisar [bisßi'sar], **bisbisear** [bisßise'ar] *vt* to mutter, mumble.

bisbiseo [bisßi'seo] *nm* muttering.

biselar [bise'lar] *vt* to bevel.

bisexual [bisek'swal] *adj*, *nm/f* bisexual.

bisiesto [bi'sjesto] *adj*: **año** ~ leap year.

bisnieto, a [bis'njeto, a] *nm/f* great-grandson/daughter; ~**s** *nmpl* great-grandchildren.

bisonte [bi'sonte] *nm* bison.

bisoñé [biso'ɲe] *nm* toupée.

bisoño, a [bi'soɲo, a] *adj* green, inexperienced.

bistec [bis'tek], **bisté** [bis'te] *nm* steak.

bisturí [bistu'ri] *nm* scalpel.

bisutería [bisute'ria] *nf* imitation *o* costume jewellery.

bit [bit] *nm* (*INFORM*) bit; ~ **de parada** stop bit; ~ **de paridad** parity bit.

bitácora [bi'takora] *nf*: **cuaderno de** ~ logbook, ship's log.

bitio ['bitjo] *nm* (*INFORM*) bit.

bizantino, a [biθan'tino, a] *adj* Byzantine; (*fig*) pointless.

bizarría [biθa'rria] *nf* (*valor*) bravery; (*generosidad*) generosity.

bizarro, a [bi'θarro, a] *adj* brave; generous.

bizco, a ['biθko, a] *adj* cross-eyed.

bizcocho [biθ'kotʃo] *nm* (*CULIN*) sponge cake.

biznieto, a [biθ'nieto, a] *nm/f* = **bisnieto**.

bizquear [biθke'ar] *vi* to squint.

blanco, a ['blanko, a] *adj* white ♦ *nm/f* white man/woman, white ♦ *nm* (*color*) white; (*en texto*) blank; (*MIL, fig*) target ♦ *nf* (*MUS*) minim; **en** ~ blank; **cheque en** ~ blank cheque; **votar en** ~ to spoil one's vote; **quedarse en** ~ to be disappointed; **noche en** ~ sleepless night; **ser el** ~ **de las burlas** to be the butt of jokes; **estar sin blanca** to be broke.

blancura [blan'kura] *nf* whiteness.

blandengue [blan'denge] *adj* (*fam*) soft, weak.

blandir [blan'dir] *vt* to brandish.

blando, a ['blando, a] *adj* soft; (*tierno*) tender, gentle; (*carácter*) mild; (*fam*) cowardly ♦ *nm/f* (*POL etc*) soft-liner.

blandura [blan'dura] *nf* softness; tenderness; mildness.

blanquear [blanke'ar] *vt* to whiten; (*fachada*) to whitewash; (*paño*) to bleach; (*dinero*) to launder ♦ *vi* to turn white.

blanquecino, a [blanke'θino, a] *adj* whitish.

blanqueo [blan'keo] *nm* (*de pared*) whitewashing; (*de dinero*) laundering.

blasfemar [blasfe'mar] *vi* to blaspheme; (*fig*) to curse.

blasfemia [blas'femja] *nf* blasphemy.

blasfemo, a [blas'femo, a] *adj* blasphemous ♦ *nm/f* blasphemer.

blasón [bla'son] *nm* coat of arms; (*fig*) honour.

blasonar [blaso'nar] *vt* to emblazon ♦ *vi* to boast, brag.

bledo ['bleðo] *nm*: **(no) me importa un** ~ I couldn't care less.

blindado, a [blin'daðo, a] *adj* (*MIL*) armour-plated; (*antibalas*) bulletproof; **coche** *o* (*AM*) **carro** ~ armoured car; **puertas blindadas** security doors.

blindaje [blin'daxe] *nm* armour, armour-plating.

bloc, *pl* **blocs** [blok, blos] *nm* writing pad; (*ESCOL*) jotter; ~ **de dibujos** sketch pad.

bloque ['bloke] *nm* (*tb INFORM*) block; (*POL*) bloc; ~ **de cilindros** cylinder block.

bloquear [bloke'ar] *vt* (*NAUT etc*) to blockade; (*aislar*) to cut off; (*COM, ECON*) to freeze; **fondos bloqueados** frozen assets.

bloqueo [blo'keo] *nm* blockade; (*COM*) freezing, blocking.

bluejean [blu'jin] *nm* (*AM*) jeans *pl*, denims *pl*.

blusa ['blusa] *nf* blouse.

B.º *abr* (*FINANZAS*: = *banco*) bank; (*COM*: = *beneficiario*) beneficiary.

boa ['boa] *nf* boa.

boato [bo'ato] *nm* show, ostentation.

bobada [bo'ßaða] *nf* foolish action (*o* statement); **decir** ~**s** to talk nonsense.

bobalicón, ona [boßali'kon, ona] *adj* utterly stupid.

bobería [boße'ria] *nf* = **bobada**.

bobina [bo'ßina] *nf* (*TEC*) bobbin; (*FOTO*) spool; (*ELEC*) coil, winding.

bobo, a ['boßo, a] *adj* (*tonto*) daft, silly; (*cándido*) naïve ♦ *nm/f* fool, idiot ♦ *nm* (*TEAT*) clown, funny man.

boca ['boka] *nf* mouth; (*de crustáceo*)

pincer; (*de cañón*) muzzle; (*entrada*)
mouth, entrance; (*INFORM*) slot; ~s *nfpl*
(*de río*) mouth *sg*; ~ **abajo/arriba** face
down/up; **a ~ jarro** point-blank; **se me
hace la ~ agua** my mouth is watering;
todo salió a pedir de ~ it all turned out
perfectly; **en ~ de** (*esp AM*) according
to; **la cosa anda de ~ en ~** the story is
going the rounds; **¡cállate la ~!** (*fam*)
shut up!; **quedarse con la ~ abierta** to be
dumbfounded; **no abrir la ~** to keep
quiet; ~ **del estómago** pit of the
stomach; ~ **de metro** tube (*BRIT*) o
subway (*US*) entrance.

bocacalle [boka'kaʎe] *nf* side street; **la
primera ~** the first turning o street.

bocadillo [boka'ðiʎo] *nm* sandwich.

bocado [bo'kaðo] *nm* mouthful, bite; (*de
caballo*) bridle; ~ **de Adán** Adam's apple.

bocajarro [boka'xarro]: **a ~** *adv* (*MIL*) at
point-blank range; **decir algo a ~** to say
sth bluntly.

bocanada [boka'naða] *nf* (*de vino*)
mouthful, swallow; (*de aire*) gust, puff.

bocata [bo'kata] *nm* (*fam*) sandwich.

bocazas [bo'kaθas] *nm/f inv* (*fam*) bigmouth.

boceto [bo'θeto] *nm* sketch, outline.

bocha ['botʃa] *nf* bowl; ~**s** *nfpl* bowls *sg*.

bochinche [bo'tʃintʃe] *nm* (*fam*) uproar.

bochorno [bo'tʃorno] *nm* (*vergüenza*)
embarrassment; (*calor*): **hace ~** it's very
muggy.

bochornoso, a [botʃor'noso, a] *adj* muggy;
embarrassing.

bocina [bo'θina] *nf* (*MUS*) trumpet; (*AUTO*)
horn; (*para hablar*) megaphone; **tocar la
~** (*AUTO*) to sound o blow one's horn.

bocinazo [boθi'naθo] *nm* (*AUTO*) toot.

bocio [bo'θjo] *nm* (*MED*) goitre.

boda ['boða] *nf* (*tb*: ~**s**) wedding, marriage; (*fiesta*) wedding reception; ~**s de
plata/de oro** silver/golden wedding *sg*.

bodega [bo'ðeɣa] *nf* (*de vino*) (wine)
cellar; (*bar*) bar; (*restaurante*) restaurant;
(*depósito*) storeroom; (*de barco*) hold.

bodegón [boðe'ɣon] *nm* (*ARTE*) still life.

bodrio [bo'ðrio] *nm*: **el libro es un ~** the
book is awful o rubbish.

B.O.E. ['boe] *nm abr* = **Boletín Oficial del
Estado.**

bofe ['bofe] *nm* (*tb*: ~**s**: *de res*) lights *pl*;
echar los ~s to slave (away).

bofetada [bofe'taða] *nf* slap (in the face);
dar de ~s a algn to punch sb.

bofetón [bofe'ton] *nm* = **bofetada.**

boga ['boɣa] *nf*: **en ~** in vogue.

bogar [bo'ɣar] *vi* (*remar*) to row; (*navegar*)
to sail.

bogavante [boɣa'ßante] *nm* (*NAUT*) stroke,
first rower; (*ZOOL*) lobster.

Bogotá [boɣo'ta] *n* Bogota.

bogotano, a [boɣo'tano, a] *adj* of o from
Bogota ♦ *nm/f* native o inhabitant of
Bogota.

bogue ['boɣe] *etc vb* V **bogar.**

bohemio, a [bo'emjo, a] *adj, nm/f* Bohemian.

boicot, *pl* **boicots** [boi'ko(t)] *nm* boycott.

boicotear [boikote'ar] *vt* to boycott.

boicoteo [boiko'teo] *nm* boycott.

boina ['boina] *nf* beret.

bola ['bola] *nf* ball; (*canica*) marble;
(*NAIPES*) (grand) slam; (*betún*) shoe
polish; (*mentira*) tale, story; ~**s** *nfpl* (*AM*)
bolas; ~ **de billar** billiard ball; ~ **de
nieve** snowball.

bolchevique [boltʃe'ßike] *adj, nm/f*
Bolshevik.

boleadoras [bolea'ðoras] *nfpl* (*AM*) bolas *sg*.

bolera [bo'lera] *nf* skittle o bowling alley.

bolero [bo'lero] *nm* bolero.

boleta [bo'leta] *nf* (*AM*: *permiso*) pass,
permit; (: *para votar*) ballot.

boletería [bolete'ria] *nf* (*AM*) ticket office.

boletero, a [bole'tero, a] *nm/f* (*AM*) ticket
seller.

boletín [bole'tin] *nm* bulletin; (*periódico*)
journal, review; ~ **escolar** (*ESP*) school
report; ~ **de noticias** news bulletin; **B~
Oficial del Estado** (*ESP*) ≈ Hansard
(*BRIT*), ≈ The Congressional Record
(*US*); ~ **de pedido** application form; ~ **de
precios** price list; ~ **de prensa** press
release; *see boxed note.*

BOLETÍN OFICIAL DEL ESTADO

The **Boletín Oficial del Estado**, *or "BOE"*,
*is the official government record of all
laws and resolutions passed by "las
Cortes"* (*the Spanish Parliament*). *It is
widely consulted, mainly because it also
publishes details of the "oposiciones"*
(*competitive public service examinations*).

---

boleto [bo'leto] *nm* (*esp AM*) ticket; ~ **de
apuestas** betting slip.

boli ['boli] *nm* Biro ®.

boliche [bo'litʃe] *nm* (*bola*) jack; (*juego*)
bowls *sg*; (*lugar*) bowling alley; (*AM*:
tienda) small grocery store.

bólido ['boliðo] *nm* meteorite; (*AUTO*)
racing car.

bolígrafo [bo'liɣrafo] *nm* ball-point pen,
biro ®.

bolillo [bo'liʎo] *nm* (*COSTURA*) bobbin (for
lacemaking).

bolívar [bo'lißar] nm monetary unit of Venezuela.

Bolivia [bo'lißja] nf Bolivia.

boliviano, a [boli'ßjano, a] adj, nm/f Bolivian.

bollo ['boʎo] nm (pan) roll; (dulce) scone; (bulto) bump, lump; (abolladura) dent; ~s nmpl (AM) troubles.

bolo ['bolo] nm skittle; (píldora) (large) pill; (juego de) ~s skittles sg.

Bolonia [bo'lonja] nf Bologna.

bolsa ['bolsa] nf (cartera) purse; (saco) bag; (AM) pocket; (ANAT) cavity, sac; (COM) stock exchange; (MINERÍA) pocket; ~ de agua caliente hot water bottle; ~ de aire air pocket; ~ de (la) basura bin-liner; ~ de dormir (AM) sleeping bag; ~ de papel paper bag; ~ de plástico plastic (o carrier) bag; "B~ de la propiedad" "Property Mart"; ~ de trabajo employment bureau; jugar a la ~ to play the market.

bolsillo [bol'siʎo] nm pocket; (cartera) purse; de ~ pocket cpd; meterse a algn en el ~ to get sb eating out of one's hand.

bolsista [bol'sista] nm/f stockbroker.

bolso ['bolso] nm (bolsa) bag; (de mujer) handbag.

boludo, a [bo'luðo, a] (AM fam!) adj stupid ♦ nm/f prat (!)

bomba ['bomba] nf (MIL) bomb; (TEC) pump; (AM: borrachera) drunkenness ♦ adj (fam): noticia ~ bombshell ♦ adv (fam): pasarlo ~ to have a great time; ~ atómica/de humo/de retardo atomic/smoke/time bomb; ~ de gasolina petrol pump; ~ de incendios fire engine.

bombacho, a [bom'batʃo, a] adj baggy.

bombardear [bombarðe'ar] vt to bombard; (MIL) to bomb.

bombardeo [bombar'ðeo] nm bombardment; bombing.

bombardero [bombar'ðero] nm bomber.

bombear [bombe'ar] vt (agua) to pump (out o up); (MIL) to bomb; (FÚTBOL) to lob; ~se vr to warp.

bombero [bom'bero] nm fireman; (cuerpo de) ~s fire brigade.

bombilla [bom'biʎa] nf (ESP), **bombillo** [bom'biʎo] nm (AM) (light) bulb.

bombín [bom'bin] nm bowler hat.

bombo ['bombo] nm (MUS) bass drum; (TEC) drum; (fam) exaggerated praise; hacer algo a ~ y platillo to make a great song and dance about sth; tengo la cabeza hecha un ~ I've got a splitting headache.

bombón [bom'bon] nm chocolate; (belleza) gem.

bombona [bom'bona] nf: ~ de butano gas cylinder.

bombonería [bombone'ria] nf sweetshop.

bonachón, ona [bona'tʃon, ona] adj good-natured.

bonaerense [bonae'rense] adj of o from Buenos Aires ♦ nm/f native o inhabitant of Buenos Aires.

bonancible [bonan'θißle] adj (tiempo) fair, calm.

bonanza [bo'nanθa] nf (NAUT) fair weather; (fig) bonanza; (MINERÍA) rich pocket o vein.

bondad [bon'dað] nf goodness, kindness; tenga la ~ de (please) be good enough to.

bondadoso, a [bonda'ðoso, a] adj good, kind.

bongo ['bonɣo] nm large canoe.

boniato [bo'njato] nm sweet potato, yam.

bonificación [bonifika'θjon] nf (COM) allowance, discount; (pago) bonus; (DEPORTE) extra points pl.

bonito, a [bo'nito, a] adj (lindo) pretty; (agradable) nice ♦ adv (AM fam) well ♦ nm (atún) tuna (fish).

bono ['bono] nm voucher; (FIN) bond; ~ de billetes de metro booklet of metro tickets; ~ del Tesoro treasury bill.

bonobús [bono'ßus] nm (ESP) bus pass.

Bono Loto, bonoloto [bono'loto] nm o f (ESP) state-run weekly lottery; V tb lotería.

boom, pl **booms** ['bum, 'bums] nm boom.

boquear [boke'ar] vi to gasp.

boquerón [boke'ron] nm (pez) (kind of) anchovy; (agujero) large hole.

boquete [bo'kete] nm gap, hole.

boquiabierto, a [bokia'ßjerto, a] adj open-mouthed (in astonishment); quedar ~ to be left aghast.

boquilla [bo'kiʎa] nf (para riego) nozzle; (para cigarro) cigarette holder; (MUS) mouthpiece.

borbollar [borßo'ʎar], **borbollear** [borßoʎe'ar] vi to bubble.

borbollón [borßo'ʎon] nm bubbling; hablar a borbollones to gabble; salir a borbollones (agua) to gush out.

borbotar [borßo'tar] vi = borbollar.

borbotón [borßo'ton] nm: salir a borbotones to gush out.

borda ['borða] nf (NAUT) gunwale; echar o tirar algo por la ~ to throw sth overboard.

bordado [bor'ðaðo] nm embroidery.

bordar [bor'ðar] *vt* to embroider.
borde ['borðe] *nm* edge, border; (*de camino etc*) side; (*en la costura*) hem; **al ~ de** (*fig*) on the verge *o* brink of; **ser ~** (*ESP fam*) to be a pain in the neck.
bordear [borðe'ar] *vt* to border.
bordillo [bor'ðiʎo] *nm* kerb (*BRIT*), curb (*US*).
bordo ['borðo] *nm* (*NAUT*) side; **a ~ on** board.
Borgoña [bor'ɣoɲa] *nf* Burgundy.
borgoña [bor'ɣoɲa] *nm* burgundy.
boricua [bo'rikwa], **borinqueño, a** [borin'keɲo, a] *adj*, *nm/f* Puerto Rican.
borla ['borla] *nf* (*gen*) tassel; (*de gorro*) pompon.
borra ['borra] *nf* (*pelusa*) fluff; (*sedimento*) sediment.
borrachera [borra'tʃera] *nf* (*ebriedad*) drunkenness; (*orgía*) spree, binge.
borracho, a [bo'rratʃo, a] *adj* drunk ♦ *nm/f* (*que bebe mucho*) drunkard, drunk; (*temporalmente*) drunk, drunk man/woman ♦ *nm* (*CULIN*) cake soaked in liqueur or spirit.
borrador [borra'ðor] *nm* (*escritura*) first draft, rough sketch; (*cuaderno*) scribbling pad; (*goma*) rubber (*BRIT*), eraser; (*COM*) daybook; (*para pizarra*) duster; **hacer un nuevo ~ de** (*COM*) to redraft.
borrar [bo'rrar] *vt* to erase, rub out; (*tachar*) to delete; (*cinta*) to wipe out; (*INFORM: archivo*) to delete, erase; (*POL etc: eliminar*) to deal with.
borrasca [bo'rraska] *nf* (*METEOROLOGÍA*) storm.
borrascoso, a [borras'koso, a] *adj* stormy.
borrego, a [bo'rreɣo, a] *nm/f* lamb; (*oveja*) sheep; (*fig*) simpleton.
borricada [borri'kaða] *nf* foolish action/statement.
borrico, a [bo'rriko, a] *nm* donkey; (*fig*) stupid man ♦ *nf* she-donkey; (*fig*) stupid woman.
borrón [bo'rron] *nm* (*mancha*) stain; **~ y cuenta nueva** let bygones be bygones.
borroso, a [bo'rroso, a] *adj* vague, unclear; (*escritura*) illegible; (*escrito*) smudgy; (*FOTO*) blurred.
Bósforo ['bosforo] *nm*: **el (Estrecho del) ~** the Bosp(h)orus.
Bosnia ['bosnja] *nf* Bosnia.
bosnio, a ['bosnjo, a] *adj*, *nm/f* Bosnian.
bosque ['boske] *nm* wood; (*grande*) forest.
bosquejar [boske'xar] *vt* to sketch.
bosquejo [bos'kexo] *nm* sketch.
bosta ['bosta] *nf* dung, manure.

bostece [bos'teθe] *etc vb* V **bostezar**.
bostezar [boste'θar] *vi* to yawn.
bostezo [bos'teθo] *nm* yawn.
bota ['bota] *nf* (*calzado*) boot; (*saco*) leather wine bottle; **ponerse las ~s** (*fam*) to strike it rich.
botadura [bota'ðura] *nf* launching.
botanas [bo'tanas] *nfpl* (*AM*) hors d'œuvres.
botánico, a [bo'taniko, a] *adj* botanical ♦ *nm/f* botanist ♦ *nf* botany.
botar [bo'tar] *vt* to throw, hurl; (*NAUT*) to launch; (*esp AM fam*) to throw out ♦ *vi* to bounce.
botarate [bota'rate] *nm* (*imbécil*) idiot.
bote ['bote] *nm* (*salto*) bounce; (*golpe*) thrust; (*vasija*) tin, can; (*embarcación*) boat; **de ~ en ~** packed, jammed full; **~ salvavidas** lifeboat; **dar un ~** to jump; **dar ~s** (*AUTO etc*) to bump; **~ de la basura** (*AM*) dustbin (*BRIT*), trashcan (*US*).
botella [bo'teʎa] *nf* bottle; **~ de vino** (*contenido*) bottle of wine; (*recipiente*) wine bottle.
botellero [bote'ʎero] *nm* wine rack.
botellín [bote'ʎin] *nm* small bottle.
botica [bo'tika] *nf* chemist's (shop) (*BRIT*), pharmacy.
boticario, a [boti'karjo, a] *nm/f* chemist (*BRIT*), pharmacist.
botijo [bo'tixo] *nm* (earthenware) jug; (*tren*) excursion train.
botín [bo'tin] *nm* (*calzado*) half boot; (*polaina*) spat; (*MIL*) booty; (*de ladrón*) loot.
botiquín [boti'kin] *nm* (*armario*) medicine chest; (*portátil*) first-aid kit.
botón [bo'ton] *nm* button; (*BOT*) bud; (*de florete*) tip; **~ de arranque** (*AUTO etc*) starter; **~ de oro** buttercup; **pulsar el ~** to press the button.
botones [bo'tones] *nm inv* bellboy, bellhop (*US*).
botulismo [botu'lismo] *nm* botulism, food poisoning.
bóveda ['boβeða] *nf* (*ARQ*) vault.
bovino, a [bo'βino, a] *adj* bovine; (*AGR*): **ganado ~** cattle.
box ['boks] *nm* (*AM*) boxing.
boxeador [boksea'ðor] *nm* boxer.
boxear [bokse'ar] *vi* to box.
boxeo [bok'seo] *nm* boxing.
boya ['boja] *nf* (*NAUT*) buoy; (*flotador*) float.
boyante [bo'jante] *adj* (*NAUT*) buoyant; (*feliz*) buoyant; (*próspero*) prosperous.
bozal [bo'θal] *nm* (*de caballo*) halter; (*de perro*) muzzle.

bozo ['boθo] *nm* (*pelusa*) fuzz; (*boca*) mouth.

bracear [braθe'ar] *vi* (*agitar los brazos*) to wave one's arms.

bracero [bra'θero] *nm* labourer; (*en el campo*) farmhand.

braga ['braɣa] *nf* (*cuerda*) sling, rope; (*de bebé*) nappy, diaper (*US*); ~**s** *nfpl* (*de mujer*) panties.

braguero [bra'ɣero] *nm* (*MED*) truss.

bragueta [bra'ɣeta] *nf* fly (*BRIT*), flies *pl* (*BRIT*), zipper (*US*).

braguetazo [braɣe'taθo] *nm* marriage of convenience.

braille [breil] *nm* braille.

bramante [bra'mante] *nm* twine, string.

bramar [bra'mar] *vi* to bellow, roar.

bramido [bra'miðo] *nm* bellow, roar.

branquias ['brankjas] *nfpl* gills.

brasa ['brasa] *nf* live *o* hot coal; **carne a la** ~ grilled meat.

brasero [bra'sero] *nm* brazier; (*AM*: *chimenea*) fireplace.

Brasil [bra'sil] *nm*: (**el**) ~ Brazil.

brasileño, a [brasi'leɲo, a] *adj*, *nm/f* Brazilian.

bravata [bra'βata] *nf* boast.

braveza [bra'βeθa] *nf* (*valor*) bravery; (*ferocidad*) ferocity.

bravío, a [bra'βio, a] *adj* wild; (*feroz*) fierce.

bravo, a ['braβo, a] *adj* (*valiente*) brave; (*bueno*) fine, splendid; (*feroz*) ferocious; (*salvaje*) wild; (*mar etc*) rough, stormy; (*CULIN*) hot, spicy ♦ *excl* bravo!

bravucón, ona [braβu'kon, ona] *adj* swaggering ♦ *nm/f* braggart.

bravura [bra'βura] *nf* bravery; ferocity; (*pey*) boast.

braza ['braθa] *nf* fathom; **nadar a la** ~ to swim (the) breast-stroke.

brazada [bra'θaða] *nf* stroke.

brazalete [braθa'lete] *nm* (*pulsera*) bracelet; (*banda*) armband.

brazo ['braθo] *nm* arm; (*ZOOL*) foreleg; (*BOT*) limb, branch; ~**s** *nmpl* (*braceros*) hands, workers; ~ **derecho** (*fig*) right-hand man; **a** ~ **partido** hand-to-hand; **cogidos** *etc* **del** ~ arm in arm; **no dar su** ~ **a torcer** not to give way easily; **huelga de** ~**s caídos** sit-down strike.

brea ['brea] *nf* pitch, tar.

brebaje [bre'βaxe] *nm* potion.

brecha ['bretʃa] *nf* breach; (*hoyo vacío*) gap, opening.

brécol ['brekol] *nm* broccoli.

brega ['breɣa] *nf* (*lucha*) struggle; (*trabajo*) hard work.

bregar [bre'ɣar] *vi* (*luchar*) to struggle;

(*trabajar mucho*) to slog away.

bregue ['breɣe] *etc vb V* **bregar**.

breña ['breɲa] *nf* rough ground.

Bretaña [bre'taɲa] *nf* Brittany.

brete ['brete] *nm* (*cepo*) shackles *pl*; (*fig*) predicament; **estar en un** ~ to be in a jam.

breteles [bre'teles] *nmpl* (*AM*) straps.

bretón, ona [bre'ton, ona] *adj*, *nm/f* Breton.

breva ['breβa] *nf* (*BOT*) early fig; (*puro*) flat cigar; **¡no caerá esa** ~**!** no such luck!

breve ['breβe] *adj* short, brief; **en** ~ (*pronto*) shortly; (*en pocas palabras*) in short ♦ *nf* (*MUS*) breve.

brevedad [breβe'ðað] *nf* brevity, shortness; **con** *o* **a la major** ~ as soon as possible.

breviario [bre'βjarjo] *nm* (*REL*) breviary.

brezal [bre'θal] *nm* moor(land), heath.

brezo ['breθo] *nm* heather.

bribón, ona [bri'βon, ona] *adj* idle, lazy ♦ *nm/f* (*vagabundo*) vagabond; (*pícaro*) rascal, rogue.

bricolaje [briko'laxe] *nm* do-it-yourself, DIY.

brida ['briða] *nf* bridle, rein; (*TEC*) clamp; **a toda** ~ at top speed.

bridge [britʃ] *nm* (*NAIPES*) bridge.

brigada [bri'ɣaða] *nf* (*unidad*) brigade; (*trabajadores*) squad, gang ♦ *nm* warrant officer.

brigadier [briɣa'ðjer] *nm* brigadier (-general).

brillante [bri'ʎante] *adj* brilliant; (*color*) bright; (*joya*) sparkling ♦ *nm* diamond.

brillantez [briʎan'teθ] *nf* (*color etc*) brightness; (*fig*) brilliance.

brillar [bri'ʎar] *vi* (*tb fig*) to shine; (*joyas*) to sparkle; ~ **por su ausencia** to be conspicuous by one's absence.

brillo ['briʎo] *nm* shine; (*brillantez*) brilliance; (*fig*) splendour; **sacar** ~ **a** to polish.

brilloso, a [bri'ʎoso, a] *adj* (*AM*) = **brillante**.

brincar [brin'kar] *vi* to skip about, hop about, jump about; **está que brinca** he's hopping mad.

brinco ['brinko] *nm* jump, leap; **a** ~**s** by fits and starts; **de un** ~ at one bound.

brindar [brin'dar] *vi*: ~ **a** *o* **por** to drink (a toast) to ♦ *vt* to offer, present; **le brinda la ocasión de** it offers *o* affords him the opportunity to; ~**se** *vr*: ~**se a hacer algo** to offer to do sth.

brindis ['brindis] *nm inv* toast; (*TAUR*) (ceremony of) dedication.

brinque ['brinke] *etc vb V* **brincar**.

brío ['brio] *nm* spirit, dash.

brioso, a [bri'oso, a] *adj* spirited, dashing.
brisa ['brisa] *nf* breeze.
británico, a [bri'taniko, a] *adj* British ♦ *nm/f*
  Briton, British person; **los ~s** the
  British.
brizna ['briθna] *nf (hebra)* strand, thread;
  (de hierba) blade; *(trozo)* piece.
broca ['broka] *nf (COSTURA)* bobbin; *(TEC)*
  drill bit; *(clavo)* tack.
brocado [bro'kaðo] *nm* brocade.
brocal [bro'kal] *nm* rim.
brocha ['brotʃa] *nf (large)* paintbrush; **~**
  de afeitar shaving brush; **pintor de ~**
  gorda painter and decorator; *(fig)* poor
  painter.
brochazo [bro'tʃaθo] *nm* brush-stroke; **a**
  grandes ~s *(fig)* in general terms.
broche ['brotʃe] *nm* brooch.
broma ['broma] *nf* joke; *(inocentada)*
  practical joke; **en ~** in fun, as a joke;
  gastar una ~ a algn to play a joke on sb;
  tomar algo a ~ to take sth as a joke.
bromear [brome'ar] *vi* to joke.
bromista [bro'mista] *adj* fond of joking
  ♦ *nm/f* joker, wag.
bromuro [bro'muro] *nm* bromide.
bronca ['bronka] *nf* row; *(regañada)*
  ticking-off; **armar una ~** to kick up a
  fuss; **echar una ~ a algn** to tell sb off.
bronce ['bronθe] *nm* bronze; *(latón)* brass.
bronceado, a [bronθe'aðo, a] *adj* bronze
  cpd; *(por el sol)* tanned ♦ *nm* (sun)tan;
  (TEC) bronzing.
bronceador [bronθea'ðor] *nm* suntan
  lotion.
broncearse [bronθe'arse] *vr* to get a
  suntan.
bronco, a ['bronko, a] *adj (manera)* rude,
  surly; *(voz)* harsh.
bronquios ['bronkjos] *nmpl* bronchial
  tubes.
bronquitis [bron'kitis] *nf inv* bronchitis.
brotar [bro'tar] *vt (tierra)* to produce ♦ *vi*
  (BOT) to sprout; *(aguas)* to gush (forth);
  (lágrimas) to well up; *(MED)* to break out.
brote ['brote] *nm (BOT)* shoot; *(MED, fig)*
  outbreak.
broza ['broθa] *nf (BOT)* dead leaves *pl*; *(fig)*
  rubbish.
bruces ['bruθes]: **de ~** *adv*: **caer** *o* **dar de ~**
  to fall headlong, fall flat.
bruja ['bruxa] *nf* witch.
Brujas ['bruxas] *nf* Bruges.
brujería [bruxe'ria] *nf* witchcraft.
brujo ['bruxo] *nm* wizard, magician.
brújula ['bruxula] *nf* compass.
bruma ['bruma] *nf* mist.
brumoso, a [bru'moso, a] *adj* misty.

bruñendo [bru'ɲendo] *etc vb* V **bruñir**.
bruñido [bru'ɲiðo] *nm* polish.
bruñir [bru'ɲir] *vt* to polish.
brusco, a ['brusko, a] *adj (súbito)* sudden;
  (áspero) brusque.
Bruselas [bru'selas] *nf* Brussels.
brusquedad [bruske'ðað] *nf* suddenness;
  brusqueness.
brutal [bru'tal] *adj* brutal.
brutalidad [brutali'ðað] *nf* brutality.
bruto, a ['bruto, a] *adj (idiota)* stupid;
  (bestial) brutish; *(peso)* gross ♦ *nm* brute;
  a la bruta, a lo ~ roughly; **en ~** raw,
  unworked.
Bs. *abr* = **bolívares**.
Bs.As. *abr* = **Buenos Aires**.
bucal [bu'kal] *adj* oral; **por vía ~** orally.
bucanero [buka'nero] *nm* buccaneer.
bucear [buθe'ar] *vi* to dive ♦ *vt* to explore.
buceo [bu'θeo] *nm* diving; *(fig)*
  investigation.
buche ['butʃe] *nm (de ave)* crop; *(ZOOL)*
  maw; *(fam)* belly.
bucle ['bukle] *nm* curl; *(INFORM)* loop.
budín [bu'ðin] *nm* pudding.
budismo [bu'ðismo] *nm* Buddhism.
budista [bu'ðista] *adj, nm/f* Buddhist.
buen [bwen] *adj* V **bueno**.
buenamente [bwena'mente] *adv*
  (fácilmente) easily; *(voluntariamente)*
  willingly.
buenaventura [bwenaβen'tura] *nf (suerte)*
  good luck; *(adivinación)* fortune; **decir** *o*
  echar la ~ a algn to tell sb's fortune.

═══════════════════ *PALABRA CLAVE*

bueno, a ['bweno, a] *(antes de nmsg:* **buen)**
  adj **1** *(excelente etc)* good; *(MED)* well; **es**
  un libro ~, **es un buen libro** it's a good
  book; **hace ~**, **hace buen tiempo** the
  weather is fine, it is fine; **es ~a persona**
  he's a good sort; **el ~ de Paco** good old
  Paco; **fue muy ~ conmigo** he was very
  nice *o* kind to me; **ya está ~** he's fine
  now
  2 *(apropiado)*: **ser ~ para** to be good for;
  creo que vamos por buen camino I think
  we're on the right track
  3 *(irónico)*: **le di un buen rapapolvo** I
  gave him a good *o* real ticking off;
  ¡buen conductor estás hecho! some
  driver *o* a fine driver you are!; **¡estaría**
  ~ que ...! a fine thing it would be if ...!
  4 *(atractivo, sabroso)*: **está ~ este**
  bizcocho this sponge is delicious; **Julio**
  está muy ~ *(fam)* Julio is a bit of alright
  5 *(grande)* good, big; **un buen número**
  de ... a good number of ...; **un buen trozo**

de ... a nice big piece of ...
6 (*saludos*): **¡buen día!** (*AM*), **¡~s días!**
(good) morning!; **¡buenas (tardes)!** good
afternoon!; (*más tarde*) good evening!;
¡buenas noches! good night!
7 (*otras locuciones*): **estar de buenas** to
be in a good mood; **por las buenas o por
las malas** by hook or by crook; **de
buenas a primeras** all of a sudden
♦ *excl*: **¡~!** all right!; **~, ¿y qué?** well, so
what?; **~, lo que pasa es que** ... well, the
thing is ...; **pero ¡~!** well, I like that!; **~,
pues** ... right, (then) ...

Buenos Aires [bweno'saires] *nm* Buenos
Aires.
buey [bwei] *nm* ox.
búfalo ['bufalo] *nm* buffalo.
bufanda [bu'fanda] *nf* scarf.
bufar [bu'far] *vi* to snort.
bufete [bu'fete] *nm* (*despacho de abogado*)
lawyer's office; **establecer su ~** to set up
in legal practice.
buffer ['bufer] *nm* (*INFORM*) buffer.
bufón [bu'fon] *nm* clown.
bufonada [bufo'naða] *nf* (*dicho*) jest;
(*hecho*) piece of buffoonery; (*TEAT*)
farce.
buhardilla [buar'ðiʎa] *nf* attic.
búho ['buo] *nm* owl; (*fig*) hermit, recluse.
buhonero [buo'nero] *nm* pedlar.
buitre ['bwitre] *nm* vulture.
bujía [bu'xia] *nf* (*vela*) candle; (*ELEC*)
candle (power); (*AUTO*) spark plug.
bula ['bula] *nf* (*papal*) bull.
bulbo ['bulßo] *nm* (*BOT*) bulb.
bulevar [bule'ßar] *nm* boulevard.
Bulgaria [bul'ɣarja] *nf* Bulgaria.
búlgaro, a ['bulɣaro, a] *adj*, *nm/f* Bulgarian.
bulimia [bu'limja] *nf* bulimia.
bulla ['buʎa] *nf* (*ruido*) uproar; (*de gente*)
crowd; **armar o meter ~** to kick up a
row.
bullendo [bu'ʎendo] *etc vb V* **bullir**.
bullicio [bu'ʎiθjo] *nm* (*ruido*) uproar;
(*movimiento*) bustle.
bullicioso, a [buʎi'θjoso, a] *adj* (*ruidoso*)
noisy, (*calle etc*) busy; (*situación*)
turbulent.
bullir [bu'ʎir] *vi* (*hervir*) to boil; (*burbujear*)
to bubble; (*mover*) to move, stir;
(*insectos*) to swarm; **~ de** (*fig*) to teem o
seethe with.
bulo ['bulo] *nm* false rumour.
bulto ['bulto] *nm* (*paquete*) package; (*fardo*)
bundle; (*tamaño*) size, bulkiness; (*MED*)
swelling, lump; (*silueta*) vague shape;
(*estatua*) bust, statue; **hacer ~** to take up

space; **escurrir el ~** to make o.s. scarce;
(*fig*) to dodge the issue.
buñuelo [bu'ɲwelo] *nm* ≈ doughnut, donut
(*US*).
BUP [bup] *nm abr* (*ESP ESCOL*:= *Bachillerato
Unificado y Polivalente*) *secondary
education for 14-17 age group*; V *tb*
sistema educativo.
buque ['buke] *nm* ship, vessel; **~ de guerra**
warship; **~ mercante** merchant ship; **~
de vela** sailing ship.
burbuja [bur'ßuxa] *nf* bubble; **hacer ~s** to
bubble; (*gaseosa*) to fizz.
burbujear [burßuxe'ar] *vi* to bubble.
burdel [bur'ðel] *nm* brothel.
Burdeos [bur'ðeos] *nm* Bordeaux.
burdo, a ['burðo, a] *adj* coarse, rough.
burgalés, esa [burɣa'les, esa] *adj* of o from
Burgos ♦ *nm/f* native o inhabitant of
Burgos.
burgués, esa [bur'ɣes, esa] *adj* middle-
class, bourgeois; **pequeño ~** lower
middle-class; (*POL*, *pey*) petty bourgeois.
burguesía [burɣe'sia] *nf* middle class,
bourgeoisie.
burla ['burla] *nf* (*mofa*) gibe; (*broma*) joke;
(*engaño*) trick; **hacer ~ de** to make fun
of.
burladero [burla'ðero] *nm* (bullfighter's)
refuge.
burlador, a [burla'ðor, a] *adj* mocking
♦ *nm/f* mocker; (*bromista*) joker ♦ *nm*
(*libertino*) seducer.
burlar [bur'lar] *vt* (*engañar*) to deceive;
(*seducir*) to seduce ♦ *vi*, **~se** *vr* to joke;
~se de to make fun of.
burlesco, a [bur'lesko, a] *adj* burlesque.
burlón, ona [bur'lon, ona] *adj* mocking.
buró [bu'ro] *nm* bureau.
burocracia [buro'kraθja] *nf* bureaucracy.
burócrata [bu'rokrata] *nm/f* bureaucrat.
buromática [buro'matika] *nf* office
automation.
burrada [bu'rraða] *nf* stupid act; **decir ~s**
to talk nonsense.
burro, a ['burro, a] *nm/f* (*ZOOL*) donkey;
(*fig*) ass, idiot ♦ *adj* stupid; **caerse del ~**
to realise one's mistake; **no ver tres en
un ~** to be as blind as a bat.
bursátil [bur'satil] *adj* stock-exchange *cpd*.
bus [bus] *nm* bus.
busca ['buska] *nf* search, hunt ♦ *nm*
bleeper, pager; **en ~ de** in search of.
buscador, a [buska'ðor, a] *nm/f* searcher.
buscapiés [buska'pjes] *nm inv* jumping
jack (*BRIT*), firecracker (*US*).
buscapleitos [buska'pleitos] *nm/f inv*
troublemaker.

buscar [bus'kar] *vt* to look for; (*objeto perdido*) to have a look for; (*beneficio*) to seek; (*enemigo*) to seek out; (*traer*) to bring, fetch; (*provocar*) to provoke; (*INFORM*) to search ♦ *vi* to look, search, seek; **ven a ~me a la oficina** come and pick me up at the office; **~le 3 o 4 pies al gato** to split hairs; **"~ y reemplazar"** (*INFORM*) "search and replace"; **se busca secretaria** secretary wanted; **se la buscó** he asked for it.

buscavidas [buska'βiðas] *nm/f inv* snooper; (*persona ambiciosa*) go-getter.

buscona [bus'kona] *nf* whore.

busilis [bu'silis] *nm inv* (*fam*) snag.

busque ['buske] *etc vb V* **buscar**.

búsqueda ['buskeða] *nf* = **busca**.

busto ['busto] *nm* (*ANAT, ARTE*) bust.

butaca [bu'taka] *nf* armchair; (*de cine, teatro*) stall, seat.

butano [bu'tano] *nm* butane (gas); **bombona de ~** gas cylinder.

butifarra [buti'farra] *nf* Catalan sausage.

buzo ['buθo] *nm* diver; (*AM: chandal*) tracksuit.

buzón [bu'θon] *nm* (*gen*) letter box; (*en la calle*) pillar box (*BRIT*); (*TELEC*) mailbox; **echar al ~** to post.

buzonear [buθone'ar] *vt* to leaflet.

byte [bait] *nm* (*INFORM*) byte.

Cc

C, c [θe, se (*esp AM*)] *nf* (*letra*) C, c; **C de Carmen** C for Charlie.

C. *abr* (= *centígrado*) C.; (= *compañía*) Co.

c. *abr* (= *capítulo*) ch.

C/ *abr* (= *calle*) St, Rd.

c/ *abr* (*COM*: = *cuenta*) a/c.

ca [ka] *excl* not a bit of it!

c.a. *abr* (= *corriente alterna*) A.C.

cabal [ka'βal] *adj* (*exacto*) exact; (*correcto*) right, proper; (*acabado*) finished, complete; **~es** *nmpl*: **estar en sus ~es** to be in one's right mind.

cábala ['kaβala] *nf* (*REL*) cab(b)ala; (*fig*) cabal, intrigue; **~s** *nfpl* guess *sg*, supposition *sg*.

cabalgadura [kaβalɣa'ðura] *nf* mount, horse.

cabalgar [kaβal'ɣar] *vt, vi* to ride.

cabalgata [kaβal'ɣata] *nf* procession; *V tb* **Reyes Magos**.

cabalgue [ka'βalɣe] *etc vb V* **cabalgar**.

cabalístico, a [kaβa'listiko, a] *adj* (*fig*) mysterious.

caballa [ka'βaʎa] *nf* mackerel.

caballeresco, a [kaβaʎe'resko, a] *adj* noble, chivalrous.

caballería [kaβaʎe'ria] *nf* mount; (*MIL*) cavalry.

caballeriza [kaβaʎe'riθa] *nf* stable.

caballerizo [kaβaʎe'riθo] *nm* groom, stableman.

caballero [kaβa'ʎero] *nm* gentleman; (*de la orden de caballería*) knight; (*trato directo*) sir; **"C~s"** "Gents".

caballerosidad [kaβaʎerosi'ðað] *nf* chivalry.

caballete [kaβa'ʎete] *nm* (*AGR*) ridge; (*ARTE*) easel.

caballito [kaβa'ʎito] *nm* (*caballo pequeño*) small horse, pony; (*juguete*) rocking horse; **~s** *nmpl* merry-go-round *sg*; **~ de mar** seahorse; **~ del diablo** dragonfly.

caballo [ka'βaʎo] *nm* horse; (*AJEDREZ*) knight; (*NAIPES*) ≈ queen; **~ de vapor** *o* **de fuerza** horsepower; **es su ~ de batalla** it's his hobby-horse; **~ blanco** (*COM*) backer; *V tb* **Baraja Española**.

cabaña [ka'βaɲa] *nf* (*casita*) hut, cabin.

cabaré, cabaret, *pl* **cabarets** [kaβa're, kaβa'res] *nm* cabaret.

cabecear [kaβeθe'ar] *vi* to nod.

cabecera [kaβe'θera] *nf* (*gen*) head; (*de distrito*) chief town; (*de cama*) headboard; (*IMPRENTA*) headline.

cabecilla [kaβe'θiʎa] *nm* ringleader.

cabellera [kaβe'ʎera] *nf* (head of) hair; (*de cometa*) tail.

cabello [ka'βeʎo] *nm* (*tb*: **~s**) hair *sg*.

cabelludo [kaβe'ʎuðo] *adj V* **ouoro**.

caber [ka'βer] *vi* (*entrar*) to fit, go; **caben 3 más** there's room for 3 more; **cabe preguntar si...** one might ask whether...; **cabe que venga más tarde** he may come later.

cabestrillo [kaβes'triʎo] *nm* sling.

cabestro [ka'βestro] *nm* halter.

cabeza [ka'βeθa] *nf* head; (*POL*) chief, leader ♦ *nm/f*: **~ rapada** skinhead; **caer de ~** to fall head first; **sentar la ~** to settle down; **~ de lectura/escritura** read/write head; **~ impresora** *o* **de impresión** printhead.

cabezada [kaβe'θaða] *nf* (*golpe*) butt; **dar una ~** to nod off.

cabezal [kaβe'θal] *nm*: **~ impresor** print head.

cabezazo [kaβe'θaθo] *nm* (*golpe*) headbutt; (*FÚTBOL*) header.

cabezón, ona [kaβe'θon, ona] *adj* with a big head; (*vino*) heady; (*obstinado*) obstinate, stubborn.

cabezota [kaβe'θota] *adj inv* obstinate, stubborn.

cabezudo, a [kaβe'θuðo, a] *adj* with a big head; (*obstinado*) obstinate, stubborn.

cabida [ka'βiða] *nf* space; **dar** ~ **a** to make room for; **tener** ~ **para** to have room for.

cabildo [ka'βildo] *nm* (*de iglesia*) chapter; (*POL*) town council.

cabina [ka'βina] *nf* (*de camión*) cabin; ~ **telefónica** (tele)phone box (*BRIT*) o booth.

cabizbajo, a [kaβiθ'βaxo, a] *adj* crestfallen, dejected.

cable ['kaβle] *nm* cable; (*de aparato*) lead; ~ **aéreo** (*ELEC*) overhead cable; **conectar con** ~ (*INFORM*) to hardwire.

cabo ['kaβo] *nm* (*de objeto*) end, extremity; (*MIL*) corporal; (*NAUT*) rope, cable; (*GEO*) cape; (*TEC*) thread; **al** ~ **de 3 días** after 3 days; **de** ~ **a rabo** o ~ from beginning to end; (*libro: leer*) from cover to cover; **llevar a** ~ to carry out; **atar** ~**s** to tie up the loose ends; **C**~ **de Buena Esperanza** Cape of Good Hope; **C**~ **de Hornos** Cape Horn; **las Islas de C**~ **Verde** the Cape Verde Islands.

cabra ['kaβra] *nf* goat; **estar como una** ~ (*fam*) to be nuts.

cabré [ka'βre] *etc vb* V **caber**.

cabrear [kaβre'ar] *vt* to annoy; ~**se** *vr* to fly off the handle.

cabrío, a [ka'βrio, a] *adj* goatish; **macho** ~ (he-)goat, billy goat.

cabriola [ka'βrjola] *nf* caper.

cabritilla [kaβri'tiʎa] *nf* kid, kidskin.

cabrito [ka'βrito] *nm* kid.

cabrón [ka'βron] *nm* (*fig: fam!*) bastard (!).

cabronada [kaβro'naða] *nf* (*fam!*): **hacer una** ~ **a algn** to be a bastard to sb.

caca ['kaka] *nf* (*palabra de niños*) pooh ♦ *excl*: **no toques, ¡**~**!** don't touch, it's dirty!

cacahuete [kaka'wete] *nm* (*ESP*) peanut.

cacao [ka'kao] *nm* cocoa; (*BOT*) cacao.

cacarear [kakare'ar] *vi* (*persona*) to boast; (*gallina*) to cackle.

cacatúa [kaka'tua] *nf* cockatoo.

cacereño, a [kaθe'reɲo, a] *adj* of o from Cáceres ♦ *nm/f* native o inhabitant of Cáceres.

cacería [kaθe'ria] *nf* hunt.

cacerola [kaθe'rola] *nf* pan, saucepan.

cacha ['katʃa] *nf* (*mango*) handle; (*nalga*) buttock.

cachalote [katʃa'lote] *nm* sperm whale.

cacharro [ka'tʃarro] *nm* (*vasija*) (earthenware) pot; (*cerámica*) piece of pottery; (*fam*) useless object; ~**s** *nmpl* pots and pans.

cachear [katʃe'ar] *vt* to search, frisk.

cachemir [katʃe'mir] *nm* cashmere.

cacheo [ka'tʃeo] *nm* searching, frisking.

cachete [ka'tʃete] *nm* (*ANAT*) cheek; (*bofetada*) slap (in the face).

cachimba [ka'tʃimba] *nf*, **cachimbo** [ka'tʃimbo] *nm* (*AM*) pipe.

cachiporra [katʃi'porra] *nf* truncheon.

cachivache [katʃi'βatʃe] *nm* piece of junk; ~**s** *nmpl* trash *sg*, junk *sg*.

cacho, a ['katʃo, a] *nm* (small) bit; (*AM: cuerno*) horn.

cachondearse [katʃonde'arse] *vr*: ~ **de algn** to tease sb.

cachondeo [katʃon'deo] *nm* (*fam*) farce, joke; (*guasa*) laugh.

cachondo, a [ka'tʃondo, a] *adj* (*ZOOL*) on heat; (*persona*) randy, sexy; (*gracioso*) funny.

cachorro, a [ka'tʃorro, a] *nm/f* (*perro*) pup, puppy; (*león*) cub.

cacique [ka'θike] *nm* chief, local ruler; (*POL*) local party boss; (*fig*) despot.

caco ['kako] *nm* pickpocket.

cacofonía [kakofo'nia] *nf* cacophony.

cacto ['kakto] *nm*, **cactus** ['kaktus] *nm inv* cactus.

cada ['kaða] *adj inv* each; (*antes de número*) every; ~ **día** each day, every day; ~ **dos días** every other day; ~ **uno/a** each one, every one; ~ **vez más/menos** more and more/less and less; **uno de** ~ **diez** one out of every ten; ¿~ **cuánto?** how often?

cadalso [ka'ðalso] *nm* scaffold.

cadáver [ka'ðaβer] *nm* (dead) body, corpse.

cadavérico, a [kaða'βeriko, a] *adj* cadaverous; (*pálido*) deathly pale.

cadena [ka'ðena] *nf* chain; (*TV*) channel; **reacción en** ~ chain reaction; **trabajo en** ~ assembly line work; ~ **midi/mini** (*MUS*) midi/mini system; ~ **perpetua** (*JUR*) life imprisonment; ~ **de caracteres** (*INFORM*) character string.

cadencia [ka'ðenθja] *nf* cadence, rhythm.

cadera [ka'ðera] *nf* hip.

cadete [ka'ðete] *nm* cadet.

Cádiz ['kaðiθ] *nm* Cadiz.

caducar [kaðu'kar] *vi* to expire.

caducidad [kaðuθi'ðað] *nf*: **fecha de** ~ expiry date; (*de comida*) sell-by date.

caduco, a [ka'ðuko, a] *adj* (*idea etc*) outdated, outmoded; **de hoja caduca**

deciduous.

caduque [ka'ðuke] *etc vb* V **caducar.**

C.A.E. *abr* (= *cóbrese al entregar*) COD.

caer [ka'er] *vi* to fall; (*premio*) to go; (*sitio*) to be, lie; (*pago*) to fall due; ~**se** to fall (down); **dejar** ~ to drop; **estar al** ~ to be due to happen; (*persona*) to be about to arrive; **me cae bien/mal** I like/don't like him; ~ **en la cuenta** to catch on; **su cumpleaños cae en viernes** her birthday falls on a Friday; **se me ha caído el guante** I've dropped my glove.

café, *pl* **cafés** [ka'fe, ka'fes] *nm* (*bebida, planta*) coffee; (*lugar*) café ♦ *adj* (*color*) brown; ~ **con leche** white coffee; ~ **solo**, ~ **negro** (*AM*) (small) black coffee.

cafeína [kafe'ina] *nf* caffein(e).

cafetal [kafe'tal] *nm* coffee plantation.

cafetera [kafe'tera] *nf* V **cafetero.**

cafetería [kafete'ria] *nf* cafe.

cafetero, a [kafe'tero, a] *adj* coffee *cpd* ♦ *nf* coffee pot; **ser muy** ~ to be a coffee addict.

cafre ['kafre] *nmlf*: **como** ~**s** (*fig*) like savages.

cagalera [kaɣa'lera] *nf* (*fam!*): **tener** ~ to have the runs.

cagar [ka'ɣar] (*fam!*) *vt* to shit (*!*); (*fig*) to bungle, mess up ♦ *vi* to have a shit (*!*); ~**se** *vr*: **¡me cago en diez** (*etc*)! Christ! (*!*).

cague ['kaɣe] *etc vb* V **cagar.**

caído, a [ka'iðo, a] *adj* fallen; (*INFORM*) down ♦ *nf* fall; (*declive*) slope; (*disminución*) fall, drop; ~ **del cielo** out of the blue; **a la caída del sol** at sunset; **sufrir una caída** to have a fall.

caiga ['kaiɣa] *etc vb* V **caer.**

caimán [kai'man] *nm* alligator.

Cairo ['kairo] *nm*: **el** ~ Cairo.

caja ['kaxa] *nf* box; (*ataúd*) coffin, casket (*US*); (*para reloj*) case; (*de ascensor*) shaft; (*COM*) cashbox; (*ECON*) fund; (*donde se hacen los pagos*) cashdesk; (*en supermercado*) checkout, till; (*TIP*) case; ~ **de ahorros** savings bank; ~ **de cambios** gearbox; ~ **fuerte,** ~ **de caudales** safe, strongbox; **ingresar en** ~ to be paid in.

cajero, a [ka'xero, a] *nmlf* cashier; (*en banco*) (bank) teller ♦ *nm*: ~ **automático** cash dispenser, automatic telling machine, A.T.M.

cajetilla [kaxe'tiʎa] *nf* (*de cigarrillos*) packet.

cajista [ka'xista] *nmlf* typesetter.

cajón [ka'xon] *nm* big box; (*de mueble*) drawer.

cal [kal] *nf* lime; **cerrar algo a** ~ **y canto** to shut sth firmly.

cala ['kala] *nf* (*GEO*) cove, inlet; (*de barco*) hold.

calabacín [kalaßa'θin] *nm* (*BOT*) baby marrow, courgette, zucchini (*US*).

calabaza [kala'ßaθa] *nf* (*BOT*) pumpkin; **dar** ~**s a** (*candidato*) to fail.

calabozo [kala'ßoθo] *nm* (*cárcel*) prison; (*celda*) cell.

calado, a [ka'laðo, a] *adj* (*prenda*) lace *cpd* ♦ *nm* (*TEC*) fretwork; (*NAUT*) draught ♦ *nf* (*de cigarrillo*) puff; **estar** ~ (**hasta los huesos**) to be soaked (to the skin).

calamar [kala'mar] *nm* squid.

calambre [ka'lambre] *nm* (*tb*: ~**s**) cramp.

calamidad [kalami'ðað] *nf* calamity, disaster; (*persona*): **es una** ~ he's a dead loss.

calamina [kala'mina] *nf* calamine.

cálamo ['kalamo] *nm* (*BOT*) stem; (*MUS*) reed.

calaña [ka'laɲa] *nf* model, pattern; (*fig*) nature, stamp.

calar [ka'lar] *vt* to soak, drench; (*penetrar*) to pierce, penetrate; (*comprender*) to see through; (*vela, red*) to lower; ~**se** *vr* (*AUTO*) to stall; ~**se las gafas** to stick one's glasses on.

calavera [kala'ßera] *nf* skull.

calcañal [kalka'ɲal], **calcañar** [kalka'ɲar] *nm* heel.

calcar [kal'kar] *vt* (*reproducir*) to trace; (*imitar*) to copy.

calce ['kalθe] *etc vb* V **calzar.**

calceta [kal'θeta] *nf* (*knee-length*) stocking; **hacer** ~ to knit.

calcetín [kalθe'tin] *nm* sock.

calcinar [kalθi'nar] *vt* to burn, blacken.

calcio ['kalθjo] *nm* calcium.

calco ['kalko] *nm* tracing.

calcomanía [kalkoma'nia] *nf* transfer.

calculador, a [kalkula'ðor, a] *adj* calculating ♦ *nf* calculator.

calcular [kalku'lar] *vt* (*MAT*) to calculate, compute; ~ **que ...** to reckon that ....

cálculo ['kalkulo] *nm* calculation; (*MED*) (gall)stone; (*MAT*) calculus; ~ **de costo** costing; ~ **diferencial** differential calculus; **obrar con mucho** ~ to act cautiously.

caldear [kalde'ar] *vt* to warm (up), heat (up); (*metales*) to weld.

caldera [kal'dera] *nf* boiler.

calderero [kalde'rero] *nm* boilermaker.

calderilla [kalde'riʎa] *nf* (*moneda*) small change.

caldero [kal'dero] *nm* small boiler.

caldo ['kaldo] *nm* stock; (*consomé*)

consommé; ~ **de cultivo** (*BIO*) culture medium; **poner a** ~ **a algn** to tear sb off a strip; **los** ~**s jerezanos** sherries.

caldoso, a [kal'doso, a] *adj* (*guisado*) juicy; (*sopa*) thin.

calé [ka'le] *adj* gipsy *cpd*.

calefacción [kalefak'θjon] *nf* heating; ~ **central** central heating.

caleidoscopio [kaleiðos'kopjo] *nm* kaleidoscope.

calendario [kalen'darjo] *nm* calendar.

calentador [kalenta'ðor] *nm* heater.

calentamiento [kalenta'mjento] *nm* (*DEPORTE*) warm-up.

calentar [kalen'tar] *vt* to heat (up); (*fam: excitar*) to turn on; (*AM: enfurecer*) to anger; ~**se** *vr* to heat up, warm up; (*fig: discusión etc*) to get heated.

calentura [kalen'tura] *nf* (*MED*) fever, (high) temperature; (*de boca*) mouth sore.

calenturiento, a [kalentu'rjento, a] *adj* (*mente*) overactive.

calibrar [kali'ßrar] *vt* to gauge, measure.

calibre [ka'lißre] *nm* (*de cañón*) calibre, bore; (*diámetro*) diameter; (*fig*) calibre.

calidad [kali'ðað] *nf* quality; **de** ~ quality *cpd*; ~ **de borrador** (*INFORM*) draft quality; ~ **de carta** *o* **de correspondencia** (*INFORM*) letter quality; ~ **texto** (*INFORM*) text quality; ~ **de vida** quality of life; **en** ~ **de** in the capacity of.

cálido, a ['kaliðo, a] *adj* hot; (*fig*) warm.

caliente [ka'ljente] *etc vb V* **calentar** ♦ *adj* hot; (*fig*) fiery; (*disputa*) heated; (*fam: cachondo*) randy.

califa [ka'lifa] *nm* caliph.

calificación [kalifika'θjon] *nf* qualification; (*de alumno*) grade, mark; ~ **de sobresaliente** first-class mark.

calificar [kalifi'kar] *vt* to qualify; (*alumno*) to grade, mark; ~ **de** to describe as.

calificativo, a [kalifika'tißo, a] *adj* qualifying ♦ *nm* qualifier, epithet.

califique [kali'fike] *etc vb V* **calificar**.

californiano, a [kalifor'njano, a] *adj*, *nm/f* Californian.

caligrafía [kaliɣra'fia] *nf* calligraphy.

calima [ka'lima] *nf* mist.

calina [ka'lina] *nf* haze.

cáliz ['kaliθ] *nm* (*BOT*) calyx; (*REL*) chalice.

caliza [ka'liθa] *nf* limestone.

callado, a [ka'ʎaðo, a] *adj* quiet, silent.

callar [ka'ʎar] *vt* (*asunto delicado*) to keep quiet about, say nothing about; (*omitir*) to pass over in silence; (*persona, oposición*) to silence ♦ *vi*, ~**se** *vr* to keep quiet, be silent; (*dejar de hablar*) to stop

talking; ¡**calla**!, be quiet!; ¡**cállate**!, ¡**cállese**! shut up!; ¡**cállate la boca**! shut your mouth!

calle ['kaʎe] *nf* street; (*DEPORTE*) lane; ~ **arriba/abajo** up/down the street; ~ **de sentido único** one-way street; **poner a algn (de patitas) en la** ~ to kick sb out.

calleja [ka'ʎexa] *nf* alley, narrow street.

callejear [kaʎexe'ar] *vi* to wander (about) the streets.

callejero, a [kaʎe'xero, a] *adj* street *cpd* ♦ *nm* street map.

callejón [kaʎe'xon] *nm* alley, passage; (*GEO*) narrow pass; ~ **sin salida** cul-de-sac; (*fig*) blind alley.

callejuela [kaʎe'xwela] *nf* side-street, alley.

callista [ka'ʎista] *nm/f* chiropodist.

callo ['kaʎo] *nm* callus; (*en el pie*) corn; ~**s** *nmpl* (*CULIN*) tripe *sg*.

callosidad [kaʎosi'ðað] *nf* (*de pie*) corn; (*de mano*) callus.

calloso, a [ka'ʎoso, a] *adj* horny, rough.

calma ['kalma] *nf* calm; (*pachorra*) slowness; (*COM, ECON*) calm, lull; ~ **chicha** dead calm; ¡~!, ¡**con** ~! take it easy!

calmante [kal'mante] *adj* soothing ♦ *nm* sedative, tranquillizer.

calmar [kal'mar] *vt* to calm, calm down; (*dolor*) to relieve ♦ *vi*, ~**se** *vr* (*tempestad*) to abate; (*mente etc*) to become calm.

calmoso, a [kal'moso, a] *adj* calm, quiet.

caló [ka'lo] *nm* (*de gitanos*) gipsy language, Romany; (*argot*) slang.

calor [ka'lor] *nm* heat; (~ *agradable*) warmth; **entrar en** ~ to get warm; **tener** ~ to be *o* feel hot.

caloría [kalo'ria] *nf* calorie.

calorífero, a [kalo'rifero, a] *adj* heat-producing, heat-giving ♦ *nm* heating system.

calque ['kalke] *etc vb V* **calcar**.

calumnia [ka'lumnja] *nf* slander; (*por escrito*) libel.

calumniar [kalum'njar] *vt* to slander; to libel.

calumnioso, a [kalum'njoso, a] *a* slanderous; libellous.

caluroso, a [kalu'roso, a] *adj* hot; (*sin exceso*) warm; (*fig*) enthusiastic.

calva ['kalßa] *nf* bald patch; (*en bosque*) clearing.

calvario [kal'ßarjo] *nm* stations *pl* of the cross; (*fig*) cross, heavy burden.

calvicie [kal'ßiθje] *nf* baldness.

calvo, a ['kalßo, a] *adj* bald; (*terreno*) bare, barren; (*tejido*) threadbare ♦ *nm* bald man.

calza ['kalθa] *nf* wedge, chock.

calzado, a [kal'θaðo, a] *adj* shod ♦ *nm* footwear ♦ *nf* roadway, highway.

calzador [kalθa'ðor] *nm* shoehorn.

calzar [kal'θar] *vt* (*zapatos etc*) to wear; (*un mueble*) to put a wedge under; (*TEC: rueda etc*) to scotch; **~se** *vr*: **~se los zapatos** to put on one's shoes; **¿qué (número) calza?** what size do you take?

calzón [kal'θon] *nm* (*tb*: **calzones**) shorts *pl*; (*AM: de hombre*) pants *pl*; (: *de mujer*) panties *pl*.

calzoncillos [kalθon'θiʎos] *nmpl* underpants.

cama ['kama] *nf* bed; (*GEO*) stratum; **~ individual/de matrimonio** single/double bed; **guardar ~** to be ill in bed.

camada [ka'maða] *nf* litter; (*de personas*) gang, band.

camafeo [kama'feo] *nm* cameo.

camaleón [kamale'on] *nm* chameleon.

cámara ['kamara] *nf* (*POL, TEC*) chamber; (*habitación*) room; (*sala*) hall; (*CINE*) cine camera; (*fotográfica*) camera; **~ de aire** inner tube; **~ alta/baja** upper/lower house; **~ de comercio** chamber of commerce; **~ digital** digital camera; **~ de gas** gas chamber; **~ de vídeo** video camera; **a ~ lenta** in slow motion.

camarada [kama'raða] *nm* comrade, companion.

camaradería [kamaraðe'ria] *nf* comradeship.

camarero, a [kama'rero, a] *nm* waiter ♦ *nf* (*en restaurante*) waitress; (*en casa, hotel*) maid.

camarilla [kama'riʎa] *nf* (*clan*) clique; (*POL*) lobby.

camarín [kama'rin] *nm* (*TEAT*) dressing room.

camarón [kama'ron] *nm* shrimp.

camarote [kama'rote] *nm* (*NAUT*) cabin.

cambiable [kam'bjaßle] *adj* (*variable*) changeable, variable; (*intercambiable*) interchangeable.

cambiante [kam'bjante] *adj* variable.

cambiar [kam'bjar] *vt* to change; (*trocar*) to exchange ♦ *vi* to change; **~se** *vr* (*mudarse*) to move; (*de ropa*) to change; **~(se) de ...** to change one's ...; **~ de idea/de ropa** to change one's mind/clothes.

cambiazo [kam'bjaθo] *nm*: **dar el ~ a algn** to swindle sb.

cambio ['kambjo] *nm* change; (*trueque*) exchange; (*COM*) rate of exchange; (*oficina*) bureau de change; (*dinero menudo*) small change; **en ~** on the other hand; (*en lugar de eso*) instead; **~ de divisas** (*COM*) foreign exchange; **~ de línea** (*INFORM*) line feed; **~ de página** (*INFORM*) form feed; **~ a término** (*COM*) forward exchange; **~ de velocidades** gear lever; **~ de vía** points *pl*.

cambista [kam'bista] *nm* (*COM*) exchange broker.

Camboya [kam'boja] *nf* Cambodia, Kampuchea.

camboyano, a [kambo'jano, a] *a*, *nm/f* Cambodian, Kampuchean.

camelar [kame'lar] *vt* (*con mujer*) to flirt with; (*persuadir*) to cajole.

camelia [ka'melia] *nf* camellia.

camello [ka'meʎo] *nm* camel; (*fam: traficante*) pusher.

camelo [ka'melo] *nm*: **me huele a ~** it smells fishy.

camerino [kame'rino] *nm* (*TEAT*) dressing room.

camilla [ka'miʎa] *nf* (*MED*) stretcher.

caminante [kami'nante] *nm/f* traveller.

caminar [kami'nar] *vi* (*marchar*) to walk, go; (*viajar*) to travel, journey ♦ *vt* (*recorrer*) to cover, travel.

caminata [kami'nata] *nf* long walk.

camino [ka'mino] *nm* way, road; (*sendero*) track; **a medio ~** halfway (there); **en el ~** on the way, en route; **~ de** on the way to; **~ particular** private road; **~ vecinal** country road; **C~s, Canales y Puertos** (*UNIV*) Civil Engineering; **C~ de Santiago** *see boxed note*; **ir por buen ~** (*fig*) to be on the right track.

CAMINO DE SANTIAGO

The **Camino de Santiago** *is a medieval pilgrim route stretching from the Pyrenees to Santiago de Compostela in north-west Spain, where tradition has it that the body of the Apostle James is buried. Nowadays it is a popular tourist route too. The "concha" (cockleshell) symbolizes the* **Camino de Santiago,** *because it is said that when St James's body was found it was covered in shells.*

---

camión [ka'mjon] *nm* lorry, truck (*US*); (*AM: autobús*) bus; **~ de bomberos** fire engine.

camionero [kamjo'nero] *nm* lorry *o* truck (*US*) driver, trucker (*esp US*).

camioneta [kamjo'neta] *nf* van, transit ®.

camisa [ka'misa] *nf* shirt; (*BOT*) skin; **~ de dormir** nightdress; **~ de fuerza**

straitjacket.
camisería [kamise'ria] *nf* outfitter's (shop).
camiseta [kami'seta] *nf* tee-shirt; (*ropa interior*) vest; (*de deportista*) top.
camisón [kami'son] *nm* nightdress, nightgown.
camomila [kamo'mila] *nf* camomile.
camorra [ka'morra] *nf*: **armar** ~ to kick up a row; **buscar** ~ to look for trouble.
camorrista [kamo'rrista] *nm/f* thug.
camote [ka'mote] *nm* (*AM*) sweet potato.
campal [kam'pal] *adj*: **batalla** ~ pitched battle.
campamento [kampa'mento] *nm* camp.
campana [kam'pana] *nf* bell.
campanada [kampa'naða] *nf* peal.
campanario [kampa'narjo] *nm* belfry.
campanilla [kampa'niʎa] *nf* (*campana*) small bell.
campante [kam'pante] *adj*: **siguió tan** ~ he went on as if nothing had happened.
campaña [kam'paɲa] *nf* (*MIL, POL*) campaign; **hacer** ~ (**en pro de/contra**) to campaign (for/against); ~ **de venta** sales campaign.
campechano, a [kampe'tʃano, a] *adj* open.
campeón, ona [kampe'on, ona] *nm/f* champion.
campeonato [kampeo'nato] *nm* championship.
campesino, a [kampe'sino, a] *adj* country *cpd*, rural; (*gente*) peasant *cpd* ♦ *nm/f* countryman/woman; (*agricultor*) farmer.
campestre [kam'pestre] *adj* country *cpd*, rural.
camping ['kampin] *nm* camping; (*lugar*) campsite; **ir de** *o* **hacer** ~ to go camping.
campiña [kam'piɲa] *nf* countryside.
campista [kam'pista] *nm/f* camper.
campo ['kampo] *nm* (*fuera de la ciudad*) country, countryside; (*AGR, ELEC, INFORM*) field; (*de fútbol*) pitch; (*de golf*) course; (*MIL*) camp; ~ **de batalla** battlefield; ~ **de minas** minefield; ~ **petrolífero** oilfield; ~ **visual** field of vision; ~ **de concentración/de internación/de trabajo** concentration/internment/labour camp.
camposanto [kampo'santo] *nm* cemetery.
CAMPSA ['kampsa] *nf abr* (*ESP COM*) = *Compañía Arrendataria del Monopolio de Petróleos, S.A.*
campus ['kampus] *nm inv* (*UNIV*) campus.
camuflaje [kamu'flaxe] *nm* camouflage.
camuflar [kamu'flar] *vt* to camouflage.
can [kan] *nm* dog, mutt (*fam*).
cana ['kana] *nf V* **cano**.
Canadá [kana'ða] *nm* Canada.

canadiense [kana'ðjense] *adj, nm/f* Canadian ♦ *nf* fur-lined jacket.
canal [ka'nal] *nm* canal; (*GEO*) channel, strait; (*de televisión*) channel; (*de tejado*) gutter; **C**~ **de la Mancha** English Channel; **C**~ **de Panamá** Panama Canal.
canalice [kana'liθe] *etc vb V* **canalizar**.
canalizar [kanali'θar] *vt* to channel.
canalla [ka'naʎa] *nf* rabble, mob ♦ *nm* swine.
canallada [kana'ʎaða] *nf* (*hecho*) dirty trick.
canalón [kana'lon] *nm* (*conducto vertical*) drainpipe; (*del tejado*) gutter; **canalones** *nmpl* (*CULIN*) cannelloni.
canapé, *pl* **canapés** [kana'pe, kana'pes] *nm* sofa, settee; (*CULIN*) canapé.
Canarias [ka'narjas] *nfpl*: **las** (**Islas**) ~ the Canaries, the Canary Isles.
canario, a [ka'narjo, a] *adj* of *o* from the Canary Isles ♦ *nm/f* native *o* inhabitant of the Canary Isles ♦ *nm* (*ZOOL*) canary.
canasta [ka'nasta] *nf* (round) basket.
canastilla [kanas'tiʎa] *nf* small basket; (*de niño*) layette.
canasto [ka'nasto] *nm* large basket.
cancela [kan'θela] *nf* (wrought-iron) gate.
cancelación [kanθela'θjon] *nf* cancellation.
cancelar [kanθe'lar] *vt* to cancel; (*una deuda*) to write off.
cáncer ['kanθer] *nm* (*MED*) cancer; **C**~ (*ASTRO*) Cancer.
cancerígeno, a [kanθe'rixeno, a] *adj* carcinogenic.
cancha ['kantʃa] *nf* (*de baloncesto, tenis etc*) court; (*AM*: *de fútbol etc*) pitch.
canciller [kanθi'ʎer] *nm* chancellor; **C**~ (*AM*) Foreign Minister, ≈ Foreign Secretary (*BRIT*).
Cancillería [kansiʎe'ria] *nf* (*AM*) Foreign Ministry, ≈ Foreign Office (*BRIT*).
canción [kan'θjon] *nf* song; ~ **de cuna** lullaby.
cancionero [kanθjo'nero] *nm* song book.
candado [kan'daðo] *nm* padlock.
candela [kan'dela] *nf* candle.
candelabro [kande'laßro] *nm* candelabra.
candelero [kande'lero] *nm* (*para vela*) candlestick; (*de aceite*) oil lamp.
candente [kan'dente] *adj* red-hot; (*tema*) burning.
candidato, a [kandi'ðato, a] *nm/f* candidate; (*para puesto*) applicant.
candidatura [kandiða'tura] *nf* candidature.
candidez [kandi'ðeθ] *nf* (*sencillez*) simplicity; (*simpleza*) naiveté.
cándido, a ['kandiðo, a] *adj* simple; naive.
candil [kan'dil] *nm* oil lamp.

candilejas [kandi'lexas] *nfpl* (*TEAT*)
footlights.

candor [kan'dor] *nm* (*sinceridad*)
frankness; (*inocencia*) innocence.

canela [ka'nela] *nf* cinnamon.

canelo [ka'nelo] *nm*: **hacer el** ~ to act the
fool.

canelones [kane'lones] *nmpl* cannelloni.

cangrejo [kan'grexo] *nm* crab.

canguro [kan'guro] *nm* (*ZOOL*) kangaroo;
(*de niños*) baby-sitter; **hacer de** ~ to
baby-sit.

caníbal [ka'niβal] *adj, nm/f* cannibal.

canica [ka'nika] *nf* marble.

caniche [ka'nitʃe] *nm* poodle.

canícula [ka'nikula] *nf* midsummer heat.

canijo, a [ka'nixo, a] *adj* frail, sickly.

canilla [ka'niʎa] *nf* (*TEC*) bobbin.

canino, a [ka'nino, a] *adj* canine ♦ *nm*
canine (tooth).

canje [kan'xe] *nm* exchange; (*trueque*)
swap.

canjear [kanxe'ar] *vt* to exchange; (*trocar*)
to swap.

cano, a ['kano, a] *adj* grey-haired, white-
haired ♦ *nf* (*tb*: **canas**) white *o* grey hair;
tener canas to be going grey.

canoa [ka'noa] *nf* canoe.

canon ['kanon] *nm* canon; (*pensión*) rent;
(*COM*) tax.

canonice [kano'niθe] *etc vb* V **canonizar**.

canónico, a [ka'noniko, a] *adj*: **derecho** ~
canon law.

canónigo [ka'noniγo] *nm* canon.

canonizar [kanoni'θar] *vt* to canonize.

canoro, a [ka'noro, a] *adj* melodious.

canoso, a [ka'noso, a] *adj* (*pelo*) grey
(*BRIT*), gray (*US*); (*persona*) grey-haired.

cansado, a [kan'saðo, a] *adj* tired, weary;
(*tedioso*) tedious, boring; **estoy** ~ **de**
hacerlo I'm sick of doing it.

cansancio [kan'sanθjo] *nm* tiredness,
fatigue.

cansar [kan'sar] *vt* (*fatigar*) to tire, tire out;
(*aburrir*) to bore; (*fastidiar*) to bother; ~**se**
vr to tire, get tired; (*aburrirse*) to get
bored.

cantábrico, a [kan'taβriko, a] *adj*
Cantabrian; **Mar C**~ Bay of Biscay;
(**Montes**) **C**~**s, Cordillera Cantábrica**
Cantabrian Mountains.

cántabro, a ['kantaβro, a] *adj, nm/f*
Cantabrian.

cantante [kan'tante] *adj* singing ♦ *nm/f*
singer.

cantaor, a [kanta'or, a] *nm/f* Flamenco
singer.

cantar [kan'tar] *vt* to sing ♦ *vi* to sing;

(*insecto*) to chirp; (*rechinar*) to squeak;
(*fam*: *criminal*) to squeal ♦ *nm* (*acción*)
singing; (*canción*) song; (*poema*) poem; ~
a algn las cuarenta to tell sb a few home
truths; ~ **a dos voces** to sing a duet.

cántara ['kantara] *nf* large pitcher.

cántaro ['kantaro] *nm* pitcher, jug.

cantautor, a [kantau'tor, a] *nm/f* singer-
songwriter.

cante ['kante] *nm*: ~ **jondo** flamenco
singing.

cantera [kan'tera] *nf* quarry.

cántico ['kantiko] *nm* (*REL*) canticle; (*fig*)
song.

cantidad [kanti'ðað] *nf* quantity, amount;
(*ECON*) sum ♦ *adv* (*fam*) a lot; ~ **alzada**
lump sum; ~ **de** lots of.

cantilena [kanti'lena] *nf* = **cantinela**.

cantimplora [kantim'plora] *nf* (*frasco*)
water bottle, canteen.

cantina [kan'tina] *nf* canteen; (*de estación*)
buffet; (*esp AM*) bar.

cantinela [kanti'nela] *nf* ballad, song.

canto ['kanto] *nm* singing; (*canción*) song;
(*borde*) edge, rim; (*de un cuchillo*) back;
~ **rodado** boulder.

cantón [kan'ton] *nm* canton.

cantor, a [kan'tor, a] *nm/f* singer.

canturrear [kanturre'ar] *vi* to sing softly.

canutas [ka'nutas] *nfpl*: **pasarlas** ~ (*fam*) to
have a rough time (of it).

canuto [ka'nuto] *nm* (*tubo*) small tube;
(*fam*: *droga*) joint.

caña ['kaɲa] *nf* (*BOT*: *tallo*) stem, stalk;
(*carrizo*) reed; (*vaso*) tumbler; (*de
cerveza*) glass of beer; (*ANAT*) shinbone;
(*AM*: *aguardiente*) cane liquor; ~ **de**
azúcar sugar cane; ~ **de pescar** fishing
rod.

cañada [ka'ɲaða] *nf* (*entre dos montañas*)
gully, ravine; (*camino*) cattle track.

cáñamo ['kaɲamo] *nm* (*BOT*) hemp.

cañaveral [kaɲaβe'ral] *nm* (*BOT*) reedbed;
(*AGR*) sugar-cane field.

cañería [kaɲe'ria] *nf* piping; (*tubo*) pipe.

caño ['kaɲo] *nm* (*tubo*) tube, pipe; (*de
aguas servidas*) sewer; (*MUS*) pipe;
(*NAUT*) navigation channel; (*de fuente*)
jet.

cañón [ka'ɲon] *nm* (*MIL*) cannon; (*de fusil*)
barrel; (*GEO*) canyon, gorge.

cañonazo [kaɲo'naθo] *nm* (*MIL*) gunshot.

cañonera [kaɲo'nera] *nf* (*tb*: **lancha** ~)
gunboat.

caoba [ka'oβa] *nf* mahogany.

caos ['kaos] *nm* chaos.

caótico, a [ka'otiko, a] *adj* chaotic.

C.A.P. *nm abr* (= *Certificado de Aptitud*

Pedagógica) teaching certificate.

cap. *abr* (= *capítulo*) ch.

capa ['kapa] *nf* cloak, cape; (*CULIN*) coating; (*GEO*) layer, stratum; (*de pintura*) coat; **de ~ y espada** cloak-and-dagger; **so ~ de** under the pretext of; **~ de ozono** ozone layer; **~s sociales** social groups.

capacho [ka'patʃo] *nm* wicker basket.

capacidad [kapaθi'ðað] *nf* (*medida*) capacity; (*aptitud*) capacity, ability; **una sala con ~ para 900** a hall seating 900; **~ adquisitiva** purchasing power.

capacitación [kapaθita'θjon] *nf* training.

capacitar [kapaθi'tar] *vt*: **~ a algn para algo** to qualify sb for sth; (*TEC*) to train sb for sth.

capar [ka'par] *vt* to castrate, geld.

caparazón [kapara'θon] *nm* (*ZOOL*) shell.

capataz [kapa'taθ] *nm* foreman, chargehand.

capaz [ka'paθ] *adj* able, capable; (*amplio*) capacious, roomy; **es ~ que venga mañana** (*AM*) he'll probably come tomorrow.

capcioso, a [kap'θjoso, a] *adj* wily, deceitful; **pregunta capciosa** trick question.

capea [ka'pea] *nf* (*TAUR*) bullfight with young bulls.

capear [kape'ar] *vt* (*dificultades*) to dodge; **~ el temporal** to weather the storm.

capellán [kape'ʎan] *nm* chaplain; (*sacerdote*) priest.

caperuza [kape'ruθa] *nf* hood; (*de bolígrafo*) cap.

capi ['kapi] *nf* (*esp AM fam*) capital (city).

capicúa [kapi'kua] *nm* reversible number, *e.g.* 1441.

capilar [kapi'lar] *adj* hair *cpd.*

capilla [ka'piʎa] *nf* chapel.

capital [kapi'tal] *adj* capital ♦ *nm* (*COM*) capital ♦ *nf* (*de nación*) capital (city); (*tb*: **~ de provincia**) provincial capital, ≈ county town; **~ activo/en acciones** working/share *o* equity capital; **~ arriesgado** venture capital; **~ autorizado** authorised capital; **~ emitido** issued capital; **~ improductivo** idle money; **~ invertido** *o* **utilizado** capital employed; **~ pagado** paid-up capital; **~ de riesgo** risk capital; **~ social** authorized *o* share capital; **inversión de ~es** capital investment; *V tb* **provincia.**

capitalice [kapita'liθe] *etc vb V* **capitalizar.**

capitalino, a [kapita'lino, a] *adj* (*AM*) of *o* from the capital ♦ *nm/f* native *o* inhabitant of the capital.

capitalismo [kapita'lismo] *nm* capitalism.

capitalista [kapita'lista] *adj, nm/f* capitalist.

capitalizar [kapitali'θar] *vt* to capitalize.

capitán [kapi'tan] *nm* captain; (*fig*) leader.

capitana [kapi'tana] *nf* flagship.

capitanear [kapitane'ar] *vt* to captain.

capitanía [kapita'nia] *nf* captaincy.

capitel [kapi'tel] *nm* (*ARQ*) capital.

capitolio [kapi'toljo] *nm* capitol.

capitulación [kapitula'θjon] *nf* (*rendición*) capitulation, surrender; (*acuerdo*) agreement, pact; **capitulaciones matrimoniales** marriage contract *sg.*

capitular [kapitu'lar] *vi* to come to terms, make an agreement; (*MIL*) to surrender.

capítulo [ka'pitulo] *nm* chapter.

capo [ka'po] *nm* drugs baron.

capó [ka'po] *nm* (*AUTO*) bonnet (*BRIT*), hood (*US*).

capón [ka'pon] *nm* capon.

caporal [kapo'ral] *nm* chief, leader.

capota [ka'pota] *nf* (*de mujer*) bonnet; (*AUTO*) hood (*BRIT*), top (*US*).

capote [ka'pote] *nm* (*abrigo: de militar*) greatcoat; (*de torero*) cloak.

capricho [ka'pritʃo] *nm* whim, caprice.

caprichoso, a [kapri'tʃoso, a] *adj* capricious.

Capricornio [kapri'kornjo] *nm* Capricorn.

cápsula ['kapsula] *nf* capsule; **~ espacial** space capsule.

captar [kap'tar] *vt* (*comprender*) to understand; (*RADIO*) to pick up; (*atención, apoyo*) to attract.

captura [kap'tura] *nf* capture; (*JUR*) arrest.

capturar [kaptu'rar] *vt* to capture; (*JUR*) to arrest; (*datos*) to input.

capucha [ka'putʃa] *nf* hood, cowl.

capullo [ka'puʎo] *nm* (*ZOOL*) cocoon; (*BOT*) bud; (*fam!*) berk (*BRIT*), jerk (*US*).

caqui ['kaki] *nm* khaki.

cara ['kara] *nf* (*ANAT, de moneda*) face; (*aspecto*) appearance; (*de disco*) side; (*fig*) boldness; (*descara*) cheek, nerve ♦ *prep*: **~ a** facing; **de ~ a** opposite, facing; **dar la ~** to face the consequences; **echar algo en ~ a algn** to reproach sb for sth; **¿~ o cruz?** heads or tails?; **¡qué ~ más dura!** what a nerve!; **de una ~** (*disquete*) single-sided.

carabina [kara'ßina] *nf* carbine, rifle; (*persona*) chaperone.

carabinero [karaßi'nero] *nm* (*de aduana*) customs officer; (*AM*) gendarme.

Caracas [ka'rakas] *nm* Caracas.

caracol [kara'kol] *nm* (*ZOOL*) snail; (*concha*) (sea)shell; **escalera de ~** spiral staircase.

caracolear [karakole'ar] vi (caballo) to prance about.

carácter, pl caracteres [ka'rakter, karak'teres] nm character; ~ de cambio de página (INFORM) form feed character; caracteres de imprenta (TIP) type(face) sg; ~ libre (INFORM) wildcard character; tener buen/mal ~ to be good-natured/bad tempered.

caracterice [karakte'riθe] etc vb V caracterizar.

característico, a [karakte'ristiko, a] adj characteristic ♦ nf characteristic.

caracterizar [karakteri'θar] vt (distinguir) to characterize, typify; (honrar) to confer (a) distinction on.

caradura [kara'ðura] nm/f cheeky person; es un ~ he's got a nerve.

carajillo [kara'xiʎo] nm black coffee with brandy.

carajo [ka'raxo] nm (esp AM fam!): ¡~! shit!(!); ¡qué ~! what the hell!; me importa un ~ I don't give a damn.

caramba [ka'ramba] excl well!, good gracious!

carámbano [ka'rambano] nm icicle.

carambola [karam'bola] nf: por ~ by a fluke.

caramelo [kara'melo] nm (dulce) sweet; (azúcar fundido) caramel.

carantoñas [karan'toɲas] nfpl: hacer ~ a algn to (try to) butter sb up.

caraqueño, a [kara'keɲo, a] adj of o from Caracas ♦ nm/f native o inhabitant of Caracas.

carátula [ka'ratula] nf (máscara) mask; (TEAT): la ~ the stage.

caravana [kara'ßana] nf caravan; (fig) group; (de autos) tailback.

carbón [kar'ßon] nm coal; ~ de leña charcoal; papel ~ carbon paper.

carbonatado, a [karßono'taðo, a] adj carbonated.

carbonato [karßo'nato] nm carbonate; ~ sódico sodium carbonate.

carboncillo [karßon'θiʎo] nm (ARTE) charcoal.

carbonice [karßo'niθe] etc vb V carbonizar.

carbonilla [karßo'niʎa] nf coal dust.

carbonizar [karßoni'θar] vt to carbonize; (quemar) to char; quedar carbonizado (ELEC) to be electrocuted.

carbono [kar'ßono] nm carbon.

carburador [karßura'ðor] nm carburettor.

carburante [karßu'rante] nm fuel.

carca ['karka] adj, nm/f inv reactionary.

carcajada [karka'xaða] nf (loud) laugh, guffaw.

carcajearse [karkaxe'arse] vr to roar with laughter.

cárcel ['karθel] nf prison, jail; (TEC) clamp.

carcelero, a [karθe'lero, a] adj prison cpd ♦ nm/f warder.

carcoma [kar'koma] nf woodworm.

carcomer [karko'mer] vt to bore into, eat into; (fig) to undermine; ~se vr to become worm-eaten; (fig) to decay.

carcomido, a [karko'miðo, a] adj worm-eaten; (fig) rotten.

cardar [kar'ðar] vt (TEC) to card, comb.

cardenal [karðe'nal] nm (REL) cardinal; (MED) bruise.

cárdeno, a ['karðeno, a] adj purple; (lívido) livid.

cardiaco, a [kar'ðjako, a], cardíaco, a [kar'ðiako, a] adj cardiac; (ataque) heart cpd.

cardinal [karði'nal] adj cardinal.

cardiólogo, a [karðj'oloɣo, a] nm/f cardiologist.

cardo ['karðo] nm thistle.

carear [kare'ar] vt to bring face to face; (comparar) to compare; ~se vr to come face to face, meet.

carecer [kare'θer] vi: ~ de to lack, be in need of.

carencia [ka'renθja] nf lack; (escasez) shortage; (MED) deficiency.

carente [ka'rente] adj: ~ de lacking in, devoid of.

carestía [kares'tia] nf (escasez) scarcity, shortage; (COM) high cost; época de ~ period of shortage.

careta [ka'reta] nf mask.

carey [ka'rei] nm (tortuga) turtle; (concha) tortoiseshell.

carezca [ka'reθka] etc vb V carecer.

carga ['karɣa] nf (peso, ELEC) load; (de barco) cargo, freight; (FINANZAS) tax, duty; (MIL) charge; (INFORM) loading; (obligación, responsabilidad) duty, obligation; ~ aérea (COM) air cargo; ~ útil (COM) payload; la ~ fiscal the tax burden.

cargadero [karɣa'ðero] nm goods platform, loading bay.

cargado, a [kar'ɣaðo, a] adj loaded; (ELEC) live; (café, té) strong; (cielo) overcast.

cargador, a [karɣa'ðor, a] nm/f loader; (NAUT) docker ♦ nm (INFORM): ~ de discos disk pack.

cargamento [karɣa'mento] nm (acción) loading; (mercancías) load, cargo.

cargante [kar'ɣante] adj (persona) trying.

cargar [kar'ɣar] vt (barco, arma) to load; (ELEC) to charge; (impuesto) to impose;

(*COM: algo en cuenta*) to charge, debit; (*MIL: enemigo*) to charge ♦ *vi* (*AUTO*) to load (up); (*inclinarse*) to lean; (*INFORM*) to load; ~ **con** to pick up, carry away; ~**se** *vr* (*fam: estropear*) to break; (: *matar*) to bump off; (*ELEC*) to become charged.

cargo ['karɣo] *nm* (*COM etc*) charge, debit; (*puesto*) post, office; (*responsabilidad*) duty, obligation; (*fig*) weight, burden; (*JUR*) charge; **altos** ~**s** high-ranking officials; **una cantidad en** ~ **a algn** a sum chargeable to sb; **hacerse** ~ **de** to take charge of *o* responsibility for.

cargue ['karɣe] *etc vb V* **cargar**.

Caribe [ka'riβe] *nm*: **el** ~ the Caribbean.

caribeño, a [kari'βeɲo, a] *adj* Caribbean.

caricatura [karika'tura] *nf* caricature.

caricia [ka'riθja] *nf* caress; (*a animal*) pat, stroke.

caridad [kari'ðað] *nf* charity.

caries ['karjes] *nf inv* (*MED*) tooth decay.

cariño [ka'riɲo] *nm* affection, love; (*caricia*) caress; (*en carta*) love ....

cariñoso, a [kari'ɲoso, a] *adj* affectionate.

carioca [ka'rjoka] *adj* (*AM*) of *o* from Rio de Janeiro ♦ *nm/f* native *o* inhabitant of Rio de Janeiro.

carisma [ka'risma] *nm* charisma.

carismático, a [karis'matiko, a] *adj* charismatic.

caritativo, a [karita'tiβo, a] *adj* charitable.

cariz [ka'riθ] *nm*: **tener** *o* **tomar buen/mal** ~ to look good/bad.

carmesí [karme'si] *adj, nm* crimson.

carmín [kar'min] *nm* (*color*) carmine; ~ **(de labios)** lipstick.

carnal [kar'nal] *adj* carnal; **primo** ~ first cousin.

carnaval [karna'βal] *nm* carnival; *see boxed note*.

CARNAVAL

The three days before "miércoles de ceniza" (Ash Wednesday), when fasting for Lent traditionally starts, are the signal for **carnaval,** *an exuberant celebration which dates back to pre-Christian times. Although in decline during the Franco years in Spain,* **carnaval** *has recently grown in popularity, Cádiz and Tenerife being particularly well known for their celebrations. "Martes de carnaval" (Shrove Tuesday) is the most important day, with colourful street parades, fancy dress, fireworks and a general party atmosphere.*

---

carne ['karne] *nf* flesh; (*CULIN*) meat; ~ **de cerdo/de cordero/de ternera/de vaca** pork/lamb/veal/beef; ~ **picada** mince; ~ **de gallina** (*fig*) gooseflesh.

carné [kar'ne] *nm* = **carnet**.

carnero [kar'nero] *nm* sheep, ram; (*carne*) mutton.

carnet, *pl* **carnets** [kar'ne, kar'nes] *nm*: ~ **de conducir** driving licence; ~ **de identidad** identity card; *V tb* **Documento Nacional de Identidad**.

carnicería [karniθe'ria] *nf* butcher's (shop); (*fig: matanza*) carnage, slaughter.

carnicero, a [karni'θero, a] *adj* carnivorous ♦ *nm/f* (*tb fig*) butcher ♦ *nm* carnivore.

carnívoro, a [kar'niβoro, a] *adj* carnivorous ♦ *nm* carnivore.

carnoso, a [kar'noso, a] *adj* beefy, fat.

caro, a ['karo, a] *adj* dear; (*COM*) dear, expensive ♦ *adv* dear, dearly; **vender** ~ to sell at a high price.

carpa ['karpa] *nf* (*pez*) carp; (*de circo*) big top; (*AM: de camping*) tent.

carpeta [kar'peta] *nf* folder, file.

carpintería [karpinte'ria] *nf* carpentry.

carpintero [karpin'tero] *nm* carpenter; **pájaro** ~ woodpecker.

carraca [ka'rraka] *nf* (*DEPORTE*) rattle.

carraspear [karraspe'ar] *vi* (*aclararse*) to clear one's throat.

carraspera [karras'pera] *nf* hoarseness.

carrera [ka'rrera] *nf* (*acción*) run(ning); (*espacio recorrido*) run; (*certamen*) race; (*trayecto*) course; (*profesión*) career; (*ESCOL, UNIV*) course; (*de taxi*) ride; (*en medias*) ladder; **a la** ~ at (full) speed; **caballo de** ~**(s)** racehorse; ~ **de armamentos** arms race.

carrerilla [karre'riʎa] *nf*: **decir algo de** ~ to reel sth off; **tomar** ~ to get up speed.

carreta [ka'rreta] *nf* wagon, cart.

carrete [ka'rrete] *nm* reel, spool; (*TEC*) coil.

carretera [karre'tera] *nf* (main) road, highway; ~ **nacional** ≈ A road (*BRIT*), state highway (*US*); ~ **de circunvalación** ring road.

carretilla [karre'tiʎa] *nf* trolley; (*AGR*) (wheel)barrow.

carril [ka'rril] *nm* furrow; (*de autopista*) lane; (*FERRO*) rail.

carril-bici, *pl* **carriles-bici** [karil'βiθi, kariles'βiθi] *nm* cycle lane, bikeway (*US*).

carrillo [ka'rriʎo] *nm* (*ANAT*) cheek; (*TEC*) pulley.

carro ['karro] *nm* cart, wagon; (*MIL*) tank; (*AM: coche*) car; (*TIP*) carriage; ~ **blindado** armoured car.

carrocería [karroθe'ria] *nf* body, bodywork *no pl* (*BRIT*).

carroña [ka'rroɲa] *nf* carrion *no pl*.

carroza [ka'rroθa] *nf* (*vehículo*) coach ♦ *nm/f* (*fam*) old fogey.

carruaje [ka'rrwaxe] *nm* carriage.

carrusel [karru'sel] *nm* merry-go-round, roundabout (*BRIT*).

carta ['karta] *nf* letter; (*CULIN*) menu; (*naipe*) card; (*mapa*) map; (*JUR*) document; ~ **de crédito** credit card; ~ **de crédito documentaria** (*COM*) documentary letter of credit; ~ **de crédito irrevocable** (*COM*) irrevocable letter of credit; ~ **certificada/urgente** registered/special delivery letter; ~ **marítima** chart; ~ **de pedido** (*COM*) order; ~ **verde** (*AUTO*) green card; ~ **de vinos** wine list; **echar una** ~ **al correo** to post a letter; **echar las** ~**s a algn** to tell sb's fortune.

cartabón [karta'βon] *nm* set square.

cartearse [karte'arse] *vr* to correspond.

cartel [kar'tel] *nm* (*anuncio*) poster, placard; (*ESCOL*) wall chart; (*COM*) cartel.

cartelera [karte'lera] *nf* hoarding, billboard; (*en periódico etc*) listings *pl*, entertainments guide; **"en** ~**"** "showing".

cartera [kar'tera] *nf* (*de bolsillo*) wallet; (*de colegial, cobrador*) satchel; (*AM: de señora*) handbag (*BRIT*), purse (*US*); (*para documentos*) briefcase; **ministro sin** ~ (*POL*) minister without portfolio; **ocupa la** ~ **de Agricultura** he is Minister of Agriculture; ~ **de pedidos** (*COM*) order book; **efectos en** ~ (*ECON*) holdings.

carterista [karte'rista] *nm/f* pickpocket.

cartero [kar'tero] *nm* postman.

cartílago [kar'tilaxo] *nm* cartilage.

cartilla [kar'tiʎa] *nf* (*ESCOL*) primer, first reading book; ~ **de ahorros** bank book.

cartografía [kartoɣra'fia] *nf* cartography.

cartón [kar'ton] *nm* cardboard.

cartucho [kar'tutʃo] *nm* (*MIL*) cartridge; (*bolsita*) paper cone; ~ **de datos** (*INFORM*) data cartridge.

cartulina [kartu'lina] *nf* fine cardboard, card.

CASA ['kasa] *nf abr* (*ESP AVIAT*) = *Construcciones Aeronáuticas S.A.*

casa ['kasa] *nf* house; (*hogar*) home; (*edificio*) building; (*COM*) firm, company; ~ **consistorial** town hall; ~ **de huéspedes** ~ guest house; ~ **de socorro** first aid post; ~ **de citas** (*fam*) brothel; **ir a** ~ to go home; **salir de** ~ to go out; (*para siempre*) to leave home; **echar la** ~ **por la ventana** (*gastar*) to spare no expense; *V tb* **hotel**.

casadero, a [kasa'ðero, a] *adj* marriageable.

casado, a [ka'saðo, a] *a* married ♦ *nm/f* married man/woman.

casamiento [kasa'mjento] *nm* marriage, wedding.

casar [ka'sar] *vt* to marry; (*JUR*) to quash, annul; ~**se** *vr* to marry, get married; ~**se por lo civil** to have a civil wedding, get married in a registry office (*BRIT*) .

cascabel [kaska'βel] *nm* (small) bell; (*ZOOL*) rattlesnake.

cascada [kas'kaða] *nf* waterfall.

cascajo [kas'kaxo] *nm* gravel, stone chippings *pl*.

cascanueces [kaska'nweθes] *nm inv*: **un** ~ **a** pair of nutcrackers.

cascar [kas'kar] *vt* to split; (*nuez*) to crack ♦ *vi* to chatter; ~**se** *vr* to crack, split, break (open).

cáscara ['kaskara] *nf* (*de huevo, fruta seca*) shell; (*de fruta*) skin; (*de limón*) peel.

cascarón [kaska'ron] *nm* (*broken*) eggshell.

cascarrabias [kaska'rraβjas] *nm/f inv* (*fam*) hothead.

casco ['kasko] *nm* (*de bombero, soldado*) helmet; (*cráneo*) skull; (*NAUT: de barco*) hull; (*ZOOL: de caballo*) hoof; (*botella*) empty bottle; (*de ciudad*): **el** ~ **antiguo** the old part; **el** ~ **urbano** the town centre; **los** ~**s azules** the UN peace-keeping force, the blue berets.

cascote [kas'kote] *nm* piece of rubble; ~**s** *nmpl* rubble *sg*.

caserío [kase'rio] *nm* hamlet, group of houses; (*casa*) country house.

casero, a [ka'sero, a] *adj*: **ser muy** ~ (*persona*) to be homeloving; **"comida casera"** "home cooking" ♦ *nm/f* (*propietario*) landlord/lady; (*COM*) house agent.

caserón [kase'ron] *nm* large (ramshackle) house.

caseta [ka'seta] *nf* hut; (*para bañista*) cubicle; (*de feria*) stall.

casete [ka'sete] *nm o f* cassette: ~ **digital** digital audio tape, DAT.

casi ['kasi] *adv* almost; ~ **nunca** hardly ever, almost never; ~ **nada** next to nothing; ~ **te caes** you almost *o* nearly fell.

casilla [ka'siʎa] *nf* (*casita*) hut, cabin; (*TEAT*) box office; (*para cartas*) pigeonhole; (*AJEDREZ*) square; **C**~ **postal**

o **de Correo(s)** (*AM*) P.O. Box; **sacar a algn de sus ~ s** to drive sb round the bend (*fam*), make sb lose his temper.
casillero [kasi'ʎero] *nm* pigeonholes.
casino [ka'sino] *nm* club; (*de juego*) casino.
caso ['kaso] *nm* case; (*suceso*) event; **en ~ de ...** in case of ...; **el ~ es que** the fact is that; **en el mejor de los ~s** at best; **en ese ~** in that case; **en todo ~** in any case; **en último ~** as a last resort; **hacer ~ a** to pay attention to; **hacer ~ omiso de** to fail to mention, pass over; **hacer o venir al ~** to be relevant.
caspa ['kaspa] *nf* dandruff.
Caspio ['kaspjo] *adj*: **Mar ~** Caspian Sea.
casque ['kaske] *etc vb V* **cascar**.
casquillo [kas'kiʎo] *nm* (*de bombilla*) fitting; (*de bala*) cartridge case.
cassette [ka'set] *nf o m* = **casete**.
casta ['kasta] *nf* caste; (*raza*) breed.
castaña [kas'taɲa] *nf V* **castaño**.
castañetear [kastaɲete'ar] *vi* (*dientes*) to chatter.
castaño, a [kas'taɲo, a] *adj* chestnut (-coloured), brown ♦ *nm* chestnut tree ♦ *nf* chestnut; (*fam: golpe*) punch; **~ de Indias** horse chestnut tree.
castañuelas [kasta'ɲwelas] *nfpl* castanets.
castellano, a [kaste'ʎano, a] *adj* Castilian; (*fam*) Spanish ♦ *nm/f* Castilian; (*fam*) Spaniard ♦ *nm* (*LING*) Castilian, Spanish; *see boxed note.*

CASTELLANO

Castellano *is now the term most widely used in Spain and Spanish America to refer to the Spanish language, since "español" is too closely associated with the concept of Spain as a nation. Some purists maintain that* **castellano** *should only refer to the variety of Spanish spoken in Castille.*

---

castellonense [kasteʎo'nense] *adj* of *o* from Castellón de la Plana ♦ *nm/f* native *o* inhabitant of Castellón de la Plana.
castidad [kasti'ðað] *nf* chastity, purity.
castigar [kasti'ɣar] *vt* to punish; (*DEPORTE*) to penalize; (*afligir*) to afflict.
castigo [kas'tiɣo] *nm* punishment; (*DEPORTE*) penalty.
castigue [kas'tiɣe] *etc vb V* **castigar**.
Castilla [kas'tiʎa] *nf* Castile.
castillo [kas'tiʎo] *nm* castle.
castizo, a [kas'tiθo, a] *adj* (*LING*) pure; (*de buena casta*) purebred, pedigree; (*auténtico*) genuine.

casto, a ['kasto, a] *adj* chaste, pure.
castor [kas'tor] *nm* beaver.
castrar [kas'trar] *vt* to castrate; (*gato*) to doctor; (*BOT*) to prune.
castrense [kas'trense] *adj* army *cpd*, military.
casual [ka'swal] *adj* chance, accidental.
casualidad [kaswali'ðað] *nf* chance, accident; (*combinación de circunstancias*) coincidence; **¡qué ~!** what a coincidence!
casualmente [kaswal'mente] *adv* by chance.
cataclismo [kata'klismo] *nm* cataclysm.
catador [kata'ðor] *nm* taster.
catadura [kata'ðura] *nf* (*aspecto*) looks *pl*.
catalán, ana [kata'lan, ana] *adj, nm/f* Catalan ♦ *nm* (*LING*) Catalan; *V tb* **lenguas cooficiales**.
catalejo [kata'lexo] *nm* telescope.
catalizador [kataliθa'ðor] *nm* catalyst; (*AUTO*) catalytic converter.
catalogar [katalo'ɣar] *vt* to catalogue; **~ (de)** (*fig*) to classify (as).
catálogo [ka'taloɣo] *nm* catalogue.
catalogue [kata'loɣe] *etc vb V* **catalogar**.
Cataluña [kata'luɲa] *nf* Catalonia.
cataplasma [kata'plasma] *nf* (*MED*) poultice.
catapulta [kata'pulta] *nf* catapult.
catar [ka'tar] *vt* to taste, sample.
catarata [kata'rata] *nf* (*GEO*) (water)fall; (*MED*) cataract.
catarro [ka'tarro] *nm* catarrh; (*constipado*) cold.
catarsis [ka'tarsis] *nf* catharsis.
catastro [ka'tastro] *nm* property register.
catástrofe [ka'tastrofe] *nf* catastrophe.
catear [kate'ar] *vt* (*fam*) to flunk.
catecismo [kate'θismo] *nm* catechism.
cátedra ['kateðra] *nf* (*UNIV*) chair, professorship; (*ESCOL*) principal teacher's post; **sentar ~ sobre un argumento** to take one's stand on an argument.
catedral [kate'ðral] *nf* cathedral.
catedrático, a [kate'ðratiko, a] *nm/f* professor; (*ESCOL*) principal teacher.
categoría [kateɣo'ria] *nf* category; (*rango*) rank, standing; (*calidad*) quality; **de ~** (*hotel*) top-class; **de baja ~** (*oficial*) low-ranking; **de segunda ~** second-rate; **no tiene ~** he has no standing.
categórico, a [kate'ɣoriko, a] *adj* categorical.
catequesis [kate'kesis] *nf* catechism lessons.
caterva [ka'terßa] *nf* throng, crowd.
cateto, a [ka'teto, a] *nm/f* yokel.
cátodo ['katoðo] *nm* cathode.

catolicismo [katoli'θismo] nm Catholicism.
católico, a [ka'toliko, a] adj, nm/f Catholic.
catorce [ka'torθe] num fourteen.
catre ['katre] nm camp bed (BRIT); cot (US); (fam) pit.
Cáucaso ['kaukaso] nm Caucasus.
cauce ['kauθe] nm (de río) riverbed; (fig) channel.
caucho ['kautʃo] nm rubber; (AM: llanta) tyre.
caución [kau'θjon] nf bail.
caucionar [kauθjo'nar] vt (JUR) to bail (out), go bail for.
caudal [kau'ðal] nm (de río) volume, flow; (fortuna) wealth; (abundancia) abundance.
caudaloso, a [kauða'loso, a] adj (río) large; (persona) wealthy, rich.
caudillaje [kauði'ʎaxe] nm leadership.
caudillo [kau'ðiʎo] nm leader, chief.
causa ['kausa] nf cause; (razón) reason; (JUR) lawsuit, case; **a o por ~ de** because of, on account of.
causar [kau'sar] vt to cause.
cáustico, a ['kaustiko, a] adj caustic.
cautela [kau'tela] nf caution, cautiousness.
cauteloso, a [kaute'loso, a] adj cautious, wary.
cautivar [kauti'βar] vt to capture; (fig) to captivate.
cautiverio [kauti'βerjo] nm, **cautividad** [kautiβi'ðað] nf captivity.
cautivo, a [kau'tiβo, a] adj, nm/f captive.
cauto, a ['kauto, a] adj cautious, careful.
cava ['kaβa] nf (bodega) (wine) cellar ♦ nm (vino) champagne-type wine.
cavar [ka'βar] vt to dig; (AGR) to dig over.
caverna [ka'βerna] nf cave, cavern.
cavernoso, a [kaβer'noso, a] adj cavernous; (voz) resounding.
caviar [ka'βjar] nm caviar(e).
cavidad [kaβi'ðað] nf cavity.
cavilación [kaβila'θjon] nf deep thought.
cavilar [kaβi'lar] vt to ponder.
cayado [ka'jaðo] nm (de pastor) crook; (de obispo) crozier.
cayendo [ka'jendo] etc vb V **caer.**
caza ['kaθa] nf (acción: gen) hunting; (: con fusil) shooting; (una ~) hunt, chase; (animales) game; **coto de ~** hunting estate ♦ nm (AVIAT) fighter.
cazabe [ka'saβe] nm (AM) cassava bread o flour.
cazador, a [kaθa'ðor, a] nm/f hunter/huntress ♦ nf jacket.
cazaejecutivos [kaθaexeku'tiβos] nm inv (COM) headhunter.
cazar [ka'θar] vt to hunt; (perseguir) to chase; (prender) to catch; **~las al vuelo** to be pretty sharp.
cazasubmarinos [kaθasuβma'rinos] nm inv (NAUT) destroyer; (AVIAT) anti-submarine craft.
cazo ['kaθo] nm saucepan.
cazuela [ka'θwela] nf (vasija) pan; (guisado) casserole.
cazurro, a [ka'θurro, a] adj surly.
CC nm abr (POL: = Comité Central) Central Committee.
c/c. abr (COM: = cuenta corriente) current account.
CC.AA. abr (ESP) = **Comunidades Autónomas.**
CCI nf abr (COM: = Cámara de Comercio Internacional) ICC.
CC.OO. nfpl abr = **Comisiones Obreras.**
CD nm abr (= compact disc) CD ♦ abr (POL: = Cuerpo Diplomático) CD.
c/d abr (= en casa de) c/o; (= con descuento) with discount.
CDN nm abr (= Centro Dramático Nacional) ≈ RADA (BRIT).
CDS nm abr (= Centro Democrático y Social) political party.
CE nm abr (= Consejo de Europa) Council of Europe ♦ nf abr (= Comunidad Europea) EC.
cebada [θe'βaða] nf barley.
cebar [θe'βar] vt (animal) to fatten (up); (anzuelo) to bait; (MIL, TEC) to prime; **~se** vr: **~se en** to vent one's fury on, take it out on.
cebo ['θeβo] nm (para animales) feed, food; (para peces, fig) bait; (de arma) charge.
cebolla [θe'βoʎa] nf onion.
cebolleta [θeβo'ʎeta] nf spring onion.
cebollino [θeβo'ʎino] nm spring onion.
cebón, ona [θe'βon, ona] adj fat, fattened.
cebra ['θeβra] nf zebra; **paso de ~** zebra crossing.
CECA ['θeka] nf abr (= Comunidad Europea del Carbón y del Acero) ECSC.
ceca ['θeka] nf: **andar o ir de la ~ a la Meca** to chase about all over the place.
cecear [θeθe'ar] vi to lisp.
ceceo [θe'θeo] nm lisp.
cecina [θe'θina] nf cured o smoked meat.
cedazo [θe'ðaθo] nm sieve.
ceder [θe'ðer] vt (entregar) to hand over; (renunciar a) to give up, part with ♦ vi (renunciar) to give in, yield; (disminuir) to diminish, decline; (romperse) to give way; (viento) to drop; (fiebre etc) to abate; **"ceda el paso"** (AUTO) "give way".
cedro ['θeðro] nm cedar.
cédula ['θeðula] nf certificate, document;

~ **de identidad** (*AM*) identity card; ~ **en blanco** blank cheque; *V tb* **Documento Nacional de Identidad.**

CEE *nf abr* (= *Comunidad Económica Europea*) EEC.

cegar [θe'ɣar] *vt* to blind; (*tubería etc*) to block up, stop up ♦ *vi* to go blind; ~**se** *vr* to be blinded (*de* by).

cegué [θe'ɣe] *etc vb V* **cegar.**

ceguemos [θe'ɣemos] *etc vb V* **cegar.**

ceguera [θe'ɣera] *nf* blindness.

CEI *nf abr* (= *Comunidad de Estados Independientes*) CIS.

Ceilán [θei'lan] *nm* Ceylon, Sri Lanka.

ceja ['θexa] *nf* eyebrow; ~**s pobladas** bushy eyebrows; **arquear las ~s** to raise one's eyebrows; **fruncir las ~s** to frown.

cejar [θe'xar] *vi* (*fig*) to back down; **no** ~ **to keep it up, stick at it.**

cejijunto, a [θexi'xunto, a] *adj* with bushy eyebrows; (*fig*) scowling.

celada [θe'laða] *nf* ambush, trap.

celador, a [θela'ðor, a] *nm/f* (*de edificio*) watchman; (*de museo etc*) attendant; (*de cárcel*) warder.

celda ['θelda] *nf* cell.

celebérrimo, a [θele'ßerrimo, a] *adj* *superlativo de* **célebre.**

celebración [θeleßra'θjon] *nf* celebration.

celebrar [θele'ßrar] *vt* to celebrate; (*alabar*) to praise ♦ *vi* to be glad; ~**se** *vr* to occur, take place.

célebre ['θeleßre] *adj* celebrated, renowned.

celebridad [θeleßri'ðað] *nf* fame; (*persona*) celebrity.

celeridad [θeleri'ðað] *nf*: **con** ~ promptly.

celeste [θe'leste] *adj* sky-blue; (*cuerpo etc*) heavenly ♦ *nm* sky blue.

celestial [θeles'tjal] *adj* celestial, heavenly.

celibato [θeli'ßato] *nm* celibacy.

célibe ['θeliße] *adj, nm/f* celibate.

celo ['θelo] *nm* zeal; (*REL*) fervour; (*pey*) envy; ~**s** *nmpl* jealousy *sg*; **dar** ~**s a algn** to make sb jealous; **tener** ~**s de algn** to be jealous of sb; **en** ~ (*animales*) on heat.

celofán [θelo'fan] *nm* Cellophane ®.

celosía [θelo'sia] *nf* lattice (window).

celoso, a [θe'loso, a] *adj* (*envidioso*) jealous; (*trabajador*) zealous; (*desconfiado*) suspicious.

celta ['θelta] *adj* Celtic ♦ *nm/f* Celt.

célula ['θelula] *nf* cell.

celular [θelu'lar] *adj*: **tejido** ~ cell tissue.

celulitis [θelu'litis] *nf* (*enfermedad*) cellulitis; (*grasa*) cellulite.

celuloide [θelu'loiðe] *nm* celluloid.

celulosa [θelu'losa] *nf* cellulose.

cementerio [θemen'terjo] *nm* cemetery, graveyard; ~ **de coches** scrapyard.

cemento [θe'mento] *nm* cement; (*hormigón*) concrete; (*AM: cola*) glue.

CEN *nm abr* (*ESP*) = *Consejo de Economía Nacional.*

cena ['θena] *nf* evening meal, dinner.

cenagal [θena'ɣal] *nm* bog, quagmire.

cenar [θe'nar] *vt* to have for dinner, dine on ♦ *vi* to have dinner, dine.

cencerro [θen'θerro] *nm* cowbell; **estar como un** ~ (*fam*) to be round the bend.

cenicero [θeni'θero] *nm* ashtray.

ceniciento, a [θeni'θjento, a] *adj* ash-coloured, ashen.

cenit [θe'nit] *nm* zenith.

ceniza [θe'niθa] *nf* ash, ashes *pl.*

censar [θen'sar] *vt* to take a census of.

censo ['θenso] *nm* census; ~ **electoral** electoral roll.

censor [θen'sor] *nm* censor; ~ **de cuentas** (*COM*) auditor; ~ **jurado de cuentas** chartered (*BRIT*) *ou* certified public (*US*) accountant.

censura [θen'sura] *nf* (*POL*) censorship; (*moral*) censure, criticism.

censurable [θensu'raßle] *adj* reprehensible.

censurar [θensu'rar] *vt* (*idea*) to censure; (*cortar: película*) to censor.

centavo [θen'taßo] *nm* hundredth (part); (*AM*) cent.

centella [θen'teʎa] *nf* spark.

centellear [θenteʎe'ar] *vi* (*metal*) to gleam; (*estrella*) to twinkle; (*fig*) to sparkle.

centelleo [θente'ʎeo] *nm* gleam(ing); twinkling; sparkling.

centena [θen'tena] *nf* hundred.

centenar [θente'nar] *nm* hundred.

centenario, a [θente'narjo, a] *adj* one hundred years old ♦ *nm* centenary.

centeno [θen'teno] *nm* rye.

centésimo, a [θen'tesimo, a] *adj, nm* hundredth.

centígrado, a [θen'tiɣraðo] *adj* centigrade.

centigramo [θenti'ɣramo] *nm* centigramme.

centilitro [θenti'litro] *nm* centilitre (*BRIT*), centiliter (*US*).

centímetro [θen'timetro] *nm* centimetre (*BRIT*), centimeter (*US*).

céntimo, a ['θentimo, a] *adj* hundredth ♦ *nm* cent.

centinela [θenti'nela] *nm* sentry, guard.

centollo, a [θen'toʎo, a] *nm/f* large (*o* spider) crab.

central [θen'tral] *adj* central ♦ *nf* head

office; (*TEC*) plant; (*TELEC*) exchange; ~
nuclear nuclear power station.
centralice [θentra'liθe] *etc vb* V **centralizar.**
centralita [θentra'lita] *nf* (*TELEC*)
switchboard.
centralización [θentraliθa'θjon] *nf*
centralization.
centralizar [θentrali'θar] *vt* to centralize.
centrar [θen'trar] *vt* to centre.
céntrico, a ['θentriko, a] *adj* central.
centrifugar [θentrifu'ɣar] *vt* (*ropa*) to spin-
dry.
centrífugo, a [θen'trifuɣo, a] *adj*
centrifugal.
centrifugue [θentri'fuɣe] *etc vb* V
centrifugar.
centrista [θen'trista] *adj* centre *cpd.*
centro ['θentro] *nm* centre; **ser de** ~ (*POL*)
to be a moderate; ~ **de acogida (para
niños)** children's home; ~ **de beneficios**
(*COM*) profit centre; ~ **cívico** community
centre; ~ **comercial** shopping centre; ~
de computatión computer centre; ~ **(de
determinación) de costos** (*COM*) cost
centre; ~ **delantero** (*DEPORTE*) centre
forward; ~ **docente** teaching institution;
~ **juvenil** youth club; ~ **de llamadas** call
centre; ~ **social** community centre.
centroafricano, a [θentroafri'kano, a] *adj*:
la República Centroafricana the Central
African Republic.
centroamericano, a [θentroameri'kano, a]
adj, nm/f Central American.
centrocampista [θentrokam'pista] *nm/f*
(*DEPORTE*) midfielder.
ceñido, a [θe'ɲiðo, a] *adj* tight.
ceñir [θe'ɲir] *vt* (*rodear*) to encircle,
surround; (*ajustar*) to fit (tightly);
(*apretar*) to tighten; ~**se** *vr*: ~**se algo** to
put sth on; ~**se al asunto** to stick to the
matter in hand.
ceño ['θeɲo] *nm* frown, scowl; **fruncir el** ~
to frown, knit one's brow.
CEOE *nf abr* (= *Confederación Española de
Organizaciones Empresariales*) ≈ CBI
(*BRIT*).
cepa ['θepa] *nf* (*de vid, fig*) stock; (*BIO*)
strain.
CEPAL [θe'pal] *nf abr* (= *Comisión
Económica de las Naciones Unidas para la
América Latina*) ECLA.
cepillar [θepi'ʎar] *vt* to brush; (*madera*) to
plane (down).
cepillo [θe'piʎo] *nm* brush; (*para madera*)
plane; (*REL*) poorbox, alms box.
cepo ['θepo] *nm* (*caza*) trap.
CEPSA ['θepsa] *nf abr* (*COM*) = *Compañía
Española de Petróleos, S.A.*

CEPYME *nf abr* = *Confederación Española
de la Pequeña y Mediana Empresa.*
cera ['θera] *nf* wax; ~ **de abejas** beeswax.
cerámica [θe'ramika] *nf* pottery; (*arte*)
ceramics *sg.*
ceramista [θera'mista] *nm/f* potter.
cerbatana [θerβa'tana] *nf* blowpipe.
cerca ['θerka] *nf* fence ♦ *adv* near, nearby,
close; **por aquí** ~ nearby ♦ *prep*: ~ **de**
(*cantidad*) nearly, about; (*distancia*) near,
close to ♦ *nmpl*: ~**s** foreground *sg.*
cercado [θer'kaðo] *nm* enclosure.
cercanía [θerka'nia] *nf* nearness,
closeness; ~**s** *nfpl* outskirts, suburbs;
tren de ~**s** commuter *o* local train.
cercano, a [θer'kano, a] *adj* close, near;
(*pueblo etc*) nearby; **C**~ **Oriente** Near
East.
cercar [θer'kar] *vt* to fence in; (*rodear*) to
surround.
cerciorar [θerθjo'rar] *vt* (*asegurar*) to
assure; ~**se** *vr* (*descubrir*) to find out (*de
about*); (*asegurarse*) to make sure (*de* of).
cerco ['θerko] *nm* (*AGR*) enclosure; (*AM*)
fence; (*MIL*) siege.
cerda ['θerða] *nf* (*de cepillo*) bristle; (*ZOOL*)
sow.
cerdada [θer'ðaða] *nf* (*fam*): **hacer una** ~ **a**
algn to play a dirty trick on sb.
Cerdeña [θer'ðeɲa] *nf* Sardinia.
cerdo ['θerðo] *nm* pig; **carne de** ~ pork.
cereal [θere'al] *nm* cereal; ~**es** *nmpl*
cereals, grain *sg.*
cerebral [θere'βral] *adj* (*tb fig*) cerebral;
(*tumor*) brain *cpd.*
cerebro [θe'reβro] *nm* brain; (*fig*) brains *pl*;
ser un ~ (*fig*) to be brilliant.
ceremonia [θere'monja] *nf* ceremony;
reunión de ~ formal meeting; **hablar sin**
~ to speak plainly.
ceremonial [θeremo'njal] *adj, nm*
ceremonial.
ceremonioso, a [θeremo'njoso, a] *adj*
ceremonious; (*cumplido*) formal.
cereza [θe'reθa] *nf* cherry.
cerezo [θe'reθo] *nm* cherry tree.
cerilla [θe'riʎa] *nf*, **cerillo** [se'riʎo] *nm* (*AM*)
match.
cerner [θer'ner] *vt* to sift, sieve; ~**se** *vr* to
hover.
cero ['θero] *nm* nothing, zero; (*DEPORTE*)
nil; **8 grados bajo** ~ 8 degrees below
zero; **a partir de** ~ from scratch.
cerque ['θerke] *etc vb* V **cercar.**
cerrado, a [θe'rraðo, a] *adj* closed, shut;
(*con llave*) locked; (*tiempo*) cloudy,
overcast; (*curva*) sharp; (*acento*) thick,
broad; **a puerta cerrada** (*JUR*) in camera.

cerradura [θerra'ðura] nf (acción) closing; (mecanismo) lock.

cerrajería [θerraxe'ria] nf locksmith's craft; (tienda) locksmith's (shop).

cerrajero, a [θerra'xero, a] nm/f locksmith.

cerrar [θe'rrar] vt to close, shut; (paso, carretera) to close; (grifo) to turn off; (trato, cuenta, negocio) to close ♦ vi to close, shut; (la noche) to come down; ~ con llave to lock; ~ el sistema (INFORM) to close o shut down the system; ~ un trato to strike a bargain; ~se vr to close, shut; (herida) to heal.

cerro ['θerro] nm hill; **andar por las** ~**s de Úbeda** to wander from the point, digress.

cerrojo [θe'rroxo] nm (herramienta) bolt; (de puerta) latch.

certamen [θer'tamen] nm competition, contest.

certero, a [θer'tero, a] adj (gen) accurate.

certeza [θer'teθa], **certidumbre** [θerti'ðumbre] nf certainty.

certificación [θertifika'θjon] nf certification; (JUR) affidavit.

certificado, a [θertifi'kaðo, a] adj certified; (CORREOS) registered ♦ nm certificate.

certificar [θertifi'kar] vt (asegurar, atestar) to certify.

certifique [θerti'fike] etc vb V **certificar**.

cervatillo [θerßa'tiʎo] nm fawn.

cervecería [θerßeθe'ria] nf (fábrica) brewery; (taberna) public house.

cerveza [θer'ßeθa] nf beer; ~ **de barril** draught beer.

cervical [θerßi'kal] adj cervical.

cerviz [θer'ßiθ] nf nape of the neck.

cesación [θesa'θjon] nf cessation, suspension.

cesante [θe'sante] adj redundant; (AM) unemployed; (ministro) outgoing; (diplomático) recalled ♦ nm/f redundant worker.

cesar [θe'sar] vi to cease, stop; (de un trabajo) to leave ♦ vt (en el trabajo) to dismiss; (alto cargo) to remove from office.

cesárea [θe'sarea] nf Caesarean (section).

cese ['θese] nm (de trabajo) dismissal; (de pago) suspension.

Cesid [θe'sið] nm abr (ESP: = Centro Superior de Investigación de la Defensa Nacional) military intelligence service.

cesión [θe'sjon] nf: ~ **de bienes** surrender of property.

césped ['θespeð] nm grass, lawn.

cesta ['θesta] nf basket.

cesto ['θesto] nm (large) basket, hamper.

cetrería [θetre'ria] nf falconry.

cetrino, a [θe'trino, a] adj (tez) sallow.

cetro ['θetro] nm sceptre.

Ceuta [θe'uta] nf Ceuta.

ceutí [θeu'ti] adj of o from Ceuta ♦ nm/f native o inhabitant of Ceuta.

C.F. nm abr (= Club de Fútbol) F.C.

CFC nm abr (= clorofluorocarbono) CFC.

cfr. abr (= confróntese, compárese) cf.

cg. abr (= centígramo) cg.

CGPJ nm abr (= Consejo General del Poder Judicial) governing body of Spanish legal system.

CGS nf abr (Guatemala, El Salvador) = Confederación General de Sindicatos.

CGT nf abr (Colombia, México, Nicaragua, ESP) = Confederación General de Trabajadores; (Argentina) = Confederación General del Trabajo.

Ch, ch [tʃe] nf former letter in the Spanish alphabet.

chabacano, a [tʃaßa'kano, a] adj vulgar, coarse.

chabola [tʃa'ßola] nf shack; ~**s** nfpl shanty town sg.

chabolismo [tʃaßo'lismo] nm: **el problema del** ~ the problem of substandard housing, the shanty town problem.

chacal [tʃa'kal] nm jackal.

chacarero [tʃaka'rero] nm (AM) small farmer.

chacha ['tʃatʃa] nf (fam) maid.

cháchara ['tʃatʃara] nf chatter; **estar de** ~ to chatter away.

chacra ['tʃakra] nf (AM) smallholding.

chafar [tʃa'far] vt (aplastar) to crush, flatten; (arruinar) to ruin.

chaflán [tʃa'flan] nm (TEC) bevel.

chal [tʃal] nm shawl.

chalado, a [tʃa'laðo, a] adj (fam) crazy.

chalé, pl **chalés** [tʃa'le, tʃa'les] nm = **chalet.**

chaleco [tʃa'leko] nm waistcoat, vest (US); ~ **antibala** bulletproof vest; ~ **salvavidas** life jacket.

chalet, pl **chalets** [tʃa'le, tʃa'les] nm villa, ≈ detached house; ~ **adosado** semi-detached house.

chalupa [tʃa'lupa] nf launch, boat.

chamaco, a [tʃa'mako, a] nm/f (AM) boy/ girl.

chamarra [tʃa'marra] nf sheepskin jacket; (AM: poncho) blanket.

champán [tʃam'pan] nm, **champaña** [tʃam'paɲa] nm champagne.

champiñón [tʃampi'ɲon] nm mushroom.

champú [tʃam'pu] (pl **champúes**,

champús) *nm* shampoo.

chamuscar [tʃamus'kar] *vt* to scorch, sear, singe.

chamusque [tʃa'muske] *etc vb V* **chamuscar**.

chamusquina [tʃamus'kina] *nf* singeing.

chance ['tʃanθe] *nm* (*a veces nf*) (*AM*) chance, opportunity.

chanchada [tʃan'tʃaða] *nf* (*AM fam*) dirty trick.

chancho, a ['tʃantʃo, a] *nm/f* (*AM*) pig.

chanchullo [tʃan'tʃuʎo] *nm* (*fam*) fiddle, wangle.

chancla ['tʃankla] *nf*, **chancleta** [tʃan'kleta] *nf* flip-flop; (*zapato viejo*) old shoe.

chandal [tʃan'dal] *nm* tracksuit; ~ **(de tootel)** shellsuit.

chantaje [tʃan'taxe] *nm* blackmail; **hacer ~ a uno** to blackmail sb.

chanza ['tʃanθa] *nf* joke.

chao [tʃao] *excl* (*fam*) cheerio.

chapa ['tʃapa] *nf* (*de metal*) plate, sheet; (*de madera*) board, panel; (*de botella*) bottle top; (*insignia*) (lapel) badge; (*AM*: *AUTO*: ~ **de matrícula**) number (*BRIT*) *o* license (*US*) plate; (*AM cerradura*) lock; **de 3 ~s** (*madera*) 3-ply.

chapado, a [tʃa'paðo, a] *adj* (*metal*) plated; (*muebles etc*) finished.

chaparro, a [tʃa'parro, a] *adj* squat; (*AM*: *bajito*) short.

chaparrón [tʃapa'rron] *nm* downpour, cloudburst.

chapotear [tʃapote'ar] *vt* to sponge down ♦ *vi* (*fam*) to splash about.

chapucero, a [tʃapu'θero, a] *adj* rough, crude ♦ *nm/f* bungler.

chapurr(e)ar [tʃapurr(e)'ar] *vt* (*idioma*) to speak badly.

chapuza [tʃa'puθa] *nf* botched job.

chapuzón [tʃapu'θon] *nm*: **darse un ~** to go for a dip.

chaqué [tʃa'ke] *nm* morning coat.

chaqueta [tʃa'keta] *nf* jacket; **cambiar la ~** (*fig*) to change sides.

chaquetón [tʃake'ton] *nm* three-quarter-length coat.

charca ['tʃarka] *nf* pond, pool.

charco ['tʃarko] *nm* pool, puddle.

charcutería [tʃarkute'ria] *nf* (*tienda*) shop selling chiefly pork meat products; (*productos*) cooked pork meats *pl*.

charla ['tʃarla] *nf* talk, chat; (*conferencia*) lecture.

charlar [tʃar'lar] *vi* to talk, chat.

charlatán, ana [tʃarla'tan, ana] *nm/f* chatterbox; (*estafador*) trickster.

charol¹ [tʃa'rol] *nm* varnish; (*cuero*) patent leather.

charol² [tʃa'rol] *nm* (*AM*), **charola** [tʃa'rola] *nf* (*AM*) tray.

charqui ['tʃarki] *nm* (*AM*) dried beef, jerky (*US*).

charro, a ['tʃarro, a] *adj* Salamancan; (*AM*) Mexican; (*ropa*) loud, gaudy; (*AM*: *costumbres*) traditional ♦ *nm/f* Salamancan; Mexican.

chárter ['tʃarter] *adj inv*: **vuelo ~** charter flight.

chascarrillo [tʃaska'rriʎo] *nm* (*fam*) funny story.

chasco ['tʃasko] *nm* (*broma*) trick, joke; (*desengaño*) disappointment.

chasis ['tʃasis] *nm inv* (*AUTO*) chassis; (*FOTO*) plateholder.

chasquear [tʃaske'ar] *vt* (*látigo*) to crack; (*lengua*) to click.

chasquido [tʃas'kiðo] *nm* (*de lengua*) click; (*de látigo*) crack.

chatarra [tʃa'tarra] *nf* scrap (metal).

chato, a ['tʃato, a] *adj* flat; (*nariz*) snub ♦ *nm* wine tumbler; **beber unos ~s** to have a few drinks.

chau [tʃau], **chaucito** [tʃau'sito] *excl* (*fam*) cheerio.

chauvinismo [tʃoβi'nismo] *nm* chauvinism.

chauvinista [tʃoβi'nista] *adj*, *nm/f* chauvinist.

chaval, a [tʃa'βal, a] *nm/f* kid (*fam*), lad/lass.

chavo ['tʃaβo] *nm* (*AM*: *fam*) bloke (*BRIT*), guy.

checo, a ['tʃeko, a] *adj*, *nm/f* Czech ♦ *nm* (*LING*) Czech.

checo(e)slovaco, a [tʃeko(e)slo'βako, a] *adj*, *nm/f* Czech, Czechoslovak.

Checo(e)slovaquia [tʃeko(e)slo'βakja] *nf* Czechoslovakia.

chepa ['tʃepa] *nf* hump.

cheque ['tʃeke] *nm* cheque (*BRIT*), check (*US*); ~ **abierto/en blanco/cruzado** open/blank/crossed cheque; ~ **al portador** cheque payable to bearer; ~ **caducado** stale cheque; ~ **de viajero** traveller's cheque.

chequeo [tʃe'keo] *nm* (*MED*) check-up; (*AUTO*) service.

chequera [tʃe'kera] *nf* (*AM*) chequebook (*BRIT*), checkbook (*US*).

chévere ['tʃeβere] *adj* (*AM*) great, fabulous (*fam*).

chicano, a [tʃi'kano, a] *adj*, *nm/f* chicano, Mexican-American.

chicha ['tʃitʃa] *nf* (*AM*) maize liquor.

chícharo [tʃitʃaro] nm (AM) pea.
chicharra [tʃi'tʃarra] nf harvest bug, cicada.
chicharrón [tʃitʃa'rron] nm (pork) crackling.
chichón [tʃi'tʃon] nm bump, lump.
chicle ['tʃikle] nm chewing gum.
chico, a ['tʃiko, a] adj small, little ♦ nm/f child; (muchacho) boy; (muchacha) girl.
chicote [tʃi'kote] nm (AM) whip.
chiflado, a [tʃi'flaðo, a] adj (fam) crazy, round the bend ♦ nm/f nutcase.
chiflar [tʃi'flar] vt to hiss, boo ♦ vi (esp AM) to whistle.
Chile ['tʃile] nm Chile.
chile ['tʃile] nm chilli, pepper.
chileno, a [tʃi'leno, a] adj, nm/f Chilean.
chillar [tʃi'ʎar] vi (persona) to yell, scream; (animal salvaje) to howl; (cerdo) to squeal; (puerta) to creak.
chillido [tʃi'ʎiðo] nm (de persona) yell, scream; (de animal) howl; (de frenos) screech(ing).
chillón, ona [tʃi'ʎon, ona] adj (niño) noisy; (color) loud, gaudy.
chimenea [tʃime'nea] nf chimney; (hogar) fireplace.
chimpancé, pl **chimpancés** [tʃimpan'θe, tʃimpan'θes] nm chimpanzee.
China ['tʃina] nf: **(la)** ~ China.
china ['tʃina] nf pebble.
chinchar [tʃin'tʃar] (fam) vt to pester, annoy; ~**se** vr to get cross; ¡**chínchate!** tough!
chinche ['tʃintʃe] nf bug; (TEC) drawing pin (BRIT), thumbtack (US) ♦ nm/f nuisance, pest.
chincheta [tʃin'tʃeta] nf drawing pin (BRIT), thumbtack (US).
chinchorro [tʃin'tʃorro] nm (AM) hammock.
chingado, a [tʃin'gaðo, a] adj (esp AM fam!) lousy, bloody (!); **hijo de la** ~**a** bastard (!), son of a bitch (US!).
chingar [tʃin'gar] vt (AM: fam!) to fuck (up) (!), screw (up) (!); ~**se** vr (AM: emborracharse) to get pissed (BRIT), get plastered (!: fracasar) to fail.
chingue ['tʃinge] etc vb V **chingar**.
chino, a ['tʃino, a] adj, nm/f Chinese ♦ nm (LING) Chinese; (CULIN) chinois, conical strainer.
chip [tʃip] nm (INFORM) chip.
chipirón [tʃipi'ron] nm squid.
Chipre ['tʃipre] nf Cyprus.
chipriota [tʃi'prjota], **chipriote** [tʃi'prjote] adj Cypriot, Cyprian ♦ nm/f Cypriot.
chiquillada [tʃiki'ʎaða] nf childish prank;

(AM: chiquillos) kids pl.
chiquillo, a [tʃi'kiʎo, a] nm/f kid (fam), youngster, child.
chiquito, a [tʃi'kito, a] adj very small, tiny ♦ nm/f kid (fam).
chirigota [tʃiri'ɣota] nf joke.
chirimbolo [tʃirim'bolo] nm thingummyjig (fam).
chirimoya [tʃiri'moja] nf custard apple.
chiringuito [tʃirin'gito] nm refreshment stall o stand.
chiripa [tʃi'ripa] nf fluke; **por** ~ by chance.
chirona [tʃi'rona], (AM) **chirola** [tʃi'rola] nf (fam) clink, jail.
chirriar [tʃi'rrjar] vi (goznes) to creak, squeak; (pájaros) to chirp, sing.
chirrido [tʃi'rriðo] nm creak(ing), squeak(ing); (de pájaro) chirp(ing).
chis [tʃis] excl sh!
chisme ['tʃisme] nm (habladurías) piece of gossip; (fam: objeto) thingummyjig.
chismoso, a [tʃis'moso, a] adj gossiping ♦ nm/f gossip.
chispa ['tʃispa] nf spark; (fig) sparkle; (ingenio) wit; (fam) drunkenness.
chispeante [tʃispe'ante] adj (tb fig) sparkling.
chispear [tʃispe'ar] vi to spark; (lloviznar) to drizzle.
chisporrotear [tʃisporrote'ar] vi (fuego) to throw out sparks; (leña) to crackle; (aceite) to hiss, splutter.
chistar [tʃistar] vi: **no** ~ not to say a word.
chiste ['tʃiste] nm joke, funny story; ~ **verde** blue joke.
chistera [tʃis'tera] nf top hat.
chistoso, a [tʃis'toso, a] adj (gracioso) funny, amusing; (bromista) witty.
chistu ['tʃistu] nm = **txistu**.
chivarse [tʃi'ßarse] vr (fam) to grass.
chivatazo [tʃißa'taθo] nm (fam) tip-off; **dar** ~ to inform.
chivo, a ['tʃißo, a] nm/f (billy/nanny-)goat; ~ **expiatorio** scapegoat.
chocante [tʃo'kante] adj startling; (extraño) odd; (ofensivo) shocking.
chocar [tʃo'kar] vi (coches etc) to collide, crash; (MIL, fig) to clash ♦ vt to shock; (sorprender) to startle; ~ **con** to collide with; (fig) to run into, run up against; ¡**chócala!** (fam) put it there!
chochear [tʃotʃe'ar] vi to dodder, be senile.
chocho, a ['tʃotʃo, a] adj doddering, senile; (fig) soft, doting.
chocolate [tʃoko'late] adj chocolate ♦ nm chocolate; (fam) dope, marijuana.
chocolatería [tʃokolate'ria] nf chocolate

factory (o shop).

chófer ['tʃofer], **chofer** [tʃo'fer] (esp AM) nm driver.

chollo ['tʃoʎo] nm (fam) bargain, snip.

chomba ['tʃomba], **chompa** ['tʃompa] nf (AM) jumper, sweater.

chopo ['tʃopo] nm black poplar.

choque ['tʃoke] etc vb V **chocar** ♦ nm (impacto) impact; (golpe) jolt; (AUTO) crash; (fig) conflict.

chorizo [tʃo'riθo] nm hard pork sausage, (type of) salami; (ladrón) crook.

chorra ['tʃorra] nf luck.

chorrada [tʃo'rraða] nf (fam): ¡es una ~! that's crap! (!); **decir ~s** to talk crap (!).

chorrear [tʃorre'ar] vt to pour ♦ vi to gush (out), spout (out); (gotear) to drip, trickle.

chorreras [tʃo'rreras] nfpl (adorno) frill sg.

chorro ['tʃorro] nm jet; (caudalito) dribble, trickle; (fig) stream; **salir a ~s** to gush forth; **con propulsión a ~** jet-propelled.

chotearse [tʃote'arse] vr to joke.

choto ['tʃoto] nm (cabrito) kid.

chovinismo [tʃoβi'nismo] nm = **chauvinismo**.

chovinista [tʃoβi'nista] adj, nm/f = **chauvinista**.

choza ['tʃoθa] nf hut, shack.

chubasco [tʃu'βasko] nm squall.

chubasquero [tʃuβas'kero] nm oilskins pl.

chuchería [tʃutʃe'ria] nf trinket.

chucho ['tʃutʃo] nm (ZOOL) mongrel.

chufa ['tʃufa] nf chufa, earth almond, tiger nut; **horchata de ~s** drink made from chufas.

chuleta [tʃu'leta] nf chop, cutlet; (ESCOL etc: fam) crib.

chulo, a ['tʃulo, a] adj (encantador) charming; (aire) proud; (pey) fresh; (fam: estupendo) great, fantastic ♦ nm (pícaro) rascal; (madrileño) working-class Madrilenian; (rufián: tb: ~ **de putas**) pimp.

chumbera [tʃum'bera] nf prickly pear.

chungo, a ['tʃungo, a] (fam) adj lousy ♦ nf: **estar de chunga** to be in a merry mood.

chupa ['tʃupa] nf (fam) jacket.

chupado, a [tʃu'paðo, a] adj (delgado) skinny, gaunt; **está ~** (fam) it's simple, it's dead easy.

chupar [tʃu'par] vt to suck; (absorber) to absorb; **~se** vr to grow thin; **para ~se los dedos** mouthwatering.

chupatintas [tʃupa'tintas] nm inv penpusher.

chupe ['tʃupe] nm (AM) stew.

chupete [tʃu'pete] nm dummy (BRIT), pacifier (US).

chupetón [tʃupe'ton] nm suck.

churrasco [tʃu'rrasko] nm (AM) barbecue, barbecued meat.

churrería [tʃurre'ria] nf stall or shop which sells "churros".

churrete [tʃu'rrete] nm grease spot.

churretón [tʃurre'ton] nm stain.

churrigueresco, a [tʃurrige'resko, a] adj (ARQ) baroque; (fig) excessively ornate.

churro, a ['tʃurro, a] adj coarse ♦ nm (CULIN) (type of) fritter; (chapuza) botch, mess; see boxed note.

churruscar [tʃurrus'kar] vt to fry crisp.

churrusque [tʃu'rruske] etc vb V **churruscar**.

churumbel [tʃurum'bel] nm (fam) kid.

chus [tʃus] excl: **no decir ni ~ ni mus** not to say a word.

chusco, a ['tʃusko, a] adj funny.

chusma ['tʃusma] nf rabble, mob.

chutar [tʃu'tar] vi (DEPORTE) to shoot (at goal); **esto va que chuta** it's going fine.

chuzo ['tʃuθo] nm: **llueve a ~s, llueven ~s de punta** it's raining cats and dogs.

C.I. nm abr = **coeficiente intelectual** o **de inteligencia**.

Cía abr (= compañía) Co.

cianuro [θja'nuro] nm cyanide.

ciática ['θjatika] nf sciatica.

cibercafé [θiβerka'fe] nm cybercafe.

ciberespacio [θiβereθ'paθjo] nm cyberspace.

cibernauta [θiβer'nauta] nmf cybernaut.

cibernética [θiβer'netika] nf cybernetics sg.

cicatrice [θika'triθe] etc vb V **cicatrizar**.

cicatriz [θika'triθ] nf scar.

cicatrizar [θikatri'θar] vt to heal; **~se** vr to heal (up), form a scar.

cíclico, a ['θikliko, a] adj cyclical.

ciclismo [θi'klismo] nm cycling.

ciclista [θi'klista] nm/f cyclist.

ciclo ['θiklo] nm cycle.

ciclomotor [θiklomo'tor] nm moped.

ciclón [θi'klon] nm cyclone.

cicloturismo [θiklotu'rismo] nm touring by bicycle.

cicuta [θi'kuta] nf hemlock.

ciego, a ['θjeɣo, a] etc vb V **cegar** ♦ adj blind ♦ nm/f blind man/woman; **a ciegas** blindly; **me puse ~ a mariscos** (fam) I stuffed myself with seafood.

ciegue ['θjeɣe] *etc vb* V **cegar.**

cielo ['θjelo] *nm* sky; (*REL*) heaven; (*ARQ*: *tb*: ~ **raso**) ceiling; ¡~**s**! good heavens!; **ver el** ~ **abierto** to see one's chance.

ciempiés [θjem'pjes] *nm inv* centipede.

cien [θjen] *num* V **ciento.**

ciénaga ['θjenaɣa] *nf* marsh, swamp.

ciencia ['θjenθja] *nf* science; ~**s** *nfpl* science *sg*; **saber algo a** ~ **cierta** to know sth for certain.

ciencia-ficción ['θjenθjafik'θjon] *nf* science fiction.

cieno ['θjeno] *nm* mud, mire.

científico, a [θjen'tifiko, a] *adj* scientific ♦ *nm/f* scientist.

ciento ['θjento], **cien** *num* hundred; **pagar al 10 por ciento** to pay at 10 per cent.

cierne ['θjerne] *etc vb* V **cerner** ♦ *nm*: **en** ~ in blossom; **en** ~**(s)** (*fig*) in its infancy.

cierre ['θjerre] *etc vb* V **cerrar** ♦ *nm* closing, shutting; (*con llave*) locking; (*RADIO, TV*) close-down; ~ **de cremallera** zip (fastener); **precios de** ~ (*BOLSA*) closing prices; ~ **del sistema** (*INFORM*) system shutdown.

cierto, a ['θjerto, a] *adj* sure, certain; (*un tal*) a certain; (*correcto*) right, correct; ~ **hombre** a certain man; **ciertas personas** certain *o* some people; **sí, es** ~ yes, that's correct; **por** ~ by the way; **lo** ~ **es que** ... the fact is that ...; **estar en lo** ~ to be right.

ciervo ['θjerβo] *nm* (*ZOOL*) deer; (: *macho*) stag.

cierzo ['θjerθo] *nm* north wind.

CIES *nm abr* = *Consejo Interamericano Económico y Social.*

cifra ['θifra] *nf* number, figure; (*cantidad*) number, quantity; (*secreta*) code; ~ **global** lump sum; ~ **de negocios** (*COM*) turnover; **en** ~**s redondas** in round figures; ~ **de referencia** (*COM*) bench mark; ~ **de ventas** (*COM*) sales figures.

cifrado, a [θi'fraðo, a] *adj* in code.

cifrar [θi'frar] *vt* to code, write in code; (*resumir*) to abridge; (*calcular*) to reckon.

cigala [θi'ɣala] *nf* Norway lobster.

cigarra [θi'ɣarra] *nf* cicada.

cigarrera [θiɣa'rrera] *nf* cigar case.

cigarrillo [θiɣa'rriʎo] *nm* cigarette.

cigarro [θi'ɣarro] *nm* cigarette; (*puro*) cigar.

cigüeña [θi'ɣweɲa] *nf* stork.

cilíndrico, a [θi'lindriko, a] *adj* cylindrical.

cilindro [θi'lindro] *nm* cylinder.

cima ['θima] *nf* (*de montaña*) top, peak; (*de árbol*) top; (*fig*) height.

címbalo ['θimbalo] *nm* cymbal.

cimbrear [θimbre'ar] *vt* to brandish; ~**se** *vr* to sway.

cimentar [θimen'tar] *vt* to lay the foundations of; (*fig*: *reforzar*) to strengthen; (: *fundar*) to found.

cimiento [θi'mjento] *etc vb* V **cimentar** ♦ *nm* foundation.

cinc [θink] *nm* zinc.

cincel [θin'θel] *nm* chisel.

cincelar [θinθe'lar] *vt* to chisel.

cincha ['θintʃa] *nf* girth, saddle strap.

cincho ['θintʃo] *nm* sash, belt.

cinco ['θinko] *num* five; (*fecha*) fifth; **las** ~ five o'clock; **no estar en sus** ~ (*fam*) to be off one's rocker.

cincuenta [θin'kwenta] *num* fifty.

cincuentón, ona [θinkwen'ton, ona] *adj*, *nm/f* fifty-year-old.

cine ['θine] *nm* cinema; **el** ~ **mudo** silent films *pl*; **hacer** ~ to make films.

cineasta [θine'asta] *nm/f* (*director de cine*) film-maker *o* director.

cine-club ['θine'klub] *nm* film club.

cinéfilo, a [θi'nefilo, a] *nm/f* film buff.

cinematográfico, a [θinemato'ɣrafiko, a] *adj* cine-, film *cpd*.

cínico, a ['θiniko, a] *adj* cynical; (*descarado*) shameless ♦ *nm/f* cynic.

cinismo [θi'nismo] *nm* cynicism.

cinta ['θinta] *nf* band, strip; (*de tela*) ribbon; (*película*) reel; (*de máquina de escribir*) ribbon; (*métrica*) tape measure; (*magnetofónica*) tape; ~ **adhesiva** sticky tape; ~ **aislante** insulating tape; ~ **de carbón** carbon ribbon; ~ **magnética** (*INFORM*) magnetic tape; ~ **métrica** tape measure; ~ **de múltiples impactos** (*en impresora*) multistrike ribbon; ~ **de tela** (*para máquina de escribir*) fabric ribbon; ~ **transportadora** conveyor belt.

cinto ['θinto] *nm* belt, girdle.

cintura [θin'tura] *nf* waist; (*medida*) waistline.

cinturón [θintu'ron] *nm* belt; (*fig*) belt, zone; ~ **salvavidas** lifebelt; ~ **de seguridad** safety belt.

ciña ['θiɲa] *etc*, **ciñendo** [θi'ɲendo] *etc vb* V **ceñir.**

CIP [θip] *nm abr* = *Club Internacional de Prensa (Madrid).*

ciprés [θi'pres] *nm* cypress (tree).

circo ['θirko] *nm* circus.

circuito [θir'kwito] *nm* circuit; (*DEPORTE*) lap; **TV por** ~ **cerrado** closed-circuit TV; ~ **experimental** (*INFORM*) breadboard; ~ **impreso** printed circuit; ~ **lógico** (*INFORM*) logical circuit.

circulación [θirkula'θjon] *nf* circulation;

(*AUTO*) traffic; **"cerrado a la ~ rodada"** "closed to vehicles".

circular [θirku'lar] *adj*, *nf* circular ♦ *vt* to circulate ♦ *vi* to circulate; (*dinero*) to be in circulation; (*AUTO*) to drive; (*autobús*) to run.

círculo ['θirkulo] *nm* circle; (*centro*) clubhouse; (*POL*) political group.

circuncidar [θirkunθi'dar] *vt* to circumcise.

circunciso, a [θirkun'θiso, a] *pp de* **circuncidar.**

circundante [θirkun'dante] *adj* surrounding.

circundar [θirkun'dar] *vt* to surround.

circunferencia [θirkunfe'renθja] *nf* circumference.

circunloquio [θirkun'lokjo] *nm* circumlocution.

circunscribir [θirkunskri'ßir] *vt* to circumscribe; **~se** *vr* to be limited.

circunscripción [θirkunskrip'θjon] *nf* division; (*POL*) constituency.

circunscrito [θirkuns'krito] *pp de* **circunscribir.**

circunspección [θirkunspek'θjon] *nf* circumspection, caution.

circunspecto, a [θirkuns'pekto, a] *adj* circumspect, cautious.

circunstancia [θirkuns'tanθja] *nf* circumstance; **~s agravantes/extenuantes** aggravating/extenuating circumstances; **estar a la altura de las ~s** to rise to the occasion.

circunvalación [θirkumbala'θjon] *nf*: **carretera de ~** ring road.

cirio ['θirjo] *nm* (wax) candle.

cirrosis [θi'rrosis] *nf* cirrhosis (of the liver).

ciruela [θi'rwela] *nf* plum; **~ pasa** prune.

ciruelo [θi'rwelo] *nm* plum tree.

cirugía [θiru'xia] *nf* surgery; **~ estética** *o* **plástica** plastic surgery.

cirujano [θiru'xano] *nm* surgeon.

cisco ['θisko] *nm*: **armar un ~** to kick up a row; **estar hecho ~** to be a wreck.

cisma ['θisma] *nm* schism; (*POL etc*) split.

cisne ['θisne] *nm* swan; **canto de ~** swan song.

cisterna [θis'terna] *nf* cistern, tank.

cistitis [θis'titis] *nf* cystitis.

cita ['θita] *nf* appointment, meeting; (*de novios*) date; (*referencia*) quotation; **acudir/faltar a una ~** to turn up for/miss an appointment.

citación [θita'θjon] *nf* (*JUR*) summons *sg*.

citadino, a [sita'ðino, a] (*AM*) *adj* urban ♦ *nm/f* urban *o* city dweller.

citar [θi'tar] *vt* to make an appointment

with, arrange to meet; (*JUR*) to summons; (*un autor, texto*) to quote; **~se** *vr*: **~se con algn** to arrange to meet sb; **se citaron en el cine** they arranged to meet at the cinema.

cítara ['θitara] *nf* zither.

citología [θitolo'xia] *nf* smear test.

cítrico, a ['θitriko, a] *adj* citric ♦ *nm*: **~s** citrus fruits.

CiU *nm abr* (*POL*) = *Convergència i Unió.*

ciudad [θju'ðað] *nf* town; (*capital de país etc*) city; **~ universitaria** university campus; **C~ del Cabo** Cape Town; **la C~ Condal** Barcelona.

ciudadanía [θjuðaða'nia] *nf* citizenship.

ciudadano, a [θjuða'ðano, a] *adj* civic ♦ *nm/f* citizen.

ciudadrealeño, a [θjuðaðrea'leɲo, a] *adj* of *o* from Ciudad Real ♦ *nm/f* native *o* inhabitant of Ciudad Real.

cívico, a ['θißiko, a] *adj* civic; (*fig*) public-spirited.

civil [θi'ßil] *adj* civil ♦ *nm* (*guardia*) policeman.

civilice [θißi'liθe] *etc vb V* **civilizar.**

civilización [θißiliθa'θjon] *nf* civilization.

civilizar [θißili'θar] *vt* to civilize.

civismo [θi'ßismo] *nm* public spirit.

cizaña [θi'θaɲa] *nf* (*fig*) discord; **sembrar ~** to sow discord.

cl. *abr* (= *centilitro*) cl.

clamar [kla'mar] *vt* to clamour for, cry out for ♦ *vi* to cry out, clamour.

clamor [kla'mor] *nm* (*grito*) cry, shout; (*fig*) clamour, protest.

clamoroso, a [klamo'roso, a] *adj* (*éxito etc*) resounding.

clan ['klan] *nm* clan; (*de gángsters*) gang.

clandestinidad [klandestini'ðað] *nf* secrecy.

clandestino, a [klandes'tino, a] *adj* clandestine; (*POL*) underground.

clara ['klara] *nf* (*de huevo*) eggwhite.

claraboya [klara'ßoja] *nf* skylight.

clarear [klare'ar] *vi* (*el día*) to dawn; (*el cielo*) to clear up, brighten up; **~se** *vr* to be transparent.

clarete [kla'rete] *nm* rosé (wine).

claridad [klari'ðað] *nf* (*del día*) brightness; (*de estilo*) clarity.

clarificar [klarifi'kar] *vt* to clarify.

clarifique [klari'fike] *etc vb V* **clarificar.**

clarín [kla'rin] *nm* bugle.

clarinete [klari'nete] *nm* clarinet.

clarividencia [klarißi'ðenθja] *nf* clairvoyance; (*fig*) far-sightedness.

claro, a ['klaro, a] *adj* clear; (*luminoso*) bright; (*color*) light; (*evidente*) clear, evident; (*poco espeso*) thin ◊ *nm* (*en bosque*) clearing ◊ *adv* clearly ◊ *excl* of course!; **hablar** ~ (*fig*) to speak plainly; **a las claras** openly; **no sacamos nada en** ~ we couldn't get anything definite.

clase ['klase] *nf* class; (*tipo*) kind, sort; (*ESCOL etc*) class; (: *aula*) classroom; ~ **alta/media/obrera** upper/middle/ working class; **dar** ~**s** to teach.

clásico, a ['klasiko, a] *adj* classical; (*fig*) classic.

clasificable [klasifi'kaßle] *adj* classifiable.

clasificación [klasifika'θjon] *nf* classification; (*DEPORTE*) league (table); (*COM*) ratings *pl*.

clasificador [klasifika'ðor] *nm* filing cabinet.

clasificar [klasifi'kar] *vt* to classify; (*INFORM*) to sort; ~**se** *vr* (*DEPORTE: torneo*) to qualify.

clasifique [klasi'fike] *etc vb V* **clasificar.**

clasista [kla'sista] *adj* (*fam: actitud*) snobbish.

claudia ['klauðja] *nf* greengage.

claudicar [klauði'kar] *vi* (*fig*) to back down.

claudique [klau'ðike] *etc vb V* **claudicar.**

claustro ['klaustro] *nm* cloister; (*UNIV*) staff; (*junta*) senate.

claustrofobia [klaustro'foßja] *nf* claustrophobia.

cláusula ['klausula] *nf* clause; ~ **de exclusión** (*COM*) exclusion clause.

clausura [klau'sura] *nf* closing, closure.

clausurar [klausu'rar] *vt* (*congreso etc*) to close, bring to a close; (*POL etc*) to adjourn; (*cerrar*) to close (down).

clavado, a [kla'ßaðo, a] *adj* nailed ◊ *excl* exactly!, precisely!

clavar [kla'ßar] *vt* (*tablas etc*) to nail (together); (*con alfiler*) to pin; (*clavo*) to hammer in; (*cuchillo*) to stick, thrust; (*mirada*) to fix; (*fam: estafar*) to cheat.

clave ['klaße] *nf* key; (*MUS*) clef ◊ *adj inv* key *cpd*; ~ **de búsqueda** (*INFORM*) search key; ~ **de clasificación** (*INFORM*) sort key.

clavel [kla'ßel] *nm* carnation.

clavicémbalo [klaßi'θembalo] *nm* harpsichord.

clavicordio [klaßikor'ðjo] *nm* clavicord.

clavícula [kla'ßikula] *nf* collar bone.

clavija [kla'ßixa] *nf* peg, pin; (*MUS*) peg; (*ELEC*) plug.

clavo ['klaßo] *nm* (*de metal*) nail; (*BOT*) clove; **dar en el** ~ (*fig*) to hit the nail on the head.

claxon ['klakson], *pl* **claxons** *nm* horn; **tocar el** ~ to sound one's horn.

clemencia [kle'menθja] *nf* mercy,

clemency.

clemente [kle'mente] *adj* merciful, clement.

cleptómano, a [klep'tomano, a] *nm/f* kleptomaniac.

clerical [kleri'kal] *adj* clerical.

clérigo ['kleriɣo] *nm* priest, clergyman.

clero ['klero] *nm* clergy.

clic [klik] *nm* click; **hacer** ~/**doble** ~ **en algo** to click/double-click on sth.

cliché [kli'tʃe] *nm* cliché; (*TIP*) stencil; (*FOTO*) negative.

cliente, a ['kljente, a] *nm/f* client, customer.

clientela [kljen'tela] *nf* clientele, customers *pl*; (*COM*) goodwill; (*MED*) patients *pl*.

clima ['klima] *nm* climate.

climatizado, a [klimati'θaðo, a] *adj* air-conditioned.

clímax ['klimaks] *nm inv* climax.

clínico, a ['kliniko, a] *adj* clinical ◊ *nf* clinic; (*particular*) private hospital.

clip, *pl* **clips** [klip, klis] *nm* paper clip.

clítoris ['klitoris] *nm inv* clitoris.

cloaca [klo'aka] *nf* sewer, drain.

clonación [klona'θjon] *nf* cloning.

clorhídrico, a [klo'ridriko, a] *adj* hydrochloric.

cloro ['kloro] *nm* chlorine.

clorofila [kloro'fila] *nf* chlorophyl(l).

cloroformo [kloro'formo] *nm* chloroform.

cloruro [klo'ruro] *nm* chloride; ~ **sódico** sodium chloride.

club, *pl* **clubs** *o* **clubes** [klub, klus, 'klußes] *nm* club; ~ **de jóvenes** youth club.

cm *abr* (= *centímetro*) cm.

C.N.T. *nf abr* (*ESP: Confederación Nacional de Trabajo*) *Anarchist Union Confederation*; (*AM*) = *Confederación Nacional de Trabajadores.*

coacción [koak'θjon] *nf* coercion, compulsion.

coaccionar [koakθjo'nar] *vt* to coerce, compel.

coagular [koaɣu'lar] *vt*, ~**se** *vr* (*sangre*) to clot; (*leche*) to curdle.

coágulo [ko'aɣulo] *nm* clot.

coalición [koali'θjon] *nf* coalition.

coartada [koar'taða] *nf* alibi.

coartar [koar'tar] *vt* to limit, restrict.

coba ['koßa] *nf*: **dar** ~ **a algn** to soft-soap sb.

cobarde [ko'ßarðe] *adj* cowardly ◊ *nm/f* coward.

cobardía [koßar'ðia] *nf* cowardice.

cobaya [ko'ßaja] *nf* guinea pig.

cobertizo [koßer'tiθo] *nm* shelter.

cobertor [koßer'tor] *nm* bedspread.

cobertura [koßer'tura] *nf* cover; (*COM*)

coverage; ~ **de dividendo** (*COM*) dividend cover.

cobija [ko'βixa] *nf* (*AM*) blanket.

cobijar [koβi'xar] *vt* (*cubrir*) to cover; (*abrigar*) to shelter; ~**se** *vr* to take shelter.

cobijo [ko'βixo] *nm* shelter.

cobra ['koβra] *nf* cobra.

cobrador, a [koβra'ðor, a] *nm/f* (*de autobús*) conductor/conductress; (*de impuestos, gas*) collector.

cobrar [ko'βrar] *vt* (*cheque*) to cash; (*sueldo*) to collect, draw; (*objeto*) to recover; (*precio*) to charge; (*deuda*) to collect ♦ *vi* to draw one's pay; ~**se** *vr* to recover, get on well; **cóbrese al entregar cash on delivery (COD)** (*BRIT*), collect on delivery (COD) (*US*); **a** ~ (*COM*) receivable; **cantidades por** ~ sums due.

cobre ['koβre] *nm* copper; (*AM fam*) cent; ~**s** *nmpl* brass instruments.

cobrizo, a [ko'βriθo, a] *adj* coppery.

cobro ['koβro] *nm* (*de cheque*) cashing; (*pago*) payment; **presentar al** ~ to cash; *V tb* **llamada**.

coca ['koka] *nf* coca; (*droga*) coke.

Coca-Cola ® ['koka'kola] *nf* Coca-Cola ®.

cocaína [koka'ina] *nf* cocaine.

cocainómano, a [kokai'nomano, a] *nm/f* cocaine addict.

cocción [kok'θjon] *nf* (*CULIN*) cooking; (*el hervir*) boiling.

cocear [koθe'ar] *vi* to kick.

cocer [ko'θer] *vt*, *vi* to cook; (*en agua*) to boil; (*en horno*) to bake.

coche ['kotʃe] *nm* (*AUTO*) car, automobile (*US*); (*de tren, de caballos*) coach, carriage; (*para niños*) pram (*BRIT*), baby carriage (*US*); ~ **de bomberos** fire engine; ~ **celular** Black Maria, prison van; ~ (**comedor**) (*FERRO*) (dining) car; ~ **fúnebre** hearse.

coche-bomba ['kotʃe'βomba], *pl* **coches-bomba** *nm* car bomb.

coche-cama ['kotʃe'kama], *pl* **coches-cama** *nm* (*FERRO*) sleeping car, sleeper.

cochera [ko'tʃera] *nf* garage; (*de autobuses, trenes*) depot.

coche-restaurante, *pl* **coches-restaurante** ['kotʃerestau'rante] *nm* (*FERRO*) dining-car, diner.

cochinada [kotʃi'naða] *nf* dirty trick.

cochinillo [kotʃi'niʎo] *nm* piglet, suckling pig.

cochino, a [ko'tʃino, a] *adj* filthy, dirty ♦ *nm/f* pig.

cocido, a [ko'θiðo, a] *adj* boiled; (*fam*) plastered ♦ *nm* stew.

cociente [ko'θjente] *nm* quotient.

cocina [ko'θina] *nf* kitchen; (*aparato*) cooker, stove; (*acto*) cookery; ~ **casera** home cooking; ~ **eléctrica** electric cooker; ~ **francesa** French cuisine; ~ **de gas** gas cooker.

cocinar [koθi'nar] *vt*, *vi* to cook.

cocinero, a [koθi'nero, a] *nm/f* cook.

coco ['koko] *nm* coconut; (*fantasma*) bogeyman; (*fam: cabeza*) nut; **comer el** ~ **a algn** (*fam*) to brainwash sb.

cocodrilo [koko'ðrilo] *nm* crocodile.

cocotero [koko'tero] *nm* coconut palm.

cóctel ['koktel] *nm* (*bebida*) cocktail; (*reunión*) cocktail party; ~ **Molotov** Molotov cocktail, petrol bomb.

coctelera [kokte'lera] *nf* cocktail shaker.

cod. *abr* (= *código*) code.

codazo [ko'ðaθo] *nm*: **dar un** ~ **a algn** to nudge sb.

codear [koðe'ar] *vi* to elbow, jostle; ~**se** *vr*: ~**se con** to rub shoulders with.

códice ['koðiθe] *nm* manuscript, codex.

codicia [ko'ðiθja] *nf* greed; (*fig*) lust.

codiciar [koðiθ'jar] *vt* to covet.

codicioso, a [koðiθ'joso, a] *adj* covetous.

codificador [koðifika'ðor] *nm* (*INFORM*) encoder; ~ **digital** digitizer.

codificar [koðifi'kar] *vt* (*mensaje*) to (en)code; (*leyes*) to codify.

código ['koðiyo] *nm* code; ~ **de barras** (*COM*) bar code; ~ **binario** binary code; ~ **de caracteres** (*INFORM*) character code; ~ **de (la) circulación** highway code; ~ **civil** common law; ~ **de control** (*INFORM*) control code; ~ **máquina** (*INFORM*) machine code; ~ **militar** military law; ~ **de operación** (*INFORM*) operational *o* machine code; ~ **penal** penal code; ~ **de práctica** code of practice.

codillo [ko'ðiʎo] *nm* (*ZOOL*) knee; (*TEC*) elbow (joint).

codo [ko'ðo] *nm* (*ANAT, de tubo*) elbow; (*ZOOL*) knee; **hablar por los** ~**s** to talk nineteen to the dozen.

codorniz [koðor'niθ] *nf* quail.

coeficiente [koefi'θjente] *nm* (*MAT*) coefficient; (*ECON etc*) rate; ~ **intelectual** *o* **de inteligencia** I.Q.

coerción [koer'θjon] *nf* coercion.

coercitivo, a [koerθi'tiβo, a] *adj* coercive.

coetáneo, a [koe'taneo, a] *nm/f*: ~**s** contemporaries.

coexistencia [koeksis'tenθja] *nf* coexistence.

coexistir [koeksis'tir] *vi* to coexist.

cofia ['kofja] *nf* (*de enfermera*) (white) cap.

cofradía [kofra'ðia] *nf* brotherhood, fraternity; V *tb* **Semana Santa**.

cofre ['kofre] *nm* (*baúl*) trunk; (*de joyas*) box; (*AM AUTO*) bonnet (*BRIT*), hood (*US*).

cogedor [koxe'ðor] *nm* dustpan.

coger [ko'xer] *vt* (*ESP*) to take (hold of); (*objeto caído*) to pick up; (*frutas*) to pick, harvest; (*resfriado, ladrón, pelota*) to catch; (*AM fam!*) to lay (*!*) ♦ *vi*: ~ **por el buen camino** to take the right road; ~**se** *vr* (*el dedo*) to catch; ~ **a algn desprevenido** to take sb unawares; ~**se a algo** to get hold of sth.

cogida [ko'xiða] *nf* gathering, harvesting; (*de peces*) catch; (*TAUR*) goring.

cogollo [ko'yoʎo] *nm* (*de lechuga*) heart; (*fig*) core, nucleus.

cogorza [ko'yorθa] *nf* (*fam*): **agarrar una** ~ to get smashed.

cogote [ko'yote] *nm* back of the neck.

cohabitar [koaßi'tar] *vi* to live together, cohabit.

cohecho [ko'etʃo] *nm* (*acción*) bribery; (*soborno*) bribe.

coherencia [koe'renθja] *nf* coherence.

coherente [koe'rente] *adj* coherent.

cohesión [koe'sjon] *nm* cohesion.

cohete [ko'ete] *nm* rocket.

cohibido, a [koi'ßiðo, a] *adj* (*PSICO*) inhibited; (*tímido*) shy; **sentirse** ~ to feel embarrassed.

cohibir [koi'ßir] *vt* to restrain, restrict; ~**se** *vr* to feel inhibited.

COI *nm abr* (= *Comité Olímpico Internacional*) IOC.

coima ['koima] *nf* (*AM fam*) bribe.

coincidencia [koinθi'ðenθja] *nf* coincidence.

coincidir [koinθi'ðir] *vi* (*en idea*) to coincide, agree; (*en lugar*) to coincide.

coito ['koito] *nm* intercourse, coitus.

cojear [koxe'ar] *vi* (*persona*) to limp, hobble; (*mueble*) to wobble, rock.

cojera [ko'xera] *nf* lameness; (*andar cojo*) limp.

cojín [ko'xin] *nm* cushion.

cojinete [koxi'nete] *nm* small cushion, pad; (*TEC*) (ball) bearing.

cojo, a ['koxo, a] *etc vb V* **coger** ♦ *adj* (*que no puede andar*) lame, crippled; (*mueble*) wobbly ♦ *nm/f* lame person, cripple.

cojón [ko'xon] *nm* (*fam!*) ball (*!*), testicle; **¡cojones!** shit! (*!*).

cojonudo, a [koxo'nuðo, a] *adj* (*ESP fam*) great, fantastic.

col [kol] *nf* cabbage; ~**es de Bruselas** Brussels sprouts.

col., col.ᵃ *abr* (= *columna*) col.

cola ['kola] *nf* tail; (*de gente*) queue; (*lugar*) end, last place; (*para pegar*) glue, gum; (*de vestido*) train; **hacer** ~ to queue (up).

colaboración [kolaßora'θjon] *nf* collaboration; (*en periódico*) contribution.

colaborador, a [kolaßora'ðor, a] *nm/f* collaborator; contributor.

colaborar [kolaßo'rar] *vi* to collaborate.

colación [kola'θjon] *nf*: **sacar a** ~ to bring up.

colado, a [ko'laðo, a] *adj* (*metal*) cast ♦ *nf*: **hacer la colada** to do the washing.

colador [kola'ðor] *nm* (*de té*) strainer; (*para verduras etc*) colander.

colapsar [kolap'sar] *vt* (*tráfico etc*) to bring to a standstill.

colapso [ko'lapso] *nm* collapse; ~ **nervioso** nervous breakdown.

colar [ko'lar] *vt* (*líquido*) to strain off; (*metal*) to cast ♦ *vi* to ooze, seep (through); ~**se** *vr* to jump the queue; (*en mitin*) to sneak in; (*equivocarse*) to slip up; ~**se en** to get into without paying; (*en una fiesta*) to gatecrash.

colateral [kolate'ral] *nm* collateral.

colcha ['koltʃa] *nf* bedspread.

colchón [kol'tʃon] *nm* mattress; ~ **inflable** inflatable mattress.

colchoneta [koltʃo'neta] *nf* (*en gimnasio*) mattress; ~ **hinchable** airbed.

colear [kole'ar] *vi* (*perro*) to wag its tail.

colección [kolek'θjon] *nf* collection.

coleccionar [kolekθjo'nar] *vt* to collect.

coleccionista [kolekθjo'nista] *nm/f* collector.

colecta [ko'lekta] *nf* collection.

colectivo, a [kolek'tißo, a] *adj* collective, joint ♦ *nm* (*AM*: *autobús*) (small) bus; (: *taxi*) collective taxi.

colector [kolek'tor] *nm* collector; (*sumidero*) sewer.

colega [ko'leya] *nm/f* colleague.

colegiado, a [kole'xjaðo, a] *adj* (*profesional*) registered ♦ *nm/f* referee.

colegial, a [kole'xjal, a] *adj* (*ESCOL etc*) school *cpd*, college *cpd* ♦ *nm/f* schoolboy/girl.

colegio [ko'lexjo] *nm* college; (*escuela*) school; (*de abogados etc*) association; ~ **de internos** boarding school; **ir al** ~ to go to school; *see boxed note.*

COLEGIO

A **colegio** *is normally a private school, either primary or secondary. Within the state system, however, the word indicates primary school, although these are also referred to as "escuelas". State secondary*

> schools are called "institutos". Extra-
> curricular subjects, such as computing or
> foreign languages, are taught in private
> schools called "academias".

colegir [kole'xir] vt (juntar) to collect,
gather; (deducir) to infer, conclude.

cólera ['kolera] nf (ira) anger; **montar en** ~
to get angry ♦ nm (MED) cholera.

colérico, a [ko'leriko, a] adj angry, furious.

colesterol [koleste'rol] nm cholesterol.

coleta [ko'leta] nf pigtail.

coletazo [kole'taθo] nm: **dar un** ~ (animal)
to flap its tail; **los últimos** ~**s** death
throes.

coletilla [kole'tiʎa] nf (en carta) postscript;
(en conversación) filler phrase.

colgado, a [kol'ɣaðo, a] pp de **colgar** ♦ adj
hanging; (ahorcado) hanged; **dejar** ~ **a**
algn to let sb down.

colgajo [kol'ɣaxo] nm tatter.

colgante [kol'ɣante] adj hanging; V **puente**
♦ nm (joya) pendant.

colgar [kol'ɣar] vt to hang (up); (tender:
ropa) to hang out ♦ vi to hang; (teléfono)
to hang up.

colgué [kol'ɣe], **colguemos** [kol'ɣemos]
etc vb V **colgar**.

colibrí [koli'ßri] nm hummingbird.

cólico ['koliko] nm colic.

coliflor [koli'flor] nf cauliflower.

coligiendo [koli'xjenðo] etc vb V **colegir**.

colija [ko'lixa] etc vb V **colegir**.

colilla [ko'liʎa] nf cigarette end, butt.

colina [ko'lina] nf hill.

colindante [kolin'dante] adj adjacent,
neighbouring.

colindar [kolin'dar] vi to adjoin, be
adjacent.

colisión [koli'sjon] nf collision; ~ **de frente**
head-on crash.

colitis [ko'litis] nf inv: **tener** ~ to have
diarrhoea.

collar [ko'ʎar] nm necklace; (de perro)
collar.

colmado, a [kol'maðo, a] adj full ♦ nm
grocer's (shop) (BRIT), grocery store
(US).

colmar [kol'mar] vt to fill to the brim; (fig)
to fulfil, realize.

colmena [kol'mena] nf beehive.

colmillo [kol'miʎo] nm (diente) eye tooth;
(de elefante) tusk; (de perro) fang.

colmo ['kolmo] nm height, summit; **para** ~
de desgracias to cap it all; **¡eso es ya el**
~**!** that's beyond a joke!

colocación [koloka'θjon] nf (acto) placing;
(empleo) job, position; (situación) place,

position; (COM) placement.

colocar [kolo'kar] vt to place, put, position;
(poner en empleo) to find a job for; ~
dinero to invest money; ~**se** vr to place
o.s.; (conseguir trabajo) to find a job.

colofón [kolo'fon] nm: **como** ~ **de las**
conversaciones as a sequel to o
following the talks.

Colombia [ko'lombja] nf Colombia.

colombiano, a [kolom'bjano, a] adj, nm/f
Colombian.

colon ['kolon] nm colon.

colón [ko'lon] nm (AM) monetary unit of
Costa Rica and El Salvador.

Colonia [ko'lonja] nf Cologne.

colonia [ko'lonja] nf colony; (de casas)
housing estate; (agua de ~) cologne; ~
escolar summer camp (for
schoolchildren).

colonice [kolo'niθe] etc vb V **colonizar**.

colonización [koloniθa'θjon] nf
colonization.

colonizador, a [koloniθa'ðor, a] adj
colonizing ♦ nm/f colonist, settler.

colonizar [koloni'θar] vt to colonize.

colono [ko'lono] nm (POL) colonist, settler;
(AGR) tenant farmer.

coloque [ko'loke] etc vb V **colocar**.

coloquial [kolo'kjal] adj colloquial.

coloquio [ko'lokjo] nm conversation;
(congreso) conference; (INFORM)
handshake.

color [ko'lor] nm colour; **a todo** ~ in full
colour; **verlo todo** ~ **de rosa** to see
everything through rose-coloured
spectacles; **le salieron los** ~**es** she
blushed.

colorado, a [kolo'raðo, a] adj (rojo) red;
(AM: chiste) rude, blue; **ponerse** ~ to
blush.

colorante [kolo'rante] nm colouring
(matter).

colorar [kolo'rar] vt to colour; (teñir) to
dye.

colorear [kolore'ar] vt to colour.

colorete [kolo'rete] nm blusher.

colorido [kolo'riðo] nm colour(ing).

coloso [ko'loso] nm colossus.

columbrar [kolum'brar] vt to glimpse, spy.

columna [ko'lumna] nf column; (pilar)
pillar; (apoyo) support; ~ **blindada** (MIL)
armoured column; ~ **vertebral** spine,
spinal column.

columpiar [kolum'pjar] vt, ~**se** vr to swing.

columpio [ko'lumpjo] nm swing.

colza ['kolθa] nf rape; **aceite de** ~ rapeseed
oil.

coma ['koma] nf comma ♦ nm (MED) coma.

comadre [ko'maðre] _nf_ (_madrina_) godmother; (_vecina_) neighbour; (_chismosa_) gossip.

comadrear [komaðre'ar] _vi_ (_esp AM_) to gossip.

comadreja [koma'ðrexa] _nf_ weasel.

comadrona [koma'ðrona] _nf_ midwife.

comandancia [koman'danθja] _nf_ command.

comandante [koman'dante] _nm_ commandant; (_grado_) major.

comandar [koman'dar] _vt_ to command.

comando [ko'mando] _nm_ (_MIL: mando_) command; (: _grupo_) commando unit; (_INFORM_) command; ~ **de búsqueda** search command.

comarca [ko'marka] _nf_ region; V _tb_ **provincia.**

comarcal [komar'kal] _adj_ local.

comba ['komba] _nf_ (_curva_) curve; (_en viga_) warp; (_cuerda_) skipping rope; **saltar a la** ~ to skip.

combar [kom'bar] _vt_ to bend, curve.

combate [kom'bate] _nm_ fight; (_fig_) battle; **fuera de** ~ out of action.

combatiente [komba'tjente] _nm_ combatant.

combatir [komba'tir] _vt_ to fight, combat.

combatividad [kombatiβi'ðað] _nf_ (_actitud_) fighting spirit; (_agresividad_) aggressiveness.

combativo, a [komba'tiβo, a] _adj_ full of fight.

combi ['kombi] _nm_ fridge-freezer.

combinación [kombina'θjon] _nf_ combination; (_QUÍMICA_) compound; (_bebida_) cocktail; (_plan_) scheme, setup; (_prenda_) slip.

combinado, a [kombi'naðo, a] _adj_: **plato** ~ _main course served with vegetables._

combinar [kombi'nar] _vt_ to combine; (_colores_) to match.

combustible [kombus'tiβle] _nm_ fuel.

combustión [kombus'tjon] _nf_ combustion.

comedia [ko'meðja] _nf_ comedy; (_TEAT_) play, drama; (_fig_) farce.

comediante [kome'ðjante] _nm/f_ (_comic_) actor/actress.

comedido, a [kome'ðiðo, a] _adj_ moderate.

comedirse [kome'ðirse] _vr_ to behave moderately; (_ser cortés_) to be courteous.

comedor, a [kome'ðor, a] _nm/f_ (_persona_) glutton ♦ _nm_ (_habitación_) dining room; (_restaurante_) restaurant; (_cantina_) canteen.

comencé [komen'θe], **comencemos** [komen'θemos] _etc vb_ V **comenzar.**

comensal [komen'sal] _nm/f_ fellow guest/

diner.

comentar [komen'tar] _vt_ to comment on; (_fam_) to discuss; **comentó que...** he made the comment that....

comentario [komen'tarjo] _nm_ comment, remark; (_LIT_) commentary; ~**s** _nmpl_ gossip _sg_; **dar lugar a** ~**s** to cause gossip.

comentarista [komenta'rista] _nm/f_ commentator.

comenzar [komen'θar] _vt, vi_ to begin, start, commence; ~ **a hacer algo** to begin _o_ start doing _o_ to do sth.

comer [ko'mer] _vt_ to eat; (_DAMAS, AJEDREZ_) to take, capture; (_párrafo etc_) to skip ♦ _vi_ to eat; (_almorzar_) to have lunch; ~**se** _vr_ to eat up; ~ **el coco a** (_fam_) to brainwash; **¡a** ~! food's ready!

comercial [komer'θjal] _adj_ commercial; (_relativo al negocio_) business _cpd_.

comerciante [komer'θjante] _nm/f_ trader, merchant; (_tendero_) shopkeeper; ~ **exclusivo** (_COM_) sole trader.

comerciar [komer'θjar] _vi_ to trade, do business.

comercio [ko'merθjo] _nm_ commerce, trade; (_negocio_) business; (_grandes empresas_) big business; (_fig_) dealings _pl_; ~ **autorizado** (_COM_) licensed trade; ~ **electrónico** e-commerce; ~ **exterior** foreign trade.

comestible [komes'tiβle] _adj_ eatable, edible ♦ _nm_: ~**s** food _sg_, foodstuffs; (_COM_) groceries.

cometa [ko'meta] _nm_ comet ♦ _nf_ kite.

cometer [kome'ter] _vt_ to commit.

cometido [kome'tiðo] _nm_ (_misión_) task, assignment; (_deber_) commitment.

comezón [kome'θon] _nf_ itch, itching.

cómic, _pl_ **cómics** ['komik, 'komiks] _nm_ comic.

comicios [ko'miθjos] _nmpl_ elections; (_voto_) voting _sg_.

cómico, a ['komiko, a] _adj_ comic(al) ♦ _nm/f_ comedian; (_de teatro_) (comic) actor/actress.

comida [ko'miða] _etc vb_ V **comedirse** ♦ _nf_ (_alimento_) food; (_almuerzo, cena_) meal; (_de mediodía_) lunch; (_AM_) dinner.

comidilla [komi'ðiʎa] _nf_: **ser la** ~ **de la ciudad** to be the talk of the town.

comience [ko'mjenθe] _etc vb_ V **comenzar.**

comienzo [ko'mjenθo] _etc vb_ V **comenzar** ♦ _nm_ beginning, start; **dar** ~ **a un acto** to begin a ceremony; ~ **del archivo** (_INFORM_) top-of-file.

comillas [ko'miʎas] _nfpl_ quotation marks.

comilón, ona [komi'lon, ona] _adj_ greedy ♦ _nf_ (_fam_) blow-out.

comino [ko'mino] _nm_ cumin (seed); **no me**

importa un ~ I don't give a damn.
comisaría [komisa'ria] *nf* police station,
precinct (*US*); (*MIL*) commissariat.
comisario [komi'sarjo] *nm* (*MIL etc*)
commissary; (*POL*) commissar.
comisión [komi'sjon] *nf* (*COM*: *pago*)
commission, rake-off (*fam*); (: *junta*)
board; (*encargo*) assignment; ~ **mixta/**
permanente joint/standing committee;
Comisiones Obreras (*ESP*) *formerly*
Communist Union Confederation.
comisura [komi'sura] *nf*: ~ **de los labios**
corner of the mouth.
comité, *pl* **comités** *nm* [komi'te, komi'tes]
committee; ~ **de empresa** works
council.
comitiva [komi'tißa] *nf* suite, retinue.
como ['komo] *adv* as; (*tal* ~) like;
(*aproximadamente*) about, approximately
♦ *conj* (*ya que, puesto que*) as, since; (*en*
seguida que) as soon as; (*si*: +*subjun*) if;
¡~ **no!** of course!; ~ **no lo haga hoy**
unless he does it today; ~ **si** as if; **es tan**
alto ~ **ancho** it is as high as it is wide.
cómo ['komo] *adv* how?, why? ♦ *excl* what?,
I beg your pardon? ♦ *nm*: **el** ~ **y el porqué**
the whys and wherefores; ¿~ **está Ud?**
how are you?; ¿~ **no?** why not?; ¡~ **no!**
(*esp AM*) of course!; ¿~ **son?** what are
they like?
cómoda ['komoða] *nf* chest of drawers.
comodidad [komoði'ðað] *nf* comfort;
venga a su ~ come at your convenience.
comodín [komo'ðin] *nm* joker; (*INFORM*)
wild card; **símbolo** ~ wild card
character.
cómodo, a ['komoðo, a] *adj* comfortable;
(*práctico, de fácil uso*) convenient.
comodón, ona [komo'ðon, ona] *adj*
comfort-loving ♦ *nm/f*: **ser un(a)** ~ to like
one's home comforts.
comoquiera [como'kjera] *conj*: ~ **que**
(+ *subjun*) in whatever way; ~ **que sea**
eso however that may be.
comp. *abr* (= *compárese*) cp.
compacto, a [kom'pakto, a] *adj* compact.
compadecer [kompaðe'θer] *vt* to pity, be
sorry for; ~**se** *vr*: ~**se de** to pity, be
sorry for.
compadezca [kompa'ðeθka] *etc vb V*
compadecer.
compadre [kom'paðre] *nm* (*padrino*)
godfather; (*esp AM*: *amigo*) friend, pal.
compaginar [kompaxi'nar] *vt*: ~ **A con B** to
bring A into line with B; ~**se** *vr*: ~**se con**
to tally with, square with.
compañerismo [kompaɲe'rismo] *nm*
comradeship.

compañero, a [kompa'ɲero, a] *nm/f*
companion; (*novio*) boyfriend/girlfriend;
~ **de clase** classmate.
compañía [kompa'ɲia] *nf* company; ~
afiliada associated company; ~
concesionadora franchiser; ~ **(no)**
cotizable (un)listed company; ~
inversionista investment trust; **hacer** ~ **a**
algn to keep sb company.
comparación [kompara'θjon] *nf*
comparison; **en** ~ **con** in comparison
with.
comparar [kompa'rar] *vt* to compare.
comparativo, a [kompara'tißo, a] *adj*
comparative.
comparecencia [kompare'θenθja] *nf* (*JUR*)
appearance (in court); **orden de** ~
summons *sg.*
comparecer [kompare'θer] *vi* to appear (in
court).
comparezca [kompa'reθka] *etc vb V*
comparecer.
comparsa [kom'parsa] *nm/f* extra.
compartimento [komparti'mento],
compartimiento [komparti'mjento] *nm*
(*FERRO*) compartment; (*de mueble, cajón*)
section; ~ **estanco** (*fig*) watertight
compartment.
compartir [kompar'tir] *vt* to divide (up),
share (out).
compás [kom'pas] *nm* (*MUS*) beat, rhythm;
(*MAT*) compasses *pl*; (*NAUT etc*) compass;
al ~ in time.
compasión [kompa'sjon] *nf* compassion,
pity.
compasivo, a [kompa'sißo, a] *adj*
compassionate.
compatibilidad [kompatißili'ðað] *nf* (*tb*
INFORM) compatibility.
compatible [kompa'tißle] *adj* compatible.
compatriota [kompa'trjota] *nm/f*
compatriot, fellow countryman/woman.
compendiar [kompen'djar] *vt* to
summarize; (*libro*) to abridge.
compendio [kom'pendjo] *nm* summary;
abridgement.
compenetración [kompenetra'θjon] *nf* (*fig*)
mutual understanding.
compenetrarse [kompene'trarse] *vr* (*fig*):
~ **(muy) bien** to get on (very) well
together.
compensación [kompensa'θjon] *nf*
compensation; (*JUR*) damages *pl*; (*COM*)
clearing.
compensar [kompen'sar] *vt* to
compensate; (*pérdida*) to make up for.
competencia [kompe'tenθja] *nf*
(*incumbencia*) domain, field; (*COM*)

receipt; (*JUR, habilidad*) competence; (*rivalidad*) competition.

competente [kompe'tente] *adj* (*JUR, persona*) competent; (*conveniente*) suitable.

competer [kompe'ter] *vi*: ~ **a** to be the responsibility of, fall to.

competición [kompeti'θjon] *nf* competition.

competidor, a [kompeti'ðor, a] *nm/f* competitor.

competir [kompe'tir] *vi* to compete.

competitivo, a [kompeti'tißo, a] *adj* competitive.

compilación [kompila'θjon] *nf* compilation; **tiempo de** ~ (*INFORM*) compile time.

compilador [kompila'ðor] *nm* compiler.

compilar [kompi'lar] *vt* to compile.

compinche [kom'pintʃe] *nm/f* (*fam*) crony.

compita [kom'pita] *etc vb V* **competir**.

complacencia [kompla'θenθja] *nf* (*placer*) pleasure; (*satisfacción*) satisfaction; (*buena voluntad*) willingness.

complacer [kompla'θer] *vt* to please; ~**se** *vr* to be pleased.

complaciente [kompla'θjente] *adj* kind, obliging, helpful.

complazca [kom'plaθka] *etc vb V* **complacer**.

complejo, a [kom'plexo, a] *adj, nm* complex.

complementario, a [komplemen'tarjo, a] *adj* complementary.

complemento [komple'mento] *nm* (*de moda, diseño*) accessory; (*LING*) complement.

completar [komple'tar] *vt* to complete.

completo, a [kom'pleto, a] *adj* complete; (*perfecto*) perfect; (*lleno*) full ♦ *nm* full complement.

complexión [komple'ksjon] *nf* constitution.

complicación [komplika'θjon] *nf* complication.

complicado, a [kompli'kaðo, a] *adj* complicated; **estar** ~ **en** to be involved in.

complicar [kompli'kar] *vt* to complicate.

cómplice ['kompliθe] *nm/f* accomplice.

complique [kom'plike] *etc vb V* **complicar**.

complot, *pl* **complots** [kom'plo(t), kom'plos] *nm* plot; (*conspiración*) conspiracy.

compondré [kompon'dre] *etc vb V* **componer**.

componenda [kompo'nenda] *nf* compromise; (*pey*) shady deal.

componente [kompo'nente] *adj, nm* component.

componer [kompo'ner] *vt* to make up, put together; (*MUS, LIT, IMPRENTA*) to compose; (*algo roto*) to mend, repair; (*adornar*) to adorn; (*arreglar*) to arrange; (*reconciliar*) to reconcile; ~**se** *vr*: ~**se de** to consist of; **componérselas para hacer algo** to manage to do sth.

componga [kom'ponga] *etc vb V* **componer**.

comportamiento [komporta'mjento] *nm* behaviour, conduct.

comportarse [kompor'tarse] *vr* to behave.

composición [komposi'θjon] *nf* composition.

compositor, a [komposi'tor, a] *nm/f* composer.

compostelano, a [komposte'lano, a] *adj* of *o* from Santiago de Compostela ♦ *nm/f* native *o* inhabitant of Santiago de Compostela.

compostura [kompos'tura] *nf* (*reparación*) mending, repair; (*composición*) composition; (*acuerdo*) agreement; (*actitud*) composure.

compota [kom'pota] *nf* compote, preserve.

compra ['kompra] *nf* purchase; ~**s** *nfpl* purchases, shopping *sg*; **hacer la** ~/**ir de** ~**s** to do the/go shopping; ~ **a granel** (*COM*) bulk buying; ~ **proteccionista** (*COM*) support buying.

comprador, a [kompra'ðor, a] *nm/f* buyer, purchaser.

comprar [kom'prar] *vt* to buy, purchase; ~ **deudas** (*COM*) to factor.

compraventa [kompra'ßenta] *nf* (*JUR*) contract of sale.

comprender [kompren'der] *vt* to understand; (*incluir*) to comprise, include.

comprensible [kompren'sißle] *adj* understandable.

comprensión [kompren'sjon] *nf* understanding; (*totalidad*) comprehensiveness.

comprensivo, a [kompren'sißo, a] *adj* comprehensive; (*actitud*) understanding.

compresa [kom'presa] *nf* compress; ~ **higiénica** sanitary towel (*BRIT*) *o* napkin (*US*).

compresión [kompre'sjon] *nf* compression.

comprimido, a [kompri'miðo, a] *adj* compressed ♦ *nm* (*MED*) pill, tablet; **en caracteres** ~**s** (*TIP*) condensed.

comprimir [kompri'mir] *vt* to compress;

(*fig*) to control; (*INFORM*) to pack.

comprobación [komproßa'θjon] *nf*: ~ **general de cuentas** (*COM*) general audit.

comprobante [kompro'ßante] *nm* proof; (*COM*) voucher; ~ **(de pago)** receipt.

comprobar [kompro'ßar] *vt* to check; (*probar*) to prove; (*TEC*) to check, test.

comprometedor, a [kompromete'ðor, a] *adj* compromising.

comprometer [komprome'ter] *vt* to compromise; (*exponer*) to endanger; ~**se** *vr* to compromise o.s.; (*involucrarse*) to get involved.

comprometido, a [komprome'tiðo, a] *a* (*situación*) awkward; (*escritor etc*) committed.

compromiso [kompro'miso] *nm* (*obligación*) obligation; (*cita*) engagement, date; (*cometido*) commitment; (*convenio*) agreement; (*dificultad*) awkward situation; **libre de** ~ (*COM*) without obligation.

comprueba [kom'prweßa] *etc vb* V **comprobar.**

compuerta [kom'pwerta] *nf* (*en canal*) sluice, floodgate; (*INFORM*) gate.

compuesto, a [kom'pwesto, a] *pp de* **componer** ♦ *adj*: ~ **de** composed of, made up of ♦ *nm* compound; (*MED*) preparation.

compulsar [kompul'sar] *vt* (*cotejar*) to collate, compare; (*JUR*) to make an attested copy of.

compulsivo, a [kompul'sißo, a] *adj* compulsive.

compungido, a [kompun'xiðo, a] *adj* remorseful.

compuse [kom'puse] *etc vb* V **componer.**

computador [komputa'ðor] *nm*, **computadora** [komputa'ðora] *nf* computer; ~ **central** mainframe computer; ~ **especializado** dedicated computer; ~ **personal** personal computer.

computar [kompu'tar] *vt* to calculate, compute.

cómputo ['komputo] *nm* calculation.

comulgar [komul'ɣar] *vi* to receive communion.

comulgue [ko'mulɣe] *etc vb* V **comulgar.**

común [ko'mun] *adj* (*gen*) common; (*corriente*) ordinary; **por lo** ~ generally ♦ *nm*: **el** ~ the community.

comuna [ko'muna] *nf* commune; (*AM*) district.

comunicación [komunika'θjon] *nf* communication; (*informe*) report.

comunicado [komuni'kaðo] *nm* announcement; ~ **de prensa** press release.

comunicar [komuni'kar] *vt* to communicate; (*ARQ*) to connect ♦ *vi* to communicate; to send a report; ~**se** *vr* to communicate; **está comunicando** (*TELEC*) the line's engaged (*BRIT*) o busy (*US*).

comunicativo, a [komunika'tißo, a] *adj* communicative.

comunidad [komuni'ðað] *nf* community; ~ **autónoma** autonomous region; ~ **de vecinos** residents' association; **C~ Económica Europea (CEE)** European Economic Community (EEC); *see boxed note.*

comunión [komu'njon] *nf* communion.

comunique [komu'nike] *etc vb* V **comunicar.**

comunismo [komu'nismo] *nm* communism.

comunista [komu'nista] *adj, nm/f* communist.

comunitario, a [komuni'tarjo, a] *adj* (*de la CE*) Community *cpd*, EC *cpd*.

═══════════════ *PALABRA CLAVE*

con [kon] *prep* **1** (*medio, compañía, modo*) with; **comer** ~ **cuchara** to eat with a spoon; **café** ~ **leche** white coffee; **estoy** ~ **un catarro** I've got a cold; **pasear** ~ **algn** to go for a walk with sb; ~ **habilidad** skilfully

2 (*a pesar de*): ~ **todo, merece nuestros respetos** all the same o even so, he deserves our respect

3 (*para* ~): **es muy bueno para** ~ **los niños** he's very good with (the) children

4 (+*infin*): ~ **llegar tan tarde se quedó sin comer** by arriving o because he arrived so late he missed out on eating;

~ **estudiar un poco apruebas** with a bit of studying you should pass **5** (*queja*): ¡~ **las ganas que tenía de ir!** and I really wanted to go (too)! ♦ *conj*: ~ **que: será suficiente ~ que le escribas** it will be enough if you write to her.

conato [ko'nato] *nm* attempt; ~ **de robo** attempted robbery.
cóncavo, a ['konkaβo, a] *adj* concave.
concebir [konθe'βir] *vt* to conceive; (*imaginar*) to imagine ♦ *vi* to conceive.
conceder [konθe'ðer] *vt* to concede.
concejal, a [konθe'xal, a] *nm/f* town councillor.
concejo [kon'θexo] *nm* council.
concentración [konθentra'θjon] *nf* concentration.
concentrar [konθen'trar] *vt*, ~**se** *vr* to concentrate.
concéntrico, a [kon'θentriko, a] *adj* concentric.
concepción [konθep'θjon] *nf* conception.
concepto [kon'θepto] *nm* concept; **por ~ de** as, by way of; **tener buen ~ de algn** to think highly of sb; **bajo ningún ~** under no circumstances.
conceptuar [konθep'twar] *vt* to judge.
concernir [konθer'nir] *vi*: **en lo que concierne a** concerning.
concertar [konθer'tar] *vt* (*MUS*) to harmonize; (*acordar: precio*) to agree; (: *tratado*) to conclude; (*trato*) to arrange, fix up; (*combinar: esfuerzos*) to coordinate; (*reconciliar: personas*) to reconcile ♦ *vi* to harmonize, be in tune.
concesión [konθe'sjon] *nf* concession; (*COM: fabricación*) licence.
concesionario, a [konθesjo'narjo, a] *nm/f* (*COM*) (licensed) dealer, agent, concessionaire; (: *de venta*) franchisee; (: *de transportes etc*) contractor.
concha ['kontʃa] *nf* shell; (*AM fam!*) cunt (!)
conchabarse [kontʃa'βarse] *vr*: ~ **contra** to gang up on.
conciencia [kon'θjenθja] *nf* (*moral*) conscience; (*conocimiento*) awareness; **libertad de ~** freedom of worship; **tener/tomar ~ de** to be/become aware of; **tener la ~ limpia** *o* **tranquila** to have a clear conscience; **tener plena ~ de** to be fully aware of.
concienciar [konθjen'θjar] *vt* to make aware; ~**se** *vr* to become aware.
concienzudo, a [konθjen'θuðo, a] *adj* conscientious.

concierne [kon'θjerne] *etc vb V* **concernir.**
concierto [kon'θjerto] *etc vb V* **concertar** ♦ *nm* concert; (*obra*) concerto.
conciliación [konθilja'θjon] *nf* conciliation.
conciliar [konθi'ljar] *vt* to reconcile ♦ *adj* (*REL*) of a council; ~ **el sueño** to get to sleep.
concilio [kon'θiljo] *nm* council.
concisión [konθi'sjon] *nf* conciseness.
conciso, a [kon'θiso, a] *adj* concise.
conciudadano, a [konθjuða'ðano, a] *nm/f* fellow citizen.
concluir [konklu'ir] *vt* (*acabar*) to conclude; (*inferir*) to infer, deduce ♦ *vi*, ~**se** *vr* to conclude; **todo ha concluido** it's all over.
conclusión [konklu'sjon] *nf* conclusion; **llegar a la ~ de que ...** to come to the conclusion that ....
concluya [kon'kluja] *etc vb V* **concluir.**
concluyente [konklu'jente] *adj* (*prueba, información*) conclusive.
concordancia [konkor'ðanθja] *nf* agreement.
concordar [konkor'ðar] *vt* to reconcile ♦ *vi* to agree, tally.
concordia [kon'korðja] *nf* harmony.
concretamente [konkreta'mente] *adv* specifically, to be exact.
concretar [konkre'tar] *vt* to make concrete, make more specific; (*problema*) to pinpoint; ~**se** *vr* to become more definite.
concreto, a [kon'kreto, a] *adj, nm* (*AM*) concrete; **en ~** (*en resumen*) to sum up; (*especificamente*) specifically; **no hay nada en ~** there's nothing definite.
concubina [konku'βina] *nf* concubine.
concuerde [kon'kwerðe] *etc vb V* **concordar.**
concupiscencia [konkupis'θenθja] *nf* (*avancia*) greed; (*lujuria*) lustfulness.
concurrencia [konku'rrenθja] *nf* turnout.
concurrido, a [konku'rriðo, a] *a* (*calle*) busy; (*local, reunión*) crowded.
concurrir [konku'rrir] *vi* (*juntarse: ríos*) to meet, come together; (: *personas*) to gather, meet.
concursante [konkur'sante] *nm* competitor.
concursar [konkur'sar] *vi* to compete.
concurso [kon'kurso] *nm* (*de público*) crowd; (*ESCOL, DEPORTE, competencia*) competition; (*COM*) invitation to tender; (*examen*) open competition; (*TV etc*) quiz; (*ayuda*) help, cooperation.
condado [kon'daðo] *nm* county.
condal [kon'dal] *adj*: **la ciudad ~** Barcelona.

conde ['konde] nm count.
condecoración [kondekora'θjon] nf (MIL) medal, decoration.
condecorar [kondeko'rar] vt to decorate.
condena [kon'dena] nf sentence; **cumplir una** ~ to serve a sentence.
condenación [kondena'θjon] nf condemnation; (REL) damnation.
condenado, a [konde'naðo, a] adj (JUR) condemned; (fam: maldito) damned ♦ nm/f (JUR) convicted person.
condenar [konde'nar] vt to condemn; (JUR) to convict; ~**se** vr (JUR) to confess (one's guilt); (REL) to be damned.
condensar [konden'sar] vt to condense.
condesa [kon'desa] nf countess.
condescendencia [kondesθen'denθja] nf condescension; **aceptar algo por** ~ to accept sth so as not to hurt feelings.
condescender [kondesθen'der] vi to acquiesce, comply.
condescienda [kondes'θjenda] etc vb V **condescender**.
condición [kondi'θjon] nf (gen) condition; (rango) social class; **condiciones** nfpl (cualidades) qualities; (estado) condition; **a** ~ **de que** ... on condition that ...; **las condiciones del contrato** the terms of the contract; **condiciones de trabajo** working conditions; **condiciones de venta** conditions of sale.
condicional [kondi'θjo'nal] adj conditional.
condicionamiento [kondiθjona'mjento] nm conditioning.
condicionar [kondiθjo'nar] vt (acondicionar) to condition; ~ **algo a algo** to make sth conditional o dependent on sth.
condimento [kondi'mento] nm seasoning.
condiscípulo, a [kondis'θipulo, a] nm/f fellow student.
condolerse [kondo'lerse] vr to sympathize.
condominio [kondo'minjo] nm (COM) joint ownership; (AM) condominium, apartment.
condón [kon'don] nm condom.
condonar [kondo'nar] vt (JUR: reo) to reprieve; (COM: deuda) to cancel.
cóndor ['kondor] nm condor.
conducente [kondu'θente] adj: ~ **a** conducive to, leading to.
conducir [kondu'θir] vt to take, convey; (ELEC etc) to carry; (AUTO) to drive; (negocio) to manage ♦ vi to drive; (fig) to lead; ~**se** vr to behave.
conducta [kon'dukta] nf conduct, behaviour.
conducto [kon'dukto] nm pipe, tube; (fig)

channel; (ELEC) lead; **por** ~ **de** through.
conductor, a [konduk'tor, a] adj leading, guiding ♦ nm (FÍSICA) conductor; (de vehículo) driver.
conduela [kon'dwela] etc vb V **condolerse**.
conduje [kon'duxe] etc vb V **conducir**.
conduzca [kon'duθka] etc vb V **conducir**.
conectado, a [konek'taðo, a] a (ELEC) connected, plugged in; (INFORM) on-line.
conectar [konek'tar] vt to connect (up), plug in; (INFORM) to toggle on; ~**se** vr (INFORM) to log in (on).
conejillo [kone'xiʎo] nm: ~ **de Indias** guinea pig.
conejo [ko'nexo] nm rabbit.
conexión [konek'sjon] nf connection; (INFORM) logging in (on).
confabularse [konfaβu'larse] vr: ~ **(para hacer algo)** to plot, conspire (to do sth).
confección [konfek'θjon] nf (preparación) preparation, making-up; (industria) clothing industry; (producto) article; **de** ~ (ropa) off-the-peg.
confeccionar [konfe(k)θjo'nar] vt to make (up).
confederación [konfeðera'θjon] nf confederation.
conferencia [konfe'renθja] nf conference; (lección) lecture; (TELEC) call; ~ **de cobro revertido** (TELEC) reversed-charge (BRIT) o collect (US) call; ~ **cumbre** summit (conference).
conferenciante [konferen'θjante] nm/f lecturer.
conferir [konfe'rir] vt to award.
confesar [konfe'sar] vt (admitir) to confess, admit; (error) to acknowledge; (crimen) to own up to.
confesión [konfe'sjon] nf confession.
confesionario [konfesjo'narjo] nm confessional.
confeso, a [kon'feso, a] adj (JUR etc) self-confessed.
confeti [kon'feti] nm confetti.
confiado, a [kon'fjaðo, a] adj (crédulo) trusting; (seguro) confident; (presumido) conceited, vain.
confianza [kon'fjanθa] nf trust; (aliento, confidencia) confidence; (familiaridad) intimacy, familiarity; (pey) vanity, conceit; **margen de** ~ credibility gap; **tener** ~ **con algn** to be on close terms with sb.
confiar [kon'fjar] vt to entrust ♦ vi (fiarse) to trust; (contar con) to rely; ~**se** vr to put one's trust.
confidencia [konfi'ðenθja] nf confidence.
confidencial [konfiðen'θjal] adj

confidential.
confidente [konfi'ðente] *nm/f* confidant/e; (*policía*) informer.
confiera [kon'fjera] *etc vb V* **conferir.**
confiese [kon'fjese] *etc vb V* **confesar.**
configuración [konfiɣura'θjon] *nf* (*tb* INFORM) configuration; **la ~ del terreno** the lie of the land; **~ de bits** (INFORM) bit pattern.
configurar [konfiɣu'rar] *vt* to shape, form.
confín [kon'fin] *nm* limit; **confines** *nmpl* confines, limits.
confinar [konfi'nar] *vi* to confine; (*desterrar*) to banish.
confiriendo [konfi'rjendo] *etc vb V* **conferir.**
confirmación [konfirma'θjon] *nf* confirmation; (REL) Confirmation.
confirmar [konfir'mar] *vt* to confirm; (JUR *etc*) to corroborate; **la excepción confirma la regla** the exception proves the rule.
confiscar [konfis'kar] *vt* to confiscate.
confisque [kon'fiske] *etc vb V* **confiscar.**
confitado, a [konfi'taðo, a] *adj*: **fruta confitada** crystallized fruit.
confite [kon'fite] *nm* sweet (BRIT), candy (US).
confitería [konfite'ria] *nf* confectionery; (*tienda*) confectioner's (shop).
confitura [konfi'tura] *nf* jam.
conflagración [konflaɣra'θjon] *nf* conflagration.
conflictivo, a [konflik'tiβo, a] *adj* (*asunto, propuesta*) controversial; (*país, situación*) troubled.
conflicto [kon'flikto] *nm* conflict; (*fig*) clash; (: *dificultad*): **estar en un ~** to be in a jam; **~ laboral** labour dispute.
confluir [konflu'ir] *vi* (*ríos etc*) to meet; (*gente*) to gather.
confluya [kon'fluja] *etc vb V* **confluir.**
conformar [konfor'mar] *vt* to shape, fashion ♦ *vi* to agree; **~se** *vr* to conform; (*resignarse*) to resign o.s.
conforme [kon'forme] *adj* alike, similar; (*de acuerdo*) agreed, in agreement; (*satisfecho*) satisfied ♦ *adv* as ♦ *excl* agreed! ♦ *nm* agreement ♦ *prep*: **~ a** in accordance with.
conformidad [konformi'ðað] *nf* (*semejanza*) similarity; (*acuerdo*) agreement; (*resignación*) resignation; **de/en ~ con** in accordance with; **dar su ~** to consent.
conformismo [konfor'mismo] *nm* conformism.
conformista [konfor'mista] *nm/f* conformist.

confort, pl conforts [kon'for, kon'for(t)s] *nm* comfort.
confortable [konfor'taβle] *adj* comfortable.
confortar [konfor'tar] *vt* to comfort.
confraternidad [konfraterni'ðað] *nf* brotherhood; **espíritu de ~** feeling of unity.
confraternizar [konfraterni'θar] *vi* to fraternize.
confrontación [konfronta'θjon] *nf* confrontation.
confrontar [konfron'tar] *vt* to confront; (*dos personas*) to bring face to face; (*cotejar*) to compare ♦ *vi* to border.
confundir [konfun'dir] *vt* (*borrar*) to blur; (*equivocar*) to mistake, confuse; (*mezclar*) to mix; (*turbar*) to confuse; **~se** *vr* (*hacerse borroso*) to become blurred; (*turbarse*) to get confused; (*equivocarse*) to make a mistake; (*mezclarse*) to mix.
confusión [konfu'sjon] *nf* confusion.
confusionismo [konfusjo'nismo] *nm* confusion, uncertainty.
confuso, a [kon'fuso, a] *adj* (*gen*) confused; (*recuerdo*) hazy; (*estilo*) obscure.
congelación [konxela'θjon] *nf* freezing; **~ de créditos** credit freeze.
congelado, a [konxe'laðo, a] *adj* frozen ♦ *nmpl*: **~s** frozen food *sg* o foods.
congelador [konxela'ðor] *nm* freezer, deep freeze.
congelar [konxe'lar] *vt* to freeze; **~se** *vr* (*sangre, grasa*) to congeal.
congénere [kon'xenere] *nm/f*: **sus ~s** his peers.
congeniar [konxe'njar] *vi* to get on (BRIT) o along (US) (well).
congénito, a [kon'xenito, a] *adj* congenital.
congestión [konxes'tjon] *nf* congestion.
congestionado, a [konxestjo'naðo, a] *adj* congested.
congestionar [konxestjo'nar] *vt* to congest; **~se** *vr* to become congested; **se le congestionó la cara** his face became flushed.
conglomerado [konglome'raðo] *nm* conglomerate.
Congo ['kongo] *nm*: **el ~** the Congo.
congoja [kon'goxa] *nf* distress, grief.
congraciarse [kongra'θjarse] *vr* to ingratiate o.s.
congratular [kongratu'lar] *vt* to congratulate.
congregación [kongreɣa'θjon] *nf* congregation.

congregar [kongre'xar] *vt*, **~se** *vr* to gather together.

congregue [kon'grexe] *etc vb V* **congregar**.

congresista [kongre'sista] *nm/f* delegate, congressman/woman.

congreso [kon'greso] *nm* congress; **C~ de los Diputados** (*ESP POL*) ≈ House of Commons (*BRIT*), House of Representatives (*US*); *V tb* **Las Cortes (españolas)**.

congrio ['kongrjo] *nm* conger (eel).

congruente [kon'grwente] *adj* congruent, congruous.

conífera [ko'nifera] *nf* conifer.

conjetura [konxe'tura] *nf* guess; (*COM*) guesstimate.

conjeturar [konxetu'rar] *vt* to guess.

conjugación [konxuxa'θjon] *nf* conjugation.

conjugar [konxu'xar] *vt* to combine, fit together; (*LING*) to conjugate.

conjugue [kon'xuxe] *etc vb V* **conjugar**.

conjunción [konxun'θjon] *nf* conjunction.

conjuntivitis [konxunti'βitis] *nf* conjunctivitis.

conjunto, a [kon'xunto, a] *adj* joint, united ♦ *nm* whole; (*MUS*) band; (*vestido*) ensemble; (*INFORM*) set; **en ~** as a whole; **~ integrado de programas** (*INFORM*) integrated software suite.

conjura [kon'xura] *nf* plot, conspiracy.

conjurar [konxu'rar] *vt* (*REL*) to exorcise; (*peligro*) to ward off ♦ *vi* to plot.

conjuro [kon'xuro] *nm* spell.

conllevar [konʎe'βar] *vt* to bear; (*Implicar*) to imply, involve.

conmemoración [konmemora'θjon] *nf* commemoration.

conmemorar [konmemo'rar] *vt* to commemorate.

conmigo [kon'mixo] *pron* with me.

conminar [konmi'nar] *vt* to threaten.

conmiseración [konmisera'θjon] *nf* pity, commiseration.

conmoción [konmo'θjon] *nf* shock; (*POL*) disturbance; (*fig*) upheaval; **~ cerebral** (*MED*) concussion.

conmovedor, a [konmoβe'ðor, a] *adj* touching, moving; (*emocionante*) exciting.

conmover [konmo'βer] *vt* to shake, disturb; (*fig*) to move; **~se** *vr* (*fig*) to be moved.

conmueva [kon'mweβa] *etc vb V* **conmover**.

conmutación [konmuta'θjon] *nf* (*INFORM*) switching; **~ de mensajes** message switching; **~ por paquetes** packet switching.

conmutador [konmuta'ðor] *nm* switch; (*AM TELEC*) switchboard.

conmutar [konmu'tar] *vt* (*JUR*) to commute.

connivencia [konni'βenθja] *nf*: **estar en ~ con** to be in collusion with.

connotación [konnota'θjon] *nf* connotation.

cono ['kono] *nm* cone; **C~ Sur** Southern Cone.

conocedor, a [konoθe'ðor, a] *adj* expert, knowledgeable ♦ *nm/f* expert, connoisseur.

conocer [kono'θer] *vt* to know; (*por primera vez*) to meet, get to know; (*entender*) to know about; (*reconocer*) to recognize; **~se** *vr* (*una persona*) to know o.s.; (*dos personas*) to (get to) know each other; **darse a ~** (*presentarse*) to make o.s. known; **se conoce que ...** (*parece*) apparently ....

conocido, a [kono'θiðo, a] *adj* (well-)known ♦ *nm/f* acquaintance.

conocimiento [konoθi'mjento] *nm* knowledge; (*MED*) consciousness; (*NAUT: tb*: **~ de embarque**) bill of lading; **~s** *nmpl* (*personas*) acquaintances; (*saber*) knowledge *sg*; **hablar con ~ de causa** to speak from experience; **~ (de embarque) aéreo** (*COM*) air waybill.

conozca [ko'noθka] *etc vb V* **conocer**.

conque ['konke] *conj* and so, so then.

conquense [kon'kense] *adj* of o from Cuenca ♦ *nm/f* native o inhabitant of Cuenca.

conquista [kon'kista] *nf* conquest.

conquistador, a [konkista'ðor, a] *adj* conquering ♦ *nm* conqueror.

conquistar [konkis'tar] *vt* (*MIL*) to conquer; (*puesto, simpatía*) to win; (*enamorar*) to win the heart of.

consabido, a [konsa'βiðo, a] *adj* (*frase etc*) old; (*pey*) **las consabidas excusas** the same old excuses.

consagrado, a [konsa'xraðo, a] *adj* (*REL*) consecrated; (*actor*) established.

consagrar [konsa'xrar] *vt* (*REL*) to consecrate; (*fig*) to devote.

consciente [kons'θjente] *adj* conscious; **ser o estar ~ de** to be aware of.

consecución [konseku'θjon] *nf* acquisition; (*de fin*) attainment.

consecuencia [konse'kwenθja] *nf* consequence, outcome; (*firmeza*) consistency; **de ~** of importance.

consecuente [konse'kwente] *adj* consistent.

consecutivo, a [konseku'tiβo, a] *adj* consecutive.

conseguir [konse'ɣir] *vt* to get, obtain; (*sus fines*) to attain.

consejería [konsexe'ria] *nf* (*POL*) ministry (*in a regional government*).

consejero, a [konse'xero, a] *nm/f* adviser, consultant; (*POL*) minister (*in a regional government*); (*COM*) director; (*en comisión*) member.

consejo [kon'sexo] *nm* advice; (*POL*) council; (*COM*) board; **un ~** a piece of advice; **~ de administración** board of directors; **~ de guerra** court-martial; **C~ de Europa** Council of Europe.

consenso [kon'senso] *nm* consensus.

consentido, a [konsen'tiðo, a] *adj* (*mimado*) spoiled.

consentimiento [konsenti'mjento] *nm* consent.

consentir [konsen'tir] *vt* (*permitir, tolerar*) to consent to; (*mimar*) to pamper, spoil ♦ *vi* to agree, consent; **~ que algn haga algo** to allow sb to do sth.

conserje [kon'serxe] *nm* caretaker; (*portero*) porter.

conserva [kon'serβa] *nf*: **en ~** (*alimentos*) tinned (*BRIT*), canned; **~s** tinned *o* canned foods.

conservación [konserβa'θjon] *nf* conservation; (*de alimentos, vida*) preservation.

conservador, a [konserβa'ðor, a] *adj* (*POL*) conservative ♦ *nm/f* conservative.

conservadurismo [konserβaðu'rismo] *nm* (*POL etc*) conservatism.

conservante [konser'ßante] *nm* preservative.

conservar [konser'ßar] *vt* (*gen*) to preserve; (*recursos*) to conserve, keep; (*alimentos, vida*) to preserve; **~se** *vr* to survive.

conservas [kon'serßas] *nfpl*: **~ (alimenticias)** tinned (*BRIT*) *o* canned goods.

conservatorio [konserßa'torjo] *nm* (*MUS*) conservatoire; (*AM*) greenhouse.

considerable [konsiðe'raßle] *adj* considerable.

consideración [konsiðera'θjon] *nf* consideration; (*estimación*) respect; **de ~** important; **De mi** *o* **nuestra (mayor) ~** (*AM*) Dear Sir(s) *o* Madam; **tomar en ~** to take into account.

considerado, a [konsiðe'raðo, a] *adj* (*atento*) considerate; (*respetado*) respected.

considerar [konsiðe'rar] *vt* (*gen*) to

consider; (*meditar*) to think about; (*tener en cuenta*) to take into account.

consienta [kon'sjenta] *etc vb V* **consentir**.

consigna [kon'siɣna] *nf* (*orden*) order, instruction; (*para equipajes*) left-luggage office (*BRIT*), checkroom (*US*).

consignación [konsiɣna'θjon] *nf* consignment; **~ de créditos** allocation of credits.

consignador [konsiɣna'ðor] *nm* (*COM*) consignor.

consignar [konsiɣ'nar] *vt* (*COM*) to send; (*créditos*) to allocate.

consignatario, a [konsiɣna'tarjo, a] *nm/f* (*COM*) consignee.

consigo [kon'siɣo] *etc vb V* **conseguir** ♦ *pron* (*m*) with him; (*f*) with her; (*usted*) with you; (*reflexivo*) with o.s.

consiguiendo [konsi'ɣjendo] *etc vb V* **conseguir**.

consiguiente [konsi'ɣjente] *adj* consequent; **por ~** and so, therefore, consequently.

consintiendo [konsin'tjendo] *etc vb V* **consentir**.

consistente [konsis'tente] *adj* consistent; (*sólido*) solid, firm; (*válido*) sound; **~ en** consisting of.

consistir [konsis'tir] *vi*: **~ en** (*componerse de*) to consist of; (*ser resultado de*) to be due to.

consola [kon'sola] *nf* console, control panel; (*mueble*) console table; **~ de juegos** games console; **~ de mando** (*INFORM*) control console; **~ de visualización** visual display console.

consolación [konsola'θjon] *nf* consolation.

consolar [konso'lar] *vt* to console.

consolidar [konsoli'ðar] *vt* to consolidate.

consomé, *pl* **consomés** [konso'me, konso'mes] *nm* consommé, clear soup.

consonancia [konso'nanθja] *nf* harmony; **en ~ con** in accordance with.

consonante [konso'nante] *adj* consonant, harmonious ♦ *nf* consonant.

consorcio [kon'sorθjo] *nm* (*COM*) consortium, syndicate.

consorte [kon'sorte] *nm/f* consort.

conspicuo, a [kons'pikwo, a] *adj* conspicuous.

conspiración [konspira'θjon] *nf* conspiracy.

conspirador, a [konspira'ðor, a] *nm/f* conspirator.

conspirar [konspi'rar] *vi* to conspire.

constancia [kons'tanθja] *nf* (*gen*) constancy; (*certeza*) certainly; **dejar ~ de algo** to put sth on record.

constante [kons'tante] *adj, nf* constant.

constar [kons'tar] *vi* (*evidenciarse*) to be clear *o* evident; ~ **(en)** to appear (in); ~ **de** to consist of; **hacer** ~ to put on record; **me consta que ...** I have evidence that ...; **que conste que lo hice por ti** believe me, I did it for your own good.

constatar [konsta'tar] *vt* (*controlar*) to check; (*observar*) to note.

constelación [konstela'θjon] *nf* constellation.

consternación [konsterna'θjon] *nf* consternation.

constipado, a [konsti'paðo, a] *adj*: **estar** ~ to have a cold ♦ *nm* cold.

constiparse [konsti'parse] *vr* to catch a cold.

constitución [konstitu'θjon] *nf* constitution; **Día de la C**~ (*ESP*) Constitution Day (*6th December*).

constitucional [konstituθjo'nal] *adj* constitutional.

constituir [konstitu'ir] *vt* (*formar, componer*) to constitute, make up; (*fundar, erigir, ordenar*) to constitute, establish; (*ser*) to be; ~**se** *vr* (*POL etc: cuerpo*) to be composed; (: *fundarse*) to be established.

constitutivo, a [konstitu'tiβo, a] *adj* constitutive, constituent.

constituya [konsti'tuja] *etc vb V* **constituir**.

constituyente [konstitu'jente] *adj* constituent.

constreñir [konstre'ɲir] *vt* (*obligar*) to compel, oblige; (*restringir*) to restrict.

constriño [kons'triɲo] *etc*, **constriñendo** [konstri'ɲendo] *etc vb V* **constreñir**.

construcción [konstruk'θjon] *nf* construction, building.

constructivo, a [konstruk'tiβo, a] *adj* constructive.

constructor, a [konstruk'tor, a] *nm/f* builder.

construir [konstru'ir] *vt* to build, construct.

construyendo [konstru'jendo] *etc vb V* **construir**.

consuelo [kon'swelo] *etc vb V* **consolar** ♦ *nm* consolation, solace.

consuetudinario, a [konswetuði'narjo, a] *adj* customary; **derecho** ~ common law.

cónsul ['konsul] *nm* consul.

consulado [konsu'laðo] *nm* (*sede*) consulate; (*cargo*) consulship.

consulta [kon'sulta] *nf* consultation; (*MED: consultorio*) consulting room; (*INFORM*) enquiry; **horas de** ~ surgery hours; **obra de** ~ reference book.

consultar [konsul'tar] *vt* to consult; ~ **un archivo** (*INFORM*) to interrogate a file.

consultor, a [konsul'tor, a] *nm*: ~ **en dirección de empresas** management consultant.

consultorio [konsul'torjo] *nm* (*MED*) surgery.

consumado, a [konsu'maðo, a] *adj* perfect; (*bribón*) out-and-out.

consumar [konsu'mar] *vt* to complete, carry out; (*crimen*) to commit; (*sentencia*) to carry out.

consumición [konsumi'θjon] *nf* consumption; (*bebida*) drink; (*comida*) food; ~ **mínima** cover charge.

consumido, a [konsu'miðo, a] *adj* (*flaco*) skinny.

consumidor, a [konsumi'ðor, a] *nm/f* consumer.

consumir [konsu'mir] *vt* to consume; ~**se** *vr* to be consumed; (*persona*) to waste away.

consumismo [konsu'mismo] *nm* (*COM*) consumerism.

consumo [kon'sumo] *nm* consumption; **bienes de** ~ consumer goods.

contabilice [kontaβi'liθe] *etc vb V* **contabilizar**.

contabilidad [kontaβili'ðað] *nf* accounting, book-keeping; (*profesión*) accountancy; (*COM*): ~ **analítica** variable costing; ~ **de costos** cost accounting; ~ **de doble partida** double-entry book-keeping; ~ **de gestión** management accounting; ~ **por partida simple** single-entry book-keeping.

contabilizar [kontaβili'θar] *vt* to enter in the accounts.

contable [kon'taβle] *nm/f* bookkeeper; (*licenciado*) accountant; ~ **de costos** (*COM*) cost accountant.

contactar [kontak'tar] *vi*: ~ **con algn** to contact sb.

contacto [kon'takto] *nm* contact; **lentes de** ~ contact lenses; **estar en** ~ **con** to be in touch with.

contado, a [kon'taðo, a] *adj*: ~**s** (*escasos*) numbered, scarce, few ♦ *nm*: **al** ~ for cash; **pagar al** ~ to pay (in) cash; **precio al** ~ cash price.

contador [konta'ðor] *nm* (*aparato*) meter; (*AM: contable*) accountant.

contaduría [kontaðu'ria] *nf* accountant's office.

contagiar [konta'xjar] *vt* (*enfermedad*) to pass on, transmit; (*persona*) to infect; ~**se** *vr* to become infected.

contagio [kon'taxjo] *nm* infection.
contagioso, a [konta'xjoso, a] *adj* infectious; (*fig*) catching.
contaminación [kontamina'θjon] *nf* (*gen*) contamination; (*del ambiente etc*) pollution.
contaminar [kontami'nar] *vt* (*gen*) to contaminate; (*aire, agua*) to pollute; (*fig*) to taint.
contante [kon'tante] *adj*: **dinero ~ (y sonante)** hard cash.
contar [kon'tar] *vt* (*páginas, dinero*) to count; (*anécdota etc*) to tell ♦ *vi* to count; **~se** *vr* to be counted, figure; **~ con** to rely on, count on; **sin ~** not to mention; **le cuento entre mis amigos** I reckon him among my friends.
contemplación [kontempla'θjon] *nf* contemplation; **no andarse con contemplaciones** not to stand on ceremony.
contemplar [kontem'plar] *vt* to contemplate; (*mirar*) to look at.
contemporáneo, a [kontempo'raneo, a] *adj, nm/f* contemporary.
contemporizar [kontempori'θar] *vi*: **~ con** to keep in with.
contención [konten'θjon] *nf* (*JUR*) suit; **muro de ~** retaining wall.
contencioso, a [konten'θjoso, a] *adj* (*JUR etc*) contentious ♦ *nm* (*POL*) conflict, dispute.
contender [konten'der] *vi* to contend; (*en un concurso*) to compete.
contendiente [konten'djente] *nm/f* contestant.
contendrá [konten'dra] *etc vb* V **contener**.
contenedor [kontene'ðor] *nm* container; (*de escombros*) skip; **~ de (la) basura** wheelie-bin (*BRIT*); **~ de vidrio** bottle bank.
contener [konte'ner] *vt* to contain, hold; (*risa etc*) to hold back, contain; **~se** *vr* to control o restrain o.s.
contenga [kon'tenga] *etc vb* V **contener**.
contenido, a [konte'niðo, a] *adj* (*moderado*) restrained; (*risa etc*) suppressed ♦ *nm* contents *pl*, content.
contentar [konten'tar] *vt* (*satisfacer*) to satisfy; (*complacer*) to please; (*COM*) to endorse; **~se** *vr* to be satisfied.
contento, a [kon'tento, a] *adj* contented, content; (*alegre*) pleased; (*feliz*) happy.
contestación [kontesta'θjon] *nf* answer, reply; **~ a la demanda** (*JUR*) defence plea.
contestador [kontesta'ðor] *nm*: **~ automático** answering machine.

contestar [kontes'tar] *vt* to answer (back), reply; (*JUR*) to corroborate, confirm.
contestatario, a [kontes'tarjo, a] *adj* anti-establishment, nonconformist.
contexto [kon'teksto] *nm* context.
contienda [kon'tjenda] *nf* contest, struggle.
contiene [kon'tjene] *etc vb* V **contener**.
contigo [kon'tiɣo] *pron* with you.
contiguo, a [kon'tiɣwo, a] *adj* (*de al lado*) next; (*vecino*) adjacent, adjoining.
continental [kontinen'tal] *adj* continental.
continente [konti'nente] *adj, nm* continent.
contingencia [kontin'xenθja] *nf* contingency; (*riesgo*) risk; (*posibilidad*) eventuality.
contingente [kontin'xente] *adj* contingent ♦ *nm* contingent; (*COM*) quota.
continuación [kontinwa'θjon] *nf* continuation; **a ~** then, next.
continuamente [kon'tinwamente] *adv* (*sin interrupción*) continuously; (*a todas horas*) constantly.
continuar [konti'nwar] *vt* to continue, go on with; (*reanudar*) to resume ♦ *vi* to continue, go on; **~ hablando** to continue talking o to talk.
continuidad [kontinwi'ðað] *nf* continuity.
continuo, a [kon'tinwo, a] *adj* (*sin interrupción*) continuous; (*acción perseverante*) continual.
contonearse [kontone'arse] *vr* (*hombre*) to swagger; (*mujer*) to swing her hips.
contorno [kon'torno] *nm* outline; (*GEO*) contour; **~s** *nmpl* neighbourhood *sg*, surrounding area *sg*.
contorsión [kontor'sjon] *nf* contortion.
contra ['kontra] *prep* against; (*COM: giro*) on ♦ *adv* against ♦ *adj, nm/f* (*POL fam*) counter-revolutionary ♦ *nm* con ♦ *nf*: **la C~ (nicaragüense)** the Contras *pl*.
contraalmirante [kontraalmi'rante] *nm* rear admiral.
contraataque [kontraa'take] *nm* counterattack.
contrabajo [kontra'ßaxo] *nm* double bass.
contrabandista [kontraßan'dista] *nm/f* smuggler.
contrabando [kontra'ßando] *nm* (*acción*) smuggling; (*mercancías*) contraband; **~ de armas** gun-running.
contracción [kontrak'θjon] *nf* contraction.
contrachapado [kontratʃa'paðo] *nm* plywood.
contracorriente [kontrako'rrjente] *nf* cross-current.
contradecir [kontraðe'θir] *vt* to contradict.
contradicción [kontraðik'θjon] *nf*

contradiction; **espíritu de** ~ contrariness.

contradicho [kontra'ðitʃo] pp de **contradecir**.

contradiciendo [kontraði'θjendo] etc vb V **contradecir**.

contradictorio, a [kontraðik'torjo, a] adj contradictory.

contradiga [kontra'ðiɣa] etc, **contradije** [kontra'ðixe], **contradirá** [kontraði'ra] etc vb V **contradecir**.

contraer [kontra'er] vt to contract; (hábito) to acquire; (limitar) to restrict; ~**se** vr to contract; (limitarse) to limit o.s.

contraespionage [kontraespjo'naxe] nm counter-espionage.

contrafuerte [kontra'fwerte] nm (ARQ) buttress.

contragolpe [kontra'ɣolpe] nm backlash.

contrahaga [kontra'aɣa] etc, **contraharé** [kontraa're] etc vb V **contrahacer**.

contrahecho, a [kontra'etʃo, a] pp de **contrahacer** ♦ adj fake; (ANAT) hunchbacked.

contrahice [kontra'iθe] etc vb V **contrahacer**.

contraiga [kon'traiɣa] etc vb V **contraer**.

contraindicaciones [kontraindika'θjones] nfpl (MED) contraindications.

contraje [kon'traxe] etc vb V **contraer**.

contralor [kontra'lor] nm (AM) government accounting inspector.

contraluz [kontra'luθ] nf (FOTO etc) back lighting; **a** ~ against the light.

contramaestre [kontrama'estre] nm foreman.

contraofensiva [kontraofen'siβa] nf counteroffensive.

contraorden [kontra'orðen] nf counter-order, countermand.

contrapartida [kontrapar'tiða] nf (COM) balancing entry; **como** ~ **(de)** in return (for), as o in compensation (for).

contrapelo [kontra'pelo]: **a** ~ adv the wrong way.

contrapesar [kontrape'sar] vt to counterbalance; (fig) to offset.

contrapeso [kontra'peso] nm counterweight; (fig) counterbalance; (COM) makeweight.

contrapondré [kontrapon'dre] etc vb V **contraponer**.

contraponer [kontrapo'ner] vt (cotejar) to compare; (oponer) to oppose.

contraponga [kontra'ponga] etc vb V **contraponer**.

contraportada [kontrapor'taða] nf (de revista) back page.

contraproducente [kontraproðu'θente] adj counterproductive.

contrapuesto [kontra'pwesto] pp de **contraponer**.

contrapunto [kontra'punto] nm counterpoint.

contrapuse [kontra'puse] etc vb V **contraponer**.

contrariar [kontra'rjar] vt (oponerse) to oppose; (poner obstáculo) to impede; (enfadar) to vex.

contrariedad [kontrarje'ðað] nf (oposición) opposition; (obstáculo) obstacle, setback; (disgusto) vexation, annoyance.

contrario, a [kon'trarjo, a] adj contrary; (persona) opposed; (sentido, lado) opposite ♦ nm/f enemy, adversary; (DEPORTE) opponent; **al** ~, **por el** ~ on the contrary; **de lo** ~ otherwise.

Contrarreforma [kontrarre'forma] nf Counter-Reformation.

contrarreloj [kontrarre'lo(x)] nf (tb: **prueba** ~) time trial.

contrarrestar [kontrarres'tar] vt to counteract.

contrarrevolución [kontrarreβolu'θjon] nf counter-revolution.

contrasentido [kontrasen'tiðo] nm contradiction; **es un** ~ **que él ...** it doesn't make sense for him to ... .

contraseña [kontra'seɲa] nf countersign; (frase) password.

contrastar [kontras'tar] vt to resist ♦ vi to contrast.

contraste [kon'traste] nm contrast.

contrata [kon'trata] nf (JUR) written contract; (empleo) hiring.

contratar [kontra'tar] vt (firmar un acuerdo para) to contract for; (empleados, obreros) to hire, engage; (DEPORTE) to sign up; ~**se** vr to sign on.

contratiempo [kontra'tjempo] nm (revés) setback; (accidente) mishap; **a** ~ (MUS) off-beat.

contratista [kontra'tista] nm/f contractor.

contrato [kon'trato] nm contract; ~ **de compraventa** contract of sale; ~ **a precio fijo** fixed-price contract; ~ **a término** forward contract; ~ **de trabajo** contract of employment o service.

contravalor [kontraβa'lor] nm exchange value.

contravención [kontraβen'θjon] nf contravention, violation.

contravendré [kontraβen'dre] etc, **contravenga** [kontra'βenga] etc vb V **contravenir**.

contravenir [kontraβe'nir] vi: ~ **a** to

contravene, violate.
contraventana [kontraßen'tana] _nf_
shutter.
contraviene [kontra'ßjene] _etc_,
contraviniendo [kontraßi'njendo] _etc vb_
V **contravenir**.
contrayendo [kontra'jendo] _vb_ V **contraer**.
contribución [kontrißu'θjon] _nf_ (_municipal
etc_) tax; (_ayuda_) contribution; **exento de
contribuciones** tax-free.
contribuir [kontrißu'ir] _vt, vi_ to contribute;
(_COM_) to pay (in taxes).
contribuyendo [kontrißu'jendo] _etc vb_ V
contribuir.
contribuyente [kontrißu'jente] _nm/f_ (_COM_)
taxpayer; (_que ayuda_) contributor.
contrincante [kontrin'kante] _nm_ opponent,
rival.
control [kon'trol] _nm_ control; (_inspección_)
inspection, check; (_COM_): ~ **de calidad**
quality control; ~ **de cambios** exchange
control; ~ **de costos** cost control; ~ **de
créditos** credit control; ~ **de existencias**
stock control; ~ **de precios** price
control.
controlador, a [kontrola'ðor, a] _nm/f_
controller; ~ **aéreo** air-traffic
controller.
controlar [kontro'lar] _vt_ to control; to
inspect, check; (_COM_) to audit.
controversia [kontro'ßersja] _nf_
controversy.
contubernio [kontu'ßernjo] _nm_ ring,
conspiracy.
contumaz [kontu'maθ] _adj_ obstinate,
stubbornly disobedient.
contundente [kontun'dente] _adj_ (_prueba_)
conclusive; (_fig: argumento_) convincing;
instrumento ~ blunt instrument.
contusión [kontu'sjon] _nf_ bruise.
contuve [kon'tuße] _etc vb_ V **contener**.
convalecencia [kombale'θenθja] _nf_
convalescence.
convalecer [kombale'θer] _vi_ to convalesce,
get better.
convaleciente [kombale'θjente] _adj, nm/f_
convalescent.
convalezca [kombα'leθka] _etc vb_ V
convalecer.
convalidar [kombali'ðar] _vt_ (_título_) to
recognize.
convencer [komben'θer] _vt_ to convince;
(_persuadir_) to persuade.
convencimiento [kombenθi'mjento] _nm_
(_acción_) convincing; (_persuasión_)
persuasion; (_certidumbre_) conviction;
tener el ~ **de que** ... to be convinced
that ... .

convención [komben'θjon] _nf_ convention.
convencional [kombenθjo'nal] _adj_
conventional.
convendré [komben'dre] _etc_, **convenga**
[kom'benga] _etc vb_ V **convenir**.
conveniencia [kombe'njenθja] _nf_
suitability; (_conformidad_) agreement;
(_utilidad, provecho_) usefulness; ~**s** _nfpl_
conventions; (_COM_) property _sg_; **ser de la
~ de algn** to suit sb.
conveniente [kombe'njente] _adj_ suitable;
(_útil_) useful; (_correcto_) fit, proper;
(_aconsejable_) advisable.
convenio [kom'benjo] _nm_ agreement,
treaty; ~ **de nivel crítico** threshold
agreement.
convenir [kombe'nir] _vi_ (_estar de acuerdo_)
to agree; (_ser conveniente_) to suit, be
suitable; **"sueldo a ~"** "salary to be
agreed"; **conviene recordar que** ... it
should be remembered that ....
convento [kom'bento] _nm_ monastery; (_de
monjas_) convent.
convenza [kom'benθa] _etc vb_ V **convencer**.
convergencia [komber'xenθja] _nf_
convergence.
converger [komber'xer], **convergir**
[komber'xir] _vi_ to converge; **sus esfuerzos
convergen a un fin común** their efforts
are directed towards the same
objective.
converja [kom'berxa] _etc vb_ V **converger,
convergir**.
conversación [kombersa'θjon] _nf_
conversation.
conversar [komber'sar] _vi_ to talk,
converse.
conversión [komber'sjon] _nf_ conversion.
converso, a [kom'berso, a] _nm/f_ convert.
convertir [komber'tir] _vt_ to convert;
(_transformar_) to transform, turn; (_COM_)
to (ex)change; ~**se** _vr_ (_REL_) to convert.
convexo, a [kom'bekso, a] _adj_ convex.
convicción [kombik'θjon] _nf_ conviction.
convicto , a [kom'bikto, a] _adj_ convicted;
(_condenado_) condemned.
convidado, a [kombi'ðaðo, a] _nm/f_ guest.
convidar [kombi'ðar] _vt_ to invite.
conviene [kom'bjene] _etc vb_ V **convenir**.
convierta [kom'bjerta] _etc vb_ V **convertir**.
convincente [kombin'θente] _adj_
convincing.
conviniendo [kombi'njendo] _etc vb_ V
convenir.
convirtiendo [kombir'tjendo] _etc vb_ V
convertir.
convite [kom'bite] _nm_ invitation;
(_banquete_) banquet.

convivencia [kombi'ßenθja] *nf* coexistence, living together.

convivir [kombi'ßir] *vi* to live together; (*POL*) to coexist.

convocar [kombo'kar] *vt* to summon, call (together).

convocatoria [komboka'torja] *nf* summons *sg*; (*anuncio*) notice of meeting; (*ESCOL*) examination session.

convoque [kom'boke] *etc vb* V **convocar**.

convoy [kom'boj] *nm* (*FERRO*) train.

convulsión [kombul'sjon] *nf* convulsion; (*POL etc*) upheaval.

conyugal [konju'val] *adj* conjugal; **vida** ~ married life.

cónyuge ['konyuxe] *nm/f* spouse, partner.

coña ['koɲa] *nf*: **tomar algo a** ~ (*fam!*) to take sth as a joke.

coñac, *pl* **coñacs** ['koɲa(k), 'koɲas] *nm* cognac, brandy.

coñazo [ko'ɲaθo] *nm* (*fam*) pain; **dar el** ~ to be a real pain.

coño ['koɲo] (*fam!*) *nm* cunt (*!*); (*AM pey*) Spaniard ♦ *excl* (*enfado*) shit (*!*); (*sorpresa*) bloody hell (*!*); ¡**qué** ~! what a pain in the arse (*!*).

cooperación [koopera'θjon] *nf* cooperation.

cooperar [koope'rar] *vi* to cooperate.

cooperativo, a [koopera'tißo, a] *adj* cooperative ♦ *nf* cooperative.

coordenada [koorðe'naða] *nf* (*MAT*) coordinate; (*fig*): ~**s** *nfpl* guidelines, framework *sg*.

coordinación [koorðina'θjon] *nf* coordination.

coordinador, a [koorðina'ðor, a] *nm/f* coordinator ♦ *nf* coordinating committee.

coordinar [koorði'nar] *vt* to coordinate.

copa ['kopa] *nf* (*tb DEPORTE*) cup; (*vaso*) glass; (*de árbol*) top; (*de sombrero*) crown; ~**s** *nfpl* (*NAIPES*) *one of the suits in the Spanish card deck*; (**tomar una**) ~ (to have a) drink; **ir de** ~**s** to go out for a drink; V *tb* **Baraja Española**.

copar [ko'par] *vt* (*puestos*) to monopolize.

coparticipación [kopartiθipa'θjon] *nf* (*COM*) co-ownership.

COPE *nf abr* (= *Cadena de Ondas Populares Españolas*) *Spanish radio network*.

Copenhague [kope'naxe] *n* Copenhagen.

copete [ko'pete] *nm* tuft (of hair); **de alto** ~ aristocratic, upper-crust (*fam*).

copia ['kopja] *nf* copy; (*ARTE*) replica; (*COM etc*) duplicate; (*INFORM*): ~ **impresa** hard copy; ~ **de respaldo** *o* **de seguridad** backup copy; **hacer** ~ **de seguridad** to

back up; ~ **de trabajo** working copy; ~ **vaciada** dump.

copiadora [kopja'ðora] *nf* photocopier; ~ **al alcohol** spirit duplicator.

copiar [ko'pjar] *vt* to copy; ~ **al pie de la letra** to copy word for word.

copiloto [kopi'loto] *nm* (*AVIAT*) co-pilot; (*AUTO*) co-driver.

copioso, a [ko'pjoso, a] *adj* copious, plentiful.

copita [ko'pita] *nf* (small) glass; (*GOLF*) tee.

copla ['kopla] *nf* verse; (*canción*) (*popular*) song.

copo ['kopo] *nm*: ~**s de maíz** cornflakes; ~ **de nieve** snowflake.

coprocesador [koproθesa'ðor] *nm* (*INFORM*) co-processor.

coproducción [koproðuk'θjon] *nf* (*CINE etc*) joint production.

copropietarios [kopropje'tarjos] *nmpl* (*COM*) joint owners.

cópula ['kopula] *nf* copulation.

copular [kopu'lar] *vi* to copulate.

coqueta [ko'keta] *adj* flirtatious, coquettish ♦ *nf* (*mujer*) flirt.

coquetear [kokete'ar] *vi* to flirt.

coraje [ko'raxe] *nm* courage; (*ánimo*) spirit; (*ira*) anger.

coral [ko'ral] *adj* choral ♦ *nf* choir ♦ *nm* (*ZOOL*) coral.

Corán [ko'ran] *nm*: **el** ~ the Koran.

coraza [ko'raθa] *nf* (*armadura*) armour; (*blindaje*) armour-plating.

corazón [kora'θon] *nm* heart; (*BOT*) core; **corazones** *nmpl* (*NAIPES*) hearts; **de buen** ~ kind-hearted; **de todo** ~ wholeheartedly; **estar mal del** ~ to have heart trouble.

corazonada [koraθo'naða] *nf* impulse; (*presentimiento*) presentiment, hunch.

corbata [kor'ßata] *nf* tie.

corbeta [kor'ßeta] *nf* corvette.

Córcega [kor'θexa] *nf* Corsica.

corcel [kor'θel] *nm* steed.

corchea [kor'tʃea] *nf* quaver.

corchete [kor'tʃete] *nm* catch, clasp; ~**s** *nmpl* (*TIP*) square brackets.

corcho ['kortʃo] *nm* cork; (*PESCA*) float.

corcovado, a [korko'ßaðo, a] *adj* hunchbacked ♦ *nm/f* hunchback.

cordel [kor'ðel] *nm* cord, line.

cordero [kor'ðero] *nm* lamb; (*piel*) lambskin.

cordial [kor'ðjal] *adj* cordial ♦ *nm* cordial, tonic.

cordialidad [korðjali'ðað] *nf* warmth, cordiality.

cordillera [korði'ʎera] *nf* range (of mountains).

Córdoba ['korðoβa] *nf* Cordova.

cordobés, esa [korðo'ßes, esa] *adj, nm/f* Cordovan.

cordón [kor'ðon] *nm* (*cuerda*) cord, string; (*de zapatos*) lace; (*ELEC*) flex, wire (*US*); (*MIL etc*) cordon.

cordura [kor'ðura] *nf* (*MED*) sanity; (*fig*) good sense.

Corea [ko'rea] *nf* Korea; ~ **del Norte/Sur** North/South Korea.

coreano, a [kore'ano, a] *adj, nm/f* Korean.

corear [kore'ar] *vt* to chorus.

coreografía [koreoɣra'fia] *nf* choreography.

corista [ko'rista] *nf* (*TEAT etc*) chorus girl.

cornada [kor'naða] *nf* (*TAUR etc*) butt, goring.

córner, *pl* **córners** ['korner, 'korners] *nm* corner (kick).

corneta [kor'neta] *nf* bugle.

cornisa [kor'nisa] *nf* cornice.

Cornualles [kor'nwaʎes] *nm* Cornwall.

cornudo, a [kor'nuðo, a] *adj* (*ZOOL*) horned; (*marido*) cuckolded.

coro ['koro] *nm* chorus; (*conjunto de cantores*) choir.

corolario [koro'larjo] *nm* corollary.

corona [ko'rona] *nf* crown; (*de flores*) garland.

coronación [korona'θjon] *nf* coronation.

coronar [koro'nar] *vt* to crown.

coronel [koro'nel] *nm* colonel.

coronilla [koro'niʎa] *nf* (*ANAT*) crown (of the head); **estar hasta la ~ (de)** to be utterly fed up (with).

corpiño [korpiɲo] *nm* bodice; (*AM: sostén*) bra.

corporación [korpora'θjon] *nf* corporation.

corporal [korpo'ral] *adj* corporal, bodily.

corporativo, a [korpora'tiβo, a] *adj* corporate.

corpulento, a [korpu'lento, a] *adj* (*persona*) well-built.

corral [ko'rral] *nm* (*patio*) farmyard; (*AGR: de aves*) poultry yard; (*redil*) pen.

correa [ko'rrea] *nf* strap; (*cinturón*) belt; (*de perro*) lead, leash; ~ **transportadora** conveyor belt.

correaje [korre'axe] *nm* (*AGR*) harness.

corrección [korrek'θjon] *nf* correction; (*reprensión*) rebuke; (*cortesía*) good manners; (*INFORM*): ~ **por líneas** line editing; ~ **en pantalla** screen editing; ~ **(de pruebas)** (*TIP*) proofreading.

correccional [korrekθjo'nal] *nm* reformatory.

correcto, a [ko'rrekto, a] *adj* correct; (*persona*) well-mannered.

corrector, a [korrek'tor, a] *nm/f:* ~ **de pruebas** proofreader.

corredera [korre'ðera] *nf:* **puerta de ~** sliding door.

corredizo, a [korre'ðiθo, a] *adj* (*puerta etc*) sliding; (*nudo*) running.

corredor, a [korre'ðor, a] *adj* running; (*rápido*) fast ♦ *nm/f* (*DEPORTE*) runner ♦ *nm* (*pasillo*) corridor; (*balcón corrido*) gallery; (*COM*) agent, broker; (*pasillo*) corridor, passage; ~ **de bienes raíces** real-estate broker; ~ **de bolsa** stockbroker; ~ **de seguros** insurance broker.

corregir [korre'xir] *vt* (*error*) to correct; (*amonestar, reprender*) to rebuke, reprimand; ~**se** *vr* to reform.

correo [ko'rreo] *nm* post, mail; (*persona*) courier; **C~s** *nmpl* Post Office *sg*; ~ **aéreo** airmail; ~ **certificado** registered mail; ~ **electrónico** E-mail, electronic mail; ~ **urgente** special delivery; **a vuelta de ~** by return (of post).

correr [ko'rrer] *vt* to run; (*viajar*) to cover, travel; (*riesgo*) to run; (*aventura*) to have; (*cortinas*) to draw; (*cerrojo*) to shoot ♦ *vi* to run; (*líquido*) to run, flow; (*rumor*) to go round; ~**se** *vr* to slide, move; (*colores*) to run; (*fam: tener orgasmo*) to come; **echar a ~** to break into a run; ~ **con los gastos** to pay the expenses; **eso corre de mi cuenta** I'll take care of that.

correspondencia [korrespon'denθja] *nf* correspondence; (*FERRO*) connection; (*reciprocidad*) return; ~ **directa** (*COM*) direct mail.

corresponder [korrespon'der] *vi* to correspond; (*convenir*) to be suitable; (*pertenecer*) to belong; (*tocar*) to concern; (*favor*) to repay; ~**se** *vr* (*por escrito*) to correspond; (*amarse*) to love one another; **"a quien corresponda"** "to whom it may concern".

correspondiente [korrespon'djente] *adj* corresponding; (*respectivo*) respective.

corresponsal [korrespon'sal] *nm/f* (newspaper) correspondent; (*COM*) agent.

corretaje [korre'taxe] *nm* (*COM*) brokerage.

corretear [korrete'ar] *vi* to loiter.

corrido, a [ko'rriðo, a] *adj* (*avergonzado*) abashed; (*fluido*) fluent ♦ *nf* run, dash; (*de toros*) bullfight; **de ~** fluently; **3 noches corridas** 3 nights running; **un kilo ~** a good kilo.

corriente [ko'rrjente] *adj* (*agua*) running;

(*fig*) flowing; (*dinero, cuenta etc*) current; (*común*) ordinary, normal ♦ *nf* current; (*fig: tendencia*) course ♦ *nm* current month; ~ *f* de aire draught; ~ eléctrica electric current; las ~s modernas del arte modern trends in art; estar al ~ de to be informed about.

corrigiendo [korri'xjendo] *etc vb* V corregir.

corrija [ko'rrixa] *etc vb* V corregir.

corrillo [ko'rriʎo] *nm* ring, circle (of people); (*fig*) clique.

corro ['korro] *nm* ring, circle (of people); (*baile*) ring-a-ring-a-roses; la gente hizo ~ the people formed a ring.

corroborar [korroßo'rar] *vt* to corroborate.

corroer [korro'er] *vt* (*tb fig*) to corrode, eat away; (*GEO*) to erode.

corromper [korrom'per] *vt* (*madera*) to rot; (*fig*) to corrupt.

corrompido, a [korrom'piðo, a] *adj* corrupt.

corrosivo, a [korro'sißo, a] *adj* corrosive.

corroyendo [korro'jendo] *etc vb* V corroer.

corrupción [korrup'θjon] *nf* rot, decay; (*fig*) corruption.

corrupto, a [ko'rrupto, a] *adj* corrupt.

corsario [kor'sarjo] *nm* privateer, corsair.

corsé [kor'se] *nm* corset.

corso, a ['korso, a] *adj, nm/f* Corsican.

cortacésped [korta'θespeð] *nm* lawn mower.

cortado, a [kor'taðo, a] *adj* (*con cuchillo*) cut; (*leche*) sour; (*confuso*) confused; (*desconcertado*) embarrassed; (*tímido*) shy ♦ *nm* white coffee (with a little milk).

cortadora [korta'ðora] *nf* cutter, slicer.

cortadura [korta'ðura] *nf* cut.

cortante [kor'tante] *adj* (*viento*) biting; (*frío*) bitter.

cortapisa [korta'pisa] *nf* (*restricción*) restriction; (*traba*) snag.

cortar [kor'tar] *vt* to cut; (*suministro*) to cut off; (*un pasaje*) to cut out; (*comunicación, teléfono*) to cut off ♦ *vi* to cut; (*AM TELEC*) to hang up; ~se *vr* (*turbarse*) to become embarrassed; (*leche*) to turn, curdle; ~ por lo sano to settle things once and for all; ~se el pelo to have one's hair cut; se cortó la línea *o* el teléfono I got cut off.

cortauñas [korta'uɲas] *nm inv* nail clippers *pl*.

corte ['korte] *nm* cut, cutting; (*filo*) edge; (*do tela*) piccc, length, (*COSTURA*) tailoring ♦ *nf* (*real*) (royal) court; ~ y confección dressmaking; ~ de corriente *o* luz power cut; me da ~ pedírselo I'm

embarrassed to ask him for it; ¡qué ~ le di! I left him with no comeback!; C~ Internacional de Justicia International Court of Justice; las C~s the Spanish Parliament *sg*; hacer la ~ a to woo, court; *see boxed note.*

LAS CORTES

The Spanish Parliament, las Cortes (Españolas), *has a lower and an upper chamber, the "Congreso de los Diputados" and the "Senado" respectively. Members of the lower house are called "diputados" and are chosen in general elections by a system of proportional representation. Some Senate members, "senadores", are voted in during general elections, while others are appointed by the regional parliaments.*

---

cortejar [korte'xar] *vt* to court.

cortejo [kor'texo] *nm* entourage; ~ fúnebre funeral procession, cortège.

cortés [kor'tes] *adj* courteous, polite.

cortesano, a [korte'sano, a] *adj* courtly.

cortesía [korte'sia] *nf* courtesy.

corteza [kor'teθa] *nf* (*de árbol*) bark; (*de pan*) crust; (*de fruta*) peel, skin; (*de queso*) rind.

cortijo [kor'tixo] *nm* farmhouse.

cortina [kor'tina] *nf* curtain; ~ de humo smoke screen.

corto, a ['korto, a] *adj* (*breve*) short; (*tímido*) bashful; ~ de luces not very bright; ~ de oído hard of hearing; ~ de vista short-sighted; estar ~ de fondos to be short of funds.

cortocircuito [kortoθir'kwito] *nm* short-circuit.

cortometraje [kortome'traxe] *nm* (*CINE*) short.

Coruña [ko'ruɲa] *nf*: La ~ Corunna.

coruñés, esa [koru'ɲes, esa] *adj* of *o* from Corunna ♦ *nm/f* native *o* inhabitant of Corunna.

corvo, a ['korßo, a] *adj* curved; (*nariz*) hooked ♦ *nf* back of knee.

cosa ['kosa] *nf* thing; (*asunto*) affair; ~ de about; eso es ~ mía that's my business; es poca ~ it's not important; ¡qué ~ más rara! how strange.

cosaco, a [ko'sako, a] *adj, nm/f* Cossack.

coscorrón [kosko'rron] *nm* bump on the head.

cosecha [ko'setʃa] *nf* (*AGR*) harvest; (*acto*) harvesting; (*de vino*) vintage; (*producción*) yield.

cosechadora [koset∫a'ðora] nf combine harvester.

cosechar [kose'tʃar] vt to harvest, gather (in).

coser [ko'ser] vt to sew; (MED) to stitch (up).

cosido [ko'siðo] nm sewing.

cosmético, a [kos'metiko, a] adj, nm cosmetic ♦ nf cosmetics pl.

cosmopolita [kosmopo'lita] adj cosmopolitan.

cosmos ['kosmos] nm cosmos.

coso ['koso] nm bullring.

cosquillas [kos'kiʎas] nfpl: **hacer** ~ to tickle; **tener** ~ to be ticklish.

cosquilleo [koski'ʎeo] nm tickling (sensation).

costa ['kosta] nf (GEO) coast; **C~ Brava** Costa Brava; **C~ Cantábrica** Cantabrian Coast; **C~ de Marfil** Ivory Coast; **C~ del Sol** Costa del Sol; **a** ~ (COM) at cost; **a** ~ **de** at the expense of; **a toda** ~ at any price.

costado [kos'taðo] nm side; **de** ~ (dormir) on one's side; **español por los 4 ~s** Spanish through and through.

costal [kos'tal] nm sack.

costalada [kosta'laða] nf bad fall.

costanera [kosta'nera] nf (AM) (seaside) promenade.

costar [kos'tar] vt (valer) to cost; **me cuesta hablarle** I find it hard to talk to him; **¿cuánto cuesta?** how much does it cost?

Costa Rica [kosta'rika] nf Costa Rica.

costarricense [kostarri'θense], **costarriqueño, a** [kostarri'keɲo, a] adj, nm/f Costa Rican.

coste ['koste] nm (COM): ~ **promedio** average cost; ~**s fijos** fixed costs; V tb **costo**.

costear [koste'ar] vt to pay for; (COM etc) to finance; (NAUT) to sail along the coast of; ~**se** vr (negocio) to pay for itself, cover its costs.

costeño, a [kos'teɲo, a] adj coastal.

costero, a [kos'tero, a] adj coastal, coast cpd.

costilla [kos'tiʎa] nf rib; (CULIN) cutlet.

costo ['kosto] nm cost, price; ~ **directo** direct cost; ~ **de expedición** shipping charges; ~ **de sustitución** replacement cost; ~ **unitario** unit cost; ~ **de la vida** cost of living.

costoso, a [kos'toso, a] adj costly, expensive.

costra ['kostra] nf (corteza) crust; (MED) scab.

costumbre [kos'tumbre] nf custom, habit;

como de ~ as usual.

costura [kos'tura] nf sewing, needlework; (confección) dressmaking; (zurcido) seam.

costurera [kostu'rera] nf dressmaker.

costurero [kostu'rero] nm sewing box o case.

cota ['kota] nf (GEO) height above sea level; (fig) height.

cotarro [ko'tarro] nm: **dirigir el** ~ (fam) to rule the roost.

cotejar [kote'xar] vt to compare.

cotejo [ko'texo] nm comparison.

cotice [ko'tiθe] etc vb V **cotizar**.

cotidiano, a [koti'ðjano, a] adj daily, day to day.

cotilla [ko'tiʎa] nf busybody, gossip.

cotillear [kotiʎe'ar] vi to gossip.

cotilleo [koti'ʎeo] nm gossip(ing).

cotización [kotiθa'θjon] nf (COM) quotation, price; (de club) dues pl.

cotizado, a [koti'θaðo, a] adj (fig) highly-prized.

cotizar [koti'θar] vt (COM) to quote, price; ~**se** vr (fig) to be highly prized; ~**se a** to sell at, fetch; (BOLSA) to stand at, be quoted at.

coto ['koto] nm (terreno cercado) enclosure; (de caza) reserve; (COM) price-fixing agreement; **poner** ~ **a** to put a stop to.

cotorra [ko'torra] nf (ZOOL: loro) parrot; (fam: persona) windbag.

COU [kou] nm abr (ESP: = Curso de Orientación Universitario) one year course leading to final school leaving certificate and university entrance examinations; V tb **sistema educativo**.

coyote [ko'jote] nm coyote, prairie wolf.

coyuntura [kojun'tura] nf (ANAT) joint; (fig) juncture, occasion; **esperar una** ~ **favorable** to await a favourable moment.

coz [koθ] nf kick.

CP nm abr (= computador personal) PC.

C.P. abr (ESP) = Caja Postal.

C.P.A. nf abr (= Caja Postal de Ahorros) Post Office Savings Bank.

CP/M nm abr (= Programa de control para microprocesadores) CP/M.

CPN nm abr (ESP) = Cuerpo de la Policía Nacional.

cps abr (= caracteres por segundo) c.p.s.

crac [krak] nm (ECON) crash.

cráneo ['kraneo] nm skull, cranium.

crápula ['krapula] nf drunkenness.

cráter ['krater] nm crater.

creación [krea'θjon] nf creation.

creador, a [krea'ðor, a] adj creative ♦ nm/f creator.

crear [kre'ar] *vt* to create, make; (*originar*) to originate; (*INFORM*: *archivo*) to create; ~**se** *vr* (*comité etc*) to be set up.
creativo, a [krea'tißo, a] *adj* creative.
crecer [kre'θer] *vi* to grow; (*precio*) to rise; ~**se** *vr* (*engreírse*) to get cocky.
creces ['kreθes]: **con** ~ *adv* amply, fully.
crecido, a [kre'θiðo, a] *adj* (*persona, planta*) full-grown; (*cantidad*) large ♦ *nf* (*de río*) spate, flood.
creciente [kre'θjente] *adj* growing; (*cantidad*) increasing; (*luna*) crescent ♦ *nm* crescent.
crecimiento [kreθi'mjento] *nm* growth; (*aumento*) increase; (*COM*) rise.
credenciales [kreðen'θjales] *nfpl* credentials.
crédito ['kreðito] *nm* credit; **a** ~ on credit; **dar** ~ **a** to believe (in); ~ **al consumidor** consumer credit; ~ **rotativo** *o* **renovable** revolving credit.
credo ['kreðo] *nm* creed.
crédulo, a ['kreðulo, a] *adj* credulous.
creencia [kre'enθja] *nf* belief.
creer [kre'er] *vt, vi* to think, believe; (*considerar*) to think, consider; ~**se** *vr* to believe o.s. (to be); ~ **en** to believe in; ¡**ya lo creo!** I should think so!
creíble [kre'ißle] *adj* credible, believable.
creído, a [kre'iðo, a] *adj* (*engreído*) conceited.
crema ['krema] *adj inv* cream (coloured) ♦ *nf* cream; (*natillas*) custard; **la** ~ **de la sociedad** the cream of society.
cremallera [krema'ʎera] *nf* zip (fastener) (*BRIT*), zipper (*US*).
crematorio [krema'torjo] *nm* crematorium (*BRIT*), crematory (*US*).
cremoso, a [kre'moso, a] *adj* creamy.
crepitar [krepi'tar] *vi* (*fuego*) to crackle.
crepúsculo [kre'puskulo] *nm* twilight, dusk.
crespo, a ['krespo, a] *adj* (*pelo*) curly.
crespón [kres'pon] *nm* crêpe.
cresta ['kresta] *nf* (*GEO, ZOOL*) crest.
Creta ['kreta] *nf* Crete.
cretino, a [kre'tino, a] *adj* cretinous ♦ *nm/f* cretin.
creyendo [kre'jendo] *etc vb V* **creer**.
creyente [kre'jente] *nm/f* believer.
crezca ['kreθka] *etc vb V* **crecer**.
cría ['kria] *etc vb V* **criar** ♦ *nf V* **crío, a**.
criada [kri'aða] *nf V* **criado, a**.
criadero [kria'ðero] *nm* nursery; (*ZOOL*) breeding place.
criadillas [kria'ðiʎas] *nfpl* (*CULIN*) bull's (*o* sheep's) testicles.
criado, a [kri'aðo, a] *nm* servant ♦ *nf*

servant, maid.
criador [kria'ðor] *nm* breeder.
crianza [kri'anθa] *nf* rearing, breeding; (*fig*) breeding; (*MED*) lactation.
criar [kri'ar] *vt* (*amamantar*) to suckle, feed; (*educar*) to bring up; (*producir*) to grow, produce; (*animales*) to breed; ~**se** *vr* to grow (up); ~ **cuervos** to nourish a viper in one's bosom; **Dios los cría y ellos se juntan** birds of a feather flock together.
criatura [kria'tura] *nf* creature; (*niño*) baby, (small) child.
criba ['krißa] *nf* sieve.
cribar [kri'ßar] *vt* to sieve.
crimen ['krimen] *nm* crime; ~ **pasional** crime of passion.
criminal [krimi'nal] *adj, nm/f* criminal.
crin [krin] *nf* (*tb*: ~**es**) mane.
crío, a ['krio, a] *nm/f* (*fam*: *chico*) kid ♦ *nf* (*de animales*) rearing, breeding; (*animal*) young.
criollo, a [kri'oʎo, a] *adj* (*gen*) Creole; (*AM*) native (to America), national ♦ *nm/f* (*gen*) Creole; (*AM*) native American.
cripta ['kripta] *nf* crypt.
crisis ['krisis] *nf inv* crisis; ~ **nerviosa** nervous breakdown.
crisma ['krisma] *nf*: **romperle la** ~ **a algn** (*fam*) to knock sb's block off.
crisol [kri'sol] *nm* (*TEC*) crucible; (*fig*) melting pot.
crispación [krispa'θjon] *nf* tension.
crispar [kris'par] *vt* (*músculo*) to cause to contract; (*nervios*) to set on edge.
cristal [kris'tal] *nm* crystal; (*de ventana*) glass, pane; (*lente*) lens; **de** ~ glass *cpd*; ~ **ahumado/tallado** smoked/cut glass.
cristalería [kristale'ria] *nf* (*tienda*) glassware shop; (*objetos*) glassware.
cristalice [krista'liθe] *etc vb V* **cristalizar**.
cristalino, a [krista'lino, a] *adj* crystalline, (*fig*) clear ♦ *nm* lens of the eye.
cristalizar [kristali'θar] *vt, vi* to crystallize.
cristiandad [kristjan'dað] *nf*,
cristianismo [kristja'nismo] *nm* Christianity.
cristiano, a [kris'tjano, a] *adj, nm/f* Christian; **hablar en** ~ to speak proper Spanish; (*fig*) to speak clearly.
Cristo ['kristo] *nm* (*dios*) Christ; (*crucifijo*) crucifix.
Cristóbal [kris'toßal] *nm*: ~ **Colón** Christopher Columbus.
criterio [kri'terjo] *nm* criterion; (*juicio*) judgement; (*enfoque*) attitude, approach; (*punto de vista*) view, opinion; ~ **de clasificación** (*INFORM*) sort criterion.
criticar [kriti'kar] *vt* to criticize.

crítico, a ['kritiko, a] *adj* critical ♦ *nm* critic ♦ *nf* criticism; (*TEAT etc*) review, notice; **la crítica** the critics *pl.*

critique [kri'tike] *etc vb* V **criticar.**

Croacia [kro'aθja] *nf* Croatia.

croar [kro'ar] *vi* to croak.

croata [kro'ata] *adj, nm/f* Croat(ian) ♦ *nm* (*LING*) Croat(ian).

croissan(t) [krwa'san] *nm* croissant.

crol ['krol] *nm* crawl.

cromado [kro'maðo] *nm* chromium plating, chrome.

cromo ['kromo] *nm* chrome; (*TIP*) coloured print.

cromosoma [kromo'soma] *nm* chromosome.

crónico, a ['kroniko, a] *adj* chronic ♦ *nf* chronicle, account; (*de periódico*) feature, article.

cronología [kronolo'xia] *nf* chronology.

cronológico, a [krono'loxiko, a] *adj* chronological.

cronometraje [kronome'traxe] *nm* timing.

cronometrar [kronome'trar] *vt* to time.

cronómetro [kro'nometro] *nm* (*DEPORTE*) stopwatch; (*TEC etc*) chronometer.

croqueta [kro'keta] *nf* croquette, rissole.

croquis ['krokis] *nm inv* sketch.

cruce ['kruθe] *etc vb* V **cruzar** ♦ *nm* crossing; (*de carreteras*) crossroads; (*AUTO etc*) junction, intersection; (*BIO*: *proceso*) crossbreeding; **luces de ~** dipped headlights.

crucero [kru'θero] *nm* (*NAUT*: *barco*) cruise ship; (: *viaje*) cruise.

crucial [kru'θjal] *adj* crucial.

crucificar [kruθifi'kar] *vt* to crucify; (*fig*) to torment.

crucifijo [kruθi'fixo] *nm* crucifix.

crucifique [kruθi'fike] *etc vb* V **crucificar.**

crucigrama [kruθi'ɣrama] *nm* crossword (puzzle).

crudeza [kru'ðeθa] *nf* (*rigor*) harshness; (*aspereza*) crudeness.

crudo, a ['kruðo, a] *adj* raw; (*no maduro*) unripe; (*petróleo*) crude; (*rudo, cruel*) cruel; (*agua*) hard; (*clima etc*) harsh ♦ *nm* crude (oil).

cruel [krwel] *adj* cruel.

crueldad [krwel'ðað] *nf* cruelty.

cruento, a ['krwento, a] *adj* bloody.

crujido [kru'xiðo] *nm* (*de madera etc*) creak.

crujiente [kru'xjente] *adj* (*galleta etc*) crunchy.

crujir [kru'xir] *vi* (*madera etc*) to creak; (*dedos*) to crack; (*dientes*) to grind; (*nieve, arena*) to crunch.

cruz [kruθ] *nf* cross; (*de moneda*) tails *sg*; (*fig*) burden; ~ **gamada** swastika; **C~ Roja** Red Cross.

cruzado, a [kru'θaðo, a] *adj* crossed ♦ *nm* crusader ♦ *nf* crusade.

cruzar [kru'θar] *vt* to cross; (*palabras*) to exchange; ~**se** *vr* (*líneas etc*) to cross, intersect; (*personas*) to pass each other; ~**se de brazos** to fold one's arms; (*fig*) not to lift a finger to help; ~**se con algn en la calle** to pass sb in the street.

c.s.f. *abr* (= *costo, seguro y flete*) c.i.f.

CSIC [θe'sik] *nm abr* (*ESP ESCOL*) = *Consejo Superior de Investigaciones Científicas.*

cta, c.ᵗᵃ *nf abr* (= *cuenta*) a/c.

cta. cto. *abr* (= *carta de crédito*) L.C.

cte. *abr* (= *corriente, de los corrientes*) inst.

CTNE *nf abr* (*TELEC*) = *Compañía Telefónica Nacional de España.*

c/u *abr* (= *cada uno*) ea.

cuaco ['kwako] *nm* (*AM*) nag.

cuaderno [kwa'ðerno] *nm* notebook; (*de escuela*) exercise book; (*NAUT*) logbook.

cuadra ['kwaðra] *nf* (*caballeriza*) stable; (*AM*) (city) block.

cuadrado, a [kwa'ðraðo, a] *adj* square ♦ *nm* (*MAT*) square.

cuadragésimo, a [kwaðra'xesimo, a] *num* fortieth.

cuadrángulo [kwa'ðrangulo, a] *nm* quadrangle.

cuadrante [kwa'ðrante] *nm* quadrant.

cuadrar [kwa'ðrar] *vt* to square; (*TIP*) to justify ♦ *vi*: ~ **con** (*cuenta*) to square with, tally with; ~**se** *vr* (*soldado*) to stand to attention; ~ **por la derecha/izquierda** to right-/left-justify.

cuadrícula [kwa'ðrikula] *nf* (*TIP etc*) grid, ruled squares.

cuadriculado, a [kwaðriku'laðo, a] *adj*: **papel** ~ squared *o* graph paper.

cuadrilátero [kwaðri'latero] *nm* (*DEPORTE*) boxing ring; (*GEOM*) quadrilateral.

cuadrilla [kwa'ðriʎa] *nf* (*amigos*) party, group; (*pandilla*) gang; (*obreros*) team.

cuadro ['kwaðro] *nm* square; (*PINTURA*) painting; (*TEAT*) scene; (*diagrama*: *tb*: ~ **sinóptico**) chart, table, diagram; (*DEPORTE, MED*) team; (*POL*) executive; ~ **de mandos** control panel; **a ~s** check *cpd.*

cuadruplicarse [kwaðrupli'karse] *vr* to quadruple.

cuádruplo, a ['kwaðruplo, a], **cuádruple** ['kwaðruple] *adj* quadruple.

cuajado, a [kwa'xaðo, a] *adj*: ~ **de** (*fig*) full of ♦ *nf* (*de leche*) curd.

cuajar [kwa'xar] *vt* to thicken; (*leche*) to curdle; (*sangre*) to congeal; (*adornar*) to adorn; (*CULIN*) to set ♦ *vi* (*nieve*) to lie; (*fig*) to become set, become established; (*idea*) to be received, be acceptable; ~se *vr* to curdle; to congeal; (*llenarse*) to fill up.

cuajo ['kwaxo] *nm*: **arrancar algo de** ~ to tear sth out by its roots.

cual [kwal] *adv* like, as ♦ *pron*: **el** ~ *etc* which; (*persona: sujeto*) who; (*: objeto*) whom; **lo** ~ (*relativo*) which; **allá cada** ~ every man to his own taste; **son a** ~ **más gandul** each is as idle as the other; **cada** ~ each one ♦ *adj* such as; **tal** ~ just as it is.

cuál [kwal] *pron interrogativo* which (one), what.

cualesquier(a) [kwales'kjer(a)] *pl de* **cualquier(a)**.

cualidad [kwali'ðað] *nf* quality.

cualificado, a [kwalifi'kaðo, a] *adj* (*obrero*) skilled, qualified.

cualquiera [kwal'kjera], **cualquier** [kwal'kjer], *pl* **cualesquier(a)** *adj* any ♦ *pron* anybody, anyone; (*quienquiera*) whoever; **en cualquier momento** any time; **en cualquier parte** anywhere; **cualquiera que sea** whichever it is; (*persona*) whoever it is.

cuán [kwan] *adv* how.

cuando ['kwando] *adv* when; (*aún si*) if, even if ♦ *conj* (*puesto que*) since ♦ *prep*: **yo,** ~ **niño** ... when I was a child *o* as a child I ...; ~ **no sea así** even if it is not so; ~ **más** at (the) most; ~ **menos** at least; ~ **no** if not, otherwise; **de** ~ **en** ~ from time to time; **ven** ~ **quieras** come when(ever) you like.

cuándo ['kwando] *adv* when; **¿desde** ~**?**, **¿de** ~ **acá?** since when?

cuantía [kwan'tia] *nf* (*alcance*) extent; (*importancia*) importance.

cuantioso, a [kwan't]oso, a] *adj* substantial.

==================== *PALABRA CLAVE*

cuanto, a ['kwanto, a] *adj* **1** (*todo*): **tiene todo** ~ **desea** he's got everything he wants; **le daremos** ~**s ejemplares necesite** we'll give him as many copies as *o* all the copies he needs; ~**s hombres la ven** all the men who see her

2: **unos** ~**s**: **había unos** ~**s periodistas** there were (quite) a few journalists

3 (+*más*): ~ **más vino bebas peor te sentirás** the more wine you drink the worse you'll feel; ~**s más, mejor** the more the merrier

♦ *pron*: **tiene** ~ **desea** he has everything he wants; **tome** ~**/**~**s quiera** take as much/many as you want

♦ *adv*: **en** ~: **en** ~ **profesor** as a teacher; **en** ~ **a mí** as for me; *V tb* **antes**

♦ *conj* **1**: ~ **más gana menos gasta** the more he earns the less he spends; ~ **más joven se es más se es confiado** the younger you are the more trusting you are

2: **en** ~: **en** ~ **llegue/llegué** as soon as I arrive/arrived.

────────────────────

cuánto, a ['kwanto, a] *adj* (*exclamación*) what a lot of; (*interrogativo: sg*) how much?; (*: pl*) how many? ♦ *pron, adv* how; (*interrogativo: sg*) how much?; (*: pl*) how many? ♦ *excl:* **¡**~ **me alegro!** I'm so glad!; **¡cuánta gente!** what a lot of people!; **¿**~ **tiempo?** how long?; **¿**~ **cuesta?** how much does it cost?; **¿a** ~**s estamos?** what's the date?; **¿**~ **hay de aquí a Bilbao?** how far is it from here to Bilbao?; **Señor no sé** ~**s** Mr. So-and-So.

cuarenta [kwa'renta] *num* forty.

cuarentena [kwaren'tena] *nf* (*MED etc*) quarantine; (*conjunto*) forty(-odd).

cuarentón, ona [kwaren'ton, ona] *adj* forty-year-old, fortyish ♦ *nm/f* person of about forty.

cuaresma [kwa'resma] *nf* Lent.

cuarta ['kwarta] *nf V* **cuarto**.

cuartear [kwarte'ar] *vt* to quarter; (*dividir*) to divide up; ~**se** *vr* to crack, split.

cuartel [kwar'tel] *nm* (*de ciudad*) quarter, district; (*MIL*) barracks *pl*; ~ **general** headquarters *pl*.

cuartelazo [kwarte'laθo] *nm* coup, military uprising.

cuarteto [kwar'teto] *nm* quartet.

cuartilla [kwar'tiʎa] *nf* (*hoja*) sheet (of paper); ~**s** *nfpl* (*TIP*) copy *sg*.

cuarto, a ['kwarto, a] *adj* fourth ♦ *nm* (*MAT*) quarter, fourth; (*habitación*) room ♦ *nf* (*MAT*) quarter, fourth; (*palmo*) span; ~ **de baño** bathroom; ~ **de estar** living room; ~ **de hora** quarter (of an) hour; ~ **de kilo** quarter kilo; **no tener un** ~ to be broke (*fam*).

cuarzo ['kwarθo] *nm* quartz.

cuatrero [kwa'trero] *nm* (*AM*) rustler, stock thief.

cuatrimestre [kwatri'mestre] *nm* four-month period.

cuatro ['kwatro] *num* four; **las** ~ four o'clock; **el** ~ **de octubre** (on) the fourth of October; *V tb* **seis**.

cuatrocientos, as [kwatro'θjentos, as] *num* four hundred; *V tb* **seiscientos**.

Cuba ['kußa] *nf* Cuba.

cuba ['kußa] *nf* cask, barrel; **estar como una** ~ (*fam*) to be sloshed.

cubalibre [kußa'lißre] *nm* (white) rum and coke ®.

cubano, a [ku'ßano, a] *adj, nm/f* Cuban.

cubata [ku'ßata] *nm* = **cubalibre**.

cubertería [kußerte'ria] *nf* cutlery.

cúbico, a ['kußiko, a] *adj* cubic.

cubierto, a [ku'ßjerto, a] *pp de* **cubrir** ♦ *adj* covered; (*cielo*) overcast ♦ *nm* cover; (*en la mesa*) place ♦ *nf* cover, covering; (*neumático*) tyre; (*NAUT*) deck; ~**s** *nmpl* cutlery *sg*; **a** ~ **de** covered with *o* in; **precio del** ~ cover charge.

cubil [ku'ßil] *nm* den.

cubilete [kußi'lete] *nm* (*en juegos*) cup.

cubito [ku'ßito] *nm*:~ **de hielo** ice cube.

cubo ['kußo] *nm* cube; (*balde*) bucket, tub; (*TEC*) drum; ~ **de (la) basura** dustbin.

cubrecama [kußre'kama] *nm* bedspread.

cubrir [ku'ßrir] *vt* to cover; (*vacante*) to fill; (*BIO*) to mate with; (*gastos*) to meet; ~**se** *vr* (*cielo*) to become overcast; (*COM: gastos*) to be met *o* paid; (: *deuda*) to be covered; ~ **las formas** to keep up appearances; **lo cubrieron las aguas** the waters closed over it; **el agua casi me cubría** I was almost out of my depth.

cucaracha [kuka'ratʃa] *nf* cockroach.

cuchara [ku'tʃara] *nf* spoon; (*TEC*) scoop.

cucharada [kutʃa'raða] *nf* spoonful; ~ **colmada** heaped spoonful.

cucharadita [kutʃara'ðita] *nf* teaspoonful.

cucharilla [kutʃa'riʎa] *nf* teaspoon.

cucharita [kutʃa'rita] *nf* teaspoon.

cucharón [kutʃa'ron] *nm* ladle.

cuchichear [kutʃitʃe'ar] *vi* to whisper.

cuchicheo [kutʃi'tʃeo] *nm* whispering.

cuchilla [ku'tʃiʎa] *nf* (*large*) knife; (*de arma blanca*) blade; ~ **de afeitar** razor blade; **pasar a** ~ to put to the sword.

cuchillada [kutʃi'ʎaða] *nf* (*golpe*) stab; (*herida*) knife *o* stab wound.

cuchillo [ku'tʃiʎo] *nm* knife.

cuchitril [kutʃi'tril] *nm* hovel; (*habitación etc*) pigsty.

cuclillas [ku'kliʎas] *nfpl*: **en** ~ squatting.

cuco, a ['kuko, a] *adj* pretty; (*astuto*) sharp ♦ *nm* cuckoo.

cucurucho [kuku'rutʃo] *nm* paper cone, cornet.

cuece ['kweθe] *etc vb V* **cocer**.

cuele ['kwele] *etc vb V* **colar**.

cuelgue ['kwelɣe] *etc vb V* **colgar**.

cuello ['kweʎo] *nm* (*ANAT*) neck; (*de vestido, camisa*) collar.

cuenca ['kwenka] *nf* (*ANAT*) eye socket; (*GEO*: *valle*) bowl, deep valley; (: *fluvial*) basin.

cuenco ['kwenko] *nm* (earthenware) bowl.

cuenta ['kwenta] *etc vb V* **contar** ♦ *nf* (*cálculo*) count, counting; (*en café, restaurante*) bill; (*COM*) account; (*de collar*) bead; (*fig*) account; **a fin de** ~**s** in the end; **en resumidas** ~**s** in short; **caer en la** ~ to catch on; **dar** ~ **a algn de sus actos** to account to sb for one's actions; **darse** ~ **de** to realize; **tener en** ~ to bear in mind; **echar** ~**s** to take stock; ~ **atrás** countdown; ~ **corriente/de ahorros/a plazo (fijo)** current/savings/ deposit account; ~ **de asignación** appropriation account; ~ **de caja** cash account; ~ **de capital** capital account; ~ **por cobrar** account receivable; ~ **de crédito** credit *o* loan account; ~ **de gastos e ingresos** income and expenditure account; ~ **por pagar** account payable; **abonar una cantidad en** ~ **a algn** to credit a sum to sb's account; **ajustar** *o* **liquidar una** ~ to settle an account; **pasar la** ~ to send the bill.

cuentagotas [kwenta'ɣotas] *nm inv* (*MED*) dropper; **a** *o* **con** ~ (*fam, fig*) drop by drop, bit by bit.

cuentakilómetros [kwentaki'lometros] *nm inv* (*de distancias*) ≈ milometer, clock; (*velocímetro*) speedometer.

cuentista [kwen'tista] *nm/f* gossip; (*LIT*) short-story writer.

cuento ['kwento] *etc vb V* **contar** ♦ *nm* story; (*LIT*) short story; ~ **de hadas** fairy story; **es el** ~ **de nunca acabar** it's an endless business; **eso no viene a** ~ that's irrelevant.

cuerda ['kwerða] *nf* rope; (*hilo*) string; (*de reloj*) spring; (*MUS*: *de violín etc*) string; (*MAT*) chord; (*ANAT*) cord; ~ **floja** tightrope; ~**s vocales** vocal cords; **dar** ~ **a un reloj** to wind up a clock.

cuerdo, a ['kwerðo, a] *adj* sane; (*prudente*) wise, sensible.

cuerear [kwere'ar] *vt* (*AM*) to skin.

cuerno ['kwerno] *nm* (*ZOOL*: *gen*) horn; (: *de ciervo*) antler; **poner los** ~**s a** (*fam*) to cuckold; **saber a** ~ **quemado** to leave a nasty taste.

cuero ['kwero] *nm* (*ZOOL*) skin, hide; (*TEC*) leather; **en** ~**s** stark naked; ~ **cabelludo** scalp.

cuerpo ['kwerpo] *nm* body; (*cadáver*) corpse; (*fig*) main part; ~ **de bomberos** fire brigade; ~ **diplomático** diplomatic corps; **luchar** ~ **a** ~ to fight hand-to-hand; **tomar** ~ (*plan etc*) to take shape.

cuervo ['kwerßo] *nm* (*ZOOL*) raven, crow; *V* **criar**.

cuesta ['kwesta] *etc vb V* **costar ♦** *nf* slope; (*en camino etc*) hill; ~ **arriba/abajo** uphill/downhill; **a** ~**s** on one's back.

cuestión [kwes'tjon] *nf* matter, question, issue; (*riña*) quarrel, dispute; **eso es otra** ~ that's another matter.

cuestionar [kwestjo'nar] *vt* to question.

cuestionario [kwestjo'narjo] *nm* questionnaire.

cueva ['kweßa] *nf* cave.

cueza ['kweθa] *etc vb V* **cocer**.

cuidado [kwi'ðaðo] *nm* care, carefulness; (*preocupación*) care, worry **♦** *excl* ¡cuidado!, look out!; **eso me tiene sin** ~ I'm not worried about that.

cuidadoso, a [kwiða'ðoso, a] *adj* careful; (*preocupado*) anxious.

cuidar [kwi'ðar] *vt* (*MED*) to care for; (*ocuparse de*) to take care of, look after; (*detalles*) to pay attention to **♦** *vi*: ~ **de** to take care of, look after; ~**se** *vr* to look after o.s.; ~**se de hacer algo** to take care to do something.

cuita ['kwita] *nf* (*preocupación*) worry, trouble; (*pena*) grief.

culata [ku'lata] *nf* (*de fusil*) butt.

culatazo [kula'taθo] *nm* kick, recoil.

culebra [ku'leßra] *nf* snake; ~ **de cascabel** rattlesnake.

culebrear [kuleßre'ar] *vi* to wriggle along; (*río*) to meander.

culebrón [kule'ßron] *nm* (*fam*) soap (opera).

culinario, a [kuli'narjo, a] *adj* culinary, cooking *cpd*.

culminación [kulmina'θjon] *nf* culmination.

culminante [kulmi'nante] *adj*: **momento** ~ climax, highlight, highspot.

culminar [kulmi'nar] *vi* to culminate.

culo ['kulo] *nm* (*fam: asentaderas*) bottom, backside, bum (*BRIT*); (: *ano*) arse(hole) (*BRIT!*), ass(hole) (*US!*); (*de vaso*) bottom.

culpa ['kulpa] *nf* fault; (*JUR*) guilt; ~**s** *nfpl* sins; **por** ~ **de** through, because of; **tener la** ~ **(de)** to be to blame (for).

culpabilidad [kulpaßili'ðað] *nf* guilt.

culpable [kul'paßle] *adj* guilty **♦** *nm/f* culprit; **confesarse** ~ to plead guilty; **declarar** ~ **a algn** to find sb guilty.

culpar [kul'par] *vt* to blame; (*acusar*) to accuse.

cultivadora [kultißa'ðora] *nf* cultivator.

cultivar [kulti'ßar] *vt* to cultivate; (*cosecha*)

to raise; (*talento*) to develop.

cultivo [kul'tißo] *nm* (*acto*) cultivation; (*plantas*) crop; (*BIO*) culture.

culto, a ['kulto, a] *adj* (*cultivado*) cultivated; (*que tiene cultura*) cultured, educated **♦** *nm* (*homenaje*) worship; (*religión*) cult; (*POL etc*) cult.

cultura [kul'tura] *nf* culture.

cultural [kultu'ral] *adj* cultural.

culturismo [kultu'rismo] *nm* body-building.

cumbre ['kumbre] *nf* summit, top; (*fig*) top, height; **conferencia (en la)** ~ summit (*conférence*).

cumpleaños [kumple'aɲos] *nm inv* birthday.

cumplido, a [kum'pliðo, a] *adj* complete, perfect; (*abundante*) plentiful; (*cortés*) courteous **♦** *nm* compliment; **visita de** ~ courtesy call.

cumplidor, a [kumpli'ðor, a] *adj* reliable.

cumplimentar [kumplimen'tar] *vt* to congratulate; (*órdenes*) to carry out.

cumplimiento [kumpli'mjento] *nm* (*de un deber*) fulfilment, execution, performance; (*acabamiento*) completion; (*COM*) expiry, end.

cumplir [kum'plir] *vt* (*orden*) to carry out, obey; (*promesa*) to carry out, fulfil; (*condena*) to serve; (*años*) to reach, attain **♦** *vi* (*pago*) to fall due; (*plazo*) to expire; ~**se** *vr* (*plazo*) to expire; (*plan etc*) to be fulfilled; (*vaticinio*) to come true; **hoy cumple dieciocho años** he is eighteen today; ~ **con** (*deberes*) to carry out, fulfil.

cúmulo ['kumulo] *nm* (*montón*) heap; (*nube*) cumulus.

cuna ['kuna] *nf* cradle, cot; **canción de** ~ lullaby.

cundir [kun'dir] *vi* (*noticia, rumor, pánico*) to spread; (*rendir*) to go a long way.

cuneta [ku'neta] *nf* ditch.

cuña ['kuɲa] *nf* (*TEC*) wedge; (*COM*) advertising spot; (*MED*) bedpan; **tener** ~**s** to have influence.

cuñado, a [ku'ɲaðo, a] *nm/f* brother/sister-in-law.

cuño ['kuɲo] *nm* (*TEC*) die-stamp; (*fig*) stamp.

cuota ['kwota] *nf* (*parte proporcional*) share; (*cotización*) fee, dues *pl*; ~ **inicial** (*COM*) down payment.

cupo ['kupo] *etc vb V* **caber ♦** *nm* quota, share; (*COM*): ~ **de importación** import quota; ~ **de ventas** sales quota.

cupón [ku'pon] *nm* coupon; ~ **de la ONCE** *o* **de los ciegos** ONCE lottery ticket; *V tb* lotería.

cúpula ['kupula] *nf* (*ARQ*) dome.

cura ['kura] *nf* (*curación*) cure; (*método curativo*) treatment ♦ *nm* priest; ~ **de emergencia** emergency treatment.

curación [kura'θjon] *nf* cure; (*acción*) curing.

curado, a [ku'raðo, a] *adj* (*CULIN*) cured; (*pieles*) tanned.

curandero, a [kuran'dero, a] *nm/f* healer.

curar [ku'rar] *vt* (*MED*: *herida*) to treat, dress; (: *enfermo*) to cure; (*CULIN*) to cure, salt; (*cuero*) to tan ♦ *vi*, ~**se** *vr* to get well, recover.

curda ['kurða] (*fam*) *nm* drunk ♦ *nf*: **agarrar una/estar** ~ to get/be sloshed.

curiosear [kurjose'ar] *vt* to glance at, look over ♦ *vi* to look round, wander round; (*explorar*) to poke about.

curiosidad [kurjosi'ðað] *nf* curiosity.

curioso, a [ku'rjoso, a] *adj* curious; (*aseado*) neat ♦ *nm/f* bystander, onlooker; ¡qué ~! how odd!

curita [ku'rita] *nf* (*AM*) sticking plaster.

currante [ku'rrante] *nm/f* (*fam*) worker.

currar [ku'rrar] *vi* (*fam*), **currelar** [kurre'lar] *vi* (*fam*) to work.

currículo [ku'rrikulo] *nm*, **currículum** [ku'rrikulum] *nm* curriculum vitae.

curro ['kurro] *nm* (*fam*) work, job.

cursar [kur'sar] *vt* (*ESCOL*) to study.

cursi ['kursi] *adj* (*fam*) pretentious; (: *amanerado*) affected.

cursilada [kursi'laða] *nf*: ¡qué ~! how tacky!

cursilería [kursile'ria] *nf* (*vulgaridad*) bad taste; (*amaneramiento*) affectation.

cursillo [kur'siʎo] *nm* short course.

cursiva [kur'sißa] *nf* italics *pl*.

curso ['kurso] *nm* (*dirección*) course; (*fig*) progress; (*ESCOL*) school year; (*UNIV*) academic year; **en** ~ (*año*) current; (*proceso*) going on, under way; **moneda de** ~ **legal** legal tender.

cursor [kur'sor] *nm* (*INFORM*) cursor; (*TEC*) slide.

curtido, a [kur'tiðo, a] *adj* (*cara etc*) weather-beaten; (*fig*: *persona*) experienced.

curtir [kur'tir] *vt* (*piel*) to tan; (*fig*) to harden.

curvo, a ['kurßo, a] *adj* (*gen*) curved; (*torcido*) bent ♦ *nf* (*gen*) curve, bend; **curva de rentabilidad** (*COM*) break-even chart.

cúspide ['kuspiðe] *nf* (*GEO*) summit, peak; (*fig*) top, pinnacle.

custodia [kus'toðja] *nf* (*cuidado*) safekeeping; (*JUR*) custody.

custodiar [kusto'ðjar] *vt* (*conservar*) to keep, take care of; (*vigilar*) to guard.

custodio [kus'toðjo] *nm* guardian, keeper.

cutáneo, a [ku'taneo, a] *adj* skin *cpd*.

cutícula [ku'tikula] *nf* cuticle.

cutis ['kutis] *nm inv* skin, complexion.

cutre ['kutre] *adj* (*fam*: *lugar*) grotty; (: *persona*) naff.

cuyo, a ['kujo, a] *pron* (*de quien*) whose; (*de que*) whose, of which; **la señora en cuya casa me hospedé** the lady in whose house I stayed; **el asunto cuyos detalles conoces** the affair the details of which you know; **por** ~ **motivo** for which reason.

C.V. *abr* (= *caballos de vapor*) H.P.

C y F *abr* (= *costo y flete*) C & F.

D d

D, d [de] *nf* (*letre*) D, d; **D de Dolores** D for David (*BRIT*), D for Dog (*US*).

D. *abr* = **Don.**

D.ª *abr* = **Doña.**

dactilar [dakti'lar] *adj*: **huellas** ~**es** fingerprints.

dactilógrafo, a [dakti'loɣrafo, a] *nm/f* typist.

dádiva ['daðißa] *nf* (*donación*) donation; (*regalo*) gift.

dadivoso, a [daði'ßoso, a] *adj* generous.

dado, a ['daðo, a] *pp de* **dar** ♦ *nm* die; ~**s** *nmpl* dice ♦ *adj*: **en un momento** ~ at a certain point; **ser** ~ **a** (*hacer algo*) to be very fond of (doing sth); ~ **que** *conj* given that.

daga ['daɣa] *nf* dagger.

daltónico, a [dal'toniko, a] *adj* colour-blind.

daltonismo [dalto'nismo] *nm* colour blindness.

dama ['dama] *nf* (*gen*) lady; (*AJEDREZ*) queen; ~**s** *nfpl* draughts; **primera** ~ (*TEAT*) leading lady; (*POL*) president's wife, first lady (*US*); ~ **de honor** (*de reina*) lady-in-waiting; (*de novia*) bridesmaid.

damasco [da'masko] *nm* (*tela*) damask; (*AM*: *árbol*) apricot tree; (: *fruta*) apricot.

damnificado, a [damnifi'kaðo, a] *nm/f*: **los**

~s the victims.
damnificar [damnifi'kar] *vt* to harm;
(*persona*) to injure.
damnifique [damni'fike] *etc vb* V
damnificar.
dance ['danθe] *etc vb* V danzar.
danés, esa [da'nes, esa] *adj* Danish ♦ *nm/f*
Dane ♦ *nm* (*LING*) Danish.
Danubio [da'nuβjo] *nm* Danube.
danza ['danθa] *nf* (*gen*) dancing; (*una* ~)
dance.
danzar [dan'θar] *vt, vi* to dance.
danzarín, ina [danθa'rin, ina] *nm/f* dancer.
dañar [da'ɲar] *vt* (*objeto*) to damage;
(*persona*) to hurt; (*estropear*) to spoil;
~**se** *vr* (*objeto*) to get damaged.
dañino, a [da'ɲino, a] *adj* harmful.
daño ['daɲo] *nm* (*a un objeto*) damage; (*a
una persona*) harm, injury; ~**s y
perjuicios** (*JUR*) damages; **hacer** ~ **a** to
damage; (*persona*) to hurt, injure;
hacerse ~ to hurt o.s.
DAO *abr* (=*Diseño Asistido por Ordenador*)
CAD.

═══════════════ PALABRA CLAVE

dar [dar] *vt* **1** (*gen*) to give; (*obra de teatro*)
to put on; (*film*) to show; (*fiesta*) to have;
~ **algo a algn** to give sb sth *o* sth to sb;
~ **una patada a algn/algo** to kick sb/sth,
give sb/sth a kick; ~ **un susto a algn** to
give sb a fright; ~ **de beber a algn** to
give sb a drink
2 (*producir: intereses*) to yield; (*fruta*) to
produce
3 (*locuciones* +*n*): **da gusto escucharle**
it's a pleasure to listen to him; **me da
pena/asco** it frightens/sickens me; V *tb*
paseo *y otros sustantivos*
4 (*considerar*): ~ **algo por descontado/
entendido** to take sth for granted/as
read; ~ **algo por concluido** to consider
sth finished; **le dieron por desaparecido**
they gave him up as lost
5 (*hora*): **el reloj dio las 6** the clock
struck 6 (o'clock)
6: **me da lo mismo** it's all the same to
me; V *tb* **igual, más**
7: **¡y dale!** (*¡otra vez!*) not again!; **estar/
seguir dale que dale** *o* **dale que te pego** *o*
(*AM*) **dale y dale** to go/keep on and on
♦ *vi* **1**: ~ **a** (*habitación*) to overlook, look
on to; (*accionar: botón etc*) to press, hit
2: ~ **con: dimos con él dos horas más
tarde** we came across him two hours
later; **al final di con la solución** I
eventually came up with the answer
3: ~ **en** (*blanco, suelo*) to hit; **el sol me da**

en la cara the sun is shining (right) in
my face
4: ~ **de sí** (*zapatos etc*) to stretch, give
5: ~ **para** to be enough for; **nuestro
presupuesto no da para más** our
budget's really tight
6: ~ **por: le ha dado por estudiar música**
now he's into studying music
7: ~ **que hablar** to set people talking;
una película que da que pensar a
thought-provoking film
♦ ~**se** *vr* **1**: ~**se un baño** to have a bath;
~**se un golpe** to hit o.s.
2: ~**se por vencido** to give up; **con eso
me doy por satisfecho** I'd settle for that
3 (*ocurrir*): **se han dado muchos casos**
there have been a lot of cases
4: ~**se a: se ha dado a la bebida** he's
taken to drinking
5: **se me dan bien/mal las ciencias** I'm
good/bad at science
6: **dárselas de: se las da de experto** he
fancies himself *o* poses as an expert.

dardo ['darðo] *nm* dart.
dársena ['darsena] *nf* (*NAUT*) dock.
datar [da'tar] *vi*: ~ **de** to date from.
dátil ['datil] *nm* date.
dativo [da'tiβo] *nm* (*LING*) dative.
dato ['dato] *nm* fact, piece of information;
(*MAT*) datum; ~**s** *nmpl* (*INFORM*) data; ~**s
de entrada/salida** input/output data; ~**s
personales** personal particulars.
dcha. *abr* (= derecha) r.h.
d. de J. C. *abr* (= después de Jesucristo)
A.D.

═══════════════ PALABRA CLAVE

de [de] *prep* (*de*+*el* = *del*) **1** (*posesión,
pertenencia*) of; **la casa** ~ **Isabel/mis
padres** Isabel's/my parents' house; **es** ~
ellos/ella it's theirs/hers; **un libro** ~
Unamuno a book by Unamuno
2 (*origen, distancia, con números*) from;
soy ~ **Gijón** I'm from Gijón; ~ **8 a 20**
from 8 to 20; **5 metros** ~ **largo** 5 metres
long; **salir del cine** to go out of *o* leave
the cinema; ~ ... **en** ... from ... to ...; ~ **2
en 2** 2 by 2, 2 at a time; **9** ~ **cada 10** 9 out
of every 10
3 (*valor descriptivo*): **una copa** ~ **vino** a
glass of wine; **una silla** ~ **madera** a
wooden chair; **la mesa** ~ **la cocina** the
kitchen table; **un viaje** ~ **dos días** a two-
day journey; **un billete** ~ **1000 pesetas** a
1000 peseta note; **un niño** ~ **tres años** a
three-year-old (child); **una máquina** ~
coser a sewing machine; **la ciudad** ~

Madrid the city of Madrid; **el tonto** ~ **Juan** that idiot Juan; **ir vestido** ~ **gris** to be dressed in grey; **la niña del vestido azul** the girl in the blue dress; **la chica del pelo largo** the girl with long hair; **trabaja** ~ **profesora** she works as a teacher; ~ **lado** sideways; ~ **atrás/ delante** rear/front
4 (*hora, tiempo*): **a las 8** ~ **la mañana** at 8 o'clock in the morning; ~ **día/noche** by day/night; ~ **hoy en ocho días** a week from now; ~ **niño era gordo** as a child he was fat
5 (*comparaciones*): **más/menos** ~ **cien personas** more/less than a hundred people; **el más caro** ~ **la tienda** the most expensive in the shop; **menos/más** ~ **lo pensado** less/more than expected
6 (*causa*): **del calor** from the heat; ~ **puro tonto** out of sheer stupidity
7 (*tema*) about; **clases** ~ **inglés** English classes; **¿sabes algo** ~ **él?** do you know anything about him?; **un libro** ~ **física** a physics book
8 (*adj* + *de* + *infin*): **fácil** ~ **entender** easy to understand
9 (*oraciones pasivas*): **fue respetado** ~ **todos** he was loved by all
10 (*condicional* + *infin*) if; ~ **ser posible** if possible; ~ **no terminarlo hoy** if I *etc* don't finish it today.

dé [de] *vb V* **dar**.
deambular [deambu'lar] *vi* to stroll, wander.
debajo [de'ßaxo] *adv* underneath; ~ **de** below, under; **por** ~ **de** beneath.
debate [de'ßate] *nm* debate.
debatir [deßa'tir] *vt* to debate; ~**se** *vr* to struggle.
debe ['deße] *nm* (*en cuenta*) debit side; ~ **y haber** debit and credit.
deber [de'ßer] *nm* duty ♦ *vt* to owe ♦ *vi*: **debe (de)** it must, it should; ~**se** *vr*: ~**se a** to be owing *o* due to; ~**es** *nmpl* (*ESCOL*) homework *sg*; **debo hacerlo** I must do it; **debe de ir** he should go; **¿qué** *o* **cuánto le debo?** how much is it?
debidamente [deßiða'mente] *adv* properly; (*rellenar: documento, solicitud*) duly.
debido, a [de'ßiðo, a] *adj* proper, due; ~ **a** due to, because of; **en debida forma** duly.
débil ['deßil] *adj* weak; (*persona: físicamente*) feeble; (*salud*) poor; (*voz, ruido*) faint; (*luz*) dim.
debilidad [deßili'ðað] *nf* weakness; feebleness; dimness; **tener** ~ **por algn** to

have a soft spot for sb.
debilitar [deßili'tar] *vt* to weaken; ~**se** *vr* to grow weak.
débito ['deßito] *nm* debit; (*deuda*) debt.
debutante [deßu'tante] *nm/f* beginner.
debutar [deßu'tar] *vi* to make one's debut.
década ['dekaða] *nf* decade.
decadencia [deka'ðenθja] *nf* (*estado*) decadence; (*proceso*) decline, decay.
decadente [deka'ðente] *adj* decadent.
decaer [deka'er] *vi* (*declinar*) to decline; (*debilitarse*) to weaken; (*salud*) to fail; (*negocio*) to fall off.
decaído, a [deka'iðo, a] *adj*: **estar** ~ (*persona*) to be down.
decaiga [de'kaiɣa] *etc vb V* **decaer**.
decaimiento [dekai'mjento] *nm* (*declinación*) decline; (*desaliento*) discouragement; (*MED: depresión*) depression.
decanato [deka'nato] *nm* (*cargo*) deanship; (*despacho*) dean's office.
decano, a [de'kano, a] *nm/f* (*UNIV etc*) dean; (*de grupo*) senior member.
decantar [dekan'tar] *vt* (*vino*) to decant.
decapitar [dekapi'tar] *vt* to behead.
decayendo [deka'jendo] *etc vb V* **decaer**.
decena [de'θena] *nf*: **una** ~ ten (or so).
decencia [de'θenθja] *nf* (*modestia*) modesty; (*honestidad*) respectability.
decenio [de'θenjo] *nm* decade.
decente [de'θente] *adj* (*correcto*) proper; (*honesto*) respectable.
decepción [deθep'θjon] *nf* disappointment.
decepcionante [deθepθjo'nante] *adj* disappointing.
decepcionar [deθepθjo'nar] *vt* to disappoint.
decibelio [deθi'ßeljo] *nm* decibel.
decidido, a [deθi'ðiðo, a] *a* decided; (*resuelto*) resolute.
decidir [deθi'ðir] *vt* (*persuadir*) to convince, persuade; (*resolver*) to decide ♦ *vi* to decide; ~**se** *vr*: ~**se a** to make up one's mind to; ~**se por** to decide *o* settle on, choose.
decimal [deθi'mal] *adj, nm* decimal.
décimo, a ['deθimo, a] *num* tenth ♦ *nf* (*MAT*) tenth; **tiene unas** ~**as de fiebre** he has a slight temperature.
decimoctavo, a [deθimok'taßo, a] *num* eighteenth; *V tb* **sexto**.
decimocuarto, a [deθimo'kwarto, a] *num* fourteenth; *V tb* **sexto**.
decimonoveno, a [deθimono'ßeno, a] *num* nineteenth; *V tb* **sexto**.
decimoquinto, a [deθimo'kinto, a] *num* fifteenth; *V tb* **sexto**.

decimoséptimo, a [deθimo'septimo, a] *num* seventeenth; *V tb* **sexto**.

decimosexto, a [deθimo'seksto, a] *num* sixteenth; *V tb* **sexto**.

decimotercero, a [deθimoter'θero, a] *num* thirteenth; *V tb* **sexto**.

decir [de'θir] *vt* (*expresar*) to say; (*contar*) to tell; (*hablar*) to speak; (*indicar*) to show; (*revelar*) to reveal; (*fam: nombrar*) to call ♦ *nm* saying; **~se** *vr*: **se dice** it is said, they say; (*se cuenta*) the story goes; **¿cómo se dice en inglés "cursi"?** what's the English for "cursi"?; **~ para** *o* **entre sí** to say to o.s.; **~ por ~** to talk for talking's sake; **dar que ~ (a la gente)** to make people talk; **querer ~** to mean; **es ~** that is to say, namely; **ni que ~ tiene que** ... it goes without saying that ...; **como quien dice** so to speak; **¡quién lo diría!** would you believe it!; **el qué dirán** gossip; **¡diga!, ¡dígame!** (*en tienda etc*) can I help you?; (*TELEC*) hello?; **le dije que fuera más tarde** I told her to go later; **es un ~** it's just a phrase.

decisión [deθi'sjon] *nf* decision; (*firmeza*) decisiveness; (*voluntad*) determination.

decisivo, a [deθi'siβo, a] *adj* decisive.

declamar [dekla'mar] *vt, vi* to declaim; (*versos etc*) to recite.

declaración [deklara'θjon] *nf* (*manifestación*) statement; (*explicación*) explanation; (*JUR: testimonio*) evidence; **~ de derechos** (*POL*) bill of rights; **~ de impuestos** (*COM*) tax return; **~ de ingresos** *o* **de la renta** income tax return; **~ jurada** affidavit; **falsa ~** (*JUR*) misrepresentation.

declarar [dekla'rar] *vt* to declare ♦ *vi* to declare; (*JUR*) to testify; **~se** *vr* (*opinión*) to make one's opinion known; (*a una chica*) to propose; (*guerra, incendio*) to break out; **~ culpable/inocente a algn** to find sb guilty/not guilty; **~se culpable/inocente** to plead guilty/not guilty.

declinación [deklina'θjon] *nf* (*decaimiento*) decline; (*LING*) declension.

declinar [dekli'nar] *vt* (*gen, LING*) to decline; (*JUR*) to reject ♦ *vi* (*el día*) to draw to a close.

declive [de'kliβe] *nm* (*cuesta*) slope; (*inclinación*) incline; (*fig*) decline; (*COM: tb:* **~ económico**) slump.

decodificador [dekoðifika'ðor] *nm* (*INFORM*) decoder.

decolorarse [dekolo'rarse] *vr* to become discoloured.

decomisar [dekomi'sar] *vt* to seize, confiscate.

decomiso [deko'miso] *nm* seizure.

decoración [dekora'θjon] *nf* decoration; (*TEAT*) scenery, set; **~ de escaparates** window dressing.

decorado [deko'raðo] *nm* (*CINE, TEAT*) scenery, set.

decorador, a [dekora'ðor, a] *nm/f* (*de interiores*) (interior) decorator; (*TEAT*) stage *o* set designer.

decorar [deko'rar] *vt* to decorate.

decorativo, a [dekora'tiβo, a] *adj* ornamental, decorative.

decoro [de'koro] *nm* (*respeto*) respect; (*dignidad*) decency; (*recato*) propriety.

decoroso, a [deko'roso, a] *adj* (*decente*) decent; (*modesto*) modest; (*digno*) proper.

decrecer [dekre'θer] *vi* to decrease, diminish; (*nivel de agua*) to go down; (*días*) to draw in.

decrépito, a [de'krepito, a] *adj* decrepit.

decretar [dekre'tar] *vt* to decree.

decreto [de'kreto] *nm* decree; (*POL*) act.

decreto-ley [dekreto'lei], *pl* **decretos-leyes** *nm* decree.

decrezca [de'kreθka] *etc vb V* **decrecer**.

decúbito [de'kuβito] *nm* (*MED*): **~ prono/supino** prone/supine position.

dedal [de'ðal] *nm* thimble.

dedalera [deða'lera] *nf* foxglove.

dédalo [deðalo] *nm* (*laberinto*) labyrinth; (*fig*) tangle, mess.

dedicación [deðika'θjon] *nf* dedication; **con ~ exclusiva** *o* **plena** full-time.

dedicar [deði'kar] *vt* (*libro*) to dedicate; (*tiempo, dinero*) to devote; **~se** *vr*: **~se a** to devote o.s. to (*hacer algo* doing sth); (*carrera, estudio*) to go in for, take up; **¿a qué se dedica usted?** what do you do (for a living)?

dedicatoria [deðika'torja] *nf* (*de libro*) dedication.

dedillo [de'ðiʎo] *nm*: **saber algo al ~** to have sth at one's fingertips.

dedique [de'ðike] *etc vb V* **dedicar**.

dedo ['deðo] *nm* finger; (*de vino etc*) drop; **~ (del pie)** toe; **~ pulgar** thumb; **~ índice** index finger; **~ mayor** *o* **cordial** middle finger; **~ anular** ring finger; **~ meñique** little finger; **contar con los ~s** to count on one's fingers; **comerse los ~s** to get very impatient; **entrar a ~** to get a job by pulling strings; **hacer ~** (*fam*) to hitch (a lift); **poner el ~ en la llaga** to put one's finger on it; **no tiene dos ~s de frente** he's pretty dim.

deducción [deðuk'θjon] *nf* deduction.

deducir [deðu'θir] *vt* (*concluir*) to deduce,

infer; (*COM*) to deduct.

deduje [de'ðuxe] *etc*, **dedujera** [deðu'xera] *etc*, **deduzca** [de'ðuθka] *etc vb V* **deducir**.

defección [defek'θjon] *nf* defection, desertion.

defecto [de'fekto] *nm* defect, flaw; (*de cara*) imperfection; ~ **de pronunciación** speech defect; **por** ~ (*INFORM*) default; ~ **latente** (*COM*) latent defect.

defectuoso, a [defek'twoso, a] *adj* defective, faulty.

defender [defen'der] *vt* to defend; (*ideas*) to uphold; (*causa*) to champion; (*amigos*) to stand up for; ~**se** *vr* to defend o.s.; ~**se bien** to give a good account of o.s.; **me defiendo en inglés** (*fig*) I can get by in English.

defendible [defen'diβle] *adj* defensible.

defensa [de'fensa] *nf* defence; (*NAUT*) fender ♦ *nm* (*DEPORTE*) back; **en** ~ **propia** in self-defence.

defensivo, a [defen'siβo, a] *adj* defensive ♦ *nf*: **a la defensiva** on the defensive.

defensor, a [defen'sor, a] *adj* defending ♦ *nm/f* (*abogado* ~) defending counsel; (*protector*) protector; ~ **del pueblo** (*ESP*) ≈ ombudsman.

deferente [defe'rente] *adj* deferential.

deferir [defe'rir] *vt* (*JUR*) to refer, delegate ♦ *vi*: ~ **a** to defer to.

deficiencia [defi'θjenθja] *nf* deficiency.

deficiente [defi'θjente] *adj* (*defectuoso*) defective; ~ **en** lacking *o* deficient in ♦ *nm/f*: **ser un** ~ **mental** to be mentally handicapped.

déficit, ~s ['defiθit] *nm* (*COM*) deficit; (*fig*) lack, shortage; ~ **presupuestario** budget deficit.

deficitario, a [defiθi'tarjo, a] *adj* (*COM*) in deficit; (*empresa*) loss-making.

defienda [de'fjenda] *etc vb V* **defender**.

defiera [de'fjera] *etc vb V* **deferir**.

definición [defini'θjon] *nf* definition; (*INFORM*: *de pantalla*) resolution.

definido, a [defi'niðo, a] *adj* (*tb LING*) definite; **bien** ~ clearly defined; ~ **por el usuario** (*INFORM*) user-defined.

definir [defi'nir] *vt* (*determinar*) to determine, establish; (*decidir*, *INFORM*) to define; (*aclarar*) to clarify.

definitivo, a [defini'tiβo, a] *adj* (*edición*, *texto*) definitive; (*fecha*) definite; **en definitiva** definitively; (*en conclusión*) finally; (*en resumen*) in short.

defiriendo [defi'rjendo] *etc vb V* **deferir**.

deflacionario, a [deflaθjo'narjo, a], **deflacionista** [deflaθjo'nista] *adj*

deflationary.

deflector [deflek'tor] *nm* (*TEC*) baffle.

deforestación [deforesta'θjon] *nf* deforestation.

deformación [deforma'θjon] *nf* (*alteración*) deformation; (*RADIO etc*) distortion.

deformar [defor'mar] *vt* (*gen*) to deform; ~**se** *vr* to become deformed.

deforme [de'forme] *adj* (*informe*) deformed; (*feo*) ugly; (*mal hecho*) misshapen.

deformidad [deformi'ðað] *nf* (*forma anormal*) deformity; (*fig*: *defecto*) (moral) shortcoming.

defraudar [defrau'ðar] *vt* (*decepcionar*) to disappoint; (*estafar*) to cheat; to defraud; ~ **impuestos** to evade tax.

defunción [defun'θjon] *nf* decease, demise.

degeneración [dexenera'θjon] *nf* (*de las células*) degeneration; (*moral*) degeneracy.

degenerar [dexene'rar] *vi* to degenerate; (*empeorar*) to get worse.

deglutir [deɣlu'tir] *vt*, *vi* to swallow.

degolladero [deɣoʎa'ðero] *nm* (*ANAT*) throat; (*cadalso*) scaffold; (*matadero*) slaughterhouse.

degollar [deɣo'ʎar] *vt* to slaughter.

degradar [deɣra'ðar] *vt* to debase, degrade; (*INFORM*: *datos*) to corrupt; ~**se** *vr* to demean o.s.

degüelle [de'ɣweʎe] *etc vb V* **degollar**.

degustación [deɣusta'θjon] *nf* sampling, tasting.

deificar [deifi'kar] *vt* (*persona*) to deify.

deifique [dei'fike] *etc vb V* **deificar**.

dejadez [dexa'ðeθ] *nf* (*negligencia*) neglect; (*descuido*) untidiness, carelessness.

dejado, a [de'xaðo, a] *adj* (*desaliñado*) slovenly; (*negligente*) careless; (*indolente*) lazy.

dejar [de'xar] *vt* (*gen*) to leave; (*permitir*) to allow, let; (*abandonar*) to abandon, forsake; (*actividad*, *empleo*) to give up; (*beneficios*) to produce, yield ♦ *vi*: ~ **de** (*parar*) to stop; ~**se** *vr* (*abandonarse*) to let o.s. go; **no puedo** ~ **de fumar** I can't give up smoking; **no dejes de visitarles** don't fail to visit them; **no dejes de comprar un billete** make sure you buy a ticket; ~ **a un lado** to leave *o* set aside; ~ **caer** to drop; ~ **entrar/salir** to let in/out; ~ **pasar** to let through; **¡déjalo!** (*no te preocupes*) don't worry about it; **te dejo en tu casa** I'll drop you off at your place; **deja mucho que desear** it leaves a lot to be desired; ~**se persuadir** to allow o.s. to *o* let o.s. be persuaded; ¡**déjate de tonterías!** stop messing about!

deje ['dexe] *nm* (trace of) accent.

dejo ['dexo] *nm* (*LING*) accent.

del [del] = **de** + **el**; *V* **de**.

del. *abr* (*ADMIN*: = *Delegación*) district office.

delantal [delan'tal] *nm* apron.

delante [de'lante] *adv* in front; (*enfrente*) opposite; (*adelante*) ahead ♦ *prep*: ~ **de** in front of, before; **la parte de** ~ the front part; **estando otros** ~ with others present.

delantero, a [delan'tero, a] *adj* front; (*patas de animal*) fore ♦ *nm* (*DEPORTE*) forward ♦ *nf* (*de vestido, casa etc*) front part; (*TEAT*) front row; (*DEPORTE*) forward line; **llevar la delantera (a algn)** to be ahead (of sb).

delatar [dela'tar] *vt* to inform on *o* against, betray; **los delató a la policía** he reported them to the police.

delator, a [dela'tor, a] *nm/f* informer.

delegación [deleɣa'θjon] *nf* (*acción, delegados*) delegation; (*COM*: *oficina*) district office, branch; ~ **de poderes** (*POL*) devolution; ~ **de policía** police station.

delegado, a [dele'ɣaðo, a] *nm/f* delegate; (*COM*) agent.

delegar [dele'ɣar] *vt* to delegate.

delegue [de'leɣe] *etc vb V* **delegar**.

deleitar [delei'tar] *vt* to delight; ~**se** *vr*: ~**se con** *o* **en** to delight in, take pleasure in.

deleite [de'leite] *nm* delight, pleasure.

deletrear [deletre'ar] *vt* (*tb fig*) to spell (out).

deletreo [dele'treo] *nm* spelling; (*fig*) interpretation, decipherment.

deleznable [deleθ'naβle] *adj* (*frágil*) fragile; (*fig*: *malo*) poor; (*excusa*) feeble.

delfín [del'fin] *nm* dolphin.

delgadez [delɣa'ðeθ] *nf* thinness, slimness.

delgado, a [del'ɣaðo, a] *adj* thin; (*persona*) slim, thin; (*tierra*) poor; (*tela etc*) light, delicate ♦ *adv*: **hilar (muy)** ~ (*fig*) to split hairs.

deliberación [deliβera'θjon] *nf* deliberation.

deliberar [deliβe'rar] *vt* to debate, discuss ♦ *vi* to deliberate.

delicadeza [delika'ðeθa] *nf* delicacy; (*refinamiento, sutileza*) refinement.

delicado, a [deli'kaðo, a] *adj* delicate; (*sensible*) sensitive; (*rasgos*) dainty; (*gusto*) refined; (*situación: difícil*) tricky; (: *violento*) embarrassing; (*punto, tema*) sore; (*persona: difícil de contentar*) hard to

please; (: *sensible*) touchy, hypersensitive; (: *atento*) considerate.

delicia [de'liθja] *nf* delight.

delicioso, a [deli'θjoso, a] *adj* (*gracioso*) delightful; (*exquisito*) delicious.

delictivo, a [delik'tiβo, a] *adj* criminal *cpd*.

delimitar [delimi'tar] *vt* to delimit.

delincuencia [delin'kwenθja] *nf*: ~ **juvenil** juvenile delinquency; **cifras de la** ~ crime rate.

delincuente [delin'kwente] *nm/f* delinquent; (*criminal*) criminal; ~ **sin antecedentes** first offender; ~ **habitual** hardened criminal.

delineante [deline'ante] *nm/f* draughtsman.

delinear [deline'ar] *vt* to delineate; (*dibujo*) to draw; (*contornos, fig*) to outline; ~ **un proyecto** to outline a project.

delinquir [delin'kir] *vi* to commit an offence.

delirante [deli'rante] *adj* delirious.

delirar [deli'rar] *vi* to be delirious, rave; (*fig*: *desatinar*) to talk nonsense.

delirio [de'lirjo] *nm* (*MED*) delirium; (*palabras insensatas*) ravings *pl*; ~ **de grandeza** megalomania; ~ **de persecución** persecution mania; **con** ~ (*fam*) madly; **¡fue el** ~! (*fam*) it was great!

delito [de'lito] *nm* (*gen*) crime; (*infracción*) offence.

delta ['delta] *nm* delta.

demacrado, a [dema'kraðo, a] *adj* emaciated.

demagogia [dema'ɣoxja] *nf* demagogy, demagoguery.

demagogo [dema'ɣoɣo] *nm* demagogue.

demanda [de'manda] *nf* (*pedido, COM*) demand; (*petición*) request; (*pregunta*) inquiry; (*reivindicación*) claim; (*JUR*) action, lawsuit; (*TEAT*) call; (*ELEC*) load; ~ **de pago** demand for payment; **escribir en** ~ **de ayuda** to write asking for help; **entablar** ~ (*JUR*) to sue; **presentar** ~ **de divorcio** to sue for divorce; ~ **final** final demand; ~ **indirecta** derived demand; ~ **de mercado** market demand.

demandado, a [deman'daðo, a] *nm/f* defendant; (*en divorcio*) respondent.

demandante [deman'dante] *nm/f* claimant; (*JUR*) plaintiff.

demandar [deman'dar] *vt* (*gen*) to demand; (*JUR*) to sue, file a lawsuit against, start proceedings against; ~ **a algn por calumnia/daños y perjuicios** to sue sb for libel/damages.

demarcación [demarka'θjon] *nf* (*de terreno*) demarcation.

demás [de'mas] *adj*: los ~ niños the other children, the remaining children ♦ *pron*: los/las ~ the others, the rest (of them); lo ~ the rest (of it); por ~ moreover; (*en vano*) in vain; y ~ etcetera.

demasía [dema'sia] *nf* (*exceso*) excess, surplus; comer en ~ to eat to excess.

demasiado, a [dema'sjaðo, a] *adj*: ~ vino too much wine ♦ *adv* (*antes de adj, adv*) too; ~s libros too many books; ¡es ~! it's too much!; es ~ pesado para levantar it is too heavy to lift; ~ lo sé I know it only too well; hace ~ calor it's too hot.

demencia [de'menθja] *nf* (*locura*) madness.

demencial [demen'θjal] *adj* crazy.

demente [de'mente] *adj* mad, insane ♦ *nm/f* lunatic.

democracia [demo'kraθja] *nf* democracy.

demócrata [de'mokrata] *nm/f* democrat.

democratacristiano, a [demokrata kris'tjano, a], **democristiano, a** [demokris'tjano, a] *adj, nm/f* Christian Democrat.

democrático, a [demo'kratiko, a] *adj* democratic.

demográfico, a [demo'ɣrafiko, a] *adj* demographic, population *cpd*; la explosión demográfica the population explosion.

demoledor, a [demole'ðor, a] *adj* (*fig*: *argumento*) overwhelming; (: *ataque*) shattering.

demoler [demo'ler] *vt* to demolish; (*edificio*) to pull down.

demolición [demoli'θjon] *nf* demolition.

demonio [de'monjo] *nm* devil, demon; ¡~s! hell!; ¿cómo ~s? how the hell?; ¿qué ~s será? what the devil can it be?; ¿dónde ~ lo habré dejado? where the devil can I have left it?; tener el ~ en el cuerpo (*no parar*) to be always on the go.

demora [de'mora] *nf* delay.

demorar [demo'rar] *vt* (*retardar*) to delay, hold back; (*dilatar*) to hold up ♦ *vi* to linger, stay on; ~se *vr* to linger, stay on; (*retrasarse*) to take a long time; ~se en hacer algo (*esp AM*) to take time doing sth.

demos ['demos] *vb* V dar.

demostración [demostra'θjon] *nf* (*gen*, *MAT*) demonstration; (*de cariño, fuerza*) show; (*de teorema*) proof; (*de amistad*) gesture; (*de cólera, gimnasia*) display; ~ comercial commercial exhibition.

demostrar [demos'trar] *vt* (*probar*) to prove; (*mostrar*) to show; (*manifestar*) to demonstrate.

demostrativo, a [demostra'tiβo, a] *adj* demonstrative.

demudado, a [demu'ðaðo, a] *adj* (*rostro*) pale; (*fig*) upset; tener el rostro ~ to look pale.

demudar [demu'ðar] *vt* to change, alter; ~se *vr* (*expresión*) to alter; (*perder color*) to change colour.

demuela [de'mwela] *etc vb* V demoler.

demuestre [de'mwestre] *etc vb* V demostrar.

den [den] *vb* V dar.

denegación [deneɣa'θjon] *nf* refusal.

denegar [dene'ɣar] *vt* (*rechazar*) to refuse; (*negar*) to deny; (*JUR*) to reject.

denegué [dene'ɣe], **deneguemos** [dene'ɣemos] *etc*, **deniego** [de'njeɣo] *etc*, **deniegue** [de'njeɣe] *etc vb* V denegar.

dengue ['denɣe] *nm* dengue o breakbone fever.

denigrante [deni'ɣrante] *adj* (*injurioso*) insulting; (*deshonroso*) degrading.

denigrar [deni'ɣrar] *vt* (*desacreditar*) to denigrate; (*injuriar*) to insult.

denodado, a [deno'ðaðo, a] *adj* bold, brave.

denominación [denomina'θjon] *nf* (*acto*) naming; (*clase*) denomination; ~ de origen *see boxed note*.

DENOMINACIÓN DE ORIGEN

The **denominación de origen**, *often abbreviated to DO, is a prestigious classification awarded to food and wine from designated regions by the Consejo Regulador de la Denominación de Origen. Produce must meet the required standards concerning quality and production methods. It is often associated with "manchego" cheeses and many of the wines from the Rioja and Ribera de Duero regions.*

---

denominador [denomina'ðor] *nm*: ~ común common denominator.

denostar [denos'tar] *vt* to insult.

denotar [deno'tar] *vt* (*indicar*) to indicate, denote.

densidad [densi'ðað] *nf* (*FÍSICA*) density; (*fig*) thickness.

denso, a ['denso, a] *adj* (*apretado*) solid; (*espeso, pastoso*) thick; (*fig*) heavy.

dentado, a [den'taðo, a] *adj* (*rueda*) cogged; (*filo*) jagged; (*sello*) perforated; (*BOT*) dentate.

dentadura [denta'ðura] *nf* (set of) teeth *pl*; ~ postiza false teeth *pl*.

dental [den'tal] *adj* dental.

dentellada [dente'ʎaða] *nf* (*mordisco*) bite, nip; (*señal*) tooth mark; partir algo a ~s to sever sth with one's teeth.

dentera [den'tera] *nf* (*sensación desagradable*) the shivers *pl*.

dentición [denti'θjon] *nf* (*acto*) teething; (*ANAT*) dentition; **estar con la** ~ to be teething.

dentífrico, a [den'tifriko, a] *adj* dental, tooth *cpd* ♦ *nm* toothpaste; **pasta dentífrica** toothpaste.

dentista [den'tista] *nm/f* dentist.

dentro ['dentro] *adv* inside ♦ *prep*: ~ **de** in, inside, within; **allí** ~ in there; **mirar por** ~ to look inside; ~ **de lo posible** as far as possible; ~ **de todo** all in all; ~ **de tres meses** within three months.

denuedo [de'nweðo] *nm* boldness, daring.

denuesto [de'nwesto] *nm* insult.

denuncia [de'nunθja] *nf* (*delación*) denunciation; (*acusación*) accusation; (*de accidente*) report; **hacer** *o* **poner una** ~ to report an incident to the police.

denunciable [denun'θjaßle] *adj* indictable, punishable.

denunciante [denun'θjante] *nm/f* accuser; (*delator*) informer.

denunciar [denun'θjar] *vt* to report; (*delatar*) to inform on *o* against.

Dep. *abr* (= *Departamento*) Dept.; (= *Depósito*) dep.

deparar [depa'rar] *vt* (*brindar*) to provide *o* furnish with; (*suj: futuro, destino*) to have in store for; **los placeres que el viaje nos deparó** the pleasures which the trip afforded us.

departamento [departa'mento] *nm* (*sección administrativa*) department, section; (*AM: piso*) flat (*BRIT*), apartment (*US*); (*distrito*) department, province; ~ **de envíos** (*COM*) dispatch department; ~ **de máquinas** (*NAUT*) engine room.

departir [depar'tir] *vi* to talk, converse.

dependencia [depen'denθja] *nf* dependence; (*POL*) dependency; (*COM*) office, section; (*sucursal*) branch office; (*ARQ: cuarto*) room; ~**s** *nfpl* outbuildings.

depender [depen'der] *vi*: ~ **de** to depend on; (*contar con*) to rely on; (*de autoridad*) to be under, be answerable to; **depende** it (all) depends; **no depende de mí** it's not up to me.

dependienta [depen'djenta] *nf* saleswoman, shop assistant.

dependiente [depen'djente] *adj* dependent ♦ *nm* salesman, shop assistant.

depilación [depila'θjon] *nf* hair removal.

depilar [depi'lar] *vt* (*con cera: piernas*) to wax; (*cejas*) to pluck.

depilatorio, a [depila'torjo, a] *adj*

depilatory ♦ *nm* hair remover.

deplorable [deplo'raßle] *adj* deplorable.

deplorar [deplo'rar] *vt* to deplore.

depondré [depon'dre] *etc vb V* **deponer**.

deponer [depo'ner] *vt* (*armas*) to lay down; (*rey*) to depose; (*gobernante*) to oust; (*ministro*) to remove from office ♦ *vi* (*JUR*) to give evidence; (*declarar*) to make a statement.

deponga [de'ponga] *etc vb V* **deponer**.

deportación [deporta'θjon] *nf* deportation.

deportar [depor'tar] *vt* to deport.

deporte [de'porte] *nm* sport.

deportista [depor'tista] *adj* sports *cpd* ♦ *nm/f* sportsman/woman.

deportivo, a [depor'tißo, a] *adj* (*club, periódico*) sports *cpd* ♦ *nm* sports car.

deposición [deposi'θjon] *nf* (*de funcionario etc*) removal from office; (*JUR: testimonio*) evidence.

depositante [deposi'tante] *nm/f* depositor.

depositar [deposi'tar] *vt* (*dinero*) to deposit; (*mercaderías*) to put away, store; ~**se** *vr* to settle; ~ **la confianza en algn** to place one's trust in sb.

depositario, a [deposi'tarjo, a] *nm/f* trustee; ~ **judicial** official receiver.

depósito [de'posito] *nm* (*gen*) deposit; (*de mercaderías*) warehouse, store; (*de animales, coches*) pound; (*de agua, gasolina etc*) tank; (*en retrete*) cistern; ~ **afianzado** bonded warehouse; ~ **bancario** bank deposit; ~ **de cadáveres** mortuary; ~ **de maderas** timber yard; ~ **de suministro** feeder bin.

depravar [depra'ßar] *vt* to deprave, corrupt; ~**se** *vr* to become depraved.

depreciación [depreθja'θjon] *nf* depreciation.

depreciar [depre'θjar] *vt* to depreciate, reduce the value of; ~**se** *vr* to depreciate, lose value.

depredador, a [depreða'ðor, a] (*ZOOL*) *adj* predatory ♦ *nm* predator.

depredar [depre'ðar] *vt* to pillage.

depresión [depre'sjon] *nf* (*gen, MED*) depression; (*hueco*) hollow; (*en horizonte, camino*) dip; (*merma*) drop; (*ECON*) slump, recession; ~ **nerviosa** nervous breakdown.

deprimente [depri'mente] *adj* depressing.

deprimido, a [depri'miðo, a] *adj* depressed.

deprimir [depri'mir] *vt* to depress; ~**se** *vr* (*persona*) to become depressed.

deprisa [de'prisa] *adv V* **prisa**.

depuesto [de'pwesto] *pp de* **deponer**.

depuración [depura'θjon] *nf* purification; (*POL*) purge; (*INFORM*) debugging.

depurador [depura'ðor] *nm* purifier.

depuradora [depura'ðora] *nf* (*de agua*) water-treatment plant; (*tb*: ~ **de aguas residuales**) sewage farm.

depurar [depu'rar] *vt* to purify; (*purgar*) to purge; (*INFORM*) to debug.

depuse [de'puse] *etc vb V* **deponer**.

der., der.º *abr* (= *derecho*) r.

derecha [de'retʃa] *nf V* **derecho, a**.

derechazo [dere'tʃaθo] *nm* (*BOXEO*) right; (*TENIS*) forehand drive; (*TAUR*) *a pass with the cape*.

derechista [dere'tʃista] (*POL*) *adj* right-wing ♦ *nm/f* right-winger.

derecho, a [de'retʃo, a] *adj* right, right-hand ♦ *nm* (*privilegio*) right; (*título*) claim, title; (*lado*) right(-hand) side; (*leyes*) law ♦ *nf* right(-hand) side ♦ *adv* straight, directly; ~**s** *nmpl* dues; (*profesionales*) fees; (*impuestos*) taxes; (*de autor*) royalties; **la(s) derecha(s)** (*pl*) (*POL*) the Right; ~**s civiles** civil rights; ~**s de muelle** (*COM*) dock dues; ~**s de patente** patent rights; ~**s portuarios** (*COM*) harbour dues; ~ **de propiedad literaria** copyright; ~ **de retención** (*COM*) lien; ~ **de timbre** (*COM*) stamp duty; ~ **de votar** right to vote; ~ **a voto** voting right; **Facultad de D**~ Faculty of Law; **a derechas** rightly, correctly; **de derechas** (*POL*) right-wing; "**reservados todos los** ~**s**" "all rights reserved"; **¡no hay** ~**!** it's not fair!; **tener** ~ **a** to have a right to; **a la derecha** on the right; (*dirección*) to the right.

deriva [de'rißa] *nf*: **ir** *o* **estar a la** ~ to drift, be adrift.

derivación [derißa'θjon] *nf* derivation.

derivado, a [deri'ßaðo, a] *adj* derived ♦ *nm* (*LING*) derivative; (*INDUSTRIA, QUÍMICA*) by-product.

derivar [deri'ßar] *vt* to derive; (*desviar*) to direct ♦ *vi*, ~**se** *vr* to derive, be derived; ~**(se) de** (*consecuencia*) to spring from.

dermatólogo, a [derma'toloxo, a] *nm/f* dermatologist.

dérmico, a ['dermiko, a] *adj* skin *cpd*.

dermoprotector, a [dermoprotek'tor, a] *adj* protective.

derogación [deroxa'θjon] *nf* repeal.

derogar [dero'xar] *vt* (*ley*) to repeal; (*contrato*) to revoke.

derogue [de'roxe] *etc vb V* **derogar**.

derramamiento [derrama'mjento] *nm* (*dispersión*) spilling; (*fig*) squandering; ~ **de sangre** bloodshed.

derramar [derra'mar] *vt* to spill; (*verter*) to pour out; (*esparcir*) to scatter; ~**se** *vr* to pour out; ~ **lágrimas** to weep.

derrame [de'rrame] *nm* (*de líquido*) spilling; (*de sangre*) shedding; (*de tubo etc*) overflow; (*perdida*) leakage; (*MED*) discharge; (*declive*) slope; ~ **cerebral** brain haemorrhage; ~ **sinovial** water on the knee.

derrapar [derra'par] *vi* to skid.

derredor [derre'ðor] *adv*: **al** *o* **en** ~ **de** around, about.

derrengado, a [derren'gaðo, a] *adj* (*torcido*) bent; (*cojo*) crippled; **estar** ~ (*fig*) to ache all over; **dejar** ~ **a algn** (*fig*) to wear sb out.

derretido, a [derre'tiðo, a] *adj* melted; (*metal*) molten; **estar** ~ **por algn** (*fig*) to be crazy about sb.

derretir [derre'tir] *vt* (*gen*) to melt; (*nieve*) to thaw; (*fig*) to squander; ~**se** *vr* to melt.

derribar [derri'ßar] *vt* to knock down; (*construcción*) to demolish; (*persona, gobierno, político*) to bring down.

derribo [de'rrißo] *nm* (*de edificio*) demolition; (*LUCHA*) throw; (*AVIAT*) shooting down; (*POL*) overthrow; ~**s** *nmpl* rubble *sg*, debris *sg*.

derrita [de'rrita] *etc vb V* **derretir**.

derrocar [derro'kar] *vt* (*gobierno*) to bring down, overthrow; (*ministro*) to oust.

derrochador, a [derrotʃa'ðor, a] *adj*, *nm/f* spendthrift.

derrochar [derro'tʃar] *vt* (*dinero, recursos*) to squander; (*energía, salud*) to be bursting with *o* full of.

derroche [de'rrotʃe] *nm* (*despilfarro*) waste, squandering; (*exceso*) extravagance; **con un** ~ **de buen gusto** with a fine display of good taste.

derroque [de'rroke] *etc vb V* **derrocar**.

derrota [de'rrota] *nf* (*NAUT*) course; (*MIL*) defeat, rout; **sufrir una grave** ~ (*fig*) to suffer a grave setback.

derrotar [derro'tar] *vt* (*gen*) to defeat.

derrotero [derro'tero] *nm* (*rumbo*) course; **tomar otro** ~ (*fig*) to adopt a different course.

derrotista [derro'tista] *adj*, *nm/f* defeatist.

derruir [derru'ir] *vt* to demolish, tear down.

derrumbamiento [derrumba'mjento] *nm* (*caída*) plunge; (*demolición*) demolition; (*desplome*) collapse; ~ **de tierra** landslide.

derrumbar [derrum'bar] *vt* to throw down; (*despeñar*) to fling *o* hurl down; (*volcar*) to upset; ~**se** *vr* (*hundirse*) to collapse; (: *techo*) to fall in, cave in; (*fig: esperanzas*) to collapse.

derrumbe [de'rrumbe] *nm*
= **derrumbamiento**.

derruyendo [derru'jendo] *etc vb V* **derruir**.

des [des] *vb V* **dar**.

desabastecido, a [desaßaste'θiðo, a] *adj*:
estar ~ de algo to be short of *o* out of
sth.

desabotonar [desaßoto'nar] *vt* to
unbutton, undo ♦ *vi* (*flores*) to blossom;
~se *vr* to come undone.

desabrido, a [desa'ßriðo, a] *adj* (*comida*)
insipid, tasteless; (*persona: soso*) dull;
(: *antipático*) rude, surly; (*respuesta*)
sharp; (*tiempo*) unpleasant.

desabrigado, a [desaßri'ɣaðo, a] *adj* (*sin
abrigo*) not sufficiently protected; (*fig*)
exposed.

desabrigar [desaßri'ɣar] *vt* (*quitar ropa a*) to
remove the clothing of; (*descubrir*) to
uncover; (*fig*) to deprive of protection;
~se *vr*: **me desabrigué en la cama** the
bedclothes came off.

desabrigue [desa'ßriɣe] *etc vb V*
desabrigar.

desabrochar [desaßro't ʃar] *vt* (*botones,
broches*) to undo, unfasten; **~se** *vr* (*ropa
etc*) to come undone.

desacatar [desaka'tar] *vt* (*ley*) to disobey.

desacato [desa'kato] *nm* (*falta de respeto*)
disrespect; (*JUR*) contempt.

desacertado, a [desaθer'taðo, a] *adj*
(*equivocado*) mistaken; (*inoportuno*)
unwise.

desacierto [desa'θjerto] *nm* (*error*)
mistake, error; (*dicho*) unfortunate
remark.

desaconsejable [desakonse'xaßle] *adj*
inadvisable.

desaconsejado, a [desakonse'xaðo, a] *adj*
ill-advised.

desaconsejar [desakonse'xar] *vt*: **~ algo a
algn** to advise sb against sth.

desacoplar [desako'plar] *vt* (*ELEC*) to
disconnect; (*TEC*) to take apart.

desacorde [desa'korðe] *adj* (*MUS*)
discordant; (*fig: opiniones*) conflicting;
estar ~ con algo to disagree with sth.

desacreditar [desakreði'tar] *vt*
(*desprestigiar*) to discredit, bring into
disrepute; (*denigrar*) to run down.

desactivar [desakti'ßar] *vt* to deactivate;
(*bomba*) to defuse.

desacuerdo [desa'kwerðo] *nm* (*conflicto*)
disagreement, discord; (*error*) error,
blunder; **en ~** out of keeping.

desafiante [desa'fjante] *adj* (*insolente*)
defiant; (*retador*) challenging ♦ *nm/f*

challenger.

desafiar [desa'fjar] *vt* (*retar*) to challenge;
(*enfrentarse a*) to defy.

desafilado, a [desafi'laðo, a] *adj* blunt.

desafinado, a [desafi'naðo, a] *adj*: **estar ~**
to be out of tune.

desafinar [desafi'nar] *vi* to be out of tune;
~se *vr* to go out of tune.

desafío [desa'fio] *nm* (*reto*) challenge;
(*combate*) duel; (*resistencia*) defiance.

desaforadamente [desaforaða'mente] *adv*:
gritar ~ to shout one's head off.

desaforado, a [desafo'raðo, a] *adj* (*grito*)
ear-splitting; (*comportamiento*)
outrageous.

desafortunadamente [desafortunaða
'mente] *adv* unfortunately.

desafortunado, a [desafortu'naðo, a] *adj*
(*desgraciado*) unfortunate, unlucky.

desagradable [desaɣra'ðaßle] *adj*
(*fastidioso, enojoso*) unpleasant; (*irritante*)
disagreeable; **ser ~ con algn** to be rude
to sb.

desagradar [desaɣra'ðar] *vi* (*disgustar*) to
displease; (*molestar*) to bother.

desagradecido, a [desaɣraðe'θiðo, a] *adj*
ungrateful.

desagrado [desa'ɣraðo] *nm* (*disgusto*)
displeasure; (*contrariedad*)
dissatisfaction; **con ~** unwillingly.

desagraviar [desaɣra'ßjar] *vt* to make
amends to.

desagravio [desa'ɣraßjo] *nm* (*satisfacción*)
amends; (*compensación*) compensation.

desaguadero [desaɣwa'ðero] *nm* drain.

desagüe [de'saɣwe] *nm* (*de un líquido*)
drainage; (*cañería: tb:* **tubo de ~**)
drainpipe; (*salida*) outlet, drain.

desaguisado, a [desaɣi'saðo, a] *adj* illegal
♦ *nm* outrage.

desahogado, a [desao'ɣaðo, a] *adj*
(*holgado*) comfortable; (*espacioso*)
roomy.

desahogar [desao'ɣar] *vt* (*aliviar*) to ease,
relieve; (*ira*) to vent; **~se** *vr* (*distenderse*)
to relax; (*desfogarse*) to let off steam
(*fam*); (*confesarse*) to confess, get sth off
one's chest (*fam*).

desahogo [desa'oɣo] *nm* (*alivio*) relief;
(*comodidad*) comfort, ease; **vivir con ~** to
be comfortably off.

desahogue [desa'oɣe] *etc vb V* **desahogar**.

desahuciado, a [desau'θjaðo, a] *adj*
hopeless.

desahuciar [desau'θjar] *vt* (*enfermo*) to
give up hope for; (*inquilino*) to evict.

desahucio [de'sauθjo] *nm* eviction.

desairado, a [desai'raðo, a] *adj*

(*menospreciado*) disregarded; (*desgarbado*) shabby; (*sin éxito*) unsuccessful; **quedar** ~ to come off badly.

desairar [desai'rar] *vt* (*menospreciar*) to slight, snub; (*cosa*) to disregard; (*COM*) to default on.

desaire [des'aire] *nm* (*menosprecio*) slight; (*falta de garbo*) unattractiveness; **dar** *o* **hacer un** ~ **a algn** to offend sb; ¿**me va usted a hacer ese** ~? I won't take no for an answer!

desajustar [desaxus'tar] *vt* (*desarreglar*) to disarrange; (*desconcertar*) to throw off balance; (*fig: planes*) to upset; ~**se** *vr* to get out of order; (*aflojarse*) to loosen.

desajuste [desa'xuste] *nm* (*de máquina*) disorder; (*avería*) breakdown; (*situación*) imbalance; (*desacuerdo*) disagreement.

desalentador, a [desalenta'ðor, a] *adj* discouraging.

desalentar [desalen'tar] *vt* (*desanimar*) to discourage; ~**se** *vr* to get discouraged.

desaliento [desa'ljento] *etc vb V* **desalentar** ♦ *nm* discouragement; (*abatimiento*) depression.

desaliñado, a [desali'ɲaðo, a] *adj* (*descuidado*) slovenly; (*raído*) shabby; (*desordenado*) untidy; (*negligente*) careless.

desaliño [desa'liɲo] *nm* (*descuido*) slovenliness; (*negligencia*) carelessness.

desalmado, a [desal'maðo, a] *adj* (*cruel*) cruel, heartless.

desalojar [desalo'xar] *vt* (*gen*) to remove, expel; (*expulsar, echar*) to eject; (*abandonar*) to move out of ♦ *vi* to move out; **la policía desalojó el local** the police cleared people out of the place.

desalquilar [desalki'lar] *vt* to vacate, move out; ~**se** *vr* to become vacant.

desamarrar [desama'rrar] *vt* to untie; (*NAUT*) to cast off.

desamor [desa'mor] *nm* (*frialdad*) indifference; (*odio*) dislike.

desamparado, a [desampa'raðo, a] *adj* (*persona*) helpless; (*lugar: expuesto*) exposed; (: *desierto*) deserted.

desamparar [desampa'rar] *vt* (*abandonar*) to desert, abandon; (*JUR*) to leave defenceless; (*barco*) to abandon.

desamparo [desam'paro] *nm* (*acto*) desertion; (*estado*) helplessness.

desamueblado, a [desamwe'ßlaðo, a] *adj* unfurnished.

desandar [desan'dar] *vt*: ~ **lo andado** *o* **el camino** to retrace one's steps.

desanduve [desan'duße] *etc*,

desanduviera [desandu'ßjera] *etc vb V* **desandar**.

desangelado, a [desanxe'laðo, a] *adj* (*habitación, edificio*) lifeless.

desangrar [desan'grar] *vt* to bleed; (*fig: persona*) to bleed dry; (*lago*) to drain; ~**se** *vr* to lose a lot of blood; (*morir*) to bleed to death.

desanimado, a [desani'maðo, a] *adj* (*persona*) downhearted; (*espectáculo, fiesta*) dull.

desanimar [desani'mar] *vt* (*desalentar*) to discourage; (*deprimir*) to depress; ~**se** *vr* to lose heart.

desánimo [de'sanimo] *nm* despondency; (*abatimiento*) dejection; (*falta de animación*) dullness.

desanudar [desanu'ðar] *vt* to untie; (*fig*) to clear up.

desapacible [desapa'θißle] *adj* unpleasant.

desaparecer [desapare'θer] *vi* to disappear; (*el sol, la luz*) to vanish; (~ **de vista**) to drop out of sight; (*efectos, señales*) to wear off ♦ *vt* (*esp AM POL*) to cause to disappear; (: *eufemismo*) to murder.

desaparecido, a [desapare'θiðo, a] *adj* missing; (*especie*) extinct ♦ *nm/f* (*AM POL*) kidnapped *o* missing person.

desaparezca [desapa'reθka] *etc vb V* **desaparecer**.

desaparición [desapari'θjon] *nf* disappearance; (*de especie etc*) extinction.

desapasionado, a [desapasjo'naðo, a] *adj* dispassionate, impartial.

desapego [desa'pexo] *nm* (*frialdad*) coolness; (*distancia*) detachment.

desapercibido, a [desaperθi'ßiðo, a] *adj* unnoticed; (*desprevenido*) unprepared; **pasar** ~ to go unnoticed.

desaplicado, a [desapli'kaðo, a] *adj* slack, lazy.

desaprensivo, a [desapren'sißo, a] *adj* unscrupulous.

desaprobar [desapro'ßar] *vt* (*reprobar*) to disapprove of; (*condenar*) to condemn; (*no consentir*) to reject.

desaprovechado, a [desaproße't ʃaðo, a] *adj* (*oportunidad, tiempo*) wasted; (*estudiante*) slack.

desaprovechar [desaproße't ʃar] *vt* to waste; (*talento*) not to use to the full ♦ *vi* (*perder terreno*) to lose ground.

desapruebe [desa'prweße] *etc vb V* **desaprobar**.

desarmar [desar'mar] *vt* (*MIL, fig*) to disarm; (*TEC*) to take apart, dismantle.

desarme [de'sarme] *nm* disarmament.

desarraigado, a [desarrai'xaðo, a] *adj* (*persona*) without roots, rootless.

desarraigar [desarrai'xar] *vt* to uproot; (*fig: costumbre*) to root out; (: *persona*) to banish.

desarraigo [desa'rraixo] *nm* uprooting.

desarraigue [desa'rraixe] *etc vb V* **desarraigar**.

desarreglado, a [desarre'xlaðo, a] *adj* (*desordenado*) disorderly, untidy; (*hábitos*) irregular.

desarreglar [desarre'xlar] *vt* to mess up; (*desordenar*) to disarrange; (*trastocar*) to upset, disturb.

desarreglo [desa'rrexlo] *nm* (*de casa, persona*) untidiness; (*desorden*) disorder; (*TEC*) trouble; (*MED*) upset; **viven en el mayor ~** they live in complete chaos.

desarrollado, a [desarro'ʎaðo, a] *adj* developed.

desarrollar [desarro'ʎar] *vt* (*gen*) to develop; (*extender*) to unfold; (*teoría*) to explain; **~se** *vr* to develop; (*extenderse*) to open (out); (*film*) to develop; (*fig*) to grow; (*tener lugar*) to take place; **aquí desarrollan un trabajo muy importante** they carry on *o* out very important work here; **la acción se desarrolla en Roma** (*CINE etc*) the scene is set in Rome.

desarrollo [desa'rroʎo] *nm* development; (*de acontecimientos*) unfolding; (*de industria, mercado*) expansion, growth; **país en vías de ~** developing country; **la industria está en pleno ~** industry is expanding steadily.

desarrugar [desarru'xar] *vt* (*alisar*) to smooth (out); (*ropa*) to remove the creases from.

desarrugue [desa'rruxe] *etc vb V* **desarrugar**.

desarticulado, a [desartiku'laðo, a] *adj* disjointed.

desarticular [desartiku'lar] *vt* (*huesos*) to dislocate, put out of joint; (*objeto*) to take apart; (*grupo terrorista etc*) to break up.

desaseado, a [desase'aðo, a] *adj* (*sucio*) dirty; (*desaliñado*) untidy.

desaseo [desa'seo] *nm* (*suciedad*) dirtiness; (*desarreglo*) untidiness.

desasga [de'sasxa] *etc vb V* **desasir**.

desasir [desa'sir] *vt* to loosen; **~se** *vr* to extricate o.s.; **~se de** to let go, give up.

desasosegar [desasose'xar] *vt* (*inquietar*) to disturb, make uneasy; **~se** *vr* to become uneasy.

desasosegué [desasose'xe], **desasoseguemos** [desasose'xemos] *etc vb V* **desasosegar**.

desasosiego [desaso'sjexo] *etc vb V* **desasosegar** ♦ *nm* (*intranquilidad*) uneasiness, restlessness; (*ansiedad*) anxiety; (*POL etc*) unrest.

desasosiegue [desaso'sjexue] *etc vb V* **desasosegar**.

desastrado, a [desas'traðo, a] *adj* (*desaliñado*) shabby; (*sucio*) dirty.

desastre [de'sastre] *nm* disaster; **¡un ~!** how awful!; **la función fue un ~** the show was a shambles.

desastroso, a [desas'troso, a] *adj* disastrous.

desatado, a [desa'taðo, a] *adj* (*desligado*) untied; (*violento*) violent, wild.

desatar [desa'tar] *vt* (*nudo*) to untie; (*paquete*) to undo; (*perro, odio*) to unleash; (*misterio*) to solve; (*separar*) to detach; **~se** *vr* (*zapatos*) to come untied; (*tormenta*) to break; (*perder control de sí*) to lose self-control; **~se en injurias** to pour out a stream of insults.

desatascar [desatas'kar] *vt* (*cañería*) to unblock, clear; (*carro*) to pull out of the mud; **~ a algn** (*fig*) to get sb out of a jam.

desatasque [desa'taske] *etc vb V* **desatascar**.

desatención [desaten'θjon] *nf* (*descuido*) inattention; (*distracción*) absent-mindedness.

desatender [desaten'der] *vt* (*no prestar atención a*) to disregard; (*abandonar*) to neglect.

desatento, a [desa'tento, a] *adj* (*distraído*) inattentive; (*descortés*) discourteous.

desatienda [desa'tjenda] *etc vb V* **desatender**.

desatinado, a [desati'naðo, a] *adj* foolish, silly.

desatino [desa'tino] *nm* (*idiotez*) foolishness, folly; (*error*) blunder; **~s** *nmpl* nonsense *sg*; **¡qué ~!** how silly!, what rubbish!

desatornillar [desatorni'ʎar] *vt* to unscrew.

desatrancar [desatran'kar] *vt* (*puerta*) to unbolt; (*cañería*) to unblock.

desatranque [desa'tranke] *etc vb V* **desatrancar**.

desautorice [desauto'riθe] *etc vb V* **desautorizar**.

desautorizado, a [desautori'θaðo, a] *adj* unauthorized.

desautorizar [desautori'θar] *vt* (*oficial*) to

deprive of authority; (*informe*) to deny.

desavendré [desaßen'dre] *etc vb V* **desavenir**.

desavenencia [desaße'nenθja] *nf* (*desacuerdo*) disagreement; (*discrepancia*) quarrel.

desavenga [desa'ßenga] *etc vb V* **desavenir**.

desavenido, a [desaße'niðo, a] *adj* (*opuesto*) contrary; (*reñidos*) in disagreement; **ellos están ~s** they are at odds.

desavenir [desaße'nir] *vt* (*enemistar*) to make trouble between; **~se** *vr* to fall out.

desaventajado, a [desaßenta'xaðo, a] *adj* (*inferior*) inferior; (*poco ventajoso*) disadvantageous.

desaviene [desa'ßjene] *etc*, **desaviniendo** [desaßi'njendo] *etc vb V* **desavenir**.

desayunar [desaju'nar] *vi*, **~se** *vr* to have breakfast ♦ *vt* to have for breakfast; **~ con café** to have coffee for breakfast; **~ con algo** (*fig*) to get the first news of sth.

desayuno [desa'juno] *nm* breakfast.

desazón [desa'θon] *nf* (*angustia*) anxiety; (*MED*) discomfort; (*fig*) annoyance.

desazonar [desaθo'nar] *vt* (*fig*) to annoy, upset; **~se** *vr* (*enojarse*) to be annoyed; (*preocuparse*) to worry, be anxious.

desbancar [desßan'kar] *vt* (*quitar el puesto a*) to oust; (*suplantar*) to supplant (in sb's affections).

desbandada [desßan'daða] *nf* rush; **~ general** mass exodus; **a la ~** in disorder.

desbandarse [desßan'darse] *vr* (*MIL*) to disband; (*fig*) to flee in disorder.

desbanque [des'ßanke] *etc vb V* **desbancar**.

desbarajuste [desßara'xuste] *nm* confusion, disorder; **¡qué ~!** what a mess!

desbaratar [desßara'tar] *vt* (*gen*) to mess up; (*plan*) to spoil; (*deshacer, destruir*) to ruin ♦ *vi* to talk nonsense; **~se** *vr* (*máquina*) to break down; (*persona*: *irritarse*) to fly off the handle (*fam*).

desbarrar [desßa'rrar] *vi* to talk nonsense.

desbloquear [desßloke'ar] *vt* (*negociaciones, tráfico*) to get going again; (*COM*: *cuenta*) to unfreeze.

desbocado, a [desßo'kaðo, a] *adj* (*caballo*) runaway; (*herramienta*) worn.

desbocar [desßo'kar] *vt* (*vasija*) to break the rim of; **~se** *vr* (*caballo*) to bolt; (*persona*: *soltar injurias*) to let out a stream of insults.

desboque [des'ßoke] *etc vb V* **desbocar**.

desbordamiento [desßorða'mjento] *nm* (*de río*) overflowing; (*INFORM*) overflow; (*de cólera*) outburst; (*de entusiasmo*) upsurge.

desbordar [desßor'ðar] *vt* (*sobrepasar*) to go beyond; (*exceder*) to exceed ♦ *vi*, **~se** *vr* (*líquido, río*) to overflow; (*entusiasmo*) to erupt; (*persona*: *exaltarse*) to get carried away.

desbravar [desßra'ßar] *vt* (*caballo*) to break in; (*animal*) to tame.

descabalgar [deskaßal'ɣar] *vi* to dismount.

descabalgue [deska'ßalɣe] *etc vb V* **descabalgar**.

descabellado, a [deskaße'ʎaðo, a] *adj* (*disparatado*) wild, crazy; (*insensato*) preposterous.

descabellar [deskaße'ʎar] *vt* to ruffle; (*TAUR*: *toro*) to give the coup de grace to.

descabezado, a [deskaße'θaðo, a] *adj* (*sin cabeza*) headless; (*insensato*) wild.

descafeinado, a [deskafei'naðo, a] *adj* decaffeinated ♦ *nm* decaffeinated coffee, de-caf.

descalabrar [deskala'ßrar] *vt* to smash; (*persona*) to hit; (: *en la cabeza*) to hit on the head; (*NAUT*) to cripple; (*dañar*) to harm, damage; **~se** *vr* to hurt one's head.

descalabro [deska'laßro] *nm* blow; (*desgracia*) misfortune.

descalce [des'kalθe] *etc vb V* **descalzar**.

descalificación [deskalifika'θjon] *nf* disqualification; **descalificaciones** *nfpl* discrediting *sg*.

descalificar [deskalifi'kar] *vt* to disqualify; (*desacreditar*) to discredit.

descalifique [deskali'fike] *etc vb V* **descalificar**.

descalzar [deskal'θar] *vt* (*zapato*) to take off.

descalzo, a [des'kalθo, a] *adj* barefoot(ed); (*fig*) destitute; **estar (con los pies) ~(s)** to be barefooted.

descambiar [deskam'bjar] *vt* to exchange.

descaminado, a [deskami'naðo, a] *adj* (*equivocado*) on the wrong road; (*fig*) misguided; **en eso no anda usted muy ~** you're not far wrong there.

descamisado, a [deskami'saðo, a] *adj* bare-chested.

descampado [deskam'paðo] *nm* open space, piece of empty ground; **comer al ~** to eat in the open air.

descansado, a [deskan'saðo, a] *adj* (*gen*) rested; (*que tranquiliza*) restful.

descansar [deskan'sar] *vt* (*gen*) to rest; (*apoyar*): **~ (sobre)** to lean (on) ♦ *vi* to rest, have a rest; (*echarse*) to lie down;

(*cadáver, restos*) to lie; **¡que usted descanse!** sleep well!; ~ **en** (*argumento*) to be based on.

descansillo [deskan'siʎo] *nm* (*de escalera*) landing.

descanso [des'kanso] *nm* (*reposo*) rest; (*alivio*) relief; (*pausa*) break; (*DEPORTE*) interval, half time; **día de** ~ day off; ~ **de enfermedad/maternidad** sick/maternity leave; **tomarse unos días de** ~ to take a few days' leave *o* rest.

descapitalizado, a [deskapitali'θaðo, a] *adj* undercapitalized.

descapotable [deskapo'taßle] *nm* (*tb*: **coche** ~) convertible.

descarado, a [deska'raðo, a] *adj* (*sin vergüenza*) shameless, (*insolente*) cheeky.

descarga [des'karɣa] *nf* (*ARQ, ELEC, MIL*) discharge; (*NAUT*) unloading.

descargador [deskarɣa'ðor] *nm* (*de barcos*) docker.

descargar [deskar'ɣar] *vt* to unload; (*golpe*) to let fly; (*arma*) to fire; (*ELEC*) to discharge; (*pila*) to run down; (*conciencia*) to relieve; (*COM*) to take up; (*persona: de una obligación*) to release; (: *de una deuda*) to free; (*JUR*) to clear ♦ *vi* (*río*): ~ **(en)** to flow (into); ~**se** *vr* to unburden o.s.; ~**se de algo** to get rid of sth.

descargo [des'karɣo] *nm* (*de obligación*) release; (*COM: recibo*) receipt; (: *de deuda*) discharge; (*JUR*) evidence; ~ **de una acusación** acquittal on a charge.

descargue [des'karɣe] *etc vb V* **descargar**.

descarnado, a [deskar'naðo, a] *adj* scrawny; (*fig*) bare; (*estilo*) straightforward.

descaro [des'karo] *nm* nerve.

descarriar [deska'rrjar] *vt* (*descaminar*) to misdirect; (*fig*) to lead astray; ~**se** *vr* (*perderse*) to lose one's way; (*separarse*) to stray; (*pervertirse*) to err, go astray.

descarrilamiento [deskarrila'mjento] *nm* (*de tren*) derailment.

descarrilar [deskarri'lar] *vi* to be derailed.

descartable [deskar'taßle] *adj* (*INFORM*) temporary.

descartar [deskar'tar] *vt* (*rechazar*) to reject; (*eliminar*) to rule out; ~**se** *vr* (*NAIPES*) to discard; ~**se de** to shirk.

descascarar [deskaska'rar] *vt* (*naranja, limón*) to peel; (*nueces, huevo duro*) to shell; ~**se** *vr* to peel (off).

descascarillado, a [deskaskari'ʎaðo, a] *adj* (*paredes*) peeling.

descendencia [desθen'denθja] *nf* (*origen*) origin, descent; (*hijos*) offspring; **morir**

sin dejar ~ to die without issue.

descendente [desθen'dente] *adj* (*cantidad*) diminishing; (*INFORM*) top-down.

descender [desθen'der] *vt* (*bajar: escalera*) to go down ♦ *vi* to descend; (*temperatura, nivel*) to fall, drop; (*líquido*) to run; (*cortina etc*) to hang; (*fuerzas, persona*) to fail, get weak; ~ **de** to be descended from.

descendiente [desθen'djente] *nm/f* descendant.

descenso [des'θenso] *nm* descent; (*de temperatura*) drop; (*de producción*) downturn; (*de calidad*) decline; (*MINERÍA*) collapse; (*bajada*) slope; (*fig: decadencia*) decline; (*de empleado etc*) demotion.

descentrado, a [desθen'traðo, a] *adj* (*pieza de una máquina*) off-centre; (*rueda*) out of true; (*persona*) bewildered; (*desequilibrado*) unbalanced; (*problema*) out of focus; **todavía está algo** ~ he is still somewhat out of touch.

descentralice [desθentra'liθe] *etc vb V* **descentralizar**.

descentralizar [desθentrali'θar] *vt* to decentralize.

descerrajar [desθerra'xar] *vt* (*puerta*) to break open.

descienda [des'θjenda] *etc vb V* **descender**.

descifrable [desθi'fraßle] *adj* (*gen*) decipherable; (*letra*) legible.

descifrar [desθi'frar] *vt* (*escritura*) to decipher; (*mensaje*) to decode; (*problema*) to puzzle out; (*misterio*) to solve.

descocado, a [desko'kaðo, a] *adj* (*descarado*) cheeky; (*desvergonzado*) brazen.

descoco [des'koko] *nm* (*descaro*) cheek; (*atrevimiento*) brazenness.

descodificador [deskoðifika'ðor] *nm* decoder.

descodificar [deskoðifi'kar] *vt* to decode.

descolgar [deskol'ɣar] *vt* (*bajar*) to take down; (*desde una posición alta*) to lower; (*de una pared etc*) to unhook; (*teléfono*) to pick up; ~**se** *vr* to let o.s. down; ~**se por** (*bajar escurriéndose*) to slip down; (*pared*) to climb down; **dejó el teléfono descolgado** he left the phone off the hook.

descolgué [deskol'xe], **descolguemos** [deskol'xemos] *etc vb V* **descolgar**.

descollar [desko'ʎar] *vi* (*sobresalir*) to stand out; (*montaña etc*) to rise; **la obra que más descuella de las suyas** his most outstanding work.

descolocado, a [deskolo'kaðo, a] *adj*: **estar**

~ (*cosa*) to be out of place; (*criada*) to be unemployed.

descolorido, a [deskolo'riðo, a] *adj* (*color, tela*) faded; (*pálido*) pale; (*fig: estilo*) colourless.

descompaginar [deskompaxi'nar] *vt* (*desordenar*) to disarrange, mess up.

descompasado, a [deskompa'saðo, a] *adj* (*sin proporción*) out of all proportion; (*excesivo*) excessive; (*hora*) unearthly.

descompensar [deskompen'sar] *vt* to unbalance.

descompondré [deskompon'dre] *etc vb V* **descomponer**.

descomponer [deskompo'ner] *vt* (*gen, LING, MAT*) to break down; (*desordenar*) to disarrange, disturb; (*materia orgánica*) to rot, decompose; (*TEC*) to put out of order; (*facciones*) to distort; (*estómago etc*) to upset; (*planes*) to mess up; (*persona: molestar*) to upset; (: *irritar*) to annoy; ~**se** *vr* (*corromperse*) to rot, decompose; (*estómago*) to get upset; (*el tiempo*) to change (for the worse); (*TEC*) to break down.

descomponga [deskom'ponga] *etc vb V* **descomponer**.

descomposición [deskomposi'θjon] *nf* (*gen*) breakdown; (*de fruta etc*) decomposition; (*putrefacción*) rotting; (*de cara*) distortion; ~ **de vientre** (*MED*) stomach upset, diarrhoea.

descompostura [deskompos'tura] *nf* (*TEC*) breakdown; (*desorganización*) disorganization; (*desorden*) untidiness.

descompuesto, a [deskom'pwesto, a] *pp de* **descomponer** ♦ *adj* (*corrompido*) decomposed; (*roto*) broken (down).

descompuse [deskom'puse] *etc vb V* **descomponer**.

descomunal [deskomu'nal] *adj* (*enorme*) huge; (*fam: excelente*) fantastic.

desconcertado, a [deskonθer'taðo, a] *adj* disconcerted, bewildered.

desconcertar [deskonθer'tar] *vt* (*confundir*) to baffle; (*incomodar*) to upset, put out; (*orden*) to disturb; ~**se** *vr* (*turbarse*) to be upset; (*confundirse*) to be bewildered.

desconchado, a [deskon'tʃaðo, a] *adj* (*pintura*) peeling.

desconchar [deskon'tʃar] *vt* (*pared*) to strip off; (*loza*) to chip off.

desconcierto [deskon'θjerto] *etc vb V* **desconcertar** ♦ *nm* (*gen*) disorder; (*desorientación*) uncertainty; (*inquietud*) uneasiness; (*confusión*) bewilderment.

desconectado, a [deskonek'taðo, a] *adj* (*ELEC*) disconnected, switched off;

(*INFORM*) offline; **estar** ~ **de** (*fig*) to have no contact with.

desconectar [deskonek'tar] *vt* to disconnect; (*desenchufar*) to unplug; (*radio, televisión*) to switch off; (*INFORM*) to toggle off.

desconfiado, a [deskon'fjaðo, a] *adj* suspicious.

desconfianza [deskon'fjanθa] *nf* distrust.

desconfiar [deskon'fjar] *vi* to be distrustful; ~ **de** (*sospechar*) to mistrust, suspect; (*no tener confianza en*) to have no faith *o* confidence in; **desconfío de ello** I doubt it; **desconfíe de las imitaciones** (*COM*) beware of imitations.

desconforme [deskon'forme] *adj* = **disconforme**.

descongelar [deskonxe'lar] *vt* (*nevera*) to defrost; (*comida*) to thaw; (*AUTO*) to de-ice; (*COM, POL*) to unfreeze.

descongestionar [deskonxestjo'nar] *vt* (*cabeza, tráfico*) to clear; (*calle, ciudad*) to relieve congestion in; (*fig: despejar*) to clear.

desconocer [deskono'θer] *vt* (*ignorar*) not to know, be ignorant of; (*no aceptar*) to deny; (*repudiar*) to disown.

desconocido, a [deskono'θiðo, a] *adj* unknown; (*que no se conoce*) unfamiliar; (*no reconocido*) unrecognized ♦ *nm/f* stranger; (*recién llegado*) newcomer; **está ~** he is hardly recognizable.

desconocimiento [deskonoθi'mjento] *nm* (*falta de conocimientos*) ignorance; (*repudio*) disregard.

desconozca [desko'noθka] *etc vb V* **desconocer**.

desconsiderado, a [deskonsiðe'raðo, a] *adj* inconsiderate; (*insensible*) thoughtless.

desconsolado, a [deskonso'laðo, a] *adj* (*afligido*) disconsolate; (*cara*) sad; (*desanimado*) dejected.

desconsolar [deskonso'lar] *vt* to distress; ~**se** *vr* to despair.

desconsuelo [deskon'swelo] *etc vb V* **desconsolar** ♦ *nm* (*tristeza*) distress; (*desesperación*) despair.

descontado, a [deskon'taðo, a] *adj*: **por ~** of course; **dar por ~ (que)** to take it for granted (that).

descontar [deskon'tar] *vt* (*deducir*) to take away, deduct; (*rebajar*) to discount.

descontento, a [deskon'tento, a] *adj* dissatisfied ♦ *nm* dissatisfaction, discontent.

descontrol [deskon'trol] *nm* (*fam*) lack of control.

descontrolado, a [deskontro'laðo, a] *adj* uncontrolled.

descontrolarse [deskontro'larse] *vr* (*persona*) to lose control.

desconvenir [deskombe'nir] *vi* (*personas*) to disagree; (*no corresponder*) not to fit; (*no convenir*) to be inconvenient.

desconvocar [deskombo'kar] *vt* to call off.

descorazonar [deskoraθo'nar] *vt* to discourage, dishearten; ~**se** *vr* to get discouraged, lose heart.

descorchador [deskortʃa'ðor] *nm* corkscrew.

descorchar [deskor'tʃar] *vt* to uncork, open.

descorrer [desko'rrer] *vt* (*cortina, cerrojo*) to draw back; (*velo*) to remove.

descortés [deskor'tes] *adj* (*mal educado*) discourteous; (*grosero*) rude.

descortesía [deskorte'sia] *nf* discourtesy; (*grosería*) rudeness.

descoser [desko'ser] *vt* to unstitch; ~**se** *vr* to come apart (at the seams); (*fam*: *descubrir un secreto*) to blurt out a secret; ~**se de risa** to split one's sides laughing.

descosido, a [desko'siðo, a] *adj* (*costura*) unstitched; (*desordenado*) disjointed ♦ *nm*: **como un** ~ (*obrar*) wildly; (*beber, comer*) to excess; (*estudiar*) like mad.

descoyuntar [deskojun'tar] *vt* (ANAT) to dislocate; (*hechos*) to twist; ~**se** *vr*: ~**se un hueso** (ANAT) to put a bone out of joint; ~**se de risa** (*fam*) to split one's sides laughing; **estar descoyuntado** (*persona*) to be double-jointed.

descrédito [des'kreðito] *nm* discredit; **caer en** ~ to fall into disrepute; **ir en** ~ **de** to be to the discredit of.

descreído, a [deskre'iðo, a] *adj* (*incrédulo*) incredulous; (*falto de fe*) unbelieving.

descremado, a [deskre'maðo, a] *adj* skimmed.

descremar [deskre'mar] *vt* (*leche*) to skim.

describir [deskri'ßir] *vt* to describe.

descripción [deskrip'θjon] *nf* description.

descrito [des'krito] *pp de* **describir**.

descuajar [deskwa'xar] *vt* (*disolver*) to melt; (*planta*) to pull out by the roots; (*extirpar*) to eradicate, wipe out; (*desanimar*) to dishearten.

descuajaringarse [deskwaxarin'garse] *vr* to fall to bits.

descuajaringue [deskwaxa'ringe] *etc vb V* **descuajaringarse**.

descuartice [deskwar'tiθe] *etc vb V* **descuartizar**.

descuartizar [deskwarti'θar] *vt* (*animal*) to carve up, cut up; (*fig*: *hacer pedazos*) to tear apart.

descubierto, a [desku'ßjerto, a] *pp de* **descubrir** ♦ *adj* uncovered, bare; (*persona*) bare-headed; (*cielo*) clear; (*coche*) open; (*campo*) treeless ♦ *nm* (*lugar*) open space; (COM: *en el presupuesto*) shortage; (: *bancario*) overdraft; **al** ~ in the open; **poner al** ~ to lay bare; **quedar al** ~ to be exposed; **estar en** ~ to be overdrawn.

descubridor, a [deskußri'ðor, a] *nm/f* discoverer.

descubrimiento [deskußri'mjento] *nm* (*hallazgo*) discovery; (*de criminal, fraude*) detection; (*revelación*) revelation; (*de secreto etc*) disclosure; (*de estatua etc*) unveiling.

descubrir [desku'ßrir] *vt* to discover, find; (*petróleo*) to strike; (*inaugurar*) to unveil; (*vislumbrar*) to detect; (*sacar a luz*: *crimen*) to bring to light; (*revelar*) to reveal, show; (*poner al descubierto*) to expose to view; (*naipes*) to lay down; (*quitar la tapa de*) to uncover; (*cacerola*) to take the lid off; (*enterarse de*: *causa, solución*) to find out; (*divisar*) to see, make out; (*delatar*) to give away, betray; ~**se** *vr* to reveal o.s.; (*quitarse sombrero*) to take off one's hat; (*confesar*) to confess; (*fig*: *salir a luz*) to come out o to light.

descuelga [des'kwelɣa] *etc*, **descuelgue** [des'kwelɣe] *etc vb V* **descolgar**.

descuelle [des'kweʎe] *etc vb V* **descollar**.

descuento [des'kwento] *etc vb V* **descontar** ♦ *nm* discount; ~ **del 3%** 3% off; **con** ~ at a discount; ~ **por pago al contado** (COM) cash discount; ~ **por volumen de compras** (COM) volume discount.

descuidado, a [deskwi'ðaðo, a] *adj* (*sin cuidado*) careless; (*desordenado*) untidy; (*olvidadizo*) forgetful; (*dejado*) neglected; (*desprevenido*) unprepared.

descuidar [deskwi'ðar] *vt* (*dejar*) to neglect; (*olvidar*) to overlook ♦ *vi*, ~**se** *vr* (*distraerse*) to be careless; (*estar desaliñado*) to let o.s. go; (*desprevenirse*) to drop one's guard; ¡**descuida!** don't worry!

descuido [des'kwiðo] *nm* (*dejadez*) carelessness; (*olvido*) negligence; (*un* ~) oversight; **al** ~ casually; (*sin cuidado*) carelessly; **al menor** ~ if my *etc* attention wanders for a minute; **con** ~ thoughtlessly; **por** ~ by an oversight.

======================= PALABRA CLAVE

desde ['desðe] *prep* **1** (*lugar*) from; ~
Burgos hasta mi casa hay 30 km it's 30
kms from Burgos to my house; ~ **lejos**
from a distance
2 (*posición*): **hablaba** ~ **el balcón** she
was speaking from the balcony
3 (*tiempo*: +*adv*, *n*): ~ **ahora** from now
on; ~ **entonces/la boda** since then/the
wedding; ~ **niño** since I *etc* was a child;
~ **3 años atrás** since 3 years ago
4 (*tiempo*: +*vb*) since; for; **nos**
conocemos ~ **1978/** ~ **hace 20 años**
we've known each other since 1978/for
20 years; **no le veo** ~ **1983/** ~ **hace 5**
años I haven't seen him since 1983/for 5
years; ¿~ **cuándo vives aquí?** how long
have you lived here?
5 (*gama*): ~ **los más lujosos hasta los**
más económicos from the most
luxurious to the most reasonably priced
6: ~ **luego (que no)** of course (not)
♦ *conj*: ~ **que**: ~ **que recuerdo** for as long
as I can remember; ~ **que llegó no ha**
salido he hasn't been out since he
arrived.

desdecir [desðe'θir] *vi*: ~ **de** (*no merecer*)
to be unworthy of; (*no corresponder*) to
clash with; ~**se** *vr*: ~**se de** to go back on.
desdén [des'ðen] *nm* scorn.
desdentado, a [desðen'taðo, a] *adj*
toothless.
desdeñable [desðe'ɲaßle] *adj*
contemptible; **nada** ~ far from
negligible, considerable.
desdeñar [desðe'ɲar] *vt* (*despreciar*) to
scorn.
desdeñoso, a [desðe'ɲoso, a] *adj* scornful.
desdibujar [desðißu'xar] *vt* to blur (the
outlines of); ~**se** *vr* to get blurred, fade
(away); **el recuerdo se ha desdibujado**
the memory has become blurred.
desdichado, a [desði'tʃaðo, a] *adj* (*sin*
suerte) unlucky; (*infeliz*) unhappy; (*día*)
ill-fated ♦ *nm/f* (*pobre desgraciado*) poor
devil.
desdicho, a [des'ðitʃo, a] *pp de* **desdecir**
♦ *nf* (*desgracia*) misfortune; (*infelicidad*)
unhappiness.
desdiciendo [desði'θjendo] *etc vb V*
desdecir.
desdiga [des'ðixa] *etc*, **desdije** [des'dixe]
etc vb V **desdecir**.
desdoblado, a [desðo'ßlaðo, a] *adj*
(*personalidad*) split.
desdoblar [desðo'ßlar] *vt* (*extender*) to

spread out; (*desplegar*) to unfold.
deseable [dese'aßle] *adj* desirable.
desear [dese'ar] *vt* to want, desire, wish
for; ¿**qué desea la señora?** (*tienda etc*)
what can I do for you, madam?; **estoy**
deseando que esto termine I'm longing
for this to finish.
desecar [dese'kar] *vt*, **desecarse** *vr* to dry
up.
desechable [dese'tʃaßle] *adj* (*envase etc*)
disposable.
desechar [dese'tʃar] *vt* (*basura*) to throw
out *o* away; (*ideas*) to reject, discard;
(*miedo*) to cast aside; (*plan*) to drop.
desecho [de'setʃo] *nm* (*desprecio*)
contempt; (*lo peor*) dregs *pl*; ~**s** *nmpl*
rubbish *sg*, waste *sg*; **de** ~ (*hierro*) scrap;
(*producto*) waste; (*ropa*) cast-off.
desembalar [desemba'lar] *vt* to unpack.
desembarace [desemba'raθe] *etc vb V*
desembarazar.
desembarazado, a [desembara'θaðo, a]
adj (*libre*) clear, free; (*desenvuelto*) free
and easy.
desembarazar [desembara'θar] *vt*
(*desocupar*) to clear; (*desenredar*) to free;
~**se** *vr*: ~**se de** to free o.s. of, get rid of.
desembarazo [desemba'raθo] *nm* (*acto*)
clearing; (*AM*: *parto*) birth; (*desenfado*)
ease.
desembarcadero [desembarka'ðero] *nm*
quay.
desembarcar [desembar'kar] *vt* (*personas*)
to land; (*mercancías etc*) to unload ♦ *vi*,
~**se** *vr* (*de barco, avión*) to disembark.
desembarco [desem'barko] *nm* landing.
desembargar [desembar'ɣar] *vt* (*gen*) to
free; (*JUR*) to remove the embargo on.
desembargue [desem'ßarɣe] *etc vb V*
desembargar.
desembarque [desem'barke] *etc vb V*
desembarcar ♦ *nm* disembarkation; (*de*
pasajeros) landing; (*de mercancías*)
unloading.
desembocadura [desemboka'ðura] *nf* (*de*
río) mouth; (*de calle*) opening.
desembocar [desembo'kar] *vi*: ~ **en** to flow
into; (*fig*) to result in.
desemboce [desem'boθe] *etc vb V*
desembozar.
desembolsar [desembol'sar] *vt* (*pagar*) to
pay out; (*gastar*) to lay out.
desembolso [desem'bolso] *nm* payment.
desemboque [desem'boke] *etc vb V*
desembocar.
desembozar [desembo'θar] *vt* to unmask.
desembragar [desembra'ɣar] *vt* (*TEC*) to
disengage; (*embrague*) to release ♦ *vi*

(*AUTO*) to declutch.

desembrague [desem'Braɣe] *etc vb* V **desembragar**.

desembrollar [desembro'ʎar] *vt* (*madeja*) to unravel; (*asunto, malentendido*) to sort out.

desembuchar [desembu't∫ar] *vt* to disgorge; (*fig*) to come out with ♦ *vi* (*confesar*) to spill the beans (*fam*); ¡**desembucha!** out with it!

desemejante [deseme'xante] *adj* dissimilar; ~ **de** different from, unlike.

desemejanza [deseme'xanθa] *nf* dissimilarity.

desempacar [desempa'kar] *vt* (*esp AM*) to unpack.

desempañar [desempa'ɲar] *vt* (*cristal*) to clean, demist.

desempaque [desem'pake] *etc vb* V **desempacar**.

desempaquetar [desempake'tar] *vt* to unpack, unwrap.

desempatar [desempa'tar] *vi* to break a tie; **volvieron a jugar para** ~ they held a play-off.

desempate [desem'pate] *nm* (*FÚTBOL*) play-off; (*TENIS*) tie-break(er).

desempeñar [desempe'ɲar] *vt* (*cargo*) to hold; (*papel*) to play; (*deber, función*) to perform, carry out; (*lo empeñado*) to redeem; ~**se** *vr* to get out of debt; ~ **un papel** (*fig*) to play (a role).

desempeño [desem'peɲo] *nm* occupation; (*de lo empeñado*) redeeming; **de mucho** ~ very capable.

desempleado, a [desemple'aðo, a] *adj* unemployed, out of work ♦ *nm/f* unemployed person.

desempleo [desem'pleo] *nm* unemployment.

desempolvar [desempol'Bar] *vt* (*muebles etc*) to dust; (*lo olvidado*) to revive.

desencadenar [desenkaðe'nar] *vt* to unchain; (*ira*) to unleash; (*provocar*) to cause, set off; ~**se** *vr* to break loose; (*tormenta*) to burst; (*guerra*) to break out; **se desencadenó una lucha violenta** a violent struggle ensued.

desencajar [desenka'xar] *vt* (*hueso*) to put out of joint; (*mandíbula*) to dislocate; (*mecanismo, pieza*) to disconnect, disengage.

desencantar [desenkan'tar] *vt* to disillusion, disenchant.

desencanto [desen'kanto] *nm* disillusionment, disenchantment.

desenchufar [desent∫u'far] *vt* to unplug, disconnect.

desenfadado, a [desenfa'ðaðo, a] *adj* (*desenvuelto*) uninhibited; (*descarado*) forward; (*en el vestir*) casual.

desenfado [desen'faðo] *nm* (*libertad*) freedom; (*comportamiento*) free and easy manner; (*descaro*) forwardness; (*desenvoltura*) self-confidence.

desenfocado, a [desenfo'kaðo, a] *adj* (*FOTO*) out of focus.

desenfrenado, a [desenfre'naðo, a] *adj* (*descontrolado*) uncontrolled; (*inmoderado*) unbridled.

desenfrenarse [desenfre'narse] *vr* (*persona: desmandarse*) to lose all self-control; (*multitud*) to run riot; (*tempestad*) to burst; (*viento*) to rage.

desenfreno [desen'freno] *nm* (*vicio*) wildness; (*falta de control*) lack of self-control; (*de pasiones*) unleashing.

desenganchar [desengan't∫ar] *vt* (*gen*) to unhook; (*FERRO*) to uncouple; (*TEC*) to disengage.

desengañar [desenga'ɲar] *vt* to disillusion; (*abrir los ojos a*) to open the eyes of; ~**se** *vr* to become disillusioned; ¡**desengáñate!** don't you believe it!

desengaño [desen'gaɲo] *nm* disillusionment; (*decepción*) disappointment; **sufrir un** ~ **amoroso** to be disappointed in love.

desengrasar [desengra'sar] *vt* to degrease.

desenlace [desen'laθe] *etc vb* V **desenlazar**.

desenlazar [desenla'θar] *vt* (*desatar*) to untie; (*problema*) to solve; (*aclarar: asunto*) to unravel; ~**se** *vr* (*desatarse*) to come undone; (*LIT*) to end.

desenmarañar [desenmara'ɲar] *vt* (*fig*) to unravel.

desenmascarar [desenmaska'rar] *vt* to unmask, expose.

desenredar [desenre'ðar] *vt* to resolve.

desenrollar [desenro'ʎar] *vt* to unroll, unwind.

desenroscar [desenros'kar] *vt* (*tornillo etc*) to unscrew.

desenrosque [desen'roske] *etc vb* V **desenroscar**.

desentenderse [desenten'derse] *vr*: ~ **de** to pretend not to know about; (*apartarse*) to have nothing to do with.

desentendido, a [desenten'diðo, a] *adj*: **hacerse el** ~ to pretend not to notice; **se hizo el** ~ he didn't take the hint.

desenterrar [desente'rrar] *vt* to exhume; (*tesoro, fig*) to unearth, dig up.

desentierre [desen'tjerre] *etc vb* V **desenterrar**.

desentonar [desento'nar] *vi* (*MUS*) to sing (*o* play) out of tune; (*no encajar*) to be out of place; (*color*) to clash.

desentorpecer [desentorpe'θer] *vt* (*miembro*) to stretch; (*fam*: *persona*) to polish up.

desentorpezca [desentor'peθka] *etc vb* V **desentorpecer**.

desentrañar [desentra'ɲar] *vt* (*misterio*) to unravel.

desentrenado, a [desentre'naðo, a] *adj* out of training.

desentumecer [desentume'θer] *vt* (*pierna etc*) to stretch; (*DEPORTE*) to loosen up.

desentumezca [desentu'meθka] *etc vb* V **desentumecer**.

desenvainar [desembai'nar] *vt* (*espada*) to draw, unsheathe.

desenvoltura [desembol'tura] *nf* (*libertad, gracia*) ease; (*descaro*) free and easy manner; (*al hablar*) fluency.

desenvolver [desembol'ßer] *vt* (*paquete*) to unwrap; (*fig*) to develop; ~**se** *vr* (*desarrollarse*) to unfold, develop; (*suceder*) to go off; (*prosperar*) to prosper; (*arreglárselas*) to cope.

desenvolvimiento [desembolßi'mjento] *nm* (*desarrollo*) development; (*de idea*) exposition.

desenvuelto, a [desem'bwelto, a] *pp de* **desenvolver** ♦ *adj* (*suelto*) easy; (*desenfadado*) confident; (*al hablar*) fluent; (*pey*) forward.

desenvuelva [desem'buelßa] *etc vb* V **desenvolver**.

deseo [de'seo] *nm* desire, wish; ~ **de saber** thirst for knowledge; **buen** ~ good intentions *pl*; **arder en** ~**s de algo** to yearn for sth.

deseoso, a [dese'oso, a] *adj*: **estar** ~ **de hacer** to be anxious to do.

deseque [de'seke] *etc vb* V **desecar**.

desequilibrado, a [desekili'ßraðo, a] *adj* unbalanced ♦ *nm/f* unbalanced person; ~ **mental** mentally disturbed person.

desequilibrar [desekili'ßrar] *vt* (*mente*) to unbalance; (*objeto*) to throw out of balance; (*persona*) to throw off balance.

desequilibrio [deseki'lißrio] *nm* (*de mente*) unbalance; (*entre cantidades*) imbalance; (*MED*) unbalanced mental condition.

desertar [deser'tar] *vt* (*JUR*: *derecho de apelación*) to forfeit ♦ *vi* to desert; ~ **de sus deberes** to neglect one's duties.

desértico, a [de'sertiko, a] *adj* desert *cpd*; (*vacío*) deserted.

desertor, a [deser'tor, a] *nm/f* deserter.

desesperación [desespera'θjon] *nf* desperation, despair; (*irritación*) fury; **es una** ~ it's maddening; **es una** ~ **tener que ...** it's infuriating to have to ....

desesperado, a [desespe'raðo, a] *adj* (*persona*: *sin esperanza*) desperate; (*caso, situación*) hopeless; (*esfuerzo*) furious ♦ *nm*: **como un** ~ like mad ♦ *nf*: **hacer algo a la desesperada** to do sth as a last resort *o* in desperation.

desesperance [desespe'ranθe] *etc vb* V **desesperanzar**.

desesperante [desespe'rante] *adj* (*exasperante*) infuriating; (*persona*) hopeless.

desesperanzar [desesperan'θar] *vt* to drive to despair; ~**se** *vr* to lose hope, despair.

desesperar [desespe'rar] *vt* to drive to despair; (*exasperar*) to drive to distraction ♦ *vi*: ~ **de** to despair of; ~**se** *vr* to despair, lose hope.

desespero [deses'pero] *nm* (*AM*) despair.

desestabilice [desestaßi'liθe] *etc vb* V **desestabilizar**.

desestabilizar [desestaßili'θar] *vt* to destabilize.

desestimar [desesti'mar] *vt* (*menospreciar*) to have a low opinion of; (*rechazar*) to reject.

desfachatez [desfatʃa'teθ] *nf* (*insolencia*) impudence; (*descaro*) rudeness.

desfalco [des'falko] *nm* embezzlement.

desfallecer [desfaʎe'θer] *vi* (*perder las fuerzas*) to become weak; (*desvanecerse*) to faint.

desfallecido, a [desfaʎe'θiðo, a] *adj* (*débil*) weak.

desfallezca [desfa'ʎeθka] *etc vb* V **desfallecer**.

desfasado, a [desfa'saðo, a] *adj* (*anticuado*) old-fashioned; (*TEC*) out of phase.

desfasar [desfa'sar] *vt* to phase out.

desfase [des'fase] *nm* (*diferencia*) gap.

desfavorable [desfaßo'raßle] *adj* unfavourable.

desfavorecer [desfaßore'θer] *vt* (*sentar mal*) not to suit.

desfavorezca [desfaßo'reθka] *etc vb* V **desfavorecer**.

desfiguración [desfiɣura'θjon] *nf*, **desfiguramiento** [desfiɣura'mjento] *nm* (*de persona*) disfigurement; (*de monumento*) defacement; (*FOTO*) blurring.

desfigurar [desfiɣu'rar] *vt* (*cara*) to disfigure; (*cuerpo*) to deform; (*cuadro, monumento*) to deface; (*FOTO*) to blur; (*sentido*) to twist; (*suceso*) to misrepresent.

desfiladero [desfila'ðero] *nm* gorge, defile.

desfilar [desfi'lar] *vi* to parade; **desfilaron ante el general** they marched past the general.

desfile [des'file] *nm* procession; (*MIL*) parade; ~ **de modelos** fashion show.

desflorar [desflo'rar] *vt* (*mujer*) to deflower; (*arruinar*) to tarnish; (*asunto*) to touch on.

desfogar [desfo'ɣar] *vt* (*fig*) to vent ♦ *vi* (*NAUT*: *tormenta*) to burst; ~**se** *vr* (*fig*) to let off steam.

desfogue [des'foɣe] *etc vb* V **desfogar**.

desgajar [desɣa'xar] *vt* (*arrancar*) to tear off; (*romper*) to break off; (*naranja*) to split into segments; ~**se** *vr* to come off.

desgana [des'ɣana] *nf* (*falta de apetito*) loss of appetite; (*renuencia*) unwillingness; **hacer algo a** ~ to do sth unwillingly.

desganado, a [desɣa'naðo, a] *adj*: **estar** ~ (*sin apetito*) to have no appetite; (*sin entusiasmo*) to have lost interest.

desgañitarse [desɣaɲi'tarse] *vr* to shout o.s. hoarse.

desgarbado, a [desɣar'ßaðo, a] *adj* (*sin gracia*) clumsy, ungainly.

desgarrador, a [desɣarra'ðor, a] *adj* heartrending.

desgarrar [desɣa'rrar] *vt* to tear (up); (*fig*) to shatter.

desgarro [des'ɣarro] *nm* (*en tela*) tear; (*aflicción*) grief; (*descaro*) impudence.

desgastar [desɣas'tar] *vt* (*deteriorar*) to wear away o down; (*estropear*) to spoil; ~**se** *vr* to get worn out.

desgaste [des'ɣaste] *nm* wear (and tear); (*de roca*) erosion; (*de cuerda*) fraying; (*de metal*) corrosion; ~ **económico** drain on one's resources.

desglosar [desɣlo'sar] *vt* to detach.

desgobierno [desɣo'ßjerno] *etc vb* V **desgobernar** ♦ *nm* (*POL*) misgovernment, misrule.

desgracia [des'ɣraθja] *nf* misfortune; (*accidente*) accident; (*vergüenza*) disgrace; (*contratiempo*) setback; **por** ~ unfortunately; **en el accidente no hay que lamentar** ~**s personales** there were no casualties in the accident; **caer en** ~ to fall from grace; **tener la** ~ **de** to be unlucky enough to.

desgraciadamente [desɣraθjaða'mente] *adv* unfortunately.

desgraciado, a [desɣra'θjaðo, a] *adj* (*sin suerte*) unlucky, unfortunate; (*miserable*) wretched; (*infeliz*) miserable ♦ *nm/f* (*malo*) swine; (*infeliz*) poor creature; **¡esa radio desgraciada!** (*esp AM*) that lousy radio!

desgraciar [desɣra'θjar] *vt* (*estropear*) to spoil; (*ofender*) to displease.

desgranar [desɣra'nar] *vt* (*trigo*) to thresh; (*guisantes*) to shell; ~ **un racimo** to pick the grapes from a bunch; ~ **mentiras** to come out with a string of lies.

desgravación [desɣraßa'θjon] *nf* (*COM*): ~ **de impuestos** tax relief; ~ **personal** personal allowance.

desgravar [desɣra'ßar] *vt* (*producto*) to reduce the tax o duty on.

desgreñado, a [desɣre'ɲaðo, a] *adj* dishevelled.

desguace [des'ɣwaθe] *nm* (*de coches*) scrapping; (*lugar*) scrapyard.

desguazar [desɣwa'θar] *vt* (*coche*) to scrap.

deshabitado, a [desaßi'taðo, a] *adj* uninhabited.

deshabitar [desaßi'tar] *vt* (*casa*) to leave empty; (*despoblar*) to depopulate.

deshacer [desa'θer] *vt* (*lo hecho*) to undo, unmake; (*proyectos*: *arruinar*) to spoil; (*casa*) to break up; (*TEC*) to take apart; (*enemigo*) to defeat; (*diluir*) to melt; (*contrato*) to break; (*intriga*) to solve; (*cama*) to strip; (*maleta*) to unpack; (*paquete*) to unwrap; (*nudo*) to untie; (*costura*) to unpick; ~**se** *vr* (*desatarse*) to come undone; (*estropearse*) to be spoiled; (*descomponerse*) to fall to pieces; (*disolverse*) to melt; (*despedazarse*) to come apart o undone; ~**se de** to get rid of; (*COM*) to dump, unload; ~**se en** (*cumplidos, elogios*) to be lavish with; ~**se en lágrimas** to burst into tears; ~**se por algo** to be crazy about sth.

deshaga [de'saɣa] *etc*, **desharé** [desa're] *etc vb* V **deshacer**.

des(h)arrapado, a [desarra'paðo, a] *adj* ragged, (**de aspecto**) ~ shabby.

deshecho, a [de'setʃo, a] *pp de* **deshacer** ♦ *adj* (*lazo, nudo*) undone; (*roto*) smashed; (*despedazado*) in pieces; (*cama*) unmade; (*MED*: *persona*) weak, emaciated; (: *salud*) broken; **estoy** ~ I'm shattered.

deshelar [dese'lar] *vt* (*cañería*) to thaw; (*heladera*) to defrost.

desheredar [desere'ðar] *vt* to disinherit.

deshice [de'siθe] *etc vb* V **deshacer**.

deshidratación [desiðrata'θjon] *nf* dehydration.

deshidratar [desiðra'tar] *vt* to dehydrate.

deshielo [des'jelo] *etc vb* V **deshelar** ♦ *nm* thaw.

deshilachar [desila'tʃar] *vt*, **deshilacharse** *vr* to fray.

deshilar [desi'lar] *vt* (*tela*) to unravel.

deshilvanado, a [desilßa'naðo, a] _adj_ (_fig_) disjointed, incoherent.

deshinchar [desin'tʃar] _vt_ (_neumático_) to let down; (_herida etc_) to reduce (the swelling of); ~**se** _vr_ (_neumático_) to go flat; (_hinchazón_) to go down.

deshojar [deso'xar] _vt_ (_árbol_) to strip the leaves off; (_flor_) to pull the petals off; ~**se** _vr_ to lose its leaves _etc._

deshollinar [desoʎi'nar] _vt_ (_chimenea_) to sweep.

deshonesto, a [deso'nesto, a] _adj_ (_no honrado_) dishonest; (_indecente_) indecent.

deshonor [deso'nor] _nm_ dishonour, disgrace; (_un_ ~) insult, affront.

deshonra [de'sonra] _nf_ (_deshonor_) dishonour; (_vergüenza_) shame.

deshonrar [deson'rar] _vt_ to dishonour.

deshonroso, a [deson'roso, a] _adj_ dishonourable, disgraceful.

deshora [de'sora]: **a** ~ _adv_ at the wrong time; (_llegar_) unexpectedly; (_acostarse_) at some unearthly hour.

deshuesar [deswe'sar] _vt_ (_carne_) to bone; (_fruta_) to stone.

desidia [de'siðja] _nf_ (_pereza_) idleness.

desierto, a [de'sjerto, a] _adj_ (_casa, calle, negocio_) deserted; (_paisaje_) bleak ♦ _nm_ desert.

designación [desiɤna'θjon] _nf_ (_para un cargo_) appointment; (_nombre_) designation.

designar [desiɤ'nar] _vt_ (_nombrar_) to designate; (_indicar_) to fix.

designio [de'siɤnjo] _nm_ plan; **con el** ~ **de** with the intention of.

desigual [desi'ɤwal] _adj_ (_lucha_) unequal; (_diferente_) different; (_terreno_) uneven; (_tratamiento_) unfair; (_cambiadizo: tiempo_) changeable; (: _carácter_) unpredictable.

desigualdad [desiɤwal'ðað] _nf_ (_ECON, POL_) inequality; (_de carácter, tiempo_) unpredictability; (_de escritura_) unevenness; (_de terreno_) roughness.

desilusión [desilu'sjon] _nf_ disillusionment; (_decepción_) disappointment.

desilusionar [desilusjo'nar] _vt_ to disillusion; (_decepcionar_) to disappoint; ~**se** _vr_ to become disillusioned.

desinencia [desi'nenθja] _nf_ (_LING_) ending.

desinfectar [desinfek'tar] _vt_ to disinfect.

desinfestar [desinfes'tar] _vt_ to decontaminate.

desinflación [desinfla'θjon] _nf_ (_COM_) disinflation.

desinflar [desin'flar] _vt_ to deflate; ~**se** _vr_ (_neumático_) to go down o flat.

desintegración [desinteɤra'θjon] _nf_ disintegration; ~ **nuclear** nuclear fission.

desintegrar [desinte'ɤrar] _vt_ (_gen_) to disintegrate; (_átomo_) to split; (_grupo_) to break up; ~**se** _vr_ to disintegrate; to split; to break up.

desinterés [desinte'res] _nm_ (_objetividad_) disinterestedness; (_altruismo_) unselfishness.

desinteresado, a [desintere'saðo, a] _adj_ (_imparcial_) disinterested; (_altruista_) unselfish.

desintoxicar [desintoksi'kar] _vt_ to detoxify; ~**se** _vr_ (_drogadicto_) to undergo treatment for drug addiction; ~**se de** (_rutina, trabajo_) to get away from.

desintoxique [desintok'sike] _etc vb V_ **desintoxicar**.

desistir [desis'tir] _vi_ (_renunciar_) to stop, desist; ~ **de** (_empresa_) to give up; (_derecho_) to waive.

deslavazado, a [deslaßa'θaðo, a] _adj_ (_lacio_) limp; (_desteñido_) faded; (_insípido_) colourless; (_incoherente_) disjointed.

desleal [desle'al] _adj_ (_infiel_) disloyal; (_COM: competencia_) unfair.

deslealtad [desleal'tað] _nf_ disloyalty.

desleído, a [desle'iðo, a] _adj_ weak, woolly.

desleír [desle'ir] _vt_ (_líquido_) to dilute; (_sólido_) to dissolve.

deslenguado, a [deslen'gwaðo, a] _adj_ (_grosero_) foul-mouthed.

deslía [des'lia] _etc vb V_ **desleír**.

desliar [des'ljar] _vt_ (_desatar_) to untie; (_paquete_) to open; ~**se** _vr_ to come undone.

deslice [des'liθe] _etc vb V_ **deslizar**.

desliendo [desli'endo] _etc vb V_ **desleír**.

desligar [desli'ɤar] _vt_ (_desatar_) to untie, undo; (_separar_) to separate; ~**se** _vr_ (_de un compromiso_) to extricate o.s.

desligue [des'liɤe] _etc vb V_ **desligar**.

deslindar [deslin'dar] _vt_ (_señalar las lindes de_) to mark out, fix the boundaries of; (_fig_) to define.

desliz [des'liθ] _nm_ (_fig_) lapse; ~ **de lengua** slip of the tongue; **cometer un** ~ to slip up.

deslizar [desli'θar] _vt_ to slip, slide; ~**se** _vr_ (_escurrirse: persona_) to slip, slide; (: _coche_) to skid; (_aguas mansas_) to flow gently; (_error_) to creep in; (_tiempo_) to pass; (_persona: irse_) to slip away; ~**se en un cuarto** to slip into a room.

deslomar [deslo'mar] _vt_ (_romper el lomo de_) to break the back of; (_fig_) to wear out; ~**se** _vr_ (_fig fam_) to work one's guts out.

deslucido, a [deslu'θiðo, a] _adj_ dull; (_torpe_)

awkward, graceless; (*deslustrado*)
tarnished; (*fracasado*) unsuccessful;
quedar ~ to make a poor impression.

deslucir [deslu'θir] *vt* (*deslustrar*) to
tarnish; (*estropear*) to spoil, ruin;
(*persona*) to discredit; **la lluvia deslució
el acto** the rain ruined the ceremony.

deslumbrar [deslum'brar] *vt* (*con la luz*) to
dazzle; (*cegar*) to blind; (*impresionar*) to
dazzle; (*dejar perplejo a*) to puzzle,
confuse.

deslustrar [deslus'trar] *vt* (*vidrio*) to frost;
(*quitar lustre a*) to dull; (*reputación*) to
sully.

desluzca [des'luθka] *etc vb V* **deslucir**.

desmadrarse [desma'ðrarse] *vr* (*fam*) to
run wild.

desmadre [des'maðre] *nm* (*fam*:
desorganización) chaos; (: *jaleo*)
commotion.

desmán [des'man] *nm* (*exceso*) outrage;
(*abuso de poder*) abuse.

desmandarse [desman'darse] *vr* (*portarse
mal*) to behave badly; (*excederse*) to get
out of hand; (*caballo*) to bolt.

desmano [des'mano]: **a** ~ *adv*: **me coge** o
pilla a ~ it's out of my way.

desmantelar [desmante'lar] *vt* (*deshacer*)
to dismantle; (*casa*) to strip;
(*organización*) to disband; (*MIL*) to raze;
(*andamio*) to take down; (*NAUT*) to unrig.

desmaquillador [desmakiʎa'ðor] *nm*
make-up remover.

desmaquillarse [desmaki'ʎarse] *vr* to take
off one's make up.

desmarcarse [desmar'karse] *vr*: ~ **de**
(*DEPORTE*) to get clear of; (*fig*) to
distance o.s. from.

desmayado, a [desma'jaðo, a] *adj* (*sin
sentido*) unconscious; (*carácter*) dull;
(*débil*) faint, weak; (*color*) pale.

desmayar [desma'jar] *vi* to lose heart; ~**se**
vr (*MED*) to faint.

desmayo [des'majo] *nm* (*MED*: *acto*) faint;
(*estado*) unconsciousness; (*depresión*)
dejection; (*de voz*) faltering; **sufrir un** ~
to have a fainting fit.

desmedido, a [desme'ðiðo, a] *adj*
excessive; (*ambición*) boundless.

desmejorado, a [desmexo'raðo, a] *adj*:
está muy desmejorada (*MED*) she's not
looking too well.

desmejorar [desmexo'rar] *vt* (*dañar*) to
impair, spoil; (*MED*) to weaken.

desmembración [desmembra'θjon] *nf*
dismemberment; (*fig*) break-up.

desmembrar [desmem'brar] *vt* (*MED*) to
dismember; (*fig*) to separate.

desmemoriado, a [desmemo'rjaðo, a] *adj*
forgetful, absent-minded.

desmentir [desmen'tir] *vt* (*contradecir*) to
contradict; (*refutar*) to deny; (*rumor*) to
scotch ♦ *vi*: ~ **de** to refute; ~**se** *vr* to
contradict o.s.

desmenuce [desme'nuθe] *etc vb V*
desmenuzar.

desmenuzar [desmenu'θar] *vt* (*deshacer*) to
crumble; (*carne*) to chop; (*examinar*) to
examine closely.

desmerecer [desmere'θer] *vt* to be
unworthy of ♦ *vi* (*deteriorarse*) to
deteriorate.

desmerezca [desme'reθka] *etc vb V*
desmerecer.

desmesurado, a [desmesu'raðo, a] *adj*
(*desmedido*) disproportionate; (*enorme*)
enormous; (*ambición*) boundless;
(*descarado*) insolent.

desmiembre [des'mjembre] *etc vb V*
desmembrar.

desmienta [des'mjenta] *etc vb V*
desmentir.

desmigajar [desmiɣa'xar], **desmigar**
[desmi'ɣar] *vt* to crumble.

desmigue [des'miɣe] *etc vb V* **desmigar**.

desmilitarice [desmilita'riθe] *etc vb V*
desmilitarizar.

desmilitarizar [desmilitari'θar] *vt* to
demilitarize.

desmintiendo [desmin'tjendo] *etc vb V*
desmentir.

desmochar [desmo'tʃar] *vt* (*árbol*) to lop;
(*texto*) to cut, hack about.

desmontable [desmon'taβle] *adj* (*que se
quita*) detachable; (*en compartimientos*)
sectional; (*que se puede plegar etc*)
collapsible.

desmontar [desmon'tar] *vt* (*deshacer*) to
dismantle; (*motor*) to strip down,
(*máquina*) to take apart; (*escopeta*) to
uncock; (*tienda de campaña*) to take
down; (*tierra*) to level; (*quitar los árboles
a*) to clear; (*jinete*) to throw ♦ *vi* to
dismount.

desmonte [des'monte] *nm* (*de tierra*)
levelling; (*de árboles*) clearing; (*terreno*)
levelled ground; (*FERRO*) cutting.

desmoralice [desmora'liθe] *etc vb V*
desmoralizar.

desmoralizador, a [desmoraliθa'ðor, a] *adj*
demoralizing.

desmoralizar [desmorali'θar] *vt* to
demoralize.

desmoronado, a [desmoro'naðo, a] *adj*
(*casa, edificio*) dilapidated.

desmoronamiento [desmorona'mjento]

_nm_ (_tb fig_) crumbling.

desmoronar [desmoro'nar] _vt_ to wear away, erode; ~**se** _vr_ (_edificio, dique_) to fall into disrepair; (_economía_) to decline.

desmovilice [desmoßi'liθe] _etc vb V_ **desmovilizar**.

desmovilizar [desmoßili'θar] _vt_ to demobilize.

desnacionalización [desnaθjonaliθa'θjon] _nf_ denationalization.

desnacionalizado, a [desnaθjonali'θaðo, a] _adj_ (_industria_) denationalized; (_persona_) stateless.

desnatado, a [desna'taðo, a] _adj_ skimmed; (_yogur_) low fat.

desnatar [desna'tar] _vt_ (_leche_) to skim; **leche sin** ~ whole milk.

desnaturalice [desnatura'liθe] _etc vb V_ **desnaturalizar**.

desnaturalizado, a [desnaturali'θaðo, a] _adj_ (_persona_) unnatural; **alcohol** ~ methylated spirits.

desnaturalizar [desnaturali'θar] _vt_ (_QUÍMICA_) to denature; (_corromper_) to pervert; (_sentido de algo_) to distort; ~**se** _vr_ (_perder la nacionalidad_) to give up one's nationality.

desnivel [desni'ßel] _nm_ (_de terreno_) unevenness; (_POL_) inequality; (_diferencia_) difference.

desnivelar [desniße'lar] _vt_ (_terreno_) to make uneven; (_fig: desequilibrar_) to unbalance; (_balanza_) to tip.

desnuclearizado, a [desnukleari'θaðo, a] _adj_: **región desnuclearizada** nuclear-free zone.

desnudar [desnu'ðar] _vt_ (_desvestir_) to undress; (_despojar_) to strip; ~**se** _vr_ (_desvestirse_) to get undressed.

desnudez [desnu'ðeθ] _nf_ (_de persona_) nudity; (_fig_) bareness.

desnudo, a [des'nuðo, a] _adj_ (_cuerpo_) naked; (_árbol, brazo_) bare; (_paisaje_) flat; (_estilo_) unadorned; (_verdad_) plain ♦ _nm/f_ nude; ~ **de** devoid _o_ bereft of; **la retrató al** ~ he painted her in the nude; **poner al** ~ to lay bare.

desnutrición [desnutri'θjon] _nf_ malnutrition.

desnutrido, a [desnu'triðo, a] _adj_ undernourished.

desobedecer [desoßeðe'θer] _vt, vi_ to disobey.

desobedezca [desoße'ðeθka] _etc vb V_ **desobedecer**.

desobediencia [desoße'ðjenθja] _nf_ disobedience.

desocupación [desokupa'θjon] _nf_ (_AM_) unemployment.

desocupado, a [desoku'paðo, a] _adj_ at leisure; (_desempleado_) unemployed; (_deshabitado_) empty, vacant.

desocupar [desoku'par] _vt_ to vacate; ~**se** _vr_ (_quedar libre_) to be free; **se ha desocupado aquella mesa** that table's free now.

desodorante [desoðo'rante] _nm_ deodorant.

desoiga [de'soiɣa] _etc vb V_ **desoír**.

desoír [deso'ir] _vt_ to ignore, disregard.

desolación [desola'θjon] _nf_ (_de lugar_) desolation; (_fig_) grief.

desolar [deso'lar] _vt_ to ruin, lay waste.

desollar [deso'ʎar] _vt_ (_quitar la piel a_) to skin; (_criticar_): ~ **vivo a** to criticize unmercifully.

desorbitado, a [desorßi'taðo, a] _adj_ (_excesivo_) excessive; (_precio_) exorbitant; **con los ojos** ~**s** pop-eyed.

desorbitar [desorßi'tar] _vt_ (_exagerar_) to exaggerate; (_interpretar mal_) to misinterpret; ~**se** _vr_ (_persona_) to lose one's sense of proportion; (_asunto_) to get out of hand.

desorden [de'sorðen] _nm_ confusion; (_de casa, cuarto_) mess; (_político_) disorder; **desórdenes** _nmpl_ (_alborotos_) disturbances; (_excesos_) excesses; **en** ~ (_gente_) in confusion.

desordenado, a [desorðe'naðo, a] _adj_ (_habitación, persona_) untidy; (_objetos: revueltos_) in a mess, jumbled; (_conducta_) disorderly.

desordenar [desorðe'nar] _vt_ (_gen_) to disarrange; (_pelo_) to mess up; (_cuarto_) to make a mess in; (_causar confusión a_) to throw into confusion.

desorganice [desorɣa'niθe] _etc vb V_ **desorganizar**.

desorganizar [desorɣani'θar] _vt_ to disorganize.

desorientar [desorjen'tar] _vt_ (_extraviar_) to mislead; (_confundir, desconcertar_) to confuse; ~**se** _vr_ (_perderse_) to lose one's way.

desovar [deso'ßar] _vi_ (_peces_) to spawn; (_insectos_) to lay eggs.

desoyendo [deso'jendo] _etc vb V_ **desoír**.

despabilado, a [despaßi'laðo, a] _adj_ (_despierto_) wide-awake; (_fig_) alert, sharp.

despabilar [despaßi'lar] _vt_ (_despertar_) to wake up; (_fig: persona_) to liven up; (_trabajo_) to get through quickly ♦ _vi_, ~**se** _vr_ to wake up; (_fig_) to get a move on.

despachar [despa't ʃar] _vt_ (_negocio_) to do, complete; (_resolver: problema_) to settle; (_correspondencia_) to deal with; (_fam:

comida) to polish off; (: *bebida*) to knock back; (*enviar*) to send, dispatch; (*vender*) to sell, deal in; (*COM: cliente*) to attend to; (*billete*) to issue; (*mandar ir*) to send away ♦ *vi* (*decidirse*) to get things settled; (*apresurarse*) to hurry up; ~**se** *vr* to finish off; (*apresurarse*) to hurry up; ~**se de algo** to get rid of sth; ~**se a su gusto con algn** to give sb a piece of one's mind; **¿quién despacha?** is anybody serving?

despacho [des'patʃo] *nm* (*oficina*) office; (: *en una casa*) study; (*de paquetes*) dispatch; (*COM: venta*) sale (of goods); (*comunicación*) message; ~ **de billetes** *o* **boletos** (*AM*) booking office; ~ **de localidades** box office; **géneros sin** ~ unsaleable goods; **tener buen** ~ to find a ready sale.

despachurrar [despatʃu'rrar] *vt* (*aplastar*) to crush; (*persona*) to flatten.

despacio [des'paθjo] *adv* (*lentamente*) slowly; (*esp AM: en voz baja*) softly; ¡~! take it easy!

despacito [despa'θito] *adv* (*fam*) slowly; (*suavemente*) softly.

despampanante [despampa'nante] *adj* (*fam: chica*) stunning.

desparejado, a [despare'xaðo, a] *adj* odd.

desparpajo [despar'paxo] *nm* (*desenvoltura*) self-confidence; (*pey*) nerve.

desparramar [desparra'mar] *vt* (*esparcir*) to scatter; (*líquido*) to spill.

despatarrarse [despata'rrarse] *vr* (*abrir las piernas*) to open one's legs wide; (*caerse*) to tumble; (*fig*) to be flabbergasted.

despavorido, a [despaβo'riðo, a] *adj* terrified.

despecho [des'petʃo] *nm* spite; **a** ~ **de** in spite of; **por** ~ out of (sheer) spite.

despectivo, a [despek'tiβo, a] *adj* (*despreciativo*) derogatory; (*LING*) pejorative.

despedace [despe'ðaθe] *etc vb V* **despedazar**.

despedazar [despeða'θar] *vt* to tear to pieces.

despedida [despe'ðiða] *nf* (*adiós*) goodbye, farewell; (*antes de viaje*) send-off; (*en carta*) closing formula; (*de obrero*) sacking; (*INFORM*) logout; **cena/función de** ~ farewell dinner/performance; **regalo de** ~ parting gift; ~ **de soltero/ soltera** stag/hen party.

despedir [despe'ðir] *vt* (*visita*) to see off, show out; (*empleado*) to dismiss; (*inquilino*) to evict; (*objeto*) to hurl, (*olor etc*) to give out *o* off; ~**se** *vr* (*dejar un*

empleo) to give up one's job; (*INFORM*) to log out *o* off; ~**se de** to say goodbye to; **se despidieron** they said goodbye to each other.

despegado, a [despe'ɣaðo, a] *adj* (*separado*) detached; (*persona: poco afectuoso*) cold, indifferent ♦ *nm/f*: **es un** ~ he has cut himself off from his family.

despegar [despe'ɣar] *vt* to unstick; (*sobre*) to open ♦ *vi* (*avión*) to take off; (*cohete*) to blast off; ~**se** *vr* to come loose, come unstuck; **sin** ~ **los labios** without uttering a word.

despego [des'peɣo] *nm* detachment.

despegue [des'peɣe] *etc vb V* **despegar** ♦ *nm* takeoff, (*de cohete*) blastoff.

despeinado, a [despei'naðo, a] *adj* dishevelled, unkempt.

despeinar [despei'nar] *vt* (*pelo*) to ruffle; **¡me has despeinado todo!** you've completely ruined my hairdo!

despejado, a [despe'xaðo, a] *adj* (*lugar*) clear, free; (*cielo*) clear; (*persona*) wide-awake, bright.

despejar [despe'xar] *vt* (*gen*) to clear; (*misterio*) to clarify, clear up; (*MAT: incógnita*) to find ♦ *vi* (*el tiempo*) to clear; ~**se** *vr* (*tiempo, cielo*) to clear (up); (*misterio*) to become clearer; (*cabeza*) to clear; **¡despejen!** (*moverse*) move along!; (*salirse*) everybody out!

despeje [des'pexe] *nm* (*DEPORTE*) clearance.

despellejar [despeʎe'xar] *vt* (*animal*) to skin; (*criticar*) to criticize unmercifully; (*fam: arruinar*) to fleece.

despelotarse [despelo'tarse] *vr* (*fam*) to strip off; (*fig*) to let one's hair down.

despelote [despe'lote] (*fam*) *nm* (*AM: lío*) mess; **¡qué** *o* **vaya** ~! what a riot *o* laugh!

despenalizar [despenali'θar] *vt* to decriminalize.

despensa [des'pensa] *nf* (*armario*) larder; (*NAUT*) storeroom; (*provisión de comestibles*) stock of food.

despeñadero [despeɲa'ðero] *nm* (*GEO*) cliff, precipice.

despeñar [despe'ɲar] *vt* (*arrojar*) to fling down; ~**se** *vr* to fling o.s. down; (*caer*) to fall headlong.

desperdiciar [desperði'θjar] *vt* (*comida, tiempo*) to waste; (*oportunidad*) to throw away.

desperdicio [desper'ðiθjo] *nm* (*despilfarro*) squandering; (*residuo*) waste; ~**s** *nmpl* (*basura*) rubbish *sg*, refuse *sg*, garbage *sg*

(_US_); (_residuos_) waste _sg_; ~**s de cocina** kitchen scraps; **el libro no tiene** ~ the book is excellent from beginning to end.

desperdigar [desperði'xar] _vt_ (_esparcir_) to scatter; (_energía_) to dissipate; ~**se** _vr_ to scatter.

desperdigue [desper'ðixe] _etc vb_ V **desperdigar.**

desperece [despe'reθe] _etc vb_ V **desperezarse.**

desperezarse [despere'θarse] _vr_ to stretch.

desperfecto [desper'fekto] _nm_ (_deterioro_) slight damage; (_defecto_) flaw, imperfection.

despertador [desperta'ðor] _nm_ alarm clock; ~ **de viaje** travelling clock.

despertar [desper'tar] _vt_ (_persona_) to wake up; (_recuerdos_) to revive; (_esperanzas_) to raise; (_sentimiento_) to arouse ♦ _vi_, ~**se** _vr_ to awaken, wake up ♦ _nm_ awakening; ~**se a la realidad** to wake up to reality.

despiadado a [despja'ðaðo, a] _adj_ (_ataque_) merciless; (_persona_) heartless.

despido [des'piðo] _etc vb_ V **despedir** ♦ _nm_ dismissal, sacking; ~ **improcedente** _o_ **injustificado** wrongful dismissal; ~ **injusto** unfair dismissal; ~ **libre** right to hire and fire; ~ **voluntario** voluntary redundancy.

despierto, a [des'pjerto, a] _etc vb_ V **despertar** ♦ _adj_ awake; (_fig_) sharp, alert.

despilfarrar [despilfa'rrar] _vt_ (_gen_) to waste; (_dinero_) to squander.

despilfarro [despil'farro] _nm_ (_derroche_) squandering; (_lujo desmedido_) extravagance.

despintar [despin'tar] _vt_ (_quitar pintura a_) to take the paint off; (_hechos_) to distort ♦ _vi_: **A no despinta a B** A is in no way inferior to B; ~**se** _vr_ (_desteñir_) to fade.

despiojar [despjo'xar] _vt_ to delouse.

despistado, a [despis'taðo, a] _adj_ (_distraído_) vague, absent-minded; (_poco práctico_) unpractical; (_confuso_) confused; (_desorientado_) off the track ♦ _nm/f_ (_tipo: distraído_) scatterbrain, absent-minded person.

despistar [despis'tar] _vt_ to throw off the track _o_ scent; (_fig_) to mislead, confuse; ~**se** _vr_ to take the wrong road; (_fig_) to become confused.

despiste [des'piste] _nm_ (_AUTO etc_) swerve; (_error_) slip; (_distracción_) absent-mindedness; **tiene un terrible** ~ he's terribly absent-minded.

desplace [des'plaθe] _etc vb_ V **desplazar.**

desplante [des'plante] _nm_: **hacer un** ~ **a algn** to be rude to sb.

desplazado, a [despla'θaðo, a] _adj_ (_pieza_) wrongly placed ♦ _nm/f_ (_inadaptado_) misfit; **sentirse un poco** ~ to feel rather out of place.

desplazamiento [desplaθa'mjento] _nm_ displacement; (_viaje_) journey; (_de opinión, votos_) shift, swing; (_INFORM_) scrolling; ~ **hacia arriba/abajo** (_INFORM_) scroll up/down.

desplazar [despla'θar] _vt_ (_gen_) to move; (_FÍSICA, NAUT, TEC_) to displace; (_tropas_) to transfer; (_suplantar_) to take the place of; (_INFORM_) to scroll; ~**se** _vr_ (_persona, vehículo_) to travel, go; (_objeto_) to move, shift; (_votos, opinión_) to shift, swing.

desplegar [desple'xar] _vt_ (_tela, papel_) to unfold, open out; (_bandera_) to unfurl; (_alas_) to spread; (_MIL_) to deploy; (_manifestar_) to display.

desplegué [desple'xe], **despleguemos** [desple'xemos] _etc vb_ V **desplegar.**

despliegue [des'pljexe] _etc vb_ V **desplegar** ♦ _nm_ unfolding, opening; deployment, display.

desplomarse [desplo'marse] _vr_ (_edificio, gobierno, persona_) to collapse; (_derrumbarse_) to topple over; (_precios_) to slump; **se ha desplomado el techo** the ceiling has fallen in.

desplumar [desplu'mar] _vt_ (_ave_) to pluck; (_fam: estafar_) to fleece.

despoblado, a [despo'βlaðo, a] _adj_ (_sin habitantes_) uninhabited; (_con pocos habitantes_) depopulated; (_con insuficientes habitantes_) underpopulated ♦ _nm_ deserted spot.

despojar [despo'xar] _vt_ (_alguien: de sus bienes_) to divest of, deprive of; (_casa_) to strip, leave bare; (_de su cargo_) to strip of; ~**se** _vr_ (_desnudarse_) to undress; ~**se de** (_ropa, hojas_) to shed; (_poderes_) to relinquish.

despojo [des'poxo] _nm_ (_acto_) plundering; (_objetos_) plunder, loot; ~**s** _nmpl_ (_de ave, res_) offal _sg._

desposado, a [despo'saðo, a] _adj, nm/f_ newly-wed.

desposar [despo'sar] _vt_ (_suj: sacerdote: pareja_) to marry; ~**se** _vr_ (_casarse_) to marry, get married.

desposeer [despose'er] _vt_ (_despojar_) to dispossess; ~ **a algn de su autoridad** to strip sb of his authority.

desposeído, a [despose'iðo, a] _nm/f_: **los** ~**s** the have-nots.

desposeyendo [despose'jendo] _etc vb_ V **desposeer.**

desposorios [despo'sorjos] _nmpl_

(*esponsales*) betrothal *sg*; (*boda*) marriage ceremony *sg*.

déspota ['despota] *nm/f* despot.

despotismo [despo'tismo] *nm* despotism.

despotricar [despotri'kar] *vi*: ~ **contra** to moan *o* complain about.

despotrique [despo'trike] *etc vb* V **despotricar**.

despreciable [despre'θjaßle] *adj* (*moralmente*) despicable; (*objeto*) worthless; (*cantidad*) negligible.

despreciar [despre'θjar] *vt* (*desdeñar*) to despise, scorn; (*afrentar*) to slight.

despreciativo, a [despreθja'tißo, a] *adj* (*observación, tono*) scornful, contemptuous; (*comentario*) derogatory.

desprecio [des'preθjo] *nm* scorn, contempt; slight.

desprender [despren'der] *vt* (*soltar*) to loosen; (*separar*) to separate; (*desatar*) to unfasten; (*olor*) to give off; ~**se** *vr* (*botón: caerse*) to fall off; (: *abrirse*) to unfasten; (*olor, perfume*) to be given off; ~**se de** to follow from; ~**se de algo** (*ceder*) to give sth up, (*desembarazarse*) to get rid of sth; **se desprende que** it transpires that.

desprendido, a [despren'dido, a] *adj* (*pieza*) loose; (*sin abrochar*) unfastened; (*desinteresado*) disinterested; (*generoso*) generous.

desprendimiento [desprendi'mjento] *nm* (*gen*) loosening; (*generosidad*) disinterestedness; (*indiferencia*) detachment; (*de gas*) leak; (*de tierra, rocas*) landslide.

despreocupado, a [despreoku'paðo, a] *adj* (*sin preocupación*) unworried, unconcerned; (*tranquilo*) nonchalant; (*en el vestir*) casual; (*negligente*) careless.

despreocuparse [despreoku'parse] *vr* to be carefree; (*dejar de inquietarse*) to stop worrying; (*ser indiferente*) to be unconcerned; ~ **de** to have no interest in.

desprestigiar [despresti'xjar] *vt* (*criticar*) to run down, disparage; (*desacreditar*) to discredit.

desprestigio [despres'tixjo] *nm* (*denigración*) disparagement; (*impopularidad*) unpopularity.

desprevenido, a [despreße'niðo, a] *adj* (*no preparado*) unprepared, unready; **coger** (*ESP*) *o* **agarrar** (*AM*) **a algn** ~ to catch sb unawares.

desproporción [despropor'θjon] *nf* disproportion, lack of proportion.

desproporcionado, a [despropor0jo'naðo, a] *adj* disproportionate, out of proportion.

despropósito [despro'posito] *nm* (*salida de tono*) irrelevant remark; (*disparate*) piece of nonsense.

desprovisto, a [despro'ßisto, a] *adj*: ~ **de** devoid of; **estar** ~ **de** to lack.

después [des'pwes] *adv* afterwards, later; (*desde entonces*) since (then); (*próximo paso*) next; **poco** ~ soon after; **un año** ~ a year later; ~ **se debatió el tema** next the matter was discussed ♦ *prep*: ~ **de** (*tiempo*) after, since; (*orden*) next (to); ~ **de comer** after lunch; ~ **de corregido el texto** after the text had been corrected; ~ **de esa fecha** (*pasado*) since that date; (*futuro*) from *o* after that date; ~ **de todo** after all; ~ **de verlo** after seeing it, after I *etc* saw it; **mi nombre está** ~ **del tuyo** my name comes next to yours ♦ *conj*: ~ **(de) que** after; ~ **(de) que lo escribí** after *o* since I wrote it, after writing it.

despuntar [despun'tar] *vt* (*lápiz*) to blunt ♦ *vi* (*BOT: plantas*) to sprout; (: *flores*) to bud; (*alba*) to break; (*día*) to dawn; (*persona: descollar*) to stand out.

desquiciar [deski'θjar] *vt* (*puerta*) to take off its hinges; (*descomponer*) to upset; (*persona: turbar*) to disturb; (: *volver loco a*) to unhinge.

desquitarse [deski'tarse] *vr* to obtain satisfaction; (*COM*) to recover a debt; (*fig: vengarse de*) to get one's own back; ~ **de una pérdida** to make up for a loss.

desquite [des'kite] *nm* (*satisfacción*) satisfaction; (*venganza*) revenge.

Dest. *abr* = **destinatario**.

destacado, a [desta'kaðo, a] *adj* outstanding.

destacamento [destaka'mento] *nm* (*MIL*) detachment.

destacar [desta'kar] *vt* (*ARTE: hacer resaltar*) to make stand out; (*subrayar*) to emphasize, point up; (*MIL*) to detach, detail; (*INFORM*) to highlight ♦ *vi*, ~**se** *vr* (*resaltarse*) to stand out; (*persona*) to be outstanding *o* exceptional; **quiero** ~ **que...** I wish to emphasize that...; ~**(se) contra** *o* **en** *o* **sobre** to stand out *o* be outlined against.

destajo [des'taxo] *nm*: **a** ~ (*por pieza*) by the job; (*con afán*) eagerly; **trabajar a** ~ to do piecework; (*fig*) to work one's fingers to the bone.

destapar [desta'par] *vt* (*botella*) to open; (*cacerola*) to take the lid off; (*descubrir*) to uncover; ~**se** *vr* (*descubrirse*) to get uncovered; (*revelarse*) to reveal one's true character.

destape [des'tape] nm nudity; (fig)
permissiveness; **el ~ español** the
process of liberalization in Spain after
Franco's death.

destaque [des'take] etc vb V **destacar**.

destartalado, a [destarta'laðo, a] adj
(desordenado) untidy; (casa etc: grande)
rambling; (: ruinoso) tumbledown.

destellar [deste'ʎar] vi (diamante) to
sparkle; (metal) to glint; (estrella) to
twinkle.

destello [des'teʎo] nm (de diamante)
sparkle; (de metal) glint; (de estrella)
twinkle; (de faro) signal light; **no tiene
un ~ de verdad** there's not a grain of
truth in it.

destemplado, a [destem'plaðo, a] adj
(MUS) out of tune; (voz) harsh; (MED) out
of sorts; (METEOROLOGÍA) unpleasant,
nasty.

destemplar [destem'plar] vt (MUS) to put
out of tune; (alterar) to upset; **~se** vr
(MUS) to lose its pitch; (descomponerse)
to get out of order; (persona: irritarse) to
get upset; (MED) to get out of sorts.

desteñir [deste'ɲir] vt to fade ♦ vi, **~se** vr to
fade; **esta tela no destiñe** this fabric will
not run.

desternillarse [desterni'ʎarse] vr: **~ de risa**
to split one's sides laughing.

desterrado, a [deste'rraðo, a] nm/f
(exiliado) exile.

desterrar [deste'rrar] vt (exilar) to exile;
(fig) to banish, dismiss.

destetar [deste'tar] vt to wean.

destiempo [des'tjempo]: **a ~** adv at the
wrong time.

destierro [des'tjerro] etc vb V **desterrar**
♦ nm exile; **vivir en el ~** to live in exile.

destilar [desti'lar] vt to distil; (pus, sangre)
to ooze; (fig: rebosar) to exude; (: revelar)
to reveal ♦ vi (gotear) to drip.

destilería [destile'ria] nf distillery; **~ de
petróleo** oil refinery.

destinar [desti'nar] vt (funcionario) to
appoint, assign; (fondos) to set aside; **es
un libro destinado a los niños** it is a book
(intended o meant) for children; **una
carta que viene destinada a usted** a
letter for you, a letter addressed to you.

destinatario, a [destina'tarjo, a] nm/f
addressee; (COM) payee.

destino [des'tino] nm (suerte) destiny; (de
viajero) destination; (función) use;
(puesto) post, placement; **~ público**
public appointment; **salir con ~ a** to
leave for; **con ~ a Londres** (avión, barco)
(bound) for London; (carta) to London.

destiña [des'tiɲa] etc, **destiñendo**
[desti'ɲeðo] etc vb V **desteñir**.

destitución [destitu'θjon] nf dismissal,
removal.

destituir [destitu'ir] vt (despedir) to
dismiss; (: ministro, funcionario) to
remove from office.

destituyendo [destitu'jendo] etc vb V
destituir.

destornillador [destorniʎa'ðor] nm
screwdriver.

destornillar [destorni'ʎar] vt, **~se** vr
(tornillo) to unscrew.

destreza [des'treθa] nf (habilidad) skill;
(maña) dexterity.

destripar [destri'par] vt (animal) to gut;
(reventar) to mangle.

destroce [de'stroθe] etc vb V **destrozar**.

destronar [destro'nar] vt (rey) to dethrone;
(fig) to overthrow.

destroncar [destron'kar] vt (árbol) to chop
off, lop; (proyectos) to ruin; (discurso) to
interrupt.

destronque [des'tronke] etc vb V
destroncar.

destrozar [destro'θar] vt (romper) to
smash, break (up); (estropear) to ruin;
(nervios) to shatter; **~ a algn en una
discusión** to crush sb in an argument.

destrozo [des'troθo] nm (acción)
destruction; (desastre) smashing; **~s**
nmpl (pedazos) pieces; (daños) havoc sg.

destrucción [destruk'θjon] nf destruction.

destructor, a [destruk'tor, a] adj
destructive ♦ nm (NAUT) destroyer.

destruir [destru'ir] vt to destroy; (casa) to
demolish; (equilibrio) to upset; (proyecto)
to spoil; (esperanzas) to dash; (argumento)
to demolish.

destruyendo [destru'jendo] etc vb V
destruir.

desuelle [de'sweʎe] etc vb V **desollar**.

desueve [de'sweβe] etc vb V **desovar**.

desunión [desu'njon] nf (separación)
separation; (discordia) disunity.

desunir [desu'nir] vt to separate; (TEC) to
disconnect; (fig) to cause a quarrel o rift
between.

desuso [de'suso] nm disuse; **caer en ~** to
fall into disuse, become obsolete; **una
expresión caída en ~** an obsolete
expression.

desvaído, a [desβa'iðo, a] adj (color) pale;
(contorno) blurred.

desvalido, a [desβa'liðo, a] adj
(desprotegido) destitute; (sin fuerzas)
helpless; **niños ~s** waifs and strays.

desvalijar [desβali'xar] vt (persona) to rob;

(*casa, tienda*) to burgle; (*coche*) to break into.

desvalorice [desßalo'riθe] *etc vb V* **desvalorizar**.

desvalorizar [desßalori'θar] *vt* to devalue.

desván [des'ßan] *nm* attic.

desvanecer [desßane'θer] *vt* (*disipar*) to dispel; (*recuerdo, temor*) to banish; (*borrar*) to blur; **~se** *vr* (*humo etc*) to vanish, disappear; (*duda*) to be dispelled; (*color*) to fade; (*recuerdo, sonido*) to fade away; (*MED*) to pass out.

desvanecido, a [desßane'θiðo, a] *adj* (*MED*) faint; **caer ~** to fall in a faint.

desvanecimiento [desßaneθi'mjento] *nm* (*desaparición*) disappearance; (*de dudas*) dispelling; (*de coloreo*) fading; (*evaporación*) evaporation; (*MED*) fainting fit.

desvanezca [desßa'neθka] *etc vb V* **desvanecer**.

desvariar [desßa'rjar] *vi* (*enfermo*) to be delirious; (*delirar*) to talk nonsense.

desvarío [desßa'rio] *nm* delirium; (*desatino*) absurdity; **~s** *nmpl* ravings.

desvelar [desße'lar] *vt* to keep awake; **~se** *vr* (*no poder dormir*) to stay awake; (*vigilar*) to be vigilant *o* watchful; **~se por algo** (*inquietarse*) to be anxious about sth; (*poner gran cuidado*) to take great care over sth.

desvelo [des'ßelo] *nm* lack of sleep; (*insomnio*) sleeplessness; (*fig*) vigilance; **~s** *nmpl* (*preocupación*) anxiety *sg*, effort *sg*.

desvencijado, a [desßenθi'xaðo, a] *adj* (*silla*) rickety; (*máquina*) broken-down.

desvencijar [desßenθi'xar] *vt* (*romper*) to break; (*soltar*) to loosen; (*persona: agotar*) to exhaust; **~se** *vr* to come apart.

desventaja [desßen'taxa] *nf* disadvantage; (*inconveniente*) drawback.

desventajoso, a [desßenta'xoso, a] *adj* disadvantageous, unfavourable.

desventura [desßen'tura] *nf* misfortune.

desventurado, a [desßentu'raðo, a] *adj* (*desgraciado*) unfortunate; (*de poca suerte*) ill-fated.

desvergonzado, a [desßervon'θaðo, a] *adj* (*sin vergüenza*) shameless; (*descarado*) insolent ♦ *nm/f* shameless person.

desvergüenza [desßer'ɣwenθa] *nf* (*descaro*) shamelessness; (*insolencia*) impudence; (*mala conducta*) effrontery; **esto es una ~** this is disgraceful; **¡qué ~!** what a nerve!

desvestir [desßes'tir] *vt*, **desvestirse** *vr* to undress.

desviación [desßja'θjon] *nf* deviation; (*AUTO: rodeo*) diversion, detour; (: *carretera de circunvalación*) ring road (*BRIT*), circular route (*US*); **~ de la circulación** traffic diversion; **es una ~ de sus principios** it is a departure from his usual principles.

desviar [des'ßjar] *vt* to turn aside; (*balón, flecha, golpe*) to deflect; (*pregunta*) to parry; (*ojos*) to avert, turn away; (*río*) to alter the course of; (*navío*) to divert, re-route; (*conversación*) to sidetrack; **~se** *vr* (*apartarse del camino*) to turn aside; (: *barco*) to go off course; (*AUTO: dar un rodeo*) to make a detour; **~se de un tema** to get away from the point.

desvincular [desßinku'lar] *vt* to free, release; **~se** *vr* (*aislarse*) to be cut off; (*alejarse*) to cut o.s. off.

desvío [des'ßio] *etc vb V* **desviar** ♦ *nm* (*desviación*) detour, diversion; (*fig*) indifference.

desvirgar [desßir'ɣar] *vt* to deflower.

desvirtuar [desßir'twar] *vt* (*estropear*) to spoil; (*argumento, razonamiento*) to detract from; (*efecto*) to counteract; (*sentido*) to distort; **~se** *vr* to spoil.

desvistiendo [desßis'tjendo] *etc vb V* **desvestir**.

desvitalizar [desßitali'θar] *vt* (*nervio*) to numb.

desvivirse [desßi'ßirse] *vr*: **~ por** to long for, crave for; **~ por los amigos** to do anything for one's friends.

detalladamente [detaʎaða'mente] *adv* (*con detalles*) in detail; (*extensamente*) at great length.

detallar [deta'ʎar] *vt* to detail; (*asunto por asunto*) to itemize.

detalle [de'taʎe] *nm* detail; (*fig*) gesture, token; **al ~** in detail; (*COM*) retail *cpd*; **comercio al ~** retail trade; **vender al ~** to sell retail; **no pierde ~** he doesn't miss a trick; **me observaba sin perder ~** he watched my every move; **tiene muchos ~s** she is very considerate.

detallista [deta'ʎista] *nm/f* retailer ♦ *adj* (*meticuloso*) meticulous; **comercio ~** retail trade.

detectar [detek'tar] *vt* to detect.

detective [detek'tiße] *nm/f* detective; **~ privado** private detective.

detector [detek'tor] *nm* (*NAUT, TEC etc*) detector; **~ de mentiras/de minas** lie/mine detector.

detención [deten'θjon] *nf* (*acción*) stopping; (*estancamiento*) stoppage; (*retraso*) holdup, delay; (*JUR: arresto*) arrest; (*cuidado*) care; ~ **de juego** (*DEPORTE*) stoppage of play; ~ **ilegal** unlawful detention.

detendré [deten'dre] *etc vb V* **detener**.

detener [dete'ner] *vt* (*gen*) to stop; (*JUR*: *arrestar*) to arrest; (: *encarcelar*) to detain; (*objeto*) to keep; (*retrasar*) to hold up, delay; (*aliento*) to hold; ~**se** *vr* to stop; ~**se en** (*demorarse*) to delay over, linger over.

detenga [de'tenga] *etc vb V* **detener**.

detenidamente [deteniða'mente] *adv* (*minuciosamente*) carefully; (*extensamente*) at great length.

detenido, a [dete'niðo, a] *adj* (*arrestado*) under arrest; (*minucioso*) detailed; (*examen*) thorough; (*tímido*) timid ♦ *nm/f* person under arrest, prisoner.

detenimiento [deteni'mjento] *nm* care; **con** ~ thoroughly.

detentar [deten'tar] *vt* to hold; (*sin derecho*: *título*) to hold unlawfully; (: *puesto*) to occupy unlawfully.

detergente [deter'xente] *adj, nm* detergent.

deteriorado, a [deterjo'raðo, a] *adj* (*estropeado*) damaged; (*desgastado*) worn.

deteriorar [deterjo'rar] *vt* to spoil, damage; ~**se** *vr* to deteriorate.

deterioro [dete'rjoro] *nm* deterioration.

determinación [determina'θjon] *nf* (*empeño*) determination; (*decisión*) decision; (*de fecha, precio*) settling, fixing.

determinado, a [determi'naðo, a] *adj* (*preciso*) fixed, set; (*LING*: *artículo*) definite; (*persona*: *resuelto*) determined; **un día** ~ on a certain day; **no hay ningún tema** ~ there is no particular theme.

determinar [determi'nar] *vt* (*plazo*) to fix; (*precio*) to settle; (*daños, impuestos*) to assess; (*pleito*) to decide; (*causar*) to cause; ~**se** *vr* to decide; **el reglamento determina que ...** the rule lays it down *o* states that ...; **aquello determinó la caída del gobierno** that brought about the fall of the government; **esto le determinó** this decided him.

detestable [detes'taβle] *adj* (*persona*) hateful; (*acto*) detestable.

detestar [detes'tar] *vt* to detest.

detonación [detona'θjon] *nf* detonation; (*sonido*) explosion.

detonante [deto'nante] *nm* (*fig*) trigger.

detonar [deto'nar] *vi* to detonate.

detractor, a [detrak'tor, a] *adj* disparaging ♦ *nm/f* detractor.

detrás [de'tras] *adv* behind; (*atrás*) at the back ♦ *prep*: ~ **de** behind; **por** ~ **de algn** (*fig*) behind sb's back; **salir de** ~ to come out from behind; **por** ~ behind.

detrasito [detra'sito] *adv* (*AM fam*) behind.

detrimento [detri'mento] *nm*: **en** ~ **de** to the detriment of.

detuve [de'tuβe] *etc vb V* **detener**.

deuda [de'uða] *nf* (*condición*) indebtedness, debt; (*cantidad*) debt; ~ **a largo plazo** long-term debt; ~ **exterior/pública** foreign/national debt; ~ **incobrable** *o* **morosa** bad debt; ~**s activas/pasivas** assets/liabilities; **contraer** ~**s** to get into debt.

deudor, a [deu'ðor, a] *nm/f* debtor; ~ **hipotecario** mortgager; ~ **moroso** slow payer.

devaluación [deβalwa'θjon] *nf* devaluation.

devaluar [deβalu'ar] *vt* to devalue.

devanar [deβa'nar] *vt* (*hilo*) to wind; ~**se** *vr*: ~**se los sesos** to rack one's brains.

devaneo [deβa'neo] *nm* (*MED*) delirium; (*desatino*) nonsense; (*fruslería*) idle pursuit; (*amorío*) flirtation.

devastar [deβas'tar] *vt* (*destruir*) to devastate.

devendré [deβen'dre] *etc*, **devenga** [de'βenga] *etc vb V* **devenir**.

devengar [deβen'gar] *vt* (*salario*: *ganar*) to earn; (: *tener que cobrar*) to be due; (*intereses*) to bring in, accrue, earn.

devengue [de'βenge] *etc vb V* **devengar**.

devenir [deβe'nir] *vi*: ~ **en** to become, turn into ♦ *nm* (*movimiento progresivo*) process of development; (*transformación*) transformation.

deviene [de'βjene] *etc*, **deviniendo** [deβi'njendo] *etc vb V* **devenir**.

devoción [deβo'θjon] *nf* devotion; (*afición*) strong attachment.

devolución [deβolu'θjon] *nf* (*reenvío*) return, sending back; (*reembolso*) repayment; (*JUR*) devolution.

devolver [deβol'βer] *vt* (*lo extraviado, prestado*) to give back; (*a su sitio*) to put back; (*carta al correo*) to send back; (*COM*) to repay, refund; (*visita, la palabra*) to return; (*salud, vista*) to restore; (*fam*: *vomitar*) to throw up ♦ *vi* (*fam*) to be sick; ~**se** *vr* (*AM*) to return; ~ **mal por bien** to return ill for good; ~ **la pelota a algn** to give sb tit for tat.

devorar [deβo'rar] *vt* to devour; (*comer ávidamente*) to gobble up; (*fig*: *fortuna*) to run through; **todo lo devoró el fuego** the

fire consumed everything; **le devoran
los celos** he is consumed with jealousy.
devoto, a [de'ßoto, a] *adj* (*REL*: *persona*)
devout; (: *obra*) devotional; (*amigo*): ~
(de algn) devoted (to sb) ◊ *nm/f* admirer;
los ~s (*REL*) the faithful; **su muy** ~ your
devoted servant.
devuelto [de'ßwelto], **devuelva**
[de'ßwelßa] *etc vb V* **devolver**.
D.F. *abr* (*México*) = *Distrito Federal*.
dg. *abr* (= *decigramo*) dg.
D.G. *abr* = *Dirección General*; (= *Director
General*) D.G.
DGT *nf abr* = *Dirección General de Tráfico*;
= *Dirección General de Turismo*.
di [di] *vb V* **dar**; **decir**.
día ['dia] *nm* day; ~ **de asueto** day off;
feriado (*AM*) *o* **festivo** (public) holiday; ~
hábil/inhábil working/non-working day;
~ **domingo,** ~ **lunes** (*AM*) Sunday,
Monday; ~ **lectivo** teaching day; ~ **libre**
day off; **D~ de Reyes** Epiphany (*6
January*); **¿qué** ~ **es?** what's the date?;
estar/poner al ~ to be/keep up to date; **el**
~ **de hoy/de mañana** today/tomorrow; **el**
~ **menos pensado** when you least
expect it; **al** ~ **siguiente** on the following
day; **todos los ~s** every day; **un** ~ **sí y
otro no** every other day; **vivir al** ~ to
live from hand to mouth; **de** ~ during
the day, by day; **es de** ~ it's daylight;
del ~ (*estilos*) fashionable; (*menú*)
today's; **de un** ~ **para otro** any day now;
en pleno ~ in full daylight; **en su** ~ in
due time; **¡hasta otro** ~! so long!
diabetes [dja'betes] *nf* diabetes *sg*.
diabético, a [dja'betiko, a] *adj*, *nm/f*
diabetic.
diablo ['djaßlo] *nm* (*tb fig*) devil; **pobre** ~
poor devil; **hace un frío de todos los ~s**
it's hellishly cold.
diablura [dja'ßlura] *nf* prank; (*travesura*)
mischief.
diabólico, a [dja'ßoliko, a] *adj* diabolical.
diadema [dja'ðema] *nf* (*para el pelo*) Alice
band, headband; (*joya*) tiara.
diáfano, a ['djafano, a] *adj* (*tela*)
diaphanous; (*agua*) crystal-clear.
diafragma [dja'fraxma] *nm* diaphragm.
diagnosis [djax'nosis] *nf inv*, **diagnóstico**
[diax'nostiko] *nm* diagnosis.
diagnosticar [djaxnosti'kar] *vt* to
diagnose.
diagonal [djaxo'nal] *adj* diagonal ◊ *nf*
(*GEOM*) diagonal; **en** ~ diagonally.
diagrama [dja'xrama] *nm* diagram; ~ **de
barras** (*COM*) bar chart; ~ **de dispersión**
(*COM*) scatter diagram; ~ **de flujo**

(*INFORM*) flowchart.
dial [di'al] *nm* dial.
dialecto [dja'lekto] *nm* dialect.
dialogar [djalo'xar] *vt* to write in dialogue
form ◊ *vi* (*conversar*) to have a
conversation; ~ **con** (*POL*) to hold talks
with.
diálogo ['djaloxo] *nm* dialogue.
dialogue [dja'loxe] *etc vb V* **dialogar**.
diamante [dja'mante] *nm* diamond.
diametralmente [djametral'mente] *adv*
diametrically; ~ **opuesto a**
diametrically opposed to.
diámetro [di'ametro] *nm* diameter; ~ **de
giro** (*AUTO*) turning circle; **faros de gran**
~ wide-angle headlights.
diana ['djana] *nf* (*MIL*) reveille; (*de blanco*)
centre, bull's-eye.
diantre ['djantre] *nm*: **¡~!** (*fam*) oh hell!
diapasón [djapa'son] *nm* (*instrumento*)
tuning fork; (*de violín etc*) fingerboard;
(*de voz*) tone.
diapositiva [djaposi'tißa] *nf* (*FOTO*) slide,
transparency.
diario, a ['djarjo, a] *adj* daily ◊ *nm*
newspaper; (*libro diario*) diary; (: *COM*)
daybook; (*COM*: *gastos*) daily expenses;
~ **de navegación** (*NAUT*) logbook; ~
hablado (*RADIO*) news (bulletin); ~ **de
sesiones** parliamentary report; **a** ~
daily; **de** *o* **para** ~ everyday.
diarrea [dja'rrea] *nf* diarrhoea.
diatriba [dja'trißa] *nf* diatribe, tirade.
dibujante [dißu'xante] *nm/f* (*de bosquejos*)
sketcher; (*de dibujos animados*)
cartoonist; (*de moda*) designer; ~ **de
publicidad** commercial artist.
dibujar [dißu'xar] *vt* to draw, sketch; ~**se**
vr (*emoción*) to show; ~**se contra** to be
outlined against.
dibujo [di'ßuxo] *nm* drawing; (*TEC*) design;
(*en papel, tela*) pattern; (*en periódico*)
cartoon; (*fig*) description; ~**s animados**
cartoons; ~ **del natural** drawing from
life.
dic., dic.ᵉ *abr* (= *diciembre*) Dec.
diccionario [dikθjo'narjo] *nm* dictionary.
dicharachero, a [ditʃara'tʃero, a] *adj*
talkative ◊ *nm/f* (*ingenioso*) wit;
(*parlanchín*) chatterbox.
dicho, a ['ditʃo, a] *pp de* **decir** ◊ *adj*
(*susodicho*) aforementioned ◊ *nm* saying;
(*proverbio*) proverb; (*ocurrencia*) bright
remark ◊ *nf* (*buena suerte*) good luck;
mejor ~ rather; ~ **y hecho** no sooner
said than done.
dichoso, a [di'tʃoso, a] *adj* (*feliz*) happy;
(*afortunado*) lucky; **¡aquel** ~ **coche!** (*fam*)

that blessed car!

diciembre [di'θjembre] nm December.

diciendo [di'θjendo] etc vb V **decir.**

dictado [dik'taðo] nm dictation; **escribir al ~** to take dictation; **los ~s de la conciencia** (fig) the dictates of conscience.

dictador [dikta'ðor] nm dictator.

dictadura [dikta'ðura] nf dictatorship.

dictáfono ® [dik'tafono] nm Dictaphone ®.

dictamen [dik'tamen] nm (opinión) opinion; (informe) report; **~ contable** auditor's report; **~ facultativo** (MED) medical report.

dictar [dik'tar] vt (carta) to dictate; (JUR: sentencia) to pass; (decreto) to issue; (AM: clase) to give; (: conferencia) to deliver.

didáctico, a [di'ðaktiko, a] adj didactic; (material) teaching cpd; (juguete) educational.

diecinueve [djeθinu'eße] num nineteen; (fecha) nineteenth; V tb **seis.**

dieciochesco, a [djeθio'tʃesko, a] adj eighteenth-century.

dieciocho [djeθi'otʃo] num eighteen; (fecha) eighteenth; V tb **seis.**

dieciséis [djeθi'seis] num sixteen; (fecha) sixteenth; V tb **seis.**

diecisiete [djeθi'sjete] num seventeen; (fecha) seventeenth; V tb **seis.**

diente ['djente] nm (ANAT, TEC) tooth; (ZOOL) fang; (: de elefante) tusk; (de ajo) clove; **~ de león** dandelion; **~s postizos** false teeth; **enseñar los ~s** (fig) to show one's claws; **hablar entre ~s** to mutter, mumble; **hincar el ~ en** (comida) to bite into.

diera ['djera] etc vb V **dar.**

diéresis [di'eresis] nf diaeresis.

dieron ['djeron] vb V **dar.**

diesel ['disel] adj: **motor ~** diesel engine.

diestro, a ['djestro, a] adj (derecho) right; (hábil) skilful; (: con las manos) handy ♦ nm (TAUR) matador ♦ nf right hand; **a ~ y siniestro** (sin método) wildly.

dieta ['djeta] nf diet; **~s** nfpl expenses; **estar a ~** to be on a diet.

dietético, a [dje'tetiko, a] adj dietetic ♦ nm/f dietician ♦ nf dietetics sg.

dietista [dje'tista] nm/f dietician.

diez [djeθ] num ten; (fecha) tenth; **hacer las ~ de últimas** (NAIPES) to sweep the board; V tb **seis.**

diezmar [djeθ'mar] vt to decimate.

difamación [difama'θjon] nf slander; libel.

difamar [difa'mar] vt (JUR: hablando) to slander; (: por escrito) to libel.

difamatorio, a [difama'torjo, a] adj

slanderous; libellous.

diferencia [dife'renθja] nf difference; **a ~ de** unlike; **hacer ~ entre** to make a distinction between; **~ salarial** (COM) wage differential.

diferencial [diferen'θjal] nm (AUTO) differential.

diferenciar [diferen'θjar] vt to differentiate between ♦ vi to differ; **~se** vr to differ, be different; (distinguirse) to distinguish o.s.

diferente [dife'rente] adj different.

diferido [dife'riðo] nm: **en ~** (TV etc) recorded.

diferir [dife'rir] vt to defer.

difícil [di'fiθil] adj difficult; (tiempos, vida) hard; (situación) delicate; **es un hombre ~** he's a difficult man to get on with.

difícilmente [di'fiθilmente] adv (con dificultad) with difficulty; (apenas) hardly.

dificultad [difikul'taθ] nf difficulty; (problema) trouble; (objeción) objection.

dificultar [difikul'tar] vt (complicar) to complicate, make difficult; (estorbar) to obstruct; **las restricciones dificultan el comercio** the restrictions hinder trade.

dificultoso, a [difikul'toso, a] adj (difícil) difficult, hard; (fam: cara) odd, ugly; (persona) awkward; fussy.

difiera [di'fjera] etc, **difiriendo** [difi'rjendo] etc vb V **diferir.**

difuminar [difumi'nar] vt to blur.

difundir [difun'dir] vt (calor, luz) to diffuse; (RADIO) to broadcast; **~se** vr to spread (out); **~ una noticia** to spread a piece of news.

difunto, a [di'funto, a] adj dead, deceased ♦ nm/f: **el ~** the deceased.

difusión [difu'sjon] nf (de calor, luz) diffusion; (de noticia, teoría) dissemination; (de programa) broadcasting; (programa) broadcast.

difuso, a [di'fuso, a] adj (luz) diffused; (conocimientos) widespread; (estilo, explicación) wordy.

diga ['diva] etc vb V **decir.**

digerir [dixe'rir] vt to digest; (fig) to absorb; (reflexionar sobre) to think over.

digestión [dixes'tjon] nf digestion; **corte de ~** indigestion.

digestivo, a [dixes'tißo, a] adj digestive ♦ nm (bebida) liqueur, digestif.

digiera [di'xjera] etc, **digiriendo** [dixi'rjendo] etc vb V **digerir.**

digital [dixi'tal] adj (INFORM) digital; (dactilar) finger cpd ♦ nf (BOT) foxglove; (droga) digitalis.

digitalizador [dixitaliθa'ðor] *nm* (*INFORM*) digitizer.

dignarse [dix'narse] *vr* to deign to.

dignidad [dixni'ðað] *nf* dignity; (*honra*) honour; (*rango*) rank; (*persona*) dignitary; **herir la ~ de algn** to hurt sb's pride.

dignificar [dixnifi'kar] *vt* to dignify.

dignifique [dixni'fike] *etc vb V* **dignificar.**

digno, a ['dixno, a] *adj* worthy; (*persona*: *honesto*) honourable; **~ de elogio** praiseworthy; **~ de mención** worth mentioning; **es ~ de verse** it is worth seeing; **poco ~** unworthy.

digresión [dixre'sjon] *nf* digression.

dije ['dixe] *etc*, **dijera** [di'xera] *etc vb V* **dooir.**

dilación [dila'θjon] *nf* delay; **sin ~** without delay, immediately.

dilapidar [dilapi'ðar] *vt* to squander, waste.

dilatación [dilata'θjon] *nf* (*expansión*) dilation.

dilatado, a [dila'taðo, a] *adj* dilated; (*período*) long drawn-out; (*extenso*) extensive.

dilatar [dila'tar] *vt* (*gen*) to dilate; (*prolongar*) to prolong; (*aplazar*) to delay; **~se** *vr* (*pupila etc*) to dilate; (*agua*) to expand.

dilema [di'lema] *nm* dilemma.

diligencia [dili'xenθja] *nf* diligence; (*rapidez*) speed; (*ocupación*) errand, job; (*carruaje*) stagecoach; **~s** *nfpl* (*JUR*) formalities; **~s judiciales** judicial proceedings; **~s previas** inquest *sg*.

diligente [dili'xente] *adj* diligent; **poco ~** slack.

dilucidar [diluθi'ðar] *vt* (*aclarar*) to elucidate, clarify; (*misterio*) to clear up.

diluir [dilu'ir] *vt* to dilute; (*aguar*, *fig*) to water down.

diluviar [dilu'ßjar] *vi* to pour with rain.

diluvio [di'lußjo] *nm* deluge, flood; **un ~ de cartas** (*fig*) a flood of letters.

diluyendo [dilu'jendo] *etc vb V* **diluir.**

dimanar [dima'nar] *vi*: **~ de** to arise *o* spring from.

dimensión [dimen'sjon] *nf* dimension; **dimensiones** *nfpl* size *sg*; **tomar las dimensiones de** to take the measurements of.

dimes ['dimes] *nmpl*: **andar en ~ y diretes con algn** to bicker *o* squabble with sb.

diminutivo [diminu'tißo] *nm* diminutive.

diminuto, a [dimi'nuto, a] *adj* tiny, diminutive.

dimisión [dimi'sjon] *nf* resignation.

dimitir [dimi'tir] *vt* (*cargo*) to give up; (*despedir*) to sack ♦ *vi* to resign.

dimos ['dimos] *vb V* **dar.**

Dinamarca [dina'marka] *nf* Denmark.

dinamarqués, esa [dinamar'kes, esa] *adj* Danish ♦ *nm/f* Dane ♦ *nm* (*LING*) Danish.

dinámico, a [di'namiko, a] *adj* dynamic ♦ *nf* dynamics *sg*.

dinamita [dina'mita] *nf* dynamite.

dinamitar [dinami'tar] *vt* to dynamite.

dinamo [di'namo], **dínamo** ['dinamo] *nf* (*nm en AM*) dynamo.

dinastía [dinas'tia] *nf* dynasty.

dineral [dine'ral] *nm* fortune.

dinero [di'nero] *nm* money; (**~ en circulación**) currency; **~ caro** (*COM*) dear money; **~ contante (y sonante)** hard cash; **~ de curso legal** legal tender; **~ efectivo** cash, ready cash; **es hombre de ~** he is a man of means; **andar mal de ~** to be short of money; **ganar ~ a espuertas** to make money hand over fist.

dinosaurio [dino'saurjo] *nm* dinosaur.

dintel [din'tel] *nm* lintel; (*umbral*) threshold.

diñar [di'ɲar] *vt* (*fam*) to give; **~la** to kick the bucket.

dio [djo] *vb V* **dar.**

diócesis ['djoθesis] *nf inv* diocese.

Dios [djos] *nm* God; **~ mediante** God willing; **a ~ gracias** thank heaven; **a la buena de ~** any old how; **una de ~ es Cristo** an almighty row; **~ los cría y ellos se juntan** birds of a feather flock together; **como ~ manda** as is proper; **¡~ mío!** (oh,) my God!; **¡por ~!** for God's sake!; **¡válgame ~!** bless my soul!

dios [djos] *nm* god.

diosa ['djosa] *nf* goddess.

Dip. *abr* (= *Diputación*) ≈ CC.

diploma [di'ploma] *nm* diploma.

diplomacia [diplo'maθja] *nf* diplomacy; (*fig*) tact.

diplomado, a [diplo'maðo, a] *adj* qualified ♦ *nm/f* holder of a diploma; (*UNIV*) graduate; *V tb* **licenciado.**

diplomático, a [diplo'matiko, a] *adj* (*cuerpo*) diplomatic; (*que tiene tacto*) tactful ♦ *nm/f* diplomat.

diptongo [dip'tongo] *nm* diphthong.

diputación [diputa'θjon] *nf* deputation; **~ permanente** (*POL*) standing committee; **~ provincial** ≈ county council.

diputado, a [dipu'taðo, a] *nm/f* delegate; (*POL*) ≈ member of parliament (*BRIT*), ≈ representative (*US*); *V tb* **Las Cortes (españolas).**

dique ['dike] *nm* dyke; (*rompeolas*)

breakwater; ~ **de contención** dam.

Dir. abr = **dirección**; (= director) dir.

diré [di're] etc vb V **decir.**

dirección [direk'θjon] nf direction; (fig: tendencia) trend; (señas, tb INFORM) address; (AUTO) steering; (gerencia) management; (de periódico) editorship; (en escuela) headship; (POL) leadership; (junta) board of directors; (despacho) director's/manager's/headmaster's/ editor's office; ~ **absoluta** (INFORM) absolute address; ~ **administrativa** office management; ~ **asistida** power-assisted steering; **D~ General de Seguridad/Turismo** State Security/ Tourist Office; ~ **relativa** (INFORM) relative address; ~ **única** o **prohibida** one-way; **tomar la ~ de una empresa** to take over the running of a company.

direccionamiento [direkθjona'mjento] nm (INFORM) addressing.

directivo, a [direk'tiβo, a] adj (junta) managing; (función) administrative ♦ nm/f (COM) manager ♦ nf (norma) directive; (tb: **junta directiva**) board of directors.

directo, a [di'rekto, a] adj direct; (línea) straight; (inmediato) immediate; (tren) through; (TV) live; **en ~** (INFORM) on line; **transmitir en ~** to broadcast live.

director, a [direk'tor, a] adj leading ♦ nm/f director; (ESCOL) head (teacher) (BRIT), principal (US); (gerente) manager(ess); (de compañía) president; (jefe) head; (PRENSA) editor; (de prisión) governor; (MUS) conductor; ~ **adjunto** assistant manager; ~ **de cine** film director; ~ **comercial** marketing manager; ~ **ejecutivo** executive director; ~ **de empresa** company director; ~ **general** general manager; ~ **gerente** managing director; ~ **de sucursal** branch manager.

directorio [direk'torjo] nm (INFORM) directory.

directrices [direk'triθes] nfpl guidelines.

dirigente [diri'xente] adj leading ♦ nm/f (POL) leader; **los ~s del partido** the party leaders.

dirigible [diri'xiβle] adj (AVIAT, NAUT) steerable ♦ nm airship.

dirigir [diri'xir] vt to direct; (acusación) to level; (carta) to address; (obra de teatro, film) to produce, direct; (MUS) to conduct; (comercio) to manage; (expedición) to lead; (sublevación) to head; (periódico) to edit; (guiar) to guide; ~**se** vr: ~**se a** to go towards, make one's

way towards; (hablar con) to speak to; ~**se a algn solicitando algo** to apply to sb for sth; **"diríjase a ..."** "apply to ...".

dirigismo [diri'xismo] nm management, control; ~ **estatal** state control.

dirija [di'rixa] etc vb V **dirigir.**

dirimir [diri'mir] vt (contrato, matrimonio) to dissolve.

discado [dis'kaðo] nm: ~ **automático** autodial.

discernir [disθer'nir] vt to discern ♦ vi to distinguish.

discierna [dis'θjerna] etc vb V **discernir.**

disciplina [disθi'plina] nf discipline.

disciplinar [disθipli'nar] vt to discipline; (enseñar) to school; (MIL) to drill; (azotar) to whip.

discípulo, a [dis'θipulo, a] nm/f disciple; (seguidor) follower; (ESCOL) pupil.

disco ['disko] nm disc (BRIT), disk (US); (DEPORTE) discus; (TELEC) dial; (AUTO: semáforo) light; (MUS) record; (INFORM) disk; ~ **de arranque** boot disk; ~ **compacto** compact disc; ~ **de densidad sencilla/doble** single/double density disk; ~ **de larga duración** long-playing record (LP); ~ **flexible** o **floppy** floppy disk; ~ **de freno** brake disc; ~ **maestro** master disk; ~ **de reserva** backup disk; ~ **rígido** hard disk; ~ **de una cara/dos caras** single-/double-sided disk; ~ **virtual** ramdisk.

discóbolo [dis'koβolo] nm discus thrower.

discográfico, a [disko'xrafiko, a] adj record cpd; **casa discográfica** record company; **sello** ~ label.

díscolo, a ['diskolo, a] adj (rebelde) unruly.

disconforme [diskon'forme] adj differing; **estar** ~ **(con)** to be in disagreement (with).

discontinuo, a [diskon'tinwo, a] adj discontinuous; (AUTO: línea) broken.

discordar [diskor'ðar] vi (MUS) to be out of tune; (estar en desacuerdo) to disagree; (colores, opiniones) to clash.

discorde [dis'korðe] adj (sonido) discordant; (opiniones) clashing.

discordia [dis'korðja] nf discord.

discoteca [disko'teka] nf disco(theque).

discreción [diskre'θjon] nf discretion; (reserva) prudence; **¡a ~!** (MIL) stand easy!; **añadir azúcar a** ~ (CULIN) add sugar to taste; **comer a** ~ to eat as much as one wishes.

discrecional [diskreθjo'nal] adj (facultativo) discretionary; **parada** ~ request stop.

discrepancia [diskre'panθja] nf (diferencia) discrepancy; (desacuerdo) disagreement.

discrepante [diskre'pante] *adj* divergent; **hubo varias voces ~s** there were some dissenting voices.

discrepar [diskre'par] *vi* to disagree.

discreto, a [dis'kreto, a] *adj* (*diplomático*) discreet; (*sensato*) sensible; (*reservado*) quiet; (*sobrio*) sober; (*mediano*) fair, fairly good; **le daremos un plazo ~** we'll allow him a reasonable time.

discriminación [diskrimina'θjon] *nf* discrimination.

discriminar [diskrimi'nar] *vt* to discriminate against; (*diferenciar*) to discriminate between.

discuerde [dis'kwerðe] *etc vb* V **discordar**.

disculpa [dis'kulpa] *nf* excuse; (*pedir perdón*) apology; **pedir ~s a/por** to apologize to/for.

disculpar [diskul'par] *vt* to excuse, pardon; **~se** *vr* to excuse o.s.; to apologize.

discurrir [disku'rrir] *vt* to contrive, think up ♦ *vi* (*pensar, reflexionar*) to think, meditate; (*recorrer*) to roam, wander; (*río*) to flow; (*el tiempo*) to pass, flow by.

discurso [dis'kurso] *nm* speech; **~ de clausura** closing speech; **pronunciar un ~** to make a speech; **en el ~ del tiempo** with the passage of time.

discusión [disku'sjon] *nf* (*diálogo*) discussion; (*riña*) argument; **tener una ~** to have an argument.

discutible [disku'tißle] *adj* debatable; **de mérito ~** of dubious worth.

discutido, a [disku'tiðo, a] *adj* controversial.

discutir [disku'tir] *vt* (*debatir*) to discuss; (*pelear*) to argue about; (*contradecir*) to argue against ♦ *vi* to discuss; (*disputar*) to argue; **~ de política** to argue about politics; **¡no discutas!** don't argue!

disecar [dise'kar] *vt* (*para conservar: animal*) to stuff; (: *planta*) to dry.

diseminar [disemi'nar] *vt* to disseminate, spread.

disentir [disen'tir] *vi* to dissent, disagree.

diseñador, a [diseɲa'dor, a] *nm/f* designer.

diseñar [dise'ɲar] *vt* to design.

diseño [di'seɲo] *nm* (*TEC*) design; (*ARTE*) drawing; (*COSTURA*) pattern; **de ~ italiano** Italian-designed; **~ asistido por ordenador** computer-assisted design, CAD.

diseque [di'seke] *etc vb* V **disecar**.

disertar [diser'tar] *vi* to speak.

disfrace [dis'fraθe] *etc vb* V **disfrazar**.

disfraz [dis'fraθ] *nm* (*máscara*) disguise; (*traje*) fancy dress; (*excusa*) pretext; **bajo el ~ de** under the cloak of.

disfrazado, a [disfra'θaðo, a] *adj* disguised; **ir ~ de** to masquerade as.

disfrazar [disfra'θar] *vt* to disguise; **~se** *vr* to dress (o.s.) up; **~se de** to disguise o.s. as.

disfrutar [disfru'tar] *vt* to enjoy ♦ *vi* to enjoy o.s.; **¡que disfrutes!** have a good time; **~ de** to enjoy, possess; **~ de buena salud** to enjoy good health.

disfrute [dis'frute] *nm* (*goce*) enjoyment; (*aprovechamiento*) use.

disgregar [disɣre'ɣar] *vt* (*desintegrar*) to disintegrate; (*manifestantes*) to disperse; **~se** *vr* to disintegrate, break up.

disgregue [dis'ɣreɣe] *etc vb* V **disgregar**.

disgustar [disɣus'tar] *vt* (*no gustar*) to displease; (*contrariar, enojar*) to annoy; to upset; **~se** *vr* to be annoyed; (*dos personas*) to fall out; **estaba muy disgustado con el asunto** he was very upset about the affair.

disgusto [dis'ɣusto] *nm* (*repugnancia*) disgust; (*contrariedad*) annoyance; (*desagrado*) displeasure; (*tristeza*) grief; (*riña*) quarrel; (*avería*) misfortune; **hacer algo a ~** to do sth unwillingly; **matar a algn a ~s** to drive sb to distraction.

disidente [disi'ðente] *nm* dissident.

disienta [di'sjenta] *etc vb* V **disentir**.

disimulado, a [disimu'laðo, a] *adj* (*solapado*) furtive, underhand; (*oculto*) covert; **hacerse el ~** to pretend not to notice.

disimular [disimu'lar] *vt* (*ocultar*) to hide, conceal ♦ *vi* to dissemble.

disimulo [disi'mulo] *nm* (*fingimiento*) dissimulation; **con ~** cunningly.

disipar [disi'par] *vt* (*duda, temor*) to dispel; (*esperanza*) to destroy; (*fortuna*) to squander; **~se** *vr* (*nubes*) to vanish; (*dudas*) to be dispelled; (*indisciplinarse*) to dissipate.

diskette [dis'ket] *nm* (*INFORM*) diskette, floppy disk.

dislate [dis'late] *nm* (*absurdo*) absurdity; **~s** *nmpl* nonsense *sg*.

dislexia [dis'leksja] *nf* dyslexia.

dislocar [dislo'kar] *vt* (*gen*) to dislocate; (*tobillo*) to sprain.

disloque [dis'loke] *etc vb* V **dislocar** ♦ *nm*: **es el ~** (*fam*) it's the last straw.

disminución [disminu'θjon] *nf* diminution.

disminuido, a [disminu'iðo, a] *nm/f*: **~ mental/físico** mentally/physically-handicapped person.

disminuir [disminu'ir] *vt* to decrease, diminish; (*estrechar*) to lessen; (*temperatura*) to lower; (*gastos, raciones*) to cut down; (*dolor*) to relieve; (*autoridad, prestigio*) to weaken; (*entusiasmo*) to damp ♦ *vi* (*días*) to grow shorter; (*precios, temperatura*) to drop, fall; (*velocidad*) to slacken; (*población*) to decrease; (*beneficios, número*) to fall off; (*memoria, vista*) to fail.

disminuyendo [disminu'jendo] *etc vb* V **disminuir**.

disociar [diso'θjar] *vt* to disassociate; ~**se** *vr* to disassociate o.s.

disoluble [diso'luβle] *adj* soluble.

disolución [disolu'θjon] *nf* (*acto*) dissolution; (*QUÍMICA*) solution; (*COM*) liquidation; (*moral*) dissoluteness.

disoluto, a [diso'luto, a] *adj* dissolute.

disolvente [disol'βente] *nm* (*solvent*) thinner.

disolver [disol'βer] *vt* (*gen*) to dissolve; (*manifestación*) to break up; ~**se** *vr* to dissolve; (*COM*) to go into liquidation.

dispar [dis'par] *adj* (*distinto*) different; (*irregular*) uneven.

disparado, a [dispa'raðo, a] *adj*: **entrar** ~ to shoot in; **salir** ~ to shoot out; **ir** ~ to go like mad.

disparador [dispara'ðor] *nm* (*de arma*) trigger; (*FOTO, TEC*) release; ~ **atómico** aerosol; ~ **de bombas** bomb release.

disparar [dispa'rar] *vt, vi* to shoot, fire; ~**se** *vr* (*arma de fuego*) to go off; (*persona: marcharse*) to rush off; (*caballo*) to bolt; (*enojarse*) to lose control.

disparatado, a [dispara'taðo, a] *adj* crazy.

disparate [dispa'rate] *nm* (*tontería*) foolish remark; (*error*) blunder; **decir** ~**s** to talk nonsense; **¡qué** ~**!** how absurd!; **costar un** ~ to cost a hell of a lot.

disparo [dis'paro] *nm* shot; (*acto*) firing; ~**s** *nmpl* shooting *sg*, (exchange of) shots (*sg*); ~ **inicial** (*de cohete*) blastoff.

dispendio [dis'pendjo] *nm* waste.

dispensar [dispen'sar] *vt* to dispense; (*ayuda*) to give; (*honores*) to grant; (*disculpar*) to excuse; **¡usted dispense!** I beg your pardon!; ~ **a algn de hacer algo** to excuse sb from doing sth.

dispensario [dispen'sarjo] *nm* (*clínica*) community clinic; (*de hospital*) outpatients' department.

dispersar [disper'sar] *vt* to disperse; (*manifestación*) to break up; ~**se** *vr* to scatter.

disperso, a [dis'perso, a] *adj* scattered.

displicencia [displi'θenθja] *nf* (*mal humor*) peevishness; (*desgana*) lack of enthusiasm.

displicente [displi'θente] *adj*

(*malhumorado*) peevish; (*poco entusiasta*) unenthusiastic.

dispondré [dispon'dre] *etc vb* V **disponer**.

disponer [dispo'ner] *vt* (*arreglar*) to arrange; (*ordenar*) to put in order; (*preparar*) to prepare, get ready ♦ *vi*: ~ **de** to have, own; ~**se** *vr*: ~**se para** to prepare to, prepare for; **la ley dispone que ...** the law provides that ...; **no puede** ~ **de esos bienes** she cannot dispose of those properties.

disponga [dis'ponga] *etc vb* V **disponer**.

disponibilidad [disponiβili'ðað] *nf* availability; ~**es** *nfpl* (*COM*) resources, financial assets.

disponible [dispo'niβle] *adj* available; (*tiempo*) spare; (*dinero*) on hand.

disposición [disposi'θjon] *nf* arrangement, disposition; (*de casa, INFORM*) layout; (*ley*) order; (*cláusula*) provision; (*aptitud*) aptitude; ~ **de ánimo** attitude of mind; **última** ~ last will and testament; **a la** ~ **de** at the disposal of; **a su** ~ at your service.

dispositivo [disposi'tiβo] *nm* device, mechanism; ~ **de alimentación** hopper; ~ **de almacenaje** storage device; ~ **periférico** peripheral (device); ~ **de seguridad** safety catch; (*fig*) security measure.

dispuesto, a [dis'pwesto, a] *pp de* **disponer** ♦ *adj* (*arreglado*) arranged; (*preparado*) disposed; (*persona: dinámico*) bright; **estar** ~**/poco** ~ **a hacer algo** to be inclined/reluctant to do sth.

dispuse [dis'puse] *etc vb* V **disponer**.

disputa [dis'puta] *nf* (*discusión*) dispute, argument; (*controversia*) controversy.

disputar [dispu'tar] *vt* (*discutir*) to dispute, question; (*contender*) to contend for ♦ *vi* to argue.

disquete [dis'kete] *nm* (*INFORM*) diskette, floppy disk.

disquetera [diske'tera] *nf* disk drive.

Dist. *abr* (= *distancia, Distrito*) dist.

distancia [dis'tanθja] *nf* distance; (*de tiempo*) interval; ~ **de parada** braking distance; ~ **del suelo** (*AUTO etc*) height off the ground; **a gran** *o* **a larga** ~ long-distance; **mantenerse a** ~ to keep one's distance; (*fig*) to remain aloof; **guardar las** ~**s** to keep one's distance.

distanciado, a [distan'θjaðo, a] *adj* (*remoto*) remote; (*fig: alejado*) far apart; **estamos** ~**s en ideas** our ideas are poles apart.

distanciamiento [distanθja'mjento] *nm* (*acto*) spacing out; (*estado*) remoteness;

(*fig*) distance.
distanciar [distan'θjar] *vt* to space out;
~**se** *vr* to become estranged.
distante [dis'tante] *adj* distant.
distar [dis'tar] *vi*: **dista 5 kms de aquí** it is 5
kms from here; **¿dista mucho?** is it far?;
dista mucho de la verdad it's very far
from the truth.
diste ['diste], **disteis** ['disteis] *vb V* **dar**.
distensión [disten'sjon] *nf* distension;
(*POL*) détente; ~ **muscular** (*MED*)
muscular strain.
distinción [distin'θjon] *nf* distinction;
(*elegancia*) elegance; (*honor*) honour; **a** ~
de unlike; **sin** ~ indiscriminately; **sin** ~
de edades irrespective of age.
distinga [dis'tinga] *etc vb V* **distinguir**.
distinguido, a [distin'giðo, a] *adj*
distinguished; (*famoso*) prominent,
well-known; (*elegante*) elegant.
distinguir [distin'gir] *vt* to distinguish;
(*divisar*) to make out; (*escoger*) to single
out; (*caracterizar*) to mark out; ~**se** *vr* to
be distinguished; (*destacarse*) to
distinguish o.s.; **a lo lejos no se distingue**
it's not visible from a distance.
distintivo, a [distin'tiβo, a] *adj* distinctive;
(*signo*) distinguishing ♦ *nm* (*de policía etc*)
badge; (*fig*) characteristic.
distinto, a [dis'tinto, a] *adj* different;
(*claro*) clear; ~**s** several, various.
distorsión [distor'sjon] *nf* (*ANAT*) twisting;
(*RADIO etc*) distortion.
distorsionar [distorsjo'nar] *vt, vi* to distort.
distracción [distrak'θjon] *nf* distraction;
(*pasatiempo*) hobby, pastime; (*olvido*)
absent-mindedness, distraction.
distraer [distra'er] *vt* (*atención*) to distract;
(*divertir*) to amuse; (*fondos*) to embezzle
♦ *vi* to be relaxing; ~**se** *vr* (*entretenerse*)
to amuse o.s.; (*perder la concentración*) to
allow one's attention to wander; ~ **a**
algn de su pensamiento to divert sb
from his train of thought; **el pescar**
distrae fishing is a relaxation.
distraído, a [distra'iðo, a] *adj* (*gen*)
absent-minded; (*desatento*) inattentive;
(*entretenido*) amusing ♦ *nm*: **hacerse el** ~
to pretend not to notice; **con aire** ~ idly;
me miró distraída she gave me a casual
glance.
distraiga [dis'traixa] *etc*, **distraje**
[dis'traxe] *etc*, **distrajera** [distra'xera]
etc, **distrayendo** [distra'jendo] *vb V*
distraer.
distribución [distriβu'θjon] *nf* distribution;
(*entrega*) delivery; (*en estadística*)
distribution, incidence; (*ARQ*) layout; ~

de premios prize giving; **la** ~ **de los**
impuestos the incidence of taxes.
distribuidor, a [distriβui'ðor, a] *nm/f*
(*persona: gen*) distributor; (: *CORREOS*)
sorter; (: *COM*) dealer; **su** ~ **habitual**
your regular dealer.
distribuir [distriβu'ir] *vt* to distribute;
(*prospectos*) to hand out; (*cartas*) to
deliver; (*trabajo*) to allocate; (*premios*) to
award; (*dividendos*) to pay; (*peso*) to
distribute; (*ARQ*) to plan.
distribuyendo [distriβu'jendo] *etc vb V*
distribuir.
distrito [dis'trito] *nm* (*sector, territorio*)
region; (*barrio*) district; ~ **electoral**
constituency; ~ **postal** postal district.
disturbio [dis'turβjo] *nm* disturbance;
(*desorden*) riot; **los** ~**s** the troubles.
disuadir [diswa'ðir] *vt* to dissuade.
disuasión [diswa'sjon] *nf* dissuasion; (*MIL*)
deterrent; ~ **nuclear** nuclear deterrent.
disuasivo, a [diswa'siβo, a] *adj* dissuasive;
arma disuasiva deterrent.
disuasorio, a [diswa'sorjo, a] *adj*
= **disuasivo**.
disuelto [di'swelto] *pp de* **disolver**.
disuelva [di'swelβa] *etc vb V* **disolver**.
disuene [di'swene] *etc vb V* **disonar**.
disyuntiva [disjun'tiβa] *nf* (*dilema*)
dilemma.
DIU ['diu] *nm abr* (= *dispositivo intrauterino*)
I.U.D.
diurno, a ['djurno, a] *adj* day *cpd*, diurnal.
diva ['diβa] *nf* prima donna.
divagar [diβa'xar] *vi* (*desviarse*) to digress.
divague [di'βaxe] *etc vb V* **divagar**.
diván [di'βan] *nm* divan.
divergencia [diβer'xenθja] *nf* divergence.
divergir [diβer'xir] *vi* (*líneas*) to diverge;
(*opiniones*) to differ; (*personas*) to
disagree.
diverja [di'βerxa] *etc vb V* **divergir**.
diversidad [diβersi'ðað] *nf* diversity,
variety.
diversificación [diβersifika'θjon] *nf* (*COM*)
diversification.
diversificar [diβersifi'kar] *vt* to diversify.
diversifique [diβersi'fike] *etc vb V*
diversificar.
diversión [diβer'sjon] *nf* (*gen*)
entertainment; (*actividad*) hobby,
pastime.
diverso, a [di'βerso, a] *adj* diverse;
(*diferente*) different ♦ *nm*: ~**s** (*COM*)
sundries; ~**s libros** several books.
divertido, a [diβer'tiðo, a] *adj* (*chiste*)
amusing, funny; (*fiesta etc*) enjoyable;
(*película, libro*) entertaining; **está** ~

(*irónico*) this is going to be fun.
divertir [dißer'tir] *vt* (*entretener, recrear*) to amuse; **~se** *vr* (*pasarlo bien*) to have a good time; (*distraerse*) to amuse o.s.
dividendo [dißi'ðendo] *nm* (*COM*): **~s** *nmpl* dividends; **~s por acción** earnings per share; **~ definitivo** final dividend.
dividir [dißi'ðir] *vt* (*gen*) to divide; (*separar*) to separate; (*distribuir*) to distribute.
divierta [di'ßjerta] *etc vb V* **divertir.**
divinidad [dißini'ðað] *nf* (*esencia divina*) divinity; **la D~** God.
divino, a [di'ßino, a] *adj* divine; (*fig*) lovely.
divirtiendo [dißir'tjendo] *etc vb V* **divertir.**
divisa [di'ßisa] *nf* (*emblema, moneda*) emblem, badge; **~s** *nfpl* currency *sg*; (*COM*) foreign exchange *sg*; **control de ~s** exchange control; **~ de reserva** reserve currency.
divisar [dißi'sar] *vt* to make out.
división [dißi'sjon] *nf* division; (*de partido*) split; (*de país*) partition.
divisorio, a [dißi'sorjo, a] *adj* (*línea*) dividing; **línea divisoria de las aguas** watershed.
divorciado, a [dißor'θjaðo, a] *adj* divorced; (*opinion*) split ♦ *nm/f* divorcé(e).
divorciar [dißor'θjar] *vt* to divorce; **~se** *vr* to get divorced.
divorcio [di'ßorθjo] *nm* divorce; (*fig*) split.
divulgación [dißulɣa'θjon] *nf* (*difusión*) spreading; (*popularización*) popularization.
divulgar [dißul'ɣar] *vt* (*desparramar*) to spread; (*popularizar*) to popularize; (*hacer circular*) to divulge, circulate; **~se** *vr* (*secreto*) to leak out; (*rumor*) to get about.
divulgue [di'ßulɣe] *etc vb V* **divulgar.**
dizque ['diske] *adv* (*AM fam*) apparently.
Dls., dls *abr* (*AM*) = **dólares.**
DM *abr* = **decimal.**
dm. *abr* = **decímetro**) dm.
DNI *nm abr* (*ESP*) = **Documento Nacional de Identidad.**
Dña. *abr* = **Doña.**
do [do] *nm* (*MUS*) C.
D.O. *abr* = **Denominación de Origen.**
dobladillo [doßla'ðiʎo] *nm* (*de vestido*) hem; (*de pantalón: vuelta*) turn-up (*BRIT*), cuff (*US*).
doblaje [do'ßlaxe] *nm* (*CINE*) dubbing.
doblar [do'ßlar] *vt* to double; (*papel*) to fold; (*caño*) to bend; (*la esquina*) to turn, go round; (*film*) to dub ♦ *vi* to turn; (*campana*) to toll; **~se** *vr* (*plegarse*) to fold (up), crease; (*encorvarse*) to bend.
doble ['doßle] *adj* (*gen*) double; (*de dos*

aspectos) dual; (*cuerda*) thick; (*fig*) two-faced ♦ *nm* double ♦ *nm/f* (*TEAT*) double, stand-in; **~s** *nmpl* (*DEPORTE*) doubles *sg*; **~ o nada** double or quits; **~ página** double-page spread; **con ~ sentido** with a double meaning; **el ~** twice the quantity *o* as much; **su sueldo es el ~ del mío** his salary is twice (as much as) mine; (*INFORM*): **~ cara** double-sided; **~ densidad** double density.
doblegar [doßle'ɣar] *vt* to fold, crease; **~se** *vr* to yield.
doblegue [do'ßleɣe] *etc vb V* **doblegar.**
doblez [do'ßleθ] *nm* (*pliegue*) fold, hem ♦ *nf* (*falsedad*) duplicity.
doc. *abr* (= *docena*) doz.; (= *documento*) doc.
doce ['doθe] *num* twelve; (*fecha*) twelfth; **las ~** twelve o'clock; *V tb* **seis.**
docena [do'θena] *nf* dozen; **por ~s** by the dozen.
docente [do'θente] *adj*: **centro/personal ~** teaching institution/staff.
dócil ['doθil] *adj* (*pasivo*) docile; (*manso*) gentle; (*obediente*) obedient.
docto, a ['dokto, a] *adj* learned, erudite ♦ *nm/f* scholar.
doctor, a [dok'tor, a] *nm/f* doctor; **~ en filosofía** Doctor of Philosophy.
doctorado [dokto'raðo] *nm* doctorate.
doctorarse [dokto'rarse] *vr* to get a doctorate.
doctrina [dok'trina] *nf* doctrine, teaching.
documentación [dokumenta'θjon] *nf* documentation; (*de identidad etc*) papers *pl*.
documental [dokumen'tal] *adj, nm* documentary.
documentar [dokumen'tar] *vt* to document; **~se** *vr* to gather information.
documento [doku'mento] *nm* (*certificado*) document; (*JUR*) exhibit; **~s** *nmpl* papers; **~ justificativo** voucher; **D~ Nacional de Identidad** national identity card; *see boxed note.*

DOCUMENTO NACIONAL DE IDENTIDAD

A laminated plastic ID card with the holder's personal details and photograph, the **Documento Nacional de Identidad** *is renewed every ten years. People are required to carry it at all times and to produce it on request for the police. In Spain it is commonly known as a "DNI" or "carnet de identidad". In Spanish America a similar card is called a "cédula (de identidad)".*

dogma ['doɣma] *nm* dogma.
dogmático, a [doɣ'matiko, a] *adj* dogmatic.
dogo ['doɣo] *nm* bulldog.
dólar ['dolar] *nm* dollar.
dolencia [do'lenθja] *nf* (*achaque*) ailment; (*dolor*) ache.
doler [do'ler] *vt, vi* to hurt; (*fig*) to grieve; **~se** *vr* (*de su situación*) to grieve, feel sorry; (*de las desgracias ajenas*) to sympathize; (*quejarse*) to complain; **me duele el brazo** my arm hurts; **no me duele el dinero** I don't mind about the money; **¡ahí le duele!** you've put your finger on it!
doliente [do'ljente] *adj* (*enfermo*) sick; (*dolorido*) aching; (*triste*) sorrowful; **la familia ~** the bereaved family.
dolor [do'lor] *nm* pain; (*fig*) grief, sorrow; **~ de cabeza** headache; **~ de estómago** stomach ache; **~ de oídos** earache; **~ sordo** dull ache.
dolorido, a [dolo'riðo, a] *adj* (*MED*) sore, aching; **la parte dolorida** the part which hurts.
doloroso, a [dolo'roso, a] *adj* (*MED*) painful; (*fig*) distressing.
domar [do'mar] *vt* to tame.
domesticado, a [domesti'kaðo, a] *adj* (*amansado*) tame.
domesticar [domesti'kar] *vt* to tame.
doméstico, a [do'mestiko, a] *adj* domestic ♦ *nm/f* servant; **economía doméstica** home economy; **gastos ~s** household expenses.
domestique [domes'tike] *etc vb V* **domesticar**.
domiciliación [domiθilja'θjon] *nf*: **~ de pagos** (*COM*) standing order, direct debit.
domiciliar [domiθi'ljar] *vt* to domicile; **~se** *vr* to take up (one's) residence.
domiciliario, a [domiθi'ljarjo, a] *adj*: **arresto ~** house arrest.
domicilio [domi'θiljo] *nm* home; **~ particular** private residence; **~ social** (*COM*) head office, registered office; **servicio a ~** delivery service; **sin ~ fijo** of no fixed abode.
dominante [domi'nante] *adj* dominant; (*person*) domineering.
dominar [domi'nar] *vt* (*gen*) to dominate; (*países*) to rule over; (*adversario*) to overpower; (*caballo, nervios, emoción*) to control; (*incendio, epidemia*) to bring under control; (*idiomas*) to be fluent in ♦ *vi* to dominate, prevail; **~se** *vr* to control o.s.

domingo [do'mingo] *nm* Sunday; **D~ de Ramos** Palm Sunday; **D~ de Resurrección** Easter Sunday; *V tb* **sábado**; **Semana Santa**.
dominguero, a [domin'gero, a] *adj* Sunday *cpd*.
dominical [domini'kal] *adj* Sunday *cpd*; **periódico ~** Sunday newspaper.
dominicano, a [domini'kano, a] *adj, nm/f* Dominican.
dominio [do'minjo] *nm* (*tierras*) domain; (*POL*) dominion; (*autoridad*) power, authority; (*supremacía*) supremacy; (*de las pasiones*) grip, hold; (*de idioma*) command; **ser del ~ público** to be widely known.
dominó [domi'no] *nm* (*pieza*) domino; (*juego*) dominoes.
dom.° *abr* (= *domingo*) Sun.
don [don] *nm* (*talento*) gift; **D~ Juan Gómez** Mr Juan Gómez, Juan Gómez Esq. (*BRIT*); **tener ~ de gentes** to known how to handle people; **~ de lenguas** gift for languages; **~ de mando** (qualities of) leadership; **~ de palabra** gift of the gab; *see boxed note*.

DON

The title **don** *or* **doña** *is used before a person's first name – for example, Don Diego, Doña Inés – as a mark of respect or politeness to someone of superior social standing or an older person. Its use is dying out but it continues to be found in official documents and correspondence: for example, Sr. D. Pedro Rodríguez Hernández, Sra. Dña Inés Rodríguez Hernández.*

---

donación [dona'θjon] *nf* donation.
donaire [do'naire] *nm* charm.
donante [do'nante] *nm/f* donor; **~ de sangre** blood donor.
donar [do'nar] *vt* to donate.
donativo [dona'tiβo] *nm* donation.
doncella [don'θeʎa] *nf* (*criada*) maid.
donde ['donde] *adv* where ♦ *prep*: **el coche está allí ~ el farol** the car is over there by the lamppost *o* where the lamppost is; **por ~** through which; **a ~** to where, to which; **en ~** where, in which; **es a ~ vamos nosotros** that's where we're going.
dónde ['donde] *adv interrogativo* where?; **¿a ~ vas?** where are you going (to)?; **¿de ~ vienes?** where have you come from?; **¿en ~?** where?; **¿por ~?** where?,

whereabouts?; ¿**por** ~ **se va al estadio?** how do you get to the stadium?

dondequiera [donde'kjera] *adv* anywhere ♦ *conj*: ~ **que** wherever; **por** ~ everywhere, all over the place.

donostiarra [donos'tjarra] *adj* of *o* from San Sebastián ♦ *nmf* native *o* inhabitant of San Sebastián.

doña ['doɲa] *nf*: **D**~ **Carmen Gómez** Mrs Carmen Gómez; *V tb* **don.**

dopar [do'par] *vt* to dope, drug.

doping ['dopin] *nm* doping, drugging.

doquier [do'kjer] *adv*: **por** ~ all over, everywhere.

dorado, a [do'raðo, a] *adj* (*color*) golden; (*TEC*) gilt.

dorar [do'rar] *vt* (*TEC*) to gild; (*CULIN*) to brown, cook lightly; ~ **la píldora** to sweeten the pill.

dormilón, ona [dormi'lon, ona] *adj* fond of sleeping ♦ *nmf* sleepyhead.

dormir [dor'mir] *vt*: ~ **la siesta por la tarde** to have an afternoon nap ♦ *vi* to sleep; ~**se** *vr* (*persona, brazo, pierna*) to fall asleep; ~**la** (*fam*) to sleep it off; ~ **la mona** (*fam*) to sleep off a hangover; ~ **como un lirón** *o* **tronco** to sleep like a log; ~ **a pierna suelta** to sleep soundly.

dormitar [dormi'tar] *vi* to doze.

dormitorio [dormi'torjo] *nm* bedroom; ~ **común** dormitory.

dorsal [dor'sal] *adj* dorsal ♦ *nm* (*DEPORTE*) number.

dorso ['dorso] *nm* back; **escribir algo al** ~ to write sth on the back; **"vease al** ~**"** "see other side", "please turn over".

DOS *nm abr* (= *sistema operativo de disco*) DOS.

dos [dos] *num* two; (*fecha*) second; **los** ~ the two of them, both of them; **cada** ~ **por tres** every five minutes; **de** ~ **en** ~ in twos; **estamos a** ~ (*TENIS*) the score is deuce; *V tb* **seis.**

doscientos, as [dos'θjentos, as] *num* two hundred.

dosel [do'sel] *nm* canopy.

dosificar [dosifi'kar] *vt* (*CULIN, MED, QUÍMICA*) to measure out; (*no derrochar*) to be sparing with.

dosifique [dosi'fike] *etc vb V* **dosificar.**

dosis ['dosis] *nf inv* dose, dosage.

dossier [do'sjer] *nm* dossier, file.

dotación [dota'θjon] *nf* (*acto, dinero*) endowment; (*plantilla*) staff; (*NAUT*) crew; **la** ~ **es insuficiente** we are under staffed.

dotado, a [do'taðo, a] *adj* gifted; ~ **de** (*persona*) endowed with; (*máquina*)

equipped with.

dotar [do'tar] *vt* to endow; (*TEC*) to fit; (*barco*) to man; (*oficina*) to staff.

dote ['dote] *nf* (*de novia*) dowry; ~**s** *nfpl* (*talentos*) gifts.

doy [doj] *vb V* **dar.**

Dpto. *abr* (= *Departamento*) dept.

Dr(a). *abr* (= *Doctor, Doctora*) Dr.

draga ['draxa] *nf* dredge.

dragado [dra'xaðo] *nm* dredging.

dragar [dra'xar] *vt* to dredge; (*minas*) to sweep.

dragón [dra'xon] *nm* dragon.

drague ['draxe] *etc vb V* **dragar.**

drama ['drama] *nm* drama; (*obra*) play.

dramático, a [dra'matiko, a] *adj* dramatic ♦ *nmf* dramatist; (*actor*) actor; **obra dramática** play.

dramaturgo, a [drama'turxo, a] *nmf* dramatist, playwright.

dramón [dra'mon] *nm* (*TEAT*) melodrama; ¡**qué** ~! what a scene!

drástico, a ['drastiko, a] *adj* drastic.

drenaje [dre'naxe] *nm* drainage.

drenar [dre'nar] *vt* to drain.

droga ['droxa] *nf* drug; (*DEPORTE*) dope; **el problema de la** ~ the drug problem.

drogadicto, a [droxa'ðikto, a] *nmf* drug addict.

drogar [dro'xar] *vt* to drug; (*DEPORTE*) to dope; ~**se** *vr* to take drugs.

drogodependencia [droxoðepen'denθja] *nf* drug addiction.

drogue ['droxe] *etc vb V* **drogar.**

droguería [droxe'ria] *nf* ≈ hardware shop (*BRIT*) *o* store (*US*).

dromedario [drome'ðarjo] *nm* dromedary.

Dto., D.to *abr* = **descuento.**

Dtor(a). *abr* (= *Director, Directora*) Dir.

ducado [du'kaðo] *nm* duchy, dukedom.

ducha ['dutʃa] *nf* (*baño*) shower; (*MED*) douche.

ducharse [du'tʃarse] *vr* to take a shower.

ducho, a ['dutʃo, a] *adj*: ~ **en** (*experimentado*) experienced in; (*hábil*) skilled at.

dúctil ['duktil] *adj* (*metal*) ductile; (*persona*) easily influenced.

duda ['duða] *nf* doubt; **sin** ~ no doubt, doubtless; ¡**sin** ~! of course!; **no cabe** ~ there is no doubt about it; **no le quepa** ~ make no mistake about it; **no quiero poner en** ~ **su conducta** I don't want to call his behaviour into question; **sacar a algn de la** ~ to settle sb's doubts; **tengo una** ~ I have a query.

dudar [du'ðar] *vt* to doubt ♦ *vi* to doubt, have doubts; ~ **acerca de algo** to be uncertain about sth; **dudó en comprarlo** he hesitated to buy it; **dudan que sea verdad** they doubt whether *o* if it's true.

dudoso, a [du'ðoso, a] *adj* (*incierto*) hesitant; (*sospechoso*) doubtful; (*conducta*) dubious.

duelo ['dwelo] *etc vb V* **doler** ♦ *nm* (*combate*) duel; (*luto*) mourning; **batirse en ~** to fight a duel.

duende ['dwende] *nm* imp, goblin; **tiene ~** he's got real soul.

dueño, a ['dweɲo, a] *nm/f* (*propietario*) owner; (*de pensión, taberna*) landlord/ lady; (*de casa, perro*) master/mistress; (*empresario*) employer; **ser ~ de sí mismo** to have self-control; (*libre*) to be one's own boss, **eres ~ de hacer como te parezca** you're free to do as you think fit; **hacerse ~ de una situación** to take command of a situation.

duerma ['dwerma] *etc vb V* **dormir.**

duermevela [dwerme'ßela] *nf* (*fam*) nap, snooze.

Duero ['dwero] *nm* Douro.

dulce ['dulθe] *adj* sweet; (*carácter, clima*) gentle, mild ♦ *adv* gently, softly ♦ *nm* sweet.

dulcificar [dulθifi'kar] *vt* (*fig*) to soften.

dulcifique [dulθi'fike] *etc vb V* **dulcificar.**

dulzón, ona [dul'θon, ona] *adj* (*alimento*) sickly-sweet, too sweet; (*canción etc*) gooey.

dulzura [dul'θura] *nf* sweetness; (*ternura*) gentleness.

duna ['duna] *nf* dune.

Dunquerque [dun'kerke] *nm* Dunkirk.

dúo ['duo] *nm* duet, duo.

duodécimo, a [duo'deθimo, a] *adj* twelfth; *V tb* **sexto, a.**

dup., dup.do *abr* (= *duplicado*) duplicated.

dúplex ['dupleks] *nm inv* (*piso*) flat on two floors; (*TELEC*) link-up; (*INFORM*): **~ integral** full duplex.

duplicar [dupli'kar] *vt* (*hacer el doble de*) to duplicate; (*cantidad*) to double; **~se** *vr* to double.

duplique [du'plike] *etc vb V* **duplicar.**

duque ['duke] *nm* duke.

duquesa [du'kesa] *nf* duchess.

duración [dura'θjon] *nf* duration, length; (*de máquina*) life; **~ media de la vida** average life expectancy; **de larga ~** (*enfermedad*) lengthy; (*pila*) long-life; (*disco*) long-playing; **de poca ~** short.

duradero, a [dura'ðero, a] *adj* (*tela*) hard-wearing; (*fe, paz*) lasting.

durante [du'rante] *adv* during; **~ toda la noche** all night long; **habló ~ una hora** he spoke for an hour.

durar [du'rar] *vi* (*permanecer*) to last; (*recuerdo*) to remain; (*ropa*) to wear (well).

durazno [du'rasno] *nm* (*AM: fruta*) peach; (: *árbol*) peach tree.

durex ['dureks] *nm* (*AM: tira adhesiva*) Sellotape ® (*BRIT*), Scotch tape ® (*US*).

dureza [du'reθa] *nf* (*cualidad*) hardness; (*de carácter*) toughness.

durmiendo [dur'mjendo] *etc vb V* **dormir.**

durmiente [dur'mjente] *adj* sleeping ♦ *nm/f* sleeper.

duro, a ['duro, a] *adj* hard; (*carácter*) hard; (*pan*) stale; (*cuello, puerta*) stiff; (*clima, luz*) harsh ♦ *adv* hard ♦ *nm* (*moneda*) five peseta coin; **el sector ~ del partido** the hardliners *pl* in the party; **ser ~ con algn** to be tough with *o* hard on sb; **~ de mollera** (*torpe*) dense; **~ de oído** hard of hearing; **trabajar ~** to work hard; **estar sin un ~** to be broke.

DVD *nm abr* (= *disco de vídeo digital*) DVD.

E e

E, e [e] *nf* (*letra*) E, e; **E de Enrique** E for Edward (*BRIT*) *o* Easy (*US*).

E *abr* (= *este*) E.

e [e] *conj* (*delante de* i- *e* hi-, *pero no* hie-) and; *V tb* **y.**

e/ *abr* (*COM*: = *envío*) shpt.

ebanista [eßa'nista] *nm/f* cabinetmaker.

ébano ['eßano] *nm* ebony.

ebrio, a ['eßrjo, a] *adj* drunk.

Ebro ['eßro] *nm* Ebro.

ebullición [eßuʎi'θjon] *nf* boiling; **punto de ~** boiling point.

eccema [ek'θema] *nm* (*MED*) eczema.

echar [e'tʃar] *vt* to throw; (*agua, vino*) to pour (out); (*CULIN*) to put in, add; (*dientes*) to cut; (*discurso*) to give; (*empleado: despedir*) to fire, sack; (*hojas*) to sprout; (*cartas*) to post; (*humo*) to emit, give out; (*reprimenda*) to deal out; (*cuenta*) to make up; (*freno*) to put on ♦ *vi*: **~ a correr/llorar** to break into a run/burst into tears; **~ a reír** to burst out laughing; **~se** *vr* to lie down; **~ abajo** (*gobierno*) to overthrow; (*edificio*) to demolish; **~ la buenaventura a algn** to tell sb's fortune; **~ la culpa a** to lay the

blame on; ~ **de menos** to miss; ~**se atrás**
to throw o.s. back(wards); (_fig_) to go
back on what one has said; ~**se una
novia** to get o.s. a girlfriend; ~**se una
siestecita** to have a nap.
echarpe [e'tʃarpe] _nm_ (woman's) stole.
eclesiástico, a [ekle'sjastiko, a] _adj_
ecclesiastical; (_autoridades etc_) church
cpd ♦ _nm_ clergyman.
eclipsar [eklip'sar] _vt_ to eclipse; (_fig_) to
outshine, overshadow.
eclipse [e'klipse] _nm_ eclipse.
eco ['eko] _nm_ echo; **encontrar un** ~ **en** to
produce a response from; **hacerse** ~ **de
una opinión** to echo an opinion; **tener** ~
to catch on.
ecografía [ekoɣra'fia] _nf_ ultrasound.
ecología [ekolo'xia] _nf_ ecology.
ecológico, a [eko'loxiko, a] _adj_ ecological;
(_producto, método_) environmentally-
friendly; (_agricultura_) organic.
ecologista [ekolo'xista] _adj_ environmental, conservation _cpd_ ♦ _nm/f_ environmentalist.
economato [ekono'mato] _nm_ cooperative
store.
economía [ekono'mia] _nf_ (_sistema_)
economy; (_cualidad_) thrift; ~ **dirigida**
planned economy; ~ **doméstica**
housekeeping; ~ **de mercado** market
economy; ~ **mixta** mixed economy; ~
sumergida black economy; **hacer** ~**s** to
economize; ~**s de escala** economies of
scale.
economice [ekono'miθe] _etc vb_ V
economizar.
económico, a [eko'nomiko, a] _adj_ (_barato_)
cheap, economical; (_persona_) thrifty;
(_COM: año etc_) financial; (: _situación_)
economic.
economista [ekono'mista] _nm/f_ economist.
economizar [ekonomi'θar] _vt_ to economize
on ♦ _vi_ (_ahorrar_) to save up; (_pey_) to be
miserly.
ecosistema [ekosis'tema] _nm_ ecosystem.
ecu ['eku] _nm_ ecu.
ecuación [ekwa'θjon] _nf_ equation.
ecuador [ekwa'ðor] _nm_ equator; **(el) E**~
Ecuador.
ecuánime [e'kwanime] _adj_ (_carácter_) level-
headed; (_estado_) calm.
ecuatorial [ekwato'rjal] _adj_ equatorial.
ecuatoriano, a [ekwato'rjano, a] _adj, nm/f_
Ecuador(i)an.
ecuestre [e'kwestre] _adj_ equestrian.
eczema [ek'θema] _nm_ = **eccema.**
ed. _abr_ (= _edición_) ed.
edad [e'ðað] _nf_ age; **¿qué** ~ **tienes?** how

old are you?; **tiene ocho años de** ~ he is
eight (years old); **de** ~ **corta** young; **ser
de** ~ **mediana/avanzada** to be middle-
aged/getting on; **ser mayor de** ~ to be of
age; **llegar a mayor** ~ to come of age; **ser
menor de** ~ to be under age; **la E**~
Media the Middle Ages; **la E**~ **de Oro** the
Golden Age.
Edén [e'ðen] _nm_ Eden.
edición [eði'θjon] _nf_ (_acto_) publication;
(_ejemplar_) edition; **"al cerrar la** ~**"** (_TIP_)
"stop press".
edicto [e'ðikto] _nm_ edict, proclamation.
edificante [eðifi'kante] _adj_ edifying.
edificar [eðifi'kar] _vt_ (_ARQ_) to build.
edificio [eði'fiθjo] _nm_ building; (_fig_)
edifice, structure.
edifique [eði'fike] _etc vb_ V **edificar.**
Edimburgo [eðim'burɣo] _nm_ Edinburgh.
editar [eði'tar] _vt_ (_publicar_) to publish;
(_preparar textos, tb INFORM_) to edit.
editor, a [eði'tor, a] _nm/f_ (_que publica_)
publisher; (_redactor_) editor ♦ _adj:_ **casa** ~**a**
publishing company.
editorial [eðito'rjal] _adj_ editorial ♦ _nm_
leading article, editorial ♦ _nf_ (_tb:_ **casa** ~)
publishers.
editorialista [eðitorja'lista] _nm/f_ leader-
writer.
Edo. _abr_ (_AM_) = **Estado.**
edredón [eðre'ðon] _nm_ eiderdown, quilt; ~
nórdico continental quilt, duvet.
educación [eðuka'θjon] _nf_ education;
(_crianza_) upbringing; (_modales_) (good)
manners _pl_; (_formación_) training; **sin** ~
ill-mannered; **¡qué falta de** ~**!** how rude!
educado, a [eðu'kaðo, a] _adj_ well-
mannered; **mal** ~ ill-mannered.
educar [eðu'kar] _vt_ to educate; (_criar_) to
bring up; (_voz_) to train.
educativo, a [eðuka'tiβo, a] _adj_
educational; (_política_) education _cpd_.
eduque [e'ðuke] _etc vb_ V **educar.**
EE.UU. _nmpl abr_ (= _Estados Unidos_) USA.
efectista [efek'tista] _adj_ sensationalist.
efectivamente [efektiβa'mente] _adv_ (_como
respuesta_) exactly, precisely; (_verdadera-
mente_) really; (_de hecho_) in fact.
efectivo, a [efek'tiβo, a] _adj_ effective;
(_real_) actual, real ♦ _nm:_ **pagar en** ~ to pay
(in) cash; **hacer** ~ **un cheque** to cash a
cheque.
efecto [e'fekto] _nm_ effect, result; (_objetivo_)
purpose, end; ~**s** _nmpl_ (_personales_) effects;
(_bienes_) goods; (_COM_) assets; (_ECON_) bills,
securities; ~ **2000** millennium bug; ~
invernadero greenhouse effect; ~**s de
consumo** consumer goods; ~**s a cobrar**

bills receivable; ~s **especiales** special
effects; ~s **personales** personal effects;
~s **secundarios** (*COM*) spin-off effects; ~s
sonoros sound effects; **hacer** *o* **surtir** ~
to have the desired effect; **hacer** ~
(*impresionar*) to make an impression;
llevar algo a ~ to carry sth out; **en** ~
in fact; (*respuesta*) exactly, indeed.

efectuar [efek'twar] *vt* to carry out; (*viaje*)
to make.

efervescente [eferβes'θente] *adj* (*bebida*)
fizzy, bubbly.

eficacia [efi'kaθja] *nf* (*de persona*)
efficiency, (*de medicamento etc*)
effectiveness.

eficaz [efi'kaθ] *adj* (*persona*) efficient;
(*acción*) effective.

eficiencia [efi'θjenθja] *nf* efficiency.

eficiente [efi'θjente] *adj* efficient.

efigie [e'fixje] *nf* effigy.

efímero, a [e'fimero, a] *adj* ephemeral.

efusión [efu'sjon] *nf* outpouring; (*en el
trato*) warmth; **con** ~ effusively.

efusivo, a [efu'siβo, a] *adj* effusive; **mis
más efusivas gracias** my warmest
thanks.

EGB *nf abr* (*ESP ESCOL*: = *Educación General
Básica*) *primary education for 6-14 year
olds*; *V tb* **sistema educativo.**

Egeo [e'xeo] *nm*: (**Mar**) ~ Aegean (Sea).

egipcio, a [e'xipθjo, a] *adj, nm/f* Egyptian.

Egipto [e'xipto] *nm* Egypt.

egocéntrico, a [exo'θentriko, a] *adj* self-
centred.

egoísmo [exo'ismo] *nm* egoism.

egoísta [exo'ista] *adj* egoistical, selfish
♦ *nm/f* egoist.

ególatra [e'xolatra] *adj* big-headed.

egregio, a [e'xrexjo, a] *adj* eminent,
distinguished.

egresado, a [exre'saðo, a] *nm/f* (*AM*)
graduate.

egresar [exre'sar] *vi* (*AM*) to graduate.

eh [e] *excl* hey!, hi!

Eire ['eire] *nm* Eire.

ej. *abr* (= *ejemplo*) ex.

eje ['exe] *nm* (*GEO, MAT*) axis; (*POL, fig*)
axis, main line; (*de rueda*) axle; (*de
máquina*) shaft, spindle.

ejecución [exeku'θjon] *nf* execution;
(*cumplimiento*) fulfilment; (*actuación*)
performance; (*JUR*: *embargo de deudor*)
attachment.

ejecutar [exeku'tar] *vt* to execute, carry
out; (*matar*) to execute; (*cumplir*) to fulfil;
(*MUS*) to perform; (*JUR*: *embargar*) to
attach, distrain; (*deseos*) to fulfil;
(*INFORM*) to run.

ejecutivo, a [exeku'tiβo, a] *adj, nm/f* executive; **el** (**poder**) ~ the Executive (Power).

ejecutor [exeku'tor] *nm* (*tb*: ~
testamentario) executor.

ejecutoria [exeku'torja] *nf* (*JUR*) final
judgment.

ejemplar [exem'plar] *adj* exemplary ♦ *nm*
example; (*ZOOL*) specimen; (*de libro*)
copy; (*de periódico*) number, issue; ~ **de
regalo** complimentary copy; **sin** ~
unprecedented.

ejemplificar [exemplifi'kar] *vt* to
exemplify, illustrate.

ejemplifique [exempli'fike] *etc vb V*
ejemplificar.

ejemplo [e'xemplo] *nm* example; (*caso*)
instance; **por** ~ for example; **dar** ~ to
set an example.

ejercer [exer'θer] *vt* to exercise; (*funciones*)
to perform; (*negocio*) to manage;
(*influencia*) to exert; (*un oficio*) to
practise; (*poder*) to wield ♦ *vi*: ~ **de** to
practise as.

ejercicio [exer'θiθjo] *nm* exercise; (*MIL*)
drill; (*COM*) fiscal *o* financial year;
(*período*) tenure; ~ **acrobático** (*AVIAT*)
stunt; ~ **comercial** business year; ~s
espirituales (*REL*) retreat *sg*; **hacer** ~ to
take exercise.

ejercitar [exerθi'tar] *vt* to exercise; (*MIL*) to
drill.

ejército [e'xerθito] *nm* army; **E~ del Aire/
de Tierra** Air Force/Army; ~ **de
ocupación** army of occupation; ~
permanente standing army; **entrar en el**
~ to join the army, join up.

ejerza [e'xerθa] *etc vb V* **ejercer.**

ejote [e'xote] *nm* (*AM*) green bean.

=================== *PALABRA CLAVE*

el [el] (*f* **la**, *pl* **los, las,** *neutro* **lo**) *art def* **1** the;
**el libro/la mesa/los estudiantes/las
flores** the book/table/students/flowers;
me gusta el fútbol I like football; **está en
la cama** she's in bed

2 (*con n abstracto o propio: no se traduce*):
el amor/la juventud love/youth; ~ **Conde
Drácula** Count Dracula

3 (*posesión: se traduce a menudo por adj
posesivo*): **romperse el brazo** to break
one's arm; **levantó la mano** he put his
hand up; **se puso el sombrero** she put
her hat on

4 (*valor descriptivo*): **tener la boca
grande/los ojos azules** to have a big
mouth/blue eyes

5 (*con días*) on; **me iré el viernes** I'll
leave on Friday; **los domingos suelo ir a**

nadar on Sundays I generally go
swimming
6 (*lo* + *adj*): **lo difícil/caro** what is
difficult/expensive; (= *cuán*): **no se da
cuenta de lo pesado que es** he doesn't
realise how boring he is
♦ *pron demos* **1**: **mi libro y el de usted** my
book and yours; **las de Pepe son mejores**
Pepe's are better; **no la(s) blanca(s) sino
la(s) gris(es)** not the white one(s) but the
grey one(s)
2: **lo de**: **lo de ayer** what happened
yesterday; **lo de las facturas** that
business about the invoices
♦ *pron relativo*: **el que** *etc* **1** (*indef*): **el (los)
que quiera(n) que se vaya(n)** anyone who
wants to can leave; **llévese el/la que más
le guste** take the one you like best
2 (*def*): **el que compré ayer** the one I
bought yesterday; **los que se van** those
who leave
3: **lo que**: **lo que pienso yo/más me gusta**
what I think/like most
♦ *conj*: **el que**: **el que lo diga** the fact that
he says so; **el que sea tan vago me
molesta** his being so lazy bothers me
♦ *excl*: **¡el susto que me diste!** what a
fright you gave me!
♦ *pron personal* **1** (*persona*: *m*) him; (: *f*) her;
(: *pl*) them; **lo/las veo** I can see him/them
2 (*animal, cosa*: *sg*) it; (: *pl*) them; **lo** (*o* **la**)
veo I can see it; **los** (*o* **las**) **veo** I can see
them
3: **lo** (*como sustituto de frase*): **no lo sabía**
I didn't know; **ya lo entiendo** I
understand now.

él [el] *pron* (*persona*) he; (*cosa*) it; (*después
de prep*: *persona*) him; (: *cosa*) it; **mis
libros y los de** ~ my books and his.
elaboración [elaβora'θjon] *nf* (*producción*)
manufacture; ~ **de presupuestos** (*COM*)
budgeting.
elaborar [elaβo'rar] *vt* (*producto*) to make,
manufacture; (*preparar*) to prepare;
(*madera, metal etc*) to work; (*proyecto etc*)
to work on *o* out.
elasticidad [elastiθi'ðað] *nf* elasticity.
elástico, a [e'lastiko, a] *adj* elastic;
(*flexible*) flexible ♦ *nm* elastic; (*gomita*)
elastic band.
elección [elek'θjon] *nf* election; (*selección*)
choice, selection; **elecciones parciales**
by-election *sg*; **elecciones generales**
general election *sg*.
electo, a [e'lekto, a] *adj* elect; **el presidente**
~ the president-elect.
electorado [elekto'raðo] *nm* electorate,

voters *pl*.
electoral [elekto'ral] *adj* electoral.
electrice [elek'triθe] *etc vb* V **electrizar**.
electricidad [elektriθi'ðað] *nf* electricity.
electricista [elektri'θista] *nm/f* electrician.
eléctrico, a [e'lektriko, a] *adj* electric.
electrificar [elektrifi'kar] *vt* to electrify.
electrizar [elektri'θar] *vt* (*FERRO, fig*) to
electrify.
electro... [elektro] *pref* electro....
electrocardiograma
[elektrokarðjo'ɣrama] *nm*
electrocardiogram.
electrocución [elektroku'θjon] *nf*
electrocution.
electrocutar [elektroku'tar] *vt* to
electrocute.
electrodo [elek'troðo] *nm* electrode.
electrodomésticos [elektroðo'mestikos]
nmpl (electrical) household appliances;
(*COM*) white goods.
electroimán [electroi'man] *nm*
electromagnet.
electromagnético, a [elektromaɣ'netiko,
a] *adj* electromagnetic.
electrón [elek'tron] *nm* electron.
electrónico, a [elek'troniko, a] *adj*
electronic ♦ *nf* electronics *sg*; **proceso** ~
de datos (*INFORM*) electronic data
processing.
electrotecnia [elektro'teknja] *nf* electrical
engineering.
electrotécnico, a [elektro'tekniko, a] *nm/f*
electrical engineer.
elefante [ele'fante] *nm* elephant.
elegancia [ele'ɣanθja] *nf* elegance, grace;
(*estilo*) stylishness.
elegante [ele'ɣante] *adj* elegant, graceful;
(*traje etc*) smart, fashionable; (*decoración*)
tasteful.
elegía [ele'xia] *nf* elegy.
elegir [ele'xir] *vt* (*escoger*) to choose,
select; (*optar*) to opt for; (*presidente*) to
elect.
elemental [elemen'tal] *adj* (*claro, obvio*)
elementary; (*fundamental*) elemental,
fundamental.
elemento [ele'mento] *nm* element; (*fig*)
ingredient; (*AM*) person, individual; (*tipo
raro*) odd person; (*de pila*) cell; ~**s** *nmpl*
elements, rudiments; **estar en su** ~ to be
in one's element; **vino a verle un** ~
someone came to see you.
elenco [e'lenko] *nm* catalogue, list; (*TEAT*)
cast; (*AM*: *equipo*) team.
elepé [ele'pe] *nm* LP.
elevación [eleβa'θjon] *nf* elevation; (*acto*)
raising, lifting; (*de precios*) rise; (*GEO*

etc) height, altitude.

elevador [eleβa'ðor] *nm* (*AM*) lift (*BRIT*), elevator (*US*).

elevar [ele'βar] *vt* to raise, lift (up); (*precio*) to put up; (*producción*) to step up; (*informe etc*) to present; ~**se** *vr* (*edificio*) to rise; (*precios*) to go up; (*transportarse, enajenarse*) to get carried away; **la cantidad se eleva a** ... the total amounts to ... .

eligiendo [eli'xjenðo] *etc*, **elija** [e'lixa] *etc vb V* **elegir**.

eliminar [elimi'nar] *vt* to eliminate, remove; (*olor, persona*) to get rid of; (*DEPORTE*) to eliminate, knock out.

eliminatoria [elimina'torja] *nf* heat, preliminary (round).

elite [e'lite], **élite** ['elite] *nf* elite, élite.

elitista [eli'tista] *adj* elitist.

elixir [elik'sir] *nm* elixir; (*tb*: ~ **bucal**) mouthwash.

ella ['eʎa] *pron* (*persona*) she; (*cosa*) it; (*después de prep: persona*) her; (: *cosa*) it; **de** ~ hers.

ellas ['eʎas] *pron V* **ellos**.

ello ['eʎo] *pron neutro* it; **es por** ~ **que** ... that's why ... .

ellos, as ['eʎos, as] *pron personal pl* they; (*después de prep*) them; **de** ~ theirs.

elocuencia [elo'kwenθja] *nf* eloquence.

elocuente [elo'kwente] *adj* cloquent; (*fig*) significant; **un dato** ~ a fact which speaks for itself.

elogiar [elo'xjar] *vt* to praise, eulogize.

elogio [e'loxjo] *nm* praise; **queda por encima de todo** ~ it's beyond praise; **hacer** ~ **de** to sing the praises of.

elote [e'lote] *nm* (*AM*) corn on the cob.

El Salvador *nm* El Salvador.

eludir [elu'ðir] *vt* (*evitar*) to avoid, evade; (*escapar*) to escape, elude.

E.M. *abr* (*MIL*: = *Estado Mayor*) G.S.

Em.ª *abr* = **Eminencia**.

emanar [ema'nar] *vi*: ~ **de** to emanate from, come from; (*derivar de*) to originate in.

emancipar [emanθi'par] *vt* to emancipate; ~**se** *vr* to become emancipated, free o.s.

embadurnar [embaður'nar] *vt* to smear.

embajada [emba'xaða] *nf* embassy.

embajador, a [embaxa'ðor, a] *nm/f* ambassador/ambassadress.

embaladura [embala'ðura] *nf* (*AM*), **embalaje** [emba'laxe] *nm* packing.

embalar [emba'lar] *vt* (*envolver*) to parcel, wrap (up); (*envasar*) to package ♦ *vi* to sprint.

embalsamar [embalsa'mar] *vt* to embalm.

embalsar [embal'sar] *vt* (*río*) to dam (up); (*agua*) to retain.

embalse [em'balse] *nm* (*presa*) dam; (*lago*) reservoir.

embarace [emba'raθe] *etc vb V* **embarazar**.

embarazada [embara'θaða] *adj f* pregnant ♦ *nf* pregnant woman.

embarazar [embara'θar] *vt* to obstruct, hamper; ~**se** *vr* (*aturdirse*) to become embarrassed; (*confundirse*) to get into a mess.

embarazo [emba'raθo] *nm* (*de mujer*) pregnancy; (*impedimento*) obstacle, obstruction; (*timidez*) embarrassment.

embarazoso, a [embara'θoso, a] *adj* (*molesto*) awkward; (*violento*) embarrassing.

embarcación [embarka'θjon] *nf* (*barco*) boat, craft; (*acto*) embarkation; ~ **de arrastre** trawler; ~ **de cabotaje** coasting vessel.

embarcadero [embarka'ðero] *nm* pier, landing stage.

embarcar [embar'kar] *vt* (*cargamento*) to ship, stow; (*persona*) to embark, put on board; (*fig*): ~ **a algn en una empresa** to involve sb in an undertaking; ~**se** *vr* to embark, go on board; (*marinero*) to sign on; (*AM*: *en tren etc*) to get on, get in.

embargar [embar'jar] *vt* (*frenar*) to restrain; (*sentidos*) to overpower; (*JUR*) to seize, impound.

embargo [em'barxo] *nm* (*JUR*) seizure; (*COM etc*) embargo; **sin** ~ still, however, nonetheless.

embargue [em'barxe] *etc vb V* **embargar**.

embarque [em'barke] *etc vb V* **embarcar** ♦ *nm* shipment, loading.

embarrancar [embarran'kar] *vt, vi* (*NAUT*) to run aground; (*AUTO etc*) to run into a ditch.

embarranque [emba'rranke] *etc vb V* **embarrancar**.

embarullar [embaru'ʎar] *vt* to make a mess of.

embate [em'bate] *nm* (*de mar, viento*) beating, violence.

embaucador, a [embauka'ðor, a] *nm/f* (*estafador*) trickster; (*impostor*) impostor.

embaucar [embau'kar] *vt* to trick, fool.

embauque [em'bauke] *etc vb V* **embaucar**.

embeber [embe'βer] *vt* (*absorber*) to absorb, soak up; (*empapar*) to saturate ♦ *vi* to shrink; ~**se** *vr*: ~ **se en un libro** to be engrossed *o* absorbed in a book.

embelesado, a [embele'saðo, a] *adj* spellbound.

embelesar [embele'sar] *vt* to enchant; ~**se** *vr*: ~**se (con)** to be enchanted (by).

embellecer [embeʎe'θer] *vt* to embellish, beautify.

embellezca [embe'ʎeθka] *etc vb V* **embellecer**.

embestida [embes'tiða] *nf* attack, onslaught; (*carga*) charge.

embestir [embes'tir] *vt* to attack, assault; to charge, attack ♦ *vi* to attack.

embistiendo [embis'tjendo] *etc vb V* **embestir**.

emblanquecer [emblanke'θer] *vt* to whiten, bleach; ~**se** *vr* to turn white.

emblanquezca [emblan'keθka] *etc vb V* **emblanquecer**.

emblema [em'blema] *nm* emblem.

embobado, a [embo'ßaðo, a] *adj* (*atontado*) stunned, bewildered.

embobar [embo'ßar] *vt* (*asombrar*) to amaze; (*fascinar*) to fascinate; ~**se** *vr*: ~**se con** *o* **de** *o* **en** to be amazed at; to be fascinated by.

embocadura [emboka'ðura] *nf* narrow entrance; (*de río*) mouth; (*MUS*) mouthpiece.

embolado [embo'laðo] *nm* (*TEAT*) bit part, minor role; (*fam*) trick.

embolia [em'bolja] *nf* (*MED*) embolism; ~ **cerebral** clot on the brain.

émbolo ['embolo] *nm* (*AUTO*) piston.

embolsar [embol'sar] *vt* to pocket, put in one's pocket.

emboquillado, a [emboki'ʎaðo, a] *adj* (*cigarrillo*) tipped, filter *cpd*.

emborrachar [emborra'tʃar] *vt* to make drunk; ~**se** *vr* to get drunk.

emboscada [embos'kaða] *nf* (*celada*) ambush.

embotar [embo'tar] *vt* to blunt, dull; ~**se** *vr* (*adormecerse*) to go numb.

embotellamiento [emboteʎa'mjento] *nm* (*AUTO*) traffic jam.

embotellar [embote'ʎar] *vt* to bottle; ~**se** *vr* (*circulación*) to get into a jam.

embozo [em'boθo] *nm* muffler, mask; (*de sábana*) turn over.

embragar [embra'ɣar] *vt* (*AUTO, TEC*) to engage; (*partes*) to connect ♦ *vi* to let in the clutch.

embrague [em'braɣe] *etc vb V* **embragar** ♦ *nm* (*tb*: **pedal de** ~) clutch.

embravecer [embraße'θer] *vt* to enrage, infuriate; ~**se** *vr* to become furious; (*mar*) to get rough; (*tormenta*) to rage.

embravecido, a [embraße'θiðo, a] *adj* (*mar*) rough; (*persona*) furious.

embriagador, a [embrjaɣa'ðor, a] *adj* intoxicating.

embriagar [embrja'ɣar] *vt* (*emborrachar*) to make drunk; (*alegrar*) to delight; ~**se** *vr* (*emborracharse*) to get drunk.

embriague [em'brjaɣe] *etc vb V* **embriagar**.

embriaguez [embrja'ɣeθ] *nf* (*borrachera*) drunkenness.

embrión [em'brjon] *nm* embryo.

embrionario, a [embrjo'narjo, a] *adj* embryonic.

embrollar [embro'ʎar] *vt* (*asunto*) to confuse, complicate; (*persona*) to involve, embroil; ~**se** *vr* (*confundirse*) to get into a muddle *o* mess.

embrollo [em'broʎo] *nm* (*enredo*) muddle, confusion; (*aprieto*) fix, jam.

embromado, a [embro'maðo, a] *adj* (*AM fam*) tricky, difficult.

embromar [embro'mar] *vt* (*burlarse de*) to tease, make fun of; (*AM fam: molestar*) to annoy.

embrujado, a [embru'xaðo, a] *adj* (*persona*) bewitched; **casa embrujada** haunted house.

embrujo [em'bruxo] *nm* (*de mirada etc*) charm, magic.

embrutecer [embrute'θer] *vt* (*atontar*) to stupefy; ~**se** *vr* to be stupefied.

embrutezca [embru'teθka] *etc vb V* **embrutecer**.

embudo [em'buðo] *nm* funnel.

embuste [em'buste] *nm* trick; (*mentira*) lie; (*hum*) fib.

embustero, a [embus'tero, a] *adj* lying, deceitful ♦ *nm/f* (*tramposo*) cheat; (*mentiroso*) liar; (*hum*) fibber.

embutido [embu'tiðo] *nm* (*CULIN*) sausage; (*TEC*) inlay.

embutir [embu'tir] *vt* to insert; (*TEC*) to inlay; (*llenar*) to pack tight, cram.

emergencia [emer'xenθja] *nf* emergency; (*surgimiento*) emergence.

emergente [emer'xente] *adj* resultant, consequent; (*nación*) emergent.

emerger [emer'xer] *vi* to emerge, appear.

emeritense [emeri'tense] *adj* of *o* from Mérida ♦ *nm/f* native *o* inhabitant of Mérida.

emerja [e'merxa] *etc vb V* **emerger**.

emigración [emiɣra'θjon] *nf* emigration; (*de pájaros*) migration.

emigrado, a [emi'ɣraðo, a] *nm/f* emigrant; (*POL etc*) émigré(e).

emigrante [emi'ɣrante] *adj, nm/f* emigrant.

emigrar [emi'ɣrar] *vi* (*personas*) to emigrate; (*pájaros*) to migrate.

eminencia [emi'nenθja] *nf* eminence; (*en títulos*): **Su E**~ His Eminence; **Vuestra**

E~ Your Eminence.
eminente [emi'nente] *adj* eminent, distinguished; (*elevado*) high.
emisario [emi'sarjo] *nm* emissary.
emisión [emi'sjon] *nf* (*acto*) emission; (*COM etc*) issue; (*RADIO, TV: acto*) broadcasting; (: *programa*) broadcast, programme, program (*US*); ~ **de acciones** (*COM*) share issue; ~ **gratuita de acciones** (*COM*) rights issue; ~ **de valores** (*COM*) flotation.
emisor, a [emi'sor, a] *nm* transmitter ♦ *nf* radio *o* broadcasting station.
emitir [emi'tir] *vt* (*olor etc*) to emit, give off; (*moneda etc*) to issue; (*opinión*) to express; (*voto*) to cast; (*señal*) to send out; (*RADIO*) to broadcast; ~ **una señal sonora** to beep.
emoción [emo'θjon] *nf* emotion; (*excitación*) excitement; (*sentimiento*) feeling; ¡**qué** ~! how exciting!; (*irónico*) what a thrill!
emocionado, a [emoθjo'naðo, a] *adj* deeply moved, stirred.
emocionante [emoθjo'nante] *adj* (*excitante*) exciting, thrilling.
emocionar [emoθjo'nar] *vt* (*excitar*) to excite, thrill; (*conmover*) to move, touch; (*impresionar*) to impress; ~**se** *vr* to get excited.
emotivo, a [emo'tißo, a] *adj* emotional.
empacar [empa'kar] *vt* (*gen*) to pack; (*en caja*) to bale, crate.
empacharse [empa'tʃarse] *vr* (*MED*) to get indigestion.
empacho [em'patʃo] *nm* (*MED*) indigestion; (*fig*) embarrassment.
empadronamiento [empaðrona'mjento] *nm* census; (*de electores*) electoral register.
empadronarse [empaðro'narse] *vr* (*POL: como elector*) to register.
empalagar [empala'xar] *vt* (*suj: comida*) to cloy; (*hartar*) to pall on ♦ *vi* to pall.
empalagoso, a [empala'xoso, a] *adj* cloying; (*fig*) tiresome.
empalague [empa'laxe] *etc vb V* **empalagar**.
empalizada [empali'θaða] *nf* fence; (*MIL*) palisade.
empalmar [empal'mar] *vt* to join, connect ♦ *vi* (*dos caminos*) to meet, join.
empalme [em'palme] *nm* joint, connection; (*de vías*) junction; (*de trenes*) connection.
empanada [empa'naða] *nf* pie, pasty.
empanar [empa'nar] *vt* (*CULIN*) to cook *o* roll in breadcrumbs *o* pastry.
empantanarse [empanta'narse] *vr* to get

swamped; (*fig*) to get bogged down.
empañarse [empa'narse] *vr* (*nublarse*) to get misty, steam up.
empapar [empa'par] *vt* (*mojar*) to soak, saturate; (*absorber*) to soak up, absorb; ~**se** *vr*: ~**se de** to soak up.
empapelar [empape'lar] *vt* (*paredes*) to paper.
empaque [em'pake] *etc vb V* **empacar**.
empaquetar [empake'tar] *vt* to pack, parcel up; (*COM*) to package.
emparedado [empare'ðaðo] *nm* sandwich.
emparejar [empare'xar] *vt* to pair ♦ *vi* to catch up.
emparentar [emparen'tar] *vi*: ~ **con** to marry into.
empariente [empa'rjente] *etc vb V* **emparentar**.
empastar [empas'tar] *vt* (*embadurnar*) to paste; (*diente*) to fill.
empaste [em'paste] *nm* (*de diente*) filling.
empatar [empa'tar] *vi* to draw, tie.
empate [em'pate] *nm* draw, tie; **un** ~ **a cero** a no-score draw.
empecé [empe'θe], **empecemos** [empe'θemos] *etc vb V* **empezar**.
empecinado, a [empeθi'naðo, a] *adj* stubborn.
empedernido, a [empeðer'niðo, a] *adj* hard, heartless; (*fijado*) hardened, inveterate; **un fumador** ~ a heavy smoker.
empedrado, a [empe'ðraðo, a] *adj* paved ♦ *nm* paving.
empedrar [empe'ðrar] *vt* to pave.
empeine [em'peine] *nm* (*de pie, zapato*) instep.
empellón [empe'ʎon] *nm* push, shove; **abrirse paso a empellones** to push *o* shove one's way past *o* through.
empeñado, a [empe'naðo, a] *adj* (*persona*) determined; (*objeto*) pawned.
empeñar [empe'nar] *vt* (*objeto*) to pawn, pledge; (*persona*) to compel; ~**se** *vr* (*obligarse*) to bind o.s., pledge o.s.; (*endeudarse*) to get into debt; ~**se en hacer** to be set on doing, be determined to do.
empeño [em'peno] *nm* (*determinación*) determination; (*cosa prendada*) pledge; **casa de** ~**s** pawnshop; **con** ~ insistently; (*con celo*) eagerly; **tener** ~ **en hacer algo** to be bent on doing sth.
empeoramiento [empeora'mjento] *nm* worsening.
empeorar [empeo'rar] *vt* to make worse, worsen ♦ *vi* to get worse, deteriorate.
empequeñecer [empekene'θer] *vt* to

dwarf; (*fig*) to belittle.

empequeñezca [empeke'ɲeθka] *etc vb V* **empequeñecer.**

emperador [empera'ðor] *nm* emperor.

emperatriz [empera'triθ] *nf* empress.

emperrarse [empe'rrarse] *vr* to get stubborn; ~ **en algo** to persist in sth.

empezar [empe'θar] *vt, vi* to begin, start; **empezó a llover** it started to rain; **bueno, para** ~ well, to start with.

empiece [em'pjeθe] *etc vb V* **empezar.**

empiedre [em'pjeðre] *etc vb V* **empedrar.**

empiezo [em'pjeθo] *etc vb V* **empezar.**

empinado, a [empi'naðo, a] *adj* steep.

empinar [empi'nar] *vt* to raise; (*botella*) to tip up; ~**se** *vr* (*persona*) to stand on tiptoe; (*animal*) to rear up; (*camino*) to climb steeply; ~ **el codo** to booze (*fam*).

empingorotado, a [empingoro'taðo, a] *adj* (*fam*) stuck-up.

empírico, a [em'piriko, a] *adj* empirical.

emplace [em'plaθe] *etc vb V* **emplazar.**

emplaste [em'plaste], **emplasto** [em'plasto] *nm* (*MED*) plaster.

emplazamiento [emplaθa'mjento] *nm* site, location; (*JUR*) summons *sg.*

emplazar [empla'θar] *vt* (*ubicar*) to site, place, locate; (*JUR*) to summons; (*convocar*) to summon.

empleado, a [emple'aðo, a] *nm/f* (*gen*) employee; (*de banco etc*) clerk; ~ **público** civil servant.

emplear [emple'ar] *vt* (*usar*) to use, employ; (*dar trabajo a*) to employ; ~**se** *vr* (*conseguir trabajo*) to be employed; (*ocuparse*) to occupy o.s.; ~ **mal el tiempo** to waste time; **¡te está bien empleado!** it serves you right!

empleo [em'pleo] *nm* (*puesto*) job; (*puestos: colectivamente*) employment; (*uso*) use, employment; **"modo de ~"** "instructions for use".

emplumar [emplu'mar] *vt* (*estafar*) to swindle.

empobrecer [empoßre'θer] *vt* to impoverish; ~**se** *vr* to become poor *o* impoverished.

empobrecimiento [empoßreθi'mjento] *nm* impoverishment.

empobrezca [empo'ßreθka] *etc vb V* **empobrecer.**

empollar [empo'ʎar] *vt* to incubate; (*ESCOL fam*) to swot (up) ♦ *vi* (*gallina*) to brood; (*ESCOL fam*) to swot.

empollón, ona [empo'ʎon, ona] *nm/f* (*ESCOL fam*) swot.

empolvar [empol'ßar] *vt* (*cara*) to powder; ~**se** *vr* to powder one's face; (*superficie*)

to get dusty.

emponzoñar [emponθo'ɲar] *vt* (*esp fig*) to poison.

emporio [em'porjo] *nm* emporium, trading centre; (*AM: gran almacén*) department store.

empotrado, a [empo'traðo, a] *adj* (*armario etc*) built-in.

empotrar [empo'trar] *vt* to embed; (*armario etc*) to build in.

emprendedor, a [emprende'ðor, a] *adj* enterprising.

emprender [empren'der] *vt* to undertake; (*empezar*) to begin, embark on; (*acometer*) to tackle, take on; ~ **marcha a** to set out for.

empresa [em'presa] *nf* enterprise; (*COM: sociedad*) firm, company; (: *negocio*) business; (*esp TEAT*) management; ~ **filial** (*COM*) affiliated company; ~ **matriz** (*COM*) parent company.

empresario, a [empre'sarjo, a] *nm/f* (*COM*) businessman/woman, entrepreneur; (*TEC*) manager; (*MUS: de ópera etc*) impresario; ~ **de pompas fúnebres** undertaker (*BRIT*), mortician (*US*).

empréstito [em'prestito] *nm* (public) loan; (*COM*) loan capital.

empujar [empu'xar] *vt* to push, shove.

empuje [em'puxe] *nm* thrust; (*presión*) pressure; (*fig*) vigour, drive.

empujón [empu'xon] *nm* push, shove; **abrirse paso a empujones** to shove one's way through.

empuñadura [empuɲa'ðura] *nf* (*de espada*) hilt; (*de herramienta etc*) handle.

empuñar [empu'ɲar] *vt* (*asir*) to grasp, take (firm) hold of; ~ **las armas** (*fig*) to take up arms.

emulación [emula'θjon] *nf* emulation.

emular [emu'lar] *vt* to emulate; (*rivalizar*) to rival.

émulo, a ['emulo, a] *nm/f* rival, competitor.

emulsión [emul'sjon] *nf* emulsion.

═══════════════════════ *PALABRA CLAVE*

en [en] *prep* **1** (*posición*) in; (: *sobre*) on; **está** ~ **el cajón** it's in the drawer; ~ **Argentina/La Paz** in Argentina/La Paz; ~ **el colegio/la oficina** at school/the office; ~ **casa** at home; **está** ~ **el suelo/quinto piso** it's on the floor/the fifth floor; ~ **el periódico** in the paper

2 (*dirección*) into; **entró** ~ **el aula** she went into the classroom; **meter algo** ~ **el bolso** to put sth into one's bag; **ir de puerta** ~ **puerta** to go from door to door

3 (*tiempo*) in; on; ~ **1605/3 semanas/ invierno** in 1605/3 weeks/winter; ~ **(el mes de) enero** in (the month of) January; ~ **aquella ocasión/época** on that occasion/at that time
4 (*precio*) for; **lo vendió ~ 20 dólares** he sold it for 20 dollars
5 (*diferencia*) by; **reducir/aumentar ~ una tercera parte/un 20 por ciento** to reduce/increase by a third/20 per cent
6 (*manera, forma*): ~ **avión/autobús** by plane/bus; **escrito ~ inglés** written in English; ~ **serio** seriously; ~ **espiral/ círculo** in a spiral/circle
7 (*después de vb que indica gastar etc*) on; **han cobrado demasiado ~ dietas** they've charged too much to expenses; **se le va la mitad del sueldo ~ comida** half his salary goes on food
8 (*tema, ocupación*): **experto ~ la materia** expert on the subject; **trabaja ~ la construcción** he works in the building industry
9 (*adj* + ~ + *infin*): **lento ~ reaccionar** slow to react.

enagua(s) [enaɣwa(s)] *nf(pl)* (*esp AM*) petticoat.
enajenación [enaxena'θjon] *nf*, **enajenamiento** [enaxena'mjento] *nm* alienation; (*fig: distracción*) absent-mindedness; (: *embelesamiento*) rapture, trance; ~ **mental** mental derangement.
enajenar [enaxe'nar] *vt* to alienate; (*fig*) to carry away.
enamorado, a [enamo'raðo, a] *adj* in love ♦ *nm/f* lover; **estar ~ (de)** to be in love (with).
enamorar [enamo'rar] *vt* to win the love of; ~**se** *vr*: ~**se (de)** to fall in love (with).
enano, a [e'nano, a] *adj* tiny, dwarf ♦ *nm/f* dwarf; (*pey*) runt.
enarbolar [enarβo'lar] *vt* (*bandera etc*) to hoist; (*espada etc*) to brandish.
enardecer [enarðe'θer] *vt* (*pasiones*) to fire, inflame; (*persona*) to fill with enthusiasm; ~**se** *vr* to get excited; ~**se por** to get enthusiastic about.
enardezca [enar'deθka] *etc vb V* **enardecer**.
encabece [enka'βeθe] *etc vb V* **encabezar**.
encabezado [enkaβe'θaðo] *nm* (*COM*) header.
encabezamiento [enkaβeθa'mjento] *nm* (*de carta*) heading; (*COM*) billhead, letterhead; (*de periódico*) headline; (*preámbulo*) foreword, preface; ~ **normal** (*TIP etc*) running head.
encabezar [enkaβe'θar] *vt* (*movimiento,*

revolución) to lead, head; (*lista*) to head; (*carta*) to put a heading to; (*libro*) to entitle.
encadenar [enkaðe'nar] *vt* to chain (together); (*fig*) to shackle.
encajar [enka'xar] *vt* (*ajustar*): ~ **en** to fit (into); (*meter a la fuerza*) to push in; (*máquina etc*) to house; (*partes*) to join; (*fam: golpe*) to give, deal; (*entrometer*) to insert ♦ *vi* to fit (well); (*fig: corresponder a*) to match; ~**se** *vr*: ~**se en un sillón** to squeeze into a chair.
encaje [en'kaxe] *nm* (*labor*) lace.
encajonar [enkaxo'nar] *vt* to box (up), put in a box.
encalar [enka'lar] *vt* (*pared*) to whitewash.
encallar [enka'ʎar] *vi* (*NAUT*) to run aground.
encaminado, a [enkami'naðo, a] *adj*: **medidas encaminadas a ... measures designed to** *o* **aimed at ....**
encaminar [enkami'nar] *vt* to direct, send; ~**se** *vr*: ~**se a** to set out for; ~ **por** (*expedición etc*) to route via.
encandilar [enkandi'lar] *vt* to dazzle; (*persona*) to daze, bewilder.
encanecer [enkane'θer] *vi*, **encanecerse** *vr* (*pelo*) to go grey.
encanezca [enka'neθka] *etc vb V* **encanecer**.
encantado, a [enkan'taðo, a] *adj* delighted; ¡~! how do you do!, pleased to meet you.
encantador, a [enkanta'ðor, a] *adj* charming, lovely ♦ *nm/f* magician, enchanter/enchantress.
encantar [enkan'tar] *vt* to charm, delight; (*cautivar*) to fascinate; (*hechizar*) to bewitch, cast a spell on.
encanto [en'kanto] *nm* (*magia*) spell, charm; (*fig*) charm, delight; (*expresion de ternura*) sweetheart; **como por ~** as if by magic.
encapotado, a [enkapo'taðo, a] *adj* (*cielo*) overcast.
encapricharse [enkapri'tʃarse] *vr*: **se ha encaprichado con ir** he's taken it into his head to go; **se ha encaprichado** he's digging his heels in.
encaramar [enkara'mar] *vt* (*subir*) to raise, lift up; ~**se** *vr* (*subir*) to perch; ~**se a** (*árbol etc*) to climb.
encararse [enka'rarse] *vr*: ~ **a** *o* **con** to confront, come face to face with.
encarcelar [enkarθe'lar] *vt* to imprison, jail.
encarecer [enkare'θer] *vt* to put up the price of ♦ *vi*, ~**se** *vr* to get dearer.

encarecidamente [enkareθiða'mente] *adv* earnestly.

encarecimiento [enkareθi'mjento] *nm* price increase.

encarezca [enka'reθka] *etc vb* V **encarecer**.

encargado, a [enkar'ɣaðo, a] *adj* in charge ♦ *nmlf* agent, representative; (*responsable*) person in charge.

encargar [enkar'ɣar] *vt* to entrust; (*COM*) to order; (*recomendar*) to urge, recommend; ~**se** *vr*: ~**se de** to look after, take charge of; ~ **algo a algn** to put sb in charge of sth.

encargo [en'karɣo] *nm* (*pedido*) assignment, job; (*responsabilidad*) responsibility; (*recomendación*) recommendation; (*COM*) order.

encargue [en'karɣe] *etc vb* V **encargar**.

encariñarse [enkari'narse] *vr*: ~ **con** to grow fond of, get attached to.

encarnación [enkarna'θjon] *nf* incarnation, embodiment.

encarnado, a [enkar'naðo, a] *adj* (*color*) red; **ponerse** ~ to blush.

encarnar [enkar'nar] *vt* to personify; (*TEAT*: *papel*) to play ♦ *vi* (*REL etc*) to become incarnate.

encarnizado, a [enkarni'θaðo, a] *adj* (*lucha*) bloody, fierce.

encarrilar [enkarri'lar] *vt* (*tren*) to put back on the rails; (*fig*) to correct, put on the right track.

encasillar [enkasi'ʎar] *vt* (*TEAT*) to typecast; (*clasificar*: *pey*) to pigeonhole.

encasquetar [enkaske'tar] *vt* (*sombrero*) to pull down *o* on; ~**se** *vr*: ~**se el sombrero** to pull one's hat down *o* on; ~ **algo a algn** to offload sth onto sb.

encauce [en'kauθe] *etc vb* V **encauzar**.

encausar [enkau'sar] *vt* to prosecute, sue.

encauzar [enkau'θar] *vt* to channel; (*fig*) to direct.

encendedor [enθende'ðor] *nm* lighter.

encender [enθen'der] *vt* (*con fuego*) to light; (*incendiar*) to set fire to; (*luz, radio*) to put on, switch on; (*INFORM*) to toggle on, switch on; (*avivar*: *pasiones etc*) to inflame; (*despertar*: *entusiasmo*) to arouse; (*odio*) to awaken; ~**se** *vr* to catch fire; (*excitarse*) to get excited; (*de cólera*) to flare up; (*el rostro*) to blush.

encendidamente [enθendiða'mente] *adv* passionately.

encendido, a [enθen'diðo, a] *adj* alight; (*aparato*) (switched) on; (*mejillas*) glowing; (*cara*: *por el vino etc*) flushed; (*mirada*) passionate ♦ *nm* (*AUTO*) ignition; (*de faroles*) lighting.

encerado, a [enθe'raðo, a] *adj* (*suelo*) waxed, polished ♦ *nm* (*ESCOL*) blackboard; (*hule*) oilcloth.

encerar [enθe'rar] *vt* (*suelo*) to wax, polish.

encerrar [enθe'rrar] *vt* (*confinar*) to shut in *o* up; (*con llave*) to lock in *o* up; (*comprender, incluir*) to include, contain; ~**se** *vr* to shut *o* lock o.s. up *o* in.

encerrona [enθe'rrona] *nf* trap.

encestar [enθes'tar] *vi* to score a basket.

encharcar [entʃar'kar] *vt* to swamp, flood; ~**se** *vr* to become flooded.

encharque [en'tʃarke] *etc vb* V **encharcar**.

enchufar [entʃu'far] *vt* (*ELEC*) to plug in; (*TEC*) to connect, fit together; (*COM*) to merge.

enchufe [en'tʃufe] *nm* (*ELEC*: *clavija*) plug; (: *toma*) socket; (*de dos tubos*) joint, connection; (*fam*: *influencia*) contact, connection; (: *puesto*) cushy job; ~ **de clavija** jack plug; **tiene un** ~ **en el ministerio** he can pull strings at the ministry.

encía [en'θia] *nf* (*ANAT*) gum.

enciclopedia [enθiklo'peðja] *nf* encyclopaedia.

encienda [en'θjenda] *etc vb* V **encender**.

encierro [en'θjerro] *etc vb* V **encerrar** ♦ *nm* shutting in *o* up; (*calabozo*) prison; (*AGR*) pen; (*TAUR*) penning.

encima [en'θima] *adv* (*sobre*) above, over; (*además*) besides; ~ **de** (*en*) on, on top of; (*sobre*) above, over; (*además de*) besides, on top of; **por** ~ **de** over; ¿**llevas dinero** ~? have you (got) any money on you?; **se me vino** ~ it took me by surprise.

encina [en'θina] *nf* (holm) oak.

encinta [en'θinta] *adj f* pregnant.

enclave [en'klaße] *nm* enclave.

enclenque [en'klenke] *adj* weak, sickly.

encoger [enko'xer] *vt* (*gen*) to shrink, contract; (*fig*: *asustar*) to scare; (: *desanimar*) to discourage; ~**se** *vr* to shrink, contract; (*fig*) to cringe; ~**se de hombros** to shrug one's shoulders.

encoja [en'koxa] *etc vb* V **encoger**.

encolar [enko'lar] *vt* (*engomar*) to glue, paste; (*pegar*) to stick down.

encolerice [enkole'riθe] *etc vb* V **encolerizar**.

encolerizar [enkoleri'θar] *vt* to anger, provoke; ~**se** *vr* to get angry.

encomendar [enkomen'dar] *vt* to entrust, commend; ~**se** *vr*: ~**se a** to put one's trust in.

encomiar [enko'mjar] *vt* to praise, pay tribute to.

encomienda [enko'mjenda] *etc vb* V

encomendar ♦ *nf* (*encargo*) charge, commission; (*elogio*) tribute; (*AM*) parcel, package; ~ **postal** (*AM*) parcel post.

encomio [en'komjo] *nm* praise, tribute.

encono [en'kono] *nm* (*rencor*) rancour, spite.

encontrado, a [enkon'traðo, a] *adj* (*contrario*) contrary, conflicting; (*hostil*) hostile.

encontrar [enkon'trar] *vt* (*hallar*) to find; (*inesperadamente*) to meet, run into; ~**se** *vr* to meet (each other); (*situarse*) to be (situated); (*persona*) to find o.s., be; (*entrar en conflicto*) to crash, collide; ~**se con** to meet; ~**se bien (de salud)** to feel well; **no se encuentra aquí en este momento** he's not in at the moment.

encontronazo [enkontro'naθo] *nm* collision, crash.

encorvar [enkor'ßar] *vt* to curve; (*inclinar*) to bend (down); ~**se** *vr* to bend down, bend over.

encrespado, a [enkres'paðo, a] *adj* (*pelo*) curly; (*mar*) rough.

encrespar [enkres'par] *vt* (*cabellos*) to curl; (*fig*) to anger, irritate; ~**se** *vr* (*el mar*) to get rough; (*fig*) to get cross o irritated.

encrucijada [enkruθi'xaða] *nf* crossroads *sg*; (*empalme*) junction.

encuadernación [enkwaðerna'θjon] *nf* binding; (*taller*) binder's.

encuadernador, a [enkwaðerna'ðor, a] *nm/f* bookbinder.

encuadrar [enkwa'ðrar] *vt* (*retrato*) to frame; (*ajustar*) to fit, insert; (*encerrar*) to contain.

encubierto [enku'ßjerto] *pp de* **encubrir**.

encubrir [enku'ßrir] *vt* (*ocultar*) to hide, conceal; (*criminal*) to harbour, shelter; (*ayudar*) to be an accomplice in.

encuentro [en'kwentro] *etc vb V* **encontrar** ♦ *nm* (*de personas*) meeting; (*AUTO etc*) collision, crash; (*DEPORTE*) match, game; (*MIL*) encounter.

encuesta [en'kwesta] *nf* inquiry, investigation; (*sondeo*) public opinion poll; ~ **judicial** post mortem.

encumbrado, a [enkum'braðo, a] *adj* eminent, distinguished.

encumbrar [enkum'brar] *vt* (*persona*) to exalt; ~**se** *vr* (*fig*) to become conceited.

endeble [en'deßle] *adj* (*argumento, excusa, persona*) weak.

endémico, a [en'demiko, a] *adj* endemic.

endemoniado, a [endemo'njaðo, a] *adj* possessed (of the devil); (*travieso*) devilish.

enderece [ende're θe] *etc vb V* **enderezar**.

enderezar [endere'θar] *vt* (*poner derecho*) to straighten (out); (: *verticalmente*) to set upright; (*fig*) to straighten o sort out; (*dirigir*) to direct; ~**se** *vr* (*persona sentada*) to sit up straight.

endeudarse [endeu'ðarse] *vr* to get into debt.

endiablado, a [endja'ßlaðo, a] *adj* devilish, diabolical; (*hum*) mischievous.

endibia [en'dißja] *nf* endive.

endilgar [endil'xar] *vt* (*fam*): ~ **algo a algn** to lumber sb with sth; ~ **un sermón a algn** to give sb a lecture.

endilgue [en'dilxe] *etc vb V* **endilgar**.

endiñar [endi'ɲar] *vt*: ~ **algo a algn** to land sth on sb.

endomingarse [endomin'garse] *vr* to dress up, put on one's best clothes.

endomingue [endo'minge] *etc vb V* **endomingarse**.

endosar [endo'sar] *vt* (*cheque etc*) to endorse.

endulce [en'dulθe] *etc vb V* **endulzar**.

endulzar [endul'θar] *vt* to sweeten; (*suavizar*) to soften.

endurecer [endure'θer] *vt* to harden; ~**se** *vr* to harden, grow hard.

endurecido, a [endure'θiðo, a] *adj* (*duro*) hard; (*fig*) hardy, tough; **estar** ~ **a algo** to be hardened o used to sth.

endurezca [endu're θka] *etc vb V* **endurecer**.

ene. *abr* (= *enero*) Jan.

enemigo, a [ene'mixo, a] *adj* enemy, hostile ♦ *nm/f* enemy ♦ *nf* enmity, hostility; **ser** ~ **de** (*persona*) to dislike; (*suj: tendencia*) to be inimical to.

enemistad [enemis'tað] *nf* enmity.

enemistar [enemis'tar] *vt* to make enemies of, cause a rift between; ~**se** *vr* to become enemies; (*amigos*) to fall out.

energético, a [ener'xetiko, a] *adj*: **política energética** energy policy.

energía [ener'xia] *nf* (*vigor*) energy, drive; (*TEC, ELEC*) energy, power; ~ **atómica/ eléctrica/eólica** atomic/electric/wind power.

enérgico, a [e'nerxiko, a] *adj* (*gen*) energetic; (*ataque*) vigorous; (*ejercicio*) strenuous; (*medida*) bold; (*voz, modales*) forceful.

energúmeno, a [ener'xumeno, a] *nm/f* madman/woman; **ponerse como un** ~ **con algn** to get furious with sb.

enero [e'nero] *nm* January.

enervar [ener'ßar] *vt* (*poner nervioso a*) to get on sb's nerves.

enésimo, a [e'nesimo, a] *adj* (*MAT*) nth; **por enésima vez** (*fig*) for the umpteenth time.

enfadado, a [enfa'ðaðo, a] *adj* angry, annoyed.

enfadar [enfa'ðar] *vt* to anger, annoy; ~**se** *vr* to get angry o annoyed.

enfado [en'faðo] *nm* (*enojo*) anger, annoyance; (*disgusto*) trouble, bother.

énfasis ['enfasis] *nm* emphasis, stress; **poner** ~ **en** to stress.

enfático, a [en'fatiko, a] *adj* emphatic.

enfatizado, a [enfati'θaðo, a] *adj*: **en caracteres** ~**s** (*INFORM*) emphasized.

enfermar [enfer'mar] *vt* to make ill ♦ *vi* to fall ill, be taken ill; **su actitud me enferma** his attitude makes me sick; ~ **del corazón** to develop heart trouble.

enfermedad [enferme'ðað] *nf* illness; ~ **venérea** venereal disease.

enfermera [enfer'mera] *nf V* **enfermero**.

enfermería [enferme'ria] *nf* infirmary; (*de colegio etc*) sick bay.

enfermero, a [enfer'mero, a] *nm* (*male*) nurse ♦ *nf* nurse; **enfermera jefa** matron.

enfermizo, a [enfer'miθo, a] *adj* (*persona*) sickly, unhealthy; (*fig*) unhealthy.

enfermo, a [en'fermo, a] *adj* ill, sick ♦ *nm/f* invalid, sick person; (*en hospital*) patient.

enfilar [enfi'lar] *vt* (*aguja*) to thread; (*calle*) to go down.

enflaquecer [enflake'θer] *vt* (*adelgazar*) to make thin; (*debilitar*) to weaken.

enflaquezca [enfla'keθka] *etc vb V* **enflaquecer**.

enfocar [enfo'kar] *vt* (*foto etc*) to focus; (*problema etc*) to consider, look at.

enfoque [en'foke] *etc vb V* **enfocar** ♦ *nm* focus; (*acto*) focusing; (*óptica*) approach.

enfrascado, a [enfras'kaðo, a] *adj*: **estar** ~ **en algo** (*fig*) to be wrapped up in sth.

enfrascarse [enfras'karse] *vr*: ~ **en un libro** to bury o.s. in a book.

enfrasque [en'fraske] *etc vb V* **enfrascar**.

enfrentamiento [enfrenta'mjento] *nm* confrontation.

enfrentar [enfren'tar] *vt* (*peligro*) to face (up to), confront; (*oponer*) to bring face to face; ~**se** *vr* (*dos personas*) to face o confront each other; (*DEPORTE: dos equipos*) to meet; ~**se a** o **con** to face up to, confront.

enfrente [en'frente] *adv* opposite; ~ **de** *prep* opposite, facing; **la casa de** ~ the house opposite, the house across the street.

enfriamiento [enfria'mjento] *nm* chilling, refrigeration; (*MED*) cold, chill.

enfriar [enfri'ar] *vt* (*alimentos*) to cool, chill; (*algo caliente*) to cool down;

(*habitación*) to air, freshen; (*entusiasmo*) to dampen; ~**se** *vr* to cool down; (*MED*) to catch a chill; (*amistad*) to cool.

enfurecer [enfure'θer] *vt* to enrage, madden; ~**se** *vr* to become furious, fly into a rage; (*mar*) to get rough.

enfurezca [enfu'reθka] *etc vb V* **enfurecer**.

engalanar [engala'nar] *vt* (*adornar*) to adorn; (*ciudad*) to decorate; ~**se** *vr* to get dressed up.

enganchar [engan't∫ar] *vt* to hook; (*ropa*) to hang up; (*dos vagones*) to hitch up; (*TEC*) to couple, connect; (*MIL*) to recruit; (*fam: atraer: persona*) to rope into; ~**se** *vr* (*MIL*) to enlist, join up; ~**se (a)** (*drogas*) to get hooked (on).

enganche [en'gant∫e] *nm* hook; (*TEC*) coupling, connection; (*acto*) hooking (up); (*MIL*) recruitment, enlistment; (*AM: depósito*) deposit.

engañar [enga'nar] *vt* to deceive; (*estafar*) to cheat, swindle ♦ *vi*: **las apariencias engañan** appearances are deceptive; ~**se** *vr* (*equivocarse*) to be wrong; (*asimismo*) to deceive o kid o.s.; **engaña a su mujer** he's unfaithful to o cheats on his wife.

engaño [en'gano] *nm* deceit; (*estafa*) trick, swindle; (*error*) mistake, misunderstanding; (*ilusión*) delusion.

engañoso, a [enga'noso, a] *adj* (*tramposo*) crooked; (*mentiroso*) dishonest, deceitful; (*aspecto*) deceptive; (*consejo*) misleading.

engarce [en'garθe] *etc vb V* **engarzar**.

engarzar [engar'θar] *vt* (*joya*) to set, mount; (*fig*) to link, connect.

engatusar [engatu'sar] *vt* (*fam*) to coax.

engendrar [enxen'drar] *vt* to breed; (*procrear*) to beget; (*fig*) to cause, produce.

engendro [en'xendro] *nm* (*BIO*) foetus; (*fig*) monstrosity; (*idea*) brainchild.

englobar [englo'βar] *vt* (*comprender*) to include, comprise; (*incluir*) to lump together.

engomar [engo'mar] *vt* to glue, stick.

engordar [engor'ðar] *vt* to fatten ♦ *vi* to get fat, put on weight.

engorro [en'gorro] *nm* bother, nuisance.

engorroso, a [engo'rroso, a] *adj* bothersome, trying.

engranaje [engra'naxe] *nm* (*AUTO*) gear; (*juego*) gears *pl*.

engrandecer [engrande'θer] *vt* to enlarge, magnify; (*alabar*) to praise, speak highly of; (*exagerar*) to exaggerate.

engrandezca [engran'deθka] *etc vb V*

engrandecer.

engrasar [engra'sar] *vt* (*TEC: poner grasa*) to grease; (: *lubricar*) to lubricate, oil; (*manchar*) to make greasy.

engrase [en'grase] *nm* greasing, lubrication.

engreído, a [engre'iðo, a] *adj* vain, conceited.

engrosar [engro'sar] *vt* (*ensanchar*) to enlarge; (*aumentar*) to increase; (*hinchar*) to swell.

engrudo [en'gruðo] *nm* paste.

engruese [en'grwese] *etc vb V* **engrosar.**

engullir [engu'ʎir] *vt* to gobble, gulp (down).

enhebrar [ene'ßrar] *vt* to thread.

enhiesto, a [e'njesto, a] *adj* (*derecho*) erect; (*bandera*) raised; (*edificio*) lofty.

enhorabuena [enora'ßwena] *excl* congratulations.

enigma [e'niɣma] *nm* enigma; (*problema*) puzzle; (*misterio*) mystery.

enigmático, a [eniɣ'matiko, a] *adj* enigmatic.

enjabonar [enxaßo'nar] *vt* to soap; (*barba*) to lather; (*fam: adular*) to soft-soap; (: *regañar*) to tick off.

enjalbegar [enxalße'ɣar] *vt* (*pared*) to whitewash.

enjalbegue [enxal'ßeɣe] *etc vb V* **enjalbegar.**

enjambre [en'xamßre] *nm* swarm.

enjaular [enxau'lar] *vt* to (put in a) cage; (*fam*) to jail, lock up.

enjuagar [enxwa'ɣar] *vt* (*ropa*) to rinse (out).

enjuague [en'xwaɣe] *etc vb V* **enjuagar** ♦ *nm* (*MED*) mouthwash; (*de ropa*) rinse, rinsing.

enjugar [enxu'ɣar] *vt* to wipe (off); (*lágrimas*) to dry; (*déficit*) to wipe out.

enjugue [en'xuɣe] *etc vb V* **enjugar.**

enjuiciar [enxwi'θjar] *vt* (*JUR: procesar*) to prosecute, try; (*fig*) to judge.

enjuto, a [en'xuto, a] *adj* dry, dried up; (*fig*) lean, skinny.

enlace [en'laθe] *etc vb V* **enlazar** ♦ *nm* link, connection; (*relación*) relationship; (*tb*: ~ **matrimonial**) marriage; (*de trenes*) connection; ~ **de datos** data link; ~ **sindical** shop steward; ~ **telefónico** telephone link-up.

enlazar [enla'θar] *vt* (*unir con lazos*) to bind together; (*atar*) to tie; (*conectar*) to link, connect; (*AM*) to lasso.

enlodar [enlo'ðar] *vt* to cover in mud; (*fig: manchar*) to stain; (: *rebajar*) to debase.

enloquecer [enloke'θer] *vt* to drive mad

♦ *vi*, ~**se** *vr* to go mad.

enloquezca [enlo'keθka] *etc vb V* **enloquecer.**

enlutado, a [enlu'taðo, a] *adj* (*persona*) in mourning.

enlutar [enlu'tar] *vt* to dress in mourning; ~**se** *vr* to go into mourning.

enmarañar [enmara'ɲar] *vt* (*enredar*) to tangle up, entangle; (*complicar*) to complicate; (*confundir*) to confuse; ~**se** *vr* (*enredarse*) to become entangled; (*confundirse*) to get confused.

enmarcar [enmar'kar] *vt* (*cuadro*) to frame; (*fig*) to provide a setting for.

enmarque [en'marke] *etc vb V* **enmarcar.**

enmascarar [enmaska'rar] *vt* to mask; (*intenciones*) to disguise; ~**se** *vr* to put on a mask.

enmendar [enmen'dar] *vt* to emend, correct; (*constitución etc*) to amend; (*comportamiento*) to reform; ~**se** *vr* to reform, mend one's ways.

enmienda [en'mjenda] *etc vb V* **enmendar** ♦ *nf* correction; amendment; reform.

enmohecerse [enmoe'θerse] *vr* (*metal*) to rust, go rusty; (*muro, plantas*) to go mouldy.

enmohezca [enmo'eθka] *etc vb V* **enmohecerse.**

enmudecer [enmuðe'θer] *vt* to silence ♦ *vi*, ~**se** *vr* (*perder el habla*) to fall silent; (*guardar silencio*) to remain silent; (*por miedo*) to be struck dumb.

enmudezca [enmu'ðeθka] *etc vb V* **enmudecer.**

ennegrecer [enneɣre'θer] *vt* (*poner negro*) to blacken; (*oscurecer*) to darken; ~**se** *vr* to turn black; (*oscurecerse*) to get dark, darken.

ennegrezca [enne'ɣreθka] *etc vb V* **ennegrecer.**

ennoblecer [ennoßle'θer] *vt* to ennoble.

ennoblezca [enno'ßleθka] *etc vb V* **ennoblecer.**

en.º *abr* (= *enero*) Jan.

enojadizo, a [enoxa'ðiθo, a] *adj* irritable, short-tempered.

enojar [eno'xar] (*esp AM*) *vt* (*encolerizar*) to anger; (*disgustar*) to annoy, upset; ~**se** *vr* to get angry; to get annoyed.

enojo [e'noxo] (*esp AM*) *nm* (*cólera*) anger; (*irritación*) annoyance; ~**s** *nmpl* trials, problems.

enojoso, a [eno'xoso, a] *adj* annoying.

enorgullecerse [enorɣuʎe'θerse] *vr* to be proud; ~ **de** to pride o.s. on, be proud of.

enorgullezca [enorɣu'ʎeθka] *etc vb V* **enorgullecerse.**

enorme [e'norme] *adj* enormous, huge; (*fig*) monstrous.

enormidad [enormi'ðað] *nf* hugeness, immensity.

enraice [en'raiθe] *etc vb* V **enraizar**.

enraizar [enrai'θar] *vi* to take root.

enrarecido, a [enrare'θiðo, a] *adj* rarefied.

enredadera [enreða'ðera] *nf* (*BOT*) creeper, climbing plant.

enredar [enre'ðar] *vt* (*cables, hilos etc*) to tangle (up), entangle; (*situación*) to complicate, confuse; (*meter cizaña*) to sow discord among *o* between; (*implicar*) to embroil, implicate; **~se** *vr* to get entangled, get tangled (up); (*situación*) to get complicated; (*persona*) to get embroiled.

enredo [en'reðo] *nm* (*maraña*) tangle; (*confusión*) mix-up, confusion; (*intriga*) intrigue; (*apuro*) jam; (*amorío*) love affair.

enrejado [enre'xaðo] *nm* grating; (*de ventana*) lattice; (*en jardín*) trellis.

enrevesado, a [enreβe'saðo, a] *adj* (*asunto*) complicated, involved.

enriquecer [enrike'θer] *vt* to make rich; (*fig*) to enrich; **~se** *vr* to get rich.

enriquezca [enri'keθka] *etc vb* V **enriquecer**.

enrojecer [enroxe'θer] *vt* to redden ♦ *vi*, **~se** *vr* (*persona*) to blush.

enrojezca [enro'xeθka] *etc vb* V **enrojecer**.

enrolar [enro'lar] *vt* (*MIL*) to enlist; (*reclutar*) to recruit; **~se** *vr* (*MIL*) to join up; (*afiliarse*) to enrol, sign on.

enrollar [enro'ʎar] *vt* to roll (up), wind (up); **~se** *vr*: **~se con algn** to get involved with sb.

enroque [en'roke] *nm* (*AJEDREZ*) castling.

enroscar [enros'kar] *vt* (*torcer, doblar*) to twist; (*arrollar*) to coil (round), wind; (*tornillo, rosca*) to screw in; **~se** *vr* to coil, wind.

enrosque [en'roske] *etc vb* V **enroscar**.

ensalada [ensa'laða] *nf* salad; (*lío*) mix-up.

ensaladilla [ensala'ðiʎa] *nf* (*tb*: **~ rusa**) ≈ Russian salad.

ensalce [en'salθe] *etc vb* V **ensalzar**.

ensalzar [ensal'θar] *vt* (*alabar*) to praise, extol; (*exaltar*) to exalt.

ensamblador [ensambla'ðor] *nm* (*INFORM*) assembler.

ensambladura [ensambla'ðura] *nf*, **ensamblaje** [ensam'blaxe] *nm* assembly; (*TEC*) joint.

ensamblar [ensam'blar] *vt* (*montar*) to assemble; (*madera etc*) to join.

ensanchar [ensan't∫ar] *vt* (*hacer más*

ancho*) to widen; (*agrandar*) to enlarge, expand; (*COSTURA*) to let out; **~se** *vr* to get wider, expand; (*pey*) to give o.s. airs.

ensanche [en'sant∫e] *nm* (*de calle*) widening; (*de negocio*) expansion.

ensangrentado, a [ensangren'taðo, a] *adj* bloodstained, covered with blood.

ensangrentar [ensangren'tar] *vt* to stain with blood.

ensangriente [ensan'grjente] *etc vb* V **ensangrentar**.

ensañarse [ensa'ɲarse] *vr*: **~ con** to treat brutally.

ensartar [ensar'tar] *vt* (*gen*) to string (together); (*carne*) to spit, skewer.

ensayar [ensa'jar] *vt* to test, try (out); (*TEAT*) to rehearse.

ensayista [ensa'jista] *nm/f* essayist.

ensayo [en'sajo] *nm* test, trial; (*QUÍMICA*) experiment; (*TEAT*) rehearsal; (*DEPORTE*) try; (*ESCOL, LITERATURA*) essay; **pedido de ~** (*COM*) trial order; **~ general** (*TEAT*) dress rehearsal; (*MUS*) full rehearsal.

enseguida [ense'ɣuiða] *adv* at once, right away; **~ termino** I've nearly finished, I shan't be long now.

ensenada [ense'naða] *nf* inlet, cove.

enseña [en'seɲa] *nf* ensign, standard.

enseñante [ense'ɲante] *nm/f* teacher.

enseñanza [ense'nanθa] *nf* (*educación*) education; (*acción*) teaching; (*doctrina*) teaching, doctrine; **~ primaria/ secundaria/superior** primary/ secondary/higher education.

enseñar [ense'ɲar] *vt* (*educar*) to teach; (*instruir*) to teach, instruct; (*mostrar, señalar*) to show.

enseres [en'seres] *nmpl* belongings.

ENSIDESA [ensi'ðesa] *abr* (*ESP COM*) = *Empresa Nacional Siderúrgica, S. A.*

ensillar [ensi'ʎar] *vt* to saddle (up).

ensimismarse [ensimis'marse] *vr* (*abstraerse*) to become lost in thought; (*estar absorto*) to be lost in thought; (*AM*) to become conceited.

ensopar [enso'par] *vt* (*AM*) to soak.

ensordecer [ensorðe'θer] *vt* to deafen ♦ *vi* to go deaf.

ensordezca [ensor'ðeθka] *etc vb* V **ensordecer**.

ensortijado, a [ensorti'xaðo, a] *adj* (*pelo*) curly.

ensuciar [ensu'θjar] *vt* (*manchar*) to dirty, soil; (*fig*) to defile; **~se** *vr* (*mancharse*) to get dirty; (*niño*) to dirty (*o* wet) o.s.

ensueño [en'sweɲo] *nm* (*sueño*) dream, fantasy; (*ilusión*) illusion; (*soñando despierto*) daydream; **de ~** dream-like.

entablado [enta'ßlaðo] nm (*piso*)
floorboards pl; (*armazón*) boarding.
entablar [enta'ßlar] vt (*recubrir*) to board
(up); (*AJEDREZ, DAMAS*) to set up;
(*conversación*) to strike up; (*JUR*) to file
♦ vi to draw.
entablillar [entaßli'ʎar] vt (*MED*) to (put in
a) splint.
entallado, a [enta'ʎaðo, a] adj waisted.
entallar [enta'ʎar] vt (*traje*) to tailor ♦ vi: **el
traje entalla bien** the suit fits well.
ente ['ente] nm (*organización*) body,
organization; (*compañía*) company; (*fam:
persona*) odd character; (*ser*) being; **~
público** (*ESP*) state(-owned) body.
entender [enten'der] vt (*comprender*) to
understand; (*darse cuenta*) to realize;
(*querer decir*) to mean ♦ vi to understand;
(*creer*) to think, believe ♦ nm: **a mi ~** in
my opinion; **~ de** to know all about; **~
algo de** to know a little about; **~ en** to
deal with, have to do with; **~se** vr
(*comprenderse*) to be understood; (*2
personas*) to get on together; (*ponerse de
acuerdo*) to agree, reach an agreement;
dar a ~ que ... to lead to believe that ...;
~se mal to get on badly; **¿entiendes?** (do
you) understand?
entendido, a [enten'diðo, a] adj
(*comprendido*) understood; (*hábil*)
skilled; (*inteligente*) knowledgeable
♦ nm/f (*experto*) expert ♦ excl agreed!
entendimiento [entendi'mjento] nm
(*comprensión*) understanding;
(*inteligencia*) mind, intellect; (*juicio*)
judgement.
enterado, a [ente'raðo, a] adj well-
informed; **estar ~ de** to know about, be
aware of; **no darse por ~** to pretend not
to understand.
enteramente [entera'mente] adv entirely,
completely.
enterarse [ente'rarse] vr: **~ (de)** to find out
(about); **para que te enteres ...** (*fam*) for
your information ....
entereza [ente're θa] nf (*totalidad*) entirety;
(*fig: carácter*) strength of mind; (*honradez*)
integrity.
enternecedor, a [enterneθe'ðor, a] adj
touching.
enternecer [enterne'θer] vt (*ablandar*) to
soften; (*apiadar*) to touch, move; **~se** vr
to be touched, be moved.
enternezca [enter'neθka] etc vb V
enternecer.
entero, a [en'tero, a] adj (*total*) whole,
entire; (*fig: recto*) honest; (: *firme*) firm,
resolute ♦ nm (*MAT*) integer; (*COM: punto*)

point; (*AM: pago*) payment; **las acciones
han subido dos ~s** the shares have gone
up two points.
enterrador [enterra'ðor] nm gravedigger.
enterrar [ente'rrar] vt to bury; (*fig*) to
forget.
entibiar [enti'ßjar] vt (*enfriar*) to cool;
(*calentar*) to warm; **~se** vr (*fig*) to
cool.
entidad [enti'ðað] nf (*empresa*) firm,
company; (*organismo*) body; (*sociedad*)
society; (*FILOSOFÍA*) entity.
entienda [en'tjenda] etc vb V entender.
entierro [en'tjerro] etc vb V enterrar ♦ nm
(*acción*) burial; (*funeral*) funeral.
entomología [entomolo'xia] nf
entomology.
entomólogo, a [ento'moloɣo, a] nm/f
entomologist.
entonación [entona'θjon] nf (*LING*)
intonation; (*fig*) conceit.
entonar [ento'nar] vt (*canción*) to intone;
(*colores*) to tone; (*MED*) to tone up ♦ vi to
be in tune; **~se** vr (*engreírse*) to give o.s.
airs.
entonces [en'tonθes] adv then, at that
time; **desde ~** since then; **en aquel ~** at
that time; **(pues) ~** and so; **el ~
embajador de España** the then Spanish
ambassador.
entornar [entor'nar] vt (*puerta, ventana*) to
half close, leave ajar; (*los ojos*) to screw
up.
entorno [en'torno] nm setting,
environment; **~ de redes** (*INFORM*)
network environment.
entorpecer [entorpe'θer] vt (*entendimiento*)
to dull; (*impedir*) to obstruct, hinder;
(: *tránsito*) to slow down, delay.
entorpezca [entor'peθka] etc vb V
entorpecer.
entrado, a [en'traðo, a] adj: **~ en años**
elderly; **(una vez) ~ el verano** in the
summer(time), when summer comes
♦ nf (*acción*) entry, access; (*sitio*)
entrance, way in; (*principio*) beginning;
(*COM*) receipts pl, takings pl; (*CULIN*)
entrée; (*DEPORTE*) innings sg; (*TEAT*)
house, audience; (*para el cine etc*) ticket;
(*INFORM*) input; (*ECON*): **entradas** nfpl
income sg; **entradas brutas** gross
receipts; **entradas y salidas** (*COM*)
income and expenditure; **entrada de aire**
(*TEC*) air intake o inlet; **de entrada** right
away; **"entrada gratis"** "admission
free"; **entrada de datos vocal** (*INFORM*)
voice input; **tiene entradas** he's losing
his hair.

entrante [en'trante] *adj* next, coming; (*POL*) incoming ♦ *nm* inlet; (*CULIN*) starter; **mes/año** ~ next month/year.

entraña [en'traɲa] *nf* (*fig*: *centro*) heart, core; (*raíz*) root; ~**s** *nfpl* (*ANAT*) entrails; (*fig*) heart *sg*.

entrañable [entra'ɲaβle] *adj* (*persona, lugar*) dear; (*relación*) close; (*acto*) intimate.

entrañar [entra'ɲar] *vt* to entail.

entrar [en'trar] *vt* (*introducir*) to bring in; (*persona*) to show in; (*INFORM*) to input ♦ *vi* (*meterse*) to go *o* come in, enter; (*comenzar*): ~ **diciendo** to begin by saying; **entré en** *o* **a** (*AM*) **la casa** I went into the house; **le entraron ganas de reír** he felt a sudden urge to laugh; **no me entra** I can't get the hang of it.

entre ['entre] *prep* (*dos*) between; (*en medio de*) among(st); (*por*): **se abrieron paso** ~ **la multitud** they forced their way through the crowd; ~ **una cosa y otra** what with one thing and another; ~ **más estudia más aprende** (*AM*) the more he studies the more he learns.

entreabierto [entrea'βjerto] *pp de* **entreabrir**.

entreabrir [entrea'βrir] *vt* to half-open, open halfway.

entreacto [entre'akto] *nm* interval.

entrecano, a [entre'kano, a] *a* greying; **ser** ~ (*persona*) to be going grey.

entrecejo [entre'θexo] *nm*: **fruncir el** ~ to frown.

entrechocar [entretʃo'kar] *vi* (*dientes*) to chatter.

entrechoque [entre'tʃoke] *etc vb V* **entrechocar**.

entrecomillado, a [entrekomi'ʎaðo, a] *adj* in inverted commas.

entrecortado, a [entrekor'taðo, a] *adj* (*respiración*) laboured, difficult; (*habla*) faltering.

entrecot [entre'ko(t)] *nm* (*CULIN*) sirloin steak.

entrecruce [entre'kruθe] *etc vb V* **entrecruzarse**.

entrecruzarse [entrekru'θarse] *vr* (*BIO*) to interbreed.

entredicho [entre'ðitʃo] *nm* (*JUR*) injunction; **poner en** ~ to cast doubt on; **estar en** ~ to be in doubt.

entrega [en'treɣa] *nf* (*de mercancías*) delivery; (*de premios*) presentation; (*de novela etc*) instalment; "~ **a domicilio**" "door-to-door delivery service".

entregar [entre'ɣar] *vt* (*dar*) to hand (over), deliver; (*ejercicios*) to hand in;

~**se** *vr* (*rendirse*) to surrender, give in, submit; ~**se a** (*dedicarse*) to devote o.s. to; **a** ~ (*COM*) to be supplied.

entregue [en'treɣe] *etc vb V* **entregar**.

entrelace [entre'laθe] *etc vb V* **entrelazar**.

entrelazar [entrela'θar] *vt* to entwine.

entremedias [entre'meðjas] *adv* (*en medio*) in between, halfway.

entremeses [entre'meses] *nmpl* hors d'œuvres.

entremeter [entreme'ter] *vt* to insert, put in; ~**se** *vr* to meddle, interfere.

entremetido, a [entreme'tiðo, a] *adj* meddling, interfering.

entremezclar [entremeθ'klar] *vt*, ~**se** *vr* to intermingle.

entrenador, a [entrena'ðor, a] *nm/f* trainer, coach.

entrenamiento [entrena'mjento] *nm* training.

entrenar [entre'nar] *vt* (*DEPORTE*) to train; (*caballo*) to exercise ♦ *vi*, ~**se** *vr* to train.

entrepierna [entre'pjerna] *nf* (*tb*: ~**s**) crotch, crutch.

entresacar [entresa'kar] *vt* to pick out, select.

entresaque [entre'sake] *etc vb V* **entresacar**.

entresuelo [entre'swelo] *nm* mezzanine, entresol; (*TEAT*) dress *o* first circle.

entretanto [entre'tanto] *adv* meanwhile, meantime.

entretejer [entrete'xer] *vt* to interweave.

entretela [entre'tela] *nf* (*de ropa*) interlining; ~**s** *nfpl* heart-strings.

entretención [entreten'sjon] *nf* (*AM*) entertainment.

entretendré [entreten'dre] *etc vb V* **entretener**.

entretener [entrete'ner] *vt* (*divertir*) to entertain, amuse; (*detener*) to hold up, delay; (*mantener*) to maintain; ~**se** *vr* (*divertirse*) to amuse o.s.; (*retrasarse*) to delay, linger; **no le entretengo más** I won't keep you any longer.

entretenga [entre'tenga] *etc vb V* **entretener**.

entretenido, a [entrete'niðo, a] *adj* entertaining, amusing.

entretenimiento [entreteni'mjento] *nm* entertainment, amusement; (*mantenimiento*) upkeep, maintenance.

entretiempo [entre'tjempo] *nm*: **ropa de** ~ clothes for spring and autumn.

entretiene [entre'tjene] *etc*, **entretuve** [entre'tuβe] *etc vb V* **entretener**.

entreveía [entreβe'ia] *etc vb V* **entrever**.

entrever [entre'βer] *vt* to glimpse, catch a

glimpse of.

entrevista [entre'βista] *nf* interview.

entrevistar [entreβis'tar] *vt* to interview;
~**se** *vr*: ~**se con** to have an interview
with, see; **el ministro se entrevistó con el
Rey ayer** the minister had an audience
with the King yesterday.

entrevisto [entre'βisto] *pp de* **entrever**.

entristecer [entriste'θer] *vt* to sadden,
grieve; ~**se** *vr* to grow sad.

entristezca [entris'teθka] *etc vb V*
entristecer.

entrometerse [entrome'terse] *vr*: ~ (**en**) to
interfere (in *o* with).

entrometido, a [entrome'tiðo, a] *adj*
interfering, meddlesome.

entroncar [entron'kar] *vi* to be connected
o related.

entronque [en'tronke] *etc vb V* **entroncar.**

entuerto [en'twerto] *nm* wrong, injustice;
~**s** *nmpl* (*MED*) afterpains.

entumecer [entume'θer] *vt* to numb,
benumb; ~**se** *vr* (*por el frío*) to go *o*
become numb.

entumecido, a [entume'θiðo, a] *adj* numb,
stiff.

entumezca [entu'meθka] *etc vb V*
entumecer.

enturbiar [entur'βjar] *vt* (*el agua*) to make
cloudy; (*fig*) to confuse; ~**se** *vr*
(*oscurecerse*) to become cloudy, (*fig*) to
get confused, become obscure.

entusiasmar [entusjas'mar] *vt* to excite,
fill with enthusiasm; (*gustar mucho*) to
delight; ~**se** *vr*: ~**se con** *o* **por** to get
enthusiastic *o* excited about.

entusiasmo [entu'sjasmo] *nm* enthusiasm;
(*excitación*) excitement.

entusiasta [entu'sjasta] *adj* enthusiastic
♦ *nm/f* enthusiast.

enumerar [enume'rar] *vt* to enumerate.

enunciación [enunθja'θjon] *nf*,
enunciado [enun'θjaðo] *nm* enunciation;
(*declaración*) declaration, statement.

enunciar [enun'θjar] *vt* to enunciate; to
declare, state.

envainar [embai'nar] *vt* to sheathe.

envalentonar [embalento'nar] *vt* to give
courage to; ~**se** *vr* (*pey: jactarse*) to boast,
brag.

envanecer [embane'θer] *vt* to make
conceited; ~**se** *vr* to grow conceited.

envanezca [emba'neθka] *etc vb V*
envanecer.

envasar [emba'sar] *vt* (*empaquetar*) to
pack, wrap; (*enfrascar*) to bottle; (*enlatar*)
to can; (*embolsar*) to pocket.

envase [em'base] *nm* packing, wrapping;

bottling; canning; pocketing; (*recipiente*)
container; (*paquete*) package; (*botella*)
bottle; (*lata*) tin (*BRIT*), can.

envejecer [embexe'θer] *vt* to make old, age
♦ *vi* (*volverse viejo*) to grow old;
(*parecer viejo*) to age.

envejecido, a [embexe'θiðo, a] *adj* old,
aged; (*de aspecto*) old-looking.

envejezca [embe'xeθka] *etc vb V* **envejecer.**

envenenar [embene'nar] *vt* to poison; (*fig*)
to embitter.

envergadura [emberɣa'ðura] *nf* (*expansión*)
expanse; (*NAUT*) breadth; (*fig*) scope; **un
programa de gran** ~ a wide-ranging
programme.

envés [em'bes] *nm* (*de tela*) back, wrong
side.

enviado, a [em'bjaðo, a] *nm/f* (*POL*) envoy;
~ **especial** (*de periódico, TV*) special
correspondent.

enviar [em'bjar] *vt* to send.

enviciar [embi'θjar] *vt* to corrupt ♦ *vi*
(*trabajo etc*) to be addictive; ~**se** *vr*: ~**se
(con *o* en)** to get addicted (to).

envidia [em'biðja] *nf* envy; **tener** ~ **a** to
envy, be jealous of.

envidiar [embi'ðjar] *vt* (*desear*) to envy;
(*tener celos de*) to be jealous of.

envidioso, a [embi'ðjoso, a] *adj* envious,
jealous.

envío [em'bio] *nm* (*acción*) sending; (*de
mercancías*) consignment; (*de dinero*)
remittance; (*en barco*) shipment; **gastos
de** ~ postage and packing; ~ **contra
reembolso** COD shipment.

enviudar [embju'ðar] *vi* to be widowed.

envoltura [embol'tura] *nf* (*cobertura*)
cover; (*embalaje*) wrapper, wrapping.

envolver [embol'βer] *vt* to wrap (up);
(*cubrir*) to cover; (*enemigo*) to surround;
(*implicar*) to involve, implicate.

envuelto [em'bwelto], **envuelva**
[em'bwelßa] *etc vb V* **envolver.**

enyesar [enje'sar] *vt* (*pared*) to plaster;
(*MED*) to put in plaster.

enzarzarse [enθar'θarse] *vr*: ~ **en algo** to
get mixed up in sth.

epa ['epa], **épale** ['epale] (*AM*) *excl* hey!,
wow!

E.P.D. *abr* (= *en paz descanse*) R.I.P.

epicentro [epi'θentro] *nm* epicentre.

épico, a ['epiko, a] *adj* epic ♦ *nf* epic
(poetry).

epidemia [epi'ðemja] *nf* epidemic.

epidémico, a [epi'ðemiko, a] *adj* epidemic.

epidermis [epi'ðermis] *nf* epidermis.

epifanía [epifa'nia] *nf* Epiphany.

epilepsia [epi'lepsja] *nf* epilepsy.

epiléptico, a [epi'leptiko, a] *adj*, *nm/f* epileptic.
epílogo [e'piloɣo] *nm* epilogue.
episcopado [episko'paðo] *nm* (*cargo*) bishopric; (*obispos*) bishops *pl* (*collectively*).
episodio [epi'soðjo] *nm* episode; (*suceso*) incident.
epístola [e'pistola] *nf* epistle.
epitafio [epi'tafjo] *nm* epitaph.
epíteto [e'piteto] *nm* epithet.
época ['epoka] *nf* period, time; (*temporada*) season; (*HISTORIA*) age, epoch; **hacer ~** to be epoch-making.
equidad [eki'ðað] *nf* equity, fairness.
equilibrar [ekili'ßrar] *vt* to balance.
equilibrio [eki'lißrjo] *nm* balance, equilibrium; **~ político** balance of power.
equilibrista [ekili'ßrista] *nm/f* (*funámbulo*) tightrope walker; (*acróbata*) acrobat.
equinoccio [eki'nokθjo] *nm* equinox.
equipaje [eki'paxe] *nm* luggage (*BRIT*), baggage (*US*); (*avíos*) equipment, kit; **~ de mano** hand luggage; **hacer el ~** to pack.
equipar [eki'par] *vt* (*proveer*) to equip.
equiparar [ekipa'rar] *vt* (*igualar*) to put on the same level; (*comparar*) to compare (*con* with); **~se** *vr*: **~se con** to be on a level with.
equipo [e'kipo] *nm* (*conjunto de cosas*) equipment; (*DEPORTE*, *grupo*) team; (*de obreros*) shift; (*de máquinas*) plant; (*turbinas etc*) set; **~ de caza** hunting gear; **~ físico** (*INFORM*) hardware; **~ médico** medical team; **~ de música** music centre.
equis ['ekis] *nf* (the letter) X.
equitación [ekita'θjon] *nf* (*acto*) riding; (*arte*) horsemanship.
equitativo, a [ekita'tißo, a] *adj* equitable, fair.
equivaldré [ekißal'dre] *etc vb V* **equivaler**.
equivalencia [ekißa'lenθja] *nf* equivalence.
equivalente [ekißa'lente] *adj*, *nm* equivalent.
equivaler [ekißa'ler] *vi*: **~ a** to be equivalent *o* equal to; (*en rango*) to rank as.
equivalga [eki'ßalɣa] *etc vb V* **equivaler**.
equivocación [ekißoka'θjon] *nf* mistake, error; (*malentendido*) misunderstanding.
equivocado, a [ekißo'kaðo, a] *adj* wrong, mistaken.
equivocarse [ekißo'karse] *vr* to be wrong, make a mistake; **~ de camino** to take the wrong road.

equívoco, a [e'kißoko, a] *adj* (*dudoso*) suspect; (*ambiguo*) ambiguous ♦ *nm* ambiguity; (*malentendido*) misunderstanding.
equivoque [eki'ßoke] *etc vb V* **equivocar**.
era ['era] *vb V* **ser** ♦ *nf* era, age; (*AGR*) threshing floor.
erais ['erais], **éramos** ['eramos], **eran** ['eran] *vb V* **ser**.
erario [e'rarjo] *nm* exchequer, treasury.
eras ['eras], **eres** ['eres] *vb V* **ser**.
erección [erek'θjon] *nf* erection.
ergonomía [erɣono'mia] *nf* ergonomics *sg*, human engineering.
erguir [er'ɣir] *vt* to raise, lift; (*poner derecho*) to straighten; **~se** *vr* to straighten up.
erice [e'riθe] *etc vb V* **erizarse**.
erigir [eri'xir] *vt* to erect, build; **~se** *vr*: **~se en** to set o.s. up as.
erija [e'rixa] *etc vb V* **erigir**.
erizado, a [eri'θaðo, a] *adj* bristly.
erizarse [eri'θarse] *vr* (*pelo*: *de perro*) to bristle; (: *de persona*) to stand on end.
erizo [e'riθo] *nm* hedgehog; **~ de mar** sea urchin.
ermita [er'mita] *nf* hermitage.
ermitaño, a [ermi'taɲo, a] *nm/f* hermit.
erosión [ero'sjon] *nf* erosion.
erosionar [erosjo'nar] *vt* to erode.
erótico, a [e'rotiko, a] *adj* erotic.
erotismo [ero'tismo] *nm* eroticism.
erradicar [erraði'kar] *vt* to eradicate.
erradique [erra'ðike] *etc vb V* **erradicar**.
errado, a [e'rraðo, a] *adj* mistaken, wrong.
errante [e'rrante] *adj* wandering, errant.
errar [e'rrar] *vi* (*vagar*) to wander, roam; (*equivocarse*) to be mistaken ♦ *vt*: **~ el camino** to take the wrong road; **~ el tiro** to miss.
errata [e'rrata] *nf* misprint.
erre ['erre] *nf* (the letter) R; **~ que ~** stubbornly.
erróneo, a [e'rroneo, a] *adj* (*equivocado*) wrong, mistaken; (*falso*) false, untrue.
error [e'rror] *nm* error, mistake; (*INFORM*) bug; **~ de imprenta** misprint; **~ de lectura/escritura** (*INFORM*) read/write error; **~ sintáctico** syntax error; **~ judicial** miscarriage of justice.
Ertzaintza [er't∫ant∫a] *nf* Basque police; *V tb* **policía**.
eructar [eruk'tar] *vt* to belch, burp.
eructo [e'rukto] *nm* belch.
erudición [eruði'θjon] *nf* erudition, learning.
erudito, a [eru'ðito, a] *adj* erudite, learned ♦ *nm/f* scholar; **los ~s en esta materia** the

experts in this field.

erupción [erup'θjon] *nf* eruption; (*MED*) rash; (*de violencia*) outbreak; (*de ira*) outburst.

es [es] *vb V* **ser**.

E/S *abr* (*INFORM*: *entrada/salida*) I/O.

esa ['esa], **esas** ['esas] *adj demostrativo V* **ese**.

ésa ['esa], **ésas** ['esas] *pron V* **ése**.

esbelto, a [es'βelto, a] *adj* slim, slender.

esbirro [es'βirro] *nm* henchman.

esbozar [esβo'θar] *vt* to sketch, outline.

esbozo [es'βoθo] *nm* sketch, outline.

escabeche [eska'βetʃe] *nm* brine; (*de aceitunas etc*) pickle; **en ~** pickled.

escabechina [eskaβe'tʃina] *nf* (*batalla*) massacre; **hacer una ~** (*ESCOL*) to fail a lot of students.

escabroso, a [eska'βroso, a] *adj* (*accidentado*) rough, uneven; (*fig*) tough, difficult; (: *atrevido*) risqué.

escabullirse [eskaβu'ʎirse] *vr* to slip away; (*largarse*) to clear out.

escacharrar [eskatʃa'rrar] *vt* (*fam*) to break; **~se** *vr* to get broken.

escafandra [eska'fandra] *nf* (*buzo*) diving suit; (**~ espacial**) spacesuit.

escala [es'kala] *nf* (*proporción, MUS*) scale; (*de mano*) ladder; (*AVIAT*) stopover; (*de colores etc*) range; **~ de tiempo** time scale; **~ de sueldos** salary scale; **una investigación a ~ nacional** a nationwide inquiry; **reproducir según ~** to reproduce to scale; **hacer ~ en** to stop off *o* over at.

escalada [eska'laða] *nf* (*de montaña*) climb; (*de pared*) scaling.

escalafón [eskala'fon] *nm* (*escala de salarios*) salary scale, wage scale.

escalar [eska'lar] *vt* to climb, scale ♦ *vi* (*MIL, POL*) to escalate.

escaldar [eskal'dar] *vt* (*quemar*) to scald; (*escarmentar*) to teach a lesson.

escalera [eska'lera] *nf* stairs *pl*, staircase; (*escala*) ladder; (*NAIPES*) run; (*de camión*) tailboard; **~ mecánica** escalator; **~ de caracol** spiral staircase; **~ de incendios** fire escape.

escalerilla [eskale'riʎa] *nf* (*de avión*) steps *pl*.

escalfar [eskal'far] *vt* (*huevos*) to poach.

escalinata [eskali'nata] *nf* staircase.

escalofriante [eskalo'frjante] *adj* chilling.

escalofrío [eskalo'frio] *nm* (*MED*) chill; **~s** *nmpl* (*fig*) shivers.

escalón [eska'lon] *nm* step, stair; (*de escalera*) rung; (*fig*: *paso*) step; (*al éxito*) ladder.

escalonar [eskalo'nar] *vt* to spread out;

(*tierra*) to terrace; (*horas de trabajo*) to stagger.

escalope [eska'lope] *nm* (*CULIN*) escalope.

escama [es'kama] *nf* (*de pez, serpiente*) scale; (*de jabón*) flake; (*fig*) resentment.

escamar [eska'mar] *vt* (*pez*) to scale; (*producir recelo*) to make wary.

escamotear [eskamote'ar] *vt* (*fam*: *robar*) to lift, swipe; (*hacer desaparecer*) to make disappear.

escampar [eskam'par] *vb impersonal* to stop raining.

escanciar [eskan'θjar] *vt* (*vino*) to pour (out).

escandalice [eskanda'liθe] *etc vb V* **escandalizar**.

escandalizar [eskandali'θar] *vt* to scandalize, shock; **~se** *vr* to be shocked; (*ofenderse*) to be offended.

escándalo [es'kandalo] *nm* scandal; (*alboroto, tumulto*) row, uproar; **armar un ~** to make a scene; **¡es un ~!** it's outrageous!

escandaloso, a [eskanda'loso, a] *adj* scandalous, shocking; (*risa*) hearty; (*niño*) noisy.

Escandinavia [eskandi'naβja] *nf* Scandinavia.

escandinavo, a [eskandi'naβo, a] *adj, nm/f* Scandinavian.

escáner [es'kaner] *nm* scanner.

escaño [es'kaɲo] *nm* bench; (*POL*) seat.

escapada [eska'paða] *nf* (*huida*) escape, flight; (*deportes*) breakaway; (*viaje*) quick trip.

escapar [eska'par] *vi* (*gen*) to escape, run away; (*DEPORTE*) to break away; **~se** *vr* to escape, get away; (*agua, gas, noticias*) to leak (out); **se me escapa su nombre** his name escapes me.

escaparate [eskapa'rate] *nm* shop window; (*COM*) showcase.

escapatoria [eskapa'torja] *nf*: **no tener ~** (*fig*) to have no way out.

escape [es'kape] *nm* (*huida*) escape; (*de agua, gas*) leak; (*de motor*) exhaust; **salir a ~** to rush out.

escapismo [eska'pismo] *nm* escapism.

escaquearse [eskake'arse] *vr* (*fam*) to duck out.

escarabajo [eskara'βaxo] *nm* beetle.

escaramuza [eskara'muθa] *nf* skirmish; (*fig*) brush.

escarbar [eskar'βar] *vt* (*gallina*) to scratch; (*fig*) to inquire into, investigate.

escarceos [eskar'θeos] *nmpl*: **en sus ~ con la política** in his occasional forays into politics; **~ amorosos** flirtations.

escarcha [es'kartʃa] *nf* frost.

escarlata [eskar'lata] *adj inv* scarlet.

escarlatina [eskarla'tina] *nf* scarlet fever.

escarmentar [eskarmen'tar] *vt* to punish severely ♦ *vi* to learn one's lesson; ¡para que escarmientes! that'll teach you!

escarmiento [eskar'mjento] *etc vb* V **escarmentar** ♦ *nm* (*ejemplo*) lesson; (*castigo*) punishment.

escarnio [es'karnjo] *nm* mockery; (*injuria*) insult.

escarola [eska'rola] *nf* (*BOT*) endive.

escarpado, a [eskar'paðo, a] *adj* (*pendiente*) sheer, steep; (*rocas*) craggy.

escasamente [eskasa'mente] *adv* (*insuficientemente*) scantily; (*apenas*) scarcely.

escasear [eskase'ar] *vi* to be scarce.

escasez [eska'seθ] *nf* (*falta*) shortage, scarcity; (*pobreza*) poverty; **vivir con ~** to live on the breadline.

escaso, a [es'kaso, a] *adj* (*poco*) scarce; (*raro*) rare; (*ralo*) thin, sparse; (*limitado*) limited; (*recursos*) scanty; (*público*) sparse; (*posibilidad*) slim; (*visibilidad*) poor.

escatimar [eskati'mar] *vt* (*limitar*) to skimp (on), be sparing with; **no ~ esfuerzos (para)** to spare no effort (to).

escayola [eska'jola] *nf* plaster.

escayolar [eskajo'lar] *vt* to put in plaster.

escena [es'θena] *nf* scene; (*decorado*) scenery; (*escenario*) stage; **poner en ~** to put on.

escenario [esθe'narjo] *nm* (*TEAT*) stage; (*CINE*) set; (*fig*) scene; **el ~ del crimen** the scene of the crime; **el ~ político** the political scene.

escenografía [esθenoɣra'fia] *nf* set o stage design.

escepticismo [esθepti'θismo] *nm* scepticism.

escéptico, a [es'θeptiko, a] *adj* sceptical ♦ *nm/f* sceptic.

escindir [esθin'dir] *vt* to split; **~se** *vr* (*facción*) to split off; **~se en** to split into.

escisión [esθi'sjon] *nf* (*MED*) excision; (*fig, POL*) split; **~ nuclear** nuclear fission.

esclarecer [esklare'θer] *vt* (*iluminar*) to light up, illuminate; (*misterio, problema*) to shed light on.

esclarezca [eskla'reθka] *etc vb* V **esclarecer**.

esclavice [eskla'ßiθe] *etc vb* V **esclavizar**.

esclavitud [esklaßi'tuð] *nf* slavery.

esclavizar [esklaßi'θar] *vt* to enslave.

esclavo, a [es'klaßo, a] *nm/f* slave.

esclusa [es'klusa] *nf* (*de canal*) lock; (*compuerta*) floodgate.

escoba [es'koßa] *nf* broom; **pasar la ~** to sweep up.

escobazo [esko'ßaθo] *nm* (*golpe*) blow with a broom; **echar a algn a ~s** to kick sb out.

escobilla [esko'ßiʎa] *nf* brush.

escocer [esko'θer] *vi* to burn, sting; **~se** *vr* to chafe, get chafed.

escocés, esa [esko'θes, esa] *adj* Scottish; (*whisky*) Scotch ♦ *nm/f* Scotsman/woman, Scot ♦ *nm* (*LING*) Scots *sg*; **tela escocesa** tartan.

Escocia [es'koθja] *nf* Scotland.

escoger [esko'xer] *vt* to choose, pick, select.

escogido, a [esko'xiðo, a] *adj* chosen, selected; (*calidad*) choice, select; (*persona*): **ser muy ~** to be very fussy.

escoja [es'koxa] *etc vb* V **escoger**.

escolar [esko'lar] *adj* school *cpd* ♦ *nm/f* schoolboy/girl, pupil.

escolaridad [eskolari'ðað] *nf* schooling; **libro de ~** school record.

escolarización [eskolariθa'θjon] *nf*: **~ obligatoria** compulsory education.

escolarizado, a [eskolari'θaðo, a] *adj, nm/f*: **los ~s** those in o attending school.

escollo [es'koʎo] *nm* (*arrecife*) reef, rock; (*fig*) pitfall.

escolta [es'kolta] *nf* escort.

escoltar [eskol'tar] *vt* to escort; (*proteger*) to guard.

escombros [es'kombros] *nmpl* (*basura*) rubbish *sg*; (*restos*) debris *sg*.

esconder [eskon'der] *vt* to hide, conceal; **~se** *vr* to hide.

escondidas [eskon'diðas] *nfpl* (*AM*) hide-and-seek *sg*; **a ~** secretly; **hacer algo a ~ de algn** to do sth behind sb's back.

escondite [eskon'dite] *nm* hiding place; (*juego*) hide-and-seek.

escondrijo [eskon'drixo] *nm* hiding place, hideout.

escopeta [esko'peta] *nf* shotgun; **~ de aire comprimido** air gun.

escoria [es'korja] *nf* (*desecho mineral*) slag; (*fig*) scum, dregs *pl*.

Escorpio [es'korpjo] *nm* (*ASTRO*) Scorpio.

escorpión [eskor'pjon] *nm* scorpion.

escotado, a [esko'taðo, a] *adj* low-cut.

escotar [esko'tar] *vt* (*vestido: ajustar*) to cut to fit; (*cuello*) to cut low.

escote [es'kote] *nm* (*de vestido*) low neck; **pagar a ~** to share the expenses.

escotilla [esko'tiʎa] *nf* (*NAUT*) hatchway.

escotillón [eskoti'ʎon] *nm* trapdoor.

escozor [esko'θor] *nm* (*dolor*) sting(ing).

escribano, a [eskri'ßano, a], **escribiente**

[eskri'ßjente] *nm/f* clerk; (*secretario judicial*) court *o* lawyer's clerk.

escribir [eskri'ßir] *vt*, *vi* to write; ~ **a máquina** to type; **¿cómo se escribe?** how do you spell it?

escrito, a [es'krito, a] *pp de* **escribir** ♦ *adj* written, in writing; (*examen*) written ♦ *nm* (*documento*) document; (*manuscrito*) text, manuscript; **por** ~ in writing.

escritor, a [eskri'tor, a] *nm/f* writer.

escritorio [eskri'torjo] *nm* desk; (*oficina*) office.

escritura [eskri'tura] *nf* (*acción*) writing; (*caligrafía*) (hand)writing; (*JUR: documento*) deed; (*COM*) indenture; ~ **de propiedad** title deed; **Sagrada E**~ (Holy) Scripture; ~ **social** articles *pl* of association.

escroto [es'kroto] *nm* scrotum.

escrúpulo [es'krupulo] *nm* scruple; (*minuciosidad*) scrupulousness.

escrupuloso, a [eskrupu'loso, a] *adj* scrupulous.

escrutar [eskru'tar] *vt* to scrutinize, examine; (*votos*) to count.

escrutinio [eskru'tinjo] *nm* (*examen atento*) scrutiny; (*POL: recuento de votos*) count(ing).

escuadra [es'kwaðra] *nf* (*TEC*) square; (*MIL etc*) squad; (*NAUT*) squadron; (*de coches etc*) fleet.

escuadrilla [eskwa'ðriʎa] *nf* (*de aviones*) squadron.

escuadrón [eskwa'ðron] *nm* squadron.

escuálido, a [es'kwaliðo, a] *adj* skinny, scraggy; (*sucio*) squalid.

escucha [es'kutʃa] *nf* (*acción*) listening ♦ *nm* (*TELEC: sistema*) monitor; (*oyente*) listener; **estar a la** ~ to listen in; **estar de** ~ **to spy**; ~**s teléfonicas** (phone) tapping *sg*.

escuchar [esku'tʃar] *vt* to listen to; (*consejo*) to heed, (*esp AM: oir*) to hear ♦ *vi* to listen; ~**se** *vr*: **se escucha muy mal** (*TELEC*) it's a very bad line.

escudarse [esku'ðarse] *vr*: ~ **en** (*fig*) to hide behind.

escudería [eskuðe'ria] *nf*: **la** ~ **Ferrari** the Ferrari team.

escudero [esku'ðero] *nm* squire.

escudilla [esku'ðiʎa] *nf* bowl, basin.

escudo [es'kuðo] *nm* shield; ~ **de armas** coat of arms.

escudriñar [eskuðri'ɲar] *vt* (*examinar*) to investigate, scrutinize; (*mirar de lejos*) to scan.

escuece [es'kweθe] *etc vb V* **escocer**.

escuela [es'kwela] *nf* (*tb fig*) school; ~ **normal** teacher training college; ~

técnica superior *university offering 5-year courses in engineering and technical subjects*; ~ **universitaria** *university offering 3-year diploma courses*; ~ **de párvulos** kindergarten; *V tb* **colegio**.

escueto, a [es'kweto, a] *adj* plain; (*estilo*) simple; (*explicación*) concise.

escueza [es'kweθa] *etc vb V* **escocer**.

escuincle [es'kwinkle] *nm* (*AM fam*) kid.

esculpir [eskul'pir] *vt* to sculpt; (*grabar*) to engrave; (*tallar*) to carve.

escultor, a [eskul'tor, a] *nm/f* sculptor.

escultura [eskul'tura] *nf* sculpture.

escupidera [eskupi'ðera] *nf* spittoon.

escupir [esku'pir] *vt* to spit (out) ♦ *vi* to spit.

escupitajo [eskupi'taxo] *nm* (*fam*) gob of spit.

escurreplatos [eskurre'platos] *nm inv* plate rack.

escurridizo, a [eskurri'ðiθo, a] *adj* slippery.

escurrir [esku'rrir] *vt* (*ropa*) to wring out; (*verduras, platos*) to drain ♦ *vi* (*los líquidos*) to drip; ~**se** *vr* (*secarse*) to drain; (*resbalarse*) to slip, slide; (*escaparse*) to slip away.

ese[1] ['ese] *nf* (the letter) S; **hacer** ~**s** (*carretera*) to zigzag; (*borracho*) to reel about.

ese[2] ['ese], **esa** ['esa], **esos** ['esos], **esas** ['esas] *adj demostrativo* (*sg*) that; (*pl*) those.

ése ['ese], **ésa** ['esa], **ésos** ['esos], **ésas** ['esas] *pron* (*sg*) that (one); (*pl*) those (ones); **ése** ... **éste** ... the former ... the latter ...; **¡no me vengas con ésas!** don't give me any more of that nonsense!

esencia [e'senθja] *nf* essence.

esencial [esen'θjal] *adj* essential; (*principal*) chief; **lo** ~ the main thing.

esfera [es'fera] *nf* sphere; (*de reloj*) face; ~ **de acción** scope; ~ **terrestre** globe.

esférico, a [es'feriko, a] *adj* spherical.

esfinge [es'finxe] *nf* sphinx.

esforcé [esfor'θe], **esforcemos** [esfor'θemos] *etc vb V* **esforzar**.

esforzado, a [esfor'θaðo, a] *adj* (*enérgico*) energetic, vigorous.

esforzarse [esfor'θarse] *vr* to exert o.s., make an effort.

esfuerce [es'fwerθe] *etc vb V* **esforzar**.

esfuerzo [es'fwerθo] *etc vb V* **esforzar** ♦ *nm* effort; **sin** ~ effortlessly.

esfumarse [esfu'marse] *vr* (*apoyo, esperanzas*) to fade away; (*persona*) to vanish.

esgrima [es'ɣrima] *nf* fencing.

esgrimidor [esɣrimi'ðor] *nm* fencer.

esgrimir [esɣri'mir] *vt* (*arma*) to brandish; (*argumento*) to use ♦ *vi* to fence.

esguince [es'ɣinθe] *nm* (*MED*) sprain.

eslabón [esla'ßon] *nm* link; ~ **perdido** (*BIO*, *fig*) missing link.

eslabonar [eslaßo'nar] *vt* to link, connect.

eslálom [es'lalom] *nm* slalom.

eslavo, a [es'laßo, a] *adj* Slav, Slavonic ♦ *nm/f* Slav ♦ *nm* (*LING*) Slavonic.

eslogan [es'loɣan] *nm, pl* **eslogans** slogan.

eslora [es'lora] *nf* (*NAUT*) length.

eslovaco, a [eslo'ßako, a] *adj, nm/f* Slovak, Slovakian ♦ *nm* (*LING*) Slovak, Slovakian.

Eslovaquia [eslo'ßakja] *nf* Slovakia.

Eslovenia [eslo'ßenja] *nf* Slovenia.

esloveno, a [eslo'ßeno, a] *adj, nm/f* Slovene, Slovenian ♦ *nm* (*LING*) Slovene, Slovenian.

esmaltar [esmal'tar] *vt* to enamel.

esmalte [es'malte] *nm* enamel; ~ **de uñas** nail varnish *o* polish.

esmerado, a [esme'raðo, a] *adj* careful, neat.

esmeralda [esme'ralda] *nf* emerald.

esmerarse [esme'rarse] *vr* (*aplicarse*) to take great pains, exercise great care; (*afanarse*) to work hard; (*hacer lo mejor*) to do one's best.

esmero [es'mero] *nm* (great) care.

esmirriado, a [esmi'rrjaðo, a] *adj* puny.

esmoquin [es'mokin] *nm* dinner jacket (*BRIT*), tuxedo (*US*).

esnob [es'nob] *adj inv* (*persona*) snobbish; (*coche etc*) posh ♦ *nm/f* snob.

esnobismo [esno'ßismo] *nm* snobbery.

eso ['eso] *pron* that, that thing *o* matter; ~ **de su coche** that business about his car; ~ **de ir al cine** all that about going to the cinema; **a ~ de las cinco** at about five o'clock; **en ~** thereupon, at that point; **por ~** therefore; ~ **es** that's it; **nada de** ~ far from it; **¡~ sí que es vida!** now this is really living!; **por ~ te lo dije** that's why I told you; **y ~ que llovía** in spite of the fact it was raining.

esófago [e'sofaɣo] *nm* (*ANAT*) oesophagus.

esos ['esos] *adj demostrativo* V **ese**.

ésos ['esos] *pron* V **ése**.

esotérico, a [eso'teriko, a] *adj* esoteric.

esp. *abr* (= *español*) Sp., Span.

espabilado, a [espaßi'laðo, a] *adj* quick-witted.

espabilar [espaßi'lar] *vt*, **espabilarse** *vr* = **despabilar(se)**.

espachurrar [espatʃu'rrar] *vt* to squash; ~**se** *vr* to get squashed.

espaciado [espa'θjaðo] *nm* (*INFORM*) spacing.

espacial [espa'θjal] *adj* (*del espacio*) space *cpd*.

espaciar [espa'θjar] *vt* to space (out).

espacio [es'paθjo] *nm* space; (*MUS*) interval; (*RADIO*, *TV*) programme, program (*US*); **el** ~ space; **ocupar mucho** ~ to take up a lot of room; **a dos** ~**s, a doble** ~ (*TIP*) double-spaced; **por** ~ **de** during, for.

espacioso, a [espa'θjoso, a] *adj* spacious, roomy.

espada [es'paða] *nf* sword ♦ *nm* swordsman; (*TAUR*) matador; ~**s** *nfpl* (*NAIPES*) one of the suits in the Spanish card deck; **estar entre la** ~ **y la pared** to be between the devil and the deep blue sea; V tb **baraja española**.

espadachín [espaða'tʃin] *nm* (*esgrimidor*) skilled swordsman.

espaguetis [espa'ɣetis] *nmpl* spaghetti *sg*.

espalda [es'palda] *nf* (*gen*) back; (*NATACIÓN*) backstroke; ~**s** *nfpl* (*hombros*) shoulders; **a** ~**s de algn** behind sb's back; **estar de** ~**s** to have one's back turned; **tenderse de** ~**s** to lie (down) on one's back; **volver la** ~ **a algn** to cold-shoulder sb.

espaldarazo [espalda'raθo] *nm* (*tb fig*) slap on the back.

espaldilla [espal'ðiʎa] *nf* shoulder blade.

espantadizo, a [espanta'ðiθo, a] *adj* timid, easily frightened.

espantajo [espan'taxo] *nm*, **espantapájaros** [espanta'paxaros] *nm inv* scarecrow.

espantar [espan'tar] *vt* (*asustar*) to frighten, scare; (*ahuyentar*) to frighten off; (*asombrar*) to horrify, appal; ~**se** *vr* to get frightened *o* scared; to be appalled.

espanto [es'panto] *nm* (*susto*) fright; (*terror*) terror; (*asombro*) astonishment; **¡qué** ~**!** how awful!

espantoso, a [espan'toso, a] *adj* frightening, terrifying; (*ruido*) dreadful.

España [es'paɲa] *nf* Spain; **la** ~ **de pandereta** touristy Spain.

español, a [espa'ɲol, a] *adj* Spanish ♦ *nm/f* Spaniard ♦ *nm* (*LING*) Spanish; V tb **castellano**.

españolice [espaɲo'liθe] *etc vb* V **españolizar**.

españolizar [espaɲoli'θar] *vt* to make Spanish, Hispanicize; ~**se** *vr* to adopt Spanish ways.

esparadrapo [espara'ðrapo] *nm* (sticking)

plaster, Band-Aid ® (US).
esparcido, a [espar'θiðo, a] adj scattered.
esparcimiento [esparθi'mjento] nm
(dispersión) spreading; (derramamiento)
scattering; (fig) cheerfulness.
esparcir [espar'θir] vt to spread; (derramar)
to scatter; ~**se** vr to spread (out); to
scatter; (divertirse) to enjoy o.s.
espárrago [es'parraγo] nm (tb: ~**s**)
asparagus; **estar hecho un** ~ to be as
thin as a rake; ¡**vete a freír** ~**s!** (fam) go
to hell!
esparto [es'parto] nm esparto (grass).
esparza [es'parθa] etc vb V **esparcir.**
espasmo [es'pasmo] nm spasm.
espátula [es'patula] nf (MED) spatula;
(ARTF) palette knife; (CULIN) fish slice.
especia [es'peθja] nf spice.
especial [espe'θjal] adj special.
especialidad [espeθjali'ðað] nf speciality,
specialty (US); (ESCOL: ramo) specialism.
especialista [espeθja'lista] nm/f specialist;
(CINE) stuntman/woman.
especializado, a [espeθjali'θaðo, a] adj
specialized; (obrero) skilled.
especialmente [espeθjal'mente] adv
particularly, especially.
especie [es'peθje] nf (BIO) species; (clase)
kind, sort; **pagar en** ~ to pay in kind.
especificar [espeθifi'kar] vt to specify.
específico, a [espe'θifiko, a] adj specific.
especifique [espeθi'fike] etc vb V
especificar.
espécimen [es'peθimen], pl **especímenes**
nm specimen.
espectáculo [espek'takulo] nm (gen)
spectacle; (TEAT etc) show; (función)
performance; **dar un** ~ to make a scene.
espectador, a [espekta'ðor, a] nm/f
spectator; (de incidente) onlooker; **los**
~**es** (TEAT) the audience sg.
espectro [es'pektro] nm ghost; (fig)
spectre.
especulación [espekula'θjon] nf
speculation; ~ **bursátil** speculation on
the Stock Market.
especular [espeku'lar] vt, vi to speculate.
especulativo, a [espekula'tiβo, a] adj
speculative.
espejismo [espe'xismo] nm mirage.
espejo [es'pexo] nm mirror; (fig) model; ~
retrovisor rear-view mirror; **mirarse al**
~ to look (at o.s.) in the mirror.
espeleología [espeleolo'xia] nf potholing.
espeluznante [espeluθ'nante] adj
horrifying, hair-raising.
espera [es'pera] nf (pausa, intervalo) wait;
(JUR: plazo) respite; **en** ~ **de** waiting for;

(con expectativa) expecting; **en** ~ **de su**
contestación awaiting your reply.
esperance [espe'ranθe] etc vb V
esperanzar.
esperanza [espe'ranθa] nf (confianza) hope;
(expectativa) expectation; **hay pocas** ~**s**
de que venga there is little prospect of
his coming.
esperanzador, a [esperanθa'ðor, a] adj
hopeful, encouraging.
esperanzar [esperan'θar] vt to give hope
to.
esperar [espe'rar] vt (aguardar) to wait for;
(tener expectativa de) to expect; (desear)
to hope for ♦ vi to wait; to expect; to
hope; ~**se** vr: **como podía** ~**se** as was to
be expected; **hacer** ~ **a uno** to keep sb
waiting; **ir a** ~ **a uno** to go and meet sb;
~ **un bebé** to be expecting (a baby).
esperma [es'perma] nf sperm.
espermatozoide [espermato'θoiðe] nm
spermatozoid.
esperpento [esper'pento] nm (persona)
sight (fam); (disparate) (piece of)
nonsense.
espesar [espe'sar] vt to thicken; ~**se** vr to
thicken, get thicker.
espeso, a [es'peso, a] adj thick; (bosque)
dense; (nieve) deep; (sucio) dirty.
espesor [espe'sor] nm thickness; (de nieve)
depth.
espesura [espe'sura] nf (bosque) thicket.
espetar [espe'tar] vt (reto, sermón) to give.
espía [es'pia] nm/f spy.
espiar [espi'ar] vt (observar) to spy on ♦ vi:
~ **para** to spy for.
espiga [es'piγa] nf (BOT: de trigo etc) ear;
(: de flores) spike.
espigado, a [espi'γaðo, a] adj (BOT) ripe;
(fig) tall, slender.
espigón [espi'γon] nm (BOT) ear; (NAUT)
breakwater.
espina [es'pina] nf thorn; (de pez) bone; ~
dorsal (ANAT) spine; **me da mala** ~ I
don't like the look of it.
espinaca [espi'naka] nf (tb: ~**s**) spinach.
espinar [espi'nar] nm (matorral) thicket.
espinazo [espi'naθo] nm spine, backbone.
espinilla [espi'niʎa] nf (ANAT: tibia)
shin(bone); (: en la piel) blackhead.
espino [es'pino] nm hawthorn.
espinoso, a [espi'noso, a] adj (planta)
thorny, prickly; (fig) bony; (problema)
knotty.
espionaje [espjo'naxe] nm spying,
espionage.
espiral [espi'ral] adj, nf spiral; **la** ~
inflacionista the inflationary spiral.

espirar [espi'rar] _vt, vi_ to breathe out, exhale.

espiritista [espiri'tista] _adj, nm/f_ spiritualist.

espíritu [es'piritu] _nm_ spirit; (_mente_) mind; (_inteligencia_) intelligence; (_REL_) spirit, soul; **E~ Santo** Holy Ghost; **con ~ amplio** with an open mind.

espiritual [espiri'twal] _adj_ spiritual.

espita [es'pita] _nf_ tap (_BRIT_), faucet (_US_).

esplendidez [esplendi'ðeθ] _nf_ (_abundancia_) lavishness; (_magnificencia_) splendour.

espléndido, a [es'plendiðo, a] _adj_ (_magnífico_) magnificent, splendid; (_generoso_) generous, lavish.

esplendor [esplen'dor] _nm_ splendour.

espliego [es'pljeʝo] _nm_ lavender.

espolear [espole'ar] _vt_ to spur on.

espoleta [espo'leta] _nf_ (_de bomba_) fuse.

espolvorear [espolßore'ar] _vt_ to dust, sprinkle.

esponja [es'ponxa] _nf_ sponge; (_fig_) sponger.

esponjoso, a [espon'xoso, a] _adj_ spongy.

esponsales [espon'sales] _nmpl_ betrothal _sg_.

espontaneidad [espontanei'ðað] _nf_ spontaneity.

espontáneo, a [espon'taneo, a] _adj_ spontaneous; (_improvisado_) impromptu; (_persona_) natural.

espora [es'pora] _nf_ spore.

esporádico, a [espo'raðiko, a] _adj_ sporadic.

esposa [es'posa] _nf_ V **esposo**.

esposar [espo'sar] _vt_ to handcuff.

esposo, a [es'poso, a] _nm_ husband ♦ _nf_ wife; **esposas** _nfpl_ handcuffs.

espuela [es'pwela] _nf_ spur; (_fam: trago_) one for the road.

espuerta [es'pwerta] _nf_ basket, pannier.

espuma [es'puma] _nf_ foam; (_de cerveza_) froth, head; (_de jabón_) lather; (_de olas_) surf.

espumadera [espuma'ðera] _nf_ skimmer.

espumarajo [espuma'raxo] _nm_ froth, foam; **echar ~s (de rabia)** to splutter with rage.

espumoso, a [espu'moso, a] _adj_ frothy, foamy; (_vino_) sparkling.

esputo [es'puto] _nm_ (_saliva_) spit; (_MED_) sputum.

esqueje [es'kexe] _nm_ (_BOT_) cutting.

esquela [es'kela] _nf_: **~ mortuoria** announcement of death.

esquelético, a [eske'letiko, a] _adj_ (_fam_) skinny.

esqueleto [eske'leto] _nm_ skeleton; (_lo esencial_) bare bones (of a matter); **en ~**

unfinished.

esquema [es'kema] _nm_ (_diagrama_) diagram; (_dibujo_) plan; (_plan_) scheme; (_FILOSOFÍA_) schema.

esquemático, a [eske'matiko, a] _adj_ schematic; **un resumen ~** a brief outline.

esquí [es'ki], _pl_ **esquís** _nm_ (_objeto_) ski; (_deporte_) skiing; **~ acuático** water-skiing; **hacer ~** to go skiing.

esquiador, a [eskja'ðor, a] _nm/f_ skier.

esquiar [es'kjar] _vi_ to ski.

esquila [es'kila] _nf_ (_campanilla_) small bell; (_encerro_) cowbell.

esquilar [eski'lar] _vt_ to shear.

esquimal [eski'mal] _adj, nm/f_ Eskimo.

esquina [es'kina] _nf_ corner; **doblar la ~** to turn the corner.

esquinazo [eski'naθo] _nm_: **dar ~ a algn** to give sb the slip.

esquirla [es'kirla] _nf_ splinter.

esquirol [eski'rol] _nm_ blackleg.

esquivar [eski'ßar] _vt_ to avoid; (_evadir_) to dodge, elude.

esquivo, a [es'kißo, a] _adj_ (_altanero_) aloof; (_desdeñoso_) scornful, disdainful.

esquizofrenia [eskiθo'frenja] _nf_ schizophrenia.

esta ['esta] _adj demostrativo_ V **este**.

ésta ['esta] _pron_ V **éste**.

está [es'ta] _vb_ V **estar**.

estabilice [estaßi'liθe] _etc vb_ V **estabilizar**.

estabilidad [estaßili'ðað] _nf_ stability.

estabilización [estaßiliθa'θjon] _nf_ (_COM_) stabilization.

estabilizar [estaßili'θar] _vt_ to stabilize; (_fijar_) to make steady; (_precios_) to peg; **~se** _vr_ to become stable.

estable [es'taßle] _adj_ stable.

establecer [estaßle'θer] _vt_ to establish; (_fundar_) to set up; (_colonos_) to settle; (_récord_) to set (up); **~se** _vr_ to establish o.s.; (_echar raíces_) to settle (down); (_COM_) to start up.

establecimiento [estaßleθi'mjento] _nm_ establishment; (_fundación_) institution; (_de negocio_) start-up; (_de colonias_) settlement; (_local_) establishment; **~ comercial** business house.

establezca [esta'ßleθka] _etc vb_ V **establecer**.

establo [es'taßlo] _nm_ (_AGR_) stall; (: _esp AM_) barn.

estaca [es'taka] _nf_ stake, post; (_de tienda de campaña_) peg.

estacada [esta'kaða] _nf_ (_cerca_) fence, fencing; (_palenque_) stockade; **dejar a algn en la ~** to leave sb in the lurch.

estación [esta'θjon] *nf* station; (*del año*) season; ~ **de autobuses/ferrocarril** bus/railway station; ~ **balnearia (de turistas)** seaside resort; ~ **de servicio** service station; ~ **terminal** terminus; ~ **de trabajo** (*COM*) work station; ~ **transmisora** transmitter; ~ **de visualización** display unit.

estacionamiento [estaθjona'mjento] *nm* (*AUTO*) parking; (*MIL*) stationing.

estacionar [estaθjo'nar] *vt* (*AUTO*) to park; (*MIL*) to station.

estacionario, a [estaθjo'narjo, a] *adj* stationary; (*COM: mercado*) slack.

estada [es'taða], **estadía** [esta'ðia] *nf* (*AM*) stay.

estadio [es'taðjo] *nm* (*fase*) stage, phase; (*DEPORTE*) stadium.

estadista [esta'ðista] *nm* (*POL*) statesman; (*ESTADÍSTICA*) statistician.

estadística [esta'ðistika] *nf* (*una* ~) figure, statistic; (*ciencia*) statistics *sg*.

estado [es'taðo] *nm* (*POL: condición*) state; ~ **civil** marital status; ~ **de cuenta(s)** bank statement, statement of accounts; ~ **de excepción** (*POL*) state of emergency; ~ **financiero** (*COM*) financial statement; ~ **mayor** (*MIL*) staff; ~ **de pérdidas y ganancias** (*COM*) profit and loss statement, operating statement; **E~s Unidos (EE.UU.)** United States (of America) (USA); **estar en** ~ (**de buena esperanza**) to be pregnant.

estadounidense [estaðouni'ðense] *adj* United States *cpd*, American ♦ *nm/f* United States citizen, American.

estafa [es'tafa] *nf* swindle, trick; (*COM etc*) racket.

estafar [esta'far] *vt* to swindle, defraud.

estafeta [esta'feta] *nf* (*oficina de correos*) post office; ~ **diplomática** diplomatic bag.

estalactita [estalak'tita] *nf* stalactite.

estalagmita [estalaɣ'mita] *nf* stalagmite.

estallar [esta'ʎar] *vi* to burst; (*bomba*) to explode, go off; (*volcán*) to erupt; (*vidrio*) to shatter; (*látigo*) to crack; (*epidemia, guerra, rebelión*) to break out; ~ **en llanto** to burst into tears.

estallido [esta'ʎiðo] *nm* explosion; (*de látigo, trueno*) crack; (*fig*) outbreak.

estambre [es'tambre] *nm* (*tela*) worsted; (*BOT*) stamen.

Estambul [estam'bul] *nm* Istanbul.

estamento [esta'mento] *nm* (social) class.

estampa [es'tampa] *nf* (*impresión, imprenta*) print, engraving; (*imagen, figura: de persona*) appearance.

estampado, a [estam'paðo, a] *adj* printed ♦ *nm* (*impresión: acción*) printing;

(: *efecto*) print; (*marca*) stamping.

estampar [estam'par] *vt* (*imprimir*) to print; (*marcar*) to stamp; (*metal*) to engrave; (*poner sello en*) to stamp; (*fig*) to stamp, imprint.

estampida [estam'piða] *nf* stampede.

estampido [estam'piðo] *nm* bang, report.

estampilla [estam'piʎa] *nf* (*sello de goma*) (rubber) stamp; (*AM*) (postage) stamp.

están [es'tan] *vb* V **estar**.

estancado, a [estan'kaðo, a] *adj* (*agua*) stagnant.

estancamiento [estanka'mjento] *nm* stagnation.

estancar [estan'kar] *vt* (*aguas*) to hold up, hold back; (*COM*) to monopolize; (*fig*) to block, hold up; ~**se** *vr* to stagnate.

estancia [es'tanθja] *nf* (*permanencia*) stay; (*sala*) room; (*AM*) farm, ranch.

estanciero [estan'sjero] *nm* (*AM*) farmer, rancher.

estanco, a [es'tanko, a] *adj* watertight ♦ *nm* tobacconist's (shop); *see boxed note*.

ESTANCO

Cigarettes, tobacco, postage stamps and official forms are all sold under a state monopoly and are usually purchased at a shop called an **estanco**. *Tobacco products are also sold in "quioscos" and bars but are generally more expensive. The number of* **estanco** *licences is regulated by the state.*

---

estándar [es'tandar] *adj, nm* standard.

estandarice [estanda'riθe] *etc vb V* **estandarizar**.

estandarizar [estandari'θar] *vt* to standardize.

estandarte [estan'darte] *nm* banner, standard.

estanque [es'tanke] *etc vb V* **estancar** ♦ *nm* (*lago*) pool, pond; (*AGR*) reservoir.

estanquero, a [estan'kero, a] *nm/f* tobacconist.

estante [es'tante] *nm* (*armario*) rack, stand; (*biblioteca*) bookcase; (*anaquel*) shelf; (*AM*) prop.

estantería [estante'ria] *nf* shelving, shelves *pl*.

estaño [es'taɲo] *nm* tin.

=========== *PALABRA CLAVE*

estar [es'tar] *vi* **1** (*posición*) to be; **está en la plaza** it's in the square; **¿está Juan?** is Juan in?; **estamos a 30 km de Junín** we're 30 kms from Junín

2 (*+ adj o adv: estado*) to be; ~ **enfermo**

to be ill; **está muy elegante** he's looking very smart; ~ **lejos** to be far (away); **¿cómo estás?** how are you keeping?
3 (+*gerundio*) to be; **estoy leyendo** I'm reading
4 (*uso pasivo*): **está condenado a muerte** he's been condemned to death; **está envasado en ...** it's packed in ...
5: ~ **a**: **¿a cuántos estamos?** what's the date today?; **estamos a 5 de mayo** it's the 5th of May; **las manzanas están a 200 ptas** apples are (selling at) 200 pesetas; **estamos a 25 grados** it's 25 degrees today
6 (*locuciones*): **¿estamos?** (*¿de acuerdo?*) okay?; (*¿listo?*) ready?; **¡ya está bien!** that's enough!; **¿está la comida?** is dinner ready?; **¡ya está!**, (*AM*) **¡ya estuvo!** that's it!
7: ~ **con**: **está con gripe** he's got (the) flu
8: ~ **de**: ~ **de vacaciones/viaje** to be on holiday/away *o* on a trip; **está de camarero** he's working as a waiter
9: ~ **para**: **está para salir** he's about to leave; **no estoy para bromas** I'm not in the mood for jokes
10: ~ **por** (*propuesta etc*) to be in favour of; (*persona etc*) to support, side with; **está por limpiar** it still has to be cleaned; **¡estoy por dejarlo!** I think I'm going to leave this!
11 (+*que*): **está que rabia** (*fam*) he's hopping mad (*fam*); **estoy que me caigo de sueño** I'm terribly sleepy, I can't keep my eyes open
12: ~ **sin**: ~ **sin dinero** to have no money; **está sin terminar** it isn't finished yet
♦ ~**se** *vr*: **se estuvo en la cama toda la tarde** he stayed in bed all afternoon; **¡estáte quieto!** stop fidgeting!

estárter [es'tarter] *nm* (*AUTO*) choke.
estas ['estas] *adj demostrativo* V **este**.
éstas ['estas] *pron* V **éste**.
estás [es'tas] *vb* V **estar**.
estatal [esta'tal] *adj* state *cpd*.
estático, a [es'tatiko, a] *adj* static.
estatua [es'tatwa] *nf* statue.
estatura [esta'tura] *nf* stature, height.
estatus [es'tatus] *nm inv* status.
estatutario, a [estatu'tarjo, a] *adj* statutory.
estatuto [esta'tuto] *nm* (*JUR*) statute; (*de ciudad*) bye-law; (*de comité*) rule; ~**s sociales** (*COM*) articles of association.
este¹ ['este] *adj* (*lado*) east; (*dirección*) easterly ♦ *nm* east; **en la parte del** ~ in

the eastern part.
este² ['este], **esta** ['esta], **estos** ['estos], **estas** ['estas] *adj demostrativo* (*sg*) this; (*pl*) these; (*AM*: *como muletilla*) er, um.
éste ['este], **ésta** ['esta], **éstos** ['estos], **éstas** ['estas] *pron* (*sg*) this (one); (*pl*) these (ones); **ése ... éste ...** the former ... the latter ....
esté [es'te] *vb* V **estar**.
estela [es'tela] *nf* wake, wash; (*fig*) trail.
estelar [este'lar] *adj* (*ASTRO*) stellar; (*TEAT*) star *cpd*.
estén [es'ten] *vb* V **estar**.
estenografía [estenoɣra'fia] *nf* shorthand.
estentóreo, a [esten'toreo, a] *adj* (*sonido*) strident; (*voz*) booming.
estepa [es'tepa] *nf* (*GEO*) steppe.
estera [es'tera] *nf* (*alfombra*) mat; (*tejido*) matting.
estercolero [esterko'lero] *nm* manure heap, dunghill.
estéreo [es'tereo] *adj inv, nm* stereo.
estereofónico, a [estereo'foniko, a] *adj* stereophonic.
estereotipar [estereoti'par] *vt* to stereotype.
estereotipo [estereo'tipo] *nm* stereotype.
estéril [es'teril] *adj* sterile, barren; (*fig*) vain, futile.
esterilice [esteri'liθe] etc *vb* V **esterilizar**.
esterilizar [esterili'θar] *vt* to sterilize.
esterilla [este'riʎa] *nf* (*alfombrilla*) small mat.
esterlina [ester'lina] *adj*: **libra** ~ pound sterling.
esternón [ester'non] *nm* breastbone.
estero [es'tero] *nm* (*AM*) swamp.
estertor [ester'tor] *nm* death rattle.
estés [es'tes] *vb* V **estar**.
esteta [es'teta] *nm/f* aesthete.
esteticienne [esteti'θjen] *nf* beautician.
estético, a [es'tetiko, a] *adj* aesthetic ♦ *nf* aesthetics *sg*.
estetoscopio [estetos'kopjo] *nm* stethoscope.
estibador [estiβa'ðor] *nm* stevedore.
estibar [esti'ßar] *vt* (*NAUT*) to stow.
estiércol [es'tjerkol] *nm* dung, manure.
estigma [es'tiɣma] *nm* stigma.
estigmatice [estiɣma'tiθe] etc *vb* V **estigmatizar**.
estigmatizar [estiɣmati'θar] *vt* to stigmatize.
estilarse [esti'larse] *vr* (*estar de moda*) to be in fashion; (*usarse*) to be used.
estilice [esti'liθe] etc *vb* V **estilizar**.
estilizar [estili'θar] *vt* to stylize; (*TEC*) to design.

estilo [es'tilo] nm style; (TEC) stylus; (NATACIÓN) stroke; ~ **de vida** lifestyle; **al ~ de** in the style of; **algo por el ~** something along those lines.

estilográfica [estilo'ɣrafika] nf fountain pen.

estima [es'tima] nf esteem, respect.

estimación [estima'θjon] nf (evaluación) estimation; (aprecio, afecto) esteem, regard.

estimado, a [esti'maðo, a] adj esteemed; "E~ Señor" "Dear Sir".

estimar [esti'mar] vt (evaluar) to estimate; (valorar) to value; (apreciar) to esteem, respect; (pensar, considerar) to think, reckon.

estimulante [estimu'lante] adj stimulating ♦ nm stimulant.

estimular [estimu'lar] vt to stimulate; (excitar) to excite; (animar) to encourage.

estímulo [es'timulo] nm stimulus; (ánimo) encouragement; (INFORM) prompt.

estío [es'tio] nm summer.

estipendio [esti'pendjo] nm salary; (COM) stipend.

estipulación [estipula'θjon] nf stipulation, condition.

estipular [estipu'lar] vt to stipulate.

estirado, a [esti'raðo, a] adj (tenso) (stretched o drawn) tight; (fig: persona) stiff, pompous; (engreído) stuck-up.

estirar [esti'rar] vt to stretch; (dinero, suma etc) to stretch out; (cuello) to crane; (dinero) to eke out; (discurso) to spin out; ~ **la pata** (fam) to kick the bucket; ~**se** vr to stretch.

estirón [esti'ron] nm pull, tug; (crecimiento) spurt, sudden growth; **dar un ~** (niño) to shoot up.

estirpe [es'tirpe] nf stock, lineage.

estival [esti'ßal] adj summer cpd.

esto ['esto] pron this, this thing o matter; (como muletilla) er, um; ~ **de la boda** this business about the wedding; **en ~** at this o that point; **por ~** for this reason.

estocada [esto'kaða] nf (acción) stab; (TAUR) death blow.

Estocolmo [esto'kolmo] nm Stockholm.

estofa [es'tofa] nf: **de baja ~** poor-quality.

estofado [esto'faðo] nm stew.

estofar [esto'far] vt (bordar) to quilt; (CULIN) to stew.

estoico, a [es'toiko, a] adj (FILOSOFÍA) stoic(al); (fig) cold, indifferent.

estomacal [estoma'kal] adj stomach cpd; **trastorno ~** stomach upset.

estómago [es'tomaɣo] nm stomach; **tener ~** to be thick-skinned.

Estonia [es'tonja] nf Estonia.

estonio, a [es'tonjo, a] adj, nm/f Estonian ♦ nm (LING) Estonian.

estoque [es'toke] nm rapier, sword.

estorbar [estor'ßar] vt to hinder, obstruct; (fig) to bother, disturb ♦ vi to be in the way.

estorbo [es'torßo] nm (molestia) bother, nuisance; (obstáculo) hindrance, obstacle.

estornino [estor'nino] nm starling.

estornudar [estornu'ðar] vi to sneeze.

estornudo [estor'nuðo] nm sneeze.

estos ['estos] adj demostrativo V **este**.

éstos ['estos] pron V **éste**.

estoy [es'toi] vb V **estar**.

estrabismo [estra'ßismo] nm squint.

estrado [es'traðo] nm (tarima) platform; (MUS) bandstand; ~**s** nmpl law courts.

estrafalario, a [estrafa'larjo, a] adj odd, eccentric; (desarreglado) slovenly, sloppy.

estrago [es'traɣo] nm ruin, destruction; **hacer ~s en** to wreak havoc among.

estragón [estra'ɣon] nm (CULIN) tarragon.

estrambótico, a [estram'botiko, a] adj odd, eccentric.

estrangulación [estrangula'θjon] nf strangulation.

estrangulador, a [estrangula'ðor, a] nm/f strangler ♦ nm (TEC) throttle; (AUTO) choke.

estrangulamiento [estrangula'mjento] nm (AUTO) bottleneck.

estrangular [estrangu'lar] vt (persona) to strangle; (MED) to strangulate.

estraperlista [estraper'lista] nm/f black marketeer.

estraperlo [estra'perlo] nm black market.

estratagema [estrata'xema] nf (MIL) stratagem; (astucia) cunning.

estratega [estra'texa] nm/f strategist.

estrategia [estra'texja] nf strategy.

estratégico, a [estra'texiko, a] adj strategic.

estratificar [estratifi'kar] vt to stratify.

estratifique [estrati'fike] etc vb V **estratificar**.

estrato [es'trato] nm stratum, layer.

estratosfera [estratos'fera] nf stratosphere.

estrechar [estre'tʃar] vt (reducir) to narrow; (vestido) to take in; (persona) to hug, embrace; ~**se** vr (reducirse) to narrow, grow narrow, (2 personas) to embrace; ~ **la mano** to shake hands.

estrechez [estre'tʃeθ] nf narrowness; (de ropa) tightness; (intimidad) intimacy;

(*COM*) want *o* shortage of money; **estrecheces** *nfpl* financial difficulties.

estrecho, a [es'tretʃo, a] *adj* narrow; (*apretado*) tight; (*íntimo*) close, intimate; (*miserable*) mean ♦ *nm* strait; ~ **de miras** narrow-minded; **E~ de Gibraltar** Straits of Gibraltar.

estrella [es'treʎa] *nf* star; ~ **fugaz** shooting star; ~ **de mar** starfish; **tener (buena)/ mala** ~ to be lucky/unlucky.

estrellado, a [estre'ʎaðo, a] *adj* (*forma*) star-shaped; (*cielo*) starry; (*huevos*) fried.

estrellar [estre'ʎar] *vt* (*hacer añicos*) to smash (to pieces); (*huevos*) to fry; ~**se** *vr* to smash; (*chocarse*) to crash; (*fracasar*) to fail.

estrellato [estre'ʎato] *nm* stardom.

estremecer [estreme'θer] *vt* to shake; ~**se** *vr* to shake, tremble; ~ **de** (*horror*) to shudder with; (*frío*) to shiver with.

estremecimiento [estremeθi'mjento] *nm* (*temblor*) trembling, shaking.

estremezca [estre'meθka] *etc vb* V **estremecer.**

estrenar [estre'nar] *vt* (*vestido*) to wear for the first time; (*casa*) to move into; (*película, obra de teatro*) to present for the first time; ~**se** *vr* (*persona*) to make one's début; (*película*) to have its premiere; (*TEAT*) to open.

estreno [es'treno] *nm* (*primer uso*) first use; (*CINE etc*) premiere.

estreñido, a [estre'ɲiðo, a] *adj* constipated.

estreñimiento [estreɲi'mjento] *nm* constipation.

estreñir [estre'ɲir] *vt* to constipate.

estrépito [es'trepito] *nm* noise, racket; (*fig*) fuss.

estrepitoso, a [estrepi'toso, a] *adj* noisy; (*fiesta*) rowdy.

estrés [es'tres] *nm* stress.

estresante [estre'sante] *adj* stressful.

estría [es'tria] *nf* groove; ~**s (en el cutis)** stretchmarks.

estribación [estriβa'θjon] *nf* (*GEO*) spur; **estribaciones** *nfpl* foothills.

estribar [estri'βar] *vi*: ~ **en** to rest on, be supported by; **la dificultad estriba en el texto** the difficulty lies in the text.

estribillo [estri'βiʎo] *nm* (*LITERATURA*) refrain; (*MUS*) chorus.

estribo [es'triβo] *nm* (*de jinete*) stirrup; (*de coche, tren*) step; (*de puente*) support; (*GEO*) spur; **perder los** ~**s** to fly off the handle.

estribor [estri'βor] *nm* (*NAUT*) starboard.

estricnina [estrik'nina] *nf* strychnine.

estricto, a [es'trikto, a] *adj* (*riguroso*) strict; (*severo*) severe.

estridente [estri'ðente] *adj* (*color*) loud; (*voz*) raucous.

estro ['estro] *nm* inspiration.

estrofa [es'trofa] *nf* verse.

estropajo [estro'paxo] *nm* scourer.

estropeado, a [estrope'aðo, a] *adj*: **está** ~ it's not working.

estropear [estrope'ar] *vt* (*arruinar*) to spoil; (*dañar*) to damage; (: *máquina*) to break; ~**se** *vr* (*objeto*) to get damaged; (*coche*) to break down; (*la piel etc*) to be ruined.

estropicio [estro'piθjo] *nm* (*rotura*) breakage; (*efectos*) harmful effects *pl*.

estructura [estruk'tura] *nf* structure.

estruendo [es'trwendo] *nm* (*ruido*) racket, din; (*fig: alboroto*) uproar, turmoil.

estrujar [estru'xar] *vt* (*apretar*) to squeeze; (*aplastar*) to crush; (*fig*) to drain, bleed.

estuario [es'twarjo] *nm* estuary.

estuche [es'tutʃe] *nm* box, case.

estudiante [estu'ðjante] *nmlf* student.

estudiantil [estuðjan'til] *adj inv* student *cpd*.

estudiantina [estuðjan'tina] *nf* student music group.

estudiar [estu'ðjar] *vt* to study; (*propuesta*) to think about *o* over; ~ **para abogado** to study to become a lawyer.

estudio [es'tuðjo] *nm* study; (*encuesta*) research; (*proyecto*) plan; (*piso*) studio flat; (*CINE, ARTE, RADIO*) studio; ~**s** *nmpl* studies; (*erudición*) learning *sg*; **cursar** *o* **hacer** ~**s** to study; ~ **de casos prácticos** case study; ~ **de desplazamientos y tiempos** (*COM*) time and motion study; ~**s de motivación** motivational research *sg*; ~ **del trabajo** (*COM*) work study; ~ **de viabilidad** (*COM*) feasibility study.

estudioso, a [estu'ðjoso, a] *adj* studious.

estufa [es'tufa] *nf* heater, fire.

estulticia [estul'tiθja] *nf* foolishness.

estupefaciente [estupefa'θjente] *adj, nm* narcotic.

estupefacto, a [estupe'fakto, a] *adj* speechless, thunderstruck.

estupendamente [estupenda'mente] *adv* (*fam*): **estoy** ~ I feel great; **le salió** ~ he did it very well.

estupendo, a [estu'pendo, a] *adj* wonderful, terrific; (*fam*) great; ¡~! that's great!, fantastic!

estupidez [estupi'ðeθ] *nf* (*torpeza*) stupidity; (*acto*) stupid thing (to do); **fue una** ~ **mía** that was a silly thing for me to do *o* say.

estúpido, a [es'tupiðo, a] *adj* stupid, silly.

estupor [estu'por] *nm* stupor; (*fig*) astonishment, amazement.

estupro [es'tupro] *nm* rape.

estuve [es'tuße] *etc*, **estuviera** [estu'ßjera] *etc vb V* **estar**.

esvástica [es'ßastika] *nf* swastika.

ET *abr* = *Ejército de Tierra.*

ETA ['eta] *nf abr* (*POL*: = *Euskadi Ta Askatasuna*) ETA.

etapa [e'tapa] *nf* (*de viaje*) stage; (*DEPORTE*) leg; (*parada*) stopping place; (*fig*) stage, phase; **por ~s** gradually *o* in stages.

etarra [e'tarra] *adj* ETA *cpd* ♦ *nm/f* member of ETA.

etc. *abr* (= *etcétera*) etc.

etcétera [et'θetera] *adv* etcetera.

etéreo, a [e'tereo, a] *adj* ethereal.

eternice [eter'niθe] *etc vb V* **eternizar**.

eternidad [eterni'ðað] *nf* eternity.

eternizarse [eterni'θarse] *vr*: **~ en hacer algo** to take ages to do sth.

eterno, a [e'terno, a] *adj* eternal, everlasting; (*despectivo*) never-ending.

ético, a ['etiko, a] *adj* ethical ♦ *nf* ethics.

etimología [etimolo'xia] *nf* etymology.

etiqueta [eti'keta] *nf* (*modales*) etiquette; (*rótulo*) label, tag; **de ~** formal.

etnia ['etnja] *nf* ethnic group.

étnico, a ['etniko, a] *adj* ethnic.

EU(A) *abr* (*esp AM*) = **Estados Unidos (de América)**.

eucalipto [euka'lipto] *nm* eucalyptus.

Eucaristía [eukaris'tia] *nf* Eucharist.

eufemismo [eufe'mismo] *nm* euphemism.

euforia [eu'forja] *nf* euphoria.

eufórico, a [eu'foriko, a] *adj* euphoric.

eunuco [eu'nuko] *nm* eunuch.

euro ['euro] *sm* (*moneda*) euro.

eurodiputado, a [euroðipu'taðo, a] *nm/f* Euro MP, MEP.

Eurolandia [euro'landja] *nf* Euroland.

Europa [eu'ropa] *nf* Europe.

europeice [euro'peiθe] *etc vb V* **europeizar**.

europeizar [europei'θar] *vt* to Europeanize; **~se** *vr* to become Europeanized.

europeo, a [euro'peo, a] *adj, nm/f* European.

Euskadi [eus'kaði] *nm* the Basque Provinces *pl*.

euskera, eusquera [eus'kera] *nm* (*LING*) Basque; *V tb* **lenguas cooficiales**.

eutanasia [euta'nasja] *nf* euthanasia.

evacuación [eßakwa'θjon] *nf* evacuation.

evacuar [eßa'kwar] *vt* to evacuate.

evadir [eßa'ðir] *vt* to evade, avoid; **~se** *vr* to escape.

evaluación [eßalwa'θjon] *nf* evaluation,

assessment.

evaluar [eßa'lwar] *vt* to evaluate, assess.

evangélico, a [eßan'xeliko, a] *adj* evangelical.

evangelio [eßan'xeljo] *nm* gospel.

evaporación [eßapora'θjon] *nf* evaporation.

evaporar [eßapo'rar] *vt* to evaporate; **~se** *vr* to vanish.

evasión [eßa'sjon] *nf* escape, flight; (*fig*) evasion; **~ fiscal** *o* **tributaria** tax evasion.

evasivo, a [eßa'sißo, a] *adj* evasive, non-committal ♦ *nf* (*pretexto*) excuse; **contestar con evasivas** to avoid giving a straight answer.

evento [e'ßento] *nm* event; (*eventualidad*) eventuality.

eventual [eßen'twal] *adj* possible, conditional (upon circumstances); (*trabajador*) casual, temporary.

Everest [eße'rest] *nm*: **el (Monte) ~** (Mount) Everest.

evidencia [eßi'ðenθja] *nf* evidence, proof; **poner en ~** to make clear; **ponerse en ~** (*persona*) to show o.s. up.

evidenciar [eßiðen'θjar] *vt* (*hacer patente*) to make evident; (*probar*) to prove, show; **~se** *vr* to be evident.

evidente [eßi'ðente] *adj* obvious, clear, evident.

evitar [eßi'tar] *vt* (*evadir*) to avoid; (*impedir*) to prevent; (*peligro*) to escape; (*molestia*) to save; (*tentación*) to shun; **si puedo ~lo** if I can help it.

evocador, a [eßoka'ðor, a] *adj* (*sugestivo*) evocative.

evocar [eßo'kar] *vt* to evoke, call forth.

evolución [eßolu'θjon] *nf* (*desarrollo*) evolution, development; (*cambio*) change; (*MIL*) manoeuvre.

evolucionar [eßoluθjo'nar] *vi* to evolve; (*MIL, AVIAT*) to manoeuvre.

evoque [e'ßoke] *etc vb V* **evocar**.

ex [eks] *adj* ex-; **el ~ ministro** the former minister, the ex-minister.

exabrupto [eksa'ßrupto] *nm* interjection.

exacción [eksak'θjon] *nf* (*acto*) exaction; (*de impuestos*) demand.

exacerbar [eksaθer'ßar] *vt* to irritate, annoy.

exactamente [eksakta'mente] *adv* exactly.

exactitud [eksakti'tuð] *nf* exactness; (*precisión*) accuracy; (*puntualidad*) punctuality.

exacto, a [ek'sakto, a] *adj* exact; accurate; punctual; **¡~!** exactly!; **eso no es del todo ~** that's not quite right; **para ser ~** to be precise.

exageración [eksaxera'θjon] *nf* exaggeration.

exagerado, a [eksaxe'raðo, a] *adj (relato)* exaggerated; *(precio)* excessive; *(persona)* over-demonstrative; *(gesto)* theatrical.

exagerar [eksaxe'rar] *vt* to exaggerate; *(exceder)* to overdo.

exaltado, a [eksal'taðo, a] *adj (apasionado)* over-excited, worked up; *(exagerado)* extreme; *(fanático)* hot-headed; *(discurso)* impassioned ♦ *nm/f (fanático)* hothead; *(POL)* extremist.

exaltar [eksal'tar] *vt* to exalt, glorify; ~**se** *vr (excitarse)* to get excited o worked up.

examen [ek'samen] *nm* examination; *(de problema)* consideration; ~ **de** *(encuesta)* inquiry into; ~ **de ingreso** entrance examination; ~ **de conducir** driving test; ~ **eliminatorio** qualifying examination.

examinar [eksami'nar] *vt* to examine; *(poner a prueba)* to test; *(inspeccionar)* to inspect; ~**se** *vr* to be examined, take an examination.

exánime [ek'sanime] *adj* lifeless; *(fig)* exhausted.

exasperar [eksaspe'rar] *vt* to exasperate; ~**se** *vr* to get exasperated, lose patience.

Exc.ª *abr* = **Excelencia.**

excarcelar [ekskarθe'lar] *vt* to release (from prison).

excavador, a [ekskaßa'ðor, a] *nm/f (persona)* excavator ♦ *nf (TEC)* digger.

excavar [ekska'ßar] *vt* to excavate, dig (out).

excedencia [eksθe'ðenθja] *nf (MIL)* leave; *(ESCOL)* sabbatical.

excedente [eksθe'ðente] *adj, nm* excess, surplus.

exceder [eksθe'ðer] *vt* to exceed, surpass; ~**se** *vr (extralimitarse)* to go too far; *(sobrepasarse)* to excel o.s.

excelencia [eksθe'lenθja] *nf* excellence; E~ Excellency; **por** ~ par excellence.

excelente [eksθe'lente] *adj* excellent.

excelso, a [eks'θelso, a] *adj* lofty, sublime.

excentricidad [eksθentriθi'ðað] *nf* eccentricity.

excéntrico, a [eks'θentriko, a] *adj, nm/f* eccentric.

excepción [eksθep'θjon] *nf* exception; **la** ~ **confirma la regla** the exception proves the rule.

excepcional [eksθepθjo'nal] *adj* exceptional.

excepto [eks'θepto] *adv* excepting, except (for).

exceptuar [eksθep'twar] *vt* to except, exclude.

excesivo, a [eksθe'sißo, a] *adj* excessive.

exceso [eks'θeso] *nm* excess; *(COM)* surplus; ~ **de equipaje/peso** excess luggage/weight; ~ **de velocidad** speeding; **en** o **por** ~ excessively.

excitación [eksθita'θjon] *nf (sensación)* excitement; *(acción)* excitation.

excitado, a [eksθi'taðo, a] *adj* excited; *(emociones)* aroused.

excitante [eksθi'tante] *adj* exciting; *(MED)* stimulating ♦ *nm* stimulant.

excitar [eksθi'tar] *vt* to excite; *(incitar)* to urge; *(emoción)* to stir up; *(esperanzas)* to raise; *(pasión)* to arouse; ~**se** *vr* to get excited.

exclamación [eksklama'θjon] *nf* exclamation.

exclamar [ekskla'mar] *vi* to exclaim; ~**se** *vr*: ~**se (contra)** to complain (about).

excluir [eksklu'ir] *vt* to exclude; *(dejar fuera)* to shut out; *(solución)* to reject; *(posibilidad)* to rule out.

exclusión [eksklu'sjon] *nf* exclusion.

exclusiva [eksklu'sißa] *nf* V **exclusivo.**

exclusive [eksklu'siße] *prep* exclusive of, not counting.

exclusivo, a [eksklu'sißo, a] *adj* exclusive ♦ *nf (PRENSA)* exclusive, scoop; *(COM)* sole right o agency; **derecho** ~ sole o exclusive right.

excluyendo [eksklu'jendo] *etc vb* V **excluir.**

Excma., Excmo. *abr* (= *Excelentísima, Excelentísimo) courtesy title.*

excombatiente [ekskomba't jente] *nm* ex-serviceman, war veteran *(US).*

excomulgar [ekskomul'ɣar] *vt (REL)* to excommunicate.

excomulgue [eksko'mulɣe] *etc vb* V **excomulgar.**

excomunión [ekskomu'njon] *nf* excommunication.

excoriar [eksko'rjar] *vt* to flay, skin.

excremento [ekskre'mento] *nm* excrement.

exculpar [ekskul'par] *vt* to exonerate; *(JUR)* to acquit; ~**se** *vr* to exonerate o.s.

excursión [ekskur'sjon] *nf* excursion, outing; **ir de** ~ to go (off) on a trip.

excursionista [ekskursjo'nista] *nm/f (turista)* sightseer.

excusa [eks'kusa] *nf* excuse; *(disculpa)* apology; **presentar sus** ~**s** to excuse o.s.

excusado, a [eksku'saðo, a] *adj* unnecessary; *(disculpado)* excused, forgiven.

excusar [eksku'sar] *vt* to excuse; *(evitar)* to avoid, prevent; ~**se** *vr (disculparse)* to apologize.

execrable [ekse'kraßle] *adj* appalling.

exención [eksen'θjon] *nf* exemption.

exento, a [ek'sento, a] *pp de* **eximir** ♦ *adj* exempt.

exequias [ek'sekjas] *nfpl* funeral rites.

exfoliar [eksfo'ljar] *vt* to exfoliate.

exhalación [eksala'θjon] *nf* (*del aire*) exhalation; (*vapor*) fumes *pl*, vapour; (*rayo*) shooting star; **salir como una** ~ to shoot out.

exhalar [eksa'lar] *vt* to exhale, breathe out; (*olor etc*) to give off; (*suspiro*) to breathe, heave.

exhaustivo, a [eksaus'tiβo, a] *adj* exhaustive.

exhausto, a [ek'saust̥o, a] *adj* exhausted, worn-out.

exhibición [eksiβi'θjon] *nf* exhibition; (*demostración*) display, show; (*de película*) showing; (*de equipo*) performance.

exhibicionista [eksiβiθjo'nista] *adj, nmf* exhibitionist.

exhibir [eksi'βir] *vt* to exhibit; to display, show; (*cuadros*) to exhibit; (*artículos*) to display; (*pasaporte*) to show; (*película*) to screen; (*mostrar con orgullo*) to show off; ~**se** *vr* (*mostrarse en público*) to show o.s. off; (*fam: indecentemente*) to expose o.s.

exhortación [eksorta'θjon] *nf* exhortation.

exhortar [eksor'tar] *vt*: ~ **a** to exhort to.

exhumar [eksu'mar] *vt* to exhume.

exigencia [eksi'xenθja] *nf* demand, requirement.

exigente [eksi'xente] *adj* demanding; (*profesor*) strict; **ser** ~ **con algn** to be hard on sb.

exigir [eksi'xir] *vt* (*gen*) to demand, require; (*impuestos*) to exact, levy; ~ **el pago** to demand payment.

exiguo, a [ek'siχwo, a] *adj* (*cantidad*) meagre; (*objeto*) tiny.

exija [e'ksixa] *etc vb V* **exigir**.

exiliado, a [eksi'ljaðo, a] *adj* exiled, in exile ♦ *nmf* exile.

exiliar [eksi'ljar] *vt* to exile; ~**se** *vr* to go into exile.

exilio [ek'siljo] *nm* exile.

eximio, a [ek'simjo, a] *adj* (*eminente*) distinguished, eminent.

eximir [eksi'mir] *vt* to exempt.

existencia [eksis'tenθja] *nf* existence; ~**s** *nfpl* stock *sg*; ~ **de mercancías** (*COM*) stock-in-trade; **tener en** ~ to have in stock; **amargar la** ~ **a algn** to make sb's life a misery.

existir [eksis'tir] *vi* to exist, be.

éxito ['eksito] *nm* (*resultado*) result, outcome; (*triunfo*) success; (*MUS, TEAT*) hit; ~ **editorial** bestseller; ~ **rotundo** smash hit; **tener** ~ to be successful.

exitoso, a [eksi'toso, a] *adj* (*esp AM*) successful.

éxodo ['eksoðo] *nm* exodus; **el** ~ **rural** the drift from the land.

ex oficio [ekso'fiθjo] *adj, adv* ex officio.

exonerar [eksone'rar] *vt* to exonerate; ~ **de una obligación** to free from an obligation.

exorcice [eksor'θiθe] *etc vb V* **exorcizar**.

exorcismo [eksor'θismo] *nm* exorcism.

exorcizar [eksorθi'θar] *vt* to exorcize.

exótico, a [ek'sotiko, a] *adj* exotic.

expandido, a [ekspan'diðo, a] *adj*: **en caracteres** ~**s** (*INFORM*) double width.

expandir [ekspan'dir] *vt* to expand; (*COM*) to expand, enlarge, ~**se** *vr* to expand, spread.

expansión [ekspan'sjon] *nf* expansion; (*recreo*) relaxation; **la** ~ **económica** economic growth; **economía en** ~ expanding economy.

expansionarse [ekspansjo'narse] *vr* (*dilatarse*) to expand; (*recrearse*) to relax.

expansivo, a [ekspan'siβo, a] *adj* expansive; (*efusivo*) communicative.

expatriado, a [ekspa'trjaðo, a] *nmf* (*emigrado*) expatriate; (*exiliado*) exile.

expatriarse [ekspa'trjarse] *vr* to emigrate; (*POL*) to go into exile.

expectación [ekspekta'θjon] *nf* (*esperanza*) expectation; (*ilusión*) excitement.

expectativa [ekspekta'tiβa] *nf* (*espera*) expectation; (*perspectiva*) prospect; ~ **de vida** life expectancy; **estar a la** ~ to wait and see (what will happen).

expedición [ekspeði'θjon] *nf* (*excursión*) expedition; **gastos de** ~ shipping charges.

expedientar [ekspeðjen'tar] *vt* to open a file on; (*funcionario*) to discipline, start disciplinary proceedings against.

expediente [ekspe'ðjente] *nm* expedient; (*JUR: procedimento*) action, proceedings *pl*; (: *papeles*) dossier, file, record; ~ **judicial** court proceedings *pl*; ~ **académico** (student's) record.

expedir [ekspe'ðir] *vt* (*despachar*) to send, forward; (*pasaporte*) to issue; (*cheque*) to make out.

expedito, a [ekspe'ðito, a] *adj* (*libre*) clear, free.

expeler [ekspe'ler] *vt* to expel, eject.

expendedor, a [ekspende'ðor, a] *nmf* (*vendedor*) dealer; (*TEAT*) ticket agent ♦ *nm* (*aparato*) vending machine; ~ **de cigarrillos** cigarette machine.

expendeduría [ekspendedu'ria] *nf* (*estanco*)

tobacconist's (shop) (*BRIT*), cigar store (*US*).

expendio [eks'pendjo] *nm* (*AM*) small shop (*BRIT*) o store (*US*).

expensas [eks'pensas] *nfpl* (*JUR*) costs; **a ~ de** at the expense of.

experiencia [ekspe'rjenθja] *nf* experience.

experimentado, a [eksperimen'taðo, a] *adj* experienced.

experimentar [eksperimen'tar] *vt* (*en laboratorio*) to experiment with; (*probar*) to test, try out; (*notar, observar*) to experience; (*deterioro, pérdida*) to suffer; (*aumento*) to show; (*sensación*) to feel.

experimento [eksperi'mento] *nm* experiment.

experto, a [eks'perto, a] *adj* expert ♦ *nm/f* expert.

expiar [ekspi'ar] *vt* to atone for.

expida [eks'piða] *etc vb V* **expedir**.

expirar [ekspi'rar] *vi* to expire.

explanada [ekspla'naða] *nf* (*paseo*) esplanade; (*a orillas del mar*) promenade.

explayarse [ekspla'jarse] *vr* (*en discurso*) to speak at length; **~ con algn** to confide in sb.

explicación [eksplika'θjon] *nf* explanation.

explicar [ekspli'kar] *vt* to explain; (*teoría*) to expound; (*UNIV*) to lecture in; **~se** *vr* to explain (o.s.); **no me lo explico** I can't understand it.

explícito, a [eks'pliθito, a] *adj* explicit.

explique [eks'plike] *etc vb V* **explicar**.

exploración [eksplora'θjon] *nf* exploration; (*MIL*) reconnaissance.

explorador, a [eksplora'ðor, a] *nm/f* (*pionero*) explorer; (*MIL*) scout ♦ *nm* (*MED*) probe; (*radar*) (radar) scanner.

explorar [eksplo'rar] *vt* to explore; (*MED*) to probe; (*radar*) to scan.

explosión [eksplo'sjon] *nf* explosion.

explosivo, a [eksplo'sißo, a] *adj* explosive.

explotación [eksplota'θjon] *nf* exploitation; (*de planta etc*) running; (*de mina*) working; (*de recurso*) development; **~ minera** mine; **gastos de ~** operating costs.

explotar [eksplo'tar] *vt* to exploit; (*planta*) to run, operate; (*mina*) to work ♦ *vi* (*bomba etc*) to explode, go off.

expondré [ekspon'dre] *etc vb V* **exponer**.

exponer [ekspo'ner] *vt* to expose; (*cuadro*) to display; (*vida*) to risk; (*idea*) to explain; (*teoría*) to expound; (*hechos*) to set out; **~se** *vr*: **~se a (hacer) algo** to run the risk of (doing) sth.

exponga [eks'ponga] *etc vb V* **exponer**.

exportación [eksporta'θjon] *nf* (*acción*)

export; (*mercancías*) exports *pl*.

exportador, a [eksporta'ðor, a] *adj* (*país*) exporting ♦ *nm/f* exporter.

exportar [ekspor'tar] *vt* to export.

exposición [eksposi'θjon] *nf* (*gen*) exposure; (*de arte*) show, exhibition; (*COM*) display; (*feria*) show, fair; (*explicación*) explanation; (*de teoría*) exposition; (*narración*) account, statement.

exprés [eks'pres] *adj inv* (*café*) espresso ♦ *nm* (*FERRO*) express (train).

expresamente [ekspresa'mente] *adv* (*concretamente*) expressly; (*a propósito*) on purpose.

expresar [ekspre'sar] *vt* to express; (*redactar*) to phrase, put; (*emoción*) to show; **~se** *vr* to express o.s.; (*dato*) to be stated; **como abajo se expresa** as stated below.

expresión [ekspre'sjon] *nf* expression; **~ familiar** colloquialism.

expresivo, a [ekspre'sißo, a] *adj* expressive; (*cariñoso*) affectionate.

expreso, a [eks'preso, a] *adj* (*explícito*) express; (*claro*) specific, clear; (*tren*) fast ♦ *nm* (*FERRO*) fast train ♦ *adv*: **mandar ~** to send by express (delivery).

exprimidor [eksprimi'ðor] *nm* (*lemon*) squeezer.

exprimir [ekspri'mir] *vt* (*fruta*) to squeeze; (*zumo*) to squeeze out.

ex profeso [ekspro'feso] *adv* expressly.

expropiar [ekspro'pjar] *vt* to expropriate.

expuesto, a [eks'pwesto, a] *pp de* **exponer** ♦ *adj* exposed; (*cuadro etc*) on show, on display; **según lo ~ arriba** according to what has been stated above.

expulsar [ekspul'sar] *vt* (*echar*) to eject, throw out; (*alumno*) to expel; (*despedir*) to sack, fire; (*DEPORTE*) to send off.

expulsión [ekspul'sjon] *nf* expulsion; sending-off.

expurgar [ekspur'ɣar] *vt* to expurgate.

expuse [eks'puse] *etc vb V* **exponer**.

exquisito, a [ekski'sito, a] *adj* exquisite; (*comida*) delicious; (*afectado*) affected.

Ext. *abr* (= *Exterior*) ext.; (= *Extensión*) ext.

éxtasis ['ekstasis] *nm* (*tb droga*) ecstasy.

extemporáneo, a [ekstempo'raneo, a] *adj* unseasonal.

extender [eksten'der] *vt* to extend; (*los brazos*) to stretch out, hold out; (*mapa, tela*) to spread (out), open (out); (*mantequilla*) to spread; (*certificado*) to issue; (*cheque, recibo*) to make out; (*documento*) to draw up; **~se** *vr* to extend; (*terreno*) to stretch o spread (out); (*persona: en el suelo*) to stretch out; (*en el tiempo*) to extend, last; (*costumbre, epidemia*) to spread; (*guerra*) to escalate; ~**se sobre un tema** to enlarge on a subject.

extendido, a [eksten'diðo, a] *adj* (*abierto*) spread out, open; (*brazos*) outstretched; (*costumbre etc*) widespread.

extensible [eksten'sißle] *adj* extending.

extensión [eksten'sjon] *nf* (*de terreno, mar*) expanse, stretch; (*MUS*) range; (*de conocimientos*) extent; (*de programa*) scope; (*de tiempo*) length, duration; (*TELEC*) extension; ~ **de plazo** (*COM*) extension; **en toda la** ~ **de la palabra** in every sense of the word; **de** ~ (*INFORM*) add-on.

extenso, a [eks'tenso, a] *adj* extensive.

extenuar [ekste'nwar] *vt* (*debilitar*) to weaken.

exterior [ekste'rjor] *adj* (*de fuera*) external; (*afuera*) outside, exterior; (*apariencia*) outward; (*deuda, relaciones*) foreign ♦ *nm* exterior, outside; (*aspecto*) outward appearance; (*DEPORTE*) wing(er); (*países extranjeros*) abroad; **asuntos** ~**es** foreign affairs; **al** ~ outwardly, on the outside; **en el** ~ abroad; **noticias del** ~ foreign *o* overseas news.

exteriorice [eksterjo'riθe] *etc vb V* **exteriorizar.**

exteriorizar [eksterjori'θar] *vt* (*emociones*) to show, reveal.

exteriormente [eksterjor'mente] *adv* outwardly.

exterminar [ekstermi'nar] *vt* to exterminate.

exterminio [ekster'minjo] *nm* extermination.

externo, a [eks'terno, a] *adj* (*exterior*) external, outside; (*superficial*) outward ♦ *nm/f* day pupil.

extienda [eks'tjenda] *etc vb V* **extender.**

extinción [ekstin'θjon] *nf* extinction.

extinga [eks'tinga] *etc vb V* **extinguir.**

extinguido, a [ekstin'giðo, a] *adj* (*animal, volcán*) extinct; (*fuego*) out, extinguished.

extinguir [ekstin'gir] *vt* (*fuego*) to extinguish, put out; (*raza, población*) to wipe out; ~**se** *vr* (*fuego*) to go out; (*BIO*) to die out, become extinct.

extinto, a [eks'tinto, a] *adj* extinct.

extintor [ekstin'tor] *nm* (fire) extinguisher.

extirpar [ekstir'par] *vt* (*vicios*) to eradicate, stamp out; (*MED*) to remove (surgically).

extorsión [ekstor'sjon] *nf* blackmail.

extra ['ekstra] *adj inv* (*tiempo*) extra; (*vino*)

vintage; (*chocolate*) good-quality; (*gasolina*) high-octane ♦ *nm/f* extra ♦ *nm* (*bono*) bonus; (*periódico*) special edition.

extracción [ekstrak'θjon] *nf* extraction; (*en lotería*) draw; (*de carbón*) mining.

extracto [eks'trakto] *nm* extract.

extractor [ekstrak'tor] *nm* (*tb:* ~ **de humos**) extractor fan.

extradición [ekstraði'θjon] *nf* extradition.

extraditar [ekstraði'tar] *vt* to extradite.

extraer [ekstra'er] *vt* to extract, take out.

extrafino, a [ekstra'fino, a] *adj* extra-fine; **azúcar** ~ caster sugar.

extraiga [eks'traiɣa] *etc*, **extraje** [eks'traxe] *etc*, **extrajera** [ekstra'xera] *etc vb V* **extraer.**

extralimitarse [ekstralimi'tarse] *vr* to go too far.

extranjerismo [ekstranxe'rismo] *nm* foreign word *o* phrase *etc*.

extranjero, a [ekstran'xero, a] *adj* foreign ♦ *nm/f* foreigner ♦ *nm* foreign lands *pl*; **en el** ~ abroad.

extrañamiento [ekstraɲa'mjento] *nm* estrangement.

extrañar [ekstra'ɲar] *vt* (*sorprender*) to find strange *o* odd; (*echar de menos*) to miss; ~**se** *vr* (*sorprenderse*) to be amazed, be surprised; (*distanciarse*) to become estranged, grow apart; **me extraña** I'm surprised.

extrañeza [ekstra'ɲeθa] *nf* (*rareza*) strangeness, oddness; (*asombro*) amazement, surprise.

extraño, a [eks'traɲo, a] *adj* (*extranjero*) foreign; (*raro, sorprendente*) strange, odd.

extraoficial [ekstraofi'θjal] *adj* unofficial, informal.

extraordinario, a [ekstraorði'narjo, a] *adj* extraordinary; (*edición, número*) special ♦ *nm* (*de periódico*) special edition; **horas extraordinarias** overtime *sg*.

extrarradio [ekstra'rraðjo] *nm* suburbs *pl*.

extrasensorial [ekstrasenso'rjal] *adj*: **percepción** ~ extrasensory perception.

extraterrestre [ekstrate'rrestre] *adj* of *o* from outer space ♦ *nm/f* creature from outer space.

extravagancia [ekstraßa'ɣanθja] *nf* oddness; outlandishness; (*rareza*) peculiarity; ~**s** *nfpl* (*tonterías*) nonsense *sg*.

extravagante [ekstraßa'ɣante] *adj* (*excéntrico*) eccentric; (*estrafalario*) outlandish.

extraviado, a [ekstra'ßjaðo, a] *adj* lost, missing.

extraviar [ekstra'ßjar] *vt* to mislead, misdirect; (*perder*) to lose, misplace; ~**se** *vr* to lose one's way, get lost; (*objeto*) to go missing, be mislaid.

extravío [ekstra'ßio] *nm* loss; (*fig*) misconduct.

extrayendo [ekstra'jendo] *vb* V **extraer**.

extremado, a [ekstre'maðo, a] *adj* extreme, excessive.

Extremadura [ekstrema'ðura] *nf* Estremadura.

extremar [ekstre'mar] *vt* to carry to extremes; ~**se** *vr* to do one's utmost, make every effort.

extremaunción [ekstremaun'θjon] *nf* extreme unction, last rites *pl*.

extremidad [ekstremi'ðað] *nf* (*punta*) extremity; (*fila*) edge; ~**es** *nfpl* (*ANAT*) extremities.

extremista [ekstre'mista] *adj, nm/f* extremist.

extremo, a [eks'tremo, a] *adj* extreme; (*más alejado*) furthest; (*último*) last ♦ *nm* end; (*situación*) extreme; **E~ Oriente** Far East; **en último** ~ as a last resort; **pasar de un** ~ **a otro** (*fig*) to go from one extreme to the other; **con** ~ in the extreme; **la extrema derecha** (*POL*) the far right; ~ **derecho/izquierdo** (*DEPORTE*) outside right/left.

extrínseco, a [eks'trinseko, a] *adj* extrinsic.

extrovertido, a [ekstroßer'tiðo, a] *adj* extrovert, outgoing ♦ *nm/f* extrovert.

exuberancia [eksuße'ranθja] *nf* exuberance.

exuberante [eksuße'rante] *adj* exuberant; (*fig*) luxuriant, lush.

exudar [eksu'ðar] *vt, vi* to exude.

exultar [eksul'tar] *vi*: ~ **(en)** to exult (in); (*pey*) to gloat (over).

exvoto [eks'ßoto] *nm* votive offering.

eyaculación [ejakula'θjon] *nf* ejaculation.

eyacular [ejaku'lar] *vt, vi* to ejaculate.

F f

F, f ['efe] *nf* (*letra*) F, f; **F de Francia** F for Frederick (*BRIT*), F for Fox (*US*).

fa [fa] *nm* (*MUS*) F.

f.ª *abr* (*COM*: = *factura*) Inv.

f.a.b. *abr* (= *franco a bordo*) f.o.b.

fabada [fa'ßaða] *nf* bean and sausage stew.

fábrica ['faßrika] *nf* factory; ~ **de moneda** mint; **marca de** ~ trademark; **precio de** ~ factory price.

fabricación [faßrika'θjon] *nf* (*manufactura*) manufacture; (*producción*) production; **de** ~ **casera** home-made; **de** ~ **nacional** home produced; ~ **en serie** mass production.

fabricante [faßri'kante] *nm/f* manufacturer.

fabricar [faßri'kar] *vt* (*manufacturar*) to manufacture, make; (*construir*) to build; (*cuento*) to fabricate, devise; ~ **en serie** to mass-produce.

fabril [fa'ßril] *adj*: **industria** ~ manufacturing industry.

fabrique [fa'ßrike] *etc vb* V **fabricar**.

fábula ['faßula] *nf* (*cuento*) fable; (*chisme*) rumour; (*mentira*) fib.

fabuloso, a [faßu'loso, a] *adj* fabulous, fantastic.

FACA ['faka] *nm abr* (*ESP AVIAT*) = Futuro Avión de Combate y Ataque.

facción [fak'θjon] *nf* (*POL*) faction; **facciones** *nfpl* (*del rostro*) features.

faceta [fa'θeta] *nf* facet.

facha ['fatʃa] (*fam*) *nm/f* fascist, right-wing extremist ♦ *nf* (*aspecto*) look; (*cara*) face; **¡qué** ~ **tienes!** you look a sight!

fachada [fa'tʃaða] *nf* (*ARQ*) façade, front; (*TIP*) title page; (*fig*) façade, outward show.

facial [fa'θjal] *adj* facial.

fácil ['faθil] *adj* (*simple*) easy; (*sencillo*) simple, straightforward; (*probable*) likely; (*respuesta*) facile; ~ **de usar** (*INFORM*) user-friendly.

facilidad [faθili'ðað] *nf* (*capacidad*) ease; (*sencillez*) simplicity; (*de palabra*) fluency; ~**es** *nfpl* facilities; "~**es de pago**" (*COM*) "credit facilities", "payment terms".

facilitar [faθili'tar] *vt* (*hacer fácil*) to make easy; (*proporcionar*) to provide; (*documento*) to issue; **le agradecería me facilitara ...** I would be grateful if you could let me have ....

fácilmente ['faθilmente] *adv* easily.

facsímil [fak'simil] *nm* (*documento*) facsimile; **enviar por ~** to fax.

factible [fak'tiβle] *adj* feasible.

factor [fak'tor] *nm* factor; (*COM*) agent; (*FERRO*) freight clerk.

factoría [fakto'ria] *nf* (*COM: agencia*) agency; (: *fábrica*) factory.

factura [fak'tura] *nf* (*cuenta*) bill; (*nota de pago*) invoice; (*hechura*) manufacture; **presentar ~ a** to invoice.

facturación [faktura'θjon] *nf* (*COM*) invoicing; (: *ventas*) turnover; **~ de equipajes** luggage check-in.

facturar [faktu'rar] *vt* (*COM*) to invoice, charge for; (*AVIAT*) to check in; (*equipaje*) to register, check (*US*).

facultad [fakul'tað] *nf* (*aptitud, ESCOL etc*) faculty; (*poder*) power.

facultativo, a [fakulta'tiβo, a] *adj* optional; (*de un oficio*) professional; **prescripción facultativa** medical prescription.

FAD *nm abr* (*ESP*) = Fondo de Ayuda y Desarrollo.

faena [fa'ena] *nf* (*trabajo*) work; (*quehacer*) task, job; **~s domésticas** housework *sg*.

faenar [fae'nar] *vi* to fish.

fagot [fa'ɣot] *nm* (*MUS*) bassoon.

faisán [fai'san] *nm* pheasant.

faja ['faxa] *nf* (*para la cintura*) sash; (*de mujer*) corset; (*de tierra*) strip.

fajo ['faxo] *nm* (*de papeles*) bundle; (*de billetes*) role, wad.

falange [fa'lanxe] *nf*: **la F~** (*POL*) the Falange.

falda ['falda] *nf* (*prenda de vestir*) skirt; (*GEO*) foothill; **~ escocesa** kilt.

fálico, a ['faliko, a] *adj* phallic.

falla ['faʎa] *nf* (*defecto*) fault, flaw.

fallar [fa'ʎar] *vt* (*JUR*) to pronounce sentence on; (*NAIPES*) to trump ♦ *vi* (*memoria*) to fail; (*plan*) to go wrong; (*motor*) to miss; **~ a algn** to let sb down.

Fallas ['faʎas] *nfpl see boxed note.*

FALLAS

In the week of 19 March (the feast of St Joseph, San José), Valencia honours its patron saint with a spectacular "fiesta" called **las Fallas.** *The Fallas are, more precisely, huge figures made of wood,*

---

cardboard, paper and cloth, depicting famous politicians and other prime targets of ridicule. At the end of the festival, these figures are set on fire by the "falleros", members of competing local groups who will have spent months working on them.

---

fallecer [faʎe'θer] *vi* to pass away, die.

fallecido, a [faʎe'θiðo, a] *adj* late ♦ *nm/f* deceased.

fallecimiento [faʎeθi'mjento] *nm* decease, demise.

fallero, a [fa'ʎero, a] *nm/f* maker of "Fallas".

fallezca [fa'ʎeθka] *etc vb V* **fallecer.**

fallido, a [fa'ʎiðo, a] *adj* vain; (*intento*) frustrated, unsuccessful.

fallo ['faʎo] *nm* (*JUR*) verdict, ruling; (*decisión*) decision; (*de jurado*) findings; (*fracaso*) failure; (*DEPORTE*) miss; (*INFORM*) bug.

falo ['falo] *nm* phallus.

falsear [false'ar] *vt* to falsify; (*firma etc*) to forge ♦ *vi* (*MUS*) to be out of tune.

falsedad [false'ðað] *nf* falseness; (*hipocresía*) hypocrisy; (*mentira*) falsehood.

falsificación [falsifika'θjon] *nf* (*acto*) falsification; (*objeto*) forgery.

falsificar [falsifi'kar] *vt* (*firma etc*) to forge; (*voto etc*) to rig; (*moneda*) to counterfeit.

falsifique [falsi'fike] *etc vb V* **falsificar.**

falso, a ['falso, a] *adj* false; (*erróneo*) wrong, mistaken; (*firma, documento*) forged; (*documento, moneda etc*) fake; **en ~** falsely; **dar un paso en ~** to trip; (*fig*) to take a false step.

falta ['falta] *nf* (*defecto*) fault, flaw; (*privación*) lack, want; (*ausencia*) absence; (*carencia*) shortage; (*equivocación*) mistake; (*JUR*) default; (*DEPORTE*) foul; (*TENIS*) fault; **~ de ortografía** spelling mistake; **~ de respeto** disrespect; **echar en ~** to miss; **hacer ~ hacer algo** to be necessary to do sth; **me hace ~ una pluma** I need a pen; **sin ~** without fail; **por ~ de** through *o* for lack of.

faltar [fal'tar] *vi* (*escasear*) to be lacking, be wanting; (*ausentarse*) to be absent, be missing; **¿falta algo?** is anything missing?; **faita mucho todavía** there's plenty of time yet; **¿falta mucho?** is there long to go?; **faltan 2 horas para llegar** there are 2 hours to go till arrival; **~ (al respeto) a algn** to be disrespectful to sb; **~ a una cita** to miss an appointment; **~ a la verdad** to lie; **¡no faltaba más!** that's the last straw!

falto, a ['falto, a] *adj* (*desposeído*) deficient,

lacking; (*necesitado*) poor, wretched;
estar ~ de to be short of.
fama ['fama] *nf* (*renombre*) fame;
(*reputación*) reputation.
famélico, a [fa'meliko, a] *adj* starving.
familia [fa'milja] *nf* family; ~ **política** in-
laws *pl*.
familiar [fami'ljar] *adj* (*relativo a la familia*)
family *cpd*; (*conocido, informal*) familiar;
(*estilo*) informal; (*LING*) colloquial ♦ *nm/f*
relative, relation.
familiarice [familja'riθe] *etc vb V*
familiarizarse.
familiaridad [familjari'ðað] *nf* familiarity;
(*informalidad*) homeliness.
familiarizarse [familjari'θarse] *vr*: ~ **con** to
familiarize o.s. with.
famoso, a [fa'moso, a] *adj* (*renombrado*)
famous.
fan, *pl* fans [fan, fans] *nm* fan.
fanático, a [fa'natiko, a] *adj* fanatical
♦ *nm/f* fanatic; (*CINE, DEPORTE etc*) fan.
fanatismo [fana'tismo] *nm* fanaticism.
fanfarrón, ona [fanfa'rron, ona] *adj*
boastful; (*pey*) showy.
fanfarronear [fanfarrone'ar] *vi* to boast.
fango ['fango] *nm* mud.
fangoso, a [fan'goso, a] *adj* muddy.
fantasear [fantase'ar] *vi* to fantasize; ~
con una idea to toy with an idea.
fantasía [fanta'sia] *nf* fantasy,
imagination; (*MUS*) fantasia; (*capricho*)
whim; **joyas de** ~ imitation jewellery *sg*.
fantasma [fan'tasma] *nm* (*espectro*) ghost,
apparition; (*presumido*) show-off.
fantástico, a [fan'tastiko, a] *adj* (*irreal,
fam*) fantastic.
fanzine [fan'θine] *nm* fanzine.
FAO ['fao] *nf abr* (= *Organización de las
Naciones Unidas para la Agricultura y la
Alimentación*) FAO.
faquir [fa'kir] *nm* fakir.
faraón [fara'on] *nm* Pharaoh.
faraónico, a [fara'oniko, a] *adj* Pharaonic;
(*fig*) grandiose.
fardar [far'ðar] *vi* to show off; ~ **de** to
boast about.
fardo ['farðo] *nm* bundle; (*fig*) burden.
faringe [fa'rinxe] *nf* pharynx.
faringitis [farin'xitis] *nf* pharyngitis.
farmacéutico, a [farma'θeutiko, a] *adj*
pharmaceutical ♦ *nm/f* chemist (*BRIT*),
pharmacist.
farmacia [far'maθja] *nf* (*ciencia*) pharmacy;
(*tienda*) chemist's (shop) (*BRIT*),
pharmacy, drugstore (*US*); ~ **de turno**
duty chemist.
fármaco ['farmako] *nm* medicine, drug.

faro ['faro] *nm* (*NAUT*: *torre*) lighthouse;
(*señal*) beacon; (*AUTO*) headlamp; ~**s
antiniebla** fog lamps; ~**s delanteros/
traseros** headlights/rear lights.
farol [fa'rol] *nm* (*luz*) lantern, lamp; (*FERRO*)
headlamp; (*poste*) lamppost; **echarse un
~** (*fam*) to show off.
farola [fa'rola] *nf* street lamp (*BRIT*) o light
(*US*), lamppost.
farruco, a [fa'rruko, a] *adj* (*fam*): **estar** o
ponerse ~ to get aggressive.
farsa ['farsa] *nf* (*gen*) farce.
farsante [far'sante] *nm/f* fraud, fake.
FASA ['fasa] *nf abr* (*ESP AUTO*) = *Fábrica de
Automóviles, S.A.*
fascículo [fas'θikulo] *nm* (*gen*) part,
instalment (*BRIT*), installment (*US*).
fascinante [fasθi'nante] *adj* fascinating.
fascinar [fasθi'nar] *vt* to fascinate;
(*encantar*) to captivate.
fascismo [fas'θismo] *nm* fascism.
fascista [fas'θista] *adj, nm/f* fascist.
fase ['fase] *nf* phase.
fastidiar [fasti'ðjar] *vt* (*disgustar*) to annoy,
bother; (*estropear*) to spoil; ~**se** *vr*
(*disgustarse*) to get annoyed o cross; **¡no
fastidies!** you're joking!; **¡que se
fastidie!** (*fam*) he'll just have to put up
with it!
fastidio [fas'tiðjo] *nm* (*disgusto*)
annoyance.
fastidioso, a [fasti'ðjoso, a] *adj* (*molesto*)
annoying.
fastuoso, a [fas'twoso, a] *adj* (*espléndido*)
magnificent; (*banquete etc*) lavish.
fatal [fa'tal] *adj* (*gen*) fatal; (*desgraciado*)
ill-fated; (*fam: malo, pésimo*) awful ♦ *adv*
terribly; **lo pasó** ~ he had a terrible
time (of it).
fatalidad [fatali'ðað] *nf* (*destino*) fate; (*mala
suerte*) misfortune.
fatídico, a [fa'tiðiko, a] *adj* fateful.
fatiga [fa'tiɣa] *nf* (*cansancio*) fatigue,
weariness; ~**s** *nfpl* hardships.
fatigar [fati'ɣar] *vt* to tire, weary; ~**se** *vr* to
get tired.
fatigoso, a [fati'ɣoso, a] *adj* (*cansador*)
tiring.
fatigue [fati'ɣe] *etc vb V* **fatigar**.
fatuo, a ['fatwo, a] *adj* (*vano*) fatuous;
(*presuntuoso*) conceited.
fauces ['fauθes] *nfpl* (*ANAT*) gullet *sg*; (*fam*)
jaws.
fauna ['fauna] *nf* fauna.
favor [fa'ßor] *nm* favour (*BRIT*), favor (*US*);
haga el ~ de ... would you be so good as
to ..., kindly ...; **por** ~ please; **a** ~ in
favo(u)r; **a** ~ **de** to be in favo(u)r of;

(COM) to the order of.
favorable [faßo'raßle] adj favourable (BRIT), favorable (US); (condiciones etc) advantageous.
favorecer [faßore'θer] vt to favour (BRIT), favor (US); (amparar) to help; (vestido etc) to become, flatter; **este peinado le favorece** this hairstyle suits him.
favorezca [faßo'reθka] etc vb V **favorecer**.
favorito, a [faßo'rito, a] adj, nm/f favourite (BRIT), favorite (US).
fax [faks] nm inv fax; **mandar por** ~ to fax.
faz [faθ] nf face; **la** ~ **de la tierra** the face of the earth.
F.C., f.c. abr = **ferrocarril**.
FE nf abr = Falange Española.
fe [fe] nf (REL) faith; (confianza) belief; (documento) certificate; **de buena** ~ (JUR) bona fide; **prestar** ~ **a** to believe, credit; **actuar con buena/mala** ~ to act in good/bad faith; **dar** ~ **de** to bear witness to; ~ **de erratas** errata.
fealdad [feal'daθ] nf ugliness.
feb., feb.º abr (= febrero) Feb.
febrero [fe'ßrero] nm February.
febril [fe'ßril] adj feverish; (movido) hectic.
fecha ['fetʃa] nf date; ~ **límite** o **tope** closing o last date; ~ **límite de venta** (de alimentos) sell-by date; ~ **de caducidad** (de alimentos) sell-by date; (de contrato) expiry date; **en** ~ **próxima** soon; **hasta la** ~ to date, so far; ~ **de vencimiento** (COM) due date; ~ **de vigencia** (COM) effective date.
fechar [fe'tʃar] vt to date.
fechoría [fetʃo'ria] nf misdeed.
fécula ['fekula] nf starch.
fecundación [fekunda'θjon] nf fertilization; ~ **in vitro** in vitro fertilization, I.V.F.
fecundar [fekun'dar] vt (generar) to fertilize, make fertile.
fecundidad [fekundi'ðað] nf fertility; (fig) productiveness.
fecundo, a [fe'kundo, a] adj (fértil) fertile; (fig) prolific; (productivo) productive.
FED nm abr (= Fondo Europeo de Desarrollo) EDF.
FEDER nm abr (= Fondo Europeo de Desarrollo Regional) ERDF.
federación [feðera'θjon] nf federation.
federal [feðe'ral] adj federal.
federalismo [feðera'lismo] nm federalism.
FEF nf abr = Federación Española de Fútbol.
felicidad [feliθi'ðað] nf (satisfacción, contento) happiness; ~**es** nfpl best wishes, congratulations.

felicitación [feliθita'θjon] nf (tarjeta) greetings card; **felicitaciones** nfpl (enhorabuena) congratulations; ~ **navideña** o **de Navidad** Christmas Greetings.
felicitar [feliθi'tar] vt to congratulate.
feligrés, esa [feli'ɣres, esa] nm/f parishioner.
felino, a [fe'lino, a] adj cat-like; (ZOOL) feline ♦ nm feline.
feliz [fe'liθ] adj (contento) happy; (afortunado) lucky.
felonía [felo'nia] nf felony, crime.
felpa ['felpa] nf (terciopelo) plush; (toalla) towelling.
felpudo [fel'puðo] nm doormat.
femenino, a [feme'nino, a] adj feminine; (ZOOL etc) female ♦ nm (LING) feminine.
feminismo [femi'nismo] nm feminism.
feminista [femi'nista] adj, nm/f feminist.
fenomenal [fenome'nal] adj phenomenal; (fam) great, terrific.
fenómeno [fe'nomeno] nm phenomenon; (fig) freak, accident ♦ adv: **lo pasamos** ~ we had a great time ♦ excl great!, marvellous!
feo, a ['feo, a] adj (gen) ugly; (desagradable) bad, nasty ♦ nm insult; **hacer un** ~ **a algn** to offend sb; **más** ~ **que Picio** as ugly as sin.
féretro ['feretro] nm (ataúd) coffin; (sarcófago) bier.
feria ['ferja] nf (gen) fair; (AM: mercado) market; (descanso) holiday, rest day; (AM: cambio) small change; ~ **comercial** trade fair; ~ **de muestras** trade show.
feriado, a [fe'rjaðo, a] (AM) adj: **día** ~ (public) holiday ♦ nm (public) holiday.
fermentar [fermen'tar] vi to ferment.
fermento [fer'mento] nm leaven, leavening.
ferocidad [feroθi'ðað] nf fierceness, ferocity.
ferocísimo, a [fero'θisimo, a] adj superlativo de **feroz**.
feroz [fe'roθ] adj (cruel) cruel; (salvaje) fierce.
férreo, a ['ferreo, a] adj iron cpd; (TEC) ferrous; (fig) (of) iron.
ferretería [ferrete'ria] nf (tienda) ironmonger's (shop) (BRIT), hardware store.
ferrocarril [ferroka'rril] nm railway, railroad (US); ~ **de vía estrecha/única** narrow-gauge/single-track railway o line.
ferroviario, a [ferrovja'rjo, a] adj rail cpd, railway cpd (BRIT), railroad cpd (US) ♦ nm:

~s railway (*BRIT*) *o* railroad (*US*) workers.

fértil ['fertil] *adj* (*productivo*) fertile; (*rico*) rich.

fertilice [ferti'liθe] *etc vb* V **fertilizar**.

fertilidad [fertili'ðað] *nf* (*gen*) fertility; (*productividad*) fruitfulness.

fertilizante [fertili'θante] *nm* fertilizer.

fertilizar [fertili'θar] *vt* to fertilize.

ferviente [fer'ßjente] *adj* fervent.

fervor [fer'ßor] *nm* fervour (*BRIT*), fervor (*US*).

fervoroso, a [ferßo'roso, a] *adj* fervent.

festejar [feste'xar] *vt* (*agasajar*) to wine and dine, fête; (*galantear*) to court; (*celebrar*) to celebrate.

festejo [fes'texo] *nm* (*diversión*) entertainment; (*galanteo*) courtship; (*fiesta*) celebration.

festín [fes'tin] *nm* feast, banquet.

festival [festi'ßal] *nm* festival.

festividad [festißi'ðað] *nf* festivity.

festivo, a [fes'tißo, a] *adj* (*de fiesta*) festive; (*fig*) witty; (*CINE, LIT*) humorous; **día** ~ holiday.

fetiche [fe'titʃe] *nm* fetish.

fetichista [feti'tʃista] *adj* fetishistic ♦ *nm/f* fetishist.

fétido, a ['fetiðo, a] *adj* (*hediondo*) foul-smelling.

feto ['feto] *nm* foetus; (*fam*) monster.

F.E.V.E. *nf abr* (= *Ferrocarriles Españoles de Vía Estrecha*) *Spanish narrow-gauge railways.*

FF.AA. *nfpl abr* (*MIL*) = **Fuerzas Armadas**.

FF.CC. *nmpl abr* = **Ferrocarriles**.

fiable [fi'aßle] *adj* (*persona*) trustworthy; (*máquina*) reliable.

fiado [fi'aðo] *nm*: **comprar al** ~ to buy on credit; **en** ~ on bail.

fiador, a [fia'ðor, a] *nm/f* (*JUR*) surety, guarantor; (*COM*) backer; **salir** ~ **por algn** to stand bail for sb.

fiambre ['fjambre] *adj* (*CULIN*) (served) cold ♦ *nm* (*CULIN*) cold meat (*BRIT*), cold cut (*US*); (*fam*) corpse, stiff.

fiambrera [fjam'brera] *nf* ≈ lunch box, dinner pail (*US*).

fianza ['fjanθa] *nf* surety; (*JUR*): **libertad bajo** ~ release on bail.

fiar [fi'ar] *vt* (*salir garante de*) to guarantee; (*JUR*) to stand bail *o* bond (*US*) for; (*vender a crédito*) to sell on credit; (*secreto*) to confide ♦ *vi*: ~ **(de)** to trust (in); **ser de** ~ to be trustworthy; ~**se** *vr*: ~ **de** to trust (in), rely on.

fiasco [fi'asko] *nm* fiasco.

fibra ['fißra] *nf* fibre (*BRIT*), fiber (*US*); (*fig*)

vigour (*BRIT*), vigor (*US*); ~ **óptica** (*INFORM*) optical fibre (*BRIT*) *o* fiber (*US*).

ficción [fik'θjon] *nf* fiction.

ficha ['fitʃa] *nf* (*TELEC*) token; (*en juegos*) counter, marker; (*en casino*) chip; (*COM, ECON*) tally, check (*US*); (*INFORM*) file; (*tarjeta*) (index) card; (*ELEC*) plug; (*en hotel*) registration form; ~ **policíaca** police dossier.

fichaje [fi'tʃaxe] *nm* signing(-up).

fichar [fi'tʃar] *vt* (*archivar*) to file, index; (*DEPORTE*) to sign (up) ♦ *vi* (*deportista*) to sign (up); (*obrero*) to clock in *o* on; **estar fichado** to have a record.

fichero [fi'tʃero] *nm* card index; (*archivo*) filing cabinet; (*COM*) box file; (*INFORM*) file, archive; (*de policía*) criminal records; ~ **activo** (*INFORM*) active file; ~ **archivado** (*INFORM*) archived file; ~ **indexado** (*INFORM*) index file; ~ **de reserva** (*INFORM*) backup file; ~ **de tarjetas** card index; **nombre de** ~ filename.

ficticio, a [fik'tiθjo, a] *adj* (*imaginario*) fictitious; (*falso*) fabricated.

ficus ['fikus] *nm inv* (*BOT*) rubber plant.

fidedigno, a [fiðe'ðiɣno, a] *adj* reliable.

fideicomiso [fiðeiko'miso] *nm* (*COM*) trust.

fidelidad [fiðeli'ðað] *nf* (*lealtad*) fidelity, loyalty; (*exactitud: de dato etc*) accuracy; **alta** ~ high fidelity, hi-fi.

fidelísimo, a [fiðe'lisimo, a] *adj superlativo de* **fiel**.

fideos [fi'ðeos] *nmpl* noodles.

fiduciario, a [fiðu'θjarjo, a] *nm/f* fiduciary.

fiebre ['fjeßre] *nf* (*MED*) fever; (*fig*) fever, excitement; ~ **amarilla/del heno** yellow/hay fever; ~ **palúdica** malaria; **tener** ~ to have a temperature.

fiel [fjel] *adj* (*leal*) faithful, loyal; (*fiable*) reliable; (*exacto*) accurate ♦ *nm* (*aguja*) needle, pointer; **los** ~**es** the faithful.

fieltro ['fjeltro] *nm* felt.

fiera ['fjera] *nf* V **fiero**.

fiereza [fje'reθa] *nf* (*ZOOL*) wildness; (*bravura*) fierceness.

fiero, a ['fjero, a] *adj* (*cruel*) cruel; (*feroz*) fierce; (*duro*) harsh ♦ *nm/f* (*fig*) fiend ♦ *nf* (*animal feroz*) wild animal *o* beast; (*fig*) dragon.

fierro ['fjerro] *nm* (*AM*) iron.

fiesta ['fjesta] *nf* party; (*de pueblo*) festival; **la** ~ **nacional** bullfighting; (*día de*) ~ (public) holiday; **mañana es** ~ it's a holiday tomorrow; ~ **de guardar** (*REL*) day of obligation; *see boxed note.*

FIESTA

Fiestas can be national public holidays (such as the *Día de la Constitución*), or special regional ones for each autonomous region, many of which are religious feast days. All over Spain there are also special local **fiestas** in honour of a patron saint or the Virgin Mary. These often last several days and can include religious processions, carnival parades, bullfights, dancing and feasting on local produce.

FIFA *nf abr* (= *Federación Internacional de Fútbol Asociación*) FIFA.

figura [fi'ɣura] *nf* (*gen*) figure; (*forma, imagen*) shape, form; (*NAIPES*) face card.

figurado, a [fiɣu'raðo, a] *adj* figurative.

figurante [fiɣu'rante] *nm/f* (*TEAT*) walk-on part; (*CINE*) extra.

figurar [fiɣu'rar] *vt* (*representar*) to represent; (*fingir*) to feign ♦ *vi* to figure; ~**se** *vr* (*imaginarse*) to imagine; (*suponer*) to suppose; **ya me lo figuraba** I thought as much.

fijador [fixa'ðor] *nm* (*FOTO etc*) fixative; (*de pelo*) gel.

fijar [fi'xar] *vt* (*gen*) to fix; (*cartel*) to post, put up; (*estampilla*) to affix, stick (on); (*pelo*) to set; (*fig*) to settle (on), decide; ~**se** *vr*: ~**se en** to notice; **¡fíjate!** just imagine!; **¿te fijas?** see what I mean?

fijo, a ['fixo, a] *adj* (*gen*) fixed; (*firme*) firm; (*permanente*) permanent; (*trabajo*) steady; (*color*) fast ♦ *adv*: **mirar** ~ to stare.

fila ['fila] *nf* row; (*MIL*) rank; (*cadena*) line; (*MIL*) rank; (*en marcha*) file; ~ **india** single file; **ponerse en** ~ to line up, get into line; **primera** ~ front row.

filántropo, a [fi'lantropo, a] *nm/f* philanthropist.

filarmónico, a [filar'moniko, a] *adj, nf* philharmonic.

filatelia [fila'telja] *nf* philately, stamp collecting.

filatelista [filate'lista] *nm/f* philatelist, stamp collector.

filete [fi'lete] *nm* (*carne*) fillet steak; (*de cerdo*) tenderloin; (*pescado*) fillet; (*MEC: rosca*) thread.

filiación [filja'θjon] *nf* (*POL etc*) affiliation; (*señas*) particulars *pl*; (*MIL, POLICÍA*) records *pl*.

filial [fi'ljal] *adj* filial ♦ *nf* subsidiary; (*sucursal*) branch.

Filipinas [fili'pinas] *nfpl*: **las (Islas)** ~ the Philippines.

filipino, a [fili'pino, a] *adj, nm/f* Philippine.

film [film], *pl* **films** *nm* = **filme**.

filmación [filma'θjon] *nf* filming, shooting.

filmar [fil'mar] *vt* to film, shoot.

filme ['filme] *nm* film, movie (*US*).

filmoteca [filmo'teka] *nf* film library.

filo ['filo] *nm* (*gen*) edge; **sacar** ~ **a** to sharpen; **al** ~ **del medio día** at about midday; **de doble** ~ double-edged.

filología [filolo'xia] *nf* philology.

filólogo, a [fi'loloɣo, a] *nm/f* philologist.

filón [fi'lon] *nm* (*MINERÍA*) vein, lode; (*fig*) gold mine.

filoso, a [fi'loso, a] *adj* (*AM*) sharp.

filosofía [filoso'fia] *nf* philosophy.

filosófico, a [filo'sofiko, a] *adj* philosophic(al).

filósofo, a [fi'losofo, a] *nm/f* philosopher.

filtración [filtra'θjon] *nf* (*TEC*) filtration; (*INFORM*) sorting; (*fig: de fondos*) misappropriation; (*de datos*) leak.

filtrar [fil'trar] *vt, vi* to filter, strain; (*información*) to leak; ~**se** *vr* to filter; (*fig: dinero*) to dwindle.

filtro ['filtro] *nm* (*TEC, utensilio*) filter.

filudo, a [fi'luðo, a] *adj* (*AM*) sharp.

fin [fin] *nm* end; (*objetivo*) aim, purpose; **a** ~ **de cuentas** at the end of the day; **al** ~ **y al cabo** when all's said and done; **a** ~ **de** in order to; **por** ~ finally; **en** ~ (*resumiendo*) in short; **¡en** ~! (*resignación*) oh, well!; ~ **de archivo** (*INFORM*) end-of-file; ~ **de semana** weekend; **sin** ~ endless(ly).

final [fi'nal] *adj* final ♦ *nm* end, conclusion ♦ *nf* (*DEPORTE*) final.

finalice [fina'liθe] *etc vb V* **finalizar**.

finalidad [finali'ðað] *nf* finality; (*propósito*) purpose, aim.

finalista [fina'lista] *nm/f* finalist.

finalizar [finali'θar] *vt* to end, finish ♦ *vi* to end, come to an end; ~ **la sesión** (*INFORM*) to log out *o* off.

financiación [finanθja'θjon] *nf* financing.

financiar [finan'θjar] *vt* to finance.

financiero, a [finan'θjero, a] *adj* financial ♦ *nm/f* financier.

financista [finan'sista] *nm/f* (*AM*) financier.

finanzas [fi'nanθas] *nfpl* finances.

finca ['finka] *nf* country estate.

fineza [fi'neθa] *nf* (*cualidad*) fineness; (*modales*) refinement.

fingir [fin'xir] *vt* (*simular*) to simulate, feign; (*pretextar*) to sham, fake ♦ *vi* (*aparentar*) to pretend; ~**se** *vr*: ~**se dormido** to pretend to be asleep.

finiquitar [finiki'tar] *vt* (*ECON: cuenta*) to settle and close.

Finisterre [finis'terre] *nm*: **el cabo de ~** Cape Finisterre.

finja ['finxa] *etc vb* V **fingir**.

finlandés, esa [finlan'des, esa] *adj* Finnish ♦ *nm/f* Finn ♦ *nm* (LING) Finnish.

Finlandia [fin'landja] *nf* Finland.

fino, a ['fino, a] *adj* fine; (*delgado*) slender; (*de buenas maneras*) polite, refined; (*inteligente*) shrewd; (*punta*) sharp; (*gusto*) discriminating; (*oído*) sharp; (*jerez*) fino, dry ♦ *nm* (*jerez*) dry sherry.

finura [fi'nura] *nf* (*calidad*) fineness; (*cortesía*) politeness; (*elegancia*) elegance; (*agudeza*) shrewdness.

FIP [fip] *nf abr* (ESP) = *Formación Intensiva Profesional*.

firma ['firma] *nf* signature; (COM) firm, company.

firmamento [firma'mento] *nm* firmament.

firmante [fir'mante] *adj, nm/f* signatory; **los abajo ~s** the undersigned.

firmar [fir'mar] *vt* to sign; **~ un contrato** (COM: *colocarse*) to sign on; **firmado y sellado** signed and sealed.

firme ['firme] *adj* firm; (*estable*) stable; (*sólido*) solid; (*constante*) steady; (*decidido*) resolute; (*duro*) hard; ¡**~s!** (MIL) attention!; **oferta en ~** (COM) firm offer ♦ *nm* road (surface).

firmemente [firme'mente] *adv* firmly.

firmeza [fir'meθa] *nf* firmness; (*constancia*) steadiness; (*solidez*) solidity.

fiscal [fis'kal] *adj* fiscal ♦ *nm* (JUR) ≈ Crown Prosecutor, Procurator Fiscal (*Escocia*), district attorney (US).

fiscalice [fiska'liθe] *etc vb* V **fiscalizar**.

fiscalizar [fiskali'θar] *vt* (*controlar*) to control; (*registrar*) to inspect (officially); (*fig*) to criticize.

fisco ['fisko] *nm* (*hacienda*) treasury, exchequer; **declarar algo al ~** to declare sth for tax purposes.

fisgar [fis'ɣar] *vt* to pry into.

fisgón, ona [fis'ɣon, ona] *adj* nosey.

fisgue ['fisɣe] *etc vb* V **fisgar**.

físico, a ['fisiko, a] *adj* physical ♦ *nm* physique; (*aspecto*) appearance, looks ♦ *nm/f* physicist ♦ *nf* physics *sg*.

fisioterapeuta [fisjotera'peuta] *nm/f* physiotherapist.

fisioterapia [fisjote'rapja] *nf* physiotherapy.

fisioterapista [fisjotera'pista] *nm/f* (AM) physiotherapist.

fisonomía [fisono'mia] *nf* physiognomy, features *pl*.

fisonomista [fisono'mista] *nm/f*: **ser buen ~** to have a good memory for faces.

flac(c)idez [fla(k)θi'ðeθ] *nf* softness, flabbiness.

flác(c)ido, a ['fla(k)θiðo, a] *adj* flabby.

flaco, a ['flako, a] *adj* (*muy delgado*) skinny, thin; (*débil*) weak, feeble.

flagrante [fla'ɣrante] *adj* flagrant.

flamante [fla'mante] *adj* (*fam*) brilliant; (: *nuevo*) brand-new.

flamear [flame'ar] *vt* (CULIN) to flambé.

flamenco, a [fla'menko, a] *adj* (*de Flandes*) Flemish; (*baile, música*) gipsy ♦ *nm/f* Fleming; **los ~s** the Flemish ♦ *nm* (LING) Flemish; (*baile, música*) flamenco; (ZOOL) flamingo.

flan [flan] *nm* creme caramel.

flanco ['flanko] *nm* side; (MIL) flank.

Flandes ['flandes] *nm* Flanders.

flanquear [flanke'ar] *vt* to flank; (MIL) to outflank.

flaquear [flake'ar] *vi* (*debilitarse*) to weaken; (*persona*) to slack.

flaqueza [fla'keθa] *nf* (*delgadez*) thinness, leanness; (*fig*) weakness.

flaquísimo, a [fla'kisimo, a] *adj superlativo de* **flaco**.

flash [flas] *pl* **flashes** [flas] *nm* (FOTO) flash.

flato ['flato] *nm*: **el** (*o* **un**) **~** the (*o* a) stitch.

flauta ['flauta] (MUS) *nf* flute ♦ *nm/f* flautist, flute player; ¡**la gran ~!** (AM) my God!; **hijo de la gran ~** (AM *fam!*) bastard (!), son of a bitch (US!).

flecha ['fletʃa] *nf* arrow.

flechazo [fle'tʃaθo] *nm* (*acción*) bowshot; (*fam*): **fue un ~** it was love at first sight.

fleco ['fleko] *nm* fringe.

flema ['flema] *nm* phlegm.

flemático, a [fle'matiko, a] *adj* phlegmatic; (*tono etc*) matter-of-fact.

flemón [fle'mon] *nm* (MED) gumboil.

flequillo [fle'kiʎo] *nm* (*pelo*) fringe.

fletar [fle'tar] *vt* (COM) to charter; (*embarcar*) to load; (AUTO) to lease (-purchase).

flete ['flete] *nm* (*carga*) freight; (*alquiler*) charter; (*precio*) freightage; **~ debido** (COM) freight forward; **~ sobre compras** (COM) freight inward.

flexible [flek'siβle] *adj* flexible; (*individuo*) compliant.

flexión [flek'sjon] *nf* (DEPORTE) bend; (: *en el suelo*) press-up.

flexo ['flekso] *nm* adjustable table lamp.

flipper ['fliper] *nm* pinball machine.

flirtear [flirte'ar] *vi* to flirt.

FLN *nm abr* (POL: ESP, Perú, Venezuela) = *Frente de Liberación Nacional*.

flojear [floxe'ar] *vi* (*piernas: al andar*) to

give way; (*alumno*) to do badly; (*cosecha, mercado*) to be poor.

flojera [flo'xera] *nf* (*AM*) laziness; **me da ~** I can't be bothered.

flojo, a ['floxo, a] *adj* (*gen*) loose; (*sin fuerzas*) limp; (*débil*) weak; (*viento*) light; (*bebida*) weak; (*trabajo*) poor; (*actitud*) slack; (*precio*) low; (*COM: mercado*) dull, slack; (*AM*) lazy.

flor [flor] *nf* flower; (*piropo*) compliment; **la ~ y nata de la sociedad** (*fig*) the cream of society; **en la ~ de la vida** in the prime of life; **a ~ de** on the surface of.

flora ['flora] *nf* flora.

florecer [flore'θer] *vi* (*BOT*) to flower, bloom; (*fig*) to flourish.

floreciente [florc'θjcntc] *udj* (*BOT*) in flower, flowering; (*fig*) thriving.

Florencia [flo'renθja] *nf* Florence.

florero [flo'rero] *nm* vase.

florezca [flo'reθka] *etc vb V* **florecer**.

florista [flo'rista] *nm/f* florist.

floristería [floriste'ria] *nf* florist's (shop).

flota ['flota] *nf* fleet.

flotación [flota'θjon] *nf* (*COM*) flotation.

flotador [flota'ðor] *nm* (*gen*) float; (*para nadar*) rubber ring; (*de cisterna*) ballcock.

flotante [flo'tante] *adj* floating; (*INFORM*): **de coma ~** floating-point.

flotar [flo'tar] *vi* to float.

flote ['flote] *nm*: **a ~** afloat; **ponerse a ~** (*fig*) to get back on one's feet.

FLS *nm abr* (*POL: Nicaragua*) = *Frente de Liberación Sandinista.*

fluctuación [fluktwa'θjon] *nf* fluctuation.

fluctuante [fluk'twante] *adj* fluctuating.

fluctuar [fluk'twar] *vi* (*oscilar*) to fluctuate.

fluidez [flui'ðeθ] *nf* fluidity; (*fig*) fluency.

fluido, a ['flwiðo, a] *adj* fluid; (*lenguaje*) fluent; (*estilo*) smooth ♦ *nm* (*líquido*) fluid.

fluir [flu'ir] *vi* to flow.

flujo ['fluxo] *nm* flow; (*POL*) swing; (*NAUT*) rising tide; **~ y reflujo** ebb and flow; **~ de sangre** (*MED*) haemorrhage (*BRIT*), hemorrhage (*US*); **~ positivo/negativo de efectivo** (*COM*) positive/negative cash flow.

flúor ['fluor] *nm* fluorine; (*en dentífrico*) fluoride.

fluorescente [flwores'θente] *adj* fluorescent ♦ *nm* (*tb*: **tubo ~**) fluorescent tube.

fluoruro [flwo'ruro] *nm* fluoride.

fluvial [fluβi'al] *adj* fluvial, river *cpd*.

fluyendo [flu'jendo] *etc vb V* **fluir**.

F.M. *nf abr* (= *Frecuencia Modulada*) F.M.

FMI *nm abr* (= *Fondo Monetario Internacional*) I.M.F.

F.N. *nf abr* (*ESP POL*) = *Fuerza Nueva* ♦ *nm*

= *Frente Nacional.*

FNPT *nm abr* (*ESP*) = *Fondo Nacional de Protección del Trabajo.*

f.º *abr* (= *folio*) fo., fol.

foca ['foka] *nf* seal.

foco ['foko] *nm* focus; (*centro*) focal point; (*fuente*) source; (*de incendio*) seat; (*ELEC*) floodlight; (*TEAT*) spotlight; (*AM*) (light) bulb, light.

fofo, a ['fofo, a] *adj* (*esponjoso*) soft, spongy; (*músculo*) flabby.

fogata [fo'γata] *nf* (*hoguera*) bonfire.

fogón [fo'γon] *nm* (*de cocina*) ring, burner.

fogoso, a [fo'γoso, a] *adj* spirited.

foja ['foxa] *nf* (*AM*) sheet (of paper); **~ de servicios** record (file).

fol. *abr* (= *folio*) fo., fol.

folder, fólder ['folder] *nm* (*AM*) folder.

folio ['foljo] *nm* folio; (*hoja*) leaf.

folklore [fol'klore] *nm* folklore.

folklórico, a [fol'kloriko, a] *adj* traditional.

follaje [fo'ʎaxe] *nm* foliage.

follar [fo'ʎar] *vt, vi* (*fam!*) to fuck (*!*).

folletinesco, a [foʎetin'esko, a] *adj* melodramatic.

folleto [fo'ʎeto] *nm* pamphlet; (*COM*) brochure; (*prospecto*) leaflet; (*ESCOL etc*) handout.

follón [fo'ʎon] *nm* (*fam: lío*) mess; (: *conmoción*) fuss, rumpus, shindy; **armar un ~** to kick up a fuss; **se armó un ~** there was a hell of a row.

fomentar [fomen'tar] *vt* (*MED*) to foment; (*fig: promover*) to promote, foster; (*odio etc*) to stir up.

fomento [fo'mento] *nm* (*fig: ayuda*) fostering; (*promoción*) promotion.

fonda ['fonda] *nf* ≈ guest house; *V tb* **hotel**.

fondear [fonde'ar] *vt* (*NAUT: sondear*) to sound; (*barco*) to search.

fondo ['fondo] *nm* (*de caja etc*) bottom; (*medida*) depth; (*de coche, sala*) back; (*ARTE etc*) background; (*reserva*) fund; (*fig: carácter*) nature; **~s** *nmpl* (*COM*) funds, resources; **~ de amortización** (*COM*) sinking fund; **F~ Monetario Internacional** International Monetary Fund; **~ del mar** sea bed *o* floor; **una investigación a ~** a thorough investigation; **en el ~** at bottom, deep down; **tener buen ~** to be good natured.

fonética [fo'netika] *nf* phonetics *sg*.

fono ['fono] *nm* (*AM*) telephone (number).

fonobuzón [fonoβu'θon] *nm* voice mail.

fonógrafo [fo'noγrafo] *nm* (*esp AM*) gramophone, phonograph (*US*).

fonología [fonolo'xia] *nf* phonology.

fontanería [fontane'ria] *nf* plumbing.

fontanero [fonta'nero] nm plumber.
footing ['futin] nm jogging; **hacer** ~ to jog.
F.O.P. [fop] nfpl abr (ESP) = **Fuerzas del Orden Público**.
forajido [fora'xiðo] nm outlaw.
foráneo, a [fo'raneo, a] adj foreign ♦ nmlf outsider.
forastero, a [foras'tero, a] nmlf stranger.
forcé [for'θe] vb V **forzar**.
forcejear [forθexe'ar] vi (luchar) to struggle.
forcemos [for'θemos] etc vb V **forzar**.
fórceps ['forθeps] nm inv forceps.
forense [fo'rense] adj forensic ♦ nmlf pathologist.
forestal [fores'tal] adj forest cpd.
forjar [for'xar] vt to forge; (formar) to form.
forma ['forma] nf (figura) form, shape; (molde) mould, pattern; (MED) fitness; (método) way, means; **estar en** ~ to be fit; ~ **de pago** (COM) method of payment; **las** ~**s** the conventions; **de** ~ **que** ... so that ...; **de todas** ~**s** in any case.
formación [forma'θjon] nf (gen) formation; (enseñanza) training; ~ **profesional** vocational training; ~ **fuera del trabajo** off-the-job training; ~ **en el trabajo** o **sobre la práctica** on-the-job training.
formal [for'mal] adj (gen) formal; (fig: persona) serious; (: de fiar) reliable; (conducta) steady.
formalice [forma'liθe] etc vb V **formalizar**.
formalidad [formali'ðað] nf formality; seriousness; reliability; steadiness.
formalizar [formali'θar] vt (JUR) to formalize; (plan) to draw up; (situación) to put in order, regularize; ~**se** vr (situación) to be put in order, be regularized.
formar [for'mar] vt (componer) to form, shape; (constituir) to make up, constitute; (ESCOL) to train, educate ♦ vi (MIL) to fall in; (DEPORTE) to line up; ~**se** vr (ESCOL) to be trained (o educated); (cobrar forma) to form, take form; (desarrollarse) to develop.
formatear [formate'ar] vt (INFORM) to format.
formateo [forma'teo] nm (INFORM) formatting.
formato [for'mato] nm (INFORM): **sin** ~ (disco, texto) unformatted; ~ **de registro** record format.
formica ® [for'mika] nf Formica ®.
formidable [formi'ðaßle] adj (temible) formidable; (asombroso) tremendous.
fórmula ['formula] nf formula.
formular [formu'lar] vt (queja) to lodge;

(petición) to draw up; (pregunta) to pose, formulate; (idea) to formulate.
formulario [formu'larjo] nm form; ~ **de solicitud/de pedido** (COM) application/ order form; **llenar un** ~ to fill in a form; ~ **contínuo desplegable** (INFORM) fanfold paper.
fornicar [forni'kar] vi to fornicate.
fornido, a [for'niðo, a] adj well-built.
fornique [for'nike] etc vb V **fornicar**.
foro ['foro] nm (gen) forum; (JUR) court.
forofo, a [fo'rofo, a] nmlf fan.
FORPPA ['forpa] nm abr (ESP) = Fondo de Ordenación y Regulación de Productos y Precios Agrarios.
FORPRONU [for'pronu] nf abr (= Fuerza de Protección de las Naciones Unidas) UNPROFOR.
forrado, a [fo'rraðo, a] adj (ropa) lined; (fam) well-heeled.
forrar [fo'rrar] vt (abrigo) to line; (libro) to cover; (coche) to upholster; ~**se** vr (fam) to line one's pockets.
forro ['forro] nm (de cuaderno) cover; (costura) lining; (de sillón) upholstery.
fortalecer [fortale'θer] vt to strengthen; ~**se** vr to fortify o.s.; (opinión etc) to become stronger.
fortaleza [forta'leθa] nf (MIL) fortress, stronghold; (fuerza) strength; (determinación) resolution.
fortalezca [forta'leθka] etc vb V **fortalecer**.
fortificar [fortifi'kar] vt to fortify; (fig) to strengthen.
fortifique [forti'fike] etc vb V **fortificar**.
fortísimo, a [for'tisimo, a] adj superlativo de **fuerte**.
fortuito, a [for'twito, a] adj accidental, chance cpd.
fortuna [for'tuna] nf (suerte) fortune, (good) luck; (riqueza) fortune, wealth.
forzar [for'θar] vt (puerta) to force (open); (compeler) to compel; (violar) to rape; (ojos etc) to strain.
forzoso, a [for'θoso, a] adj necessary; (inevitable) inescapable; (obligatorio) compulsory.
forzudo, a [for'θuðo, a] adj burly.
fosa ['fosa] nf (sepultura) grave; (en tierra) pit; (MED) cavity; ~**s nasales** nostrils.
fosfato [fos'fato] nm phosphate.
fosforescente [fosfores'θente] adj phosphorescent.
fósforo ['fosforo] nm (QUÍMICA) phosphorus; (esp AM: cerilla) match.
fósil [fosil] adj fossil, fossilized ♦ nm fossil.
foso ['foso] nm ditch; (TEAT) pit; (AUTO): ~

de reconocimiento inspection pit.
foto ['foto] *nf* photo, snap(shot); **sacar una**
~ to take a photo *o* picture.
fotocopia [foto'kopja] *nf* photocopy.
fotocopiadora [fotokopja'ðora] *nf*
photocopier.
fotocopiar [fotoko'pjar] *vt* to photocopy.
fotogénico, a [foto'xeniko, a] *adj*
photogenic.
fotografía [fotoxra'fia] *nf* (*arte*)
photography; (*una* ~) photograph.
fotografiar [fotoxra'fjar] *vt* to photograph.
fotógrafo, a [fo'toxrafo, a] *nm/f*
photographer.
fotomatón [fotoma'ton] *nm* (*cabina*) photo
booth.
fotómetro [fo'tometro] *nm* (*FOTO*) light
meter.
fotonovela [fotono'ßela] *nf* photo-story.
foulard [fu'lar] *nm* (head)scarf.
FP *nf abr* (*ESP: ESCOL, COM*) = *Formación
Profesional* ♦ *nm abr* (*POL*) = *Frente Popular.*
FPLP *nm abr* (*POL:* = *Frente Popular para la
Liberación de Palestina*) PFLP.
Fr. *abr* (= *Fray, franco*) Fr.
frac [frak], *pl* **fracs** *o* **fraques** ['frakes] *nm*
dress coat, tails.
fracasar [fraka'sar] *vi* (*gen*) to fail; (*plan
etc*) to fall through.
fracaso [fra'kaso] *nm* (*desgracia, revés*)
failure; (*de negociaciones etc*) collapse,
breakdown.
fracción [frak'θjon] *nf* fraction; (*POL*)
faction, splinter group.
fraccionamiento [fraksjona'mjento] *nm*
(*AM*) housing estate.
fractura [frak'tura] *nf* fracture, break.
fragancia [fra'xanθja] *nf* (*olor*) fragrance,
perfume.
fragante [fra'xante] *adj* fragrant, scented.
fraganti [fra'xanti]: **in** ~ *adv*: **coger a algn
in** ~ to catch sb red-handed.
fragata [fra'xata] *nf* frigate.
frágil ['fraxil] *adj* (*débil*) fragile; (*COM*)
breakable; (*fig*) frail, delicate.
fragilidad [fraxili'ðað] *nf* fragility; (*de
persona*) frailty.
fragmento [fra'xmento] *nm* fragment;
(*pedazo*) piece; (*de discurso*) excerpt; (*de
canción*) snatch.
fragor [fra'xor] *nm* (*ruido intenso*) din.
fragua ['fraxwa] *nf* forge.
fraguar [fra'xwar] *vt* to forge; (*fig*) to
concoct ♦ *vi* to harden.
fragüe ['fraxwe] *etc vb V* **fraguar.**
fraile ['fraile] *nm* (*REL*) friar; (: *monje*)
monk.
frambuesa [fram'bwesa] *nf* raspberry.

francés, esa [fran'θes, esa] *adj* French
♦ *nm/f* Frenchman/woman ♦ *nm* (*LING*)
French.
Francia ['franθja] *nf* France.
franco, a ['franko, a] *adj* (*cándido*) frank,
open; (*COM: exento*) free ♦ *nm* (*moneda*)
franc; ~ **de derechos** duty-free; ~ **al
costado del buque** (*COM*) free alongside
ship; ~ **puesto sobre vagón** (*COM*) free
on rail; ~ **a bordo** free on board.
francotirador, a [frankotira'ðor, a] *nm/f*
sniper.
franela [fra'nela] *nf* flannel.
franja ['franxa] *nf* fringe; (*de uniforme*)
stripe; (*de tierra etc*) strip.
franquear [franke'ar] *vt* (*camino*) to clear;
(*carta, paquete*) to frank, stamp; (*obstáculo*) to overcome; (*COM etc*) to free, exempt.
franqueo [fran'keo] *nm* postage.
franqueza [fran'keθa] *nf* frankness.
franquicia [fran'kiθja] *nf* exemption; ~ **aduanera** exemption from customs duties.
franquismo [fran'kismo] *nm*: **el** ~ (*sistema*)
the Franco system; (*período*) the Franco
years; *see boxed note.*

FRANQUISMO

*Both the political reign and style of
government of Francisco Franco (from the
end of the Spanish Civil War in 1939 until
his death in 1975) are commonly called*
franquismo. *The General was a powerful,
authoritarian, right-wing dictator, who
promoted traditional Catholic values and
self-sufficiency. From the 1960s on, Spain
gradually opened its doors to the outside
world and this coincided with a period of
economic growth and the rise of internal
political opposition. On Franco's death
Spain became a democratic constitutional
monarchy.*

---

franquista [fran'kista] *adj* pro-Franco
♦ *nm/f* supporter of Franco.
frasco ['frasko] *nm* bottle, flask; ~ **al vacío**
(vacuum) flask.
frase ['frase] *nf* sentence; (*locución*)
phrase, expression; ~ **hecha** set phrase.
fraternal [frater'nal] *adj* brotherly,
fraternal.
fraude ['frauðe] *nm* (*cualidad*) dishonesty;
(*acto*) fraud, swindle.
fraudulento, a [frauðu'lento, a] *adj*
fraudulent.
frazada [fra'saða] *nf* (*AM*) blanket.
frecuencia [fre'kwenθja] *nf* frequency; **con**
~ frequently, often; ~ **de red** (*INFORM*)

mains frequency; ~ **del reloj** (*INFORM*) clock speed; ~ **telefónica** voice frequency.

frecuentar [frekwen'tar] *vt* (*lugar*) to frequent; (*persona*) to see frequently *o* often; ~ **la buena sociedad** to mix in high society.

frecuente [fre'kwente] *adj* frequent; (*costumbre*) common; (*vicio*) rife.

fregadero [freɣa'ðero] *nm* (kitchen) sink.

fregado, a [fre'ɣaðo, a] *adj* (*AM fam!*) damn, bloody (*!*).

fregar [fre'ɣar] *vt* (*frotar*) to scrub; (*platos*) to wash (up); (*AM*) to annoy.

fregón, ona [fre'ɣon, ona] *adj* = **fregado** ♦ *nf* (*utensilio*) mop; (*pey: sirvienta*) skivvy.

fregué [fre'ɣe], **freguemos** [fre'ɣemos] *etc vb V* **fregar**.

freidora [frei'ðora] *nf* deep-fat fryer.

freír [fre'ir] *vt* to fry.

fréjol ['frexol] *nm* = **fríjol**.

frenar [fre'nar] *vt* to brake; (*fig*) to check.

frenazo [fre'naθo] *nm*: **dar un** ~ to brake sharply.

frenesí [frene'si] *nm* frenzy.

frenético, a [fre'netiko, a] *adj* frantic; **ponerse** ~ to lose one's head.

freno ['freno] *nm* (*TEC, AUTO*) brake; (*de cabalgadura*) bit; (*fig*) check.

frente ['frente] *nm* (*ARQ, MIL, POL*) front; (*de objeto*) front part ♦ *nf* forehead, brow; ~ **de batalla** battle front; **hacer** ~ **común con algn** to make common cause with sb; ~ **a** in front of; (*en situación opuesta de*) opposite; **chocar de** ~ to crash head-on; **hacer** ~ **a** to face up to.

fresa ['fresa] *nf* (*ESP: fruta*) strawberry; (*de dentista*) drill.

fresco, a ['fresko, a] *adj* (*nuevo*) fresh; (*huevo*) newly-laid; (*frío*) cool; (*descarado*) cheeky, bad-mannered ♦ *nm* (*aire*) fresh air; (*ARTE*) fresco; (*AM: bebida*) fruit juice *o* drink ♦ *nm/f* (*fam*) shameless person; (*persona insolente*) impudent person; **tomar el** ~ to get some fresh air; **¡qué** ~! what a cheek!

frescor [fres'kor] *nm* freshness.

frescura [fres'kura] *nf* freshness; (*descaro*) cheek, nerve; (*calma*) calmness.

fresno ['fresno] *nm* ash (tree).

fresón [fre'son] *nm* strawberry.

frialdad [frjal'dað] *nf* (*gen*) coldness; (*indiferencia*) indifference.

fricción [frik'θjon] *nf* (*gen*) friction; (*acto*) rub(bing); (*MED*) massage; (*POL, fig etc*) friction, trouble.

friega ['frjeɣa] *etc*, **friegue** ['frjeɣe] *etc vb V* **fregar**.

friendo [fri'endo] *etc vb V* **freír**.

frigidez [frixi'ðeθ] *nf* frigidity.

frígido, a ['frixiðo, a] *adj* frigid.

frigorífico, a [friɣo'rifiko, a] *adj* refrigerating ♦ *nm* refrigerator; (*camión*) freezer lorry *o* truck (*US*); **instalación frigorífica** cold-storage plant.

frijol [fri'xol], **fríjol** ['frixol] *nm* kidney bean.

frió [fri'o] *vb V* **freír**.

frío, a ['frio, a] *etc vb V* **freír** ♦ *adj* cold; (*fig: indiferente*) unmoved, indifferent; (*poco entusiasta*) chilly ♦ *nm* cold(ness); indifference; **¡qué** ~! how cold it is!

friolento, a [frjo'lento, a] (*AM*), **friolero, a** [frjo'lero, a] *adj* sensitive to cold.

frito, a ['frito, a] *pp de* **freír** ♦ *adj* fried ♦ *nm* fry; **me trae** ~ **ese hombre** I'm sick and tired of that man; ~**s variados** mixed grill.

frívolo, a ['friβolo, a] *adj* frivolous.

frondoso, a [fron'doso, a] *adj* leafy.

frontal [fron'tal] *nm*: **choque** ~ head-on collision.

frontera [fron'tera] *nf* frontier; (*línea divisoria*) border; (*zona*) frontier area.

fronterizo, a [fronte'riθo, a] *adj* frontier *cpd*; (*contiguo*) bordering.

frontón [fron'ton] *nm* (*DEPORTE: cancha*) pelota court; (: *juego*) pelota.

frotar [fro'tar] *vt* to rub; (*fósforo*) to strike; ~**se** *vr*: ~**se las manos** to rub one's hands.

frs. *abr* (= *francos*) fr.

fructífero, a [fruk'tifero, a] *adj* productive, fruitful.

frugal [fru'ɣal] *adj* frugal.

fruncir [frun'θir] *vt* (*COSTURA*) to gather; (*ceño*) to frown; (*labios*) to purse.

frunza ['frunθa] *etc vb V* **fruncir**.

frustración [frustra'θjon] *nf* frustration.

frustrar [frus'trar] *vt* to frustrate; ~**se** *vr* to be frustrated; (*plan etc*) to fail.

fruta ['fruta] *nf* fruit.

frutal [fru'tal] *adj* fruit-bearing, fruit *cpd* ♦ *nm*: (*árbol*) ~ fruit tree.

frutería [frute'ria] *nf* fruit shop.

frutero, a [fru'tero, a] *adj* fruit *cpd* ♦ *nm/f* fruiterer ♦ *nm* fruit dish *o* bowl.

frutilla [fru'tiʎa] *nf* (*AM*) strawberry.

fruto ['fruto] *nm* (*BOT*) fruit; (*fig: resultado*) result, outcome; ~**s secos** ≈ nuts and raisins.

FSLN *nm abr* (*POL: Nicaragua*) = *Frente Sandinista de Liberación Nacional*.

fue [fwe] *vb V* **ser, ir**.

fuego ['fweɣo] *nm* (*gen*) fire; (*CULIN*: *gas*) burner, ring; (*MIL*) fire; (*fig*: *pasión*) fire, passion; ~**s artificiales** *o* **de artificio** fireworks; **prender** ~ **a** to set fire to; **a** ~ **lento** on a low flame *o* gas; **¡alto el** ~**!** cease fire!; **estar entre dos** ~**s** to be in the crossfire; **¿tienes** ~**?** have you (got) a light?

fuelle ['fweʎe] *nm* bellows *pl*.

fuel-oil [fuel'oil] *nm* paraffin (*BRIT*), kerosene (*US*).

fuente ['fwente] *nf* fountain; (*manantial*, *fig*) spring; (*origen*) source; (*plato*) large dish; ~ **de alimentación** (*INFORM*) power supply; **de** ~ **desconocida/fidedigna** from an unknown/reliable source.

fuera ['fwera] *etc vb V* **cor, ir** ♦ *adv* out(side); (*en otra parte*) away; (*excepto, salvo*) except, save ♦ *prep*: ~ **de** outside; (*fig*) besides; ~ **de alcance** out of reach; ~ **de combate** out of action; (*boxeo*) knocked out; ~ **de sí** beside o.s.; **por** ~ (on the) outside; **los de** ~ strangers, newcomers; **estar** ~ (*en el extranjero*) to be abroad.

fuera-borda [fwera'ɓorða] *nm inv* outboard engine *o* motor.

fuerce ['fwerθe] *etc vb V* **forzar**.

fuereño, a [fwe'reɲo, a] *nm/f* (*AM*) outsider.

fuero ['fwero] *nm* (*carta municipal*) municipal charter; (*leyes locales*) local *o* regional law code; (*privilegio*) privilege; (*autoridad*) jurisdiction; (*fig*): **en mi** *etc* ~ **interno** in my *etc* heart of hearts ..., deep down ....

fuerte ['fwerte] *adj* strong; (*golpe*) hard; (*ruido*) loud; (*comida*) rich; (*lluvia*) heavy; (*dolor*) intense ♦ *adv* strongly; hard; loud(ly) ♦ *nm* (*MIL*) fort, strongpoint; (*fig*): **el canto no es mi** ~ singing is not my strong point.

fuerza ['fwerθa] *etc vb V* **forzar** ♦ *nf* (*fortaleza*) strength; (*TEC, ELEC*) power; (*coacción*) force; (*violencia*) violence; (*MIL*: *tb*: ~**s**) forces *pl*; ~ **de arrastre** (*TEC*) pulling power; ~ **de brazos** manpower; ~ **mayor** force majeure; ~ **bruta** brute force; ~**s armadas** (FF.AA.) armed forces; ~ **de Orden Público** (F.O.P.) police (forces); ~ **vital** vitality; **a** ~ **de** by (dint of); **cobrar** ~**s** to recover one's strength; **tener** ~**s para** to have the strength to; **hacer algo a la** ~ to be forced to do sth; **con** ~ **legal** (*COM*) legally binding; **a la** ~, **por** ~ of necessity; ~ **de voluntad** willpower.

fuete ['fwete] *nm* (*AM*) whip.

fuga ['fuɣa] *nf* (*huida*) flight, escape; (*de enamorados*) elopement; (*de gas etc*) leak; ~ **de cerebros** (*fig*) brain drain.

fugarse [fu'ɣarse] *vr* to flee, escape.

fugaz [fu'ɣaθ] *adj* fleeting.

fugitivo, a [fuxi'tiβo, a] *adj* fugitive, fleeing ♦ *nm/f* fugitive.

fugue ['fuɣe] *etc vb V* **fugarse**.

fui [fwi] *etc vb V* **ser, ir**.

fulano, a [fu'lano, a] *nm/f* so-and-so, what's-his-name.

fulgor [ful'ɣor] *nm* brilliance.

fulminante [fulmi'nante] *adj* (*pólvora*) fulminating; (*fig*: *mirada*) withering; (*MED*) fulminant; (*fam*) terrific, tremendous.

fulminar [fulmi'nar] *vt*: **caer fulminado por un rayo** to be struck down by lightning; ~ **a algn con la mirada** to look daggers at sb.

fumador, a [fuma'ðor, a] *nm/f* smoker; **no** ~ non-smoker.

fumar [fu'mar] *vt, vi* to smoke; ~**se** *vr* (*disipar*) to squander; ~ **en pipa** to smoke a pipe.

fumigar [fumi'ɣar] *vt* to fumigate.

funámbulo, a [fu'nambulo, a], **funambulista** [funambu'lista] *nm/f* tightrope walker.

función [fun'θjon] *nf* function; (*de puesto*) duties *pl*; (*TEAT etc*) show; **entrar en funciones** to take up one's duties; ~ **de tarde/de noche** matinée/evening performance.

funcional [funθjo'nal] *adj* functional.

funcionamiento [funθjona'mjento] *nm* functioning; (*TEC*) working; **en** ~ (*COM*) on stream; **entrar en** ~ to come into operation.

funcionar [funθjo'nar] *vi* (*gen*) to function; (*máquina*) to work; "**no funciona**" "out of order".

funcionario, a [funθjo'narjo, a] *nm/f* official; (*público*) civil servant.

funda ['funda] *nf* (*gen*) cover; (*de almohada*) pillowcase; ~ **protectora del disco** (*INFORM*) disk-jacket.

fundación [funda'θjon] *nf* foundation.

fundado, a [fun'daðo, a] *adj* (*justificado*) well-founded.

fundamental [fundamen'tal] *adj* fundamental, basic.

fundamentalismo [fundamenta'lismo] *nm* fundamentalism.

fundamentalista [fundamenta'lista] *adj*, *nm/f* fundamentalist.

fundamentar [fundamen'tar] *vt* (*poner base*) to lay the foundations of; (*establecer*) to found; (*fig*) to base.

fundamento [funda'mento] *nm* (*base*)
foundation; (*razón*) grounds; **eso carece
de** ~ that is groundless.
fundar [fun'dar] *vt* to found; (*crear*) to set
up; (*fig: basar*): ~ **(en)** to base *o* found
(on); **~se** *vr*: **~se en** to be founded on.
fundición [fundi'θjon] *nf* (*acción*) smelting;
(*fábrica*) foundry; (*TIP*) fount (*BRIT*), font.
fundir [fun'dir] *vt* (*gen*) to fuse; (*metal*) to
smelt, melt down; (*COM*) to merge;
(*estatua*) to cast; **~se** *vr* (*colores etc*) to
merge, blend; (*unirse*) to fuse together;
(*ELEC: fusible, lámpara etc*) to blow; (*nieve
etc*) to melt.
fúnebre ['funeßre] *adj* funeral *cpd*,
funereal.
funeral [fune'ral] *nm* funeral.
funeraria [fune'rarja] *nf* undertaker's
(*BRIT*), mortician's (*US*).
funesto, a [fu'nesto, a] *adj* ill-fated;
(*desastroso*) fatal.
fungir [fun'xir] *vi*: ~ **de** (*AM*) to act as.
furgón [fur'xon] *nm* wagon.
furgoneta [furxo'neta] *nf* (*AUTO, COM*)
(transit) van (*BRIT*), pickup (truck) (*US*).
furia ['furja] *nf* (*ira*) fury; (*violencia*)
violence.
furibundo, a [furi'ßundo, a] *adj* furious.
furioso, a [fu'rjoso, a] *adj* (*iracundo*)
furious; (*violento*) violent.
furor [fu'ror] *nm* (*cólera*) rage; (*pasión*)
frenzy, passion; **hacer** ~ to be a
sensation.
furtivo, a [fur'tißo, a] *adj* furtive ♦ *nm*
poacher.
furúnculo [fu'runkulo] *nm* (*MED*) boil.
fuselaje [fuse'laxe] *nm* fuselage.
fusible [fu'sißle] *nm* fuse.
fusil [fu'sil] *nm* rifle.
fusilamiento [fusila'mjento] *nm* (*JUR*)
execution by firing squad.
fusilar [fusi'lar] *vt* to shoot.
fusión [fu'sjon] *nf* (*gen*) melting; (*unión*)
fusion; (*COM*) merger, amalgamation.
fusionar [fusjo'nar] *vt* to fuse (together);
(*COM*) to merge; **~se** *vr* (*COM*) to merge,
amalgamate.
fusta ['fusta] *nf* (*látigo*) riding crop.
fútbol ['futßol] *nm* football.
futbolín [futßo'lin] *nm* table football.
futbolista [futßo'lista] *nm/f* footballer.
fútil ['futil] *adj* trifling.
futilidad [futili'ðað], **futileza** [futi'leθa] *nf*
triviality.
futón [fu'ton] *nm* futon.
futuro, a [fu'turo, a] *adj* future ♦ *nm*
future; (*LING*) future tense; **~s** *nmpl*
(*COM*) futures.

Gg

G, g [xe] *nf* (*letra*) G, g; **G de Gerona** G for
George.
g/ *abr* = **giro**.
gabacho, a [ga'ßatʃo, a] *adj* Pyrenean;
(*fam*) Frenchified ♦ *nm/f* Pyrenean
villager; (*fam*) Frenchy.
gabán [ga'ßan] *nm* overcoat.
gabardina [gaßar'ðina] *nf* (*tela*) gabardine;
(*prenda*) raincoat.
gabinete [gaßi'nete] *nm* (*POL*) cabinet;
(*estudio*) study; (*de abogados etc*) office;
~ **de consulta/de lectura** consulting/
reading room.
gacela [ga'θela] *nf* gazelle.
gaceta [ga'θeta] *nf* gazette.
gacetilla [gaθe'tiʎa] *nf* (*en periódico*) news
in brief; (*de personalidades*) gossip
column.
gachas ['gatʃas] *nfpl* porridge *sg*.
gacho, a ['gatʃo, a] *adj* (*encorvado*) bent
down; (*orejas*) drooping.
gaditano, a [gaði'tano, a] *adj* of *o* from
Cadiz ♦ *nm/f* native *o* inhabitant of Cadiz.
GAE *nm abr* (*ESP MIL*) = **Grupo Aéreo
Embarcado.**
gaélico, a [ga'eliko, a] *adj* Gaelic ♦ *nm/f*
Gael ♦ *nm* (*LING*) Gaelic.
gafar [ga'far] *vt* (*fam: traer mala suerte*) to
put a jinx on.
gafas ['gafas] *nfpl* glasses; ~ **oscuras** dark
glasses; ~ **de sol** sunglasses.
gafe ['gafe] *adj*: **ser** ~ to be jinxed ♦ *nm*
(*fam*) jinx.
gaita ['gaita] *nf* flute; (~ *gallega*) bagpipes
pl; (*dificultad*) bother; (*cosa engorrosa*)
tough job.
gajes ['gaxes] *nmpl* (*salario*) pay *sg*; **los** ~
del oficio occupational hazards; ~ **y
emolumentos** perquisites.
gajo ['gaxo] *nm* (*gen*) bunch; (*de árbol*)
bough; (*de naranja*) segment.
gala ['gala] *nf* full dress; (*fig: lo mejor*)
cream, flower; **~s** *nfpl* finery *sg*; **estar de**
~ to be in one's best clothes; **hacer** ~ **de**
to display, show off; **tener algo a** ~ to be
proud of sth.
galaico, a [ga'laiko, a] *adj* Galician.
galán [ga'lan] *nm* lover, gallant; (*hombre*

atractivo) ladies' man; (*TEAT*): **primer ~** leading man.

galante [ga'lante] *adj* gallant; (*atento*) charming; (*cortés*) polite.

galantear [galante'ar] *vt* (*hacer la corte a*) to court, woo.

galanteo [galan'teo] *nm* (*coquetea*) flirting; (*de pretendiente*) wooing.

galantería [galante'ria] *nf* (*caballerosidad*) gallantry; (*cumplido*) politeness; (*piropo*) compliment.

galápago [ga'lapaɣo] *nm* (*ZOOL*) freshwater tortoise.

galardón [galar'ðon] *nm* award, prize.

galardonar [galarðo'nar] *vt* (*premiar*) to reward; (*una obra*) to award a prize for.

galaxia [ga'laksja] *nf* galaxy.

galbana [gal'ßana] *nf* (*pereza*) sloth, laziness.

galeote [gale'ote] *nm* galley slave.

galera [ga'lera] *nf* (*nave*) galley; (*carro*) wagon; (*MED*) hospital ward; (*TIP*) galley.

galería [gale'ria] *nf* (*gen*) gallery; (*balcón*) veranda(h); (*de casa*) corridor; (*fam: publico*) audience; **~ secreta** secret passage.

Gales ['galeo] *nm*: (**el País de**) ~ Wales.

galés, esa [ga'les, esa] *adj* Welsh ♦ *nm/f* Welshman/woman ♦ *nm* (*LING*) Welsh.

galgo, a ['galɣo, a] *nm/f* greyhound.

Galia ['galja] *nf* Gaul.

Galicia [ga'liθja] *nf* Galicia.

galicismo [gali'θismo] *nm* gallicism.

Galilea [gali'lea] *nf* Galilee.

galimatías [galima'tias] *nm inv* (*asunto*) rigmarole; (*lenguaje*) gibberish, nonsense.

gallardía [gaʎar'ðia] *nf* (*galantería*) dash; (*gracia*) gracefulness; (*valor*) bravery; (*elegancia*) elegance; (*nobleza*) nobleness.

gallego, a [ga'ʎeɣo, a] *adj* Galician; (*AM pey*) Spanish ♦ *nm/f* Galician; (*AM pey*) Spaniard ♦ *nm* (*LING*) Galician; **V tb lenguas cooficiales.**

galleta [ga'ʎeta] *nf* biscuit; (*fam: bofetada*) whack, slap.

gallina [ga'ʎina] *nf* hen ♦ *nm* (*fam*) coward; **~ ciega** blind man's buff; **~ clueca** broody hen.

gallinazo [gaʎi'naso] *nm* (*AM*) turkey buzzard.

gallinero [gaʎi'nero] *nm* (*criadero*) henhouse; (*TEAT*) gods *sg*, top gallery; (*voces*) hubbub.

gallo ['gaʎo] *nm* cock, rooster; (*MUS*) false *o* wrong note; (*cambio de voz*) break in the voice; **en menos que canta un ~** in an instant.

galo, a ['galo, a] *adj* Gallic; (= *francés*) French ♦ *nm/f* Gaul.

galón [ga'lon] *nm* (*COSTURA*) braid; (*MIL*) stripe; (*medida*) gallon.

galopante [galo'pante] *adj* galloping.

galopar [galo'par] *vi* to gallop.

galope [ga'lope] *nm* gallop; **al ~** (*fig*) in great haste; **a ~ tendido** at full gallop.

galvanice [galßa'niθe] *etc vb* V **galvanizar.**

galvanizar [galßani'θar] *vt* to galvanize.

gama ['gama] *nf* (*MUS*) scale; (*fig*) range; (*ZOOL*) doe.

gamba ['gamba] *nf* prawn.

gamberrada [gambe'rraða] *nf* act of hooliganism.

gamberro, a [gam'berro, a] *nm/f* hooligan, lout.

gamo ['gamo] *nm* (*ZOOL*) buck.

gamuza [ga'muθa] *nf* chamois; (*bayeta*) duster; (*AM: piel*) suede.

gana ['gana] *nf* (*deseo*) desire, wish; (*apetito*) appetite; (*voluntad*) will; (*añoranza*) longing; **de buena ~** willingly; **de mala ~** reluctantly; **me dan ~s de** I feel like, I want to; **tener ~s de** to feel like; **no me da la (real) ~** I don't (damned well) want to; **son ~s de molestar** they're just trying to be awkward.

ganadería [ganaðe'ria] *nf* (*ganado*) livestock; (*ganado vacuno*) cattle *pl*; (*cría, comercio*) cattle raising.

ganadero, a [gana'ðero, a] *adj* stock *cpd* ♦ *nm* stockman.

ganado [ga'naðo] *nm* livestock; **~ caballar/cabrío** horses *pl*/goats *pl*; **~ lanar** *u* **ovejuno** sheep *pl*; **~ porcino/vacuno** pigs *pl*/cattle *pl*.

ganador, a [gana'ðor, a] *adj* winning ♦ *nm/f* winner; (*ECON*) earner.

ganancia [ga'nanθja] *nf* (*lo ganado*) gain; (*aumento*) increase; (*beneficio*) profit; **~s** *nfpl* (*ingresos*) earnings; (*beneficios*) profit *sg*, winnings; **~s y pérdidas** profit and loss; **~ bruta/líquida** gross/net profit; **~s de capital** capital gains; **sacar ~ de** to draw profit from.

ganapán [gana'pan] *nm* (*obrero casual*) odd-job man; (*individuo tosco*) lout.

ganar [ga'nar] *vt* (*obtener*) to get, obtain; (*sacar ventaja*) to gain; (*COM*) to earn; (*DEPORTE, premio*) to win; (*derrotar*) to beat; (*alcanzar*) to reach; (*MIL: objetivo*) to take; (*apoyo*) to gain, win ♦ *vi* (*DEPORTE*) to win; **~se** *vr*: **~se la vida** to earn one's living; **se lo ha ganado** he deserves it; **~ tiempo** to gain time.

ganchillo [gan'tʃiʎo] *nm* (*para croché*)

crochet hook; (*arte*) crochet work.

gancho ['gantʃo] *nm* (*gen*) hook; (*colgador*) hanger; (*pey: revendedor*) tout; (*fam: atractivo*) sex appeal; (*BOXEO: golpe*) hook.

gandul, a [gan'dul, a] *adj, nm/f* good-for-nothing.

ganga ['ganga] *nf* (*cosa*) bargain; (*buena situación*) cushy job.

Ganges ['ganxes] *nm*: **el (Río)** ~ the Ganges.

ganglio ['gangljo] *nm* (*ANAT*) ganglion; (*MED*) swelling.

gangrena [gan'grena] *nf* gangrene.

gansada [gan'saða] *nf* (*fam*) stupid thing (to do).

ganso, a ['ganso, a] *nm/f* (*ZOOL*) gander/goose; (*fam*) idiot.

Gante ['gante] *nm* Ghent.

ganzúa [gan'θua] *nf* skeleton key ♦ *nm/f* burglar.

gañán [ga'ɲan] *nm* farmhand, farm labourer.

garabatear [garaβate'ar] *vt* to scribble, scrawl.

garabato [gara'ßato] *nm* (*gancho*) hook; (*garfio*) grappling iron; (*escritura*) scrawl, scribble; (*fam*) sex appeal.

garaje [ga'raxe] *nm* garage.

garante [ga'rante] *adj* responsible ♦ *nm/f* guarantor.

garantía [garan'tia] *nf* guarantee; (*seguridad*) pledge; (*compromiso*) undertaking; (*JUR: caución*) warranty; **de máxima** ~ absolutely guaranteed; ~ **de trabajo** job security.

garantice [garan'tiθe] *etc vb* V **garantizar**.

garantizar [garanti'θar] *vt* (*hacerse responsable de*) to vouch for; (*asegurar*) to guarantee.

garbanzo [gar'ßanθo] *nm* chickpea.

garbeo [gar'ßeo] *nm*: **darse un** ~ to go for a walk.

garbo ['garßo] *nm* grace, elegance; (*aire*) jauntiness; (*de mujer*) glamour; **andar con** ~ to walk gracefully.

garboso, a [gar'ßoso, a] *adj* graceful, elegant.

garete [ga'rete] *nm*: **irse al** ~ to go to the dogs.

garfio ['garfjo] *nm* grappling iron; (*gancho*) hook; (*ALPINISMO*) climbing iron.

gargajo [gar'ɣaxo] *nm* phlegm, sputum.

garganta [gar'ɣanta] *nf* (*interna*) throat; (*externa, de botella*) neck; (*GEO: barranco*) ravine; (*desfiladero*) narrow pass.

gargantilla [garɣan'tiʎa] *nf* necklace.

gárgara ['garɣara] *nf* gargle, gargling;

hacer ~s to gargle; **¡vete a hacer** ~s!** (*fam*) go to blazes!

gárgola ['garɣola] *nf* gargoyle.

garita [ga'rita] *nf* cabin, hut; (*MIL*) sentry box; (*puesto de vigilancia*) lookout post.

garito [ga'rito] *nm* (*lugar*) gaming house *o* den.

garra ['garra] *nf* (*de gato, TEC*) claw; (*de ave*) talon; (*fam*) hand, paw; (*fig: de canción etc*) bite; **caer en las** ~s de algn to fall into sb's clutches.

garrafa [ga'rrafa] *nf* carafe, decanter.

garrafal [garra'fal] *adj* enormous, terrific; (*error*) terrible.

garrapata [garra'pata] *nf* (*ZOOL*) tick.

garrotazo [garro'taθo] *nm* blow with a stick *o* club.

garrote [ga'rrote] *nm* (*palo*) stick; (*porra*) club, cudgel; (*suplicio*) garrotte.

garza ['garθa] *nf* heron.

gas [gas] *nm* gas; (*vapores*) fumes *pl*; ~**es de escape** exhaust (fumes).

gasa ['gasa] *nf* gauze; (*de pañal*) nappy liner.

gaseoso, a [gase'oso, a] *adj* gassy, fizzy ♦ *nf* lemonade, pop (*fam*).

gasoducto [gaso'ðukto] *nm* gas pipeline.

gasoil [ga'soil], **gasóleo** [ga'soleo] *nm* diesel (oil).

gasolina [gaso'lina] *nf* petrol, gas(oline) (*US*); ~ **sin plomo** unleaded petrol.

gasolinera [gasoli'nera] *nf* petrol (*BRIT*) *o* gas (*US*) station.

gastado, a [gas'taðo, a] *adj* (*ropa*) worn out; (*usado: frase etc*) trite.

gastar [gas'tar] *vt* (*dinero, tiempo*) to spend; (*consumir*) to use (up), consume; (*desperdiciar*) to waste; (*llevar*) to wear; ~**se** *vr* to wear out; (*terminarse*) to run out; (*estropearse*) to waste; ~ **bromas** to crack jokes; **¿qué número gastas?** what size (shoe) do you take?

gasto ['gasto] *nm* (*desembolso*) expenditure, spending; (*cantidad gastada*) outlay, expense; (*consumo, uso*) use; (*desgaste*) waste; ~**s** *nmpl* (*desembolsos*) expenses; (*cargos*) charges, costs; ~ **corriente** (*COM*) revenue expenditure; ~ **fijo** (*COM*) fixed charge; ~**s bancarios** bank charges; ~**s corrientes** running expenses; ~**s de distribución** (*COM*) distribution costs; ~**s generales** overheads; ~**s de mantenimiento** maintenance expenses; ~**s operacionales** operating costs; ~**s de tramitación** (*COM*) handling charge *sg*; ~**s vencidos** (*COM*) accrued charges; **cubrir** ~**s** to cover expenses; **meterse en**

~s to incur expense.

gastronomía [gastro'mia] *nf* gastronomy.

gata ['gata] *nf* (*ZOOL*) she-cat; **andar a** ~s to go on all fours.

gatear [gate'ar] *vi* to go on all fours.

gatillo [ga'tiʎo] *nm* (*de arma de fuego*) trigger; (*de dentista*) forceps.

gato ['gato] *nm* (*ZOOL*) cat; (*TEC*) jack; ~ **de Angora** Angora cat; ~ **montés** wildcat; **dar a algn** ~ **por liebre** to take sb in; **aquí hay** ~ **encerrado** there's something fishy here.

gatuno, a [ga'tuno, a] *adj* feline.

gaucho, a ['gautʃo, a] *adj, nm/f* gaucho.

gaveta [ga'ßeta] *nf* drawer.

gavilán [gaßi'lan] *nm* sparrowhawk.

gavilla [ga'ßiʎa] *nf* sheaf.

gaviota [ga'ßjota] *nf* seagull.

gay [ge] *adj, nm* gay, homosexual.

gazapo [ga'θapo] *nm* young rabbit.

gaznate [gaθ'nate] *nm* (*pescuezo*) gullet; (*garganta*) windpipe.

gazpacho [gaθ'patʃo] *nm* gazpacho.

gel [xel] *nm* gel.

gelatina [xela'tina] *nf* jelly; (*polvos etc*) gelatine.

gema ['xema] *nf* gem.

gemelo, a [xe'melo, a] *adj, nm/f* twin; ~s *nmpl* (*de camisa*) cufflinks; ~s **de campo** field glasses, binoculars; ~s **de teatro** opera glasses.

gemido [xe'miðo] *nm* (*quejido*) moan, groan; (*lamento*) wail, howl.

Géminis ['xeminis] *nm* (*ASTRO*) Gemini.

gemir [xe'mir] *vi* (*quejarse*) to moan, groan; (*animal*) to whine; (*viento*) to howl.

gen [xen] *nm* gene.

gen. *abr* (*LING*) = **género; genitivo.**

gendarme [xen'darme] *nm* (*AM*) policeman.

genealogía [xeneaio'xia] *nf* genealogy.

generación [xenera'θjon] *nf* generation; **primera/segunda/tercera/cuarta** ~ (*INFORM*) first/second/third/fourth generation.

generado, a [xene'raðo, a] *adj* (*INFORM*): ~ **por ordenador** computer generated.

generador [xenera'ðor] *nm* generator; ~ **de programas** (*INFORM*) program generator.

general [xene'ral] *adj* general; (*común*) common; (*pey: corriente*) rife; (*frecuente*) usual ♦ *nm* general; ~ **de brigada/de división** brigadier-/major-general; **por lo o en** ~ in general.

generalice [xenera'liθe] *etc vb V* **generalizar.**

generalidad [xenerali'ðað] *nf* generality.

Generalitat [jenerali'tat] *nf regional government of Catalonia*; ~ **Valenciana** *regional government of Valencia.*

generalización [xenerali θa'θjon] *nf* generalization.

generalizar [xenerali'θar] *vt* to generalize; ~**se** *vr* to become generalized, spread; (*difundirse*) to become widely known.

generalmente [xeneral'mente] *adv* generally.

generar [xene'rar] *vt* to generate.

genérico, a [xe'neriko, a] *adj* generic.

género ['xenero] *nm* (*clase*) kind, sort; (*tipo*) type; (*BIO*) genus; (*LING*) gender; (*COM*) material; ~s *nmpl* (*productos*) goods; ~ **humano** human race; ~ **chico** (*zarzuela*) Spanish operetta; ~s **de punto** knitwear *sg.*

generosidad [xenerosi'ðað] *nf* generosity.

generoso, a [xene'roso, a] *adj* generous.

genético, a [xe'netiko, a] *adj* genetic ♦ *nf* genetics *sg.*

genial [xe'njal] *adj* inspired; (*idea*) brilliant; (*afable*) genial.

genialidad [xenjali'ðað] *nf* (*singularidad*) genius; (*acto genial*) stroke of genius; **es una** ~ **suya** it's one of his brilliant ideas.

genio ['xenjo] *nm* (*carácter*) nature, disposition; (*humor*) temper; (*facultad creadora*) genius; **mal** ~ bad temper; ~ **vivo** quick o hot temper; **de mal** ~ bad-tempered.

genital [xeni'tal] *adj* genital ♦ *nm*: ~**es** genitals, genital organs.

genocidio [xeno'θiðjo] *nm* genocide.

Génova ['xenoßa] *nf* Genoa.

genovés, esa [xeno'ßes, esa] *adj, nm/f* Genoese.

gente ['xente] *nf* (*personas*) people *pl*; (*raza*) race; (*nación*) nation; (*parientes*) relatives *pl*; ~ **bien/baja** posh/lower-class people *pl*; ~ **menuda** (*niños*) children *pl*; **es buena** ~ (*fam: esp AM*) he's a good sort; **una** ~ **como Vd** (*AM*) a person like you.

gentil [xen'til] *adj* (*elegante*) graceful; (*encantador*) charming; (*REL*) gentile.

gentileza [xenti'leθa] *nf* grace; charm; (*cortesía*) courtesy; **por** ~ **de** by courtesy of.

gentilicio, a [xenti'liθjo, a] *adj* (*familiar*) family *cpd.*

gentío [xen'tio] *nm* crowd, throng.

gentuza [xen'tuθa] *nf* (*pey: plebe*) rabble; (: *chusma*) riffraff.

genuflexión [xenuflek'sjon] *nf* genuflexion.

genuino, a [xe'nwino, a] adj genuine.
GEO ['xeo] nmpl abr (ESP: = Grupos
　Especiales de Operaciones) Special Police
　Units used in anti-terrorist operations
　etc.
geografía [xeoɣra'fia] nf geography.
geográfico, a [xeo'ɣrafiko, a] adj
　geographic(al).
geología [xeolo'xia] nf geology.
geólogo, a [xe'oloɣo, a] nm/f geologist.
geometría [xeome'tria] nf geometry.
geométrico, a [xeo'metriko, a] adj
　geometric(al).
Georgia [xe'orxja] nf Georgia.
georgiano, a [xeor'xjano, a] adj, nm/f
　Georgian ♦ nm (LING) Georgian.
geranio [xe'ranjo] nm (BOT) geranium.
gerencia [xe'renθja] nf management;
　(cargo) post of manager; (oficina)
　manager's office.
gerente [xe'rente] nm/f (supervisor)
　manager; (jefe) director.
geriatría [xerja'tria] nf (MED) geriatrics sg.
geriátrico, a [xer'jatriko, a] adj geriatric.
germano, a [xer'mano, a] adj German,
　Germanic ♦ nm/f German.
germen ['xermen] nm germ.
germinar [xermi'nar] vi to germinate;
　(brotar) to sprout.
gerundense [xerun'dense] adj of o from
　Gerona ♦ nm/f native o inhabitant of
　Gerona.
gerundio [xe'rundjo] nm (LING) gerund.
gestación [xesta'θjon] nf gestation.
gesticulación [xestikula'θjon] nf (ademán)
　gesticulation; (mueca) grimace.
gesticular [xestiku'lar] vi (con ademanes)
　to gesture; (con muecas) to make faces.
gestión [xes'tjon] nf management;
　(diligencia, acción) negotiation; **hacer las
　gestiones preliminares** to do the
　groundwork; ~ **de cartera** (COM)
　portfolio management; ~ **financiera**
　(COM) financial management; ~ **interna**
　(INFORM) housekeeping; ~ **de personal**
　personnel management; ~ **de riesgos**
　(COM) risk management.
gestionar [xestjo'nar] vt (lograr) to try to
　arrange; (llevar) to manage.
gesto ['xesto] nm (mueca) grimace;
　(ademán) gesture; **hacer ~s** to make
　faces.
gestor, a [xes'tor, a] adj managing ♦ nm/f
　manager; (promotor) promoter; (agente)
　business agent.
gestoría [xesto'ria] nf agency undertaking
　business with government departments,
　insurance companies etc.

Gibraltar [xißral'tar] nm Gibraltar.
gibraltareño, a [xißralta'reɲo, a] adj of o
　from Gibraltar ♦ nm/f native o inhabitant
　of Gibraltar.
gigante [xi'ɣante] adj, nm/f giant.
gijonés [xixo'nes, esa] adj of o from Gijón
　♦ nm/f native o inhabitant of Gijón.
gilipollas [xili'poʎas] (fam) adj inv daft
　♦ nm/f berk.
gilipollez [xilipo'ʎez] nf (fam): **es una** ~
　that's a load of crap (!); **decir gilipolleces**
　to talk crap (!).
gima ['xima] etc vb V gemir.
gimnasia [xim'nasja] nf gymnastics pl;
　confundir la ~ **con la magnesia** to get
　things mixed up.
gimnasio [xim'nasjo] nm gym(nasium).
gimnasta [xim'nasta] nm/f gymnast.
gimotear [ximote'ar] vi to whine,
　whimper; (lloriquear) to snivel.
Ginebra [xi'neßra] n Geneva.
ginebra [xi'neßra] nf gin.
ginecología [xinekolo'xia] nf
　gyn(a)ecology.
ginecológico, a [xineko'loxiko, a] adj
　gyn(a)ecological.
ginecólogo, a [xine'koloɣo, a] nm/f
　gyn(a)ecologist.
gira ['xira] nf tour, trip.
girar [xi'rar] vt (dar la vuelta) to turn
　(around); (: rápidamente) to spin; (COM:
　giro postal) to draw; (comerciar: letra de
　cambio) to issue ♦ vi to turn (round); (dar
　vueltas) to rotate; (rápido) to spin; **la
　conversación giraba en torno a las
　elecciones** the conversation centred on
　the election; ~ **en descubierto** to
　overdraw.
giratorio, a [xira'torjo, a] adj (gen)
　revolving; (puente) swing cpd; (silla)
　swivel cpd.
giro ['xiro] nm (movimiento) turn,
　revolution; (LING) expression; (COM)
　draft; (de sucesos) trend, course; ~
　bancario money order, bank giro; ~ **de
　existencias** (COM) stock turnover; ~
　postal postal order; ~ **a la vista** (COM)
　sight draft.
gis [xis] nm (AM) chalk.
gitano, a [xi'tano, a] adj, nm/f gypsy.
glacial [gla'θjal] adj icy, freezing.
glaciar [gla'θjar] nm glacier.
glándula ['glandula] nf (ANAT, BOT) gland.
glicerina [gliθe'rina] nf (TEC) glycerin(e).
global [glo'ßal] adj (en conjunto) global;
　(completo) total; (investigación) full;
　(suma) lump cpd.
globo ['gloßo] nm (esfera) globe, sphere;

(*aeróstato, juguete*) balloon.

glóbulo ['gloβulo] *nm* globule; (*ANAT*) corpuscle; ~ **blanco/rojo** white/red corpuscle.

gloria ['glorja] *nf* glory; (*fig*) delight; (*delicia*) bliss.

glorieta [glo'rjeta] *nf* (*de jardín*) bower, arbour, (*US*) arbor; (*AUTO*) roundabout (*BRIT*), traffic circle (*US*); (*plaza redonda*) circus; (*cruce*) junction.

glorificar [glorifi'kar] *vt* (*enaltecer*) to glorify, praise.

glorifique [glori'fike] *etc vb* V **glorificar**.

glorioso, a [glo'rjoso, a] *adj* glorious.

glosa ['glosa] *nf* comment; (*explicación*) gloss.

glosar [glo'sar] *vt* (*comentar*) to comment on.

glosario [glo'sarjo] *nm* glossary.

glotón, ona [glo'ton, ona] *adj* gluttonous, greedy ♦ *nm/f* glutton.

glotonería [glotone'ria] *nf* gluttony, greed.

glúteo ['gluteo] *nm* (*fam: nalga*) buttock.

gnomo ['nomo] *nm* gnome.

gobernación [goβerna'θjon] *nf* government, governing; (*POL*) Provincial Governor's office; **Ministro de la G~** Minister of the Interior, Home Secretary (*BRIT*).

gobernador, a [goβerna'ðor, a] *adj* governing ♦ *nm/f* governor.

gobernanta [goβer'nanta] *nf* (*esp AM: niñera*) governess.

gobernante [goβer'nante] *adj* governing ♦ *nm* ruler, governor ♦ *nf* (*en hotel etc*) housekeeper.

gobernar [goβer'nar] *vt* (*dirigir*) to guide, direct; (*POL*) to rule, govern ♦ *vi* to govern; (*NAUT*) to steer; ~ **mal** to misgovern.

gobierno [go'βjerno] *etc vb* V **gobernar** ♦ *nm* (*POL*) government; (*gestión*) management; (*dirección*) guidance, direction; (*NAUT*) steering; (*puesto*) governorship.

goce ['goθe] *etc vb* V **gozar** ♦ *nm* enjoyment.

godo, a ['goðo, a] *nm/f* Goth; (*AM pey*) Spaniard.

gol [gol] *nm* goal.

golear [gole'ar] *vt* (*marcar*) to score a goal against.

golf [golf] *nm* golf.

golfo, a ['golfo, a] *nm/f* (*pilluelo*) street urchin; (*vago*) tramp; (*gorrón*) loafer; (*gamberro*) lout ♦ *nm* (*GEO*) gulf ♦ *nf* (*fam: prostituta*) slut, whore, hooker (*US*).

golondrina [golon'drina] *nf* swallow.

golosina [golo'sina] *nf* titbit; (*dulce*) sweet.

goloso, a [go'loso, a] *adj* sweet-toothed; (*fam: glotón*) greedy.

golpe ['golpe] *nm* blow; (*de puño*) punch; (*de mano*) smack; (*de remo*) stroke; (*FÚTBOL*) kick; (*TENIS etc*) hit, shot; (*mala suerte*) misfortune; (*fam: atraco*) job, heist (*US*); (*fig: choque*) clash; **no dar** ~ to be bone idle; **de un** ~ with one blow; **de** ~ suddenly; ~ (**de estado**) coup (d'état); ~ **de gracia** coup de grâce (*tb fig*); ~ **de fortuna/maestro** stroke of luck/genius; **cerrar una puerta de** ~ to slam a door.

golpear [golpe'ar] *vt, vi* to strike, knock; (*asestar*) to beat; (*de puño*) to punch; (*golpetear*) to tap; (*mesa*) to bang.

golpista [gol'pista] *adj:* **intentona** ~ coup attempt ♦ *nm/f* participant in a coup (d'état).

golpiza [gol'pisa] *nf:* **dar una** ~ **a algn** (*AM*) to beat sb up.

goma ['goma] *nf* (*caucho*) rubber; (*elástico*) elastic; (*tira*) rubber *o* elastic (*BRIT*) band; (*fam: preservativo*) condom; (*droga*) hashish; (*explosivo*) plastic explosive; ~ (**de borrar**) eraser, rubber (*BRIT*); ~ **de mascar** chewing gum; ~ **de pegar** gum, glue.

goma-espuma [gomaes'puma] *nf* foam rubber.

gomina [go'mina] *nf* hair gel.

gomita [go'mita] *nf* rubber *o* elastic (*BRIT*) band.

góndola ['gondola] *nf* (*barco*) gondola; (*de tren*) goods wagon.

gordo, a ['gorðo, a] *adj* (*gen*) fat; (*persona*) plump; (*agua*) hard; (*fam*) enormous ♦ *nm/f* fat man *o* woman; **el (premio)** ~ (*en lotería*) first prize; **¡~!** (*fam*) fatty!

gordura [gor'ðura] *nf* fat; (*corpulencia*) fatness, stoutness.

gorgojo [gor'xoxo] *nm* (*insecto*) grub.

gorgorito [gorɣo'rito] *nm* (*gorjeo*) trill, warble.

gorila [go'rila] *nm* gorilla; (*fam*) tough, thug; (*guardaespaldas*) bodyguard.

gorjear [gorxe'ar] *vi* to twitter, chirp.

gorjeo [gor'xeo] *nm* twittering, chirping.

gorra ['gorra] *nf* (*gen*) cap; (*de niño*) bonnet; (*militar*) bearskin; ~ **de montar/ de paño/de punto/de visera** riding/ cloth/knitted/peaked cap; **andar** *o* **ir** *o* **vivir de** ~ to sponge, scrounge; **entrar de** ~ (*fam*) to gatecrash.

gorrión [go'rrjon] *nm* sparrow.

gorro ['gorro] *nm* cap; (*de niño, mujer*) bonnet; **estoy hasta el** ~ I am fed up.

gorrón, ona [go'rron, ona] *nm* pebble;

(*TEC*) pivot ♦ *nm/f* scrounger.

gorronear [gorroneˈar] *vi* (*fam*) to sponge, scrounge.

gota [ˈgota] *nf* (*gen*) drop; (*de pintura*) blob; (*de sudor*) bead; (*MED*) gout; ~ **a** ~ drop by drop; **caer a** ~**s** to drip.

gotear [goteˈar] *vi* to drip; (*escurrir*) to trickle; (*salirse*) to leak; (*cirio*) to gutter; (*lloviznar*) to drizzle.

gotera [goˈtera] *nf* leak.

gótico, a [ˈgotiko, a] *adj* Gothic.

gozar [goˈθar] *vi* to enjoy o.s.; ~ **de** (*disfrutar*) to enjoy; (*poseer*) to possess; ~ **de buena salud** to enjoy good health.

gozne [ˈgoθne] *nm* hinge.

gozo [ˈgoθo] *nm* (*alegría*) joy; (*placer*) pleasure; ¡**mi** ~ **en el pozo**! that's torn it!, just my luck!

g.p. *nm abr* (= *giro postal*) m.o.

gr. *abr* (= *gramo(s)*) g.

grabación [graβaˈθjon] *nf* recording.

grabado, a [graˈβaðo, a] *adj* (*MUS*) recorded; (*en cinta*) taped, on tape ♦ *nm* print, engraving; ~ **al agua fuerte** etching; ~ **al aguatinta** aquatint; ~ **en cobre** copperplate; ~ **en madera** woodcut; ~ **rupestre** rock carving.

grabador, a [graβaˈðor, a] *nm/f* engraver ♦ *nf* tape-recorder; ~**a de cassettes** cassette recorder.

grabar [graˈβar] *vt* to engrave; (*discos, cintas*) to record; (*impresionar*) to impress.

gracejo [graˈθexo] *nm* (*humor*) wit, humour; (*elegancia*) grace.

gracia [ˈgraθja] *nf* (*encanto*) grace, gracefulness; (*REL*) grace; (*chiste*) joke; (*humor*) humour, wit; ¡**muchas** ~**s**! thanks very much!; ~**s a** thanks to; **tener** ~ (*chiste etc*) to be funny; ¡**qué** ~! how funny!; (*irónico*) what a nerve!; **no me hace** ~ (*broma*) it's not funny; (*plan*) I am not too keen; **con** ~**s anticipadas/repetidas** thanking you in advance/again; **dar las** ~**s a algn por algo** to thank sb for sth.

grácil [ˈgraθil] *adj* (*sutil*) graceful; (*delgado*) slender; (*delicado*) delicate.

gracioso, a [graˈθjoso, a] *adj* (*garboso*) graceful; (*chistoso*) funny; (*cómico*) comical; (*agudo*) witty; (*título*) gracious ♦ *nm/f* (*TEAT*) comic character, fool; **su graciosa Majestad** His/Her Gracious Majesty.

grada [ˈgraða] *nf* (*de escalera*) step; (*de anfiteatro*) tier, row; ~**s** *nfpl* (*de estadio*) terraces.

gradación [graðaˈθjon] *nf* gradation; (*serie*) graded series.

gradería [graðeˈria] *nf* (*gradas*) (flight of) steps *pl*; (*de anfiteatro*) tiers *pl*, rows *pl*; ~ **cubierta** covered stand.

grado [ˈgraðo] *nm* degree; (*etapa*) stage, step; (*nivel*) rate; (*de parentesco*) order of lineage; (*de aceite, vino*) grade; (*grada*) step; (*ESCOL*) class, year, grade (*US*); (*UNIV*) degree; (*LING*) degree of comparison; (*MIL*) rank; **de buen** ~ willingly; **en sumo** ~, **en** ~ **superlativo** in the highest degree.

graduación [graðwaˈθjon] *nf* (*acto*) gradation; (*clasificación*) rating; (*del alcohol*) proof, strength; (*ESCOL*) graduation; (*MIL*) rank; **de alta** ~ high-ranking.

gradual [graˈðwal] *adj* gradual.

graduar [graˈðwar] *vt* (*gen*) to graduate; (*medir*) to gauge; (*TEC*) to calibrate; (*UNIV*) to confer a degree on; (*MIL*) to commission; ~**se** *vr* to graduate; ~**se la vista** to have one's eyes tested.

grafía [graˈfia] *nf* (*escritura*) writing; (*ortografía*) spelling.

gráfico, a [ˈgrafiko, a] *adj* graphic; (*fig: vívido*) vivid, lively ♦ *nm* diagram ♦ *nf* graph; ~ **de barras** (*COM*) bar chart; ~ **de sectores** o **de tarta** (*COM*) pie chart; ~**s** *nmpl* (*tb INFORM*) graphics; ~**s empresariales** (*COM*) business graphics.

grafito [graˈfito] *nm* (*TEC*) graphite, black lead.

grafología [grafoloˈxia] *nf* graphology.

gragea [graˈxea] *nf* (*MED*) pill; (*caramelo*) dragée.

grajo [ˈgraxo] *nm* rook.

Gral. *abr* (*MIL*: = *General*) Gen.

gramático, a [graˈmatiko, a] *nm/f* (*persona*) grammarian ♦ *nf* grammar.

gramo [ˈgramo] *nm* gramme (*BRIT*), gram (*US*).

gran [gran] *adj V* **grande**.

grana [ˈgrana] *nf* (*BOT*) seedling; (*color*) scarlet; **ponerse como la** ~ to go as red as a beetroot.

granada [graˈnaða] *nf* pomegranate; (*MIL*) grenade; ~ **de mano** hand grenade; ~ **de metralla** shrapnel shell.

granadilla [granaˈðiʎa] *nf* (*AM*) passion fruit.

granadino, a [granaˈðino, a] *adj* of o from Granada ♦ *nm/f* native o inhabitant of Granada ♦ *nf* grenadine.

granar [graˈnar] *vi* to seed.

granate [graˈnate] *adj inv* maroon ♦ *nm* garnet; (*color*) maroon.

Gran Bretaña [grambreˈtaɲa] *nf* Great

Britain.

Gran Canaria [granka'narja] *nf* Grand Canary.

grancanario, a [granka'narjo, a] *adj* of o from Grand Canary ♦ *nm/f* native o inhabitant of Grand Canary.

grande ['grande], **gran** *adj* (*de tamaño*) big, large; (*alto*) tall; (*distinguido*) great; (*impresionante*) grand ♦ *nm* grandee; ¿cómo es de ~? how big is it?, what size is it?; **pasarlo en** ~ to have a tremendous time.

grandeza [gran'deθa] *nf* greatness; (*tamaño*) bigness; (*esplendidez*) grandness; (*nobleza*) nobility.

grandioso, a [gran'djoso, a] *adj* magnificent, grand.

grandullón, ona [granðu'ʎon, ona] *adj* oversized.

granel [gra'nel] *nm* (*montón*) heap; **a** ~ (*COM*) in bulk.

granero [gra'nero] *nm* granary, barn.

granice [gra'niθe] *etc vb* V **granizar**.

granito [gra'nito] *nm* (*AGR*) small grain; (*roca*) granite.

granizada [grani'θaða] *nf* hailstorm; (*fig*) hail; **una** ~ **de balas** a hail of bullets.

granizado [grani'θaðo] *nm* iced drink; ~ **de café** iced coffee.

granizar [grani'θar] *vi* to hail.

granizo [gra'niθo] *nm* hail.

granja ['granxa] *nf* (*gen*) farm; ~ **avícola** chicken o poultry farm.

granjear [granxe'ar] *vt* (*cobrar*) to earn; (*ganar*) to win; (*avanzar*) to gain; ~**se** *vr* (*amistad etc*) to gain for o.s.

granjero, a [gran'xero, a] *nm/f* farmer.

grano ['grano] *nm* grain; (*semilla*) seed; (*baya*) berry; (*MED*) pimple, spot; (*partícula*) particle; (*punto*) speck; ~**s** *nmpl* cereals; ~ **de café** coffee bean; **ir al** ~ to get to the point.

granuja [gra'nuxa] *nm* rogue; (*golfillo*) urchin.

grapa ['grapa] *nf* staple; (*TEC*) clamp; (*sujetador*) clip, fastener; (*ARQ*) cramp.

grapadora [grapa'ðora] *nf* stapler.

GRAPO ['grapo] *nm abr* (*ESP POL*) = Grupo de Resistencia Antifascista Primero de Octubre.

grasa ['grasa] *nf* V **graso**.

grasiento, a [gra'sjento, a] *adj* greasy; (*de aceite*) oily; (*mugriento*) filthy.

graso, a ['graso, a] *adj* fatty; (*aceitoso*) greasy, oily ♦ *nf* (*gen*) grease; (*de cocina*) fat, lard; (*sebo*) suet; (*mugre*) filth; (*AUTO*) oil, (*lubricante*) grease; ~ **de ballena** blubber; ~ **de pescado** fish oil.

grasoso, a [gra'soso, a] *adj* (*AM*) greasy, sticky.

gratificación [gratifika'θjon] *nf* (*propina*) tip; (*aguinaldo*) gratuity; (*bono*) bonus; (*recompensa*) reward.

gratificar [gratifi'kar] *vt* (*dar propina*) to tip; (*premiar*) to reward; **"se gratificará"** "a reward is offered".

gratifique [grati'fike] *etc vb* V **gratificar**.

gratinar [grati'nar] *vt* to cook au gratin.

gratis ['gratis] *adv* free, for nothing.

gratitud [grati'tuð] *nf* gratitude.

grato, a ['grato, a] *adj* (*agradable*) pleasant, agreeable; (*bienvenido*) welcome; **nos es** ~ **informarle que** ... we are pleased to inform you that ....

gratuito, a [gra'twito, a] *adj* (*gratis*) free; (*sin razón*) gratuitous; (*acusación*) unfounded.

grava ['graβa] *nf* (*guijos*) gravel; (*piedra molida*) crushed stone; (*en carreteras*) road metal.

gravamen [gra'βamen] *nm* (*carga*) burden; (*impuesto*) tax; **libre de** ~ (*ECON*) free from encumbrances.

gravar [gra'βar] *vt* to burden; (*COM*) to tax; (*ECON*) to assess for tax; ~ **con impuestos** to burden with taxes.

grave ['graβe] *adj* heavy; (*fig, MED*) grave, serious; (*importante*) important; (*herida*) severe; (*MUS*) low, deep; (*LING*: *acento*) grave; **estar** ~ to be seriously ill.

gravedad [graβe'ðað] *nf* gravity; (*fig*) seriousness; (*grandeza*) importance; (*dignidad*) dignity; (*MUS*) depth.

grávido, a ['graβiðo, a] *adj* (*preñada*) pregnant.

gravilla [gra'βiʎa] *nf* gravel.

gravitación [graβita'θjon] *nf* gravitation.

gravitar [graβi'tar] *vi* to gravitate; ~ **sobre** to rest on.

gravoso, a [gra'βoso, a] *adj* (*pesado*) burdensome; (*costoso*) costly.

graznar [graθ'nar] *vi* (*cuervo*) to squawk; (*pato*) to quack; (*hablar ronco*) to croak.

graznido [graθ'niðo] *nm* squawk; croak.

Grecia ['greθja] *nf* Greece.

gregario, a [gre'xarjo, a] *adj* gregarious; **instinto** ~ herd instinct.

gremio ['gremjo] *nm* (*asociación*) professional association, guild.

greña ['greɲa] *nf* (*cabellos*) shock of hair; (*maraña*) tangle; **andar a la** ~ to bicker, squabble.

greñudo, a [gre'ɲuðo, a] *adj* (*persona*) dishevelled; (*pelo*) tangled.

gresca ['greska] *nf* uproar; (*trifulca*) row.

griego, a ['grjexo, a] *adj* Greek, Grecian

♦ nm/f Greek ♦ nm (LING) Greek.
grieta ['grjeta] nf crack; (hendidura) chink; (quiebra) crevice; (MED) chap; (POL) rift.
grifa ['grifa] nf (fam: droga) marijuana.
grifo ['grifo] nm tap (BRIT), faucet (US); (AM) petrol (BRIT) o gas (US) station.
grilletes [gri'ʎetes] nmpl fetters, shackles.
grillo ['griʎo] nm (ZOOL) cricket; (BOT) shoot; ~s nmpl shackles, irons.
grima ['grima] nf (horror) loathing; (desagrado) reluctance; (desazón) uneasiness; **me da** ~ it makes me sick.
gringo, a ['gringo, a] (AM) adj (pey: extranjero) foreign; (: norteamericano) Yankee; (idioma) foreign ♦ nm/f foreigner; Yank.
gripa ['gripa] nf (AM) flu, influenza.
gripe ['gripe] nf flu, influenza.
gris [gris] adj grey.
grisáceo, a [gri'saθeo, a] adj greyish.
grisoso, a [gri'soso, a] adj (AM) greyish, grayish (esp US).
gritar [gri'tar] vt, vi to shout, yell; ¡no grites! stop shouting!
grito ['grito] nm shout, yell; (de horror) scream; **a** ~ **pelado** at the top of one's voice; **poner el** ~ **en el cielo** to scream blue murder; **es el último** ~ (de moda) it's all the rage.
groenlandés, esa [groenlan'des, esa] adj Greenland cpd ♦ nm/f Greenlander.
Groenlandia [groen'landja] nf Greenland.
grosella [gro'seʎa] nf (red)currant; ~ **negra** blackcurrant.
grosería [grose'ria] nf (actitud) rudeness; (comentario) vulgar comment; (palabrota) swearword.
grosero, a [gro'sero, a] adj (poco cortés) rude, bad-mannered; (ordinario) vulgar, crude.
grosor [gro'sor] nm thickness.
grotesco, a [gro'tesko, a] adj grotesque; (absurdo) bizarre.
grúa ['grua] nf (TEC) crane; (de petróleo) derrick; ~ **corrediza** o **móvil/de pescante/puente/de torre** travelling/jib/overhead/tower crane.
grueso, a ['grweso, a] adj thick; (persona) stout; (calidad) coarse ♦ nm bulk; (espesor) thickness; (densidad) density; (de gente) main body, mass; **el** ~ **de** the bulk of.
grulla ['gruʎa] nf (ZOOL) crane.
grumete [gru'mete] nm (NAUT) cabin o ship's boy.
grumo ['grumo] nm (coágulo) clot, lump; (masa) dollop.
gruñido [gru'niðo] nm grunt, growl; (fig)

grumble.
gruñir [gru'nir] vi (animal) to grunt, growl; (fam) to grumble.
gruñón, ona [gru'non, ona] adj grumpy ♦ nm/f grumbler.
grupa ['grupa] nf (ZOOL) rump.
grupo ['grupo] nm group; (TEC) unit, set; (de árboles) cluster; ~ **sanguíneo** blood group.
gruta ['gruta] nf grotto.
Gta. abr (AUTO) = **Glorieta**.
guaca ['gwaka] nf Indian tomb.
guacamole [gwaka'mole] nm (AM) avocado salad.
guachimán [gwatʃi'man] nm (AM) night watchman.
guadalajareño, a [gwaðalaxa'reno, a] adj of o from Guadalajara ♦ nm/f native o inhabitant of Guadalajara.
Guadalquivir [gwaðalki'ßir] nm: **el (Río)** ~ the Guadalquivir.
guadaña [gwa'ðana] nf scythe.
guadañar [gwaða'nar] vt to scythe, mow.
Guadiana [gwa'ðjana] nm: **el (Río)** ~ the Guadiana.
guagua ['gwaɣwa] nf (AM, Canarias) bus; (AM: criatura) baby.
guajolote [gwaxo'lote] nm (AM) turkey.
guano ['gwano] nm guano.
guantada [gwan'taða] nf, **guantazo** [gwan'taθo] nm slap.
guante ['gwante] nm glove; **se ajusta como un** ~ it fits like a glove; **echar el** ~ **a algn** to catch hold of sb; (fig: policía) to catch sb.
guapo, a ['gwapo, a] adj good-looking; (mujer) pretty, attractive; (hombre) handsome; (elegante) smart ♦ nm lover, gallant; (AM fam) tough guy, bully.
guaraní [gwara'ni] adj, nm/f Guarani ♦ nm (moneda) monetary unit of Paraguay.
guarapo [gwa'rapo] nm (AM) fermented cane juice.
guarda ['gwarða] nm/f (persona) warden, keeper ♦ nf (acto) guarding; (custodia) custody; (TIP) flyleaf, endpaper; ~ **forestal** game warden.
guarda(a)gujas [gwarða'ɣuxas] nm inv (FERRO) switchman.
guardabarros [gwarða'ßarros] nm inv mudguard (BRIT), fender (US).
guardabosques [gwarða'ßoskes] nm inv gamekeeper.
guardacoches [gwarða'kotʃes] nm/f inv (celador) parking attendant.
guardacostas [gwarða'kostas] nm inv coastguard vessel.
guardador, a [gwarða'ðor, a] adj protective; (tacaño) mean, stingy ♦ nm/f

guardian, protector.
guardaespaldas [gwardaes'paldas] *nm/f inv* bodyguard.
guardameta [gwarða'meta] *nm* goalkeeper.
guardapolvo [gwarda'polßo] *nm* dust cover; (*prenda de vestir*) overalls *pl*.
guardar [gwar'ðar] *vt* (*gen*) to keep; (*vigilar*) to guard, watch over; (*conservar*) to put away; (*dinero: ahorrar*) to save; (*promesa etc*) to keep; (*ley*) to observe; (*rencor*) to bear, harbour; (*INFORM: archivo*) to save; ~**se de algo** (*evitar*) to avoid sth; (*abstenerse*) to refrain from sth; ~**se de hacer algo** to be careful not to do sth; **guardársela a algn** to have it in for sb.
guardarropa [gwarða'rropa] *nm* (*armario*) wardrobe; (*en establecimiento público*) cloakroom.
guardería [gwarðe'ria] *nf* nursery.
guardia ['gwarðja] *nf* (*MIL*) guard; (*cuidado*) care, custody ♦ *nm/f* guard; (*policía*) policeman/woman; **estar de** ~ to be on guard; **montar** ~ to mount guard; **la G**~ **Civil** the Civil Guard; ~ **municipal** *o* **urbana** municipal police; **un** ~ **civil** a Civil Guard(sman); **un(a)** ~ **nacional** a policeman/woman; ~ **urbano** traffic policeman; *see boxed note.*

GUARDIA CIVIL

The **Guardia Civil** *is a branch of the army, or "Ejército de Tierra", and is run along military lines. It has a policing role outside large towns and cities and comes under the joint control of the Spanish Ministry of Defence and the Ministry of the Interior. It is also known as "La Benemérita".*

---

guardián, ana [gwar'ðjan, ana] *nm/f* (*gen*) guardian, keeper.
guarecer [gware'θer] *vt* (*proteger*) to protect; (*abrigar*) to shelter; ~**se** *vr* to take refuge.
guarezca [gwa're θka] *etc vb V* **guarecer.**
guarida [gwa'riða] *nf* (*de animal*) den, lair; (*de persona*) haunt, hideout; (*refugio*) refuge.
guarnecer [gwarne'θer] *vt* (*equipar*) to provide; (*adornar*) to adorn; (*TEC*) to reinforce.
guarnezca [gwar'neθka] *etc vb V* **guarnecer.**
guarnición [gwarni'θjon] *nf* (*de vestimenta*) trimming; (*de piedra*) mount; (*CULIN*) garnish; (*arneses*) harness; (*MIL*) garrison.

guarrada [gwa'rraða] (*fam*) *nf* (*cosa sucia*) dirty mess; (*acto o dicho obsceno*) obscenity; **hacer una** ~ **a algn** to do the dirty on sb.
guarrería [gwarre'ria] *nf* = **guarrada.**
guarro, a ['gwarro, a] *nm/f* (*fam*) pig; (*fig*) dirty *o* slovenly person.
guasa ['gwasa] *nf* joke; **con** *o* **de** ~ jokingly, in fun.
guasón, ona [gwa'son, ona] *adj* witty; (*bromista*) joking ♦ *nm/f* wit; joker.
Guatemala [gwate'mala] *nf* Guatemala.
guatemalteco, a [gwatemal'teko, a] *adj*, *nm/f* Guatemalan.
guateque [gwa'teke] *nm* (*fiesta*) party.
guay [gwai] *adj* (*fam*) super, great.
guayaba [gwa'jaßa] *nf* (*BOT*) guava.
Guayana [gwa'jana] *nf* Guyana, Guiana.
gubernamental [gußernamen'tal], **gubernativo, a** [gußerna'tißo, a] *adj* governmental.
guedeja [ge'ðexa] *nf* long hair.
guerra ['gerra] *nf* war; (*arte*) warfare; (*pelea*) struggle; ~ **atómica/ bacteriológica/nuclear/de guerrillas** atomic/germ/nuclear/guerrilla warfare; **Primera/Segunda G**~ **Mundial** First/ Second World War; ~ **de precios** (*COM*) price war; ~ **civil/fría** civil/cold war; ~ **a muerte** fight to the death; **de** ~ military, war *cpd*; **estar en** ~ to be at war; **dar** ~ to be annoying.
guerrear [gerre'ar] *vi* to wage war.
guerrero, a [ge'rrero, a] *adj* fighting; (*carácter*) warlike ♦ *nm/f* warrior.
guerrilla [ge'rriʎa] *nf* guerrilla warfare; (*tropas*) guerrilla band *o* group.
guerrillero, a [gerri'ʎero, a] *nm/f* guerrilla (fighter); (*contra invasor*) partisan.
gueto ['geto] *nm* ghetto.
guía ['gia] *etc vb V* **guiar** ♦ *nm/f* (*persona*) guide ♦ *nf* (*libro*) guidebook; (*manual*) handbook; (*INFORM*) prompt; ~ **de ferrocarriles** railway timetable; ~ **telefónica** telephone directory; ~ **del turista/del viajero** tourist/traveller's guide.
guiar [gi'ar] *vt* to guide, direct; (*dirigir*) to lead; (*orientar*) to advise; (*AUTO*) to steer; ~**se** *vr*: ~**se por** to be guided by.
guijarro [gi'xarro] *nm* pebble.
guillotina [giʎo'tina] *nf* guillotine.
guinda ['ginda] *nf* morello cherry; (*licor*) cherry liqueur.
guindar [gin'dar] *vt* to hoist; (*fam: robar*) to nick.
guindilla [gin'diʎa] *nf* chil(l)i pepper.
Guinea [gi'nea] *nf* Guinea.

guineo, a [gi'neo, a] *adj* Guinea *cpd*,
Guinean ♦ *nm/f* Guinean.
guiñapo [gi'ɲapo] *nm* (*harapo*) rag;
(*persona*) rogue.
guiñar [gi'ɲar] *vi* to wink.
guiño ['giɲo] *nm* (*parpadeo*) wink; (*muecas*)
grimace; **hacer ~s a** (*enamorados*) to
make eyes at.
guiñol [gi'ɲol] *nm* (*TEAT*) puppet theatre.
guión [gi'on] *nm* (*LING*) hyphen, dash;
(*esquema*) summary, outline; (*CINE*)
script.
guionista [gjo'nista] *nm/f* scriptwriter.
guipuzcoano, a [gipuθko'ano, a] *adj* of *o*
from Guipúzcoa ♦ *nm/f* native *o*
inhabitant of Guipúzcoa.
guiri ['giri] *nm/f* (*fam, pey*) foreigner.
guirigay [giri'gai] *nm* (*griterío*) uproar;
(*confusión*) chaos.
guirnalda [gir'nalda] *nf* garland.
guisa ['gisa] *nf*: **a ~ de** as, like.
guisado [gi'saðo] *nm* stew.
guisante [gi'sante] *nm* pea.
guisar [gi'sar] *vt, vi* to cook; (*fig*) to
arrange.
guiso ['giso] *nm* cooked dish.
guita ['gita] *nf* twine; (*fam: dinero*) dough.
guitarra [gi'tarra] *nf* guitar.
guitarrista [gita'rrista] *nm/f* guitarist.
gula ['gula] *nf* gluttony, greed.
gusano [gu'sano] *nm* maggot, worm; (*de
mariposa, polilla*) caterpillar; (*fig*) worm;
(*ser despreciable*) creep; **~ de seda** silk-
worm.
gustar [gus'tar] *vt* to taste, sample ♦ *vi* to
please, be pleasing; **~ de algo** to like *o*
enjoy sth; **me gustan las uvas** I like
grapes; **le gusta nadar** she likes *o* enjoys
swimming; **¿gusta Ud?** would you like
some?; **como Ud guste** as you wish.
gusto ['gusto] *nm* (*sentido, sabor*) taste;
(*agrado*) liking; (*placer*) pleasure; **tiene
un ~ amargo** it has a bitter taste; **tener
buen ~** to have good taste; **sobre ~s no
hay nada escrito** there's no accounting
for tastes; **de buen/mal ~** in good/bad
taste; **sentirse a ~** to feel at ease;
¡mucho *o* tanto ~ (en conocerle)! how do
you do?, pleased to meet you; **el ~ es
mío** the pleasure is mine; **tomar ~ a** to
take a liking to; **con ~** willingly, gladly.
gustoso, a [gus'toso, a] *adj* (*sabroso*) tasty;
(*agradable*) pleasant; (*con voluntad*)
willing, glad; **lo hizo ~** he did it gladly.
gutural [gutu'ral] *adj* guttural.
guyanés, esa [gwaja'nes, esa] *adj, nm/f*
Guyanese.

H h

H, h ['atʃe] *nf* (*letra*) H, h; **H de Historia** H
for Harry (*BRIT*) *o* How (*US*).
H. *abr* (*QUÍMICA*: = *Hidrógeno*) H;
(= *Hectárea(s)*) ha.; (*COM*: = *Haber*) cr.
h. *abr* (= *hora(s)*) h., hr(s).; (= *hacia*) c.
♦ *nmpl abr* (= *habitantes*) pop.
ha [a] *vb* V **haber**.
Ha. *abr* (= *Hectárea(s)*) ha.
haba ['aβa] *nf* bean; **son ~s contadas** it
goes without saying; **en todas partes
cuecen ~s** it's the same (story) the
whole world over.
Habana [a'βana] *nf*: **la ~** Havana.
habanero, a [aβa'nero, a] *adj* of *o* from
Havana ♦ *nm/f* native *o* inhabitant of
Havana ♦ *nf* (*MUS*) habanera.
habano [a'βano] *nm* Havana cigar.
habeas corpus [a'βeas'korpus] *nm* (*LAW*)
habeas corpus.

—————————— *PALABRA CLAVE*

haber [a'βer] *vb aux* **1** (*tiempos compuestos*)
to have; **había comido** I have/had eaten;
antes/después de ~lo visto before
seeing/after seeing *o* having seen it; **si
lo hubiera sabido habría ido** if I had
known I would have gone
2: **¡~lo dicho antes!** you should have
said so before!; **¿habráse visto (cosa
igual)?** have you ever seen anything like
it?
3: **~ de**: **he de hacerlo** I must do it; **ha de
llegar mañana** it should arrive
tomorrow
♦ *vb impers* **1** (*existencia: sg*) there is; (: *pl*)
there are; **hay un hermano/dos
hermanos** there is one brother/there are
two brothers; **¿cuánto hay de aquí a
Sucre?** how far is it from here to
Sucre?; **habrá unos 4 grados** it must be
about 4 degrees; **no hay quien te
entienda** there's no understanding you
2 (*obligación*): **hay que hacer algo**
something must be done; **hay que
apuntarlo para acordarse** you have to
write it down to remember
3: **¡hay que ver!** well I never!
4: **¡no hay de *o* por (*AM*) qué!** don't

mention it!, not at all!
5: ¿qué hay? (*¿qué pasa?*) what's up?,
what's the matter?; (*¿qué tal?*) how's it
going?
♦ **~se** *vr*: **habérselas con algn** to have it
out with sb
♦ *vt*: **he aquí unas sugerencias** here are
some suggestions; **todos los inventos
habidos y por ~** all inventions present
and future; **en el encuentro habido ayer**
in yesterday's game
♦ *nm* (*en cuenta*) credit side; **~es** *nmpl*
assets; **¿cuánto tengo en el ~?** how
much do I have in my account?; **tiene
varias novelas en su ~** he has several
novels to his credit.

habichuela [aβi'tʃwela] *nf* kidney bean.
hábil ['aβil] *adj* (*listo*) clever, smart; (*capaz*)
fit, capable; (*experto*) expert; **día ~**
working day.
habilidad [aβili'ðað] *nf* (*gen*) skill, ability;
(*inteligencia*) cleverness; (*destreza*)
expertness, expertise; (*JUR*)
competence; **~ (para)** fitness (for); **tener
~ manual** to be clever with one's hands.
habilitación [aβilita'θjon] *nf* qualification;
(*colocación de muebles*) fitting out;
(*financiamiento*) financing; (*oficina*)
paymaster's office.
habilitado [aβili'taðo] *nm* paymaster.
habilitar [aβili'tar] *vt* to qualify; (*autorizar*)
to authorize; (*capacitar*) to enable; (*dar
instrumentos*) to equip; (*financiar*) to
finance.
hábilmente [aβil'mente] *adv* skilfully,
expertly.
habitable [aβi'taβle] *adj* inhabitable.
habitación [aβita'θjon] *nf* (*cuarto*) room;
(*casa*) dwelling, abode; (*BIO: morada*)
habitat; **~ sencilla** *o* **individual** single
room; **~ doble** *o* **de matrimonio** double
room.
habitante [aβi'tante] *nm/f* inhabitant.
habitar [aβi'tar] *vt* (*residir en*) to inhabit;
(*ocupar*) to occupy ♦ *vi* to live.
hábitat, *pl* **hábitats** ['aβitat, 'aβitats] *nm*
habitat.
hábito ['aβito] *nm* habit; **tener el ~ de
hacer algo** to be in the habit of doing
sth.
habitual [aβi'twal] *adj* habitual.
habituar [aβi'twar] *vt* to accustom; **~se** *vr*:
~se a to get used to.
habla ['aβla] *nf* (*capacidad de hablar*)
speech; (*idioma*) language; (*dialecto*)
dialect; **perder el ~** to become
speechless; **de ~ francesa** French-

speaking; **estar al ~** to be in contact;
(*TELEC*) to be on the line; **¡González al ~!**
(*TELEC*) Gonzalez speaking!
hablador, a [aβla'ðor, a] *adj* talkative
♦ *nm/f* chatterbox.
habladuría [aβlaðu'ria] *nf* rumour; **~s** *nfpl*
gossip *sg*.
hablante [a'βlante] *adj* speaking ♦ *nm/f*
speaker.
hablar [a'βlar] *vt* to speak, talk ♦ *vi* to
speak; **~se** *vr* to speak to each other; **~
con** to speak to; **¡hable!, ¡puede ~!**
(*TELEC*) you're through!; **de eso ni ~** no
way, that's not on; **~ alto/bajo/claro** to
speak loudly/quietly/plainly *o* bluntly; **~
de** to speak of *o* about; **"se habla inglés"**
"English spoken here"; **no se hablan**
they are not on speaking terms.
habré [a'βre] *etc vb* V **haber**.
hacedor, a [aθe'ðor, a] *nm/f* maker.
hacendado, a [aθen'daðo, a] *adj* property-
owning ♦ *nm* (*terrateniente*) large
landowner.
hacendoso, a [aθen'doso, a] *adj*
industrious, hard-working.

========= *PALABRA CLAVE*

hacer [a'θer] *vt* **1** (*fabricar, producir,
conseguir*) to make; (*construir*) to build; **~
una película/un ruido** to make a film/
noise; **el guisado lo hizo yo** I made *o*
cooked the stew; **~ amigos** to make
friends
2 (*ejecutar: trabajo etc*) to do; **~ la colada**
to do the washing; **~ la comida** to do the
cooking; **¿qué haces?** what are you
doing?; **¡eso está hecho!** you've got it!;
~ el tonto/indio to act the fool/clown; **~
el malo** *o* **el papel del malo** (*TEAT*) to play
the villain
3 (*estudios, algunos deportes*) to do; **~
español/económicas** to do *o* study
Spanish/economics; **~ yoga/gimnasia** to
do yoga/go to gym
4 (*transformar, incidir en*): **esto lo hará
más difícil** this will make it more
difficult; **salir te hará sentir mejor** going
out will make you feel better; **te hace
más joven** it makes you look younger
5 (*cálculo*): **2 y 2 hacen 4** 2 and 2 make 4;
éste hace 100 this one makes 100
6 (+*sub*): **esto hará que ganemos** this
will make us win; **harás que no quiera
venir** you'll stop him wanting to come
7 (*como sustituto de vb*) to do; **él bebió y
yo hice lo mismo** he drank and I did
likewise
8: no hace más que criticar all he does is

criticize
♦ *vb semi-aux*: ~ +*infin* 1 (*directo*): **les hice
venir** I made *o* had them come; **~
trabajar a los demás** to get others to
work
2 (*por intermedio de otros*): ~ **reparar
algo** to get sth repaired
♦ *vi* 1: **haz como que no lo sabes** act as if
you don't know; **hiciste bien en
decírmelo** you were right to tell me
2 (*ser apropiado*): **si os hace** if it's alright
with you
3: ~ **de**: ~ **de madre para uno** to be like a
mother to sb; (*TEAT*): ~ **de Otelo** to play
Othello; **la tabla hace de mesa** the board
does as a table
♦ *vb impers* 1: **hace calor/frío** it's hot/cold;
V tb **bueno; sol; tiempo**
2 (*tiempo*): **hace 3 años** 3 years ago;
hace un mes que voy/no voy I've been
going/I haven't been for a month; **no le
veo desde hace mucho** I haven't seen
him for a long time
3: **¿cómo has hecho para llegar tan
rápido?** how did you manage to get here
so quickly?
♦ **~se** *vr* 1 (*volverse*) to become; **se
hicieron amigos** they became friends;
~se viejo to get *o* grow old; **se hace
tarde** it's getting late
2: **~se algo: me hice un traje** I got a suit
made
3 (*acostumbrarse*): **~se a** to get used to;
~se a la idea to get used to the idea
4: **se hace con huevos y leche** it's made
out of eggs and milk; **eso no se hace**
that's not done
5 (*obtener*): **~se de** *o* **con algo** to get
hold of sth
6 (*fingirse*): **~se el sordo/sueco** to turn a
deaf ear/pretend not to notice.

hacha ['atʃa] *nf* axe; (*antorcha*) torch.
hachazo [a'tʃaθo] *nm* axe blow.
hache ['atʃe] *nf* (the letter) H; **llámele
usted** ~ call it what you will.
hachís [a'tʃis] *nm* hashish.
hacia ['aθja] *prep* (*en dirección de, actitud*)
towards; (*cerca de*) near; ~ **arriba/abajo**
up(wards)/down(wards); ~ **mediodía**
about noon.
hacienda [a'θjenda] *nf* (*propiedad*)
property; (*finca*) farm; (*AM*) ranch; ~
pública public finance; **(Ministerio de)
H~** Exchequer (*BRIT*), Treasury
Department (*US*).
hacinar [aθi'nar] *vt* to pile (up); (*AGR*) to
stack; (*fig*) to overcrowd.

hada ['aða] *nf* fairy; ~ **madrina** fairy
godmother.
hado ['aðo] *nm* fate, destiny.
haga ['aɣa] *etc vb V* **hacer.**
Haití [ai'ti] *nm* Haiti.
haitiano, a [ai'tjano, a] *adj, nm/f* Haitian.
hala ['ala] *excl* (*vamos*) come on!; (*anda*)
get on with it!
halagar [ala'ɣar] *vt* (*lisonjear*) to flatter.
halago [a'laɣo] *nm* (*adulación*) flattery.
halague [a'laɣe] *etc vb V* **halagar.**
halagüeño, a [ala'ɣweɲo, a] *adj* flattering.
halcón [al'kon] *nm* falcon, hawk.
hálito ['alito] *nm* breath.
halitosis [ali'tosis] *nf* halitosis, bad breath.
hallar [a'ʎar] *vt* (*gen*) to find; (*descubrir*) to
discover; (*toparse con*) to run into; **~se** *vr*
to be (situated); (*encontrarse*) to find o.s.;
se halla fuera he is away; **no se halla** he
feels out of place.
hallazgo [a'ʎaθɣo] *nm* discovery; (*cosa*)
find.
halo ['alo] *nm* halo.
halógeno, a [a'loxeno, a] *adj*: **faro** ~
halogen lamp.
halterofilia [altero'filja] *nf* weightlifting.
hamaca [a'maka] *nf* hammock.
hambre ['ambre] *nf* hunger; (*carencia*)
famine; (*inanición*) starvation; (*fig*)
longing; **tener** ~ to be hungry.
hambriento, a [am'brjento, a] *adj* hungry,
starving ♦ *nm/f* starving person; **los ~s**
the hungry; ~ **de** hungry *o* longing for.
hambruna [am'bruna] *nf* famine.
Hamburgo [am'burɣo] *nm* Hamburg.
hamburguesa [ambur'ɣesa] *nf*
hamburger, burger.
hampa ['ampa] *nf* underworld.
hampón [am'pon] *nm* thug.
han [an] *vb V* **haber.**
haragán, ana [ara'ɣan, ana] *adj, nm/f* good-
for-nothing.
haraganear [araɣane'ar] *vi* to idle, loaf
about.
harapiento, a [ara'pjento, a] *adj* tattered,
in rags.
harapo [a'rapo] *nm* rag.
hardware ['xardwer] *nm* (*INFORM*)
hardware.
haré [a're] *etc vb V* **hacer.**
harén [a'ren] *nm* harem.
harina [a'rina] *nf* flour; **eso es** ~ **de otro
costal** that's another kettle of fish.
harinero, a [ari'nero, a] *nm/f* flour
merchant.
harinoso, a [ari'noso, a] *adj* floury.
hartar [ar'tar] *vt* to satiate, glut; (*fig*) to
tire, sicken; **~se** *vr* (*de comida*) to fill o.s.,

gorge o.s.; (*cansarse*) to get fed up (*de* with).

hartazgo [ar'taθɣo] *nm* surfeit, glut.

harto, a ['arto, a] *adj* (*lleno*) full; (*cansado*) fed up ♦ *adv* (*bastante*) enough; (*muy*) very; **estar ~ de** to be fed up with; **¡estoy ~ de decírtelo!** I'm sick and tired of telling you (so)!

hartura [ar'tura] *nf* (*exceso*) surfeit; (*abundancia*) abundance; (*satisfacción*) satisfaction.

has [as] *vb* V **haber**.

Has. *abr* (= *Hectáreas*) ha.

hasta ['asta] *adv* even ♦ *prep* (*alcanzando a*) as far as, up/down to; (*de tiempo: a tal hora*) till, until; (: *antes de*) before ♦ *conj*: **~ que** until; **~ luego** *o* **ahora** (*fam*)/**el sábado** see you soon/on Saturday; **~ la fecha** (up) to date; **~ nueva orden** until further notice; **~ en Valencia hiela a veces** even in Valencia it freezes sometimes.

hastiar [as'tjar] *vt* (*gen*) to weary; (*aburrir*) to bore; **~se** *vr*: **~se de** to get fed up with.

hastío [as'tio] *nm* weariness; boredom.

hatajo [a'taxo] *nm*: **un ~ de gamberros** a bunch of hooligans.

hatillo [a'tiʎo] *nm* belongings *pl*, kit; (*montón*) bundle, heap.

Hawai [a'wai] *nm* (*tb*: **las Islas ~**) Hawaii.

hawaianas [awa'janas] *nfpl* (*esp AM*) flip-flops (*BRIT*), thongs.

hawaiano, a [awa'jano, a] *adj, nm/f* Hawaiian.

hay [ai] *vb* V **haber**.

Haya ['aja] *nf*: **la ~** The Hague.

haya ['aja] *etc vb* V **haber** ♦ *nf* beech tree.

hayal [a'jal] *nm* beech grove.

haz [aθ] *vb* V **hacer** ♦ *nm* bundle, bunch; (*rayo: de luz*) beam ♦ *nf*: **~ de la tierra** face of the earth.

hazaña [a'θaɲa] *nf* feat, exploit; **sería una ~** it would be a great achievement.

hazmerreír [aθmerre'ir] *nm inv* laughing stock.

HB *abr* (= *Herri Batasuna*) *Basque political party.*

he [e] *vb* V **haber** ♦ *adv*: **~ aquí** here is, here are; **~ aquí por qué** ... that is why ....

hebilla [e'βiʎa] *nf* buckle, clasp.

hebra ['eβra] *nf* thread; (*BOT: fibra*) fibre, grain.

hebreo, a [e'βreo, a] *adj, nm/f* Hebrew ♦ *nm* (*LING*) Hebrew.

Hébridas ['eβriðas] *nfpl*: **las ~** the Hebrides.

hechice [e'tʃiθe] *etc vb* V **hechizar**.

hechicero, a [etʃi'θero, a] *nm/f* sorcerer/sorceress.

hechizar [etʃi'θar] *vt* to cast a spell on, bewitch.

hechizo [e'tʃiθo] *nm* witchcraft, magic; (*acto de magia*) spell, charm.

hecho, a ['etʃo, a] *pp de* **hacer** ♦ *adj* complete; (*maduro*) mature; (*COSTURA*) ready-to-wear ♦ *nm* deed, act; (*dato*) fact; (*cuestión*) matter; (*suceso*) event ♦ *excl* agreed!, done!; **¡bien ~!** well done!; **de ~** in fact, as a matter of fact; (*POL etc*: *adj, adv*) de facto; **de ~ y de derecho** de facto and de jure; **~ a la medida** made-to-measure; **a lo ~, pecho** it's no use crying over spilt milk.

hechura [e'tʃura] *nf* making, creation; (*producto*) product; (*forma*) form, shape; (*de persona*) build; (*TEC*) craftsmanship.

hectárea [ek'tarea] *nf* hectare.

heder [e'ðer] *vi* to stink, smell; (*fig*) to be unbearable.

hediondez [eðjon'deθ] *nf* stench, stink; (*cosa*) stinking thing.

hediondo, a [e'ðjondo, a] *adj* stinking.

hedor [e'ðor] *nm* stench.

hegemonía [exemo'nia] *nf* hegemony.

helada [e'laða] *nf* frost.

heladera [ela'ðera] *nf* (*AM: refrigerador*) refrigerator.

heladería [elaðe'ria] *nf* ice-cream stall (*o* parlour).

helado, a [e'laðo, a] *adj* frozen; (*glacial*) icy; (*fig*) chilly, cold ♦ *nm* ice-cream; **dejar ~ a algn** to dumbfound sb.

helador, a [ela'ðor, a] *adj* (*viento etc*) icy, freezing.

helar [e'lar] *vt* to freeze, ice (up); (*dejar atónito*) to amaze; (*desalentar*) to discourage ♦ *vi*, **~se** *vr* to freeze; (*AVIAT, FERRO etc*) to ice (up), freeze up; (*líquido*) to set.

helecho [e'letʃo] *nm* bracken, fern.

helénico, a [e'leniko, a] *adj* Hellenic, Greek.

heleno, a [e'leno, a] *nm/f* Hellene, Greek.

hélice ['eliθe] *nf* spiral; (*TEC*) propeller; (*MAT*) helix.

helicóptero [eli'koptero] *nm* helicopter.

helio ['eljo] *nm* helium.

helmántico, a [el'mantiko, a] *adj* of *o* from Salamanca.

helvético, a [el'βetiko, a] *adj, nm/f* Swiss.

hematoma [ema'toma] *nm* bruise.

hembra ['embra] *nf* (*BOT, ZOOL*) female; (*mujer*) woman; (*TEC*) nut; **un elefante ~** a she-elephant.

hemeroteca [emero'teka] *nf* newspaper

library.

hemiciclo [emi'θiklo] *nm*: **el** ~ (*POL*) the floor.

hemisferio [emis'ferjo] *nm* hemisphere.

hemofilia [emo'filja] *nf* haemophilia (*BRIT*), hemophilia (*US*).

hemorragia [emo'rraxja] *nf* haemorrhage (*BRIT*), hemorrhage (*US*).

hemorroides [emo'rroiðes] *nfpl* haemorrhoids (*BRIT*), hemorrhoids (*US*).

hemos ['emos] *vb V* **haber.**

henar [e'nar] *nm* meadow, hayfield.

henchir [en't∫ir] *vt* to fill, stuff; ~**se** *vr* (*llenarse de comida*) to stuff o.s. (with food); (*inflarse*) to swell (up).

Hendaya [en'daja] *nf* Hendaye.

hender [en'der] *vt* to cleave, split.

hendidura [endi'ðura] *nf* crack, split; (*GEO*) fissure.

henequén [ene'ken] *nm* (*AM*) henequen.

heno ['eno] *nm* hay.

hepatitis [epa'titis] *nf inv* hepatitis.

herbario, a [er'βarjo, a] *adj* herbal ♦ *nm* (*colección*) herbarium; (*especialista*) herbalist; (*botánico*) botanist.

herbicida [erβi'θiða] *nm* weedkiller.

herbívoro, a [er'βiβoro, a] *adj* herbivorous.

herboristería [erβoriste'ria] *nf* herbalist's shop.

heredad [ere'ðað] *nf* landed property; (*granja*) farm.

heredar [ere'ðar] *vt* to inherit.

heredero, a [ere'ðero, a] *nm/f* heir(ess); ~ **del trono** heir to the throne.

hereditario, a [ereði'tarjo, a] *adj* hereditary.

hereje [e'rexe] *nm/f* heretic.

herejía [ere'xia] *nf* heresy.

herencia [e'renθja] *nf* inheritance; (*fig*) heritage; (*BIO*) heredity.

herético, a [e'retiko, a] *adj* heretical.

herido, a [e'riðo, a] *adj* injured, wounded; (*fig*) offended ♦ *nm/f* casualty ♦ *nf* wound, injury.

herir [e'rir] *vt* to wound, injure; (*fig*) to offend; (*conmover*) to touch, move.

hermana [er'mana] *nf V* **hermano.**

hermanar [erma'nar] *vt* to match; (*unir*) to join; (*ciudades*) to twin.

hermanastro, a [erma'nastro, a] *nm/f* stepbrother/sister.

hermandad [erman'dað] *nf* brotherhood; (*de mujeres*) sisterhood; (*sindicato etc*) association.

hermano, a [er'mano, a] *adj* similar ♦ *nm* brother ♦ *nf* sister; ~ **gemelo** twin brother; ~ **político** brother-in-law; ~ **primo** first cousin; **mis** ~**s** my brothers,

my brothers and sisters; **hermana política** sister-in-law.

hermético, a [er'metiko, a] *adj* hermetic; (*fig*) watertight.

hermoso, a [er'moso, a] *adj* beautiful, lovely; (*estupendo*) splendid; (*guapo*) handsome.

hermosura [ermo'sura] *nf* beauty; (*de hombre*) handsomeness.

hernia ['ernja] *nf* hernia, rupture; ~ **discal** slipped disc.

herniarse [er'njarse] *vr* to rupture o.s.; (*fig*) to break one's back.

héroe ['eroe] *nm* hero.

heroicidad [eroiθi'ðað] *nf* heroism; (*una* ~) heroic deed.

heroico, a [e'roiko, a] *adj* heroic.

heroína [ero'ina] *nf* (*mujer*) heroine; (*droga*) heroin.

heroinómano, a [eroi'nomano, a] *nm/f* heroin addict.

heroísmo [ero'ismo] *nm* heroism.

herpes ['erpes] *nmpl o nfpl* (*MED*: *gen*) herpes *sg*; (: *de la piel*) shingles *sg*.

herradura [erra'ðura] *nf* horseshoe.

herraje [e'rraxe] *nm* (*trabajos*) ironwork.

herramienta [erra'mjenta] *nf* tool.

herrería [erre'ria] *nf* smithy; (*TEC*) forge.

herrero [e'rrero] *nm* blacksmith.

herrumbre [e'rrumbre] *nf* rust.

herrumbroso, a [errum'broso, a] *adj* rusty.

hervidero [erβi'ðero] *nm* (*fig*) swarm; (*POL etc*) hotbed.

hervir [er'βir] *vi* to boil; (*burbujear*) to bubble; (*fig*): ~ **de** to teem with; ~ **a fuego lento** to simmer.

hervor [er'βor] *nm* boiling; (*fig*) ardour, fervour.

heterogéneo, a [etero'xeneo, a] *adj* heterogeneous.

heterosexual [eterosek'swal] *adj, nm/f* heterosexual.

hez [eθ] *nf* (*tb*: **heces** *pl*) dregs.

hibernar [iβer'nar] *vi* to hibernate.

híbrido, a ['iβriðo, a] *adj* hybrid.

hice ['iθe] *etc vb V* **hacer.**

hidalgo, a [i'ðalxo, a] *adj* noble; (*honrado*) honourable (*BRIT*), honorable (*US*) ♦ *nm/f* noble(man/woman).

hidratante [iðra'tante] *adj*: **crema** ~ moisturizing cream, moisturizer.

hidratar [iðra'tar] *vt* to moisturize.

hidrato [i'ðrato] *nm* hydrate; ~ **de carbono** carbohydrate.

hidráulico, a [i'ðrauliko, a] *adj* hydraulic ♦ *nf* hydraulics *sg*.

hidro... [iðro] *pref* hydro..., water-....

hidroavión [iðroa'βjon] *nm* seaplane.

hidroeléctrico, a [iðroe'lektriko, a] *adj* hydroelectric.

hidrófilo, a [i'ðrofilo, a] *adj* absorbent; **algodón** ~ cotton wool (*BRIT*), absorbent cotton (*US*).

hidrofobia [iðro'foßja] *nf* hydrophobia, rabies.

hidrófugo, a [i'ðrofuɣo, a] *adj* damp-proof.

hidrógeno [i'ðroxeno] *nm* hydrogen.

hieda ['jeða] *etc vb V* **heder.**

hiedra ['jeðra] *nf* ivy.

hiel [jel] *nf* gall, bile; (*fig*) bitterness.

hielo ['jelo] *etc vb V* **helar** ♦ *nm* (*gen*) ice; (*escarcha*) frost; (*fig*) coldness, reserve; **romper el** ~ (*fig*) to break the ice.

hiena ['jena] *nf* (*ZOOL*) hyena.

hiera ['jera] *etc vb V* **herir.**

hierba ['jerßa] *nf* (*pasto*) grass; (*CULIN, MED: planta*) herb; **mala** ~ weed; (*fig*) evil influence.

hierbabuena [jerßa'ßwena] *nf* mint.

hierro ['jerro] *nm* (*metal*) iron; (*objeto*) iron object; ~ **acanalado** corrugated iron; ~ **colado** *o* **fundido** cast iron; **de** ~ iron *cpd*.

hierva ['jerßa] *etc vb V* **hervir.**

hígado ['iɣaðo] *nm* liver; ~**s** *nmpl* (*fig*) guts; **echar los** ~**s** to wear o.s. out.

higiene [i'xjene] *nf* hygiene.

higiénico, a [i'xjeniko, a] *adj* hygienic.

higo ['iɣo] *nm* fig; ~ **seco** dried fig; ~ **chumbo** prickly pear; **de** ~**s a brevas** once in a blue moon.

higuera [i'ɣera] *nf* fig tree.

hijastro, a [i'xastro, a] *nm/f* stepson/ daughter.

hijo, a ['ixo, a] *nm/f* son/daughter, child; (*uso vocativo*) dear; ~**s** *nmpl* children, sons and daughters; **sin** ~**s** childless; ~**/hija político/a** son-/daughter-in-law; ~ **pródigo** prodigal son; ~ **de papá/mamá** daddy's/mummy's boy; ~ **de puta** (*fam!*) bastard (*!*), son of a bitch (*!*); **cada** ~ **de vecino** any Tom, Dick or Harry.

hilacha [i'latʃa] *nf* ravelled thread; ~ **de acero** steel wool.

hilado, a [i'laðo, a] *adj* spun.

hilandero, a [ilan'dero, a] *nm/f* spinner.

hilar [i'lar] *vt* to spin; (*fig*) to reason, infer; ~ **delgado** to split hairs.

hilera [i'lera] *nf* row, file.

hilo ['ilo] *nm* thread; (*BOT*) fibre; (*tela*) linen; (*metal*) wire; (*de agua*) trickle, thin stream; (*de luz*) beam, ray; (*de conversación*) thread, theme; (*de pensamientos*) train; ~ **dental** dental floss; **colgar de un** ~ (*fig*) to hang by a thread; **traje de** ~ linen suit.

hilvanar [ilßa'nar] *vt* (*COSTURA*) to tack

(*BRIT*), baste (*US*); (*fig*) to do hurriedly.

Himalaya [ima'laja] *nm*: **el** ~, **los Montes** ~ the Himalayas.

himno ['imno] *nm* hymn; ~ **nacional** national anthem.

hincapié [inka'pje] *nm*: **hacer** ~ **en** to emphasize, stress.

hincar [in'kar] *vt* to drive (in), thrust (in); (*diente*) to sink; ~**se** *vr*: ~**se de rodillas** (*esp AM*) to kneel down.

hincha ['intʃa] *nm/f* (*fam: DEPORTE*) fan.

hinchado, a [in'tʃaðo, a] *adj* (*gen*) swollen; (*persona*) pompous ♦ *nf* (group of) supporters *o* fans.

hinchar [in'tʃar] *vt* (*gen*) to swell; (*inflar*) to blow up, inflate; (*fig*) to exaggerate; ~**se** *vr* (*inflarse*) to swell up; (*fam: llenarse*) to stuff o.s.; (*fig*) to get conceited; ~**se de reír** to have a good laugh.

hinchazón [intʃa'θon] *nf* (*MED*) swelling; (*protuberancia*) bump, lump; (*altivez*) arrogance.

hindú [in'du] *adj, nm/f* Hindu.

hinojo [i'noxo] *nm* fennel.

hinque ['inke] *etc vb V* **hincar.**

hipar [i'par] *vi* to hiccup.

hiper... [iper] *pref* hyper....

hiperactivo, a [iperak'tißo, a] *adj* hyperactive.

hipermercado [ipermer'kaðo] *nm* hypermarket, superstore.

hipersensible [ipersen'sißle] *adj* hypersensitive.

hipertensión [iperten'sjon] *nf* high blood pressure, hypertension.

hípico, a ['ipiko, a] *adj* horse *cpd*, equine; **club** ~ riding club.

hipnosis [ip'nosis] *nf inv* hypnosis.

hipnotice [ipno'tiθe] *etc vb V* **hipnotizar.**

hipnotismo [ipno'tismo] *nm* hypnotism.

hipnotizar [ipnoti'θar] *vt* to hypnotize.

hipo ['ipo] *nm* hiccups *pl*; **quitar el** ~ **a algn** to cure sb's hiccups.

hipocondría [ipokon'dria] *nf* hypochondria.

hipocondríaco, a [ipokon'driako, a] *adj, nm/f* hypochondriac.

hipocresía [ipokre'sia] *nf* hypocrisy.

hipócrita [i'pokrita] *adj* hypocritical ♦ *nm/f* hypocrite.

hipodérmico, a [ipo'ðermiko, a] *adj*: **aguja hipodérmica** hypodermic needle.

hipódromo [i'poðromo] *nm* racetrack.

hipopótamo [ipo'potamo] *nm* hippopotamus.

hipoteca [ipo'teka] *nf* mortgage; **redimir una** ~ to pay off a mortgage.

hipotecar [ipote'kar] *vt* to mortgage; (*fig*)

to jeopardize.

hipotecario, a [ipote'karjo, a] *adj* mortgage *cpd*.

hipótesis [i'potesis] *nf inv* hypothesis; **es una ~ (nada más)** that's just a theory.

hipotético, a [ipo'tetiko, a] *adj* hypothetic(al).

hiriendo [i'rjendo] *etc vb V* **herir**.

hiriente [i'rjente] *adj* offensive, wounding.

hirsuto, a [ir'suto, a] *adj* hairy.

hirviendo [ir'ßjendo] *etc vb V* **hervir**.

hisopo [i'sopo] *nm* (*REL*) sprinkler; (*BOT*) hyssop; (*de algodón*) swab.

hispánico, a [is'paniko, a] *adj* Hispanic, Spanish.

hispanidad [ispani'ðað] *nf* (*cualidad*) Spanishness; (*POL*) Spanish *o* Hispanic world.

hispanista [ispa'nista] *nm/f* (*UNIV etc*) Hispan(ic)ist.

hispano, a [is'pano, a] *adj* Hispanic, Spanish, Hispano- ♦ *nm/f* Spaniard.

Hispanoamérica [ispanoa'merika] *nf* Spanish *o* Latin America.

hispanoamericano, a [ispanoameri'kano, a] *adj, nm/f* Spanish *o* Latin American.

hispanohablante [ispanoa'ßlante], **hispanoparlante** [ispanopar'lante] *adj* Spanish-speaking.

histeria [is'terja] *nf* hysteria.

histérico, a [is'teriko, a] *adj* hysterical.

histerismo [iste'rismo] *nm* (*MED*) hysteria; (*fig*) hysterics.

histograma [isto'xrama] *nm* histogram.

historia [is'torja] *nf* history; (*cuento*) story, tale; **~s** *nfpl* (*chismes*) gossip *sg*; **dejarse de ~s** to come to the point; **pasar a la ~** to go down in history.

historiador, a [istorja'ðor, a] *nm/f* historian.

historial [isto'rjal] *nm* record; (*profesional*) curriculum vitae, c.v., résumé (*US*); (*MED*) case history.

histórico, a [is'toriko, a] *adj* historical; (*fig*) historic.

historieta [isto'rjeta] *nf* tale, anecdote; (*dibujos*) comic strip.

histrionismo [istrjo'nismo] *nm* (*TEAT*) acting; (*fig*) histrionics *pl*.

hito ['ito] *nm* (*fig*) landmark; (*objetivo*) goal, target; (*fig*) milestone.

hizo ['iθo] *vb V* **hacer**.

Hna(s). *abr* (= *Hermana(s)*) Sr(s).

Hno(s). *abr* (= *Hermano(s)*) Bro(s).

hocico [o'θiko] *nm* snout; (*fig*) grimace.

hockey ['xoki] *nm* hockey; **~ sobre hielo** ice hockey.

hogar [o'xar] *nm* fireplace, hearth; (*casa*) home; (*vida familiar*) home life.

hogareño, a [oxa'reɲo, a] *adj* home *cpd*; (*persona*) home-loving.

hogaza [o'xaθa] *nf* (*pan*) large loaf.

hoguera [o'xera] *nf* (*gen*) bonfire; (*para herejes*) stake.

hoja ['oxa] *nf* (*gen*) leaf; (*de flor*) petal; (*de hierba*) blade; (*de papel*) sheet; (*página*) page; (*formulario*) form; (*de puerta*) leaf; **~ de afeitar** razor blade; **~ de cálculo electrónico** spreadsheet; **~ de trabajo** (*INFORM*) worksheet; **de ~ ancha** broad-leaved; **de ~ caduca/perenne** deciduous/evergreen.

hojalata [oxa'lata] *nf* tin(plate).

hojaldre [o'xaldre] *nm* (*CULIN*) puff pastry.

hojarasca [oxa'raska] *nf* (*hojas*) dead *o* fallen leaves *pl*; (*fig*) rubbish.

hojear [oxe'ar] *vt* to leaf through, turn the pages of.

hola ['ola] *excl* hello!

Holanda [o'landa] *nf* Holland.

holandés, esa [olan'des, esa] *adj* Dutch ♦ *nm/f* Dutchman/woman; **los holandeses** the Dutch ♦ *nm* (*LING*) Dutch.

holgado, a [ol'xaðo, a] *adj* loose, baggy; (*rico*) well-to-do.

holgar [ol'xar] *vi* (*descansar*) to rest; (*sobrar*) to be superfluous; **huelga decir que** it goes without saying that.

holgazán, ana [olxa'θan, ana] *adj* idle, lazy ♦ *nm/f* loafer.

holgazanear [olxaθane'ar] *vi* to laze *o* loaf around.

holgura [ol'xura] *nf* looseness, bagginess; (*TEC*) play, free movement; (*vida*) comfortable living, luxury.

hollar [o'ʎar] *vt* to tread (on), trample.

hollín [o'ʎin] *nm* soot.

hombre ['ombre] *nm* man; (*raza humana*): **el ~** man(kind) ♦ *excl*: **¡sí ~!** (*claro*) of course!; (*para énfasis*) man, old chap; **~ de negocios** businessman; **~-rana** frogman; **~ de bien** *o* **pro** honest man; **~ de confianza** right-hand man; **~ de estado** statesman; **el ~ medio** the average man.

hombrera [om'brera] *nf* shoulder strap.

hombro ['ombro] *nm* shoulder; **arrimar el ~** to lend a hand; **encogerse de ~s** to shrug one's shoulders.

hombruno, a [om'bruno, a] *adj* mannish.

homenaje [ome'naxe] *nm* (*gen*) homage; (*tributo*) tribute; **un partido ~** a benefit match.

homeopatía [omeopa'tia] *nf* hom(o)eopathy.

homeopático, a [omeo'patiko, a] *adj*

hom(o)eopathic.

homicida [omi'θiða] *adj* homicidal ♦ *nm/f* murderer.

homicidio [omi'θiðjo] *nm* murder, homicide; (*involuntario*) manslaughter.

homologación [omoloɣa'θjon] *nf* (*de sueldo, condiciones*) parity.

homologar [omolo'ɣar] *vt* (*COM*) to standardize; (*ESCOL*) to officially approve; (*DEPORTE*) to officially recognize; (*sueldos*) to equalize.

homólogo, a [o'moloɣo, a] *nm/f* counterpart, opposite number.

homónimo [o'monimo] *nm* (*tocayo*) namesake.

homosexual [omosek'swal] *adj, nm/f* homosexual.

hondo, a ['ondo, a] *adj* deep; **lo** ~ the depth(s) (*pl*), the bottom; **con ~ pesar** with deep regret.

hondonada [ondo'naða] *nf* hollow, depression; (*cañón*) ravine; (*GEO*) lowland.

hondura [on'dura] *nf* depth, profundity.

Honduras [on'duras] *nf* Honduras.

hondureño, a [ondu'reɲo, a] *adj, nm/f* Honduran.

honestidad [onesti'ðað] *nf* purity, chastity; (*decencia*) decency.

honesto, a [o'nesto, a] *adj* chaste; decent, honest; (*justo*) just.

hongo ['oŋgo] *nm* (*BOT: gen*) fungus; (: *comestible*) mushroom; (: *venenoso*) toadstool; (*sombrero*) bowler (hat) (*BRIT*), derby (*US*); **~s del pie** footrot *sg*, athlete's foot *sg*.

honor [o'nor] *nm* (*gen*) honour (*BRIT*), honor (*US*); (*gloria*) glory; **~ profesional** professional etiquette; **en ~ a la verdad** to be fair.

honorable [ono'raβle] *adj* honourable (*BRIT*), honorable (*US*).

honorario, a [ono'rarjo, a] *adj* honorary ♦ *nm*: **~s** fees.

honorífico, a [ono'rifiko, a] *adj* honourable (*BRIT*), honorable (*US*); **mención honorífica** hono(u)rable mention.

honra ['onra] *nf* (*gen*) honour; (*renombre*) good name; **~s fúnebres** funeral rites; **tener algo a mucha ~** to be proud of sth.

honradez [onra'ðeθ] *nf* honesty; (*de persona*) integrity.

honrado, a [on'raðo, a] *adj* honest, upright.

honrar [on'rar] *vt* to honour; **~se** *vr*: **~se con algo/de hacer algo** to be honoured by sth/to do sth.

honroso, a [on'roso, a] *adj* (*honrado*)

honourable; (*respetado*) respectable.

hora ['ora] *nf* hour; (*tiempo*) time; **¿qué ~ es?** what time is it?; **¿a qué ~?** at what time?; **media ~** half an hour; **a la ~ de comer/de recreo** at lunchtime/at playtime; **a primera ~** first thing (in the morning); **a última ~** at the last moment; **"última ~"** "stop press"; **noticias de última ~** last-minute news; **a altas ~s** in the small hours; **a la ~ en punto** on the dot; **¡a buena ~!** about time, too!; **en mala ~** unluckily; **dar la ~** to strike the hour; **poner el reloj en ~** to set one's watch; **~s de oficina/de trabajo** office/working hours; **~s de visita** visiting times; **~s extras** *o* **extraordinarias** overtime *sg*; **~s punta** rush hours; **no ver la ~ de** to look forward to; **¡ya era ~!** and about time too!

horadar [ora'ðar] *vt* to drill, bore.

horario, a [o'rarjo, a] *adj* hourly, hour *cpd* ♦ *nm* timetable; **~ comercial** business hours.

horca ['orka] *nf* gallows *sg*; (*AGR*) pitchfork.

horcajadas [orka'xaðas]: **a ~** *adv* astride.

horchata [or'tʃata] *nf* cold drink made from tiger nuts and water, tiger nut milk.

horda ['orða] *nf* horde.

horizontal [oriθon'tal] *adj* horizontal.

horizonte [ori'θonte] *nm* horizon.

horma ['orma] *nf* mould; **~ (de calzado)** last; **~ de sombrero** hat block.

hormiga [or'miɣa] *nf* ant; **~s** *nfpl* (*MED*) pins and needles.

hormigón [ormi'ɣon] *nm* concrete; **~ armado/pretensado** reinforced/prestressed concrete.

hormigueo [ormi'ɣeo] *nm* (*comezón*) itch; (*fig*) uneasiness.

hormiguero [ormi'ɣero] *nm* (*ZOOL*) ant's nest; **era un ~** it was swarming with people.

hormona [or'mona] *nf* hormone.

hornada [or'naða] *nf* batch of loaves (*etc*).

hornillo [or'niʎo] *nm* (*cocina*) portable stove.

horno ['orno] *nm* (*CULIN*) oven; (*TEC*) furnace; (*para cerámica*) kiln; **~ microondas** microwave (oven); **alto ~** blast furnace; **~ crematorio** crematorium.

horóscopo [o'roskopo] *nm* horoscope.

horquilla [or'kiʎa] *nf* hairpin; (*AGR*) pitchfork.

horrendo, a [o'rrendo, a] *adj* horrendous,

horrible – huerto

frightful.
horrible [o'rriβle] *adj* horrible, dreadful.
horripilante [orripi'lante] *adj* hair-raising, horrifying.
horripilar [orripi'lar] *vt*: ~ **a algn** to horrify sb; ~**se** *vr* to be horrified.
horror [o'rror] *nm* horror, dread; (*atrocidad*) atrocity; ¡**qué** ~! (*fam*) how awful!; **estudia horrores** he studies a hell of a lot.
horrorice [orro'riθe] *etc vb* V **horrorizar.**
horrorizar [orrori'θar] *vt* to horrify, frighten; ~**se** *vr* to be horrified.
horroroso, a [orro'roso, a] *adj* horrifying, ghastly.
hortaliza [orta'liθa] *nf* vegetable.
hortelano, a [orte'lano, a] *nm/f* (market) gardener.
hortera [or'tera] *adj* (*fam*) vulgar, naff.
horterada [orte'raða] *nf* (*fam*): **es una** ~ it's really naff.
hortícola [or'tikola] *adj* horticultural.
horticultura [ortikul'tura] *nf* horticulture.
hortofrutícola [ortofru'tikola] *adj* fruit and vegetable *cpd.*
hosco, a ['osko, a] *adj* dark; (*persona*) sullen, gloomy.
hospedaje [ospe'ðaxe] *nm* (cost of) board and lodging.
hospedar [ospe'ðar] *vt* to put up; ~**se** *vr*: ~**se (con/en)** to stay *o* lodge (with/at).
hospedería [ospeðe'ria] *nf* (*edificio*) inn; (*habitación*) guest room.
hospicio [os'piθjo] *nm* (*para niños*) orphanage.
hospital [ospi'tal] *nm* hospital.
hospitalario, a [ospita'larjo, a] *adj* (*acogedor*) hospitable.
hospitalice [ospita'liθe] *etc vb* V **hospitalizar.**
hospitalidad [ospitali'ðað] *nf* hospitality.
hospitalizar [ospitali'θar] *vt* to send *o* take to hospital, hospitalize.
hosquedad [oske'ðað] *nf* sullenness.
hostal [os'tal] *nm* small hotel; V *tb* **hotel.**
hostelería [ostele'ria] *nf* hotel business *o* trade.
hostia ['ostja] *nf* (*REL*) host, consecrated wafer; (*fam: golpe*) whack, punch ♦ *excl*: ¡~(**s**)! (*fam!*) damn!
hostigar [osti'ɣar] *vt* to whip; (*fig*) to harass, pester.
hostigue [os'tiɣe] *etc vb* V **hostigar.**
hostil [os'til] *adj* hostile.
hostilidad [ostili'ðað] *nf* hostility.
hotel [o'tel] *nm* hotel; *see boxed note.*

HOTEL

In Spain you can choose from the following categories of accommodation, in descending order of quality and price: **hotel** *(from five stars down to one),* "hostal", "pensión", "casa de huéspedes" *or* "fonda". *Standards can vary widely even within these categories. The state also runs luxury hotels called* "paradores", *which are usually sited in places of particular historical interest and are often architecturally important buildings themselves.*

---

hotelero, a [ote'lero, a] *adj* hotel *cpd* ♦ *nm/f* hotelier.
hoy [oi] *adv* (*este día*) today; (*en la actualidad*) now(adays) ♦ *nm* present time; ~ (**en**) **día** now(adays); **el día de** ~, ~ **día** (*AM*) this very day; ~ **por** ~ right now; **de** ~ **en ocho días** a week today; **de** ~ **en adelante** from now on.
hoya ['oja] *nf* pit; (*sepulcro*) grave; (*GEO*) valley.
hoyo ['ojo] *nm* hole, pit; (*tumba*) grave; (*GOLF*) hole; (*MED*) pockmark.
hoyuelo [oj'welo] *nm* dimple.
hoz [oθ] *nf* sickle.
hube ['uβe] *etc vb* V **haber.**
hucha ['utʃa] *nf* money box.
hueco, a ['weko, a] *adj* (*vacío*) hollow, empty; (*resonante*) booming; (*sonido*) resonant; (*persona*) conceited; (*estilo*) pompous ♦ *nm* hollow, cavity; (*agujero*) hole; (*de escalera*) well; (*de ascensor*) shaft; (*vacante*) vacancy; ~ **de la mano** hollow of the hand.
huela ['wela] *etc vb* V **oler.**
huelga ['welɣa] *etc vb* V **holgar** ♦ *nf* strike; **declararse en** ~ to go on strike, come out on strike; ~ **general** general strike; ~ **de hambre** hunger strike; ~ **oficial** official strike.
huelgue ['welɣe] *etc vb* V **holgar.**
huelguista [wel'ɣista] *nm/f* striker.
huella ['weʎa] *nf* (*acto de pisar, pisada*) tread(ing); (*marca del paso*) footprint, footstep; (: *de animal, máquina*) track; ~ **digital** fingerprint; **sin dejar** ~ without leaving a trace.
huérfano, a ['werfano, a] *adj* orphan(ed); (*fig*) unprotected ♦ *nm/f* orphan.
huerta ['werta] *nf* market garden (*BRIT*), truck farm (*US*); (*Murcia, Valencia*) irrigated region.
huerto ['werto] *nm* kitchen garden; (*de*

árboles frutales) orchard.
hueso ['weso] *nm* (*ANAT*) bone; (*de fruta*) stone, pit (*US*); **sin ~** (*carne*) boned; **estar en los ~s** to be nothing but skin and bone; **ser un ~** (*profesor*) to be terribly strict; **un ~ duro de roer** a hard nut to crack.
huesoso, a [we'soso, a] *adj* (*esp AM*) bony.
huésped, a ['wespeð, a] *nm/f* (*invitado*) guest; (*habitante*) resident; (*anfitrión*) host(ess).
huesudo, a [we'suðo, a] *adj* bony, big-boned.
huevas ['weßas] *nfpl* eggs, roe *sg*; (*AM*: *fam!*) balls (*!*).
huevera [we'ßera] *nf* eggcup.
huevo ['weßo] *nm* egg, (*fam!*) ball (*!*), testicle; ~ **duro/escalfado/estrellado** *o* **frito/pasado por agua** hard-boiled/poached/fried/soft-boiled egg; ~**s revueltos** scrambled eggs; **me costó un ~** (*fam!*) it was hard work; **tener ~s** (*fam!*) to have guts.
huevón, ona [we'ßon, ona] *nm/f* (*AM fam!*) stupid bastard (*!*), stupid idiot.
huida [u'iða] *nf* escape, flight; ~ **de capitales** (*COM*) flight of capital.
huidizo, a [ui'ðiθo, a] *adj* (*tímido*) shy; (*pasajero*) fleeting.
huir [u'ir] *vt* (*escapar*) to flee, escape; (*evadir*) to avoid ♦ *vi* to flee, run away; ~**se** *vr* (*escaparse*) to escape.
hule ['ule] *nm* (*encerado*) oilskin; (*esp AM*) rubber.
hulla ['uʎa] *nf* bituminous coal.
humanice [uma'niθe] *etc vb V* **humanizar**.
humanidad [umani'ðað] *nf* (*género humano*) man(kind); (*cualidad*) humanity; (*fam: gordura*) corpulence.
humanitario, a [umani'tarjo, a] *adj* humanitarian; (*benévolo*) humane.
humanizar [umani'θar] *vt* to humanize; ~**se** *vr* to become more human.
humano, a [u'mano, a] *adj* (*gen*) human; (*humanitario*) humane ♦ *nm* human; **ser ~** human being.
humareda [uma'reða] *nf* cloud of smoke.
humeante [ume'ante] *adj* smoking, smoky.
humedad [ume'ðað] *nf* (*del clima*) humidity; (*de pared etc*) dampness; **a prueba de ~** damp-proof.
humedecer [umeðe'θer] *vt* to moisten, wet; ~**se** *vr* to get wet.
humedezca [ume'ðeθka] *etc vb V* **humedecer**.
húmedo, a ['umeðo, a] *adj* (*mojado*) damp, wet; (*tiempo etc*) humid.
humildad [umil'dað] *nf* humility,

humbleness.
humilde [u'milde] *adj* humble, modest; (*clase etc*) low, modest.
humillación [umiʎa'θjon] *nf* humiliation.
humillante [umi'ʎante] *adj* humiliating.
humillar [umi'ʎar] *vt* to humiliate; ~**se** *vr* to humble o.s., grovel.
humo ['umo] *nm* (*de fuego*) smoke; (*gas nocivo*) fumes *pl*; (*vapor*) steam, vapour; ~**s** *nmpl* (*fig*) conceit *sg*; **irse todo en ~** (*fig*) to vanish without trace; **bajar los ~s a algn** to take sb down a peg or two.
humor [u'mor] *nm* (*disposición*) mood, temper; (*lo que divierte*) humour; **de buen/mal ~** in a good/bad mood.
humorismo [umo'rismo] *nm* humour.
humorista [umo'rista] *nm/f* comic.
humorístico, a [umo'ristiko, a] *adj* funny, humorous.
hundimiento [undi'mjento] *nm* (*gen*) sinking; (*colapso*) collapse.
hundir [un'dir] *vt* to sink; (*edificio, plan*) to ruin, destroy; ~**se** *vr* to sink, collapse; (*fig: arruinarse*) to be ruined; (*desaparecer*) to disappear; **se hundió la economía** the economy collapsed; **se hundieron los precios** prices slumped.
húngaro, a ['ungaro, a] *adj*, *nm/f* Hungarian ♦ *nm* (*LING*) Hungarian, Magyar.
Hungría [un'gria] *nf* Hungary.
huracán [ura'kan] *nm* hurricane.
huraño, a [u'raɲo, a] *adj* shy; (*antisocial*) unsociable.
hurgar [ur'ɣar] *vt* to poke, jab; (*remover*) to stir (up); ~**se** *vr*: ~**se (las narices)** to pick one's nose.
hurgonear [urɣone'ar] *vt* to poke.
hurgue ['urɣe] *etc vb V* **hurgar**.
hurón [u'ron] *nm* (*ZOOL*) ferret.
hurra ['urra] *excl* hurray!, hurrah!
hurtadillas [urta'ðiʎas]: **a ~** *adv* stealthily, on the sly.
hurtar [ur'tar] *vt* to steal; ~**se** *vr* to hide, keep out of the way.
hurto ['urto] *nm* theft, stealing; (*lo robado*) (piece of) stolen property, loot.
husmear [usme'ar] *vt* (*oler*) to sniff out, scent; (*fam*) to pry into ♦ *vi* to smell bad.
huso ['uso] *nm* (*TEC*) spindle; (*de torno*) drum.
huy ['ui] *excl* (*dolor*) ow!, ouch!; (*sorpresa*) well!; (*alivio*) phew!; **¡~, perdona!** oops, sorry!
huyendo [u'jendo] *etc vb V* **huir**.

I i

I, i [i] *nf* (*letra*) I, i; **I de Inés** I for Isaac (*BRIT*) *o* Item (*US*).

I.A. *abr* = **inteligencia artificial**.

iba ['iβa] *etc vb V* **ir**.

Iberia [i'βerja] *nf* Iberia.

ibérico, a [i'βeriko, a] *adj* Iberian; **la Península ibérica** the Iberian Peninsula.

ibero, a [i'βero, a], **íbero, a** ['iβero, a] *adj*, *nm/f* Iberian.

iberoamericano, a [iβeroameri'kano, a] *adj*, *nm/f* Latin American.

íbice ['iβiθe] *nm* ibex.

ibicenco, a [iβi'θenko, a] *adj* of *o* from Ibiza ♦ *nm/f* native *o* inhabitant of Ibiza.

Ibiza [i'βiθa] *nf* Ibiza.

ice ['iθe] *etc vb V* **izar**.

iceberg [iθe'ber] *nm* iceberg.

ICONA [i'kona] *nm abr* (*ESP*) = *Instituto Nacional para la Conservación de la Naturaleza*.

icono [i'kono] *nm* (*tb INFORM*) icon.

iconoclasta [ikono'klasta] *adj* iconoclastic ♦ *nm/f* iconoclast.

ictericia [ikte'riθja] *nf* jaundice.

íd. *abr* = **ídem**.

I+D *abr* (= *Investigación y Desarrollo*) R&D.

ida ['iða] *nf* going, departure; **~ y vuelta** round trip, return; **~s y venidas** comings and goings.

IDE [iðe] *nf abr* (= *Iniciativa de Defensa Estratégica*) SDI.

idea [i'ðea] *nf* idea; (*impresión*) opinion; (*propósito*) intention; **~ genial** brilliant idea; **a mala ~** out of spite; **no tengo la menor ~** I haven't a clue.

ideal [iðe'al] *adj*, *nm* ideal.

idealice [iðea'liθe] *etc vb V* **idealizar**.

idealista [iðea'lista] *adj* idealistic ♦ *nm/f* idealist.

idealizar [iðeali'θar] *vt* to idealize.

idear [iðe'ar] *vt* to think up; (*aparato*) to invent; (*viaje*) to plan.

ídem ['iðem] *pron* ditto.

idéntico, a [i'ðentiko, a] *adj* identical.

identidad [iðenti'ðað] *nf* identity; **~ corporativa** corporate identity *o* image.

identificación [iðentifika'θjon] *nf* identification.

identificar [iðentifi'kar] *vt* to identify; **~se** *vr*: **~se con** to identify with.

identifique [iðenti'fike] *etc vb V* **identificar**.

ideología [iðeolo'xia] *nf* ideology.

ideológico, a [iðeo'loxiko, a] *adj* ideological.

idílico, a [i'ðiliko, a] *adj* idyllic.

idilio [i'ðiljo] *nm* love affair.

idioma [i'ðjoma] *nm* language.

idiomático, a [iðjo'matiko, a] *adj* idiomatic.

idiota [i'ðjota] *adj* idiotic ♦ *nm/f* idiot.

idiotez [iðjo'teθ] *nf* idiocy.

idolatrar [iðola'trar] *vt* (*fig*) to idolize.

ídolo ['iðolo] *nm* (*tb fig*) idol.

idoneidad [iðonei'ðað] *nf* suitability; (*capacidad*) aptitude.

idóneo, a [i'ðoneo, a] *adj* suitable.

iglesia [i'xlesja] *nf* church; **~ parroquial** parish church; **¡con la ~ hemos topado!** now we're really up against it!

iglú [i'xlu] *nm* igloo; (*contenedor*) bottle bank.

ignición [ixni'θjon] *nf* ignition.

ignominia [ixno'minja] *nf* ignominy.

ignominioso, a [ixnomi'njoso, a] *adj* ignominious.

ignorado, a [ixno'raðo, a] *adj* unknown; (*dato*) obscure.

ignorancia [ixno'ranθja] *nf* ignorance; **por ~** through ignorance.

ignorante [ixno'rante] *adj* ignorant, uninformed ♦ *nm/f* ignoramus.

ignorar [ixno'rar] *vt* not to know, be ignorant of; (*no hacer caso a*) to ignore; **ignoramos su paradero** we don't know his whereabouts.

ignoto, a [ix'noto, a] *adj* unknown.

igual [i'xwal] *adj* equal; (*similar*) like, similar; (*mismo*) (the) same; (*constante*) constant; (*temperatura*) even ♦ *nm/f* equal; **al ~ que** *prep, conj* like, just like; **~ que** the same as; **sin ~** peerless; **me da o es ~** I don't care, it makes no difference; **no tener ~** to be unrivalled; **son ~es** they're the same.

iguala [i'xwala] *nf* equalization; (*COM*) agreement.

igualada [ixwa'laða] *nf* equalizer.

igualar [ixwa'lar] *vt* (*gen*) to equalize, make equal; (*terreno*) to make even; (*COM*) to agree upon; **~se** *vr* (*platos de balanza*) to balance out; **~se (a)** (*equivaler*) to be equal (to).

igualdad [ixwal'dað] *nf* equality; (*similaridad*) sameness; (*uniformidad*) uniformity; **en ~ de condiciones** on an equal basis.

igualmente [iɣwal'mente] *adv* equally;
(*también*) also, likewise ♦ *excl* the same
to you!

iguana [i'ɣwana] *nf* iguana.

ikurriña [iku'rriɲa] *nf* Basque flag.

ilegal [ile'ɣal] *adj* illegal.

ilegitimidad [ilexitimi'ðað] *nf* illegitimacy.

ilegítimo, a [ile'xitimo, a] *adj* illegitimate.

ileso, a [i'leso, a] *adj* unhurt, unharmed.

ilícito, a [i'liθito, a] *adj* illicit.

ilimitado, a [ilimi'taðo, a] *adj* unlimited.

Ilma., Ilmo. *abr* (= *Ilustrísima, Ilustrísimo*)
courtesy title.

ilógico, a [i'loxiko, a] *adj* illogical.

iluminación [ilumina'θjon] *nf* illumination;
(*alumbrado*) lighting; (*fig*)
enlightenment.

iluminar [ilumi'nar] *vt* to illuminate, light
(up); (*fig*) to enlighten.

ilusión [ilu'sjon] *nf* illusion; (*quimera*)
delusion; (*esperanza*) hope; (*emoción*)
excitement, thrill; **hacerse ilusiones** to
build up one's hopes; **no te hagas
ilusiones** don't build up your hopes o get
too excited.

ilusionado, a [ilusjo'naðo, a] *adj* excited.

ilusionar [ilusjo'nar] *vt*: ~ **a alguien**
(*falsamente*) to build up sb's hopes; ~**se**
vr (*falsamente*) to build up one's hopes;
(*entusiasmarse*) to get excited; **me
ilusiona mucho el viaje** I'm really
excited about the trip.

ilusionista [ilusjo'nista] *nm/f* conjurer.

iluso, a [i'luso, a] *adj* gullible, easily
deceived ♦ *nm/f* dreamer, visionary.

ilusorio, a [ilu'sorjo, a] *adj* (*de ilusión*)
illusory, deceptive; (*esperanza*) vain.

ilustración [ilustra'θjon] *nf* illustration;
(*saber*) learning, erudition; **la I**~ the
Enlightenment.

ilustrado, a [ilus'traðo, a] *adj* illustrated,
learned.

ilustrar [ilus'trar] *vt* to illustrate; (*instruir*)
to instruct; (*explicar*) to explain, make
clear; ~**se** *vr* to acquire knowledge.

ilustre [i'lustre] *adj* famous, illustrious.

imagen [i'maxen] *nf* (*gen*) image; (*dibujo,
TV*) picture; (*REL*) statue; **ser la viva ~ de**
to be the spitting o living image of; **a su
~** in one's own image.

imaginación [imaxina'θjon] *nf*
imagination; (*fig*) fancy; **ni por ~** on no
account; **no se me pasó por la ~ que ...**
it never even occurred to me that ....

imaginar [imaxi'nar] *vt* (*gen*) to imagine;
(*idear*) to think up; (*suponer*) to suppose;
~**se** *vr* to imagine; **¡imagínate!** just
imagine!, just fancy!; **imagínese que ...**

suppose that ...; **me imagino que sí** I
should think so.

imaginario, a [imaxi'narjo, a] *adj*
imaginary.

imaginativo, a [imaxina'tiβo, a] *adj*
imaginative ♦ *nf* imagination.

imán [i'man] *nm* magnet.

iman(t)ar [ima'n(t)ar] *vt* to magnetize.

imbécil [im'beθil] *nm/f* imbecile, idiot.

imbecilidad [imbeθili'ðað] *nf* imbecility,
stupidity.

imberbe [im'berβe] *adj* beardless.

imborrable [imbo'rraβle] *adj* indelible;
(*inolvidable*) unforgettable.

imbuir [imbu'ir] *vi* to imbue.

imbuyendo [imbu'jendo] *etc vb V* **imbuir.**

imitación [imita'θjon] *nf* imitation;
(*parodia*) mimicry; **a ~ de** in imitation
of; **desconfíe de las imitaciones** (*COM*)
beware of copies o imitations.

imitador, a [imita'ðor, a] *adj* imitative
♦ *nm/f* imitator; (*TEAT*) mimic.

imitar [imi'tar] *vt* to imitate; (*parodiar,
remedar*) to mimic, ape; (*copiar*) to
follow.

impaciencia [impa'θjenθja] *nf* impatience.

impacientar [impaθjen'tar] *vt* to make
impatient; (*enfadar*) to irritate; ~**se** *vr* to
get impatient; (*inquietarse*) to fret.

impaciente [impa'θjente] *adj* impatient;
(*nervioso*) anxious.

impacto [im'pakto] *nm* impact; (*esp AM:
fig*) shock.

impagado, a [impa'ɣaðo, a] *adj* unpaid,
still to be paid.

impar [im'par] *adj* odd ♦ *nm* odd number.

imparable [impa'raβle] *adj* unstoppable.

imparcial [impar'θjal] *adj* impartial, fair.

imparcialidad [imparθjali'ðað] *nf*
impartiality, fairness.

impartir [impar'tir] *vt* to impart, give.

impasible [impa'siβle] *adj* impassive.

impávido, a [im'paβiðo, a] *adj* fearless,
intrepid.

IMPE ['impe] *nm abr* (*ESP COM*) = *Instituto de
la Mediana y Pequeña Empresa.*

impecable [impe'kaβle] *adj* impeccable.

impedido, a [impe'ðiðo, a] *adj*: **estar ~** to
be an invalid ♦ *nm/f*: **ser un ~ físico** to be
an invalid.

impedimento [impeði'mento] *nm*
impediment, obstacle.

impedir [impe'ðir] *vt* (*obstruir*) to impede,
obstruct; (*estorbar*) to prevent; ~ **el
tráfico** to block the traffic.

impeler [impe'ler] *vt* to drive, propel; (*fig*)
to impel.

impenetrabilidad [impenetraβili'ðað] *nf*

impenetrability.

impenetrable [impene'traßle] *adj*
impenetrable; (*fig*) incomprehensible.

impensable [impen'saßle] *adj* unthinkable.

impepinable [impepi'naßle] *adj* (*fam*)
certain, inevitable.

imperante [impe'rante] *adj* prevailing.

imperar [impe'rar] *vi* (*reinar*) to rule, reign;
(*fig*) to prevail, reign; (*precio*) to be
current.

imperativo, a [impera'tißo, a] *adj* (*persona*)
imperious; (*urgente, LING*) imperative.

imperceptible [imperθep'tißle] *adj*
imperceptible.

imperdible [imper'ðißle] *nm* safety pin.

imperdonable [imperðo'naßle] *adj*
unforgivable, inexcusable.

imperecedero, a [impereθe'ðero, a] *adj*
undying.

imperfección [imperfek'θjon] *nf*
imperfection; (*falla*) flaw, fault.

imperfecto, a [imper'fekto, a] *adj* faulty,
imperfect ♦ *nm* (*LING*) imperfect tense.

imperial [impe'rjal] *adj* imperial.

imperialismo [imperja'lismo] *nm*
imperialism.

imperialista [imperja'lista] *adj*
imperialist(ic) ♦ *nm/f* imperialist.

impericia [impe'riθja] *nf* (*torpeza*)
unskilfulness; (*inexperiencia*)
inexperience.

imperio [im'perjo] *nm* empire; (*autoridad*)
rule, authority; (*fig*) pride, haughtiness;
vale un ~ (*fig*) it's worth a fortune.

imperioso, a [impe'rjoso, a] *adj* imperious;
(*urgente*) urgent; (*imperativo*)
imperative.

impermeable [imperme'aßle] *adj* (*a prueba
de agua*) waterproof ♦ *nm* raincoat, mac
(*BRIT*).

impersonal [imperso'nal] *adj* impersonal.

impertérrito, a [imper'territo, a] *adj*
undaunted.

impertinencia [imperti'nenθja] *nf*
impertinence.

impertinente [imperti'nente] *adj*
impertinent.

imperturbable [impertur'ßaßle] *adj*
imperturbable; (*sereno*) unruffled;
(*impasible*) impassive.

ímpetu ['impetu] *nm* (*impulso*) impetus,
impulse; (*impetuosidad*) impetuosity;
(*violencia*) violence.

impetuosidad [impetwosi'ðað] *nf*
impetuousness; (*violencia*) violence.

impetuoso, a [impe'twoso, a] *adj*
impetuous; (*río*) rushing; (*acto*) hasty.

impida [im'piða] *etc vb V* **impedir**.

impío, a [im'pio, a] *adj* impious, ungodly;
(*cruel*) cruel, pitiless.

implacable [impla'kaßle] *adj* implacable,
relentless.

implantación [implanta'θjon] *nf*
introduction; (*BIO*) implantation.

implantar [implan'tar] *vt* (*costumbre*) to
introduce; (*BIO*) to implant; ~**se** *vr* to be
introduced.

implicar [impli'kar] *vt* to involve; (*entrañar*)
to imply; **esto no implica que ...** this does
not mean that ....

implícito, a [im'pliθito, a] *adj* (*tácito*)
implicit; (*sobreentendido*) implied.

implique [im'plike] *etc vb V* **implicar**.

implorar [implo'rar] *vt* to beg,
implore.

impondré [impon'dre] *etc vb V* **imponer**.

imponente [impo'nente] *adj*
(*impresionante*) impressive, imposing;
(*solemne*) grand ♦ *nm/f* (*COM*) depositor.

imponer [impo'ner] *vt* (*gen*) to impose;
(*tarea*) to set; (*exigir*) to exact; (*miedo*) to
inspire; (*COM*) to deposit; ~**se** *vr* to
assert o.s.; (*prevalecer*) to prevail;
(*costumbre*) to grow up; ~**se un deber** to
assume a duty.

imponga [im'ponga] *etc vb V* **imponer**.

imponible [impo'nißle] *adj* (*COM*) taxable,
subject to tax; (*importación*) dutiable,
subject to duty; **no** ~ tax-free, tax-
exempt (*US*).

impopular [impopu'lar] *adj* unpopular.

importación [importa'θjon] *nf* (*acto*)
importing; (*mercancías*) imports *pl*.

importancia [impor'tanθja] *nf* importance;
(*valor*) value, significance; (*extensión*)
size, magnitude; **no dar** ~ **a** to consider
unimportant; (*fig*) to make light of; **no
tiene** ~ it's nothing.

importante [impor'tante] *adj* important;
valuable, significant.

importar [impor'tar] *vt* (*del extranjero*) to
import; (*costar*) to amount to; (*implicar*)
to involve ♦ *vi* to be important, matter;
me importa un bledo I don't give a
damn; **¿le importa que fume?** do you
mind if I smoke?; **¿te importa
prestármelo?** would you mind lending it
to me?; **¿qué importa?** what difference
does it make?; **no importa** it doesn't
matter; **no le importa** he doesn't care, it
doesn't bother him; **"no importa precio"**
"cost no object".

importe [im'porte] *nm* (*total*) amount;
(*valor*) value.

importunar [importu'nar] *vt* to bother,
pester.

importuno, a [impor'tuno, a] *adj*
(*inoportuno, molesto*) inopportune;
(*indiscreto*) troublesome.

imposibilidad [imposiβili'ðað] *nf*
impossibility; **mi ~ para hacerlo** my
inability to do it.

imposibilitado, a [imposiβili'taðo, a] *adj*:
verse ~ para hacer algo to be unable to
do sth.

imposibilitar [imposiβili'tar] *vt* to make
impossible, prevent.

imposible [impo'siβle] *adj* impossible;
(*insoportable*) unbearable, intolerable; **es
~** it's out of the question; **es ~ de
predecir** it's impossible to forecast *o*
predict.

imposición [imposi'θjon] *nf* imposition;
(*COM*) tax; (*inversión*) deposit; **efectuar
una ~** to make a deposit.

impostor, a [impos'tor, a] *nm/f* impostor.

impostura [impos'tura] *nf* fraud,
imposture.

impotencia [impo'tenθja] *nf* impotence.

impotente [impo'tente] *adj* impotent.

impracticable [imprakti'kaβle] *adj*
(*irrealizable*) impracticable; (*intransitable*)
impassable.

imprecar [impre'kar] *vi* to curse.

imprecisión [impreθi'sjon] *nf* lack of
precision, vagueness.

impreciso, a [impre'θiso, a] *adj* imprecise,
vague.

impredecible [impreðe'θiβle],
impredictible [impreðik'tiβle] *adj*
unpredictable.

impregnar [imprex'nar] *vt* to impregnate;
(*fig*) to pervade; **~se** *vr* to become
impregnated.

imprenta [im'prenta] *nf* (*acto*) printing;
(*aparato*) press; (*casa*) printer's; (*letra*)
print.

impreque [im'preke] *etc vb V*
imprecar.

imprescindible [impresθin'diβle] *adj*
essential, vital.

impresión [impre'sjon] *nf* impression;
(*IMPRENTA*) printing; (*edición*) edition;
(*FOTO*) print; (*marca*) imprint; **~ digital**
fingerprint.

impresionable [impresjo'naβle] *adj*
(*sensible*) impressionable.

impresionado, a [impresjo'naðo, a] *adj*
impressed; (*FOTO*) exposed.

impresionante [impresjo'nante] *adj*
impressive; (*tremendo*) tremendous;
(*maravilloso*) great, marvellous.

impresionar [impresjo'nar] *vt* (*conmover*)
to move; (*afectar*) to impress, strike;

(*película fotográfica*) to expose; **~se** *vr* to
be impressed; (*conmoverse*) to be
moved.

impresionista [impresjo'nista] *adj*
impressionist(ic); (*ARTE*) impressionist
♦ *nm/f* impressionist.

impreso, a [im'preso, a] *pp de* **imprimir**
♦ *adj* printed ♦ *nm* printed paper/book
etc; **~s** *nmpl* printed matter *sg*; **~ de
solicitud** application form.

impresora [impre'sora] *nf* (*INFORM*)
printer; **~ de chorro de tinta** ink-jet
printer; **~ (por) láser** laser printer; **~ de
línea** line printer; **~ de matriz (de
agujas)** dot-matrix printer; **~ de rueda** *o*
de margarita daisy-wheel printer.

imprevisible [impreβi'siβle] *adj*
unforeseeable; (*individuo*) unpredictable.

imprevisión [impreβi'sjon] *nf* short-
sightedness; (*irreflexión*)
thoughtlessness.

imprevisto, a [impre'βisto, a] *adj*
unforeseen; (*inesperado*) unexpected
♦ *nm*: **~s** (*dinero*) incidentals, unforeseen
expenses.

imprimir [impri'mir] *vt* to stamp; (*textos*) to
print; (*INFORM*) to output, print out.

improbabilidad [improβaβili'ðað] *nf*
improbability, unlikelihood.

improbable [impro'βaβle] *adj* improbable;
(*inverosímil*) unlikely.

improcedente [improθe'ðente] *adj*
inappropriate; (*JUR*) inadmissible.

improductivo, a [improðuk'tiβo, a] *adj*
unproductive.

impronunciable [impronun'θjaβle] *adj*
unpronounceable.

improperio [impro'perjo] *nm* insult; **~s**
nmpl abuse *sg*.

impropiedad [impropje'ðað] *nf*
impropriety (of language).

impropio, a [im'propjo, a] *adj* improper;
(*inadecuado*) inappropriate.

improvisación [improβisa'θjon] *nf*
improvization.

improvisado, a [improβi'saðo, a] *adj*
improvised, impromptu.

improvisar [improβi'sar] *vt* to improvise;
(*comida*) to rustle up ♦ *vi* to improvise;
(*MUS*) to extemporize; (*TEAT etc*) to ad-
lib.

improviso [impro'βiso] *adv* **de ~**
unexpectedly, suddenly; (*MUS etc*)
impromptu.

imprudencia [impru'ðenθja] *nf*
imprudence; (*indiscreción*) indiscretion;
(*descuido*) carelessness.

imprudente [impru'ðente] *adj* imprudent;

indiscreet.

Impte. abr (= Importe) amt.

impúdico, a [im'puðiko, a] adj shameless; (lujurioso) lecherous.

impudor [impu'ðor] nm shamelessness; (lujuria) lechery.

impuesto, a [im'pwesto, a] pp de **imponer** ♦ adj imposed ♦ nm tax; (derecho) duty; **anterior al** ~ pre-tax; **sujeto a** ~ taxable; ~ **de lujo** luxury tax; ~ **de plusvalía** capital gains tax; ~ **sobre la propiedad** property tax; ~ **sobre la renta** income tax; ~ **sobre la renta de las personas físicas (IRPF)** personal income tax; ~ **sobre la riqueza** wealth tax; ~ **de transferencia de capital** capital transfer tax; ~ **de venta** sales tax; ~ **sobre el valor añadido (IVA)** value added tax (VAT).

impugnar [impuɣ'nar] vt to oppose, contest; (refutar) to refute, impugn.

impulsar [impul'sar] vt to promote.

impulsivo, a [impul'siβo, a] adj impulsive.

impulso [im'pulso] nm impulse; (fuerza, empuje) thrust, drive; (fig: sentimiento) urge, impulse; **a ~s del miedo** driven on by fear.

impune [im'pune] adj unpunished.

impunemente [impune'mente] adv with impunity.

impureza [impu'reθa] nf impurity; (fig) lewdness.

impuro, a [im'puro, a] adj impure; lewd.

impuse [im'puse] etc vb V **imponer**.

imputación [imputa'θjon] nf imputation.

imputar [impu'tar] vt: ~ **a** to attribute to, to impute to.

inabordable [inaβor'ðaβle] adj unapproachable.

inacabable [inaka'βaβle] adj (infinito) endless; (interminable) interminable.

inaccesible [inakθe'siβle] adj inaccessible; (fig: precio) beyond one's reach, prohibitive; (individuo) aloof.

inacción [inak'θjon] nf inactivity.

inaceptable [inaθep'taβle] adj unacceptable.

inactividad [inaktiβi'ðað] nf inactivity; (COM) dullness.

inactivo, a [inak'tiβo, a] adj inactive; (COM) dull; (población) non-working.

inadaptación [inaðapta'θjon] nf maladjustment.

inadaptado, a [inaðap'taðo, a] adj maladjusted ♦ nm/f misfit.

inadecuado, a [inaðe'kwaðo, a] adj (insuficiente) inadequate; (inapto) unsuitable.

inadmisible [inaðmi'siβle] adj inadmissible.

inadvertido, a [inaðβer'tiðo, a] adj (no visto) unnoticed.

inagotable [inaɣo'taβle] adj inexhaustible.

inaguantable [inaɣwan'taβle] adj unbearable.

inalámbrico, a [ina'lambriko, a] adj cordless.

inalcanzable [inalkan'θaβle] adj unattainable.

inalterable [inalte'raβle] adj immutable, unchangeable.

inamovible [inamo'βiβle] adj fixed, immovable; (TEC) undetachable.

inanición [inani'θjon] nf starvation.

inanimado, a [inani'maðo, a] adj inanimate.

inapelable [inape'laβle] adj (JUR) unappealable; (fig) irremediable.

inapetencia [inape'tenθja] nf lack of appetite.

inaplicable [inapli'kaβle] adj not applicable.

inapreciable [inapre'θjaβle] adj invaluable.

inarrugable [inarru'ɣaβle] adj crease-resistant.

inasequible [inase'kiβle] adj unattainable.

inaudito, a [inau'ðito, a] adj unheard-of.

inauguración [inauɣura'θjon] nf inauguration; (de exposición) opening.

inaugurar [inauɣu'rar] vt to inaugurate; to open.

I.N.B. abr (= Instituto Nacional de Bachillerato) ≈ comprehensive school (BRIT), high school (US).

I.N.B.A. abr (AM) = Instituto Nacional de Bellas Artes.

inca ['inka] nm/f Inca.

INCAE [in'kae] nm abr = Instituto Centroamericano de Administración de Empresas.

incaico, a [in'kaiko, a] adj Inca.

incalculable [inkalku'laβle] adj incalculable.

incandescente [inkandes'θente] adj incandescent.

incansable [inkan'saβle] adj tireless, untiring.

incapacidad [inkapaθi'ðað] nf incapacity; (incompetencia) incompetence; ~ **física/mental** physical/mental disability.

incapacitar [inkapaθi'tar] vt (inhabilitar) to incapacitate, handicap; (descalificar) to disqualify.

incapaz [inka'paθ] adj incapable; ~ **de hacer algo** unable to do sth.

incautación [inkauta'θjon] nf seizure,

confiscation.
incautarse [inkau'tarse] *vr*: ~ **de** to seize, confiscate.
incauto, a [in'kauto, a] *adj* (*imprudente*) incautious, unwary.
incendiar [inθen'djar] *vt* to set fire to; (*fig*) to inflame; ~**se** *vr* to catch fire.
incendiario, a [inθen'djarjo, a] *adj* incendiary ♦ *nm/f* fire-raiser, arsonist.
incendio [in'θendjo] *nm* fire; ~ **intencionado** arson.
incentivo [inθen'tiβo] *nm* incentive.
incertidumbre [inθerti'ðumbre] *nf* (*inseguridad*) uncertainty; (*duda*) doubt.
incesante [inθe'sante] *adj* incessant.
incesto [in'θesto] *nm* incest.
incidencia [inθi'ðenθja] *nf* (*MAT*) incidence; (*fig*) effect.
incidente [inθi'ðente] *nm* incident.
incidir [inθi'ðir] *vi*: ~ **en** (*influir*) to influence; (*afectar*) to affect; ~ **en un error** to be mistaken.
incienso [in'θjenso] *nm* incense.
incierto, a [in'θjerto, a] *adj* uncertain.
incineración [inθinera'θjon] *nf* incineration; (*de cadáveres*) cremation.
incinerar [inθine'rar] *vt* to burn; to cremate.
incipiente [inθi'pjente] *adj* incipient.
incisión [inθi'sjon] *nf* incision.
incisivo, a [inθi'siβo, a] *adj* sharp, cutting; (*fig*) incisive.
inciso [in'θiso] *nm* (*LING*) clause, sentence; (*coma*) comma; (*JUR*) subsection.
incitante [inθi'tante] *adj* (*estimulante*) exciting; (*provocativo*) provocative.
incitar [inθi'tar] *vt* to incite, rouse.
incivil [inθi'βil] *adj* rude, uncivil.
inclemencia [inkle'menθja] *nf* (*severidad*) harshness, severity; (*del tiempo*) inclemency.
inclemente [inkle'mente] *adj* harsh, severe; inclement.
inclinación [inklina'θjon] *nf* (*gen*) inclination; (*de tierras*) slope, incline; (*de cabeza*) nod, bow; (*fig*) leaning, bent.
inclinado, a [inkli'naðo, a] *adj* (*objeto*) leaning; (*superficie*) sloping.
inclinar [inkli'nar] *vt* to incline; (*cabeza*) to nod, bow; ~**se** *vr* to lean, slope; (*en reverencia*) to bow; (*encorvarse*) to stoop; ~**se a** (*parecerse*) to take after, resemble; ~**se ante** to bow down to; **me inclino a pensar que** ... I'm inclined to think that ....
incluir [inklu'ir] *vt* to include; (*incorporar*) to incorporate; (*meter*) to enclose; **todo incluido** (*COM*) inclusive, all-in.

inclusive [inklu'siβe] *adv* inclusive ♦ *prep* including.
incluso, a [in'kluso, a] *adj* included ♦ *adv* inclusively; (*hasta*) even.
incluyendo [inklu'jendo] *etc vb V* **incluir**.
incobrable [inko'βraβle] *adj* irrecoverable; (*deuda*) bad.
incógnita [in'koɣnita] *nf* (*fig*) mystery.
incógnito [in'koɣnito]: **de** ~ *adv* incognito.
incoherencia [inkoe'renθja] *nf* incoherence; (*falta de conexión*) disconnectedness.
incoherente [inkoe'rente] *adj* incoherent.
incoloro, a [inko'loro, a] *adj* colourless.
incólume [in'kolume] *adj* safe; (*indemne*) unhurt, unharmed.
incombustible [inkombus'tiβle] *adj* (*gen*) fire-resistant; (*telas*) fireproof.
incomodar [inkomo'ðar] *vt* to inconvenience; (*molestar*) to bother, trouble; (*fastidiar*) to annoy; ~**se** *vr* to put o.s. out; (*fastidiarse*) to get annoyed; **no se incomode** don't bother.
incomodidad [inkomoði'ðað] *nf* inconvenience; (*fastidio, enojo*) annoyance; (*de vivienda*) discomfort.
incómodo, a [in'komoðo, a] *adj* (*inconfortable*) uncomfortable; (*molesto*) annoying; (*inconveniente*) inconvenient; **sentirse** ~ to feel ill at ease.
incomparable [inkompa'raβle] *adj* incomparable.
incomparecencia [inkompare'θenθja] *nf* (*JUR etc*) failure to appear.
incompatible [inkompa'tiβle] *adj* incompatible.
incompetencia [inkompe'tenθja] *nf* incompetence.
incompetente [inkompe'tente] *adj* incompetent.
incompleto, a [inkom'pleto, a] *adj* incomplete, unfinished.
incomprendido, a [inkompren'diðo, a] *adj* misunderstood.
incomprensible [inkompren'siβle] *adj* incomprehensible.
incomunicado, a [inkomuni'kaðo, a] *adj* (*aislado*) cut off, isolated; (*confinado*) in solitary confinement.
incomunicar [inkomuni'kar] *vt* (*gen*) to cut off; (*preso*) to put into solitary confinement; ~**se** *vr* (*fam*) to go into one's shell.
incomunique [inkomu'nike] *etc vb V* **incomunicar**.
inconcebible [inkonθe'βiβle] *adj* inconceivable.
inconcluso, a [inkon'kluso, a] *adj*

(_inacabado_) unfinished.
incondicional [inkondiθjo'nal] _adj_
unconditional; (_apoyo_) wholehearted;
(_partidario_) staunch.
inconexo, a [inko'nekso, a] _adj_
unconnected; (_desunido_) disconnected;
(_incoherente_) incoherent.
inconfeso, a [inkon'feso, a] _adj_
unconfessed; **un homosexual** ~ a closet
homosexual.
inconformista [inkonfor'mista] _adj, nm/f_
nonconformist.
inconfundible [inkonfun'diβle] _adj_
unmistakable.
incongruente [inkon'grwente] _adj_
incongruous.
inconmensurable [inkonmensu'raβle] _adj_
immeasurable, vast.
inconsciencia [inkons'θjenθja] _nf_
unconsciousness; (_fig_) thoughtlessness.
inconsciente [inkons'θjente] _adj_
unconscious; thoughtless; (_ignorante_)
unaware; (_involuntario_) unwitting.
inconsecuencia [inkonse'kwenθja] _nf_
inconsistency.
inconsecuente [inkonse'kwente] _adj_
inconsistent.
inconsiderado, a [inkonsiðe'raðo, a] _adj_
inconsiderate.
inconsistente [inkonsis'tente] _adj_
inconsistent; (_CULIN_) lumpy; (_endeble_)
weak; (_tela_) flimsy.
inconstancia [inkons'tanθja] _nf_
inconstancy; (_de tiempo_) changeability;
(_capricho_) fickleness.
inconstante [inkons'tante] _adj_ inconstant;
changeable; fickle.
incontable [inkon'taβle] _adj_ countless,
innumerable.
incontestable [inkontes'taβle] _adj_
unanswerable; (_innegable_) undeniable.
incontinencia [inkonti'nenθja] _nf_
incontinence.
incontrolado, a [inkontro'laðo, a] _adj_
uncontrolled.
incontrovertible [inkontroβer'tiβle] _adj_
undeniable, incontrovertible.
inconveniencia [inkombe'njenθja] _nf_
unsuitability, inappropriateness;
(_descortesía_) impoliteness.
inconveniente [inkombe'njente] _adj_
unsuitable; impolite ♦ _nm_ obstacle;
(_desventaja_) disadvantage; **el** ~ **es que** ...
the trouble is that ...; **no hay** ~ **en** _o_ **para**
hacer eso there is no objection to doing
that; **no tengo** ~ I don't mind.
incordiar [inkor'ðjar] _vt_ (_fam_) to hassle.
incorporación [inkorpora'θjon] _nf_

incorporation; (_fig_) inclusion.
incorporado, a [inkorpo'raðo, a] _adj_ (_TEC_)
built-in.
incorporar [inkorpo'rar] _vt_ to incorporate;
(_abarcar_) to embody; (_CULIN_) to mix; ~**se**
_vr_ to sit up; ~**se a** to join.
incorrección [inkorrek'θjon] _nf_
incorrectness, inaccuracy; (_descortesía_)
bad-mannered behaviour.
incorrecto, a [inko'rrekto, a] _adj_ incorrect,
wrong; (_comportamiento_) bad-mannered.
incorregible [inkorre'xiβle] _adj_
incorrigible.
incorruptible [inkorrup'tiβle] _adj_
incorruptible.
incorrupto, a [inko'rrupto, a] _adj_
uncorrupted; (_fig_) pure.
incredulidad [inkreðuli'ðað] _nf_ incredulity;
(_escepticismo_) scepticism.
incrédulo, a [in'kreðulo, a] _adj_
incredulous, unbelieving; sceptical.
increíble [inkre'iβle] _adj_ incredible.
incrementar [inkremen'tar] _vt_ (_aumentar_)
to increase; (_alzar_) to raise; ~**se** _vr_ to
increase.
incremento [inkre'mento] _nm_ increment;
(_aumento_) rise, increase; ~ **de precio**
rise in price.
increpar [inkre'par] _vt_ to reprimand.
incriminar [inkrimi'nar] _vt_ (_JUR_) to
incriminate.
incruento, a [in'krwento, a] _adj_ bloodless.
incrustar [inkrus'tar] _vt_ to incrust; (_piedras:_
en joya) to inlay; (_fig_) to graft; (_TEC_) to
set.
incubar [inku'ßar] _vt_ to incubate; (_fig_) to
hatch.
incuestionable [inkwestjo'naßle] _adj_
unchallengeable.
inculcar [inkul'kar] _vt_ to inculcate.
inculpar [inkul'par] _vt:_ ~ **de** (_acusar_) to
accuse of; (_achacar, atribuir_) to charge
with, blame for.
inculque [in'kulke] _etc vb_ V **inculcar.**
inculto, a [in'kulto, a] _adj_ (_persona_)
uneducated, uncultured; (_fig: grosero_)
uncouth ♦ _nm/f_ ignoramus.
incumbencia [inkum'benθja] _nf_ obligation;
no es de mi ~ it is not my field.
incumbir [inkum'bir] _vi:_ ~ **a** to be
incumbent upon; **no me incumbe a mí** it
is no concern of mine.
incumplimiento [inkumpli'mjento] _nm_
non-fulfilment; (_COM_) repudiation; ~ **de**
contrato breach of contract; **por** ~ by
default.
incurable [inku'raßle] _adj_ (_enfermedad_)
incurable; (_paciente_) incurably ill.

incurrir [inku'rrir] vi: ~ **en** to incur;
(crimen) to commit; ~ **en un error** to
make a mistake.

indagación [indaɣa'θjon] nf investigation;
(búsqueda) search; (JUR) inquest.

indagar [inda'ɣar] vt to investigate; to
search; (averiguar) to ascertain.

indague [in'daɣe] etc vb V **indagar**.

indebido, a [inde'βiðo, a] adj undue;
(dicho) improper.

indecencia [inde'θenθja] nf indecency;
(dicho) obscenity.

indecente [inde'θente] adj indecent,
improper; (lascivo) obscene.

indecible [inde'θiβle] adj unspeakable;
(indescriptible) indescribable.

indeciso, a [inde'θiso, a] adj (por decidir)
undecided; (vacilante) hesitant.

indefenso, a [inde'fenso, a] adj
defenceless.

indefinido, a [indefi'niðo, a] adj indefinite;
(vago) vague, undefined.

indeleble [inde'leβle] adj indelible.

indemne [in'demne] adj (objeto)
undamaged; (persona) unharmed,
unhurt.

indemnice [indem'niθe] etc vb V
indemnizar.

indemnización [indemniθa'θjon] nf (acto)
indemnification; (suma) indemnity; ~ **de**
cese redundancy payment; ~ **de despido**
severance pay; **doble** ~ double
indemnity.

indemnizar [indemni'θar] vt to indemnify;
(compensar) to compensate.

independencia [indepen'denθja] nf
independence.

independice [indepen'diθe] etc vb V
independizar.

independiente [indepen'djente] adj (libre)
independent; (autónomo) self-sufficient;
(INFORM) stand-alone.

independizar [independi'θar] vt to make
independent; ~**se** vr to become
independent.

indescifrable [indesθi'fraβle] adj (MIL:
código) indecipherable; (fig: misterio)
impenetrable.

indeseable [indese'aβle] adj, nm/f
undesirable.

indeterminado, a [indetermi'naðo, a] adj
(tb LING) indefinite; (desconocido)
indeterminate.

India ['indja] nf: **la** ~ India.

indiano, a [in'djano, a] adj (Spanish-)
American ♦ nm Spaniard who has made
good in America.

indicación [indika'θjon] nf indication;

(dato) piece of information; (señal) sign;
(sugerencia) suggestion, hint;
indicaciones nfpl (COM) instructions.

indicado, a [indi'kaðo, a] adj (apto) right,
appropriate.

indicador [indika'ðor] nm indicator; (TEC)
gauge, meter; (aguja) hand, pointer; (de
carretera) roadsign; ~ **de encendido**
(INFORM) power-on indicator.

indicar [indi'kar] vt (mostrar) to indicate,
show; (suj: termómetro etc) to read,
register; (señalar) to point to.

indicativo, a [indika'tiβo, a] adj indicative
♦ nm (RADIO) call sign; ~ **de nacionalidad**
(AUTO) national identification plate.

índice ['indiθe] nm index; (catálogo)
catalogue; (ANAT) index finger,
forefinger; ~ **del coste de (la) vida** cost-
of-living index; ~ **de crédito** credit rating;
~ **de materias** table of contents; ~ **de**
natalidad birth rate; ~ **de precios al por**
menor (IPM) (COM) retail price index
(RPI).

indicio [in'diθjo] nm indication, sign; (en
pesquisa etc) clue; (INFORM) marker,
mark.

indiferencia [indife'renθja] nf
indifference; (apatía) apathy.

indiferente [indife'rente] adj indifferent;
me es ~ it makes no difference to me.

indígena [in'dixena] adj indigenous, native
♦ nm/f native.

indigencia [indi'xenθja] nf poverty, need.

indigenista [indixe'nista] (AM) adj pro-
Indian ♦ nm/f (estudiante) student of
Indian cultures; (POL etc) promoter of
Indian cultures.

indigestar [indixes'tar] vt to cause
indigestion to; ~**se** vr to get indigestion.

indigestión [indixes'tjon] nf indigestion.

indigesto, a [indi'xesto, a] adj undigested;
(indigestible) indigestible; (fig) turgid.

indignación [indiɣna'θjon] nf indignation.

indignante [indix'nante] adj outrageous,
infuriating.

indignar [indix'nar] vt to anger, make
indignant; ~**se** vr: ~**se por** to get
indignant about.

indigno, a [in'dixno, a] adj (despreciable)
low, contemptible; (inmerecido)
unworthy.

indio, a ['indjo, a] adj, nm/f Indian.

indique [in'dike] etc vb V **indicar**.

indirecto, a [indi'rekto, a] adj indirect ♦ nf
insinuation, innuendo; (sugerencia) hint.

indisciplina [indisθi'plina] nf (gen) lack of
discipline; (MIL) insubordination.

indiscreción [indiskre'θjon] nf

(*imprudencia*) indiscretion; (*irreflexión*) tactlessness; (*acto*) gaffe, faux pas; ..., **si no es** ~ ..., if I may say so.
indiscreto, a [indis'kreto, a] *adj* indiscreet.
indiscriminado, a [indiskrimi'naðo, a] *adj* indiscriminate.
indiscutible [indisku'tißle] *adj* indisputable, unquestionable.
indispensable [indispen'saßle] *adj* indispensable.
indispondré [indispon'dre] *etc vb V* **indisponer**.
indisponer [indispo'ner] *vt* to spoil, upset; (*salud*) to make ill; ~**se** *vr* to fall ill; ~**se con algn** to fall out with sb.
indisponga [indis'ponga] *etc vb V* **indisponer**.
indisposición [indisposi'θjon] *nf* indisposition; (*desgana*) unwillingness.
indispuesto, a [indis'pwesto, a] *pp de* **indisponer** ♦ *adj* indisposed; **sentirse** ~ to feel unwell *o* indisposed.
indispuse [indis'puse] *etc vb V* **indisponer**.
indistinto, a [indis'tinto, a] *adj* indistinct; (*vago*) vague.
individual [indißi'ðwal] *adj* individual; (*habitación*) single ♦ *nm* (*DEPORTE*) singles *sg*.
individuo, a [indi'ßiðwo, a] *adj* individual ♦ *nm* individual.
Indochina [indo'tʃina] *nf* Indochina.
indocumentado, a [indokumen'taðo, a] *adj* without identity papers.
indoeuropeo, a [indoeuro'peo, a] *adj, nm/f* Indo-European.
índole ['indole] *nf* (*naturaleza*) nature; (*clase*) sort, kind.
indolencia [indo'lenθja] *nf* indolence, laziness.
indoloro, a [in'doloro, a] *adj* painless.
indomable [indo'maßle] *adj* (*animal*) untameable; (*espíritu*) indomitable.
indómito, a [in'domito, a] *adj* indomitable.
Indonesia [indo'nesja] *nf* Indonesia.
indonesio, a [indo'nesjo, a] *adj, nm/f* Indonesian.
inducción [induk'θjon] *nf* (*FILOSOFÍA, ELEC*) induction; **por** ~ by induction.
inducir [indu'θir] *vt* to induce; (*inferir*) to infer; (*persuadir*) to persuade; ~ **a algn en el error** to mislead sb.
indudable [indu'ðaßle] *adj* undoubted; (*incuestionable*) unquestionable; **es** ~ **que** ... there is no doubt that ....
indulgencia [indul'xenθja] *nf* indulgence; (*JUR etc*) leniency; **proceder sin** ~ **contra** to proceed ruthlessly against.
indultar [indul'tar] *vt* (*perdonar*) to pardon,

reprieve; (*librar de pago*) to exempt.
indulto [in'dulto] *nm* pardon; exemption.
indumentaria [indumen'tarja] *nf* (*ropa*) clothing, dress.
industria [in'dustrja] *nf* industry; (*habilidad*) skill; ~ **agropecuaria** farming and fishing; ~ **pesada** heavy industry; ~ **petrolífera** oil industry.
industrial [indus'trjal] *adj* industrial ♦ *nm* industrialist.
industrializar [industrjali'θar] *vt* to industrialize; ~**se** *vr* to become industrialized.
INE ['ine] *nm abr* (*ESP*) = *Instituto Nacional de Estadística*.
inédito, a [i'neðito, a] *adj* (*libro*) unpublished; (*nuevo*) unheard-of.
inefable [ine'faßle] *adj* ineffable, indescribable.
ineficacia [inefi'kaθja] *nf* (*de medida*) ineffectiveness; (*de proceso*) inefficiency.
ineficaz [inefi'kaθ] *adj* (*inútil*) ineffective; (*ineficiente*) inefficient.
ineludible [inelu'ðißle] *adj* inescapable, unavoidable.
INEM, Inem [i'nem] *nm abr* (*ESP*: = *Instituto Nacional de Empleo*) ≈ Department of Employment (*BRIT*).
INEN ['inen] *nm abr* (*México*) = *Instituto Nacional de Energía Nuclear*.
inenarrable [inena'rraßle] *adj* inexpressible.
ineptitud [inepti'tuð] *nf* ineptitude, incompetence.
inepto, a [i'nepto, a] *adj* inept, incompetent.
inequívoco, a [ine'kißoko, a] *adj* unequivocal; (*inconfundible*) unmistakable.
inercia [i'nerθja] *nf* inertia; (*pasividad*) passivity.
inerme [i'nerme] *adj* (*sin armas*) unarmed; (*indefenso*) defenceless.
inerte [i'nerte] *adj* inert; (*inmóvil*) motionless.
inescrutable [ineskru'taßle] *adj* inscrutable.
inesperado, a [inespe'raðo, a] *adj* unexpected, unforeseen.
inestable [ines'taßle] *adj* unstable.
inestimable [inesti'maßle] *adj* inestimable; **de valor** ~ invaluable.
inevitable [ineßi'taßle] *adj* inevitable.
inexactitud [ineksakti'tuð] *nf* inaccuracy.
inexacto, a [inek'sakto, a] *adj* inaccurate; (*falso*) untrue.
inexistente [ineksis'tente] *adj* non-

existent.

inexorable [inekso'raßle] *adj* inexorable.

inexperiencia [inekspe'rjenθja] *nf* inexperience, lack of experience.

inexperto, a [ineks'perto, a] *adj* (*novato*) inexperienced.

inexplicable [inekspli'kaßle] *adj* inexplicable.

inexpresable [inekspre'saßle] *adj* inexpressible.

inexpresivo, a [inekspre'sißo, a] *adj* inexpressive; (*ojos*) dull; (*cara*) wooden.

inexpugnable [inekspuɣ'naßle] *adj* (*MIL*) impregnable; (*fig*) firm.

infalible [infa'lißle] *adj* infallible; (*indefectible*) certain, sure; (*plan*) foolproof.

infame [in'fame] *adj* infamous.

infamia [in'famja] *nf* infamy; (*deshonra*) disgrace.

infancia [in'fanθja] *nf* infancy, childhood; **jardín de la ~** nursery school.

infanta [in'fanta] *nf* (*hija del rey*) infanta, princess.

infante [in'fante] *nm* (*hijo del rey*) infante, prince.

infantería [infante'ria] *nf* infantry.

infantil [infan'til] *adj* child's, children's; (*pueril, aniñado*) infantile; (*cándido*) childlike.

infarto [in'farto] *nm* (*tb*: **~ de miocardio**) heart attack.

infatigable [infati'ɣaßle] *adj* tireless, untiring.

infección [infek'θjon] *nf* infection.

infeccioso, a [infek'θjoso, a] *adj* infectious.

infectar [infek'tar] *vt* to infect; **~se** *vr*: **~se (de)** (*tb fig*) to become infected (with).

infecundidad [infekundi'ðað] *nf* (*de tierra*) infertility, barrenness; (*de mujer*) sterility.

infecundo, a [infe'kundo, a] *adj* infertile, barren; sterile.

infeliz [infe'liθ] *adj* (*desgraciado*) unhappy, wretched; (*inocente*) gullible ♦ *nmlf* (*desgraciado*) wretch; (*inocentón*) simpleton.

inferior [infe'rjor] *adj* inferior; (*situación, MAT*) lower ♦ *nmlf* inferior, subordinate; **cualquier número ~ a 9** any number less than *o* under *o* below 9; **una cantidad ~ a** a lesser quantity.

inferioridad [inferjori'ðað] *nf* inferiority; **estar en ~ de condiciones** to be at a disadvantage.

inferir [infe'rir] *vt* (*deducir*) to infer, deduce; (*causar*) to cause.

infernal [infer'nal] *adj* infernal.

infértil [in'fertil] *adj* infertile.

infestar [infes'tar] *vt* to infest.

infidelidad [infiðeli'ðað] *nf* (*gen*) infidelity, unfaithfulness.

infiel [in'fjel] *adj* unfaithful, disloyal; (*falso*) inaccurate ♦ *nmlf* infidel, unbeliever.

infiera [in'fjera] *etc vb* V **inferir**.

infierno [in'fjerno] *nm* hell; **¡vete al ~!** go to hell; **está en el quinto ~** it's at the back of beyond.

infiltrar [infil'trar] *vt* to infiltrate; **~se** *vr* to infiltrate, filter; (*líquidos*) to percolate.

ínfimo, a ['infimo, a] *adj* (*vil*) vile, mean; (*más bajo*) lowest; (*peor*) worst; (*miserable*) wretched.

infinidad [infini'ðað] *nf* infinity; (*abundancia*) great quantity; **~ de** vast numbers of; **~ de veces** countless times.

infinitivo [infini'tißo] *nm* infinitive.

infinito, a [infi'nito, a] *adj* infinite; (*fig*) boundless ♦ *adv* infinitely ♦ *nm* infinite; (*MAT*) infinity; **hasta lo ~** ad infinitum.

infiriendo [infi'rjendo] *etc vb* V **inferir**.

inflación [infla'θjon] *nf* (*hinchazón*) swelling; (*monetaria*) inflation; (*fig*) conceit.

inflacionario, a [inflaθjo'narjo, a] *adj* inflationary.

inflacionismo [inflaθjo'nismo] *nm* (*ECON*) inflation.

inflacionista [inflaθjo'nista] *adj* inflationary.

inflamar [infla'mar] *vt* to set on fire; (*MED, fig*) to inflame; **~se** *vr* to catch fire; to become inflamed.

inflar [in'flar] *vt* (*hinchar*) to inflate, blow up; (*fig*) to exaggerate; **~se** *vr* to swell (up); (*fig*) to get conceited.

inflexible [inflek'sißle] *adj* inflexible; (*fig*) unbending.

infligir [infli'xir] *vt* to inflict.

inflija [in'flixa] *etc vb* V **infligir**.

influencia [in'flwenθja] *nf* influence.

influenciar [inflwen'θjar] *vt* to influence.

influir [influ'ir] *vt* to influence ♦ *vi* to have influence, carry weight; (*contribuir a*) to have a hand in.

influjo [in'fluxo] *nm* influence; **~ de capitales** (*ECON etc*) capital influx.

influyendo [influ'jendo] *etc vb* V **influir**.

influyente [influ'jente] *adj* influential.

información [informa'θjon] *nf* information; (*noticias*) news *sg*; (*informe*) report; (*INFORM: datos*) data; (*JUR*) inquiry; **I~** (*oficina*) Information; (*TELEC*)

Directory Enquiries (*BRIT*), Directory Assistance (*US*); (*mostrador*) Information Desk; **una** ~ a piece of information; **abrir una** ~ (*JUR*) to begin proceedings; ~ **deportiva** (*en periódico*) sports section.

informal [infor'mal] *adj* (*gen*) informal.

informante [infor'mante] *nmlf* informant.

informar [infor'mar] *vt* (*gen*) to inform; (*revelar*) to reveal, make known ♦ *vi* (*JUR*) to plead; (*denunciar*) to inform; (*dar cuenta de*) to report on; ~**se** *vr* to find out; ~**se de** to inquire into.

informática [infor'matika] *nf* V **informático**.

informatice [informa'tiθe] *etc vb* V **informatizar**.

informático, a [infor'matiko, a] *adj* computer *cpd* ♦ *nf* (*TEC*) information technology; computing; (*ESCOL*) computer science *o* studies; ~ **de gestión** commercial computing.

informativo, a [informa'tiβo, a] *adj* (*libro*) informative; (*folleto*) information *cpd*; (*RADIO, TV*) news *cpd* ♦ *nm* (*RADIO, TV*) news programme.

informatización [informatiθa'θjon] *nf* computerization.

informatizar [informati'θar] *vt* to computerize.

informe [in'forme] *adj* shapeless ♦ *nm* report; (*dictamen*) statement; (*MIL*) briefing; (*JUR*) plea; ~**s** *nmpl* information *sg*; (*datos*) data; ~ **anual** annual report; ~ **del juez** summing-up.

infortunio [infor'tunjo] *nm* misfortune.

infracción [infrak'θjon] *nf* infraction, infringement; (*AUTO*) offence.

infraestructura [infraestruk'tura] *nf* infrastructure.

in fraganti [infra'ɣanti] *adv*: **pillar a algn** ~ to catch sb red-handed.

infranqueable [infranke'aβle] *adj* impassable; (*fig*) insurmountable.

infrarrojo, a [infra'rroxo, a] *adj* infrared.

infravalorar [infraβalo'rar] *vt* to undervalue; (*FIN*) to underestimate.

infringir [infrin'xir] *vt* to infringe, contravene.

infrinja [in'frinxa] *etc vb* V **infringir**.

infructuoso, a [infruk'twoso, a] *adj* fruitless, unsuccessful.

infundado, a [infun'daðo, a] *adj* groundless, unfounded.

infundir [infun'dir] *vt* to infuse, instil; ~ **ánimo a algn** to encourage sb; ~ **miedo a algn** to intimidate sb.

infusión [infu'sjon] *nf* infusion; ~ **de manzanilla** camomile tea.

Ing. *abr* = **Ingeniero**.

ingeniar [inxe'njar] *vt* to think up, devise; ~**se** *vr* to manage; ~**se para** to manage to.

ingeniería [inxenje'ria] *nf* engineering; ~ **genética** genetic engineering; ~ **de sistemas** (*INFORM*) systems engineering.

ingeniero, a [inxe'njero, a] *nmlf* engineer; ~ **de sonido** sound engineer; ~ **de caminos** civil engineer.

ingenio [in'xenjo] *nm* (*talento*) talent; (*agudeza*) wit; (*habilidad*) ingenuity, inventiveness; (*TEC*): ~ **azucarero** sugar refinery.

ingenioso, a [inxe'njoso, a] *adj* ingenious, clever; (*divertido*) witty.

ingente [in'xente] *adj* huge, enormous.

ingenuidad [inxenwi'ðað] *nf* ingenuousness; (*sencillez*) simplicity.

ingenuo, a [in'xenwo, a] *adj* ingenuous.

ingerir [inxe'rir] *vt* to ingest; (*tragar*) to swallow; (*consumir*) to consume.

ingiera [in'xjera] *etc*, **ingiriendo** [inxi'rjenðo] *etc vb* V **ingerir**.

Inglaterra [ingla'terra] *nf* England.

ingle ['ingle] *nf* groin.

inglés, esa [in'gles, esa] *adj* English ♦ *nmlf* Englishman/woman ♦ *nm* (*LING*) English; **los ingleses** the English.

ingratitud [ingrati'tuð] *nf* ingratitude.

ingrato, a [in'grato, a] *adj* ungrateful; (*tarea*) thankless.

ingravidez [ingraβi'ðeθ] *nf* weightlessness.

ingrediente [ingre'ðjente] *nm* ingredient; ~**s** *nmpl* (*AM: tapas*) titbits.

ingresar [ingre'sar] *vt* (*dinero*) to deposit ♦ *vi* to come *o* go in; ~ **a** (*espAM*) to enter; ~ **en** (*club*) to join; (*MIL, ESCOL*) to enrol in; ~ **en el hospital** to go into hospital.

ingreso [in'greso] *nm* (*entrada*) entry; (*: en hospital etc*) admission; (*MIL, ESCOL*) enrolment; ~**s** *nmpl* (*dinero*) income *sg*; (*: COM*) takings *pl*; ~ **gravable** taxable income *sg*; ~**s accesorios** fringe benefits; ~**s brutos** gross receipts; ~**s devengados** earned income *sg*; ~**s exentos de impuestos** non-taxable income *sg*; ~**s personales disponibles** disposable personal income *sg*.

íngrimo, a ['ingrimo, a] *adj* (*AM: tb* ~ **y solo**) all alone.

inhábil [i'naβil] *adj* unskilful, clumsy.

inhabilitar [inaβili'tar] *vt* (*POL, MED*): ~ **a algn (para hacer algo)** to disqualify sb (from doing sth).

inhabitable [inaβi'taβle] *adj* uninhabitable.

inhabituado, a [inaβi'twaðo, a] *adj* unaccustomed.

inhalador [inala'ðor] nm (MED) inhaler.
inhalar [ina'lar] vt to inhale.
inherente [ine'rente] adj inherent.
inhibición [iniβi'θjon] nf inhibition.
inhibir [ini'βir] vt to inhibit; (REL) to restrain; ~se vr to keep out.
inhospitalario, a [inospita'larjo, a], **inhóspito, a** [i'nospito, a] adj inhospitable.
inhumación [inuma'θjon] nf burial, interment.
inhumano, a [inu'mano, a] adj inhuman.
INI ['ini] nm abr = Instituto Nacional de Industria.
inicial [ini'θjal] adj, nf initial.
inicialice [iniθja'liθe] etc vb V inicializar.
inicializar [iniθjali'θar] vt (INFORM) to initialize.
iniciar [ini'θjar] vt (persona) to initiate; (empezar) to begin, commence; (conversación) to start up; ~ a algn en un secreto to let sb into a secret; ~ la sesión (INFORM) to log in o on.
iniciativa [iniθja'tiβa] nf initiative; (liderazgo) leadership; la ~ privada private enterprise.
inicio [i'niθjo] nm start, beginning.
inicuo, a [i'nikwo, a] adj iniquitous.
inigualado, a [iniɣwa'laðo, a] adj unequalled.
ininteligible [ininteli'xiβle] adj unintelligible.
ininterrumpido, a [ininterrum'piðo, a] adj uninterrupted; (proceso) continuous; (progreso) steady.
injerencia [inxe'renθja] nf interference.
injertar [inxer'tar] vt to graft.
injerto [in'xerto] nm graft; ~ de piel skin graft.
injuria [in'xurja] nf (agravio, ofensa) offence; (insulto) insult; ~s nfpl abuse sg.
injuriar [inxu'rjar] vt to insult.
injurioso, a [inxu'rjoso, a] adj offensive; insulting.
injusticia [inxus'tiθja] nf injustice, unfairness; con ~ unjustly.
injusto, a [in'xusto, a] adj unjust, unfair.
inmaculado, a [inmaku'laðo, a] adj immaculate, spotless.
inmadurez [inmaðu'reθ] nf immaturity.
inmaduro, a [inma'ðuro, a] adj immature; (fruta) unripe.
inmediaciones [inmeðja'θjones] nfpl neighbourhood sg, environs.
inmediatez [inmeðja'teθ] nf immediacy.
inmediato, a [inme'ðjato, a] adj immediate; (contiguo) adjoining; (rápido) prompt; (próximo) neighbouring, next;

de ~ (esp AM) immediately.
inmejorable [inmexo'raβle] adj unsurpassable; (precio) unbeatable.
inmemorable [inmemo'raβle], **inmemorial** [inmemo'rjal] adj immemorial.
inmenso, a [in'menso, a] adj immense, huge.
inmerecido, a [inmere'θiðo, a] adj undeserved.
inmersión [inmer'sjon] nf immersion; (buzo) dive.
inmigración [inmiɣra'θjon] nf immigration.
inmigrante [inmi'ɣrante] adj, nm/f immigrant.
inminente [inmi'nente] adj imminent, impending.
inmiscuirse [inmisku'irse] vr to interfere, meddle.
inmiscuyendo [inmisku'jendo] etc vb V inmiscuirse.
inmobiliario, a [inmoβi'ljarjo, a] adj real-estate cpd, property cpd ♦ nf estate agency.
inmolar [inmo'lar] vt to immolate, sacrifice.
inmoral [inmo'ral] adj immoral.
inmortal [inmor'tal] adj immortal.
inmortalice [inmorta'liθe] etc vb V inmortalizar.
inmortalizar [inmortali'θar] vt to immortalize.
inmotivado, a [inmoti'βaðo, a] adj motiveless; (sospecha) groundless.
inmóvil [in'moβil] adj immobile.
inmovilizar [inmoβili'θar] vt to immobilize; (paralizar) to paralyse; ~se vr: se le ha inmovilizado la pierna her leg was paralysed.
inmueble [in'mweβle] adj: bienes ~s real estate sg, landed property sg ♦ nm property.
inmundicia [inmun'diθja] nf filth.
inmundo, a [in'mundo, a] adj filthy.
inmune [in'mune] adj (MED) immune.
inmunidad [inmuni'ðað] nf immunity; (fisco) exemption; ~ diplomática/ parlamentaria diplomatic/parliamentary immunity.
inmunitario, a [inmuni'tarjo, a] adj: sistema ~ immune system.
inmunización [inmuniθa'θjon] nf immunization.
inmunizar [inmuni'θar] vt to immunize.
inmutable [inmu'taβle] adj immutable; permaneció ~ he didn't flinch.
inmutarse [inmu'tarse] vr: siguió sin ~ he

carried on unperturbed.

innato, a [in'nato, a] *adj* innate.

innecesario, a [inneθe'sarjo, a] *adj* unnecessary.

innegable [inne'ɣaβle] *adj* undeniable.

innoble [in'noβle] *adj* ignoble.

innovación [innoβa'θjon] *nf* innovation.

innovador, a [innoβa'ðor, a] *adj* innovatory, innovative ♦ *nm/f* innovator.

innovar [inno'βar] *vt* to introduce.

innumerable [innume'raβle] *adj* countless.

inocencia [ino'θenθja] *nf* innocence.

inocentada [inoθen'taða] *nf* practical joke.

inocente [ino'θente] *adj* (*ingenuo*) naive, innocent; (*inculpable*) innocent; (*sin malicia*) harmless ♦ *nm/f* simpleton; **día de los (Santos) I~s** ≈ April Fool's Day; *see boxed note*.

DÍA DE LOS SANTOS INOCENTES

El día de los (Santos) Inocentes, 28 December, is when the Church commemorates Herod's slaughter of the innocent children of Judea in biblical times. On this day Spaniards play "inocentadas" (practical jokes) on each other, much like British April Fools' Day pranks, perhaps sticking a "monigote" (cut-out paper figure) on someone's back or broadcasting unlikely news stories.

---

inocuidad [inokwi'ðað] *nf* harmlessness.

inocular [inoku'lar] *vt* to inoculate.

inocuo, a [i'nokwo, a] *adj* (*sustancia*) harmless.

inodoro, a [ino'ðoro, a] *adj* odourless ♦ *nm* toilet (*BRIT*), lavatory (*BRIT*), washroom (*US*).

inofensivo, a [inofen'siβo, a] *adj* inoffensive.

inolvidable [inolβi'ðaβle] *adj* unforgettable.

inoperante [inope'rante] *adj* ineffective.

inopinado, a [inopi'naðo, a] *adj* unexpected.

inoportuno, a [inopor'tuno, a] *adj* untimely; (*molesto*) inconvenient; (*inapropiado*) inappropriate.

inoxidable [inoksi'ðaβle] *adj* stainless; **acero ~** stainless steel.

inquebrantable [inkeβran'taβle] *adj* unbreakable; (*fig*) unshakeable.

inquiera [in'kjera] *etc vb V* **inquirir**.

inquietante [inkje'tante] *adj* worrying.

inquietar [inkje'tar] *vt* to worry, trouble; **~se** *vr* to worry, get upset.

inquieto, a [in'kjeto, a] *adj* anxious,

worried; **estar ~ por** to be worried about.

inquietud [inkje'tuð] *nf* anxiety, worry.

inquilino, a [inki'lino, a] *nm/f* tenant; (*COM*) lessee.

inquiriendo [inki'rjendo] *etc vb V* **inquirir**.

inquirir [inki'rir] *vt* to enquire into, investigate.

insaciable [insa'θjaβle] *adj* insatiable.

insalubre [insa'luβre] *adj* unhealthy; (*condiciones*) insanitary.

INSALUD [insa'luð] *nm abr* (*ESP*) = Instituto Nacional de la Salud.

insano, a [in'sano, a] *adj* (*loco*) insane; (*malsano*) unhealthy.

insatisfacción [insatisfak'θjon] *nf* dissatisfaction.

insatisfecho, a [insatis'fetʃo, a] *adj* (*condición*) unsatisfied; (*estado de ánimo*) dissatisfied.

inscribir [inskri'βir] *vt* to inscribe; (*en lista*) to put; (*en censo*) to register; **~se** *vr* to register; (*ESCOL etc*) to enrol.

inscripción [inskrip'θjon] *nf* inscription; (*ESCOL etc*) enrolment; (*en censo*) registration.

inscrito [ins'krito] *pp de* **inscribir**.

insecticida [insekti'θiða] *nm* insecticide.

insecto [in'sekto] *nm* insect.

inseguridad [inseɣuri'ðað] *nf* insecurity.

inseguro, a [inse'ɣuro, a] *adj* insecure; (*inconstante*) unsteady; (*incierto*) uncertain.

inseminación [insemina'θjon] *nf*: **~ artificial** artificial insemination (A.I.).

inseminar [insemi'nar] *vt* to inseminate, fertilize.

insensato, a [insen'sato, a] *adj* foolish, stupid.

insensibilice [insensiβi'liθe] *etc vb V* **insensibilizar**.

insensibilidad [insensiβili'ðað] *nf* (*gen*) insensitivity; (*dureza de corazón*) callousness.

insensibilizar [insensiβili'θar] *vt* to desensitize; (*MED*) to anaesthetize (*BRIT*), anesthetize (*US*); (*eufemismo*) to knock out *o* unconscious.

insensible [insen'siβle] *adj* (*gen*) insensitive; (*movimiento*) imperceptible; (*sin sentido*) numb.

inseparable [insepa'raβle] *adj* inseparable.

INSERSO [in'serso] *nm abr* (= Instituto Nacional de Servicios Sociales) *branch of social services*.

insertar [inser'tar] *vt* to insert.

inservible [inser'βiβle] *adj* useless.

insidioso, a [insi'ðjoso, a] *adj* insidious.

insigne [in'siɣne] *adj* distinguished; (*famoso*) notable.

insignia [in'siɣnja] *nf* (*señal distintiva*) badge; (*estandarte*) flag.

insignificante [insiɣnifi'kante] *adj* insignificant.

insinuar [insi'nwar] *vt* to insinuate, imply; ~**se** *vr*: ~**se con algn** to ingratiate o.s. with sb.

insípido, a [in'sipiðo, a] *adj* insipid.

insistencia [insis'tenθja] *nf* insistence.

insistir [insis'tir] *vi* to insist; ~ **en algo** to insist on sth; (*enfatizar*) to stress sth.

in situ [in'situ] *adv* on the spot, in situ.

insobornable [insoβor'naβle] *adj* incorruptible.

insociable [inso'θjaβle] *adj* unsociable.

insolación [insola'θjon] *nf* (*MED*) sunstroke.

insolencia [inso'lenθja] *nf* insolence.

insolente [inso'lente] *adj* insolent.

insólito, a [in'solito, a] *adj* unusual.

insoluble [inso'luβle] *adj* insoluble.

insolvencia [insol'βenθja] *nf* insolvency.

insomne [in'somne] *adj* sleepless ♦ *nm/f* insomniac.

insomnio [in'somnjo] *nm* insomnia.

insondable [inson'daβle] *adj* bottomless.

insonorización [insonoriθa'θjon] *nf* soundproofing.

insonorizado, a [insonori'θaðo, a] *adj* (*cuarto etc*) soundproof.

insoportable [insopor'taβle] *adj* unbearable.

insoslayable [insosla'jaβle] *adj* unavoidable.

insospechado, a [insospe't∫aðo, a] *adj* (*inesperado*) unexpected.

insostenible [insoste'niβle] *adj* untenable.

inspección [inspek'θjon] *nf* inspection, check; **I**~ inspectorate; ~ **técnica** (**de vehículos**) ~ MOT (test) (*BRIT*).

inspeccionar [inspekθjo'nar] *vt* (*examinar*) to inspect, examine; (*controlar*) to check; (*INFORM*) to peek.

inspector, a [inspek'tor, a] *nm/f* inspector.

inspectorado [inspekto'raðo] *nm* inspectorate.

inspiración [inspira'θjon] *nf* inspiration.

inspirador, a [inspira'ðor, a] *adj* inspiring.

inspirar [inspi'rar] *vt* to inspire; (*MED*) to inhale; ~**se** *vr*: ~**se en** to be inspired by.

instalación [instala'θjon] *nf* (*equipo*) fittings *pl*, equipment; ~ **eléctrica** wiring.

instalar [insta'lar] *vt* (*establecer*) to instal; (*erguir*) to set up, erect; ~**se** *vr* to establish o.s.; (*en una vivienda*) to move into.

instancia [ins'tanθja] *nf* (*solicitud*) application; (*ruego*) request; (*JUR*) petition; **a** ~ **de** at the request of; **en última** ~ in the last resort.

instantáneo, a [instan'taneo, a] *adj* instantaneous ♦ *nf* snap(shot); **café** ~ instant coffee.

instante [ins'tante] *nm* instant, moment; **en un** ~ in a flash.

instar [ins'tar] *vt* to press, urge.

instaurar [instau'rar] *vt* (*establecer*) to establish, set up.

instigador, a [instiɣa'ðor, a] *nm/f* instigator; ~ **de un delito** (*JUR*) accessory before the fact.

instigar [insti'ɣar] *vt* to instigate.

instigue [ins'tiɣe] *etc vb V* **instigar.**

instintivo, a [instin'tiβo, a] *adj* instinctive.

instinto [ins'tinto] *nm* instinct; **por** ~ instinctively.

institución [institu'θjon] *nf* institution, establishment; ~ **benéfica** charitable foundation.

instituir [institu'ir] *vt* to establish; (*fundar*) to found.

instituto [insti'tuto] *nm* (*gen*) institute; **I**~ **Nacional de Enseñanza** (*ESP*) ≈ comprehensive (*BRIT*) *o* high (*US*) school; **I**~ **Nacional de Industria (INI)** (*ESP COM*) ≈ National Enterprise Board (*BRIT*) .

institutriz [institu'triθ] *nf* governess.

instituyendo [institu'jendo] *etc vb V* **instituir.**

instrucción [instruk'θjon] *nf* instruction; (*enseñanza*) education, teaching; (*JUR*) proceedings *pl*; (*MIL*) training; (*DEPORTE*) coaching; (*conocimientos*) knowledge; (*INFORM*) statement; **instrucciones para el uso** directions for use; **instrucciones de funcionamiento** operating instructions.

instructivo, a [instruk'tiβo, a] *adj* instructive.

instruir [instru'ir] *vt* (*gen*) to instruct; (*enseñar*) to teach, educate; (*JUR: proceso*) to prepare, draw up; ~**se** *vr* to learn, teach o.s.

instrumento [instru'mento] *nm* (*gen*, *MUS*) instrument; (*herramienta*) tool, implement; (*COM*) indenture; (*JUR*) legal document; ~ **de percusión/cuerda/ viento** percussion/string(ed)/wind instrument.

instruyendo [instru'jendo] *etc vb V* **instruir**

insubordinarse [insuβorði'narse] *vr* to rebel.

insuficiencia [insufi'θjenθja] *nf* (*carencia*)

lack; (*inadecuación*) inadequacy; ~ **cardíaca/renal** heart/kidney failure.

insuficiente [insufi'θjente] *adj* (*gen*) insufficient; (*ESCOL: nota*) unsatisfactory.

insufrible [insu'friβle] *adj* insufferable.

insular [insu'lar] *adj* insular.

insulina [insu'lina] *nf* insulin.

insulso, a [in'sulso, a] *adj* insipid; (*fig*) dull.

insultar [insul'tar] *vt* to insult.

insulto [in'sulto] *nm* insult.

insumisión [insumi'sjon] *nf* refusal to do military service or community service.

insumiso, a [insu'miso, a] *adj* (*rebelde*) rebellious ♦ *nm/f* (*POL*) person who refuses to do military service or community service; V *tb* **mili**.

insuperable [insupe'raβle] *adj* (*excelente*) unsurpassable; (*problema etc*) insurmountable.

insurgente [insur'xente] *adj*, *nm/f* insurgent.

insurrección [insurrek'θjon] *nf* insurrection, rebellion.

insustituible [insusti'twiβle] *adj* irreplaceable.

intachable [inta'tʃaβle] *adj* irreproachable.

intacto, a [in'takto, a] *adj* (*sin tocar*) untouched; (*entero*) intact.

integrado, a [inte'xraðo, a] *adj* (*INFORM*): **circuito** ~ integrated circuit.

integral [inte'xral] *adj* integral; (*completo*) complete; (*TEC*) built-in; **pan** ~ wholemeal bread.

integrante [inte'xrante] *adj* integral ♦ *nm/f* member.

integrar [inte'xrar] *vt* to make up, compose; (*MAT, fig*) to integrate.

integridad [intexri'ðað] *nf* wholeness; (*carácter, tb INFORM*) integrity; **en su** ~ completely.

integrismo [inte'xrismo] *nm* fundamentalism.

integrista [inte'xrista] *adj*, *nm/f* fundamentalist.

íntegro, a ['intexro, a] *adj* whole, entire; (*texto*) uncut, unabridged; (*honrado*) honest.

intelectual [intelek'twal] *adj*, *nm/f* intellectual.

intelectualidad [intelektwali'ðað] *nf* intelligentsia, intellectuals *pl*.

inteligencia [inteli'xenθja] *nf* intelligence; (*ingenio*) ability; ~ **artificial** artificial intelligence.

inteligente [inteli'xente] *adj* intelligent.

inteligible [inteli'xiβle] *adj* intelligible.

intemperancia [intempe'ranθja] *nf* excess, intemperance.

intemperie [intem'perje] *nf*: **a la** ~ outdoors, in the open air.

intempestivo, a [intempes'tiβo, a] *adj* untimely.

intención [inten'θjon] *nf* (*gen*) intention, purpose; **con segundas intenciones** maliciously; **con** ~ deliberately.

intencionado, a [intenθjo'naðo, a] *adj* deliberate; **bien** ~ well-meaning; **mal** ~ ill-disposed, hostile.

intendencia [inten'denθja] *nf* management, administration; (*MIL: tb*: **cuerpo de** ~) ≈ service corps.

intensidad [intensi'ðað] *nf* (*gen*) intensity; (*ELEC, TEC*) strength; (*de recuerdo*) vividness; **llover con** ~ to rain hard.

intensificar [intensifi'kar] *vt*, **intensificarse** *vr* to intensify.

intensifique [intensi'fike] *etc vb V* **intensificar**.

intensivo, a [inten'siβo, a] *adj* intensive; **curso** ~ crash course.

intenso, a [in'tenso, a] *adj* intense; (*impresión*) vivid; (*sentimiento*) profound, deep.

intentar [inten'tar] *vt* (*tratar*) to try, attempt.

intento [in'tento] *nm* (*intención*) intention, purpose; (*tentativa*) attempt.

intentona [inten'tona] *nf* (*POL*) attempted coup.

interaccionar [interakθjo'nar] *vi* (*INFORM*) to interact.

interactivo, a [interak'tiβo, a] *adj* interactive; (*INFORM*): **computación interactiva** interactive computing.

intercalación [interkala'θjon] *nf* (*INFORM*) merging.

intercalar [interka'lar] *vt* to insert; (*INFORM: archivos, texto*) to merge.

intercambiable [interkam'bjaβle] *adj* interchangeable.

intercambio [inter'kambjo] *nm* (*canje*) exchange; (*trueque*) swap.

interceder [interθe'ðer] *vi* to intercede.

interceptar [interθep'tar] *vt* to intercept, cut off; (*AUTO*) to hold up.

interceptor [interθep'tor] *nm* interceptor; (*TEC*) trap.

intercesión [interθe'sjon] *nf* intercession.

interés [inte'res] *nm* (*gen, COM*) interest; (*importancia*) concern; (*parte*) share, part; (*pey*) self-interest; ~ **compuesto** compound interest; ~ **simple** simple interest; **con un** ~ **de 9 por ciento** at an interest of 9%; **dar a** ~ to lend at interest; **tener ~ en** (*COM*) to hold a share in; **intereses acumulados** accrued interest *sg*; **intereses por cobrar** interest receivable *sg*; **intereses creados** vested interests; **intereses por pagar** interest payable *sg*.

interesado, a [intere'saðo, a] *adj* interested; (*prejuiciado*) prejudiced; (*pey*) mercenary, self-seeking ♦ *nm/f* person concerned; (*firmante*) the undersigned.

interesante [intere'sante] *adj* interesting.

interesar [intere'sar] *vt* to interest, be of interest to ♦ *vi* to interest, be of interest; (*importar*) to be important; **~se** *vr*: **~se en** *o* **por** to take an interest in; **no me interesan los toros** bullfighting does not appeal to me.

interestatal [interesta'tal] *adj* inter-state.

interface [inter'faθe], **interfase** [inter'fase] *nm* (*INFORM*) interface; **~ hombre/máquina/por menús** man/machine/menu interface.

interfaz [inter'faθ] *nm* = **interface**.

interferencia [interfe'renθja] *nf* interference.

interferir [interfe'rir] *vt* to interfere with; (*TELEC*) to jam ♦ *vi* to interfere.

interfiera [inter'fjera] *etc*, **interfiriendo** [interfi'rjendo] *etc vb V* **interferir**.

interfono [inter'fono] *nm* intercom.

ínterin ['interin] *adv* meanwhile ♦ *nm* interim; **en el ~** in the meantime.

interino, a [inte'rino, a] *adj* temporary; (*empleado etc*) provisional ♦ *nm/f* temporary holder of a post; (*MED*) locum; (*ESCOL*) supply teacher; (*TEAT*) stand-in.

interior [inte'rjor] *adj* inner, inside; (*COM*) domestic, internal ♦ *nm* interior, inside; (*fig*) soul, mind; (*DEPORTE*) inside forward; **Ministerio del I~** ≈ Home Office (*BRIT*), Ministry of the Interior; **dije para mi ~** I said to myself.

interjección [interxek'θjon] *nf* interjection.

interlínea [inter'linea] *nf* (*INFORM*) line feed.

interlocutor, a [interloku'tor, a] *nm/f* speaker; (*al teléfono*) person at the other end (of the line); **mi ~** the person I was speaking to.

intermediario, a [interme'ðjarjo, a] *adj* (*mediador*) mediating ♦ *nm/f* intermediary, go-between; (*mediador*) mediator.

intermedio, a [inter'meðjo, a] *adj* intermediate; (*tiempo*) intervening ♦ *nm* interval; (*POL*) recess.

interminable [intermi'naßle] *adj* endless,

interminable.

intermitente [intermi'tente] *adj* intermittent ♦ *nm* (*AUTO*) indicator.

internacional [internaθjo'nal] *adj* international.

internado [inter'naðo] *nm* boarding school.

internamiento [interna'mjento] *nm* internment.

internar [inter'nar] *vt* to intern; (*en un manicomio*) to commit; **~se** *vr* (*penetrar*) to penetrate; **~se en** to go into *o* right inside; **~se en un estudio** to study a subject in depth.

internauta [inter'nauta] *nmf* Internet user.

Internet [inter'net] *nm o nf* Internet.

interno, a [in'terno, a] *adj* internal, interior; (*POL etc*) domestic ♦ *nm/f* (*alumno*) boarder.

interpelación [interpela'θjon] *nf* appeal, plea.

interpelar [interpe'lar] *vt* (*rogar*) to implore; (*hablar*) to speak to; (*POL*) to ask for explanations, question formally.

interpondré [interpon'dre] *etc vb V* **interponer**.

interponer [interpo'ner] *vt* to interpose, put in; **~se** *vr* to intervene.

interponga [inter'ponga] *etc vb V* **interponer**.

interposición [interposi'θjon] *nf* insertion.

interpretación [interpreta'θjon] *nf* interpretation; (*MUS, TEAT*) performance; **mala ~** misinterpretation.

interpretar [interpre'tar] *vt* to interpret.

intérprete [in'terprete] *nm/f* (*LING*) interpreter, translator; (*MUS, TEAT*) performer, artist(e).

interpuesto [inter'pwesto], **interpuse** [inter'puse] *etc vb V* **interponer**.

interrogación [interroɣa'θjon] *nf* interrogation; (*LING: tb*: **signo de ~**) question mark; (*TELEC*) polling.

interrogante [interro'ɣante] *adj* questioning ♦ *nm* question mark; (*fig*) question mark, query.

interrogar [interro'ɣar] *vt* to interrogate, question.

interrogatorio [interroɣa'torjo] *nm* interrogation; (*MIL*) debriefing; (*JUR*) examination.

interrogue [inte'rroɣe] *etc vb V* **interrogar**.

interrumpir [interrum'pir] *vt* to interrupt; (*vacaciones*) to cut short; (*servicio*) to cut off; (*tráfico*) to block.

interrupción [interrup'θjon] *nf* interruption.

interruptor [interrup'tor] _nm_ (_ELEC_) switch.
intersección [intersek'θjon] _nf_
intersection; (_AUTO_) junction.
interurbano, a [interur'ßano, a] _adj_ inter
city; (_TELEC_) long-distance.
intervalo [inter'ßalo] _nm_ interval;
(_descanso_) break; **a ~s** at intervals,
every now and then.
intervención [interßen'θjon] _nf_
supervision; (_COM_) audit(ing); (_MED_)
operation; (_TELEC_) tapping; (_participación_)
intervention; **~ quirúrgica** surgical
operation; **la política de no ~** the policy
of non-intervention.
intervencionista [interßenθjo'nista] _adj_: **no
~** (_COM_) laissez-faire.
intervendré [interßen'dre] _etc_, **inter-
venga** [inter'ßenga] _etc vb V_ **intervenir**.
intervenir [interße'nir] _vt_ (_controlar_) to
control, supervise; (_COM_) to audit; (_MED_)
to operate on; (_TELEC_) to tap ♦ _vi_
(_participar_) to take part, participate;
(_mediar_) to intervene.
interventor, a [interßen'tor, a] _nm/f_
inspector; (_COM_) auditor.
interviniendo [interßi'njendo] _etc vb V_
intervenir.
interviú [inter'ßju] _nf_ interview.
intestino [intes'tino] _nm_ intestine.
inti ['inti] _nm monetary unit of Peru_.
intimar [inti'mar] _vt_ to intimate, announce;
(_mandar_) to order ♦ _vi_, **~se** _vr_ to become
friendly.
intimidad [intimi'ðað] _nf_ intimacy;
(_familiaridad_) familiarity; (_vida privada_)
private life; (_JUR_) privacy.
intimidar [intimi'ðar] _vt_ to intimidate,
scare.
íntimo, a ['intimo, a] _adj_ intimate;
(_pensamientos_) innermost; (_vida_)
personal, private; **una boda íntima** a
quiet wedding.
intolerable [intole'raßle] _adj_ intolerable,
unbearable.
intolerancia [intole'ranθja] _nf_ intolerance.
intoxicación [intoksika'θjon] _nf_ poisoning;
~ alimenticia food poisoning.
intraducible [intraðu'θißle] _adj_
untranslatable.
intranet [intra'net] _nf_ intranet.
intranquilice [intranki'liθe] _etc vb V_
intranquilizarse.
intranquilizarse [intrankili'θarse] _vr_ to get
worried _o_ anxious.
intranquilo, a [intran'kilo, a] _adj_ worried.
intranscendente [intransθen'dente] _adj_
unimportant.
intransferible [intransfe'rißle] _adj_ not

transferable.
intransigente [intransi'xente] _adj_
intransigent.
intransitable [intransi'taßle] _adj_
impassable.
intransitivo, a [intransi'tißo, a] _adj_
intransitive.
intratable [intra'taßle] _adj_ (_problema_)
intractable; (_dificultad_) awkward;
(_individuo_) unsociable.
intrepidez [intrepi'ðeθ] _nf_ courage,
bravery.
intrépido, a [in'trepiðo, a] _adj_ intrepid,
fearless.
intriga [in'triɣa] _nf_ intrigue; (_plan_) plot.
intrigar [intri'ɣar] _vt_, _vi_ to intrigue.
intrigue [in'triɣe] _etc vb V_ **intrigar**.
intrincado, a [intrin'kaðo, a] _adj_ intricate.
intrínseco, a [in'trinseko, a] _adj_ intrinsic.
introducción [introðuk'θjon] _nf_
introduction; (_de libro_) foreword;
(_INFORM_) input.
introducir [introðu'θir] _vt_ (_gen_) to
introduce; (_moneda_) to insert; (_INFORM_)
to input, enter.
introduje [intro'ðuxe] _etc_, **introduzca**
[intro'ðuθka] _etc vb V_ **introducir**.
intromisión [intromi'sjon] _nf_ interference,
meddling.
introvertido, a [introßer'tiðo, a] _adj_, _nm/f_
introvert.
intruso, a [in'truso, a] _adj_ intrusive ♦ _nm/f_
intruder.
intuición [intwi'θjon] _nf_ intuition.
intuir [intu'ir] _vt_ to know by intuition,
intuit.
intuyendo [intu'jendo] _etc vb V_ **intuir**.
inundación [inunda'θjon] _nf_ flood(ing).
inundar [inun'dar] _vt_ to flood; (_fig_) to
swamp, inundate.
inusitado, a [inusi'taðo, a] _adj_ unusual.
inútil [i'nutil] _adj_ useless; (_esfuerzo_) vain,
fruitless.
inutilice [inuti'liθe] _etc vb V_ **inutilizar**.
inutilidad [inutili'ðað] _nf_ uselessness.
inutilizar [inutili'θar] _vt_ to make unusable,
put out of action; (_incapacitar_) to disable;
~se _vr_ to become useless.
invadir [imba'ðir] _vt_ to invade.
invalidar [imbali'ðar] _vt_ to invalidate.
invalidez [imbali'ðeθ] _nf_ (_MED_)
disablement; (_JUR_) invalidity.
inválido, a [im'baliðo, a] _adj_ invalid; (_JUR_)
null and void ♦ _nm/f_ invalid.
invariable [imba'rjable] _adj_ invariable.
invasión [imba'sjon] _nf_ invasion.
invasor, a [imba'sor, a] _adj_ invading ♦ _nm/f_
invader.

invencible [imben'θißle] *adj* invincible; (*timidez, miedo*) unsurmountable.
invención [imben'θjon] *nf* invention.
inventar [imben'tar] *vt* to invent.
inventario [imben'tarjo] *nm* inventory; (*COM*) stocktaking.
inventiva [imben'tißa] *nf* inventiveness.
invento [im'bento] *nm* invention; (*fig*) brainchild; (*pey*) silly idea.
inventor, a [imben'tor, a] *nm/f* inventor.
invernadero [imberna'ðero] *nm* greenhouse.
invernal [imber'nal] *adj* wintry, winter *cpd.*
invernar [imber'nar] *vi* (*ZOOL*) to hibernate.
inverosímil [imbero'simil] *adj* implausible.
inversión [imber'sjon] *nf* (*COM*) investment; ~ **de capitales** capital investment; **inversiones extranjeras** foreign investment *sg.*
inverso, a [im'berso, a] *adj* inverse, opposite; **en el orden** ~ in reverse order; **a la inversa** inversely, the other way round.
inversor, a [imber'sor, a] *nm/f* (*COM*) investor.
invertebrado, a [imberte'ßraðo, a] *adj, nm* invertebrate.
invertido, a [imber'tiðo, a] *adj* inverted; (*al revés*) reversed; (*homosexual*) homosexual ♦ *nm/f* homosexual.
invertir [imber'tir] *vt* (*COM*) to invest; (*volcar*) to turn upside down; (*tiempo etc*) to spend.
investigación [imbestiɣa'θjon] *nf* investigation; (*indagación*) inquiry; (*UNIV*) research; ~ **y desarrollo** (*COM*) research and development (R & D); ~ **de los medios de publicidad** media research; ~ **del mercado** market research.
investigador, a [imbestiɣa'ðor, a] *nm/f* investigator; (*UNIV*) research fellow.
investigar [imbesti'ɣar] *vt* to investigate; (*estudiar*) to do research into.
investigue [imbes'tiɣe] *etc vb V* **investigar.**
investir [imbes'tir] *vt*: ~ **a algn con algo** to confer sth on sb; **fue investido Doctor Honoris Causa** he was awarded an honorary doctorate.
invicto, a [im'bikto, a] *adj* unconquered.
invidente [imbi'ðente] *adj* sightless ♦ *nm/f* blind person; **los** ~**s** the sightless.
invierno [im'bjerno] *nm* winter.
invierta [im'bjerta] *etc vb V* **invertir.**
inviolabilidad [imbjolaßili'ðað] *nf* inviolability; ~ **parlamentaria** parliamentary immunity.
invirtiendo [imbir'tjendo] *etc vb V* **invertir.**

invisible [imbi'sißle] *adj* invisible; **exportaciones/importaciones** ~**s** invisible exports/imports.
invitación [imbita'θjon] *nf* invitation.
invitado, a [imbi'taðo, a] *nm/f* guest.
invitar [imbi'tar] *vt* to invite; (*incitar*) to entice; ~ **a algn a hacer algo** to invite sb to do sth; ~ **a algo** to pay for sth; **nos invitó a cenar fuera** she took us out for dinner; **invito yo** it's on me.
in vitro [im'bitro] *adv* in vitro.
invocar [imbo'kar] *vt* to invoke, call on; (*INFORM*) to call.
involucrar [imbolu'krar] *vt*: ~ **algo en un discurso** to bring something irrelevant into a discussion; ~ **a algn en algo** to involve sb in sth; ~**se** *vr* (*interesarse*) to get involved.
involuntario, a [imbolun'tarjo, a] *adj* involuntary; (*ofensa etc*) unintentional.
invoque [im'boke] *etc vb V* **invocar.**
inyección [injek'θjon] *nf* injection.
inyectar [injek'tar] *vt* to inject.
ión [i'on] *nm* ion.
IPC *nm abr* (*ESP*: = *índice de precios al consumo*) CPI.
IPM *nm abr* (= *índice de precios al por menor*) RPI.

═══════════════ *PALABRA CLAVE*

ir [ir] *vi* **1** to go; (*a pie*) to walk; (*viajar*) to travel; ~ **caminando** to walk; **fui en tren** I went *o* travelled by train; **voy a la calle** I'm going out; ~ **en coche/en bicicleta** to drive/cycle; ~ **a pie** to walk, go on foot; ~ **de pesca** to go fishing; **¡(ahora) voy!** (I'm just) coming!
2: ~ **(a) por**: ~ **(a) por el médico** to fetch the doctor
3 (*progresar: persona, cosa*) to go; **el trabajo va muy bien** work is going very well; **¿cómo te va?** how are things going?; **me va muy bien** I'm getting on very well; **le fue fatal** it went awfully badly for him
4 (*funcionar*): **el coche no va muy bien** the car isn't running very well
5 (*sentar*): **me va estupendamente** (*ropa, color*) it suits me really well; (*medicamento*) it works really well for me; ~ **bien con algo** to go well with sth
6 (*aspecto*): **iba muy bien vestido** he was very well dressed; ~ **con zapatos negros** to wear black shoes
7 (*locuciones*): **¿vino? – ¡que va!** did he come? – of course not!; **vamos, no llores** come on, don't cry; **¡vaya coche!** (*admiración*) what a car!, that's some

car!; (*desprecio*) that's a terrible car!; ¡**vaya**! (*regular*) so so; (*desagrado*) come on!; ¡**vamos**! come on!; ¡**que le vaya bien**! (*adiós*) take care! **8**: **no vaya a ser: tienes que correr, no vaya a ser que pierdas el tren** you'll have to run so as not to miss the train **9**: **no me** *etc* **va ni me viene** I *etc* don't care

♦ *vb aux* **1**: ~ **a: voy/iba a hacerlo hoy** I am/was going to do it today **2** (+*gerundio*): **iba anocheciendo** it was getting dark; **todo se me iba aclarando** everything was gradually becoming clearer to me **3** (+*pp* = *pasivo*): **van vendidos 300 ejemplares** 300 copies have been sold so far

♦ ~**se** *vr* **1**: ¿**por dónde se va al zoológico?** which is the way to the zoo? **2** (*marcharse*) to leave; **ya se habrán ido** they must already have left *o* gone; ¡**vámonos**!, (*AM*) ¡**nos fuimos**! let's go!; ¡**vete**! go away!; ¡**vete a saber**! your guess is as good as mine!, who knows!

ira ['ira] *nf* anger, rage.
iracundo, a [ira'kundo, a] *adj* irascible.
Irak [i'rak] *nm* = **Iraq**.
Irán [i'ran] *nm* Iran.
iraní [ira'ni] *adj*, *nm/f* Iranian.
Iraq [i'rak] *nm* Iraq.
iraquí [ira'ki] *adj*, *nm/f* Iraqui.
irascible [iras'θiβle] *adj* irascible.
irguiendo [ir'ɣjendo] *etc vb V* **erguir**.
iris ['iris] *nm inv* (*arco* ~) rainbow; (*ANAT*) iris.
Irlanda [ir'landa] *nf* Ireland; ~ **del Norte** Northern Ireland, Ulster.
irlandés, esa [irlan'des, esa] *adj* Irish ♦ *nm/f* Irishman/woman ♦ *nm* (*LING*) Gaelic, Irish; **los irlandeses** *npl* the Irish.
ironía [iro'nia] *nf* irony.
irónico, a [i'roniko, a] *adj* ironic(al).
IRPF *nm abr* (*ESP*) = *impuesto sobre la renta de las personas físicas*.
irracional [irraθjo'nal] *adj* irrational.
irrazonable [irraθo'naβle] *adj* unreasonable.
irreal [irre'al] *adj* unreal.
irrealizable [irreali'θaβle] *adj* (*gen*) unrealizable; (*meta*) unrealistic.
irrebatible [irreβa'tiβle] *adj* irrefutable.
irreconocible [irrekono'θiβle] *adj* unrecognizable.
irrecuperable [irrekupe'raβle] *adj* irrecoverable, irretrievable.
irreembolsable [irreembol'saβle] *adj* (*COM*)

non-returnable.
irreflexión [irreflek'sjon] *nf* thoughtlessness; (*ímpetu*) rashness.
irregular [irreɣu'lar] *adj* irregular; (*situación*) abnormal, anomalous; **margen izquierdo/derecho** ~ (*texto*) ragged left/ right (margin).
irregularidad [irreɣulari'ðað] *nf* irregularity.
irremediable [irreme'ðjaβle] *adj* irremediable; (*vicio*) incurable.
irreprochable [irrepro'tʃaβle] *adj* irreproachable.
irresistible [irresis'tiβle] *adj* irresistible.
irresoluto, a [irreso'luto, a] *adj* irresolute, hesitant; (*sin resolver*) unresolved.
irrespetuoso, a [irrespe'twoso, a] *adj* disrespectful.
irresponsable [irrespon'saβle] *adj* irresponsible.
irreverente [irreβe'rente] *adj* disrespectful.
irreversible [irreβer'siβle] *adj* irreversible.
irrevocable [irreβo'kaβle] *adj* irrevocable.
irrigar [irri'ɣar] *vt* to irrigate.
irrigue [i'rriɣe] *etc vb V* **irrigar**.
irrisorio, a [irri'sorjo, a] *adj* derisory, ridiculous; (*precio*) bargain *cpd*.
irritación [irrita'θjon] *nf* irritation.
irritar [irri'tar] *vt* to irritate, annoy; ~**se** *vr* to get angry, lose one's temper.
irrompible [irrom'piβle] *adj* unbreakable.
irrumpir [irrum'pir] *vi*: ~ **en** to burst *o* rush into.
irrupción [irrup'θjon] *nf* irruption; (*invasión*) invasion.
IRTP *nm abr* (*ESP*: = *impuesto sobre el rendimiento del trabajo personal*) ≈ PAYE.
isla ['isla] *nf* (*GEO*) island; **I~s Británicas** British Isles; **I~s Filipinas/Malvinas/ Canarias** Philippines/Falklands/ Canaries.
Islam [is'lam] *nm* Islam.
islámico, a [is'lamiko, a] *adj* Islamic.
islandés, esa [islan'des, esa] *adj* Icelandic ♦ *nm/f* Icelander ♦ *nm* (*LING*) Icelandic.
Islandia [is'landja] *nf* Iceland.
isleño, a [is'leɲo, a] *adj* island *cpd* ♦ *nm/f* islander.
islote [is'lote] *nm* small island.
isotónico, a [iso'toniko, a] *adj* isotonic.
isótopo [i'sotopo] *nm* isotope.
Israel [isra'el] *nm* Israel.
israelí [israe'li] *adj*, *nm/f* Israeli.
istmo ['istmo] *nm* isthmus; **el I~ de Panamá** the Isthmus of Panama.
Italia [i'talja] *nf* Italy.
italiano, a [ita'ljano, a] *adj*, *nm/f* Italian

◆ *nm* (*LING*) Italian.
itinerante [itine'rante] *adj* travelling;
(*embajador*) roving.
itinerario [itine'rarjo] *nm* itinerary, route.
ITV *nf abr* (= *Inspección Técnica de
Vehículos*) ≈ MOT (test) (*BRIT*).
IVA ['ißa] *nm abr* (*ESP COM*: = *Impuesto sobre
el Valor Añadido*) VAT.
IVP *nm abr* = *Instituto Venezolano de
Petroquímica*.
izada [i'saða] *nf* (*AM*) lifting, raising.
izar [i'θar] *vt* to hoist.
izda, izq.ª *abr* = **izquierda**.
izdo, izq, izq.º *abr* – **izquierdo**.
izquierda [iθ'kjerða] *nf V* **izquierdo**.
izquierdista [iθkjer'ðista] *adj* leftist, left-
wing ◆ *nm/f* left-winger, leftist
izquierdo, a [iθ'kjerðo, a] *adj* left ◆ *nf* left;
(*POL*) left (wing); **a la ~** on the left; **es un
cero a la ~** (*fam*) he is a nonentity;
conducción por la ~ left-hand drive.

Jj

J, j ['xota] *nf* (*letra*) J, j; **J de José** J for
Jack (*BRIT*) o Jig (*US*).
jabalí [xaßa'li] *nm* wild boar.
jabalina [xaßa'lina] *nf* javelin.
jabato, a [xa'ßato, a] *adj* brave, bold ◆ *nm*
young wild boar.
jabón [xa'ßon] *nm* soap; (*fam*: *adulación*)
flattery; **~ de afeitar** shaving soap; **~ de
tocador** toilet soap; **dar ~ a algn** to soft-
soap sb.
jabonar [xaßo'nar] *vt* to soap.
jaca ['xaka] *nf* pony.
jacinto [xa'θinto] *nm* hyacinth.
jactancia [xak'tanθja] *nf* boasting,
boastfulness.
jactarse [xak'tarse] *vr*: **~ (de)** to boast o
brag (about o of).
jadear [xaðe'ar] *vi* to pant, gasp for
breath.
jadeo [xa'ðeo] *nm* panting, gasping.
jaguar [xa'ɣwar] *nm* jaguar.
jalar [xa'lar] *vt* (*AM*) to pull.
jalbegue [xal'ßeɣe] *nm* (*pintura*)
whitewash.
jalea [xa'lea] *nf* jelly.
jaleo [xa'leo] *nm* racket, uproar; **armar un
~** to kick up a racket.

jalón [xa'lon] *nm* (*AM*) tug.
jalonar [xalo'nar] *vt* to stake out; (*fig*) to
mark.
Jamaica [xa'maika] *nf* Jamaica.
jamaicano, a [xamai'kano, a] *adj, nm/f*
Jamaican.
jamás [xa'mas] *adv* never, not ... ever;
(*interrogativo*) ever; **¿~ se vio tal cosa?**
did you ever see such a thing?
jamón [xa'mon] *nm* ham; **~ dulce/serrano**
boiled/cured ham.
Japón [xa'pon] *nm*: **el ~** Japan.
japonés, esa [xapo'nes, esa] *adj, nm/f*
Japanese ◆ *nm* (*LING*) Japanese.
jaque ['xake] *nm*: **~ mate** checkmate.
jaqueca [xa'keka] *nf* (very bad) headache,
migraine.
jarabe [xa'raße] *nm* syrup; **~ para la tos**
cough syrup o mixture.
jarana [xa'rana] *nf* (*juerga*) spree (*fam*);
andar/ir de ~ to be/go on a spree.
jarcia ['xarθja] *nf* (*NAUT*) ropes *pl*, rigging.
jardín [xar'ðin] *nm* garden; **~ botánico**
botanical garden; **~ de (la) infancia** (*ESP*)
o **de niños** (*AM*) o **infantil** (*AM*)
kindergarten, nursery school.
jardinería [xarðine'ria] *nf* gardening.
jardinero, a [xarði'nero, a] *nm/f* gardener.
jarra ['xarra] *nf* jar; (*jarro*) jug; (*de leche*)
churn; (*de cerveza*) mug; **de** o **en ~s** with
arms akimbo.
jarro ['xarro] *nm* jug.
jarrón [xa'rron] *nm* vase; (*ARQUEOLOGÍA*)
urn.
jaspeado, a [xaspe'ado, a] *adj* mottled,
speckled.
jaula ['xaula] *nf* cage; (*embalaje*) crate.
jauría [xau'ria] *nf* pack of hounds.
jazmín [xaθ'min] *nm* jasmine.
J. C. *abr* = **Jesucristo**.
jeep, *pl* **jeeps** ® [jip, jips] *nm* jeep ®.
jefa ['xefa] *nf V* **jefe**.
jefatura [xefa'tura] *nf* (*liderato*) leadership;
(*sede*) central office; **J~ de la aviación
civil** ≈ Civil Aviation Authority; **~ de
policía** police headquarters *sg*.
jefazo [xe'faθo] *nm* bigwig.
jefe, a ['xefe, a] *nm/f* (*gen*) chief, head;
(*patrón*) boss; (*POL*) leader; (*COM*)
manager(ess); **~ de camareros** head
waiter; **~ de cocina** chef; **~ ejecutivo**
(*COM*) chief executive; **~ de estación**
stationmaster; **~ de estado** head of
state; **~ de oficina** (*COM*) office manager;
~ de producción (*COM*) production
manager; **~ supremo** commander-in-
chief; **ser el ~** (*fig*) to be the boss.
JEN [xen] *nf abr* (*ESP*) = *Junta de Energía*

Nuclear.
jengibre [xen'xiβre] nm ginger.
jeque ['xeke] nm sheik(h).
jerarquía [xerar'kia] nf (orden) hierarchy; (rango) rank.
jerárquico, a [xe'rarkiko, a] adj hierarchic(al).
jerez [xe'reθ] nm sherry; **J~ de la Frontera** Jerez.
jerezano, a [xere'θano, a] adj of o from Jerez ♦ nm/f native o inhabitant of Jerez.
jerga ['xerɣa] nf (tela) coarse cloth; (lenguaje) jargon; **~ informática** computer jargon.
jerigonza [xeri'ɣonθa] nf (jerga) jargon, slang; (galimatías) nonsense, gibberish.
jeringa [xe'ringa] nf syringe; (AM) annoyance, bother; **~ de engrase** grease gun.
jeringar [xerin'gar] vt to annoy, bother.
jeringue [xe'ringe] etc vb V **jeringar**.
jeringuilla [xerin'guiʎa] nf hypodermic (syringe).
jeroglífico [xero'ɣlifiko] nm hieroglyphic.
jersey [xer'sei], pl **jerseys** nm jersey, pullover, jumper.
Jerusalén [xerusa'len] n Jerusalem.
Jesucristo [xesu'kristo] nm Jesus Christ.
jesuita [xe'swita] adj, nm Jesuit.
Jesús [xe'sus] nm Jesus; ¡~! good heavens!; (al estornudar) bless you!
jet, pl **jets** [jet, jet] nm jet (plane) ♦ nf: **la ~** the jet set.
jeta ['xeta] nf (ZOOL) snout; (fam: cara) mug; ¡**que ~ tienes!** (fam: insolencia) you've got a nerve!
jíbaro, a ['xiβaro, a] adj, nm/f Jíbaro (Indian).
jícara ['xikara] nf small cup.
jiennense [xjen'nense] adj of o from Jaén ♦ nm/f native o inhabitant of Jaén.
jilguero [xil'ɣero] nm goldfinch.
jinete, a [xi'nete, a] nm/f horseman/woman.
jipijapa [xipi'xapa] nm (AM) straw hat.
jira ['xira] nf (de tela) strip; (excursión) picnic.
jirafa [xi'rafa] nf giraffe.
jirón [xi'ron] nm rag, shred.
JJ.OO. nmpl abr = **Juegos Olímpicos**.
jocosidad [xokosi'ðað] nf humour; (chiste) joke.
jocoso, a [xo'koso, a] adj humorous, jocular.
joder [xo'ðer] (fam!) vt to fuck (!), screw (!); (fig: fastidiar) to piss off (!), bug; **~se** vr (fracasar) to fail; ¡~! damn it!; **se jodió todo** everything was ruined.
jodido, a [xo'ðiðo, a] adj (fam!: difícil) awkward; **estoy ~** I'm knackered.

jofaina [xo'faina] nf washbasin.
jojoba [xo'xoβa] nf jojoba.
jolgorio [xol'ɣorjo] nm (juerga) fun, revelry.
jonrón [xon'ron] nm home run.
Jordania [xor'ðanja] nf Jordan.
jornada [xor'naða] nf (viaje de un día) day's journey; (camino o viaje entero) journey; (día de trabajo) working day; **~ de 8 horas** 8-hour day; (trabajar a) **~ partida** (to work a) split shift.
jornal [xor'nal] nm (day's) wage.
jornalero, a [xorna'lero, a] nm/f (day) labourer.
joroba [xo'roβa] nf hump.
jorobado, a [xoro'βaðo, a] adj hunchbacked ♦ nm/f hunchback.
jorobar [xoro'βar] vt to annoy, pester, bother; **~se** vr to get cross; ¡**hay que ~se!** to hell with it!; **esto me joroba** I'm fed up with this!
jota ['xota] nf letter J; (danza) Aragonese dance; (fam) jot, iota; **no saber ni ~** to have no idea.
joven ['xoβen] adj young ♦ nm young man, youth ♦ nf young woman, girl.
jovencito, a [xoβen'θito, a] nm/f youngster.
jovial [xo'βjal] adj cheerful, jolly.
jovialidad [xoβjali'ðað] nf cheerfulness.
joya ['xoxa] nf jewel, gem; (fig: persona) gem; **~s de fantasía** imitation jewellery sg.
joyería [xoxe'ria] nf (joyas) jewellery; (tienda) jeweller's (shop).
joyero [xo'xero] nm (persona) jeweller; (caja) jewel case.
Juan [xwan] nm: **Noche de San ~** see boxed note.

NOCHE DE SAN JUAN

The **Noche de San Juan** (evening of the Feast of Saint John) on 24 June coincides with the summer solstice; the "fiesta" has in fact replaced other more ancient pagan festivals. Traditionally fire plays a major part in these festivities, which can last for days in certain areas. Celebrations, fireworks and dancing centre around "hogueras" (bonfires) in towns and villages across Spain.

---

juanete [xwa'nete] nm (del pie) bunion.
jubilación [xuβila'θjon] nf (retiro) retirement.
jubilado, a [xuβi'laðo, a] adj retired ♦ nm/f retired person, pensioner (BRIT), senior citizen.
jubilar [xuβi'lar] vt to pension off, retire;

(*fam*) to discard; ~**se** *vr* to retire.
jubileo [xuβi'leo] *nm* jubilee.
júbilo ['xuβilo] *nm* joy, rejoicing.
jubiloso, a [xuβi'loso, a] *adj* jubilant.
judaísmo [xuða'ismo] *nm* Judaism.
judía [xu'ðia] *nf* V **judío**.
judicatura [xuðika'tura] *nf* (*cargo de juez*)
office of judge; (*cuerpo de jueces*)
judiciary.
judicial [xuði'θjal] *adj* judicial.
judío, a [xu'ðio, a] *adj* Jewish ♦ *nm* Jew ♦ *nf*
Jewess, Jewish woman; (*CULIN*) bean;
judía blanca haricot bean; **judía verde**
French o string bean.
juego ['xweɣo] *etc vb* V **jugar** ♦ *nm* (*gen*)
play; (*pasatiempo, partido*) game; (*en
casino*) gambling; (*deporte*) sport;
(*conjunto*) set; (*herramientas*) kit; ~ **de
azar** game of chance; ~ **de café** coffee
set; ~ **de caracteres** (*INFORM*) font; ~
limpio/sucio fair/foul o dirty play; **J~s
Olímpicos** Olympic Games; ~ **de
programas** (*INFORM*) suite of programs;
fuera de ~ (*DEPORTE: persona*) offside;
(: *pelota*) out of play; **por** ~ in fun, for fun.
juegue ['xweɣe] *etc vb* V **jugar**.
juerga ['xwerɣa] *nf* binge; (*fiesta*) party; **ir
de** ~ to go out on a binge.
juerguista [xwer'ɣista] *nm/f* reveller.
jueves ['xweβes] *nm inv* Thursday.
juez [xweθ] *nm/f* (*f tb*: **jueza**) judge; (*TENIS*)
umpire; ~ **de línea** linesman; ~ **de paz**
justice of the peace; ~ **de salida** starter.
jugada [xu'ɣaða] *nf* play; **buena** ~ good
move (o shot o stroke) *etc*.
jugador, a [xuɣa'ðor, a] *nm/f* player; (*en
casino*) gambler.
jugar [xu'ɣar] *vt* to play; (*en casino*) to
gamble; (*apostar*) to bet ♦ *vi* to play; to
gamble; (*COM*) to speculate; ~**se** *vr* to
gamble (away); ~**se el todo por el todo**
to stake one's all, go for bust; **¿quién
juega?** whose move is it?; **¡me la han
jugado!** (*fam*) I've been had!
jugarreta [xuɣa'rreta] *nf* (*mala jugada*) bad
move; (*trampa*) dirty trick; **hacer una** ~ **a
algn** to play a dirty trick on sb.
juglar [xu'ɣlar] *nm* minstrel.
jugo ['xuɣo] *nm* (*BOT, de fruta*) juice; (*fig*)
essence, substance; ~ **de naranja** (*esp
AM*) orange juice.
jugoso, a [xu'ɣoso, a] *adj* juicy; (*fig*)
substantial, important.
jugué [xu'ɣe], **juguemos** [xu'ɣemos] *etc
vb* V **jugar**.
juguete [xu'ɣete] *nm* toy.
juguetear [xuɣete'ar] *vi* to play.
juguetería [xuɣete'ria] *nf* toyshop.

juguetón, ona [xuɣe'ton, ona] *adj* playful.
juicio ['xwiθjo] *nm* judgement; (*sana razón*)
sanity, reason; (*opinión*) opinion; (*JUR:
proceso*) trial; **estar fuera de** ~ to be out
of one's mind; **a mi** ~ in my opinion.
juicioso, a [xwi'θjoso, a] *adj* wise,
sensible.
JUJEM [xu'xem] *nf abr* (*ESP MIL*) = *Junta de
Jefes del Estado Mayor*.
jul. *abr* (= *julio*) Jul.
julio ['xuljo] *nm* July.
jumento, a [xu'mento, a] *nm/f* donkey.
jun. *abr* (= *junio*) Jun.
junco ['xunko] *nm* rush, reed.
jungla ['xungla] *nf* jungle.
junio ['xunjo] *nm* June.
junta ['xunta] *nf* V **junto**.
juntar [xun'tar] *vt* to join, unite; (*maquinaria*) to assemble, put together; (*dinero*) to
collect; ~**se** *vr* to join, meet; (*reunirse:
personas*) to meet, assemble; (*arrimarse*)
to approach, draw closer; ~**se con algn**
to join sb.
junto, a ['xunto, a] *adj* joined; (*unido*)
united; (*anexo*) near, close; (*contiguo,
próximo*) next, adjacent ♦ *nf* (*asamblea*)
meeting, assembly; (*comité, consejo*)
board, council, committee; (*MIL, POL*)
junta; (*articulación*) joint ♦ *adv*: **todo** ~ all
at once ♦ *prep*: ~ **a** near (to), next to; ~**s**
together; **junta constitutiva** (*COM*)
statutory meeting; **junta directiva** (*COM*)
board of management; **junta general
extraordinaria** (*COM*) extraordinary
general meeting.
juntura [xun'tura] *nf* (*punto de unión*) join,
junction; (*articulación*) joint.
jura ['xura] *nf* oath, pledge; ~ **de bandera**
(ceremony of taking the) oath of
allegiance.
jurado [xu'raðo] *nm* (*JUR: individuo*) juror;
(: *grupo*) jury; (*de concurso: grupo*) panel
(of judges); (: *individuo*) member of a
panel.
juramentar [xuramen'tar] *vt* to swear in,
administer the oath to; ~**se** *vr* to be
sworn in, take the oath.
juramento [xura'mento] *nm* oath;
(*maldición*) oath, curse; **bajo** ~ on oath;
prestar ~ to take the oath; **tomar** ~ **a** to
swear in, administer the oath to.
jurar [xu'rar] *vt, vi* to swear; ~ **en falso** to
commit perjury; **jurárselas a algn** to
have it in for sb.
jurídico, a [xu'riðiko, a] *adj* legal,
juridical.
jurisdicción [xurisðik'θjon] *nf* (*poder,
autoridad*) jurisdiction; (*territorio*)

district.

jurisprudencia [xurispru'ðenθja] *nf* jurisprudence.

jurista [xu'rista] *nm/f* jurist.

justamente [xusta'mente] *adv* justly, fairly; (*precisamente*) just, exactly.

justicia [xus'tiθja] *nf* justice; (*equidad*) fairness, justice; **de** ~ deservedly.

justiciero, a [xusti'θjero, a] *adj* just, righteous.

justificable [xustifi'kaßle] *adj* justifiable.

justificación [xustifika'θjon] *nf* justification; ~ **automática** (*INFORM*) automatic justification.

justificado, a [xustifi'kaðo, a] *adj* (*TIP*): **(no)** ~ (un)justified.

justificante [xustifi'kante] *nm* voucher; ~ **médico** sick note.

justificar [xustifi'kar] *vt* (*tb TIP*) to justify; (*probar*) to verify.

justifique [xusti'fike] *etc vb V* **justificar**.

justo, a ['xusto, a] *adj* (*equitativo*) just, fair, right; (*preciso*) exact, correct; (*ajustado*) tight ♦ *adv* (*precisamente*) exactly, precisely; (*apenas a tiempo*) just in time; ¡~! that's it!, correct!; **llegaste muy** ~ you just made it; **vivir muy** ~ to be hard up.

juvenil [xuße'nil] *adj* youthful.

juventud [xußen'tuð] *nf* (*adolescencia*) youth; (*jóvenes*) young people *pl.*

juzgado [xuθ'ɣaðo] *nm* tribunal; (*JUR*) court.

juzgar [xuθ'ɣar] *vt* to judge; **a** ~ **por** ... to judge by ..., judging by ...; ~ **mal** to misjudge; **júzguelo usted mismo** see for yourself.

kepí, kepis [ke'pi, 'kepis] *nm* (*esp AM*) kepi, military hat.

kerosene [kero'sene] *nm* kerosene.

kg. *abr* (= *kilogramo(s)*) kg.

kilate [ki'late] *nm* = **quilate.**

kilo ['kilo] *nm* kilo.

kilobyte ['kiloßait] *nm* (*INFORM*) kilobyte.

kilogramo [kilo'ɣramo] *nm* kilogramme (*BRIT*), kilogram (*US*).

kilolitro [kilo'litro] *nm* kilolitre (*BRIT*), kiloliter (*US*).

kilometraje [kilome'traxe] *nm* distance in kilometres, ≈ mileage.

kilométrico, a [kilo'metriko, a] *adj* kilometric; (*fam*) very long; **(billete)** ~ (*FERRO*) mileage ticket.

kilómetro [ki'lometro] *nm* kilometre (*BRIT*), kilometer (*US*).

kiloocteto [kilook'teto] *nm* (*INFORM*) kilobyte.

kilovatio [kilo'ßatjo] *nm* kilowatt.

kiosco ['kjosko] *nm* = **quiosco.**

Kirguizistán [kirɣiθis'tan] *nm* Kirghizia.

kiwi ['kiwi] *nm* kiwi (fruit).

km *abr* (= *kilómetro(s)*) km.

km/h *abr* (= *kilómetros por hora*) km/h.

knock-out ['nokau], **K.O.** ['kao] *nm* knockout; (*golpe*) knockout blow; **dejar** o **poner a algn** ~ to knock sb out.

kosovar [koso'ßar] *adj* Kosovan.

Kosovo ['kosoßo] *nm* Kosovo.

k.p.h. *abr* (= *kilómetros por hora*) km/h.

k.p.l. *abr* (= *kilómetros por litro*) ≈ m.p.g.

kurdo, a ['kurðo, a] *adj* Kurdish ♦ *nm/f* Kurd ♦ *nm* (*LING*) Kurdish.

kuwaití [kußai'ti] *adj, nm/f* Kuwaiti.

kv *abr* (= *kilovatio*) kw.

kv/h *abr* (= *kilovatios-hora*) kw-h.

Kk

K, k [ka] *nf* (*letra*) K, k; **K de Kilo** K for King.

K *abr* (= *1.000*) K; (*INFORM*: = *1.024*) K.

Kampuchea [kampu't ʃea] *nf* Kampuchea.

karaoke [kara'oke] *nm* karaoke.

kárate ['karate] *nm*, **karate** [ka'rate] *nm* karate.

KAS *nf abr* (= *Koordinadora Abertzale Sozialista*) *Basque nationalist umbrella group.*

Kazajstán [kaθaxs'tan] *nm* Kazakhstan.

k/c. *abr* (= *kilociclos*) kc.

Kenia ['kenja] *nf* Kenya.

keniata [ke'njata] *adj, nm/f* Kenyan.

Ll

L, l ['ele] *nf* (*letra*) L, l; **L de Lorenzo** L for Lucy (*BRIT*) o Love (*US*).

l. *abr* (= *litro(s)*) l.; (*JUR*) = **ley**; (*LITERATURA:* = *libro*) bk.

L/ *abr* (*COM*) = **letra.**

la [la] *artículo definido fsg* the ♦ *pron* her; (*usted*) you; (*cosa*) it ♦ *nm* (*MUS*) A; **está en** ~ **cárcel** he's in jail; ~ **del sombrero rojo** the woman/girl/one in the red hat.

laberinto [laße'rinto] nm labyrinth.

labia ['laßja] nf fluency; (pey) glibness;
tener mucha ~ to have the gift of the
gab.

labial [la'ßjal] adj labial.

labio ['laßjo] nm lip; (de vasija etc) edge,
rim; ~ inferior/superior lower/upper lip.

labor [la'ßor] nf labour; (AGR) farm work;
(tarea) job, task; (COSTURA) needlework,
sewing; (punto) knitting; ~ de equipo
teamwork; ~ de ganchillo crochet.

laborable [laßo'raßle] adj (AGR) workable;
día ~ working day.

laboral [laßo'ral] adj (accidente,
conflictividad) industrial; (jornada)
working; (derecho, relaciones) labour cpd.

laboralista [laßora'lista] adj: abogado ~
labour lawyer.

laborar [laßo'rar] vi to work.

laboratorio [laßora'torjo] nm laboratory.

laborioso, a [laßo'rjoso, a] a (persona)
hard-working; (trabajo) tough.

laborista [laßo'rista] (BRIT POL) adj: Partido
L~ Labour Party ♦ nm/f Labour Party
member o supporter.

labrado, a [la'ßraðo, a] adj worked;
(madera) carved; (metal) wrought ♦ nm
(AGR) cultivated field.

Labrador [laßra'ðor] nm Labrador.

labrador, a [laßra'ðor, a] nm/f farmer.

labranza [la'ßranθa] nf (AGR) cultivation.

labrar [la'ßrar] vt (gen) to work; (madera
etc) to carve; (fig) to cause, bring about.

labriego, a [la'ßrjeɣo, a] nm/f peasant.

laca ['laka] nf lacquer; (de pelo) hairspray;
~ de uñas nail varnish.

lacayo [la'kajo] nm lackey.

lacerar [laθe'rar] vt to lacerate.

lacio, a ['laθjo, a] adj (pelo) lank, straight.

lacón [la'kon] nm shoulder of pork.

lacónico, a [la'koniko, a] adj laconic.

lacra ['lakra] nf (defecto) blemish; ~ social
social disgrace.

lacrar [la'krar] vt (cerrar) to seal (with
sealing wax).

lacre ['lakre] nm sealing wax.

lacrimógeno, a [lakri'moxeno, a] adj (fig)
sentimental; gas ~ tear gas.

lacrimoso, a [lakri'moso, a] adj tearful.

lactancia [lak'tanθja] nf breast-feeding.

lactar [lak'tar] vt, vi to suckle, breast-feed.

lácteo, a ['lakteo, a] adj: productos ~s
dairy products.

ladear [laðe'ar] vt to tip, tilt ♦ vi to tilt; ~se
vr to lean; (DEPORTE) to swerve; (AVIAT)
to bank, turn.

ladera [la'ðera] nf slope.

ladino, a [la'ðino, a] adj cunning.

lado ['laðo] nm (gen) side; (fig) protection;
(MIL) flank; ~ izquierdo left(-hand) side;
~ a ~ side by side; al ~ de next to,
beside; hacerse a un ~ to stand aside;
poner de ~ to put on its side; poner a un
~ to put aside; me da de ~ I don't care;
por un ~ ..., por otro ~ ... on the one
hand ..., on the other (hand), ...; por
todos ~s on all sides, all round (BRIT).

ladrar [la'ðrar] vi to bark.

ladrido [la'ðriðo] nm bark, barking.

ladrillo [la'ðriʎo] nm (gen) brick; (azulejo)
tile.

ladrón, ona [la'ðron, ona] nm/f thief.

lagar [la'ɣar] nm (wine/oil) press.

lagartija [laɣar'tixa] nf (small) lizard, wall
lizard.

lagarto [la'ɣarto] nm (ZOOL) lizard; (AM)
alligator.

lago ['laɣo] nm lake.

Lagos ['laɣos] nm Lagos.

lágrima ['laɣrima] nf tear.

lagrimal [laɣri'mal] nm (inner) corner of
the eye.

lagrimear [laɣrime'ar] vi to weep; (ojos) to
water.

laguna [la'ɣuna] nf (lago) lagoon; (en
escrito, conocimientos) gap.

laico, a ['laiko, a] adj lay ♦ nm/f layman/
woman.

laja ['laxa] nf rock.

lamber [lam'ber] vt (AM) to lick.

lambiscón, ona [lambis'kon, ona] adj
flattering ♦ nm/f flatterer.

lameculos [lame'kulos] nm/f inv (fam)
arselicker (!), crawler.

lamentable [lamen'taßle] adj lamentable,
regrettable; (miserable) pitiful.

lamentación [lamenta'θjon] nf
lamentation; ahora no sirven
lamentaciones it's no good crying over
spilt milk.

lamentar [lamen'tar] vt (sentir) to regret;
(deplorar) to lament; ~se vr to lament; lo
lamento mucho I'm very sorry.

lamento [la'mento] nm lament.

lamer [la'mer] vt to lick.

lámina ['lamina] nf (plancha delgada) sheet;
(para estampar, estampa) plate; (grabado)
engraving.

laminar [lami'nar] vt (en libro) to laminate;
(TEC) to roll.

lámpara ['lampara] nf lamp; ~ de alcohol/
gas spirit/gas lamp; ~ de pie standard
lamp.

lamparilla [lampa'riʎa] nf nightlight.

lamparón [lampa'ron] nm (MED) scrofula;
(mancha) (large) grease spot.

lampiño, a [lam'piɲo, a] _adj (sin pelo)_ hairless.

lana ['lana] _nf_ wool; _(tela)_ woollen _(BRIT)_ o woolen _(US)_ cloth; _(AM fam: dinero)_ dough; **(hecho) de** ~ wool _cpd._

lance ['lanθe] _etc vb_ V **lanzar** ♦ _nm (golpe)_ stroke; _(suceso)_ event, incident.

lanceta [lan'seta] _nf (AM)_ sting.

lancha ['lantʃa] _nf_ launch; ~ **motora** motorboat; ~ **de pesca** fishing boat; ~ **salvavidas/torpedera** lifeboat/torpedo boat; ~ **neumática** rubber dinghy.

lanero, a [la'nero, a] _adj_ wool _cpd._

langosta [lan'gosta] _nf (insecto)_ locust; _(crustáceo)_ lobster (: _de río)_ crayfish.

langostino [langos'tino] _nm_ prawn; _(de agua dulce)_ crayfish.

languidecer [langiðe'θer] _vi_ to languish.

languidez [langi'ðeθ] _nf_ languor.

languidezca [langi'ðeθka] _etc vb_ V **languidecer.**

lánguido, a ['langiðo, a] _adj (gen)_ languid; _(sin energía)_ listless.

lanilla [la'niʎa] _nf_ nap; _(tela)_ thin flannel cloth.

lanolina [lano'lina] _nf_ lanolin(e).

lanudo, a [la'nuðo, a] _adj_ woolly, fleecy.

lanza ['lanθa] _nf (arma)_ lance, spear; **medir** ~**s** to cross swords.

lanzacohetes [lanθako'etes] _nm inv_ rocket launcher.

lanzadera [lanθa'ðera] _nf_ shuttle.

lanzado, a [lan'θaðo, a] _adj (atrevido)_ forward; _(decidido)_ determined; **ir** ~ _(rápido)_ to fly along.

lanzallamas [lanθa'ʎamas] _nm inv_ flamethrower.

lanzamiento [lanθa'mjento] _nm (gen)_ throwing; _(NAUT, COM)_ launch, launching; ~ **de pesos** putting the shot.

lanzar [lan'θar] _vt (gen)_ to throw; _(con violencia)_ to fling; _(DEPORTE: pelota)_ to bowl; (: _US)_ to pitch; _(NAUT, COM)_ to launch; _(JUR)_ to evict; _(grito)_ to give, utter; ~**se** _vr_ to throw o.s.; _(fig)_ to take the plunge; ~**se a** _(fig)_ to embark upon.

Lanzarote [lanθa'rote] _nm_ Lanzarote.

lanzatorpedos [lanθator'peðos] _nm inv_ torpedo tube.

lapa ['lapa] _nf_ limpet.

La Paz _nf_ La Paz.

lapicero [lapi'θero] _nm_ pencil; _(AM)_ propelling _(BRIT)_ o mechanical _(US)_ pencil; (: _bolígrafo)_ Biro ®.

lápida ['lapiða] _nf_ stone; ~ **conmemorativa** memorial stone; ~ **mortuoria** headstone.

lapidar [lapi'ðar] _vt_ to stone; _(TEC)_ to

polish, lap.

lapidario, a [lapi'ðarjo, a] _adj, nm_ lapidary.

lápiz ['lapiθ] _nm_ pencil; ~ **de color** coloured pencil; ~ **de labios** lipstick; ~ **óptico** o **luminoso** light pen.

lapón, ona [la'pon, ona] _adj_ Lapp ♦ _nm/f_ Laplander, Lapp ♦ _nm (LING)_ Lapp.

Laponia [la'ponja] _nf_ Lapland.

lapso ['lapso] _nm_ lapse; _(error)_ error; ~ **de tiempo** interval of time.

lapsus ['lapsus] _nm inv_ error, mistake.

LAR [lar] _nf abr (ESP JUR)_ = _Ley de Arrendamientos Rústicos._

largamente [larɤa'mente] _adv_ for a long time; _(relatar)_ at length.

largar [lar'ɤar] _vt (soltar)_ to release; _(aflojar)_ to loosen; _(lanzar)_ to launch; _(fam)_ to let fly; _(velas)_ to unfurl; _(AM)_ to throw; ~**se** _vr (fam)_ to beat it; ~**se a** _(AM)_ to start to.

largo, a ['larɤo, a] _adj (longitud)_ long; _(tiempo)_ lengthy; _(persona: alta)_ tall; (: _fig)_ generous ♦ _nm_ length; _(MUS)_ largo; **dos años** ~**s** two long years; **a** ~ **plazo** in the long term; **tiene 9 metros de** ~ it is 9 metres long; **a lo** ~ _(posición)_ lengthways; **a lo** ~ **de** along; _(tiempo)_ all through, throughout; **a la larga** in the long run; **me dio largas con una promesa** she put me off with a promise; **¡**~ **de aquí!** _(fam)_ clear off!

largometraje [larɤome'traxe] _nm_ full-length o feature film.

largue ['larɤe] _etc vb_ V **largar.**

larguero [lar'ɤero] _nm (ARQ)_ main beam, chief support; _(de puerta)_ jamb; _(DEPORTE)_ crossbar; _(en cama)_ bolster.

largueza [lar'ɤeθa] _nf_ generosity.

larguirucho, a [larɤi'rutʃo, a] _adj_ lanky, gangling.

larguísimo, a [lar'ɤisimo, a] _adj superlativo de_ **largo.**

largura [lar'ɤura] _nf_ length.

laringe [la'rinxe] _nf_ larynx.

laringitis [larin'xitis] _nf_ laryngitis.

larva ['larβa] _nf_ larva.

las [las] _artículo definido fpl_ the ♦ _pron_ them; ~ **que cantan** the ones/women/girls who sing.

lasaña [la'saɲa] _nf_ lasagne, lasagna.

lasca ['laska] _nf_ chip of stone.

lascivia [las'θiβja] _nf_ lewdness; _(lujuria)_ lust; _(fig)_ playfulness.

lascivo, a [las'θiβo, a] _adj_ lewd.

láser ['laser] _nm_ laser.

Las Palmas _nf_ Las Palmas.

lástima ['lastima] _nf (pena)_ pity; **dar** ~ to be pitiful; **es una** ~ **que** it's a pity that;

¡qué ~! what a pity!; **estar hecho una ~** to be a sorry sight.

lastimar [lasti'mar] *vt* (*herir*) to wound; (*ofender*) to offend; **~se** *vr* to hurt o.s.

lastimero, a [lasti'mero,͵a] *adj* pitiful, pathetic.

lastre ['lastre] *nm* (*TEC, NAUT*) ballast; (*fig*) dead weight.

lata ['lata] *nf* (*metal*) tin; (*envase*) tin, can; (*fam*) nuisance; **en ~** tinned; **dar (la) ~** to be a nuisance.

latente [la'tente] *adj* latent.

lateral [late'ral] *adj* side, lateral ♦ *nm* (*TEAT*) wings *pl*.

latido [la'tiðo] *nm* (*del corazón*) beat; (*de herida*) throb(bing).

latifundio [lati'fundjo] *nm* large estate.

latifundista [latifun'dista] *nm/f* owner of a large estate.

latigazo [lati'ɣaθo] *nm* (*golpe*) lash; (*sonido*) crack; (*fig: regaño*) dressing-down.

látigo ['latiɣo] *nm* whip.

latiguillo [lati'ɣiʎo] *nm* (*TEAT*) hamming.

latín [la'tin] *nm* Latin; **saber (mucho) ~** (*fam*) to be pretty sharp.

latinajo [lati'naxo] *nm* dog Latin; **echar ~s** to come out with Latin words.

latino, a [la'tino, a] *adj* Latin.

Latinoamérica [latinoa'merika] *nf* Latin America.

latinoamericano, a [latinoameri'kano, a] *adj, nm/f* Latin American.

latir [la'tir] *vi* (*corazón, pulso*) to beat.

latitud [lati'tuð] *nf* (*GEO*) latitude; (*fig*) breadth, extent.

lato, a ['lato, a] *adj* broad.

latón [la'ton] *nm* brass.

latoso, a [la'toso, a] *adj* (*molesto*) annoying; (*aburrido*) boring.

latrocinio [latro'θinjo] *nm* robbery.

LAU *nf abr* (*ESP JUR*) = *Ley de Arrendamientos Urbanos.*

laúd [la'uð] *nm* lute.

laudatorio, a [lauða'torjo, a] *adj* laudatory.

laudo ['lauðo] *nm* (*JUR*) decision, finding.

laurear [laure'ar] *vt* to honour, reward.

laurel [lau'rel] *nm* (*BOT*) laurel; (*CULIN*) bay.

Lausana [lau'sana] *nf* Lausanne.

lava ['laβa] *nf* lava.

lavable [la'βaβle] *adj* washable.

lavabo [la'βaβo] *nm* (*jofaina*) washbasin; (*retrete*) lavatory (*BRIT*), toilet (*BRIT*), washroom (*US*).

lavadero [laβa'ðero] *nm* laundry.

lavado [la'βaðo] *nm* washing; (*de ropa*) wash, laundry; (*ARTE*) wash; **~ de**

cerebro brainwashing.

lavadora [laβa'ðora] *nf* washing machine.

lavanda [la'βanda] *nf* lavender.

lavandería [laβande'ria] *nf* laundry; **~ automática** launderette.

lavaparabrisas [laβapara'βrisas] *nm inv* windscreen washer.

lavaplatos [laβa'platos] *nm inv* dishwasher.

lavar [la'βar] *vt* to wash; (*borrar*) to wipe away; **~se** *vr* to wash o.s.; **~se las manos** to wash one's hands; (*fig*) to wash one's hands of it; **~ y marcar** (*pelo*) to shampoo and set; **~ en seco** to dry-clean.

lavativa [laβa'tiβa] *nf* (*MED*) enema.

lavavajillas [laβaβa'xiʎas] *nm inv* dishwasher.

laxante [lak'sante] *nm* laxative.

laxitud [laksi'tuð] *nf* laxity, slackness.

lazada [la'θaða] *nf* bow.

lazarillo [laθa'riʎo] *nm*: **perro de ~** guide dog.

lazo ['laθo] *nm* knot; (*lazada*) bow; (*para animales*) lasso; (*trampa*) snare; (*vínculo*) tie; **~ corredizo** slipknot.

LBE *nf abr* (*ESP JUR*) = *Ley Básica de Empleo.*

lb(s) *abr* = **libra(s).**

L/C *abr* (= *Letra de Crédito*) B/E.

Lda., Ldo. *abr* = **Licenciado, a.**

le [le] *pron* (*directo*) him (*o* her); (: *usted*) you; (*indirecto*) to him (*o* her *o* it); (: *usted*) to you.

leal [le'al] *adj* loyal.

lealtad [leal'tað] *nf* loyalty.

lebrel [le'βrel] *nm* greyhound.

lección [lek'θjon] *nf* lesson; **~ práctica** object lesson; **dar lecciones** to teach, give lessons; **dar una ~ a algn** (*fig*) to teach sb a lesson.

leche ['letʃe] *nf* milk; (*fam!*) semen, spunk (*!*); **dar una ~ a algn** (*fam*) to belt sb; **estar de mala ~** (*fam*) to be in a foul mood; **tener mala ~** (*fam*) to be a nasty piece of work; **~ condensada/en polvo** condensed/powdered milk; **~ desnatada** skimmed milk; **~ de magnesia** milk of magnesia; **¡~!** hell!

lechera [le'tʃera] *nf V* **lechero.**

lechería [letʃe'ria] *nf* dairy.

lechero, a [le'tʃero, a] *adj* milk *cpd* ♦ *nm* milkman ♦ *nf* (*vendedora*) milkmaid; (*recipiente*) milk pan; (*para servir*) milk churn.

lecho ['letʃo] *nm* (*cama, de río*) bed; (*GEO*) layer; **~ mortuorio** deathbed.

lechón [le'tʃon] *nm* sucking (*BRIT*) *o* suckling (*US*) pig.

lechoso, a [le'tʃoso, a] *adj* milky.

lechuga [le'tʃuɣa] *nf* lettuce.
lechuza [le'tʃuθa] *nf* (barn) owl.
lectivo, a [lek'tißo, a] *adj* (*horas*) teaching *cpd*; **año** *o* **curso** ~ (*ESCOL*) school year; (*UNIV*) academic year.
lector, a [lek'tor, a] *nm/f* reader; (*ESCOL, UNIV*) (conversation) assistant ♦ *nm*: ~ **óptico de caracteres** (*INFORM*) optical character reader ♦ *nf*: ~**a de fichas** (*INFORM*) card reader.
lectura [lek'tura] *nf* reading; ~ **de marcas sensibles** (*INFORM*) mark sensing.
leer [le'er] *vt* to read; ~ **entre líneas** to read between the lines.
legación [leɣa'θjon] *nf* legation.
legado [le'ɣaðo] *nm* (*don*) bequest; (*herencia*) legacy; (*enviado*) legate.
legajo [le'ɣaxo] *nm* file, bundle (of papers).
legal [le'ɣal] *adj* legal, lawful; (*persona*) trustworthy.
legalice [leɣa'liθe] *etc vb V* **legalizar**.
legalidad [leɣali'ðað] *nf* legality.
legalizar [leɣali'θar] *vt* to legalize; (*documento*) to authenticate.
legaña [le'ɣaɲa] *nf* sleep (*in eyes*).
legar [le'ɣar] *vt* to bequeath, leave.
legatario, a [leɣa'tarjo, a] *nm/f* legatee.
legendario, a [lexen'darjo, a] *adj* legendary.
legible [le'xißle] *adj* legible; ~ **por máquina** (*INFORM*) machine-readable.
legión [le'xjon] *nf* legion.
legionario, a [lexjo'narjo, a] *adj* legionary ♦ *nm* legionnaire.
legislación [lexisla'θjon] *nf* legislation; (*leyes*) laws *pl*; ~ **antimonopolio** (*COM*) anti-trust legislation.
legislar [lexis'lar] *vt* to legislate.
legislativo, a [lexisla'tißo, a] *adj*: **(elecciones) legislativas** ≈ general election.
legislatura [lexisla'tura] *nf* (*POL*) period of office.
legitimar [lexiti'mar] *vt* to legitimize.
legítimo, a [le'xitimo, a] *adj* (*genuino*) authentic; (*legal*) legitimate, rightful.
lego, a ['leɣo, a] *adj* (*REL*) secular; (*ignorante*) ignorant ♦ *nm* layman.
legua ['leɣwa] *nf* league; **se ve** (*o* **nota) a la** ~ you can tell (it) a mile off.
legue ['leɣe] *etc vb V* **legar**.
leguleyo [leɣu'lejo] *nm* (*pey*) petty *o* shyster (*US*) lawyer.
legumbres [le'ɣumbres] *nfpl* pulses.
leído, a [le'iðo, a] *adj* well-read.
lejanía [lexa'nia] *nf* distance.
lejano, a [le'xano, a] *adj* far-off; (*en el tiempo*) distant; (*fig*) remote; **L~ Oriente** Far East.

lejía [le'xia] *nf* bleach.
lejísimos [le'xisimos] *adv* a long, long way.
lejos ['lexos] *adv* far, far away; **a lo** ~ **in** the distance; **de** *o* **desde** ~ from a distance; **está muy** ~ it's a long way (away); **¿está** ~**?** is it far?; ~ **de** *prep* far from.
lelo, a ['lelo, a] *adj* silly ♦ *nm/f* idiot.
lema ['lema] *nm* motto; (*POL*) slogan.
lencería [lenθe'ria] *nf* (*telas*) linen, drapery; (*ropa interior*) lingerie.
lendakari [lenda'kari] *nm* head of the Basque Autonomous Government.
lengua ['lengwa] *nf* tongue; ~ **cooficial** *see boxed note*; ~ **materna** mother tongue; ~ **oficial** official language; ~ **de tierra** (*GEO*) spit *o* tongue of land; **dar a la** ~ to chatter; **morderse la** ~ to hold one's tongue; **sacar la** ~ **a algn** (*fig*) to cock a snook at sb.

lenguado [len'gwaðo] *nm* sole.
lenguaje [len'gwaxe] *nm* language; (*forma de hablar*) (mode of) speech; ~ **comercial** business language; ~ **ensamblador** *o* **de alto nivel** (*INFORM*) high-level language; ~ **máquina** (*INFORM*) machine language; ~ **original** source language; ~ **periodístico** journalese; ~ **de programación** (*INFORM*) programming language; **en** ~ **llano** ≈ in plain English.
lenguaraz [lengwa'raθ] *adj* talkative; (*pey*) foul-mouthed.
lengüeta [len'gweta] *nf* (*ANAT*) epiglottis; (*de zapatos, MUS*) tongue.
lenidad [leni'ðað] *nf* lenience.
Leningrado [lenin'graðo] *nm* Leningrad.
lente ['lente] *nm* *o* *nf* lens; (*lupa*) magnifying glass; ~**s** *pl* glasses; ~**s de contacto** contact lenses.
lenteja [len'texa] *nf* lentil.
lentejuela [lente'xwela] *nf* sequin.
lentilla [len'tiʎa] *nf* contact lens.
lentitud [lenti'tuð] *nf* slowness; **con** ~

slowly.
lento, a ['lento, a] *adj* slow.
leña ['leɲa] *nf* firewood; **dar ~ a** to thrash; **echar ~ al fuego** to add fuel to the flames.
leñador, a [leɲa'ðor, a] *nm/f* woodcutter.
leño ['leɲo] *nm* (*trozo de árbol*) log; (*madera*) timber; (*fig*) blockhead.
Leo ['leo] *nm* (*ASTRO*) Leo.
león [le'on] *nm* lion; **~ marino** sea lion.
leonera [leo'nera] *nf* (*jaula*) lion's cage; **parece una ~** it's shockingly dirty.
leonés, esa [leo'nes, esa] *adj, nm/f* Leonese ♦ *nm* (*LING*) Leonese.
leonino, a [leo'nino, a] *adj* leonine.
leopardo [leo'parðo] *nm* leopard.
leotardos [leo'tarðos] *nmpl* tights.
lepra ['lepra] *nf* leprosy.
leprosería [leprose'ria] *nf* leper colony.
leproso, a [le'proso, a] *nm/f* leper.
lerdo, a ['lerðo, a] *adj* (*lento*) slow; (*patoso*) clumsy.
leridano, a [leri'ðano, a] *adj* of *o* from Lérida ♦ *nm/f* native *o* inhabitant of Lérida.
les [les] *pron* (*directo*) them; (: *ustedes*) you; (*indirecto*) to them; (: *ustedes*) to you.
lesbiana [les'ßjana] *nf* lesbian.
lesión [le'sjon] *nf* wound, lesion; (*DEPORTE*) injury.
lesionado, a [lesjo'naðo, a] *adj* injured ♦ *nm/f* injured person.
lesionar [lesjo'nar] *vt* (*dañar*) to hurt; (*herir*) to wound; **~se** *vr* to get hurt.
letal [le'tal] *adj* lethal.
letanía [leta'nia] *nf* litany; (*retahíla*) long list.
letárgico, a [le'tarxiko, a] *adj* lethargic.
letargo [le'tarɣo] *nm* lethargy.
letón, ona [le'ton, ona] *adj, nm/f* Latvian ♦ *nm* (*LING*) Latvian.
Letonia [le'tonja] *nf* Latvia.
letra ['letra] *nf* letter; (*escritura*) handwriting; (*COM*) letter, bill, draft; (*MUS*) lyrics *pl*; **~s** *nfpl* (*UNIV*) arts; **~ bastardilla/negrilla** italics *pl*/bold type; **~ de cambio** bill of exchange; **~ de imprenta** print; **~ inicial/mayúscula/minúscula** initial/capital/small letter; **lo tomó al pie de la ~** he took it literally; **~ bancaria** (*COM*) bank draft; **~ de patente** (*COM*) letters patent *pl*; **escribir 4 ~s a algn** to drop a line to sb.
letrado, a [le'traðo, a] *adj* learned; (*fam*) pedantic ♦ *nm/f* lawyer.
letrero [le'trero] *nm* (*cartel*) sign; (*etiqueta*) label.
letrina [le'trina] *nf* latrine.

leucemia [leu'θemja] *nf* leukaemia.
leucocito [leuko'θito] *nm* white blood cell, leucocyte.
leva ['leßa] *nf* (*NAUT*) weighing anchor; (*MIL*) levy; (*TEC*) lever.
levadizo, a [leßa'ðiθo, a] *adj*: **puente ~** drawbridge.
levadura [leßa'ðura] *nf* yeast, leaven; **~ de cerveza** brewer's yeast.
levantamiento [leßanta'mjento] *nm* raising, lifting; (*rebelión*) revolt, rising; (*GEO*) survey; **~ de pesos** weightlifting.
levantar [leßan'tar] *vt* (*gen*) to raise; (*del suelo*) to pick up; (*hacia arriba*) to lift (up); (*plan*) to make, draw up; (*mesa*) to clear; (*campamento*) to strike; (*fig*) to cheer up, hearten, **~se** *vr* to get up; (*enderezarse*) to straighten up; (*rebelarse*) to rebel; (*sesión*) to be adjourned; (*niebla*) to lift; (*viento*) to rise; **~se (de la cama)** to get up, get out of bed; **~ el ánimo** to cheer up.
levante [le'ßante] *nm* east; (*viento*) east wind; **el L~** *region of Spain extending from Castellón to Murcia*.
levantino, a [leßan'tino, a] *adj* of *o* from the *Levante* ♦ *nm/f*: **los ~s** the people of the *Levante*.
levar [le'ßar] *vi* to weigh anchor.
leve ['leße] *adj* light; (*fig*) trivial; (*mínimo*) slight.
levedad [leße'ðað] *nf* lightness; (*fig*) levity.
levita [le'ßita] *nf* frock coat.
léxico, a ['leksiko, a] *adj* lexical ♦ *nm* (*vocabulario*) vocabulary; (*LING*) lexicon.
ley [lei] *nf* (*gen*) law; (*metal*) standard; **decreto-~** decree law; **de buena ~** (*fig*) genuine; **según la ~** in accordance with the law, by law, in law.
leyenda [le'jenda] *nf* legend; (*TIP*) inscription.
leyendo [le'jendo] *etc vb V* **leer**.
liar [li'ar] *vt* to tie (up); (*unir*) to bind; (*envolver*) to wrap (up); (*enredar*) to confuse; (*cigarrillo*) to roll; **~se** *vr* (*fam*) to get involved; (*confundirse*) to get mixed up; **~se a palos** to get involved in a fight.
lib. *abr* (= *libro*) bk.
libanés, esa [lißa'nes, esa] *adj, nm/f* Lebanese.
Líbano ['lißano] *nm*: **el ~** the Lebanon.
libar [li'ßar] *vt* to suck.
libelo [li'ßelo] *nm* satire, lampoon; (*JUR*) petition.
libélula [li'ßelula] *nf* dragonfly.
liberación [lißera'θjon] *nf* liberation; (*de la cárcel*) release.

liberado, a [liße'raðo, a] *adj* liberated; (*COM*) paid-up, paid-in (*US*).
liberal [liße'ral] *adj, nm/f* liberal.
liberar [liße'rar] *vt* to liberate.
libertad [lißer'tað] *nf* liberty, freedom; ~ **de asociación/de culto/de prensa/de comercio/de palabra** freedom of association/of worship/of the press/of trade/of speech; ~ **condicional** probation; ~ **bajo palabra** parole; ~ **bajo fianza** bail; **estar en** ~ to be free; **poner a algn en** ~ to set sb free.
libertador, a [lißerta'ðor, a] *adj* liberating ♦ *nm/f* liberator; **El L**~ (*AM*) The Liberator.
libertar [lißer'tar] *vt* (*preso*) to set free; (*de una obligación*) to release; (*eximir*) to exempt.
libertinaje [lißerti'naxe] *nm* licentiousness.
libertino, a [lißer'tino, a] *adj* permissive ♦ *nm/f* permissive person.
Libia ['lißja] *nf* Libya.
libidinoso, a [lißiði'noso, a] *adj* lustful; (*viejo*) lecherous.
libido [li'ßiðo] *nf* libido.
libio, a ['lißjo, a] *adj, nm/f* Libyan.
libra ['lißra] *nf* pound; **L**~ (*ASTRO*) Libra; ~ **esterlina** pound sterling.
librador, a [lißra'ðor, a] *nm/f* drawer.
libranza [li'ßranθa] *nf* (*COM*) draft; (*letra de cambio*) bill of exchange.
librar [li'ßrar] *vt* (*de peligro*) to save; (*batalla*) to wage, fight; (*de impuestos*) to exempt; (*cheque*) to make out; (*JUR*) to exempt; ~**se** *vr*: ~**se de** to escape from, free o.s. from; **de buena nos hemos librado** we're well out of that.
libre ['lißre] *adj* (*gen*) free; (*lugar*) unoccupied; (*tiempo*) spare; (*asiento*) vacant; (*COM*): ~ **a bordo** free on board; ~ **de franqueo** post-free; ~ **de impuestos** free of tax; **tiro** ~ free kick; **los 100 metros** ~ the 100 metres freestyle (race); **al aire** ~ in the open air; **¿estás** ~? are you free?
librecambio [lißre'kambjo] *nm* free trade.
librecambista [lißrekam'bista] *adj* free-trade *cpd* ♦ *nm* free-trader.
librería [lißre'ria] *nf* (*tienda*) bookshop; (*estante*) bookcase; ~ **de ocasión** secondhand bookshop.
librero, a [li'ßrero, a] *nm/f* bookseller.
libreta [li'ßreta] *nf* notebook; (*pan*) one-pound loaf; ~ **de ahorros** savings book.
libro ['lißro] *nm* book; ~ **de actas** minute book; ~ **de bolsillo** paperback; ~ **de cabecera** bedside book; ~ **de caja** (*COM*) cashbook; ~ **de caja auxiliar** (*COM*) petty

cash book; ~ **de cocina** cookery book (*BRIT*), cookbook (*US*); ~ **de consulta** reference book; ~ **de cuentas** account book; ~ **de cuentos** storybook; ~ **de cheques** cheque (*BRIT*) *o* check (*US*) book; ~ **diario** journal; ~ **de entradas y salidas** (*COM*) daybook; ~ **de honor** visitors' book; ~ **mayor** (*COM*) general ledger; ~ **de reclamaciones** complaints book; ~ **de texto** textbook.
Lic. *abr* = **Licenciado, a.**
licencia [li'θenθja] *nf* (*gen*) licence; (*permiso*) permission; ~ **por enfermedad/con goce de sueldo** sick/paid leave; ~ **de armas/de caza** gun/game licence; ~ **de exportación** (*COM*) export licence; ~ **poética** poetic licence.
licenciado, a [liθen'θjaðo, a] *adj* licensed ♦ *nm/f* graduate; **L**~ **en Filosofía y Letras** ≈ Bachelor of Arts; *see boxed note.*

LICENCIADO

After an average of five years at Spanish universities, successful students are awarded a degree called a **licenciado**. *If they have done a shorter three-year course, such as nursing, or if they choose not to stay on for another two years to specialize, they are awarded a "diplomado" instead. "Cursos de posgrado", postgraduate courses, are becoming increasingly popular, especially one-year specialist courses called "masters".*

licenciar [liθen'θjar] *vt* (*empleado*) to dismiss; (*permitir*) to permit, allow; (*soldado*) to discharge; (*estudiante*) to confer a degree upon; ~**se** *vr*: ~**se en letras** to get an arts degree.
licenciatura [liθenθja'tura] *nf* (*título*) degree; (*estudios*) degree course.
licencioso, a [liθen'θjoso, a] *adj* licentious.
liceo [li'θeo] *nm* (*esp AM*) (high) school.
licitación [liθita'θjon] *nf* bidding; (*oferta*) tender, offer.
licitador [liθita'ðor] *nm* bidder.
licitar [liθi'tar] *vt* to bid for ♦ *vi* to bid.
lícito, a ['liθito, a] *adj* (*legal*) lawful; (*justo*) fair, just; (*permisible*) permissible.
licor [li'kor] *nm* spirits *pl* (*BRIT*), liquor (*US*); (*con hierbas etc*) liqueur.
licra ® ['likra] *nf* Lycra ®.
licuadora [likwa'ðora] *nf* blender.
licuar [li'kwar] *vt* to liquidize.
lid [lið] *nf* combat; (*fig*) controversy.
líder ['liðer] *nm/f* leader.

liderato [liðe'rato] *nm* = **liderazgo**.

liderazgo [liðe'raθγo] *nm* leadership.

lidia ['liðja] *nf* bullfighting; (*una* ~) bullfight; **toros de** ~ fighting bulls.

lidiar [li'ðjar] *vt, vi* to fight.

liebre ['ljeβre] *nf* hare; **dar gato por** ~ to con.

Lieja ['ljexa] *nf* Liège.

lienzo ['ljenθo] *nm* linen; (*ARTE*) canvas; (*ARQ*) wall.

lifting ['liftin] *nm* facelift.

liga ['liγa] *nf* (*de medias*) garter, suspender; (*confederación*) league; (*AM: gomita*) rubber band.

ligadura [liγa'ðura] *nf* bond, tie; (*MED, MUS*) ligature.

ligamento [liγa'mento] *nm* (*ANAT*) ligament; (*atadura*) tie; (*unión*) bond.

ligar [li'γar] *vt* (*atar*) to tie; (*unir*) to join; (*MED*) to bind up; (*MUS*) to slur; (*fam*) to get off with, pick up ♦ *vi* to mix, blend; (*fam*) to get off with sb; (*2 personas*) to get off with one another; ~**se** *vr* (*fig*) to commit o.s.; ~ **con** (*fam*) to get off with, pick up; ~**se a algn** to get off with o pick up sb.

ligereza [lixe'reθa] *nf* lightness; (*rapidez*) swiftness; (*agilidad*) agility; (*superficialidad*) flippancy.

ligero, a [li'xero, a] *adj* (*de peso*) light; (*tela*) thin; (*rápido*) swift, quick; (*ágil*) agile, nimble; (*de importancia*) slight; (*de carácter*) flippant, superficial ♦ *adv* quickly, swiftly; **a la ligera** superficially; **juzgar a la ligera** to jump to conclusions.

light ['lait] *adj inv* (*cigarrillo*) low-tar; (*comida*) diet *cpd*.

ligón [li'γon] *nm* (*fam*) Romeo.

ligue ['liγe] *etc vb V* **ligar** ♦ *nm/f* boyfriend/ girlfriend ♦ *nm* (*persona*) pick-up.

liguero [li'γero] *nm* suspender (*BRIT*) o garter (*US*) belt.

lija ['lixa] *nf* (*ZOOL*) dogfish; (**papel de**) ~ sandpaper.

lijar [li'xar] *vt* to sand.

lila ['lila] *adj inv, nf* lilac ♦ *nm* (*fam*) twit.

lima ['lima] *nf* file; (*BOT*) lime; ~ **de uñas** nail file; **comer como una** ~ to eat like a horse.

limar [li'mar] *vt* to file; (*alisar*) to smooth over; (*fig*) to polish up.

limbo ['limbo] *nm* (*REL*) limbo; **estar en el** ~ to be on another planet.

limitación [limita'θjon] *nf* limitation, limit; ~ **de velocidad** speed limit.

limitado, a [limi'taðo, a] *adj* limited; **sociedad limitada** (*COM*) limited company.

limitar [limi'tar] *vt* to limit; (*reducir*) to reduce, cut down ♦ *vi*: ~ **con** to border on; ~**se** *vr*: ~**se a** to limit o confine o.s. to.

límite ['limite] *nm* (*gen*) limit; (*fin*) end; (*frontera*) border; **como** ~ at (the) most; (*fecha*) at the latest; **no tener** ~**s** to know no bounds; ~ **de crédito** (*COM*) credit limit; ~ **de página** (*INFORM*) page break; ~ **de velocidad** speed limit.

limítrofe [li'mitrofe] *adj* bordering, neighbouring.

limón [li'mon] *nm* lemon ♦ *adj*: **amarillo** ~ lemon-yellow.

limonada [limo'naða] *nf* lemonade.

limonero [limo'nero] *nm* lemon tree.

limosna [li'mosna] *nf* alms *pl*; **pedir** ~ to beg; **vivir de** ~ to live on charity.

limpiabotas [limpja'βotas] *nm/f inv* bootblack (*BRIT*), shoeshine boy/girl.

limpiacristales [limpjakris'tales] *nm inv* (*detergente*) window cleaner.

limpiador, a [limpja'ðor, a] *adj* cleaning, cleansing ♦ *nm/f* cleaner.

limpiaparabrisas [limpjapara'βrisas] *nm inv* windscreen (*BRIT*) o windshield (*US*) wiper.

limpiar [lim'pjar] *vt* to clean; (*con trapo*) to wipe; (*quitar*) to wipe away; (*zapatos*) to shine, polish; (*casa*) to tidy up; (*fig*) to clean up; (: *purificar*) to cleanse, purify; (*MIL*) to mop up; ~ **en seco** to dry-clean.

limpieza [lim'pjeθa] *nf* (*estado*) cleanliness; (*acto*) cleaning; (: *de las calles*) cleansing; (: *de zapatos*) polishing; (*habilidad*) skill; (*fig: POLICÍA*) clean-up; (*pureza*) purity; (*MIL*): **operación de** ~ mopping-up operation; ~ **étnica** ethnic cleansing; ~ **en seco** dry cleaning.

limpio, a ['limpjo, a] *adj* clean; (*moralmente*) pure; (*ordenado*) tidy; (*despejado*) clear; (*COM*) clear, net; (*fam*) honest ♦ *adv*: **jugar** ~ to play fair; **pasar a** ~ to make a fair copy; **sacar algo en** ~ to get benefit from sth; ~ **de** free from.

linaje [li'naxe] *nm* lineage, family.

linaza [li'naθa] *nf* linseed; **aceite de** ~ linseed oil.

lince ['linθe] *nm* lynx; **ser un** ~ (*fig: observador*) to be very observant; (: *astuto*) to be shrewd.

linchar [lin't∫ar] *vt* to lynch.

lindante [lin'dante] *adj* adjoining; ~ **con** bordering on.

lindar [lin'dar] *vi* to adjoin; ~ **con** to border on; (*ARQ*) to abut on.

linde ['linde] *nm* o *nf* boundary.

lindero, a [lin'dero, a] *adj* adjoining ♦ *nm*

boundary.

lindo, a ['lindo, a] *adj* pretty, lovely ♦ *adv*
(*esp AM*: *fam*) nicely, very well; **canta
muy** ~ (*AM*) he sings beautifully; **se
divertían de lo** ~ they enjoyed
themselves enormously.

línea ['linea] *nf* (*gen*, *moral*, *POL etc*) line;
(*talle*) figure; (*INFORM*): **en** ~ on line;
fuera de ~ off line; ~ **de estado** status
line; ~ **de formato** format line; ~ **aérea**
airline; ~ **de alto el fuego** ceasefire line;
~ **de fuego** firing line; ~ **de meta** goal
line; (*de carrera*) finishing line; ~ **de
montaje** assembly line; ~ **dura** (*POL*)
hard line; ~ **recta** straight line; **la** ~ **de
1995** (*moda*) the 1995 look.

lineal [line'al] *adj* linear; (*INFORM*) on-line.

lingote [lin'gote] *nm* ingot.

lingüista [lin'gwista] *nmf* linguist.

lingüística [lin'gwistika] *nf* linguistics *sg*.

linimento [lini'mento] *nm* liniment.

lino ['lino] *nm* linen; (*BOT*) flax.

linóleo [li'noleo] *nm* lino, linoleum.

linterna [lin'terna] *nf* lantern, lamp; ~
eléctrica *o* **a pilas** torch (*BRIT*), flashlight
(*US*).

lío ['lio] *nm* bundle; (*desorden*) muddle,
mess; (*fam*: *follón*) fuss; (: *relación
amorosa*) affair; **armar un** ~ to make a
fuss; **meterse en un** ~ to get into a jam;
tener un ~ **con algn** to be having an
affair with sb.

lipotimia [lipo'timja] *nf* blackout.

liquen ['liken] *nm* lichen.

liquidación [likiða'θjon] *nf* liquidation;
(*cuenta*) settlement; **venta de** ~
clearance sale.

liquidar [liki'ðar] *vt* (*QUÍMICA*) to liquefy;
(*COM*) to liquidate; (*deudas*) to pay off;
(*empresa*) to wind up; ~ **a algn** to bump
sb off, rub sb out (*fam*).

liquidez [liki'ðeθ] *nf* liquidity.

líquido, a ['likiðo, a] *adj* liquid; (*ganancia*)
net ♦ *nm* liquid; (*COM*: *efectivo*) ready
cash *o* money; (: *ganancia*) net amount *o*
profit; ~ **imponible** net taxable income.

lira ['lira] *nf* (*MUS*) lyre; (*moneda*) lira.

lírico, a ['liriko, a] *adj* lyrical.

lirio ['lirjo] *nm* (*BOT*) iris.

lirismo [li'rismo] *nm* lyricism;
(*sentimentalismo*) sentimentality.

lirón [li'ron] *nm* (*ZOOL*) dormouse; (*fig*)
sleepyhead.

Lisboa [lis'βoa] *nf* Lisbon.

lisboeta [lisβo'eta] *adj* of *o* from Lisbon
♦ *nmf* native *o* inhabitant of Lisbon.

lisiado, a [li'sjaðo, a] *adj* injured ♦ *nmf*
cripple.

lisiar [li'sjar] *vt* to maim; ~**se** *vr* to injure
o.s.

liso, a ['liso, a] *adj* (*terreno*) flat; (*cabello*)
straight; (*superficie*) even; (*tela*) plain;
lisa y llanamente in plain language,
plainly.

lisonja [li'sonxa] *nf* flattery.

lisonjear [lisonxe'ar] *vt* to flatter; (*fig*) to
please.

lisonjero, a [lison'xero, a] *adj* flattering;
(*agradable*) gratifying, pleasing ♦ *nmf*
flatterer.

lista ['lista] *nf* list; (*de alumnos*) school
register; (*de libros*) catalogue; (*de
correos*) poste restante; (*de platos*) menu;
(*de precios*) price list; **pasar** ~ to call the
roll; (*ESCOL*) to call the register; ~ **de
correos** poste restante; ~ **de direcciones**
mailing list; ~ **electoral** electoral roll; ~
de espera waiting list; **tela a** ~**s** striped
material.

listado, a [lis'taðo, a] *adj* striped ♦ *nm*
(*COM*, *INFORM*) listing; ~ **paginado**
(*INFORM*) paged listing.

listar [lis'tar] *vt* (*INFORM*) to list.

listo, a ['listo, a] *adj* (*perspicaz*) smart,
clever; (*preparado*) ready; ~ **para usar**
ready-to-use; **¿estás** ~**?** are you ready?;
pasarse de ~ to be too clever by half.

listón [lis'ton] *nm* (*tela*) ribbon; (*de madera*,
metal) strip.

litera [li'tera] *nf* (*en barco*, *tren*) berth; (*en
dormitorio*) bunk, bunk bed.

literal [lite'ral] *adj* literal.

literario, a [lite'rarjo, a] *adj* literary.

literato, a [lite'rato, a] *nmf* writer.

literatura [litera'tura] *nf* literature.

litigante [liti'xante] *nmf* litigant, claimant.

litigar [liti'xar] *vt* to fight ♦ *vi* (*JUR*) to go to
law; (*fig*) to dispute, argue.

litigio [li'tixjo] *nm* (*JUR*) lawsuit; (*fig*): **en** ~
con in dispute with.

litigue [li'tixe] *etc vb V* **litigar**.

litografía [litoxra'fia] *nf* lithography; (*una
*~) lithograph.

litoral [lito'ral] *adj* coastal ♦ *nm* coast,
seaboard.

litro ['litro] *nm* litre, liter (*US*).

Lituania [li'twanja] *nf* Lithuania.

lituano, a [li'twano, a] *adj*, *nmf* Lithuanian
♦ *nm* (*LING*) Lithuanian.

liturgia [li'turxja] *nf* liturgy.

liviano, a [li'βjano, a] *adj* (*persona*) fickle;
(*cosa*, *objeto*) trivial; (*AM*) light.

lívido, a ['liβiðo, a] *adj* livid.

living ['liβin], *pl* **livings** *nm* (*esp AM*) sitting
room.

Ll, ll ['eʎe] *nf* *former letter in the Spanish*

alphabet.

llaga ['ʎaɣa] nf wound.

llagar [ʎa'ɣar] vt to make sore; (herir) to wound.

llague ['ʎaɣe] etc vb V **llagar**.

llama ['ʎama] nf flame; (fig) passion; (ZOOL) llama; **en ~s** burning, ablaze.

llamada [ʎa'maða] nf call; (a la puerta) knock; (: timbre) ring; **~ a cobro revertido** reverse-charge call; **~ al orden** call to order; **~ a pie de página** reference note; **~ a procedimiento** (INFORM) procedure call; **~ interurbana** trunk call.

llamado [ʎa'maðo] nm (AM) (telephone) call; (llamamiento) appeal, call.

llamamiento [ʎama'mjento] nm call; **hacer un ~ a algn para que haga algo** to appeal to sb to do sth.

llamar [ʎa'mar] vt to call; (convocar) to summon; (invocar) to invoke; (atraer con gesto) to beckon; (atención) to attract; (TELEC: tb: **~ por teléfono**) to call, ring up, telephone; (MIL) to call up ♦ vi (por teléfono) to phone; (a la puerta) to knock (o ring); (por señas) to beckon; **~se** vr to be called, be named; **¿cómo se llama usted?** what's your name?; **¿quién llama?** (TELEC) who's calling?, who's that?; **no me llama la atención** (fam) I don't fancy it.

llamarada [ʎama'raða] nf (llamas) blaze; (rubor) flush; (fig) flare-up.

llamativo, a [ʎama'tiβo, a] adj showy; (color) loud.

llamear [ʎame'ar] vi to blaze.

llanamente [ʎana'mente] adv (lisamente) smoothly; (sin ostentaciones) plainly; (sinceramente) frankly; V **liso**.

llaneza [ʎa'neθa] nf (gen) simplicity; (honestidad) straightforwardness, frankness.

llano, a ['ʎano, a] adj (superficie) flat; (persona) straightforward; (estilo) clear ♦ nm plain, flat ground.

llanta ['ʎanta] nf (wheel) rim; (AM: neumático) tyre; (: cámara) (inner) tube.

llanto ['ʎanto] nm weeping; (fig) lamentation; (canción) dirge, lament.

llanura [ʎa'nura] nf (lisura) flatness, smoothness; (GEO) plain.

llave ['ʎaβe] nf key; (de gas, agua) tap (BRIT), faucet (US); (MECÁNICA) spanner; (de la luz) switch; (MUS) key; **~ inglesa** monkey wrench; **~ maestra** master key; **~ de contacto** (AUTO) ignition key; **~ de paso** stopcock; **echar ~ a** to lock up.

llavero [ʎa'βero] nm keyring.

llavín [ʎa'βin] nm latchkey.

llegada [ʎe'ɣaða] nf arrival.

llegar [ʎe'ɣar] vt to bring up, bring over ♦ vi to arrive; (bastar) to be enough; **~se** vr: **~ se a** to approach; **~ a** (alcanzar) to reach; to manage to, succeed in; **~ a saber** to find out; **~ a ser famoso/el jefe** to become famous/the boss; **~ a las manos** to come to blows; **~ a las manos de** to come into the hands of; **no llegues tarde** don't be late; **esta cuerda no llega** this rope isn't long enough.

llegue ['ʎeɣe] etc vb V **llegar**.

llenar [ʎe'nar] vt to fill; (superficie) to cover; (espacio, tiempo) to fill, take up; (formulario) to fill in o out; (deber) to fulfil; (fig) to heap; **~se** vr to fill (up); **~se de** (fam) to stuff o.s. with.

lleno, a ['ʎeno, a] adj full, filled; (repleto) full up ♦ nm (abundancia) abundance; (TEAT) full house; **dar de ~ contra un muro** to hit a wall head-on.

llevadero, a [ʎeβa'ðero, a] adj bearable, tolerable.

llevar [ʎe'βar] vt to take; (ropa) to wear; (cargar) to carry; (quitar) to take away; (en coche) to drive; (transportar) to transport; (ruta) to follow, keep to; (traer: dinero) to carry; (suj: camino etc): **~ a** to lead to; (MAT) to carry; (aguantar) to bear; (negocio) to conduct, direct; to manage; **~se** vr to carry off, take away; **llevamos dos días aquí** we have been here for two days; **él me lleva 2 años** he's 2 years older than me; **~ adelante** (fig) to carry forward; **~ por delante a uno** (en coche etc) to run sb over; (fig) to ride roughshod over sb; **~ la ventaja** to be winning o in the lead; **~ los libros** (COM) to keep the books; **llevo las de perder** I'm likely to lose; **no las lleva todas consigo** he's not all there; **nos llevó a cenar fuera** she took us out for a meal; **~se a uno por delante** (atropellar) to run sb over; **~se bien** to get on well (together).

llorar [ʎo'rar] vt to cry, weep ♦ vi to cry, weep; (ojos) to water; **~ a moco tendido** to sob one's heart out; **~ de risa** to cry with laughter.

lloriquear [ʎorike'ar] vi to snivel, whimper.

lloro ['ʎoro] nm crying, weeping.

llorón, ona [ʎo'ron, ona] adj tearful ♦ nm/f cry-baby.

lloroso, a [ʎo'roso, a] adj (gen) weeping, tearful; (triste) sad, sorrowful.

llover [ʎo'ßer] *vi* to rain; ~ **a cántaros** *o* **a cubos** *o* **a mares** to rain cats and dogs, pour (down); **ser una cosa llovida del cielo** to be a godsend; **llueve sobre mojado** it never rains but it pours.

llovizna [ʎo'ßiθna] *nf* drizzle.

lloviznar [ʎoßiθ'nar] *vi* to drizzle.

llueve ['ʎweße] *etc vb V* **llover**.

lluvia ['ʎußja] *nf* rain; (*cantidad*) rainfall; (*fig: balas etc*) hail, shower; ~ **radioactiva** radioactive fallout; **día de** ~ rainy day; **una** ~ **de regalos** a shower of gifts.

lluvioso, a [ʎu'ßjoso, a] *adj* rainy.

lo [lo] *artículo definido neutro:* ~ **bueno** the good ♦ *pron* (*persona*) him; (*cosa*) it; ~ **mío** what is mine; ~ **difícil es que** ... the difficult thing about it is that ...; **no saben** ~ **aburrido que es** they don't know how boring it is; **viste a** ~ **americano** he dresses in the American style; ~ **de** that matter of; ~ **que** what, that which; **toma** ~ **que quieras** take what(ever) you want; ~ **que sea** whatever; **¡toma** ~ **que he dicho!** I stand by what I said!

loa ['loa] *nf* praise.

loable [lo'aßle] *adj* praiseworthy.

LOAPA [lo'apa] *nf abr* (*ESP JUR*) = *Ley Orgánica de Armonización del Proceso Autónomo.*

loar [lo'ar] *vt* to praise.

lobato [lo'ßato] *nm* (*ZOOL*) wolf cub.

lobo ['loßo] *nm* wolf; ~ **de mar** (*fig*) sea dog; ~ **marino** seal.

lóbrego, a ['loßreɣo, a] *adj* dark; (*fig*) gloomy.

lóbulo ['loßulo] *nm* lobe.

LOC *nm abr* (= *lector óptico de caracteres*) OCR.

local [lo'kal] *adj* local ♦ *nm* place, site; (*oficinas*) premises *pl*.

localice [loka'liθe] *etc vb V* **localizar**.

localidad [lokali'ðað] *nf* (*barrio*) locality; (*lugar*) location; (*TEAT*) seat, ticket.

localizar [lokali'θar] *vt* (*ubicar*) to locate, find; (*encontrar*) to find, track down; (*restringir*) to localize; (*situar*) to place.

loción [lo'θjon] *nf* lotion, wash.

loco, a ['loko, a] *adj* mad; (*fig*) wild, mad ♦ *nm/f* lunatic, madman/woman; ~ **de atar**, ~ **de remate**, ~ **rematado** raving mad; **a lo** ~ without rhyme or reason; **ando** ~ **con el examen** the exam is driving me crazy; **estar** ~ **de alegría** to be overjoyed *o* over the moon.

locomoción [lokomo'θjon] *nf* locomotion.

locomotora [lokomo'tora] *nf* engine, locomotive.

locuaz [lo'kwaθ] *adj* loquacious, talkative.

locución [loku'θjon] *nf* expression.

locura [lo'kura] *nf* madness; (*acto*) crazy act.

locutor, a [loku'tor, a] *nm/f* (*RADIO*) announcer; (*comentarista*) commentator; (*TV*) newscaster, newsreader.

locutorio [loku'torjo] *nm* (*TELEC*) telephone box *o* booth.

lodo ['loðo] *nm* mud.

logia ['loxja] *nf* (*MIL, de masones*) lodge; (*ARQ*) loggia.

lógico, a ['loxiko, a] *adj* logical; (*correcto*) natural; (*razonable*) reasonable ♦ *nm* logician ♦ *nf* logic; **es** ~ **que** ... it stands to reason that ...; **ser de una lógica aplastante** to be as clear as day.

logístico, a [lo'xistiko, a] *adj* logistical ♦ *nf* logistics *pl*.

logotipo [loɣo'tipo] *nm* logo.

logrado, a [lo'ɣraðo, a] *adj* accomplished.

lograr [lo'ɣrar] *vt* (*obtener*) to get, obtain; (*conseguir*) to achieve, attain; ~ **hacer** to manage to do; ~ **que algn venga** to manage to get sb to come; ~ **acceso a** (*INFORM*) to access.

logro ['loɣro] *nm* achievement, success; (*COM*) profit.

logroñés, esa [loɣro'ɲes, esa] *adj* of *o* from Logroño ♦ *nm/f* native *o* inhabitant of Logroño.

LOGSE *nf abr* (= *Ley Orgánica de Ordenación General del Sistema Educativo*) *educational reform act.*

Loira ['loira] *nm* Loire.

loma ['loma] *nf* hillock, low ridge.

Lombardía [lombar'ðia] *nf* Lombardy.

lombriz [lom'briθ] *nf* (earth)worm.

lomo ['lomo] *nm* (*de animal*) back; (*CULIN: de cerdo*) pork loin; (: *de vaca*) rib steak; (*de libro*) spine.

lona ['lona] *nf* canvas.

loncha ['lontʃa] *nf* = **lonja**.

lonche ['lontʃe] *nm* (*AM*) lunch.

lonchería [lontʃe'ria] *nf* (*AM*) snack bar, diner (*US*).

londinense [londi'nense] *adj* London *cpd*, of *o* from London ♦ *nm/f* Londoner.

Londres ['londres] *nm* London.

longaniza [longa'niθa] *nf* pork sausage.

longevidad [lonxeßi'ðað] *nf* longevity.

longitud [lonxi'tuð] *nf* length; (*GEO*) longitude; **tener 3 metros de** ~ to be 3 metres long; ~ **de onda** wavelength; **salto de** ~ long jump.

longitudinal [lonxituði'nal] *adj* longitudinal.

lonja ['lonxa] *nf* slice; (*de tocino*) rasher; (*COM*) market, exchange; ~ **de pescado**

fish market.
lontananza [lonta'nanθa] *nf* background;
en ~ far away, in the distance.
Lorena [lo'rena] *nf* Lorraine.
loro ['loro] *nm* parrot.
los [los] *artículo definido mpl* the ♦ *pron* them;
(*ustedes*) you; **mis libros y ~ de usted** my
books and yours.
losa ['losa] *nf* stone; **~ sepulcral**
gravestone.
lote ['lote] *nm* portion, share; (*COM*) lot;
(*INFORM*) batch.
lotería [lote'ria] *nf* lottery; (*juego*) lotto; **le
tocó la ~** he won a big prize in the
lottery; (*fig*) he struck lucky; **~ nacional**
national lottery; **~ primitiva** (*ESP*) *type
of state-run lottery; see boxed note.*

LOTERÍA

*Millions of pounds are spent in Spain
every year on* **loterías**, *or lotteries. The
weekly "Lotería Nacional" is very popular,
especially at Christmas. Other weekly
lotteries include the Bono Loto and the
(Lotería) Primitiva. One of the best known
is run by the wealthy and influential
society for the blind, "la ONCE"; their form
is called "el cupón de la ONCE" or "el
cupón de los ciegos".*

---

lotero, a [lo'tero, a] *nm/f* seller of lottery
tickets.
Lovaina [lo'βaina] *nf* Louvain.
loza ['loθa] *nf* crockery; **~ fina** china.
lozanía [loθa'nia] *nf* (*lujo*) luxuriance.
lozano, a [lo'θano, a] *adj* luxuriant;
(*animado*) lively.
lubina [lu'βina] *nf* (*ZOOL*) sea bass.
lubricante [luβri'kante] *adj, nm* lubricant.
lubricar [luβri'kar], **lubrificar** [luβrifi'kar]
vt to lubricate.
lubrifique [luβri'fike] *etc vb V* **lubrificar**.
lubrique [lu'βrike] *etc vb V* **lubricar**.
lucense [lu'θense] *adj* of o from Lugo ♦ *nm/f*
native o inhabitant of Lugo.
Lucerna [lu'θerna] *nf* Lucerne.
lucero [lu'θero] *nm* (*ASTRO*) bright star;
(*fig*) brilliance; **~ del alba/de la tarde**
morning/evening star.
luces ['luθes] *nfpl de* **luz**.
lucha ['lutʃa] *nf* fight, struggle; **~ de clases**
class struggle; **~ libre** wrestling.
luchar [lu'tʃar] *vi* to fight.
lucidez [luθi'ðeθ] *nf* lucidity.
lucido, a [lu'θiðo, a] *adj* (*espléndido*)
splendid, brilliant; (*elegante*) elegant;
(*exitoso*) successful.

lúcido, a ['luθiðo, a] *adj* lucid.
luciérnaga [lu'θjernaɣa] *nf* glow-worm.
lucimiento [luθi'mjento] *nm* (*brillo*)
brilliance; (*éxito*) success.
lucio ['luθjo] *nm* (*ZOOL*) pike.
lucir [lu'θir] *vt* to illuminate, light (up);
(*ostentar*) to show off ♦ *vi* (*brillar*) to
shine; (*AM: parecer*) to look, seem; **~se** *vr*
(*irónico*) to make a fool of o.s.;
(*ostentarse*) to show off; **la casa luce
limpia** the house looks clean.
lucrativo, a [lukra'tiβo, a] *adj* lucrative,
profitable; **institución no lucrativa** non
profit-making institution.
lucro ['lukro] *nm* profit, gain; **~s y daños**
(*COM*) profit and loss *sg.*
luctuoso, a [luk'twoso, a] *adj* mournful.
lúdico, a ['luðiko, a] *adj* playful; (*actividad*)
recreational.
ludopatía [luðopa'tia] *nf* addiction to
gambling (*o* videogames).
luego ['lweɣo] *adv* (*después*) next; (*más
tarde*) later, afterwards; (*AM fam: en
seguida*) at once, immediately; **desde ~**
of course; **¡hasta ~!** see you later!, so
long!; **¿y ~?** what next?
lugar [lu'ɣar] *nm* place; (*sitio*) spot; (*pueblo*)
village, town; **en ~ de** instead of; **en
primer ~** in the first place, firstly; **dar ~
a** to give rise to; **hacer ~** to make room;
fuera de ~ out of place; **tener ~** to take
place; **~ común** commonplace; **yo en su
~** if I were him; **no hay ~ para preocupaciones** there is no cause for concern.
lugareño, a [luɣa'reɲo, a] *adj* village *cpd*
♦ *nm/f* villager.
lugarteniente [luɣarte'njente] *nm* deputy.
lúgubre ['luɣuβre] *adj* mournful.
lujo ['luxo] *nm* luxury; (*fig*) profusion,
abundance; **de ~** luxury *cpd*, de luxe.
lujoso, a [lu'xoso, a] *adj* luxurious.
lujuria [lu'xurja] *nf* lust.
lumbago [lum'baɣo] *nm* lumbago.
lumbre ['lumbre] *nf* (*luz*) light; (*fuego*) fire;
cerca de la ~ near the fire, at the
fireside; **¿tienes ~?** (*para cigarro*) have
you got a light?
lumbrera [lum'brera] *nf* luminary; (*fig*)
leading light.
luminoso, a [lumi'noso, a] *adj* luminous,
shining; (*idea*) bright, brilliant.
luna ['luna] *nf* moon; (*vidrio: escaparate*)
plate glass; (: *de un espejo*) glass; (: *de
gafas*) lens; (*fig*) crescent; **~ creciente/
llena/menguante/nueva** crescent/full/
waning/new moon; **~ de miel**
honeymoon; **estar en la ~** to have one's
head in the clouds.

lunar [lu'nar] *adj* lunar ♦ *nm* (*ANAT*) mole; **tela a ~es** spotted material.

lunes ['lunes] *nm inv* Monday.

luneta [lu'neta] *nf* lens.

lupa ['lupa] *nf* magnifying glass.

lusitano, a [lusi'tano, a], **luso, a** ['luso, a] *adj, nm/f* Portuguese.

lustrador [lustra'ðor] *nm* (*AM*) bootblack.

lustrar [lus'trar] *vt* (*esp AM*) (*mueble*) to polish; (*zapatos*) to shine.

lustre ['lustre] *nm* polish; (*fig*) lustre; **dar ~ a** to polish.

lustro ['lustro] *nm* period of five years.

lustroso, a [lus'troso, a] *adj* shining.

luterano, a [lute'rano, a] *adj* Lutheran.

luto ['luto] *nm* mourning; (*congoja*) grief, sorrow; **llevar el o vestirse de ~** to be in mourning.

luxación [luksa'θjon] *nf* (*MED*) dislocation; **tener una ~ de tobillo** to have a dislocated ankle.

Luxemburgo [luksem'burɣo] *nm* Luxembourg.

luz [luθ], *pl* **luces** *nf* (*tb fig*) light; (*fam*) electricity; **dar a ~ un niño** to give birth to a child; **sacar a la ~** to bring to light; **dar la ~** to switch on the light; **encender** (*ESP*) *o* **prender** (*AM*)/**apagar la ~** to switch the light on/off; **les cortaron la ~** their (electricity) supply was cut off; **a la ~ de** in the light of; **a todas luces** by any reckoning; **hacer la ~ sobre** to shed light on; **tener pocas luces** to be dim *o* stupid; **~ de la luna/del sol** *o* **solar** moonlight/sunlight; **~ eléctrica** electric light; **~ roja/verde** red/green light; **~ de cruce** (*AUTO*) dipped headlight; **~ de freno** brake light; **~ intermitente/trasera** flashing/rear light; **luces de tráfico** traffic lights; **el Siglo de las Luces** the Age of Enlightenment; **traje de luces** bullfighter's costume.

M m

M, m ['eme] *nf* (*letra*) M, m; **M de Madrid** M for Mike.

M. *abr* (*FERRO*) = **Metro.**

m. *abr* (= *metro(s)*) m; (= *minuto(s)*) min., m; (= *masculino*) m., masc.

M.ª *abr* = **María.**

macabro, [ma'kaßro, a] *adj* macabre.

macaco [ma'kako] *nm* (*ZOOL*) rhesus monkey; (*fam*) runt, squirt.

macana [ma'kana] *nf* (*AM*: *porra*) club; (: *mentira*) lie, fib; (: *tontería*) piece of nonsense.

macanudo, a [maka'nuðo, a] *adj* (*AM fam*) great.

macarra [ma'karra] *nm* (*fam*) thug.

macarrones [maka'rrones] *nmpl* macaroni *sg*.

Macedonia [maθe'ðonja] *nf* Macedonia.

macedonia [maθe'ðonja] *nf*: **~ de frutas** fruit salad.

macedonio [maθe'ðonjo] *adj, nm/f* Macedonian ♦ *nm* (*LING*) Macedonian.

macerar [maθe'rar] *vt* (*CULIN*) to soak, macerate; **~se** *vr* to soak, soften.

maceta [ma'θeta] *nf* (*de flores*) pot of flowers; (*para plantas*) flowerpot.

macetero [maθe'tero] *nm* flowerpot stand *o* holder.

machacar [matʃa'kar] *vt* to crush, pound; (*moler*) to grind (up); (*aplastar*) to mash ♦ *vi* (*insistir*) to go on, keep on.

machacón, ona [matʃa'kon, ona] *adj* (*pesado*) tiresome; (*insistente*) insistent; (*monótono*) monotonous.

machamartillo [matʃamar'tiʎo]: **a ~** *adv*: **creer a ~** (*firmemente*) to believe firmly.

machaque [ma'tʃake] *etc vb V* **machacar.**

machete [ma'tʃete] *nm* machete, (large) knife.

machismo [ma'tʃismo] *nm* sexism; male chauvinism.

machista [ma'tʃista] *adj, nm* sexist; male chauvinist.

macho ['matʃo] *adj* male; (*fig*) virile ♦ *nm* male; (*fig*) he-man, tough guy (*US*); (*TEC*: *perno*) pin, peg; (*ELEC*) pin, plug; (*COSTURA*) hook.

macilento, a [maθi'lento, a] adj (*pálido*) pale; (*ojeroso*) haggard.

macizo, a [ma'θiθo, a] adj (*grande*) massive; (*fuerte, sólido*) solid ♦ nm mass, chunk; (*GEO*) massif.

macramé [makra'me] nm macramé.

macrobiótico, a [makro'ßjotiko, a] adj macrobiotic.

macro-comando [makroko'mando] nm (*INFORM*) macro (command).

macroeconomía [makroekono'mia] nf (*COM*) macroeconomics sg.

mácula ['makula] nf stain, blemish.

macuto [ma'kuto] nm (*MIL*) knapsack.

Madagascar [maðaɣas'kar] nm Madagascar.

madeja [ma'ðexa] nf (*de lana*) skein, hank.

madera [ma'ðera] nf wood; (*fig*) nature, character; (: *aptitud*) aptitude; **una ~ a** piece of wood; **~ contrachapada** o **laminada** plywood; **tiene buena ~** he's made of solid stuff; **tiene ~ de futbolista** he's got the makings of a footballer.

maderaje [maðe'raxe], **maderamen** [maðe'ramen] nm timber; (*trabajo*) woodwork, timbering.

maderero [maðe'rero] nm timber merchant.

madero [ma'ðero] nm beam; (*fig*) ship.

madrastra [ma'ðrastra] nf stepmother.

madre ['maðre] adj mother cpd; (*AM*) tremendous ♦ nf mother; (*de vino etc*) dregs pl; **~ adoptiva/política/soltera** foster mother/mother-in-law/unmarried mother; **la M~ Patria** the Mother Country; **sin ~** motherless; **¡~ mía!** oh dear!; **¡tu ~!** (*fam!*) fuck off! (*!*); **salirse de ~** (*río*) to burst its banks; (*persona*) to lose all self-control.

madreperla [maðre'perla] nf mother-of-pearl.

madreselva [maðre'selßa] nf honeysuckle.

Madrid [ma'ðrið] n Madrid.

madriguera [maðri'ɣera] nf burrow.

madrileño, a [maðri'leɲo, a] adj of o from Madrid ♦ nm/f native o inhabitant of Madrid.

Madriles [ma'ðriles] nmpl: **Los ~** (*fam*) Madrid sg.

madrina [ma'ðrina] nf godmother; (*ARQ*) prop, shore; (*TEC*) brace; **~ de boda** bridesmaid.

madroño [ma'ðroɲo] nm (*BOT*) strawberry tree, arbutus.

madrugada [maðru'ɣaða] nf early morning, small hours; (*alba*) dawn, daybreak; **a las 4 de la ~** at 4 o'clock in the morning.

madrugador, a [maðruɣa'ðor, a] adj early-rising.

madrugar [maðru'ɣar] vi to get up early; (*fig*) to get a head start.

madrugue [ma'ðruɣe] etc vb V **madrugar.**

madurar [maðu'rar] vt, vi (*fruta*) to ripen; (*fig*) to mature.

madurez [maðu'reθ] nf ripeness; (*fig*) maturity.

maduro, a [ma'ðuro, a] adj ripe; (*fig*) mature; **poco ~** unripe.

MAE nm abr (*ESP POL*) = Ministerio de Asuntos Exteriores.

maestra [ma'estra] nf V **maestro.**

maestría [maes'tria] nf mastery; (*habilidad*) skill, expertise; (*AM*) Master's Degree.

maestro, a [ma'estro, a] adj masterly, (*perito*) skilled, expert; (*principal*) main; (*educado*) trained ♦ nm/f master/mistress; (*profesor*) teacher ♦ nm (*autoridad*) authority; (*MUS*) maestro; (*obrero*) skilled workman; **~ albañil** master mason; **~ de obras** foreman.

mafia ['mafja] nf mafia; **la M~** the Mafia.

mafioso [ma'fjoso] nm gangster.

Magallanes [maɣa'ʎanes] nm: **Estrecho de ~** Strait of Magellan.

magia ['maxja] nf magic.

mágico, a ['maxiko, a] adj magic(al) ♦ nm/f magician.

magisterio [maxis'terjo] nm (*enseñanza*) teaching; (*profesión*) teaching profession; (*maestros*) teachers pl.

magistrado [maxis'traðo] nm magistrate; **Primer M~** (*AM*) President, Prime Minister.

magistral [maxis'tral] adj magisterial; (*fig*) masterly.

magistratura [maxistra'tura] nf magistracy; **M~ del Trabajo** (*ESP*) ≈ Industrial Tribunal.

magnánimo, a [maɣ'nanimo, a] adj magnanimous.

magnate [maɣ'nate] nm magnate, tycoon; **~ de la prensa** press baron.

magnesio [maɣ'nesjo] nm (*QUÍMICA*) magnesium.

magnetice [maɣne'tiθe] etc vb V **magnetizar.**

magnético, a [maɣ'netiko, a] adj magnetic.

magnetismo [maɣne'tismo] nm magnetism.

magnetizar [maɣneti'θar] vt to magnetize.

magnetofón [maɣneto'fon], **magnetófono** [maɣne'tofono] nm tape recorder.

magnetofónico, a [maɣneto'foniko, a] adj:

cinta magnetofónica recording tape.

magnicidio [maɣni'θiðjo] nm assassination (of an important person).

magnífico, a [maɣ'nifiko, a] adj splendid, magnificent.

magnitud [maɣni'tuð] nf magnitude.

mago, a ['maɣo, a] nm/f magician, wizard; **los Reyes M~s** the Magi, the Three Wise Men; V tb **Reyes Magos**.

magrear [maɣre'ar] vt (fam) to touch up.

magro, a ['maɣro, a] adj (persona) thin, lean; (carne) lean.

maguey [ma'ɣei] nm (BOT) agave.

magulladura [maɣuʎa'ðura] nf bruise.

magullar [maɣu'ʎar] vt (amoratar) to bruise; (dañar) to damage; (fam: golpear) to bash, beat.

Maguncia [ma'ɣunθja] nf Mainz.

mahometano, a [maome'tano, a] adj Mohammedan.

mahonesa [mao'nesa] nf = **mayonesa**.

maicena [mai'θena] nf cornflour, corn starch (US).

maillot [ma'jot] nm swimming costume; (DEPORTE) vest.

maître ['metre] nm head waiter.

maíz [ma'iθ] nm maize (BRIT), corn (US); sweet corn.

maizal [mai'θal] nm maize field, cornfield.

majadero, a [maxa'ðero, a] adj silly, stupid.

majar [ma'xar] vt to crush, grind.

majareta [maxa'reta] adj (fam) cracked, potty.

majestad [maxes'tað] nf majesty; **Su M~** His/Her Majesty; **(Vuestra) M~** Your Majesty.

majestuoso, a [maxes'twoso, a] adj majestic.

majo, a ['maxo, a] adj nice; (guapo) attractive, good-looking; (elegante) smart.

mal [mal] adv badly; (equivocadamente) wrongly; (con dificultad) with difficulty ♦ adj = **malo, a** ♦ nm evil; (desgracia) misfortune; (daño) harm, damage; (MED) illness ♦ conj: **~ que le pese** whether he likes it or not; **me entendió ~** he misunderstood me; **hablar ~ de algn** to speak ill of sb; **huele ~** it smells bad; **ir de ~ en peor** to go from bad to worse; **oigo/veo ~** I can't hear/see very well; **si ~ no recuerdo** if my memory serves me right; **¡menos ~!** just as well!; **~ que bien** rightly or wrongly; **no hay ~ que por bien no venga** every cloud has a silver lining; **~ de ojo** evil eye.

malabarismo [malaßa'rismo] nm juggling.

malabarista [malaßa'rista] nm/f juggler.

malaconsejado, a [malakonse'xaðo, a] adj ill-advised.

malacostumbrado, a [malakostum'braðo, a] adj (consentido) spoiled.

malacostumbrar [malakostum'brar] vt: **~ a algn** to get sb into bad habits.

malagueño, a [mala'ɣeɲo, a] adj of o from Málaga ♦ nm/f native o inhabitant of Málaga.

Malaisia [ma'laisja] nf Malaysia.

malaria [ma'larja] nf malaria.

Malasia [ma'lasja] nf Malaysia.

malavenido, a [malaße'niðo, a] adj incompatible.

malayo, a [ma'lajo, a] adj Malay(an) ♦ nm/f Malay ♦ nm (LING) Malay.

Malaysia [ma'laisia] nf Malaysia.

malcarado, a [malka'raðo, a] adj ugly, grim-faced.

malcriado, a [mal'krjaðo, a] adj (consentido) spoiled.

malcriar [mal'krjar] vt to spoil, pamper.

maldad [mal'dað] nf evil, wickedness.

maldecir [malde'θir] vt to curse ♦ vi: **~ de** to speak ill of.

maldiciendo [maldi'θjendo] etc vb V **maldecir**.

maldición [maldi'θjon] nf curse; **¡~!** curse it!, damn!

maldiga [mal'diɣa] etc, **maldije** [mal'dixe] etc vb V **maldecir**.

maldito, a [mal'dito, a] adj (condenado) damned; (perverso) wicked ♦ nm: **el ~** the devil; **¡~ sea!** damn it!; **no le hace ~ (el) caso** he doesn't take a blind bit of notice.

maleable [male'aßle] adj malleable.

maleante [male'ante] adj wicked ♦ nm/f criminal, crook.

malecón [male'kon] nm pier, jetty.

maledicencia [maleði'θenθja] nf slander, scandal.

maleducado, a [maleðu'kaðo, a] adj bad-mannered, rude.

maleficio [male'fiθjo] nm curse, spell.

malentendido [malenten'diðo] nm misunderstanding.

malestar [males'tar] nm (gen) discomfort; (enfermedad) indisposition; (fig: inquietud) uneasiness; (POL) unrest; **siento un ~ en el estómago** my stomach is upset.

maleta [ma'leta] nf case, suitcase; (AUTO) boot (BRIT), trunk (US); **hacer la ~** to pack.

maletera [male'tera] nf (AM AUTO) boot (BRIT), trunk (US).

maletero [male'tero] nm (AUTO) boot

(*BRIT*), trunk (*US*); (*persona*) porter.
maletín [male'tin] *nm* small case, bag;
(*portafolio*) briefcase.
malevolencia [maleßo'lenθja] *nf* malice,
spite.
malévolo, a [ma'leßolo, a] *adj* malicious,
spiteful.
maleza [ma'leθa] *nf* (*hierbas malas*) weeds
pl; (*arbustos*) thicket.
malgache [mal'ɣatʃe] *adj* of *o* from
Madagascar ♦ *nm/f* native *o* inhabitant of
Madagascar.
malgastar [malɣas'tar] *vt* (*tiempo, dinero*)
to waste; (*recursos*) to squander; (*salud*)
to ruin.
malhaya [ma'laja] *excl* (*esp AM: fam!*) damn
(it)! (*!*); ¡~ **sea/sean!** damn it/them! (*!*)
malhechor, a [male'tʃor, a] *nm/f*
delinquent; (*criminal*) criminal.
malherido, a [male'riðo, a] *adj* badly
injured.
malhumorado, a [malumo'raðo, a] *adj*
bad-tempered.
malicia [ma'liθja] *nf* (*maldad*) wickedness;
(*astucia*) slyness, guile; (*mala intención*)
malice, spite; (*carácter travieso*)
mischievousness.
malicioso, a [mali'θjoso, a] *adj* wicked,
evil; sly, crafty; malicious, spiteful;
mischievous.
malignidad [maliɣni'ðað] *nf* (*MED*)
malignancy; (*malicia*) malice.
maligno, a [ma'liɣno, a] *adj* evil; (*dañino*)
pernicious, harmful; (*malévolo*)
malicious; (*MED*) malignant ♦ *nm*: **el ~**
the devil.
malintencionado, a [malintenθjo'naðo, a]
adj (*comentario*) hostile; (*persona*)
malicious.
malla ['maʎa] *nf* (*de una red*) mesh; (*red*)
network; (*AM: de baño*) swimsuit; (*de
ballet, gimnasia*) leotard; ~**s** *nfpl* tights; ~
de alambre wire mesh.
Mallorca [ma'ʎorka] *nf* Majorca.
mallorquín, ina [maʎor'kin, ina] *adj, nm/f*
Majorcan ♦ *nm* (*LING*) Majorcan.
malnutrido, a [malnu'triðo, a] *adj*
undernourished.
malo, a ['malo, a] *adj* (**mal** before *nmsg*)
bad; (*calidad*) poor; (*falso*) false;
(*espantoso*) dreadful; (*niño*) naughty
♦ *nm/f* villain ♦ *nm* (*CINE fam*) bad guy
♦ *nf* spell of bad luck; **estar ~** to be ill;
andar a malas con algn to be on bad
terms with sb; **estar de malas** (*mal
humor*) to be in a bad mood; **lo ~ es
que ...** the trouble is that ....
malograr [malo'ɣrar] *vt* to spoil; (*plan*) to

upset; (*ocasión*) to waste; ~**se** *vr* (*plan etc*)
to fail, come to grief; (*persona*) to die
before one's time.
maloliente [malo'ljente] *adj* stinking,
smelly.
malparado, a [malpa'raðo, a] *adj*: **salir ~** to
come off badly.
malpensado, a [malpen'saðo, a] *adj* evil-
minded.
malquerencia [malke'renθja] *nf* dislike.
malquistar [malkis'tar] *vt*: ~ **a dos
personas** to cause a rift between two
people; ~**se** *vr* to fall out.
malsano, a [mal'sano, a] *adj* unhealthy.
malsonante [malso'nante] *adj* (*palabra*)
nasty, rude.
Malta ['malta] *nf* Malta.
malta ['malta] *nf* malt.
malteada [malte'aða] *nf* (*AM*) milk shake.
maltés, esa [mal'tes, esa] *adj, nm/f* Maltese.
maltraer [maltra'er] *vt* (*abusar*) to insult,
abuse; (*maltratar*) to ill-treat.
maltratar [maltra'tar] *vt* to ill-treat,
mistreat.
maltrecho, a [mal'tretʃo, a] *adj* battered,
damaged.
malva ['malßa] *nf* mallow; ~ **loca**
hollyhock; (**de color de**) ~ mauve.
malvado, a [mal'ßaðo, a] *adj* evil,
villainous.
malvavisco [malßa'ßisko] *nm*
marshmallow.
malvender [malßen'der] *vt* to sell off
cheap *o* at a loss.
malversación [malßersa'θjon] *nf*
embezzlement, misappropriation.
malversar [malßer'sar] *vt* to embezzle,
misappropriate.
Malvinas [mal'ßinas] *nfpl*: **Islas ~** Falkland
Islands.
mama ['mama], *pl* **mamás** *nf* (*de animal*)
teat; (*de mujer*) breast.
mamá [ma'ma] *nf* (*fam*) mum, mummy.
mamacita [mama'sita] *nf* (*AM fam*) mum,
mummy.
mamadera [mama'dera] *nf* (*AM*) baby's
bottle.
mamagrande [mama'grande] *nf* (*AM*)
grandmother.
mamar [ma'mar] *vt* (*pecho*) to suck; (*fig*) to
absorb, assimilate ♦ *vi* to suck; **dar de ~**
to (breast-)feed; (*animal*) to suckle.
mamarracho [mama'rratʃo] *nm* sight,
mess.
mambo ['mambo] *nf* (*MUS*) mambo.
mamífero, a [ma'mifero, a] *adj*
mammalian, mammal *cpd* ♦ *nm* mammal.
mamón, ona [ma'mon, ona] *adj* small,

baby *cpd* ◊ *nm/f* small baby; (*fam!*)
wanker (*!*).

mamotreto [mamo'treto] *nm* hefty
volume; (*fam*) whacking great thing.

mampara [mam'para] *nf* (*entre
habitaciones*) partition; (*biombo*) screen.

mamporro [mam'porro] *nm* (*fam*): **dar un** ~
a to clout.

mampostería [mamposte'ria] *nf* masonry.

mamut [ma'mut] *nm* mammoth.

maná [ma'na] *nm* manna.

manada [ma'naða] *nf* (*ZOOL*) herd; (: *de
leones*) pride; (: *de lobos*) pack; **llegaron
en** ~**s** (*fam*) they came in droves.

Managua [ma'naɣwa] *n* Managua.

manantial [manan'tjal] *nm* spring; (*fuente*)
fountain; (*fig*) source.

manar [ma'nar] *vt* to run with, flow with
◊ *vi* to run, flow; (*abundar*) to abound.

manaza [ma'naθa] *nf* big hand ◊ *adj, nm/f inv*:
~**s: ser un** ~**s** to be clumsy.

mancebo [man'θeßo] *nm* (*joven*) young
man.

mancha ['mantʃa] *nf* stain, mark; (*de tinta*)
blot; (*de vegetación*) patch; (*imperfección*)
stain, blemish, blot; (*boceto*) sketch,
outline; **la M**~ La Mancha.

manchado, a [man'tʃaðo, a] *adj* (*sucio*)
dirty; (*animal*) spotted; (*ave*) speckled;
(*tinta*) smudged.

manchar [man'tʃar] *vt* to stain, mark;
(*ZOOL*) to patch; (*ensuciar*) to soil, dirty;
~**se** *vr* to get dirty; (*fig*) to dirty one's
hands.

manchego, a [man'tʃeɣo, a] *adj* of *o* from
La Mancha ◊ *nm/f* native *o* inhabitant of
La Mancha.

mancilla [man'θiʎa] *nf* stain, blemish.

mancillar [manθi'ʎar] *vt* to stain, sully.

manco, a ['manko, a] *adj* one-armed; one-
handed; (*fig*) defective, faulty; **no ser** ~
to be useful *o* active.

mancomunar [mankomu'nar] *vt* to unite,
bring together; (*recursos*) to pool; (*JUR*)
to make jointly responsible.

mancomunidad [mankomuni'ðað] *nf*
union, association; (*comunidad*)
community; (*JUR*) joint responsibility.

mandado [man'daðo] *nm* (*orden*) order;
(*recado*) commission, errand.

mandamás [manda'mas] *adj, nm/f inv* boss;
ser un ~ to be very bossy.

mandamiento [manda'mjento] *nm* (*orden*)
order, command; (*REL*) commandment;
~ **judicial** warrant.

mandar [man'dar] *vt* (*ordenar*) to order;
(*dirigir*) to lead, command; (*país*) to rule
over; (*enviar*) to send; (*pedir*) to order,

ask for ◊ *vi* to be in charge; (*pey*) to be
bossy; ~**se** *vr*: ~**se mudar** (*AM fam*) to go
away, clear off; **¿mande?** pardon?,
excuse me? (*US*); **¿manda usted algo
más?** is there anything else?; ~ **a algn a
paseo** *o* **a la porra** to tell sb to go to hell;
se lo mandaremos por correo we'll post
it to you; ~ **hacer un traje** to have a suit
made.

mandarín [manda'rin] *nm* petty
bureaucrat.

mandarina [manda'rina] *nf* (*fruta*)
tangerine, mandarin (orange).

mandatario, a [manda'tarjo, a] *nm/f*
(*representante*) agent; **primer** ~ (*esp AM*)
head of state.

mandato [man'dato] *nm* (*orden*) order;
(*POL: período*) term of office; (: *territorio*)
mandate; (*INFORM*) command; ~ **judicial**
(*search*) warrant.

mandíbula [man'dißula] *nf* jaw.

mandil [man'dil] *nm* (*delantal*) apron.

Mandinga [man'dinɣa] *nm* (*AM*) Devil.

mandioca [man'djoka] *nf* cassava.

mando ['mando] *nm* (*MIL*) command; (*de
país*) rule; (*el primer lugar*) lead; (*POL*)
term of office; (*TEC*) control; ~ **a la
izquierda** left-hand drive; **los altos** ~**s**
the high command *sg*; ~ **por botón**
push-button control; **al** ~ **de** in charge
of; **tomar el** ~ to take the lead.

mandolina [mando'lina] *nf* mandolin(e).

mandón, ona [man'don, ona] *adj* bossy,
domineering.

manecilla [mane'θiʎa] *nf* (*TEC*) pointer; (*de
reloj*) hand.

manejable [mane'xaßle] *adj* manageable;
(*fácil de usar*) handy.

manejar [mane'xar] *vt* to manage;
(*máquina*) to work, operate; (*caballo etc*)
to handle; (*casa*) to run, manage; (*AM
AUTO*) to drive ◊ *vi* (*AM AUTO*) to drive;
~**se** *vr* (*comportarse*) to act, behave;
(*arreglárselas*) to manage; "~ **con
cuidado**" "handle with care".

manejo [ma'nexo] *nm* management;
handling; running; driving; (*facilidad de
trato*) ease, confidence; (*de idioma*)
command; ~**s** *nmpl* intrigues; **tengo** ~
del francés I have a good command of
French.

manera [ma'nera] *nf* way, manner,
fashion; (*ARTE, LITERATURA etc: estilo*)
manner, style; ~**s** *nfpl* (*modales*)
manners; **su** ~ **de ser** the way he is;
(*aire*) his manner; **de mala** ~ (*fam*) badly,
unwillingly; **de ninguna** ~ no way, by no
means; **de otra** ~ otherwise; **de todas** ~**s**

at any rate; **en gran** ~ to a large extent;
sobre ~ exceedingly; **a mi** ~ **de ver** in
my view; **no hay** ~ **de persuadirle**
there's no way of convincing him.

manga ['manga] *nf* (*de camisa*) sleeve; (*de
riego*) hose; **de** ~ **corta/larga** short-/
long-sleeved; **andar** ~ **por hombro**
(*desorden*) to be topsy-turvy; **tener** ~
ancha to be easy-going.

mangante [man'gante] *adj* (*descarado*)
brazen ♦ *nm* (*mendigo*) beggar.

mangar [man'gar] *vt* (*unir*) to plug in; (*fam:
birlar*) to pinch, nick, swipe; (*mendigar*)
to beg.

mango ['mango] *nm* handle; (*BOT*) mango;
~ **de escoba** broomstick.

mangonear [mangone'ar] *vt* to boss about
♦ *vi* to be bossy.

mangue ['mange] *etc vb V* **mangar**.

manguera [man'gera] *nf* (*de riego*) hose;
(*tubo*) pipe; ~ **de incendios** fire hose.

maní [ma'ni] *nm, pl* **maníes** *o* **manises**
(*AM: cacahuete*) peanut; (: *planta*)
groundnut plant.

manía [ma'nia] *nf* (*MED*) mania; (*fig: moda*)
rage, craze; (*disgusto*) dislike; (*malicia*)
spite; **tiene** ~ **s** she's a bit fussy; **tener** ~
a algn to dislike sb.

maníaco, a [ma'niako, a] *adj* maniac(al)
♦ *nm/f* maniac.

maniatar [manja'tar] *vt* to tie the hands of.

maniático, a [ma'njatiko, a] *adj*
maniac(al); (*loco*) crazy; (*tiquismiquis*)
fussy ♦ *nm/f* maniac.

manicomio [mani'komjo] *nm* mental
hospital (*BRIT*), insane asylum (*US*).

manicuro, a [mani'kuro, a] *nm/f* manicurist
♦ *nf* manicure.

manido, a [ma'niðo, a] *adj* (*tema etc*) trite,
stale.

manifestación [manifesta'θjon] *nf*
(*declaración*) statement, declaration;
(*demostración*) show, display; (*POL*)
demonstration.

manifestante [manifes'tante] *nm/f*
demonstrator.

manifestar [manifes'tar] *vt* to show,
manifest; (*declarar*) to state, declare;
~**se** *vr* to show, become apparent; (*POL:
desfilar*) to demonstrate; (: *reunirse*) to
hold a mass meeting.

manifiesto, a [mani'fjesto, a] *etc vb V*
manifestar ♦ *adj* clear, manifest ♦ *nm*
manifesto; (*ANAT, NAUT*) manifest; **poner
algo de** ~ (*aclarar*) to make sth clear;
(*revelar*) to reveal sth; **quedar** ~ to be
plain *o* clear.

manija [ma'nixa] *nf* handle.

manilla [ma'niʎa] *nf* (*de reloj*) hand; (*AM*)
handle, lever; ~**s** (**de hierro**) *nfpl*
handcuffs.

manillar [mani'ʎar] *nm* handlebars *pl*.

maniobra [ma'njoβra] *nf* manœuvring;
(*maneja*) handling; (*fig: movimiento*)
manœuvre, move; (: *estratagema*) trick,
stratagem; ~**s** *nfpl* manœuvres.

maniobrar [manjo'βrar] *vt* to manœuvre;
(*manejar*) to handle ♦ *vi* to manœuvre.

manipulación [manipula'θjon] *nf*
manipulation; (*COM*) handling.

manipular [manipu'lar] *vt* to manipulate;
(*manejar*) to handle.

maniquí [mani'ki] *nm/f* model ♦ *nm* dummy.

manirroto, a [mani'rroto, a] *adj* lavish,
extravagant ♦ *nm/f* spendthrift.

manita [ma'nita] *nf* little hand; ~**s de plata**
artistic hands.

manitas [ma'nitas] *adj inv* good with one's
hands ♦ *nm/f inv*: **ser un** ~ to be very good
with one's hands.

manito [ma'nito] *nm* (*AM: en conversación*)
mate (*fam*), chum.

manivela [mani'βela] *nf* crank.

manjar [man'xar] *nm* (tasty) dish.

mano[1] ['mano] *nf* hand; (*ZOOL*) foot, paw;
(*de pintura*) coat; (*serie*) lot, series; **a** ~
by hand; **a** ~ **derecha/izquierda** on (*o* to)
the right(-hand side)/left(-hand side);
hecho a ~ handmade; **a** ~**s llenas**
lavishly, generously; **de primera** ~ (at)
first hand; **de segunda** ~ (at) second
hand; **robo a** ~ **armada** armed robbery;
Pedro es mi ~ **derecha** Pedro is my
right-hand man; ~ **de obra** labour,
manpower; ~ **de santo** sure remedy;
darse la(s) ~**(s)** to shake hands; **echar
una** ~ to lend a hand; **echar una** ~ **a** to
lay hands on; **echar** ~ **de** to make use of;
estrechar la ~ **a algn** to shake sb's hand;
traer *o* **llevar algo entre** ~**s** to deal *o* be
busy with sth; **está en tus** ~**s** it's up to
you; **se le fue la** ~ his hand slipped; (*fig*)
he went too far; **¡** ~**s a la obra!** to work!

mano[2] ['mano] *nm* (*AM fam*) friend, mate.

manojo [ma'noxo] *nm* handful, bunch; ~
de llaves bunch of keys.

manómetro [ma'nometro] *nm* (pressure)
gauge.

manopla [ma'nopla] *nf* (*paño*) flannel; ~**s**
nfpl mittens.

manoseado, a [manose'aðo, a] *adj* well-
worn.

manosear [manose'ar] *vt* (*tocar*) to handle,
touch; (*desordenar*) to mess up, rumple;
(*insistir en*) to overwork; (*acariciar*) to
caress, fondle; (*pey: persona*) to feel *o*

touch up.

manotazo [mano'taθo] _nm_ slap, smack.

mansalva [man'salßa]: **a ~** _adv_ indiscriminately.

mansedumbre [manse'ðumbre] _nf_ gentleness, meekness; (_de animal_) tameness.

mansión [man'sjon] _nf_ mansion.

manso, a ['manso, a] _adj_ gentle, mild; (_animal_) tame.

manta ['manta] _nf_ blanket; (_AM_) poncho.

manteca [man'teka] _nf_ fat; (_AM_) butter; **~ de cacahuete/cacao** peanut/cocoa butter; **~ de cerdo** lard.

mantecado [mante'kaðo] _nm_ ice cream.

mantecoso, a [mante'koso, a] _adj_ fat, greasy; **queso ~** soft cheese.

mantel [man'tel] _nm_ tablecloth.

mantelería [mantele'ria] _nf_ table linen.

mantendré [manten'dre] _etc vb_ V **mantener**.

mantener [mante'ner] _vt_ to support, maintain; (_alimentar_) to sustain; (_conservar_) to keep; (_TEC_) to maintain, service; **~se** _vr_ (_seguir de pie_) to be still standing; (_no ceder_) to hold one's ground; (_subsistir_) to sustain o.s., keep going; **~ algo en equilibrio** to keep sth balanced; **~se a distancia** to keep one's distance; **~se firme** to hold one's ground.

mantenga [man'tenga] _etc vb_ V **mantener**.

mantenimiento [manteni'mjento] _nm_ maintenance; sustenance; (_sustento_) support.

mantequería [manteke'ria] _nf_ (_ultramarinos_) grocer's (shop).

mantequilla [manteˈkiʎa] _nf_ butter.

mantilla [man'tiʎa] _nf_ mantilla; **~s** _nfpl_ baby clothes; **estar en ~s** (_persona_) to be terribly innocent; (_proyecto_) to be in its infancy.

manto ['manto] _nm_ (_capa_) cloak; (_de ceremonia_) robe, gown.

mantón [man'ton] _nm_ shawl.

mantuve [man'tuße] _etc vb_ V **mantener**.

manual [ma'nwal] _adj_ manual ♦ _nm_ manual, handbook; **habilidad ~** manual skill.

manubrio [ma'nußrio] _nm_ (_AM AUTO_) steering wheel.

manufactura [manufak'tura] _nf_ manufacture; (_fábrica_) factory.

manufacturado, a [manufaktu'raðo, a] _adj_ manufactured.

manuscrito, a [manus'krito, a] _adj_ handwritten ♦ _nm_ manuscript.

manutención [manuten'θjon] _nf_ maintenance; (_sustento_) support.

manzana [man'θana] _nf_ apple; (_ARQ_) block; **~ de la discordia** (_fig_) bone of contention.

manzanal [manθa'nal] _nm_ apple orchard.

manzanilla [manθa'niʎa] _nf_ (_planta_) camomile; (_infusión_) camomile tea; (_vino_) manzanilla.

manzano [man'θano] _nm_ apple tree.

maña ['maɲa] _nf_ (_gen_) skill, dexterity; (_pey_) guile; (_costumbre_) habit; (_una ~_) trick, knack; **con ~** craftily.

mañana [ma'ɲana] _adv_ tomorrow ♦ _nm_ future ♦ _nf_ morning; **de** _o_ **por la ~** in the morning; **¡hasta ~!** see you tomorrow!; **pasado ~** the day after tomorrow; **~ por la ~** tomorrow morning.

mañanero, a [maɲa'nero, a] _adj_ early-rising.

maño, a ['maɲo, a] _adj_ Aragonese ♦ _nm/f_ native _o_ inhabitant of Aragon.

mañoso, a [ma'ɲoso, a] _adj_ (_hábil_) skilful; (_astuto_) smart, clever.

mapa ['mapa] _nm_ map.

mapuche, a [ma'putʃhe, a] _adj_, _nm/f_ Mapuche, Araucanian.

maqueta [ma'keta] _nf_ (scale) model.

maquiavélico, a [makja'ßeliko, a] _adj_ Machiavellian.

maquillador, a [makiʎa'ðor, a] _nm/f_ (_TEAT etc_) make-up artist.

maquillaje [maki'ʎaxe] _nm_ make-up; (_acto_) making up.

maquillar [maki'ʎar] _vt_ to make up; **~se** _vr_ to put on (some) make-up.

máquina ['makina] _nf_ machine; (_de tren_) locomotive, engine; (_FOTO_) camera; (_AM: coche_) car; (_fig_) machinery; (: _proyecto_) plan, project; **a toda ~** at full speed; **escrito a ~** typewritten; **~ de escribir** typewriter; **~ de coser/lavar** sewing/washing machine; **~ de facsímil** facsimile (machine), fax; **~ de franqueo** franking machine; **~ tragaperras** fruit machine; (_COM_) slot machine.

maquinación [makina'θjon] _nf_ machination, plot.

maquinal [maki'nal] _adj_ (_fig_) mechanical, automatic.

maquinar [maki'nar] _vt, vi_ to plot.

maquinaria [maki'narja] _nf_ (_máquinas_) machinery; (_mecanismo_) mechanism, works _pl_.

maquinilla [maki'niʎa] _nf_ small machine; (_torno_) winch; **~ de afeitar** razor; **~ eléctrica** electric razor.

maquinista [maki'nista] _nm_ (_FERRO_) engine driver (_BRIT_), engineer (_US_); (_TEC_) operator; (*NAUT*) engineer.

mar [mar] *nm* sea; ~ **de fondo**
groundswell; ~ **llena** high tide; ~
adentro *o* **afuera** out at sea; **en alta** ~ on
the high seas; **por** ~ by sea *o* boat;
hacerse a la ~ to put to sea; **a** ~**es** in
abundance; **un** ~ **de** lots of; **es la** ~ **de**
guapa she is ever so pretty; **el M**~
Negro/Báltico the Black/Baltic Sea; **el**
M~ **Muerto/Rojo** the Dead/Red Sea; **el**
M~ **del Norte** the North Sea.

mar. *abr* (= *marzo*) Mar.

maraca [ma'raka] *nf* maraca.

maraña [ma'raɲa] *nf* (*maleza*) thicket;
(*confusión*) tangle.

maravilla [mara'ßiʎa] *nf* marvel, wonder;
(*BOT*) marigold; **hacer** ~**s** to work
wonders; **a (las mil)** ~**s** wonderfully
well.

maravillar [maraßi'ʎar] *vt* to astonish,
amaze; ~**se** *vr* to be astonished, be
amazed.

maravilloso, a [maraßi'ʎoso, a] *adj*
wonderful, marvellous.

marbellí [marße'ʎi] *adj* of *o* from Marbella
♦ *nm/f* native *o* inhabitant of Marbella.

marca ['marka] *nf* mark; (*sello*) stamp;
(*COM*) make, brand; (*de ganado*) brand;
(: *acto*) branding; (*NAUT*) seamark;
(: *boya*) marker; (*DEPORTE*) record; **de** ~
excellent, outstanding; ~ **de fábrica**
trademark; ~ **propia** own brand; ~
registrada registered trademark.

marcación [marka'θjon] *nf* (*TELEC*): ~
automática autodial.

marcado, a [mar'kaðo, a] *adj* marked,
strong.

marcador [marka'ðor] *nm* marker;
(*rotulador*) marker (pen); (*de libro*)
bookmark; (*DEPORTE*) scoreboard;
(: *persona*) scorer.

marcapasos [marka'pasos] *nm inv*
pacemaker.

marcar [mar'kar] *vt* to mark; (*número de
teléfono*) to dial; (*gol*) to score; (*números*)
to record, keep a tally of; (*el pelo*) to set;
(*ganado*) to brand; (*suj: termómetro*) to
read, register; (: *reloj*) to show; (*tarea*) to
assign; (*COM*) to put a price on ♦ *vi*
(*DEPORTE*) to score; (*TELEC*) to dial; **mi
reloj marca las 2** it's 2 o'clock by my
watch; ~ **el compás** (*MUS*) to keep time;
~ **el paso** (*MIL*) to mark time.

marcha ['martʃa] *nf* march; (*DEPORTE*)
walk; (*TEC*) running, working; (*AUTO*)
gear; (*velocidad*) speed; (*fig*) progress;
(*dirección*) course; **dar** ~ **atrás** to
reverse, put into reverse; **estar en** ~ to

be under way, be in motion; **hacer algo
sobre la** ~ to do sth as you *etc* go along;
poner en ~ to put into gear; **ponerse en**
~ to start, get going; **a** ~**s forzadas** (*fig*)
with all speed; **¡en** ~**!** (*MIL*) forward
march!; (*fig*) let's go!; **"**~ **moderada"**
(*AUTO*) "drive slowly"; **que tiene** *o* **de
mucha** ~ (*fam*) very lively.

marchante, a [mar'tʃante, a] *nm/f* dealer,
merchant.

marchar [mar'tʃar] *vi* (*ir*) to go; (*funcionar*)
to work, go; (*fig*) to go, proceed; ~**se** *vr*
to go (away), leave; **todo marcha bien**
everything is going well.

marchitar [martʃi'tar] *vt* to wither, dry up;
~**se** *vr* (*BOT*) to wither; (*fig*) to fade away.

marchito, a [mar'tʃito, a] *adj* withered,
faded; (*fig*) in decline.

marchoso, a [mar'tʃoso, a] *adj* (*fam*:
animado) lively; (: *moderno*) modern.

marcial [mar'θjal] *adj* martial, military.

marciano, a [mar'θjano, a] *adj* Martian, of
o from Mars.

marco ['marko] *nm* frame; (*DEPORTE*)
goalposts *pl*; (*moneda*) mark; (*fig*)
setting; (*contexto*) framework; ~ **de
chimenea** mantelpiece.

marea [ma'rea] *nf* tide; (*llovizna*) drizzle; ~
alta/baja high/low tide; ~ **negra** oil slick.

mareado, a [mare'aðo, a] *adj*: **estar** ~ (*con
náuseas*) to feel sick; (*aturdido*) to feel
dizzy.

marear [mare'ar] *vt* (*fig: irritar*) to annoy,
upset; (*MED*): ~ **a algn** to make sb feel
sick; ~**se** *vr* (*tener náuseas*) to feel sick;
(*desvanecerse*) to feel faint; (*aturdirse*) to
feel dizzy; (*fam: emborracharse*) to get
tipsy.

marejada [mare'xaða] *nf* (*NAUT*) swell,
heavy sea.

maremágnum [mare'maɣnum] *nm* (*fig*)
ocean, abundance.

maremoto [mare'moto] *nm* tidal wave.

mareo [ma'reo] *nm* (*náusea*) sick feeling;
(*aturdimiento*) dizziness; (*fam: lata*)
nuisance.

marfil [mar'fil] *nm* ivory.

margarina [marɣa'rina] *nf* margarine.

margarita [marɣa'rita] *nf* (*BOT*) daisy;
(*rueda*) ~ (*en máquina impresora*) daisy
wheel.

margen ['marxen] *nm* (*borde*) edge,
border; (*fig*) margin, space ♦ *nf* (*de río
etc*) bank; ~ **de beneficio** *o* **de ganancia**
profit margin; ~ **comercial** mark-up; ~
de confianza credibility gap; **dar** ~ **para**
to give an opportunity for; **dejar a algn
al** ~ to leave sb out (in the cold);

mantenerse al ~ to keep out (of things);
al ~ de lo que digas despite what you
say.

marginado, a [marxi'naðo, a] nm/f outcast.

marginal [marxi'nal] adj (tema, error)
minor; (grupo) fringe cpd; (anotación)
marginal.

marginar [marxi'nar] vt to exclude.

maría [ma'ria] nf (fam: mujer) housewife.

mariachi [ma'rjatʃi] nm (música) mariachi
music; (grupo) mariachi band; (persona)
mariachi player.

marica [ma'rika] nm (fam) sissy;
(homosexual) queer.

Maricastaña [marikas'taɲa] nf: **en los días**
o **en tiempos de** ~ way back, in the good
old days.

maricón [mari'kon] nm (fam) queer.

marido [ma'riðo] nm husband.

marihuana [mari'wənə] nf marijuana,
cannabis.

marimacho [mari'matʃo] nf (fam) mannish
woman.

marimorena [marimo'rena] nf fuss, row;
armar una ~ to kick up a row.

marina [ma'rina] nf navy; ~ **mercante**
merchant navy.

marinero, a [mari'nero, a] adj sea cpd;
(barco) seaworthy ♦ nm sailor, seaman.

marino, a [ma'rino, a] adj sea cpd, marine
♦ nm sailor; ~ **de agua dulce/de**
cubierta/de primera landlubber/
deckhand/able seaman.

marioneta [marjo'neta] nf puppet.

mariposa [mari'posa] nf butterfly.

mariposear [maripose'ar] vi (revolotear) to
flutter about; (ser inconstante) to be
fickle; (coquetear) to flirt.

mariquita [mari'kita] nm (fam) sissy;
(homosexual) queer ♦ nf (ZOOL) ladybird
(BRIT), ladybug (US).

marisco [ma'risko] nm (tb: ~s) shellfish,
seafood.

marisma [ma'risma] nf marsh, swamp.

marisquería [mariske'ria] nf shellfish bar,
seafood restaurant.

marítimo, a [ma'ritimo, a] adj sea cpd,
maritime.

marmita [mar'mita] nf pot.

mármol ['marmol] nm marble.

marmóreo, a [mar'moreo, a] adj marble.

marmota [mar'mota] nf (ZOOL) marmot;
(fig) sleepyhead.

maroma [ma'roma] nf rope.

marque ['marke] etc vb V **marcar.**

marqués, esa [mar'kes, esa] nm/f
marquis/marchioness.

marquesina [marke'sina] nf (de parada)
bus-shelter.

marquetería [markete'ria] nf marquetry,
inlaid work.

marranada [marra'naða] nf (fam): **es una** ~
that's disgusting; **hacer una** ~ **a algn** to
do the dirty on sb.

marrano, a [ma'rrano, a] adj filthy, dirty
♦ nm (ZOOL) pig; (malo) swine; (sucio)
dirty pig.

marras ['marras]: **de** ~ adv: **es el problema**
de ~ it's the same old problem.

marrón [ma'rron] adj brown.

marroquí [marro'ki] adj, nm/f Moroccan
♦ nm Morocco (leather).

Marruecos [ma'rrwekos] nm Morocco.

marta ['marta] nf (animal) (pine) marten;
(piel) sable.

Marte ['marte] nm Mars.

martes ['martes] nm inv Tuesday; ~ **de**
carnaval Shrove Tuesday; V tb **Carnaval.**

martillar [marti'ʎar], **martillear**
[martiʎe'ar] vt to hammer.

martilleo [marti'ʎeo] nm hammering.

martillo [mar'tiʎo] nm hammer; (de
presidente de asamblea, comité) gavel; ~
neumático pneumatic drill (BRIT),
jackhammer (US).

Martinica [marti'nika] nf Martinique.

mártir ['martir] nm/f martyr.

martirice [marti'riθe] etc vb V **martirizar.**

martirio [mar'tirjo] nm martyrdom; (fig)
torture, torment.

martirizar [martiri'θar] vt (REL) to martyr;
(fig) to torture, torment.

maruja [ma'ruxa] nf (fam) = **maría.**

marxismo [mark'sismo] nm Marxism.

marxista [mark'sista] adj, nm/f Marxist.

marzo ['marθo] nm March.

mas [mas] conj but.

═══════════════ PALABRA CLAVE

más [mas] adj, adv **1**: ~ **(que, de)** (compar)
more (than), ...+er (than); ~ **grande/**
inteligente bigger/more intelligent;
trabaja ~ **(que yo)** he works more (than
me); ~ **de 6** more than 6; **es** ~ **de**
medianoche it's after midnight; **durar** ~
to last longer; V tb **cada**

2 (superl): **el** ~ the most, ...+est; **el** ~
grande/inteligente (de) the biggest/most
intelligent (in)

3 (negativo): **no tengo** ~ **dinero** I haven't
got any more money; **no viene** ~ **por**
aquí he doesn't come round here any
more; **no sé** ~ I don't know any more,
that's all I know

4 (adicional): **un kilómetro** ~ one more
kilometre; **no le veo** ~ **solución que** ... I

see no other solution than to ...; ¿algo ~?
anything else?; (*en tienda*) will that be
all?; ¿quién ~? anybody else?
5 (+ *adj: valor intensivo*): ¡qué perro ~
sucio! what a filthy dog!; ¡es ~ tonto!
he's so stupid!
6 (*locuciones*): ~ o menos more or less;
los ~ most people; es ~ in fact,
furthermore; ~ bien rather; ¡qué ~ da!
what does it matter!; *V tb* no
7: por ~: por ~ que lo intento no matter
how much *o* hard I try; por ~ que
quisiera ayudar
much as I should like to help
8: de ~: veo que aquí estoy de ~ I can
see I'm not needed here; tenemos uno
de ~ we've got one extra
9: (*AM*): no ~ only, just; ayer no ~ just
yesterday
♦ *prep*: **2 ~ 2 son 4** 2 and *o* plus 2 are 4
♦ *nm inv*: este trabajo tiene sus ~ y sus
menos this job's got its good points and
its bad points.

masa ['masa] *nf* (*mezcla*) dough; (*volumen*)
volume, mass; (*FÍSICA*) mass; en ~ en
masse; las ~s (*POL*) the masses.
masacrar [masa'krar] *vt* to massacre.
masacre [ma'sakre] *nf* massacre.
masaje [ma'saxe] *nm* massage; dar ~ a to
massage.
masajista [masa'xista] *nm/f* masseur/
masseuse.
mascar [mas'kar] *vt, vi* to chew; (*fig*) to
mumble, mutter.
máscara ['maskara] *nf* (*tb INFORM*) mask ♦
nm/f masked person; ~ antigás gas mask.
mascarada [maska'raða] *nf* masquerade.
mascarilla [maska'riʎa] *nf* mask; (*vaciado*)
deathmask; (*maquillaje*) face pack.
mascarón [maska'ron] *nm* large mask; ~
de proa figurehead.
mascota [mas'kota] *nf* mascot.
masculino, a [masku'lino, a] *adj*
masculine; (*BIO*) male ♦ *nm* (*LING*)
masculine.
mascullar [masku'ʎar] *vt* to mumble,
mutter.
masificación [masifika'θjon] *nf*
overcrowding.
masilla [ma'siʎa] *nf* putty.
masivo, a [ma'sißo, a] *adj* (*en masa*) mass.
masón [ma'son] *nm* (free)mason.
masonería [masone'ria] *nf* (free)masonry.
masoquista [maso'kista] *adj* masochistic
♦ *nm/f* masochist.
masque ['maske] *etc vb V* mascar.
mastectomía [mastekto'mia] *nf*

mastectomy.
máster, *pl* **masters** ['master, 'masters] *nm*
postgraduate degree; *V tb* licenciado.
masticar [masti'kar] *vt* to chew; (*fig*) to
ponder over.
mástil ['mastil] *nm* (*de navío*) mast; (*de
guitarra*) neck.
mastín [mas'tin] *nm* mastiff.
mastique [mas'tike] *etc vb V* masticar.
masturbación [masturßa'θjon] *nf*
masturbation.
masturbarse [mastur'ßarse] *vr* to
masturbate.
Mat. *abr* = **Matemáticas.**
mata ['mata] *nf* (*arbusto*) bush, shrub; (*de
hierbas*) tuft; (*campo*) field; (*manojo*) tuft,
blade; ~s *nfpl* scrub *sg*; ~ de pelo mop of
hair; a salto de ~ (*día a día*) from day to
day; (*al azar*) haphazardly.
matadero [mata'ðero] *nm* slaughterhouse,
abattoir.
matador, a [mata'ðor, a] *adj* killing ♦ *nm/f*
killer ♦ *nm* (*TAUR*) matador, bullfighter.
matamoscas [mata'moskas] *nm inv* (*palo*)
fly swat.
matanza [ma'tanθa] *nf* slaughter.
matar [ma'tar] *vt* to kill; (*tiempo, pelota*) to
kill ♦ *vi* to kill; ~se *vr* (*suicidarse*) to kill
o.s., commit suicide; (*morir*) to be *o* get
killed; (*gastarse*) to wear o.s. out; ~ el
hambre to stave off hunger; ~ a algn a
disgustos to make sb's life a misery;
~las callando to go about things slyly;
~se trabajando to kill o.s. with work;
~se por hacer algo to struggle to do sth.
matarife [mata'rife] *nm* slaughterman.
matasanos [mata'sanos] *nm inv* quack.
matasellos [mata'seʎos] *nm inv* postmark.
mate ['mate] *adj* (*sin brillo: color*) dull, matt
♦ *nm* (*en ajedrez*) (check)mate; (*AM:
hierba*) maté; (: *vasija*) gourd.
matemático, a [mate'matiko, a] *adj*
mathematical ♦ *nm/f* mathematician
♦ **matemáticas** *nfpl* mathematics *sg*.
materia [ma'terja] *nf* (*gen*) matter; (*TEC*)
material; (*ESCOL*) subject; en ~ de on
the subject of; (*en cuanto a*) as regards;
~ prima raw material; entrar en ~ to get
down to business.
material [mate'rjal] *adj* material; (*dolor*)
physical; (*real*) real; (*literal*) literal ♦ *nm*
material; (*TEC*) equipment; ~ de
construcción building material; ~es de
derribo rubble *sg*.
materialismo [materja'lismo] *nm*
materialism.
materialista [materja'lista] *adj*
materialist(ic).

materialmente [materjal'mente] *adv* materially; (*fig*) absolutely.

maternal [mater'nal] *adj* motherly, maternal.

maternidad [materni'ðað] *nf* motherhood, maternity.

materno, a [ma'terno, a] *adj* maternal; (*lengua*) mother *cpd*.

matice [ma'tiθe] *etc vb V* **matizar.**

matinal [mati'nal] *adj* morning *cpd*.

matiz [ma'tiθ] *nm* shade; (*de sentido*) shade, nuance; (*ironía etc*) touch.

matizar [mati'θar] *vt* (*variar*) to vary; (*ARTE*) to blend; ~ **de** to tinge with.

matón [ma'ton] *nm* bully.

matorral [mato'rral] *nm* thicket.

matraca [ma'traka] *nf* rattle; (*fam*) nuisance.

matraz [ma'traθ] *nm* (*QUÍMICA*) flask.

matriarcado [matrjar'kaðo] *nm* matriarchy.

matrícula [ma'trikula] *nf* (*registro*) register; (*ESCOL: inscripción*) registration; (*AUTO*) registration number; (: *placa*) number plate.

matricular [matriku'lar] *vt* to register, enrol.

matrimonial [matrimo'njal] *adj* matrimonial.

matrimonio [matri'monjo] *nm* (*pareja*) (married) couple; (*acto*) marriage; ~ **civil/clandestino** civil/secret marriage; **contraer** ~ **(con)** to marry.

matriz [ma'triθ] *nf* (*ANAT*) womb; (*TEC*) mould; (*MAT*) matrix; **casa** ~ (*COM*) head office.

matrona [ma'trona] *nf* (*persona de edad*) matron.

matutino, a [matu'tino, a] *adj* morning *cpd*.

maula ['maula] *adj* (*persona*) good-for-nothing ♦ *nm/f* (*vago*) idler, slacker ♦ *nf* (*persona*) dead loss (*fam*).

maullar [mau'ʎar] *vi* to mew, miaow.

maullido [mau'ʎiðo] *nm* mew(ing), miaow(ing).

Mauricio [mau'riθjo] *nm* Mauritius.

Mauritania [mauri'tanja] *nf* Mauritania.

mausoleo [mauso'leo] *nm* mausoleum.

maxilar [maksi'lar] *nm* jaw(bone).

máxima ['maksima] *nf V* **máximo.**

máxime ['maksime] *adv* especially.

máximo, a ['maksimo, a] *adj* maximum; (*más alto*) highest; (*más grande*) greatest ♦ *nm* maximum ♦ *nf* maxim; ~ **jefe** *o* **líder** (*AM*) President, leader; **como** ~ at most; **al** ~ to the utmost.

maxisingle [maksi'singel] *nm* twelve-inch (single).

maya ['maja] *adj* Mayan ♦ *nm/f* Maya(n).

mayo ['majo] *nm* May.

mayonesa [majo'nesa] *nf* mayonnaise.

mayor [ma'jor] *adj* main, chief; (*adulto*) grown-up, adult; (*JUR*) of age; (*de edad avanzada*) elderly; (*MUS*) major; (*comparativo: de tamaño*) bigger; (: *de edad*) older; (*superlativo: de tamaño*) biggest; (*tb: fig*) greatest; (: *de edad*) oldest ♦ *nm* chief, boss; (*adulto*) adult; **al por** ~ wholesale; ~ **de edad** adult; *V tb* **mayores.**

mayoral [majo'ral] *nm* foreman.

mayordomo [major'ðomo] *nm* butler.

mayoreo [majo'reo] *nm* (*AM*) wholesale (trade).

mayores [ma'jores] *nmpl* grown-ups; **llegar a** ~**es** to get out of hand.

mayoría [majo'ria] *nf* majority, greater part; **en la** ~ **de los casos** in most cases; **en su** ~ on the whole.

mayorista [majo'rista] *nm/f* wholesaler.

mayoritario, a [majori'tarjo, a] *adj* majority *cpd*; **gobierno** ~ majority government.

mayúsculo, a [ma'juskulo, a] *adj* (*fig*) big, tremendous ♦ *nf* capital (letter); **mayúsculas** *nfpl* capitals; (*TIP*) upper case *sg*.

maza ['maθa] *nf* (*arma*) mace; (*DEPORTE*) bat; (*POLO*) stick.

mazacote [maθa'kote] *nm* hard mass; (*CULIN*) dry doughy food; (*ARTE, LITERATURA etc*) mess, hotchpotch.

mazapán [maθa'pan] *nm* marzipan.

mazmorra [maθ'morra] *nf* dungeon.

mazo ['maθo] *nm* (*martillo*) mallet; (*de mortero*) pestle; (*de flores*) bunch; (*DEPORTE*) bat.

mazorca [ma'θorka] *nf* (*BOT*) spike; (*de maíz*) cob, ear.

MCAC *nm abr = Mercado Común de la América Central.*

MCI *nm abr = Mercado Común Iberoamericano.*

me [me] *pron* (*directo*) me; (*indirecto*) (to) me; (*reflexivo*) (to) myself; **¡dámelo!** give it to me!; ~ **lo compró** (*de mí*) he bought it from me; (*para mí*) he bought it for me.

meandro [me'andro] *nm* meander.

mear [me'ar] (*fam*) *vt* to piss on (*!*) ♦ *vi* to pee, piss (*!*), have a piss (*!*); ~**se** *vr* to wet o.s.

Meca ['meka] *nf*: **La** ~ Mecca.

mecánica [me'kanika] *nf V* **mecánico.**

mecanice [meka'niθe] *etc vb V* **mecanizar.**

mecánico, a [me'kaniko, a] *adj*

mechanical; (*repetitivo*) repetitive ♦ *nm/f*
mechanic ♦ *nf* (*estudio*) mechanics *sg*;
(*mecanismo*) mechanism.
mecanismo [meka'nismo] *nm* mechanism;
(*engranaje*) gear.
mecanizar [mekani'θar] *vt* to mechanize.
mecanografía [mekanoɣra'fia] *nf*
typewriting.
mecanografiado, a [mekanoɣra'fjaðo, a]
adj typewritten ♦ *nm* typescript.
mecanógrafo, a [meka'noɣrafo, a] *nm/f*
(copy) typist.
mecate [me'kate] *nm* (*AM*) rope.
mecedor [mɔsc'ðor] *nm* (*AM*), **mecedora**
[meθe'ðora] *nf* rocking chair.
mecenas [me'θenas] *nm inv* patron.
mecenazgo [meθe'naθɣo] *nm* patronage.
mecer [me'θer] *vt* (*cuna*) to rock; **~se** *vr* to
rock; (*rama*) to sway.
mecha ['metʃa] *nf* (*de vela*) wick; (*de
bomba*) fuse; **a toda ~** at full speed;
ponerse ~s to streak one's hair.
mechero [me'tʃero] *nm* (*cigarette*) lighter.
mechón [me'tʃon] *nm* (*gen*) tuft; (*manojo*)
bundle; (*de pelo*) lock.
medalla [me'ðaʎa] *nf* medal.
media ['meðja] *nf* V **medio**.
mediación [meða'θjon] *nf* mediation; **por
~ de** through.
mediado, a [me'ðjaðo, a] *adj* half-full;
(*trabajo*) half-completed; **a ~s de** in the
middle of, halfway through.
medianamente [meðjana'mente] *adv*
(*moderadamente*) moderately, fairly;
(*regularmente*) moderately well.
mediano, a [me'ðjano, a] *adj* (*regular*)
medium, average; (*mediocre*) mediocre
♦ *nf* (*AUT*) central reservation, median
(*US*); (**de tamaño**) ~ medium-sized.
medianoche [meðja'notʃe] *nf* midnight.
mediante [me'ðjante] *adv* by (means of),
through.
mediar [me'ðjar] *vi* (*tiempo*) to elapse;
(*interceder*) to mediate, intervene;
(*existir*) to exist; **media el hecho de que
...** there is the fact that ....
medicación [meðika'θjon] *nf* medication,
treatment.
medicamento [meðika'mento] *nm*
medicine, drug.
medicina [meði'θina] *nf* medicine.
medicinal [meðiθi'nal] *adj* medicinal.
medición [meði'θjon] *nf* measurement.
médico, a ['meðiko, a] *adj* medical ♦ *nm/f*
doctor; **~ de cabecera** family doctor; **~
pediatra** paediatrician; **~ residente**
house physician, intern (*US*).
medida [me'ðiða] *nf* measure; (*medición*)

measurement; (*de camisa, zapato etc*)
size, fitting; (*prudencia*) moderation,
prudence; **en cierta/gran ~** up to a
point/to a great extent; **un traje a la ~**
made-to-measure suit; **~ de cuello** collar
size; **a ~ de** in proportion to; (*de acuerdo
con*) in keeping with; **con ~** with
restraint; **sin ~** immoderately; **a ~ que
...** (at the same time) as ...; **tomar ~s** to
take steps.
medieval [meðje'ßal] *adj* medieval.
medio, a ['meðjo, a] *adj* half (a); (*punto*)
mid, middle; (*promedio*) average ♦ *adv*
half-; (*esp AM*: *un tanto*) rather, quite
♦ *nm* (*centro*) middle, centre; (*promedio*)
average; (*método*) means, way;
(*ambiente*) environment ♦ *nf* (*prenda de
vestir*) stocking, (*AM*) sock; (*promedio*)
average; **~s** *nfpl* tights; **media hora** half
an hour; **~ litro** half a litre; **las tres y
media** half past three; **M~ Oriente**
Middle East; **a ~ camino** halfway
(there); **~ dormido** half asleep; **~
enojado** (*esp AM*) rather annoyed; **lo dejó
a ~s** he left it half-done; **ir a ~s** to go
fifty-fifty; **a ~ terminar** half finished; **en
~ in** the middle; (*entre*) in between; **por
~ de** by (means of), through; **en los ~s
financieros** in financial circles;
encontrarse en su ~ to be in one's
element; **~ circulante** (*COM*) money
supply; *V tb* **medios**.
medioambiental [meðjoambjen'tal] *adj*
environmental.
mediocre [me'ðjokre] *adj* middling,
average; (*pey*) mediocre.
mediocridad [meðjokri'ðað] *nf* middling
quality; (*pey*) mediocrity.
mediodía [meðjo'ðia] *nm* midday, noon.
mediopensionista [meðjopensjo'nista]
nm/f day boy/girl.
medios ['meðjos] *nmpl* means, resources;
los ~ de comunicación the media.
medir [me'ðir] *vt* (*gen*) to measure ♦ *vi* to
measure; **~se** *vr* (*moderarse*) to be
moderate, act with restraint; **¿cuánto
mides?** — **mido 1.50 m** how tall are you?
— I am 1.50 m tall.
meditabundo, a [meðita'ßundo, a] *adj*
pensive.
meditar [meði'tar] *vt* to ponder, think
over, meditate on; (*planear*) to think out
♦ *vi* to ponder, think, meditate.
mediterráneo, a [meðite'rraneo, a] *adj*
Mediterranean ♦ *nm*: **el (mar) M~** the
Mediterranean (Sea).
medrar [me'ðrar] *vi* to increase, grow;
(*mejorar*) to improve; (*prosperar*) to

prosper, thrive; (*animal, planta etc*) to grow.

medroso, a [me'ðroso, a] *adj* fearful, timid.

médula ['meðula] *nf* (*ANAT*) marrow; (*BOT*) pith; ~ **espinal** spinal cord; **hasta la** ~ (*fig*) to the core.

medusa [me'ðusa] *nf* (*ESP*) jellyfish.

megabyte ['meɣaβait] *nm* (*INFORM*) megabyte.

megafonía [meɣafo'nia] *nf* PA *o* public address system.

megáfono [me'ɣafono] *nm* public address system.

megalomanía [meɣaloma'nia] *nf* megalomania.

megalómano, a [meɣa'lomano, a] *nm/f* megalomaniac.

megaocteto [meɣaok'teto] *nm* (*INFORM*) megabyte.

mejicano, a [mexi'kano, a] *adj, nm/f* Mexican.

Méjico ['mexiko] *nm* Mexico.

mejilla [me'xiʎa] *nf* cheek.

mejillón [mexi'ʎon] *nm* mussel.

mejor [me'xor] *adj, adv* (*comparativo*) better; (*superlativo*) best; **lo** ~ the best thing; **lo** ~ **de la vida** the prime of life; **a lo** ~ probably; (*quizá*) maybe; ~ **dicho** rather; **tanto** ~ so much the better; **es el** ~ **de todos** he's the best of all.

mejora [me'xora] *nf,* **mejoramiento** [mexora'mjento] *nm* improvement.

mejorar [mexo'rar] *vt* to improve, make better ♦ *vi,* ~**se** *vr* to improve, get better; (*COM*) to do well, prosper; ~ **a** to be better than; **los negocios mejoran** business is picking up.

mejoría [mexo'ria] *nf* improvement; (*restablecimiento*) recovery.

mejunje [me'xunxe] *nm* (*pey*) concoction.

melancolía [melanko'lia] *nf* melancholy.

melancólico, a [melan'koliko, a] *adj* (*triste*) sad, melancholy; (*soñador*) dreamy.

melena [me'lena] *nf* (*de persona*) long hair; (*ZOOL*) mane.

melillense [meli'ʎense] *adj* of *o* from Melilla ♦ *nm/f* native *o* inhabitant of Melilla.

mella ['meʎa] *nf* (*rotura*) notch, nick; **hacer** ~ (*fig*) to make an impression.

mellizo, a [me'ʎiθo, a] *adj, nm/f* twin.

melocotón [meloko'ton] *nm* (*ESP*) peach.

melodía [melo'ðia] *nf* melody; (*aire*) tune.

melodrama [melo'ðrama] *nm* melodrama.

melodramático, a [meloðra'matiko, a] *adj* melodramatic.

melón [me'lon] *nm* melon.

melopea [melo'pea] *nf* (*fam*): **tener una** ~ to be sloshed.

meloso, a [me'loso, a] *adj* honeyed, sweet; (*empalagoso*) sickly, cloying; (*voz*) sweet; (*zalamero*) smooth.

membrana [mem'brana] *nf* membrane.

membrete [mem'brete] *nm* letterhead; **papel con** ~ headed notepaper.

membrillo [mem'briʎo] *nm* quince; **carne de** ~ quince jelly.

memo, a ['memo, a] *adj* silly, stupid ♦ *nm/f* idiot.

memorable [memo'raβle] *adj* memorable.

memorándum [memo'randum] *nm* (*libro*) notebook; (*comunicación*) memorandum.

memoria [me'morja] *nf* (*gen*) memory; (*artículo*) (learned) paper; ~**s** *nfpl* (*de autor*) memoirs; ~ **anual** annual report; **aprender algo de** ~ to learn sth by heart; **si tengo buena** ~ if my memory serves me right; **venir a la** ~ to come to mind; (*INFORM*): ~ **de acceso aleatorio** random access memory, RAM; ~ **auxiliar** backing storage; ~ **fija** read-only memory, ROM; ~ **fija programable** programmable memory; ~ **del teclado** keyboard memory.

memorice [memo'riθe] *etc vb V* **memorizar**.

memorizar [memori'θar] *vt* to memorize.

menaje [me'naxe] *nm* (*muebles*) furniture; (*utensilios domésticos*) household equipment; ~ **de cocina** kitchenware.

mención [men'θjon] *nf* mention; **digno de** ~ noteworthy; **hacer** ~ **de** to mention.

mencionar [menθjo'nar] *vt* to mention; (*nombrar*) to name; **sin** ~ ... let alone ....

mendicidad [mendiθi'ðað] *nf* begging.

mendigar [mendi'ɣar] *vt* to beg (for).

mendigo, a [men'diɣo, a] *nm/f* beggar.

mendigue [men'diɣe] *etc vb V* **mendigar**.

mendrugo [men'druɣo] *nm* crust.

menear [mene'ar] *vt* to move; (*cola*) to wag; (*cadera*) to swing; (*fig*) to handle; ~**se** *vr* to shake; (*balancearse*) to sway; (*moverse*) to move; (*fig*) to get a move on.

menester [menes'ter] *nm* (*necesidad*) necessity; ~**es** *nmpl* (*deberes*) duties; **es** ~ **hacer algo** it is necessary to do sth, sth must be done.

menestra [me'nestra] *nf*: ~ **de verduras** vegetable stew.

mengano, a [men'gano, a] *nm/f* Mr (*o* Mrs *o* Miss) So-and-so.

mengua ['mengwa] *nf* (*disminución*) decrease; (*falta*) lack; (*pobreza*) poverty; (*fig*) discredit; **en** ~ **de** to the detriment of.

menguante [men'gwante] *adj* decreasing, diminishing; (*luna*) waning; (*marea*) ebb *cpd*.

menguar [men'gwar] *vt* to lessen, diminish; (*fig*) to discredit ♦ *vi* to diminish, decrease; (*fig*) to decline.

mengüe ['mengwe] *etc vb* V **menguar.**

menopausia [meno'pausja] *nf* menopause.

menor [me'nor] *adj* (*más pequeño*: *comparativo*) smaller; (*número*) less, lesser; (: *superlativo*) smallest; (*número*) least; (*más joven*: *comparativo*) younger; (: *superlativo*) youngest; (*MUS*) minor ♦ *nm/f* (*joven*) young person, juvenile; **Juanito es ~ que Pepe** Juanito is younger than Pepe; **ella es la ~ de todas** she is the youngest of all; **no tengo la ~ idea** I haven't the faintest idea; **al por ~** retail; **~ de edad** under age.

Menorca [me'norka] *nf* Minorca.

menorquín, ina [menor'kin, ina] *adj, nm/f* Minorcan.

══════ PALABRA CLAVE

menos [menos] *adj* **1**: **~ (que, de)** (*compar*: *cantidad*) less (than); (: *número*) fewer (than); **con ~ entusiasmo** with less enthusiasm; **~ gente** fewer people; V tb **cada**

2 (*superl*): **es el que ~ culpa tiene** he is the least to blame; **donde ~ problemas hay** where there are fewest problems ♦ *adv* **1** (*compar*): **~ (que, de)** less (than); **me gusta ~ que el otro** I like it less than the other one; **~ de 5** less than 5; **~ de lo que piensas** less than you think

2 (*superl*): **es el ~ listo (de su clase)** he's the least bright (in his class); **de todas ellas es la que ~ me agrada** out of all of them she's the one I like least; **(por) lo ~** at (the very) least; **es lo ~ que puedo hacer** it's the least I can do; **lo ~ posible** as little as possible

3 (*locuciones*): **no quiero verle y ~ visitarle** I don't want to see him let alone visit him; **tenemos 7 (de) ~** we're 7 short; **eso es lo de ~** that's the least of it; **¡todo ~ eso!** anything but that!; **al/por lo ~** at (the very) least; **si al ~** if only

♦ *prep* except; (*cifras*) minus; **todos ~ él** everyone except (for) him; **5 ~ 2** 5 minus 2; **las 7 ~ 20** (*hora*) 20 to 7

♦ *conj*: **a ~ que: a ~ que venga mañana** unless he comes tomorrow.

menoscabar [menoska'ßar] *vt* (*estropear*) to damage, harm; (*fig*) to discredit.

menospreciar [menospre'θjar] *vt* to underrate, undervalue; (*despreciar*) to scorn, despise.

menosprecio [menos'preθjo] *nm* underrating, undervaluation; scorn, contempt.

mensaje [men'saxe] *nm* message; **~ de error** (*INFORM*) error message.

mensajero, a [mensa'xero, a] *nm/f* messenger.

menstruación [menstrwa'θjon] *nf* menstruation.

menstruar [mens'trwar] *vi* to menstruate.

mensual [men'swal] *adj* monthly; **100 ptas ~es** 100 ptas. a month.

mensualidad [menswali'ðað] *nf* (*salario*) monthly salary; (*COM*) monthly payment *o* instalment.

menta ['menta] *nf* mint.

mentado, a [men'taðo, a] *adj* (*mencionado*) aforementioned; (*famoso*) well-known ♦ *nf*: **hacerle una mentada a algn** (*AM fam*) to (seriously) insult sb.

mental [men'tal] *adj* mental.

mentalidad [mentali'ðað] *nf* mentality, way of thinking.

mentalizar [mentali'θar] *vt* (*sensibilizar*) to make aware; (*convencer*) to convince; (*preparar mentalmente*) to psych up; **~se** *vr* (*concienciarse*) to become aware; (*prepararse mentalmente*) to get psyched up; **~se de que ...** (*convencerse*) to get it into one's head that ...

mentar [men'tar] *vt* to mention, name; **~ la madre a algn** to swear at sb.

mente ['mente] *nf* mind; (*inteligencia*) intelligence; **no tengo en ~ hacer eso** it is not my intention to do that.

mentecato, a [mente'kato, a] *adj* silly, stupid ♦ *nm/f* fool, idiot.

mentir [men'tir] *vi* to lie; **¡miento!** sorry, I'm wrong!

mentira [men'tira] *nf* (*una ~*) lie; (*acto*) lying; (*invención*) fiction; **~ piadosa** white lie; **una ~ como una casa** a whopping great lie (*fam*); **parece ~ que ...** it seems incredible that ..., I can't believe that ....

mentiroso, a [menti'roso, a] *adj* lying; (*falso*) deceptive ♦ *nm/f* liar.

mentís [men'tis] *nm inv* denial; **dar el ~ a** to deny.

mentón [men'ton] *nm* chin.

menú [me'nu] *nm* (*tb INFORM*) menu; (*en restaurante*) set meal; **guiado por ~** (*INFORM*) menu-driven.

menudear [menuðe'ar] *vt* (*repetir*) to repeat frequently ♦ *vi* (*ser frecuente*) to be frequent; (*detallar*) to go into great detail.

menudencia [menu'ðenθja] *nf* (*bagatela*) trifle; ~**s** *nfpl* odds and ends.

menudeo [menu'ðeo] *nm* retail sales *pl.*

menudillos [menu'ðiʎos] *nmpl* giblets.

menudo, a [me'nuðo, a] *adj* (*pequeño*) small, tiny; (*sin importancia*) petty, insignificant; ¡~ **negocio!** (*fam*) some deal!; **a** ~ often, frequently.

meñique [me'nike] *nm* little finger.

meollo [me'oʎo] *nm* (*fig*) essence, core.

mequetrefe [meke'trefe] *nm* good-for-nothing, whippersnapper.

mercader [merka'ðer] *nm* merchant.

mercadería [merkaðe'ria] *nf* commodity; ~**s** goods, merchandise *sg.*

mercado [mer'kaðo] *nm* market; ~ **en baja** falling market; **M~ Común** Common Market; ~ **de demanda/de oferta** seller's/buyer's market; ~ **laboral** labour market; ~ **objetivo** target market; ~ **de productos básicos** commodity market; ~ **de valores** stock market; ~ **exterior/interior** *o* **nacional/libre** overseas/home/free market.

mercancía [merkan'θia] *nf* commodity; ~**s** *nfpl* goods, merchandise *sg*; ~**s en depósito** bonded goods; ~**s perecederas** perishable goods.

mercancías [merkan'θias] *nm inv* goods train, freight train (*US*).

mercantil [merkan'til] *adj* mercantile, commercial.

mercenario, a [merθe'narjo, a] *adj, nm* mercenary.

mercería [merθe'ria] *nf* (*artículos*) haberdashery (*BRIT*), notions *pl* (*US*); (*tienda*) haberdasher's shop (*BRIT*), drapery (*BRIT*), notions store (*US*).

Mercosur [merko'sur] *nm abr* = Mercado Común del Sur.

mercurio [mer'kurjo] *nm* mercury.

merecedor, a [mereθe'ðor, a] *adj* deserving; ~ **de confianza** trustworthy.

merecer [mere'θer] *vt* to deserve, merit ♦ *vi* to be deserving, be worthy; **merece la pena** it's worthwhile.

merecido, a [mere'θiðo, a] *adj* (well) deserved; **llevarse su** ~ to get one's deserts.

merendar [meren'dar] *vt* to have for tea ♦ *vi* to have tea; (*en el campo*) to have a picnic.

merendero [meren'dero] *nm* (*café*) tearoom; (*en el campo*) picnic spot.

merengue [me'renge] *nm* meringue.

merezca [me'reθka] *etc vb V* **merecer.**

meridiano [meri'ðjano] *nm* (*ASTRO, GEO*) meridian; **la explicación es de una claridad meridiana** the explanation is as clear as day.

meridional [meriðjo'nal] *adj* Southern ♦ *nm/f* Southerner.

merienda [me'rjenda] *etc vb V* **merendar** ♦ *nf* (light) tea, afternoon snack; (*de campo*) picnic; ~ **de negros** free-for-all.

mérito ['merito] *nm* merit; (*valor*) worth, value; **hacer** ~**s** to make a good impression; **restar** ~ **a** to detract from.

meritorio, a [meri'torjo, a] *adj* deserving.

merluza [mer'luθa] *nf* hake; **coger una** ~ (*fam*) to get sozzled.

merma ['merma] *nf* decrease; (*pérdida*) wastage.

mermar [mer'mar] *vt* to reduce, lessen ♦ *vi* to decrease, dwindle.

mermelada [merme'laða] *nf* jam; ~ **de naranja** marmalade.

mero, a ['mero, a] *adj* mere, simple; (*AM fam*) real ♦ *adv* (*AM*) just, right ♦ *nm* (*ZOOL*) grouper; **el** ~ ~ (*AM fam*) the boss.

merodear [meroðe'ar] *vi* (*MIL*) to maraud; (*de noche*) to prowl (about); (*curiosear*) to snoop around.

mes [mes] *nm* month; (*salario*) month's pay; **el** ~ **corriente** this *o* the current month.

mesa ['mesa] *nf* table; (*de trabajo*) desk; (*COM*) counter; (*en mitin*) platform; (*GEO*) plateau; (*ARQ*) landing; ~ **de noche/de tijera/de operaciones** *u* **operatoria** bedside/folding/operating table; ~ **redonda** (*reunión*) round table; ~ **digitalizadora** (*INFORM*) graph pad; ~ **directiva** board; ~ **y cama** bed and board; **poner/quitar la** ~ to lay/clear the table.

mesarse [me'sarse] *vr*: ~ **el pelo** *o* **los cabellos** to tear one's hair.

mesera [me'sera] *nf* (*AM*) waitress.

mesero [me'sero] *nm* (*AM*) waiter.

meseta [me'seta] *nf* (*GEO*) meseta, tableland; (*ARQ*) landing.

mesilla [me'siʎa], **mesita** [me'sita] *nf*: ~ **de noche** bedside table.

mesón [me'son] *nm* inn.

mestizo, a [mes'tiθo, a] *adj* half-caste, of mixed race; (*ZOOL*) crossbred ♦ *nm/f* half-caste.

mesura [me'sura] *nf* (*calma*) calm; (*moderación*) moderation, restraint; (*cortesía*) courtesy.

mesurar [mesu'rar] *vt* (*contener*) to restrain; ~**se** *vr* to restrain o.s.

meta ['meta] *nf* goal; (*de carrera*) finish; (*fig*) goal, aim, objective.

metabolismo [metaßo'lismo] *nm* metabolism.

metafísico, a [meta'fisiko, a] *adj* metaphysical ♦ *nf* metaphysics *sg*.

metáfora [me'tafora] *nf* metaphor.

metafórico, a [meta'foriko, a] *adj* metaphorical.

metal [me'tal] *nm* (*materia*) metal; (*MUS*) brass.

metálico, a [me'taliko, a] *adj* metallic; (*de metal*) metal ♦ *nm* (*dinero contante*) cash.

metalurgia [meta'lurxja] *nf* metallurgy.

metalúrgico, a [meta'lurxiko, a] *adj* metallurgic(al); **industria ~a** engineering industry

metamorfosear [metamorfose'ar] *vt*: **~ (en)** to metamorphose *o* transform (into).

metamorfosis [metamor'fosis] *nf inv* metamorphosis, transformation.

metedura [mete'ðura] *nf*: **~ de pata** (*fam*) blunder.

meteorito [meteo'rito] *nm* meteorite.

meteoro [mete'oro] *nm* meteor.

meteorología [meteorolo'xia] *nf* meteorology.

meteorólogo, a [meteo'roloɣo, a] *nm/f* meteorologist; (*RADIO, TV*) weather reporter.

meter [me'ter] *vt* (*colocar*) to put, place; (*introducir*) to put in, insert; (*involucrar*) to involve; (*causar*) to make, cause; **~se** *vr*: **~se en** to go into, enter; (*fig*) to interfere in, meddle in; **~se a** to start; **~se a escritor** to become a writer; **~se con algn** to provoke sb, pick a quarrel with sb; **~ prisa a algn** to hurry sb up.

meticuloso, a [metiku'loso, a] *adj* meticulous, thorough.

metido, a [me'tiðo, a] *adj*: **estar muy ~ en un asunto** to be deeply involved in a matter; **~ en años** elderly; **~ en carne** plump.

metódico, a [me'toðiko, a] *adj* methodical.

metodismo [meto'ðismo] *nm* Methodism.

método ['metoðo] *nm* method.

metodología [metoðolo'xia] *nf* methodology.

metomentodo [metomen'toðo] *nm inv* meddler, busybody.

metraje [me'traxe] *nm* (*CINE*) length; **cinta de largo/corto ~** full-length film/short.

metralla [me'traʎa] *nf* shrapnel.

metralleta [metra'ʎeta] *nf* sub-machine-gun.

métrico, a ['metriko, a] *adj* metric ♦ *nf*

metrics *pl*; **cinta métrica** tape measure.

metro ['metro] *nm* metre; (*tren: tb:* **metropolitano**) underground (*BRIT*), subway (*US*); (*instrumento*) rule; **~ cuadrado/cúbico** square/cubic metre.

metrópoli [me'tropoli], **metrópolis** [me'tropolis] *nf* (*ciudad*) metropolis; (*colonial*) mother country.

mexicano, a [mexi'kano, a] *adj, nm/f* (*AM*) Mexican.

México ['mexiko] *nm* (*AM*) Mexico; **Ciudad de ~** Mexico City.

mezcla ['meθkla] *nf* mixture; (*fig*) blend.

mezclar [meθ'klar] *vt* to mix (up); (*armonizar*) to blend; (*combinar*) to merge; **~se** *vr* to mix, mingle; **~ en** to get mixed up in, get involved in.

mezcolanza [meθko'lanθa] *nf* hotchpotch, jumble.

mezquindad [meθkin'dað] *nf* (*cicatería*) meanness; (*miras estrechas*) pettiness; (*acto*) mean action.

mezquino, a [meθ'kino, a] *adj* (*cicatero*) mean ♦ *nm/f* (*avaro*) mean person; (*miserable*) petty individual.

mezquita [meθ'kita] *nf* mosque.

MF *abr* (= *Modulación de Frecuencia*) FM.

mg. *abr* (= *miligramo(s)*) mg.

mi [mi] *adj posesivo* my ♦ *nm* (*MUS*) E.

mí [mi] *pron* me, myself; **¿y a ~ qué?** so what?

miaja ['mjaxa] *nf* crumb; **ni una ~** (*fig*) not the least little bit.

miau [mjau] *nm* miaow.

michelín [mitʃe'lin] *nm* (*fam*) spare tyre.

mico ['miko] *nm* monkey.

micro ['mikro] *nm* (*RADIO*) mike, microphone; (*AM: pequeño*) minibus; (: *grande*) coach, bus.

microbio [mi'kroßjo] *nm* microbe.

microbús [mikro'ßus] *nm* minibus.

microchip [mikro'tʃip] *nm* microchip.

microcomputador [mikrokomputa'ðor] *nm*, **microcomputadora** [mikrokomputa'ðora] *nf* micro(computer).

microeconomía [mikroekono'mia] *nf* microeconomics *sg*.

microficha [mikro'fitʃa] *nf* microfiche.

microfilm, pl microfilms [mikro'film, mikro'films] *nm* microfilm.

micrófono [mi'krofono] *nm* microphone.

microinformática [mikroinfor'matika] *nf* microcomputing.

micrómetro [mi'krometro] *nm* micrometer.

microonda [mikro'onda] *nf* microwave, **(horno) ~s** microwave (oven).

microordenador [mikroordena'ðor] *nm*

microcomputer.

micropastilla [mikropas'tiʎa],
microplaqueta [mikropla'keta] _nf_
(_INFORM_) chip, wafer.

microplaquita [mikropla'kita] _nf_: ~ **de
silicio** silicon chip.

microprocesador [mikroprocesa'ðor] _nm_
microprocessor.

microscópico, a [mikros'kopiko, a] _adj_
microscopic.

microscopio [mikros'kopjo] _nm_
microscope.

midiendo [mi'ðjendo] _etc vb_ V **medir.**

miedo ['mjeðo] _nm_ fear; (_nerviosismo_)
apprehension, nervousness; **meter** ~ **a**
to scare, frighten; **tener** ~ to be afraid;
de ~ wonderful, marvellous; **¡qué** ~!
(_fam_) how awful!; **me da** ~ it scares me;
hace un frío de ~ (_fam_) it's terribly cold.

miedoso, a [mje'ðoso, a] _adj_ fearful,
timid.

miel [mjel] _nf_ honey; **no hay** ~ **sin hiel**
there's no rose without a thorn.

miembro ['mjembro] _nm_ limb; (_socio_)
member; (_de institución_) fellow; ~ **viril**
penis.

mientes ['mjentes] _etc vb_ V **mentar; mentir**
♦ _nfpl_: **no parar** ~ **en** to pay no attention
to; **traer a las** ~ to recall.

mientras ['mjentras] _conj_ while; (_duración_)
as long as ♦ _adv_ meanwhile; ~ **(que)**
whereas; ~ **tanto** meanwhile; ~ **más
tiene, más quiere** the more he has, the
more he wants.

miérc. _abr_ (= _miércoles_) Wed.

miércoles ['mjerkoles] _nm inv_ Wednesday;
~ **de ceniza** Ash Wednesday; V _tb_
Carnaval.

mierda ['mjerða] _nf_ (_fam!_) shit (_!_), crap (_!_);
(_fig_) filth, dirt; **¡vete a la** ~! go to hell!

mies [mjes] _nf_ (ripe) corn, wheat, grain.

miga ['miɣa] _nf_ crumb; (_fig: meollo_)
essence; **hacer buenas** ~**s** (_fam_) to get on
well; **esto tiene su** ~ there's more to this
than meets the eye.

migaja [mi'ɣaxa] _nf_: **una** ~ **de** (_un poquito_)
a little; ~**s** _nfpl_ crumbs; (_pey_) left-overs.

migración [miɣra'θjon] _nf_ migration.

migratorio, a [miɣra'torjo, a] _adj_
migratory.

mil [mil] _num_ thousand; **dos** ~ **libras** two
thousand pounds.

milagro [mi'laɣro] _nm_ miracle; **hacer** ~**s**
(_fig_) to work wonders.

milagroso, a [mila'ɣroso, a] _adj_
miraculous.

Milán [mi'lan] _nm_ Milan.

milenario, a [mile'narjo, a] _adj_ millennial;

(_fig_) very ancient.

milenio [mi'lenjo] _nm_ millennium.

milésimo, a [mi'lesimo, a] _num_ thousandth.

mili ['mili] _nf_: **hacer la** ~ (_fam_) to do one's
military service; _see boxed note._

MILI

La mili, _military service, is compulsory in
Spain, although the number of months'
service has been reduced and recruits are
now posted close to their home town.
There continues to be strong opposition
from conscientious objectors, who are
obliged to do "Prestación Social
Sustitutoria" instead; this usually involves
doing some form of community service
and lasts longer. Those who refuse to do
either of these, "los insumisos", can be
sent to prison._

---

milicia [mi'liθja] _nf_ (_MIL_) militia; (_servicio
militar_) military service.

miligramo [mili'ɣramo] _nm_ milligram.

milímetro [mi'limetro] _nm_ millimetre
(_BRIT_), millimeter (_US_).

militante [mili'tante] _adj_ militant.

militar [mili'tar] _adj_ military ♦ _nm/f_ soldier
♦ _vi_ to serve in the army; (_fig_) to
militate, fight.

militarismo [milita'rismo] _nm_ militarism.

milla ['miʎa] _nf_ mile; ~ **marina** nautical
mile.

millar [mi'ʎar] _num_ thousand; **a** ~**es** in
thousands.

millón [mi'ʎon] _num_ million.

millonario, a [miʎo'narjo, a] _nm/f_
millionaire.

millonésima, a [miʎo'nesimo, a] _num_
millionth.

mimado, a [mi'maðo, a] _adj_ spoiled.

mimar [mi'mar] _vt_ to spoil, pamper.

mimbre ['mimbre] _nm_ wicker; **de** ~ wicker
cpd, wickerwork.

mimetismo [mime'tismo] _nm_ mimicry.

mímica ['mimika] _nf_ (_para comunicarse_)
sign language; (_imitación_) mimicry.

mimo ['mimo] _nm_ (_caricia_) caress; (_de niño_)
spoiling; (_TEAT_) mime; (_: actor_) mime
artist.

mina ['mina] _nf_ mine; (_pozo_) shaft; (_de
lápiz_) lead refill; **hullera** _o_ ~ **de carbón**
coalmine.

minar [mi'nar] _vt_ to mine; (_fig_) to
undermine.

mineral [mine'ral] _adj_ mineral ♦ _nm_ (_GEO_)
mineral; (_mena_) ore.

minería [mine'ria] _nf_ mining.

minero, a [mi'nero, a] adj mining cpd ♦ nm/f miner.
miniatura [minja'tura] adj inv, nf miniature.
minicadena [minika'ðena] nf (MUS) mini hi-fi.
minicomputador [minikomputa'ðor] nm minicomputer.
MiniDisc ® [mini'ðisk] nm MiniDisc ®.
minidisco [mini'ðisko] nm diskette.
minifalda [mini'falda] nf miniskirt.
minifundio [mini'fundjo] nm smallholding, small farm.
minimizar [minimi'θar] vt to minimize.
mínimo, a ['minimo, a] adj minimum; (insignificante) minimal ♦ nm minimum; **precio/salario** ~ minimum price/wage; **lo** ~ **que pueden hacer** the least they can do.
minino, a [mi'nino, a] nm/f (fam) puss, pussy.
ministerio [minis'terjo] nm ministry (BRIT), department (US); **M~ de Asuntos Exteriores** Foreign Office (BRIT), State Department (US); **M~ del Comercio e Industria** Department of Trade and Industry; **M~ de (la) Gobernación** o **del Interior** ≈ Home Office (BRIT), Ministry of the Interior; **M~ de Hacienda** Treasury (BRIT), Treasury Department (US).
ministro, a [mi'nistro, a] nm/f minister, secretary (esp US); **M~ de Hacienda** Chancellor of the Exchequer, Secretary of the Treasury (US); **M~ de (la) Gobernación** o **del Interior** ≈ Home Secretary (BRIT), Secretary of the Interior (US).
minoría [mino'ria] nf minority.
minorista [mino'rista] nm retailer.
mintiendo [min'tjendo] etc vb V **mentir**.
minucia [mi'nuθja] nf (detalle insignificante) trifle; (bagatela) mere nothing.
minuciosidad [minuθjosi'ðað] nf (meticulosidad) thoroughness, meticulousness.
minucioso, a [minu'θjoso, a] adj thorough, meticulous; (prolijo) very detailed.
minúsculo, a [mi'nuskulo, a] adj tiny, minute ♦ nf small letter; **minúsculas** nfpl (TIP) lower case sg.
minusvalía [minusßa'lia] nf physical handicap; (COM) depreciation, capital loss.
minusválido, a [minus'ßaliðo, a] adj (physically) handicapped o disabled ♦ nm/f disabled person.
minuta [mi'nuta] nf (de comida) menu; (de abogado etc) fee.
minutero [minu'tero] nm minute hand.
minuto [mi'nuto] nm minute.

Miño ['miɲo] nm: **el (río)** ~ the Miño.
mío, a ['mio, a] adj, pron: **el** ~ mine; **un amigo** ~ a friend of mine; **lo** ~ what is mine; **los** ~**s** my people, my relations.
miope ['mjope] adj short-sighted.
miopía [mjo'pia] nf near- o short-sightedness.
MIR [mir] nm abr (POL) = Movimiento de Izquierda Revolucionaria; (ESP MED) = Médico Interno y Residente.
mira ['mira] nf (de arma) sight(s) (pl); (fig) aim, intention; **de amplias/estrechas** ~**s** broad-/narrow-minded.
mirada [mi'raða] nf look, glance; (expresión) look, expression; ~ **de soslayo** sidelong glance; ~ **fija** stare, gaze; ~ **perdida** distant look; **echar una** ~ **a** to glance at; **levantar/bajar la** ~ to look up/down; **resistir la** ~ **de algn** to stare sb out.
mirado, a [mi'raðo, a] adj (sensato) sensible; (considerado) considerate; **bien/mal** ~ well/not well thought of.
mirador [mira'ðor] nm viewpoint, vantage point.
miramiento [mira'mjento] nm (consideración) considerateness; **tratar sin** ~**s a algn** to ride roughshod over sb.
mirar [mi'rar] vt to look at; (observar) to watch; (considerar) to consider, think over; (vigilar, cuidar) to watch, look after ♦ vi to look; (ARQ) to face; ~**se** vr (dos personas) to look at each other; ~ **algo/a algn de reojo** o **de través** to look askance at sth/sb; ~ **algo/a algn por encima del hombro** to look down on sth/sb; ~ **bien/mal** to think highly of/have a poor opinion of; ~ **fijamente** to stare o gaze at; ~ **por** (fig) to look after; ~ **por la ventana** to look out of the window; ~**se al espejo** to look at o.s. in the mirror; ~**se a los ojos** to look into each other's eyes.
mirilla [mi'riʎa] nf (agujero) spyhole, peephole.
mirlo ['mirlo] nm blackbird.
misa ['misa] nf mass; ~ **del gallo** midnight mass (on Christmas Eve); ~ **de difuntos** requiem mass; **como en** ~ in dead silence; **estos datos van a** ~ (fig) these facts are utterly trustworthy.
misántropo [mi'santropo] nm misanthrope, misanthropist.
miscelánea [misθe'lanea] nf miscellany.
miserable [mise'raßle] adj (avaro) mean, stingy; (nimio) miserable, paltry; (lugar) squalid; (fam) vile, despicable ♦ nm/f (malvado) rogue.

miseria [mi'serja] *nf* misery; (*pobreza*) poverty; (*tacañería*) meanness, stinginess; (*condiciones*) squalor; **una ~** a pittance.

misericordia [miseri'korðja] *nf* (*compasión*) compassion, pity; (*perdón*) forgiveness, mercy.

misil [mi'sil] *nm* missile.

misión [mi'sjon] *nf* mission; (*tarea*) job, duty; (*POL*) assignment; **misiones** *nfpl* (*REL*) overseas missions.

misionero, a [misjo'nero, a] *nm/f* missionary.

mismamente [misma'mente] *adv* (*fam:* *sólo*) only, just.

mismísimo, a [mis'misimo, a] *adj superlativo* selfsame, very (same).

mismo, a ['mismo, a] *adj* (*semejante*) same; (*después de pronombre*) -self; (*para* *énfasis*) very ♦ *adv:* **aquí/ayer/hoy ~** right here/only yesterday/this very day; **ahora ~** right now ♦ *conj:* **lo ~ que** just like, just as; **por lo ~** for the same reason; **el ~ traje** the same suit; **en ese ~ momento** at that very moment; **vino el ~ Ministro** the Minister himself came; **yo ~ lo vi** I saw it myself; **lo hizo por sí ~** he did it by himself; **lo ~ the** same (thing); **da lo ~** it's all the same; **quedamos en las mismas** we're no further forward.

misógino [mi'soxino] *nm* misogynist.

miss [mis] *nf* beauty queen.

misterio [mis'terjo] *nm* mystery; (*lo* *secreto*) secrecy.

misterioso, a [miste'rjoso, a] *adj* mysterious; (*inexplicable*) puzzling.

misticismo [misti'θismo] *nm* mysticism.

místico, a ['mistiko, a] *adj* mystic(al) ♦ *nm/f* mystic ♦ *nf* mysticism.

mitad [mi'tað] *nf* (*medio*) half; (*centro*) middle; **~ (y) ~** half-and-half; (*fig*) yes and no; **a ~ de precio** (at) half-price; **en** *o* **a ~ del camino** halfway along the road; **cortar por la ~** to cut through the middle.

mítico, a ['mitiko, a] *adj* mythical.

mitigar [miti'ɣar] *vt* to mitigate; (*dolor*) to relieve; (*sed*) to quench; (*ira*) to appease; (*preocupación*) to allay; (*soledad*) to alleviate.

mitigue [mi'tiɣe] *etc vb* V **mitigar**.

mitin ['mitin] *nm* (*esp POL*) meeting.

mito ['mito] *nm* myth.

mitología [mitolo'xia] *nf* mythology.

mitológico, a [mito'loxiko, a] *adj* mythological.

mixto, a ['miksto, a] *adj* mixed; (*comité*) joint.

ml. *abr* (= *mililitro*) ml.

mm. *abr* (= *milímetro*) mm.

m/n *abr* (*ECON*) = *moneda nacional.*

M.° *abr* (*POL:* = *Ministerio*) Min.

m/o *abr* (*COM*) = *mi orden.*

mobiliario [moβi'ljarjo] *nm* furniture.

MOC *nm abr* = *Movimiento de Objeción de Conciencia.*

mocasín [moka'sin] *nm* moccasin.

mocedad [moθe'ðað] *nf* youth.

mochila [mo'tʃila] *nf* rucksack (*BRIT*), backpack.

moción [mo'θjon] *nf* motion; **~ compuesta** (*POL*) composite motion.

moco ['moko] *nm* mucus; **limpiarse los ~s** to blow one's nose; **no es ~ de pavo** it's no trifle.

mocoso, a [mo'koso, a] *adj* snivelling; (*fig*) ill-bred ♦ *nm/f* (*fam*) brat.

moda ['moða] *nf* fashion; (*estilo*) style; **de** *o* **a la ~** in fashion, fashionable; **pasado de ~** out of fashion; **vestido a la última ~** trendily dressed.

modal [mo'ðal] *adj* modal ♦ *nm:* **~es** *nmpl* manners.

modalidad [moðali'ðað] *nf* (*clase*) kind, variety; (*manera*) way; (*INFORM*) mode; **~ de texto** (*INFORM*) text mode.

modelar [moðe'lar] *vt* to model.

modelo [mo'ðelo] *adj inv* model ♦ *nm/f* model ♦ *nm* (*patrón*) pattern; (*norma*) standard.

módem ['moðem] *nm* (*INFORM*) modem.

moderado, a [moðe'raðo, a] *adj* moderate.

moderar [moðe'rar] *vt* to moderate; (*violencia*) to restrain, control; (*velocidad*) to reduce; **~se** *vr* to restrain o.s., control o.s.

modernice [moðer'niθe] *etc vb* V **modernizar**.

modernizar [moðerni'θar] *vt* to modernize; (*INFORM*) to upgrade.

moderno, a [mo'ðerno, a] *adj* modern; (*actual*) present-day; (*equipo etc*) up-to-date.

modestia [mo'ðestja] *nf* modesty.

modesto, a [mo'ðesto, a] *adj* modest.

módico, a ['moðiko, a] *adj* moderate, reasonable.

modificar [moðifi'kar] *vt* to modify.

modifique [moði'fike] *etc vb* V **modificar**.

modismo [mo'ðismo] *nm* idiom.

modisto, a [mo'ðisto, a] *nm/f* dressmaker.

modo ['moðo] *nm* (*manera, forma*) way, manner; (*INFORM, MUS*) mode; (*LING*) mood; **~s** *nmpl* manners; **"~ de empleo"** "instructions for use"; **~ de gobierno**

form of government; **a ~ de** like; **de este ~** in this way; **de ningún ~** in no way; **de todos ~s** at any rate; **de un ~ u otro** (in) one way or another.

modorra [mo'ðorra] nf drowsiness.

modoso, a [mo'ðoso, a] adj (educado) quiet, well-mannered.

modulación [moðula'θjon] nf modulation; **~ de frecuencia** (RADIO) frequency modulation, FM.

módulo ['moðulo] nm module; (de mueble) unit.

mofarse [mo'farse] vr: **~ de** to mock, scoff at.

moflete [mo'flete] nm fat cheek, chubby cheek.

mogollón [moɣo'ʎon] (fam) nm: **~ de discos** etc loads of records etc ♦ adv: **un ~** a hell of a lot.

mohín [mo'in] nm (mueca) (wry) face; (pucheros) pout.

mohino, a [mo'ino, a] adj (triste) gloomy, depressed; (enojado) sulky.

moho ['moo] nm (BOT) mould, mildew; (en metal) rust.

mohoso, a [mo'oso, a] adj mouldy; rusty.

mojado, a [mo'xaðo, a] adj wet; (húmedo) damp; (empapado) drenched.

mojar [mo'xar] vt to wet; (humedecer) to damp(en), moisten; (calar) to soak; **~se** vr to get wet; **~ el pan en el café** to dip o dunk one's bread in one's coffee.

mojigato, a [moxi'ɣato, a] adj (hipócrita) hypocritical; (santurrón) sanctimonious; (gazmoño) prudish ♦ nm/f hypocrite; sanctimonious person; prude.

mojón [mo'xon] nm (hito) landmark; (en un camino) signpost; (~ kilométrico) milestone.

mol. abr (= molécula) mol.

molar [mo'lar] nm molar ♦ vt (fam): **lo que más me mola es ...** what I'm really into is ...; **¿te mola un pitillo?** do you fancy a smoke?

Moldavia [mol'ðaβja], **Moldova** [mol'ðoβa] nf Moldavia, Moldova.

moldavo, a [mol'ðaβo, a] adj, nm/f Moldavian, Moldovan.

molde ['molde] nm mould; (vaciado) cast; (de costura) pattern; (fig) model.

moldear [molde'ar] vt to mould; (en yeso etc) to cast.

mole ['mole] nf mass, bulk; (edificio) pile.

molécula [mo'lekula] nf molecule.

moler [mo'ler] vt to grind, crush; (pulverizar) to pound; (trigo etc) to mill; (cansar) to tire out, exhaust; **~ a algn a palos** to give sb a beating.

molestar [moles'tar] vt to bother; (fastidiar) to annoy; (incomodar) to inconvenience, put out; (perturbar) to trouble, upset ♦ vi to be a nuisance; **~se** vr to bother; (incomodarse) to go to a lot of trouble; (ofenderse) to take offence; **¿le molesta el ruido?** do you mind the noise?; **siento ~le** I'm sorry to trouble you.

molestia [mo'lestja] nf bother, trouble; (incomodidad) inconvenience; (MED) discomfort; **no es ninguna ~** it's no trouble at all.

molesto, a [mo'lesto, a] adj (que fastidia) annoying; (incómodo) inconvenient; (inquieto) uncomfortable, ill at ease; (enfadado) annoyed; **estar ~** (MED) to be in some discomfort, estar **~ con algn** (fig) to be cross with sb; **me sentí ~** I felt embarrassed.

molido, a [mo'liðo, a] adj (machacado) ground; (pulverizado) powdered; **estar ~** (fig) to be exhausted o dead beat.

molinero [moli'nero] nm miller.

molinillo [moli'niʎo] nm hand mill; **~ de carne/café** mincer/coffee grinder.

molino [mo'lino] nm (edificio) mill; (máquina) grinder.

mollera [mo'ʎera] nf (ANAT) crown of the head; (fam: seso) brains pl; **duro de ~** (estúpido) thick.

Molucas [mo'lukas] nfpl: **las (Islas) ~** the Moluccas, the Molucca Islands.

molusco [mo'lusko] nm mollusc.

momentáneo, a [momen'taneo, a] adj momentary.

momento [mo'mento] nm (gen) moment; (TEC) momentum; **de ~** at the moment, for the moment; **en ese ~** at that moment, just then; **por el ~** for the time being.

momia ['momja] nf mummy.

mona ['mona] nf V **mono**.

Mónaco ['monako] nm Monaco.

monada [mo'naða] nf (de niño) charming habit; (cosa primorosa) lovely thing; (chica) pretty girl; **¡qué ~!** isn't it cute?

monaguillo [mona'ɣiʎo] nm altar boy.

monarca [mo'narka] nm/f monarch, ruler.

monarquía [monar'kia] nf monarchy.

monárquico, a [mo'narkiko, a] nm/f royalist, monarchist.

monasterio [monas'terjo] nm monastery.

Moncloa [mon'kloa] nf: **la ~** official residence of the Spanish Prime Minister.

monda ['monda] nf (poda) pruning; (: de árbol) lopping; (: de fruta) peeling; (cáscara) skin; **¡es la ~!** (fam: fantástico)

it's great!; (: *el colmo*) it's the limit!;
(: *persona*: *gracioso*) he's a knockout!

mondadientes [monda'ðjentes] *nm inv*
toothpick.

mondar [mon'dar] *vt* (*limpiar*) to clean;
(*pelar*) to peel; ~**se** *vr*: ~**se de risa** (*fam*)
to split one's sides laughing.

moneda [mo'neða] *nf* (*tipo de dinero*)
currency, money; (*pieza*) coin; **una** ~ **de
5 pesetas** a 5 peseta coin; ~ **de curso
legal** tender; ~ **extranjera** foreign
exchange; ~ **única** single currency; **es** ~
corriente (*fig*) it's common knowledge.

monedero [mone'ðero] *nm* purse.

monegasco, a [mone'ɣasko, a] *adj* of *o*
from Monaco, Monegasque ♦ *nm/f*
Monegasque.

monetario, a [mone'tarjo, a] *adj*
monetary, financial.

monetarista [moneta'rista] *adj*, *nm/f*
monetarist.

mongólico, a [mon'goliko, a] *adj*, *nm/f*
Mongol.

monigote [moni'ɣote] *nm* (*dibujo*) doodle;
(*de papel*) cut-out figure; (*pey*) wimp; *V tb*
Día de los (Santos) Inocentes.

monitor [moni'tor] *nm* (*INFORM*) monitor;
~ **en color** colour monitor; ~ **fósfor
verde** green screen.

monja ['monxa] *nf* nun.

monje ['monxe] *nm* monk.

mono, a ['mono, a] *adj* (*bonito*) lovely,
pretty; (*gracioso*) nice, charming ♦ *nm/f*
monkey, ape ♦ *nm* dungarees *pl*; (*overo-
les*) overalls *pl*; (*fam*: *de droges*) cold
turkey; **una chica muy mona** a very
pretty girl; **dormir la** ~ to sleep it off.

monóculo [mo'nokulo] *nm* monocle.

monografía [monoɣra'fia] *nf* monograph.

monolingüe [mono'lingwe] *adj*
monolingual.

monólogo [mo'noloɣo] *nm* monologue.

monomando [mono'mando] *nm* (*tb*: **grifo**
~) mixer tap.

monoparental [monoparen'tal] *adj*: **familia**
~ single-parent family.

monopatín [monopa'tin] *nm* skateboard.

monopolice [monopo'liθe] *etc vb V*
monopolizar.

monopolio [mono'poljo] *nm* monopoly; ~
total absolute monopoly.

monopolista [monopo'lista] *adj*, *nm/f*
monopolist.

monopolizar [monopoli'θar] *vt* to
monopolize.

monosílabo, a [mono'silaßo, a] *adj*
monosyllabic ♦ *nm* monosyllable.

monotonía [monoto'nia] *nf* (*sonido*)

monotone; (*fig*) monotony.

monótono, a [mo'notono, a] *adj*
monotonous.

mono-usuario, a [monou'swarjo, a] *adj*
(*INFORM*) single-user.

monóxido [mo'noksiðo] *nm* monoxide; ~
de carbono carbon monoxide.

Mons. *abr* (*REL*) = **Monseñor**.

monseñor [monse'ɲor] *nm* monsignor.

monserga [mon'serɣa] *nf* (*lenguaje
confuso*) gibberish; (*tonterías*) drivel.

monstruo ['monstrwo] *nm* monster ♦ *adj
inv* fantastic.

monstruoso, a [mons'trwoso, a] *adj*
monstrous.

monta ['monta] *nf* total, sum; **de poca** ~
unimportant, of little account.

montacargas [monta'karɣas] *nm inv*
service lift (*BRIT*), freight elevator (*US*).

montador [monta'ðor] *nm* (*para montar*)
mounting block; (*profesión*) fitter; (*CINE*)
film editor.

montaje [mon'taxe] *nm* assembly;
(*organización*) fitting up; (*TEAT*) décor;
(*CINE*) montage.

montante [mon'tante] *nm* (*poste*) upright;
(*soporte*) stanchion; (*ARQ*: *de puerta*)
transom; (: *de ventana*) mullion; (*suma*)
amount, total.

montaña [mon'taɲa] *nf* (*monte*) mountain;
(*sierra*) mountains *pl*, mountainous area;
(*AM*: *selva*) forest; ~ **rusa** roller coaster.

montañero, a [monta'ɲero, a] *adj*
mountain *cpd* ♦ *nm/f* mountaineer,
climber.

montañés, esa [monta'ɲes, esa] *adj*
mountain *cpd*; (*de Santander*) of *o* from
the Santander region ♦ *nm/f* highlander;
native *o* inhabitant of the Santander
region.

montañismo [monta'ɲismo] *nm*
mountaineering, climbing.

montañoso, a [monta'ɲoso, a] *adj*
mountainous.

montar [mon'tar] *vt* (*subir a*) to mount, get
on; (*caballo etc*) to ride; (*TEC*) to
assemble, put together; (*negocio*) to set
up; (*colocar*) to lift on to; (*CINE*: *película*)
to edit; (*TEAT*: *obra*) to stage, put on;
(*CULIN*: *batir*) to whip, beat
♦ *vi* to mount, get on; (*sobresalir*) to
overlap; ~ **en cólera** to get angry; ~ **un
número** *o* **numerito** to make a scene;
tanto monta it makes no odds.

montaraz [monta'raθ] *adj* mountain *cpd*,
highland *cpd*; (*pey*) uncivilized.

monte ['monte] *nm* (*montaña*) mountain;
(*bosque*) woodland; (*área sin cultivar*) wild

area, wild country; ~ **de piedad**
pawnshop; ~ **alto** forest; ~ **bajo**
scrub(land).

montera [mon'tera] nf (sombrero) cloth
cap; (de torero) bullfighter's hat.

monto ['monto] nm total, amount.

montón [mon'ton] nm heap, pile; **un ~ de**
(fig) heaps of, lots of; **a montones** by the
score, galore.

montura [mon'tura] nf (cabalgadura)
mount; (silla) saddle; (arreos) harness;
(de joya) mounting; (de gafas) frame.

monumental [monumen'tal] adj (tb fig)
monumental; **zona ~** area of historical
interest.

monumento [monu'mento] nm monument;
(de conmemoración) memorial.

monzón [mon'θon] nm monsoon.

moña ['mona] nf hair ribbon.

moño ['mono] nm (de pelo) bun; **estar
hasta el ~** (fam) to be fed up to the back
teeth.

MOPTMA nm abr = Ministerio de Obras
Públicas, Transporte y Medio Ambiente.

moqueta [mo'keta] nf fitted carpet.

moquillo [mo'kiʎo] nm (enfermedad)
distemper.

mora ['mora] nf (BOT) mulberry;
(: zarzamora) blackberry; (COM): **en ~** in
arrears.

morado, a [mo'raðo, a] adj purple, violet
♦ nm bruise ♦ nf (casa) dwelling, abode;
pasarlas moradas to have a tough time
of it.

moral [mo'ral] adj moral ♦ nf (ética) ethics
pl; (moralidad) morals pl, morality;
(ánimo) morale; **tener baja la ~** to be in
low spirits.

moraleja [mora'lexa] nf moral.

moralice [mora'liθe] etc vb V **moralizar.**

moralidad [morali'ðað] nf morals pl,
morality.

moralizar [morali'θar] vt to moralize.

morar [mo'rar] vi to live, dwell.

moratón [mora'ton] nm bruise.

moratoria [mora'torja] nf moratorium.

morbo ['morβo] nm (fam) morbid pleasure.

morbosidad [morβosi'ðað] nf morbidity.

morboso, a [mor'βoso, a] adj morbid.

morcilla [mor'θiʎa] nf blood sausage,
≈ black pudding (BRIT).

mordaz [mor'ðaθ] adj (crítica) biting,
scathing.

mordaza [mor'ðaθa] nf (para la boca) gag;
(TEC) clamp.

morder [mor'ðer] vt to bite; (mordisquear)
to nibble; (fig: consumir) to eat away, eat
into ♦ vi, ~**se** vr to bite; **está que muerde**

he's hopping mad; ~**se la lengua** to hold
one's tongue.

mordida [mor'ðiða] nf (AM fam) bribe.

mordisco [mor'ðisko] nm bite.

mordisquear [morðiske'ar] vt to nibble at.

moreno, a [mo'reno, a] adj (color) (dark)
brown; (de tez) dark; (de pelo ~) dark-
haired; (negro) black ♦ nm/f (de tez) dark-
skinned man/woman; (de pelo) dark-
haired man/woman.

morfina [mor'fina] nf morphine.

morfinómano, a [morfi'nomano, a] adj
addicted to hard drugs ♦ nm/f drug
addict.

morgue ['morgue] nf (AM) mortuary (BRIT),
morgue (US).

moribundo, a [mori'βundo, a] adj dying
♦ nm/f dying person.

morir [mo'rir] vi to die; (fuego) to die
down; (luz) to go out; ~**se** vr to die; (fig)
to be dying; (FERRO etc: vías) to end;
(calle) to come out; **fue muerto a tiros/en
un accidente** he was shot (dead)/was
killed in an accident; ~ **de frío/hambre**
to die of cold/starve to death; **¡me
muero de hambre!** (fig) I'm starving!;
~**se por algo** to be dying for sth; ~**se
por algn** to be crazy about sb.

mormón, ona [mor'mon, ona] nm/f
Mormon.

moro, a ['moro, a] adj Moorish ♦ nm/f
Moor; **¡hay ~s en la costa!** watch out!

moroso, a [mo'roso, a] adj (lento) slow
♦ nm (COM) bad debtor, defaulter;
deudor ~ (COM) slow payer.

morral [mo'rral] nm haversack.

morriña [mo'rrina] nf homesickness; **tener
~** to be homesick.

morro ['morro] nm (ZOOL) snout, nose;
(AUTO, AVIAT) nose; (fam: labio) (thick)
lip; **beber a ~** to drink from the bottle;
caer de ~ to nosedive; **estar de ~s (con
algn)** to be in a bad mood (with sb);
tener ~ to have a nerve.

morrocotudo, a [morroko'tuðo, a] adj
(fam) (fantástico) smashing; (riña, golpe)
tremendous; (fuerte) strong; (pesado)
heavy; (difícil) awkward.

morsa ['morsa] nf walrus.

morse ['morse] nm Morse (code).

mortadela [morta'ðela] nf mortadella,
bologna sausage.

mortaja [mor'taxa] nf shroud; (TEC)
mortise; (AM) cigarette paper.

mortal [mor'tal] adj mortal; (golpe) deadly.

mortalidad [mortali'ðað], **mortandad**
[mortan'dað] nf mortality.

mortecino, a [morte'θino, a] adj (débil)

weak; (_luz_) dim; (_color_) dull.

mortero [mor'tero] _nm_ mortar.

mortífero, a [mor'tifero, a] _adj_ deadly, lethal.

mortificar [mortifi'kar] _vt_ to mortify; (_atormentar_) to torment.

mortifique [morti'fike] _etc vb_ V **mortificar**.

mortuorio, a [mor'tworjo, a] _adj_ mortuary, death _cpd_.

Mosa ['mosa] _nm_: **el (Río)** ~ the Meuse.

mosaico [mo'saiko] _nm_ mosaic.

mosca ['moska] _nf_ fly; **por si las** ~**s** just in case; **estar** ~ (_desconfiar_) to smell a rat; **tener la** ~ **en** _o_ **detrás de la oreja** to be wary.

moscovita [mosko'βita] _adj_ Muscovite, Moscow _cpd_ ♦ _nm/f_ Muscovite.

Moscú [mos'ku] _nm_ Moscow.

mosquear [moske'ar] (_fam_) _vt_ (_hacer sospechar_) to make suspicious; (_fastidiar_) to annoy; ~**se** _vr_ (_enfadarse_) to get annoyed; (_ofenderse_) to take offence.

mosquita [mos'kita] _nf_: **parece una** ~ **muerta** he looks as though butter wouldn't melt in his mouth.

mosquitero [moski'tero] _nm_ mosquito net.

mosquito [mos'kito] _nm_ mosquito.

Mossos ['mosos] _nmpl_: ~ **d'Esquadra** Catalan police; V _tb_ **policía**.

mostaza [mos'taθa] _nf_ mustard.

mosto ['mosto] _nm_ unfermented grape juice.

mostrador [mostra'ðor] _nm_ (_de tienda_) counter; (_de café_) bar.

mostrar [mos'trar] _vt_ to show; (_exhibir_) to display, exhibit; (_explicar_) to explain; ~**se** _vr_: ~**se amable** to be kind; to prove to be kind; **no se muestra muy inteligente** he doesn't seem (to be) very intelligent; ~ **en pantalla** (_INFORM_) to display.

mota ['mota] _nf_ speck, tiny piece; (_en diseño_) dot.

mote ['mote] _nm_ (_apodo_) nickname.

motín [mo'tin] _nm_ (_del pueblo_) revolt, rising; (_del ejército_) mutiny.

motivación [motiβa'θjon] _nf_ motivation.

motivar [moti'βar] _vt_ (_causar_) to cause, motivate; (_explicar_) to explain, justify.

motivo [mo'tiβo] _nm_ motive, reason; (_ARTE, MUS_) motif; **con** ~ **de** (_debido a_) because of; (_en ocasión de_) on the occasion of; (_con el fin de_) in order to; **sin** ~ for no reason at all.

moto ['moto] _nf_, **motocicleta** [motoθi'kleta] _nf_ motorbike (_BRIT_),

motorcycle.

motoneta [moto'neta] _nf_ (_AM_) Vespa ®.

motor, a [mo'tor, a] _adj_ (_TEC_) motive; (_ANAT_) motor ♦ _nm_ motor, engine; ~ **a chorro** _o_ **de reacción/de explosión** jet engine/internal combustion engine ♦ _nf_ motorboat.

motorismo [moto'rismo] _nm_ motorcycling.

motorista [moto'rista] _nm/f_ (_esp AM_: _automovilista_) motorist; (: _motociclista_) motorcyclist.

motorizado, a [motori'θaðo, a] _adj_ motorized.

motosierra [moto'sjerra] _nf_ mechanical saw.

motriz [mo'triz] _adj_: **fuerza** ~ motive power; (_fig_) driving force.

movedizo, a [moβe'ðiθo, a] _adj_ (_inseguro_) unsteady; (_fig_) unsettled, changeable; (_persona_) fickle.

mover [mo'βer] _vt_ to move; (_cambiar de lugar_) to shift; (_cabeza: para negar_) to shake; (: _para asentir_) to nod; (_accionar_) to drive; (_fig_) to cause, provoke; ~**se** _vr_ to move; (_mar_) to get rough; (_viento_) to rise; (_fig: apurarse_) to get a move on; (: _transformarse_) to be on the move.

movible [mo'βiβle] _adj_ (_no fijo_) movable; (_móvil_) mobile; (_cambiadizo_) changeable.

movido, a [mo'βiðo, a] _adj_ (_FOTO_) blurred; (_persona: activo_) active; (_mar_) rough; (_día_) hectic ♦ _nf_ move; **la movida madrileña** the Madrid scene.

móvil ['moβil] _adj_ mobile; (_pieza de máquina_) moving; (_mueble_) movable ♦ _nm_ motive.

movilice [moβi'liθe] _etc vb_ V **movilizar**.

movilidad [moβili'ðað] _nf_ mobility.

movilizar [moβili'θar] _vt_ to mobilize.

movimiento [moβi'mjento] _nm_ (_gen_, _LITERATURA, POL_) movement; (_TEC_) motion; (_actividad_) activity; (_MUS_) tempo; **el M**~ the Falangist Movement; ~ **de bloques** (_INFORM_) block move; ~ **de mercancías** (_COM_) turnover, volume of business; ~ **obrero/sindical** workers'/ trade union movement; ~ **sísmico** earth tremor.

Mozambique [moθam'bike] _nm_ Mozambique.

mozambiqueño, a [moθambi'keɲo, a] _adj_, _nm/f_ Mozambican.

mozo, a ['moθo, a] _adj_ (_joven_) young; (_soltero_) single, unmarried ♦ _nm/f_ (_joven_) youth, young man/girl; (_camarero_) waiter; (_camarera_) waitress; ~ **de**

estación porter.
MPAIAC [emepa'jak] *nm abr* (*ESP POL*)
= *Movimiento para la Autodeterminación y la Independencia del Archipiélago Canario.*
mucama [mu'kama] *nf* (*AM*) maid.
muchacho, a [mu'tʃatʃo, a] *nm/f* (*niño*) boy/girl; (*criado*) servant/servant *o* maid.
muchedumbre [mutʃe'ðumbre] *nf* crowd.
muchísimo, a [mu'tʃisimo, a] *adj* (*superlativo de* **mucho**) lots and lots of, ever so much ♦ *adv* ever so much.

══════════════ PALABRA CLAVE

mucho, a ['mutʃo, a] *adj* **1** (*cantidad*) a lot of, much; (*número*) lots of, a lot of, many; · dinero a lot of money; **hace ~ calor** it's very hot; **muchas amigas** lots *o* a lot of *o* many friends
2 (*sg: fam*): **ésta es mucha casa para él** this house is much too big for him; **había ~ borracho** there were a lot *o* lots of drunks
♦ *pron:* **tengo ~ que hacer** I've got a lot to do; **~s dicen que ...** a lot of people say that ...; *V tb* **tener**
♦ *adv* **1**: **me gusta ~** I like it a lot *o* very much; **lo siento ~** I'm very sorry; **come ~** he eats a lot; **trabaja ~** he works hard; **¿te vas a quedar ~?** are you going to be staying long?; **~ más/menos** much *o* a lot more/less
2 (*respuesta*) very; **¿estás cansado? – ¡~!** are you tired? – very!
3 (*locuciones*): **como ~** at (the) most; **el mejor con ~** by far the best; **¡ni ~ menos!** far from it!; **no es rico ni ~ menos** he's far from being rich
4: **por ~ que: por ~ que le creas** however much *o* no matter how much you believe him

muda ['muða] *nf* (*de ropa*) change of clothing; (*ZOOL*) moult; (*de serpiente*) slough.
mudanza [mu'ðanθa] *nf* (*cambio*) change; (*de casa*) move; **estar de ~** to be moving.
mudar [mu'ðar] *vt* to change; (*ZOOL*) to shed ♦ *vi* to change; **~se** *vr* (*la ropa*) to change; **~se de casa** to move house.
mudo, a ['muðo, a] *adj* dumb; (*callado, película*) silent; (*LING: letra*) mute; (: *consonante*) voiceless; **quedarse ~ (de)** (*fig*) to be dumb with; **quedarse ~ de asombro** to be speechless.
mueble ['mweßle] *nm* piece of furniture; **~s** *nmpl* furniture *sg*.

mueble-bar [mweßle'ßar] *nm* cocktail cabinet.
mueca ['mweka] *nf* face, grimace; **hacer ~s a** to make faces at.
muela ['mwela] *etc vb V* **moler** ♦ *nf* (*diente*) tooth; (: *de atrás*) molar; (*de molino*) millstone; (*de afilar*) grindstone; **~ del juicio** wisdom tooth.
muelle ['mweʎe] *adj* (*blando*) soft; (*fig*) soft, easy ♦ *nm* spring; (*NAUT*) wharf; (*malecón*) jetty.
muera ['mwera] *etc vb V* **morir**.
muerda ['mwerða] *etc vb V* **morder**.
muermo ['mwermo] *nm* (*fam*) wimp.
muerte ['mwerte] *nf* death; (*homicidio*) murder; **dar ~ a** to kill; **de mala ~** (*fam*) lousy, rotten; **es la ~** (*fam*) it's deadly boring.
muerto, a ['mwerto, a] *pp de* **morir** ♦ *adj* dead; (*color*) dull ♦ *nm/f* dead man/woman; (*difunto*) deceased; (*cadáver*) corpse; **cargar con el ~** (*fam*) to carry the can; **echar el ~ a algn** to pass the buck; **hacer el ~** (*nadando*) to float; **estar ~ de cansancio** to be dead tired.
muesca ['mweska] *nf* nick.
muestra ['mwestra] *etc vb V* **mostrar** ♦ *nf* (*señal*) indication, sign; (*demostración*) demonstration; (*prueba*) proof; (*estadística*) sample; (*modelo*) model, pattern; (*testimonio*) token; **dar ~s de** to show signs of; **~ al azar** (*COM*) random sample.
muestrario [mwes'trarjo] *nm* collection of samples; (*exposición*) showcase.
muestreo [mwes'treo] *nm* sample, sampling.
mueva ['mweßa] *etc vb V* **mover**.
mugir [mu'xir] *vi* (*vaca*) to moo.
mugre ['muɣre] *nf* dirt, filth, muck.
mugriento, a [mu'ɣrjento, a] *adj* dirty, filthy mucky.
mugroso, a [muɣ'roso, a] *adj* (*AM*) filthy, grubby.
muja ['muxa] *etc vb V* **mugir**.
mujer [mu'xer] *nf* woman; (*esposa*) wife.
mujeriego [muxe'rjexo] *nm* womaniser.
mula ['mula] *nf* mule.
muladar [mula'ðar] *nm* dungheap, dunghill.
mulato, a [mu'lato, a] *adj, nm/f* mulatto.
muleta [mu'leta] *nf* (*para andar*) crutch; (*TAUR*) stick with red cape attached.
muletilla [mule'tiʎa] *nf* (*palabra*) pet word, tag; (*de cómico*) catch phrase.
mullido, a [mu'ʎiðo, a] *adj* (*cama*) soft; (*hierba*) soft, springy.
multa ['multa] *nf* fine; **echar** *o* **poner una ~**

a to fine.

multar [mul'tar] *vt* to fine; (*DEPORTE*) to penalize.

multiacceso [multjak'θeso] *adj* (*INFORM*) multi-access.

multicine [multi'θine] *nm* multiscreen cinema.

multicolor [multiko'lor] *adj* multicoloured.

multicopista [multiko'pista] *nm* duplicator.

multimillonario, a [multimiʎo'narjo, a] *adj* (*contrato*) multimillion pound *o* dollar *cpd* ♦ *nm/f* multimillionaire/-millionairess.

multinacional [multinaθjo'nal] *adj, nf* multinational.

múltiple ['multiple] *adj* multiple; (*pl*) many, numerous; **de tarea** ~ (*INFORM*) multi-tasking; **de usuario** ~ (*INFORM*) multi-user.

multiplicar [multipli'kar] *vt* (*MAT*) to multiply; (*fig*) to increase; ~**se** *vr* (*BIO*) to multiply; (*fig*) to be everywhere at once.

multiplique [multi'plike] *etc vb* V **multiplicar**.

múltiplo ['multiplo] *adj, nm* multiple.

multitud [multi'tuð] *nf* (*muchedumbre*) crowd; ~ **de** lots of.

multitudinario, a [multituði'narjo, a] *adj* (*numeroso*) multitudinous; (*de masa*) mass *cpd*.

mundanal [munda'nal] *adj* worldly; **lejos del** ~ **ruido** far from the madding crowd.

mundano, a [mun'dano, a] *adj* worldly; (*de moda*) fashionable.

mundial [mun'djal] *adj* world-wide, universal; (*guerra, récord*) world *cpd*.

mundialmente [mundjal'mente] *adv* worldwide; ~ **famoso** world-famous.

mundo ['mundo] *nm* world; (*ámbito*) world, circle; **el otro** ~ the next world; **el** ~ **del espectáculo** show business; **todo el** ~ everybody; **tener** ~ to be experienced, know one's way around; **el** ~ **es un pañuelo** it's a small world; **no es nada del otro** ~ it's nothing special; **se le cayó el** ~ **(encima)** his world fell apart.

Munich ['munitʃ] *nm* Munich.

munición [muni'θjon] *nf* (*MIL: provisiones*) stores *pl*, supplies *pl*; (: *de armas*) ammunition.

municipal [muniθi'pal] *adj* (*elección*) municipal; (*concejo*) town *cpd*, local; (*piscina etc*) public ♦ *nm* (*guardia*) policeman.

municipio [muni'θipjo] *nm* (*ayuntamiento*) town council, corporation; (*territorio administrativo*) town, municipality.

muñeca [mu'ɲeka] *nf* (*ANAT*) wrist; (*juguete*) doll.

muñeco [mu'ɲeko] *nm* (*figura*) figure; (*marioneta*) puppet; (*fig*) puppet, pawn; (*niño*) pretty little boy; ~ **de nieve** snowman.

muñequera [muɲe'kera] *nf* wristband.

muñón [mu'ɲon] *nm* (*ANAT*) stump.

mural [mu'ral] *adj* mural, wall *cpd* ♦ *nm* mural.

muralla [mu'raʎa] *nf* (city) wall(s) (*pl*).

murciano, a [mur'θjano, a] *adj* of *o* from Murcia ♦ *nm/f* native *o* inhabitant of Murcia.

murciélago [mur'θjelaɣo] *nm* bat.

murga ['murɣa] *nf* (*banda*) band of street musicians; **dar la** ~ to be a nuisance.

murmullo [mur'muʎo] *nm* murmur(ing); (*cuchicheo*) whispering; (*de arroyo*) murmur, rippling; (*de hojas, viento*) rustle, rustling; (*ruido confuso*) hum(ming).

murmuración [murmura'θjon] *nf* gossip; (*críticas*) backbiting.

murmurador, a [murmura'ðor, a] *adj* gossiping; (*criticón*) backbiting ♦ *nm/f* gossip; backbiter.

murmurar [murmu'rar] *vi* to murmur, whisper; (*criticar*) to criticize; (*cotillear*) to gossip.

muro ['muro] *nm* wall; ~ **de contención** retaining wall.

mus [mus] *nm* card game.

musaraña [musa'raɲa] *nf* (*ZOOL*) shrew; (*insecto*) creepy-crawly; **pensar en las** ~**s** to daydream.

muscular [musku'lar] *adj* muscular.

músculo ['muskulo] *nm* muscle.

musculoso, a [musku'loso, a] *adj* muscular.

museo [mu'seo] *nm* museum; ~ **de arte** *o* **de pintura** art gallery; ~ **de cera** waxworks.

musgo ['musɣo] *nm* moss.

musical [musi'kal] *adj, nm* musical.

músico, a ['musiko, a] *adj* musical ♦ *nm/f* musician ♦ *nf* music; **irse con la música a otra parte** to clear off.

musitar [musi'tar] *vt, vi* to mutter, mumble.

muslo ['muslo] *nm* thigh; (*de pollo*) leg, drumstick.

mustio, a ['mustjo, a] *adj* (*persona*) depressed, gloomy; (*planta*) faded, withered.

musulmán, ana [musul'man, ana] *nm/f* Moslem, Muslim.

mutación [muta'θjon] *nf* (*BIO*) mutation;

(: *cambio*) (sudden) change.
mutilar [muti'lar] *vt* to mutilate; (*a una persona*) to maim.
mutis ['mutis] *nm inv* (*TEAT*) exit; **hacer ~** (*TEAT*: *retirarse*) to exit, go off; (*fig*) to say nothing.
mutismo [mu'tismo] *nm* silence.
mutualidad [mutwali'ðað] *nf* (*reciprocidad*) mutual character; (*asociación*) friendly o benefit (*US*) society.
mutuamente [mutwa'mente] *adv* mutually.
mutuo, a ['mutwo, a] *adj* mutual.
muy [mwi] *adv* very; (*demasiado*) too; **M~ Señor mío** Dear Sir; **~ bien** (*de acuerdo*) all right; **~ de noche** very late at night; **eso es ~ de él** that's just like him; **eso es ~ español** that's typically Spanish.

$$N n$$

N, n ['ene] *nf* (*letra*) N, n; **N de Navarra** N for Nellie (*BRIT*) o Nan (*US*).
N *abr* (= *norte*) N.
N. *abr* (= *noviembre*) Nov; (*AM*: = *moneda nacional*) local currency; **le entregaron sólo N.$2.000** they only gave him $2000 pesos.
N.º *abr* (= *número*) No.
n. *abr* (*LING*: = *nombre*) n; (= *nacido*) b.
n/ *abr* = **nuestro, a.**
nabo ['naβo] *nm* turnip.
nácar ['nakar] *nm* mother-of-pearl.
nacer [na'θer] *vi* to be born; (*huevo*) to hatch; (*vegetal*) to sprout; (*río*) to rise; (*fig*) to begin, originate, have its origins; **nació para poeta** he was born to be a poet; **nadie nace enseñado** we all have to learn; **nació una sospecha en su mente** a suspicion formed in her mind.
nacido, a [na'θiðo, a] *adj* born; **recién ~** newborn.
naciente [na'θjente] *adj* new, emerging; (*sol*) rising.
nacimiento [naθi'mjento] *nm* birth; (*fig*) birth, origin; (*de Navidad*) Nativity; (*linaje*) descent, family; (*de río*) source; **ciego de ~** blind from birth.
nación [na'θjon] *nf* nation; (*pueblo*) people; **Naciones Unidas** United Nations.
nacional [naθjo'nal] *adj* national; (*COM,*

ECON) domestic, home *cpd*.
nacionalice [naθjona'liθe] *etc vb V* **nacionalizar.**
nacionalidad [naθjonali'ðað] *nf* nationality; (*ESP POL*) autonomous region.
nacionalismo [naθjona'lismo] *nm* nationalism.
nacionalista [naθjona'lista] *adj, nm/f* nationalist.
nacionalizar [naθjonali'θar] *vt* to nationalize; **~se** *vr* (*persona*) to become naturalized.
nada ['naða] *pron* nothing ♦ *adv* not at all, in no way ♦ *nf* nothingness; **no decir ~** (*más*) to say nothing (else), not to say anything (else); **¡~ más!** that's all; **de ~** don't mention it; **~ de eso** nothing of the kind; **antes de ~** right away; **como si ~** as if it didn't matter; **no ha sido ~** it's nothing; **la ~** the void.
nadador, a [naða'ðor, a] *nm/f* swimmer.
nadar [na'ðar] *vi* to swim; **~ en la abundancia** (*fig*) to be rolling in money.
nadie ['naðje] *pron* nobody, no-one; **~ habló** nobody spoke; **no había ~** there was nobody there, there wasn't anybody there; **es un don ~** he's a nobody o nonentity.
nadita [na'ðita] (*esp AM*: *fam*) = **nada.**
nado ['naðo]: **a ~** *adv*: **pasar a ~** to swim across.
nafta ['nafta] *nf* (*AM*) petrol (*BRIT*), gas(oline) (*US*).
naftalina [nafta'lina] *nf*: **bolas de ~** mothballs.
náhuatl ['nawatl] *adj, nm* Nahuatl.
naipe ['naipe] *nm* (playing) card; **~s** *nmpl* cards.
nal. *abr* (= *nacional*) nat.
nalgas ['nalɣas] *nfpl* buttocks.
Namibia [na'miβja] *nf* Namibia.
nana ['nana] *nf* lullaby.
napias ['napjas] *nfpl* (*fam*) conk *sg*.
Nápoles ['napoles] *nf* Naples.
napolitano, a [napoli'tano, a] *adj* of o from Naples, Neapolitan ♦ *nm/f* Neapolitan.
naranja [na'ranxa] *adj inv, nf* orange; **media ~** (*fam*) better half; **¡~s de la China!** nonsense!
naranjada [naran'xaða] *nf* orangeade.
naranjo [na'ranxo] *nm* orange tree.
Narbona [nar'βona] *nf* Narbonne.
narcisista [narθi'sista] *adj* narcissistic.
narciso [nar'θiso] *nm* narcissus.
narcotice [narko'tiθe] *etc vb V* **narcotizar.**
narcótico, a [nar'kotiko, a] *adj, nm* narcotic.

narcotizar [narkoti'θar] *vt* to drug.
narcotraficante [narkotrafi'kante] *nm/f*
   narcotics *o* drug trafficker.
narcotráfico [narko'trafiko] *nm* narcotics *o*
   drug trafficking.
nardo ['narðo] *nm* lily.
narices [na'riθes] *nfpl* V **nariz**.
narigón, ona [nari'ɣon, ona], **narigudo, a**
   [nari'ɣuðo, a] *adj* big-nosed.
nariz [na'riθ] *nf* nose; **narices** *nfpl* nostrils;
   ¡**narices!** (*fam*) rubbish!; **delante de las**
   narices de algn under one's (very) nose;
   estar hasta las narices to be completely
   fed up; **meter las narices en algo** to poke
   one's nose into sth.
narración [narra'θjon] *nf* narration.
narrador, a [narra'ðor, a] *nm/f* narrator.
narrar [na'rrar] *vt* to narrate, recount.
narrativo, a [narra'tiβo, a] *adj* narrative
   ♦ *nf* narrative, story.
nasal [na'sal] *adj* nasal.
N.ª S.ra *abr* = *Nuestra Señora*.
nata ['nata] *nf* cream (*tb fig*); (*en leche cocida etc*) skin; ~ **batida** whipped cream.
natación [nata'θjon] *nf* swimming.
natal [na'tal] *adj* natal; (*país*) native; **ciudad**
   ~ home town.
natalicio [nata'liθjo] *nm* birthday.
natalidad [natali'ðað] *nf* birth rate.
natillas [na'tiʎas] *nfpl* (egg) custard *sg*.
natividad [natiβi'ðað] *nf* nativity.
nativo, a [na'tiβo, a] *adj*, *nm/f* native.
nato, a ['nato, a] *adj* born; **un músico** ~ a
   born musician.
natural [natu'ral] *adj* natural; (*fruta etc*)
   fresh ♦ *nm/f* native ♦ *nm* disposition,
   temperament; **buen** ~ good nature; **fruta**
   al ~ fruit in its own juice.
naturaleza [natura'leθa] *nf* nature; (*género*)
   nature, kind; ~ **muerta** still life.
naturalice [natura'liθe] *etc vb* V
   naturalizarse.
naturalidad [naturali'ðað] *nf* naturalness.
naturalización [naturaliθa'θjon] *nf*
   naturalization.
naturalizarse [naturali'θarse] *vr* to become
   naturalized; (*aclimatarse*) to become
   acclimatized.
naturalmente [natural'mente] *adv*
   naturally; ¡~! of course!
naturista [natu'rista] *adj* (*MED*)
   naturopathic ♦ *nm/f* naturopath.
naufragar [naufra'ɣar] *vi* (*barco*) to sink;
   (*gente*) to be shipwrecked; (*fig*) to fail.
naufragio [nau'fraxjo] *nm* shipwreck.
náufrago, a ['naufraxo, a] *nm/f* castaway,
   shipwrecked person.
naufrague [nau'fraxe] *etc vb* V **naufragar**.

náusea ['nausea] *nf* nausea; **me da** ~**s** it
   makes me feel sick.
nauseabundo, a [nausea'βundo, a] *adj*
   nauseating, sickening.
náutico, a ['nautiko, a] *adj* nautical; **club** ~
   sailing *o* yacht club ♦ *nf* navigation,
   seamanship.
navaja [na'βaxa] *nf* (*cortaplumas*) clasp knife
   (*BRIT*), penknife; ~ (**de afeitar**) razor.
navajazo [naβa'xaθo] *nm* (*herida*) gash;
   (*golpe*) slash.
naval [na'βal] *adj* (*MIL*) naval; **construcción**
   ~ shipbuilding; **sector** ~ shipbuilding
   industry.
Navarra [na'βarra] *nf* Navarre.
navarro, a [na'βarro, a] *adj* of *o* from
   Navarre, Navarrese ♦ *nm/f* Navarrese
   ♦ *nm* (*LING*) Navarrese.
nave ['naβe] *nf* (*barco*) ship, vessel; (*ARQ*)
   nave; ~ **espacial** spaceship; **quemar las**
   ~**s** to burn one's boats.
navegación [naβeɣa'θjon] *nf* navigation;
   (*viaje*) sea journey; ~ **aérea** air traffic; ~
   costera coastal shipping; ~ **fluvial** river
   navigation.
navegador [naβeɣa'ðor] *nm* (*INFORM*)
   browser.
navegante [naβe'ɣante] *nm/f* navigator.
navegar [naβe'ɣar] *vi* (*barco*) to sail; (*avión*)
   to fly ♦ *vt* to sail; to fly; (*dirigir el rumbo*
   de) to navigate.
navegue [na'βeɣe] *etc vb* V **navegar**.
Navidad [naβi'ðað] *nf* Christmas; ~**es** *nfpl*
   Christmas time *sg*; **día de** ~ Christmas
   Day; **por** ~**es** at Christmas (time);
   ¡**felices** ~**es**! Merry Christmas.
navideño, a [naβi'ðeɲo, a] *adj* Christmas
   cpd.
navío [na'βio] *nm* ship.
nazi ['naθi] *adj*, *nm/f* Nazi.
nazismo [na'θismo] *nm* Nazism.
n/cta *abr* (*COM*) = *nuestra cuenta*.
N. de la R. *abr* (= *nota de la redacción*)
   editor's note.
N. de la T./del T. *abr* (= *nota de la*
   traductora/del traductor) translator's note.
NE *abr* (= *nor(d)este*) NE.
neblina [ne'βlina] *nf* mist.
nebuloso, a [neβu'loso, a] *adj* foggy;
   (*calinoso*) misty; (*indefinido*) nebulous,
   vague ♦ *nf* nebula.
necedad [neθe'ðað] *nf* foolishness; (*una* ~)
   foolish act.
necesario, a [neθe'sarjo, a] *adj* necessary;
   si fuera *o* **fuese** ~ if need(s) be.
neceser [neθe'ser] *nm* vanity case; (*bolsa*
   grande) holdall.
necesidad [neθesi'ðað] *nf* need; (*lo*

inevitable) necessity; (*miseria*) poverty, need; **en caso de** ~ in case of need *o* emergency; **hacer sus** ~**es** to relieve o.s.

necesitado, a [neθesi'taðo, a] *adj* needy, poor; ~ **de** in need of.

necesitar [neθesi'tar] *vt* to need, require ♦ *vi*: ~ **de** to have need of; ~**se** *vr* to be needed; (*anuncios*) **"necesítase coche"** "car wanted".

necio, a ['neθjo, a] *adj* foolish ♦ *nm/f* fool.

necrología [nekrolo'xia] *nf* obituary.

necrópolis [ne'kropolis] *nf inv* cemetery.

néctar ['nektar] *nm* nectar.

nectarina [nekta'rina] *nf* nectarine.

neerlandés, esa [neerlan'des, esa] *adj* Dutch ♦ *nm/f* Dutchman/woman ♦ *nm* (*LING*) Dutch; **los neerlandeses** the Dutch.

nefando, a [ne'fando, a] *adj* unspeakable.

nefasto, a [ne'fasto, a] *adj* ill-fated, unlucky.

negación [neɣa'θjon] *nf* negation; (*LING*) negative; (*rechazo*) refusal, denial.

negado, a [ne'ɣaðo, a] *adj*: ~ **para** inept at, unfitted for.

negar [ne'ɣar] *vt* (*renegar, rechazar*) to refuse; (*prohibir*) to refuse, deny; (*desmentir*) to deny; ~**se** *vr*: ~**se a hacer algo** to refuse to do sth.

negativo, a [neɣa'tiβo, a] *adj* negative ♦ *nm* (*FOTO*) negative; (*MAT*) minus ♦ *nf* (*gen*) negative; (*rechazo*) refusal, denial; **negativa rotunda** flat refusal.

negligencia [neɣli'xenθja] *nf* negligence.

negligente [neɣli'xente] *adj* negligent.

negociable [neɣo'θjaβle] *adj* (*COM*) negotiable.

negociación [neɣoθja'θjon] *nf* negotiation.

negociado [neɣo'θjaðo] *nm* department, section.

negociante [neɣo'θjante] *nm/f* businessman/woman.

negociar [neɣo'θjar] *vt, vi* to negotiate; ~ **en** to deal in, trade in.

negocio [ne'ɣoθjo] *nm* (*COM*) business; (*asunto*) affair, business; (*operación comercial*) deal, transaction; (*AM*) shop, store; (*lugar*) place of business; **los** ~**s** business *sg*; **hacer** ~ to do business; **el** ~ **del libro** the book trade; ~ **autorizado** licensed trade; **hombre de** ~**s** businessman; ~ **sucio** shady deal; **hacer un buen** ~ to pull off a profitable deal; **¡mal** ~! it looks bad!

negra ['neɣra] *nf V* **negro** ♦ *nf* (*MUS*) crotchet.

negrita [ne'ɣrita] *nf* (*TIP*) bold face; **en** ~ in bold (type).

negro, a ['neɣro, a] *adj* black; (*suerte*) awful, atrocious; (*humor etc*) sad; (*lúgubre*) gloomy ♦ *nm* (*color*) black ♦ *nm/f* Negro/Negress, black ♦ *nf* (*MUS*) crotchet; ~ **como la boca del lobo** pitch-black; **estoy** ~ **con esto** I'm getting desperate about it; **ponerse** ~ (*fam*) to get cross.

negrura [ne'ɣrura] *nf* blackness.

negué [ne'ɣe], **neguemos** [ne'ɣemos] *etc vb V* **negar**.

nene, a ['nene, a] *nm/f* baby, small child.

nenúfar [ne'nufar] *nm* water lily.

neologismo [neolo'xismo] *nm* neologism.

neón [ne'on] *nm* neon.

neoyorquino, a [neojor'kino, a] *adj* New York *cpd* ♦ *nm/f* New Yorker.

neozelandés, esa [neoθelan'des, esa] *adj* New Zealand *cpd* ♦ *nm/f* New Zealander.

nepotismo [nepo'tismo] *nm* nepotism.

nervio ['nerβjo] *nm* (*ANAT*) nerve; (: *tendón*) tendon; (*fig*) vigour; (*TEC*) rib; **crispar los** ~**s a algn, poner los** ~**s de punta a algn** to get on sb's nerves.

nerviosismo [nerβjo'sismo] *nm* nervousness, nerves *pl*.

nervioso, a [ner'βjoso, a] *adj* nervous; (*sensible*) nervy, highly-strung; (*impaciente*) restless; **¡no te pongas** ~! take it easy!

nervudo, a [ner'βuðo, a] *adj* tough; (*mano*) sinewy.

neto, a ['neto, a] *adj* clear; (*limpio*) clean; (*COM*) net.

neumático, a [neu'matiko, a] *adj* pneumatic ♦ *nm* (*ESP*) tyre (*BRIT*), tire (*US*); ~ **de recambio** spare tyre.

neumonía [neumo'nia] *nf* pneumonia.

neura ['neura] (*fam*) *nm/f* (*persona*) neurotic ♦ *nf* (*obsesión*) obsession.

neuralgia [neu'ralxja] *nf* neuralgia.

neurálgico, a [neu'ralxiko, a] *adj* neuralgic; (*fig: centro*) nerve *cpd*.

neurastenia [neuras'tenja] *nf* neurasthenia; (*fig*) excitability.

neurasténico, a [neuras'teniko, a] *adj* neurasthenic; excitable.

neurólogo, a [neu'roloɣo, a] *nm/f* neurologist.

neurona [neu'rona] *nf* neuron.

neurosis [neu'rosis] *nf inv* neurosis.

neurótico, a [neu'rotiko, a] *adj, nm/f* neurotic.

neutral [neu'tral] *adj* neutral.

neutralice [neutra'liθe] *etc vb V* **neutralizar**.

neutralizar [neutrali'θar] *vt* to neutralize; (*contrarrestar*) to counteract.

neutro, a ['neutro, a] *adj* (*BIO, LING*) neuter.

neutrón [neu'tron] *nm* neutron.
nevado, a [ne'ßaðo, a] *adj* snow-covered; (*montaña*) snow-capped; (*fig*) snowy, snow-white ♦ *nf* snowstorm; (*caída de nieve*) snowfall.
nevar [ne'ßar] *vi* to snow ♦ *vt* (*fig*) to whiten.
nevera [ne'ßera] *nf* (*ESP*) refrigerator (*BRIT*), icebox (*US*).
nevisca [ne'ßiska] *nf* flurry of snow.
nexo ['nekso] *nm* link, connection.
n/f *abr* (*COM*) = *nuestro favor*.
ni [ni] *conj* nor, neither; (*tb*: ~ **siquiera**) not even; ~ **que** not even if; ~ **blanco** ~ **negro** neither white nor black; ~ **el uno** ~ **el otro** neither one nor the other.
Nicaragua [nika'raɣwa] *nf* Nicaragua.
nicaragüense [nikara'ɣwense] *adj, nm/f* Nicaraguan.
nicho ['nitʃo] *nm* niche.
nicotina [niko'tina] *nf* nicotine.
nido ['niðo] *nm* nest; (*fig*) hiding place; ~ **de ladrones** den of thieves.
niebla ['njeßla] *nf* fog; (*neblina*) mist; **hay** ~ it is foggy.
niego ['njeɣo] *etc*, **niegue** ['njeɣe] *etc vb V* negar.
nieto, a ['njeto, a] *nm/f* grandson/daughter; ~**s** *nmpl* grandchildren.
nieve ['njeße] *etc vb V* **nevar** ♦ *nf* snow; (*AM*) ice cream; **copo de** ~ snowflake.
N.I.F. *nm abr* (= *Número de Identificación Fiscal*) ID number used for tax purposes.
Nigeria [ni'xerja] *nf* Nigeria.
nigeriano, a [nixe'rjano, a] *adj, nm/f* Nigerian.
nigromancia [nixro'manθja] *nf* necromancy, black magic.
nihilista [nii'lista] *adj* nihilistic ♦ *nm* nihilist.
Nilo ['nilo] *nm*: **el (Río)** ~ the Nile.
nimbo ['nimbo] *nm* (*aureola*) halo; (*nube*) nimbus.
nimiedad [nimje'ðað] *nf* small-mindedness; (*trivialidad*) triviality; (*una* ~) trifle, tiny detail.
nimio, a ['nimjo, a] *adj* trivial, insignificant.
ninfa ['ninfa] *nf* nymph.
ninfómana [nin'fomana] *nf* nymphomaniac.
ninguno, a [nin'guno, a] *adj* (**ningún** *delante de nmsg*) no ♦ *pron* (*nadie*) nobody; (*ni uno*) none, not one; (*ni uno ni otro*) neither; **de ninguna manera** by no means, not at all; **no voy a ninguna parte** I'm not going anywhere.
niña ['niɲa] *nf V* niño.

niñera [ni'ɲera] *nf* nursemaid, nanny.
niñería [niɲe'ria] *nf* childish act.
niñez [ni'ɲeθ] *nf* childhood; (*infancia*) infancy.
niño, a ['niɲo, a] *adj* (*joven*) young; (*inmaduro*) immature ♦ *nm* (*chico*) boy, child ♦ *nf* girl, child; (*ANAT*) pupil; **los** ~**s** the children; ~ **bien** rich kid; ~ **expósito** foundling; ~ **de pecho** babe-in-arms; ~ **prodigio** child prodigy; **de** ~ as a child; **ser el** ~ **mimado de algn** to be sb's pet; **ser la niña de los ojos de algn** to be the apple of sb's eye.
nipón, ona [ni'pon, ona] *adj, nm/f* Japanese; **los nipones** the Japanese.
níquel ['nikel] *nm* nickel.
niquelar [nike'lar] *vt* (*TEC*) to nickel-plate.
níspero ['nispero] *nm* medlar.
nitidez [niti'ðeθ] *nf* (*claridad*) clarity; (: *de atmósfera*) brightness; (: *de imagen*) sharpness.
nítido, a ['nitiðo, a] *adj* bright; (*fig*) pure; (*imagen*) clear, sharp.
nitrato [ni'trato] *nm* nitrate.
nitrógeno [ni'troxeno] *nm* nitrogen.
nitroglicerina [nitroɣliθe'rina] *nf* nitroglycerine.
nivel [ni'ßel] *nm* (*GEO*) level; (*norma*) level, standard; (*altura*) height; ~ **de aceite** oil level; ~ **de aire** spirit level; ~ **de vida** standard of living; **al** ~ **de** on a level with, at the same height as; (*fig*) on a par with; **a 900m sobre el** ~ **del mar** at 900m above sea level.
nivelado, a [niße'laðo, a] *adj* level, flat; (*TEC*) flush.
nivelar [niße'lar] *vt* to level out; (*fig*) to even up; (*COM*) to balance.
Niza ['niθa] *nf* Nice.
n/l. *abr* (*COM*) = *nuestra letra*.
NNE *abr* (= *nornordeste*) NNE.
NNO *abr* (= *nornoroeste*) NNW.
NN. UU. *nfpl abr* (= *Naciones Unidas*) UN *sg*.
NO *abr* (= *noroeste*) NW.
no [no] *adv* no; (*con verbo*) not ♦ *excl* no!; ~ **tengo nada** I don't have anything, I have nothing; ~ **es el mío** it's not mine; **ahora** ~ not now; ¿~ **lo sabes?** don't you know?; ~ **mucho** not much; ~ **bien termine, lo entregaré** as soon as I finish I'll hand it over; **¡a que** ~ **lo sabes!** I bet you don't know!; **¡cómo** ~! of course!; **pacto de** ~ **agresión** non-aggression pact; **los países** ~ **alineados** the non-aligned countries; **el** ~ **va más** the ultimate; **la** ~ **intervención** non-intervention.

n/o abr (COM) = nuestra orden.

noble ['noβle] adj, nmf noble; **los ~s** the nobility sg.

nobleza [noβ'leθa] nf nobility.

noche ['notʃe] nf night, night-time; (la tarde) evening; (fig) darkness; **de ~, por la ~** at night; **ayer por la ~** last night; **esta ~** tonight; **(en) toda la ~** all night; **hacer ~ en un sitio** to spend the night in a place; **se hace de ~** it's getting dark.

Nochebuena [notʃe'βwena] nf Christmas Eve; see boxed note.

NOCHEBUENA

On **Nochebuena** in Spanish homes family members normally gather together for a large supper and the more religiously inclined attend "la misa del gallo" at midnight. The tradition of receiving Christmas presents from Santa Claus on Christmas Eve is becoming more and more widespread and is gradually replacing the visit of "los Reyes Magos" (the Three Wise Men) who bring gifts on 6 January.

Nochevieja [notʃe'βjexa] nf New Year's Eve; V tb **uvas**.

noción [no'θjon] nf notion; **nociones** nfpl elements, rudiments.

nocivo, a [no'θiβo, a] adj harmful.

noctambulismo [noktambu'lismo] nm sleepwalking.

noctámbulo, a [nok'tambulo, a] nmf sleepwalker.

nocturno, a [nok'turno, a] adj (de la noche) nocturnal, night cpd; (de la tarde) evening cpd ♦ nm nocturne.

Noé [no'e] nm Noah.

nogal [no'ɣal] nm walnut tree; (madera) walnut.

nómada ['nomaða] adj nomadic ♦ nmf nomad.

nomás [no'mas] adv: (AM: gen) just; (: tan sólo) only; **así ~** (AM fam) just like that; **ayer ~** only yesterday ♦ conj (AM: en cuanto) ~ **se fue se acordó** no sooner had she left than she remembered.

nombramiento [nombra'mjento] nm naming; (a un empleo) appointment; (POL etc) nomination; (MIL) commission.

nombrar [nom'brar] vt (gen) to name; (mencionar) to mention; (designar) to appoint, nominate; (MIL) to commission.

nombre ['nombre] nm name; (sustantivo) noun; (fama) renown; ~ **y apellidos** name in full; ~ **común/propio** common/proper

noun; ~ **de pila/de soltera** Christian/ maiden name; ~ **de fichero** (INFORM) file name; **en ~ de** in the name of, on behalf of; **sin ~** nameless; **su conducta no tiene** ~ his behaviour is utterly despicable.

nomenclatura [nomenkla'tura] nf nomenclature.

nomeolvides [nomeol'βiðes] nm inv forget-me-not.

nómina ['nomina] nf (lista) list; (COM: tb: ~s) payroll.

nominal [nomi'nal] adj nominal; (valor) face cpd; (LING) noun cpd, substantival.

nominar [nomi'nar] vt to nominate.

nominativo, a [nomina'tiβo, a] adj (LING) nominative; (COM): **un cheque ~ a X** a cheque made out to X.

non [non] adj odd, uneven ♦ nm odd number; **pares y ~es** odds and evens.

nonagésimo, a [nona'xesimo, a] num ninetieth.

nono, a ['nono, a] num ninth.

nordeste [nor'ðeste] adj north-east, north-eastern, north-easterly ♦ nm north-east; (viento) north-east wind, north-easterly.

nórdico, a ['norðiko, a] adj (del norte) northern, northerly; (escandinavo) Nordic, Norse ♦ nmf northerner; (escandinavo) Norseman/woman ♦ nm (LING) Norse.

noreste [no'reste] adj, nm = **nordeste**.

noria ['norja] nf (AGR) waterwheel; (de carnaval) big (BRIT) o Ferris (US) wheel.

norma ['norma] nf standard, norm, rule; (patrón) pattern; (método) method.

normal [nor'mal] adj (corriente) normal; (habitual) usual, natural; (TEC) standard; **Escuela N~** teacher training college; (gasolina) ~ two-star petrol.

normalice [norma'liθe] etc vb V **normalizar**.

normalidad [normali'ðað] nf normality.

normalización [normaliθa'θjon] nf (COM) standardization.

normalizar [normali'θar] vt (reglamentar) to normalize; (COM, TEC) to standardize; **~se** vr to return to normal.

normalmente [normal'mente] adv (con normalidad) normally; (habitualmente) usually.

Normandía [norman'dia] nf Normandy.

normando, a [nor'mando, a] adj, nmf Norman.

normativo, a [norma'tiβo, a] adj: **es ~ en todos los coches nuevos** it is standard in all new cars ♦ nf regulations pl.

noroeste [noro'este] adj north-west, north-western, north-westerly ♦ nm north-west; (*viento*) north-west wind, north-westerly.

norte ['norte] *adj* north, northern, northerly ♦ *nm* north; (*fig*) guide.

Norteamérica [nortea'merika] *nf* North America.

norteamericano, a [norteameri'kano, a] *adj, nm/f* (North) American.

norteño, a [nor'teɲo, a] *adj* northern ♦ *nm/f* northerner.

Noruega [no'rweɣa] *nf* Norway.

noruego, a [no'rweɣo, a] *adj, nm/f* Norwegian ♦ *nm* (*LING*) Norwegian.

nos [nos] *pron* (*directo*) us; (*indirecto*) (to) us; (*reflexivo*) (to) ourselves; (*recíproco*) (to) each other; ~ **levantamos a las 7** we get up at 7.

nosocomio [noso'komio] *nm* (*AM*) hospital.

nosotros, as [no'sotros, as] *pron* (*sujeto*) we; (*después de prep*) us; ~ **(mismos)** ourselves.

nostalgia [nos'talxja] *nf* nostalgia, homesickness.

nostálgico, a [nos'talxiko, a] *adj* nostalgic, homesick.

nota ['nota] *nf* note; (*ESCOL*) mark; (*de fin de año*) report; (*UNIV etc*) footnote; (*COM*) account; ~ **de aviso** advice note; ~ **de crédito/débito** credit/debit note; ~ **de gastos** expenses claim; ~ **de sociedad** gossip column; **tomar** ~**s** to take notes.

notable [no'taβle] *adj* noteworthy, notable; (*ESCOL etc*) outstanding ♦ *nm/f* notable.

notar [no'tar] *vt* to notice, note; (*percibir*) to feel; (*ver*) to see; ~**se** *vr* to be obvious; **se nota que ...** one observes that ....

notaría [nota'ria] *nf* (*profesión*) profession of notary; (*despacho*) notary's office.

notarial [nota'rjal] *adj* (*estilo*) legal; **acta** ~ affidavit.

notario [no'tarjo] *nm* notary; (*abogado*) solicitor.

noticia [no'tiθja] *nf* (*información*) piece of news; (*TV etc*) news item; **las** ~**s** the news *sg*; **según nuestras** ~**s** according to our information; **tener** ~**s de algn** to hear from sb.

noticiario [noti'θjarjo] *nm* (*CINE*) newsreel; (*TV*) news bulletin.

noticiero [noti'θjero] *nm* newspaper, gazette; (*AM: tb:* ~ **telediario**) news bulletin.

notificación [notifika'θjon] *nf* notification.

notificar [notifi'kar] *vt* to notify, inform.

notifique [noti'fike] *etc vb V* **notificar**.

notoriedad [notorje'ðað] *nf* fame, renown.

notorio, a [no'torjo, a] *adj* (*público*) well-known; (*evidente*) obvious.

nov. *abr* (= **noviembre**) Nov.

novatada [noβa'taða] *nf* (*burla*) teasing, hazing (*US*); **pagar la** ~ to learn the hard way.

novato, a [no'βato, a] *adj* inexperienced ♦ *nm/f* beginner, novice.

novecientos, as [noβe'θjentos, as] *num* nine hundred.

novedad [noβe'ðað] *nf* (*calidad de nuevo*) newness, novelty; (*noticia*) piece of news; (*cambio*) change, (new) development; (*sorpresa*) surprise; ~**es** *nfpl* (*noticia*) latest (news) *sg*.

novedoso, a [noβe'ðoso, a] *adj* novel.

novel [no'βel] *adj* new; (*inexperto*) inexperienced ♦ *nm/f* beginner.

novela [no'βela] *nf* novel; ~ **policíaca** detective story.

novelero, a [noβe'lero, a] *adj* highly imaginative.

novelesco, a [noβe'lesko, a] *adj* fictional; (*romántico*) romantic; (*fantástico*) fantastic.

novelista [noβe'lista] *nm/f* novelist.

novelística [noβe'listika] *nf*: **la** ~ fiction, the novel.

noveno, a [no'βeno, a] *num* ninth.

noventa [no'βenta] *num* ninety.

novia ['noβja] *nf V* **novio**.

noviazgo [no'βjaɣo] *nm* engagement.

novicio, a [no'βiθjo, a] *nm/f* novice.

noviembre [no'βjembre] *nm* November.

novilla [no'βiʎa] *nf* heifer.

novillada [noβi'ʎaða] *nf* (*TAUR*) bullfight with young bulls.

novillero [noβi'ʎero] *nm* novice bullfighter.

novillo [no'βiʎo] *nm* young bull, bullock; **hacer** ~**s** (*fam*) to play truant (*BRIT*) o hooky (*US*).

novio, a ['noβjo, a] *nm/f* boyfriend/girlfriend; (*prometido*) fiancé/fiancée; (*recién casado*) bridegroom/bride; **los** ~**s** the newly-weds.

novísimo, a [no'βisimo, a] *adj superlativo de* **nuevo, a**.

NPI *nm abr* (*INFORM:* = *número personal de identificación*) PIN.

N. S. *abr* = *Nuestro Señor*.

ntra., ntro. *abr* = *nuestra, nuestro*.

NU *nfpl abr* (= *Naciones Unidas*) UN *sg*.

nubarrón [nuβa'rron] *nm* storm cloud.

nube ['nuβe] *nf* cloud; (*MED: ocular*) cloud, film; (*fig*) mass; **una** ~ **de críticas** a storm of criticism; **los precios están por las** ~**s** prices are sky-high; **estar en las** ~**s** to be away with the fairies.

nublado, a [nu'βlaðo, a] *adj* cloudy ♦ *nm* storm cloud.

nublar [nu'βlar] *vt* (*oscurecer*) to darken;

(*confundir*) to cloud; ~**se** *vr* to cloud over.
nuca ['nuka] *nf* nape of the neck.
nuclear [nukle'ar] *adj* nuclear.
nuclearizado, a [nukleari'θaðo, a] *adj*:
países ~**s** countries possessing nuclear
weapons.
núcleo ['nukleo] *nm* (*centro*) core; (*FÍSICA*)
nucleus.
nudillo [nu'ðiʎo] *nm* knuckle.
nudista [nu'dista] *adj, nm/f* nudist.
nudo ['nuðo] *nm* knot; (*unión*) bond; (*de*
problema) crux; (*FERRO*) junction; (*fig*)
lump; ~ **corredizo** slipknot; **con un** ~ **en**
la garganta with a lump in one's throat.
nudoso, a [nu'ðoso, a] *adj* knotty; (*tronco*)
gnarled; (*bastón*) knobbly.
nueces ['nweθes] *nfpl de* **nuez**.
nuera ['nwera] *nf* daughter-in-law.
nuestro, a ['nwestro, a] *adj posesivo* our
♦ *pron* ours; ~ **padre** our father; **un**
amigo ~ a friend of ours; **es el** ~ it's
ours; **los** ~**s** our people; (*DEPORTE*) our *o*
the local team *o* side.
nueva ['nweβa] *nf* V **nuevo**.
Nueva Esoocia *nf* Nova Scotia.
nuevamente [nweβa'mente] *adv* (*otra vez*)
again; (*de nuevo*) anew.
Nueva York [-'jork] *nf* New York.
Nueva Zeland(i)a [-θe'land(j)a] *nf* New
Zealand.
nueve ['nweβe] *num* nine.
nuevo, a ['nweβo, a] *adj* (*gen*) new ♦ *nf*
piece of news; **¿qué hay de** ~? (*fam*)
what's new?; **de** ~ again.
Nuevo Méjico *nm* New Mexico.
nuez [nweθ], *pl* **nueces** *nf* (*del nogal*)
walnut; (*fruto*) nut; ~ **de Adán** Adam's
apple; ~ **moscada** nutmeg.
nulidad [nuli'ðað] *nf* (*incapacidad*)
incompetence; (*abolición*) nullity;
(*individuo*) nonentity; **es una** ~ he's a
dead loss.
nulo, a ['nulo, a] *adj* (*inepto, torpe*) useless;
(*inválido*) (null and) void; (*DEPORTE*)
drawn, tied.
núm. *abr* (= *número*) no.
numen ['numen] *nm* inspiration.
numeración [numera'θjon] *nf* (*cifras*)
numbers *pl*; (*arábiga, romana etc*)
numerals *pl*; ~ **de línea** (*INFORM*) line
numbering.
numerador [numera'ðor] *nm* (*MAT*)
numerator.
numeral [nume'ral] *nm* numeral.
numerar [nume'rar] *vt* to number; ~**se** *vr*
(*MIL etc*) to number off.
numerario, a [nume'rarjo, a] *adj*
numerary; **profesor** ~ permanent *o*

tenured member of teaching staff ♦ *nm*
hard cash.
numérico, a [nu'meriko, a] *adj* numerical.
número ['numero] *nm* (*gen*) number;
(*tamaño: de zapato*) size; (*ejemplar: de*
diario) number, issue; (*TEAT etc*) turn,
act, number; **sin** ~ numberless,
unnumbered; ~ **binario** (*INFORM*) binary
number; ~ **de matrícula/de teléfono**
registration/telephone number; ~
personal de identificación (*INFORM etc*)
personal identification number; ~ **de**
serie (*COM*) serial number; ~ **atrasado**
back number.
numeroso, a [nume'roso, a] *adj* numerous;
familia numerosa large family.
numerus ['numerus] *nm*: ~ **clausus** (*UNIV*)
restricted *o* selective entry.
nunca ['nunka] *adv* (*jamás*) never; (*con*
verbo negativo) ever; ~ **lo pensé** I never
thought it; **no viene** ~ he never comes;
~ **más** never again.
nuncio ['nunθjo] *nm* (*REL*) nuncio.
nupcial [nup'θjal] *adj* wedding *cpd*.
nupcias ['nupθjas] *nfpl* wedding *sg*,
nuptials.
nutria ['nutrja] *nf* otter.
nutrición [nutri'θjon] *nf* nutrition.
nutrido, a [nu'triðo, a] *adj* (*alimentado*)
nourished; (*fig: grande*) large;
(*abundante*) abundant; **mal** ~
undernourished; ~ **de** full of.
nutrir [nu'trir] *vt* to feed, nourish; (*fig*) to
feed, strengthen.
nutritivo, a [nutri'tiβo, a] *adj* nourishing,
nutritious.
nylon [ni'lon] *nm* nylon.

Ñ ñ

Ñ, ñ ['eɲe] *nf* (*letra*) Ñ, ñ.
ñato, a ['ɲato, a] *adj* (*AM*) snub-nosed.
ñoñería [ɲoɲe'ria], **ñoñez** [ɲo'ɲeθ] *nf*
insipidness.
ñoño, a ['ɲoɲo, a] *adj* (*soso*) insipid;
(*persona: débil*) spineless.
ñoquis ['ɲokis] *nmpl* (*CULIN*) gnocchi.

O o

O, o [o] *nf* (*letra*) O, o; **O de Oviedo** O for
Oliver (*BRIT*) o Oboe (*US*).
O *abr* (= *oeste*) W.
o [o] *conj* or; ~ ... ~ either ... or; ~ **sea** that
is.
ó [o] *conj* (*en números para evitar confusión*)
or; **5** ~ **6** 5 or 6.
o/ *nm* (*COM*: = *orden*) o.
OACI *nf abr* (= *Organización de la Aviación
Civil Internacional*) ICAO.
oasis [o'asis] *nm inv* oasis.
obcecado, a [oßθe'kaðo, a] *adj* blind;
(*terco*) stubborn.
obcecarse [oßθe'karse] *vr* to be obstinate;
~ **en hacer** to insist on doing.
obceque [oß'θeke] *etc vb V* **obcecarse**.
obedecer [oßeðe'θer] *vt* to obey; ~ **a** (*MED
etc*) to yield to; (*fig*) ~ **a** ..., ~ **al hecho de
que** ... to be due to ..., arise from ....
obedezca [oße'ðeθka] *etc vb V* **obedecer**.
obediencia [oße'ðjenθja] *nf* obedience.
obediente [oße'ðjente] *adj* obedient.
obertura [oßer'tura] *nf* overture.
obesidad [oßesi'ðað] *nf* obesity.
obeso, a [o'ßeso, a] *adj* obese.
óbice ['oßiθe] *nm* obstacle, impediment.
obispado [oßis'paðo] *nm* bishopric.
obispo [o'ßispo] *nm* bishop.
óbito ['oßito] *nm* demise.
objeción [oßxe'θjon] *nf* objection; **hacer
una** ~, **poner objeciones** to raise
objections, object.
objetar [oßxe'tar] *vt, vi* to object.
objetivo, a [oßxe'tißo, a] *adj* objective ♦ *nm*
objective; (*fig*) aim; (*FOTO*) lens.
objeto [oß'xeto] *nm* (*cosa*) object; (*fin*) aim.
objetor, a [oßxe'tor, a] *nm/f* objector; ~ **de
conciencia** conscientious objector; *V tb*
mili.
oblea [o'ßlea] *nf* (*REL, fig*) wafer; (*INFORM*)
chip, wafer.
oblicuo, a [o'ßlikwo, a] *adj* oblique;
(*mirada*) sidelong.
obligación [oßliɣa'θjon] *nf* obligation;
(*COM*) bond, debenture.
obligar [oßli'ɣar] *vt* to force; ~**se** *vr*: ~**se a**
to commit o.s. to.
obligatorio, a [oßliɣa'torjo, a] *adj*
compulsory, obligatory.
obligue [o'ßliɣe] *etc vb V* **obligar**.
oboe [o'ßoe] *nm* oboe; (*músico*) oboist.
Ob.ᵖᵒ *abr* (= *Obispo*) Bp.
obra ['oßra] *nf* work; (*hechura*) piece of
work; (*ARQ*) construction, building;
(*libro*) book; (*MUS*) opus; (*TEAT*) play; ~
de arte work of art; ~ **maestra**
masterpiece; ~ **de consulta** reference
book; ~**s** complete works; ~
benéfica charity; "~**s**" (*en carretera*)
"men at work"; ~**s públicas** public
works; **por** ~ **de** thanks to (the efforts
of); ~**s son amores y no buenas razones**
actions speak louder than words.
obrar [o'ßrar] *vt* to work; (*tener efecto*) to
have an effect on ♦ *vi* to act, behave;
(*tener efecto*) to have an effect; **la carta
obra en su poder** the letter is in his/her
possession.
obr. cit. *abr* (= *obra citada*) op. cit.
obrero, a [o'ßrero, a] *adj* working;
(*movimiento*) labour *cpd*; **clase obrera**
working class ♦ *nm/f* (*gen*) worker; (*sin
oficio*) labourer.
obscenidad [oßsθeni'ðað] *nf* obscenity.
obsceno, a [oßs'θeno, a] *adj* obscene.
obscu... = **oscu...**
obsequiar [oßse'kjar] *vt* (*ofrecer*) to
present; (*agasajar*) to make a fuss of,
lavish attention on.
obsequio [oß'sekjo] *nm* (*regalo*) gift;
(*cortesía*) courtesy, attention.
obsequioso, a [oßse'kjoso, a] *adj*
attentive.
observación [oßserßa'θjon] *nf* observation;
(*reflexión*) remark; (*objeción*) objection.
observador, a [oßserßa'ðor, a] *adj*
observant ♦ *nm/f* observer.
observancia [oßser'ßanθja] *nf* observance.
observar [oßser'ßar] *vt* to observe; (*notar*)
to notice; (*leyes*) to observe, respect;
(*reglas*) to abide by.
observatorio [oßserßa'torjo] *nm*
observatory; ~ **del tiempo** weather
station.
obsesión [oßse'sjon] *nf* obsession.
obsesionar [oßsesjo'nar] *vt* to obsess.
obseso, a [oß'seso, a] *nm/f* (*sexual*) sex
maniac.
obsolescencia [oßsoles'θenθja] *nf*: ~
incorporada (*COM*) built-in obsolescence.
obsoleto, a [oßso'leto, a] *adj* obsolete.
obstaculice [oßstaku'liθe] *etc vb V*
obstaculizar.
obstaculizar [oßstakuli'θar] *vt* (*dificultar*) to
hinder, hamper.
obstáculo [oßs'takulo] *nm* (*gen*) obstacle;

(*impedimento*) hindrance, drawback.
obstante [oßs'tante]: **no** ~ *adv*
nevertheless; (*de todos modos*) all the
same ⧫ *prep* in spite of.
obstetra [oßs'tetra] *nm/f* obstetrician.
obstetricia [oßste'triθja] *nf* obstetrics *sg*.
obstinado, a [oßsti'naðo, a] *adj* (*gen*)
obstinate; (*terco*) stubborn.
obstinarse [oßsti'narse] *vr* to dig one's
heels in; ~ **en** to persist in.
obstrucción [oßstruk'θjon] *nf* obstruction.
obstruir [oßstru'ir] *vt* to obstruct;
(*bloquear*) to block; (*estorbar*) to hinder.
obstruyendo [oßstru'jendo] *etc vb V*
obstruir.
obtención [oßten'θjon] *nf* (*COM*)
procurement.
obtendré [oßten'dre] *etc vb V* **obtener**.
obtener [oßte'ner] *vt* (*conseguir*) to obtain;
(*ganar*) to gain.
obtenga [oß'tenga] *etc vb V* **obtener**.
obturación [oßtura'θjon] *nf* plugging,
stopping; (*FOTO*): **velocidad de** ~ shutter
speed.
obturador [oßtura'ðor] *nm* (*FOTO*) shutter.
obtuso, a [oß'tuso, a] *adj* (*filo*) blunt; (*MAT*,
fig) obtuse.
obtuve [oß'tuße] *etc vb V* **obtener**.
obús [o'ßus] *nm* (*MIL*) shell.
obviar [oß'ßjar] *vt* to obviate, remove.
obvio, a [o'ßßjo, a] *adj* obvious.
oca [oka] *nf* goose; (*tb*: **juego de la** ~)
≈ snakes and ladders.
ocasión [oka'sjon] *nf* (*oportunidad*)
opportunity, chance; (*momento*)
occasion, time; (*causa*) cause; **de** ~
secondhand; **con** ~ **de** on the occasion
of; **en algunas ocasiones** sometimes;
aprovechar la ~ to seize one's
opportunity.
ocasionar [okasjo'nar] *vt* to cause.
ocaso [o'kaso] *nm* sunset; (*fig*) decline.
occidental [okθiðen'tal] *adj* western ⧫ *nm/f*
westerner ⧫ *nm* west.
occidente [okθi'ðente] *nm* west; **el O**~ the
West.
occiso, a [ok'θiso, a] *nm/f*: **el** ~ the
deceased; (*de asesinato*) the victim.
O.C.D.E. *nf abr* (= *Organización de
Cooperación y Desarrollo Económicos*)
OECD.
océano [o'θeano] *nm* ocean; **el** ~ **Índico** the
Indian Ocean.
ochenta [o'tʃenta] *num* eighty.
ocho [o'tʃo] *num* eight; (*fecha*) eighth; ~
días a week.
ochocientos, as [otʃo'θjentos, as] *num*
eight hundred.

OCI ['oθi] *nf abr* (*POL: Venezuela, Perú*)
= *Oficina Central de Información*.
ocio [o'θjo] *nm* (*tiempo*) leisure; (*pey*)
idleness; "**guía del** ~" "what's on".
ociosidad [oθjosi'ðað] *nf* idleness.
ocioso, a [o'θjoso, a] *adj* (*inactivo*) idle;
(*inútil*) useless.
oct. *abr* (= *octubre*) Oct.
octanaje [okta'naxe] *nm*: **de alto** ~ high
octane.
octano [ok'tano] *nm* octane.
octavilla [okta'ßiʎa] *nm* leaflet, pamphlet.
octavo, a [ok'taßo, a] *num* eighth.
octeto [ok'teto] *nm* (*INFORM*) byte.
octogenario, a [oktoxe'narjo, a] *adj*, *nm/f*
octogenarian.
octubre [ok'tußre] *nm* October.
OCU ['oku] *nf abr* (*ESP.* = *Organización de
Consumidores y Usuarios*) ≈ Consumers'
Association.
ocular [oku'lar] *adj* ocular, eye *cpd*; **testigo**
~ eyewitness.
oculista [oku'lista] *nm/f* oculist.
ocultar [okul'tar] *vt* (*esconder*) to hide;
(*callar*) to conceal; (*disfrazar*) to screen;
~**se** *vr* to hide (o.s.); ~**se a la vista** to
keep out of sight.
oculto, a [o'kulto, a] *adj* hidden; (*fig*)
secret.
ocupación [okupa'θjon] *nf* occupation;
(*tenencia*) occupancy.
ocupado, a [oku'paðo, a] *adj* (*persona*)
busy; (*plaza*) occupied, taken; (*teléfono*)
engaged; **¿está ocupada la silla?** is that
seat taken?
ocupar [oku'par] *vt* (*gen*) to occupy;
(*puesto*) to hold, fill; (*individuo*) to
engage; (*obreros*) to employ; (*confiscar*)
to seize; ~**se** *vr*: ~**se de o en** to concern
o.s. with; (*cuidar*) to look after; ~**se de lo
suyo** to mind one's own business.
ocurrencia [oku'rrenθja] *nf* (*ocasión*)
occurrence; (*agudeza*) witticism.
ocurrir [oku'rrir] *vi* to happen; ~**se** *vr*: **se
me ocurrió que** ... it occurred to me that
...; **¿se te ocurre algo?** can you think of o
come up with anything? **¿qué ocurre?**
what's going on?
oda ['oða] *nf* ode.
ODECA [o'ðeka] *nf abr* = *Organización de
Estados Centroamericanos*.
odiar [o'ðjar] *vt* to hate.
odio [o'ðjo] *nm* (*gen*) hate, hatred;
(*disgusto*) dislike.
odioso, a [o'ðjoso, a] *adj* (*gen*) hateful;
(*malo*) nasty.
odisea [oði'sea] *nf* odyssey.
odontología [oðontolo'xia] *nf* dentistry,

dental surgery.

odontólogo, a [oðon'toloɣo, a] *nm/f* dentist, dental surgeon.

odre ['oðre] *nm* wineskin.

O.E.A. *nf abr* (= *Organización de Estados Americanos*) O.A.S.

OECE *nf abr* (= *Organización Europea de Cooperación Económica*) OEEC.

OELA [o'ela] *nf abr* = *Organización de Estados Latinoamericanos*.

oeste [o'este] *nm* west; **una película del** ~ a western.

ofender [ofen'der] *vt* (*agraviar*) to offend; (*insultar*) to insult; ~**se** *vr* to take offence.

ofensa [o'fensa] *nf* offence; (*insulto*) slight.

ofensivo, a [ofen'siβo, a] *adj* (*insultante*) insulting; (*MIL*) offensive ♦ *nf* offensive.

oferta [o'ferta] *nf* offer; (*propuesta*) proposal; (*para contrato*) bid, tender; **la** ~ **y la demanda** supply and demand; **artículos en** ~ goods on offer; ~ **excedentaria** (*COM*) excess supply; ~ **monetaria** money supply; ~ **pública de adquisición (OPA)** (*COM*) takeover bid; ~**s de trabajo** (*en periódicos*) situations vacant column.

offset ['ofset] *nm* offset.

oficial [ofi'θjal] *adj* official ♦ *nm* official; (*MIL*) officer.

oficialista [ofisja'lista] *adj* (*AM*) (pro-) government; **el candidato** ~ the governing party's candidate.

oficiar [ofi'θjar] *vt* to inform officially ♦ *vi* (*REL*) to officiate.

oficina [ofi'θina] *nf* office; ~ **de colocación** employment agency; ~ **de información** information bureau; ~ **de objetos perdidos** lost property office (*BRIT*), lost-and-found department (*US*); ~ **de turismo** tourist office.

oficinista [ofiθi'nista] *nm/f* clerk; **los** ~**s** white-collar workers.

oficio [o'fiθjo] *nm* (*profesión*) profession; (*puesto*) post; (*REL*) service; (*función*) function; (*comunicado*) official letter; **ser del** ~ to be an old hand; **tener mucho** ~ to have a lot of experience; ~ **de difuntos** funeral service; **de** ~ officially.

oficioso, a [ofi'θjoso, a] *adj* (*pey*) officious; (*no oficial*) unofficial, informal.

ofimática [ofi'matika] *nf* office automation.

ofrecer [ofre'θer] *vt* (*dar*) to offer; (*proponer*) to propose; ~**se** *vr* (*persona*) to offer o.s., volunteer; (*situación*) to present itself; **¿qué se le ofrece?, ¿se le ofrece algo?** what can I do for you?, can I get you anything?

ofrecimiento [ofreθi'mjento] *nm* offer, offering.

ofrendar [ofren'dar] *vt* to offer, contribute.

ofrezca [o'freθka] *etc vb V* **ofrecer**.

oftalmología [oftalmolo'xia] *nf* ophthalmology.

oftalmólogo, a [oftal'moloɣo, a] *nm/f* ophthalmologist.

ofuscación [ofuska'θjon] *nf*, **ofuscamiento** [ofuska'mjento] *nm* (*fig*) bewilderment.

ofuscar [ofus'kar] *vt* (*confundir*) to bewilder; (*enceguecer*) to dazzle, blind.

ofusque [o'fuske] *etc vb V* **ofuscar**.

ogro ['oɣro] *nm* ogre.

OIC *nf abr* = *Organización Interamericana del Café*; (*COM*) = *Organización Internacional del Comercio*.

oída [o'iða] *nf*: **de** ~**s** by hearsay.

oído [o'iðo] *nm* (*ANAT, MUS*) ear; (*sentido*) hearing; ~ **interno** inner ear; **de** ~ by ear; **apenas pude dar crédito a mis** ~**s** I could scarcely believe my ears; **hacer** ~**s sordos a** to turn a deaf ear to.

OIEA *nm abr* (= *Organismo Internacional de Energía Atómica*) IAEA.

oiga ['oiɣa] *etc vb V* **oír**.

OIR [o'ir] *nf abr* (= *Organización Internacional para los Refugiados*) IRO.

oír [o'ir] *vt* (*gen*) to hear; (*esp AM: escuchar*) to listen to; **¡oye!** (*sorpresa*) I say!, say! (*US*); **¡oiga!** (*TELEC*) hullo?; ~ **misa** to attend mass; **como quien oye llover** without paying (the slightest) attention.

O.I.T. *nf abr* (= *Organización Internacional del Trabajo*) ILO.

ojal [o'xal] *nm* buttonhole.

ojalá [oxa'la] *excl* if only (it were so)!, some hope! ♦ *conj* if only...!, would that...!; ~ **que venga hoy** I hope he comes today; **¡**~ **pudiera!** I wish I could!

ojeada [oxe'aða] *nf* glance; **echar una** ~ **a** to take a quick look at.

ojera [o'xera] *nf*: **tener** ~**s** to have bags under one's eyes.

ojeriza [oxe'riθa] *nf* ill-will; **tener** ~ **a** to have a grudge against, have it in for.

ojeroso, a [oxe'roso, a] *adj* haggard.

ojete [o'xete] *nm* eye(let).

ojo ['oxo] *nm* eye; (*de puente*) span; (*de cerradura*) keyhole ♦ *excl* careful!; **tener** ~ **para** to have an eye for; ~**s saltones** bulging *o* goggle eyes; ~ **de buey** porthole; ~ **por** ~ an eye for an eye; **en un abrir y cerrar de** ~**s** in the twinkling of an eye; **a** ~**s vistas** openly; (*crecer etc*) before one's (very) eyes; **a ~ (de buen cubero)** roughly; **~s que no ven, corazón que no siente** out of sight, out of mind; **ser el ~ derecho de algn** (*fig*) to be the apple of sb's eye.

okupa [o'kupa] *nm/f* (*fam*) squatter.

ola ['ola] *nf* wave; **~ de calor/frío** heatwave/cold spell; **la nueva ~** the latest fashion; (*CINE, MUS*) (the) new wave.

OLADE [o'laðe] *nf abr* = *Organización Latinoamericana de Energía.*

olé [o'le] *excl* bravo!, olé!

oleada [ole'aða] *nf* big wave, swell; (*fig*) wave.

oleaje [ole'axe] *nm* swell.

óleo ['oleo] *nm* oil.

oleoducto [oleo'ðukto] *nm* (oil) pipeline.

oler [o'ler] *vt* (*gen*) to smell; (*inquirir*) to pry into; (*fig: sospechar*) to sniff out ♦ *vi* to smell; **~ a** to smell of; **huele mal** it smells bad, it stinks.

olfatear [olfate'ar] *vt* to smell; (*fig: sospechar*) to sniff out; (*inquirir*) to pry into.

olfato [ol'fato] *nm* sense of smell.

oligarquía [oliɣar'kia] *nf* oligarchy.

olimpiada [olim'piaða] *nf*: **la ~ o las ~s** the Olympics.

olímpicamente [o'limpikamente] *adv*: **pasar ~ de algo** to totally ignore sth.

olímpico, a [o'limpiko, a] *adj* Olympian; (*deportes*) Olympic.

oliva [o'lißa] *nf* (*aceituna*) olive; **aceite de ~** olive oil.

olivar [oli'ßar] *nm* olive grove *o* plantation.

olivo [o'lißo] *nm* olive tree.

olla ['oʎa] *nf* pan; (*para hervir agua*) kettle; (*comida*) stew; **~ a presión** pressure cooker.

olmo ['olmo] *nm* elm (tree).

olor [o'lor] *nm* smell.

oloroso, a [olo'roso, a] *adj* scented.

OLP *nf abr* (= *Organización para la Liberación de Palestina*) PLO.

olvidadizo, a [olßiða'ðiθo, a] *adj* (*desmemoriado*) forgetful; (*distraído*) absent-minded.

olvidar [olßi'ðar] *vt* to forget; (*omitir*) to omit; (*abandonar*) to leave behind; **~se** *vr* (*fig*) to forget o.s.; **se me olvidó** I forgot.

olvido [ol'ßiðo] *nm* oblivion; (*acto*) oversight; (*descuido*) slip; **caer en el ~** to fall into oblivion.

O.M. *abr* (*POL*) = *Orden Ministerial.*

ombligo [om'blixo] *nm* navel.

OMI *nf abr*(= *Organización Marítima Internacional*) IMO.

ominoso, a [omi'noso, a] *adj* ominous.

omisión [omi'sjon] *nf* (*abstención*) omission; (*descuido*) neglect.

omiso, a [o'miso, a] *adj*: **hacer caso ~ de** to ignore, pass over.

omitir [omi'tir] *vt* to leave *o* miss out, omit.

ómnibus ['omnißus] *nm* (*AM*) bus.

omnipotente [omnipo'tente] *adj* omnipotent.

omnipresente [omnipre'sente] *adj* omnipresent.

omnívoro, a [om'nißoro, a] *adj* omnivorous.

omoplato [omo'plato], **omóplato** [o'moplato] *nm* shoulder-blade.

OMS *nf abr* (= *Organización Mundial de la Salud*) WHO.

ONCE ['onθe] *nf abr* (= *Organización Nacional de Ciegos Españoles*) *charity for the blind.*

once ['onθe] *num* eleven ♦ *nm* (*AM*): **~s** *nfpl* tea break *sg*.

onda ['onda] *nf* wave; **~ corta/larga/media** short/long/medium wave; **~s acústicas/hertzianas** acoustic/Hertzian waves; **~ sonora** sound wave.

ondear [onde'ar] *vi* to wave; (*tener ondas*) to be wavy; (*agua*) to ripple; **~se** *vr* to swing, sway.

ondulación [ondula'θjon] *nf* undulation.

ondulado, a [ondu'laðo, a] *adj* wavy ♦ *nm* wave.

ondulante [ondu'lante] *adj* undulating.

ondular [ondu'lar] *vt* (*el pelo*) to wave ♦ *vi*, **~se** *vr* to undulate.

oneroso, a [one'roso, a] *adj* onerous.

ONG *nf abr* (= *organización no gubernamental*) NGO.

onomástico, a [ono'mastiko, a] *adj*: **fiesta onomástica** saint's day ♦ *nm* saint's day.

ONU ['onu] *nf abr* V **Organización de las Naciones Unidas**.

onubense [onu'ßense] *adj* of *o* from Huelva ♦ *nm/f* native *o* inhabitant of Huelva.

ONUDI [o'nuði] *nf abr* (= *Organización de las Naciones Unidas para el Desarrollo Industrial*) UNIDO (*United Nations Industrial Development Organization*).

onza ['onθa] *nf* ounce.

O.P. *nfpl abr* = **obras públicas**; (*COM*) = *Oficina Principal.*

OPA *nf abr* (= *oferta pública de adquisición*) takeover bid.

opaco, a [o'pako, a] *adj* opaque; (*fig*) dull.

ópalo ['opalo] *nm* opal.

opción [op'θjon] *nf* (*gen*) option; (*derecho*) right, option; **no hay ~** there is no alternative.

opcional [opθjo'nal] _adj_ optional.

O.P.E.P. [o'pep] _nf abr_ (= _Organización de Países Exportadores de Petróleo_) OPEC.

ópera ['opera] _nf_ opera; ~ **bufa** o **cómica** comic opera.

operación [opera'θjon] _nf_ (_gen_) operation; (_COM_) transaction, deal; ~ **"llave en manos"** (_INFORM_) turnkey operation; ~ **a plazo** (_COM_) forward transaction; **operaciones accesorias** (_INFORM_) housekeeping; **operaciones a término** (_COM_) futures.

operador, a [opera'ðor, a] _nm/f_ operator; (_CINE_: _proyección_) projectionist; (: _rodaje_) cameraman.

operar [ope'rar] _vt_ (_producir_) to produce, bring about; (_MED_) to operate on ♦ _vi_ (_COM_) to operate, deal; ~**se** _vr_ to occur; (_MED_) to have an operation; **se han operado grandes cambios** great changes have been made o have taken place.

operario, a [ope'rarjo, a] _nm/f_ worker.

opereta [ope'reta] _nf_ operetta.

opinar [opi'nar] _vt_ (_estimar_) to think ♦ _vi_ (_enjuiciar_) to give one's opinion; ~ **bien de** to think well of.

opinión [opi'njon] _nf_ (_creencia_) belief; (_criterio_) opinion; **la** ~ **pública** public opinion.

opio ['opjo] _nm_ opium.

opíparo, a [o'piparo, a] _adj_ sumptuous.

opondré [opon'dre] _etc vb_ V **oponer**.

oponente [opo'nente] _nm/f_ opponent.

oponer [opo'ner] _vt_ (_resistencia_) to put up, offer; (_negativa_) to raise; ~**se** _vr_ (_objetar_) to object; (_estar frente a frente_) to be opposed; (_dos personas_) to oppose each other; ~ **A a B** to set A against B; **me opongo a pensar que ...** I refuse to believe o think that ....

oponga [o'ponga] _etc vb_ V **oponer**.

Oporto [o'porto] _nm_ Oporto.

oporto [o'porto] _nm_ port.

oportunidad [oportuni'ðað] _nf_ (_ocasión_) opportunity; (_posibilidad_) chance.

oportunismo [oportu'nismo] _nm_ opportunism.

oportunista [oportu'nista] _nm/f_ opportunist; (_infección_) opportunistic.

oportuno, a [opor'tuno, a] _adj_ (_en su tiempo_) opportune, timely; (_respuesta_) suitable; **en el momento** ~ at the right moment.

oposición [oposi'θjon] _nf_ opposition; **oposiciones** _nfpl_ public examinations; **ganar un puesto por oposiciones** to win a post by public competitive examination; **hacer oposiciones a, presentarse a**

unas oposiciones a to sit a competitive examination for; _see boxed note._

opositar [oposi'tar] _vi_ to sit a public entrance examination.

opositor, a [oposi'tor, a] _nm/f_ (_ADMIN_) candidate to a public examination; (_adversario_) opponent.

opresión [opre'sjon] _nf_ oppression.

opresivo, a [opre'sißo, a] _adj_ oppressive.

opresor, a [opre'sor, a] _nm/f_ oppressor.

oprimir [opri'mir] _vt_ to squeeze; (_asir_) to grasp; (_pulsar_) to press; (_fig_) to oppress.

optar [op'tar] _vi_ (_elegir_) to choose; ~ **a** o **por** to opt for.

optativo, a [opta'tißo, a] _adj_ optional.

óptico, a ['optiko, a] _adj_ optic(al) ♦ _nm/f_ optician ♦ _nf_ optics _sg_; (_fig_) viewpoint.

optimismo [opti'mismo] _nm_ optimism.

optimista [opti'mista] _nm/f_ optimist.

óptimo, a ['optimo, a] _adj_ (_el mejor_) very best.

opuesto, a [o'pwesto, a] _pp de_ **oponer** ♦ _adj_ (_contrario_) opposite; (_antagónico_) opposing.

opulencia [opu'lenθja] _nf_ opulence.

opulento, a [opu'lento, a] _adj_ opulent.

opuse [o'puse] _etc vb_ V **oponer**.

ORA ['ora] _nf abr_ (_ESP_: = _Operación de Regulación de Aparcamientos_) parking regulations.

ora ['ora] _adv_: ~ **tú** ~ **yo** now you, now me.

oración [ora'θjon] _nf_ (_discurso_) speech; (_REL_) prayer; (_LING_) sentence.

oráculo [o'rakulo] _nm_ oracle.

orador, a [ora'ðor, a] _nm/f_ orator; (_conferenciante_) speaker.

oral [o'ral] _adj_ oral; **por vía** ~ (_MED_) orally.

orangután [orangu'tan] _nm_ orang-utan.

orar [o'rar] _vi_ (_REL_) to pray.

oratoria [ora'torja] _nf_ oratory.

orbe ['orβe] nm orb, sphere; (fig) world; **en todo el** ~ all over the globe.

órbita ['orβita] nf orbit; (ANAT: ocular) (eye-)socket.

orden ['orðen] nm (gen) order; (INFORM) command; ~ **público** public order, law and order; (números) **del** ~ **de** about; **de primer** ~ first-rate; **en** ~ **de prioridad** in order of priority ♦ nf (gen) order; ~ **bancaria** banker's order; ~ **de compra** (COM) purchase order; ~ **del día** agenda; **eso ahora está a la** ~ **del día** that is now the order of the day; **a la** ~ **de usted** at your service; **dar la** ~ **de hacer algo** to give the order to do sth.

ordenación [orðena'θjon] nf (estado) order; (acto) ordering; (REL) ordination.

ordenado, a [orðe'naðo, a] adj (metódico) methodical; (arreglado) orderly.

ordenador [orðena'ðor] nm computer; ~ **central** mainframe computer; ~ **de gestión** business computer; ~ **portátil** laptop (computer); ~ **de sobremesa** desktop computer.

ordenamiento [orðena'mjento] nm legislation.

ordenanza [orðe'nanθa] nf ordinance; ~**s municipales** by-laws ♦ nm (COM etc) messenger; (MIL) orderly; (bedel) porter.

ordenar [orðe'nar] vt (mandar) to order; (poner orden) to put in order, arrange; ~**se** vr (REL) to be ordained.

ordeñadora [orðeɲa'ðora] nf milking machine.

ordeñar [orðe'ɲar] vt to milk.

ordinariez [orðina'rjeθ] nf (cualidad) coarseness, vulgarity; (una ~) coarse remark o joke etc.

ordinario, a [orði'narjo, a] adj (común) ordinary, usual; (vulgar) vulgar, common.

ordinograma [orðino'ɣrama] nm flowchart.

orear [ore'ar] vt to air; ~**se** vr (ropa) to air.

orégano [o'reɣano] nm oregano.

oreja [o'rexa] nf ear; (MECÁNICA) lug, flange.

orensano, a [oren'sano, a] adj of o from Orense ♦ nm/f native o inhabitant of Orense.

orfanato [orfa'nato] nm, **orfanatorio** [orfana'torjo] nm orphanage.

orfandad [orfan'dað] nf orphanhood.

orfebre [or'feβre] nm gold-/silversmith.

orfebrería [orfeβre'ria] nf gold/silver work.

orfelinato [orfeli'nato] nm orphanage.

orfeón [orfe'on] nm (MUS) choral society.

organice [orɣa'niθe] etc vb V **organizar**.

orgánico, a [or'ɣaniko, a] adj organic.

organigrama [orɣani'ɣrama] nm flow chart; (de organización) organization chart.

organillo [orɣa'niʎo] nm barrel organ.

organismo [orɣa'nismo] nm (BIO) organism; (POL) organization; **O**~ **Internacional de Energía Atómica** International Atomic Energy Agency.

organista [orɣa'nista] nm/f organist.

organización [orɣaniθa'θjon] nf organization; **O**~ **de las Naciones Unidas (ONU)** United Nations Organization **O**~ **del Tratado del Atlántico Norte (OTAN)** North Atlantic Treaty Organization (NATO).

organizador, a [orɣaniθa'ðor, a] adj organizing; **el comité** ~ the organizing committee ♦ nm/f organizer.

organizar [orɣani'θar] vt to organize.

órgano ['orɣano] nm organ.

orgasmo [or'ɣasmo] nm orgasm.

orgía [or'xia] nf orgy.

orgullo [or'ɣuʎo] nm (altanería) pride; (autorespeto) self-respect.

orgulloso, a [orɣu'ʎoso, a] adj (gen) proud; (altanero) haughty.

orientación [orjenta'θjon] nf (posición) position; (dirección) direction; ~ **profesional** occupational guidance.

oriental [orjen'tal] adj oriental; (región etc) eastern ♦ nm/f oriental.

orientar [orjen'tar] vt (situar) to orientate; (señalar) to point; (dirigir) to direct; (guiar) to guide; ~**se** vr to get one's bearings; (decidirse) to decide on a course of action.

oriente [o'rjente] nm east; **el O**~ the East, the Orient; **Cercano/Medio/Lejano O**~ Near/ Middle/Far East.

orificio [ori'fiθjo] nm orifice.

origen [o'rixen] nm origin; (nacimiento) lineage, birth; **dar** ~ **a** to cause, give rise to.

original [orixi'nal] adj (nuevo) original; (extraño) odd, strange ♦ nm original; (TIP) manuscript; (TEC) master (copy).

originalidad [orixinali'ðað] nf originality.

originar [orixi'nar] vt to originate; ~**se** vr to originate.

originario, a [orixi'narjo, a] adj (nativo) native; (primordial) original; **ser** ~ **de** to originate from; **país** ~ country of origin.

orilla [o'riʎa] nf (borde) border; (de río) bank; (de bosque, tela) edge; (de mar) shore; **a** ~**s de** on the banks of.

orillar [ori'ʎar] vt (bordear) to skirt, go round; (COSTURA) to edge; (resolver) to wind up; (*tocar: asunto*) to touch briefly on; (*dificultad*) to avoid.

orín [o'rin] *nm* ɪ ust.

orina [o'rina] *nf* ʋrine.

orinal [ori'nal] *nm* (*chamber*) pot.

orinar [ori'nar] *vi* to urinate; ~**se** *vr* to wet o.s.

orines [o'rines] *nmpl* urine *sg*.

oriundo, a [o'rjundo, a] *adj*: ~ **de** native of.

orla ['orla] *nf* edge, border; (*ESCOL*) graduation photograph.

ornamentar [ornamen'tar] *vt* (*adornar, ataviar*) to adorn; (*revestir*) to bedeck.

ornar [or'nar] *vt* to adorn.

ornitología [ornitolo'xia] *nf* ornithology, bird watching.

ornitólogo, a [orni'toloɣo, a] *nm/f* ornithologist.

oro ['oro] *nm* gold; ~ **en barras** gold ingots; **de** ~ gold, golden; **no es** ~ **todo lo que reluce** all that glitters is not gold; **hacerse de** ~ to make a fortune; *V tb* **oros**.

orondo, a [o'rondo, a] *adj* (*vasija*) rounded; (*individuo*) smug, self-satisfied.

oropel [oro'pel] *nm* tinsel.

oros ['oros] *nmpl* (*NAIPES*) *one of the suits in the Spanish card deck*; *V tb* **Baraja Española**.

orquesta [or'kesta] *nf* orchestra; ~ **de cámara/sinfónica** chamber/symphony orchestra; ~ **de jazz** jazz band.

orquestar [orkes'tar] *vt* to orchestrate.

orquídea [or'kiðea] *nf* orchid.

ortiga [or'tiɣa] *nf* nettle.

ortodoncia [orto'ðonθja] *nf* orthodontics *sg*.

ortodoxo, a [orto'ðokso, a] *adj* orthodox.

ortografía [ortoɣra'fia] *nf* spelling.

ortopedia [orto'peðja] *nf* orthop(a)edics *sg*.

ortopédico, a [orto'peðiko, a] *adj* orthop(a)edic.

oruga [o'ruɣa] *nf* caterpillar.

orujo [o'ruxo] *nm type of strong grape liqueur made from grape pressings*.

orzuelo [or'θwelo] *nm* (*MED*) stye.

os [os] *pron* (*gen*) you; (*a vosotros*) (to) you; (*reflexivo*) (to) yourselves; (*mutuo*) (to) each other; **vosotros** ~ **laváis** you wash yourselves; **¡callar**~! (*fam*) shut up!

osa ['osa] *nf* (she-)bear; **O**~ **Mayor/Menor** Great/Little Bear, Ursa Major/Minor.

osadía [osa'ðia] *nf* daring; (*descaro*) impudence.

osamenta [osa'menta] *nf* skeleton.

osar [o'sar] *vi* to dare.

oscense [os'θense] *adj* of *o* from Huesca. ♦ *nm/f* native *o* inhabitant of Huesca.

oscilación [osθila'θjon] *nf* (*movimiento*) oscillation; (*fluctuación*) fluctuation; (*vacilación*) hesitation; (*columpio*) swinging, movement to and fro.

oscilar [osθi'lar] *vi* to oscillate; to fluctuate; to hesitate.

ósculo ['oskulo] *nm* kiss.

oscurecer [oskure'θer] *vt* to darken ♦ *vi* to grow dark; ~**se** *vr* to grow *o* get dark.

oscurezca [osku'reθka] *etc vb V* **oscurecer**.

oscuridad [oskuri'ðað] *nf* obscurity; (*tinieblas*) darkness.

oscuro, a [os'kuro, a] *adj* dark; (*fig*) obscure; (*indefinido*) confused; (*cielo*) overcast, cloudy; (*futuro etc*) uncertain; **a oscuras** in the dark.

óseo, a ['oseo, a] *adj* bony; (*MED etc*) bone *cpd*.

oso ['oso] *nm* bear; ~ **blanco/gris/pardo** polar/grizzly/brown bear; ~ **de peluche** teddy bear; ~ **hormiguero** anteater; **hacer el** ~ to play the fool.

Ostende [os'tende] *nm* Ostend.

ostensible [osten'siβle] *adj* obvious.

ostensiblemente [ostensiβle'mente] *adv* perceptibly, visibly.

ostentación [ostenta'θjon] *nf* (*gen*) ostentation; (*acto*) display.

ostentar [osten'tar] *vt* (*gen*) to show; (*pey*) to flaunt, show off; (*poseer*) to have, possess.

ostentoso, a [osten'toso, a] *adj* ostentatious, showy.

osteópata [oste'opata] *nm/f* osteopath.

ostra ['ostra] *nf* oyster ♦ *excl*: **¡**~**s!** (*fam*) sugar!

ostracismo [ostra'θismo] *nm* ostracism.

OTAN ['otan] *nf abr V* **Organización del Tratado del Atlántico Norte**.

OTASE [o'tase] *nf abr* (= *Organización del Tratado del Sudeste Asiático*) SEATO.

otear [ote'ar] *vt* to observe; (*fig*) to look into.

otero [o'tero] *nm* low hill, hillock.

otitis [o'titis] *nf* earache.

otoñal [oto'nal] *adj* autumnal.

otoño [o'tono] *nm* autumn, fall (*US*).

otorgamiento [otorɣa'mjento] *nm* conferring, granting; (*JUR*) execution.

otorgar [otor'ɣar] *vt* (*conceder*) to concede; (*dar*) to grant; (*poderes*) to confer; (*premio*) to award.

otorgue [o'torɣe] *etc vb V* **otorgar**.

otorrinolaringólogo, a [otorrinolarin'go loɣo, a] *nm/f* (*MED*: *tb*: **otorrino**) ear, nose and throat specialist.

═══════════ PALABRA CLAVE

otro, a ['otro, a] adj **1** (distinto: sg) another;
(: pl) other; **otra cosa/persona**
something/someone else; **con ~s amigos**
with other o different friends; **a/en otra
parte** elsewhere, somewhere else
2 (adicional): **tráigame ~ café (más), por
favor** can I have another coffee please;
~s 10 días más another 10 days
♦ pron **1** (sg) another one; **el ~** the other
one; **(los) ~s** (the) others; **¡otra!** (MUS)
more!; **de ~** somebody o someone else's;
que lo haga ~ let somebody o someone
else do it; **ni uno ni ~** neither one nor
the other
2 (recíproco): **se odian (la) una a (la) otra**
they hate one another o each other
3: ~ tanto: comer ~ tanto to eat the
same o as much again; **recibió una
decena de telegramas y otras tantas
llamadas** he got about ten telegrams and
as many calls.

otrora [o'trora] adv formerly; **el ~ señor
del país** the one-time ruler of the
country.
OUA nf abr (= Organización de la Unidad
Africana) OAU.
ovación [oβa'θjon] nf ovation.
ovacionar [oβaθjo'nar] vt to cheer.
oval [o'βal], **ovalado, a** [oβa'laðo, a] adj
oval.
óvalo ['oβalo] nm oval.
ovario [o'βarjo] nm ovary.
oveja [o'βexa] nf sheep; **~ negra** (fig) black
sheep (of the family).
overol [oβe'rol] nm (AM) overalls pl.
ovetense [oβe'tense] adj of o from Oviedo
♦ nm/f native o inhabitant of Oviedo.
ovillo [o'βiʎo] nm (de lana) ball; (fig) tangle;
hacerse un ~ to curl up (into a ball).
OVNI ['oβni] nm abr (= objeto volante no
identificado) UFO.
ovulación [oβula'θjon] nf ovulation.
óvulo ['oβulo] nm ovum.
oxidación [oksiða'θjon] nf rusting.
oxidar [oksi'ðar] vt to rust; **~se** vr to go
rusty; (TEC) to oxidize.
óxido ['oksiðo] nm oxide.
oxigenado, a [oksixe'naðo, a] adj
(QUÍMICA) oxygenated; (pelo) bleached.
oxigenar [oksixe'nar] vt to oxygenate; **~se**
vr to become oxygenated; (fam) to get
some fresh air.
oxígeno [ok'sixeno] nm oxygen.
oyendo [o'jendo] etc vb V **oír**.
oyente [o'jente] nm/f listener, hearer;

(ESCOL) unregistered o occasional
student.

═══════════ *P p*

P, p [pe] nf (letra) P, p; **P de París** P for
Peter.
P abr (REL = padre) Fr.; = **papa**.
p. abr (= página) p.
p.a. abr = **por autorización**.
pabellón [paβe'ʎon] nm bell tent; (ARQ)
pavilion; (de hospital etc) block, section;
(bandera) flag; **~ de conveniencia** (COM)
flag of convenience; **~ de la oreja** outer
ear.
pábilo ['paβilo] nm wick.
pábulo ['paβulo] nm food; **dar ~ a** to feed,
encourage.
PAC nf abr (= Política Agrícola Común) CAP.
pacense [pa'θense] adj of o from Badajoz
♦ nm/f native o inhabitant of Badajoz.
paceño, a [pa'θeɲo, a] adj of o from La
Paz ♦ nm/f native o inhabitant of La Paz.
pacer [pa'θer] vi to graze ♦ vt to graze on.
pachá [pa'tʃa] nm: **vivir como un ~** to live
like a king.
pachanguero, a [patʃan'gero, a] adj (pey:
música) noisy and catchy.
pachorra [pa'tʃorra] nf (indolencia)
slowness; (tranquilidad) calmness.
pachucho, a [pa'tʃutʃo, a] adj (fruta)
overripe; (persona) off-colour, poorly.
paciencia [pa'θjenθja] nf patience; **¡~! be
patient!; ¡~ y barajar!** don't give up!;
perder la ~ to lose one's temper.
paciente [pa'θjente] adj, nm/f patient.
pacificación [paθifika'θjon] nf pacification.
pacificar [paθifi'kar] vt to pacify;
(tranquilizar) to calm.
pacífico, a [pa'θifiko, a] adj peaceful;
(persona) peace-loving; (existencia)
pacific; **el (Océano) P~** the Pacific
(Ocean).
pacifique [paθi'fike] etc vb V **pacificar**.
pacifismo [paθi'fismo] nm pacifism.
pacifista [paθi'fista] nm/f pacifist.
pacotilla [pako'tiʎa] nf trash; **de ~** shoddy.
pactar [pak'tar] vt to agree to, agree on
♦ vi to come to an agreement.
pacto ['pakto] nm (tratado) pact; (acuerdo)
agreement.

padecer [paðe'θer] *vt* (*sufrir*) to suffer; (*soportar*) to endure, put up with; (*ser víctima de*) to be a victim of ♦ *vi*: ~ **de** to suffer from.

padecimiento [paðeθi'mjento] *nm* suffering.

padezca [pa'ðeθka] *etc vb* V **padecer**.

padrastro [pa'ðrastro] *nm* stepfather.

padre ['paðre] *nm* father ♦ *adj* (*fam*): **un éxito** ~ a tremendous success; ~**s** *nmpl* parents; ~ **espiritual** confessor; **P~ Nuestro** Lord's Prayer; ~ **político** father-in-law; **García** ~ García senior; **¡tu** ~! (*fam!*) up yours! (*!*).

padrino [pa'ðrino] *nm* godfather; (*fig*) sponsor, patron; ~**s** *nmpl* godparents; ~ **de boda** best man.

padrón [pa'ðron] *nm* (*censo*) census, roll; (*de socios*) register.

paella [pa'eʎa] *nf* paella, *dish of rice with meat, shellfish etc.*

paga ['paχa] *nf* (*dinero pagado*) payment; (*sueldo*) pay, wages *pl*.

pagadero, a [paχa'ðero, a] *adj* payable; ~ **a la entrega/a plazos** payable on delivery/in instalments.

pagano, a [pa'χano, a] *adj, nm/f* pagan, heathen.

pagar [pa'χar] *vt* (*gen*) to pay; (*las compras, crimen*) to pay for; (*deuda*) to pay (off); (*fig: favor*) to repay ♦ *vi* to pay; ~**se** *vr*: ~**se con algo** to be content with sth; **¡me las pagarás!** I'll get you for this!

pagaré [paχa're] *nm* I.O.U.

página ['paxina] *nf* page; ~ **de inicio** (*INFORM*) home page; ~**s amarillas** Yellow Pages ®.

paginación [paxina'θjon] *nf* (*INFORM, TIP*) pagination.

paginar [paxi'nar] *vt* (*INFORM, TIP*) to paginate.

pago ['paχo] *nm* (*dinero*) payment; (*fig*) return; ~ **anticipado/a cuenta/a la entrega/en especie/inicial** advance payment/payment on account/cash on delivery/payment in kind/down payment; ~ **a título gracioso** ex gratia payment; **en** ~ **de** in return for.

pág(s). *abr* (= *página(s)*) p(p).

pague ['paχe] *etc vb* V **pagar**.

paila ['paila] *nf* (*AM*) frying pan.

país [pa'is] *nm* (*gen*) country; (*región*) land; **los Países Bajos** the Low Countries; **el P~ Vasco** the Basque Country.

paisaje [pai'saxe] *nm* countryside, landscape; (*vista*) scenery.

paisano, a [pai'sano, a] *adj* of the same country ♦ *nm/f* (*compatriota*) fellow

countryman/woman; **vestir de** ~ (*soldado*) to be in civilian clothes; (*guardia*) to be in plain clothes.

paja ['paxa] *nf* straw; (*fig*) trash, rubbish; (*en libro, ensayo*) padding, waffle; **riñeron por un quítame allá esas** ~**s** they quarrelled over a trifle.

pajar [pa'xar] *nm* hay loft.

pajarita [paxa'rita] *nf* bow tie.

pájaro ['paxaro] *nm* bird; (*fam: astuto*) clever fellow; **tener la cabeza a** ~**s** to be featherbrained.

pajita [pa'xita] *nf* (*drinking*) straw.

pajizo, a [pa'xiθo, a] *adj* (*de paja*) straw *cpd*; (*techo*) thatched; (*color*) straw-coloured.

pakistaní [pakista'ni] *adj, nm/f* Pakistani.

pala ['pala] *nf* (*de mango largo*) spade; (*de mango corto*) shovel; (*raqueta etc*) bat; (: *de tenis*) racquet; (*CULIN*) slice; ~ **matamoscas** fly swat.

palabra [pa'laβra] *nf* (*gen, promesa*) word; (*facultad*) (power of) speech; (*derecho de hablar*) right to speak; **faltar a su** ~ to go back on one's word; **quedarse con la** ~ **en la boca** to stop short; (*en reunión, comité etc*) **tomar la** ~ to speak, take the floor; **pedir la** ~ to ask to be allowed to speak; **tener la** ~ to have the floor; **no encuentro** ~**s para expresarme** words fail me.

palabrería [palaβre'ria] *nf* hot air.

palabrota [pala'βrota] *nf* swearword.

palacio [pa'laθjo] *nm* palace; (*mansión*) mansion, large house; ~ **de justicia** courthouse; ~ **municipal** town/city hall.

palada [pa'laða] *nf* shovelful, spadeful; (*de remo*) stroke.

paladar [pala'ðar] *nm* palate.

paladear [palaðe'ar] *vt* to taste.

palanca [pa'lanka] *nf* lever; (*fig*) pull, influence; ~ **de cambio** (*AUTO*) gear lever, gearshift (*US*); ~ **de freno** (*AUTO*) brake lever; ~ **de gobierno** *o* **de control** (*INFORM*) joystick.

palangana [palan'gana] *nf* washbasin.

palco ['palko] *nm* box.

palenque [pa'lenke] *nm* (*cerca*) stockade, fence; (*área*) arena, enclosure; (*de gallos*) pit.

palentino, a [palen'tino, a] *adj* of *o* from Palencia ♦ *nm/f* native *o* inhabitant of Palencia.

paleolítico, a [paleo'litiko, a] *adj* paleolithic.

paleontología [paleontolo'xia] *nf* paleontology.

Palestina [pales'tina] *nf* Palestine.

palestino, a [pales'tino, a] *adj, nm/f* Palestinian.

palestra [pa'lestra] *nf*: **salir** *o* **saltar a la** ~ to come into the spotlight.

paleto, a [pa'leto, a] *nm/f* yokel, hick (*US*) ♦ *nf* (*pala*) small shovel; (*ARTE*) palette; (*ANAT*) shoulder blade; (*AM*) ice lolly.

paliar [pa'ljar] *vt* (*mitigar*) to mitigate; (*disfrazar*) to conceal.

paliativo [palja'tiβo] *nm* palliative.

palidecer [paliðe'θer] *vi* to turn pale.

palidez [pali'ðeθ] *nf* paleness.

palidezca [pali'ðeθka] *etc vb V* **palidecer**.

pálido, a ['paliðo, a] *adj* pale.

palillo [pa'liʎo] *nm* small stick; (*para dientes*) toothpick; ~**s** (**chinos**) chopsticks; **estar hecho un** ~ to be as thin as a rake.

palio ['paljo] *nm* canopy

palique [pa'like] *nm*: **estar de** ~ (*fam*) to have a chat.

paliza [pa'liθa] *nf* beating, thrashing; **dar** *o* **propinar** (*fam*) **una** ~ **a algn** to give sb a thrashing.

palma ['palma] *nf* (*ANAT*) palm; (*árbol*) palm tree; **batir** *o* **dar** ~**s** to clap, applaud; **llevarse la** ~ to triumph, win.

palmada [pal'maða] *nf* slap; ~**s** *nfpl* clapping *sg*, applause *sg*.

Palma de Mallorca *nf* Palma.

palmar [pal'mar] *vi* (*tb*: ~**la**) to die, kick the bucket.

palmarés [palma'res] *nm* (*lista*) list of winners; (*historial*) track record.

palmear [palme'ar] *vi* to clap.

palmero, a [pal'mero, a] *adj* of the island of Palma ♦ *nm/f* native *o* inhabitant of the island of Palma ♦ *nm* (*AM*), *nf* palm tree.

palmo ['palmo] *nm* (*medida*) span; (*fig*) small amount; ~ **a** ~ inch by inch.

palmotear [palmote'ar] *vi* to clap, applaud.

palmoteo [palmo'teo] *nm* clapping, applause.

palo ['palo] *nm* stick; (*poste*) post, pole; (*mango*) handle, shaft; (*golpe*) blow, hit; (*de golf*) club; (*de béisbol*) bat; (*NAUT*) mast; (*NAIPES*) suit; **vermut a** ~ **seco** straight vermouth; **de tal** ~ **tal astilla** like father like son.

paloma [pa'loma] *nf* dove, pigeon; ~ **mensajera** carrier *o* homing pigeon.

palomilla [palo'miʎa] *nf* moth; (*TEC*: *tuerca*) wing nut; (*soporte*) bracket.

palomitas [palo'mitas] *nfpl* popcorn *sg*.

palpable [pal'paβle] *adj* palpable; (*fig*) tangible.

palpar [pal'par] *vt* to touch, feel.

palpitación [palpita'θjon] *nf* palpitation.

palpitante [palpi'tante] *adj* palpitating; (*fig*) burning.

palpitar [palpi'tar] *vi* to palpitate; (*latir*) to beat.

palta ['palta] *nf* (*AM*) avocado.

palúdico, a [pa'luðiko, a] *adj* marshy.

paludismo [palu'ðismo] *nm* malaria.

palurdo, a [pa'lurðo, a] *adj* coarse, uncouth ♦ *nm/f* yokel, hick (*US*).

pamela [pa'mela] *nf* sun hat.

pampa ['pampa] *nf* (*AM*) pampa(s), prairie.

pamplinas [pam'plinas] *nfpl* nonsense *sg*.

pamplonés, esa [pamplo'nes, esa], **pamplonica** [pamplo'nika] *adj* of *o* from Pamplona ♦ *nm/f* native *o* inhabitant of Pamplona.

pan [pan] *nm* bread; (*una barra*) loaf; ~ **de molde** sliced loaf; ~ **integral** wholemeal bread; ~ **rallado** breadcrumbs *pl*; **eso es** ~ **comido** it's a cinch; **llamar al** ~ ~ **y al vino vino** to call a spade a spade.

pana ['pana] *nf* corduroy.

panadería [panaðe'ria] *nf* baker's (shop).

panadero, a [pana'ðero, a] *nm/f* baker.

panal [pa'nal] *nm* honeycomb.

Panamá [pana'ma] *nm* Panama.

panameño, a [pana'meɲo, a] *adj* Panamanian.

pancarta [pan'karta] *nf* placard, banner.

pancho, a ['pantʃo, a] *adj*: **estar tan** ~ to remain perfectly calm.

pancito [pan'sito] *nm* (*AM*) (bread) roll.

páncreas ['pankreas] *nm* pancreas.

panda ['panda] *nm* panda ♦ *nf* gang.

pandereta [pande'reta] *nf* tambourine.

pandilla [pan'diʎa] *nf* set, group; (*de criminales*) gang; (*pey*) clique.

pando, a ['pando, a] *adj* sagging.

panel [pa'nel] *nm* panel; ~ **acústico** acoustic screen.

panera [pa'nera] *nf* bread basket.

panfleto [pan'fleto] *nm* (*POL etc*) pamphlet; lampoon.

pánico ['paniko] *nm* panic.

panificadora [panifika'ðora] *nf* bakery.

panorama [pano'rama] *nm* panorama; (*vista*) view.

panqué [pan'ke] *nm* (*AM*) pancake.

pantaletas [panta'letas] *nfpl* (*AM*) panties.

pantalla [pan'taʎa] *nf* (*de cine*) screen; (*cubreluz*) lampshade; (*INFORM*) screen, display; **servir de** ~ **a** to be a blind for; ~ **de cristal líquido** liquid crystal display; ~ **táctil** touch-sensitive screen; ~ **de ayuda** help screen; ~ **plana** plane screen.

pantalón [panta'lon] *nm*, **pantalones** [panta'lones] *nmpl* trousers *pl*, pants *pl* (*US*); **pantalones vaqueros** jeans *pl*.

pantano [pan'tano] *nm* (*ciénaga*) marsh,

swamp; (_depósito: de agua_) reservoir; (_fig_) jam, fix, difficulty.

pantera [pan'tera] _nf_ panther.

pantis ['pantis] _nmpl_ tights.

pantomima [panto'mima] _nf_ pantomime.

pantorrilla [panto'rriʎa] _nf_ calf (of the leg).

pantufla [pan'tufla] _nf_ slipper.

panty ['panti] _nm_ = **pantis**.

panza ['panθa] _nf_ belly, paunch.

panzón, ona [pan'θon, ona], **panzudo, a** [pan'θuðo, a] _adj_ fat, potbellied.

pañal [pa'ɲal] _nm_ nappy, diaper (_US_); **estar todavía en ~es** to be still wet behind the ears.

pañería [paɲe'ria] _nf_ (_artículos_) drapery; (_tienda_) draper's (shop), dry-goods store (_US_).

paño ['paɲo] _nm_ (_tela_) cloth; (_pedazo de tela_) (piece of) cloth; (_trapo_) duster, rag; **~ de cocina** dishcloth; **~ higiénico** sanitary towel; **~s menores** underclothes; **~s calientes** (_fig_) half-measures; **no andarse con ~s calientes** to pull no punches.

pañuelo [pa'ɲwelo] _nm_ handkerchief, hanky (_fam_); (_para la cabeza_) (head)scarf.

papa ['papa] _nf_ (_AM_) potato ♦ _nm_: **el P~** the Pope.

papá [pa'pa] _nm_, _pl_ **papás** (_fam_) dad, daddy, pop (_US_); **~s** _nmpl_ parents; **hijo de ~** Hooray Henry (_fam_).

papada [pa'paða] _nf_ double chin.

papagayo [papa'ɣajo] _nm_ parrot.

papanatas [papa'natas] _nm inv_ (_fam_) sucker, simpleton.

paparrucha [papa'rrutʃa] _nf_ (_tontería_) piece of nonsense.

papaya [pa'paja] _nf_ papaya.

papear [pape'ar] _vt_, _vi_ (_fam_) to eat.

papel [pa'pel] _nm_ (_gen_) paper; (_hoja de papel_) sheet of paper; (_TEAT_) part, role; **~es** _nmpl_ identification papers; **~ de calco/carbón/de cartas** tracing paper/carbon paper/stationery; **~ contínuo** (_INFORM_) continuous stationery; **~ de envolver/empapelar** brown paper, wrapping paper/wallpaper; **~ de aluminio/higiénico** tinfoil/toilet paper; **~ del** _o_ **de pagos al Estado** government bonds _pl_; **~ de lija** sandpaper; **~ moneda** paper money; **~ plegado (en abanico** _o_ **en acordeón)** fanfold paper; **~ secante** blotting paper; **~ térmico** thermal paper.

papeleo [pape'leo] _nm_ red tape.

papelera [pape'lera] _nf_ (_cesto_) wastepaper basket; (_escritorio_) desk.

papelería [papele'ria] _nf_ (_tienda_) stationer's (shop).

papeleta [pape'leta] _nf_ (_pedazo de papel_) slip _o_ bit of paper; (_POL_) ballot paper; (_ESCOL_) report; **¡vaya ~!** this is a tough one!

paperas [pa'peras] _nfpl_ mumps _sg_.

papilla [pa'piʎa] _nf_ (_de bebé_) baby food; (_pey_) mush; **estar hecho ~** to be dog-tired.

paquete [pa'kete] _nm_ (_caja_) packet; (_bulto_) parcel; (_AM fam_) nuisance, bore; (_INFORM_) package (_of software_); (_vacaciones_) package tour; **~ de aplicaciones** (_INFORM_) applications package; **~ integrado** (_INFORM_) integrated package; **~ de gestión integrado** combined management suite; **~s postales** parcel post _sg_.

paquistaní [pakista'ni] = **pakistaní**.

par [par] _adj_ (_igual_) like, equal; (_MAT_) even ♦ _nm_ equal; (_de guantes_) pair; (_de veces_) couple; (_dignidad_) peer; (_GOLF, COM_) par ♦ _nf_ par; **~es** _o_ **nones** odds or evens; **abrir de ~ en ~** to open wide; **a la ~** par; **sobre/bajo la ~** above/below par.

para ['para] _prep_ (_gen_) for; **no es ~ comer** it's not for eating; **decir ~ sí** to say to o.s.; **¿~ qué lo quieres?** what do you want it for?; **se casaron ~ separarse otra vez** they married only to separate again; **~ entonces** by then _o_ that time; **lo tendré ~ mañana** I'll have it for tomorrow; **ir ~ casa** to go home, head for home; **~ profesor es muy estúpido** he's very stupid for a teacher; **¿quién es usted ~ gritar así?** who are you to shout like that?; **tengo bastante ~ vivir** I have enough to live on.

parabellum [para'ßelum] _nm_ (automatic) pistol.

parabién [para'ßjen] _nm_ congratulations _pl._

parábola [pa'raßola] _nf_ parable; (_MAT_) parabola.

parabólica [para'ßolika] _nf_ (_tb_: **antena ~**) satellite dish.

parabrisas [para'ßrisas] _nm inv_ windscreen, windshield (_US_).

paracaídas [paraka'iðas] _nm inv_ parachute.

paracaidista [parakai'ðista] _nm/f_ parachutist; (_MIL_) paratrooper.

parachoques [para'tʃokes] _nm inv_ bumper, fender (_US_); shock absorber.

parada [pa'raða] _nf_ V **parado**.

paradero [para'ðero] _nm_ stopping-place; (_situación_) whereabouts.

parado, a [pa'raðo, a] _adj_ (_persona_) motionless, standing still; (_fábrica_) closed, at a standstill; (*coche*) stopped; (*AM: de pie*) standing (up); (*sin empleo*) unemployed, idle; (*confuso*) confused ♦ *nf* (*gen*) stop; (*acto*) stopping; (*de industria*) shutdown, stoppage; (*lugar*) stopping-place; **salir bien** ~ to come off well; **parada de autobús** bus stop; **parada discrecional** request stop; **parada en seco** sudden stop; **parada de taxis** taxi rank.

paradoja [para'ðoxa] *nf* paradox.

paradójico, a [para'ðoxiko, a] *adj* paradoxical.

parador [para'ðor] *nm* (luxury) hotel.

parafrasear [parafrase'ar] *vt* to paraphrase.

paráfrasis [pa'rafrasis] *nf inv* paraphrase.

paraguas [pa'raɣwas] *nm inv* umbrella.

Paraguay [para'ɣwai] *nm*: **el** ~ Paraguay.

paraguayo, a [para'ɣwajo, a] *adj, nm/f* Paraguayan.

paraíso [para'iso] *nm* paradise, heaven; ~ **fiscal** (*COM*) tax haven.

paraje [pa'raxe] *nm* place, spot.

paralelo, a [para'lelo, a] *adj, nm* parallel; **en** ~ (*ELEC, INFORM*) (in) parallel.

paralice [para'liθe] *etc vb V* **paralizar**.

parálisis [pa'ralisis] *nf inv* paralysis; ~ **cerebral** cerebral palsy; ~ **progresiva** creeping paralysis.

paralítico, a [para'litiko, a] *adj, nm/f* paralytic.

paralizar [parali'θar] *vt* to paralyse; ~**se** *vr* to become paralysed; (*fig*) to come to a standstill.

parámetro [pa'rametro] *nm* parameter.

paramilitar [paramili'tar] *adj* paramilitary.

páramo ['paramo] *nm* bleak plateau.

parangón [paran'gon] *nm*: **sin** ~ incomparable.

paraninfo [para'ninfo] *nm* (*ESCOL*) assembly hall.

paranoia [para'noia] *nf* paranoia.

paranoico, a [para'noiko, a] *adj, nm/f* paranoid.

paranormal [paranor'mal] *adj* paranormal.

parapetarse [parape'tarse] *vr* to shelter.

parapléjico, a [para'plexiko, a] *adj, nm/f* paraplegic.

parar [pa'rar] *vt* to stop; (*progreso etc*) to check, halt; (*golpe*) to ward off ♦ *vi* to stop; (*hospedarse*) to stay, put up; ~**se** *vr* to stop; (*AM*) to stand up; **no** ~ **de hacer algo** to keep on doing sth; **ha parado de llover** it has stopped raining; **van a** ~ **en la comisaría** they're going to end up in the police station, **no sabemos en qué va a** ~ **todo esto** we don't know where all

this is going to end; ~**se a hacer algo** to stop to do sth; ~**se en** to pay attention to.

pararrayos [para'rrajos] *nm inv* lightning conductor.

parásito, a [pa'rasito, a] *nm/f* parasite.

parasol [para'sol] *nm* parasol, sunshade.

parcela [par'θela] *nf* plot, piece of ground, smallholding.

parche ['partʃe] *nm* patch.

parchís [par'tʃis] *nm* ludo.

parcial [par'θjal] *adj* (*pago*) part-; (*eclipse*) partial; (*juez*) prejudiced, biased.

parcialidad [parθjali'ðað] *nf* (*prejuicio*) prejudice, bias.

parco, a ['parko, a] *adj* (*frugal*) sparing; (*moderado*) moderate.

pardillo, a [par'ðiʎo, a] *adj* (*pey*) provincial ♦ *nm/f* (*pey*) country bumpkin ♦ *nm* (*ZOOL*) linnet.

pardo, a ['parðo, a] *adj* (*color*) brown; (*cielo*) overcast; (*voz*) flat, dull.

parear [pare'ar] *vt* (*juntar, hacer par*) to match, put together; (*calcetines*) to put into pairs; (*BIO*) to mate, pair.

parecer [pare'θer] *nm* (*opinión*) opinion, view; (*aspecto*) looks *pl* ♦ *vi* (*tener apariencia*) to seem, look; (*asemejarse*) to look like, seem like; (*aparecer, llegar*) to appear; ~**se** *vr* to look alike, resemble each other; ~**se a** to look like, resemble; **al** ~ apparently; **me parece que** I think (that), it seems to me that.

parecido, a [pare'θiðo, a] *adj* similar ♦ *nm* similarity, likeness, resemblance; ~ **a** like, similar to; **bien** ~ good-looking, nice-looking.

pared [pa'reð] *nf* wall; ~ **divisoria/ medianera** dividing/party wall; **subirse por las** ~**es** (*fam*) to go up the wall.

paredón [pare'ðon] *nm*: **llevar a algn al** ~ to put sb up against a wall, shoot sb.

parejo, a [pa'rexo, a] *adj* (*igual*) equal; (*liso*) smooth, even ♦ *nf* (*dos*) pair; (*: de personas*) couple; (*el otro: de un par*) other one (of a pair); (*: persona*) partner; (*Guardias*) Civil Guard patrol.

parentela [paren'tela] *nf* relations *pl*.

parentesco [paren'tesko] *nm* relationship.

paréntesis [pa'rentesis] *nm inv* parenthesis; (*digresión*) digression; (*en escrito*) bracket.

parezca [pa'reθka] *etc vb V* **parecer**.

parida [pa'riða] *nf*: ~ **mental** (*fam*) dumb idea.

paridad [pari'ðað] *nf* (*ECON*) parity.

pariente, a [pa'rjente, a] *nm/f* relative, relation.

parihuela [pari'wela] *nf* stretcher.
paripé [pari'pe] *nm*: **hacer el** ~ to put on an act.
parir [pa'rir] *vt* to give birth to ♦ *vi* (*mujer*) to give birth, have a baby; (*yegua*) to foal; (*vaca*) to calve.
París [pa'ris] *nm* Paris.
parisiense [pari'sjense] *adj, nm/f* Parisian.
paritario, a [pari'tarjo, a] *adj* equal.
parking ['parkin] *nm* car park, parking lot (*US*).
parlamentar [parlamen'tar] *vi* (*negociar*) to parley.
parlamentario, a [parlamen'tarjo, a] *adj* parliamentary ♦ *nm/f* member of parliament.
parlamento [parla'mento] *nm* (*POL*) parliament; (*JUR*) speech.
parlanchín, ina [parlan'tʃin, ina] *adj* loose-tongued, indiscreet ♦ *nm/f* chatterbox.
parlante [par'lante] *nm* (*AM*) loudspeaker.
parlar [par'lar] *vi* to chatter (away).
parlotear [parlote'ar] *vi* to chatter, prattle.
parloteo [parlo'teo] *nm* chatter, prattle.
parné [par'ne] *nm* (*fam: dinero*) dough.
paro ['paro] *nm* (*huelga*) stoppage (of work), strike; (*desempleo*) unemployment; ~ **cardiaco** cardiac arrest; **subsidio de** ~ unemployment benefit; **hay** ~ **en la industria** work in the industry is at a standstill; ~ **del sistema** (*INFORM*) system shutdown.
parodia [pa'roðja] *nf* parody.
parodiar [paro'ðjar] *vt* to parody.
parpadear [parpaðe'ar] *vi* (*los ojos*) to blink; (*luz*) to flicker.
parpadeo [parpa'ðeo] *nm* (*de ojos*) blinking, winking; (*de luz*) flickering.
párpado ['parpaðo] *nm* eyelid.
parque ['parke] *nm* (*lugar verde*) park; ~ **de atracciones/de bomberos/zoológico** fairground/fire station/zoo.
parqué, parquet [par'ke] *nm* parquet.
parqueadero [parkea'ðero] *nm* (*AM*) car park, parking lot (*US*).
parquímetro [par'kimetro] *nm* parking meter.
parra ['parra] *nf* grapevine.
párrafo ['parrafo] *nm* paragraph; **echar un** ~ (*fam*) to have a chat.
parranda [pa'rranda] *nf* (*fam*) spree, binge.
parrilla [pa'rriʎa] *nf* (*CULIN*) grill; (*AM AUTO*) roof-rack; ~ (**de salida**) (*AUTO*) starting grid; **carne a la** ~ grilled meat.
parrillada [parri'ʎaða] *nf* barbecue.
párroco ['parroko] *nm* parish priest.
parroquia [pa'rrokja] *nf* parish; (*iglesia*) parish church; (*COM*) clientele,

customers *pl.*
parroquiano, a [parro'kjano, a] *nm/f* parishioner; client, customer.
parsimonia [parsi'monja] *nf* (*frugalidad*) sparingness; (*calma*) deliberateness; **con** ~ calmly.
parte ['parte] *nm* message; (*informe*) report; ~ **meteorológico** weather forecast ♦ *nf* part; (*lado, cara*) side; (*de reparto*) share; (*JUR*) party; **en alguna** ~ **de Europa** somewhere in Europe; **en cualquier** ~ anywhere; **por ahí no se va a ninguna** ~ that leads nowhere; (*fig*) this is getting us nowhere; **en gran** ~ to a large extent; **la mayor** ~ **de los españoles** most Spaniards; **de algún tiempo a esta** ~ for some time past; **de** ~ **de algn** on sb's behalf; **¿de** ~ **de quién?** (*TELEC*) who is speaking?; **por** ~ **de** on the part of; **yo por mi** ~ I for my part; **por una** ~ ... **por otra** ~ on the one hand, ... on the other (hand); **dar** ~ **a algn** to report to sb; **tomar** ~ to take part.
partera [par'tera] *nf* midwife.
parterre [par'terre] *nm* (*de flores*) (flower)bed.
partición [parti'θjon] *nf* division, sharing-out; (*POL*) partition.
participación [partiθipa'θjon] *nf* (*acto*) participation, taking part; (*parte*) share; (*COM*) share, stock (*US*); (*de lotería*) shared prize; (*aviso*) notice, notification; ~ **en los beneficios** profit-sharing; ~ **minoritaria** minority interest.
participante [partiθi'pante] *nm/f* participant.
participar [partiθ'par] *vt* to notify, inform ♦ *vi* to take part, participate; ~ **en una empresa** (*COM*) to invest in an enterprise; **le participo que** ... I have to tell you that ....
partícipe [par'tiθipe] *nm/f* participant; **hacer** ~ **a algn de algo** to inform sb of sth.
participio [parti'θipjo] *nm* participle; ~ **de pasado/presente** past/present participle.
partícula [par'tikula] *nf* particle.
particular [partiku'lar] *adj* (*especial*) particular, special; (*individual, personal*) private, personal ♦ *nm* (*punto, asunto*) particular, point; (*individuo*) individual; **tiene coche** ~ he has a car of his own; **no dijo mucho sobre el** ~ he didn't say much about the matter.
particularice [partikula'riθe] *etc vb V* **particularizar**.

particularidad [partikulari'ðað] *nf* peculiarity; **tiene la ~ de que ...** one of its special features is (that) ....

particularizar [partikulari'θar] *vt* to distinguish; (*especificar*) to specify; (*detallar*) to give details about.

partida [par'tiða] *nf* (*salida*) departure; (*COM*) entry, item; (*juego*) game; (*grupo, bando*) band, group; **mala ~** dirty trick; **~ de nacimiento/matrimonio/defunción** birth/marriage/death certificate; **echar una ~** to have a game.

partidario, a [parti'ðarjo, a] *adj* partisan ♦ *nm/f* (*DEPORTE*) supporter; (*POL*) partisan.

partidismo [parti'ðismo] *nm* (*JUR*) partisanship, bias; (*POL*) party politics.

partido [par'tiðo] *nm* (*POL*) party; (*encuentro*) game, match; (*apoyo*) support; (*equipo*) team; **~ amistoso** (*DEPORTE*) friendly (game); **~ de fútbol** football match; **sacar ~ de** to profit from, benefit from; **tomar ~** to take sides.

partir [par'tir] *vt* (*dividir*) to split, divide; (*compartir, distribuir*) to share (out), distribute; (*romper*) to break open, split open; (*rebanada*) to cut (off) ♦ *vi* (*tomar camino*) to set off, set out; (*comenzar*) to start (off *o* out); **~se** *vr* to crack *o* split *o* break (in two *etc*); **a ~ de** (starting) from; **~se de risa** to split one's sides (laughing).

partitura [parti'tura] *nf* score.

parto ['parto] *nm* birth, delivery; (*fig*) product, creation; **estar de ~** to be in labour.

parvulario [parβu'larjo] *nm* nursery school, kindergarten.

párvulo, a ['parβulo, a] *nm/f* infant.

pasa ['pasa] *nf V* **paso**.

pasable [pa'saβle] *adj* passable.

pasada [pa'saða] *nf V* **pasado**.

pasadizo [pasa'ðiθo] *nm* (*pasillo*) passage, corridor; (*callejuela*) alley.

pasado, a [pa'saðo, a] *adj* past; (*malo: comida, fruta*) bad; (*muy cocido*) overdone; (*anticuado*) out of date ♦ *nm* past; (*LING*) past (tense) ♦ *nf* passing, passage; (*acción de pulir*) rub, polish; **~ mañana** the day after tomorrow; **el mes ~** last month; **~s dos días** after two days; **lo ~, ~** let bygones be bygones; **~ de moda** old-fashioned; **~ por agua** (*huevo*) boiled; **de pasada** in passing, incidentally; **una mala pasada** a dirty trick.

pasador [pasa'ðor] *nm* (*gen*) bolt; (*de pelo*) pin, grip, slide; **~es** *nmpl* (*AM: cordones*) shoelaces.

pasaje [pa'saxe] *nm* (*gen*) passage; (*pago de viaje*) fare; (*los pasajeros*) passengers *pl*; (*pasillo*) passageway.

pasajero, a [pasa'xero, a] *adj* passing; (*ave*) migratory ♦ *nm/f* passenger; (*viajero*) traveller.

pasamanos [pasa'manos] *nm inv* rail, handrail; (*de escalera*) banister.

pasamontañas [pasamon'taɲas] *nm inv* balaclava (helmet).

pasaporte [pasa'porte] *nm* passport.

pasar [pa'sar] *vt* (*gen*) to pass; (*tiempo*) to spend; (*durezas*) to suffer, endure; (*noticia*) to give, pass on; (*película*) to show; (*persona*) to take, conduct; (*río*) to cross; (*barrera*) to pass through; (*falta*) to overlook, tolerate; (*contrincante*) to surpass, do better than; (*coche*) to overtake; (*contrabando*) to smuggle (in/out); (*enfermedad*) to give, infect with ♦ *vi* (*gen*) to pass, go; (*terminarse*) to be over; (*ocurrir*) to happen; **~se** *vr* (*efectos*) to pass, be over; (*flores*) to fade; (*comida*) to go bad, go off; (*fig*) to overdo it, go too far *o* over the top; **~ de** to go beyond, exceed; **¡pase!** come in!; **nos hicieron ~** they showed us in; **~ por** to fetch; **~ por alto** to skip; **~ por una crisis** to go through a crisis; **se hace ~ por médico** he passes himself off as a doctor; **~lo bien/bomba** *o* **de maravilla** to have a good/great time; **~se al enemigo** to go over to the enemy; **~se de la raya** to go too far; **¡no te pases!** don't try me!; **se me pasó** I forgot; **se me pasó el turno** I missed my turn; **no se le pasa nada** nothing escapes him, he misses nothing; **ya se te pasará** you'll get over it; **¿qué pasa?** what's happening?, what's going on?, what's up?; **¡cómo pasa el tiempo!** time just flies!; **pase lo que pase** come what may; **el autobús pasa por nuestra casa** the bus goes past our house.

pasarela [pasa'rela] *nf* footbridge; (*en barco*) gangway.

pasatiempo [pasa'tjempo] *nm* pastime, hobby; (*distracción*) amusement.

Pascua, pascua ['paskwa] *nf*: **~ (de Resurrección)** Easter; **~ de Navidad** Christmas; **~s** *nfpl* Christmas time *sg*; **¡felices ~s!** Merry Christmas; **de ~s a Ramos** once in a blue moon; **hacer la ~ a** (*fam*) to annoy, bug.

pase ['pase] *nm* pass; (*CINE*) performance, showing; (*COM*) permit; (*JUR*) licence.

pasear [pase'ar] *vt* to take for a walk;

(*exhibir*) to parade, show off ♦ *vi*, ~**se** *vr* to walk, go for a walk; ~ **en coche** to go for a drive.

paseo [pa'seo] *nm* (*avenida*) avenue; (*distancia corta*) short walk; ~ **marítimo** promenade; **dar un** ~ to go for a walk; **mandar a algn a** ~ to tell sb to go to blazes; **¡vete a** ~! get lost!

pasillo [pa'siʎo] *nm* passage, corridor.

pasión [pa'sjon] *nf* passion.

pasional [pasjo'nal] *adj* passionate; **crimen** ~ crime of passion.

pasivo, a [pa'siβo, a] *adj* passive; (*inactivo*) inactive ♦ *nm* (*COM*) liabilities *pl*, debts *pl*; (*de cuenta*) debit side; ~ **circulante** current liabilities.

pasma ['pasma] *nm* (*fam*) cop.

pasmado, a [pas'maðo, a] *adj* (*asombrado*) astonished; (*atontado*) bewildered.

pasmar [pas'mar] *vt* (*asombrar*) to amaze, astonish; ~**se** *vr* to be amazed *o* astonished.

pasmo ['pasmo] *nm* amazement, astonishment; (*fig*) wonder, marvel.

pasmoso, a [pas'moso, a] *adj* amazing, astonishing.

paso, a ['paso, a] *adj* dried ♦ *nm* (*gen, de baile*) step; (*modo de andar*) walk; (*huella*) footprint; (*rapidez*) speed, pace, rate; (*camino accesible*) way through, passage; (*cruce*) crossing; (*pasaje*) passing, passage; (*REL*) *religious float or sculpture*; (*GEO*) pass; (*estrecho*) strait; (*fig*) step, measure; (*apuro*) difficulty ♦ *nf* raisin; **pasa de Corinto/de Esmirna** currant/sultana; ~ **a** ~ step by step; **a ese** ~ (*fig*) at that rate; **salir al** ~ **de** *o* **a** to waylay; **salir del** ~ to get out of trouble; **dar un** ~ **en falso** to trip; (*fig*) to take a false step; **estar de** ~ to be passing through; ~ **atrás** step backwards; (*fig*) backward step; ~ **elevado/subterráneo** flyover/subway, underpass (*US*); **prohibido el** ~ no entry; **ceda el** ~ give way; *V tb* **Semana Santa**.

pasota [pa'sota] *adj, nm/f* (*fam*) ≈ dropout; **ser un (tipo)** ~ to be a bit of a dropout; (*ser indiferente*) not to care about anything.

pasotismo [paso'tismo] *nm* underground *o* alternative culture.

pasta ['pasta] *nf* (*gen*) paste; (*CULIN: masa*) dough; (: *de bizcochos etc*) pastry; (*fam*) money, dough; (*encuadernación*) hardback; ~**s** *nfpl* (*bizcochos*) pastries, small cakes; (*fideos, espaguetis etc*) noodles, spaghetti *sg etc*; ~ **de dientes** *o* **dentífrica** toothpaste; ~ **de madera** wood pulp.

pastar [pas'tar] *vt, vi* to graze.

pastel [pas'tel] *nm* (*dulce*) cake; (*de carne*) pie; (*ARTE*) pastel; (*fig*) plot; ~**es** *nmpl* pastry *sg*, confectionery *sg*.

pastelería [pastele'ria] *nf* cake shop, pastry shop.

pasteurizado, a [pasteuri'θaðo, a] *adj* pasteurized.

pastilla [pas'tiʎa] *nf* (*de jabón, chocolate*) cake, bar; (*píldora*) tablet, pill.

pastizal [pasti'θal] *nm* pasture.

pasto ['pasto] *nm* (*hierba*) grass; (*lugar*) pasture, field; (*fig*) food, nourishment.

pastor, a [pas'tor, a] *nm/f* shepherd(ess) ♦ *nm* clergyman, pastor; (*ZOOL*) sheepdog; ~ **alemán** Alsatian.

pastoso, a [pas'toso, a] *adj* (*material*) doughy, pasty; (*lengua*) furry; (*voz*) mellow.

pat. *abr* (= *patente*) pat.

pata ['pata] *nf* (*pierna*) leg; (*pie*) foot; (*de muebles*) leg; ~**s arriba** upside down; **a cuatro** ~**s** on all fours; **meter la** ~ to put one's foot in it; ~ **de cabra** (*TEC*) crowbar; ~**s de gallo** crow's feet; **tener buena/mala** ~ to be lucky/unlucky.

patada [pa'taða] *nf* stamp; (*puntapié*) kick; **a** ~**s** in abundance; (*trato*) roughly; **echar a algn a** ~**s** to kick sb out.

patagón, ona [pata'ɣon, ona] *adj, nm/f* Patagonian.

Patagonia [pata'ɣonja] *nf*: **la** ~ Patagonia.

patalear [patale'ar] *vi* to stamp one's feet.

pataleo [pata'leo] *nm* stamping.

patán [pa'tan] *nm* rustic, yokel.

patata [pa'tata] *nf* potato; ~**s fritas** *o* **a la española** chips, French fries; ~**s a la inglesa** crisps; **ni** ~ (*fam*) nothing at all; **no entendió ni** ~ he didn't understand a single word.

paté [pa'te] *nm* pâté.

patear [pate'ar] *vt* (*pisar*) to stamp on, trample (on); (*pegar con el pie*) to kick ♦ *vi* to stamp (with rage), stamp one's foot.

patentar [paten'tar] *vt* to patent.

patente [pa'tente] *adj* obvious, evident; (*COM*) patent ♦ *nf* patent.

patera [pa'tera] *nf* boat.

paternal [pater'nal] *adj* fatherly, paternal.

paternalista [paterna'lista] *adj* (*tono, actitud etc*) patronizing.

paternidad [paterni'ðað] *nf* fatherhood, parenthood; (*JUR*) paternity.

paterno, a [pa'terno, a] *adj* paternal.

patético, a [pa'tetiko, a] *adj* pathetic, moving.

patíbulo [pa'tiβulo] *nm* scaffold,

gallows *sg.*
patilla [pa'tiʎa] *nf* (*de gafas*) arm; (*de pelo*)
sideburn.
patín [pa'tin] *nm* skate; (*de tobogán*)
runner; ~ **de hielo** ice skate; ~ **de
ruedas** roller skate.
patinaje [pati'naxe] *nm* skating.
patinar [pati'nar] *vi* to skate; (*resbalarse*) to
skid, slip; (*fam*) to slip up, blunder.
patinazo [pati'naθo] *nm* (*AUTO*) skid; **dar
un** ~ (*fam*) to blunder.
patio ['patjo] *nm* (*de casa*) patio,
courtyard; ~ **de recreo** playground.
pato ['pato] *nm* duck; **pagar el** ~ (*fam*) to
take the blame, carry the can.
patológico, a [pato'loxiko, a] *adj*
pathological.
patoso, a [pa'toso, a] *adj* awkward,
clumsy.
patraña [pa'traɲa] *nf* story, fib.
patria ['patrja] *nf* native land, mother
country; ~ **chica** home town.
patrimonio [patri'monjo] *nm* inheritance;
(*fig*) heritage; (*COM*) net worth.
patriota [pa'trjota] *nmlf* patriot.
patriotero, a [patrjo'tero, a] *adj*
chauvinistic.
patriótico, a [pa'trjotiko, a] *adj* patriotic.
patriotismo [patrjo'tismo] *nm* patriotism.
patrocinador, a [patroθina'ðor, a] *nmlf*
sponsor.
patrocinar [patroθi'nar] *vt* to sponsor;
(*apoyar*) to back, support.
patrocinio [patro'θinjo] *nm* sponsorship;
backing, support.
patrón, ona [pa'tron, ona] *nmlf* (*jefe*) boss,
chief, master/mistress; (*propietario*)
landlord/lady; (*REL*) patron saint ♦ *nm*
(*COSTURA*) pattern; (*TEC*) standard; ~ **oro**
gold standard.
patronal [patro'nal] *adj*: **la clase** ~
management; **cierre** ~ lockout.
patronato [patro'nato] *nm* sponsorship;
(*acto*) patronage; (*COM*) employers'
association; (*fundación*) trust; **el** ~ **de
turismo** the tourist board.
patrulla [pa'truʎa] *nf* patrol.
patrullar [patru'ʎar] *vi* to patrol.
paulatino, a [paula'tino, a] *adj* gradual,
slow.
paupérrimo, a [pau'perrimo, a] *adj* very
poor, poverty-stricken.
pausa ['pausa] *nf* pause; (*intervalo*) break;
(*interrupción*) interruption; (*TEC: en
videograbadora*) hold; **con** ~ slowly.
pausado, a [pau'saðo, a] *adj* slow,
deliberate.
pauta ['pauta] *nf* line, guide line.

pavimento [paβi'mento] *nm* (*ARQ*) flooring.
pavo ['paβo] *nm* turkey; (*necio*) silly thing,
idiot; ~ **real** peacock; ¡**no seas** ~! don't
be silly!
pavonearse [paβone'arse] *vr* to swagger,
show off.
pavor [pa'βor] *nm* dread, terror.
payasada [paja'saða] *nf* ridiculous thing
(to do); ~**s** *nfpl* clowning *sg.*
payaso, a [pa'jaso, a] *nmlf* clown.
payo, a ['pajo, a] *adj, nmlf* non-gipsy.
paz [paθ] *nf* peace; (*tranquilidad*)
peacefulness, tranquillity; **dejar a algn
en** ~ to leave sb alone *o* in peace; **hacer
las paces** to make peace; (*fig*) to make
up; ¡**haya** ~! stop it!
pazca ['paθka] *etc vb* V **pacer.**
PC *nm abr* (*POL*: = *Partido Comunista*) CP.
P.C.E. *nm abr* = *Partido Comunista Español.*
PCL *nf abr* (= *pantalla de cristal líquido*)
LCD.
PCUS [pe'kus] *nm abr* (= *Partido Comunista
de la Unión Soviética*) Soviet Communist
Party.
P.D. *abr* (= *posdata*) P.S.
pdo. *abr* (= *pasado*) ult.
peaje [pe'axe] *nm* toll; **autopista de** ~ toll
motorway, turnpike (*US*).
peatón [pea'ton] *nm* pedestrian; **paso de
peatones** pedestrian crossing,
crosswalk (*US*).
peca ['peka] *nf* freckle.
pecado [pe'kaðo] *nm* sin.
pecador, a [peka'ðor, a] *adj* sinful ♦ *nmlf*
sinner.
pecaminoso, a [pekami'noso, a] *adj* sinful.
pecar [pe'kar] *vi* (*REL*) to sin; (*fig*): ~ **de
generoso** to be too generous.
pecera [pe'θera] *nf* goldfish bowl.
pecho ['petʃo] *nm* (*ANAT*) chest; (*de mujer*)
breast(s) (*pl*), bosom; (*corazón*) heart,
breast; (*valor*) courage, spirit; **dar el** ~ **a**
to breast-feed; **tomar algo a** ~ to take
sth to heart; **no le cabía en el** ~ he was
bursting with happiness.
pechuga [pe'tʃuʀa] *nf* breast (of chicken
etc).
pecoso, a [pe'koso, a] *adj* freckled.
peculiar [peku'ljar] *adj* special, peculiar;
(*característico*) typical, characteristic.
peculiaridad [pekuljari'ðað] *nf* peculiarity;
special feature, characteristic.
pedagogía [peðaʀo'xia] *nf* education.
pedagogo [peða'ʀoʀo] *nm* pedagogue,
teacher.
pedal [pe'ðal] *nm* pedal; ~ **de embrague**
clutch (pedal); ~ **de freno** footbrake.
pedalear [peðale'ar] *vi* to pedal.

pedante [pe'ðante] _adj_ pedantic ♦ _nm/f_ pedant.

pedantería [peðante'ria] _nf_ pedantry.

pedazo [pe'ðaθo] _nm_ piece, bit; **hacerse ~s** to fall to pieces; (_romperse_) to smash, shatter; **un ~ de pan** a scrap of bread; (_fig_) a terribly nice person.

pedernal [peðer'nal] _nm_ flint.

pedestal [peðes'tal] _nm_ base; **tener/poner a algn en un ~** to put sb on a pedestal.

pedestre [pe'ðestre] _adj_ pedestrian; **carrera ~** foot race.

pediatra [pe'ðjatra] _nm/f_ paediatrician (_BRIT_), pediatrician (_US_).

pediatría [peðja'tria] _nf_ paediatrics _sg_ (_BRIT_), pediatrics _sg_ (_US_).

pedicuro, a [peði'kuro, a] _nm/f_ chiropodist (_BRIT_), podiatrist (_US_).

pedido [pe'ðiðo] _nm_ (_COM: mandado_) order; (_petición_) request; **~s en cartera** (_COM_) backlog _sg_.

pedigrí [peði'ɣri] _nm_ pedigree.

pedir [pe'ðir] _vt_ to ask for, request; (_comida, COM: mandar_) to order; (_exigir: precio_) to ask; (_necesitar_) to need, demand, require ♦ _vi_ to ask; **~ prestado** to borrow; **~ disculpas** to apologize; **me pidió que cerrara la puerta** he asked me to shut the door; **¿cuánto piden por el coche?** how much are they asking for the car?

pedo ['peðo] (_fam_) _adj inv_: **estar ~** to be pissed (_!_) ♦ _nm_ fart (_!_).

pedrada [pe'ðraða] _nf_ throw of a stone; (_golpe_) blow from a stone; **herir a algn de una ~** to hit sb with a stone.

pedrea [pe'ðrea] _nf_ (_granizada_) hailstorm; (_de lotería_) minor prizes.

pedrisco [pe'ðrisko] _nm_ (_granizo_) hail; (_granizada_) hailstorm.

Pedro ['peðro] _nm_ Peter; **entrar como ~ por su casa** to come in as if one owned the place.

pega ['peɣa] _nf_ (_dificultad_) snag; **de ~** false, dud; **poner ~s** to raise objections.

pegadizo, a [peɣa'ðiθo, a] _adj_ (_canción etc_) catchy.

pegajoso, a [peɣa'xoso, a] _adj_ sticky, adhesive.

pegamento [peɣa'mento] _nm_ gum.

pegar [pe'ɣar] _vt_ (_papel, sellos_) to stick (on); (_con cola_) to glue; (_cartel_) to post, stick up; (_coser_) to sew (on); (_unir: partes_) to join, fix together; (_MED_) to give, infect with; (_dar: golpe_) to give, deal ♦ _vi_ (_adherirse_) to stick, adhere; (_ir juntos: colores_) to match, go together; (_golpear_) to hit; (_quemar: el sol_) to strike hot, burn

(_fig_); **~se** _vr_ (_gen_) to stick; (_dos personas_) to hit each other, fight; **~le a algo** to be a great one for sth; **~ un grito** to let out a yell; **~ un salto** to jump (with fright); **~ fuego** to catch fire; **~ en** to touch; **~se un tiro** to shoot o.s.; **no pega** that doesn't seem right; **ese sombrero no pega con el abrigo** that hat doesn't go with the coat.

pegatina [peɣa'tina] _nf_ (_POL etc_) sticker.

pego ['peɣo] _nm_: **dar el ~** (_pasar por verdadero_) to look like the real thing.

pegote [pe'ɣote] _nm_ (_fig_) patch, ugly mend; **tirarse ~s** (_fam_) to come on strong.

pegue ['peɣe] _etc vb_ V **pegar**.

peinado [pei'naðo] _nm_ (_en peluquería_) hairdo; (_estilo_) hair style.

peinar [pei'nar] _vt_ to comb sb's hair; (_hacer estilo_) to style; **~se** _vr_ to comb one's hair.

peine ['peine] _nm_ comb.

peineta [pei'neta] _nf_ ornamental comb.

p.ej. _abr_ (= _por ejemplo_) e.g.

Pekín [pe'kin] _n_ Peking.

pela ['pela] _nf_ (_ESP fam_) peseta; V _tb_ **pelas**.

pelado, a [pe'laðo, a] _adj_ (_cabeza_) shorn; (_fruta_) peeled; (_campo, fig_) bare; (_fam: sin dinero_) broke.

pelaje [pe'laxe] _nm_ (_ZOOL_) fur, coat; (_fig_) appearance.

pelambre [pe'lambre] _nm_ long hair, mop.

pelar [pe'lar] _vt_ (_fruta, patatas_) to peel; (_cortar el pelo a_) to cut the hair of; (_quitar la piel: animal_) to skin; (_ave_) to pluck; (_habas etc_) to shell; **~se** _vr_ (_la piel_) to peel off; **corre que se las pela** (_fam_) he runs like nobody's business.

pelas ['pelas] _nfpl_ (_ESP fam_) dough.

peldaño [pel'daɲo] _nm_ step; (_de escalera portátil_) rung.

pelea [pe'lea] _nf_ (_lucha_) fight; (_discusión_) quarrel, row.

peleado, a [pele'aðo, a] _adj_: **estar ~ (con algn)** to have fallen out (with sb).

pelear [pele'ar] _vi_ to fight; **~se** _vr_ to fight; (_reñirse_) to fall out, quarrel.

pelele [pe'lele] _nm_ (_figura_) guy, dummy; (_fig_) puppet.

peletería [pelete'ria] _nf_ furrier's, fur shop.

peliagudo, a [pelja'ɣuðo, a] _adj_ tricky.

pelícano [pe'likano] _nm_ pelican.

película [pe'likula] _nf_ (_CINE_) film, movie (_US_); (_cobertura ligera_) film, thin covering; (_FOTO: rollo_) roll _o_ reel of film; **~ de dibujos (animados)** cartoon film; **~ muda** silent film; **de ~** (_fam_) astonishing, out of this world.

peligrar [peli'ɣrar] _vi_ to be in danger.

peligro [pe'liɣro] _nm_ danger; (_riesgo_) risk;

"~ **de muerte**" "danger"; **correr** ~ **de** to be in danger of; **con** ~ **de la vida** at the risk of one's life.

peligrosidad [peliɣrosi'ðað] *nf* danger, riskiness.

peligroso, a [peli'ɣroso, a] *adj* dangerous; risky.

pelirrojo, a [peli'rroxo, a] *adj* red-haired, red-headed.

pellejo [pe'ʎexo] *nm* (*de animal*) skin, hide; **salvar el** ~ to save one's skin.

pellizcar [peʎiθ'kar] *vt* to pinch, nip.

pellizco [pe'ʎiθko] *nm* (*gen*) pinch.

pellizque [pe'ʎiθke] *etc vb V* **pellizcar**.

pelma ['pelma] *nm/f*, **pelmazo** [pel'maθo] *nm* (*fam*) pest.

pelo ['pelo] *nm* (*cabellos*) hair; (*de barba, bigote*) whisker; (*de animal: pellejo*) fur, coat; (*de perro etc*) hair, coat; (*de ave*) down; (*de tejido*) nap; (*TEC*) fibre; **a** ~ bareheaded; (*desnudo*) naked; **al** ~ just right; **venir al** ~ to be exactly what one needs; **por los** ~**s** by the skin of one's teeth; **escaparse por un** ~ to have a close shave; **se me pusieron los** ~**s de punta** my hair stood on end; **no tener** ~**s en la lengua** to be outspoken, not mince words; **tomar el** ~ **a algn** to pull sb's leg.

pelón, ona [pe'lon, ona] *adj* hairless, bald.

pelota [pe'lota] *nf* ball; (*fam: cabeza*) nut (*fam*); **en** ~**(s)** stark naked; ~ **vasca** pelota; **devolver la** ~ **a algn** (*fig*) to turn the tables on sb; **hacer la** ~ **(a algn)** to creep (to sb).

pelotera [pelo'tera] *nf* (*fam*) barney.

pelotón [pelo'ton] *nm* (*MIL*) squad, detachment.

peluca [pe'luka] *nf* wig.

peluche [pe'lutʃe] *nm*: **muñeco de** ~ soft toy.

peludo, a [pe'luðo, a] *adj* hairy, shaggy.

peluquería [peluke'ria] *nf* hairdresser's; (*para hombres*) barber's (shop).

peluquero, a [pelu'kero, a] *nm/f* hairdresser; barber.

peluquín [pelu'kin] *nm* toupée.

pelusa [pe'lusa] *nf* (*BOT*) down; (*COSTURA*) fluff.

pelvis ['pelßis] *nf* pelvis.

PEMEX [pe'meks] *nm abr* = *Petróleos Mejicanos*.

PEN [pen] *nm abr* (*ESP*) = *Plan Energético Nacional*.

pena ['pena] *nf* (*congoja*) grief, sadness; (*remordimiento*) regret; (*dificultad*) trouble; (*dolor*) pain; (*AM: vergüenza*) shame; (*JUR*) sentence; (*DEPORTE*) penalty; ~ **capital** capital punishment; ~

de muerte death penalty; ~ **pecuniaria** fine; **merecer** *o* **valer la** ~ to be worthwhile; **a duras** ~**s** with great difficulty; **so** ~ **de** on pain of; **me dan** ~ I feel sorry for them; **¿no te da** ~ **hacerlo?** (*AM*) aren't you embarrassed doing that?; **¡qué** ~! what a shame *o* pity!

penal [pe'nal] *adj* penal ♦ *nm* (*cárcel*) prison.

penalidad [penali'ðað] *nf* (*problema, dificultad*) trouble, hardship; (*JUR*) penalty, punishment.

penalizar [penali'θar] *vt* to penalize.

penalti, penalty [pe'nalti] *nm* (*DEPORTE*) penalty.

penar [pe'nar] *vt* to penalize; (*castigar*) to punish ♦ *vi* to suffer.

pendejo, a [pen'dexo, a] *nm/f* (*AM fam!*) wanker (*BRIT!*), jerk (*US!*).

pender [pen'der] *vi* (*colgar*) to hang; (*JUR*) to be pending.

pendiente [pen'djente] *adj* pending, unsettled ♦ *nm* earring ♦ *nf* hill, slope; **tener una asignatura** ~ to have to resit a subject.

pendón [pen'don] *nm* banner, standard.

péndulo ['pendulo] *nm* pendulum.

pene ['pene] *nm* penis.

penene [pe'nene] *nm/f* = PNN.

penetración [penetra'θjon] *nf* (*acto*) penetration; (*agudeza*) sharpness, insight.

penetrante [pene'trante] *adj* (*herida*) deep; (*persona, arma*) sharp; (*sonido*) penetrating, piercing; (*mirada*) searching; (*viento, ironía*) biting.

penetrar [pene'trar] *vt* to penetrate, pierce; (*entender*) to grasp ♦ *vi* to penetrate, go in; (*líquido*) to soak in; (*emoción*) to pierce.

penicilina [peniθi'lina] *nf* penicillin.

península [pe'ninsula] *nf* peninsula; **P**~ **Ibérica** Iberian Peninsula.

peninsular [peninsu'lar] *adj* peninsular.

penique [pe'nike] *nm* penny; ~**s** *nmpl* pence.

penitencia [peni'tenθja] *nf* (*remordimiento*) penitence; (*castigo*) penance; **en** ~ as a penance.

penitencial [peniten'θjal] *adj* penitential.

penitenciaría [penitenθja'ria] *nf* prison, penitentiary.

penitenciario, a [peniten'θjarjo, a] *adj* prison *cpd*.

penoso, a [pe'noso, a] *adj* laborious, difficult.

pensado, a [pen'saðo, a] *adj*: **bien/mal** ~

well intentioned/cynical; **en el momento menos** ~ when least expected.

pensador, a [pensa'ðor, a] *nm/f* thinker.

pensamiento [pensa'mjento] *nm* (*gen*) thought; (*mente*) mind; (*idea*) idea; (*BOT*) pansy; **no se le pasó por el** ~ it never occurred to him.

pensar [pen'sar] *vt* to think; (*considerar*) to think over, think out; (*proponerse*) to intend, plan, propose; (*imaginarse*) to think up, invent ♦ *vi* to think; ~ **en** to think of *o* about; (*anhelar*) to aim at, aspire to; **dar que** ~ **a algn** to give sb food for thought.

pensativo, a [pensa'tißo, a] *adj* thoughtful, pensive.

pensión [pen'sjon] *nf* (*casa*) ≈ guest house; (*dinero*) pension; (*cama y comida*) board and lodging; ~ **de jubilación** retirement pension; ~ **escalada** graduated pension; ~ **completa** full board; **media** ~ half board.

pensionista [pensjo'nista] *nm/f* (*jubilado*) (old-age) pensioner; (*quien vive en pensión*) lodger; (*ESCOL*) boarder.

pentágono [pen'tayono] *nm* pentagon: **el P**~ (*US*) the Pentagon.

pentagrama [penta'yrama] *nm* (*MUS*) stave, staff.

penúltimo, a [pe'nultimo, a] *adj* penultimate, second last.

penumbra [pe'numbra] *nf* half-light, semi-darkness.

penuria [pe'nurja] *nf* shortage, want.

peña ['peɲa] *nf* (*roca*) rock; (*cuesta*) cliff, crag; (*grupo*) group, circle; (*DEPORTE*) supporters' club.

peñasco [pe'ɲasko] *nm* large rock, boulder.

peñón [pe'ɲon] *nm* crag; **el P**~ the Rock (of Gibraltar).

peón [pe'on] *nm* labourer; (*AM*) farm labourer, farmhand; (*TEC*) spindle, shaft; (*AJEDREZ*) pawn.

peonza [pe'onθa] *nf* spinning top.

peor [pe'or] *adj* (*comparativo*) worse; (*superlativo*) worst ♦ *adv* worse; worst; **de mal en** ~ from bad to worse; **tanto** ~ so much the worse; **A es** ~ **que B** A is worse than B; **Z es el** ~ **de todos** Z is the worst of all.

pepenar [pepe'nar] *vi* (*AM*) to sift through rubbish *o* garbage.

pepinillo [pepi'niʎo] *nm* gherkin.

pepino [pe'pino] *nm* cucumber; **(no) me importa un** ~ I don't care two hoots.

pepita [pe'pita] *nf* (*BOT*) pip; (*MINERÍA*) nugget.

pepito [pe'pito] *nm* meat sandwich.

peque ['peke] *etc vb V* **pecar**.

pequeñez [peke'ɲeθ] *nf* smallness, littleness; (*trivialidad*) trifle, triviality.

pequeño, a [pe'keɲo, a] *adj* small, little; (*cifra*) small, low; (*bajo*) short; ~ **burgués** lower middle-class.

pequinés, esa [peki'nes, esa] *adj, nm/f* Pekinese.

pera ['pera] *adj inv* classy; **niño** ~ spoiled upper-class brat ♦ *nf* pear; **eso es pedir** ~**s al olmo** that's asking the impossible.

peral [pe'ral] *nm* pear tree.

percance [per'kanθe] *nm* setback, misfortune.

per cápita [per'kapita] *adj*: **renta** ~ per capita income.

percatarse [perka'tarse] *vr*: ~ **de** to notice, take note of.

percebe [per'θeße] *nm* (*ZOOL*) barnacle; (*fam*) idiot.

percepción [perθep'θjon] *nf* (*vista*) perception; (*idea*) notion, idea; (*COM*) collection.

perceptible [perθep'tißle] *adj* perceptible, noticeable; (*COM*) payable, receivable.

percha ['pertʃa] *nf* (*poste*) pole, support; (*gancho*) peg; (*de abrigos*) coat stand; (*colgador*) coat hanger; (*de ave*) perch.

perchero [per'tʃero] *nm* clothes rack.

percibir [perθi'ßir] *vt* to perceive, notice; (*ver*) to see; (*peligro etc*) to sense; (*COM*) to earn, receive, get.

percusión [perku'sjon] *nf* percussion.

percusor [perku'sor], **percutor** [perku'tor] *nm* (*TEC*) hammer; (*de arma*) firing pin.

perdedor, a [perðe'ðor, a] *adj* losing ♦ *nm/f* loser.

perder [per'ðer] *vt* to lose; (*tiempo, palabras*) to waste; (*oportunidad*) to lose, miss; (*tren*) to miss ♦ *vi* to lose; ~**se** *vr* (*extraviarse*) to get lost; (*desaparecer*) to disappear, be lost to view; (*arruinarse*) to be ruined; **echar a** ~ (*comida*) to spoil, ruin; (*oportunidad*) to waste; **tener buen** ~ to be a good loser; **¡no te lo pierdas!** don't miss it!; **he perdido la costumbre** I have got out of the habit.

perdición [perði'θjon] *nf* perdition; (*fig*) ruin.

pérdida ['perðiða] *nf* loss; (*de tiempo*) waste; (*COM*) net loss; ~**s** *nfpl* (*COM*) losses; **¡no tiene** ~! you can't go wrong!; ~ **contable** (*COM*) book loss.

perdido, a [per'ðiðo, a] *adj* lost; **estar** ~ **por** to be crazy about; **es un caso** ~ he is a hopeless case.

perdigón [perði'yon] *nm* pellet.

perdiz [per'ðiθ] *nf* partridge.
perdón [per'ðon] *nm* (*disculpa*) pardon, forgiveness; (*clemencia*) mercy; ¡~! sorry!, I beg your pardon!; **con** ~ if I may, if you don't mind.
perdonar [perðo'nar] *vt* to pardon, forgive; (*la vida*) to spare; (*excusar*) to exempt, excuse ♦ *vi* to pardon, forgive; ¡**perdone (usted)!** sorry!, I beg your pardon!; **perdone, pero me parece que ...** excuse me, but I think ...
perdurable [perðu'raßle] *adj* lasting; (*eterno*) everlasting.
perdurar [perðu'rar] *vi* (*resistir*) to last, endure; (*seguir existiendo*) to stand, still exist.
perecedero, a [pereθe'ðero, a] *adj* perishable.
perecer [pere'θer] *vi* to perish, die.
peregrinación [pereɣrina'θjon] *nf* (*REL*) pilgrimage.
peregrino, a [pere'ɣrino] *adj* (*extraño*) strange; (*singular*) rare ♦ *nm/f* pilgrim.
perejil [pere'xil] *nm* parsley.
perenne [pe'renne] *adj* everlasting, perennial.
perentorio, a [peren'torjo, a] *adj* (*urgente*) urgent; (*terminante*) peremptory; (*fijo*) set, fixed.
pereza [pe're θa] *nf* (*flojera*) laziness; (*lentitud*) sloth, slowness.
perezca [pe'reθka] *etc vb* V **perecer**.
perezoso, a [pere'θoso, a] *adj* lazy; slow, sluggish.
perfección [perfek'θjon] *nf* perfection; **a la** ~ to perfection.
perfeccionar [perfekθjo'nar] *vt* to perfect; (*acabar*) to complete, finish.
perfecto, a [per'fekto, a] *adj* perfect ♦ *nm* (*LING*) perfect (tense).
perfidia [per'fiðja] *nf* perfidy, treachery.
pérfido, a ['perfiðo, a] *adj* perfidious, treacherous.
perfil [per'fil] *nm* (*parte lateral*) profile; (*silueta*) silhouette, outline; (*TEC*) (cross) section; ~**es** *nmpl* features; (*fig*) social graces; ~ **del cliente** (*COM*) customer profile; **en** ~ from the side, in profile.
perfilado, a [perfi'laðo, a] *adj* (*bien formado*) well-shaped; (*largo: cara*) long.
perfilar [perfi'lar] *vt* (*trazar*) to outline; (*dar carácter a*) to shape, give character to; ~**se** *vr* to be silhouetted (*en* against); **el proyecto se va perfilando** the project is taking shape.
perforación [perfora'θjon] *nf* perforation; (*con taladro*) drilling.
perforadora [perfora'ðora] *nf* drill; ~ **de**

fichas card-punch.
perforar [perfo'rar] *vt* to perforate; (*agujero*) to drill, bore; (*papel*) to punch a hole in ♦ *vi* to drill, bore.
perfumado, a [perfu'maðo, a] *adj* scented, perfumed.
perfumar [perfu'mar] *vt* to scent, perfume.
perfume [per'fume] *nm* perfume, scent.
pergamino [perɣa'mino] *nm* parchment.
pericia [pe'riθja] *nf* skill, expertise.
periferia [peri'ferja] *nf* periphery; (*de ciudad*) outskirts *pl*.
periférico, a [peri'feriko, a] *adj* peripheral ♦ *nm* (*INFORM*) peripheral; (*AM: AUTO*) ring road; **barrio** ~ outlying district.
perilla [pe'riʎa] *nf* goatee.
perímetro [pe'rimetro] *nm* perimeter.
periódico, a [pe'rjoðiko, a] *adj* periodic(al) ♦ *nm* (news)paper; ~ **dominical** Sunday (news)paper.
periodismo [perjo'ðismo] *nm* journalism.
periodista [perjo'ðista] *nm/f* journalist.
periodístico, a [perjo'ðistiko, a] *adj* journalistic.
periodo [pe'rjoðo], **período** [pe'rioðo] *nm* period; ~ **contable** (*COM*) accounting period.
peripecias [peri'peθjas] *nfpl* adventures.
peripuesto, a [peri'pwesto, a] *adj* dressed up; **tan** ~ all dressed up (to the nines).
perito, a [pe'rito, a] *adj* (*experto*) expert; (*diestro*) skilled, skilful ♦ *nm/f* expert; skilled worker; (*técnico*) technician.
perjudicar [perxuði'kar] *vt* (*gen*) to damage, harm; (*fig*) to prejudice.
perjudicial [perxuði'θjal] *adj* damaging, harmful; (*en detrimento*) detrimental.
perjudique [perxu'ðike] *etc vb* V **perjudicar**.
perjuicio [per'xwiθjo] *nm* damage, harm; **en/sin** ~ **de** to the detriment of/without prejudice to.
perjurar [perxu'rar] *vi* to commit perjury.
perla ['perla] *nf* pearl; **me viene de** ~**s** it suits me fine.
permanecer [permane'θer] *vi* (*quedarse*) to stay, remain; (*seguir*) to continue to be.
permanencia [perma'nenθja] *nf* (*duración*) permanence; (*estancia*) stay.
permanente [perma'nente] *adj* (*que queda*) permanent; (*constante*) constant; (*comisión etc*) standing ♦ *nf* perm; **hacerse una** ~ to have one's hair permed.
permanezca [perma'ncθka] *etc vb* V **permanecer**.
permisible [permi'sißle] *adj* permissible, allowable.

permiso [per'miso] *nm* permission;
(*licencia*) permit, licence (*BRIT*), license
(*US*); **con ~** excuse me; **estar de ~** (*MIL*)
to be on leave; **~ de conducir** *o*
conductor driving licence (*BRIT*),
driver's license (*US*); **~ de exportación/
importación** export/import licence; **~
por asuntos familiares** compassionate
leave.

permitir [permi'tir] *vt* to permit, allow;
~se *vr:* **~se algo** to allow o.s. sth; **no me
puedo ~ ese lujo** I can't afford that; **¿me
permite?** may I?; **si lo permite el tiempo**
weather permitting.

permuta [per'muta] *nf* exchange.

permutar [permu'tar] *vt* to switch,
exchange; **~ destinos con algn** to swap *o*
exchange jobs with sb.

pernicioso, a [perni'θjoso, a] *adj* (*maligno,
MED*) pernicious; (*persona*) wicked.

perno ['perno] *nm* bolt.

pernoctar [pernok'tar] *vi* to stay for the
night.

pero ['pero] *conj* but; (*aún*) yet ♦ *nm*
(*defecto*) flaw, defect; (*reparo*) objection;
¡no hay ~ que valga! there are no buts
about it.

perogrullada [peroɣru'ʎaða] *nf* platitude,
truism.

perol [pe'rol] *nm,* **perola** [pe'rola] *nf* pan.

peronista [pero'nista] *adj, nm/f* Peronist.

perorata [pero'rata] *nf* long-winded
speech.

perpendicular [perpendiku'lar] *adj*
perpendicular; **el camino es ~ al río** the
road is at right angles to the river.

perpetrar [perpe'trar] *vt* to perpetrate.

perpetuamente [perpetwa'mente] *adv*
perpetually.

perpetuar [perpe'twar] *vt* to perpetuate.

perpetuo, a [per'petwo, a] *adj* perpetual;
(*JUR etc: condena*) life *cpd.*

Perpiñán [perpi'ɲan] *nm* Perpignan.

perplejo, a [per'plexo, a] *adj* perplexed,
bewildered.

perra ['perra] *nf* bitch; (*fam: dinero*) money;
(: *manía*) mania, crazy idea; (: *rabieta*)
tantrum; **estar sin una ~** to be flat broke.

perrera [pe'rrera] *nf* kennel.

perro ['perro] *nm* dog; **~ caliente** hot dog;
"~ peligroso" "beware of the dog"; **ser
~ viejo** to be an old hand; **tiempo de ~s**
filthy weather; **~ que ladra no muerde**
his bark is worse than his bite.

persa ['persa] *adj, nm/f* Persian ♦ *nm* (*LING*)
Persian.

persecución [perseku'θjon] *nf* pursuit,
hunt, chase; (*REL, POL*) persecution.

perseguir [perse'ɣir] *vt* to pursue, hunt;
(*cortejar*) to chase after; (*molestar*) to
pester, annoy; (*REL, POL*) to persecute;
(*JUR*) to prosecute.

perseverante [perseße'rante] *adj*
persevering, persistent.

perseverar [perseve'rar] *vi* to persevere,
persist; **~ en** to persevere in, persist
with.

persiana [per'sjana] *nf* (Venetian) blind.

persiga [per'siɣa] *etc vb V* **perseguir.**

persignarse [persiɣ'narse] *vr* to cross o.s.

persiguiendo [persi'ɣjenðo] *etc vb V*
perseguir.

persistente [persis'tente] *adj* persistent.

persistir [persis'tir] *vi* to persist.

persona [per'sona] *nf* person; **10 ~s** 10
people; **tercera ~** third party; (*LING*)
third person; **en ~** in person *o* the flesh;
por ~ a head; **es buena ~** he's a good
sort.

personaje [perso'naxe] *nm* important
person, celebrity; (*TEAT*) character.

personal [perso'nal] *adj* (*particular*)
personal; (*para una persona*) single, for
one person ♦ *nm* (*plantilla*) personnel,
staff; (*NAUT*) crew; (*fam: gente*) people.

personalidad [personali'ðað] *nf*
personality; (*JUR*) status.

personalizar [personali'θar] *vt* to
personalize ♦ *vi* (*al hablar*) to name
names.

personarse [perso'narse] *vr* to appear in
person; **~ en** to present o.s. at, report to.

personero, a [perso'nero, a] *nm/f* (*AM*)
(government) official.

personificar [personifi'kar] *vt* to personify.

personifique [personi'fike] *etc vb V*
personificar.

perspectiva [perspek'tißa] *nf* perspective;
(*vista, panorama*) view, panorama;
(*posibilidad futura*) outlook, prospect;
tener algo en ~ to have sth in view.

perspicacia [perspi'kaθja] *nf* discernment,
perspicacity.

perspicaz [perspi'kaθ] *adj* shrewd.

persuadir [perswa'ðir] *vt* (*gen*) to
persuade; (*convencer*) to convince; **~se**
vr to become convinced.

persuasión [perswa'sjon] *nf* (*acto*)
persuasion; (*convicción*) conviction.

persuasivo, a [perwa'sißo, a] *adj*
persuasive; convincing.

pertenecer [pertene'θer] *vi:* **~ a** to belong
to; (*fig*) to concern.

perteneciente [pertene'θjente] *adj:* **~ a**
belonging to.

pertenencia [perte'nenθja] *nf* ownership;

~s *nfpl* possessions, property *sg*.

pertenezca [perte'neθka] *etc vb* V pertenecer.

pértiga ['pertiɣa] *nf* pole; **salto de** ~ pole vault.

pertinaz [perti'naθ] *adj* (*persistente*) persistent; (*terco*) obstinate.

pertinente [perti'nente] *adj* relevant, pertinent; (*apropiado*) appropriate; ~ **a** concerning, relevant to.

pertrechar [pertre't ʃar] *vt* (*gen*) to supply; (*MIL*) to supply with ammunition and stores; ~**se** *vr*: ~**se de algo** to provide o.s. with sth.

pertrechos [per'tret ʃos] *nmpl* (*gen*) implements; (*MIL*) supplies and stores.

perturbación [perturβa'θjon] *nf* (*POL*) disturbance; (*MED*) upset, disturbance; ~ **del orden público** breach of the peace.

perturbador, a [perturβa'ðor, a] *adj* (*que perturba*) perturbing, disturbing; (*subversivo*) subversive.

perturbar [pertur'βar] *vt* (*el orden*) to disturb; (*MED*) to upset, disturb; (*mentalmente*) to perturb.

Perú [pe'ru] *nm*: **el** ~ Peru.

peruano, a [pe'rwano, a] *adj, nm/f* Peruvian.

perversión [perβer'sjon] *nf* perversion.

perverso, a [perβerso, a] *adj* perverse; (*depravado*) depraved.

pervertido, a [perβer'tiðo, a] *adj* perverted ♦ *nm/f* pervert.

pervertir [perβer'tir] *vt* to pervert, corrupt.

pervierta [per'βjerta] *etc*, **pervirtiendo** [perβir'tjendo] *etc vb* V pervertir.

pesa ['pesa] *nf* weight; (*DEPORTE*) shot.

pesadez [pesa'ðeθ] *nf* (*calidad de pesado*) heaviness; (*lentitud*) slowness; (*aburrimiento*) tediousness; **es una** ~ **tener que** ... it's a bind having to ....

pesadilla [pesa'ðiʎa] *nf* nightmare, bad dream; (*fig*) worry, obsession.

pesado, a [pe'saðo, a] *adj* (*gen*) heavy; (*lento*) slow; (*difícil, duro*) tough, hard; (*aburrido*) tedious, boring; (*bochornoso*) sultry ♦ *nm/f* bore; **tener el estómago** ~ to feel bloated; ¡**no seas** ~! come off it!

pesadumbre [pesa'ðumbre] *nf* grief, sorrow.

pésame ['pesame] *nm* expression of condolence, message of sympathy; **dar el** ~ to express one's condolences.

pesar [pe'sar] *vt* to weigh; (*fig*) to weigh heavily on; (*afligir*) to grieve ♦ *vi* to weigh; (*ser pesado*) to weigh a lot, be heavy; (*fig: opinión*) to carry weight ♦ *nm* (*sentimiento*) regret; (*pena*) grief,

sorrow; **a** ~ **de (que)** in spite of, despite; **no me pesa haberlo hecho** I'm not sorry I did it.

pesca ['peska] *nf* (*acto*) fishing; (*cantidad de pescado*) catch; ~ **de altura/en bajura** deep sea/coastal fishing; **ir de** ~ to go fishing.

pescadería [peskaðe'ria] *nf* fish shop, fishmonger's.

pescadilla [peska'ðiʎa] *nf* whiting.

pescado [pes'kaðo] *nm* fish.

pescador, a [peska'ðor, a] *nm/f* fisherman/ woman.

pescar [pes'kar] *vt* (*coger*) to catch; (*tratar de coger*) to fish for; (*fam: lograr*) to get hold of, land; (*conseguir: trabajo*) to manage to get; (*sorprender*) to catch unawares ♦ *vi* to fish, go fishing.

pescuezo [pes'kweθo] *nm* neck.

pese ['pese] *prep*: ~ **a** despite, in spite of.

pesebre [pe'seβre] *nm* manger.

peseta [pe'seta] *nf* peseta.

pesetero, a [pese'tero, a] *adj* money-grubbing.

pesimismo [pesi'mismo] *nm* pessimism.

pesimista [pesi'mista] *adj* pessimistic ♦ *nm/f* pessimist.

pésimo, a ['pesimo, a] *adj* abominable, vile.

peso ['peso] *nm* weight; (*balanza*) scales *pl*; (*AM COM*) monetary unit; (*moneda*) peso; (*DEPORTE*) shot; ~ **bruto/neto** gross/net weight; ~ **mosca/pesado** fly-/ heavyweight; **de poco** ~ light(weight); **levantamiento de** ~**s** weightlifting; **vender a** ~ to sell by weight; **argumento de** ~ weighty argument; **eso cae de su** ~ that goes without saying.

pesque ['peske] *etc vb* V pescar.

pesquero, a [pes'kero, a] *adj* fishing *cpd*.

pesquisa [pes'kisa] *nf* inquiry, investigation.

pestaña [pes'taɲa] *nf* (*ANAT*) eyelash; (*borde*) rim.

pestañear [pestaɲe'ar] *vi* to blink.

peste ['peste] *nf* plague; (*fig*) nuisance; (*mal olor*) stink, stench; ~ **negra** Black Death; **echar** ~**s** to swear, fume.

pesticida [pesti'θiða] *nm* pesticide.

pestilencia [pesti'lenθja] *nf* (*mal olor*) stink, stench.

pestillo [pes'tiʎo] *nm* bolt, latch; (*cerrojo*) catch; (*picaporte*) (door) handle.

petaca [pe'taka] *nf* (*de cigarrillos*) cigarette case; (*de pipa*) tobacco pouch; (*AM: maleta*) suitcase.

pétalo ['petalo] *nm* petal.

petanca [pe'tanka] *nf* a game in which

metal bowls are thrown at a target bowl.

petardo [pe'tarðo] *nm* firework, firecracker.

petición [peti'θjon] *nf (pedido)* request, plea; *(memorial)* petition; *(JUR)* plea; **a ~ de** at the request of; **~ de aumento de salarios** wage demand *o* claim.

petirrojo [peti'rroxo] *nm* robin.

peto ['peto] *nm (corpiño)* bodice; *(TAUR)* horse's padding.

pétreo, a ['petreo, a] *adj* stony, rocky.

petrificar [petrifi'kar] *vt* to petrify.

petrifique [petri'fike] *etc vb V* **petrificar.**

petrodólar [petro'ðolar] *nm* petrodollar.

petróleo [pe'troleo] *nm* oil, petroleum.

petrolero, a [petro'lero, a] *adj* petroleum *cpd* ♦ *nm (COM)* oil man; *(buque)* (oil) tanker.

petulancia [petu'lanθja] *nf (insolencia)* vanity, opinionated nature.

peyorativo, a [pejora'tiβo, a] *adj* pejorative.

pez [peθ] *nm* fish; **~ de colores** goldfish; **~ espada** swordfish; **estar como ~ en el agua** to feel completely at home.

pezón [pe'θon] *nm* teat, nipple.

pezuña [pe'θuɲa] *nf* hoof.

piadoso, a [pja'ðoso, a] *adj (devoto)* pious, devout; *(misericordioso)* kind, merciful.

Piamonte [pja'monte] *nm* Piedmont.

pianista [pja'nista] *nm/f* pianist.

piano ['pjano] *nm* piano; **~ de cola** grand piano.

piar [pjar] *vi* to cheep.

piara ['pjara] *nf (manada)* herd, drove.

PIB *nm abr (ESP COM: = Producto Interno Bruto)* GDP.

pibe, a ['piβe, a] *nm/f (AM)* boy/girl, kid, child.

pica ['pika] *nf (MIL)* pike; *(TAUR)* goad; **poner una ~ en Flandes** to bring off something difficult.

picadero [pika'ðero] *nm* riding school.

picadillo [pika'ðiʎo] *nm* mince, minced meat.

picado, a [pi'kaðo, a] *adj* pricked, punctured; *(mar)* choppy; *(diente)* bad; *(tabaco)* cut; *(enfadado)* cross.

picador [pika'ðor] *nm (TAUR)* picador; *(minero)* faceworker.

picadora [pika'ðora] *nf* mincer.

picadura [pika'ðura] *nf (pinchazo)* puncture; *(de abeja)* sting; *(de mosquito)* bite; *(tabaco picado)* cut tobacco.

picana [pi'kana] *(AM) nf (AGR)* cattle prod; *(POL: para tortura)* electric prod.

picante [pi'kante] *adj (comida, sabor)* hot;

(comentario) racy, spicy.

picaporte [pika'porte] *nm (tirador)* handle; *(pestillo)* latch.

picar [pi'kar] *vt (agujerear, perforar)* to prick, puncture; *(billete)* to punch, clip; *(abeja)* to sting; *(mosquito, serpiente)* to bite; *(persona)* to nibble (at); *(incitar)* to incite, goad; *(dañar, irritar)* to annoy, bother; *(quemar: lengua)* to burn, sting ♦ *vi (pez)* to bite, take the bait; *(el sol)* to burn, scorch; *(abeja, MED)* to sting; *(mosquito)* to bite; **~se** *vr (agriarse)* to turn sour, go off; *(mar)* to get choppy; *(ofenderse)* to take offence; **me pican los ojos** my eyes sting; **me pica el brazo** my arm itches.

picardía [pikar'ðia] *nf* villainy; *(astucia)* slyness, craftiness; *(una ~)* dirty trick; *(palabra)* rude/bad word *o* expression.

picaresco, a [pika'resko, a] *adj (travieso)* roguish, rascally; *(LIT)* picaresque.

pícaro, a ['pikaro, a] *adj (malicioso)* villainous; *(travieso)* mischievous ♦ *nm (astuto)* sly sort; *(sinvergüenza)* rascal, scoundrel.

picazón [pika'θon] *nf (comezón)* itch; *(ardor)* sting(ing feeling); *(remordimiento)* pang of conscience.

pichón, ona [pi'tʃon, ona] *nm/f (paloma)* young pigeon; *(apelativo)* darling, dearest.

pico ['piko] *nm (de ave)* beak; *(punto agudo)* peak, sharp point; *(TEC)* pick, pickaxe; *(GEO)* peak, summit; *(labia)* talkativeness; **no abrir el ~** to keep quiet; **~ parásito** *(ELEC)* spike; **y ~** and a bit; **son las 3 y ~** it's just after 3; **tiene 50 libros y ~** he has 50-odd books; **me costó un ~** it cost me quite a bit.

picor [pi'kor] *nm* itch; *(ardor)* sting(ing feeling).

picota [pi'kota] *nf* pillory; **poner a algn en la ~** *(fig)* to ridicule sb.

picotada [piko'taða] *nf*, **picotazo** [piko'taθo] *nm (de pájaro)* peck; *(de insecto)* sting, bite.

picotear [pikote'ar] *vt* to peck ♦ *vi* to nibble, pick.

pictórico, a [pik'toriko, a] *adj* pictorial; **tiene dotes pictóricas** she has a talent for painting.

picudo, a [pi'kuðo, a] *adj* pointed, with a point.

pidiendo [pi'ðjendo] *etc vb V* **pedir.**

pie [pje] *(pl ~s) nm (gen, MAT)* foot; *(de cama, página, escalera)* foot, bottom; *(TEAT)* cue; *(fig: motivo)* motive, basis; *(: fundamento)* foothold; **~s planos** flat feet; **ir a ~** to go on foot, walk; **estar de ~** to be standing (up); **ponerse de ~** to stand up; **al ~ de la letra** (*citar*) literally, verbatim; (*copiar*) exactly, word for word; **de ~s a cabeza** from head to foot; **en ~ de guerra** on a war footing; **sin ~s ni cabeza** pointless, absurd; **dar ~ a** to give cause for; **no dar ~ con bola** to be no good at anything; **saber de qué ~ cojea algn** to know sb's weak spots.

piedad [pje'ðað] *nf* (*lástima*) pity, compassion; (*clemencia*) mercy; (*devoción*) piety, devotion; **tener ~ de** to take pity on.

piedra ['pjeðra] *nf* stone; (*roca*) rock; (*de mechero*) flint; (*METEOROLOGÍA*) hailstone; **primera ~** foundation stone; **~ de afilar** grindstone, **~ arenisca/caliza** sand-/limestone.

piel [pjel] *nf* (*ANAT*) skin; (*ZOOL*) skin, hide; (*de oso*) fur; (*cuero*) leather; (*BOT*) skin, peel ♦ *nm/f*: **~ roja** redskin.

pienso ['pjenso] *etc vb V* **pensar** ♦ *nm* (*AGR*) feed.

pierda ['pjerða] *etc vb V* **perder**.

pierna ['pjerna] *nf* leg; **en ~s** bare-legged.

pieza ['pjeθa] *nf* piece; (*esp AM*: *habitación*) room; (*MUS*) piece, composition; (*TEAT*) work, play; **~ de recambio** *o* **repuesto** spare (part), extra (*US*); **~ de ropa** article of clothing; **quedarse de una ~** to be dumbfounded.

pigmento [pix'mento] *nm* pigment.

pigmeo, a [pix'meo, a] *adj, nm/f* pigmy.

pijama [pi'xama] *nm* pyjamas *pl*.

pijo, a ['pixo, a] *nm/f* (*fam*) upper-class twit.

pijotada [pixo'taða] *nf* nuisance.

pila ['pila] *nf* (*ELEC*) battery; (*montón*) heap, pile; (*fuente*) sink; (*REL*: *tb*: **~ bautismal**) font; **nombre de ~** Christian *o* first name; **tengo una ~ de cosas que hacer** (*fam*) I have heaps *o* stacks of things to do; **~ de discos** (*INFORM*) disk pack.

pilar [pi'lar] *nm* pillar; (*de puente*) pier; (*fig*) prop, mainstay.

píldora ['pildora] *nf* pill; **la ~ (anticonceptiva)** the pill; **tragarse la ~** to be taken in.

pileta [pi'leta] *nf* basin, bowl; (*AM*: *de cocina*) sink; (: *piscina*) swimming pool.

pillaje [pi'ʎaxe] *nm* pillage, plunder.

pillar [pi'ʎar] *vt* (*fam*: *coger*) to catch; (: *agarrar*) to grasp, seize; (: *entender*) to grasp, catch on to; (*suj*: *coche etc*) to run over; **~ un resfriado** (*fam*) to catch a cold.

pillo, a ['piʎo, a] *adj* villainous; (*astuto*) sly,

crafty ♦ *nm/f* rascal, rogue, scoundrel.

pilón [pi'lon] *nm* pillar, post; (*ELEC*) pylon; (*bebedero*) drinking trough; (*de fuente*) basin.

pilotar [pilo'tar] *vt* (*avión*) to pilot; (*barco*) to steer.

piloto [pi'loto] *nm* pilot; (*AUTO*) rear light, tail light; (*conductor*) driver ♦ *adj inv*: **planta ~** pilot plant; **luz ~** side light.

piltrafa [pil'trafa] *nf* (*carne*) poor quality meat; (*fig*) worthless object; (: *individuo*) wretch.

pimentón [pimen'ton] *nm* (*polvo*) paprika.

pimienta [pi'mjenta] *nf* pepper.

pimiento [pi'mjento] *nm* pepper, pimiento.

pimpante [pim'pante] *adj* (*encantador*) charming; (*tb*: **tan ~**) smug, self-satisfied.

PIN *nm abr* (*ESP COM*: = *Producto Interior Neto*) net domestic product.

pin, *pl* **pins** [pin, pins] *nm* badge.

pinacoteca [pinako'teka] *nf* art gallery.

pinar [pi'nar] *nm* pinewood.

pincel [pin'θel] *nm* paintbrush.

pincelada [pinθe'laða] *nf* brushstroke; **última ~** (*fig*) finishing touch.

pinchadiscos [pintʃa'diskos] *nm/f inv* disc jockey, DJ.

pinchar [pin'tʃar] *vt* (*perforar*) to prick, pierce; (*neumático*) to puncture; (*incitar*) to prod ♦ *vi* (*MUS fam*) to be DJ; **~se** *vr* (*con droga*) to inject o.s.; (*neumático*) to burst, puncture; **no ~ ni cortar** (*fam*) to cut no ice; **tener un neumático pinchado** to have a puncture *o* a flat tyre.

pinchazo [pin'tʃaθo] *nm* (*perforación*) prick; (*de llanta*) puncture, flat (*US*).

pinche ['pintʃe] *nm* (*de cocina*) kitchen boy, scullion.

pinchito [pin'tʃito] *nm* shish kebab.

pincho ['pintʃo] *nm* point; (*aguijón*) spike; (*CULIN*) savoury (snack); **~ moruno** shish kebab; **~ de tortilla** small slice of omelette.

ping-pong ['pimpon] *nm* table tennis.

pingüe ['pingwe] *adj* (*grasoso*) greasy; (*cosecha*) bumper *cpd*; (*negocio*) lucrative.

pingüino [pin'gwino] *nm* penguin.

pinitos [pi'nitos] *nmpl*: **hacer sus primeros ~** to take one's first steps.

pino ['pino] *nm* pine (tree); **vivir en el quinto ~** to live at the back of beyond.

pinta ['pinta] *nf* spot; (*gota*) spot, drop; (*aspecto*) appearance, look(s) (*pl*); (*medida*) pint; **tener buena ~** to look good, look well; **por la ~** by the look of it.

pintado, a [pin'taðo, a] *adj* spotted; (*de muchos colores*) colourful ♦ *nf* piece of political graffiti; ~**s** *nfpl* political graffiti *sg*; **me sienta que ni ~, me viene que ni ~** it suits me a treat.

pintar [pin'tar] *vt* to paint ♦ *vi* to paint; (*fam*) to count, be important; ~**se** *vr* to put on make-up; **pintárselas solo para hacer algo** to manage to do sth by o.s.; **no pinta nada** (*fam*) he has no say.

pintor, a [pin'tor, a] *nm/f* painter; ~ **de brocha gorda** house painter; (*fig*) bad painter.

pintoresco, a [pinto'resko, a] *adj* picturesque.

pintura [pin'tura] *nf* painting; ~ **a la acuarela** watercolour; ~ **al óleo** oil painting; ~ **rupestre** cave painting.

pinza ['pinθa] *nf* (*ZOOL*) claw; (*para colgar ropa*) clothes peg, clothespin (*US*); (*TEC*) pincers *pl*; ~**s** *nfpl* (*para depilar*) tweezers.

piña ['piɲa] *nf* (*fruto del pino*) pine cone; (*fruta*) pineapple; (*fig*) group.

piñón [pi'ɲon] *nm* (*BOT*) pine nut; (*TEC*) pinion.

PIO *nm abr* (*ESP*: = *Patronato de Igualdad de Oportunidades*) ≈ Equal Opportunities Board.

pío, a ['pio, a] *adj* (*devoto*) pious, devout; (*misericordioso*) merciful ♦ *nm*: **no decir ni** ~ not to breathe a word.

piojo ['pjoxo] *nm* louse.

piojoso, a [pjo'xoso, a] *adj* lousy; (*sucio*) dirty.

piolet [pjo'le], *pl* ~**s** [-s] *nm* ice axe.

pionero, a [pjo'nero, a] *adj* pioneering ♦ *nm/f* pioneer.

pipa ['pipa] *nf* pipe; (*BOT*) seed, pip.

pipí [pi'pi] *nm* (*fam*): **hacer** ~ to have a wee(-wee).

pipiolo [pi'pjolo] *nm* youngster; (*novato*) novice, greenhorn.

pique ['pike] *etc vb V* **picar** ♦ *nm* (*resentimiento*) pique, resentment; (*rivalidad*) rivalry, competition; **irse a** ~ to sink; (*familia*) to be ruined; **tener un** ~ **con algn** to have a grudge against sb.

piqueta [pi'keta] *nf* pick(axe).

piquete [pi'kete] *nm* (*agujerito*) small hole; (*MIL*) squad, party; (*de obreros*) picket; ~ **secundario** secondary picket.

pirado, a [pi'raðo, a] *adj* (*fam*) round the bend.

piragua [pi'raɣwa] *nf* canoe.

piragüismo [pira'ɣwismo] *nm* (*DEPORTE*) canoeing.

pirámide [pi'ramiðe] *nf* pyramid.

piraña [pi'raɲa] *nf* piranha.

pirarse [pi'rarse] *vr*: ~**(las)** (*largarse*) to beat it (*fam*); (*ESCOL*) to cut class.

pirata [pi'rata] *adj*: **edición/disco** ~ pirate edition/bootleg record ♦ *nm* pirate; (*tb*: ~ **informático**) hacker.

pirenaico, a [pire'naiko, a] *adj* Pyrenean.

Pirineo(s) [piri'neo(s)] *nm(pl)* Pyrenees *pl*.

pirómano, a [pi'romano, a] *nm/f* (*PSICO*) pyromaniac; (*JUR*) arsonist.

piropo [pi'ropo] *nm* compliment, (piece of) flattery; **echar** ~**s a** to make flirtatious remarks to.

pirueta [pi'rweta] *nf* pirouette.

piruleta [piru'leta] *nf* lollipop.

pirulí [piru'li] *nm* lollipop.

pis [pis] *nm* (*fam*) pee; **hacer** ~ to have a pee.

pisada [pi'saða] *nf* (*paso*) footstep; (*huella*) footprint.

pisar [pi'sar] *vt* (*caminar sobre*) to walk on, tread on; (*apretar con el pie*) to press; (*fig*) to trample on, walk all over ♦ *vi* to tread, step, walk; ~ **el acelerador** to step on the accelerator; ~ **fuerte** (*fig*) to act determinedly.

piscifactoría [pisθifakto'ria] *nf* fish farm.

piscina [pis'θina] *nf* swimming pool.

Piscis ['pisθis] *nm* (*ASTRO*) Pisces.

piso ['piso] *nm* (*suelo, de edificio*) floor; (*AM*) ground; (*apartamento*) flat, apartment; **primer** ~ (*ESP*) first *o* second (*US*) floor; (*AM*) ground *o* first (*US*) floor.

pisotear [pisote'ar] *vt* to trample (on *o* underfoot); (*fig: humillar*) to trample on.

pisotón [piso'ton] *nm* (*con el pie*) stamp.

pista ['pista] *nf* track, trail; (*indicio*) clue; (*INFORM*) track; ~ **de auditoría** (*COM*) audit trail; ~ **de aterrizaje** runway; ~ **de baile** dance floor; ~ **de tenis** tennis court; ~ **de hielo** ice rink; **estar sobre la** ~ **de algn** to be on sb's trail.

pisto ['pisto] *nm* (*CULIN*) ratatouille; **darse** ~ (*fam*) to show off.

pistola [pis'tola] *nf* pistol; (*TEC*) spray-gun.

pistolero, a [pisto'lero, a] *nm/f* gunman, gangster ♦ *nf* holster.

pistón [pis'ton] *nm* (*TEC*) piston; (*MUS*) key.

pitar [pi'tar] *vt* (*hacer sonar*) to blow; (*partido*) to referee; (*rechiflar*) to whistle at, boo; (*actor, obra*) to hiss ♦ *vi* to whistle; (*AUTO*) to sound *o* toot one's horn; (*AM*) to smoke; **salir pitando** to beat it.

pitido [pi'tiðo] *nm* whistle; (*sonido agudo*) beep; (*sonido corto*) pip.

pitillera [piti'ʎera] *nf* cigarette case.

pitillo [pi'tiʎo] *nm* cigarette.

pito ['pito] *nm* whistle; (*de coche*) horn;

(*cigarrillo*) cigarette; (*fam: de marijuana*) joint; (*fam!*) prick (*!*); **me importa un** ~ I don't care two hoots.
pitón [pi'ton] *nm* (*ZOOL*) python.
pitonisa [pito'nisa] *nf* fortune-teller.
pitorrearse [pitorre'arse] *vr*: ~ **de** to scoff at, make fun of.
pitorreo [pito'rreo] *nm* joke, laugh; **estar de** ~ to be in a joking mood.
píxel ['piksel] *nm* (*INFORM*) pixel.
piyama [pi'jama] *nm* (*AM*) pyjamas *pl*, pajamas (*US*) *pl*.
pizarra [pi'θarra] *nf* (*piedra*) slate; (*encerado*) blackboard.
pizca ['piθka] *nf* pinch, spot; (*fig*) spot, speck, trace; **ni** ~ not a bit.
pizza ['pitsa] *nf* pizza.
placa ['plaka] *nf* plate; (*MED*) dental plate; (*distintivo*) badge; ~ **de matrícula** number plate; ~ **madre** (*INFORM*) mother board.
placaje [pla'kaxe] *nm* tackle.
placard [pla'kar] *nm* (*AM*) built-in cupboard, (clothes) closet (*US*).
placenta [pla'θenta] *nf* placenta; (*tras el parto*) afterbirth.
placentero, a [plaθen'tero, a] *adj* pleasant, agreeable ♦ *vt* to please.
placer [pla'θer] *nm* pleasure; **a** ~ at one's pleasure.
plácido, a ['plaθiðo, a] *adj* placid.
plafón [pla'fon] *nm* (*AM*) ceiling.
plaga ['plaɣa] *nf* pest; (*MED*) plague; (*fig*) swarm.
plagar [pla'ɣar] *vt* to infest, plague; (*llenar*) to fill; **plagado de** riddled with; **han plagado la ciudad de carteles** they have plastered the town with posters.
plagiar [pla'ɣjar] *vt* to plagiarize; (*AM*) to kidnap.
plagiario, a [pla'ɣjario, a] *nm/f* plagiarist; (*AM*) kidnapper.
plagio ['plaxjo] *nm* plagiarism; (*AM*) kidnap.
plague ['plaɣe] *etc vb V* **plagar**.
plan [plan] *nm* (*esquema, proyecto*) plan; (*idea, intento*) idea, intention; (*de curso*) programme; ~ **cotizable de jubilación** contributory pension scheme; ~ **de estudios** curriculum, syllabus; ~ **de incentivos** (*COM*) incentive scheme; **tener** ~ (*fam*) to have a date; **tener un** ~ (*fam*) to have an affair; **en** ~ **de cachondeo** for a laugh; **en** ~ **económico** (*fam*) on the cheap; **vamos en** ~ **de turismo** we're going as tourists; **si te pones en ese** ~ ... if that's your attitude ...
plana ['plana] *nf V* **plano**.

plancha ['plantʃa] *nf* (*para planchar*) iron; (*rótulo*) plate, sheet; (*NAUT*) gangway; (*CULIN*) grill; **pescado a la** ~ grilled fish.
planchado, a [plan'tʃaðo, a] *adj* (*ropa*) ironed; (*traje*) pressed ♦ *nm* ironing.
planchar [plan'tʃar] *vt* to iron ♦ *vi* to do the ironing.
planeador [planea'ðor] *nm* glider.
planear [plane'ar] *vt* to plan ♦ *vi* to glide.
planeta [pla'neta] *nm* planet.
planetario, a [plane'tarjo, a] *adj* planetary ♦ *nm* planetarium.
planicie [pla'niθje] *nf* plain.
planificación [planifika'θjon] *nf* planning; ~ **corporativa** (*COM*) corporate planning; ~ **familiar** family planning; **diagrama de** ~ (*COM*) planner.
planilla [pla'niʎa] *nf* (*AM*) form.
plano, a ['plano, a] *adj* flat, level, even; (*liso*) smooth ♦ *nm* (*MAT, TEC, AVIAT*) plane; (*FOTO*) shot; (*ARQ*) plan; (*GEO*) map; (*de ciudad*) map, street plan ♦ *nf* sheet of paper, page; (*TEC*) trowel **primer** ~ close-up; **caer de** ~ to fall flat; **rechazar algo de** ~ to turn sth down flat; **le daba el sol de** ~ (*fig*) the sun shone directly on it; **en primera plana** on the front page; **plana mayor** staff.
planta ['planta] *nf* (*BOT, TEC*) plant; (*ANAT*) sole of the foot, foot; ~ **baja** ground floor.
plantación [planta'θjon] *nf* (*AGR*) plantation; (*acto*) planting.
plantar [plan'tar] *vt* (*BOT*) to plant; (*puesto*) to put in; (*levantar*) to erect, set up; ~**se** *vr* to stand firm; ~ **a algn en la calle** to chuck sb out; **dejar plantado a algn** (*fam*) to stand sb up; ~**se en** to reach, get to.
plantear [plante'ar] *vt* (*problema*) to pose; (*dificultad*) to raise; **se lo plantearé** I'll put it to him.
plantel [plan'tel] *nm* (*fig*) group, set.
plantilla [plan'tiʎa] *nf* (*de zapato*) insole; (*personal*) personnel; **ser de** ~ to be on the staff.
plantío [plan'tio] *nm* (*acto*) planting; (*lugar*) plot, bed, patch.
plantón [plan'ton] *nm* (*MIL*) guard, sentry; (*fam*) long wait; **dar (un)** ~ **a algn** to stand sb up.
plañir [pla'ɲir] *vi* to mourn.
plasma ['plasma] *nm* plasma.
plasmar [plas'mar] *vt* (*dar forma*) to mould, shape; (*representar*) to represent ♦ *vi*: ~ **en** to take the form of.
plasta ['plasta] *nf* soft mass, lump; (*desastre*) botch, mess.

plasticidad [plastiθi'ðað] nf (fig) expressiveness.

plástico, a ['plastiko, a] adj plastic ♦ nf (art of) sculpture, modelling ♦ nm plastic.

plastificar [plastifi'kar] vt (documento) to laminate.

plastifique [plasti'fike] etc vb V **plastificar**.

plastilina [plasti'lina] nf Plasticine ®.

plata ['plata] nf (metal) silver; (cosas hechas de plata) silverware; (AM) cash, dough (fam); **hablar en** ~ to speak bluntly o frankly.

plataforma [plata'forma] nf platform; ~ **de lanzamiento/perforación** launch(ing) pad/drilling rig.

plátano ['platano] nm (fruta) banana; (árbol) plane tree.

platea [pla'tea] nf (TEAT) pit.

plateado, a [plate'aðo, a] adj silver; (TEC) silver-plated.

platense [pla'tense] (fam) = **ríoplatense**.

plática ['platika] nf (AM) talk, chat; (REL) sermon.

platicar [plati'kar] vi (AM) to talk, chat.

platillo [pla'tiʎo] nm saucer; (de limosnas) collecting bowl; ~**s** nmpl cymbals; ~ **volador** o **volante** flying saucer; **pasar el** ~ to pass the hat round.

platina [pla'tina] nf (MUS) tape deck.

platino [pla'tino] nm platinum; ~**s** nmpl (AUTO) (contact) points.

platique [pla'tike] etc vb V **platicar**.

plato ['plato] nm plate, dish; (parte de comida) course; (guiso) dish; ~ **frutero/sopero** fruit/soup dish; **pagar los** ~**s rotos** (fam) to carry the can (fam).

plató [pla'to] nm set.

platónico, a [pla'toniko, a] adj platonic.

playa ['plaja] nf beach; (costa) seaside; ~ **de estacionamiento** (AM) car park.

playero, a [pla'jero, a] adj beach cpd ♦ nf (AM: camiseta) T-shirt; ~**s** nfpl canvas shoes; (TENIS) tennis shoes.

plaza ['plaθa] nf square; (mercado) market(place); (sitio) room, space; (en vehículo) seat, place; (colocación) post, job; ~ **de abastos** food market; ~ **mayor** main square; ~ **de toros** bullring; **hacer la** ~ to do the daily shopping; **reservar una** ~ to reserve a seat; **el hotel tiene 100** ~**s** the hotel has 100 beds.

plazca ['plaθka] etc vb V **placer**.

plazo ['plaθo] nm (lapso de tiempo) time, period, term; (fecha de vencimiento) expiry date; (pago parcial) instalment; **a corto/largo** ~ short-/long-term; **comprar a** ~**s** to buy on hire purchase, pay for in instalments; **nos dan un** ~ **de 8 días** they

allow us a week.

plazoleta [plaθo'leta], **plazuela** [pla'θwela] nf small square.

pleamar [plea'mar] nf high tide.

plebe ['pleβe] nf: **la** ~ the common people pl, the masses pl; (pey) the plebs pl.

plebeyo, a [ple'βejo, a] adj plebeian; (pey) coarse, common.

plebiscito [pleβis'θito] nm plebiscite.

pleca ['pleka] nf (INFORM) backslash.

plegable [ple'xaβle] adj pliable; (silla) folding.

plegar [ple'xar] vt (doblar) to fold, bend; (COSTURA) to pleat; ~**se** vr to yield, submit.

plegaria [ple'xarja] nf (oración) prayer.

plegué [ple'xe], **pleguemos** [ple'xemos] etc vb V **plegar**.

pleitear [pleite'ar] vi (JUR) to plead, conduct a lawsuit; (litigar) to go to law.

pleito ['pleito] nm (JUR) lawsuit, case; (fig) dispute, feud; ~**s** nmpl litigation sg; **entablar** ~ to bring an action o a lawsuit; **poner** ~ to sue.

plenario, a [ple'narjo, a] adj plenary, full.

plenilunio [pleni'lunjo] nm full moon.

plenitud [pleni'tuð] nf plenitude, fullness; (abundancia) abundance.

pleno, a ['pleno, a] adj full; (completo) complete ♦ nm plenum; **en** ~ as a whole; (por unanimidad) unanimously; **en** ~ **día** in broad daylight; **en** ~ **verano** at the height of summer; **en plena cara** full in the face.

pletina nf (MUS) tape deck.

pleuresía [pleure'sia] nf pleurisy.

plexiglás [pleksi'ylas] nm acrylic.

pliego ['pljexo] etc vb V **plegar** ♦ nm (hoja) sheet (of paper); (carta) sealed letter/document; ~ **de condiciones** details pl, specifications pl.

pliegue ['pljexe] etc vb V **plegar** ♦ nm fold, crease; (de vestido) pleat.

plisado [pli'saðo] nm pleating.

plomero [plo'mero] nm (AM) plumber.

plomizo, a [plo'miθo, a] adj leaden, lead-coloured.

plomo ['plomo] nm (metal) lead; (ELEC) fuse; **caer a** ~ to fall heavily o flat.

pluma ['pluma] nf (ZOOL) feather; ~ **estilográfica**, ~ **fuente** (AM) fountain pen.

plumazo [plu'maθo] nm (lit, fig) stroke of the pen.

plumero [plu'mero] nm (quitapolvos) feather duster; **ya te veo el** ~ I know what you're up to.

plumón [plu'mon] nm (AM) felt-tip pen.

plural [plu'ral] *adj* plural ♦ *nm*: **en** ~ **in the plural.**

pluralidad [plurali'ðað] *nf* plurality; **una** ~ **de votos** a majority of votes.

pluriempleo [pluriem'pleo] *nm* moonlighting.

plus [plus] *nm* bonus.

plusmarquista [plusmar'kista] *nm/f* (*DEPORTE*) record holder.

plusvalía [plusßa'lia] *nf* (*mayor valor*) appreciation, added value; (*COM*) goodwill.

plutocracia [pluto'kraθja] *nf* plutocracy.

PM *nf abr* (*MIL*: = *Policía Militar*) MP.

p.m. *abr* (= *post meridiem*) p.m.; (= *por minuto*) per minute.

PMA *nm abr* (= *Programa Mundial de Alimentos*) World Food Programme.

pmo. *abr* (= *próximo*) prox.

PN *nf abr* (*MIL*: = *Policía Naval*) Naval Police.

PNB *nm abr* (*ESP COM*: = *producto nacional bruto*) GNP.

P.N.D. *nm abr* (*ESCOL*: = *personal no docente*) non-teaching staff.

PNN *nm/f abr* (= *profesor no numerario*) untenured teacher; (*ESP COM*: = *producto nacional neto*) net national product.

PNUD *nm abr* (= *Programa de las Naciones Unidas para el Desarrollo*) United Nations Development Programme.

PNV *nm abr* (*ESP POL*) = *Partido Nacional Vasco.*

P.º *abr* (= *Paseo*) Av(e).

p.o. *abr* = *por orden.*

p.º n.º *abr* (= *peso neto*) nt. wt.

población [poßla'θjon] *nf* population; (*pueblo, ciudad*) town, city; ~ **activa** working population.

poblado, a [po'ßlaðo, a] *adj* inhabited; (*barba*) thick; (*cejas*) bushy ♦ *nm* (*aldea*) village; (*pueblo*) (small) town; ~ **de** (*lleno*) filled with; **densamente** ~ densely populated.

poblador, a [poßla'ðor, a] *nm/f* settler, colonist.

poblar [po'ßlar] *vt* (*colonizar*) to colonize; (*fundar*) to found; (*habitar*) to inhabit; ~**se de** to fill up with; (*irse cubriendo*) to become covered with.

pobre ['poßre] *adj* poor ♦ *nm/f* poor person; (*mendigo*) beggar; **los** ~**s** the poor; ¡~! poor thing!; ~ **diablo** (*fig*) poor wretch *o* devil.

pobreza [po'ßreθa] *nf* poverty.

pocho, a ['potʃo, a] *adj* (*flor, color*) faded, discoloured; (*persona*) pale; (*fruta*) overripe; (*deprimido*) depressed.

pocilga [po'θilɣa] *nf* pigsty.

pocillo [po'siʎo] *nm* (*AM*) coffee cup.

pócima ['poθima], **poción** [po'θjon] *nf* potion; (*brebaje*) concoction, nasty drink.

━━━━━━━━━━━ *PALABRA CLAVE*

poco, a ['poko, a] *adj* **1** (*sg*) little, not much; ~ **tiempo** little *o* not much time; **de** ~ **interés** of little interest, not very interesting; **poca cosa** not much
2 (*pl*) few, not many; **unos** ~**s** a few, some; ~**s niños comen lo que les conviene** few children eat what they should
♦ *adv* **1** little, not much; **cuesta** ~ it doesn't cost much; ~ **más o menos** more or less
2 (+*adj*: = *negativo, antónimo*): ~ **amable/inteligente** not very nice/ intelligent
3: **por** ~ **me caigo** I almost fell
4 (*tiempo*): ~ **después** soon after that; **dentro de** ~ shortly; **hace** ~ a short time ago, not long ago; **a** ~ **de haberse casado** shortly after getting married
5: ~ **a** ~ little by little
6 (*AM*): **¿a** ~ **no está divino?** isn't it just divine?; **de a** ~ gradually
♦ *nm* a little, a bit; **un** ~ **triste/de dinero** a little sad/money.

poda ['poða] *nf* (*acto*) pruning; (*temporada*) pruning season.

podar [po'ðar] *vt* to prune.

podenco [po'ðenko] *nm* hound.

━━━━━━━━━━━ *PALABRA CLAVE*

poder [po'ðer] *vi* **1** (*capacidad*) can, be able to; **no puedo hacerlo** I can't do it, I'm unable to do it
2 (*permiso*) can, may, be allowed to; **¿se puede?** may I (*o* we)?; **puedes irte ahora** you may go now; **no se puede fumar en este hospital** smoking is not allowed in this hospital
3 (*posibilidad*) may, might, could; **puede llegar mañana** he may *o* might arrive tomorrow; **pudiste haberte hecho daño** you might *o* could have hurt yourself; **¡podías habérmelo dicho antes!** you might have told me before!
4: **puede (ser)** perhaps; **puede que lo sepa Tomás** Tomás may *o* might know
5: **¡no puedo más!** I've had enough!; **no pude menos que dejarlo** I couldn't help but leave it; **es tonto a más no** ~ he's as stupid as they come
6: ~ **con: ¿puedes con eso?** can you manage that?; **no puedo con este crío**

this kid's too much for me
7: **él me puede** (*fam*) he's stronger than me
♦ *nm* power; **el** ~ the Government; ~ **adquisitivo** purchasing power; **detentar** *u* **ocupar** *o* **estar en el** ~ to be in power *o* office; **estar** *u* **obrar en** ~ **de** to be in the hands *o* possession of; **por** ~**(es)** by proxy.

poderío [poðe'rio] *nm* power; (*autoridad*) authority.
poderoso, a [poðe'roso, a] *adj* powerful.
podio ['poðjo] *nm* podium.
podólogo, a [po'ðoloɣo, a] *nm/f* chiropodist (*BRIT*), podiatrist (*US*).
podré [po'ðre] *etc vb* V **poder.**
podrido, a [po'ðriðo, a] *adj* rotten, bad; (*fig*) rotten, corrupt.
podrir [po'ðrir] = **pudrir.**
poema [po'ema] *nm* poem.
poesía [poe'sia] *nf* poetry.
poeta [po'eta] *nm* poet.
poético, a [po'etiko, a] *adj* poetic(al).
poetisa [poe'tisa] *nf* (woman) poet.
póker ['poker] *nm* poker.
polaco, a [po'lako, a] *adj* Polish ♦ *nm/f* Pole ♦ *nm* (*LING*) Polish.
polar [po'lar] *adj* polar.
polarice [pola'riθe] *etc vb* V **polarizar.**
polaridad [polari'ðað] *nf* polarity.
polarizar [polari'θar] *vt* to polarize.
polea [po'lea] *nf* pulley.
polémica [po'lemika] *nf* polemics *sg*; (*una* ~) controversy.
polemice [pole'miθe] *etc vb* V **polemizar.**
polémico, a [po'lemiko, a] *adj* polemic(al).
polemizar [polemi'θar] *vi* to argue.
polen ['polen] *nm* pollen.
poleo [po'leo] *nm* pennyroyal.
poli ['poli] *nm* (*fam*) cop (*fam*) ♦ *nf*: **la** ~ the cops *pl* (*fam*).
policía [poli'θia] *nm/f* policeman/woman ♦ *nf* police; ~ **municipal** local police; ~ **nacional** national police; *see boxed note.*

POLICÍA

There are two branches of the Spanish police, both of which are armed. The **policía nacional** *is in charge of national security and public order in general, while the remit of the* **policía municipal** *is mainly to deal with traffic offences, and police the local community. Catalonia and the Basque Country have their own police forces, the "Mossos d'Esquadra" and the "Ertzaintza" respectively.*

policíaco, a [poli'θiako, a] *adj* police *cpd*; **novela policíaca** detective story.
polideportivo [poliðepor'tiβo] *nm* sports centre.
poliéster [poli'ester] *nm* polyester.
polietileno [polieti'leno] *nm* polythene (*BRIT*), polyethylene (*US*).
polifacético, a [polifa'θetiko, a] *adj* (*persona, talento*) many-sided, versatile.
poligamia [poli'ɣamja] *nf* polygamy.
polígamo, a [po'liɣamo, a] *adj* polygamous ♦ *nm* polygamist.
polígono [po'liɣono] *nm* (*MAT*) polygon; (*solar*) building lot; (*zona*) area; (*unidad vecina*) housing estate; ~ **industrial** industrial estate.
polígrafo [po'liɣrafo] *nm* polygraph.
polilla [po'liʎa] *nf* moth.
Polinesia [poli'nesja] *nf* Polynesia.
polinesio, a [poli'nesjo, a] *adj, nm/f* Polynesian.
polio ['poljo] *nf* polio.
Polisario [poli'sarjo] *nm abr* (*POL: tb*: **Frente** ~) = *Frente Político de Liberación del Sáhara y Río de Oro.*
politécnico [poli'tekniko] *nm* polytechnic.
político, a [po'litiko, a] *adj* political; (*discreto*) tactful; (*pariente*) in-law ♦ *nm/f* politician ♦ *nf* politics *sg*; (*económica, agraria*) policy; **padre** ~ father-in-law; **política exterior/de ingresos y precios** foreign/prices and incomes policy.
póliza ['poliθa] *nf* certificate, voucher; (*impuesto*) tax *o* fiscal stamp; ~ **de seguro(s)** insurance policy.
polizón [poli'θon] *nm* (*AVIAT, NAUT*) stowaway.
pollera [po'ʎera] *nf* (*criadero*) hencoop; (*AM*) skirt, overskirt.
pollería [poʎe'ria] *nf* poulterer's (shop).
pollo ['poʎo] *nm* chicken; (*joven*) young man; (*señorito*) playboy; ~ **asado** roast chicken.
polo ['polo] *nm* (*GEO, ELEC*) pole; (*helado*) ice lolly; (*DEPORTE*) polo; (*suéter*) polo-neck; **P**~ **Norte/Sur** North/South Pole; **esto es el** ~ **opuesto de lo que dijo antes** this is the exact opposite of what he said before.
Polonia [po'lonja] *nf* Poland.
poltrona [pol'trona] *nf* reclining chair, easy chair.
polución [polu'θjon] *nf* pollution; ~ **ambiental** environmental pollution.
polvera [pol'βera] *nf* powder compact.
polvo ['polβo] *nm* dust; (*QUÍMICA, CULIN, MED*) powder; (*fam!*) screw(*!*); **en** ~ powdered; ~ **de talco** talcum powder;

estar hecho ~ to be worn out *o* exhausted; **hacer algo** ~ to smash sth; **hacer** ~ **a algn** to shatter sb; *V tb* **polvos.**

pólvora ['polßora] *nf* gunpowder; (*fuegos artificiales*) fireworks *pl*; **propagarse como la** ~ (*noticia*) to spread like wildfire.

polvoriento, a [polßo'rjento, a] *adj* (*superficie*) dusty; (*sustancia*) powdery.

polvorín [polßo'rin] *nm* (*fig*) powder keg.

polvorosa [polßo'rosa] *adj* (*fam*): **poner pies en** ~ to beat it.

polvos ['polßos] *nmpl* powder *sg*.

polvoso, a [pol'ßoso, a] *adj* (*AM*) dusty.

pomada [po'maða] *nf* pomade.

pomelo [po'melo] *nm* grapefruit.

pómez ['pomeθ] *nf*: **piedra** ~ pumice stone.

pomo ['pomo] *nm* handle.

pompa ['pompa] *nf* (*burbuja*) bubble; (*bomba*) pump; (*esplendor*) pomp, splendour; ~**s fúnebres** funeral *sg*.

pomposo, a [pom'poso, a] *adj* splendid, magnificent; (*pey*) pompous.

pómulo ['pomulo] *nm* cheekbone.

ponche ['pontʃe] *nm* punch.

poncho ['pontʃo] *nm* (*AM*) poncho, cape.

ponderar [ponde'rar] *vt* (*considerar*) to weigh up, consider; (*elogiar*) to praise highly, speak in praise of.

pondré [pon'dre] *etc vb V* **poner.**

ponencia [po'nenθja] *nf* (*exposición*) (learned) paper, communication; (*informe*) report.

===================== *PALABRA CLAVE*

poner [po'ner] *vt* **1** to put; (*colocar*) to place, set; (*ropa*) to put on; (*problema, la mesa*) to set; (*interés*) to show; (*telegrama*) to send; (*obra de teatro*) to put on; (*película*) to show; **ponlo más alto** turn it up; **¿qué ponen en el Excelsior?** what's on at the Excelsior?; ~ **algo a secar** to put sth (out) to dry; **¡no pongas esa cara!** don't look at me like that!

2 (*tienda*) to open; (*instalar: gas etc*) to put in; (*radio, TV*) to switch *o* turn on

3 (*suponer*): **pongamos que ...** let's suppose that ...

4 (*contribuir*): **el gobierno ha puesto otro millón** the government has contributed another million

5 (*TELEC*): **póngame con el Sr. López** can you put me through to Mr. López?

6 (*estar escrito*) to say; **¿qué pone aquí?** what does it say here?

7: ~ **de**: **le han puesto de director general** they've appointed him general manager

8 (+*adj*) to make; **me estás poniendo nerviosa** you're making me nervous

9 (*dar nombre*): **al hijo le pusieron Diego** they called their son Diego

♦ *vi* (*gallina*) to lay

♦ ~**se** *vr* **1** (*colocarse*): **se puso a mi lado** he came and stood beside me; **tú ponte en esa silla** you go and sit on that chair

2 (*vestido, cosméticos*) to put on; **¿por qué no te pones el vestido nuevo?** why don't you put on *o* wear your new dress?

3 (*sol*) to set

4 (+*adj*) to get, become; to turn; ~**se enfermo/gordo/triste** to get ill/fat/sad; **se puso muy serio** he got very serious; **después de lavarla la tela se puso azul** after washing it the material turned blue; **¡no te pongas así!** don't be like that!; ~**se cómodo** to make o.s. comfortable

5: ~**se a**: **se puso a llorar** he started to cry; **tienes que** ~**te a estudiar** you must get down to studying

6: ~**se a bien con algn** to make it up with sb, ~**se a mal con algn** to get on the wrong side of sb

7 (*AM*): **se me pone que ...** it seems to me that ..., I think that ....

ponga ['ponga] *etc vb V* **poner.**

poniente [po'njente] *nm* west.

pontevedrés, esa [ponteße'ðres, esa] *adj* of *o* from Pontevedra ♦ *nm/f* native *o* inhabitant of Pontevedra.

pontificado [pontifi'kaðo] *nm* papacy, pontificate.

pontífice [pon'tifiθe] *nm* pope, pontiff; **el Sumo P**~ His Holiness the Pope.

pontón [pon'ton] *nm* pontoon.

ponzoña [pon'θoɲa] *nf* poison, venom.

ponzonoso, a [ponθo'ɲoso, a] *adj* poisonous, venomous.

pop [pop] *adj inv, nm* (*MUS*) pop.

popa ['popa] *nf* stern; **a** ~ astern, abaft; **de** ~ **a proa** fore and aft.

popular [popu'lar] *adj* popular; (*del pueblo*) of the people.

popularice [popula'riθe] *etc vb V* **popularizarse.**

popularidad [populari'ðað] *nf* popularity.

popularizarse [populari'θarse] *vr* to become popular.

poquísimo, a [po'kisimo, a] *adj* (*superlativo de* **poco**) very little; (*pl*) very few; (*casi nada*) hardly any.

poquito [po'kito] *nm*: **un** ~ a little bit ♦ *adv* a little, a bit; **a** ~**s** bit by bit.

═══════════ PALABRA CLAVE

por [por] *prep* **1** (*objetivo*) for; **luchar ~ la patria** to fight for one's country; **hazlo ~ mí** do it for my sake
2 (+*infin*): **~ no llegar tarde** so as not to arrive late; **~ citar unos ejemplos** to give a few examples
3 (*causa*) out of, because of; **no es ~ eso** that's not the reason; **~ escasez de fondos** through *o* for lack of funds
4 (*tiempo*): **~ la mañana/noche** in the morning/at night; **se queda ~ una semana** she's staying (for) a week
5 (*lugar*): **pasar ~ Madrid** to pass through Madrid; **ir a Guayaquil ~ Quito** to go to Guayaquil via Quito; **caminar ~ la calle** to walk along the street; **~ allí** over there; **se va ~ ahí** we have to go that way; **¿~ dónde?** which way?; **está ~ el norte** it's somewhere in the north; **~ todo el país** throughout the country
6 (*cambio, precio*): **te doy uno nuevo ~ el que tienes** I'll give you a new one (in return) for the one you've got; **lo vendí ~ 15 dólares** I sold it for 15 dollars
7 (*valor distributivo*): **550 pesetas ~ hora/cabeza** 550 pesetas an *o* per hour/a *o* per head; **10 ~ ciento** 10 per cent; **80 (kms) ~ hora** 80 (km) an *o* per hour
8 (*modo, medio*) by; **~ correo/avión** by post/air; **día ~ día** day by day; **~ orden** in order; **entrar ~ la entrada principal** to go in through the main entrance
9 (*agente*) by; **hecho ~ él** done by him; **"dirigido ~"** "directed by"
10: **10 ~ 10 son 100** 10 by 10 is 100
11 (*en lugar de*): **vino él ~ su jefe** he came instead of his boss
12: **~ mí que revienten** as far as I'm concerned they can drop dead
13 (*evidencia*): **~ lo que dicen** judging by *o* from what they say
14: **estar/quedar ~ hacer** to be still *o* remain to be done
15: **~ (muy) difícil que sea** however hard it is *o* may be; **~ más que lo intente** no matter how *o* however hard I try
16: **~ qué** why; **¿~ qué?** why?; **¿~?** (*fam*) why (do you ask)?

porcelana [porθe'lana] *nf* porcelain; (*china*) china.
porcentaje [porθen'taxe] *nm* percentage; **~ de actividad** (*INFORM*) hit rate.
porche ['portʃe] *nm* (*de una plaza*) arcade; (*de casa*) porch.
porción [por'θjon] *nf* (*parte*) portion, share;

(*cantidad*) quantity, amount.
pordiosero, a [porðjo'sero, a] *nm/f* beggar.
porfía [por'fia] *nf* persistence; (*terquedad*) obstinacy.
porfiado, a [por'fjaðo, a] *adj* persistent; obstinate.
porfiar [por'fjar] *vi* to persist, insist; (*disputar*) to argue stubbornly.
pormenor [porme'nor] *nm* detail, particular.
pormenorice [pormeno'riθe] *etc vb* V **pormenorizar.**
pormenorizar [pormenori'θar] *vt* to (set out in) detail ♦ *vi* to go into detail.
porno ['porno] *adj inv* porno ♦ *nm* porn.
pornografía [pornoɣra'fia] *nf* pornography.
poro ['poro] *nm* pore.
poroso, a [po'roso, a] *adj* porous.
poroto [po'roto] *nm* (*AM*) kidney bean.
porque ['porke] *conj* (*a causa de*) because; (*ya que*) since; **~ sí** because I feel like it.
porqué [por'ke] *nm* reason, cause.
porquería [porke'ria] *nf* (*suciedad*) filth, muck, dirt; (*acción*) dirty trick; (*objeto*) small thing, trifle; (*fig*) rubbish.
porqueriza [porke'riθa] *nf* pigsty.
porra ['porra] *nf* (*arma*) stick, club; (*cachiporra*) truncheon; **¡~s!** oh heck!; **¡vete a la ~!** go to heck!
porrazo [po'rraθo] *nm* (*golpe*) blow; (*caída*) bump; **de un ~** in one go.
porro ['porro] *nm* joint.
porrón [po'rron] *nm* glass wine jar with a long spout.
port [por(t)] *nm* (*INFORM*) port.
portaaviones [port(a)a'ßjones] *nm inv* aircraft carrier.
portada [por'taða] *nf* (*TIP*) title page; (: *de revista*) cover.
portador, a [porta'ðor, a] *nm/f* carrier, bearer; (*COM*) bearer, payee; (*MED*) carrier; **ser ~ del virus del sida** to be HIV-positive.
portaequipajes [portaeki'paxes] *nm inv* boot (*BRIT*), trunk (*US*); (*baca*) luggage rack.
portafolio(s) [porta'foljo(s)] *nm* (*AM*) briefcase; **~ de inversiones** (*COM*) investment portfolio.
portal [por'tal] *nm* (*entrada*) vestibule, hall; (*pórtico*) porch, doorway; (*puerta de entrada*) main door; (*DEPORTE*) goal; **~es** *nmpl* arcade *sg*.
portaligas [porta'liɣas] *nm inv* (*AM*) suspender belt.
portamaletas [portama'letas] *nm inv* roof rack.

portamonedas [portamo'neðas] *nm inv* purse.

portar [por'tar] *vt* to carry, bear; ~**se** *vr* to behave, conduct o.s.; ~**se mal** to misbehave; **se portó muy bien conmigo** he treated me very well.

portátil [por'tatil] *adj* portable.

portaviones [porta'ßjones] *nm inv* aircraft carrier.

portavoz [porta'ßoθ] *nm/f* spokesman/ woman.

portazo [por'taθo] *nm:* **dar un** ~ to slam the door.

porte ['porte] *nm (COM)* transport; (*precio*) transport charges *pl*; (*CORREOS*) postage; ~ **debido** (*COM*) carriage forward; ~ **pagado** (*COM*) carriage paid, post-paid.

portento [por'tento] *nm* marvel, wonder.

portentoso, a [porten'toso, a] *adj* marvellous, extraordinary.

porteño, a [por'teɲo, a] *adj* of o from Buenos Aires ♦ *nm/f* native o inhabitant of Buenos Aires.

portería [porte'ria] *nf (oficina)* porter's office; (*gol*) goal.

portero, a [por'tero, a] *nm/f* porter; (*conserje*) caretaker; (*DEPORTE*) goalkeeper.

pórtico ['portiko] *nm (porche)* portico, porch; (*fig*) gateway; (*arcada*) arcade.

portilla [por'tiʎa] *nf*, **portillo** [por'tiʎo] *nm* gate.

portón [pro'ton] *nm* proton.

portorriqueño, a [portorri'keɲo, a] *adj, nm/f* Puerto Rican.

portuario, a [por'twarjo] *adj (del puerto)* port *cpd*, harbour *cpd*; (*del muelle*) dock *cpd*; **trabajador** ~ docker.

Portugal [portu'ɣal] *nm* Portugal.

portugués, esa [portu'ɣes, esa] *adj, nm/f* Portuguese ♦ *nm (LING)* Portuguese.

porvenir [porße'nir] *nm* future.

pos [pos]: **en** ~ **de:** *prep* after, in pursuit of.

posada [po'saða] *nf (refugio)* shelter, lodging; (*mesón*) guest house; **dar** ~ **a** to give shelter to, take in.

posaderas [posa'ðeras] *nfpl* backside *sg*, buttocks.

posar [po'sar] *vt (en el suelo)* to lay down, put down; (*la mano*) to place, put gently ♦ *vi* to sit, pose; ~**se** *vr* to settle; (*pájaro*) to perch; (*avión*) to land, come down.

posdata [pos'ðata] *nf* postscript.

pose ['pose] *nf (ARTE, afectación)* pose.

poseedor, a [posee'ðor, a] *nm/f* owner, possessor; (*de récord, puesto*) holder.

poseer [pose'er] *vt* to have, possess, own;

(*ventaja*) to enjoy; (*récord, puesto*) to hold.

poseído, a [pose'iðo, a] *adj* possessed; **estar muy** ~ **de** to be very vain about.

posesión [pose'sjon] *nf* possession; **tomar** ~ **(de)** to take over.

posesionarse [posesjo'narse] *vr:* ~ **de** to take possession of, take over.

posesivo, a [pose'sißo, a] *adj* possessive.

poseyendo [pose'jendo] *etc vb V* **poseer.**

posgrado [pos'ɣraðo] *nm* = **postgrado.**

posgraduado, a [posɣra'ðwaðo, a] *adj, nm/f* = **postgraduado.**

posibilidad [posißili'ðað] *nf* possibility; (*oportunidad*) chance.

posibilitar [posißili'tar] *vt* to make possible, permit; (*hacer factible*) to make feasible.

posible [po'sißle] *adj* possible; (*factible*) feasible ♦ *nm:* ~**s** means; (*bienes*) funds, assets; **de ser** ~ if possible; **en** o **dentro de lo** ~ as far as possible; **lo antes** ~ as quickly as possible.

posición [posi'θjon] *nf (gen)* position; (*rango social*) status.

positivo, a [posi'tißo, a] *adj* positive ♦ *nf (FOTO)* print.

poso ['poso] *nm* sediment.

posoperatorio, a [posopera'torjo, a] *adj, nm* = **postoperatorio.**

posponer [pospo'ner] *vt* to put behind o below; (*aplazar*) to postpone.

posponga [pos'ponga] *etc*, **pospuesto** [pos'pwesto], **pospuse** [pos'puse] *etc vb V* **posponer.**

posta ['posta] *nf (de caballos)* relay, team; **a** ~ on purpose, deliberately.

postal [pos'tal] *adj* postal ♦ *nf* postcard.

poste ['poste] *nm (de telégrafos)* post, pole; (*columna*) pillar.

póster ['poster], *pl* **posters** ['posters] *nm* poster.

postergar [poster'ɣar] *vt (esp AM)* to put off, postpone, delay.

postergue [pos'terɣe] *etc vb V* **postergar.**

posteridad [posteri'ðað] *nf* posterity.

posterior [poste'rjor] *adj* back, rear; (*siguiente*) following, subsequent; (*más tarde*) later; **ser** ~ **a** to be later than.

posterioridad [posterjori'ðað] *nf:* **con** ~ later, subsequently.

postgrado [post'ɣraðo] *nm:* **curso de** ~ postgraduate course.

postgraduado, a [postɣra'ðwaðo, a] *adj, nm/f* postgraduate.

pos(t)guerra [pos(t)'ɣerra] *nf* postwar period; **en la** ~ after the war.

postigo [pos'tiɣo] *nm (portillo)* postern;

(*contraventana*) shutter.

postín [pos'tin] *nm* (*fam*) elegance; **de** ~ posh; **darse** ~ to show off.

postizo, a [pos'tiθo, a] *adj* false, artificial; (*sonrisa*) false, phoney ♦ *nm* hairpiece.

postoperatorio, a [postopera'torjo, a] *adj* postoperative ♦ *nm* postoperative period.

postor, a [pos'tor, a] *nm/f* bidder; **mejor** ~ highest bidder.

postrado, a [pos'traðo, a] *adj* prostrate.

postrar [pos'trar] *vt* (*derribar*) to cast down, overthrow; (*humillar*) to humble; (*MED*) to weaken, exhaust; ~**se** *vr* to prostrate o.s.

postre ['postre] *nm* sweet, dessert ♦ *nf*: **a la** ~ in the end, when all is said and done; **para** ~ (*fam*) to crown it all; **llegar a los** ~**s** (*fig*) to come too late.

postrero, a [pos'trero, a] *adj* (*delante de nmsg*: **postrer**: *último*) last; (: *que viene detrás*) rear.

postrimerías [postrime'rias] *nfpl* final stages.

postulado [postu'laðo] *nm* postulate.

postulante [postu'lante] *nm/f* petitioner; (*REL*) postulant.

póstumo, a ['postumo, a] *adj* posthumous.

postura [pos'tura] *nf* (*del cuerpo*) posture, position; (*fig*) attitude, position.

post-venta [pos'ßenta] *adj* (*COM*) after-sales.

potable [po'taßle] *adj* drinkable.

potaje [po'taxe] *nm* thick vegetable soup.

pote ['pote] *nm* pot, jar.

potencia [po'tenθja] *nf* power; (*capacidad*) capacity; ~ **(en caballos)** horsepower; **en** ~ potential, in the making; **las grandes** ~**s** the great powers.

potencial [poten'θjal] *adj, nm* potential.

potenciar [poten'θjar] *vt* (*promover*) to promote; (*fortalecer*) to boost.

potente [po'tente] *adj* powerful.

potestad [potes'tað] *nf* authority; **patria** ~ paternal authority.

potosí [poto'si] *nm* fortune; **cuesta un** ~ it costs the earth.

potra ['potra] *nf* (*ZOOL*) filly; **tener** ~ to be lucky.

potro ['potro] *nm* (*ZOOL*) colt; (*DEPORTE*) vaulting horse.

pozo ['poθo] *nm* well; (*de río*) deep pool; (*de mina*) shaft; ~ **negro** cesspool; **ser un** ~ **de ciencia** (*fig*) to be deeply learned.

PP *abr* (= *por poderes*) pp; (= *porte pagado*) carriage paid.

p.p.m. *abr* (= *palabras por minuto*) wpm.

práctica ['praktika] *nf* V **práctico**.

practicable [prakti'kaßle] *adj* practicable; (*camino*) passable, usable.

prácticamente ['praktikamente] *adv* practically.

practicante [prakti'kante] *nm/f* (*MED*: *ayudante de doctor*) medical assistant; (: *enfermero*) nurse; (*quien practica algo*) practitioner ♦ *adj* practising.

practicar [prakti'kar] *vt* to practise; (*deporte*) to go in for, play; (*ejecutar*) to carry out, perform.

práctico, a ['praktiko, a] *adj* (*gen*) practical; (*conveniente*) handy; (*instruído*: *persona*) skilled, expert ♦ *nf* practice; (*método*) method; (*arte, capacidad*) skill; **en la práctica** in practice.

practique [prak'tike] *etc vb* V **practicar**.

pradera [pra'ðera] *nf* meadow; (*de Canadá*) prairie.

prado ['praðo] *nm* (*campo*) meadow, field; (*pastizal*) pasture; (*AM*) lawn.

Praga ['praɣa] *nf* Prague.

pragmático, a [praɣ'matiko, a] *adj* pragmatic.

preámbulo [pre'ambulo] *nm* preamble, introduction; **decir algo sin** ~**s** to say sth without beating about the bush.

precalentamiento [prekalenta'mjento] *nm* (*DEPORTE*) warm-up.

precalentar [prekalen'tar] *vt* to preheat.

precaliente [preka'ljente] *etc vb* V **precalentar**.

precario, a [pre'karjo, a] *adj* precarious.

precaución [prekau'θjon] *nf* (*medida preventiva*) preventive measure, precaution; (*prudencia*) caution, wariness.

precaver [preka'ßer] *vt* to guard against; (*impedir*) to forestall; ~**se** *vr*: ~**se de** *o* **contra algo** to (be on one's) guard against sth.

precavido, a [preka'ßiðo, a] *adj* cautious, wary.

precedencia [preθe'ðenθja] *nf* precedence; (*prioridad*) priority; (*superioridad*) greater importance, superiority.

precedente [preθe'ðente] *adj* preceding; (*anterior*) former ♦ *nm* precedent; **sin** ~**(s)** unprecedented; **establecer** *o* **sentar un** ~ to establish *o* set a precedent.

preceder [preθe'ðer] *vt, vi* to precede, go/come before.

precepto [pre'θepto] *nm* precept.

preceptor [preθep'tor] *nm* (*maestro*) teacher; (: *particular*) tutor.

preciado, a [pre'θjaðo, a] *adj* (*estimado*) esteemed, valuable.

preciar [pre'θjar] *vt* to esteem, value; ~**se**

vr to boast; **~se de** to pride o.s. on.

precintar [preθin'tar] *vt* (*local*) to seal off; (*producto*) to seal.

precinto [pre'θinto] *nm* (*COM*: *tb*: ~ **de garantía**) seal.

precio ['preθjo] *nm* (*de mercado*) price; (*costo*) cost; (*valor*) value, worth; (*de viaje*) fare; ~ **de coste** *o* **de cobertura** cost price; ~ **al contado** cash price; ~ **al detalle** *o* **al por menor** retail price; ~ **al detallista** trade price; ~ **de entrega inmediata** spot price; ~ **de oferta** offer price; ~ **de oportunidad** bargain price; ~ **de salida** upset price; ~ **tope** top price; ~ **unitario** unit price; **no tener** ~ (*fig*) to be priceless; **"no importa ~"** "cost no object".

preciosidad [preθjosi'ðað] *nf* (*valor*) (high) value, (great) worth; (*encanto*) charm; (*cosa bonita*) beautiful thing; **es una** ~ it's lovely, it's really beautiful.

precioso, a [pre'θjoso, a] *adj* precious; (*de mucho valor*) valuable; (*fam*) lovely, beautiful.

precipicio [preθi'pjeθjo] *nm* cliff, precipice; (*fig*) abyss.

precipitación [preθipita'θjon] *nf* (*prisa*) haste; (*lluvia*) rainfall; (*QUÍMICA*) precipitation.

precipitado, a [preθipi'taðo, a] *adj* hasty, rash; (*salida*) hasty, sudden ♦ *nm* (*QUÍMICA*) precipitate.

precipitar [preθipi'tar] *vt* (*arrojar*) to hurl, throw; (*apresurar*) to hasten; (*acelerar*) to speed up, accelerate; (*QUÍMICA*) to precipitate; **~se** *vr* to throw o.s.; (*apresurarse*) to rush; (*actuar sin pensar*) to act rashly; **~se hacia** to rush towards.

precisado, a [preθi'saðo, a] *adj*: **verse** ~ **a hacer algo** to be obliged to do sth.

precisamente [preθisa'mente] *adv* precisely; (*justo*) precisely, exactly, just; ~ **por eso** for that very reason; ~ **fue él quien lo dijo** as a matter of fact he said it; **no es eso** ~ it's not really that.

precisar [preθi'sar] *vt* (*necesitar*) to need, require; (*fijar*) to determine exactly, fix; (*especificar*) to specify; (*señalar*) to pinpoint.

precisión [preθi'sjon] *nf* (*exactitud*) precision.

preciso, a [pre'θiso, a] *adj* (*exacto*) precise; (*necesario*) necessary, essential; (*estilo, lenguaje*) concise; **es** ~ **que lo hagas** you must do it.

precocidad [prekoθi'ðað] *nf* precociousness, precocity.

preconcebido, a [prekonθe'ßiðo, a] *adj*

preconceived.

preconice [preko'niθe] *etc vb V* **preconizar**.

preconizar [prekoni'θar] *vt* (*aconsejar*) to advise; (*prever*) to foresee.

precoz [pre'koθ] *adj* (*persona*) precocious; (*calvicie*) premature.

precursor, a [prekur'sor, a] *nm/f* precursor.

predecesor, a [preðeθe'sor, a] *nm/f* predecessor.

predecir [preðe'θir] *vt* to predict, foretell, forecast.

predestinado, a [preðesti'naðo, a] *adj* predestined.

predeterminar [preðetermi'nar] *vt* to predetermine.

predicado [preði'kaðo] *nm* predicate.

predicador, a [preðika'ðor, a] *nm/f* preacher.

predicar [preði'kar] *vt, vi* to preach.

predicción [preðik'θjon] *nf* prediction; (*pronóstico*) forecast; ~ **del tiempo** weather forecast(ing).

predicho [pre'ðitʃo], **prediga** [pre'ðiɣa] *etc*, **predije** [pre'ðixe] *etc vb V* **predecir**.

predilecto, a [preði'lekto, a] *adj* favourite.

predique [pre'ðike] *etc vb V* **predicar**.

prediré [preði're] *etc vb V* **predecir**.

predispondré [preðispon'dre] *etc vb V* **predisponer**.

predisponer [preðispo'ner] *vt* to predispose; (*pey*) to prejudice.

predisponga [preðis'ponga] *etc vb V* **predisponer**.

predisposición [preðisposi'θjon] *nf* predisposition, inclination; prejudice, bias; (*MED*) tendency.

predispuesto [preðis'pwesto], **predispuse** [preðis'puse] *etc vb V* **predisponer**.

predominante [preðomi'nante] *adj* predominant; (*preponderante*) prevailing; (*interés*) controlling.

predominar [preðomi'nar] *vt* to dominate ♦ *vi* to predominate; (*prevalecer*) to prevail.

predominio [preðo'minjo] *nm* predominance; prevalence.

preescolar [preesko'lar] *adj* preschool.

preestreno [prees'treno] *nm* preview, press view.

prefabricado, a [prefaßri'kaðo, a] *adj* prefabricated.

prefacio [pre'faθjo] *nm* preface.

preferencia [prefe'renθja] *nf* preference; **de** ~ preferably, for preference; **localidad de** ~ reserved seat.

preferible [prefe'rißle] *adj* preferable.

preferir [prefe'rir] *vt* to prefer.
prefiera [pre'fjera] *etc vb* V **preferir**.
prefijo [pre'fixo] *nm* prefix.
prefiriendo [prefi'rjendo] *etc vb* V **preferir**.
pregón [pre'ɣon] *nm* proclamation, announcement.
pregonar [preɣo'nar] *vt* to proclaim, announce; (*mercancía*) to hawk.
pregonero [preɣo'nero] *nm* town crier.
pregunta [pre'ɣunta] *nf* question; ~ **capciosa** catch question; **hacer una** ~ to ask a question.
preguntar [preɣun'tar] *vt* to ask; (*cuestionar*) to question ♦ *vi* to ask; ~**se** *vr* to wonder; ~ **por algn** to ask for sb; ~ **por la salud de algn** to ask after sb's health.
preguntón, ona [preɣun'ton, ona] *adj* inquisitive.
prehistórico, a [preis'toriko, a] *adj* prehistoric.
prejuicio [pre'xwiθjo] *nm* prejudgement; (*preconcepción*) preconception; (*pey*) prejudice, bias.
prejuzgar [prexuθ'ɣar] *vt* (*predisponer*) to prejudge.
prejuzgue [pre'xuθɣe] *etc vb* V **prejuzgar**.
preliminar [prelimi'nar] *adj, nm* preliminary.
preludio [pre'luðjo] *nm* (*MUS, fig*) prelude.
premamá [prema'ma] *adj*: **vestido** ~ maternity dress.
prematrimonial [prematrimo'njal] *adj*: **relaciones** ~**es** premarital sex.
prematuro, a [prema'turo, a] *adj* premature.
premeditación [premeðita'θjon] *nf* premeditation.
premeditado, a [premeði'taðo, a] *adj* premeditated, deliberate; (*intencionado*) wilful.
premeditar [premeði'tar] *vt* to premeditate.
premiar [pre'mjar] *vt* to reward; (*en un concurso*) to give a prize to.
premio ['premjo] *nm* reward; prize; (*COM*) premium; ~ **gordo** first prize.
premisa [pre'misa] *nf* premise.
premonición [premoni'θjon] *nf* premonition.
premura [pre'mura] *nf* (*prisa*) haste, urgency.
prenatal [prena'tal] *adj* antenatal, prenatal.
prenda ['prenda] *nf* (*ropa*) garment, article of clothing; (*garantía*) pledge; (*fam*) darling!; ~**s** *nfpl* talents, gifts; **dejar algo en** ~ to pawn sth; **no soltar** ~ to give

nothing away; (*fig*) not to say a word.
prendar [pren'dar] *vt* to captivate, enchant; ~**se de algo** to fall in love with sth.
prendedor [prende'ðor] *nm* brooch.
prender [pren'der] *vt* (*captar*) to catch, capture; (*detener*) to arrest; (*coser*) to pin, attach; (*sujetar*) to fasten; (*AM*) to switch on ♦ *vi* to catch; (*arraigar*) to take root; ~**se** *vr* (*encenderse*) to catch fire.
prendido, a [pren'diðo, a] *adj* (*AM: luz etc*) on.
prensa ['prensa] *nf* press; **la P**~ the press; **tener mala** ~ to have *o* get a bad press; **la** ~ **nacional** the national press.
prensar [pren'sar] *vt* to press.
preñado, a [pre'ɲaðo, a] *adj* (*mujer*) pregnant; ~ **de** pregnant with, full of.
preocupación [preokupa'θjon] *nf* worry, concern; (*ansiedad*) anxiety.
preocupado, a [preoku'paðo, a] *adj* worried, concerned; anxious.
preocupar [preoku'par] *vt* to worry; ~**se** *vr* to worry; ~**se de algo** (*hacerse cargo*) to take care of sth; ~**se por algo** to worry about sth.
preparación [prepara'θjon] *nf* (*acto*) preparation; (*estado*) preparedness, readiness; (*entrenamiento*) training.
preparado, a [prepa'raðo, a] *adj* (*dispuesto*) prepared; (*CULIN*) ready (to serve) ♦ *nm* (*MED*) preparation; ¡~**s, listos, ya!** ready, steady, go!
preparar [prepa'rar] *vt* (*disponer*) to prepare, get ready; (*TEC: tratar*) to prepare, process, treat; (*entrenar*) to teach, train; ~**se** *vr*: ~**se a** *o* **para hacer algo** to prepare *o* get ready to do sth.
preparativo, a [prepara'tiβo] *adj* preparatory, preliminary ♦ *nm*: ~**s** *nmpl* preparations.
preparatoria [prepara'torja] *nf* (*AM*) sixth form college (*BRIT*), senior high school (*US*).
preposición [preposi'θjon] *nf* preposition.
prepotencia [prepo'tenθja] *nf* abuse of power; (*POL*) high-handedness; (*soberbia*) arrogance.
prepotente [prepo'tente] *adj* (*POL*) high-handed; (*soberbio*) arrogant.
prerrogativa [prerroɣa'tiβa] *nf* prerogative, privilege.
presa ['presa] *nf* (*cosa apresada*) catch; (*víctima*) victim; (*de animal*) prey; (*de agua*) dam; **hacer** ~ **en** to clutch (on to), seize; **ser** ~ **de** (*fig*) to be a prey to.
presagiar [presa'xjar] *vt* to threaten.
presagio [pre'saxjo] *nm* omen.

presbítero [pres'ßitero] *nm* priest.

prescindir [presθin'dir] *vi:* ~ **de** (*privarse de*) to do without, go without; (*descartar*) to dispense with; **no podemos** ~ **de él** we can't manage without him.

prescribir [preskri'ßir] *vt* to prescribe.

prescripción [preskrip'θjon] *nf* prescription; ~ **facultativa** medical prescription.

prescrito [pres'krito] *pp de* **prescribir**.

preseleccionar [preselekθjo'nar] *vt* (*DEPORTE*) to seed.

presencia [pre'senθja] *nf* presence; **en** ~ **de** in the presence of.

presencial [presen'θjal] *adj:* **testigo** ~ eyewitness.

presenciar [presen'θjar] *vt* to be present at; (*asistir a*) to attend; (*ver*) to see, witness.

presentación [presenta'θjon] *nf* presentation; (*introducción*) introduction.

presentador, a [presenta'ðor, a] *nm/f* compère.

presentar [presen'tar] *vt* to present; (*ofrecer*) to offer; (*mostrar*) to show, display; (*renuncia*) to tender; (*moción*) to propose; (*a una persona*) to introduce; ~**se** *vr* (*llegar inesperadamente*) to appear, turn up; (*ofrecerse: como candidato*) to run, stand; (*aparecer*) to show, appear; (*solicitar empleo*) to apply; ~ **al cobro** (*COM*) to present for payment; ~**se a la policía** to report to the police.

presente [pre'sente] *adj* present ♦ *nm* present; (*LING*) present (tense); (*regalo*) gift; **los** ~**s** those present; **hacer** ~ to state, declare; **tener** ~ to remember, bear in mind; **la carta** ~, **la** ~ this letter.

presentimiento [presenti'mjento] *nm* premonition, presentiment.

presentir [presen'tir] *vt* to have a premonition of.

preservación [preserßa'θjon] *nf* protection, preservation.

preservar [preser'ßar] *vt* to protect, preserve.

preservativo [preserßa'tißo] *nm* sheath, condom.

presidencia [presi'ðenθja] *nf* presidency; (*de comité*) chairmanship; **ocupar la** ~ to preside, be in *o* take the chair.

presidente [presi'ðente] *nm/f* president; chairman/woman; (*en parlamento*) speaker; (*JUR*) presiding magistrate.

presidiario [presi'ðjarjo] *nm* convict.

presidio [pre'siðjo] *nm* prison, penitentiary.

presidir [presi'ðir] *vt* (*dirigir*) to preside at,

preside over; (: *comité*) to take the chair at; (*dominar*) to dominate, rule ♦ *vi* to preside; to take the chair.

presienta [pre'sjenta] *etc*, **presintiendo** [presin'tjendo] *etc vb* V **presentir**.

presión [pre'sjon] *nf* pressure; ~ **arterial** *o* **sanguínea** blood pressure; **a** ~ under pressure.

presionar [presjo'nar] *vt* to press; (*botón*) to push, press; (*fig*) to press, put pressure on ♦ *vi:* ~ **para** *o* **por** to press for.

preso, a ['preso, a] *adj:* **estar** ~ **de terror** *o* **pánico** to be panic-stricken ♦ *nm/f* prisoner; **tomar** *o* **llevar** ~ **a algn** to arrest sb, take sb prisoner.

prestación [presta'θjon] *nf* (*aportación*) lending; (*INFORM*) capability; (*servicio*) service; (*subsidio*) benefit; **prestaciones** *nfpl* (*AUTO*) performance features; ~ **de juramento** oath-taking; ~ **personal** obligatory service; **P**~ **Social Sustitutoria** community service for conscientious objectors; *V tb* **mili.**

prestado, a [pres'taðo, a] *adj* on loan; **dar algo** ~ to lend sth; **pedir** ~ to borrow.

prestamista [presta'mista] *nm/f* moneylender.

préstamo ['prestamo] *nm* loan; ~ **con garantía** loan against collateral; ~ **hipotecario** mortgage.

prestar [pres'tar] *vt* to lend, loan; (*atención*) to pay; (*ayuda*) to give; (*servicio*) to do, render; (*juramento*) to take, swear; ~**se** *vr* (*ofrecerse*) to offer *o* volunteer.

prestatario, a [presta'tarjo, a] *nm/f* borrower.

presteza [pres'teθa] *nf* speed, promptness.

prestidigitador [prestiðixita'ðor] *nm* conjurer.

prestigio [pres'tixjo] *nm* prestige; (*reputación*) face; (*renombre*) good name.

prestigioso, a [presti'xjoso, a] *adj* (*honorable*) prestigious; (*famoso, renombrado*) renowned, famous.

presto, a ['presto, a] *adj* (*rápido*) quick, prompt; (*dispuesto*) ready ♦ *adv* at once, right away.

presumido, a [presu'miðo, a] *adj* conceited.

presumir [presu'mir] *vt* to presume ♦ *vi* (*tener aires*) to be conceited; **según cabe** ~ as may be presumed, presumably; ~ **de listo** to think o.s. very smart.

presunción [presun'θjon] *nf* presumption; (*sospecha*) suspicion; (*vanidad*) conceit.

presunto, a [pre'sunto, a] *adj* (*supuesto*)

supposed, presumed; (*así llamado*) so-called.

presuntuoso, a [presun'twoso, a] *adj* conceited, presumptuous.

presupondré [presupon'dre] *etc vb V* **presuponer**.

presuponer [presupo'ner] *vt* to presuppose.

presuponga [presu'ponga] *etc vb V* **presuponer**.

presupuestar [presupwes'tar] *vi* to budget ♦ *vt*: ~ **algo** to budget for sth.

presupuestario, a [presupwes'tarjo, a] *adj* (*FINANZAS*) budgetary, budget *cpd*.

presupuesto [presu'pwesto] *pp de* **presuponer** ♦ *nm* (*FINANZAS*) budget; (*estimación: de costo*) estimate; **asignación de** ~ (*COM*) budget appropriation.

presupuse [presu'puse] *etc vb V* **presuponer**.

presuroso, a [presu'roso, a] *adj* (*rápido*) quick, speedy; (*que tiene prisa*) hasty.

pretencioso, a [preten'θjoso, a] *adj* pretentious.

pretender [preten'der] *vt* (*intentar*) to try to, seek to; (*reivindicar*) to claim; (*buscar*) to seek, try for; (*cortejar*) to woo, court; ~ **que** to expect that; **¿qué pretende usted?** what are you after?

pretendiente [preten'djente] *nm/f* (*candidato*) candidate, applicant; (*amante*) suitor.

pretensión [preten'sjon] *nf* (*aspiración*) aspiration; (*reivindicación*) claim; (*orgullo*) pretension.

pretérito, a [pre'terito, a] *adj* (*LING*) past; (*fig*) past, former.

pretextar [preteks'tar] *vt* to plead, use as an excuse.

pretexto [pre'teksto] *nm* pretext; (*excusa*) excuse; **so** ~ **de** under pretext of.

pretil [pre'til] *nm* (*valla*) parapet; (*baranda*) handrail.

prevalecer [preβale'θer] *vi* to prevail.

prevaleciente [preβale'θjente] *adj* prevailing, prevalent.

prevalezca [preβa'leθka] *etc vb V* **prevalecer**.

prevención [preβen'θjon] *nf* (*preparación*) preparation; (*estado*) preparedness, readiness; (*medida*) prevention; (*previsión*) foresight, forethought; (*precaución*) precaution.

prevendré [preβen'dre] *etc*, **prevenga** [pre'βenga] *etc vb V* **prevenir**.

prevenido, a [preβe'niðo, a] *adj* prepared, ready; (*cauteloso*) cautious; **estar** ~ (*preparado*) to be ready; **ser** ~ (*cuidadoso*) to be cautious; **hombre** ~ **vale por dos** forewarned is forearmed.

prevenir [preβe'nir] *vt* (*impedir*) to prevent; (*prever*) to foresee, anticipate; (*predisponer*) to prejudice, bias; (*avisar*) to warn; (*preparar*) to prepare, get ready; ~**se** *vr* to get ready, prepare; ~**se contra** to take precautions against.

preventivo, a [preβen'tiβo, a] *adj* preventive, precautionary.

prever [pre'βer] *vt* to foresee; (*anticipar*) to anticipate.

previniendo [preβi'njendo] *etc vb V* **prevenir**.

previo, a ['preβjo, a] *adj* (*anterior*) previous, prior ♦ *prep*: ~ **acuerdo de los otros** subject to the agreement of the others; ~ **pago de los derechos** on payment of the fees.

previsible [preβi'siβle] *adj* foreseeable.

previsión [preβi'sjon] *nf* (*perspicacia*) foresight; (*predicción*) forecast; (*prudencia*) caution; ~ **de ventas** (*COM*) sales forecast.

previsor, a [preβi'sor, a] *adj* (*precavido*) far-sighted; (*prudente*) thoughtful.

previsto [pre'βisto] *pp de* **prever**.

P.R.I. *nm abr* (*AM*) = **Partido Revolucionario Institucional**.

prieto, a ['prjeto, a] *adj* (*oscuro*) dark; (*AM*) dark(-skinned); (*fig*) mean; (*comprimido*) tight, compressed.

prima ['prima] *nf V* **primo**.

primacía [prima'θia] *nf* primacy.

primar [pri'mar] *vi* (*tener primacía*) to occupy first place; ~ **sobre** to have priority over.

primario, a [pri'marjo, a] *adj* primary ♦ *nf* primary education; *V tb* **sistema educativo**.

primavera [prima'βera] *nf* (*temporada*) spring; (*período*) springtime.

primaveral [primaβe'ral] *adj* spring *cpd*, springlike.

primero, a [pri'mero, a] *adj* (*delante de nmsg: primer*) first; (*fig*) prime; (*anterior*) former; (*básico*) fundamental ♦ *adv* first; (*más bien*) sooner, rather ♦ *nf* (*AUTO*) first gear; (*FERRO*) first class; **de primera** (*fam*) first-class, first-rate; **de buenas a primeras** suddenly; **primera dama** (*TEAT*) leading lady.

primicia [pri'miθja] *nf* (*PRENSA*) scoop; ~**s** *nfpl* (*tb fig*) first fruits.

primitivo, a [primi'tiβo, a] *adj* primitive; (*original*) original; (*COM: acción*) ordinary ♦ *nf*: **(Lotería) Primitiva** *weekly state-run*

lottery; v *tb* **lotería**.
primo, a ['primo, a] *adj* (*MAT*) prime ♦ *nm/f* cousin; (*fam*) fool, dupe ♦ *nf* (*COM*) bonus; (*seguro*) premium; (*a la exportación*) subsidy; ~ **hermano** first cousin; **materias primas** raw materials; **hacer el** ~ to be taken for a ride.
primogénito, a [primo'xenito, a] *adj* first-born.
primor [pri'mor] *nm* (*cuidado*) care; **es un** ~ it's lovely.
primordial [primor'ðjal] *adj* basic, fundamental.
primoroso, a [primo'roso, a] *adj* exquisite, fine.
princesa [prin'θesa] *nf* princess.
principado [prinθi'paðo] *nm* principality.
principal [prinθi'pal] *adj* principal, main; (*más destacado*) foremost; (*piso*) first, second (*US*); (*INFORM*) foreground ♦ *nm* (*jefe*) chief, principal.
príncipe ['prinθipe] *nm* prince; ~ **heredero** crown prince; **P~ de Asturias** *King's son and heir to the Spanish throne*; ~ **de gales** (*tela*) check.
principiante [prinθi'pjante] *nm/f* beginner; (*novato*) novice.
principio [prin'θipjo] *nm* (*comienzo*) beginning, start; (*origen*) origin; (*base*) rudiment, basic idea; (*moral*) principle; **a ~s de** at the beginning of; **desde el** ~ from the first; **en un** ~ at first.
pringar [prin'gar] *vt* (*CULIN*: *pan*) to dip; (*ensuciar*) to dirty; ~**se** *vr* to get splashed *o* soiled; ~ **a algn en un asunto** (*fam*) to involve sb in a matter.
pringoso, a [prin'goso, a] *adj* greasy; (*pegajoso*) sticky.
pringue ['pringe] *etc vb* V **pringar** ♦ *nm* (*grasa*) grease, fat, dripping.
prioridad [priori'ðað] *nf* priority; (*AUTO*) right of way.
prioritario, a [priori'tarjo, a] *adj* (*INFORM*) foreground.
prisa ['prisa] *nf* (*apresuramiento*) hurry, haste; (*rapidez*) speed; (*urgencia*) (sense of) urgency; **correr** ~ to be urgent; **darse** ~ to hurry up; **estar de** *o* **tener** ~ to be in a hurry.
prisión [pri'sjon] *nf* (*cárcel*) prison; (*período de cárcel*) imprisonment.
prisionero, a [prisjo'nero, a] *nm/f* prisoner.
prismáticos [pris'matikos] *nmpl* binoculars.
privación [priβa'θjon] *nf* deprivation; (*falta*) want, privation; **privaciones** *nfpl* hardships, privations.
privado, a [pri'βaðo, a] *adj* (*particular*)

private; (*POL*: *favorito*) favourite (*BRIT*), favorite (*US*); **en** ~ privately, in private; "~ **y confidencial**" "private and confidential".
privar [pri'βar] *vt* to deprive; ~**se** *vr*: ~**se de** (*abstenerse*) to deprive o.s. of; (*renunciar*) to give up.
privativo, a [priβa'tiβo, a] *adj* exclusive.
privatizar [priβati'θar] *vt* to privatize.
privilegiado, a [priβile'xjaðo, a] *adj* privileged; (*memoria*) very good ♦ *nm/f* (*afortunado*) privileged person.
privilegiar [priβile'xjar] *vt* to grant a privilege to; (*favorecer*) to favour.
privilegio [priβi'lexjo] *nm* privilege; (*concesión*) concession.
pro [pro] *nm o nf* profit, advantage ♦ *prep*. **asociación** ~ **ciegos** association for the blind ♦ *pref*: ~ **soviético/americano** pro-Soviet/-American; **en** ~ **de** on behalf of, for; **los** ~**s y los contras** the pros and cons.
proa ['proa] *nf* (*NAUT*) bow, prow.
probabilidad [proβaβili'ðað] *nf* probability, likelihood; (*oportunidad, posibilidad*) chance, prospect.
probable [pro'βaβle] *adj* probable, likely; **es** ~ **que** + *subjun* it is probable *o* likely that; **es** ~ **que no venga** he probably won't come.
probador [proβa'ðor] *nm* (*persona*) taster (*of wine etc*); (*en una tienda*) fitting room.
probar [pro'βar] *vt* (*demostrar*) to prove; (*someter a prueba*) to test, try out; (*ropa*) to try on; (*comida*) to taste ♦ *vi* to try; ~**se** *vr*: ~**se un traje** to try on a suit.
probeta [pro'βeta] *nf* test tube.
problema [pro'βlema] *nm* problem.
procaz [pro'kaθ] *adj* insolent, impudent.
procedencia [proθe'ðenθja] *nf* (*principio*) source, origin; (*lugar de salida*) point of departure.
procedente [proθe'ðente] *adj* (*razonable*) reasonable; (*conforme a derecho*) proper, fitting; ~ **de** coming from, originating in.
proceder [proθe'ðer] *vi* (*avanzar*) to proceed; (*actuar*) to act; (*ser correcto*) to be right (and proper), be fitting ♦ *nm* (*comportamiento*) behaviour, conduct; **no procede obrar así** it is not right to act like that; ~ **de** to come from, originate in.
procedimiento [proθeði'mjento] *nm* procedure; (*proceso*) process; (*método*) means, method; (*trámite*) proceedings *pl*.
prócer ['proθer] *nm* (*persona eminente*) worthy; (*líder*) great man, leader; (*esp*

AM) national hero.

procesado, a [proθe'saðo, a] *nm/f* accused (person).

procesador [proθesa'ðor] *nm*: ~ **de textos** (*INFORM*) word processor.

procesamiento [proθesa'mjento] *nm* (*INFORM*) processing; ~ **de datos** data processing; ~ **por lotes** batch processing; ~ **solapado** multiprogramming; ~ **de textos** word processing.

procesar [proθe'sar] *vt* to try, put on trial; (*INFORM*) to process.

procesión [proθe'sjon] *nf* procession; **la ~ va por dentro** he keeps his troubles to himself.

proceso [pro'θeso] *nm* process; (*JUR*) trial; (*lapso*) course (of time); (*INFORM*): ~ **(automático) de datos** (automatic) data processing; ~ **no prioritario** background process; ~ **por pasadas** batch processing; ~ **en tiempo real** real-time programming.

proclama [pro'klama] *nf* (*acto*) proclamation; (*cartel*) poster.

proclamar [prokla'mar] *vt* to proclaim.

proclive [pro'kliβe] *adj*: ~ **(a)** inclined *o* prone (to).

procreación [prokrea'θjon] *nf* procreation.

procrear [prokre'ar] *vt, vi* to procreate.

procurador, a [prokura'ðor, a] *nm/f* attorney, solicitor.

procurar [proku'rar] *vt* (*intentar*) to try, endeavour; (*conseguir*) to get, obtain; (*asegurar*) to secure; (*producir*) to produce.

prodigar [proði'ɣar] *vt* to lavish; ~**se** *vr*: ~**se en** to be lavish with.

prodigio [pro'ðixjo] *nm* prodigy; (*milagro*) wonder, marvel; **niño ~** child prodigy.

prodigioso, a [proði'xjoso, a] *adj* prodigious, marvellous.

pródigo, a ['proðiɣo, a] *adj* (*rico*) rich, productive; **hijo ~** prodigal son.

producción [proðuk'θjon] *nf* production; (*suma de productos*) output; (*producto*) product; ~ **en serie** mass production.

producir [proðu'θir] *vt* to produce; (*generar*) to cause, bring about; (*impresión*) to give; (*COM: interés*) to bear; ~**se** *vr* (*gen*) to come about, happen; (*hacerse*) to be produced, be made; (*estallar*) to break out; (*accidente*) to take place.

productividad [proðuktiβi'ðað] *nf* productivity.

productivo, a [proðuk'tiβo, a] *adj* productive; (*provechoso*) profitable.

producto [pro'ðukto] *nm* (*resultado*)

product; *producción*) production; ~ **alimenticio** foodstuff; ~ (**nacional) bruto** gross (national) product; ~ **interno bruto** gross domestic product.

productor, a [proðuk'tor, a] *adj* productive, producing ♦ *nm/f* producer.

produje [pro'ðuxe], **produjera** [proðu'xera], **produzca** [pro'ðuθka] *etc vb* V **producir**.

proeza [pro'eθa] *nf* exploit, feat.

profanar [profa'nar] *vt* to desecrate, profane.

profano, a [pro'fano, a] *adj* profane ♦ *nm/f* (*inexperto*) layman/woman; **soy ~ en música** I don't know anything about music.

profecía [profe'θia] *nf* prophecy.

proferir [profe'rir] *vt* (*palabra, sonido*) to utter; (*injuria*) to hurl, let fly.

profesar [profe'sar] *vt* (*declarar*) to profess; (*practicar*) to practise.

profesión [profe'sjon] *nf* profession; (*confesión*) avowal; **abogado de ~, de ~ abogado** a lawyer by profession.

profesional [profesjo'nal] *adj* professional.

profesor, a [profe'sor, a] *nm/f* teacher; (*instructor*) instructor; (~ *de universidad*) lecturer; ~ **adjunto** assistant lecturer, associate professor (*US*).

profesorado [profeso'raðo] *nm* (*profesión*) teaching profession; (*cuerpo*) teaching staff, faculty (*US*); (*cargo*) professorship.

profeta [pro'feta] *nm/f* prophet.

profetice [profe'tiθe] *etc vb* V **profetizar**.

profetizar [profeti'θar] *vt, vi* to prophesy.

profiera [pro'fjera] *etc*, **profiriendo** [profi'rjendo] *etc vb* V **proferir**.

profilaxis [profi'laksis] *nf inv* prevention.

prófugo, a ['profuɣo, a] *nm/f* fugitive; (*desertor*) deserter.

profundice [profun'diθe] *etc vb* V **profundizar**.

profundidad [profundi'ðað] *nf* depth; **tener una ~ de 30 cm** to be 30 cm deep.

profundizar [profundi'θar] *vt* (*fig*) to go deeply into, study in depth.

profundo, a [pro'fundo, a] *adj* deep; (*misterio, pensador*) profound; **poco ~** shallow.

profusión [profu'sjon] *nf* (*abundancia*) profusion; (*prodigalidad*) wealth.

progenie [pro'xenje] *nf* offspring.

progenitor [proxeni'tor] *nm* ancestor; ~**es** *nmpl* (*fam*) parents.

programa [pro'ɣrama] *nm* programme; (*INFORM*) program; ~ **de estudios** curriculum, syllabus; ~ **verificador de**

ortografía (*INFORM*) spelling checker.
programación [proɣrama'θjon] *nf*
(*INFORM*) programming; ~ **estructurada**
structured programming.
programador, a [proɣrama'ðor, a] *nm/f*
(*computer*) programmer; ~ **de**
aplicaciones applications programmer.
programar [proɣra'mar] *vt* (*INFORM*) to
programme.
programería [proɣrame'ria] *nf* (*INFORM*): ~
fija firmware.
progre ['proɣre] *adj* (*fam*) liberal.
progresar [proɣre'sar] *vi* to progress,
make progress.
progresión [proɣres'jon] *nf*: ~
geométrica/aritmética geometric/
arithmetic progression.
progresista [proɣre'sista] *adj, nm/f*
progressive.
progresivo, a [proɣre'siβo, a] *adj*
progressive; (*gradual*) gradual;
(*continuo*) continuous.
progreso [pro'ɣreso] *nm* (*tb*: ~**s**) progress;
hacer ~**s** to progress, advance.
prohibición [proiβi'θjon] *nf* prohibition,
ban; **levantar la** ~ **de** to remove the ban
on.
prohibir [proi'βir] *vt* to prohibit, ban,
forbid; **se prohíbe fumar** no smoking.
prohibitivo, a [proiβi'tiβo, a] *adj*
prohibitive.
prójimo, a ['proximo, a] *nm* fellow man
♦ *nm/f* (*vecino*) neighbour.
prole ['prole] *nf* (*descendencia*) offspring.
proletariado [proleta'rjaðo] *nm*
proletariat.
proletario, a [prole'tarjo, a] *adj, nm/f*
proletarian.
proliferación [prolifera'θjon] *nf*
proliferation; ~ **de armas nucleares**
spread of nuclear arms.
proliferar [prolife'rar] *vi* to proliferate.
prolífico, a [pro'lifiko, a] *adj* prolific.
prolijo, a [pro'lixo, a] *adj* long-winded,
tedious; (*AM*) neat.
prólogo ['proloɣo] *nm* prologue;
(*preámbulo*) preface, introduction.
prolongación [prolonga'θjon] *nf*
extension.
prolongado, a [prolon'gaðo, a] *adj* (*largo*)
long; (*alargado*) lengthy.
prolongar [prolon'gar] *vt* (*gen*) to extend;
(*en el tiempo*) to prolong; (*calle, tubo*) to
make longer, extend; ~**se** *vr* (*alargarse*)
to extend, go on.
prolongue [pro'longe] *etc vb V* **prolongar**.
prom. *abr* (= *promedio*) av.
promedio [pro'meðjo] *nm* average; (*de*

distancia) middle, mid-point.
promesa [pro'mesa] *nf* promise ♦ *adj*:
jugador ~ promising player; **faltar a una**
~ to break a promise.
prometer [prome'ter] *vt* to promise ♦ *vi* to
show promise; ~**se** *vr* (*dos personas*) to
get engaged.
prometido, a [prome'tiðo, a] *adj* promised;
engaged ♦ *nm/f* fiancé/fiancée.
prominente [promi'nente] *adj* prominent.
promiscuidad [promiskwi'ðað] *nf*
promiscuity.
promiscuo, a [pro'miskwo, a] *adj*
promiscuous.
promoción [promo'θjon] *nf* promotion;
(*año*) class, year; ~ **por correspondencia**
directa (*COM*) direct mailshot; ~ **de**
ventas sales promotion *o* drive.
promocionar [promoθjo'nar] *vt* (*COM*: *dar*
publicidad) to promote.
promontorio [promon'torjo] *nm*
promontory.
promotor [promo'tor] *nm* promoter;
(*instigador*) instigator.
promover [promo'βer] *vt* to promote;
(*causar*) to cause; (*juicio*) to bring;
(*motín*) to instigate, stir up.
promueva [pro'mweβa] *etc vb V* **promover**.
promulgar [promul'ɣar] *vt* to promulgate;
(*fig*) to proclaim.
promulgue [pro'mulɣe] *etc vb V*
promulgar.
pronombre [pro'nombre] *nm* pronoun.
pronosticar [pronosti'kar] *vt* to predict,
foretell, forecast.
pronóstico [pro'nostiko] *nm* prediction,
forecast; (*profecía*) omen; (*MED*:
diagnóstico) prognosis; **de** ~ **leve** slight,
not serious; ~ **del tiempo** weather
forecast.
pronostique [pronos'tike] *etc vb V*
pronosticar.
prontitud [pronti'tuð] *nf* speed, quickness.
pronto, a ['pronto, a] *adj* (*rápido*) prompt,
quick; (*preparado*) ready ♦ *adv* quickly,
promptly; (*en seguida*) at once, right
away; (*dentro de poco*) soon; (*temprano*)
early ♦ *nm* urge, sudden feeling; **tener**
~**s de enojo** to be quick-tempered; **al** ~
at first; **de** ~ suddenly; **¡hasta** ~**!** see
you soon!; **lo más** ~ **posible** as soon as
possible; **por lo** ~ meanwhile, for the
present; **tan** ~ **como** as soon as.
pronunciación [pronunθja'θjon] *nf*
pronunciation.
pronunciado, a [pronun'θjaðo, a] *adj*
(*marcado*) pronounced; (*curva etc*) sharp;
(*facciones*) marked.

pronunciamiento [pronunθja'mjento] *nm* (*rebelión*) insurrection.

pronunciar [pronun'θjar] *vt* to pronounce; (*discurso*) to make, deliver; (*JUR: sentencia*) to pass, pronounce; ~**se** *vr* to revolt, rise, rebel; (*declararse*) to declare o.s.; ~**se sobre** to pronounce on.

propagación [propaɣa'θjon] *nf* propagation; (*difusión*) spread(ing).

propaganda [propa'ɣanda] *nf* (*política*) propaganda; (*comercial*) advertising; **hacer** ~ **de** (*COM*) to advertise.

propagar [propa'ɣar] *vt* to propagate; (*difundir*) to spread, disseminate; ~**se** *vr* (*BIO*) to propagate; (*fig*) to spread.

propague [pro'paɣe] *etc vb V* **propagar**.

propalar [propa'lar] *vt* (*divulgar*) to divulge; (*publicar*) to publish an account of.

propano [pro'pano] *nm* propane.

propasarse [propa'sarse] *vr* (*excederse*) to go too far; (*sexualmente*) to take liberties.

propensión [propen'sjon] *nf* inclination, propensity.

propenso, a [pro'penso, a] *adj*: ~ **a** prone o inclined to; **ser** ~ **a hacer algo** to be inclined o have a tendency to do sth.

propiamente [propja'mente] *adv* properly; (*realmente*) really, exactly; ~ **dicho** real, true.

propicio, a [pro'piθjo, a] *adj* favourable, propitious.

propiedad [propje'ðað] *nf* property; (*posesión*) possession, ownership; (*conveniencia*) suitability; (*exactitud*) accuracy; ~ **particular** private property; ~ **pública** (*COM*) public ownership; **ceder algo a algn en** ~ to transfer to sb the full rights over sth.

propietario, a [propje'tarjo, a] *nm/f* owner, proprietor.

propina [pro'pina] *nf* tip; **dar algo de** ~ to give something extra.

propinar [propi'nar] *vt* (*golpe*) to strike; (*azotes*) to give.

propio, a ['propjo, a] *adj* own, of one's own; (*característico*) characteristic, typical; (*conveniente*) proper; (*mismo*) selfsame, very; **el** ~ **ministro** the minister himself; **¿tienes casa propia?** have you a house of your own?; **eso es muy** ~ **de él** that's just like him; **tiene un olor muy** ~ it has a smell of its own.

propondré [propon'dre] *etc vb V* **proponer**.

proponente [propo'nente] *nm* proposer, mover.

proponer [propo'ner] *vt* to propose, put forward; (*candidato*) to propose, nominate; (*problema*) to pose; ~**se** *vr* to propose, plan, intend.

proponga [pro'ponga] *etc vb V* **proponer**.

proporción [propor'θjon] *nf* proportion; (*MAT*) ratio; (*razón, porcentaje*) rate; **proporciones** *nfpl* dimensions; (*fig*) size *sg*; **en** ~ **con** in proportion to.

proporcionado, a [proporθjo'naðo, a] *adj* proportionate; (*regular*) medium, middling; (*justo*) just right; **bien** ~ well-proportioned.

proporcional [proporθjo'nal] *adj* proportional; ~ **a** proportional to.

proporcionar [proporθjo'nar] *vt* (*dar*) to give, supply, provide; **esto le proporciona una renta anual de ...** this brings him in a yearly income of ....

proposición [proposi'θjon] *nf* proposition; (*propuesta*) proposal.

propósito [pro'posito] *nm* (*intención*) purpose; (*intento*) aim, intention ♦ *adv*: **a** ~ by the way, incidentally; **a** ~ **de** about, with regard to.

propuesto, a [pro'pwesto, a] *pp de* **proponer** ♦ *nf* proposal.

propugnar [propuɣ'nar] *vt* to uphold.

propulsar [propul'sar] *vt* to drive, propel; (*fig*) to promote, encourage.

propulsión [propul'sjon] *nf* propulsion; ~ **a chorro** o **por reacción** jet propulsion.

propuse [pro'puse] *etc vb V* **proponer**.

prorrata [pro'rrata] *nf* (*porción*) share, quota, prorate (*US*) ♦ *adv* (*COM*) pro rata.

prorratear [prorrate'ar] *vt* (*dividir*) to share out, prorate (*US*).

prórroga ['prorroɣa] *nf* (*gen*) extension; (*JUR*) stay; (*COM*) deferment.

prorrogable [prorro'ɣaβle] *adj* which can be extended.

prorrogar [prorro'ɣar] *vt* (*período*) to extend; (*decisión*) to defer, postpone.

prorrogue [pro'rroɣe] *etc vb V* **prorrogar**.

prorrumpir [prorrum'pir] *vi* to burst forth, break out; ~ **en gritos** to start shouting; ~ **en lágrimas** to burst into tears.

prosa ['prosa] *nf* prose.

prosaico, a [pro'saiko, a] *adj* prosaic, dull.

proscribir [proskri'βir] *vt* to prohibit, ban; (*desterrar*) to exile, banish; (*partido*) to proscribe.

proscripción [proskrip'θjon] *nf* prohibition, ban; banishment; proscription.

proscrito, a [pros'krito, a] *pp de* **proscribir** ♦ *adj* (*prohibido*) banned; (*desterrado*) outlawed ♦ *nm/f* (*exilado*) exile; (*bandido*) outlaw.

prosecución [proseku'θjon] *nf*
continuation; (*persecución*) pursuit.
proseguir [prose'ɣir] *vt* to continue, carry
on, proceed with; (*investigación, estudio*)
to pursue ♦ *vi* to continue, go on.
prosiga [pro'siɣa] *etc*, **prosiguiendo**
[prosi'ɣjenðo] *etc vb V* **proseguir**.
prosista [pro'sista] *nm/f* (*escritor*) prose
writer.
prospección [prospek'θjon] *nf* exploration;
(*del petróleo, del oro*) prospecting.
prospecto [pros'pekto] *nm* prospectus;
(*folleto*) leaflet, sheet of instructions.
prosperar [prospe'rar] *vi* to prosper,
thrive, flourish.
prosperidad [prosperi'ðað] *nf* prosperity;
(*éxito*) success.
próspero, a ['prospero, a] *adj* prosperous;
(*que tiene éxito*) successful.
prostíbulo [pros'tiβulo] *nm* brothel.
prostitución [prostitu'θjon] *nf*
prostitution.
prostituir [prosti'twir] *vt* to prostitute; **~se**
vr to prostitute o.s., become a prostitute.
prostituta [prosti'tuta] *nf* prostitute.
prostituyendo [prostitu'jendo] *etc vb V*
prostituir.
protagonice [protaɣo'niθe] *etc vb V*
protagonizar.
protagonista [protaɣo'nista] *nm/f*
protagonist; (*LIT: personaje*) main
character, hero(ine).
protagonizar [protaɣoni'θar] *vt* to head,
take the chief role in.
protección [protek'θjon] *nf* protection.
proteccionismo [protekθjo'nismo] *nm*
(*COM*) protectionism.
protector, a [protek'tor, a] *adj* protective,
protecting; (*tono*) patronizing ♦ *nm/f*
protector; (*bienhechor*) patron; (*de la
tradición*) guardian.
proteger [prote'xer] *vt* to protect; **~ contra
grabación** *o* **contra escritura** (*INFORM*) to
write-protect.
protegido, a [prote'xiðo, a] *nm/f* protégé/
protégée.
proteína [prote'ina] *nf* protein.
proteja [pro'texa] *etc vb V* **proteger**.
prótesis ['protesis] *nf* (*MED*) prosthesis.
protesta [pro'testa] *nf* protest.
protestante [protes'tante] *adj* Protestant.
protestar [protes'tar] *vt* to protest,
declare; (*fe*) to protest ♦ *vi* to protest;
(*objetar*) to object; **cheque protestado
por falta de fondos** cheque referred to
drawer.
protocolo [proto'kolo] *nm* protocol, **sin ~s**
(*formalismo*) informal(ly).

protón [pro'ton] *nm* proton.
prototipo [proto'tipo] *nm* prototype; (*ideal*)
model.
protuberancia [protuβe'ranθja] *nf*
protuberance.
prov. *abr* (= *provincia*) prov.
provecho [pro'βetʃo] *nm* advantage,
benefit; (*FINANZAS*) profit; ¡**buen ~**! bon
appétit!; **en ~ de** to the benefit of; **sacar
~ de** to benefit from, profit by.
provechoso, a [proβe'tʃoso, a] *adj*
(*ventajoso*) advantageous; (*beneficioso*)
beneficial, useful; (*FINANZAS: lucrativo*)
profitable.
proveedor, a [proβee'ðor, a] *nm/f*
(*abastecedor*) supplier; (*distribuidor*)
dealer; **~ de (acceso a) Internet** Internet
Service Provider.
proveer [proβe'er] *vt* to provide, supply;
(*preparar*) to provide, get ready;
(*vacante*) to fill; (*negocio*) to transact,
dispatch ♦ *vi*: **~ a** to provide for; **~se** *vr*:
~se de to provide o.s. with.
provendré [proβen'dre] *etc*, **provenga**
[pro'βenɡa] *etc vb V* **provenir**.
provenir [proβe'nir] *vi*: **~ de** to come from.
Provenza [pro'βenθa] *nf* Provence.
proverbial [proβer'βjal] *adj* proverbial;
(*fig*) notorious.
proverbio [pro'βerβjo] *nm* proverb.
proveyendo [proβe'jendo] *etc vb V* **proveer**.
providencia [proβi'ðenθja] *nf* providence;
(*previsión*) foresight; **~s** *nfpl* measures,
steps.
provincia [pro'βinθja] *nf* province; (*ESP.
ADMIN*) ≈ county, ≈ region (*Scot*); **un
pueblo de ~(s)** a country town; *see boxed
note*.

PROVINCIA

Spain is divided up into 55 administrative
provincias, *including the islands and also
the territories in North Africa. Each one
has a "capital de provincia", which
generally bears the same name. Provinces
are grouped together by way of
geographical, historical and cultural links
into "comunidades autónomas". The term
"comarca" (region) normally has purely
geographical connotations, but in
Catalonia designates administrative
boundaries.*

---

provinciano, a [proβin'θjano, a] *adj*
provincial; (*del campo*) country *cpd*.
proviniendo [proβi'njendo] *etc vb V*
provenir.

provisión [proßi'sjon] _nf_ provision; (_abastecimiento_) provision, supply; (_medida_) measure, step.

provisional [proßisjo'nal] _adj_ provisional.

provisorio, a [proßi'sorjo, a] _adj_ (_esp AM_) provisional.

provisto, a [pro'ßisto, a] _adj_: ~ **de** provided _o_ supplied with; (_que tiene_) having, possessing.

provocación [proßoka'θjon] _nf_ provocation.

provocador, a [proßoka'ðor, a] _adj_ provocative, provoking.

provocar [proßo'kar] _vt_ to provoke; (_alentar_) to tempt, invite; (_causar_) to bring about, lead to; (_promover_) to promote; (_estimular_) to rouse, stir, stimulate; (_protesta, explosión_) to cause, spark off; (_AM_): **¿te provoca un café?** would you like a coffee?

provocativo, a [proßoka'tißo, a] _adj_ provocative.

provoque [pro'ßoke] _etc vb_ V **provocar.**

proxeneta [prokse'neta] _nm/f_ go-between; (_de prostitutas_) pimp/procuress.

próximamente [proksima'mente] _adv_ shortly, soon.

proximidad [proksimi'ðað] _nf_ closeness, proximity.

próximo, a ['proksimo, a] _adj_ near, close; (_vecino_) neighbouring; (_el que viene_) next; **en fecha próxima** at an early date; **el mes** ~ next month.

proyección [projek'θjon] _nf_ projection; (_CINE_) showing; (_diapositiva_) slide, transparency; (_influencia_) influence; **el tiempo de ~ es de 35 minutos** the film runs for 35 minutes.

proyectar [projek'tar] _vt_ (_objeto_) to hurl, throw; (_luz_) to cast, shed; (_CINE_) to screen, show; (_planear_) to plan.

proyectil [projek'til] _nm_ projectile, missile; ~ **(tele)dirigido** guided missile.

proyecto [pro'jekto] _nm_ plan; (_idea_) project; (_estimación de costo_) detailed estimate; **tener algo en** ~ to be planning sth; ~ **de ley** (_POL_) bill.

proyector [projek'tor] _nm_ (_CINE_) projector.

prudencia [pru'ðenθja] _nf_ (_sabiduría_) wisdom, prudence; (_cautela_) care.

prudente [pru'ðente] _adj_ sensible, wise, prudent; (_cauteloso_) careful.

prueba ['prweßa] _etc vb_ V **probar** ♦ _nf_ proof; (_ensayo_) test, trial; (_cantidad_) taste, sample; (_saboreo_) testing, sampling; (_de ropa_) fitting; (_DEPORTE_) event; **a** ~ on trial; (_COM_) on approval; **a** ~ **de** proof against; **a** ~ **de agua/fuego** waterproof/

fireproof; ~ **de capacitación** (_COM_) proficiency test; ~ **de fuego** (_fig_) acid test; ~ **de vallas** hurdles; **someter a** ~ to put to the test; **¿tiene usted** ~ **de ello?** can you prove it?, do you have proof?

prurito [pru'rito] _nm_ itch; (_de bebé_) nappy rash; (_anhelo_) urge.

psico... [siko] _pref_ psycho...

psicoanálisis [sikoa'nalisis] _nm_ psychoanalysis.

psicoanalista [sikoana'lista] _nm/f_ psychoanalyst.

psicología [sikolo'xia] _nf_ psychology.

psicológico, a [siko'loxiko, a] _adj_ psychological.

psicólogo, a [si'koloγo, a] _nm/f_ psychologist.

psicópata [si'kopata] _nm/f_ psychopath.

psicosis [si'kosis] _nf inv_ psychosis.

psicosomático, a [sikoso'matiko, a] _adj_ psychosomatic.

psicoterapia [sikote'rapja] _nf_ psychotherapy.

psiquiatra [si'kjatra] _nm/f_ psychiatrist.

psiquiátrico, a [si'kjatriko, a] _adj_ psychiatric ♦ _nm_ mental hospital.

psíquico, a ['sikiko, a] _adj_ psychic(al).

PSOE [pe'soe] _nm abr_ = _Partido Socialista Obrero Español._

PSS _nf abr_ (= _Prestación Social Sustitutoria_) community service for conscientious objectors.

Pta. _abr_ (_GEO_: = _Punta_) Pt.

pta(s). _abr_ = **peseta(s).**

ptmo. _abr_ (_COM_) = **préstamo.**

pts. _abr_ = **pesetas.**

púa ['pua] _nf_ sharp point; (_para guitarra_) plectrum; **alambre de ~s** barbed wire.

pub [puß/paß/paf] _nm_ pub.

púber, a ['pußer, a] _adj, nm/f_ adolescent.

pubertad [pußer'tað] _nf_ puberty.

publicación [pußlika'θjon] _nf_ publication.

publicar [pußli'kar] _vt_ (_editar_) to publish; (_hacer público_) to publicize; (_divulgar_) to make public, divulge.

publicidad [pußliθi'ðað] _nf_ publicity; (_COM_) advertising; **dar** ~ **a** to publicize, give publicity to; ~ **gráfica** display advertising; ~ **en el punto de venta** point-of-sale advertising.

publicitar [pußliθi'tar] _vt_ to publicize.

publicitario, a [pußliθi'tarjo, a] _adj_ publicity _cpd_; advertising _cpd_.

público, a ['pußliko, a] _adj_ public ♦ _nm_ public; (_TEAT etc_) audience; (_DEPORTE_) spectators _pl_, crowd; (_restaurantes etc_) clients _pl_; **el gran** ~ the general public; **hacer** ~ to publish; (_difundir_) to disclose;

~ **objetivo** (*COM*) target audience.
publique [pu'ßlike] *etc vb V* **publicar**.
pucherazo [putʃe'raθo] *nm* (*fraude*)
electoral fiddle; **dar** ~ to rig an election.
puchero [pu'tʃero] *nm* (*CULIN: olla*) cooking
pot; (: *guiso*) stew; **hacer** ~**s** to pout.
pudibundo, a [puði'ßundo, a] *adj* bashful.
púdico, a ['puðiko, a] *adj* modest;
(*pudibundo*) bashful.
pudiendo [pu'ðjendo] *etc vb V* **poder**.
pudiente [pu'ðjente] *adj* (*opulento*)
wealthy; (*poderoso*) powerful.
pudín [pu'ðin] *nm* pudding.
pudor [pu'ðor] *nm* modesty; (*vergüenza*)
(sense of) shame.
pudoroso, a [puðo'roso, a] *adj* (*modesto*)
modest; (*casto*) chaste.
pudrir [pu'ðrir] *vt* to rot; (*fam*) to upset,
annoy; ~**se** *vr* to rot, decay; (*fig*) to rot,
languish.
pueblerino, a [pweßle'rino, a] *adj*
(*lugareño*) small-town *cpd*; (*persona*)
rustic, provincial ♦ *nm/f* (*aldeano*)
country person.
pueblo ['pweßlo] *etc vb V* **poblar** ♦ *nm*
people; (*nación*) nation; (*aldea*) village;
(*plebe*) common people; (*población
pequeña*) small town, country town.
pueda ['pweða] *etc vb V* **poder**.
puente ['pwente] *nm* (*gen*) bridge; (*NAUT*:
tb: ~ **de mando**) bridge; (: *cubierta*) deck;
~ **aéreo** airlift; ~ **colgante** suspension
bridge; ~ **levadizo** drawbridge; **hacer
(el)** ~ (*fam*) to take a long weekend.
puenting ['pwentin] *nm* bungee jumping.
puerco, a ['pwerko, a] *adj* (*sucio*) dirty,
filthy; (*obsceno*) disgusting ♦ *nm/f* pig/
sow.
pueril [pwe'ril] *adj* childish.
puerro ['pwerro] *nm* leek.
puerta ['pwerta] *nf* door; (*de jardín*) gate;
(*portal*) doorway; (*fig*) gateway; (*gol*)
goal; (*INFORM*) port; **a la** ~ at the door; **a**
~ **cerrada** behind closed doors; ~
corredera/giratoria sliding/swing o
revolving door; ~ **principal/trasera** o **de
servicio** front/back door; ~ **(de
transmisión en) paralelo/serie** (*INFORM*)
parallel/serial port; **tomar la** ~ (*fam*) to
leave.
puerto ['pwerto] *nm* (*tb INFORM*) port; (*de
mar*) seaport; (*paso*) pass; (*fig*) haven,
refuge; **llegar a** ~ (*fig*) to get over a
difficulty.
Puerto Rico [pwerto'riko] *nm* Puerto Rico.
puertorriqueño, a [pwertorri'keɲo, a] *adj,
nm/f* Puerto Rican.
pues [pwes] *adv* (*entonces*) then;

(¡*entonces*!) well, well then; (*así que*) so
♦ *conj* (*porque*) since; ~ ... **no sé** well ... I
don't know.
puesto, a ['pwesto, a] *pp de* **poner** ♦ *adj*
dressed ♦ *nm* (*lugar, posición*) place;
(*trabajo*) post, job; (*MIL*) post; (*COM*) stall;
(*quiosco*) kiosk ♦ *conj*: ~ **que** since, as ♦ *nf*
(*apuesta*) bet, stake; ~ **de mercado**
market stall; ~ **de policía** police station;
~ **de socorro** first aid post; **puesta en
escena** staging; **puesta en marcha**
starting; **puesta del sol** sunset; **puesta a
cero** (*INFORM*) reset.
pugna ['puɣna] *nf* battle, conflict.
pugnar [puɣ'nar] *vi* (*luchar*) to struggle,
fight; (*pelear*) to fight.
puja ['puxa] *nf* (*esfuerzo*) attempt; (*en una
subasta*) bid.
pujante [pu'xante] *adj* strong, vigorous.
pujar [pu'xar] *vt* (*precio*) to raise, push up
♦ *vi* (*en licitación*) to bid, bid up; (*fig:
esforzarse*) to struggle, strain.
pulcro, a ['pulkro, a] *adj* neat, tidy.
pulga ['pulɣa] *nf* flea; **tener malas** ~**s** to be
short-tempered.
pulgada [pul'ɣaða] *nf* inch.
pulgar [pul'ɣar] *nm* thumb.
pulgón [pul'ɣon] *nm* plant louse, greenfly.
pulir [pu'lir] *vt* to polish; (*alisar*) to smooth;
(*fig*) to polish up, touch up.
pulla ['puʎa] *nf* cutting remark.
pulmón [pul'mon] *nm* lung; **a pleno** ~
(*respirar*) deeply; (*gritar*) at the top of
one's voice; ~ **de acero** iron lung.
pulmonía [pulmo'nia] *nf* pneumonia.
pulpa ['pulpa] *nf* pulp; (*de fruta*) flesh, soft
part.
pulpería [pulpe'ria] *nf* (*AM*) small grocery
store.
púlpito ['pulpito] *nm* pulpit.
pulpo ['pulpo] *nm* octopus.
pulsacion [pulsa'θjon] *nf* beat, pulsation;
(*ANAT*) throb(bing); (*en máquina de
escribir*) tap; (*de pianista, mecanógrafo*)
touch; ~ **(de una tecla)** (*INFORM*)
keystroke; ~ **doble** (*INFORM*) strikeover.
pulsador [pulsa'ðor] *nm* button, push
button.
pulsar [pul'sar] *vt* (*tecla*) to touch, tap;
(*MUS*) to play; (*botón*) to press, push ♦ *vi*
to pulsate; (*latir*) to beat, throb.
pulsera [pul'sera] *nf* bracelet; **reloj de** ~
wristwatch.
pulso ['pulso] *nm* (*MED*) pulse; **hacer algo a**
~ to do sth unaided o by one's own
efforts.
pulular [pulu'lar] *vi* (*estar plagado*). ~ **(de)**
to swarm (with).

pulverice [pulße'riθe] *etc vb V* **pulverizar.**

pulverizador [pulßeriθa'ðor] *nm* spray, spray gun.

pulverizar [pulßeri'θar] *vt* to pulverize; (*líquido*) to spray.

puna ['puna] *nf* (*AM MED*) mountain sickness.

punce ['punθe] *etc vb V* **punzar.**

punción [pun'θjon] *nf* (*MED*) puncture.

pundonor [pundo'nor] *nm* (*dignidad*) self-respect.

punición [puni'θjon] *nf* punishment.

punitivo, a [puni'tißo, a] *adj* punitive.

punki ['punki] *adj, nm/f* punk.

punta ['punta] *nf* point, tip; (*extremidad*) end; (*promontorio*) headland; (*COSTURA*) corner; (*TEC*) small nail; (*fig*) touch, trace; **horas ~s** peak hours, rush hours; **sacar ~ a** to sharpen; **de ~** on end; **de ~ a ~** from one end to the other; **estar de ~** to be edgy; **ir de ~ en blanco** to be all dressed up to the nines; **tener algo en la ~ de la lengua** to have sth on the tip of one's tongue; **se le pusieron los pelos de ~** her hair stood on end.

puntada [pun'taða] *nf* (*COSTURA*) stitch.

puntal [pun'tal] *nm* prop, support.

puntapié [punta'pje], *pl* **puntapiés** *nm* kick; **echar a algn a ~s** to kick sb out.

punteado, a [punte'aðo, a] *adj* (*moteado*) dotted; (*diseño*) of dots ♦ *nm* (*MUS*) twang.

puntear [punte'ar] *vt* to tick, mark; (*MUS*) to pluck.

puntería [punte'ria] *nf* (*de arma*) aim, aiming; (*destreza*) marksmanship.

puntero, a [pun'tero, a] *adj* leading ♦ *nm* (*señal, INFORM*) pointer; (*dirigente*) leader.

puntiagudo, a [puntja'ɣuðo, a] *adj* sharp, pointed.

puntilla [pun'tiʎa] *nf* (*TEC*) tack, braid; (*COSTURA*) lace edging; **(andar) de ~s** (to walk) on tiptoe.

puntilloso, a [punti'ʎoso, a] *adj* (*pundonoroso*) punctilious; (*susceptible*) touchy.

punto ['punto] *nm* (*gen*) point; (*señal diminuta*) spot, dot; (*lugar*) spot, place; (*momento*) point, moment; (*en un examen*) mark; (*tema*) item; (*COSTURA*) stitch; (*INFORM*: *impresora*) pitch; (: *pantalla*) pixel; **a ~** ready; **estar a ~ de** to be on the point of *o* about to; **llegar a ~** to come just at the right moment; **al ~** at once; **en ~** on the dot; **estar en su ~** (*CULIN*) to be done to a turn; **hasta cierto ~** to some extent; **hacer ~** to knit; **poner**

un motor en ~ to tune an engine; **~ de partida/de congelación/de fusión** starting/freezing/melting point; **~ de vista** point of view, viewpoint; **~ muerto** dead centre; (*AUTO*) neutral (gear); **~s a tratar** matters to be discussed, agenda *sg*; **~ final** full stop; **dos ~s** colon; **~ y coma** semicolon; **~ acápite** (*AM*) full stop, new paragraph; **~ de interrogación** question mark; **~s suspensivos** suspension points; **~ de equilibrio/de pedido** (*COM*) breakeven/reorder point; **~ inicial** *o* **de partida** (*INFORM*) home; **~ de referencia/de venta** (*COM*) benchmark point/point-of-sale.

puntuación [puntwa'θjon] *nf* punctuation; (*puntos: en examen*) mark(s) (*pl*); (: *DEPORTE*) score.

puntual [pun'twal] *adj* (*a tiempo*) punctual; (*cálculo*) exact, accurate; (*informe*) reliable.

puntualice [puntwa'liθe] *etc vb V* **puntualizar.**

puntualidad [puntwali'ðað] *nf* punctuality; exactness, accuracy; reliability.

puntualizar [puntwali'θar] *vt* to fix, specify.

puntuar [pun'twar] *vt* (*LING, TIP*) to punctuate; (*examen*) to mark ♦ *vi* (*DEPORTE*) to score, count.

punzada [pun'θaða] *nf* (*puntura*) prick; (*MED*) stitch; (*dolor*) twinge (of pain).

punzante [pun'θante] *adj* (*dolor*) shooting, sharp; (*herramienta*) sharp; (*comentario*) biting.

punzar [pun'θar] *vt* to prick, pierce ♦ *vi* to shoot, stab.

punzón [pun'θon] *nm* (*TEC*) punch.

puñado [pu'ɲaðo] *nm* handful (*tb fig*); **a ~s** by handfuls.

puñal [pu'ɲal] *nm* dagger.

puñalada [puɲa'laða] *nf* stab.

puñeta [pu'ɲeta] *nf*: **¡~!**, **¡qué ~(s)!** (*fam!*) hell!; **mandar a algn a hacer ~s** (*fam*) to tell sb to go to hell.

puñetazo [puɲe'taθo] *nm* punch.

puño ['puɲo] *nm* (*ANAT*) fist; (*cantidad*) fistful, handful; (*COSTURA*) cuff; (*de herramienta*) handle; **como un ~** (*verdad*) obvious; (*palpable*) tangible, visible; **de ~ y letra del poeta** in the poet's own handwriting.

pupila [pu'pila] *nf* (*ANAT*) pupil.

pupitre [pu'pitre] *nm* desk.

puré [pu're], *pl* **purés** *nm* puree; (*sopa*) (thick) soup; **~ de patatas** mashed potatoes; **estar hecho ~** (*fig*) to be knackered.

pureza [pu'reθa] *nf* purity.
purga ['purxa] *nf* purge.
purgante [pur'xante] *adj, nm* purgative.
purgar [pur'xar] *vt* to purge; (*POL: depurar*) to purge, liquidate; **~se** *vr* (*MED*) to take a purge.
purgatorio [purxa'torjo] *nm* purgatory.
purgue ['purxe] *etc vb V* **purgar**.
purificar [purifi'kar] *vt* to purify; (*refinar*) to refine.
purifique [puri'fike] *etc vb V* **purificar**.
puritano, a [puri'tano, a] *adj* (*actitud*) puritanical; (*iglesia, tradición*) puritan ♦ *nm/f* puritan.
puro, a ['puro, a] *adj* pure; (*depurado*) unadulterated; (*oro*) solid; (*cielo*) clear; (*verdad*) simple, plain ♦ *adv*: **de ~ cansado** out of sheer tiredness ♦ *nm* cigar; **por pura casualidad** by sheer chance.
púrpura ['purpura] *nf* purple.
purpúreo, a [pur'pureo, a] *adj* purple.
pus [pus] *nm* pus.
puse ['puse] *etc vb V* **poner**.
pústula ['pustula] *nf* pimple, sore.
puta ['puta] *nf* whore, prostitute.
putada [pu'taða] *nf* (*fam!*): **hacer una ~ a algn** to play a dirty trick on sb; **¡qué ~!** what a pain in the arse!(*!*).
putería [pute'ria] *nf* (*prostitución*) prostitution; (*prostíbulo*) brothel.
putrefacción [putrefak'θjon] *nf* rotting, putrefaction.
pútrido, a ['putriðo, a] *adj* rotten.
puzzle ['puθle] *nm* puzzle.
PVP *abr* (*ESP: = Precio Venta al Público*) ≈ RRP.
PYME *nf abr* (= *Pequeña y Mediana Empresa*) SME.

Q q

Q, q [ku] *nf* (*letra*) Q, q; **Q de Querido** Q for Queen.
q.e.g.e. *abr* (= *que en gloria esté*) R.I.P.
q.e.p.d. *abr* (= *que en paz descanse*) R.I.P.
q.e.s.m. *abr* (= *que estrecha su mano*) *courtesy formula*.
qm. *abr* = **quintal(es) métrico(s)**.
qts. *abr* = **quilates**.

que [ke] *conj* **1** (*con oración subordinada: muchas veces no se traduce*) that; **dijo ~ vendría** he said (that) he would come; **espero ~ lo encuentres** I hope (that) you find it; **dile ~ me llame** ask him to call me; *V tb* **el**
2 (*en oración independiente*): **¡~ entre!** send him in; **¡que se mejore tu padre!** I hope your father gets better; **¡~ lo haga él!** he can do it!; (*orden*) get him to do it!
3 (*enfático*): **¿me quieres? – ¡~ sí!** do you love me? – of course!; **te digo ~ sí** I'm telling you
4 (*consecutivo: muchas veces no se traduce*) that; **es tan grande ~ no lo puedo levantar** it's so big (that) I can't lift it
5 (*comparaciones*) than; **yo ~ tú/él** if I were you/him; *V tb* **más; menos**
6 (*valor disyuntivo*): **~ le guste o no** whether he likes it or not; **~ venga o ~ no venga** whether he comes or not
7 (*porque*): **no puedo, ~ tengo ~ quedarme en casa** I can't, I've got to stay in
8: **siguió toca ~ toca** he kept on playing
♦ *pron* **1** (*cosa*) that, which; (*+prep*) which; **el sombrero ~ te compraste** the hat (that *o* which) you bought; **la cama en ~ dormí** the bed (that *o* which) I slept in; **el día (en) ~ ella nació** the day (when) she was born
2 (*persona: suj*) that, who; (: *objeto*) that, whom; **el amigo ~ me acompañó al museo** the friend that *o* who went to the museum with me: **la chica ~ invité** the girl (that *o* whom) I invited.

qué [ke] *adj* what?, which? ♦ *pron* what?; **¡~ divertido/asco!** how funny/revolting!; **¡~ día más espléndido!** what a glorious day!; **¿~ edad tienes?** how old are you?; **¿de ~ me hablas?** what are you saying to me?; **¿~ tal?** how are you?, how are things?; **¿~ hay (de nuevo)?** what's new?; **¿~ más?** anything else?
quebrada [ke'Braða] *nf V* **quebrado**.
quebradero [keBra'ðero] *nm*: **~ de cabeza** headache, worry.
quebradizo, a [keBra'ðiθo, a] *adj* fragile; (*persona*) frail.
quebrado, a [ke'Braðo, a] *adj* (*roto*) broken; (*terreno*) rough, uneven ♦ *nm/f* bankrupt ♦ *nm* (*MAT*) fraction ♦ *nf* ravine; **~ rehabilitado** discharged bankrupt.
quebradura [keBra'ðura] *nf* (*fisura*) fissure;

(*MED*) rupture.

quebrantamiento [keβranta'mjento] *nm*
(*acto*) breaking; (*de ley*) violation;
(*estado*) exhaustion.

quebrantar [keβran'tar] *vt* (*infringir*) to
violate, transgress; ~**se** *vr* (*persona*) to
fail in health.

quebranto [ke'βranto] *nm* damage, harm;
(*decaimiento*) exhaustion; (*dolor*) grief,
pain.

quebrar [ke'βrar] *vt* to break, smash ♦ *vi* to
go bankrupt; ~**se** *vr* to break, get
broken; (*MED*) to be ruptured.

quechua ['ketʃua] *adj, nm/f* Quechua.

queda ['keða] *nf:* (**toque de**) ~ curfew.

quedar [ke'ðar] *vi* to stay, remain;
(*encontrarse*) to be; (*restar*) to remain, be
left; ~**se** *vr* to remain, stay (behind); ~
en (*acordar*) to agree on/to; (*acabar
siendo*) to end up as; ~ **por hacer** to be
still to be done; ~ **ciego/mudo** to be left
blind/dumb; **no te queda bien ese
vestido** that dress doesn't suit you;
quedamos a las seis we agreed to meet
at six; **eso queda muy lejos** that's a long
way (away); **nos quedan 12 kms para
llegar al pueblo** there are still 12 kms
before we get to the village; **no queda
otra** there's no alternative; ~**se (con)
algo** to keep sth; ~**se con algn** (*fam*) to
swindle sb; ~**se en nada** to come to
nothing *o* nought; ~**se sin** to run out of.

quedo, a ['keðo, a] *adj* still ♦ *adv* softly,
gently.

quehacer [kea'θer] *nm* task, job; ~**es
(domésticos)** household chores.

queja ['kexa] *nf* complaint.

quejarse [ke'xarse] *vr* (*enfermo*) to moan,
groan; (*protestar*) to complain; ~ **de que**
... to complain (about the fact) that ....

quejica [ke'xika] *adj* grumpy, complaining
♦ *nm/f* grumbler, whinger.

quejido [ke'xiðo] *nm* moan.

quejoso, a [ke'xoso, a] *adj* complaining.

quema ['kema] *nf* fire; (*combustión*)
burning.

quemado, a [ke'maðo, a] *adj* burnt;
(*irritado*) annoyed.

quemadura [kema'ðura] *nf* burn, scald;
(*de sol*) sunburn; (*de fusible*) blow-out.

quemar [ke'mar] *vt* to burn; (*fig: malgastar*)
to burn up, squander; (*COM: precios*) to
slash, cut; (*fastidiar*) to annoy, bug ♦ *vi* to
be burning hot; ~**se** *vr* (*consumirse*) to
burn (up); (*del sol*) to get sunburnt.

quemarropa [kema'rropa]: **a** ~ *adv* point-
blank.

quemazón [kema'θon] *nf* burn; (*calor*)

intense heat; (*sensación*) itch.

quena ['kena] *nf* (*AM*) Indian flute.

quepo ['kepo] *etc vb V* **caber**.

querella [ke'reʎa] *nf* (*JUR*) charge;
(*disputa*) dispute.

querellarse [kere'ʎarse] *vr* to file a
complaint.

querencia [ke'renθja] *nf* (*ZOOL*) homing
instinct; (*fig*) homesickness.

═══════════════════ *PALABRA CLAVE*

querer [ke'rer] *vt* **1** (*desear*) to want; **quiero
más dinero** I want more money; **quisiera**
o **querría un té** I'd like a tea; **quiero
ayudar/que vayas** I want to help/you to
go; **como Vd quiera** as you wish, as you
please; **ven cuando quieras** come when
you like; **lo hizo sin** ~ he didn't mean to
do it; **no quiero** I don't want to; **le pedí
que me dejara ir pero no quiso** I asked
him to let me go but he refused

2 (*preguntas: para pedir u ofrecer algo*):
¿quiere abrir la ventana? could you open
the window?; **¿quieres echarme una
mano?** can you give me a hand?; **¿quiere
un café?** would you like some coffee?

3 (*amar*) to love; (*tener cariño a*) to be
fond of; **quiere mucho a sus hijos** he's
very fond of his children

4 (*requerir*): **esta planta quiere más luz**
this plant needs more light

5: ~ **decir** to mean; **¿qué quieres decir?**
what do you mean?

querido, a [ke'riðo, a] *adj* dear ♦ *nm/f*
darling; (*amante*) lover; **nuestra querida
patria** our beloved country.

querosén [kero'sen], **querosene**
[kero'sene] *nm* (*AM*) kerosene, paraffin.

querré [ke'rre] *etc vb V* **querer**.

quesería [kese'ria] *nf* dairy; (*fábrica*)
cheese factory.

quesero, a [ke'sero, a] *adj:* **la industria
quesera** the cheese industry ♦ *nm/f*
cheesemaker ♦ *nf* cheese dish.

queso ['keso] *nm* cheese; ~ **rallado** grated
cheese; ~ **crema** cream cheese; **dárselas
con** ~ **a algn** (*fam*) to take sb in.

quetzal [ket'sal] *nm* monetary unit of
Guatemala.

quicio ['kiθjo] *nm* hinge; **estar fuera de** ~
to be beside o.s.; **sacar a algn de** ~ to
drive sb up the wall.

quid [kið] *nm* gist, crux; **dar en el** ~ to hit
the nail on the head.

quiebra ['kjeβra] *nf* break, split; (*COM*)
bankruptcy; (*ECON*) slump.

quiebro ['kjeβro] *etc vb V* **quebrar** ♦ *nm* (*del*

cuerpo) swerve.

quien [kjen] *pron relativo* (*suj*) who; (*complemento*) whom; (*indefinido*): ~ **dice eso es tonto** whoever says that is a fool; **hay ~ piensa que** there are those who think that; **no hay ~ lo haga** no-one will do it; ~ **más,** ~ **menos tiene sus problemas** everybody has problems.

quién [kjen] *pron interrogativo* who; (*complemento*) whom; ¿~ **es?** who is it?, who's there?; (*TELEC*) who's calling?

quienquiera [kjen'kjera] (*pl* **quienesquiera**) *pron* whoever.

quiera ['kjera] *etc vb V* **querer.**

quieto, a ['kjeto, a] *adj* still; (*carácter*) placid; ¡**estáte ~!** keep still!

quietud [kje'tuð] *nf* stillness.

quijada [ki'xaða] *nf* jaw, jawbone.

quijote [ki'xote] *nm* dreamer; **Don Q~** Don Quixote.

quil. *abr* = **quilates.**

quilate [ki'late] *nm* carat.

quilla ['kiʎa] *nf* keel.

quilo... ['kilo] = **kilo...**

quimera [ki'mera] *nf* (*sueño*) pipe dream.

quimérico, a [ki'meriko, a] *adj* fantastic.

químico, a ['kimiko, a] *adj* chemical ♦ *nm/f* chemist ♦ *nf* chemistry.

quimioterapia [kimiote'rapja] *nf* chemotherapy.

quina ['kina] *nf* quinine.

quincallería [kinkaʎe'ria] *nf* ironmonger's (shop), hardware store (*US*).

quince ['kinθe] *num* fifteen; ~ **días** a fortnight.

quinceañero, a [kinθea'ɲero, a] *adj* fifteen-year-old; (*adolescente*) teenage ♦ *nm/f* fifteen-year-old; (*adolescente*) teenager.

quincena [kin'θena] *nf* fortnight; (*pago*) fortnightly pay.

quincenal [kinθe'nal] *adj* fortnightly.

quincuagésimo, a [kinkwa'xesimo, a] *num* fiftieth.

quiniela [ki'njela] *nf* football pools *pl*; ~**s** *nfpl* pools coupon *sg*.

quinientos, as [ki'njentos, as] *num* five hundred.

quinina [ki'nina] *nf* quinine.

quinqué [kin'ke] *nm* oil lamp.

quinquenal [kinke'nal] *adj* five-year *cpd*.

quinqui ['kinki] *nm* delinquent.

quinta ['kinta] *nf V* **quinto.**

quintaesencia [kintae'senθja] *nf* quintessence.

quintal [kin'tal] *nm* (*Castilla: peso*) = *46kg*; ~ **métrico** – *100kg*.

quinteto [kin'teto] *nm* quintet.

quinto, a ['kinto, a] *adj* fifth ♦ *nm* (*MIL*) conscript, draftee ♦ *nf* country house; (*MIL*) call-up, draft.

quíntuplo, a ['kintuplo, a] *adj* quintuple, five-fold.

quiosco ['kjosko] *nm* (*de música*) bandstand; (*de periódicos*) news stand (*also selling sweets, cigarettes etc*).

quirófano [ki'rofano] *nm* operating theatre.

quiromancia [kiro'manθja] *nf* palmistry.

quirúrgico, a [ki'rurxiko, a] *adj* surgical.

quise ['kise] *etc vb V* **querer.**

quisque ['kiske] *pron* (*fam*): **cada** *o* **todo ~** (absolutely) everyone.

quisquilloso [kiski'ʎoso, a] *adj* (*susceptible*) touchy; (*meticuloso*) pernickety.

quiste ['kiste] *nm* cyst.

quitaesmalte [kitaes'malte] *nm* nail polish remover.

quitamanchas [kita'mantʃas] *nm inv* stain remover.

quitanieves [kita'njeßes] *nm inv* snowplough (*BRIT*), snowplow (*US*).

quitar [ki'tar] *vt* to remove, take away; (*ropa*) to take off; (*dolor*) to relieve; (*vida*) to take; (*valor*) to reduce; (*hurtar*) to remove, steal ♦ *vi*: ¡**quita de ahí!** get away!; ~**se** *vr* to withdraw; (*mancha*) to come off *o* out; (*ropa*) to take off; **me quita mucho tiempo** it takes up a lot of my time; **el café me quita el sueño** coffee stops me sleeping; ~ **de en medio a algn** to get rid of sb; ~**se algo de encima** to get rid of sth; ~**se del tabaco** to give up smoking; **se quitó el sombrero** he took off his hat.

quitasol [kita'sol] *nm* sunshade (*BRIT*), parasol.

quite ['kite] *nm* (*esgrima*) parry; (*evasión*) dodge; **estar al ~** to be ready to go to sb's aid.

Quito ['kito] *n* Quito.

quizá(s) [ki'θa(s)] *adv* perhaps, maybe.

quórum ['kworum] *pl* **quórums** ['kworum] *nm* quorum.

Rr

R, r ['erre] *nf* (*letra*) R, r; **R de Ramón** R for Robert (*BRIT*) *o* Roger (*US*).
R. *abr* = **Remite, Remitente**.
rabadilla [raβa'ðiʎa] *nf* base of the spine.
rábano ['raβano] *nm* radish; **me importa un ~** I don't give a damn.
rabia ['raβja] *nf* (*MED*) rabies *sg*; (*fig: ira*) fury, rage; **¡qué ~!** isn't it infuriating!; **me da ~** it maddens me; **tener ~ a algn** to have a grudge against sb.
rabiar [ra'βjar] *vi* to have rabies; to rage, be furious; **~ por algo** to long for sth.
rabieta [ra'βjeta] *nf* tantrum, fit of temper.
rabino [ra'βino] *nm* rabbi.
rabioso, a [ra'βjoso, a] *adj* rabid; (*fig*) furious.
rabo ['raβo] *nm* tail.
racanear [rakane'ar] *vi* (*fam*) to skive.
rácano ['rakano] *nm* (*fam*) slacker, skiver.
RACE *nm abr* (= *Real Automóvil Club de España*) ≈ RAC.
racha ['ratʃa] *nf* gust of wind; (*serie*) string, series; **buena/mala ~** spell of good/bad luck.
racial [ra'θjal] *adj* racial, race *cpd*.
racimo [ra'θimo] *nm* bunch.
raciocinio [raθjo'θinjo] *nm* reason; (*razonamiento*) reasoning.
ración [ra'θjon] *nf* portion; **raciones** *nfpl* rations.
racional [raθjo'nal] *adj* (*razonable*) reasonable; (*lógico*) rational.
racionalice [raθjona'liθe] *etc vb V* **racionalizar**.
racionalizar [raθjonali'θar] *vt* to rationalize; (*COM*) to streamline.
racionamiento [raθjona'mjento] *nm* (*COM*) rationing.
racionar [raθjo'nar] *vt* to ration (out).
racismo [ra'θismo] *nm* racialism, racism.
racista [ra'θista] *adj, nm/f* racist.
radar [ra'ðar] *nm* radar.
radiación [raðja'θjon] *nf* radiation; (*TELEC*) broadcasting.
radiactividad [raðjaktiβi'ðað] *nf* radioactivity.
radiado, a [ra'ðjaðo, a] *adj* radio *cpd*, broadcast.

radiador [raðja'ðor] *nm* radiator.
radial [ra'ðjal] *adj* (*AM*) radio *cpd*.
radiante [ra'ðjante] *adj* radiant.
radiar [ra'ðjar] *vt* to radiate; (*TELEC*) to broadcast; (*MED*) to give radiotherapy to.
radical [raði'kal] *adj, nm/f* radical ♦ *nm* (*LING*) root; (*MAT*) square-root sign.
radicar [raði'kar] *vi* to take root; **~ en** to lie *o* consist in; **~se** *vr* to establish o.s., put down (one's) roots.
radio ['raðjo] *nf* radio; (*aparato*) radio (set) ♦ *nm* (*MAT*) radius; (*AM*) radio; (*QUÍMICA*) radium; **~ de acción** extent of one's authority, sphere of influence.
radioactivo, a [raðjoak'tiβo, a] *adj* radioactive.
radioaficionado, a [raðjoafiθjo'naðo, a] *nm/f* radio ham.
radiocasete [raðjoka'sete] *nm* radiocassette (player).
radiodifusión [raðjodifu'sjon] *nf* broadcasting.
radioemisora [raðjoemi'sora] *nf* transmitter, radio station.
radiofónico, a [raðjo'foniko, a] *adj* radio *cpd*.
radiografía [raðjoɣra'fia] *nf* X-ray.
radiólogo, a [ra'ðjoloɣo, a] *nm/f* radiologist.
radionovela [raðjono'βela] *nf* radio series.
radiotaxi [raðjo'taksi] *nm* radio taxi.
radioterapia [raðjote'rapja] *nf* radiotherapy.
radioyente [raðjo'jente] *nm/f* listener.
radique [ra'ðike] *etc vb V* **radicar**.
RAE *nf abr* = **Real Academia Española**.
ráfaga ['rafaɣa] *nf* gust; (*de luz*) flash; (*de tiros*) burst.
raído, a [ra'iðo, a] *adj* (*ropa*) threadbare; (*persona*) shabby.
raigambre [rai'ɣambre] *nf* (*BOT*) roots *pl*; (*fig*) tradition.
raíz [ra'iθ] (*pl* **raíces**) *nf* root; **~ cuadrada** square root; **a ~ de** as a result of; (*después de*) immediately after.
raja ['raxa] *nf* (*de melón etc*) slice; (*hendedura*) slit, split; (*grieta*) crack.
rajar [ra'xar] *vt* to split; (*fam*) to slash; **~se** *vr* to split, crack; **~se de** to back out of.
rajatabla [raxa'taβla]: **a ~** *adv* (*estrictamente*) strictly, to the letter.
ralea [ra'lea] *nf* (*pey*) kind, sort.
ralentí [ra'lenti] *nm* (*TV etc*) slow motion; (*AUTO*) neutral; **al ~** in slow motion; (*AUTO*) ticking over.
rallador [raʎa'ðor] *nm* grater.
rallar [ra'ʎar] *vt* to grate.

ralo, a ['ralo, a] *adj* thin, sparse.

RAM [ram] *nf abr* (= *random access memory*) RAM.

rama ['rama] *nf* bough, branch; **andarse por las ~s** (*fig, fam*) to beat about the bush.

ramaje [ra'maxe] *nm* branches *pl*, foliage.

ramal [ra'mal] *nm* (*de cuerda*) strand; (*FERRO*) branch line; (*AUTO*) branch (road).

rambla ['rambla] *nf* (*avenida*) avenue.

ramera [ra'mera] *nf* whore, hooker (*US*).

ramificación [ramifika'θjon] *nf* ramification.

ramificarse [ramifi'karse] *vr* to branch out.

ramifique [rami'fike] *etc vb V* **ramificarse**.

ramillete [rami'ʎete] *nm* bouquet; (*fig*) select group.

ramo ['ramo] *nm* branch, twig; (*sección*) department, section; (*sector*) field, sector.

rampa ['rampa] *nf* ramp.

ramplón, ona [ram'plon, ona] *adj* uncouth, coarse.

rana ['rana] *nf* frog; **salto de ~** leapfrog; **cuando las ~s críen pelos** when pigs fly.

ranchero [ran'tʃero] *nm* (*AM*) rancher; (*pequeño propietario*) smallholder.

rancho ['rantʃo] *nm* (*MIL*) food; (*AM: grande*) ranch; (: *pequeño*) small farm.

rancio, a ['ranθjo, a] *adj* (*comestibles*) stale, rancid; (*vino*) aged, mellow; (*fig*) ancient.

rango ['rango] *nm* rank; (*prestigio*) standing.

ranura [ra'nura] *nf* groove; (*de teléfono etc*) slot; **~ de expansión** (*INFORM*) expansion slot.

rap [rap] *nm* (*MUS*) rap.

rapacidad [rapaθi'ðað] *nf* rapacity.

rapapolvo [rapa'polβo] *nm:* **echar un ~ a algn** to give sb a ticking off.

rapar [ra'par] *vt* to shave; (*los cabellos*) to crop.

rapaz [ra'paθ] *adj* (*ZOOL*) predatory ♦ *nm/f* (*f:* **rapaza**) young boy/girl.

rape ['rape] *nm* quick shave; (*pez*) angler (fish); **al ~** cropped.

rapé [ra'pe] *nm* snuff.

rapidez [rapi'ðeθ] *nf* speed, rapidity.

rápido, a ['rapiðo, a] *adj* fast, quick ♦ *adv* quickly ♦ *nm* (*FERRO*) express; **~s** *nmpl* rapids.

rapiña [ra'piɲa] *nm* robbery; **ave de ~** bird of prey.

rap(p)el [ra'pel] *nm* (*DEPORTE*) abseiling.

raptar [rap'tar] *vt* to kidnap.

rapto ['rapto] *nm* kidnapping; (*impulso*) sudden impulse; (*éxtasis*) ecstasy, rapture.

raqueta [ra'keta] *nf* racquet.

raquítico, a [ra'kitiko, a] *adj* stunted; (*fig*) poor, inadequate.

raquitismo [raki'tismo] *nm* rickets *sg*.

rareza [ra'reθa] *nf* rarity; (*fig*) eccentricity.

raro, a ['raro, a] *adj* (*poco común*) rare; (*extraño*) odd, strange; (*excepcional*) remarkable; **¡qué ~!** how (very) odd!; **¡(qué) cosa más rara!** how strange!

ras [ras] *nm:* **a ~ de** level with; **a ~ de tierra** at ground level.

rasar [ra'sar] *vt* to level.

rascacielos [raska'θjelos] *nm inv* skyscraper.

rascar [ras'kar] *vt* (*con las uñas etc*) to scratch; (*raspar*) to scrape; **~se** *vr* to scratch (o.s.).

rasgar [ras'ɣar] *vt* to tear, rip (up).

rasgo ['rasɣo] *nm* (*con pluma*) stroke; **~s** *nmpl* features, characteristics; **a grandes ~s** in outline, broadly.

rasgue ['rasɣe] *etc vb V* **rasgar**.

rasguear [rasɣe'ar] *vt* (*MUS*) to strum.

rasguñar [rasɣu'ɲar] *vt* to scratch; (*bosquejar*) to sketch.

rasguño [ras'ɣuɲo] *nm* scratch.

raso, a ['raso, a] *adj* (*liso*) flat, level; (*a baja altura*) very low ♦ *nm* satin; (*campo llano*) flat country; **cielo ~** clear sky; **al ~** in the open.

raspado [ras'paðo] *nm* (*MED*) scrape.

raspador [raspa'ðor] *nm* scraper.

raspadura [raspa'ðura] *nf* (*acto*) scrape, scraping; (*marca*) scratch; **~s** *nfpl* scrapings.

raspar [ras'par] *vt* to scrape; (*arañar*) to scratch; (*limar*) to file ♦ *vi* (*manos*) to be rough; (*vino*) to be sharp, have a rough taste.

rasque ['raske] *etc vb V* **rascar**.

rastra ['rastra] *nf:* **a ~s** by dragging; (*fig*) unwillingly.

rastreador [rastrea'ðor] *nm* tracker; **~ de minas** minesweeper.

rastrear [rastre'ar] *vt* (*seguir*) to track; (*minas*) to sweep.

rastrero, a [ras'trero, a] *adj* (*BOT, ZOOL*) creeping; (*fig*) despicable, mean.

rastrillar [rastri'ʎar] *vt* to rake.

rastrillo [ras'triʎo] *nm* rake; (*AM*) safety razor.

rastro ['rastro] *nm* (*AGR*) rake; (*pista*) track, trail; (*vestigio*) trace; (*mercado*) fleamarket; **el R~** *the Madrid fleamarket*; **perder el ~** to lose the scent; **desaparecer sin ~** to vanish without

trace.
rastrojo [ras'troxo] *nm* stubble.
rasurador [rasura'ðor] *nm*, (*AM*)
　rasuradora [rasura'ðora] *nf* electric
　shaver *o* razor.
rasurarse [rasu'rarse] *vr* to shave.
rata ['rata] *nf* rat.
ratear [rate'ar] *vt* (*robar*) to steal.
ratero, a [ra'tero, a] *adj* light-fingered
　♦ *nm/f* pickpocket; (*AM: de casas*) burglar.
ratificar [ratifi'kar] *vt* to ratify.
ratifique [rati'fike] *etc vb V* **ratificar**.
rato ['rato] *nm* while, short time; **a ~s**
　from time to time; **al poco ~** shortly
　after, soon afterwards; **~s libres** *o* **de**
　ocio leisure *sg*, spare *o* free time *sg*; **hay**
　para ~ there's still a long way to go;
　pasar el ~ to kill time; **pasar un buen/**
　mal ~ to have a good/rough time.
ratón [ra'ton] *nm* (*tb INFORM*) mouse.
ratonera [rato'nera] *nf* mousetrap.
RAU *nf abr* (= *República Árabe Unida*) UAR.
raudal [rau'ðal] *nm* torrent; **a ~es** in
　abundance; **entrar a ~es** to pour in.
raya ['raja] *nf* line; (*marca*) scratch; (*en*
　tela) stripe; (*TIP*) hyphen; (*de pelo*)
　parting; (*límite*) boundary; (*pez*) ray; **a**
　~s striped; **pasarse de la ~** to overstep
　the mark; **tener a ~** to keep in check.
rayado, a [ra'jaðo, a] *adj* (*papel*) ruled;
　(*tela, diseño*) striped.
rayar [ra'jar] *vt* to line; to scratch;
　(*subrayar*) to underline ♦ *vi*: **~ en** *o* **con** to
　border on; **al ~ el alba** at first light.
rayo ['rajo] *nm* (*del sol*) ray, beam; (*de luz*)
　shaft; (*en una tormenta*) (flash of)
　lightning; **~ solar** *o* **de sol** sunbeam; **~s**
　infrarrojos infrared rays; **~s X** X-rays;
　como un ~ like a shot; **la noticia cayó**
　como un ~ the news was a bombshell;
　pasar como un ~ to flash past.
raza ['raθa] *nf* race; (*de animal*) breed; **~**
　humana human race; **de pura ~** (*caballo*)
　thoroughbred; (*perro etc*) pedigree.
razón [ra'θon] *nf* reason; (*justicia*) right,
　justice; (*razonamiento*) reasoning;
　(*motivo*) reason, motive; (*proporción*)
　rate; (*MAT*) ratio; **a ~ de 10 cada día** at
　the rate of 10 a day; **"~: ..."** "inquiries
　to ..."; **en ~ de** with regard to; **perder la**
　~ to go out of one's mind; **dar ~ a algn**
　to agree that sb is right; **dar ~ de** to
　give an account of, report on; **tener/no**
　tener ~ to be right/wrong; **~ directa/**
　inversa direct/inverse proportion; **~ de**
　ser raison d'être.
razonable [raθo'naßle] *adj* reasonable;
　(*justo, moderado*) fair.

razonamiento [raθona'mjento] *nm* (*juicio*)
　judgement; (*argumento*) reasoning.
razonar [raθo'nar] *vt, vi* to reason, argue.
RDA *nf* = **República Democrática Alemana**.
Rdo. *abr* (*REL*: = *Reverendo*) Rev.
RDSI *nf abr* (= *Red Digital de Servicios*
　Integrados) ISDN.
re [re] *nm* (*MUS*) D.
reabierto [rea'ßjerto] *pp de* **reabrir**.
reabrir [rea'ßrir] *vt*, **~se** *vr* to reopen.
reacción [reak'θjon] *nf* reaction; **avión a ~**
　jet plane; **~ en cadena** chain reaction.
reaccionar [reakθjo'nar] *vi* to react.
reaccionario, a [reakθjo'narjo, a] *adj*
　reactionary.
reacio, a [re'aθjo, a] *adj* stubborn; **ser** *o*
　estar ~ a to be opposed to.
reactivar [reakti'ßar] *vt* to reactivate; **~se**
　vr (*economía*) to be on the upturn.
reactor [reak'tor] *nm* reactor; (*avión*) jet
　plane; **~ nuclear** nuclear reactor.
readaptación [reaðapta'θjon] *nf*: **~**
　profesional industrial retraining.
readmitir [reaðmi'tir] *vt* to readmit.
reafirmar [reafir'mar] *vt* to reaffirm.
reagrupar [reaɣru'par] *vt* to regroup.
reajustar [reaxus'tar] *vt* (*INFORM*) to reset.
reajuste [rea'xuste] *nm* readjustment; **~**
　salarial wage increase; **~ de plantilla**
　rationalization.
real [re'al] *adj* real; (*del rey, fig*) royal;
　(*espléndido*) grand ♦ *nm* (*de feria*)
　fairground; **la R~ Academia Española** *see*
　boxed note.

┌───┐
│ **REAL ACADEMIA ESPAÑOLA**

The **Real Academia Española** *(RAE), dating*
back to 1713, is the regulatory body for the
Spanish language in Spain. It produces its
own dictionaries and grammars, and is
considered to be the leading authority on
the language, although it has been
criticized in the past for being too
conservative. In 1994, along with the
Spanish American "academias", it
approved a fundamental change to the
Spanish alphabet: "ch" and "ll" are no
longer treated as separate letters,
although. "ñ" continues to follow "n" as a
new letter.
└───┘

realce [re'alθe] *etc vb V* **realzar** ♦ *nm* (*TEC*)
　embossing; **poner de ~** to emphasize.
real-decreto [re'alde'kreto] (*pl* **~es-~s**) *nm*
　royal decree.
realeza [rea'leθa] *nf* royalty.
realice [rea'liθe] *etc vb V* **realizar**.

realidad [reali'ðað] *nf* reality; (*verdad*) truth; ~ **virtual** virtual reality; **en** ~ in fact.

realismo [rea'lismo] *nm* realism.

realista [rea'lista] *nmf* realist.

realización [realiθa'θjon] *nf* fulfilment, realization; (*COM*) selling up (*BRIT*), conversion into money (*US*); ~ **de plusvalías** profit-taking.

realizador, a [realiθa'ðor, a] *nmf* (*TV etc*) producer.

realizar [reali'θar] *vt* (*objetivo*) to achieve; (*plan*) to carry out; (*viaje*) to make, undertake; (*COM*) to realize; ~**se** *vr* to come about, come true; ~**se como persona** to fulfil one's aims in life.

realmente [real'mente] *adv* really.

realojar [realo'xar] *vt* to rehouse.

realquilar [realki'lar] *vt* (*subarrendar*) to sublet; (*alquilar de nuevo*) to relet.

realzar [real'θar] *vt* (*TEC*) to raise; (*embellecer*) to enhance; (*acentuar*) to highlight.

reanimar [reani'mar] *vt* to revive; (*alentar*) to encourage; ~**se** *vr* to revive.

reanudar [reanu'ðar] *vt* (*renovar*) to renew; (*historia, viaje*) to resume.

reaparición [reapari'θjon] *nf* reappearance; (*vuelta*) return.

reapertura [reaper'tura] *nf* reopening.

rearme [re'arme] *nm* rearmament.

reata [re'ata] *nf* (*AM*) lasso.

reavivar [reaβi'βar] *vt* (*persona*) to revive; (*fig*) to rekindle.

rebaja [re'βaxa] *nf* reduction, lowering; (*COM*) discount; "**grandes ~s**" "big reductions", "sale".

rebajar [reβa'xar] *vt* (*bajar*) to lower; (*reducir*) to reduce; (*precio*) to cut; (*disminuir*) to lessen; (*humillar*) to humble; ~**se** *vr*: ~**se a hacer algo** to stoop to doing sth.

rebanada [reβa'naða] *nf* slice.

rebañar [reβa'ɲar] *vt* to scrape clean.

rebaño [re'βaɲo] *nm* herd; (*de ovejas*) flock.

rebasar [reβa'sar] *vt* (*tb*: ~ **de**) to exceed; (*AUTO*) to overtake.

rebatir [reβa'tir] *vt* to refute; (*rebajar*) to reduce; (*ataque*) to repel.

rebato [re'βato] *nm* alarm; (*ataque*) surprise attack; **llamar** *o* **tocar a** ~ (*fig*) to sound the alarm.

rebeca [re'βeka] *nf* cardigan.

rebelarse [reβe'larse] *vr* to rebel, revolt.

rebelde [re'βelde] *adj* rebellious; (*niño*) unruly ♦ *nmf* rebel; **ser** ~ **a** to be in revolt against, rebel against.

rebeldía [reβel'dia] *nf* rebelliousness; (*desobediencia*) disobedience; (*JUR*) default.

rebelión [reβe'ljon] *nf* rebellion.

rebenque [re'βenke] *nm* (*AM*) whip.

reblandecer [reβlande'θer] *vt* to soften.

reblandezca [reβlan'deθka] *etc vb V* **reblandecer**.

rebobinar [reβoβi'nar] *vt* to rewind.

reboce [re'βoθe] *etc vb V* **rebozar**.

rebosante [reβo'sante] *adj*: ~ **de** (*fig*) brimming *o* overflowing with.

rebosar [reβo'sar] *vi* to overflow; (*abundar*) to abound, be plentiful; ~ **de salud** to be bursting *o* brimming with health.

rebotar [reβo'tar] *vt* to bounce; (*rechazar*) to repel.

rebote [re'βote] *nm* rebound; **de** ~ on the rebound.

rebozado, a [reβo'θaðo, a] *adj* (*CULIN*) fried in batter *o* breadcrumbs *o* flour.

rebozar [reβo'θar] *vt* to wrap up; (*CULIN*) to fry in batter *etc*.

rebozo [re'βoθo] *nm*: **sin** ~ openly.

rebuscado, a [reβus'kaðo, a] *adj* affected.

rebuscar [reβus'kar] *vi* (*en bolsillo, cajón*) to fish; (*en habitación*) to search high and low.

rebuznar [reβuθ'nar] *vi* to bray.

recabar [reka'βar] *vt* (*obtener*) to manage to get; ~ **fondos** to collect money.

recadero [reka'ðero] *nm* messenger.

recado [re'kaðo] *nm* message; **dejar/tomar un** ~ (*TELEC*) to leave/take a message.

recaer [reka'er] *vi* to relapse; ~ **en** to fall to *o* on; (*criminal etc*) to fall back into, relapse into; (*premio*) to go to.

recaída [reka'iða] *nf* relapse.

recaiga [re'kaiɣa] *etc vb V* **recaer**.

recalcar [rekal'kar] *vt* (*fig*) to stress, emphasize.

recalcitrante [rekalθi'trante] *adj* recalcitrant.

recalentamiento [rekalenta'mjento] *nm*: ~ **global** global warming.

recalentar [rekalen'tar] *vt* (*comida*) to warm up, reheat; (*demasiado*) to overheat; ~**se** *vr* to overheat, get too hot.

recaliente [reka'ljente] *etc vb V* **recalentar**.

recalque [re'kalke] *etc vb V* **recalcar**.

recámara [re'kamara] *nf* side room; (*AM*) bedroom.

recamarera [rekama'rera] *nf* (*AM*) maid.

recambio [re'kambjo] *nm* spare; (*de pluma*) refill; **piezas de** ~ spares.

recapacitar [rekapaθi'tar] *vi* to reflect.

recapitular [rekapitu'lar] *vt* to recap.

recargable [rekar'ɣaβle] *adj* (*batería, pila*)

rechargeable; (_mechero, pluma_) refillable.

recargado, a [rekar'xaðo, a] _adj_ overloaded; (_exagerado_) over-elaborate.

recargar [rekar'xar] _vt_ to overload; (_batería_) to recharge; (_mechero, pluma_) to refill.

recargo [re'karxo] _nm_ surcharge; (_aumento_) increase.

recargue [re'karxe] _etc vb V_ **recargar**.

recatado, a [reka'taðo, a] _adj_ (_modesto_) modest, demure; (_prudente_) cautious.

recato [re'kato] _nm_ (_modestia_) modesty, demureness; (_cautela_) caution.

recauchutado, a [rekautʃu'taðo, a] _adj_ remould _cpd_.

recaudación [rekauða'θjon] _nf_ (_acción_) collection; (_cantidad_) takings _pl_; (_en deporte_) gate; (_oficina_) tax office.

recaudador, a [rekauða'ðor, a] _nm/f_ tax collector.

recaudar [rekau'ðar] _vt_ to collect.

recaudo [re'kauðo] _nm_ (_impuestos_) collection; (_JUR_) surety; **estar a buen ~** to be in safekeeping; **poner algo a buen ~** to put sth in a safe place.

recayendo [reka'jendo] _etc vb V_ **recaer**.

rece ['reθe] _etc vb V_ **rezar**.

recelar [reθe'lar] _vt_: **~ que** (_sospechar_) to suspect that; (_temer_) to fear that ♦ _vi_: **~(se) de** to distrust.

recelo [re'θelo] _nm_ distrust, suspicion.

receloso, a [reθe'loso, a] _adj_ distrustful, suspicious.

recepción [reθep'θjon] _nf_ reception; (_acto de recibir_) receipt.

recepcionista [reθepθjo'nista] _nm/f_ receptionist.

receptáculo [reθep'takulo] _nm_ receptacle.

receptivo, a [reθep'tiβo, a] _adj_ receptive.

receptor, a [reθep'tor, a] _nm/f_ recipient ♦ _nm_ (_TELEC_) receiver; **descolgar el ~** to pick up the receiver.

recesión [reθe'sjon] _nf_ (_COM_) recession.

receta [re'θeta] _nf_ (_CULIN_) recipe; (_MED_) prescription.

recetar [reθe'tar] _vt_ to prescribe.

rechace [re'tʃaθe] _etc vb V_ **rechazar**.

rechazar [retʃa'θar] _vt_ to repel, drive back; (_idea_) to reject; (_oferta_) to turn down.

rechazo [re'tʃaθo] _nm_ (_de fusil_) recoil; (_rebote_) rebound; (_negación_) rebuff.

rechifla [re'tʃifla] _nf_ hissing, booing; (_fig_) derision.

rechinar [retʃi'nar] _vi_ to creak; (_dientes_) to grind; (_máquina_) to clank, clatter; (_metal seco_) to grate; (_motor_) to hum.

rechistar [retʃis'tar] _vi_: **sin ~** without complaint.

rechoncho, a [re'tʃontʃo, a] _adj_ (_fam_) stocky, thickset (_BRIT_), heavy-set (_US_).

rechupete [retʃu'pete]: **de ~** _adj_ (_comida_) delicious.

recibidor [reθiβi'ðor] _nm_ entrance hall.

recibimiento [reθiβi'mjento] _nm_ reception, welcome.

recibir [reθi'βir] _vt_ to receive; (_dar la bienvenida_) to welcome; (_salir al encuentro de_) to go and meet ♦ _vi_ to entertain; **~se** _vr_: **~se de** to qualify as.

recibo [re'θiβo] _nm_ receipt; **acusar ~ de** to acknowledge receipt of.

reciclaje [reθi'klaxe] _nm_ recycling; (_de trabajadores_) retraining; **cursos de ~** refresher courses.

reciclar [reθi'klar] _vt_ to recycle; (_trabajador_) to retrain.

recién [re'θjen] _adv_ recently, newly; (_AM_) just, recently; **~ casado** newly-wed; **el ~ llegado** the newcomer; **el ~ nacido** the newborn child; **~ a las seis** only at six o'clock.

reciente [re'θjente] _adj_ recent; (_fresco_) fresh.

recientemente [reθjente'mente] _adv_ recently.

recinto [re'θinto] _nm_ enclosure; (_área_) area, place.

recio, a ['reθjo, a] _adj_ strong, tough; (_voz_) loud ♦ _adv_ hard; loud(ly).

recipiente [reθi'pjente] _nm_ (_objeto_) container; receptacle; (_persona_) recipient.

reciprocidad [reθiproθi'ðað] _nf_ reciprocity.

recíproco, a [re'θiproko, a] _adj_ reciprocal.

recital [reθi'tal] _nm_ (_MUS_) recital; (_LIT_) reading.

recitar [reθi'tar] _vt_ to recite.

reclamación [reklama'θjon] _nf_ claim, demand; (_queja_) complaint; **~ salarial** pay claim.

reclamar [rekla'mar] _vt_ to claim, demand ♦ _vi_: **~ contra** to complain about; **~ a algn en justicia** to take sb to court.

reclamo [re'klamo] _nm_ (_anuncio_) advertisement; (_tentación_) attraction.

reclinar [rekli'nar] _vt_ to recline, lean; **~se** _vr_ to lean back.

recluir [reklu'ir] _vt_ to intern, confine.

reclusión [reklu'sjon] _nf_ (_prisión_) prison; (_refugio_) seclusion; **~ perpetua** life imprisonment.

recluso, a [re'kluso, a] _adj_ imprisoned; **población reclusa** prison population ♦ _nm/f_ (_solitario_) recluse; (_JUR_) prisoner.

recluta [re'kluta] _nm/f_ recruit ♦ _nf_

recruitment.
reclutamiento [rekluta'mjento] *nm*
recruitment.
recluyendo [reklu'jendo] *etc vb V* **recluir.**
recobrar [reko'ßrar] *vt (recuperar)* to
recover; *(rescatar)* to get back; *(ciudad)*
to recapture; *(tiempo)* to make up (for);
~**se** *vr* to recover.
recochineo [rekotʃi'neo] *nm (fam)*
mickey-taking.
recodo [re'koðo] *nm (de río, camino)* bend.
recogedor, a [rekoxe'ðor, a] *nm/f* picker,
harvester.
recoger [reko'xer] *vt* to collect; *(AGR)* to
harvest; *(fruta)* to pick; *(levantar)* to pick
up; *(juntar)* to gather; *(pasar a buscar)* to
come for, get; *(dar asilo)* to give shelter
to; *(faldas)* to gather up; *(mangas)* to roll
up; *(pelo)* to put up; ~**se** *vr (retirarse)* to
retire; **me recogieron en la estación** they
picked me up at the station.
recogido, a [reko'xiðo, a] *adj (lugar)* quiet,
secluded; *(pequeño)* small ♦ *nf (CORREOS)*
collection; *(AGR)* harvest; **recogida de
datos** *(INFORM)* data capture.
recogimiento [rekoxi'mjento] *nm*
collection; *(AGR)* harvesting.
recoja [re'koxa] *etc vb V* **recoger.**
recolección [rekolek'θjon] *nf (AGR)*
harvesting; *(colecta)* collection.
recomencé [rekomen'θe],
recomencemos [rekomen'θemos] *etc vb
V* **recomenzar.**
recomendable [rekomen'daßle] *adj*
recommendable; **poco** ~ inadvisable.
recomendación [rekomenda'θjon] *nf*
(sugerencia) suggestion,
recommendation; *(referencia)* reference;
carta de ~ **para** letter of introduction to.
recomendar [rekomen'dar] *vt* to suggest,
recommend; *(confiar)* to entrust.
recomenzar [rekomen'θar] *vt, vi* to begin
again, recommence.
recomience [reko'mjenθe] *etc vb V*
recomenzar.
recomiende [reko'mjende] *etc vb V*
recomendar.
recomienzo [reko'mjenθo] *etc vb V*
recomenzar.
recompensa [rekom'pensa] *nf* reward,
recompense; *(compensación)*: ~ **(de una
pérdida)** compensation (for a loss);
como *o* **en** ~ **por** in return for.
recompensar [rekompen'sar] *vt* to reward,
recompense.
recompondré [rekompon'dre] *etc vb V*
recomponer.
recomponer [rekompo'ner] *vt* to mend;

(INFORM: texto) to reformat.
recomponga [rekom'ponga] *etc*,
recompuesto [rekom'pwesto],
recompuse [rekom'puse] *etc vb V*
recomponer.
reconciliación [rekonθilja'θjon] *nf*
reconciliation.
reconciliar [rekonθi'ljar] *vt* to reconcile;
~**se** *vr* to become reconciled.
recóndito, a [re'kondito, a] *adj (lugar)*
hidden, secret.
reconfortar [rekonfor'tar] *vt* to comfort.
reconocer [rekono'θer] *vt* to recognize; ~
los hechos to face the facts.
reconocido, a [rekono'θiðo, a] *adj*
recognized; *(agradecido)* grateful.
reconocimiento [rekonoθi'mjento] *nm*
recognition; *(registro)* search;
(inspección) examination; *(gratitud)*
gratitude; *(confesión)* admission; ~
óptico de caracteres *(INFORM)* optical
character recognition; ~ **de la voz**
(INFORM) speech recognition.
reconozca [rekono'θka] *etc vb V* **reconocer.**
reconquista [rekon'kista] *nf* reconquest.
reconquistar [rekonkis'tar] *vt (MIL)* to
reconquer; *(fig)* to recover, win back.
reconstituyente [rekonstitu'jente] *nm*
tonic.
reconstruir [rekonstru'ir] *vt* to reconstruct.
reconstruyendo [rekonstru'jendo] *etc vb V*
reconstruir.
reconversión [rekomber'sjon] *nf*
restructuring, reorganization; *(tb:* ~
industrial) rationalization.
recopilación [rekopila'θjon] *nf (resumen)*
summary; *(compilación)* compilation.
recopilar [rekopi'lar] *vt* to compile.
récord ['rekorð] *adj inv* record; **cifras** ~
record figures ♦ *nm, pl* **records, récords**
['rekorð] record; **batir el** ~ to break the
record.
recordar [rekor'ðar] *vt (acordarse de)* to
remember; *(traer a la memoria)* to recall;
(acordar a otro) to remind ♦ *vi* to
remember; **recuérdale que me debe 5
dólares** remind him that he owes me 5
dollars; **que yo recuerde** as far as I can
remember; **creo** ~**, si mal no recuerdo** if
my memory serves me right.
recordatorio [rekorða'torjo] *nm (de
fallecimiento)* in memoriam card; *(de
bautizo, comunión)* commemorative card.
recorrer [reko'rrer] *vt (país)* to cross,
travel through; *(distancia)* to cover;
(registrar) to search; *(repasar)* to look
over.
recorrido [reko'rriðo] *nm* run, journey;

tren de largo ~ main-line *o* inter-city (*BRIT*) train.

recortado, a [rekor'taðo, a] *adj* uneven, irregular.

recortar [rekor'tar] *vt* (*papel*) to cut out; (*el pelo*) to trim; (*dibujar*) to draw in outline; ~**se** *vr* to stand out, be silhouetted.

recorte [re'korte] *nm* (*acción, de prensa*) cutting; (*de telas, chapas*) trimming; ~ **presupuestario** budget cut; ~ **salarial** wage cut.

recostado, a [rekos'taðo, a] *adj* leaning; **estar** ~ to be lying down.

recostar [rekos'tar] *vt* to lean; ~**se** *vr* to lie down.

recoveco [reko'ßeko] *nm* (*de camino, río etc*) bend; (*en casa*) cubbyhole.

recreación [rekrea'θjon] *nf* recreation.

recrear [rekre'ar] *vt* (*entretener*) to entertain; (*volver a crear*) to recreate.

recreativo, a [rekrea'tißo, a] *adj* recreational.

recreo [re'kreo] *nm* recreation; (*ESCOL*) break, playtime.

recriminar [rekrimi'nar] *vt* to reproach ♦ *vi* to recriminate; ~**se** *vr* to reproach each other.

recrudecer [rekruðe'θer] *vt, vi,* **recrudecerse** *vr* to worsen.

recrudecimiento [rekruðeθi'mjento] *nm* upsurge.

recrudezca [recru'ðeθka] *etc vb V* **recrudecer.**

recta ['rekta] *nf V* **recto.**

rectangular [rektaŋgu'lar] *adj* rectangular.

rectángulo, a [rek'taŋgulo, a] *adj* rectangular ♦ *nm* rectangle.

rectificable [rektifi'kaßle] *adj* rectifiable; **fácilmente** ~ easily rectified.

rectificación [rektifika'θjon] *nf* correction.

rectificar [rektifi'kar] *vt* to rectify; (*volverse recto*) to straighten ♦ *vi* to correct o.s.

rectifique [rekti'fike] *etc vb V* **rectificar.**

rectitud [rekti'tuð] *nf* straightness; (*fig*) rectitude.

recto, a ['rekto, a] *adj* straight; (*persona*) honest, upright; (*estricto*) strict; (*juez*) fair; (*juicio*) sound ♦ *nm* rectum; (*ATLETISMO*) straight ♦ *nf* straight line; **en el sentido** ~ **de la palabra** in the proper sense of the word; **recta final** *o* **de llegada** home straight.

rector, a [rek'tor, a] *adj* governing ♦ *nm/f* head, chief; (*ESCOL*) rector, president (*US*).

rectorado [rekto'raðo] *nm* (*cargo*) rectorship, presidency (*US*); (*oficina*) rector's office.

recuadro [re'kwaðro] *nm* box; (*TIP*) inset.

recubrir [reku'ßir] *vt* to cover.

recuento [re'kwento] *nm* inventory; **hacer el** ~ **de** to count *o* reckon up.

recuerdo [re'kwerðo] *etc vb V* **recordar** ♦ *nm* souvenir; ~**s** *nmpl* memories; **¡**~**s a tu madre!** give my regards to your mother!; **"R**~ **de Mallorca"** "a present from Majorca"; **contar los** ~**s** to reminisce.

recueste [re'kweste] *etc vb V* **recostar.**

recular [reku'lar] *vi* to back down.

recuperable [rekupe'raßle] *adj* recoverable.

recuperación [rekupera'θjon] *nf* recovery; ~ **de datos** (*INFORM*) data retrieval.

recuperar [rekupe'rar] *vt* to recover; (*tiempo*) to make up; (*INFORM*) to retrieve; ~**se** *vr* to recuperate.

recurrir [reku'rrir] *vi* (*JUR*) to appeal; ~ **a** to resort to; (*persona*) to turn to.

recurso [re'kurso] *nm* resort; (*medio*) means *pl*, resource; (*JUR*) appeal; **como último** ~ as a last resort; ~**s económicos** economic resources; ~**s naturales** natural resources.

recusar [reku'sar] *vt* to reject, refuse.

red [reð] *nf* net, mesh; (*FERRO, INFORM*) network; (*ELEC, de agua*) mains, supply system; (*de tiendas*) chain; (*trampa*) trap; **la R**~ (*Internet*) the Net; **estar conectado con la** ~ to be connected to the mains; ~ **local** (*INFORM*) local area network; ~ **de transmisión** (*INFORM*) data network.

redacción [reðak'θjon] *nf* (*acción*) writing; (*ESCOL*) essay, composition; (*limpieza de texto*) editing; (*personal*) editorial staff.

redactar [reðak'tar] *vt* to draw up, draft; (*periódico, INFORM*) to edit.

redactor, a [reðak'tor, a] *nm/f* writer; (*en periódico*) editor.

redada [re'ðaða] *nf* (*PESCA*) cast, throw; (*fig*) catch; ~ **policial** police raid, round-up.

redención [reðen'θjon] *nf* redemption.

redentor, a [reðen'tor, a] *adj* redeeming ♦ *nm/f* (*COM*) redeemer.

redescubierto [reðesku'ßjerto] *pp de* **redescubrir.**

redescubrir [reðesku'ßrir] *vt* to rediscover.

redesignar [reðesix'nar] *vt* (*INFORM*) to rename.

redicho, a [re'ðitʃo, a] *adj* affected.

redil [re'ðil] *nm* sheepfold.

redimir [reði'mir] *vt* to redeem; (*rehén*) to ransom.

redistribución [reðistrißu'θjon] *nf* (*COM*)

redeployment.

rédito ['reðito] *nm* interest, yield.

redoblar [reðo'ßlar] *vt* to redouble ♦ *vi* (*tambor*) to play a roll on the drums.

redoble [re'ðoßle] *nm* (*MUS*) drumroll, drumbeat; (*de trueno*) roll.

redomado, a [reðo'maðo, a] *adj* (*astuto*) sly, crafty; (*perfecto*) utter.

redonda [re'ðonda] *nf V* **redondo**.

redondear [reðonde'ar] *vt* to round, round off; (*cifra*) to round up.

redondel [reðon'del] *nm* (*círculo*) circle; (*TAUR*) bullring, arena; (*AUTO*) roundabout.

redondo, a [re'ðondo, a] *adj* (*circular*) round; (*completo*) complete ♦ *nf*: **a la redonda** around, round about; **en muchas millas a la redonda** for many miles around; **rehusar en ~** to give a flat refusal.

reducción [reðuk'θjon] *nf* reduction; **~ del activo** (*COM*) divestment; **~ de precios** (*COM*) price-cutting.

reducido, a [reðu'θiðo, a] *adj* reduced; (*limitado*) limited; (*pequeño*) small; **quedar ~ a** to be reduced to.

reducir [reðu'θir] *vt* to reduce, limit; (*someter*) to bring under control; **~se** *vr* to diminish; (*MAT*): **~ (a)** to reduce (to), convert (into); **~ las millas a kilómetros** to convert miles into kilometres; **~se a** (*fig*) to come o boil down to.

reducto [re'ðukto] *nm* redoubt.

reduje [re'ðuxe] *etc vb V* **reducir**.

redundancia [reðun'danθja] *nf* redundancy.

reduzca [re'ðuθka] *etc vb V* **reducir**.

reedición [re(e)ði'θjon] *nf* reissue.

reeditar [re(e)ði'tar] *vt* to reissue.

reelección [re(e)lek'θjon] *nf* re-election.

reelegir [re(e)le'xir] *vt* to re-elect.

reembolsable [re(e)mbol'saßle] *adj* (*COM*) redeemable, refundable.

reembolsar [re(e)mbol'sar] *vt* (*persona*) to reimburse; (*dinero*) to repay, pay back; (*depósito*) to refund.

reembolso [re(e)m'bolso] *nm* reimbursement; refund; **enviar algo contra ~** to send sth cash on delivery; **contra ~ del flete** freight forward; **~ fiscal** tax rebate.

reemplace [re(e)m'plaθe] *etc vb V* **reemplazar**.

reemplazar [re(e)mpla'θar] *vt* to replace.

reemplazo [re(e)m'plaθo] *nm* replacement; **de ~** (*MIL*) reserve.

reencuentro [re(e)n'kwentro] *nm* reunion.

reengancharse [re(e)ngan'tʃarse] *vr* (*MIL*)

to re-enlist.

reestreno [re(e)s'treno] *nm* rerun.

reestructurar [re(e)struktu'rar] *vt* to restructure.

reexportación [re(e)ksporta'θjon] *nf* (*COM*) re-export.

reexportar [re(e)kspor'tar] *vt* (*COM*) to re-export.

REF *nm abr* (*ESP ECON*) = **Régimen Económico Fiscal**.

Ref.ª *abr* (= *referencia*) ref.

refacción [refak'θjon] *nf* (*AM*) repair(s); **refacciones** *nfpl* (*piezas de repuesto*) spare parts.

referencia [refe'renθja] *nf* reference; **con ~ a** with reference to; **hacer ~ a** to refer o allude to; **~ comercial** (*COM*) trade reference.

referéndum [refe'rendum], *pl* **referéndums** *nm* referendum.

referente [refe'rente] *adj*: **~ a** concerning, relating to.

referir [refe'rir] *vt* (*contar*) to tell, recount; (*relacionar*) to refer, relate; **~se** *vr*: **~se a** to refer to; **~ al lector a un apéndice** to refer the reader to an appendix; **~ a** (*COM*) to convert into; **por lo que se refiere a eso** as for that, as regards that.

refiera [re'fjera] *etc vb V* **referir**.

refilón [refi'lon]: **de ~** *adv* obliquely; **mirar a algn de ~** to look out of the corner of one's eye at sb.

refinado, a [refi'naðo, a] *adj* refined.

refinamiento [refina'mjento] *nm* refinement; **~ por pasos** (*INFORM*) stepwise refinement.

refinar [refi'nar] *vt* to refine.

refinería [refine'ria] *nf* refinery.

refiriendo [refi'rjendo] *etc vb V* **referir**.

reflector [reflek'tor] *nm* reflector; (*ELEC*) spotlight; (*AVIAT, MIL*) searchlight.

reflejar [refle'xar] *vt* to reflect; **~se** *vr* to be reflected.

reflejo, a [re'flexo, a] *adj* reflected; (*movimiento*) reflex ♦ *nm* reflection; (*ANAT*) reflex; (*en el pelo*): **~s** *nmpl* highlights; **tiene el pelo castaño con ~s rubios** she has chestnut hair with blond streaks.

reflexión [reflek'sjon] *nf* reflection.

reflexionar [refleksjo'nar] *vt* to reflect on ♦ *vi* (*detenerse*) to pause (to think); **¡reflexione!** you think it over!

reflexivo, a [reflek'sißo, a] *adj* thoughtful; (*LING*) reflexive.

refluir [reflu'ir] *vi* to flow back.

reflujo [re'fluxo] *nm* ebb.

refluyendo [reflu'jendo] *etc vb V* **refluir**.

reforcé [refor'θe], **reforcemos** [refor'θemos] _etc vb_ V **reforzar**.

reforma [re'forma] _nf_ reform; (_ARQ etc_) repair; ~ **agraria** agrarian reform.

reformar [refor'mar] _vt_ to reform; (_modificar_) to change, alter; (_texto_) to revise; (_ARQ_) to repair; ~**se** _vr_ to mend one's ways.

reformatear [reformate'ar] _vt_ (_INFORM_: _disco_) to reformat.

reformatorio [reforma'torjo] _nm_ reformatory; ~ **de menores** remand home.

reformista [refor'mista] _adj_, _nm/f_ reformist.

reforzamiento [reforθa'mjento] _nm_ reinforcement.

reforzar [refor'θar] _vt_ to strengthen; (_ARQ_) to reinforce; (_fig_) to encourage.

refractario, a [refrak'tarjo, a] _adj_ (_TEC_) heat-resistant; **ser** ~ **a una reforma** to resist _o_ be opposed to a reform.

refrán [re'fran] _nm_ proverb, saying.

refregar [refre'ɣar] _vt_ to scrub.

refrenar [refre'nar] _vt_ to check, restrain.

refrendar [refren'dar] _vt_ (_firma_) to endorse, countersign; (_ley_) to approve.

refrescante [refres'kante] _adj_ refreshing, cooling.

refrescar [refres'kar] _vt_ to refresh ♦ _vi_ to cool down; ~**se** _vr_ to get cooler; (_tomar aire fresco_) to go out for a breath of fresh air; (_beber_) to have a drink.

refresco [re'fresko] _nm_ soft drink, cool drink; "~**s**" "refreshments".

refresque [re'freske] _etc vb_ V **refrescar**.

refriega [re'frjeɣa] _etc vb_ V **refregar** ♦ _nf_ scuffle, brawl.

refriegue [re'frjeɣe] _etc vb_ V **refregar**.

refrigeración [refrixera'θjon] _nf_ refrigeration; (_de casa_) air-conditioning.

refrigerado, a [refrixe'raðo, a] _adj_ cooled; (_sala_) air-conditioned.

refrigerador [refrixera'ðor] _nm_, (_AM_) **refrigeradora** [refrixera'ðora] _nf_ refrigerator, icebox (_US_).

refrigerar [refrixe'rar] _vt_ to refrigerate; (_sala_) to air-condition.

refrito [re'frito] _nm_ (_CULIN_): **un** ~ **de cebolla y tomate** sautéed onions and tomatoes; **un** ~ (_fig_) a rehash.

refuerce [re'fwerθe] _etc vb_ V **reforzar**.

refuerzo [re'fwerθo] _etc vb_ V **reforzar** ♦ _nm_ reinforcement; (_TEC_) support.

refugiado, a [refu'xjaðo, a] _nm/f_ refugee.

refugiarse [refu'xjarse] _vr_ to take refuge, shelter.

refugio [re'fuxjo] _nm_ refuge; (_protección_) shelter; (_AUTO_) street _o_ traffic island; ~

alpino _o_ **de montaña** mountain hut; ~ **subterráneo** (_MIL_) underground shelter.

refulgencia [reful'xenθja] _nf_ brilliance.

refulgir [reful'xir] _vi_ to shine, be dazzling.

refulja [re'fulxa] _etc vb_ V **refulgir**.

refundir [refun'dir] _vt_ to recast; (_escrito etc_) to adapt, rewrite.

refunfuñar [refunfu'ɲar] _vi_ to grunt, growl; (_quejarse_) to grumble.

refunfuñón, ona [refunfu'ɲon, ona] (_fam_) _adj_ grumpy ♦ _nm/f_ grouch.

refutación [refuta'θjon] _nf_ refutation.

refutar [refu'tar] _vt_ to refute.

regadera [reɣa'ðera] _nf_ watering can; (_AM_) shower; **estar como una** ~ (_fam_) to be as mad as a hatter.

regadío [reɣa'ðio] _nm_ irrigated land.

regalado, a [reɣa'laðo, a] _adj_ comfortable, luxurious; (_gratis_) free, for nothing; **lo tuvo** ~ it was handed to him on a plate.

regalar [reɣa'lar] _vt_ (_dar_) to give (as a present); (_entregar_) to give away; (_mimar_) to pamper, make a fuss of; ~**se** _vr_ to treat o.s. to.

regalía [reɣa'lia] _nf_ privilege, prerogative; (_COM_) bonus; (_de autor_) royalty.

regaliz [reɣa'liθ] _nm_ liquorice.

regalo [re'ɣalo] _nm_ (_obsequio_) gift, present; (_gusto_) pleasure; (_comodidad_) comfort.

regañadientes [reɣaɲa'ðjentes]: **a** ~ _adv_ reluctantly.

regañar [reɣa'ɲar] _vt_ to scold ♦ _vi_ to grumble; (_dos personas_) to fall out, quarrel.

regañón, ona [reɣa'ɲon, ona] _adj_ nagging.

regar [re'ɣar] _vt_ to water, irrigate; (_fig_) to scatter, sprinkle.

regata [re'ɣata] _nf_ (_NAUT_) race.

regatear [reɣate'ar] _vt_ (_COM_) to bargain over; (_escatimar_) to be mean with ♦ _vi_ to bargain, haggle; (_DEPORTE_) to dribble; **no** ~ **esfuerzo** to spare no effort.

regateo [reɣa'teo] _nm_ bargaining; (_DEPORTE_) dribbling; (_del cuerpo_) swerve, dodge.

regazo [re'ɣaθo] _nm_ lap.

regencia [re'xenθja] _nf_ regency.

regeneración [rexenera'θjon] _nf_ regeneration.

regenerar [rexene'rar] _vt_ to regenerate.

regentar [rexen'tar] _vt_ to direct, manage; (_puesto_) to hold in an acting capacity; (_negocio_) to be in charge of.

regente, a [re'xente, a] _adj_ (_príncipe_) regent; (_director_) managing ♦ _nm_ (_COM_) manager; (_POL_) regent.

régimen ['reximen], _pl_ **regímenes**

[re'ximenes] *nm* regime; (*reinado*) rule; (*MED*) diet; (*reglas*) (set of) rules *pl*; (*manera de vivir*) lifestyle; **estar a** ~ to be on a diet.

regimiento [rexi'mjento] *nm* regiment.

regio, a ['rexjo, a] *adj* royal, regal; (*fig: suntuoso*) splendid; (*AM fam*) great, terrific.

región [re'xjon] *nf* region; (*área*) area.

regional [rexjo'nal] *adj* regional.

regir [re'xir] *vt* to govern, rule; (*dirigir*) to manage, run; (*ECON, JUR, LING*) to govern ♦ *vi* to apply, be in force.

registrador [rexistra'ðor] *nm* registrar, recorder.

registrar [rexis'trar] *vt* (*buscar*) to search; (*en cajón*) to look through; (*inspeccionar*) to inspect, (*anotar*) to register, record; (*INFORM, MUS*) to record; ~**se** *vr* to register; (*ocurrir*) to happen.

registro [re'xistro] *nm* (*acto*) registration; (*MUS, libro*) register; (*lista*) list, record; (*INFORM*) record; (*inspección*) inspection, search; ~ **civil** registry office; ~ **electoral** voting register; ~ **de la propiedad** land registry (office).

regla ['rexla] *nf* (*ley*) rule, regulation; (*de medir*) ruler, rule; (*MED: período*) period; (~ *científica*) law, principle; **no hay** ~ **sin excepción** every rule has its exception.

reglamentación [rexlamenta'θjon] *nf* (*acto*) regulation; (*lista*) rules *pl*.

reglamentar [rexlamen'tar] *vt* to regulate.

reglamentario, a [rexlamen'tarjo, a] *adj* statutory; **en la forma reglamentaria** in the properly established way.

reglamento [rexla'mento] *nm* rules *pl*, regulations *pl*; ~ **del tráfico** highway code.

reglar [re'xlar] *vt* (*acciones*) to regulate; ~**se** *vr*: ~**se por** to be guided by.

regocijarse [rexoθi'xarse] *vr*: ~ **de** *o* **por** to rejoice at, be glad about.

regocijo [rexo'θixo] *nm* joy, happiness.

regodearse [rexoðe'arse] *vr* to be glad, be delighted; (*pey*): ~ **con** *o* **en** to gloat over.

regodeo [rexo'ðeo] *nm* delight; (*pey*) perverse pleasure.

regresar [rexre'sar] *vi* to come/go back, return; ~**se** *vr* (*AM*) to return.

regresivo, a [rexre'sißo, a] *adj* backward; (*fig*) regressive.

regreso [re'xreso] *nm* return; **estar de** ~ to be back, be home.

regué [re'xe], **reguemos** [re'xemos] *etc vb* V **regar**.

reguero [re'xero] *nm* (*de sangre*) trickle;

(*de humo*) trail.

regulación [rexula'θjon] *nf* regulation; (*TEC*) adjustment; (*control*) control; ~ **de empleo** redundancies *pl*; ~ **del tráfico** traffic control.

regulador [rexula'ðor] *nm* (*TEC*) regulator; (*de radio etc*) knob, control.

regular [rexu'lar] *adj* regular; (*normal*) normal, usual; (*común*) ordinary; (*organizado*) regular, orderly; (*mediano*) average; (*fam*) not bad, so-so ♦ *adv*: **estar** ~ to be so-so *o* alright ♦ *vt* (*controlar*) to control, regulate; (*TEC*) to adjust; **por lo** ~ as a rule.

regularice [rexula'riθe] *etc vb* V **regularizar**.

regularidad [rexulari'ðað] *nf* regularity; **con** ~ regularly.

regularizar [rexulari'θar] *vt* to regularize.

regusto [re'xusto] *nm* aftertaste.

rehabilitación [reaßilita'θjon] *nf* rehabilitation; (*ARQ*) restoration.

rehabilitar [reaßili'tar] *vt* to rehabilitate; (*ARQ*) to restore; (*reintegrar*) to reinstate.

rehacer [rea'θer] *vt* (*reparar*) to mend, repair; (*volver a hacer*) to redo, repeat; ~**se** *vr* (*MED*) to recover.

rehaga [re'axa] *etc*, **reharé** [rea're] *etc*, **rehaz** [re'aθ], **rehecho** [re'etʃo] *vb* V **rehacer**.

rehén [re'en] *nm/f* hostage.

rehice [re'iθe] *etc*, **rehizo** [re'iθo] *vb* V **rehacer**.

rehogar [reo'xar] *vt* to sauté, toss in oil.

rehuir [rcu'ir] *vt* to avoid, shun.

rehusar [reu'sar] *vt, vi* to refuse.

rehuyendo [reu'jendo] *etc vb* V **rehuir**.

reina ['reina] *nf* queen.

reinado [rei'naðo] *nm* reign.

reinante [rei'nante] *adj* (*fig*) prevailing.

reinar [rei'nar] *vi* to reign; (*fig: prevalecer*) to prevail, be general.

reincidir [reinθi'ðir] *vi* to relapse; (*criminal*) to repeat an offence.

reincorporarse [reinkorpo'rarse] *vr*: ~ **a** to rejoin.

reinicializar [reiniθjali'θar] *vt* (*INFORM*) to reset.

reino ['reino] *nm* kingdom; **el R**~ **Unido** the United Kingdom.

reinserción [reinser'θjon] *nf* rehabilitation.

reinsertar [reinser'tar] *vt* to rehabilitate.

reintegración [reintexra'θjon] *nf* (*COM*) reinstatement.

reintegrar [reinte'xrar] *vt* (*reconstituir*) to reconstruct; (*persona*) to reinstate; (*dinero*) to refund, pay back; ~**se** *vr*: ~**se a** to return to.

reintegro [rein'texro] *nm* refund,

reimbursement; (*en banco*) withdrawal.

reír [re'ir] *vi*, **reírse** *vr* to laugh; ~**se de** to laugh at.

reiterado, a [reite'raðo, a] *adj* repeated.

reiterar [reite'rar] *vt* to reiterate; (*repetir*) to repeat.

reivindicación [reißindika'θjon] *nf* (*demanda*) claim, demand; (*justificación*) vindication.

reivindicar [reißindi'kar] *vt* to claim.

reivindique [reißin'dike] *etc vb V* **reivindicar**.

reja ['rexa] *nf* (*de ventana*) grille, bars *pl*; (*en la calle*) grating.

rejamos [re'xamos] *etc vb V* **regir**.

rejilla [re'xiʎa] *nf* grating, grille; (*muebles*) wickerwork; (*de ventilación*) vent; (*de coche etc*) luggage rack.

rejuvenecer [rexußene'θer] *vt*, *vi* to rejuvenate.

rejuvenezca [rexuße'neθka] *etc vb V* **rejuvenecer**.

relación [rela'θjon] *nf* relation, relationship; (*MAT*) ratio; (*lista*) list; (*narración*) report; ~ **costo-efectivo** *o* **costo-rendimiento** (*COM*) cost-effectiveness; **relaciones** *nfpl* (*enchufes*) influential friends, connections; **relaciones carnales** sexual relations; **relaciones comerciales** business connections; **relaciones empresariales/ humanas** industrial/human relations; **relaciones laborales/públicas** labour/ public relations; **con** ~ **a, en** ~ **con** in relation to; **estar en** *o* **tener buenas relaciones con** to be on good terms with.

relacionar [relaθjo'nar] *vt* to relate, connect; ~**se** *vr* to be connected *o* linked.

relajación [relaxa'θjon] *nf* relaxation.

relajado, a [rela'xaðo, a] *adj* (*disoluto*) loose; (*cómodo*) relaxed; (*MED*) ruptured.

relajante [rela'xante] *adj* relaxing; (*MED*) sedative.

relajar [rela'xar] *vt*, **relajarse** *vr* to relax.

relamerse [rela'merse] *vr* to lick one's lips.

relamido, a [rela'miðo, a] *adj* (*pulcro*) overdressed; (*afectado*) affected.

relámpago [re'lampaxo] *nm* flash of lightning ♦ *adj* lightning *cpd*; **como un** ~ as quick as lightning, in a flash; **visita/ huelga** ~ lightning visit/strike.

relampaguear [relampaxe'ar] *vi* to flash.

relanzar [relan'θar] *vt* to relaunch.

relatar [rela'tar] *vt* to tell, relate.

relatividad [relatißi'ðað] *nf* relativity.

relativo, a [rela'tißo, a] *adj* relative; **en lo** ~ **a** concerning.

relato [re'lato] *nm* (*narración*) story, tale.

relax [re'las] *nm* rest; "**R**~" (*en anuncio*) "Personal services".

relegar [rele'xar] *vt* to relegate; ~ **algo al olvido** to banish sth from one's mind.

relegue [re'lexe] *etc vb V* **relegar**.

relevante [rele'ßante] *adj* eminent, outstanding.

relevar [rele'ßar] *vt* (*sustituir*) to relieve; ~**se** *vr* to relay; ~ **a algn de un cargo** to relieve sb of his post.

relevo [re'leßo] *nm* relief; **carrera de** ~**s** relay race; ~ **con cinta** (*INFORM*) tape relay; **coger** *o* **tomar el** ~ to take over, stand in.

relieve [re'ljeße] *nm* (*ARTE, TEC*) relief; (*fig*) prominence, importance; **bajo** ~ bas-relief; **un personaje de** ~ an important man; **dar** ~ **a** to highlight.

religión [reli'xjon] *nf* religion.

religioso, a [reli'xjoso, a] *adj* religious ♦ *nm/f* monk/nun.

relinchar [relin't ʃar] *vi* to neigh.

relincho [re'lint ʃo] *nm* neigh; (*acto*) neighing.

reliquia [re'likja] *nf* relic; ~ **de familia** heirloom.

rellano [re'ʎano] *nm* (*ARQ*) landing.

rellenar [reʎe'nar] *vt* (*llenar*) to fill up; (*CULIN*) to stuff; (*COSTURA*) to pad; (*formulario etc*) to fill in *o* out.

relleno, a [re'ʎeno, a] *adj* full up; (*CULIN*) stuffed ♦ *nm* stuffing; (*de tapicería*) padding.

reloj [re'lo(x)] *nm* clock; ~ **de pie** grandfather clock; ~ **(de pulsera)** wristwatch; ~ **de sol** sundial; ~ **despertador** alarm (clock); **como un** ~ like clockwork; **contra (el)** ~ against the clock.

relojería [reloxe'ria] *nf* (*tienda*) watchmaker's (shop); **aparato de** ~ clockwork; **bomba de** ~ time bomb.

relojero, a [relo'xero, a] *nm/f* clockmaker; watchmaker.

reluciente [relu'θjente] *adj* brilliant, shining.

relucir [relu'θir] *vi* to shine; (*fig*) to excel; **sacar algo a** ~ to show sth off.

relumbrante [relum'brante] *adj* dazzling.

relumbrar [relum'brar] *vi* to dazzle, shine brilliantly.

reluzca [re'luθka] *etc vb V* **relucir**.

remachar [rema't ʃar] *vt* to rivet; (*fig*) to hammer home, drive home.

remache [re'mat ʃe] *nm* rivet.

remanente [rema'nente] *nm* remainder; (*COM*) balance; (*de producto*) surplus.

remangarse [reman'garse] *vr* to roll one's

sleeves up.

remanso [re'manso] *nm* pool.

remar [re'mar] *vi* to row.

rematado, a [rema'taðo, a] *adj* complete, utter; **es un loco** ~ he's a raving lunatic.

rematar [rema'tar] *vt* to finish off; (*animal*) to put out of its misery; (*COM*) to sell off cheap ♦ *vi* to end, finish off; (*DEPORTE*) to shoot.

remate [re'mate] *nm* end, finish; (*punta*) tip; (*DEPORTE*) shot; (*ARQ*) top; (*COM*) auction sale; **de** *o* **para** ~ to crown it all (*BRIT*), to top it off.

remediable [reme'ðjaßle] *adj*: **fácilmente** ~ easily remedied.

remediar [reme'ðjar] *vt* (*gen*) to remedy; (*subsanar*) to make good, repair; (*evitar*) to avoid; **sin poder** ~**lo** without being able to prevent it.

remedio [re'meðjo] *nm* remedy; (*JUR*) recourse, remedy; **poner** ~ **a** to correct, stop; **no tener más** ~ to have no alternative; **¡qué** ~**!** there's no other way; **como último** ~ as a last resort; **sin** ~ inevitable; (*MED*) hopeless.

remedo [re'meðo] *nm* imitation; (*pey*) parody.

remendar [remen'dar] *vt* to repair; (*con parche*) to patch; (*fig*) to correct.

remesa [re'mesa] *nf* remittance; (*COM*) shipment.

remiendo [re'mjendo] *etc vb V* **remendar** ♦ *nm* mend; (*con parche*) patch; (*cosido*) darn; (*fig*) correction.

remilgado, a [remil'xaðo, a] *adj* prim; (*afectado*) affected.

remilgo [re'milxo] *nm* primness; (*afectación*) affectation.

reminiscencia [reminis'θenθja] *nf* reminiscence.

remirar [remi'rar] *vt* (*volver a mirar*) to look at again; (*examinar*) to look hard at.

remisión [remi'sjon] *nf* (*acto*) sending, shipment; (*REL*) forgiveness, remission; **sin** ~ hopelessly.

remiso, a [re'miso, a] *adj* remiss.

remite [re'mite] *nm* (*en sobre*) name and address of sender.

remitente [remi'tente] *nm/f* (*CORREOS*) sender.

remitir [remi'tir] *vt* to remit, send ♦ *vi* to slacken.

remo ['remo] *nm* (*de barco*) oar; (*DEPORTE*) rowing; **cruzar un río a** ~ to row across a river.

remoce [re'moθe] *etc vb V* **remozar**.

remodelación [remodela'θjon] *nf* (*POL*): ~ **del gobierno** cabinet reshuffle.

remojar [remo'xar] *vt* to steep, soak; (*galleta etc*) to dip, dunk; (*fam*) to celebrate with a drink.

remojo [re'moxo] *nm* steeping, soaking; (*por la lluvia*) drenching, soaking; **dejar la ropa en** ~ to leave clothes to soak.

remojón [remo'xon] *nm* soaking; **darse un** ~ (*fam*) to go (in) for a dip.

remolacha [remo'latʃa] *nf* beet, beetroot (*BRIT*).

remolcador [remolka'ðor] *nm* (*NAUT*) tug; (*AUTO*) breakdown lorry.

remolcar [remol'kar] *vt* to tow.

remolino [remo'lino] *nm* eddy; (*de agua*) whirlpool; (*de viento*) whirlwind; (*de gente*) crowd.

remolón, ona [remo'lon, ona] *adj* lazy ♦ *nm/f* slacker, shirker.

remolque [re'molke] *etc vb V* **remolcar** ♦ *nm* tow, towing; (*cuerda*) towrope; **llevar a** ~ to tow.

remontar [remon'tar] *vt* to mend; (*obstáculo*) to negotiate, get over; ~**se** *vr* to soar; ~**se a** (*COM*) to amount to; (*en tiempo*) to go back to, date from; ~ **el vuelo** to soar.

rémora ['remora] *nf* hindrance.

remorder [remor'ðer] *vt* to distress, disturb.

remordimiento [remorði'mjento] *nm* remorse.

remotamente [remota'mente] *adv* vaguely.

remoto, a [re'moto, a] *adj* remote.

remover [remo'ßer] *vt* to stir; (*tierra*) to turn over; (*objetos*) to move round.

remozar [remo'θar] *vt* (*ARQ*) to refurbish; (*fig*) to brighten *o* polish up.

remuerda [re'mwerða] *etc vb V* **remorder**.

remueva [re'mweßa] *etc vb V* **remover**.

remuneración [remunera'θjon] *nf* remuneration.

remunerado, a [remune'raðo, a] *adj*: **trabajo bien/mal** ~ well-/badly-paid job.

remunerar [remune'rar] *vt* to remunerate; (*premiar*) to reward.

renacer [rena'θer] *vi* to be reborn; (*fig*) to revive.

renacimiento [renaθi'mjento] *nm* rebirth; **el R**~ the Renaissance.

renacuajo [rena'kwaxo] *nm* (*ZOOL*) tadpole.

renal [re'nal] *adj* renal, kidney *cpd*.

Renania [re'nanja] *nf* Rhineland.

renazca [re'naθka] *etc vb V* **renacer**.

rencilla [ren'θiʎa] *nf* quarrel; ~**s** *nfpl* bickering *sg*.

rencor [ren'kor] *nm* rancour, bitterness; (*resentimiento*) ill feeling, resentment;

guardar ~ **a** to have a grudge against.
rencoroso, a [renko'roso, a] _adj_ spiteful.
rendición [rendi'θjon] _nf_ surrender.
rendido, a [ren'diðo, a] _adj_ (_sumiso_)
submissive; (_agotado_) worn-out,
exhausted; (_enamorado_) devoted.
rendija [ren'dixa] _nf_ (_hendedura_) crack;
(_abertura_) aperture; (_fig_) rift, split; (_JUR_)
loophole.
rendimiento [rendi'mjento] _nm_
(_producción_) output; (_COM_) yield,
profit(s) (_pl_); (_TEC, COM_) efficiency; ~ **de**
capital (_COM_) return on capital.
rendir [ren'dir] _vt_ (_vencer_) to defeat;
(_producir_) to produce; (_dar beneficio_) to
yield; (_agotar_) to exhaust ♦ _vi_ to pay;
(_COM_) to yield, produce; ~**se** _vr_
(_someterse_) to surrender; (_ceder_) to
yield; (_cansarse_) to wear o.s. out; ~
homenaje _o_ **culto a** to pay homage to; **el**
negocio no rinde the business doesn't
pay.
renegado, a [rene'xaðo, a] _adj, nm/f_
renegade.
renegar [rene'xar] _vt_ (_negar_) to deny
vigorously ♦ _vi_ (_blasfemar_) to blaspheme;
~ **de** (_renunciar_) to renounce; (_quejarse_)
to complain about.
renegué [rene'xe], **reneguemos**
[rene'xemos] _etc vb V_ **renegar**.
RENFE ['renfe] _nf abr ESP._ = _Red Nacional de_
Ferrocarriles Españoles.
renglón [ren'glon] _nm_ (_línea_) line; (_COM_)
item, article; **a** ~ **seguido** immediately
after.
rengo, a ['rengo, a] _adj_ (_AM_) lame.
reniego [re'njexo] _etc_, **reniegue**
[re'njexe] _etc vb V_ **renegar**.
reno ['reno] _nm_ reindeer.
renombrado, a [renom'braðo, a] _adj_
renowned.
renombre [re'nombre] _nm_ renown.
renovable [reno'ßaßle] _adj_ renewable.
renovación [renoßa'θjon] _nf_ (_de contrato_)
renewal; (_ARQ_) renovation.
renovar [reno'ßar] _vt_ to renew; (_ARQ_) to
renovate; (_sala_) to redecorate.
renquear [renke'ar] _vi_ to limp; (_fam_) to get
along, scrape by.
renta ['renta] _nf_ (_ingresos_) income;
(_beneficio_) profit; (_alquiler_) rent; ~
gravable _o_ **imponible** taxable income; ~
nacional (bruta) (gross) national income;
~ **no salarial** unearned income; ~ **sobre**
el terreno (_COM_) ground rent; ~ **vitalicia**
annuity; **política de** ~**s** incomes policy;
vivir de sus ~**s** to live on one's private
income.

rentabilizar [rentaßili'θar] _vt_ to make
profitable.
rentable [ren'taßle] _adj_ profitable; **no** ~
unprofitable.
rentar [ren'tar] _vt_ to produce, yield; (_AM_)
to rent.
rentista [ren'tista] _nm/f_ (_accionista_)
shareholder (_BRIT_), stockholder (_US_).
renuencia [re'nwenθja] _nf_ reluctance.
renuente [re'nwente] _adj_ reluctant.
renueve [re'nweße] _etc vb V_ **renovar**.
renuncia [re'nunθja] _nf_ resignation.
renunciar [renun'θjar] _vt_ to renounce, give
up ♦ _vi_ to resign; ~ **a hacer algo** to give
up doing sth.
reñido, a [re'ɲiðo, a] _adj_ (_batalla_) bitter,
hard-fought; **estar** ~ **con algn** to be on
bad terms with sb; **está** ~ **con su familia**
he has fallen out with his family.
reñir [re'ɲir] _vt_ (_regañar_) to scold ♦ _vi_ (_estar_
peleado) to quarrel, fall out; (_combatir_) to
fight.
reo ['reo] _nm/f_ culprit, offender; (_JUR_)
accused.
reojo [re'oxo]: **de** ~ _adv_ out of the corner
of one's eye.
reorganice [reorxa'niθe] _etc vb V_
reorganizar.
reorganizar [reorxani'θar] _vt_ to
reorganize.
Rep _abr_ = **República**.
reparación [repara'θjon] _nf_ (_acto_) mending,
repairing; (_TEC_) repair; (_fig_) amends,
reparation; **"reparaciones en el acto"**
"repairs while you wait".
reparar [repa'rar] _vt_ to repair; (_fig_) to make
amends for; (_suerte_) to retrieve;
(_observar_) to observe ♦ _vi_: ~ **en** (_darse_
cuenta de) to notice; (_poner atención en_) to
pay attention to; **sin** ~ **en los gastos**
regardless of the cost.
reparo [re'paro] _nm_ (_advertencia_)
observation; (_duda_) doubt; (_dificultad_)
difficulty; (_escrúpulo_) scruple, qualm;
poner ~**s (a)** to raise objections (to);
(_criticar_) to criticize; **no tuvo** ~ **en**
hacerlo he did not hesitate to do it.
repartición [reparti'θjon] _nf_ distribution;
(_división_) division.
repartidor, a [reparti'ðor, a] _nm/f_
distributor; ~ **de leche** milkman.
repartir [repar'tir] _vt_ to distribute, share
out; (_COM, CORREOS_) to deliver; (_MIL_) to
partition; (_libros_) to give out; (_comida_) to
serve out; (_NAIPES_) to deal.
reparto [re'parto] _nm_ distribution; (_COM,_
CORREOS) delivery; (_TEAT, CINE_) cast;
(_AM: urbanización_) housing estate (_BRIT_),

real estate development (*US*); "~ **a domicilio**" "home delivery service".

repasar [repa'sar] *vt* (*ESCOL*) to revise; (*MECÁNICA*) to check, overhaul; (*COSTURA*) to mend.

repaso [re'paso] *nm* revision; (*MECÁNICA*) overhaul, checkup; (*COSTURA*) mending; ~ **general** servicing, general overhaul; **curso de** ~ refresher course.

repatriar [repa'trjar] *vt* to repatriate; ~**se** *vr* to return home.

repelente [repe'lente] *adj* repellent, repulsive.

repeler [repe'ler] *vt* to repel; (*idea, oferta*) to reject.

repensar [repen'sar] *vt* to reconsider.

repente [re'pente] *nm* sudden movement; (*fig*) impulse; **de** ~ suddenly; ~ **de ira** fit of anger.

repentice [repen'tiθe] *etc vb V* **repentizar**.

repentino, a [repen'tino, a] *adj* sudden; (*imprevisto*) unexpected.

repentizar [repenti'θar] *vi* (*MUS*) to sight-read.

repercusión [reperku'sjon] *nf* repercussion; **de amplia** *o* **ancha** ~ far-reaching.

repercutir [reperku'tir] *vi* (*objeto*) to rebound; (*sonido*) to echo; ~ **en** (*fig*) to have repercussions *o* effects on.

repertorio [reper'torjo] *nm* list; (*TEAT*) repertoire.

repesca [re'peska] *nf* (*ESCOL fam*) resit.

repetición [repeti'θjon] *nf* repetition.

repetido, a [repe'tiðo, a] *adj* repeated; **repetidas veces** repeatedly.

repetir [repe'tir] *vt* to repeat; (*plato*) to have a second helping of; (*TEAT*) to give as an encore, sing *etc* again ♦ *vi* to repeat; (*sabor*) to come back; ~**se** *vr* to repeat o.s.; (*suceso*) to recur.

repetitivo, a [repeti'tißo, a] *adj* repetitive, repetitious.

repicar [repi'kar] *vi* (*campanas*) to ring (out).

repiense [re'pjense] *etc vb V* **repensar**.

repipi [re'pipi] *adj* la-di-da ♦ *nf*: **es una** ~ she's a little madam.

repique [re'pike] *etc vb V* **repicar** ♦ *nm* pealing, ringing.

repiqueteo [repike'teo] *nm* pealing; (*de tambor*) drumming.

repisa [re'pisa] *nf* ledge, shelf; ~ **de chimenea** mantelpiece; ~ **de ventana** windowsill.

repitiendo [repi'tjendo] *etc vb V* **repetir**.

replantear [replante'ar] *vt* (*cuestión pública*) to readdress; (*problema personal*)

to reconsider; (*en reunión*) to raise again; ~**se** *vr*: ~**se algo** to reconsider sth.

replegarse [reple'ɣarse] *vr* to fall back, retreat.

replegué [reple'ɣe], **repleguemos** [reple'ɣemos] *etc vb V* **replegarse**.

repleto, a [re'pleto, a] *adj* replete, full up; ~ **de** filled *o* crammed with.

réplica ['replika] *nf* answer; (*ARTE*) replica; **derecho de** ~ right of *o* to reply.

replicar [repli'kar] *vi* to answer; (*objetar*) to argue, answer back.

repliego [re'pljeɣo] *etc vb V* **replegarse**.

repliegue [re'pljeɣe] *etc vb V* **replegarse** ♦ *nm* (*MIL*) withdrawal.

replique [re'plike] *etc vb V* **replicar**.

repoblación [repoßla'θjon] *nf* repopulation; (*de río*) restocking; ~ **forestal** reafforestation.

repoblar [repo'ßlar] *vt* to repopulate; to restock.

repollo [re'poʎo] *nm* cabbage.

repondré [repon'dre] *etc vb V* **reponer**.

reponer [repo'ner] *vt* to replace, put back; (*máquina*) to re-set; (*TEAT*) to revive; ~**se** *vr* to recover; ~ **que** to reply that.

reponga [re'ponga] *etc vb V* **reponer**.

reportaje [repor'taxe] *nm* report, article; ~ **gráfico** illustrated report.

reportar [repor'tar] *vt* (*traer*) to bring, carry; (*conseguir*) to obtain; (*fig*) to check; ~**se** *vr* (*contenerse*) to control o.s.; (*calmarse*) to calm down; **la cosa no le reportó sino disgustos** the affair brought him nothing but trouble.

reportero, a [repor'tero, a] *nm/f* reporter; ~ **gráfico/a** news photographer.

reposacabezas [reposaka'ßeθas] *nm inv* headrest.

reposado, a [repo'saðo, a] *adj* (*descansado*) restful; (*tranquilo*) calm.

reposar [repo'sar] *vi* to rest, repose; (*muerto*) to lie, rest.

reposición [reposi'θjon] *nf* replacement; (*CINE*) second showing; (*TEAT*) revival.

reposo [re'poso] *nm* rest.

repostar [repos'tar] *vt* to replenish; (*AUTO*) to fill up (with petrol *o* gasoline).

repostería [reposte'ria] *nf* (*arte*) confectionery, pastry-making; (*tienda*) confectioner's (shop).

repostero, a [repos'tero, a] *nm/f* confectioner.

reprender [repren'der] *vt* to reprimand; (*niño*) to scold.

reprensión [repren'sjon] *nf* rebuke, reprimand; (*de niño*) telling-off,

scolding.
represa [re'presa] *nf* dam; (*lago artificial*) lake, pool.
represalia [repre'salja] *nf* reprisal; **tomar ~s** to take reprisals, retaliate.
representación [representa'θjon] *nf* representation; (*TEAT*) performance; **en ~ de** representing; **por ~** by proxy; **~ visual** (*INFORM*) display.
representante [represen'tante] *nm/f* (*POL, COM*) representative; (*TEAT*) performer.
representar [represen'tar] *vt* to represent; (*significar*) to mean; (*TEAT*) to perform; (*edad*) to look; **~se** *vr* to imagine; **tal acto representaría la guerra** such an act would mean war.
representativo, a [representa'tiβo, a] *adj* representative.
represión [repre'sjon] *nf* repression.
represivo, a [repre'siβo, a] *adj* repressive.
reprimenda [repri'menda] *nf* reprimand, rebuke.
reprimir [repri'mir] *vt* to repress; **~se** *vr*: **~se de hacer algo** to stop o.s. from doing sth.
reprobación [reproβa'θjon] *nf* reproval; (*culpa*) blame.
reprobar [repro'βar] *vt* to censure, reprove.
réprobo, a ['reproβo, a] *nm/f* reprobate.
reprochar [repro't∫ar] *vt* to reproach; (*censurar*) to condemn, censure.
reproche [re'prot∫e] *nm* reproach.
reproducción [reproδuk'θjon] *nf* reproduction.
reproducir [reproδu'θir] *vt* to reproduce; **~se** *vr* to breed; (*situación*) to recur.
reproductor, a [reproδuk'tor, a] *adj* reproductive ♦ *nm*: **~ de discos compactos** CD player.
reproduje [repro'δuxe], **reprodujera** [reproδu'xera] *etc*, **reproduzca** [repro'δuθka] *etc vb V* **reproducir**.
repruebe [re'prweβe] *etc vb V* **reprobar**.
reptar [rep'tar] *vi* to creep, crawl.
reptil [rep'til] *nm* reptile.
república [re'puβlika] *nf* republic; **R~ Dominicana** Dominican Republic; **R~ Democrática Alemana (RDA)** German Democratic Republic; **R~ Federal Alemana (RFA)** Federal Republic of Germany; **R~ Árabe Unida** United Arab Republic.
republicano, a [repuβli'kano, a] *adj, nm/f* republican.
repudiar [repu'δjar] *vt* to repudiate; (*fe*) to renounce.
repudio [re'puδjo] *nm* repudiation.

repueble [re'pweβle] *etc vb V* **repoblar**.
repuesto [re'pwesto] *pp de* **reponer** ♦ *nm* (*pieza de recambio*) spare (part); (*abastecimiento*) supply; **rueda de ~** spare wheel; **y llevamos otro de ~** and we have another as a spare *o* in reserve.
repugnancia [repuɣ'nanθja] *nf* repugnance.
repugnante [repuɣ'nante] *adj* repugnant, repulsive.
repugnar [repuɣ'nar] *vt* to disgust ♦ *vi*, **~se** *vr* (*contradecirse*) to contradict each other; (*dar asco*) to be disgusting.
repujar [repu'xar] *vt* to emboss.
repulsa [re'pulsa] *nf* rebuff.
repulsión [repul'sjon] *nf* repulsion, aversion.
repulsivo, a [repul'siβo, a] *adj* repulsive.
repuse [re'puse] *etc vb V* **reponer**.
reputación [reputa'θjon] *nf* reputation.
reputar [repu'tar] *vt* to consider, deem.
requemado, a [reke'maδo, a] *adj* (*quemado*) scorched; (*bronceado*) tanned.
requemar [reke'mar] *vt* (*quemar*) to scorch; (*secar*) to parch; (*CULIN*) to overdo, burn; (*la lengua*) to burn, sting.
requerimiento [rekeri'mjento] *nm* request; (*demanda*) demand; (*JUR*) summons.
requerir [reke'rir] *vt* (*pedir*) to ask, request; (*exigir*) to require; (*ordenar*) to call for; (*llamar*) to send for, summon.
requesón [reke'son] *nm* cottage cheese.
requete... [rekete] *pref* extremely.
requiebro [re'kjeβro] *nm* (*piropo*) compliment, flirtatious remark.
réquiem ['rekjem] *nm* requiem.
requiera [re'kjera] *etc*, **requiriendo** [reki'rjendo] *etc vb V* **requerir**.
requisa [re'kisa] *nf* (*inspección*) survey, inspection; (*MIL*) requisition.
requisar [reki'sar] *vt* (*MIL*) to requisition; (*confiscar*) to seize, confiscate.
requisito [reki'sito] *nm* requirement, requisite; **~ previo** prerequisite; **tener los ~s para un cargo** to have the essential qualifications for a post.
res [res] *nf* beast, animal.
resabio [re'saβjo] *nm* (*maña*) vice, bad habit; (*dejo*) (unpleasant) aftertaste.
resaca [re'saka] *nf* (*en el mar*) undertow, undercurrent; (*fig*) backlash; (*fam*) hangover.
resaltar [resal'tar] *vi* to project, stick out; (*fig*) to stand out.
resarcir [resar'θir] *vt* to compensate; (*pagar*) to repay; **~se** *vr* to make up for; **~ a algn de una pérdida** to compensate sb for a loss; **~ a algn de una cantidad** to

repay sb a sum.

resarza [re'sarθa] *etc vb V* **resarcir**.

resbalada [resβa'laða] *nf (AM)* slip.

resbaladizo, a [resβala'ðiθo, a] *adj* slippery.

resbalar [resβa'lar] *vi*, **resbalarse** *vr* to slip, slide; (*fig*) to slip (up); **le resbalaban las lágrimas por las mejillas** tears were trickling down his cheeks.

resbalón [resβa'lon] *nm* (*acción*) slip; (*deslizamiento*) slide; (*fig*) slip.

rescatar [reska'tar] *vt* (*salvar*) to save, rescue; (*objeto*) to get back, recover; (*cautivos*) to ransom.

rescate [res'kate] *nm* rescue; (*objeto*) recovery; **pagar un** ~ to pay a ransom.

rescindir [resθin'dir] *vt* (*contrato*) to annul, rescind.

rescisión [resθi'sjon] *nf* cancellation.

rescoldo [res'koldo] *nm* embers *pl*.

resecar [rese'kar] *vt* to dry off, dry thoroughly; (*MED*) to cut out, remove; **~se** *vr* to dry up.

reseco, a [re'seko, a] *adj* very dry; (*fig*) skinny.

resentido, a [resen'tiðo, a] *adj* resentful; **es un** ~ he's bitter.

resentimiento [resenti'mjento] *nm* resentment, bitterness.

resentirse [resen'tirse] *vr* (*debilitarse: persona*) to suffer; ~ **con** to resent; ~ **de** (*consecuencias*) to feel the effects of.

reseña [re'seɲa] *nf* (*cuenta*) account; (*informe*) report; (*LIT*) review.

reseñar [rese'ɲar] *vt* to describe; (*LIT*) to review.

reseque [re'seke] *etc vb V* **resecar**.

reserva [re'serβa] *nf* reserve; (*reservación*) reservation; **a** ~ **de que** ... unless ...; **con toda** ~ in strictest confidence; **de** ~ spare; **tener algo de** ~ to have sth in reserve; ~ **de indios** Indian reservation; (*COM*): ~ **para amortización** depreciation allowance; ~ **de caja** *o* **en efectivo** cash reserves; ~**s del Estado** government stock; ~**s en oro** gold reserves.

reservado, a [reser'βaðo, a] *adj* reserved; (*retraído*) cold, distant ♦ *nm* private room; (*FERRO*) reserved compartment.

reservar [reser'βar] *vt* (*guardar*) to keep; (*FERRO, TEAT etc*) to reserve, book; ~**se** *vr* to save o.s.; (*callar*) to keep to o.s.; ~ **con exceso** to overbook.

resfriado [res'friaðo] *nm* cold.

resfriarse [res'friarse] *vr* to cool off; (*MED*) to catch (a) cold.

resfrío [res'frio] *nm* (*esp AM*) cold.

resguardar [resɣwar'ðar] *vt* to protect,

shield; ~**se** *vr*: ~**se de** to guard against.

resguardo [res'ɣwarðo] *nm* defence; (*vale*) voucher; (*recibo*) receipt, slip.

residencia [resi'ðenθja] *nf* residence; (*UNIV*) hall of residence; ~ **para ancianos** *o* **jubilados** rest home.

residencial [resiðen'θjal] *adj* residential ♦ *nf* (*urbanización*) housing estate (*BRIT*), real estate development (*US*).

residente [resi'ðente] *adj, nm/f* resident.

residir [resi'ðir] *vi* to reside, live; ~ **en** to reside *o* lie in; (*consistir en*) to consist of.

residual [resi'ðwal] *adj* residual; **aguas** ~**es** sewage.

residuo [re'siðwo] *nm* residue; ~**s atmosféricos** *o* **radiactivos** fallout *sg*.

resienta [re'sjenta] *etc vb V* **resentir**.

resignación [resiɣna'θjon] *nf* resignation.

resignarse [resiɣ'narse] *vr*: ~ **a** *o* **con** to resign o.s. to, be resigned to.

resina [re'sina] *nf* resin.

resintiendo [resin'tjendo] *etc vb V* **resentir**.

resistencia [resis'tenθja] *nf* (*dureza*) endurance, strength; (*oposición, FÍSC*) resistance; **la R**~ (*MIL*) the Resistance.

resistente [resis'tente] *adj* strong, hardy; (*TEC*) resistant; ~ **al calor** heat-resistant.

resistir [resis'tir] *vt* (*soportar*) to bear; (*oponerse a*) to resist, oppose; (*aguantar*) to put up with ♦ *vi* to resist; (*aguantar*) to last, endure; ~**se** *vr*: ~**se a** to refuse to, resist; **no puedo** ~ **este frío** I can't bear *o* stand this cold; **me resisto a creerlo** I refuse to believe it; **se le resiste la química** chemistry escapes her.

resol [re'sol] *nm* glare of the sun.

resollar [reso'ʎar] *vi* to breathe noisily, wheeze.

resolución [resolu'θjon] *nf* resolution; (*decisión*) decision; (*moción*) motion; ~ **judicial** legal ruling; **tomar una** ~ to take a decision.

resoluto, a [reso'luto, a] *adj* resolute.

resolver [resol'βer] *vt* to resolve; (*solucionar*) to solve, resolve; (*decidir*) to decide, settle; ~**se** *vr* to make up one's mind.

resonancia [reso'nanθja] *nf* (*del sonido*) resonance; (*repercusión*) repercussion; (*fig*) wide effect, impact.

resonante [reso'nante] *adj* resonant, resounding; (*fig*) tremendous.

resonar [reso'nar] *vi* to ring, echo.

resoplar [reso'plar] *vi* to snort; (*por cansancio*) to puff.

resoplido [reso'pliðo] *nm* heavy breathing.

resorte [re'sorte] *nm* spring; (*fig*) lever.

respaldar [respal'dar] *vt* to back (up),

support; (*INFORM*) to back up; ~**se** *vr* to lean back; ~**se con** *o* **en** (*fig*) to take one's stand on.

respaldo [res'paldo] *nm* (*de sillón*) back; (*fig*) support, backing.

respectivo, a [respek'tißo, a] *adj* respective; **en lo** ~ **a** with regard to.

respecto [res'pekto] *nm*: **al** ~ on this matter; **con** ~ **a,** ~ **de** with regard to, in relation to.

respetable [respe'taßle] *adj* respectable.

respetar [respe'tar] *vt* to respect.

respeto [res'peto] *nm* respect; (*acatamiento*) deference; ~**s** *nmpl* respects; **por** ~ **a** out of consideration for; **presentar sus** ~**s a** to pay one's respects to.

respetuoso, a [respe'twoso, a] *adj* respectful.

respingo [res'pingo] *nm* start, jump.

respiración [respira'θjon] *nf* breathing; (*MED*) respiration; (*ventilación*) ventilation.

respirar [respi'rar] *vt, vi* to breathe; **no dejar** ~ **a algn** to keep on at sb; **estuvo escuchándole sin** ~ he listened to him in complete silence.

respiratorio, a [respira'torjo, a] *adj* respiratory.

respiro [res'piro] *nm* breathing; (*fig: descanso*) respite, rest; (*COM*) period of grace.

resplandecer [resplande'θer] *vi* to shine.

resplandeciente [resplande'θjente] *adj* resplendent, shining.

resplandezca [resplan'deθka] *etc vb V* **resplandecer**.

resplandor [resplan'dor] *nm* brilliance, brightness; (*del fuego*) blaze.

responder [respon'der] *vt* to answer ♦ *vi* to answer; (*fig*) to respond; (*pey*) to answer back; (*corresponder*) to correspond; ~ **a** (*situación etc*) to respond to; ~ **a una pregunta** to answer a question; ~ **a una descripción** to fit a description; ~ **de** *o* **por** to answer for.

respondón, ona [respon'don, ona] *adj* cheeky.

responsabilice [responsaßi'liθe] *etc vb V* **responsabilizarse**.

responsabilidad [responsaßili'ðað] *nf* responsibility; **bajo mi** ~ on my authority; ~ **ilimitada** (*COM*) unlimited liability.

responsabilizarse [responsaßili'θarse] *vr* to make o.s. responsible, take charge.

responsable [respon'sable] *adj* responsible; **la persona** ~ the person in charge; **hacerse** ~ **de algo** to assume responsibility for sth.

respuesta [res'pwesta] *nf* answer, reply; (*reacción*) response.

resquebrajar [reskeßra'xar] *vt,* **resquebrajarse** *vr* to crack, split.

resquemor [reske'mor] *nm* resentment.

resquicio [res'kiθjo] *nm* chink; (*hendedura*) crack.

resta ['resta] *nf* (*MAT*) remainder.

restablecer [restaßle'θer] *vt* to re-establish, restore; ~**se** *vr* to recover.

restablecimiento [restaßleθi'mjento] *nm* re-establishment; (*restauración*) restoration; (*MED*) recovery.

restablezca [resta'ßleθka] *etc vb V* **restablecer**.

restallar [resta'ʎar] *vi* to crack.

restante [res'tante] *adj* remaining; **lo** ~ the remainder; **los** ~**s** the rest, those left (over).

restar [res'tar] *vt* (*MAT*) to subtract; (*descontar*) to deduct; (*fig*) to take away ♦ *vi* to remain, be left.

restauración [restaura'θjon] *nf* restoration.

restaurador, a [restaura'ðor, a] *nm/f* (*persona*) restorer.

restaurante [restau'rante] *nm* restaurant.

restaurar [restau'rar] *vt* to restore.

restitución [restitu'θjon] *nf* return, restitution.

restituir [restitu'ir] *vt* (*devolver*) to return, give back; (*rehabilitar*) to restore.

restituyendo [restitu'jendo] *etc vb V* **restituir**.

resto ['resto] *nm* (*residuo*) rest, remainder; (*apuesta*) stake; ~**s** *nmpl* remains; (*CULIN*) leftovers, scraps; ~**s mortales** mortal remains.

restregar [restre'xar] *vt* to scrub, rub.

restregué [restre'xe], **restreguemos** [restre'xemos] *etc vb V* **restregar**.

restricción [restrik'θjon] *nf* restriction; **sin** ~ **de** without restrictions on *o* as to; **hablar sin restricciones** to talk freely.

restrictivo, a [restrik'tißo, a] *adj* restrictive.

restriego [res'trjexo] *etc,* **restriegue** [res'trjexe] *etc vb V* **restregar**.

restringir [restrin'xir] *vt* to restrict, limit.

restrinja [res'trinxa] *etc vb V* **restringir**.

resucitar [resuθi'tar] *vt, vi* to resuscitate, revive.

resuello [re'sweʎo] *etc vb V* **resollar** ♦ *nm* (*aliento*) breath.

resuelto, a [re'swelto, a] *pp de* **resolver** ♦ *adj* resolute, determined; **estar** ~ **a**

algo to be set on sth; **estar ~ a hacer algo** to be determined to do sth.
resuelva [re'swelßa] *etc vb V* **resolver**.
resuene [re'swene] *etc vb V* **resonar**.
resulta [re'sulta] *nf* result; **de ~s de** as a result of.
resultado [resul'taðo] *nm* result; (*conclusión*) outcome; **~s** *nmpl* (*INFORM*) output *sg*; **dar ~** to produce results.
resultante [resul'tante] *adj* resulting, resultant.
resultar [resul'tar] *vi* (*ser*) to be; (*llegar a ser*) to turn out to be; (*salir bien*) to turn out well; (*seguir*) to ensue; **~ a** (*COM*) to amount to; **~ de** to stem from; **~ en** to result in, produce; **resulta que ...** (*por consecuencia*) it follows that ...; (*parece que*) it seems that ...; **el conductor resultó muerto** the driver was killed; **no resultó** it didn't work o come off; **me resulta difícil hacerlo** it's difficult for me to do it.
resumen [re'sumen] *nm* summary, résumé; **en ~** in short.
resumir [resu'mir] *vt* to sum up; (*condensar*) to summarize; (*cortar*) to abridge, cut down; (*condensar*) to summarize; **~se** *vr*: **la situación se resume en pocas palabras** the situation can be summed up in a few words.
resurgir [resur'xir] *vi* (*reaparecer*) to reappear.
resurrección [resurrek'θjon] *nf* resurrection.
retablo [re'taßlo] *nm* altarpiece.
retaguardia [reta'ywarðja] *nf* rearguard.
retahíla [reta'ila] *nf* series, string; (*de injurias*) volley, stream.
retal [re'tal] *nm* remnant.
retar [re'tar] *vt* (*gen*) to challenge; (*desafiar*) to defy, dare.
retardar [retar'ðar] *vt* (*demorar*) to delay; (*hacer más lento*) to slow down; (*retener*) to hold back.
retardo [re'tarðo] *nm* delay.
retazo [re'taθo] *nm* snippet (*BRIT*), fragment.
RETD *nf abr* (*ESP TELEC*) = Red Especial de Transmisión de Datos.
rete... ['rete] *pref* very, extremely.
retén [re'ten] *nm* (*AM*) roadblock, checkpoint.
retención [reten'θjon] *nf* retention; (*de pago*) deduction; **~ de llamadas** (*TELEC*) hold facility.
retendré [reten'dre] *etc vb V* **retener**.
retener [rete'ner] *vt* (*guardar*) to retain, keep; (*intereses*) to withhold.

retenga [re'tenga] *etc vb V* **retener**.
reticencia [reti'θenθja] *nf* (*sugerencia*) insinuation, (malevolent) suggestion; (*engaño*) half-truth.
reticente [reti'θente] *adj* (*insinuador*) insinuating; (*engañoso*) deceptive.
retiene [re'tjene] *etc vb V* **retener**.
retina [re'tina] *nf* retina.
retintín [retin'tin] *nm* jangle, jingle; **decir algo con ~** to say sth sarcastically.
retirado, a [reti'raðo, a] *adj* (*lugar*) remote; (*vida*) quiet; (*jubilado*) retired ♦ *nf* (*MIL*) retreat; (*de dinero*) withdrawal; (*de embajador*) recall; (*refugio*) safe place; **batirse en retirada** to retreat.
retirar [reti'rar] *vt* to withdraw; (*la mano*) to draw back, (*quitar*) to remove; (*dinero*) to take out, withdraw; (*jubilar*) to retire, pension off; **~se** *vr* to retreat, withdraw; (*jubilarse*) to retire; (*acostarse*) to retire, go to bed.
retiro [re'tiro] *nm* retreat; (*jubilación, tb DEPORTE*) retirement; (*pago*) pension; (*lugar*) quiet place.
reto ['reto] *nm* dare, challenge.
retocar [reto'kar] *vt* to touch up, retouch.
retoce [re'toθe] *etc vb V* **retozar**.
retoño [re'toɲo] *nm* sprout, shoot; (*fig*) offspring, child.
retoque [re'toke] *etc vb V* **retocar** ♦ *nm* retouching.
retorcer [retor'θer] *vt* to twist; (*argumento*) to turn, twist; (*manos, lavado*) to wring; **~se** *vr* to become twisted; (*persona*) to writhe; **~se de dolor** to writhe in o squirm with pain.
retorcido, a [retor'θiðo, a] *adj* (*tb fig*) twisted.
retorcimiento [retorθi'mjento] *nm* twist, twisting; (*fig*) deviousness.
retórico, a [re'toriko, a] *adj* rhetorical; (*pey*) affected, windy ♦ *nf* rhetoric; (*pey*) affectedness.
retornable [retor'naßle] *adj* returnable.
retornar [retor'nar] *vt* to return, give back ♦ *vi* to return, go/come back.
retorno [re'torno] *nm* return; **~ del carro** (*INFORM, TIP*) carriage return; **~ del carro automático** (*INFORM*) wordwrap, word wraparound.
retortero [retor'tero] *nm*: **andar al ~** to bustle about, have heaps of things to do; **andar al ~ por algn** to be madly in love with sb.
retortijón [retorti'xon] *nm* twist, twisting; **~ de tripas** stomach cramp.
retorzamos [retor'θamos] *etc vb V* **retorcer**.

retozar [reto'θar] *vi* (*juguetear*) to frolic, romp; (*saltar*) to gambol.

retozón, ona [reto'θon, ona] *adj* playful.

retracción [retrak'θjon] *nf* retraction.

retractarse [retrak'tarse] *vr* to retract; **me retracto** I take that back.

retraerse [retra'erse] *vr* to retreat, withdraw.

retraído, a [retra'iðo, a] *adj* shy, retiring.

retraiga [re'traiχa] *etc vb V* **retraerse**.

retraimiento [retrai'mjento] *nm* retirement; (*timidez*) shyness.

retraje [re'traxe] *etc*, **retrajera** [retra'xera] *etc vb V* **retraerse**.

retransmisión [retransmi'sjon] *nf* repeat (broadcast).

retransmitir [retransmi'tir] *vt* (*mensaje*) to relay; (*TV etc*) to repeat, retransmit; (: *en vivo*) to broadcast live.

retrasado, a [retra'saðo, a] *adj* late; (*MED*) mentally retarded; (*país etc*) backward, underdeveloped; **estar ~** (*reloj*) to be slow; (*persona, industria*) to be o lag behind.

retrasar [retra'sar] *vt* (*demorar*) to postpone, put off; (*retardar*) to slow down ♦ *vi*, **~se** *vr* (*atrasarse*) to be late; (*reloj*) to be slow; (*producción*) to fall (away); (*quedarse atrás*) to lag behind.

retraso [re'traso] *nm* (*demora*) delay; (*lentitud*) slowness; (*tardanza*) lateness; (*atraso*) backwardness; **~s** *nmpl* (*COM*) arrears; (*deudas*) deficit *sg*, debts; **llegar con ~** to arrive late; **llegar con 25 minutos de ~** to be 25 minutes late; **llevo un ~ de 6 semanas** I'm 6 weeks behind (with my work *etc*); **~ mental** mental deficiency.

retratar [retra'tar] *vt* (*ARTE*) to paint the portrait of; (*fotografiar*) to photograph; (*fig*) to depict, describe; **~se** *vr* to have one's portrait painted; to have one's photograph taken.

retratista [retra'tista] *nm/f* (*pintura*) (portrait) painter; (*FOTO*) photographer.

retrato [re'trato] *nm* portrait; (*FOTO*) photograph; (*descripción*) portrayal, depiction; (*fig*) likeness; **ser el vivo ~ de** to be the spitting image of.

retrato-robot [re'tratoro'ßo(t)], *pl* **retratos-robot** *nm* identikit picture.

retrayendo [retra'jendo] *etc vb V* **retraerse**.

retreta [re'treta] *nf* retreat.

retrete [re'trete] *nm* toilet.

retribución [retrißu'θjon] *nf* (*recompensa*) reward; (*pago*) pay, payment.

retribuir [retrißu'ir] *vt* (*recompensar*) to reward; (*pagar*) to pay.

retribuyendo [retrißu'jendo] *etc vb V* **retribuir**.

retro... [retro] *pref* retro....

retroactivo, a [retroak'tißo, a] *adj* retroactive, retrospective; **dar efecto ~ a un pago** to backdate a payment.

retroalimentación [retroalimenta'θjon] *nf* (*INFORM*) feedback.

retroceder [retroθe'ðer] *vi* (*echarse atrás*) to move back(wards); (*fig*) to back down; **no ~ to stand firm; la policía hizo ~ a la multitud** the police forced the crowd back.

retroceso [retro'θeso] *nm* backward movement; (*MED*) relapse; (*COM*) recession, depression; (*fig*) backing down.

retrógrado, a [re'troχraðo, a] *adj* retrograde, retrogressive; (*POL*) reactionary.

retropropulsión [retropropul'sjon] *nf* jet propulsion.

retrospectivo, a [retrospek'tißo, a] *adj* retrospective; **mirada retrospectiva** backward glance.

retrovisor [retroßi'sor] *nm* rear-view mirror.

retuerce [re'twerθe] *etc*, **retuerza** [re'twerθa] *etc vb V* **retorcer**.

retumbante [retum'bante] *adj* resounding.

retumbar [retum'bar] *vi* to echo, resound; (*continuamente*) to reverberate.

retuve [re'tuße] *etc vb V* **retener**.

reuma ['reuma] *nm* rheumatism.

reumático, a [reu'matiko, a] *adj* rheumatic.

reumatismo [reuma'tismo] *nm* rheumatism.

reunificar [reunifi'kar] *vt* to reunify.

reunifique [reuni'fike] *etc vb V* **reunificar**.

reunión [reu'njon] *nf* (*asamblea*) meeting; (*fiesta*) party; **~ en la cumbre** summit meeting; **~ de ventas** (*COM*) sales meeting.

reunir [reu'nir] *vt* (*juntar*) to reunite, join (together); (*recoger*) to gather (together); (*personas*) to bring o get together; (*cualidades*) to combine; **~se** *vr* (*personas: en asamblea*) to meet, gather; **reunió a sus amigos para discutirlo** he got his friends together to talk it over.

reválida [re'ßaliða] *nf* (*ESCOL*) final examination.

revalidar [reßali'ðar] *vt* (*ratificar*) to confirm, ratify.

revalorar [reßalo'rar] *vt* to revalue, reassess.

revalor(iz)ación [reßalor(iθ)a'θjon] *nf*

revaluation; (*ECON*) reassessment.

revancha [re'ßantʃa] *nf* revenge; (*DEPORTE*) return match; (*BOXEO*) return fight.

revelación [reßela'θjon] *nf* revelation.

revelado [reße'laðo] *nm* developing.

revelador, a [reßela'ðor, a] *adj* revealing.

revelar [ɹeße'lar] *vt* to reveal; (*secreto*) to disclose; (*mostrar*) to show; (*FOTO*) to develop.

revendedor, a [reßende'ðor, a] *nm/f* retailer; (*pey*) ticket tout.

revendré [reßen'dre] *etc*, **revenga** [re'ßenga] *etc vb V* **revenirse**.

revenirse [reße'nirse] *vr* to shrink; (*comida*) to go bad *o* off; (*vino*) to sour; (*CULIN*) to get tough.

reventa [re'ßenta] *nf* resale; (*especulación*) speculation; (*de entradas*) touting.

reventar [reßen'tar] *vt* to burst, explode; (*molestar*) to annoy, rile ♦ *vi*, ~**se** *vr* (*estallar*) to burst, explode; **me revienta tener que ponérmelo** I hate having to wear it; ~ **de** (*fig*) to be bursting with; ~ **por** to be bursting to.

reventón [reßen'ton] *nm* (*AUTO*) blow-out (*BRIT*), flat (*US*).

reverberación [reßerßera'θjon] *nf* reverberation.

reverberar [reßerße'rar] *vi* (*luz*) to play, be reflected; (*superficie*) to shimmer; (*nieve*) to glare; (*sonido*) to reverberate.

reverbero [reßer'ßero] *nm* play; shimmer, shine; glare; reverberation.

reverencia [reße'renθja] *nf* reverence; (*inclinación*) bow.

reverenciar [reßeren'θjar] *vt* to revere.

reverendo, a [reße'rendo, a] *adj* reverend; (*fam*) big, awful; **un ~ imbécil** an awful idiot.

reverente [reße'rente] *adj* reverent.

reversible [reßer'sißle] *adj* reversible.

reverso [re'ßeɹso] *nm* back, other side; (*de moneda*) reverse.

revertir [reßer'tir] *vi* to revert; ~ **en beneficio de** to be to the advantage of; ~ **en perjuicio de** to be to the detriment of.

revés [re'ßes] *nm* back, wrong side; (*fig*) reverse, setback; (*DEPORTE*) backhand; **al** ~ the wrong way round; (*de arriba abajo*) upside down; (*ropa*) inside out; **y al** ~ and vice versa; **volver algo al** ~ to turn sth round; (*ropa*) to turn sth inside out; **los reveses de la fortuna** the blows of fate.

revestir [reßes'tir] *vt* (*poner*) to put on; (*cubrir*) to cover, coat; (*cualidad*) to have, possess; ~**se** *vr* (*REL*) to put on one's vestments; (*ponerse*) to put on; ~ **con** *o*

de to arm o.s. with; **el acto revestía gran solemnidad** the ceremony had great dignity.

reviejo, a [re'ßjexo, a] *adj* very old, ancient.

reviene [re'ßjene] *etc vb V* **revenirse**.

reviente [re'ßjente] *etc vb V* **reventar**.

revierta [re'ßjerta] *etc vb V* **revertir**.

reviniendo [reßi'njendo] *etc vb V* **revenirse**.

revirtiendo [reßir'tjendo] *etc vb V* **revertir**.

revisar [reßi'sar] *vt* (*examinar*) to check; (*texto etc*) to revise; (*JUR*) to review.

revisión [reßi'sjon] *nf* revision; ~ **aduanera** customs inspection; ~ **de cuentas** audit.

revisor, a [reßi'sor, a] *nm/f* inspector; (*FERRO*) ticket collector; ~ **de cuentas** auditor.

revista [re'ßista] *etc vb V* **revestir** ♦ *nf* magazine, review; (*sección*) section, page; (*TEAT*) revue; (*inspección*) inspection; ~ **literaria** literary review; ~ **de libros** book reviews (page); **pasar** ~ **a** to review, inspect.

revivir [reßi'ßir] *vt* (*recordar*) to revive memories of ♦ *vi* to revive.

revocación [reßoka'θjon] *nf* repeal.

revocar [reßo'kar] *vt* (*decisión*) to revoke; (*ARQ*) to plaster.

revolcar [reßol'kar] *vt* to knock down, send flying; ~**se** *vr* to roll about.

revolcón [reßol'kon] *nm* tumble.

revolotear [reßolote'ar] *vi* to flutter.

revoloteo [reßolo'teo] *nm* fluttering.

revolqué [reßol'ke], **revolquemos** [reßol'kemos] *etc vb V* **revolcar**.

revoltijo [reßol'tixo] *nm* mess, jumble.

revoltoso, a [reßol'toso, a] *adj* (*travieso*) naughty, unruly.

revolución [reßolu'θjon] *nf* revolution.

revolucionar [reßoluθjo'nar] *vt* to revolutionize

revolucionario, a [reßoluθjo'narjo, a] *adj*, *nm/f* revolutionary.

revolver [reßol'ßer] *vt* (*desordenar*) to disturb, mess up; (*agitar*) to shake; (*líquido*) to stir; (*mover*) to move about; (*POL*) to stir up ♦ *vi*: ~ **en** to go through, rummage (about) in; ~**se** *vr* (*en cama*) to toss and turn; (*METEOROLOGÍA*) to break, turn stormy; ~**se contra** to turn on *o* against; **han revuelto toda la casa** they've turned the whole house upside down.

revólver [re'ßolßer] *nm* revolver.

revoque [re'ßoke] *etc vb V* **revocar**.

revuelco [re'ßwelko] *etc vb V* **revolcar**.

revuelo [re'ßwelo] *nm* fluttering; (*fig*) commotion; **armar** *o* **levantar un gran ~**

to cause a great stir.

revuelque [re'ßwelke] *etc vb V* **revolcar.**

revuelto, a [re'ßwelto, a] *pp de* **revolver** ♦ *adj* (*mezclado*) mixed-up, in disorder; (*mar*) rough; (*tiempo*) unsettled ♦ *nf* (*motín*) revolt; (*agitación*) commotion; **todo estaba** ~ everything was in disorder *o* was topsy-turvy.

revuelva [re'ßwelßa] *etc vb V* **revolver.**

revulsivo [reßul'sißo] *nm*: **servir de** ~ to have a salutary effect.

rey [rei] *nm* king; **los R~es** the King and Queen; **los R~es Magos** the Magi; *see boxed note.*

REYES MAGOS

On the night before 6 January (Epiphany), a holiday in Spain, children go to bed expecting **los Reyes Magos**, *the Three Wise Men, to bring them presents. Twelfth Night processions, known as "cabalgatas", take place that evening too; three people dressed as* **los Reyes Magos** *arrive in town by land or sea to the delight of the local children.*

---

reyerta [re'jerta] *nf* quarrel, brawl.

rezagado, a [reθa'ɣaðo, a] *adj*: **quedar** ~ to be left behind; (*estar retrasado*) to be late, be behind ♦ *nm/f* straggler.

rezagar [reθa'ɣar] *vt* (*dejar atrás*) to leave behind; (*retrasar*) to delay, postpone; **~se** *vr* (*atrasarse*) to fall behind.

rezague [re'θaɣe] *etc vb V* **rezagar.**

rezar [re'θar] *vi* to pray; ~ **con** (*fam*) to concern, have to do with.

rezo ['reθo] *nm* prayer.

rezongar [reθon'gar] *vi* to grumble; (*murmurar*) to mutter; (*refunfuñar*) to growl.

rezongue [re'θonge] *etc vb V* **rezongar.**

rezumar [reθu'mar] *vt* to ooze ♦ *vi* to leak; **~se** *vr* to leak out.

RFA *nf abr* = **República Federal Alemana.**

ría ['ria] *nf* estuary.

riachuelo [rja'tʃwelo] *nm* stream.

riada [ri'aða] *nf* flood.

ribera [ri'ßera] *nf* (*de río*) bank; (: *área*) riverside.

ribete [ri'ßete] *nm* (*de vestido*) border; (*fig*) addition.

ribetear [rißete'ar] *vt* to edge, border.

rice ['riθe] *etc vb V* **rizar.**

ricino [ri'θino] *nm*: **aceite de** ~ castor oil.

rico, a ['riko, a] *adj* (*adinerado*) rich, wealthy; (*lujoso*) luxurious; (*comida*) delicious; (*niño*) lovely, cute ♦ *nm/f* rich person; **nuevo** ~ nouveau riche.

rictus ['riktus] *nm* (*mueca*) sneer, grin; ~ **de amargura** bitter smile.

ridiculez [riðiku'leθ] *nf* absurdity.

ridiculice [riðiku'liθe] *etc vb V* **ridiculizar.**

ridiculizar [riðikuli'θar] *vt* to ridicule.

ridículo, a [ri'ðikulo, a] *adj* ridiculous; **hacer el** ~ to make a fool of o.s.; **poner a algn en** ~ to make a fool of sb; **ponerse en** ~ to make a fool of o.s.

riego ['rjeɣo] *etc vb V* **regar** ♦ *nm* (*aspersión*) watering; (*irrigación*) irrigation.

riegue ['rjeɣe] *etc vb V* **regar.**

riel [rjel] *nm* rail.

rienda ['rjenda] *nf* rein; (*fig*) restraint, moderating influence; **dar** ~ **suelta a** to give free rein to; **llevar las** ~**s** to be in charge.

riendo ['rjendo] *vb V* **reír.**

riesgo ['rjesɣo] *nm* risk; **seguro a** *o* **contra todo** ~ comprehensive insurance; ~ **para la salud** health hazard; **correr el** ~ **de** to run the risk of.

Rif [rif] *nm* Rif(f).

rifa ['rifa] *nf* (*lotería*) raffle.

rifar [ri'far] *vt* to raffle.

rifeño, a [ri'feɲo, a] *adj* of the Rif(f), Rif(f)ian ♦ *nm/f* Rif(f)ian, Rif(f).

rifle ['rifle] *nm* rifle.

rigidez [rixi'ðeθ] *nf* rigidity, stiffness; (*fig*) strictness.

rígido, a ['rixiðo, a] *adj* rigid, stiff; (*moralmente*) strict, inflexible; (*cara*) wooden, expressionless.

rigiendo [ri'xjendo] *etc vb V* **regir.**

rigor [ri'ɣor] *nm* strictness, rigour; (*dureza*) toughness; (*inclemencia*) harshness; (*meticulosidad*) accuracy; **el** ~ **del verano** the hottest part of the summer; **con todo** ~ **científico** with scientific precision; **de** ~ de rigueur, essential; **después de los saludos de** ~ after the inevitable greetings.

riguroso, a [rixu'roso, a] *adj* rigorous; (*METEOROLOGÍA*) harsh; (*severo*) severe.

rija ['rixa] *etc vb V* **regir** ♦ *nf* quarrel.

rima ['rima] *nf* rhyme; ~**s** *nfpl* verse *sg*; ~ **imperfecta** assonance; ~ **rimando** (*fam*) merrily.

rimar [ri'mar] *vi* to rhyme.

rimbombante [rimbom'bante] *adj* (*fig*) pompous.

rímel, rímmel ['rimel] *nm* mascara.

rimero [ri'mero] *nm* stack, pile.

Rin [rin] *nm* Rhine.

rincón [rin'kon] *nm* corner (*inside*).

rindiendo [rin'djendo] *etc vb V* **rendir.**

ring [riŋ] *nm* (*BOXEO*) ring.

rinoceronte [rinoθe'ronte] *nm* rhinoceros.
riña ['riɲa] *nf* (*disputa*) argument; (*pelea*) brawl.
riñendo [ri'ɲendo] *etc vb V* **reñir**.
riñón [ri'ɲon] *nm* kidney; **me costó un ~** (*fam*) it cost me an arm and a leg; **tener riñones** to have guts.
río ['rio] *etc vb V* **reír** ♦ *nm* river; (*fig*) torrent, stream; **~ abajo/arriba** downstream/upstream; **cuando el ~ suena, agua lleva** there's no smoke without fire.
rió [ri'o] *vb V* **reír**.
Río de Janeiro ['rioðexa'neiro] *nm* Rio de Janeiro.
Río de la Plata ['rioðela'plata] *nm* Rio de la Plata, River Plate.
Rioja [ri'oxa] *nf*: **La ~** La Rioja ♦ *nm*: **r~** rioja wine.
riojano, a [rjo'xano, a] *adj*, *nm/f* Riojan.
rioplatense [riopla'tense] *adj* of o from the River Plate region ♦ *nm/f* native o inhabitant of the River Plate region.
riqueza [ri'keθa] *nf* wealth, riches *pl*; (*cualidad*) richness.
risa ['risa] *nf* laughter; (*una ~*) laugh; ¡**qué ~!** what a laugh!; **caerse o morirse de ~** to split one's sides laughing, die laughing; **tomar algo a ~** to laugh sth off.
risco ['risko] *nm* crag, cliff.
risible [ri'sißle] *adj* ludicrous, laughable.
risotada [riso'taða] *nf* guffaw, loud laugh.
ristra ['ristra] *nf* string.
ristre ['ristre] *nm*: **en ~** at the ready.
risueño, a [ri'sweɲo, a] *adj* (*sonriente*) smiling; (*contento*) cheerful.
ritmo ['ritmo] *nm* rhythm; **a ~ lento** slowly; **trabajar a ~ lento** to go slow.
rito ['rito] *nm* rite.
ritual [ri'twal] *adj*, *nm* ritual.
rival [ri'ßal] *adj*, *nm/f* rival.
rivalice [rißa'liθe] *etc vb V* **rivalizar**.
rivalidad [rißali'ðað] *nf* rivalry, competition.
rivalizar [rißali'θar] *vi*: **~ con** to rival, compete with.
rizado, a [ri'θaðo, a] *adj* (*pelo*) curly; (*superficie*) ridged; (*terreno*) undulating; (*mar*) choppy ♦ *nm* curls *pl*.
rizar [ri'θar] *vt* to curl; **~se** *vr* (*el pelo*) to curl; (*agua*) to ripple; (*el mar*) to become choppy.
rizo ['riθo] *nm* curl; (*agua*) ripple.
Rma. *abr* (= *Reverendísima*) courtesy title.
Rmo. *abr* (= *Reverendísimo*) Rt. Rev.
RNE *nf abr* = *Radio Nacional de España*.
R. O. *abr* (=*Real Orden*) royal order.

robar [ro'ßar] *vt* to rob; (*objeto*) to steal; (*casa etc*) to break into; (*NAIPES*) to draw; (*atención*) to steal, capture; (*paciencia*) to exhaust.
roble ['roßle] *nm* oak.
robledal [roßle'ðal], **robledo** [ro'ßleðo] *nm* oakwood.
robo ['roßo] *nm* robbery, theft; (*objeto robado*) stolen article o goods *pl*; ¡**esto es un ~!** this is daylight robbery!
robot [ro'ßo(t)], *pl* **robots** *adj*, *nm* robot ♦ *nm* (*tb*: **~ de cocina**) food processor.
robótica [ro'ßotika] *nf* robotics *sg*.
robustecer [roßuste'θer] *vt* to strengthen.
robustezca [roßus'teθka] *etc vb V* **robustecer**.
robusto, a [ro'ßusto, a] *adj* robust, strong.
ROC *abr* (*INFORM*: = *reconocimiento óptico de caracteres*) OCR.
roca ['roka] *nf* rock; **la R~** the Rock (of Gibraltar).
roce ['roθe] *etc vb V* **rozar** ♦ *nm* rub, rubbing; (*caricia*) brush; (*TEC*) friction; (*en la piel*) graze; **tener ~ con** to have a brush with.
rociar [ro'θjar] *vt* to sprinkle, spray.
rocín [ro'θin] *nm* nag, hack.
rocío [ro'θio] *nm* dew.
rock [rok] *adj inv*, *nm* (*MUS*) rock (*cpd*).
rockero, a [ro'kero, a] *adj* rock *cpd* ♦ *nm/f* rocker.
rocoso, a [ro'koso, a] *adj* rocky.
rodado, a [ro'ðaðo, a] *adj* (*con ruedas*) wheeled ♦ *nf* rut.
rodaja [ro'ðaxa] *nf* (*raja*) slice.
rodaje [ro'ðaxe] *nm* (*CINE*) shooting, filming; (*AUTO*): **en ~** running in.
rodamiento [roða'mjento] *nm* (*AUTO*) tread.
Ródano ['roðano] *nm* Rhône.
rodar [ro'ðar] *vt* (*vehículo*) to wheel (along); (*escalera*) to roll down; (*viajar por*) to travel (over) ♦ *vi* to roll; (*coche*) to go, run; (*CINE*) to shoot, film; (*persona*) to move about (from place to place), drift; **echarlo todo a ~** (*fig*) to mess it all up.
Rodas ['roðas] *nf* Rhodes.
rodear [roðe'ar] *vt* to surround ♦ *vi* to go round; **~se** *vr*: **~se de amigos** to surround o.s. with friends.
rodeo [ro'ðeo] *nm* (*ruta indirecta*) long way round, roundabout way; (*desvío*) detour; (*evasión*) evasion; (*AM*) rodeo; **dejarse de ~s** to talk straight; **hablar sin ~s** to come to the point, speak plainly.
rodilla [ro'ðiʎa] *nf* knee; **de ~s** kneeling.
rodillo [ro'ðiʎo] *nm* roller; (*CULIN*) rolling-pin; (*en máquina de escribir, impresora*)

platen.

rododendro [roðo'ðendro] *nm* rhododendron.

roedor, a [roe'ðor, a] *adj* gnawing ♦ *nm* rodent.

roer [ro'er] *vt* (*masticar*) to gnaw; (*corroer, fig*) to corrode.

rogar [ro'ɣar] *vt* (*pedir*) to beg, ask for ♦ *vi* (*suplicar*) to beg, plead; ~**se** *vr*: **se ruega no fumar** please do not smoke; ~ **que** + *subjun* to ask to ...; **ruegue a este señor que nos deje en paz** please ask this gentleman to leave us alone; **no se hace de** ~ he doesn't have to be asked twice.

rogué [ro'ɣe], **roguemos** [ro'ɣemos] *etc vb V* **rogar**.

rojizo, a [ro'xiθo, a] *adj* reddish.

rojo, a ['roxo, a] *adj* red ♦ *nm* red (colour); (*POL*) red; **ponerse** ~ to turn red, blush; **al** ~ **vivo** red-hot.

rol [rol] *nm* list, roll; (*esp AM: papel*) role.

rollizo, a [ro'ʎiθo, a] *adj* (*objeto*) cylindrical; (*persona*) plump.

rollo, a ['roʎo, a] *adj* (*fam*) boring, tedious ♦ *nm* roll; (*de cuerda*) coil; (*madera*) log; (*fam*) bore; (*discurso*) boring speech; **¡qué ~!** what a carry-on!; **la conferencia fue un** ~ the lecture was a big drag.

ROM [rom] *nf abr* (= *memoria de sólo lectura*) ROM.

Roma ['roma] *nf* Rome; **por todas partes se va a** ~ all roads lead to Rome.

romance [ro'manθe] *nm* (*LING*) Romance language; (*LIT*) ballad; **hablar en** ~ to speak plainly.

románico, a [ro'maniko, a] *adj, nm* Romanesque.

romano, a [ro'mano, a] *adj* Roman, of Rome ♦ *nm/f* Roman.

romanticismo [romanti'θismo] *nm* romanticism.

romántico, a [ro'mantiko, a] *adj* romantic.

rombo ['rombo] *nm* (*GEOM*) rhombus; (*diseño*) diamond; (*TIP*) lozenge.

romería [rome'ria] *nf* (*REL*) pilgrimage; (*excursión*) trip, outing; *see boxed note.*

ROMERÍA

Originally a pilgrimage to a shrine or church to express devotion to the Virgin Mary or a local saint, the term **romería** *has been extended to describe the rural "fiesta" which accompanies the pilgrimage. People come from all over the country to spend the day in celebration, bringing copious amounts of food and drink with them.*

---

romero, a [ro'mero, a] *nm/f* pilgrim ♦ *nm* rosemary.

romo, a ['romo, a] *adj* blunt; (*fig*) dull.

rompecabezas [rompeka'βeθas] *nm inv* riddle, puzzle; (*juego*) jigsaw (puzzle).

rompehielos [rompe'jelos] *nm inv* icebreaker.

rompeolas [rompe'olas] *nm inv* breakwater.

romper [rom'per] *vt* to break; (*hacer pedazos*) to smash; (*papel, tela etc*) to tear, rip; (*relaciones*) to break off ♦ *vi* (*olas*) to break; (*sol, diente*) to break through; ~ **un contrato** to break a contract; ~ **a** to start (suddenly) to; ~ **a llorar** to burst into tears; ~ **con algn** to fall out with sb; **ha roto con su novio** she has broken up with her fiancé.

rompimiento [rompi'mjento] *nm* (*acto*) breaking; (*fig*) break; (*quiebra*) crack; ~ **de relaciones** breaking off of relations.

ron [ron] *nm* rum.

roncar [ron'kar] *vi* (*al dormir*) to snore; (*animal*) to roar.

roncha ['rontʃa] *nf* (*cardenal*) bruise; (*hinchazón*) swelling.

ronco, a ['ronko, a] *adj* (*afónico*) hoarse; (*áspero*) raucous.

ronda ['ronda] *nf* (*de bebidas etc*) round; (*patrulla*) patrol; (*de naipes*) hand, game; **ir de** ~ to do one's round.

rondar [ron'dar] *vt* to patrol; (*a una persona*) to hang round; (*molestar*) to harass; (*a una chica*) to court ♦ *vi* to patrol; (*fig*) to prowl round; (*MUS*) to go serenading.

rondeño, a [ron'deɲo, a] *adj* of o from Ronda ♦ *nm/f* native o inhabitant of Ronda.

ronque ['ronke] *etc vb V* **roncar**.

ronquido [ron'kiðo] *nm* snore, snoring.

ronronear [ronrone'ar] *vi* to purr.

ronroneo [ronro'neo] *nm* purr.

roña ['roɲa] *nf* (*veterinaria*) mange; (*mugre*) dirt, grime; (*óxido*) rust.

roñica [ro'ɲika] *nm/f* (*fam*) skinflint.

roñoso, a [ro'ɲoso, a] *adj* (*mugriento*) filthy; (*tacaño*) mean.

ropa ['ropa] *nf* clothes *pl*, clothing; ~ **blanca** linen; ~ **de cama** bed linen; ~ **interior** underwear; ~ **lavada** o **para lavar** washing; ~ **planchada** ironing; ~ **sucia** dirty clothes *pl*, washing; ~ **usada** secondhand clothes.

ropaje [ro'paxe] *nm* gown, robes *pl*.

ropero [ro'pero] *nm* linen cupboard; (*guardarropa*) wardrobe.

rosa ['rosa] *adj inv* pink ♦ *nf* rose; (*ANAT*)

red birthmark; ~ **de los vientos** the compass; **estar como una** ~ to feel as fresh as a daisy; **(color) de** ~ pink.

rosado, a [ro'saðo, a] *adj* pink ♦ *nm* rosé.

rosal [ro'sal] *nm* rosebush.

rosaleda [rosa'leða] *nf* rose bed *o* garden.

rosario [ro'sarjo] *nm* (REL) rosary; (*fig: serie*) string; **rezar el** ~ to say the rosary.

rosbif [ros'βif] *nm* roast beef.

rosca ['roska] *nf* (*de tornillo*) thread; (*de humo*) coil, spiral; (*pan, postre*) ring-shaped roll/pastry; **hacer la** ~ **a algn** (*fam*) to suck up to sb; **pasarse de** ~ (*fig*) to go too far.

Rosellón [rose'ʎon] *nm* Roussillon.

rosetón [rose'ton] *nm* rosette; (ARQ) rose window.

rosquilla [ros'kiʎa] *nf small ring-shaped cake*; (*de humo*) ring.

rosticería [rostise'ria] *nf* (AM) *roast chicken shop*.

rostro ['rostro] *nm* (*cara*) face; (*fig*) cheek.

rotación [rota'θjon] *nf* rotation; ~ **de cultivos** crop rotation.

rotativo, a [rota'tiβo, a] *adj* rotary ♦ *nm* newspaper.

roto, a ['roto, a] *pp de* **romper** ♦ *adj* broken; (*en pedazos*) smashed; (*tela, papel*) torn; (*vida*) shattered ♦ *nm* (*en vestido*) hole, tear.

rótula ['rotula] *nf* kneecap; (TEC) ball-and-socket joint.

rotulador [rotula'ðor] *nm* felt-tip pen.

rotular [rotu'lar] *vt* (*carta, documento*) to head, entitle; (*objeto*) to label.

rótulo ['rotulo] *nm* (*título*) heading, title; (*etiqueta*) label; (*letrero*) sign.

rotundo, a [ro'tundo, a] *adj* round; (*enfático*) emphatic.

rotura [ro'tura] *nf* (*rompimiento*) breaking; (MED) fracture.

roturar [rotu'rar] *vt* to plough.

roulote [ru'lote] *nf* caravan (BRIT), trailer (US).

rozado, a [ro'θaðo, a] *adj* worn.

rozadura [roθa'ðura] *nf* abrasion, graze.

rozar [ro'θar] *vt* (*frotar*) to rub; (*ensuciar*) to dirty; (MED) to graze; (*tocar ligeramente*) to shave, skim; (*fig*) to touch *o* border on; ~**se** *vr* to rub (together); ~ **con** (*fam*) to rub shoulders with.

Rte. *abr* = **remite, remitente.**

RTVE *nf abr* (TV) = *Radiotelevisión Española.*

Ruán [ru'an] *nm* Rouen.

rubéola [ru'βeola] *nf* German measles, rubella.

rubí [ru'βi] *nm* ruby; (*de reloj*) jewel.

rubio, a ['ruβjo, a] *adj* fair-haired, blond(e)

♦ *nm/f* blond/blonde; **tabaco** ~ Virginia tobacco; (*cerveza*) **rubia** lager.

rubor [ru'βor] *nm* (*sonrojo*) blush; (*timidez*) bashfulness.

ruborice [ruβo'riθe] *etc vb V* **ruborizarse.**

ruborizarse [ruβori'θarse] *vr* to blush.

ruboroso, a [ruβo'roso, a] *adj* blushing.

rúbrica ['ruβrika] *nf* (*título*) title, heading; (*de la firma*) flourish; **bajo la** ~ **de** under the heading of.

rubricar [ruβri'kar] *vt* (*firmar*) to sign with a flourish; (*concluir*) to sign and seal.

rubrique [ru'βrike] *etc vb V* **rubricar.**

rudeza [ru'ðeθa] *nf* (*tosquedad*) coarseness; (*sencillez*) simplicity.

rudimentario, a [ruðimen'tarjo, a] *adj* rudimentary, basic.

rudo, a ['ruðo, a] *adj* (*sin pulir*) unpolished; (*grosero*) coarse; (*violento*) violent; (*sencillo*) simple.

rueda ['rweða] *nf* wheel; (*círculo*) ring, circle; (*rodaja*) slice, round; (*en impresora etc*) sprocket; ~ **delantera/trasera/de repuesto** front/back/spare wheel; ~ **impresora** (INFORM) print wheel; ~ **de prensa** press conference.

ruedo ['rweðo] *etc vb V* **rodar** ♦ *nm* (*contorno*) edge, border; (*de vestido*) hem; (*círculo*) circle; (TAUR) arena, bullring; (*esterilla*) (round) mat.

ruego ['rweɣo] *etc vb V* **rogar** ♦ *nm* request; **a** ~ **de** at the request of; **"~s y preguntas"** "question and answer session".

ruegue ['rweɣe] *etc vb V* **rogar.**

rufián [ru'fjan] *nm* scoundrel.

rugby ['ruɣβi] *nm* rugby.

rugido [ru'xiðo] *nm* roar.

rugir [ru'xir] *vi* to roar; (*toro*) to bellow; (*estómago*) to rumble.

rugoso, a [ru'xoso, a] *adj* (*arrugado*) wrinkled; (*áspero*) rough; (*desigual*) ridged.

ruibarbo [rwi'βarβo] *nm* rhubarb.

ruido ['rwiðo] *nm* noise; (*sonido*) sound; (*alboroto*) racket, row; (*escándalo*) commotion, rumpus; ~ **de fondo** background noise; **hacer** *o* **meter** ~ to cause a stir.

ruidoso, a [rwi'ðoso, a] *adj* noisy, loud; (*fig*) sensational.

ruin [rwin] *adj* contemptible, mean.

ruina ['rwina] *nf* ruin; (*colapso*) collapse; (*de persona*) ruin, downfall; **estar hecho una** ~ to be a wreck; **la empresa le llevó a la** ~ the venture ruined him (financially).

ruindad [rwin'dað] *nf* lowness, meanness;

(*acto*) low *o* mean act.
ruinoso, a [rwi'noso, a] *adj* ruinous;
(*destartalado*) dilapidated, tumbledown;
(*COM*) disastrous.
ruiseñor [rwise'ɲor] *nm* nightingale.
ruja ['ruxa] *etc vb* V **rugir**.
ruleta [ru'leta] *nf* roulette.
rulo ['rulo] *nm* (*para el pelo*) curler.
rulot(e) [ru'lot(e)] *nf* caravan (*BRIT*), trailer
(*US*).
Rumanía [ru'manja] *nf* Rumania.
rumano, a [ru'mano, a] *adj, nm/f* Rumanian.
rumba ['rumba] *nf* rumba.
rumbo ['rumbo] *nm* (*ruta*) route, direction;
(*ángulo de dirección*) course, bearing;
(*fig*) course of events; **con ~ a** in the
direction of; **ir con ~ a** to be heading
for; (*NAUT*) to be bound for.
rumboso, a [rum'boso, a] *adj* (*generoso*)
generous.
rumiante [ru'mjante] *nm* ruminant.
rumiar [ru'mjar] *vt* to chew; (*fig*) to chew
over ♦ *vi* to chew the cud.
rumor [ru'mor] *nm* (*ruido sordo*) low sound;
(*murmuración*) murmur, buzz.
rumorearse [rumore'arse] *vr*: **se rumorea
que** it is rumoured that.
rumoroso, a [rumo'roso, a] *adj* full of
sounds; (*arroyo*) murmuring.
runrún [run'run] *nm* (*voces*) murmur,
sound of voices; (*fig*) rumour; (*de una
máquina*) whirr.
rupestre [ru'pestre] *adj* rock *cpd*; **pintura ~**
cave painting.
ruptura [rup'tura] *nf* (*gen*) rupture;
(*disputa*) split; (*de contrato*) breach; (*de
relaciones*) breaking-off.
rural [ru'ral] *adj* rural.
Rusia ['rusja] *nf* Russia.
ruso, a ['ruso, a] *adj, nm/f* Russian ♦ *nm*
(*LING*) Russian.
rústico, a ['rustiko, a] *adj* rustic; (*ordinario*)
coarse, uncouth ♦ *nm/f* yokel ♦ *nf*: **libro en
rústica** paperback (book).
ruta ['ruta] *nf* route.
rutina [ru'tina] *nf* routine; **~ diaria** daily
routine; **por ~** as a matter of course.
rutinario, a [ruti'narjo, a] *adj* routine.

S s

S, s ['ese] *nf* S, s; **S de Sábado** S for Sugar.
S *abr* (= *san, santo, a*) St.; (= *sur*) S.
s. *abr* (= *siglo*) c.; (= *siguiente*) foll.
s/ *abr* (*COM*) = **su(s)**.
S.ª *abr* (= *Sierra*) Mts.
S.A. *abr* (= *Sociedad Anónima*) Ltd., Inc.
(*US*); (= *Su Alteza*) H.H.
sáb. *abr* (= *sábado*) Sat.
sábado ['saβaðo] *nm* Saturday; (*de los
judíos*) Sabbath; **del ~ en ocho días** a
week on Saturday; **un ~ sí y otro no,
cada dos ~s** every other Saturday; **S~
Santo** Holy Saturday; V *tb* **Semana
Santa**.
sabana [sa'βana] *nf* savannah.
sábana ['saβana] *nf* sheet; **se le pegan las
~s** he can't get up in the morning.
sabandija [saβan'dixa] *nf* (*bicho*) bug; (*fig*)
louse.
sabañón [saβa'ɲon] *nm* chilblain.
sabático, a [sa'βatiko, a] *adj* (*REL, UNIV*)
sabbatical.
sabelotodo [saβelo'toðo] *nm/f inv* know-all.
saber [sa'βer] *vt* to know; (*llegar a conocer*)
to find out, learn; (*tener capacidad de*) to
know how to ♦ *vi*: **~ a** to taste of, taste
like ♦ *nm* knowledge, learning; **~se** *vr*: **se
sabe que ...** it is known that ...; **no se
sabe** nobody knows; **a ~** namely; **¿sabes
conducir/nadar?** can you drive/swim?;
¿sabes francés? do you *o* can you speak
French?; **~ de memoria** to know by
heart; **lo sé** I know; **hacer ~** to inform,
let know; **que yo sepa** as far as I know;
vete *o* anda a ~ your guess is as good as
mine, who knows!; **¿sabe?** (*fam*) you
know (what I mean)?; **le sabe mal que
otro la saque a bailar** it upsets him that
anybody else should ask her to dance.
sabido, a [sa'βiðo, a] *adj* (*consabido*) well-
known; **como es ~** as we all know.
sabiduría [saβiðu'ria] *nf* (*conocimientos*)
wisdom; (*instrucción*) learning; **~ popular**
folklore.
sabiendas [sa'βjendas]: **a ~** *adv*
knowingly; **a ~ de que ...** knowing full
well that ....
sabihondo, a [sa'βjondo, a] *adj, nm/f*

know-all, know-it-all (US).
sabio, a ['saβjo,a] adj (docto) learned;
(prudente) wise, sensible.
sablazo [sa'βlaθo] nm (herida) sword
wound; (fam) sponging; **dar un ~ a algn**
to tap sb for money.
sable [sa'βle] nm sabre.
sabor [sa'βor] nm taste, flavour; (fig)
flavour; **sin ~** flavourless.
saborear [saβore'ar] vt to taste, savour;
(fig) to relish.
sabotaje [saβo'taxe] nm sabotage.
saboteador, a [saβotea'ðor, a] nm/f
saboteur.
sabotear [saβote'ar] vt to sabotage.
Saboya [sa'βoja] nf Savoy.
sabré [sa'βre] etc vb V **saber.**
sabroso, a [sa'βroso, a] adj tasty, (fig fam)
racy, salty.
saca ['saka] nf big sack; **~ de correo(s)**
mailbag; (COM) withdrawal.
sacacorchos [saka'kortʃos] nm inv
corkscrew.
sacapuntas [saka'puntas] nm inv pencil
sharpener.
sacar [sa'kar] vt to take out; (fig: extraer) to
get (out); (quitar) to remove, get out;
(hacer salir) to bring out; (fondos: de
cuenta) to draw out, withdraw; (obtener:
legado etc) to get; (demostrar) to show;
(conclusión) to draw; (novela etc) to
publish, bring out; (ropa) to take off;
(obra) to make; (premio) to receive;
(entradas) to get; (TENIS) to serve;
(FÚTBOL) to put into play; **~ adelante**
(niño) to bring up; **~ a algn a bailar** to
dance with sb; **~ a algn de sí** to infuriate
sb; **~ una foto** to take a photo; **~ la
lengua** to stick out one's tongue; **~
buenas/malas notas** to get good/bad
marks.
sacarina [saka'rina] nf saccharin(e).
sacerdote [saθer'ðote] nm priest.
saciar [sa'θjar] vt (hartar) to satiate; (fig) to
satisfy; **~se** vr (fig) to be satisfied.
saciedad [saθje'ðað] nf satiety; **hasta la ~**
(comer) one's fill; (repetir) ad nauseam.
saco ['sako] nm bag; (grande) sack; (su
contenido) bagful; (AM: chaqueta) jacket;
~ de dormir sleeping bag.
sacramento [sakra'mento] nm sacrament.
sacrificar [sakrifi'kar] vt to sacrifice;
(animal) to slaughter; (perro etc) to put to
sleep; **~se** vr to sacrifice o.s.
sacrificio [sakri'fiθjo] nm sacrifice.
sacrifique [sakri'fike] etc vb V **sacrificar.**
sacrilegio [sakri'lexjo] nm sacrilege.
sacrílego, a [sa'krilexo, a] adj sacrilegious.

sacristán [sakris'tan] nm verger.
sacristía [sakris'tia] nf sacristy.
sacro, a ['sakro, a] adj sacred.
sacudida [saku'ðiða] nf (agitación) shake,
shaking; (sacudimiento) jolt, bump; (fig)
violent change; (POL etc) upheaval; **~
eléctrica** electric shock.
sacudir [saku'ðir] vt to shake; (golpear) to
hit; (ala) to flap; (alfombra) to beat; **~ a
algn** (fam) to belt sb.
sádico, a ['saðiko, a] adj sadistic ♦ nm/f
sadist.
sadismo [sa'ðismo] nm sadism.
sadomasoquismo [saðomaso'kismo] nm
sadomasochism, S & M.
sadomasoquista [saðomaso'kista] adj
sadomasochistic ♦ nm/f sadomasochist.
saeta [sa'eta] nf (flecha) arrow; (MUS)
sacred song in flamenco style.
safari [sa'fari] nm safari.
sagacidad [saɣaθi'ðað] nf shrewdness,
cleverness.
sagaz [sa'ɣaθ] adj shrewd, clever.
Sagitario [saxi'tarjo] nm (ASTRO)
Sagittarius.
sagrado, a [sa'ɣraðo, a] adj sacred, holy.
Sáhara ['saara] nm: **el ~** the Sahara
(desert).
saharaui [saxa'rawi] adj Saharan ♦ nm/f
native o inhabitant of the Sahara.
sajón, ona [sa'xon, 'xona] adj, nm/f Saxon.
Sajonia [sa'xonja] nf Saxony.
sal [sal] vb ver **salir** ♦ nf salt; (gracia) wit;
(encanto) charm; **~es de baño** bath salts;
~ gorda o **de cocina** kitchen o cooking
salt.
sala ['sala] nf (cuarto grande) large room;
(~ de estar) living room; (TEAT) house,
auditorium; (de hospital) ward; **~ de
apelación** court; **~ de conferencias**
lecture hall; **~ de espera** waiting room;
~ de embarque departure lounge; **~ de
estar** living room; **~ de fiestas** function
room; **~ de juntas** (COM) boardroom.
salado, a [sa'laðo, a] adj salty; (fig) witty,
amusing; **agua salada** salt water.
salar [sa'lar] vt to salt, add salt to.
salarial [sala'rjal] adj (aumento, revisión)
wage cpd, salary cpd, pay cpd.
salario [sa'larjo] nm wage, pay.
salchicha [sal'tʃitʃa] nf (pork) sausage.
salchichón [saltʃi'tʃon] nm (salami-type)
sausage.
saldar [sal'dar] vt to pay; (vender) to sell
off; (fig) to settle, resolve.
saldo ['saldo] nm (pago) settlement; (de
una cuenta) balance; (lo restante)
remnant(s) (pl), remainder; (liquidación)

sale; (*COM*): ~ **anterior** balance brought forward; ~ **acreedor/deudor** *o* **pasivo** credit/debit balance; ~ **final** final balance.

saldré [sal'dre] *etc vb V* **salir**.

salero [sa'lero] *nm* salt cellar; (*ingenio*) wit; (*encanto*) charm.

salga ['salɤa] *etc vb V* **salir**.

salida [sa'liða] *nf* (*puerta etc*) exit, way out; (*acto*) leaving, going out; (*de tren, AVIAT*) departure; (*COM, TEC*) output, production; (*fig*) way out; (*resultado*) outcome; (*COM: oportunidad*) opening; (*GEO, válvula*) outlet; (*de gas*) escape; (*ocurrencia*) joke; **calle sin** ~ cul-de-sac; **a la** ~ **del teatro** after the theatre; **dar la** ~ (*DEPORTE*) to give the starting signal; ~ **de incendios** fire escape; ~ **impresa** (*INFORM*) hard copy; **no hay** ~ there's no way out of it; **no tenemos otra** ~ we have no option; **tener** ~**s** to be witty.

salido, a [sa'liðo, a] *adj* (*fam*) randy.

saliente [sa'ljente] *adj* (*ARQ*) projecting; (*sol*) rising; (*fig*) outstanding.

salina [sa'lina] *nf* salt mine; ~**s** *nfpl* saltworks *sg*.

==================== *PALABRA CLAVE*

salir [sa'lir] *vi* **1** (*persona*) to come *o* go out; (*tren, avión*) to leave; **Juan ha salido** Juan has gone out; **salió de la cocina** he came out of the kitchen; **salimos de Madrid a las 8** we left Madrid at 8 (o'clock); **salió corriendo (del cuarto)** he ran out (of the room); ~ **de un apuro** to get out of a jam

2 (*pelo*) to grow; (*diente*) to come through; (*disco, libro*) to come out; (*planta, número de lotería*) to come up; ~ **a la superficie** to come to the surface; **anoche salió en la tele** she appeared *o* was on TV last night; **salió en todos los periódicos** it was in all the papers; **le salió un trabajo** he got a job

3 (*resultar*): **la muchacha nos salió muy trabajadora** the girl turned out to be a very hard worker; **la comida te ha salido exquisita** the food was delicious; **sale muy caro** it's very expensive; **la entrevista que hice me salió bien/mal** the interview I did turned out *o* went well/badly; **nos salió a 5.000 ptas cada uno** it worked out at 5,000 pesetas each; **no salen las cuentas** it doesn't work out *o* add up; ~ **ganando** to come out on top; ~ **perdiendo** to lose out

4 (*DEPORTE*) to start; (*NAIPES*) to lead

5: ~ **con algn** to go out with sb

6: ~ **adelante: no sé como haré para** ~

adelante I don't know how I'll get by

♦ ~**se** *vr* **1** (*líquido*) to spill; (*animal*) to escape

2 (*desviarse*): ~**se de la carretera** to leave *o* go off the road; ~**se de lo normal** to be unusual; ~**se del tema** to get off the point

3: ~**se con la suya** to get one's own way

saliva [sa'lißa] *nf* saliva.

salivadera [salißa'ðera] *nf* (*AM*) spittoon.

salmantino, a [salman'tino, a] *adj* of *o* from Salamanca ♦ *nm/f* native *o* inhabitant of Salamanca.

salmo ['salmo] *nm* psalm.

salmón [sal'mon] *nm* salmon.

salmonete [salmo'nete] *nm* red mullet.

salmuera [sal'mwera] *nf* pickle, brine.

salón [sa'lon] *nm* (*de casa*) living-room, lounge; (*muebles*) lounge suite; ~ **de belleza** beauty parlour; ~ **de baile** dance hall; ~ **de sesiones** assembly hall.

salpicadero [salpika'ðero] *nm* (*AUTO*) dashboard.

salpicar [salpi'kar] *vt* (*de barro, pintura*) to splash; (*rociar*) to sprinkle, spatter; (*esparcir*) to scatter.

salpicón [salpi'kon] *nm* (*acto*) splashing; (*CULIN*) meat *o* fish salad.

salpimentar [salpimen'tar] *vt* (*CULIN*) to season.

salpique [sal'pike] *etc vb V* **salpicar**.

salsa ['salsa] *nf* sauce; (*con carne asada*) gravy; (*fig*) spice; ~ **mayonesa** mayonnaise; **estar en su** ~ (*fam*) to be in one's element.

saltamontes [salta'montes] *nm inv* grasshopper.

saltar [sal'tar] *vt* to jump (over), leap (over); (*dejar de lado*) to skip, miss out ♦ *vi* to jump, leap; (*pelota*) to bounce; (*al aire*) to fly up; (*quebrarse*) to break; (*al agua*) to dive; (*fig*) to explode, blow up; (*botón*) to come off; (*corcho*) to pop out; ~**se** *vr* (*omitir*) to skip, miss; **salta a la vista** it's obvious; ~**se todas las reglas** to break all the rules.

salteado, a [salte'aðo, a] *adj* (*CULIN*) sauté(ed).

salteador [saltea'ðor] *nm* (*tb*: ~ **de caminos**) highwayman.

saltear [salte'ar] *vt* (*robar*) to rob (in a holdup); (*asaltar*) to assault, attack; (*CULIN*) to sauté.

saltimbanqui [saltim'banki] *nm/f* acrobat.

salto ['salto] *nm* jump, leap; (*al agua*) dive; **a** ~**s** by jumping; ~ **de agua** waterfall; ~ **de altura** high jump; ~ **de cama**

negligee; ~ **mortal** somersault; (*INFORM*):
~ **de línea** line feed; ~ **de línea automático**
wordwrap; ~ **de página** formfeed.
saltón, ona [sal'ton, ona] *adj* (*ojos*)
bulging, popping; (*dientes*) protruding.
salubre [sa'lußre] *adj* healthy, salubrious.
salud [sa'luð] *nf* health; **estar bien/mal de**
~ to be in good/poor health; ¡(a su) ~!
cheers!, good health!; **beber a la ~ de** to
drink (to) the health of.
saludable [salu'ðaßle] *adj* (*de buena salud*)
healthy; (*provechoso*) good, beneficial.
saludar [salu'ðar] *vt* to greet; (*MIL*) to
salute; **ir a ~ a algn** to drop in to see sb;
salude de mi parte a X give my regards
to X; **le saluda atentamente** (*en carta*)
yours faithfully.
saludo [sa'luðo] *nm* greeting; ~**s** (*en carta*)
best wishes, regards; **un ~ afectuoso** *o*
cordial yours sincerely.
salva ['salßa] *nf* (*MIL*) salvo; **una ~ de**
aplausos thunderous applause.
salvación [salßa'θjon] *nf* salvation;
(*rescate*) rescue.
salvado [sal'ßaðo] *nm* bran.
salvador [salßa'ðor] *nm* rescuer, saviour;
el S~ the Saviour; **El S~** El Salvador;
San S~ San Salvador.
salvadoreño, a [salßaðo'reɲo, a] *adj*, *nm/f*
Salvadoran, Salvadorian.
salvaguardar [salßaɣwar'ðar] *vt* to
safeguard; (*INFORM*) to back up, make a
backup copy of.
salvajada [salßa'xaða] *nf* savage deed,
atrocity.
salvaje [sal'ßaxe] *adj* wild; (*tribu*) savage.
salvajismo [salßa'xismo] *nm* savagery.
salvamento [salßa'mento] *nm* (*acción*)
rescue; (*de naufragio*) salvage; ~ **y**
socorrismo life-saving.
salvapantallas [salßapan'taʎas] *nm inv*
screen saver.
salvar [sal'ßar] *vt* (*rescatar*) to save, rescue;
(*resolver*) to overcome, resolve; (*cubrir*
distancias) to cover, travel; (*hacer excep-*
ción) to except, exclude; (*un barco*) to salvage; ~**se** *vr* to save o.s., escape; **¡sálvese**
el que pueda! every man for himself!
salvavidas [salßa'ßiðas] *adj inv*: **bote/**
chaleco/cinturón ~ lifeboat/lifejacket/
lifebelt.
salvedad [salße'ðað] *nf* reservation,
qualification; **con la ~ de que** ... with the
proviso that ....
salvia ['salßja] *nf* sage.
salvo, a ['salßo, a] *adj* safe ♦ *prep* except
(for), save; ~ **error u omisión** (*COM*)
errors and omissions excepted; **a ~ out**

of danger; ~ **que** unless.
salvoconducto [salßokon'dukto] *nm* safe-
conduct.
samba ['samba] *nf* samba.
san [san] *nm* (*apócope de* **santo**) saint; ~
Juan St. John; *V tb* **Juan**.
sanar [sa'nar] *vt* (*herida*) to heal; (*persona*)
to cure ♦ *vi* (*persona*) to get well,
recover; (*herida*) to heal.
sanatorio [sana'torjo] *nm* sanatorium.
sanción [san'θjon] *nf* sanction.
sancionar [sanθjo'nar] *vt* to sanction.
sancocho [san'kotʃo] *nm* (*AM*) stew.
sandalia [san'dalja] *nf* sandal.
sándalo ['sandalo] *nm* sandal(wood).
sandez [san'deθ] *nf* (*cualidad*) foolishness;
(*acción*) stupid thing; **decir sandeces** to
talk nonsense.
sandía [san'dia] *nf* watermelon.
sandinista [sanði'nista] *adj*, *nm/f*
Sandinist(a).
sandwich ['sandwitʃ], *pl* **sandwichs** *o*
sandwiches *nm* sandwich.
saneamiento [sanea'mjento] *nm* sanitation.
sanear [sane'ar] *vt* to drain; (*indemnizar*) to
compensate; (*ECON*) to reorganize.
sanfermines [sanfer'mines] *nmpl see boxed*
note.

sangrar [san'grar] *vt*, *vi* to bleed; (*texto*) to
indent.
sangre ['sangre] *nf* blood; ~ **fría** sangfroid;
a ~ fría in cold blood.
sangría [san'gria] *nf* (*MED*) bleeding;
(*CULIN*) sangria, *sweetened drink of red*
wine with fruit, ≈ *fruit cup*.
sangriento, a [san'grjento, a] *adj* bloody.
sanguijuela [sangi'xwela] *nf* (*ZOOL*, *fig*)
leech.
sanguinario, a [sangi'narjo, a] *adj*
bloodthirsty.
sanguíneo, a [san'gineo, a] *adj* blood *cpd*.

sanidad [saniˈðað] *nf* sanitation; (*calidad de sano*) health, healthiness; ~ **pública** public health (department).

sanitario, a [saniˈtarjo, a] *adj* sanitary; (*de la salud*) health *cpd* ♦ *nm*: ~**s** *nmpl* toilets (*BRIT*), restroom *sg* (*US*).

San Marino [sanmaˈrino] *nm*: **(La República de)** ~ San Marino.

sano, a [ˈsano, a] *adj* healthy; (*sin daños*) sound; (*comida*) wholesome; (*entero*) whole, intact; ~ **y salvo** safe and sound.

santanderino, a [santandeˈrino, a] *adj* of o from Santander ♦ *nm/f* native o inhabitant of Santander.

Santiago [sanˈtjaɣo] *nm*: ~ **(de Chile)** Santiago.

santiamén [santjaˈmen] *nm*: **en un** ~ in no time at all.

santidad [santiˈðað] *nf* holiness, sanctity.

santificar [santifiˈkar] *vt* to sanctify.

santifique [santiˈfike] *etc vb V* **santificar**.

santiguarse [santiˈɣwarse] *vr* to make the sign of the cross.

santigüe [santiˈɣwe] *etc vb V* **santiguarse**.

santo, a [ˈsanto, a] *adj* holy; (*fig*) wonderful, miraculous ♦ *nm/f* saint ♦ *nm* saint's day; **hacer su santa voluntad** to do as one jolly well pleases; **¿a** ~ **de qué ...?** why on earth ...?; **se le fue el** ~ **al cielo** he forgot what he was about to say; ~ **y seña** password; *see boxed note*.

SANTO

As well as having a birthday, Spaniards have traditionally celebrated el santo, *their saint's day, when the saint they were called after — San Pedro or la Virgen de los Dolores, for example — is honoured in the Christian calendar. The custom is gradually dying out.*

---

santuario [sanˈtwarjo] *nm* sanctuary, shrine.

saña [ˈsaɲa] *nf* rage, fury.

sapo [ˈsapo] *nm* toad.

saque [ˈsake] *etc vb V* **sacar** ♦ *nm* (*TENIS*) service, serve; (*FÚTBOL*) throw-in; ~ **inicial** kick-off; ~ **de esquina** corner (kick); **tener buen** ~ to eat heartily.

saquear [sakeˈar] *vt* (*MIL*) to sack; (*robar*) to loot, plunder; (*fig*) to ransack.

saqueo [saˈkeo] *nm* sacking; looting, plundering; ransacking.

S.A.R. *abr* (= *Su Alteza Real*) HRH.

sarampión [saramˈpjon] *nm* measles *sg*.

sarape [saˈrape] *nm* (*AM*) blanket.

sarcasmo [sarˈkasmo] *nm* sarcasm.

sarcástico, a [sarˈkastiko, a] *adj* sarcastic.

sarcófago [sarˈkofaɣo] *nm* sarcophagus.

sardina [sarˈðina] *nf* sardine.

sardo, a [ˈsarðo, a] *adj*, *nm/f* Sardinian.

sardónico, a [sarˈðoniko, a] *adj* sardonic; (*irónico*) ironical, sarcastic.

sargento [sarˈxento] *nm* sergeant.

sarmiento [sarˈmjento] *nm* vine shoot.

sarna [ˈsarna] *nf* itch; (*MED*) scabies.

sarpullido [sarpuˈʎiðo] *nm* (*MED*) rash.

sarro [ˈsarro] *nm* deposit; (*en dientes*) tartar.

sarta [ˈsarta] *nf* (*fig*): **una** ~ **de mentiras** a pack of lies.

sartén [sarˈten] *nf* frying pan; **tener la** ~ **por el mango** to rule the roost.

sastre [ˈsastre] *nm* tailor.

sastrería [sastreˈria] *nf* (*arte*) tailoring; (*tienda*) tailor's (shop).

Satanás [sataˈnas] *nm* Satan.

satélite [saˈtelite] *nm* satellite.

satinado, a [satiˈnaðo, a] *adj* glossy ♦ *nm* gloss, shine.

sátira [ˈsatira] *nf* satire.

satírico, a [saˈtiriko, a] *adj* satiric(al).

sátiro [ˈsatiro] *nm* (*MITOLOGÍA*) satyr; (*fig*) sex maniac.

satisfacción [satisfakˈθjon] *nf* satisfaction.

satisfacer [satisfaˈθer] *vt* to satisfy; (*gastos*) to meet; (*deuda*) to pay; (*COM*: *letra de cambio*) to honour (*BRIT*), honor (*US*); (*pérdida*) to make good; ~**se** *vr* to satisfy o.s., be satisfied; (*vengarse*) to take revenge.

satisfaga [satisˈfaɣa] *etc*, **satisfaré** [satisfaˈre] *etc vb V* **satisfacer**.

satisfecho, a [satisˈfetʃo, a] *pp de* **satisfacer** ♦ *adj* satisfied; (*contento*) content(ed), happy; (*tb*: ~ **de sí mismo**) self-satisfied, smug.

satisfice [satisˈfiθe] *etc vb V* **satisfacer**.

saturación [saturaˈθjon] *nf* saturation; **llegar a la** ~ to reach saturation point.

saturar [satuˈrar] *vt* to saturate; ~**se** *vr* (*mercado, aeropuerto*) to reach saturation point; **¡estoy saturado de tanta televisión!** I can't take any more television!

sauce [ˈsauθe] *nm* willow; ~ **llorón** weeping willow.

saúco [saˈuko] *nm* (*BOT*) elder.

saudí [sauˈði] *adj*, *nm/f* Saudi.

sauna [ˈsauna] *nf* sauna.

savia [ˈsaβja] *nf* sap.

saxo [ˈsakso] *nm* sax.

saxofón [saksoˈfon] *nm* saxophone.

saya [ˈsaja] *nf* (*falda*) skirt; (*enagua*) petticoat.

sayo [ˈsajo] *nm* smock.

sazón [sa'θon] *nf* (*de fruta*) ripeness; **a la ~** then, at that time.

sazonado, a [saθo'naðo, a] *adj* (*fruta*) ripe; (*CULIN*) flavoured, seasoned.

sazonar [saθo'nar] *vt* to ripen; (*CULIN*) to flavour, season.

s/c *abr* (*COM*: = *su casa*) your firm; (: = *su cuenta*) your account.

Sdo. *abr* (*COM*: = *Saldo*) bal.

SE *abr* (= *sudeste*) SE.

════════════ *PALABRA CLAVE*

se [se] *pron* **1** (*reflexivo: sg: m*) himself; (: *f*) herself; (: *pl*) themselves; (: *cosa*) itself; (: *de Vd*) yourself; (: *de Vds*) yourselves; (*indefinido*) oneself; **~ mira en el espejo** he looks at himself in the mirror; **¡siénte~!** sit down!; **~ durmió** he fell asleep; **~ está preparando** she's getting (herself) ready; *para usos léxicos del pron ver el vb en cuestión, p.ej.* **arrepentirse**

2 (*como complemento indirecto*) to him; to her; to them; to it; to you; **~ lo dije ayer** (*a Vd*) I told you yesterday; **~ compró un sombrero** he bought himself a hat; **~ rompió la pierna** he broke his leg; **cortar~ el pelo** to get one's hair cut; (*uno mismo*) to cut one's hair; **~ comió un pastel** he ate a cake

3 (*uso recíproco*) each other, one another; **~ miraron (el uno al otro)** they looked at each other *o* one another

4 (*en oraciones pasivas*): **se han vendido muchos libros** a lot of books have been sold; **"~ vende coche"** "car for sale"

5 (*impers*): **~ dice que** people say that, it is said that; **allí ~ come muy bien** the food there is very good, you can eat very well there.

sé [se] *vb V* **saber, ser**.

sea ['sea] *etc vb V* **ser**.

SEAT ['seat] *nf abr* = *Sociedad Española de Automóviles de Turismo*.

sebo ['seβo] *nm* fat, grease.

Sec. *abr* (= *Secretario*) Sec.

seca ['seka] *nf V* **seco**.

secado [se'kaðo] *nm* drying; **~ a mano** blow-dry.

secador [seka'ðor] *nm*: **~ para el pelo** hairdryer.

secadora [seka'ðora] *nf* tumble dryer; **~ centrífuga** spin-dryer.

secano [se'kano] *nm* (*AGR: tb: tierra de ~*) dry land *o* region; **cultivo de ~** dry farming.

secante [se'kante] *adj* (*viento*) drying ♦ *nm* blotting paper.

secar [se'kar] *vt* to dry; (*superficie*) to wipe dry; (*frente, suelo*) to mop; (*líquido*) to mop up; (*tinta*) to blot; **~se** *vr* to dry (off); (*río, planta*) to dry up.

sección [sek'θjon] *nf* section; (*COM*) department; **~ deportiva** (*en periódico*) sports page(s).

seco, a ['seko, a] *adj* dry; (*fruta*) dried; (*persona: magro*) thin, skinny; (*carácter*) cold; (*antipático*) disagreeable; (*respuesta*) sharp, curt ♦ *nf* dry season; **habrá pan a secas** there will be just bread; **decir algo a secas** to say sth curtly; **parar en ~** to stop dead.

secreción [sekre'θjon] *nf* secretion.

secretaría [sekreta'ria] *nf* secretariat; (*oficina*) secretary's office.

secretariado [sekreta'rjaðo] *nm* (*oficina*) secretariat; (*cargo*) secretaryship; (*curso*) secretarial course.

secretario, a [sekre'tarjo, a] *nm/f* secretary; **~ adjunto** (*COM*) assistant secretary.

secreto, a [se'kreto, a] *adj* secret; (*información*) confidential; (*persona*) secretive ♦ *nm* secret; (*calidad*) secrecy.

secta ['sekta] *nf* sect.

sectario, a [sek'tarjo, a] *adj* sectarian.

sector [sek'tor] *nm* sector (*tb INFORM*); (*de opinión*) section; (*fig: campo*) area, field; **~ privado/público** (*COM, ECON*) private/public sector.

secuela [se'kwela] *nf* consequence.

secuencia [se'kwenθja] *nf* sequence.

secuestrar [sekwes'trar] *vt* to kidnap; (*avión*) to hijack; (*bienes*) to seize, confiscate.

secuestro [se'kwestro] *nm* kidnapping; hijack; seizure, confiscation.

secular [seku'lar] *adj* secular.

secundar [sekun'dar] *vt* to second, support.

secundario, a [sekun'darjo, a] *adj* secondary; (*carretera*) side *cpd*; (*INFORM*) background *cpd* ♦ *nf* secondary education; *V tb* **sistema educativo**.

sed [seð] *nf* thirst; (*fig*) thirst, craving; **tener ~** to be thirsty.

seda ['seða] *nf* silk; **~ dental** dental floss.

sedal [se'ðal] *nm* fishing line.

sedante [se'ðante] *nm* sedative.

sede ['seðe] *nf* (*de gobierno*) seat; (*de compañía*) headquarters *pl*, head office; **Santa S~** Holy See.

sedentario, a [seðen'tarjo, a] *adj* sedentary.

SEDIC [se'ðik] *nf abr* = *Sociedad Española de*

Documentación e Información Científica.

sedición [seði'θjon] *nf* sedition.

sediento, a [se'ðjento, a] *adj* thirsty.

sedimentar [seðimen'tar] *vt* to deposit; ~**se** *vr* to settle.

sedimento [seði'mento] *nm* sediment.

sedoso, a [se'ðoso, a] *adj* silky, silken.

seducción [seðuk'θjon] *nf* seduction.

seducir [seðu'θir] *vt* to seduce; (*sobornar*) to bribe; (*cautivar*) to charm, fascinate; (*atraer*) to attract.

seductor, a [seðuk'tor, a] *adj* seductive; charming, fascinating; attractive; (*engañoso*) deceptive, misleading ♦ *nm/f* seducer.

seduje [se'ðuxe] *etc*, **seduzca** [se'ðuθka] *etc vb V* **seducir**.

sefardí [sefar'ði], **sefardita** [sefar'ðita] *adj* Sephardi(c) ♦ *nm/f* Sephardi.

segador, a [seɣa'ðor, a] *nm/f* (*persona*) harvester ♦ *nf* (*TEC*) mower, reaper.

segadora-trilladora [seɣa'ðoratriʎa'ðora] *nf* combine harvester.

segar [se'ɣar] *vt* (*mies*) to reap, cut; (*hierba*) to mow, cut; (*esperanzas*) to ruin.

seglar [se'ɣlar] *adj* secular, lay.

segoviano, a [seɣo'βjano, a] *adj* of *o* from Segovia ♦ *nm/f* native *o* inhabitant of Segovia.

segregación [seɣreɣa'θjon] *nf* segregation; ~ **racial** racial segregation.

segregar [seɣre'ɣar] *vt* to segregate, separate.

segregue [se'ɣreɣe] *etc vb V* **segregar**.

segué [se'ɣe], **seguemos** [se'ɣemos] *etc vb V* **segar**.

seguidamente [seɣiða'mente] *adv* (*sin parar*) without a break; (*inmediatamente después*) immediately after.

seguido, a [se'ɣiðo, a] *adj* (*continuo*) continuous, unbroken; (*recto*) straight ♦ *adv* (*directo*) straight (on); (*después*) after; (*AM: a menudo*) often ♦ *nf*: **en seguida** at once, right away; **5 días ~s** 5 days running, 5 days in a row; **en seguida termino** I've nearly finished, I shan't be long now.

seguimiento [seɣi'mjento] *nm* chase, pursuit; (*continuación*) continuation.

seguir [se'ɣir] *vt* to follow; (*venir después*) to follow on, come after; (*proseguir*) to continue; (*perseguir*) to chase, pursue; (*indicio*) to follow up; (*mujer*) to court ♦ *vi* (*gen*) to follow; (*continuar*) to continue, carry *o* go on; ~**se** *vr* to follow; **a ~** to be continued; **sigo sin comprender** I still don't understand; **sigue lloviendo** it's still raining; **sigue** (*en carta*) P.T.O.; (*en libro, TV*) continued; "**hágase** ~" "please forward"; **¡siga!** (*AM: pase*) come in!

según [se'ɣun] *prep* according to ♦ *adv*: ~ (**y conforme**) it all depends ♦ *conj* as; ~ **esté el tiempo** depending on the weather; ~ **me consta** as far as I know; **está** ~ **lo dejaste** it is just as you left it.

segundo, a [se'ɣundo, a] *adj* second; (*en discurso*) secondly ♦ *nm* (*gen, medida de tiempo*) second; (*piso*) second floor ♦ *nf* (*sentido*) second meaning; ~ (**de a bordo**) (*NAUT*) first mate; **segunda (clase)** (*FERRO*) second class; **segunda (marcha)** (*AUTO*) second (gear); **de segunda mano** second hand.

seguramente [seɣura'mente] *adv* surely; (*con certeza*) for sure, with certainty; (*probablemente*) probably; **¿lo va a comprar? — ~** is he going to buy it? — I should think so.

seguridad [seɣuri'ðað] *nf* safety; (*del estado, de casa etc*) security; (*certidumbre*) certainty; (*confianza*) confidence; (*estabilidad*) stability; ~ **social** social security; ~ **incendios** fire precautions *pl*; ~ **en sí mismo** (self-) confidence.

seguro, a [se'ɣuro, a] *adj* (*cierto*) sure, certain; (*fiel*) trustworthy; (*libre de peligro*) safe; (*bien defendido, firme*) secure; (*datos etc*) reliable; (*fecha*) firm ♦ *adv* for sure, certainly ♦ *nm* (*dispositivo*) safety device; (*de cerradura*) tumbler; (*de arma*) safety catch; (*COM*) insurance; ~ **contra accidentes/incendios** fire/accident insurance; ~ **contra terceros/a todo riesgo** third party/comprehensive insurance; ~ **dotal con beneficios** with-profits endowment assurance; **S~ de Enfermedad** ≈ National Insurance; ~ **marítimo** marine insurance; ~ **mixto** endowment assurance; ~ **temporal** term insurance; ~ **de vida** life insurance.

seis [seis] *num* six; ~ **mil** six thousand; **tiene** ~ **años** she is six (years old); **unos** ~ about six; **hoy es el** ~ today is the sixth.

seiscientos, as [seis'θjentos, as] *num* six hundred.

seísmo [se'ismo] *nm* tremor, earthquake.

selección [selek'θjon] *nf* selection; ~ **múltiple** multiple choice; ~ **nacional** (*DEPORTE*) national team.

seleccionador, a [selekθjona'ðor, a] *nm/f* (*DEPORTE*) selector.

seleccionar [selekθjo'nar] *vt* to pick, choose, select.

selectividad [selektißi'ðað] *nf* (*UNIV*) entrance examination; *see boxed note*.

SELECTIVIDAD

School-leavers wishing to go on to university sit the dreaded entrance examination, the **selectividad**, *in June, with resits in September. When student numbers are too high for a particular course, only the best candidates get through. The others must wait a year to sit the examination again.*

---

selecto, a [se'lekto, a] *adj* select, choice; (*escogido*) selected.

sellado, a [se'ʎaðo, a] *adj* (*documento oficial*) sealed; (*pasaporte*) stamped.

sellar [se'ʎar] *vt* (*documento oficial*) to seal; (*pasaporte, visado*) to stamp; (*marcar*) to brand; (*pacto, labios*) to seal.

sello [se'ʎo] *nm* stamp; (*precinto*) seal; (*fig: tb:* ~ **distintivo**) hallmark; ~ **fiscal** revenue stamp; ~**s de prima** (*COM*) trading stamps.

selva ['selßa] *nf* (*bosque*) forest, woods *pl*; (*jungla*) jungle; **la S**~ **Negra** the Black Forest.

semáforo [se'maforo] *nm* (*AUTO*) traffic lights *pl*; (*FERRO*) signal.

semana [se'mana] *nf* week; ~ **inglesa** 5-day (working) week; ~ **laboral** working week; **S**~ **Santa** Holy Week; **entre** ~ during the week; *see boxed note*.

SEMANA

Semana Santa *is an important national holiday in Spain. The whole country takes "Viernes Santo" (Good Friday) "Sábado Santo", (Holy Saturday), and "Domingo de Resurrección" (Easter Sunday) off, while other days around this time of year vary according to region. There are spectacular processions all over the country, with members of "cofradías" (brotherhoods) dressing in hooded robes and parading their "pasos" (religious floats or sculptures) through the streets. Holy Week in Seville is very famous, on account of the religious fervour shown by the locals.*

---

semanal [sema'nal] *adj* weekly.

semanario [sema'narjo] *nm* weekly (magazine).

semántica [se'mantika] *nf* semantics *sg*.

semblante [sem'blante] *nm* face; (*fig*) look.

sembrar [sem'brar] *vt* to sow; (*objetos*) to sprinkle, scatter about; (*noticias etc*) to spread.

semejante [seme'xante] *adj* (*parecido*) similar; (*tal*) such; ~**s** alike, similar ♦ *nm* fellow man, fellow creature; **son muy** ~**s** they are very much alike; **nunca hizo cosa** ~ he never did such a thing.

semejanza [seme'xanθa] *nf* similarity, resemblance; **a** ~ **de** like, as.

semejar [seme'xar] *vi* to seem like, resemble; ~**se** *vr* to look alike, be similar.

semen ['semen] *nm* semen.

semental [semen'tal] *nm* (*macho*) stud.

sementera [semen'tera] *nf* (*acto*) sowing; (*temporada*) seedtime; (*tierra*) sown land.

semestral [semes'tral] *adj* half-yearly, bi-annual.

semestre [se'mestre] *nm* period of six months; (*US UNIV*) semester; (*COM*) half-yearly payment.

semicírculo [semi'θirkulo] *nm* semicircle.

semiconductor [semikonduk'tor] *nm* semiconductor.

semiconsciente [semikons'θjente] *adj* semiconscious.

semidesnatado, a [semiðesna'taðo, a] *adj* semi-skimmed.

semifinal [semifi'nal] *nf* semifinal.

semiinconsciente [semi(i)nkons'θjente] *adj* semiconscious.

semilla [se'miʎa] *nf* seed.

semillero [semi'ʎero] *nm* (*AGR etc*) seedbed; (*fig*) hotbed.

seminario [semi'narjo] *nm* (*REL*) seminary; (*ESCOL*) seminar.

semiseco [semi'seko] *nm* medium-dry.

semita [se'mita] *adj* Semitic ♦ *nm/f* Semite.

sémola ['semola] *nf* semolina.

sempiterno, a [sempi'terno, a] *adj* everlasting.

Sena ['sena] *nm*: **el** ~ the (river) Seine.

senado [se'naðo] *nm* senate; *V tb* **Las Cortes (españolas)**.

senador, a [sena'ðor, a] *nm/f* senator.

sencillez [senθi'ʎeθ] *nf* simplicity; (*de persona*) naturalness.

sencillo, a [sen'θiʎo, a] *adj* simple; (*carácter*) natural, unaffected; (*billete*) single ♦ *nm* (*disco*) single; (*AM*) small change.

senda ['senda] *nf*, **sendero** [sen'dero] *nm* path, track; **Sendero Luminoso** the Shining Path (guerrilla movement).

senderismo [sende'rismo] *nm* trekking.

sendos, as ['sendos, as] *adj pl*: **les dio** ~ **golpes** he hit both of them.

senil [se'nil] *adj* senile.

seno ['seno] *nm* (*ANAT*) bosom, bust; (*fig*)

bosom; ~s *nmpl* breasts; ~ **materno** womb.

sensación [sensa'θjon] *nf* sensation; (*sentido*) sense; (*sentimiento*) feeling; **causar** *o* **hacer** ~ to cause a sensation.

sensacional [sensaθjo'nal] *adj* sensational.

sensatez [sensa'teθ] *nf* common sense.

sensato, a [sen'sato, a] *adj* sensible.

sensibilidad [sensiβili'ðað] *nf* sensitivity; (*para el arte*) feel.

sensibilizar [sensiβili'θar] *vt:* ~ **a la población/opinión pública** to raise public awareness.

sensible [sen'sible] *adj* sensitive; (*apreciable*) perceptible, appreciable; (*pérdida*) considerable.

sensiblero, a [sensi'βlero, a] *adj* sentimental, slushy.

sensitivo, a [sensi'tiβo, a], **sensorial** [senso'rjal] *adj* sense *cpd.*

sensor [sen'sor] *nm:* ~ **de fin de papel** paper out sensor.

sensual [sen'swal] *adj* sensual.

sentado, a [sen'taðo, a] *adj* (*establecido*) settled; (*carácter*) sensible ♦ *nf* sitting; (*POL*) sit-in, sit-down protest; **dar por** ~ to take for granted, assume; **dejar algo** ~ to establish sth firmly; **estar** ~ to sit, be sitting (down); **de una sentada** at one sitting.

sentar [sen'tar] *vt* to sit, seat; (*fig*) to establish ♦ *vi* (*vestido*) to suit; (*alimento*): ~ **bien/mal a** to agree/disagree with; ~**se** *vr* (*persona*) to sit, sit down; (*el tiempo*) to settle (down); (*los depósitos*) to settle; **¡siéntese!** (do) sit down, take a seat.

sentencia [sen'tenθja] *nf* (*máxima*) maxim, saying; (*JUR*) sentence; (*INFORM*) statement; ~ **de muerte** death sentence.

sentenciar [senten'θjar] *vt* to sentence.

sentido, a [sen'tiðo, a] *adj* (*pérdida*) regrettable; (*carácter*) sensitive ♦ *nm* sense; (*sentimiento*) feeling; (*significado*) sense, meaning; (*dirección*) direction; **mi más** ~ **pésame** my deepest sympathy; ~ **del humor** sense of humour; ~ **común** common sense; **en el buen** ~ **de la palabra** in the best sense of the word; **sin** ~ meaningless; **tener** ~ to make sense; ~ **único** one-way (street).

sentimental [sentimen'tal] *adj* sentimental; **vida** ~ love life.

sentimiento [senti'mjento] *nm* (*emoción*) feeling, emotion; (*sentido*) sense; (*pesar*) regret, sorrow.

sentir [sen'tir] *vt* to feel; (*percibir*) to perceive, sense; (*esp AM*) *oír* to hear;

(*lamentar*) to regret, be sorry for; (*música etc*) to have a feeling for ♦ *vi* to feel; (*lamentarse*) to feel sorry ♦ *nm* opinion, judgement; ~**se** *vr* to feel; **lo siento** I'm sorry; ~**se mejor/mal** to feel better/ill; ~**se como en su casa** to feel at home.

seña ['sena] *nf* sign; (*MIL*) password; ~**s** *nfpl* address *sg*; ~**s personales** personal description *sg*; **por más** ~**s** moreover; **dar** ~**s de** to show signs of.

señal [se'nal] *nf* sign; (*síntoma*) symptom; (*indicio*) indication; (*FERRO, TELEC*) signal; (*marca*) mark; (*COM*) deposit; (*INFORM*) marker, mark; **en** ~ **de** as a token of, as a sign of; **dar** ~**es de** to show signs of; ~ **de auxilio/de peligro** distress/danger signal; ~ **de llamada** ringing tone; ~ **para marcar** dialling tone.

señalado, a [sena'laðo, a] *adj* (*persona*) distinguished; (*pey*) notorious.

señalar [sena'lar] *vt* to mark; (*indicar*) to point out, indicate; (*significar*) to denote; (*referirse a*) to allude to; (*fijar*) to fix, settle; (*pey*) to criticize.

señalice [sena'liθe] *etc vb* V **señalizar.**

señalización [senaliθa'θjon] *nf* signposting; signals *pl.*

señalizar [senali'θar] *vt* (*AUTO*) to put up road signs on; (*FERRO*) to put signals on; (*AUTO: ruta*): **está bien señalizada** it's well signposted.

señas ['senas] *nfpl* V **seña.**

señor, a [se'nor, a] *adj* (*fam*) lordly ♦ *nm* (*hombre*) man; (*caballero*) gentleman; (*dueño*) owner, master; (*trato: antes de nombre propio*) Mr; (: *hablando directamente*) sir ♦ *nf* (*dama*) lady; (*trato: antes de nombre propio*) Mrs; (: *hablando directamente*) madam; (*esposa*) wife; **los** ~**es González** Mr and Mrs González; **S~ Don Jacinto Benavente** (*en sobre*) Mr J. Benavente, J. Benavente Esq.; **S~ Director ...** (*de periódico*) Dear Sir ...; ~ **juez** my lord, your worship (*US*); ~ **Presidente** Mr Chairman *o* President; **Muy** ~ **mío** Dear Sir; **Muy** ~**es nuestros** Dear Sirs; **Nuestro S~** (*REL*) Our Lord; **¿está la señora?** is the lady of the house in?; **la señora de Smith** Mrs Smith; **Nuestra Señora** (*REL*) Our Lady.

señoría [seno'ria] *nf* rule; **su** *o* **vuestra S~** your *o* his/her lordship/ladyship.

señorío [seno'rio] *nm* manor; (*fig*) rule.

señorita [seno'rita] *nf* (*gen*) Miss; (*mujer joven*) young lady; (*maestra*) schoolteacher.

señorito [seno'rito] *nm* young gentleman;

(*lenguaje de criados*) master; (*pey*) toff.
señuelo [se'ɲwelo] *nm* decoy.
Sep. *abr* (= *septiembre*) Sept.
sepa ['sepa] *etc vb V* **saber.**
separable [sepa'raβle] *adj* separable; (*TEC*) detachable.
separación [separa'θjon] *nf* separation; (*división*) division; (*distancia*) gap, distance; ~ **de bienes** division of property.
separado, a [sepa'raðo, a] *adj* separate; (*TEC*) detached; **vive** ~ **de su mujer** he is separated from his wife; **por** ~ separately.
separador [separa'ðor] *nm* (*INFORM*) delimiter.
separadora [separa'ðora] *nf*: ~ **de hojas** burster.
separar [sepa'rar] *vt* to separate; (*silla de la mesa*) to move away; (*TEC: pieza*) to detach; (*persona: de un cargo*) to remove, dismiss; (*dividir*) to divide; ~**se** *vr* (*parte*) to come away; (*partes*) to come apart; (*persona*) to leave, go away; (*matrimonio*) to separate.
separata [sepa'rata] *nf* offprint.
separatismo [separa'tismo] *nm* (*POL*) separatism.
sepelio [se'peljo] *nm* burial, interment.
sepia ['sepja] *nf* cuttlefish.
Sept. *abr* (= *septiembre*) Sept.
septentrional [septentrjo'nal] *adj* north *cpd*, northern.
septiembre [sep'tjembre] *nm* September.
séptimo, a ['septimo, a] *adj, nm* seventh.
septuagésimo, a [septwa'xesimo, a] *adj* seventieth.
sepulcral [sepul'kral] *adj* sepulchral; (*fig*) gloomy, dismal.
sepulcro [se'pulkro] *nm* tomb, grave, sepulchre.
sepultar [sepul'tar] *vt* to bury; (*en accidente*) to trap; **quedaban sepultados en la caverna** they were trapped in the cave.
sepultura [sepul'tura] *nf* (*acto*) burial; (*tumba*) grave, tomb; **dar** ~ **a** to bury; **recibir** ~ to be buried.
sepulturero, a [sepultu'rero, a] *nm/f* gravedigger.
seque ['seke] *etc vb V* **secar.**
sequedad [seke'ðað] *nf* dryness; (*fig*) brusqueness, curtness.
sequía [se'kia] *nf* drought.
séquito ['sekito] *nm* (*de rey etc*) retinue; (*POL*) followers *pl*.
SER *nf abr* (= *Sociedad Española de Radiodifusión*) Spanish radio network.

───────── PALABRA CLAVE

ser [ser] *vi* **1** (*descripción, identidad*) to be; **es médica/muy alta** she's a doctor/very tall; **la familia es de Cuzco** his (*o* her *etc*) family is from Cuzco; ~ **de madera** to be made of wood; **soy Ana** it's Ana
2 (*propiedad*): **es de Joaquín** it's Joaquín's, it belongs to Joaquín
3 (*horas, fechas, números*): **es la una** it's one o'clock; **son las seis y media** it's half-past six; **es el 1 de junio** it's the first of June; **somos/son seis** there are six of us/them; **2 y 2 son 4** 2 and 2 are *o* make 4
4 (*suceso*): **¿qué ha sido eso?** what was that?; **la fiesta es en mi casa** the party's at my house; **¿qué será de mí?** what will become of me?; **"érase una vez ..."** "once upon a time ..."
5 (*en oraciones pasivas*): **ha sido descubierto ya** it's already been discovered
6: es de esperar que ... it is to be hoped *o* I *etc* hope that ...
7 (*locuciones con sub*): **o sea** that is to say; **sea él sea su hermana** either him or his sister; **tengo que irme, no sea que mis hijos estén esperándome** I have to go in case my children are waiting for me
8: a o de no ~ **por él ...** but for him ...
9: a no ~ **que: a no** ~ **que tenga uno ya** unless he's got one already
♦ *nm* being; ~ **humano** human being; ~ **vivo** living creature.

Serbia ['serβja] *nf* Serbia.
serbio, a ['serβjo, a] *adj* Serbian ♦ *nm/f* Serb.
serenarse [sere'narse] *vr* to calm down; (*mar*) to grow calm; (*tiempo*) to clear up.
serenidad [sereni'ðað] *nf* calmness.
sereno, a [se'reno, a] *adj* (*persona*) calm, unruffled; (*el tiempo*) fine, settled; (*ambiente*) calm, peaceful ♦ *nm* night watchman.
serial [se'rjal] *nm* serial.
serie ['serje] *nf* series; (*cadena*) sequence, succession; (*TV etc*) serial; (*de inyecciones*) course; **fuera de** ~ out of order; (*fig*) special, out of the ordinary; **fabricación en** ~ mass production; (*INFORM*): **interface/impresora en** ~ serial interface/printer.
seriedad [serje'ðað] *nf* seriousness; (*formalidad*) reliability; (*de crisis*) gravity, seriousness.

serigrafía [seriɣraˈfia] _nf_ silk screen printing.

serio, a [ˈserjo, a] _adj_ serious; reliable, dependable; grave, serious; **poco ~** (_actitud_) undignified; (_carácter_) unreliable; **en ~** seriously.

sermón [serˈmon] _nm_ (_REL_) sermon.

sermonear [sermoneˈar] _vt_ (_fam_) to lecture ♦ _vi_ to sermonize.

seropositivo, a [seroposiˈtiβo, a] _adj_ HIV-positive.

serpentear [serpenteˈar] _vi_ to wriggle; (_camino, río_) to wind, snake.

serpentina [serpenˈtina] _nf_ streamer.

serpiente [serˈpjente] _nf_ snake; **~ boa** boa constrictor; **~ de cascabel** rattlesnake.

serranía [serraˈnia] _nf_ mountainous area.

serrano, a [seˈrrano, a] _adj_ highland _cpd_, hill _cpd_ ♦ _nm/f_ highlander.

serrar [seˈrrar] _vt_ to saw.

serrín [seˈrrin] _nm_ sawdust.

serrucho [seˈrrutʃo] _nm_ handsaw.

Servia [ˈserβja] _nf_ Serbia.

servicial [serβiˈθjal] _adj_ helpful, obliging.

servicio [serˈβiθjo] _nm_ service; (_CULIN etc_) set; **~s** _nmpl_ toilet(s) (_pl_); **estar de ~** to be on duty; **~ aduanero o de aduana** customs service; **~ a domicilio** home delivery service; **~ incluido** (_en hotel etc_) service charge included; **~ militar** military service; **~ público** (_COM_) public utility.

servidor, a [serβiˈðor, a] _nm/f_ servant ♦ _nm_ (_INFORM_) server; **su seguro ~ (s.s.s.)** yours faithfully; **un ~** (_el que habla o escribe_) your humble servant.

servidumbre [serβiˈðumbre] _nf_ (_sujeción_) servitude; (_criados_) servants _pl_, staff.

servil [serˈβil] _adj_ servile.

servilleta [serβiˈʎeta] _nf_ serviette, napkin.

servilletero [serβiʎeˈtero] _nm_ napkin ring.

servir [serˈβir] _vt_ to serve; (_comida_) to serve out o up; (_TENIS etc_) to serve ♦ _vi_ to serve; (_camarero_) to serve, wait; (_tener utilidad_) to be of use, be useful; **~se** _vr_ to serve o help o.s.; **¿en qué puedo ~le?** how can I help you?; **~ vino a algn** to pour out wine for sb; **~ de guía** to act o serve as a guide; **no sirve para nada** it's no use at all; **~se de algo** to make use of sth, use sth; **sírvase pasar** please come in.

sesantía [θesanˈtia] _nf_ (_AM_) unemployment.

sesenta [seˈsenta] _num_ sixty.

sesentón, ona [sesenˈton, ona] _adj, nm/f_ sixty-year-old.

sesgado, a [sesˈɣaðo, a] _adj_ slanted,

slanting.

sesgo [ˈsesɣo] _nm_ slant; (_fig_) slant, twist.

sesión [seˈsjon] _nf_ (_POL_) session, sitting; (_CINE_) showing; (_TEAT_) performance; **abrir/levantar la ~** to open/close o adjourn the meeting; **la segunda ~** the second house.

seso [ˈseso] _nm_ brain; (_fig_) intelligence; **~s** _nmpl_ (_CULIN_) brains; **devanarse los ~s** to rack one's brains.

sesudo, a [seˈsuðo, a] _adj_ sensible, wise.

set, _pl_ **sets** [set, sets] _nm_ (_TENIS_) set.

Set. _abr_ (= _setiembre_) Sept.

seta [ˈseta] _nf_ mushroom; **~ venenosa** toadstool.

setecientos, as [seteˈθjentos, as] _num_ seven hundred.

setenta [seˈtenta] _num_ seventy.

setiembre [seˈtjembre] _nm_ = **septiembre**.

seto [ˈseto] _nm_ fence; **~ vivo** hedge.

seudo... [seuðo] _pref_ pseudo....

seudónimo [seuˈðonimo] _nm_ pseudonym.

Seúl [seˈul] _nm_ Seoul.

s.e.u.o. _abr_ (= _salvo error u omisión_) E & O E.

severidad [seβeriˈðað] _nf_ severity.

severo, a [seˈβero, a] _adj_ severe; (_disciplina_) strict; (_frío_) bitter.

Sevilla [seˈβiʎa] _nf_ Seville.

sevillano, a [seβiˈʎano, a] _adj_ of o from Seville ♦ _nm/f_ native o inhabitant of Seville.

sexagenario, a [seksaxeˈnarjo, a] _adj_ sixty-year-old ♦ _nm/f_ person in his/her sixties.

sexagésimo, a [seksaˈxesimo, a] _num_ sixtieth.

sexo [ˈsekso] _nm_ sex; **el ~ femenino/masculino** the female/male sex.

sexto, a [ˈseksto, a] _num_ sixth; **Juan S~** John the Sixth.

sexual [sekˈswal] _adj_ sexual; **vida ~** sex life.

sexualidad [sekswaliˈðað] _nf_ sexuality.

s.f. _abr_ (= _sin fecha_) no date.

s/f _abr_ (_COM_: = _su favor_) your favour.

sgte(s). _abr_ (= _siguiente(s)_) foll.

si [si] _conj_ if; (_en pregunta indirecta_) if, whether ♦ _nm_ (_MUS_) B; **~ ... ~ ...** whether ... or ...; **me pregunto ~ ...** I wonder if o whether ...; **~ no** if not, otherwise; **¡~ fuera verdad!** if only it were true!; **por ~ viene** in case he comes.

sí [si] _adv_ yes ♦ _nm_ consent ♦ _pron_ (_uso impersonal_) oneself; (_sg: m_) himself; (: _f_) herself; (: _de cosa_) itself; (: _de usted_) yourself; (_pl_) themselves; (: _de ustedes_) yourselves; (: _recíproco_) each other; **él no**

quiere pero yo ~ he doesn't want to but I do; **ella** ~ **vendrá** she will certainly come, she is sure to come; **claro que** ~ of course; **creo que** ~ I think so; **porque** ~ because that's the way it is; (*porque lo digo yo*) because I say so; **¡~ que lo es!** I'll say it is!; **¡eso ~ que no!** never; **se ríe de** ~ **misma** she laughs at herself; **cambiaron una mirada entre** ~ they gave each other a look; **de por** ~ in itself.

siamés, esa [sja'mes, esa] *adj, nm/f* Siamese.

sibarita [sißa'rita] *adj* sybaritic ♦ *nm/f* sybarite.

sicario [si'karjo] *nm* hired killer.

Sicilia [si'θilja] *nf* Sicily.

siciliano, a [siθi'ljano, a] *adj, nm/f* Sicilian ♦ *nm* (*LING*) Sicilian.

SIDA ['siða] *nm abr* (= *síndrome de inmunodeficiencia adquirida*) AIDS.

sida ['siða] *nm* AIDS.

siderurgia [siðe'rurxja] *nf* iron and steel industry.

siderúrgico, a [siðe'rurxico, a] *adj* iron and steel *cpd*.

sidra ['siðra] *nf* cider.

siega ['sjexa] *etc vb V* **segar** ♦ *nf* (*cosechar*) reaping; (*segar*) mowing; (*época*) harvest (time).

siegue ['sjexe] *etc vb V* **segar**.

siembra ['sjembra] *etc vb V* **sembrar** ♦ *nf* sowing.

siempre ['sjempre] *adv* always; (*todo el tiempo*) all the time; (*AM: así y todo*) still ♦ *conj*: ~ **que** ... (+ *indic*) whenever ...; (+ *subjun*) provided that ...; **es lo de** ~ it's the same old story; **como** ~ as usual; **para** ~ forever; ~ **me voy mañana** (*AM*) I'm still leaving tomorrow.

sien [sjen] *nf* (*ANAT*) temple.

siento ['sjento] *etc vb V* **sentar, sentir**.

sierra ['sjerra] *etc vb V* **serrar** ♦ *nf* (*TEC*) saw; (*GEO*) mountain range; **S~ Leona** Sierra Leone.

siervo, a ['sjerßo, a] *nm/f* slave.

siesta ['sjesta] *nf* siesta, nap; **dormir la** *o* **echarse una** *o* **tomar una** ~ to have an afternoon nap *o* a doze.

siete ['sjete] *num* seven ♦ *excl* (*AM fam*): **¡la gran ~!** wow!, hell!; **hijo de la gran ~** (*fam!*) bastard(*!*), son of a bitch (*US!*).

sífilis ['sifilis] *nf* syphilis.

sifón [si'fon] *nm* syphon; **whisky con** ~ whisky and soda.

siga ['sixa] *etc vb V* **seguir**.

sigilo [si'xilo] *nm* secrecy; (*discreción*) discretion.

sigla ['sixla] *nf* initial, abbreviation.

siglo ['sixlo] *nm* century; (*fig*) age; **S~ de las Luces** Age of Enlightenment; **S~ de Oro** Golden Age.

significación [sixnifika'θjon] *nf* significance.

significado [sixnifi'kaðo] *nm* significance; (*de palabra etc*) meaning.

significar [sixnifi'kar] *vt* to mean, signify; (*notificar*) to make known, express.

significativo, a [sixnifika'tißo, a] *adj* significant.

signifique [sixni'fike] *etc vb V* **significar**.

signo ['sixno] *nm* sign; ~ **de admiración** *o* **exclamación** exclamation mark; ~ **igual** equals sign; ~ **de interrogación** question mark; ~ **de más/de menos** plus/minus sign; ~**s de puntuación** punctuation marks.

siguiendo [si'xjendo] *etc vb V* **seguir**.

siguiente [si'xjente] *adj* following; (*próximo*) next.

silbar [sil'ßar] *vt, vi* to whistle; (*silbato*) to blow; (*TEAT etc*) to hiss.

silbato [sil'ßato] *nm* (*instrumento*) whistle.

silbido [sil'ßiðo] *nm* whistle, whistling; (*abucheo*) hiss.

silenciador [silenθja'ðor] *nm* silencer.

silenciar [silen'θjar] *vt* (*persona*) to silence; (*escándalo*) to hush up.

silencio [si'lenθjo] *nm* silence, quiet; **en el** ~ **más absoluto** in dead silence; **guardar** ~ to keep silent.

silencioso, a [silen'θjoso, a] *adj* silent, quiet.

silfide ['silfiðe] *nf* sylph.

silicio [si'liθjo] *nm* silicon.

silla ['siʎa] *nf* (*asiento*) chair; (*tb:* ~ **de montar**) saddle; ~ **de ruedas** wheelchair.

sillería [siʎe'ria] *nf* (*asientos*) chairs *pl*, set of chairs; (*REL*) choir stalls *pl*; (*taller*) chairmaker's workshop.

sillín [si'ʎin] *nm* saddle, seat.

sillón [si'ʎon] *nm* armchair, easy chair.

silueta [si'lweta] *nf* silhouette; (*de edificio*) outline; (*figura*) figure.

silvestre [sil'ßestre] *adj* (*BOT*) wild; (*fig*) rustic, rural.

sima ['sima] *nf* abyss, chasm.

simbolice [simbo'liθe] *etc vb V* **simbolizar**.

simbólico, a [sim'boliko, a] *adj* symbolic(al).

simbolizar [simboli'θar] *vt* to symbolize.

símbolo ['simbolo] *nm* symbol; ~ **gráfico** (*INFORM*) icon.

simetría [sime'tria] *nf* symmetry.

simétrico, a [si'metriko, a] *adj* symmetrical.

simiente [si'mjente] *nf* seed.

similar [simi'lar] _adj_ similar.
similitud [simili'tuð] _nf_ similarity, resemblance.
simio ['simjo] _nm_ ape.
simpatía [simpa'tia] _nf_ liking; (_afecto_) affection; (_amabilidad_) kindness; (_de ambiente_) friendliness; (_de persona, lugar_) charm, attractiveness; (_solidaridad_) mutual support, solidarity; **tener ~ a** to like; **la famosa ~ andaluza** that well-known Andalusian charm.
simpatice [simpa'tiθe] _etc vb V_ **simpatizar.**
simpático, a [sim'patiko, a] _adj_ nice, pleasant; (_bondadoso_) kind; **no le hemos caído muy ~s** she didn't much take to us.
simpatiquísimo, a [simpati'kisimo, a] _adj_ (_superl de_ **simpático**) ever so nice; ever so kind.
simpatizante [simpati'θante] _nm/f_ sympathizer.
simpatizar [simpati'θar] _vi:_ **~ con** to get on well with.
simple ['simple] _adj_ simple; (_elemental_) simple, easy; (_mero_) mere; (_puro_) pure, sheer ♦ _nm/f_ simpleton; **un ~ soldado** an ordinary soldier.
simpleza [sim'pleθa] _nf_ simpleness; (_necedad_) silly thing.
simplicidad [simpliθi'ðað] _nf_ simplicity.
simplificar [simplifi'kar] _vt_ to simplify.
simplifique [simpli'fike] _etc vb V_ **simplificar.**
simplón, ona [sim'plon, ona] _adj_ simple, gullible ♦ _nm/f_ simple soul.
simposio [sim'posjo] _nm_ symposium.
simulacro [simu'lakro] _nm_ (_apariencia_) semblance; (_fingimiento_) sham.
simular [simu'lar] _vt_ to simulate; (_fingir_) to feign, sham.
simultanear [simultane'ar] _vt:_ **~ dos cosas** to do two things simultaneously.
simultáneo, a [simul'taneo, a] _adj_ simultaneous.
sin [sin] _prep_ without; (_a no ser por_) but for ♦ _conj:_ **~ que** (+ _subjun_) without; **~ decir nada** without a word; **~ verlo yo** without my seeing it; **platos ~ lavar** unwashed _o_ dirty dishes; **la ropa está ~ lavar** the clothes are unwashed; **~ que lo sepa él** without his knowing; **~ embargo** however.
sinagoga [sina'xoxa] _nf_ synagogue.
Sinaí [sina'i] _nm:_ **El ~** Sinai, the Sinai Peninsula; **el Monte ~** Mount Sinai.
sinceridad [sinθeri'ðað] _nf_ sincerity.
sincero, a [sin'θero, a] _adj_ sincere; (_persona_) genuine; (_opinión_) frank; (_felicitaciones_) heartfelt.

síncope ['sinkope] _nm_ (_desmayo_) blackout; **~ cardíaco** (_MED_) heart failure.
sincronice [sinkro'niθe] _etc vb V_ **sincronizar.**
sincronizar [sinkroni'θar] _vt_ to synchronize.
sindical [sindi'kal] _adj_ union _cpd_, trade-union _cpd_.
sindicalista [sindika'lista] _adj_ trade-union _cpd_ ♦ _nm/f_ trade unionist.
sindicar [sindi'kar] _vt_ (_obreros_) to organize, unionize; **~se** _vr_ (_obrero_) to join a union.
sindicato [sindi'kato] _nm_ (_de trabajadores_) trade(s) _o_ labor (_US_) union; (_de negociantes_) syndicate.
sindique [sin'dike] _etc vb V_ **sindicar.**
síndrome ['sindrome] _nm_ syndrome; **~ de abstinencia** withdrawal symptoms.
sine qua non [sine'kwanon] _adj:_ **condición ~** sine qua non.
sinfín [sin'fin] _nm:_ **un ~ de** a great many, no end of.
sinfonía [sinfo'nia] _nf_ symphony.
sinfónico, a [sin'foniko, a] _adj_ (_música_) symphonic; **orquesta sinfónica** symphony orchestra.
Singapur [singa'pur] _nm_ Singapore.
singular [singu'lar] _adj_ singular; (_fig_) out-standing, exceptional; (_pey_) peculiar, odd ♦ _nm_ (_LING_) singular; **en ~** in the singular.
singularice [singula'riθe] _etc vb V_ **singularizar.**
singularidad [singulari'ðað] _nf_ singularity, peculiarity.
singularizar [singulari'θar] _vt_ to single out; **~se** _vr_ to distinguish o.s., stand out.
siniestro, a [si'njestro, a] _adj_ left; (_fig_) sinister ♦ _nm_ (_accidente_) accident; (_desastre_) natural disaster.
sinnúmero [sin'numero] _nm_ = **sinfín.**
sino ['sino] _nm_ fate, destiny ♦ _conj_ (_pero_) but; (_salvo_) except, save; **no son 8 ~ 9** there are not 8 but 9; **todos ~ él** all except him.
sinónimo, a [si'nonimo, a] _adj_ synonymous ♦ _nm_ synonym.
sinrazón [sinra'θon] _nf_ wrong, injustice.
sinsabor [sinsa'ßor] _nm_ (_molestia_) trouble; (_dolor_) sorrow; (_preocupación_) uneasiness.
sintaxis [sin'taksis] _nf_ syntax.
síntesis ['sintesis] _nf inv_ synthesis.
sintetice [sinte'tiθe] _etc vb V_ **sintetizar.**
sintético, a [sin'tetiko, a] _adj_ synthetic.
sintetizador [sintetiθa'ðor] _nm_ synthesizer.
sintetizar [sinteti'θar] _vt_ to synthesize.
sintiendo [sin'tjendo] _etc vb V_ **sentir.**
síntoma ['sintoma] _nm_ symptom.
sintomático, a [sinto'matiko, a] _adj_

symptomatic.

sintonía [sinto'nia] *nf* (*RADIO*) tuning; (*melodía*) signature tune.

sintonice [sinto'niθe] *etc vb V* **sintonizar.**

sintonizador [sintoniθa'ðor] *nm* (*RADIO*) tuner.

sintonizar [sintoni'θar] *vt* (*RADIO*) to tune (in) to, pick up.

sinuoso, a [si'nwoso, a] *adj* (*camino*) winding; (*rumbo*) devious.

sinvergüenza [simber'ɣwenθa] *nm/f* rogue, scoundrel.

sionismo [sjo'nismo] *nm* Zionism.

siquiera [si'kjera] *conj* even if, even though ♦ *adv* (*esp AM*) at least; **ni** ~ not even; ~ **bebe algo** at least drink something.

sirena [si'rena] *nf* siren, mermaid; (*bocina*) siren, hooter.

Siria ['sirja] *nf* Syria.

sirio, a ['sirjo, a] *adj, nm/f* Syrian.

sirviendo [sir'ßjendo] *etc vb V* **servir.**

sirviente, a [sir'ßjente, a] *nm/f* servant.

sisa ['sisa] *nf* petty theft; (*COSTURA*) dart; (*sobaquera*) armhole.

sisar [si'sar] *vt* (*robar*) to thieve; (*COSTURA*) to take in.

sisear [sise'ar] *vt, vi* to hiss.

sísmico, a ['sismiko, a] *adj*: **movimiento** ~ earthquake.

sismógrafo [sis'moɣrafo] *nm* seismograph.

sistema [sis'tema] *nm* system; (*método*) method; ~ **educativo** education system; ~ **impositivo** *o* **tributario** taxation, tax system; ~ **pedagógico** educational system; ~ **de alerta inmediata** early-warning system; ~ **binario** (*INFORM*) binary system; ~ **experto** expert system; ~ **de facturación** (*COM*) invoicing system; ~ **de fondo fijo** (*COM*) imprest system; ~ **de lógica compartida** (*INFORM*) shared logic system; ~ **métrico** metric system; ~ **operativo (en disco)** (*INFORM*) (disk-based) operating system; *see boxed note.*

SISTEMA EDUCATIVO

The reform of the Spanish **sistema educativo** *(education system) begun in the early 1990s, has replaced the old EGB, BUP and COU courses with the following: six years of compulsory primary education ("primaria"); four years of compulsory secondary education ("secundaria"); and a two-year "bachillerato", which is optional but a prerequisite for entry into higher education.*

---

sistemático, a [siste'matiko, a] *adj* systematic.

sitiar [si'tjar] *vt* to besiege, lay siege to.

sitio ['sitjo] *nm* (*lugar*) place; (*espacio*) room, space; (*MIL*) siege; ~ **Web** (*INFORM*) website; **¿hay ~?** is there any room?; **hay ~ de sobra** there's plenty of room.

situación [sitwa'θjon] *nf* situation, position; (*estatus*) position, standing.

situado, a [si'twaðo, a] *adj* situated, placed; **estar** ~ (*COM*) to be financially secure.

situar [si'twar] *vt* to place, put; (*edificio*) to locate, situate.

S.L. *abr* (*COM*: = *Sociedad Limitada*) Ltd.

slip [es'lip], *pl* **slips** *nm* pants *pl*, briefs *pl*.

slot [es'lot], *pl* **slots** *nm*: ~ **de expansión** expansion slot.

S.M. *abr* (= *Su Majestad*) HM.

SME *nm abr* (= *Sistema Monetario Europeo*) EMS; **(mecanismo de cambios del)** ~ ERM.

smoking [(e)'smokin] (*pl* ~**s**) *nm* dinner jacket (*BRIT*), tuxedo (*US*).

s/n *abr* (= *sin número*) no number.

snob [es'nob] = **esnob.**

SO *abr* (= *suroeste*) SW.

so [so] *excl* whoa!; **¡~ burro!** you idiot! ♦ *prep* under.

s/o *abr* (*COM*: = *su orden*) your order.

sobaco [so'ßako] *nm* armpit.

sobado, a [so'ßaðo, a] *adj* (*ropa*) worn; (*arrugado*) crumpled; (*libro*) well-thumbed; (*CULIN*: *masa*) short.

sobar [so'ßar] *vt* (*tela*) to finger; (*ropa*) to rumple, mess up; (*músculos*) to rub, massage.

soberanía [soßera'nia] *nf* sovereignty.

soberano, a [soße'rano, a] *adj* sovereign; (*fig*) supreme ♦ *nm/f* sovereign; **los** ~**s** the king and queen.

soberbio, a [so'ßerßjo, a] *adj* (*orgulloso*) proud; (*altivo*) haughty, arrogant; (*fig*) magnificent, superb ♦ *nf* pride; haughtiness, arrogance; magnificence.

sobornar [soßor'nar] *vt* to bribe.

soborno [so'ßorno] *nm* (*un* ~) bribe; (*el* ~) bribery.

sobra ['soßra] *nf* excess, surplus; ~**s** *nfpl* left-overs, scraps; **de** ~ surplus, extra; **lo sé de** ~ I'm only too aware of it; **tengo de** ~ I've more than enough.

sobradamente [soßraða'mente] *adv* amply; (*saber*) only too well.

sobrado, a [so'ßraðo, a] *adj* (*más que suficiente*) more than enough, (*superfluo*) excessive ♦ *adv* too, exceedingly;

sobradas veces repeatedly.
sobrante [so'ßrante] *adj* remaining, extra
♦ *nm* surplus, remainder.
sobrar [so'ßrar] *vt* to exceed, surpass ♦ *vi*
(*tener de más*) to be more than enough;
(*quedar*) to remain, be left (over).
sobrasada [soßra'saða] *nf* ≈ sausage
spread.
sobre ['soßre] *prep* (*gen*) on; (*encima*) on
(top of); (*por encima de, arriba de*) over,
above; (*más que*) more than; (*además*) in
addition to, besides; (*alrededor de*) about;
(*porcentaje*) in, out of; (*tema*) about, on
♦ *nm* envelope; ~ **todo** above all; **3 ~ 100**
3 in a 100, 3 out of every 100; **un libro ~
Tirso** a book about Tirso; ~ **de ventanilla**
window envelope.
sobrecama [soßre'kama] *nf* bedspread.
sobrecapitalice [soßrekapita'liθe] *etc vb V*
sobrecapitalizar.
sobrecapitalizar [soßrekapitali'θar] *vi* to
overcapitalize.
sobrecargar [soßrekar'ɣar] *vt* (*camión*) to
overload; (*COM*) to surcharge.
sobrecargue [soßre'karɣe] *etc vb V*
sobrecargar.
sobrecoger [soßreko'xer] *vt* (*sobresaltar*) to
startle; (*asustar*) to scare; ~**se** *vr*
(*sobresaltarse*) to be startled; (*asustarse*)
to get scared; (*quedar impresionado*): ~**se**
(**de**) to be overawed (by).
sobrecoja [soßre'koxa] *etc vb V*
sobrecoger.
sobredosis [soßre'ðosis] *nf inv* overdose.
sobre(e)ntender [soßre(e)nten'der] *vt* to
understand; (*adivinar*) to deduce, infer;
~**se** *vr*: **se sobre(e)ntiende que** ... it is
implied that ....
sobreescribir [soßreeskri'ßir] *vt* (*INFORM*)
to overwrite.
sobre(e)stimar [soßre(e)sti'mar] *vt* to
overestimate.
sobregiro [soßre'xiro] *nm* (*COM*) overdraft.
sobrehumano, a [soßreu'mano, a] *adj*
superhuman.
sobreimprimir [soßreimpri'mir] *vt* (*COM*) to
merge.
sobrellevar [soßreʎe'ßar] *vt* (*fig*) to bear,
endure.
sobremesa [soßre'mesa] *nf* (*después de
comer*) sitting on after a meal; (*INFORM*)
desktop; **conversación de ~** table talk.
sobremodo [soßre'moðo] *adv* very much,
enormously.
sobrenatural [soßrenatu'ral] *adj*
supernatural.
sobrenombre [soßre'nombre] *nm*
nickname.

sobrepasar [soßrepa'sar] *vt* to exceed,
surpass.
sobrepondré [soßrepon'dre] *etc vb V*
sobreponer.
sobreponer [soßrepo'ner] *vt* (*poner encima*)
to put on top; (*añadir*) to add; ~**se** *vr*: ~**se
a** to overcome.
sobreponga [soßre'ponga] *etc vb V*
sobreponer.
sobreprima [soßre'prima] *nf* (*COM*)
loading.
sobreproducción [soßreproðuk'θjon] *nf*
overproduction.
sobrepuesto [soßre'pwesto], **sobrepuse**
[soßre'puse] *etc vb V* **sobreponer**.
sobresaldré [soßresal'dre] *etc*,
sobresalga [soßre'salɣa] *etc vb V*
sobresalir.
sobresaliente [soßresa'ljente] *adj*
projecting; (*fig*) outstanding, excellent;
(*UNIV etc*) first class ♦ *nm* (*UNIV etc*) first
class (mark), distinction.
sobresalir [soßresa'lir] *vi* to project, jut
out; (*fig*) to stand out, excel.
sobresaltar [soßresal'tar] *vt* (*asustar*) to
scare, frighten; (*sobrecoger*) to startle.
sobresalto [soßre'salto] *nm* (*movimiento*)
start; (*susto*) scare; (*turbación*) sudden
shock.
sobreseer [soßrese'er] *vt*: ~ **una causa**
(*JUR*) to stop a case.
sobrestadía [soßresta'ðia] *nf* (*COM*)
demurrage.
sobretensión [soßreten'sjon] *nf* (*ELEC*): ~
transitoria surge.
sobretiempo [soßre'tjempo] *nm* (*AM*)
overtime.
sobretodo [soßre'toðo] *nm* overcoat.
sobrevendré [soßreßen'dre] *etc*,
sobrevenga [soßre'ßenga] *etc vb V*
sobrevenir.
sobrevenir [soßreße'nir] *vi* (*ocurrir*) to
happen (unexpectedly); (*resultar*) to
follow, ensue.
sobreviene [soßre'ßjene] *etc*, **sobrevine**
[soßre'ßine] *etc vb V* **sobrevenir**.
sobreviviente [soßreßi'ßjente] *adj*
surviving ♦ *nm/f* survivor.
sobrevivir [soßreßi'ßir] *vi* to survive;
(*persona*) to outlive; (*objeto etc*) to
outlast.
sobrevolar [soßreßo'lar] *vt* to fly over.
sobrevuele [soßre'ßwele] *etc vb V*
sobrevolar.
sobriedad [soßrje'ðað] *nf* sobriety,
soberness; (*moderación*) moderation,
restraint.
sobrino, a [so'ßrino, a] *nm/f* nephew/niece.

sobrio, a ['soßrjo, a] adj (moderado) moderate, restrained.

socarrón, ona [soka'rron, ona] adj (sarcástico) sarcastic, ironic(al).

socavar [soka'ßar] vt to undermine; (excavar) to dig underneath o below.

socavón [soka'ßon] nm (en mina) gallery; (hueco) hollow; (en la calle) hole.

sociable [so'θjaßle] adj (persona) sociable, friendly; (animal) social.

social [so'θjal] adj social; (COM) company cpd.

socialdemócrata [soθjalde'mokrata] adj social-democratic ♦ nm/f social democrat.

socialice [soθja'liθe] etc vb V **socializar**.

socialista [soθja'lista] adj, nm/f socialist.

socializar [soθjali'θar] vt to socialize.

sociedad [soθje'ðað] nf society; (COM) company; ~ **de ahorro y préstamo** savings and loan society; ~ **anónima** (S.A.) limited company (Ltd) (BRIT), incorporated company (Inc) (US); ~ **de beneficiencia** friendly society (BRIT), benefit association (US); ~ **de cartera** investment trust; ~ **comanditaria** (COM) co-ownership; ~ **conjunta** (COM) joint venture; ~ **inmobiliaria** building society (BRIT), savings and loan (society) (US); ~ **de responsabilidad limitada** (COM) private limited company.

socio, a ['soθjo, a] nm/f (miembro) member; (COM) partner; ~ **activo** active partner; ~ **capitalista** o **comanditario** sleeping o silent (US) partner.

socioeconómico, a [soθjoeko'nomiko, a] adj socio-economic.

sociología [soθjolo'xia] nf sociology.

sociólogo, a [so'θjoloɣo, a] nm/f sociologist.

socorrer [soko'rrer] vt to help.

socorrido, a [soko'rriðo, a] adj (tienda) well-stocked; (útil) handy; (persona) helpful.

socorrismo [soko'rrismo] nm life-saving.

socorrista [soko'rrista] nm/f first aider; (en piscina, playa) lifeguard.

socorro [so'korro] nm (ayuda) help, aid; (MIL) relief; ¡~! help!

soda ['soða] nf (sosa) soda; (bebida) soda (water).

sódico, a ['soðiko, a] adj sodium cpd.

soez [so'eθ] adj dirty, obscene.

sofá [so'fa] nm sofa, settee.

sofá-cama [so'fakama] nm studio couch, sofa bed.

Sofía ['sofja] nf Sofia.

sofisticación [sofistika'θjon] nf sophistication.

sofisticado, a [sofisti'kaðo, a] adj sophisticated.

sofocado, a [sofo'kaðo, a] adj: **estar** ~ (fig) to be out of breath; (ahogarse) to feel stifled.

sofocar [sofo'kar] vt to suffocate; (apagar) to smother, put out; ~**se** vr to suffocate; (fig) to blush, feel embarrassed.

sofoco [so'foko] nm suffocation; (azoro) embarrassment.

sofocón [sofo'kon] nm: **llevarse** o **pasar un** ~ to have a sudden shock.

sofreír [sofre'ir] vt to fry lightly.

sofría [so'fria] etc, **sofriendo** [so'frjendo] etc, **sofrito** [so'frito] vb V **sofreír**.

soft(ware) ['sof(wer)] nm (INFORM) software.

soga ['soɣa] nf rope.

sois [sois] vb V **ser**.

soja ['soxa] nf soya.

sojuzgar [soxuθ'ɣar] vt to subdue, rule despotically.

sojuzgue [so'xuθɣe] etc vb V **sojuzgar**.

sol [sol] nm sun; (luz) sunshine, sunlight; (MUS) G; ~ **naciente/poniente** rising/ setting sun; **tomar el** ~ to sunbathe; **hace** ~ it is sunny.

solace [so'laθe] etc vb V **solazar**.

solamente [sola'mente] adv only, just.

solapa [so'lapa] nf (de chaqueta) lapel; (de libro) jacket.

solapado, a [sola'paðo, a] adj sly, underhand.

solar [so'lar] adj solar, sun cpd ♦ nm (terreno) plot (of ground); (local) undeveloped site.

solaz [so'laθ] nm recreation, relaxation.

solazar [sola'θar] vt (divertir) to amuse; ~**se** vr to enjoy o.s., relax.

soldada [sol'daða] nf pay.

soldado [sol'daðo] nm soldier; ~ **raso** private.

soldador [solda'ðor] nm soldering iron; (persona) welder.

soldar [sol'dar] vt to solder, weld; (unir) to join, unite.

soleado, a [sole'aðo, a] adj sunny.

soledad [sole'ðað] nf solitude; (estado infeliz) loneliness.

solemne [so'lemne] adj solemn; (tontería) utter; (error) complete.

solemnidad [solemni'ðað] nf solemnity.

soler [so'ler] vi to be in the habit of, be accustomed to; **suele salir a las ocho** she usually goes out at 8 o'clock; **solíamos ir todos los años** we used to go every year.

solera [so'lera] *nf* (*tradición*) tradition; **vino de** ~ vintage wine.

solfeo [sol'feo] *nm* singing of scales; **ir a clases de** ~ to take singing lessons.

solicitar [soliθi'tar] *vt* (*permiso*) to ask for, seek; (*puesto*) to apply for; (*votos*) to canvass for; (*atención*) to attract; (*persona*) to pursue, chase after.

solícito, a [so'liθito, a] *adj* (*diligente*) diligent; (*cuidadoso*) careful.

solicitud [soliθi'tuð] *nf* (*calidad*) great care; (*petición*) request; (*a un puesto*) application.

solidaridad [soliðari'ðað] *nf* solidarity; **por** ~ **con** (*POL etc*) out of *o* in solidarity with.

solidario, a [soli'ðarjo, a] *adj* (*participación*) joint, common; (*compromiso*) mutually binding; **hacerse** ~ **de** to declare one's solidarity with.

solidarizarse [soliðari'θarse] *vr*: ~ **con algn** to support sb, sympathize with sb.

solidez [soli'ðeθ] *nf* solidity.

sólido, a ['soliðo, a] *adj* solid; (*TEC*) solidly made; (*bien construido*) well built.

soliloquio [soli'lokjo] *nm* soliloquy.

solista [so'lista] *nm/f* soloist.

solitario, a [soli'tarjo, a] *adj* (*persona*) lonely, solitary; (*lugar*) lonely, desolate ♦ *nm/f* (*reclusa*) recluse; (*en la sociedad*) loner ♦ *nm* solitaire ♦ *nf* tapeworm.

soliviantar [soliβjan'tar] *vt* to stir up, rouse (to revolt); (*enojar*) to anger; (*sacar de quicio*) to exasperate.

solloce [so'ʎoθe] *etc vb* ▼ **sollozar**.

sollozar [soʎo'θar] *vi* to sob.

sollozo [so'ʎoθo] *nm* sob.

solo, a ['solo, a] *adj* (*único*) single, sole; (*sin compañía*) alone; (*MUS*) solo; (*solitario*) lonely; **hay una sola dificultad** there is just one difficulty; **a solas** alone, by o.s.

sólo ['solo] *adv* only, just; (*exclusivamente*) solely; **tan** ~ only just.

solomillo [solo'miʎo] *nm* sirloin.

solsticio [sols'tiθjo] *nm* solstice.

soltar [sol'tar] *vt* (*dejar ir*) to let go of; (*desprender*) to unfasten, loosen; (*librar*) to release, set free; (*amarras*) to cast off; (*AUTO: freno etc*) to release; (*suspiro*) to heave; (*risa etc*) to let out; ~**se** *vr* (*desanudarse*) to come undone; (*desprenderse*) to come off; (*adquirir destreza*) to become expert; (*en idioma*) to become fluent.

soltero, a [sol'tero, a] *adj* single, unmarried ♦ *nm* bachelor ♦ *nf* single woman, spinster.

solterón [solte'ron] *nm* confirmed bachelor.

solterona [solte'rona] *nf* spinster, maiden lady; (*pey*) old maid.

soltura [sol'tura] *nf* looseness, slackness; (*de los miembros*) agility, ease of movement; (*en el hablar*) fluency, ease.

soluble [so'luβle] *adj* (*QUÍMICA*) soluble; (*problema*) solvable; ~ **en agua** soluble in water.

solución [solu'θjon] *nf* solution; ~ **de continuidad** break in continuity.

solucionar [soluθjo'nar] *vt* (*problema*) to solve; (*asunto*) to settle, resolve.

solvencia [sol'βenθja] *nf* (*COM: estado*) solvency; (: *acción*) settlement, payment.

solventar [solβen'tar] *vt* (*pagar*) to settle, pay; (*resolver*) to resolve.

solvente [sol'βente] *adj* solvent, free of debt.

Somalia [so'malja] *nf* Somalia.

sombra ['sombra] *nf* shadow; (*como protección*) shade; ~**s** *nfpl* darkness *sg*, shadows; **sin** ~ **de duda** without a shadow of doubt; **tener buena/mala** ~ (*suerte*) to be lucky/unlucky; (*carácter*) to be likeable/disagreeable.

sombrero [som'brero] *nm* hat; ~ **hongo** bowler (hat), derby (*US*); ~ **de copa** *o* **de pelo** (*AM*) top hat.

sombrilla [som'briʎa] *nf* parasol, sunshade.

sombrío, a [som'brio, a] *adj* (*oscuro*) shady; (*fig*) sombre, sad; (*persona*) gloomy.

somero, a [so'mero, a] *adj* superficial.

someter [some'ter] *vt* (*país*) to conquer; (*persona*) to subject to one's will; (*informe*) to present, submit; ~**se** *vr* to give in, yield, submit; ~**se a** to submit to; ~**se a una operación** to undergo an operation.

sometimiento [someti'mjento] *nm* (*estado*) submission; (*acción*) presentation.

somier [so'mjer] *pl* **somiers** *nm* spring mattress.

somnífero [som'nifero] *nm* sleeping pill *o* tablet.

somnolencia [somno'lenθja] *nf* sleepiness, drowsiness.

somos ['somos] *vb* ▼ **ser**.

son [son] *vb* ▼ **ser** ♦ *nm* sound; **en** ~ **de broma** as a joke.

sonado, a [so'naðo, a] *adj* (*comentado*) talked-of; (*famoso*) famous; (*COM: pey*) hyped(-up).

sonajero [sona'xero] *nm* (baby's) rattle.

sonambulismo [sonambu'lismo] *nm*

sleepwalking.

sonámbulo, a [so'nambulo, a] *nm/f* sleepwalker.

sonar [so'nar] *vt* (*campana*) to ring; (*trompeta, sirena*) to blow ♦ *vi* to sound; (*hacer ruido*) to make a noise; (*LING*) to be sounded, be pronounced; (*ser conocido*) to sound familiar; (*campana*) to ring; (*reloj*) to strike, chime; ~**se** *vr*: ~**se (la nariz)** to blow one's nose; **es un nombre que suena** it's a name that's in the news; **me suena ese nombre** that name rings a bell.

sonda ['sonda] *nf* (*NAUT*) sounding; (*TEC*) bore, drill; (*MED*) probe.

sondear [sonde'ar] *vt* to sound; to bore (into), drill; to probe, sound; (*fig*) to sound out.

sondeo [son'deo] *nm* sounding; boring, drilling; (*encuesta*) poll, enquiry; ~ **de la opinión pública** public opinion poll.

sónico, a ['soniko, a] *adj* sonic, sound *cpd*.

sonido [so'niðo] *nm* sound.

sonoro, a [so'noro, a] *adj* sonorous; (*resonante*) loud, resonant; (*LING*) voiced; **efectos** ~**s** sound effects.

sonreír [sonre'ir] *vi*, **sonreírse** *vr* to smile.

sonría [son'ria] *etc*, **sonriendo** [son'rjendo] *etc vb V* **sonreír**.

sonriente [son'rjente] *adj* smiling.

sonrisa [son'risa] *nf* smile.

sonrojar [sonro'xar] *vt*: ~ **a algn** to make sb blush; ~**se** *vr*: ~**se (de)** to blush (at).

sonrojo [son'roxo] *nm* blush.

sonsacar [sonsa'kar] *vt* to wheedle, coax; ~ **a algn** to pump sb for information.

sonsaque [son'sake] *etc vb V* **sonsacar**.

sonsonete [sonso'nete] *nm* (*golpecitos*) tap(ping); (*voz monótona*) monotonous delivery, singsong (voice).

soñador, a [soɲa'ðor, a] *nm/f* dreamer.

soñar [so'ɲar] *vt, vi* to dream; ~ **con** to dream about *o* of; **soñé contigo anoche** I dreamed about you last night.

soñoliento, a [soɲo'ljento, a] *adj* sleepy, drowsy.

sopa ['sopa] *nf* soup; ~ **de fideos** noodle soup.

sopero, a [so'pero, a] *adj* (*plato, cuchara*) soup *cpd* ♦ *nm* soup plate ♦ *nf* soup tureen.

sopesar [sope'sar] *vt* to try the weight of; (*fig*) to weigh up.

sopetón [sope'ton] *nm*: **de** ~ suddenly, unexpectedly.

soplar [so'plar] *vt* (*polvo*) to blow away, blow off; (*inflar*) to blow up; (*vela*) to blow out; (*ayudar a recordar*) to prompt; (*birlar*) to nick; (*delatar*) to split on ♦ *vi* to

blow; (*delatar*) to squeal; (*beber*) to booze, bend the elbow.

soplete [so'plete] *nm* blowlamp; ~ **soldador** welding torch.

soplo ['soplo] *nm* blow, puff; (*de viento*) puff, gust.

soplón, ona [so'plon, ona] *nm/f* (*fam*: *chismoso*) telltale; (: *de policía*) informer, grass.

soponcio [so'ponθjo] *nm* dizzy spell.

sopor [so'por] *nm* drowsiness.

soporífero, a [sopo'rifero, a] *adj* sleep-inducing; (*fig*) soporific ♦ *nm* sleeping pill.

soportable [sopor'taßle] *adj* bearable.

soportal [sopor'tal] *nm* porch; ~**es** *nmpl* arcade *sg*.

soportar [sopor'tar] *vt* to bear, carry; (*fig*) to bear, put up with.

soporte [so'porte] *nm* support; (*fig*) pillar, support; (*INFORM*) medium; ~ **de entrada/salida** input/output medium.

soprano [so'prano] *nf* soprano.

sor [sor] *nf*: **S**~ **María** Sister Mary.

sorber [sor'ßer] *vt* (*chupar*) to sip; (*inhalar*) to sniff, inhale; (*absorber*) to soak up, absorb.

sorbete [sor'ßete] *nm* sherbet.

sorbo ['sorßo] *nm* (*trago*) gulp, swallow; (*chupada*) sip; **beber a** ~**s** to sip.

sordera [sor'ðera] *nf* deafness.

sórdido, a ['sorðiðo, a] *adj* dirty, squalid.

sordo, a ['sorðo, a] *adj* (*persona*) deaf; (*ruido*) dull; (*LING*) voiceless ♦ *nm/f* deaf person; **quedarse** ~ to go deaf.

sordomudo, a [sorðo'muðo, a] *adj* deaf and dumb ♦ *nm/f* deaf-mute.

soriano, a [so'rjano, a] *adj* of *o* from Soria ♦ *nm/f* native *o* inhabitant of Soria.

sorna ['sorna] *nf* (*malicia*) slyness; (*tono burlón*) sarcastic tone.

soroche [so'rotʃe] *nm* (*AM MED*) mountain sickness.

sorprendente [sorpren'dente] *adj* surprising.

sorprender [sorpren'der] *vt* to surprise; (*asombrar*) to amaze; (*sobresaltar*) to startle; (*coger desprevenido*) to catch unawares; ~**se** *vr*: ~**se (de)** to be surprised *o* amazed (at).

sorpresa [sor'presa] *nf* surprise.

sorpresivo, a [sorpre'sißo, a] *adj* (*AM*) surprising; (*imprevisto*) sudden.

sortear [sorte'ar] *vt* to draw lots for; (*rifar*) to raffle; (*dificultad*) to dodge, avoid.

sorteo [sor'teo] *nm* (*en lotería*) draw; (*rifa*) raffle.

sortija [sor'tixa] *nf* ring; (*rizo*) ringlet, curl.

sortilegio [sorti'lexjo] *nm* (*hechicería*) sorcery; (*hechizo*) spell.

sosegado, a [sose'ɣaðo, a] *adj* quiet, calm.

sosegar [sose'ɣar] *vt* to quieten, calm; (*el ánimo*) to reassure ♦ *vi* to rest.

sosegué [sose'ɣe], **soseguemos** [sose'ɣemos] *etc vb V* **sosegar**.

sosiego [so'sjeɣo] *etc vb V* **sosegar** ♦ *nm* quiet(ness), calm(ness).

sosiegue [so'sjeɣe] *etc vb V* **sosegar**.

soslayar [sosla'jar] *vt* (*preguntas*) to get round.

soslayo [sos'lajo]: **de** ~ *adv* obliquely, sideways; **mirar de** ~ to look out of the corner of one's eye (at).

soso, a ['soso, a] *adj* (*CULIN*) tasteless; (*fig*) dull, uninteresting.

sospecha [sos'petʃa] *nf* suspicion.

sospechar [sospe'tʃar] *vt* to suspect ♦ *vi*: ~ **de** to be suspicious of.

sospechoso, a [sospe'tʃoso, a] *adj* suspicious; (*testimonio, opinión*) suspect ♦ *nm/f* suspect.

sostén [sos'ten] *nm* (*apoyo*) support; (*sujetador*) bra; (*alimentación*) sustenance, food.

sostendré [sosten'dre] *etc vb V* **sostener**.

sostener [soste'ner] *vt* to support; (*mantener*) to keep up, maintain; (*alimentar*) to sustain, keep going; ~**se** *vr* to support o.s.; (*seguir*) to continue, remain.

sostenga [sos'tenga] *etc vb V* **sostener**.

sostenido, adj [soste'niðo, a] *adj* continuous, sustained; (*prolongado*) prolonged; (*MUS*) sharp ♦ *nm* (*MUS*) sharp.

sostuve [sos'tuße] *etc vb V* **sostener**.

sota ['sota] *nf* (*NAIPES*) ≈ jack; *V tb* **baraja española**.

sotana [so'tana] *nf* (*REL*) cassock.

sótano ['sotano] *nm* basement.

sotavento [sota'ßento] *nm* (*NAUT*) lee, leeward.

soterrar [sote'rrar] *vt* to bury; (*esconder*) to hide away.

sotierre [so'tjerre] *etc vb V* **soterrar**.

soviético, a [so'ßjetiko, a] *adj, nm/f* Soviet; **los** ~**s** the Soviets, the Russians.

soy [soi] *vb V* **ser**.

soya ['soja] *nf* (*AM*) soya (bean).

SP *abr* (*AUTO*) = **servicio público**.

SPM *nm abr* (= *síndrome premenstrual*) PMS.

spooling [es'pulin] *nm* (*INFORM*) spooling.

sport [es'por(t)] *nm* sport.

spot [es'pot], *pl* **spot** *nm* (*publicitario*) ad.

squash [es'kwas] *nm* (*DEPORTE*) squash.

Sr. *abr* (= *Señor*) Mr.

Sra. *abr* (= *Señora*) Mrs.

S.R.C. *abr* (= *se ruega contestación*) R.S.V.P.

Sres., Srs. *abr* (= *Señores*) Messrs.

Sri Lanka [sri'lanka] *nm* Sri Lanka.

Srta. *abr* = **Señorita**.

SS *abr* (= *Santos, Santas*) SS.

ss. *abr* (= *siguientes*) foll.

S.S. *abr* (*REL*: = *Su Santidad*) H.H.

SS.MM. *abr* (= *Sus Majestades*) Their Royal Highnesses.

Sta. *abr* (= *Santa*) St; (= *Señorita*) Miss.

stand [es'tan, es'tan(s)] *nm* (*COM*) stand.

stárter [es'tarter] *nm* (*AUTO*) self-starter, starting motor.

status ['status, es'tatus] *nm inv* status.

statu(s) quo [es'tatu(s)'kuo] *nm* status quo.

Sto. *abr* (= *Santo*) St.

stop, pl stops [es'top, es'top(s)] *nm* (*AUTO*) stop sign.

su [su] *pron* (*de él*) his; (*de ella*) her; (*de una cosa*) its; (*de ellos, ellas*) their; (*de usted, ustedes*) your.

suave ['swaße] *adj* gentle; (*superficie*) smooth; (*trabajo*) easy; (*música, voz*) soft, sweet; (*clima, sabor*) mild.

suavice [swa'ßiθe] *etc vb V* **suavizar**.

suavidad [swaßi'ðað] *nf* gentleness; (*de superficie*) smoothness; (*de música*) softness, sweetness.

suavizante [swaßi'θante] *nm* conditioner.

suavizar [swaßi'θar] *vt* to soften; (*quitar la aspereza*) to smooth (out); (*pendiente*) to ease; (*colores*) to tone down; (*carácter*) to mellow; (*dureza*) to temper.

subalimentado, a [sußalimen'taðo, a] *adj* undernourished.

subalterno, a [sußal'terno, a] *adj* (*importancia*) secondary; (*personal*) minor, auxiliary ♦ *nm* subordinate.

subarrendar [sußarren'dar] *vt* (*COM*) to lease back.

subarriendo [sußa'rrjendo] *nm* (*COM*) leaseback.

subasta [su'ßasta] *nf* auction; **poner en** *o* **sacar a pública** ~ to put up for public auction; ~ **a la rebaja** Dutch auction.

subastador, a [sußasta'ðor, a] *nm/f* auctioneer.

subastar [sußas'tar] *vt* to auction (off).

subcampeón, ona [sußkampe'on, ona] *nm/f* runner-up.

subconsciente [sußkons'θjente] *adj* subconscious.

subcontratar [sußkontra'tar] *vt* (*COM*) to

subcontract.

subcontrato [sußkon'trato] *nm* (*COM*) subcontract.

subdesarrollado, a [sußðesarro'ʎaðo, a] *adj* underdeveloped.

subdesarrollo [sußðesa'rroʎo] *nm* underdevelopment.

subdirector, a [sußðirek'tor, a] *nm/f* assistant *o* deputy manager.

subdirectorio [sußðirek'torjo] *nm* (*INFORM*) subdirectory.

súbdito, a ['sußðito, a] *nm/f* subject.

subdividir [sußðißi'ðir] *vt* to subdivide.

subempleo [sußem'pleo] *nm* underemployment.

subestimar [sußesti'mar] *vt* to underestimate, underrate.

subido, a [su'ßiðo, a] *adj* (*color*) bright, strong; (*precio*) high ♦ *nf* (*de montaña etc*) ascent, climb; (*de precio*) rise, increase; (*pendiente*) slope, hill.

subíndice [su'ßindiθe] *nm* (*INFORM*, *TIP*) subscript.

subir [su'ßir] *vt* (*objeto*) to raise, lift up; (*cuesta, calle*) to go up; (*colina, montaña*) to climb; (*precio*) to raise, put up; (*empleado etc*) to promote ♦ *vi* to go/come up; (*a un coche*) to get in; (*a un autobús, tren*) to get on; (*precio*) to rise, go up; (*en el empleo*) to be promoted; (*río, marea*) to rise; ~**se** *vr* to get up, climb; ~**se a un coche** to get in(to) a car.

súbito, a ['sußito, a] *adj* (*repentino*) sudden; (*imprevisto*) unexpected.

subjetivo, a [sußxe'tißo, a] *adj* subjective.

subjuntivo [sußxun'tißo] *nm* subjunctive (mood).

sublevación [sußleßa'θjon] *nf* revolt, rising.

sublevar [sußle'ßar] *vt* to rouse to revolt; ~**se** *vr* to revolt, rise.

sublimar [sußli'mar] *vt* (*persona*) to exalt; (*deseos etc*) to sublimate.

sublime [su'ßlime] *adj* sublime.

subliminal [sußlimi'nal] *adj* subliminal.

submarinista [sußmari'nista] *nm/f* underwater explorer.

submarino, a [sußma'rino, a] *adj* underwater ♦ *nm* submarine.

subnormal [sußnor'mal] *adj* subnormal ♦ *nm/f* subnormal person.

suboficial [sußofi'θjal] *nm* non-commissioned officer.

subordinado, a [sußorði'naðo, a] *adj, nm/f* subordinate.

subproducto [sußpro'ðukto] *nm* by-product.

subrayado [sußra'jaðo] *nm* underlining.

subrayar [sußra'jar] *vt* to underline; (*recalcar*) to underline, emphasize.

subrepticio, a [sußrep'tiθjo, a] *adj* surreptitious.

subrutina [sußru'tina] *nf* (*INFORM*) subroutine.

subsanar [sußsa'nar] *vt* (*reparar*) to make good; (*perdonar*) to excuse; (*sobreponerse a*) to overcome.

subscribir [sußskri'ßir] *vt* = **suscribir**.

subscrito [sußs'krito] *pp de* **subscribir**.

subsecretario, a [sußsekre'tarjo, a] *nm/f* undersecretary, assistant secretary.

subsidiariedad [sußsiðjarie'ðað] *nf* (*POL*) subsidiarity.

subsidiario, a [sußsi'ðjarjo, a] *adj* subsidiary.

subsidio [suß'siðjo] *nm* (*ayuda*) aid, financial help; (*subvención*) subsidy, grant; (*de enfermedad, paro etc*) benefit, allowance.

subsistencia [sußsis'tenθja] *nf* subsistence.

subsistir [sußsis'tir] *vi* to subsist; (*vivir*) to live; (*sobrevivir*) to survive, endure.

subsuelo [suß'swelo] *nm* subsoil.

subterfugio [sußter'fuxjo] *nm* subterfuge.

subterráneo, a [sußte'rraneo, a] *adj* underground, subterranean ♦ *nm* underpass, underground passage; (*AM*) underground railway, subway (*US*).

subtítulo [suß'titulo] *nm* subtitle, subheading.

suburbano, a [sußur'ßano, a] *adj* suburban.

suburbio [su'ßurßjo] *nm* (*barrio*) slum quarter; (*afueras*) suburbs *pl*.

subvención [sußßen'θjon] *nf* subsidy, subvention, grant; ~ **estatal** state subsidy *o* support; ~ **para la inversión** (*COM*) investment grant.

subvencionar [sußßenθjo'nar] *vt* to subsidize.

subversión [sußßer'sjon] *nf* subversion.

subversivo, a [sußßer'sißo, a] *adj* subversive.

subyacente [sußja'θente] *adj* underlying.

subyugar [sußju'ʏar] *vt* (*país*) to subjugate, subdue; (*enemigo*) to overpower; (*voluntad*) to dominate.

subyugue [sub'juʏe] *etc vb V* **subyugar**.

succión [suk'θjon] *nf* suction.

succionar [sukθjo'nar] *vt* (*sorber*) to suck; (*TEC*) to absorb, soak up.

sucedáneo, a [suθe'ðaneo, a] *adj* substitute ♦ *nm* substitute (food).

suceder [suθe'ðer] *vi* to happen; ~ **a** (*seguir*) to succeed, follow; **lo que sucede**

es que ... the fact is that ...; ~ **al trono** to succeed to the throne.

sucesión [suθe'sjon] *nf* succession; (*serie*) sequence, series; (*hijos*) issue, offspring.

sucesivamente [suθesiβa'mente] *adv*: **y así ~** and so on.

sucesivo, a [suθe'siβo, a] *adj* successive, following; **en lo ~** in future, from now on.

suceso [su'θeso] *nm* (*hecho*) event, happening; (*incidente*) incident.

sucesor, a [suθe'sor, a] *nm/f* successor; (*heredero*) heir/heiress.

suciedad [suθje'ðað] *nf* (*estado*) dirtiness; (*mugre*) dirt, filth.

sucinto, a [su'θinto, a] *adj* (*conciso*) succinct, concise.

sucio, a ['suθjo, a] *adj* dirty; (*mugriento*) grimy; (*manchado*) grubby; (*borroso*) smudged; (*conciencia*) bad; (*conducta*) vile; (*táctica*) dirty, unfair.

Sucre ['sukre] *n* Sucre.

sucre ['sukre] *nm Ecuadorean monetary unit.*

suculento, a [suku'lento, a] *adj* (*sabroso*) tasty; (*jugoso*) succulent.

sucumbir [sukum'bir] *vi* to succumb.

sucursal [sukur'sal] *nf* branch (office); (*filial*) subsidiary.

Sudáfrica [su'ðafrika] *nf* South Africa.

sudafricano, a [suðafri'kano, a] *adj*, *nm/f* South African.

Sudamérica [suða'merika] *nf* South America.

sudamericano, a [suðameri'kano, a] *adj*, *nm/f* South American.

sudanés, esa [suða'nes, esa] *adj*, *nm/f* Sudanese.

sudar [su'ðar] *vt*, *vi* to sweat; (*BOT*) to ooze, give out *o* off.

sudeste [su'ðeste] *adj* south-east(ern); (*rumbo, viento*) south-easterly ♦ *nm* south-east; (*viento*) south-east wind.

sudoeste [suðo'este] *adj* south-west(ern); (*rumbo, viento*) south-westerly ♦ *nm* south-west; (*viento*) south-west wind.

sudor [su'ðor] *nm* sweat.

sudoroso, a [suðo'roso, a] *adj* sweaty, sweating.

Suecia ['sweθja] *nf* Sweden.

sueco, a ['sweko, a] *adj* Swedish ♦ *nm/f* Swede ♦ *nm* (*LING*) Swedish; **hacerse el ~** to pretend not to hear *o* understand.

suegro, a ['sweɣro, a] *nm/f* father-/mother-in-law; **los ~s** one's in-laws.

suela ['swela] *nf* (*de zapato, tb pescado*) sole.

sueldo ['sweldo] *etc vb V* **soldar** ♦ *nm* pay, wage(s) (*pl*).

suelo ['swelo] *etc vb V* **soler** ♦ *nm* (*tierra*) ground; (*de casa*) floor.

suelto, a ['swelto, a] *etc vb V* **soltar** ♦ *adj* loose; (*libre*) free; (*separado*) detached; (*ágil*) quick, agile; (*corriente*) fluent, flowing ♦ *nm* (loose) change, small change; **está muy ~ en inglés** he is very good at *o* fluent in English.

suene ['swene] *etc vb V* **sonar**.

sueño ['sweɲo] *etc vb V* **soñar** ♦ *nm* sleep; (*somnolencia*) sleepiness, drowsiness; (*lo soñado, fig*) dream; ~ **pesado** *o* **profundo** deep *o* heavy sleep; **tener ~** to be sleepy.

suero ['swero] *nm* (*MED*) serum; (*de leche*) whey.

suerte ['swerte] *nf* (*fortuna*) luck; (*azar*) chance; (*destino*) fate, destiny; (*condición*) lot; (*género*) sort, kind; **lo echaron a ~s** they drew lots *o* tossed up for it; **tener ~** to be lucky; **de otra ~** otherwise, if not; **de ~ que** so that, in such a way that.

suéter ['sweter], *pl* **suéters** *nm* sweater.

suficiencia [sufi'θjenθja] *nf* (*cabida*) sufficiency; (*idoneidad*) suitability; (*aptitud*) adequacy.

suficiente [sufi'θjente] *adj* enough, sufficient.

sufijo [su'fixo] *nm* suffix.

sufragar [sufra'ɣar] *vt* (*ayudar*) to help; (*gastos*) to meet; (*proyecto*) to pay for.

sufragio [su'fraxjo] *nm* (*voto*) vote; (*derecho de voto*) suffrage.

sufrague [su'fraɣe] *etc vb V* **sufragar**.

sufrido, a [su'friðo, a] *adj* (*de carácter fuerte*) tough; (*paciente*) long-suffering; (*tela*) hard-wearing; (*color*) that does not show the dirt; (*marido*) complaisant.

sufrimiento [sufri'mjento] *nm* suffering.

sufrir [su'frir] *vt* (*padecer*) to suffer; (*soportar*) to bear, stand, put up with; (*apoyar*) to hold up, support ♦ *vi* to suffer.

sugerencia [suxe'renθja] *nf* suggestion.

sugerir [suxe'rir] *vt* to suggest; (*sutilmente*) to hint; (*idea: incitar*) to prompt.

sugestión [suxes'tjon] *nf* suggestion; (*sutil*) hint; (*poder*) hypnotic power.

sugestionar [suxestjo'nar] *vt* to influence.

sugestivo, a [suxes'tiβo, a] *adj* stimulating; (*atractivo*) attractive; (*fascinante*) fascinating.

sugiera [su'xjera] *etc*, **sugiriendo** [suxi'rjendo] *etc vb V* **sugerir**.

suicida [sui'θiða] *adj* suicidal ♦ *nm/f*

suicidal person; (*muerto*) suicide, person who has committed suicide.

suicidarse [suiθi'ðarse] *vr* to commit suicide, kill o.s.

suicidio [sui'θiðjo] *nm* suicide.

Suiza ['swiθa] *nf* Switzerland.

suizo, a ['swiθo, a] *adj, nm/f* Swiss ♦ *nm* sugared bun.

sujeción [suxe'θjon] *nf* subjection.

sujetador [suxeta'ðor] *nm* fastener, clip; (*prenda femenina*) bra, brassiere.

sujetapapeles [suxetapa'peles] *nm inv* paper clip.

sujetar [suxe'tar] *vt* (*fijar*) to fasten; (*detener*) to hold down; (*fig*) to subject, subjugate; (*pelo etc*) to keep o hold in place; (*papeles*) to fasten together; ~**se** *vr* to subject o.s.

sujeto, a [su'xeto, a] *adj* fastened, secure ♦ *nm* subject; (*individuo*) individual; (*fam: tipo*) fellow, character, type, guy (*US*); ~ **a** subject to.

sulfurar [sulfu'rar] *vt* (*TEC*) to sulphurate; (*sacar de quicio*) to annoy; ~**se** *vr* (*enojarse*) to get riled, see red, blow up.

sulfuro [sul'furo] *nm* sulphide.

suma ['suma] *nf* (*cantidad*) total, sum; (*de dinero*) sum; (*acto*) adding (up), addition; **en** ~ in short; ~ **y sigue** (*COM*) carry forward.

sumador [suma'ðor] *nm* (*INFORM*) adder.

sumamente [suma'mente] *adv* extremely, exceedingly.

sumar [su'mar] *vt* to add (up); (*reunir*) to collect, gather ♦ *vi* to add up.

sumario, a [su'marjo, a] *adj* brief, concise ♦ *nm* summary.

sumergir [sumer'xir] *vt* to submerge; (*hundir*) to sink; (*bañar*) to immerse, dip; ~**se** *vr* (*hundirse*) to sink beneath the surface.

sumerja [su'merxa] *etc vb V* **sumergir**.

sumidero [sumi'ðero] *nm* drain, sewer; (*TEC*) sump.

suministrador, a [suministra'ðor, a] *nm/f* supplier.

suministrar [suminis'trar] *vt* to supply, provide.

suministro [sumi'nistro] *nm* supply; (*acto*) supplying, providing.

sumir [su'mir] *vt* to sink, submerge; (*fig*) to plunge; ~**se** *vr* (*objeto*) to sink; ~**se en el estudio** to become absorbed in one's studies.

sumisión [sumi'sjon] *nf* (*acto*) submission; (*calidad*) submissiveness, docility.

sumiso, a [su'miso, a] *adj* submissive, docile.

súmmum ['sumum] *nm inv* (*fig*) height.

sumo, a ['sumo, a] *adj* great, extreme; (*mayor*) highest, supreme ♦ *nm* sumo (wrestling); **a lo** ~ at most.

suntuoso, a [sun'twoso, a] *adj* sumptuous, magnificent; (*lujoso*) lavish.

sup. *abr* (= *superior*) sup.

supe ['supe] *etc vb V* **saber**.

supeditar [supeði'tar] *vt* to subordinate; (*sojuzgar*) to subdue; (*oprimir*) to oppress; ~**se** *vr*: ~**se a** to subject o.s. to.

super... [super] *pref* super..., over....

súper ['super] *adj* (*fam*) super, great.

superable [supe'raβle] *adj* (*dificultad*) surmountable; (*tarea*) that can be performed.

superación [supera'θjon] *nf* (*tb:* ~ **personal**) self-improvement.

superar [supe'rar] *vt* (*sobreponerse a*) to overcome; (*rebasar*) to surpass, do better than; (*pasar*) to go beyond; (*marca, récord*) to break; (*etapa: dejar atrás*) to get past; ~**se** *vr* to excel o.s.

superávit [supe'raβit], *pl* **superávits** *nm* surplus.

superchería [supertʃe'ria] *nf* fraud, trick, swindle.

superficial [superfi'θjal] *adj* superficial; (*medida*) surface *cpd*.

superficie [super'fiθje] *nf* surface; (*área*) area; **grandes** ~**s** (*COM*) superstores.

superfluo, a [su'perflwo, a] *adj* superfluous.

superíndice [supe'rindiθe] *nm* (*INFORM, TIP*) superscript.

superintendente [superinten'dente] *nm/f* supervisor, superintendent.

superior [supe'rjor] *adj* (*piso, clase*) upper; (*temperatura, número, nivel*) higher; (*mejor: calidad, producto*) superior, better ♦ *nm/f* superior.

superiora [supe'rjora] *nf* (*REL*) mother superior.

superioridad [superjori'ðað] *nf* superiority.

superlativo, a [superla'tiβo, a] *adj, nm* superlative.

supermercado [supermer'kaðo] *nm* supermarket.

superpoblación [superpoβla'θjon] *nf* overpopulation; (*congestionamiento*) overcrowding.

superponer [superpo'ner] *vt* (*INFORM*) to overstrike.

superposición [superposi'θjon] *nf* (*en impresora*) overstrike.

superpotencia [superpo'tenθja] *nf* superpower, great power.

superproducción [superproðuk'θjon] _nf_ overproduction.

supersónico, a [super'soniko, a] _adj_ supersonic.

superstición [supersti'θjon] _nf_ superstition.

supersticioso, a [supersti'θjoso, a] _adj_ superstitious.

supervisar [superßi'sar] _vt_ to supervise; (_COM_) to superintend.

supervisor, a [superßi'sor, a] _nm/f_ supervisor.

supervivencia [superßi'ßenθja] _nf_ survival.

superviviente [superßi'ßjente] _adj_ surviving ♦ _nm/f_ survivor.

suplantar [suplan'tar] _vt_ (_persona_) to supplant; (_hacerse pasar por otro_) to take the place of.

suplementario, a [suplemen'tarjo, a] _adj_ supplementary.

suplemento [suple'mento] _nm_ supplement.

suplencia [su'plenθja] _nf_ substitution, replacement; (_etapa_) period during which one deputizes _etc_.

suplente [su'plente] _adj_ substitute; (_disponible_) reserve ♦ _nm/f_ substitute.

supletorio, a [suple'torjo, a] _adj_ supplementary; (_adicional_) extra ♦ _nm_ supplement; **mesa supletoria** spare table.

súplica ['suplika] _nf_ request; (_REL_) supplication; (_JUR: instancia_) petition; ~**s** _nfpl_ entreaties.

suplicar [supli'kar] _vt_ (_cosa_) to beg (for), plead for; (_persona_) to beg, plead with; (_JUR_) to appeal to, petition.

suplicio [su'pliθjo] _nm_ torture; (_tormento_) torment; (_emoción_) anguish; (_experiencia penosa_) ordeal.

suplique [su'plike] _etc vb V_ **suplicar**.

suplir [su'plir] _vt_ (_compensar_) to make good, make up for; (_reemplazar_) to replace, substitute ♦ _vi_: ~ **a** to take the place of, substitute for.

supo ['supo] _etc vb V_ **saber**.

supondré [supon'dre] _etc vb V_ **suponer**.

suponer [supo'ner] _vt_ to suppose; (_significar_) to mean; (_acarrear_) to involve ♦ _vi_ to count, have authority; **era de ~ que** ... it was to be expected that ....

suponga [su'ponga] _etc vb V_ **suponer**.

suposición [suposi'θjon] _nf_ supposition.

supositorio [suposi'torjo] _nm_ suppository.

supremacía [suprema'θia] _nf_ supremacy.

supremo, a [su'premo, a] _adj_ supreme.

supresión [supre'sjon] _nf_ suppression; (_de derecho_) abolition; (_de dificultad_)

removal; (_de palabra etc_) deletion; (_de restricción_) cancellation, lifting.

suprimir [supri'mir] _vt_ to suppress; (_derecho, costumbre_) to abolish; (_dificultad_) to remove; (_palabra etc, INFORM_) to delete; (_restricción_) to cancel, lift.

supuestamente [supwesta'mente] _adv_ supposedly.

supuesto, a [su'pwesto, a] _pp de_ **suponer** ♦ _adj_ (_hipotético_) supposed; (_falso_) false ♦ _nm_ assumption, hypothesis ♦ _conj_: ~ **que** since; **dar por ~ algo** to take sth for granted; **por ~** of course.

supurar [supu'rar] _vi_ to fester, suppurate.

supuse [su'puse] _etc vb V_ **suponer**.

sur [sur] _adj_ southern; (_rumbo_) southerly ♦ _nm_ south; (_viento_) south wind.

Suráfrica [su'rafrika] _etc_ = **Sudáfrica** _etc_.

Suramérica [sura'merika] _etc_ = **Sudamérica** _etc_.

surcar [sur'kar] _vt_ to plough; (_superficie_) to cut, score.

surco ['surko] _nm_ (_en metal, disco_) groove; (_AGR_) furrow.

surcoreano, a [surkore'ano, a] _adj, nm/f_ South Korean.

sureño, a [su'reɲo, a] _adj_ southern ♦ _nm/f_ southerner.

sureste [su'reste] = **sudeste**.

surf [surf] _nm_ surfing.

surgir [sur'xir] _vi_ to arise, emerge; (_dificultad_) to come up, crop up.

surja ['surxa] _etc vb V_ **surgir**.

suroeste [suro'este] = **sudoeste**.

surque ['surke] _etc vb V_ **surcar**.

surrealismo [surrea'lismo] _nm_ surrealism.

surrealista [surrea'lista] _adj, nm/f_ surrealist.

surtido, a [sur'tiðo, a] _adj_ mixed, assorted ♦ _nm_ (_selección_) selection, assortment; (_abastecimiento_) supply, stock.

surtidor [surti'ðor] _nm_ (_chorro_) jet, spout; (_fuente_) fountain; ~ **de gasolina** petrol (_BRIT_) o gas (_US_) pump.

surtir [sur'tir] _vt_ to supply, provide; (_efecto_) to have, produce ♦ _vi_ to spout, spurt; ~**se** _vr_: ~**se de** to provide o.s. with.

susceptible [susθep'tiße] _adj_ susceptible; (_sensible_) sensitive; ~ **de** capable of.

suscitar [susθi'tar] _vt_ to cause, provoke; (_discusión_) to start; (_duda, problema_) to raise; (_interés, sospechas_) to arouse.

suscribir [suskri'ßir] _vt_ (_firmar_) to sign; (_respaldar_) to subscribe to, endorse; (_COM: acciones_) to take out an option on; ~**se** _vr_ to subscribe; ~ **a algn a una revista** to take out a subscription to a journal for sb.

suscripción [suskrip'θjon] *nf* subscription.

suscrito, a [sus'krito, a] *pp de* **suscribir**
♦ *adj:* ~ **en exceso** oversubscribed.

susodicho, a [suso'ditʃo, a] *adj* above-
mentioned.

suspender [suspen'der] *vt* (*objeto*) to hang
(up), suspend; (*trabajo*) to stop, suspend;
(*ESCOL*) to fail.

suspense [sus'pense] *nm* suspense.

suspensión [suspen'sjon] *nf* suspension;
(*fig*) stoppage, suspension; (*JUR*) stay; ~
de fuego *o* **de hostilidades** ceasefire,
cessation of hostilities; ~ **de pagos**
suspension of payments.

suspensivo, a [suspen'siβo, a] *adj:* **puntos**
~**s** dots, suspension points.

suspenso, a [sus'penso, a] *adj* hanging,
suspended; (*ESCOL*) failed ♦ *nm* (*ESCOL*)
fail(ure); **quedar** *o* **estar en** ~ to be
pending.

suspicacia [suspi'kaθja] *nf* suspicion,
mistrust.

suspicaz [suspi'kaθ] *adj* suspicious,
distrustful.

suspirar [suspi'rar] *vi* to sigh.

suspiro [sus'piro] *nm* sigh.

sustancia [sus'tanθja] *nf* substance; ~ **gris**
(*ANAT*) grey matter; **sin** ~ lacking in
substance, shallow.

sustancial [sustan'θjal] *adj* substantial.

sustancioso, a [sustan'θjoso, a] *adj*
substantial; (*discurso*) solid.

sustantivo, a [sustan'tiβo, a] *adj*
substantive; (*LING*) substantival, noun
cpd ♦ *nm* noun, substantive.

sustentar [susten'tar] *vt* (*alimentar*) to
sustain, nourish; (*objeto*) to hold up,
support; (*idea, teoría*) to maintain,
uphold; (*fig*) to sustain, keep going.

sustento [sus'tento] *nm* support; (*alimento*)
sustenance, food.

sustituir [sustitu'ir] *vt* to substitute,
replace.

sustituto, a [susti'tuto, a] *nm/f* substitute,
replacement.

sustituyendo [sustitu'jendo] *etc vb V*
sustituir.

susto ['susto] *nm* fright, scare; **dar un** ~ **a
algn** to give sb a fright; **darse** *o* **pegarse
un** ~ (*fam*) to get a fright.

sustraer [sustra'er] *vt* to remove, take
away; (*MAT*) to subtract.

sustraiga [sus'traiʁa] *etc*, **sustraje**
[sus'traxe] *etc*, **sustrajera** [sustra'xera]
etc vb V **sustraer.**

sustrato [sus'trato] *nm* substratum.

sustrayendo [sustra'jendo] *etc vb V*

sustraer.

susurrar [susu'rrar] *vi* to whisper.

susurro [su'surro] *nm* whisper.

sutil [su'til] *adj* (*aroma*) subtle; (*tenue*) thin;
(*hilo, hebra*) fine; (*olor*) delicate; (*brisa*)
gentle; (*diferencia*) fine, subtle;
(*inteligencia*) sharp, keen.

sutileza [suti'leθa] *nf* subtlety; (*delgadez*)
thinness; (*delicadeza*) delicacy; (*agudeza*)
keenness.

sutura [su'tura] *nf* suture.

suturar [sutu'rar] *vt* to suture; (*juntar con
puntos*) to stitch.

suyo, a ['sujo, a] *adj* (*con artículo o después
del verbo* ser: *de él*) his; (: *de ella*) hers;
(: *de ellos, ellas*) theirs; (: *de usted,
ustedes*) yours; (*después de un nombre: de
él*) of his; (: *de ella*) of hers; (: *de ellos,
ellas*) of theirs; (: *de usted, ustedes*) of
yours; **lo** ~ (what is) his; (*su parte*) his
share, what he deserves; **los** ~**s** (*familia*)
one's family *o* relations; (*partidarios*)
one's own people *o* supporters; ~
afectísimo (*en carta*) yours faithfully *o*
sincerely; **de** ~ in itself; **eso es muy** ~
that's just like him; **hacer de las suyas** to
get up to one's old tricks; **ir a la suya, ir
a lo** ~ to go one's own way; **salirse con la
suya** to get one's way.

T t

T, t [te] *nf* (*letra*) T, t; **T de Tarragona** T for
Tommy.

t *abr* = **tonelada.**

T. *abr* (= *Telefón, Telégrafo*) tel.; (*COM*)
= **Tarifa; Tasa.**

t. *abr* (= *tomo(s)*) vol(s).

Tabacalera [taβaka'lera] *nf Spanish state
tobacco monopoly.*

tabaco [ta'βako] *nm* tobacco; (*fam*)
cigarettes *pl.*

tábano ['taβano] *nm* horsefly.

tabaquería [tabake'ria] *nf* tobacconist's
(*BRIT*), cigar store (*US*).

tabarra [ta'βarra] *nf* (*fam*) nuisance; **dar la**
~ to be a pain in the neck.

taberna [ta'βerna] *nf* bar.

tabernero, a [taβer'nero, a] *nm/f*
(*encargado*) publican; (*camarero*)
barman/barmaid.

tabique [ta'βike] *nm* (*pared*) thin wall; (*para dividir*) partition.

tabla ['taβla] *nf* (*de madera*) plank; (*estante*) shelf; (*de anuncios*) board; (*lista, catálogo*) list; (*mostrador*) counter; (*de vestido*) pleat; (*ARTE*) panel; ~**s** *nfpl* (*TAUR, TEAT*) boards; **hacer** ~**s** to draw; ~ **de consulta** (*INFORM*) lookup table.

tablado [ta'βlaðo] *nm* (*plataforma*) platform; (*suelo*) plank floor; (*TEAT*) stage.

tablao [ta'βlao] *nm* (*tb*: ~ **flamenco**) flamenco show.

tablero [ta'βlero] *nm* (*de madera*) plank, board; (*pizarra*) blackboard; (*de ajedrez, damas*) board; (*AUTO*) dashboard; ~ **de gráficos** (*INFORM*) graph pad.

tableta [ta'βleta] *nf* (*MED*) tablet; (*de chocolate*) bar.

tablilla [ta'βliʎa] *nf* small board; (*MED*) splint.

tablón [ta'βlon] *nm* (*de suelo*) plank; (*de techo*) beam; (*de anuncios*) notice board.

tabú [ta'βu] *nm* taboo.

tabulación [taβula'θjon] *nf* (*INFORM*) tab(bing).

tabulador [taβula'ðor] *nm* (*INFORM, TIP*) tab.

tabuladora [taβula'ðora] *nf*: ~ **eléctrica** electric accounting machine.

tabular [taβu'lar] *vt* to tabulate; (*INFORM*) to tab.

taburete [taβu'rete] *nm* stool.

tacaño, a [ta'kaɲo, a] *adj* (*avaro*) mean; (*astuto*) crafty.

tacha ['tatʃa] *nf* (*defecto*) flaw, defect; (*TEC*) stud; **poner** ~ **a** to find fault with; **sin** ~ flawless.

tachar [ta'tʃar] *vt* (*borrar*) to cross out; (*corregir*) to correct; (*criticar*) to criticize; ~ **de** to accuse of.

tacho ['tatʃo] *nm* (*AM*) bucket, pail.

tachón [ta'tʃon] *nm* erasure; (*tachadura*) crossing-out; (*TEC*) ornamental stud; (*COSTURA*) trimming.

tachuela [ta'tʃwela] *nf* (*clavo*) tack.

tácito, a ['taθito, a] *adj* tacit; (*acuerdo*) unspoken; (*LING*) understood; (*ley*) unwritten.

taciturno, a [taθi'turno, a] *adj* (*callado*) silent; (*malhumorado*) sullen.

taco ['tako] *nm* (*BILLAR*) cue; (*libro de billetes*) book; (*manojo de billetes*) wad; (*AM*) heel; (*tarugo*) peg; (*fam: bocado*) snack; (: *palabrota*) swear word; (: *trago de vino*) swig; (*Méjico*) filled tortilla; **armarse o hacerse un** ~ to get into a mess.

tacógrafo [ta'koɣrafo] *nm* (*COM*) tachograph.

tacón [ta'kon] *nm* heel; **de** ~ **alto** high-heeled.

taconear [takone'ar] *vi* (*dar golpecitos*) to tap with one's heels; (*MIL etc*) to click one's heels.

taconeo [tako'neo] *nm* (*heel*) tapping *o* clicking.

táctico, a ['taktiko, a] *adj* tactical ♦ *nf* tactics *pl*.

tacto ['takto] *nm* touch; (*acción*) touching; (*fig*) tact.

TAE *nf abr* (= *tasa anual equivalente*) APR.

tafetán [tafe'tan] *nm* taffeta; **tafetanes** *nmpl* (*fam*) frills; ~ **adhesivo** *o* **inglés** sticking plaster.

tafilete [tafi'lete] *nm* morocco leather.

tahona [ta'ona] *nf* (*panadería*) bakery; (*molino*) flourmill.

tahúr [ta'ur] *nm* gambler; (*pey*) cheat.

tailandés, esa [tailan'des, esa] *adj, nm/f* Thai ♦ *nm* (*LING*) Thai.

Tailandia [tai'landja] *nf* Thailand.

taimado, a [tai'maðo, a] *adj* (*astuto*) sly; (*resentido*) sullen.

taita ['taita] *nm* dad, daddy.

tajada [ta'xaða] *nf* slice; (*fam*) rake-off; **sacar** ~ to get one's share.

tajante [ta'xante] *adj* sharp; (*negativa*) emphatic; **es una persona** ~ he's an emphatic person.

tajar [ta'xar] *vt* to cut, slice.

Tajo ['taxo] *nm* Tagus.

tajo ['taxo] *nm* (*corte*) cut; (*filo*) cutting edge; (*GEO*) cleft.

tal [tal] *adj* such; **un** ~ **García** a man called García; ~ **vez** perhaps ♦ *pron* (*persona*) someone, such a one; (*cosa*) something, such a thing; ~ **como** such as; ~ **para cual** tit for tat; (*dos iguales*) two of a kind; **hablábamos de que si** ~ **si cual** we were talking about this, that and the other ♦ *adv*: ~ **como** (*igual*) just as; ~ **cual** (*como es*) just as it is; ~ **el padre, cual el hijo** like father, like son; **¿qué** ~**?** how are things?; **¿qué** ~ **te gusta?** how do you like it? ♦ *conj*: **con** ~ **(de) que** provided that.

tala ['tala] *nf* (*de árboles*) tree felling.

taladradora [talaðra'ðora] *nf* drill; ~ **neumática** pneumatic drill.

taladrar [tala'ðrar] *vt* to drill; (*fig: suj: ruido*) to pierce.

taladro [ta'laðro] *nm* (*gen*) drill; (*hoyo*) drill hole; ~ **neumático** pneumatic drill.

talante [ta'lante] *nm* (*humor*) mood; (*voluntad*) will, willingness.

talar [ta'lar] *vt* to fell, cut down; (*fig*) to devastate.

talco ['talko] nm (polvos) talcum powder; (MINERALOGÍA) talc.

talega [ta'leɣa] nf sack.

talego [ta'leɣo] nm sack; **tener** ~ (fam) to have money.

talento [ta'lento] nm talent; (capacidad) ability; (don) gift.

Talgo ['talgo] nm ubr (FERRO = tren articulado ligero Goicoechea-Oriol) high-speed train.

talidomida [taliðo'miða] nm thalidomide.

talismán [talis'man] nm talisman.

talla ['taʎa] nf (estatura, fig, MED) height, stature; (de ropa) size, fitting; (palo) measuring rod; (ARTE: de madera)) carving; (de piedra) sculpture.

tallado, a [ta'ʎaðo, a] adj carved ♦ nm (de madera) carving; (de piedra) sculpture.

tallar [ta'ʎar] vt (trabajar) to work, carve; (grabar) to engrave; (medir) to measure; (repartir) to deal ♦ vi to deal.

tallarín [taʎa'rin] nm noodle.

talle ['taʎe] nm (ANAT) waist; (medida) size; (física) build; (: de mujer) figure; (fig) appearance; **de** ~ **esbelto** with a slim figure.

taller [ta'ʎer] nm (TEC) workshop; (fábrica) factory; (AUTO) garage; (de artista) studio.

tallo ['taʎo] nm (de planta) stem; (de hierba) blade; (brote) shoot; (col) cabbage; (CULIN) candied peel.

talmente [tal'mente] adv (de esta forma) in such a way; (hasta tal punto) to such an extent; (exactamente) exactly.

talón [ta'lon] nm (gen) heel; (COM) counterfoil; (TEC) rim; ~ **de Aquiles** Achilles heel.

talonario [talo'narjo] nm (de cheques) cheque book; (de billetes) book of tickets; (de recibos) receipt book.

tamaño, a [ta'maɲo, a] adj (tan grande) such a big; (tan pequeño) such a small ♦ nm size; **de** ~ **natural** full-size; ¿**de qué** ~ **es?** what size is it?

tamarindo [tama'rindo] nm tamarind.

tambaleante [tambale'ante] adj (persona) staggering; (mueble) wobbly; (vehículo) swaying.

tambalearse [tambale'arse] vr (persona) to stagger; (mueble) to wobble; (vehículo) to sway.

también [tam'bjen] adv (igualmente) also, too, as well; (además) besides; **estoy cansado — yo** ~ I'm tired — so am I o / me too.

tambor [tam'bor] nm drum; (ANAT) eardrum; ~ **del freno** brake drum; ~

magnético (INFORM) magnetic drum.

tamboril [tambo'ril] nm small drum.

tamborilear [tamborile'ar] vi (MUS) to drum; (con los dedos) to drum with one's fingers.

tamborilero [tambori'lero] nm drummer.

Támesis ['tamesis] nm Thames.

tamice [ta'miθe] etc vb V **tamizar**.

tamiz [ta'miθ] nm sieve.

tamizar [tami'θar] vt to sieve.

tampoco [tam'poko] adv nor, neither; **yo** ~ **lo compré** I didn't buy it either.

tampón [tam'pon] nm plug; (MED) tampon.

tan [tan] adv so; ~ **es así que** so much so that; ¡**qué cosa** ~ **rara!** how strange!; **no es una idea** ~ **buena** it is not such a good idea.

tanatorio [tana'torjo] nm (privado) funeral home o parlour; (público) mortuary.

tanda ['tanda] nf (gen) series; (de inyecciones) course; (juego) set; (turno) shift; (grupo) gang.

tándem ['tandem] nm tandem; (POL) duo.

tanga ['tanga] nm (bikini) tanga; (ropa interior) tanga briefs.

tangente [tan'xente] nf tangent; **salirse por la** ~ to go off at a tangent.

Tánger ['tanxer] n Tangier.

tangerino, a [tanxe'rino, a] adj of o from Tangier ♦ nm/f native o inhabitant of Tangier.

tangible [tan'xiβle] adj tangible.

tango ['tango] nm tango.

tanino [ta'nino] nm tannin.

tanque ['tanke] nm (gen) tank; (AUTO, NAUT) tanker.

tanqueta [tan'keta] nf (MIL) small tank, armoured vehicle.

tantear [tante'ar] vt (calcular) to reckon (up); (medir) to take the measure of; (probar) to test, try out; (tomar la medida: persona) to take the measurements of; (considerar) to weigh up ♦ vi (DEPORTE) to score.

tanteo [tan'teo] nm (cálculo) (rough) calculation; (prueba) test, trial; (DEPORTE) scoring; (adivinanzas) guesswork; **al** ~ by trial and error.

tantísimo, a [tan'tisimo, a] adj so much; ~**s** so many.

tanto, a ['tanto, a] adj (cantidad) so much, as much; ~**s** so many, as many; **20 y** ~**s** 20-odd ♦ adv (cantidad) so much, as much; (tiempo) so long, as long; ~ **tú como yo** both you and I; ~ **como eso** it's not as bad as that; ~ **más ... cuanto que** it's all the more ... because; ~ **mejor/ peor** so much the better/the worse; ~ **si**

viene como si va whether he comes or whether he goes; ~ **es así que** so much so that; **por ~, por lo ~** therefore; **me he vuelto ronco de** *o* **con ~ hablar** I have become hoarse with so much talking ♦ *conj*: **con ~ que** provided (that); **en ~ que** while; **hasta ~ (que)** until such time as ♦ *nm* (*suma*) certain amount; (*proporción*) so much; (*punto*) point; (*gol*) goal; ~ **alzado** agreed price; ~ **por ciento** percentage; **al ~** up to date; **estar al ~ de los acontecimientos** to be fully abreast of events; **un ~ perezoso** somewhat lazy; **al ~ de que** because of the fact that ♦ *pron*: **cado uno paga ~** each one pays so much; **uno de ~s** one of many; **a ~s de agosto** on such and such a day in August; **entre ~** meanwhile.

tañer [ta'ɲer] *vt* (*MUS*) to play; (*campana*) to ring.

T/año *abr* = toneladas por año.

TAO *nf abr* (= traducción asistida por ordenador) MAT.

tapa ['tapa] *nf* (*de caja, olla*) lid; (*de botella*) top; (*de libro*) cover; (*comida*) snack.

tapacubos [tapa'kuβos] *nm inv* hub cap.

tapadera [tapa'ðera] *nf* lid, cover.

tapado [ta'paðo] *nm* (*AM: abrigo*) coat.

tapar [ta'par] *vt* (*cubrir*) to cover; (*envolver*) to wrap *o* cover up; (*la vista*) to obstruct; (*persona, falta*) to conceal; (*AM*) to fill; ~**se** *vr* to wrap o.s. up.

tapete [ta'pete] *nm* table cover; **estar sobre el ~** (*fig*) to be under discussion.

tapia ['tapja] *nf* (garden) wall.

tapiar [ta'pjar] *vt* to wall in.

tapice [ta'piθe] *etc vb V* **tapizar**.

tapicería [tapiθe'ria] *nf* tapestry; (*para muebles*) upholstery; (*tienda*) upholsterer's (shop).

tapicero, a [tapi'θero, a] *nm/f* (*de muebles*) upholsterer.

tapiz [ta'piθ] *nm* (*alfombra*) carpet; (*tela tejida*) tapestry.

tapizar [tapi'θar] *vt* (*pared*) to wallpaper; (*suelo*) to carpet; (*muebles*) to upholster.

tapón [ta'pon] *nm* (*corcho*) stopper; (*TEC*) plug; (*MED*) tampon; ~ **de rosca** *o* **de tuerca** screw-top.

taponar [tapo'nar] *vt* (*botella*) to cork; (*tubería*) to block.

taponazo [tapo'naθo] *nm* (*de tapón*) pop.

tapujo [ta'puxo] *nm* (*embozo*) muffler; (*engaño*) deceit; **sin ~s** honestly.

taquigrafía [takiɣra'fia] *nf* shorthand.

taquígrafo, a [ta'kiɣrafo, a] *nm/f* shorthand writer.

taquilla [ta'kiʎa] *nf* (*de estación etc*) booking office; (*de teatro*) box office; (*suma recogida*) takings *pl*; (*archivador*) filing cabinet.

taquillero, a [taki'ʎero, a] *adj*: **función taquillera** box office success ♦ *nm/f* ticket clerk.

taquimecanografía [takimekanoɣra'fia] *nf* shorthand and typing.

taquímetro [ta'kimetro] *nm* speedometer; (*de control*) tachymeter.

tara ['tara] *nf* (*defecto*) defect; (*COM*) tare.

tarado, a [ta'raðo, a] *adj* (*COM*) defective, imperfect; (*idiota*) stupid; (*loco*) crazy, nuts ♦ *nm/f* idiot, cretin.

tarántula [ta'rantula] *nf* tarantula.

tararear [tarare'ar] *vi* to hum.

tardanza [tar'ðanθa] *nf* (*demora*) delay; (*lentitud*) slowness.

tardar [tar'ðar] *vi* (*tomar tiempo*) to take a long time; (*llegar tarde*) to be late; (*demorar*) to delay; **¿tarda mucho el tren?** does the train take long?; **a más ~** at the (very) latest; ~ **en hacer algo** to be slow *o* take a long time to do sth; **no tardes en venir** come soon, come before long.

tarde ['tarðe] *adv* (*hora*) late; (*fuera de tiempo*) too late ♦ *nf* (*de día*) afternoon; (*de noche*) evening; ~ **o temprano** sooner or later; **de ~ en ~** from time to time; **¡buenas ~s!** (*de día*) good afternoon!; (*de noche*) good evening!; **a** *o* **por la ~** in the afternoon; in the evening.

tardío, a [tar'ðio, a] *adj* (*retrasado*) late; (*lento*) slow (to arrive).

tardo, a ['tarðo, a] *adj* (*lento*) slow; (*torpe*) dull; ~ **de oído** hard of hearing.

tarea [ta'rea] *nf* task; ~**s** *nfpl* (*ESCOL*) homework *sg*; ~ **de ocasión** chore.

tarifa [ta'rifa] *nf* (*lista de precios*) price list; (*COM*) tariff; ~ **básica** basic rate; ~ **completa** all-in cost; ~ **a destajo** piece rate; ~ **doble** double time.

tarima [ta'rima] *nf* (*plataforma*) platform; (*taburete*) stool; (*litera*) bunk.

tarjeta [tar'xeta] *nf* card; ~ **postal/de crédito/de Navidad** postcard/credit card/Christmas card; ~ **de circuitos** (*INFORM*) circuit board; ~ **cliente** loyalty card; ~ **comercial** (*COM*) calling card; ~ **dinero** cash card; ~ **gráficos** (*INFORM*) graphics card; ~ **de multifunción** (*INFORM*) multiplication card.

tarot [ta'rot] *nm* tarot.

tarraconense [tarrako'nense] *adj* of *o* from Tarragona ♦ *nm/f* native *o* inhabitant of Tarragona.

tarro ['taɾɾo] nm jar, pot.

tarta ['taɾta] nf (pastel) cake; (torta) tart.

tartajear [taɾtaxe'aɾ] vi to stammer.

tartamudear [taɾtamuðe'aɾ] vi to stutter, stammer.

tartamudo, a [taɾta'muðo, a] adj stuttering, stammering ♦ nm/f stutterer, stammerer.

tartárico, a [taɾ'taɾiko, a] adj: **ácido** ~ tartaric acid.

tártaro ['taɾtaɾo] adj, nm Tartar ♦ nm (QUIMICA) tartar.

tarugo, a [ta'ɾuxo, a] adj stupid ♦ nm (de madera) lump.

tarumba [ta'ɾumba] adj (confuso) confused.

tasa ['tasa] nf (precio) (fixed) price, rate; (valoración) valuation; (medida, norma) measure, standard; **básica** (COM) basic rate; ~ **de cambio** exchange rate; **de** ~ **cero** (COM) zero-rated; ~ **de crecimiento** growth rate; ~ **de interés/de nacimiento** rate of interest/birth rate; ~ **de rendimiento** (COM) rate of return; ~**s universitarias** university fees.

tasación [tasa'θjon] nf assessment, valuation; (fig) appraisal.

tasador, a [tasa'ðoɾ, a] nm/f valuer; (COM: de impuestos) assessor.

tasar [ta'saɾ] vt (arreglar el precio) to fix a price for; (valorar) to value, assess; (limitar) to limit.

tasca ['taska] nf (fam) pub.

tata ['tata] nm (fam) dad(dy) ♦ nf (niñera) nanny, maid.

tatarabuelo, a [tataɾa'ßwelo, a] nm/f great-great-grandfather/mother; **los** ~**s** one's great-great-grandparents.

tatuaje [ta'twaxe] nm (dibujo) tattoo; (acto) tattooing.

tatuar [ta'twaɾ] vt to tattoo.

taumaturgo [tauma'tuɾvo] nm miracle-worker.

taurino, a [tau'ɾino, a] adj bullfighting cpd.

Tauro ['tauɾo] nm Taurus.

tauromaquia [tauɾo'makja] nf (art of) bullfighting.

tautología [tautolo'xia] nf tautology.

taxativo, a [taksa'tißo, a] adj (restringido) limited; (sentido) specific.

taxi ['taksi] nm taxi.

taxidermia [taksi'ðeɾmja] nf taxidermy.

taxímetro [tak'simetro] nm taximeter.

taxista [tak'sista] nm/f taxi driver.

Tayikistán [tajikis'tan] nm Tajikistan.

taza ['taθa] nf cup; (de retrete) bowl; ~ **para café** coffee cup.

tazón [ta'θon] nm mug, large cup;

(escudilla) basin.

TCI nf abr (= tarjeta de circuito impreso) PCB.

te [te] pron (complemento de objeto) you; (complemento indirecto) (to) you; (reflexivo) (to) yourself; ¿~ **duele mucho el brazo?** does your arm hurt a lot?; ~ **equivocas** you're wrong; ¡**cálma**~! calm yourself!

té [te], pl **tés** nm tea; (reunión) tea party.

tea ['tea] nf (antorcha) torch.

teatral [tea'tral] adj theatre cpd; (fig) theatrical.

teatro [te'atro] nm theatre; (LITERATURA) plays pl, drama; **el** ~ (carrera) the theatre, acting; ~ **de aficionados/de variedades** amateur/variety theatre, vaudeville theater (US); **hacer** ~ (fig) to make a fuss.

tebeo [te'ßeo] nm children's comic.

techado [te'tʃaðo] nm (techo) roof; **bajo** ~ under cover.

techo ['tetʃo] nm (externo) roof; (interno) ceiling.

techumbre [te'tʃumbre] nf roof.

tecla ['tekla] nf (INFORM, MUS, TIP) key; (INFORM): ~ **de anulación/de borrar** cancel/delete key; ~ **de control/de edición** control/edit key; ~ **con flecha** arrow key; ~ **programable** user-defined key; ~ **de retorno/de tabulación** return/tab key; ~ **del cursor** cursor key; ~**s de control direccional del cursor** cursor control keys.

teclado [te'klaðo] nm keyboard (tb INFORM); ~ **numérico** (INFORM) numeric keypad.

teclear [tekle'aɾ] vi to strum; (fam) to drum ♦ vt (INFORM) to key (in), type in, keyboard.

tecleo [te'kleo] nm (MUS: sonido) strumming; (: forma de tocar) fingering; (fam) drumming.

tecnicismo [tekni'θismo] nm (carácter técnico) technical nature; (LING) technical term.

técnico, a ['tekniko, a] adj technical ♦ nm technician; (experto) expert ♦ nf (procedimientos) technique; (arte, oficio) craft.

tecnicolor [tekniko'lor] nm Technicolor ®.

tecnócrata [tek'nokrata] nm/f technocrat.

tecnología [teknolo'xia] nf technology; ~ **de estado sólido** (INFORM) solid-state technology; ~ **de la información** information technology.

tecnológico, a [tekno'loxiko, a] adj technological.

tecnólogo, a [tek'noloɣo, a] nm/f
technologist.
tedio ['teðjo] nm (aburrimiento) boredom;
(apatía) apathy; (fastidio) depression.
tedioso, a [te'ðjoso, a] adj boring;
(cansado) wearisome, tedious.
Teherán [tee'ran] nm Teheran.
teja ['texa] nf (azulejo) tile; (BOT) lime (tree).
tejado [te'xaðo] nm (tiled) roof.
tejano, a [te'xano, a] adj, nm/f Texan ♦ nmpl:
~s (vaqueros) jeans.
Tejas ['texas] nm Texas.
tejemaneje [texema'nexe] nm (actividad)
bustle; (lío) fuss, to-do; (intriga) intrigue.
tejer [te'xer] vt to weave; (tela de araña) to
spin; (AM) to knit; (fig) to fabricate ♦ vi:
~ **y destejer** to chop and change.
tejido [te'xiðo] nm fabric; (estofa, tela)
(knitted) material; (ANAT) tissue;
(textura) texture.
tejo ['texo] nm (BOT) yew (tree).
tel. abr (= teléfono) tel.
tela ['tela] nf (material) material; (de fruta,
en líquido) skin; (del ojo) film; **hay ~ para
rato** there's lots to talk about; **poner en
~ de juicio** to (call in) question; ~ **de
araña** cobweb, spider's web.
telar [te'lar] nm (máquina) loom; (de teatro)
gridiron; ~**es** nmpl textile mill sg.
telaraña [tela'raɲa] nf cobweb, spider's web.
tele... [tele] pref tele...
tele ['tele] nf (fam) TV.
telecargar [telekar'ɣar] vt (INFORM) to
download.
telecomunicación [telekomunika'θjon] nf
telecommunication.
teleconferencia [telekonfe'renθja] nf
(reunión) teleconference; (sistema)
teleconferencing.
telecontrol [telekon'trol] nm remote
control.
telecopiadora [telekopja'ðora] nf: ~
facsímil fax copier.
telediario [tele'ðjarjo] nm television news.
teledifusión [teleðifu'sjon] nf (television)
broadcast.
teledirigido, a [teleðiri'xiðo, a] adj
remote-controlled.
teléf. abr (= teléfono) tel.
teleférico [tele'feriko] nm (tren) cable-
railway; (de esquí) ski-lift.
telefilm [tele'film], **telefilme** [tele'filme]
nm TV film.
telefonazo [telefo'naθo] nm (fam) telephone
call; **te daré un** ~ I'll give you a ring.
telefonear [telefone'ar] vi to telephone.
telefónicamente [tele'fonikamente] adv by
(tele)phone.

telefónico, a [tele'foniko, a] adj telephone
cpd ♦ nf: **Telefónica** (ESP) Spanish national
telephone company, ≈ British Telecom.
telefonista [telefo'nista] nm/f telephonist.
teléfono [te'lefono] nm (tele)phone; ~
móvil mobile phone; **está hablando por**
~ he's on the phone.
telefoto [tele'foto] nf telephoto.
telegrafía [teleɣra'fia] nf telegraphy.
telégrafo [te'leɣrafo] nm telegraph; (fam:
persona) telegraph boy.
telegrama [tele'ɣrama] nm telegram.
teleimpresor [teleimpre'sor] nm
teleprinter.
telemática [tele'matika] nf telematics sg.
telémetro [te'lemetro] nm rangefinder.
telenovela [teleno'ßela] nf soap (opera).
teleobjetivo [teleobxe'tißo] nm telephoto
lens.
telepatía [telepa'tia] nf telepathy.
telepático, a [tele'patiko, a] adj telepathic.
teleproceso [telepro'θeso] nm
teleprocessing.
telescópico, a [tele'skopiko, a] adj
telescopic.
telescopio [tele'skopjo] nm telescope.
telesilla [tele'siʎa] nm chairlift.
telespectador, a [telespekta'ðor, a] nm/f
viewer.
telesquí [teles'ki] nm ski-lift.
teletex(to) [tele'teks(to)] nm teletext.
teletipista [teleti'pista] nm/f teletypist.
teletipo [tele'tipo] nm teletype(writer).
teletrabajo [teletra'ßaxo] nm teleworking.
televentas [tele'ßentas] nfpl telesales.
televidente [teleßi'ðente] nm/f viewer.
televisar [teleßi'sar] vt to televise.
televisión [teleßi'sjon] nf television; ~ **en
color/por satélite** colour/satellite
television; ~ **digital** digital television.
televisivo,a [teleßi'sißo, a] adj television
cpd.
televisor [teleßi'sor] nm television set.
télex ['teleks] nm telex; **máquina** ~ telex
(machine); **enviar por** ~ to telex.
telón [te'lon] nm curtain; ~ **de boca/
seguridad** front/safety curtain; ~ **de
acero** (POL) iron curtain; ~ **de fondo**
backcloth, background.
telonero, a [telo'nero, a] nm/f support act;
los ~**s** (MUS) the support band.
tema ['tema] nm (asunto) subject, topic;
(MUS) theme; ~**s de actualidad** current
affairs ♦ nf (obsesión) obsession; (manía)
ill-will; **tener** ~ **a algn** to have a grudge
against sb.
temario [te'marjo] nm (ESCOL) set of top-
ics; (de una conferencia) agenda.

temático, a [te'matiko, a] *adj* thematic ♦ *nf* subject matter.

tembladera [tembla'ðera] *nf* shaking; (*AM*) quagmire.

temblar [tem'blar] *vi* to shake, tremble; (*de frío*) to shiver.

tembleque [tem'bleke] *adj* shaking ♦ *nm* shaking.

temblón, ona [tem'blon, ona] *adj* shaking.

temblor [tem'blor] *nm* trembling; (*AM: de tierra*) earthquake.

tembloroso, a [temblo'roso, a] *adj* trembling.

temer [te'mer] *vt* to fear ♦ *vi* to be afraid; **temo que Juan llegue tarde** I am afraid Juan may be late.

temerario, a [teme'rarjo, a] *adj* (*imprudente*) rash; (*descuidado*) reckless, (*arbitrario*) hasty.

temeridad [temeri'ðað] *nf* (*imprudencia*) rashness; (*audacia*) boldness.

temeroso, a [teme'roso, a] *adj* (*miedoso*) fearful; (*que inspira temor*) frightful.

temible [te'mißle] *adj* fearsome.

temor [te'mor] *nm* (*miedo*) fear; (*duda*) suspicion.

témpano ['tempano] *nm* (*MUS*) kettledrum; ~ **de hielo** ice floe.

temperamento [tempera'mento] *nm* temperament; **tener** ~ to be temperamental.

temperar [tempe'rar] *vt* to temper, moderate.

temperatura [tempera'tura] *nf* temperature.

tempestad [tempes'tað] *nf* storm; ~ **en un vaso de agua** (*fig*) storm in a teacup.

tempestuoso, a [tempes'twoso, a] *adj* stormy.

templado, a [tem'plaðo, a] *adj* (*moderado*) moderate; (: *en el comer*) frugal; (: *en el beber*) abstemious; (*agua*) lukewarm; (*clima*) mild; (*MUS*) in tune, well-tuned.

templanza [tem'planθa] *nf* moderation; (*en el beber*) abstemiousness; (*del clima*) mildness.

templar [tem'plar] *vt* (*moderar*) to moderate; (*furia*) to restrain; (*calor*) to reduce; (*solución*) to dilute; (*afinar*) to tune (up); (*acero*) to temper ♦ *vi* to moderate; ~**se** *vr* to be restrained.

temple ['temple] *nm* (*humor*) mood; (*coraje*) courage; (*ajuste*) tempering; (*afinación*) tuning; (*pintura*) tempera.

templo ['templo] *nm* (*iglesia*) church; (*pagano etc*) temple; ~ **metodista** Methodist chapel.

temporada [tempo'raða] *nf* time, period;

(*estación, social, DEPORTE*) season; **en plena** ~ at the height of the season.

temporal [tempo'ral] *adj* (*no permanente*) temporary; (*REL*) temporal ♦ *nm* storm.

temporario, a [tempo'rarjo, a] *adj* (*AM*) temporary.

tempranero, a [tempra'nero, a] *adj* (*BOT*) early; (*persona*) early-rising.

temprano, a [tem'prano, a] *adj* early ♦ *adv* early; (*demasiado pronto*) too soon, too early; **lo más** ~ **posible** as soon as possible.

ten [ten] *vb* V **tener**.

tenacidad [tenaθi'ðað] *nf* (*gen*) tenacity; (*dureza*) toughness; (*terquedad*) stubbornness.

tenacillas [tena'θiʎas] *nfpl* (*gen*) tongs; (*para el pelo*) curling tongs; (*MED*) forceps.

tenaz [te'naθ] *adj* (*material*) tough; (*persona*) tenacious; (*pegajoso*) sticky; (*terco*) stubborn.

tenaza(s) [te'naθa(s)] *nf(pl)* (*MED*) forceps; (*TEC*) pliers; (*ZOOL*) pincers.

tendal [ten'dal] *nm* awning.

tendedero [tende'ðero] *nm* (*para ropa*) drying-place; (*cuerda*) clothes line.

tendencia [ten'denθja] *nf* tendency; (*proceso*) trend; ~ **imperante** prevailing tendency; ~ **del mercado** run of the market; **tener** ~ **a** to tend *o* have a tendency to.

tendenciosidad [tendenθjosi'ðað] *nf* tendentiousness.

tendencioso, a [tenden'θjoso, a] *adj* tendentious.

tender [ten'der] *vt* (*extender*) to spread out; (*ropa*) to hang out; (*vía férrea, cable*) to lay; (*cuerda*) to stretch; (*trampa*) to set ♦ *vi* to tend; ~**se** *vr* to lie down; (*fig: dejarse llevar*) to let o.s. go; (: *dejar ir*) to let things go; ~ **la cama/la mesa** (*AM*) to make the bed/lay the table.

ténder ['tender] *nm* (*FERRO*) tender.

tenderete [tende'rete] *nm* (*puesto*) stall; (*carretilla*) barrow; (*exposición*) display of goods.

tendero, a [ten'dero, a] *nm/f* shopkeeper.

tendido, a [ten'diðo, a] *adj* (*acostado*) lying down, flat; (*colgado*) hanging ♦ *nm* (*ropa*) washing; (*TAUR*) front rows *pl* of seats; (*colocación*) laying; (*ARQ: enyesado*) coat of plaster; **a galope** ~ flat out.

tendón [ten'don] *nm* tendon.

tendré [ten'dre] *etc vb* V **tener**.

tenducho [ten'dutʃo] *nm* small dirty shop.

tenebroso, a [tene'ßroso, a] *adj* (*oscuro*) dark; (*fig*) gloomy; (*siniestro*) sinister.

tenedor [tene'ðor] *nm* (*CULIN*) fork;
(*poseedor*) holder; ~ **de libros** bookkeeper; ~ **de acciones** shareholder; ~ **de
póliza** policyholder.
teneduría [teneðu'ria] *nf* keeping; ~ **de
libros** book-keeping.
tenencia [te'nenθja] *nf* (*de casa*) tenancy;
(*de oficio*) tenure; (*de propiedad*)
possession; ~ **asegurada** security of
tenure; ~ **ilícita de armas** illegal
possession of weapons.

================= *PALABRA CLAVE*

tener [te'ner] *vt* **1** (*poseer, gen*) to have; (*en
la mano*) to hold; **¿tienes un boli?** have
you got a pen?; **va a ~ un niño** she's
going to have a baby; **tiene los ojos
azules** he's got blue eyes; **¡ten** (*o* **tenga**)!,
¡aquí tienes (*o* **tiene**)! here you are!
2 (*edad, medidas*) to be; **tiene 7 años**
she's 7 (years old); **tiene 15 cm de largo**
it's 15 cm long
3 (*sentimientos, sensaciones*): ~ **sed/
hambre/frío/calor** to be thirsty/hungry/
cold/hot; ~ **celos** to be jealous; ~
cuidado to be careful; ~ **razón** to be
right; ~ **suerte** to be lucky
4 (*considerar*): **lo tengo por brillante** I
consider him to be brilliant; ~ **en
mucho a algn** to think very highly of sb
5 (+ *pp*, + *adj*, + *gerundio*): **tengo
terminada ya la mitad del trabajo** I've
done half the work already; **tenía el
sombrero puesto** he had his hat on; **tenía
pensado llamarte** I had been thinking of
phoning you; **nos tiene hartos** we're fed
up with him; **me ha tenido tres horas
esperando** he kept me waiting three
hours
6: ~ **que hacer algo** to have to do sth;
tengo que acabar este trabajo hoy I have
to finish this job today
7: **¿qué tienes, estás enfermo?** what's the
matter with you, are you ill?
8 (*locuciones*): **¿conque ésas tenemos?**
so it's like that, then?; **no las tengo
todas conmigo** I'm a bit unsure (about
it); **lo tiene difícil** he'll have a hard job
♦ ~**se** *vr* **1**: ~**se en pie** to stand up
2: ~**se por** to think o.s.; **se tiene por un
gran cantante** he thinks himself a great
singer.

tenga ['tenga] *etc vb V* **tener**.
tenia ['tenja] *nf* tapeworm.
teniente [te'njente] *nm* lieutenant; ~
coronel lieutenant colonel.
tenis ['tenis] *nm* tennis; ~ **de mesa** table

tennis.
tenista [te'nista] *nm/f* tennis player.
tenor [te'nor] *nm* (*tono*) tone; (*sentido*)
meaning; (*MUS*) tenor; **a ~ de** on the
lines of.
tenorio [te'norjo] *nm* (*fam*) ladykiller, Don
Juan.
tensar [ten'sar] *vt* to tauten; (*arco*) to draw.
tensión [ten'sjon] *nf* tension; (*TEC*) stress;
(*MED*): ~ **arterial** blood pressure; ~
nerviosa nervous strain; **tener la ~ alta**
to have high blood pressure.
tenso, a ['tenso, a] *adj* tense; (*relaciones*)
strained.
tentación [tenta'θjon] *nf* temptation.
tentáculo [ten'takulo] *nm* tentacle.
tentador, a [tenta'ðor, a] *adj* tempting
♦ *nm/f* tempter/temptress.
tentar [ten'tar] *vt* (*tocar*) to touch, feel;
(*seducir*) to tempt; (*atraer*) to attract;
(*probar*) to try (out); (*MED*) to probe; ~
hacer algo to try to do sth.
tentativa [tenta'tiβa] *nf* attempt; ~ **de
asesinato** attempted murder.
tentempié [tentem'pje] *nm* (*fam*) snack.
tenue ['tenwe] *adj* (*delgado*) thin, slender;
(*alambre*) fine; (*insustancial*) tenuous;
(*sonido*) faint; (*neblina*) light; (*lazo,
vínculo*) slight.
teñir [te'ɲir] *vt* to dye; (*fig*) to tinge; ~**se el
pelo** to dye one's hair.
teología [teolo'xia] *nf* theology.
teólogo, a [te'oloyo, a] *nm/f* theologist,
theologian.
teorema [teo'rema] *nm* theorem.
teoría [teo'ria] *nf* theory; **en ~** in theory.
teóricamente [te'orikamente] *adv*
theoretically.
teorice [teo'riθe] *etc vb V* **teorizar**.
teórico, a [te'oriko, a] *adj* theoretic(al)
♦ *nm/f* theoretician, theorist.
teorizar [teori'θar] *vi* to theorize.
tequila [te'kila] *nm o f* tequila.
TER [ter] *nm abr* (*FERRO*) = *tren español
rápido*.
terapeuta [tera'peuta] *nm/f* therapist.
terapéutico, a [tera'peutiko, a] *adj*
therapeutic(al) ♦ *nf* therapeutics *sg*.
terapia [te'rapja] *nf* therapy; ~ **laboral**
occupational therapy.
tercer [ter'θer] *adj V* **tercero**.
tercermundista [terθermun'dista] *adj*
Third World *cpd*.
tercero, a [ter'θero, a] *adj* third (*delante de
nmsg*: **tercer**) ♦ *nm* (*árbitro*) mediator;
(*JUR*) third party.
terceto [ter'θeto] *nm* trio.
terciado, a [ter'θjaðo, a] *adj* slanting;

azúcar ~ brown sugar.

terciar [ter'θjar] vt (MAT) to divide into three; (inclinarse) to slope; (llevar) to wear across one's chest ♦ vi (participar) to take part; (hacer de árbitro) to mediate; ~**se** vr to arise.

terciario, a [ter'θjarjo, a] adj tertiary.

tercio ['terθjo] nm third.

terciopelo [terθjo'pelo] nm velvet.

terco, a ['terko, a] adj obstinate, stubborn; (material) tough.

tergal ® [ter'ɣal] nm Terylene ®.

tergiversación [terxiβersa'θjon] nf (deformación) distortion; (evasivas) prevarication.

tergiversar [terxiβer'sar] vt to distort ♦ vi to prevaricate.

termal [ter'mal] adj thermal.

termas ['termas] nfpl hot springs.

térmico, a ['termiko, a] adj thermic, thermal, heat cpd.

terminación [termina'θjon] nf (final) end; (conclusión) conclusion, ending.

terminal [termi'nal] adj terminal ♦ nm (ELEC, INFORM) terminal; ~ **conversacional** interactive terminal; ~ **de pantalla** visual display unit ♦ nf (AVIAT, FERRO) terminal.

terminante [termi'nante] adj (final) final, definitive; (tajante) categorical.

terminar [termi'nar] vt (completar) to complete, finish; (concluir) to end ♦ vi (llegar a su fin) to end; (parar) to stop; (acabar) to finish; ~**se** vr to come to an end; ~ **por hacer algo** to end up (by) doing sth.

término ['termino] nm end, conclusion; (parada) terminus; (límite) boundary; (en discusión) point; (LING, COM) term; ~ **medio** average; (fig) middle way; **en otros** ~s in other words; **en último** ~ (a fin de cuentas) in the last analysis; (como último recurso) as a last resort; **en** ~s **de** in terms of; **según los** ~s **del contrato** according to the terms of the contract.

terminología [terminolo'xia] nf terminology.

termita [ter'mita] nf termite.

termo ['termo] nm Thermos ® (flask).

termodinámico, a [termoði'namiko, a] adj thermodynamic ♦ nf thermodynamics sg.

termoimpresora [termoimpre'sora] nf thermal printer.

termómetro [ter'mometro] nm thermometer.

termonuclear [termonukle'ar] adj thermonuclear.

termostato [termos'tato] nm thermostat.

ternero, a [ter'nero, a] nm/f (animal) calf ♦ nf (carne) veal.

terneza [ter'neθa] nf tenderness.

ternilla [ter'niʎa] nf gristle; (cartílago) cartilage.

terno ['terno] nm (traje) three-piece suit; (conjunto) set of three.

ternura [ter'nura] nf (trato) tenderness; (palabra) endearment; (cariño) fondness.

terquedad [terke'ðað] nf obstinacy; (dureza) harshness.

terrado [te'rraðo] nm terrace.

Terranova [terra'noβa] nf Newfoundland.

terraplén [terra'plen] nm (AGR) terrace; (FERRO) embankment; (MIL) rampart; (cuesta) slope.

terráqueo, a [te'rrakeo, a] adj: **globo** ~ globe.

terrateniente [terrate'njente] nm landowner.

terraza [te'rraθa] nf (balcón) balcony; (techo) flat roof; (AGR) terrace.

terremoto [terre'moto] nm earthquake.

terrenal [terre'nal] adj earthly.

terreno, a [te'rreno, a] adj (de la tierra) earthly, worldly ♦ nm (tierra) land; (parcela) plot; (suelo) (fig) field; **un** ~ a piece of land; **sobre el** ~ on the spot; **ceder/perder** ~ to give/lose ground; **preparar el** ~ (a) (fig) to pave the way (for).

terrestre [te'rrestre] adj terrestrial; (ruta) land cpd.

terrible [te'rriβle] adj (espantoso) terrible; (aterrador) dreadful; (tremendo) awful.

territorial [territo'rjal] adj territorial.

territorio [terri'torjo] nm territory; ~ **bajo mandato** mandated territory.

terrón [te'rron] nm (de azúcar) lump; (de tierra) clod, lump; **terrones** nmpl land sg.

terror [te'rror] nm terror.

terrorífico, a [terro'rifiko, a] adj terrifying.

terrorismo [terro'rismo] nm terrorism.

terrorista [terro'rista] adj, nm/f terrorist.

terroso, a [te'rroso, a] adj earthy.

terruño [te'rruɲo] nm (pedazo) clod; (parcela) plot; (fig) native soil; **apego al** ~ attachment to one's native soil.

terso, a ['terso, a] adj (liso) smooth; (pulido) polished; (fig: estilo) flowing.

tersura [ter'sura] nf smoothness; (brillo) shine.

tertulia [ter'tulja] nf (reunión informal) social gathering; (grupo) group, circle; (sala) clubroom; ~ **literaria** literary circle.

tesina [te'sina] nf dissertation.

tesis ['tesis] _nf inv_ thesis.
tesón [te'son] _nm_ (_firmeza_) firmness; (_tenacidad_) tenacity.
tesorería [tesore'ria] _nf_ treasurership.
tesorero, a [teso'rero, a] _nm/f_ treasurer.
tesoro [te'soro] _nm_ treasure; **T~ público** (_POL_) Exchequer.
test, _pl_ **tests** [tes(t), tes(t)] _nm_ test.
testaferro [testa'ferro] _nm_ figurehead.
testamentaría [testamenta'ria] _nf_ execution of a will.
testamentario, a [testamen'tarjo, a] _adj_ testamentary ♦ _nm/f_ executor/ executrix.
testamento [testa'mento] _nm_ will.
testar [tes'tar] _vi_ to make a will.
testarada [testa'raða] _nf,_ **testarazo** [testa'raθo] _nm:_ **darse un(a) ~** (_fam_) to bump one's head.
testarudo, a [testa'ruðo, a] _adj_ stubborn.
testículo [tes'tikulo] _nm_ testicle.
testificar [testifi'kar] _vt_ to testify; (_fig_) to attest ♦ _vi_ to give evidence.
testifique [testi'fike] _etc vb V_ **testificar.**
testigo [tes'tiɣo] _nm/f_ witness; **~ de cargo/descargo** witness for the prosecution/defence; **~ ocular** eye witness; **poner a algn por ~** to cite sb as a witness.
testimonial [testimo'njal] _adj_ (_prueba_) testimonial; (_gesto_) token.
testimoniar [testimo'njar] _vt_ to testify to; (_fig_) to show.
testimonio [testi'monjo] _nm_ testimony; **en ~ de** as a token _o_ mark of; **falso ~** perjured evidence, false witness.
teta ['teta] _nf_ (_de biberón_) teat; (_ANAT_) nipple; (_fam_) breast; (_fam!_) tit (_!_).
tétanos ['tetanos] _nm_ tetanus.
tetera [te'tera] _nf_ teapot; **~ eléctrica** (electric) kettle.
tetilla [te'tiʎa] _nf_ (_ANAT_) nipple; (_de biberón_) teat.
tétrico, a ['tetriko, a] _adj_ gloomy, dismal.
textil [teks'til] _adj_ textile.
texto ['teksto] _nm_ text.
textual [teks'twal] _adj_ textual; **palabras ~es** exact words.
textura [teks'tura] _nf_ (_de tejido_) texture; (_de mineral_) structure.
tez [teθ] _nf_ (_cutis_) complexion; (_color_) colouring.
tfno. _abr_ (= _teléfono_) tel.
ti [ti] _pron_ you; (_reflexivo_) yourself.
tía ['tia] _nf_ (_pariente_) aunt; (_mujer cualquiera_) girl, bird (_col_); (_fam: pej: vieja_) old bag; (: _prostituta_) whore.
Tibet [ti'ßet] _nm:_ **El ~** Tibet.

tibetano, a [tiße'tano, a] _adj, nm/f_ Tibetan ♦ _nm_ (_LING_) Tibetan.
tibia ['tißja] _nf_ tibia.
tibieza [ti'ßjeθa] _nf_ (_temperatura_) tepidness; (_fig_) coolness.
tibio, a ['tißjo, a] _adj_ lukewarm, tepid.
tiburón [tißu'ron] _nm_ shark.
tic [tik] _nm_ (_ruido_) click; (_de reloj_) tick; **~ nervioso** (_MED_) nervous tic.
tico, a ['tiko, a] _adj, nm/f_ (_AM fam_) Costa Rican.
tictac [tik'tak] _nm_ (_de reloj_) tick tock.
tiemble ['tjemble] _etc vb V_ **temblar.**
tiempo ['tjempo] _nm_ (_gen_) time; (_época, período_) age, period; (_METEOROLOGÍA_) weather; (_LING_) tense; (_edad_) age; (_de juego_) half; **a ~** in time; **a un _o_ al mismo ~** at the same time; **al poco ~** very soon (after); **andando el ~** in due course; **cada cierto ~** every so often; **con ~** in time; **con el ~** eventually; **de ~ en ~** from time to time; **en mis ~s** in my time; **en los buenos ~s** in the good old days; **hace buen/mal ~** the weather is fine/bad; **estar a ~** to be in time; **hace ~** some time ago; **hacer ~** to while away the time; **¿qué ~ tiene?** how old is he?; **motor de 2 ~s** two-stroke engine; **~ compartido** (_INFORM_) time sharing; **~ de ejecución** (_INFORM_) run time; **~ inactivo** (_COM_) downtime; **~ libre** spare time; **~ de paro** (_COM_) idle time; **a ~ partido** (_trabajar_) part-time; **~ preferencial** (_COM_) prime time; **en ~ real** (_INFORM_) real time.
tienda ['tjenda] _etc vb V_ **tender** ♦ _nf_ shop; (_más grande_) store; (_NAUT_) awning; **~ de campaña** tent.
tiene ['tjene] _etc vb V_ **tener.**
tienta ['tjenta] _nf_ (_MED_) probe; (_fig_) tact; **andar a ~s** to grope one's way along.
tiento ['tjento] _etc vb V_ **tentar** ♦ _nm_ (_tacto_) touch; (_precaución_) wariness; (_pulso_) steady hand; (_ZOOL_) feeler, tentacle.
tierno, a ['tjerno, a] _adj_ (_blando, dulce_) tender; (_fresco_) fresh.
tierra ['tjerra] _nf_ earth; (_suelo_) soil; (_mundo_) world; (_país_) country, land; (_ELEC_) earth, ground (_US_); **~ adentro** inland; **~ natal** native land; **echar ~ a un asunto** to hush an affair up; **no es de estas ~s** he's not from these parts; **la T~ Santa** the Holy Land.
tieso, a ['tjeso, a] _adj_ (_rígido_) rigid; (_duro_) stiff; (_fig: testarudo_) stubborn; (_fam: orgulloso_) conceited ♦ _adv_ strongly.
tiesto ['tjesto] _nm_ flowerpot; (_pedazo_)

piece of pottery.

tifoidea [tifoi'ðea] *nf* typhoid.

tifón [ti'fon] *nm* (*huracán*) typhoon; (*de mar*) tidal wave.

tifus ['tifus] *nm* typhus; ~ **icteroides** yellow fever.

tigre ['tixre] *nm* tiger; (*AM*) jaguar.

tijera [ti'xera] *nf* (*una* ~) (pair of) scissors *pl*; (*ZOOL*) claw; (*persona*) gossip; **de** ~ folding; **~s** *nfpl* scissors; (*para plantas*) shears; **unas ~s** a pair of scissors.

tijeretear [tixerete'ar] *vt* to snip ♦ *vi* (*fig*) to meddle.

tila ['tila] *nf* (*BOT*) lime tree; (*CULIN*) lime flower tea.

tildar [til'dar] *vt*: ~ **de** to brand as.

tilde ['tilde] *nf* (*defecto*) defect; (*trivialidad*) triviality; (*TIP*) tilde.

tilín [ti'lin] *nm* tinkle.

tilo ['tilo] *nm* lime tree.

timador, a [tima'ðor, a] *nm/f* swindler.

timar [ti'mar] *vt* (*robar*) to steal; (*estafar*) to swindle; (*persona*) to con; **~se** *vr* (*fam*) to make eyes (*con algn* at sb).

timbal [tim'bal] *nm* small drum.

timbrar [tim'brar] *vt* to stamp; (*sellar*) to seal; (*carta*) to postmark.

timbrazo [tim'braθo] *nm* ring; **dar un** ~ to ring the bell.

timbre ['timbre] *nm* (*sello*) stamp; (*campanilla*) bell; (*tono*) timbre; (*COM*) stamp duty.

timidez [timi'ðeθ] *nf* shyness.

tímido, a ['timiðo, a] *adj* shy, timid.

timo ['timo] *nm* swindle; **dar un** ~ **a algn** to swindle sb.

timón [ti'mon] *nm* helm, rudder; (*AM*) steering wheel; **coger el** ~ (*fig*) to take charge.

timonel [timo'nel] *nm* helmsman.

timorato, a [timo'rato, a] *adj* God-fearing; (*mojigato*) sanctimonious.

tímpano ['timpano] *nm* (*ANAT*) eardrum; (*MUS*) small drum.

tina ['tina] *nf* tub; (*AM: baño*) bath(tub).

tinaja [ti'naxa] *nf* large earthen jar.

tinerfeño, a [tiner'feɲo, a] *adj* of *o* from Tenerife ♦ *nm/f* native *o* inhabitant of Tenerife.

tinglado [tin'glaðo] *nm* (*cobertizo*) shed; (*fig: truco*) trick; (*intriga*) intrigue; **armar un** ~ to lay a plot.

tinieblas [ti'njeßlas] *nfpl* darkness *sg*; (*sombras*) shadows; **estamos en** ~ **sobre sus proyectos** (*fig*) we are in the dark about his plans.

tino ['tino] *nm* (*habilidad*) skill; (*MIL*) marksmanship; (*juicio*) insight;

(*moderación*) moderation; **sin** ~ immoderately; **coger el** ~ to get the feel *o* hang of it.

tinta ['tinta] *nf* ink; (*TEC*) dye; (*ARTE*) colour; ~ **china** Indian ink; **~s** *nfpl* (*fig*) shades; **medias ~s** (*fig*) half measures; **saber algo de buena** ~ to have sth on good authority.

tinte ['tinte] *nm* (*acto*) dyeing; (*fig*) tinge; (*barniz*) veneer.

tintero [tin'tero] *nm* inkwell; **se le quedó en el** ~ he clean forgot about it.

tintinear [tintine'ar] *vt* to tinkle.

tinto, a ['tinto, a] *adj* (*teñido*) dyed; (*manchado*) stained ♦ *nm* red wine.

tintorera [tinto'rera] *nf* shark.

tintorería [tintore'ria] *nf* dry cleaner's.

tintorero [tinto'rero] *nm* dry cleaner('s).

tintura [tin'tura] *nf* (*acto*) dyeing; (*QUÍMICA*) dye; (*farmacéutico*) tincture.

tiña ['tiɲa] *etc vb V* **teñir** ♦ *nf* (*MED*) ringworm.

tío ['tio] *nm* (*pariente*) uncle; (*fam: viejo*) old fellow; (: *individuo*) bloke, chap, guy (*US*).

tiovivo [tio'ßißo] *nm* roundabout.

típico, a ['tipiko, a] *adj* typical; (*pintoresco*) picturesque.

tiple ['tiple] *nm* soprano (voice) ♦ *nf* soprano.

tipo ['tipo] *nm* (*clase*) type, kind; (*norma*) norm; (*patrón*) pattern; (*fam: hombre*) fellow, bloke, guy (*US*); (*ANAT*) build; (: *de mujer*) figure; (*IMPRENTA*) type; ~ **bancario/de descuento** bank/discount rate; ~ **de interés** interest rate; ~ **de interés vigente** (*COM*) standard rate; ~ **de cambio** exchange rate; ~ **base** (*COM*) base rate; ~ **a término** (*COM*) forward rate; **dos ~s sospechosos** two suspicious characters; ~ **de letra** (*INFORM, TIP*) typeface; ~ **de datos** (*INFORM*) data type.

tipografía [tipoɣra'fia] *nf* (*tipo*) printing; (*lugar*) printing press.

tipográfico, a [tipo'ɣrafiko, a] *adj* printing.

tipógrafo, a [ti'poɣrafo, a] *nm/f* printer.

tíque(t) ['tike], *pl* **tíque(t)s** ['tikes] *nm* ticket; (*en tienda*) cash slip.

tiquismiquis [tikis'mikis] *nm* fussy person ♦ *nmpl* (*querellas*) squabbling *sg*; (*escrúpulos*) silly scruples.

tira ['tira] *nf* strip; (*fig*) abundance ♦ *nm*: ~ **y afloja** give and take; (*cautela*) caution; **la** ~ **de ...** (*fam*) lots of ....

tirabuzón [tiraßu'θon] *nm* corkscrew; (*rizo*) curl.

tiradero [tira'ðero] *nm* (*AM*) rubbish dump.

tirado, a [ti'raðo, a] *adj* (*barato*) dirt-cheap; (*fam: fácil*) very easy ♦ *nf* (*acto*) cast, throw; (*distancia*) distance; (*serie*) series; (*TIP*) printing, edition; **de una tirada** at one go; **está** ~ (*fam*) it's a cinch.

tirador, a [tira'ðor, a] *nm/f* (*persona*) shooter ♦ *nm* (*mango*) handle; (*ELEC*) flex; ~ **certero** sniper.

tiralíneas [tira'lineas] *nm inv* ruling-pen.

tiranía [tira'nia] *nf* tyranny.

tiránico, a [ti'raniko, a] *adj* tyrannical.

tiranizar [tirani'θar] *vt* (*pueblo, empleado*) to tyrannize.

tirano, a [ti'rano, a] *adj* tyrannical ♦ *nm/f* tyrant.

tirante [ti'rante] *adj* (*cuerda*) tight, taut; (*relaciones*) strained ♦ *nm* (*ARQ*) brace; (*TEC*) stay; (*correa*) shoulder strap; ~**s** *nmpl* braces, suspenders (*US*).

tirantez [tiran'teθ] *nf* tightness; (*fig*) tension.

tirar [ti'rar] *vt* to throw; (*volcar*) to upset; (*derribar*) to knock down *o* over; (*tiro*) to fire; (*cohete*) to launch; (*bomba*) to drop; (*edificio*) to pull down; (*desechar*) to throw out *o* away; (*disipar*) to squander; (*imprimir*) to print; (*dar: golpe*) to deal ♦ *vi* (*disparar*) to shoot; (*jalar*) to pull; (*fig*) to draw; (*interesar*) to appeal; (*fam: andar*) to go; (*tender a, buscar realizar*) to tend to; (*DEPORTE*) to shoot; ~**se** *vr* to throw o.s.; (*fig*) to demean o.s.; (*fam !*) to screw (*!*); ~ **abajo** to bring down, destroy; **tira más a su padre** he takes more after his father; ~ **de algo** to pull *o* tug (on) sth; **ir tirando** to manage; ~ **a la derecha** to turn *o* go right; **a todo** ~ at the most.

tirita [ti'rita] *nf* (sticking) plaster, bandaid (*US*).

tiritar [tiri'tar] *vi* to shiver.

tiritona [tiri'tona] *nf* shivering (fit).

tiro ['tiro] *nm* (*lanzamiento*) throw; (*disparo*) shot; (*tiroteo*) shooting; (*DEPORTE*) shot; (*TENIS, GOLF*) drive; (*alcance*) range; (*de escalera*) flight (of stairs); (*golpe*) blow; (*engaño*) hoax; ~ **al blanco** target practice; **caballo de** ~ cart-horse; **andar de** ~**s largos** to be all dressed up; **al** ~ (*AM*) at once; **de a** ~ (*AM fam*) completely; **se pegó un** ~ he shot himself; **le salió el** ~ **por la culata** it backfired on him.

tiroides [ti'roiðes] *nm inv* thyroid.

Tirol [ti'rol] *nm*: **El** ~ the Tyrol.

tirolés, esa [tiro'les, esa] *adj, nm/f* Tyrolean.

tirón [ti'ron] *nm* (*sacudida*) pull, tug; **de un** ~ in one go; **dar un** ~ **a** to pull at, tug at.

tirotear [tirote'ar] *vt* to shoot at; ~**se** *vr* to exchange shots.

tiroteo [tiro'teo] *nm* exchange of shots, shooting; (*escaramuza*) skirmish.

tirria ['tirrja] *nf*: **tener una** ~ **a algn** to have a grudge against sb.

tísico, a ['tisiko, a] *adj, nm/f* consumptive.

tisis ['tisis] *nf* consumption, tuberculosis.

tít. *abr* = **título**.

titánico, a [ti'taniko, a] *adj* titanic.

titere ['titere] *nm* puppet; **no dejar** ~ **con cabeza** to turn everything upside-down.

titilar [titi'lar] *vi* (*luz, estrella*) to twinkle; (*parpado*) to flutter.

titiritero, a [titiri'tero, a] *nm/f* (*acróbata*) acrobat; (*malabarista*) juggler.

titubeante [tituße'ante] *adj* (*inestable*) shaky, tottering; (*farfullante*) stammering; (*dudoso*) hesitant.

titubear [tituße'ar] *vi* to stagger; (*tartamudear*) to stammer; (*vacilar*) to hesitate.

titubeo [titu'ßeo] *nm* staggering; stammering; hesitation.

titulado, a [titu'laðo, a] *adj* (*libro*) entitled; (*persona*) titled.

titular [titu'lar] *adj* titular ♦ *nm/f* (*de oficina*) occupant; (*de pasaporte*) holder ♦ *nm* headline ♦ *vt* to title; ~**se** *vr* to be entitled.

título ['titulo] *nm* (*gen*) title; (*de diario*) headline; (*certificado*) professional qualification; (*universitario*) university degree; (*COM*) bond; (*fig*) right; ~**s** *nmpl* qualifications; **a** ~ **de** by way of; (*en calidad de*) in the capacity of; **a** ~ **de curiosidad** as a matter of interest; ~ **de propiedad** title deed; ~**s convertibles de interés fijo** (*COM*) convertible loan stock *sg*.

tiza ['tiθa] *nf* chalk; **una** ~ a piece of chalk.

tizna ['tiθna] *nf* grime.

tiznar [tiθ'nar] *vt* to blacken; (*manchar*) to smudge, stain; (*fig*) to tarnish.

tizón [ti'θon], **tizo** ['tiθo] *nm* brand; (*fig*) stain.

TLC *nm abr* (= *Tratado de Libre Comercio*) NAFTA.

Tm. *abr* = **tonelada(s) métrica(s)**.

toalla [to'aʎa] *nf* towel.

tobillo [to'ßiʎo] *nm* ankle.

tobogán [toßo'xan] *nm* toboggan; (*montaña rusa*) switchback; (*resbaladilla*) chute, slide.

toca ['toka] *nf* headdress.

tocadiscos [toka'ðiskos] *nm inv* record player.

tocado – tonada

tocado, a [to'kaðo, a] *adj* (*fruta etc*) rotten;
♦ *nm* headdress; **estar ~ de la cabeza**
(*fam*) to be weak in the head.

tocador [toka'ðor] *nm* (*mueble*) dressing
table; (*cuarto*) boudoir; (*neceser*) toilet
case; (*fam*) ladies' room.

tocante [to'kante]: **~ a** *prep* with regard
to; **en lo ~ a** as for, so far as concerns.

tocar [to'kar] *vt* to touch; (*sentir*) to feel;
(*con la mano*) to handle; (*MUS*) to play;
(*campana*) to ring; (*tambor*) to beat;
(*trompeta*) to blow; (*topar con*) to run
into, strike; (*referirse a*) to allude to; (*ser
emparentado con*) to be related to ♦ *vi* (*a
la puerta*) to knock (on *o* at the door); (*ser
de turno*) to fall to, be the turn of; (*ser
hora*) to be due; (*atañer*) to concern; **~se**
vr (*cubrirse la cabeza*) to cover one's head;
(*tener contacto*) to touch (each other);
~le a algn to fall to sb's lot; **~ en** (*NAUT*)
to call at; **por lo que a mí me toca** as far
as I am concerned; **esto toca en la locura**
this verges on madness.

tocateja [toka'texa] (*fam*): **a ~** *adv* in
readies.

tocayo, a [to'kajo, a] *nm/f* namesake.

tocino [to'θino] *nm* (bacon) fat; **~ de
panceta** bacon.

todavía [toða'βia] *adv* (*aun*) even; (*aún*)
still, yet; **~ más** yet *o* still more; **~ no**
not yet; **~ en 1970** as late as 1970; **está
lloviendo ~** it's still raining.

toditito, a [toði'tito, a], **todito, a** [to'ðito,
a] *adj* (*AM fam*) (absolutely) all.

<hr>

================= *PALABRA CLAVE*

todo, a ['toðo, a] *adj* **1** (*sg*) all; **toda la
carne** all the meat; **toda la noche** all
night, the whole night; **~ el libro** the
whole book; **toda una botella** a whole
bottle; **~ lo contrario** quite the opposite;
está toda sucia she's all dirty; **a toda
velocidad** at full speed; **por ~ el país**
throughout the whole country; **es ~ un
hombre** he's every inch a man; **soy ~
oídos** I'm all ears
2 (*pl*) all; every; **~s los libros** all the
books; **todas las noches** every night; **~s
los que quieran salir** all those who want
to leave; **~s vosotros** all of you
♦ *pron* **1** everything, all; **~s** everyone,
everybody; **lo sabemos ~** we know
everything; **~s querían más tiempo**
everybody *o* everyone wanted more
time; **nos marchamos ~s** all of us left;
corriendo y ~, no llegaron a tiempo even
though they ran, they still didn't arrive
in time

2 (*con preposición*): **a pesar de ~** even so,
in spite of everything; **con ~ él me sigue
gustando** even so I still like him; **le
llamaron de todo** they called him all the
names under the sun; **no me agrada del
~** I don't entirely like it
♦ *adv* all; **vaya ~ seguido** keep straight
on *o* ahead
♦ *nm*: **como un ~** as a whole; **arriba del ~**
at the very top.

<hr>

todopoderoso, a [toðopoðe'roso, a] *adj* all
powerful; (*REL*) almighty.

todoterreno [toðote'rreno] *nm* (*tb:
vehículo ~*) four-by-four.

toga ['toxa] *nf* toga; (*ESCOL*) gown.

Tokio ['tokjo] *n* Tokyo.

toldo ['toldo] *nm* (*para el sol*) sunshade;
(*tienda*) marquee; (*fig*) pride.

tole ['tole] *nm* (*fam*) commotion.

toledano, a [tole'ðano, a] *adj* of *o* from
Toledo ♦ *nm/f* native *o* inhabitant of
Toledo.

tolerable [tole'raβle] *adj* tolerable.

tolerancia [tole'ranθja] *nf* tolerance.

tolerante [tole'rante] *adj* tolerant; (*fig*)
open-minded.

tolerar [tole'rar] *vt* to tolerate; (*resistir*) to
endure.

Tolón [to'lon] *nm* Toulon.

toma ['toma] *nf* (*gen*) taking; (*MED*) dose;
(*ELEC*: *tb: ~ de corriente*) socket; (*MEC*)
inlet; **~ de posesión** (*por presidente*)
taking up office; **~ de tierra** (*AVIAT*)
landing.

tomadura [toma'ðura] *nf*: **~ de pelo** hoax.

tomar [to'mar] *vt* (*gen, CINE, FOTO, TV*) to
take; (*actitud*) to adopt; (*aspecto*) to take
on; (*notas*) to take down; (*beber*) to drink
♦ *vi* to take; (*AM*) to drink; **~se** *vr* to take;
~se por to consider o.s. to be; **¡toma!**
here you are!; **~ asiento** to sit down; **~ a
algn por loco** to think sb mad; **~ a bien/a
mal** to take well/badly; **~ en serio** to
take seriously; **~ el pelo a algn** to pull
sb's leg; **~la con algn** to pick a quarrel
with sb; **~ por escrito** to write down;
toma y daca give and take.

tomate [to'mate] *nm* tomato.

tomatera [toma'tera] *nf* tomato plant.

tomavistas [toma'βistas] *nm inv* movie
camera.

tomillo [to'miʎo] *nm* thyme.

tomo ['tomo] *nm* (*libro*) volume; (*fig*)
importance.

ton [ton] *abr* = **tonelada** ♦ *nm*: **sin ~ ni son**
without rhyme or reason.

tonada [to'naða] *nf* tune.

tonalidad [tonali'ðað] nf tone.
tonel [to'nel] nm barrel.
tonelada [tone'laða] nf ton; ~ **métrica** metric ton.
tonelaje [tone'laxe] nm tonnage.
tonelero [tone'lero] nm cooper.
tongo ['tongo] nm (DEPORTE) fix.
tónico, a ['toniko, a] adj tonic ♦ nm (MED) tonic ♦ nf (MUS) tonic; (fig) keynote.
tonificador, a [tonifika'ðor, a], **tonificante** [tonifi'kante] adj invigorating, stimulating.
tonificar [tonifi'kar] vt to tone up.
tonifique [toni'fike] etc vb V tonificar.
tonillo [to'niʎo] nm monotonous voice.
tono ['tono] nm (MUS) tone; (altura) pitch; (color) shade; **fuera de** ~ inappropriate; ~ **de marcar** (TELEC) dialling tone; **darse** ~ to put on airs.
tontear [tonte'ar] vi (fam) to fool about; (enamorados) to flirt.
tontería [tonte'ria] nf (estupidez) foolishness; (una ~) silly thing; ~**s** nfpl rubbish sg, nonsense sg.
tonto, a ['tonto, a] adj stupid; (ridículo) silly ♦ nm/f fool; (payaso) clown; **a tontas y a locas** anyhow; **hacer(se) el** ~ to act the fool.
topacio [to'paθjo] nm topaz.
topar [to'par] vt (tropezar) to bump into; (encontrar) to find, come across; (cabra etc) to butt ♦ vi: ~ **contra** o **en** to run into; ~ **con** to run up against; **el problema topa en eso** that's where the problem lies.
tope ['tope] adj maximum ♦ nm (fin) end; (límite) limit; (riña) quarrel; (FERRO) buffer; (AUTO) bumper; **al** ~ end to end; **fecha** ~ closing date; **precio** ~ top price; **sueldo** ~ maximum salary; ~ **de tabulación** tab stop.
tópico, a ['topiko, a] adj topical; (MED) local ♦ nm platitude, cliché; **de uso** ~ for external application.
topo ['topo] nm (ZOOL) mole; (fig) blunderer.
topografía [topoɣra'fia] nf topography.
topógrafo, a [to'poɣrafo, a] nm/f topographer; (agrimensor) surveyor.
toponimia [topo'nimja] nf place names pl; (estudio) study of place names.
toque ['toke] etc vb V tocar ♦ nm touch; (MUS) beat; (de campana) ring, chime; (MIL) bugle call; (fig) crux; **dar un** ~ **a** to test; **dar el último** ~ **a** to put the final touch to; ~ **de queda** curfew.
toquetear [tokete'ar] vt to handle; (fam!) to touch up.

toquilla [to'kiʎa] nf (chal) shawl.
tórax ['toraks] nm inv thorax.
torbellino [torbe'ʎino] nm whirlwind; (fig) whirl.
torcedura [torθe'ðura] nf twist; (MED) sprain.
torcer [tor'θer] vt to twist; (la esquina) to turn; (MED) to sprain; (cuerda) to plait; (ropa, manos) to wring; (persona) to corrupt; (sentido) to distort ♦ vi (cambiar de dirección) to turn; ~**se** vr to twist; (doblar) to bend; (desviarse) to go astray; (fracasar) to go wrong; ~ **un pie** to twist one's foot; **el coche torció a la derecha** the car turned right.
torcido, a [tor'θiðo, a] adj twisted; (fig) crooked ♦ nm curl.
tordo, a ['torðo, a] adj dappled ♦ nm thrush.
torear [tore'ar] vt (fig: evadir) to dodge; (toro) to fight ♦ vi to fight bulls.
toreo [to'reo] nm bullfighting.
torero, a [to'rero, a] nm/f bullfighter.
toril [to'ril] nm bullpen.
tormenta [tor'menta] nf storm; (fig: confusión) turmoil.
tormento [tor'mento] nm torture; (fig) anguish.
tormentoso, a [tormen'toso, a] adj stormy.
tornar [tor'nar] vt (devolver) to return, give back; (transformar) to transform ♦ vi to go back; ~**se** vr (ponerse) to become; (volver) to return.
tornasol [torna'sol] nm (BOT) sunflower; **papel de** ~ litmus paper.
tornasolado, a [tornaso'laðo, a] adj (brillante) iridescent; (reluciente) shimmering.
torneo [tor'neo] nm tournament.
tornero, a [tor'nero, a] nm/f machinist.
tornillo [tor'niʎo] nm screw; **apretar los** ~**s a algn** to apply pressure on sb; **le falta un** ~ (fam) he's got a screw loose.
torniquete [torni'kete] nm (puerta) turnstile; (MED) tourniquet.
torno ['torno] nm (TEC: grúa) winch; (: de carpintero) lathe; (tambor) drum; ~ **de banco** vice, vise (US); **en** ~ (a) round, about.
toro ['toro] nm bull; (fam) he-man; **los** ~**s** bullfighting sg.
toronja [to'ronxa] nf grapefruit.
torpe ['torpe] adj (poco hábil) clumsy, awkward; (movimiento) sluggish; (necio) dim; (lento) slow; (indecente) crude; (no honrado) dishonest.

torpedo [tor'peðo] *nm* torpedo.

torpemente [torpe'mente] *adv* (*sin destreza*) clumsily; (*lentamente*) slowly.

torpeza [tor'peθa] *nf* (*falta de agilidad*) clumsiness; (*lentitud*) slowness; (*rigidez*) stiffness; (*error*) mistake; (*crudeza*) obscenity.

torre ['torre] *nf* tower; (*de petróleo*) derrick; (*de electricidad*) pylon; (*AJEDREZ*) rook; (*AVIAT, MIL, NAUT*) turret.

torrefacto, a [torre'fakto, a] *adj*: **café ~ high roast coffee.

torrencial [torren'θjal] *adj* torrential.

torrente [to'rrente] *nm* torrent.

tórrido, a ['torriðo, a] *adj* torrid.

torrija [to'rrixa] *nf* fried bread; ~**s** French toast *sg*.

torsión [tor'sjon] *nf* twisting.

torso ['torso] *nm* torso.

torta ['torta] *nf* cake; (*fam*) slap; ~ **de huevos** (*AM*) omelette; **no entendió ni ~** he didn't understand a word of it.

tortazo [tor'taðo] *nm* (*bofetada*) slap; (*de coche*) crash.

tortícolis [tor'tikolis] *nm inv* stiff neck.

tortilla [tor'tiʎa] *nf* omelette; (*AM*) maize pancake; ~ **francesa/española** plain/potato omelette; **cambiar** *o* **volver la ~ a algn** to turn the tables on sb.

tortillera [torti'ʎera] *nf* (*fam!*) lesbian.

tórtola ['tortola] *nf* turtledove.

tortuga [tor'tuɣa] *nf* tortoise; ~ **marina** turtle.

tortuoso, a [tor'twoso, a] *adj* winding.

tortura [tor'tura] *nf* torture.

torturar [tortu'rar] *vt* to torture.

torvo, a ['torβo, a] *adj* grim, fierce.

torzamos [tor'θamos] *etc vb V* torcer.

tos [tos] *nf inv* cough; ~ **ferina** whooping cough.

Toscana [tos'kana] *nf*: **La ~** Tuscany.

tosco, a ['tosko, a] *adj* coarse.

toser [to'ser] *vi* to cough; **no hay quien le tosa** he's in a class by himself.

tostado, a [tos'taðo, a] *adj* toasted; (*por el sol*) dark brown; (*piel*) tanned ♦ *nf* tan; (*pan*) piece of toast; **tostadas** *nfpl* toast *sg*.

tostador [tosta'ðor] *nm* toaster.

tostar [tos'tar] *vt* to toast; (*café*) to roast; (*al sol*) to tan; ~**se** *vr* to get brown.

tostón [tos'ton] *nm*: **ser un ~** to be a drag.

total [to'tal] *adj* total ♦ *adv* in short; (*al fin y al cabo*) when all is said and done ♦ *nm* total; **en ~** in all; ~ **que** to cut a long story short; ~ **de comprobación** (*INFORM*) hash total; ~ **debe/haber** (*COM*) debit/assets total.

totalidad [totali'ðað] *nf* whole.

totalitario, a [totali'tarjo, a] *adj* totalitarian.

totalmente [to'talmente] *adv* totally.

tóxico, a ['toksiko, a] *adj* toxic ♦ *nm* poison.

toxicómano, a [toksi'komano, a] *adj* addicted to drugs ♦ *nm/f* drug addict.

toxina [to'ksina] *nf* toxin.

tozudo, a [to'θuðo, a] *adj* obstinate.

traba ['traβa] *nf* bond, tie; (*cadena*) fetter; **poner ~s a** to restrain.

trabajador, a [traβaxa'ðor, a] *nm/f* worker ♦ *adj* hard-working.

trabajar [traβa'xar] *vt* to work; (*arar*) to till; (*empeñarse en*) to work at; (*empujar; persona*) to push; (*convencer*) to persuade ♦ *vi* to work; (*esforzarse*) to strive; ¡**a ~**! let's get to work!; ~ **por hacer algo** to strive to do sth.

trabajo [tra'βaxo] *nm* work; (*tarea*) task; (*POL*) labour; (*fig*) effort; **tomarse el ~ de** to take the trouble to; ~ **por turno/a destajo** shift work/piecework; ~ **en proceso** (*COM*) work-in-progress.

trabajoso, a [traβa'xoso, a] *adj* hard; (*MED*) pale.

trabalenguas [traβa'lengwas] *nm inv* tongue twister.

trabar [tra'βar] *vt* (*juntar*) to join, unite; (*atar*) to tie down, fetter; (*agarrar*) to seize; (*amistad*) to strike up; ~**se** *vr* to become entangled; (*reñir*) to squabble; **se le traba la lengua** he gets tongue-tied.

trabazón [traβa'θon] *nf* (*TEC*) joining, assembly; (*fig*) bond, link.

trabucar [traβu'kar] *vt* (*confundir*) to confuse, mix up; (*palabras*) to misplace.

trabuque [tra'βuke] *etc vb V* trabucar.

tracción [trak'θjon] *nf* traction; ~ **delantera/trasera** front-wheel/rear-wheel drive.

trace ['traθe] *etc vb V* trazar.

tractor [trak'tor] *nm* tractor.

trad. *abr* (= *traducido*) trans.

tradición [traði'θjon] *nf* tradition.

tradicional [traðiθjo'nal] *adj* traditional.

traducción [traðuk'θjon] *nf* translation; ~ **asistida por ordenador** computer-assisted translation.

traducible [traðu'θiβle] *adj* translatable.

traducir [traðu'θir] *vt* to translate; ~**se en** (*fig*) to entail, result in.

traductor, a [traðuk'tor, a] *nm/f* translator.

traduzca [tra'ðuθka] *etc vb V* traducir.

traer [tra'er] *vt* to bring; (*llevar*) to carry; (*ropa*) to wear; (*incluir*) to carry; (*fig*) to cause; ~**se** *vr*: ~**se algo** to be up to sth; ~**se bien/mal** to dress well/badly; **traérselas** to be annoying; ~ **consigo** to involve, entail; **es un problema que se**

las trae it's a difficult problem.
traficante [trafi'kante] *nm/f* trader, dealer.
traficar [trafi'kar] *vi* to trade; ~ **con** (*pey*) to deal illegally in.
tráfico ['trafiko] *nm* (*COM*) trade; (*AUTO*) traffic.
trafique [tra'fike] *etc vb V* **traficar.**
tragaderas [traɣa'ðeras] *nfpl* (*garganta*) throat *sg*, gullet *sg*; (*credulidad*) gullibility *sg*.
tragaluz [traɣa'luθ] *nm* skylight.
tragamonedas [traɣamo'neðas] *nm inv*, **tragaperras** [traɣa'perras] *nm inv* slot machine.
tragar [tra'ɣar] *vt* to swallow; (*devorar*) to devour, bolt down; ~**se** *vr* to swallow; (*tierra*) to absorb, soak up; **no le puedo** ~ (*persona*) I can't stand him.
tragedia [tra'xeðja] *nf* tragedy.
trágico, a ['traxiko, a] *adj* tragic.
trago ['traɣo] *nm* (*líquido*) drink; (*comido de golpe*) gulp; (*fam: de bebida*) swig; (*desgracia*) blow; ~ **amargo** (*fig*) hard time.
trague ['traɣe] *etc vb V* **tragar.**
traición [trai'θjon] *nf* treachery; (*JUR*) treason; (*una* ~) act of treachery.
traicionar [traiθjo'nar] *vt* to betray.
traicionero, a [traiθjo'nero, a] = **traidor, a.**
traída [tra'iða] *nf* carrying; ~ **de aguas** water supply.
traidor, a [trai'ðor, a] *adj* treacherous ♦ *nm/f* traitor.
traiga ['traiɣa] *etc vb V* **traer.**
trailer, *pl* **trailers** ['trailer, 'trailer(s)] *nm* trailer.
traje ['traxe] *etc vb V* **traer** ♦ *nm* (*gen*) dress; (*de hombre*) suit; (~ *típico*) costume; (*fig*) garb; ~ **de baño** swimsuit; ~ **de luces** bullfighter's costume; ~ **hecho a la medida** made-to-measure suit.
trajera [tra'xera] *etc vb V* **traer.**
trajín [tra'xin] *nm* haulage; (*fam: movimiento*) bustle; **trajines** *nmpl* goings-on.
trajinar [traxi'nar] *vt* (*llevar*) to carry, transport ♦ *vi* (*moverse*) to bustle about; (*viajar*) to travel around.
trama ['trama] *nf* (*fig*) link; (: *intriga*) plot; (*de tejido*) weft.
tramar [tra'mar] *vt* to plot; (*TEC*) to weave; ~**se** *vr* (*fig*): **algo se está tramando** there's something going on.
tramitar [trami'tar] *vt* (*asunto*) to transact; (*negociar*) to negotiate; (*manejar*) to handle.
trámite ['tramite] *nm* (*paso*) step; (*JUR*)

transaction; ~**s** *nmpl* (*burocracia*) paperwork *sg*, procedures; (*JUR*) proceedings.
tramo ['tramo] *nm* (*de tierra*) plot; (*de escalera*) flight; (*de vía*) section.
tramoya [tra'moja] *nf* (*TEAT*) piece of stage machinery; (*fig*) trick.
tramoyista [tramo'jista] *nm/f* scene shifter; (*fig*) trickster.
trampa ['trampa] *nf* trap; (*en el suelo*) trapdoor; (*prestidigitación*) conjuring trick; (*engaño*) trick; (*fam*) fiddle; (*de pantalón*) fly; **caer en la** ~ to fall into the trap; **hacer** ~**s** (*hacer juegos de manos*) to juggle, conjure; (*trampear*) to cheat.
trampear [trampe'ar] *vt, vi* to cheat.
trampilla [tram'piʎa] *nf* trap, hatchway.
trampolín [trampo'lin] *nm* trampoline; (*de piscina etc*) diving board.
tramposo, a [tram'poso, a] *adj* crooked, cheating ♦ *nm/f* crook, cheat.
tranca ['tranka] *nf* (*palo*) stick; (*viga*) beam; (*de puerta, ventana*) bar; (*borrachera*) binge; **a** ~**s y barrancas** with great difficulty.
trancar [tran'kar] *vt* to bar ♦ *vi* to stride along.
trancazo [tran'kaθo] *nm* (*golpe*) blow.
trance ['tranθe] *nm* (*momento difícil*) difficult moment; (*situación crítica*) critical situation; (*estado hipnotizado*) trance; **estar en** ~ **de muerte** to be at death's door.
tranco ['tranko] *nm* stride.
tranque ['tranke] *etc vb V* **trancar.**
tranquilamente [tran'kilamente] *adv* (*sin preocupaciones: leer, trabajar*) peacefully; (*sin enfadarse: hablar, discutir*) calmly.
tranquilice [tranki'liθe] *etc vb V* **tranquilizar.**
tranquilidad [trankili'ðað] *nf* (*calma*) calmness, stillness; (*paz*) peacefulness.
tranquilizador, a [trankiliθa'ðor, a] *adj* (*música*) soothing; (*hecho*) reassuring.
tranquilizante [trankili'θante] *nm* tranquillizer.
tranquilizar [trankili'θar] *vt* (*calmar*) to calm (down); (*asegurar*) to reassure.
tranquilo, a [tran'kilo, a] *adj* (*calmado*) calm; (*apacible*) peaceful; (*mar*) calm; (*mente*) untroubled.
Trans. *abr* (*COM*) = **transferencia.**
transacción [transak'θjon] *nf* transaction.
transar [tran'sar] *vi* (*AM*) = **transigir.**
transatlántico, a [transat'lantiko, a] *adj* transatlantic ♦ *nm* (ocean) liner.
transbordador [transβorða'ðor] *nm* ferry.
transbordar [transβor'ðar] *vt* to transfer;

~**se** *vr* to change.
transbordo [trans'ßorðo] *nm* transfer;
hacer ~ to change (trains).
transcender [transθen'der] *vt* = **trascender**.
transcribir [transkri'ßir] *vt* to transcribe.
transcurrir [transku'rrir] *vi* (*tiempo*) to
pass; (*hecho*) to turn out.
transcurso [trans'kurso] *nm* passing, lapse;
en el ~ de 8 días in the course of a week.
transeúnte [transe'unte] *adj* transient
♦ *nm/f* passer-by.
transexual [transe'kswal] *adj*, *nm/f*
transsexual.
transferencia [transfe'renθja] *nf*
transference; (*COM*) transfer; ~
bancaria banker's order; ~ de crédito
(*COM*) credit transfer; ~ electrónica de
fondos (*COM*) electronic funds transfer.
transferir [transfe'rir] *vt* to transfer;
(*aplazar*) to postpone.
transfiera [trans'fjera] *etc vb V* **transferir**.
transfigurar [transfixu'rar] *vt* to
transfigure.
transfiriendo [transfi'rjendo] *etc vb V*
transferir.
transformación [transforma'θjon] *nf*
transformation.
transformador [transforma'ðor] *nm*
transformer.
transformar [transfor'mar] *vt* to
transform; (*convertir*) to convert.
tránsfuga ['transfuxa] *nm/f* (*MIL*) deserter;
(*POL*) turncoat.
transfusión [transfu'sjon] *nf* (*tb*: ~ de
sangre) (blood) transfusion.
transgénico, a [trans'xeniko, a] *adj*
genetically modified.
transgredir [transxre'dir] *vt* to transgress.
transgresión [transxre'sjon] *nf*
transgression.
transición [transi'θjon] *nf* transition;
período de ~ transitional period.
transido, a [tran'siðo, a] *adj* overcome; ~
de angustia beset with anxiety; ~ de
dolor racked with pain.
transigir [transi'xir] *vi* to compromise;
(*ceder*) to make concessions.
transija [tran'sixa] *etc vb V* **transigir**.
Transilvania [transil'ßanja] *nf*
Transylvania.
transistor [transis'tor] *nm* transistor.
transitable [transi'taßle] *adj* (*camino*)
passable.
transitar [transi'tar] *vi* to go (from place to
place).
transitivo, a [transi'tißo, a] *adj* transitive.
tránsito ['transito] *nm* transit; (*AUTO*)
traffic; (*parada*) stop; horas de máximo ~

rush hours; "se prohíbe el ~" "no
thoroughfare."
transitorio, a [transi'torjo, a] *adj*
transitory.
transmisión [transmi'sjon] *nf* (*RADIO, TV*)
transmission, broadcast(ing);
(*transferencia*) transfer; ~ en circuito
hookup; ~ en directo/exterior live/
outside broadcast; ~ de datos (en
paralelo/en serie) (*INFORM*) (parallel/
serial) data transfer *o* transmission;
plena/media ~ bidireccional (*INFORM*)
full/half duplex.
transmitir [transmi'tir] *vt* to transmit;
(*RADIO, TV*) to broadcast; (*enfermedad*) to
give, pass on.
transparencia [transpa'renθja] *nf*
transparency; (*claridad*) clearness,
clarity; (*foto*) slide.
transparentar [transparen'tar] *vt* to reveal
♦ *vi* to be transparent.
transparente [transpa'rente] *adj*
transparent; (*aire*) clear; (*ligero*)
diaphanous ♦ *nm* curtain.
transpirar [transpi'rar] *vi* to perspire; (*fig*)
to transpire.
transpondré [transpon'dre] *etc vb V*
transponer.
transponer [transpo'ner] *vt* to transpose;
(*cambiar de sitio*) to move about ♦ *vi*
(*desaparecer*) to disappear; (*ir más allá*) to
go beyond; ~se *vr* to change places;
(*ocultarse*) to hide; (*sol*) to go down.
transponga [trans'ponga] *etc vb V*
transponer.
transportador [transporta'ðor] *nm*
(*MECÁNICA*): ~ de correa belt conveyor.
transportar [transpor'tar] *vt* to transport;
(*llevar*) to carry.
transporte [trans'porte] *nm* transport;
(*COM*) haulage; Ministerio de T~s
Ministry of Transport.
transpuesto [trans'pwesto], **transpuse**
[trans'puse] *etc vb V* **transponer**.
transversal [transßer'sal] *adj* transverse,
cross ♦ *nf* (*tb*: calle ~) cross street.
transversalmente [transßersal'mente] *adv*
obliquely.
tranvía [tram'bia] *nm* tram, streetcar (*US*).
trapecio [tra'peθjo] *nm* trapeze.
trapecista [trape'θista] *nm/f* trapeze artist.
trapero, a [tra'pero, a] *nm/f* ragman.
trapicheos [trapi'tʃeos] *nmpl* (*fam*)
schemes, fiddles.
trapisonda [trapi'sonda] *nf* (*jaleo*) row;
(*estafa*) swindle.
trapo ['trapo] *nm* (*tela*) rag; (*de cocina*)
cloth; ~s *nmpl* (*fam*: de mujer) clothes,

dresses; **a todo** ~ under full sail; **soltar el** ~ (*llorar*) to burst into tears.

tráquea ['trakea] *nf* trachea, windpipe.

traqueteo [trake'teo] *nm* (*crujido*) crack; (*golpeteo*) rattling.

tras [tras] *prep* (*detrás*) behind; (*después*) after; ~ **de** besides; **día** ~ **día** day after day; **uno** ~ **otro** one after the other.

trascendencia [trasθen'denθja] *nf* (*importancia*) importance; (*filosofía*) transcendence.

trascendental [trasθenden'tal] *adj* important; transcendental.

trascender [trasθen'der] *vi* (*oler*) to smell; (*noticias*) to come out, leak out; (*eventos, sentimientos*) to spread, have a wide effect; ~ **a** (*afectar*) to reach, have an effect on; (*oler a*) to smack of; **en su novela todo trasciende a romanticismo** everything in his novel smacks of romanticism.

trascienda [tras'θjenda] *etc vb V* **trascender**.

trasegar [trase'ɣar] *vt* (*mover*) to move about; (*vino*) to decant.

trasegué [trase'ɣe], **traseguemos** [trase'ɣemos] *etc vb V* **trasegar**.

trasero, a [tra'sero, a] *adj* back, rear ♦ *nm* (*ANAT*) bottom; ~**s** *nmpl* ancestors.

trasfondo [tras'fondo] *nm* background.

trasgo ['trasɣo] *nm* (*duende*) goblin.

trasgredir [trasɣre'ðir] *vt* to contravene.

trashumante [trasu'mante] *adj* migrating.

trasiego [tra'sjeɣo] *etc vb V* **trasegar** ♦ *nm* (*cambiar de sitio*) move, switch; (*de vino*) decanting; (*trastorno*) upset.

trasiegue [tra'sjeɣe] *etc vb V* **trasegar**.

trasladar [trasla'ðar] *vt* to move; (*persona*) to transfer; (*posponer*) to postpone; (*copiar*) to copy; (*interpretar*) to interpret; ~**se** *vr* (*irse*) to go; (*mudarse*) to move; ~**se a otro puesto** to move to a new job.

traslado [tras'laðo] *nm* move; (*mudanza*) move, removal; (*de persona*) transfer; (*copia*) copy; ~ **de bloque** (*INFORM*) block move, cut-and-paste.

traslucir [traslu'θir] *vt* to show; ~**se** *vr* to be translucent; (*fig*) to be revealed.

trasluz [tras'luθ] *nm* reflected light; **al** ~ against *o* up to the light.

trasluzca [tras'luθka] *etc vb V* **traslucir**.

trasmano [tras'mano]: **a** ~ *adv* (*fuera de alcance*) out of reach; (*apartado*) out of the way.

trasnochado, a [trasno'tʃaðo, a] *adj* dated.

trasnochador, a [trasnotʃa'ðor, a] *adj* given to staying up late ♦ *nm/f* (*fig*) night bird.

trasnochar [trasno'tʃar] *vi* (*acostarse tarde*) to stay up late; (*no dormir*) to have a sleepless night; (*pasar la noche*) to stay the night.

traspasar [traspa'sar] *vt* (*bala*) to pierce, go through; (*propiedad*) to sell, transfer; (*calle*) to cross over; (*límites*) to go beyond; (*ley*) to break; **"traspaso negocio"** "business for sale".

traspaso [tras'paso] *nm* transfer; (*fig*) anguish.

traspié [tras'pje], *pl* **traspiés** *nm* (*caída*) stumble; (*tropezón*) trip; (*fig*) blunder.

trasplantar [trasplan'tar] *vt* to transplant.

trasplante [tras'plante] *nm* transplant.

traspuesto, a [tras'pwesto, a] *adj*: **quedarse** ~ to doze off.

trastada [tras'taða] *nf* (*fam*) prank.

trastazo [tras'taθo] *nm* (*fam*) bump; **darse un** ~ (*persona*) to bump o.s.; (*en coche*) to have a bump.

traste ['traste] *nm* (*MUS*) fret; **dar al** ~ **con algo** to ruin sth; **ir al** ~ to fall through.

trastero [tras'tero] *nm* lumber room.

trastienda [tras'tjenda] *nf* backshop; **obtener algo por la** ~ to get sth by underhand means.

trasto ['trasto] *nm* (*mueble*) piece of furniture; (*tarro viejo*) old pot; (*pey: cosa*) piece of junk; (: *persona*) dead loss; ~**s** *nmpl* (*TEAT*) scenery *sg*; **tirar los** ~**s a la cabeza** to have a blazing row.

trastocar [trasto'kar] *vt* (*papeles*) to mix up.

trastornado, a [trastor'naðo, a] *adj* (*loco*) mad; (*agitado*) crazy.

trastornar [trastor'nar] *vt* to overturn, upset; (*fig: ideas*) to confuse; (: *nervios*) to shatter; (: *persona*) to drive crazy; ~**se** *vr* (*plan*) to fall through.

trastorno [tras'torno] *nm* (*acto*) overturning; (*confusión*) confusion; (*POL*) disturbance, upheaval; (*MED*) upset; ~ **estomacal** stomach upset; ~ **mental** mental disorder, breakdown.

trasunto [tra'sunto] *nm* copy.

trasvase [tras'ßase] *nm* (*de río*) diversion.

tratable [tra'taßle] *adj* friendly.

tratado [tra'taðo] *nm* (*POL*) treaty; (*COM*) agreement; (*LITERATURA*) treatise.

tratamiento [trata'mjento] *nm* treatment; (*TEC*) processing; (*de problema*) handling; ~ **de datos** (*INFORM*) data processing; ~ **de gráficos** (*INFORM*) graphics; ~ **de márgenes** margin settings; ~ **de textos** (*INFORM*) word processing; ~ **por lotes** (*INFORM*) batch processing; ~ **de tú** familiar address.

tratante [tra'tante] *nm/f* dealer, merchandizer.

tratar [tra'tar] *vt* (*ocuparse de*) to treat; (*manejar, TEC*) to handle; (*INFORM*) to process; (*MED*) to treat; (*dirigirse a: persona*) to address ♦ *vi*: ~ **de** (*hablar sobre*) to deal with, be about; (*intentar*) to try to; ~ **con** (*COM*) to trade in; (*negociar*) to negotiate with; (*tener contactos*) to have dealings with; ~**se** *vr* to treat each other; **se trata de la nueva piscina** it's about the new pool; **¿de qué se trata?** what's it about?

trato ['trato] *nm* dealings *pl*; (*relaciones*) relationship; (*comportamiento*) manner; (*COM, JUR*) agreement, contract; (*título*) (form of) address; **de ~ agradable** pleasant; **de fácil ~** easy to get on with; ~ **equitativo** fair deal; **¡~ hecho!** it's a deal!; **malos ~s** ill-treatment *sg*.

trauma ['trauma] *nm* trauma.

traumático, a [trau'matiko, a] *adj* traumatic.

través [tra'ßes] *nm* (*contratiempo*) reverse; **al ~** across, crossways; **a ~ de** across; (*sobre*) over; (*por*) through; **de ~** across, (*de lado*) sideways.

travesaño [traße'saɲo] *nm* (*ARQ*) crossbeam; (*DEPORTE*) crossbar.

travesía [traße'sia] *nf* (*calle*) cross-street; (*NAUT*) crossing.

travesti [tra'ßesti] *nm/f* transvestite.

travesura [traße'sura] *nf* (*broma*) prank; (*ingenio*) wit.

travieso, a [tra'ßjeso, a] *adj* (*niño*) naughty; (*adulto*) restless; (*ingenioso*) witty ♦ *nf* crossing; (*ARQ*) crossbeam; (*FERRO*) sleeper.

trayecto [tra'jekto] *nm* (*ruta*) road, way; (*viaje*) journey; (*tramo*) stretch; (*curso*) course; **final del ~** end of the line.

trayectoria [trajek'torja] *nf* trajectory; (*desarrollo*) development, path; **la ~ actual del partido** the party's present line.

trayendo [tra'jendo] *etc vb V* **traer.**

traza ['traθa] *nf* (*ARQ*) plan, design; (*aspecto*) looks *pl*; (*señal*) sign; (*engaño*) trick; (*habilidad*) skill; (*INFORM*) trace.

trazado, a [tra'θaðo, a] *adj*: **bien ~** shapely, well-formed ♦ *nm* (*ARQ*) plan, design; (*fig*) outline; (*de carretera etc*) line, route.

trazador [traθa'ðor] *nm* plotter; ~ **plano** flatbed plotter.

trazar [tra'θar] *vt* (*ARQ*) to plan; (*ARTE*) to sketch; (*fig*) to trace; (*itinerario: hacer*) to plot; (*plan*) to follow.

trazo ['traθo] *nm* (*línea*) line; (*bosquejo*) sketch; ~**s** *nmpl* (*de cara*) lines, features.

TRB *abr* = *toneladas de registro bruto.*

trébol ['treßol] *nm* (*BOT*) clover; ~**es** *nmpl* (*NAIPES*) clubs.

trece ['treθe] *num* thirteen; **estar en sus ~** to stand firm.

trecho ['tretʃo] *nm* (*distancia*) distance; (*de tiempo*) while; (*fam*) piece; **de ~ en ~** at intervals.

tregua ['treɣwa] *nf* (*MIL*) truce; (*fig*) lull; **sin ~** without respite.

treinta ['treinta] *num* thirty.

treintena [trein'tena] *nf* (about) thirty.

tremendo, a [tre'mendo, a] *adj* (*terrible*) terrible; (*imponente: cosa*) imposing; (*fam: fabuloso*) tremendous; (*divertido*) entertaining.

trémulo, a ['tremulo, a] *adj* quivering; (*luz*) flickering.

tren [tren] *nm* (*FERRO*) train; ~ **de aterrizaje** undercarriage; ~ **directo/expreso/(de) mercancías/de pasajeros/suplementario** through/fast/goods *o* freight/passenger/relief train; ~ **de vida** way of life.

trenca ['trenka] *nf* duffel coat.

trence ['trenθe] *etc vb V* **trenzar.**

trenza ['trenθa] *nf* (*de pelo*) plait.

trenzar [tren'θar] *vt* (*el pelo*) to plait ♦ *vi* (*en baile*) to weave in and out; ~**se** *vr* (*AM*) to become involved.

trepa ['trepa] *nf* (*subida*) climb; (*ardid*) trick.

trepador(a) [trepa'ðor(a)] *nm/f* (*fam*): **ser un(a) ~** to be on the make ♦ *nf* (*BOT*) climber.

trepar [tre'par] *vt, vi* to climb; (*TEC*) to drill.

trepidación [trepiða'θjon] *nf* shaking, vibration.

trepidar [trepi'ðar] *vi* to shake, vibrate.

tres [tres] *num* three; (*fecha*) third; **las ~** three o'clock.

trescientos, as [tres'θjentos, as] *num* three hundred.

tresillo [tre'siʎo] *nm* three-piece suite; (*MUS*) triplet.

treta ['treta] *nf* (*COM etc*) gimmick; (*fig*) trick.

tri... [tri] *pref* tri..., three-....

tríada ['triaða] *nf* triad.

triangular [trjangu'lar] *adj* triangular.

triángulo [tri'angulo] *nm* triangle.

tribal [tri'ßal] *adj* tribal.

tribu ['trißu] *nf* tribe.

tribuna [tri'ßuna] *nf* (*plataforma*) platform; (*DEPORTE*) stand; (*fig*) public speaking; ~ **de la prensa** press box; ~ **del acusado** (*JUR*) dock; ~ **del jurado** jury box.

tribunal [triβu'nal] *nm* (*juicio*) court; (*comisión, fig*) tribunal; (*ESCOL: examinadores*) board of examiners; **T~ Supremo** High Court, (*US*) Supreme Court; **T~ de Justicia de las Comunidades Europeas** European Court of Justice.

tributar [triβu'tar] *vt* to pay; (*las gracias*) to give; (*cariño*) to show.

tributario, a [triβu'tarjo, a] *adj* (*GEO, POL*) tributary *cpd*; (*ECON*) tax *cpd*, taxation *cpd* ♦ *nm* (*GEO*) tributary ♦ *nm/f* (*COM*) taxpayer; **sistema ~** tax system.

tributo [tri'βuto] *nm* (*COM*) tax.

trice ['triθe] *etc vb V* **trizar**.

triciclo [tri'θiklo] *nm* tricycle.

tricornio [tri'kornjo] *nm* three-cornered hat.

tricota [tri'kota] *nf* (*AM*) knitted sweater.

tricotar [triko'tar] *vi* to knit.

tridimensional [triðimensjo'nal] *adj* three-dimensional.

trienal [trje'nal] *adj* three-year.

trifulca [tri'fulka] *nf* (*fam*) row, shindy.

trigal [tri'ɣal] *nm* wheat field.

trigésimo, a [tri'xesimo, a] *num* thirtieth.

trigo ['triɣo] *nm* wheat; **~s** *nmpl* wheat field(s) (*pl*).

trigueño, a [tri'ɣeɲo, a] *adj* (*pelo*) corn-coloured; (*piel*) olive-skinned.

trillado, a [tri'ʎaðo, a] *adj* threshed; (*fig*) trite, hackneyed.

trilladora [triʎa'ðora] *nf* threshing machine.

trillar [tri'ʎar] *vt* (*AGR*) to thresh; (*fig*) to frequent.

trillizos, as [tri'ʎiθos, as] *nmpl/nfpl* triplets.

trilogía [trilo'xia] *nf* triology.

trimestral [trimes'tral] *adj* quarterly; (*ESCOL*) termly.

trimestre [tri'mestre] *nm* (*ESCOL*) term; (*COM*) quarter, financial period; (: *pago*) quarterly payment.

trinar [tri'nar] *vi* (*MUS*) to trill; (*ave*) to sing, warble; **está que trina** he's hopping mad.

trincar [trin'kar] *vt* (*atar*) to tie up; (*NAUT*) to lash; (*agarrar*) to pinion.

trinchante [trin'tʃante] *nm* (*para cortar carne*) carving knife; (*tenedor*) meat fork.

trinchar [trin'tʃar] *vt* to carve.

trinchera [trin'tʃera] *nf* (*fosa*) trench; (*para vía*) cutting; (*impermeable*) trench-coat.

trineo [tri'neo] *nm* sledge.

trinidad [trini'ðað] *nf* trio; (*REL*): **la T~** the Trinity.

trino ['trino] *nm* trill.

trinque ['trinke] *etc vb V* **trincar**.

trinquete [trin'kete] *nm* (*TEC*) pawl; (*NAUT*) foremast.

trío ['trio] *nm* trio.

tripa ['tripa] *nf* (*ANAT*) intestine; (*fig, fam*) belly; **~s** *nfpl* (*ANAT*) insides; (*CULIN*) tripe *sg*; **tener mucha ~** to be fat; **me duelen las ~s** I have a stomach ache.

tripartito, a [tripar'tito, a] *adj* tripartite.

triple ['triple] *adj* triple; (*tres veces*) threefold.

triplicado, a [tripli'kaðo, a] *adj*: **por ~** in triplicate.

triplicar [tripli'kar] *vt* to treble.

triplo ['triplo] *adj* = **triple**.

trípode ['tripoðe] *nm* tripod.

Trípoli ['tripoli] *nm* Tripoli.

tríptico ['triptiko] *nm* (*ARTE*) triptych; (*documento*) three-part document.

tripulación [tripula'θjon] *nf* crew.

tripulante [tripu'lante] *nm/f* crewman/woman.

tripular [tripu'lar] *vt* (*barco*) to man; (*AUTO*) to drive.

triquiñuela [triki'ɲwela] *nf* trick.

tris [tris] *nm* crack; **en un ~** in an instant; **estar en un ~ de hacer algo** to be within an inch of doing sth.

triste ['triste] *adj* (*afligido*) sad; (*sombrío*) melancholy, gloomy; (*desolado*) desolate; (*lamentable*) sorry, miserable; (*viejo*) old; (*único*) single; **no queda sino un ~ penique** there's just one miserable penny left.

tristeza [tris'teθa] *nf* (*aflicción*) sadness; (*melancolía*) melancholy; (*de lugar*) desolation; (*pena*) misery.

tristón, ona [tris'ton, ona] *adj* sad, downhearted.

trituradora [tritura'ðora] *nf* shredder.

triturar [tritu'rar] *vt* (*moler*) to grind; (*mascar*) to chew; (*documentos*) to shred.

triunfador, a [triunfa'ðor, a] *adj* triumphant; (*ganador*) winning ♦ *nm/f* winner.

triunfal [triun'fal] *adj* triumphant; (*arco*) triumphal.

triunfante [triun'fante] *adj* triumphant; (*ganador*) winning.

triunfar [triun'far] *vi* (*tener éxito*) to triumph; (*ganar*) to win; (*NAIPES*) to be trumps; **triunfan corazones** hearts are trumps; **~ en la vida** to succeed in life.

triunfo [tri'unfo] *nm* triumph; (*NAIPES*) trump.

trivial [tri'βjal] *adj* trivial.

trivialice [triβja'liθe] *etc vb V* **trivializar**.

trivializar [triβjali'θar] *vt* to minimize, play

down.

triza ['triθa] nf bit, piece; **hacer algo** ~s to smash sth to bits; (papel) to tear sth to shreds.

trocar [tro'kar] vt (COM) to exchange; (dinero, de lugar) to change; (palabras) to exchange; (confundir) to confuse; (vomitar) to vomit; ~se vr (confundirse) to get mixed up; (transformarse): ~se **(en)** to change (into).

trocear [troθe'ar] vt to cut up.

trocha ['trotʃa] nf (sendero) by-path; (atajo) short cut.

troche ['trotʃe]: **a ~ y moche** adv helter-skelter, pell-mell.

trofeo [tro'feo] nm (premio) trophy; (éxito) success.

trola ['trola] nf (fam) fib.

tromba ['tromba] nf whirlwind; **~ de agua** cloudburst.

trombón [trom'bon] nm trombone.

trombosis [trom'bosis] nf inv thrombosis.

trompa ['trompa] nf (MUS) horn; (de elefante) trunk; (trompo) humming top; (hocico) snout; (ANAT) tube, duct ♦ nm (MUS) horn player; **~ de Falopio** Fallopian tube; **cogerse una ~** (fam) to get tight.

trompada [trom'paða] nf, **trompazo** [trom'paθo] nm (choque) bump, bang; (puñetazo) punch.

trompeta [trom'peta] nf trumpet; (clarín) bugle ♦ nm trumpeter.

trompetilla [trompe'tiʎa] nf ear trumpet.

trompicón [trompi'kon]: **a trompicones** adv in fits and starts.

trompo ['trompo] nm spinning top.

trompón [trom'pon] nm bump.

tronado, a [tro'naðo, a] adj broken-down.

tronar [tro'nar] vt (AM) to shoot, execute ♦ vi to thunder; (fig) to rage; (fam) to go broke.

tronchar [tron'tʃar] vt (árbol) to chop down; (fig: vida) to cut short; (esperanza) to shatter; (persona) to tire out; ~se vr to fall down; ~se de risa to split one's sides with laughter.

tronco ['tronko] nm (de árbol, ANAT) trunk; (de planta) stem; **estar hecho un ~** to be sound asleep.

tronera [tro'nera] nf (MIL) loophole; (ARQ) small window.

trono ['trono] nm throne.

tropa ['tropa] nf (MIL) troop; (soldados) soldiers pl; (soldados rasos) ranks pl; (gentío) mob.

tropecé [trope'θe], **tropecemos** [trope'θemos] etc vb V **tropezar**.

tropel [tro'pel] nm (muchedumbre) crowd; (prisa) rush; (montón) throng; **acudir** etc **en ~** to come etc in a mad rush.

tropelía [trope'lia] nm outrage.

tropezar [trope'θar] vi to trip, stumble; (fig) to slip up; ~**se** vr (dos personas) to run into each other; ~ **con** (encontrar) to run into; (topar con) to bump into.

tropezón [trope'θon] nm trip; (fig) blunder; (traspié): **dar un ~** to trip.

tropical [tropi'kal] adj tropical.

trópico ['tropiko] nm tropic.

tropiece [tro'pjeθe] etc vb V **tropezar**.

tropiezo [tro'pjeθo] etc vb V **tropezar** ♦ nm (error) slip, blunder; (desgracia) misfortune; (revés) setback; (obstáculo) snag; (discusión) quarrel.

troqué [tro'ke], **troquemos** [tro'kemos] etc vb V **trocar**.

trotamundos [trota'mundos] nm inv globetrotter.

trotar [tro'tar] vi to trot; (viajar) to travel about.

trote ['trote] nm trot; (fam) travelling; **de mucho ~** hard-wearing.

Troya ['troja] nf Troy; **aquí fue ~** now there's nothing but ruins.

trozo ['troθo] nm bit, piece; (LITERATURA, MUS) passage; **a ~s** in bits.

trucha ['trutʃa] nf (pez) trout; (TEC) crane.

truco ['truko] nm (habilidad) knack; (engaño) trick; (CINE) trick effect o photography; ~**s** nmpl billiards sg; ~ **publicitario** advertising gimmick.

trueco ['trweko] etc vb V **trocar**.

trueno ['trweno] etc vb V **tronar** ♦ nm (gen) thunder; (estampido) boom; (de arma) bang.

trueque ['trweke] etc vb V **trocar** ♦ nm exchange; (COM) barter.

trufa ['trufa] nf (BOT) truffle; (fig: fam) fib.

truhán, ana [tru'an, ana] nm/f rogue.

truncado, a [trun'kaðo, a] adj truncated.

truncar [trun'kar] vt (cortar) to truncate; (la vida etc) to cut short; (el desarrollo) to stunt.

trunque ['trunke] etc vb V **truncar**.

tu [tu] adj your.

tú [tu] pron you.

tubérculo [tu'βerkulo] nm (BOT) tuber.

tuberculosis [tuβerku'losis] nf inv tuberculosis.

tubería [tuβe'ria] nf pipes pl, piping; (conducto) pipeline.

tubo ['tuβo] nm tube, pipe; ~ **de desagüe** drainpipe; ~ **de ensayo** test-tube; ~ **de escape** exhaust (pipe); ~ **digestivo** alimentary canal.

tuerca ['twerka] *nf* (*TEC*) nut.
tuerce ['twerθe] *etc vb V* **torcer**.
tuerto, a ['twerto, a] *adj* (*torcido*) twisted; (*ciego*) blind in one eye ♦ *nm/f* one-eyed person ♦ *nm* (*ofensa*) wrong; **a tuertas** upside-down.
tuerza ['twerθa] *etc vb V* **torcer**.
tueste ['tweste] *etc vb V* **tostar**.
tuétano ['twetano] *nm* (*ANAT: médula*) marrow; (*BOT*) pith; **hasta los ~s** through and through, utterly.
tufo ['tufo] *nm* vapour; (*fig: pey*) stench.
tugurio [tu'ɣurjo] *nm* slum.
tul [tul] *nm* tulle.
tulipán [tuli'pan] *nm* tulip.
tullido, a [tu'ʎiðo, a] *adj* crippled; (*cansado*) exhausted.
tumba ['tumba] *nf* (*sepultura*) tomb; (*sacudida*) shake; (*voltereta*) somersault; **ser (como) una ~** to keep one's mouth shut.
tumbar [tum'bar] *vt* to knock down; (*doblar*) to knock over; (*fam: suj: olor*) to overpower ♦ *vi* to fall down; **~se** *vr* (*echarse*) to lie down; (*extenderse*) to stretch out.
tumbo ['tumbo] *nm* (*caída*) fall; (*de vehículo*) jolt; (*momento crítico*) critical moment.
tumbona [tum'bona] *nf* lounger.
tumor [tu'mor] *nm* tumour.
tumulto [tu'multo] *nm* turmoil; (*POL: motín*) riot.
tuna ['tuna] *nf* (*MUS*) student music group; *V tb* **tuno**; *see boxed note.*

> ### TUNA
>
> A **tuna** *is a musical group made up of university students, or quite often former students, who dress up in costumes from the "Edad de Oro", the Spanish Golden Age. These musical troupes wander through town, playing guitars, lutes and tambourines and serenading young women in the halls of residence. Sometimes they make impromptu appearances at weddings or parties, singing traditional songs for a few "pesetas".*

---

tunante [tu'nante] *adj* rascally ♦ *nm* rogue, villain; **¡~!** you villain!
tunda ['tunda] *nf* (*de tela*) shearing; (*golpeo*) beating.
tundir [tun'dir] *vt* (*tela*) to shear; (*hierba*) to mow; (*fig*) to exhaust; (*fam: golpear*) to beat.
tunecino, a [tune'θino, a] *adj, nm/f* Tunisian.

túnel ['tunel] *nm* tunnel.
Túnez ['tuneθ] *nm* Tunis.
túnica ['tunika] *nf* tunic; (*vestido largo*) long dress; (*ANAT, BOT*) tunic.
Tunicia [tu'niθja] *nf* Tunisia.
tuno, a ['tuno, a] *nm/f* (*fam*) rogue ♦ *nm* (*MUS*) member of a "tuna".
tuntún [tun'tun]: **al ~** *adv* thoughtlessly.
tupamaro, a [tupa'maro, a] *adj, nm/f* (*AM*) urban guerrilla.
tupé [tu'pe] *nm* quiff.
tupí [tu'pi], **tupí-guaraní** [tupigwara'ni] *adj, nm/f* Tupi-Guarani.
tupido, a [tu'piðo, a] *adj* (*denso*) dense; (*fig: torpe*) dim; (*tela*) close-woven.
turba ['turßa] *nf* (*combustible*) turf; (*muchedumbre*) crowd.
turbación [turßa'θjon] *nf* (*molestia*) disturbance; (*preocupación*) worry.
turbado, a [tur'ßaðo, a] *adj* (*molesto*) disturbed; (*preocupado*) worried.
turbante [tur'ßante] *nm* turban.
turbar [tur'ßar] *vt* (*molestar*) to disturb; (*incomodar*) to upset; **~se** *vr* to be disturbed.
turbina [tur'ßina] *nf* turbine.
turbio, a ['turßjo, a] *adj* (*agua etc*) cloudy; (*vista*) dim, blurred; (*tema*) unclear, confused; (*negocio*) shady ♦ *adv* indistinctly.
turbión [tur'ßjon] *nf* downpour; (*fig*) shower, hail.
turbo ['turßo] *adj inv* turbo(-charged) ♦ *nm* (*tb coche*) turbo.
turbulencia [turßu'lenθja] *nf* turbulence; (*fig*) restlessness.
turbulento, a [turßu'lento, a] *adj* turbulent; (*fig: intranquilo*) restless; (: *ruidoso*) noisy.
turco, a ['turko, a] *adj* Turkish ♦ *nm/f* Turk ♦ *nm* (*LING*) Turkish.
Turena [tu'rena] *nf* Touraine.
turgente [tur'xente], **túrgido, a** ['turxiðo, a] *adj* (*hinchado*) turgid, swollen.
Turín [tu'rin] *nm* Turin.
turismo [tu'rismo] *nm* tourism; (*coche*) saloon car; **hacer ~** to go travelling (abroad).
turista [tu'rista] *nm/f* tourist; (*vacacionista*) holidaymaker (*BRIT*), vacationer (*US*).
turístico, a [tu'ristiko, a] *adj* tourist *cpd*.
Turkmenistán [turkmeni'stan] *nm* Turkmenistan.
turnar [tur'nar] *vi*, **turnarse** *vr* to take (it in) turns.
turno ['turno] *nm* (*oportunidad, orden de prioridad*) opportunity; (*DEPORTE etc*) turn; **es su ~** it's his turn (next); **~ de**

día/de noche (*INDUSTRIA*) day/night shift.
turolense [turo'lense] *adj* of *o* from Teruel
♦ *nm/f* native *o* inhabitant of Teruel.
turquesa [tur'kesa] *nf* turquoise.
Turquía [tur'kia] *nf* Turkey.
turrón [tu'rron] *nm* (*dulce*) nougat; (*fam*)
sinecure, cushy job *o* number.
tute ['tute] *nm* (*NAIPES*) card game; **darse**
un ~ to break one's back.
tutear [tute'ar] *vt* to address as familiar
"tú"; **~se** *vr* to be on familiar terms.
tutela [tu'tela] *nf* (*legal*) guardianship;
(*instrucción*) guidance; **estar bajo la ~ de**
(*fig*) to be under the protection of.
tutelar [tute'lar] *adj* tutelary ♦ *vt* to
protect.
tutor, a [tu'tor, a] *nm/f* (*legal*) guardian;
(*ESCOL*) tutor; **~ de curso** form master/
mistress.
tuve ['tuβe] *etc vb V* **tener**.
tuyo, a ['tujo, a] *adj* yours, of yours ♦ *pron*
yours; **los ~s** (*fam*) your relations, your
family.
TVE *nf abr* = *Televisión Española*.

U u

U, u [u] *nf* (*letra*) U, u; **viraje en U** U-turn; **U**
de Ulises U for Uncle.
u [u] *conj* or.
UAR [war] *nfpl abr* (*ESP*) = *Unidades*
Antiterroristas Rurales.
ubérrimo, a [u'βerrimo, a] *adj* very rich,
fertile.
ubicación [uβika'θjon] *nf* (*esp AM*) place,
position, location.
ubicado, a [uβi'kaðo, a] *adj* (*esp AM*)
situated.
ubicar [uβi'kar] *vt* (*esp AM*) to place,
situate; (: *fig*) to install in a post;
(: *encontrar*) to find; **~se** *vr* to be situated,
be located.
ubicuo, a [u'βikwo, a] *adj* ubiquitous.
ubique [u'βike] *etc vb V* **ubicar**.
ubre ['uβre] *nf* udder.
Ucrania [u'kranja] *nf* Ukraine.
ucraniano, a [ukra'njano, a] *adj*, *nm/f*
Ukrainian ♦ *nm* (*LING*) Ukrainian.
ucranio [u'kranjo] *nm* (*LING*) Ukrainian.
Ud(s) *abr* = **usted(es)**.
UE *nf abr* (= *Unión Europea*) EU.

UEFA *nf abr* (= *Unión de Asociaciones de*
Fútbol Europeo) UEFA.
UEO *nf abr* (= *Unión Europea Occidental*)
WEU.
UEP *nf abr* = *Unión Europea de Pagos*.
uf [uf] *excl* (*cansancio*) phew!; (*repugnancia*)
ugh!
ufanarse [ufa'narse] *vr* to boast; **~ de** to
pride o.s. on.
ufano, a [u'fano, a] *adj* (*arrogante*)
arrogant; (*presumido*) conceited.
UGT *nf abr V* **Unión General de**
Trabajadores.
ujier [u'xjer] *nm* usher; (*portero*)
doorkeeper.
úlcera ['ulθera] *nf* ulcer.
ulcerar [ulθe'rar] *vt* to make sore; **~se** *vr* to
ulcerate.
ulterior [ulte'rjor] *adj* (*más allá*) farther,
further; (*subsecuente, siguiente*)
subsequent.
ulteriormente [ulterjor'mente] *adv* later,
subsequently.
últimamente ['ultimamente] *adv*
(*recientemente*) lately, recently;
(*finalmente*) finally; (*como último recurso*)
as a last resort.
ultimar [ulti'mar] *vt* to finish; (*finalizar*) to
finalize; (*AM: rematar*) to finish off,
murder.
ultimátum [ulti'matum] *nm*, *pl*
ultimátums ultimatum.
último, a ['ultimo, a] *adj* last; (*más reciente*)
latest, most recent; (*más bajo*) bottom;
(*más alto*) top; (*fig*) final, extreme; **en las**
últimas on one's last legs; **por ~** finally.
ultra ['ultra] *adj* ultra ♦ *nm/f* extreme
right-winger.
ultracongelar [ultrakonxe'lar] *vt* to deep-
freeze.
ultraderecha [ultraðe'retʃa] *nf* extreme
right (wing).
ultrajar [ultra'xar] *vt* (*escandalizar*) to
outrage; (*insultar*) to insult, abuse.
ultraje [ul'traxe] *nm* outrage; insult.
ultraligero [ultrali'xero] *nm* microlight
(*BRIT*), microlite (*US*).
ultramar [ultra'mar] *nm*: **de *o* en ~** abroad,
overseas; **los países de ~** the overseas
countries.
ultramarino, a [ultrama'rino, a] *adj*
overseas, foreign ♦ *nmpl*: **~s** groceries;
tienda de ~s grocer's (shop).
ultranza [ul'tranθa]: **a ~** *adv* to the death;
(*a todo trance*) at all costs; (*completo*)
outright; (*POL etc*) out-and-out, extreme;
un nacionalista a ~ a rabid nationalist.
ultrarrojo, a [ultra'rroxo, a] *adj*

= **infrarrojo, a.**
ultrasónico, a [ultra'soniko, a] *adj*
ultrasonic.
ultratumba [ultra'tumba] *nf*: **la vida de ~**
the next life; **una voz de ~** a ghostly
voice.
ultravioleta [ultraßjo'leta] *adj inv*
ultraviolet.
ulular [ulu'lar] *vi* to howl; (*búho*) to hoot.
umbilical [umbili'kal] *adj*: **cordón ~**
umbilical cord.
umbral [um'bral] *nm* (*gen*) threshold; **~ de
rentabilidad** (*COM*) break-even point.
umbrío, a [um'brio, a] *adj* shady.
UME *nf abr* (= *Unión Monetaria y
Económica*) EMU.

=============== PALABRA CLAVE

un, una [un, 'una] *art indef* a; (*antes de vocal*)
an; **una mujer/naranja** a woman/an orange
♦ *adj* **1**: **unos** (*o* **unas**): **hay unos regalos para
ti** there are some presents for you; **hay
unas cervezas en la nevera** there are some
beers in the fridge
2 (*enfático*): **¡hace un frío!** it's so cold!;
¡tiene una casa! he's got some house!

U.N.A.M. ['unam] *nf abr* = *Universidad
Nacional Autónoma de México.*
unánime [u'nanime] *adj* unanimous.
unanimidad [unanimi'ðað] *nf* unanimity;
por ~ unanimously.
unción [un'θjon] *nf* anointing.
uncir [un'θir] *vt* to yoke.
undécimo, a [un'deθimo, a] *adj*, *nm/f* eleventh.
UNED [u'ned] *nf abr* (*ESP UNIV*: =
*Universidad Nacional de Enseñanza a
Distancia*) ≈ Open University (*BRIT*).
ungir [un'xir] *vt* to rub with ointment;
(*REL*) to anoint.
ungüento [un'gwento] *nm* ointment; (*fig*)
salve, balm.
únicamente ['unikamente] *adv* solely;
(*solamente*) only.
unicidad [uniθi'ðað] *nf* uniqueness.
único, a ['uniko, a] *adj* only; (*solo*) sole,
single; (*sin par*) unique; **hijo ~** only child.
unidad [uni'ðað] *nf* unity; (*TEC*) unit; **~
móvil** (*TV*) mobile unit; (*INFORM*): **~
central** system unit, central processing
unit; **~ de control** control unit; **~ de
disco** disk drive; **~ de entrada/salida**
input/output device; **~ de información**
data item; **~ periférica** peripheral
device; **~ de presentación visual** *o* **de
visualización** visual display unit; **~ procesadora central** central processing unit.

unido, a [u'niðo, a] *adj* joined, linked; (*fig*)
united.
unifamiliar [unifamil'jar] *adj*: **vivienda ~**
single-family home.
unificar [unifi'kar] *vt* to unite, unify.
unifique [uni'fike] *etc vb V* **unificar.**
uniformado, a [unifor'maðo, a] *adj*
uniformed, in uniform.
uniformar [unifor'mar] *vt* to make
uniform; (*TEC*) to standardize.
uniforme [uni'forme] *adj* uniform, equal;
(*superficie*) even ♦ *nm* uniform.
uniformidad [uniformi'ðað] *nf* uniformity;
(*llaneza*) levelness, evenness.
unilateral [unilate'ral] *adj* unilateral.
unión [u'njon] *nf* (*gen*) union; (*acto*)
uniting, joining; (*calidad*) unity; (*TEC*)
joint; (*fig*) closeness, togetherness; **en ~
con** (together) with, accompanied by; **~
aduanera** customs union; **U~ General de
Trabajadores (UGT)** (*ESP*) *Socialist
Union Confederation*; **U~ Europea**
European Union; **la U~ Soviética** the
Soviet Union; **punto de ~** (*TEC*) junction.
unir [u'nir] *vt* (*juntar*) to join, unite; (*atar*) to
tie, fasten; (*combinar*) to combine ♦ *vi*
(*ingredientes*) to mix well; **~se** *vr* to join
together, unite; (*empresas*) to merge; **les
une una fuerte simpatía** they are bound
by (a) strong affection; **~se en
matrimonio** to marry.
unisex [uni'seks] *adj inv* unisex.
unísono [u'nisono] *nm*: **al ~** in unison.
unitario, a [uni'tarjo, a] *adj* unitary; (*REL*)
Unitarian ♦ *nm/f* (*REL*) Unitarian.
universal [unißer'sal] *adj* universal; (*mundial*) world *cpd*; **historia ~** world history.
universidad [unißersi'ðað] *nf* university; **~
laboral** polytechnic, poly.
universitario, a [unißersi'tarjo, a] *adj*
university *cpd* ♦ *nm/f* (*profesor*) lecturer;
(*estudiante*) (university) student.
universo [uni'ßerso] *nm* universe.
unja ['unxa] *etc vb V* **ungir.**

=============== PALABRA CLAVE

uno, a ['uno, a] *adj* one; **es todo ~** it's all
one and the same; **~s pocos** a few; **~s
cien** about a hundred
♦ *pron* **1** one; **quiero sólo uno** I only want
one; **~ de ellos** one of them; **una de dos**
either one or the other; **no doy una hoy** I
can't do anything right today
2 (*alguien*) somebody, someone;
conozco a ~ que se te parece I know
somebody *o* someone who looks like
you; **~s querían quedarse** some (people)
wanted to stay

3 (*impersonal*) one; ~ **mismo** oneself; ~
nunca sabe qué hacer one never knows
what to do
4: ~**s ... otros ...** some ... others; **una y
otra son muy agradables** they're both
very nice; **(los)** ~**(s) a (los) otro(s)** each
other, one another
♦ *nf* one; **es la una** it's one o'clock
♦ *num* (number) one; **el día** ~ the first.

untar [un'tar] *vt* (*gen*) to rub; (*engrasar*) to
grease, oil; (*MED*) to rub (with
ointment); (*fig*) to bribe; ~**se** *vr* (*fig*) to be
crooked; ~ **el pan con mantequilla** to
spread butter on one's bread.
unto ['unto] *nm* animal fat; (*MED*)
ointment.
unza ['unθa] *etc vb* V **uncir.**
uña ['uɲa] *nf* (*ANAT*) nail; (*del pie*) toenail;
(*garra*) claw; (*casco*) hoof; (*arrancaclavos*)
claw; **ser** ~ **y carne** to be as thick as
thieves; **enseñar** *o* **mostrar** *o* **sacar las** ~**s**
to show one's claws.
UOE *nf abr* (*ESP MIL*) = *Unidad de
Operaciones Especiales.*
UPA *nf abr* = *Unión Panamericana.*
UPC *nf abr* (= *unidad procesadora central*)
CPU.
uperizado, a [uperi'θaðo, a] *adj*: **leche
uperizada** UHT milk.
Urales [u'rales] *nmpl* (*tb*: **Montes** ~) Urals.
uralita ® [ura'lita] *nf* corrugated asbestos
cement.
uranio [u'ranjo] *nm* uranium.
urbanidad [urβani'ðað] *nf* courtesy,
politeness.
urbanismo [urβa'nismo] *nm* town
planning.
urbanista [urβa'nista] *nm/f* town planner.
urbanización [urβaniθa'θjon] *nf* (*colonia,
barrio*) estate, housing scheme.
urbanizar [urβani'θar] *vt* to develop.
urbano, a [ur'βano, a] *adj* (*de ciudad*)
urban, town *cpd*; (*cortés*) courteous,
polite.
urbe ['urβe] *nf* large city, metropolis.
urdimbre [ur'ðimbre] *nf* (*de tejido*) warp;
(*intriga*) intrigue.
urdir [ur'ðir] *vt* to warp; (*fig*) to plot,
contrive.
urgencia [ur'xenθja] *nf* urgency; (*prisa*)
haste, rush; **salida de** ~ emergency exit;
servicios de ~ emergency services.
urgente [ur'xente] *adj* urgent; (*insistente*)
insistent; **carta** ~ registered (*BRIT*) *o*
special delivery (*US*) letter.
urgir [ur'xir] *vi* to be urgent; **me urge** I'm
in a hurry for it; **me urge terminarlo** I

must finish it as soon as I can.
urinario, a [uri'narjo, a] *adj* urinary ♦ *nm*
urinal, public lavatory, comfort station
(*US*).
urja ['urxa] *etc vb* V **urgir.**
urna ['urna] *nf* urn; (*POL*) ballot box; **acudir
a las** ~**s** (*fig: persona*) to (go and) vote;
(: *gobierno*) to go to the country.
urología [urolo'xia] *nf* urology.
urólogo, a [u'roloɣo, a] *nm/f* urologist.
urraca [u'rraka] *nf* magpie.
URSS *nf abr* (= *Unión de Repúblicas
Socialistas Soviéticas*) USSR.
Uruguay [uru'ɣwai] *nm*: **El** ~ Uruguay.
uruguayo, a [uru'ɣwajo, a] *adj, nm/f*
Uruguayan.
usado, a [u'saðo, a] *adj* (*gen*) used; (*ropa
etc*) worn; **muy** ~ worn out.
usanza [u'sanθa] *nf* custom, usage.
usar [u'sar] *vt* to use; (*ropa*) to wear; (*tener
costumbre*) to be in the habit of ♦ *vi*: ~ **de**
to make use of; ~**se** *vr* to be used; (*ropa*)
to be worn *o* in fashion.
USO *nf abr* (*ESP*. = *Unión Sindical Obrera*)
workers' union.
uso ['uso] *nm* use; (*MECÁNICA etc*) wear;
(*costumbre*) usage, custom; (*moda*)
fashion; **al** ~ in keeping with custom; **al**
~ **de** in the style of; **de** ~ **externo** (*MED*)
for external application; **estar en el** ~ **de
la palabra** to be speaking, have the floor;
~ **y desgaste** (*COM*) wear and tear.
usted [us'teð] *pron* (*sg: abr* **Ud** *o* **Vd**: *formal*)
you *sg*; ~**es** (*pl: abr* **Uds** *o* **Vds**: *formal*)
you *pl*; (*AM: formal y fam*) you *pl*.
usual [u'swal] *adj* usual.
usuario, a [usw'arjo, a] *nm/f* user; ~ **final**
(*COM*) end user.
usufructo [usu'frukto] *nm* use; ~ **vitalicio
(de)** life interest (in).
usura [u'sura] *nf* usury.
usurero, a [usu'rero, a] *nm/f* usurer.
usurpar [usur'par] *vt* to usurp.
utensilio [uten'siljo] *nm* tool; (*CULIN*)
utensil.
útero ['utero] *nm* uterus, womb.
útil ['util] *adj* useful; (*servible*) usable,
serviceable ♦ *nm* tool; **día** ~ working
day, weekday; **es muy** ~ **tenerlo aquí
cerca** it's very handy having it here
close by.
utilice [uti'liθe] *etc vb* V **utilizar.**
utilidad [utili'ðað] *nf* usefulness, utility;
(*COM*) profit; ~**es líquidas** net profit *sg*.
utilitario [utili'tarjo] *nm* (*INFORM*) utility.
utilizar [utili'θar] *vt* to use, utilize;
(*explotar*) to harness.
utopía [uto'pia] *nf* Utopia.

utópico, a [u'topiko, a] *adj* Utopian.
uva ['ußa] *nf* grape; ~ **pasa** raisin; ~ **de Corinto** currant; **estar de mala** ~ to be in a bad mood; **las (doce)** ~**s** *see boxed note.*

LAS UVAS

Las uvas *play an important part in the New Years' Eve ("Nochevieja") celebrations; on the stroke of midnight people from every part of Spain, at home, in restaurants or in the "plaza mayor", eat a grape for each stroke of the clock at the Puerta del Sol in Madrid. It is said to bring luck for the coming year.*

---

uve ['uße] *nf name of the letter V*; **en forma de** ~ V-shaped; ~ **doble** *name of the letter W.*
UVI ['ußi] *nf abr* (*ESP MED*: = *unidad de vigilancia intensiva*) ICU.

V v

V, v [(*ESP*) 'uße, (*AM*) be'lkorta, bet∫ika] *nf* (*letra*) V, v; **V de Valencia** V for Victor.
V. *abr* (= *visto*) approved, passed.
v. *abr* (= *voltio*) v.; (= *véase*) v.; (= *verso*) v.
va [ba] *vb V* **ir.**
V.A. *abr* = *Vuestra Alteza.*
vaca ['baka] *nf* (*animal*) cow; (*carne*) beef; (*cuero*) cowhide; ~**s flacas/gordas** (*fig*) bad/good times.
vacaciones [baka'θjones] *nfpl* holiday(s); **estar/irse** *o* **marcharse de** ~ to be/go (away) on holiday.
vacante [ba'kante] *adj* vacant, empty ♦ *nf* vacancy.
vaciado, a [baθja'ðaðo, a] *adj* (*hecho en molde*) cast in a mould; (*hueco*) hollow ♦ *nm* cast, mould(ing).
vaciar [ba'θjar] *vt* to empty (out); (*ahuecar*) to hollow out; (*moldear*) to cast; (*INFORM*) to dump ♦ *vi* (*río*) to flow (*en* into); ~**se** *vr* to empty; (*fig*) to blab, spill the beans.
vaciedad [baθje'ðað] *nf* emptiness.
vacilación [baθila'θjon] *nf* hesitation.
vacilante [baθi'lante] *adj* unsteady; (*habla*) faltering; (*luz*) flickering; (*fig*) hesitant.
vacilar [baθi'lar] *vi* to be unsteady; to falter; to flicker; to hesitate, waver;

(*persona*) to stagger, stumble; (*memoria*) to fail; (*esp AM*: *divertirse*) to have a great time.
vacilón [baθi'lon] *nm* (*esp AM*): **estar** *o* **ir de** ~ to have a great time.
vacío, a [ba'θio, a] *adj* empty; (*puesto*) vacant; (*desocupado*) idle; (*vano*) vain; (*charla etc*) light, superficial ♦ *nm* emptiness; (*FÍSICA*) vacuum; (*un* ~) (empty) space; **hacer el** ~ **a algn** to send sb to Coventry.
vacuna [ba'kuna] *nf* vaccine.
vacunar [baku'nar] *vt* to vaccinate; ~**se** *vr* to get vaccinated.
vacuno, a [ba'kuno, a] *adj* bovine.
vacuo, a ['bakwo, a] *adj* empty.
vadear [baðe'ar] *vt* (*río*) to ford; (*problema*) to overcome; (*persona*) to sound out.
vado ['baðo] *nm* ford; (*solución*) solution; (*descanso*) respite.
vagabundo, a [baɣa'ßundo, a] *adj* wandering; (*pey*) vagrant ♦ *nm/f* (*errante*) wanderer; (*vago*) tramp, bum (*US*).
vagamente [baɣa'mente] *adv* vaguely.
vagancia [ba'ɣanθja] *nf* vagrancy.
vagar [ba'ɣar] *vi* to wander; (*pasear*) to saunter up and down; (*no hacer nada*) to idle ♦ *nm* leisure.
vagido [ba'xiðo] *nm* wail.
vagina [ba'xina] *nf* vagina.
vago, a ['baɣo, a] *adj* vague; (*perezoso*) lazy; (*ambulante*) wandering ♦ *nm/f* (*vagabundo*) tramp, bum (*US*); (*flojo*) lazybones *sg*, idler.
vagón [ba'ɣon] *nm* (*de pasajeros*) carriage; (*de mercancías*) wagon; ~ **cama/ restaurante** sleeping/dining car.
vague ['baɣe] *etc vb V* **vagar.**
vaguear [baɣe'ar] *vi* to laze around.
vaguedad [baɣe'ðað] *nf* vagueness.
vahído [ba'iðo] *nm* dizzy spell.
vaho ['bao] *nm* (*vapor*) vapour, steam; (*olor*) smell; (*respiración*) breath; ~**s** *nmpl* (*MED*) inhalation *sg*.
vaina ['baina] *nf* sheath ♦ *nm* (*AM*) nuisance.
vainilla [bai'niʎa] *nf* vanilla.
vainita [bai'nita] *nf* (*AM*) green *o* French bean.
vais [bais] *vb V* **ir.**
vaivén [bai'ßen] *nm* to-and-fro movement; (*de tránsito*) coming and going; **vaivenes** *nmpl* (*fig*) ups and downs.
vajilla [ba'xiʎa] *nf* crockery, dishes *pl*; (*una* ~) service; ~ **de porcelana** chinaware.
val [bal], **valdré** [bal'dre] *etc vb V* **valer.**
vale ['bale] *nm* voucher; (*recibo*) receipt; (*pagaré*) I.O.U.; ~ **de regalo** gift voucher

o token.

valedero, a [bale'ðero, a] *adj* valid.

valenciano, a [balen'θjano, a] *adj, nm/f* Valencian ♦ *nm* (*LING*) Valencian.

valentía [balen'tia] *nf* courage, bravery; (*pey*) boastfulness; (*acción*) heroic deed.

valentísimo, a [balen'tisimo, a] *adj* (*superl de* **valiente**) very brave, courageous.

valentón, ona [balen'ton, ona] *adj* blustering.

valer [ba'ler] *vt* to be worth; (*MAT*) to equal; (*costar*) to cost; (*amparar*) to aid, protect ♦ *vi* (*ser útil*) to be useful; (*ser válido*) to be valid; ~**se** *vr* to defend o.s. ♦ *nm* worth, value; ~ **la pena** to be worthwhile; **¿vale?** O.K.?; **¡vale!** (*¡basta!*) that'll do!; **¡eso no vale!** that doesn't count!; **no vale nada** it's no good; (*mercancía*) it's worthless; (*argumento*) it's no use; **no vale para nada** he's no good at all; **más vale tarde que nunca** better late than never; **más vale que nos vayamos** we'd better go; ~**se de** to make use of, take advantage of; ~**se por sí mismo** to help *o* manage by o.s.

valga ['balɣa] *etc vb V* **valer.**

valía [ba'lia] *nf* worth; **de gran** ~ (*objeto*) very valuable.

validar [bali'ðar] *vt* to validate; (*POL*) to ratify.

validez [bali'ðeθ] *nf* validity; **dar** ~ **a** to validate.

válido, a ['baliðo, a] *adj* valid.

valiente [ba'ljente] *adj* brave, valiant; (*audaz*) bold; (*pey*) boastful; (*con ironía*) fine, wonderful ♦ *nm/f* brave man/ woman.

valija [ba'lixa] *nf* case; (*AM*) suitcase; (*mochila*) satchel; (*CORREOS*) mailbag; ~ **diplomática** diplomatic bag.

valioso, a [ba'ljoso, a] *adj* valuable; (*rico*) wealthy.

valla ['baʎa] *nf* fence; (*DEPORTE*) hurdle; (*fig*) barrier; ~ **publicitaria** billboard.

vallar [ba'ʎar] *vt* to fence in.

valle ['baʎe] *nm* valley, vale.

vallisoletano, a [baʎisole'tano, a] *adj* of *o* from Valladolid ♦ *nm/f* native *o* inhabitant of Valladolid.

valor [ba'lor] *nm* value, worth; (*precio*) price; (*valentía*) valour, courage; (*importancia*) importance; (*cara*) nerve, cheek (*fam*); **sin** ~ worthless; ~ **adquisitivo** *o* **de compra** purchasing power; **dar** ~ **a** to attach importance to; **quitar** ~ **a** to minimize the importance of; (*COM*): ~ **según balance** book value; ~ **comercial** *o* **de mercado** market value;

~ **contable/desglosado** asset/break-up value; ~ **de escasez** scarcity value; ~ **intrínseco** intrinsic value; ~ **a la par** par value; ~ **neto** net worth; ~ **de rescate/de sustitución** surrender/replacement value; *V tb* **valores.**

valoración [balora'θjon] *nf* valuation.

valorar [balo'rar] *vt* to value; (*tasar*) to price; (*fig*) to assess.

valores [ba'lores] *nmpl* (*COM*) securities; ~ **en cartera** *o* **habidos** investments.

vals [bals] *nm* waltz.

válvula ['balβula] *nf* valve.

vamos ['bamos] *vb V* **ir.**

vampiro, iresa [bam'piro, i'resa] *nm/f* vampire ♦ *nf* (*CINE*) vamp, femme fatale.

van [ban] *vb V* **ir.**

vanagloriarse [banaɣlo'rjarse] *vr* to boast.

vandalismo [banda'lismo] *nm* vandalism.

vándalo, a ['bandalo, a] *nm/f* vandal.

vanguardia [ban'gwardja] *nf* vanguard; **de** ~ (*ARTE*) avant-garde; **estar en** *o* **ir a la** ~ **de** (*fig*) to be in the forefront of.

vanguardista [bangwar'ðista] *adj* avant-garde.

vanidad [bani'ðað] *nf* vanity; (*inutilidad*) futility; (*irrealidad*) unreality.

vanidoso, a [bani'ðoso, a] *adj* vain, conceited.

vano, a ['bano, a] *adj* (*irreal*) unreal; (*irracional*) unreasonable; (*inútil*) vain, useless; (*persona*) vain, conceited; (*frívolo*) frivolous.

vapor [ba'por] *nm* vapour; (*vaho*) steam; (*de gas*) fumes *pl*; (*neblina*) mist; ~**es** *nmpl* (*MED*) hysterics; **al** ~ (*CULIN*) steamed.

vaporice [bapo'riθe] *etc vb V* **vaporizar.**

vaporizador [baporiθa'ðor] *nm* (*perfume etc*) spray.

vaporizar [bapori'θar] *vt* to vaporize; (*perfume*) to spray.

vaporoso, a [bapo'roso, a] *adj* vaporous; (*vahoso*) steamy; (*tela*) light, airy.

vapulear [bapule'ar] *vt* to thrash; (*fig*) to slate.

vaque ['bake] *etc vb V* **vacar.**

vaquería [bake'ria] *nf* dairy.

vaquero, a [ba'kero, a] *adj* cattle *cpd* ♦ *nm* cowboy; ~**s** *nmpl* jeans.

vaquilla [ba'kiʎa] *nf* heifer.

vara ['bara] *nf* stick, pole; (*TEC*) rod; ~ **mágica** magic wand.

varado, a [ba'raðo, a] *adj* (*NAUT*) stranded; **estar** ~ to be aground.

varar [ba'rar] *vt* to beach ♦ *vi*, ~**se** *vr* to be beached.

varear [bare'ar] *vt* to hit, beat; (*frutas*) to

knock down (with poles).

variable [ba'rjaßle] _adj, nf_ variable (_tb INFORM_).

variación [barja'θjon] _nf_ variation; **sin ~** unchanged.

variado, a [ba'rjaðo, a] _adj_ varied; (_dulces, galletas_) assorted; **entremeses ~s** a selection of starters.

variante [ba'rjante] _adj_ variant ♦ _nf_ (_alternativa_) alternative; (_AUTO_) bypass.

variar [ba'rjar] _vt_ (_cambiar_) to change; (_poner variedad_) to vary; (_modificar_) to modify; (_cambiar de posición_) to switch around ♦ _vi_ to vary; **~ de** to differ from; **~ de opinión** to change one's mind; **para ~** just for a change.

varicela [bari'θela] _nf_ chicken pox.

varices [ba'riθes] _nfpl_ varicose veins.

variedad [barje'ðað] _nf_ variety.

varilla [ba'riʎa] _nf_ stick; (_BOT_) twig; (_TEC_) rod; (_de rueda_) spoke; **~ mágica** magic wand.

vario, a ['barjo, a] _adj_ (_variado_) varied; (_multicolor_) motley; (_cambiable_) changeable; **~s** various, several.

variopinto, a [barjo'pinto, a] _adj_ diverse; **un público ~** a mixed audience.

varita [ba'rita] _nf_: **~ mágica** magic wand.

varón [ba'ron] _nm_ male, man.

varonil [baro'nil] _adj_ manly.

Varsovia [bar'soßja] _nf_ Warsaw.

vas [bas] _vb_ V **ir**.

vasco, a ['basko, a], **vascongado, a** [baskon'gaðo, a] _adj, nm/f_ Basque ♦ _nm_ (_LING_) Basque ♦ _nfpl_: **las Vascongadas** the Basque Country _sg_ o Provinces.

vascuence [bas'kwenθe] _nm_ (_LING_) Basque.

vasectomía [basekto'mia] _nf_ vasectomy.

vaselina [base'lina] _nf_ Vaseline ®.

vasija [ba'sixa] _nf_ (earthenware) vessel.

vaso ['baso] _nm_ glass, tumbler; (_ANAT_) vessel; (_cantidad_) glass(ful); **~ de vino** glass of wine; **~ para vino** wineglass.

vástago ['bastaɣo] _nm_ (_BOT_) shoot; (_TEC_) rod; (_fig_) offspring.

vasto, a ['basto, a] _adj_ vast, huge.

váter ['bater] _nm_ lavatory, W.C.

Vaticano [bati'kano] _nm_: **el ~** the Vatican; **la Ciudad del ~** the Vatican City.

vaticinar [batiθi'nar] _vt_ to prophesy, predict.

vaticinio [bati'θinjo] _nm_ prophecy.

vatio ['batjo] _nm_ (_ELEC_) watt.

vaya ['baja] _etc vb_ V **ir**.

Vda. _abr_ = **viuda**.

Vd(s) _abr_ = **usted(es)**.

ve [be] _vb_ V **ir, ver**.

vea ['bea] _etc vb_ V **ver**.

vecinal [beθi'nal] _adj_ (_camino, impuesto etc_) local.

vecindad [beθin'dað] _nf_, **vecindario** [beθin'darjo] _nm_ neighbourhood; (_habitantes_) residents _pl_.

vecino, a [be'θino, a] _adj_ neighbouring ♦ _nm/f_ neighbour; (_residente_) resident; **somos ~s** we live next door to one another.

vector [bek'tor] _nm_ vector.

veda ['beða] _nf_ prohibition; (_temporada_) close season.

vedado [be'ðaðo] _nm_ preserve.

vedar [be'ðar] _vt_ (_prohibir_) to ban, prohibit; (_idea, plan_) to veto; (_impedir_) to stop, prevent.

vedette [be'ðet] _nf_ (_TEAT, CINE_) star(let).

vega ['beɣa] _nf_ fertile plain o valley.

vegetación [bexeta'θjon] _nf_ vegetation.

vegetal [bexe'tal] _adj, nm_ vegetable.

vegetar [bexe'tar] _vi_ to vegetate.

vegetariano, a [bexeta'rjano, a] _adj, nm/f_ vegetarian.

vegetativo, a [bexeta'tißo, a] _adj_ vegetative.

vehemencia [bee'menθja] _nf_ (_insistencia_) vehemence; (_pasión_) passion; (_fervor_) fervour; (_violencia_) violence.

vehemente [bee'mente] _adj_ vehement; passionate; fervent; violent.

vehículo [be'ikulo] _nm_ vehicle; (_MED_) carrier; **~ de servicio público** public service vehicle; **~ espacial** spacecraft.

veinte ['beinte] _num_ twenty; (_orden, fecha_) twentieth; **el siglo ~** the twentieth century.

veintena [bein'tena] _nf_: **una ~** (about) twenty, a score.

vejación [bexa'θjon] _nf_ vexation; (_humillación_) humiliation.

vejamen [be'xamen] _nm_ satire.

vejar [be'xar] _vt_ (_irritar_) to annoy, vex; (_humillar_) to humiliate.

vejatorio, a [bexa'torjo, a] _adj_ humiliating, degrading.

vejez [be'xeθ] _nf_ old age.

vejiga [be'xiɣa] _nf_ (_ANAT_) bladder.

vela ['bela] _nf_ (_de cera_) candle; (_NAUT_) sail; (_insomnio_) sleeplessness; (_vigilia_) vigil; (_MIL_) sentry duty; (_fam_) snot; **a toda ~** (_NAUT_) under full sail; **estar a dos ~s** (_fam_) to be skint; **pasar la noche en ~** to have a sleepless night.

velado, a [be'laðo, a] _adj_ veiled; (_sonido_) muffled; (_FOTO_) blurred ♦ _nf_ soirée.

velador [bela'ðor] _nm_ watchman; (_candelero_) candlestick; (_AM_) bedside table.

velar [be'lar] *vt* (*vigilar*) to keep watch over; (*cubrir*) to veil ♦ *vi* to stay awake; ~ **por** to watch over, look after.

velatorio [bela'torjo] *nm* (funeral) wake.

veleidad [belei'ðað] *nf* (*ligereza*) fickleness; (*capricho*) whim.

velero [be'lero] *nm* (*NAUT*) sailing ship; (*AVIAT*) glider.

veleta [be'leta] *nm/f* fickle person ♦ *nf* weather vane.

veliz [be'lis] *nm* (*AM*) suitcase.

vello ['beʎo] *nm* down, fuzz.

vellón [be'ʎon] *nm* fleece.

velloso, a [be'ʎoso, a] *adj* fuzzy.

velludo, a [be'ʎuðo, a] *adj* shaggy ♦ *nm* plush, velvet.

velo ['belo] *nm* veil; ~ **de paladar** (*ANAT*) soft palate.

velocidad [beloθi'ðað] *nf* speed; (*TEC*) rate, pace, velocity; (*MECÁNICA*, *AUTO*) gear; **¿a qué ~?** how fast?; **de alta** ~ high-speed; **cobrar** ~ to pick up *o* gather speed; **meter la segunda** ~ to change into second gear; ~ **máxima de impresión** (*INFORM*) maximum print speed.

velocímetro [belo'θimetro] *nm* speedometer.

velódromo [be'loðromo] *nm* cycle track.

veloz [be'loθ] *adj* fast, swift.

ven [ben] *vb V* **venir**.

vena ['bena] *nf* vein; (*fig*) vein, disposition; (*GEO*) seam, vein.

venablo [be'naβlo] *nm* javelin.

venado [be'naðo] *nm* deer; (*CULIN*) venison.

venal [be'nal] *adj* (*ANAT*) venous; (*pey*) venal.

venalidad [benali'ðað] *nf* venality.

vencedor, a [benθe'ðor, a] *adj* victorious ♦ *nm/f* victor, winner.

vencer [ben'θer] *vt* (*dominar*) to defeat, beat; (*derrotar*) to vanquish; (*superar, controlar*) to overcome, master ♦ *vi* (*triunfar*) to win (through), triumph; (*pago*) to fall due; (*plazo*) to expire; **dejarse** ~ to yield, give in.

vencido, a [ben'θiðo, a] *adj* (*derrotado*) defeated, beaten; (*COM*) payable, due ♦ *adv*: **pagar** ~ to pay in arrears; **le pagan por meses** ~**s** he is paid at the end of the month; **darse por** ~ to give up.

vencimiento [benθi'mjento] *nm* collapse; (*COM: plazo*) expiration; **a su** ~ when it falls due.

venda ['benda] *nf* bandage.

vendaje [ben'daxe] *nm* bandage, dressing.

vendar [ben'dar] *vt* to bandage; ~ **los ojos** to blindfold.

vendaval [benda'βal] *nm* (*viento*) gale; (*huracán*) hurricane.

vendedor, a [bende'ðor, a] *nm/f* seller; ~ **ambulante** hawker, pedlar (*BRIT*), peddler (*US*).

vender [ben'der] *vt* to sell; (*comerciar*) to market; (*traicionar*) to sell out, betray; ~**se** *vr* to be sold; ~ **al contado/al por mayor/al por menor/a plazos** to sell for cash/wholesale/retail/on credit; "**se vende**" "for sale"; "**véndese coche**" "car for sale"; ~ **al descubierto** to sell short.

vendimia [ben'dimja] *nf* grape harvest; **la** ~ **de 1973** the 1973 vintage.

vendimiar [bendi'mjar] *vi* to pick grapes.

vendré [ben'dre] *etc vb V* **venir**.

Venecia [be'neθja] *nf* Venice.

veneciano, a [bene'θjano, a] *adj, nm/f* Venetian.

veneno [be'neno] *nm* poison, venom.

venenoso, a [bene'noso, a] *adj* poisonous.

venerable [bene'raβle] *adj* venerable.

veneración [benera'θjon] *nf* veneration.

venerar [bene'rar] *vt* (*reconocer*) to venerate; (*adorar*) to worship.

venéreo, a [be'nereo, a] *adj* venereal.

venezolano, a [beneθo'lano, a] *adj, nm/f* Venezuelan.

Venezuela [bene'θwela] *nf* Venezuela.

venga ['benga] *etc vb V* **venir**.

vengador, a [benga'ðor, a] *adj* avenging ♦ *nm/f* avenger.

venganza [ben'ganθa] *nf* vengeance, revenge.

vengar [ben'gar] *vt* to avenge; ~**se** *vr* to take revenge.

vengativo, a [benga'tiβo, a] *adj* (*persona*) vindictive.

vengue ['benge] *etc vb V* **vengar**.

venia ['benja] *nf* (*perdón*) pardon; (*permiso*) consent; **con su** ~ by your leave.

venial [be'njal] *adj* venial.

venida [be'niða] *nf* (*llegada*) arrival; (*regreso*) return; (*fig*) rashness.

venidero, a [beni'ðero, a] *adj* coming, future; **en lo** ~ in (the) future.

venir [be'nir] *vi* to come; (*llegar*) to arrive; (*ocurrir*) to happen; ~**se** *vr*: ~**se abajo** to collapse; ~ **a menos** (*persona*) to lose status; (*empresa*) to go downhill; ~ **bien** to be suitable, come just right; (*ropa, gusto*) to suit; ~ **mal** to be unsuitable *o* inconvenient, come awkwardly; **el año que viene** next year; **¡ven acá!** come (over) here!; **¡venga!** (*fam*) come on!

venta ['benta] *nf* (*COM*) sale; (*posada*) inn; ~ **a plazos** hire purchase; ~ **al contado/**

al por mayor/al por menor *o* **al detalle** cash sale/wholesale/retail; ~ **a domicilio** door-to-door selling; ~ **y arrendamiento al vendedor** sale and lease back; ~ **de liquidación** clearance sale; **estar de** *o* **en** ~ to be (up) for sale *o* on the market; ~**s brutas** gross sales; ~**s a término** forward sales.

ventaja [ben'taxa] *nf* advantage; **llevar la** ~ (*en carrera*) to be leading *o* ahead.

ventajoso, a [benta'xoso, a] *adj* advantageous.

ventana [ben'tana] *nf* window; ~ **de guillotina/galería** sash/bay window; ~ **de la nariz** nostril.

ventanilla [venta'niʎa] *nf* (*de taquilla, tb INFORM*) window.

ventearse [bente'arse] *vr* (*romperse*) to crack; (*ANAT*) to break wind.

ventilación [bentila'θjon] *nf* ventilation; (*corriente*) draught; (*fig*) airing.

ventilador [bentila'ðor] *nm* ventilator; (*eléctrico*) fan.

ventilar [benti'lar] *vt* to ventilate; (*a secar*) to put out to dry; (*fig*) to air, discuss.

ventisca [ben'tiska] *nf* blizzard.

ventisquero [bentis'kero] *nm* snowdrift.

ventolera [bento'lera] *nf* (*ráfaga*) gust of wind; (*idea*) whim, wild idea; **le dio la** ~ **de comprarlo** he had a sudden notion to buy it.

ventosear [bentose'ar] *vi* to break wind.

ventosidad [bentosi'ðað] *nf* flatulence.

ventoso, a [ben'toso, a] *adj* windy ♦ *nf* (*ZOOL*) sucker; (*instrumento*) suction pad.

ventrículo [ben'trikulo] *nm* ventricle.

ventrílocuo, a [ben'trilokwo, a] *nm/f* ventriloquist.

ventriloquia [bentri'lokja] *nf* ventriloquism.

ventura [ben'tura] *nf* (*felicidad*) happiness; (*buena suerte*) luck; (*destino*) fortune; **a la (buena)** ~ at random.

venturoso, a [bentu'roso, a] *adj* happy; (*afortunado*) lucky, fortunate.

venza ['benθa] *etc vb V* **vencer**.

ver [ber] *vt, vi* to see; (*mirar*) to look at, watch; (*investigar*) to look into; (*entender*) to see, understand; ~**se** *vr* (*encontrarse*) to meet; (*dejarse* ~) to be seen; (*hallarse*: *en un apuro*) to find o.s., be ♦ *nm* looks *pl*, appearance; **a** ~ let's see; **a** ~ **si** ... I wonder if ...; **por lo que veo** apparently; **dejarse** ~ to become apparent; **no tener nada que** ~ **con** to have nothing to do with; **a mi modo de** ~ as I see it; **merece** ~**se** it's worth seeing; **no lo veo** I can't see it; **¡nos vemos!** see you (later)!;

¡habráse visto! did you ever! (*fam*); **¡viera(n)** *o* **hubiera(n) visto qué casa!** (*AM fam*) if only you'd seen the house!, what a house!; **ya se ve que** ... it is obvious that ...; **si te vi no me acuerdo** they *etc* just don't want to know.

vera ['bera] *nf* edge, verge; (*de río*) bank; **a la** ~ **de** near, next to.

veracidad [beraθi'ðað] *nf* truthfulness.

veraneante [berane'ante] *nm/f* holidaymaker, (summer) vacationer (*US*).

veranear [berane'ar] *vi* to spend the summer.

veraneo [bera'neo] *nm*: **estar de** ~ to be away on (one's summer) holiday; **lugar de** ~ holiday resort.

veraniego, a [bera'njeɣo, a] *adj* summer *cpd*.

verano [be'rano] *nm* summer.

veras ['beras] *nfpl* truth *sg*; **de** ~ really, truly; **esto va de** ~ this is serious.

veraz [be'raθ] *adj* truthful.

verbal [ber'ßal] *adj* verbal; (*mensaje etc*) oral.

verbena [ber'ßena] *nf* street party.

verbigracia [berßi'ɣraθja] *adv* for example.

verbo ['berßo] *nm* verb.

verborrea [berßo'rrea] *nf* verbosity, verbal diarrhoea.

verboso, a [ber'ßoso, a] *adj* verbose.

verdad [ber'ðað] *nf* (*lo verídico*) truth; (*fiabilidad*) reliability ♦ *adv* really; **¿~?, ¿no es ~?** isn't it?, aren't you?, don't you? *etc*; **de** ~ *adj* real, proper; **a decir** ~, **no quiero** to tell (you) the truth, I don't want to; **la pura** ~ the plain truth.

verdaderamente [berðaðera'mente] *adv* really, indeed, truly.

verdadero, a [berða'ðero, a] *adj* (*veraz*) true, truthful; (*fiable*) reliable; (*fig*) real.

verde ['berðe] *adj* green; (*fruta etc*) green, unripe; (*chiste etc*) blue, smutty, dirty ♦ *nm* green; **viejo** ~ dirty old man; **poner** ~ **a algn** to give sb a dressing-down.

verdear [berðe'ar], **verdecer** [berðe'θer] *vi* to turn green.

verdezca [ber'ðeθka] *etc vb V* **verdecer**.

verdor [ber'ðor] *nm* (*lo verde*) greenness; (*BOT*) verdure; (*fig*) youthful vigour.

verdugo [ber'ðuɣo] *nm* executioner; (*BOT*) shoot; (*cardenal*) weal.

verdulero, a [berðu'lero, a] *nm/f* greengrocer.

verdura [ber'ðura] *nf* greenness; ~**s** *nfpl* (*CULIN*) greens.

vereda [be'reða] *nf* path; (*AM*) pavement, sidewalk (*US*); **meter a algn en** ~ to bring sb into line.

veredicto [bere'ðikto] *nm* verdict.

vergel [ber'xel] *nm* lush garden.

vergonzoso, a [berɣon'θoso, a] *adj* shameful; (*tímido*) timid, bashful.

vergüenza [ber'ɣwenθa] *nf* shame, sense of shame; (*timidez*) bashfulness; (*pudor*) modesty; **tener ~** to be ashamed; **me da ~ decírselo** I feel too shy o it embarrasses me to tell him; **¡qué ~!** (*de situación*) what a disgrace!; (*a persona*) shame on you!

vericueto [beri'kweto] *nm* rough track.

verídico, a [be'riðiko, a] *adj* true, truthful.

verificar [berifi'kar] *vt* to check; (*corroborar*) to verify (*tb* INFORM); (*testamento*) to prove; (*llevar a cabo*) to carry out; **~se** *vr* to occur, happen; (*mitin etc*) to be held; (*profecía etc*) to come o prove true.

verifique [beri'fike] *etc vb V* **verificar**.

verja ['berxa] *nf* iron gate; (*cerca*) railing(s) (*pl*); (*rejado*) grating.

vermut [ber'mu], *pl* **vermuts** *nm* vermouth ♦ *nf* (*esp AM*) matinée.

verosímil [bero'simil] *adj* likely, probable; (*relato*) credible.

verosimilitud [berosimili'tuð] *nf* likeliness, probability.

verruga [be'rruɣa] *nf* wart.

versado, a [ber'saðo, a] *adj*: **~ en** versed in.

Versalles [ber'saʎes] *nm* Versailles.

versar [ber'sar] *vi* to go round, turn; **~ sobre** to deal with, be about.

versátil [ber'satil] *adj* versatile.

versículo [ber'sikulo] *nm* (*REl*) verse.

versión [ber'sjon] *nf* version; (*traducción*) translation.

verso ['berso] *nm* (*gen*) verse; **un ~** a line of poetry; **~ libre/suelto** free/blank verse.

vértebra ['berteßra] *nf* vertebra.

vertebrado, a [berte'ßraðo, a] *adj, nm/f* vertebrate.

vertebral [berte'ßral] *adj* vertebral; **columna ~** spine.

vertedero [berte'ðero] *nm* rubbish dump, tip.

verter [ber'ter] *vt* (*vaciar*) to empty, pour (out); (*tirar*) to dump ♦ *vi* to flow.

vertical [berti'kal] *adj* vertical; (*postura, piano etc*) upright ♦ *nf* vertical.

vértice ['bertiθe] *nm* vertex, apex.

vertiente [ber'tjente] *nf* slope.

vertiginoso, a [bertixi'noso, a] *adj* giddy, dizzy.

vértigo ['bertiɣo] *nm* vertigo; (*mareo*) dizziness; (*actividad*) intense activity; **de**

~ (*fam: velocidad*) giddy; (: *ruido*) tremendous; (: *talento*) fantastic.

vesícula [be'sikula] *nf* blister; **~ biliar** gall bladder.

vespa ® ['bespa] *nf* (*motor*) scooter.

vespertino, a [besper'tino, a] *adj* evening *cpd*.

vespino ® [bes'pino] *nm o f* ≈ moped.

vestíbulo [bes'tißulo] *nm* hall; (*de teatro*) foyer.

vestido [bes'tiðo] *nm* (*ropa*) clothes *pl*, clothing; (*de mujer*) dress, frock.

vestigio [bes'tixjo] *nm* (*trazo*) trace; (*señal*) sign; **~s** *nmpl* remains.

vestimenta [besti'menta] *nf* clothing.

vestir [bes'tir] *vt* (*poner: ropa*) to put on; (*llevar: ropa*) to wear; (*cubrir*) to clothe, cover, (*pagar: la ropa*) to clothe, pay for the clothing of; (*sastre*) to make clothes for ♦ *vi* (*ponerse: ropa*) to dress; (*verse bien*) to look good; **~se** *vr* to get dressed, dress o.s.; **traje de ~** (*formal*) formal suit; **estar vestido de** to be dressed o clad in; (*como disfraz*) to be dressed as.

vestuario [bes'twarjo] *nm* clothes *pl*, wardrobe; (*TEAT: para actores*) dressing room; (: *para público*) cloakroom; (*DEPORTE*) changing room.

Vesubio [be'sußjo] *nm* Vesuvius.

veta ['beta] *nf* (*vena*) vein, seam; (*raya*) streak; (*de madera*) grain.

vetar [be'tar] *vt* to veto.

veterano, a [bete'rano, a] *adj, nm/f* veteran.

veterinario, a [beteri'narjo, a] *nm/f* vet(erinary surgeon) ♦ *nf* veterinary science.

veto ['beto] *nm* veto.

vetusto, a [be'tusto, a] *adj* ancient.

vez [beθ] *nf* time; (*turno*) turn; **a la ~ que** at the same time as; **a su ~** in its turn; **cada ~ más/menos** more and more/less and less; **una ~ once; dos veces** twice; **de una ~** in one go; **de una ~ para siempre** once and for all; **en ~ de** instead of; **a veces** sometimes; **otra ~** again; **una y otra ~** repeatedly; **pocas veces** seldom; **de ~ en cuando** from time to time; **7 veces 9** 7 times 9; **hacer las veces de** to stand in for; **tal ~** perhaps; **¿lo viste alguna ~?** did you ever see it?; **¿cuántas veces?** how often?; **érase una ~** once upon a time (there was).

v. g., v. gr. *abr* (= *verbigracia*) viz.

vía ['bia] *nf* (*calle*) road; (*ruta*) track, route; (*FERRO*) line; (*fig*) way; (*ANAT*) passage, tube ♦ *prep* via, by way of; **por ~ bucal** orally; **por ~ judicial** by legal means; **por**

~ **oficial** through official channels; **por** ~ **de** by way of; **en** ~**s de** in the process of; **un país en** ~**s de desarrollo** a developing country; ~ **aérea** airway; **V**~ **Láctea** Milky Way; ~ **pública** public highway *o* thoroughfare; ~ **única** one-way street; **el tren está en la** ~ **8** the train is (standing) at platform 8.

viable ['bjaßle] *adj* (*COM*) viable; (*plan etc*) feasible.

viaducto [bja'ðukto] *nm* viaduct.

viajante [bja'xante] *nm* commercial traveller, traveling salesman (*US*).

viajar [bja'xar] *vi* to travel, journey.

viaje ['bjaxe] *nm* journey; (*gira*) tour; (*NAUT*) voyage; (*COM: carga*) load; **los** ~**s** travel *sg*; **estar de** ~ to be on a journey; ~ **de ida y vuelta** round trip; ~ **de novios** honeymoon.

viajero, a [bja'xero, a] *adj* travelling (*BRIT*), traveling (*US*); (*ZOOL*) migratory ♦ *nm/f* (*quien viaja*) traveller; (*pasajero*) passenger.

vial [bjal] *adj* road *cpd*, traffic *cpd*.

vianda ['bjanda] *nf* (*tb:* ~**s**) food.

viáticos ['bjatikos] *nmpl* (*COM*) travelling (*BRIT*) *o* traveling (*US*) expenses.

víbora ['bißora] *nf* viper.

vibración [bißra'θjon] *nf* vibration.

vibrador [bißra'ðor] *nm* vibrator.

vibrante [bi'ßrante] *adj* vibrant, vibrating.

vibrar [bi'ßrar] *vt* to vibrate ♦ *vi* to vibrate; (*pulsar*) to throb, beat, pulsate.

vicario [bi'karjo] *nm* curate.

vicecónsul [biθe'konsul] *nm* vice-consul.

vicegerente [biθexe'rente] *nm/f* assistant manager.

vicepresidente [biθepresi'ðente] *nm/f* vice president; (*de comité etc*) vice-chairman.

viceversa [biθe'ßersa] *adv* vice versa.

viciado, a [bi'θjaðo, a] *adj* (*corrompido*) corrupt; (*contaminado*) foul, contaminated.

viciar [bi'θjar] *vt* (*pervertir*) to pervert; (*adulterar*) to adulterate; (*falsificar*) to falsify; (*JUR*) to nullify; (*estropear*) to spoil; (*sentido*) to twist; ~**se** *vr* to become corrupted; (*aire, agua*) to be(come) polluted.

vicio ['biθjo] *nm* (*libertinaje*) vice; (*mala costumbre*) bad habit; (*mimo*) spoiling; (*alabeo*) warp, warping; **de** *o* **por** ~ out of sheer habit.

vicioso, a [bi'θjoso, a] *adj* (*muy malo*) vicious; (*corrompido*) depraved; (*mimado*) spoiled ♦ *nm/f* depraved person; (*adicto*) addict.

vicisitud [biθisi'tuð] *nf* vicissitude.

víctima ['biktima] *nf* victim; (*de accidente etc*) casualty.

victimario [bikti'marjo] *nm* (*AM*) killer, murderer.

victoria [bik'torja] *nf* victory.

victorioso, a [bikto'rjoso, a] *adj* victorious.

vicuña [bi'kuɲa] *nf* vicuna.

vid [bið] *nf* vine.

vida ['biða] *nf* life; (*duración*) lifetime; (*modo de vivir*) way of life; **¡**~**!**, **¡**~ **mía!** (*saludo cariñoso*) my love!; **de por** ~ for life; **de** ~ **airada** *o* **libre** loose-living; **en la/mi** ~ never; **estar con** ~ to be still alive; **ganarse la** ~ to earn one's living; **¡esto es** ~**!** this is the life!; **le va la** ~ **en esto** his life depends on it.

vidente [bi'ðente] *nm/f* (*adivino*) clairvoyant; (*no ciego*) sighted person.

vídeo ['biðeo] *nm* video; (*aparato*) video (recorder); **cinta de** ~ videotape; **película de** ~ videofilm; **grabar en** ~ to record, (video)tape; ~ **compuesto/ inverso** (*INFORM*) composite/reverse video.

videocámara [biðeo'kamara] *nf* video camera; (*pequeña*) camcorder.

videocassette [biðeoka'set] *nm* video cassette.

videoclip [biðeo'klip] *nm* (music) video.

videoclub [biðeo'klub] *nm* video club; (*tienda*) video shop.

videodatos [biðeo'ðatos] *nmpl* (*COM*) viewdata.

videojuego [biðeo'xweɣo] *nm* video game.

videotex(o) [biðeo'teks(o)] *nm* Videotex ®.

vidriero, a [bi'ðrjero, a] *nm/f* glazier ♦ *nf* (*ventana*) stained-glass window; (*AM: de tienda*) shop window; (*puerta*) glass door.

vidrio ['biðrjo] *nm* glass; (*AM*) window; ~ **cilindrado/inastillable** plate/splinter-proof glass.

vidrioso, a [bi'ðrjoso, a] *adj* glassy; (*frágil*) fragile, brittle; (*resbaladizo*) slippery.

viejo, a ['bjexo, a] *adj* old ♦ *nm/f* old man/ woman; **mi** ~**/vieja** (*fam*) my old man/ woman; **hacerse** *o* **ponerse** ~ to grow *o* get old.

Viena ['bjena] *nf* Vienna.

viene ['bjene] *etc vb* V **venir**.

vienés, esa [bje'nes, esa] *adj, nm/f* Viennese.

viento ['bjento] *nm* wind; (*olfato*) scent; **contra** ~ **y marea** at all costs; **ir** ~ **en popa** to go splendidly; (*negocio*) to prosper.

vientre ['bjentre] *nm* belly; (*matriz*) womb; ~**s** *nmpl* bowels; **hacer de** ~ to have a movement of the bowels.

vier. *abr* (= *viernes*) Fri.

viernes ['bjernes] *nm inv* Friday; **V~ Santo** Good Friday; *V tb* **Semana Santa.**

vierta ['bjerta] *etc vb V* **verter.**

Vietnam [bjet'nam] *nm*: **el ~** Vietnam.

vietnamita [bjetna'mita] *adj, nm/f* Vietnamese.

viga ['biɣa] *nf* beam, rafter; (*de metal*) girder.

vigencia [bi'xenθja] *nf* validity; (*de contrato etc*) term, life; **estar/entrar en ~** to be in/come into effect o force.

vigente [bi'xente] *adj* valid, in force; (*imperante*) prevailing.

vigésimo, a [bi'xesimo, a] *num* twentieth.

vigía [bi'xia] *nm* look-out ♦ *nf* (*atalaya*) watchtower; (*acción*) watching.

vigilancia [bixi'lanθja] *nf* vigilance.

vigilante [bixi'lante] *adj* vigilant ♦ *nm* caretaker; (*en cárcel*) warder; (*en almacén*) shopwalker (BRIT), floor-walker (US); **~ jurado** security guard (*licensed to carry a gun*); **~ nocturno** night watchman.

vigilar [bixi'lar] *vt* to watch over; (*cuidar*) to look after, keep an eye on ♦ *vi* to be vigilant; (*hacer guardia*) to keep watch.

vigilia [vi'xilja] *nf* wakefulness; (REL) fast; **comer de ~** to fast.

vigor [bi'ɣor] *nm* vigour, vitality; **en ~** in force; **entrar/poner en ~** to take/put into effect.

vigoroso, a [bixo'roso, a] *adj* vigorous.

VIH *nm abr* (= *virus de inmunodeficiencia humana*) HIV.

vil [bil] *adj* vile, low.

vileza [bi'leθa] *nf* vileness; (*acto*) base deed.

vilipendiar [bilipen'djar] *vt* to vilify, revile.

villa ['biʎa] *nf* (*pueblo*) small town; (*municipalidad*) municipality; **la V~** (ESP) Madrid; **~ miseria** shanty town.

villancico [biʎan'θiko] *nm* (Christmas) carol.

villorrio [bi'ʎorrjo] *nm* one-horse town, dump; (AM: *barrio pobre*) shanty town.

vilo ['bilo]: **en ~** *adv* in the air, suspended; (*fig*) on tenterhooks, in suspense; **estar** o **quedar en ~** to be left in suspense.

vinagre [bi'naɣre] *nm* vinegar.

vinagrera [bina'ɣrera] *nf* vinegar bottle; **~s** *nfpl* cruet stand *sg.*

vinagreta [bina'ɣreta] *nf* French dressing.

vinatería [binate'ria] *nf* wine shop.

vinatero, a [bina'tero, a] *adj* wine *cpd* ♦ *nm* wine merchant.

vinculación [binkula'θjon] *nf* (*lazo*) link, bond; (*acción*) linking.

vincular [binku'lar] *vt* to link, bind.

vínculo ['binkulo] *nm* link, bond.

vindicar [bindi'kar] *vt* to vindicate; (*vengar*) to avenge; (JUR) to claim.

vinícola [bi'nikola] *adj* (*industria*) wine *cpd*; (*región*) wine-growing *cpd*.

vinicultura [binikul'tura] *nf* wine growing.

vino ['bino] *etc vb V* **venir** ♦ *nm* wine; **~ de solera/seco/tinto** vintage/dry/red wine; **~ de Jerez** sherry; **~ de Oporto** port (wine).

viña ['biɲa] *nf*, **viñedo** [bi'ɲeðo] *nm* vineyard.

viñeta [bi'ɲeta] *nf* (*en historieta*) cartoon.

viola ['bjola] *nf* viola.

violación [bjola'θjon] *nf* violation; (JUR) offence, infringement; (*estupro*): **~ (sexual)** rape; **~ de contrato** (COM) breach of contract.

violar [bjo'lar] *vt* to violate; (JUR) to infringe; (*cometer estupro*) to rape.

violencia [bjo'lenθja] *nf* (*fuerza*) violence, force; (*embarazo*) embarrassment; (*acto injusto*) unjust act.

violentar [bjolen'tar] *vt* to force; (*casa*) to break into; (*agredir*) to assault; (*violar*) to violate.

violento, a [bjo'lento, a] *adj* violent; (*furioso*) furious; (*situación*) embarrassing; (*acto*) forced, unnatural; (*difícil*) awkward; **me es muy ~** it goes against the grain with me.

violeta [bjo'leta] *nf* violet.

violín [bjo'lin] *nm* violin.

violón [bjo'lon] *nm* double bass.

violoncelo [bjolon'θelo] *nm* cello.

virador [bira'ðor] *nm* (*para fotocopiadora*) toner.

viraje [bi'raxe] *nm* turn; (*de vehículo*) swerve; (*de carretera*) bend; (*fig*) change of direction.

virar [bi'rar] *vi* to turn; to swerve; to change direction.

virgen ['birxen] *adj* virgin; (*cinta*) blank ♦ *nm/f* virgin; **la Santísima V~** (REL) the Blessed Virgin.

virginidad [birxini'ðað] *nf* virginity.

Virgo ['birɣo] *nm* Virgo.

viril [bi'ril] *adj* virile.

virilidad [birili'ðað] *nf* virility.

virrey [bi'rrei] *nm* viceroy.

virtual [bir'twal] *adj* (*real*) virtual; (*en potencia*) potential.

virtud [bir'tuð] *nf* virtue; **en ~ de** by virtue of.

virtuoso, a [bir'twoso, a] *adj* virtuous

◆ _nm/f_ virtuoso.
viruela [bi'rwela] _nf_ smallpox; ~s _nfpl_
pockmarks; ~s **locas** chickenpox _sg_.
virulento, a [biru'lento, a] _adj_ virulent.
virus ['birus] _nm inv_ virus.
viruta [bi'ruta] _nf_ wood _o_ metal shaving.
vis [bis] _nf_: ~ **cómica** sense of humour.
visa ['bisa] _nf_ (_AM_), **visado** [bi'saðo] _nm_
visa; ~ **de permanencia** residence
permit.
visar [bi'sar] _vt_ (_pasaporte_) to visa;
(_documento_) to endorse.
víscera ['bisθera] _nf_ internal organ; ~s _nfpl_
entrails.
visceral [bisθe'ral] _adj_ (_odio_) deep-rooted;
reacción ~ gut reaction.
viscoso, a [bis'koso, a] _adj_ viscous.
visera [bi'sera] _nf_ visor.
visibilidad [bisiβili'ðað] _nf_ visibility.
visible [bi'siβle] _adj_ visible; (_fig_) obvious;
exportaciones/importaciones ~s (_COM_)
visible exports/imports.
visillo [bi'siʎo] _nm_ lace curtain.
visión [bi'sjon] _nf_ (_ANAT_) vision,
(eye)sight; (_fantasía_) vision, fantasy;
(_panorama_) view; **ver visiones** to see _o_ be
seeing things.
visionario, a [bisjo'narjo, a] _adj_ (_que prevé_)
visionary; (_alucinado_) deluded ◆ _nm/f_
visionary; (_chalado_) lunatic.
visita [bi'sita] _nf_ call, visit; (_persona_)
visitor; **horas/tarjeta de** ~ visiting
hours/card; ~ **de cortesía/de cumplido/
de despedida** courtesy/formal/farewell
visit; **hacer una** ~ to pay a visit; **ir de** ~
to go visiting.
visitar [bisi'tar] _vt_ to visit, call on;
(_inspeccionar_) to inspect.
vislumbrar [bislum'brar] _vt_ to glimpse,
catch a glimpse of.
vislumbre [bis'lumbre] _nf_ glimpse;
(_centelleo_) gleam; (_idea vaga_) glimmer.
viso ['biso] _nm_ (_de metal_) glint, gleam; (_de
tela_) sheen; (_aspecto_) appearance; **hay un**
~ **de verdad en esto** there is an element
of truth in this.
visón [bi'son] _nm_ mink.
visor [bi'sor] _nm_ (_FOTO_) viewfinder.
víspera ['bispera] _nf_ eve, day before; **la** ~ _o_
en ~s **de** on the eve of.
vista ['bista] _nf_ sight, vision; (_capacidad de
ver_) (eye)sight; (_mirada_) look(s) (_pl_);
(_FOTO etc_) view; (_JUR_) hearing ◆ _nm_
customs officer; **a primera** ~ at first
glance; ~ **general** overview; **fijar** _o_ **clavar
la** ~ **en** to stare at; **hacer la** ~ **gorda** to
turn a blind eye; **volver la** ~ to look
back; **está a la** ~ **que** it's obvious that; **a**

la ~ (_COM_) at sight; **en** ~ **de** in view of;
en ~ **de que** in view of the fact that;
¡**hasta la** ~! so long!, see you!; **con** ~s **a**
with a view to; _V tb_ **visto, a**.
vistazo [bis'taθo] _nm_ glance; **dar** _o_ **echar
un** ~ **a** to glance at.
visto, a ['bisto, a] _etc vb V_ **vestir** ◆ _pp de_ **ver**
◆ _adj_ seen; (_considerado_) considered ◆ _nm_:
~ **bueno** approval; "~ **bueno**"
"approved"; **por lo** ~ evidently; **dar el** ~
bueno a algo to give sth the go-ahead;
está ~ **que** it's clear that; **está bien/mal**
~ it's acceptable/unacceptable; **está
muy** ~ it is very common; **estaba** ~ it
had to be; ~ **que** _conj_ since, considering
that.
vistoso, a [bis'toso, a] _adj_ colourful;
(_alegre_) gay; (_pey_) gaudy.
visual [bi'swal] _adj_ visual.
visualice [biswa'liθe] _etc vb V_ **visualizar**.
visualizador [biswaliθa'ðor] _nm_ (_INFORM_)
display screen, VDU.
visualizar [biswali'θar] _vt_ (_imaginarse_) to
visualize; (_INFORM_) to display.
vital [bi'tal] _adj_ life _cpd_, living _cpd_; (_fig_)
vital; (_persona_) lively, vivacious.
vitalicio, a [bita'liθjo, a] _adj_ for life.
vitalidad [bitali'ðað] _nf_ vitality.
vitamina [bita'mina] _nf_ vitamin.
vitaminado, a [bitami'naðo, a] _adj_ with
added vitamins.
vitamínico, a [bita'miniko, a] _adj_ vitamin
cpd; **complejos** ~s vitamin compounds.
viticultor, a [bitikul'tor, a] _nm/f_ vine
grower.
viticultura [bitikul'tura] _nf_ vine growing.
vitorear [bitore'ar] _vt_ to cheer, acclaim.
vítores ['bitores] _nmpl_ cheers.
vitoriano, a [bito'rjano, a] _adj_ of _o_ from
Vitoria ◆ _nm/f_ native _o_ inhabitant of
Vitoria.
vítreo, a ['bitreo, a] _adj_ vitreous.
vitrina [bi'trina] _nf_ glass case; (_en casa_)
display cabinet; (_AM_) shop window.
vituperar [bitupe'rar] _vt_ to condemn.
vituperio [bitu'perjo] _nm_ (_condena_)
condemnation; (_censura_) censure;
(_insulto_) insult.
viudez [bju'ðeθ] _nf_ widowhood.
viudo, a ['bjuðo, a] _adj_ widowed ◆ _nm_
widower ◆ _nf_ widow.
viva ['biβa] _excl_ hurrah! ◆ _nm_ cheer; ¡~ **el
rey**! long live the King!
vivacidad [biβaθi'ðað] _nf_ (_vigor_) vigour;
(_vida_) vivacity.
vivamente [biβa'mente] _adv_ in lively
fashion; (_descripción etc_) vividly;
(_protesta_) sharply; (_emoción_) acutely.

vivaracho, a [bi'ßa'ratʃo, a] *adj* jaunty, lively; (*ojos*) bright, twinkling.

vivaz [bi'ßaθ] *adj* (*que dura*) enduring; (*vigoroso*) vigorous; (*vivo*) lively.

vivencia [bi'ßenθja] *nf* experience.

víveres ['bißeres] *nmpl* provisions.

vivero [bi'ßero] *nm* (*HORTICULTURA*) nursery; (*para peces*) fishpond; (: *COM*) fish farm.

viveza [bi'ßeθa] *nf* liveliness; (*agudeza*) sharpness.

vividor, a [bißi'ðor, a] *adj* (*pey*) opportunistic ♦ *nm* (*aprovechado*) hustler.

vivienda [bi'ßjenda] *nf* (*alojamiento*) housing; (*morada*) dwelling; **~s protegidas** *o* **sociales** council housing *sg* (*BRIT*), public housing *sg* (*US*).

viviente [bi'ßjente] *adj* living.

vivificar [bißifi'kar] *vt* to give life to.

vivifique [bißi'fike] *etc vb V* **vivificar**.

vivir [bi'ßir] *vt* (*experimentar*) to live *o* go through ♦ *vi* (*gen, COM*): **~ (de)** to live (by, off, on) ♦ *nm* life, living; **¡viva!** hurray!; **¡viva el rey!** long live the king!

vivo, a ['bißo, a] *adj* living, live, alive; (*fig*) vivid; (*movimiento*) quick; (*color*) bright; (*protesta etc*) strong; (*astuto*) smart, clever; **en ~** (*TV etc*) live; **llegar a lo ~** to cut to the quick.

vizcaíno, a [biθka'ino, a] *adj, nm/f* Biscayan.

Vizcaya [biθ'kaja] *nf* Biscay; **el Golfo de ~** the Bay of Biscay.

V.M. *abr* = **Vuestra Majestad**.

V.O. *abr* = **versión original**.

V.ºB.º *abr* = **visto bueno**.

vocablo [bo'kaßlo] *nm* (*palabra*) word; (*término*) term.

vocabulario [bokaßu'larjo] *nm* vocabulary, word list.

vocación [boka'θjon] *nf* vocation.

vocacional [bokasjo'nal] *nf* (*AM*) ~ **technical college**.

vocal [bo'kal] *adj* vocal ♦ *nm/f* member (of a committee *etc*) ♦ *nm* non-executive director ♦ *nf* vowel.

vocalice [boka'liθe] *etc vb V* **vocalizar**.

vocalizar [bokali'θar] *vt* to vocalize.

voceador [bosea'ðor] *nm* (*AM*): ~ **de periódicos** newspaper vendor *o* seller.

vocear [boθe'ar] *vt* (*para vender*) to cry; (*aclamar*) to acclaim; (*fig*) to proclaim ♦ *vi* to yell.

vocerío [boθe'rio] *nm* shouting; (*escándalo*) hullabaloo.

vocero, a [bo'sero, a] *nm/f* (*AM*) spokesman/woman.

vociferar [boθife'rar] *vt* to shout; (*jactarse*) to proclaim boastfully ♦ *vi* to yell.

vocinglero, a [boθin'glero, a] *adj* vociferous; (*gárrulo*) garrulous; (*fig*) blatant.

vodevil [boðe'ßil] *nm* music hall, variety, (*US*) vaudeville.

vodka ['boðka] *nm* vodka.

vodú [bo'ðu] *nm* voodoo.

vol *abr* = **volumen**.

volado, a [bo'laðo, a] *adj*: **estar ~** (*fam: inquieto*) to be worried; (: *loco*) to be crazy.

volador, a [bola'ðor, a] *adj* flying.

voladura [bola'ðura] *nf* blowing up, demolition; (*MINERÍA*) blasting.

volandas [bo'landas]: **en ~** *adv* in *o* through the air; (*fig*) swiftly.

volante [bo'lante] *adj* flying ♦ *nm* (*de máquina, coche*) steering wheel; (*de reloj*) balance; (*nota*) note; **ir al ~** to be at the wheel, be driving.

volar [bo'lar] *vt* (*demolir*) to blow up, demolish ♦ *vi* to fly; (*fig: correr*) to rush, hurry; (*fam: desaparecer*) to disappear; **voy volando** I must dash; **¡cómo vuela el tiempo!** how time flies!

volátil [bo'latil] *adj* volatile; (*fig*) changeable.

volcán [bol'kan] *nm* volcano.

volcánico, a [bol'kaniko, a] *adj* volcanic.

volcar [bol'kar] *vt* to upset, overturn; (*tumbar, derribar*) to knock over; (*vaciar*) to empty out ♦ *vi* to overturn; **~se** *vr* to tip over; (*barco*) to capsize.

voleibol [bolei'ßol] *nm* volleyball.

voleo [bo'leo] *nm* volley; **a(l) ~** haphazardly; **de un ~** quickly.

Volga ['bolɣa] *nm* Volga.

volición [boli'θjon] *nf* volition.

volqué [bol'ke], **volquemos** [bol'kemos] *etc vb V* **volcar**.

volquete [bol'kete] *nm* dumper, dump truck (*US*).

voltaje [bol'taxe] *nm* voltage.

voltear [bolte'ar] *vt* to turn over; (*volcar*) to knock over; (*doblar*) to peal ♦ *vi* to roll over; **~se** *vr* (*AM*) to turn round; **~ a hacer algo** (*AM*) to do sth again.

voltereta [bolte'reta] *nf* somersault; **~ sobre las manos** handspring; **~ lateral** cartwheel.

voltio ['boltjo] *nm* volt.

voluble [bo'lußle] *adj* fickle.

volumen [bo'lumen] *nm* volume; **~ monetario** money supply; **~ de negocios** turnover; **bajar el ~** to turn down the volume; **poner la radio a todo ~** to turn the radio up full.

voluminoso, a [bolumi'noso, a] *adj*
voluminous; (*enorme*) massive.

voluntad [bolun'tað] *nf* will, willpower;
(*deseo*) desire, wish; (*afecto*) fondness; **a**
~ at will; (*cantidad*) as much as one
likes; **buena** ~ goodwill; **mala** ~ ill will,
malice; **por causas ajenas a mi** ~ for
reasons beyond my control.

voluntario, a [bolun'tarjo, a] *adj* voluntary
♦ *nm/f* volunteer.

voluntarioso, a [bolunta'rjoso, a] *adj*
headstrong.

voluptuoso, a [bolup'twoso, a] *adj*
voluptuous.

volver [bol'ßer] *vt* to turn; (*boca abajo*) to
turn (over); (*voltear*) to turn round, turn
upside down; (*poner al revés*) to turn inside
out; (*devolver*) to return; (*transformar*) to
change, transform; (*manga*) to roll up ♦ *vi*
to return, go/come back; ~**se** *vr* to turn
round; (*llegar a ser*) to become; ~ **la espalda**
to turn one's back; ~ **bien por mal** to
return good for evil; ~ **a hacer** to do again;
~ **en sí** to come to *o* round, regain
consciousness; ~ **la vista atrás** to look
back; ~ **loco a algn** to drive sb mad; ~**se**
loco to go mad.

vomitar [bomi'tar] *vt, vi* to vomit.

vómito ['bomito] *nm* (*acto*) vomiting;
(*resultado*) vomit.

voracidad [boraθi'ðað] *nf* voracity.

vorágine [bo'raxine] *nf* whirlpool; (*fig*)
maelstrom.

voraz [bo'raθ] *adj* voracious; (*fig*) fierce.

vórtice ['bortiθe] *nm* whirlpool; (*de aire*)
whirlwind.

vos [bos] *pron* (*AM*) you.

voseo [bo'seo] *nm* (*AM*) addressing a
person as "vos", *familiar usage.*

Vosgos ['bosɣos] *nmpl* Vosges.

vosotros, as [bo'sotros, as] *pron* you *pl*;
(*reflexivo*) yourselves; **entre** ~ among
yourselves.

votación [bota'θjon] *nf* (*acto*) voting; (*voto*)
vote; ~ **a mano alzada** show of hands;
someter algo a ~ to put sth to the vote.

votar [bo'tar] *vt* (*POL: partido etc*) to vote
for; (*proyecto: aprobar*) to pass; (*REL*) to
vow ♦ *vi* to vote.

voto ['boto] *nm* vote; (*promesa*) vow;
(*maldición*) oath, curse; ~**s** *nmpl* (good)
wishes; ~ **de bloque/de grupo** block/
card vote; ~ **de censura/de
(des)confianza/de gracias** vote of
censure/(no) confidence/thanks; **dar su**
~ to cast one's vote.

voy [boi] *vb V* **ir**.

voz [boθ] *nf* voice; (*grito*) shout; (*chisme*)

rumour; (*LING: palabra*) word; (: *forma*)
voice; **dar voces** to shout, yell; **llamar a**
algn a voces to shout to sb; **llevar la** ~
cantante (*fig*) to be the boss; **tener la** ~
tomada to be hoarse; **tener** ~ **y voto** to
have the right to speak; **a media** ~ in a
low voice; **a** ~ **en cuello** *o* **en grito** at the
top of one's voice; **de viva** ~ verbally; **en**
~ **alta** aloud; ~ **de mando** command.

vozarrón [boθa'rron] *nm* booming voice.

vra., vro. *abr* = **vuestra, vuestro.**

Vto. *abr* (*COM*) = **vencimiento.**

vudú [bu'ðu] *nm* voodoo.

vuelco ['bwelko] *etc vb V* **volcar** ♦ *nm* spill,
overturning; (*fig*) collapse; **mi corazón**
dio un ~ my heart missed a beat.

vuelo ['bwelo] *etc vb V* **volar** ♦ *nm* flight;
(*encaje*) lace, frill; (*de falda etc*) loose
part; (*fig*) importance; **de altos** ~**s** (*fig:*
plan) grandiose; (: *persona*) ambitious;
alzar el ~ to take flight; (*fig*) to dash off;
coger al ~ to catch in flight; ~ **en picado**
dive; ~ **libre** hang-gliding; ~ **regular**
scheduled flight; **falda de mucho** ~ full *o*
wide skirt.

vuelque ['bwelke] *etc vb V* **volcar.**

vuelta ['bwelta] *nf* turn; (*curva*) bend,
curve; (*regreso*) return; (*revolución*)
revolution; (*paseo*) stroll; (*circuito*) lap;
(*de papel, tela*) reverse; (*de pantalón*)
turn-up (*BRIT*), cuff (*US*); (*dinero*)
change; ~ **a empezar** back to square
one; ~ **al mundo** world trip; **V**~ **de**
Francia Tour de France; ~ **cerrada**
hairpin bend; **a la** ~ (*ESP*) on one's
return; **a la** ~ **de la esquina, a la** ~ (*AM*)
round the corner; **a** ~ **de correo** by
return of post; **dar** ~**s** to turn, revolve;
dar ~**s a una idea** to turn over an idea
(in one's mind); **dar una** ~ to go for a
walk; **dar media** ~ (*AUTO*) to do a U-turn;
(*fam*) to beat it; **estar de** ~ (*fam*) to be
back; **poner a algn de** ~ **y media** to heap
abuse on sb; **no tiene** ~ **de hoja** there's
no alternative.

vueltita [bwel'tita] *nf* (*esp AM fam*) (little)
walk; (: *en coche*) (little) drive.

vuelto ['bwelto] *pp de* **volver** ♦ *nm* (*AM:*
moneda) change.

vuelva ['bwelßa] *etc vb V* **volver.**

vuestro, a ['bwestro, a] *adj* your; (*después*
de n) of yours ♦ *pron*: **el** ~/**la vuestra/los**
~**s/las vuestras** yours; **lo** ~ (what is)
yours; **un amigo** ~ a friend of yours;
una idea vuestra an idea of yours.

vulgar [bul'ɣar] *adj* (*ordinario*) vulgar;
(*común*) common.

vulgarice [bulɣa'riθe] *etc vb V* **vulgarizar.**

vulgaridad [bulɣari'ðað] *nf* commonness; (*acto*) vulgarity; (*expresión*) coarse expression; ~**es** *nfpl* banalities.
vulgarismo [bulɣa'rismo] *nm* popular form of a word.
vulgarizar [bulɣari'θar] *vt* to popularize.
vulgo ['bulɣo] *nm* common people.
vulnerable [bulne'raßle] *adj* vulnerable.
vulnerar [bulne'rar] *vt* to harm, damage; (*derechos*) to interfere with; (*JUR*, *COM*) to violate.
vulva ['bulßa] *nf* vulva.

W w

W, w ['ußʹe'doßle, (*AM*) 'doßleße] *nf* (*letra*) W, w; **W de Washington** W for William.
walkie-talkie [walki'talki] *nm* walkie-talkie.
walkman ® ['wal(k)man] *nm* Walkman ®.
wáter ['bater] *nm* lavatory.
waterpolo [water'polo] *nm* waterpolo.
wátman ['watman] *adj inv* (*fam*) cool.
whisky ['wiski] *nm* whisky.
Winchester ['wintʃester] *nm* (*INFORM*): **disco** ~ Winchester disk.
windsurf ['winsurf] *nm* windsurfing.
WWW *nm* o *nf abr* (*INFORM*: = *World Wide Web*) WWW.

X x

X, x ['ekis] *nf* (*letra*) X, x; **X de Xiquena** X for Xmas.
xenofobia [seno'foßja] *nf* xenophobia.
xenófobo, a [se'nofoßo, a] *adj* xenophobic ♦ *nm/f* xenophobe.
xerografía [seroɣra'fia] *nf* xerography.
xilófono [si'lofono] *nm* xylophone.
Xunta ['shunta] *nf* (*tb* ~ **de Galicia**) *regional government of Galicia*.

Y y

Y, y [i'ɣrjeɣa] *nf* (*letra*) Y, y; **Y de Yegua** Y for Yellow (*BRIT*) o Yoke (*US*).
y [i] *conj* and; (*AM fam: pues*) well; ¿~ **eso?** why?, how so?; ¡~ **los demás?** what about the others?; ~ **bueno,** ... (*AM*) well ...
ya [ja] *adv* (*gen*) already; (*ahora*) now; (*en seguida*) at once; (*pronto*) soon ♦ *excl* all right!; (*por supuesto*) of course! ♦ *conj* (*ahora que*) now that; ~ **no** not any more, no longer; ~ **lo sé** I know; ~ **dice que sí,** ~ **dice que no** first he says yes, then he says no; ¡~, ~! yes, yes!; (*con impaciencia*) all right!, O.K.!; ¡~ **voy!** (*enfático: no se suele traducir*) coming!; ~ **que** since.
yacer [ja'θer] *vi* to lie.
yacimiento [jaθi'mjento] *nm* bed, deposit; ~ **petrolífero** oilfield.
Yakarta [ja'karta] *nf* Jakarta.
yanqui ['janki] *adj* Yankee ♦ *nm/f* Yank, Yankee.
yate ['jate] *nm* yacht.
yazca ['jaθka] *etc vb V* **yacer**.
yedra ['jeðra] *nf* ivy.
yegua ['jeɣwa] *nf* mare.
yema ['jema] *nf* (*del huevo*) yolk; (*BOT*) leaf bud; (*fig*) best part; ~ **del dedo** fingertip.
Yemen ['jemen] *nm*: **el** ~ **del Norte** Yemen; **el** ~ **del Sur** Southern Yemen.
yemení [jeme'ni] *adj, nm/f* Yemeni.
yendo ['jendo] *vb V* **ir**.
yerba ['jerßa] *nf* = **hierba**.
yerbatero, a [jerßa'tero, a] *adj* (*AM*) maté ♦ *nm/f* (*AM*) herbal healer.
yerga ['jerɣa] *etc*, **yergue** ['jerɣe] *etc vb V* **erguir**.
yermo, a ['jermo, a] *adj* barren; (*de gente*) uninhabited ♦ *nm* waste land.
yerno ['jerno] *nm* son-in-law.
yerre ['jerre] *etc vb V* **errar**.
yerto, a ['jerto, a] *adj* stiff.
yesca ['jeska] *nf* tinder.
yeso ['jeso] *nm* (*GEO*) gypsum; (*ARQ*) plaster.
yo ['jo] *pron personal* I; **soy** ~ it's me, it is I; ~ **que tú/usted** if I were you.

yodo ['joðo] nm iodine.
yoga ['joɣa] nm yoga.
yogur(t) [jo'ɣur(t)] nm yogurt.
yogurtera [joɣur'tera] nf yogurt maker.
yuca ['juka] nf yucca.
yudo ['juðo] nm judo.
yugo ['juɣo] nm yoke.
Yugoslavia [juɣos'laβja] nf Yugoslavia.
yugoslavo, a [juɣos'laβo, a] adj Yugoslavian ♦ nm/f Yugoslav.
yugular [juɣu'lar] adj jugular.
yunque ['junke] nm anvil.
yunta ['junta] nf yoke.
yuntero [jun'tero] nm ploughman.
yute ['jute] nm jute.
yuxtapondré [jukstapond're] etc vb V **yuxtaponer**.
yuxtaponer [jukstapo'ner] vt to juxtapose.
yuxtaponga [juksta'ponga] etc vb V **yuxtaponer**.
yuxtaposición [jukstaposi'θjon] nf juxtaposition.
yuxtapuesto [juksta'pwesto], **yuxtapuse** [juksta'puse] etc vb V **yuxtaponer**.

Z z

Z, z ['θeta, (esp AM) 'seta] nf (letra) Z, z; **Z de Zaragoza** Z for Zebra.
zafar [θa'far] vt (soltar) to untie; (superficie) to clear; ~**se** vr (escaparse) to escape; (ocultarse) to hide o.s. away; (TEC) to slip off; ~**se de** (persona) to get away from.
zafio, a ['θafjo, a] adj coarse.
zafiro [θa'firo] nm sapphire.
zaga ['θaɣa] nf rear; **a la** ~ behind, in the rear.
zagal [θa'ɣal] nm boy, lad.
zagala [θa'ɣala] nf girl, lass.
zaguán [θa'ɣwan] nm hallway.
zaherir [θae'rir] vt (criticar) to criticize; (fig: herir) to wound.
zahiera etc, **zahiriendo** [θa'jera, θai'rjendo] etc vb V **zaherir**.
zahorí [θao'ri] nm clairvoyant.
zaino, a ['θaino, a] adj (color de caballo) chestnut; (pérfido) treacherous; (animal) vicious.
zalamería [θalame'ria] nf flattery.
zalamero, a [θala'mero, a] adj flattering; (relamido) suave.

zamarra [θa'marra] nf (piel) sheepskin; (saco) sheepskin jacket.
Zambeze [θam'beθe] nm Zambezi.
zambo, a ['θambo, a] adj knock-kneed ♦ nm/f (AM) half-breed (of Negro and Indian parentage); (mulato) mulatto ♦ nf samba.
zambullida [θambu'ʎiða] nf dive, plunge.
zambullirse [θambu'ʎirse] vr to dive; (ocultarse) to hide o.s.
zamorano, a [θamo'rano, a] adj of o from Zamora ♦ nm/f native o inhabitant of Zamora.
zampar [θam'par] vt (esconder) to hide o put away (hurriedly); (comer) to gobble; (arrojar) to hurl ♦ vi to eat voraciously; ~**se** vr (chocar) to bump; (fig) to gatecrash.
zanahoria [θana'orja] nf carrot.
zancada [θan'kaða] nf stride.
zancadilla [θanka'ðiʎa] nf trip; (fig) stratagem; **echar la** ~ **a algn** to trip sb up.
zancajo [θan'kaxo] nm (ANAT) heel; (fig) dwarf.
zanco ['θanko] nm stilt.
zancudo, a [θan'kuðo, a] adj long-legged ♦ nm (AM) mosquito.
zángano ['θangano] nm drone; (holgazán) idler, slacker.
zanja ['θanxa] nf (fosa) ditch; (tumba) grave.
zanjar [θan'xar] vt (fosa) to ditch, trench; (problema) to surmount; (conflicto) to resolve.
zapapico [θapa'piko] nm pick, pickaxe.
zapata [θa'pata] nf half-boot; (MECÁNICA) shoe.
zapateado [θapate'aðo] nm (flamenco) tap dance.
zapatear [θapate'ar] vt (tocar) to tap with one's foot; (patear) to kick; (fam) to ill-treat ♦ vi to tap with one's feet.
zapatería [θapate'ria] nf (oficio) shoemaking; (tienda) shoe-shop; (fábrica) shoe factory.
zapatero, a [θapa'tero, a] nm/f shoemaker; ~ **remendón** cobbler.
zapatilla [θapa'tiʎa] nf slipper; (TEC) washer; (para deporte) training shoe.
zapato [θa'pato] nm shoe.
zapear [θape'ar] vi to flick through the channels.
zapping ['θapin] nm channel-hopping; **hacer** ~ to channel-hop.
zar [θar] nm tsar, czar.
zarabanda [θara'βanda] nf saraband; (fig) whirl.
Zaragoza [θara'ɣoθa] nf Saragossa.

zaragozano, a [θaraɣo'θano, a] *adj* of *o* from Saragossa ♦ *nm/f* native *o* inhabitant of Saragossa.

zaranda [θa'randa] *nf* sieve.

zarandear [θarande'ar] *vt* to sieve; (*fam*) to shake vigorously.

zarpa ['θarpa] *nf* (*garra*) claw, paw; **echar la ~ a** to claw at; (*fam*) to grab.

zarpar [θar'par] *vi* to weigh anchor.

zarpazo [θar'paθo] *nm*: **dar un ~** to claw.

zarza ['θarθa] *nf* (*BOT*) bramble.

zarzal [θar'θal] *nm* (*matorral*) bramble patch.

zarzamora [θarθa'mora] *nf* blackberry.

zarzuela [θar'θwela] *nf* Spanish light opera; **la Z~** *home of the Spanish Royal Family.*

zigzag [θiɣ'θaɣ] *adj* zigzag.

zigzaguear [θiɣθaɣe'ar] *vi* to zigzag.

zinc [θink] *nm* zinc.

zíper ['siper] *nm* (*AM*) zip, zipper (*US*).

zócalo ['θokalo] *nm* (*ARQ*) plinth, base; (*de pared*) skirting board.

zoco ['θoko] *nm* (Arab) market, souk.

zodíaco [θo'ðiako] *nm* zodiac; **signo del ~** star sign.

zona ['θona] *nf* zone; **~ fronteriza** border area; **~ del dólar** (*COM*) dollar area; **~ de fomento** *o* **de desarrollo** development area.

zonzo, a ['sonso, a] *adj* (*AM*) silly.

zoología [θoolo'xia] *nf* zoology.

zoológico, a [θoo'loxiko, a] *adj* zoological ♦ *nm* (*tb*: **parque ~**) zoo.

zoólogo, a [θo'oloɣo, a] *nm/f* zoologist.

zoom [θum] *nm* zoom lens.

zopenco, a [θo'penko, a] (*fam*) *adj* dull, stupid ♦ *nm/f* clot, nitwit.

zopilote [sopi'lote] *nm* (*AM*) buzzard.

zoquete [θo'kete] *nm* (*madera*) block; (*pan*) crust; (*fam*) blockhead.

zorro, a ['θorro, a] *adj* crafty ♦ *nm/f* fox/ vixen ♦ *nf* (*fam*) whore, tart, hooker (*US*).

zote ['θote] (*fam*) *adj* dim, stupid ♦ *nm/f* dimwit.

zozobra [θo'θoßra] *nf* (*fig*) anxiety.

zozobrar [θoθo'ßrar] *vi* (*hundirse*) to capsize; (*fig*) to fail.

zueco ['θweko] *nm* clog.

zulo ['θulo] *nm* (*de armas*) cache.

zumbar [θum'bar] *vt* (*burlar*) to tease; (*golpear*) to hit ♦ *vi* to buzz; (*fam*) to be very close; **~se** *vr*: **~se de** to tease; **me zumban los oídos** I have a buzzing *o* ringing in my ears.

zumbido [θum'biðo] *nm* buzzing; (*fam*) punch; **~ de oídos** buzzing *o* ringing in the ears.

zumo ['θumo] *nm* juice; (*ganancia*) profit; **~ de naranja** (fresh) orange juice.

zurcir [θur'θir] *vt* (*coser*) to darn; (*fig*) to put together; **¡que las zurzan!** to blazes with them!

zurdo, a ['θurðo, a] *adj* (*mano*) left; (*persona*) left-handed.

zurrar [θu'rrar] *vt* (*TEC*) to dress; (*fam*: *pegar duro*) to wallop; (: *aplastar*) to flatten; (: *criticar*) to criticize harshly.

zurriagazo [θurrja'ɣaθo] *nm* lash, stroke; (*desgracia*) stroke of bad luck.

zurrón [θu'rron] *nm* pouch.

zurza ['θurθa] *etc vb V* **zurcir**.

zutano, a [θu'tano, a] *nm/f* so-and-so.

English-Spanish
Inglés-Español

Aa

A, a [eɪ] n (*letter*) A, a; (*SCOL*: *mark*) ≈ sobresaliente; (*MUS*): **A** la m; **A for Andrew**, (*US*) **A for Able** A de Antonio; **A road** n (*BRIT AUT*) ≈ carretera nacional; **A shares** npl (*BRIT STOCK EXCHANGE*) acciones fpl de clase A.

a [ə] *indef art* (*before vowel or silent h*: **an**) **1** un(a); ~ **book** un libro; **an apple** una manzana; **she's** ~ **nurse** (ella) es enfermera; **I haven't got** ~ **car** no tengo coche

2 (*instead of the number "one"*) un(a); ~ **year ago** hace un año; ~ **hundred/ thousand pounds** cien/mil libras

3 (*in expressing ratios, prices etc*): **3** ~ **day/week** 3 al día/a la semana; **10 km an hour** 10 km por hora; **£5** ~ **person** £5 por persona; **30p** ~ **kilo** 30p el kilo; **3 times** ~ **month** 3 veces al mes.

a. *abbr* = **acre**.

AA n *abbr* (*BRIT*: = *Automobile Association*) ≈ RACE m (*SP*); (= *Alcoholics Anonymous*; (*US*: = *Associate in/of Arts*) título universitario; (= *anti-aircraft*) A.A.

AAA n *abbr* (= *American Automobile Association*) ≈ RACE m (*SP*); ['θri:'eɪz] (*BRIT*: = *Amateur Athletics Association*) asociación de atletismo amateur.

A & R n *abbr* (*MUS*) (= *artists and repertoire*) nuevos artistas y canciones; ~ **man** descubridor de jóvenes talentos.

AAUP n *abbr* (= *American Association of University Professors*) asociación de profesores universitarios.

AB *abbr* (*BRIT*) = **able-bodied seaman**;

(*Canada*) = *Alberta*.

aback [ə'bæk] *adv*: **to be taken** ~ quedar(se) desconcertado.

abandon [ə'bændən] *vt* abandonar; (*renounce*) renunciar a ♦ n abandono; (*wild behaviour*): **with** ~ con desenfreno; **to** ~ **ship** abandonar el barco.

abandoned [ə'bændənd] *adj* (*child, house etc*) abandonado; (*unrestrained: manner*) desinhibido.

abase [ə'beɪs] *vt*: **to** ~ **o.s. (so far as to do ...)** rebajarse (hasta el punto de hacer ...).

abashed [ə'bæʃt] *adj* avergonzado.

abate [ə'beɪt] *vi* moderarse; (*lessen*) disminuir; (*calm down*) calmarse.

abatement [ə'beɪtmənt] n (*of pollution, noise*) disminución f.

abattoir ['æbətwɑ:*] n (*BRIT*) matadero.

abbey ['æbɪ] n abadía.

abbot ['æbət] n abad m.

abbreviate [ə'bri:vɪeɪt] *vt* abreviar.

abbreviation [əbri:vɪ'eɪʃən] n (*short form*) abreviatura; (*act*) abreviación f.

ABC n *abbr* (= *American Broadcasting Company*) cadena de televisión.

abdicate ['æbdɪkeɪt] *vt*, *vi* abdicar.

abdication [æbdɪ'keɪʃən] n abdicación f.

abdomen ['æbdəmən] n abdomen m.

abdominal [æb'dɔmɪnl] *adj* abdominal.

abduct [æb'dʌkt] *vt* raptar, secuestrar.

abductor [æb'dʌktə*] n raptor(a) m/f, secuestrador(a) m/f.

abduction [æb'dʌkʃən] n rapto, secuestro.

Aberdonian [æbə'dəunɪən] *adj* de Aberdeen ♦ n nativo/a or habitante m/f de Aberdeen.

aberration [æbə'reɪʃən] n aberración f; **in a moment of mental** ~ en un momento de enajenación mental.

abet [ə'bɛt] *vt see* **aid.**
abeyance [ə'beɪəns] *n*: **in ~** (*law*) en desuso; (*matter*) en suspenso.
abhor [əb'hɔː*] *vt* aborrecer, abominar (de).
abhorrent [əb'hɔrənt] *adj* aborrecible, detestable.
abide [ə'baɪd] *vt*: **I can't ~ it/him** no lo/le puedo ver *or* aguantar; **to ~ by** *vt fus* atenerse a.
abiding [ə'baɪdɪŋ] *adj* (*memory etc*) perdurable.
ability [ə'bɪlɪtɪ] *n* habilidad *f*, capacidad *f*; (*talent*) talento; **to the best of my ~** lo mejor que pueda *etc*.
abject ['æbdʒɛkt] *adj* (*poverty*) sórdido; (*apology*) rastrero; (*coward*) vil.
ablaze [ə'bleɪz] *adj* en llamas, ardiendo.
able ['eɪbl] *adj* capaz; (*skilled*) hábil; **to be ~ to do sth** poder hacer algo.
able-bodied ['eɪbl'bɔdɪd] *adj* sano; **~ seaman** marinero de primera.
ably ['eɪblɪ] *adv* hábilmente.
ABM *n abbr* = **anti-ballistic missile.**
abnormal [æb'nɔːməl] *adj* anormal.
abnormality [æbnɔː'mælɪtɪ] *n* (*condition*) anormalidad *f*; (*instance*) anomalía.
aboard [ə'bɔːd] *adv* a bordo ♦ *prep* a bordo de; **~ the train** en el tren.
abode [ə'bəʊd] *n* (*old*) morada; (*LAW*) domicilio; **of no fixed ~** sin domicilio fijo.
abolish [ə'bɔlɪʃ] *vt* suprimir, abolir.
abolition [æbəʊ'lɪʃən] *n* supresión *f*, abolición *f*.
abominable [ə'bɔmɪnəbl] *adj* abominable.
aborigine [æbə'rɪdʒɪnɪ] *n* aborigen *m/f*.
abort [ə'bɔːt] *vt* abortar; (*COMPUT*) interrumpir ♦ *vi* (*COMPUT*) interrumpir el programa.
abortion [ə'bɔːʃən] *n* aborto (provocado); **to have an ~** abortar.
abortionist [ə'bɔːʃənɪst] *n* persona que practica abortos.
abortive [ə'bɔːtɪv] *adj* fracasado.
abound [ə'baʊnd] *vi*: **to ~** (**in** *or* **with**) abundar (de *or* en).

================= *KEYWORD*

about [ə'baʊt] *adv* **1** (*approximately*) más o menos, aproximadamente; **~ a hundred/ thousand** *etc* unos(unas) *or* como cien/ mil *etc*; **it takes ~ 10 hours** se tarda unas *or* más o menos 10 horas; **at ~ 2 o'clock** sobre las dos; **I've just ~ finished** casi he terminado
2 (*referring to place*) por todas partes; **to leave things lying ~** dejar las cosas (tiradas) por ahí; **to run ~** correr por todas partes; **to walk ~** pasearse, ir y venir; **is Paul ~?** ¿está por aquí Paul?; **it's the other way ~** es al revés
3: **to be ~ to do sth** estar a punto de hacer algo; **I'm not ~ to do all that for nothing** no pienso hacer todo eso para nada
♦ *prep* **1** (*relating to*) de, sobre, acerca de; **a book ~ London** un libro sobre *or* acerca de Londres; **what is it ~?** (*book, film*) ¿de qué se trata?; **we talked ~ it** hablamos de eso *or* ello; **what** *or* **how ~ doing this?** ¿qué tal si hacemos esto?
2 (*referring to place*) por; **to walk ~ the town** caminar por la ciudad.

about face, about turn *n* (*MIL*) media vuelta; (*fig*) cambio radical.
above [ə'bʌv] *adv* encima, por encima, arriba ♦ *prep* encima de; **mentioned ~** susodicho; **~ all** sobre todo; **he's not ~ a bit of blackmail** es capaz hasta de hacer chantaje.
above board *adj* legítimo.
above-mentioned [əbʌv'mɛnʃnd] *adj* susodicho.
abrasion [ə'breɪʒən] *n* (*on skin*) abrasión *f*.
abrasive [ə'breɪzɪv] *adj* abrasivo.
abreast [ə'brɛst] *adv* uno al lado de otro; **to keep ~ of** mantenerse al corriente de.
abridge [ə'brɪdʒ] *vt* abreviar.
abroad [ə'brɔːd] *adv* (*to be*) en el extranjero; (*to go*) al extranjero; **there is a rumour ~ that ...** corre el rumor de que ...
abrupt [ə'brʌpt] *adj* (*sudden: departure*) repentino; (*manner*) brusco.
abruptly [ə'brʌptlɪ] *adv* (*leave*) repentinamente; (*speak*) bruscamente.
abscess ['æbsɪs] *n* absceso.
abscond [əb'skɔnd] *vi* fugarse.
absence ['æbsəns] *n* ausencia; **in the ~ of** (*person*) en ausencia de; (*thing*) a falta de.
absent ['æbsənt] *adj* ausente; **~ without leave (AWOL)** ausente sin permiso.
absentee [æbsən'tiː] *n* ausente *m/f*.
absenteeism [æbsən'tiːɪzəm] *n* absentismo.
absent-minded [æbsənt'maɪndɪd] *adj* distraído.
absolute ['æbsəluːt] *adj* absoluto; **~ monopoly** monopolio total.
absolutely [æbsə'luːtlɪ] *adv* totalmente; **oh yes, ~!** ¡claro *or* por supuesto que sí!
absolution [æbsə'luːʃən] *n* (*REL*) absolución *f*.
absolve [əb'zɔlv] *vt*: **to ~ sb (from)** absolver a alguien (de).
absorb [əb'zɔːb] *vt* absorber; **to be ~ed in a**

book estar enfrascado en un libro.
absorbent [əb'zɔːbənt] *adj* absorbente.
absorbent cotton *n* (*US*) algodón *m* hidrófilo.
absorbing [əb'zɔːbɪŋ] *adj* absorbente; (*book etc*) interesantísimo.
absorption [əb'zɔːpʃən] *n* absorción *f*.
abstain [əb'steɪn] *vi*: **to ~ (from)** abstenerse (de).
abstemious [əb'stiːmɪəs] *adj* abstemio.
abstention [əb'stenʃən] *n* abstención *f*.
abstinence ['æbstɪnəns] *n* abstinencia.
abstract ['æbstrækt] *adj* abstracto.
abstruse [æb'struːs] *adj* abstruso, oscuro.
absurd [əb'səːd] *adj* absurdo.
absurdity [əb'səːdɪtɪ] *n* absurdo.
ABTA ['æbtə] *n abbr* = *Association of British Travel Agents*.
abundance [ə'bʌndəns] *n* abundancia.
abundant [ə'bʌndənt] *adj* abundante.
abuse [ə'bjuːs] *n* (*insults*) insultos *mpl*, improperios *mpl*; (*misuse*) abuso ♦ *vt* [ə'bjuːz] (*ill-treat*) maltratar; (*take advantage of*) abusar de; **open to ~** sujeto al abuso.
abusive [ə'bjuːsɪv] *adj* ofensivo.
abysmal [ə'bɪzməl] *adj* pésimo; (*ignorance*) supino.
abyss [ə'bɪs] *n* abismo.
AC *abbr* (= *alternating current*) corriente *f* alterna ♦ *n abbr* (*US*) = *athletic club*.
a/c *abbr* (*BANKING etc*) = *account, account current*.
academic [ækə'dɛmɪk] *adj* académico, universitario; (*pej: issue*) puramente teórico ♦ *n* estudioso/a; (*lecturer*) profesor(a) *m/f* universitario/a; **~ year** (*UNIV*) año académico.
academy [ə'kædəmɪ] *n* (*learned body*) academia; (*school*) instituto, colegio; **~ of music** conservatorio.
ACAS ['eɪkæs] *n abbr* (*BRIT*: = *Advisory, Conciliation and Arbitration Service*) ≈ Instituto de Mediación, Arbitraje y Conciliación.
accede [æk'siːd] *vi*: **to ~ to** acceder a.
accelerate [æk'sɛləreɪt] *vt* acelerar ♦ *vi* acelerarse.
acceleration [æksɛlə'reɪʃən] *n* aceleración *f*.
accelerator [æk'sɛləreɪtə*] *n* (*BRIT*) acelerador *m*.
accent ['æksɛnt] *n* acento.
accentuate [æk'sɛntjueɪt] *vt* (*syllable*) acentuar; (*need, difference etc*) recalcar, subrayar.
accept [ək'sɛpt] *vt* aceptar; (*approve*) aprobar, (*concede*) admitir.
acceptable [ək'sɛptəbl] *adj* aceptable;

admisible.
acceptance [ək'sɛptəns] *n* aceptación *f*; aprobación *f*; **to meet with general ~** recibir la aprobación general.
access ['æksɛs] *n* acceso ♦ *vt* (*COMPUT*) acceder a; **the burglars gained ~ through a window** los ladrones lograron entrar por una ventana; **to have ~ to** tener acceso a.
accessible [æk'sɛsəbl] *adj* accesible.
accession [æk'sɛʃən] *n* (*of monarch*) subida, ascenso; (*addition*) adquisición *f*.
accessory [æk'sɛsərɪ] *n* accesorio; **toilet accessories** artículos *mpl* de tocador.
access road *n* carretera de acceso; (*to motorway*) carril *m* de acceso.
access time *n* (*COMPUT*) tiempo de acceso.
accident ['æksɪdənt] *n* accidente *m*; (*chance*) casualidad *f*; **by ~** (*unintentionally*) sin querer; (*by coincidence*) por casualidad; **~s at work** accidentes *mpl* de trabajo; **to meet with** *or* **to have an ~** tener *or* sufrir un accidente.
accidental [æksɪ'dɛntl] *adj* accidental, fortuito.
accidentally [æksɪ'dɛntəlɪ] *adv* sin querer; por casualidad.
accident insurance *n* seguro contra accidentes.
accident-prone ['æksɪdənt'prəun] *adj* propenso a los accidentes.
acclaim [ə'kleɪm] *vt* aclamar, aplaudir ♦ *n* aclamación *f*, aplausos *mpl*.
acclamation [æklə'meɪʃən] *n* (*approval*) aclamación *f*; (*applause*) aplausos *mpl*; **by ~** por aclamación.
acclimatize [ə'klaɪmətaɪz], (*US*) **acclimate** [ə'klaɪmət] *vt*: **to become ~d** aclimatarse.
accolade ['ækəuleɪd] *n* (*prize*) premio; (*praise*) alabanzas *fpl*, homenaje *m*.
accommodate [ə'kɔmədeɪt] *vt* alojar, hospedar; (*oblige, help*) complacer; **this car ~s 4 people comfortably** en este coche caben 4 personas cómodamente.
accommodating [ə'kɔmədeɪtɪŋ] *adj* servicial, complaciente.
accommodation *n*, (*US*) **accommodations** *npl* [ə'kɔmə'deɪʃən(z)] alojamiento; "**~ to let**" "se alquilan habitaciones"; **seating ~** asientos *mpl*.
accompaniment [ə'kʌmpənɪmənt] *n* acompañamiento.
accompanist [ə'kʌmpənɪst] *n* (*MUS*) acompañante *m/f*.
accompany [ə'kʌmpənɪ] *vt* acompañar.
accomplice [ə'kʌmplɪs] *n* cómplice *m/f*.
accomplish [ə'kʌmplɪʃ] *vt* (*finish*) acabar;

(*aim*) realizar; (*task*) llevar a cabo.

accomplished [əˈkʌmplɪʃt] *adj* experto, hábil.

accomplishment [əˈkʌmplɪʃmənt] *n* (*ending*) conclusión *f*; (*bringing about*) realización *f*; (*skill*) talento.

accord [əˈkɔːd] *n* acuerdo ♦ *vt* conceder; **of his own ~** espontáneamente; **with one ~** de *or* por común acuerdo.

accordance [əˈkɔːdəns] *n*: **in ~ with** de acuerdo con.

according [əˈkɔːdɪŋ]: **~ to** *prep* según; (*in accordance with*) conforme a; **it went ~ to plan** salió según lo previsto.

accordingly [əˈkɔːdɪŋlɪ] *adv* (*thus*) por consiguiente.

accordion [əˈkɔːdɪən] *n* acordeón *m*.

accordionist [əˈkɔːdɪənɪst] *n* acordeonista *m/f*.

accost [əˈkɒst] *vt* abordar, dirigirse a.

account [əˈkaunt] *n* (*COMM*) cuenta, factura; (*report*) informe *m*; **~s** *npl* (*COMM*) cuentas *fpl*; "**~ payee only**" "únicamente en cuenta del beneficiario"; **your ~ is still outstanding** su cuenta está todavía pendiente; **of little ~** de poca importancia; **on ~** a crédito; **to buy sth on ~** comprar algo a crédito; **on no ~** bajo ningún concepto; **on ~ of** a causa de, por motivo de; **to take into ~, take ~ of** tener en cuenta; **to keep an ~ of** llevar la cuenta de; **to bring sb to ~ for sth/for having done sth** pedirle cuentas a algn por algo/por haber hecho algo.

▶ **account for** *vt fus* (*explain*) explicar; **all the children were ~ed for** no faltaba ningún niño.

accountability [əkauntəˈbɪlɪtɪ] *n* responsabilidad *f*.

accountable [əˈkauntəbl] *adj*: **~ (for)** responsable (de).

accountancy [əˈkauntənsɪ] *n* contabilidad *f*.

accountant [əˈkauntənt] *n* contable *m/f*, contador(a) *m/f* (*LAM*).

accounting [əˈkauntɪŋ] *n* contabilidad *f*.

accounting period *n* período contable, ejercicio financiero.

account number *n* (*at bank etc*) número de cuenta.

account payable *n* cuenta por pagar.

account receivable *n* cuenta por cobrar.

accoutrements [əˈkuːtrəmənts] *npl* equipo, pertrechos *mpl*.

accredited [əˈkrɛdɪtɪd] *adj* (*agent etc*) autorizado, acreditado.

accretion [əˈkriːʃən] *n* acumulación *f*.

accrue [əˈkruː] *vi* (*mount up*) aumentar, incrementarse; (*interest*) acumularse; **to**

~ to corresponder a; **~d charges** gastos *mpl* vencidos; **~d interest** interés *m* acumulado.

accumulate [əˈkjuːmjuleɪt] *vt* acumular ♦ *vi* acumularse.

accumulation [əkjuːmjuˈleɪʃən] *n* acumulación *f*.

accuracy [ˈækjurəsɪ] *n* exactitud *f*, precisión *f*.

accurate [ˈækjurɪt] *adj* (*number*) exacto; (*answer*) acertado; (*shot*) certero.

accurately [ˈækjurɪtlɪ] *adv* (*count, shoot, answer*) con precisión.

accursed [əˈkəːst] *adj* maldito.

accusation [ækjuˈzeɪʃən] *n* acusación *f*.

accusative [əˈkjuːzətɪv] *n* acusativo.

accuse [əˈkjuːz] *vt* acusar; (*blame*) echar la culpa a.

accused [əˈkjuːzd] *n* acusado/a.

accuser [əˈkjuːzə*] *n* acusador(a) *m/f*.

accustom [əˈkʌstəm] *vt* acostumbrar; **to ~ o.s. to sth** acostumbrarse a algo.

accustomed [əˈkʌstəmd] *adj*: **~ to** acostumbrado a.

AC/DC *abbr = alternating current/direct current.*

ACE [eɪs] *n abbr = American Council on Education.*

ace [eɪs] *n* as *m*.

acerbic [əˈsəːbɪk] *adj* acerbo; (*fig*) mordaz.

acetate [ˈæsɪteɪt] *n* acetato.

ache [eɪk] *n* dolor *m* ♦ *vi* doler; (*yearn*): **to ~ to do sth** ansiar hacer algo; **i've got stomach ~** *or* (*US*) **a stomach ~** tengo dolor de estómago, me duele el estómago; **my head ~s** me duele la cabeza.

achieve [əˈtʃiːv] *vt* (*reach*) alcanzar; (*realize*) realizar; (*victory, success*) lograr, conseguir.

achievement [əˈtʃiːvmənt] *n* (*completion*) realización *f*; (*success*) éxito *m*.

Achilles heel [əˈkɪliːz-] *n* talón *m* de Aquiles.

acid [ˈæsɪd] *adj* ácido; (*bitter*) agrio ♦ *n* ácido.

acidity [əˈsɪdɪtɪ] *n* acidez *f*; (*MED*) acedía.

acid rain *n* lluvia ácida.

acid test *n* (*fig*) prueba de fuego.

acknowledge [əkˈnɒlɪdʒ] *vt* (*letter: also:* **~ receipt of**) acusar recibo de; (*fact*) reconocer.

acknowledgement [əkˈnɒlɪdʒmənt] *n* acuse *m* de recibo; reconocimiento; **~s** (*in book*) agradecimientos *mpl*.

ACLU *n abbr* (= *American Civil Liberties Union*) *unión americana por libertades civiles.*

acme ['ækmɪ] n súmmum m.
acne ['æknɪ] n acné m.
acorn ['eɪkɔːn] n bellota.
acoustic [ə'kuːstɪk] adj acústico.
acoustic coupler [-'kʌplə*] n (COMPUT) acoplador m acústico.
acoustics [ə'kuːstɪks] n, npl acústica sg.
acquaint [ə'kweɪnt] vt: **to ~ sb with sth** (inform) poner a algn al corriente de algo; **to be ~ed with** (person) conocer; (fact) estar al corriente de.
acquaintance [ə'kweɪntəns] n conocimiento; (person) conocido/a; **to make sb's ~** conocer a algn.
acquiesce [ækwɪ'ɛs] vi (agree): **to ~ (in)** consentir (en), conformarse (con).
acquire [ə'kwaɪə*] vt adquirir.
acquired [ə'kwaɪəd] adj adquirido; **it's an ~** taste es algo a lo que uno se aficiona poco a poco.
acquisition [ækwɪ'zɪʃən] n adquisición f.
acquisitive [ə'kwɪzɪtɪv] adj codicioso.
acquit [ə'kwɪt] vt absolver, exculpar; **to ~ o.s. well** defenderse bien.
acquittal [ə'kwɪtl] n absolución f, exculpación f.
acre ['eɪkə*] n acre m.
acreage ['eɪkɔrɪdʒ] n extensión f.
acrid ['ækrɪd] adj (smell) acre; (fig) mordaz, sarcástico.
acrimonious [ækrɪ'məunɪəs] adj (remark) mordaz; (argument) reñido.
acrobat ['ækrəbæt] n acróbata m/f.
acrobatic [ækrə'bætɪk] adj acrobático.
acrobatics [ækrə'bætɪks] npl acrobacias fpl.
acronym ['ækrənɪm] n siglas fpl.
across [ə'krɔs] prep (on the other side of) al otro lado de; (crosswise) a través de ♦ adv de un lado a otro, de una parte a otra; a través, al través; **to run/swim ~** atravesar corriendo/nadando; **~ from** enfrente de; **the lake is 12 km ~** el lago tiene 12 km de ancho; **to get sth ~ to sb** (fig) hacer comprender algo a algn.
acrylic [ə'krɪlɪk] adj acrílico.
act [ækt] n acto, acción f; (THEAT) acto; (in music-hall etc) número; (LAW) decreto, ley f ♦ vi (behave) comportarse; (THEAT) actuar; (pretend) fingir; (take action) tomar medidas ♦ vt (part) hacer, representar; **~ of God** fuerza mayor; **it's only an ~** es cuento; **to catch sb in the ~** coger a algn in fraganti or con las manos en la masa; **to ~ Hamlet** hacer el papel de Hamlet; **to ~ as** actuar or hacer de; **~ing in my capacity as chairman, I ...** en mi calidad de presidente, yo ...; **it ~s as a deterrent** sirve para disuadir; **he's only ~ing** está

fingiendo nada más.
► **act on** vt: **to ~ on sth** actuar or obrar sobre algo.
► **act out** vt (event) representar; (fantasies) realizar.
acting ['æktɪŋ] adj suplente ♦ n: **to do some ~** hacer algo de teatro; **he is the ~ manager** es el gerente en funciones.
action ['ækʃən] n acción f, acto; (MIL) acción f; (LAW) proceso, demanda; **to put a plan into ~** poner un plan en acción or en marcha; **killed in ~** (MIL) muerto en acto de servicio or en combate; **out of ~** (person) fuera de combate; (thing) averiado, descompuesto; **to take ~** tomar medidas; **to bring an ~ against sb** entablar or presentar demanda contra algn.
action replay n (TV) repetición f.
activate ['æktɪveɪt] vt activar.
active ['æktɪv] adj activo, enérgico; (volcano) en actividad; **to play an ~ part in** colaborar activamente en; **~ file** (COMPUT) fichero activo.
active duty (AD) n (US MIL) servicio activo.
actively ['æktɪvlɪ] adv (participate) activamente; (discourage, dislike) enérgicamente.
active partner n (COMM) socio activo.
activist ['æktɪvɪst] n activista m/f.
activity [æk'tɪvɪtɪ] n actividad f.
actor ['æktə*] n actor m.
actress ['æktrɪs] n actriz f.
ACTT n abbr (BRIT: = Association of Cinematographic, Television and Allied Technicians) sindicato de técnicos de cine y televisión.
actual ['æktjuəl] adj verdadero, real.
actually ['æktjuəlɪ] adv realmente, en realidad.
actuary ['æktjuərɪ] n (COMM) actuario/a (de seguros).
actuate ['æktjueɪt] vt mover, impulsar.
acumen ['ækjumən] n perspicacia; **business ~** talento para los negocios.
acupuncture ['ækjupʌŋktʃə*] n acupuntura.
acute [ə'kjuːt] adj agudo.
acutely [ə'kjuːtlɪ] adv profundamente, extremadamente.
AD adv abbr (= Anno Domini) A.C. ♦ n abbr (US MIL) see **active duty**.
ad [æd] n abbr = **advertisement**.
adage ['ædɪdʒ] n refrán m, adagio.
Adam ['ædəm] n Adán m; **~'s apple** n nuez f (de la garganta).
adamant ['ædəmənt] adj firme, inflexible.

adapt [ə'dæpt] vt adaptar; (reconcile) acomodar ♦ vi: **to ~ (to)** adaptarse (a), ajustarse (a).

adaptability [ədæptə'bɪlɪtɪ] n (of person, device etc) adaptabilidad f.

adaptable [ə'dæptəbl] adj (device) adaptable; (person) acomodadizo, que se adapta.

adaptation [ædæp'teɪʃən] n adaptación f.

adapter, adaptor [ə'dæptə*] n (ELEC) adaptador m.

ADC n abbr (MIL) = aide-de-camp; (US: = Aid to Dependent Children) ayuda para niños dependientes.

add [æd] vt añadir, agregar (esp LAM); (figures: also: ~ **up**) sumar ♦ vi: **to ~ to** (increase) aumentar, acrecentar.

▶**add on** vt añadir.

▶**add up** vt (figures) sumar ♦ vi (fig): **it doesn't ~ up** no tiene sentido; **it doesn't ~ up to much** es poca cosa, no tiene gran or mucha importancia.

addendum [ə'dɛndəm] n ad(d)enda m or f.

adder ['ædə*] n víbora.

addict ['ædɪkt] n (to drugs etc) adicto/a; (enthusiast) aficionado/a, entusiasta m/f; **heroin ~** heroinómano/a.

addicted [ə'dɪktɪd] adj: **to be ~ to** ser adicto a; ser aficionado a.

addiction [ə'dɪkʃən] n (dependence) hábito morboso; (enthusiasm) afición f.

addictive [ə'dɪktɪv] adj que causa adicción.

adding machine ['ædɪŋ-] n calculadora.

Addis Ababa ['ædɪs'æbəbə] n Addis Abeba m.

addition [ə'dɪʃən] n (adding up) adición f; (thing added) añadidura, añadido; **in ~** además, por añadidura; **in ~ to** además de.

additional [ə'dɪʃənl] adj adicional.

additive ['ædɪtɪv] n aditivo.

addled ['ædld] adj (BRIT: rotten) podrido; (: fig) confuso.

address [ə'drɛs] n dirección f, señas fpl; (speech) discurso; (COMPUT) dirección f ♦ vt (letter) dirigir; (speak to) dirigirse a, dirigir la palabra a; **form of ~** tratamiento; **absolute/relative ~** (COMPUT) dirección f absoluta/relativa; **to ~ o.s. to sth** (issue, problem) abordar.

address book n agenda (de direcciones).

addressee [ædrɛ'si:] n destinatario/a.

Aden ['eɪdn] n Adén m.

adenoids ['ædɪnɔɪdz] npl vegetaciones fpl (adenoideas).

adept ['ædɛpt] adj: **~ at** experto or ducho en.

adequacy ['ædɪkwəsɪ] n idoneidad f.

adequate ['ædɪkwɪt] adj (satisfactory) adecuado; (enough) suficiente; **to feel ~ to a task** sentirse con fuerzas para una tarea.

adequately ['ædɪkwɪtlɪ] adv adecuadamente.

adhere [əd'hɪə*] vi: **to ~ to** adherirse a; (fig: abide by) observar.

adherent [əd'hɪərənt] n partidario/a.

adhesion [əd'hi:ʒən] n adherencia.

adhesive [əd'hi:zɪv] adj, n adhesivo.

adhesive tape n (BRIT) cinta adhesiva; (US: MED) esparadrapo.

ad hoc [æd'hɔk] adj (decision) ad hoc; (committee) formado con fines específicos ♦ adv ad hoc.

adieu [ə'dju:] excl ¡vaya con Dios!

ad inf ['æd'ɪnf] adv hasta el infinito.

adjacent [ə'dʒeɪsənt] adj: **~ to** contiguo a, inmediato a.

adjective ['ædʒɛktɪv] n adjetivo.

adjoin [ə'dʒɔɪn] vt estar contiguo a; (land) lindar con.

adjoining [ə'dʒɔɪnɪŋ] adj contiguo, vecino.

adjourn [ə'dʒɜːn] vt aplazar; (session) suspender, levantar; (US: end) terminar ♦ vi suspenderse; **the meeting has been ~ed till next week** se ha levantado la sesión hasta la semana que viene; **they ~ed to the pub** (col) se trasladaron al bar.

adjournment [ə'dʒɜːnmənt] n (period) suspensión f; (postponement) aplazamiento.

Adjt. abbr = **adjutant**.

adjudicate [ə'dʒuːdɪkeɪt] vi sentenciar; (contest) hacer de árbitro en, juzgar; (claim) decidir.

adjudication [ədʒuːdɪ'keɪʃən] n fallo.

adjudicator [ə'dʒuːdɪkeɪtə*] n juez m, árbitro.

adjust [ə'dʒʌst] vt (change) modificar; (arrange) arreglar; (machine) ajustar ♦ vi: **to ~ (to)** adaptarse (a).

adjustable [ə'dʒʌstəbl] adj ajustable.

adjuster [ə'dʒʌstə*] n see **loss adjuster**.

adjustment [ə'dʒʌstmənt] n modificación f; arreglo; (of prices, wages) ajuste m.

adjutant ['ædʒətənt] n ayudante m.

ad-lib [æd'lɪb] vt, vi improvisar ♦ adv: **ad lib** a voluntad, a discreción.

adman ['ædmæn] n (col) publicista m.

admin ['ædmɪn] n abbr (col) = **administration**.

administer [əd'mɪnɪstə*] vt proporcionar; (justice) administrar.

administration [ædmɪnɪ'streɪʃən] n administración f; (government) gobierno;

the A~ (*US*) la Administración.
administrative [əd'mɪnɪstrətɪv] *adj* administrativo.
administrator [əd'mɪnɪstreɪtə*] *n* administrador(a) *m/f*.
admirable ['ædmərəbl] *adj* admirable.
admiral ['ædmərəl] *n* almirante *m*.
Admiralty ['ædmərəltɪ] *n* (*BRIT*) Ministerio de Marina, Almirantazgo.
admiration [ædmə'reɪʃən] *n* admiración *f*.
admire [əd'maɪə*] *vt* admirar.
admirer [əd'maɪərə*] *n* admirador(a) *m/f*; (*suitor*) pretendiente *m*.
admiring [əd'maɪərɪŋ] *adj* (*expression*) de admiración.
admissible [əd'mɪsəbl] *adj* admisible.
admission [əd'mɪʃən] *n* (*exhibition, nightclub*) entrada; (*enrolment*) ingreso; (*confession*) confesión *f*; **"~ free"** "entrada gratis *or* libre"; **by his own ~** él mismo reconoce que.
admit [əd'mɪt] *vt* dejar entrar, dar entrada a; (*permit*) admitir; (*acknowledge*) reconocer; **"this ticket ~s two"** "entrada para 2 personas"; **children not ~ted** se prohíbe la entrada a (los) menores de edad; **I must ~ that** ... debo reconocer que ...
▶**admit of** *vt fus* admitir, permitir.
▶**admit to** *vt fus* confesarse culpable de.
admittance [əd'mɪtəns] *n* entrada; **"no ~"** "se prohíbe la entrada", "prohibida la entrada".
admittedly [əd'mɪtədlɪ] *adv* de acuerdo que.
admonish [əd'mɔnɪʃ] *vt* amonestar; (*advise*) aconsejar.
ad nauseam [æd'nɔːsɪæm] *adv* hasta la saciedad.
ado [ə'duː] *n*: **without (any) more ~** sin más (ni más).
adolescence [ædəu'lɛsns] *n* adolescencia.
adolescent [ædəu'lɛsnt] *adj, n* adolescente *m/f*.
adopt [ə'dɔpt] *vt* adoptar.
adopted [ə'dɔptɪd] *adj* adoptivo.
adoption [ə'dɔpʃən] *n* adopción *f*.
adoptive [ə'dɔptɪv] *adj* adoptivo.
adorable [ə'dɔːrəbl] *adj* adorable.
adoration [ædə'reɪʃən] *n* adoración *f*.
adore [ə'dɔː*] *vt* adorar.
adoring [ə'dɔːrɪŋ] *adj*: **to his ~ public** a un público que le adora *or* le adoraba *etc*.
adorn [ə'dɔːn] *vt* adornar.
adornment [ə'dɔːnmənt] *n* adorno.
ADP *n abbr see* **automatic data processing**.
adrenalin [ə'drɛnəlɪn] *n* adrenalina.
Adriatic [eɪdrɪ'ætɪk] *n*: **the ~ (Sea)** el (Mar)

Adriático.
adrift [ə'drɪft] *adv* a la deriva; **to come ~** (*boat*) ir a la deriva, soltarse; (*wire, rope etc*) soltarse.
adroit [ə'drɔɪt] *adj* diestro, hábil.
ADT *abbr* (*US: = Atlantic Daylight Time*) *hora de verano de Nueva York*.
adulation [ædju'leɪʃən] *n* adulación *f*.
adult ['ædʌlt] *n* adulto/a ♦ *adj*: **~ education** educación *f* para adultos.
adulterate [ə'dʌltəreɪt] *vt* adulterar.
adulterer [ə'dʌltərə*] *n* adúltero.
adulteress [ə'dʌltrɪs] *n* adúltera.
adultery [ə'dʌltərɪ] *n* adulterio.
adulthood ['ædʌlthud] *n* edad *f* adulta.
advance [əd'vɑːns] *n* adelanto, progreso; (*money*) anticipo; (*MIL*) avance *m* ♦ *vt* avanzar, adelantar; (*money*) anticipar ♦ *vi* avanzar, adelantarse; **in ~** por adelantado; (*book*) con antelación; **to make ~s to sb** (*gen*) ponerse en contacto con algn; (*amorously*) insinuarse a algn.
advanced *adj* avanzado; (*SCOL: studies*) adelantado; **~ in years** entrado en años.
advancement [əd'vɑːnsmənt] *n* progreso; (*in rank*) ascenso.
advance notice *n* previo aviso.
advance payment *n* (*part sum*) anticipo.
advantage [əd'vɑːntɪdʒ] *n* (*also TENNIS*) ventaja; **to take ~ of** aprovecharse de; **it's to our ~** es ventajoso para nosotros.
advantageous [ædvən'teɪdʒəs] *adj* ventajoso, provechoso.
advent ['ædvənt] *n* advenimiento; **A~** Adviento.
adventure [əd'vɛntʃə*] *n* aventura.
adventure playground *n* parque *m* infantil.
adventurous [əd'vɛntʃərəs] *adj* aventurero; (*bold*) arriesgado.
adverb ['ædvəːb] *n* adverbio.
adversary ['ædvəsərɪ] *n* adversario, contrario.
adverse ['ædvəːs] *adj* adverso, contrario; **~ to** adverso a.
adversity [əd'vəːsɪtɪ] *n* infortunio.
advert ['ædvəːt] *n abbr* (*BRIT*) = **advertisement**.
advertise ['ædvətaɪz] *vi* hacer propaganda; (*in newspaper etc*) poner un anuncio, anunciarse; **to ~ for** (*staff*) buscar por medio de anuncios ♦ *vt* anunciar.
advertisement [əd'vəːtɪsmənt] *n* (*COMM*) anuncio.
advertiser ['ædvətaɪzə*] *n* anunciante *m/f*.
advertising ['ædvətaɪzɪŋ] *n* publicidad *f*, propaganda; anuncios *mpl*.
advertising agency *n* agencia de

publicidad.

advertising campaign *n* campaña de publicidad.

advice [əd'vaɪs] *n* consejo, consejos *mpl*; (*notification*) aviso; **a piece of** ~ un consejo; **to take legal** ~ consultar a un abogado; **to ask (sb) for** ~ pedir consejo (a algn).

advice note *n* (*BRIT*) nota de aviso.

advisable [əd'vaɪzəbl] *adj* aconsejable, conveniente.

advise [əd'vaɪz] *vt* aconsejar; **to** ~ **sb of sth** (*inform*) informar a algn de algo; **to** ~ **sb against sth/doing sth** desaconsejar algo a algn/aconsejar a algn que no haga algo; **you will be well/ill** ~**d to go** deberías/no deberías ir.

advisedly [əd'vaɪzɪdlɪ] *adv* (*deliberately*) deliberadamente.

adviser [əd'vaɪzə*] *n* consejero/a; (*business adviser*) asesor(a) *m/f*.

advisory [əd'vaɪzərɪ] *adj* consultivo; **in an** ~ **capacity** como asesor.

advocate ['ædvəkeɪt] *vt* (*argue for*) abogar por; (*give support to*) ser partidario de ♦ *n* ['ædvəkɪt] abogado/a.

advt. *abbr* = **advertisement**.

AEA *n abbr* (*BRIT*: = *Atomic Energy Authority*) consejo de energía nuclear.

AEC *n abbr* (*US*: = *Atomic Energy Commission*) AEC *f*.

AEEU *n abbr* (*BRIT*: = *Amalgamated Engineering and Electrical Union*) sindicato mixto de ingenieros y electricistas.

Aegean [iː'dʒiːən] *n*: **the** ~ **(Sea)** el (Mar) Egeo.

aegis ['iːdʒɪs] *n*: **under the** ~ **of** bajo la tutela de.

aeon ['iːən] *n* eón *m*.

aerial ['ɛərɪəl] *n* antena ♦ *adj* aéreo.

aerie ['ɛərɪ] *n* (*US*) aguilera.

aero- ['ɛərəu] *pref* aero-.

aerobatics [ɛərəu'bætɪks] *npl* acrobacia aérea.

aerobics [ɛə'rəubɪks] *nsg* aerobic *m*, aerobismo (*LAM*).

aerodrome ['ɛərədrəum] *n* (*BRIT*) aeródromo.

aerodynamic [ɛərəudaɪ'næmɪk] *adj* aerodinámico.

aeronautics [ɛərəu'nɔːtɪks] *nsg* aeronáutica.

aeroplane ['ɛərəpleɪn] *n* (*BRIT*) avión *m*.

aerosol ['ɛərəsɔl] *n* aerosol *m*.

aerospace industry ['ɛərəuspeɪs-] *n* industria aeroespacial.

aesthetic [iːs'θetɪk] *adj* estético.

aesthetics [iːs'θetɪks] *npl* estética.

a.f. *abbr* = *audiofrequency*.

afar [ə'fɑː*] *adv* lejos; **from** ~ desde lejos.

AFB *n abbr* (*US*) = *Air Force Base*.

AFDC *n abbr* (*US*: = *Aid to Families with Dependent Children*) ayuda a familias con hijos menores.

affable ['æfəbl] *adj* afable.

affair [ə'fɛə*] *n* asunto; (*also*: **love** ~) aventura *f* amorosa; ~**s** (*business*) asuntos *mpl*; **the Watergate** ~ el asunto (de) Watergate.

affect [ə'fɛkt] *vt* afectar, influir en; (*move*) conmover.

affectation [æfɛk'teɪʃən] *n* afectación *f*.

affected [ə'fɛktɪd] *adj* afectado.

affection [ə'fɛkʃən] *n* afecto, cariño.

affectionate [ə'fɛkʃənɪt] *adj* afectuoso, cariñoso.

affectionately [ə'fɛkʃənɪtlɪ] *adv* afectuosamente.

affidavit [æfɪ'deɪvɪt] *n* (*LAW*) declaración *f* jurada.

affiliated [ə'fɪlieɪtɪd] *adj* afiliado; ~ **company** empresa *or* compañía filial *or* subsidiaria.

affinity [ə'fɪnɪtɪ] *n* afinidad *f*.

affirm [ə'fəːm] *vt* afirmar.

affirmation [æfə'meɪʃən] *n* afirmación *f*.

affirmative [ə'fəːmətɪv] *adj* afirmativo.

affix [ə'fɪks] *vt* (*signature*) estampar; (*stamp*) pegar.

afflict [ə'flɪkt] *vt* afligir.

affliction [ə'flɪkʃən] *n* enfermedad *f*, aflicción *f*.

affluence ['æfluəns] *n* opulencia, riqueza.

affluent ['æfluənt] *adj* adinerado, acaudalado; **the** ~ **society** la sociedad opulenta.

afford [ə'fɔːd] *vt* poder permitirse; (*provide*) proporcionar; **can we** ~ **a car?** ¿podemos permitirnos el gasto de comprar un coche?

affordable [ə'fɔːdəbl] *adj* asequible.

affray [ə'freɪ] *n* refriega, reyerta.

affront [ə'frʌnt] *n* afrenta, ofensa.

affronted [ə'frʌntɪd] *adj* ofendido.

Afghan ['æfgæn] *adj*, *n* afgano/a *m/f*.

Afghanistan [æf'gænɪstæn] *n* Afganistán *m*.

afield [ə'fiːld] *adv*: **far** ~ muy lejos.

AFL-CIO *n abbr* (*US*: = *American Federation of Labor and Congress of Industrial Organizations*) confederación sindicalista.

afloat [ə'fləut] *adv* (*floating*) a flote; (*at sea*) en el mar.

afoot [ə'fut] *adv*: **there is something** ~ algo se está tramando.

aforesaid [ə'fɔːsɛd] *adj* susodicho; (*COMM*) mencionado anteriormente.

afraid [ə'freɪd] *adj*: **to be ~ of** (*person*) tener miedo a; (*thing*) tener miedo de; **to be ~ to** tener miedo de, temer; **I am ~ that** me temo que; **I'm ~ so** ¡me temo que sí!, ¡lo siento, pero es así!; **I'm ~ not** me temo que no.

afresh [ə'freʃ] *adv* de nuevo, otra vez.

Africa ['æfrɪkə] *n* África.

African ['æfrɪkən] *adj*, *n* africano/a *m/f*.

Afrikaans [æfrɪ'kɑːns] *n* africaans *m*.

Afrikaner [æfrɪ'kɑːnə*] *n* africánder *m/f*.

Afro-American ['æfrəuə'merɪkən] *adj*, *n* afroamericano/a *m/f*.

AFT *n abbr* (= *American Federation of Teachers*) sindicato de profesores.

aft [ɑːft] *adv* (*to be*) en popa; (*to go*) a popa.

after ['ɑːftə*] *prep* (*time*) después de; (*place, order*) detrás de, tras ♦ *adv* después ♦ *conj* después (de) que; **what/who are you ~?** ¿qué/a quién buscas?; **the police are ~ him** la policía le está buscando; **~ having done/he left** después de haber hecho/ después de que se marchó; **~ dinner** después de cenar *or* comer; **the day ~ tomorrow** pasado mañana; **to ask ~ sb** preguntar por algn; **~ all** después de todo, al fin y al cabo; **~ you!** ¡Vd primero!; **quarter ~ two** (*US*) las 2 y cuarto.

afterbirth ['ɑːftəbə:θ] *n* placenta.

aftercare ['ɑːftəkeə*] *n* (*MED*) asistencia postoperatoria.

after-effects ['ɑːftərɪfekts] *npl* secuelas *fpl*, efectos *mpl*.

afterlife ['ɑːftəlaɪf] *n* vida después de la muerte.

aftermath ['ɑːftəmɑː:θ] *n* consecuencias *fpl*, resultados *mpl*.

afternoon [ɑːftə'nuːn] *n* tarde *f*; **good ~!** ¡buenas tardes!

afters ['ɑːftəz] *n* (*col: dessert*) postre *m*.

after-sales service [ɑːftə'seɪlz-] *n* (*BRIT COMM: for car, washing machine etc*) servicio de asistencia pos-venta.

after-shave (lotion) ['ɑːftəʃeɪv-] *n* loción *f* para después del afeitado, aftershave *m*.

aftershock ['ɑːftəʃɔk] *n* (*of earthquake*) pequeño temblor *m* posterior.

aftertaste ['ɑːftəteɪst] *n* regusto.

afterthought ['ɑːftəθɔ:t] *n* ocurrencia (tardía).

afterwards ['ɑːftəwədz] *adv* después, más tarde.

again [ə'gen] *adv* otra vez, de nuevo; **to do sth ~** volver a hacer algo; **~ and ~** una y otra vez; **now and ~** de vez en cuando.

against [ə'genst] *prep* (*opposed*) en contra de; (*close to*) contra, junto a; **I was leaning**

~ the desk estaba apoyado en el escritorio; **(as) ~** frente a.

age [eɪdʒ] *n* edad *f*; (*old ~*) vejez *f*; (*period*) época ♦ *vi* envejecer(se) ♦ *vt* envejecer; **what ~ is he?** ¿qué edad *or* cuántos años tiene?; **he is 20 years of ~** tiene 20 años; **under ~** menor de edad; **to come of ~** llegar a la mayoría de edad; **it's been ~s since I saw you** hace siglos que no te veo.

aged [eɪdʒd] *adj*: **~ 10** de 10 años de edad ♦ *npl* ['eɪdʒɪd]: **the ~** los ancianos.

age group *n*: **to be in the same ~** tener la misma edad; **the 40 to 50 ~** las personas de 40 a 50 años.

ageing ['eɪdʒɪŋ] *adj* que envejece; (*pej*) en declive ♦ *n* envejecimiento.

ageless ['eɪdʒlɪs] *adj* (*eternal*) eterno; (*ever young*) siempre joven.

age limit *n* límite *m* de edad, edad *f* tope.

agency ['eɪdʒənsɪ] *n* agencia; **through *or* by the ~ of** por medio de.

agenda [ə'dʒendə] *n* orden *m* del día; **on the ~** (*COMM*) en el orden del día.

agent ['eɪdʒənt] *n* (*gen*) agente *m/f*; (*representative*) representante *m/f*, delegado/a.

aggravate ['ægrəveɪt] *vt* agravar; (*annoy*) irritar, exasperar.

aggravating ['ægrəveɪtɪŋ] *adj* irritante, molesto.

aggravation [ægrə'veɪʃən] *n* agravamiento.

aggregate ['ægrɪgeɪt] *n* conjunto.

aggression [ə'greʃən] *n* agresión *f*.

aggressive [ə'gresɪv] *adj* agresivo; (*vigorous*) enérgico.

aggressiveness [ə'gresɪvnɪs] *n* agresividad *f*.

aggressor [ə'gresə*] *n* agresor(a) *m/f*.

aggrieved [ə'griːvd] *adj* ofendido, agraviado.

aggro ['ægrəu] *n* (*col*) (*physical violence*) bronca; (*bad feeling*) mal rollo; (*hassle*) rollo, movida.

aghast [ə'gɑːst] *adj* horrorizado.

agile ['ædʒaɪl] *adj* ágil.

agility [ə'dʒɪlɪtɪ] *n* agilidad *f*.

agitate ['ædʒɪteɪt] *vt* (*shake*) agitar; (*trouble*) inquietar; **to ~ for** hacer campaña en pro de *or* en favor de.

agitated ['ædʒɪteɪtɪd] *adj* agitado.

agitator ['ædʒɪteɪtə*] *n* agitador(a) *m/f*.

AGM *n abbr see* **annual general meeting**.

agnostic [æg'nɔstɪk] *adj*, *n* agnóstico/a *m/f*.

ago [ə'gəu] *adv*: **2 days ~** hace 2 días; **not long ~** hace poco; **how long ~?** ¿hace cuánto tiempo?; **as long ~ as 1960** ya en 1960.

agog [ə'gɔg] *adj* (*anxious*) ansioso; (*excited*):

(all) ~ **(for)** (todo) emocionado (por).
agonize ['ægənaɪz] *vi:* **to** ~ **(over)**
atormentarse (por).
agonized ['ægənaɪzd] *adj* angustioso.
agonizing ['ægənaɪzɪŋ] *adj* (*pain*) atroz;
(*suspense*) angustioso.
agony ['ægənɪ] *n* (*pain*) dolor *m* atroz;
(*distress*) angustia; **to be in** ~ retorcerse
de dolor.
agony aunt *n* (*BRIT col*) consejera
sentimental.
agony column *n* consultorio sentimental.
agree [ə'griː] *vt* (*price*) acordar, quedar en
♦ *vi* (*statements etc*) coincidir, concordar;
to ~ **(with)** (*person*) estar de acuerdo
(con), ponerse de acuerdo (con); **to** ~ **to
do** aceptar hacer; **to** ~ **to sth** consentir
en algo; **to** ~ **that** (*admit*) estar de
acuerdo en que; **it was** ~**d that ...** se
acordó que ...; **garlic doesn't** ~ **with me** el
ajo no me sienta bien.
agreeable [ə'griːəbl] *adj* agradable; (*person*)
simpático; (*willing*) de acuerdo,
conforme.
agreeably [ə'griːəblɪ] *adv* agradablemente.
agreed [ə'griːd] *adj* (*time, place*) convenido.
agreement [ə'griːmənt] *n* acuerdo; (*COMM*)
contrato; **in** ~ de acuerdo, conforme; **by
mutual** ~ de común acuerdo.
agricultural [ægrɪ'kʌltʃərəl] *adj* agrícola.
agriculture ['ægrɪkʌltʃə*] *n* agricultura.
aground [ə'graund] *adv:* **to run** ~ encallar,
embarrancar.
ahead [ə'hed] *adv* delante; ~ **of** delante de;
(*fig: schedule etc*) antes de; ~ **of time**
antes de la hora; **to be** ~ **of sb** (*fig*) llevar
ventaja *or* la delantera a algn; **go right** *or*
straight ~ siga adelante; **they were (right)**
~ **of us** iban (justo) delante de nosotros.
ahoy [ə'hɔɪ] *excl* ¡oiga!
AI *n abbr* = *Amnesty International*; (*COMPUT*)
= **artificial intelligence**.
AIB *n abbr* (*BRIT*: = *Accident Investigation
Bureau*) *oficina de investigación de
accidentes*.
AID *n abbr* (= *artificial insemination by donor*)
inseminación artificial por donante; (*US*:
= *Agency for International Development*)
Agencia Internacional para el
Desarrollo.
aid [eɪd] *n* ayuda, auxilio ♦ *vt* ayudar,
auxiliar; **in** ~ **of** a beneficio de; **with the**
~ **of** con la ayuda de; **to** ~ **and abet** (*LAW*)
ser cómplice.
aide [eɪd] *n* (*POL*) ayudante *m/f*.
AIDS [eɪdz] *n abbr* (= *acquired immune* (*or
immuno-*)*deficiency syndrome*) SIDA *m*,
sida *m*.

AIH *abbr* (= *artificial insemination by
husband*) *inseminación artificial por
esposo*.
ailing ['eɪlɪŋ] *adj* (*person, economy*)
enfermizo.
ailment ['eɪlmənt] *n* enfermedad *f*, achaque
m.
aim [eɪm] *vt* (*gun*) apuntar; (*missile, remark*)
dirigir; (*blow*) asestar ♦ *vi* (*also:* **take** ~)
apuntar ♦ *n* puntería; (*objective*)
propósito, meta; **to** ~ **at** (*objective*)
aspirar a, pretender; **to** ~ **to do** tener
como objetivo hacer, aspirar a hacer.
aimless ['eɪmlɪs] *adj* sin propósito, sin
objeto.
aimlessly ['eɪmlɪslɪ] *adv* sin rumbo fijo.
ain't [eɪnt] (*col*) = **am not; aren't; isn't**.
air [ɛə*] *n* aire *m*; (*appearance*) aspecto ♦ *vt*
(*room*) ventilar; (*clothes, bed, grievances,
ideas*) airear; (*views*) hacer público ♦ *cpd*
aéreo; **to throw sth into the** ~ (*ball etc*)
lanzar algo al aire; **by** ~ (*travel*) en avión;
to be on the ~ (*RADIO, TV: programme*)
estarse emitiendo: (: *station*) estar
emitiendo.
airbag ['ɛəbæg] *n* airbag *m inv*.
air base *n* (*MIL*) base *f* aérea.
air bed *n* (*BRIT*) colcheta inflable *or*
neumática.
airborne ['ɛəbɔːn] *adj* (*in the air*) en el aire;
(*MIL*) aerotransportado; **as soon as the
plane was** ~ tan pronto como el avión
estuvo en el aire.
air cargo *n* carga aérea.
air-conditioned ['ɛəkən'dɪʃənd] *adj*
climatizado.
air conditioning [-kən'dɪʃənɪŋ] *n* aire *m*
acondicionado.
air-cooled ['ɛəkuːld] *adj* refrigerado por
aire.
aircraft ['ɛəkrɑːft] *n, pl inv* avión *m*.
aircraft carrier *n* porta(a)viones *m inv*.
air cushion *n* cojín *m* de aire; (*AVIAT*)
colchón *m* de aire.
airdrome ['ɛədrəum] *n* (*US*) aeródromo.
airfield ['ɛəfiːld] *n* campo de aviación.
Air Force *n* fuerzas aéreas *fpl*, aviación *f*.
air freight *n* flete *m* por avión.
air freshener *n* ambientador *m*.
air gun *n* escopeta de aire comprimido.
air hostess (*BRIT*) *n* azafata, aeromoza
(*LAM*).
airily ['ɛərɪlɪ] *adv* muy a la ligera.
airing ['ɛərɪŋ] *n:* **to give an** ~ **to** (*linen*)
airear; (*room*) ventilar; (*fig: ideas etc*)
airear, someter a discusión.
air letter *n* (*BRIT*) carta aérea.
airlift ['ɛəlɪft] *n* puente *m* aéreo.

airline ['ɛəlaɪn] n línea aérea.
airliner ['ɛəlaɪnə*] n avión m de pasajeros.
airlock ['ɛəlɔk] n (in pipe) esclusa de aire.
airmail ['ɛəmeɪl] n: **by ~** por avión.
air mattress n colchón m inflable.
airplane ['ɛəpleɪn] n (US) avión m.
air pocket n bolsa de aire.
airport ['ɛəpɔːt] n aeropuerto.
air rage n conducta ugresiva de pasajeros a bordo de un avión.
air raid n ataque m aéreo.
air rifle n escopeta de aire comprimido.
airsick ['ɛəsɪk] adj: **to be ~** marearse (en avión).
airspeed ['ɛəspiːd] n velocidad f de vuelo.
airstrip ['ɛəstrɪp] n pista de aterrizaje.
air terminal n terminal f.
airtight ['ɛətaɪt] adj hermético.
air time n (RADIO, TV) tiempo en antena.
air traffic control n control m de tráfico aéreo.
air traffic controller n controlador(a) m/f aéreo/a.
airway ['ɛəweɪ] n (AVIAT) vía aérea; (ANAT) vía respiratoria.
airy ['ɛərɪ] adj (room) bien ventilado; (manners) despreocupado.
aisle [aɪl] n (of church) nave f lateral; (of theatre, plane) pasillo.
ajar [ə'dʒɑː*] adj entreabierto.
AK abbr (US) = Alaska.
aka abbr (= also known as) alias.
akin [ə'kɪn] adj: **~ to** semejante a.
AL abbr (US) = Alabama.
ALA n abbr = American Library Association.
Ala. abbr (US) = Alabama.
alabaster ['æləbɑːstə*] n alabastro.
à la carte [ælæ'kɑːt] adv a la carta.
alacrity [ə'lækrɪtɪ] n: **with ~** con la mayor prontitud.
alarm [ə'lɑːm] n alarma; (anxiety) inquietud f ♦ vt asustar, alarmar.
alarm clock n despertador m.
alarmed [ə'lɑːmd] adj (person) alarmado, asustado; (house, car etc) con alarma.
alarming [ə'lɑːmɪŋ] adj alarmante.
alarmingly [ə'lɑːmɪŋlɪ] adv de forma alarmante; **~ quickly** a una velocidad alarmante.
alarmist [ə'lɑːmɪst] n alarmista m/f.
alas [ə'læs] adv desgraciadamente ♦ excl ¡ay!
Alas. abbr (US) = Alaska.
Alaska [ə'læskə] n Alaska.
Albania [æl'beɪnɪə] n Albania.
Albanian [æl'beɪnɪən] adj albanés/esa ♦ n albanés/esa m/f; (LING) albanés m.
albatross ['ælbətrɔs] n albatros m.

albeit [ɔːl'biːɪt] conj (although) aunque.
album ['ælbəm] n álbum m; (L.P.) elepé m.
albumen ['ælbjumɪn] n albúmina f.
alchemy ['ælkɪmɪ] n alquimia.
alcohol ['ælkəhɔl] n alcohol m.
alcohol-free adj sin alcohol.
alcoholic [ælkə'hɔlɪk] adj, n alcohólico/a m/f.
alcoholism ['ælkəhɔlɪzəm] n alcoholismo.
alcove ['ælkəuv] n nicho, hueco.
Ald. abbr = alderman.
alderman ['ɔːldəmən] n concejal m.
ale [eɪl] n cerveza.
alert [ə'lɔːt] adj alerta inv; (sharp) despierto, despabilado ♦ n alerta m, alarma ♦ vt poner sobre aviso; **to ~ sb (to sth)** poner sobre aviso or alertar a algn (de algo); **to ~ sb to the dangers of sth** poner sobre aviso or alertar a algn de los peligros de algo; **to be on the ~** estar alerta or sobre aviso.
alertness [ə'lɔːtnɪs] n vigilancia.
Aleutian Islands [ə'luːʃən-] npl Islas fpl Aleutianas.
Alexandria [ælɪg'zɑːndrɪə] n Alejandría.
alfresco [æl'freskəu] adj, adv al aire libre.
algebra ['ældʒɪbrə] n álgebra.
Algeria [æl'dʒɪərɪə] n Argelia.
Algerian [æl'dʒɪərɪən] adj, n argelino/a m/f.
Algiers [æl'dʒɪəz] n Argel m.
algorithm ['ælgərɪðəm] n algoritmo.
alias ['eɪlɪəs] adv alias, conocido por ♦ n alias m.
alibi ['ælɪbaɪ] n coartada.
alien ['eɪlɪən] n (foreigner) extranjero/a ♦ adj: **~ to** ajeno a.
alienate ['eɪlɪəneɪt] vt enajenar, alejar.
alienation [eɪlɪə'neɪʃən] n alejamiento m.
alight [ə'laɪt] adj ardiendo ♦ vi apearse.
align [ə'laɪn] vt alinear.
alignment [ə'laɪnmənt] n alineación f; **the desks are out of ~** los pupitres no están bien alineados.
alike [ə'laɪk] adj ncmejantes, iguales ♦ adv igualmente, del mismo modo; **to look ~** parecerse.
alimony ['ælɪmənɪ] n (LAW) pensión f alimenticia.
alive [ə'laɪv] adj (gen) vivo; (lively) activo.
alkali ['ælkəlaɪ] n álcali m.

===================================== KEYWORD

all [ɔːl] adj (sg) todo/a; (pl) todos/as; **~ day** todo el día; **~ night** toda la noche; **~ men** todos los hombres; **~ five came** vinieron los cinco; **~ the books** todos los libros; **~ the time/his life** todo el tiempo/toda su vida; **for ~ their efforts** a pesar de todos sus esfuerzos

◆ *pron* **1** todo; **I ate it** ~, **I ate** ~ **of it** me lo comí todo; ~ **of them** todos (ellos); ~ **of us went** fuimos todos; ~ **the boys went** fueron todos los chicos; **is that** ~? ¿eso es todo?, ¿algo más?; (*in shop*) ¿algo más?, ¿alguna cosa más?
2 (*in phrases*): **above** ~ sobre todo; por encima de todo; **after** ~ después de todo; **at** ~: **anything at** ~ lo que sea; **not at** ~ (*in answer to question*) en absoluto; (*in answer to thanks*) ¡de nada!, ¡no hay de qué!; **I'm not at** ~ **tired** no estoy nada cansado/a; **anything at** ~ **will do** cualquier cosa viene bien; ~ **in** ~ a fin de cuentas
◆ *adv*: ~ **alone** completamente solo/a; **to be/feel** ~ in estar rendido; **it's not as hard as** ~ **that** no es tan difícil como lo pintas; ~ **the more/the better** tanto más/mejor; ~ **but** casi; **the score is 2** ~ están empatados a 2.

all-around ['ɔːlə'raund] *adj* (*US*) = **all-round**.
allay [ə'leɪ] *vt* (*fears*) aquietar; (*pain*) aliviar.
all clear *n* (*after attack etc*) fin *m* de la alerta; (*fig*) luz *f* verde.
allegation [ælɪ'geɪʃən] *n* alegato.
allege [ə'lɛdʒ] *vt* pretender; **he is** ~**d to have said** ... se afirma que él dijo ....
alleged [ə'lɛdʒd] *adj* supuesto, presunto.
allegedly [ə'lɛdʒɪdlɪ] *adv* supuestamente, según se afirma.
allegiance [ə'liːdʒəns] *n* lealtad *f*.
allegory ['ælɪɡərɪ] *n* alegoría.
all-embracing ['ɔːləm'breɪsɪŋ] *adj* universal.
allergic [ə'lɜːdʒɪk] *adj*: ~ **to** alérgico a.
allergy ['ælədʒɪ] *n* alergia.
alleviate [ə'liːvɪeɪt] *vt* aliviar.
alleviation [əliːvɪ'eɪʃən] *n* alivio.
alley ['ælɪ] *n* (*street*) callejuela; (*in garden*) paseo.
alleyway ['ælɪweɪ] *n* callejón *m*.
alliance [ə'laɪəns] *n* alianza.
allied ['ælaɪd] *adj* aliado; (*related*) relacionado.
alligator ['ælɪɡeɪtə*] *n* caimán *m*.
all-important ['ɔːlɪm'pɔːtənt] *adj* de suma importancia.
all-in ['ɔːlɪn] *adj* (*BRIT*) (*also adv: charge*) todo incluido.
all-in wrestling *n* lucha libre.
alliteration [əlɪtə'reɪʃən] *n* aliteración *f*.
all-night ['ɔːl'naɪt] *adj* (*café*) abierto toda la noche; (*party*) que dura toda la noche.
allocate ['æləkeɪt] *vt* (*share out*) repartir; (*devote*) asignar.
allocation [ælə'keɪʃən] *n* (*of money*) ración

f, cuota; (*distribution*) reparto.
allot [ə'lɔt] *vt* asignar; **in the** ~**ted time** en el tiempo asignado.
allotment [ə'lɔtmənt] *n* porción *f*; (*garden*) parcela.
all-out ['ɔːlaut] *adj* (*effort etc*) supremo ◆ *adv*: **all out** con todas las fuerzas, a fondo.
allow [ə'lau] *vt* (*permit*) permitir, dejar; (*a claim*) admitir; (*sum to spend, time estimated*) dar, conceder; (*concede*): **to** ~ **that** reconocer que; **to** ~ **sb to do** permitir a alguien hacer; **smoking is not** ~**ed** prohibido fumar; **he is** ~**ed to** ... se le permite ...; **we must** ~ **3 days for the journey** debemos dejar 3 días para el viaje.
▶**allow for** *vt fus* tener en cuenta.
allowance [ə'lauəns] *n* concesión *f*; (*payment*) subvención *f*, pensión *f*; (*discount*) descuento, rebaja; **to make** ~**s for** (*person*) disculpar a; (*thing: take into account*) tener en cuenta.
alloy ['ælɔɪ] *n* aleación *f*.
all right *adv* (*feel, work*) bien; (*as answer*) ¡de acuerdo!, ¡está bien!
all-round ['ɔːl'raund] *adj* completo; (*view*) amplio.
all-rounder ['ɔːl'raundə*] *n*: **to be a good** ~ ser una persona que hace de todo.
allspice ['ɔːlspaɪs] *n* pimienta inglesa *or* de Jamaica.
all-time ['ɔːl'taɪm] *adj* (*record*) de todos los tiempos.
allude [ə'luːd] *vi*: **to** ~ **to** aludir a.
alluring [ə'ljuərɪŋ] *adj* seductor(a), atractivo.
allusion [ə'luːʒən] *n* referencia, alusión *f*.
ally *n* ['ælaɪ] aliado/a ◆ *vt* [ə'laɪ]: **to** ~ **o.s. with** aliarse con.
almanac ['ɔːlmənæk] *n* almanaque *m*.
almighty [ɔːl'maɪtɪ] *adj* todopoderoso.
almond ['ɑːmənd] *n* (*fruit*) almendra; (*tree*) almendro.
almost ['ɔːlməust] *adv* casi; **he** ~ **fell** casi *or* por poco se cae.
alms [ɑːmz] *npl* limosna *sg*.
aloft [ə'lɔft] *adv* arriba.
alone [ə'ləun] *adj* solo ◆ *adv* sólo, solamente; **to leave sb** ~ dejar a algn en paz; **to leave sth** ~ no tocar algo; **let** ~ ... y mucho menos, y no digamos ...
along [ə'lɔŋ] *prep* a lo largo de, por ◆ *adv*: **is he coming** ~ **with us?** ¿viene con nosotros?; **he was limping** ~ iba cojeando; ~ **with** junto con; **all** ~ (*all the time*) desde el principio.
alongside [ə'lɔŋ'saɪd] *prep* al lado de ◆ *adv* (*NAUT*) de costado; **we brought our boat**

~ atracamos nuestro barco.
aloof [ə'luːf] adj distante ♦ adv: **to stand** ~
mantenerse a distancia.
aloud [ə'laud] adv en voz alta.
alphabet ['ælfəbɛt] n alfabeto.
alphabetical [ælfə'bɛtɪkəl] adj alfabético; **in**
~ **order** por orden alfabético.
alphanumeric [ælfənjuː'mɛrɪk] adj
alfanumérico.
alpine ['ælpaɪn] adj alpino, alpestre.
Alps [ælps] npl: **the** ~ los Alpes.
already [ɔːl'rɛdɪ] adv ya.
alright ['ɔːl'raɪt] adv (BRIT) = **all right**.
Alsatian [æl'seɪʃən] n (dog) pastor m
alemán.
also ['ɔːlsəu] adv también, además.
Alta. abbr (Canada) = Alberta.
altar ['ɔltə*] n altar m.
alter ['ɔltə*] vt cambiar, modificar ♦ vi
cambiarse, modificarse.
alteration [ɔltə'reɪʃən] n cambio,
modificación f; ~**s** npl (ARCH) reformas fpl;
(SEWING) arreglos mpl; **timetable subject
to** ~ el horario puede cambiar.
altercation [ɔltə'keɪʃən] n altercado.
alternate [ɔl'tɔːnɪt] adj alterno ♦ vi
['ɔltəneɪt]: **to** ~ **(with)** alternar (con); **on** ~
days en días alternos.
alternately [ɔl'tɔːnɪtlɪ] adv
alternativamente, por turno.
alternating ['ɔltəneɪtɪŋ] adj (current)
alterno.
alternative [ɔl'tɔːnətɪv] adj alternativo ♦ n
alternativa.
alternatively [ɔl'tɔːnətɪvlɪ] adv: ~ **one could**
... por otra parte se podría....
alternative medicine n medicina
alternativa.
alternator ['ɔltəneɪtə*] n (AUT) alternador
m.
although [ɔːl'ðəu] conj aunque, si bien.
altitude ['æltɪtjuːd] n altitud f, altura.
altitude sickness n mal m de altura,
soroche m (LAM).
alto ['æltəu] n (female) contralto f; (male)
alto.
altogether [ɔːltə'gɛðə*] adv
completamente, del todo; (on the whole, in
all) en total, en conjunto; **how much is
that** ~? ¿cuánto es todo or en total?
altruism ['æltruɪzəm] n altruismo.
altruistic [æltru'ɪstɪk] adj altruista.
aluminium [ælju'mɪnɪəm], (US) **aluminum**
[ə'luːmɪnəm] n aluminio.
always ['ɔːlweɪz] adv siempre.
Alzheimer's ['æltshaɪməz] (also: ~ **disease**)
enfermedad f de Alzheimer.
AM abbr (= amplitude modulation) A.M. f;

(POL) = **Assembly Member**.
am [æm] vb see **be**.
a.m. adv abbr (= ante meridiem) de la
mañana.
AMA n abbr = American Medical Association.
amalgam [ə'mælgəm] n amalgama.
amalgamate [ə'mælgəmeɪt] vi
amalgamarse ♦ vt amalgamar.
amalgamation [əmælgə'meɪʃən] n (COMM)
fusión f.
amass [ə'mæs] vt amontonar, acumular.
amateur ['æmətə*] n aficionado/a, amateur
m/f; ~ **dramatics** dramas mpl presentados
por aficionados.
amateurish ['æmətərɪʃ] adj (pej) torpe,
inexperto.
amaze [ə'meɪz] vt asombrar, pasmar; **to be
~d (at)** asombrarse (de).
amazement [ə'meɪzmənt] n asombro,
sorpresa; **to my** ~ para mi sorpresa.
amazing [ə'meɪzɪŋ] adj extraordinario,
asombroso; (bargain, offer) increíble.
amazingly [ə'meɪzɪŋlɪ] adv
extraordinariamente.
Amazon ['æməzən] n (GEO) Amazonas m;
(MYTHOLOGY) amazona ♦ cpd: **the** ~
basin/jungle la cuenca/selva del
Amazonas.
Amazonian [æmə'zəunɪən] adj amazónico.
ambassador [æm'bæsədə*] n embajador(a)
m/f.
amber ['æmbə*] n ámbar m; **at** ~ (BRIT AUT)
en amarillo.
ambidextrous [æmbɪ'dɛkstrəs] adj
ambidextro.
ambience ['æmbɪəns] n ambiente m.
ambiguity [æmbɪ'gjuːtɪ] n ambigüedad f;
(of meaning) doble sentido.
ambiguous [æm'bɪgjuəs] adj ambiguo.
ambition [æm'bɪʃən] n ambición f; **to
achieve one's** ~ realizar su ambición.
ambitious [æm'bɪʃəs] adj ambicioso; (plan)
grandioso.
ambivalent [æm'bɪvələnt] adj ambivalente;
(pej) equívoco.
amble ['æmbl] vi (gen: ~ **along**) deambular,
andar sin prisa.
ambulance ['æmbjuləns] n ambulancia.
ambulanceman/woman ['æmbjulənsmən/
wumən] n ambulanciero/a.
ambush ['æmbuʃ] n emboscada ♦ vt tender
una emboscada a; (fig) coger (SP) or
agarrar (LAM) por sorpresa.
ameba [ə'miːbə] n (US) = **amoeba**.
ameliorate [ə'miːlɪəreɪt] vt mejorar.
amelioration [əmiːlɪə'reɪʃən] n mejora.
amen [ɑː'mɛn] excl amén.
amenable [ə'miːnəbl] adj: ~ **to** (advice etc)

sensible a.

amend [ə'mɛnd] *vt* (*law*, *text*) enmendar; **to make ~s** (*apologize*) enmendarlo, dar cumplida satisfacción.

amendment [ə'mɛndmənt] *n* enmienda.

amenities [ə'miːnɪtɪz] *npl* comodidades *fpl*.

amenity [ə'miːnɪtɪ] *n* servicio.

America [ə'mɛrɪkə] *n* América (del Norte).

American [ə'mɛrɪkən] *adj*, *n* (norte)americano/a *m/f*, estadounidense *m/f*.

Americanism [ə'mɛrɪkənɪzəm] *n* americanismo.

americanize [ə'mɛrɪkənaɪz] *vt* americanizar.

Amerindian [æmər'ɪndɪən] *adj*, *n* amerindio/a.

amethyst ['æmɪθɪst] *n* amatista.

Amex ['æmɛks] *n abbr* = *American Stock Exchange*.

amiable ['eɪmɪəbl] *adj* (*kind*) amable, simpático.

amicable ['æmɪkəbl] *adj* amistoso, amigable.

amicably ['æmɪkəblɪ] *adv* amigablemente, amistosamente; **to part ~** separarse amistosamente.

amid(st) [ə'mɪd(st)] *prep* entre, en medio de.

amiss [ə'mɪs] *adv*: **to take sth ~** tomar algo a mal; **there's something ~** pasa algo.

ammo ['æməu] *n abbr* (*col*) = *ammunition*.

ammonia [ə'məunɪə] *n* amoníaco.

ammunition [æmju'nɪʃən] *n* municiones *fpl*; (*fig*) argumentos *mpl*.

ammunition dump *n* depósito de municiones.

amnesia [æm'niːzɪə] *n* amnesia.

amnesty ['æmnɪstɪ] *n* amnistía; **to grant an ~ to** amnistiar (a); **A~ International** Amnistía Internacional.

amoeba, (*US*) **ameba** [ə'miːbə] *n* amiba.

amok [ə'mɔk] *adv*: **to run ~** enloquecerse, desbocarse.

among(st) [ə'mʌŋ(st)] *prep* entre, en medio de.

amoral [æ'mɔrəl] *adj* amoral.

amorous ['æmərəs] *adj* cariñoso.

amorphous [ə'mɔːfəs] *adj* amorfo.

amortization [əmɔːtaɪ'zeɪʃən] *n* amortización *f*.

amount [ə'maunt] *n* (*gen*) cantidad *f*; (*of bill etc*) suma, importe *m* ♦ *vi*: **to ~ to** (*total*) sumar; (*be same as*) equivaler a, significar; **this ~s to a refusal** esto equivale a una negativa; **the total ~** (*of money*) la suma total.

amp(ère) ['æmp(ɛə*)] *n* amperio; **a 13 amp**

plug un enchufe de 13 amperios.

ampersand ['æmpəsænd] *n* signo &, "y" comercial.

amphetamine [æm'fɛtəmiːn] *n* anfetamina.

amphibian [æm'fɪbɪən] *n* anfibio.

amphibious [æm'fɪbɪəs] *adj* anfibio.

amphitheatre, (*US*) **amphitheater** ['æmfɪθɪətə*] *n* anfiteatro.

ample ['æmpl] *adj* (*spacious*) amplio; (*abundant*) abundante; **to have ~ time** tener tiempo de sobra.

amplifier ['æmplɪfaɪə*] *n* amplificador *m*.

amplify ['æmplɪfaɪ] *vt* amplificar, aumentar; (*explain*) explicar.

amply ['æmplɪ] *adv* ampliamente.

ampoule, (*US*) **ampule** ['æmpuːl] *n* (*MED*) ampolla.

amputate ['æmpjuteɪt] *vt* amputar.

amputee [æmpju'tiː] *n* persona que ha sufrido una amputación.

Amsterdam ['æmstədæm] *n* Amsterdam *m*.

amt *abbr* = *amount*.

amuck [ə'mʌk] *adv* = *amok*.

amuse [ə'mjuːz] *vt* divertir; (*distract*) distraer, entretener; **to ~ o.s. with sth/ by doing sth** distraerse con algo/ haciendo algo; **he was ~d at the joke** le divirtió el chiste.

amusement [ə'mjuːzmənt] *n* diversión *f*; (*pastime*) pasatiempo; (*laughter*) risa; **much to my ~** con gran regocijo mío.

amusement arcade *n* salón *m* de juegos.

amusement park *n* parque *m* de atracciones.

amusing [ə'mjuːzɪŋ] *adj* divertido.

an [æn, ən, n] *indef art see* **a.**

ANA *n abbr* = *American Newspaper Association; American Nurses Association.*

anachronism [ə'nækrənɪzəm] *n* anacronismo.

anaemia [ə'niːmɪə] *n* anemia.

anaemic [ə'niːmɪk] *adj* anémico; (*fig*) flojo.

anaesthetic [ænɪs'θɛtɪk] *n* anestesia; **local/ general ~** anestesia local/general.

anaesthetist [æ'niːsθɪtɪst] *n* anestesista *m/f*.

anagram ['ænəgræm] *n* anagrama *m*.

anal ['eɪnl] *adj* anal.

analgesic [ænæl'dʒiːsɪk] *adj*, *n* analgésico.

analogous [ə'næləgəs] *adj*: **~ to** *or* **with** análogo a.

analog(ue) ['ænəlɔg] *adj* (*computer*, *watch*) analógico.

analogy [ə'nælədʒɪ] *n* analogía; **to draw an ~ between** señalar la analogía entre.

analyse ['ænəlaɪz] *vt* (*BRIT*) analizar.

analysis, *pl* **analyses** [ə'næləsɪs, -siːz] *n* análisis *m inv*.

analyst ['ænəlɪst] *n* (*political ~*) analista *m/f*,

(*psycho~*) psicoanalista *m/f.*
analytic(al) [ænə'lıtık(əl)] *adj* analítico.
analyze ['ænəlaız] *vt (US)* = **analyse.**
anarchic [æ'nɑːkık] *adj* anárquico.
anarchist ['ænəkıst] *adj, n* anarquista *m/f.*
anarchy ['ænəkı] *n* anarquía, desorden *m.*
anathema [ə'næθımə] *n:* **that is ~ to him** eso es pecado para él.
anatomical [ænə'tɔmıkəl] *adj* anatómico.
anatomy [ə'nætəmı] *n* anatomía.
ANC *n abbr* = *African National Congress.*
ancestor ['ænsıstə*] *n* antepasado.
ancestral [æn'sɛstrəl] *adj* ancestral.
ancestry ['ænsıstrı] *n* ascendencia, abolengo.
anchor ['æŋkə*] *n* ancla, áncora ♦ *vi (also:* **to drop** ~) anclar, echar el ancla ♦ *vt (fig)* sujetar, afianzar; **to weigh** ~ levar anclas.
anchorage ['æŋkərıdʒ] *n* ancladero.
anchor man, anchor woman *n (RADIO, TV)* presentador(a) *m/f.*
anchovy ['æntʃəvı] *n* anchoa.
ancient ['eınʃənt] *adj* antiguo; **~ monument** monumento histórico.
ancillary [æn'sılərı] *adj (worker, staff)* auxiliar.
and [ænd] *conj* y; *(before i, hi)* e; **~ so on** etcétera; **try ~ come** procure *or* intente venir; **better ~ better** cada vez mejor.
Andalusia [ændə'luːzıə] *n* Andalucía.
Andean ['ændıən] *adj* andino/a; **~ high plateau** altiplanicie *f,* altiplano *(LAM).*
Andes ['ændiːz] *npl:* **the ~** los Andes.
anecdote ['ænıkdəut] *n* anécdota.
anemia [ə'niːmıə] *n (US)* = **anaemia.**
anemic [ə'niːmık] *adj (US)* = **anaemic.**
anemone [ə'nɛmənı] *n (BOT)* anémone *f;* **sea ~** anémona.
anesthetic [ænıs'θɛtık] *adj, n (US)* = **anaesthetic.**
anesthetist [æ'niːsθıtıst] *n (US)* = **anaesthetist.**
anew [ə'njuː] *adv* de nuevo, otra vez.
angel ['eındʒəl] *n* ángel *m.*
angel dust *n* polvo de ángel.
angelic [æn'dʒɛlık] *adj* angélico.
anger ['æŋgə*] *n* ira, cólera, enojo *(LAM)* ♦ *vt* enojar, enfurecer.
angina [æn'dʒaınə] *n* angina (del pecho).
angle ['æŋgl] *n* ángulo; **from their ~** desde su punto de vista.
angler ['æŋglə*] *n* pescador(a) *m/f* (de caña).
Anglican ['æŋglıkən] *adj, n* anglicano/a.
anglicize ['æŋglısaız] *vt* anglicanizar.
angling ['æŋglıŋ] *n* pesca con caña.
Anglo- ['æŋgləu] *pref* anglo... .

Angola [æŋ'gəulə] *n* Angola.
Angolan [æŋ'gəulən] *adj, n* angoleño/a *m/f.*
angrily ['æŋgrılı] *adv* enojado, enfadado.
angry ['æŋgrı] *adj* enfadado, enojado *(esp LAM);* **to be ~ with sb/at sth** estar enfadado con algn/por algo; **to get ~** enfadarse, enojarse *(esp LAM).*
anguish ['æŋgwıʃ] *n (physical)* tormentos *mpl;* (*mental)* angustia.
anguished ['æŋgwıʃt] *adj* angustioso.
angular ['æŋgjulə*] *adj (shape)* angular; *(features)* anguloso.
animal ['ænıməl] *adj, n* animal *m.*
animal rights [-raıts] *npl* derechos *mpl* de los animales.
animate ['ænımeıt] *vt (enliven)* animar; *(encourage)* estimular, alentar ♦ ['ænımıt] *adj* vivo, animado.
animated ['ænımeıtıd] *adj* vivo, animado.
animation [ænı'meıʃən] *n* animación *f.*
animosity [ænı'mɔsıtı] *n* animosidad *f,* rencor *m.*
aniseed ['ænısiːd] *n* anís *m.*
Ankara ['æŋkərə] *n* Ankara.
ankle ['æŋkl] *n* tobillo *m.*
ankle sock *n* calcetín *m.*
annex ['ænɛks] *n (also: Brit:* **annexe)** *(building)* edificio anexo ♦ *vt* [æ'nɛks] *(territory)* anexar.
annihilate [ə'naıəleıt] *vt* aniquilar.
annihilation [ənaıə'leıʃən] *n* aniquilación *f.*
anniversary [ænı'vəːsərı] *n* aniversario.
annotate ['ænəuteıt] *vt* anotar.
announce [ə'nauns] *vt (gen)* anunciar; *(inform)* comunicar; **he ~d that he wasn't going** declaró que no iba.
announcement [ə'naunsmənt] *n (gen)* anuncio; *(declaration)* declaración *f;* **I'd like to make an ~** quisiera anunciar algo.
announcer [ə'naunsə*] *n (RADIO, TV)* locutor(a) *m/f.*
annoy [ə'nɔı] *vt* molestar, fastidiar, fregar *(LAM),* embromar *(LAM);* **to be ~ed (at sth/with sb)** estar enfadado *or* molesto (por algo/con algn); **don't get ~ed!** ¡no se enfade!
annoyance [ə'nɔıəns] *n* enojo; *(thing)* molestia.
annoying [ə'nɔııŋ] *adj* molesto, fastidioso, fregado *(LAM),* embromado *(LAM);* *(person)* pesado.
annual ['ænjuəl] *adj* anual ♦ *n (BOT)* anual *m;* *(book)* anuario.
annual general meeting (AGM) *n* junta general anual.
annually ['ænjuəlı] *adv* anualmente, cada año.
annual report *n* informe *m or* memoria

anual.
annuity [ə'njuːɪtɪ] *n* renta *or* pensión *f* vitalicia.
annul [ə'nʌl] *vt* anular; (*law*) revocar.
annulment [ə'nʌlmənt] *n* anulación *f*.
annum ['ænəm] *n see* **per annum**.
Annunciation [ənʌnsɪ'eɪʃən] *n* Anunciación *f*.
anode ['ænəud] *n* ánodo.
anoint [ə'nɔɪnt] *vt* untar.
anomalous [ə'nɔmələs] *adj* anómalo.
anomaly [ə'nɔmælɪ] *n* anomalía.
anon. [ə'nɔn] *abbr* = **anonymous**.
anonymity [ænə'nɪmɪtɪ] *n* anonimato.
anonymous [ə'nɔnɪməs] *adj* anónimo; **to remain ~** quedar en el anonimato.
anorak ['ænəræk] *n* anorak *m*.
anorexia [ænə'rɛksɪə] *n* (*MED*) anorexia.
anorexic [ænə'rɛksɪk] *adj*, *n* anoréxico/a *m/f*.
another [ə'nʌðə*] *adj*: **~ book** otro libro; **~ beer?** ¿(quieres) otra cerveza?; **in ~ 5 years** en cinco años más ♦ *pron* otro; *see also* **one.**
ANSI *n abbr* (= *American National Standards Institution*) oficina de normalización de *EEUU*.
answer ['ɑːnsə*] *n* respuesta, contestación *f*; (*to problem*) solución *f* ♦ *vi* contestar, responder ♦ *vt* (*reply to*) contestar a, responder a; (*problem*) resolver; **to ~ the phone** contestar el teléfono; **in ~ to your letter** contestando *or* en contestación a su carta; **to ~ the door** abrir la puerta.
▶**answer back** *vi* replicar, ser respondón/ona.
▶**answer for** *vt fus* responder de *or* por.
▶**answer to** *vt fus* (*description*) corresponder a.
answerable ['ɑːnsərəbl] *adj*: **~ to sb for sth** responsable ante algn de algo.
answering machine ['ɑːnsərɪŋ-] *n* contestador *m* automático.
ant [ænt] *n* hormiga.
ANTA *n abbr* = *American National Theater and Academy*.
antagonism [æn'tægənɪzəm] *n* antagonismo *m*.
antagonist [æn'tægənɪst] *n* antagonista *m/f*, adversario/a.
antagonistic [æntægə'nɪstɪk] *adj* antagónico; (*opposed*) contrario, opuesto.
antagonize [æn'tægənaɪz] *vt* provocar la enemistad de.
Antarctic [ænt'ɑːktɪk] *adj* antártico ♦ *n*: **the ~** el Antártico.
Antarctica [æn'tɑːktɪkə] *n* Antártida.
Antarctic Circle *n* Círculo Polar Antártico.

Antarctic Ocean *n* Océano Antártico.
ante ['æntɪ] *n*: **to up the ~** subir la apuesta.
ante... ['æntɪ] *pref* ante....
anteater ['æntiːtə*] *n* oso hormiguero.
antecedent [æntɪ'siːdənt] *n* antecedente *m*.
antechamber ['æntɪtʃeɪmbə*] *n* antecámara.
antelope ['æntɪləup] *n* antílope *m*.
antenatal [æntɪ'neɪtl] *adj* prenatal.
antenatal clinic *n* clínica prenatal.
antenna [æn'tɛnə], *pl* **~e** [-niː] *n* antena.
anteroom ['æntɪrum] *n* antesala.
anthem ['ænθəm] *n*: **national ~** himno nacional.
anthology [æn'θɔlədʒɪ] *n* antología.
anthropologist [ænθrə'pɔlədʒɪst] *n* antropólogo/a.
anthropology [ænθrə'pɔlədʒɪ] *n* antropología.
anti... [æntɪ] *pref* anti....
anti-aircraft ['æntɪ'ɛəkrɑːft] *adj* antiaéreo.
antiballistic [æntɪbə'lɪstɪk] *adj* antibalístico.
antibiotic [æntɪbaɪ'ɔtɪk] *adj*, *n* antibiótico.
antibody ['æntɪbɔdɪ] *n* anticuerpo.
anticipate [æn'tɪsɪpeɪt] *vt* (*foresee*) prever; (*expect*) esperar, contar con; (*forestall*) anticiparse a, adelantarse a; **this is worse than I ~d** esto es peor de lo que esperaba; **as ~d** según se esperaba.
anticipation [æntɪsɪ'peɪʃən] *n* previsión *f*; esperanza; anticipación *f*.
anticlimax [æntɪ'klaɪmæks] *n* decepción *f*.
anticlockwise [æntɪ'klɔkwaɪz] *adv* en dirección contraria a la de las agujas del reloj.
antics ['æntɪks] *npl* payasadas *fpl*.
anticyclone [æntɪ'saɪkləun] *n* anticiclón *m*.
antidepressant ['æntɪdɪ'prɛsnt] *n* antidepresivo.
antidote ['æntɪdəut] *n* antídoto.
antifreeze ['æntɪfriːz] *n* anticongelante *m*.
antihistamine [æntɪ'hɪstəmiːn] *n* antihistamínico.
Antilles [æn'tɪliːz] *npl*: **the ~** las Antillas.
antipathy [æn'tɪpəθɪ] *n* (*between people*) antipatía; (*to person, thing*) aversión *f*.
antiperspirant ['æntɪpəːspɪrənt] *n* antitranspirante *m*.
Antipodean [æntɪpə'diːən] *adj* antípoda.
Antipodes [æn'tɪpədiːz] *npl*: **the ~** las Antípodas.
antiquarian [æntɪ'kwɛərɪən] *n* anticuario/a.
antiquated ['æntɪkweɪtɪd] *adj* anticuado.
antique [æn'tiːk] *n* antigüedad *f* ♦ *adj* antiguo.
antique dealer *n* anticuario/a.
antique shop *n* tienda de antigüedades.
antiquity [æn'tɪkwɪtɪ] *n* antigüedad *f*.
anti-Semitic ['æntɪsɪ'mɪtɪk] *adj* antisemita.

anti-Semitism [æntɪ'sɛmɪtɪzəm] *n* antisemitismo.
antiseptic [æntɪ'sɛptɪk] *adj, n* antiséptico.
antisocial [æntɪ'səʊʃəl] *adj* antisocial.
antitank [æntɪ'tæŋk] *adj* antitanque.
antithesis, *pl* **antitheses** [æn'tɪθɪsɪs, -siːz] *n* antítesis *f inv.*
antitrust [æntɪ'trʌst] *adj:* ~ **legislation** legislación *f* antimonopolio.
antlers ['æntləz] *npl* cornamenta.
anus ['eɪnəs] *n* ano.
anvil ['ænvɪl] *n* yunque *m.*
anxiety [æŋ'zaɪətɪ] *n* (*worry*) inquietud *f*; (*eagerness*) ansia, anhelo.
anxious ['æŋkʃəs] *adj* (*worried*) inquieto; (*keen*) deseoso; **I'm very** ~ **about you** me tienes muy preocupado.
anxiously ['æŋkʃəslɪ] *adv* con inquietud, de manera angustiada.

═══════════════ *KEYWORD*

any ['ɛnɪ] *adj* **1** (*in questions etc*) algún/ alguna; **have you** ~ **butter/children?** ¿tienes mantequilla/hijos?; **if there are** ~ **tickets left** si quedan billetes, si queda algún billete
2 (*with negative*): **I haven't** ~ **money/ books** no tengo dinero/libros
3 (*no matter which*) cualquier; ~ **excuse will do** valdrá *or* servirá cualquier excusa; **choose** ~ **book you like** escoge el libro que quieras; ~ **teacher you ask will tell you** cualquier profesor al que preguntes te lo dirá
4 (*in phrases*): **in** ~ **case** de todas formas, en cualquier caso; ~ **day now** cualquier día (de estos); **at** ~ **moment** en cualquier momento, de un momento a otro; **at** ~ **rate** en todo caso; ~ **time: come (at)** ~ **time** ven cuando quieras; **he might come (at)** ~ **time** podría llegar de un momento a otro
♦ *pron* **1** (*in questions etc*): **have you got** ~**?** ¿tienes alguno/a?; **can** ~ **of you sing?** ¿sabe cantar alguno de vosotros/ustedes?
2 (*with negative*): **I haven't** ~ **(of them)** no tengo ninguno
3 (*no matter which one(s)*): **take** ~ **of those books (you like)** toma el libro que quieras de ésos
♦ *adv* **1** (*in questions etc*): **do you want** ~ **more soup/sandwiches?** ¿quieres más sopa/bocadillos?; **are you feeling** ~ **better?** ¿te sientes algo mejor?
2 (*with negative*): **I can't hear him** ~ **more** ya no le oigo; **don't wait** ~ **longer** no esperes más.

anybody ['ɛnɪbɔdɪ] *pron* cualquiera, cualquier persona; (*in interrogative sentences*) alguien; (*in negative sentences*): **I don't see** ~ no veo a nadie.
anyhow ['ɛnɪhaʊ] *adv* de todos modos, de todas maneras; (*carelessly*) de cualquier manera; (*haphazardly*) de cualquier modo; **I shall go** ~ iré de todas maneras.
anyone ['ɛnɪwʌn] = **anybody.**
anyplace ['ɛnɪpleɪs] *adv* (*US*) = **anywhere.**
anything ['ɛnɪθɪŋ] *pron* (*see* **anybody**) cualquier cosa; (*in interrogative sentences*) algo; (*in negative sentences*) nada; (*everything*) todo; ~ **else?** ¿algo más?; **it can cost** ~ **between £15 and £20** puede costar entre 15 y 20 libras.
anytime ['ɛnɪtaɪm] *adv* (*at any moment*) en cualquier momento, de un momento a otro; (*whenever*) no importa cuándo, cuando quiera.
anyway ['ɛnɪweɪ] *adv* de todas maneras; de cualquier modo.
anywhere ['ɛnɪwɛə*] *adv* (*see* **anybody**) dondequiera; (*interrogative*) en algún sitio; (*negative sense*) en ningún sitio; (*everywhere*) en *or* por todas partes; **I don't see him** ~ no le veo en ningún sitio; ~ **in the world** en cualquier parte del mundo.
Anzac ['ænzæk] *n abbr* (= *Australia-New Zealand Army Corps*).
apace [ə'peɪs] *adv* aprisa.
apart [ə'pɑːt] *adv* aparte, separadamente; **10 miles** ~ separados por 10 millas; **to take** ~ desmontar; ~ **from** *prep* aparte de.
apartheid [ə'pɑːteɪt] *n* apartheid *m.*
apartment [ə'pɑːtmənt] *n* (*US*) piso, departamento (*LAM*), apartamento; (*room*) cuarto.
apartment block *or* **building** (*US*) bloque *m* de pisos.
apathetic [æpə'θɛtɪk] *adj* apático, indiferente.
apathy ['æpəθɪ] *n* apatía, indiferencia.
APB *n abbr* (*US:* = *all points bulletin*) *expresión usada por la policía que significa "descubrir y aprehender al sospechoso".*
ape [eɪp] *n* mono ♦ *vt* imitar, remedar.
Apennines ['æpənaɪnz] *npl:* **the** ~ los Apeninos *mpl.*
aperitif [ə'pɛrɪtiːf] *n* aperitivo.
aperture ['æpətʃjʊə*] *n* rendija, resquicio; (*PHOT*) abertura.
APEX ['eɪpɛks] *n abbr* (*AVIAT* = *advance purchase excursion*) APEX *m.*
apex ['eɪpɛks] *n* ápice *m*; (*fig*) cumbre *f.*
aphid ['eɪfɪd] *n* pulgón *m.*

aphorism ['æfərɪzəm] n aforismo.
aphrodisiac [æfrəu'dɪzɪæk] adj, n afrodisíaco.
API n abbr = American Press Institute.
apiece [ə'piːs] adv cada uno.
aplomb [ə'plɔm] n aplomo, confianza.
APO n abbr (US: = Army Post Office) servicio postal del ejército.
Apocalypse [ə'pɔkəlɪps] n Apocalipsis m.
apocryphal [ə'pɔkrɪfəl] adj apócrifo.
apolitical [eɪpə'lɪtɪkl] adj apolítico.
apologetic [əpɔlə'dʒetɪk] adj (look, remark) de disculpa.
apologetically [əpɔlə'dʒetɪkəlɪ] adv con aire de disculpa, excusándose, disculpándose.
apologize [ə'pɔlədʒaɪz] vi: to ~ (for sth to sb) disculparse (con algn por algo).
apology [ə'pɔlədʒɪ] n disculpa, excusa; **please accept my apologies** le ruego me disculpe.
apoplectic [æpə'plɛktɪk] adj (MED) apoplético; (col): ~ **with rage** furioso.
apoplexy ['æpəplɛksɪ] n apoplegía.
apostle [ə'pɔsl] n apóstol m/f.
apostrophe [ə'pɔstrəfɪ] n apóstrofo m.
appal [ə'pɔːl] vt horrorizar, espantar.
Appalachian Mountains [æpə'leɪʃən-] npl: **the** ~ los (Montes) Apalaches.
appalling [ə'pɔːlɪŋ] adj espantoso; (awful) pésimo; **she's an** ~ **cook** es una cocinera malísima.
apparatus [æpə'reɪtəs] n aparato; (in gymnasium) aparatos mpl.
apparel [ə'pærl] n (US) indumentaria.
apparent [ə'pærənt] adj aparente; (obvious) manifiesto, evidente; **it is** ~ **that** está claro que.
apparently [ə'pærəntlɪ] adv por lo visto, al parecer, dizque (LAM).
apparition [æpə'rɪʃən] n aparición f.
appeal [ə'piːl] vi (LAW) apelar ♦ n (LAW) apelación f; (request) llamamiento, llamado (LAM); (plea) súplica; (charm) atractivo, encanto; **to** ~ **for** solicitar; **to** ~ **to** (subj: person) rogar a, suplicar a; (: thing) atraer, interesar; **to** ~ **to sb for mercy** rogarle misericordia a alguien; **it doesn't** ~ **to me** no me atrae, no me llama la atención; **right of** ~ derecho de apelación.
appealing [ə'piːlɪŋ] adj (nice) atractivo; (touching) conmovedor(a), emocionante.
appear [ə'pɪə*] vi aparecer, presentarse; (LAW) comparecer; (publication) salir (a luz), publicarse; (seem) parecer; **it would** ~ **that** parecería que.
appearance [ə'pɪərəns] n aparición f; (look, aspect) apariencia, aspecto; **to keep up**

~**s** salvar las apariencias; **to all** ~**s** al parecer.
appease [ə'piːz] vt (pacify) apaciguar; (satisfy) satisfacer.
appeasement [ə'piːzmənt] n (POL) apaciguamiento.
append [ə'pɛnd] vt (COMPUT) añadir (al final).
appendage [ə'pɛndɪdʒ] n añadidura.
appendicitis [əpɛndɪ'saɪtɪs] n apendicitis f.
appendix, pl **appendices** [ə'pɛndɪks, -dɪsiːz] n apéndice m; **to have one's** ~ **out** operarse de apendicitis.
appetite ['æpɪtaɪt] n apetito; (fig) deseo, anhelo; **that walk has given me an** ~ ese paseo me ha abierto el apetito.
appetizer ['æpɪtaɪzə*] n (drink) aperitivo; (food) tapas fpl (SP).
appetizing ['æpɪtaɪzɪŋ] adj apetitoso.
applaud [ə'plɔːd] vt, vi aplaudir.
applause [ə'plɔːz] n aplausos mpl.
apple ['æpl] n manzana.
apple tree n manzano.
appliance [ə'plaɪəns] n aparato; **electrical** ~**s** electrodomésticos mpl.
applicable [ə'plɪkəbl] adj aplicable, pertinente; **the law is** ~ **from January** la ley es aplicable or se pone en vigor a partir de enero; **to be** ~ **to** referirse a.
applicant ['æplɪkənt] n candidato/a; solicitante m/f.
application [æplɪ'keɪʃən] n aplicación f; (for a job, a grant etc) solicitud f.
application form n solicitud f.
applications package n (COMPUT) paquete m de programas de aplicación.
applied [ə'plaɪd] adj (science, art) aplicado.
apply [ə'plaɪ] vt: to ~ (to) aplicar (a); (fig) emplear (para) ♦ vi: to ~ to (ask) dirigirse a; (be suitable for) ser aplicable a; (be relevant to) tener que ver con; **to** ~ **for** (permit, grant, job) solicitar; **to** ~ **the brakes** echar el freno; **to** ~ **o.s. to** aplicarse a, dedicarse a.
appoint [ə'pɔɪnt] vt (to post) nombrar; (date, place) fijar, señalar.
appointee [əpɔɪn'tiː] n persona nombrada.
appointment [ə'pɔɪntmənt] n (engagement) cita; (date) compromiso; (act) nombramiento; (post) puesto; **to make an** ~ **(with)** (doctor) pedir hora (con); (friend) citarse (con); **"~s (vacant)"** "ofertas de trabajo"; **by** ~ mediante cita.
apportion [ə'pɔːʃən] vt repartir.
appraisal [ə'preɪzl] n evaluación f.
appraise [ə'preɪz] vt (value) tasar, valorar; (situation etc) evaluar.
appreciable [ə'priːʃəbl] adj sensible.

appreciably [ə'pri:ʃəblı] *adv* sensiblemente, de manera apreciable.

appreciate [ə'pri:ʃıeıt] *vt* (*like*) apreciar, tener en mucho; (*be grateful for*) agradecer; (*be aware of*) comprender ♦ *vi* (*COMM*) aumentar en valor; **I ~d your help** agradecí tu ayuda.

appreciation [əpri:ʃı'eıʃən] *n* aprecio; reconocimiento, agradecimiento; aumento en valor.

appreciative [ə'pri:ʃıətıv] *adj* agradecido.

apprehend [æprı'hɛnd] *vt* percibir; (*arrest*) detener.

apprehension [æprı'hɛnʃən] *n* (*fear*) aprensión *f*.

apprehensive [æprı'hɛnsıv] *adj* aprensivo.

apprentice [ə'prɛntıs] *n* aprendiz(a) *m/f*.

apprenticeship [ə'prɛntısʃıp] *n* aprendizaje *m*; **to serve one's ~** hacer el aprendizaje.

appro. ['æprəu] *abbr* (*BRIT COMM*: *col*) = approval.

approach [ə'prəutʃ] *vi* acercarse ♦ *vt* acercarse a; (*be approximate*) aproximarse a; (*ask, apply to*) dirigirse a; (*problem*) abordar ♦ *n* acercamiento; aproximación *f*; (*access*) acceso; (*proposal*) proposición *f*; (*to problem etc*) enfoque *m*; **to ~ sb about sth** hablar con algn sobre algo.

approachable [ə'prəutʃəbl] *adj* (*person*) abordable; (*place*) accesible.

approach road *n* vía de acceso.

approbation [æprə'beıʃən] *n* aprobación *f*.

appropriate [ə'prəuprııt] *adj* apropiado, conveniente ♦ *vt* [-rıeıt] (*take*) apropiarse de; (*allot*): **to ~ sth for** destinar algo a; **~ for or to** apropiado para; **it would not be ~ for me to comment** no estaría bien or sería pertinente que yo diera mi opinión.

appropriation [əprəuprı'eıʃən] *n* asignación *f*.

approval [ə'pru:vəl] *n* aprobación *f*, visto bueno; **on ~** (*COMM*) a prueba; **to meet with sb's ~** obtener la aprobación de algn.

approve [ə'pru:v] *vt* aprobar.
▶**approve of** *vt fus* aprobar.

approved school *n* (*BRIT*) correccional *m*.

approx. *abbr* (= approximately) aprox.

approximate [ə'prɒksımıt] *adj* aproximado.

approximately [ə'prɒksımıtlı] *adv* aproximadamente, más o menos.

approximation [əprɒksı'meıʃən] *n* aproximación *f*.

Apr. *abbr* (= April) abr.

apr *n abbr* (= annual percentage rate) tasa de interés anual.

apricot ['eıprıkɔt] *n* albaricoque *m* (*SP*), damasco (*LAM*).

April ['eıprəl] *n* abril *m*; **~ Fools' Day** *n* ≈ día *m* de los (Santos) Inocentes; *ver recuadro*.

APRIL FOOLS' DAY

El 1 de abril es **April Fools' Day** en la tradición anglosajona. Tal día se les gastan bromas a los más desprevenidos, quienes reciben la denominación de "April Fool" (≈ inocente), y tanto la prensa escrita como la televisión difunden alguna historia falsa con la que sumarse al espíritu del día.

---

apron ['eıprən] *n* delantal *m*; (*AVIAT*) pista.

apse [æps] *n* (*ARCH*) ábside *m*.

APT *n abbr* (*BRIT*) = advanced passenger train.

Apt. *abbr* = apartment.

apt [æpt] *adj* (*to the point*) acertado, oportuno; (*appropriate*) apropiado; **~ to do** (*likely*) propenso a hacer.

aptitude ['æptıtju:d] *n* aptitud *f*, capacidad *f*.

aptitude test *n* prueba de aptitud.

aptly ['æptlı] *adj* acertadamente.

aqualung ['ækwəlʌŋ] *n* escafandra autónoma.

aquarium [ə'kwɛərıəm] *n* acuario.

Aquarius [ə'kwɛərıəs] *n* Acuario.

aquatic [ə'kwætık] *adj* acuático.

aqueduct ['ækwıdʌkt] *n* acueducto.

AR *abbr* (*US*) = Arkansas.

ARA *n abbr* (*BRIT*) = Associate of the Royal Academy.

Arab ['ærəb] *adj, n* árabe *m/f*.

Arabia [ə'reıbıə] *n* Arabia.

Arabian [ə'reıbıən] *adj* árabe, arábigo.

Arabian Desert *n* Desierto de Arabia.

Arabian Sea *n* Mar *m* de Omán.

Arabic ['ærəbık] *adj* (*language, manuscripts*) árabe, arábigo ♦ *n* árabe *m*; **~ numerals** numeración *f* arábiga.

arable ['ærəbl] *adj* cultivable.

Aragon ['ærəgən] *n* Aragón *m*.

ARAM *n abbr* (*BRIT*) = Associate of the Royal Academy of Music.

arbitrary ['ɑːbıtrərı] *adj* arbitrario.

arbitrate ['ɑːbıtreıt] *vi* arbitrar.

arbitration [ɑːbı'treıʃən] *n* arbitraje *m*; **the dispute went to ~** el conflicto laboral fue sometido al arbitraje.

arbitrator ['ɑːbıtreıtə*] *n* árbitro.

ARC *n abbr* = American Red Cross.

arc [ɑːk] *n* arco.

arcade [ɑː'keıd] *n* (*ARCH*) arcada; (*round a square*) soportales *mpl*; (*shopping ~*) galería comercial.

arch [ɑːtʃ] *n* arco; (*vault*) bóveda; (*of foot*) empeine *m* ♦ *vt* arquear.
archaeological [ɑːkɪə'lɒdʒɪkl] *adj* arqueológico.
archaeologist [ɑːkɪ'ɒlədʒɪst] *n* arqueólogo/a.
archaeology [ɑːkɪ'ɒlədʒɪ] *n* arqueología.
archaic [ɑː'keɪɪk] *adj* arcaico.
archangel ['ɑːkeɪndʒəl] *n* arcángel *m*.
archbishop [ɑːtʃ'bɪʃəp] *n* arzobispo.
arched [ɑːtʃt] *adj* abovedado.
archenemy ['ɑːtʃ'ɛnəmɪ] *n* enemigo jurado.
archeology [ɑːkɪ'ɒlədʒɪ] *etc* (*US*) = **archaeology** *etc.*
archer ['ɑːtʃə*] *n* arquero/a.
archery ['ɑːtʃərɪ] *n* tiro al arco.
archetypal ['ɑːkɪtaɪpəl] *adj* arquetípico.
archetype ['ɑːkɪtaɪp] *n* arquetipo.
archipelago [ɑːkɪ'pɛlɪgəu] *n* archipiélago.
architect ['ɑːkɪtɛkt] *n* arquitecto/a.
architectural [ɑːkɪ'tɛktʃərəl] *adj* arquitectónico.
architecture ['ɑːkɪtɛktʃə*] *n* arquitectura.
archive ['ɑːkaɪv] *n* (*often pl: also COMPUT*) archivo.
archive file *n* (*COMPUT*) fichero archivado.
archives ['ɑːkaɪvz] *npl* archivo *sg.*
archivist ['ɑːkɪvɪst] *n* archivero/a.
archway ['ɑːtʃweɪ] *n* arco, arcada.
ARCM *n abbr* (*BRIT*) = *Associate of the Royal College of Music.*
Arctic ['ɑːktɪk] *adj* ártico ♦ *n*: **the** ~ el Ártico.
Arctic Circle *n* Círculo Polar Ártico.
Arctic Ocean *n* Océano (Glacial) Ártico.
ARD *n abbr* (*US MED*) = *acute respiratory disease.*
ardent ['ɑːdənt] *adj* (*desire*) ardiente; (*supporter, lover*) apasionado.
ardour, (*US*) **ardor** ['ɑːdə*] *n* ardor *m*, pasión *f*.
arduous ['ɑːdjuəs] *adj* (*gen*) arduo; (*journey*) penoso.
are [ɑː*] *vb see* **be.**
area ['ɛərɪə] *n* área; (*MATH etc*) superficie *f*, extensión *f*; (*zone*) región *f*, zona; **the London** ~ la zona de Londres.
area code *n* (*US TEL*) prefijo.
arena [ə'riːnə] *n* arena; (*of circus*) pista; (*for bullfight*) plaza, ruedo.
aren't [ɑːnt] = **are not.**
Argentina [ɑːdʒən'tiːnə] *n* Argentina.
Argentinian [ɑːdʒən'tɪnɪən] *adj*, *n* argentino/a *m/f.*
arguable ['ɑːgjuəbl] *adj*: **it is** ~ **whether** ... es dudoso que + *subjun.*
arguably ['ɑːgjuəblɪ] *adv*: **it is** ~ ... es discutiblemente ....

argue ['ɑːgjuː] *vt* (*debate: case, matter*) mantener, argüir ♦ *vi* (*quarrel*) discutir; (*reason*) razonar, argumentar; **to** ~ **that** sostener que; **to** ~ **about sth (with sb)** pelearse (con algn) por algo.
argument ['ɑːgjumənt] *n* (*reasons*) argumento; (*quarrel*) discusión *f*; (*debate*) debate *m*; ~ **for/against** argumento en pro/contra de.
argumentative [ɑːgju'mɛntətɪv] *adj* discutidor(a).
aria ['ɑːrɪə] *n* (*MUS*) aria.
ARIBA *n abbr* (*BRIT*) = *Associate of the Royal Institute of British Architects.*
arid ['ærɪd] *adj* árido.
aridity [ə'rɪdɪtɪ] *n* aridez *f*.
Aries ['ɛərɪz] *n* Aries *m*.
arise [ə'raɪz], *pt* **arose,** *pp* **arisen** [ə'rɪzn] *vi* (*rise up*) levantarse, alzarse; (*emerge*) surgir, presentarse; **to** ~ **from** derivar de; **should the need** ~ si fuera necesario.
aristocracy [ærɪs'tɒkrəsɪ] *n* aristocracia.
aristocrat ['ærɪstəkræt] *n* aristócrata *m/f.*
aristocratic [ærɪstə'krætɪk] *adj* aristocrático.
arithmetic [ə'rɪθmətɪk] *n* aritmética.
arithmetical [ærɪθ'mɛtɪkl] *adj* aritmético.
Ariz. *abbr* (*US*) = *Arizona.*
Ark [ɑːk] *n*: **Noah's** ~ el Arca *f* de Noé.
Ark. *abbr* (*US*) = *Arkansas.*
arm [ɑːm] *n* (*ANAT*) brazo ♦ *vt* armar; ~ **in** ~ cogidos del brazo; *see also* **arms.**
armaments ['ɑːməmənts] *npl* (*weapons*) armamentos *mpl.*
armchair ['ɑːmtʃɛə*] *n* sillón *m*, butaca.
armed [ɑːmd] *adj* armado; **the** ~ **forces** las fuerzas armadas.
armed robbery *n* robo a mano armada.
Armenia [ɑː'miːnɪə] *n* Armenia.
Armenian [ɑː'miːnɪən] *adj* armenio ♦ *n* armenio/a; (*LING*) armenio.
armful ['ɑːmful] *n* brazada.
armistice ['ɑːmɪstɪs] *n* armisticio.
armour, (*US*) **armor** ['ɑːmə*] *n* armadura.
armo(u)red car *n* coche *m or* carro (*LAM*) blindado.
armo(u)ry ['ɑːmərɪ] *n* arsenal *m*.
armpit ['ɑːmpɪt] *n* sobaco, axila.
armrest ['ɑːmrɛst] *n* reposabrazos *m inv*, brazo.
arms [ɑːmz] *npl* (*weapons*) armas *fpl*; (*HERALDRY*) escudo *sg.*
arms control *n* control *m* de armamentos.
arms race *n* carrera de armamentos.
army ['ɑːmɪ] *n* ejército.
aroma [ə'rəumə] *n* aroma *m*, fragancia.
aromatherapy [ərəumə'θɛrəpɪ] *n* aromaterapia.

aromatic [ærə'mætɪk] *adj* aromático,
fragante.
arose [ə'rəuz] *pt of* **arise.**
around [ə'raund] *adv* alrededor; (*in the area*)
a la redonda ♦ *prep* alrededor de.
arousal [ə'rauzəl] *n* (*sexual*) excitación *f*; (*of
feelings, interest*) despertar *m*.
arouse [ə'rauz] *vt* despertar.
arrange [ə'reɪndʒ] *vt* arreglar, ordenar;
(*programme*) organizar ♦ *vi*: **we have ~d
for a taxi to pick you up** hemos
organizado todo para que le recoja un
taxi; **to ~ to do sth** quedar en hacer algo;
it was ~d that ... se quedó en que ....
arrangement [ə'reɪndʒmənt] *n* arreglo;
(*agreement*) acuerdo; **~s** *npl* (*plans*) planes
mpl, medidas *fpl*; (*preparations*)
preparativos *mpl*; **to come to an ~ (with
sb)** llegar a un acuerdo (con algn); **by ~**
convenir; **I'll make ~s for you to be met**
haré los preparativos para que le estén
esperando.
arrant ['ærənt] *adj*: **~ nonsense** una
verdadera tontería.
array [ə'reɪ] *n* (*COMPUT*) matriz *f*; **~ of**
(*things*) serie *f or* colección *f* de; (*people*)
conjunto de.
arrears [ə'rɪəz] *npl* atrasos *mpl*; **in ~** (*COMM*)
en mora; **to be in ~ with one's rent** estar
retrasado en el pago del alquiler.
arrest [ə'rest] *vt* detener; (*sb's attention*)
llamar ♦ *n* detención *f*; **under ~** detenido.
arresting [ə'restɪŋ] *adj* (*fig*) llamativo.
arrival [ə'raɪvəl] *n* llegada, arribo (*LAM*);
new ~ recién llegado/a.
arrive [ə'raɪv] *vi* llegar, arribar (*LAM*).
arrogance ['ærəgəns] *n* arrogancia,
prepotencia (*LAM*).
arrogant ['ærəgənt] *adj* arrogante,
prepotente (*LAM*).
arrow ['ærəu] *n* flecha.
arse [ɑːs] *n* (*BRIT col!*) culo, trasero.
arsenal ['ɑːsɪnl] *n* arsenal *m*.
arsenic ['ɑːsnɪk] *n* arsénico.
arson ['ɑːsn] *n* incendio provocado.
art [ɑːt] *n* arte *m*; (*skill*) destreza; (*technique*)
técnica; **A~s** *npl* (*SCOL*) Letras *fpl*; **work
of ~** obra de arte.
artefact ['ɑːtɪfækt] *n* artefacto.
arterial [ɑː'tɪərɪəl] *adj* (*ANAT*) arterial; (*road
etc*) principal.
artery ['ɑːtərɪ] *n* (*MED, road etc*)
arteria.
artful ['ɑːtful] *adj* (*cunning: person, trick*)
mañoso.
art gallery *n* pinacoteca, museo de
pintura; (*COMM*) galería de arte.
arthritis [ɑː'θraɪtɪs] *n* artritis *f*.

artichoke ['ɑːtɪtʃəuk] *n* alcachofa;
Jerusalem ~ aguaturma.
article ['ɑːtɪkl] *n* artículo, objeto, cosa; (*in
newspaper*) artículo; (*BRIT LAW: training*):
~s *npl* contrato *sg* de aprendizaje; **~s of
clothing** prendas *fpl* de vestir.
articles of association *npl* (*COMM*)
estatutos *mpl* sociales, escritura
social.
articulate *adj* [ɑː'tɪkjulɪt] (*speech*) claro;
(*person*) que se expresa bien ♦ *vi*
[ɑː'tɪkjuleɪt] articular.
articulated lorry *n* (*BRIT*) trailer *m*.
artifice ['ɑːtɪfɪs] *n* artificio, truco.
artificial [ɑːtɪ'fɪʃəl] *adj* artificial; (*teeth etc*)
postizo.
artificial insemination *n* inseminación *f*
artificial.
artificial intelligence (A.I.) *n* inteligencia
artificial (I.A.).
artificial respiration *n* respiración *f*
artificial.
artillery [ɑː'tɪləri] *n* artillería.
artisan ['ɑːtɪzæn] *n* artesano/a.
artist ['ɑːtɪst] *n* artista *m/f*; (*MUS*) intérprete
m/f.
artistic [ɑː'tɪstɪk] *adj* artístico.
artistry ['ɑːtɪstrɪ] *n* arte *m*, habilidad *f*
(artística).
artless ['ɑːtlɪs] *adj* (*innocent*) natural,
sencillo; (*clumsy*) torpe.
art school *n* escuela de bellas
artes.
artwork ['ɑːtwəːk] *n* material *m*
gráfico.
arty ['ɑːtɪ] *adj* artistoide.
ARV *n abbr* (= *American Revised Version*)
traducción americana de la Biblia.
AS *n abbr* (*US UNIV.* = *Associate in/of Science*)
título universitario ♦ *abbr* (*US*) = *American
Samoa.*

=================================== KEYWORD

as [æz] *conj* **1** (*referring to time: while*)
mientras; (: *when*) cuando; **she wept ~
she told her story** lloraba mientras
contaba lo que le ocurrió; **~ the years go
by** a medida que pasan los años, con el
paso de los años; **he came in ~ I was
leaving** entró cuando me marchaba; **~
from tomorrow** a partir de *or* desde
mañana
2 (*in comparisons*): **~ big ~** tan grande
como; **twice ~ big ~** el doble de grande
que; **~ much money/many books ~** tanto
dinero/tantos libros como; **~ soon ~** en
cuanto, no bien (*LAM*)
3 (*since, because*) como, ya que; **~ I don't**

speak German I can't understand him como no hablo alemán no le entiendo, no le entiendo ya que no hablo alemán **4** (*although*): **much ~ I like them, ...** aunque me gustan, ... **5** (*referring to manner, way*): **do ~ you wish** haz lo que quieras; **~ she said** como dijo; **he gave it to me ~ a present** me lo dio de regalo; **it's on the left ~ you go in** según se entra, a la izquierda **6** (*concerning*): **~ for** *or* **to that** por *or* en lo que respecta a eso **7**: **~ if** *or* **though** como si; **he looked ~ if he was ill** parecía como si estuviera enfermo, tenía aspecto de enfermo; *see also* **long; such; well** ♦ *prep* (*in the capacity of*): **he works ~ a barman** trabaja de barman; **~ chairman of the company, he** ... como presidente de la compañía, ...

ASA *n abbr* (= *American Standards Association*) *instituto de normalización*; (*BRIT:* = *Advertising Standards Authority*) *departamento de control de la publicidad*; (: = *Amateur Swimming Association*) *federación amateur de natación*.
a.s.a.p. *abbr* (= *as soon as possible*) cuanto antes, lo más pronto posible.
asbestos [æz'bɛstəs] *n* asbesto, amianto.
ascend [ə'sɛnd] *vt* subir, ascender.
ascendancy [ə'sɛndənsɪ] *n* ascendiente *m*, dominio.
ascendant [ə'sɛndənt] *n*: **to be in the ~** estar en auge, ir ganando predominio.
Ascension [ə'sɛnʃən] *n*: **the ~** la Ascensión.
Ascension Island *n* Isla Ascensión.
ascent [ə'sɛnt] *n* subida; (*slope*) cuesta, pendiente *f*; (*of plane*) ascenso.
ascertain [æsə'teɪn] *vt* averiguar.
ascetic [ə'sɛtɪk] *adj* ascético.
asceticism [ə'sɛtɪsɪzəm] *n* ascetismo.
ASCII ['æskiː] *n abbr* (= *American Standard Code for Information Interchange*) ASCII.
ascribe [ə'skraɪb] *vt*: **to ~ sth to** atribuir algo a.
ASCU *n abbr* (*US*) = *Association of State Colleges and Universities*.
ASE *n abbr* = *American Stock Exchange*.
ASH [æʃ] *n abbr* (*BRIT:* = *Action on Smoking and Health*) organización anti-tabaco.
ash [æʃ] *n* ceniza; (*tree*) fresno.
ashamed [ə'feɪmd] *adj* avergonzado; **to be ~ of** avergonzarse de.
ashcan ['æʃkæn] *n* (*US*) cubo *or* bote *m* (*LAM*) de la basura.
ashen ['æʃn] *adj* pálido.

ashore [ə'ʃɔː*] *adv* en tierra.
ashtray ['æʃtreɪ] *n* cenicero.
Ash Wednesday *n* miércoles *m* de ceniza.
Asia ['eɪʃə] *n* Asia.
Asian ['eɪʃən], **Asiatic** [eɪsɪ'ætɪk] *adj*, *n* asiático/a *m/f*.
aside [ə'saɪd] *adv* a un lado ♦ *n* aparte *m*; **~ from** *prep* (*as well as*) aparte *or* además de.
ask [ɑːsk] *vt* (*question*) preguntar; (*demand*) pedir; (*invite*) invitar ♦ *vi*: **to ~ about sth** preguntar acerca de algo; **to ~ sb sth/to do sth** preguntar algo a algn/pedir a algn que haga algo; **to ~ sb about sth** preguntar algo a algn; **to ~ (sb) a question** hacer una pregunta (a algn); **to ~ sb the time** preguntar la hora a algn; **to ~ sb out to dinner** invitar a cenar a algn.
▶**ask after** *vt fus* preguntar por.
▶**ask for** *vt fus* pedir; **it's just ~ing for trouble** *or* **for it** es buscarse problemas.
askance [ə'skɑːns] *adv*: **to look ~ at sb** mirar con recelo a algn.
askew [ə'skjuː] *adv* sesgado, ladeado.
asking price *n* (*COMM*) precio inicial.
asleep [ə'sliːp] *adj* dormido; **to fall ~** dormirse, quedarse dormido.
ASLEF ['æzlɛf] *n abbr* (*BRIT:* = *Associated Society of Locomotive Engineers and Firemen*) sindicato de ferroviarios.
asp [æsp] *n* áspid *m*.
asparagus [əs'pærəgəs] *n* espárragos *mpl*.
ASPCA *n abbr* = *American Society for the Prevention of Cruelty to Animals*.
aspect ['æspɛkt] *n* aspecto, apariencia; (*direction in which a building etc faces*) orientación *f*.
aspersions [əs'pɜːʃənz] *npl*: **to cast ~ on** difamar a, calumniar a.
asphalt ['æsfælt] *n* asfalto.
asphyxiate [æs'fɪksɪeɪt] *vt* asfixiar.
asphyxiation [aesfɪksɪ'eɪʃən] *n* asfixia.
aspirate ['æspəreɪt] *vt* aspirar ♦ *adj* ['æspərɪt] aspirado.
aspirations [æspə'reɪʃənz] *npl* aspiraciones *fpl*; (*ambition*) ambición *f*.
aspire [əs'paɪə*] *vi*: **to ~ to** aspirar a, ambicionar.
aspirin ['æsprɪn] *n* aspirina.
aspiring [əs'paɪərɪŋ] *adj*: **an ~ actor** un aspirante a actor.
ass [æs] *n* asno, burro; (*col*) imbécil *m/f*; (*US col!*) culo, trasero.
assailant [ə'seɪlənt] *n* agresor(a) *m/f*.
assassin [ə'sæsɪn] *n* asesino/a.
assassinate [ə'sæsɪneɪt] *vt* asesinar.
assassination [əsæsɪ'neɪʃən] *n* asesinato.
assault [ə'sɔːlt] *n* (*gen: attack*) asalto,

agresión f ♦ vt asaltar, agredir, (*sexually*)
violar.
assemble [ə'sɛmbl] vt reunir, juntar;
(*TECH*) montar ♦ vi reunirse, juntarse.
assembler [ə'sɛmblə*] n (*COMPUT*)
ensamblador m.
assembly [ə'sɛmblɪ] n (*meeting*) reunión f,
asamblea; (*construction*) montaje m.
assembly language n (*COMPUT*) lenguaje
m ensamblador.
assembly line n cadena de montaje.
assent [ə'sɛnt] n asentimiento, aprobación
f ♦ vi consentir, asentir; **to** ~ **(to sth)**
consentir (en algo).
assert [ə'sɔːt] vt afirmar; (*insist on*) hacer
valer; **to** ~ **o.s.** imponerse.
assertion [ə'sɔːʃən] n afirmación f.
assertive [ə'sɔːtɪv] adj enérgico, agresivo,
perentorio.
assess [ə'sɛs] vt valorar, calcular; (*tax,
damages*) fijar; (*property etc: for tax*)
gravar.
assessment [ə'sɛsmənt] n valoración f,
gravamen m; (*judgment*): ~ **(of)** juicio
(sobre).
assessor [ə'sɛsə*] n asesor(a) m/f; (*of tax*)
tasador(a) m/f.
asset ['æsɛt] n posesión f, (*quality*) ventaja;
~**s** npl (*funds*) activo sg, fondos mpl.
asset-stripping ['æsɛt'strɪpɪŋ] n (*COMM*)
acaparamiento de activos.
assiduous [ə'sɪdjuəs] adj asiduo.
assign [ə'saɪn] vt (*date*) fijar; (*task*) asignar;
(*resources*) destinar; (*property*) traspasar.
assignment [ə'saɪnmənt] n asignación f,
(*task*) tarea.
assimilate [ə'sɪmɪleɪt] vt asimilar.
assimilation [əsɪmɪ'leɪʃən] n asimilación f.
assist [ə'sɪst] vt ayudar.
assistance [ə'sɪstəns] n ayuda, auxilio.
assistant [ə'sɪstənt] n ayudante m/f; (*BRIT:
also:* **shop** ~) dependiente/a m/f.
assistant manager n subdirector(a) m/f.
assizes [ə'saɪzɪz] npl sesión f de un tribunal.
associate [ə'səuʃɪɪt] adj asociado ♦ n socio/
a, colega m/f; (*in crime*) cómplice m/f;
(*member*) miembro/a ♦ vb [ə'səuʃɪeɪt] vt
asociar; (*ideas*) relacionar ♦ vi: **to** ~ **with**
sb tratar con alguien; ~ **director**
subdirector/a m/f; ~**d company** compañía
afiliada.
association [əsəusɪ'eɪʃən] n asociación f;
(*COMM*) sociedad f; **in** ~ **with** en
asociación con.
association football n (*BRIT*) fútbol m.
assorted [ə'sɔːtɪd] adj surtido, variado; **in**
~ **sizes** en distintos tamaños.
assortment [ə'sɔːtmənt] n surtido.

Asst. abbr = **Assistant**.
assuage [ə'sweɪdʒ] vt mitigar.
assume [ə'sjuːm] vt (*suppose*) suponer;
(*responsibilities etc*) asumir; (*attitude,
name*) adoptar, tomar.
assumed name n nombre m falso.
assumption [ə'sʌmpʃən] n (*supposition*)
suposición f, presunción f; (*act*) asunción
f; **on the** ~ **that** suponiendo que.
assurance [ə'ʃuərəns] n garantía, promesa;
(*confidence*) confianza, aplomo; (*BRIT:
insurance*) seguro; **I can give you no** ~**s** no
puedo hacerle ninguna promesa.
assure [ə'ʃuə*] vt asegurar.
assured [ə'ʃuəd] adj seguro.
assuredly [ə'ʃuərɪdlɪ] adv indudablemente.
AST n abbr (= *Atlantic Standard Time*) hora
oficial del este del Canadá.
asterisk ['æstərɪsk] n asterisco.
astern [ə'stɔːn] adv a popa.
asteroid ['æstərɔɪd] n asteroide m.
asthma ['æsmə] n asma.
asthmatic [æs'mætɪk] adj, n asmático/a m/f.
astigmatism [ə'stɪgmətɪzəm] n
astigmatismo.
astir [ə'stɔː*] adv en acción.
astonish [ə'stɔnɪʃ] vt asombrar, pasmar.
astonishing [ə'stɔnɪʃɪŋ] adj asombroso,
pasmoso; **I find it** ~ **that** ... me asombra or
pasma que ....
astonishingly [ə'stɔnɪʃɪŋlɪ] adv
increíblemente, asombrosamente.
astonishment [ə'stɔnɪʃmənt] n asombro,
sorpresa; **to my** ~ con gran sorpresa
mía.
astound [ə'staund] vt asombrar, pasmar.
astounding [ə'staundɪŋ] adj asombroso.
astray [ə'streɪ] adv: **to go** ~ extraviarse; **to
lead** ~ llevar por mal camino; **to go** ~ **in**
one's calculations equivocarse en sus
cálculos.
astride [ə'straɪd] prep a caballo or
horcajadas sobre.
astringent [əs'trɪndʒənt] adj, n astringente
m.
astrologer [əs'trɔlədʒə*] n astrólogo/a.
astrology [əs'trɔlədʒɪ] n astrología.
astronaut ['æstrənɔːt] n astronauta m/f.
astronomer [əs'trɔnəmə*] n astrónomo/a.
astronomical [æstrə'nɔmɪkəl] adj
astronómico.
astronomy [əs'trɔnəmɪ] n astronomía.
astrophysics ['æstrəu'fɪzɪks] n astrofísica.
astute [əs'tjuːt] adj astuto.
asunder [ə'sʌndə*] adv: **to tear** ~ hacer
pedazos.
ASV n abbr (= *American Standard Version*)
traducción americana de la Biblia.

asylum [ə'saɪləm] *n* (*refuge*) asilo; (*hospital*) manicomio; **to seek political** ~ pedir asilo político.

asymmetric(al) [eɪsɪ'mɛtrɪk(l)] *adj* asimétrico.

━━━━━━━━━━━━━━━━ KEYWORD

at [æt] *prep* **1** (*referring to position*) en; (*direction*) a; ~ **the top** en lo alto; ~ **home/school** en casa/la escuela; **to look** ~ **sth/sb** mirar algo/a algn

2 (*referring to time*): ~ **4 o'clock** a las 4; ~ **night** por la noche; ~ **Christmas** en Navidad; ~ **times** a veces

3 (*referring to rates, speed etc*): ~ **£1 a kilo** a una libra el kilo; **two** ~ **a time** de dos en dos; ~ **50 km/h** a 50 km/h

4 (*referring to manner*): ~ **a stroke** de un golpe; ~ **peace** en paz

5 (*referring to activity*): **to be** ~ **work** estar trabajando; (*in the office etc*) estar en el trabajo; **to play** ~ **cowboys** jugar a los vaqueros; **to be good** ~ **sth** ser bueno en algo

6 (*referring to cause*): **shocked/surprised/annoyed** ~ **sth** asombrado/sorprendido/fastidiado por algo; **I went** ~ **his suggestion** fui a instancias suyas.

━━━━━━━━━━━━━━━━

ate [ɛt, eɪt] *pt of* eat.

atheism ['eɪθɪɪzəm] *n* ateísmo.

atheist ['eɪθɪɪst] *n* ateo/a.

Athenian [ə'θiːnɪən] *adj, n* ateniense *m/f*.

Athens ['æθɪnz] *n* Atenas *f*.

athlete ['æθliːt] *n* atleta *m/f*.

athletic [æθ'lɛtɪk] *adj* atlético.

athletics [æθ'lɛtɪks] *n* atletismo.

Atlantic [ət'læntɪk] *adj* atlántico ♦ *n*: **the** ~ **(Ocean)** el (Océano) Atlántico.

atlas ['ætləs] *n* atlas *m*.

Atlas Mountains *npl*: **the** ~ el Atlas.

A.T.M. *n abbr* (= *Automated Telling Machine*) cajero automático.

atmosphere ['ætməsfɪə*] *n* (*air*) atmósfera; (*fig*) ambiente *m*.

atom ['ætəm] *n* átomo.

atomic [ə'tɒmɪk] *adj* atómico.

atom(ic) bomb *n* bomba atómica.

atomic power *n* energía atómica.

atomizer ['ætəmaɪzə*] *n* atomizador *m*.

atone [ə'təun] *vi*: **to** ~ **for** expiar.

atonement [ə'təunmənt] *n* expiación *f*.

A to Z ® *n* guía alfabética; (*map*) callejero.

ATP *n abbr* (= *Association of Tennis Professionals*) *sindicato de jugadores de tenis profesionales.*

atrocious [ə'trəuʃəs] *adj* atroz; (*fig*) horrible, infame.

atrocity [ə'trɔsɪtɪ] *n* atrocidad *f*.

atrophy ['ætrəfɪ] *n* atrofia ♦ *vi* atrofiarse.

attach [ə'tætʃ] *vt* sujetar; (*stick*) pegar; (*document, letter*) adjuntar; **to be** ~**ed to sb/sth** (*to like*) tener cariño a algn/algo; **the** ~**ed letter** la carta adjunta.

attaché [ə'tæʃeɪ] *n* agregado/a.

attaché case *n* (*BRIT*) maletín *m*.

attachment [ə'tætʃmənt] *n* (*tool*) accesorio; (*love*): ~ **(to)** apego (a), cariño (a).

attack [ə'tæk] *vt* (*MIL*) atacar; (*criminal*) agredir, asaltar; (*task etc*) emprender ♦ *n* ataque *m*, asalto; (*on sb's life*) atentado; **heart** ~ infarto (de miocardio).

attacker [ə'tækə*] *n* agresor(a) *m/f*, asaltante *m/f*.

attain [ə'teɪn] *vt* (*also*: ~ **to**) alcanzar; (*achieve*) lograr, conseguir.

attainments [ə'teɪnmənts] *npl* (*skill*) talento *sg*.

attempt [ə'tɛmpt] *n* tentativa, intento; (*attack*) atentado ♦ *vt* intentar, tratar de; **he made no** ~ **to help** ni siquiera intentó ayudar.

attempted [ə'tɛmptɪd] *adj*: ~ **murder/burglary/suicide** tentativa *or* intento de asesinato/robo/suicidio.

attend [ə'tɛnd] *vt* asistir a; (*patient*) atender.

▶**attend to** *vt fus* (*needs, affairs etc*) ocuparse de; (*speech etc*) prestar atención a; (*customer*) atender a.

attendance [ə'tɛndəns] *n* asistencia, presencia; (*people present*) concurrencia.

attendant [ə'tɛndənt] *n* sirviente/a *m/f*, mozo/a; (*THEAT*) acomodador(a) *m/f* ♦ *adj* concomitante.

attention [ə'tɛnʃən] *n* atención *f* ♦ *excl* (*MIL*) ¡firme(s)!; **for the** ~ **of...** (*ADMIN*) a la atención de...; **it has come to my** ~ **that ...** me he enterado de que ....

attentive [ə'tɛntɪv] *adj* atento; (*polite*) cortés.

attenuate [ə'tɛnjueɪt] *vt* atenuar.

attest [ə'tɛst] *vi*: **to** ~ **to** dar fe de.

attic ['ætɪk] *n* desván *m*, altillo (*LAM*), entretecho (*LAM*).

attitude ['ætɪtjuːd] *n* (*gen*) actitud *f*; (*disposition*) disposición *f*.

attorney [ə'təːnɪ] *n* (*US: lawyer*) abogado/a; (*having proxy*) apoderado.

Attorney General *n* (*BRIT*) ≈ Presidente *m* del Consejo del Poder Judicial (*SP*); (*US*) ≈ ministro de justicia.

attract [ə'trækt] *vt* atraer; (*attention*) llamar.

attraction [ə'trækʃən] *n* (*gen*) encanto, atractivo; (*PHYSICS, towards sth*) atracción f.

attractive [ə'træktɪv] adj atractivo.

attribute ['ætrɪbjuːt] n atributo ♦ vt [ə'trɪbjuːt]: **to ~ sth to** atribuir algo a; (accuse) achacar algo a.

attrition [ə'trɪʃən] n: **war of ~** guerra de agotamiento or desgaste.

Atty. Gen. abbr = **Attorney General.**

ATV n abbr (= all terrain vehicle) vehículo todo terreno.

atypical [eɪ'tɪpɪkl] adj atípico.

aubergine ['əubəʒiːn] n (BRIT) berenjena.

auburn ['ɔːbən] adj color castaño rojizo.

auction ['ɔːkʃən] n (also: **sale by ~**) subasta ♦ vt subastar.

auctioneer [ɔːkʃə'nɪə*] n subastador(a) m/f.

auction room n sala de subastas.

audacious [ɔː'deɪʃəs] adj (bold) audaz, osado; (impudent) atrevido, descarado.

audacity [ɔː'dæsɪtɪ] n audacia, atrevimiento; (pej) descaro.

audible ['ɔːdɪbl] adj audible, que se puede oír.

audience ['ɔːdɪəns] n auditorio; (gathering) público; (interview) audiencia.

audio-typist ['ɔːdɪəu'taɪpɪst] n mecanógrafo/a de dictáfono.

audiovisual [ɔːdɪəu'vɪzjuəl] adj audiovisual.

audiovisual aid n ayuda or medio audiovisual.

audit ['ɔːdɪt] vt revisar, intervenir.

audition [ɔː'dɪʃən] n audición f ♦ vi: **to ~ for** **the part of** hacer una audición para el papel de.

auditor ['ɔːdɪtə*] n interventor(a) m/f, censor(a) m/f de cuentas.

auditorium [ɔːdɪ'tɔːrɪəm] n auditorio.

Aug. abbr (= August) ag.

augment [ɔːg'mɛnt] vt, vi aumentar.

augur ['ɔːgə*] vi: **it ~s well** es de buen agüero.

August ['ɔːgəst] n agosto.

august [ɔː'gʌst] adj augusto.

aunt [ɑːnt] n tía.

auntie, aunty ['ɑːntɪ] n diminutive of **aunt**.

au pair ['əu'pɛə*] n (also: **~ girl**) chica f au pair.

aura ['ɔːrə] n aura; (atmosphere) ambiente m.

auspices ['ɔːspɪsɪz] npl: **under the ~ of** bajo los auspicios de.

auspicious [ɔːs'pɪʃəs] adj propicio, de buen augurio.

austere [ɔs'tɪə*] adj austero; (manner) adusto.

austerity [ɔ'stɛrɪtɪ] n austeridad f.

Australasia [ɔːstrə'leɪzɪə] n Australasia.

Australia [ɔs'treɪlɪə] n Australia.

Australian [ɔs'treɪlɪən] adj, n australiano/a m/f.

Austria ['ɔstrɪə] n Austria.

Austrian ['ɔstrɪən] adj, n austríaco/a m/f.

AUT n abbr (BRIT: = Association of University Teachers) sindicato de profesores de universidad.

authentic [ɔː'θɛntɪk] adj auténtico.

authenticate [ɔː'θɛntɪkeɪt] vt autentificar.

authenticity [ɔːθɛn'tɪsɪtɪ] n autenticidad f.

author ['ɔːθə*] n autor(a) m/f.

authoritarian [ɔːθɔrɪ'tɛərɪən] adj autoritario.

authoritative [ɔː'θɔrɪtətɪv] adj autorizado; (manner) autoritario.

authority [ɔː'θɔrɪtɪ] n autoridad f; **the authorities** npl las autoridades; **to have ~ to do sth** tener autoridad para hacer algo.

authorization [ɔːθəraɪ'zeɪʃən] n autorización f.

authorize ['ɔːθəraɪz] vt autorizar.

authorized capital n (COMM) capital m autorizado or social.

autistic [ɔː'tɪstɪk] adj autista.

auto ['ɔːtəu] n (US) coche m, carro (LAM), auto (LAM), automóvil m.

autobiographical [ɔːtəbaɪə'græfɪkəl] adj autobiográfico.

autobiography [ɔːtbaɪ'ɔgrəfɪ] n autobiografía.

autocratic [ɔːtə'krætɪk] adj autocrático.

Autocue ® ['ɔːtəukjuː] n autocue m, teleapuntador m.

autograph ['ɔːtəgrɑːf] n autógrafo ♦ vt firmar; (photo etc) dedicar.

autoimmune [ɔːtəuɪ'mjuːn] adj autoinmune.

automat ['ɔːtəmæt] n (US) restaurante m de autoservicio.

automate ['ɔːtəmeɪt] vt automatizar.

automated ['ɔːtəmeɪtɪd] adj automatizado.

automatic [ɔːtə'mætɪk] adj automático ♦ n (gun) pistola automática; (washing machine) lavadora.

automatically [ɔːtə'mætɪklɪ] adv automáticamente.

automatic data processing (ADP) n proceso automático de datos.

automation [ɔːtə'meɪʃən] n automatización f.

automaton, pl **automata** [ɔː'tɔmətən, -tə] n autómata.

automobile [ɔːtəməbiːl] n (US) coche m, carro (LAM), automóvil m.

autonomous [ɔː'tɔnəməs] adj autónomo.

autonomy [ɔː'tɔnəmɪ] n autonomía.

autopsy ['ɔːtɔpsɪ] n autopsia.

autumn ['ɔːtəm] n otoño.

auxiliary [ɔːg'zɪlɪərɪ] adj auxiliar.

AV *n abbr* (= *Authorized Version*) traducción inglesa de la Biblia ♦ *abbr* = **audiovisual**.
Av. *abbr* (= *avenue*) Av., Avda.
avail [ə'veɪl] *vt*: **to ~ o.s. of** aprovechar(se) de, valerse de ♦ *n*: **to no ~** en vano, sin resultado.
availability [əveɪlə'bɪlɪtɪ] *n* disponibilidad *f*.
available [ə'veɪləbl] *adj* disponible; (*obtainable*) asequible; **to make sth ~ to sb** poner algo a la disposición de algn; **is the manager ~?** ¿está libre el gerente?
avalanche ['ævəlɑːnʃ] *n* alud *m*, avalancha.
avant-garde ['ævɑ̃ŋ'gɑːd] *adj* de vanguardia.
avarice ['ævərɪs] *n* avaricia.
avaricious [ævə'rɪʃəs] *adj* avaricioso.
avdp. *abbr* = *avoirdupois*.
Ave. *abbr* (= *avenue*) Av., Avda.
avenge [ə'vɛndʒ] *vt* vengar.
avenue ['ævənjuː] *n* avenida; (*fig*) camino, vía.
average ['ævərɪdʒ] *n* promedio, media ♦ *adj* (*mean*) medio; (*ordinary*) regular, corriente ♦ *vt* calcular el promedio de; **on ~** por término medio.
▶**average out** *vi*: **to ~ out at** salir a un promedio de.
averse [ə'vɜːs] *adj*: **to be ~ to sth/doing** sentir aversión *or* antipatía por algo/por hacer.
aversion [ə'vɜːʃən] *n* aversión *f*, repugnancia.
avert [ə'vɜːt] *vt* prevenir; (*blow*) desviar; (*one's eyes*) apartar.
aviary ['eɪvɪərɪ] *n* pajarera.
aviation [eɪvɪ'eɪʃən] *n* aviación *f*.
aviator ['eɪvɪeɪtə*] *n* aviador(a) *m/f*.
avid ['ævɪd] *adj* ávido, ansioso.
avidly ['ævɪdlɪ] *adv* ávidamente, con avidez.
avocado [ævə'kɑːdəʊ] *n* (*also: Brit:* ~ **pear**) aguacate *m*, palta (*LAM*).
avoid [ə'vɔɪd] *vt* evitar, eludir.
avoidable [ə'vɔɪdəbl] *adj* evitable, eludible.
avoidance [ə'vɔɪdəns] *n* evasión *f*.
avow [ə'vaʊ] *vt* prometer.
avowal [ə'vaʊəl] *n* promesa, voto.
avowed [ə'vaʊd] *adj* declarado.
AVP *n abbr* (*US*) = *assistant vice-president*.
avuncular [ə'vʌŋkjʊlə*] *adj* paternal.
AWACS ['eɪwæks] *n abbr* (= *airborne warning and control system*) AWACS *m*.
await [ə'weɪt] *vt* esperar, aguardar; **long ~ed** largamente esperado.
awake [ə'weɪk] *adj* despierto ♦ (*vb: pt* **awoke**, *pp* **awoken** *or* **awaked**) *vt* despertar ♦ *vi* despertarse; **to be ~** estar despierto.

awakening [ə'weɪknɪŋ] *n* despertar *m*.
award [ə'wɔːd] *n* (*prize*) premio; (*medal*) condecoración *f*; (*LAW*) fallo, sentencia; (*act*) concesión *f* ♦ *vt* (*prize*) otorgar, conceder; (*LAW: damages*) adjudicar.
aware [ə'wɛə*] *adj* consciente; (*awake*) despierto; (*informed*) enterado; **to become ~ of** darse cuenta de, enterarse de; **I am fully ~ that** sé muy bien que.
awareness [ə'wɛənɪs] *n* conciencia, conocimiento.
awash [ə'wɒʃ] *adj* inundado.
away [ə'weɪ] *adv* (*gen*) fuera; (*far* ~) lejos; **two kilometres ~** a dos kilómetros (de distancia); **two hours ~ by car** a dos horas en coche; **the holiday was two weeks ~** faltaban dos semanas para las vacaciones; **~ from** lejos de, fuera de; **he's ~ for a week** estará ausente una semana; **he's ~ in Barcelona** está en Barcelona; **to take ~** llevar(se); **to work/pedal ~** seguir trabajando/pedaleando; **to fade ~** desvanecerse; (*sound*) apagarse.
away game *n* (*SPORT*) partido de fuera.
awe [ɔː] *n* respeto, temor *m* reverencial.
awe-inspiring [ɔː'ɪnspaɪərɪŋ], **awesome** ['ɔːsəm] *adj* imponente, pasmoso.
awestruck ['ɔːstrʌk] *adj* pasmado.
awful ['ɔːfəl] *adj* terrible; **an ~ lot of** (*people, cars, dogs*) la mar de, muchísimos.
awfully ['ɔːfəlɪ] *adv* (*very*) terriblemente.
awhile [ə'waɪl] *adv* (durante) un rato, algún tiempo.
awkward ['ɔːkwəd] *adj* (*clumsy*) desmañado, torpe; (*shape, situation*) incómodo; (*difficult: question*) difícil; (*problem*) complicado.
awkwardness ['ɔːkwədnɪs] *n* (*clumsiness*) torpeza; (*of situation*) incomodidad *f*.
awl [ɔːl] *n* lezna, subilla.
awning ['ɔːnɪŋ] *n* (*of shop*) toldo; (*of window etc*) marquesina.
awoke [ə'wəʊk], **awoken** [ə'wəʊkən] *pt, pp of* **awake**.
AWOL ['eɪwɒl] *abbr* (*MIL*) *see* **absent without leave**.
awry [ə'raɪ] *adv*: **to be ~** estar descolocado *or* atravesado; **to go ~** salir mal, fracasar.
axe, (*US*) **ax** [æks] *n* hacha ♦ *vt* (*employee*) despedir; (*project etc*) cortar; (*jobs*) reducir; **to have an ~ to grind** (*fig*) tener un interés creado *or* algún fin interesado.
axes ['æksiːz] *npl of* **axis**.
axiom ['æksɪəm] *n* axioma *m*.
axiomatic [æksɪə'mætɪk] *adj* axiomático.
axis, *pl* **axes** ['æksɪs, -siːz] *n* eje *m*.

axle ['æksl] n eje m, árbol m.
ay(e) [aɪ] excl (yes) sí; **the ayes** npl los que votan a favor.
AYH n abbr = American Youth Hostels.
AZ abbr (US) = Arizona.
Azerbaijan [æzəbaɪ'dʒɑːn] n Azerbaiyán m.
Azerbaijani [æzəbaɪ'dʒɑːnɪ], **Azeri** [ə'zɛərɪ] adj, n azerbaiyano/a, azerí m/f.
Azores [ə'zɔːz] npl: **the ~** las (Islas) Azores.
Aztec ['æztɛk] adj, n azteca m/f.
azure ['eɪʒə*] adj celeste.

B b

B, b [biː] n (letter) B, b f; (SCOL: mark) N; (MUS) si m; **B for Benjamin**, (US) **B for Baker** B de Barcelona; **B road** (BRIT AUT) ≈ carretera secundaria.
BA n abbr = British Academy; (SCOL) = Bachelor of Arts; see also bachelor's degree.
babble ['bæbl] vi farfullar.
baboon [bə'buːn] n mandril m.
baby ['beɪbɪ] n bebé m/f.
baby carriage n (US) cochecito.
babyish ['beɪbɪɪʃ] adj infantil.
baby-sit ['beɪbɪsɪt] vi hacer de canguro.
baby-sitter ['beɪbɪsɪtə*] n canguro m/f.
bachelor ['bætʃələ*] n soltero; **B~ of Arts/Science (BA/BSc)** licenciado/a en Filosofía y Letras/Ciencias.
bachelor's degree n licenciatura; ver recuadro.

BACHELOR'S DEGREE

Se denomina **bachelor's degree** a la titulación que se recibe al finalizar el primer ciclo universitario, normalmente después de un período de estudio de tres o cuatro años. Las titulaciones más frecuentes son las de Letras, "BA (Bachelor of Arts)", Ciencias, "BSc (Bachelor of Science)", Educación, "BEd (Bachelor of Education)" y Derecho, "LLB (Bachelor of Laws)".

---

back [bæk] n (of person) espalda; (of animal) lomo; (of hand, page) dorso; (as opposed to front) parte f de atrás; (of room) fondo; (of chair) respaldo; (FOOTBALL) defensa m; **to have one's ~ to the wall** (fig) estar entre la espada y la pared; **to break the ~ of a** job hacer lo más difícil de un trabajo; **~ to front** al revés; **at the ~ of my mind was the thought that ...** en el fondo tenía la idea de que ... ♦ vt (candidate: also: **~ up**) respaldar, apoyar; (horse: at races) apostar a; (car) dar marcha atrás a or con ♦ vi (car etc) dar marcha atrás ♦ adj (in compounds) de atrás; **~ seats/wheels** (AUT) asientos mpl/ruedas fpl traseros/as; **~ garden/room** jardín m/habitación f de atrás; **~ payments** pagos mpl con efecto retroactivo; **~ rent** renta atrasada; **to take a ~ seat** (fig) pasar a segundo plano ♦ adv (not forward) (hacia) atrás; **he's ~** (returned) ha vuelto; **he ran ~** volvió corriendo; **throw the ball ~** (restitution) devuelve la pelota; **can I have it ~?** ¿me lo devuelve?; **he called ~** (again) volvió a llamar; **~ and forth** de acá para allá; **as far ~ as the 13th century** ya en el siglo XIII; **when will you be ~?** ¿cuándo volverá?
▶**back down** vi echarse atrás.
▶**back on** to vt fus: **the house ~s on to the golf course** por atrás la casa da al campo de golf.
▶**back out** vi (of promise) volverse atrás.
▶**back up** vt (support: person) apoyar, respaldar; (: theory) defender; (car) dar marcha atrás a; (COMPUT) hacer una copia de reserva de.
backache ['bækeɪk] n dolor m de espalda.
backbencher ['bæk'bɛntʃə*] n (BRIT) diputado sin cargo oficial en el gobierno o la oposición.
back benches npl (BRIT) ver recuadro.

BACK BENCHES

Reciben el nombre genérico de **the back benches** los escaños más alejados del pasillo central en la Cámara de los Comunes del Parlamento británico, que son ocupados por los "backbenchers", los miembros de la cámara que no tienen cargo en el gobierno o en la oposición.

---

backbiting ['bækbaɪtɪŋ] n murmuración f.
backbone ['bækbəun] n columna vertebral; **the ~ of the organization** el pilar de la organización.
backchat ['bæktʃæt] n réplicas fpl.
backcloth ['bækklɔθ] n telón m de fondo.
backcomb ['bækkəum] vt cardar.
backdate [bæk'deɪt] vt (letter) poner fecha atrasada a; **~d pay rise** aumento de sueldo con efecto retroactivo.
backdrop ['bækdrɔp] n = backcloth.
backer ['bækə*] n partidario/a; (COMM)

promotor(a) *m/f*.
backfire [bæk'faɪə*] *vi* (*AUT*) petardear;
(*plans*) fallar, salir mal.
backgammon ['bækgæmən] *n*
backgammon *m*.
background ['bækɡraund] *n* fondo; (*of
events*) antecedentes *mpl*; (*basic
knowledge*) bases *fpl*; (*experience*)
conocimientos *mpl*, educación *f* ♦ *cpd*
(*noise, music*) de fondo; (*COMPUT*)
secundario; ~ **reading** lectura de
preparación; **family** ~ origen *m*,
antecedentes *mpl* familiares.
backhand ['bækhænd] *n* (*TENNIS: also*: ~
stroke) revés *m*.
backhanded ['bæk'hændɪd] *adj* (*fig*)
ambiguo, equívoco.
backhander ['bæk'hændə*] *n* (*BRIT: bribe*)
soborno.
backing ['bækɪŋ] *n* (*fig*) apoyo, respaldo;
(*COMM*) respaldo financiero; (*MUS*)
acompañamiento.
backlash ['bæklæʃ] *n* reacción *f* (en contra).
backlog ['bæklɔg] *n*: ~ **of work** trabajo
atrasado.
back number *n* (*of magazine etc*) número
atrasado.
backpack ['bækpæk] *n* mochila.
backpacker ['bækpækə*] *n* mochilero/a.
back pay *n* atrasos *mpl*.
backpedal ['bækpɛdl] *vi* (*fig*) volverse/
echarse atrás.
backseat driver ['bæksiːt-] *n* pasajero que
se empeña en aconsejar al conductor.
backside ['bæksaɪd] *n* (*col*) trasero.
backslash ['bækslæʃ] *n* pleca, barra
inversa.
backslide ['bækslaɪd] *vi* reincidir, recaer.
backspace ['bækspeɪs] *vi* (*in typing*)
retroceder.
backstage [bæk'steɪdʒ] *adv* entre
bastidores.
back-street ['bækstriːt] *adj* de barrio; ~
abortionist persona que practica abortos
clandestinos.
backstroke ['bækstrəuk] *n* espalda.
backtrack ['bæktræk] *vi* (*fig*) = **backpedal**.
backup ['bækʌp] *adj* (*train, plane*)
suplementario; (*COMPUT: disk, file*) de
reserva ♦ *n* (*support*) apoyo; (*also*: ~ **file**)
copia de reserva; (*US: congestion*)
embotellamiento, retención *f*.
back-up lights *npl* (*US*) luces *fpl* de marcha
atrás.
backward ['bækwəd] *adj* (*movement*) hacia
atrás; (*person, country*) atrasado; (*shy*)
tímido.
backwardness ['bækwədnɪs] *n* atraso.

backwards ['bækwədz] *adv* (*move, go*)
hacia atrás; (*read a list*) al revés; (*fall*) de
espaldas; **to know sth** ~ *or* (*US*) ~ **and
forwards** (*col*) saberse algo al dedillo.
backwater ['bækwɔːtə*] *n* (*fig*) lugar *m*
atrasado *or* apartado.
backyard [bæk'jɑːd] *n* patio trasero.
bacon ['beɪkən] *n* tocino, bacon *m*, beicon
m.
bacteria [bæk'tɪərɪə] *npl* bacterias *fpl*.
bacteriology [bæktɪərɪ'ɔlədʒɪ] *n*
bacteriología.
bad [bæd] *adj* malo; (*serious*) grave; (*meat,
food*) podrido, pasado; **to go** ~ pasarse;
to have a ~ **time of it** pasarlo mal; **I feel** ~
about it (*guilty*) me siento culpable; ~
debt (*COMM*) cuenta incobrable; **in** ~ **faith**
de mala fe.
baddie, baddy ['bædɪ] *n* (*col: CINE etc*)
malo/a.
bade [bæd, beɪd] *pt of* **bid**.
badge [bædʒ] *n* insignia; (*metal* ~) chapa;
(*of policeman*) placa; (*stick-on*) pegatina.
badger ['bædʒə*] *n* tejón *m*.
badly ['bædlɪ] *adv* (*work, dress etc*) mal; ~
wounded gravemente herido; **he needs it**
~ le hace mucha falta; **to be** ~ **off (for
money)** andar mal de dinero; **things are
going** ~ las cosas van muy mal.
bad-mannered ['bæd'mænəd] *adj* mal
educado.
badminton ['bædmɪntən] *n* bádminton *m*.
bad-tempered ['bæd'tɛmpəd] *adj* de mal
genio *or* carácter; (*temporary*) de mal
humor.
baffle ['bæfl] *vt* desconcertar, confundir.
baffling ['bæflɪŋ] *adj* incomprensible.
bag [bæg] *n* bolsa; (*handbag*) bolso; (*satchel*)
mochila; (*case*) maleta; (*of hunter*) caza
♦ *vt* (*col: take*) coger (*SP*), agarrar (*LAM*),
pescar; ~**s of** (*col: lots of*) un montón de;
to pack one's ~**s** hacer las maletas.
bagful ['bægful] *n* saco (lleno).
baggage ['bægɪdʒ] *n* equipaje *m*.
baggage claim *n* recogida de equipajes.
baggy ['bægɪ] *adj* (*trousers*) ancho, holgado.
Baghdad [bæg'dæd] *n* Bagdad *m*.
bag lady *n* (*col*) *mujer sin hogar cargada
de bolsas.*
bagpipes ['bægpaɪps] *npl* gaita *sg*.
bag-snatcher ['bægsnætʃə*] *n* (*BRIT*)
ladrón/ona *m/f* de bolsos.
bag-snatching ['bægsnætʃɪŋ] *n* (*BRIT*) tirón
m (de bolsos).
Bahamas [bə'hɑːməz] *npl*: **the** ~ las (Islas)
Bahama.
Bahrain [bɑː'reɪn] *n* Bahrein *m*.
bail [beɪl] *n* fianza ♦ *vt* (*prisoner: also*: **grant**

~ to) poner en libertad bajo fianza; (boat:
also: ~ out) achicar; on ~ (prisoner) bajo
fianza; to be released on ~ ser puesto en
libertad bajo fianza; to ~ sb out pagar la
fianza de algn; see also **bale**.
bailiff ['beɪlɪf] n alguacil m.
bait [beɪt] n cebo ♦ vt poner el cebo en.
bake [beɪk] vt cocer (al horno) ♦ vi (cook)
cocerse; (be hot) hacer un calor terrible.
baked beans npl judías fpl en salsa de
tomate.
baker ['beɪkə*] n panadero/a.
baker's dozen n docena del fraile.
bakery ['beɪkərɪ] n (for bread) panadería;
(for cakes) pastelería.
baking ['beɪkɪŋ] n (act) cocción f; (batch)
hornada.
baking powder n levadura (en polvo).
baking tin n molde m (para horno).
balaclava [bælə'klɑːvə] n (also: ~ helmet)
pasamontañas m inv.
balance ['bæləns] n equilibrio; (COMM: sum)
balance m; (remainder) resto; (scales)
balanza ♦ vt equilibrar; (budget) nivelar;
(account) saldar; (compensate)
compensar; ~ of trade/payments balanza
de comercio/pagos; ~ carried forward
balance m pasado a cuenta nueva; ~
brought forward saldo de hoja anterior;
to ~ the books hacer el balance.
balanced ['bælənst] adj (personality, diet)
equilibrado.
balance sheet n balance m.
balcony ['bælkənɪ] n (open) balcón m;
(closed) galería.
bald [bɔːld] adj calvo; (tyre) liso.
baldness ['bɔːldnɪs] n calvicie f.
bale [beɪl] n (AGR) paca, fardo.
►**bale out** vi (of a plane) lanzarse en
paracaídas ♦ vt (NAUT) achicar; to ~ sb
out of a difficulty sacar a algn de un
apuro.
Balearic Islands [bælɪ'ærɪk-] npl: the ~ las
(Islas) Baleares.
baleful ['beɪlful] adj (look) triste; (sinister)
funesto, siniestro.
balk [bɔːk] vi: to ~ (at) resistirse (a);
(horse) plantarse (ante).
Balkan ['bɔːlkən] adj balcánico ♦ n: the ~s
los Balcanes.
ball [bɔːl] n (sphere) bola; (football) balón m;
(for tennis, golf etc) pelota; (dance) baile m;
to be on the ~ (fig: competent) ser un
enterado; (: alert) estar al tanto; to play ~
(with sb) jugar a la pelota (con algn); (fig)
cooperar; to start the ~ rolling (fig)
empezar; the ~ is in your court (fig) le
toca a usted.

ballad ['bæləd] n balada, romance m.
ballast ['bæləst] n lastre m.
ball bearing n cojinete m de bolas.
ballcock ['bɔːlkɔk] n llave f de bola or de
flotador.
ballerina [bælə'riːnə] n bailarina.
ballet ['bæleɪ] n ballet m.
ballet dancer n bailarín/ina m/f (de ballet).
ballistic [bə'lɪstɪk] adj balístico;
intercontinental ~ missile misil m
balístico intercontinental.
ballistics [bə'lɪstɪks] n balística.
balloon [bə'luːn] n globo; (in comic strip)
bocadillo ♦ vi dispararse.
balloonist [bə'luːnɪst] n aeróstata m/f.
ballot ['bælət] n votación f.
ballot box n urna (electoral).
ballot paper n papeleta.
ballpark ['bɔːlpɑːk] n (US) estadio de
béisbol.
ball-point pen ['bɔːlpɔɪnt-] n bolígrafo.
ballroom ['bɔːlrum] n salón m de baile.
balm [bɑːm] n (also fig) bálsamo.
balmy ['bɑːmɪ] adj (breeze, air) suave; (col)
= **barmy**.
BALPA ['bælpə] n abbr (= British Airline
Pilots' Association) sindicato de pilotos de
líneas aéreas.
balsa (wood) ['bɔːlsə-] n (madera de)
balsa.
Baltic ['bɔːltɪk] adj báltico ♦ n: the ~ (Sea) el
(Mar) Báltico.
balustrade ['bæləstreɪd] n barandilla.
bamboo [bæm'buː] n bambú m.
bamboozle [bæm'buːzl] vt (col) embaucar,
engatusar.
ban [bæn] n prohibición f ♦ vt prohibir;
(exclude) excluir; he was ~ned from
driving le retiraron el carnet de
conducir.
banal [bə'nɑːl] adj banal, vulgar.
banana [bə'nɑːnə] n plátano, banana (LAM).
band [bænd] n (group) banda; (gang)
pandilla; (strip) faja, tira; (at a dance)
orquesta; (MIL) banda; (rock ~) grupo.
►**band together** vi juntarse, asociarse.
bandage ['bændɪdʒ] n venda, vendaje m ♦ vt
vendar.
Band-Aid ® ['bændeɪd] n (US) tirita, curita
(LAM).
bandit ['bændɪt] n bandido; one-armed ~
máquina tragaperras.
bandstand ['bændstænd] n quiosco de
música.
bandwagon ['bændwægən] n: to jump on
the ~ (fig) subirse al carro.
bandy ['bændɪ] vt (jokes, insults)
intercambiar.

bandy-legged ['bændı'lɛgd] *adj* patizambo.
bane [beɪn] *n*: **it** (*or* **he** *etc*) **is the** ~ **of my life** me amarga la vida.
bang [bæŋ] *n* estallido; (*of door*) portazo; (*blow*) golpe *m* ♦ *vt* golpear ♦ *vi* estallar ♦ *adv*: **to be** ~ **on time** (*col*) llegar en punto; **to** ~ **the door** dar un portazo; **to** ~ **into sth** chocar con algo, golpearse contra algo; *see also* **bangs**.
banger ['bæŋə*] *n* (*BRIT*: *car*: *also*: **old** ~) armatoste *m*, cacharro; (*BRIT col*: *sausage*) salchicha; (*firework*) petardo.
Bangkok [bæŋ'kɔk] *n* Bangkok *m*.
Bangladesh [bæŋglə'dɛʃ] *n* Bangladesh *f*.
bangle ['bæŋgl] *n* brazalete *m*, ajorca.
bangs [bæŋz] *npl* (*US*) flequillo *sg*.
banish ['bænɪʃ] *vt* desterrar.
banister(s) ['bænɪstə(z)] *n*(*pl*) barandilla *f*, pasamanos *m inv*.
banjo, *pl* ~**es** *or* ~**s** ['bændʒəu] *n* banjo.
bank [bæŋk] *n* (*COMM*) banco; (*of river, lake*) ribera, orilla; (*of earth*) terraplén *m*.
▸**bank on** *vt fus* contar con.
bank account *n* cuenta bancaria.
bank balance *n* saldo.
bank card *n* = **banker's card**.
bank charges *npl* comisión *fsg*.
bank draft *n* letra de cambio.
banker ['bæŋkə*] *n* banquero; ~**'s card** (*BRIT*) tarjeta bancaria; ~**'s order** orden *f* bancaria.
bank giro *n* giro bancario.
bank holiday *n* (*BRIT*) día *m* festivo *or* de fiesta; *ver recuadro*.

BANK HOLIDAY

El término **bank holiday** *se aplica en el Reino Unido a todo día festivo oficial en el que cierran bancos y comercios. Los más destacados coinciden con Navidad, Semana Santa, finales de mayo y finales de agosto. Al contrario que en los países de tradición católica, no se celebran las festividades dedicadas a los santos.*

---

banking ['bæŋkɪŋ] *n* banca.
bank loan *n* préstamo bancario.
bank manager *n* director(a) *m/f* (de sucursal) de banco.
banknote ['bæŋknəut] *n* billete *m* de banco.
bank rate *n* tipo de interés bancario.
bankrupt ['bæŋkrʌpt] *n* quebrado/a ♦ *adj* quebrado, insolvente; **to go** ~ quebrar, hacer bancarrota; **to be** ~ estar en quiebra.
bankruptcy ['bæŋkrʌptsɪ] *n* quiebra, bancarrota.

bank statement *n* extracto de cuenta.
banner ['bænə*] *n* bandera; (*in demonstration*) pancarta.
banns [bænz] *npl* amonestaciones *fpl*.
banquet ['bæŋkwɪt] *n* banquete *m*.
banter ['bæntə*] *n* guasa, bromas *fpl*.
BAOR *n abbr* (= *British Army of the Rhine*) fuerzas británicas en Alemania.
baptism ['bæptɪzəm] *n* bautismo; (*act*) bautizo.
baptize [bæp'taɪz] *vt* bautizar.
bar [ba:*] *n* barra; (*on door*) tranca; (*of window, cage*) reja; (*of soap*) pastilla; (*fig*: *hindrance*) obstáculo; (*prohibition*) prohibición *f*; (*pub*) bar *m*, cantina (*esp LAM*); (*counter*: *in pub*) barra, mostrador *m*; (*MUS*) barra ♦ *vt* (*road*) obstruir; (*window, door*) atrancar; (*person*) excluir; (*activity*) prohibir; **behind** ~**s** entre rejas; **the B**~ (*LAW*: *profession*) la abogacía; (: *people*) el cuerpo de abogados; ~ **none** sin excepción.
Barbados [ba:'beɪdɔs] *n* Barbados *m*.
barbarian [ba:'bɛərɪən] *n* bárbaro/a.
barbaric [ba:'bærɪk] *adj* bárbaro.
barbarity [ba:'bærɪtɪ] *n* barbaridad *f*.
barbarous ['ba:bərəs] *adj* bárbaro.
barbecue ['ba:bɪkju:] *n* barbacoa, asado (*LAM*).
barbed wire ['ba:bd-] *n* alambre *m* de espino.
barber ['ba:bə*] *n* peluquero, barbero.
barbiturate [ba:'bɪtjurɪt] *n* barbitúrico.
Barcelona [ba:sɪ'ləunə] *n* Barcelona.
bar chart *n* gráfico de barras.
bar code *n* código de barras.
bare [bɛə*] *adj* desnudo; (*head*) descubierto ♦ *vt* desnudar; **to** ~ **one's teeth** enseñar los dientes.
bareback ['bɛəbæk] *adv* a pelo.
barefaced ['bɛəfeɪst] *adj* descarado.
barefoot ['bɛəfut] *adj*, *adv* descalzo.
bareheaded [bɛə'hedɪd] *adj* descubierto, sin sombrero.
barely ['bɛəlɪ] *adv* apenas.
bareness ['bɛənɪs] *n* desnudez *f*.
Barents Sea ['bærənts-] *n*: **the** ~ el Mar de Barents.
bargain ['ba:gɪn] *n* pacto; (*transaction*) negocio; (*good buy*) ganga ♦ *vi* negociar; (*haggle*) regatear; **into the** ~ además, por añadidura.
▸**bargain for** *vt fus* (*col*): **he got more than he** ~**ed for** le resultó peor de lo que esperaba.
bargaining ['ba:gənɪŋ] *n* negociación *f*; regateo; ~ **table** mesa de negociaciones.
bargaining position *n*: **to be in a strong/**

weak ~ estar/no estar en una posición de fuerza para negociar.
barge [bɑːdʒ] n barcaza.
▶**barge in** vi irrumpir; (conversation) entrometerse.
▶**barge into** vt fus dar contra.
baritone ['bærɪtəun] n barítono.
barium meal ['bɛərɪəm-] n (MED) sulfato de bario.
bark [bɑːk] n (of tree) corteza; (of dog) ladrido ♦ vi ladrar.
barley ['bɑːlɪ] n cebada.
barley sugar n azúcar m cande.
barmaid ['bɑːmeɪd] n camarera.
barman ['bɑːmən] n camarero, barman m.
barmy ['bɑːmɪ] adj (col) chiflado, chalado.
barn [bɑːn] n granero; (for animals) cuadra.
barnacle ['bɑːnəkl] n percebe m.
barn owl n lechuza.
barometer [bə'rɔmɪtə*] n barómetro.
baron ['bærən] n barón m; (fig) magnate m; **the press ~s** los magnates de la prensa.
baroness ['bærənɪs] n baronesa.
baroque [bə'rɔk] adj barroco.
barrack ['bærək] vt (BRIT) abuchear.
barracks ['bærəks] npl cuartel msg.
barrage ['bærɑːʒ] n (MIL) cortina de fuego; (dam) presa; (fig: of criticism etc) lluvia, aluvión m; **a ~ of questions** una lluvia de preguntas.
barrel ['bærəl] n barril m; (of wine) tonel m, cuba; (of gun) cañón m.
barren ['bærən] adj estéril.
barricade [bærɪ'keɪd] n barricada ♦ vt cerrar con barricadas.
barrier ['bærɪə*] n barrera; (crash ~) barrera.
barrier cream n crema protectora.
barring ['bɑːrɪŋ] prep excepto, salvo.
barrister ['bærɪstə*] n (BRIT) abogado/a; ver recuadro.

BARRISTER

En el sistema legal inglés **barrister** es el abogado que se ocupa de defender los casos de sus clientes en los tribunales superiores. El equivalente escocés es "advocate". Normalmente actúan según instrucciones de un "solicitor", abogado de despacho que no toma parte activa en los juicios de dichos tribunales. El título de **barrister** lo otorga el órgano colegiado correspondiente, "the Inns of Court".

---

barrow ['bærəu] n (cart) carretilla.
barstool ['bɑːstuːl] n taburete m (de bar).
Bart. abbr (BRIT) = baronet.

bartender ['bɑːtɛndə*] n (US) camarero, barman m.
barter ['bɑːtə*] vt: **to ~ sth for sth** trocar algo por algo.
base [beɪs] n base f ♦ vt: **to ~ sth on** basar or fundar algo en ♦ adj bajo, infame; **to ~ at** (troops) estacionar en; **I'm ~d in London** (work) trabajo en Londres.
baseball ['beɪsbɔːl] n béisbol m.
base camp n campamento base.
Basel ['bɑːzəl] n Basilea.
baseless ['beɪslɪs] adj infundado.
baseline ['beɪslaɪn] n (TENNIS) línea de fondo.
basement ['beɪsmənt] n sótano.
base rate n tipo base.
bases ['beɪsiːz] npl of **basis**; ['beɪsɪz] npl of **base**.
bash [bæʃ] n: **I'll have a ~ (at it)** lo intentaré ♦ vt (col) golpear.
▶**bash up** vt (col: car) destrozar; (: person) aporrear, vapulear.
bashful ['bæʃful] adj tímido, vergonzoso.
bashing ['bæʃɪŋ] n (col) paliza.
BASIC ['beɪsɪk] n BASIC m.
basic ['beɪsɪk] adj (salary etc) básico; (elementary: principles) fundamental.
basically ['beɪsɪklɪ] adv fundamentalmente, en el fondo.
basic rate n (of tax) base f mínima imponible.
basil ['bæzl] n albahaca.
basin ['beɪsn] n (vessel) cuenco, tazón m; (GEO) cuenca; (also: **wash~**) palangana, jofaina; (in bathroom) lavabo.
basis ['beɪsɪs] pl **-ses** [-siːz] n base f; **on the ~ of what you've said** en base a lo que has dicho.
bask [bɑːsk] vi: **to ~ in the sun** tomar el sol.
basket ['bɑːskɪt] n cesta, cesto.
basketball ['bɑːskɪtbɔːl] n baloncesto.
basketball player n jugador(a) m/f de baloncesto.
basketwork ['bɑːskɪtwəːk] n cestería.
Basle [bɑːl] n Basilea.
basmati rice [bəz'mætɪ-] n arroz m basmati.
Basque [bæsk] adj, n vasco/a m/f.
Basque Country n Euskadi m, País m Vasco.
bass [beɪs] n (MUS) bajo.
bass clef n clave f de fa.
bassoon [bə'suːn] n fagot m.
bastard ['bɑːstəd] n bastardo/a; (col!) cabrón m, hijo de puta (!).
baste [beɪst] vt (CULIN) rociar (con su salsa).

bastion ['bæstɪən] n bastión m, baluarte m.

bat [bæt] n (ZOOL) murciélago; (for ball games) palo; (for cricket, baseball) bate m; (BRIT: for table tennis) pala; **he didn't ~ an eyelid** ni pestañeó, ni se inmutó.

batch [bætʃ] n lote m, remesa; (of bread) hornada.

batch processing n (COMPUT) proceso por lotes.

bated ['beɪtɪd] adj: **with ~ breath** sin respirar.

bath [bɑːθ, pl bɑːðz] n (action) baño; (~tub) bañera, tina (esp LAM) ♦ vt bañar; **to have a ~** bañarse, darse un baño; see also **baths**.

bathchair ['bɑːθtʃɛə*] n silla de ruedas.

bathe [beɪð] vi bañarse; (US) darse un baño, bañarse ♦ vt (wound etc) lavar; (US) bañar, dar un baño a.

bather ['beɪðə*] n bañista m/f.

bathing ['beɪðɪŋ] n baño.

bathing cap n gorro de baño.

bathing costume, (US) **bathing suit** n bañador m, traje m de baño.

bathing trunks npl bañador msg.

bathmat ['bɑːθmæt] n alfombrilla de baño.

bathrobe ['bɑːθrəʊb] n albornoz m.

bathroom ['bɑːθrum] n (cuarto de) baño.

baths [bɑːðz] npl piscina sg.

bath towel n toalla de baño.

bathtub ['bɑːθtʌb] n bañera.

batman ['bætmən] n (BRIT) ordenanza m.

baton ['bætən] n (MUS) batuta.

battalion [bə'tælɪən] n batallón m.

batten ['bætn] n (CARPENTRY) listón m; (NAUT) junquillo, sable m.

▶**batten down** vt (NAUT): **to ~ down the hatches** atrancar las escotillas.

batter ['bætə*] vt maltratar, apalear; (subj: wind, rain) azotar ♦ n batido.

battered ['bætəd] adj (hat, pan) estropeado.

battery ['bætərɪ] n batería; (of torch) pila.

battery charger n cargador m de baterías.

battery farming n cría intensiva.

battle ['bætl] n batalla; (fig) lucha ♦ vi luchar; **that's half the ~** (col) ya hay medio camino andado; **to fight a losing ~** (fig) luchar por una causa perdida.

battlefield ['bætlfiːld] n campo m de batalla.

battlements ['bætlmənts] npl almenas fpl.

battleship ['bætlʃɪp] n acorazado.

batty ['bætɪ] adj (col: person) chiflado; (: idea) de chiflado.

bauble ['bɔːbl] n chuchería.

baud [bɔːd] n (COMPUT) baudio.

baud rate n (COMPUT) velocidad f (de transmisión) en baudios.

bauxite ['bɔːksaɪt] n bauxita.

Bavaria [bə'vɛərɪə] n Baviera.

Bavarian [bə'vɛərɪən] adj, n bávaro/a m/f.

bawdy ['bɔːdɪ] adj indecente; (joke) verde.

bawl [bɔːl] vi chillar, gritar.

bay [beɪ] n (GEO) bahía; (for parking) parking m, estacionamiento; (loading ~) patio de carga; (BOT) laurel m ♦ vi aullar; **to hold sb at ~** mantener a alguien a raya.

bay leaf n (hoja de) laurel m.

bayonet ['beɪənɪt] n bayoneta.

bay window n ventana salediza.

bazaar [bə'zɑː*] n bazar m.

bazooka [bə'zuːkə] n bazuca.

BB n abbr (BRIT: = Boys' Brigade) organización juvenil para chicos.

B. & B. n abbr = **bed and breakfast**.

BBB n abbr (US: = Better Business Bureau) organismo para la defensa del consumidor.

BBC n abbr (= British Broadcasting Corporation) BBC f; ver recuadro.

BBC

La **BBC** es el organismo público británico de radio y televisión, autónomo en cuanto a su política de programas pero regulado por un estatuto ("BBC charter") que ha de aprobar el Parlamento. Además de cadenas nacionales de televisión y de radio, transmite también un servicio informativo mundial ("BBC World Service"). A no tener publicidad, se financia a través de operaciones comerciales paralelas y del cobro de una licencia anual obligatoria ("TV licence") para los que tienen aparato de televisión.

BC ad abbr (= before Christ) a. de J.C. ♦ abbr (Canada) = British Columbia.

BCG n abbr (= Bacillus Calmette-Guérin) vacuna de la tuberculosis.

BD n abbr (= Bachelor of Divinity) Licenciado/a en Teología.

B/D abbr = **bank draft**.

BDS n abbr (= Bachelor of Dental Surgery) título universitario.

═══════════════════ KEYWORD

be [biː] (pt **was, were**, pp **been**) aux vb **1** (with present participle: forming continuous tenses): **what are you doing?** ¿qué estás haciendo?, ¿qué haces?; **they're coming tomorrow** vienen mañana; **I've been waiting for you for hours** llevo horas esperándote

2 (with pp: forming passives) ser (but often

replaced by activo or reflexive constructions); **to** ~ **murdered** ser asesinado; **the box had been opened** habían abierto la caja; **the thief was nowhere to** ~ **seen** no se veía al ladrón por ninguna parte
3 (*in tag questions*): **it was fun, wasn't it?** fue divertido, ¿no? *or* ¿verdad?; **he's good-looking, isn't he?** es guapo, ¿no te parece?; **she's back again, is she?** entonces, ¿ha vuelto?
4 (+*to* +*infin*): **the house is to** ~ **sold** (*necessity*) hay que vender la casa; (*future*) van a vender la casa; **he's not to open it** no tiene que abrirlo; **he was to have come yesterday** debía de haber venido ayer; **am I to understand that ...?** ¿debo entender que ...?
♦ *vb* +*complement* **1** (*with n or num complement*) ser; **he's a doctor** es médico; **2 and 2 are 4** 2 y 2 son 4
2 (*with adj complement: expressing permanent or inherent quality*) ser; (: *expressing state seen as temporary or reversible*) estar; **I'm English** soy inglés/esa; **she's tall/pretty** es alta/bonita; **he's young** es joven; ~ **careful/good/quiet** ten cuidado/pórtate bien/callate; **I'm tired** estoy cansado/a; **I'm warm** tengo calor; **it's dirty** está sucio/a
3 (*of health*) estar; **how are you?** ¿cómo estás?; **he's very ill** está muy enfermo; **I'm better now** ya estoy mejor
4 (*of age*) tener; **how old are you?** ¿cuántos años tienes?; **I'm sixteen (years old)** tengo dieciséis años
5 (*cost*) costar; ser; **how much was the meal?** ¿cuánto fue *or* costó la comida?; **that'll** ~ **£5.75, please** son £5.75, por favor; **this shirt is £17** esta camisa cuesta £17
♦ *vi* **1** (*exist, occur etc*) existir, haber; **the best singer that ever was** el mejor cantante que existió jamás; **is there a God?** ¿hay un Dios?, ¿existe Dios?; ~ **that as it may** sea como sea; **so** ~ **it** así sea
2 (*referring to place*) estar; **I won't** ~ **here tomorrow** no estaré aquí mañana
3 (*referring to movement*): **where have you been?** ¿dónde has estado?
♦ *impers vb* **1** (*referring to time*): **it's 5 o'clock** son las 5; **it's the 28th of April** estamos a 28 de abril
2 (*referring to distance*): **it's 10 km to the village** el pueblo está a 10 km
3 (*referring to the weather*): **it's too hot/cold** hace demasiado calor/frío; **it's windy today** hace viento hoy

4 (*emphatic*): **it's me** soy yo; **it was Maria who paid the bill** fue María la que pagó la cuenta.

B/E *abbr* = **bill of exchange.**
beach [biːtʃ] *n* playa ♦ *vt* varar.
beach buggy [-bʌgɪ] *n* buggy *m*.
beachcomber ['biːtʃkəumə*] *n* raquero/a.
beachwear ['biːtʃwɛə*] *n* ropa de playa.
beacon ['biːkən] *n* (*lighthouse*) faro; (*marker*) guía; (*radio* ~) radiofaro.
bead [biːd] *n* cuenta, abalorio; (*of dew, sweat*) gota; ~**s** *npl* (*necklace*) collar *m*.
beady ['biːdɪ] *adj* (*eyes*) pequeño y brillante.
beagle ['biːgl] *n* sabueso pequeño, beagle *m*.
beak [biːk] *n* pico.
beaker ['biːkə*] *n* vaso.
beam [biːm] *n* (ARCH) viga; (*of light*) rayo, haz *m* de luz; (*RADIO*) rayo ♦ *vi* brillar; (*smile*) sonreír; **to drive on full** *or* **main** ~ conducir con las luces largas.
beaming ['biːmɪŋ] *adj* (*sun, smile*) radiante.
bean [biːn] *n* judía, fríjol/frijol *m* (*esp LAM*); **runner/broad** ~ habichuela/haba; **coffee** ~ grano de café.
beanpole ['biːnpəul] *n* (*col*) espárrago.
beansprouts ['biːnsprauts] *npl* brotes *mpl* de soja.
bear [bɛə*] *n* oso; (*STOCK EXCHANGE*) bajista *m* ♦ (*vb*: *pt* **bore**, *pp* **borne**) *vt* (*weight etc*) llevar; (*cost*) pagar; (*responsibility*) tener; (*traces, signs*) mostrar; (*produce: fruit*) dar; (*COMM: interest*) devengar; (*endure*) soportar, aguantar; (*stand up to*) resistir a; (*children*) tener, dar a luz ♦ *vi*: **to** ~ **right/left** torcer a la derecha/izquierda; **I can't** ~ **him** no le puedo ver, no lo soporto; **to bring pressure to** ~ **on sb** ejercer presión sobre algn.
▶**bear on** *vt fus* tener que ver con, referirse a.
▶**bear out** *vt fus* (*suspicions*) corroborar, confirmar; (*person*) confirmar lo dicho por.
▶**bear up** *vi* (*cheer up*) animarse; **he bore up well under the strain** resistió bien la presión.
▶**bear with** *vt fus* (*sb's moods, temper*) tener paciencia con.
bearable ['bɛərəbl] *adj* soportable, aguantable.
beard [bɪəd] *n* barba.
bearded ['bɪədɪd] *adj* con barba.
bearer ['bɛərə*] *n* (*of news, cheque*) portador(a) *m/f*; (*of passport*) titular *m/f*.
bearing ['bɛərɪŋ] *n* porte *m*; (*connection*)

relación *f*; (**ball**) ~**s** *npl* cojinetes *mpl* a bolas; **to take a** ~ marcarse; **to find one's** ~**s** orientarse.

bearskin ['bɛəskɪn] *n* (*MIL*) gorro militar (*de piel de oso*).

beast [biːst] *n* bestia; (*col*) bruto, salvaje *m*.

beastly ['biːstlɪ] *adj* bestial; (*awful*) horrible.

beat [biːt] *n* (*of heart*) latido; (*MUS*) ritmo, compás *m*; (*of policeman*) ronda ♦ (*vb: pt* **beat**, *pp* **beaten**) *vt* (*hit*) golpear; (*eggs*) batir; (*defeat*) vencer, derrotar; (*better*) sobrepasar; (*drum*) tocar; (*rhythm*) marcar ♦ *vi* (*heart*) latir; **off the** ~**en track** aislado; **to** ~ **about the bush** andarse con rodeos; **to** ~ **it** largarse; **that** ~**s everything!** (*col*) ¡eso es el colmo!; **to** ~ **on a door** dar golpes en una puerta.

▸**beat down** *vt* (*door*) derribar a golpes; (*price*) conseguir rebajar, regatear; (*seller*) hacer rebajar el precio ♦ *vi* (*rain*) llover a cántaros; (*sun*) caer de plomo.

▸**beat off** *vt* rechazar.

▸**beat up** *vt* (*col: person*) dar una paliza a.

beater ['biːtə*] *n* (*for eggs, cream*) batidora.

beating ['biːtɪŋ] *n* paliza, golpiza (*LAM*); **to take a** ~ recibir una paliza.

beat-up ['biːt'ʌp] *adj* (*col*) destartalado.

beautiful ['bjuːtɪful] *adj* hermoso, bello, lindo (*esp LAM*).

beautifully ['bjuːtɪfəlɪ] *adv* de maravilla.

beautify ['bjuːtɪfaɪ] *vt* embellecer.

beauty ['bjuːtɪ] *n* belleza, hermosura; (*concept, person*) belleza; **the** ~ **of it is that ...** lo mejor de esto es que ....

beauty contest *n* concurso de belleza.

beauty queen *n* reina de la belleza.

beauty salon *n* salón *m* de belleza.

beauty sleep *n*: **to get one's** ~ no perder *horas de sueño*.

beauty spot *n* lunar *m* postizo; (*BRIT: TOURISM*) lugar *m* pintoresco.

beaver ['biːvə*] *n* castor *m*.

becalmed [bɪ'kɑːmd] *adj* encalmado.

became [bɪ'keɪm] *pt of* **become**.

because [bɪ'kɔz] *conj* porque; ~ **of** *prep* debido a, a causa de.

beck [bɛk] *n*: **to be at the** ~ **and call of** estar a disposición de.

beckon ['bɛkən] *vt* (*also:* ~ **to**) llamar con señas.

become [bɪ'kʌm] (*irreg: like* **come**) *vi* (+ *noun*) hacerse, llegar a ser; (+ *adj*) ponerse, volverse ♦ *vt* (*suit*) favorecer, sentar bien a; **to** ~ **fat** engordar; **to** ~ **angry** enfadarse; **it became known that ...** se descubrió que ....

becoming [bɪ'kʌmɪŋ] *adj* (*behaviour*)

decoroso; (*clothes*) favorecedor(a).

becquerel [bɛkə'rɛl] *n* becquerelio.

BEd *n abbr* (= *Bachelor of Education*) título universitario; *see also* **Bachelor's Degree**.

bed [bɛd] *n* cama; (*of flowers*) macizo; (*of sea, lake*) fondo; (*of coal, clay*) capa; **to go to** ~ acostarse.

▸**bed down** *vi* acostarse.

bed and breakfast (B & B) *n* ≈ pensión *f*; *ver recuadro*.

┌─────────────────────────────┐
│ **BED AND BREAKFAST**   │
│   │
│ *Se llama* **bed and breakfast** *a la casa de* │
│ *hospedaje particular, o granja si es en el* │
│ *campo, que ofrece cama y desayuno a* │
│ *tarifas inferiores a las de un hotel. El* │
│ *servicio se suele anunciar con carteles* │
│ *colocados en las ventanas del* │
│ *establecimiento, en el jardín o en la* │
│ *carretera y en ellos aparece a menudo* │
│ *únicamente el símbolo "B & B".* │
└─────────────────────────────┘

bedbug ['bɛdbʌg] *n* chinche *f*.

bedclothes ['bɛdkləuðz] *npl* ropa de cama.

bedding ['bɛdɪŋ] *n* ropa de cama.

bedeck [bɪ'dɛk] *vt* engalanar, adornar.

bedevil [bɪ'dɛvl] *vt* (*dog*) acosar; (*trouble*) fastidiar.

bedfellow ['bɛdfɛləu] *n*: **they are strange** ~**s** (*fig*) hacen una pareja rara.

bedlam ['bɛdləm] *n* confusión *f*.

bedpan ['bɛdpæn] *n* cuña.

bedraggled [bɪ'drægld] *adj* desastrado.

bedridden ['bɛdrɪdn] *adj* postrado (en cama).

bedrock ['bɛdrɔk] *n* (*GEO*) roca firme; (*fig*) pilar *m*.

bedroom ['bɛdrum] *n* dormitorio, alcoba.

Beds *abbr* (*BRIT*) = *Bedfordshire*.

bed settee *n* sofá-cama *m*.

bedside ['bɛdsaɪd] *n*: **at sb's** ~ a la cabecera de alguien.

bedside lamp *n* lámpara de noche.

bedsit(ter) ['bɛdsɪt(ə*)] *n* (*BRIT*) estudio.

bedspread ['bɛdsprɛd] *n* cubrecama *m*, colcha.

bedtime ['bɛdtaɪm] *n* hora de acostarse; **it's** ~ es hora de acostarse *or* de irse a la cama.

bee [biː] *n* abeja; **to have a** ~ **in one's bonnet (about sth)** tener una idea fija (de algo).

beech [biːtʃ] *n* haya.

beef [biːf] *n* carne *f* de vaca; **roast** ~ rosbif *m*.

▸**beef up** *vt* (*col*) reforzar.

beefburger ['biːfbəːgə*] *n* hamburguesa.

beefeater ['biːfiːtə*] n alabardero de la Torre de Londres.

beehive ['biːhaɪv] n colmena.

bee-keeping ['biːkiːpɪŋ] n apicultura.

beeline ['biːlaɪn] n: **to make a ~ for** ir derecho a.

been [biːn] pp of **be**.

beep [biːp] n pitido ♦ vi pitar.

beeper ['biːpə*] n (of doctor etc) busca m inv.

beer [bɪə*] n cerveza.

beer belly n (col) barriga (de bebedor de cerveza).

beer can n bote m or lata de cerveza.

beet [biːt] n (US) remolacha.

beetle ['biːtl] n escarabajo.

beetroot ['biːtruːt] n (BRIT) remolacha.

befall [bɪ'fɔːl] vi (vt) (irreg: like **fall**) acontecer (a).

befit [bɪ'fɪt] vt convenir a, corresponder a.

before [bɪ'fɔː*] prep (of time) antes de; (of space) delante de ♦ conj antes (de) que ♦ adv (time) antes; (space) delante, adelante; ~ **going** antes de marcharse; ~ **she goes** antes de que se vaya; **the week** ~ la semana anterior; **I've never seen it** ~ no lo he visto nunca.

beforehand [bɪ'fɔːhænd] adv de antemano, con anticipación.

befriend [bɪ'frɛnd] vt ofrecer amistad a.

befuddled [bɪ'fʌdld] adj aturdido, atontado.

beg [bɛg] vi pedir limosna, mendigar ♦ vt pedir, rogar; (entreat) suplicar; **I ~ your pardon** (apologising) perdóneme; (not hearing) ¿perdón?

began [bɪ'gæn] pt of **begin**.

beggar ['bɛgə*] n mendigo/a.

begin, pt **began,** pp **begun** [bɪ'gɪn, -gæn, -gʌn] vt, vi empezar, comenzar; **to ~ doing** or **to do sth** empezar a hacer algo; **I can't ~ to thank you** no encuentro palabras para agradecerle; **to ~ with, I'd like to know ...** en primer lugar, quisiera saber ...; **~ning from Monday** a partir del lunes.

beginner [bɪ'gɪnə*] n principiante m/f.

beginning [bɪ'gɪnɪŋ] n principio, comienzo; **right from the ~** desde el principio.

begrudge [bɪ'grʌdʒ] vt: **to ~ sb sth** tenerle envidia a alguien por algo.

beguile [bɪ'gaɪl] vt (enchant) seducir.

beguiling [bɪ'gaɪlɪŋ] adj seductor(a), atractivo.

begun [bɪ'gʌn] pp of **begin**.

behalf [bɪ'hɑːf] n: **on ~ of,** (US) **in ~ of** en nombre de; (for benefit of) por.

behave [bɪ'heɪv] vi (person) portarse, comportarse; (thing) funcionar; (well: also: ~ **o.s.**) portarse bien.

behaviour, (US) **behavior** [bɪ'heɪvjə*] n

comportamiento, conducta.

behead [bɪ'hɛd] vt decapitar.

beheld [bɪ'hɛld] pt, pp of **behold**.

behind [bɪ'haɪnd] prep detrás de ♦ adv detrás, por detrás, atrás ♦ n trasero; **to be ~ (schedule)** ir retrasado; ~ **the scenes** (fig) entre bastidores; **we're ~ them in technology** (fig) nos dejan atrás en tecnología; **to leave sth ~** olvidar or dejarse algo; **to be ~ with sth** estar atrasado en algo; **to be ~ with payments (on sth)** estar atrasado en el pago (de algo).

behold [bɪ'həuld] (irreg: like **hold**) vt contemplar.

beige [beɪʒ] adj (color) beige.

being ['biːɪŋ] n ser m; **to come into ~** nacer, aparecer.

Beirut [beɪ'ruːt] n Beirut m.

Belarus [bɛlə'rus] n Bielorrusia.

Belarussian [bɛlə'rʌʃən] adj, n bielorruso/a ♦ n (LING) bielorruso.

belated [bɪ'leɪtɪd] adj atrasado, tardío.

belch [bɛltʃ] vi eructar ♦ vt (also: ~ **out:** smoke etc) vomitar, arrojar.

beleaguered [bɪ'liːgəd] adj asediado.

Belfast ['bɛlfɑːst] n Belfast m.

belfry ['bɛlfrɪ] n campanario.

Belgian ['bɛldʒən] adj, n belga m/f.

Belgium ['bɛldʒəm] n Bélgica.

Belgrade [bɛl'greɪd] n Belgrado.

belie [bɪ'laɪ] vt (give false impression of) desmentir, contradecir.

belief [bɪ'liːf] n (opinion) opinión f; (trust, faith) fe f; (acceptance as true) it's **beyond ~** es increíble; **in the ~ that** creyendo que.

believable [bɪ'liːvəbl] adj creíble.

believe [bɪ'liːv] vt, vi creer; **to ~ (that)** creer (que); **to ~ in** (God, ghosts) creer en; (method) ser partidario de; **he is ~d to be abroad** se cree que está en el extranjero; **I don't ~ in corporal punishment** no soy partidario del castigo corporal.

believer [bɪ'liːvə*] n (in idea, activity) partidario/a; (REL) creyente m/f, fiel m/f.

belittle [bɪ'lɪtl] vt despreciar.

Belize [bɛ'liːz] n Belice f.

bell [bɛl] n campana; (small) campanilla; (on door) timbre m; (animal's) cencerro; (on toy etc) cascabel m; **that rings a ~** (fig) eso me suena.

bellboy ['bɛlbɔɪ] n, (US) **bellhop** ['bɛlhɔp] n botones m inv.

belligerent [bɪ'lɪdʒərənt] adj (at war) beligerante; (fig) agresivo.

bellow ['bɛləu] *vi* bramar; (*person*) rugir
♦ *vt* (*orders*) gritar.
bellows ['bɛləuz] *npl* fuelle *msg*.
bell push *n* pulsador *m* de timbre.
belly ['bɛlɪ] *n* barriga, panza.
bellyache ['bɛlɪeɪk] *n* dolor *m* de barriga *or*
de tripa ♦ *vi* (*col*) gruñir.
bellyful ['bɛlɪful] *n*: **to have had a ~ of**
(*col*) estar más que harto de ....
belong [bɪ'lɔŋ] *vi*: **to ~ to** pertenecer a;
(*club etc*) ser socio de; **this book ~s here**
este libro va aquí.
belongings [bɪ'lɔŋɪŋz] *npl*: **personal ~**
pertenencias *fpl*.
Belorussia [bɛləu'rʌʃə] *n* Bielorrusia.
Belorussian [bɛləu'rʌʃən] *adj*, *n* =
Belarussian.
beloved [bɪ'lʌvɪd] *adj*, *n* querido/a *m/f*,
amado/a *m/f*.
below [bɪ'ləu] *prep* bajo, debajo de ♦ *adv*
abajo, (por) debajo; **see ~** véase más
abajo.
belt [bɛlt] *n* cinturón *m*; (*TECH*) correa,
cinta ♦ *vt* (*thrash*) golpear con correa;
industrial ~ cinturón industrial.
►**belt out** *vt* (*song*) cantar a voz en grito *or*
a grito pelado.
►**belt up** *vi* (*AUT*) ponerse el cinturón de
seguridad; (*fig, col*) cerrar el pico.
beltway ['bɛltweɪ] *n* (*US AUT*) carretera de
circunvalación.
bemoan [bɪ'məun] *vt* lamentar.
bemused [bɪ'mjuːzd] *adj* perplejo.
bench [bɛntʃ] *n* banco; **the B~** (*LAW*) el
tribunal; (*people*) la judicatura.
bench mark *n* punto de referencia.
bend [bɛnd] *vb* (*pt, pp* **bent** [bɛnt]) *vt* doblar;
(*body, head*) inclinar ♦ *vi* inclinarse; (*road*)
curvarse ♦ *n* (*BRIT: in road, river*) recodo;
(*in pipe*) codo; *see also* **bends**.
►**bend down** *vi* inclinarse, doblarse.
►**bend over** *vi* inclinarse.
bends [bɛndz] *npl* (*MED*) apoplejía por
cambios bruscos de presión.
beneath [bɪ'niːθ] *prep* bajo, debajo de;
(*unworthy of*) indigno de ♦ *adv* abajo, (por)
debajo.
benefactor ['bɛnɪfæktə*] *n* bienhechor *m*.
benefactress ['bɛnɪfæktrɪs] *n* bienhechora.
beneficial [bɛnɪ'fɪʃəl] *adj*: **~ to** beneficioso
para.
beneficiary [bɛnɪ'fɪʃərɪ] *n* (*LAW*)
beneficiario/a.
benefit ['bɛnɪfɪt] *n* beneficio, provecho;
(*allowance of money*) subsidio ♦ *vt*
beneficiar ♦ *vi*: **he'll ~ from it** le sacará
provecho; **unemployment ~** subsidio de
desempleo.

Benelux ['bɛnɪlʌks] *n* Benelux *m*.
benevolence [bɪ'nɛvələns] *n* benevolencia.
benevolent [bɪ'nɛvələnt] *adj* benévolo.
BEng *n abbr* (= *Bachelor of Engineering*)
título universitario.
benign [bɪ'naɪn] *adj* (*person, MED*) benigno;
(*smile*) afable.
bent [bɛnt] *pt, pp of* **bend** ♦ *n* inclinación *f*
♦ *adj* (*wire, pipe*) doblado, torcido; **to be**
~ on estar empeñado en.
bequeath [bɪ'kwiːð] *vt* legar.
bequest [bɪ'kwɛst] *n* legado.
bereaved [bɪ'riːvd] *adj* afligido ♦ *n*: **the ~**
los afligidos *mpl*.
bereavement [bɪ'riːvmənt] *n* aflicción *f*.
beret ['bɛreɪ] *n* boina.
Bering Sea ['bɛərɪŋ-] *n*: **the ~** el Mar de
Bering.
berk [bəːk] *n* (*BRIT col*) capullo/a (*!*).
Berks *abbr* (*BRIT*) = *Berkshire*.
Berlin [bəː'lɪn] *n* Berlín *m*; **East/West ~**
Berlín del Este/Oeste.
berm [bəːm] *n* (*US AUT*) arcén *m*.
Bermuda [bəː'mjuːdə] *n* las (Islas)
Bermudas.
Bermuda shorts *npl* bermudas *mpl or fpl*.
Bern [bəːn] *n* Berna.
berry ['bɛrɪ] *n* baya.
berserk [bə'səːk] *adj*: **to go ~** perder los
estribos.
berth [bəːθ] *n* (*bed*) litera; (*cabin*) camarote
m; (*for ship*) amarradero ♦ *vi* atracar,
amarrar; **to give sb a wide ~** (*fig*) evitar
encontrarse con algn.
beseech, *pt, pp* **besought** [bɪ'siːtʃ, -'sɔːt] *vt*
suplicar.
beset, *pt, pp* **beset** [bɪ'sɛt] *vt* (*person*) acosar
♦ *adj*: **a policy ~ with dangers** una política
rodeada de peligros.
besetting [bɪ'sɛtɪŋ] *adj*: **his ~ sin** su
principal falta.
beside [bɪ'saɪd] *prep* junto a, al lado de;
(*compared with*) comparado con; **to be ~**
o.s. with anger estar fuera de sí; **that's ~**
the point eso no tiene nada que ver con
el asunto.
besides [bɪ'saɪdz] *adv* además ♦ *prep* (*as well*
as) además de; (*except*) excepto.
besiege [bɪ'siːdʒ] *vt* (*town*) sitiar; (*fig*)
asediar.
besmirch [bɪ'sməːtʃ] *vt* (*fig*) manchar,
mancillar.
besotted [bɪ'sɔtɪd] *adj*: **~ with** chiflado por.
bespoke [bɪ'spəuk] *adj* (*garment*) hecho a la
medida; **~ tailor** sastre *m* que
confecciona a la medida.
best [bɛst] *adj* (el/la) mejor ♦ *adv* (lo) mejor;
the ~ part of (*quantity*) la mayor parte de;

at ~ en el mejor de los casos; **to make the ~ of sth** sacar el mejor partido de algo; **to do one's ~** hacer todo lo posible; **to the ~ of my knowledge** que yo sepa; **to the ~ of my ability** como mejor puedo; **the ~ thing to do is** ... lo mejor (que se puede hacer) es ...; **he's not exactly patient at the ~ of times** no es que tenga mucha paciencia precisamente.

bestial ['bestɪəl] *adj* bestial.

best man *n* padrino de boda.

bestow [bɪ'stəu] *vt* otorgar; (*honour, praise*) dispensar; **to ~ sth on sb** conceder *or* dar algo a algn.

bestseller ['best'selə*] *n* éxito de ventas, best-seller *m*.

bet [bet] *n* apuesta ♦ *vt, vi* (*pt, pp* **bet** *or* **betted**) apostar (*on* a); **it's a safe ~** (*fig*) es cosa segura.

Bethlehem ['beθlɪhem] *n* Belén *m*.

betray [bɪ'treɪ] *vt* traicionar; (*inform on*) delatar.

betrayal [bɪ'treɪəl] *n* traición *f*.

better ['betə*] *adj* mejor ♦ *adv* mejor ♦ *vt* mejorar; (*record etc*) superar ♦ *n*: **to get the ~ of sb** quedar por encima de algn; **you had ~ do it** más vale que lo hagas; **he thought ~ of it** cambió de parecer; **to get ~** mejorar(se); (*MED*) reponerse; **that's ~!** ¡eso es!; **I had ~ go** tengo que irme; **a change for the ~** una mejora; **~ off** *adj* más acomodado.

betting ['betɪŋ] *n* juego, apuestas *fpl*.

betting shop *n* (*BRIT*) casa de apuestas.

between [bɪ'twiːn] *prep* entre ♦ *adv* (*also in* **~:** *time*) mientras tanto; (: *place*) en medio; **the road ~ here and London** la carretera de aquí a Londres; **we only had 5 ~ us** teníamos sólo 5 entre todos.

bevel ['bevəl] *n* (*also:* **~ edge**) bisel *m*, chaflán *m*.

beverage ['bevərɪdʒ] *n* bebida.

bevy ['bevɪ] *n*: **a ~ of** una bandada de.

bewail [bɪ'weɪl] *vt* lamentar.

beware [bɪ'wɛə*] *vi*: **to ~ (of)** tener cuidado (con) ♦ *excl* ¡cuidado!

bewildered [bɪ'wɪldəd] *adj* aturdido, perplejo.

bewildering [bɪ'wɪldərɪŋ] *adj* desconcertante.

bewitching [bɪ'wɪtʃɪŋ] *adj* hechicero, encantador(a).

beyond [bɪ'jɔnd] *prep* más allá de; (*exceeding*) además de, fuera de; (*above*) superior a ♦ *adv* más allá, más lejos; **~ doubt** fuera de toda duda; **~ repair** irreparable.

b/f *abbr* (= *brought forward*) saldo previo.

BFPO *n abbr* (= *British Forces Post Office*) servicio postal del ejército.

bhp *n abbr* (= *brake horsepower*) potencia al freno.

bi ... [baɪ] *pref* bi ....

biannual [baɪ'ænjuəl] *adj* semestral.

bias ['baɪəs] *n* (*prejudice*) prejuicio; (*preference*) predisposición *f*.

bias(s)ed ['baɪəst] *adj* parcial; **to be ~ against** tener perjuicios contra.

biathlon [baɪ'æθlən] *n* biatlón *m*.

bib [bɪb] *n* babero.

Bible ['baɪbl] *n* Biblia.

biblical ['bɪblɪkəl] *adj* bíblico.

bibliography [bɪblɪ'ɔgrəfɪ] *n* bibliografía.

bicarbonate of soda [baɪ'kɑːbənɪt-] *n* bicarbonato de soda.

bicentenary [baɪsen'tiːnərɪ], (*US*) **bicentennial** [baɪsen'tenɪəl] *n* bicentenario.

biceps ['baɪseps] *n* bíceps *m*.

bicker ['bɪkə*] *vi* reñir.

bickering ['bɪkərɪŋ] *n* riñas *fpl*, altercados *mpl*.

bicycle ['baɪsɪkl] *n* bicicleta.

bicycle path *n* camino para ciclistas.

bicycle pump *n* bomba de bicicleta.

bid [bɪd] *n* (*at auction*) oferta, puja, postura; (*attempt*) tentativa, conato ♦ *vi* (*pt, pp* **bid**) hacer una oferta ♦ *vt* (*pt* **bade** [bæd], *pp* **bidden** ['bɪdn]) mandar, ordenar; **to ~ sb good day** dar a algn los buenos días.

bidder ['bɪdə*] *n*: **the highest ~** el mejor postor.

bidding ['bɪdɪŋ] *n* (*at auction*) ofertas *fpl*, puja; (*order*) orden *f*, mandato.

bide [baɪd] *vt*: **to ~ one's time** esperar el momento adecuado.

bidet ['biːdeɪ] *n* bidet *m*.

bidirectional ['baɪdɪ'rekʃənl] *adj* bidireccional.

biennial [baɪ'enɪəl] *adj, n* bienal *f*.

bier [bɪə*] *n* féretro.

bifocals [baɪ'fəuklz] *npl* gafas *fpl or* anteojos *mpl* (*LAM*) bifocales.

big [bɪg] *adj* grande; **~ business** gran negocio; **to do things in a ~ way** hacer las cosas en grande.

bigamy ['bɪgəmɪ] *n* bigamia.

big dipper [-'dɪpə*] *n* montaña rusa.

big end *n* (*AUT*) cabeza de biela.

biggish ['bɪgɪʃ] *adj* más bien grande; (*man*) más bien alto.

bigheaded ['bɪg'hedɪd] *adj* engreído.

bigot ['bɪgət] *n* fanático/a, intolerante *m/f*.

bigoted ['bɪgətɪd] *adj* fanático, intolerante.

bigotry ['bɪgətrɪ] *n* fanatismo, intolerancia.

big toe *n* dedo gordo (del pie).

big top n (*circus*) circo; (*main tent*) carpa principal.
big wheel n (*at fair*) noria.
bigwig ['bɪgwɪg] n (*col*) pez m gordo.
bike [baɪk] n bici f.
bikini [bɪ'kiːnɪ] n bikini m.
bilateral [baɪ'lætərl] adj (*agreement*) bilateral.
bile [baɪl] n bilis f.
bilge [bɪldʒ] n (*water*) agua de sentina.
bilingual [baɪ'lɪŋgwəl] adj bilingüe.
bilious ['bɪlɪəs] adj bilioso (*also fig*).
bill [bɪl] n (*gen*) cuenta; (*invoice*) factura; (*POL*) proyecto de ley; (*US: banknote*) billete m; (*of bird*) pico; (*notice*) cartel m; (*THEAT*) programa m ♦ vt extender or pasar la factura a; **may I have the ~ please?** ¿puede traerme la cuenta, por favor?; **~ of exchange** letra de cambio; **~ of lading** conocimiento de embarque; **~ of sale** escritura de venta; "**post no ~s**" "prohibido fijar carteles".
billboard ['bɪlbɔːd] n (*US*) valla publicitaria.
billet ['bɪlɪt] n alojamiento ♦ vt: **to ~ sb (on sb)** alojar a algn (con algn).
billfold ['bɪlfəʊld] n (*US*) cartera.
billiards ['bɪljədz] n billar m.
billion ['bɪljən] n (*BRIT*) billón m; (*US*) mil millones mpl.
billow ['bɪləʊ] n (*of smoke*) nube f; (*of sail*) ondulación f ♦ vi (*smoke*) salir en nubes; (*sail*) ondear, ondular.
billowy ['bɪləʊɪ] adj ondulante.
billy ['bɪlɪ] n (*US*) porra.
billy goat n macho cabrío.
bimbo ['bɪmbəʊ] n (*col*) tía buena sin seso.
bin [bɪn] n (*gen*) cubo or bote m (*LAM*) de la basura; **litter~** n (*BRIT*) papelera.
binary ['baɪnərɪ] adj (*MATH*) binario; **~ code** código binario; **~ system** sistema m binario.
bind, pt, pp **bound** [baɪnd, baʊnd] vt atar, liar; (*wound*) vendar; (*book*) encuadernar; (*oblige*) obligar.
▶**bind over** vt (*LAW*) obligar por vía legal.
▶**bind up** vt (*wound*) vendar; **to be bound up in** (*work, research etc*) estar absorto en; **to be bound up with** (*person*) estar estrechamente ligado a.
binder ['baɪndə*] n (*file*) archivador m.
binding ['baɪndɪŋ] adj (*contract*) vinculante.
binge [bɪndʒ] n borrachera, juerga; **to go on a ~** ir de juerga.
bingo ['bɪŋgəʊ] n bingo m.
bin-liner ['bɪnlaɪnə*] n bolsa de la basura.
binoculars [bɪ'nɔkjʊləz] npl prismáticos mpl, gemelos mpl.

biochemistry [baɪə'kemɪstrɪ] n bioquímica.
biodegradable ['baɪəʊdɪ'greɪdəbl] adj biodegradable.
biodiversity ['baɪəʊdaɪ'vəːsɪtɪ] n biodiversidad f.
biofuel ['baɪəʊfjuəl] n biocarburante m.
biographer [baɪ'ɔgrəfə*] n biógrafo/a.
biographical [baɪə'græfɪkəl] adj biográfico.
biography [baɪ'ɔgrəfɪ] n biografía.
biological [baɪə'lɔdʒɪkəl] adj biológico.
biological clock n reloj m biológico.
biologist [baɪ'ɔlədʒɪst] n biólogo/a.
biology [baɪ'ɔlədʒɪ] n biología.
biophysics ['baɪəʊ'fɪzɪks] nsg biofísica.
biopic ['baɪəʊpɪk] n filme m biográfico.
biopsy ['baɪɔpsɪ] n biopsia.
biosphere ['baɪəsfɪə*] n biosfera.
biotechnology ['baɪəʊtɛk'nɔlədʒɪ] n biotecnología.
biped ['baɪpɛd] n bípedo.
birch [bəːtʃ] n abedul m; (*cane*) vara.
bird [bəːd] n ave f, pájaro; (*BRIT col: girl*) chica.
birdcage ['bəːdkeɪdʒ] n jaula.
bird of prey n ave f de presa.
bird's-eye view ['bəːdzaɪ-] n vista de pájaro.
bird watcher n ornitólogo/a.
Biro ® ['baɪrəʊ] n bolígrafo.
birth [bəːθ] n nacimiento; (*MED*) parto; **to give ~ to** parir, dar a luz a; (*fig*) dar origen a.
birth certificate n partida de nacimiento.
birth control n control m de natalidad; (*methods*) métodos mpl anticonceptivos.
birthday ['bəːθdeɪ] n cumpleaños m inv.
birthplace ['bəːθpleɪs] n lugar m de nacimiento.
birth rate n (tasa de) natalidad f.
Biscay ['bɪskeɪ] n: **the Bay of ~** el Mar Cantábrico, el golfo de Vizcaya.
biscuit ['bɪskɪt] n (*BRIT*) galleta.
bisect [baɪ'sɛkt] vt (*also MATH*) bisecar.
bisexual ['baɪ'sɛksjuəl] adj, n bisexual m/f.
bishop ['bɪʃəp] n obispo; (*CHESS*) alfil m.
bistro ['biːstrəʊ] n café-bar m.
bit [bɪt] pt of **bite** ♦ n trozo, pedazo, pedacito; (*COMPUT*) bit m; (*for horse*) freno, bocado; **a ~ of** un poco de; **a ~ mad** algo loco; **~ by ~** poco a poco; **to come to ~s** (*break*) hacerse pedazos; **to do one's ~** aportar su granito de arena; **bring all your ~s and pieces** trae todas tus cosas.
bitch [bɪtʃ] n (*dog*) perra; (*col!*) zorra (*!*).
bite [baɪt] vt, vi (pt **bit** [bɪt], pp **bitten** ['bɪtn]) morder; (*insect etc*) picar ♦ n (*wound: of dog, snake etc*) mordedura; (*of insect*)

picadura; (*mouthful*) bocado; **to ~ one's
nails** morderse las uñas; **let's have a ~ (to
eat)** comamos algo.
biting ['baɪtɪŋ] *adj* (*wind*) que traspasa los
huesos; (*criticism*) mordaz.
bit part *n* (*THEAT*) papel *m* sin importancia,
papelito.
bitten ['bɪtn] *pp of* **bite**.
bitter ['bɪtə*] *adj* amargo; (*wind, criticism*)
cortante, penetrante; (*icy: weather*)
glacial; (*battle*) encarnizado ♦ *n* (*BRIT:
beer*) *cerveza típica británica a base de
lúpulos.*
bitterly ['bɪtəlɪ] *adv* (*disappoint, complain,
weep*) desconsoladamente; (*oppose,
criticise*) implacablemente; (*jealous*)
agriamente; **it's ~ cold** hace un frío
glacial.
bitterness ['bɪtənɪs] *n* amargura; (*anger*)
rencor *m*.
bitty ['bɪtɪ] *adj* deshilvanado.
bitumen ['bɪtjumɪn] *n* betún *m*.
bivouac ['bɪvuæk] *n* vivac *m*, vivaque *m*.
bizarre [bɪ'zɑ:*] *adj* raro, estrafalario.
bk *abbr* = **bank, book**.
BL *n abbr* (= *Bachelor of Law(s), Bachelor of
Letters*) *título universitario*; (*US:* =
Bachelor of Literature) *título universitario.*
bl *abbr* = **bill of lading**.
blab [blæb] *vi* cantar ♦ *vt* (*also:* ~ **out**)
soltar, contar.
black [blæk] *adj* (*colour*) negro; (*dark*)
oscuro ♦ *n* (*colour*) color *m* negro;
(*person*): **B~** negro/a ♦ *vt* (*shoes*) lustrar;
(*BRIT: INDUSTRY*) boicotear; **to give sb a ~
eye** ponerle a algn el ojo morado; ~
coffee café *m* solo; **there it is in ~ and
white** (*fig*) ahí está bien claro; **to be in the
~** (*in credit*) tener saldo positivo; ~ **and
blue** *adj* amoratado.
▶**black out** *vi* (*faint*) desmayarse.
black belt *n* (*SPORT*) cinturón *m* negro; (*US:
area*) zona negra.
blackberry ['blækbərɪ] *n* zarzamora.
blackbird ['blækbəːd] *n* mirlo.
blackboard ['blækbɔːd] *n* pizarra.
black box *n* (*AVIAT*) caja negra.
Black Country *n* (*BRIT*): **the ~** *región
industrial del centro de Inglaterra.*
blackcurrant ['blæk'kʌrənt] *n* grosella
negra.
black economy *n* economía sumergida.
blacken ['blækən] *vt* ennegrecer; (*fig*)
denigrar.
Black Forest *n*: **the ~** la Selva Negra.
blackguard ['blægɑːd] *n* canalla *m*, pillo.
black hole *n* (*ASTRO*) agujero negro.
black ice *n* hielo invisible en la carretera.

blackjack ['blækdʒæk] *n* (*US*) veintiuna.
blackleg ['blækleg] *n* (*BRIT*) esquirol *m/f*.
blacklist ['blæklɪst] *n* lista negra ♦ *vt* poner
en la lista negra.
blackmail ['blækmeɪl] *n* chantaje *m* ♦ *vt*
chantajear.
blackmailer ['blækmeɪlə*] *n* chantajista *m/f*.
black market *n* mercado negro,
estraperlo.
blackness ['blæknɪs] *n* negrura.
blackout ['blækaut] *n* (*TV, ELEC*) apagón *m*;
(*fainting*) desmayo, pérdida de
conocimiento.
black pepper *n* pimienta negra.
Black Sea *n*: **the ~** el Mar Negro.
black sheep *n* oveja negra.
blacksmith ['blæksmɪθ] *n* herrero.
black spot *n* (*AUT*) punto negro.
bladder ['blædə*] *n* vejiga.
blade [bleɪd] *n* hoja; (*cutting edge*) filo; **a ~
of grass** una brizna de hierba.
blame [bleɪm] *n* culpa ♦ *vt*: **to ~ sb for sth**
echar a algn la culpa de algo; **to be to ~
(for)** tener la culpa (de); **I'm not to ~** yo
no tengo la culpa; **and I don't ~ him** y lo
comprendo perfectamente.
blameless ['bleɪmlɪs] *adj* (*person*) inocente.
blanch [blɑːntʃ] *vi* (*person*) palidecer;
(*CULIN*) escaldar.
bland [blænd] *adj* suave; (*taste*) soso.
blank [blæŋk] *adj* en blanco; (*shot*) de
fogueo; (*look*) sin expresión ♦ *n* blanco,
espacio en blanco; cartucho de fogueo; **to
draw a ~** (*fig*) no conseguir nada.
blank cheque, (*US*) **blank check** *n*
cheque *m* en blanco.
blanket ['blæŋkɪt] *n* manta, frazada (*LAM*),
cobija (*LAM*) ♦ *adj* (*statement, agreement*)
comprensivo, general; **to give ~ cover**
(*subj: insurance policy*) dar póliza a todo
riesgo.
blankly ['blæŋklɪ] *adv*: **she looked at me ~**
me miró sin comprender.
blare [bleə*] *vi* (*brass band, horns, radio*)
resonar.
blasé ['blɑːzeɪ] *adj* de vuelta de todo.
blaspheme [blæs'fiːm] *vi* blasfemar.
blasphemous ['blæsfɪməs] *adj* blasfemo.
blasphemy ['blæsfɪmɪ] *n* blasfemia.
blast [blɑːst] *n* (*of wind*) ráfaga, soplo; (*of
whistle*) toque *m*; (*of explosive*) carga
explosiva; (*force*) choque *m* ♦ *vt* (*blow up*)
volar; (*blow open*) abrir con carga
explosiva ♦ *excl* (*BRIT col*) ¡maldito sea!;
(at) full ~ (*also fig*) a toda marcha.
▶**blast off** *vi* (*spacecraft etc*) despegar.
blast furnace *n* alto horno.
blast-off ['blɑːstɔf] *n* (*SPACE*) lanzamiento.

blatant ['bleɪtənt] *adj* descarado.
blatantly ['bleɪtəntlɪ] *adv*: **it's ~ obvious** está clarísimo.
blather ['blæðə*] *vi* decir tonterías.
blaze [bleɪz] *n* (*fire*) fuego; (*flames*) llamarada; (*glow: of fire, sun etc*) resplandor *m*; (*fig*) arranque *m* ♦ *vi* (*fire*) arder con llamaradas; (*fig*) brillar ♦ *vt*: **to ~ a trail** (*fig*) abrir (un) camino; **in a ~ of publicity** bajo los focos de la publicidad.
blazer ['bleɪzə*] *n chaqueta de uniforme de colegial o de socio de club*.
bleach [bliːtʃ] *n* (*also*: **household ~**) lejía ♦ *vt* (*linen*) blanquear.
bleached [bliːtʃt] *adj* (*hair*) de colorado; (*clothes*) blanqueado.
bleachers ['bliːtʃəz] *npl* (*US SPORT*) gradas *fpl*.
bleak [bliːk] *adj* (*countryside*) desierto; (*landscape*) desolado, desierto; (*weather*) desapacible; (*smile*) triste; (*prospect, future*) poco prometedor(a).
bleary-eyed ['blɪərɪ'aɪd] *adj*: **to be ~** tener ojos de cansado.
bleat [bliːt] *vi* balar.
bleed, *pt*, *pp* **bled** [bliːd, bled] *vt* sangrar; (*brakes, radiator*) desaguar ♦ *vi* sangrar.
bleeding ['bliːdɪŋ] *adj* sangrante.
bleep [bliːp] *n* pitido ♦ *vi* pitar ♦ *vt* llamar por el busca.
bleeper ['bliːpə*] *n* (*of doctor etc*) busca *m*.
blemish ['blemɪʃ] *n* mancha, tacha.
blench [blentʃ] *vi* (*shrink back*) acobardarse; (*grow pale*) palidecer.
blend [blend] *n* mezcla ♦ *vt* mezclar ♦ *vi* (*colours etc*) combinarse, mezclarse.
blender ['blendə*] *n* (*CULIN*) batidora.
bless, *pt*, *pp* **blessed** or **blest** [bles, blest] *vt* bendecir.
blessed ['blesɪd] *adj* (*REL: holy*) santo, bendito; (: *happy*) dichoso; **every ~ day** cada santo día.
blessing ['blesɪŋ] *n* bendición *f*; (*advantage*) beneficio, ventaja; **to count one's ~s** agradecer lo que se tiene; **it was a ~ in disguise** no hay mal que por bien no venga.
blew [bluː] *pt of* **blow**.
blight [blaɪt] *vt* (*hopes etc*) frustrar, arruinar.
blimey ['blaɪmɪ] *excl* (*BRIT col*) ¡caray!
blind [blaɪnd] *adj* ciego ♦ *n* (*for window*) persiana ♦ *vt* cegar; (*dazzle*) deslumbrar.
blind alley *n* callejón *m* sin salida.
blind corner *n* (*BRIT*) esquina or curva sin visibilidad.
blind date *n* cita a ciegas.
blinders ['blaɪndəz] *npl* (*US*) anteojeras *fpl*.

blindfold ['blaɪndfəuld] *n* venda ♦ *adj, adv* con los ojos vendados ♦ *vt* vendar los ojos a.
blinding ['blaɪndɪŋ] *adj* (*flash, light*) cegador; (*pain*) intenso.
blindingly ['blaɪndɪŋlɪ] *adv*: **it's ~ obvious** salta a la vista.
blindly ['blaɪndlɪ] *adv* a ciegas, ciegamente.
blindness ['blaɪndnɪs] *n* ceguera.
blind spot *n* (*AUT*) ángulo muerto; **to have a ~ about sth** estar ciego para algo.
blink [blɪŋk] *vi* parpadear, pestañear; (*light*) oscilar; **to be on the ~** (*col*) estar estropeado.
blinkers ['blɪŋkəz] *npl* (*esp Brit*) anteojeras *fpl*.
blinking ['blɪŋkɪŋ] *adj* (*col*): **this ~...** este condenado....
blip [blɪp] *n* señal *f* luminosa; (*on graph*) pequeña desviación *f*; (*fig*) pequeña anomalía.
bliss [blɪs] *n* felicidad *f*.
blissful ['blɪsful] *adj* dichoso; **in ~ ignorance** feliz en la ignorancia.
blissfully ['blɪsfulɪ] *adv* (*sigh, smile*) con felicidad; **~ happy** sumamente feliz.
blister ['blɪstə*] *n* (*on skin, paint*) ampolla ♦ *vi* ampollarse.
blistering ['blɪstərɪŋ] *adj* (*heat*) abrasador(a).
blithely ['blaɪðlɪ] *adv* alegremente, despreocupadamente.
blithering ['blɪðərɪŋ] *adj* (*col*): **this ~ idiot** este tonto perdido.
BLit(t) *n abbr* (= *Bachelor of Literature*) *título universitario*.
blitz [blɪts] *n* bombardeo aéreo; **to have a ~ on sth** (*fig*) emprenderla con algo.
blizzard ['blɪzəd] *n* ventisca.
BLM *n abbr* (*US*) = *Bureau of Land Management*.
bloated ['bləutɪd] *adj* hinchado.
blob [blɔb] *n* (*drop*) gota; (*stain, spot*) mancha.
bloc [blɔk] *n* (*POL*) bloque *m*.
block [blɔk] *n* bloque *m* (*also COMPUT*); (*in pipes*) obstáculo; (*of buildings*) manzana ♦ *vt* (*gen*) obstruir, cerrar; (*progress*) estorbar; (*COMPUT*) agrupar; **~ of flats** (*BRIT*) bloque *m* de pisos; **mental ~** amnesia temporal; **~ and tackle** (*TECH*) aparejo de polea; **3 ~s from here** a 3 manzanas or cuadras (*LAM*) de aquí.
▶**block up** *vt* tapar, obstruir; (*pipe*) atascar.
blockade [blɔ'keɪd] *n* bloqueo ♦ *vt* bloquear.
blockage ['blɔkɪdʒ] *n* estorbo, obstrucción *f*.

block booking n reserva en grupo.
blockbuster ['blɔkbʌstə*] n (book) best-seller m; (film) éxito de público.
block capitals npl mayúsculas fpl.
block letters npl letras fpl de molde.
block release n (BRIT) exención f por estudios.
block vote n (BRIT) voto por delegación.
bloke [bləuk] n (BRIT col) tipo, tío.
blond(e) [blɔnd] adj, n rubio/a m/f.
blood [blʌd] n sangre f; **new ~** (fig) gente f nueva.
blood bank n banco de sangre.
blood count n recuento de glóbulos rojos y blancos.
blood donor n donante m/f de sangre.
blood group n grupo sanguíneo.
bloodhound ['blʌdhaund] n sabueso.
bloodless ['blʌdlɪs] adj (pale) exangüe; (revolt etc) sin derramamiento de sangre, incruento.
bloodletting ['blʌdletɪŋ] n (MED) sangría; (fig) sangría, carnicería.
blood poisoning n septicemia de la sangre.
blood pressure n tensión f sanguínea; **to have high/low ~** tener la tensión alta/baja.
bloodshed ['blʌdʃed] n baño de sangre.
bloodshot ['blʌdʃɔt] adj inyectado en sangre.
bloodstained ['blʌdsteɪnd] adj manchado de sangre.
bloodstream ['blʌdstriːm] n corriente f sanguínea.
blood test n análisis m de sangre.
bloodthirsty ['blʌdθəːstɪ] adj sanguinario.
blood transfusion n transfusión f de sangre.
blood type n grupo sanguíneo.
blood vessel n vaso sanguíneo.
bloody ['blʌdɪ] adj sangriento; (BRIT col!): **this ~...** este condenado or fregado (! AM) ... (!) ♦ adv (BRIT col!): **~ strong/good** terriblemente fuerte/bueno.
bloody-minded ['blʌdɪ'maɪndɪd] adj (BRIT col) con malas pulgas.
bloom [bluːm] n floración f; **in ~** en flor ♦ vi florecer.
blooming ['bluːmɪŋ] adj (col): **this ~...** este condenado....
blossom ['blɔsəm] n flor f ♦ vi florecer; (fig) desarrollarse; **to ~ into** (fig) convertirse en.
blot [blɔt] n borrón m ♦ vt (dry) secar; (stain) manchar; **to ~ out** vt (view) tapar; (memories) borrar; **to be a ~ on the landscape** estropear el paisaje; **to ~**

one's copy book (fig) manchar su reputación.
blotchy ['blɔtʃɪ] adj (complexion) lleno de manchas.
blotter ['blɔtə*] n secante m.
blotting paper ['blɔtɪŋ-] n papel m secante.
blotto ['blɔtəu] adj (col) mamado.
blouse [blauz] n blusa.
blow [bləu] n golpe m ♦ vb (pt **blew**, pp **blown** [bluː, bləun]) vi soplar; (fuse) fundirse ♦ vt (glass) soplar; (fuse) quemar; (instrument) tocar; **to come to ~s** llegar a golpes; **to ~ one's nose** sonarse.
▶**blow away** vt llevarse, arrancar.
▶**blow down** vt derribar.
▶**blow off** vt arrebatar.
▶**blow out** vt apagar ♦ vi apagarse; (tyre) reventar.
▶**blow over** vi amainar.
▶**blow up** vi estallar ♦ vt volar; (tyre) inflar; (PHOT) ampliar.
blow-dry ['bləudraɪ] n secado con secador de mano ♦ vt secar con secador de mano.
blowlamp ['bləulæmp] n (BRIT) soplete m, lámpara de soldar.
blow-out ['bləuaut] n (of tyre) pinchazo; (col: big meal) banquete m, festín m.
blowtorch ['bləutɔːtʃ] n = **blowlamp**.
blow-up ['bləuʌp] n (PHOT) ampliación f.
blowzy ['blauzɪ] adj (BRIT) dejado, desaliñado.
BLS n abbr (US) = Bureau of Labor Statistics.
blubber ['blʌbə*] n grasa de ballena ♦ vi (pej) lloriquear.
bludgeon ['blʌdʒən] vt: **to ~ sb into doing sth** coaccionar a algn a hacer algo.
blue [bluː] adj azul; **~ film** película porno; **~ joke** chiste verde; **once in a ~ moon** de higos a brevas; **to come out of the ~** (fig) ser completamente inesperado; see also **blues**.
blue baby n niño azul or cianótico.
bluebell ['bluːbel] n campanilla, campánula azul.
blue-blooded [bluː'blʌdɪd] adj de sangre azul.
bluebottle ['bluːbɔtl] n moscarda, mosca azul.
blue cheese n queso azul.
blue-chip ['bluːtʃɪp] n: **~ investment** inversión f asegurada.
blue-collar worker ['bluːkɔlə*-] n obrero/a.
blue jeans npl tejanos mpl, vaqueros mpl.
blueprint ['bluːprɪnt] n proyecto; **~ (for)** (fig) anteproyecto (de).
blues [bluːz] npl: **the ~** (MUS) el blues; **to have the ~** estar triste.
bluff [blʌf] vi tirarse un farol, farolear ♦ n

bluff *m*, farol *m*; (*GEO*) precipicio, despeñadero; **to call sb's** ~ coger a algn en un renuncio.

bluish ['bluːɪʃ] *adj* azulado.

blunder ['blʌndə*] *n* patinazo, metedura de pata ♦ *vi* cometer un error, meter la pata; **to** ~ **into sb/sth** tropezar con algn/algo.

blunt [blʌnt] *adj* (*knife*) desafilado; (*person*) franco, directo ♦ *vt* embotar, desafilar; **this pencil is** ~ este lápiz está despuntado; ~ **instrument** (*LAW*) instrumento contundente.

bluntly ['blʌntlɪ] *adv* (*speak*) francamente, de modo terminante.

bluntness ['blʌntnɪs] *n* (*of person*) franqueza, brusquedad *f*.

blur [bləː*] *n* aspecto borroso ♦ *vt* (*vision*) enturbiar; (*memory*) empañar.

blurb [bləːb] *n* propaganda.

blurred [bləːd] *adj* borroso.

blurt [bləːt]: **to** ~ **out** *vt* (*say*) descolgarse con, dejar escapar.

blush [blʌʃ] *vi* ruborizarse, ponerse colorado ♦ *n* rubor *m*.

blusher ['blʌʃə*] *n* colorete *m*.

bluster ['blʌstə*] *n* fanfarronada, bravata ♦ *vi* fanfarronear, echar bravatas.

blustering ['blʌstərɪŋ] *adj* (*person*) fanfarrón/ona.

blustery ['blʌstərɪ] *adj* (*weather*) tempestuoso, tormentoso.

Blvd *abbr* = **boulevard**.

BM *n abbr* = *British Museum*; (*UNIV*: = *Bachelor of Medicine*) *título universitario*.

BMA *n abbr* = *British Medical Association*.

BMJ *n abbr* = *British Medical Journal*.

BMus *n abbr* (= *Bachelor of Music*) *título universitario*.

BMX *n abbr* (= *bicycle motocross*) BMX *f*; ~ **bike** bici(cleta) *f* BMX.

BO *n abbr* (*col*: = *body odour*) olor *m* a sudor; (*US*) = **box office**.

boa ['bəuə] *n* boa.

boar [bɔː*] *n* verraco, cerdo.

board [bɔːd] *n* tabla, tablero; (*on wall*) tablón *m*; (*for chess etc*) tablero; (*committee*) junta, consejo; (*in firm*) mesa *or* junta directiva; (*NAUT, AVIAT*): **on** ~ a bordo ♦ *vt* (*ship*) embarcarse en; (*train*) subir a; **full** ~ (*BRIT*) pensión *f* completa; **half** ~ (*BRIT*) media pensión; ~ **and lodging** alojamiento y comida; **to go by the** ~ (*fig*) irse por la borda; **above** ~ (*fig*) sin tapujos; **across the** ~ (*fig: adv*) en todos los niveles; (: *adj*) general.

▶**board up** *vt* (*door*) tapar, cegar.

boarder ['bɔːdə*] *n* huésped(a) *m/f*; (*SCOL*) interno/a.

board game *n* juego de tablero.

boarding card ['bɔːdɪŋ-] *n* (*BRIT: AVIAT, NAUT*) tarjeta de embarque.

boarding house ['bɔːdɪŋ-] *n* casa de huéspedes.

boarding party ['bɔːdɪŋ-] *n* brigada de inspección.

boarding pass ['bɔːdɪŋ-] *n* (*US*) = **boarding card**.

boarding school ['bɔːdɪŋ-] *n* internado.

board meeting *n* reunión *f* de la junta directiva.

board room *n* sala de juntas.

boardwalk ['bɔːdwɔːk] *n* (*US*) paseo entablado.

boast [bəust] *vi*: **to** ~ **(about** *or* **of)** alardear (de) ♦ *vt* ostentar ♦ *n* alarde *m*, baladronada.

boastful ['bəustfəl] *adj* presumido, jactancioso.

boastfulness ['bəustfulnɪs] *n* fanfarronería, jactancia.

boat [bəut] *n* barco, buque *m*; (*small*) barca, bote *m*; **to go by** ~ ir en barco.

boater ['bəutə*] *n* (*hat*) canotié *m*.

boating ['bəutɪŋ] *n* canotaje *m*.

boatman ['bəutmən] *n* barquero.

boat people *npl refugiados que huyen en barca.*

boatswain ['bəusn] *n* contramaestre *m*.

bob [bɔb] *vi* (*boat, cork on water: also:* ~ **up and down**) menearse, balancearse ♦ *n* (*BRIT col*) = **shilling**.

▶**bob up** *vi* (re)aparecer de repente.

bobbin ['bɔbɪn] *n* (*of sewing machine*) carrete *m*, bobina.

bobby ['bɔbɪ] *n* (*BRIT col*) poli *m/f*.

bobsleigh ['bɔbsleɪ] *n* bob *m*, trineo de competición *f*.

bode [bəud] *vi*: **to** ~ **well/ill (for)** ser de buen/mal agüero (para).

bodice ['bɔdɪs] *n* corpiño.

-bodied ['bɔdɪd] *adj suff* de cuerpo ....

bodily ['bɔdɪlɪ] *adj* (*comfort, needs*) corporal; (*pain*) corpóreo ♦ *adv* (*in person*) en persona; (*carry*) corporalmente; (*lift*) en peso.

body ['bɔdɪ] *n* cuerpo; (*corpse*) cadáver *m*; (*of car*) caja, carrocería; (*also:* ~ **stocking**) body *m*; (*fig: organization*) organización *f*; (: *public*) organismo; (: *quantity*) masa; (: *of speech, document*) parte *f* principal; **ruling** ~ directiva; **in a** ~ todos juntos, en masa.

body blow *n* (*fig*) palo.

body-building ['bɔdɪˈbɪldɪŋ] *n* culturismo.

bodyguard ['bɔdɪgɑːd] *n* guardaespaldas *m inv*.

body language *n* lenguaje *m* gestual.
body search *n* cacheo; **to carry out a ~ on sb** registrar a algn; **to submit to** *or* **undergo a ~** ser registrado.
bodywork ['bɔdiwɔːk] *n* carrocería.
boffin ['bɔfɪn] *n* (*BRIT*) científico/a.
bog [bɔg] *n* pantano, ciénaga ♦ *vt*: **to get ~ged down** (*fig*) empantanarse, atascarse.
boggle ['bɔgl] *vi*: **the mind ~s!** ¡no puedo creerlo!
Bogotá [bəugə'taː] *n* Bogotá.
bogus ['bəugəs] *adj* falso, fraudulento; (*person*) fingido.
Bohemia [bə'hiːmɪə] *n* Bohemia.
Bohemian [bə'hiːmɪən] *adj*, *n* bohemio/a *m/f*.
boil [bɔɪl] *vt* cocer; (*eggs*) pasar por agua ♦ *vi* hervir ♦ *n* (*MED*) furúnculo, divieso; **to bring to the ~** calentar hasta que hierva; **to come to the** (*BRIT*) *or* **a** (*US*) **~** comenzar a hervir; **~ed egg** huevo pasado por agua; **~ed potatoes** patatas *fpl* *or* papas *fpl* (*LAM*) cocidas.
►**boil down** *vi* (*fig*): **to ~ down to** reducirse a.
►**boil over** *vi* (*liquid*) rebosar; (*anger, resentment*) llegar al colmo.
boiler ['bɔɪlə*] *n* caldera.
boiler suit *n* (*BRIT*) mono, overol *m* (*LAM*).
boiling ['bɔɪlɪŋ] *adj*: **I'm ~** (**hot**) (*col*) estoy asado.
boiling point *n* punto de ebullición *f*.
boil-in-the-bag [bɔɪlɪnðə'bæg] *adj*: **~ meals** platos que se cuecen en su misma bolsa.
boisterous ['bɔɪstərəs] *adj* (*noisy*) bullicioso; (*excitable*) exuberante; (*crowd*) tumultuoso.
bold [bəuld] *adj* (*brave*) valiente, audaz; (*pej*) descarado; (*outline*) grueso; (*colour*) vivo; **~ type** (*TYP*) negrita.
boldly ['bəuldlɪ] *adv* audazmente.
boldness ['bəuldnɪs] *n* valor *m*, audacia; (*cheek*) descaro.
Bolivia [bə'lɪvɪə] *n* Bolivia.
Bolivian [bə'lɪvɪən] *adj*, *n* boliviano/a *m/f*.
bollard ['bɔləd] *n* (*BRIT AUT*) poste *m*.
bolshy ['bɔlʃɪ] *adj* (*BRIT col*) protestón/ona; **to be in a ~ mood** tener el día protestón.
bolster ['bəulstə*] *n* travesero, cabezal *m*.
►**bolster up** *vt* reforzar; (*fig*) alentar.
bolt [bəult] *n* (*lock*) cerrojo; (*with nut*) perno, tornillo ♦ *adv*: **~ upright** rígido, erguido ♦ *vt* (*door*) echar el cerrojo a; (*food*) engullir ♦ *vi* fugarse; (*horse*) desbocarse.
bomb [bɔm] *n* bomba ♦ *vt* bombardear.
bombard [bɔm'baːd] *vt* bombardear, (*fig*) asediar.

bombardment [bɔm'baːdmənt] *n* bombardeo.
bombastic [bɔm'bæstɪk] *adj* rimbombante; (*person*) pomposo.
bomb disposal *n* desactivación *f* de explosivos.
bomb disposal expert *n* artificiero/a.
bomber ['bɔmə*] *n* (*AVIAT*) bombardero; (*terrorist*) persona que pone bombas.
bombing ['bɔmɪŋ] *n* bombardeo.
bomb scare *n* amenaza de bomba.
bombshell ['bɔmʃel] *n* obús *m*, granada; (*fig*) bomba.
bomb site *n* lugar *m* donde estalló una bomba.
bona fide ['bəunə'faɪdɪ] *adj* genuino, auténtico.
bonanza [bə'nænzə] *n* bonanza.
bond [bɔnd] *n* (*binding promise*) fianza; (*FINANCE*) bono; (*link*) vínculo, lazo; **in ~** (*COMM*) en depósito bajo fianza.
bondage ['bɔndɪdʒ] *n* esclavitud *f*.
bonded goods ['bɔndɪd-] *npl* mercancías *fpl* en depósito de aduanas.
bonded warehouse ['bɔndɪd-] *n* depósito de aduanas.
bone [bəun] *n* hueso; (*of fish*) espina ♦ *vt* deshuesar; quitar las espinas a; **~ of contention** manzana de la discordia.
bone china *n* porcelana fina.
bone-dry ['bəun'draɪ] *adj* completamente seco.
bone idle *adj* gandul.
bone marrow *n* médula; **~ transplant** transplante *m* de médula.
boner ['bəunə*] *n* (*US col*) plancha, patochada.
bonfire ['bɔnfaɪə*] *n* hoguera, fogata.
bonk [bɔŋk] *vt*, *vi* (*hum, col*) chingar (*!*).
bonkers ['bɔŋkəz] *adj* (*BRIT col*) majareta.
Bonn [bɔn] *n* Bonn *m*.
bonnet ['bɔnɪt] *n* gorra; (*BRIT: of car*) capó *m*.
bonny ['bɔnɪ] *adj* (*esp Scottish*) bonito, hermoso, lindo.
bonus ['bəunəs] *n* (*at Christmas etc*) paga extraordinaria; (*merit award*) sobrepaga, prima.
bony ['bəunɪ] *adj* (*arm, face, MED: tissue*) huesudo; (*meat*) lleno de huesos; (*fish*) lleno de espinas; (*thin: person*) flaco, delgado.
boo [buː] *vt* abuchear.
boob [buːb] *n* (*col: mistake*) disparate *m*, sandez *f*; (*: breast*) teta.
booby prize ['buːbɪ-] *n* premio de consolación (*al último*).
booby trap ['buːbɪ-] *n* (*MIL etc*) trampa

explosiva.

book [buk] *n* libro; (*notebook*) libreta; (*of stamps etc*) librillo; ~s (*COMM*) cuentas *fpl*, contabilidad *f* ♦ *vt* (*ticket, seat, room*) reservar; (*driver*) fichar; (*FOOTBALL*) amonestar; **to keep the** ~s llevar las cuentas *or* los libros; **by the** ~ según las reglas; **to throw the** ~ **at sb** echar un rapapolvo a algn.

►**book in** *vi* (*at hotel*) registrarse.

►**book up** *vt*: **all seats are** ~**ed up** todas las plazas están reservadas; **the hotel is** ~**ed up** el hotel está lleno.

bookable ['bukəbl] *adj*: **seats are** ~ los asientos se pueden reservar (de antemano).

bookcase ['bukkeɪs] *n* librería, estante *m* para libros.

booking office ['bukɪŋ-] *n* (*BRIT: RAIL*) despacho de billetes *or* boletos (*LAM*); (: *THEAT*) taquilla, boletería (*LAM*).

book-keeping ['buk'ki:pɪŋ] *n* contabilidad *f*.

booklet ['buklɪt] *n* folleto.

bookmaker ['bukmeɪkə*] *n* corredor *m* de apuestas.

bookseller ['buksɛlə*] *n* librero/a.

bookshelf ['bukʃɛlf] *n* estante *m*.

bookshop ['bukʃɔp] *n* librería.

bookstall ['bukstɔːl] *n* quiosco de libros.

book store *n* = **bookshop**.

book token *n* vale *m* para libros.

book value *n* (*COMM*) valor *m* contable.

bookworm ['bukwə:m] *n* (*fig*) ratón *m* de biblioteca.

boom [bu:m] *n* (*noise*) trueno, estampido; (*in prices etc*) alza rápida; (*ECON*) boom *m*, auge *m* ♦ *vi* (*cannon*) hacer gran estruendo, retumbar; (*ECON*) estar en alza.

boomerang ['bu:məræŋ] *n* bumerang *m* (*also fig*) ♦ *vi*: **to** ~ **on sb** (*fig*) ser contraproducente para algn.

boom town *n* ciudad *f* de crecimiento rápido.

boon [bu:n] *n* favor *m*, beneficio.

boorish ['buərɪʃ] *adj* grosero.

boost [bu:st] *n* estímulo, empuje *m* ♦ *vt* estimular, empujar; (*increase: sales, production*) aumentar; **to give a** ~ **to** (*morale*) levantar; **it gave a** ~ **to his confidence** le dio confianza en sí mismo.

booster ['bu:stə*] *n* (*MED*) reinyección *f*; (*TV*) repetidor *m*; (*ELEC*) elevador *m* de tensión; (*also*: ~ **rocket**) cohete *m*.

boot [bu:t] *n* bota; (*ankle* ~) botín *m*, borceguí *m*; (*BRIT: of car*) maleta, maletero, baúl *m* (*LAM*) ♦ *vt* dar un

puntapié a; (*COMPUT*) arrancar; **to** ~ (*in addition*) además, por añadidura; **to give sb the** ~ (*col*) despedir a algn, poner a algn en la calle.

booth [bu:ð] *n* (*at fair*) barraca; (*telephone* ~, *voting* ~) cabina.

bootleg ['bu:tlɛg] *adj* de contrabando; ~ **record** disco pirata.

booty ['bu:tɪ] *n* botín *m*.

booze [bu:z] (*col*) *n* bebida ♦ *vi* emborracharse.

boozer ['bu:zə*] *n* (*col: person*) bebedor(a) *m/f*; (: *BRIT: pub*) bar *m*.

border ['bɔ:də*] *n* borde *m*, margen *m*; (*of a country*) frontera ♦ *adj* fronterizo; **the B~s** *región fronteriza entre Escocia e Inglaterra*.

►**border on** *vt fus* lindar con; (*fig*) rayar en.

borderline ['bɔ:dəlaɪn] *n* (*fig*) frontera.

bore [bɔ:*] *pt of* **bear** ♦ *vt* (*hole*) taladrar; (*person*) aburrir ♦ *n* (*person*) pelmazo, pesado; (*of gun*) calibre *m*.

bored [bɔ:d] *adj* aburrido; **he's** ~ **to tears** *or* **to death** *or* **stiff** está aburrido como una ostra, está muerto de aburrimiento.

boredom ['bɔ:dəm] *n* aburrimiento.

boring ['bɔ:rɪŋ] *adj* aburrido, pesado.

born [bɔ:n] *adj*: **to be** ~ nacer; **I was** ~ **in 1960** nací en 1960.

born-again [bɔ:nə'gɛn] *adj*: ~ **Christian** evangelista *m/f*.

borne [bɔ:n] *pp of* **bear**.

Borneo ['bɔ:nɪəu] *n* Borneo.

borough ['bʌrə] *n* municipio.

borrow ['bɔrəu] *vt*: **to** ~ **sth (from sb)** tomar algo prestado (a alguien); **may I** ~ **your car?** ¿me prestas tu coche?

borrower ['bɔrəuə*] *n* prestatario/a.

borrowing ['bɔrəuɪŋ] *n* préstamos *mpl*.

borstal ['bɔ:stl] *n* (*BRIT*) reformatorio (de menores).

Bosnia ['bɔznɪə] *n* Bosnia.

Bosnia-Herzegovina, Bosnia-Hercegovina ['bɔ:snɪəhɛrzə'gəuvi:nə] *n* Bosnia-Herzegovina.

Bosnian ['bɔznɪən] *adj, n* bosnio/a.

bosom ['buzəm] *n* pecho; (*fig*) seno; ~ **friend** *n* amigo/a íntimo/a *or* del alma.

boss [bɔs] *n* jefe/a *m/f*; (*employer*) patrón/ona *m/f*; (*political etc*) cacique *m* ♦ *vt* (*also*: ~ **about** *or* **around**) mangonear; **stop** ~**ing everyone about!** ¡deja de dar órdenes *or* de mangonear a todos!

bossy ['bɔsɪ] *adj* mandón/ona.

bosun ['bəusn] *n* contramaestre *m*.

botanical [bə'tænɪkl] *adj* botánico.

botanist ['bɔtənɪst] *n* botanista *m/f*.

botany ['bɔtənɪ] *n* botánica.

botch [bɔtʃ] *vt* (*also*: ~ **up**) arruinar, estropear.

both [bəʊθ] *adj, pron* ambos/as, los/las dos; ~ **of us went, we** ~ **went** fuimos los dos, ambos fuimos ♦ *adv*: ~ **A and B** tanto A como B.

bother ['bɔðə*] *vt* (*worry*) preocupar; (*disturb*) molestar, fastidiar, fregar (*LAM*), embromar (*LAM*) ♦ *vi* (*gen*: ~ **o.s.**) molestarse ♦ *n*: **what a** ~! ¡qué lata! ♦ *excl* ¡maldita sea!, ¡caramba!; **I'm sorry to** ~ **you** perdona que te moleste; **to** ~ **doing** tomarse la molestia de hacer; **please don't** ~ no te molestes.

Botswana [bɔt'swɑːnə] *n* Botswana.

bottle ['bɔtl] *n* botella; (*small*) frasco; (*baby's*) biberón *m* ♦ *vt* embotellar; ~ **of wine/milk** botella de vino/de leche; **wine/milk** ~ botella de vino/de leche.

►**bottle up** *vt* (*fig*) contener, reprimir.

bottle bank *n* contenedor *m* de vidrio, iglú *m*.

bottleneck ['bɔtlnɛk] *n* embotellamiento.

bottle-opener ['bɔtləʊpnə*] *n* abrebotellas *m inv*.

bottom ['bɔtəm] *n* (*of box, sea*) fondo; (*buttocks*) trasero, culo; (*of page, mountain, tree*) pie *m*; (*of list*) final *m* ♦ *adj* (*lowest*) más bajo; (*last*) último; **to get to the** ~ **of sth** (*fig*) llegar al fondo de algo.

bottomless ['bɔtəmlɪs] *adj* sin fondo, insondable.

bottom line *n*: **the** ~ lo fundamental; **the** ~ **is he has to go** el caso es que tenemos que despedirle.

bough [baʊ] *n* rama.

bought [bɔːt] *pt, pp of* **buy**.

bouillon cube ['buːjɔn-] *n* (*US*) cubito de caldo.

boulder ['bəʊldə*] *n* canto rodado.

bounce [baʊns] *vi* (*ball*) (re)botar; (*cheque*) ser rechazado ♦ *vt* hacer (re)botar ♦ *n* (*rebound*) (re)bote *m*; **he's got plenty of** ~ (*fig*) tiene mucha energía.

bouncer ['baʊnsə*] *n* (*col*) forzudo, gorila *m*.

bouncy castle ® ['baʊnsɪ-] *n* castillo inflable.

bound [baʊnd] *pt, pp of* **bind** ♦ *n* (*leap*) salto; (*gen pl*: *limit*) límite *m* ♦ *vi* (*leap*) saltar ♦ *adj*: ~ **by** rodeado de; **to be** ~ **to do sth** (*obliged*) tener el deber de hacer algo; **he's** ~ **to come** es seguro que vendrá; **"out of** ~**s to the public"** "prohibido el paso"; ~ **for** con destino a.

boundary ['baʊndrɪ] *n* límite *m*, lindero.

boundless ['baʊndlɪs] *adj* ilimitado.

bountiful ['baʊntɪful] *adj* (*person*) liberal,

generoso; (*God*) bondadoso; (*supply*) abundante.

bouquet ['buːkeɪ] *n* (*of flowers*) ramo, ramillete *m*; (*of wine*) aroma *m*.

bourbon ['buəbən] *n* (*US*: *also*: ~ **whiskey**) whisky *m* americano, bourbon *m*.

bourgeois ['buəʒwɑː] *adj, n* burgués/esa *m/f*.

bout [baʊt] *n* (*of malaria etc*) ataque *m*; (*BOXING etc*) combate *m*, encuentro.

boutique [buː'tiːk] *n* boutique *f*, tienda de ropa.

bow [bəʊ] *n* (*knot*) lazo; (*weapon, MUS*) arco; [baʊ] (*of the head*) reverencia; (*NAUT*: *also*: ~**s**) proa ♦ *vi* [baʊ] inclinarse, hacer una reverencia; (*yield*): **to** ~ **to** *or* **before** ceder ante, someterse a; **to** ~ **to the inevitable** resignarse a lo inevitable.

bowels ['baʊəlz] *npl* intestinos *mpl*, vientre *m*.

bowl [bəʊl] *n* tazón *m*, cuenco; (*for washing*) palangana, jofaina; (*ball*) bola; (*US*: *stadium*) estadio ♦ *vi* (*CRICKET*) arrojar la pelota; *see also* **bowls**.

bow-legged ['bəʊ'lɛgɪd] *adj* estevado.

bowler ['bəʊlə*] *n* (*CRICKET*) lanzador *m* (de la pelota); (*BRIT*: *also*: ~ **hat**) hongo, bombín *m*.

bowling ['bəʊlɪŋ] *n* (*game*) bolos *mpl*, bochas *fpl*.

bowling alley *n* bolera.

bowling green *n* pista para bochas.

bowls [bəʊlz] *n* juego de los bolos, bochas *fpl*.

bow tie ['bəʊ-] *n* corbata de lazo, pajarita.

box [bɔks] *n* (*also*: **cardboard** ~) caja, cajón *m*; (*for jewels*) estuche *m*; (*for money*) cofre *m*; (*crate*) cofre *m*, arca; (*THEAT*) palco ♦ *vt* encajonar ♦ *vi* (*SPORT*) boxear.

boxer ['bɔksə*] *n* (*person*) boxeador *m*; (*dog*) bóxer *m*.

box file *n* fichero.

boxing ['bɔksɪŋ] *n* (*SPORT*) boxeo, box *m* (*LAM*).

Boxing Day *n* (*BRIT*) día *m* de San Esteban; *ver recuadro*.

BOXING DAY

El día después de Navidad es **Boxing Day**, *fiesta en todo el Reino Unido, aunque si el 26 de diciembre cae en domingo el día de descanso se traslada al lunes. En dicho día solía ser tradición entregar "Christmas boxes" (aguinaldos) a empleados, proveedores a domicilio, carteros etc.*

---

boxing gloves *npl* guantes *mpl* de boxeo.

boxing ring *n* ring *m*, cuadrilátero.

box number *n* (*for advertisements*) apartado.
box office *n* taquilla, boletería (*LAM*).
boxroom ['bɔksrum] *n* trastero.
boy [bɔɪ] *n* (*young*) niño; (*older*) muchacho.
boycott ['bɔɪkɔt] *n* boicot *m* ♦ *vt* boicotear.
boyfriend ['bɔɪfrɛnd] *n* novio.
boyish ['bɔɪʃ] *adj* de muchacho, inmaduro.
boy scout *n* boy scout *m*.
Bp *abbr* = **bishop**.
BPOE *n abbr* (*US*: = *Benevolent and Protective Order of Elks*) organización benéfica.
BR *abbr see* **British Rail**.
bra [brɑː] *n* sostén *m*, sujetador *m*, corpiño (*LAM*).
brace [breɪs] *n* refuerzo, abrazadera; (*BRIT*: *on teeth*) corrector *m*; (*tool*) berbiquí *m* ♦ *vt* asegurar, reforzar; **to ~ o.s. (for)** (*fig*) prepararse (para); *see also* **braces**.
bracelet ['breɪslɪt] *n* pulsera, brazalete *m*, pulso (*LAM*).
braces ['breɪsɪz] *npl* (*BRIT*) tirantes *mpl*, suspensores *mpl* (*LAM*); (*US*: *on teeth*) corrector *m*.
bracing ['breɪsɪŋ] *adj* vigorizante, tónico.
bracken ['brækən] *n* helecho.
bracket ['brækɪt] *n* (*TECH*) soporte *m*, puntal *m*; (*group*) clase *f*, categoría; (*also*: **brace ~**) soporte *m*, abrazadera; (*also*: **round ~**) paréntesis *m inv*; (*gen*: **square ~**) corchete *m* ♦ *vt* (*fig*: *also*: ~ **together**) agrupar; **income ~** nivel *m* económico; **in ~s** entre paréntesis.
brackish ['brækɪʃ] *adj* (*water*) salobre.
brag [bræg] *vi* jactarse.
braid [breɪd] *n* (*trimming*) galón *m*; (*of hair*) trenza.
Braille [breɪl] *n* Braille *m*.
brain [breɪn] *n* cerebro; **~s** *npl* sesos *mpl*; **she's got ~s** es muy lista.
brainchild ['breɪntʃaɪld] *n* invención *f*.
braindead ['breɪndɛd] *adj* (*MED*) clínicamente muerto; (*col*) subnormal, tarado.
brainless ['breɪnlɪs] *adj* estúpido, insensato.
brainstorm ['breɪnstɔːm] *n* (*fig*) ataque *m* de locura, frenesí *m*; (*US*: *brainwave*) idea luminosa *or* genial, inspiración *f*.
brainstorming ['breɪnstɔːmɪŋ] *n* discusión intensa para solucionar problemas.
brainwash ['breɪnwɔʃ] *vt* lavar el cerebro a.
brainwave ['breɪnweɪv] *n* idea luminosa *or* genial, inspiración *f*.
brainy ['breɪnɪ] *adj* muy listo *or* inteligente.
braise [breɪz] *vt* cocer a fuego lento.
brake [breɪk] *n* (*on vehicle*) freno ♦ *vt*, *vi* frenar.

brake drum *n* tambor *m* de freno.
brake fluid *n* líquido de frenos.
brake light *n* luz *f* de frenado.
brake pedal *n* pedal *m* de freno.
bramble ['bræmbl] *n* (*fruit*) zarza.
bran [bræn] *n* salvado.
branch [brɑːntʃ] *n* rama; (*fig*) ramo; (*COMM*) sucursal *f* ♦ *vi* ramificarse; (*fig*) extenderse.
►**branch out** *vi* ramificarse.
branch line *n* (*RAIL*) ramal *m*, línea secundaria.
branch manager *n* director(a) *m/f* de sucursal.
brand [brænd] *n* marca; (*iron*) hierro de marcar ♦ *vt* (*cattle*) marcar con hierro candente.
brandish ['brændɪʃ] *vt* blandir.
brand name *n* marca.
brand-new ['brænd'njuː] *adj* flamante, completamente nuevo.
brandy ['brændɪ] *n* coñac *m*, brandy *m*.
brash [bræʃ] *adj* (*rough*) tosco; (*cheeky*) descarado.
Brasilia [brə'zɪlɪə] *n* Brasilia.
brass [brɑːs] *n* latón *m*; **the ~** (*MUS*) los cobres.
brass band *n* banda de metal.
brassière ['bræsɪə*] *n* sostén *m*, sujetador *m*.
brass tacks *npl*: **to get down to ~** ir al grano.
brat [bræt] *n* (*pej*) mocoso/a.
bravado [brə'vɑːdəu] *n* fanfarronería.
brave [breɪv] *adj* valiente, valeroso ♦ *n* guerrero indio ♦ *vt* (*challenge*) desafiar; (*resist*) aguantar.
bravely ['breɪvlɪ] *adv* valientemente, con valor.
bravery ['breɪvərɪ] *n* valor *m*, valentía.
bravo [brɑː'vəu] *excl* ¡bravo!, ¡olé!
brawl [brɔːl] *n* pendencia, reyerta ♦ *vi* pelearse.
brawn [brɔːn] *n* fuerza muscular; (*meat*) carne *f* en gelatina.
brawny ['brɔːnɪ] *adj* fornido, musculoso.
bray [breɪ] *n* rebuzno ♦ *vi* rebuznar.
brazen ['breɪzn] *adj* descarado, cínico ♦ *vt*: **to ~ it out** echarle cara al asunto.
brazier ['breɪzɪə*] *n* brasero.
Brazil [brə'zɪl] *n* (el) Brasil.
Brazilian [brə'zɪlɪən] *adj*, *n* brasileño/a *m/f*.
breach [briːtʃ] *vt* abrir brecha en ♦ *n* (*gap*) brecha; (*estrangement*) ruptura; (*breaking*): ~ **of confidence** abuso de confianza; ~ **of contract** infracción *f* de contrato; ~ **of the peace** perturbación *f* del órden público; **in ~ of** por

incumplimiento or infracción de.

bread [brɛd] n pan m; (col: money) pasta, lana (LAM); ~ **and butter** n pan con mantequilla; (fig) pan (de cada día) ♦ adj común y corriente; **to earn one's daily** ~ ganarse el pan; **to know which side one's** ~ **is buttered (on)** saber dónde aprieta el zapato.

breadbin ['brɛdbɪn] n panera.

breadboard ['brɛdbɔːd] n (COMPUT) circuito experimental.

breadbox ['brɛdbɔks] n (US) panera.

breadcrumbs ['brɛdkrʌmz] npl migajas fpl; (CULIN) pan msg rallado.

breadline ['brɛdlaɪn] n: **on the** ~ en la miseria.

breadth [brɛtθ] n anchura; (fig) amplitud f.

breadwinner ['brɛdwɪnə*] n sostén m de la familia.

break [breɪk] vb (pt **broke** [brəuk], pp **broken** ['brəukən]) vt (gen) romper; (promise) no cumplir; (fall) amortiguar; (journey) interrumpir; (law) violar, infringir; (record) batir; (news) comunicar ♦ vi romperse, quebrarse; (storm) estallar; (weather) cambiar ♦ n (gap) abertura; (crack) grieta; (fracture) fractura; (in relations) ruptura; (rest) descanso; (time) intervalo; (: at school) (período de) recreo; (holiday) vacaciones fpl; (chance) oportunidad f; (escape) evasión f, fuga; **to** ~ **with sb** (fig) romper con algn; **to** ~ **even** vi cubrir los gastos; **to** ~ **free** or **loose** vi escaparse; **lucky** ~ (col) chiripa, racha de buena suerte; **to have** or **take a** ~ (few minutes) descansar; **without a** ~ sin descanso or descansar.

▶**break down** vt (door etc) echar abajo, derribar; (resistance) vencer, acabar con; (figures, data) analizar, descomponer; (undermine) acabar con ♦ vi estropearse; (MED) sufrir un colapso; (AUT) averiarse, descomponerse (LAM); (person) romper a llorar.

▶**break in** vt (horse etc) domar ♦ vi (burglar) forzar una entrada.

▶**break into** vt fus (house) forzar.

▶**break off** vi (speaker) pararse, detenerse; (branch) partir ♦ vt (talks) suspender; (engagement) romper.

▶**break open** vt (door etc) abrir por la fuerza, forzar.

▶**break out** vi estallar; **to** ~ **out in spots** salir a algn granos.

▶**break through** vi: **the sun broke through** asomó el sol ♦ vt fus (defences, barrier) abrirse paso por; (crowd) abrirse paso por.

▶**break up** vi (partnership) disolverse; (friends) romper ♦ vt (rocks, ice etc) partir; (crowd) disolver.

breakable ['breɪkəbl] adj quebradizo ♦ n: ~**s** cosas fpl frágiles.

breakage ['breɪkɪdʒ] n rotura; **to pay for** ~**s** pagar por los objetos rotos.

breakaway ['breɪkəweɪ] adj (group etc) disidente.

break-dancing ['breɪkdɑːnsɪŋ] n break m.

breakdown ['breɪkdaun] n (AUT) avería; (in communications) interrupción f; (MED: also: **nervous** ~) colapso, crisis f nerviosa; (of figures) desglose m.

breakdown van n (BRIT) (camión m) grúa.

breaker ['breɪkə*] n rompiente m, ola grande.

breakeven ['breɪk'iːvn] cpd: ~ **chart** gráfico del punto de equilibrio; ~ **point** punto de break-even or de equilibrio.

breakfast ['brɛkfəst] n desayuno.

breakfast cereal n cereales mpl para el desayuno.

break-in ['breɪkɪn] n robo con allanamiento de morada.

breaking and entering ['breɪkɪŋənd 'ɛntərɪŋ] n (LAW) violación f de domicilio, allanamiento de morada.

breaking point ['breɪkɪŋ-] n punto de ruptura.

breakthrough ['breɪkθruː] n ruptura; (fig) avance m, adelanto.

break-up ['breɪkʌp] n (of partnership, marriage) disolución f.

break-up value n (COMM) valor m de liquidación.

breakwater ['breɪkwɔːtə*] n rompeolas m inv.

breast [brɛst] n (of woman) pecho, seno; (chest) pecho; (of bird) pechuga.

breast-feed ['brɛstfiːd] vt, vi (irreg: like **feed**) amamantar, dar el pecho.

breaststroke ['brɛststrəuk] n braza de pecho.

breath [brɛθ] n aliento, respiración f; **out of** ~ sin aliento, sofocado; **to go out for a** ~ **of air** salir a tomar el fresco.

Breathalyser ® ['brɛθəlaɪzə*] n (BRIT) alcoholímetro m; ~ **test** n prueba de alcoholemia.

breathe [briːð] vt, vi respirar; (noisily) resollar; **I won't** ~ **a word about it** no diré ni una palabra de ello.

▶**breathe in** vt, vi aspirar.

▶**breathe out** vt, vi espirar.

breather ['briːðə*] n respiro, descanso.

breathing ['briːðɪŋ] n respiración f.

breathing space n (fig) respiro, pausa.

breathless ['brɛθlɪs] *adj* sin aliento, jadeante; (*with excitement*) pasmado.
breathtaking ['brɛθteɪkɪŋ] *adj* imponente, pasmoso.
breath test *n* prueba de la alcoholemia.
-bred [brɛd] *suff:* **to be well/ill~** estar bien/mal criado.
breed [briːd] *vb* (*pt, pp* **bred** [brɛd]) *vt* criar; (*fig: hate, suspicion*) crear, engendrar ♦ *vi* reproducirse, procrear ♦ *n* raza, casta.
breeder ['briːdə*] *n* (*person*) criador(a) *m/f*; (*PHYSICS: also:* ~ **reactor**) reactor *m*.
breeding ['briːdɪŋ] *n* (*of person*) educación *f*.
breeze [briːz] *n* brisa.
breezeblock ['briːzblɔk] *n* (*BRIT*) bovedilla.
breezy ['briːzɪ] *adj* de mucho viento, ventoso; (*person*) despreocupado.
Breton ['brɛtən] *adj* bretón/ona ♦ *n* bretón/ona *m/f*; (*LING*) bretón *m*.
brevity ['brɛvɪtɪ] *n* brevedad *f*.
brew [bruː] *vt* (*tea*) hacer; (*beer*) elaborar; (*plot*) tramar ♦ *vi* hacerse; elaborarse; tramarse; (*storm*) amenazar.
brewer ['bruːə*] *n* cervecero, fabricante *m* de cerveza.
brewery ['bruːərɪ] *n* fábrica de cerveza.
briar ['braɪə*] *n* (*thorny bush*) zarza; (*wild rose*) escaramujo, rosa silvestre.
bribe [braɪb] *n* soborno ♦ *vt* sobornar, cohechar; **to ~ sb to do sth** sobornar a algn para que haga algo.
bribery ['braɪbərɪ] *n* soborno, cohecho.
bric-a-brac ['brɪkəbræk] *n inv* baratijas *fpl.*
brick [brɪk] *n* ladrillo.
bricklayer ['brɪkleɪə*] *n* albañil *m*.
brickwork ['brɪkwɔːk] *n* enladrillado.
brickworks ['brɪkwɔːks] *n* ladrillar *m.*
bridal ['braɪdl] *adj* nupcial.
bride [braɪd] *n* novia.
bridegroom ['braɪdgruːm] *n* novio.
bridesmaid ['braɪdzmeɪd] *n* dama de honor.
bridge [brɪdʒ] *n* puente *m*; (*NAUT*) puente *m* de mando; (*of nose*) caballete *m*; (*CARDS*) bridge *m* ♦ *vt* (*river*) tender un puente sobre.
bridgehead ['brɪdʒhɛd] *n* cabeza de puente.
bridging loan ['brɪdʒɪŋ-] *n* crédito provisional.
bridle ['braɪdl] *n* brida, freno ♦ *vt* poner la brida a; (*fig*) reprimir, refrenar ♦ *vi* (*in anger etc*) picarse.
bridle path *n* camino de herradura.
brief [briːf] *adj* breve, corto ♦ *n* (*LAW*) escrito ♦ *vt* (*inform*) informar; (*instruct*) dar instrucciones a; **in ~ ...** en resumen ...; **to ~ sb (about sth)** informar a algn (sobre algo).

briefcase ['briːfkeɪs] *n* cartera, portafolio(s) *m inv* (*LAM*).
briefing ['briːfɪŋ] *n* (*PRESS*) informe *m*.
briefly *adv* (*smile, glance*) brevemente; (*explain, say*) brevemente, en pocas palabras.
briefs [briːfs] *npl* (*for men*) calzoncillos *mpl*; (*for women*) bragas *fpl.*
Brig. *abbr* = **brigadier**.
brigade [brɪ'geɪd] *n* (*MIL*) brigada.
brigadier [brɪgə'dɪə*] *n* general *m* de brigada.
bright [braɪt] *adj* claro; (*room*) luminoso; (*day*) de sol; (*person: clever*) listo, inteligente; (: *lively*) alegre, animado; (*colour*) vivo; **to look on the ~ side** mirar el lado bueno.
brighten ['braɪtn] (*also:* ~ **up**) *vt* (*room*) hacer más alegre ♦ *vi* (*weather*) despejarse; (*person*) animarse, alegrarse.
brill [brɪl] *adj* (*BRIT col*) guay.
brilliance ['brɪljəns] *n* brillo, brillantez *f*; (*fig: of person*) inteligencia.
brilliant ['brɪljənt] *adj* (*light, idea, person, success*) brillante; (*clever*) genial.
brilliantly ['brɪljəntlɪ] *adv* brillantemente.
brim [brɪm] *n* borde *m*; (*of hat*) ala.
brimful ['brɪm'ful] *adj* lleno hasta el borde; (*fig*) rebosante.
brine [braɪn] *n* (*CULIN*) salmuera.
bring, *pt, pp* **brought** [brɪŋ, brɔːt] *vt* (*thing*) traer; (*person*) conducir; **to ~ sth to an end** terminar con algo; **I can't ~ myself to sack him** no soy capaz de echarle.
► **bring about** *vt* ocasionar, producir.
► **bring back** *vt* volver a traer; (*return*) devolver.
► **bring down** *vt* bajar; (*price*) rebajar.
► **bring forward** *vt* adelantar; (*BOOKKEEPING*) sumar y seguir.
► **bring in** *vt* (*harvest*) recoger; (*person*) hacer entrar *or* pasar; (*object*) traer; (*POL: bill, law*) presentar; (*LAW: verdict*) pronunciar; (*produce: income*) producir, rendir.
► **bring off** *vt* (*task, plan*) lograr, conseguir; (*deal*) cerrar.
► **bring out** *vt* (*object*) sacar; (*new product*) sacar; (*book*) publicar.
► **bring round** *vt* (*unconscious person*) hacer volver en sí; (*convince*) convencer.
► **bring up** *vt* (*person*) educar, criar; (*carry up*) subir; (*question*) sacar a colación; (*food: vomit*) devolver, vomitar.
brink [brɪŋk] *n* borde *m*; **on the ~ of doing sth** a punto de hacer algo; **she was on the ~ of tears** estaba al borde de las lágrimas.

brisk [brɪsk] adj (walk) enérgico, vigoroso; (speedy) rápido; (wind) fresco; (trade) activo, animado; (abrupt) brusco; **business is** ~ el negocio va bien.
brisket ['brɪskɪt] n falda de vaca.
bristle ['brɪsl] n cerda ♦ vi erizarse.
bristly ['brɪslɪ] adj (beard, hair) erizado; **to have a** ~ **chin** tener la barba crecida.
Brit [brɪt] n abbr (col: = British person) británico/a.
Britain ['brɪtən] n (also: **Great** ~) Gran Bretaña.
British ['brɪtɪʃ] adj británico; **the** ~ npl los británicos; **the** ~ **Isles** npl las Islas Británicas.
British Rail (BR) n ≈ RENFE f (SP).
British Summer Time n hora de verano británica.
Briton ['brɪtən] n británico/a.
brittle ['brɪtl] adj quebradizo, frágil.
Br(o). abbr (REL) = **brother**.
broach [brəutʃ] vt (subject) abordar.
broad [brɔːd] adj ancho, amplio; (accent) cerrado ♦ n (US col) tía; **in** ~ **daylight** en pleno día; **the** ~ **outlines** las líneas generales.
broad bean n haba.
broadcast ['brɔːdkɑːst] n emisión f ♦ vb (pt, pp broadcast) vt (RADIO) emitir; (TV) transmitir ♦ vi emitir; transmitir.
broadcaster ['brɔːdkɑːstə*] n locutor(a) m/f.
broadcasting ['brɔːdkɑːstɪŋ] n radiodifusión f, difusión f.
broadcasting station n emisora.
broaden ['brɔːdn] vt ensanchar ♦ vi ensancharse.
broadly ['brɔːdlɪ] adv en general.
broad-minded ['brɔːd'maɪndɪd] adj tolerante, liberal.
broadsheet ['brɔːdʃiːt] n (BRIT) periódico de gran formato (no sensacionalista); see also **quality press**.
brocade [brə'keɪd] n brocado.
broccoli ['brɔkəlɪ] n brécol m, bróculi m.
brochure ['brəuʃjuə*] n folleto.
brogue [brəug] n (accent) acento regional; (shoe) (tipo de) zapato de cuero grueso.
broil [brɔɪl] vt (US) asar a la parrilla.
broiler ['brɔɪlə*] n (fowl) pollo (para asar).
broke [brəuk] pt of **break** ♦ adj (col) pelado, sin una perra; **to go** ~ quebrar.
broken ['brəukən] pp of **break** ♦ adj (stick) roto; (fig: marriage) deshecho; (: promise, vow) violado; ~ **leg** pierna rota; **in** ~ **English** en un inglés chapurreado.
broken-down ['brəukn'daun] adj (car) averiado; (machine) estropeado; (house) destartalado.

broken-hearted ['brəukn'hɑːtɪd] adj con el corazón destrozado.
broker ['brəukə*] n corredor(a) m/f de bolsa.
brokerage ['brəukərɪdʒ] n corretaje m.
brolly ['brɔlɪ] n (BRIT col) paraguas m inv.
bronchitis [brɔŋ'kaɪtɪs] n bronquitis f.
bronze [brɔnz] n bronce m.
bronzed [brɔnzd] adj bronceado.
brooch [brəutʃ] n broche m.
brood [bruːd] n camada, cría; (children) progenie f ♦ vi (hen) empollar; **to** ~ **over** dar vueltas a, rumiar.
broody ['bruːdɪ] adj (fig) triste, melancólico.
brook [bruk] n arroyo.
broom [brum] n escoba; (BOT) retama.
broomstick ['brumstɪk] n palo de escoba.
Bros. abbr (COMM: = Brothers) Hnos.
broth [brɔθ] n caldo.
brothel ['brɔθl] n burdel m.
brother ['brʌðə*] n hermano.
brotherhood ['brʌðəhud] n hermandad f.
brother-in-law ['brʌðərɪn'lɔː] n cuñado.
brotherly ['brʌðəlɪ] adj fraternal.
brought [brɔːt] pt, pp of **bring**.
brow [brau] n (forehead) frente f; (of hill) cumbre f.
browbeat ['braubiːt] vt (irreg: like **beat**) intimidar.
brown [braun] adj marrón; (hair) castaño; (tanned) moreno ♦ n (colour) marrón m ♦ vt (tan) poner moreno; (CULIN) dorar; **to go** ~ (person) ponerse moreno; (leaves) dorarse.
brown bread n pan m moreno.
brownie ['brauni] n niña exploradora.
brown paper n papel m de estraza.
brown rice n arroz m integral.
brown sugar n azúcar m moreno.
browse [brauz] n (animal) pacer; (among books) hojear libros; **to** ~ **through a book** hojear un libro.
browser ['brauzə*] n (COMPUT) navegador m.
bruise [bruːz] n (on person) cardenal m, hematoma m ♦ vt (leg etc) magullar; (fig: feelings) herir.
Brum [brʌm] n abbr, **Brummagem** ['brʌmədʒəm] n (col) = **Birmingham**.
Brummie ['brʌmi] n (col) habitante m/f de Birmingham.
brunch [brʌntʃ] n desayuno-almuerzo.
brunette [bruː'nɛt] n morena, morocha (LAM).
brunt [brʌnt] n: **to bear the** ~ **of** llevar el peso de.
brush [brʌʃ] n cepillo, escobilla (LAM); (large) escoba, (for painting, shaving etc)

brocha; (*artist's*) pincel *m*; (*BOT*) maleza
♦ *vt* cepillar; (*gen*: ~ **past, ~ against**)
rozar al pasar; **to have a ~ with the**
police tener un roce con la policía.
▶**brush aside** *vt* rechazar, no hacer caso
a.
▶**brush up** *vt* (*knowledge*) repasar,
refrescar.
brushed [brʌʃt] *adj* (*nylon, denim etc*)
afelpado; (*TECH*: *steel, chrome etc*)
cepillado.
brushwood ['brʌʃwud] *n* (*bushes*) maleza;
(*sticks*) leña.
brusque [bruːsk] *adj* (*person, manner*)
brusco; (*tone*) áspero.
Brussels ['brʌslz] *n* Bruselas.
Brussels sprout *n* col *f* de Bruselas.
brutal ['bruːtl] *adj* brutal.
brutality [bruː'tælɪtɪ] *n* brutalidad *f*.
brutalize ['bruːtəlaɪz] *vt* (*harden*) embrutecer; (*ill-treat*) tratar brutalmente a.
brute [bruːt] *n* bruto; (*person*) bestia ♦ *adj*:
by ~ force por la fuerza bruta.
BS *n abbr* (*US*: = *Bachelor of Science*) título
universitario.
bs *abbr* = **bill of sale**.
BSA *n abbr* = *Boy Scouts of America*.
BSc *abbr* = **Bachelor of Science**; *see also*
Bachelor's Degree.
BSE *n abbr* (= *bovine spongiform*
encephalopathy) encefalopatía
espongiforme bovina.
BSI *n abbr* (= *British Standards Institution*)
institución británica de normalización.
BST *n abbr* (= *British Summer Time*) hora de
verano británica.
Bt. *abbr* (*BRIT*) = **baronet**.
btu *n abbr* (= *British thermal unit*) ≈ 1054.2
julios.
bubble ['bʌbl] *n* burbuja; (*in paint*) ampolla
♦ *vi* burbujear, borbotar.
bubble bath *n* espuma para el baño.
bubble gum *n* chicle *m*.
bubblejet printer ['bʌbldʒet-] *n* impresora
de inyección por burbujas.
bubbly ['bʌblɪ] *adj* (*person*) vivaracho;
(*liquid*) con burbujas ♦ *n* (*col*) champán *m*.
Bucharest [buːkə'rest] *n* Bucarest *m*.
buck [bʌk] *n* macho; (*US col*) dólar *m* ♦ *vi*
corcovear; **to pass the ~ (to sb)** echar (a
algn) el muerto.
▶**buck up** *vi* (*cheer up*) animarse, cobrar
ánimo ♦ *vt*: **to ~ one's ideas up** poner más
empeño.
bucket ['bʌkɪt] *n* cubo, balde *m* (*esp LAM*)
♦ *vi*: **the rain is ~ing (down)** (*col*) está
lloviendo a cántaros.
Buckingham Palace ['bʌkɪŋəm-] *n* el

Palacio de Buckingham; *ver recuadro*.

BUCKINGHAM PALACE

Buckingham Palace *es la residencia oficial*
del monarca británico en Londres. Data de
1703 y fue en principio el palacio del Duque
de Buckingham, para pasar a manos de
Jorge III en 1762. Fue reconstruido el siglo
pasado y reformado después a principios
de este siglo. Hoy en día parte del palacio
está abierto al público.

---

buckle ['bʌkl] *n* hebilla ♦ *vt* abrochar con
hebilla ♦ *vi* torcerse, combarse.
▶**buckle down** *vi* poner empeño.
Bucks [bʌks] *abbr* (*BRIT*) = *Buckinghamshire*.
bud [bʌd] *n* brote *m*, yema; (*of flower*)
capullo ♦ *vi* brotar, echar brotes.
Budapest [bjuːdə'pest] *n* Budapest *m*.
Buddhism ['budɪzm] *n* Budismo.
Buddhist ['budɪst] *adj, n* budista *m/f*.
budding ['bʌdɪŋ] *adj* en ciernes, en
embrión.
buddy ['bʌdɪ] *n* (*US*) compañero,
compinche *m*.
budge [bʌdʒ] *vt* mover; (*fig*) hacer ceder
♦ *vi* moverse.
budgerigar ['bʌdʒərɪgaː*] *n* periquito.
budget ['bʌdʒɪt] *n* presupuesto ♦ *vi*: **to ~**
for sth presupuestar algo; **I'm on a tight**
~ no puedo gastar mucho; **she works out**
her ~ every month planea su
presupuesto todos los meses.
budgie ['bʌdʒɪ] *n* = **budgerigar**.
Buenos Aires ['bweɪnɔs'aɪrɪz] *n* Buenos
Aires *m* ♦ *adj* bonaerense, porteño (*LAM*).
buff [bʌf] *adj* (*colour*) color *m* de ante ♦ *n*
(*enthusiast*) entusiasta *m/f*.
buffalo ['bʌfələu], *pl* ~ *or* **buffaloes** *n*
(*BRIT*) búfalo; (*US*: *bison*) bisonte *m*.
buffer ['bʌfə*] *n* amortiguador *m*; (*COMPUT*)
memoria intermedia, buffer *m*.
buffer zone *n* zona (que sirve de) colchón.
buffet ['bufeɪ] *n* (*BRIT*: *bar*) bar *m*, cafetería;
(*food*) buffet *m* ♦ *vt* ['bʌfɪt] (*strike*)
abofetear; (*wind etc*) golpear.
buffet car *n* (*BRIT RAIL*) coche-restaurante
m.
buffet lunch *n* buffet *m* (almuerzo).
buffoon [bə'fuːn] *n* bufón *m*.
bug [bʌg] *n* (*insect*) chinche *m*; (: *gen*) bicho,
sabandija; (*germ*) microbio, bacilo; (*spy*
device) micrófono oculto; (*COMPUT*) fallo,
error *m* ♦ *vt* (*annoy*) fastidiar; (*room*)
poner un micrófono oculto en; (*phone*)
pinchar; **I've got the travel ~** (*fig*) me
encanta viajar; **it really ~s me** me

fastidia or molesta mucho.
bugbear ['bʌgbeə*] n pesadilla.
bugle ['bju:gl] n corneta, clarín m.
build [bɪld] n (of person) talle m, tipo ♦ vt (pt, pp **built** [bɪlt]) construir, edificar.
▶**build on** vt fus (fig) basar en.
▶**build up** vt (MED) fortalecer; (stocks) acumular; (establish: business) fomentar, desarrollar; (: reputation) crear(se); (increase: production) aumentar; **don't ~ your hopes up too soon** no te hagas demasiadas ilusiones.
builder ['bɪldə*] n constructor(a) m/f; (contractor) contratista m/f.
building ['bɪldɪŋ] n (act of) construcción f; (habitation, offices) edificio.
building contractor n contratista m/f de obras.
building industry n construcción f.
building site n solar m (SP), obra (LAM).
building society n (BRIT) sociedad f de préstamo inmobiliario; ver recuadro.

BUILDING SOCIETY

En el Reino Unido existe un tipo de entidad financiera llamada **building society** do la que sus clientes son también propietarios y cuyos servicios son similares a los de los bancos, aunque se centran fundamentalmente en créditos hipotecarios y cuentas de ahorro. Son la entidad más utilizada por el público en general a la hora de pedir créditos para la compra de la vivienda.

---

building trade n = building industry.
build-up ['bɪldʌp] n (publicity): **to give sb/sth a good ~** hacer mucha propaganda de algn/algo.
built [bɪlt] pt, pp of build.
built-in ['bɪlt'ɪn] adj (cupboard) empotrado; (device) interior, incorporado; **~ obsolescence** caducidad f programada.
built-up ['bɪltʌp] adj (area) urbanizado.
bulb [bʌlb] n (BOT) bulbo; (ELEC) bombilla, bombillo (LAM), foco (LAM).
Bulgaria [bʌl'geərɪə] n Bulgaria.
Bulgarian [bʌl'geərɪən] adj búlgaro ♦ n búlgaro/a; (LING) búlgaro.
bulge [bʌldʒ] n bombeo, pandeo; (in birth rate, sales) alza, aumento ♦ vi bombearse, pandearse; (pocket etc) hacer bulto.
bulimia [bə'lɪmɪə] n bulimia.
bulk [bʌlk] n (mass) bulto, volumen m; (major part) grueso; **in ~** (COMM) a granel; **the ~ of** la mayor parte de; **to buy in ~** comprar en grandes cantidades.
bulk buying n compra a granel.

bulk carrier n (buque m) granelero.
bulkhead ['bʌlkhed] n mamparo.
bulky ['bʌlkɪ] adj voluminoso, abultado.
bull [bul] n toro; (STOCK EXCHANGE) alcista m/f de bolsa; (REL) bula.
bulldog ['buldɔg] n dogo.
bulldoze ['buldəuz] vt mover con excavadora; **I was ~d into doing it** (fig col) me obligaron a hacerlo.
bulldozer ['buldəuzə*] n buldozer m, excavadora.
bullet ['bulɪt] n bala; **~ wound** balazo.
bulletin ['bulɪtɪn] n comunicado, parte m; (journal) boletín m.
bulletin board n (US) tablón m de anuncios; (COMPUT) tablero de noticias.
bulletproof ['bulɪtpru:f] adj a prueba de balas; **~ vest** chaleco anti-balas.
bullfight ['bulfaɪt] n corrida de toros.
bullfighter ['bulfaɪtə*] n torero.
bullfighting ['bulfaɪtɪŋ] n los toros mpl, el toreo; (art of ~) tauromaquia.
bullion ['buljən] n oro or plata en barras.
bullock ['bulək] n novillo.
bullring ['bulrɪŋ] n plaza de toros.
bull's-eye ['bulzaɪ] n blanco, diana.
bullshit ['bulʃɪt] (col!) excl chorradas ♦ n chorradas fpl ♦ vi decir chorradas ♦ vt: **to ~ sb** quedarse con algn.
bully ['bulɪ] n valentón m, matón m ♦ vt intimidar, tiranizar.
bum [bʌm] n (BRIT: col: backside) culo; (: tramp) vagabundo; (col: esp US: idler) holgazán/ana m/f, flojo/a.
bumble ['bʌmbl] vi (walk unsteadily) andar de forma vacilante; (fig) farfullar, trastabillar.
bumblebee ['bʌmblbi:] n abejorro.
bumbling ['bʌmblɪŋ] n divagación f.
bumf [bʌmf] n (col: forms etc) papeleo.
bump [bʌmp] n (blow) tope m, choque m; (jolt) sacudida; (noise) choque m, topetón m; (on road etc) bache m; (on head) chichón m ♦ vt (strike) chocar contra, topetar ♦ vi dar sacudidas.
▶**bump into** vt fus chocar contra, tropezar con; (person) topar con; (col: meet) tropezar con, toparse con.
bumper ['bʌmpə*] n (BRIT) parachoques m inv ♦ adj: **~ crop/harvest** cosecha abundante.
bumper cars npl (US) autos or coches mpl de choque.
bumph [bʌmf] n = bumf.
bumptious ['bʌmpʃəs] adj engreído, presuntuoso.
bumpy ['bʌmpɪ] adj (road) lleno de baches; (journey, flight) agitado.

bun [bʌn] n (_BRIT: cake_) pastel m; (_US: bread_) bollo; (_of hair_) moño.

bunch [bʌntʃ] n (_of flowers_) ramo; (_of keys_) manojo; (_of bananas_) piña; (_of people_) grupo; (_pej_) pandilla.

bundle ['bʌndl] n (_gen_) bulto, fardo; (_of sticks_) haz m; (_of papers_) legajo ♦ vt (_also:_ ~ **up**) atar, envolver; **to** ~ **sth/sb into** meter algo/a algn precipitadamente en.

bun fight n (_BRIT col: tea party_) merienda; (: _function_) fiesta oficial.

bung [bʌŋ] n tapón m, bitoque m ♦ vt (_throw: also:_ ~ **into**) arrojar; (_also:_ ~ **up**: _pipe, hole_) tapar; **my nose is ~ed up** (_col_) tengo la nariz atascada or taponada.

bungalow ['bʌŋgələu] n bungalow m, chalé m.

bungee jumping ['bʌndʒiː'dʒʌmpɪŋ] n puenting m, banyi m.

bungle ['bʌŋgl] vt chapucear.

bunion ['bʌnjən] n juanete m.

bunk [bʌŋk] n litera; ~ **beds** npl literas fpl.

bunker ['bʌŋkə*] n (_coal store_) carbonera; (_MIL_) refugio; (_GOLF_) bunker m.

bunk off vi: **to** ~ **school** (_BRIT col_) pirarse las clases; **I'll** ~ **at 3 this afternoon** me voy a pirar a las 3 esta tarde.

bunny ['bʌnɪ] n (_also:_ ~ **rabbit**) conejito.

Bunsen burner ['bʌnsn-] n mechero Bunsen.

bunting ['bʌntɪŋ] n empavesada, banderas fpl.

buoy [bɔɪ] n boya.

▶**buoy up** vt mantener a flote; (_fig_) animar.

buoyancy ['bɔɪənsɪ] n (_of ship_) flotabilidad f.

buoyant ['bɔɪənt] adj (_carefree_) boyante, optimista; (_COMM: market, prices etc_) sostenido.

BUPA ['buːpə] n abbr (= British United Provident Association) seguro médico privado.

burden ['bəːdn] n carga ♦ vt cargar; **to be a** ~ **to sb** ser una carga para algn.

bureau, pl ~**x** ['bjuərəu, -z] n (_BRIT: writing desk_) escritorio, buró m; (_US: chest of drawers_) cómoda; (_office_) oficina, agencia.

bureaucracy [bjuə'rɔkrəsɪ] n burocracia.

bureaucrat ['bjuərəkræt] n burócrata m/f.

bureaucratic [bjuərə'krætɪk] adj burocrático.

burgeon ['bəːdʒən] vi (_develop rapidly_) crecer, incrementarse; (_trade etc_) florecer.

burger ['bəːgə*] n hamburguesa.

burglar ['bəːglə*] n ladrón/ona m/f.

burglar alarm n alarma f contra robo.

burglarize ['bəːgləraɪz] vt (_US_) robar (con allanamiento).

burglary ['bəːglərɪ] n robo con allanamiento or fractura, robo de una casa.

burgle ['bəːgl] vt robar (con allanamiento).

burial ['bɛrɪəl] n entierro.

burial ground n cementerio.

burlesque [bəː'lɛsk] n parodia.

burly ['bəːlɪ] adj fornido, membrudo.

Burma ['bəːmə] n Birmania; _see also_ **Myanmar**.

Burmese [bəː'miːz] adj birmano ♦ n (_pl inv_) birmano/a; (_LING_) birmano.

burn [bəːn] vb (_pt, pp_ **burned** or **burnt** [bəːnt]) vt quemar; (_house_) incendiar ♦ vi quemarse, arder; incendiarse; (_sting_) escocer ♦ n (_MED_) quemadura; **the cigarette ~t a hole in her dress** se ha quemado el vestido con el cigarrillo; **I've ~t myself!** ¡me he quemado!

▶**burn down** vt incendiar.

▶**burn out** vt (_subj: writer etc_): **to** ~ **o.s. out** agotarse.

burner ['bəːnə*] n (_gas_) quemador m.

burning ['bəːnɪŋ] adj ardiente; (_building, forest_) en llamas.

Burns' Night [bəːnz-] n ver recuadro.

burp [bəːp] (_col_) n eructo ♦ vi eructar.

burrow ['bʌrəu] n madriguera ♦ vt hacer una madriguera.

bursar ['bəːsə*] n tesorero; (_BRIT: student_) becario/a.

bursary ['bəːsərɪ] n (_BRIT_) beca.

burst [bəːst] vb (_pt, pp_ **burst**) vt (_balloon, pipe_) reventar; (_banks etc_) romper ♦ vi reventarse; romperse; (_tyre_) pincharse; (_bomb_) estallar ♦ n (_explosion_) estallido; (_also:_ ~ **pipe**) reventón m; **the river has** ~ **its banks** el río se ha desbordado; **to** ~ **into flames** estallar en llamas; **to** ~ **out laughing** soltar la carcajada; **to** ~ **into tears** deshacerse en lágrimas; **to be ~ing with** reventar de; **a** ~ **of energy** una

explosión de energía; **a ~ of applause** una salva de aplausos; **a ~ of speed** una escapada; **to ~ open** *vi* abrirse de golpe.
▶**burst into** *vt fus* (*room etc*) irrumpir en.

bury ['beri] *vt* enterrar; (*body*) enterrar, sepultar; **to ~ the hatchet** enterrar el hacha (de guerra), echar pelillos a la mar.

bus [bʌs] *n* autobús *m*, camión *m* (*LAM*).

bus boy *n* (*US*) ayudante *m/f* de camarero.

bush [buʃ] *n* arbusto; (*scrub land*) monte *m* bajo; **to beat about the ~** andar(se) con rodeos.

bushed [buʃt] *adj* (*col*) molido.

bushel ['buʃl] *n* (*measure*: *Brit*) = 36,36 *litros*; (: *US*) = 35,24 *litros*.

bush fire *n* incendio en el monte.

bushy ['buʃɪ] *adj* (*beard, eyebrows*) poblado; (*hair*) espeso; (*fur*) tupido.

busily ['bɪzɪlɪ] *adv* afanosamente.

business ['bɪznɪs] *n* (*matter, affair*) asunto; (*trading*) comercio, negocios *mpl*; (*firm*) empresa, casa; (*occupation*) oficio; **to be away on ~** estar en viaje de negocios; **it's my ~ to...** me toca *or* corresponde...; **it's none of my ~** no es asunto mío; **he means ~** habla en serio; **he's in the insurance ~** se dedica a los seguros, **I'm here on ~** estoy aquí por mi trabajo; **to do ~ with sb** hacer negocios con algn.

business address *n* dirección *f* comercial.

business card *n* tarjeta de visita.

businesslike ['bɪznɪslaɪk] *adj* (*company*) serio; (*person*) eficiente.

businessman ['bɪznɪsmən] *n* hombre *m* de negocios.

business trip *n* viaje *m* de negocios.

businesswoman ['bɪznɪswumən] *n* mujer *f* de negocios.

busker ['bʌskə*] *n* (*BRIT*) músico/a ambulante.

bus route *n* recorrido del autobús.

bus station *n* estación *f* or terminal *f* de autobuses.

bus-stop ['bʌsstɔp] *n* parada de autobús, paradero (*LAM*).

bust [bʌst] *n* (*ANAT*) pecho ♦ *adj* (*col*: *broken*) roto, estropeado ♦ *vt* (*col*: *POLICE*: *arrest*) detener; **to go ~** quebrar.

bustle ['bʌsl] *n* bullicio, movimiento ♦ *vi* menearse, apresurarse.

bustling ['bʌslɪŋ] *adj* (*town*) animado, bullicioso.

bust-up ['bʌstʌp] *n* (*col*) riña.

busty ['bʌstɪ] *adj* (*col*) pechugona, con buena delantera.

busy ['bɪzɪ] *adj* ocupado, atareado; (*shop, street*) concurrido, animado ♦ *vt*: **to ~ o.s.**

with ocuparse en; **he's a ~ man** (*normally*) es un hombre muy ocupado; (*temporarily*) está muy ocupado; **the line's ~** (*esp US*) está comunicando.

busybody ['bɪzɪbɔdɪ] *n* entrometido/a.

busy signal *n* (*US TEL*) señal *f* de comunicando.

══════════ KEYWORD

but [bʌt] *conj* **1** pero; **he's not very bright, ~ he's hard-working** no es muy inteligente, pero es trabajador
2 (*in direct contradiction*) sino; **he's not English ~ French** no es inglés sino francés; **he didn't sing ~ he shouted** no cantó sino que gritó
3 (*showing disagreement, surprise etc*): **~ that's far too expensive!** ¡pero eso es carísimo!; **~ it does work!** ¡(pero) sí que funciona!
♦ *prep* (*apart from, except*) menos, salvo; **we've had nothing ~ trouble** no hemos tenido más que problemas; **no-one ~ him can do it** nadie más que él puede hacerlo; **the last ~ one** el penúltimo; **who ~ a lunatic would do such a thing?** ¡sólo un loco haría una cosa así!; **~ for you/your help** si no fuera por ti/tu ayuda; **anything ~ that** cualquier cosa menos eso
♦ *adv* (*just, only*): **she's ~ a child** no es más que una niña; **had I ~ known** si lo hubiera sabido; **I can ~ try** al menos lo puedo intentar; **it's all ~ finished** está casi acabado.

butane ['bju:teɪn] *n* (*also*: **~ gas**) (gas *m*) butano.

butch [butʃ] *adj* (*pej*: *woman*) machirula, marimacho; (*col*: *man*) muy macho.

butcher ['butʃə*] *n* carnicero/a ♦ *vt* hacer una carnicería con; (*cattle etc for meat*) matar; **~'s (shop)** carnicería.

butler ['bʌtlə*] *n* mayordomo.

butt [bʌt] *n* (*cask*) tonel *m*; (*for rain*) tina; (*thick end*) cabo, extremo; (*of gun*) culata; (*of cigarette*) colilla; (*BRIT fig*: *target*) blanco ♦ *vt* dar cabezadas contra, topetar.
▶**butt in** *vi* (*interrupt*) interrumpir.

butter ['bʌtə*] *n* mantequilla, manteca (*LAM*) ♦ *vt* untar con mantequilla.

butter bean *n* judía blanca.

buttercup ['bʌtəkʌp] *n* ranúnculo.

butterfingers ['bʌtəfɪŋgəz] *n* (*col*) torpe *m/f*.

butterfly ['bʌtəflaɪ] *n* mariposa; (*SWIMMING*: *also*: **~ stroke**) (braza de) mariposa.

buttocks ['bʌtəks] *npl* nalgas *fpl*.

button ['bʌtn] *n* botón *m* ♦ *vt* (*also*: **~ up**)

abotonar, abrochar ♦ *vi* abrocharse.
buttonhole ['bʌtnhəul] *n* ojal *m*; (*flower*)
flor *f* que se lleva en el ojal.
buttress ['bʌtrɪs] *n* contrafuerte *m*; (*fig*)
apoyo, sostén *m*.
buy [baɪ] *vb* (*pt, pp* **bought** [bɔːt]) *vt* comprar
♦ *n* compra; **to ~ sb sth/sth from sb**
comprarle algo a algn; **to ~ sb a drink**
invitar a algn a una copa; **a good/bad ~**
una buena/mala compra.
►**buy back** *vt* volver a comprar.
►**buy in** *vt* proveerse *or* abastecerse de.
►**buy into** *vt fus* comprar acciones en.
►**buy off** *vt* (*col: bribe*) sobornar.
►**buy out** *vt* (*partner*) comprar la parte de.
buyer ['baɪə*] *n* comprador(a) *m/f*; **~'s**
market mercado favorable al comprador.
buy-out ['baɪaut] *n* (*COMM*) adquisición *f* de
(la totalidad de) las acciones.
buzz [bʌz] *n* zumbido; (*col: phone call*)
llamada (telefónica) ♦ *vt* (*call on intercom*)
llamar; (*with buzzer*) hacer sonar; (*AVIAT:
plane, building*) pasar rozando ♦ *vi*
zumbar; **my head is ~ing** me zumba la
cabeza.
►**buzz off** *vi* (*BRIT col*) largarse.
buzzard ['bʌzəd] *n* (*BRIT*) águila ratonera;
(*US*) buitre *m*, gallinazo (*LAM*).
buzzer ['bʌzə*] *n* timbre *m*.
buzz word *n* palabra que está de moda.

═══════════ *KEYWORD*

by [baɪ] *prep* **1** (*referring to cause, agent*) por;
de; **abandoned ~ his mother** abandonado
por su madre; **surrounded ~ enemies**
rodeado de enemigos; **a painting ~**
Picasso un cuadro de Picasso
2 (*referring to method, manner, means*): **~**
bus/car/train en autobús/coche/tren; **to**
pay ~ cheque pagar con cheque(s); **~**
moonlight/candlelight a la luz de la luna/
una vela; **~ saving hard, he ...**
ahorrando, ...
3 (*via, through*) por; **we came ~ Dover**
vinimos por Dover
4 (*close to, past*): **the house ~ the river** la
casa junto al río; **she rushed ~ me** pasó a
mi lado como una exhalación; **I go ~ the**
post office every day paso por delante de
Correos todos los días
5 (*time: not later than*) para; (: *during*): **~**
daylight de día; **~ 4 o'clock** para las
cuatro; **~ this time tomorrow** mañana a
estas horas; **~ the time I got here it was**
too late cuando llegué ya era demasiado
tarde
6 (*amount*): **~ the metre/kilo** por metro/
kilo; **paid ~ the hour** pagado por hora

7 (*MATH, measure*): **to divide/multiply ~ 3**
dividir/multiplicar por 3; **a room 3**
metres ~ 4 una habitación de 3 metros
por 4; **it's broader ~ a metre** es un metro
más ancho; **the bus missed me ~ inches**
no me pilló el autobús por un pelo
8 (*according to*) según, de acuerdo con;
it's 3 o'clock ~ my watch según mi reloj,
son las tres; **it's all right ~ me** por mí,
está bien
9: (**all**) **~ oneself** *etc* todo solo; **he did it**
(**all**) **~ himself** lo hizo él solo; **he was**
standing (**all**) **~ himself in a corner** estaba
de pie solo en un rincón
10: **~ the way** a propósito, por cierto; **this**
wasn't my idea, ~ the way pues, no fue
idea mía
♦ *adv* **1** *see* **go**; **pass** *etc*
2: **~ and ~** finalmente; **they'll come back**
~ and ~ acabarán volviendo; **~ and large**
en líneas generales, en general.

bye(-bye) ['baɪ('baɪ)] *excl* adiós, hasta
luego, chao (*esp LAM*).
by(e)-law ['baɪlɔː] *n* ordenanza municipal.
by-election ['baɪɪlɛkʃən] *n* (*BRIT*) elección *f*
parcial; *ver recuadro*.

┌─────────────────────────────┐
│ **BY-ELECTION** │
└─────────────────────────────┘

Se celebra una **by-election** *en el Reino
Unido y otros países de la "Commonwealth" cuando es necesario reemplazar a
un parlamentario ("Member of Parliament") cesado o fallecido durante una
legislatura. Dichas elecciones tienen lugar
únicamente en el área electoral represen-
tada por el citado parlamentario, su
"constituency".*

bygone ['baɪgɔn] *adj* pasado, del pasado
♦ *n*: **let ~s be ~s** lo pasado, pasado está.
Byelorussia [bjɛləu'rʌʃə] *n* Bielorrusia.
Byelorussian [bjɛləu'rʌʃən] *adj, n* =
Belorussian.
bypass ['baɪpɑːs] *n* carretera de
circunvalación; (*MED*) (operación *f* de)
by-pass *m* ♦ *vt* evitar.
by-product ['baɪprɔdʌkt] *n* subproducto,
derivado.
bystander ['baɪstændə*] *n* espectador(a) *m/
f*.
byte [baɪt] *n* (*COMPUT*) byte *m*, octeto.
byway ['baɪweɪ] *n* camino poco
frecuentado.
byword ['baɪwəːd] *n*: **to be a ~ for** ser
sinónimo de.
by-your-leave ['baɪjɔː'liːv] *n*: **without so**

much as a ~ sin decir nada, sin dar
ningún tipo de explicación.

Cc

C, c [si:] n (letter) C, c f; (MUS): **C do** m; **C for
Charlie** C de Carmen.
C abbr (= Celsius, centigrade) C.
c abbr (= century) S.; (= circa) hacia; (US etc)
= cent(s).
CA n abbr = **Central America**; (BRIT) =
chartered accountant; (US) = California.
ca. abbr (= circa) c.
c/a abbr = capital account, credit account,
current account.
CAA n abbr (BRIT: = Civil Aviation Authority)
organismo de control y desarrollo de la
aviación civil.
CAB n abbr (BRIT: = Citizens' Advice Bureau)
≈ Servicio de Información Ciudadana.
cab [kæb] n taxi m; (of truck) cabina.
cabaret ['kæbəreɪ] n cabaret m.
cabbage ['kæbɪdʒ] n col f, berza.
cabbie, cabby ['kæbɪ] n (col) taxista m/f.
cab driver n taxista m/f.
cabin ['kæbɪn] n cabaña; (on ship) camarote
m.
cabin cruiser n yate m de motor.
cabinet ['kæbɪnɪt] n (POL) consejo de
ministros; (furniture) armario; (also:
display ~) vitrina.
cabinet-maker ['kæbɪnɪt'meɪkə*] n
ebanista m.
cabinet minister n ministro/a (del
gabinete).
cable ['keɪbl] n cable m ♦ vt cablegrafiar.
cable-car ['keɪblkɑ:*] n teleférico.
cablegram ['keɪblgræm] n cablegrama m.
cable television n televisión f por cable.
cache [kæʃ] n (drugs) alijo; (arms) zulo.
cackle ['kækl] vi cacarear.
cactus, pl **cacti** ['kæktəs, -taɪ] n cacto.
CAD n abbr (= computer-aided design) DAO
m.
caddie, caddy ['kædɪ] n (GOLF) cadi m.
cadence ['keɪdəns] n ritmo; (MUS)
cadencia.
cadet [kə'dɛt] n (MIL) cadete m; **police ~**
cadete m de policía.
cadge [kædʒ] vt gorronear.
cadger ['kædʒə*] n gorrón/ona m/f.

cadre ['kædrɪ] n cuadro.
Caesarean, (US) Cesarean [si:'zɛərɪən] adj:
~ **(section)** cesárea.
CAF abbr (BRIT: = cost and freight) C y F.
café ['kæfeɪ] n café m.
cafeteria [kæfɪ'tɪərɪə] n cafetería (con
autoservicio para comer).
caffein(e) ['kæfi:n] n cafeína.
cage [keɪdʒ] n jaula ♦ vt enjaular.
cagey ['keɪdʒɪ] adj (col) cauteloso,
reservado.
cagoule [kə'gu:l] n canguro.
cahoots [kə'hu:ts] n: **to be in** ~ **(with sb)**
estar conchabado (con algn).
CAI n abbr (= computer-aided instruction)
enseñanza asistida por ordenador.
Cairo ['kaɪərəu] n El Cairo.
cajole [kə'dʒəul] vt engatusar.
cake [keɪk] n pastel m; (of soap) pastilla; **he
wants to have his** ~ **and eat it** (fig) quiere
estar en misa y repicando; **it's a piece of**
~ (col) es pan comido.
caked [keɪkt] adj: ~ **with** cubierto de.
cake shop n pastelería.
Cal. abbr (US) = California.
calamine ['kæləmaɪn] n calamina.
calamitous [kə'læmɪtəs] adj calamitoso.
calamity [kə'læmɪtɪ] n calamidad f.
calcium ['kælsɪəm] n calcio.
calculate ['kælkjuleɪt] vt (estimate: chances,
effect) calcular.
▶**calculate on** vt fus: **to** ~ **on sth/on doing
sth** contar con algo/con hacer algo.
calculated ['kælkjuleɪtɪd] adj: **we took a** ~
risk calculamos el riesgo.
calculating ['kælkjuleɪtɪŋ] adj (scheming)
calculador(a).
calculation [kælkju'leɪʃən] n cálculo,
cómputo.
calculator ['kælkjuleɪtə*] n calculadora.
calculus ['kælkjuləs] n cálculo.
calendar ['kæləndə*] n calendario; ~
month/year n mes m/año civil.
calf, pl **calves** [kɑ:f, kɑ:vz] n (of cow)
ternero, becerro; (of other animals) cría;
(also: ~skin) piel f de becerro; (ANAT)
pantorrilla, canilla (LAM).
caliber ['kælɪbə*] n (US) = calibre.
calibrate ['kælɪbreɪt] vt (gun etc) calibrar;
(scale of measuring instrument) graduar.
calibre, (US) caliber ['kælɪbə*] n calibre m.
calico ['kælɪkəu] n calicó m.
Calif. abbr (US) = California.
California [kælɪ'fɔ:nɪə] n California.
calipers ['kælɪpəz] npl (US) = callipers.
call [kɔ:l] vt (gen, also TEL) llamar;
(announce: flight) anunciar; (meeting,
strike) convocar ♦ vi (shout) llamar;

(*telephone*) llamar (por teléfono), telefonear; (*visit: also:* ~ **in,** ~ **round**) hacer una visita ♦ *n* (*shout, TEL*) llamada, llamado (*LAM*); (*of bird*) canto; (*appeal*) llamamiento, llamado (*LAM*); (*summons: for flight etc*) llamada; (*fig: lure*) llamada; **to be** ~**ed** (*person, object*) llamarse; **to** ~ **sb names** poner verde a algn; **let's** ~ **it a day** (*col*) ¡dejémoslo!, ¡ya está bien!; **who is** ~**ing?** ¿de parte de quién?; **London** ~**ing** (*RADIO*) aquí Londres; **on** ~ (*nurse, doctor etc*) de guardia; **please give me a** ~ **at 7** llámeme a las 7, por favor; **long-distance** ~ conferencia (interurbana); **to make a** ~ llamar por teléfono; **port of** ~ puerto de escala; **to pay a** ~ **on sb** pasarse a ver a algn; **there's not much** ~ **for these items** estos artículos no tienen mucha demanda.

►**call at** *vt fus* (*ship*) hacer escala en, tocar en; (*train*) parar en.

►**call back** *vi* (*return*) volver; (*TEL*) volver a llamar.

►**call for** *vt fus* (*demand*) pedir, exigir; (*fetch*) venir por.

►**call in** *vt* (*doctor, expert, police*) llamar.

►**call off** *vt* suspender; **the strike was** ~**ed off** se desconvocó la huelga.

►**call on** *vt fus* (*visit*) ir a ver; (*turn to*) acudir a.

►**call out** *vi* gritar, dar voces ♦ *vt* (*doctor*) llamar; (*police, troops*) hacer intervenir.

►**call up** *vt* (*MIL*) llamar a filas.

Callanetics ® [kælə'nɛtɪks] *nsg gimnasia de repetición de pequeños ejercicios musculares.*

callbox ['kɔːlbɔks] *n* (*BRIT*) cabina telefónica.

call centre *n* (*BRIT*) centro de llamadas.

caller ['kɔːlə*] *n* visita *f*; (*TEL*) usuario/a; **hold the line,** ~**!** ¡no cuelgue!

call girl *n* prostituta.

call-in ['kɔːlɪn] *n* (*US*) *programa de línea abierta al público.*

calling ['kɔːlɪŋ] *n* vocación *f*; (*profession*) profesión *f*.

calling card *n* tarjeta de visita.

callipers, (*US*) **calipers** ['kælɪpəz] *npl* (*MED*) aparato ortopédico; (*MATH*) calibrador *m*.

callous ['kæləs] *adj* insensible, cruel.

callousness ['kæləsnɪs] *n* insensibilidad, crueldad *f*.

callow ['kæləu] *adj* inexperto, novato.

calm [kɑːm] *adj* tranquilo; (*sea*) tranquilo, en calma ♦ *n* calma, tranquilidad *f* ♦ *vt* calmar, tranquilizar.

►**calm down** *vi* calmarse, tranquilizarse ♦ *vt* calmar, tranquilizar.

calmly ['kɑːmlɪ] *adv* tranquilamente, con calma.

calmness ['kɑːmnɪs] *n* calma.

Calor gas ® ['kælə*-] *n* butano.

calorie ['kælərɪ] *n* caloría; **low-**~ **product** producto bajo en calorías.

calve [kɑːv] *vi* parir.

calves [kɑːvz] *npl of* **calf.**

CAM *n abbr* (= *computer-aided manufacturing*) producción *f* asistida por ordenador.

camber ['kæmbə*] *n* (*of road*) combadura.

Cambodia [kæm'bəudjə] *n* Camboya.

Cambodian [kæm'bəudjən] *adj, n* camboyano/a *m/f*.

Cambs *abbr* (*BRIT*) = *Cambridgeshire.*

camcorder ['kæmkɔːdə*] *n* videocámara.

came [keɪm] *pt of* **come.**

camel ['kæməl] *n* camello.

cameo ['kæmɪəu] *n* camafeo.

camera ['kæmərə] *n* cámara *or* máquina fotográfica; (*CINE, TV*) cámara; (*movie* ~) cámara, tomavistas *m inv*; **in** ~ a puerta cerrada.

cameraman ['kæmərəmən] *n* cámara *m*.

Cameroon, Cameroun [kæme'ruːn] *n* Camerún *m*.

camomile tea ['kæməmaɪl-] *n* manzanilla.

camouflage ['kæməflɑːʒ] *n* camuflaje *m* ♦ *vt* camuflar.

camp [kæmp] *n* campo, campamento ♦ *vi* acampar ♦ *adj* afectado, afeminado; **to go** ~**ing** ir de *or* hacer camping.

campaign [kæm'peɪn] *n* (*MIL, POL etc*) campaña ♦ *vi*: **to** ~ (**for/against**) hacer campaña (a favor de/en contra de).

campaigner [kæm'peɪnə*] *n*: ~ **for** defensor(a) *m/f* de; ~ **against** persona que hace campaña contra.

campbed ['kæmpbɛd] *n* (*BRIT*) cama plegable.

camper ['kæmpə*] *n* campista *m/f*; (*vehicle*) caravana.

camping ['kæmpɪŋ] *n* camping *m*.

campsite ['kæmpsaɪt] *n* camping *m*.

campus ['kæmpəs] *n* campus *m*.

camshaft ['kæmʃɑːft] *n* árbol *m* de levas.

can [kæn] *aux vb see next headword* ♦ *n* (*of oil, water*) bidón *m*; (*tin*) lata, bote *m* ♦ *vt* enlatar; (*preserve*) conservar en lata; **a** ~ **of beer** una lata *or* un bote de cerveza; **to carry the** ~ (*col*) pagar el pato.

━━━━━━━━━━━━━━━━━━━ *KEYWORD*

can (*negative* **cannot, can't**; *conditional and pt* **could**) *aux vb* **1** (*be able to*) poder; **you** ~ **do it if you try** puedes hacerlo si lo intentas; **I** ~**'t see you** no te veo; ~ **you hear me?**

(*not translated*) ¿me oyes?
2 (*know how to*) saber; I ~ **swim/play
tennis/drive** sé nadar/jugar al tenis/
conducir; ~ **you speak French?** ¿hablas *or*
sabes hablar francés?
3 (*may*) poder; ~ **I use your phone?** ¿me
dejas *or* puedo usar tu teléfono?; **could I
have a word with you?** ¿podría hablar
contigo un momento?
4 (*expressing disbelief, puzzlement etc*): **it
~'t be true!** ¡no puede ser (verdad)!;
what CAN he want? ¿qué querrá?
5 (*expressing possibility, suggestion etc*): **he
could be in the library** podría estar en la
biblioteca; **she could have been delayed**
puede que se haya retrasado.

Canada ['kænədə] *n* Canadá *m*.
Canadian [kə'neɪdɪən] *adj, n* canadiense *m/f*.
canal [kə'næl] *n* canal *m*.
canary [kə'neərɪ] *n* canario.
Canary Islands, Canaries [kə'neərɪz] *npl*
las (Islas) Canarias.
Canberra ['kænbərə] *n* Canberra.
cancel ['kænsəl] *vt* cancelar; (*train*)
suprimir; (*appointment, cheque*) anular;
(*cross out*) tachar.
►**cancel out** *vt* (*MATH*) anular; (*fig*)
contrarrestar; **they · each other out** se
anulan mutuamente.
cancellation [kænsə'leɪʃən] *n* cancelación *f*;
supresión *f*.
cancer ['kænsə*] *n* cáncer *m*; **C~** (*ASTRO*)
Cáncer *m*.
cancerous ['kænsərəs] *adj* canceroso.
cancer patient *n* enfermo/a *m/f* de cáncer.
cancer research *n* investigación *f* del
cáncer.
C and F *abbr* (= *cost and freight*) C y F.
candid ['kændɪd] *adj* franco, abierto.
candidacy ['kændɪdəsɪ] *n* candidatura.
candidate ['kændɪdeɪt] *n* candidato/a.
candidature ['kændɪdətʃə*] *n* (*BRIT*) =
candidacy.
candidly ['kændɪdlɪ] *adv* francamente, con
franqueza.
candle ['kændl] *n* vela; (*in church*) cirio.
candle holder *n see* **candlestick**.
candlelight ['kændllaɪt] *n*: **by ~** a la luz de
una vela.
candlestick ['kændlstɪk] *n* (*also*: **candle
holder**: *single*) candelero; (: *low*)
palmatoria; (*bigger, ornate*) candelabro.
candour, (*US*) **candor** ['kændə*] *n*
franqueza.
candy ['kændɪ] *n* azúcar *m* cande; (*US*)
caramelo ♦ *vt* (*fruit*) escarchar.
candy-floss ['kændɪflɔs] *n* (*BRIT*) algodón *m*

(azucarado).
cane [keɪn] *n* (*BOT*) caña; (*for baskets, chairs
etc*) mimbre *m*; (*stick*) vara, palmeta; (: *for
walking*) bastón *m* ♦ *vt* (*BRIT SCOL*) castigar
(con palmeta); ~ **liquor** caña.
canine ['kænaɪn] *adj* canino.
canister ['kænɪstə*] *n* bote *m*.
cannabis ['kænəbɪs] *n* canabis *m*.
canned [kænd] *adj* en lata, de lata; (*col*:
music) grabado; (: *drunk*) mamado.
cannibal ['kænɪbəl] *n* caníbal *m/f*,
antropófago/a.
cannibalism ['kænɪbəlɪzəm] *n* canibalismo.
cannon, *pl* ~ *or* ~**s** ['kænən] *n* cañón *m*.
cannonball ['kænənbɔːl] *n* bala (de cañón).
cannon fodder *n* carne *f* de cañón.
cannot ['kænɔt] = **can not**.
canny ['kænɪ] *adj* avispado.
canoe [kə'nuː] *n* canoa; (*SPORT*) piragua.
canoeing [kə'nuːɪŋ] *n* (*SPORT*) piragüismo.
canoeist [kə'nuːɪst] *n* piragüista *m/f*.
canon ['kænən] *n* (*clergyman*) canónigo;
(*standard*) canon *m*.
canonize ['kænənaɪz] *vt* canonizar.
can opener *n* abrelatas *m inv*.
canopy ['kænəpɪ] *n* dosel *m*, toldo.
can't [kænt] = **can not**.
Cantab. *abbr* (*BRIT*: = *cantabrigiensis*) = *of
Cambridge*.
cantankerous [kæn'tæŋkərəs] *adj* arisco,
malhumorado.
canteen [kæn'tiːn] *n* (*eating place*) comedor
m; (*BRIT*: *of cutlery*) juego.
canter ['kæntə*] *n* medio galope ♦ *vi* ir a
medio galope.
cantilever ['kæntɪliːvə*] *n* viga voladiza.
canvas ['kænvəs] *n* (*material*) lona; (*painting*)
lienzo; (*NAUT*) velamen *m*; **under ~**
(*camping*) en tienda de campaña.
canvass ['kænvəs] *vt* (*POL*: *district*) hacer
campaña (puerta a puerta) en; (: *person*)
hacer campaña (puerta a puerta) a favor
de; (*COMM*: *district*) sondear el mercado
en; (: *citizens, opinions*) sondear.
canvasser ['kænvəsə*] *n* (*POL*)
representante *m/f* electoral; (*COMM*)
corredor(a) *m/f*.
canyon ['kænjən] *n* cañón *m*.
CAP *n abbr* (= *Common Agricultural Policy*)
PAC *f*.
cap [kæp] *n* (*hat*) gorra; (*for swimming*)
gorro; (*of pen*) capuchón *m*; (*of bottle*)
tapón *m*; (: *metal*) chapa; (*contraceptive*)
diafragma *m* ♦ *vt* (*outdo*) superar; (*BRIT
SPORT*) seleccionar (para el equipo
nacional); **and to ~ it all, he ...** y para
colmo, él ....
capability [keɪpə'bɪlɪtɪ] *n* capacidad *f*.

capable ['keɪpəbl] *adj* capaz.
capacity [kə'pæsɪtɪ] *n* capacidad *f*; (*position*) calidad *f*; **filled to** ~ lleno a reventar; **this work is beyond my** ~ este trabajo es superior a mí; **in an advisory** ~ como asesor.
cape [keɪp] *n* capa; (*GEO*) cabo.
Cape of Good Hope *n* Cabo de Buena Esperanza.
caper ['keɪpə*] *n* (*CULIN: also:* ~s) alcaparra; (*prank*) travesura.
Cape Town *n* Ciudad *f* del Cabo.
capital ['kæpɪtl] *n* (*also:* ~ **city**) capital *f*; (*money*) capital *m*; (*also:* ~ **letter**) mayúscula.
capital account *n* cuenta de capital.
capital allowance *n* desgravación *f* sobre bienes del capital.
capital assets *n* activo fijo.
capital expenditure *n* inversión *f* de capital.
capital gains tax *n* impuesto sobre la plusvalía.
capital goods *npl* bienes *mpl* de capital.
capital-intensive [kæpɪtlɪn'tensɪv] *adj* de utilización intensiva de capital.
capital investment *n* inversión *f* de capital.
capitalism ['kæpɪtəlɪzəm] *n* capitalismo.
capitalist ['kæpɪtəlɪst] *adj, n* capitalista *m/f*.
capitalize ['kæpɪtəlaɪz] *vt* (*COMM: provide with capital*) capitalizar.
▸**capitalize on** *vt fus* (*fig*) sacar provecho de, aprovechar.
capital punishment *n* pena de muerte.
capital transfer tax *n* impuesto sobre plusvalía de cesión.
Capitol ['kæpɪtl] *n*: **the** ~ el Capitolio; *ver recuadro*.

CAPITOL

El Capitolio (Capitol) es el edificio en el que se reúne el Congreso de los Estados Unidos ("Congress"), situado en la ciudad de Washington. Por extensión, también se suele llamar así al edificio en el que tienen lugar las sesiones parlamentarias de la cámara de representantes de muchos de los estados.

---

capitulate [kə'pɪtjuleɪt] *vi* capitular, rendirse.
capitulation [kəpɪtju'leɪʃən] *n* capitulación *f*, rendición *f*.
capricious [kə'prɪʃəs] *adj* caprichoso.
Capricorn ['kæprɪkɔːn] *n* Capricornio.
caps [kæps] *abbr* (= *capital letters*) may.

capsize [kæp'saɪz] *vt* volcar, hacer zozobrar ♦ *vi* volcarse, zozobrar.
capstan ['kæpstən] *n* cabrestante *m*.
capsule ['kæpsjuːl] *n* cápsula.
Capt. *abbr* = **Captain**.
captain ['kæptɪn] *n* capitán *m* ♦ *vt* capitanear, ser el capitán de.
caption ['kæpʃən] *n* (*heading*) título; (*to picture*) leyenda, pie *m*.
captivate ['kæptɪveɪt] *vt* cautivar, encantar.
captive ['kæptɪv] *adj, n* cautivo/a *m/f*.
captivity [kæp'tɪvɪtɪ] *n* cautiverio.
captor ['kæptə*] *n* captor(a) *m/f*.
capture ['kæptʃə*] *vt* capturar; (*place*) tomar; (*attention*) captar, llamar ♦ *n* captura; toma; (*data* ~) formulación *f* de datos.
car [kɑː*] *n* coche *m*, carro (*LAM*), automóvil *m*, auto (*LAM*); (*US RAIL*) vagón *m*; **by** ~ en coche.
Caracas [kə'rækəs] *n* Caracas *m*.
carafe [kə'ræf] *n* garrafa.
caramel ['kærəməl] *n* caramelo.
carat ['kærət] *n* quilate *m*; **18-**~ **gold** oro de 18 quilates.
caravan ['kærəvæn] *n* (*BRIT*) caravana, remolque *m*; (*of camels*) caravana.
caravan site *n* (*BRIT*) camping *m* para caravanas.
caraway ['kærəweɪ] *n*: ~ **seed** carvi *m*.
carbohydrates [kɑːbəu'haɪdreɪts] *npl* (*foods*) hidratos *mpl* de carbono.
car bomb *n* coche-bomba *m*.
carbon ['kɑːbən] *n* carbono.
carbonated ['kɑːbəneɪtɪd] *adj* (*drink*) con gas.
carbon copy *n* copia al carbón.
carbon dioxide *n* dióxido de carbono, anhídrido carbónico.
carbon monoxide *n* monóxido de carbono.
carbon paper *n* papel *m* carbón.
carbon ribbon *n* cinta de carbón.
car boot sale *n* mercadillo (*de objetos usados expuestos en el maletero del coche*).
carburettor, (*US*) **carburetor** [kɑːbju'retə*] *n* carburador *m*.
carcass ['kɑːkəs] *n* (*animal*) res *f* muerta; (*dead body*) cadáver *m*.
carcinogenic [kɑːsɪnə'dʒɛnɪk] *adj* cancerígeno.
card [kɑːd] *n* (*thin cardboard*) cartulina; (*playing* ~) carta, naipe *m*; (*visiting* ~, *greetings* ~ *etc*) tarjeta; (*index* ~) ficha; **membership** ~ carnet *m*; **to play** ~s jugar a las cartas *or* los naipes.
cardamom ['kɑːdəməm] *n* cardamomo.

cardboard ['kɑːdbɔːd] n cartón m, cartulina.
cardboard box n caja de cartón.
cardboard city n zona de marginados sin hogar (*que se refugian entre cartones*).
card-carrying member ['kɑːdkærɪɪŋ-] n miembro con carnet.
card game n juego de naipes or cartas.
cardiac ['kɑːdɪæk] adj cardíaco.
cardigan ['kɑːdɪɡən] n chaqueta (de punto), rebeca.
cardinal ['kɑːdɪnl] adj cardinal ♦ n cardenal m.
cardinal number n número cardinal.
card index n fichero.
cardphone ['kɑːdfəun] n cabina que funciona con tarjetas telefónicas.
cardsharp ['kɑːdʃɑːp] n fullero/a.
card vote n voto por delegación.
CARE [kɛə*] n abbr (= Cooperative for American Relief Everywhere) sociedad benéfica.
care [kɛə*] n cuidado; (*worry*) preocupación f; (*charge*) cargo, custodia ♦ vi: **to ~ about** preocuparse por; **~ of (c/o)** en casa de, al cuidado de; (: *on letter*) para (entregar a); **in sb's ~** a cargo de algn, **the child has been taken into ~** pusieron al niño bajo custodia del gobierno; **"with ~"** "¡frágil!"; **to take ~ to** cuidarse de, tener cuidado de; **to take ~ of** vt cuidar; (*details, arrangements*) encargarse de; **I don't ~** no me importa; **I couldn't ~ less** me trae sin cuidado.
►**care for** vt fus cuidar; (*like*) querer.
careen [kəˈriːn] vi (*ship*) inclinarse, escorar ♦ vt carenar.
career [kəˈrɪə*] n carrera (profesional); (*occupation*) profesión f ♦ vi (*also*: ~ **along**) correr a toda velocidad.
career girl n mujer f dedicada a su profesión.
careers officer n consejero/a de orientación profesional.
carefree ['kɛəfriː] adj despreocupado.
careful ['kɛəful] adj cuidadoso; (*cautious*) cauteloso; **(be) ~!** ¡ten cuidado!; **he's very ~ with his money** mira mucho el dinero; (*pej*) es muy tacaño.
carefully ['kɛəfəlɪ] adv con cuidado, cuidadosamente.
careless ['kɛəlɪs] adj descuidado; (*heedless*) poco atento.
carelessly ['kɛəlɪslɪ] adv sin cuidado, a la ligera.
carelessness ['kɛəlɪsnɪs] n descuido, falta de atención.
carer ['kɛərə*] n persona que cuida de

enfermos, ancianos o disminuidos.
caress [kəˈrɛs] n caricia ♦ vt acariciar.
caretaker ['kɛəteɪkə*] n portero/a, conserje m/f.
caretaker government n gobierno provisional.
car-ferry ['kɑːfɛrɪ] n transbordador m para coches.
cargo, pl ~es ['kɑːɡəu] n cargamento, carga.
cargo boat n buque m de carga, carguero.
cargo plane n avión m de carga.
car hire n alquiler m de coches.
Caribbean [kærɪˈbiːən] adj caribe, caribeño; **the ~ (Sea)** el (Mar) Caribe.
caricature ['kærɪkətjuə*] n caricatura.
caring ['kɛərɪŋ] adj humanitario.
carnage ['kɑːnɪdʒ] n matanza, carnicería.
carnal ['kɑːnl] adj carnal.
carnation [kɑːˈneɪʃən] n clavel m.
carnival ['kɑːnɪvəl] n carnaval m; (*US*) parque m de atracciones.
carnivore ['kɑːnɪvɔː*] n carnívoro/a.
carnivorous [kɑːˈnɪvrəs] adj carnívoro.
carol ['kærəl] n: **(Christmas) ~** villancico.
carouse [kəˈrauz] vi estar de juerga.
carousel [kærəˈsɛl] n (*US*) tiovivo, caballitos mpl.
carp [kɑːp] n (*fish*) carpa.
►**carp at** or **about** vt fus sacar faltas de.
car park n (*BRIT*) aparcamiento, parking m, playa de estacionamiento (*LAM*).
carpenter ['kɑːpɪntə*] n carpintero.
carpentry ['kɑːpɪntrɪ] n carpintería.
carpet ['kɑːpɪt] n alfombra ♦ vt alfombrar; **fitted ~** moqueta.
carpet bombing n bombardeo de arrasamiento.
carpet slippers npl zapatillas fpl.
carpet sweeper [-ˈswiːpə*] n cepillo mecánico.
car phone n teléfono de coche.
carping ['kɑːpɪŋ] adj (*critical*) criticón/ona.
carriage ['kærɪdʒ] n coche m; (*BRIT RAIL*) vagón m; (*for goods*) transporte m; (*of typewriter*) carro; (*bearing*) porte m; **~ forward** porte m debido; **~ free** franco de porte; **~ paid** porte pagado; **~ inwards/ outwards** gastos mpl de transporte a cargo del comprador/vendedor.
carriage return n (*on typewriter etc*) tecla de regreso.
carriageway ['kærɪdʒweɪ] n (*BRIT*: part of road*) calzada; **dual ~** autovía.
carrier ['kærɪə*] n transportista m/f; (*company*) empresa de transportes; (*MED*) portador(a) m/f.
carrier bag n (*BRIT*) bolsa de papel or

plástico.
carrier pigeon *n* paloma mensajera.
carrion ['kærɪən] *n* carroña.
carrot ['kærət] *n* zanahoria.
carry ['kærɪ] *vt* (*subj: person*) llevar;
(*transport*) transportar; (*a motion, bill*)
aprobar; (*involve: responsibilities etc*)
entrañar, conllevar; (*COMM: stock*) tener
en existencia; (: *interest*) llevar; (*MATH:*
figure) llevarse ♦ *vi* (*sound*) oírse; **to get**
carried away (*fig*) entusiasmarse; **this**
loan carries 10% interest este empréstito
devenga un interés del 10 por ciento.
▶**carry forward** *vt* (*MATH, COMM*) pasar a
la página/columna siguiente.
▶**carry on** *vi* (*continue*) seguir (adelante),
continuar; (*fam: complain*) montar el
número ♦ *vt* seguir, continuar.
▶**carry out** *vt* (*orders*) cumplir;
(*investigation*) llevar a cabo, realizar.
carrycot ['kærɪkɔt] *n* (*BRIT*) cuna portátil,
capazo.
carry-on ['kærɪ'ɔn] *n* (*col*) follón *m*.
cart [kɑːt] *n* carro, carreta ♦ *vt* cargar con.
carte blanche ['kɑːt'blɔnʃ] *n*: **to give sb** ~
dar carta blanca a algn.
cartel [kɑː'tɛl] *n* (*COMM*) cartel *m*.
cartilage ['kɑːtɪlɪdʒ] *n* cartílago.
cartographer [kɑː'tɔgrəfə*] *n* cartógrafo/a.
carton ['kɑːtən] *n* caja (de cartón); (*of*
cigarettes) cartón *m*.
cartoon [kɑː'tuːn] *n* (*PRESS*) chiste *m*;
(*comic strip*) historieta, tira cómica; (*film*)
dibujos *mpl* animados.
cartoonist [kɑː'tuːnɪst] *n* humorista *m/f*
gráfico.
cartridge ['kɑːtrɪdʒ] *n* cartucho.
cartwheel ['kɑːtwiːl] *n*: **to turn a** ~ dar una
voltereta lateral.
carve [kɑːv] *vt* (*meat*) trinchar; (*wood*)
tallar; (*stone*) cincelar, esculpir; (*on tree*)
grabar.
▶**carve up** *vt* dividir, repartir; (*meat*)
trinchar.
carving ['kɑːvɪŋ] *n* (*in wood etc*) escultura,
talla.
carving knife *n* trinchante *m*.
car wash *n* túnel *m* de lavado.
Casablanca [kæsə'blæŋkə] *n* Casablanca.
cascade [kæs'keɪd] *n* salto de agua,
cascada; (*fig*) chorro ♦ *vi* caer a chorros.
case [keɪs] *n* (*container*) caja; (*MED*) caso;
(*for jewels etc*) estuche *m*; (*LAW*) causa,
proceso; (*BRIT: also: suit~*) maleta;
lower/upper ~ (*TYP*) caja baja/alta; **in** ~
of en caso de; **in any** ~ en todo caso; **just**
in ~ por si acaso; **to have a good** ~ tener
buenas razones; **there's a strong** ~ **for**

reform hay razones sólidas para exigir
una reforma.
case history *n* (*MED*) historial *m* médico,
historia clínica.
case study *n* estudio de casos prácticos.
cash [kæʃ] *n* (dinero) efectivo; (*col: money*)
dinero ♦ *vt* cobrar, hacer efectivo; **to pay**
(in) ~ pagar al contado; ~ **on delivery**
(COD) entrega contra reembolso; ~ **with**
order paga al hacer el pedido; **to be short**
of ~ estar pelado, estar sin blanca.
▶**cash in** *vt* (*insurance policy etc*) cobrar
♦ *vi*: **to** ~ **in on sth** sacar partido or
aprovecharse de algo.
cash account *n* cuenta de caja.
cash and carry *n* cash and carry *m*,
autoservicio mayorista.
cashbook ['kæʃbuk] *n* libro de caja.
cash box *n* hucha.
cash card *n* tarjeta *f* de(l) cajero
(automático).
cash desk *n* (*BRIT*) caja.
cash discount *n* descuento por pago al
contado.
cash dispenser *n* cajero automático.
cashew [kæ'ʃuː] *n* (*also:* ~ **nut**) anacardo.
cash flow *n* flujo de fondos, cash-flow *m*,
movimiento de efectivo.
cashier [kæ'ʃɪə*] *n* cajero/a ♦ *vt* (*MIL*)
destituir, expulsar.
cashmere ['kæʃmɪə*] *n* cachemir *m*,
cachemira.
cash payment *n* pago al contado.
cash price *n* precio al contado.
cash register *n* caja.
cash reserves *npl* reserva en efectivo.
cash sale *n* venta al contado.
casing ['keɪsɪŋ] *n* revestimiento.
casino [kə'siːnəu] *n* casino.
cask [kɑːsk] *n* tonel *m*, barril *m*.
casket ['kɑːskɪt] *n* cofre *m*, estuche *m*; (*US:*
coffin) ataúd *m*.
Caspian Sea ['kæspɪən-] *n*: **the** ~ el Mar
Caspio.
cassava [kə'sɑːvə] *n* mandioca.
casserole ['kæsərəul] *n* (*food, pot*) cazuela.
cassette [kæ'sɛt] *n* cas(s)et(t)e *m or f*.
cassette deck *n* platina.
cassette player, cassette recorder *n*
cas(s)et(t)e *m*.
cassock ['kæsək] *n* sotana.
cast [kɑːst] *vb* (*pt, pp* **cast**) *vt* (*throw*) echar,
arrojar, lanzar; (*skin*) mudar, perder;
(*metal*) fundir; (*THEAT*): **to** ~ **sb as Othello**
dar a algn el papel de Otelo ♦ *n* (*THEAT*)
reparto; (*mould*) forma, molde *m*; (*also:*
plaster ~) vaciado; **to** ~ **loose** soltar; **to** ~
one's vote votar.

►**cast aside** *vt* (*reject*) descartar, desechar.
►**cast away** *vt* desechar.
►**cast down** *vt* derribar.
►**cast off** *vi* (*NAUT*) soltar amarras; (*KNITTING*) cerrar los puntos ♦ *vt* (*KNITTING*) cerrar; **to ~ sb off** abandonar a algn, desentenderse de algn.
►**cast on** *vt* (*KNITTING*) montar.
castanets [kæstə'nɛts] *npl* castañuelas *fpl.*
castaway ['kɑːstəwəɪ] *n* náufrago/a.
caste [kɑːst] *n* casta.
caster sugar ['kɑːstə*-] *n* (*BRIT*) azúcar *m* en polvo.
Castile [kæs'tiːl] *n* Castilla.
Castilian [kæs'tɪlɪən] *adj, n* castellano/a ♦ *n* (*LING*) castellano.
casting vote ['kɑːstɪŋ-] *n* (*BRIT*) voto decisivo.
cast iron *n* hierro fundido *or* colado ♦ *adj* (*fig: alibi*) irrebatible; (*will*) férreo.
castle ['kɑːsl] *n* castillo; (*CHESS*) torre *f.*
castor ['kɑːstə*] *n* (*wheel*) ruedecilla.
castor oil *n* aceite *m* de ricino.
castrate [kæs'treɪt] *vt* castrar.
casual ['kæʒjul] *adj* (*by chance*) fortuito; (*irregular: work etc*) eventual, temporero; (*unconcerned*) despreocupado, (*informal: clothes*) de sport.
casually ['kæʒjulɪ] *adv* por casualidad; de manera despreocupada.
casualty ['kæʒjultɪ] *n* víctima, herido; (*dead*) muerto; (*MIL*) baja; **heavy casualties** numerosas bajas *fpl.*
casualty ward *n* urgencias *fpl.*
cat [kæt] *n* gato.
catacombs ['kætəkuːmz] *npl* catacumbas *fpl.*
Catalan ['kætəlæn] *adj, n* catalán/ana *m/f.*
catalogue, (*US*) **catalog** ['kætəlɔg] *n* catálogo ♦ *vt* catalogar.
Catalonia [kætə'ləunɪə] *n* Cataluña.
catalyst ['kætəlɪst] *n* catalizador *m.*
catalytic converter [kætə'lɪtɪkkən'vəːtə*] *n* catalizador *m.*
catapult ['kætəpʌlt] *n* tirachinas *m inv.*
cataract ['kætərækt] *n* (*MED*) cataratas *fpl.*
catarrh [kə'tɑː*] *n* catarro.
catastrophe [kə'tæstrəfɪ] *n* catástrofe *f.*
catastrophic [kætə'strɔfɪk] *adj* catastrófico.
catcall ['kætkɔːl] *n* (*at meeting etc*) rechifla, silbido.
catch [kætʃ] *vb* (*pt, pp* **caught** [kɔːt]) *vt* coger (*SP*), agarrar (*LAM*); (*arrest*) atrapar, coger (*SP*); (*grasp*) asir; (*breath*) recobrar; (*person: by surprise*) pillar; (*attract: attention*) captar; (*MED*) pillar, coger; (*also: ~ up*) alcanzar ♦ *vi* (*fire*)

encenderse; (*in branches etc*) engancharse ♦ *n* (*fish etc*) captura; (*act of catching*) cogida; (*trick*) trampa; (*of lock*) pestillo, cerradura; **to ~ fire** prenderse; (*house*) incendiarse; **to ~ sight of** divisar.
►**catch on** *vi* (*understand*) caer en la cuenta; (*grow popular*) tener éxito, cuajar.
►**catch out** *vt* (*fig: with trick question*) hundir.
►**catch up** *vi* (*fig*) ponerse al día.
catching ['kætʃɪŋ] *adj* (*MED*) contagioso.
catchment area ['kætʃmənt-] *n* (*BRIT*) zona de captación.
catch phrase *n* frase *f* de moda.
catch-22 ['kætʃtwɛntɪ'tuː] *n*: **it's a ~ situation** es un callejón sin salida, es un círculo vicioso.
catchy ['kætʃɪ] *adj* (*tune*) pegadizo.
catechism ['kætɪkɪzəm] *n* (*REL*) catecismo.
categoric(al) [kætɪ'gɔrɪk(əl)] *adj* categórico, terminante.
categorically [kætɪ'gɔrɪkəlɪ] *adv* categóricamente, terminantemente.
categorize ['kætɪgəraɪz] *vt* clasificar.
category ['kætɪgɔrɪ] *n* categoría.
cater ['keɪtə*] *vi*: **to ~ for** (*BRIT*) abastecer a; (*needs*) atender a; (*consumers*) proveer a.
caterer ['keɪtərə*] *n* abastecedor(a) *m/f,* proveedor(a) *m/f.*
catering ['keɪtərɪŋ] *n* (*trade*) hostelería.
caterpillar ['kætəpɪlə*] *n* oruga.
caterpillar track *n* rodado de oruga.
cat flap *n* gatera.
cathedral [kə'θiːdrəl] *n* catedral *f.*
cathode-ray tube ['kæθəudreɪ'tjuːb] *n* tubo de rayos catódicos.
catholic ['kæθəlɪk] *adj* católico; **C~** *adj, n* (*REL*) católico/a *m/f.*
CAT scanner [kæt-] (*MED*) *n abbr* (= *computerized axial tomography scanner*) escáner *m* TAC.
cat's-eye ['kætsaɪ] *n* (*BRIT AUT*) catafaro.
catsup ['kætsəp] *n* (*US*) ketchup, catsup *m.*
cattle ['kætl] *npl* ganado *sg.*
catty ['kætɪ] *adj* malicioso.
catwalk ['kætwɔːk] *n* pasarela.
Caucasian [kɔː'keɪzɪən] *adj, n* caucásico/a *m/f.*
Caucasus ['kɔːkəsəs] *n* Cáucaso.
caucus ['kɔːkəs] *n* (*POL: local committee*) comité *m* local; (: *US: to elect candidates*) comité *m* electoral; (: *group*) camarilla política.
caught [kɔːt] *pt, pp of* **catch.**
cauliflower ['kɔlɪflauə*] *n* coliflor *f.*
cause [kɔːz] *n* causa; (*reason*) motivo,

razón f ♦ vt causar; (*provoke*) provocar; **to ~ sb to do sth** hacer que algn haga algo.

causeway ['kɔ:zweɪ] n (*road*) carretera elevada; (*embankment*) terraplén m.

caustic ['kɔ:stɪk] adj cáustico; (*fig*) mordaz.

cauterize ['kɔ:təraɪz] vt cauterizar.

caution ['kɔ:ʃən] n cautela, prudencia; (*warning*) advertencia, amonestación f ♦ vt amonestar.

cautious ['kɔ:ʃəs] adj cauteloso, prudente, precavido.

cautiously ['kɔ:ʃəslɪ] adv con cautela.

cautiousness ['kɔ:ʃəsnɪs] n cautela.

cavalcade [kævəl'keɪd] n cabalgata.

cavalier [kævə'lɪə*] n (*knight*) caballero ♦ adj (*pej: offhand: person, attitude*) arrogante, desdeñoso.

cavalry ['kævəlrɪ] n caballería.

cave [keɪv] n cueva, caverna ♦ vi: **to go caving** ir en una expedición espeleológica.

▶**cave in** vi (*roof etc*) derrumbarse, hundirse.

caveman ['keɪvmæn] n cavernícola m.

cavern ['kævən] n caverna.

cavernous ['kævənəs] adj (*cheeks, eyes*) hundido.

caviar(e) ['kævɪɑ:*] n caviar m.

cavity ['kævɪtɪ] n hueco, cavidad f.

cavity wall insulation n aislamiento térmico.

cavort [kə'vɔ:t] vi hacer cabrioladas.

cayenne [keɪ'ɛn] n: **~ pepper** pimentón m picante.

CB n abbr (= *Citizens' Band (Radio)*) frecuencias de radio usadas para la comunicación privada; (*BRIT:* = *Companion of (the Order of) the Bath*) título de nobleza.

CBC n abbr (= *Canadian Broadcasting Corporation*) cadena de radio y televisión.

CBE n abbr (= *Companion of (the Order of) the British Empire*) título de nobleza.

CBI n abbr (= *Confederation of British Industry*) ≈ C.E.O.E. f (*SP*).

CBS n abbr (*US:* = *Columbia Broadcasting System*) cadena de radio y televisión.

CC abbr (*BRIT*) = *County Council*.

cc abbr (= *cubic centimetres*) cc, cm³; (*on letter etc*) = **carbon copy**.

CCA n abbr (*US:* = *Circuit Court of Appeals*) tribunal de apelación itinerante.

CCTV n abbr = **closed-circuit television**.

CCU n abbr (*US:* = *coronary care unit*) unidad f de cuidados cardiológicos.

CD n abbr (= *compact disc*) CD m; **~ player** reproductor m de compact disc; (*MIL*) = *Civil Defence (Corps)* (*BRIT*), *Civil Defense*

(*US*) ♦ abbr (*BRIT:* = *Corps Diplomatique*) CD.

CDC n abbr (*US*) = *center for disease control*.

CD-I ® n (= *Compact Disc Interactive*) CD-I m, disco m compacto interactivo.

Cdr. abbr = **Commander**.

CD-ROM n abbr (= *compact disc read-only memory*) CD-ROM m.

CDT n abbr (*US:* = *Central Daylight Time*) hora de verano del centro.

cease [si:s] vt cesar.

ceasefire ['si:sfaɪə*] n alto m el fuego.

ceaseless ['si:slɪs] adj incesante.

ceaselessly ['si:slɪslɪ] adv sin cesar.

CED n abbr (*US*) = *Committee for Economic Development*.

cedar ['si:də*] n cedro.

cede [si:d] vt ceder.

CEEB n abbr (*US:* = *College Entrance Examination Board*) tribunal para las pruebas de acceso a la universidad.

ceilidh ['keɪlɪ] n baile con música y danzas tradicionales escocesas o irlandesas.

ceiling ['si:lɪŋ] n techo; (*fig: upper limit*) límite m, tope m.

celebrate ['sɛlɪbreɪt] vt celebrar; (*have a party*) festejar ♦ vi: **let's ~!** ¡vamos a celebrarlo!

celebrated ['sɛlɪbreɪtɪd] adj célebre.

celebration [sɛlɪ'breɪʃən] n celebración f.

celebrity [sɪ'lɛbrɪtɪ] n celebridad f.

celeriac [sə'lɛrɪæk] n apio-nabo.

celery ['sɛlərɪ] n apio.

celestial [sɪ'lɛstɪəl] adj (*of sky*) celeste; (*divine*) celestial.

celibacy ['sɛlɪbəsɪ] n celibato.

cell [sɛl] n celda; (*BIOL*) célula; (*ELEC*) elemento.

cellar ['sɛlə*] n sótano; (*for wine*) bodega.

cellist ['tʃɛlɪst] n violoncelista m/f.

cello ['tʃɛləu] n violoncelo.

cellophane ['sɛləfeɪn] n celofán m.

cellphone ['sɛlfəun] n teléfono celular.

cellular ['sɛljulə*] adj celular.

celluloid ['sɛljulɔɪd] n celuloide m.

cellulose ['sɛljuləus] n celulosa.

Celsius ['sɛlsɪəs] adj centígrado.

Celt [kɛlt, sɛlt] n celta m/f.

Celtic ['kɛltɪk, 'sɛltɪk] adj celta, céltico ♦ n (*LING*) celta m.

cement [sə'mɛnt] n cemento ♦ vt cementar; (*fig*) cimentar.

cement mixer n hormigonera.

cemetery ['sɛmɪtrɪ] n cementerio.

cenotaph ['sɛnətɑ:f] n cenotafio.

censor ['sɛnsə*] n censor(a) m/f ♦ vt (*cut*) censurar.

censorship ['sɛnsəʃɪp] n censura.

censure ['sɛnʃə*] vt censurar.
census ['sɛnsəs] n censo.
cent [sɛnt] n (unit of dollar) centavo; (unit of euro) céntimo; see also **per**.
centenary [sɛn'tiːnərɪ], (US) **centennial** [sɛn'tɛnɪəl] n centenario.
center ['sɛntə*] n (US) = **centre**.
centigrade ['sɛntɪgreɪd] adj centígrado.
centilitre, (US) **centiliter** ['sɛntɪliːtə*] n centilitro.
centimetre, (US) **centimeter** ['sɛntɪmiːtə*] n centímetro.
centipede ['sɛntɪpiːd] n ciempiés m inv.
central ['sɛntrəl] adj central; (of house etc) céntrico.
Central African Republic n República Centroafricana.
Central America n Centroamérica.
Central American adj, n centroamericano/a m/f.
central heating n calefacción f central.
centralize ['sɛntrəlaɪz] vt centralizar.
central processing unit (CPU) n (COMPUT) unidad f procesadora central, unidad f central de proceso.
central reservation n (BRIT AUT) mediana.
centre, (US) **center** ['sɛntə*] n centro ♦ vt centrar; **to ~ (on)** (concentrate) concentrar (en).
centrefold, (US) **centerfold** ['sɛntəfəuld] n página central plegable.
centre-forward ['sɛntə'fɔːwəd] n (SPORT) delantero centro.
centre-half ['sɛntə'hɑːf] n (SPORT) medio centro.
centrepiece, (US) **centerpiece** ['sɛntəpiːs] n punto central.
centre spread n (BRIT) páginas fpl centrales.
centre-stage n: **to take ~** pasar a primer plano.
centrifuge ['sɛntrɪfjuːdʒ] n centrifugadora.
century ['sɛntjurɪ] n siglo; **in the twentieth ~** en el siglo veinte.
CEO n abbr (US) = **chief executive officer**.
ceramic [sɪ'ræmɪk] adj de cerámica.
ceramics [sɪ'ræmɪks] n cerámica.
cereal ['siːrɪəl] n cereal m.
cerebral ['sɛrɪbrəl] adj cerebral.
ceremonial [sɛrɪ'məunɪəl] n ceremonial.
ceremony ['sɛrɪmənɪ] n ceremonia; **to stand on ~** hacer ceremonias, andarse con cumplidos.
cert [sɜːt] n (BRIT col): **it's a dead ~** ¡es cosa segura!
certain ['sɜːtən] adj seguro; (correct) cierto; (particular) cierto; **for ~** a ciencia cierta.
certainly ['sɜːtənlɪ] aav desde luego, por

supuesto.
certainty ['sɜːtəntɪ] n certeza, certidumbre f, seguridad f.
certificate [sə'tɪfɪkɪt] n certificado.
certified ['sɜːtɪfaɪd] adj: **~ mail** (US) correo certificado.
certified public accountant (CPA) n (US) contable m/f diplomado/a.
certify ['sɜːtɪfaɪ] vt certificar.
cervical ['sɜːvɪkl] adj: **~ cancer** cáncer m cervical; **~ smear** citología.
cervix ['sɜːvɪks] n cerviz f, cuello del útero.
Cesarean [sɪ'zɛərɪən] adj, n (US) = **Caesarean**.
cessation [sə'seɪʃən] n cese m, suspensión f.
cesspit ['sɛspɪt] n pozo negro.
CET n abbr (= Central European Time) hora de Europa central.
Ceylon [sɪ'lɔn] n Ceilán m.
cf. abbr (= compare) cfr.
CFC n abbr (= chlorofluorocarbon) CFC m.
c/f abbr (COMM) = carried forward.
CG n abbr (= coastguard.
cg abbr (= centigram) cg.
CH n abbr (BRIT: = Companion of Honour) título de nobleza.
ch abbr (BRIT: = central heating) cal. cen.
ch. abbr (= chapter) cap.
Chad [tʃæd] n Chad m.
chafe [tʃeɪf] vt (rub) rozar; (irritate) irritar; **to ~ (against)** (fig) irritarse or enojarse (con).
chaffinch ['tʃæfɪntʃ] n pinzón m (vulgar).
chagrin ['ʃægrɪn] n (annoyance) disgusto; (disappointment) desazón f.
chain [tʃeɪn] n cadena ♦ vt (also: ~ **up**) encadenar.
chain reaction n reacción f en cadena.
chain-smoke ['tʃeɪnsməuk] vi fumar un cigarrillo tras otro.
chain store n tienda de una cadena, **~** grandes almacenes mpl.
chair [tʃeə*] n silla; (armchair) sillón m; (of university) cátedra ♦ vt (meeting) presidir; **the ~** (US: electric ~) la silla eléctrica; **please take a ~** siéntese or tome asiento, por favor.
chairlift ['tʃeəlɪft] n telesilla m.
chairman ['tʃeəmən] n presidente m.
chairperson ['tʃeəpɜːsn] n presidente/a m/f.
chairwoman ['tʃeəwumən] n presidenta.
chalet ['ʃæleɪ] n chalet m (de madera).
chalice ['tʃælɪs] n cáliz m.
chalk [tʃɔːk] n (GEO) creta; (for writing) tiza, gis m (LAM).
▶**chalk up** vt apuntar; (fig: success, victory) apuntarse.
challenge ['tʃælɪndʒ] n desafío, reto ♦ vt

desafiar, retar; (*statement, right*) poner en duda; **to ~ sb to do sth** retar a algn a que haga algo.

challenger ['tʃælɪndʒə�*] n (*SPORT*) contrincante *m/f.*

challenging ['tʃælɪndʒɪŋ] adj que supone un reto; (*tone*) de desafío.

chamber ['tʃeɪmbə*] n cámara, sala; ~ **of commerce** cámara de comercio.

chambermaid ['tʃeɪmbəmeɪd] n camarera.

chamber music n música de cámara.

chamberpot ['tʃeɪmbəpɔt] n orinal *m.*

chameleon [kə'miːlɪən] n camaleón *m.*

chamois ['ʃæmwɑː] n gamuza.

champagne [ʃæm'peɪn] n champaña *m,* champán *m.*

champers ['ʃæmpəz] *nsg* (*col*) champán *m.*

champion ['tʃæmpɪən] n campeón/ona *m/f;* (*of cause*) defensor(a) *m/f,* paladín *m/f* ♦ vt defender, apoyar.

championship ['tʃæmpɪənʃɪp] n campeonato.

chance [tʃɑːns] n (*coincidence*) casualidad *f;* (*luck*) suerte *f;* (*fate*) azar *m;* (*opportunity*) ocasión *f,* oportunidad *f,* chance *m* or *f* (*LAM*); (*likelihood*) posibilidad *f;* (*risk*) riesgo ♦ vt arriesgar, probar ♦ adj fortuito, casual; **to ~ it** arriesgarse, intentarlo; **to take a ~** arriesgarse; **by ~** por casualidad; **it's the ~ of a lifetime** es la oportunidad de su vida; **the ~s are that ...** lo más probable es que ...; **to ~ to do sth** (*happen*) hacer algo por casualidad.

▶**chance (up)on** *vt fus* tropezar(se) con.

chancel ['tʃɑːnsəl] n coro y presbiterio.

chancellor ['tʃɑːnsələ*] n canciller *m;* **C~ of the Exchequer** (*BRIT*) Ministro de Economía y Hacienda; *see also* **Downing Street.**

chancy ['tʃɑːnsɪ] adj (*col*) arriesgado.

chandelier [ʃændə'lɪə*] n araña (de luces).

change [tʃeɪndʒ] vt cambiar; (*clothes, house*) cambiarse de, mudarse de; (*transform*) transformar ♦ vi cambiar(se); (*trains*) hacer transbordo; (*be transformed*): **to ~ into** transformarse en ♦ n cambio; (*alteration*) modificación *f,* transformación *f;* (*coins*) suelto; (*money returned*) vuelta, vuelto (*LAM*); **to ~ one's mind** cambiar de opinión *or* idea; **to ~ gear** (*AUT*) cambiar de marcha; **she ~d into an old skirt** se puso una falda vieja; **for a ~** para variar; **can you give me ~ for £1?** ¿tiene cambio de una libra?; **keep the ~** quédese con la vuelta.

changeable ['tʃeɪndʒəbl] adj (*weather*) cambiable; (*person*) variable.

changeless ['tʃeɪndʒlɪs] adj inmutable.

change machine n máquina de cambio.

changeover ['tʃeɪndʒəuvə*] n (*to new system*) cambio.

changing ['tʃeɪndʒɪŋ] adj cambiante.

changing room n (*BRIT*) vestuario.

channel ['tʃænl] n (*TV*) canal *m;* (*of river*) cauce *m;* (*of sea*) estrecho; (*groove, fig: medium*) conducto, medio ♦ vt (*river etc*) encauzar; **to ~ into** (*fig: interest, energies*) encauzar a, dirigir a; **the (English) C~** el Canal (de la Mancha); **the C~ Islands** las Islas Anglonormandas; **~s of communication** canales *mpl* de comunicación; **green/red ~** (*CUSTOMS*) pasillo verde/rojo.

Channel Tunnel n: **the ~** el túnel del Canal de la Mancha, el Eurotúnel.

chant [tʃɑːnt] n canto; (*of crowd*) gritos *mpl* ♦ vt cantar; **the demonstrators ~ed their disapproval** los manifestantes corearon su desaprobación.

chaos ['keɪɔs] n caos *m.*

chaos theory n teoría del caos.

chaotic [keɪ'ɔtɪk] adj caótico.

chap [tʃæp] n (*BRIT col: man*) tío, tipo; **old ~** amigo (mío).

chapel ['tʃæpəl] n capilla.

chaperone ['ʃæpərəun] n carabina.

chaplain ['tʃæplɪn] n capellán *m.*

chapped [tʃæpt] adj agrietado.

chapter ['tʃæptə*] n capítulo.

char [tʃɑː*] vt (*burn*) carbonizar, chamuscar ♦ n (*BRIT*) = **charlady.**

character ['kærɪktə*] n carácter *m,* naturaleza, índole *f;* (*in novel, film*) personaje *m;* (*role*) papel *m;* (*individuality, COMPUT*) carácter *m;* **a person of good ~** una persona de buena reputación.

character code n código de caracteres.

characteristic [kærɪktə'rɪstɪk] adj característico ♦ n característica.

characterize ['kærɪktəraɪz] vt caracterizar.

charade [ʃə'rɑːd] n farsa, comedia; **~s** (*game*) charadas *fpl.*

charcoal ['tʃɑːkəul] n carbón *m* vegetal; (*ART*) carboncillo.

charge [tʃɑːdʒ] n carga; (*LAW*) cargo, acusación *f;* (*cost*) precio, coste *m;* (*responsibility*) cargo; (*task*) encargo ♦ vt (*LAW*) acusar (*with* de); (*gun, battery, MIL: enemy*) cargar; (*price*) pedir; (*customer*) cobrar; (*sb with task*) encargar ♦ vi precipitarse; (*make pay*) cobrar; **~s** *npl:* **bank ~s** comisiones *fpl* bancarias; **extra ~** recargo, suplemento; **free of ~** gratis; **to reverse the ~s** (*BRIT TEL*) llamar a cobro revertido; **to take ~ of** hacerse cargo de, encargarse de; **to be in ~ of** estar

encargado de; **how much do you ~?**
¿cuánto cobra usted?; **to ~ an expense
(up) to sb's account** cargar algo a cuenta
de algn; **~ it to my account** póngalo *or*
cárguelo a mi cuenta.
charge account *n* (*US*) cuenta abierta *or* a
crédito.
charge card *n* tarjeta de cuenta.
chargé d'affaires [ˈʃɑːʒeɪdæˈfɛə*] *n*
encargado de negocios.
chargehand [ˈtʃɑːdʒhænd] *n* capataz *m*.
charger [ˈtʃɑːdʒə*] *n* (*also*: **battery ~**)
cargador *m* (de baterías); (*old*: *warhorse*)
caballo de batalla.
chariot [ˈtʃærɪət] *n* carro.
charisma [kæˈrɪzmə] *n* carisma *m*.
charitable [ˈtʃærɪtəbl] *adj* caritativo.
charity [ˈtʃærɪtɪ] *n* (*gen*) caridad *f*;
(*organization*) organización *f* benéfica.
charlady [ˈtʃɑːleɪdɪ] *n* (*BRIT*) mujer *f* de la
limpieza.
charlatan [ˈʃɑːlətən] *n* charlatán *m*.
charm [tʃɑːm] *n* encanto, atractivo; (*spell*)
hechizo; (*object*) amuleto ♦ *vt* encantar;
hechizar.
charm bracelet *n* pulsera amuleto.
charming [ˈtʃɑːmɪŋ] *adj* encantador(a);
(*person*) simpático.
chart [tʃɑːt] *n* (*table*) cuadro; (*graph*)
gráfica; (*map*) carta de navegación;
(*weather ~*) mapa *m* meteorológico ♦ *vt*
(*course*) trazar; (*sales, progress*) hacer una
gráfica de; **to be in the ~s** (*record, pop
group*) estar en la lista de éxitos.
charter [ˈtʃɑːtə*] *vt* (*bus*) alquilar; (*plane,
ship*) fletar ♦ *n* (*document*) estatuto, carta;
on ~ en alquiler, alquilado.
chartered accountant (CA) *n* (*BRIT*)
contable *m/f* diplomado/a.
charter flight *n* vuelo chárter.
charwoman [ˈtʃɑːwumən] *n* = **charlady**.
chase [tʃeɪs] *vt* (*pursue*) perseguir; (*hunt*)
cazar ♦ *n* persecución *f*; caza; **to ~ after**
correr tras.
▶**chase up** *vt* (*information*) tratar de
conseguir; **to ~ sb up about sth** recordar
algo a algn.
chasm [ˈkæzəm] *n* abismo.
chassis [ˈʃæsɪ] *n* chasis *m*.
chaste [tʃeɪst] *adj* casto.
chastened [ˈtʃeɪsənd] *adj* escarmentado.
chastening [ˈtʃeɪsnɪŋ] *adj* aleccionador(a).
chastity [ˈtʃæstɪtɪ] *n* castidad *f*.
chat [tʃæt] *vi* (*also*: **have a ~**) charlar ♦ *n*
charla.
▶**chat up** *vt* (*col*: *girl*) ligar con, enrollarse
con.
chatline [ˈtʃætlaɪn] *n* línea (telefónica)

múltiple, party line *f*.
chat show *n* (*BRIT*) programa *m* de
entrevistas.
chattel [ˈtʃætl] *n* bien *m* mueble.
chatter [ˈtʃætə*] *vi* (*person*) charlar; (*teeth*)
castañetear ♦ *n* (*of birds*) parloteo; (*of
people*) charla, cháchara.
chatterbox [ˈtʃætəbɔks] *n* parlanchín/ina
m/f.
chattering classes [ˈtʃætərɪŋˈklɑːsɪz] *npl*:
the ~ (*col: pej*) los intelectualillos.
chatty [ˈtʃætɪ] *adj* (*style*) informal; (*person*)
hablador(a).
chauffeur [ˈʃəufə*] *n* chófer *m*.
chauvinist [ˈʃəuvɪnɪst] *n* (*male ~*) machista
m; (*nationalist*) chovinista *m/f*, patriotero/a
m/f.
ChE *abbr* = *chemical engineer*.
cheap [tʃiːp] *adj* barato; (*joke*) de mal
gusto, chabacano; (*poor quality*) malo;
(*reduced*: *ticket*) económico, (: *fare*) barato
♦ *adv* barato.
cheapen [ˈtʃiːpn] *vt* rebajar el precio de,
abaratar.
cheaply [ˈtʃiːplɪ] *adv* barato, a bajo precio.
cheat [tʃiːt] *vi* hacer trampa; (*in exam*)
copiar ♦ *vt* estafar, timar ♦ *n* trampa;
estafa; (*person*) tramposo/a *m/f*; **he's been
~ing on his wife** ha estado engañando a
su esposa.
cheating [ˈtʃiːtɪŋ] *n* trampa.
check [tʃɛk] *vt* comprobar; (*count*) contar;
(*halt*) frenar; (*restrain*) refrenar,
restringir ♦ *vi*: **to ~ with sb** consultar con
algn; (*official etc*) informarse por ♦ *n*
(*inspection*) control *m*, inspección *f*; (*curb*)
freno; (*bill*) nota, cuenta; (*US*) = **cheque**;
(*pattern*: *gen pl*) cuadro ♦ *adj* (*also*: **~ed**:
pattern, cloth) a cuadros; **to keep a ~ on
sth/sb** controlar algo/a algn.
▶**check in** *vi* (*in hotel*) registrarse; (*at
airport*) facturar ♦ *vt* (*luggage*) facturar.
▶**check out** *vi* (*of hotel*) desocupar la
habitación ♦ *vt* (*investigate*: *story*)
comprobar; (: *person*) informarse sobre.
▶**check up** *vi*: **to ~ up on sth** comprobar
algo; **to ~ up on sb** investigar a algn.
checkbook [ˈtʃɛkbuk] *n* (*US*) =
chequebook.
checkered [ˈtʃɛkəd] *adj* (*US*) = **chequered**.
checkers [ˈtʃɛkəz] *n* (*US*) damas *fpl*.
check-in [ˈtʃɛkɪn] *n* (*also*: **~ desk**: *at airport*)
mostrador *m* de facturación.
checking account [ˈtʃɛkɪŋ-] *n* (*US*) cuenta
corriente.
checklist [ˈtʃɛklɪst] *n* lista.
checkmate [ˈtʃɛkmeɪt] *n* jaque *m* mate.
checkout [ˈtʃɛkaut] *n* (*in supermarket*) caja.

checkpoint ['tʃɛkpɔɪnt] n (punto de) control m, retén m (_LAM_).

checkroom ['tʃɛkrum] n (_US_) consigna.

checkup ['tʃɛkʌp] n (_MED_) reconocimiento general; (_of machine_) revisión f.

cheek [tʃiːk] n mejilla; (_impudence_) descaro.

cheekbone ['tʃiːkbəun] n pómulo.

cheeky ['tʃiːkɪ] adj fresco, descarado.

cheep [tʃiːp] n (_of bird_) pío ♦ vi piar.

cheer [tʃɪə*] vt vitorear, ovacionar; (_gladden_) alegrar, animar ♦ vi dar vivas ♦ n viva m; ~s npl vítores mpl; ~s! ¡salud!

►**cheer on** vt (_person etc_) animar con aplausos or gritos.

►**cheer up** vi animarse ♦ vt alegrar, animar.

cheerful ['tʃɪəful] adj alegre.

cheerfulness ['tʃɪəfulnɪs] n alegría.

cheering ['tʃɪərɪŋ] n ovaciones fpl, vítores mpl.

cheerio [tʃɪərɪ'əu] excl (_BRIT_) ¡hasta luego!

cheerleader ['tʃɪəliːdə*] n animador(a) m/f.

cheerless ['tʃɪəlɪs] adj triste, sombrío.

cheese [tʃiːz] n queso.

cheeseboard ['tʃiːzbɔːd] n tabla de quesos.

cheeseburger ['tʃiːzbəːgə*] n hamburguesa con queso.

cheesecake ['tʃiːzkeɪk] n pastel m de queso.

cheetah ['tʃiːtə] n guepardo.

chef [ʃɛf] n jefe/a m/f de cocina.

chemical ['kɛmɪkəl] adj químico ♦ n producto químico.

chemist ['kɛmɪst] n (_BRIT: pharmacist_) farmacéutico/a; (_scientist_) químico/a; ~'s (shop) n (_BRIT_) farmacia.

chemistry ['kɛmɪstrɪ] n química.

chemotherapy [kiːməu'θɛrəpɪ] n quimioterapia.

cheque, (_US_) **check** [tʃɛk] n (_BRIT_) cheque m; **to pay by** ~ pagar con cheque.

chequebook, (_US_) **checkbook** ['tʃɛkbuk] n talonario (de cheques), chequera (_LAM_).

cheque card n (_BRIT_) tarjeta de identificación bancaria.

chequered, (_US_) **checkered** ['tʃɛkəd] adj (_fig_) accidentado; (_pattern_) de cuadros.

cherish ['tʃɛrɪʃ] vt (_love_) querer, apreciar; (_protect_) cuidar; (_hope etc_) abrigar.

cheroot [ʃə'ruːt] n puro (_cortado en los dos extremos_).

cherry ['tʃɛrɪ] n cereza.

Ches abbr (_BRIT_) = Cheshire.

chess [tʃɛs] n ajedrez m.

chessboard ['tʃɛsbɔːd] n tablero (de ajedrez).

chessman ['tʃɛsmən] n pieza (de ajedrez).

chest [tʃɛst] n (_ANAT_) pecho; (_box_) cofre m; **to get sth off one's** ~ (_col_) desahogarse; ~ **of drawers** n cómoda.

chest measurement n talla (_de chaqueta etc_).

chestnut ['tʃɛsnʌt] n castaña; (_also:_ ~ **tree**) castaño; (_colour_) castaño ♦ adj (color) castaño inv.

chesty ['tʃɛstɪ] adj (_cough_) de bronquios, de pecho.

chew [tʃuː] vt mascar, masticar.

chewing gum ['tʃuːɪŋ-] n chicle m.

chic [ʃiːk] adj elegante.

chicanery [ʃɪ'keɪnərɪ] n embustes mpl, sofismas mpl.

Chicano [tʃɪ'kɑːnəu] adj, n chicano/a.

chick [tʃɪk] n pollito, polluelo; (_US col_) chica.

chicken ['tʃɪkɪn] n gallina, pollo; (_food_) pollo; (_col: coward_) gallina m/f.

►**chicken out** vi (_col_) rajarse; **to** ~ **out of doing sth** rajarse y no hacer algo.

chickenpox ['tʃɪkɪnpɔks] n varicela.

chickpea ['tʃɪkpiː] n garbanzo.

chicory ['tʃɪkərɪ] n (_for coffee_) achicoria; (_salad_) escarola.

chide [tʃaɪd] vt: **to** ~ **sb for sth** reprender a algn por algo.

chief [tʃiːf] n jefe/a m/f ♦ adj principal, máximo (_esp LAM_); **C**~ **of Staff** (_MIL_) Jefe m del Estado mayor.

chief executive, (_US_) **chief executive officer** n director m general.

chiefly ['tʃiːflɪ] adv principalmente.

chieftain ['tʃiːftən] n jefe m, cacique m.

chiffon ['ʃɪfɔn] n gasa.

chilblain ['tʃɪlbleɪn] n sabañón m.

child, pl ~**ren** [tʃaɪld, 'tʃɪldrən] n niño/a; (_offspring_) hijo/a.

child benefit n (_BRIT_) subsidio por cada hijo pequeño.

childbirth ['tʃaɪldbəːθ] n parto.

childhood ['tʃaɪldhud] n niñez f, infancia.

childish ['tʃaɪldɪʃ] adj pueril, infantil.

childless ['tʃaɪldlɪs] adj sin hijos.

childlike ['tʃaɪldlaɪk] adj de niño, infantil.

child minder n (_BRIT_) niñera, madre f de día.

child prodigy n niño/a prodigio inv.

children's home n centro de acogida para niños.

child's play n (_fig_): **this is** ~ esto es coser y cantar.

Chile ['tʃɪlɪ] n Chile m.

Chilean ['tʃɪlɪən] adj, n chileno/a m/f.

chill [tʃɪl] n frío; (_MED_) resfriado ♦ adj frío ♦ vt enfriar; (_CULIN_) refrigerar.

►**chill out** vi (_esp US col_) tranquilizarse.

chil(l)i ['tʃɪlɪ] n (BRIT) chile m, ají m (LAM).
chilling ['tʃɪlɪŋ] adj escalofriante.
chilly ['tʃɪlɪ] adj frío.
chime [tʃaɪm] n repique m, campanada ♦ vi repicar, sonar.
chimney ['tʃɪmnɪ] n chimenea.
chimney sweep n deshollinador m.
chimpanzee [tʃɪmpæn'ziː] n chimpancé m.
chin [tʃɪn] n mentón m, barbilla.
China ['tʃaɪnə] n China.
china ['tʃaɪnə] n porcelana; (crockery) loza.
Chinese [tʃaɪ'niːz] adj chino ♦ n (pl inv) chino/a; (LING) chino.
chink [tʃɪŋk] n (opening) rendija, hendedura; (noise) tintineo.
chintz [tʃɪnts] n cretona.
chip [tʃɪp] n (gen pl: CULIN: BRIT) patata or papa (LAM) frita; (: US: also: potato ~) patata or papa (LAM) frita; (of wood) astilla; (stone) lasca; (in gambling) ficha; (COMPUT) chip m ♦ vt (cup, plate) desconchar; **when the ~s are down** (fig) a la hora de la verdad.
▶**chip in** vi (col: interrupt) interrumpir, meterse; (: contribute) contribuir.
chipboard ['tʃɪpbɔːd] n madera aglomerada.
chipmunk ['tʃɪpmʌŋk] n ardilla listada.
chip shop n ver recuadro.

CHIP SHOP

Se denomina **chip shop** o "fish-and-chip shop" a un tipo de tienda popular de comida rápida en la que se despachan platos tradicionales británicos, principalmente filetes de pescado rebozado frito y patatas fritas.

---

chiropodist [kɪ'rɔpədɪst] n (BRIT) podólogo/a.
chiropody [kɪ'rɔpədɪ] n podología.
chirp [tʃəːp] vi gorjear; (cricket) cantar ♦ n (of cricket) canto.
chirpy ['tʃəːpɪ] adj alegre, animado.
chisel ['tʃɪzl] n (for wood) escoplo; (for stone) cincel m.
chit [tʃɪt] n nota.
chitchat ['tʃɪttʃæt] n chismes mpl, habladurías fpl.
chivalrous ['ʃɪvəlrəs] adj caballeroso.
chivalry ['ʃɪvəlrɪ] n caballerosidad f.
chives [tʃaɪvz] npl cebollinos mpl.
chloride ['klɔːraɪd] n cloruro.
chlorine ['klɔːriːn] n cloro.
chock-a-block ['tʃɔkə'blɔk], **chock-full** [tʃɔk'ful] adj atestado.
chocolate ['tʃɔklɪt] n chocolate m.

choice [tʃɔɪs] n elección f; (preference) preferencia ♦ adj escogido; **I did it by** or **from** ~ lo hice de buena gana; **a wide** ~ un gran surtido, una gran variedad.
choir ['kwaɪə*] n coro.
choirboy ['kwaɪəbɔɪ] n niño de coro.
choke [tʃəuk] vi ahogarse; (on food) atragantarse ♦ vt ahogar; (block) atascar ♦ n (AUT) estárter m.
choker ['tʃəukə*] n (necklace) gargantilla.
cholera ['kɔlərə] n cólera m.
cholesterol [kɔ'lɛstərəl] n colesterol m.
choose [tʃuːz], pt **chose**, pp **chosen** [tʃəuz, 'tʃəuzn] vt escoger, elegir; (team) seleccionar; **to** ~ **between** elegir or escoger entre; **to** ~ **from** escoger entre.
choosy ['tʃuːzɪ] adj remilgado.
chop [tʃɔp] vt (wood) cortar, talar; (CULIN: also: ~ up) picar ♦ n tajo, golpe m cortante; (CULIN) chuleta; **~s** npl (jaws) boca sg; **to get the** ~ (col: project) ser suprimido; (: person: be sacked) ser despedido.
chopper ['tʃɔpə*] n (helicopter) helicóptero.
choppy ['tʃɔpɪ] adj (sea) picado, agitado.
chopsticks ['tʃɔpstɪks] npl palillos mpl.
choral ['kɔːrəl] adj coral.
chord [kɔːd] n (MUS) acorde m.
chore [tʃɔː*] n faena, tarea; (routine task) trabajo rutinario.
choreographer [kɔrɪ'ɔgrəfə*] n coreógrafo/a.
choreography [kɔrɪ'ɔgrəfɪ] n coreografía.
chorister ['kɔrɪstə*] n corista m/f; (US) director(a) m/f de un coro.
chortle ['tʃɔːtl] vi reírse satisfecho.
chorus ['kɔːrəs] n coro; (repeated part of song) estribillo.
chose [tʃəuz] pt of **choose**.
chosen ['tʃəuzn] pp of **choose**.
chow [tʃau] n (dog) perro chino.
chowder ['tʃaudə*] n (esp US) sopa de pescado.
Christ [kraɪst] n Cristo.
christen ['krɪsn] vt bautizar.
christening ['krɪsnɪŋ] n bautizo.
Christian ['krɪstɪən] adj, n cristiano/a m/f.
Christianity [krɪstɪ'ænɪtɪ] n cristianismo.
Christian name n nombre m de pila.
Christmas ['krɪsməs] n Navidad f; **Merry** ~! ¡Felices Navidades!, ¡Felices Pascuas!
Christmas card n crisma m inv, tarjeta de Navidad.
Christmas Day n día m de Navidad.
Christmas Eve n Nochebuena.
Christmas Island n Isla Christmas.
Christmas tree n árbol m de Navidad.
chrome [krəum] n = **chromium plating**.

chromium ['krəumıəm] *n* cromo; (*also*: ~ **plating**) cromado.
chromosome ['krəuməsəum] *n* cromosoma *m*.
chronic ['krɒnɪk] *adj* crónico; (*fig*: *liar*, *smoker*) empedernido.
chronicle ['krɒnɪkl] *n* crónica.
chronological [krɒnə'lɒdʒɪkəl] *adj* cronológico.
chrysalis ['krɪsəlɪs] *n* (*BIO*) crisálida.
chrysanthemum [krɪ'sænθəməm] *n* crisantemo.
chubby ['tʃʌbɪ] *adj* rechoncho.
chuck [tʃʌk] *vt* tirar; **to** ~ **(up** *or* **in)** *vt* (*BRIT*) dejar, mandar a paseo.
chuckle ['tʃʌkl] *vi* reírse entre dientes.
chuffed [tʃʌft] *adj* (*col*): **to be** ~ **(about sth)** estar encantado (con algo).
chug [tʃʌg] *vi* (*also*: ~ **along**: *train*) ir despacio; (: *fig*) ir tirando.
chum [tʃʌm] *n* amiguete/a *m/f*, coleguilla *m/f*.
chump [tʃʌmp] *n* (*col*) tonto/a, estúpido/a.
chunk [tʃʌŋk] *n* pedazo, trozo.
chunky ['tʃʌŋkɪ] *adj* (*furniture etc*) achaparrado; (*person*) fornido; (*knitwear*) de lana gorda, grueso.
Chunnel [tʃʌnl] *n* = **Channel Tunnel**.
church [tʃɔːtʃ] *n* iglesia; **the C**~ **of England** la Iglesia Anglicana.
churchyard ['tʃɔːtʃjɑːd] *n* cementerio, camposanto.
churlish ['tʃɔːlɪʃ] *adj* grosero; (*mean*) arisco.
churn [tʃɔːn] *n* (*for butter*) mantequera; (*for milk*) lechera.
▶**churn out** *vt* producir en serie.
chute [ʃuːt] *n* (*also*: **rubbish** ~) vertedero; (*BRIT*: *children's slide*) tobogán *m*.
chutney ['tʃʌtnɪ] *n salsa picante de frutas y especias*.
CIA *n abbr* (*US*: = *Central Intelligence Agency*) CIA *f*, Agencia Central de Inteligencia.
cicada [sɪ'kɑːdə] *n* cigarra.
CID *n abbr* (*BRIT*: = *Criminal Investigation Department*) ≈ B.I.C. *f* (*SP*).
cider ['saɪdə*] *n* sidra.
C.I.F. *abbr* (= *cost, insurance and freight*) c.s.f.
cigar [sɪ'gɑː*] *n* puro.
cigarette [sɪgə'rɛt] *n* cigarrillo, pitillo.
cigarette case *n* pitillera.
cigarette end *n* colilla.
cigarette holder *n* boquilla.
C-in-C *abbr* = **commander-in-chief**.
cinch [sɪntʃ] *n*: **it's a** ~ está tirado.
Cinderella [sɪndə'rɛlə] *n* Cenicienta.
cinders ['sɪndəz] *npl* cenizas *fpl*.

cine-camera ['sɪnɪ'kæmərə] *n* (*BRIT*) cámara cinematográfica.
cine-film ['sɪnɪfɪlm] *n* (*BRIT*) película de cine.
cinema ['sɪnəmə] *n* cine *m*.
cinnamon ['sɪnəmən] *n* canela.
cipher ['saɪfə*] *n* clave *f*; (*fig*) cero; **in** ~ en clave.
circle ['sɔːkl] *n* círculo; (*in theatre*) anfiteatro ♦ *vi* dar vueltas ♦ *vt* (*surround*) rodear, cercar; (*move round*) dar la vuelta a.
circuit ['sɔːkɪt] *n* circuito; (*track*) pista; (*lap*) vuelta.
circuit board *n* tarjeta de circuitos.
circuitous [sɔː'kjuɪtəs] *adj* indirecto.
circular ['sɔːkjulə*] *adj* circular ♦ *n* circular *f*; (*as advertisement*) panfleto.
circulate ['sɔːkjuleɪt] *vi* circular; (*person*: *socially*) alternar, circular ♦ *vt* poner en circulación.
circulation [sɔːkju'leɪʃən] *n* circulación *f*; (*of newspaper etc*) tirada.
circumcise ['sɔːkəmsaɪz] *vt* circuncidar.
circumference [sə'kʌmfərəns] *n* circunferencia.
circumscribe ['sɔːkəmskraɪb] *vt* circunscribir.
circumspect ['sɔːkəmspɛkt] *adj* circunspecto, prudente.
circumstances ['sɔːkəmstənsɪz] *npl* circunstancias *fpl*; (*financial condition*) situación *f* económica; **in the** ~ en *or* dadas las circunstancias; **under no** ~ de ninguna manera, bajo ningún concepto.
circumstantial [sɔːkəm'stænʃəl] *adj* detallado; ~ **evidence** prueba indiciaria.
circumvent [sɔːkəmvɛnt] *vt* (*rule etc*) burlar.
circus ['sɔːkəs] *n* circo; (*also*: **C**~: *in place names*) Plaza.
cirrhosis [sɪ'rəusɪs] *n* (*also*: ~ **of the liver**) cirrosis *f inv*.
CIS *n abbr* (= *Commonwealth of Independent States*) CEI *f*.
cissy ['sɪsɪ] *n* = **sissy**.
cistern ['sɪstən] *n* tanque *m*, depósito; (*in toilet*) cisterna.
citation [saɪ'teɪʃən] *n* cita; (*LAW*) citación *f*; (*MIL*) mención *f*.
cite [saɪt] *vt* citar.
citizen ['sɪtɪzn] *n* (*POL*) ciudadano/a; (*of city*) habitante *m/f*.
Citizens' Advice Bureau *n* (*BRIT*) *organización voluntaria británica que aconseja especialmente en temas legales o financieros.*
citizenship ['sɪtɪznʃɪp] *n* ciudadanía.

citric ['sɪtrɪk] adj: ~ **acid** ácido cítrico.
citrus fruits ['sɪtrəs-] npl cítricos mpl.
city ['sɪtɪ] n ciudad f; **the C~** centro financiero de Londres.
city centre n centro de la ciudad.
City Hall n (US) ayuntamiento.
City Technology College n (BRIT) ≈ Centro de formación profesional.
civic ['sɪvɪk] adj cívico; (authorities) municipal.
civic centre n (BRIT) centro de administración municipal.
civil ['sɪvɪl] adj civil; (polite) atento, cortés; (well-bred) educado.
civil defence n protección f civil.
civil engineer n ingeniero/a de caminos.
civil engineering n ingeniería de caminos.
civilian [sɪ'vɪlɪən] adj civil; (clothes) de paisano ♦ n civil m/f.
civilization [sɪvɪlaɪ'zeɪʃən] n civilización f.
civilized ['sɪvɪlaɪzd] adj civilizado.
civil law n derecho civil.
civil liberties npl libertades fpl civiles.
civil rights npl derechos mpl civiles.
civil servant n funcionario/a (del Estado).
Civil Service n administración f pública.
civil war n guerra civil.
civvies ['sɪvɪz] npl: **in ~** (col) de paisano.
cl abbr (= centilitre) cl.
clad [klæd] adj: ~ **(in)** vestido (de).
claim [kleɪm] vt exigir, reclamar; (rights etc) reivindicar; (assert) pretender ♦ vi (for insurance) reclamar ♦ n (for expenses) reclamación f; (LAW) demanda; (pretension) pretensión f; **to put in a ~ for** sth presentar una demanda por algo.
claimant ['kleɪmənt] n (ADMIN, LAW) demandante m/f.
claim form n solicitud f.
clairvoyant [kleə'vɔɪənt] n clarividente m/f.
clam [klæm] n almeja.
▶**clam up** vi (col) cerrar el pico.
clamber ['klæmbə*] vi trepar.
clammy ['klæmɪ] adj (cold) frío y húmedo; (sticky) pegajoso.
clamour, (US) **clamor** ['klæmə*] n (noise) clamor m; (protest) protesta ♦ vi: **to ~ for** sth clamar por algo, pedir algo a voces.
clamp [klæmp] n abrazadera; (laboratory ~) grapa; (wheel ~) cepo ♦ vt afianzar (con abrazadera).
▶**clamp down on** vt fus (subj: government, police) poner coto a.
clampdown ['klæmpdaun] n restricción f; **there has been a ~ on terrorism** se ha puesto coto al terrorismo.
clan [klæn] n clan m.

clandestine [klæn'dɛstɪn] adj clandestino.
clang [klæŋ] n estruendo ♦ vi sonar con estruendo.
clanger [klæŋə*] n: **to drop a ~** (BRIT col) meter la pata.
clansman ['klænzmən] n miembro del clan.
clap [klæp] vi aplaudir ♦ vt (hands) batir ♦ n (of hands) palmada; **to ~ one's hands** dar palmadas, batir las palmas; **a ~ of thunder** un trueno.
clapping ['klæpɪŋ] n aplausos mpl.
claptrap ['klæptræp] n (col) gilipolleces fpl.
claret ['klærət] n burdeos m inv.
clarification [klærɪfɪ'keɪʃən] n aclaración f.
clarify ['klærɪfaɪ] vt aclarar.
clarinet [klærɪ'nɛt] n clarinete m.
clarity ['klærɪtɪ] n claridad f.
clash [klæʃ] n estruendo; (fig) choque m ♦ vi enfrentarse; (personalities, interests) oponerse, chocar; (colours) desentonar; (dates, events) coincidir.
clasp [klɑːsp] n broche m; (on jewels) cierre m ♦ vt abrochar; (hand) apretar; (embrace) abrazar.
class [klɑːs] n (gen) clase f; (group, category) clase f, categoría ♦ cpd de clase ♦ vt clasificar.
class-conscious ['klɑːs'kɔnʃəs] adj clasista, con conciencia de clase.
classic ['klæsɪk] adj clásico ♦ n (work) obra clásica, clásico; **~s** npl (UNIV) clásicas fpl.
classical ['klæsɪkəl] adj clásico; ~ **music** música clásica.
classification [klæsɪfɪ'keɪʃən] n clasificación f.
classified ['klæsɪfaɪd] adj (information) reservado.
classified advertisement n anuncio por palabras.
classify ['klæsɪfaɪ] vt clasificar.
classless ['klɑːslɪs] adj: ~ **society** sociedad f sin clases.
classmate ['klɑːsmeɪt] n compañero/a de clase.
classroom ['klɑːsrum] n aula.
classy ['klɑːsɪ] adj (col) elegante, con estilo.
clatter ['klætə*] n ruido, estruendo; (of hooves) trápala ♦ vi hacer ruido or estruendo.
clause [klɔːz] n cláusula; (LING) oración f.
claustrophobia [klɔːstrə'fəubɪə] n claustrofobia.
claustrophobic [klɔːstrə'fəubɪk] adj claustrofóbico; **I feel ~** me entra claustrofobia.
claw [klɔː] n (of cat) uña; (of bird of prey) garra; (of lobster) pinza; (TECH) garfio ♦ vi: **to ~ at** arañar; (tear) desgarrar.

clay [kleɪ] *n* arcilla.
clean [kliːn] *adj* limpio; (*copy*) en limpio; (*lines*) bien definido ♦ *vt* limpiar ♦ *adv*: he ~ forgot lo olvidó por completo; **to come** ~ (*col: admit guilt*) confesarlo todo; **to have a** ~ **driving licence** tener el carnet de conducir sin sanciones; **to** ~ **one's teeth** lavarse los dientes.
►**clean off** *vt* limpiar.
►**clean out** *vt* limpiar (a fondo).
►**clean up** *vt* limpiar, asear ♦ *vi* (*fig: make profit*): **to** ~ **up on** sacar provecho de.
clean-cut ['kliːn'kʌt] *adj* bien definido; (*outline*) nítido; (*person*) de buen parecer.
cleaner ['kliːnə*] *n* encargado/a *m/f* de la limpieza; (*also: dry* ~) tintorero/a.
cleaning ['kliːnɪŋ] *n* limpieza.
cleaning lady *n* señora de la limpieza, asistenta.
cleanliness ['klɛnlɪnɪs] *n* limpieza.
cleanse [klɛnz] *vt* limpiar.
cleanser ['klɛnzə*] *n* detergente *m*; (*cosmetic*) loción *f or* crema limpiadora.
clean-shaven ['kliːn'ʃeɪvn] *adj* bien afeitado.
cleansing department ['klɛnzɪŋ-] *n* (*BRIT*) servicio municipal de limpieza.
clean sweep *n*: **to make a** ~ (*SPORT*) arrasar, barrer.
clear [klɪə*] *adj* claro; (*road, way*) libre; (*profit*) neto; (*majority*) absoluto ♦ *vt* (*space*) despejar, limpiar; (*LAW: suspect*) absolver; (*obstacle*) salvar, saltar por encima de; (*debt*) liquidar; (*cheque*) aceptar; (*site, woodland*) desmontar ♦ *vi* (*fog etc*) despejarse ♦ *n*: **to be in the** ~ (*out of debt*) estar libre de deudas; (*out of suspicion*) estar fuera de toda sospecha; (*out of danger*) estar fuera de peligro ♦ *adv*: ~ **of** a distancia de; **to make o.s.** ~ explicarse claramente; **to make it** ~ **to sb that ...** hacer entender a algn que ...; **I have a** ~ **day tomorrow** mañana tengo el día libre; **to keep** ~ **of sth/sb** evitar algo/a algn; **to** ~ **a profit of ...** sacar una ganancia de ...; **to** ~ **the table** recoger *or* quitar la mesa.
►**clear off** *vi* (*col: leave*) marcharse, mandarse mudar (*LAM*).
►**clear up** *vt* limpiar; (*mystery*) aclarar, resolver.
clearance ['klɪərəns] *n* (*removal*) despeje *m*; (*permission*) acreditación *f*.
clear-cut ['klɪə'kʌt] *adj* bien definido, claro.
clearing ['klɪərɪŋ] *n* (*in wood*) claro.
clearing bank *n* (*BRIT*) banco central.
clearing house *n* (*COMM*) cámara de compensación.

clearly ['klɪəlɪ] *adv* claramente.
clearway ['klɪəweɪ] *n* (*BRIT*) *carretera en la que no se puede estacionar.*
cleaver ['kliːvə] *n* cuchilla (de carnicero).
clef [klɛf] *n* (*MUS*) clave *f*.
cleft [klɛft] *n* (*in rock*) grieta, hendedura.
clemency ['klɛmənsɪ] *n* clemencia.
clement ['klɛmənt] *adj* (*weather*) clemente.
clench [klɛntʃ] *vt* apretar, cerrar.
clergy ['klɜːdʒɪ] *n* clero.
clergyman ['klɜːdʒɪmən] *n* clérigo.
clerical ['klɛrɪkəl] *adj* de oficina; (*REL*) clerical; (*error*) de copia.
clerk [klɑːk, (*US*) klɜːrk] *n* oficinista *m/f*; (*US*) dependiente/a *m/f*, vendedor(a) *m/f*; **C~ of the Court** secretario/a de juzgado.
clever ['klɛvə*] *adj* (*mentally*) inteligente, listo; (*skilful*) hábil; (*device, arrangement*) ingenioso.
cleverly ['klɛvəlɪ] *adv* ingeniosamente.
clew [kluː] *n* (*US*) = **clue**.
cliché ['kliːʃeɪ] *n* cliché *m*, frase *f* hecha.
click [klɪk] *vt* (*tongue*) chasquear ♦ *vi* (*COMPUT*) hacer clic; **to** ~ **one's heels** taconear.
client ['klaɪənt] *n* cliente *m/f*.
clientele [kliːɑːn'tɛl] *n* clientela.
cliff [klɪf] *n* acantilado.
cliffhanger ['klɪfhæŋə*] *n*: **it was a** ~ estuvimos en ascuas hasta el final.
climactic [klaɪ'mæktɪk] *adj* culminante.
climate ['klaɪmɪt] *n* clima *m*; (*fig*) clima *m*, ambiente *m*.
climax ['klaɪmæks] *n* punto culminante; (*of play etc*) clímax *m*; (*sexual* ~) orgasmo.
climb [klaɪm] *vi* subir, trepar; (*plane*) elevarse, remontar el vuelo ♦ *vt* (*stairs*) subir; (*tree*) trepar a; (*mountain*) escalar ♦ *n* subida, ascenso; **to** ~ **over a wall** saltar una tapia.
►**climb down** *vi* (*fig*) volverse atrás.
climbdown ['klaɪmdaun] *n* vuelta atrás.
climber ['klaɪmə*] *n* escalador(a) *m/f*.
climbing ['klaɪmɪŋ] *n* escalada.
clinch [klɪntʃ] *vt* (*deal*) cerrar; (*argument*) rematar.
clincher ['klɪntʃə*] *n* (*col*): **that was the** ~ **for me** eso me hizo decidir.
cling, *pt*, *pp* **clung** [klɪŋ, klʌŋ] *vi*: **to** ~ **(to)** agarrarse (a); (*clothes*) pegarse (a).
clingfilm ['klɪŋfɪlm] *n* plástico adherente.
clinic ['klɪnɪk] *n* clínica.
clinical ['klɪnɪkl] *adj* clínico; (*fig*) frío, impasible.
clink [klɪŋk] *vi* tintinear.
clip [klɪp] *n* (*for hair*) horquilla; (*also: paper* ~) sujetapapeles *m inv*, clip *m*; (*clamp*) grapa ♦ *vt* (*cut*) cortar; (*hedge*) podar;

(*also*: ~ **together**) unir.
clippers ['klɪpəz] *npl* (*for gardening*) tijeras *fpl* de podar; (*for hair*) maquinilla *sg*; (*for nails*) cortauñas *m inv*.
clipping ['klɪpɪŋ] *n* (*from newspaper*) recorte *m*.
clique [kliːk] *n* camarilla.
cloak [kləuk] *n* capa, manto ♦ *vt* (*fig*) encubrir, disimular.
cloakroom ['kləukrum] *n* guardarropa *m*; (*BRIT*: *WC*) lavabo, aseos *mpl*, baño (*esp LAM*).
clobber ['klɔbə*] *n* (*col*) bártulos *mpl*, trastos *mpl* ♦ *vt* dar una paliza a.
clock [klɔk] *n* reloj *m*; (*in taxi*) taxímetro; **to work against the** ~ trabajar contra reloj; **around the** ~ las veinticuatro horas; **to sleep round the** ~ dormir un día entero; **30,000 on the** ~ (*AUT*) treinta mil millas en el cuentakilómetros.
▶**clock in, clock on** *vi* fichar, picar.
▶**clock off, clock out** *vi* fichar *or* picar la salida.
▶**clock up** *vt* hacer.
clockwise ['klɔkwaɪz] *adv* en el sentido de las agujas del reloj.
clockwork ['klɔkwəːk] *n* aparato de relojería ♦ *adj* (*toy, train*) de cuerda.
clog [klɔg] *n* zueco, chanclo ♦ *vt* atascar ♦ *vi* atascarse.
cloister ['klɔɪstə*] *n* claustro.
clone [kləun] *n* clon *m*.
close *adj*, *adv and derivatives* [kləus] *adj* cercano, próximo; (*near*): ~ **(to)** cerca (de); (*print, weave*) tupido, compacto; (*friend*) íntimo; (*connection*) estrecho; (*examination*) detallado, minucioso; (*weather*) bochornoso; (*atmosphere*) sofocante; (*room*) mal ventilado ♦ *adv* cerca; ~ **by**, ~ **at hand** *adj*, *adv* muy cerca; ~ **to** *prep* cerca de; **to have a** ~ **shave** (*fig*) escaparse por un pelo; **how** ~ **is Edinburgh to Glasgow?** ¿qué distancia hay de Edimburgo a Glasgow?; **at** ~ **quarters** de cerca ♦ *vb and derivatives* [kləuz] *vt* cerrar; (*end*) concluir, terminar ♦ *vi* (*shop etc*) cerrar; (*end*) concluir(se), terminar(se) ♦ *n* (*end*) fin *m*, final *m*, conclusión *f*; **to bring sth to a** ~ terminar algo.
▶**close down** *vi* cerrar definitivamente.
▶**close in** *vi* (*hunters*) acercarse rodeando, rodear; (*evening, night*) caer; (*fog*) cerrarse; **to** ~ **in on sb** rodear *or* cercar a algn; **the days are closing in** los días son cada vez más cortos.
▶**close off** *vt* (*area*) cerrar al tráfico *or* al público.

closed [kləuzd] *adj* (*shop etc*) cerrado.
closed-circuit ['kləuzd'səːkɪt] *adj*: ~ **television** televisión *f* por circuito cerrado.
closed shop *n* empresa en la que todo el personal está afiliado a un sindicato.
close-knit ['kləus'nɪt] *adj* (*fig*) muy unido.
closely ['kləuslɪ] *adv* (*study*) con detalle; (*listen*) con atención; (*watch*: *person, events*) de cerca; **we are** ~ **related** somos parientes cercanos; **a** ~ **guarded secret** un secreto rigurosamente guardado.
close season [kləuz-] *n* (*FOOTBALL*) temporada de descanso; (*HUNTING*) veda.
closet ['klɔzɪt] *n* (*cupboard*) armario, placar(d) *m* (*LAM*).
close-up ['kləusʌp] *n* primer plano.
closing ['kləuzɪŋ] *adj* (*stages, remarks*) último, final; ~ **price** (*STOCK EXCHANGE*) cotización *f* de cierre.
closing time *n* hora de cierre.
closure ['kləuʒə*] *n* cierre *m*.
clot [klɔt] *n* (*gen*: *blood* ~) embolia; (*col*: *idiot*) imbécil *m/f* ♦ *vi* (*blood*) coagularse.
cloth [klɔθ] *n* (*material*) tela, paño; (*table* ~) mantel *m*; (*rag*) trapo.
clothe [kləuð] *vt* vestir; (*fig*) revestir.
clothes [kləuðz] *npl* ropa *sg*; **to put one's** ~ **on** vestirse, ponerse la ropa; **to take one's** ~ **off** desvestirse, desnudarse.
clothes brush *n* cepillo (para la ropa).
clothes line *n* cuerda (para tender la ropa).
clothes peg, (*US*) **clothes pin** *n* pinza.
clothing ['kləuðɪŋ] *n* = **clothes**.
clotted cream ['klɔtɪd-] *n* nata muy espesa.
cloud [klaud] *n* nube *f*; (*storm* ~) nubarrón *m* ♦ *vt* (*liquid*) enturbiar; **every** ~ **has a silver lining** no hay mal que por bien no venga; **to** ~ **the issue** empañar el problema.
▶**cloud over** *vi* (*also fig*) nublarse.
cloudburst ['klaudbəːst] *n* chaparrón *m*.
cloud-cuckoo-land ['klaud'kuku:'lænd] *n* Babia.
cloudy ['klaudɪ] *adj* nublado; (*liquid*) turbio.
clout [klaut] *n* (*fig*) influencia, peso ♦ *vt* dar un tortazo a.
clove [kləuv] *n* clavo; ~ **of garlic** diente *m* de ajo.
clover ['kləuvə*] *n* trébol *m*.
clown [klaun] *n* payaso ♦ *vi* (*also*: ~ **about**, ~ **around**) hacer el payaso.
cloying ['klɔɪɪŋ] *adj* (*taste*) empalagoso.
club [klʌb] *n* (*society*) club *m*; (*weapon*) porra, cachiporra; (*also*: **golf** ~) palo ♦ *vt* aporrear ♦ *vi*: **to** ~ **together** (*join forces*)

unir fuerzas; ~**s** *npl* (*CARDS*) tréboles *mpl*.
club car *n* (*US RAIL*) coche *m* salón.
club class *n* (*AVIAT*) clase *f* preferente.
clubhouse ['klʌbhaus] *n local social, sobre todo en clubs deportivos.*
club soda *n* (*US*) soda.
cluck [klʌk] *vi* cloquear.
clue [kluː] *n* pista; (*in crosswords*) indicación *f*; **I haven't a** ~ no tengo ni idea.
clued up, (*US*) **clued in** [kluːd-] *adj* (*col*) al tanto, al corriente.
clueless ['kluːlɪs] *adj* (*col*) desorientado.
clump [klʌmp] *n* (*of trees*) grupo.
clumsy ['klʌmzɪ] *adj* (*person*) torpe; (*tool*) difícil de manejar.
clung [klʌŋ] *pt, pp of* **cling**.
cluster ['klʌstə*] *n* grupo; (*BOT*) racimo ♦ *vi* agruparse, apiñarse.
clutch [klʌtʃ] *n* (*AUT*) embrague *m*; (*pedal*) (pedal *m* de) embrague *m*; **to fall into sb's** ~**es** caer en las garras de algn ♦ *vt* agarrar.
clutter ['klʌtə*] *vt* (*also:* ~ **up**) atestar, llenar desordenadamente ♦ *n* desorden *m*, confusión *f*.
CM *abbr* (*US*) = *North Mariana Islands.*
cm *abbr* (= *centimetre*) cm.
CNAA *n abbr* (*BRIT*: = *Council for National Academic Awards*) *organismo no universitario que otorga diplomas.*
CND *n abbr* (= *Campaign for Nuclear Disarmament*) *plataforma pro desarme nuclear.*
CO *n abbr* = **commanding officer**; (*BRIT*) = *Commonwealth Office* ♦ *abbr* (*US*) = *Colorado.*
Co. *abbr* = **county**; = **company**.
c/o *abbr* (= *care of*) c/a, a/c.
coach [kəutʃ] *n* (*bus*) autocar *m* (*SP*), autobús *m*; (*horse-drawn*) coche *m*; (*ceremonial*) carroza; (*of train*) vagón *m*, coche *m*; (*SPORT*) entrenador(a) *m/f*, instructor(a) *m/f* ♦ *vt* (*SPORT*) entrenar; (*student*) preparar, enseñar.
coach trip *n* excursión *f* en autocar.
coagulate [kəu'ægjuleɪt] *vi* coagularse.
coal [kəul] *n* carbón *m*.
coal face *n* frente *m* de carbón.
coalfield ['kəulfiːld] *n* yacimiento de carbón.
coalition [kəuə'lɪʃən] *n* coalición *f*.
coal man *n* carbonero.
coalmine ['kəulmaɪn] *n* mina de carbón.
coalminer ['kəulmaɪnə*] *n* minero (de carbón).
coalmining ['keulmaɪnɪŋ] *n* minería (de carbón).

coarse [kɔːs] *adj* basto, burdo; (*vulgar*) grosero, ordinario.
coast [kəust] *n* costa, litoral *m* ♦ *vi* (*AUT*) ir en punto muerto.
coastal ['kəustl] *adj* costero.
coaster ['kəustə*] *n* buque *m* costero, barco de cabotaje.
coastguard ['kəustgɑːd] *n* guardacostas *m inv*.
coastline ['kəustlaɪn] *n* litoral *m*.
coat [kəut] *n* (*jacket*) chaqueta, saco (*LAM*); (*overcoat*) abrigo; (*of animal*) pelo, lana; (*of paint*) mano *f*, capa ♦ *vt* cubrir, revestir.
coat hanger *n* percha, gancha (*LAM*).
coating ['kəutɪŋ] *n* capa, baño.
coat of arms *n* escudo de armas.
co-author ['kəu'ɔːθə*] *n* coautor(a) *m/f*.
coax [kəuks] *vt* engatusar.
cob [kɔb] *n see* **corn**.
cobbler ['kɔblə*] *n* zapatero (remendón).
cobbles ['kɔblz], **cobblestones** ['kɔblstəunz] *npl* adoquines *mpl*.
COBOL ['kəubɔl] *n* COBOL *m*.
cobra ['kəubrə] *n* cobra.
cobweb ['kɔbwɛb] *n* telaraña.
cocaine [kə'keɪn] *n* cocaína.
cock [kɔk] *n* (*rooster*) gallo; (*male bird*) macho ♦ *vt* (*gun*) amartillar.
cock-a-hoop [kɔkə'huːp] *adj*: **to be** ~ estar más contento que unas pascuas.
cockatoo [kɔkə'tuː] *n* cacatúa.
cockerel ['kɔkərl] *n* gallito, gallo joven.
cock-eyed ['kɔkaɪd] *adj* bizco; (*fig: crooked*) torcido; (*: idea*) disparatado.
cockle ['kɔkl] *n* berberecho.
cockney ['kɔknɪ] *n* habitante de ciertos barrios de Londres.
cockpit ['kɔkpɪt] *n* (*in aircraft*) cabina.
cockroach ['kɔkrəutʃ] *n* cucaracha.
cocktail ['kɔkteɪl] *n* combinado, cóctel *m*; **prawn** ~ cóctel *m* de gambas.
cocktail cabinet *n* mueble-bar *m*.
cocktail party *n* cóctel *m*.
cocktail shaker [-ʃeɪkə*] *n* coctelera.
cocky ['kɔkɪ] *adj* farruco, flamenco.
cocoa ['kəukəu] *n* cacao; (*drink*) chocolate *m*.
coconut ['kəukənʌt] *n* coco.
cocoon [kə'kuːn] *n* capullo.
cod [kɔd] *n* bacalao.
COD *abbr see* **cash on delivery**, **collect on delivery** (*US*).
code [kəud] *n* código; (*cipher*) clave *f*; (*TEL*) prefijo; ~ **of behaviour** código de conducta; ~ **of practice** código profesional.
codeine ['kəudiːn] *n* codeína.

codger [ˈkɔdʒə*] n (BRII col): **an old** ~ un abuelo.

codicil [ˈkɔdɪsɪl] n codicilo.

codify [ˈkəudɪfaɪ] vt codificar.

cod-liver oil [ˈkɔdlɪvə*-] n aceite m de hígado de bacalao.

co-driver [ˈkəuˈdraɪvə*] n (in race) copiloto m/f; (of lorry) segundo conductor m.

co-ed [ˈkəuɛd] adj abbr = **coeducational ♦** n abbr (US: = female student) alumna de una universidad mixta; (BRIT: school) colegio mixto.

coeducational [kəuɛdjuˈkeɪʃənl] adj mixto.

coerce [kəuˈəːs] vt forzar, coaccionar.

coercion [kəuˈəːʃən] n coacción f.

coexistence [ˈkəuɪgˈzɪstəns] n coexistencia.

C. of C. n abbr = **chamber of commerce.**

C of E abbr = **Church of England.**

coffee [ˈkɔfɪ] n café m; **white** ~, (US) ~ **with cream** café con leche.

coffee bar n (BRIT) cafetería.

coffee bean n grano de café.

coffee break n descanso (para tomar café).

coffee cup n taza de café, pocillo (LAM).

coffeepot [ˈkɔfɪpɔt] n cafetera.

coffee table n mesita baja.

coffin [ˈkɔfɪn] n ataúd m.

C of I abbr = Church of Ireland.

C of S abbr = Church of Scotland.

cog [kɔg] n diente m.

cogent [ˈkəudʒənt] adj lógico, convincente.

cognac [ˈkɔnjæk] n coñac m.

cogwheel [ˈkɔgwiːl] n rueda dentada.

cohabit [kəuˈhæbɪt] vi (formal): **to** ~ **(with sb)** cohabitar (con algn).

coherent [kəuˈhɪərənt] adj coherente.

cohesion [kəuˈhiːʒən] n cohesión f.

cohesive [kəuˈhiːsɪv] adj (fig) cohesivo, unido.

COI n abbr (BRIT: = Central Office of Information) servicio de información gubernamental.

coil [kɔɪl] n rollo; (of rope) vuelta; (of smoke) espiral f; (AUT, ELEC) bobina, carrete m; (contraceptive) DIU m ♦ vt enrollar.

coin [kɔɪn] n moneda ♦ vt acuñar; (word) inventar, acuñar.

coinage [ˈkɔɪnɪdʒ] n moneda.

coin-box [ˈkɔɪnbɔks] n (BRIT) caja recaudadora.

coincide [kəuɪnˈsaɪd] vi coincidir.

coincidence [kəuˈɪnsɪdəns] n casualidad f, coincidencia.

coin-operated [ˈkɔɪnˈɔpəreɪtɪd] adj (machine) que funciona con monedas.

Coke ® [kəuk] n Coca Cola ® f.

coke [kəuk] n (coal) coque m.

Col. abbr (= colonel) col; (US) = Colorado.

COLA n abbr (US: = cost-of-living adjustment) reajuste salarial de acuerdo con el coste de la vida.

colander [ˈkɔləndə*] n escurridor m.

cold [kəuld] adj frío ♦ n frío; (MED) resfriado; **it's** ~ hace frío; **to be** ~ tener frío; **to catch a** ~ coger un catarro, resfriarse, acatarrarse; **in** ~ **blood** a sangre fría; **the room's getting** ~ está empezando a hacer frío en la habitación; **to give sb the** ~ **shoulder** tratar a algn con frialdad.

cold-blooded [ˈkəuldˈblʌdɪd] adj (ZOOL) de sangre fría.

cold cream n crema.

coldly [ˈkəuldlɪ] adj fríamente.

cold sore n calentura, herpes m labial.

cold sweat n: **to be in a** ~ (about sth) tener sudores fríos (por algo).

cold turkey n (col) mono.

Cold War n: **the** ~ la guerra fría.

coleslaw [ˈkəulslɔː] n ensalada de col con zanahoria.

colic [ˈkɔlɪk] n cólico.

colicky [ˈkɔlɪkɪ] adj: **to be** ~ tener un cólico.

collaborate [kəˈlæbəreɪt] vi colaborar.

collaboration [kəlæbəˈreɪʃən] n colaboración f; (POL) colaboracionismo.

collaborator [kəˈlæbəreɪtə*] n colaborador(a) m/f; (POL) colaboracionista m/f.

collage [kɔˈlɑːʒ] n collage m.

collagen [ˈkɔlədʒən] n colágeno.

collapse [kəˈlæps] vi (gen) hundirse, derrumbarse; (MED) sufrir un colapso ♦ n (gen) hundimiento; (MED) colapso; (of government) caída; (of plans, scheme) fracaso; (of business) ruina.

collapsible [kəˈlæpsəbl] adj plegable.

collar [ˈkɔlə*] n (of coat, shirt) cuello; (for dog, TECH) collar m ♦ vt (col: person) agarrar; (: object) birlar.

collarbone [ˈkɔləbəun] n clavícula.

collate [kɔˈleɪt] vt cotejar.

collateral [kɔˈlætərəl] n (COMM) garantía subsidiaria.

collation [kəˈleɪʃən] n colación f.

colleague [ˈkɔliːg] n colega m/f, compañero/a m/f.

collect [kəˈlɛkt] vt reunir; (as a hobby) coleccionar; (BRIT: call and pick up) recoger; (wages) cobrar; (debts) recaudar; (donations, subscriptions) colectar ♦ vi (crowd) reunirse ♦ adv: **to call** ~ (US TEL) llamar a cobro revertido; **to** ~ **one's thoughts** reponerse, recobrar el dominio de sí mismo; ~ **on delivery** (COD) (US) entrega contra reembolso.

collection – come

collection [kə'lɛkʃən] n colección f; (of
fares, wages) cobro; (of post) recogida.
collective [kə'lɛktɪv] adj colectivo.
collective bargaining n negociación f del
convenio colectivo.
collector [kə'lɛktə*] n coleccionista m/f; (of
taxes etc) recaudador(a) m/f; ~'s **item** or
piece pieza de coleccionista.
college ['kɔlɪdʒ] n colegio; (of technology,
agriculture etc) escuela.
collide [kə'laɪd] vi chocar.
collie ['kɔlɪ] n (dog) collie m, perro pastor
escocés.
colliery ['kɔlɪərɪ] n (BRIT) mina de carbón.
collision [kə'lɪʒən] n choque m, colisión f; **to
be on a ~ course** (also fig) ir rumbo al
desastre.
colloquial [kə'ləukwɪəl] adj coloquial.
collusion [kə'luːʒən] n confabulación f,
connivencia; **in ~ with** en connivencia
con.
Colo. abbr (US) = Colorado.
cologne [kə'ləun] n (also: **eau de ~**) (agua
de) colonia.
Colombia [kə'lɔmbɪə] n Colombia.
Colombian [kə'lɔmbɪən] adj, n colombiano/a
m/f.
colon ['kəulən] n (sign) dos puntos; (MED)
colon m.
colonel ['kɜːnl] n coronel m.
colonial [kə'ləunɪəl] adj colonial.
colonize ['kɔlənaɪz] vt colonizar.
colonnade [kɔlə'neɪd] n columnata.
colony ['kɔlənɪ] n colonia.
color ['kʌlə*] etc (US) = **colour.**
Colorado beetle [kɔlə'rɑːdəu-] n
escarabajo de la patata.
colossal [kə'lɔsl] adj colosal.
colour, (US) color ['kʌlə*] n color m ♦ vt
colorear, pintar; (dye) teñir ♦ vi (blush)
sonrojarse; ~**s** npl (of party, club) colores
mpl.
colo(u)r bar n segregación f racial.
colo(u)r-blind ['kʌləblaɪnd] adj daltónico.
colo(u)red ['kʌləd] adj de color; (photo) en
color; (of race) de color.
colo(u)r film n película en color.
colo(u)rful ['kʌləful] adj lleno de color;
(person) pintoresco.
colo(u)ring ['kʌlərɪŋ] n colorido, color;
(substance) colorante m.
colo(u)rless ['kʌlələs] adj incoloro, sin
color.
colo(u)r scheme n combinación f de
colores.
colour supplement n (BRIT PRESS)
suplemento semanal or dominical.
colo(u)r television n televisión f en color.

colt [kəult] n potro.
column ['kɔləm] n columna; (fashion ~,
sports ~ etc) sección f, columna; **the
editorial ~** el editorial.
columnist ['kɔləmnɪst] n columnista m/f.
coma ['kəumə] n coma m.
comb [kəum] n peine m; (ornamental)
peineta ♦ vt (hair) peinar; (area) registrar
a fondo, peinar.
combat ['kɔmbæt] n combate m ♦ vt
combatir.
combination [kɔmbɪ'neɪʃən] n (gen)
combinación f.
combination lock n cerradura de
combinación.
combine [kəm'baɪn] vt combinar; (qualities)
reunir ♦ vi combinarse ♦ n ['kɔmbaɪn]
(ECON) cartel m; **a ~d effort** un esfuerzo
conjunto.
combine (harvester) n cosechadora.
combo ['kɔmbəu] n (JAZZ etc) conjunto.
combustion [kəm'bʌstʃən] n combustión f.

═══════════════════════════ KEYWORD

come [kʌm] (pt **came**, pp **come**) vi **1**
(movement towards) venir; **to ~ running**
venir corriendo; ~ **with me** ven conmigo
2 (arrive) llegar; **he's ~ here to work** ha
venido aquí para trabajar; **to ~ home**
volver a casa; **we've just ~ from Seville**
acabamos de llegar de Sevilla; **coming!**
¡voy!
3 (reach): **to ~ to** llegar a; **the bill came
to £40** la cuenta ascendía a cuarenta
libras
4 (occur): **an idea came to me** se me
ocurrió una idea; **if it ~s to it** llegado el
caso
5 (be, become): **to ~ loose/undone** etc
aflojarse/desabrocharse, desatarse etc;
I've ~ to like him por fin ha llegado a
gustarme
►**come about** vi suceder, ocurrir
►**come across** vt fus (person) encontrarse
con; (thing) encontrar ♦ vi: **to ~ across
well/badly** causar buena/mala impresión
►**come away** vi (leave) marcharse;
(become detached) desprenderse
►**come back** vi (return) volver; (reply): **can
I ~ back to you on that one?** volvamos
sobre ese punto
►**come by** vt fus (acquire) conseguir
►**come down** vi (price) bajar; (building)
derrumbarse; (: be demolished) ser
derribado
►**come forward** vi presentarse
►**come from** vt fus (place, source) ser de
►**come in** vi (visitor) entrar; (train, report)

llegar; (*fashion*) ponerse de moda; (*on deal etc*) entrar
►**come in for** *vt fus* (*criticism etc*) recibir
►**come into** *vt fus* (*money*) heredar; (*be involved*) tener que ver con; **to ~ into fashion** ponerse de moda
►**come off** *vi* (*button*) soltarse, desprenderse; (*attempt*) salir bien
►**come on** *vi* (*pupil, work, project*) marchar; (*lights*) encenderse; (*electricity*) volver; **~ on!** ¡vamos!
►**come out** *vi* (*fact*) salir a la luz; (*book, sun*) salir; (*stain*) quitarse; **to ~ out (on strike)** declararse en huelga; **to ~ out for/against** declararse a favor/en contra de
►**come over** *vt fus*: **I don't know what's ~ over him!** ¡no sé lo que le pasa!
►**come round** *vi* (*after faint, operation*) volver en sí
►**come through** *vi* (*survive*) sobrevivir; (*telephone call*): **the call came through** recibimos la llamada
►**come to** *vi* (*wake*) volver en sí; (*total*) sumar; **how much does it ~ to?** ¿cuánto es en total?, ¿a cuánto asciende?
►**come under** *vt fus* (*heading*) entrar dentro de, (*influence*) estar bajo
►**come up** *vi* (*sun*) salir; (*problem*) surgir; (*event*) aproximarse; (*in conversation*) mencionarse
►**come up against** *vt fus* (*resistance etc*) tropezar con
►**come up to** *vt fus* llegar hasta; **the film didn't ~ up to our expectations** la película no fue tan buena como esperábamos
►**come up with** *vt fus* (*idea*) sugerir; (*money*) conseguir
►**come upon** *vt fus* (*find*) dar con.

comeback [ˈkʌmbæk] *n* (*reaction*) reacción *f*; (*response*) réplica; **to make a ~** (*THEAT*) volver a las tablas.
Comecon [ˈkɔmɪkɔn] *n abbr* (= *Council for Mutual Economic Aid*) COMECON *m*.
comedian [kəˈmiːdɪən] *n* humorista *m*.
comedienne [kəmiːdɪˈɛn] *n* humorista.
comedown [ˈkʌmdaun] *n* revés *m*.
comedy [ˈkɔmɪdɪ] *n* comedia.
comet [ˈkɔmɪt] *n* cometa *m*.
comeuppance [kʌmˈʌpəns] *n*: **to get one's ~** llevar su merecido.
comfort [ˈkʌmfət] *n* comodidad *f*, confort *m*; (*well-being*) bienestar *m*; (*solace*) consuelo; (*relief*) alivio ♦ *vt* consolar; *see also* **comforts**.
comfortable [ˈkʌmfətəbl] *adj* cómodo;

(*income*) adecuado; (*majority*) suficiente; **I don't feel very ~ about it** la cosa me tiene algo preocupado.
comfortably [ˈkʌmfətəblɪ] *adv* (*sit*) cómodamente; (*live*) holgadamente.
comforter [ˈkʌmfətə*] *n* (*US: pacifier*) chupete *m*; (: *bed cover*) colcha.
comforts [ˈkʌmfəts] *npl* comodidades *fpl*.
comfort station *n* (*US*) servicios *mpl*.
comic [ˈkɔmɪk] *adj* (*also:* **~al**) cómico, gracioso ♦ *n* (*magazine*) tebeo; (*for adults*) cómic *m*.
comic strip *n* tira cómica.
coming [ˈkʌmɪŋ] *n* venida, llegada ♦ *adj* que viene; (*next*) próximo; (*future*) venidero; **~(s) and going(s)** *n(pl)* ir y venir *m*, ajetreo; **in the ~ weeks** en las próximas semanas.
Comintern [ˈkɔmɪntɔːn] *n* Comintern *m*.
comma [ˈkɔmə] *n* coma.
command [kəˈmɑːnd] *n* orden *f*, mandato; (*MIL: authority*) mando; (*mastery*) dominio; (*COMPUT*) orden *f*, comando ♦ *vt* (*troops*) mandar; (*give orders to*) mandar, ordenar; (*be able to get*) disponer de; (*deserve*) merecer; **to have at one's ~** (*money, resources etc*) disponer de; **to have/take ~ of** estar al/asumir el mando de.
command economy *n* economía dirigida.
commandeer [kɔmənˈdɪə*] *vt* requisar.
commander [kəˈmɑːndə*] *n* (*MIL*) comandante *m/f*, jefe/a *m/f*.
commanding [kəˈmɑːndɪŋ] *adj* (*appearance*) imponente; (*voice, tone*) imperativo; (*lead*) abrumador(a); (*position*) dominante.
commanding officer *n* comandante *m*.
commandment [kəˈmɑːndmənt] *n* (*REL*) mandamiento.
command module *n* módulo de mando.
commando [kəˈmɑːndəu] *n* comando.
commemorate [kəˈmɛməreɪt] *vt* conmemorar.
commemoration [kəmɛməˈreɪʃən] *n* conmemoración *f*.
commemorative [kəˈmɛmərətɪv] *adj* conmemorativo.
commence [kəˈmɛns] *vt, vi* comenzar.
commend [kəˈmɛnd] *vt* (*praise*) elogiar, alabar; (*recommend*) recomendar; (*entrust*) encomendar.
commendable [kəˈmɛndəbl] *adj* encomiable.
commendation [kɔmɛnˈdeɪʃən] *n* (*for bravery etc*) elogio, encomio.
commensurate [kəˈmɛnʃərɪt] *adj*: **~ with** en proporción a.
comment [ˈkɔmɛnt] *n* comentario ♦ *vi*: **to ~**

that comentar *or* observar que ♦ *vi:* **to ~ (on)** comentar, hacer comentarios (sobre); **"no ~"** "no tengo nada que decir", "sin comentarios".

commentary ['kɔməntərɪ] *n* comentario.

commentator ['kɔmənteɪtə*] *n* comentarista *m/f.*

commerce ['kɔmɔːs] *n* comercio.

commercial [kə'mɜːʃəl] *adj* comercial ♦ *n* (*TV*) anuncio.

commercial bank *n* banco comercial.

commercial break *n* intermedio para publicidad.

commercialism [kə'mɜːʃəlɪzəm] *n* comercialismo.

commercial television *n* televisión *f* comercial.

commercial vehicle *n* vehículo comercial.

commiserate [kə'mɪzəreɪt] *vi:* **to ~ with** compadecerse de, condolerse de.

commission [kə'mɪʃən] *n* (*committee, fee, order for work of art etc*) comisión *f*; (*act*) perpetración *f* ♦ *vt* (*MIL*) nombrar; (*work of art*) encargar; **out of ~** (*machine*) fuera de servicio; **~ of inquiry** comisión *f* investigadora; **I get 10% ~** me dan el diez por ciento de comisión; **to ~ sb to do sth** encargar a algn que haga algo; **to ~ sth from sb** (*painting etc*) encargar algo a algn.

commissionaire [kəmɪʃə'nɛə*] *n* (*BRIT*) portero, conserje *m.*

commissioner [kə'mɪʃənə*] *n* comisario; (*POLICE*) comisario *m* de policía.

commit [kə'mɪt] *vt* (*act*) cometer; (*to sb's care*) entregar; **to ~ o.s. (to do)** comprometerse (a hacer); **to ~ suicide** suicidarse; **to ~ sb for trial** remitir a algn al tribunal.

commitment [kə'mɪtmənt] *n* compromiso.

committed [kə'mɪtɪd] *adj* (*writer, politician etc*) comprometido.

committee [kə'mɪtɪ] *n* comité *m*; **to be on a ~** ser miembro/a de un comité.

committee meeting *n* reunión *f* del comité.

commodious [kə'məʊdɪəs] *adj* grande, espacioso.

commodity [kə'mɒdɪtɪ] *n* mercancía.

commodity exchange *n* bolsa de productos *or* de mercancías.

commodity market *n* mercado de productos básicos.

commodore ['kɒmədɔː*] *n* comodoro.

common ['kɒmən] *adj* (*gen*) común; (*pej*) ordinario ♦ *n* campo común; **in ~** en común; **in ~ use** de uso corriente.

common cold *n:* **the ~** el resfriado.

common denominator *n* común denominador *m.*

commoner ['kɒmənə*] *n* plebeyo/a.

common land *n* campo comunal, ejido.

common law *n* ley *f* consuetudinaria.

common-law ['kɒmənlɔː] *adj:* **~ wife** esposa de hecho.

commonly ['kɒmənlɪ] *adv* comúnmente.

Common Market *n* Mercado Común.

commonplace ['kɒmənpleɪs] *adj* corriente.

commonroom ['kɒmənrum] *n* sala de reunión.

Commons ['kɒmənz] *npl* (*BRIT POL*): **the ~** (la Cámara de) los Comunes.

common sense *n* sentido común.

Commonwealth ['kɒmənwɛlθ] *n:* **the ~** la Comunidad (Británica) de Naciones, la Commonwealth; *ver recuadro.*

COMMONWEALTH

La **Commonwealth** *es la asociación de estados soberanos independientes y territorios asociados que formaban parte del antiguo Imperio Británico. Éste pasó a llamarse así después de la Segunda Guerra Mundial, aunque ya desde 1931 se le conocía como "British Commonwealth of Nations". Todos los estados miembros reconocen al monarca británico como "Head of the Commonwealth".*

---

commotion [kə'məʊʃən] *n* tumulto, confusión *f.*

communal ['kɒmjuːnl] *adj* comunal; (*kitchen*) común.

commune ['kɒmjuːn] *n* (*group*) comuna ♦ *vi* [kə'mjuːn]: **to ~ with** comunicarse con.

communicate [kə'mjuːnɪkeɪt] *vt* comunicar ♦ *vi:* **to ~ (with)** comunicarse (con).

communication [kəmjuːnɪ'keɪʃən] *n* comunicación *f.*

communications network *n* red *f* de comunicaciones.

communications satellite *n* satélite *m* de comunicaciones.

communicative [kə'mjuːnɪkətɪv] *adj* comunicativo.

communion [kə'mjuːnɪən] *n* (*also:* **Holy C~**) comunión *f.*

communiqué [kə'mjuːnɪkeɪ] *n* comunicado, parte *m.*

communism ['kɒmjunɪzəm] *n* comunismo.

communist ['kɒmjunɪst] *adj, n* comunista *m/f.*

community [kə'mjuːnɪtɪ] *n* comunidad *f*; (*large group*) colectividad *f*; (*local*)

vecindario.
community centre n centro social.
community chest n (US) fondo social.
community health centre n centro
médico, casa de salud.
community spirit n civismo.
commutation ticket [kɔmju'teɪʃən-] n (US)
billete m de abono.
commute [kə'mjuːt] vi viajar a diario de
casa al trabajo ♦ vt conmutar.
commuter [kə'mjuːtə*] n persona que
viaja a diario de casa al trabajo.
compact [kəm'pækt] adj compacto; (style)
conciso; (packed) apretado ♦ n ['kɔmpækt]
(pact) pacto; (also: **powder** ~) polvera.
compact disc n compact disc m, disco
compacto.
compact disc player n lector m or
reproductor m de discos compactos.
companion [kəm'pænɪən] n compañero/a.
companionship [kəm'pænjənʃɪp] n
compañerismo.
companionway [kəm'pænjənweɪ] n (NAUT)
escalerilla.
company ['kʌmpənɪ] n (gen) compañía;
(COMM) empresa, compañía; **to keep sb** ~
acompañar a algn; **Smith and C**~ Smith y
Compañía.
company car n coche m de la empresa.
company director n director(a) m/f de
empresa.
company secretary n (BRIT)
administrador(a) m/f de empresa.
comparable ['kɔmpərəbl] adj comparable.
comparative [kəm'pærətɪv] adj (freedom,
luxury, cost) relativo; (study, linguistics)
comparado.
comparatively [kəm'pærətɪvlɪ] adv
(relatively) relativamente.
compare [kəm'pɛə*] vt comparar ♦ vi: **to** ~
(with) poder compararse (con); ~**d with**
or **to** comparado con or a; **how do the
prices** ~? ¿cómo son los precios en
comparación?
comparison [kəm'pærɪsn] n comparación f;
in ~ **(with)** en comparación (con).
compartment [kəm'pɑːtmənt] n
compartim(i)ento; (RAIL) departamento,
compartimento.
compass ['kʌmpəs] n brújula; ~**es** npl
compás m; **within the** ~ **of** al alcance de.
compassion [kəm'pæʃən] n compasión f.
compassionate [kəm'pæʃənɪt] adj
compasivo; **on** ~ **grounds** por compasión.
compassionate leave n permiso por
asuntos familiares.
compatibility [kəmpætɪ'bɪlɪtɪ] n
compatibilidad f.

compatible [kəm'pætɪbl] adj compatible.
compel [kəm'pɛl] vt obligar.
compelling [kəm'pɛlɪŋ] adj (fig: argument)
convincente.
compendium [kəm'pɛndɪəm] n compendio.
compensate ['kɔmpənseɪt] vt compensar
♦ vi: **to** ~ **for** compensar.
compensation [kɔmpən'seɪʃən] n (for loss)
indemnización f.
compère ['kɔmpɛə*] n presentador(a) m/f.
compete [kəm'piːt] vi (take part) competir;
(vie with) competir, hacer la
competencia.
competence ['kɔmpɪtəns] n capacidad f,
aptitud f.
competent ['kɔmpɪtənt] adj competente,
capaz.
competing [kəm'piːtɪŋ] adj (rival)
competidor(a); (ideas) contrapuesto.
competition [kɔmpɪ'tɪʃən] n (contest)
concurso; (SPORT) competición f; (ECON,
rivalry) competencia; **in** ~ **with** en
competencia con.
competitive [kəm'pɛtɪtɪv] adj (ECON, SPORT)
competitivo; (spirit) competidor(a), de
competencia; (selection) por concurso.
competitor [kəm'pɛtɪtə*] n (rival)
competidor(a) m/f; (participant)
concursante m/f.
compile [kəm'paɪl] vt recopilar.
complacency [kəm'pleɪsnsɪ] n
autosatisfacción f.
complacent [kəm'pleɪsənt] adj
autocomplaciente.
complain [kəm'pleɪn] vi (gen) quejarse;
(COMM) reclamar.
complaint [kəm'pleɪnt] n (gen) queja;
(COMM) reclamación f; (LAW) demanda,
querella; (MED) enfermedad f.
complement ['kɔmplɪmənt] n
complemento; (esp ship's crew) dotación f
♦ vt ['kɔmplɪmɛnt] (enhance)
complementar.
complementary [kɔmplɪ'mɛntərɪ] adj
complementario.
complete [kəm'pliːt] adj (full) completo;
(finished) acabado ♦ vt (fulfil) completar;
(finish) acabar; (a form) rellenar; **it's a** ~
disaster es un desastre total.
completely [kəm'pliːtlɪ] adv
completamente.
completion [kəm'pliːʃən] n (gen)
conclusión f, terminación f; **to be nearing**
~ estar a punto de terminarse; **on** ~ **of
contract** cuando se realice el contrato.
complex ['kɔmplɛks] adj complejo ♦ n (gen)
complejo.
complexion [kəm'plɛkʃən] n (of face) tez f,

cutis *m*; (*fig*) aspecto.
complexity [kəm'plɛksɪtɪ] *n* complejidad
f.
compliance [kəm'plaɪəns] *n* (*submission*)
sumisión *f*; (*agreement*) conformidad *f*; **in**
~ **with** de acuerdo con.
compliant [kəm'plaɪənt] *adj* sumiso;
conforme.
complicate ['kɔmplɪkeɪt] *vt* complicar.
complicated ['kɔmplɪkeɪtɪd] *adj*
complicado.
complication [kɔmplɪ'keɪʃən] *n*
complicación *f*.
complicity [kəm'plɪsɪtɪ] *n* complicidad *f*.
compliment ['kɔmplɪmənt] *n* (*formal*)
cumplido; (*flirtation*) piropo ♦ *vt* felicitar;
~**s** *npl* saludos *mpl*; **to pay sb a** ~ (*formal*)
hacer cumplidos a algn; (*flirt*) piropear,
echar piropos a algn; **to** ~ **sb** (**on sth/on
doing sth**) felicitar a algn (por algo/por
haber hecho algo).
complimentary [kɔmplɪ'mɛntərɪ] *adj*
elogioso; (*copy*) de regalo; ~ **ticket**
invitación *f*.
compliments slip *n* saluda *m*.
comply [kəm'plaɪ] *vi*: **to** ~ **with** acatar.
component [kəm'pəunənt] *adj* componente
♦ *n* (*TECH*) pieza, componente *m*.
compose [kəm'pəuz] *vt* componer; **to be**
~**d of** componerse de, constar de; **to** ~
o.s. tranquilizarse.
composed [kəm'pəuzd] *adj* sosegado.
composer [kəm'pəuzə*] *n* (*MUS*)
compositor(a) *m/f*.
composite ['kɔmpəzɪt] *adj* compuesto; ~
motion (*COMM*) moción *f* compuesta.
composition [kɔmpə'zɪʃən] *n* composición
f.
compos mentis ['kɔmpəs'mɛntɪs] *adj*: **to be**
~ estar en su sano juicio.
compost ['kɔmpɔst] *n* abono.
compost heap *n montón de basura
orgánica para abono.*
composure [kəm'pəuʒə*] *n* serenidad *f*,
calma.
compound ['kɔmpaund] *n* (*CHEM*)
compuesto; (*LING*) término compuesto;
(*enclosure*) recinto ♦ *adj* (*gen*) compuesto;
(*fracture*) complicado ♦ *vt* [kəm'paund] (*fig*:
problem, difficulty) agravar.
comprehend [kɔmprɪ'hɛnd] *vt* comprender.
comprehension [kɔmprɪ'hɛnʃən] *n*
comprensión *f*.
comprehensive [kɔmprɪ'hɛnsɪv] *adj* (*broad*)
extenso; (*general*) de conjunto; ~ (**school**)
*n centro estatal de enseñanza
secundaria*, ≈ Instituto Nacional de
Bachillerato (*SP*); *ver recuadro*.

COMPREHENSIVE SCHOOL

*En los años 60 se creó un nuevo tipo de
centro educativo de enseñanza secundaria
(aproximadamente de los once años en
adelante) denominado* **comprehensive
school**, *abierto a todos los alumnos
independientemente de sus capacidades,
con el que se intentó poner fin a la división
tradicional entre centros de enseñanzas
teóricas para acceder a la educación
superior ("grammar schools") y otros de
enseñanzas básicamente profesionales
("secondary modern schools").*

---

comprehensive insurance policy *n*
seguro a todo riesgo.
compress [kəm'prɛs] *vt* comprimir ♦ *n*
['kɔmprɛs] (*MED*) compresa.
comprise [kəm'praɪz] *vt* (*also*: **be** ~**d of**)
comprender, constar de.
compromise ['kɔmprəmaɪz] *n* solución *f* intermedia; (*agreement*) arreglo ♦ *vt* comprometer ♦ *vi* transigir, transar (*LAM*) ♦ *cpd*
(*decision, solution*) de término medio.
compulsion [kəm'pʌlʃən] *n* obligación *f*;
under ~ a la fuerza, por obligación.
compulsive [kəm'pʌlsɪv] *adj* compulsivo.
compulsory [kəm'pʌlsərɪ] *adj* obligatorio.
compulsory purchase *n* expropiación *f*.
compunction [kəm'pʌŋkʃən] *n* escrúpulo;
to have no ~ **about doing sth** no tener
escrúpulos en hacer algo.
computer [kəm'pjuːtə*] *n* ordenador *m*,
computador *m*, computadora.
computer game *n* juego de ordenador.
computerize [kəm'pjuːtəraɪz] *vt* (*data*)
computerizar; (*system*) informatizar.
computer language *n* lenguaje *m* de
ordenador *or* computadora.
computer literate *adj*: **to be** ~ tener
conocimientos de informática a nivel de
usuario.
computer peripheral *n* periférico.
computer program *n* programa *m*
informático *or* de ordenador.
computer programmer *n*
programador(a) *m/f*.
computer programming *n* programación
f.
computer science *n* informática.
computing [kəm'pjuːtɪŋ] *n* (*activity*)
informática.
comrade ['kɔmrɪd] *n* compañero/a.
comradeship ['kɔmrɪdʃɪp] *n* camaradería,
compañerismo.
comsat ® ['kɔmsæt] *n abbr*

= **communications satellite**.
con [kɔn] vt timar, estafar ♦ n timo, estafa;
to ~ sb into doing sth (col) engañar a
algn para que haga algo.
concave ['kɔn'keɪv] adj cóncavo.
conceal [kən'siːl] vt ocultar; (thoughts etc)
disimular.
concede [kən'siːd] vt reconocer; (game)
darse por vencido en; (territory) ceder ♦ vi
darse por vencido.
conceit [kən'siːt] n orgullo,
presunción f.
conceited [kən'siːtɪd] adj orgulloso.
conceivable [kən'siːvəbl] adj concebible; **it
is ~ that** ... es posible que ....
conceivably [kən'siːvəblɪ] adv: **he may ~ be
right** es posible que tenga razón.
conceive [kən'siːv] vt, vi concebir; **to ~ of
sth/of doing sth** imaginar algo/
imaginarse haciendo algo.
concentrate ['kɔnsəntreɪt] vi concentrarse
♦ vt concentrar.
concentration [kɔnsən'treɪʃən] n
concentración f.
concentration camp n campo de
concentración.
concentric [kən'sɛntrɪk] adj concéntrico.
concept ['kɔnsɛpt] n concepto.
conception [kən'sɛpʃən] n (idea) concepto,
idea; (BIOL) concepción f.
concern [kən'səːn] n (matter) asunto;
(COMM) empresa; (anxiety) preocupación f
♦ vt tener que ver con; (affect) atañer,
concernir; **to be ~ed (about)** interesarse
(por), preocuparse (por); **to be ~ed with**
tratar de; "**to whom it may ~**" "a quien
corresponda"; **the department ~ed**
(under discussion) el departamento en
cuestión; (relevant) el departamento
competente; **as far as I am ~ed** en cuanto
a mí, por lo que a mí se refiere.
concerning [kən'səːnɪŋ] prep sobre, acerca
de.
concert ['kɔnsət] n concierto.
concerted [kən'səːtəd] adj (efforts etc)
concertado.
concert hall n sala de conciertos.
concertina [kɔnsə'tiːnə] n concertina.
concerto [kən'tʃəːtəu] n concierto.
concession [kən'sɛʃən] n concesión f; (price
~) descuento; **tax ~** privilegio fiscal.
concessionaire [kənsɛʃə'nɛə*] n
concesionario/a.
concessionary [kən'sɛʃənərɪ] adj (ticket,
fare) con descuento, a precio reducido.
conciliation [kənsɪlɪ'eɪʃən] n conciliación f.
conciliatory [kən'sɪlɪətrɪ] adj
conciliador(a).

concise [kən'saɪs] adj conciso.
conclave ['kɔnkleɪv] n cónclave m.
conclude [kən'kluːd] vt (finish) concluir;
(treaty etc) firmar; (agreement) llegar a;
(decide): **to ~ that** ... llegar a la
conclusión de que ... ♦ vi (events)
concluir, terminar.
concluding [kən'kluːdɪŋ] adj (remarks etc)
final.
conclusion [kən'kluːʒən] n conclusión f; **to
come to the ~ that** llegar a la conclusión
de que.
conclusive [kən'kluːsɪv] adj decisivo,
concluyente.
conclusively [kən'kluːsɪvlɪ] adv
concluyentemente.
concoct [kən'kɔkt] vt (food, drink) preparar;
(story) inventar; (plot) tramar.
concoction [kən'kɔkʃən] n (food) mezcla;
(drink) brebaje m.
concord ['kɔnkɔːd] n (harmony) concordia;
(treaty) acuerdo.
concourse ['kɔnkɔːs] n (hall) vestíbulo.
concrete ['kɔnkriːt] n hormigón m ♦ adj
concreto.
concrete mixer n hormigonera.
concur [kən'kəː*] vi estar de acuerdo.
concurrently [kən'kʌrntlɪ] adv al mismo
tiempo.
concussion [kən'kʌʃən] n conmoción f
cerebral.
condemn [kən'dɛm] vt condenar.
condemnation [kɔndɛm'neɪʃən] n (gen)
condena; (blame) censura.
condensation [kɔndɛn'seɪʃən] n
condensación f.
condense [kən'dɛns] vi condensarse ♦ vt
condensar; (text) abreviar.
condensed milk n leche f condensada.
condescend [kɔndɪ'sɛnd] vi condescender;
to ~ to sb tratar a algn con
condescendencia; **to ~ to do sth** dignarse
hacer algo.
condescending [kɔndɪ'sɛndɪŋ] adj
superior.
condition [kən'dɪʃən] n condición f; (of
health) estado; (disease) enfermedad f ♦ vt
condicionar; **on ~ that** a condición (de)
que; **weather ~s** condiciones
atmosféricas; **in good/poor ~** en buenas/
malas condiciones, en buen/mal estado;
~s of sale condiciones de venta.
conditional [kən'dɪʃənl] adj condicional.
conditioned reflex [kən'dɪʃənd-] n reflejo
condicionado.
conditioner [kən'dɪʃənə*] n (for hair)
suavizante m, acondicionador m.
condo ['kɔndəu] n (US col) = **condominium**.

condolences [kən'dəulənsız] *npl* pésame *msg.*

condom ['kɔndəm] *n* condón *m.*

condominium [kɔndə'mınıəm] *n* (*US: building*) bloque *m* de pisos *or* apartamentos (*propiedad de quienes lo habitan*), condominio (*LAM*); (: *apartment*) piso *or* apartamento (en propiedad), condominio (*LAM*).

condone [kən'dəun] *vt* condonar.

conducive [kən'djuːsıv] *adj:* ~ **to** conducente a.

conduct ['kɔndʌkt] *n* conducta, comportamiento ♦ *vt* [kən'dʌkt] (*lead*) conducir; (*manage*) llevar, dirigir; (*MUS*) dirigir ♦ *vi* (*MUS*) llevar la batuta; **to** ~ **o.s.** comportarse.

conducted tour *n* (*BRIT*) visita con guía.

conductor [kən'dʌktə*] *n* (*of orchestra*) director(a) *m/f*; (*US: on train*) revisor(a) *m/ f*; (*on bus*) cobrador *m*; (*ELEC*) conductor *m.*

conductress [kən'dʌktrıs] *n* (*on bus*) cobradora.

cone [kəun] *n* cono; (*pine* ~) piña; (*for ice cream*) cucurucho.

confectioner [kən'fɛkʃənə*] *n* (*of cakes*) pastelero/a; (*of sweets*) confitero/a; ~'**s (shop)** *n* pastelería; confitería.

confectionery [kən'fɛkʃənrı] *n* pasteles *mpl*; dulces *mpl.*

confederate [kən'fɛdrıt] *adj* confederado ♦ *n* (*pej*) cómplice *m/f*; (*US: HISTORY*) confederado/a.

confederation [kənfɛdə'reıʃən] *n* confederación *f.*

confer [kən'fəː*] *vt* otorgar (*on* a) ♦ *vi* conferenciar; **to** ~ **(with sb about sth)** consultar (con algn sobre algo).

conference ['kɔnfərns] *n* (*meeting*) reunión *f*; (*convention*) congreso; **to be in** ~ estar en una reunión.

conference room *n* sala de conferencias.

confess [kən'fɛs] *vt* confesar ♦ *vi* confesar; (*REL*) confesarse.

confession [kən'fɛʃən] *n* confesión *f.*

confessional [kən'fɛʃənl] *n* confesionario.

confessor [kən'fɛsə*] *n* confesor *m.*

confetti [kən'fɛtı] *n* confeti *m.*

confide [kən'faıd] *vi:* **to** ~ **in** confiar en.

confidence ['kɔnfıdns] *n* (*gen, also:* **self-**~) confianza; (*secret*) confidencia; **in** ~ (*speak, write*) en confianza; **to have (every)** ~ **that** estar seguro *or* confiado de que; **motion of no** ~ moción *f* de censura; **to tell sb sth in strict** ~ decir algo a algn de manera confidencial.

confidence trick *n* timo.

confident ['kɔnfıdənt] *adj* seguro de sí mismo.

confidential [kɔnfı'dɛnʃəl] *adj* confidencial; (*secretary*) de confianza.

confidentiality [kɔnfıdɛnʃı'ælıtı] *n* confidencialidad *f.*

configuration [kənfıgju'reıʃən] *n* (*also COMPUT*) configuración *f.*

confine [kən'faın] *vt* (*limit*) limitar; (*shut up*) encerrar; **to** ~ **o.s. to doing sth** limitarse a hacer algo.

confined [kən'faınd] *adj* (*space*) reducido.

confinement [kən'faınmənt] *n* (*prison*) reclusión *f*; (*MED*) parto; **in solitary** ~ incomunicado.

confines ['kɔnfaınz] *npl* confines *mpl.*

confirm [kən'fəːm] *vt* confirmar.

confirmation [kɔnfə'meıʃən] *n* confirmación *f.*

confirmed [kən'fəːmd] *adj* empedernido.

confiscate ['kɔnfıskeıt] *vt* confiscar.

confiscation [kɔnfıs'keıʃən] *n* incautación *f.*

conflagration [kɔnflə'greıʃən] *n* conflagración *f.*

conflict ['kɔnflıkt] *n* conflicto ♦ *vi* [kən'flıkt] (*opinions*) estar reñido; (*reports, evidence*) contradecirse.

conflicting [kən'flıktıŋ] *adj* (*reports, evidence, opinions*) contradictorio.

conform [kən'fɔːm] *vi:* **to** ~ **to** (*laws*) someterse a; (*usages, mores*) amoldarse a; (*standards*) ajustarse a.

conformist [kən'fɔːmıst] *n* conformista *m/f.*

confound [kən'faund] *vt* confundir; (*amaze*) pasmar.

confounded [kən'faundıd] *adj* condenado.

confront [kən'frʌnt] *vt* (*problems*) hacer frente a; (*enemy, danger*) enfrentarse con.

confrontation [kɔnfrən'teıʃən] *n* enfrentamiento, confrontación *f.*

confrontational [kɔnfrən'teıʃənəl] *adj* conflictivo.

confuse [kən'fjuːz] *vt* (*perplex*) desconcertar; (*mix up*) confundir.

confused [kən'fjuːzd] *adj* confuso; (*person*) desconcertado; **to get** ~ desconcertarse; (*muddled up*) hacerse un lío.

confusing [kən'fjuːzıŋ] *adj* confuso.

confusion [kən'fjuːʒən] *n* confusión *f.*

congeal [kən'dʒiːl] *vi* coagularse.

congenial [kən'dʒiːnıəl] *adj* agradable.

congenital [kən'dʒɛnıtl] *adj* congénito.

congested [kən'dʒɛstıd] *adj* (*gen*) atestado; (*telephone lines*) saturado.

congestion [kən'dʒɛstʃən] *n* congestión *f.*

conglomerate [kən'glɔmərət] *n* (*COMM, GEO*) conglomerado.

conglomeration [kənglɔmə'reɪʃən] n conglomeración f.
Congo ['kɔŋgəu] n (state) Congo.
congratulate [kən'grætjuleɪt] vt felicitar.
congratulations [kəngrætju'leɪʃənz] npl: ~ (on) felicitaciones fpl (por); ~! ¡enhorabuena!, ¡felicidades!
congregate ['kɔŋgrɪgeɪt] vi congregarse.
congregation [kɔŋgrɪ'geɪʃən] n (in church) fieles mpl.
congress ['kɔŋgrɛs] n congreso; (US POL): C~ el Congreso (de los Estados Unidos); ver recuadro.

CONGRESS

En el Congreso de los Estados Unidos (**Congress**) se elaboran y aprueban las leyes federales. Consta de dos cámaras: la Cámara de Representantes ("House of Representatives"), cuyos 435 miembros son elegidos cada dos años por voto popular directo y en número proporcional a los habitantes de cada estado, y el Senado ("Senate"), con 100 senadores ("senators"), 2 por estado, de los que un tercio se elige cada dos años y el resto cada seis.

---

congressman ['kɔŋgrɛsmən] n (US) diputado, miembro del Congreso.
congresswoman ['kɔŋgrɛswumən] n (US) diputada, miembro f del Congreso.
conical ['kɔnɪkl] adj cónico.
conifer ['kɔnɪfə*] n conífera.
coniferous [kə'nɪfərəs] adj (forest) conífero.
conjecture [kən'dʒɛktʃə*] n conjetura.
conjugal ['kɔndʒugl] adj conyugal.
conjugate ['kɔndʒugeɪt] vt conjugar.
conjunction [kən'dʒʌŋkʃən] n conjunción f; **in ~ with** junto con.
conjunctivitis [kəndʒʌŋktɪ'vaɪtɪs] n conjuntivitis f.
conjure ['kʌndʒə*] vi hacer juegos de manos.
▶**conjure up** vt (ghost, spirit) hacer aparecer; (memories) evocar.
conjurer ['kʌndʒərə*] n ilusionista m/f.
conjuring trick ['kʌndʒərɪŋ-] n juego de manos.
conker ['kɔŋkə*] n (BRIT) castaño de Indias.
conk out [kɔŋk-] vi (col) estropearse, fastidiarse, descomponerse (LAM).
con man n timador m.
Conn. abbr (US) = Connecticut.
connect [kə'nɛkt] vt juntar, unir; (ELEC) conectar; (pipes) empalmar; (fig) relacionar, asociar ♦ vi: **to ~ with** (train)

enlazar con; **to be ~ed with** (associated) estar relacionado con; (related) estar emparentado con; **I am trying to ~ you** (TEL) estoy intentando ponerle al habla.
connection [kə'nɛkʃən] n juntura, unión f; (ELEC) conexión f; (TECH) empalme m; (RAIL) enlace m; (TEL) comunicación f; (fig) relación f; **what is the ~ between them?** ¿qué relación hay entre ellos?; **in ~ with** con respecto a, en relación a; **she has many business ~s** tiene muchos contactos profesionales; **to miss/make a ~** perder/coger el enlace.
connoisseur [kɔnɪ'səː*] n experto/a, entendido/a.
connotation [kɔnə'teɪʃən] n connotación f.
conquer ['kɔŋkə*] vt (territory) conquistar; (enemy, feelings) vencer.
conqueror ['kɔŋkərə*] n conquistador(a) m/f.
conquest ['kɔŋkwɛst] n conquista.
cons [kɔnz] npl see **convenience, pro.**
conscience ['kɔnʃəns] n conciencia; **in all ~** en conciencia.
conscientious [kɔnʃɪ'ɛnʃəs] adj concienzudo; (objection) de conciencia.
conscientious objector n objetor m de conciencia.
conscious ['kɔnʃəs] adj consciente; (deliberate: insult, error) premeditado, intencionado; **to become ~ of sth/that** darse cuenta de algo/de que.
consciousness ['kɔnʃəsnɪs] n conciencia; (MED) conocimiento.
conscript ['kɔnskrɪpt] n recluta m/f.
conscription [kən'skrɪpʃən] n servicio militar (obligatorio).
consecrate ['kɔnsɪkreɪt] vt consagrar.
consecutive [kən'sɛkjutɪv] adj consecutivo; **on 3 ~ occasions** en 3 ocasiones consecutivas.
consensus [kən'sɛnsəs] n consenso; **the ~ of opinion** el consenso general.
consent [kən'sɛnt] n consentimiento ♦ vi: **to ~ to** consentir en; **by common ~** de común acuerdo.
consequence ['kɔnsɪkwəns] n consecuencia; **in ~** por consiguiente.
consequently ['kɔnsɪkwəntlɪ] adv por consiguiente.
conservation [kɔnsə'veɪʃən] n conservación f; (of nature) conservación, protección f.
conservationist [kɔnsə'veɪʃnɪst] n conservacionista m/f.
conservative [kən'səːvətɪv] adj conservador(a); (cautious) moderado; C~ adj, n (BRIT POL) conservador(a) m/f; **the**

C~ Party el partido conservador (británico).

conservatory [kən'sɔːvətrɪ] *n (greenhouse)* invernadero.

conserve [kən'sɔːv] *vt* conservar ♦ *n* conserva.

consider [kən'sɪdə*] *vt* considerar; *(take into account)* tomar en cuenta; *(study)* estudiar, examinar; **to ~ doing sth** pensar en (la posibilidad de) hacer algo; **all things ~ed** pensándolo bien; **~ yourself lucky** ¡date por satisfecho!

considerable [kən'sɪdərəbl] *adj* considerable.

considerably [kən'sɪdərəblɪ] *adv* bastante, considerablemente.

considerate [kən'sɪdərɪt] *adj* considerado.

consideration [kənsɪdə'reɪʃən] *n* consideración *f*; *(reward)* retribución *f*; **to be under ~** estar estudiándose; **my first ~ is my family** mi primera consideración es mi familia.

considered [kən'sɪdəd] *adj*: **it's my ~ opinion that ...** depués de haber reflexionado mucho, pienso que ....

considering [kən'sɪdərɪŋ] *prep*: **~ (that)** teniendo en cuenta (que).

consign [kən'saɪn] *vt* consignar.

consignee [kɔnsaɪ'niː] *n* consignatario/a.

consignment [kən'saɪnmənt] *n* envío.

consignment note *n (COMM)* talón *m* de expedición.

consist [kən'sɪst] *vi*: **to ~ of** consistir en.

consistency [kən'sɪstənsɪ] *n (of person etc)* consecuencia, coherencia; *(thickness)* consistencia.

consistent [kən'sɪstənt] *adj (person, argument)* consecuente, coherente; *(results)* constante.

consolation [kɔnsə'leɪʃən] *n* consuelo.

console [kən'səul] *vt* consolar ♦ *n* ['kɔnsəul] *(control panel)* consola.

consolidate [kən'sɔlɪdeɪt] *vt* consolidar.

consols ['kɔnsɔlz] *npl (BRIT STOCK EXCHANGE)* valores *mpl* consolidados.

consommé [kən'sɔmeɪ] *n* consomé *m*, caldo.

consonant ['kɔnsənənt] *n* consonante *f*.

consort ['kɔnsɔːt] *n* consorte *m/f* ♦ *vi* [kən'sɔːt]: **to ~ with sb** *(often pej)* asociarse con algn; **prince ~** príncipe *m* consorte.

consortium [kən'sɔːtɪəm] *n* consorcio.

conspicuous [kən'spɪkjuəs] *adj (visible)* visible; *(garish etc)* llamativo; *(outstanding)* notable; **to make o.s. ~** llamar la atención.

conspiracy [kən'spɪrəsɪ] *n* conjura, complot

m.

conspire [kən'spaɪə*] *vi* conspirar.

constable ['kʌnstəbl] *n (BRIT)* agente *m/f* (de policía); **chief ~** ≈ jefe *m/f* de policía.

constabulary [kən'stæbjulərɪ] *n* ≈ policía.

constancy ['kɔnstənsɪ] *n* constancia; fidelidad *f*.

constant ['kɔnstənt] *adj (gen)* constante; *(loyal)* leal, fiel.

constantly ['kɔnstəntlɪ] *adv* constantemente.

constellation [kɔnstə'leɪʃən] *n* constelación *f*.

consternation [kɔnstə'neɪʃən] *n* consternación *f*.

constipated ['kɔnstɪpeɪtəd] *adj* estreñido.

constipation [kɔnstɪ'peɪʃən] *n* estreñimiento.

constituency [kən'stɪtjuənsɪ] *n (POL)* distrito electoral; *(people)* electorado; *ver recuadro*.

CONSTITUENCY

Constituency *es la denominación que recibe un distrito o circunscripción electoral y el grupo de electores registrados en ella en el sistema electoral británico. Cada circunscripción elige a un diputado ("Member of Parliament"), el cual se halla disponible semanalmente para las consultas y peticiones de sus electores durante ciertas horas a la semana, tiempo al que se llama "surgery".*

---

constituency party *n* partido local.

constituent [kən'stɪtjuənt] *n (POL)* elector(a) *m/f*; *(part)* componente *m*.

constitute ['kɔnstɪtjuːt] *vt* constituir.

constitution [kɔnstɪ'tjuːʃən] *n* constitución *f*.

constitutional [kɔnstɪ'tjuːʃənl] *adj* constitucional; **~ monarchy** monarquía constitucional.

constrain [kən'streɪn] *vt* obligar.

constrained [kən'streɪnd] *adj*: **to feel ~ to ...** sentirse obligado a ....

constraint [kən'streɪnt] *n (force)* fuerza; *(limit)* restricción *f*; *(restraint)* reserva; *(embarrassment)* cohibición *f*.

constrict [kən'strɪkt] *vt* oprimir.

constriction [kən'strɪkʃən] *n* constricción *f*, opresión *f*.

construct [kən'strʌkt] *vt* construir.

construction [kən'strʌkʃən] *n* construcción *f*; *(fig: interpretation)* interpretación *f*; **under ~** en construcción.

construction industry *n* industria de la

construcción.
constructive [kən'strʌktɪv] *adj*
constructivo.
construe [kən'struː] *vt* interpretar.
consul ['kɔnsl] *n* cónsul *m/f*.
consulate ['kɔnsjulɪt] *n* consulado.
consult [kən'sʌlt] *vt, vi* consultar; **to ~ sb**
(about sth) consultar a algn (sobre algo).
consultancy [kən'sʌltənsɪ] *n (COMM)*
consultoría; *(MED)* puesto de especialista.
consultant [kən'sʌltənt] *n (BRIT MED)*
especialista *m/f*; *(other specialist)* asesor(a)
m/f, consultor(a) *m/f*.
consultation [kɔnsəl'teɪʃən] *n* consulta; **in**
~ with en consulta con.
consultative [kən'sʌltətɪv] *adj* consultivo.
consulting room *n (BRIT)* consulta,
consultorio.
consume [kən'sjuːm] *vt (eat)* comerse;
(drink) beberse; *(fire etc, COMM)* consumir.
consumer [kən'sjuːmə*] *n (of electricity, gas*
etc) consumidor(a) *m/f*.
consumer association *n* asociación *f* de
consumidores.
consumer credit *n* crédito al consumidor.
consumer durables *npl* bienes *mpl* de
consumo duraderos.
consumer goods *npl* bienes *mpl* de
consumo.
consumerism [kən'sjuːmərɪzəm] *n*
consumismo.
consumer society *n* sociedad *f* de
consumo.
consumer watchdog *n* organización *f*
protectora del consumidor.
consummate ['kɔnsʌmeɪt] *vt* consumar.
consumption [kən'sʌmpʃən] *n* consumo;
(MED) tisis *f*; **not fit for human ~** no apto
para el consumo humano.
cont. *abbr (= continued)* sigue.
contact ['kɔntækt] *n* contacto; *(person: pej)*
enchufe *m* ♦ *vt* ponerse en contacto con;
~ lenses *npl* lentes *fpl* de contacto; **to be in**
~ with sb/sth estar en contacto con
algn/algo; **business ~s** relaciones *fpl*
comerciales.
contagious [kən'teɪdʒəs] *adj* contagioso.
contain [kən'teɪn] *vt* contener; **to ~ o.s.**
contenerse.
container [kən'teɪnə*] *n* recipiente *m*; *(for*
shipping etc) contenedor *m*.
containerize [kən'teɪnəraɪz] *vt* transportar
en contenedores.
container ship *n* buque *m* contenedor,
portacontenedores *m inv*.
contaminate [kən'tæmɪneɪt] *vt* contaminar.
contamination [kəntæmɪ'neɪʃən] *n*
contaminación *f*.

cont'd *abbr (= continued)* sigue.
contemplate ['kɔntəmpleɪt] *vt (gen)*
contemplar; *(reflect upon)* considerar;
(intend) pensar.
contemplation [kɔntəm'pleɪʃən] *n*
contemplación *f*.
contemporary [kən'tempərərɪ] *adj, n (of the*
same age) contemporáneo/a *m/f*.
contempt [kən'tempt] *n* desprecio; **~ of**
court *(LAW)* desacato (a los tribunales *or*
a la justicia).
contemptible [kən'temptɪbl] *adj*
despreciable, desdeñable.
contemptuous [kən'temptjuəs] *adj*
desdeñoso.
contend [kən'tend] *vt (argue)* afirmar ♦ *vi*
(struggle) luchar; **he has a lot to ~ with**
tiene que hacer frente a muchos
problemas.
contender [kən'tendə*] *n (SPORT)*
contendiente *m/f*.
content [kən'tent] *adj (happy)* contento;
(satisfied) satisfecho ♦ *vt* contentar;
satisfacer ♦ *n* ['kɔntent] contenido; **~s** *npl*
contenido *msg*; **(table of) ~s** índice *m* de
materias; *(in magazine)* sumario; **to be ~**
with conformarse con; **to ~ o.s. with**
sth/with doing sth conformarse con
algo/con hacer algo.
contented [kən'tentɪd] *adj* contento;
satisfecho.
contentedly [kən'tentɪdlɪ] *adv* con aire
satisfecho.
contention [kən'tenʃən] *n* discusión *f*;
(belief) argumento; **bone of ~** manzana de
la discordia.
contentious [kən'tenʃəs] *adj* discutible.
contentment [kən'tentmənt] *n* satisfacción
f.
contest ['kɔntest] *n* contienda; *(competition)*
concurso ♦ *vt* [kən'test] *(dispute)*
impugnar; *(LAW)* disputar, litigar; *(POL:*
election, seat) presentarse como
candidato/a a.
contestant [kən'testənt] *n* concursante *m/f*;
(in fight) contendiente *m/f*.
context ['kɔntekst] *n* contexto; **in/out of ~**
en/fuera de contexto.
continent ['kɔntɪnənt] *n* continente *m*; **the**
C~ *(BRIT)* el continente europeo, Europa;
on the C~ en el continente europeo, en
Europa.
continental [kɔntɪ'nentl] *adj* continental;
(BRIT: European) europeo.
continental breakfast *n* desayuno estilo
europeo.
continental quilt *n (BRIT)* edredón *m*.
contingency [kən'tɪndʒənsɪ] *n*

contingencia.
contingent [kən'tɪndʒənt] n (*group*)
representación f.
continual [kən'tɪnjuəl] *adj* continuo.
continually [kən'tɪnjuəlɪ] *adv*
continuamente.
continuation [kəntɪnju'eɪʃən] n
prolongación f; (*after interruption*)
reanudación f; (*story, episode*)
continuación f.
continue [kən'tɪnjuː] vi, vt seguir,
continuar; ~**d on page 10** sigue en la
página 10.
continuing education [kən'tɪnjuɪŋ] n
educación f continua de adultos.
continuity [kɒntɪ'njuːtɪ] n (*also CINE*)
continuidad f.
continuity girl n (*CINE*) secretaria de
continuidad.
continuous [kən'tɪnjuəs] *adj* continuo; ~
performance (*CINE*) sesión f continua; ~
stationery papel m continuo.
continuously [kən'tɪnjuəslɪ] *adv*
continuamente.
contort [kən'tɔːt] vt retorcer.
contortion [kən'tɔːʃən] n (*movement*)
contorsión f.
contortionist [kən'tɔːʃənɪst] n
contorsionista m/f.
contour ['kɒntuə*] n contorno; (*also*: ~ **line**)
curva de nivel.
contraband ['kɒntrəbænd] n contrabando
♦ *adj* de contrabando.
contraception [kɒntrə'sɛpʃən] n
contracepción f.
contraceptive [kɒntrə'sɛptɪv] *adj, n*
anticonceptivo.
contract ['kɒntrækt] n contrato ♦ *cpd*
['kɒntrækt] (*price, date*) contratado, de
contrato; (*work*) bajo contrato ♦ *vb*
[kən'trækt] vi (*COMM*): **to** ~ **to do sth**
comprometerse por contrato a hacer
algo; (*become smaller*) contraerse,
encogerse ♦ vt contraer; **to be under** ~ **to
do sth** estar bajo contrato para hacer
algo; ~ **of employment** or **of service**
contrato de trabajo.
▶**contract in** vi tomar parte.
▶**contract out** vi: **to** ~ **out (of)** optar por
no tomar part (en); **to** ~ **out of a pension
scheme** dejar de cotizar en un plan de
jubilación.
contraction [kən'trækʃən] n contracción f.
contractor [kən'træktə*] n contratista m/f.
contractual [kən'træktjuəl] *adj* contractual.
contradict [kɒntrə'dɪkt] vt (*declare to be
wrong*) desmentir; (*be contrary to*)
contradecir.

contradiction [kɒntrə'dɪkʃən] n
contradicción f; **to be in** ~ **with**
contradecir.
contradictory [kɒntrə'dɪktərɪ] *adj*
(*statements*) contradictorio; **to be** ~ **to**
contradecir.
contralto [kən'træltəu] n contralto f.
contraption [kən'træpʃən] n (*pej*) artilugio
m.
contrary ['kɒntrərɪ] *adj* (*opposite, different*)
contrario; [kən'trɛərɪ] (*perverse*) terco ♦ n:
on the ~ al contrario; **unless you hear to
the** ~ a no ser que le digan lo contrario;
~ **to what we thought** al contrario de lo
que pensábamos.
contrast ['kɒntrɑːst] n contraste m ♦ vt
[kən'trɑːst] contrastar; **in** ~ **to** or **with** a
diferencia de.
contrasting [kən'trɑːstɪŋ] *adj* (*opinion*)
opuesto; (*colour*) que hace contraste.
contravene [kɒntrə'viːn] vt contravenir.
contravention [kɒntrə'vɛnʃən] n: ~ **(of)**
contravención f (de).
contribute [kən'trɪbjuːt] vi contribuir ♦ vt:
to ~ **to** (*gen*) contribuir a; (*newspaper*)
colaborar en; (*discussion*) intervenir en.
contribution [kɒntrɪ'bjuːʃən] n (*money*)
contribución f; (*to debate*) intervención f;
(*to journal*) colaboración f.
contributor [kən'trɪbjutə*] n (*to newspaper*)
colaborador(a) m/f.
contributory [kən'trɪbjutərɪ] *adj* (*cause*)
contribuyente; **it was a** ~ **factor in** ... fue
un factor que contribuyó en ....
contributory pension scheme n plan m
cotizable de jubilación.
contrivance [kən'traɪvəns] n (*machine,
device*) aparato, dispositivo.
contrive [kən'traɪv] vt (*invent*) idear ♦ vi: **to**
~ **to do** lograr hacer; (*try*) procurar
hacer.
control [kən'trəul] vt controlar; (*traffic etc*)
dirigir; (*machinery*) manejar; (*temper*)
dominar; (*disease, fire*) dominar,
controlar ♦ n (*command*) control m; (*of
car*) conducción f; (*check*) freno; ~**s** npl
mandos mpl; **to** ~ **o.s.** controlarse,
dominarse; **everything is under** ~ todo
está bajo control; **to be in** ~ **of** estar al
mando de; **the car went out of** ~ el coche
se descontroló.
control group n (*MED, PSYCH etc*) grupo de
control.
control key n (*COMPUT*) tecla de control.
controlled economy n economía dirigida.
controller [kən'trəulə*] n controlador(a)
m/f.
controlling interest [kən'trəulɪŋ-] n

participación *f* mayoritaria.
control panel *n* (*on aircraft, ship, TV etc*)
tablero de instrumentos.
control point *n* (puesto de) control *m*.
control room *n* (*NAUT, MIL*) sala de
mandos; (*RADIO, TV*) sala de control.
control tower *n* (*AVIAT*) torre *f* de control.
control unit *n* (*COMPUT*) unidad *f* de
control.
controversial [kɔntrə'vəːʃl] *adj* polémico.
controversy ['kɔntrəvəːsɪ] *n* polémica.
conurbation [kɔnəː'beɪʃən] *n* conurbación *f*.
convalesce [kɔnvə'lɛs] *vi* convalecer.
convalescence [kɔnvə'lɛsns] *n*
convalecencia.
convalescent [kɔnvə'lɛsnt] *adj, n*
convaleciente *m/f*.
convector [kən'vɛktə'] *n* calentador *m* de
convección.
convene [kən'viːn] *vt* (*meeting*) convocar
♦ *vi* reunirse.
convenience [kən'viːnɪəns] *n* (*comfort*)
comodidad *f*; (*advantage*) ventaja; **at your
earliest** ~ (*COMM*) tan pronto como le sea
posible; **all modern** ~**s**, (*BRIT*) **all mod
cons** todo confort.
convenience foods *npl* platos *mpl*
preparados.
convenient [kən'viːnɪənt] *adj* (*useful*) útil;
(*place*) conveniente; (*time*) oportuno; **if it
is** ~ **for you** si le viene bien.
conveniently [kən'viːnɪəntlɪ] *adv* (*happen*)
oportunamente; (*situated*)
convenientemente.
convent ['kɔnvənt] *n* convento.
convent school *n* colegio de monjas.
convention [kən'vɛnʃən] *n* convención *f*;
(*meeting*) asamblea.
conventional [kən'vɛnʃənl] *adj*
convencional.
converge [kən'vəːdʒ] *vi* converger.
conversant [kən'vəːsnt] *adj*: **to be** ~ **with**
estar familiarizado con.
conversation [kɔnvə'seɪʃən] *n*
conversación *f*.
conversational [kɔnvə'seɪʃənl] *adj* (*familiar*)
familiar; (*talkative*) locuaz; ~ **mode**
(*COMPUT*) modo de conversación.
converse ['kɔnvəːs] *n* inversa ♦ *vi* [kən'vəːs]
conversar; **to** ~ **(with sb about sth)**
conversar *or* platicar (*LAM*) (con algn de
algo).
conversely [kɔn'vəːslɪ] *adv* a la inversa.
conversion [kən'vəːʃən] *n* conversión *f*;
(*house* ~) reforma, remodelación *f*.
conversion table *n* tabla de
equivalencias.
convert [kən'vəːt] *vt* (*REL, COMM*) convertir;

(*alter*) transformar ♦ *n* ['kɔnvəːt]
converso/a.
convertible [kən'vəːtəbl] *adj* convertible
♦ *n* descapotable *m*; ~ **loan stock**
obligaciones *fpl* convertibles.
convex ['kɔn'vɛks] *adj* convexo.
convey [kən'veɪ] *vt* transportar; (*thanks*)
comunicar; (*idea*) expresar.
conveyance [kən'veɪəns] *n* (*of goods*)
transporte *m*; (*vehicle*) vehículo, medio de
transporte.
conveyancing [kən'veɪənsɪŋ] *n* (*LAW*)
preparación *f* de escrituras de traspaso.
conveyor belt [kən'veɪə*-] *n* cinta
transportadora.
convict [kən'vɪkt] *vt* (*gen*) condenar; (*find
guilty*) declarar culpable a ♦ *n* ['kɔnvɪkt]
presidiario/a.
conviction [kən'vɪkʃən] *n* condena; (*belief*)
creencia, convicción *f*.
convince [kən'vɪns] *vt* convencer; **to** ~ **sb
(of sth/that)** convencer a algn (de algo/de
que).
convinced [kən'vɪnst] *adj*: ~ **of/that**
convencido de/de que.
convincing [kən'vɪnsɪŋ] *adj* convincente.
convincingly [kən'vɪnsɪŋlɪ] *adv* de modo
convincente, convincentemente.
convivial [kən'vɪvɪəl] *adj* (*person*) sociable;
(*atmosphere*) alegre.
convoluted ['kɔnvəluːtɪd] *adj* (*argument etc*)
enrevesado; (*shape*) enrollado,
enroscado.
convoy ['kɔnvɔɪ] *n* convoy *m*.
convulse [kən'vʌls] *vt* convulsionar; **to be
~d with laughter** dislocarse de risa.
convulsion [kən'vʌlʃən] *n* convulsión *f*.
coo [kuː] *vi* arrullar.
cook [kuk] *vt* cocinar; (*stew etc*) guisar;
(*meal*) preparar ♦ *vi* hacerse; (*person*)
cocinar ♦ *n* cocinero/a.
► **cook up** *vt* (*col: excuse, story*) inventar.
cookbook ['kukbuk] *n* libro de cocina.
cooker ['kukə*] *n* cocina.
cookery ['kukərɪ] *n* cocina.
cookery book *n* (*BRIT*) = **cookbook**.
cookie ['kukɪ] *n* (*US*) galleta.
cooking ['kukɪŋ] *n* cocina ♦ *cpd* (*apples*)
para cocinar; (*utensils, salt, foil*) de cocina.
cooking chocolate *n* chocolate *m* fondant
or de hacer.
cookout ['kukaut] *n* (*US*) comida al aire
libre.
cool [kuːl] *adj* fresco; (*not hot*) tibio; (*not
afraid*) tranquilo; (*unfriendly*) frío ♦ *vt*
enfriar ♦ *vi* enfriarse; (*weather*)
hace fresco; **to keep sth** ~ *or* **in a** ~ **place**
conservar algo fresco *or* en un sitio

fresco.
►**cool down** *vi* enfriarse; (*fig: person, situation*) calmarse.
coolant ['kuːlənt] *n* refrigerante *m.*
cool box, (*US*) **cooler** ['kuːlə*] *n* nevera portátil.
cooling ['kuːlɪŋ] *adj* refrescante.
cooling-off period [kuːlɪŋ'ɔf-] *n* (*INDUSTRY*) plazo de negociaciones.
cooling tower *n* torre *f* de refrigeración.
coolly ['kuːlɪ] *adv* (*calmly*) con tranquilidad; (*audaciously*) descaradamente; (*unenthusiastically*) fríamente, con frialdad.
coolness ['kuːlnɪs] *n* frescura; tranquilidad *f*; (*hostility*) frialdad *f*; (*indifference*) falta de entusiasmo.
coop [kuːp] *n* gallinero ♦ *vt*: **to ~ up** (*fig*) encerrar.
co-op ['kəuɔp] *n abbr* (= *Cooperative* (*Society*)) cooperativa.
cooperate [kəu'ɔpəreɪt] *vi* cooperar, colaborar; **will he ~?** ¿querrá cooperar?
cooperation [kəuɔpə'reɪʃən] *n* cooperación *f*, colaboración *f.*
cooperative [kəu'ɔpərətɪv] *adj* cooperativo; (*person*) dispuesto a colaborar ♦ *n* cooperativa.
co-opt [kəu'ɔpt] *vt*: **to ~ sb into sth** nombrar a algn para algo.
coordinate [kəu'ɔːdɪneɪt] *vt* coordinar ♦ *n* [kəu'ɔːdɪnət] (*MATH*) coordenada; **~s** *npl* (*clothes*) coordinados *mpl.*
coordination [kəuɔːdɪ'neɪʃən] *n* coordinación *f.*
coot [kuːt] *n* focha *f* (común).
co-ownership [kəu'əunəʃɪp] *n* co-propiedad *f.*
cop [kɔp] *n* (*col*) poli *m.*
cope [kəup] *vi*: **to ~ with** poder con; (*problem*) hacer frente a.
Copenhagen [kəupən'heɪɡən] *n* Copenhague *m.*
copier ['kɔpɪə*] *n* (*photo~*) (foto)copiadora.
co-pilot ['kəu'paɪlət] *n* copiloto *m/f.*
copious ['kəupɪəs] *adj* copioso, abundante.
copper ['kɔpə*] *n* (*metal*) cobre *m*; (*col: policeman*) poli *m*; **~s** *npl* perras *fpl*; (*small change*) calderilla.
coppice ['kɔpɪs], **copse** [kɔps] *n* bosquecillo.
copulate ['kɔpjuleɪt] *vi* copular.
copulation [kɔpju'leɪʃən] *n* cópula.
copy ['kɔpɪ] *n* copia; (*of book*) ejemplar *m*; (*of magazine*) número; (*material: for printing*) original *m* ♦ *vt* copiar (*also COMPUT*); (*imitate*) copiar, imitar; **to make good ~** (*fig*) ser una noticia de interés;

rough **~** borrador *m*; **fair ~** copia en limpio.
►**copy out** *vt* copiar.
copycat ['kɔpɪkæt] *n* (*pej*) imitador(a) *m/f.*
copyright ['kɔpɪraɪt] *n* derechos *mpl* de autor.
copy typist *n* mecanógrafo/a.
coral ['kɔrəl] *n* coral *m.*
coral reef *n* arrecife *m* (de coral).
Coral Sea *n*: **the ~** el Mar del Coral.
cord [kɔːd] *n* cuerda; (*ELEC*) cable *m*; (*fabric*) pana; **~s** *npl* (*trousers*) pantalones *mpl* de pana.
cordial ['kɔːdɪəl] *adj* cordial ♦ *n* cordial *m.*
cordless ['kɔːdlɪs] *adj* sin hilos.
cordon ['kɔːdn] *n* cordón *m.*
►**cordon off** *vt* acordonar.
Cordova ['kɔːdəvə] *n* Córdoba.
corduroy ['kɔːdərɔɪ] *n* pana.
CORE [kɔː*] *n abbr* (*US*) = *Congress of Racial Equality.*
core [kɔː*] *n* (*of earth, nuclear reactor*) centro, núcleo; (*of fruit*) corazón *m*; (*of problem etc*) esencia, meollo ♦ *vt* quitar el corazón de.
Corfu [kɔː'fuː] *n* Corfú *m.*
coriander [kɔrɪ'ændə*] *n* culantro, cilantro.
cork [kɔːk] *n* corcho; (*tree*) alcornoque *m.*
corkage ['kɔːkɪdʒ] *n precio que se cobra en un restaurante por una botella de vino traída de fuera.*
corked [kɔːkt] *adj* (*wine*) con sabor a corcho.
corkscrew ['kɔːkskruː] *n* sacacorchos *m inv.*
cormorant ['kɔːmərnt] *n* cormorán *m.*
Corn *abbr* (*BRIT*) = *Cornwall.*
corn [kɔːn] *n* (*BRIT: wheat*) trigo; (*US: maize*) maíz *m*, choclo (*LAM*); (*on foot*) callo; **~ on the cob** (*CULIN*) maíz en la mazorca.
cornea ['kɔːnɪə] *n* córnea.
corned beef ['kɔːnd-] *n* carne *f* de vaca acecinada.
corner ['kɔːnə*] *n* (*outside*) esquina; (*inside*) rincón *m*; (*in road*) curva; (*FOOTBALL*) córner *m*, saque *m* de esquina ♦ *vt* (*trap*) arrinconar; (*COMM*) acaparar ♦ *vi* (*in car*) tomar las curvas; **to cut ~s** atajar.
corner flag *n* (*FOOTBALL*) banderola de esquina.
corner kick *n* (*FOOTBALL*) córner *m*, saque *m* de esquina.
cornerstone ['kɔːnəstəun] *n* piedra angular.
cornet ['kɔːnɪt] *n* (*MUS*) corneta; (*BRIT: of ice cream*) cucurucho.
cornflakes ['kɔːnfleɪks] *npl* copos *mpl* de maíz, cornflakes *mpl.*
cornflour ['kɔːnflauə*] *n* (*BRIT*) harina de

maíz.
cornice ['kɔːnɪs] n cornisa.
Cornish ['kɔːnɪʃ] adj de Cornualles.
corn oil n aceite m de maíz.
cornstarch ['kɔːnstɑːtʃ] n (US) = **cornflour.**
cornucopia [kɔːnjuˈkəupɪə] n cornucopia.
Cornwall ['kɔːnwəl] n Cornualles m.
corny ['kɔːnɪ] adj (col) gastado.
corollary [kəˈrɔlərɪ] n corolario.
coronary ['kɔrənərɪ] n: ~ **(thrombosis)**
infarto.
coronation [kɔrəˈneɪʃən] n coronación f.
coroner ['kɔrənə*] n juez m/f de instrucción.
coronet ['kɔrənɪt] n corona.
Corp. abbr = **corporation.**
corporal ['kɔːpərl] n cabo ♦ adj: ~
punishment castigo corporal.
corporate ['kɔːpərɪt] adj corporativo.
corporate hospitality n obsequios a los
clientes por cortesía de la empresa.
corporate identity, corporate image n
(of organization) identidad f corporativa.
corporation [kɔːpəˈreɪʃən] n (of town)
ayuntamiento; (COMM) corporación f.
corps [kɔː*], pl **corps** [kɔːz] n cuerpo; **press**
~ gabinete m de prensa.
corpse [kɔːps] n cadáver m.
corpulent ['kɔːpjulənt] adj corpulento/a.
Corpus Christi ['kɔːpəsˈkrɪstɪ] n Corpus m
(Christi).
corpuscle ['kɔːpʌsl] n corpúsculo.
corral [kəˈrɑːl] n corral m.
correct [kəˈrɛkt] adj correcto, (accurate)
exacto ♦ vt corregir; **you are** ~ tiene
razón.
correction [kəˈrɛkʃən] n rectificación f;
(erasure) tachadura.
correlate ['kɔrɪleɪt] vi: **to** ~ **with** tener
correlación con.
correlation [kɔrɪˈleɪʃən] n correlación f.
correspond [kɔrɪsˈpɔnd] vi (write)
escribirse; (be equal to) corresponder.
correspondence [kɔrɪsˈpɔndəns] n
correspondencia.
correspondence course n curso por
correspondencia.
correspondent [kɔrɪsˈpɔndənt] n
corresponsal m/f.
corresponding [kɔrɪsˈpɔndɪŋ] adj
correspondiente.
corridor ['kɔrɪdɔː*] n pasillo.
corroborate [kəˈrɔbəreɪt] vt corroborar.
corroboration [kərɔbəˈreɪʃən] n
corroboración f, confirmación f.
corrode [kəˈrəud] vt corroer ♦ vi corroerse.
corrosion [kəˈrəuʒən] n corrosión f.
corrosive [kəˈrəusɪv] adj corrosivo.
corrugated ['kɔrəgeɪtɪd] adj ondulado.

corrugated cardboard n cartón m
ondulado.
corrugated iron n chapa ondulada.
corrupt [kəˈrʌpt] adj corrompido; (person)
corrupto ♦ vt corromper; (bribe)
sobornar; (data) degradar; ~ **practices**
(dishonesty, bribery) corrupción f.
corruption [kəˈrʌpʃən] n corrupción f; (of
data) alteración f.
corset ['kɔːsɪt] n faja; (old-style) corsé m.
Corsica ['kɔːsɪkə] n Córcega.
Corsican ['kɔːsɪkən] adj, n corso/a m/f.
cortège [kɔːˈteɪʒ] n cortejo, comitiva.
cortisone ['kɔːtɪzəun] n cortisona.
c.o.s. abbr (= cash on shipment) pago al
embarcar.
cosh [kɔʃ] n (BRIT) cachiporra.
cosignatory ['kəuˈsɪgnətərɪ] n
cosignatario/a.
cosine ['kəusaɪn] n coseno.
cosiness ['kəuzɪnɪs] n comodidad f;
(atmosphere) lo acogedor.
cos lettuce [kɔs-] n lechuga romana.
cosmetic [kɔzˈmetɪk] n cosmético ♦ adj
(also fig) cosmético; (surgery) estético.
cosmic ['kɔzmɪk] adj cósmico.
cosmonaut ['kɔzmənɔːt] n cosmonauta m/f.
cosmopolitan [kɔzməˈpɔlɪtn] adj
cosmopolita.
cosmos ['kɔzmɔs] n cosmos m.
cosset ['kɔsɪt] vt mimar.
cost [kɔst] n (gen) coste m, costo; (price)
precio; ~**s** npl (LAW) costas fpl ♦ vb (pt, pp
cost) vi costar, valer ♦ vt preparar el
presupuesto de; **how much does it** ~**?**
¿cuánto cuesta?, ¿cuánto vale?; **what will**
it ~ **to have it repaired?** ¿cuánto costará
repararlo?; **the** ~ **of living** el coste or
costo de la vida; **at all** ~**s** cueste lo que
cueste.
cost accountant n contable m de costos.
co-star ['kəustɑː*] n coprotagonista m/f.
Costa Rica ['kɔstəˈriːkə] n Costa Rica.
Costa Rican ['kɔstəˈriːkən] adj, n
costarriqueño/a m/f, costarricense m/f.
cost centre n centro (de determinación)
de coste.
cost control n control m de costes.
cost-effective [kɔstɪˈfɛktɪv] adj (COMM)
rentable.
cost-effectiveness ['kɔstɪˈfɛktɪvnɪs] n
relación f coste-rendimiento.
costing ['kɔstɪŋ] n cálculo del coste.
costly ['kɔstlɪ] adj (expensive) costoso.
cost-of-living [kɔstəvˈlɪvɪŋ] adj: ~
allowance n plus m de carestía de vida; ~
index n índice m del coste de vida.
cost price n (BRIT) precio de coste.

costume ['kɔstjuːm] n traje m; (BRIT: also: swimming ~) traje de baño.
costume jewellery n bisutería.
cosy, (US) **cozy** ['kəuzɪ] adj cómodo, a gusto; (room, atmosphere) acogedor(a).
cot [kɔt] n (BRIT: child's) cuna; (US: folding bed) cama plegable.
cot death n muerte f en la cuna.
Cotswolds ['kɔtswəuldz] npl región de colinas del suroeste inglés.
cottage ['kɔtɪdʒ] n casita de campo.
cottage cheese n requesón m.
cottage industry n industria artesanal.
cottage pie n pastel de carne cubierta de puré de patatas.
cotton ['kɔtn] n algodón m; (thread) hilo.
►**cotton on** vi (col): **to ~ on (to sth)** caer en la cuenta (de algo).
cotton candy n (US) algodón m (azucarado).
cotton wool n (BRIT) algodón m (hidrófilo).
couch [kautʃ] n sofá m; (in doctor's surgery) camilla.
couchette [kuːˈʃɛt] n litera.
couch potato n (col) persona comodona que no se mueve en todo el día.
cough [kɔf] vi toser ♦ n tos f.
►**cough up** vt escupir.
cough drop n pastilla para la tos.
cough mixture n jarabe m para la tos.
could [kud] pt of **can**.
couldn't ['kudnt] = **could not**.
council ['kaunsl] n consejo; **city** or **town ~** ayuntamiento; **C~ of Europe** Consejo de Europa.
council estate n (BRIT) barriada de viviendas sociales de alquiler.
council house n (BRIT) vivienda social de alquiler.
councillor ['kaunslə*] n concejal m/f.
council tax n (BRIT) contribución f municipal (dependiente del valor de la vivienda).
counsel ['kaunsl] n (advice) consejo; (lawyer) abogado/a ♦ vt aconsejar; **~ for the defence/the prosecution** abogado/a defensor(a)/fiscal; **to ~ sth/sb to do sth** aconsejar algo/a algn que haga algo.
counsellor, (US) **counselor** ['kaunslə*] n consejero/a; (US LAW) abogado/a.
count [kaunt] vt (gen) contar; (include) incluir ♦ vi contar ♦ n cuenta; (of votes) escrutinio; (nobleman) conde m; (sum) total m, suma; **to ~ the cost of** calcular el coste de; **not ~ing the children** niños aparte; **10 ~ing him** diez incluyéndolo a él, diez con él; **~ yourself lucky** date por satisfecho; **that doesn't ~!** ¡eso no vale!;

to ~ (up) to 10 contar hasta diez; **it ~s for very little** cuenta poco; **to keep ~ of sth** llevar la cuenta de algo.
►**count on** vt fus contar con; **to ~ on doing sth** contar con hacer algo.
►**count up** vt contar.
countdown ['kauntdaun] n cuenta atrás.
countenance ['kauntɪnəns] n semblante m, rostro ♦ vt (tolerate) aprobar, consentir.
counter ['kauntə*] n (in shop) mostrador m; (position: in post office, bank) ventanilla; (in games) ficha; (TECH) contador m ♦ vt contrarrestar; (blow) parar; (attack) contestar a ♦ adv: **~ to** contrario a; **to buy under the ~** (fig) comprar de estraperlo or bajo mano; **to ~ sth with sth/by doing sth** contestar algo con algo/haciendo algo.
counteract ['kauntər'ækt] vt contrarrestar.
counterattack ['kauntərə'tæk] n contraataque m ♦ vi contraatacar.
counterbalance ['kauntə'bæləns] n contrapeso.
counter-clockwise ['kauntə'klɔkwaɪz] adv en sentido contrario al de las agujas del reloj.
counter-espionage ['kauntər'ɛspɪənɑːʒ] n contraespionaje m.
counterfeit ['kauntəfɪt] n falsificación f ♦ vt falsificar ♦ adj falso, falsificado.
counterfoil ['kauntəfɔɪl] n (BRIT) matriz f, talón m.
counterintelligence ['kauntərɪn'tɛlɪdʒəns] n contraespionaje m.
countermand ['kauntəmɑːnd] vt revocar.
counter-measure ['kauntəmɛʒə*] n contramedida.
counteroffensive ['kauntərə'fɛnsɪv] n contraofensiva.
counterpane ['kauntəpeɪn] n colcha.
counterpart ['kauntəpɑːt] n (of person) homólogo/a.
counter-productive [kauntəprə'dʌktɪv] adj contraproducente.
counterproposal ['kauntəprə'pəuzl] n contrapropuesta.
countersign ['kauntəsaɪn] vt ratificar, refrendar.
countess ['kauntɪs] n condesa.
countless ['kauntlɪs] adj innumerable.
countrified ['kʌntrɪfaɪd] adj rústico.
country ['kʌntrɪ] n país m; (native land) patria; (as opposed to town) campo; (region) región f, tierra; **in the ~** en el campo; **mountainous ~** región f montañosa.
country and western (music) n música country.

country dancing n (BRIT) baile m regional.
country house n casa de campo.
countryman ['kʌntrɪmən] n (national) compatriota m; (rural) hombre m del campo.
countryside ['kʌntrɪsaɪd] n campo.
countrywide ['kʌntrɪ'waɪd] adj nacional ♦ adv por todo el país.
county ['kauntɪ] n condado; see also **district council**.
county council n (BRIT) ≈ diputación f provincial.
county town n cabeza de partido.
coup, ~s [kuː, -z] n golpe m; (triumph) éxito; (also: ~ d'état) golpe de estado.
coupé ['kuːpeɪ] n cupé m.
couple ['kʌpl] n (of things) par m; (of people) pareja; (married ~) matrimonio ♦ vt (ideas, names) unir, juntar; (machinery) acoplar; **a ~ of** un par de.
couplet ['kʌplɪt] n pareado.
coupling ['kʌplɪŋ] n (RAIL) enganche m.
coupon ['kuːpɔn] n cupón m; (pools ~) boleto (de quiniela).
courage ['kʌrɪdʒ] n valor m, valentía.
courageous [kə'reɪdʒəs] adj valiente.
courgette [kuə'ʒet] n (BRIT) calabacín m.
courier ['kurɪə*] n mensajero/a; (diplomatic) correo; (for tourists) guía m/f (de turismo).
course [kɔːs] n (direction) dirección f; (of river, SCOL) curso; (of ship) rumbo; (fig) proceder m; (GOLF) campo; (part of meal) plato; **of ~** adv desde luego, naturalmente; **of ~!** ¡claro!, ¡cómo no! (LAM); **(no) of ~ not!** ¡claro que no!, ¡por supuesto que no!; **in due ~** a su debido tiempo; **in the ~ of the next few days** durante los próximos días; **we have no other ~ but to ...** no tenemos más remedio que ...; **there are 2 ~s open to us** se nos ofrecen dos posibilidades; **the best ~ would be to ...** lo mejor sería ...; **~ of treatment** (MED) tratamiento.
court [kɔːt] n (royal) corte f; (LAW) tribunal m, juzgado; (TENNIS) pista, cancha (LAM) ♦ vt (woman) cortejar; (fig: favour, popularity) solicitar, buscar; (: death, disaster, danger etc) buscar; **to take to ~** demandar; **~ of appeal** tribunal m de apelación.
courteous ['kɜːtɪəs] adj cortés.
courtesan [kɔːtɪ'zæn] n cortesana.
courtesy ['kɜːtəsɪ] n cortesía; **by ~ of** (por) cortesía de.
courtesy light n (AUT) luz f interior.
court-house ['kɔːthaus] n (US) palacio de justicia.
courtier ['kɔːtɪə*] n cortesano.

court martial, pl **courts martial** ['kɔːt'mɑːʃəl] n consejo de guerra ♦ vt someter a consejo de guerra.
courtroom ['kɔːtrum] n sala de justicia.
court shoe n zapato de mujer de estilo clásico.
courtyard ['kɔːtjɑːd] n patio.
cousin ['kʌzn] n primo/a; **first ~** primo/a carnal.
cove [kəuv] n cala, ensenada.
covenant ['kʌvənənt] n convenio ♦ vt: **to ~ £20 per year to a charity** concertar el pago de veinte libras anuales a una sociedad benéfica.
Coventry ['kɔvəntrɪ] n: **to send sb to ~** (fig) hacer el vacío a algn.
cover ['kʌvə*] vt cubrir; (with lid) tapar; (chairs etc) revestir; (distance) cubrir, recorrer; (include) abarcar; (protect) abrigar; (journalist) investigar; (issues) tratar ♦ n cubierta; (lid) tapa; (for chair etc) funda; (for bed) cobertor m; (envelope) sobre m; (of magazine) portada; (shelter) abrigo; (insurance) cobertura; **to take ~** (shelter) protegerse, resguardarse; **under ~** (indoors) bajo techo; **under ~ of darkness** al amparo de la oscuridad; **under separate ~** (COMM) por separado; **£10 will ~ everything** con diez libras cubriremos todos los gastos.
▶**cover up** vt (child, object) cubrir completamente, tapar; (fig: hide: truth, facts) ocultar; **to ~ up for sb** (fig) encubrir a algn.
coverage ['kʌvərɪdʒ] n alcance m; (in media) reportaje m; (INSURANCE) cobertura.
coveralls ['kʌvərɔːlz] npl (US) mono sg.
cover charge n precio del cubierto.
covering ['kʌvərɪŋ] n cubierta, envoltura.
covering letter, (US) **cover letter** n carta de explicación.
cover note n (INSURANCE) póliza provisional.
cover price n precio de cubierta.
covert ['kəuvət] adj (secret) secreto, encubierto; (dissembled) furtivo.
cover-up ['kʌvərʌp] n encubrimiento.
covet ['kʌvɪt] vt codiciar.
covetous ['kʌvɪtəs] adj codicioso.
cow [kau] n vaca ♦ vt intimidar.
coward ['kauəd] n cobarde m/f.
cowardice ['kauədɪs] n cobardía.
cowardly ['kauədlɪ] adj cobarde.
cowboy ['kaubɔɪ] n vaquero.
cower ['kauə*] vi encogerse (de miedo).
co-worker ['kəuwɜːkə*] n colaborador(a) m/f.

cowshed ['kauʃɛd] n establo.
cowslip ['kauslɪp] n (*BOT*) primavera, prímula.
coxswain ['kɔksn] n (*abbr:* **cox**) timonel m.
coy [kɔɪ] adj tímido.
coyote [kɔɪ'əutɪ] n coyote m.
cozy ['kəuzɪ] adj (*US*) = **cosy**.
CP n abbr (= *Communist Party*) PC m.
cp. abbr (= *compare*) cfr.
c/p abbr (*BRIT*) = **carriage paid**.
CPA n abbr (*US*) = **certified public accountant**.
CPI n abbr (= *Consumer Price Index*) IPC m.
Cpl. abbr (*MIL*) = **corporal**.
CP/M n abbr (= *Central Program for Microprocessors*) CP/M m.
c.p.s. abbr (= *characters per second*) c.p.s.
CPSA n abbr (*BRIT*: = *Civil and Public Services Association*) sindicato de funcionarios.
CPU n abbr = **central processing unit**.
cr. abbr = **credit, creditor**.
crab [kræb] n cangrejo.
crab apple n manzana silvestre.
crack [kræk] n grieta; (*noise*) crujido; (: *of whip*) chasquido; (*joke*) chiste m; (*col: drug*) crack m; (*attempt*): **to have a ~ at sth** intentar algo ♦ vt agrietar, romper; (*nut*) cascar; (*safe*) forzar; (*whip etc*) chasquear; (*knuckles*) crujir; (*joke*) contar; (*case: solve*) resolver; (*code*) descifrar ♦ adj (*athlete*) de primera clase; **to ~ jokes** (*col*) bromear.
►**crack down on** vt fus reprimir fuertemente, adoptar medidas severas contra.
►**crack up** vi sufrir una crisis nerviosa.
crackdown ['krækdaun] n: ~ (**on**) (*on crime*) campaña (contra); (*on spending*) reducción f (en).
cracker ['krækə*] n (*biscuit*) galleta salada, crácker m; (*Christmas ~*) sorpresa (navideña).
crackle ['krækl] vi crepitar.
crackling ['kræklɪŋ] n (*on radio, telephone*) interferencia; (*of fire*) chisporroteo, crepitación f; (*of leaves etc*) crujido; (*of pork*) chicharrón m.
crackpot ['krækpɔt] (*col*) n pirado/a ♦ adj de pirado.
cradle ['kreɪdl] n cuna ♦ vt (*child*) mecer, acunar; (*object*) abrazar.
craft [krɑːft] n (*skill*) arte m; (*trade*) oficio; (*cunning*) astucia; (*boat*) embarcación f.
craftsman ['krɑːftsmən] n artesano.
craftsmanship ['krɑːftsmənʃɪp] n artesanía.
crafty ['krɑːftɪ] adj astuto.
crag [kræg] n peñasco.

craggy ['krægɪ] adj escarpado.
cram [kræm] vt (*fill*): **to ~ sth with** llenar algo (a reventar) de; (*put*): **to ~ sth into** meter algo a la fuerza en ♦ vi (*for exams*) empollar.
crammed [kræmd] adj atestado.
cramp [kræmp] n (*MED*) calambre m; (*TECH*) grapa ♦ vt (*limit*) poner trabas a.
cramped [kræmpt] adj apretado; (*room*) minúsculo.
crampon ['kræmpən] n crampón m.
cranberry ['krænbərɪ] n arándano.
crane [kreɪn] n (*TECH*) grúa; (*bird*) grulla ♦ vt, vi: **to ~ forward, to ~ one's neck** estirar el cuello.
cranium ['kreɪnɪəm] n cráneo.
crank [kræŋk] n manivela; (*person*) chiflado/a.
crankshaft ['kræŋkʃɑːft] n cigüeñal m.
cranky ['kræŋkɪ] adj (*eccentric*) maniático; (*bad-tempered*) de mal genio.
cranny ['krænɪ] n see **nook**.
crap [kræp] n (*col!*) mierda (!).
crappy ['kræpɪ] adj (*col*) chungo.
craps [kræps] n (*US*) dados mpl.
crash [kræʃ] n (*noise*) estrépito; (*of cars, plane*) accidente m; (*of business*) quiebra; (*STOCK EXCHANGE*) crac m ♦ vt (*plane*) estrellar ♦ vi (*plane*) estrellarse; (*two cars*) chocar; (*fall noisily*) caer con estrépito; **he ~ed the car into a wall** estrelló el coche contra una pared or tapia.
crash barrier n (*AUT*) barrera de protección.
crash course n curso acelerado.
crash helmet n casco (protector).
crash landing n aterrizaje m forzoso.
crass [kræs] adj grosero, maleducado.
crate [kreɪt] n caja, cajón m de embalaje; (*col*) armatoste m.
crater ['kreɪtə*] n cráter m.
cravat(e) [krə'væt] n pañuelo.
crave [kreɪv] vt, vi: **to ~ (for)** ansiar, anhelar.
craving ['kreɪvɪŋ] n (*for food, cigarettes, etc*) ansias fpl; (*during pregnancy*) antojo.
crawl [krɔːl] vi (*drag o.s.*) arrastrarse; (*child*) andar a gatas, gatear; (*vehicle*) avanzar (lentamente); (*col*): **to ~ to sb** dar coba a algn, hacerle la pelota a algn ♦ n (*SWIMMING*) crol m.
crawler lane [krɔːlə-] n (*BRIT AUT*) carril m para tráfico lento.
crayfish ['kreɪfɪʃ] n, pl inv (*freshwater*) cangrejo (de río); (*saltwater*) cigala.
crayon ['kreɪən] n lápiz m de color.
craze [kreɪz] n manía; (*fashion*) moda.
crazed [kreɪzd] adj (*look, person*) loco,

demente; (*pottery*, *glaze*) agrietado, cuarteado.

crazy ['kreɪzɪ] *adj* (*person*) loco; (*idea*) disparatado; **to go** ~ volverse loco; **to be** ~ **about sb/sth** (*col*) estar loco por algn/algo.

crazy paving *n* pavimento de baldosas irregulares.

creak [kriːk] *vi* crujir; (*hinge etc*) chirriar, rechinar.

cream [kriːm] *n* (*of milk*) nata, crema; (*lotion*) crema; (*fig*) flor *f* y nata ♦ *adj* (*colour*) color *m* crema; **whipped** ~ nata batida.

▶**cream off** *vt* (*fig*) (*best talents, part of profits*) separar lo mejor de.

cream cake *n* pastel *m* de nata

cream cheese *n* queso fresco cremoso.

creamery ['kriːmərɪ] *n* (*shop*) quesería; (*factory*) central *f* lechera.

creamy ['kriːmɪ] *adj* cremoso.

crease [kriːs] *n* (*fold*) pliegue *m*; (*in trousers*) raya; (*wrinkle*) arruga ♦ *vt* (*fold*) doblar, plegar; (*wrinkle*) arrugar ♦ *vi* (*wrinkle up*) arrugarse.

crease-resistant ['kriːsrɪzɪstənt] *adj* inarrugable.

create [kriː'eɪt] *vt* (*also COMPUT*) crear; (*impression*) dar; (*fuss, noise*) hacer.

creation [kriː'eɪʃən] *n* creación *f*.

creative [kriː'eɪtɪv] *adj* creativo.

creativity [kriːeɪ'tɪvɪtɪ] *n* creatividad *f*.

creator [kriː'eɪtə*] *n* creador(a) *m/f*.

creature ['kriːtʃə*] *n* (*living thing*) criatura; (*animal*) animal *m*; (*insect*) bicho

creature comforts *npl* comodidades *fpl* materiales.

crèche, creche [krɛʃ] *n* (*BRIT*) guardería (infantil).

credence ['kriːdəns] *n*: **to lend** *or* **give** ~ **to** creer en, dar crédito a.

credentials [krɪ'dɛnʃlz] *npl* credenciales *fpl*; (*letters of reference*) referencias *fpl*.

credibility [krɛdɪ'bɪlɪtɪ] *n* credibilidad *f*.

credible ['krɛdɪbl] *adj* creíble; (*witness, source*) fidedigno.

credit ['krɛdɪt] *n* (*gen*) crédito; (*merit*) honor *m*, mérito ♦ *vt* (*COMM*) abonar; (*believe*) creer, dar crédito a ♦ *adj* crediticio; **to be in** ~ (*person, bank account*) tener saldo a favor; **on** ~ a crédito; (*col*) al fiado; **he's a** ~ **to his family** hace honor a su familia; **to** ~ **sb with** (*fig*) reconocer a algn el mérito de; *see also* **credits**.

creditable ['krɛdɪtəbl] *adj* estimable, digno de elogio.

credit account *n* cuenta de crédito.

credit agency *n* agencia de informes comerciales.

credit balance *n* saldo acreedor.

credit card *n* tarjeta de crédito.

credit control *n* control *m* de créditos.

credit facilities *npl* facilidades *fpl* de crédito.

credit limit *n* límite *m* de crédito.

credit note *n* nota de crédito.

creditor ['krɛdɪtə*] *n* acreedor(a) *m/f*.

credits ['krɛdɪts] *npl* (*CINE*) títulos *mpl* or rótulos *mpl* de crédito, créditos *mpl*.

credit transfer *n* transferencia de crédito.

creditworthy ['krɛdɪtwəɪðɪ] *adj* solvente.

credulity [krɪ'djuːlɪtɪ] *n* credulidad *f*.

creed [kriːd] *n* credo.

creek [kriːk] *n* cala, ensenada; (*US*) riachuelo.

creel [kriːl] *n* nasa.

creep, *pt, pp* **crept** [kriːp, krɛpt] *vi* (*animal*) deslizarse; (*plant*) trepar; **to** ~ **up on sb** acercarse sigilosamente a algn; (*fig: old age etc*) acercarse ♦ *n* (*col*): **he's a** ~ ¡qué lameculos es!; **it gives me the** ~**s** me da escalofríos.

creeper ['kriːpə*] *n* enredadera.

creepers ['kriːpəz] *npl* (*US: for baby*) pelele *msg*.

creepy ['kriːpɪ] *adj* (*frightening*) horripilante.

creepy-crawly ['kriːpɪ'krɔːlɪ] *n* (*col*) bicho.

cremate [krɪ'meɪt] *vt* incinerar.

cremation [krɪ'meɪʃən] *n* incineración *f*, cremación *f*.

crematorium, *pl* **crematoria** [krɛmə'tɔːrɪəm, -'tɔːrɪə] *n* crematorio.

creosote ['krɪəsəut] *n* creosota.

crêpe [kreɪp] *n* (*fabric*) crespón *m*; (*also*: ~ **rubber**) crep(é) *m*.

crêpe bandage *n* (*BRIT*) venda elástica.

crêpe paper *n* papel *m* crep(é).

crêpe sole *n* (*on shoes*) suela de crep(é).

crept [krɛpt] *pt, pp of* **creep**.

crescent ['krɛsnt] *n* media luna; (*street*) calle *f* (*en forma de semicírculo*).

cress [krɛs] *n* berro.

crest [krɛst] *n* (*of bird*) cresta; (*of hill*) cima, cumbre *f*; (*of helmet*) cimera; (*of coat of arms*) blasón *m*.

crestfallen ['krɛstfɔːlən] *adj* alicaído.

Crete [kriːt] *n* Creta.

cretin ['krɛtɪn] *n* cretino/a.

crevasse [krɪ'væs] *n* grieta.

crevice ['krɛvɪs] *n* grieta, hendedura.

crew [kruː] *n* (*of ship etc*) tripulación *f*; (*CINE etc*) equipo; (*gang*) pandilla, banda; (*MIL*) dotación *f*.

crew-cut ['kruːkʌt] *n* corte *m* al rape.

crew-neck ['kru:nɛk] n cuello de caja.
crib [krɪb] n pesebre m ♦ vt (col) plagiar; (SCOL) copiar.
crick [krɪk] n: ~ **in the neck** tortícolis f inv.
cricket ['krɪkɪt] n (insect) grillo; (game) críquet m.
cricketer ['krɪkɪtə*] n jugador(a) m/f de críquet.
crime [kraɪm] n crimen m; (less serious) delito.
crime wave n ola de crímenes or delitos.
criminal ['krɪmɪnl] n criminal m/f, delincuente m/f ♦ adj criminal; (law) penal.
Criminal Investigation Department (CID) n ≈ Brigada de Investigación Criminal (B.I.C. f) (SP).
crimp [krɪmp] vt (hair) rizar.
crimson ['krɪmzn] adj carmesí.
cringe [krɪndʒ] vi encogerse.
crinkle ['krɪŋkl] vt arrugar.
crinkly ['krɪŋklɪ] adj (hair) rizado, crespo.
cripple ['krɪpl] n lisiado/a, cojo/a ♦ vt lisiar, mutilar; (ship, plane) inutilizar; (production, exports) paralizar; ~**d with arthritis** paralizado por la artritis.
crippling ['krɪplɪŋ] adj (injury etc) debilitador(a); (prices, taxes) devastador(a).
crisis, pl **crises** ['kraɪsɪs, -si:z] n crisis f.
crisp [krɪsp] adj fresco; (toast, snow) crujiente; (manner) seco.
crisps [krɪsps] npl (BRIT) patatas fpl fritas.
crisscross ['krɪskrɔs] adj entrelazado, entrecruzado ♦ vt entrecruzar(se).
criterion, pl **criteria** [kraɪ'tɪərɪən, -'tɪərɪə] n criterio.
critic ['krɪtɪk] n crítico/a.
critical ['krɪtɪkl] adj (gen) crítico; (illness) grave; **to be** ~ **of sb/sth** criticar a algn/algo.
critically ['krɪtɪklɪ] adv (speak etc) en tono crítico; (ill) gravemente.
criticism ['krɪtɪsɪzm] n crítica.
criticize ['krɪtɪsaɪz] vt criticar.
critique [krɪ'tiːk] n crítica.
croak [krəuk] vi (frog) croar; (raven) graznar ♦ n (of raven) graznido.
Croat ['krəuæt] adj, n = **Croatian.**
Croatia [krəu'eɪʃə] n Croacia.
Croatian [krəu'eɪʃən] adj, n croata m/f ♦ n (LING) croata m.
crochet ['krəuʃeɪ] n ganchillo.
crock [krɔk] n cántaro; (col: person: also: **old** ~) carcamal m/f, vejestorio; (: car etc) cacharro.
crockery ['krɔkərɪ] n (plates, cups etc) loza, vajilla.
crocodile ['krɔkədaɪl] n cocodrilo.

crocus ['krəukəs] n azafrán m.
croft [krɔft] n granja pequeña.
crofter ['krɔftə*] n pequeño granjero.
croissant ['krwasã] n croissant m, medialuna (esp LAM).
crone [krəun] n arpía, bruja.
crony ['krəunɪ] n compinche m/f.
crook [kruk] n (fam) ladrón/ona m/f; (of shepherd) cayado; (of arm) pliegue m.
crooked ['krukɪd] adj torcido; (path) tortuoso; (fam) sucio.
crop [krɔp] n (produce) cultivo; (amount produced) cosecha; (riding ~) látigo de montar; (of bird) buche m ♦ vt cortar, recortar; (subj: animals: grass) pacer.
▶**crop up** vi surgir, presentarse.
crop spraying [-'spreɪɪŋ] n fumigación f de los cultivos.
croquet ['krəukeɪ] n croquet m.
croquette [krə'kɛt] n croqueta (de patata).
cross [krɔs] n cruz f ♦ vt (street etc) cruzar, atravesar; (thwart: person) contrariar, ir contra ♦ vi: **the boat** ~**es from Santander to Plymouth** el barco hace la travesía de Santander a Plymouth ♦ adj de mal humor, enojado; **it's a** ~ **between geography and sociology** es una mezcla de geografía y sociología; **to** ~ **o.s.** santiguarse; **they've got their lines** ~**ed** (fig) hay un malentendido entre ellos; **to be/get** ~ **with sb (about sth)** estar enfadado/enfadarse con algn (por algo).
▶**cross out** vt tachar.
▶**cross over** vi cruzar.
crossbar ['krɔsbɑː*] n travesaño; (of bicycle) barra.
crossbow ['krɔsbəu] n ballesta.
cross-Channel ferry ['krɔs'tʃænl-] n transbordador m que cruza el Canal de la Mancha.
cross-check ['krɔstʃɛk] n verificación f ♦ vt verificar.
cross-country (race) ['krɔs'kʌntrɪ-] n carrera a campo traviesa, cross m.
cross-dressing [krɔs'drɛsɪŋ] n travestismo.
cross-examination ['krɔsɪgzæmɪ'neɪʃən] n interrogatorio.
cross-examine ['krɔsɪg'zæmɪn] vt interrogar.
cross-eyed ['krɔsaɪd] adj bizco.
crossfire ['krɔsfaɪə*] n fuego cruzado.
crossing ['krɔsɪŋ] n (road) cruce m; (rail) paso a nivel; (sea passage) travesía; (also: **pedestrian** ~) paso de peatones.
crossing guard n (US) persona encargada de ayudar a los niños a cruzar la calle.
crossing point n paso; (at border) paso fronterizo.

cross purposes npl: to be at ~ with sb tener un malentendido con algn.

cross-question ['krɔs'kwestʃən] vt interrogar.

cross-reference ['krɔs'refrəns] n remisión f.

crossroads ['krɔsrəudz] nsg cruce m; (fig) encrucijada.

cross section n corte m transversal; (of population) muestra (representativa).

crosswalk ['krɔswɔːk] n (US) paso de peatones.

crosswind ['krɔswɪnd] n viento de costado.

crossword ['krɔswɔːd] n crucigrama m.

crotch [krɔtʃ] n (of garment) entrepierna.

crotchet ['krɔtʃɪt] n (BRIT MUS) negra.

crotchety ['krɔtʃɪtɪ] adj (person) arisco.

crouch [krautʃ] vi agacharse.

crouton ['kruːtɔn] n cubito de pan frito.

crow [krəu] n (bird) cuervo; (of cock) canto, cacareo ♦ vi (cock) cantar; (fig) jactarse.

crowbar ['krəubɑː*] n palanca.

crowd [kraud] n muchedumbre f; (SPORT) público; (common herd) vulgo ♦ vt (gather) amontonar; (fill) llenar ♦ vi (gather) reunirse; (pile up) amontonarse; ~s of people gran cantidad de gente.

crowded ['kraudɪd] adj (full) atestado; (well-attended) concurrido.

crowd scene n (CINE, THEAT) escena con muchos comparsas.

crown [kraun] n corona; (of head) coronilla; (of hat) copa; (of hill) cumbre f ♦ vt (also tooth) coronar; **and to ~ it all ...** (fig) y para colmo or remate ....

crown court n (LAW) tribunal m superior; ver recuadro.

CROWN COURT

En el sistema legal inglés los delitos graves como asesinato, violación o atraco son juzgados por un jurado en un tribunal superior llamado **crown court** con sede en noventa ciudades. Los jueces de paz ("Justice of the Peace"), juzgan delitos menores e infracciones de la ley en juzgados llamados "Magistrates' Courts". Es el juez de paz quien decide remitir los casos pertinentes a la **crown court**, que en caso de recursos se remite al tribunal de apelación, "Court of Appeal".

---

crowning ['kraunɪŋ] adj (achievement, glory) máximo.

crown jewels npl joyas fpl reales.

crown prince n príncipe m heredero.

crow's feet ['krəuzfiːt] npl patas fpl de gallo.

crucial ['kruːʃl] adj crucial, decisivo; **his approval is ~ to the success of the project** su aprobación es crucial para el éxito del proyecto.

crucifix ['kruːsɪfɪks] n crucifijo.

crucifixion [kruːsɪ'fɪkʃən] n crucifixión f.

crucify ['kruːsɪfaɪ] vt crucificar; (fig) martirizar.

crude [kruːd] adj (materials) bruto; (fig: basic) tosco; (: vulgar) ordinario.

crude (oil) n (petróleo) crudo.

cruel ['kruəl] adj cruel.

cruelty ['kruəltɪ] n crueldad f.

cruet ['kruːɪt] n vinagreras fpl.

cruise [kruːz] n crucero ♦ vi (ship) navegar; (holidaymakers) hacer un crucero; (car) ir a velocidad constante.

cruise missile n misil m de crucero.

cruiser ['kruːzə*] n crucero.

cruising speed ['kruːzɪŋ-] n velocidad f de crucero.

crumb [krʌm] n miga, migaja.

crumble ['krʌmbl] vt desmenuzar ♦ vi (gen) desmenuzarse; (building) desmoronarse.

crumbly ['krʌmblɪ] adj desmenuzable.

crummy ['krʌmɪ] adj (col: poor quality) pésimo, cutre (SP); (: unwell) fatal.

crumpet ['krʌmpɪt] n ≈ bollo para tostar.

crumple ['krʌmpl] vt (paper) estrujar; (material) arrugar.

crunch [krʌntʃ] vt (with teeth) ronzar; (underfoot) hacer crujir ♦ n (fig) hora de la verdad.

crunchy ['krʌntʃɪ] adj crujiente.

crusade [kruː'seɪd] n cruzada ♦ vi: **to ~ for/ against** (fig) hacer una campaña en pro de/en contra de.

crusader [kruː'seɪdə*] n (fig) paladín m/f.

crush [krʌʃ] n (crowd) aglomeración f ♦ vt (gen) aplastar; (paper) estrujar; (cloth) arrugar; (grind, break up: garlic, ice) picar; (fruit) exprimir; (grapes) exprimir, prensar; **to have a ~ on sb** estar enamorado de algn.

crushing ['krʌʃɪŋ] adj aplastante; (burden) agobiante.

crust [krʌst] n corteza.

crustacean [krʌs'teɪʃən] n crustáceo.

crusty ['krʌstɪ] adj (bread) crujiente; (person) de mal carácter; (remark) brusco.

crutch [krʌtʃ] n (MED) muleta; (support) apoyo.

crux [krʌks] n: **the ~** lo esencial, el quid.

cry [kraɪ] vi llorar; (shout: also: ~ out) gritar ♦ n grito; (of animal) aullido; (weep): **she had a good ~** lloró a lágrima viva; **what are you ~ing about?** ¿por qué lloras?; **to ~ for help** pedir socorro a voces; **it's a far**

~ **from** ... *(fig)* dista mucho de ....
▶**cry off** *vi* retirarse.
crypt [krɪpt] *n* cripta.
cryptic ['krɪptɪk] *adj* enigmático.
crystal ['krɪstl] *n* cristal *m*.
crystal-clear ['krɪstl'klɪə*] *adj* claro como el agua; *(fig)* cristalino.
crystallize ['krɪstəlaɪz] *vt (fig)* cristalizar ♦ *vi* cristalizarse; ~**d fruits** frutas *fpl* escarchadas.
CSA *n abbr* = *Confederate States of America*; (= *Child Support Agency*) *organismo que supervisa el pago de la pensión a hijos de padres separados.*
CSC *n abbr* (= *Civil Service Commission*) *comisión para la contratación de funcionarios.*
CSE *n abbr* (*BRIT*: = *Certificate of Secondary Education*) ≈ título de BUP.
CS gas *n* (*BRIT*) gas *m* lacrimógeno.
CST *n abbr* (*US*: = *Central Standard Time*) *huso horario.*
CT, Ct. *abbr* (*US*) = *Connecticut.*
ct *abbr* = **carat.**
CTC *n abbr* (*BRIT*: *city technology college*) ≈ centro de formación profesional.
cu. *abbr* = **cubic.**
cub [kʌb] *n* cachorro; (*also*: ~ **scout**) niño explorador.
Cuba ['kju:bə] *n* Cuba.
Cuban ['kju:bən] *adj*, *n* cubano/a *m/f*.
cubbyhole ['kʌbɪhəul] *n* cuchitril *m*.
cube [kju:b] *n* cubo; (*of sugar*) terrón *m* ♦ *vt* (*MATH*) elevar al cubo.
cube root *n* raíz *f* cúbica.
cubic ['kju:bɪk] *adj* cúbico; ~ **capacity** (*AUT*) capacidad *f* cúbica.
cubicle ['kju:bɪkl] *n* (*at pool*) caseta; (*for bed*) cubículo.
cubism ['kju:bɪzəm] *n* cubismo.
cuckoo ['kuku:] *n* cuco.
cuckoo clock *n* reloj *m* de cuco.
cucumber ['kju:kʌmbə*] *n* pepino.
cuddle ['kʌdl] *vt* abrazar ♦ *vi* abrazarse.
cuddly ['kʌdlɪ] *adj* mimoso; (*toy*) de peluche.
cudgel ['kʌdʒəl] *vt*: **to** ~ **one's brains** devanarse los sesos.
cue [kju:] *n* (*snooker* ~) taco; (*THEAT etc*) entrada.
cuff [kʌf] *n* (*BRIT*: *of shirt, coat etc*) puño; (*US*: *of trousers*) vuelta; (*blow*) bofetada ♦ *vt* bofetear; **off the** ~ *adv* improvisado.
cufflinks ['kʌflɪŋks] *npl* gemelos *mpl*.
cu. in. *abbr* = *cubic inches.*
cuisine [kwɪ'zi:n] *n* cocina.
cul-de-sac ['kʌldəsæk] *n* callejón *m* sin salida.

culinary ['kʌlɪnərɪ] *adj* culinario.
cull [kʌl] *vt* (*select*) entresacar; (*kill selectively*: *animals*) matar selectivamente ♦ *n* matanza selectiva; **seal** ~ matanza selectiva de focas.
culminate ['kʌlmɪneɪt] *vi*: **to** ~ **in** culminar en.
culmination [kʌlmɪ'neɪʃən] *n* culminación *f*, colmo.
culottes [ku:'lɔts] *npl* falda *f* pantalón.
culpable ['kʌlpəbl] *adj* culpable.
culprit ['kʌlprɪt] *n* culpable *m/f*.
cult [kʌlt] *n* culto; **a** ~ **figure** un ídolo.
cultivate ['kʌltɪveɪt] *vt* (*also fig*) cultivar.
cultivated ['kʌltɪveɪtɪd] *adj* culto.
cultivation [kʌltɪ'veɪʃən] *n* cultivo; (*fig*) cultura.
cultural ['kʌltʃərəl] *adj* cultural.
culture ['kʌltʃə*] *n* (*also fig*) cultura.
cultured ['kʌltʃəd] *adj* culto.
cumbersome ['kʌmbəsəm] *adj* voluminoso.
cumin ['kʌmɪn] *n* (*spice*) comino.
cummerbund ['kʌməbʌnd] *n* faja, fajín *m*.
cumulative ['kju:mjulətɪv] *adj* cumulativo.
cunning ['kʌnɪŋ] *n* astucia ♦ *adj* astuto; (*clever: device, idea*) ingenioso.
cunt [kʌnt] *n* (*col!*) *n* coño (*!*); (*insult*) mamonazo/a (*!*).
cup [kʌp] *n* taza; (*prize, event*) copa; **a** ~ **of tea** una taza de té.
cupboard ['kʌbəd] *n* armario, placar(d) *m* (*LAM*).
cup final *n* (*FOOTBALL*) final *f* de copa.
cupful ['kʌpful] *n* taza.
Cupid ['kju:pɪd] *n* Cupido.
cupola ['kju:pələ] *n* cúpula.
cuppa ['kʌpə] *n* (*BRIT col*) (taza de) té *m*.
cup-tie ['kʌptaɪ] *n* (*BRIT*) partido de copa.
cur [kə:*] *n* perro de mala raza; (*person*) canalla *m*.
curable ['kjuərəbl] *adj* curable.
curate ['kjuərɪt] *n* coadjutor *m*.
curator [kjuə'reɪtə*] *n* director(a) *m/f*.
curb [kə:b] *vt* refrenar; (*powers, spending*) limitar ♦ *n* freno; (*US*: *kerb*) bordillo.
curd cheese [kə:d-] *n* requesón *m*.
curdle ['kə:dl] *vi* cuajarse.
curds [kə:dz] *npl* requesón *msg*.
cure [kjuə*] *vt* curar ♦ *n* cura, curación *f*; **to be** ~**d of sth** curarse de algo; **to take a** ~ tomar un remedio.
cure-all ['kjuərɔ:l] *n* (*also fig*) panacea.
curfew ['kə:fju:] *n* toque *m* de queda.
curio ['kjuərɪəu] *n* curiosidad *f*.
curiosity [kjuərɪ'ɔsɪtɪ] *n* curiosidad *f*.
curious ['kjuərɪəs] *adj* curioso; **I'm** ~ **about him** me intriga.
curiously ['kjuərɪəslɪ] *adv* curiosamente; ~

enough, ... aunque parezca extraño ....

curl [kə:l] n rizo; (of smoke etc) espiral f, voluta ♦ vt (hair) rizar; (paper) arrollar; (lip) fruncir ♦ vi rizarse; arrollarse.
► **curl up** vi arrollarse; (person) hacerse un ovillo; (fam) morirse de risa.

curler ['kə:lə*] n bigudí m.

curlew ['kə:lu:] n zarapito.

curling tongs, (US) **curling irons** ['kə:lɪŋ-] npl tenacillas fpl.

curly ['kə:lɪ] adj rizado.

currant ['kʌrnt] n pasa; (black, red) grosella.

currency ['kʌrnsɪ] n moneda; **to gain** ~ (fig) difundirse.

current ['kʌrnt] n corriente f ♦ adj actual; **direct/alternating** ~ corriente directa/ alterna; **the** ~ **issue of a magazine** el último número de una revista; **in** ~ **use** de uso corriente.

current account n (BRIT) cuenta corriente.

current affairs npl (noticias fpl de) actualidad f.

current assets npl (COMM) activo disponible.

current liabilities npl (COMM) pasivo circulante.

currently ['kʌrntlɪ] adv actualmente.

curriculum, pl ~**s** or **curricula** [kə'rɪkjuləm, -lə] n plan m de estudios.

curriculum vitae (CV) [-'vi:taɪ] n currículum m (vitae).

curry ['kʌrɪ] n curry m ♦ vt: **to** ~ **favour with** buscar el favor de.

curry powder n curry m en polvo.

curse [kə:s] vi echar pestes ♦ vt maldecir ♦ n maldición f; (swearword) palabrota.

cursor ['kə:sə*] n (COMPUT) cursor m.

cursory ['kə:sərɪ] adj rápido, superficial.

curt [kə:t] adj seco.

curtail [kə:'teɪl] vt (cut short) acortar; (restrict) restringir.

curtain ['kə:tn] n cortina; (THEAT) telón m; **to draw the** ~**s** (together) cerrar las cortinas; (apart) abrir las cortinas.

curtain call n (THEAT) llamada a escena.

curtain ring n anilla.

curts(e)y ['kə:tsɪ] n reverencia ♦ vi hacer una reverencia.

curvature ['kə:vətʃə*] n curvatura.

curve [kə:v] n curva ♦ vt, vi torcer.

curved [kə:vd] adj curvo.

cushion ['kuʃən] n cojín m; (SNOOKER) banda ♦ vt (seat) acolchar; (shock) amortiguar.

cushy ['kuʃɪ] adj (col): **a** ~ **job** un chollo; **to have a** ~ **time** tener la vida arreglada.

custard ['kʌstəd] n (for pouring) natillas fpl.

custard powder n polvos mpl para natillas.

custodial sentence [kʌs'təudɪəl-] n pena de prisión.

custodian [kʌs'təudɪən] n guardián/ana m/f; (of museum etc) conservador(a) m/f.

custody ['kʌstədɪ] n custodia; **to take sb into** ~ detener a algn; **in the** ~ **of** al cuidado or cargo de.

custom ['kʌstəm] n costumbre f; (COMM) clientela; see also **customs**.

customary ['kʌstəmərɪ] adj acostumbrado; **it is** ~ **to do** ... es la costumbre hacer ....

custom-built ['kʌstəm'bɪlt] adj = **custom-made**.

customer ['kʌstəmə*] n cliente m/f; **he's an awkward** ~ (col) es un tipo difícil.

customer profile n perfil m del cliente.

customized ['kʌstəmaɪzd] adj (car etc) hecho a encargo.

custom-made ['kʌstəm'meɪd] adj hecho a la medida.

customs ['kʌstəmz] npl aduana sg; **to go through (the)** ~ pasar la aduana.

Customs and Excise n (BRIT) Aduanas fpl y Arbitrios.

customs officer n aduanero/a, funcionario/a de aduanas.

cut [kʌt] vb (pt, pp **cut**) vt cortar; (price) rebajar; (record) grabar; (reduce) reducir; (col: avoid: class, lecture) fumarse, faltar a ♦ vi cortar; (intersect) cruzarse ♦ n corte m; (in skin) corte, cortadura; (with sword) tajo; (of knife) cuchillada; (in salary etc) recorte m; (slice of meat) tajada; **to** ~ **one's finger** cortarse un dedo; **to get one's hair** ~ cortarse el pelo; **to** ~ **sb dead** negarle el saludo or cortarle (LAM) a algn; **it** ~**s both ways** (fig) tiene doble filo; **to** ~ **a tooth** echar un diente; **power** ~ (BRIT) apagón m.
► **cut back** vt (plants) podar; (production, expenditure) reducir.
► **cut down** vt (tree) cortar, derribar; (consumption, expenses) reducir; **to** ~ **sb down to size** (fig) bajarle los humos a algn.
► **cut in** vi: **to** ~ **in (on)** (interrupt: conversation) interrumpir, intervenir (en); (AUT) cerrar el paso (a).
► **cut off** vt cortar; (fig) aislar; (troops) cercar; **we've been** ~ **off** (TEL) nos han cortado la comunicación.
► **cut out** vt (shape) recortar; (delete) suprimir.
► **cut up** vt cortar (en pedazos); (chop: food) trinchar, cortar.

cut-and-dried ['kʌtən'draɪd] adj (also: **cut-and-dry**) arreglado de antemano, seguro.

cutback ['kʌtbæk] *n* reducción *f*.
cute [kjuːt] *adj* lindo, mono; (*shrewd*) listo.
cuticle ['kjuːtɪkl] *n* cutícula.
cutlery ['kʌtlərɪ] *n* cubiertos *mpl*.
cutlet ['kʌtlɪt] *n* chuleta.
cutoff ['kʌtɔf] *n* (*also*: ~ **point**) límite *m*.
cutout ['kʌtaut] *n* (*shape*) recortable *m*.
cut-price ['kʌt'praɪs], (*US*) **cut-rate**
['kʌt'reɪt] *adj* a precio reducido.
cutthroat ['kʌtθrəut] *n* asesino/a ♦ *adj*
feroz; ~ **competition** competencia
encarnizada *or* despiadada.
cutting ['kʌtɪŋ] *adj* (*gen*) cortante; (*remark*)
mordaz ♦ *n* (*BRIT: from newspaper*) recorte
m; (: *RAIL*) desmonte *m*; (*CINE*) montaje *m*.
cutting edge *n* (*of knife*) filo; (*fig*)
vanguardia; **a country on** *or* **at the** ~ **of**
space technology un país puntero en
tecnología del espacio.
CV *n abbr see* **curriculum vitae**.
C & W *n abbr* = **country and western**
(**music**).
cwo *abbr* (*COMM*) = **cash with order**.
cwt. *abbr* = **hundredweight(s)**.
cyanide ['saɪənaɪd] *n* cianuro.
cybercafé ['saɪbə,kæfeɪ] *n* cibercafé *m*.
cybernetics [saɪbə'netɪks] *nsg* cibernética.
cyberspace ['saɪbəspeɪs] *n* ciberespacio.
cyclamen ['sɪkləmən] *n* ciclamen *m*.
cycle ['saɪkl] *n* ciclo; (*bicycle*) bicicleta ♦ *vi*
ir en bicicleta.
cycle race *n* carrera ciclista.
cycle rack *n* soporte *m* para bicicletas.
cycling ['saɪklɪŋ] *n* ciclismo.
cycling holiday *n* vacaciones *fpl* en
bicicleta.
cyclist ['saɪklɪst] *n* ciclista *m/f*.
cyclone ['saɪkləun] *n* ciclón *m*.
cygnet ['sɪgnɪt] *n* pollo de cisne.
cylinder ['sɪlɪndə*] *n* cilindro.
cylinder block *n* bloque *m* de cilindros.
cylinder capacity *n* cilindrada.
cylinder head *n* culata de cilindro.
cylinder-head gasket *n* junta de culata.
cymbals ['sɪmblz] *npl* platillos *mpl*,
címbalos *mpl*.
cynic ['sɪnɪk] *n* cínico/a.
cynical ['sɪnɪkl] *adj* cínico.
cynicism ['sɪnɪsɪzəm] *n* cinismo.
CYO *n abbr* (*US*) = *Catholic Youth Organization*.
cypress ['saɪprɪs] *n* ciprés *m*.
Cypriot ['sɪprɪət] *adj, n* chipriota *m/f*.
Cyprus ['saɪprəs] *n* Chipre *f*.
cyst [sɪst] *n* quiste *m*.
cystitis [sɪs'taɪtɪs] *n* cistitis *f*.
CZ *n abbr* (*US*: = *Central Zone*) *zona del*
Canal de Panamá.
czar [zɑː*] *n* zar *m*.

czarina [zɑː'riːnə] *n* zarina.
Czech [tʃek] *adj* checo ♦ *n* checo/a; (*LING*)
checo; **the** ~ **Republic** la República
Checa.
Czechoslovak [tʃekə'sləuvæk] *adj, n* =
Czechoslovakian.
Czechoslovakia [tʃekəslə'vækɪə] *n*
Checoslovaquia.
Czechoslovakian [tʃekəslə'vækɪən] *adj, n*
checoslovaco/a *m/f*.

D d

D, d [diː] *n* (*letter*) D, d; (*MUS*): **D** re *m*; **D for**
David, (*US*) **D for Dog** D de Dolores.
D *abbr* (*US POL*) = **democrat(ic)**.
d *abbr* (*BRIT*: *old*) = **penny**.
d. *abbr* = **died**.
DA *n abbr* (*US*) = **district attorney**.
dab [dæb] *v*: **to** ~ **ointment onto a wound**
aplicar pomada sobre una herida; **to** ~
with paint dar unos toques de pintura ♦ *n*
(*light stroke*) toque *m*; (*small amount*)
pizca.
dabble ['dæbl] *vi*: **to** ~ **in** hacer por
afición.
Dacca ['dækə] *n* Dacca.
dachshund ['dækshund] *n* perro tejonero.
Dacron ® ['deɪkrɔn] *n* (*US*) terylene *m*.
dad [dæd], **daddy** ['dædɪ] *n* papá *m*.
daddy-long-legs [dædɪ'lɔŋlegz] *n* típula.
daffodil ['dæfədɪl] *n* narciso.
daft [dɑːft] *adj* chiflado.
dagger ['dægə*] *n* puñal *m*, daga; **to look**
~**s at sb** fulminar a algn con la mirada.
dahlia ['deɪljə] *n* dalia.
daily ['deɪlɪ] *adj* diario, cotidiano ♦ *n* (*paper*)
diario; (*domestic help*) asistenta ♦ *adv*
todos los días, cada día; **twice** ~ dos
veces al día.
dainty ['deɪntɪ] *adj* delicado.
dairy ['dɛərɪ] *n* (*shop*) lechería; (*on farm*)
vaquería ♦ *adj* (*cow etc*) lechero.
dairy cow *n* vaca lechera.
dairy farm *n* vaquería.
dairy produce *n* productos *mpl* lácteos.
dais ['deɪɪs] *n* estrado.
daisy ['deɪzɪ] *n* margarita.
daisy wheel *n* (*on printer*) (rueda)
margarita.
daisy-wheel printer *n* impresora de

margarita.
Dakar ['dækə*] n Dakar m.
dale [deɪl] n valle m.
dally ['dælɪ] vi entretenerse.
dalmatian [dæl'meɪʃən] n (dog) (perro) dálmata m.
dam [dæm] n presa; (reservoir) embalse ♦ vt embalsar.
damage ['dæmɪdʒ] n daño; (fig) perjuicio; (to machine) avería ♦ vt dañar; perjudicar; averiar; ~ **to property** daños materiales.
damages ['dæmɪdʒɪz] npl (LAW) daños y perjuicios; **to pay £5000 in** ~ pagar £5000 por daños y perjuicios.
damaging ['dæmɪdʒɪŋ] adj: ~ **(to)** perjudicial (a).
Damascus [də'mɑːskəs] n Damasco.
dame [deɪm] n (title) dama; (US col) tía; (THEAT) vieja; see also **pantomime**.
damn [dæm] vt condenar; (curse) maldecir ♦ n (col): **I don't give a** ~ me importa un pito ♦ adj (col: also: ~ed) maldito, fregado (LAM); ~ **(it)!** ¡maldito sea!
damnable ['dæmnəbl] adj (col: behaviour) detestable; (: weather) horrible.
damnation [dæm'neɪʃən] n (REL) condenación f ♦ excl (col) ¡maldición!, ¡maldito sea!
damning ['dæmɪŋ] adj (evidence) irrecusable.
damp [dæmp] adj húmedo, mojado ♦ n humedad f ♦ vt (also: ~en) (cloth, rag) mojar; (enthusiasm) enfriar.
dampcourse ['dæmpkɔːs] n aislante m hidrófugo.
damper ['dæmpə*] n (MUS) sordina; (of fire) regulador m de tiro; **to put a** ~ **on things** ser un jarro de agua fría.
dampness ['dæmpnɪs] n humedad f.
damson ['dæmzən] n ciruela damascena.
dance [dɑːns] n baile m ♦ vi bailar; **to** ~ **about** saltar.
dance hall n salón m de baile.
dancer ['dɑːnsə*] n bailador(a) m/f; (professional) bailarín/ina m/f.
dancing ['dɑːnsɪŋ] n baile m.
D and C n abbr (MED: = dilation and curettage) raspado.
dandelion ['dændɪlaɪən] n diente m de león.
dandruff ['dændrəf] n caspa.
dandy ['dændɪ] n dandi ♦ adj (US col) estupendo.
Dane [deɪn] n danés/esa m/f.
danger ['deɪndʒə*] n peligro; (risk) riesgo; ~**!** (on sign) ¡peligro!; **to be in** ~ **of** correr riesgo de; **out of** ~ fuera de peligro.
danger list n (MED): **to be on the** ~ estar grave.

dangerous ['deɪndʒərəs] adj peligroso.
dangerously ['deɪndʒərəslɪ] adv peligrosamente; ~ **ill** gravemente enfermo.
danger zone n área or zona de peligro.
dangle ['dæŋgl] vt colgar ♦ vi pender, estar colgado.
Danish ['deɪnɪʃ] adj danés/esa ♦ n (LING) danés m.
Danish pastry n pastel m de almendra.
dank [dæŋk] adj húmedo y malsano.
Danube ['dænjuːb] n Danubio.
dapper ['dæpə*] adj pulcro, apuesto.
Dardanelles [dɑːdə'nɛlz] npl Dardanelos mpl.
dare [dɛə*] vt: **to** ~ **sb to do** desafiar a algn a hacer ♦ vi: **to** ~ **(to) do sth** atreverse a hacer algo; **I** ~ **say** (I suppose) puede ser, a lo mejor; **I** ~ **say he'll turn up** puede ser que or quizás venga; **I** ~**n't tell him** no me atrevo a decírselo.
daredevil ['dɛədɛvl] n temerario/a, atrevido/a.
Dar-es-Salaam ['dɑːrɛssə'lɑːm] n Dar es Salaam m.
daring ['dɛərɪŋ] adj (person) osado; (plan, escape) atrevido ♦ n atrevimiento, osadía.
dark [dɑːk] adj oscuro; (hair, complexion) moreno; (fig: cheerless) triste, sombrío ♦ n (gen) oscuridad f; (night) tinieblas fpl; ~ **chocolate** chocolate m amargo; **it is/is getting** ~ es de noche/está oscureciendo; **in the** ~ **about** (fig) ignorante de; **after** ~ después del anochecer.
darken ['dɑːkn] vt oscurecer; (colour) hacer más oscuro ♦ vi oscurecerse; (cloud over) nublarse.
dark glasses npl gafas fpl oscuras.
dark horse n (fig) incógnita.
darkly ['dɑːklɪ] adv (gloomily) tristemente; (sinisterly) siniestramente.
darkness ['dɑːknɪs] n (in room) oscuridad f; (night) tinieblas fpl.
darkroom ['dɑːkrum] n cuarto oscuro.
darling ['dɑːlɪŋ] adj, n querido/a m/f.
darn [dɑːn] vt zurcir.
dart [dɑːt] n dardo; (in sewing) pinza ♦ vi precipitarse; **to** ~ **away/along** vi salir/ marchar disparado.
dartboard ['dɑːtbɔːd] n diana.
darts [dɑːts] n dardos mpl.
dash [dæʃ] n (small quantity: of liquid) gota, chorrito; (: of solid) pizca; (sign) guión m; (: long) raya ♦ vt (break) romper, estrellar; (hopes) defraudar ♦ vi precipitarse, ir de prisa; **a** ~ **of soda** un poco or chorrito de sifón or soda.
►**dash away, dash off** vi marcharse

apresuradamente.

dashboard ['dæʃbɔːd] n (AUT) salpicadero.

dashing ['dæʃɪŋ] adj gallardo.

dastardly ['dæstədlɪ] adj ruin, vil.

DAT n abbr (= digital audio tape) cas(s)et(t)e m or f digital.

data ['deɪtə] npl datos mpl.

database ['deɪtəbeɪs] n base f de datos.

data capture n recogida de datos.

data link n enlace m de datos.

data processing n proceso or procesamiento de datos.

data transmission n transmisión f de datos.

date [deɪt] n (day) fecha; (with friend) cita; (fruit) dátil m ♦ vt fechar; (col: girl etc) salir con; **what's the ~ today?** ¿qué fecha es hoy?; **~ of birth** fecha de nacimiento; **closing ~** fecha tope; **to ~** adv hasta la fecha; **out of ~** pasado de moda; **up to ~** moderno; puesto al día; **to bring up to ~** (correspondence, information) poner al día; (method) actualizar; **to bring sb up to ~** poner a algn al corriente; **letter ~d 5th July** or (US) **July 5th** carta fechada el 5 de julio.

dated ['deɪtɪd] adj anticuado.

date rape n violación ocurrida durante una cita con un conocido.

date stamp n matasellos m inv; (on fresh foods) sello de fecha.

dative ['deɪtɪv] n dativo.

daub [dɔːb] vt embadurnar.

daughter ['dɔːtə*] n hija.

daughter-in-law ['dɔːtərɪnlɔː] n nuera, hija política.

daunting ['dɔːntɪŋ] adj desalentador(a).

davenport ['dævnpɔːt] n escritorio; (US: sofa) sofá m.

dawdle ['dɔːdl] vi (waste time) perder el tiempo; (go slowly) andar muy despacio; **to ~ over one's work** trabajar muy despacio.

dawn [dɔːn] n alba, amanecer m ♦ vi amanecer; (fig): **it ~ed on him that ...** cayó en la cuenta de que ...; **at ~** al amanecer; **from ~ to dusk** de sol a sol.

dawn chorus n canto de los pájaros al amanecer.

day [deɪ] n día m; (working ~) jornada; **the ~ before** el día anterior; **the ~ after tomorrow** pasado mañana; **the ~ before yesterday** anteayer, antes de ayer; **the ~ after, the following ~** el día siguiente; **by ~ de día; ~ by ~** día a día; **(on) the ~ that ...** el día que ...; **to work an 8-hour ~** trabajar 8 horas diarias or al día; **he works 8 hours a ~** trabaja 8 horas al día;

paid by the ~ pagado por día; **these ~s, in the present ~** hoy en día.

daybook ['deɪbuk] n (BRIT) diario or libro de entradas y salidas.

daybreak ['deɪbreɪk] n amanecer m.

day-care centre ['deɪkɛə-] n centro de día; (for children) guardería infantil.

daydream ['deɪdriːm] n ensueño ♦ vi soñar despierto.

daylight ['deɪlaɪt] n luz f (del día).

daylight robbery n: **it's ~!** (fig, col) ¡es un robo descarado!

Daylight Saving Time n (US) hora de verano.

day-release course [deɪrɪ'liːs-] n curso de formación de un día a la semana.

day return (ticket) n (BRIT) billete m de ida y vuelta (en un día).

day shift n turno de día.

daytime ['deɪtaɪm] n día m.

day-to-day ['deɪtə'deɪ] adj cotidiano, diario; (expenses) diario; **on a ~ basis** día por día.

day trip n excursión f (de un día).

day tripper n excursionista m/f.

daze [deɪz] vt (stun) aturdir ♦ n: **in a ~** aturdido.

dazed [deɪzd] adj aturdido.

dazzle ['dæzl] vt deslumbrar.

dazzling ['dæzlɪŋ] adj (light, smile) deslumbrante; (colour) fuerte.

DBS n abbr (= direct broadcasting by satellite) transmisión vía satélite.

DC abbr (ELEC) = **direct current**; (US) = **District of Columbia**.

DCC ® n abbr (= digital compact cassette) cas(s)et(t)e m digital compacto.

DD n abbr (= Doctor of Divinity) título universitario.

dd. abbr (COMM) = **delivered**.

D/D abbr = **direct debit**.

D-day ['diːdeɪ] n (fig) día m clave.

DDS n abbr (US: = Doctor of Dental Science; Doctor of Dental Surgery) títulos universitarios.

DDT n abbr (= dichlorodiphenyltrichloroethane) DDT m.

DE abbr (US) = **Delaware**.

DEA n abbr (US: = Drug Enforcement Administration) brigada especial dedicada a la lucha contra el tráfico de estupefacientes.

deacon ['diːkən] n diácono.

dead [dɛd] adj muerto; (limb) dormido; (battery) agotado ♦ adv totalmente; (exactly) justo; **he was ~ on arrival** ingresó cadáver; **to shoot sb ~** matar a algn a tiros; **~ tired** muerto (de cansancio); **to stop** ~ parar en seco; **the line has gone** ~ (*TEL*) se ha cortado la línea; **the** ~ *npl* los muertos.

dead beat *adj*: **to be** ~ (*col*) estar hecho polvo.

deaden ['dɛdn] *vt* (*blow, sound*) amortiguar; (*pain*) calmar, aliviar.

dead end *n* callejón *m* sin salida.

dead-end ['dɛdend] *adj*: **a** ~ **job** un trabajo sin porvenir.

dead heat *n* (*SPORT*) empate *m*.

deadline ['dɛdlaɪn] *n* fecha tope; **to work to a** ~ trabajar con una fecha tope.

deadlock ['dɛdlɔk] *n* punto muerto.

dead loss *n* (*col*): **to be a** ~ (*person*) ser un inútil; (*thing*) ser una birria.

deadly ['dɛdlɪ] *adj* mortal, fatal; ~ **dull** aburridísimo.

deadly nightshade [-'naɪtʃeɪd] *n* belladona.

deadpan ['dɛdpæn] *adj* sin expresión.

Dead Sea *n*: **the** ~ el Mar Muerto.

dead season *n* (*TOURISM*) temporada baja.

deaf [dɛf] *adj* sordo; **to turn a** ~ **ear to sth** hacer oídos sordos a algo.

deaf-aid ['dɛfeɪd] *n* audífono.

deaf-and-dumb ['dɛfən'dʌm] *adj* (*person*) sordomudo; (*alphabet*) para sordomudos.

deafen ['dɛfn] *vt* ensordecer.

deafening ['dɛfnɪŋ] *adj* ensordecedor(a).

deaf-mute ['dɛfmjuːt] *n* sordomudo/a.

deafness ['dɛfnɪs] *n* sordera.

deal [diːl] *n* (*agreement*) pacto, convenio; (*business*) negocio, transacción *f*; (*CARDS*) reparto ♦ *vt* (*pt, pp* **dealt**) (*gen*) dar; **a great** ~ **(of)** bastante, mucho; **it's a** ~! (*col*) ¡trato hecho!, ¡de acuerdo!; **to do a** ~ **with sb** hacer un trato con algn; **he got a bad/fair** ~ **from them** le trataron mal/bien.

▶**deal in** *vt fus* tratar en, comerciar en.

▶**deal with** *vt fus* (*people*) tratar con; (*problem*) ocuparse de; (*subject*) tratar de.

dealer ['diːlə*] *n* comerciante *m/f*; (*CARDS*) mano *f*.

dealership ['diːləʃɪp] *n* concesionario.

dealings ['diːlɪŋz] *npl* (*COMM*) transacciones *fpl*; (*relations*) relaciones *fpl*.

dealt [dɛlt] *pt, pp of* **deal**.

dean [diːn] *n* (*REL*) deán *m*; (*SCOL*) decano/a.

dear [dɪə*] *adj* querido; (*expensive*) caro ♦ *n*: **my** ~ querido/a; ~ **me!** ¡Dios mío!; **D**~ **Sir/Madam** (*in letter*) Muy señor mío, Estimado señor/Estimada señora, De mi/nuestra (mayor) consideración (*esp LAM*); **D**~ **Mr/Mrs X** Estimado/a señor(a) X.

dearly ['dɪəlɪ] *adv* (*love*) mucho; (*pay*) caro.

dearth [dəːθ] *n* (*of food, resources, money*) escasez *f*.

death [dɛθ] *n* muerte *f*.

deathbed ['dɛθbɛd] *n* lecho de muerte.

death certificate *n* partida de defunción.

death duties *npl* (*BRIT*) derechos *mpl* de sucesión.

deathly ['dɛθlɪ] *adj* mortal; (*silence*) profundo.

death penalty *n* pena de muerte.

death rate *n* tasa de mortalidad.

death row *n*: **to be on** ~ (*US*) estar condenado a muerte.

death sentence *n* condena a muerte.

death squad *n* escuadrón *m* de la muerte.

deathtrap ['dɛθtræp] *n* lugar *m* (*or* vehículo *etc*) muy peligroso.

deb [dɛb] *n abbr* (*col*) = **debutante**.

debacle [deɪ'bɑːkl] *n* desastre *m*, catástrofe *f*.

debar [dɪ'bɑː*] *vt*: **to** ~ **sb from doing** prohibir a algn hacer.

debase [dɪ'beɪs] *vt* degradar.

debatable [dɪ'beɪtəbl] *adj* discutible; **it is** ~ **whether ...** es discutible si ....

debate [dɪ'beɪt] *n* debate *m* ♦ *vt* discutir.

debauched [dɪ'bɔːtʃt] *adj* vicioso.

debauchery [dɪ'bɔːtʃərɪ] *n* libertinaje *m*.

debenture [dɪ'bɛntʃə*] *n* (*COMM*) bono, obligación *f*.

debenture capital *n* capital *m* hipotecario.

debilitate [dɪ'bɪlɪteɪt] *vt* debilitar.

debilitating [dɪ'bɪlɪteɪtɪŋ] *adj* (*illness etc*) debilitante.

debit ['dɛbɪt] *n* debe *m* ♦ *vt*: **to** ~ **a sum to sb** *or* **to sb's account** cargar una suma en cuenta a algn.

debit balance *n* saldo deudor *or* pasivo.

debit note *n* nota de débito *or* cargo.

debonair [dɛbə'nɛə*] *adj* jovial, cortés/esa.

debrief [diː'briːf] *vt* hacer dar parte.

debriefing [diː'briːfɪŋ] *n* relación *f* (de un informe).

debris ['dɛbriː] *n* escombros *mpl*.

debt [dɛt] *n* deuda; **to be in** ~ tener deudas; ~**s of £5000** deudas de cinco mil libras; **bad** ~ deuda incobrable.

debt collector *n* cobrador(a) *m/f* de deudas.

debtor ['dɛtə*] *n* deudor(a) *m/f*.

debug ['diː'bʌg] *vt* (*COMPUT*) depurar.

debunk [diː'bʌŋk] *vt* (*col*: *theory*) desprestigiar, desacreditar; (: *claim*) desacreditar; (: *person, institution*) desenmascarar.

début ['deɪbjuː] *n* presentación *f*.

debutante ['dɛbjutænt] *n* debutante *f*.

Dec. *abbr* (= *December*) dic.

decade ['dɛkeɪd] *n* década, decenio.
decadence ['dɛkədəns] *n* decadencia.
decadent ['dɛkədənt] *adj* decadente.
de-caff ['diːkæf] *n* (*col*) descafeinado.
decaffeinated [dɪ'kæfɪneɪtɪd] *adj*
  descafeinado.
decamp [dɪ'kæmp] *vi* (*col*) escaparse,
  largarse, rajarse (*LAM*).
decant [dɪ'kænt] *vt* decantar.
decanter [dɪ'kæntə*] *n* jarra, decantador *m*.
decathlon [dɪ'kæθlən] *n* decatlón *m*.
decay [dɪ'keɪ] *n* (*fig*) decadencia; (*of
  building*) desmoronamiento; (*of tooth*)
  caries *f inv* ♦ *vi* (*rot*) pudrirse; (*fig*) decaer.
decease [dɪ'siːs] *n* fallecimiento ♦ *vi*
  fallecer.
deceased [dɪ'siːst] *adj* difunto.
deceit [dɪ'siːt] *n* engaño.
deceitful [dɪ'siːtful] *adj* engañoso.
deceive [dɪ'siːv] *vt* engañar.
decelerate [diː'sɛləreɪt] *vt* moderar la
  marcha de ♦ *vi* decelerar.
December [dɪ'sɛmbə*] *n* diciembre *m*.
decency ['diːsənsɪ] *n* decencia.
decent ['diːsənt] *adj* (*proper*) decente;
  (*person*) amable, bueno.
decently ['diːsəntlɪ] *adv* (*respectably*)
  decentemente; (*kindly*) amablemente.
decentralization [diːsɛntrəlaɪ'zeɪʃən] *n*
  descentralización *f*.
decentralize [diː'sɛntrəlaɪz] *vt*
  descentralizar.
deception [dɪ'sɛpʃən] *n* engaño.
deceptive [dɪ'sɛptɪv] *adj* engañoso.
decibel ['dɛsɪbɛl] *n* decibel(io) *m*.
decide [dɪ'saɪd] *vt* (*person*) decidir;
  (*question, argument*) resolver ♦ *vi*: **to ~ to
  do/that** decidir hacer/que; **to ~ on sth**
  tomar una decisión sobre algo; **to ~
  against doing sth** decidir en contra de
  hacer algo.
decided [dɪ'saɪdɪd] *adj* (*resolute*) decidido;
  (*clear, definite*) indudable.
decidedly [dɪ'saɪdɪdlɪ] *adv* decididamente.
deciding [dɪ'saɪdɪŋ] *adj* decisivo.
deciduous [dɪ'sɪdjuəs] *adj* de hoja caduca.
decimal ['dɛsɪməl] *adj* decimal ♦ *n* decimal
  f; **to 3 ~ places** con 3 cifras decimales.
decimalize ['dɛsɪmələɪz] *vt* convertir al
  sistema decimal.
decimal point *n* coma decimal.
decimal system *n* sistema *m* métrico
  decimal.
decimate ['dɛsɪmeɪt] *vt* diezmar.
decipher [dɪ'saɪfə*] *vt* descifrar.
decision [dɪ'sɪʒən] *n* decisión *f*; **to make a ~**
  tomar una decisión.
decisive [dɪ'saɪsɪv] *adj* (*influence*) decisivo;

(*manner, person*) decidido; (*reply*) tajante.
deck [dɛk] *n* (*NAUT*) cubierta; (*of bus*) piso;
  (*of cards*) baraja; **cassette ~** platina; **to go
  up on ~** subir a (la) cubierta; **below ~** en
  la bodega.
deckchair ['dɛktʃɛə*] *n* tumbona.
deckhand ['dɛkhænd] *n* marinero de
  cubierta.
declaration [dɛklə'reɪʃən] *n* declaración *f*.
declare [dɪ'klɛə*] *vt* (*gen*) declarar.
declassify [diː'klæsɪfaɪ] *vt* permitir que
  salga a la luz.
decline [dɪ'klaɪn] *n* decaimiento,
  decadencia; (*lessening*) disminución *f* ♦ *vt*
  rehusar ♦ *vi* decaer; disminuir; **~ in living
  standards** disminución *f* del nivel de vida;
  to ~ to do sth rehusar hacer algo.
declutch ['diː'klʌtʃ] *vi* desembragar.
decode [diː'kəud] *vt* descifrar.
decoder [diː'kəudə*] *n* (*COMPUT, TV*)
  de(s)codificador *m*.
decompose [diːkəm'pəuz] *vi*
  descomponerse.
decomposition [diːkɔmpə'zɪʃən] *n*
  descomposición *f*.
decompression [diːkəm'prɛʃən] *n*
  descompresión *f*.
decompression chamber *n* cámara de
  descompresión.
decongestant [diːkən'dʒɛstənt] *n*
  descongestionante.
decontaminate [diːkən'tæmɪneɪt] *vt*
  descontaminar.
decontrol [diːkən'trəul] *vt* (*trade*) quitar
  controles a; (*prices*) descongelar.
décor ['deɪkɔː*] *n* decoración *f*; (*THEAT*)
  decorado.
decorate ['dɛkəreɪt] *vt* (*paint*) pintar;
  (*paper*) empapelar; (*adorn*): **to ~ (with)**
  adornar (de), decorar (de).
decoration [dɛkə'reɪʃən] *n* adorno; (*act*)
  decoración *f*; (*medal*) condecoración *f*.
decorative ['dɛkərətɪv] *adj* decorativo.
decorator ['dɛkəreɪtə*] *n* (*workman*) pintor
  m decorador.
decorum [dɪ'kɔːrəm] *n* decoro.
decoy ['diːkɔɪ] *n* señuelo; **police ~** trampa
  or señuelo policial.
decrease ['diːkriːs] *n* disminución *f* ♦ (*vb*:
  [dɪ'kriːs]) *vt* disminuir, reducir ♦ *vi*
  reducirse; **to be on the ~** ir
  disminuyendo.
decreasing [dɪ'kriːsɪŋ] *adj* decreciente.
decree [dɪ'kriː] *n* decreto ♦ *vt*: **to ~ (that)**
  decretar (que); **~ absolute/nisi** sentencia
  absoluta/provisional de divorcio.
decrepit [dɪ'krɛpɪt] *adj* (*person*) decrépito;
  (*building*) ruinoso.

decry [dɪ'kraɪ] *vt* criticar, censurar.
dedicate ['dɛdɪkeɪt] *vt* dedicar.
dedicated ['dɛdɪkeɪtɪd] *adj* dedicado;
(*COMPUT*) especializado; ~ **word**
processor procesador *m* de textos
especializado *or* dedicado.
dedication [dɛdɪ'keɪʃən] *n* (*devotion*)
dedicación *f*; (*in book*) dedicatoria.
deduce [dɪ'djuːs] *vt* deducir.
deduct [dɪ'dʌkt] *vt* restar; (*from wage etc*)
descontar, deducir.
deduction [dɪ'dʌkʃən] *n* (*amount deducted*)
descuento; (*conclusion*) deducción *f*,
conclusión *f*.
deed [diːd] *n* hecho, acto; (*feat*) hazaña;
(*LAW*) escritura; ~ **of covenant** escritura
de contrato.
deem [diːm] *vt* (*formal*) juzgar, considerar;
to ~ it wise to do considerar prudente
hacer.
deep [diːp] *adj* profundo; (*voice*) bajo;
(*breath*) profundo, a pleno pulmón ♦ *adv*:
the spectators stood 20 ~ los
espectadores se formaron de 20 en
fondo; **to be 4 metres** ~ tener 4 metros
de profundidad.
deepen ['diːpn] *vt* ahondar, profundizar
♦ *vi* (*darkness*) intensificarse.
deep-freeze ['diːp'friːz] *n* arcón *m*
congelador.
deep-fry ['diːp'fraɪ] *vt* freír en aceite
abundante.
deeply ['diːplɪ] *adv* (*breathe*)
profundamente, a pleno pulmón;
(*interested, moved, grateful*)
profundamente, hondamente; **to regret**
sth ~ sentir algo profundamente.
deep-rooted ['diːp'ruːtɪd] *adj* (*prejudice,
habit*) profundamente arraigado;
(*affection*) profundo.
deep-sea ['diːp'siː] *adj*: ~ **diver** buzo; ~
diving buceo de altura.
deep-seated ['diːp'siːtɪd] *adj* (*beliefs*)
(profundamente) arraigado.
deep-set ['diːpsɛt] *adj* (*eyes*) hundido.
deer [dɪə*] *n, pl inv* ciervo.
deerstalker ['dɪəstɔːkə*] *n* (*hat*) gorro de
cazador.
deface [dɪ'feɪs] *vt* desfigurar, mutilar.
defamation [dɛfə'meɪʃən] *n* difamación *f*.
defamatory [dɪ'fæmətrɪ] *adj* difamatorio.
default [dɪ'fɔːlt] *vi* faltar al pago; (*SPORT*)
no presentarse, no comparecer ♦ *n*
(*COMPUT*) defecto; **by** ~ (*LAW*) en
rebeldía; (*SPORT*) por incomparecencia;
to ~ **on a debt** dejar de pagar una deuda.
defaulter [dɪ'fɔːltə*] *n* (*in debt*) moroso/a.
default option *n* (*COMPUT*) opción *f* por

defecto.
defeat [dɪ'fiːt] *n* derrota ♦ *vt* derrotar,
vencer; (*fig: efforts*) frustrar.
defeatism [dɪ'fiːtɪzəm] *n* derrotismo.
defeatist [dɪ'fiːtɪst] *adj, n* derrotista *m/f*.
defecate ['dɛfəkeɪt] *vi* defecar.
defect ['diːfɛkt] *n* defecto ♦ *vi* [dɪ'fɛkt]: **to** ~
to the enemy pasarse al enemigo;
physical ~ defecto físico; **mental** ~
deficiencia mental.
defective [dɪ'fɛktɪv] *adj* (*gen*) defectuoso;
(*person*) anormal.
defector [dɪ'fɛktə*] *n* tránsfuga *m/f*.
defence, (*US*) **defense** [dɪ'fɛns] *n* defensa;
the Ministry of D~ el Ministerio de
Defensa; **witness for the** ~ testigo de
descargo.
defenceless [dɪ'fɛnslɪs] *adj* indefenso.
defence spending *n* gasto militar.
defend [dɪ'fɛnd] *vt* defender; (*decision,
action*) defender; (*opinion*) mantener.
defendant [dɪ'fɛndənt] *n* acusado/a; (*in civil
case*) demandado/a.
defender [dɪ'fɛndə*] *n* defensor(a) *m/f*.
defending champion [dɪ'fɛndɪŋ-] *n*
(*SPORT*) defensor(a) *m/f* del título.
defending counsel *n* (*LAW*) abogado
defensor.
defense [dɪ'fɛns] *n* (*US*) = **defence**.
defensive [dɪ'fɛnsɪv] *adj* defensivo ♦ *n*
defensiva; **on the** ~ a la defensiva.
defer [dɪ'fəː*] *vt* (*postpone*) aplazar; **to** ~ **to**
diferir a; (*submit*): **to** ~ **to sb/sb's opinion**
someterse a algn/a la opinión de algn.
deference ['dɛfərəns] *n* deferencia,
respeto; **out of** *or* **in** ~ **to** por respeto a.
deferential [dɛfə'rɛnʃəl] *adj* respetuoso.
deferred [dɪ'fəːd] *adj*: ~ **creditor** acreedor
m diferido.
defiance [dɪ'faɪəns] *n* desafío; **in** ~ **of** en
contra de.
defiant [dɪ'faɪənt] *adj* (*insolent*) insolente;
(*challenging*) retador(a).
defiantly [dɪ'faɪəntlɪ] *adv* con aire de
desafío.
deficiency [dɪ'fɪʃənsɪ] *n* (*lack*) falta; (*COMM*)
déficit *m*; (*defect*) defecto.
deficient [dɪ'fɪʃənt] *adj* (*lacking*)
insuficiente; (*incomplete*) incompleto;
(*defective*) defectuoso; (*mentally*) anormal;
~ **in** deficiente en.
deficit ['dɛfɪsɪt] *n* déficit *m*.
defile [dɪ'faɪl] *vt* manchar; (*violate*) violar.
define [dɪ'faɪn] *vt* (*also COMPUT*) definir.
definite ['dɛfɪnɪt] *adj* (*fixed*) determinado;
(*clear, obvious*) claro; **he was** ~ **about it**
no dejó lugar a dudas (sobre ello).
definitely ['dɛfɪnɪtlɪ] *adv*: **he's** ~ **mad** no

cabe duda de que está loco.
definition [dɛfɪ'nɪʃən] *n* definición *f.*
definitive [dɪ'fɪnɪtɪv] *adj* definitivo.
deflate [diː'fleɪt] *vt* (*gen*) desinflar;
(*pompous person*) quitar *or* rebajar los
humos a; (*ECON*) deflacionar.
deflation [diː'fleɪʃən] *n* (*ECON*) deflación *f.*
deflationary [diː'fleɪʃənrɪ] *adj* (*ECON*)
deflacionario.
deflect [dɪ'flɛkt] *vt* desviar.
defog [diː'fɔg] *vt* desempañar.
defogger [diː'fɔgə*] *n* (*US AUT*) dispositivo
antivaho.
deform [dɪ'fɔːm] *vt* deformar.
deformed [dɪ'fɔːmd] *adj* deformado.
deformity [dɪ'fɔːmɪtɪ] *n* deformación *f.*
defraud [dɪ'frɔːd] *vt* estafar; **to** ~ **sb of sth**
estafar algo a algn.
defray [dɪ'freɪ] *vt*: **to** ~ **sb's expenses**
reembolsar a algn los gastos.
defrost [diː'frɔst] *vt* (*frozen food, fridge*)
descongelar.
defroster [diː'frɔstə*] *n* (*US*) eliminador *m*
de vaho.
deft [dɛft] *adj* diestro, hábil.
defunct [dɪ'fʌŋkt] *adj* difunto; (*organization
etc*) ya desaparecido.
defuse [diː'fjuːz] *vt* desarmar; (*situation*)
calmar, apaciguar.
defy [dɪ'faɪ] *vt* (*resist*) oponerse a;
(*challenge*) desafiar; (*order*) contravenir.
degenerate [dɪ'dʒɛnəreɪt] *vi* degenerar
♦ *adj* [dɪ'dʒɛnərɪt] degenerado.
degradation [dɛgrə'deɪʃən] *n* degradación
f.
degrade [dɪ'greɪd] *vt* degradar.
degrading [dɪ'greɪdɪŋ] *adj* degradante.
degree [dɪ'griː] *n* grado; (*SCOL*) título; **10**
~**s below freezing** 10 grados bajo cero; **to
have a** ~ **in maths** ser licenciado/a en
matemáticas; **by** ~**s** (*gradually*) poco a
poco, por etapas; **to some** ~, **to a certain**
~ hasta cierto punto; **a considerable** ~ **of
risk** un gran índice de riesgo.
dehydrated [diːhaɪ'dreɪtɪd] *adj*
deshidratado; (*milk*) en polvo.
dehydration [diːhaɪ'dreɪʃən] *n*
deshidratación *f.*
de-ice [diː'aɪs] *vt* (*windscreen*) deshelar.
de-icer [diː'aɪsə*] *n* descongelador *m.*
deign [deɪn] *vi*: **to** ~ **to do** dignarse hacer.
deity [ˈdiːɪtɪ] *n* deidad *f,* divinidad *f.*
déjà vu [deɪʒɑː'vuː] *n*: **I had a sense of** ~
sentía como si lo hubiera vivido.
dejected [dɪ'dʒɛktɪd] *adj* abatido,
desanimado.
dejection [dɪ'dʒɛkʃən] *n* abatimiento.
Del. *abbr* (*US*) = *Delaware.*

del. *abbr* = **delete**.
delay [dɪ'leɪ] *vt* demorar, aplazar; (*person*)
entretener; (*train*) retrasar; (*payment*)
aplazar ♦ *vi* tardar ♦ *n* demora, retraso;
without ~ en seguida, sin tardar.
delayed-action [dɪleɪd'ækʃən] *adj* (*bomb
etc*) de acción retardada.
delectable [dɪ'lɛktəbl] *adj* (*person*)
encantador(a); (*food*) delicioso.
delegate ['dɛlɪgɪt] *n* delegado/a ♦ *vt*
['dɛlɪgeɪt] delegar; **to** ~ **sth to sb/sb to do
sth** delegar algo en algn/en algn para
hacer algo.
delegation [dɛlɪ'geɪʃən] *n* (*of work etc*)
delegación *f.*
delete [dɪ'liːt] *vt* suprimir, tachar;
(*COMPUT*) suprimir, borrar.
Delhi ['dɛlɪ] *n* Delhi *m.*
deli ['dɛlɪ] *n* = **delicatessen**.
deliberate [dɪ'lɪbərɪt] *adj* (*intentional*)
intencionado; (*slow*) pausado, lento ♦ *vi*
[dɪ'lɪbəreɪt] deliberar.
deliberately [dɪ'lɪbərɪtlɪ] *adv* (*on purpose*) a
propósito; (*slowly*) pausadamente.
deliberation [dɪlɪbə'reɪʃən] *n* (*consideration*)
reflexión *f,* (*discussion*) deliberación *f,*
discusión *f.*
delicacy ['dɛlɪkəsɪ] *n* delicadeza; (*choice
food*) manjar *m.*
delicate ['dɛlɪkɪt] *adj* (*gen*) delicado;
(*fragile*) frágil.
delicately ['dɛlɪkɪtlɪ] *adv* con delicadeza,
delicadamente; (*act, express*) con
discreción.
delicatessen [dɛlɪkə'tɛsn] *n* tienda
especializada en comida exótica.
delicious [dɪ'lɪʃəs] *adj* delicioso, rico.
delight [dɪ'laɪt] *n* (*feeling*) placer *m,* deleite
m; (*object*) encanto, delicia ♦ *vt* encantar,
deleitar; **to take** ~ **in** deleitarse en.
delighted [dɪ'laɪtɪd] *adj*: ~ (**at** *or* **with/to
do**) encantado (con/de hacer); **to be** ~
that estar encantado de que; **I'd be** ~ con
mucho *or* todo gusto.
delightful [dɪ'laɪtful] *adj* encantador(a),
delicioso.
delimit [diː'lɪmɪt] *vt* delimitar.
delineate [dɪ'lɪnɪeɪt] *vt* delinear.
delinquency [dɪ'lɪŋkwənsɪ] *n* delincuencia.
delinquent [dɪ'lɪŋkwənt] *adj, n* delincuente
m/f.
delirious [dɪ'lɪrɪəs] *adj* (*MED, fig*) delirante;
to be ~ delirar, desvariar.
delirium [dɪ'lɪrɪəm] *n* delirio.
deliver [dɪ'lɪvə*] *vt* (*distribute*) repartir;
(*hand over*) entregar; (*message*)
comunicar; (*speech*) pronunciar; (*blow*)
lanzar, dar; (*MED*) asistir al parto de.

deliverance [dɪ'lɪvrəns] n liberación f.

delivery [dɪ'lɪvərɪ] n reparto; entrega; (of speaker) modo de expresarse; (MED) parto, alumbramiento; **to take ~ of** recibir.

delivery note n nota de entrega.

delivery van n furgoneta de reparto.

delta ['dɛltə] n delta m.

delude [dɪ'luːd] vt engañar.

deluge ['dɛljuːdʒ] n diluvio ♦ vt (fig): **to ~ (with)** inundar (de).

delusion [dɪ'luːʒən] n ilusión f, engaño.

de luxe [də'lʌks] adj de lujo.

delve [dɛlv] vi: **to ~ into** hurgar en.

Dem. abbr (US POL) = **democrat(ic).**

demand [dɪ'mɑːnd] vt (gen) exigir; (rights) reclamar; (need) requerir ♦ n (gen) exigencia; (claim) reclamación f; (ECON) demanda; **to ~ sth (from or of sb)** exigir algo (a algn); **to be in ~** ser muy solicitado; **on ~** a solicitud.

demanding [dɪ'mɑːndɪŋ] adj (boss) exigente; (work) absorbente.

demarcation [diːmɑːˈkeɪʃən] n demarcación f.

demarcation dispute n conflicto de definición or demarcación del trabajo.

demean [dɪ'miːn] vt: **to ~ o.s.** rebajarse.

demeanour, (US) demeanor [dɪ'miːnə*] n porte m, conducta, comportamiento.

demented [dɪ'mɛntɪd] adj demente.

demi- ['dɛmɪ] pref semi..., medio....

demilitarize [diːˈmɪlɪtəraɪz] vt desmilitarizar; **~d zone** zona desmilitarizada.

demise [dɪ'maɪz] n (death) fallecimiento.

demist [diːˈmɪst] vt (AUT) eliminar el vaho de.

demister [diːˈmɪstə*] n (AUT) eliminador m de vaho.

demo ['dɛməʊ] n abbr (col: = demonstration) manifestación f.

demobilization [diːˌməʊbɪlaɪˈzeɪʃən] n desmovilización f.

democracy [dɪ'mɒkrəsɪ] n democracia.

democrat ['dɛməkræt] n demócrata m/f.

democratic [dɛmə'krætɪk] adj democrático; **the D~ Party** el partido demócrata (estadounidense).

demography [dɪ'mɒgrəfɪ] n demografía.

demolish [dɪ'mɒlɪʃ] vt derribar, demoler.

demolition [dɛmə'lɪʃən] n derribo, demolición f.

demon ['diːmən] n (evil spirit) demonio ♦ cpd temible.

demonstrate ['dɛmənstreɪt] vt demostrar ♦ vi manifestarse; **to ~ (for/against)** manifestarse (a favor de/en contra de).

demonstration [dɛmən'streɪʃən] n (POL) manifestación f; (proof) prueba, demostración f; **to hold a ~ (POL)** hacer una manifestación.

demonstrative [dɪ'mɒnstrətɪv] adj (person) expresivo; (LING) demostrativo.

demonstrator ['dɛmənstreɪtə*] n (POL) manifestante m/f.

demoralize [dɪ'mɒrəlaɪz] vt desmoralizar.

demote [dɪ'məʊt] vt degradar.

demotion [dɪ'məʊʃən] n degradación f; (COMM) descenso.

demur [dɪ'mɜː*] vi: **to ~ (at)** hacer objeciones (a), vacilar (ante) ♦ n: **without ~** sin objeción.

demure [dɪ'mjʊə*] adj recatado.

demurrage [dɪ'mʌrɪdʒ] n sobrestadía.

den [dɛn] n (of animal) guarida; (study) estudio.

denationalization [diːnæʃnəlaɪˈzeɪʃən] n desnacionalización f.

denationalize [diːˈnæʃnəlaɪz] vt desnacionalizar.

denatured alcohol [diːˈneɪtʃəd-] n (US) alcohol m desnaturalizado.

denial [dɪ'naɪəl] n (refusal) negativa; (of report etc) denegación f.

denier ['dɛnɪə*] n denier m.

denim ['dɛnɪm] n tela vaquera; see also **denims.**

denim jacket n chaqueta vaquera, saco vaquero (LAM).

denims ['dɛnɪmz] npl vaqueros mpl.

denizen ['dɛnɪzn] n (inhabitant) habitante m/f; (foreigner) residente m/f extranjero/a.

Denmark ['dɛnmɑːk] n Dinamarca.

denomination [dɪnɒmɪ'neɪʃən] n valor m; (REL) confesión f.

denominator [dɪ'nɒmɪneɪtə*] n denominador m.

denote [dɪ'nəʊt] vt indicar, significar.

denounce [dɪ'naʊns] vt denunciar.

dense [dɛns] adj (thick) espeso; (: foliage etc) tupido; (stupid) torpe.

densely [dɛnslɪ] adv: **~ populated** con una alta densidad de población.

density ['dɛnsɪtɪ] n densidad f; **single/double-~ disk** n disco de densidad sencilla/de doble densidad.

dent [dɛnt] n abolladura ♦ vt (also: **make a ~ in**) abollar.

dental ['dɛntl] adj dental.

dental floss [-flɒs] n seda dental.

dental surgeon n odontólogo/a.

dentifrice ['dɛntɪfrɪs] n dentífrico.

dentist ['dɛntɪst] n dentista m/f; **~'s surgery** (BRIT) consultorio dental.

dentistry ['dɛntɪstrɪ] n odontología.

dentures ['dɛntʃəz] npl dentadura sg (postiza).
denude [dɪ'njuːd] vt: **to ~ of** despojar de.
denunciation [dɪnʌnsɪ'eɪʃən] n denuncia, denunciación f.
deny [dɪ'naɪ] vt negar; (charge) rechazar; (report) desmentir; **to ~ o.s.** privarse (de); **he denies having said it** niega haberlo dicho.
deodorant [diː'əudərənt] n desodorante m.
depart [dɪ'pɑːt] vi irse, marcharse; (train) salir; **to ~ from** (fig: differ from) apartarse de.
departed [dɪ'pɑːtɪd] adj (bygone: days, glory) pasado; (dead) difunto ♦ n: **the (dear) ~** el/la/los/las difunto/a/os/as.
department [dɪ'pɑːtmənt] n (COMM) sección f; (SCOL) departamento; (POL) ministerio; **that's not my ~** (fig) no tiene que ver conmigo; **D~ of State** (US) Ministerio de Asuntos Exteriores.
departmental [diːpɑːt'mɛntl] adj (dispute) departamental; (meeting) departamental, de departamento; **~ manager** jefe/a m/f de sección or de departamento or de servicio.
department store n gran almacén m.
departure [dɪ'pɑːtʃə*] n partida, ida; (of train) salida; **a new ~** un nuevo rumbo.
departure lounge n (at airport) sala de embarque.
depend [dɪ'pɛnd] vi: **to ~ (up)on** (be dependent upon) depender de; (rely on) contar con; **it ~s** depende, según; **~ing on the result** según el resultado.
dependable [dɪ'pɛndəbl] adj (person) formal, serio.
dependant [dɪ'pɛndənt] n dependiente m/f.
dependence [dɪ'pɛndəns] n dependencia.
dependent [dɪ'pɛndənt] adj: **to be ~ (on)** depender (de) ♦ n = **dependant**.
depict [dɪ'pɪkt] vt (in picture) pintar; (describe) representar.
depilatory [dɪ'pɪlətrɪ] n (also: ~ **cream**) depilatorio.
depleted [dɪ'pliːtɪd] adj reducido.
deplorable [dɪ'plɔːrəbl] adj deplorable.
deplore [dɪ'plɔː*] vt deplorar.
deploy [dɪ'plɔɪ] vt desplegar.
depopulate [diː'pɔpjuleɪt] vt despoblar.
depopulation ['diːpɔpju'leɪʃən] n despoblación f.
deport [dɪ'pɔːt] vt deportar.
deportation [diːpɔː'teɪʃən] n deportación f.
deportation order n orden f de expulsión or deportación.
deportee [diːpɔː'tiː] n deportado/a.
deportment [dɪ'pɔːtmənt] n

comportamiento.
depose [dɪ'pəuz] vt deponer.
deposit [dɪ'pɔzɪt] n depósito; (CHEM) sedimento; (of ore, oil) yacimiento ♦ vt (gen) depositar; **to put down a ~ of £50** dejar un depósito de 50 libras.
deposit account n (BRIT) cuenta de ahorros.
depositor [dɪ'pɔzɪtə*] n depositante m/f, cuentacorrentista m/f.
depository [dɪ'pɔzɪtərɪ] n almacén m depositario.
depot ['dɛpəu] n (storehouse) depósito; (for vehicles) parque m.
deprave [dɪ'preɪv] vt depravar.
depraved [dɪ'preɪvd] adj depravado, vicioso.
depravity [dɪ'prævɪtɪ] n depravación f, vicio.
deprecate ['dɛprɪkeɪt] vt desaprobar, lamentar.
deprecating ['dɛprɪkeɪtɪŋ] adj (disapproving) de desaprobación; (apologetic): **a ~ smile** una sonrisa de disculpa.
depreciate [dɪ'priːʃɪeɪt] vi depreciarse, perder valor.
depreciation [dɪpriːʃɪ'eɪʃən] n depreciación f.
depress [dɪ'prɛs] vt deprimir; (press down) apretar.
depressant [dɪ'prɛsnt] n (MED) calmante m, sedante m.
depressed [dɪ'prɛst] adj deprimido; (COMM: market, economy) deprimido; (area) deprimido (económicamente); **to get ~** deprimirse.
depressing [dɪ'prɛsɪŋ] adj deprimente.
depression [dɪ'prɛʃən] n depresión f; **the economy is in a state of ~** la economía está deprimida.
deprivation [dɛprɪ'veɪʃən] n privación f; (loss) pérdida.
deprive [dɪ'praɪv] vt: **to ~ sb of** privar a algn de.
deprived [dɪ'praɪvd] adj necesitado.
dept. abbr (= department) dto.
depth [dɛpθ] n profundidad f; **at a ~ of 3 metres** a 3 metros de profundidad; **to be out of one's ~** (swimmer) perder pie; (fig) estar perdido; **to study sth in ~** estudiar algo a fondo; **in the ~s of** en lo más hondo de.
depth charge n carga de profundidad.
deputation [dɛpju'teɪʃən] n delegación f.
deputize ['dɛpjutaɪz] vi: **to ~ for sb** sustituir a algn.
deputy ['dɛpjutɪ] adj: **~ head**

subdirector(a) *m/f* ♦ *n* sustituto/a, suplente *m/f*; (*POL*) diputado/a; (*agent*) representante *m/f*.

deputy leader *n* (*POL*) vicepresidente/a *m/f*.

derail [dɪ'reɪl] *vt*: **to ~ed** descarrilarse.

derailment [dɪ'reɪlmənt] *n* descarrilamiento.

deranged [dɪ'reɪndʒd] *adj* trastornado.

derby ['dəːbɪ] *n* (*US*) hongo.

Derbys *abbr* (*BRIT*) = **Derbyshire**.

deregulate [diː'regjuleɪt] *vt* desreglamentar.

deregulation [diːregju'leɪʃən] *n* desreglamentación *f*.

derelict ['derɪlɪkt] *adj* abandonado.

deride [dɪ'raɪd] *vt* ridiculizar, mofarse de.

derision [dɪ'rɪʒən] *n* irrisión *f*, mofas *fpl*.

derisive [dɪ'raɪsɪv] *adj* burlón/ona.

derisory [dɪ'raɪzərɪ] *adj* (*sum*) irrisorio; (*laughter*, *person*) burlón/ona, irónico.

derivation [derɪ'veɪʃən] *n* derivación *f*.

derivative [dɪ'rɪvətɪv] *n* derivado ♦ *adj* (*work*) poco original.

derive [dɪ'raɪv] *vt* derivar ♦ *vi*: **to ~ from** derivarse de.

derived [dɪ'raɪvd] *adj* derivado.

dermatitis [dəːmə'taɪtɪs] *n* dermatitis *f*.

dermatology [dəːmə'tɔlədʒɪ] *n* dermatología.

derogatory [dɪ'rɔgətərɪ] *adj* despectivo.

derrick ['derɪk] *n* torre *f* de perforación.

derv [dəːv] *n* (*BRIT*) gasoil *m*.

DES *n abbr* (*BRIT*: = *Department of Education and Science*) ministerio de educación y ciencia.

descend [dɪ'send] *vt*, *vi* descender, bajar; **to ~ from** descender de; **in ~ing order of importance** de mayor a menor importancia.

▶**descend on** *vt fus* (*subj*: *enemy*, *angry person*) caer sobre; (: *misfortune*) sobrevenir; (*fig*: *gloom*, *silence*) invadir; **visitors ~ed (up)on us** las visitas nos invadieron.

descendant [dɪ'sendənt] *n* descendiente *m/f*.

descent [dɪ'sent] *n* descenso; (*GEO*) pendiente *f*, declive *m*; (*origin*) descendencia.

describe [dɪs'kraɪb] *vt* describir.

description [dɪs'krɪpʃən] *n* descripción *f*; (*sort*) clase *f*, género; **of every ~** de toda clase.

descriptive [dɪs'krɪptɪv] *adj* descriptivo.

desecrate ['desɪkreɪt] *vt* profanar.

desegregation [diːsegrɪ'geɪʃən] *n* desegregación *f*.

desert ['dezət] *n* desierto ♦ *vb* [dɪ'zəːt] *vt* abandonar, desamparar ♦ *vi* (*MIL*) desertar; *see also* **deserts**.

deserter [dɪ'zəːtə*] *n* desertor(a) *m/f*.

desertion [dɪ'zəːʃən] *n* deserción *f*.

desert island *n* isla desierta.

deserts [dɪ'zəːts] *npl*: **to get one's just ~** llevarse su merecido.

deserve [dɪ'zəːv] *vt* merecer, ser digno de, ameritar (*LAM*).

deservedly [dɪ'zəːvɪdlɪ] *adv* con razón.

deserving [dɪ'zəːvɪŋ] *adj* (*person*) digno; (*action*, *cause*) meritorio.

desiccated ['desɪkeɪtɪd] *adj* desecado.

design [dɪ'zaɪn] *n* (*sketch*) bosquejo; (*of dress*, *car*) diseño; (*pattern*) dibujo ♦ *vt* (*gen*) diseñar; **industrial ~** diseño industrial; **to have ~s on sb** tener la(s) mira(s) puesta(s) en algn; **to be ~ed for sb/sth** estar hecho para algn/algo.

designate ['dezɪgneɪt] *vt* (*appoint*) nombrar; (*destine*) designar ♦ *adj* ['dezɪgnɪt] designado.

designation [dezɪg'neɪʃən] *n* (*appointment*) nombramiento; (*name*) denominación *f*.

designer [dɪ'zaɪnə*] *n* diseñador(a) *m/f*; (*fashion ~*) modisto/a.

desirability [dɪzaɪərə'bɪlɪtɪ] *n* ventaja, atractivo.

desirable [dɪ'zaɪərəbl] *adj* (*proper*) deseable; (*attractive*) atractivo; **it is ~ that** es conveniente que.

desire [dɪ'zaɪə*] *n* deseo ♦ *vt* desear; **to ~ sth/to do sth/that** desear algo/hacer algo/que.

desirous [dɪ'zaɪərəs] *adj* deseoso.

desist [dɪ'zɪst] *vi*: **to ~ (from)** desistir (de).

desk [desk] *n* (*in office*) escritorio; (*for pupil*) pupitre *m*; (*in hotel*, *at airport*) recepción *f*; (*BRIT*: *in shop*, *restaurant*) caja.

desktop computer ['desktɔp] *n* ordenador *m* de sobremesa.

desktop publishing ['desktɔp-] *n* autoedición *f*.

desolate ['desəlɪt] *adj* (*place*) desierto; (*person*) afligido.

desolation [desə'leɪʃən] *n* (*of place*) desolación *f*; (*of person*) aflicción *f*.

despair [dɪs'peə*] *n* desesperación *f* ♦ *vi*: **to ~ of** desesperar de; **in ~** desesperado.

despatch [dɪs'pætʃ] *n*, *vt* = **dispatch**.

desperate ['despərɪt] *adj* desesperado; (*fugitive*) peligroso; (*measures*) extremo; **we are getting ~** estamos al borde de desesperación

desperately ['despərɪtlɪ] *adv* desesperadamente; (*very*) terriblemente, gravemente; **~ ill** gravemente enfermo.

desperation [dɛspə'reɪʃən] n desesperación
f; **in** ~ desesperado.
despicable [dɪs'pɪkəbl] adj vil,
despreciable.
despise [dɪs'paɪz] vt despreciar.
despite [dɪs'paɪt] prep a pesar de, pese a.
despondent [dɪs'pɔndənt] adj deprimido,
abatido.
despot ['dɛspɔt] n déspota m/f.
dessert [dɪ'zəːt] n postre m.
dessertspoon [dɪ'zəːtspuːn] n cuchara (de
postre).
destabilize [diː'steɪbɪlaɪz] vt desestabilizar.
destination [dɛstɪ'neɪʃən] n destino.
destine ['dɛstɪn] vt destinar.
destined ['dɛstɪnd] adj: ~ **for London** con
destino a Londres.
destiny ['dɛstɪnɪ] n destino.
destitute ['dɛstɪtjuːt] adj desamparado,
indigente.
destitution [dɛstɪ'tjuːʃən] n indigencia,
miseria.
destroy [dɪs'trɔɪ] vt destruir; (finish) acabar
con.
destroyer [dɪs'trɔɪə*] n (NAUT) destructor
m.
destruction [dɪs'trʌkʃən] n destrucción f;
(fig) ruina.
destructive [dɪs'trʌktɪv] adj destructivo,
destructor(a).
desultory ['dɛsəltərɪ] adj (reading) poco
metódico; (conversation) inconexo;
(contact) intermitente.
detach [dɪ'tætʃ] vt separar; (unstick)
despegar.
detachable [dɪ'tætʃəbl] adj separable;
(TECH) desmontable.
detached [dɪ'tætʃt] adj (attitude) objetivo,
imparcial.
detached house n chalé m, chalet m.
detachment [dɪ'tætʃmənt] n separación f;
(MIL) destacamento; (fig) objetividad f,
imparcialidad f.
detail ['diːteɪl] n detalle m; (MIL)
destacamento ♦ vt detallar; (MIL)
destacar; **in** ~ detalladamente; **to go into**
~(s) entrar en detalles.
detailed ['diːteɪld] adj detallado.
detain [dɪ'teɪn] vt retener; (in captivity)
detener.
detainee [diːteɪ'niː] n detenido/a.
detect [dɪ'tɛkt] vt (discover) descubrir;
(MED, POLICE) identificar; (MIL, RADAR,
TECH) detectar; (notice) percibir.
detection [dɪ'tɛkʃən] n descubrimiento,
identificación f; **crime** ~ investigación f;
to escape ~ (criminal) escaparse sin ser
descubierto; (mistake) pasar inadvertido.

detective [dɪ'tɛktɪv] n detective m.
detective story n novela policíaca.
detector [dɪ'tɛktə*] n detector m.
détente [deɪ'taːnt] n distensión f, detente f.
detention [dɪ'tɛnʃən] n detención f,
arresto.
deter [dɪ'təː*] vt (dissuade) disuadir;
(prevent) impedir; **to** ~ **sb from doing sth**
disuadir a algn de que haga algo.
detergent [dɪ'təːdʒənt] n detergente m.
deteriorate [dɪ'tɪərɪəreɪt] vi deteriorarse.
deterioration [dɪtɪərɪə'reɪʃən] n deterioro.
determination [dɪtəːmɪ'neɪʃən] n
resolución f.
determine [dɪ'təːmɪn] vt determinar; **to** ~
to do sth decidir hacer algo.
determined [dɪ'təːmɪnd] adj: **to be** ~ **to do**
sth estar decidido or resuelto a hacer
algo; **a** ~ **effort** un esfuerzo enérgico.
deterrence [dɪ'tɛrns] n disuasión f.
deterrent [dɪ'tɛrənt] n fuerza de disuasión;
to act as a ~ servir para prevenir.
detest [dɪ'tɛst] vt aborrecer.
detestable [dɪ'tɛstəbl] adj aborrecible.
dethrone [diː'θrəun] vt destronar.
detonate ['dɛtəneɪt] vi estallar ♦ vt hacer
detonar.
detonator ['dɛtəneɪtə*] n detonador m,
fulminante m.
detour ['diːtuə*] n (gen, US AUT: diversion)
desvío ♦ vt (US: traffic) desviar; **to make a**
~ dar un rodeo.
detract [dɪ'trækt] vt: **to** ~ **from** quitar
mérito a, restar valor a.
detractor [dɪ'træktə*] n detractor(a) m/f.
detriment ['dɛtrɪmənt] n: **to the** ~ **of** en
perjuicio de; **without** ~ **to** sin detrimento
de, sin perjuicio para.
detrimental [dɛtrɪ'mɛntl] adj perjudicial.
deuce [djuːs] n (TENNIS) cuarenta iguales.
devaluation [dɪvælju'eɪʃən] n devaluación
f.
devalue [dɪ'væljuː] vt devaluar.
devastate ['dɛvəsteɪt] vt devastar; **he was**
~**d by the news** las noticias le dejaron
desolado.
devastating ['dɛvəsteɪtɪŋ] adj
devastador(a); (fig) arrollador(a).
devastation [dɛvəs'teɪʃən] n devastación f,
ruina.
develop [dɪ'vɛləp] vt desarrollar; (PHOT)
revelar; (disease) contraer; (habit)
adquirir ♦ vi desarrollarse; (advance)
progresar; **this land is to be** ~**ed** se va a
construir en este terreno; **to** ~ **a taste for**
sth tomar gusto a algo; **to** ~ **into**
transformarse or convertirse en.
developer [dɪ'vɛləpə*] n (property ~)

promotor(a) *m/f*.
developing country *n* país *m* en (vías de) desarrollo.
development [dɪ'vɛləpmənt] *n* desarrollo; (*advance*) progreso; (*of affair, case*) desenvolvimiento; (*of land*) urbanización *f*.
development area *n* zona de fomento *or* desarrollo.
deviant ['diːvɪənt] *adj* anómalo, pervertido.
deviate ['diːvɪeɪt] *vi*: **to ~ (from)** desviarse (de).
deviation [diːvɪ'eɪʃən] *n* desviación *f*.
device [dɪ'vaɪs] *n* (*scheme*) estratagema, recurso; (*apparatus*) aparato, mecanismo; (*explosive ~*) artefacto explosivo.
devil ['dɛvl] *n* diablo, demonio.
devilish ['dɛvlɪʃ] *adj* diabólico.
devil-may-care ['dɛvlmeɪ'kɛə*] *adj* despreocupado.
devil's advocate *n*: **to play (the) ~** hacer de abogado del diablo.
devious ['diːvɪəs] *adj* intricado, enrevesado; (*person*) taimado.
devise [dɪ'vaɪz] *vt* idear, inventar.
devoid [dɪ'vɔɪd] *adj*: **~ of** desprovisto de.
devolution [diːvə'luːʃən] *n* (*POL*) descentralización *f*.
devolve [dɪ'vɔlv] *vi*: **to ~ (up)on** recaer sobre.
devote [dɪ'vəut] *vt*: **to ~ sth to** dedicar algo a.
devoted [dɪ'vəutɪd] *adj* (*loyal*) leal, fiel; **the book is ~ to politics** el libro trata de política.
devotee [dɛvəu'tiː] *n* devoto/a.
devotion [dɪ'vəuʃən] *n* dedicación *f*; (*REL*) devoción *f*.
devour [dɪ'vauə*] *vt* devorar.
devout [dɪ'vaut] *adj* devoto.
dew [djuː] *n* rocío.
dexterity [dɛks'tɛrɪtɪ] *n* destreza.
dext(e)rous ['dɛkstrəs] *adj* (*skilful*) diestro, hábil; (*movement*) ágil.
dg *abbr* (= *decigram*) dg.
diabetes [daɪə'biːtiːz] *n* diabetes *f*.
diabetic [daɪə'bɛtɪk] *n* diabético/a ♦ *adj* diabético; (*chocolate, jam*) para diabéticos.
diabolical [daɪə'bɔlɪkəl] *adj* diabólico; (*col*: *dreadful*) horrendo, horroroso.
diagnose ['daɪəgnəuz] *vt* diagnosticar.
diagnosis, *pl* **diagnoses** [daɪəg'nəusɪs, -siːz] *n* diagnóstico.
diagonal [daɪ'ægənl] *adj* diagonal ♦ *n* diagonal *f*.
diagram ['daɪəgræm] *n* diagrama *m*, esquema *m*.

dial ['daɪəl] *n* esfera; (*of radio*) dial *m*; (: *tuner*) sintonizador *m*; (*of phone*) disco ♦ *vt* (*number*) marcar, discar (*LAM*); **to ~ a wrong number** equivocarse de número; **can I ~ London direct?** ¿puedo marcar un número de Londres directamente?
dial. *abbr* = **dialect**.
dial code *n* (*US*) prefijo.
dialect ['daɪəlɛkt] *n* dialecto.
dialling code ['daɪəlɪŋ-] *n* (*BRIT*) prefijo.
dialling tone *n* (*BRIT*) señal *f or* tono de marcar.
dialogue, (*US*) **dialog** ['daɪəlɔg] *n* diálogo.
dial tone *n* (*US*) señal *f or* tono de marcar.
dialysis [daɪ'ælɪsɪs] *n* diálisis *f*.
diameter [daɪ'æmɪtə*] *n* diámetro.
diametrically [daɪə'mɛtrɪklɪ] *adv*: **~ opposed (to)** diametralmente opuesto (a).
diamond ['daɪəmənd] *n* diamante *m*; **~s** *npl* (*CARDS*) diamantes *mpl*.
diamond ring *n* anillo *or* sortija de diamantes.
diaper ['daɪəpə*] *n* (*US*) pañal *m*.
diaphragm ['daɪəfræm] *n* diafragma *m*.
diarrhoea, (*US*) **diarrhea** [daɪə'riːə] *n* diarrea.
diary ['daɪərɪ] *n* (*daily account*) diario; (*book*) agenda; **to keep a ~** escribir un diario.
diatribe ['daɪətraɪb] *n*: **~ (against)** diatriba (contra).
dice [daɪs] *n*, *pl inv* dados *mpl* ♦ *vt* (*CULIN*) cortar en cuadritos.
dicey ['daɪsɪ] *adj* (*col*): **it's a bit ~** (*risky*) es un poco arriesgado; (*doubtful*) es un poco dudoso.
dichotomy [daɪ'kɔtəmɪ] *n* dicotomía.
dickhead ['dɪkhɛd] *n* (*BRIT col!*) gilipollas *m inv*.
Dictaphone ® ['dɪktəfəun] *n* dictáfono ®.
dictate [dɪk'teɪt] *vt* dictar ♦ *n* ['dɪkteɪt] dictado.
▶**dictate to** *vt fus* (*person*) dar órdenes a; **I won't be ~d to** no recibo órdenes de nadie.
dictation [dɪk'teɪʃən] *n* (*to secretary etc*) dictado; **at ~ speed** para tomar al dictado.
dictator [dɪk'teɪtə*] *n* dictador *m*.
dictatorship [dɪk'teɪtəʃɪp] *n* dictadura.
diction ['dɪkʃən] *n* dicción *f*.
dictionary ['dɪkʃənrɪ] *n* diccionario.
did [dɪd] *pt of* **do**.
didactic [daɪ'dæktɪk] *adj* didáctico.
diddle ['dɪdl] *vt* estafar, timar.
didn't ['dɪdnt] = **did not**.
die [daɪ] *vi* morir; **to ~ (of or from)** morirse (de); **to be dying** morirse, estar muriéndose; **to be dying for sth/to do sth**

morirse por algo/de ganas de hacer algo.
►**die away** vi (sound, light) desvanecerse.
►**die down** vi (gen) apagarse; (wind)
amainar.
►**die out** vi desaparecer, extinguirse.
diehard ['daɪhɑːd] n intransigente m/f.
diesel ['diːzl] n diesel m.
diesel engine n motor m diesel.
diesel fuel, diesel oil n gas-oil m.
diet ['daɪət] n dieta; (restricted food)
régimen m ♦ vi (also: be on a ~) estar a
dieta, hacer régimen; to live on a ~ of
alimentarse de.
dietician [daɪə'tɪʃən] n dietista m/f.
differ ['dɪfə*] vi (be different) ser distinto,
diferenciarse; (disagree) discrepar.
difference ['dɪfrəns] n diferencia; (quarrel)
desacuerdo; **it makes no ~ to me** me da
igual or lo mismo; **to settle one's ~s**
arreglarse.
different ['dɪfrənt] adj diferente, distinto.
differential [dɪfə'renʃəl] n diferencial f.
differentiate [dɪfə'renʃɪeɪt] vt distinguir
♦ vi diferenciarse; **to ~ between**
distinguir entre.
differently ['dɪfrəntlɪ] adv de otro modo, en
forma distinta.
difficult ['dɪfɪkəlt] adj difícil; **~ to
understand** difícil de entender.
difficulty ['dɪfɪkəltɪ] n dificultad f; **to have
difficulties with** (police, landlord etc) tener
problemas con; **to be in ~** estar en
apuros.
diffidence ['dɪfɪdəns] n timidez f, falta de
confianza en sí mismo.
diffident ['dɪfɪdənt] adj tímido.
diffuse [dɪ'fjuːs] adj difuso ♦ vt [dɪ'fjuːz]
difundir.
dig [dɪg] vt (pt, pp **dug** [dʌg]) (hole) cavar;
(ground) remover; (coal) extraer; (nails
etc) hincar ♦ n (prod) empujón m;
(archaeological) excavación f; (remark)
indirecta; **to ~ into** (savings) consumir; **to
~ one's pockets for sth** hurgar en el
bolsillo buscando algo; **to ~ one's nails
into** clavar las uñas en; see also **digs**.
►**dig in** vi (also: ~ o.s. in: MIL)
atrincherarse; (col: eat) hincar los
dientes ♦ vt (compost) añadir al suelo;
(knife, claw) clavar; **to ~ in one's heels**
(fig) mantenerse en sus trece.
►**dig out** vt (hole) excavar; (survivors, car
from snow) sacar.
►**dig up** vt desenterrar; (plant)
desarraigar.
digest [daɪ'dʒest] vt (food) digerir; (facts)
asimilar ♦ n ['daɪdʒest] resumen m.
digestible [daɪ'dʒestəbl] adj digerible.

digestion [dɪ'dʒestʃən] n digestión f.
digestive [daɪ'dʒestɪv] adj (juices, system)
digestivo.
digit ['dɪdʒɪt] n (number) dígito; (finger)
dedo.
digital ['dɪdʒɪtl] adj digital.
digital camera n cámara digital.
digital compact cassette n cas(s)et(t)e m
or f digital compacto.
digital TV n televisión f digital.
dignified ['dɪgnɪfaɪd] adj grave, solemne;
(action) decoroso.
dignify ['dɪgnɪfaɪ] vt dignificar.
dignitary ['dɪgnɪtərɪ] n dignatario/a.
dignity ['dɪgnɪtɪ] n dignidad f.
digress [daɪ'gres] vi: **to ~ from** apartarse
de.
digression [daɪ'greʃən] n digresión f.
digs [dɪgz] npl (BRIT: col) alojamiento.
dike [daɪk] n = **dyke**.
dilapidated [dɪ'læpɪdeɪtɪd] adj
desmoronado, ruinoso.
dilate [daɪ'leɪt] vt dilatar ♦ vi dilatarse.
dilatory ['dɪlətərɪ] adj (person) lento; (action)
dilatorio.
dilemma [daɪ'lemə] n dilema m; **to be in a ~**
estar en un dilema.
dilettante [dɪlɪ'tæntɪ] n diletante m/f.
diligence ['dɪlɪdʒəns] n diligencia.
diligent ['dɪlɪdʒənt] adj diligente.
dill [dɪl] n eneldo.
dilly-dally ['dɪlɪ'dælɪ] vi (hesitate) vacilar;
(dawdle) entretenerse.
dilute [daɪ'luːt] vt diluir.
dim [dɪm] adj (light) débil; (sight) turbio;
(outline) borroso; (stupid) lerdo; (room)
oscuro ♦ vt (light) bajar; **to take a ~ view
of sth** tener una pobre opinión de algo.
dime [daɪm] n (US) moneda de diez
centavos.
dimension [dɪ'menʃən] n dimensión f.
-dimensional [dɪ'menʃənl] adj suff: **two~** de
dos dimensiones.
dimensions [dɪ'menʃənz] npl dimensiones
fpl.
diminish [dɪ'mɪnɪʃ] vt, vi disminuir.
diminished [dɪ'mɪnɪʃt] adj: **~ responsibility**
(LAW) responsabilidad f disminuida.
diminutive [dɪ'mɪnjutɪv] adj diminuto ♦ n
(LING) diminutivo.
dimly ['dɪmlɪ] adv débilmente; (not clearly)
vagamente.
dimmer ['dɪmə*] n (also: ~ **switch**)
regulador m (de intensidad); (US AUT)
interruptor m.
dimple ['dɪmpl] n hoyuelo.
dimwitted ['dɪm'wɪtɪd] adj (col) lerdo, de
pocas luces.

din [dɪn] n estruendo, estrépito ♦ vt: **to ~ sth into sb** (col) meter algo en la cabeza a algn.

dine [daɪn] vi cenar.

diner ['daɪnə*] n (person: in restaurant) comensal m/f; (BRIT RAIL) = **dining car**; (US) restaurante económico.

dinghy ['dɪŋɡɪ] n bote m; (also: **rubber ~**) lancha (neumática).

dingy ['dɪndʒɪ] adj (room) sombrío; (dirty) sucio; (dull) deslucido.

dining car ['daɪnɪŋ-] n (BRIT) coche-restaurante m.

dining room ['daɪnɪŋ-] n comedor m.

dinner ['dɪnə*] n (evening meal) cena, comida (LAM); (lunch) comida; (public) cena, banquete m; ~ **'s ready!** ¡la cena está servida!

dinner jacket n smoking m.

dinner party n cena.

dinner time n hora de cenar or comer.

dinosaur ['daɪnəsɔ:*] n dinosaurio.

dint [dɪnt] n: **by ~ of (doing) sth** a fuerza de (hacer) algo.

diocese ['daɪəsɪs] n diócesis f.

dioxide [daɪ'ɔksaɪd] n bióxido; **carbon ~** bióxido de carbono.

Dip. abbr (BRIT) = **diploma**.

dip [dɪp] n (slope) pendiente f; (in sea) chapuzón m ♦ vt (in water) mojar; (ladle etc) meter; (BRIT AUT): **to ~ one's lights** poner la luz de cruce ♦ vi inclinarse hacia abajo.

diphtheria [dɪf'θɪərɪə] n difteria.

diphthong ['dɪfθɒŋ] n diptongo.

diploma [dɪ'pləumə] n diploma m.

diplomacy [dɪ'pləuməsɪ] n diplomacia.

diplomat ['dɪpləmæt] n diplomático/a m/f.

diplomatic [dɪplə'mætɪk] adj diplomático; **to break off ~ relations** romper las relaciones diplomáticas.

diplomatic corps n cuerpo diplomático.

diplomatic immunity n inmunidad f diplomática.

dipstick ['dɪpstɪk] n (AUT) varilla de nivel (del aceite).

dipswitch ['dɪpswɪtʃ] n (BRIT AUT) interruptor m.

dire [daɪə*] adj calamitoso.

direct [daɪ'rɛkt] adj (gen) directo; (manner, person) franco ♦ vt dirigir; **can you ~ me to...?** ¿puede indicarme dónde está...?; **to ~ sb to do sth** mandar a algn hacer algo.

direct access n (COMPUT) acceso directo.

direct cost n costo directo.

direct current n corriente f continua.

direct debit n domiciliación f bancaria de recibos; **to pay by ~** domiciliar el pago.

direct dialling n servicio automático de llamadas.

direction [dɪ'rɛkʃən] n dirección f; **sense of ~** sentido de la orientación; **~s** npl (advice) órdenes fpl, instrucciones fpl; (to a place) señas fpl; **in the ~ of** hacia, en dirección a; **~s for use** modo de empleo; **to ask for ~s** preguntar el camino.

directional [dɪ'rɛkʃənl] adj direccional.

directive [daɪ'rɛktɪv] n orden f, instrucción f; **a government ~** una orden del gobierno.

direct labour n mano f de obra directa.

directly [dɪ'rɛktlɪ] adv (in straight line) directamente; (at once) en seguida.

direct mail n correspondencia personalizada.

direct mailshot n (BRIT) promoción f por correspondencia personalizada.

directness [dɪ'rɛktnɪs] n (of person, speech) franqueza.

director [dɪ'rɛktə*] n director(a) m/f; **managing ~** director(a) m/f gerente.

Director of Public Prosecutions n ≈ fiscal m/f general del Estado.

directory [dɪ'rɛktərɪ] n (TEL) guía (telefónica); (street ~) callejero; (trade ~) directorio de comercio; (COMPUT) directorio.

directory enquiries, (US) **directory assistance** n (service) (servicio de) información f.

dirt [də:t] n suciedad f.

dirt-cheap ['də:t'tʃi:p] adj baratísimo.

dirt road n (US) camino sin firme.

dirty ['də:tɪ] adj sucio; (joke) verde, colorado (LAM) ♦ vt ensuciar; (stain) manchar.

dirty trick n mala jugada, truco sucio.

disability [dɪsə'bɪlɪtɪ] n incapacidad f.

disability allowance n pensión f de invalidez.

disable [dɪs'eɪbl] vt (subj: illness, accident) dejar incapacitado or inválido; (tank, gun) inutilizar; (LAW: disqualify) incapacitar.

disabled [dɪs'eɪbld] adj minusválido.

disabuse [dɪsə'bju:z] vt desengañar.

disadvantage [dɪsəd'vɑ:ntɪdʒ] n desventaja, inconveniente m.

disadvantaged [dɪsəd'vɑ:ntɪdʒd] adj (person) desventajado.

disadvantageous [dɪsædvən'teɪdʒəs] adj desventajoso.

disaffected [dɪsə'fɛktɪd] adj descontento; **to be ~ (to or towards)** estar descontento (de).

disaffection [dɪsə'fɛkʃən] n desafecto, descontento.

disagree [dɪsə'griː] *vi* (*differ*) discrepar; **to ~ (with)** no estar de acuerdo (con); **I ~ with you** no estoy de acuerdo contigo.

disagreeable [dɪsə'grɪəbl] *adj* desagradable.

disagreement [dɪsə'griːmənt] *n* (*gen*) desacuerdo; (*quarrel*) riña; **to have a ~ with sb** estar en desacuerdo con algn.

disallow ['dɪsə'lau] *vt* (*goal*) anular; (*claim*) rechazar.

disappear [dɪsə'pɪə*] *vi* desaparecer.

disappearance [dɪsə'pɪərəns] *n* desaparición *f*.

disappoint [dɪsə'pɔɪnt] *vt* decepcionar; (*hopes*) defraudar.

disappointed [dɪsə'pɔɪntɪd] *adj* decepcionado.

disappointing [dɪsə'pɔɪntɪŋ] *adj* decepcionante.

disappointment [dɪsə'pɔɪntmənt] *n* decepción *f*.

disapproval [dɪsə'pruːvəl] *n* desaprobación *f*.

disapprove [dɪsə'pruːv] *vi*: **to ~ of** desaprobar.

disapproving [dɪsə'pruːvɪŋ] *adj* de desaprobación, desaprobador(a).

disarm [dɪs'ɑːm] *vt* desarmar.

disarmament [dɪs'ɑːməmənt] *n* desarme *m*.

disarmament talks *npl* conversaciones *fpl* de *or* sobre desarme.

disarming [dɪs'ɑːmɪŋ] *adj* (*smile*) que desarma, encantador(a).

disarray [dɪsə'reɪ] *n*: **in ~** (*troops*) desorganizado; (*thoughts*) confuso; (*hair, clothes*) desarreglado; **to throw into ~** provocar el caos.

disaster [dɪ'zɑːstə*] *n* desastre *m*.

disaster area *n* zona catastrófica.

disastrous [dɪ'zɑːstrəs] *adj* desastroso.

disband [dɪs'bænd] *vt* disolver ♦ *vi* desbandarse.

disbelief [dɪsbə'liːf] *n* incredulidad *f*; **in ~** con incredulidad.

disbelieve ['dɪsbə'liːv] *vt* (*person, story*) poner en duda, no creer.

disc [dɪsk] *n* disco; (*COMPUT*) = **disk**.

disc. *abbr* (*COMM*) = **discount**.

discard [dɪs'kɑːd] *vt* (*old things*) tirar; (*fig*) descartar.

discern [dɪ'sɔːn] *vt* percibir, discernir; (*understand*) comprender.

discernible [dɪ'sɔːnəbl] *adj* perceptible.

discerning [dɪ'sɔːnɪŋ] *adj* perspicaz.

discharge [dɪs'tʃɑːdʒ] *vt* (*task, duty*) cumplir; (*ship etc*) descargar; (*patient*) dar de alta; (*employee*) despedir; (*soldier*) licenciar; (*defendant*) poner en libertad;

(*settle: debt*) saldar ♦ *n* ['dɪstʃɑːdʒ] (*ELEC*) descarga; (*vaginal ~*) emisión *f* vaginal; (*dismissal*) despedida; (*of duty*) desempeño; (*of debt*) pago, descargo; (*of gas, chemicals*) escape *m*; **~d bankrupt** quebrado/a rehabilitado/a.

disciple [dɪ'saɪpl] *n* discípulo/a.

disciplinary ['dɪsɪplɪnərɪ] *adj*: **to take ~ action against sb** disciplinar a algn.

discipline ['dɪsɪplɪn] *n* disciplina ♦ *vt* disciplinar; **to ~ o.s. to do sth** obligarse a hacer algo.

disc jockey (DJ) *n* pinchadiscos *m/f inv*.

disclaim [dɪs'kleɪm] *vt* negar tener.

disclaimer [dɪs'kleɪmə*] *n* rectificación *f*; **to issue a ~** hacer una rectificación.

disclose [dɪs'kləuz] *vt* revelar.

disclosure [dɪs'kləuʒə*] *n* revelación *f*.

disco ['dɪskəu] *n abbr* = **discothèque**.

discolouration, (*US*) **discoloration** [dɪskʌlə'reɪʃən] *n* descoloramiento, decoloración *f*.

discolo(u)red [dɪs'kʌləd] *adj* descolorido.

discomfort [dɪs'kʌmfət] *n* incomodidad *f*; (*unease*) inquietud *f*; (*physical*) malestar *m*.

disconcert [dɪskən'sɔːt] *vt* desconcertar.

disconnect [dɪskə'nɛkt] *vt* (*gen*) separar; (*ELEC etc*) desconectar; (*supply*) cortar (el suministro) a.

disconsolate [dɪs'kɔnsəlɪt] *adj* desconsolado.

discontent [dɪskən'tɛnt] *n* descontento.

discontented [dɪskən'tɛntɪd] *adj* descontento.

discontinue [dɪskən'tɪnjuː] *vt* interrumpir; (*payments*) suspender.

discord ['dɪskɔːd] *n* discordia; (*MUS*) disonancia.

discordant [dɪs'kɔːdənt] *adj* disonante.

discothèque ['dɪskəutɛk] *n* discoteca.

discount ['dɪskaunt] *n* descuento ♦ *vt* [dɪs'kaunt] descontar; (*report etc*) descartar; **at a ~** con descuento; **~ for cash** descuento por pago en efectivo; **to give sb a ~ on sth** hacer un descuento a algn en algo.

discount house *n* (*FINANCE*) banco de descuento; (*COMM: also:* **discount store**) ≈ tienda de saldos.

discount rate *n* (*COMM*) tipo de descuento.

discount store *n* ≈ tienda de saldos.

discourage [dɪs'kʌrɪdʒ] *vt* desalentar; (*oppose*) oponerse a; (*dissuade, deter*) desanimar, disuadir.

discouragement [dɪs'kʌrɪdʒmənt] *n* (*dissuasion*) disuasión *f*; (*depression*) desánimo, desaliento; **to act as a ~ to**

servir para disuadir.
discouraging [dɪs'kʌrɪdʒɪŋ] *adj*
desalentador(a).
discourteous [dɪs'kə:tɪəs] *adj* descortés.
discover [dɪs'kʌvə*] *vt* descubrir.
discovery [dɪs'kʌvərɪ] *n* descubrimiento.
discredit [dɪs'krɛdɪt] *vt* desacreditar.
discreet [dɪ'skri:t] *adj* (*tactful*) discreto;
(*careful*) circunspecto, prudente.
discreetly [dɪ'skri:tlɪ] *adv* discretamente.
discrepancy [dɪ'skrɛpənsɪ] *n* (*difference*)
diferencia; (*disagreement*) discrepancia.
discretion [dɪ'skrɛʃən] *n* (*tact*) discreción *f*;
(*care*) prudencia, circunspección *f*; **use
your own** ~ haz lo que creas oportuno.
discretionary [dɪ'skrɛʃənrɪ] *adj* (*powers*)
discrecional.
discriminate [dɪ'skrɪmɪneɪt] *vi*: **to** ~
between distinguir entre; **to** ~ **against**
discriminar contra.
discriminating [dɪ'skrɪmɪneɪtɪŋ] *adj*
entendido.
discrimination [dɪskrɪmɪ'neɪʃən] *n*
(*discernment*) perspicacia; (*bias*)
discriminación *f*; **racial/sexual** ~
discriminación racial/sexual.
discus ['dɪskəs] *n* disco.
discuss [dɪ'skʌs] *vt* (*gen*) discutir; (*a theme*)
tratar.
discussion [dɪ'skʌʃən] *n* discusión *f*; **under**
~ en discusión.
disdain [dɪs'deɪn] *n* desdén *m* ♦ *vt* desdeñar.
disease [dɪ'zi:z] *n* enfermedad *f*.
diseased [dɪ'zi:zd] *adj* enfermo.
disembark [dɪsɪm'bɑ:k] *vt, vi* desembarcar.
disembarkation [dɪsɛmbɑ:'keɪʃən] *n*
desembarque *m*.
disenchanted [dɪsɪn'tʃɑ:ntɪd] *adj*: ~ (**with**)
desilusionado (con).
disenfranchise ['dɪsɪn'fræntʃaɪz] *vt* privar
del derecho al voto; (*COMM*) privar de
franquicias.
disengage [dɪsɪn'geɪdʒ] *vt* soltar; **to** ~ **the
clutch** (*AUT*) desembragar.
disentangle [dɪsɪn'tæŋgl] *vt* desenredar.
disfavour, (*US*) **disfavor** [dɪs'feɪvə*] *n*
desaprobación *f*.
disfigure [dɪs'fɪgə*] *vt* desfigurar.
disgorge [dɪs'gɔ:dʒ] *vt* verter.
disgrace [dɪs'greɪs] *n* ignominia; (*downfall*)
caída; (*shame*) vergüenza, escándalo ♦ *vt*
deshonrar.
disgraceful [dɪs'greɪsful] *adj* vergonzoso;
(*behaviour*) escandaloso.
disgruntled [dɪs'grʌntld] *adj* disgustado,
descontento.
disguise [dɪs'gaɪz] *n* disfraz *m* ♦ *vt*
disfrazar; (*voice*) disimular; (*feelings etc*)

ocultar; **in** ~ disfrazado; **to** ~ **o.s. as**
disfrazarse de; **there's no disguising the
fact that** ... no puede ocultarse el hecho
de que ....
disgust [dɪs'gʌst] *n* repugnancia ♦ *vt*
repugnar, dar asco a.
disgusting [dɪs'gʌstɪŋ] *adj* repugnante,
asqueroso.
dish [dɪʃ] *n* (*gen*) plato; **to do** *or* **wash the**
~**es** fregar los platos.
▶**dish out** *vt* (*money, exam papers*)
repartir; (*food*) servir; (*advice*) dar.
▶**dish up** *vt* servir.
dishcloth ['dɪʃklɔθ] *n* paño de cocina,
bayeta.
dishearten [dɪs'hɑ:tn] *vt* desalentar.
dishevelled, (*US*) **disheveled** [dɪ'ʃɛvəld]
adj (*hair*) despeinado; (*clothes, appearance*)
desarreglado.
dishonest [dɪs'ɔnɪst] *adj* (*person*) poco
honrado, tramposo; (*means*) fraudulento.
dishonesty [dɪs'ɔnɪstɪ] *n* falta de honradez.
dishonour, (*US*) **dishonor** [dɪs'ɔnə*] *n*
deshonra.
dishono(u)rable [dɪs'ɔnərəbl] *adj*
deshonroso.
dish soap *n* (*US*) lavavajillas *m inv*.
dishtowel ['dɪʃtauəl] *n* (*US*) trapo de
fregar.
dishwasher ['dɪʃwɔʃə*] *n* lavaplatos *m inv*;
(*person*) friegaplatos *m/f inv*.
dishy ['dɪʃɪ] *adj* (*BRIT col*) buenón/ona.
disillusion [dɪsɪ'lu:ʒən] *vt* desilusionar; **to
become** ~**ed** (**with**) quedar desilusionado
(con).
disillusionment [dɪsɪ'lu:ʒənmənt] *n*
desilusión *f*.
disincentive [dɪsɪn'sɛntɪv] *n* freno; **to act
as a** ~ (**to**) actuar de freno (a); **to be a** ~
to ser un freno a.
disinclined ['dɪsɪn'klaɪnd] *adj*: **to be** ~ **to do
sth** estar poco dispuesto a hacer algo.
disinfect [dɪsɪn'fɛkt] *vt* desinfectar.
disinfectant [dɪsɪn'fɛktənt] *n* desinfectante
m.
disinflation [dɪsɪn'fleɪʃən] *n* desinflación *f*.
disinformation [dɪsɪnfə'meɪʃən] *n*
desinformación *f*.
disingenuous [dɪsɪn'dʒɛnjuəs] *adj* poco
sincero, falso.
disinherit [dɪsɪn'hɛrɪt] *vt* desheredar.
disintegrate [dɪs'ɪntɪgreɪt] *vi* disgregarse,
desintegrarse.
disinterested [dɪs'ɪntrəstɪd] *adj*
desinteresado.
disjointed [dɪs'dʒɔɪntɪd] *adj* inconexo.
disk [dɪsk] *n* (*COMPUT*) disco, disquete *m*;
single-/double-sided ~ disco de una

cara/dos caras.

disk drive *n* disc drive *m*.

diskette [dɪs'kɛt] *n* diskette *m*, disquete *m*, disco flexible.

disk operating system (DOS) *n* sistema *m* operativo de discos (DOS).

dislike [dɪs'laɪk] *n* antipatía, aversión *f* ♦ *vt* tener antipatía a; **to take a ~ to sb/sth** cogerle *or* agarrarle (*LAM*) antipatía a algn/algo; **I ~ the idea** no me gusta la idea.

dislocate ['dɪsləkeɪt] *vt* dislocar; **he ~d his shoulder** se dislocó el hombro.

dislodge [dɪs'lɔdʒ] *vt* sacar; (*enemy*) desalojar.

disloyal [dɪs'lɔɪəl] *adj* desleal.

dismal ['dɪzml] *adj* (*dark*) sombrío; (*depressing*) triste; (*very bad*) fatal.

dismantle [dɪs'mæntl] *vt* desmontar, desarmar.

dismay [dɪs'meɪ] *n* consternación *f* ♦ *vt* consternar; **much to my ~** para gran consternación mía.

dismiss [dɪs'mɪs] *vt* (*worker*) despedir; (*official*) destituir; (*idea, LAW*) rechazar; (*possibility*) descartar ♦ *vi* (*MIL*) romper filas.

dismissal [dɪs'mɪsl] *n* despedida; destitución *f*.

dismount [dɪs'maunt] *vi* apearse; (*rider*) desmontar.

disobedience [dɪsə'biːdɪəns] *n* desobediencia.

disobedient [dɪsə'biːdɪənt] *adj* desobediente.

disobey [dɪsə'beɪ] *vt* desobedecer; (*rule*) infringir.

disorder [dɪs'ɔːdə*] *n* desorden *m*; (*rioting*) disturbio; (*MED*) trastorno; (*disease*) enfermedad *f*; **civil ~** desorden *m* civil.

disorderly [dɪs'ɔːdəlɪ] *adj* (*untidy*) desordenado; (*meeting*) alborotado; **~ conduct** (*LAW*) conducta escandalosa.

disorganized [dɪs'ɔːgənaɪzd] *adj* desorganizado.

disorientated [dɪs'ɔːrɪɛnteɪtəd] *adj* desorientado.

disown [dɪs'əun] *vt* renegar de.

disparaging [dɪs'pærɪdʒɪŋ] *adj* despreciativo; **to be ~ about sth/sb** menospreciar algo/a algn.

disparate ['dɪspərɪt] *adj* dispar.

disparity [dɪs'pærɪtɪ] *n* disparidad *f*.

dispassionate [dɪs'pæʃənɪt] *adj* (*unbiased*) imparcial; (*unemotional*) desapasionado.

dispatch [dɪs'pætʃ] *vt* enviar; (*kill*) despachar; (*deal with: business*) despachar ♦ *n* (*sending*) envío; (*speed*)

prontitud *f*; (*PRESS*) informe *m*; (*MIL*) parte *m*.

dispatch department *n* (*COMM*) departamento de envíos.

dispatch rider *n* (*MIL*) correo.

dispel [dɪs'pɛl] *vt* disipar, dispersar.

dispensary [dɪs'pɛnsərɪ] *n* dispensario.

dispensation [dɪspɛn'seɪʃən] *n* (*REL*) dispensa.

dispense [dɪs'pɛns] *vt* dispensar, repartir; (*medicine*) preparar.

▶**dispense with** *vt fus* (*make unnecessary*) prescindir de.

dispenser [dɪs'pɛnsə*] *n* (*container*) distribuidor *m* automático.

dispensing chemist [dɪs'pɛnsɪŋ-] *n* (*BRIT*) farmacia.

dispersal [dɪs'pɔːsl] *n* dispersión *f*.

disperse [dɪs'pɔːs] *vt* dispersar ♦ *vi* dispersarse.

dispirited [dɪ'spɪrɪtɪd] *adj* desanimado, desalentado.

displace [dɪs'pleɪs] *vt* (*person*) desplazar; (*replace*) reemplazar.

displaced person *n* (*POL*) desplazado/a.

displacement [dɪs'pleɪsmənt] *n* cambio de sitio.

display [dɪs'pleɪ] *n* (*exhibition*) exposición *f*; (*COMPUT*) visualización *f*; (*MIL*) desfile *m*; (*of feeling*) manifestación *f*; (*pej*) aparato, pompa ♦ *vt* exponer; manifestar; (*ostentatiously*) lucir; **on ~** (*exhibits*) expuesto, exhibido; (*goods*) en el escaparate.

display advertising *n* publicidad *f* gráfica.

displease [dɪs'pliːz] *vt* (*offend*) ofender; (*annoy*) fastidiar; **~d with** disgustado con.

displeasure [dɪs'plɛʒə*] *n* disgusto.

disposable [dɪs'pəuzəbl] *adj* (*not reusable*) desechable; **~ personal income** ingresos *mpl* personales disponibles.

disposable nappy *n* pañal *m* desechable.

disposal [dɪs'pəuzl] *n* (*sale*) venta; (*of house*) traspaso; (*by giving away*) donación *f*; (*arrangement*) colocación *f*; (*of rubbish*) destrucción *f*; **at one's ~** a la disposición de algn; **to put sth at sb's ~** poner algo a disposición de algn.

disposed [dɪs'pəuzd] *adj*: **~ to do** dispuesto a hacer.

dispose of [dɪs'pəuz] *vt fus* (*time, money*) disponer de; (*unwanted goods*) deshacerse de; (*COMM: sell*) traspasar, vender; (*throw away*) tirar.

disposition [dɪspə'zɪʃən] *n* disposición *f*; (*temperament*) carácter *m*.

dispossess ['dɪspə'zɛs] *vt*: **to ~ sb (of)**

desposeer a algn (de).
disproportion [dɪsprə'pɔːʃən] *n*
desproporción *f*.
disproportionate [dɪsprə'pɔːʃənət] *adj*
desproporcionado.
disprove [dɪs'pruːv] *vt* refutar.
dispute [dɪs'pjuːt] *n* disputa; (*verbal*)
discusión *f*; (*also*: **industrial** ~) conflicto
(laboral) ♦ *vt* (*argue*) disputar; (*question*)
cuestionar; **to be in** *or* **under** ~ (*matter*)
discutirse; (*territory*) estar en disputa;
(*JUR*) estar en litigio.
disqualification [dɪskwɔlɪfɪ'keɪʃən] *n*
inhabilitación *f*; (*SPORT, from driving*)
descalificación *f*.
disqualify [dɪs'kwɔlɪfaɪ] *vt* (*SPORT*)
desclasificar; **to** ~ **sb for sth/from doing
sth** incapacitar a algn para algo/hacer
algo.
disquiet [dɪs'kwaɪət] *n* preocupación *f*,
inquietud *f*.
disquieting [dɪs'kwaɪətɪŋ] *adj* inquietante.
disregard [dɪsrɪ'gɑːd] *vt* desatender;
(*ignore*) no hacer caso de ♦ *n* (*indifference*:
to feelings, danger, money): ~ **(for)**
indiferencia (a); ~ **(of)** (*non-observance*: *of
law, rules*) violación *f* (de).
disrepair [dɪsrɪ'pɛə*] *n*: **to fall into** ~
(*building*) desmoronarse; (*street*)
deteriorarse.
disreputable [dɪs'rɛpjutəbl] *adj* (*person,
area*) de mala fama; (*behaviour*)
vergonzoso.
disrepute ['dɪsrɪ'pjuːt] *n* descrédito,
ignominia; **to bring into** ~ desacreditar.
disrespectful [dɪsrɪ'spɛktful] *adj*
irrespetuoso.
disrupt [dɪs'rʌpt] *vt* (*meeting, public
transport, conversation*) interrumpir;
(*plans*) desbaratar, alternar, trastornar.
disruption [dɪs'rʌpʃən] *n* trastorno;
desbaratamiento; interrupción *f*.
disruptive [dɪs'rʌptɪv] *adj* (*influence*)
disruptivo; (*strike action*) perjudicial.
dissatisfaction [dɪssætɪs'fækʃən] *n*
disgusto, descontento.
dissatisfied [dɪs'sætɪsfaɪd] *adj* insatisfecho.
dissect [dɪ'sɛkt] *vt* (*also fig*) disecar.
disseminate [dɪ'sɛmɪneɪt] *vt* divulgar,
difundir.
dissent [dɪ'sɛnt] *n* disensión *f*.
dissenter [dɪ'sɛntə*] *n* (*REL, POL etc*)
disidente *m/f*.
dissertation [dɪsə'teɪʃən] *n* (*UNIV*) tesina;
see also **master's degree**.
disservice [dɪs'səːvɪs] *n*: **to do sb a** ~
perjudicar a alguien.
dissident ['dɪsɪdnt] *adj, n* disidente *m/f*.

dissimilar [dɪ'sɪmɪlə*] *adj* distinto.
dissipate ['dɪsɪpeɪt] *vt* disipar; (*waste*)
desperdiciar.
dissipated ['dɪsɪpeɪtɪd] *adj* disoluto.
dissipation [dɪsɪ'peɪʃən] *n* disipación *f*;
(*moral*) libertinaje *m*, vicio; (*waste*)
derroche *m*.
dissociate [dɪ'səuʃɪeɪt] *vt* disociar; **to** ~ **o.s.
from** disociarse de.
dissolute ['dɪsəluːt] *adj* disoluto.
dissolution [dɪsə'luːʃən] *n* (*of organization,
marriage, POL*) disolución *f*.
dissolve [dɪ'zɔlv] *vt* (*gen, COMM*) disolver
♦ *vi* disolverse.
dissuade [dɪ'sweɪd] *vt*: **to** ~ **sb (from)**
disuadir a algn (de).
distaff ['dɪstæf] *n*: ~ **side** rama femenina.
distance ['dɪstns] *n* distancia; **in the** ~ a lo
lejos; **what** ~ **is it to London?** ¿qué
distancia hay de aquí a Londres?; **it's
within walking** ~ se puede ir andando.
distant ['dɪstnt] *adj* lejano; (*manner*)
reservado, frío.
distaste [dɪs'teɪst] *n* repugnancia.
distasteful [dɪs'teɪstful] *adj* repugnante,
desagradable.
Dist. Atty. *abbr* (*US*) = **district attorney**.
distemper [dɪs'tɛmpə*] *n* (*of dogs*)
moquillo.
distend [dɪ'stɛnd] *vt* dilatar, hinchar ♦ *vi*
dilatarse, hincharse.
distended [dɪ'stɛndɪd] *adj* (*stomach*)
hinchado.
distil, (*US*) **distill** [dɪs'tɪl] *vt* destilar.
distillery [dɪs'tɪlərɪ] *n* destilería.
distinct [dɪs'tɪŋkt] *adj* (*different*) distinto;
(*clear*) claro; (*unmistakeable*) inequívoco;
as ~ **from** a diferencia de.
distinction [dɪs'tɪŋkʃən] *n* distinción *f*; (*in
exam*) sobresaliente *m*; **a writer of** ~ un
escritor destacado; **to draw a** ~ **between**
hacer una distinción entre.
distinctive [dɪs'tɪŋktɪv] *adj* distintivo.
distinctly [dɪs'tɪŋktlɪ] *adv* claramente.
distinguish [dɪs'tɪŋgwɪʃ] *vt* distinguir ♦ *vi*:
to ~ **(between)** distinguir (entre).
distinguished [dɪs'tɪŋgwɪʃt] *adj* (*eminent*)
distinguido; (*career*) eminente; (*refined*)
distinguido, de categoría.
distinguishing [dɪs'tɪŋgwɪʃɪŋ] *adj* (*feature*)
distintivo.
distort [dɪs'tɔːt] *vt* torcer, retorcer;
(*account, news*) desvirtuar, deformar.
distortion [dɪs'tɔːʃən] *n* deformación *f*; (*of
sound*) distorsión *f*; (*of truth etc*)
tergiversación *f*; (*of facts*) falseamiento *m*.
distract [dɪs'trækt] *vt* distraer.
distracted [dɪs'træktɪd] *adj* distraído.

distracting [dɪs'træktɪŋ] *adj* que distrae la atención, molesto.

distraction [dɪs'trækʃən] *n* distracción *f*; (*confusion*) aturdimiento; (*amusement*) diversión *f*; **to drive sb to** ~ (*distress, anxiety*) volver loco a algn.

distraught [dɪs'trɔːt] *adj* turbado, enloquecido.

distress [dɪs'trɛs] *n* (*anguish*) angustia; (*want*) miseria; (*pain*) dolor *m*; (*danger*) peligro ♦ *vt* afligir; (*pain*) doler; **in** ~ (*ship etc*) en peligro.

distressing [dɪs'trɛsɪŋ] *adj* angustioso; doloroso.

distress signal *n* señal *f* de socorro.

distribute [dɪs'trɪbjuːt] *vt* (*gen*) distribuir; (*share out*) repartir.

distribution [dɪstrɪ'bjuːʃən] *n* distribución *f*.

distribution cost *n* gastos *mpl* de distribución.

distributor [dɪs'trɪbjutə*] *n* (*AUT*) distribuidor *m*; (*COMM*) distribuidora.

district ['dɪstrɪkt] *n* (*of country*) zona, región *f*; (*of town*) barrio; (*ADMIN*) distrito.

district attorney *n* (*US*) fiscal *m/f*.

district council *n* ≈ municipio; *ver recuadro*.

DISTRICT COUNCIL

En Inglaterra y Gales, con la excepción de Londres, la administración local corre a cargo del **district council**, *responsable de los servicios municipales como vivienda, urbanismo, recolección de basuras, salud medioambiental etc. La mayoría de sus miembros son elegidos a nivel local cada cuatro años. Hay un total de 369 "districts" (distritos), repartidos en 53 "counties" (condados), que se financian a través de los impuestos municipales y partidas presupuestarias del Estado. Éste controla sus gastos a través de una comisión independiente.*

---

district manager *n* representante *m/f* regional.

district nurse *n* (*BRIT*) enfermera que atiende a pacientes a domicilio.

distrust [dɪs'trʌst] *n* desconfianza ♦ *vt* desconfiar de.

distrustful [dɪs'trʌstful] *adj* desconfiado.

disturb [dɪs'təːb] *vt* (*person*: *bother, interrupt*) molestar; (*meeting*) interrumpir; (*disorganize*) desordenar; **sorry to** ~ **you** perdone la molestia.

disturbance [dɪs'təːbəns] *n* (*political etc*) disturbio; (*violence*) alboroto; (*of mind*)

trastorno; **to cause a** ~ causar alboroto; ~ **of the peace** alteración *f* del orden público.

disturbed [dɪs'təːbd] *adj* (*worried, upset*) preocupado, angustiado; **to be emotionally/mentally** ~ tener problemas emocionales/ser un trastornado mental.

disturbing [dɪs'təːbɪŋ] *adj* inquietante, perturbador(a).

disuse [dɪs'juːs] *n*: **to fall into** ~ caer en desuso.

disused [dɪs'juːzd] *adj* abandonado.

ditch [dɪtʃ] *n* zanja; (*irrigation* ~) acequia ♦ *vt* (*col*) deshacerse de.

dither ['dɪðə*] *vi* vacilar.

ditto ['dɪtəu] *adv* ídem, lo mismo.

divan [dɪ'væn] *n* diván *m*.

divan bed *n* cama turca.

dive [daɪv] *n* (*from board*) salto; (*underwater*) buceo; (*of submarine*) inmersión *f*; (*AVIAT*) picada ♦ *vi* saltar; bucear; sumergirse; picar.

diver ['daɪvə*] *n* (*SPORT*) saltador(a) *m/f*; (*underwater*) buzo.

diverge [daɪ'vəːdʒ] *vi* divergir.

divergent [daɪ'vəːdʒənt] *adj* divergente.

diverse [daɪ'vəːs] *adj* diversos/as, varios/as.

diversification [daɪvəːsɪfɪ'keɪʃən] *n* diversificación *f*.

diversify [daɪ'vəːsɪfaɪ] *vt* diversificar.

diversion [daɪ'vəːʃən] *n* (*BRIT AUT*) desviación *f*; (*distraction, MIL*) diversión *f*.

diversity [daɪ'vəːsɪtɪ] *n* diversidad *f*.

divert [daɪ'vəːt] *vt* (*BRIT*: *train, plane, traffic*) desviar; (*amuse*) divertir.

divest [daɪ'vɛst] *vt*: **to** ~ **sb of sth** despojar a alguien de algo.

divide [dɪ'vaɪd] *vt* dividir; (*separate*) separar ♦ *vi* dividirse; (*road*) bifurcarse; **to** ~ (**between, among**) repartir *or* dividir (entre); **40** ~**d by 5** 40 dividido por 5.

▶**divide out** *vt*: **to** ~ **out (between, among)** (*sweets, tasks etc*) repartir (entre).

divided [dɪ'vaɪdɪd] *adj* (*country, couple*) dividido, separado; (*opinions*) en desacuerdo.

divided highway *n* (*US*) carretera de doble calzada.

dividend ['dɪvɪdɛnd] *n* dividendo; (*fig*) beneficio.

dividend cover *n* cobertura de dividendo.

dividers [dɪ'vaɪdəz] *npl* compás *m* de puntas.

divine [dɪ'vaɪn] *adj* divino ♦ *vt* (*future*) vaticinar; (*truth*) alumbrar; (*water, metal*) descubrir, detectar.

diving ['daɪvɪŋ] *n* (*SPORT*) salto; (*underwater*) buceo.

diving board n trampolín m.

diving suit n escafandra.

divinity [dɪ'vɪnɪtɪ] n divinidad f; (SCOL) teología.

divisible [dɪ'vɪzɪbl] adj divisible.

division [dɪ'vɪʒən] n (also BRIT FOOTBALL) división f; (sharing out) repartimiento; (BRIT POL) votación f; ~ **of labour** división f del trabajo.

divisive [dɪ'vaɪsɪv] adj divisivo.

divorce [dɪ'vɔːs] n divorcio ♦ vt divorciarse de.

divorced [dɪ'vɔːst] adj divorciado.

divorcee [dɪvɔː'siː] n divorciado/a.

divot ['dɪvət] n (GOLF) chuleta.

divulge [daɪ'vʌldʒ] vt divulgar, revelar.

D.I.Y. adj, n abbr (BRIT) = **do-it-yourself**.

dizziness ['dɪzɪnɪs] n vértigo.

dizzy ['dɪzɪ] adj (person) mareado; (height) vertiginoso; **to feel** ~ marearse; **I feel** ~ estoy mareado.

DJ n abbr see **disc jockey**.

d.j. n abbr = **dinner jacket**.

Djakarta [dʒə'kɑːtə] n Yakarta.

DJIA n abbr (US STOCK EXCHANGE) = Dow Jones Industrial Average.

dl abbr (= decilitre(s)) dl.

DLit(t) abbr (= Doctor of Literature, Doctor of Letters) título universitario.

DLO n abbr (= dead-letter office) oficina de Correos que se encarga de las cartas que no llegan a su destino.

dm abbr (= decimetre(s)) dm.

DMus abbr (= Doctor of Music) título universitario.

DMZ n abbr (= demilitarized zone) zona desmilitarizada.

DNA n abbr (= deoxyribonucleic acid) ADN m.

═══════════════ KEYWORD

do [duː] (pt **did**, pp **done**) n **1** (inf: party etc): **we're having a little** ~ **on Saturday** damos una fiestecita el sábado; **it was rather a grand** ~ fue un acontecimiento a lo grande

2: **the** ~**s and don'ts** lo que se debe y no se debe hacer

♦ aux vb **1** (in negative constructions: not translated) **I don't understand** no entiendo

2 (to form questions: not translated) ~ **you speak English?** ¿habla (usted) inglés?; **didn't you know?** ¿no lo sabías?; **what** ~ **you think?** ¿qué opinas?

3 (for emphasis, in polite expressions): **people** ~ **make mistakes sometimes** a veces sí se cometen errores; **she does seem rather late** a mí también me parece que se ha retrasado; ~ **sit down/help yourself** siéntate/sírvete por favor; ~ **take care!** ¡ten cuidado! ¿eh?; **I DO wish I could ...** ojalá (que) pudiera ...; **but I DO like it** pero, sí (que) me gusta

4 (used to avoid repeating vb): **she sings better than I** ~ canta mejor que yo; ~ **you agree?** — **yes, I** ~/**no, I don't** ¿estás de acuerdo? — sí (lo estoy)/no (lo estoy); **she lives in Glasgow** — **so** ~ **I** vive en Glasgow — yo también; **he didn't like it and neither did we** no le gustó y a nosotros tampoco; **who made this mess?** — **I did** ¿quién hizo esta chapuza? — yo; **he asked me to help him and I did** me pidió que le ayudara y lo hice

5 (in question tags): **you like him, don't you?** te gusta, ¿verdad? or ¿no?; **I don't know him,** ~ **I?** creo que no le conozco; **he laughed, didn't he?** se rió ¿no?

♦ vt **1** (gen, carry out, perform etc): **what are you** ~**ing tonight?** ¿qué haces esta noche?; **what can I** ~ **for you?** (in shop) ¿en qué puedo servirle?; **what does he** ~ **for a living?** ¿a qué se dedica?; **I'll** ~ **all I can** haré todo lo que pueda; **what have you done with my slippers?** ¿qué has hecho con mis zapatillas?; **to** ~ **the washing-up/cooking** fregar los platos/cocinar; **to** ~ **one's teeth/hair/nails** lavarse los dientes/arreglarse el pelo/arreglarse las uñas

2 (AUT etc): **the car was** ~**ing 100** el coche iba a 100; **we've done 200 km already** ya hemos hecho 200 km; **he can** ~ **100 in that car** puede ir a 100 en ese coche

3 (visit: city, museum) visitar, recorrer

4 (cook): **a steak – well done please** un filete bien hecho, por favor

♦ vi **1** (act, behave) hacer; ~ **as I** ~ haz como yo

2 (get on, fare): **he's** ~**ing well/badly at school** va bien/mal en la escuela; **the firm is** ~**ing well** la empresa anda or va bien; **how** ~ **you** ~**?** mucho gusto; (less formal) ¿qué tal?

3 (suit): **will it** ~**?** ¿sirve?, ¿está or va bien?; **it doesn't** ~ **to upset her** cuidado en ofenderla

4 (be sufficient) bastar; **will £10** ~**?** ¿será bastante con £10?; **that'll** ~ así está bien; **that'll** ~**!** (in annoyance) ¡ya está bien!, ¡basta ya!; **to make** ~ **(with)** arreglárselas (con)

►**do away with** vt fus (kill, disease) eliminar; (abolish: law etc) abolir; (withdraw) retirar

►**do out of** vt fus: **to** ~ **sb out of sth** pisar

algo a algn
►**do up** *vt* (*laces*) atar; (*zip, dress, shirt*) abrochar; (*renovate: room, house*) renovar
►**do with** *vt fus* (*need*): **I could ~ with a drink/some help** no me vendría mal un trago/un poco de ayuda; (*be connected*) tener que ver con; **what has it got to ~ with you?** ¿qué tiene que ver contigo?
►**do without** *vi*: **if you're late for dinner then you'll ~ without** si llegas tarde tendrás que quedarte sin cenar ♦ *vt fus* pasar sin; **I can ~ without a car** puedo pasar sin coche.

do. *abbr* = **ditto**.
DOA *abbr* = **dead on arrival**.
d.o.b. *abbr* = **date of birth**.
doc [dɔk] *n* (*col*) médico/a.
docile ['dəusaɪl] *adj* dócil.
dock [dɔk] *n* (*NAUT: wharf*) dársena, muelle *m*; (*LAW*) banquillo (de los acusados); **~s** *npl* muelles *mpl*, puerto *sg* ♦ *vi* (*enter~*) atracar (en el muelle) ♦ *vt* (*pay etc*) descontar.
dock dues *npl* derechos *mpl* de muelle.
docker ['dɔkə*] *n* trabajador *m* portuario, estibador *m*.
docket ['dɔkɪt] *n* (*on parcel etc*) etiqueta.
dockyard ['dɔkjɑːd] *n* astillero.
doctor ['dɔktə*] *n* médico; (*Ph.D. etc*) doctor(a) *m/f* ♦ *vt* (*fig*) arreglar, falsificar; (*drink etc*) adulterar.
doctorate ['dɔktərɪt] *n* doctorado; *ver recuadro*.

```
┌─────────────────────────────────────┐
│ DOCTORATE                           │
│                                     │
│ El grado más alto que conceden las  │
│ universidades es el doctorado       │
│ (doctorate), tras un período de     │
│ estudio e investigación             │
│ original no inferior a tres años que│
│ culmina con la exposición de una    │
│ tesis ("thesis")                    │
│ en la que se exponen los resultados.│
│ El título más frecuente es el de    │
│ "PhD"                               │
│ ("Doctor of Philosophy"), que se    │
│ obtiene en Letras, Ciencias e       │
│ Ingeniería, aunque también existen  │
│ otros doctorados específicos en     │
│ Música, Derecho etc.                │
└─────────────────────────────────────┘
```

Doctor of Philosophy (Ph.D.) *n* Doctor *m* (en Filosofía y Letras).
doctrinaire [dɔktrɪ'nɛə*] *adj* doctrinario.
doctrine ['dɔktrɪn] *n* doctrina.
docudrama [dɔkju'drɑːmə] *n* (*TV*) docudrama *m*.
document ['dɔkjumənt] *n* documento ♦ *vt* documentar.
documentary [dɔkju'mɛntərɪ] *adj* documental ♦ *n* documental *m*.

documentation [dɔkjumɛn'teɪʃən] *n* documentación *f*.
DOD *n abbr* (*US*: = *Department of Defense*) Ministerio de Defensa.
doddering ['dɔdərɪŋ] *adj*, **doddery** ['dɔdərɪ] *adj* vacilante.
doddle ['dɔdl] *n*: **it's a ~** (*BRIT col*) es pan comido.
dodge [dɔdʒ] *n* (*of body*) regate *m*; (*fig*) truco ♦ *vt* (*gen*) evadir; (*blow*) esquivar ♦ *vi* escabullirse; (*SPORT*) hacer una finta; **to ~ out of the way** echarse a un lado; **to ~ through the traffic** esquivar el tráfico.
dodgems ['dɔdʒəmz] *npl* (*BRIT*) autos *or* coches *mpl* de choque.
dodgy ['dɔdʒɪ] (*col*) *adj* (*uncertain*) dudoso; (*shady*) sospechoso; (*risky*) arriesgado.
DOE *n abbr* (*BRIT*) = **Department of the Environment**; (*US*) = *Department of Energy*.
doe [dəu] *n* (*deer*) cierva, gama; (*rabbit*) coneja.
does [dʌz] *vb see* **do**.
doesn't ['dʌznt] = **does not**.
dog [dɔg] *n* perro ♦ *vt* seguir (de cerca); (*fig: memory etc*) perseguir; **to go to the ~s** (*person*) echarse a perder; (*nation etc*) ir a la ruina.
dog biscuit *n* galleta de perro.
dog collar *n* collar *m* de perro; (*fig*) alzacuello(s) *msg*.
dog-eared ['dɔgɪəd] *adj* sobado; (*page*) con la esquina doblada.
dogfish ['dɔgfɪʃ] *n* cazón *m*, perro marino.
dog food *n* comida para perros.
dogged ['dɔgɪd] *adj* tenaz, obstinado.
doggy ['dɔgɪ] *n* (*col*) perrito.
doggy bag *n* bolsa para llevarse las sobras de la comida.
dogma ['dɔgmə] *n* dogma *m*.
dogmatic [dɔg'mætɪk] *adj* dogmático.
do-gooder [duː'gudə*] *n* (*col pej*): **to be a ~** ser una persona bien intencionada *or* un filantropista.
dogsbody ['dɔgzbɔdɪ] *n* (*BRIT*) burro de carga.
doily ['dɔɪlɪ] *n* pañito de adorno.
doing ['duːɪŋ] *n*: **this is your ~** esto es obra tuya.
doings ['duːɪŋz] *npl* (*events*) sucesos *mpl*; (*acts*) hechos *mpl*.
do-it-yourself [duːɪtjɔː'sɛlf] *n* bricolaje *m*.
doldrums ['dɔldrəmz] *npl*: **to be in the ~** (*person*) estar abatido; (*business*) estar estancado.
dole [dəul] *n* (*BRIT: payment*) subsidio de paro; **on the ~** ~ parado.
►**dole out** *vt* repartir.
doleful ['dəulful] *adj* triste, lúgubre.

doll [dɔl] *n* muñeca.
▶**doll up** *vt*: **to ~ o.s. up** ataviarse.
dollar ['dɔlə*] *n* dólar *m*.
dollop ['dɔləp] *n* buena cucharada.
dolly ['dɔlɪ] *n* muñeca.
dolphin ['dɔlfɪn] *n* delfín *m*.
domain [də'meɪn] *n* (*fig*) campo,
competencia; (*land*) dominios *mpl*.
dome [dəum] *n* (*ARCH*) cúpula; (*shape*)
bóveda.
domestic [də'mɛstɪk] *adj* (*animal, duty*)
doméstico; (*flight, news, policy*) nacional.
domesticated [də'mɛstɪkeɪtɪd] *adj*
domesticado; (*person: home-loving*)
casero, hogareño.
domesticity [dəumɛs'tɪsɪtɪ] *n* vida casera.
domestic servant *n* sirviente/a *m/f*.
domicile ['dɔmɪsaɪl] *n* domicilio.
dominant ['dɔmɪnənt] *adj* dominante.
dominate ['dɔmɪneɪt] *vt* dominar.
domination [dɔmɪ'neɪʃən] *n* dominación *f*.
domineering [dɔmɪ'nɪərɪŋ] *adj* dominante.
Dominican Republic [də'mɪnɪkən-] *n*
República Dominicana.
dominion [də'mɪnɪən] *n* dominio.
domino, *pl* ~**es** ['dɔmɪnəu] *n* ficha de
dominó.
dominoes ['dɔmɪnəuz] *n* (*game*) dominó.
don [dɔn] *n* (*BRIT*) profesor(a) *m/f* de
universidad.
donate [də'neɪt] *vt* donar.
donation [də'neɪʃən] *n* donativo.
done [dʌn] *pp of* **do**.
donkey ['dɔŋkɪ] *n* burro.
donkey-work ['dɔŋkɪwəːk] *n* (*BRIT col*)
trabajo pesado.
donor ['dəunə*] *n* donante *m/f*.
donor card *n* carnet *m* de donante de
órganos.
don't [dəunt] = **do not**.
donut ['dəunʌt] *n* (*US*) = **doughnut**.
doodle ['duːdl] *n* garabato ♦ *vi* pintar
dibujitos *or* garabatos.
doom [duːm] *n* (*fate*) suerte *f*; (*death*)
muerte *f* ♦ *vt*: **to be ~ed to failure** estar
condenado al fracaso.
doomsday ['duːmzdeɪ] *n* día *m* del juicio
final.
door [dɔː*] *n* puerta; (*of car*) portezuela;
(*entry*) entrada; **from ~ to ~** de puerta en
puerta.
doorbell ['dɔːbɛl] *n* timbre *m*.
door handle *n* tirador *m*; (*of car*) manija.
door knocker *n* aldaba.
doorman ['dɔːmən] *n* (*in hotel*) portero.
doormat ['dɔːmæt] *n* felpudo, estera.
doorstep ['dɔːstɛp] *n* peldaño; **on your ~**
en la puerta de casa; (*fig*) al lado de casa.

door-to-door ['dɔːtə'dɔː*] *adj*: ~ **selling**
venta a domicilio.
doorway ['dɔːweɪ] *n* entrada, puerta; **in the
~** en la puerta.
dope [dəup] *n* (*col: person*) imbécil *m/f*;
(: *information*) información *f*, informes *mpl*
♦ *vt* (*horse etc*) drogar.
dopey ['dəupɪ] *adj* atontado.
dormant ['dɔːmənt] *adj* inactivo; (*latent*)
latente.
dormer ['dɔːmə*] *n* (*also:* ~ **window**)
buhardilla.
dormitory ['dɔːmɪtrɪ] *n* (*BRIT*) dormitorio;
(*US: hall of residence*) residencia, colegio
mayor.
dormouse, *pl* **dormice** ['dɔːmaus, -maɪs] *n*
lirón *m*.
Dors *abbr* (*BRIT*) = **Dorset**.
DOS *n abbr see* **disk operating system**.
dosage ['dəusɪdʒ] *n* (*on medicine bottle*)
dosis *f inv*, dosificación *f*.
dose [dəus] *n* (*of medicine*) dosis *f inv*; **a ~ of
flu** un ataque de gripe ♦ *vt*: **to ~ o.s. with**
automedicarse con
dosser ['dɔsə*] *n* (*BRIT col*) mendigo/a; (*lazy
person*) vago/a.
doss house ['dɔs-] *n* (*BRIT*) pensión *f* de
mala muerte.
dossier ['dɔsɪeɪ] *n*: ~ (**on**) expediente *m*
(sobre).
DOT *n abbr* (*US*: = *Department of
Transportation*) *ministerio de transporte*.
dot [dɔt] *n* punto; ~**ted with** salpicado de;
on the ~ en punto.
dot command *n* (*COMPUT*) instrucción *f*
(precedida) de punto.
dote [dəut]: **to ~ on** *vt fus* adorar, idolatrar.
dot-matrix printer [dɔt'meɪtrɪks-] *n*
impresora matricial *or* de matriz.
dotted line ['dɔtɪd-] *n* línea de puntos; **to
sign on the ~** firmar.
dotty ['dɔtɪ] *adj* (*col*) disparatado, chiflado.
double ['dʌbl] *adj* doble ♦ *adv* (*twice*): **to
cost ~** costar el doble ♦ *n* (*gen*) doble *m*
♦ *vt* doblar; (*efforts*) redoblar ♦ *vi*
doblarse; (*have two uses etc*): **to ~ as**
hacer las veces de; ~ **five two six (5526)**
(*TELEC*) cinco cinco dos seis; **spelt with a
~ "s"** escrito con dos "eses"; **on the ~**,
(*BRIT*) **at the ~** corriendo.
▶**double back** *vi* (*person*) volver sobre sus
pasos.
▶**double up** *vi* (*bend over*) doblarse; (*share
bedroom*) compartir.
double bass *n* contrabajo.
double bed *n* cama matrimonial.
double-breasted ['dʌbl'brɛstɪd] *adj*
cruzado.

double-check ['dʌblt∫ɛk] *vt* volver a revisar ♦ *vi*: **I'll** ~ voy a revisarlo otra vez.

double-click ['dʌbl,klɪk] *vi* (*COMPUT*) hacer doble clic.

double cream *n* nata enriquecida.

doublecross ['dʌbl'krɔs] *vt* (*trick*) engañar; (*betray*) traicionar.

doubledecker ['dʌbl'dɛkə*] *n* autobús *m* de dos pisos.

double glazing *n* (*BRIT*) doble acristalamiento.

double indemnity *n* doble indemnización *f*.

double-page ['dʌblpeɪdʒ] *adj*: ~ **spread** doble página.

double room *n* cuarto para dos.

doubles ['dʌblz] *n* (*TENNIS*) juego de dobles.

double time *n* tarifa doble.

double whammy [-'wæmɪ] *n* (*col*) palo doble.

doubly ['dʌblɪ] *adv* doblemente.

doubt [daut] *n* duda ♦ *vt* dudar; (*suspect*) dudar de; **to** ~ **that** dudar que; **there is no** ~ **that** no cabe duda de que; **without (a)** ~ sin duda (alguna); **beyond** ~ fuera de duda; **I** ~ **it very much** lo dudo mucho.

doubtful ['dautful] *adj* dudoso; (*person*) sospechoso; **to be** ~ **about sth** tener dudas sobre algo; **I'm a bit** ~ no estoy convencido.

doubtless ['dautlɪs] *adv* sin duda.

dough [dəu] *n* masa, pasta; (*col*: *money*) pasta, lana (*LAM*).

doughnut ['dəunʌt] *n* buñuelo.

douse [daus] *vt* (*drench*: *with water*) mojar; (*extinguish*: *flames*) apagar.

dove [dʌv] *n* paloma.

dovetail ['dʌvteɪl] *vi* (*fig*) encajar.

dowager ['dauɪdʒə*] *n*: ~ **duchess** duquesa viuda.

dowdy ['daudɪ] *adj* desaliñado; (*inelegant*) poco elegante.

Dow-Jones average ['daudʒəunz-] *n* (*US*) índice *m* Dow-Jones.

down [daun] *n* (*fluff*) pelusa; (*feathers*) plumón *m*, flojel *m*; (*hill*) loma ♦ *adv* (~*wards*) abajo, hacia abajo; (*on the ground*) por/en tierra ♦ *prep* abajo ♦ *vt* (*col*: *drink*) beberse, tragar(se); ~ **with X!** ¡abajo X!; ~ **here** aquí abajo; **I'll be** ~ **in a minute** ahora bajo; **England is two goals** ~ Inglaterra está perdiendo por dos tantos; **I've been** ~ **with flu** he estado con gripe; **the price of meat is** ~ ha bajado el precio de la carne; **I've got it** ~ **in my diary** lo he apuntado en

mi agenda; **to pay £2** ~ dejar £2 de depósito; **he went** ~ **the hill** fue cuesta abajo; ~ **under** (*in Australia etc*) en Australia/Nueva Zelanda; **to** ~ **tools** (*fig*) declararse en huelga.

down-and-out ['daunəndaut] *n* (*tramp*) vagabundo/a.

down-at-heel ['daunət'hiːl] *adj* venido a menos; (*appearance*) desaliñado.

downbeat ['daunbiːt] *n* (*MUS*) compás *m* ♦ *adj* (*gloomy*) pesimista.

downcast ['daunkɑːst] *adj* abatido.

downfall ['daunfɔːl] *n* caída, ruina.

downgrade [daun'greɪd] *vt* (*job*) degradar; (*hotel*) bajar de categoría a.

downhearted [daun'hɑːtɪd] *adj* desanimado.

downhill [daun'hɪl] *adv*: **to go** ~ ir cuesta abajo; (*business*) estar en declive.

Downing Street ['daunɪŋ-] *n* (*BRIT*) Downing Street *f*; *ver recuadro*.

DOWNING STREET

Downing Street *es la calle de Londres en la que tienen su residencia oficial tanto el Primer Ministro ("Prime Minister") como el Ministro de Economía ("Chancellor of the Exchequer"). El primero vive en el nº10 y el segundo en el nº11. Es una calle cerrada al público que se encuentra en el barrio de Westminster, en el centro de Londres.* **Downing Street** *se usa también en lenguaje periodístico para referirse al jefe del gobierno británico.*

---

download ['daunləud] *vt* (*COMPUT*) transferir, telecargar.

down-market ['daun'mɑːkɪt] *adj* de escasa calidad.

down payment *n* entrada, pago al contado.

downplay ['daunpleɪ] *vt* (*US*) quitar importancia a.

downpour ['daunpɔː*] *n* aguacero.

downright ['daunraɪt] *adj* (*nonsense, lie*) manifiesto; (*refusal*) terminante.

downsize [daun'saɪz] *vt* reducir la plantilla de.

Down's syndrome [daunz-] *n* síndrome *m* de Down.

downstairs [daun'stɛəz] *adv* (*below*) (en el piso de) abajo; (*motion*) escaleras abajo; **to come** (*or* **go**) ~ bajar la escalera.

downstream [daun'striːm] *adv* aguas *or* río abajo.

downtime ['dauntaɪm] *n* (*COMM*) tiempo inactivo.

down-to-earth [dauntu'ɔ:θ] *adj* práctico.
downtown [daun'taun] *adv* en el centro de la ciudad.
downtrodden ['dauntrɔdn] *adj* oprimido.
downward ['daunwəd] *adv* hacia abajo
♦ *adj*: **a ~ trend** una tendencia descendente.
downward(s) ['daunwəd(z)] *adv* hacia abajo; **face ~s** (*person*) boca abajo; (*object*) cara abajo.
dowry ['daurɪ] *n* dote *f*.
doz. *abbr* = **dozen**.
doze [dəuz] *vi* dormitar.
►**doze off** *vi* echar una cabezada.
dozen ['dʌzn] *n* docena; **a ~ books** una docena de libros; **~s of** cantidad de; **~s of times** cantidad de veces; **80p a ~** 80 peniques la docena.
DPh., D. Phil. *n abbr* (= *Doctor of Philosophy*) título universitario.
DPP *n abbr* (*BRIT*) = **Director of Public Prosecutions**.
DPT *n abbr* (= *diphtheria, pertussis, tetanus*) vacuna trivalente.
DPW *n abbr* (*US*: = *Department of Public Works*) ministerio de obras públicas.
Dr, Dr. *abbr* (= *doctor*) Dr.
Dr. *abbr* (*in street names*) = **Drive**.
dr *abbr* (*COMM*) = **debtor**.
drab [dræb] *adj* gris, monótono.
draft [drɑːft] *n* (*first copy: of document, report*) borrador *m*; (*COMM*) giro; (*US: call-up*) quinta ♦ *vt* (*write roughly*) hacer un borrador de; *see also* **draught**.
draftsman ['drɑːftsmən] *etc* (*US*) = **draughtsman** *etc*.
drag [dræg] *vt* arrastrar; (*river*) dragar, rastrear ♦ *vi* arrastrarse por el suelo ♦ *n* (*AVIAT: resistance*) resistencia aerodinámica; (*col*) lata; (*women's clothing*): **in ~** travestido.
►**drag away** *vt*: **to ~ away (from)** separar a rastras (de).
►**drag on** *vi* ser interminable.
dragnet ['drægnɛt] *n* (*NAUT*) rastra; (*fig*) emboscada.
dragon ['drægən] *n* dragón *m*.
dragonfly ['drægənflaɪ] *n* libélula.
dragoon [drə'guːn] *n* (*cavalryman*) dragón *m* ♦ *vt*: **to ~ sb into doing sth** forzar a algn a hacer algo.
drain [dreɪn] *n* desaguadero; (*in street*) sumidero; (*~ cover*) rejilla del sumidero ♦ *vt* (*land, marshes*) desecar; (*MED*) drenar; (*reservoir*) desecar; (*fig*) agotar ♦ *vi* escurrirse; **to be a ~ on** consumir, agotar; **to feel ~ed (of energy)** (*fig*) sentirse agotado.
drainage ['dreɪnɪdʒ] *n* (*act*) desagüe *m*;

(*MED, AGR*) drenaje *m*; (*sewage*) alcantarillado.
draining board ['dreɪnɪŋ-], (*US*) **drainboard** ['dreɪnbɔːd] *n* escurridero, escurridor *m*.
drainpipe ['dreɪnpaɪp] *n* tubo de desagüe.
drake [dreɪk] *n* pato (macho).
dram [dræm] *n* (*drink*) traguito, copita.
drama ['drɑːmə] *n* (*art*) teatro; (*play*) drama *m*.
dramatic [drə'mætɪk] *adj* dramático.
dramatist ['dræmətɪst] *n* dramaturgo/a.
dramatize ['dræmətaɪz] *vt* (*events etc*) dramatizar; (*adapt: novel: for TV, cinema*) adaptar.
drank [dræŋk] *pt* de **drink**.
drape [dreɪp] *vt* cubrir.
draper ['dreɪpə*] *n* (*BRIT*) pañero, mercero.
drapes [dreɪps] *npl* (*US*) cortinas *fpl*.
drastic ['dræstɪk] *adj* (*measure, reduction*) severo; (*change*) radical.
draught, (*US*) **draft** [drɑːft] *n* (*of air*) corriente *f* de aire; (*drink*) trago; (*NAUT*) calado; **on ~** (*beer*) de barril.
draught beer *n* cerveza de barril.
draughtboard ['drɑːftbɔːd] (*BRIT*) *n* tablero de damas.
draughts [drɑːfts] *n* (*BRIT*) juego de damas.
draughtsman, (*US*) **draftsman** ['drɑːftsmən] *n* proyectista *m*, delineante *m*.
draughtsmanship, (*US*) **draftsmanship** ['drɑːftsmənʃɪp] *n* (*drawing*) dibujo lineal; (*skill*) habilidad *f* para el dibujo.
draw [drɔː] *vb* (*pt* **drew**, *pp* **drawn** [druː, drɔːn]) *vt* (*pull*) tirar; (*take out*) sacar; (*attract*) atraer; (*picture*) dibujar; (*money*) retirar; (*formulate: conclusion*): **to ~ (from)** sacar (de); (*comparison, distinction*): **to ~ (between)** hacer (entre) ♦ *vi* (*SPORT*) empatar ♦ *n* (*SPORT*) empate *m*; (*lottery*) sorteo; (*attraction*) atracción *f*; **to ~ near** *vi* acercarse.
►**draw back** *vi*: **to ~ back (from)** echarse atrás (de).
►**draw in** *vi* (*car*) aparcar; (*train*) entrar en la estación.
►**draw on** *vt* (*resources*) utilizar, servirse de; (*imagination, person*) recurrir a.
►**draw out** *vi* (*lengthen*) alargarse.
►**draw up** *vi* (*stop*) pararse ♦ *vt* (*document*) redactar; (*plans*) trazar.
drawback ['drɔːbæk] *n* inconveniente *m*, desventaja.
drawbridge ['drɔːbrɪdʒ] *n* puente *m* levadizo.
drawee [drɔː'iː] *n* girado, librado.
drawer [drɔː*] *n* cajón *m*; (*of cheque*)

librador(a) *m/f.*
drawing ['drɔːɪŋ] *n* dibujo.
drawing board *n* tablero (de dibujante).
drawing pin *n* (*BRIT*) chincheta *m.*
drawing room *n* salón *m.*
drawl [drɔːl] *n* habla lenta y cansina.
drawn [drɔːn] *pp of* draw ♦ *adj* (*haggard*: *with tiredness*) ojeroso; (: *with pain*) macilento.
drawstring ['drɔːstrɪŋ] *n* cordón *m.*
dread [drɛd] *n* pavor *m*, terror *m* ♦ *vt* temer, tener miedo *or* pavor a.
dreadful ['drɛdful] *adj* espantoso; **I feel** ~!
(*ill*) ¡me siento fatal *or* malísimo!;
(*ashamed*) ¡qué vergüenza!
dream [driːm] *n* sueño ♦ *vt, vi* (*pt, pp*
dreamed *or* **dreamt** [drɛmt]) soñar; **to have a** ~ **about sb/sth** soñar con algn/algo; **sweet** ~**s!** ¡que sueñes con los angelitos!
▶**dream up** *vt* (*reason, excuse*) inventar;
(*plan, idea*) idear.
dreamer ['driːmə*] *n* soñador(a) *m/f.*
dream world *n* mundo imaginario *or* de ensueño.
dreamy ['driːmɪ] *adj* (*person*) soñador(a), distraído; (*music*) de sueño.
dreary ['drɪərɪ] *adj* monótono, aburrido.
dredge [drɛdʒ] *vt* dragar.
▶**dredge up** *vt* sacar con draga; (*fig: unpleasant facts*) pescar, sacar a luz.
dredger ['drɛdʒə*] *n* (*ship, machine*) draga;
(*CULIN*) tamiz *m.*
dregs [drɛgz] *npl* heces *fpl.*
drench [drɛntʃ] *vt* empapar; ~**ed to the skin** calado hasta los huesos.
dress [drɛs] *n* vestido; (*clothing*) ropa ♦ *vt*
vestir; (*wound*) vendar; (*CULIN*) aliñar;
(*shop window*) decorar, arreglar ♦ *vi*
vestirse; **to** ~ **o.s., get** ~**ed** vestirse; **she**
~**es very well** se viste muy bien.
▶**dress up** *vi* vestirse de etiqueta; (*in fancy dress*) disfrazarse.
dress circle *n* (*BRIT*) principal *m.*
dress designer *n* modisto/a.
dresser ['drɛsə*] *n* (*furniture*) aparador *m*;
(: *US*) tocador *m*; (*THEAT*) camarero/a.
dressing ['drɛsɪŋ] *n* (*MED*) vendaje *m*;
(*CULIN*) aliño.
dressing gown *n* (*BRIT*) bata.
dressing room *n* (*THEAT*) camarín *m*;
(*SPORT*) vestidor *m.*
dressing table *n* tocador *m.*
dressmaker ['drɛsmeɪkə*] *n* modista, costurera.
dressmaking ['drɛsmeɪkɪŋ] *n* costura.
dress rehearsal *n* ensayo general.
dress shirt *n* camisa de frac.
dressy ['drɛsɪ] *adj* (*col*) elegante.

drew [druː] *pt of* **draw.**
dribble ['drɪbl] *vi* gotear, caer gota a gota;
(*baby*) babear ♦ *vt* (*ball*) driblar, regatear.
dried [draɪd] *adj* (*gen*) seco; (*fruit*) paso;
(*milk*) en polvo.
drier ['draɪə*] *n* = **dryer.**
drift [drɪft] *n* (*of current etc*) velocidad *f*; (*of sand*) montón *m*; (*of snow*) ventisquero;
(*meaning*) significado ♦ *vi* (*boat*) ir a la deriva; (*sand, snow*) amontonarse; **to catch sb's** ~ cogerle el hilo a algn; **to let things** ~ dejar las cosas como están; **to** ~
apart (*friends*) seguir su camino; (*lovers*) disgustarse, romper.
drifter ['drɪftə*] *n* vagabundo/a.
driftwood ['drɪftwud] *n* madera flotante.
drill [drɪl] *n* taladro; (*bit*) broca; (*of dentist*) fresa; (*for mining etc*) perforadora, barrena; (*MIL*) instrucción *f* ♦ *vt* perforar, taladrar; (*soldiers*) ejercitar; (*pupils: in grammar*) hacer ejercicios con ♦ *vi* (*for oil*) perforar.
drilling ['drɪlɪŋ] *n* (*for oil*) perforación *f.*
drilling rig *n* (*on land*) torre *f* de perforación; (*at sea*) plataforma de perforación.
drily ['draɪlɪ] *adv* secamente.
drink [drɪŋk] *n* bebida ♦ *vt, vi* (*pt* **drank,** *pp*
drunk) beber, tomar (*LAM*); **to have a** ~
tomar algo; tomar una copa *or* un trago;
a ~ **of water** un trago de agua; **to invite sb for** ~**s** invitar a algn a tomar unas copas; **there's food and** ~ **in the kitchen**
hay de comer y de beber en la cocina;
would you like something to ~**?** ¿quieres beber *or* tomar algo?
▶**drink in** *vt* (*subj: person: fresh air*)
respirar; (*story, sight*) beberse.
drinkable ['drɪŋkəbl] *adj* (*not poisonous*)
potable; (*palatable*) aguantable.
drink-driving [drɪŋk'draɪvɪŋ] *n:* **to be charged with** ~ ser acusado de conducir borracho *or* en estado de embriaguez.
drinker ['drɪŋkə*] *n* bebedor(a) *m/f.*
drinking ['drɪŋkɪŋ] *n* (*drunkenness*) beber *m.*
drinking fountain *n* fuente *f* de agua potable.
drinking water *n* agua potable.
drip [drɪp] *n* (*act*) goteo; (*one* ~) gota; (*MED*)
gota a gota *m*; (*sound: of water etc*) goteo;
(*col: spineless person*) soso/a ♦ *vi* gotear, caer gota a gota.
drip-dry ['drɪp'draɪ] *adj* (*shirt*) de lava y pon.
dripping ['drɪpɪŋ] *n* (*animal fat*) pringue *m*
♦ *adj:* ~ **wet** calado.
drive [draɪv] *n* paseo (en coche); (*journey*)
viaje *m* (en coche); (*also:* ~**way**) entrada;
(*street*) calle; (*energy*) energía, vigor *m*;

(*PSYCH*) impulso; (*SPORT*) ataque *m*;
(*COMPUT*: *also*: **disk** ~) disc drive *m* ♦ *vb* (*pt*
drove, *pp* **driven** [drəuv, 'drɪvn]) *vt* (*car*)
conducir, manejar (*LAM*); (*nail*) clavar;
(*push*) empujar; (*TECH*: *motor*) impulsar
♦ *vi* (*AUT*: *at controls*) conducir; (: *travel*)
pasearse en coche; **to go for a** ~ dar una
vuelta en coche; **it's 3 hours'** ~ **from
London** es un viaje de 3 horas en coche
desde Londres; **left-/right-hand** ~
conducción *f* a la izquierda/derecha;
front-/rear-wheel ~ tracción *f* delantera/
trasera; **sales** ~ promoción *f* de ventas; **to
~ sb mad** volverle loco a algn; **to ~ sb to
(do) sth** empujar a algn a (hacer) algo; **he
~s a taxi** es taxista; **he ~s a Mercedes**
tiene un Mercedes; **can you ~?** ¿sabes
conducir *or* (*LAM*) manejar?; **to ~ at 50
km an hour** ir a 50km por hora.
▶**drive at** *vt fus* (*fig*: *intend, mean*) querer
decir, insinuar.
▶**drive on** *vi* no parar, seguir adelante ♦ *vt*
(*incite, encourage*) empujar.
drive-by ['draɪvbaɪ] *n*: ~ **shooting** tiroteo
desde el coche.
drive-in ['draɪvɪn] *adj* (*esp US*): ~ **cinema**
autocine *m*.
drivel ['drɪvl] *n* (*col*) tonterías *fpl*.
driven ['drɪvn] *pp of* **drive**.
driver ['draɪvə*] *n* conductor(a) *m/f*, chofer
m (*LAM*); (*of taxi*) taxista *m/f*.
driver's license *n* (*US*) carnet *m or*
permiso de conducir.
driveway ['draɪvweɪ] *n* camino de entrada.
driving ['draɪvɪŋ] *n* conducir *m*, manejar *m*
(*LAM*) ♦ *adj* (*force*) impulsor(a).
driving instructor *n* instructor(a) *m/f* de
autoescuela.
driving lesson *n* clase *f* de conducir.
driving licence *n* (*BRIT*) carnet *m or*
permiso de conducir.
driving school *n* autoescuela.
driving test *n* examen *m* de conducir.
drizzle ['drɪzl] *n* llovizna, garúa (*LAM*) ♦ *vi*
lloviznar.
droll [drəul] *adj* gracioso.
dromedary ['drɔmɪdərɪ] *n* dromedario.
drone [drəun] *vi* (*bee, aircraft, engine*)
zumbar; (: *also*: ~ **on**) murmurar sin
interrupción ♦ *n* zumbido; (*male bee*)
zángano.
drool [dru:l] *vi* babear; **to ~ over sb/sth**
caérsele la baba por algn/algo.
droop [dru:p] *vi* (*fig*) decaer, desanimarse.
drop [drɔp] *n* (*of water*) gota; (*fall*: *in price*)
bajada; (: *in salary*) disminución *f* ♦ *vt*
(*allow to fall*) dejar caer; (*voice, eyes, price*)
bajar; (*set down from car*) dejar ♦ *vi* (*price,*

temperature) bajar; (*wind*) calmarse,
amainar; (*numbers, attendance*) disminuir;
~s *npl* (*MED*) gotas *fpl*; **cough ~s** pastillas
fpl para la tos; **a ~ of 10%** una bajada del
10 por ciento; **to ~ anchor** echar el ancla;
to ~ sb a line mandar unas líneas a algn.
▶**drop in** *vi* (*col*: *visit*): **to ~ in (on)** pasar
por casa (de).
▶**drop off** *vi* (*sleep*) dormirse ♦ *vt*
(*passenger*) bajar, dejar.
▶**drop out** *vi* (*withdraw*) retirarse.
droplet ['drɔplɪt] *n* gotita.
dropout ['drɔpaut] *n* (*from society*)
marginado/a; (*from university*) estudiante
m/f que ha abandonado los estudios.
dropper ['drɔpə*] *n* (*MED*) cuentagotas *m
inv*.
droppings ['drɔpɪŋz] *npl* excremento *sg*.
dross [drɔs] *n* (*coal, fig*) escoria.
drought [draut] *n* sequía.
drove [drəuv] *pt of* **drive**.
drown [draun] *vt* (*also*: ~ **out**: *sound*)
ahogar ♦ *vi* ahogarse.
drowse [drauz] *vi* estar medio dormido.
drowsy ['drauzɪ] *adj* soñoliento; **to be** ~
tener sueño.
drudge [drʌdʒ] *n* esclavo del trabajo.
drudgery ['drʌdʒərɪ] *n* trabajo pesado *or*
monótono.
drug [drʌg] *n* (*MED*) medicamento, droga;
(*narcotic*) droga ♦ *vt* drogar; **to be on ~s**
drogarse; **he's on ~s** se droga.
drug addict *n* drogadicto/a.
druggist ['drʌgɪst] *n* (*US*) farmacéutico/a.
drug peddler *n* traficante *m/f* de drogas.
drugstore ['drʌgstɔ:*] *n* (*US*) tienda (*de
comestibles, periódicos y medicamentos*).
drug trafficker *n* narcotraficante *m/f*.
drum [drʌm] *n* tambor *m*; (*large*) bombo;
(*for oil, petrol*) bidón *m* ♦ *vi* tocar el
tambor; (*with fingers*) tamborilear ♦ *vt*: **to
~ one's fingers on the table** tamborilear
con los dedos sobre la mesa; **~s** *npl*
batería *sg*.
▶**drum up** *vt* (*enthusiasm, support*)
movilizar, fomentar.
drummer ['drʌmə*] *n* (*in military band*)
tambor *m/f*; (*in jazz/pop group*) batería *m/f*.
drumstick ['drʌmstɪk] *n* (*MUS*) palillo,
baqueta; (*chicken leg*) muslo (de pollo).
drunk [drʌŋk] *pp of* **drink** ♦ *adj* borracho
♦ *n* (*also*: ~**ard**) borracho/a; **to get** ~
emborracharse.
drunken ['drʌŋkən] *adj* borracho.
drunkenness ['drʌŋkənnɪs] *n* embriaguez *f*.
dry [draɪ] *adj* seco; (*day*) sin lluvia; (*climate*)
árido, seco; (*humour*) agudo;
(*uninteresting*: *lecture*) aburrido, pesado

♦ *vt* secar; (*tears*) enjugarse ♦ *vi* secarse; **on ~ land** en tierra firme; **to ~ one's hands/hair/eyes** secarse las manos/el pelo/las lágrimas.

►**dry up** *vi* (*supply, imagination etc*) agotarse; (*in speech*) atascarse.

dry-clean ['draɪ'kliːn] *vt* limpiar *or* lavar en seco; "**~ only**" (*on label*) "limpieza *or* lavado en seco".

dry-cleaner's ['draɪ'kliːnəz] *n* tintorería.

dry-cleaning ['draɪ'kliːnɪŋ] *n* lavado en seco.

dry dock *n* (*NAUT*) dique *m* seco.

dryer ['draɪə*] *n* (*for hair*) secador *m*; (*for clothes*) secadora.

dry goods *npl* (*COMM*) mercería *sg.*

dry goods store *n* (*US*) mercería.

dry ice *n* nieve *f* carbónica, hielo seco.

dryness ['draɪnɪs] *n* sequedad *f.*

dry rot *n* putrefacción *f.*

dry run *n* (*fig*) ensayo.

dry ski slope *n* pista artificial de esquí.

DSc *n abbr* (= *Doctor of Science*) título universitario.

DST *n abbr* (*US*: = *Daylight Saving Time*) hora de verano.

DT *n abbr* (*COMPUT*) = **data transmission.**

DTI *n abbr* (*BRIT*) = *Department of Trade and Industry.*

DTP *n abbr* = **desktop publishing.**

DT's *n abbr* (*col*: = *delirium tremens*) delirium *m* tremens.

dual ['djuəl] *adj* doble.

dual carriageway *n* (*BRIT*) ≈ autovía.

dual-control ['djuəlkən'trəul] *adj* de doble mando.

dual nationality *n* doble nacionalidad *f.*

dual-purpose ['djuəl'pɜːpəs] *adj* de doble uso.

dubbed [dʌbd] *adj* (*CINE*) doblado.

dubious ['djuːbɪəs] *adj* indeciso; (*reputation, company*) dudoso; (*character*) sospechoso; **I'm very ~ about it** tengo mis dudas sobre ello.

Dublin ['dʌblɪn] *n* Dublín.

Dubliner ['dʌblɪnə*] *n* dublinés/esa *m/f.*

duchess ['dʌtʃɪs] *n* duquesa.

duck [dʌk] *n* pato ♦ *vi* agacharse ♦ *vt* (*plunge in water*) zambullir.

duckling ['dʌklɪŋ] *n* patito.

duct [dʌkt] *n* conducto, canal *m.*

dud [dʌd] *n* (*shell*) obús *m* que no estalla; (*object, tool*): **it's a ~** es una filfa ♦ *adj*: **~ cheque** (*BRIT*) cheque *m* sin fondos.

due [djuː] *adj* (*proper*) debido; (*fitting*) conveniente ♦ *adv*: **~ north** derecho al norte; **~s** *npl* (*for club, union*) cuota *sg*; (*in harbour*) derechos *mpl*; **in ~**

course a su debido tiempo; **~ to** debido a; **to be ~ to** deberse a; **the train is ~ to arrive at 8.00** el tren tiene (prevista) la llegada a las ocho; **the rent's ~ on the 30th** hay que pagar el alquiler el día 30; **I am ~ 6 days' leave** me deben 6 días de vacaciones; **she is ~ back tomorrow** ella debe volver mañana.

due date *n* fecha de vencimiento.

duel ['djuəl] *n* duelo.

duet [djuːˈet] *n* dúo.

duff [dʌf] *adj* sin valor.

duffel bag ['dʌfl-] *n* macuto.

duffel coat ['dʌfl-] *n* trenca.

dug [dʌg] *pt, pp of* **dig.**

dugout ['dʌgaut] *n* (*canoe*) piragua (*hecha de un solo tronco*); (*SPORT*) banquillo; (*MIL*) refugio subterráneo.

duke [djuːk] *n* duque *m.*

dull [dʌl] *adj* (*light*) apagado; (*stupid*) torpe; (*boring*) pesado; (*sound, pain*) sordo; (*weather, day*) gris ♦ *vt* (*pain, grief*) aliviar; (*mind, senses*) entorpecer.

duly ['djuːlɪ] *adv* debidamente; (*on time*) a su debido tiempo.

dumb [dʌm] *adj* mudo; (*stupid*) estúpido; **to be struck ~** (*fig*) quedar boquiabierto.

dumbbell ['dʌmbɛl] *n* (*SPORT*) pesa.

dumbfounded [dʌmˈfaundɪd] *adj* pasmado.

dummy ['dʌmɪ] *n* (*tailor's model*) maniquí *m*; (*BRIT*: *for baby*) chupete *m* ♦ *adj* falso, postizo; **~ run** ensayo.

dump [dʌmp] *n* (*heap*) montón *m* de basura; (*place*) basurero, vertedero; (*col*) tugurio; (*MIL*) depósito; (*COMPUT*) copia vaciada ♦ *vt* (*put down*) dejar; (*get rid of*) deshacerse de; (*COMPUT*) vaciar; (*COMM*: *goods*) inundar el mercado de; **to be (down) in the ~s** (*col*) tener murria, estar deprimido.

dumping ['dʌmpɪŋ] *n* (*ECON*) dumping *m*; (*of rubbish*): "**no ~**" "prohibido verter basura".

dumpling ['dʌmplɪŋ] *n bola de masa hervida.*

dumpy ['dʌmpɪ] *adj* regordete/a.

dunce [dʌns] *n* zopenco.

dune [djuːn] *n* duna.

dung [dʌŋ] *n* estiércol *m.*

dungarees [dʌŋgəˈriːz] *npl* mono *sg*, overol *msg* (*LAM*).

dungeon ['dʌndʒən] *n* calabozo.

dunk [dʌŋk] *vt* mojar.

duo ['djuːəu] *n* (*gen, MUS*) dúo.

duodenal [djuːəˈdiːnl] *adj* (*ulcer*) de duodeno.

duodenum [djuːəˈdiːnəm] *n* duodeno.

dupe [djuːp] *n* (*victim*) víctima ♦ *vt* engañar.

duplex ['dju:plɛks] n (US: also: ~ **apartment**) dúplex m.

duplicate ['dju:plɪkət] n duplicado; (copy of letter etc) copia ♦ adj (copy) duplicado ♦ vt ['dju:plɪkeɪt] duplicar; (on machine) multicopiar; **in** ~ por duplicado.

duplicate key n duplicado de una llave.

duplicating machine ['dju:plɪkeɪtɪŋ-], **duplicator** ['dju:plɪkeɪtə*] n multicopista m.

duplicity [dju:'plɪsɪtɪ] n doblez f.

Dur abbr (BRIT) = Durham.

durability [djuərə'bɪlɪtɪ] n durabilidad f.

durable ['djuərəbl] adj duradero.

duration [djuə'reɪʃən] n duración f.

duress [djuə'rɛs] n: **under** ~ por coacción.

Durex ® ['djuərɛks] n (BRIT) preservativo.

during ['djuərɪŋ] prep durante.

dusk [dʌsk] n crepúsculo, anochecer m.

dusky ['dʌskɪ] adj oscuro; (complexion) moreno.

dust [dʌst] n polvo ♦ vt (furniture) desempolvar; (cake etc): **to** ~ **with** espolvorear de.

►**dust off** vt (also fig) desempolvar, quitar el polvo de.

dustbin ['dʌstbɪn] n (BRIT) cubo de la basura, balde m (LAM).

dustbin liner n bolsa de basura.

duster ['dʌstə*] n paño, trapo; (feather ~) plumero.

dust jacket n sobrecubierta.

dustman ['dʌstmən] n (BRIT) basurero.

dustpan ['dʌstpæn] n cogedor m.

dust storm n vendaval m de polvo.

dusty ['dʌstɪ] adj polvoriento.

Dutch [dʌtʃ] adj holandés/esa ♦ n (LING) holandés m ♦ adv: **to go** ~ pagar a escote; **the** ~ npl los holandeses.

Dutch auction n subasta a la rebaja.

Dutchman ['dʌtʃmən], **Dutchwoman** ['dʌtʃwumən] n holandés/esa m/f.

dutiful ['dju:tɪful] adj (child) obediente; (husband) sumiso; (employee) cumplido.

duty ['dju:tɪ] n deber m; (tax) derechos mpl de aduana; **on** ~ de servicio; (at night etc) de guardia; **off** ~ libre (de servicio); **to make it one's** ~ **to do sth** encargarse de hacer algo sin falta; **to pay** ~ **on sth** pagar los derechos sobre algo.

duty-free [dju:tɪ'fri:] adj libre de derechos de aduana; ~ **shop** tienda libre de impuestos.

duty officer n (MIL etc) oficial m/f de guardia.

duvet ['du:veɪ] n (BRIT) edredón m (nórdico).

DV abbr (= Deo volente) Dios mediante.

DVD n abbr (= digital versatile or video disc) DVD m.

DVLA n abbr (BRIT: = Driver and Vehicle Licensing Agency) organismo encargado de la expedición de permisos de conducir y matriculación de vehículos.

DVM n abbr (US: = Doctor of Veterinary Medicine) título universitario.

dwarf [dwɔ:f], pl **dwarves** [dwɔ:vz] n enano ♦ vt empequeñecer.

dwell [dwɛl], pt, pp **dwelt** [dwɛlt] vi morar.

►**dwell on** vt fus explayarse en.

dweller ['dwɛlə*] n habitante m; **city** ~ habitante m de la ciudad.

dwelling ['dwɛlɪŋ] n vivienda.

dwelt [dwɛlt] pt, pp of dwell.

dwindle ['dwɪndl] vi menguar, disminuir.

dwindling ['dwɪndlɪŋ] adj (strength, interest) menguante; (resources, supplies) en disminución.

dye [daɪ] n tinte m ♦ vt teñir; **hair** ~ tinte m para el pelo.

dying ['daɪɪŋ] adj moribundo, agonizante; (moments) final; (words) último.

dyke [daɪk] n (BRIT) dique m; (channel) arroyo, acequia; (causeway) calzada.

dynamic [daɪ'næmɪk] adj dinámico.

dynamics [daɪ'næmɪks] n or npl dinámica sg.

dynamite ['daɪnəmaɪt] n dinamita ♦ vt dinamitar.

dynamo ['daɪnəməu] n dinamo f or m (LAM).

dynasty ['dɪnəstɪ] n dinastía.

dysentery ['dɪsɪntrɪ] n disentería.

dyslexia [dɪs'lɛksɪə] n dislexia.

dyslexic [dɪs'lɛksɪk] adj, n disléxico/a m/f.

dyspepsia [dɪs'pɛpsɪə] n dispepsia.

dystrophy ['dɪstrəfɪ] n distrofia; **muscular** ~ distrofia muscular.

E e

E, e [i:] n (letter) E, e f; (MUS) mi m; **E for Edward**, (US) **E for Easy** E de Enrique.

E abbr (= east) E ♦ n abbr (= Ecstasy) éxtasis m.

E111 n abbr (also: **form** ~) impreso E111.

ea. abbr = each.

E.A. abbr (US: = educational age) nivel escolar.

each [i:tʃ] adj cada inv ♦ pron cada uno; ~ **other** el uno al otro; **they hate** ~ **other** se odian (entre ellos *or* mutuamente); ~ **day** cada día; **they have 2 books** ~ tienen 2 libros cada uno; **they cost £5** ~ cuestan cinco libras cada uno; ~ **of us** cada uno de nosotros.

eager ['i:gə*] *adj* (*gen*) impaciente; (*hopeful*) ilusionado; (*keen*) entusiasmado; (: *pupil*) apasionado; **to be** ~ **to do sth** estar deseoso de hacer algo; **to be** ~ **for** ansiar, anhelar.

eagerly ['i:gəlɪ] *adv* con impaciencia; con ilusión; con entusiasmo.

eagerness ['i:gənɪs] *n* impaciencia; ilusión *f*; entusiasmo.

eagle ['i:gl] *n* águila.

E and OE *abbr* = **errors and omissions excepted.**

ear [ɪə*] *n* oreja; (*sense of hearing*) oído; (*of corn*) espiga; **up to the** ~**s in debt** abrumado de deudas.

earache ['ɪəreɪk] *n* dolor *m* de oídos.

eardrum ['ɪədrʌm] *n* tímpano.

earful ['ɪəful] *n*: **to give sb an** ~ (*col*) echar una bronca a algn.

earl [ə:l] *n* conde *m*.

early ['ə:lɪ] *adv* (*gen*) temprano; (*ahead of time*) con tiempo, con anticipación ♦ *adj* (*gen*) temprano; (*reply*) pronto; (*man*) primitivo; (*first: Christians, settlers*) primero; **to have an** ~ **night** acostarse temprano; **in the** ~ *or* ~ **in the spring/ 19th century** a principios de primavera/ del siglo diecinueve; **you're** ~! ¡has llegado temprano *or* pronto!; ~ **in the morning/afternoon** a primeras horas de la mañana/tarde; **she's in her** ~ **forties** tiene poco más de cuarenta años; **at your earliest convenience** (*COMM*) con la mayor brevedad posible; **I can't come any earlier** no puedo llegar antes.

early retirement *n* jubilación *f* anticipada.

early warning system *n* sistema *m* de alerta inmediata.

earmark ['ɪəmɑ:k] *vt*: **to** ~ **for** reservar para, destinar a.

earn [ə:n] *vt* (*gen*) ganar; (*interest*) devengar; (*praise*) ganarse; **to** ~ **one's living** ganarse la vida.

earned income *n* renta del trabajo.

earnest ['ə:nɪst] *adj* serio, formal ♦ *n* (*also*: ~ **money**) anticipo, señal *f*; **in** ~ *adv* en serio.

earnings ['ə:nɪŋz] *npl* (*personal*) ingresos *mpl*; (*of company etc*) ganancias *fpl*.

earphones ['ɪəfəunz] *npl* auriculares *mpl*.

earplugs ['ɪəplʌgz] *npl* tapones *mpl* para los oídos.

earring ['ɪərɪŋ] *n* pendiente *m*, arete *m* (*esp*

LAM).

earshot ['ɪəʃɒt] *n*: **out of/within** ~ fuera del/al alcance del oído.

earth [ə:θ] *n* (*gen*) tierra; (*BRIT: ELEC*) toma de tierra ♦ *vt* (*BRIT: ELEC*) conectar a tierra.

earthenware ['ə:θnwɛə*] *n* loza (de barro).

earthly ['ə:θlɪ] *adj* terrenal, mundano; ~ **paradise** paraíso terrenal; **there is no** ~ **reason to think** ... no existe razón para pensar ....

earthquake ['ə:θkweɪk] *n* terremoto.

earth-shattering ['ə:θʃætərɪŋ] *adj* trascendental.

earthworm ['ə:θwə:m] *n* lombriz *f*.

earthy ['ə:θɪ] *adj* (*fig: uncomplicated*) sencillo; (: *coarse*) grosero.

earwig ['ɪəwɪg] *n* tijereta.

ease [i:z] *n* facilidad *f*; (*comfort*) comodidad *f* ♦ *vt* (*task*) facilitar; (*pain*) aliviar; (*loosen*) soltar; (*relieve: pressure, tension*) aflojar; (*weight*) aligerar; (*help pass*): **to** ~ **sth in/ out** meter/sacar algo con cuidado ♦ *vi* (*situation*) relajarse; **with** ~ con facilidad; **to feel at** ~/**ill at** ~ sentirse a gusto/a disgusto; **at** ~! (*MIL*) ¡descansen!
▶**ease off, ease up** *vi* (*work, business*) aflojar; (*person*) relajarse.

easel ['i:zl] *n* caballete *m*.

easily ['i:zɪlɪ] *adv* fácilmente.

easiness ['i:zɪnɪs] *n* facilidad *f*; (*of manners*) soltura.

east [i:st] *n* este *m*, oriente *m* ♦ *adj* del este, oriental ♦ *adv* al este, hacia el este; **the E**~ el Oriente; (*POL*) el Este.

Easter ['i:stə*] *n* Pascua (de Resurrección).

Easter egg *n* huevo de Pascua.

Easter holidays *npl* Semana Santa *sg*.

Easter Island *n* Isla de Pascua.

easterly ['i:stəlɪ] *adj* (*to the east*) al este; (*from the east*) del este.

Easter Monday *n* lunes *m* de Pascua.

eastern ['i:stən] *adj* del este, oriental; **E**~ **Europe** Europa del Este; **the E**~ **bloc** (*POL*) los países del Este.

Easter Sunday *n* Domingo de Resurrección.

East Germany *n* (*formerly*) Alemania Oriental *or* del Este.

eastward(s) ['i:stwəd(z)] *adv* hacia el este.

easy ['i:zɪ] *adj* (*life*) fácil, holgado, cómodo; (*relaxed*) natural ♦ *adv*: **to take it** *or* **things** ~ (*not worry*) no preocuparse; (*go slowly*) tomarlo con calma; (*rest*) descansar; **payment on** ~ **terms** (*COMM*) facilidades de pago; **I'm** ~ (*col*) me da igual, no me importa; **easier said than done** del dicho al hecho hay buen trecho.

easy chair n butaca.
easy-going ['iːzɪ'gəʊɪŋ] adj acomodadizo.
easy touch [iːzɪ'tʌtʃ] n: **he's an ~** (col) es fácil de convencer.
eat, pt **ate**, pp **eaten** [iːt, eɪt, 'iːtn] vt comer.
▶**eat away** vt (subj: sea) desgastar; (: acid) corroer.
▶**eat into, eat away at** vt fus corroer.
▶**eat out** vi comer fuera.
▶**eat up** vt (meal etc) comerse; **it ~s up electricity** devora la electricidad.
eatable ['iːtəbl] adj comestible.
eau de Cologne [əʊdəkə'ləʊn] n (agua de) colonia.
eaves [iːvz] npl alero sg.
eavesdrop ['iːvzdrɔp] vi: **to ~ (on sb)** escuchar a escondidas (a algn).
ebb [ɛb] n reflujo ♦ vi bajar; (fig: also: ~ **away**) decaer; **~ and flow** el flujo y reflujo; **to be at a low ~** (fig: person) estar de capa caída.
ebb tide n marea menguante.
ebony ['ɛbənɪ] n ébano.
ebullient [ɪ'bʌlɪənt] adj entusiasta, animado.
EC n abbr (= European Community) CE f.
ECB n abbr (= European Central Bank) BCE m.
eccentric [ɪk'sɛntrɪk] adj, n excéntrico/a.
ecclesiastical [ɪkliːzɪ'æstɪkəl] adj eclesiástico.
ECG n abbr (= electrocardiogram) E.C. m.
ECGD n abbr (= Export Credits Guarantee Department) servicio de garantía financiera a la exportación.
echo, ~**es** ['ɛkəʊ] n eco m ♦ vt (sound) repetir ♦ vi resonar, hacer eco.
ECLA n abbr (= Economic Commission for Latin America) CEPAL f.
éclair ['eɪkleə*] n petisú m.
eclipse [ɪ'klɪps] n eclipse m ♦ vt eclipsar.
ECM n abbr (US: = European Common Market) MCE m.
eco- ['iːkəʊ] pref eco-.
eco-friendly ['iːkəʊfrɛndlɪ] adj ecológico.
ecological [iːkə'lɔdʒɪkl] adj ecológico.
ecologist [ɪ'kɔlədʒɪst] n ecologista m/f; (scientist) ecólogo/a m/f.
ecology [ɪ'kɔlədʒɪ] n ecología.
e-commerce n abbr (= electronic commerce) comercio electrónico.
economic [iːkə'nɔmɪk] adj (profitable: price) económico; (: business etc) rentable.
economical [iːkə'nɔmɪkl] adj económico.
economically [iːkə'nɔmɪklɪ] adv económicamente.
economics [iːkə'nɔmɪks] n economía ♦ npl (financial aspects) finanzas fpl.
economist [ɪ'kɔnəmɪst] n economista m/f.

economize [ɪ'kɔnəmaɪz] vi economizar, ahorrar.
economy [ɪ'kɔnəmɪ] n economía; **economies of scale** economías fpl de escala.
economy class n (AVIAT etc) clase f turista.
economy size n tamaño familiar.
ecosystem ['iːkəʊsɪstəm] n ecosistema m.
eco-tourism [iːkəʊ'tuərɪzm] n turismo verde or ecológico.
ECSC n abbr (= European Coal and Steel Community) CECA f.
ecstasy ['ɛkstəsɪ] n éxtasis m inv.
ecstatic [ɛks'tætɪk] adj extático, extasiado.
ECT n abbr see **electroconvulsive therapy**.
ECU, ecu n abbr (= European Currency Unit) ECU, ecu m.
Ecuador ['ɛkwədɔː*] n Ecuador m.
Ecuador(i)an [ɛkwə'dɔːr(ɪ)ən] adj, n ecuatoriano/a m/f.
ecumenical [iːkju'mɛnɪkl] adj ecuménico.
eczema ['ɛksɪmə] n eczema m.
eddy ['ɛdɪ] n remolino.
Eden ['iːdn] n Edén m.
edge [ɛdʒ] n (of knife etc) filo; (of object) borde m; (of lake etc) orilla ♦ vt (SEWING) ribetear ♦ vi: **to ~ past** pasar con dificultad; **on ~** (fig) = **edgy; to ~ away from** alejarse poco a poco de; **to ~ forward** avanzar poco a poco.
edgeways ['ɛdʒweɪz] adv: **he couldn't get a word in ~** no pudo meter baza.
edging ['ɛdʒɪŋ] n (SEWING) ribete m; (of path) borde m.
edgy ['ɛdʒɪ] adj nervioso, inquieto.
edible ['ɛdɪbl] adj comestible.
edict ['iːdɪkt] n edicto.
edifice ['ɛdɪfɪs] n edificio.
edifying ['ɛdɪfaɪɪŋ] adj edificante.
Edinburgh ['ɛdɪnbərə] n Edimburgo.
edit ['ɛdɪt] vt (be editor of) dirigir; (re-write) redactar; (cut) cortar; (COMPUT) editar.
edition [ɪ'dɪʃən] n (gen) edición f; (number printed) tirada.
editor ['ɛdɪtə*] n (of newspaper) director(a) m/f; (of book) redactor(a) m/f; (film ~) montador(a) m/f.
editorial [ɛdɪ'tɔːrɪəl] adj editorial ♦ n editorial m; ~ **staff** redacción f.
EDP n abbr (= electronic data processing) PED m.
EDT n abbr (US: = Eastern Daylight Time) hora de verano de Nueva York.
educate ['ɛdjukeɪt] vt (gen) educar; (instruct) instruir.
educated guess ['ɛdjukeɪtɪd-] n hipótesis f sólida.
education [ɛdju'keɪʃən] n educación f;

(*schooling*) enseñanza; (*SCOL: subject etc*) pedagogía; **primary/secondary** ~ enseñanza primaria/secundaria.

educational [ɛdju'keɪʃənl] *adj* (*policy etc*) de educación, educativo; (*teaching*) docente; (*instructive*) educativo; ~ **technology** tecnología educacional.

Edwardian [ɛd'wɔːdɪən] *adj* eduardiano.

E.E. *abbr* = **electrical engineer**.

EEC *n abbr* (= *European Economic Community*) CEE *f*.

EEG *n abbr see* **electroencephalogram**.

eel [iːl] *n* anguila.

EENT *n abbr* (*US MED*) = *eye, ear, nose and throat*.

EEOC *n abbr* (*US*: = *Equal Employment Opportunities Commission*) comisión que investiga discriminación racial o sexual en el empleo.

eerie ['ɪərɪ] *adj* (*sound, experience*) espeluznante.

EET *n abbr* (= *Eastern European Time*) hora de Europa oriental.

efface [ɪ'feɪs] *vt* borrar.

effect [ɪ'fɛkt] *n* efecto ♦ *vt* efectuar, llevar a cabo; ~**s** *npl* (*property*) efectos *mpl*; **to take** ~ (*law*) entrar en vigor *or* vigencia; (*drug*) surtir efecto; **in** ~ en realidad; **to have an** ~ **on sb/sth** hacerle efecto a algn/afectar algo; **to put into** ~ (*plan*) llevar a la práctica; **his letter is to the** ~ **that...** su carta viene a decir que....

effective [ɪ'fɛktɪv] *adj* (*gen*) eficaz; (*striking: display, outfit*) impresionante; (*real*) efectivo; **to become** ~ (*LAW*) entrar en vigor; ~ **date** fecha de vigencia.

effectively [ɪ'fɛktɪvlɪ] *adv* (*efficiently*) eficazmente; (*strikingly*) de manera impresionante; (*in reality*) en efecto.

effectiveness [ɪ'fɛktɪvnɪs] *n* eficacia.

effeminate [ɪ'fɛmɪnɪt] *adj* afeminado.

effervescent [ɛfə'vɛsnt] *adj* efervescente.

efficacy ['ɛfɪkəsɪ] *n* eficacia.

efficiency [ɪ'fɪʃənsɪ] *n* (*gen*) eficiencia; (*of machine*) rendimiento.

efficient [ɪ'fɪʃənt] *adj* eficiente; (*remedy, product, system*) eficaz; (*machine, car*) de buen rendimiento.

effigy ['ɛfɪdʒɪ] *n* efigie *f*.

effluent ['ɛfluənt] *n* vertidos *mpl*.

effort ['ɛfət] *n* esfuerzo; **to make an** ~ **to do sth** estar deseoso de hacer algo.

effortless ['ɛfətlɪs] *adj* sin ningún esfuerzo.

effrontery [ɪ'frʌntərɪ] *n* descaro.

effusive [ɪ'fjuːsɪv] *adj* efusivo.

EFL *n abbr* (*SCOL*) = *English as a foreign language*.

EFTA ['ɛftə] *n abbr* (= *European Free Trade*

Association) EFTA *f*.

e.g. *adv abbr* (= *exempli gratia*) p.ej.

egg [ɛg] *n* huevo; **hard-boiled/soft-boiled/poached** ~ huevo duro *or* a la copa (*LAM*) *or* tibio (*LAM*)/pasado por agua/escalfado; **scrambled** ~**s** huevos revueltos.

▶**egg on** *vt* incitar.

eggcup ['ɛgkʌp] *n* huevera.

eggnog [ɛg'nɔg] *n* ponche *m* de huevo.

eggplant ['ɛgplɑːnt] *n* (*esp US*) berenjena.

eggshell ['ɛgʃɛl] *n* cáscara de huevo.

egg-timer ['ɛgtaɪmə*] *n* reloj *m* de arena (*para cocer huevos*).

egg white *n* clara de huevo.

egg yolk *n* yema de huevo.

ego ['iːgəu] *n* ego.

egotism ['ɛgəutɪzəm] *n* egoísmo.

egotist ['ɛgəutɪst] *n* egoísta *m/f*.

ego trip *n*: **to be on an** ~ creerse el centro del mundo.

Egypt ['iːdʒɪpt] *n* Egipto.

Egyptian [ɪ'dʒɪpʃən] *adj, n* egipcio/a *m/f*.

eiderdown ['aɪdədaun] *n* edredón *m*.

eight [eɪt] *num* ocho.

eighteen [eɪ'tiːn] *num* dieciocho.

eighth [eɪtθ] *num* octavo.

eighty ['eɪtɪ] *num* ochenta.

Eire ['ɛərə] *n* Eire *m*.

EIS *n abbr* (= *Educational Institute of Scotland*) sindicato de profesores escoceses.

either ['aɪðə*] *adj* cualquiera de los dos ...; (*both, each*) cada ♦ *pron*: ~ (**of them**) cualquiera (de los dos) ♦ *adv* tampoco ♦ *conj*: ~ **yes or no** o sí o no; **on** ~ **side** en ambos lados; **I don't like** ~ no me gusta ninguno de los dos; **no, I don't** ~ no, yo tampoco.

eject [ɪ'dʒɛkt] *vt* echar; (*tenant*) desahuciar ♦ *vi* eyectarse.

ejector seat [ɪ'dʒɛktə-] *n* asiento proyectable.

eke out [iːk-] *vt fus* (*money*) hacer que llegue.

EKG *n abbr* (*US*) *see* **electrocardiogram**.

el [ɛl] *n abbr* (*US col*) = **elevated railroad**.

elaborate *adj* [ɪ'læbərɪt] (*design, pattern*) complicado ♦ *vb* [ɪ'læbəreɪt] *vt* elaborar ♦ *vi* explicarse con muchos detalles.

elaborately [ɪ'læbərɪtlɪ] *adv* de manera complicada; (*decorated*) profusamente.

elaboration [ɪlæbə'reɪʃən] *n* elaboración *f*.

elapse [ɪ'læps] *vi* transcurrir.

elastic [ɪ'læstɪk] *adj, n* elástico.

elastic band *n* (*BRIT*) gomita.

elated [ɪ'leɪtɪd] *adj*: **to be** ~ estar eufórico.

elation [ɪ'leɪʃən] *n* euforia.

elbow ['ɛlbəu] *n* codo ♦ *vt*: **to** ~ **one's way through the crowd** abrirse paso a

codazos por la muchedumbre.
elbow grease n (col): **to use some** or **a bit of** ~ menearse.
elder ['ɛldə*] adj mayor ♦ n (tree) saúco; (person) mayor; (of tribe) anciano.
elderly ['ɛldəlɪ] adj de edad, mayor ♦ npl: **the** ~ la gente mayor, los ancianos.
eldest ['ɛldɪst] adj, n el/la mayor.
elect [ɪ'lɛkt] vt elegir; (choose): **to** ~ **to do** optar por hacer.
election [ɪ'lɛkʃən] n elección f; **to hold an** ~ convocar elecciones.
election campaign n campaña electoral.
electioneering [ɪlɛkʃə'mɪərɪŋ] n campaña electoral.
elector [ɪ'lɛktə*] n elector(a) m/f.
electoral [ɪ'lɛktərəl] adj electoral.
electoral college n colegio electoral.
electoral roll n censo electoral.
electorate [ɪ'lɛktərɪt] n electorado.
electric [ɪ'lɛktrɪk] adj eléctrico.
electrical [ɪ'lɛktrɪkl] adj eléctrico.
electrical engineer n ingeniero/a electricista.
electrical failure n fallo eléctrico.
electric blanket n manta eléctrica.
electric chair n silla eléctrica.
electric cooker n cocina eléctrica.
electric current n corriente f eléctrica.
electric fire n estufa eléctrica.
electrician [ɪlɛk'trɪʃən] n electricista m/f.
electricity [ɪlɛk'trɪsɪtɪ] n electricidad f; **to switch on/off the** ~ conectar/desconectar la electricidad.
electricity board n (BRIT) compañía eléctrica (estatal).
electric light n luz f eléctrica.
electric shock n electrochoque m.
electrify [ɪ'lɛktrɪfaɪ] vt (RAIL) electrificar; (fig: audience) electrizar.
electro... [ɪ'lɛktrəʊl] pref electro.
electrocardiogram (ECG, (US) EKG) [ɪ'lɛktrə'kɑːdɪəgræm] n electrocardiograma m.
electrocardiograph [ɪ'lɛktrəʊ'kɑːdɪəgræf] n electrocardiógrafo.
electro-convulsive therapy (ECT) [ɪ'lɛktrəkən'vʌlsɪv-] n electroterapia.
electrocute [ɪ'lɛktrəʊkjuːt] vt electrocutar.
electrode [ɪ'lɛktrəʊd] n electrodo.
electroencephalogram (EEG) [ɪ'lɛktrəʊɛn'sɛfələgræm] n electroencefalograma m.
electrolysis [ɪlɛk'trɒlɪsɪs] n electrólisis f inv.
electromagnetic [ɪ'lɛktrəmæg'nɛtɪk] adj electromagnético.
electron [ɪ'lɛktrɒn] n electrón m.
electronic [ɪlɛk'trɒnɪk] adj electrónico.

electronic data processing (EDP) n tratamiento or proceso electrónico de datos.
electronic mail n correo electrónico.
electronics [ɪlɛk'trɒnɪks] n electrónica.
electron microscope n microscopio electrónico.
electroplated [ɪ'lɛktrə'pleɪtɪd] adj galvanizado.
electrotherapy [ɪ'lɛktrə'θɛrəpɪ] n electroterapia.
elegance ['ɛlɪgəns] n elegancia.
elegant ['ɛlɪgənt] adj elegante.
elegy ['ɛlɪdʒɪ] n elegía.
element ['ɛlɪmənt] n (gen) elemento; (of heater, kettle etc) resistencia.
elementary [ɛlɪ'mɛntərɪ] adj elemental; (primitive) rudimentario; (school, education) primario.
elementary school n (US) escuela de enseñanza primaria; ver recuadro.

ELEMENTARY SCHOOL

En Estados Unidos y Canadá se llama **elementary school** al centro estatal en el que los niños reciben los primeros seis u ocho años de su educación, también llamado "grade school" o "grammar school".

---

elephant ['ɛlɪfənt] n elefante m.
elevate ['ɛlɪveɪt] vt (gen) elevar; (in rank) ascender.
elevated railroad n (US) ferrocarril m urbano elevado.
elevation [ɛlɪ'veɪʃən] n elevación f; (rank) ascenso; (height) altitud f.
elevator ['ɛlɪveɪtə*] n (US) ascensor m, elevador m (LAM).
eleven [ɪ'lɛvn] num once.
elevenses [ɪ'lɛvnzɪz] npl (BRIT) ≈ café m de media mañana.
eleventh [ɪ'lɛvnθ] adj undécimo; **at the** ~ **hour** (fig) a última hora.
elf, pl **elves** [ɛlf, ɛlvz] n duende m.
elicit [ɪ'lɪsɪt] vt: **to** ~ **sth (from sb)** obtener algo (de algn).
eligible ['ɛlɪdʒəbl] adj cotizado; **to be** ~ **for a pension** tener derecho a una pensión.
eliminate [ɪ'lɪmɪneɪt] vt eliminar; (score out) suprimir; (a suspect, possibility) descartar.
elimination [ɪlɪmɪ'neɪʃən] n eliminación f; supresión f; **by process of** ~ por eliminación.
elite [eɪ'liːt] n élite f.
elitist [eɪ'liːtɪst] adj (pej) elitista.

elixir [ɪ'lɪksɪə*] n elixir m.
Elizabethan [ɪlɪzə'biːθən] adj isabelino.
elm [ɛlm] n olmo.
elocution [ɛlə'kjuːʃən] n elocución f.
elongated ['iːlɔŋgeɪtɪd] adj alargado.
elope [ɪ'ləup] vi fugarse.
elopement [ɪ'ləupmənt] n fuga.
eloquence ['ɛləkwəns] n elocuencia.
eloquent ['ɛləkwənt] adj elocuente.
else [ɛls] adv: **or** ~ si no; **something** ~ otra
cosa or algo más; **somewhere** ~ en otra
parte; **everywhere** ~ en los demás sitios;
everyone ~ todos los demás; **nothing** ~
nada más; **is there anything** ~ **I can do?**
¿puedo hacer algo más?; **where** ~?
¿dónde más?, ¿en qué otra parte?; **there
was little** ~ **to do** apenas quedaba otra
cosa que hacer; **nobody** ~ **spoke** no habló
nadie más.
elsewhere [ɛls'wɛə*] adv (be) en otra parte;
(go) a otra parte.
ELT n abbr (SCOL) = English Language
Teaching.
elucidate [ɪ'luːsɪdeɪt] vt esclarecer,
elucidar.
elude [ɪ'luːd] vt eludir; (blow, pursuer)
esquivar.
elusive [ɪ'luːsɪv] adj escurridizo; (answer)
difícil de encontrar; **he is very** ~ no es
fácil encontrarlo.
elves [ɛlvz] npl of **elf.**
emaciated [ɪ'meɪsɪeɪtɪd] adj escuálido.
E-Mail, e-mail ['iːmeɪl] n abbr (= electronic
mail) correo electrónico ♦ vt: **to** ~ **sb**
mandar un mensaje por correo
electrónico a algn.
emanate ['ɛməneɪt] vi emanar, provenir.
emancipate [ɪ'mænsɪpeɪt] vt emancipar.
emancipated [ɪ'mænsɪpeɪtɪd] adj liberado.
emancipation [ɪmænsɪ'peɪʃən] n
emancipación f, liberación f.
emasculate [ɪ'mæskjuleɪt] vt castrar; (fig)
debilitar.
embalm [ɪm'bɑːm] vt embalsamar.
embankment [ɪm'bæŋkmənt] n (of railway)
terraplén m; (riverside) dique m.
embargo, pl ~**es** [ɪm'bɑːgəu] n prohibición
f; (COMM, NAUT) embargo; **to put an** ~ **on
sth** poner un embargo en algo.
embark [ɪm'bɑːk] vi embarcarse ♦ vt
embarcar; **to** ~ **on** (journey) comenzar,
iniciar; (fig) emprender.
embarkation [ɛmbɑː'keɪʃən] n (people)
embarco; (goods) embarque m.
embarkation card n tarjeta de embarque.
embarrass [ɪm'bærəs] vt avergonzar, dar
vergüenza a; (financially etc) poner en un
aprieto.

embarrassed [ɪm'baerəst] adj azorado,
violento; **to be** ~ sentirse azorado or
violento.
embarrassing [ɪm'bærəsɪŋ] adj (situation)
violento; (question) embarazoso.
embarrassment [ɪm'bærəsmənt] n
vergüenza, azoramiento; (financial)
apuros mpl.
embassy ['ɛmbəsɪ] n embajada; **the
Spanish E**~ la embajada española.
embed [ɪm'bɛd] vt (jewel) empotrar; (teeth
etc) clavar.
embellish [ɪm'bɛlɪʃ] vt embellecer; (fig:
story, truth) adornar.
embers ['ɛmbəz] npl rescoldo sg, ascuas.
embezzle [ɪm'bɛzl] vt desfalcar,
malversar.
embezzlement [ɪm'bɛzlmənt] n desfalco,
malversación f.
embezzler [ɪm'bɛzlə*] n malversador(a)
m/f.
embitter [ɪm'bɪtə*] vt (person) amargar;
(relationship) envenenar.
embittered [ɪm'bɪtəd] adj resentido,
amargado.
emblem ['ɛmbləm] n emblema m.
embody [ɪm'bɔdɪ] vt (spirit) encarnar;
(ideas) expresar.
embolden [ɪm'bəuldən] vt envalentonar;
(TYP) poner en negrita.
embolism ['ɛmbəlɪzəm] n embolia.
emboss [ɪm'bɔs] vt estampar en relieve;
(metal, leather) repujar.
embossed [ɪm'bɔst] adj realzado; ~ **with** ...
con ... en relieve.
embrace [ɪm'breɪs] vt abrazar, dar un
abrazo a; (include) abarcar; (adopt: idea)
adherirse a ♦ vi abrazarse ♦ n abrazo.
embroider [ɪm'brɔɪdə*] vt bordar; (fig:
story) adornar, embellecer.
embroidery [ɪm'brɔɪdərɪ] n bordado.
embroil [ɪm'brɔɪl] vt: **to become** ~**ed** (in
sth) enredarse (en algo).
embryo ['ɛmbrɪəu] n (also fig) embrión m.
emcee [ɛm'siː] n (US) presentador(a) m/f.
emend [ɪ'mɛnd] vt (text) enmendar.
emerald ['ɛmərəld] n esmeralda.
emerge [ɪ'məːdʒ] vi (gen) salir; (arise)
surgir; **it** ~**s that** resulta que.
emergence [ɪ'məːdʒəns] n (of nation)
surgimiento.
emergency [ɪ'məːdʒənsɪ] n (event)
emergencia; (crisis) crisis f inv; **in an** ~ en
caso de urgencia; **(to declare a) state of** ~
(declarar) estado de emergencia or de
excepción.
emergency cord n (US) timbre m de
alarma.

emergency exit n salida de emergencia.
emergency landing n aterrizaje m forzoso.
emergency lane n (US) arcén m.
emergency meeting n reunión f extraordinaria.
emergency service n servicio de urgencia.
emergency stop n (AUT) parada en seco.
emergent [ɪ'mɜːdʒənt] adj (nation) recientemente independizado.
emery board ['ɛmərɪ-] n lima de uñas.
emetic [ɪ'mɛtɪk] n vomitivo, emético.
emigrant ['ɛmɪgrənt] n emigrante m/f.
emigrate ['ɛmɪgreɪt] vi emigrar.
emigration [ɛmɪ'greɪʃən] n emigración f.
émigré ['ɛmɪgreɪ] n emigrado/a.
eminence ['ɛmɪnəns] n eminencia; **to gain** or **win** ~ ganarse fama.
eminent ['ɛmɪnənt] adj eminente.
eminently ['ɛmɪnəntlɪ] adv eminentemente.
emirate ['ɛmɪrɪt] n emirato.
emission [ɪ'mɪʃən] n emisión f.
emit [ɪ'mɪt] vt emitir; (smell, smoke) despedir.
emolument [ɪ'mɒljʊmənt] n (often pl: formal) honorario, emolumento.
emotion [ɪ'məʊʃən] n emoción f.
emotional [ɪ'məʊʃənl] adj (person) sentimental; (scene) conmovedor(a), emocionante.
emotionally [ɪ'məʊʃnəlɪ] adv (behave, speak) con emoción; (be involved) sentimentalmente.
emotive [ɪ'məʊtɪv] adj emotivo.
empathy ['ɛmpəθɪ] n empatía; **to feel** ~ **with sb** sentirse identificado con algn.
emperor ['ɛmpərə*] n emperador m.
emphasis ['ɛmfəsɪs], pl **emphases** ['ɛmfəsiːz, -sɪz] n énfasis m inv; **to lay** or **place** ~ **on sth** (fig) hacer hincapié en algo; **the** ~ **is on sport** se da mayor importancia al deporte.
emphasize ['ɛmfəsaɪz] vt (word, point) subrayar, recalcar; (feature) hacer resaltar.
emphatic [ɛm'fætɪk] adj (condemnation) enérgico; (denial) rotundo.
emphatically [ɛm'fætɪklɪ] adv con énfasis.
emphysema [ɛmfɪ'siːmə] n (MED) enfisema m.
empire ['ɛmpaɪə*] n imperio.
empirical [ɛm'pɪrɪkl] adj empírico.
employ [ɪm'plɔɪ] vt (give job to) emplear; (make use of: thing, method) emplear, usar; **he's ~ed in a bank** está empleado en un banco.
employee [ɪmplɔɪ'iː] n empleado/a.
employer [ɪm'plɔɪə*] n patrón/ona m/f;

(businessman) empresario/a.
employment [ɪm'plɔɪmənt] n empleo; **full** ~ pleno empleo; **without** ~ sin empleo; **to find** ~ encontrar trabajo; **place of** ~ lugar m de trabajo.
employment agency n agencia de colocaciones or empleo.
employment exchange n bolsa de trabajo.
empower [ɪm'paʊə*] vt: **to** ~ **sb to do sth** autorizar a algn para hacer algo.
empress ['ɛmprɪs] n emperatriz f.
emptiness ['ɛmptɪnɪs] n vacío.
empty ['ɛmptɪ] adj vacío; (street, area) desierto; (threat) vano ♦ n (bottle) envase m ♦ vt vaciar; (place) dejar vacío ♦ vi vaciarse; (house) quedar(se) vacío or desocupado; (place) quedar(se) desierto; **to** ~ **into** (river) desembocar en.
empty-handed ['ɛmptɪ'hændɪd] adj con las manos vacías.
empty-headed ['ɛmptɪ'hɛdɪd] adj casquivano.
EMS n abbr (= European Monetary System) SME m.
EMT n abbr = emergency medical technician.
EMU n abbr (= Economic and Monetary Union) UME f.
emulate ['ɛmjuleɪt] vt emular.
emulsion [ɪ'mʌlʃən] n emulsión f.
enable [ɪ'neɪbl] vt: **to** ~ **sb to do sth** (allow) permitir a algn hacer algo; (prepare) capacitar a algn para hacer algo.
enact [ɪn'ækt] vt (law) promulgar; (play, scene, role) representar.
enamel [ɪ'næməl] n esmalte m.
enamel paint n esmalte m.
enamoured [ɪ'næməd] adj: **to be** ~ **of** (person) estar enamorado de; (activity etc) tener gran afición a; (idea) aferrarse a.
encampment [ɪn'kæmpmənt] n campamento.
encase [ɪn'keɪs] vt: **to** ~ **in** (contain) encajar; (cover) cubrir.
encased [ɪn'keɪst] adj: ~ **in** (covered) revestido de.
enchant [ɪn'tʃɑːnt] vt encantar.
enchanting [ɪn'tʃɑːntɪŋ] adj encantador(a).
encircle [ɪn'sɜːkl] vt (gen) rodear; (waist) ceñir.
encl. abbr (= enclosed) adj.
enclave ['ɛnkleɪv] n enclave m.
enclose [ɪn'kləʊz] vt (land) cercar; (with letter etc) adjuntar; (in receptacle): **to** ~ **(with)** encerrar (con); **please find ~d** le mandamos adjunto.
enclosure [ɪn'kləʊʒə*] n cercado, recinto; (COMM) carta adjunta.

encoder [ɪn'kəʊdə*] n (*COMPUT*) codificador m.

encompass [ɪn'kʌmpəs] vt abarcar.

encore [ɔŋ'kɔː*] excl ¡otra!, ¡bis! ♦ n bis m.

encounter [ɪn'kauntə*] n encuentro ♦ vt encontrar, encontrarse con; (*difficulty*) tropezar con.

encourage [ɪn'kʌrɪdʒ] vt alentar, animar; (*growth*) estimular; **to ~ sb (to do sth)** animar a algn (a hacer algo).

encouragement [ɪn'kʌrɪdʒmənt] n estímulo; (*of industry*) fomento.

encouraging [ɪn'kʌrɪdʒɪŋ] adj alentador(a).

encroach [ɪn'krəʊtʃ] vi: **to ~ (up)on** (*gen*) invadir; (*time*) adueñarse de.

encrust [ɪn'krʌst] vt incrustar.

encrusted [ɪn'krʌstəd] adj: **~ with** recubierto de.

encumber [ɪn'kʌmbə*] vt: **to be ~ed with** (*carry*) estar cargado de; (*debts*) estar gravado de.

encyclop(a)edia [ɛnsaɪkləʊ'piːdɪə] n enciclopedia.

end [ɛnd] n (*gen, also aim*) fin m; (*of table*) extremo; (*of line, rope etc*) cabo; (*of pointed object*) punta; (*of town*) barrio; (*of street*) final m; (*SPORT*) lado ♦ vt terminar, acabar; (*also*: **bring to an ~, put an ~ to**) acabar con ♦ vi terminar, acabar; **to ~ (with)** terminar (con); **in the ~** al final; **to be at an ~** llegar a su fin; **at the ~ of the day** (*fig*) al fin y al cabo, a fin de cuentas; **to this ~, with this ~ in view** con este propósito; **from ~ to ~** de punta a punta; **on ~** (*object*) de punta, de cabeza; **to stand on ~** (*hair*) erizarse, ponerse de punta; **for hours on ~** hora tras hora.

▶**end up** vi: **to ~ up in** terminar en; (*place*) ir a parar a.

endanger [ɪn'deɪndʒə*] vt poner en peligro; **an ~ed species** (*of animal*) una especie en peligro de extinción.

endear [ɪn'dɪə*] vt: **to ~ o.s. to sb** ganarse la simpatía de algn.

endearing [ɪn'dɪərɪŋ] adj entrañable.

endearment [ɪn'dɪərmənt] n cariño, palabra cariñosa; **to whisper ~s** decir unas palabras cariñosas al oído; **term of ~** nombre m cariñoso.

endeavour, (*US*) **endeavor** [ɪn'dɛvə*] n esfuerzo; (*attempt*) tentativa ♦ vi: **to ~ to do** esforzarse por hacer; (*try*) procurar hacer.

endemic [ɛn'dɛmɪk] adj (*poverty, disease*) endémico.

ending ['ɛndɪŋ] n fin m, final m; (*of book*) desenlace m; (*LING*) terminación f.

endive ['ɛndaɪv] n (*curly*) escarola; (*smooth, flat*) endibia.

endless ['ɛndlɪs] adj interminable, inacabable; (*possibilities*) infinito.

endorse [ɪn'dɔːs] vt (*cheque*) endosar; (*approve*) aprobar.

endorsee [ɪndɔː'siː] n endosatario/a.

endorsement [ɪn'dɔːsmənt] n (*approval*) aprobación f; (*signature*) endoso; (*BRIT: on driving licence*) nota de sanción.

endorser [ɪn'dɔːsə*] n avalista m/f.

endow [ɪn'dau] vt (*provide with money*) dotar; (*found*) fundar; **to be ~ed with** (*fig*) estar dotado de.

endowment [ɪn'daumənt] adj (*amount*) donación f.

endowment mortgage n hipoteca dotal.

endowment policy n póliza dotal.

end product n (*INDUSTRY*) producto final; (*fig*) resultado.

end result n resultado.

endurable [ɪn'djuərəbl] adj soportable, tolerable.

endurance [ɪn'djuərəns] n resistencia.

endurance test n prueba de resistencia.

endure [ɪn'djuə*] vt (*bear*) aguantar, soportar; (*resist*) resistir ♦ vi (*last*) perdurar; (*resist*) resistir.

enduring [ɪn'djuərɪŋ] adj duradero.

end user n (*COMPUT*) usuario final.

enema ['ɛnɪmə] n (*MED*) enema m.

enemy ['ɛnəmɪ] adj, n enemigo/a m/f; **to make an ~ of sb** enemistarse con algn.

energetic [ɛnə'dʒɛtɪk] adj enérgico.

energy ['ɛnədʒɪ] n energía.

energy crisis n crisis f energética.

energy-saving ['ɛnədʒɪseɪvɪŋ] adj (*policy*) para ahorrar energía; (*device*) que ahorra energía ♦ n ahorro de energía.

enervating ['ɛnəveɪtɪŋ] adj deprimente.

enforce [ɪn'fɔːs] vt (*LAW*) hacer cumplir.

enforced [ɪn'fɔːst] adj forzoso, forzado.

enfranchise [ɪn'fræntʃaɪz] vt (*give vote to*) conceder el derecho de voto a; (*set free*) emancipar.

engage [ɪn'geɪdʒ] vt (*attention*) captar; (*in conversation*) abordar; (*worker, lawyer*) contratar ♦ vi (*TECH*) engranar; **to ~ in** dedicarse a, ocuparse en; **to ~ sb in conversation** entablar conversación con algn; **to ~ the clutch** embragar.

engaged [ɪn'geɪdʒd] adj (*BRIT: busy, in use*) ocupado; (*betrothed*) prometido; **to get ~** prometerse; **he is ~ in research** se dedica a la investigación.

engaged tone n (*BRIT TEL*) señal f de comunicado.

engagement [ɪn'geɪdʒmənt] n

(*appointment*) compromiso, cita; (*battle*) combate *m*; (*to marry*) compromiso; (*period*) noviazgo; **I have a previous** ~ ya tengo un compromiso.

engagement ring *n* anillo de pedida.

engaging [ɪn'geɪdʒɪŋ] *adj* atractivo, simpático.

engender [ɪn'dʒendə*] *vt* engendrar.

engine ['endʒɪn] *n* (*AUT*) motor *m*; (*RAIL*) locomotora.

engine driver *n* (*BRIT*: *of train*) maquinista *m/f*.

engineer [endʒɪ'nɪə*] *n* ingeniero/a; (*BRIT*: *for repairs*) técnico/a; (*US RAIL*) maquinista *m/f*; **civil/mechanical** ~ ingeniero/a de caminos, canales y puertos/industrial.

engineering [endʒɪ'nɪərɪŋ] *n* ingeniería ♦ *cpd* (*works, factory*) de componentes mecánicos.

engine failure, engine trouble *n* avería del motor.

England ['ɪŋglənd] *n* Inglaterra.

English ['ɪŋglɪʃ] *adj* inglés/esa ♦ *n* (*LING*) el inglés; **the** ~ *npl* los ingleses.

English Channel *n*: **the** ~ el Canal de la Mancha.

Englishman ['ɪŋglɪʃmən], **Englishwoman** ['ɪŋglɪʃwumən] *n* inglés/esa *m/f*.

English-speaker ['ɪŋglɪʃspi:kə*] *n* persona de habla inglesa.

English-speaking ['ɪŋglɪʃspi:kɪŋ] *adj* de habla inglesa.

engraving [ɪn'greɪvɪŋ] *n* grabado.

engrossed [ɪn'grəust] *adj*: ~ **in** absorto en.

engulf [ɪn'gʌlf] *vt* sumergir, hundir; (*subj*: *fire*) devorar.

enhance [ɪn'hɑ:ns] *vt* (*gen*) aumentar; (*beauty*) realzar; (*position, reputation*) mejorar.

enigma [ɪ'nɪgmə] *n* enigma *m*.

enigmatic [enɪg'mætɪk] *adj* enigmático.

enjoy [ɪn'dʒɔɪ] *vt* (*have*: *health, fortune*) disfrutar de, gozar de; (*food*) comer con gusto; **I** ~ **doing...** me gusta hacer...; **to** ~ **o.s.** divertirse, pasarlo bien.

enjoyable [ɪn'dʒɔɪəbl] *adj* (*pleasant*) agradable; (*amusing*) divertido.

enjoyment [ɪn'dʒɔɪmənt] *n* (*use*) disfrute *m*; (*joy*) placer *m*.

enlarge [ɪn'lɑ:dʒ] *vt* aumentar; (*broaden*) extender; (*PHOT*) ampliar ♦ *vi*: **to** ~ **on** (*subject*) tratar con más detalles.

enlarged [ɪn'lɑ:dʒd] *adj* (*edition*) aumentado; (*MED*: *organ, gland*) dilatado.

enlargement [ɪn'lɑ:dʒmənt] *n* (*PHOT*) ampliación *f*.

enlighten [ɪn'laɪtn] *vt* informar, instruir.

enlightened [ɪn'laɪtnd] *adj* iluminado;

(*tolerant*) comprensivo.

enlightening [ɪn'laɪtnɪŋ] *adj* informativo, instructivo.

Enlightenment [ɪn'laɪtnmənt] *n* (*HISTORY*): **the** ~ la Ilustración, el Siglo de las Luces.

enlist [ɪn'lɪst] *vt* alistar; (*support*) conseguir ♦ *vi* alistarse; ~**ed man** (*US*: *MIL*) soldado raso.

enliven [ɪn'laɪvn] *vt* (*people*) animar; (*events*) avivar, animar.

enmity ['enmɪtɪ] *n* enemistad *f*.

ennoble [ɪ'nəubl] *vt* ennoblecer.

enormity [ɪ'nɔːmɪtɪ] *n* enormidad *f*.

enormous [ɪ'nɔːməs] *adj* enorme.

enough [ɪ'nʌf] *adj*: ~ **time/books** bastante tiempo/bastantes libros ♦ *n*: **have you got** ~? ¿tiene usted bastante? ♦ *adv*: **big** ~ bastante grande; **he has not worked** ~ no ha trabajado bastante; (**that's**) ~! ¡basta ya!, ¡ya está bien!; **that's** ~, **thanks** con eso basta, gracias; **will 5 be** ~? ¿bastará con 5?; **I've had** ~ estoy harto; **he was kind** ~ **to lend me the money** tuvo la bondad *o* amabilidad de prestarme el dinero; ... **which, funnily** ~ ... ... lo que, por extraño que parezca ... .

enquire [ɪn'kwaɪə*] *vt*, *vi* = **inquire**.

enrage [ɪn'reɪdʒ] *vt* enfurecer.

enrich [ɪn'rɪtʃ] *vt* enriquecer.

enrol, (*US*) **enroll** [ɪn'rəul] *vt* (*members*) inscribir; (*SCOL*) matricular ♦ *vi* inscribirse; (*SCOL*) matricularse.

enrol(l)ment [ɪn'rəulmənt] *n* inscripción *f*; matriculación *f*.

en route [ɔn'ru:t] *adv* durante el viaje; ~ **for/from/to** camino de/de/a.

ensconce [ɪn'skɔns] *vt*: **to** ~ **o.s.** instalarse cómodamente, acomodarse.

ensemble [ɔn'sɔmbl] *n* (*MUS*) conjunto.

enshrine [ɪn'ʃraɪn] *vt* recoger.

ensign ['ensaɪn] *n* (*flag*) bandera; (*NAUT*) alférez *m*.

enslave [ɪn'sleɪv] *vt* esclavizar.

ensue [ɪn'sju:] *vi* seguirse; (*result*) resultar.

ensuing [ɪn'sju:ɪŋ] *adj* subsiguiente.

ensure [ɪn'ʃuə*] *vt* asegurar.

ENT *n* *abbr* (= *Ear, Nose and Throat*) otorrinolaringología.

entail [ɪn'teɪl] *vt* (*imply*) suponer; (*result in*) acarrear.

entangle [ɪn'tæŋgl] *vt* (*thread etc*) enredar, enmarañar; **to become** ~**d in sth** (*fig*) enredarse en algo.

entanglement [ɪn'tæŋglmənt] *n* enredo.

enter ['entə*] *vt* (*room, profession*) entrar en; (*club*) hacerse socio de; (*army*) alistarse en; (*sb for a competition*)

inscribir; (*write down*) anotar, apuntar;
(*COMPUT*) introducir ♦ *vi* entrar; **to ~ for**
vt fus presentarse a; **to ~ into** *vt fus*
(*relations*) establecer; (*plans*) formar
parte de; (*debate*) tomar parte en;
(*negotiations*) entablar; (*agreement*) llegar
a, firmar; **to ~ (up)on** *vt fus* (*career*)
emprender.
enteritis [ɛntə'raɪtɪs] *n* enteritis *f*.
enterprise ['ɛntəpraɪz] *n* empresa; (*spirit*)
iniciativa; **free ~** la libre empresa;
private ~ la iniciativa privada.
enterprising ['ɛntəpraɪzɪŋ] *adj*
emprendedor(a).
entertain [ɛntə'teɪn] *vt* (*amuse*) divertir;
(*receive: guest*) recibir (en casa); (*idea*)
abrigar.
entertainer [ɛntə'teɪnə*] *n* artista *m/f*.
entertaining [ɛntə'teɪnɪŋ] *adj* divertido,
entretenido ♦ *n*: **to do a lot of ~** dar
muchas fiestas, tener muchos invitados.
entertainment [ɛntə'teɪnmənt] *n*
(*amusement*) diversión *f*; (*show*)
espectáculo; (*party*) fiesta.
entertainment allowance *n* (*COMM*)
gastos *mpl* de representación.
enthral [ɪn'θrɔ:l] *vt* embelesar, cautivar.
enthralled [ɪn'θrɔ:ld] *adj* cautivado.
enthralling [ɪn'θrɔ:lɪŋ] *adj* cautivador(a).
enthuse [ɪn'θu:z] *vi*: **to ~ about** *or* **over**
entusiasmarse por.
enthusiasm [ɪn'θu:zɪæzəm] *n* entusiasmo.
enthusiast [ɪn'θu:zɪæst] *n* entusiasta *m/f*.
enthusiastic [ɪnθu:zɪ'æstɪk] *adj* entusiasta;
to be ~ about sb/sth estar entusiasmado
con algn/algo.
entice [ɪn'taɪs] *vt* tentar; (*seduce*) seducir.
entire [ɪn'taɪə*] *adj* entero, todo.
entirely [ɪn'taɪəlɪ] *adv* totalmente.
entirety [ɪn'taɪərətɪ] *n*: **in its ~** en su
totalidad.
entitle [ɪn'taɪtl] *vt*: **to ~ sb to sth** dar a algn
derecho a algo.
entitled [ɪn'taɪtld] *adj* (*book*) titulado; **to be
~ to sth/to do sth** tener derecho a algo/a
hacer algo.
entity ['ɛntɪtɪ] *n* entidad *f*.
entourage [ɔntu'rɑ:ʒ] *n* séquito.
entrails ['ɛntreɪlz] *npl* entrañas *fpl*; (*US*)
asadura *sg*, menudos *mpl*.
entrance ['ɛntrəns] *n* entrada ♦ *vt* [ɪn'trɑ:ns]
encantar, hechizar; **to gain ~ to**
(*university etc*) ingresar en.
entrance examination *n* (*to school*)
examen *m* de ingreso.
entrance fee *n* entrada.
entrance ramp *n* (*US AUT*) rampa de
acceso.

entrancing [ɪn'trɑ:nsɪŋ] *adj* encantador(a).
entrant ['ɛntrənt] *n* (*in race, competition*)
participante *m/f*; (*in exam*) candidato/a.
entreat [ɛn'tri:t] *vt* rogar, suplicar.
entrenched [ɛn'trɛntʃd] *adj*: **~ interests**
intereses *mpl* creados.
entrepreneur [ɔntrəprə'nə:*] *n*
empresario/a, capitalista *m/f*.
entrepreneurial [ɔntrəprə'nə:rɪəl] *adj*
empresarial.
entrust [ɪn'trʌst] *vt*: **to ~ sth to sb** confiar
algo a algn.
entry ['ɛntrɪ] *n* entrada; (*permission to enter*)
acceso; (*in register, diary, ship's log*) apunte
m; (*in account book, ledger, list*) partida; **no
~** prohibido el paso; (*AUT*) dirección
prohibida; **single/double ~ book-keeping**
contabilidad *f* simple/por partida doble.
entry form *n* boletín *m* de inscripción.
entry phone *n* (*BRIT*) portero automático.
E-number ['i:nʌmbə*] *n* número E.
enumerate [ɪ'nju:məreɪt] *vt* enumerar.
enunciate [ɪ'nʌnsɪeɪt] *vt* pronunciar;
(*principle etc*) enunciar.
envelop [ɪn'vɛləp] *vt* envolver.
envelope ['ɛnvələup] *n* sobre *m*.
enviable ['ɛnvɪəbl] *adj* envidiable.
envious ['ɛnvɪəs] *adj* envidioso; (*look*) de
envidia.
environment [ɪn'vaɪərnmənt] *n* medio
ambiente; (*surroundings*) entorno;
Department of the E~ ministerio del
medio ambiente.
environmental [ɪnvaɪərn'mɛntl] *adj*
(*medio*) ambiental; **~ studies** (*in school
etc*) ecología *sg*.
environmentalist [ɪnvaɪərn'mɛntlɪst] *n*
ecologista *m/f*.
environmentally [ɪnvaɪərn'mɛntlɪ] *adv*: **~
sound/friendly** ecológico.
envisage [ɪn'vɪzɪdʒ] *vt* (*foresee*) prever;
(*imagine*) concebir.
envision [ɪn'vɪʒən] *vt* imaginar.
envoy ['ɛnvɔɪ] *n* enviado/a.
envy ['ɛnvɪ] *n* envidia ♦ *vt* tener envidia a;
to ~ sb sth envidiar algo a algn.
enzyme ['ɛnzaɪm] *n* enzima *m or f*.
EPA *n abbr* (*US*: = *Environmental Protection
Agency*) Agencia del Medio Ambiente.
ephemeral [ɪ'fɛmərəl] *adj* efímero.
epic ['ɛpɪk] *n* epopeya ♦ *adj* épico.
epicentre, (*US*) **epicenter** ['ɛpɪsɛntə*] *n*
epicentro.
epidemic [ɛpɪ'dɛmɪk] *n* epidemia.
epigram ['ɛpɪgræm] *n* epigrama *m*.
epilepsy ['ɛpɪlɛpsɪ] *n* epilepsia.
epileptic [ɛpɪ'lɛptɪk] *adj, n* epiléptico/a *m/f*.
epilogue ['ɛpɪlɔg] *n* epílogo.

episcopal [ɪˈpɪskəpl] *adj* episcopal.
episode [ˈɛpɪsəud] *n* episodio.
epistle [ɪˈpɪsl] *n* epístola.
epitaph [ˈɛpɪtɑːf] *n* epitafio.
epithet [ˈɛpɪθɛt] *n* epíteto.
epitome [ɪˈpɪtəmɪ] *n* arquetipo.
epitomize [ɪˈpɪtəmaɪz] *vt* representar.
epoch [ˈiːpɔk] *n* época.
eponymous [ɪˈpɔnɪməs] *adj* epónimo.
equable [ˈɛkwəbl] *adj* (*climate*) estable;
(*character*) ecuánime.
equal [ˈiːkwl] *adj* (*gen*) igual; (*treatment*)
equitativo ♦ *n* igual *m/f* ♦ *vt* ser igual a;
(*fig*) igualar; **to be ~ to** (*task*) estar a la
altura de; **the E~ Opportunities
Commission** (*BRIT*) comisión para la
igualdad de la mujer en el trabajo.
equality [iːˈkwɔlɪtɪ] *n* igualdad *f*.
equalize [ˈiːkwəlaɪz] *vt, vi* igualar; (*SPORT*)
empatar.
equalizer [ˈiːkwəlaɪzə*] *n* igualada.
equally [ˈiːkwəlɪ] *adv* igualmente; (*share etc*)
a partes iguales; **they are ~ clever** son
tan listos uno como otro.
equals sign *n* signo igual.
equanimity [ɛkwəˈnɪmɪtɪ] *n* ecuanimidad *f*.
equate [ɪˈkweɪt] *vt*: **to ~ sth with** equiparar
algo con.
equation [ɪˈkweɪʒən] *n* (*MATH*) ecuación *f*.
equator [ɪˈkweɪtə*] *n* ecuador *m*.
equatorial [ɛkwəˈtɔːrɪəl] *adj* ecuatorial.
Equatorial Guinea *n* Guinea Ecuatorial.
equestrian [ɪˈkwɛstrɪən] *adj* ecuestre ♦ *n*
jinete *m/f*.
equilibrium [iːkwɪˈlɪbrɪəm] *n* equilibrio.
equinox [ˈiːkwɪnɔks] *n* equinoccio.
equip [ɪˈkwɪp] *vt* (*gen*) equipar; (*person*)
proveer; **~ped with** (*machinery etc*)
provisto de; **to be well ~ped** estar bien
equipado; **he is well ~ped for the job** está
bien preparado para este puesto.
equipment [ɪˈkwɪpmənt] *n* equipo.
equitable [ˈɛkwɪtəbl] *adj* equitativo.
equities [ˈɛkwɪtɪz] *npl* (*BRIT COMM*) acciones
fpl ordinarias.
equity [ˈɛkwɪtɪ] *n* (*fairness*) equidad *f*;
(*ECON*: *of debtor*) valor *m* líquido.
equity capital *n* capital *m* propio,
patrimonio neto.
equivalent [ɪˈkwɪvəlnt] *adj, n* equivalente *m*;
to be ~ to equivaler a.
equivocal [ɪˈkwɪvəkl] *adj* equívoco.
equivocate [ɪˈkwɪvəkeɪt] *vi* andarse con
ambigüedades.
equivocation [ɪkwɪvəˈkeɪʃən] *n*
ambigüedad *f*.
ER *abbr* (*BRIT*: = Elizabeth Regina) *la reina
Isabel.*

er [əː] *interj* (*col*: *in hesitation*) esto, este
(*LAM*).
ERA *n abbr* (*US POL*: = Equal Rights
Amendment) *enmienda sobre la igualdad
de derechos de la mujer.*
era [ˈɪərə] *n* era, época.
eradicate [ɪˈrædɪkeɪt] *vt* erradicar,
extirpar.
erase [ɪˈreɪz] *vt* (*also COMPUT*) borrar.
eraser [ɪˈreɪzə*] *n* goma de borrar.
erect [ɪˈrɛkt] *adj* erguido ♦ *vt* erigir,
levantar; (*assemble*) montar.
erection [ɪˈrɛkʃən] *n* (*of building*)
construcción *f*; (*of machinery*) montaje *m*;
(*structure*) edificio; (*MED*) erección *f*.
ergonomics [əːgəˈnɔmɪks] *n* ergonomía.
ERISA *n abbr* (*US*: = Employee Retirement
Income Security Act*) ley que regula las
pensiones de jubilados.*
Eritrea [ɛrɪˈtreɪə] *n* Eritrea.
ERM *n abbr* (= Exchange Rate Mechanism)
(mecanismo de cambios del) SME *m*.
ermine [ˈəːmɪn] *n* armiño.
ERNIE [ˈəːnɪ] *n abbr* (*BRIT*: = Electronic
Random Number Indicating Equipment)
*ordenador que elige al azar los números
ganadores de los bonos del Estado.*
erode [ɪˈrəud] *vt* (*GEO*) erosionar; (*metal*)
corroer, desgastar.
erogenous zone [ɪˈrɔdʒənəs-] *n* zona
erógena.
erosion [ɪˈrəuʒən] *n* erosión *f*; desgaste *m*.
erotic [ɪˈrɔtɪk] *adj* erótico.
eroticism [ɪˈrɔtɪsɪzm] *n* erotismo.
err [əː*] *vi* errar; (*REL*) pecar.
errand [ˈɛrnd] *n* recado, mandado; **to run
~s** hacer recados; **~ of mercy** misión *f* de
caridad.
errand boy *n* recadero.
erratic [ɪˈrætɪk] *adj* variable; (*results etc*)
desigual, poco uniforme.
erroneous [ɪˈrəunɪəs] *adj* erróneo.
error [ˈɛrə*] *n* error *m*, equivocación *f*;
typing/spelling ~ error *m* de
mecanografía/ortografía; **in ~** por
equivocación; **~s and omissions excepted**
salvo error u omisión.
error message *n* (*COMPUT*) mensaje *m* de
error.
erstwhile [ˈəːstwaɪl] *adj* antiguo, previo.
erudite [ˈɛrudaɪt] *adj* erudito.
erudition [ɛruˈdɪʃən] *n* erudición *f*.
erupt [ɪˈrʌpt] *vi* entrar en erupción; (*MED*)
hacer erupción; (*fig*) estallar.
eruption [ɪˈrʌpʃən] *n* erupción *f*; (*fig*: *of
anger, violence*) explosión *f*, estallido.
ESA *n abbr* (= European Space Agency)
Agencia Espacial Europea.

escalate ['ɛskəleɪt] *vi* extenderse, intensificarse; (*costs*) aumentar vertiginosamente.

escalation clause [ɛskə'leɪʃən-] *n* cláusula de reajuste de los precios.

escalator ['ɛskəleɪtə*] *n* escalera mecánica.

escapade [ɛskə'peɪd] *n* aventura.

escape [ɪ'skeɪp] *n* (*gen*) fuga; (*TECH*) escape *m*; (*from duties*) escapatoria; (*from chase*) evasión *f* ♦ *vi* (*gen*) escaparse; (*flee*) huir, evadirse ♦ *vt* evitar, eludir; (*consequences*) escapar a; **to ~ from** (*place*) escaparse de; (*person*) huir de; (*clutches*) librarse de; **to ~ to** (*another place, freedom, safety*) huir a; **to ~ notice** pasar desapercibido.

escape artist *n* artista *m/f* de la evasión.

escape clause *n* (*fig: in agreement*) cláusula de excepción.

escapee [ɪskeɪ'piː] *n* fugado/a.

escape hatch *n* (*in submarine, space rocket*) escotilla de salvamento.

escape key *n* (*COMPUT*) tecla de escape.

escape route *n* (*from fire*) vía de escape.

escapism [ɪ'skeɪpɪzəm] *n* escapismo, evasión *f*.

escapist [ɪ'skeɪpɪst] *adj* escapista, de evasión ♦ *n* escapista *m/f*.

escapologist [ɛskə'pɒlədʒɪst] *n* (*BRIT*) = **escape artist**.

escarpment [ɪ'skɑːpmənt] *n* escarpa.

eschew [ɪs'tʃuː] *vt* evitar, abstenerse de.

escort ['ɛskɔːt] *n* acompañante *m/f*; (*MIL*) escolta; (*NAUT*) convoy *m* ♦ *vt* [ɪ'skɔːt] acompañar; (*MIL, NAUT*) escoltar.

escort agency *n* agencia de acompañantes.

Eskimo ['ɛskɪməu] *adj* esquimal ♦ *n* esquimal *m/f*; (*LING*) esquimal *m*.

ESL *n abbr* (*SCOL*) = *English as a Second Language.*

esophagus [iː'sɒfəgəs] *n* (*US*) = **oesophagus.**

esoteric [ɛsəu'tɛrɪk] *adj* esotérico.

ESP *n abbr* = **extrasensory perception**; (*SCOL:* = *English for Special Purposes*) inglés especializado.

esp. *abbr* = **especially.**

especially [ɪ'spɛʃlɪ] *adv* (*gen*) especialmente; (*above all*) sobre todo; (*particularly*) en especial.

espionage ['ɛspɪɒnɑːʒ] *n* espionaje *m.*

esplanade [ɛsplə'neɪd] *n* (*by sea*) paseo marítimo.

espouse [ɪ'spauz] *vt* adherirse a.

Esq. *abbr* (= *Esquire*) D.

Esquire [ɪ'skwaɪə*] *n:* **J. Brown, ~**

Sr. D. J. Brown.

essay ['ɛseɪ] *n* (*SCOL*) redacción *f*; (: *longer*) trabajo.

essayist ['ɛseɪɪst] *n* ensayista *m/f.*

essence ['ɛsns] *n* esencia; **in ~** esencialmente; **speed is of the ~** es esencial hacerlo con la mayor prontitud.

essential [ɪ'sɛnʃl] *adj* (*necessary*) imprescindible; (*basic*) esencial ♦ *n* (*often pl*) lo esencial; **it is ~ that** es imprescindible que.

essentially [ɪ'sɛnʃlɪ] *adv* esencialmente.

EST *n abbr* (*US:* = *Eastern Standard Time*) hora de invierno de Nueva York.

est. *abbr* (= *established*) fundado; (= *estimated*) aprox.

establish [ɪ'stæblɪʃ] *vt* establecer; (*prove: fact, identity*) comprobar, verificar; (*prove*) demostrar; (*relations*) entablar.

established [ɪ'stæblɪʃt] *adj* (*business*) de buena reputación; (*staff*) de plantilla.

establishment [ɪ'stæblɪʃmənt] *n* (*also business*) establecimiento; **the E~** la clase dirigente; **a teaching ~** un centro de enseñanza.

estate [ɪ'steɪt] *n* (*land*) finca, hacienda; (*property*) propiedad *f*; (*inheritance*) herencia; (*POL*) estado; **housing ~** (*BRIT*) urbanización *f*; **industrial ~** polígono industrial.

estate agency *n* (*BRIT*) agencia inmobiliaria.

estate agent *n* (*BRIT*) agente *m/f* inmobiliario/a.

estate car *n* (*BRIT*) ranchera.

esteem [ɪ'stiːm] *n:* **to hold sb in high ~** estimar en mucho a algn ♦ *vt* estimar.

esthetic [iːs'θɛtɪk] *adj* (*US*) = **aesthetic.**

estimate ['ɛstɪmət] *n* estimación *f*; (*assessment*) tasa, cálculo; (*COMM*) presupuesto ♦ *vt* ['ɛstɪmeɪt] estimar; tasar, calcular; **to give sb an ~ of** presentar a algn un presupuesto de; **at a rough ~** haciendo un cálculo aproximado; **to ~ for** (*COMM*) hacer un presupuesto de, presupuestar.

estimation [ɛstɪ'meɪʃən] *n* opinión *f*, juicio; (*esteem*) aprecio; **in my ~** a mi juicio.

Estonia [ɛ'stəunɪə] *n* Estonia.

Estonian [ɛ'stəunɪən] *adj* estonio ♦ *n* estonio/a; (*LING*) estonio.

estranged [ɪ'streɪndʒd] *adj* separado.

estrangement [ɪ'streɪndʒmənt] *n* alejamiento, distanciamiento.

estrogen ['iːstrəudʒən] *n* (*US*) = **oestrogen.**

estuary ['ɛstjuərɪ] *n* estuario, ría.

ET *n abbr* (*BRIT:* = *Employment Training*) *plan estatal de formación para los*

desempleados ♦ *abbr* (*US*) = Eastern Time.
et al. *abbr* (= *et alii*: and others) et al.
etc *abbr* (= *et cetera*) etc.
etch [ɛtʃ] *vt* grabar al aguafuerte.
etching ['etʃɪŋ] *n* aguafuerte *m or f.*
ETD *n abbr* = estimated time of departure.
eternal [ɪ'tə:nl] *adj* eterno.
eternity [ɪ'tə:nɪtɪ] *n* eternidad *f.*
ether ['i:θə*] *n* éter *m.*
ethereal [ɪ'θɪərɪəl] *adj* etéreo.
ethical ['ɛθɪkl] *adj* ético; (*honest*) honrado.
ethics ['ɛθɪks] *n* ética ♦ *npl* moralidad *f.*
Ethiopia [i:θɪ'əupɪə] *n* Etiopía.
Ethiopian [i:θɪ'əupɪən] *adj, n* etiope *m/f.*
ethnic ['ɛθnɪk] *adj* étnico.
ethnic cleansing [-klɛnzɪŋ] *n* limpieza étnica.
ethos ['i:θɔs] *n* (*of culture, group*) sistema *m* de valores.
etiquette ['ɛtɪkɛt] *n* etiqueta.
ETV *n abbr* (*US*: = Educational Television) televisión *f* escolar.
etymology [ɛtɪ'mɔlədʒɪ] *n* etimología.
EU *n abbr* (= European Union) UE *f.*
eucalyptus [ju:kə'lɪptəs] *n* eucalipto.
Eucharist ['ju:kərɪst] *n* Eucaristía.
eulogy ['ju:lədʒɪ] *n* elogio, encomio.
euphemism ['ju:fəmɪzm] *n* eufemismo.
euphemistic [ju:fə'mɪstɪk] *adj* eufemístico.
euphoria [ju:'fɔːrɪə] *n* euforia.
Eurasia [juə'reɪʃə] *n* Eurasia.
Eurasian [juə'reɪʃən] *adj, n* eurasiático/a *m/f.*
Euratom [juə'rætəm] *n abbr* (= European Atomic Energy Commission) Euratom *m.*
Euro- *pref* euro-.
euro ['juərəu] *n* (*currency*) euro.
Eurocheque ['juərəutʃɛk] *n* Eurocheque *m.*
Eurocrat ['juərəukræt] *n* eurócrata *m/f.*
Eurodollar ['juərəudɔlə*] *n* eurodólar *m.*
Euroland ['juərəulænd] *n* Eurolandia.
Europe ['juərəp] *n* Europa.
European [juərə'pi:ən] *adj, n* europeo/a *m/f.*
European Court of Justice *n* Tribunal *m* de Justicia de las Comunidades Europeas.
European Economic Community *n* Comunidad *f* Económica Europea.
Euro-sceptic [juərəu'skɛptɪk] *n* euroescéptico/a.
euthanasia [ju:θə'neɪzɪə] *n* eutanasia.
evacuate [ɪ'vækjueɪt] *vt* evacuar; (*place*) desocupar.
evacuation [ɪvækju'eɪʃən] *n* evacuación *f.*
evacuee [ɪvækju'i:] *n* evacuado/a.
evade [ɪ'veɪd] *vt* evadir, eludir.
evaluate [ɪ'væljueɪt] *vt* evaluar; (*value*) tasar; (*evidence*) interpretar.
evangelical [i:væn'dʒɛlɪkəl] *adj* evangélico.

evangelist [ɪ'vændʒəlɪst] *n* evangelista *m*; (*preacher*) evangelizador(a) *m/f.*
evaporate [ɪ'væpəreɪt] *vi* evaporarse; (*fig*) desvanecerse ♦ *vt* evaporar.
evaporated milk [ɪ'væpəreɪtɪd-] *n* leche *f* evaporada.
evaporation [ɪvæpə'reɪʃən] *n* evaporación *f.*
evasion [ɪ'veɪʒən] *n* evasión *f.*
evasive [ɪ'veɪsɪv] *adj* evasivo.
eve [i:v] *n*: on the ~ of en vísperas de.
even ['i:vn] *adj* (*level*) llano; (*smooth*) liso; (*speed, temperature*) uniforme; (*number*) par; (*SPORT*) igual(es) ♦ *adv* hasta, incluso; ~ **if**, ~ **though** aunque + *subjun*, así + *subjun* (*LAM*); ~ **more** aun más; ~ **so** aun así; **not** ~ ni siquiera; ~ **he was there** hasta él estaba allí; ~ **on Sundays** incluso los domingos; ~ **faster** aún más rápido; **to break** ~ cubrir los gastos; **to get** ~ **with sb** ajustar cuentas con algn; **to** ~ **out** *vi* nivelarse.
even-handed [i:vn'hændɪd] *adj* imparcial.
evening ['i:vnɪŋ] *n* tarde *f*; (*dusk*) atardecer *m*; (*night*) noche *f*; **in the** ~ por la tarde; **this** ~ esta tarde *or* noche; **tomorrow/ yesterday** ~ mañana/ayer por la tarde *or* noche.
evening class *n* clase *f* nocturna.
evening dress *n* (*man's*) traje *m* de etiqueta; (*woman's*) traje *m* de noche.
evenly ['i:vnlɪ] *adv* de modo uniforme; (*divide*) equitativamente.
evensong ['i:vnsɔŋ] *n* vísperas *fpl.*
event [ɪ'vɛnt] *n* suceso, acontecimiento; (*SPORT*) prueba; **in the** ~ **of** en caso de; **in the** ~ en realidad; **in the course of** ~s en el curso de los acontecimientos; **at all** ~s, **in any** ~ en cualquier caso.
eventful [ɪ'vɛntful] *adj* azaroso; (*game etc*) lleno de emoción.
eventing [ɪ'vɛntɪŋ] *n* (*HORSERIDING*) competición *f.*
eventual [ɪ'vɛntʃuəl] *adj* final.
eventuality [ɪvɛntʃu'ælɪtɪ] *n* eventualidad *f.*
eventually [ɪ'vɛntʃuəlɪ] *adv* (*finally*) por fin; (*in time*) con el tiempo.
ever ['ɛvə*] *adv* nunca, jamás; (*at all times*) siempre; **for** ~ (para) siempre; **the best** ~ lo nunca visto; **did you** ~ **meet him?** ¿llegaste a conocerle?; **have you** ~ **been there?** ¿has estado allí alguna vez?; **have you** ~ **seen it?** ¿lo has visto alguna vez?; **better than** ~ mejor que nunca; **thank you** ~ **so much** muchísimas gracias; **yours** ~ (*in letters*) un abrazo de; ~ **since** *adv* desde entonces ♦ *conj* después de que.
Everest ['ɛvərɪst] *n* (*also*: Mount ~) el Everest *m.*

evergreen ['ɛvəgriːn] *n* árbol *m* de hoja perenne.
everlasting [ɛvə'lɑːstɪŋ] *adj* eterno, perpetuo.

=================== *KEYWORD*

every ['ɛvrɪ] *adj* **1** (*each*) cada; ~ **one of them** (*persons*) todos ellos/as; (*objects*) cada uno de ellos/as; ~ **shop in the town was closed** todas las tiendas de la ciudad estaban cerradas
2 (*all possible*) todo/a; **I gave you ~ assistance** te di toda la ayuda posible; **I have ~ confidence in him** tiene toda mi confianza; **we wish you ~ success** te deseamos toda suerte de éxitos
3 (*showing recurrence*) todo/a; ~ **day/ week** todos los días/todas las semanas; ~ **other car had been broken into** habían forzado uno de cada dos coches; **she visits me ~ other/third day** me visita cada dos/tres días; ~ **now and then** de vez en cuando.

everybody ['ɛvrɪbɔdɪ] *pron* todos *pl*, todo el mundo; ~ **knows about it** todo el mundo lo sabe; ~ **else** todos los demás.
everyday ['ɛvrɪdeɪ] *adj* (*daily: use, occurrence, experience*) diario, cotidiano; (*usual: expression*) corriente; (*common*) vulgar; (*routine*) rutinario.
everyone ['ɛvrɪwʌn] = **everybody**.
everything ['ɛvrɪθɪŋ] *pron* todo; ~ **is ready** todo está dispuesto; **he did ~ possible** hizo todo lo posible.
everywhere ['ɛvrɪwɛə*] *adv* (*be*) en todas partes; (*go*) a *or* por todas partes; ~ **you go you meet...** en todas partes encontrarás....
evict [ɪ'vɪkt] *vt* desahuciar.
eviction [ɪ'vɪkʃən] *n* desahucio.
eviction notice *n* orden *f* de desahucio *or* desalojo (*LAM*).
evidence ['ɛvɪdəns] *n* (*proof*) prueba; (*of witness*) testimonio; (*facts*) datos *mpl*, hechos *mpl*; **to give ~** prestar declaración, dar testimonio.
evident ['ɛvɪdənt] *adj* evidente, manifiesto.
evidently ['ɛvɪdəntlɪ] *adv* (*obviously*) obviamente, evidentemente; (*apparently*) por lo visto.
evil ['iːvl] *adj* malo; (*influence*) funesto; (*smell*) horrible ♦ *n* mal *m*.
evildoer ['iːvlduːə*] *n* malhechor(a) *m/f*.
evince [ɪ'vɪns] *vt* mostrar, dar señales de.
evocative [ɪ'vɔkətɪv] *adj* sugestivo, evocador(a).
evoke [ɪ'vəuk] *vt* evocar; (*admiration*)

provocar.
evolution [iːvə'luːʃən] *n* evolución *f*, desarrollo.
evolve [ɪ'vɔlv] *vt* desarrollar ♦ *vi* evolucionar, desarrollarse.
ewe [juː] *n* oveja.
ex- [ɛks] *pref* (*former: husband, president etc*) ex-; (*out of*): **the price ~ works** precio de fábrica.
exacerbate [ɛk'sæsəbeɪt] *vt* exacerbar.
exact [ɪg'zækt] *adj* exacto ♦ *vt*: **to ~ sth (from)** exigir algo (de).
exacting [ɪg'zæktɪŋ] *adj* exigente; (*conditions*) arduo.
exactitude [ɪg'zæktɪtjuːd] *n* exactitud *f*.
exactly [ɪg'zæktlɪ] *adv* exactamente; (*time*) en punto; ~! ¡exacto!
exactness [ɪg'zæktnɪs] *n* exactitud *f*.
exaggerate [ɪg'zædʒəreɪt] *vt, vi* exagerar.
exaggerated [ɪg'zædʒəreɪtɪd] *adj* exagerado.
exaggeration [ɪgzædʒə'reɪʃən] *n* exageración *f*.
exalt [ɪg'zɔːlt] *vt* (*praise*) ensalzar; (*elevate*) elevar.
exalted [ɪg'zɔːltɪd] *adj* (*position*) elevado; (*elated*) enardecido.
exam [ɪg'zæm] *n abbr* (*SCOL*) = **examination**.
examination [ɪgzæmɪ'neɪʃən] *n* (*gen*) examen *m*; (*LAW*) interrogación *f*; (*inquiry*) investigación *f*; **to take** *or* **sit an ~** hacer un examen; **the matter is under ~** se está examinando el asunto.
examine [ɪg'zæmɪn] *vt* (*gen*) examinar; (*inspect: machine, premises*) inspeccionar; (*SCOL, LAW: person*) interrogar; (*at customs: luggage, passport*) registrar; (*MED*) hacer un reconocimiento médico de, examinar.
examiner [ɪg'zæmɪnə*] *n* examinador(a) *m/f*.
example [ɪg'zɑːmpl] *n* ejemplo; **for ~** por ejemplo; **to set a good/bad ~** dar buen/ mal ejemplo.
exasperate [ɪg'zɑːspəreɪt] *vt* exasperar, irritar; ~**d by** *or* **at** *or* **with** exasperado por *or* con.
exasperating [ɪg'zɑːspəreɪtɪŋ] *adj* irritante.
exasperation [ɪgzɑːspə'reɪʃən] *n* exasperación *f*, irritación *f*.
excavate ['ɛkskəveɪt] *vt* excavar.
excavation [ɛkskə'veɪʃən] *n* excavación *f*.
excavator ['ɛkskəveɪtə*] *n* excavadora.
exceed [ɪk'siːd] *vt* exceder; (*number*) pasar de; (*speed limit*) sobrepasar; (*limits*) rebasar; (*powers*) excederse en; (*hopes*) superar.
exceedingly [ɪk'siːdɪŋlɪ] *adv* sumamente,

sobremanera.
excel [ɪk'sɛl] vi sobresalir; **to** ~ **o.s.** lucirse.
excellence ['ɛksələns] n excelencia.
Excellency ['ɛksələnsɪ] n: **His** ~ Su
Excelencia.
excellent ['ɛksələnt] adj excelente.
except [ɪk'sɛpt] prep (also: ~ **for**, ~**ing**)
excepto, salvo ♦ vt exceptuar, excluir; ~
if/when excepto si/cuando; ~ **that** salvo
que.
exception [ɪk'sɛpʃən] n excepción f; **to take**
~ **to** ofenderse por; **with the** ~ **of** a
excepción de; **to make an** ~ hacer una
excepción.
exceptional [ɪk'sɛpʃənl] adj excepcional.
excerpt ['ɛksə:pt] n extracto.
excess [ɪk'sɛs] n exceso; **in** ~ **of** superior a;
see also **excesses**.
excess baggage n exceso de equipaje.
excesses npl excesos mpl.
excess fare n suplemento.
excessive [ɪk'sɛsɪv] adj excesivo.
excess supply n exceso de oferta.
excess weight n exceso de peso.
exchange [ɪks'tʃeɪndʒ] n cambio; (of
prisoners) canje m; (of ideas) intercambio;
(also: **telephone** ~) central f (telefónica)
♦ vt intercambiar; **to** ~ **(for)** cambiar
(por); **in** ~ **for** a cambio de; **foreign** ~
(COMM) divisas fpl.
exchange control n control m de divisas.
exchange rate n tipo de cambio.
exchequer [ɪks'tʃɛkə*] n: **the** ~ (BRIT)
Hacienda.
excisable [ɛk'saɪzəbl] adj sujeto al pago de
impuestos sobre el consumo.
excise ['ɛksaɪz] n impuestos mpl sobre el
consumo interior.
excitable [ɪk'saɪtəbl] adj excitable.
excite [ɪk'saɪt] vt (stimulate) entusiasmar;
(anger) suscitar, provocar; (move)
emocionar; **to get** ~**d** emocionarse.
excitement [ɪk'saɪtmənt] n emoción f.
exciting [ɪk'saɪtɪŋ] adj emocionante.
excl. abbr = **excluding; exclusive (of)**.
exclaim [ɪk'skleɪm] vi exclamar.
exclamation [ɛksklə'meɪʃən] n
exclamación f.
exclamation mark n signo de admiración.
exclude [ɪk'sklu:d] vt excluir; (except)
exceptuar.
excluding [ɪks'klu:dɪŋ] prep: ~ **VAT** IVA no
incluido.
exclusion [ɪk'sklu:ʒən] n exclusión f; **to the**
~ **of** con exclusión de.
exclusion clause n cláusula de exclusión.
exclusion zone n zona de exclusión.
exclusive [ɪk'sklu:sɪv] adj exclusivo; (club,

district) selecto; ~ **of tax** excluyendo
impuestos; ~ **of postage/service**
franqueo/servicio no incluido; **from 1st
to 13th March** ~ del 1 al 13 de marzo
exclusive.
exclusively [ɪk'sklu:sɪvlɪ] adv únicamente.
excommunicate [ɛkskə'mju:nɪkeɪt] vt
excomulgar.
excrement ['ɛkskrəmənt] n excremento.
excrete [ɪk'skri:t] vi excretar.
excruciating [ɪk'skru:ʃɪeɪtɪŋ] adj (pain)
agudísimo, atroz.
excursion [ɪk'skɔ:ʃən] n excursión f.
excursion ticket n billete m (especial) de
excursión.
excusable [ɪk'skju:səbl] adj perdonable.
excuse n [ɪk'skju:s] disculpa, excusa;
(evasion) pretexto ♦ vt [ɪk'skju:z]
disculpar, perdonar; (justify) justificar; **to
make** ~**s for sb** presentar disculpas por
algn; **to** ~ **sb from doing sth** dispensar a
algn de hacer algo; **to** ~ **o.s. (for (doing)
sth)** pedir disculpas a algn (por (hacer)
algo), ~ **me!** ¡perdone!; (attracting
attention) ¡oiga(, por favor)!; **if you will** ~
me con su permiso.
ex-directory ['ɛksdɪ'rɛktərɪ] adj (BRIT): ~
(phone) number número que no figura en
la guía (telefónica).
execrable ['ɛksɪkrəbl] adj execrable,
abominable; (manners) detestable.
execute ['ɛksɪkju:t] vt (plan) realizar;
(order) cumplir; (person) ajusticiar,
ejecutar.
execution [ɛksɪ'kju:ʃən] n realización f;
cumplimiento; ejecución f.
executioner [ɛksɪ'kju:ʃənə*] n verdugo.
executive [ɪg'zɛkjutɪv] n (COMM)
ejecutivo/a; (POL) poder m ejecutivo ♦ adj
ejecutivo; (car, plane, position) de
ejecutivo; (offices, suite) de la dirección;
(secretary) de dirección.
executive director n director(a) m/f
ejecutivo/a.
executor [ɪg'zɛkjutə*] n albacea m,
testamentario.
exemplary [ɪg'zɛmplərɪ] adj ejemplar.
exemplify [ɪg'zɛmplɪfaɪ] vt ejemplificar.
exempt [ɪg'zɛmpt] adj: ~ **from** exento de
♦ vt: **to** ~ **sb from** eximir a algn de.
exemption [ɪg'zɛmpʃən] n exención f;
(immunity) inmunidad f.
exercise ['ɛksəsaɪz] n ejercicio ♦ vt ejercer;
(patience etc) proceder con; (dog) sacar
de paseo ♦ vi hacer ejercicio.
exercise bike n bicicleta estática.
exercise book n cuaderno de ejercicios.
exert [ɪg'zə:t] vt ejercer; (strength, force)

emplear; **to ~ o.s.** esforzarse.
exertion [ɪɡ'zɔːʃən] *n* esfuerzo.
exfoliant [ɛks'fəʊlɪənt] *n* exfoliante *m*.
ex gratia ['ɛks'ɡreɪʃə] *adj*: **~ payment** pago
a título voluntario.
exhale [ɛks'heɪl] *vt* despedir, exhalar ♦ *vi*
espirar.
exhaust [ɪɡ'zɔːst] *n* (*pipe*) (tubo de) escape
m; (*fumes*) gases *mpl* de escape ♦ *vt* agotar;
to ~ o.s. agotarse.
exhausted [ɪɡ'zɔːstɪd] *adj* agotado.
exhausting [ɪɡ'zɔːstɪŋ] *adj*: **an ~ journey/
day** un viaje/día agotador.
exhaustion [ɪɡ'zɔːstʃən] *n* agotamiento;
nervous ~ agotamiento nervioso.
exhaustive [ɪɡ'zɔːstɪv] *adj* exhaustivo.
exhibit [ɪɡ'zɪbɪt] *n* (*ART*) obra expuesta;
(*LAW*) objeto expuesto ♦ *vt* (*show:
emotions*) manifestar; (: *courage, skill*)
demostrar; (*paintings*) exponer.
exhibition [ɛksɪ'bɪʃən] *n* exposición *f*.
exhibitionist [ɛksɪ'bɪʃənɪst] *n*
exhibicionista *m/f*.
exhibitor [ɪɡ'zɪbɪtə*] *n* expositor(a) *m/f*.
exhilarating [ɪɡ'zɪləreɪtɪŋ] *adj* estimulante,
tónico.
exhilaration [ɪɡzɪlə'reɪʃən] *n* júbilo.
exhort [ɪɡ'zɔːt] *vt* exhortar.
exile ['ɛksaɪl] *n* exilio; (*person*) exiliado/a
♦ *vt* desterrar, exiliar.
exist [ɪɡ'zɪst] *vi* existir.
existence [ɪɡ'zɪstəns] *n* existencia.
existentialism [ɛɡzɪs'tɛnʃəlɪzəm] *n*
existencialismo.
existing [ɪɡ'zɪstɪŋ] *adj* existente, actual.
exit ['ɛksɪt] *n* salida ♦ *vi* (*THEAT*) hacer
mutis; (*COMPUT*) salir (del sistema).
exit poll *n* encuesta a la salida de los
colegios electorales.
exit ramp *n* (*US AUT*) vía de acceso.
exit visa *n* visado de salida.
exodus ['ɛksədəs] *n* éxodo.
ex officio ['ɛksə'fɪʃɪəu] *adj* de pleno
derecho ♦ *adv* ex oficio.
exonerate [ɪɡ'zɔnəreɪt] *vt*: **to ~ from**
exculpar de.
exorbitant [ɪɡ'zɔːbɪtənt] *adj* (*price,
demands*) exorbitante, excesivo.
exorcize ['ɛksɔːsaɪz] *vt* exorcizar.
exotic [ɪɡ'zɒtɪk] *adj* exótico.
expand [ɪk'spænd] *vt* ampliar, extender;
(*number*) aumentar ♦ *vi* (*trade etc*)
ampliarse, expandirse; (*gas, metal*)
dilatarse; **to ~ on** (*notes, story etc*)
ampliar.
expanse [ɪk'spæns] *n* extensión *f*.
expansion [ɪk'spænʃən] *n* ampliación *f*;
aumento; (*of trade*) expansión *f*.

expansionism [ɪk'spænʃənɪzəm] *n*
expansionismo.
expansionist [ɪk'spænʃənɪst] *adj*
expansionista.
expatriate [ɛks'pætrɪət] *n* expatriado/a.
expect [ɪk'spɛkt] *vt* (*gen*) esperar; (*count
on*) contar con; (*suppose*) suponer ♦ *vi*: **to
be ~ing** estar encinta; **to ~ to do sth**
esperar hacer algo; **as ~ed** como era de
esperar; **I ~ so** supongo que sí.
expectancy [ɪk'spɛktənsɪ] *n* (*anticipation*)
expectación *f*; **life ~** esperanza de vida.
expectantly [ɪk'spɛktəntlɪ] *adv* (*look, listen*)
con expectación.
expectant mother [ɪk'spɛktənt-] *n* futura
madre *f*.
expectation [ɛkspɛk'teɪʃən] *n* esperanza,
expectativa; **in ~ of** esperando; **against**
or **contrary to all ~(s)** en contra de todas
las previsiones; **to come** *or* **live up to sb's
~s** resultar tan bueno como se esperaba;
to fall short of sb's ~s no cumplir las
esperanzas de algn, decepcionar a algn.
expedience [ɪk'spiːdɪəns], **expediency**
[ɪk'spiːdɪənsɪ] *n* conveniencia.
expedient [ɪk'spiːdɪənt] *adj* conveniente,
oportuno ♦ *n* recurso, expediente *m*.
expedite ['ɛkspɪdaɪt] *vt* (*speed up*) acelerar;
(: *progress*) facilitar.
expedition [ɛkspə'dɪʃən] *n* expedición *f*.
expeditionary force [ɛkspə'dɪʃnrɪ-] *n*
cuerpo expedicionario.
expel [ɪk'spɛl] *vt* expulsar.
expend [ɪk'spɛnd] *vt* gastar; (*use up*)
consumir.
expendable [ɪk'spɛndəbl] *adj* prescindible.
expenditure [ɪk'spɛndɪtʃə*] *n* gastos *mpl*,
desembolso; (*of time, effort*) gasto.
expense [ɪk'spɛns] *n* gasto, gastos *mpl*;
(*high cost*) coste *m*; **~s** *npl* (*COMM*) gastos
mpl; **at the ~ of** a costa de; **to meet the ~**
of hacer frente a los gastos de.
expense account *n* cuenta de gastos (de
representación).
expensive [ɪk'spɛnsɪv] *adj* caro, costoso.
experience [ɪk'spɪərɪəns] *n* experiencia ♦ *vt*
experimentar; (*suffer*) sufrir; **to learn by
~** aprender con la experiencia.
experienced [ɪk'spɪərɪənst] *adj*
experimentado.
experiment [ɪk'spɛrɪmənt] *n* experimento
♦ *vi* hacer experimentos, experimentar;
to perform *or* **carry out an ~** realizar un
experimento; **as an ~** como experimento;
to ~ with a new vaccine experimentar
con una vacuna nueva.
experimental [ɪkspɛrɪ'mɛntl] *adj*
experimental; **the process is still at the ~**

stage el proceso está todavía en prueba.
expert ['ɛkspəːt] *adj* experto, perito ♦ *n*
experto/a, perito/a; (*specialist*)
especialista *m/f*; ~ **witness** (*LAW*) testigo
pericial; ~ **in** *or* **at doing sth** experto *or*
perito en hacer algo; **an ~ on sth** un
experto en algo.
expertise [ɛkspəːˈtiːz] *n* pericia.
expiration [ɛkspɪˈreɪʃən] *n* (*gen*) expiración
f, vencimiento.
expire [ɪkˈspaɪə*] *vi* (*gen*) caducar,
vencerse.
expiry [ɪkˈspaɪərɪ] *n* caducidad *f*,
vencimiento.
explain [ɪkˈspleɪn] *vt* explicar; (*mystery*)
aclarar.
►**explain away** *vt* justificar.
explanation [ɛkspləˈneɪʃən] *n* explicación *f*;
aclaración *f*; **to find an ~ for sth**
encontrarle una explicación a algo.
explanatory [ɪkˈsplænətrɪ] *adj* explicativo;
aclaratorio.
expletive [ɪkˈspliːtɪv] *n* imprecación *f*.
explicable [ɪkˈsplɪkəbl] *adj* explicable.
explicit [ɪkˈsplɪsɪt] *adj* explícito.
explicitly [ɪkˈsplɪsɪtlɪ] *adv* explícitamente.
explode [ɪkˈspləud] *vi* estallar, explotar;
(*with anger*) reventar ♦ *vt* hacer explotar;
(*fig: theory, myth*) demoler.
exploit ['ɛksplɔɪt] *n* hazaña ♦ *vt* [ɪkˈsplɔɪt]
explotar.
exploitation [ɛksplɔɪˈteɪʃən] *n* explotación
f.
exploration [ɛkspləˈreɪʃən] *n* exploración *f*.
exploratory [ɪkˈsplɔrətrɪ] *adj* (*fig: talks*)
exploratorio, preliminar.
explore [ɪkˈsplɔː*] *vt* explorar; (*fig*)
examinar, sondear.
explorer [ɪkˈsplɔːrə*] *n* explorador(a) *m/f*.
explosion [ɪkˈspləuʒən] *n* explosión *f*.
explosive [ɪkˈspləusɪv] *adj*, *n* explosivo.
exponent [ɪkˈspəunənt] *n* partidario/a; (*of
skill, activity*) exponente *m/f*.
export *vt* [ɛkˈspɔːt] exportar ♦ *n* ['ɛkspɔːt]
exportación *f* ♦ *cpd* de exportación.
exportation [ɛkspɔːˈteɪʃən] *n* exportación *f*.
export drive *n* campaña de exportación.
exporter [ɛkˈspɔːtə*] *n* exportador(a) *m/f*.
export licence *n* licencia de exportación.
export manager *n* gerente *m/f* de
exportación.
export trade *n* comercio exterior.
expose [ɪkˈspəuz] *vt* exponer; (*unmask*)
desenmascarar.
exposé [ɪkˈspəuzeɪ] *n* relevación *f*.
exposed [ɪkˈspəuzd] *adj* expuesto; (*land,
house*) desprotegido; (*ELEC: wire*) al aire;
(*pipe, beam*) al descubierto.

exposition [ɛkspəˈzɪʃən] *n* exposición *f*.
exposure [ɪkˈspəuʒə*] *n* exposición *f*;
(*PHOT: speed*) (tiempo *m* de) exposición *f*;
(: *shot*) fotografía; **to die from ~** (*MED*)
morir de frío.
exposure meter *n* fotómetro.
expound [ɪkˈspaund] *vt* exponer; (*theory,
text*) comentar; (*one's views*) explicar.
express [ɪkˈsprɛs] *adj* (*definite*) expreso,
explícito; (*BRIT: letter etc*) urgente ♦ *n*
(*train*) rápido ♦ *adv* (*send*) por correo
extraordinario ♦ *vt* expresar; (*squeeze*)
exprimir; **to send sth ~** enviar algo por
correo urgente; **to ~ o.s.** expresarse.
expression [ɪkˈsprɛʃən] *n* expresión *f*.
expressionism [ɪkˈsprɛʃənɪzm] *n*
expresionismo.
expressive [ɪkˈsprɛsɪv] *adj* expresivo.
expressly [ɪkˈsprɛslɪ] *adv* expresamente.
expressway [ɪkˈsprɛsweɪ] *n* (*US: urban
motorway*) autopista.
expropriate [ɛksˈprəuprɪeɪt] *vt* expropiar.
expulsion [ɪkˈspʌlʃən] *n* expulsión *f*.
expurgate ['ɛkspəgeɪt] *vt* expurgar.
exquisite [ɛkˈskwɪzɪt] *adj* exquisito.
exquisitely [əkˈokwɪzɪtlɪ] *adv*
exquisitamente.
ex-serviceman ['ɛksˈsəːvɪsmən] *n*
ex-combatiente *m*.
ext. *abbr* (*TEL*) = **extension**.
extemporize [ɪkˈstɛmpəraɪz] *vi* improvisar.
extend [ɪkˈstɛnd] *vt* (*visit, street*) prolongar;
(*building*) ampliar; (*thanks, friendship etc*)
extender; (*COMM: credit*) conceder;
(*deadline*) prorrogar ♦ *vi* (*land*)
extenderse; **the contract ~s to/for ...** el
contrato se prolonga hasta/por ....
extension [ɪkˈstɛnʃən] *n* extensión *f*;
(*building*) ampliación *f*; (*TEL: line*)
extensión *f*; (: *telephone*) supletorio *m*; (*of
deadline*) prórroga, ~ **3718** extensión
3718.
extension cable *n* (*ELEC*) alargador *m*.
extensive [ɪkˈstɛnsɪv] *adj* (*gen*) extenso;
(*damage*) importante; (*knowledge*) amplio.
extensively [ɪkˈstɛnsɪvlɪ] *adv* (*altered,
damaged etc*) extensamente; **he's travelled
~** ha viajado por muchos países.
extent [ɪkˈstɛnt] *n* (*breadth*) extensión *f*;
(*scope: of knowledge, activities*) alcance *m*;
(*degree: of damage, loss*) grado; **to some ~**
hasta cierto punto; **to a certain ~** hasta
cierto punto; **to a large ~** en gran parte;
to the ~ of... hasta el punto de...; **to such
an ~ that...** hasta tal punto que...; **to what
~?** ¿hasta qué punto?; **debts to the ~ of
£5000** deudas por la cantidad de £5000.
extenuating [ɪkˈstɛnjueɪtɪŋ] *adj*: ~

circumstances circunstancias *fpl*
atenuantes.
exterior [ɛk'stɪərɪə*] *adj* exterior, externo
♦ *n* exterior *m*.
exterminate [ɪk'stə:mɪneɪt] *vt* exterminar.
extermination [ɪkstə:mɪ'neɪʃən] *n*
exterminio.
external [ɛk'stə:nl] *adj* externo, exterior
♦ *the* ~s la apariencia exterior; ~
affairs asuntos *mpl* exteriores; **for** ~ **use
only** (*MED*) para uso tópico.
externally [ɛk'stə:nəlɪ] *adv* por fuera.
extinct [ɪk'stɪŋkt] *adj* (*volcano*) extinguido,
apagado; (*race*) extinguido.
extinction [ɪk'stɪŋkʃən] *n* extinción *f*.
extinguish [ɪk'stɪŋgwɪʃ] *vt* extinguir,
apagar.
extinguisher [ɪk'stɪŋgwɪʃə*] *n* extintor *m*.
extol, (*US*) **extoll** [ɪk'stəul] *vt* (*merits,
virtues*) ensalzar, alabar; (*person*) alabar,
elogiar.
extort [ɪk'stɔ:t] *vt* sacar a la fuerza;
(*confession*) arrancar.
extortion [ɪk'stɔ:ʃən] *n* extorsión *f*.
extortionate [ɪk'stɔ:ʃnət] *adj* excesivo,
exorbitante.
extra ['ɛkstrə] *adj* adicional ♦ *adv* (*in
addition*) más ♦ *n* (*addition*) extra *m*,
suplemento; (*THEAT*) extra *m/f*, comparsa
m/f; (*newspaper*) edición *f* extraordinaria;
wine will cost ~ el vino se paga aparte; ~
large sizes tallas extragrandes; *see also*
extras.
extra... ['ɛkstrə] *pref* extra... .
extract *vt* [ɪk'strækt] sacar; (*tooth*) extraer;
(*confession*) arrancar ♦ *n* ['ɛkstrækt]
fragmento; (*CULIN*) extracto.
extraction [ɪk'strækʃən] *n* extracción *f*;
(*origin*) origen *m*.
extractor fan [ɪk'stræktə-] *n* extractor *m* de
humos.
extracurricular [ɛkstrəkə'rɪkjulə*] *adj*
(*SCOL*) extraescolar.
extradite ['ɛkstrədaɪt] *vt* extraditar.
extradition [ɛkstrə'dɪʃən] *n* extradición *f*.
extramarital [ɛkstrə'mærɪtl] *adj*
extramatrimonial.
extramural [ɛkstrə'mjuərl] *adj* extra-
académico.
extraneous [ɪk'streɪnɪəs] *adj* extraño,
ajeno.
extraordinary [ɪk'strɔ:dnrɪ] *adj*
extraordinario; (*odd*) raro; **the** ~ **thing is
that** ... lo más extraordinario es que ....
extraordinary general meeting *n* junta
general extraordinaria.
extrapolation [ɪkstræpə'leɪʃən] *n*
extrapolación *f*.

extras *npl* (*additional expense*) extras *mpl*.
extrasensory perception (ESP)
['ɛkstrə'sɛnsərɪ-] *n* percepción *f*
extrasensorial.
extra time *n* (*FOOTBALL*) prórroga.
extravagance [ɪk'strævəgəns] *n* (*excessive
spending*) derroche *m*; (*thing bought*)
extravagancia.
extravagant [ɪk'strævəgənt] *adj* (*wasteful*)
derrochador(a); (*taste, gift*)
excesivamente caro; (*price*) exorbitante;
(*praise*) excesivo.
extreme [ɪk'stri:m] *adj* extremo; (*poverty
etc*) extremado; (*case*) excepcional ♦ *n*
extremo; **the** ~ **left/right** (*POL*) la
extrema izquierda/derecha; ~**s of
temperature** temperaturas extremas.
extremely [ɪk'stri:mlɪ] *adv* sumamente,
extremadamente.
extremist [ɪk'stri:mɪst] *adj, n* extremista *m/f*.
extremity [ɪk'strɛmətɪ] *n* extremidad *f*,
punta; (*need*) apuro, necesidad *f*;
extremities *npl* (*hands and feet*)
extremidades *fpl*.
extricate ['ɛkstrɪkeɪt] *vt*: **to** ~ **o.s. from**
librarse de.
extrovert ['ɛkstrəvə:t] *n* extrovertido/a.
exuberance [ɪg'zju:bərns] *n* exuberancia.
exuberant [ɪg'zju:bərnt] *adj* (*person*)
eufórico; (*style*) exuberante.
exude [ɪg'zju:d] *vt* rezumar.
exult [ɪg'zʌlt] *vi* regocijarse.
exultant [ɪg'zʌltənt] *adj* (*person*)
regocijado, jubiloso; (*shout, expression,
smile*) de júbilo.
exultation [ɛgzʌl'teɪʃən] *n* regocijo, júbilo.
eye [aɪ] *n* ojo ♦ *vt* mirar; **to keep an** ~ **on**
vigilar; **as far as the** ~ **can see** hasta
donde alcanza la vista; **with an** ~ **to
doing sth** con vistas *or* miras a hacer
algo; **to have an** ~ **for sth** tener mucha
vista *or* buen ojo para algo; **there's more
to this than meets the** ~ esto tiene su
miga.
eyeball ['aɪbɔ:l] *n* globo ocular.
eyebath ['aɪbɑ:θ] *n* baño ocular, lavaojos *m
inv*.
eyebrow ['aɪbrau] *n* ceja.
eyebrow pencil *n* lápiz *m* de cejas.
eye-catching ['aɪkætʃɪŋ] *adj* llamativo.
eye cup *n* (*US*) = **eyebath.**
eyedrops ['aɪdrɔps] *npl* gotas *fpl* para los
ojos.
eyeful ['aɪful] *n* (*col*): **to get an** ~ **of sth** ver
bien algo.
eyelash ['aɪlæʃ] *n* pestaña.
eyelet ['aɪlɪt] *n* ojete *m*.
eye-level ['aɪlɛvl] *adj* a la altura de los ojos.

eyelid ['aɪlɪd] n párpado.
eyeliner ['aɪlaɪnə*] n lápiz m de ojos.
eye-opener ['aɪəupnə*] n revelación f, gran sorpresa.
eyeshadow ['aɪʃædəu] n sombra de ojos.
eyesight ['aɪsaɪt] n vista.
eyesore ['aɪsɔ:*] n monstruosidad f.
eyestrain ['aɪstreɪn] n: **to get** ~ cansar la vista or los ojos.
eyetooth, pl **eyeteeth** ['aɪtu:θ, -ti:θ] n colmillo; **to give one's eyeteeth for sth/to do sth** (col, fig) dar un ojo de la cara por algo/por hacer algo.
eyewash ['aɪwɔʃ] n (fig) disparates mpl, tonterías fpl.
eye witness n testigo m/f ocular.
eyrie ['ɪərɪ] n aguilera.

Ff

F, f [ɛf] n (letter) F, f f; (MUS) fa m; **F for Frederick,** (US) **F for Fox** F de Francia.
F. abbr = **Fahrenheit.**
FA n abbr (BRIT: = Football Association) ≈ AFE f (SP).
FAA n abbr (US) = Federal Aviation Administration.
fable ['feɪbl] n fábula.
fabric ['fæbrɪk] n tejido, tela.
fabricate ['fæbrɪkeɪt] vt fabricar; (fig) inventar.
fabrication [fæbrɪ'keɪʃən] n fabricación f; (fig) invención f.
fabric ribbon n (for typewriter) cinta de tela.
fabulous ['fæbjuləs] adj fabuloso.
façade [fə'sɑ:d] n fachada.
face [feɪs] n (ANAT) cara, rostro; (of clock) esfera, cara; (side) cara; (surface) superficie f ♦ vt mirar a; (fig) enfrentarse a; ~ **down** (person, card) boca abajo; **to lose** ~ desprestigiarse; **to save** ~ salvar las apariencias; **to make** or **pull a** ~ hacer muecas; **in the** ~ **of** (difficulties etc) en vista de, ante; **on the** ~ **of it** a primera vista; ~ **to** ~ cara a cara; **to** ~ **the fact that ...** reconocer que ....
▶**face up to** vt fus hacer frente a, enfrentarse a.
face cloth n (BRIT) toallita.
face cream n crema (de belleza).

faceless ['feɪslɪs] adj (fig) anónimo.
face lift n lifting m, estirado facial.
face powder n polvos mpl para la cara.
face-saving ['feɪsseɪvɪŋ] adj para salvar las apariencias.
facet ['fæsɪt] n faceta.
facetious [fə'si:ʃəs] adj chistoso.
facetiously [fə'si:ʃəslɪ] adv chistosamente.
face value n (of stamp) valor m nominal; **to take sth at** ~ (fig) tomar algo en sentido literal, aceptar las apariencias de algo.
facial ['feɪʃəl] adj de la cara ♦ n (also: **beauty** ~) tratamiento facial, limpieza.
facile ['fæsaɪl] adj superficial.
facilitate [fə'sɪlɪteɪt] vt facilitar.
facility [fə'sɪlɪtɪ] n facilidad f; **facilities** npl instalaciones fpl; **credit** ~ facilidades de crédito.
facing ['feɪsɪŋ] prep frente a ♦ adj de enfrente.
facsimile [fæk'sɪmɪlɪ] n facsímil(e) m.
fact [fækt] n hecho; **in** ~ en realidad; **to know for a** ~ **that ...** saber a ciencia cierta que ....
fact-finding ['fæktfaɪndɪŋ] adj: **a** ~ **tour/mission** un viaje/una misión de reconocimiento.
faction ['fækʃən] n facción f.
factional ['fækʃənl] adj (fighting) entre distintas facciones.
factor ['fæktə*] n factor m; (COMM: person) agente m/f comisionado/a ♦ vi (COMM) comprar deudas; **safety** ~ factor de seguridad.
factory ['fæktərɪ] n fábrica.
factory farming n cría industrial.
factory floor n (workers) trabajadores mpl, mano f de obra directa; (area) talleres mpl.
factory ship n buque m factoría.
factual ['fæktjuəl] adj basado en los hechos.
faculty ['fækəltɪ] n facultad f; (US: teaching staff) personal m docente.
fad [fæd] n novedad f, moda.
fade [feɪd] vi descolorarse, desteñirse; (sound, hope) desvanecerse; (light) apagarse; (flower) marchitarse.
▶**fade away** vi (sound) apagarse.
▶**fade in** vt (TV, CINE) fundir; (RADIO: sound) mezclar ♦ vi (TV, CINE) fundirse; (RADIO) oírse por encima.
▶**fade out** vt (TV, CINE) fundir; (RADIO) apagar, disminuir el volumen de ♦ vi (TV, CINE) desvanecerse; (RADIO) apagarse, dejarse de oír.
faded ['feɪdɪd] adj (clothes, colour) descolorido; (flower) marchito.
faeces, (US) **feces** ['fi:si:z] npl excremento

sg, heces *fpl*.

fag [fæg] *n* (*BRIT col: cigarette*) pitillo (*SP*), cigarro; (*US col: homosexual*) maricón *m*.

fag end *n* (*BRIT col*) colilla.

fagged [fægd] *adj* (*BRIT col: exhausted*) rendido, agotado.

Fahrenheit ['fɑːrənhaɪt] *n* Fahrenheit *m*.

fail [feɪl] *vt* suspender; (*subj: memory etc*) fallar a ♦ *vi* suspender; (*be unsuccessful*) fracasar; (*strength, brakes, engine*) fallar; **to ~ to do sth** (*neglect*) dejar de hacer algo; (*be unable*) no poder hacer algo; **without ~** sin falta; **words ~ me!** ¡no sé qué decir!

failing ['feɪlɪŋ] *n* falta, defecto ♦ *prep* a falta de; **~ that** de no ser posible eso.

failsafe ['feɪlseɪf] *adj* (*device etc*) de seguridad.

failure ['feɪljə*] *n* fracaso; (*person*) fracasado/a; (*mechanical etc*) fallo; (*in exam*) suspenso; (*of crops*) pérdida, destrucción *f*; **it was a complete ~** fue un fracaso total.

faint [feɪnt] *adj* débil; (*smell, breeze, trace*) leve; (*recollection*) vago; (*mark*) apenas visible ♦ *n* desmayo ♦ *vi* desmayarse; **to feel ~** estar mareado, marearse.

faintest ['feɪntɪst] *adj*: **I haven't the ~ idea** no tengo la más remota idea.

faint-hearted [feɪnt'hɑːtɪd] *adj* apocado.

faintly ['feɪntlɪ] *adv* débilmente; (*vaguely*) vagamente.

faintness ['feɪntnɪs] *n* debilidad *f*; vaguedad *f*.

fair [fɛə*] *adj* justo; (*hair, person*) rubio; (*weather*) bueno; (*good enough*) suficiente; (*sizeable*) considerable ♦ *adv*: **to play ~** jugar limpio ♦ *n* feria; (*BRIT: funfair*) parque *m* de atracciones; **it's not ~!** ¡no es justo!, ¡no hay derecho!; **~ copy** copia en limpio; **~ play** juego limpio; **a ~ amount of** bastante; **~ wear and tear** desgaste *m* natural; **trade ~** feria de muestras.

fair game *n*: **to be ~** ser presa fácil.

fairground ['fɛəɡraʊnd] *n* recinto ferial.

fair-haired [fɛə'hɛəd] *adj* (*person*) rubio.

fairly ['fɛəlɪ] *adv* (*justly*) con justicia; (*equally*) equitativamente; (*quite*) bastante; **I'm ~ sure** estoy bastante seguro.

fairness ['fɛənɪs] *n* justicia; (*impartiality*) imparcialidad *f*; **in all ~** a decir verdad.

fairy ['fɛərɪ] *n* hada.

fairy godmother *n* hada madrina.

fairyland ['fɛərɪlænd] *n* el país de ensueño.

fairy lights *npl* bombillas *fpl* de colores.

fairy tale *n* cuento de hadas.

faith [feɪθ] *n* fe *f*; (*trust*) confianza; (*sect*) religión *f*; **to have ~ in sb/sth** confiar en algn/algo.

faithful ['feɪθful] *adj* fiel.

faithfully ['feɪθfulɪ] *adv* fielmente; **yours ~** (*BRIT: in letters*) le saluda atentamente.

faith healer *n* curador(a) *m/f* por fe.

fake [feɪk] *n* (*painting etc*) falsificación *f*; (*person*) impostor(a) *m/f* ♦ *adj* falso ♦ *vt* fingir; (*painting etc*) falsificar.

falcon ['fɔːlkən] *n* halcón *m*.

Falkland Islands ['fɔːlklənd-] *npl* Islas *fpl* Malvinas.

fall [fɔːl] *n* caída; (*US*) otoño; (*decrease*) disminución *f* ♦ *vi*, *pt* **fell**, *pp* **fallen** ['fɔːlən] caer; (*accidentally*) caerse; (*price*) bajar; **~s** *npl* (*waterfall*) cataratas *fpl*, salto *sg* de agua; **a ~ of earth** un desprendimiento de tierra; **a ~ of snow** una nevada; **to ~ flat** *vi* (*on one's face*) caerse de bruces; (*joke, story*) no hacer gracia; **to ~ short of sb's expectations** decepcionar a algn; **to ~ in love (with sb/sth)** enamorarse (de algn/algo).

▶**fall apart** *vi* deshacerse.

▶**fall back** *vi* retroceder.

▶**fall back on** *vt fus* (*remedy etc*) recurrir a; **to have sth to ~ back on** tener algo a que recurrir.

▶**fall behind** *vi* quedarse atrás; (*fig: with payments*) retrasarse.

▶**fall down** *vi* (*person*) caerse; (*building, hopes*) derrumbarse.

▶**fall for** *vt fus* (*trick*) tragar; (*person*) enamorarse de.

▶**fall in** *vi* (*roof*) hundirse; (*MIL*) alinearse.

▶**fall in with** *vt fus*: **to ~ in with sb's plans** acomodarse con los planes de algn.

▶**fall off** *vi* caerse; (*diminish*) disminuir.

▶**fall out** *vi* (*friends etc*) reñir; (*MIL*) romper filas.

▶**fall over** *vi* caer(se).

▶**fall through** *vi* (*plan, project*) fracasar.

fallacy ['fæləsɪ] *n* error *m*.

fallback position ['fɔːlbæk-] *n* posición *f* de repliegue.

fallen ['fɔːlən] *pp of* **fall**.

fallible ['fæləbl] *adj* falible.

falling ['fɔːlɪŋ] *adj*: **~ market** mercado en baja.

falling-off ['fɔːlɪŋ'ɔf] *n* (*reduction*) disminución *f*.

Fallopian tube [fə'ləʊpɪən-] *n* (*ANAT*) trompa de Falopio.

fallout ['fɔːlaʊt] *n* lluvia radioactiva.

fallout shelter *n* refugio antinuclear.

fallow ['fæləʊ] *adj* (*land, field*) en barbecho.

false [fɔːls] *adj* (*gen*) falso; (*teeth etc*)

postizo; (*disloyal*) desleal, traidor(a);
under ~ pretences con engaños.
false alarm *n* falsa alarma.
falsehood ['fɔːlshud] *n* falsedad *f*.
falsely ['fɔːlslɪ] *adv* falsamente.
false teeth *npl* (*BRIT*) dentadura *sg* postiza.
falsify ['fɔːlsɪfaɪ] *vt* falsificar.
falter ['fɔːltə*] *vi* vacilar.
fame [feɪm] *n* fama.
familiar [fə'mɪlɪə*] *adj* familiar; (*well-known*) conocido; (*tone*) de confianza; **to be ~ with** (*subject*) estar enterado de; **to make o.s. ~ with** familiarizarse con; **to be on ~ terms with sb** tener confianza con algn.
familiarity [fəmɪlɪ'ærɪtɪ] *n* familiaridad *f*.
familiarize [fə'mɪlɪəraɪz] *vt*: **to ~ o.s. with** familiarizarse con.
family ['fæmɪlɪ] *n* familia.
family allowance *n* subsidio que se recibe por cada hijo.
family business *n* negocio familiar.
family credit *n* (*BRIT*) ≈ ayuda familiar.
family doctor *n* médico/a de cabecera.
family life *n* vida doméstica *or* familiar.
family man *n* (*home-loving*) hombre *m* casero; (*having family*) padre *m* de familia.
family planning *n* planificación *f* familiar.
family planning clinic *n* clínica de planificación familiar.
family tree *n* árbol *m* genealógico.
famine ['fæmɪn] *n* hambre *f*, hambruna.
famished ['fæmɪʃt] *adj* hambriento; **I'm ~!** (*col*) ¡estoy muerto de hambre!, ¡tengo un hambre canina!
famous ['feɪməs] *adj* famoso, célebre.
famously ['feɪməslɪ] *adv* (*get on*) estupendamente.
fan [fæn] *n* abanico; (*ELEC*) ventilador *m*; (*person*) aficionado/a; (*SPORT*) hincha *m/f*; (*of pop star*) fan *m/f* ♦ *vt* abanicar; (*fire, quarrel*) atizar.
►**fan out** *vi* desplegarse.
fanatic [fə'nætɪk] *n* fanático/a.
fanatical [fə'nætɪkəl] *adj* fanático.
fan belt *n* correa de ventilador.
fancied ['fænsɪd] *adj* imaginario.
fanciful ['fænsɪful] *adj* (*gen*) fantástico; (*imaginary*) fantasioso; (*design*) rebuscado.
fan club *n* club *m* de fans.
fancy ['fænsɪ] *n* (*whim*) capricho, antojo; (*imagination*) imaginación *f* ♦ *adj* (*luxury*) de lujo; (*price*) exorbitado ♦ *vt* (*feel like, want*) tener ganas de; (*imagine*) imaginarse, figurarse; **to take a ~ to sb** tomar cariño a algn; **when the ~ takes him** cuando se le antoja; **it took** *or* **caught**

my ~ me cayó en gracia; **to ~ that** ... imaginarse que ...; **he fancies her** le gusta (ella) mucho.
fancy dress *n* disfraz *m*.
fancy-dress ball ['fænsɪdrɛs-] *n* baile *m* de disfraces.
fancy goods *n* artículos *mpl* de fantasía.
fanfare ['fænfɛə*] *n* fanfarria (de trompeta).
fanfold paper ['fænfəuld-] *n* papel *m* plegado en abanico *or* en acordeón.
fang [fæŋ] *n* colmillo.
fan heater *n* calefactor *m* de aire.
fanlight ['fænlaɪt] *n* (montante *m* en) abanico.
fanny ['fænɪ] *n* (*BRIT col!*) chocho (*!*); (*US col*) pompis *m*, culo.
fantasize ['fæntəsaɪz] *vi* fantasear, hacerse ilusiones.
fantastic [fæn'tæstɪk] *adj* fantástico.
fantasy ['fæntəzɪ] *n* fantasía.
fanzine ['fænziːn] *n* fanzine *m*.
FAO *n abbr* (= *Food and Agriculture Organization*) FAO *f*, OAA *f*.
FAQ *abbr* (= *free alongside quay*) franco sobre muelle.
far [faː*] *adj* (*distant*) lejano ♦ *adv* lejos; **the ~ left/right** (*POL*) la extrema izquierda/derecha; **~ away, ~ off** (a lo) lejos; **~ better** mucho mejor; **~ from** lejos de; **by ~** con mucho; **it's by ~ the best** es con mucho el mejor; **go as ~ as the farm** vaya hasta la granja; **is it ~ to London?** ¿a cuánto está Londres?; **it's not ~ (from here)** no está lejos (de aquí); **as ~ as I know** que yo sepa; **how ~ have you got with your work?** ¿hasta dónde has llegado en tu trabajo?
faraway ['fɑːrəweɪ] *adj* remoto; (*look*) ausente, perdido.
farce [fɑːs] *n* farsa.
farcical ['fɑːsɪkəl] *adj* absurdo.
fare [fɛə*] *n* (*on trains, buses*) precio (del billete); (*in taxi: cost*) tarifa; (*: passenger*) pasajero; (*food*) comida; **half/full ~** medio billete *m*/billete *m* completo.
Far East *n*: **the ~** el Extremo *or* Lejano Oriente.
farewell [fɛə'wɛl] *excl*, *n* adiós *m*.
far-fetched [fɑː'fɛtʃt] *adj* inverosímil.
farm [fɑːm] *n* granja, finca, estancia (*LAM*), chacra (*LAM*), rancho (*LAM*) ♦ *vt* cultivar.
►**farm out** *vt* (*work*): **to ~ out (to sb)** mandar hacer fuera (a algn).
farmer ['fɑːmə*] *n* granjero/a, estanciero/a (*LAM*).
farmhand ['fɑːmhænd] *n* peón *m*.
farmhouse ['fɑːmhaus] *n* granja, casa de

hacienda (*LAM*).

farming ['fɑːmɪŋ] *n* (*gen*) agricultura; (*tilling*) cultivo; **sheep** ~ cría de ovejas.

farm labourer *n* = **farmhand**.

farmland ['fɑːmlænd] *n* tierra de cultivo.

farm produce *n* productos *mpl* agrícolas.

farm worker *n* = **farmhand**.

farmyard ['fɑːmjɑːd] *n* corral *m*.

Faroe Islands ['fɛərəu-], **Faroes** ['fɛərəuz] *npl*: **the** ~ las Islas Feroe.

far-reaching [fɑːˈriːtʃɪŋ] *adj* (*reform, effect*) de gran alcance.

far-sighted [fɑːˈsaɪtɪd] *adj* previsor(a).

fart [fɑːt] (*col!*) *n* pedo (*!*) ♦ *vi* tirarse un pedo (*!*).

farther ['fɑːðə*] *adv* más lejos, más allá ♦ *adj* más lejano.

farthest ['fɑːðɪst] *superlative of* **far**.

FAS *abbr* (= *free alongside ship*) franco al costado del buque.

fascinate ['fæsɪneɪt] *vt* fascinar.

fascinating ['fæsɪneɪtɪŋ] *adj* fascinante.

fascination [fæsɪˈneɪʃən] *n* fascinación *f*.

fascism ['fæʃɪzəm] *n* fascismo.

fascist ['fæʃɪst] *adj, n* fascista *m/f*.

fashion ['fæʃən] *n* moda; (*manner*) manera ♦ *vt* formar; **in** ~ a la moda; **out of** ~ pasado de moda; **in the Greek** ~ a la griega, al estilo griego; **after a** ~ (*finish, manage etc*) en cierto modo.

fashionable ['fæʃnəbl] *adj* de moda; (*writer*) de moda, popular; **it is** ~ **to do** ... está de moda hacer ....

fashion designer *n* diseñador(a) *m/f* de modas, modisto/a.

fashion show *n* desfile *m* de modelos.

fast [fɑːst] *adj* (*also PHOT: film*) rápido; (*dye, colour*) sólido; (*clock*): **to be** ~ estar adelantado ♦ *adv* rápidamente, de prisa; (*stuck, held*) firmemente ♦ *n* ayuno ♦ *vi* ayunar; ~ **asleep** profundamente dormido; **in the** ~ **lane** (*AUT*) en el carril de adelantamiento; **my watch is 5 minutes** ~ mi reloj está adelantado 5 minutos; **as** ~ **as I** *etc* **can** lo más rápido posible; **to make a boat** ~ amarrar una barca.

fasten ['fɑːsn] *vt* asegurar, sujetar; (*coat, belt*) abrochar ♦ *vi* cerrarse.

▶**fasten (up)on** *vt fus* (*idea*) aferrarse a.

fastener ['fɑːsnə*] *n* cierre *m*; (*of door etc*) cerrojo; (*BRIT: zip* ~) cremallera.

fastening ['fɑːsnɪŋ] *n* = **fastener**.

fast food *n* comida rápida, platos *mpl* preparados.

fastidious [fæsˈtɪdɪəs] *adj* (*fussy*) delicado; (*demanding*) exigente.

fat [fæt] *adj* gordo; (*meat*) con mucha grasa;

(*greasy*) grasiento ♦ *n* grasa; (*on person*) carnes *fpl*; (*lard*) manteca; **to live off the** ~ **of the land** vivir a cuerpo de rey.

fatal ['feɪtl] *adj* (*mistake*) fatal; (*injury*) mortal; (*consequence*) funesto.

fatalism ['feɪtəlɪzəm] *n* fatalismo.

fatality [fəˈtælɪtɪ] *n* (*road death etc*) víctima *f* mortal.

fatally ['feɪtəlɪ] *adv*: ~ **injured** herido de muerte.

fate [feɪt] *n* destino, sino.

fated ['feɪtɪd] *adj* predestinado.

fateful ['feɪtful] *adj* fatídico.

fat-free ['fætfriː] *adj* sin grasa.

father ['fɑːðə*] *n* padre *m*.

Father Christmas *n* Papá *m* Noel.

fatherhood ['fɑːðəhud] *n* paternidad *f*.

father-in-law ['fɑːðərɪnlɔː] *n* suegro.

fatherland ['fɑːðəlænd] *n* patria.

fatherly ['fɑːðəlɪ] *adj* paternal.

fathom ['fæðəm] *n* braza ♦ *vt* (*unravel*) desentrañar; (*understand*) explicarse.

fatigue [fəˈtiːg] *n* fatiga, cansancio; **metal** ~ fatiga del metal.

fatness ['fætnɪs] *n* gordura.

fatten ['fætn] *vt*, *vi* engordar; **chocolate is** ~**ing** el chocolate engorda.

fatty ['fætɪ] *adj* (*food*) graso ♦ *n* (*fam*) gordito/a, gordinflón/ona *m/f*.

fatuous ['fætjuəs] *adj* fatuo, necio.

faucet ['fɔːsɪt] *n* (*US*) grifo, llave *f*, canilla (*LAM*).

fault [fɔːlt] *n* (*blame*) culpa; (*defect: in character*) defecto; (*in manufacture*) desperfecto; (*GEO*) falla ♦ *vt* criticar; **it's my** ~ es culpa mía; **to find** ~ **with** criticar, poner peros a; **at** ~ culpable.

faultless ['fɔːltlɪs] *adj* (*action*) intachable; (*person*) sin defectos.

faulty ['fɔːltɪ] *adj* defectuoso.

fauna ['fɔːnə] *n* fauna.

faux pas ['fəuˈpɑː] *n* desacierto.

favour, (*US*) **favor** ['feɪvə*] *n* favor *m*; (*approval*) aprobación *f* ♦ *vt* (*proposition*) estar a favor de, aprobar; (*person etc*) preferir; (*assist*) favorecer; **to ask a** ~ **of** pedir un favor a; **to do sb a** ~ hacer un favor a algn; **to find** ~ **with sb** (*subj: person*) caerle bien a algn; (: *suggestion*) tener buena acogida por parte de algn; **in** ~ **of** a favor de; **to be in** ~ **of sth/of doing sth** ser partidario *or* estar a favor de algo/de hacer algo.

favo(u)rable ['feɪvərəbl] *adj* favorable.

favo(u)rably ['feɪvərəblɪ] *adv* favorablemente.

favo(u)rite ['feɪvərɪt] *adj, n* favorito/a *m/f*, preferido/a *m/f*.

favo(u)ritism ['feɪvərɪtɪzəm] n favoritismo.
fawn [fɔːn] n cervato ♦ adj (also: ~-coloured) de color cervato, leonado ♦ vi: to ~ (up)on adular.
fax [fæks] n fax m ♦ vt mandar or enviar por fax.
FBI n abbr (US: =Federal Bureau of Investigation) FBI m.
FCC n abbr (US) = Federal Communications Commission.
FCO n abbr (BRIT: = Foreign and Commonwealth Office) ≈ Min. de AA. EE.
FD n abbr (US) = fire department.
FDA n abbr (US: = Food and Drug Administration) oficina que se ocupa del control de los productos alimentarios y farmacéuticos.
FE n abbr = further education.
fear [fɪə*] n miedo, temor m ♦ vt temer; for ~ of por temor a; ~ of heights vértigo; to ~ for/that temer por/que.
fearful ['fɪəful] adj temeroso; (awful) espantoso; to be ~ of (frightened) tener miedo de.
fearfully ['fɪəfulɪ] adv (timidly) con miedo; (col: very) terriblemente.
fearless ['fɪəlɪs] adj (gen) sin miedo or temor; (bold) audaz.
fearlessly ['fɪəlɪslɪ] adv temerariamente.
fearlessness ['fɪəlɪsnɪs] n temeridad f.
fearsome ['fɪəsəm] adj (opponent) temible; (sight) espantoso.
feasibility [fiːzə'bɪlɪtɪ] n factibilidad f, viabilidad f.
feasibility study n estudio de viabilidad.
feasible ['fiːzəbl] adj factible, viable.
feast [fiːst] n banquete m; (REL: also: ~ day) fiesta ♦ vi banquetear.
feat [fiːt] n hazaña.
feather ['feðə*] n pluma ♦ vt: to ~ one's nest (fig) hacer su agosto, sacar tajada ♦ cpd (mattress, bed, pillow) de plumas.
feather-weight ['feðəweɪt] n (BOXING) peso pluma.
feature ['fiːtʃə*] n (gen) característica; (ANAT) rasgo; (article) reportaje m ♦ vt (subj: film) presentar ♦ vi figurar; ~s npl (of face) facciones fpl; a (special) ~ on sth/sb un reportaje (especial) sobre algo/algn; it ~d prominently in ... tuvo un papel destacado en ....
feature film n largometraje m.
Feb. abbr (= February) feb.
February ['fɛbruərɪ] n febrero.
feces ['fiːsiːz] npl (US) = faeces.
feckless ['fɛklɪs] adj irresponsable, irreflexivo.
Fed abbr (US) = federal, federation.

fed [fɛd] pt, pp of feed.
Fed. [fɛd] n abbr (US col) = Federal Reserve Board.
federal ['fɛdərəl] adj federal.
Federal Republic of Germany n República Federal de Alemania.
federation [fɛdə'reɪʃən] n federación f.
fed-up [fɛd'ʌp] adj: to be ~ (with) estar harto (de).
fee [fiː] n (professional) honorarios mpl; (for examination) derechos mpl; (of school) matrícula; (membership ~) cuota; (entrance ~) entrada; for a small ~ por poco dinero.
feeble ['fiːbl] adj débil.
feeble-minded [fiːbl'maɪndɪd] adj imbécil.
feed [fiːd] n (gen, of baby) comida; (of animal) pienso; (on printer) dispositivo de alimentación ♦ vt (pt, pp fed) (gen) alimentar; (BRIT: breastfeed) dar el pecho a; (animal, baby) dar de comer a ♦ vi (baby, animal) comer.
▶**feed back** vt (results) pasar.
▶**feed in** vt (COMPUT) introducir.
▶**feed into** vt (data, information) suministrar a; to ~ sth into a machine introducir algo en una máquina.
▶**feed on** vt fus alimentarse de.
feedback ['fiːdbæk] n (from person) reacción f; (TECH) realimentación f, feedback m.
feeder ['fiːdə*] n (bib) babero.
feeding bottle ['fiːdɪŋ-] n (BRIT) biberón m.
feel [fiːl] n (sensation) sensación f; (sense of touch) tacto ♦ vt (pt, pp felt) tocar; (cold, pain etc) sentir; (think, believe) creer; to get the ~ of sth (fig) acostumbrarse a algo; to ~ hungry/cold tener hambre/frío; to ~ lonely/better sentirse solo/mejor; I don't ~ well no me siento bien; it ~s soft es suave al tacto; it ~s colder out here se siente más frío aquí fuera; to ~ like (want) tener ganas de; I'm still ~ing my way (fig) todavía me estoy orientando; I ~ that you ought to do it creo que debes hacerlo; to ~ about or around in one's pocket tantear.
feeler ['fiːlə*] n (of insect) antena; to put out ~s (fig) tantear el terreno.
feeling ['fiːlɪŋ] n (physical) sensación f; (foreboding) presentimiento; (impression) impresión f; (emotion) sentimiento; what are your ~s about the matter? ¿qué opinas tú del asunto?; to hurt sb's ~s herir los sentimientos de algn; ~s ran high about it causó mucha controversia; I got the ~ that ... me dio la impresión de que ...; there was a general ~ that ... la

opinión general fue que ....
fee-paying school ['fiːpeɪɪŋ-] *n* colegio de pago.
feet [fiːt] *npl of* **foot**.
feign [feɪn] *vt* fingir.
feigned [feɪnd] *adj* fingido.
feline ['fiːlaɪn] *adj* felino.
fell [fɛl] *pt of* **fall** ♦ *vt* (*tree*) talar ♦ *adj*: **with one ~ blow** con un golpe feroz; **at one ~ swoop** de un solo golpe ♦ *n* (*BRIT*: *mountain*) montaña; (: *moorland*): **the ~s** los páramos.
fellow ['fɛləu] *n* tipo, tío (*SP*); (*of learned society*) socio/a; (*UNIV*) *miembro de la junta de gobierno de un colegio* ♦ *cpd*: **~ students** compañeros/as *m/fpl* de curso, condiscípulos/as *m/fpl*.
fellow citizen *n* conciudadano/a.
fellow countryman *n* compatriota *m*.
fellow feeling *n* compañerismo.
fellow men *npl* semejantes *mpl*.
fellowship ['fɛləuʃɪp] *n* compañerismo; (*grant*) beca.
fellow traveller *n* compañero/a de viaje; (*POL*: *with communists*) simpatizante *m/f*.
fellow worker *n* colega *m/f*.
felon ['fɛlən] *n* criminal *m/f*.
felony ['fɛlənɪ] *n* crimen *m*, delito mayor.
felt [fɛlt] *pt, pp of* **feel** ♦ *n* fieltro.
felt-tip pen ['fɛlttɪp-] *n* rotulador *m*.
female ['fiːmeɪl] *n* (*woman*) mujer *f*; (*ZOOL*) hembra ♦ *adj* femenino.
feminine ['fɛmɪnɪn] *adj* femenino.
femininity [fɛmɪ'nɪnɪtɪ] *n* feminidad *f*.
feminism ['fɛmɪnɪzəm] *n* feminismo.
feminist ['fɛmɪnɪst] *n* feminista *m/f*.
fence [fɛns] *n* valla, cerca; (*RACING*) valla ♦ *vt* (*also*: ~ **in**) cercar ♦ *vi* hacer esgrima; **to sit on the ~** (*fig*) nadar entre dos aguas.
►**fence in** *vt* cercar.
►**fence off** *vt* separar con cerca.
fencing ['fɛnsɪŋ] *n* esgrima.
fend [fɛnd] *vi*: **to ~ for o.s.** valerse por sí mismo.
►**fend off** *vt* (*attack, attacker*) rechazar, repeler; (*blow*) desviar; (*awkward question*) esquivar.
fender ['fɛndə*] *n* pantalla; (*US*: *AUT*) parachoques *m inv*; (: *RAIL*) trompa.
fennel ['fɛnl] *n* hinojo.
Fens [fɛnz] *npl* (*BRIT*): **the ~** *las tierras bajas de Norfolk* (*antiguamente zona de marismas*).
ferment *vi* [fə'mɛnt] fermentar ♦ *n* ['fəːmɛnt] (*fig*) agitación *f*.
fermentation [fəːmɛn'teɪʃən] *n* fermentación *f*.

fern [fəːn] *n* helecho.
ferocious [fə'rəuʃəs] *adj* feroz.
ferociously [fə'rəuʃəslɪ] *adv* ferozmente, con ferocidad.
ferocity [fə'rɔsɪtɪ] *n* ferocidad *f*.
ferret ['fɛrɪt] *n* hurón *m*.
►**ferret about, ferret around** *vi* rebuscar.
►**ferret out** *vt* (*secret, truth*) desentrañar.
ferry ['fɛrɪ] *n* (*small*) barca (de pasaje), balsa; (*large*: *also*: ~**boat**) transbordador *m*, ferry *m* ♦ *vt* transportar; **to ~ sth/sb across** *or* **over** transportar algo/a algn a la otra orilla; **to ~ sb to and fro** llevar a algn de un lado para otro.
ferryman ['fɛrɪmən] *n* barquero.
fertile ['fəːtaɪl] *adj* fértil; (*BIOL*) fecundo.
fertility [fə'tɪlɪtɪ] *n* fertilidad *f*; fecundidad *f*.
fertility drug *n* medicamento contra la infertilidad.
fertilization [fəːtɪlaɪ'zeɪʃən] *n* fertilización *f*; (*BIOL*) fecundación *f*.
fertilize ['fəːtɪlaɪz] *vt* fertilizar; (*BIOL*) fecundar; (*AGR*) abonar.
fertilizer ['fəːtɪlaɪzə*] *n* abono, fertilizante *m*.
fervent ['fəːvənt] *adj* ferviente.
fervour, (*US*) **fervor** ['fəːvə*] *n* fervor *m*, ardor *m*.
fester ['fɛstə*] *vi* supurar.
festival ['fɛstɪvəl] *n* (*REL*) fiesta; (*ART, MUS*) festival *m*.
festive ['fɛstɪv] *adj* festivo; **the ~ season** (*BRIT*: *Christmas*) las Navidades.
festivities [fɛs'tɪvɪtɪz] *npl* festejos *mpl*.
festoon [fɛs'tuːn] *vt*: **to ~ with** festonear *or* engalanar de.
fetch [fɛtʃ] *vt* ir a buscar; (*BRIT*: *sell for*) venderse por; **how much did it ~?** ¿por cuánto se vendió?
►**fetch up** *vi* ir a parar.
fetching ['fɛtʃɪŋ] *adj* atractivo.
fête [feɪt] *n* fiesta.
fetid ['fɛtɪd] *adj* fétido.
fetish ['fɛtɪʃ] *n* fetiche *m*.
fetter ['fɛtə*] *vt* (*person*) encadenar, poner grillos a; (*horse*) trabar; (*fig*) poner trabas a.
fetters ['fɛtəz] *npl* grillos *mpl*.
fettle ['fɛtl] *n*: **in fine ~** en buenas condiciones.
fetus ['fiːtəs] *n* (*US*) = **foetus**.
feud [fjuːd] *n* (*hostility*) enemistad *f*; (*quarrel*) disputa; **a family ~** una pelea familiar.
feudal ['fjuːdl] *adj* feudal.
feudalism ['fjuːdəlɪzəm] *n* feudalismo.
fever ['fiːvə*] *n* fiebre *f*; **he has a ~** tiene

fiebre.
feverish ['fiːvərɪʃ] *adj* febril.
feverishly ['fiːvərɪʃlɪ] *adv* febrilmente.
few [fjuː] *adj* (*not many*) pocos; (*some*)
algunos, unos ♦ *pron* algunos; **a** ~ *adj* unos
pocos; ~ **people** poca gente; **a good** ~,
quite a ~ bastantes; **in** *or* **over the next** ~
days en los próximos días; **every** ~ **weeks**
cada 2 o 3 semanas; **a** ~ **more days** unos
días más.
fewer ['fjuːə*] *adj* menos.
fewest ['fjuːɪst] *adj* los/las menos.
FFA *n abbr* = *Future Farmers of America.*
FH *abbr* (*BRIT*) = **fire hydrant**.
FHA *n abbr* (*US*: = *Federal Housing
Association*) *oficina federal de la
vivienda.*
fiancé [fɪˈɑːŋseɪ] *n* novio, prometido.
fiancée [fɪˈɑːŋseɪ] *n* novia, prometida.
fiasco [fɪˈæskəu] *n* fiasco.
fib [fɪb] *n* mentirijilla ♦ *vi* decir
mentirijillas.
fibre, (*US*) **fiber** ['faɪbə*] *n* fibra.
fibreboard, (*US*) **fiberboard** ['faɪbəbɔːd] *n*
fibra vulcanizada.
fibreglass, (*US*) **fiberglass** ['faɪbəglɑːs] *n*
fibra de vidrio.
fibrositis [faɪbrəˈsaɪtɪs] *n* fibrositis *f inv*.
FICA *n abbr* (*US*) = *Federal Insurance
Contributions Act.*
fickle ['fɪkl] *adj* inconstante.
fiction ['fɪkʃən] *n* (*gen*) ficción *f*.
fictional ['fɪkʃənl] *adj* novelesco.
fictionalize ['fɪkʃənəlaɪz] *vt* novelar.
fictitious [fɪkˈtɪʃəs] *adj* ficticio.
fiddle ['fɪdl] *n* (*MUS*) violín *m*; (*cheating*)
trampa ♦ *vt* (*BRIT*: *accounts*) falsificar; **tax**
~ evasión *f* fiscal; **to work a** ~ hacer
trampa.
▶**fiddle with** *vt fus* juguetear con.
fiddler ['fɪdlə*] *n* violinista *m/f*.
fiddly ['fɪdlɪ] *adj* (*task*) delicado, mañoso;
(*object*) enrevesado.
fidelity [fɪˈdɛlɪtɪ] *n* fidelidad *f*.
fidget ['fɪdʒɪt] *vi* moverse (nerviosamente).
fidgety ['fɪdʒɪtɪ] *adj* nervioso.
fiduciary [fɪˈduːʃɪərɪ] *n* fiduciario/a.
field [fiːld] *n* (*gen*, *COMPUT*) campo; (*fig*)
campo, esfera; (*SPORT*) campo, cancha
(*LAM*); (*competitors*) competidores *mpl*
♦ *cpd*: **to have a** ~ **day** (*fig*) ponerse las
botas; **to lead the** ~ (*SPORT*, *COMM*) llevar
la delantera; **to give sth a year's trial in
the** ~ (*fig*) sacar algo al mercado a
prueba por un año; **my particular** ~ mi
especialidad.
field glasses *npl* gemelos *mpl*.
field hospital *n* hospital *m* de campaña.

field marshal *n* mariscal *m*.
fieldwork ['fiːldwɜːk] *n* (*ARCHAEOLOGY,
GEO*) trabajo de campo.
fiend [fiːnd] *n* demonio.
fiendish ['fiːndɪʃ] *adj* diabólico.
fierce [fɪəs] *adj* feroz; (*wind, attack*) violento;
(*heat*) intenso; (*fighting, enemy*)
encarnizado.
fiercely ['fɪəslɪ] *adv* con ferocidad;
violentamente; intensamente;
encarnizadamente.
fierceness ['fɪəsnɪs] *n* ferocidad *f*;
violencia; intensidad *f*; encarnizamiento.
fiery ['faɪərɪ] *adj* (*burning*) ardiente;
(*temperament*) apasionado.
FIFA ['fiːfə] *n abbr* (= *Fédération
Internationale de Football Association*)
FIFA *f*.
fifteen [fɪfˈtiːn] *num* quince.
fifth [fɪfθ] *num* quinto.
fiftieth ['fɪftɪθ] *num* quincuagésimo.
fifty ['fɪftɪ] *num* cincuenta; **the fifties** los
años cincuenta; **to be in one's fifties**
andar por los cincuenta.
fifty-fifty ['fɪftɪ'fɪftɪ] *adv*: **to go** ~ **with sb** ir
a medias con algn ♦ *adj*: **we have a** ~
chance of success tenemos un cincuenta
por ciento de posibilidades de tener
éxito.
fig [fɪg] *n* higo.
fight [faɪt] *n* (*gen*) pelea; (*MIL*) combate *m*;
(*struggle*) lucha ♦ *vb* (*pt, pp* **fought**) *vt*
luchar contra; (*cancer, alcoholism*)
combatir; (*LAW*): **to** ~ **a case** defenderse;
(*quarrel*): **to** ~ (**with sb**) pelear (con algn)
♦ *vi* pelear, luchar; (*fig*): **to** ~ (**for/against**)
luchar por/contra.
▶**fight back** *vi* defenderse; (*after illness*)
recuperarse ♦ *vt* (*tears*) contener.
▶**fight down** *vt* (*anger, anxiety, urge*)
reprimir.
▶**fight off** *vt* (*attack, attacker*) rechazar;
(*disease, sleep, urge*) luchar contra.
▶**fight out** *vt*: **to** ~ **it out** decidirlo en una
pelea.
fighter ['faɪtə*] *n* combatiente *m/f*; (*fig*)
luchador(a) *m/f*; (*plane*) caza *m*.
fighter-bomber ['faɪtəbɔmə*] *n*
cazabombardero.
fighter pilot *n* piloto de caza.
fighting ['faɪtɪŋ] *n* (*gen*) el luchar; (*battle*)
combate *m*; (*in streets*) disturbios *mpl*.
figment ['fɪgmənt] *n*: **a** ~ **of the
imagination** un producto de la
imaginación.
figurative ['fɪgjurətɪv] *adj* (*meaning*)
figurado; (*ART*) figurativo.
figure ['fɪgə*] *n* (*DRAWING, GEOM*) figura,

dibujo; (*number, cipher*) cifra; (*person, outline*) figura; (*body shape*) línea; (: *attractive*) tipo ♦ *vt* (*esp US: think, calculate*) calcular, imaginarse ♦ *vi* (*appear*) figurar; (*esp US: make sense*) ser lógico; ~ **of speech** (*LING*) figura retórica; **public** ~ personaje *m*.
►**figure on** *vt fus* (*US*) contar con.
►**figure out** *vt* (*understand*) comprender.
figurehead ['fɪgəhɛd] *n* (*fig*) figura decorativa.
figure skating *n* patinaje *m* artístico.
Fiji (Islands) ['fiːdʒiː-] *n(pl)* (Islas *fpl*) Fiji *fpl*.
filament ['fɪləmənt] *n* (*ELEC*) filamento.
filch [fɪltʃ] *vt* (*col: steal*) birlar.
file [faɪl] *n* (*tool*) lima; (*for nails*) lima de uñas; (*dossier*) expediente *m*; (*folder*) carpeta; (*in cabinet*) archivo; (*COMPUT*) fichero; (*row*) fila ♦ *vt* limar; (*papers*) clasificar; (*LAW: claim*) presentar; (*store*) archivar; **to open/close a** ~ (*COMPUT*) abrir/cerrar un fichero; **to** ~ **in/out** *vi* entrar/salir en fila; **to** ~ **a suit against sb** entablar pleito contra algn; **to** ~ **past** desfilar ante.
file name *n* (*COMPUT*) nombre *m* de fichero.
filibuster ['fɪlɪbʌstə*] (*esp US: POL*) *n* obstruccionista *m/f*, filibustero/a ♦ *vi* usar maniobras obstruccionistas.
filing ['faɪlɪŋ] *n*: **to do the** ~ llevar los archivos.
filing cabinet *n* fichero, archivo.
filing clerk *n* oficinista *m/f*.
fill [fɪl] *vt* llenar; (*tooth*) empastar; (*vacancy*) cubrir ♦ *n*: **to eat one's** ~ comer hasta hartarse; **we've already** ~**ed that vacancy** ya hemos cubierto esa vacante; ~**ed with admiration (for)** lleno de admiración (por).
►**fill in** *vt* rellenar; (*details, report*) completar; **to** ~ **sb in on sth** (*col*) poner a algn al corriente *or* al día sobre algo.
►**fill out** *vt* (*form, receipt*) rellenar.
►**fill up** *vt* llenar (hasta el borde) ♦ *vi* (*AUT*) echar gasolina.
fillet ['fɪlɪt] *n* filete *m*.
fillet steak *n* filete *m* de ternera.
filling ['fɪlɪŋ] *n* (*CULIN*) relleno; (*for tooth*) empaste *m*.
filling station *n* estación *f* de servicio.
fillip ['fɪlɪp] *n* estímulo.
filly ['fɪlɪ] *n* potra.
film [fɪlm] *n* película ♦ *vt* (*scene*) filmar ♦ *vi* rodar.
film script *n* guión *m*.
film star *n* estrella de cine.
filmstrip ['fɪlmstrɪp] *n* tira de diapositivas.

film studio *n* estudio de cine.
Filofax ® ['faɪləufæks] *n* agenda (profesional).
filter ['fɪltə*] *n* filtro ♦ *vt* filtrar.
►**filter in, filter through** *vi* filtrarse.
filter coffee *n* café *m* (molido) para filtrar.
filter lane *n* (*BRIT*) carril *m* de selección.
filter-tipped ['fɪltətɪpt] *adj* con filtro.
filth [fɪlθ] *n* suciedad *f*.
filthy ['fɪlθɪ] *adj* sucio; (*language*) obsceno.
fin [fɪn] *n* (*gen*) aleta.
final ['faɪnl] *adj* (*last*) final, último; (*definitive*) definitivo ♦ *n* (*SPORT*) final *f*; ~**s** *npl* (*SCOL*) exámenes *mpl* finales; ~ **demand** (*on invoice etc*) último aviso; ~ **dividend** dividendo final.
finale [fɪ'nɑːlɪ] *n* final *m*.
finalist ['faɪnəlɪst] *n* (*SPORT*) finalista *m/f*.
finality [faɪ'nælɪtɪ] *n* finalidad *f*; **with an air of** ~ en tono resuelto, de modo terminante.
finalize ['faɪnəlaɪz] *vt* ultimar.
finally ['faɪnəlɪ] *adv* (*lastly*) por último, finalmente; (*eventually*) por fin; (*irrevocably*) de modo definitivo; (*once and for all*) definitivamente.
finance [faɪ'næns] *n* (*money, funds*) fondos *mpl*; ~**s** *npl* finanzas *fpl* ♦ *cpd* (*page, section, company*) financiero ♦ *vt* financiar.
financial [faɪ'nænʃəl] *adj* financiero.
financially [faɪ'nænʃəlɪ] *adv* económicamente.
financial management *n* gestión *f* financiera.
financial statement *n* estado financiero.
financial year *n* ejercicio (financiero).
financier [faɪ'nænsɪə*] *n* financiero/a.
find [faɪnd] *vt* (*pt, pp* **found** [faund]) (*gen*) encontrar, hallar; (*come upon*) descubrir ♦ *n* hallazgo; descubrimiento; **to** ~ **sb guilty** (*LAW*) declarar culpable a algn; **I** ~ **it easy** me resulta fácil.
►**find out** *vt* averiguar; (*truth, secret*) descubrir ♦ *vi*: **to** ~ **out about** enterarse de.
findings ['faɪndɪŋz] *npl* (*LAW*) veredicto *sg*, fallo *sg*; (*of report*) recomendaciones *fpl*.
fine [faɪn] *adj* (*delicate*) fino; (*beautiful*) hermoso ♦ *adv* (*well*) bien ♦ *n* (*LAW*) multa ♦ *vt* (*LAW*) multar; **the weather is** ~ hace buen tiempo; **he's** ~ está muy bien; **you're doing** ~ no lo estás haciendo muy bien; **to cut it** ~ (*of time, money*) calcular muy justo; **to get a** ~ **for (doing) sth** recibir una multa por (hacer) algo.
fine arts *npl* bellas artes *fpl*.
finely ['faɪnlɪ] *adv* (*splendidly*) con elegancia; (*chop*) en trozos pequeños,

fino; (*adjust*) con precisión.

fineness ['faɪnnɪs] *n* (*of cloth*) finura; (*of idea*) sutilidad *f*.

fine print *n*: **the** ~ la letra pequeña *or* menuda.

finery ['faɪnərɪ] *n* galas *fpl*.

finesse [fɪ'nɛs] *n* sutileza.

fine-tooth comb ['faɪntu:θ-] *n*: **to go through sth with a** ~ revisar algo a fondo.

finger ['fɪŋgə*] *n* dedo ♦ *vt* (*touch*) manosear; (*MUS*) puntear; **little/index** ~ (dedo) meñique *m*/índice *m*.

fingernail ['fɪŋgəneɪl] *n* uña.

fingerprint ['fɪŋgəprɪnt] *n* huella dactilar ♦ *vt* tomar las huellas dactilares de.

fingertip ['fɪŋgətɪp] *n* yema del dedo; **to have sth at one's** ~**s** saberse algo al dedillo.

finicky ['fɪnɪkɪ] *adj* (*fussy*) delicado.

finish ['fɪnɪʃ] *n* (*end*) fin *m*; (*SPORT*) meta; (*polish etc*) acabado ♦ *vt, vi* acabar, terminar; **to** ~ **doing sth** acabar de hacer algo; **to** ~ **first/second/third** (*SPORT*) llegar el primero/segundo/tercero; **I've** ~ **ed with the paper** he terminado con el periódico; **she's** ~**ed with him** ha roto *or* acabado con él.

► **finish off** *vt* acabar, terminar; (*kill*) rematar.

► **finish up** *vt* acabar, terminar ♦ *vi* ir a parar, terminar.

finished ['fɪnɪʃt] *adj* (*product*) acabado; (*performance*) pulido; (*col: tired*) rendido, hecho polvo.

finishing ['fɪnɪʃɪŋ] *adj*: ~ **touches** toque *m* final.

finishing line *n* línea de llegada *or* meta.

finishing school *n* colegio para la educación social de señoritas.

finite ['faɪnaɪt] *adj* finito.

Finland ['fɪnlənd] *n* Finlandia.

Finn [fɪn] *n* finlandés/esa *m/f*.

Finnish ['fɪnɪʃ] *adj* finlandés/esa ♦ *n* (*LING*) finlandés *m*.

fiord [fjɔːd] *n* fiordo.

fir [fəː*] *n* abeto.

fire ['faɪə*] *n* fuego; (*accidental, damaging*) incendio ♦ *vt* (*gun*) disparar; (*set fire to*) incendiar; (*excite*) exaltar; (*interest*) despertar; (*dismiss*) despedir ♦ *vi* encenderse; (*AUT: subj: engine*) encender; **electric/gas** ~ estufa eléctrica/de gas; **on** ~ ardiendo, en llamas; **to be on** ~ estar ardiendo; **to catch** ~ prenderse fuego; **to set** ~ **to sth, set sth on** ~ prender fuego a algo; **insured against** ~ asegurado contra incendios; **to be/come under** ~ estar/caer bajo el fuego enemigo.

fire alarm *n* alarma de incendios.

firearm ['faɪərɑːm] *n* arma de fuego.

fire brigade, (*US*) **fire department** *n* (cuerpo de) bomberos *mpl*.

fire door *n* puerta contra incendios.

fire drill *n* (ejercicio de) simulacro de incendio.

fire engine *n* coche *m* de bomberos.

fire escape *n* escalera de incendios.

fire extinguisher *n* extintor *m*.

fireguard ['faɪəgɑːd] *n* pantalla (guardallama).

fire hazard *n* = **fire risk**.

fire hydrant *n* boca de incendios.

fire insurance *n* seguro contra incendios.

fireman ['faɪəmən] *n* bombero.

fireplace ['faɪəpleɪs] *n* chimenea.

fireplug ['faɪəplʌg] *n* (*US*) boca de incendios.

fire practice *n* = **fire drill**.

fireproof ['faɪəpruːf] *adj* a prueba de fuego; (*material*) incombustible.

fire regulations *npl* reglamentos *mpl* contra incendios.

fire risk *n* peligro de incendio.

firescreen ['faɪəskriːn] *n* pantalla refractaria.

fireside ['faɪəsaɪd] *n*: **by the** ~ al lado de la chimenea.

fire station *n* parque *m* de bomberos.

firewood ['faɪəwud] *n* leña.

fireworks ['faɪəwəːks] *npl* fuegos *mpl* artificiales.

firing ['faɪərɪŋ] *n* (*MIL*) disparos *mpl*, tiroteo.

firing line *n* línea de fuego; **to be in the** ~ (*fig: liable to be criticised*) estar en la línea de fuego.

firing squad *n* pelotón *m* de ejecución.

firm [fəːm] *adj* firme; (*offer, decision*) en firme ♦ *n* empresa; **to be a** ~ **believer in sth** ser un partidario convencido de algo; **to stand** ~ *or* **take a** ~ **stand on sth** (*fig*) mantenerse firme ante algo.

firmly ['fəːmlɪ] *adv* firmemente.

firmness ['fəːmnɪs] *n* firmeza.

first [fəːst] *adj* primero ♦ *adv* (*before others*) primero; (*when listing reasons etc*) en primer lugar, primeramente ♦ *n* (*person: in race*) primero/a; (*AUT: also:* ~ **gear**) primera; **at** ~ al principio; ~ **of all** ante todo; **the** ~ **of January** el uno *or* primero de enero; **in the** ~ **instance** en primer lugar; **I'll do it** ~ **thing tomorrow** lo haré mañana a primera hora; **for the** ~ **time** por primera vez; **head** ~ de cabeza; **from the (very)** ~ desde el principio.

first aid *n* primeros auxilios *mpl*.

first aid kit *n* botiquín *m*.
first aid post, (*US*) **first aid station** *n* puesto de auxilio.
first-class ['fɜːstklɑːs] *adj* de primera clase; ~ **ticket** (*RAIL etc*) billete *m or* boleto (*LAM*) de primera clase; ~ **mail** correo de primera clase.
first-hand [fɜːst'hænd] *adj* de primera mano.
first lady *n* (*esp US*) primera dama.
firstly ['fɜːstlɪ] *adv* en primer lugar.
first name *n* nombre *m* de pila.
first night *n* estreno.
first-rate [fɜːst'reɪt] *adj* de primera (clase).
first-time buyer [fɜːsttaɪm-] *n persona que compra su primera vivienda*.
fir tree *n* abeto.
FIS *n abbr* (*BRIT: = Family Income Supplement*) *ayuda estatal familiar*.
fiscal ['fɪskəl] *adj* fiscal; ~ **year** año fiscal, ejercicio.
fish [fɪʃ] *n, pl inv* pez *m*; (*food*) pescado ♦ *vt* pescar en ♦ *vi* pescar; **to go** ~**ing** ir de pesca.
▶**fish out** *vt* (*from water, box etc*) sacar.
fish-and-chip shop *n* = **chip shop**.
fishbone ['fɪʃbəun] *n* espina.
fisherman ['fɪʃəmən] *n* pescador *m*.
fishery ['fɪʃərɪ] *n* pesquería.
fish factory *n* fábrica de elaboración de pescado.
fish farm *n* piscifactoría.
fish fingers *npl* (*BRIT*) palitos *mpl* de pescado (empanado).
fishing boat ['fɪʃɪŋ-] *n* barca de pesca.
fishing industry *n* industria pesquera.
fishing line *n* sedal *m*.
fishing net *n* red *f* de pesca.
fishing rod *n* caña (de pescar).
fishing tackle *n* aparejo (de pescar).
fish market *n* mercado de pescado.
fishmonger ['fɪʃmʌŋgə*] *n* (*BRIT*) pescadero/a.
fishmonger's (shop) *n* (*BRIT*) pescadería.
fishseller ['fɪʃsɛlə*] *n* (*US*) = **fishmonger**.
fish slice *n* paleta para pescado.
fish sticks *npl* (*US*) = **fish fingers**.
fishstore ['fɪʃstɔː*] *n* (*US*) = **fishmonger's (shop)**.
fishy ['fɪʃɪ] *adj* (*fig*) sospechoso.
fission ['fɪʃən] *n* fisión *f*; **atomic/nuclear** ~ fisión *f* atómica/nuclear.
fissure ['fɪʃə*] *n* fisura.
fist [fɪst] *n* puño.
fistfight ['fɪstfaɪt] *n* lucha a puñetazos.
fit [fɪt] *adj* (*MED, SPORT*) en (buena) forma; (*proper*) adecuado, apropiado ♦ *vt* (*subj: clothes*) quedar bien a; (*try on: clothes*)

probar; (*match: facts*) cuadrar *or* corresponder *or* coincidir con; (*description*) estar de acuerdo con; (*accommodate*) ajustar, adaptar ♦ *vi* (*clothes*) quedar bien; (*in space, gap*) caber; (*facts*) coincidir ♦ *n* (*MED*) ataque *m*; (*outburst*) arranque *m*; ~ **to** apto para; ~ **for** apropiado para; **do as you think** *or* **see** ~ haz lo que te parezca mejor; **to keep** ~ mantenerse en forma; **to be** ~ **for work** (*after illness*) estar en condiciones para trabajar; ~ **of coughing** acceso de tos; ~ **of anger/enthusiasm** arranque de cólera/entusiasmo; **to have** *or* **suffer a** ~ tener un ataque *or* acceso; **this dress is a good** ~ este vestido me queda bien; **by** ~**s and starts** a rachas.
▶**fit in** *vi* encajar ♦ *vt* (*object*) acomodar; (*fig: appointment, visitor*) encontrar un hueco para; **to** ~ **in with sb's plans** acomodarse a los planes de algn.
▶**fit out** *vt* (*BRIT: also:* **fit up**) equipar.
fitful ['fɪtful] *adj* espasmódico, intermitente.
fitfully ['fɪtfəlɪ] *adv* irregularmente; **to sleep** ~ dormir a rachas.
fitment ['fɪtmənt] *n* mueble *m*.
fitness ['fɪtnɪs] *n* (*MED*) forma física; (*of remark*) conveniencia.
fitted carpet ['fɪtɪd-] *n* moqueta.
fitted cupboards ['fɪtɪd-] *npl* armarios *mpl* empotrados.
fitted kitchen ['fɪtɪd-] *n* cocina amueblada.
fitter ['fɪtə*] *n* ajustador(a) *m/f*.
fitting ['fɪtɪŋ] *adj* apropiado ♦ *n* (*of dress*) prueba; *see also* **fittings**.
fitting room *n* (*in shop*) probador *m*.
fittings ['fɪtɪŋz] *npl* instalaciones *fpl*.
five [faɪv] *num* cinco; **she is** ~ **(years old)** tiene cinco años (de edad); **it costs** ~ **pounds** cuesta cinco libras; **it's** ~ **(o'clock)** son las cinco.
five-day week ['faɪvdeɪ] *n* semana inglesa.
fiver ['faɪvə*] *n* (*col: BRIT*) billete *m* de cinco libras; (: *US*) billete *m* de cinco dólares.
fix [fɪks] *vt* (*secure*) fijar, asegurar; (*mend*) arreglar; (*make ready: meal, drink*) preparar ♦ *n*: **to be in a** ~ estar en un aprieto; **to** ~ **sth in one's mind** fijar algo en la memoria; **the fight was a** ~ (*col*) la pelea estaba amañada.
▶**fix on** *vt* (*decide on*) fijar.
▶**fix up** *vt* (*arrange: date, meeting*) arreglar; **to** ~ **sb up with sth** conseguirle algo a algn.
fixation [fɪk'seɪʃən] *n* (*PSYCH, fig*) fijación *f*.
fixative ['fɪksətɪv] *n* fijador *m*.
fixed [fɪkst] *adj* (*prices etc*) fijo; **how are you**

~ **for money?** (col) ¿qué tal andas de dinero?

fixed assets npl activo sg fijo.

fixed charge n gasto fijo.

fixed-price contract ['fɪkstpraɪs-] n contrato a precio fijo.

fixture ['fɪkstʃə*] n (SPORT) encuentro; ~s npl instalaciones fpl fijas.

fizz [fɪz] vi burbujear.

fizzle out ['fɪzl-] vi apagarse; (enthusiasm, interest) decaer; (plan) quedar en agua de borrajas.

fizzy ['fɪzɪ] adj (drink) gaseoso.

fjord [fjɔːd] n = fiord.

FL abbr (US) = Florida.

Fla. abbr (US) = Florida.

flabbergasted ['flæbəgɑːstɪd] adj pasmado.

flabby ['flæbɪ] adj flojo (de carnes); (skin) fofo.

flag [flæg] n bandera; (stone) losa ♦ vi decaer; ~ **of convenience** pabellón m de conveniencia.

▶**flag down** vt: **to** ~ **sb down** hacer señas a algn para que se pare.

flagpole ['flægpəul] n asta de bandera.

flagrant ['fleɪgrənt] adj flagrante.

flagship ['flægʃɪp] n buque m insignia or almirante.

flagstone ['flægstəun] n losa.

flag stop n (US) parada discrecional.

flair [fleə*] n aptitud f especial.

flak [flæk] n (MIL) fuego antiaéreo; (col: criticism) lluvia de críticas.

flake [fleɪk] n (of rust, paint) desconchón m; (of snow) copo; (of soap powder) escama ♦ vi (also: ~ off) (paint) desconcharse; (skin) descamarse.

flaky ['fleɪkɪ] adj (paintwork) desconchado; (skin) escamoso.

flaky pastry n (CULIN) hojaldre m.

flamboyant [flæm'bɔɪənt] adj (dress) vistoso; (person) extravagante.

flame [fleɪm] n llama; **to burst into** ~**s** incendiarse; **old** ~ (col) antiguo amor m/f.

flamingo [flə'mɪŋgəu] n flamenco.

flammable ['flæməbl] adj inflamable.

flan [flæn] n (BRIT) tarta.

flank [flæŋk] n flanco; (of person) costado ♦ vt flanquear.

flannel ['flænl] n (BRIT: also: **face** ~) toallita; (fabric) franela; ~**s** npl pantalones mpl de franela.

flannelette [flænə'lɛt] n franela de algodón.

flap [flæp] n (of pocket, envelope) solapa; (of table) hoja (plegadiza); (wing movement) aletazo, (AVIAT) flap m ♦ vt (wings) batir ♦ vi (sail, flag) ondear.

flapjack ['flæpdʒæk] n (US: pancake) torta, panqueque m (LAM).

flare [fleə*] n llamarada; (MIL) bengala; (in skirt etc) vuelo.

▶**flare up** vi encenderse; (fig: person) encolerizarse; (: revolt) estallar.

flash [flæʃ] n relámpago; (also: **news** ~) noticias fpl de última hora; (PHOT) flash m; (US: torch) linterna ♦ vt (light, headlights) lanzar destellos con; (torch) encender ♦ vi destellar; **in a** ~ en un santiamén; ~ **of inspiration** ráfaga de inspiración; **to** ~ **sth about** (fig, col: flaunt) ostentar algo, presumir con algo; **he** ~**ed by** or **past** pasó como un rayo.

flashback ['flæʃbæk] n flashback m, escena retrospectiva.

flashbulb ['flæʃbʌlb] n bombilla de flash.

flash card n (SCOL) tarjeta.

flash cube n cubo m de flash.

flasher ['flæʃə*] n exhibicionista m.

flashlight ['flæʃlaɪt] n (US: torch) linterna.

flashpoint ['flæʃpɔɪnt] n punto de inflamación; (fig) punto de explosión.

flashy ['flæʃɪ] adj (pej) ostentoso.

flask [flɑːsk] n petaca; (also: **vacuum** ~) termo.

flat [flæt] adj llano; (smooth) liso; (tyre) desinflado; (battery) descargado; (beer) sin gas; (MUS: instrument) desafinado ♦ n (BRIT: apartment) piso (SP), departamento (LAM), apartamento; (AUT) pinchazo; (MUS) bemol m; **(to work)** ~ **out** (trabajar) a tope; ~ **rate of pay** sueldo fijo.

flatfooted [flæt'futɪd] adj de pies planos.

flatly ['flætlɪ] adv rotundamente, de plano.

flatmate ['flætmeɪt] n compañero/a de piso.

flatness ['flætnɪs] n (of land) llanura, lo llano.

flat-screen ['flætskriːn] adj de pantalla plana.

flatten ['flætn] vt (also: ~ **out**) allanar; (smooth out) alisar; (house, city) arrasar.

flatter ['flætə*] vt adular, halagar; (show to advantage) favorecer.

flatterer ['flætərə*] n adulador(a) m/f.

flattering ['flætərɪŋ] adj halagador(a); (clothes etc) que favorece, favorecedor(a).

flattery ['flætərɪ] n adulación f.

flatulence ['flætjuləns] n flatulencia.

flaunt [flɔːnt] vt ostentar, lucir.

flavour, (US) **flavor** ['fleɪvə*] n sabor m, gusto ♦ vt sazonar, condimentar; **strawberry** ~**ed** con sabor a fresa.

flavo(u)ring ['fleɪvərɪŋ] n (in product) aromatizante m.

flaw [flɔː] n defecto.
flawless ['flɔːlɪs] adj intachable.
flax [flæks] n lino.
flaxen ['flæksən] adj muy rubio.
flea [fliː] n pulga.
flea market n rastro, mercadillo.
fleck [flɛk] n mota ♦ vt (with blood, mud etc) salpicar; **brown ~ed with white** marrón con motas blancas.
fledg(e)ling ['flɛdʒlɪŋ] n (fig) novato/a, principiante m/f.
flee [fliː], pt, pp **fled** [flɛd] vt huir de, abandonar ♦ vi huir.
fleece [fliːs] n vellón m; (wool) lana ♦ vt (col) desplumar.
fleecy ['fliːsɪ] adj (blanket) lanoso, lanudo; (cloud) aborregado.
fleet [fliːt] n flota; (of cars, lorries etc) parque m.
fleeting ['fliːtɪŋ] adj fugaz.
Flemish ['flɛmɪʃ] adj flamenco ♦ n (LING) flamenco; **the ~** los flamencos.
flesh [flɛʃ] n carne f; (of fruit) pulpa; **of ~ and blood** de carne y hueso.
flesh wound n herida superficial.
flew [fluː] pt of **fly**.
flex [flɛks] n cable m ♦ vt (muscles) tensar.
flexibility [flɛksɪ'bɪlɪtɪ] n flexibilidad f.
flexible ['flɛksəbl] adj (gen, disk) flexible; **~ working hours** horario sg flexible.
flexitime ['flɛksɪtaɪm] n horario flexible.
flick [flɪk] n golpecito; (with finger) capirotazo; (BRIT: col: film) película ♦ vt dar un golpecito a.
▶**flick off** vt quitar con el dedo.
▶**flick through** vt fus hojear.
flicker ['flɪkə*] vi (light) parpadear; (flame) vacilar ♦ n parpadeo.
flick knife n navaja de muelle.
flier ['flaɪə*] n aviador(a) m/f.
flies [flaɪz] npl of **fly**.
flight [flaɪt] n vuelo; (escape) huida, fuga; (also: ~ **of steps**) tramo (de escaleras); **to take ~** huir, darse a la fuga; **to put to ~** ahuyentar; **how long does the ~ take?** ¿cuánto dura el vuelo?
flight attendant n (US) auxiliar m/f de vuelo.
flight deck n (AVIAT) cabina de mandos.
flight path n trayectoria de vuelo.
flight recorder n registrador m de vuelo.
flighty ['flaɪtɪ] adj caprichoso.
flimsy ['flɪmzɪ] adj (thin) muy ligero; (excuse) flojo.
flinch [flɪntʃ] vi encogerse.
fling [flɪŋ] vt (pt, pp **flung** [flʌŋ]) arrojar ♦ n (love affair) aventura amorosa.
flint [flɪnt] n pedernal m; (in lighter) piedra.

flip [flɪp] vt: **to ~ a coin** echar a cara o cruz.
▶**flip over** vt dar la vuelta a.
▶**flip through** vt fus (book) hojear; (records) ver de pasada.
flippancy ['flɪpənsɪ] n ligereza.
flippant ['flɪpənt] adj poco serio.
flipper ['flɪpə*] n (of seal etc, for swimming) aleta.
flip side n (of record) cara B.
flirt [flɜːt] vi coquetear, flirtear ♦ n coqueta f.
flirtation [flɜː'teɪʃən] n coqueteo, flirteo.
flit [flɪt] vi revolotear.
float [fləʊt] n flotador m; (in procession) carroza; (sum of money) (dinero suelto para) cambio ♦ vi (also COMM: currency) flotar ♦ vt (gen) hacer flotar; (company) lanzar; **to ~ an idea** plantear una idea.
floating ['fləʊtɪŋ] adj: **~ vote** voto indeciso; **~ voter** votante m/f indeciso/a.
flock [flɒk] n (of sheep) rebaño; (of birds) bandada; (of people) multitud f.
floe [fləʊ] n: **ice ~** témpano de hielo.
flog [flɒg] vt azotar; (col) vender.
flood [flʌd] n inundación f; (of words, tears etc) torrente m ♦ vt (also AUT: carburettor) inundar; **to ~ the market** (COMM) inundar el mercado.
flooding ['flʌdɪŋ] n inundación f.
floodlight ['flʌdlaɪt] n foco ♦ vt (irreg: like **light**) iluminar con focos.
floodlit ['flʌdlɪt] pt, pp of **floodlight** ♦ adj iluminado.
flood tide n pleamar f.
floodwater ['flʌdwɔːtə*] n aguas fpl (de la inundación).
floor [flɔː*] n suelo, piso (LAM); (storey) piso; (of sea, valley) fondo; (dance ~) pista ♦ vt (fig: baffle) dejar anonadado; **ground ~**, (US) **first ~** planta baja; **first ~**, (US) **second ~** primer piso; **top ~** último piso; **to have the ~** (speaker) tener la palabra.
floorboard ['flɔːbɔːd] n tabla.
flooring ['flɔːrɪŋ] n suelo; (material) solería.
floor lamp n (US) lámpara de pie.
floor show n cabaret m.
floorwalker ['flɔːwɔːkə*] n (US COMM) supervisor(a) m/f.
flop [flɒp] n fracaso ♦ vi (fail) fracasar.
floppy ['flɒpɪ] adj flojo ♦ n = **floppy disk**.
floppy disk n (COMPUT) floppy m, floppy-disk m, disco flexible.
flora ['flɔːrə] n flora.
floral ['flɔːrl] adj floral; (dress, wallpaper) de flores.
Florence ['flɒrəns] n Florencia.
Florentine ['flɒrəntaɪn] adj, n florentino/a m/f.

florid ['flɔrɪd] *adj* (*style*) florido.
florist ['flɔrɪst] *n* florista *m/f*; ~'s (**shop**) *n* floristería.
flotation [fləu'teɪʃən] *n* (*of shares*) emisión *f*; (*of company*) lanzamiento.
flounce [flauns] *n* volante *m*.
▶**flounce in** *vi* entrar con gesto exagerado.
▶**flounce out** *vi* salir con gesto airado.
flounder ['flaundə*] *vi* tropezar ♦ *n* (*ZOOL*) platija.
flour ['flauə*] *n* harina.
flourish ['flʌrɪʃ] *vi* florecer ♦ *n* ademán *m*, movimiento (ostentoso).
flourishing ['flʌrɪʃɪŋ] *adj* floreciente.
flout [flaut] *vt* burlarse de; (*order*) no hacer caso de, hacer caso omiso de.
flow [fləu] *n* (*movement*) flujo; (*direction*) curso; (*of river, also ELEC*) corriente *f* ♦ *vi* correr, fluir.
flow chart *n* organigrama *m*.
flow diagram *n* organigrama *m*.
flower ['flauə*] *n* flor *f* ♦ *vi* florecer; **in** ~ en flor.
flower bed *n* macizo.
flowerpot ['flauəpɔt] *n* tiesto.
flowery ['flauərɪ] *adj* florido; (*perfume, pattern*) de flores.
flowing ['fləuɪŋ] *adj* (*hair, clothes*) suelto; (*style*) fluido.
flown [fləun] *pp of* **fly**.
flu [flu:] *n* gripe *f*.
fluctuate ['flʌktjueɪt] *vi* fluctuar.
fluctuation [flʌktju'eɪʃən] *n* fluctuación *f*.
flue [flu:] *n* cañón *m*.
fluency ['flu:ənsɪ] *n* fluidez *f*, soltura.
fluent ['flu:ənt] *adj* (*speech*) elocuente; **he speaks ~ French, he's ~ in French** domina el francés.
fluently ['flu:əntlɪ] *adv* con soltura.
fluff [flʌf] *n* pelusa.
fluffy ['flʌfɪ] *adj* lanoso.
fluid ['flu:ɪd] *adj, n* fluido, líquido; (*in diet*) líquido.
fluke [flu:k] *n* (*col*) chiripa.
flummox ['flʌməks] *vt* desconcertar.
flung [flʌŋ] *pt, pp of* **fling**.
flunky ['flʌŋkɪ] *n* lacayo.
fluorescent [fluə'resnt] *adj* fluorescente.
fluoride ['fluəraɪd] *n* fluoruro.
fluoride toothpaste *n* pasta de dientes con flúor.
flurry ['flʌrɪ] *n* (*of snow*) ventisca; (*haste*) agitación *f*; ~ **of activity** frenesí *m* de actividad.
flush [flʌʃ] *n* (*on face*) rubor *m*; (*fig: of youth, beauty*) resplandor *m* ♦ *vt* limpiar con agua; (*also*: ~ **out**) (*game, birds*) levantar;

(*fig: criminal*) poner al descubierto ♦ *vi* ruborizarse ♦ *adj*: ~ **with** a ras de; **to** ~ **the toilet** tirar de la cadena (del wáter); **hot ~es** (*MED*) sofocos *mpl*.
flushed [flʌʃt] *adj* ruborizado.
fluster ['flʌstə*] *n* aturdimiento ♦ *vt* aturdir.
flustered ['flʌstəd] *adj* aturdido.
flute [flu:t] *n* flauta travesera.
flutter ['flʌtə*] *n* (*of wings*) revoloteo, aleteo; (*fam: bet*) apuesta ♦ *vi* revolotear; **to be in a** ~ estar nervioso.
flux [flʌks] *n* flujo; **in a state of** ~ cambiando continuamente.
fly [flaɪ] *n* (*insect*) mosca; (*on trousers: also*: **flies**) bragueta ♦ *vb* (*pt* **flew**, *pp* **flown**) *vt* (*plane*) pilotar; (*cargo*) transportar (en avión); (*distances*) recorrer (en avión) ♦ *vi* volar; (*passengers*) ir en avión; (*escape*) evadirse; (*flag*) ondear.
▶**fly away** *vi* (*bird, insect*) irse volando.
▶**fly in** *vi* (*person*) llegar en avión; (*plane*) aterrizar; **he flew in from Bilbao** llegó en avión desde Bilbao.
▶**fly off** *vi* irse volando.
▶**fly out** *vi* irse en avión.
fly-fishing ['flaɪfɪʃɪŋ] *n* pesca con mosca.
flying ['flaɪɪŋ] *n* (*activity*) (el) volar ♦ *adj*: ~ **visit** visita relámpago; **with ~ colours** con lucimiento.
flying buttress *n* arbotante *m*.
flying picket *n* piquete *m* volante.
flying saucer *n* platillo volante.
flying squad *n* (*POLICE*) brigada móvil.
flying start *n*: **to get off to a** ~ empezar con buen pie.
flyleaf, *pl* **flyleaves** ['flaɪli:f, -li:vz] *n* (hoja de) guarda.
flyover ['flaɪəuvə*] *n* (*BRIT: bridge*) paso elevado *or* a desnivel (*LAM*).
flypast ['flaɪpɑ:st] *n* destile *m* aéreo.
flysheet ['flaɪʃi:t] *n* (*for tent*) doble techo.
flyswatter ['flaɪswɔtə*] *n* matamoscas *m inv*.
flyweight ['flaɪweɪt] *adj* de peso mosca ♦ *n* peso mosca.
flywheel ['flaɪwi:l] *n* volante *m* (de motor).
FM *abbr* (*BRIT MIL*) = **field marshal**; (*RADIO*: = frequency modulation) FM.
FMB *n abbr* (*US*) = *Federal Maritime Board*.
FMCS *n abbr* (*US*: = *Federal Mediation and Conciliation Services*) organismo de conciliación en conflictos laborales.
FO *n abbr* (*BRIT*: = *Foreign Office*) ≈ Min. de AA. EE.
foal [fəul] *n* potro.
foam [fəum] *n* espuma ♦ *vi* hacer espuma.
foam rubber *n* goma espuma.

FOB *abbr* (= *free on board*) f.a.b.
fob [fɔb] *n* (*also:* **watch** ~) leontina ♦ *vt:* **to ~ sb off with sth** deshacerse de algn con algo.
foc *abbr* (*BRIT:* = *free of charge*) gratis.
focal ['fəukəl] *adj* focal; ~ **point** punto focal; (*fig*) centro de atención.
focus ['fəukəs] (*pl:* ~**es**) *n* foco ♦ *vt* (*field glasses etc*) enfocar ♦ *vi:* **to ~ (on)** enfocar (a); (*issue etc*) centrarse en; **in/out of** ~ enfocado/desenfocado.
fodder ['fɔdə*] *n* pienso.
FOE *n abbr* (= *Friends of the Earth*) Amigos *mpl* de la Tierra; (*US:* = *Fraternal Order of Eagles*) *organización benéfica*.
foe [fəu] *n* enemigo.
foetus, (*US*) **fetus** ['fiːtəs] *n* feto.
fog [fɔg] *n* niebla.
fogbound ['fɔgbaund] *adj* inmovilizado por la niebla.
foggy ['fɔgɪ] *adj:* **it's** ~ hay niebla.
fog lamp, (*US*) **fog light** *n* (*AUT*) faro antiniebla.
foible ['fɔɪbl] *n* manía.
foil [fɔɪl] *vt* frustrar ♦ *n* hoja; (*kitchen* ~) papel *m* (de) aluminio; (*FENCING*) florete *m*.
foist [fɔɪst] *vt:* **to ~ sth on sb** endilgarle algo a algn.
fold [fəuld] *n* (*bend, crease*) pliegue *m*; (*AGR*) redil *m* ♦ *vt* doblar; (*map etc*) plegar; **to ~ one's arms** cruzarse de brazos.
►**fold up** *vi* plegarse, doblarse; (*business*) quebrar.
folder ['fəuldə*] *n* (*for papers*) carpeta; (*binder*) carpeta de anillas; (*brochure*) folleto.
folding ['fəuldɪŋ] *adj* (*chair, bed*) plegable.
foliage ['fəulɪɪdʒ] *n* follaje *m*.
folio ['fəulɪəu] *n* folio.
folk [fəuk] *npl* gente *f* ♦ *adj* popular, folklórico; ~**s** *npl* familia, parientes *mpl*.
folklore ['fəuklɔː*] *n* folklore *m*.
folk music *n* música folk.
folk singer *n* cantante *m/f* de música folk.
folk song *n* canción *f* popular *or* folk.
follow ['fɔləu] *vt* seguir ♦ *vi* seguir; (*result*) resultar; **he** ~**ed suit** hizo lo mismo; **to ~ sb's advice** seguir el consejo de algn; **I don't quite ~ you** no te comprendo muy bien; **to ~ in sb's footsteps** seguir los pasos de algn; **it doesn't ~ that** ... no se deduce que ....
►**follow on** *vi* seguir; (*continue*): **to ~ on from** ser la consecuencia lógica de.
►**follow out** *vt* (*implement: idea, plan*) realizar, llevar a cabo.
►**follow through** *vt* llevar hasta el fin ♦ *vi*

(*SPORT*) dar el remate.
►**follow up** *vt* (*letter, offer*) responder a; (*case*) investigar.
follower ['fɔləuə*] *n* seguidor(a) *m/f*; (*POL*) partidario/a.
following ['fɔləuɪŋ] *adj* siguiente ♦ *n* seguidores *mpl*.
follow-up ['fɔləuʌp] *n* continuación *f*.
follow-up letter *n* carta recordatoria.
folly ['fɔlɪ] *n* locura.
fond [fɔnd] *adj* (*loving*) cariñoso; **to be ~ of sb** tener cariño a algn; **she's ~ of swimming** tiene afición a la natación, le gusta nadar.
fondle ['fɔndl] *vt* acariciar.
fondly ['fɔndlɪ] *adv* (*lovingly*) con cariño; **he ~ believed that** ... creía ingenuamente que ....
fondness ['fɔndnɪs] *n* (*for things*) afición *f*; (*for people*) cariño.
font [fɔnt] *n* pila bautismal.
food [fuːd] *n* comida.
food chain *n* cadena alimenticia.
food mixer *n* batidora.
food poisoning *n* intoxicación *f* alimentaria.
food processor *n* robot *m* de cocina.
food stamp *n* (*US*) vale *m* para comida.
foodstuffs ['fuːdstʌfs] *npl* comestibles *mpl*.
fool [fuːl] *n* tonto/a; (*CULIN*) mousse *m* de frutas ♦ *vt* engañar; **to make a ~ of o.s.** ponerse en ridículo; **you can't ~ me** a mí no me engañas; *see also* **April Fool's Day**.
►**fool about, fool around** *vi* hacer el tonto.
foolhardy ['fuːlhɑːdɪ] *adj* temerario.
foolish ['fuːlɪʃ] *adj* tonto; (*careless*) imprudente.
foolishly ['fuːlɪʃlɪ] *adv* tontamente, neciamente.
foolproof ['fuːlpruːf] *adj* (*plan etc*) infalible.
foolscap ['fuːlskæp] *n* ≈ papel *m* tamaño folio.
foot [fut], *pl* **feet** *n* (*gen, also: of page, stairs etc*) pie *m*; (*measure*) pie (= 304 *mm*); (*of animal, table*) pata ♦ *vt* (*bill*) pagar; **on ~** a pie; **to find one's feet** acostumbrarse; **to put one's ~ down** (*say no*) plantarse; (*AUT*) pisar el acelerador.
footage ['futɪdʒ] *n* (*CINE*) imágenes *fpl*.
foot-and-mouth (disease) [futənd'mauθ-] *n* fiebre *f* aftosa.
football ['futbɔːl] *n* balón *m*; (*game: BRIT*) fútbol *m*; (*: US*) fútbol *m* americano.
footballer ['futbɔːlə*] *n* (*BRIT*) = **football player**.
football match *n* partido de fútbol.
football player *n* futbolista *m/f*, jugador(a)

m/f de fútbol.

footbrake ['futbreɪk] *n* freno de pie.

footbridge ['futbrɪdʒ] *n* pasarela, puente *m* para peatones.

foothills ['futhɪlz] *npl* estribaciones *fpl.*

foothold ['futhəuld] *n* pie *m* firme.

footing ['futɪŋ] *n* (*fig*) nivel *m*; **to lose one's** ~ perder el equilibrio; **on an equal** ~ en pie de igualdad.

footlights ['futlaɪts] *npl* candilejas *fpl.*

footman ['futmən] *n* lacayo.

footnote ['futnəut] *n* nota (de pie de página).

footpath ['futpɑːθ] *n* sendero.

footprint ['futprɪnt] *n* huella, pisada.

footrest ['futrest] *n* apoyapiés *m inv.*

footsie ['futsɪ] *n*; **to play** ~ **with sb** (*col*) juguetear con los pies de algn.

footsore ['futsɔː*] *adj* con los pies doloridos.

footstep ['futstep] *n* paso.

footwear ['futwɛə*] *n* calzado.

FOR *abbr* (= *free on rail*) franco (puesto sobre) vagón.

===================== KEYWORD

for [fɔː] *prep* **1** (*indicating destination, intention*) para; **the train** ~ **London** el tren para Londres; (*in announcements*) el tren con destino a Londres; **he left** ~ **Rome** marchó para Roma; **he went** ~ **the paper** fue por el periódico; **is this** ~ **me?** ¿es esto para mí?; **it's time** ~ **lunch** es la hora de comer

2 (*indicating purpose*) para; **what('s it)** ~**?** ¿para qué (es)?; **what's this button** ~**?** ¿para qué sirve este botón?; **to pray** ~ **peace** rezar por la paz

3 (*on behalf of, representing*): **the MP** ~ **Hove** el diputado por Hove; **he works** ~ **the government/a local firm** trabaja para el gobierno/en una empresa local; **I'll ask him** ~ **you** se lo pediré por ti; **G** ~ **George** G de Gerona

4 (*because of*) por esta razón; ~ **fear of being criticized** por temor a ser criticado

5 (*with regard to*) para; **it's cold** ~ **July** hace frío para julio; **he has a gift** ~ **languages** tiene don de lenguas

6 (*in exchange for*) por; **I sold it** ~ **£5** lo vendí por £5; **to pay 50 pence** ~ **a ticket** pagar 50 peniques por un billete

7 (*in favour of*): **are you** ~ **or against us?** ¿estás con nosotros o contra nosotros?; **I'm all** ~ **it** estoy totalmente a favor; **vote** ~ **X** vote (a) X

8 (*referring to distance*): **there are roadworks** ~ **5 km** hay obras en 5 km; **we**

walked ~ **miles** caminamos kilómetros y kilómetros

9 (*referring to time*): **he was away** ~ **2 years** estuvo fuera (durante) dos años; **it hasn't rained** ~ **3 weeks** no ha llovido durante *or* en 3 semanas; **I have known her** ~ **years** la conozco desde hace años; **can you do it** ~ **tomorrow?** ¿lo podrás hacer para mañana?

10 (*with infinitive clauses*): **it is not** ~ **me to decide** la decisión no es cosa mía; **it would be best** ~ **you to leave** sería mejor que te fueras; **there is still time** ~ **you to do it** todavía te queda tiempo para hacerlo; ~ **this to be possible** ... para que esto sea posible ...

11 (*in spite of*) a pesar de; ~ **all his complaints** a pesar de sus quejas

♦ *conj* (*since, as: rather formal*) puesto que.

forage ['fɒrɪdʒ] *n* forraje *m.*

foray ['fɒreɪ] *n* incursión *f.*

forbid, *pt* **forbad(e)**, *pp* **forbidden** [fə'bɪd, -'bæd, -'bɪdn] *vt* prohibir; **to** ~ **sb to do sth** prohibir a algn hacer algo.

forbidding [fə'bɪdɪŋ] *adj* (*landscape*) inhóspito; (*severe*) severo.

force [fɔːs] *n* fuerza ♦ *vt* obligar, forzar; **to** ~ **o.s. to do** hacer un esfuerzo por hacer; **the F~s** *npl* (*BRIT*) las Fuerzas Armadas; **sales** ~ (*COMM*) personal *m* de ventas; **a** ~ **5 wind** un viento fuerza 5; **to join** ~**s** unir fuerzas; **in** ~ (*law etc*) en vigor; **to** ~ **sb to do sth** obligar a algn a hacer algo.

▶**force back** *vt* (*crowd, enemy*) hacer retroceder; (*tears*) reprimir.

▶**force down** *vt* (*food*) tragar con esfuerzo.

forced [fɔːst] *adj* (*smile*) forzado; (*landing*) forzoso.

force-feed ['fɔːsfiːd] *vt* (*animal, prisoner*) alimentar a la fuerza.

forceful ['fɔːsful] *adj* enérgico.

forcemeat ['fɔːsmiːt] *n* (*CULIN*) relleno.

forceps ['fɔːseps] *npl* fórceps *m inv.*

forcible ['fɔːsəbl] *adj* (*violent*) a la fuerza; (*telling*) convincente.

forcibly ['fɔːsəblɪ] *adv* a la fuerza.

ford [fɔːd] *n* vado ♦ *vt* vadear.

fore [fɔː*] *n*: **to bring to the** ~ sacar a la luz pública; **to come to the** ~ empezar a destacar.

forearm ['fɔːrɑːm] *n* antebrazo.

forebear ['fɔːbɛə*] *n* antepasado.

foreboding [fɔː'bəudɪŋ] *n* presentimiento.

forecast ['fɔːkɑːst] *n* pronóstico ♦ *vt* (*irreg: like* **cast**) pronosticar; **weather** ~ previsión *f* meteorológica.

foreclose [fɔː'kləuz] *vt* (*LAW: also:* ~ **on**) extinguir el derecho de redimir.

foreclosure [fɔː'kləuʒə*] *n* apertura de un juicio hipotecario.

forecourt ['fɔːkɔːt] *n* (*of garage*) área de entrada.

forefathers ['fɔːfɑːðəz] *npl* antepasados *mpl*.

forefinger ['fɔːfɪŋgə*] *n* (dedo) índice *m*.

forefront ['fɔːfrʌnt] *n*: **in the** ~ **of** en la vanguardia de.

forego, *pt* **forewent**, *pp* **foregone** [fɔː'gəu, -'wɛnt, -'gɔn] *vt* = **forgo**.

foregoing ['fɔːgəuɪŋ] *adj* anterior, precedente.

foregone ['fɔːgɔn] *pp of* **forego** ♦ *adj*: **it's a** ~ **conclusion** es una conclusión inevitable.

foreground ['fɔːgraund] *n* primer plano.

forehand ['fɔːhænd] *n* (*TENNIS*) derechazo directo.

forehead ['fɔrɪd] *n* frente *f*.

foreign ['fɔrɪn] *adj* extranjero; (*trade*) exterior.

foreign currency *n* divisas *fpl*.

foreigner ['fɔrɪnə*] *n* extranjero/a.

foreign exchange *n* (*system*) cambio de divisas; (*money*) divisas *fpl*, moneda extranjera.

foreign investment *n* inversión *f* en el extranjero; (*money, stock*) inversiones *fpl* extranjeras.

Foreign Minister *n* Ministro/a de Asuntos Exteriores, Canciller *m* (*LAM*).

Foreign Office *n* Ministerio de Asuntos Exteriores.

Foreign Secretary *n* (*BRIT*) Ministro/a de Asuntos Exteriores, Canciller *m* (*LAM*).

foreleg ['fɔːlɛg] *n* pata delantera.

foreman ['fɔːmən] *n* capataz *m*; (*LAW: of jury*) presidente *m/f*.

foremost ['fɔːməust] *adj* principal ♦ *adv*: **first and** ~ ante todo, antes que nada.

forename ['fɔːneɪm] *n* nombre *m* (de pila).

forensic [fə'rɛnsɪk] *adj* forense; ~ **scientist** forense *m/f*.

foreplay ['fɔːpleɪ] *n* preámbulos *mpl* (*de estimulación sexual*).

forerunner ['fɔːrʌnə*] *n* precursor(a) *m/f*.

foresee, *pt* **foresaw**, *pp* **foreseen** [fɔː'siː, -'sɔː, -'siːn] *vt* prever.

foreseeable [fɔː'siːəbl] *adj* previsible.

foreshadow [fɔː'ʃædəu] *vt* prefigurar, anunciar.

foreshore ['fɔːʃɔː*] *n* playa.

foreshorten [fɔː'ʃɔːtn] *vt* (*figure, scene*) escorzar.

foresight ['fɔːsaɪt] *n* previsión *f*.

foreskin ['fɔːskɪn] *n* (*ANAT*) prepucio.

forest ['fɔrɪst] *n* bosque *m*.

forestall [fɔː'stɔːl] *vt* anticiparse a.

forestry ['fɔrɪstrɪ] *n* silvicultura.

foretaste ['fɔːteɪst] *n* anticipo.

foretell, *pt*, *pp* **foretold** [fɔː'tɛl, -'təuld] *vt* predecir, pronosticar.

forethought ['fɔːθɔːt] *n* previsión *f*.

forever [fə'rɛvə*] *adv* siempre; (*for good*) para siempre.

forewarn [fɔː'wɔːn] *vt* avisar, advertir.

forewent [fɔː'wɛnt] *pt of* **forego**.

foreword ['fɔːwəːd] *n* prefacio.

forfeit ['fɔːfɪt] *n* (*in game*) prenda ♦ *vt* perder (derecho a).

forgave [fə'geɪv] *pt of* **forgive**.

forge [fɔːdʒ] *n* fragua; (*smithy*) herrería ♦ *vt* (*signature: BRIT: money*) falsificar; (*metal*) forjar.

►**forge ahead** *vi* avanzar mucho.

forger ['fɔːdʒə*] *n* falsificador(a) *m/f*.

forgery ['fɔːdʒərɪ] *n* falsificación *f*.

forget, *pt* **forgot**, *pp* **forgotten** [fə'gɛt, -'gɔt, -'gɔtn] *vt* olvidar, olvidarse de ♦ *vi* olvidarse.

forgetful [fə'gɛtful] *adj* olvidadizo.

forget-me-not [fə'gɛtmɪnɔt] *n* nomeolvides *f inv*.

forgive, *pt* **forgave**, *pp* **forgiven** [fə'gɪv, -'geɪv, -'gɪvn] *vt* perdonar; **to** ~ **sb for sth/ for doing sth** perdonar algo a algn/a algn por haber hecho algo.

forgiveness [fə'gɪvnɪs] *n* perdón *m*.

forgiving [fə'gɪvɪŋ] *adj* compasivo.

forgo, *pt* **forwent**, *pp* **forgone** [fɔː'gəu, -'wɛnt, -'gɔn] *vt* (*give up*) renunciar a; (*go without*) privarse de.

forgot [fə'gɔt] *pt of* **forget**.

forgotten [fə'gɔtn] *pp of* **forget**.

fork [fɔːk] *n* (*for eating*) tenedor *m*; (*for gardening*) horca; (*of roads*) bifurcación *f*; (*in tree*) horcadura ♦ *vi* (*road*) bifurcarse.

►**fork out** *vt* (*col: pay*) soltar.

forked [fɔːkt] *adj* (*lightning*) en zigzag.

fork-lift truck ['fɔːklɪft-] *n* máquina elevadora.

forlorn [fə'lɔːn] *adj* (*person*) triste, melancólico; (*deserted: cottage*) abandonado; (*desperate: attempt*) desesperado.

form [fɔːm] *n* forma; (*BRIT SCOL*) curso; (*document*) formulario, planilla (*LAM*) ♦ *vt* formar; **in the** ~ **of** en forma de; **in top** ~ en plena forma; **to be in good** ~ (*SPORT, fig*) estar en plena forma; **to** ~ **part of sth** formar parte de algo; **to** ~ **a circle/a queue** hacer una curva/una cola.

formal ['fɔːməl] *adj* (*offer, receipt*) por escrito; (*person etc*) correcto; (*occasion, dinner*) ceremonioso; ~ **dress** traje *m* de

vestir; (*evening dress*) traje *m* de etiqueta.
formalities [fɔː'mælɪtɪz] *npl* formalidades
fpl.
formality [fɔː'mælɪtɪ] *n* ceremonia.
formalize ['fɔːməlaɪz] *vt* formalizar.
formally ['fɔːməlɪ] *adv* oficialmente.
format ['fɔːmæt] *n* formato ♦ *vt* (*COMPUT*)
formatear.
formation [fɔː'meɪʃən] *n* formación *f.*
formative ['fɔːmətɪv] *adj* (*years*) de
formación.
format line *n* (*COMPUT*) línea de formato.
former ['fɔːmə*] *adj* anterior; (*earlier*)
antiguo; (*ex*) ex; **the ~ ... the latter ...**
aquél ... éste ...; **the ~ president** el
antiguo *or* ex presidente; **the ~**
Yugoslavia/Soviet Union la antigua *or* ex
Yugoslavia/Unión Soviética.
formerly ['fɔːməlɪ] *adv* antiguamente.
form feed *n* (*on printer*) salto de página.
Formica ® [fɔː'maɪkə] *n* formica ®.
formidable ['fɔːmɪdəbl] *adj* formidable.
formula ['fɔːmjulə] *n* fórmula; **F~ One**
(*AUT*) Fórmula Uno.
formulate ['fɔːmjuleɪt] *vt* formular.
fornicate ['fɔːnɪkeɪt] *vi* fornicar.
forsake, *pt* **forsook,** *pp* **forsaken** [fə'seɪk,
-'suk, -'seɪkən] *vt* (*gen*) abandonar; (*plan*)
renunciar a.
fort [fɔːt] *n* fuerte *m*; **to hold the ~** (*fig*)
quedarse a cargo.
forte ['fɔːtɪ] *n* fuerte *m.*
forth [fɔːθ] *adv:* **back and ~** de acá para
allá; **and so ~** y así sucesivamente.
forthcoming [fɔːθ'kʌmɪŋ] *adj* próximo,
venidero; (*character*) comunicativo.
forthright ['fɔːθraɪt] *adj* franco.
forthwith ['fɔːθ'wɪθ] *adv* en el acto, acto
seguido.
fortification [fɔːtɪfɪ'keɪʃən] *n* fortificación *f.*
fortified wine ['fɔːtɪfaɪd-] *n* vino
encabezado.
fortify ['fɔːtɪfaɪ] *vt* fortalecer.
fortitude ['fɔːtɪtjuːd] *n* fortaleza.
fortnight ['fɔːtnaɪt] *n* (*BRIT*) quincena; **it's a**
~ since ... hace quince días que ....
fortnightly ['fɔːtnaɪtlɪ] *adj* quincenal ♦ *adv*
quincenalmente.
FORTRAN ['fɔːtræn] *n* FORTRAN *m.*
fortress ['fɔːtrɪs] *n* fortaleza.
fortuitous [fɔː'tjuːɪtəs] *adj* fortuito.
fortunate ['fɔːtʃənɪt] *adj:* **it is ~ that ...** (es
una) suerte que ....
fortunately ['fɔːtʃənɪtlɪ] *adv*
afortunadamente.
fortune ['fɔːtʃən] *n* suerte *f*; (*wealth*)
fortuna; **to make a ~** hacer un dineral.
fortuneteller ['fɔːtʃəntɛlə*] *n* adivino/a.

forty ['fɔːtɪ] *num* cuarenta.
forum ['fɔːrəm] *n* (*also fig*) foro.
forward ['fɔːwəd] *adj* (*position*) avanzado;
(*movement*) hacia delante; (*front*)
delantero; (*not shy*) atrevido ♦ *n* (*SPORT*)
delantero ♦ *vt* (*letter*) remitir; (*career*)
promocionar; **to move ~** avanzar;
"please ~" "remítase al destinatario".
forward contract *n* contrato a término.
forward exchange *n* cambio a término.
forward planning *n* planificación *f* por
anticipado.
forward rate *n* tipo a término.
forward(s) ['fɔːwəd(z)] *adv* (hacia)
adelante.
forward sales *npl* ventas *fpl* a término.
forwent [fɔː'wɛnt] *pt of* **forgo.**
fossil ['fɔsl] *n* fósil *m*; **~ fuel** combustible *m*
fósil.
foster ['fɔstə*] *vt* (*child*) acoger en familia;
(*idea*) fomentar.
foster brother *n* hermano de leche.
foster child *n* hijo/a adoptivo/a.
foster mother *n* madre *f* adoptiva.
fought [fɔːt] *pt, pp of* **fight.**
foul [faul] *adj* (*gen*) sucio, puerco; (*weather,
smell etc*) asqueroso ♦ *n* (*FOOTBALL*) falta
♦ *vt* (*dirty*) ensuciar; (*block*) atascar;
(*entangle: anchor, propeller*) atascar,
enredarse en; (*football player*) cometer
una falta contra.
foul play *n* (*SPORT*) mala jugada; (*LAW*)
muerte *f* violenta.
found [faund] *pt, pp of* **find** ♦ *vt* (*establish*)
fundar.
foundation [faun'deɪʃən] *n* (*act*) fundación
f; (*basis*) base *f*; (*also:* **~ cream**) base *f* de
maquillaje.
foundations [faun'deɪʃənz] *npl* (*of building*)
cimientos *mpl*; **to lay the ~** poner los
cimientos.
foundation stone *n:* **to lay the ~** poner la
primera piedra.
founder ['faundə*] *n* fundador(a) *m/f* ♦ *vi*
irse a pique.
founding ['faundɪŋ] *adj:* **~ fathers** (*esp US*)
fundadores *mpl*, próceres *mpl*; **~ member**
miembro fundador.
foundry ['faundrɪ] *n* fundición *f.*
fountain ['fauntɪn] *n* fuente *f.*
fountain pen *n* (pluma) estilográfica,
(*LAM*) plumafuente *f.*
four [fɔː*] *num* cuatro; **on all ~s** a gatas.
four-footed [fɔː'futɪd] *adj* cuadrúpedo.
four-letter word ['fɔːlɛtə-] *n* taco.
four-poster ['fɔː'pəustə*] *n* (*also:* **~ bed**)
cama de columnas.
foursome ['fɔːsəm] *n* grupo de cuatro

personas.
fourteen ['fɔː'tiːn] *num* catorce.
fourteenth [fɔː'tiːnθ] *num* decimocuarto.
fourth [fɔːθ] *num* cuarto ♦ *n* (*AUT*: *also*: ~
  gear) cuarta (velocidad).
four-wheel drive ['fɔːwiːl-] *n* tracción ƒ a
  las cuatro ruedas.
fowl [faul] *n* ave ƒ (de corral).
fox [fɔks] *n* zorro ♦ *vt* confundir.
fox fur *n* piel ƒ de zorro.
foxglove ['fɔksglʌv] *n* (*BOT*) dedalera.
fox-hunting ['fɔkshʌntɪŋ] *n* caza de zorros.
foxtrot ['fɔkstrɔt] *n* fox(trot) *m*.
foyer ['fɔɪeɪ] *n* vestíbulo.
FP *n abbr* (*BRIT*) = *former pupil*; (*US*)
  = **fireplug.**
FPA *n abbr* (*BRIT*: = *Family Planning
  Association*) *asociación de planificación
  familiar.*
Fr. *abbr* (*REL*) (= *Father*) P.; (= *friar*) Fr.
fr. *abbr* (= *franc*) f.
fracas ['frækɑː] *n* gresca, refriega.
fraction ['frækʃən] *n* fracción ƒ.
fractionally ['frækʃnəlɪ] *adv* ligeramente.
fractious ['frækʃəs] *adj* (*person, mood*)
  irascible.
fracture ['fræktʃə*] *n* fractura ♦ *vt*
  fracturar.
fragile ['frædʒaɪl] *adj* frágil.
fragment ['frægmənt] *n* fragmento.
fragmentary ['fræg'mentərɪ] *adj*
  fragmentario.
fragrance ['freɪgrəns] *n* fragancia.
fragrant ['freɪgrənt] *adj* fragante, oloroso.
frail [freɪl] *adj* (*fragile*) frágil, quebradizo;
  (*weak*) delicado.
frame [freɪm] *n* (*TECH*) armazón ƒ; (*of
  picture, door etc*) marco; (*of spectacles*:
  also: ~**s**) montura ♦ *vt* encuadrar; (*picture*)
  enmarcar; (*reply*) formular; **to** ~ **sb** (*col*)
  inculpar por engaños a algn.
frame of mind *n* estado de ánimo.
framework ['freɪmwəːk] *n* marco.
France [frɑːns] *n* Francia.
franchise ['fræntʃaɪz] *n* (*POL*) derecho al
  voto, sufragio; (*COMM*) licencia,
  concesión ƒ.
franchisee [fræntʃaɪ'ziː] *n* concesionario/a.
franchiser ['fræntʃaɪzə*] *n* compañía
  concesionaria.
frank [fræŋk] *adj* franco ♦ *vt* (*BRIT*: *letter*)
  franquear.
frankfurter ['fræŋkfəːtə*] *n* salchicha de
  Frankfurt.
frankincense ['fræŋkɪnsɛns] *n* incienso.
franking machine ['fræŋkɪŋ-] *n* máquina
  de franqueo.
frankly ['fræŋklɪ] *adv* francamente.

frankness ['fræŋknɪs] *n* franqueza.
frantic ['fræntɪk] *adj* (*desperate*: *need, desire*)
  desesperado; (: *search*) frenético;
  (: *person*) desquiciado.
fraternal [frə'təːnl] *adj* fraterno.
fraternity [frə'təːnɪtɪ] *n* (*club*) fraternidad ƒ;
  (*US*) club *m* de estudiantes; (*guild*)
  gremio.
fraternization [frætənaɪ'zeɪʃən] *n*
  fraternización ƒ.
fraternize ['frætənaɪz] *vi* confraternizar.
fraud [frɔːd] *n* fraude *m*; (*person*)
  impostor(a) *m/f*.
fraudulent ['frɔːdjulənt] *adj* fraudulento.
fraught [frɔːt] *adj* (*tense*) tenso; ~ **with**
  cargado de.
fray [freɪ] *n* combate *m*, lucha, refriega ♦ *vi*
  deshilacharse; **tempers were** ~**ed** el
  ambiente se ponía tenso.
FRB *n abbr* (*US*) = *Federal Reserve Board*.
FRCM *n abbr* (*BRIT*) = *Fellow of the Royal
  College of Music*.
FRCO *n abbr* (*BRIT*) = *Fellow of the Royal
  College of Organists*.
FRCP *n abbr* (*BRIT*) = *Fellow of the Royal
  College of Physicians*.
FRCS *n abbr* (*BRIT*) = *Fellow of the Royal
  College of Surgeons*.
freak [friːk] *n* (*person*) fenómeno; (*event*)
  suceso anormal; (*col*: *enthusiast*) adicto/a
  ♦ *adj* (*storm, conditions*) anormal; **health** ~
  (*col*) maniático/a en cuestión de salud.
▶**freak out** *vi* (*col*: *on drugs*) flipar.
freakish ['friːkɪʃ] *adj* (*result*) inesperado;
  (*appearance*) estrambótico; (*weather*)
  cambiadizo.
freckle ['frɛkl] *n* peca.
freckled ['frɛkld] *adj* pecoso, lleno de
  pecas.
free [friː] *adj* (*person*: *at liberty*) libre; (*not
  fixed*) suelto; (*gratis*) gratuito;
  (*unoccupied*) desocupado; (*liberal*)
  generoso ♦ *vt* (*prisoner etc*) poner en
  libertad; (*jammed object*) soltar; **to give sb
  a** ~ **hand** dar carta blanca a algn; ~ **and
  easy** despreocupado; **is this seat** ~? ¿está
  libre este asiento?; ~ **of tax** libre de
  impuestos; **admission** ~ entrada libre; ~
  (**of charge**), **for** ~ *adv* gratis.
freebie ['friːbɪ] *n* (*col*): **it's a** ~ es gratis.
freedom ['friːdəm] *n* libertad ƒ; ~ **of
  association** libertad ƒ de asociación.
freedom fighter *n* luchador(a) *m/f* por la
  libertad.
free enterprise *n* libre empresa.
Freefone ® ['friːfəun] *n* (*BRIT*) número
  gratuito.
free-for-all ['friːfərɔːl] *n* riña general.

free gift n regalo.
freehold ['friːhəuld] n propiedad f absoluta.
free kick n tiro libre.
freelance ['friːlɑːns] adj, adv por cuenta
propia; **to do ~ work** trabajar por su
cuenta.
freely ['friːlɪ] adv libremente; (liberally)
generosamente.
free-market economy ['friːˈmɑːkɪt-] n
economía de libre mercado.
freemason ['friːmeɪsn] n francmasón m.
freemasonry ['friːmeɪsnrɪ] n
(franc)masonería.
freepost ['friːpəust] n porte m pagado.
free-range ['friːˈreɪndʒ] adj (hen, eggs) de
granja.
free sample n muestra gratuita.
freesia ['friːʒə] n fresia.
free speech n libertad f de expresión.
free trade n libre comercio.
freeway ['friːweɪ] n (US) autopista.
freewheel [friːˈwiːl] vi ir en punto muerto.
freewheeling [friːˈwiːlɪŋ] adj libre,
espontáneo; (careless) irresponsable.
free will n libre albedrío; **of one's own ~**
por su propia voluntad.
freeze [friːz] vb (pt **froze**, pp **frozen** [frəuz,
frəuzn]) vi helarse, congelarse ♦ vt
(prices, food, salaries) congelar ♦ n helada;
congelación f.
►**freeze over** vi (lake, river) helarse,
congelarse; (window, windscreen)
cubrirse de escarcha.
►**freeze up** vi helarse, congelarse.
freeze-dried ['friːzdraɪd] adj liofilizado.
freezer ['friːzə*] n congelador m,
congeladora.
freezing ['friːzɪŋ] adj helado.
freezing point n punto de congelación; **3
degrees below ~** tres grados bajo cero.
freight [freɪt] n (goods) carga, (money
charged) flete m; **~ forward** contra
reembolso del flete, flete por pagar; **~
inward** flete sobre compras.
freight car n vagón m de mercancías.
freighter ['freɪtə*] n buque m de carga;
(AVIAT) avión m de transporte de
mercancías.
freight forwarder [-ˈfɔːwədə*] n agente m
expedidor.
freight train n (US) tren m de mercancías.
French [frentʃ] adj francés/esa ♦ n (LING)
francés m; **the ~** npl los franceses.
French bean n judía verde.
French bread n pan m francés.
French Canadian adj, n francocanadiense
m/f.
French dressing n (CULIN) vinagreta.

French fried potatoes, (US) **French fries**
npl patatas fpl or papas fpl (LAM) fritas.
French Guiana [-gaɪˈænə] n la Guayana
Francesa.
French loaf n barra de pan.
Frenchman ['frentʃmən] n francés m.
French Riviera n: **the ~** la Riviera, la
Costa Azul.
French stick n barra de pan.
French window n puertaventana.
Frenchwoman ['frentʃwumən] n francesa.
frenetic [frəˈnetɪk] adj frenético.
frenzy ['frenzɪ] n frenesí m.
frequency ['friːkwənsɪ] n frecuencia.
frequency modulation (FM) n
frecuencia modulada.
frequent adj ['friːkwənt] frecuente ♦ vt
[frɪˈkwent] frecuentar.
frequently ['friːkwəntlɪ] adv
frecuentemente, a menudo.
fresco ['freskəu] n fresco.
fresh [freʃ] adj (gen) fresco; (new) nuevo;
(water) dulce; **to make a ~ start** empezar
de nuevo.
freshen ['freʃən] vi (wind) arreciar; (air)
refrescar.
►**freshen up** vi (person) refrescarse.
freshener ['freʃnə*] n: **air ~** ambientador m;
skin ~ tónico.
fresher ['freʃə*] n (BRIT SCOL: col)
estudiante m/f de primer año.
freshly ['freʃlɪ] adv: **~ painted/arrived**
recién pintado/llegado.
freshman ['freʃmən] n (US: SCOL) = **fresher**.
freshness ['freʃnɪs] n frescura.
freshwater ['freʃwɔːtə*] adj (fish) de agua
dulce.
fret [fret] vi inquietarse.
fretful ['fretful] adj (child) quejumbroso.
Freudian ['frɔɪdɪən] adj freudiano; **~ slip**
lapsus m (freudiano).
FRG n abbr (= Federal Republic of Germany)
RFA f.
Fri. abbr (= Friday) vier.
friar ['fraɪə*] n fraile m; (before name) fray.
friction ['frɪkʃən] n fricción f.
friction feed n (on printer) avance m por
fricción.
Friday ['fraɪdɪ] n viernes m inv.
fridge [frɪdʒ] n (BRIT) nevera, frigo,
refrigeradora (LAM), heladera (LAM).
fridge-freezer ['frɪdʒ'friːzə*] n frigorífico-
congelador m, combi m.
fried [fraɪd] pt, pp of **fry** ♦ adj: **~ egg** huevo
frito, huevo estrellado.
friend [frend] n amigo/a.
friendliness ['frendlɪnɪs] n simpatía.
friendly ['frendlɪ] adj simpático.

friendly fire *n* fuego amigo, disparos *mpl* del propio bando.
friendship ['frɛndʃɪp] *n* amistad *f*.
frieze [friːz] *n* friso.
frigate ['frɪgɪt] *n* fragata.
fright [fraɪt] *n* susto; **to take** ~ asustarse.
frighten ['fraɪtn] *vt* asustar.
▶**frighten away, frighten off** *vt* (*birds, children etc*) espantar, ahuyentar.
frightened ['fraɪtnd] *adj* asustado.
frightening ['fraɪtnɪŋ] *adj*: **it's** ~ da miedo.
frightful ['fraɪtful] *adj* espantoso, horrible.
frightfully ['fraɪtfulɪ] *adv* terriblemente; **I'm** ~ **sorry** lo siento muchísimo.
frigid ['frɪdʒɪd] *adj* (*MED*) frígido.
frigidity [frɪ'dʒɪdɪtɪ] *n* (*MED*) frigidez *f*.
frill [frɪl] *n* volante *m*; **without** ~s (*fig*) sin adornos.
frilly ['frɪlɪ] *adj* con volantes.
fringe [frɪndʒ] *n* (*BRIT: of hair*) flequillo; (*edge: of forest etc*) borde *m*, margen *m*.
fringe benefits *npl* ventajas *fpl* complementarias.
fringe theatre *n* teatro experimental.
Frisbee ® ['frɪzbɪ] *n* frisbee ® *m*.
frisk [frɪsk] *vt* cachear, registrar.
frisky ['frɪskɪ] *adj* juguetón/ona.
fritter ['frɪtə*] *n* buñuelo.
▶**fritter away** *vt* desperdiciar.
frivolity [frɪ'vɔlɪtɪ] *n* frivolidad *f*.
frivolous ['frɪvələs] *adj* frívolo.
frizzy ['frɪzɪ] *adj* crespo.
fro [frəu] *see* **to**.
frock [frɔk] *n* vestido.
frog [frɔg] *n* rana; **to have a** ~ **in one's throat** tener carraspera.
frogman ['frɔgmən] *n* hombre-rana *m*.
frogmarch ['frɔgmɑːtʃ] *vt*: **to** ~ **sb in/out** meter/sacar a algn a rastras.
frolic ['frɔlɪk] *vi* juguetear.

=== *KEYWORD* ===

from [frɔm] *prep* **1** (*indicating starting place*) de, desde; **where do you come** ~?, **where are you** ~? ¿de dónde eres?; **where has he come** ~? ¿de dónde ha venido?; ~ **London to Glasgow** de Londres a Glasgow; **to escape** ~ **sth/sb** escaparse de algo/algn
2 (*indicating origin etc*) de; **a letter/ telephone call** ~ **my sister** una carta/ llamada de mi hermana; **tell him** ~ **me that ...** dígale de mi parte que ...
3 (*indicating time*): ~ **one o'clock to** *or* **until** *or* **till nine** de la una a las nueve, desde la una hasta las nueve; ~ **January (on)** a partir de enero; **(as)** ~ **Friday** a partir del viernes

4 (*indicating distance*) de; **the hotel is 1 km from the beach** el hotel está a 1 km de la playa
5 (*indicating price, number etc*) de; **prices range** ~ **£10 to £50** los precios van desde £10 a *or* hasta £50; **the interest rate was increased** ~ **9% to 10%** el tipo de interés fue incrementado de un 9% a un 10%
6 (*indicating difference*) de; **he can't tell red** ~ **green** no sabe distinguir el rojo del verde; **to be different** ~ **sb/sth** ser diferente a algn/algo
7 (*because of, on the basis of*): ~ **what he says** por lo que dice; **weak** ~ **hunger** debilitado por el hambre.

frond [frɔnd] *n* fronda.
front [frʌnt] *n* (*foremost part*) parte *f* delantera; (*of house*) fachada; (*promenade: also: sea* ~) paseo marítimo; (*MIL, POL, METEOROLOGY*) frente *m*; (*fig: appearances*) apariencia ♦ *adj* (*wheel, leg*) delantero; (*row, line*) primero ♦ *vi*: **to** ~ **onto sth** dar a algo; **in** ~ (**of**) delante (de).
frontage ['frʌntɪdʒ] *n* (*of building*) fachada.
front bench *n* (*BRIT POL*) *ver recuadro*.

┌─────────────────────────┐
│ **FRONT BENCH** │
└─────────────────────────┘

El término genérico **front bench** *se usa para referirse a los escaños situados en primera fila a ambos lados del Presidente* (*"Speaker"*) *de la Cámara de los Comunes* (*"House of Commons"*) *del Parlamento británico. Dichos escaños son ocupados por los miembros del gobierno a un lado y los del gobierno en la oposición* (*"shadow cabinet"*) *al otro. Por esta razón a todos ellos se les denomina "frontbenchers".*

frontbencher ['frʌnt'bɛntʃə*] *n* (*BRIT*) *see* **front bench**.
front desk *n* (*US*) recepción *f*.
front door *n* puerta principal.
frontier ['frʌntɪə*] *n* frontera.
front page *n* primera plana.
front room *n* (*BRIT*) salón *m*, sala.
front runner *n* favorito/a.
front-wheel drive ['frʌntwiːl-] *n* tracción *f* delantera.
frost [frɔst] *n* (*gen*) helada; (*also:* **hoar**~) escarcha ♦ *vt* (*US CULIN*) escarchar.
frostbite ['frɔstbaɪt] *n* congelación *f*.
frosted ['frɔstɪd] *adj* (*glass*) esmerilado; (*esp US: cake*) glaseado.
frosting ['frɔstɪŋ] *n* (*esp US: icing*) glaseado.
frosty ['frɔstɪ] *adj* (*surface*) cubierto de

escarcha; (*welcome etc*) glacial.
froth [frɔθ] *n* espuma.
frothy ['frɔθɪ] *adj* espumoso.
frown [fraun] *vi* fruncir el ceño ♦ *n*: **with a**
~ frunciendo el entrecejo.
▶**frown on** *vt fus* desaprobar.
froze [frəuz] *pt of* **freeze**.
frozen ['frəuzn] *pp of* **freeze** ♦ *adj* (*food*)
congelado; (*COMM*): ~ **assets** activos *mpl*
congelados *or* bloqueados.
FRS *n* (*BRIT*: = *Fellow of the Royal Society*)
miembro de la principal asociación de
investigación científica; (*US*: = *Federal
Reserve System*) banco central de
los EE. UU.
frugal ['fruːgəl] *adj* (*person*) frugal.
fruit [fruːt] *n* (*pl inv*) fruta.
fruiterer ['fruːtərə*] *n* frutero/a; ~'s **(shop)**
frutería.
fruit fly *n* mosca de la fruta.
fruitful ['fruːtful] *adj* provechoso.
fruition [fruː'ɪʃən] *n*: **to come to** ~
realizarse.
fruit juice *n* jugo *or* zumo (*SP*) de fruta.
fruitless ['fruːtlɪs] *adj* (*fig*) infructuoso,
inútil.
fruit machine *n* (*BRIT*) máquina
tragaperras.
fruit salad *n* macedonia *or* ensalada (*LAM*)
de frutas.
frump [frʌmp] *n* espantajo, adefesio.
frustrate [frʌs'treɪt] *vt* frustrar.
frustrated [frʌs'treɪtɪd] *adj* frustrado.
frustrating [frʌs'treɪtɪŋ] *adj* (*job, day*)
frustrante.
frustration [frʌs'treɪʃən] *n* frustración *f*.
fry, *pt, pp* **fried** [fraɪ, -d] *vt* freír ♦ *n*: **small** ~
gente *f* menuda.
frying pan ['fraɪɪŋ-] *n* sartén *f or m* (*LAM*).
FT *n abbr* (*BRIT*: = *Financial Times*) periódico
financiero; **the** ~ **index** el índice de
valores del Financial Times.
ft. *abbr* = **foot, feet**.
FTC *n abbr* (*US*) = *Federal Trade Commission.*
FTSE 100 Index *n abbr* (= *Financial Times
Stock Exchange 100 Index*) índice bursátil
del Financial Times.
fuchsia ['fjuːʃə] *n* fucsia.
fuck [fʌk] (*col!*) *vt* joder (*SP!*), coger (*LAM!*)
♦ *vi* joder (*SP!*), coger (*LAM!*); ~ **off!** ¡vete
a tomar por culo! (*!*).
fuddled ['fʌdld] *adj* (*muddled*) confuso,
aturdido; (*col: tipsy*) borracho.
fuddy-duddy ['fʌdɪdʌdɪ] (*pej*) *n* carcamal
m, carroza *m/f* ♦ *adj* chapado a la antigua.
fudge [fʌdʒ] *n* (*CULIN*) caramelo blando ♦ *vt*
(*issue, problem*) rehuir, esquivar.
fuel [fjuəl] *n* (*for heating*) combustible *m*;

(*coal*) carbón *m*; (*wood*) leña; (*for engine*)
carburante *m* ♦ *vt* (*furnace etc*) alimentar;
(*aircraft, ship etc*) aprovisionar de
combustible.
fuel oil *n* fuel oil *m*.
fuel pump *n* (*AUT*) surtidor *m* de gasolina.
fuel tank *n* depósito de combustible.
fug [fʌg] *n* aire *m* viciado.
fugitive ['fjuːdʒɪtɪv] *n* (*from prison*)
fugitivo/a.
fulfil, (*US*) **fulfill** [ful'fɪl] *vt* (*function*)
desempeñar; (*condition*) cumplir; (*wish,
desire*) realizar.
fulfilled [ful'fɪld] *adj* (*person*) realizado.
fulfil(l)ment [ful'fɪlmənt] *n* realización *f*; (*of
promise*) cumplimiento.
full [ful] *adj* lleno, (*fig*) pleno; (*complete*)
completo; (*information*) detallado; (*price*)
íntegro, sin descuento ♦ *adv*: ~ **well**
perfectamente; **we're** ~ **up for July**
estamos completos para julio; **I'm** ~ **(up)**
estoy lleno; ~ **employment** pleno empleo;
~ **name** nombre *m* completo; **a** ~ **two
hours** dos horas enteras; **at** ~ **speed** a
toda velocidad; **in** ~ (*reproduce, quote*)
íntegramente; **to write sth in** ~ escribir
algo por extenso; **to pay in** ~ pagar la
deuda entera.
fullback ['fulbæk] *n* (*FOOTBALL*) defensa *m*;
(*RUGBY*) zaguero.
full-blooded ['ful'blʌdɪd] *adj* (*vigorous:
attack*) vigoroso; (*pure*) puro.
full-cream ['ful'kriːm] *adj*: ~ **milk** leche *f*
entera.
full driving licence *n* (*BRIT AUT*) carnet *m*
de conducir (*definitivo*); *see also* **L-plates**.
full-fledged ['fulfledʒd] *adj* (*US*) = **fully-
fledged**.
full-grown ['ful'grəun] *adj* maduro.
full-length ['ful'leŋθ] *adj* (*portrait*) de
cuerpo entero; (*film*) de largometraje.
full moon *n* luna llena, plenilunio.
fullness ['fulnɪs] *n* plenitud *f*, amplitud *f*.
full-scale ['fulskeɪl] *adj* (*attack, war, search,
retreat*) en gran escala; (*plan, model*) de
tamaño natural.
full stop *n* punto.
full-time ['fultaɪm] *adj* (*work*) de tiempo
completo ♦ *adv*: **to work** ~ trabajar a
tiempo completo.
fully ['fulɪ] *adv* completamente; (*at least*) al
menos.
fully-fledged ['fulɪ'fledʒd], (*US*) **full-
fledged** *adj* (*teacher, barrister*) diplomado;
(*bird*) con todas sus plumas, capaz de
volar; (*fig*) de pleno derecho.
fully-paid ['fulɪpeɪd] *adj*: ~ **share** acción *f*
liberada.

fulsome ['fulsəm] *adj* (*pej: praise, gratitude*) excesivo, exagerado; (: *manner*) obsequioso.

fumble with ['fʌmbl-] *vt fus* manosear.

fume [fju:m] *vi* humear, echar humo.

fumes [fju:mz] *npl* humo *sg*, gases *mpl*.

fumigate ['fju:mɪgeɪt] *vt* fumigar.

fun [fʌn] *n* (*amusement*) diversión *f*; (*joy*) alegría; **to have** ~ divertirse; **for** ~ por gusto; **to make** ~ **of** reírse de.

function ['fʌŋkʃən] *n* función *f* ♦ *vi* funcionar; **to** ~ **as** hacer (las veces) de, fungir de (*LAM*).

functional ['fʌŋkʃənl] *adj* funcional.

function key *n* (*COMPUT*) tecla de función.

fund [fʌnd] *n* fondo; (*reserve*) reserva; ~**s** *npl* fondos *mpl*.

fundamental [fʌndə'mɛntl] *adj* fundamental ♦ *n*: ~**s** fundamentos *mpl*.

fundamentalism [fʌndə'mɛntəlɪzəm] *n* fundamentalismo, integrismo.

fundamentalist [fʌndə'mɛntəlɪst] *n* fundamentalista *m/f*, integrista *m/f*.

fundamentally [fʌndə'mɛntəlɪ] *adv* fundamentalmente.

funding ['fʌndɪŋ] *n* financiación *f*.

fund-raising ['fʌndreɪzɪŋ] *n* recaudación *f* de fondos.

funeral ['fju:nərəl] *n* (*burial*) entierro; (*ceremony*) funerales *mpl*.

funeral director *n* director(a) *m/f* de pompas fúnebres.

funeral parlour *n* (*BRIT*) funeraria.

funeral service *n* misa de cuerpo presente.

funereal [fju:'nɪərɪəl] *adj* fúnebre.

funfair ['fʌnfɛə*] *n* (*BRIT*) parque *m* de atracciones; (*travelling*) feria.

fungus, *pl* **fungi** ['fʌŋgəs, -gaɪ] *n* hongo.

funicular [fju:'nɪkjulə*] *n* (*also*: ~ **railway**) funicular *m*.

funky ['fʌŋkɪ] *adj* (*music*) funky; (*col: good*) guay.

funnel ['fʌnl] *n* embudo; (*of ship*) chimenea.

funnily ['fʌnɪlɪ] *adv* de modo divertido, graciosamente; (*oddly*) de una manera rara; ~ **enough** aunque parezca extraño.

funny ['fʌnɪ] *adj* gracioso, divertido; (*strange*) curioso, raro.

funny bone *n* hueso de la alegría.

fun run *n* maratón *m* popular.

fur [fə:*] *n* piel *f*; (*BRIT: on tongue etc*) sarro.

fur coat *n* abrigo de pieles.

furious ['fjuərɪəs] *adj* furioso; (*effort, argument*) violento; **to be** ~ **with sb** estar furioso con algn.

furiously ['fjuərɪəslɪ] *adv* con furia.

furl [fə:l] *vt* (*sail*) recoger.

furlong ['fə:lɔŋ] *n* octava parte de una milla.

furlough ['fə:ləu] *n* (*MIL*, *US*) permiso.

furnace ['fə:nɪs] *n* horno.

furnish ['fə:nɪʃ] *vt* amueblar; (*supply*) proporcionar; (*information*) facilitar.

furnished ['fə:nɪʃt] *adj*: ~ **flat** *or* (*US*) **apartment** piso amueblado.

furnishings ['fə:nɪʃɪŋz] *npl* mobiliario *sg*.

furniture ['fə:nɪtʃə*] *n* muebles *mpl*; **piece of** ~ mueble *m*.

furniture polish *n* cera para muebles.

furore [fjuə'rɔ:rɪ] *n* (*protests*) escándalo.

furrier ['fʌrɪə*] *n* peletero/a.

furrow ['fʌrəu] *n* surco ♦ *vt* (*forehead*) arrugar.

furry ['fə:rɪ] *adj* peludo; (*toy*) de peluche.

further ['fə:ðə*] *adj* (*new*) nuevo; (*place*) más lejano ♦ *adv* más lejos; (*more*) más; (*moreover*) además ♦ *vt* hacer avanzar; **how much** ~ **is it?** ¿a qué distancia queda?; ~ **to your letter of ...** (*COMM*) con referencia a su carta de ...; **to** ~ **one's interests** fomentar sus intereses.

further education *n* educación *f* postescolar.

furthermore [fə:ðə'mɔ:*] *adv* además.

furthermost ['fə:ðəməust] *adj* más lejano.

furthest ['fə:ðɪst] *superlative of* **far**.

furtive ['fə:tɪv] *adj* furtivo.

furtively ['fə:tɪvlɪ] *adv* furtivamente, a escondidas.

fury ['fjuərɪ] *n* furia.

fuse, (*US*) **fuze** [fju:z] *n* fusible *m*; (*for bomb etc*) mecha ♦ *vt* (*metal*) fundir; (*fig*) fusionar ♦ *vi* fundirse; fusionarse; (*BRIT: ELEC*): **to** ~ **the lights** fundir los plomos; **a** ~ **has blown** se ha fundido un fusible.

fuse box *n* caja de fusibles.

fuselage ['fju:zəlɑ:ʒ] *n* fuselaje *m*.

fuse wire *n* hilo fusible.

fusillade [fju:zɪ'leɪd] *n* descarga cerrada; (*fig*) lluvia.

fusion ['fju:ʒən] *n* fusión *f*.

fuss [fʌs] *n* (*noise*) bulla; (*dispute*) lío, jaleo; (*complaining*) protesta ♦ *vi* preocuparse (por pequeñeces) ♦ *vt* (*person*) molestar; **to make a** ~ armar jaleo.

► **fuss over** *vt fus* (*person*) contemplar, mimar.

fusspot ['fʌspɔt] *n* (*col*) quisquilloso/a.

fussy ['fʌsɪ] *adj* (*person*) quisquilloso; **I'm not** ~ (*col*) me da igual.

fusty ['fʌstɪ] *adj* (*pej*) rancio; **to smell** ~ oler a cerrado.

futile ['fju:taɪl] *adj* vano.

futility [fju:'tɪlɪtɪ] *n* inutilidad *f*.

futon ['fu:tɔn] *n* futón *m*.

future ['fjuːtʃə*] adj (gen) futuro; (coming) venidero ♦ n futuro, porvenir; **in** ~ de ahora en adelante.

futures ['fjuːtʃəz] npl (COMM) operaciones fpl a término, futuros mpl.

futuristic [fjuːtʃə'rıstık] adj futurista.

fuze [fjuːz] (US) = **fuse**.

fuzzy ['fʌzı] adj (PHOT) borroso; (hair) muy rizado.

fwd. abbr = **forward**.

fwy abbr (US) = **freeway**.

FY abbr = **fiscal year**.

FYI abbr = **for your information**.

G g

G, g [dʒiː] n (letter) G, g f; **G** (MUS) sol m; **G for George** G de Gerona.

G n abbr (BRIT SCOL: = good) N; (US CINE: = general audience) todos los públicos.

g. abbr (= gram(s), gravity) g.

G7 n abbr (POL = Group of Seven) G7 m.

GA abbr (US) = **Georgia**.

gab [gæb] n: **to have the gift of the** ~ (col) tener mucha labia.

gabble ['gæbl] vi hablar atropelladamente; (gossip) cotorrear.

gaberdine [gæbə'diːn] n gabardina.

gable ['geıbl] n aguilón m.

Gabon [gə'bɔn] n Gabón m.

gad about [gæd-] vi (col) moverse mucho.

gadget ['gædʒıt] n aparato.

gadgetry ['gædʒıtrı] n chismes mpl.

Gaelic ['geılık] adj, n (LING) gaélico.

gaffe [gæf] n plancha, patinazo, metedura de pata.

gaffer ['gæfə*] n (BRIT col) jefe m; ((old) man) vejete m.

gag [gæg] n (on mouth) mordaza; (joke) chiste m ♦ vt (prisoner etc) amordazar ♦ vi (choke) tener arcadas.

gaga ['gɑːgɑː] adj: **to go** ~ (senile) chochear; (ecstatic) caérsele a algn la baba.

gage [geıdʒ] n, vt (US) = **gauge**.

gaiety ['geıtı] n alegría.

gaily ['geılı] adv alegremente.

gain [geın] n ganancia ♦ vt ganar ♦ vi (watch) adelantarse; **to** ~ **by sth** ganar con algo; **to** ~ **ground** ganar terreno; **to** ~ **3 lbs (in weight)** engordar 3 libras.

▶**gain (up)on** vt fus alcanzar.

gainful ['geınful] adj (employment) remunerado.

gainfully ['geınfulı] adv: **to be** ~ **employed** tener un trabajo remunerado.

gait [geıt] n forma de andar, andares mpl.

gala ['gɑːlə] n gala; **swimming** ~ certamen m de natación.

Galapagos Islands [gə'læpəgəs-] npl: **the** ~ las Islas Galápagos.

galaxy ['gæləksı] n galaxia.

gale [geıl] n (wind) vendaval m; ~ **force 10** vendaval de fuerza 10.

gall [gɔːl] n (ANAT) bilis f, hiel f; (fig: impudence) descaro, caradura ♦ vt molestar.

gal(l). abbr = **gallon(s)**.

gallant ['gælənt] adj valeroso; (towards ladies) galante.

gallantry ['gæləntrı] n valentía; (courtesy) galantería.

gall bladder n vesícula biliar.

galleon ['gælıən] n galeón m.

gallery ['gælərı] n (also THEAT) galería; (for spectators) tribuna; (also: **art** ~: state-owned) pinacoteca or museo de arte; (: private) galería de arte.

galley ['gælı] n (ship's kitchen) cocina; (ship) galera.

galley proof n (TYP) prueba de galera, galerada.

Gallic ['gælık] adj galo.

gallon ['gæln] n galón m (= 8 pints; BRIT = 4,546 litros, US = 3,785 litros).

gallop ['gæləp] n galope m ♦ vi galopar; ~**ing inflation** inflación f galopante.

gallows ['gæləuz] n horca.

gallstone ['gɔːlstəun] n cálculo biliar.

Gallup poll ['gæləp-] n sondeo de opinión.

galore [gə'lɔː*] adv en cantidad, en abundancia.

galvanize ['gælvənaız] vt (metal) galvanizar; (fig): **to** ~ **sb into action** mover or impulsar a algn a actuar.

Gambia ['gæmbıə] n Gambia.

gambit ['gæmbıt] n (fig): **opening** ~ táctica inicial.

gamble ['gæmbl] n (risk) jugada arriesgada; (bet) apuesta ♦ vt: **to** ~ **on** apostar a; (fig) confiar en que ♦ vi jugar; (COMM) especular; **to** ~ **on the Stock Exchange** jugar a la bolsa.

gambler ['gæmblə*] n jugador(a) m/f.

gambling ['gæmblıŋ] n juego.

gambol ['gæmbl] vi brincar, juguetear.

game [geım] n (gen) juego; (match) partido; (of cards) partida; (HUNTING) caza ♦ adj valiente; (ready): **to be** ~ **for anything**

estar dispuesto a todo; ~s (SCOL)
deportes mpl; **big** ~ caza mayor.
game bird n ave f de caza.
gamekeeper ['geɪmki:pə*] n guardabosque
m/f.
gamely ['geɪmlɪ] adv con decisión.
game reserve n coto de caza.
games console [geɪmz-] n consola de
juegos.
game show n programa m concurso inv,
concurso.
gamesmanship ['geɪmzmənʃɪp] n (uso de)
artimañas fpl para ganar.
gaming ['geɪmɪŋ] n juego.
gammon ['gæmən] n (bacon) tocino
ahumado; (ham) jamón m ahumado.
gamut ['gæmət] n (MUS) gama; **to run the
(whole)** ~ **of emotions** (fig) recorrer toda
la gama de emociones.
gander ['gændə*] n ganso.
gang [gæŋ] n pandilla; (of criminals etc)
banda; (of kids) pandilla; (of colleagues)
peña; (of workmen) brigada ♦ vi: **to** ~ **up
on sb** conchabarse contra algn.
Ganges ['gændʒi:z] n: **the** ~ el Ganges.
gangland ['gæŋglænd] adj: ~ **bosses**
cabecillas mafiosos; ~ **killings** asesinatos
entre bandas.
gangling ['gæŋglɪŋ] adj larguirucho.
gangly ['gæŋglɪ] adj desgarbado.
gangplank ['gæŋplæŋk] n pasarela,
plancha.
gangrene ['gæŋgri:n] n gangrena.
gangster ['gæŋstə*] n gángster m.
gang warfare n guerra entre bandas.
gangway ['gæŋweɪ] n (BRIT: in theatre, bus
etc) pasillo; (on ship) pasarela.
gantry ['gæntrɪ] n (for crane, railway signal)
pórtico; (for rocket) torre f de
lanzamiento.
GAO n abbr (US: = General Accounting Office)
tribunal de cuentas.
gaol [dʒeɪl] n, vt (BRIT) = **jail**.
gap [gæp] n hueco; (in trees, traffic) claro; (in
market, records) laguna; (in time)
intervalo.
gape [geɪp] vi mirar boquiabierto.
gaping ['geɪpɪŋ] adj (hole) muy abierto.
garage ['gærɑ:ʒ] n garaje m.
garb [gɑ:b] n atuendo.
garbage ['gɑ:bɪdʒ] n (US) basura;
(nonsense) bobadas fpl; (fig: film, book etc)
basura.
garbage can n (US) cubo or balde m (LAM)
or bote m (LAM) de la basura.
garbage collector n (US) basurero/a.
garbage disposal unit n triturador m (de
basura).

garbage man n basurero.
garbage truck n (US) camión m de la
basura.
garbled ['gɑ:bld] adj (account, explanation)
confuso.
garden ['gɑ:dn] n jardín m; ~**s** npl (public)
parque m, jardines mpl; (private) huertos
mpl.
garden centre n centro de jardinería.
garden city n (BRIT) ciudad f jardín.
gardener ['gɑ:dnə*] n jardinero/a.
gardening ['gɑ:dnɪŋ] n jardinería.
garden party n recepción f al aire libre.
gargle ['gɑ:gl] vi hacer gárgaras,
gargarear (LAM).
gargoyle ['gɑ:gɔɪl] n gárgola.
garish ['gɛərɪʃ] adj chillón/ona.
garland ['gɑ:lənd] n guirnalda.
garlic ['gɑ:lɪk] n ajo.
garment ['gɑ:mənt] n prenda (de vestir).
garner ['gɑ:nə*] vt hacer acopio de.
garnish ['gɑ:nɪʃ] vt adornar; (CULIN)
aderezar.
garret ['gærɪt] n desván m, buhardilla.
garrison ['gærɪsn] n guarnición f ♦ vt
guarnecer.
garrulous ['gærjuləs] adj charlatán/ana.
garter ['gɑ:tə*] n (US) liga.
garter belt n (US) liguero, portaligas m inv.
gas [gæs] n gas m; (US: gasoline) gasolina
♦ vt asfixiar con gas; **Calor** ~ ® (gas m)
butano.
gas chamber n cámara de gas.
Gascony ['gæskənɪ] n Gascuña.
gas cooker n (BRIT) cocina de gas.
gas cylinder n bombona de gas.
gaseous ['gæsɪəs] adj gaseoso.
gas fire n estufa de gas.
gas-fired ['gæsfaɪəd] adj de gas.
gash [gæʃ] n brecha, raja; (from knife)
cuchillada ♦ vt rajar; (with knife)
acuchillar.
gasket ['gæskɪt] n (AUT) junta.
gas mask n careta antigás.
gas meter n contador m de gas.
gasoline ['gæsəli:n] n (US) gasolina.
gasp [gɑ:sp] n grito sofocado ♦ vi (pant)
jadear.
▶**gasp out** vt (say) decir jadeando.
gas pedal n (esp US) acelerador m.
gas ring n hornillo de gas.
gas station n (US) gasolinera.
gas stove n cocina de gas.
gassy ['gæsɪ] adj con mucho gas.
gas tank n (US AUT) depósito (de gasolina).
gas tap n llave f del gas.
gastric ['gæstrɪk] adj gástrico.
gastric ulcer n úlcera gástrica.

gastroenteritis ['gæstrəuɛntə'raıtıs] n gastroenteritis f.

gasworks ['gæswɔ:ks] nsg or npl fábrica de gas.

gate [geıt] n (also at airport) puerta; (RAIL: at level crossing) barrera; (metal) verja.

gâteau, pl ~x ['gætəu, z] n tarta.

gatecrash ['geıtkræʃ] vt colarse en.

gatecrasher ['geıtkræʃə*] n intruso/a.

gatehouse ['geıthaus] n casa del guarda.

gateway ['geıtweı] n puerta.

gather ['gæðə*] vt (flowers, fruit) coger (SP), recoger (LAM); (assemble) reunir; (pick up) recoger; (SEWING) fruncir; (understand) sacar en consecuencia ♦ vi (assemble) reunirse; (dust) acumularse; (clouds) cerrarse; **to ~ speed** ganar velocidad; **to ~ (from/that)** deducir (por/que); **as far as I can ~** por lo que tengo entendido.

gathering ['gæðərıŋ] n reunión f, asamblea.

GATT [gæt] n abbr (= General Agreement on Tariffs and Trade) GATT m.

gauche [gəuʃ] adj torpe.

gaudy ['gɔ:dı] adj chillón/ona.

gauge, (US) **gage** [geıdʒ] n calibre m; (RAIL) ancho de vía, entrevía; (instrument) indicador m ♦ vt medir; (fig: sb's capabilities, character) juzgar, calibrar; **petrol ~** indicador m (del nivel) de gasolina; **to ~ the right moment** elegir el momento (oportuno).

Gaul [gɔ:l] n Galia.

gaunt [gɔ:nt] adj descarnado; (fig) adusto.

gauntlet ['gɔ:ntlıt] n (fig): **to run the ~ of sth** exponerse a algo; **to throw down the ~** arrojar el guante.

gauze [gɔ:z] n gasa.

gave [geıv] pt of **give.**

gawk [gɔ:k] vi mirar pasmado.

gawky ['gɔ:kı] adj desgarbado.

gay [geı] adj (colour, person) alegre; (homosexual) gay.

gaze [geız] n mirada fija ♦ vi: **to ~ at sth** mirar algo fijamente.

gazelle [gə'zɛl] n gacela.

gazette [gə'zɛt] n (newspaper) gaceta; (official publication) boletín m oficial.

gazetteer [gæzə'tıə*] n índice geográfico.

gazump [gə'zʌmp] vti (BRIT) echarse atrás en la venta ya acordada de una casa por haber una oferta más alta.

GB abbr (= Great Britain) G.B.

GBH n abbr (BRIT LAW: col) = **grievous bodily harm.**

GC n abbr (BRIT: = George Cross) distinción honorífica.

GCE n abbr (BRIT: = General Certificate of

Education) ≈ certificado de bachillerato.

GCHQ n abbr (BRIT: = Government Communications Headquarters) centro de intercepción de las telecomunicaciones internacionales.

GCSE n abbr (BRIT: = General Certificate of Secondary Education) ≈ certificado de bachillerato.

Gdns. abbr (= gardens) jdns.

GDP n abbr (= gross domestic product) PIB m.

GDR n abbr (= German Democratic Republic) RDA f.

gear [gıə*] n equipo; (TECH) engranaje m; (AUT) velocidad f, marcha ♦ vt (fig: adapt): **to ~ sth to** adaptar or ajustar algo a; **top** or (US) **high/low ~** cuarta/primera; **in ~** con la marcha metida; **our service is ~ed to meet the needs of the disabled** nuestro servicio va enfocado a responder a las necesidades de los minusválidos.

▶**gear up** vi prepararse.

gear box n caja de cambios.

gear lever, (US) **gear shift** n palanca de cambio.

gear wheel n rueda dentada.

GED n abbr (US SCOL) = general educational development.

geese [gi:s] npl of **goose.**

geezer ['gi:zə*] n (BRIT col) tipo, maromo (SP).

Geiger counter ['gaıgə-] n contador m Geiger.

gel [dʒɛl] n gel m.

gelatin(e) ['dʒɛlətı:n] n gelatina.

gelignite ['dʒɛlıgnaıt] n gelignita.

gem [dʒɛm] n gema, piedra preciosa; (fig) joya.

Gemini ['dʒɛmınaı] n Géminis m.

gen [dʒɛn] n (BRIT col): **to give sb the ~ on sth** poner a algn al tanto de algo.

Gen. abbr (MIL: = General) Gen., Gral.

gen. abbr (= general) grl.; = **generally.**

gender ['dʒɛndə*] n género.

gene [dʒı:n] n gen(e) m.

genealogy [dʒı:nı'ælədʒı] n genealogía.

general ['dʒɛnərl] n general m ♦ adj general; **in ~** en general; **~ audit** auditoría general; **the ~ public** el gran público.

general anaesthetic, (US) **general anesthetic** n anestesia general.

general delivery n (US) lista de correos.

general election n elecciones fpl generales.

generalization [dʒɛnrəlaı'zeıʃən] n generalización f.

generalize ['dʒɛnrəlaız] vi generalizar.

generally ['dʒɛnrəlı] adv generalmente, en

general.
general manager n director(a) m/f general.
general practitioner (GP) n médico/a de medicina general.
general strike n huelga general.
generate ['dʒɛnəreɪt] vt generar.
generation [dʒɛnə'reɪʃən] n (of electricity etc) generación f; **first/second/third/ fourth** ~ (of computer) primera/segunda/ tercera/cuarta generación.
generator ['dʒɛnəreɪtə*] n generador m.
generic [dʒɪ'nɛrɪk] adj genérico.
generosity [dʒɛnə'rɔsɪtɪ] n generosidad f.
generous ['dʒɛnərəs] adj generoso; (copious) abundante.
generously ['dʒɛnərəslɪ] adv generosamente; abundantemente.
genesis ['dʒɛnɪsɪs] n génesis f.
genetic [dʒɪ'nɛtɪk] adj genético.
genetic engineering n ingeniería genética.
genetic fingerprinting [-'fɪŋɡəprɪntɪŋ] n identificación f genética.
genetics [dʒɪ'nɛtɪks] n genética.
Geneva [dʒɪ'niːvə] n Ginebra.
genial ['dʒiːnɪəl] adj afable.
genitals ['dʒɛnɪtlz] npl (órganos mpl) genitales mpl.
genitive ['dʒɛnɪtɪv] n genitivo.
genius ['dʒiːnɪəs] n genio.
Genoa ['dʒɛnəuə] n Génova.
genocide ['dʒɛnəusaɪd] n genocidio.
gent [dʒɛnt] n abbr (BRIT col) = **gentleman**.
genteel [dʒɛn'tiːl] adj fino, distinguido.
Gentile ['dʒɛntaɪl] n gentil m/f.
gentle ['dʒɛntl] adj (sweet) dulce; (touch etc) ligero, suave.
gentleman ['dʒɛntlmən] n señor m; (well-bred man) caballero; ~**'s agreement** acuerdo entre caballeros.
gentlemanly ['dʒɛntlmənlɪ] adj caballeroso.
gentleness ['dʒɛntlnɪs] n dulzura; (of touch) suavidad f.
gently ['dʒɛntlɪ] adv suavemente.
gentrification [dʒɛntrɪfɪ'keɪʃən] n aburguesamiento.
gentry ['dʒɛntrɪ] npl pequeña nobleza sg.
gents [dʒɛnts] n servicios mpl (de caballeros).
genuine ['dʒɛnjuɪn] adj auténtico; (person) sincero.
genuinely ['dʒɛnjuɪnlɪ] adv sinceramente.
geographer [dʒɪ'ɔɡrəfə*] n geográfo/a.
geographic(al) [dʒɪə'ɡræfɪk(l)] adj geográfico.
geography [dʒɪ'ɔɡrəfɪ] n geografía.
geological [dʒɪə'lɔdʒɪkl] adj geológico.

geologist [dʒɪ'ɔlədʒɪst] n geólogo/a.
geology [dʒɪ'ɔlədʒɪ] n geología.
geometric(al) [dʒɪə'mɛtrɪk(l)] adj geométrico.
geometry [dʒɪ'ɔmətrɪ] n geometría.
Geordie ['dʒɔːdɪ] n habitante m/f de Tyneside.
Georgia ['dʒɔːdʒə] n Georgia.
Georgian ['dʒɔːdʒən] adj georgiano ♦ n georgiano/a; (LING) georgiano.
geranium [dʒɪ'reɪnjəm] n geranio.
geriatric [dʒɛrɪ'ætrɪk] adj, n geriátrico/a m/f.
germ [dʒəːm] n (microbe) microbio, bacteria; (seed, fig) germen m.
German ['dʒəːmən] adj alemán/ana ♦ n alemán/ana m/f; (LING) alemán m.
German Democratic Republic n República Democrática Alemana.
germane [dʒəː'meɪn] adj: ~ **(to)** pertinente (a).
German measles n rubeola, rubéola.
German Shepherd n (dog) pastor m alemán.
Germany ['dʒəːmənɪ] n Alemania; **East/ West** ~ Alemania Oriental or Democrática/Occidental or Federal.
germination [dʒəːmɪ'neɪʃən] n germinación f.
germ warfare n guerra bacteriológica.
gesticulate [dʒɛs'tɪkjuleɪt] vi gesticular.
gesticulation [dʒɛstɪkju'leɪʃən] n gesticulación f.
gesture ['dʒɛstjə*] n gesto; **as a** ~ **of friendship** en señal de amistad.

═══════════════ KEYWORD

get [ɡɛt] (pt, pp **got**, pp **gotten** (US)) vi **1** (become, be) ponerse, volverse; **to** ~ **old/ tired** envejecer/cansarse; **to** ~ **drunk** emborracharse; **to** ~ **dirty** ensuciarse; **to** ~ **ready/washed** prepararse/lavarse; **to** ~ **married** casarse; **when do I** ~ **paid?** ¿cuándo me pagan or se me paga?; **it's** ~**ting late** se está haciendo tarde
2 (go): **to** ~ **to/from** llegar a/de; **to** ~ **home** llegar a casa; **he got under the fence** pasó por debajo de la barrera
3 (begin) empezar a; **to** ~ **to know sb** (llegar a) conocer a algn; **I'm** ~**ting to like him** me está empezando a gustar; **let's** ~ **going** or **started** ¡vamos (a empezar)!
4 (modal aux vb): **you've got to do it** tienes que hacerlo
♦ vt **1**: **to** ~ **sth done** (finish) hacer algo; (have done) mandar hacer algo; **to** ~ **one's hair cut** cortarse el pelo; **to** ~ **the car going** or **to go** arrancar el coche; **to** ~

sb to do sth conseguir *or* hacer que algn haga algo; **to ~ sth/sb ready** preparar algo/a algn
2 (*obtain: money, permission, results*) conseguir; (*find: job, flat*) encontrar; (*fetch: person, doctor*) buscar; (*object*) ir a buscar, traer; **to ~ sth for sb** conseguir algo para algn; **~ me Mr Jones, please** (*TEL*) póngame *or* comuníqueme (*LAM*) con el Sr. Jones, por favor; **can I ~ you a drink?** ¿quieres algo de beber?
3 (*receive: present, letter*) recibir; (*acquire: reputation*) alcanzar; (: *prize*) ganar; **what did you ~ for your birthday?** ¿qué te regalaron por tu cumpleaños?; **how much did you ~ for the painting?** ¿cuánto sacaste por el cuadro?
4 (*catch*) coger (*SP*), agarrar (*LAM*); (*hit: target etc*) dar en; **to ~ sb by the arm/ throat** coger *or* agarrar a algn por el brazo/cuello; **~ him!** ¡cógelo! (*SP*), ¡atrápalo! (*LAM*); **the bullet got him in the leg** la bala le dio en la pierna
5 (*take, move*) llevar; **to ~ sth to sb** hacer llegar algo a algn; **do you think we'll ~ it through the door?** ¿crees que lo podremos meter por la puerta?
6 (*catch, take: plane, bus etc*) coger (*SP*), tomar (*LAM*); **where do I ~ the train for Birmingham?** ¿dónde se coge *or* se toma el tren para Birmingham?
7 (*understand*) entender; (*hear*) oír; **I've got it!** ¡ya lo tengo!, ¡eureka!; **I don't ~ your meaning** no te entiendo; **I'm sorry, I didn't ~ your name** lo siento, no me he enterado de tu nombre
8 (*have, possess*): **to have got** tener
9 (*col: annoy*) molestar; (: *thrill*) chiflar
▸**get about** *vi* salir mucho; (*news*) divulgarse
▸**get across** *vt* (*message, meaning*) lograr comunicar ♦ *vi*: **to ~ across to sb** hacer que algn comprenda
▸**get along** *vi* (*agree*) llevarse bien; (*depart*) marcharse; (*manage*) = **get by**
▸**get at** *vt fus* (*attack*) meterse con; (*reach*) alcanzar; (*the truth*) descubrir; **what are you ~ting at?** ¿qué insinúas?
▸**get away** *vi* marcharse; (*escape*) escaparse
▸**get away with** *vt fus* hacer impunemente
▸**get back** *vi* (*return*) volver ♦ *vt* recobrar
▸**get back at** *vt fus* (*col*): **to ~ back at sb (for sth)** vengarse de algn (por algo)
▸**get by** *vi* (*pass*) (lograr) pasar; (*manage*) arreglárselas; **I can ~ by in Dutch** me defiendo en holandés
▸**get down** *vi* bajar(se) ♦ *vt fus* bajar ♦ *vt*

bajar; (*depress*) deprimir
▸**get down to** *vt fus* (*work*) ponerse a
▸**get in** *vi* entrar; (*train*) llegar; (*arrive home*) volver a casa, regresar; (*political party*) salir ♦ *vt* (*bring in: harvest*) recoger; (: *coal, shopping, supplies*) comprar, traer; (*insert*) meter
▸**get into** *vt fus* entrar en; (*vehicle*) subir a; **to ~ into a rage** enfadarse
▸**get off** *vi* (*from train etc*) bajar(se); (*depart: person, car*) marcharse ♦ *vt* (*remove*) quitar; (*send off*) mandar; (*have as leave: day, time*) tener libre ♦ *vt fus* (*train, bus*) bajar(se) de; **to ~ off to a good start** (*fig*) empezar muy bien *or* con buen pie
▸**get on** *vi* (*at oxam otc*): **how are you ~ting on?** ¿cómo te va?; (*agree*): **to ~ on (with)** llevarse bien (con) ♦ *vt fus* subir(se) a
▸**get on to** *vt fus* (*deal with*) ocuparse de; (*col: contact: on phone etc*) hablar con
▸**get out** *vi* salir; (*of vehicle*) bajar(se); (*news*) saberse ♦ *vt* sacar
▸**get out of** *vt fus* salir de; (*duty etc*) escaparse de; (*gain from: pleasure, benefit*) sacar de
▸**get over** *vt fus* (*illness*) recobrarse de
▸**get round** *vt fus* rodear; (*fig: person*) engatusar ♦ *vi*: **to ~ round to doing sth** encontrar tiempo para hacer algo
▸**get through** *vt fus* (*finish*) acabar ♦ *vi* (*TEL*) (lograr) comunicar
▸**get through to** *vt fus* (*TEL*) lograr comunicar con
▸**get together** *vi* reunirse ♦ *vt* reunir, juntar
▸**get up** *vi* (*rise*) levantarse ♦ *vt fus* subir; **to ~ up enthusiasm for sth** cobrar entusiasmo por algo
▸**get up to** *vt fus* (*reach*) llegar a; (*prank*) hacer.

getaway [ˈgɛtəweɪ] *n* fuga.
getaway car *n*: **the thieves' ~** el coche en que huyeron los ladrones.
get-together [ˈgɛtəgɛðə*] *n* reunión *f*; (*party*) fiesta.
get-up [ˈgɛtʌp] *n* (*BRIT col: outfit*) atavío, atuendo.
get-well card [gɛtˈwɛl-] *n* tarjeta en la que se desea a un enfermo que se mejore.
geyser [ˈgiːzə*] *n* (*water heater*) calentador *m* de agua; (*GEO*) géiser *m*.
Ghana [ˈgɑːnə] *n* Ghana.
Ghanaian [gɑːˈneɪən] *adj, n* ghanés/esa *m/f*.
ghastly [ˈgɑːstlɪ] *adj* horrible; (*pale*) pálido.
gherkin [ˈgəːkɪn] *n* pepinillo.
ghetto [ˈgɛtəu] *n* gueto.

ghetto blaster [-'blɑːstə*] n
radiocas(s)et(t)e m portátil (de gran
tamaño).
ghost [gəust] n fantasma m ♦ vt (book)
escribir por otro.
ghostly ['gəustlɪ] adj fantasmal.
ghost story n cuento de fantasmas.
ghostwriter ['gəustraɪtə*] n negro/a.
ghoul [guːl] n espíritu m necrófago.
GHQ n abbr (MIL: = general headquarters)
E.M.
GI n abbr (US col: = government issue)
soldado del ejército norteamericano.
giant ['dʒaɪənt] n gigante m/f ♦ adj
gigantesco, gigante; ~ **(size) packet**
paquete m (de tamaño) gigante or
familiar.
giant killer n (SPORT) matagigantes m inv.
gibber ['dʒɪbə*] vi farfullar.
gibberish ['dʒɪbərɪʃ] n galimatías m.
gibe [dʒaɪb] n pulla.
giblets ['dʒɪblɪts] npl menudillos mpl.
Gibraltar [dʒɪ'brɔːltə*] n Gibraltar m.
giddiness ['gɪdɪnɪs] n mareo.
giddy ['gɪdɪ] adj (dizzy) mareado; (height,
speed) vertiginoso; **it makes me** ~ me
marea; **I feel** ~ me siento mareado.
gift [gɪft] n (gen) regalo; (COMM: also: **free**
~) obsequio; (ability) don m; **to have a** ~
for sth tener dotes para algo.
gifted ['gɪftɪd] adj dotado.
gift token, gift voucher n vale-regalo m.
gig [gɪg] n (col: concert) actuación f.
gigabyte ['dʒɪgəbaɪt] n gigabyte m.
gigantic [dʒaɪ'gæntɪk] adj gigantesco.
giggle ['gɪgl] vi reírse tontamente ♦ n
risilla.
GIGO ['gaɪgəu] abbr (COMPUT: col) = garbage
in, garbage out.
gill [dʒɪl] n (measure) = 0.25 pints (BRIT
= 0.148 l, US = 0.118 l).
gills [gɪlz] npl (of fish) branquias fpl, agallas
fpl.
gilt [gɪlt] adj, n dorado.
gilt-edged ['gɪltɛdʒd] adj (COMM: stocks,
securities) de máxima garantía.
gimlet ['gɪmlɪt] n barrena de mano.
gimmick ['gɪmɪk] n reclamo; **sales** ~
reclamo promocional.
gimmicky ['gɪmɪkɪ] adj de reclamo.
gin [dʒɪn] n (liquor) ginebra.
ginger ['dʒɪndʒə*] n jengibre m.
ginger ale n ginger ale m.
ginger beer n refresco m de jengibre.
gingerbread ['dʒɪndʒəbrɛd] n pan m de
jengibre.
ginger-haired [dʒɪndʒə'hɛəd] adj pelirrojo.
gingerly ['dʒɪndʒəlɪ] adv con pies de plomo.

ginseng ['dʒɪnsɛŋ] n ginseng m.
gipsy ['dʒɪpsɪ] n gitano/a.
giraffe [dʒɪ'rɑːf] n jirafa.
girder ['gəːdə*] n viga.
girdle ['gəːdl] n (corset) faja ♦ vt ceñir.
girl [gəːl] n (small) niña; (young woman)
chica, joven f, muchacha; **an English** ~
una (chica) inglesa.
girlfriend ['gəːlfrɛnd] n (of girl) amiga; (of
boy) novia.
Girl Guide n exploradora.
girlish ['gəːlɪʃ] adj de niña.
Girl Scout n (US) = **Girl Guide**.
giro ['dʒaɪrəu] n (BRIT: bank ~) giro
bancario; (post office ~) giro postal.
girth [gəːθ] n circunferencia; (of saddle)
cincha.
gist [dʒɪst] n lo esencial.
give [gɪv] vb (pt **gave**, pp **given** [geɪv, 'gɪvn])
vt dar; (deliver) entregar; (as gift) regalar
♦ vi (break) romperse; (stretch: fabric) dar
de sí; **to** ~ **sb sth,** ~ **sth to sb** dar algo a
algn; **how much did you** ~ **for it?** ¿cuánto
pagaste por él?; **12 o'clock,** ~ **or take a
few minutes** más o menos las doce; ~
them my regards dales recuerdos de mi
parte; **I can** ~ **you 10 minutes** le puedo
conceder 10 minutos; **to** ~ **way** (BRIT AUT)
ceder el paso; **to** ~ **way to despair** ceder
a la desesperación.
▶**give away** vt (give free) regalar; (betray)
traicionar; (disclose) revelar.
▶**give back** vt devolver.
▶**give in** vi ceder ♦ vt entregar.
▶**give off** vt despedir.
▶**give out** vt distribuir ♦ vi (be exhausted:
supplies) agotarse; (fail: engine) averiarse;
(strength) fallar.
▶**give up** vi rendirse, darse por vencido
♦ vt renunciar a; **to** ~ **up smoking** dejar
de fumar; **to** ~ **o.s. up** entregarse.
give-and-take ['gɪvənd'teɪk] n (col) toma y
daca m.
giveaway ['gɪvəweɪ] n (col): **her expression
was a** ~ su expresión la delataba; **the
exam was a** ~! ¡el examen estaba tirado!
♦ cpd: ~ **prices** precios mpl de regalo.
given ['gɪvn] pp of **give** ♦ adj (fixed: time,
amount) determinado ♦ conj: ~ **(that)** ...
dado (que) ...; ~ **the circumstances** ...
dadas las circunstancias ....
glacial ['gleɪsɪəl] adj glacial.
glacier ['glæsɪə*] n glaciar m.
glad [glæd] adj contento; **to be** ~ **about
sth/that** alegrarse de algo/de que; **I was**
~ **of his help** agradecí su ayuda.
gladden ['glædn] vt alegrar.
glade [gleɪd] n claro.

gladiator ['glædɪeɪtə*] n gladiador m.
gladioli [glædɪ'əʊlaɪ] npl gladiolos mpl.
gladly ['glædlɪ] adv con mucho gusto.
glamorous ['glæmərəs] adj con encanto, atractivo.
glamour ['glæmə*] n encanto, atractivo.
glance [glɑːns] n ojeada, mirada ♦ vi: **to ~ at** echar una ojeada a.
▶**glance off** vt fus (bullet) rebotar en.
glancing ['glɑːnsɪŋ] adj (blow) oblicuo.
gland [glænd] n glándula.
glandular ['glændjʊlə*] adj: **~ fever** mononucleosis f infecciosa.
glare [glɛə*] n deslumbramiento, brillo ♦ vi deslumbrar; **to ~ at** mirar con odio.
glaring ['glɛərɪŋ] adj (mistake) manifiesto.
glasnost ['glæznɔst] n glasnost f.
glass [glɑːs] n vidrio, cristal m; (for drinking) vaso; (: with stem) copa; (also: **looking ~**) espejo.
glass-blowing ['glɑːsbləʊɪŋ] n soplado de vidrio.
glass ceiling n (fig) techo or barrera invisible (que impide ascender profesionalmente a las mujeres o miembros de minorías étnicas).
glasses ['glɑːsəs] npl gafas fpl, anteojos mpl (LAM).
glass fibre, (US) **glass fiber** n fibra de vidrio.
glasshouse ['glɑːshaʊs] n invernadero.
glassware ['glɑːswɛə*] n cristalería.
glassy ['glɑːsɪ] adj (eyes) vidrioso.
Glaswegian [glæs'wiːdʒən] adj de Glasgow ♦ n nativo/a (or habitante m/f) de Glasgow.
glaze [gleɪz] vt (window) acristalar; (pottery) vidriar; (CULIN) glasear ♦ n barniz m; (CULIN) vidriado.
glazed [gleɪzd] adj (eye) vidrioso; (pottery) vidriado.
glazier ['gleɪzɪə*] n vidricro/a.
gleam [gliːm] n destello ♦ vi relucir; **a ~ of hope** un rayo de esperanza.
gleaming ['gliːmɪŋ] adj reluciente.
glean [gliːn] vt (gather: information) recoger.
glee [gliː] n alegría, regocijo.
gleeful ['gliːful] adj alegre.
glen [glɛn] n cañada.
glib [glɪb] adj (person) de mucha labia; (comment) fácil.
glibly ['glɪblɪ] adv (explain) con mucha labia.
glide [glaɪd] vi deslizarse; (AVIAT, birds) planear.
glider ['glaɪdə*] n (AVIAT) planeador m.
gliding ['glaɪdɪŋ] n (AVIAT) vuelo sin motor.
glimmer ['glɪmə*] n luz f tenue.
glimpse [glɪmps] n vislumbre m ♦ vt vislumbrar, entrever; **to catch a ~ of** vislumbrar.

glint [glɪnt] n destello; (in the eye) chispa ♦ vi centellear.
glisten ['glɪsn] vi relucir, brillar.
glitter ['glɪtə*] vi relucir, brillar ♦ n brillo.
glittering ['glɪtərɪŋ] adj reluciente, brillante.
glitz [glɪts] n (col) vistosidad f.
gloat [gləʊt] vi: **to ~ over** regodearse con.
global ['gləʊbl] adj (world-wide) mundial; (comprehensive) global.
global warming [-'wɔːmɪŋ] n (re)calentamiento global or de la tierra.
globe [gləʊb] n globo, esfera; (model) bola del mundo; globo terráqueo.
globetrotter ['gləʊbtrɔtə*] n trotamundos m inv.
globule ['glɔbjuːl] n glóbulo.
gloom [gluːm] n penumbra; (sadness) desaliento, melancolía.
gloomily ['gluːmɪlɪ] adv tristemente; de modo pesimista.
gloomy ['gluːmɪ] adj (dark) oscuro; (sad) triste; (pessimistic) pesimista; **to feel ~** sentirse pesimista.
glorification [glɔːrɪfɪ'keɪʃən] n glorificación f.
glorify ['glɔːrɪfaɪ] vt glorificar.
glorious ['glɔːrɪəs] adj glorioso; (weather, sunshine) espléndido.
glory ['glɔːrɪ] n gloria.
glory hole n (col) trastero.
Glos abbr (BRIT) = Gloucestershire.
gloss [glɔs] n (shine) brillo; (also: **~ paint**) (pintura) esmalte m.
▶**gloss over** vt fus restar importancia a; (omit) pasar por alto.
glossary ['glɔsərɪ] n glosario.
glossy ['glɔsɪ] adj (hair) brillante; (photograph) con brillo; (magazine) de papel satinado or cuché.
glove [glʌv] n guante m.
glove compartment n (AUT) guantera.
glow [gləʊ] vi (shine) brillar ♦ n brillo.
glower ['glaʊə*] vi: **to ~ at** mirar con ceño.
glowing ['gləʊɪŋ] adj (fire) vivo; (complexion) encendido; (fig: report, description) entusiasta.
glow-worm ['gləʊwəːm] n luciérnaga.
glucose ['gluːkəʊs] n glucosa.
glue [gluː] n pegamento, cemento (LAM) ♦ vt pegar.
glue-sniffing ['gluːsnɪfɪŋ] n inhalación f de pegamento or cemento (LAM).
glum [glʌm] adj (mood) abatido; (person, tone) melancólico.
glut [glʌt] n superabundancia.
glutinous ['gluːtɪnəs] adj glutinoso,

pegajoso.

glutton ['glʌtn] *n* glotón/ona *m/f*; ~ **for punishment** masoquista *m/f*.

gluttony ['glʌtənı] *n* gula, glotonería.

glycerin(e) ['glısərı:n] *n* glicerina.

GM *adj abbr* (= *genetically modified*) transgénico.

gm *abbr* (= *gram*) g.

GMAT *n abbr* (*US:* = *Graduate Management Admissions Test*) examen de admisión al segundo ciclo de la enseñanza superior.

GMB *n abbr* (*BRIT:* = *General Municipal and Boilermakers (Union)*) sindicato obrero.

GMT *abbr* (= *Greenwich Mean Time*) GMT.

gnarled [nɑ:ld] *adj* nudoso.

gnash [næʃ] *vt:* **to ~ one's teeth** hacer rechinar los dientes.

gnat [næt] *n* mosquito.

gnaw [nɔ:] *vt* roer.

gnome [nəum] *n* gnomo.

GNP *n abbr* (= *gross national product*) PNB *m*.

go [gəu] *vb* (*pt* **went**, *pp* **gone** [wɛnt, gɔn]) *vi* ir; (*travel*) viajar; (*depart*) irse, marcharse; (*work*) funcionar, marchar; (*be sold*) venderse; (*time*) pasar; (*become*) ponerse; (*break etc*) estropearse, romperse; (*fit, suit*): **to ~ with** hacer juego con ♦ *n* (*pl* **~es**): **to have a ~ (at)** probar suerte (con); **to be on the ~** no parar; **whose ~ is it?** ¿a quién le toca?; **to ~ by car/on foot** ir en coche/a pie; **he's ~ing to do it** va a hacerlo; **to ~ for a walk** ir a dar un paseo; **to ~ dancing** ir a bailar; **to ~ looking for sth/sb** ir a buscar algo/a algn; **to make sth ~, get sth ~ing** poner algo en marcha; **my voice has gone** he perdido la voz; **the cake is all gone** se acabó la tarta; **the money will ~ towards our holiday** el dinero es para (ayuda de) nuestras vacaciones; **how did it ~?** ¿qué tal salió *or* resultó?, ¿cómo ha ido?; **the meeting went well** la reunión salió bien; **to ~ and see sb, ~ to see sb** ir a ver a algn; **to ~ to sleep** dormirse; **I'll take whatever is ~ing** acepto lo que haya; ... **to ~** (*US: food*) ... para llevar; **to ~ round the back** pasar por detrás.

▶**go about** *vi* (*rumour*) propagarse; (*also:* **~ round**: *wander about*) andar (de un sitio para otro) ♦ *vt fus:* **how do I ~ about this?** ¿cómo me las arreglo para hacer esto?; **to ~ about one's business** ocuparse de sus asuntos.

▶**go after** *vt fus* (*pursue*) perseguir; (*job, record etc*) andar tras.

▶**go against** *vt fus* (*be unfavourable to:* *results*) ir en contra de; (*be contrary to:*

principles) ser contrario a.

▶**go ahead** *vi* seguir adelante.

▶**go along** *vi* ir; **as you ~ along** sobre la marcha ♦ *vt fus* bordear.

▶**go along with** *vt fus* (*accompany*) acompañar; (*agree with:* *idea*) estar de acuerdo con.

▶**go around** *vi* = **go round**.

▶**go away** *vi* irse, marcharse.

▶**go back** *vi* volver.

▶**go back on** *vt fus* (*promise*) faltar a.

▶**go by** *vi* (*time*) pasar ♦ *vt fus* guiarse por.

▶**go down** *vi* bajar; (*ship*) hundirse; (*sun*) ponerse ♦ *vt fus* bajar por; **that should ~ down well with him** eso le va a gustar; **she's gone down with the flu** ha cogido la gripe.

▶**go for** *vt fus* (*fetch*) ir por; (*like*) gustar; (*attack*) atacar.

▶**go in** *vi* entrar.

▶**go in for** *vt fus* (*competition*) presentarse a.

▶**go into** *vt fus* entrar en; (*investigate*) investigar; (*embark on*) dedicarse a.

▶**go off** *vi* irse, marcharse; (*food*) pasarse; (*lights etc*) apagarse; (*explode*) estallar; (*event*) realizarse ♦ *vt fus* perder el interés por; **the party went off well** la fiesta salió bien.

▶**go on** *vi* (*continue*) seguir, continuar; (*lights*) encenderse; (*happen*) pasar, ocurrir; (*be guided by*) partir de; **to ~ on doing sth** seguir haciendo algo; **what's ~ing on here?** ¿qué pasa aquí?

▶**go on at** *vt fus* (*nag*) soltarle el rollo a.

▶**go out** *vi* salir; (*fire, light*) apagarse; (*ebb:* *tide*) bajar, menguar; **to ~ out with sb** salir con algn.

▶**go over** *vi* (*ship*) zozobrar ♦ *vt fus* (*check*) revisar; **to ~ over sth in one's mind** repasar algo mentalmente.

▶**go round** *vi* (*circulate:* *news, rumour*) correr; (*suffice*) alcanzar, bastar; (*revolve*) girar, dar vueltas; (*visit*): **to ~ round (to sb's)** pasar a ver (a algn); **to ~ round (by)** (*make a detour*) dar la vuelta (por).

▶**go through** *vt fus* (*town etc*) atravesar; (*search through*) revisar; (*perform:* *ceremony*) realizar; (*examine:* *list, book*) repasar.

▶**go through with** *vt fus* (*plan, crime*) llevar a cabo; **I couldn't ~ through with it** no pude llevarlo a cabo.

▶**go together** *vi* (*harmonize:* *people etc*) entenderse.

▶**go under** *vi* (*sink:* *ship, person*) hundirse; (*fig:* *business, firm*) quebrar.

▶**go up** *vi* subir; **to ~ up in flames** estallar

en llamas.

▶**go without** *vt fus* pasarse sin.

goad [gəud] *vt* aguijonear.

go-ahead ['gəuəhɛd] *adj* emprendedor(a) ♦ *n* luz *f* verde; **to give sth/sb the** ~ dar luz verde a algo/algn.

goal [gəul] *n* meta, arco (*LAM*); (*score*) gol *m*.

goal difference *n* diferencia por goles.

goalie ['gəulɪ] *n* (*col*) portero, guardameta *m/f*, arquero (*LAM*).

goalkeeper ['gəulkiːpə*] *n* portero, guardameta *m/f*, arquero (*LAM*).

goal post *n* poste *m* (de la portería).

goat [gəut] *n* cabra *f*.

gobble ['gɔbl] *vt* (*also*: ~ **down**, ~ **up**) engullir.

go-between ['gəubɪtwiːn] *n* intermediario/a.

Gobi Desert ['gəubɪ-] *n* Desierto de Gobi.

goblet ['gɔblɪt] *n* copa.

goblin ['gɔblɪn] *n* duende *m*.

go-cart ['gəukɑːt] *n* = **go-kart**.

god [gɔd] *n* dios *m*; **G~** Dios *m*.

god-awful [gɔd'ɔːfəl] *adj* (*col*) de puta pena.

godchild ['gɔdtʃaɪld] *n* ahijado/a.

goddamn ['gɔddæm] *adj* (*col*: *also*: **goddamned**) maldito, puñetero ♦ *excl*: ~! ¡cagüen diez!

goddess ['gɔdɪs] *n* diosa.

godfather ['gɔdfɑːðə*] *n* padrino.

god-fearing ['gɔdfɪərɪŋ] *adj* temeroso de Dios.

god-forsaken ['gɔdfəseɪkən] *adj* dejado de la mano de Dios.

godmother ['gɔdmʌðə*] *n* madrina.

godparents ['gɔdpɛərənts] *npl*: **the** ~ los padrinos.

godsend ['gɔdsɛnd] *n*: **to be a** ~ venir como llovido del cielo.

godson ['gɔdsʌn] *n* ahijado.

goes [gəuz] *vb see* **go**.

gofer ['gəufə*] *n* (*col*) chico/a para todo.

go-getter ['gəugɛtə*] *n* ambicioso/a.

goggle ['gɔgl] *vi*: **to** ~ **(at)** mirar con ojos desorbitados.

goggles ['gɔglz] *npl* (*AUT*) gafas *fpl*, anteojos *mpl* (*LAM*); (*diver's*) gafas *fpl* submarinas.

going ['gəuɪŋ] *n* (*conditions*) cosas *fpl* ♦ *adj*: **the** ~ **rate** la tarifa corriente *or* en vigor; **it was slow** ~ las cosas iban lentas.

going-over [gəuɪŋ'əuvə*] *n* revisión *f*; (*col*: *beating*) paliza.

goings-on ['gəuɪŋz'ɔn] *npl* (*col*) tejemanejes *mpl*.

go-kart ['gəukɑːt] *n* kart *m*.

gold [gəuld] *n* oro ♦ *adj* (*reserves*) de oro.

golden ['gəuldn] *adj* (*made of gold*) de oro; (~ *in colour*) dorado.

Golden Age *n* Siglo de Oro.

golden handshake *n* cuantiosa gratificación por los servicios prestados.

golden rule *n* regla de oro.

goldfish ['gəuldfɪʃ] *n* pez *m* de colores.

gold leaf *n* pan *m* de oro.

gold medal *n* (*SPORT*) medalla de oro.

goldmine ['gəuldmaɪn] *n* mina de oro.

gold-plated ['gəuld'pleɪtɪd] *adj* chapado en oro.

goldsmith ['gəuldsmɪθ] *n* orfebre *m/f*.

gold standard *n* patrón *m* oro.

golf [gɔlf] *n* golf *m*.

golf ball *n* (*for game*) pelota de golf; (*on typewriter*) esfera impresora.

golf club *n* club *m* de golf; (*stick*) palo (de golf).

golf course *n* campo de golf.

golfer ['gɔlfə*] *n* jugador(a) *m/f* de golf, golfista *m/f*.

golfing ['gɔlfɪŋ] *n*: **to go** ~ jugar al golf.

gondola ['gɔndələ] *n* góndola.

gondolier [gɔndə'lɪə*] *n* gondolero.

gone [gɔn] *pp of* **go**.

goner ['gɔnə*] *n* (*col*): **to be a** ~ estar en las últimas.

gong [gɔŋ] *n* gong *m*.

gonorrhea [gɔnə'rɪə] *n* gonorrea.

good [gud] *adj* bueno, (*before m sing n* buen); (*well-behaved*) educado ♦ *n* bien *m*; ~! ¡qué bien!; **he's** ~ **at it** se le da bien; **to be** ~ **for** servir para; **it's** ~ **for you** te hace bien; **would you be** ~ **enough to...?** ¿podría hacerme el favor de...?, ¿sería tan amable de...?; **that's very** ~ **of you** es usted muy amable; **to feel** ~ sentirse bien; **it's** ~ **to see you** me alegro de verte; **a** ~ **deal (of)** mucho; **a** ~ **many** muchos, **to make** ~ reparar; **it's no** ~ **complaining** no sirve de nada quejarse; **is this any** ~? (*will it do?*) ¿sirve esto?; (*what's it like?*) ¿qué tal es esto?; **it's a** ~ **thing you were there** menos mal que estabas allí; **for** ~ (*for ever*) para siempre, definitivamente; ~ **morning/afternoon** ¡buenos días/buenas tardes!; ~ **evening!** ¡buenas noches!; ~ **night!** ¡buenas noches!; **he's up to no** ~ está tramando algo; **for the common** ~ para el bien común; *see also* **goods**.

goodbye [gud'baɪ] *excl* ¡adiós!; **to say** ~ **(to)** (*person*) despedirse (de).

good faith *n* buena fe *f*.

good-for-nothing ['gudfənʌθɪŋ] *n* inútil *m/f*.

Good Friday *n* Viernes *m* Santo.

good-humoured ['gud'hju:məd] *adj*
(*person*) afable, de buen humor; (*remark,
joke*) bien intencionado.

good-looking ['gud'lukɪŋ] *adj* guapo.

good-natured ['gud'neɪtʃəd] *adj* (*person*) de
buen carácter; (*discussion*) cordial.

goodness ['gudnɪs] *n* (*of person*) bondad *f*;
for ~ sake! ¡por Dios!; **~ gracious!**
¡madre mía!

goods [gudz] *npl* bienes *mpl*; (*COMM etc*)
géneros *mpl*, mercancías *fpl*, artículos *mpl*;
all his ~ and chattels todos sus bienes.

goods train *n* (*BRIT*) tren *m* de mercancías.

goodwill [gud'wɪl] *n* buena voluntad *f*;
(*COMM*) fondo de comercio; (*customer
connections*) clientela.

goody-goody ['gudɪgudɪ] *n* (*pej*)
santurrón/ona *m/f*.

gooey ['gu:ɪ] *adj* (*BRIT col*) pegajoso; (*cake,
behaviour*) empalagoso.

goose, *pl* **geese** [gu:s, gi:s] *n* ganso, oca.

gooseberry ['guzbərɪ] *n* grosella espinosa
or silvestre.

gooseflesh ['gu:sfleʃ] *n*, **goosepimples**
['gu:spɪmplz] *npl* carne *f* de gallina.

goose step *n* (*MIL*) paso de la oca.

GOP *n abbr* (*US POL: col* = Grand Old Party)
Partido Republicano.

gopher ['gəufə*] *n* = **gofer**.

gore [gɔ:*] *vt* dar una cornada a, cornear
♦ *n* sangre *f*.

gorge [gɔ:dʒ] *n* garganta ♦ *vr*: **to ~ o.s. (on)**
atracarse (de).

gorgeous ['gɔ:dʒəs] *adj* precioso; (*weather*)
estupendo; (*person*) guapísimo.

gorilla [gə'rɪlə] *n* gorila *m*.

gormless ['gɔ:mlɪs] *adj* (*col*) ceporro,
zoquete.

gorse [gɔ:s] *n* tojo.

gory ['gɔ:rɪ] *adj* sangriento.

go-slow ['gəu'sləu] *n* (*BRIT*) huelga de celo.

gospel ['gɔspl] *n* evangelio.

gossamer ['gɔsəmə*] *n* gasa.

gossip ['gɔsɪp] *n* cotilleo; (*person*) cotilla *m/f*
♦ *vi* cotillear, comadrear (*LAM*); **a piece of
~** un cotilleo.

gossip column *n* ecos *mpl* de sociedad.

got [gɔt] *pt, pp of* **get**.

Gothic ['gɔθɪk] *adj* gótico.

gotten ['gɔtn] (*US*) *pp of* **get**.

gouge [gaudʒ] *vt* (*also:* ~ **out**: *hole etc*)
excavar; (: *initials*) grabar; **to ~ sb's eyes
out** sacar los ojos a algn.

goulash ['gu:læʃ] *n* g(o)ulash *m*.

gourd [guəd] *n* calabaza.

gourmet ['guəmeɪ] *n* gastrónomo/a *m/f*.

gout [gaut] *n* gota.

govern ['gʌvən] *vt* (*gen*) gobernar; (*event,*

conduct) regir.

governess ['gʌvənɪs] *n* institutriz *f*.

governing ['gʌvənɪŋ] *adj* (*POL*) de gobierno,
gubernamental; **~ body** organismo de
gobierno.

government ['gʌvnmənt] *n* gobierno; **local
~** administración *f* municipal.

governmental [gʌvn'mɛntl] *adj*
gubernamental.

government stock *n* papel *m* del Estado.

governor ['gʌvənə*] *n* gobernador(a) *m/f*;
(*of jail*) director(a) *m/f*.

Govt. *abbr* (= *Government*) gobno.

gown [gaun] *n* vestido; (*of teacher, BRIT: of
judge*) toga.

GP *n abbr see* **general practitioner**.

GPMU *n abbr* (*BRIT:* = Graphical, Paper and
Media Union) *sindicato de trabajadores
del sector editorial*.

GPO *n abbr* (*BRIT: old*) = General Post Office;
(*US*) = Government Printing Office.

gr. *abbr* (*COMM:* = gross) bto.

grab [græb] *vt* coger (*SP*) *or* agarrar; **to ~
at** intentar agarrar.

grace [greɪs] *n* (*REL*) gracia; (*gracefulness*)
elegancia, gracia; (*graciousness*) cortesía,
gracia ♦ *vt* (*favour*) honrar; (*adorn*)
adornar; **5 days' ~** un plazo de 5 días; **to
say ~** bendecir la mesa; **his sense of
humour is his saving ~** lo que le salva es
su sentido del humor.

graceful ['greɪsful] *adj* elegante.

gracious ['greɪʃəs] *adj* amable ♦ *excl*: **good
~!** ¡Dios mío!

grade [greɪd] *n* (*quality*) clase *f*, calidad *f*; (*in
hierarchy*) grado; (*US: SCOL*) curso
(: *gradient*) pendiente *f*, cuesta ♦ *vt*
clasificar; **to make the ~** (*fig*) dar el
nivel; *see also* **high school**.

grade crossing *n* (*US*) paso a nivel.

grade school *n* (*US*) escuela primaria; *see
also* **elementary school**.

gradient ['greɪdɪənt] *n* pendiente *f*.

gradual ['grædjuəl] *adj* gradual.

gradually ['grædjuəlɪ] *adv* gradualmente.

graduate *n* ['grædjuɪt] licenciado/a,
graduado/a, egresado/a (*LAM*); (*US: SCOL*)
bachiller *m/f* ♦ *vi* ['grædjueɪt] licenciarse,
graduarse, recibirse (*LAM*); (*US*) obtener
el título de bachillerato.

graduated pension ['grædjueɪtɪd-] *n*
pensión *f* escalonada.

graduation [grædju'eɪʃən] *n* graduación *f*;
(*US SCOL*) entrega de los títulos de
bachillerato.

graffiti [grə'fi:tɪ] *npl* pintadas *fpl*.

graft [gra:ft] *n* (*AGR, MED*) injerto; (*bribery*)
corrupción *f* ♦ *vt* injertar; **hard ~** (*col*)

trabajo duro.

grain [greɪn] n (single particle) grano; (no pl: cereals) cereales mpl; (US: corn) trigo; (in wood) veta.

gram [græm] n (US) gramo.

grammar ['græmə*] n gramática.

grammar school n (BRIT) ≈ instituto (de segunda enseñanza); (US) escuela primaria; see also **comprehensive school**.

grammatical [grə'mætɪkl] adj gramatical.

gramme [græm] n = **gram**.

gramophone ['græməfəun] n (BRIT) gramófono.

granary ['grænərɪ] n granero.

grand [grænd] adj grandioso ♦ n (US: col) mil dólares mpl.

grandchildren ['grænt∫ɪldrən] npl nietos mpl.

granddad ['grændæd] n yayo, abuelito.

granddaughter ['grændɔːtə*] n nieta.

grandeur ['grændjə*] n grandiosidad f.

grandfather ['grænfɑːðə*] n abuelo.

grandiose ['grændɪəuz] adj grandioso; (pej) pomposo.

grand jury n (US) jurado de acusación.

grandma ['grænmɑː] n yaya, abuelita.

grandmother ['grænmʌðə*] n abuela.

grandpa ['grænpɑː] n = **granddad**.

grandparents ['grændpeərənts] npl abuelos mpl.

grand piano n piano de cola.

Grand Prix ['grɑ̃:'pri:] n (AUT) gran premio, Grand Prix m.

grandson ['grænsʌn] n nieto.

grandstand ['grændstænd] n (SPORT) tribuna.

grand total n suma total, total m.

granite ['grænɪt] n granito.

granny ['grænɪ] n abuelita, yaya.

grant [grɑːnt] vt (concede) conceder; (admit): **to ~ (that)** reconocer (que) ♦ n (SCOL) beca; **to take sth for ~ed** dar algo por sentado.

granulated sugar ['grænjuleɪtɪd-] n (BRIT) azúcar m granulado.

granule ['grænjuːl] n gránulo.

grape [greɪp] n uva; **sour ~s** (fig) envidia sg; **a bunch of ~s** un racimo de uvas.

grapefruit ['greɪpfruːt] n pomelo, toronja.

grape juice n jugo or zumo (SP) de uva.

grapevine ['greɪpvaɪn] n vid f, parra; **I heard it on the ~** (fig) me enteré, me lo contaron.

graph [grɑːf] n gráfica.

graphic ['græfɪk] adj gráfico.

graphic designer n diseñador(a) m/f gráfico/a.

graphic equalizer n ecualizador m gráfico.

graphics ['græfɪks] n (art, process) artes fpl gráficas ♦ npl (drawings: also COMPUT) gráficos mpl.

graphite ['græfaɪt] n grafito.

graph paper n papel m cuadriculado.

grapple ['græpl] vi: **to ~ with a problem** enfrentarse a un problema.

grappling iron ['græplɪŋ-] n (NAUT) rezón m.

grasp [grɑːsp] vt agarrar, asir; (understand) comprender ♦ n (grip) asimiento; (reach) alcance m; (understanding) comprensión f; **to have a good ~ of** (subject) dominar.

▶**grasp at** vt fus (rope etc) tratar de agarrar; (fig: opportunity) aprovechar.

grasping ['grɑːspɪŋ] adj avaro.

grass [grɑːs] n hierba, grama (LAM), (lawn) césped m; (pasture) pasto; (col: informer) soplón/ona m/f.

grasshopper ['grɑːshɔpə*] n saltamontes m inv.

grassland ['grɑːslænd] n pradera, pampa (LAM).

grass roots adj de base ♦ npl (POL) bases fpl.

grass snake n culebra.

grassy ['grɑːsɪ] adj cubierto de hierba.

grate [greɪt] n parrilla ♦ vi chirriar, rechinar ♦ vt (CULIN) rallar.

grateful ['greɪtful] adj agradecido.

gratefully ['greɪtfəlɪ] adv con agradecimiento.

grater ['greɪtə*] n rallador m.

gratification [grætɪfɪ'keɪ∫ən] n satisfacción f.

gratify ['grætɪfaɪ] vt complacer; (whim) satisfacer.

gratifying ['grætɪfaɪɪŋ] adj gratificante.

grating ['greɪtɪŋ] n (iron bars) rejilla ♦ adj (noise) chirriante.

gratitude ['grætɪtjuːd] n agradecimiento.

gratuitous [grə'tjuːɪtəs] adj gratuito.

gratuity [grə'tjuːɪtɪ] n gratificación f.

grave [greɪv] n tumba ♦ adj serio, grave.

gravedigger ['greɪvdɪgə*] n sepulturero/a.

gravel ['grævl] n grava.

gravely ['greɪvlɪ] adv seriamente; **~ ill** muy grave.

gravestone ['greɪvstəun] n lápida.

graveyard ['greɪvjɑːd] n cementerio, camposanto.

gravitate ['grævɪteɪt] vi gravitar.

gravitation [grævɪ'teɪ∫ən] n gravitación f.

gravity ['grævɪtɪ] n gravedad f; (seriousness) seriedad f.

gravy ['greɪvɪ] n salsa de carne.

gravy boat n salsera.

gravy train n (esp US: col): **to get on the ~** coger un chollo.

gray [greɪ] _adj_ (_US_) = **grey**.
graze [greɪz] _vi_ pacer ♦ _vt_ (_touch lightly,_
scrape) rozar ♦ _n_ (_MED_) rozadura.
grazing ['greɪzɪŋ] _n_ (_for livestock_) pastoreo.
grease [griːs] _n_ (_fat_) grasa; (_lubricant_)
lubricante _m_ ♦ _vt_ engrasar; **to ~ the skids**
(_US_: _fig_) engrasar el mecanismo.
grease gun _n_ pistola engrasadora.
greasepaint ['griːspeɪnt] _n_ maquillaje _m_.
greaseproof ['griːspruːf] _adj_ a prueba de
grasa; (_BRIT_: _paper_) de grasa.
greasy ['griːsɪ] _adj_ (_hands, clothes_)
grasiento; (_road, surface_) resbaladizo.
great [greɪt] _adj_ grande, (_before n sing_)
gran; (_col_) estupendo, macanudo (_LAM_),
regio (_LAM_), chévere (_LAM_); (_pain, heat_)
intenso; **we had a ~ time** nos lo pasamos
muy bien; **they're ~ friends** son íntimos
_or_ muy amigos; **the ~ thing is that ...** lo
bueno es que ...; **it was ~!** ¡fue
estupendo!
Great Barrier Reef _n_ Gran Barrera de
Coral.
Great Britain _n_ Gran Bretaña.
greater ['greɪtə*] _adj_ mayor; **G~ London** el
área metropolitana de Londres.
greatest ['greɪtɪst] _adj_ (el/la) mayor.
great-grandchild, _pl_ **-children**
[greɪt'grændtʃaɪld, 'tʃɪldrən] _n_ bisnieto/a.
great-grandfather [greɪt'grændfɑːðə*] _n_
bisabuelo.
great-grandmother [greɪt'grændmʌðə*] _n_
bisabuela.
Great Lakes _npl_: **the ~** los Grandes Lagos.
greatly ['greɪtlɪ] _adv_ sumamente, muy.
greatness ['greɪtnɪs] _n_ grandeza.
Greece [griːs] _n_ Grecia.
greed [griːd] _n_ (_also_: **~iness**) codicia; (_for_
food) gula.
greedily ['griːdɪlɪ] _adv_ con avidez.
greedy ['griːdɪ] _adj_ codicioso; (_for food_)
glotón/ona.
Greek [griːk] _adj_ griego ♦ _n_ griego/a; (_LING_)
griego; **ancient/modern ~** griego
antiguo/moderno.
green [griːn] _adj_ verde; (_inexperienced_)
novato ♦ _n_ verde _m_; (_stretch of grass_)
césped _m_; (_of golf course_) campo, "green"
_m_; **the G~ party** (_POL_) el partido verde; **~s**
npl verduras _fpl_; **to have ~ fingers** (_fig_)
tener buena mano para las plantas.
green belt _n_ cinturón _m_ verde.
green card _n_ (_AUT_) carta verde.
greenery ['griːnərɪ] _n_ vegetación _f_.
greenfly ['griːnflaɪ] _n_ pulgón _m_.
greengage ['griːngeɪdʒ] _n_ (ciruela)
claudia.
greengrocer ['griːngrəʊsə*] _n_ (_BRIT_)

frutero/a, verdulero/a.
greenhouse ['griːnhaus] _n_ invernadero.
greenhouse effect _n_: **the ~** el efecto
invernadero.
greenhouse gas _n_ gas _m_ que produce el
efecto invernadero.
greenish ['griːnɪʃ] _adj_ verdoso.
Greenland ['griːnlənd] _n_ Groenlandia.
Greenlander ['griːnləndə*] _n_ groenlandés/
esa/_m/f_.
green light _n_ luz _f_ verde.
green pepper _n_ pimiento verde.
greet [griːt] _vt_ saludar; (_news_) recibir.
greeting ['griːtɪŋ] _n_ (_gen_) saludo; (_welcome_)
bienvenida; **~s** saludos _mpl_; **season's ~s**
Felices Pascuas.
greeting(s) card _n_ tarjeta de felicitación.
gregarious [grə'gɛərɪəs] _adj_ gregario.
grenade [grə'neɪd] _n_ (_also_: **hand ~**)
granada.
grew [gruː] _pt of_ **grow**.
grey [greɪ] _adj_ gris; **to go ~** salirle canas.
grey-haired [greɪ'hɛəd] _adj_ canoso.
greyhound ['greɪhaund] _n_ galgo.
grid [grɪd] _n_ rejilla; (_ELEC_) red _f_.
griddle ['grɪdl] _n_ (_esp US_) plancha.
gridiron ['grɪdaɪən] _n_ (_CULIN_) parrilla.
gridlock ['grɪdlɔk] _n_ (_esp US_) retención _f_.
grief [griːf] _n_ dolor _m_, pena; **to come to ~**
(_plan_) fracasar, ir al traste; (_person_)
acabar mal, desgraciarse.
grievance ['griːvəns] _n_ (_cause for complaint_)
motivo de queja, agravio.
grieve [griːv] _vi_ afligirse, acongojarse ♦ _vt_
afligir, apenar; **to ~ for** llorar por; **to ~**
for sb (_dead person_) llorar la pérdida de
algn.
grievous ['griːvəs] _adj_ grave; (_loss_) cruel; **~**
bodily harm (_LAW_) daños _mpl_ corporales
graves.
grill [grɪl] _n_ (_on cooker_) parrilla ♦ _vt_ (_BRIT_)
asar a la parrilla; (_question_) interrogar;
~ed meat carne _f_ (asada) a la parrilla _or_
plancha.
grille [grɪl] _n_ rejilla.
grim [grɪm] _adj_ (_place_) lúgubre; (_person_)
adusto.
grimace [grɪ'meɪs] _n_ mueca ♦ _vi_ hacer
muecas.
grime [graɪm] _n_ mugre _f_.
grimly ['grɪmlɪ] _adv_ (_say_) sombríamente.
grimy ['graɪmɪ] _adj_ mugriento.
grin [grɪn] _n_ sonrisa abierta ♦ _vi_: **to ~ (at)**
sonreír abiertamente (a).
grind [graɪnd] _vb_ (_pt, pp_ **ground** [graund]) _vt_
(_coffee, pepper etc_) moler; (_US_: _meat_)
picar; (_make sharp_) afilar; (_polish_: _gem,_
lens) esmerilar ♦ _vi_ (_car gears_) rechinar

♦ *n*: **the daily ~** (*col*) la rutina diaria; **to ~ one's teeth** hacer rechinar los dientes; **to ~ to a halt** (*vehicle*) pararse con gran estruendo de frenos; (*fig*: *talks, scheme*) interrumpirse; (*work, production*) paralizarse.

grinder ['graɪndə*] *n* (*machine*: *for coffee*) molinillo.

grindstone ['graɪndstəun] *n*: **to keep one's nose to the ~** trabajar sin descanso.

grip [grɪp] *n* (*hold*) asimiento; (*of hands*) apretón *m*; (*handle*) asidero; (*of racquet etc*) mango; (*understanding*) comprensión *f* ♦ *vt* agarrar; **to get to ~s with** enfrentarse con; **to lose one's ~** (*fig*) perder el control; **he lost his ~ of the situation** la situación se le fue de las manos.

gripe [graɪp] *n* (*col*: *complaint*) queja ♦ *vi* (*col*: *complain*): **to ~** (**about**) quejarse (de); **~s** *npl* retortijones *mpl*.

gripping ['grɪpɪŋ] *adj* absorbente.

grisly ['grɪzlɪ] *adj* horripilante, horrible.

gristle ['grɪsl] *n* cartílago.

grit [grɪt] *n* gravilla; (*courage*) valor *m* ♦ *vt* (*road*) poner gravilla en; **I've got a piece of ~ in my eye** tengo una arenilla en el ojo; **to ~ one's teeth** apretar los dientes.

grits [grɪts] *npl* (*US*) maíz *msg* a medio moler.

grizzle ['grɪzl] *vi* (*cry*) lloriquear.

grizzly ['grɪzlɪ] *n* (*also*: **~ bear**) oso pardo.

groan [grəun] *n* gemido, quejido ♦ *vi* gemir, quejarse.

grocer ['grəusə*] *n* tendero (de ultramarinos); **~'s (shop)** *n* tienda de ultramarinos *or* de abarrotes (*LAM*).

groceries ['grəusərɪz] *npl* comestibles *mpl*.

grocery ['grəusərɪ] *n* (*shop*) tienda de ultramarinos.

grog [grɔg] *n* (*BRIT*) grog *m*.

groggy ['grɔgɪ] *adj* atontado.

groin [grɔɪn] *n* ingle *f*.

groom [gru:m] *n* mozo/a de cuadra; (*also*: **bride~**) novio ♦ *vt* (*horse*) almohazar; **well-~ed** acicalado.

groove [gru:v] *n* ranura; (*of record*) surco.

grope [grəup] *vi* ir a tientas; **to ~ for** buscar a tientas.

gross [grəus] *adj* grueso; (*COMM*) bruto ♦ *vt* (*COMM*) recaudar en bruto.

gross domestic product (GDP) *n* producto interior bruto (PIB).

gross income *n* ingresos *mpl* brutos.

grossly ['grəuslɪ] *adv* (*greatly*) enormemente.

gross national product (GNP) *n* producto nacional bruto (PNB).

gross profit *n* beneficios *mpl* brutos.

gross sales *npl* ventas *fpl* brutas.

grotesque [grə'tɛsk] *adj* grotesco.

grotto ['grɔtəu] *n* gruta.

grotty ['grɔtɪ] *adj* asqueroso.

grouch [grautʃ] *vi* (*col*) refunfuñar ♦ *n* (*col*: *person*) refunfuñón/ona *m/f*.

ground [graund] *pt, pp of* **grind** ♦ *n* suelo, tierra; (*SPORT*) campo, terreno; (*reason*: *gen pl*) motivo, razón *f*; (*US*: *also*: **~ wire**) tierra ♦ *vt* (*plane*) mantener en tierra; (*US*: *ELEC*) conectar con tierra ♦ *vi* (*ship*) varar, encallar ♦ *adj* (*coffee etc*) molido; **~s** *npl* (*of coffee etc*) poso *sg*; (*gardens etc*) jardines *mpl*, parque *m*; **on the ~** en el suelo; **common ~** terreno común; **to gain/lose ~** ganar/perder terreno; **to the ~** al suelo; **below ~** bajo tierra; **he covered a lot of ~ in his lecture** abarcó mucho en la clase.

ground cloth *n* (*US*) = **groundsheet**.

ground control *n* (*AVIAT, SPACE*) control *m* desde tierra.

ground floor *n* (*BRIT*) planta baja.

grounding ['graundɪŋ] *n* (*in education*) conocimientos *mpl* básicos.

groundkeeper ['graundki:pə*] *n* = **groundsman**.

groundless ['graundlɪs] *adj* infundado, sin fundamento.

groundnut ['graundnʌt] *n* cacahuete *m*.

ground rent *n* alquiler *m* del terreno.

ground rules *npl* normas básicas.

groundsheet ['graundʃi:t] (*BRIT*) *n* tela impermeable.

groundsman ['graundzmən], (*US*) **groundskeeper** ['graundzki:pə*] *n* (*SPORT*) encargado de pista de deportes.

ground staff *n* personal *m* de tierra.

ground swell *n* mar *m or f* de fondo; (*fig*) ola.

ground-to-air ['grauntə'ɛə] *adj* tierra-aire.

ground-to-ground ['grauntə'graund] *adj* tierra-tierra.

groundwork ['graundwə:k] *n* trabajo preliminar.

group [gru:p] *n* grupo; (*MUS*: *pop* **~**) conjunto, grupo ♦ (*vb*: *also*: **~ together**) *vt* agrupar ♦ *vi* agruparse.

groupie ['gru:pɪ] *n* groupie *f*.

group therapy *n* terapia de grupo.

grouse [graus] *n* (*pl inv*) (*bird*) urogallo ♦ *vi* (*complain*) quejarse.

grove [grəuv] *n* arboleda.

grovel ['grɔvl] *vi* (*fig*) arrastrarse.

grow, *pt* **grew,** *pp* **grown** [grəu, gru:, grəun] *vi* crecer; (*increase*) aumentar; (*expand*) desarrollarse; (*become*) volverse ♦ *vt* cultivar; (*hair, beard*) dejar crecer; **to ~ rich/weak** enriquecerse/debilitarse; **to ~ tired of waiting** cansarse de esperar.

►**grow apart** *vi* (*fig*) alejarse uno del otro.

►**grow away from** *vt fus* (*fig*) alejarse de.

►**grow on** *vt fus*: **that painting is ~ing on me** ese cuadro me gusta cada vez más.

►**grow out of** *vt fus* (*clothes*): **I've grown out of this shirt** esta camisa se me ha quedado pequeña; (*habit*) perder.

►**grow up** *vi* crecer, hacerse hombre/mujer.

grower ['grəuə*] *n* (*AGR*) cultivador(a) *m/f*, productor(a) *m/f*.

growing ['grəuɪŋ] *adj* creciente; **~ pains** (*also fig*) problemas *mpl* de crecimiento.

growl [graul] *vi* gruñir.

grown [grəun] *pp of* **grow**.

grown-up [grəun'ʌp] *n* adulto/a, mayor *m/f*.

growth [grəuθ] *n* crecimiento, desarrollo; (*what has grown*) brote *m*; (*MED*) tumor *m*.

growth rate *n* tasa de crecimiento.

GRSM *n abbr* (*BRIT*) = *Graduate of the Royal Schools of Music.*

grub [grʌb] *n* gusano; (*col: food*) comida.

grubby ['grʌbɪ] *adj* sucio, mugriento, mugroso (*LAM*).

grudge [grʌdʒ] *n* rencor ♦ *vt*: **to ~ sb sth** dar algo a algn de mala gana; **to bear sb a ~** guardar rencor a algn; **he ~s (giving) the money** da el dinero de mala gana.

grudgingly ['grʌdʒɪŋlɪ] *adv* de mala gana.

gruelling, (*US*) **grueling** ['gruəlɪŋ] *adj* agotador.

gruesome ['gru:səm] *adj* horrible.

gruff [grʌf] *adj* (*voice*) ronco; (*manner*) brusco.

grumble ['grʌmbl] *vi* refunfuñar, quejarse.

grumpy ['grʌmpɪ] *adj* gruñón/ona.

grunge [grʌndʒ] *n* (*MUS, fashion*) grunge *m*.

grunt [grʌnt] *vi* gruñir ♦ *n* gruñido.

G-string ['dʒi:strɪŋ] *n* tanga *m*.

GSUSA *n abbr* = *Girl Scouts of the United States of America.*

GT *abbr* (*AUT*: = *gran turismo*) GT.

GU *abbr* (*US*) = *Guam.*

guarantee [gærən'ti:] *n* garantía ♦ *vt* garantizar; **he can't ~ (that) he'll come** no está seguro de poder venir.

guarantor [gærən'tɔ:*] *n* garante *m/f*, fiador(a) *m/f*.

guard [gɑ:d] *n* guardia; (*person*) guarda *m/f*; (*BRIT RAIL*) jefe *m* de tren; (*safety device: on machine*) cubierta de protección; (*protection*) protección *f*; (*fire~*) pantalla; (*mud~*) guardabarros *m inv* ♦ *vt* guardar; **to ~ (against** *or* **from)** proteger (de); **to be on one's ~** (*fig*) estar en guardia.

►**guard against** *vi*: **to ~ against doing sth** guardarse de hacer algo.

guard dog *n* perro guardián.

guarded ['gɑ:dɪd] *adj* (*fig*) cauteloso.

guardian ['gɑ:dɪən] *n* guardián/ana *m/f*; (*of minor*) tutor(a) *m/f*.

guardrail ['gɑ:dreɪl] *n* pretil *m*.

guard's van *n* (*BRIT RAIL*) furgón *m* del jefe de tren.

Guatemala [gwɑ:tə'mɑ:lə] *n* Guatemala.

Guatemalan [gwɑ:tə'mɑ:lən] *adj, n* guatemalteco/a *m/f*.

Guernsey ['gə:nzɪ] *n* Guernsey *m*.

guerrilla [gə'rɪlə] *n* guerrillero/a.

guerrilla warfare *n* guerra de guerrillas.

guess [gɛs] *vi, vt* (*gen*) adivinar; (*suppose*) suponer ♦ *n* suposición *f*, conjetura; **I ~ you're right** (*esp US*) supongo que tienes razón; **to keep sb ~ing** mantener a algn a la expectativa; **to take** *or* **have a ~** tratar de adivinar; **my ~ is that ...** yo creo que ....

guesstimate ['gɛstɪmɪt] *n* cálculo aproximado.

guesswork ['gɛswə:k] *n* conjeturas *fpl*; **I got the answer by ~** acerté a ojo de buen cubero.

guest [gɛst] *n* invitado/a; (*in hotel*) huésped(a) *m/f*; **be my ~** (*col*) estás en tu casa.

guest-house ['gɛsthaus] *n* casa de huéspedes, pensión *f*.

guest room *n* cuarto de huéspedes.

guff [gʌf] *n* (*col*) bobadas *fpl*.

guffaw [gʌ'fɔ:] *n* carcajada ♦ *vi* reírse a carcajadas.

guidance ['gaɪdəns] *n* (*gen*) dirección *f*; (*advice*) consejos *mpl*; **marriage/vocational ~** orientación *f* matrimonial/profesional.

guide [gaɪd] *n* (*person*) guía *m/f*; (*book, fig*) guía *f*; (*also:* **girl ~**) exploradora ♦ *vt* guiar; **to be ~d by sb/sth** dejarse guiar por algn/algo.

guidebook ['gaɪdbuk] *n* guía.

guided missile ['gaɪdɪd-] *n* misil *m* teledirigido.

guide dog *n* perro guía.

guidelines ['gaɪdlaɪnz] *npl* (*fig*) directrices *fpl*.

guild [gɪld] *n* gremio.

guildhall ['gɪldhɔ:l] *n* (*BRIT*: *town hall*) ayuntamiento.

guile [gaɪl] *n* astucia.

guileless ['gaɪllɪs] *adj* cándido.

guillotine ['gɪləti:n] *n* guillotina.

guilt [gɪlt] *n* culpabilidad *f*.

guilty ['gɪltɪ] *adj* culpable; **to feel ~ (about)** sentirse culpable (de); **to plead ~/not ~**

declararse culpable/inocente.

Guinea ['gɪnɪ] n: **Republic of** ~ República de Guinea.

guinea ['gɪnɪ] n (BRIT: old) guinea (= 21 chelines: en la actualidad ya no se usa esta moneda).

guinea pig n cobaya; (fig) conejillo de Indias.

guise [gaɪz] n: **in** or **under the** ~ **of** bajo la apariencia de.

guitar [gɪ'tɑ:*] n guitarra.

guitarist [gɪ'tɑːrɪst] n guitarrista m/f.

gulch [gʌltʃ] n (US) barranco.

gulf [gʌlf] n golfo; (abyss) abismo; **the G**~ el Golfo (Pérsico).

Gulf States npl: **the** ~ los países del Golfo.

Gulf Stream n: **the** ~ la Corriente del Golfo.

gull [gʌl] n gaviota.

gullet ['gʌlɪt] n esófago.

gullibility [gʌlɪ'bɪlɪtɪ] n credulidad f.

gullible ['gʌlɪbl] adj crédulo.

gully ['gʌlɪ] n barranco.

gulp [gʌlp] vi tragar saliva ♦ vt (also: ~ **down**) tragarse ♦ n (of liquid) trago; (of food) bocado; **in** or **at one** ~ de un trago.

gum [gʌm] n (ANAT) encía; (glue) goma, cemento (LAM); (sweet) gominola; (also: **chewing-**~) chicle m ♦ vt pegar con goma.

▶**gum up** vt: **to** ~ **up the works** (col) entorpecerlo todo.

gumboots ['gʌmbuːts] npl (BRIT) botas fpl de goma.

gum tree n árbol m gomero.

gun [gʌn] n (small) pistola; (shotgun) escopeta; (rifle) fusil m; (cannon) cañón m ♦ vt (also: ~ **down**) abatir a tiros; **to stick to one's** ~**s** (fig) mantenerse firme or en sus trece.

gunboat ['gʌnbəut] n cañonero.

gun dog n perro de caza.

gunfire ['gʌnfaɪə*] n disparos mpl.

gung-ho [gʌŋ'həu] adj (col) patriotero.

gunk [gʌŋk] n (col) masa viscosa.

gunman ['gʌnmən] n pistolero.

gunner ['gʌnə*] n artillero.

gunpoint ['gʌnpɔɪnt] n: **at** ~ a mano armada.

gunpowder ['gʌnpaudə*] n pólvora.

gunrunning ['gʌnrʌnɪŋ] n tráfico de armas.

gunshot ['gʌnʃɔt] n disparo.

gunsmith ['gʌnsmɪθ] n armero.

gurgle ['gəːgl] vi gorgotear.

guru ['guːruː] n guru m.

gush [gʌʃ] vi chorrear; (fig) deshacerse en efusiones.

gushing ['gʌʃɪŋ] adj efusivo.

gusset ['gʌsɪt] n (in tights, pants) escudete

m.

gust [gʌst] n (of wind) ráfaga.

gusto ['gʌstəu] n entusiasmo.

gusty ['gʌstɪ] adj racheado.

gut [gʌt] n intestino; (MUS etc) cuerda de tripa ♦ vt (poultry, fish) destripar; (building): **the blaze** ~**ted the entire building** el fuego destruyó el edificio entero.

gut reaction n reacción f instintiva.

guts [gʌts] npl (courage) agallas fpl, valor m; (col: innards: of people, animals) tripas fpl; **to hate sb's** ~ odiar a algn (a muerte).

gutsy ['gʌtsɪ] adj: **to be** ~ (col) tener agallas.

gutted ['gʌtɪd] adj (col: disappointed): **I was** ~ me quedé hecho polvo.

gutter ['gʌtə*] n (of roof) canalón m; (in street) cuneta; **the** ~ (fig) el arroyo.

gutter press n (col): **the** ~ la prensa sensacionalista or amarilla; see also **tabloid press**.

guttural ['gʌtərl] adj gutural.

guy [gaɪ] n (also: ~**rope**) viento, cuerda; (col: man) tío (SP), tipo.

Guyana [gaɪ'ænə] n Guayana.

Guy Fawkes' Night [gaɪ'fɔːks-] n ver recuadro.

GUY FAWKES' NIGHT

La noche del cinco de noviembre, **Guy Fawkes' Night**, se celebra el fracaso de la conspiración de la pólvora ("Gunpowder Plot"), el intento fallido de volar el parlamento de Jaime 1 en 1605. Esa noche se lanzan fuegos artificiales y se queman en muchas hogueras muñecos de trapo que representan a "Guy Fawkes", uno de los cabecillas. Días antes los niños tienen por costumbre pedir a los viandantes "a penny for the guy", dinero para comprar los cohetes.

---

guzzle ['gʌzl] vi tragar ♦ vt engullir.

gym [dʒɪm] n (also: **gymnasium**) gimnasio; (also: **gymnastics**) gimnasia.

gymkhana [dʒɪm'kɑːnə] n gincana.

gymnast ['dʒɪmnæst] n gimnasta m/f.

gymnastics [dʒɪm'næstɪks] n gimnasia.

gym shoes npl zapatillas fpl de gimnasia.

gym slip n (BRIT) pichi m.

gynaecologist, (US) **gynecologist** [gaɪnɪ'kɔlədʒɪst] n ginecólogo/a.

gynaecology, (US) **gynecology** [gaɪnə'kɔlədʒɪ] n ginecología.

gypsy ['dʒɪpsɪ] n = **gipsy**.

gyrate [dʒaɪ'reɪt] vi girar.

gyroscope ['dʒaɪrəskəup] n giroscopio.

H h

H, h [eɪtʃ] n (letter) H, h f; **H for Harry,** (US) **H for How** H de Historia.
habeas corpus ['heɪbɪəs'kɔːpəs] n (LAW) hábeas corpus m.
haberdashery ['hæbə'dæʃərɪ] n (BRIT) mercería; (US: men's clothing) prendas fpl de caballero.
habit ['hæbɪt] n hábito, costumbre f; **to get out of/into the ~ of doing sth** perder la costumbre de/acostumbrarse a hacer algo.
habitable ['hæbɪtəbl] adj habitable.
habitat ['hæbɪtæt] n hábitat m.
habitation [hæbɪ'teɪʃən] n habitación f.
habitual [hə'bɪtjuəl] adj acostumbrado, habitual; (drinker, liar) empedernido.
habitually [hə'bɪtjuəlɪ] adv por costumbre.
hack [hæk] vt (cut) cortar; (slice) tajar ♦ n corte m; (axe blow) hachazo; (pej: writer) escritor(a) m/f a sueldo; (old horse) jamelgo.
hacker ['hækə*] n (COMPUT) pirata m informático.
hackles ['hæklz] npl: **to make sb's ~ rise** (fig) poner furioso a algn.
hackney cab ['hæknɪ-] n coche m de alquiler.
hackneyed ['hæknɪd] adj trillado, gastado.
hacksaw ['hæksɔː] n sierra para metales.
had [hæd] pt, pp of **have**.
haddock, pl **~** or **~s** ['hædək] n especie de merluza.
hadn't ['hædnt] = **had not**.
haematology, (US) **hematology** ['hiːmə'tɔlədʒɪ] n hematología.
haemoglobin, (US) **hemoglobin** ['hiːmə'gləubɪn] n hemoglobina.
haemophilia, (US) **hemophilia** ['hiːmə'fɪlɪə] n hemofilia.
haemorrhage, (US) **hemorrhage** ['hɛmərɪdʒ] n hemorragia.
haemorrhoids, (US) **hemorrhoids** ['hɛmərɔɪdz] npl hemorroides fpl, almorranas fpl.
hag [hæg] n (ugly) vieja fea, tarasca; (nasty) bruja; (witch) hechicera.
haggard ['hægəd] adj ojeroso.

haggis ['hægɪs] n (Scottish) asadura de cordero cocida; see also **Burns' Night**.
haggle ['hægl] vi (argue) discutir; (bargain) regatear.
haggling ['hæglɪŋ] n regateo.
Hague [heɪg] n: **The ~** La Haya.
hail [heɪl] n (weather) granizo ♦ vt saludar; (call) llamar a ♦ vi granizar; **to ~ (as)** aclamar (como), celebrar (como); **he ~s from Scotland** es natural de Escocia.
hailstone ['heɪlstəun] n (piedra de) granizo.
hailstorm ['heɪlstɔːm] n granizada.
hair [hɛə*] n (gen) pelo, cabellos mpl; (one ~) pelo, cabello; (head of ~) pelo, cabellera; (on legs etc) vello; **to do one's ~** arreglarse el pelo; **grey ~** canas fpl.
hairbrush ['hɛəbrʌʃ] n cepillo (para el pelo).
haircut ['hɛəkʌt] n corte m de pelo.
hairdo ['hɛəduː] n peinado.
hairdresser ['hɛədrɛsə*] n peluquero/a; **~'s** peluquería.
hair-dryer ['hɛədraɪə*] n secador m (de pelo).
-haired [hɛəd] adj suff: **fair/long~** (de pelo) rubio or güero (LAM)/de pelo largo.
hairgrip ['hɛəgrɪp] n horquilla.
hairline ['hɛəlaɪn] n nacimiento del pelo.
hairline fracture n fractura muy fina.
hairnet ['hɛənɛt] n redecilla.
hair oil n brillantina.
hairpiece ['hɛəpiːs] n trenza postiza.
hairpin ['hɛəpɪn] n horquilla.
hairpin bend, (US) **hairpin curve** n curva muy cerrada.
hair-raising ['hɛəreɪzɪŋ] adj espeluznante.
hair remover n depilatorio.
hair's breadth n: **by a ~** por un pelo.
hair spray n laca.
hairstyle ['hɛəstaɪl] n peinado.
hairy ['hɛərɪ] adj peludo, velludo.
Haiti ['heɪtɪ] n Haití m.
hake [heɪk] n merluza.
halcyon ['hælsɪən] adj feliz.
hale [heɪl] adj: **~ and hearty** sano y fuerte.
half [hɑːf] n (pl halves [hɑːvz]) mitad f; (SPORT: of match) tiempo, parte f; (: of ground) campo ♦ adj medio ♦ adv medio, a medias; **~-an-hour** media hora; **two and a ~** dos y media; **~ a dozen** media docena; **~ a pound** media libra, ≈ 250 gr.; **to cut sth in ~** cortar algo por la mitad; **to go halves (with sb)** ir a medias (con algn); **~empty/closed** medio vacío/ entreabierto; **~ asleep** medio dormido; **~ past 3** las 3 y media.
half-back ['hɑːfbæk] n (SPORT) medio.
half-baked ['hɑːf'beɪkt] adj (col: idea,

scheme) mal concebido *or* pensado.

half-breed ['hɑːfbriːd] *n* = **half-caste**.

half-brother ['hɑːfbrʌðə*] *n* hermanastro.

half-caste ['hɑːfkɑːst] *n* mestizo/a.

half-hearted ['hɑːf'hɑːtɪd] *adj* indiferente, poco entusiasta.

half-hour [hɑːf'auə*] *n* media hora.

half-mast ['hɑːf'mɑːst] *n*: **at** ~ (*flag*) a media asta.

halfpenny ['heɪpnɪ] *n* medio penique *m*.

half-price ['hɑːf'praɪs] *adj* a mitad de precio.

half term *n* (*BRIT SCOL*) *vacaciones de mediados del trimestre*.

half-time [hɑːf'taɪm] *n* descanso.

halfway ['hɑːf'weɪ] *adv* a medio camino, to **meet sb** ~ (*fig*) llegar a un acuerdo con algn.

halfway house *n centro de readaptación de antiguos presos*; (*fig*) solución *f* intermedia.

half-wit ['hɑːfwɪt] *n* (*col*) zoquete *m*.

half-yearly [hɑːf'jɪəlɪ] *adv* semestralmente ♦ *adj* semestral.

halibut ['hælɪbət] *n*, *pl inv* halibut *m*.

halitosis [hælɪ'təusɪs] *n* halitosis *f*.

hall [hɔːl] *n* (*for concerts*) sala; (*entrance way*) entrada, vestíbulo.

hallmark ['hɔːlmɑːk] *n* (*mark*) rasgo distintivo; (*seal*) sello.

hallo [hə'ləu] *excl* = **hello**.

hall of residence *n* (*BRIT*) colegio mayor, residencia universitaria.

Hallowe'en [hæləu'iːn] *n* víspera de Todos los Santos; *ver recuadro*.

HALLOWE'EN

La tradición anglosajona dice que en la noche del 31 de octubre, **Hallowe'en**, *víspera de Todos los Santos, es fácil ver a brujas y fantasmas. Es una ocasión festiva en la que los niños se disfrazan y van de puerta en puerta llevando un farol hecho con una calabaza en forma de cabeza humana. Cuando se les abre la puerta gritan "trick or treat" para indicar que gastarán una broma a quien no les dé un pequeño regalo (como golosinas o dinero).*

---

hallucination [həluːsɪ'neɪʃən] *n* alucinación *f*.

hallway ['hɔːlweɪ] *n* vestíbulo.

halo ['heɪləu] *n* (*of saint*) aureola.

halt [hɔːlt] *n* (*stop*) alto, parada; (*RAIL*) apeadero ♦ *vt* parar ♦ *vi* pararse; (*process*) interrumpirse; **to call a** ~ (**to sth**) (*fig*) poner fin (a algo).

halter ['hɔːltə*] *n* (*for horse*) cabestro.

halterneck ['hɔːltənɛk] *adj* de espalda escotada.

halve [hɑːv] *vt* partir por la mitad.

halves [hɑːvz] *pl of* **half**.

ham [hæm] *n* jamón *m* (cocido); (*col: also*: **radio** ~) radioaficionado/a *m/f*; (: *also*: ~ **actor**) comicastro.

hamburger ['hæmbəːgə*] *n* hamburguesa.

ham-fisted ['hæm'fɪstɪd] *adj* torpe, desmañado.

hamlet ['hæmlɪt] *n* aldea.

hammer ['hæmə*] *n* martillo ♦ *vt* (*nail*) clavar; **to** ~ **a point home to sb** remacharle un punto a algn.

►**hammer out** *vt* (*metal*) forjar a martillo; (*fig: solution, agreement*) elaborar (trabajosamente).

hammock ['hæmək] *n* hamaca.

hamper ['hæmpə*] *vt* estorbar ♦ *n* cesto.

hamster ['hæmstə*] *n* hámster *m*.

hand [hænd] *n* mano *f*; (*of clock*) aguja, manecilla; (*writing*) letra; (*worker*) obrero; (*measurement of horse*) palmo ♦ *vt* (*give*) dar, pasar; (*deliver*) entregar; **to give sb a** ~ echar una mano a algn, ayudar a algn; **to force sb's** ~ forzarle la mano a algn; **at** ~ a mano; **in** ~ entre manos; **we have the matter in** ~ tenemos el asunto entre manos; **to have in one's** ~ (*knife, victory*) tener en la mano; **to have a free** ~ tener carta blanca; **on** ~ (*person, services*) a mano, al alcance; **to** ~ (*information etc*) a mano; **on the one** ~ ..., **on the other** ~ ... por una parte ... por otra (parte) ....

►**hand down** *vt* pasar, bajar; (*tradition*) transmitir; (*heirloom*) dejar en herencia; (*US: sentence, verdict*) imponer.

►**hand in** *vt* entregar.

►**hand out** *vt* (*leaflets, advice*) repartir, distribuir.

►**hand over** *vt* (*deliver*) entregar; (*surrender*) ceder.

►**hand round** *vt* (*BRIT: information, papers*) pasar (de mano en mano); (: *chocolates etc*) ofrecer.

handbag ['hændbæg] *n* bolso, cartera (*LAM*).

hand baggage *n* = **hand luggage**.

handball ['hændbɔːl] *n* balonmano.

handbasin ['hændbeɪsn] *n* lavabo.

handbook ['hændbuk] *n* manual *m*.

handbrake ['hændbreɪk] *n* freno de mano.

hand cream *n* crema para las manos.

handcuffs ['hændkʌfs] *npl* esposas *fpl*.

handful ['hændful] *n* puñado.

hand-held ['hænd'hɛld] *adj* de mano.

handicap ['hændɪkæp] *n* desventaja;

(SPORT) hándicap m ♦ vt estorbar.

handicapped ['hændɪkæpt] adj: **to be mentally** ~ ser deficiente m/f mental; **to be physically** ~ ser minusválido/a.

handicraft ['hændɪkrɑːft] n artesanía.

handiwork ['hændɪwɔːk] n manualidad(es) f(pl); (fig) obra; **this looks like his** ~ (pej) es obra de él, parece.

handkerchief ['hæŋkətʃɪf] n pañuelo.

handle ['hændl] n (of door etc) pomo; (of cup etc) asa; (of knife etc) mango; (for winding) manivela ♦ vt (touch) tocar; (deal with) encargarse de; (treat: people) manejar; "~ **with care**" "(manéjese) con cuidado"; **to fly off the** ~ perder los estribos.

handlebar(s) ['hændlbɑː(z)] n(pl) manillar msg.

handling ['hændlɪŋ] n (AUT) conducción f; **his** ~ **of the matter** su forma de llevar el asunto.

handling charges npl gastos mpl de tramitación.

hand luggage n equipaje m de mano.

handmade ['hændmeɪd] adj hecho a mano.

handout ['hændaut] n (distribution) repartición f; (charity) limosna; (leaflet) folleto, octavilla; (press ~) nota.

hand-picked ['hænd'pɪkt] adj (produce) escogido a mano; (staff etc) seleccionado cuidadosamente.

handrail ['hændreɪl] n (on staircase etc) pasamanos m inv, barandilla.

handset ['hændset] n (TEL) auricular m.

handshake ['hændʃeɪk] n apretón m de manos; (COMPUT) coloquio.

handsome ['hænsəm] adj guapo.

hands-on ['hændz'ɔn] adj práctico; **she has a very** ~ **approach** le gusta tomar parte activa; ~ **experience** (COMPUT) experiencia práctica.

handstand ['hændstænd] n voltereta, salto mortal.

hand-to-mouth ['hændtə'mauθ] adj (existence) precario.

handwriting ['hændraɪtɪŋ] n letra.

handwritten ['hændrɪtn] adj escrito a mano, manuscrito.

handy ['hændɪ] adj (close at hand) a mano; (useful: machine, tool etc) práctico; (skilful) hábil, diestro; **to come in** ~ venir bien.

handyman ['hændɪmæn] n manitas m inv.

hang, pt, pp **hung** [hæŋ, hʌŋ] vt colgar; (head) bajar; (criminal: pt, pp **hanged**) ahorcar; **to get the** ~ **of sth** (col) coger el tranquillo a algo.

▶**hang about** vi haraganear.

▶**hang back** vi (hesitate): **to** ~ **back (from doing)** vacilar (en hacer).

▶**hang on** vi (wait) esperar ♦ vt fus (depend on: decision etc) depender de; **to** ~ **on to** (keep hold of) agarrarse or aferrarse a; (keep) guardar, quedarse con.

▶**hang out** vt (washing) tender, colgar ♦ vi (col: live) vivir; (: often be found) moverse; **to** ~ **out of sth** colgar fuera de algo.

▶**hang together** vi (cohere: argument etc) sostenerse.

▶**hang up** vt (coat) colgar ♦ vi (TEL) colgar; **to** ~ **up on sb** colgarle a algn.

hangar ['hæŋə*] n hangar m.

hangdog ['hæŋdɔg] adj (guilty: look, expression) avergonzado.

hanger ['hæŋə*] n percha.

hanger-on [hæŋər'ɔn] n parásito.

hang-glider ['hæŋglaɪdə*] n ala delta.

hang-gliding ['hæŋglaɪdɪŋ] n vuelo con ala delta.

hanging ['hæŋɪŋ] n (execution) ejecución f (en la horca).

hangman ['hæŋmən] n verdugo.

hangover ['hæŋəuvə*] n (after drinking) resaca.

hang-up ['hæŋʌp] n complejo.

hanker ['hæŋkə*] vi: **to** ~ **after** (miss) echar de menos; (long for) añorar.

hankie, hanky ['hæŋkɪ] n abbr = **handkerchief**.

Hansard ['hænsɑːd] n actas oficiales de las sesiones del parlamento británico.

Hants abbr (BRIT) = Hampshire.

haphazard [hæp'hæzəd] adj fortuito.

hapless ['hæplɪs] adj desventurado.

happen ['hæpən] vi suceder, ocurrir; (take place) tener lugar, realizarse; **as it** ~**s** da la casualidad de que; **what's** ~**ing?** ¿qué pasa?

▶**happen (up)on** vt fus tropezar or dar con.

happening ['hæpnɪŋ] n suceso, acontecimiento.

happily ['hæpɪlɪ] adv (luckily) afortunadamente; (cheerfully) alegremente.

happiness ['hæpɪnɪs] n (contentment) felicidad f; (joy) alegría.

happy ['hæpɪ] adj feliz; (cheerful) alegre; **to be** ~ **(with)** estar contento (con); **yes, I'd be** ~ **to** sí, con mucho gusto; **H**~ **Christmas/New Year!** ¡Feliz Navidad!/ ¡Feliz Año Nuevo!; ~ **birthday!** ¡felicidades!, ¡feliz cumpleaños!

happy-go-lucky ['hæpɪgəu'lʌkɪ] adj despreocupado.

happy hour n horas en las que la bebida es más barata en un bar.

harangue [hə'ræŋ] vt arengar.

harass ['hærəs] *vt* acosar, hostigar.
harassed ['hærəst] *adj* agobiado,
presionado.
harassment ['hærəsmənt] *n* persecución *f*,
acoso; (*worry*) preocupación *f*.
harbour, (*US*) **harbor** ['hɑːbə*] *n* puerto
♦ *vt* (*hope etc*) abrigar; (*hide*) dar abrigo a;
(*retain: grudge etc*) guardar.
harbo(u)r dues *npl* derechos *mpl*
portuarios.
hard [hɑːd] *adj* duro; (*difficult*) difícil;
(*person*) severo ♦ *adv* (*work*) mucho, duro;
(*think*) profundamente; **to look ~ at sb/
sth** clavar los ojos en algn/algo; **to try ~**
esforzarse; **no ~ feelings!** ¡sin
rencor(es)!; **to be ~ of hearing** ser duro
de oído; **to be ~ done by** ser tratado
injustamente; **to be ~ on sb** ser muy
duro con algn; **I find it ~ to believe that ...**
me cuesta trabajo creer que ....
hard-and-fast ['hɑːdən'fɑːst] *adj* rígido,
definitivo.
hardback ['hɑːdbæk] *n* libro de tapas
duras.
hard cash *n* dinero en efectivo.
hard copy *n* (*COMPUT*) copia impresa.
hard-core ['hɑːd'kɔː*] *adj* (*pornography*)
duro; (*supporters*) incondicional.
hard court *n* (*TENNIS*) pista *or* cancha (de
tenis) de cemento.
hard disk *n* (*COMPUT*) disco duro.
harden ['hɑːdn] *vt* endurecer; (*steel*)
templar; (*fig*) curtir; (: *determination*)
fortalecer ♦ *vi* (*substance*) endurecerse.
hardened ['hɑːdnd] *adj* (*criminal*) habitual;
to be ~ to sth estar acostumbrado a algo.
hard-headed ['hɑːd'hedɪd] *adj* poco
sentimental, realista.
hard-hearted ['hɑːd'hɑːtɪd] *adj* insensible.
hard-hitting ['hɑːd'hɪtɪŋ] *adj* (*speech,
article*) contundente.
hard labour *n* trabajos *mpl* forzados.
hardliner [hɑːd'laɪnə*] *n* partidario/a de la
línea dura.
hard-luck story ['hɑːdlʌk-] *n* dramón *m*.
hardly ['hɑːdlɪ] *adv* (*scarcely*) apenas; **that
can ~ be true** eso difícilmente puede ser
cierto; **~ ever** casi nunca; **I can ~ believe
it** apenas me lo puedo creer.
hardness ['hɑːdnɪs] *n* dureza.
hard-nosed ['hɑːd'nəuzd] *adj* duro, sin
contemplaciones.
hard-pressed ['hɑːd'prest] *adj* en apuros.
hard sell *n* publicidad *f* agresiva; **~
techniques** técnicas *fpl* agresivas de
venta.
hardship ['hɑːdʃɪp] *n* (*troubles*) penas *fpl*;
(*financial*) apuro.

hard shoulder *n* (*AUT*) arcén *m*.
hard-up [hɑːd'ʌp] *adj* (*col*) sin un duro (*SP*)
or plata (*LAM*).
hardware ['hɑːdwɛə*] *n* ferretería;
(*COMPUT*) hardware *m*.
hardware shop *n* ferretería.
hard-wearing [hɑːd'wɛərɪŋ] *adj* resistente,
duradero; (*shoes*) resistente.
hard-won ['hɑːd'wʌn] *adj* ganado con
esfuerzo.
hard-working [hɑːd'wɜːkɪŋ] *adj*
trabajador(a).
hardy ['hɑːdɪ] *adj* fuerte; (*plant*) resistente.
hare [hɛə*] *n* liebre *f*.
hare-brained ['hɛəbreɪnd] *adj* atolondrado.
harelip ['hɛəlɪp] *n* labio leporino.
harem [hɑː'riːm] *n* harén *m*.
haricot (bean) ['hærɪkəu-] *n* alubia.
hark back [hɑːk-] *vi*: **to ~ back to** (*former
days, earlier occasion*) recordar.
harm [hɑːm] *n* daño, mal *m* ♦ *vt* (*person*)
hacer daño a; (*health, interests*)
perjudicar; (*thing*) dañar; **out of ~'s way**
a salvo; **there's no ~ in trying** no se
pierde nada con intentar.
harmful ['hɑːmful] *adj* (*gen*) dañino;
(*reputation*) perjudicial.
harmless ['hɑːmlɪs] *adj* (*person*) inofensivo;
(*drugs*) inocuo.
harmonica [hɑː'mɔnɪkə] *n* armónica.
harmonious [hɑː'məunɪəs] *adj* armonioso.
harmonize ['hɑːmənaɪz] *vt*, *vi* armonizar.
harmony ['hɑːmənɪ] *n* armonía.
harness ['hɑːnɪs] *n* arreos *mpl* ♦ *vt* (*horse*)
enjaezar; (*resources*) aprovechar.
harp [hɑːp] *n* arpa ♦ *vi*: **to ~ on (about)**
machacar (con).
harpoon [hɑː'puːn] *n* arpón *m*.
harrow ['hærəu] *n* grada ♦ *vt* gradar.
harrowing ['hærəuɪŋ] *adj* angustioso.
harry ['hærɪ] *vt* (*MIL*) acosar; (*person*)
hostigar.
harsh [hɑːʃ] *adj* (*cruel*) duro, cruel; (*severe*)
severo; (*words*) hosco; (*colour*) chillón/
ona; (*contrast*) violento.
harshly ['hɑːʃlɪ] *adv* (*say*) con aspereza;
(*treat*) con mucha dureza.
harshness ['hɑːʃnɪs] *n* dureza.
harvest ['hɑːvɪst] *n* cosecha; (*of grapes*)
vendimia ♦ *vt*, *vi* cosechar.
harvester ['hɑːvɪstə*] *n* (*machine*)
cosechadora; (*person*) segador(a) *m/f*;
combine ~ segadora trilladora.
has [hæz] *vb see* **have**.
has-been ['hæzbiːn] *n* (*col: person*) persona
acabada; (: *thing*) vieja gloria.
hash [hæʃ] *n* (*CULIN*) picadillo; (*fig: mess*)
lío.

hashish ['hæʃɪʃ] n hachís m.
hasn't ['hæznt] = **has not.**
hassle ['hæsl] n (col) lío, rollo ♦ vt incordiar.
haste [heɪst] n prisa.
hasten ['heɪsn] vt acelerar ♦ vi darse prisa; I ~ **to add that...** me apresuro a añadir que ....
hastily ['heɪstɪlɪ] adv de prisa.
hasty ['heɪstɪ] adj apresurado.
hat [hæt] n sombrero.
hatbox ['hætbɔks] n sombrerera.
hatch [hætʃ] n (NAUT: also: ~**way**) escotilla ♦ vi salir del cascarón ♦ vt incubar; (fig: scheme, plot) idear, tramar.
hatchback ['hætʃbæk] n (AUT) tres or cinco puertas m.
hatchet ['hætʃɪt] n hacha.
hatchet job n (col) varapalo.
hatchet man n (col) ejecutor m de faenas desagradables por cuenta de otro.
hate [heɪt] vt odiar, aborrecer ♦ n odio; I ~ **to trouble you, but ...** siento or lamento molestarle, pero ....
hateful ['heɪtful] adj odioso.
hatred ['heɪtrɪd] n odio.
hat trick n: **to score a** ~ (BRIT SPORT) marcar tres tantos (or triunfos) seguidos.
haughtily ['hɔːtɪlɪ] adv con arrogancia.
haughty ['hɔːtɪ] adj altanero, arrogante.
haul [hɔːl] vt tirar, jalar (LAM); (by lorry) transportar ♦ n (of fish) redada; (of stolen goods etc) botín m.
haulage ['hɔːlɪdʒ] n (BRIT) transporte m; (costs) gastos mpl de transporte.
haulage contractor n (firm) empresa de transportes; (person) transportista m/f.
haulier ['hɔːlɪə*], (US) **hauler** ['hɔːlə*] n transportista m/f.
haunch [hɔːntʃ] n anca; (of meat) pierna.
haunt [hɔːnt] vt (subj: ghost) aparecer en; (frequent) frecuentar; (obsess) obsesionar ♦ n guarida.
haunted ['hɔːntɪd] adj (castle etc) embrujado; (look) de angustia.
haunting ['hɔːntɪŋ] adj (sight, music) evocativo.
Havana [hə'vɑːnə] n La Habana.

━━━━━━━━━━━━━━ KEYWORD

have [hæv] (pt, pp **had**) aux vb **1** (gen) haber; **to** ~ **arrived/eaten** haber llegado/comido; **having finished** or **when he had finished, he left** cuando hubo acabado, se fue

2 (in tag questions): **you've done it,** ~**n't you?** lo has hecho, ¿verdad? or ¿no?
3 (in short answers and questions): **I** ~**n't** no; **so I** ~ pues, es verdad; **we** ~**n't paid** — **yes we** ~**!** no hemos pagado — ¡sí que hemos pagado!; **I've been there before,** ~ **you?** he estado allí antes, ¿y tú?
♦ modal aux vb (be obliged): **to** ~ (**got**) **to do sth** tener que hacer algo; **you** ~**n't to tell her** no hay que or no debes decírselo
♦ vt **1** (possess) tener; **he has (got) blue eyes/dark hair** tiene los ojos azules/el pelo negro
2 (referring to meals etc): **to** ~ **breakfast/lunch/dinner** desayunar/comer/cenar; **to** ~ **a drink/a cigarette** tomar algo/fumar un cigarrillo
3 (receive) recibir; (obtain) obtener; **may I** ~ **your address?** ¿puedes darme tu dirección?; **you can** ~ **it for £5** te lo puedes quedar por £5; **I must** ~ **it by tomorrow** lo necesito para mañana; **to** ~ **a baby** tener un niño or bebé
4 (maintain, allow): **I won't** ~ **it/this nonsense!** ¡no lo permitiré!/¡no permitiré estas tonterías!; **we can't** ~ **that** no podemos permitir eso
5: **to** ~ **sth done** hacer or mandar hacer algo; **to** ~ **one's hair cut** cortarse el pelo; **to** ~ **sb do sth** hacer que algn haga algo
6 (experience, suffer): **to** ~ **a cold/flu** tener un resfriado/la gripe; **she had her bag stolen/her arm broken** le robaron el bolso/se rompió un brazo; **to** ~ **an operation** operarse
7 (+noun): **to** ~ **a swim/walk/bath/rest** nadar/dar un paseo/darse un baño/descansar; **let's** ~ **a look** vamos a ver; **to** ~ **a meeting/party** celebrar una reunión/una fiesta; **let me** ~ **a try** déjame intentarlo
▶**have in** vt: **to** ~ **it in for sb** (col) tenerla tomada con algn
▶**have on** vt: ~ **you anything on tomorrow?** ¿vas a hacer algo mañana?; **I don't** ~ **any money on me** no llevo dinero (encima); **to** ~ **sb on** (BRIT col) tomarle el pelo a algn
▶**have out** vt: **to** ~ **it out with sb** (settle a problem etc) dejar las cosas en claro con algn.

haven ['heɪvn] n puerto; (fig) refugio.
haven't ['hævnt] = **have not.**
haversack ['hævəsæk] n macuto.
haves [hævz] npl: **the** ~ **and the have-nots** los ricos y los pobres.
havoc ['hævək] n estragos mpl; **to play** ~

with sth hacer estragos en algo.
Hawaii [hə'waɪiː] n (Islas fpl) Hawai m.
Hawaiian [hə'waɪjən] adj, n hawaiano/a m/f.
hawk [hɔːk] n halcón m ♦ vt (goods for sale) pregonar.
hawkish ['hɔːkɪʃ] adj beligerante.
hawthorn ['hɔːθɔːn] n espino.
hay [heɪ] n heno.
hay fever n fiebre f del heno.
haystack ['heɪstæk] n almiar m.
haywire ['heɪwaɪə*] adj (col): **to go ~** (person) volverse loco; (plan) irse al garete.
hazard ['hæzəd] n riesgo; (danger) peligro ♦ vt (remark) aventurar; (one's life) arriesgar; **to be a health ~** ser un peligro para la salud; **to ~ a guess** aventurar una respuesta or hipótesis.
hazardous ['hæzədəs] adj (dangerous) peligroso; (risky) arriesgado.
hazard warning lights npl (AUT) señales fpl de emergencia.
haze [heɪz] n neblina.
hazel ['heɪzl] n (tree) avellano ♦ adj (eyes) color m de avellano.
hazelnut ['heɪzlnʌt] n avellana.
hazy ['heɪzɪ] adj brumoso; (idea) vago.
H-bomb ['eɪtʃbɒm] n bomba H.
h & c abbr (BRIT) = hot and cold (water).
HE abbr = **high explosive**; (REL, DIPLOMACY: = His (or Her) Excellency) S. Excª.
he [hiː] pron él; **~ who...** aquél que..., quien....
head [hɛd] n cabeza; (leader) jefe/a m/f; (COMPUT) cabeza (grabadora) ♦ vt (list) encabezar; (group) capitanear; **~s (or tails)** cara (o cruz); **~ first** de cabeza; **~ over heels** patas arriba; **~ over heels in love** perdidamente enamorado; **on your ~ be it!** ¡allá tú!; **they went over my ~ to the manager** fueron directamente al gerente sin hacerme caso; **it was above** or **over their ~s** no alcanzaron a entenderlo; **to come to a ~** (fig: situation etc) llegar a un punto crítico; **to have a ~ for business** tener talento para los negocios; **to have no ~ for heights** no resistir las alturas; **to lose/keep one's ~** perder la cabeza/mantener la calma; **to sit at the ~ of the table** sentarse a la cabecera de la mesa; **to ~ the ball** cabecear (el balón).
► **head for** vt fus dirigirse a.
► **head off** vt (threat, danger) evitar.
headache ['hɛdeɪk] n dolor m de cabeza; **to have a ~** tener dolor de cabeza.
headband ['hɛdbænd] n cinta (para la cabeza), vincha (LAM).

headboard ['hɛdbɔːd] n cabecera.
headdress ['hɛddrɛs] n (of bride, Indian) tocado.
headed notepaper ['hɛdɪd-] n papel m con membrete.
header ['hɛdə*] n (BRIT col: FOOTBALL) cabezazo; (: fall) caída de cabeza.
headfirst [hɛd'fɜːst] adv de cabeza.
headhunt ['hɛdhʌnt] vt: **to be ~ed** ser seleccionado por un cazatalentos.
headhunter ['hɛdhʌntə*] n (fig) cazaejecutivos m inv.
heading ['hɛdɪŋ] n título.
headlamp ['hɛdlæmp] n (BRIT) = **headlight**.
headland ['hɛdlənd] n promontorio.
headlight ['hɛdlaɪt] n faro.
headline ['hɛdlaɪn] n titular m.
headlong ['hɛdlɒŋ] adv (fall) de cabeza; (rush) precipitadamente.
headmaster/mistress [hɛd'mɑːstə*/mɪstrɪs] n director(a) m/f (de escuela).
head office n oficina central, central f.
head-on [hɛd'ɒn] adj (collision) de frente.
headphones ['hɛdfəʊnz] npl auriculares mpl.
headquarters (HQ) ['hɛdkwɔːtəz] npl sede f central; (MIL) cuartel m general.
head-rest ['hɛdrɛst] n reposa-cabezas m inv.
headroom ['hɛdrum] n (in car) altura interior; (under bridge) (límite m de) altura.
headscarf ['hɛdskɑːf] n pañuelo.
headset ['hɛdsɛt] n cascos mpl.
headstone ['hɛdstəʊn] n lápida.
headstrong ['hɛdstrɒŋ] adj testarudo.
head waiter n maître m.
headway ['hɛdweɪ] n: **to make ~** (fig) hacer progresos.
headwind ['hɛdwɪnd] n viento contrario.
heady ['hɛdɪ] adj (experience, period) apasionante; (wine) fuerte.
heal [hiːl] vt curar ♦ vi cicatrizar.
health [hɛlθ] n salud f.
health care n asistencia sanitaria.
health centre n ambulatorio, centro médico.
health food(s) n(pl) alimentos mpl orgánicos.
health hazard n riesgo para la salud.
Health Service n (BRIT) servicio de salud pública, ≈ Insalud m (SP).
healthy ['hɛlθɪ] adj (gen) sano; (economy, bank balance) saludable.
heap [hiːp] n montón m ♦ vt amontonar; (plate) colmar; **~s (of)** (col: lots) montones (de); **to ~ favours/praise/gifts** etc **on sb** colmar a algn de favores/elogios/regalos etc.

hear, *pt, pp* **heard** [hɪə*, hɔːd] *vt* oír; (*perceive*) sentir; (*listen to*) escuchar; (*lecture*) asistir a; (*LAW: case*) ver ♦ *vi* oír; **to ~ about** oír hablar de; **to ~ from sb** tener noticias de alguien; **I've never heard of that book** nunca he oído hablar de ese libro.

►**hear out** *vt*: **to ~ sb out** dejar que algn termine de hablar.

hearing ['hɪərɪŋ] *n* (*sense*) oído; (*LAW*) vista; **to give sb a ~** dar a algn la oportunidad de hablar, escuchar a algn.

hearing aid *n* audífono.

hearsay ['hɪəseɪ] *n* rumores *mpl*, habladurías *fpl*.

hearse [hɔːs] *n* coche *m* fúnebre.

heart [hɑːt] *n* corazón *m*; **~s** *npl* (*CARDS*) corazones *mpl*; **at ~** en el fondo; **by ~** (*learn, know*) de memoria; **to have a weak ~** tener el corazón débil; **to set one's ~ on sth/on doing sth** anhelar algo/hacer algo; **I did not have the ~ to tell her** no tuve valor para decírselo; **to take ~** cobrar ánimos; **the ~ of the matter** lo esencial *or* el meollo del asunto.

heartache ['hɑːteɪk] *n* angustia.

heart attack *n* infarto (de miocardio).

heartbeat ['hɑːtbiːt] *n* latido (del corazón).

heartbreak ['hɑːtbreɪk] *n* angustia, congoja.

heartbreaking ['hɑːtbreɪkɪŋ] *adj* desgarrador(a).

heartbroken ['hɑːtbrəukən] *adj*: **she was ~ about it** le partió el corazón.

heartburn ['hɑːtbɔːn] *n* acedía.

-hearted ['hɑːtɪd] *adj suff*: **a kind~ person** una persona bondadosa.

heartening ['hɑːtnɪŋ] *adj* alentador(a).

heart failure *n* (*MED*) paro cardíaco.

heartfelt ['hɑːtfɛlt] *adj* (*cordial*) cordial; (*deeply felt*) sincero.

hearth [hɑːθ] *n* (*gen*) hogar *m*; (*fireplace*) chimenea.

heartily ['hɑːtɪlɪ] *adv* sinceramente, cordialmente; (*laugh*) a carcajadas; (*eat*) con buen apetito; **to be ~ sick of** estar completamente harto de.

heartland ['hɑːtlænd] *n* zona interior *or* central; (*fig*) corazón *m*.

heartless ['hɑːtlɪs] *adj* despiadado.

heartstrings ['hɑːtstrɪŋz] *npl*: **to tug (at) sb's ~** tocar la fibra sensible de algn.

heart-throb ['hɑːtθrɔb] *n* ídolo.

heart-to-heart ['hɑːttə'hɑːt] *n* (*also*: **~ talk**) conversación *f* íntima.

heart transplant *n* transplante *m* de corazón.

hearty ['hɑːtɪ] *adj* cordial.

heat [hiːt] *n* (*gen*) calor *m*; (*SPORT: also*: **qualifying ~**) prueba eliminatoria; (*ZOOL*): **in** *or* **on ~** en celo ♦ *vt* calentar.

►**heat up** *vi* (*gen*) calentarse.

heated ['hiːtɪd] *adj* caliente; (*fig*) acalorado.

heater ['hiːtə*] *n* calentador *m*.

heath [hiːθ] *n* (*BRIT*) brezal *m*.

heathen ['hiːðn] *adj, n* pagano/a *m/f*.

heather ['hɛðə*] *n* brezo.

heating ['hiːtɪŋ] *n* calefacción *f*.

heat-resistant ['hiːtrɪzɪstənt] *adj* refractario.

heart-seeking ['hiːtsiːkɪŋ-] *adj* guiado por infrarrojos, termoguiado.

heatstroke ['hiːtstrəuk] *n* insolación *f*.

heatwave ['hiːtweɪv] *n* ola de calor.

heave [hiːv] *vt* (*pull*) tirar; (*push*) empujar con esfuerzo; (*lift*) levantar (con esfuerzo) ♦ *vi* (*water*) subir y bajar ♦ *n* tirón *m*; empujón *m*; (*effort*) esfuerzo; (*throw*) echada; **to ~ a sigh** dar *or* echar un suspiro, suspirar.

►**heave to** *vi* (*NAUT*) ponerse al pairo.

heaven ['hɛvn] *n* cielo; (*REL*) paraíso; **thank ~!** ¡gracias a Dios!; **for ~'s sake!** (*pleading*) ¡por el amor de Dios!, ¡por lo que más quiera!; (*protesting*) ¡por Dios!

heavenly ['hɛvnlɪ] *adj* celestial; (*REL*) divino.

heavenly body *n* cuerpo celeste.

heavily ['hɛvɪlɪ] *adv* pesadamente; (*drink, smoke*) en exceso; (*sleep, sigh*) profundamente.

heavy ['hɛvɪ] *adj* pesado; (*work*) duro; (*sea, rain, meal*) fuerte; (*drinker, smoker*) empedernido; (*eater*) comilón/ona.

heavy-duty ['hɛvɪ'djuːtɪ] *adj* resistente.

heavy goods vehicle (HGV) *n* (*BRIT*) vehículo pesado.

heavy-handed ['hɛvɪ'hændɪd] *adj* (*clumsy, tactless*) torpe.

heavy industry *n* industria pesada.

heavy metal *n* (*MUS*) heavy *m* (metal).

heavy-set [hevɪ'sɛt] *adj* (*esp US*) corpulento, fornido.

heavy user *n* consumidor *m* intensivo.

heavyweight ['hɛvɪweɪt] *n* (*SPORT*) peso pesado.

Hebrew ['hiːbruː] *adj, n* (*LING*) hebreo.

Hebrides ['hɛbrɪdiːz] *npl*: **the ~** las Hébridas.

heck [hɛk] *n* (*col*): **why the ~ ...?** ¿por qué porras ...?; **a ~ of a lot of** cantidad de.

heckle ['hɛkl] *vt* interrumpir.

heckler ['hɛklə*] *n* el/la que interrumpe a un orador.

hectare ['hɛktɑː*] *n* (*BRIT*) hectárea.

hectic ['hɛktɪk] *adj* agitado; (*busy*) ocupado.

hector ['hɛktə*] vt intimidar con bravatas.

he'd [hi:d] = **he would**; **he had**.

hedge [hɛdʒ] n seto ♦ vt cercar (con un seto) ♦ vi contestar con evasivas; **as a ~ against inflation** como protección contra la inflación; **to ~ one's bets** (fig) cubrirse.

hedgehog ['hɛdʒhɔg] n erizo.

hedgerow ['hɛdʒrəu] n seto vivo.

hedonism ['hi:dənɪzəm] n hedonismo.

heed [hi:d] vt (also: **take ~ of**) (pay attention) hacer caso de; (bear in mind) tener en cuenta; **to pay (no) ~ to, take (no) ~ of** (no) hacer caso a, (no) tener en cuenta.

heedless ['hi:dlɪs] adj desatento.

heel [hi:l] n talón m ♦ vt (shoe) poner tacón a; **to take to one's ~s** (col) poner pies en polvorosa; **to bring to ~** meter en cintura.

hefty ['hɛftɪ] adj (person) fornido; (piece) grande; (price) alto.

heifer ['hɛfə*] n novilla, ternera.

height [haɪt] n (of person) talla f; (of building) altura; (high ground) cerro; (altitude) altitud f; **what ~ are you?** ¿cuánto mides?; **of average ~** de estatura mediana; **to be afraid of ~s** tener miedo a las alturas; **it's the ~ of fashion** es el último grito en moda.

heighten ['haɪtn] vt elevar; (fig) aumentar.

heinous ['heɪnəs] adj atroz, nefasto.

heir [ɛə*] n heredero.

heir apparent n presunto heredero.

heiress ['ɛərɛs] n heredera.

heirloom ['ɛəlu:m] n reliquia de familia.

heist [haɪst] n (col: hold-up) atraco a mano armada.

held [hɛld] pt, pp of **hold**.

helicopter ['hɛlɪkɔptə*] n helicóptero.

heliport ['hɛlɪpɔ:t] n (AVIAT) helipuerto.

helium ['hi:lɪəm] n helio.

hell [hɛl] n infierno; **oh ~!** (col) ¡demonios!, ¡caramba!

he'll [hi:l] = **he will, he shall**.

hellbent [hɛl'bɛnt] adj (col): **he was ~ on going** se le metió entre ceja y ceja ir.

hellish ['hɛlɪʃ] adj infernal; (col) horrible.

hello [hə'ləu] excl ¡hola!; (surprise) ¡caramba!; (TEL) ¡dígame! (esp SP), ¡aló! (LAM).

helm [hɛlm] n (NAUT) timón m.

helmet ['hɛlmɪt] n casco.

helmsman ['hɛlmzmən] n timonel m.

help [hɛlp] n ayuda; (charwoman) criada, asistenta ♦ vt ayudar; **~!** ¡socorro!; **with the ~ of** con la ayuda de; **can I ~ you?** (in shop) ¿qué desea?; **to be of ~ to sb** servir a algn; **to ~ sb (to) do sth** echarle una mano or ayudar a algn a hacer algo; **~**

yourself sírvete; **he can't ~ it** no lo puede evitar.

helper ['hɛlpə*] n ayudante m/f.

helpful ['hɛlpful] adj útil; (person) servicial.

helping ['hɛlpɪŋ] n ración f.

helping hand n: **to give sb a ~** echar una mano a algn.

helpless ['hɛlplɪs] adj (incapable) incapaz; (defenceless) indefenso.

helpline ['hɛlplaɪn] n teléfono de asistencia al público.

Helsinki ['hɛlsɪŋkɪ] n Helsinki m.

helter-skelter ['hɛltə'skɛltə*] n (in funfair) tobogán m.

hem [hɛm] n dobladillo ♦ vt poner or coser el dobladillo a.

▸**hem in** vt cercar; **to feel ~med in** (fig) sentirse acosado.

he-man ['hi:mæn] n macho.

hematology [hi:mə'tɔlədʒɪ] n (US) = **haematology**.

hemisphere ['hɛmɪsfɪə*] n hemisferio.

hemline ['hɛmlaɪn] n bajo (del vestido).

hemlock ['hɛmlɔk] n cicuta.

hemoglobin [hi:mə'gləubɪn] n (US) = **haemoglobin**.

hemophilia [hi:mə'fɪlɪə] n (US) = **haemophilia**.

hemorrhage ['hɛmərɪdʒ] n (US) = **haemorrhage**.

hemorrhoids ['hɛmərɔɪdz] npl (US) = **haemorrhoids**.

hemp [hɛmp] n cáñamo.

hen [hɛn] n gallina; (female bird) hembra.

hence [hɛns] adv (therefore) por lo tanto; **2 years ~** de aquí a 2 años.

henceforth [hɛns'fɔ:θ] adv de hoy en adelante.

henchman ['hɛntʃmən] n (pej) secuaz m.

henna ['hɛnə] n alheña.

hen night n (col) despedida de soltera.

hen party n (col) reunión f de mujeres.

henpecked ['hɛnpɛkt] adj: **to be ~** ser un calzonazos.

hepatitis [hɛpə'taɪtɪs] n hepatitis f inv.

her [hə:*] pron (direct) la; (indirect) le; (stressed, after prep) ella ♦ adj su; see also **me; my**.

herald ['hɛrəld] n (forerunner) precursor(a) m/f ♦ vt anunciar.

heraldic [hɛ'rældɪk] adj heráldico.

heraldry ['hɛrəldrɪ] n heráldica.

herb [hə:b] n hierba.

herbaceous [hə:'beɪʃəs] adj herbáceo.

herbal ['hə:bl] adj de hierbas.

herbicide ['hə:bɪsaɪd] n herbicida m.

herd [hə:d] n rebaño; (of wild animals, swine) piara ♦ vt (drive, gather: animals) llevar en

manada; (: *people*) reunir.
▸**herd together** *vt* agrupar, reunir ♦ *vi*
apiñarse, agruparse.
here [hɪə*] *adv* aquí; ~! (*present*)
¡presente!; ~ **is/are** aquí está/están; ~
she is aquí está; **come** ~! ¡ven aquí *or*
acá!; ~ **and there** aquí y allá.
hereabouts ['hɪərə'bauts] *adv* por aquí
(cerca).
hereafter [hɪər'ɑːftə*] *adv* en el futuro ♦ *n*:
the ~ el más allá.
hereby [hɪə'baɪ] *adv* (*in letter*) por la
presente.
hereditary [hɪ'redɪtrɪ] *adj* hereditario.
heredity [hɪ'redɪtɪ] *n* herencia.
heresy ['herəsɪ] *n* herejía.
heretic ['herətɪk] *n* hereje *m/f*.
heretical [hɪ'retɪkəl] *adj* herético.
herewith [hɪə'wɪð] *adv*: **I send you** ~ ... le
mando adjunto ....
heritage ['herɪtɪdʒ] *n* (*gen*) herencia; (*fig*)
patrimonio; **our national** ~ nuestro
patrimonio nacional.
hermetically [hɜː'metɪkəlɪ] *adv*: ~ **sealed**
herméticamente cerrado.
hermit ['hɜːmɪt] *n* ermitaño/a.
hernia ['hɜːnɪə] *n* hernia.
hero, *pl* ~**es** ['hɪərəu] *n* héroe *m*; (*in book,
film*) protagonista *m*.
heroic [hɪ'rəuɪk] *adj* heroico.
heroin ['herəuɪn] *n* heroína.
heroin addict *n* heroinómano/a, adicto/a a
la heroína.
heroine ['herəuɪn] *n* heroína; (*in book, film*)
protagonista.
heroism ['herəuɪzm] *n* heroísmo.
heron ['herən] *n* garza.
hero worship *n* veneración *f*.
herring ['herɪŋ] *n* arenque *m*.
hers [hɜːz] *pron* (el) suyo/(la) suya *etc*; **a
friend of** ~ un amigo suyo; **this is** ~ esto
es suyo *or* de ella; *see also* **mine**.
herself [hɜː'self] *pron* (*reflexive*) se;
(*emphatic*) ella misma; (*after prep*) sí
(misma); *see also* **oneself**.
Herts *abbr* (*BRIT*) = **Hertfordshire**.
he's [hiːz] = **he is; he has**.
hesitant ['hezɪtənt] *adj* indeciso; **to be** ~
about doing sth no decidirse a hacer
algo.
hesitate ['hezɪteɪt] *vi* dudar, vacilar; **don't**
~ **to ask (me)** no dudes en pedírmelo.
hesitation [hezɪ'teɪʃən] *n* indecisión *f*; **I
have no** ~ **in saying (that)** ... no tengo el
menor reparo en afirmar que ....
hessian ['hesɪən] *n* arpillera.
heterogeneous ['hetərə'dʒiːnɪəs] *adj*
heterogéneo.

heterosexual [hetərəu'seksjuəl] *adj, n*
heterosexual *m/f*.
het up [het'ʌp] *adj* (*col*) agitado, nervioso.
HEW *n abbr* (*US*: = *Department of Health,
Education and Welfare*) *ministerio de
sanidad, educación y bienestar público*.
hew [hjuː] *vt* cortar.
hex [heks] (*US*) *n* maleficio, mal *m* de ojo
♦ *vt* embrujar.
hexagon ['heksəgən] *n* hexágono.
hexagonal [hek'sægənl] *adj* hexagonal.
hey [heɪ] *excl* ¡oye!, ¡oiga!
heyday ['heɪdeɪ] *n*: **the** ~ **of** el apogeo de.
HF *n abbr* = *high frequency*.
HGV *n abbr see* **heavy goods vehicle**.
HI *abbr* (*US*) = *Hawaii*.
hi [haɪ] *excl* ¡hola!
hiatus [haɪ'eɪtəs] *n* vacío, interrupción *f*;
(*LING*) hiato.
hibernate ['haɪbəneɪt] *vi* invernar.
hibernation [haɪbə'neɪʃən] *n* hibernación *f*.
hiccough, hiccup ['hɪkʌp] *vi* hipar; ~**s** *npl*
hipo *sg*.
hid [hɪd] *pt of* **hide**.
hick [hɪk] *n* (*US col*) paleto/a.
hidden ['hɪdn] *pp of* **hide** ♦ *adj*: **there are no**
~ **extras** no hay suplementos ocultos; ~
agenda plan *m* encubierto.
hide [haɪd] *n* (*skin*) piel *f* ♦ *vb* (*pt* **hid,** *pp*
hidden [hɪd, 'hɪdn]) *vt* esconder, ocultar;
(*feelings, truth*) encubrir, ocultar ♦ *vi*: **to** ~
(**from sb**) esconderse *or* ocultarse (de
algn).
hide-and-seek [haɪdən'siːk] *n* escondite *m*.
hideaway ['haɪdəweɪ] *n* escondite *m*.
hideous ['hɪdɪəs] *adj* horrible.
hideously ['hɪdɪəslɪ] *adv* horriblemente.
hide-out ['haɪdaut] *n* escondite *m*, refugio.
hiding ['haɪdɪŋ] *n* (*beating*) paliza; **to be in**
~ (*concealed*) estar escondido.
hiding place *n* escondrijo.
hierarchy ['haɪərɑːkɪ] *n* jerarquía.
hieroglyphic [haɪərə'glɪfɪk] *adj* jeroglífico
♦ *n*: ~**s** jeroglíficos *mpl*.
hi-fi ['haɪfaɪ] *abbr* (= *high fidelity*) *n* estéreo,
hifi *m* ♦ *adj* de alta fidelidad.
higgledy-piggledy ['hɪgldɪ'pɪgldɪ] *adv* en
desorden, de cualquier modo.
high [haɪ] *adj* alto; (*speed, number*) grande,
alto; (*price*) elevado; (*wind*) fuerte; (*voice*)
agudo; (*col: on drugs*) colocado; (: *on drink*)
borracho; (*CULIN: meat, game*) pasado;
(: *spoilt*) estropeado ♦ *adv* alto, a gran
altura ♦ *n*: **exports have reached a new** ~
las exportaciones han alcanzado niveles
inusitados; **it is 20 m** ~ tiene 20 m de
altura; ~ **in the air** en las alturas; **to pay a**
~ **price for sth** pagar algo muy caro.

highball ['hɔːbɔːl] n (US: drink) whisky m soda, highball m (LAM), jaibol m (LAM).
highboy ['haɪbɔɪ] n (US) cómoda alta.
highbrow ['haɪbrau] adj culto.
highchair ['haɪtʃɛə*] n silla alta (para niños).
high-class ['haɪ'klɑːs] adj (neighbourhood) de alta sociedad; (hotel) de lujo; (person) distinguido; (food) de alta categoría.
High Court n (LAW) tribunal m supremo; ver recuadro.

HIGH COURT

En el sistema legal de Inglaterra y Gales **High Court** es la forma abreviada de "High Court of Justice", tribunal superior que junto con el de apelación ("Court of Appeal") forma el Tribunal Supremo ("Supreme Court of Judicature"). En el sistema legal escocés es la forma abreviada de "High Court of Justiciary" tribunal con jurado que juzga los delitos más serios, que pueden dar lugar a una pena de gran severidad.

higher ['haɪə*] adj (form of life, study etc) superior ♦ adv más alto.
higher education n educación f or enseñanza superior.
high explosive n explosivo de gran potencia.
highfalutin [haɪfə'luːtɪn] adj (col) de altos vuelos, encopetado.
high finance n altas finanzas fpl.
high-flier, high-flyer [haɪ'flaɪə*] n ambicioso/a.
high-handed [haɪ'hændɪd] adj despótico.
high-heeled [haɪ'hiːld] adj de tacón alto.
highjack ['haɪdʒæk] = hijack.
high jump n (SPORT) salto de altura.
highlands ['haɪləndz] npl tierras fpl altas; **the H~** (in Scotland) las Tierras Altas de Escocia.
high-level ['haɪlɛvl] adj (talks etc) de alto nivel; **~ language** (COMPUT) lenguaje m de alto nivel.
highlight ['haɪlaɪt] n (fig: of event) punto culminante ♦ vt subrayar.
highly ['haɪlɪ] adv sumamente; **~ paid** muy bien pagado; **to speak ~ of** hablar muy bien de.
highly-strung ['haɪlɪ'strʌŋ] adj muy excitable.
highness ['haɪnɪs] n altura; **Her** or **His H~** Su Alteza.
high-pitched [haɪ'pɪtʃt] adj agudo.
high point n: **the ~** el punto culminante.

high-powered ['haɪ'pauəd] adj (engine) de gran potencia; (fig: person) importante.
high-pressure ['haɪprɛʃə*] adj de alta presión; (fig: salesman etc) enérgico.
high-rise ['haɪraɪz] n (also: **~ block**, **~ building**) torre f de pisos.
high school n centro de enseñanza secundaria, ≈ Instituto Nacional de Bachillerato (SP), liceo (LAM); ver recuadro.

HIGH SCHOOL

El término **high school** se aplica en Estados Unidos a dos tipos de centros de educación secundaria: "Junior High Schools", en los que se imparten normalmente del 7º al 9º curso (llamado "grade") y "Senior High Schools", que abarcan los cursos 10º, 11º y 12º y en ocasiones el 9º. Aquí pueden estudiarse asignaturas tanto de contenido académico como profesional. En Gran Bretaña también se llaman **high school** algunos centros de enseñanza secundaria.

high season n (BRIT) temporada alta.
high-speed ['haɪspiːd] adj de alta velocidad.
high-spirited [haɪ'spɪrɪtɪd] adj animado.
high spirits npl ánimos mpl.
high street n (BRIT) calle f mayor.
high tide n marea alta.
highway ['haɪweɪ] n carretera; (US) autopista; **the information ~** la autopista de la información.
Highway Code n (BRIT) código de la circulación.
hijack ['haɪdʒæk] vt secuestrar ♦ n (also: **~ing**) secuestro.
hijacker ['haɪdʒækə*] n secuestrador(a) m/f.
hike [haɪk] vi (go walking) ir de excursión (a pie); (tramp) caminar ♦ n caminata, (col: in prices etc) aumento.
▶**hike up** vt (raise) aumentar.
hiker ['haɪkə*] n excursionista m/f.
hilarious [hɪ'lɛərɪəs] adj divertidísimo.
hilarity [hɪ'lærɪtɪ] n (laughter) risas fpl, carcajadas fpl.
hill [hɪl] n colina; (high) montaña; (slope) cuesta.
hillbilly ['hɪlbɪlɪ] n (US) rústico/a montañés/esa; (pej) palurdo/a.
hillside ['hɪlsaɪd] n ladera.
hilltop ['hɪltɔp] n cumbre f.
hilly ['hɪlɪ] adj montañoso; (uneven) accidentado.
hilt [hɪlt] n (of sword) empuñadura; **to the ~** (fig: support) incondicionalmente; **to be in debt up to the ~** estar hasta el cuello de

deudas.
him [hɪm] *pron (direct)* le, lo; *(indirect)* le; *(stressed, after prep)* él; *see also* **me**.
Himalayas [hɪmə'leɪəz] *npl:* **the ~** el Himalaya.
himself [hɪm'sɛlf] *pron (reflexive)* se; *(emphatic)* él mismo; *(after prep)* sí (mismo); *see also* **oneself**.
hind [haɪnd] *adj* posterior ♦ *n* cierva.
hinder ['hɪndə*] *vt* estorbar, impedir.
hindquarters ['haɪndkwɔːtəz] *npl (ZOOL)* cuartos *mpl* traseros.
hindrance ['hɪndrəns] *n* estorbo, obstáculo.
hindsight ['haɪndsaɪt] *n* percepción *f* tardía *or* retrospectiva; **with the benefit of ~** con la perspectiva del tiempo transcurrido.
Hindu ['hɪnduː] *n* hindú *m/f.*
hinge [hɪndʒ] *n* bisagra, gozne *m* ♦ *vi (fig):* **to ~ on** depender de.
hint [hɪnt] *n* indirecta; *(advice)* consejo ♦ *vt:* **to ~ that** insinuar que ♦ *vi:* **to ~ at** aludir a; **to drop a ~** soltar *or* tirar una indirecta; **give me a ~** dame una pista.
hip [hɪp] *n* cadera; *(BOT)* escaramujo.
hip flask *n* petaca.
hip-hop ['hɪphɔp] *n* hip hop *m.*
hippie ['hɪpɪ] *n* hippie *m/f,* jipi *m/f.*
hip pocket *n* bolsillo de atrás.
hippopotamus, *pl* **~es** *or* **hippopotami** [hɪpə'pɔtəməs, -'pɔtəmaɪ] hipopótamo.
hippy ['hɪpɪ] *n* = **hippie**.
hire ['haɪə*] *vt (BRIT: car, equipment)* alquilar; *(worker)* contratar ♦ *n* alquiler *m;* **for ~** se alquila; *(taxi)* libre; **on ~** de alquiler.
▶**hire out** *vt* alquilar, arrendar.
hire(d) car *n (BRIT)* coche *m* de alquiler.
hire purchase (H.P.) *n (BRIT)* compra a plazos; **to buy sth on ~** comprar algo a plazos.
his [hɪz] *pron* (el) suyo/(la) suya *etc* ♦ *adj* su; **this is ~** esto es suyo *or* de él; *see also* **my**, **mine**.
Hispanic [hɪs'pænɪk] *adj* hispánico.
hiss [hɪs] *vi* sisear; *(in protest)* silbar ♦ *n* siseo; silbido.
histogram ['hɪstəgræm] *n* histograma *m.*
historian [hɪ'stɔːrɪən] *n* historiador(a) *m/f.*
historic(al) [hɪ'stɔrɪk(l)] *adj* histórico.
history ['hɪstərɪ] *n* historia; **there's a long ~ of that illness in his family** esa enfermedad corre en su familia.
histrionics [hɪstrɪ'ɔnɪks] *npl* histrionismo.
hit [hɪt] *vt (pt, pp* **hit)** *(strike)* golpear, pegar; *(reach: target)* alcanzar; *(collide with: car)* chocar contra; *(fig: affect)* afectar ♦ *n* golpe *m;* *(success)* éxito; **to ~ the**

headlines salir en primera plana; **to ~ the road** *(col)* largarse; **to ~ it off with sb** llevarse bien con algn.
▶**hit back** *vi* defenderse; *(fig)* devolver golpe por golpe.
▶**hit out at** *vt fus* asestar un golpe a; *(fig)* atacar.
▶**hit (up)on** *vt fus (answer)* dar con; *(solution)* hallar, encontrar.
hit and miss *adj:* **it's very ~**, **it's a ~ affair** es cuestión de suerte.
hit-and-run driver ['hɪtən'rʌn-] *n* conductor(a) que tras atropellar a algn se da a la fuga.
hitch [hɪtʃ] *vt (fasten)* atar, amarrar; *(also:* **~ up)** arremangarse ♦ *n (difficulty)* problema, pega; **to ~ a lift** hacer autostop; **technical ~** problema *m* técnico.
▶**hitch up** *vt (horse, cart)* enganchar, uncir.
hitch-hike ['hɪtʃhaɪk] *vi* hacer autostop.
hitch-hiker ['hɪtʃhaɪkə*] *n* autostopista *m/f.*
hi-tech [haɪ'tɛk] *adj* de alta tecnología.
hitherto ['hɪðə'tuː] *adv* hasta ahora, hasta aquí.
hit list *n* lista negra.
hitman ['hɪtmæn] *n* asesino a sueldo.
hit or miss ['hɪtə'mɪs] *adj* = **hit and miss**.
hit parade *n:* **the ~** los cuarenta principales.
HIV *n abbr (= human immunodeficiency virus)* VIH *m;* **~-negative** no portador(a) del virus del sida, no seropositivo; **~-positive** portador(a) del virus del sida, seropositivo.
hive [haɪv] *n* colmena; **the shop was a ~ of activity** *(fig)* la tienda era una colmena humana.
▶**hive off** *vt (col: separate)* separar; *(: privatize)* privatizar.
hl *abbr (= hectolitre)* hl.
HM *abbr (= His (or Her) Majesty)* S.M.
HMG *abbr = His (or Her) Majesty's Government.*
HMI *n abbr (BRIT SCOL) = His (or Her) Majesty's Inspector.*
HMO *n abbr (US: = health maintenance organization)* seguro médico global.
HMS *abbr = His (or Her) Majesty's Ship.*
HMSO *n abbr (BRIT = His (or Her) Majesty's Stationery Office) distribuidor oficial de las publicaciones del gobierno del Reino Unido.*
HNC *n abbr (BRIT: = Higher National Certificate) título académico.*
HND *n abbr (BRIT: = Higher National Diploma) título académico.*
hoard [hɔːd] *n (treasure)* tesoro; *(stockpile)* provisión *f* ♦ *vt* acumular.

hoarding ['hɔːdɪŋ] n (for posters) valla publicitaria.
hoarfrost ['hɔːfrɒst] n escarcha.
hoarse [hɔːs] adj ronco.
hoax [həuks] n engaño.
hob [hɒb] n quemador m.
hobble ['hɒbl] vi cojear.
hobby ['hɒbɪ] n pasatiempo, afición f.
hobby-horse ['hɒbɪhɔːs] n (fig) tema preferido.
hobnob ['hɒbnɒb] vi: **to ~ (with)** alternar (con).
hobo ['həubəu] n (US) vagabundo.
hock [hɒk] n (of animal, CULIN) corvejón m; (col): **to be in ~** (person) estar empeñado or endeudado; (object) estar empeñado.
hockey ['hɒkɪ] n hockey m.
hocus-pocus [həukəs'pəukəs] n (trickery) engañifa; (words: of magician) abracadabra m.
hod [hɒd] n capacho.
hodge-podge ['hɒdʒpɒdʒ] n (US) = **hotchpotch**.
hoe [həu] n azadón m ♦ vt azadonar.
hog [hɒg] n cerdo, puerco ♦ vt (fig) acaparar; **to go the whole ~** echar el todo por el todo.
Hogmanay [hɒgmə'neɪ] n (Scottish) Nochevieja.
hoist [hɔɪst] n (crane) grúa ♦ vt levantar, alzar.
hoity-toity [hɔɪtɪ'tɔɪtɪ] adj (col): **to be ~** darse humos.
hold [həuld] vb (pt, pp **held** [held]) vt tener; (contain) contener; (keep back) retener; (believe) sostener; (take ~ of) coger (SP), agarrar (LAM); (take weight) soportar; (meeting) celebrar ♦ vi (withstand pressure) resistir; (be valid) ser válido; (stick) pegarse ♦ n (grasp) asimiento; (fig) dominio; (WRESTLING) presa; (NAUT) bodega; **~ the line!** (TEL) ¡no cuelgue!; **to ~ one's own** (fig) defenderse; **to ~ office** (POL) ocupar un cargo; **to ~ firm** or **fast** mantenerse firme; **he ~s the view that ...** opina or es su opinión que ...; **to ~ sb responsible for sth** culpar or echarle la culpa a algn de algo; **where can I get ~ of ...?** ¿dónde puedo encontrar (a) ...?; **to catch** or **get (a) ~ of** agarrarse or asirse de.
►**hold back** vt retener; (secret) ocultar; **to ~ sb back from doing sth** impedir a algn hacer algo, impedir que algn haga algo.
►**hold down** vt (person) sujetar; (job) mantener.
►**hold forth** vi perorar.
►**hold off** vt (enemy) rechazar ♦ vi: **if the**

rain **~s off** si no llueve.
►**hold on** vi agarrarse bien; (wait) esperar.
►**hold on to** vt fus agarrarse a; (keep) guardar.
►**hold out** vt ofrecer ♦ vi (resist) resistir; **to ~ out (against)** resistir (a), sobrevivir.
►**hold over** vt (meeting etc) aplazar.
►**hold up** vt (raise) levantar; (support) apoyar; (delay) retrasar; (: traffic) demorar; (rob: bank) asaltar, atracar.
holdall ['həuldɔːl] n (BRIT) bolsa.
holder ['həuldə*] n (of ticket, record) poseedor(a) m/f; (of passport, post, office, title etc) titular m/f.
holding ['həuldɪŋ] n (share) participación f.
holding company n holding m.
holdup ['həuldʌp] n (robbery) atraco; (delay) retraso; (BRIT: in traffic) embotellamiento.
hole [həul] n agujero ♦ vt agujerear; **~ in the heart** (MED) boquete m en el corazón; **to pick ~s in** (fig) encontrar defectos en; **the ship was ~d** se abrió una vía de agua en el barco.
►**hole up** vi esconderse.
holiday ['hɒlədɪ] n vacaciones fpl; (day off) (día m de) fiesta, día m festivo or feriado (LAM); **on ~** de vacaciones; **to be on ~** estar de vacaciones.
holiday camp n colonia or centro vacacional; (for children) colonia veraniega infantil.
holidaymaker ['hɒlədɪmeɪkə*] n (BRIT) turista m/f.
holiday pay n paga de las vacaciones.
holiday resort n centro turístico.
holiday season n temporada de vacaciones.
holiness ['həulɪnɪs] n santidad f.
holistic [həu'lɪstɪk] adj holístico.
Holland ['hɒlənd] n Holanda.
holler ['hɒlə*] vi (col) gritar, vocear.
hollow ['hɒləu] adj hueco; (fig) vacío; (eyes) hundido; (sound) sordo ♦ n (gen) hueco; (in ground) hoyo ♦ vt: **to ~ out** ahuecar.
holly ['hɒlɪ] n acebo.
hollyhock ['hɒlɪhɒk] n malva loca.
holocaust ['hɒləkɔːst] n holocausto.
hologram ['hɒləgræm] n holograma m.
hols [hɒlz] npl (col): **the ~** las vacaciones.
holster ['həulstə*] n pistolera.
holy ['həulɪ] adj (gen) santo, sagrado; (water) bendito; **the H~ Father** el Santo Padre.
Holy Communion n Sagrada Comunión f.
Holy Ghost, Holy Spirit n Espíritu m Santo.
homage ['hɒmɪdʒ] n homenaje m; **to pay ~ to** rendir homenaje a.

home [həum] *n* casa; (*country*) patria; (*institution*) asilo; (*COMPUT*) punto inicial ♦ *adj* (*domestic*) casero, de casa; (*ECON, POL*) nacional; (*SPORT: team*) de casa; (: *match, win*) en casa ♦ *adv* (*direction*) a casa; **at** ~ en casa; **to go/come** ~ ir/volver a casa; **make yourself at** ~ ¡estás en tu casa!; **it's near my** ~ está cerca de mi casa.
►**home in on** *vt fus* (*missiles*) dirigirse hacia.
home address *n* domicilio.
home-brew [həum'bru:] *n* cerveza *etc* casera.
homecoming ['həumkʌmɪŋ] *n* regreso (al hogar).
home computer *n* ordenador *m* doméstico.
Home Counties *npl* condados que rodean Londres.
home economics *n* economía doméstica.
home ground *n*: **to be on** ~ estar en su *etc* terreno.
home-grown ['həumgrəun] *adj* de cosecha propia.
home help *n* (*BRIT*) trabajador(a) *m/f* del servicio de atención domiciliaria.
homeland ['həumlænd] *n* tierra natal.
homeless ['həumlɪs] *adj* sin hogar, sin casa ♦ *npl*: **the** ~ las personas sin hogar.
home loan *n* préstamo para la vivienda.
homely ['həumlɪ] *adj* (*domestic*) casero; (*simple*) sencillo.
home-made [həum'meɪd] *adj* hecho en casa.
Home Office *n* (*BRIT*) Ministerio del Interior.
homeopathy [həumɪ'ɔpəθɪ] *etc* (*US*) = **homoeopathy** *etc*.
home page *n* (*COMPUT*) página de inicio.
home rule *n* autonomía.
Home Secretary *n* (*BRIT*) Ministro del Interior.
homesick ['həumsɪk] *adj*: **to be** ~ tener morriña *or* nostalgia.
home town *n* ciudad *f* natal.
home truth *n*: **to tell sb a few** ~s decir cuatro verdades a algn.
homeward ['həumwəd] *adj* (*journey*) de vuelta.
homeward(s) ['həumwəd(z)] *adv* hacia casa.
homework ['həumwə:k] *n* deberes *mpl*.
homicidal [hɔmɪ'saɪdl] *adj* homicida.
homicide ['hɔmɪsaɪd] *n* (*US*) homicidio.
homing ['həumɪŋ] *adj* (*device, missile*) buscador(a); ~ **pigeon** paloma mensajera.
homoeopath, (*US*) **homeopath**

['həumɪəupæθ] *n* homeópata *m/f*.
homoeopathic, (*US*) **homeopathic** [həumɪəu'pæθɪk] *adj* homeopático.
homoeopathy, (*US*) **homeopathy** [həumɪ'ɔpəθɪ] *n* homeopatía.
homogeneous [hɔmə'dʒiːnɪəs] *adj* homogéneo.
homogenize [hə'mɔdʒənaɪz] *vt* homogeneizar.
homosexual [hɔməu'sɛksjuəl] *adj, n* homosexual *m/f*.
Hon. *abbr* (= *honourable, honorary*) en *títulos*.
Honduras [hɔn'djuərəs] *n* Honduras *fpl*.
hone [həun] *vt* (*sharpen*) afilar; (*fig*) perfeccionar.
honest ['ɔnɪst] *adj* honrado; (*sincere*) franco, sincero; **to be quite** ~ **with you** ... para serte franco ....
honestly ['ɔnɪstlɪ] *adv* honradamente; francamente, de verdad.
honesty ['ɔnɪstɪ] *n* honradez *f*.
honey ['hʌnɪ] *n* miel *f*; (*US col*) cariño; (: *to strangers*) guapo, linda.
honeycomb ['hʌnɪkəum] *n* panal *m*; (*fig*) laberinto.
honeymoon ['hʌnɪmuːn] *n* luna de miel.
honeysuckle ['hʌnɪsʌkl] *n* madreselva.
Hong Kong ['hɔŋ'kɔŋ] *n* Hong-Kong *m*.
honk [hɔŋk] *vi* (*AUT*) tocar la bocina.
Honolulu [hɔnə'luːluː] *n* Honolulú *m*.
honorary ['ɔnərərɪ] *adj* no remunerado; (*duty, title*) honorario.
honour, (*US*) **honor** ['ɔnə*] *vt* honrar ♦ *n* honor *m*, honra; **in** ~ **of** en honor de; **it's a great** ~ es un gran honor.
hono(u)rable ['ɔnərəbl] *adj* honrado, honorable.
hono(u)r-bound ['ɔnə'baund] *adj* moralmente obligado.
honours degree *n* (*UNIV*) licenciatura superior; *ver recuadro*.

HONOURS DEGREE

Tras un período de estudios de tres años normalmente (cuatro en Escocia), los universitarios obtienen una licenciatura llamada **honours degree**. *La calificación global que se recibe, en una escala de mayor a menor es la siguiente: "first class" (I), "upper-second class" (II:1), "lower-second class" (II:2) y "third class" (III). El licenciado puede añadir las letras "Hons" al título obtenido tras su nombre y apellidos, por ejemplo "BA Hons"; ver también "ordinary degree".*

honours list n (BRIT) lista de distinciones honoríficas que entrega la reina; ver recuadro.

HONOURS LIST

A la lista con los títulos honoríficos y condecoraciones que el monarca británico otorga en Año Nuevo y en el día de su cumpleaños se la conoce con el nombre de **honours list**. Las personas que reciben dichas distinciones suelen ser miembros destacados de la vida pública (ámbito empresarial, ejército, deportes, espectáculos), aunque últimamente también se reconoce con ellas el trabajo abnegado y anónimo de la gente de la calle.

Hons. abbr (UNIV) = **hono(u)rs degree.**
hood [hud] n capucha; (BRIT AUT) capota; (US AUT) capó m; (US col) matón m.
hooded ['hudɪd] adj (robber) encapuchado.
hoodlum ['huːdləm] n matón m.
hoodwink ['hudwɪŋk] vt (BRIT) timar.
hoof, pl ~**s** or **hooves** [huːf, huːvz] n pezuña.
hook [huk] n gancho; (on dress) corchete m, broche m; (for fishing) anzuelo ♦ vt enganchar; ~**s and eyes** corchetes mpl, macho y hembra m; **by** ~ **or by crook** por las buenas o por las malas, cueste lo que cueste; **to be** ~**ed on** (col) estar enganchado a.
▶**hook up** vt (RADIO, TV) transmitir en cadena.
hooligan ['huːlɪgən] n gamberro.
hooliganism ['huːlɪgənɪzəm] n gamberrismo.
hoop [huːp] n aro.
hoot [huːt] vi (BRIT AUT) tocar la bocina; (siren) sonar la sirena; (owl) ulular ♦ n bocinazo, toque m de sirena; **to** ~ **with laughter** morirse de risa.
hooter ['huːtə*] n (BRIT AUT) bocina; (of ship, factory) sirena.
hoover ® ['huːvə*] (BRIT) n aspiradora ♦ vt pasar la aspiradora por.
hooves [huːvz] pl of **hoof.**
hop [hɔp] vi saltar, brincar; (on one foot) saltar con un pie ♦ n salto, brinco; see also **hops.**
hope [həup] vt, vi esperar ♦ n esperanza; **I** ~ **so/not** espero que sí/no.
hopeful ['həupful] adj (person) optimista; (situation) prometedor(a); **I'm** ~ **that she'll manage to come** confío en que podrá venir.
hopefully ['həupfulɪ] adv con optimismo, con esperanza.

hopeless ['həuplɪs] adj desesperado.
hopelessly ['həuplɪslɪ] adv (live etc) sin esperanzas; **I'm** ~ **confused/lost** estoy totalmente despistado/perdido.
hopper ['hɔpə*] n (chute) tolva.
hops [hɔps] npl lúpulo sg.
horde [hɔːd] n horda.
horizon [hə'raɪzn] n horizonte m.
horizontal [hɔrɪ'zɔntl] adj horizontal.
hormone ['hɔːməun] n hormona.
hormone replacement therapy n terapia hormonal sustitutiva.
horn [hɔːn] n cuerno, cacho (LAM); (MUS: also: **French** ~) trompa; (AUT) bocina, claxon m.
horned [hɔːnd] adj con cuernos.
hornet ['hɔːnɪt] n avispón m.
horny ['hɔːnɪ] adj (material) córneo; (hands) calloso; (US col) cachondo.
horoscope ['hɔrəskəup] n horóscopo.
horrendous [hɔ'rendəs] adj horrendo.
horrible ['hɔrɪbl] adj horrible.
horribly ['hɔrɪblɪ] adv horriblemente.
horrid ['hɔrɪd] adj horrible, horroroso.
horridly ['hɔrɪdlɪ] adv (behave) tremendamente mal.
horrific [hɔ'rɪfɪk] adj (accident) horroroso; (film) horripilante.
horrify ['hɔrɪfaɪ] vt horrorizar.
horrifying ['hɔrɪfaɪɪŋ] adj horroroso.
horror ['hɔrə*] n horror m.
horror film n película de terror or miedo.
horror-struck ['hɔrəstrʌk], **horror-stricken** ['hɔrəstrɪkn] adj horrorizado.
hors d'œuvre [ɔː'dəːvrə] n entremeses mpl.
horse [hɔːs] n caballo.
horseback ['hɔːsbæk] n: **on** ~ a caballo.
horsebox ['hɔːsbɔks] n remolque m para transportar caballos.
horse chestnut n (tree) castaño de Indias.
horsedrawn ['hɔːsdrɔːn] adj de tracción animal.
horsefly ['hɔːsflaɪ] n tábano.
horseman ['hɔːsmən] n jinete m.
horseplay ['hɔːspleɪ] n pelea amistosa.
horsepower (hp) ['hɔːspauə*] n caballo (de fuerza), potencia en caballos.
horse-racing ['hɔːsreɪsɪŋ] n carreras fpl de caballos.
horseradish ['hɔːsrædɪʃ] n rábano picante.
horseshoe ['hɔːsʃuː] n herradura.
horse show n concurso hípico.
horse-trader ['hɔːstreɪdə*] n chalán/ana m/f.
horse trials npl = **horse show.**
horsewhip ['hɔːswɪp] vt azotar.
horsewoman ['hɔːswumən] n amazona.
horsey ['hɔːsɪ] adj (col: person) aficionado a los caballos.

horticulture ['hɔːtɪkʌltʃə*] _n_ horticultura.
hose [həuz] _n_ (_also_: ~**pipe**) manguera.
▶**hose down** _vt_ limpiar con manguera.
hosiery ['həuzɪərɪ] _n_ calcetería.
hospice ['hɔspɪs] _n_ hospicio.
hospitable ['hɔspɪtəbl] _adj_ hospitalario.
hospital ['hɔspɪtl] _n_ hospital _m_.
hospitality [hɔspɪ'tælɪtɪ] _n_ hospitalidad _f_.
hospitalize ['hɔspɪtəlaɪz] _vt_ hospitalizar.
host [həust] _n_ anfitrión _m_; (_TV, RADIO_) presentador(a) _m/f_; (_of inn etc_) mesonero; (_REL_) hostia; (_large number_): **a** ~ **of** multitud de.
hostage ['hɔstɪdʒ] _n_ rehén _m_.
hostel ['hɔstl] _n_ hostal _m_; (_for students, nurses etc_) residencia; (_also_: **youth** ~) albergue _m_ juvenil; (_for homeless people_) hospicio.
hostelling ['hɔstlɪŋ] _n_: **to go (youth)** ~ hospedarse en albergues.
hostess ['həustɪs] _n_ anfitriona; (_BRIT_: _air_ ~) azafata; (_in night-club_) señorita de compañía.
hostile ['hɔstaɪl] _adj_ hostil.
hostility [hɔ'stɪlɪtɪ] _n_ hostilidad _f_.
hot [hɔt] _adj_ caliente; (_weather_) caluroso, de calor; (_as opposed to only warm_) muy caliente; (_spicy_) picante; (_fig_) ardiente, acalorado; **to be** ~ (_person_) tener calor; (_object_) estar caliente; (_weather_) hacer calor.
▶**hot up** _vi_ (_col: situation_) ponerse difícil _or_ apurado; (: _party_) animarse ♦ _vt_ (_col: pace_) apretar; (: _engine_) aumentar la potencia de.
hot air _n_ (_col_) palabras _fpl_ huecas.
hot-air balloon [hɔt'ɛə-] _n_ (_AVIAT_) globo aerostático _or_ de aire caliente.
hotbed ['hɔtbɛd] _n_ (_fig_) semillero.
hot-blooded [hɔt'blʌdɪd] _adj_ impetuoso.
hotchpotch ['hɔtʃpotʃ] _n_ mezcolanza, baturrillo.
hot dog _n_ perrito caliente.
hotel [həu'tɛl] _n_ hotel _m_.
hotelier [həu'tɛlɪə*] _n_ hotelero.
hotel industry _n_ industria hotelera.
hotel room _n_ habitación _f_ de hotel.
hot flush _n_ (_BRIT_) sofoco.
hotfoot ['hɔtfut] _adv_ a toda prisa.
hothead ['hɔthɛd] _n_ (_fig_) exaltado/a.
hotheaded [hɔt'hɛdɪd] _adj_ exaltado.
hothouse ['hɔthaus] _n_ invernadero.
hot line _n_ (_POL_) teléfono rojo, línea directa.
hotly ['hɔtlɪ] _adv_ con pasión, apasionadamente.
hotplate ['hɔtpleɪt] _n_ (_on cooker_) hornillo.
hotpot ['hɔtpɔt] _n_ (_BRIT CULIN_) estofado.

hot potato _n_ (_BRIT col_) asunto espinoso; **to drop sth/sb like a** ~ no querer saber ya nada de algo/algn.
hot seat _n_ primera fila.
hot spot _n_ (_trouble spot_) punto caliente; (_night club etc_) lugar _m_ popular.
hot spring _n_ terma, fuente _f_ de aguas termales.
hot-tempered ['hɔt'tɛmpəd] _adj_ de mal genio _or_ carácter.
hot-water bottle [hɔt'wɔːtə-] _n_ bolsa de agua caliente.
hot-wire ['hɔtwaɪə*] _vt_ (_col: car_) hacer el puente en.
hound [haund] _vt_ acosar ♦ _n_ perro de caza.
hour ['auə*] _n_ hora; **at 30 miles an** ~ a 30 millas por hora; **lunch** ~ la hora del almuerzo _or_ de comer; **to pay sb by the** ~ pagar a algn por horas.
hourly ['auəlɪ] _adj_ (de) cada hora; (_rate_) por hora ♦ _adv_ cada hora.
house _n_ [haus] (_pl_ ~**s** ['hauzɪz]) (_also firm_) casa; (_POL_) cámara; (_THEAT_) sala ♦ _vt_ [hauz] (_person_) alojar; **at/to my** ~ en/a mi casa; **the H**~ (**of Commons/Lords**) (_BRIT_) la Cámara de los Comunes/Lores; **the H**~ (**of Representatives**) (_US_) la Cámara de Representantes; **on the** ~ (_fig_) la casa invita.
house arrest _n_ arresto domiciliario.
houseboat ['hausbəut] _n_ casa flotante.
housebound ['hausbaund] _adj_ confinado en casa.
housebreaking ['hausbreɪkɪŋ] _n_ allanamiento de morada.
house-broken ['hausbrəukən] _adj_ (_US_) = **house-trained**.
housecoat ['hauskəut] _n_ bata.
household ['haushəuld] _n_ familia.
householder ['haushəuldə*] _n_ propietario/a; (_head of house_) cabeza de familia.
househunting ['haushʌntɪŋ] _n_: **to go** ~ ir en busca de vivienda.
housekeeper ['hauskiːpə*] _n_ ama de llaves.
housekeeping ['hauskiːpɪŋ] _n_ (_work_) trabajos _mpl_ domésticos; (_COMPUT_) gestión _f_ interna; (_also_: ~ **money**) dinero para gastos domésticos.
houseman ['hausmən] _n_ (_BRIT MED_) médico residente.
house-owner ['hausəunə*] _n_ propietario/a de una vivienda.
house plant _n_ planta de interior.
house-proud ['hauspraud] _adj_ preocupado por el embellecimiento de la casa.
house-to-house ['haustə'haus] _adj_ (_collection_) de casa en casa; (_search_) casa por casa.

house-train ['haʊstreɪn] vt (pet) enseñar (a hacer sus necesidades en el sitio apropiado).
house-trained ['haʊstreɪnd] adj (BRIT: animal) enseñado.
house-warming ['haʊswɔːmɪŋ] n (also: ~ party) fiesta de estreno de una casa.
housewife ['haʊswaɪf] n ama de casa.
housework ['haʊswɜːk] n faenas fpl (de la casa).
housing ['haʊzɪŋ] n (act) alojamiento; (houses) viviendas fpl ♦ cpd (problem, shortage) de (la) vivienda.
housing association n asociación f de la vivienda.
housing benefit n (BRIT) subsidio por alojamiento.
housing conditions npl condiciones fpl de habitabilidad.
housing development, (BRIT) housing estate n urbanización f.
hovel ['hɒvl] n casucha.
hover ['hɒvə*] vi flotar (en el aire); (helicopter) cernerse; **to ~ on the brink of disaster** estar al borde mismo del desastre.
hovercraft ['hɒvəkrɑːft] n aerodeslizador m, hovercraft m.
hoverport ['hɒvəpɔːt] n puerto de aerodeslizadores.
how [haʊ] adv cómo; **~ are you?** ¿cómo está usted?, ¿cómo estás?; **~ do you do?** encantado, mucho gusto; **~ far is it to ...?** ¿qué distancia hay de aquí a ...?; **~ long have you been here?** ¿cuánto (tiempo) hace que estás aquí?, ¿cuánto (tiempo) llevas aquí?; **~ lovely!** ¡qué bonito!; **~ many/much?** ¿cuántos/cuánto?; **~ old are you?** ¿cuántos años tienes?; **~ is school?** ¿qué tal la escuela?; **~ about a drink?** ¿te gustaría algo de beber?, ¿qué te parece una copa?
however [haʊ'ɛvə*] adv de cualquier manera; (+ adjective) por muy ... que; (in questions) cómo ♦ conj sin embargo, no obstante.
howitzer ['haʊɪtsə*] n (MIL) obús m.
howl [haʊl] n aullido ♦ vi aullar.
howler ['haʊlə*] n plancha, falta garrafal.
howling ['haʊlɪŋ] adj (wind) huracanado.
HP n abbr see **hire purchase**.
hp abbr see **horsepower**.
HQ n abbr see **headquarters**.
HR n abbr (US) = House of Representatives.
HRH abbr (= His (or Her) Royal Highness) S.A.R.
hr(s) abbr (= hour(s)) h.
HRT n abbr see **hormone replacement therapy**.

HS abbr (US) = high school.
HST abbr (US: = Hawaiian Standard Time) hora de Hawai.
HTML n abbr (= Hypertext Mark-up Language) HTML m.
hub [hʌb] n (of wheel) cubo; (fig) centro.
hubbub ['hʌbʌb] n barahúnda, barullo.
hubcap ['hʌbkæp] n tapacubos m inv.
HUD n abbr (US: = Department of Housing and Urban Development) ministerio de la vivienda y urbanismo.
huddle ['hʌdl] vi: **to ~ together** amontonarse.
hue [hjuː] n color m, matiz m; **~ and cry** n protesta.
huff [hʌf] n: **in a ~** enojado.
huffy ['hʌfɪ] adj (col) mosqueado.
hug [hʌg] vt abrazar ♦ n abrazo.
huge [hjuːdʒ] adj enorme.
hulk [hʌlk] n (ship) barco viejo; (person, building etc) mole f.
hulking ['hʌlkɪŋ] adj pesado.
hull [hʌl] n (of ship) casco.
hullabaloo ['hʌləbə'luː] n (col: noise) algarabía, jaleo.
hullo [hə'ləʊ] excl = **hello**.
hum [hʌm] vt tararear, canturrear ♦ vi tararear, canturrear; (insect) zumbar ♦ n (also ELEC) zumbido; (of traffic, machines) zumbido, ronroneo; (of voices etc) murmullo.
human ['hjuːmən] adj humano ♦ n (also: ~ being) ser m humano.
humane [hjuː'meɪn] adj humano, humanitario.
humanism ['hjuːmənɪzəm] n humanismo.
humanitarian [hjuːmænɪ'tɛərɪən] adj humanitario.
humanity [hjuː'mænɪtɪ] n humanidad f.
humanly ['hjuːmənlɪ] adv humanamente.
human relations npl relaciones fpl humanas.
human rights npl derechos mpl humanos.
humble ['hʌmbl] adj humilde ♦ vt humillar.
humbly ['hʌmblɪ] adv humildemente.
humbug ['hʌmbʌg] n patrañas fpl; (BRIT: sweet) caramelo de menta.
humdrum ['hʌmdrʌm] adj (boring) monótono, aburrido; (routine) rutinario.
humid ['hjuːmɪd] adj húmedo.
humidifier [hjuː'mɪdɪfaɪə*] n humectador m.
humidity [hjuː'mɪdɪtɪ] n humedad f.
humiliate [hjuː'mɪlɪeɪt] vt humillar.
humiliation [hjuːmɪlɪ'eɪʃən] n humillación f.
humility [hjuː'mɪlɪtɪ] n humildad f.
humorist ['hjuːmərɪst] n humorista m/f.
humorous ['hjuːmərəs] adj gracioso,

divertido.

humour, (*US*) **humor** ['hju:mə*] *n*
humorismo, sentido del humor; (*mood*)
humor *m* ♦ *vt* (*person*) complacer; **sense of**
~ sentido del humor; **to be in a good/bad**
~ estar de buen/mal humor.

humo(u)rless ['hju:məlıs] *adj* serio.

hump [hʌmp] *n* (*in ground*) montículo;
(*camel's*) giba.

humus ['hju:məs] *n* (*BIO*) humus *m*.

hunch [hʌntʃ] *n* (*premonition*)
presentimiento; **I have a** ~ **that** tengo la
corazonada *or* el presentimiento de que.

hunchback ['hʌntʃbæk] *n* jorobado/a.

hunched [hʌntʃt] *adj* jorobado.

hundred ['hʌndrəd] *num* ciento; (*before n*)
cien; **about a** ~ **people** unas cien
personas, alrededor de cien personas; **~s**
of centenares de; **~s of people**
centenares de personas; **I'm a** ~ **per cent**
sure estoy completamente seguro.

hundredweight ['hʌndrədweɪt] *n* (*BRIT*)
= *50.8 kg*; *112 lb*; (*US*) = *45.3 kg*; *100 lb*.

hung [hʌŋ] *pt, pp of* **hang.**

Hungarian [hʌŋ'gɛərɪən] *adj* húngaro ♦ *n*
húngaro/a *m/f*; (*LING*) húngaro.

Hungary ['hʌŋgərɪ] *n* Hungría.

hunger ['hʌŋgə*] *n* hambre *f* ♦ *vi*: **to** ~ **for**
(*fig*) tener hambre de, anhelar.

hunger strike *n* huelga de hambre.

hungover [hʌŋ'əuvə*] *adj* (*col*): **to be** ~
tener resaca.

hungrily ['hʌŋgrəlɪ] *adv* ávidamente, con
ganas.

hungry ['hʌŋgrɪ] *adj* hambriento; **to be** ~
tener hambre; ~ **for** (*fig*) sediento de.

hunk [hʌŋk] *n* (*of bread etc*) trozo, pedazo.

hunt [hʌnt] *vt* (*seek*) buscar; (*SPORT*) cazar
♦ *vi* cazar ♦ *n* caza, cacería.

►**hunt down** *vt* acorralar, seguir la pista
a.

hunter ['hʌntə*] *n* cazador(a) *m/f*; (*horse*)
caballo de caza.

hunting ['hʌntɪŋ] *n* caza.

hurdle ['hə:dl] *n* (*SPORT*) valla; (*fig*)
obstáculo.

hurl [hə:l] *vt* lanzar, arrojar.

hurling ['hə:lɪŋ] *n* (*SPORT*) *juego irlandés*
semejante al hockey.

hurly-burly ['hə:lɪ'bə:lɪ] *n* jaleo, follón *m*.

hurrah [hu'rɑ:], **hurray** [hu'reɪ] *n* ¡viva!,
¡hurra!

hurricane ['hʌrɪkən] *n* huracán *m*.

hurried ['hʌrɪd] *adj* (*fast*) apresurado;
(*rushed*) hecho de prisa.

hurriedly ['hʌrɪdlɪ] *adv* con prisa,
apresuradamente.

hurry ['hʌrɪ] *n* prisa ♦ *vb* (*also*: ~ **up**) *vi*

apresurarse, darse prisa, apurarse (*LAM*)
♦ *vt* (*person*) dar prisa a; (*work*)
apresurar, hacer de prisa; **to be in a** ~
tener prisa, tener apuro (*LAM*), estar
apurado (*LAM*); **to** ~ **back/home** darse
prisa en volver/volver a casa.

►**hurry along** *vi* pasar de prisa.

►**hurry away, hurry off** *vi* irse corriendo.

►**hurry on** *vi*: **to** ~ **on to say** apresurarse a
decir.

►**hurry up** *vi* darse prisa, apurarse (*esp*
LAM).

hurt [hə:t] *vb* (*pt, pp* **hurt**) *vt* hacer daño a;
(*business, interests etc*) perjudicar ♦ *vi*
doler ♦ *adj* lastimado; **I** ~ **my arm** me
lastimé el brazo; **where does it** ~**?**
¿dónde te duele?

hurtful ['hə:tful] *adj* (*remark etc*) hiriente,
dañino.

hurtle ['hə:tl] *vi*: **to** ~ **past** pasar como un
rayo.

husband ['hʌzbənd] *n* marido.

hush [hʌʃ] *n* silencio ♦ *vt* hacer callar;
(*cover up*) encubrir; ~**!** ¡chitón!, ¡cállate!

►**hush up** *vt* (*fact*) encubrir, callar.

hushed [hʌʃt] *adj* (*voice*) bajo.

hush-hush [hʌʃ'hʌʃ] *adj* (*col*) muy secreto.

husk [hʌsk] *n* (*of wheat*) cáscara.

husky ['hʌskɪ] *adj* ronco; (*burly*) fornido ♦ *n*
perro esquimal.

hustings ['hʌstɪŋz] *npl* (*POL*) mitin *msg*
preelectoral.

hustle ['hʌsl] *vt* (*push*) empujar; (*hurry*) dar
prisa a ♦ *n* bullicio, actividad *f* febril; ~
and bustle ajetreo.

hut [hʌt] *n* cabaña; (*shed*) cobertizo.

hutch [hʌtʃ] *n* conejera.

hyacinth ['haɪəsınθ] *n* jacinto.

hybrid ['haɪbrɪd] *adj, n* híbrido.

hydrant ['haɪdrənt] *n* (*also*: **fire** ~) boca de
incendios.

hydraulic [haɪ'drɔ:lɪk] *adj* hidráulico.

hydraulics [haɪ'drɔ:lɪks] *n* hidráulica.

hydrochloric ['haɪdrəu'klɔrɪk] *adj*: ~ **acid**
ácido clorhídrico.

hydroelectric [haɪdrəu'lɛktrɪk] *adj*
hidroeléctrico.

hydrofoil ['haɪdrəfɔɪl] *n* aerodeslizador *m*.

hydrogen ['haɪdrədʒən] *n* hidrógeno.

hydrogen bomb *n* bomba de hidrógeno.

hydrophobia [haɪdrə'fəubɪə] *n* hidrofobia.

hydroplane ['haɪdrəpleɪn] *n* hidroavión *m*,
hidroavioneta.

hyena [haɪ'i:nə] *n* hiena.

hygiene ['haɪdʒi:n] *n* higiene *f*.

hygienic [haɪ'dʒi:nɪk] *adj* higiénico.

hymn [hɪm] *n* himno.

hype [haɪp] *n* (*col*) bombo.

hyperactive [haɪpər'æktɪv] *adj* hiperactivo.
hypermarket ['haɪpəmɑːkɪt] *n* hipermercado.
hypertension ['haɪpə'tɛnʃən] *n* hipertensión *f*.
hyphen ['haɪfn] *n* guión *m*.
hypnosis [hɪp'nəʊsɪs] *n* hipnosis *f*.
hypnotic [hɪp'nɔtɪk] *adj* hipnótico.
hypnotism ['hɪpnətɪzəm] *n* hipnotismo.
hypnotist ['hɪpnətɪst] hipnotista *m/f*.
hypnotize ['hɪpnətaɪz] *vt* hipnotizar.
hypoallergenic ['haɪpəuælə'dʒɛnɪk] *adj* hipoalérgeno.
hypochondriac [haɪpəu'kɔndrɪæk] *n* hipocondríaco/a.
hypocrisy [hɪ'pɔkrɪsɪ] *n* hipocresía.
hypocrite ['hɪpəkrɪt] *n* hipócrita *m/f*.
hypocritical [hɪpə'krɪtɪkl] *adj* hipócrita.
hypodermic [haɪpə'dɜːmɪk] *adj* hipodérmico ♦ *n* (*syringe*) aguja hipodérmica.
hypotenuse [haɪ'pɔtɪnjuːz] *n* hipotenusa.
hypothermia [haɪpəu'θɜːmɪə] *n* hipotermia.
hypothesis, *pl* **hypotheses** [haɪ'pɔθɪsɪs, -siːz] *n* hipótesis *f inv*.
hypothetical [haɪpə'θɛtɪkl] *adj* hipotético.
hysterectomy [hɪstə'rɛktəmɪ] *n* histerectomía.
hysteria [hɪ'stɪərɪə] *n* histeria.
hysterical [hɪ'stɛrɪkl] *adj* histérico.
hysterics [hɪ'stɛrɪks] *npl* histeria *sg*, histerismo *sg*; **to have** ~ ponerse histérico.
Hz *abbr* (= *Hertz*) Hz.

I i

I, i [aɪ] *n* (*letter*) I, i *f*; **I for Isaac**, (*US*) **I for Item** I de Inés, I de Israel.
I [aɪ] *pron* yo ♦ *abbr* = **island**; **isle**.
IA, Ia. *abbr* (*US*) = *Iowa*.
IAEA *n abbr see* **International Atomic Energy Agency**.
IBA *n abbr* (*BRIT*) = **Independent Broadcasting Authority**; *see* **ITV**.
Iberian [aɪ'bɪərɪən] *adj* ibero, ibérico.
Iberian Peninsula *n*: **the** ~ la Península Ibérica.
IBEW *n abbr* (*US*: = *International Brotherhood of Electrical Workers*) sindicato internacional de electricistas.

ib(id). *abbr* (= *ibidem*: *from the same source*) ibídem.
i/c *abbr* (*BRIT*) = *in charge*.
ICBM *n abbr* (= *intercontinental ballistic missile*) misil *m* balístico intercontinental.
ICC *n abbr* (= *International Chamber of Commerce*) CCI *f*; (*US*) = *Interstate Commerce Commission*.
ice [aɪs] *n* hielo ♦ *vt* (*cake*) alcorzar ♦ *vi* (*also*: ~ **over**, ~ **up**) helarse; **to keep sth on** ~ (*fig*: *plan*, *project*) tener algo en reserva.
ice age *n* período glaciar.
ice axe *n* piqueta (de alpinista).
iceberg ['aɪsbɜːg] *n* iceberg *m*; **the tip of the** ~ la punta del iceberg.
icebox ['aɪsbɔks] *n* (*BRIT*) congelador *m*; (*US*) nevera, refrigeradora (*LAM*).
icebreaker ['aɪsbreɪkə*] *n* rompehielos *m inv*.
ice bucket *n* cubo para el hielo.
icecap ['aɪskæp] *n* casquete *m* polar.
ice-cold [aɪs'kəuld] *adj* helado.
ice cream *n* helado.
ice-cream soda *n* soda mezclada con helado.
ice cube *n* cubito de hielo.
iced [aɪst] *adj* (*drink*) con hielo; (*cake*) escarchado.
ice hockey *n* hockey *m* sobre hielo.
Iceland ['aɪslənd] *n* Islandia.
Icelander ['aɪsləndə*] *n* islandés/esa *m/f*.
Icelandic [aɪs'lændɪk] *adj* islandés/esa ♦ *n* (*LING*) islandés *m*.
ice lolly *n* (*BRIT*) polo.
ice pick *n* piolet *m*.
ice rink *n* pista de hielo.
ice-skate ['aɪsskeɪt] *n* patín *m* de hielo ♦ *vi* patinar sobre hielo.
ice-skating ['aɪsskeɪtɪŋ] *n* patinaje *m* sobre hielo.
icicle ['aɪsɪkl] *n* carámbano.
icing ['aɪsɪŋ] *n* (*CULIN*) alcorza; (*AVIAT etc*) formación *f* de hielo.
icing sugar *n* (*BRIT*) azúcar *m* glas(eado).
ICJ *n abbr see* **International Court of Justice**.
icon ['aɪkɔn] *n* (*gen*, *COMPUT*) icono.
ICR *n abbr* (*US*) = *Institute for Cancer Research*.
ICRC *n abbr* (= *International Committee of the Red Cross*) CICR.
ICU *n abbr* (= *intensive care unit*) UVI *f*.
icy ['aɪsɪ] *adj* (*road*) helado; (*fig*) glacial.
ID *abbr* (*US*) = *Idaho*.
I'd [aɪd] = **I would**; **I had**.
Ida. *abbr* (*US*) – *Idaho*.
ID card *n* (= *identity card*) DNI *m*.
IDD *n abbr* (*BRIT TEL*: = *international direct dialling*) servicio automático

internacional.
idea [aɪ'dɪə] *n* idea; **good** ~! ¡buena idea!; **to have an** ~ **that** ... tener la impresión de que ...; **I haven't the least** ~ no tengo ni (la más remota) idea.
ideal [aɪ'dɪəl] *n* ideal *m* ♦ *adj* ideal.
idealism [aɪ'dɪəlɪzəm] *n* idealismo.
idealist [aɪ'dɪəlɪst] *n* idealista *m/f.*
ideally [aɪ'dɪəlɪ] *adv* perfectamente; ~, **the book should have** ... idealmente, el libro debería tener ....
identical [aɪ'dɛntɪkl] *adj* idéntico.
identification [aɪdɛntɪfɪ'keɪʃən] *n* identificación *f*; **means of** ~ documentos *mpl* personales.
identify [aɪ'dɛntɪfaɪ] *vt* identificar ♦ *vi*: **to** ~ **with** identificarse con.
Identikit ® [aɪ'dɛntɪkɪt] *n*: ~ **(picture)** retrato-robot *m.*
identity [aɪ'dɛntɪtɪ] *n* identidad *f.*
identity card *n* carnet *m* de identidad, cédula (de identidad) (*LAM*).
identity papers *npl* documentos *mpl* (de identidad), documentación *fsg.*
identity parade *n* identificación *f* de acusados.
ideological [aɪdɪə'lɔdʒɪkəl] *adj* ideológico.
ideology [aɪdɪ'ɔlədʒɪ] *n* ideología.
idiocy ['ɪdɪəsɪ] *n* idiotez *f*; (*stupid act*) estupidez *f.*
idiom ['ɪdɪəm] *n* modismo; (*style of speaking*) lenguaje *m.*
idiomatic [ɪdɪə'mætɪk] *adj* idiomático.
idiosyncrasy [ɪdɪəu'sɪŋkrəsɪ] *n* idiosincrasia.
idiot ['ɪdɪət] *n* (*gen*) idiota *m/f*; (*fool*) tonto/a.
idiotic [ɪdɪ'ɔtɪk] *adj* idiota; tonto.
idle ['aɪdl] *adj* (*lazy*) holgazán/ana; (*unemployed*) parado, desocupado; (*talk*) frívolo ♦ *vi* (*machine*) funcionar *or* marchar en vacío; ~ **capacity** (*COMM*) capacidad *f* sin utilizar; ~ **money** (*COMM*) capital *m* improductivo; ~ **time** (*COMM*) tiempo de paro.
▶**idle away** *vt*: **to** ~ **away one's time** malgastar *or* desperdiciar el tiempo.
idleness ['aɪdlnɪs] *n* holgazanería; paro, desocupación *f.*
idler ['aɪdlə*] *n* holgazán/ana *m/f*, vago/a.
idol ['aɪdl] *n* ídolo.
idolize ['aɪdəlaɪz] *vt* idolatrar.
idyllic [ɪ'dɪlɪk] *adj* idílico.
i.e. *abbr* (= *id est: that is*) es decir.
if [ɪf] *conj* si ♦ *n*: **there are a lot of** ~**s and buts** hay muchas dudas sin resolver; **(even)** ~ aunque, si bien; **I'd be pleased** ~ **you could do it** yo estaría contento si pudieras hacerlo; ~ **necessary** si

resultase necesario; ~ **only** si solamente; **as** ~ como si.
iffy ['ɪfɪ] *adj* (*col*) dudoso.
igloo ['ɪgluː] *n* iglú *m.*
ignite [ɪg'naɪt] *vt* (*set fire to*) encender ♦ *vi* encenderse.
ignition [ɪg'nɪʃən] *n* (*AUT*) encendido; **to switch on/off the** ~ arrancar/apagar el motor.
ignition key *n* (*AUT*) llave *f* de contacto.
ignoble [ɪg'nəubl] *adj* innoble, vil.
ignominious [ɪgnə'mɪnɪəs] *adj* ignominioso, vergonzoso.
ignoramus [ɪgnə'reɪməs] *n* ignorante *m/f*, inculto/a.
ignorance ['ɪgnərəns] *n* ignorancia; **to keep sb in** ~ **of sth** ocultarle algo a algn.
ignorant ['ɪgnərənt] *adj* ignorante; **to be** ~ **of** (*subject*) desconocer; (*events*) ignorar.
ignore [ɪg'nɔː*] *vt* (*person*) no hacer caso de; (*fact*) pasar por alto.
ikon ['aɪkɔn] *n* = **icon.**
IL *abbr* (*US*) = *Illinois.*
ILA *n abbr* (*US*: = *International Longshoremen's Association*) *sindicato internacional de trabajadores portuarios.*
ill [ɪl] *adj* enfermo, malo ♦ *n* mal *m*; (*fig*) infortunio ♦ *adv* mal; **to take** *or* **be taken** ~ caer *or* ponerse enfermo; **to feel** ~ **(with)** encontrarse mal (de); **to speak/ think** ~ **of sb** hablar/pensar mal de algn; *see also* **ills.**
Ill. *abbr* (*US*) = *Illinois.*
I'll [aɪl] = **I will, I shall.**
ill-advised [ɪləd'vaɪzd] *adj* poco recomendable; **he was** ~ **to go** se equivocaba al ir.
ill-at-ease [ɪlət'iːz] *adj* incómodo.
ill-considered [ɪlkən'sɪdəd] *adj* (*plan*) poco pensado.
ill-disposed [ɪldɪs'pəuzd] *adj*: **to be** ~ **towards sb/sth** estar maldispuesto hacia algn/algo.
illegal [ɪ'liːgl] *adj* ilegal.
illegible [ɪ'lɛdʒɪbl] *adj* ilegible.
illegitimate [ɪlɪ'dʒɪtɪmət] *adj* ilegítimo.
ill-fated [ɪl'feɪtɪd] *adj* malogrado.
ill-favoured, (*US*) **ill-favored** [ɪl'feɪvəd] *adj* poco agraciado.
ill feeling *n* rencor *m.*
ill-gotten ['ɪlgɔtn] *adj* (*gains etc*) mal adquirido.
ill health *n* mala salud *f*; **to be in** ~ estar mal de salud.
illicit [ɪ'lɪsɪt] *adj* ilícito.
ill-informed [ɪlɪn'fɔːmd] *adj* (*judgement*) erróneo; (*person*) mal informado.

illiterate [ɪ'lɪtərət] adj analfabeto.
ill-mannered [ɪl'mænəd] adj mal educado.
illness ['ɪlnɪs] n enfermedad f.
illogical [ɪ'lɔdʒɪkl] adj ilógico.
ills [ɪlz] npl males mpl.
ill-suited [ɪl'suːtɪd] adj (couple)
incompatible; **he is ~ to the job** no es la
persona indicada para el trabajo.
ill-timed [ɪl'taɪmd] adj inoportuno.
ill-treat [ɪl'triːt] vt maltratar.
ill-treatment [ɪl'triːtmənt] n malos tratos
mpl.
illuminate [ɪ'luːmɪneɪt] vt (room, street)
iluminar, alumbrar; (subject) aclarar; **~d
sign** letrero luminoso.
illuminating [ɪ'luːmɪneɪtɪŋ] adj
revelador(a).
illumination [ɪluːmɪ'neɪʃən] n alumbrado;
~s npl luminarias fpl, luces fpl.
illusion [ɪ'luːʒən] n ilusión f; **to be under the
~ that**... estar convencido de que ....
illusive [ɪ'luːsɪv], **illusory** [ɪ'luːsərɪ] adj
ilusorio.
illustrate ['ɪləstreɪt] vt ilustrar.
illustration [ɪlə'streɪʃən] n (example)
ejemplo, ilustración f; (in book) lámina,
ilustración f.
illustrator ['ɪləstreɪtə*] n ilustrador(a) m/f.
illustrious [ɪ'lʌstrɪəs] adj ilustre.
ill will n rencor m.
ILO n abbr (= International Labour
Organization) OIT f.
ILWU n abbr (US: = International
Longshoremen's and Warehousemen's
Union) sindicato internacional de
trabajadores portuarios y almacenistas.
I'm [aɪm] = **I am**.
image ['ɪmɪdʒ] n imagen f.
imagery ['ɪmɪdʒərɪ] n imágenes fpl.
imaginable [ɪ'mædʒɪnəbl] adj imaginable.
imaginary [ɪ'mædʒɪnərɪ] adj imaginario.
imagination [ɪmædʒɪ'neɪʃən] n imaginación
f; (inventiveness) inventiva; (illusion)
fantasía.
imaginative [ɪ'mædʒɪnətɪv] adj
imaginativo.
imagine [ɪ'mædʒɪn] vt imaginarse;
(suppose) suponer.
imbalance [ɪm'bæləns] n desequilibrio.
imbecile ['ɪmbəsiːl] n imbécil m/f.
imbue [ɪm'bjuː] vt: **to ~ sth with** imbuir
algo de.
IMF n abbr see **International Monetary Fund**.
imitate ['ɪmɪteɪt] vt imitar.
imitation [ɪmɪ'teɪʃən] n imitación f; (copy)
copia; (pej) remedo.
imitator ['ɪmɪteɪtə*] n imitador(a) m/f.
immaculate [ɪ'mækjulət] adj limpísimo,

inmaculado; (REL) inmaculado.
immaterial [ɪmə'tɪərɪəl] adj incorpóreo; **it is
~ whether**... no importa si... .
immature [ɪmə'tjuə*] adj (person)
inmaduro; (of one's youth) joven.
immaturity [ɪmə'tjuərɪtɪ] n inmadurez f.
immeasurable [ɪ'mɛʒrəbl] adj
inconmensurable.
immediacy [ɪ'miːdɪəsɪ] n urgencia,
proximidad f.
immediate [ɪ'miːdɪət] adj inmediato;
(pressing) urgente, apremiante; **in the ~
future** en un futuro próximo.
immediately [ɪ'miːdɪətlɪ] adv (at once) en
seguida; **~ next to** justo al lado de.
immense [ɪ'mens] adj inmenso, enorme.
immensely [ɪ'menslɪ] adv enormemente.
immensity [ɪ'mensɪtɪ] n (of size, difference)
inmensidad f; (of problem) enormidad f.
immerse [ɪ'məːs] vt (submerge) sumergir;
to be ~d in (fig) estar absorto en.
immersion heater [ɪ'məːʃən-] n (BRIT)
calentador m de inmersión.
immigrant ['ɪmɪgrənt] n inmigrante m/f.
immigrate ['ɪmɪgreɪt] vi inmigrar.
immigration [ɪmɪ'greɪʃən] n inmigración f.
immigration authorities npl servicio sg
de inmigración.
immigration laws npl leyes fpl de
inmigración.
imminent ['ɪmɪnənt] adj inminente.
immobile [ɪ'məubaɪl] adj inmóvil.
immobilize [ɪ'məubɪlaɪz] vt inmovilizar.
immoderate [ɪ'mɔdərɪt] adj (person)
desmesurado; (opinion, reaction, demand)
excesivo.
immodest [ɪ'mɔdɪst] adj (indecent)
desvergonzado, impúdico; (boasting)
jactancioso.
immoral [ɪ'mɔrl] adj inmoral.
immorality [ɪmə'rælɪtɪ] n inmoralidad f.
immortal [ɪ'mɔːtl] adj inmortal.
immortality [ɪmɔː'tælɪtɪ] n inmortalidad f.
immortalize [ɪ'mɔːtlaɪz] vt inmortalizar.
immovable [ɪ'muːvəbl] adj (object)
imposible de mover; (person)
inconmovible.
immune [ɪ'mjuːn] adj: **~ (to)** inmune (a).
immune system n sistema m inmunitario.
immunity [ɪ'mjuːnɪtɪ] n (MED, of diplomat)
inmunidad f; (COMM) exención f.
immunization [ɪmjunaɪ'zeɪʃən] n
inmunización f.
immunize ['ɪmjunaɪz] vt inmunizar.
imp [ɪmp] n (small devil, also fig: child)
diablillo.
impact ['ɪmpækt] n (gen) impacto.
impair [ɪm'pɛə*] vt perjudicar.

-impaired [ɪmˈpɛəd] *suff*: **visually**~ con defectos de visión.
impale [ɪmˈpeɪl] *vt* (*with sword*) atravesar.
impart [ɪmˈpɑːt] *vt* comunicar; (*make known*) participar; (*bestow*) otorgar.
impartial [ɪmˈpɑːʃl] *adj* imparcial.
impartiality [ɪmpɑːʃɪˈælɪtɪ] *n* imparcialidad *f*.
impassable [ɪmˈpɑːsəbl] *adj* (*barrier*) infranqueable; (*road*) intransitable.
impasse [ɪmˈpɑːs] *n* callejón *m* sin salida; **to reach an** ~ llegar a un punto muerto.
impassioned [ɪmˈpæʃənd] *adj* apasionado, exaltado.
impassive [ɪmˈpæsɪv] *adj* impasible.
impatience [ɪmˈpeɪʃəns] *n* impaciencia.
impatient [ɪmˈpeɪʃənt] *adj* impaciente; **to get** *or* **grow** ~ impacientarse.
impatiently [ɪmˈpeɪʃəntlɪ] *adv* con impaciencia.
impeachment [ɪmˈpiːtʃmənt] *n* denuncia, acusación *f*.
impeccable [ɪmˈpɛkəbl] *adj* impecable.
impecunious [ɪmpɪˈkjuːnɪəs] *adj* sin dinero.
impede [ɪmˈpiːd] *vt* estorbar, dificultar.
impediment [ɪmˈpɛdɪmənt] *n* obstáculo, estorbo; (*also*: **speech** ~) defecto (del habla).
impel [ɪmˈpɛl] *vt* (*force*): **to** ~ **sb** (**to do sth**) obligar a algn (a hacer algo).
impending [ɪmˈpɛndɪŋ] *adj* inminente.
impenetrable [ɪmˈpɛnɪtrəbl] *adj* (*jungle, fortress*) impenetrable; (*unfathomable*) insondable.
imperative [ɪmˈpɛrətɪv] *adj* (*tone*) imperioso; (*necessary*) imprescindible ♦ *n* (*LING*) imperativo.
imperceptible [ɪmpəˈsɛptɪbl] *adj* imperceptible.
imperfect [ɪmˈpəːfɪkt] *adj* imperfecto; (*goods etc*) defectuoso.
imperfection [ɪmpəˈfɛkʃən] *n* (*blemish*) desperfecto; (*fault, flaw*) defecto.
imperial [ɪmˈpɪərɪəl] *adj* imperial.
imperialism [ɪmˈpɪərɪəlɪzəm] *n* imperialismo.
imperil [ɪmˈpɛrɪl] *vt* poner en peligro.
imperious [ɪmˈpɪərɪəs] *adj* señorial, apremiante.
impersonal [ɪmˈpəːsənl] *adj* impersonal.
impersonate [ɪmˈpəːsəneɪt] *vt* hacerse pasar por.
impersonation [ɪmpəːsəˈneɪʃən] *n* imitación *f*.
impersonator [ɪmˈpəːsəneɪtə*] *n* (*THEAT etc*) imitador(a) *m/f*.
impertinence [ɪmˈpəːtɪnəns] *n* impertinencia, insolencia.

impertinent [ɪmˈpəːtɪnənt] *adj* impertinente, insolente.
imperturbable [ɪmpəˈtəːbəbl] *adj* imperturbable, impasible.
impervious [ɪmˈpəːvɪəs] *adj* impermeable; (*fig*): ~ **to** insensible a.
impetuous [ɪmˈpɛtjuəs] *adj* impetuoso.
impetus [ˈɪmpətəs] *n* ímpetu *m*; (*fig*) impulso.
impinge [ɪmˈpɪndʒ]: **to** ~ **on** *vt fus* (*affect*) afectar a.
impish [ˈɪmpɪʃ] *adj* travieso.
implacable [ɪmˈplækəbl] *adj* implacable.
implant [ɪmˈplɑːnt] *vt* (*MED*) injertar, implantar; (*fig*: *idea, principle*) inculcar.
implausible [ɪmˈplɔːzɪbl] *adj* implausible.
implement *n* [ˈɪmplɪmənt] instrumento, herramienta ♦ *vt* [ˈɪmplɪment] hacer efectivo; (*carry out*) realizar.
implicate [ˈɪmplɪkeɪt] *vt* (*compromise*) comprometer; (*involve*) enredar; **to** ~ **sb in sth** comprometer a algn en algo.
implication [ɪmplɪˈkeɪʃən] *n* consecuencia; **by** ~ indirectamente.
implicit [ɪmˈplɪsɪt] *adj* (*gen*) implícito; (*complete*) absoluto.
implicitly [ɪmˈplɪsɪtlɪ] *adv* implícitamente.
implore [ɪmˈplɔː*] *vt* (*person*) suplicar.
imploring [ɪmˈplɔːrɪŋ] *adj* de súplica.
imply [ɪmˈplaɪ] *vt* (*involve*) implicar, suponer; (*hint*) insinuar.
impolite [ɪmpəˈlaɪt] *adj* mal educado.
impolitic [ɪmˈpɔlɪtɪk] *adj* poco diplomático.
imponderable [ɪmˈpɔndərəbl] *adj* imponderable.
import *vt* [ɪmˈpɔːt] importar ♦ *n* [ˈɪmpɔːt] (*COMM*) importación *f*; (*meaning*) significado, sentido ♦ *cpd* (*duty, licence etc*) de importación.
importance [ɪmˈpɔːtəns] *n* importancia; **to be of great/little** ~ tener mucha/poca importancia.
important [ɪmˈpɔːtənt] *adj* importante; **it's not** ~ no importa, no tiene importancia; **it is** ~ **that** es importante que.
importantly [ɪmˈpɔːtəntlɪ] *adv* (*pej*) dándose importancia; **but, more** ~ ... pero, lo que es aún más importante ....
import duty *n* derechos *mpl* de importación.
imported [ɪmˈpɔːtɪd] *adj* importado.
importer [ɪmˈpɔːtə*] *n* importador(a) *m/f*.
import licence, (*US*) **import license** *n* licencia de importación.
impose [ɪmˈpəʊz] *vt* imponer ♦ *vi*: **to** ~ **on sb** abusar de algn.
imposing [ɪmˈpəʊzɪŋ] *adj* imponente, impresionante.

imposition [ɪmpə'zɪʃn] *n* (*of tax etc*) imposición *f*; **to be an ~** (*on person*) molestar.

impossibility [ɪmpɔsə'bɪlɪtɪ] *n* imposibilidad *f*.

impossible [ɪm'pɔsɪbl] *adj* imposible; (*person*) insoportable; **it is ~ for me to leave now** me es imposible salir ahora.

impossibly [ɪm'pɔsɪblɪ] *adv* imposiblemente.

impostor [ɪm'pɔstə*] *n* impostor(a) *m/f*.

impotence ['ɪmpətəns] *n* impotencia.

impotent ['ɪmpətənt] *adj* impotente.

impound [ɪm'paund] *vt* embargar.

impoverished [ɪm'pɔvərɪʃt] *adj* necesitado; (*land*) agotado.

impracticable [ɪm'præktɪkəbl] *adj* no factible, irrealizable.

impractical [ɪm'præktɪkl] *adj* (*person*) poco práctico.

imprecise [ɪmprɪ'saɪs] *adj* impreciso.

impregnable [ɪm'prɛgnəbl] *adj* invulnerable; (*castle*) inexpugnable.

impregnate ['ɪmprɛgneɪt] *vt* (*gen*) impregnar; (*soak*) empapar; (*fertilize*) fecundar.

impresario [ɪmprɪ'saːrɪəu] *n* empresario/a.

impress [ɪm'prɛs] *vt* impresionar; (*mark*) estampar ♦ *vi* causar buena impresión; **to ~ sth on sb** convencer a algn de la importancia de algo.

impression [ɪm'prɛʃən] *n* impresión *f*; (*footprint etc*) huella; (*print run*) edición *f*; **to be under the ~ that** tener la idea de que; **to make a good/bad ~ on sb** causar buena/mala impresión a algn.

impressionable [ɪm'prɛʃnəbl] *adj* impresionable.

impressionist [ɪm'prɛʃənɪst] *n* impresionista *m/f*.

impressive [ɪm'prɛsɪv] *adj* impresionante.

imprint ['ɪmprɪnt] *n* (*PUBLISHING*) pie *m* de imprenta; (*fig*) sello.

imprison [ɪm'prɪzn] *vt* encarcelar.

imprisonment [ɪm'prɪznmənt] *n* encarcelamiento; (*term of ~*) cárcel *f*; **life ~** cadena perpetua.

improbable [ɪm'prɔbəbl] *adj* improbable, inverosímil.

impromptu [ɪm'prɔmptjuː] *adj* improvisado ♦ *adv* de improviso.

improper [ɪm'prɔpə*] *adj* (*incorrect*) impropio; (*unseemly*) indecoroso; (*indecent*) indecente.

impropriety [ɪmprə'praɪətɪ] *n* falta de decoro; (*indecency*) indecencia; (*of language*) impropiedad *f*.

improve [ɪm'pruːv] *vt* mejorar; (*foreign language*) perfeccionar ♦ *vi* mejorar.

▶**improve (up)on** *vt fus* (*offer*) mejorar.

improvement [ɪm'pruːvmənt] *n* mejora; perfeccionamiento; **to make ~s to** mejorar.

improvise ['ɪmprəvaɪz] *vt, vi* improvisar.

imprudence [ɪm'pruːdns] *n* imprudencia.

imprudent [ɪm'pruːdnt] *adj* imprudente.

impudent ['ɪmpjudnt] *adj* descarado, insolente.

impugn [ɪm'pjuːn] *vt* impugnar.

impulse ['ɪmpʌls] *n* impulso; **to act on ~** sin reflexión dejarse llevar por el impulso.

impulse buying *n* compra impulsiva.

impulsive [ɪm'pʌlsɪv] *adj* irreflexivo, impulsivo.

impunity [ɪm'pjuːnɪtɪ] *n*: **with ~** impunemente.

impure [ɪm'pjuə*] *adj* (*adulterated*) adulterado; (*morally*) impuro.

impurity [ɪm'pjuərɪtɪ] *n* impureza.

IN *abbr* (*US*) = *Indiana*.

KEYWORD

in [ɪn] *prep* **1** (*indicating place, position, with place names*) en; **~ the house/garden** en (la) casa/el jardín; **~ here/there** aquí/ahí *or* allí dentro; **~ London/England** en Londres/Inglaterra; **~ town** en el centro (de la ciudad)

2 (*indicating time*) en; **~ spring** en (la) primavera; **in 1888/May** en 1888/mayo; **~ the afternoon** por la tarde; **at 4 o'clock ~ the afternoon** a las 4 de la tarde; **I did it ~ 3 hours/days** lo hice en 3 horas/días; **I'll see you ~ 2 weeks** *or* **~ 2 weeks' time** te veré dentro de 2 semanas; **once ~ a hundred years** una vez cada cien años

3 (*indicating manner etc*) en; **~ a loud/soft voice** en voz alta/baja; **~ pencil/ink** a lápiz/bolígrafo; **the boy ~ the blue shirt** el chico de la camisa azul; **~ writing** por escrito; **to pay ~ dollars** pagar en dólares

4 (*indicating circumstances*): **~ the sun/ shade** al sol/a la sombra; **~ the rain** bajo la lluvia; **a change ~ policy** un cambio de política; **a rise ~ prices** un aumento de precios

5 (*indicating mood, state*): **~ tears** llorando; **~ anger/despair** enfadado/ desesperado; **to live ~ luxury** vivir lujosamente

6 (*with ratios, numbers*): **1 ~ 10 households, 1 household ~ 10** una de cada 10 familias; **20 pence ~ the pound** 20 peniques por libra; **they lined up ~ twos** se alinearon de dos en dos; **~**

hundreds a *or* por centenares
7 (*referring to people, works*) en; entre; **the
disease is common** ~ **children** la
enfermedad es común entre los niños; ~
(**the works of**) **Dickens** en (las obras de)
Dickens
8 (*indicating profession etc*): **to be** ~
teaching dedicarse a la enseñanza
9 (*after superlative*) de; **the best pupil** ~
the class el/la mejor alumno/a de la clase
10 (*with present participle*): ~ **saying this**
al decir esto
♦ *adv*: **to be** ~ (*person: at home*) estar en
casa; (: *work*) estar; (*train, ship, plane*)
haber llegado; (*in fashion*) estar de moda;
she'll be ~ **later today** llegará más tarde
hoy; **to ask sb** ~ hacer pasar a algn; **to
run/limp** *etc* ~ entrar corriendo/
cojeando *etc*
♦ ~ **that** *conj* ya que
♦ *npl*: **the** ~**s and outs** (*of proposal,
situation etc*) los detalles.

in., ins *abbr* = **inch(es)**.
inability [ɪnəˈbɪlɪtɪ] *n* incapacidad *f*; ~ **to
pay** insolvencia en el pago.
inaccessible [ɪnəkˈsɛsɪbl] *adj* inaccesible.
inaccuracy [ɪnˈækjʊrəsɪ] *n* inexactitud *f*.
inaccurate [ɪnˈækjʊrət] *adj* inexacto,
incorrecto.
inaction [ɪnˈækʃən] *n* inacción *f*.
inactive [ɪnˈæktɪv] *adj* inactivo.
inactivity [ɪnækˈtɪvɪtɪ] *n* inactividad *f*.
inadequacy [ɪnˈædɪkwəsɪ] *n* insuficiencia;
incapacidad *f*.
inadequate [ɪnˈædɪkwət] *adj* (*insufficient*)
insuficiente; (*unsuitable*) inadecuado;
(*person*) incapaz.
inadmissible [ɪnədˈmɪsəbl] *adj*
improcedente, inadmisible.
inadvertent [ɪnədˈvɜːtənt] *adj* descuidado,
involuntario.
inadvertently [ɪnədˈvɜːtntlɪ] *adv* por
descuido.
inadvisable [ɪnədˈvaɪzəbl] *adj* poco
aconsejable.
inane [ɪˈneɪn] *adj* necio, fatuo.
inanimate [ɪnˈænɪmət] *adj* inanimado.
inapplicable [ɪnˈæplɪkəbl] *adj* inaplicable.
inappropriate [ɪnəˈprəʊprɪət] *adj*
inadecuado.
inapt [ɪnˈæpt] *adj* impropio.
inaptitude [ɪnˈæptɪtjuːd] *n* incapacidad *f*.
inarticulate [ɪnɑːˈtɪkjʊlət] *adj* (*person*)
incapaz de expresarse; (*speech*) mal
pronunciado.
inartistic [ɪnɑːˈtɪstɪk] *adj* antiestético.
inasmuch as [ɪnəzˈmʌtʃ-] *adv* en la medida

en que.
inattention [ɪnəˈtɛnʃən] *n* desatención *f*.
inattentive [ɪnəˈtɛntɪv] *adj* distraído.
inaudible [ɪnˈɔːdɪbl] *adj* inaudible.
inaugural [ɪˈnɔːgjʊrəl] *adj* inaugural;
(*speech*) de apertura.
inaugurate [ɪˈnɔːgjʊreɪt] *vt* inaugurar;
(*president, official*) investir.
inauguration [ɪnɔːgjuˈreɪʃən] *n*
inauguración *f*; (*of official*) investidura; (*of
event*) ceremonia de apertura.
inauspicious [ɪnɔːsˈpɪʃəs] *adj* poco
propicio, inoportuno.
in-between [ɪnbɪˈtwiːn] *adj* intermedio.
inborn [ɪnˈbɔːn] *adj* (*feeling*) innato.
inbred [ɪnˈbrɛd] *adj* innato; (*family*)
consanguíneo.
inbreeding [ɪnˈbriːdɪŋ] *n* endogamia.
Inc. *abbr* = **incorporated**.
Inca [ˈɪŋkə] *adj* (*also*: ~**n**) inca, de los incas
♦ *n* inca *m/f*.
incalculable [ɪnˈkælkjʊləbl] *adj*
incalculable.
incapability [ɪnkeɪpəˈbɪlɪtɪ] *n* incapacidad *f*.
incapable [ɪnˈkeɪpəbl] *adj*: ~ (**of doing sth**)
incapaz (de hacer algo).
incapacitate [ɪnkəˈpæsɪteɪt] *vt*: **to** ~ **sb**
incapacitar a algn.
incapacitated [ɪnkəˈpæsɪteɪtɪd] *adj*
incapacitado.
incapacity [ɪnkəˈpæsɪtɪ] *n* (*inability*)
incapacidad *f*.
incarcerate [ɪnˈkɑːsəreɪt] *vt* encarcelar.
incarnate *adj* [ɪnˈkɑːnɪt] en persona ♦ *vt*
[ˈɪnkɑːneɪt] encarnar.
incarnation [ɪnkɑːˈneɪʃən] *n* encarnación *f*.
incendiary [ɪnˈsɛndɪərɪ] *adj* incendiario ♦ *n*
(*bomb*) bomba incendiaria.
incense *n* [ˈɪnsɛns] incienso ♦ *vt* [ɪnˈsɛns]
(*anger*) indignar, encolerizar.
incentive [ɪnˈsɛntɪv] *n* incentivo, estímulo.
incentive bonus *n* prima.
incentive scheme *n* plan *m* de incentivos.
inception [ɪnˈsɛpʃən] *n* comienzo,
principio.
incessant [ɪnˈsɛsnt] *adj* incesante,
continuo.
incessantly [ɪnˈsɛsəntlɪ] *adv*
constantemente.
incest [ˈɪnsɛst] *n* incesto.
inch [ɪntʃ] *n* pulgada; **to be within an** ~ **of**
estar a dos dedos de; **he didn't give an** ~
no hizo la más mínima concesión; **a few**
~**es** unas pulgadas.
▶**inch forward** *vi* avanzar palmo a palmo.
incidence [ˈɪnsɪdns] *n* (*of crime, disease*)
incidencia.
incident [ˈɪnsɪdnt] *n* incidente *m*; (*in book*)

episodio.

incidental [ɪnsɪ'dɛntl] *adj* circunstancial, accesorio; (*unplanned*) fortuito; ~ **to** relacionado con; ~ **expenses** (gastos *mpl*) imprevistos *mpl*.

incidentally [ɪnsɪ'dɛntəlɪ] *adv* (*by the way*) por cierto.

incidental music *n* música de fondo.

incident room *n* (*POLICE*) centro de coordinación.

incinerate [ɪn'sɪnəreɪt] *vt* incinerar, quemar.

incinerator [ɪn'sɪnəreɪtə*] *n* incinerador *m*, incineradora.

incipient [ɪn'sɪpɪənt] *adj* incipiente.

incision [ɪn'sɪʒən] *n* incisión *f*.

incisive [ɪn'saɪsɪv] *adj* (*mind*) penetrante; (*remark etc*) incisivo.

incisor [ɪn'saɪzə*] *n* incisivo.

incite [ɪn'saɪt] *vt* provocar, incitar.

incl. *abbr* = **including; inclusive (of)**.

inclement [ɪn'klɛmənt] *adj* inclemente.

inclination [ɪnklɪ'neɪʃən] *n* (*tendency*) tendencia, inclinación *f*.

incline *n* ['ɪnklaɪn] pendiente *f*, cuesta ♦ *vb* [ɪn'klaɪn] *vt* (*slope*) inclinar; (*head*) poner de lado ♦ *vi* inclinarse; **to be ~d to** (*tend*) ser propenso a; (*be willing*) estar dispuesto a.

include [ɪn'kluːd] *vt* incluir, comprender; (*in letter*) adjuntar; **the tip is/is not ~d** la propina está/no está incluida.

including [ɪn'kluːdɪŋ] *prep* incluso, inclusive; ~ **tip** propina incluida.

inclusion [ɪn'kluːʒən] *n* inclusión *f*.

inclusive [ɪn'kluːsɪv] *adj* inclusivo ♦ *adv* inclusive; ~ **of tax** incluidos los impuestos; **$50, ~ of all surcharges** 50 dólares, incluidos todos los recargos.

incognito [ɪnkɔg'niːtəu] *adv* de incógnito.

incoherent [ɪnkəu'hɪərənt] *adj* incoherente.

income ['ɪnkʌm] *n* (*personal*) ingresos *mpl*; (*from property etc*) renta; (*profit*) rédito; **gross/net** ~ ingresos *mpl* brutos/netos; ~ **and expenditure account** cuenta de gastos e ingresos.

income bracket *n* categoría económica.

income support *n* (*BRIT*) ≈ ayuda familiar.

income tax *n* impuesto sobre la renta.

income tax inspector *n* inspector(a) *m/f* de Hacienda.

income tax return *n* declaración *f* de ingresos.

incoming ['ɪnkʌmɪŋ] *adj* (*passengers, flight*) de llegada; (*government*) entrante; (*tenant*) nuevo.

incommunicado ['ɪnkəmjunɪ'kɑːdəu] *adj*: **to**

hold sb ~ mantener incomunicado a algn.

incomparable [ɪn'kɔmpərəbl] *adj* incomparable, sin par.

incompatible [ɪnkəm'pætɪbl] *adj* incompatible.

incompetence [ɪn'kɔmpɪtəns] *n* incompetencia.

incompetent [ɪn'kɔmpɪtənt] *adj* incompetente.

incomplete [ɪnkəm'pliːt] *adj* incompleto; (*unfinished*) sin terminar.

incomprehensible [ɪnkɔmprɪ'hɛnsɪbl] *adj* incomprensible.

inconceivable [ɪnkən'siːvəbl] *adj* inconcebible.

inconclusive [ɪnkən'kluːsɪv] *adj* sin resultado (definitivo); (*argument*) poco convincente.

incongruity [ɪnkɔŋ'gruːɪtɪ] *n* incongruencia.

incongruous [ɪn'kɔŋgruəs] *adj* discordante.

inconsequential [ɪnkɔnsɪ'kwɛnʃl] *adj* intranscendente.

inconsiderable [ɪnkən'sɪdərəbl] *adj* insignificante.

inconsiderate [ɪnkən'sɪdərət] *adj* desconsiderado; **how ~ of him!** ¡qué falta de consideración (de su parte)!

inconsistency [ɪnkən'sɪstənsɪ] *n* inconsecuencia; (*of actions etc*) falta de lógica; (*of work*) carácter *m* desigual, inconsistencia; (*of statement etc*) contradicción *f*.

inconsistent [ɪnkən'sɪstnt] *adj* inconsecuente; ~ **with** que no concuerda con.

inconsolable [ɪnkən'səuləbl] *adj* inconsolable.

inconspicuous [ɪnkən'spɪkjuəs] *adj* (*discreet*) discreto; (*person*) que llama poco la atención.

inconstancy [ɪn'kɔnstənsɪ] *n* inconstancia.

inconstant [ɪn'kɔnstənt] *adj* inconstante.

incontinence [ɪn'kɔntɪnəns] *n* incontinencia.

incontinent [ɪn'kɔntɪnənt] *adj* incontinente.

incontrovertible [ɪnkɔntrə'vəːtəbl] *adj* incontrovertible.

inconvenience [ɪnkən'viːnjəns] *n* (*gen*) inconvenientes *mpl*; (*trouble*) molestia ♦ *vt* incomodar; **to put sb to great** ~ causar mucha molestia a algn; **don't** ~ **yourself** no se moleste.

inconvenient [ɪnkən'viːnjənt] *adj* incómodo, poco práctico; (*time, place*) inoportuno; **that time is very** ~ **for me** esa hora me es muy inconveniente.

incorporate [ɪn'kɔːpəreɪt] *vt* incorporar; (*contain*) comprender; (*add*) agregar.
incorporated [ɪn'kɔːpəreɪtɪd] *adj*: ~ **company** (*US: abbr* **Inc.**) ≈ Sociedad *f* Anónima (S.A.).
incorrect [ɪnkə'rɛkt] *adj* incorrecto.
incorrigible [ɪn'kɔrɪdʒəbl] *adj* incorregible.
incorruptible [ɪnkə'rʌptɪbl] *adj* incorruptible.
increase *n* ['ɪnkriːs] aumento ♦ *vb* [ɪn'kriːs] *vi* aumentar; (*grow*) crecer; (*price*) subir ♦ *vt* aumentar; **an** ~ **of 5%** un aumento de 5%; **to be on the** ~ ir en aumento.
increasing [ɪn'kriːsɪŋ] *adj* (*number*) creciente, que va en aumento.
increasingly [ɪn'kriːsɪŋlɪ] *adv* cada vez más.
incredible [ɪn'krɛdɪbl] *adj* increíble.
incredibly [ɪn'krɛdɪblɪ] *adv* increíblemente.
incredulous [ɪn'krɛdjuləs] *adj* incrédulo.
increment ['ɪnkrɪmənt] *n* aumento, incremento.
incriminate [ɪn'krɪmɪneɪt] *vt* incriminar.
incriminating [ɪn'krɪmɪneɪtɪŋ] *adj* incriminatorio.
incrust [ɪn'krʌst] *vt* = **encrust**.
incubate ['ɪnkjubeɪt] *vt* (*eggs*) incubar, empollar ♦ *vi* (*egg, disease*) incubar.
incubation [ɪnkju'beɪʃən] *n* incubación *f*.
incubation period *n* período de incubación.
incubator ['ɪnkjubeɪtə*] *n* incubadora.
inculcate ['ɪnkʌlkeɪt] *vt*: **to** ~ **sth in sb** inculcar algo en algn.
incumbent [ɪn'kʌmbənt] *n* ocupante *m/f* ♦ *adj*: **it is** ~ **on him to...** le incumbe....
incur [ɪn'kə:*] *vt* (*expenses*) incurrir en; (*loss*) sufrir.
incurable [ɪn'kjuərəbl] *adj* incurable.
incursion [ɪn'kə:ʃən] *n* incursión *f*.
Ind. *abbr* (*US*) = Indiana.
indebted [ɪn'dɛtɪd] *adj*: **to be** ~ **to sb** estar agradecido a algn.
indecency [ɪn'diːsnsɪ] *n* indecencia.
indecent [ɪn'diːsnt] *adj* indecente.
indecent assault *n* (*BRIT*) atentado contra el pudor.
indecent exposure *n* exhibicionismo.
indecipherable [ɪndɪ'saɪfərəbl] *adj* indescifrable.
indecision [ɪndɪ'sɪʒən] *n* indecisión *f*.
indecisive [ɪndɪ'saɪsɪv] *adj* indeciso; (*discussion*) no resuelto, inconcluyente.
indeed [ɪn'diːd] *adv* efectivamente, en realidad; **yes** ~! ¡claro que sí!
indefatigable [ɪndɪ'fætɪgəbl] *adj* incansable, infatigable.
indefensible [ɪndɪ'fɛnsəbl] *adj* (*conduct*) injustificable.

indefinable [ɪndɪ'faɪnəbl] *adj* indefinible.
indefinite [ɪn'dɛfɪnɪt] *adj* indefinido; (*uncertain*) incierto.
indefinitely [ɪn'dɛfɪnɪtlɪ] *adv* (*wait*) indefinidamente.
indelible [ɪn'dɛlɪbl] *adj* imborrable.
indelicate [ɪn'dɛlɪkɪt] *adj* (*tactless*) indiscreto, inoportuno; (*not polite*) poco delicado.
indemnify [ɪn'dɛmnɪfaɪ] *vt* indemnizar, resarcir.
indemnity [ɪn'dɛmnɪtɪ] *n* (*insurance*) indemnidad *f*; (*compensation*) indemnización *f*.
indent [ɪn'dɛnt] *vt* (*text*) sangrar.
indentation [ɪndɛn'teɪʃən] *n* mella; (*TYP*) sangría.
independence [ɪndɪ'pɛndns] *n* independencia.
Independence Day *n* Día *m* de la Independencia; *ver recuadro*.

INDEPENDENCE DAY

El cuatro de julio es la fiesta nacional de los Estados Unidos, **Independence Day,** *en conmemoración de la Declaración de Independencia escrita por Thomas Jefferson y adoptada en 1776. En ella se proclamaba la ruptura total con Gran Bretaña de las trece colonias americanas que fueron el origen de los Estados Unidos de América.*

independent [ɪndɪ'pɛndənt] *adj* independiente; **to become** ~ independizarse.
in-depth ['ɪndɛpθ] *adj* en profundidad, a fondo.
indescribable [ɪndɪ'skraɪbəbl] *adj* indescriptible.
indestructible [ɪndɪs'trʌktəbl] *adj* indestructible.
indeterminate [ɪndɪ'tə:mɪnɪt] *adj* indeterminado.
index ['ɪndɛks] *n* (*pl*: ~**es**: *in book*) índice *m*; (: *in library etc*) catálogo; (*pl*: **indices** ['ɪndɪsiːz]: *ratio, sign*) exponente *m*.
index card *n* ficha.
index finger *n* índice *m*.
index-linked ['ɪndɛks'lɪŋkt], (*US*) **indexed** ['ɪndɛkst] *adj* indexado.
India ['ɪndɪə] *n* la India.
Indian ['ɪndɪən] *adj*, *n* indio/a *m/f*; (*American* ~) indio/a *m/f* de América, amerindio/a *m/f*; **Red** ~ piel roja *m/f*.
Indian Ocean *n*: **the** ~ el Océano Índico, el Mar de las Indias.
Indian summer *n* (*fig*) veranillo de San

Martín.

india rubber *n* caucho.

indicate ['ɪndɪkeɪt] *vt* indicar ♦ *vi* (*BRIT AUT*): **to ~ left/right** indicar a la izquierda/a la derecha.

indication [ɪndɪ'keɪʃən] *n* indicio, señal *f*.

indicative [ɪn'dɪkətɪv] *adj*: **to be ~ of sth** indicar algo ♦ *n* (*LING*) indicativo.

indicator ['ɪndɪkeɪtə*] *n* (*gen*) indicador *m*; (*AUT*) intermitente *m*, direccional *m* (*LAM*).

indices ['ɪndɪsiːz] *npl of* **index**.

indict [ɪn'daɪt] *vt* acusar.

indictable [ɪn'daɪtəbl] *adj*: **~ offence** delito procesable.

indictment [ɪn'daɪtmənt] *n* acusación *f*.

indifference [ɪn'dɪfrəns] *n* indiferencia.

indifferent [ɪn'dɪfrənt] *adj* indiferente; (*poor*) regular.

indigenous [ɪn'dɪdʒɪnəs] *adj* indígena.

indigestible [ɪndɪ'dʒɛstɪbl] *adj* indigesto.

indigestion [ɪndɪ'dʒɛstʃən] *n* indigestión *f*.

indignant [ɪn'dɪgnənt] *adj*: **to be ~ about sth** indignarse por algo.

indignation [ɪndɪg'neɪʃən] *n* indignación *f*.

indignity [ɪn'dɪgnɪtɪ] *n* indignidad *f*.

indigo ['ɪndɪgəʊ] *adj* (*colour*) (de color) añil ♦ *n* añil *m*.

indirect [ɪndɪ'rɛkt] *adj* indirecto.

indirectly [ɪndɪ'rɛktlɪ] *adv* indirectamente.

indiscernible [ɪndɪ'səːnəbl] *adj* imperceptible.

indiscreet [ɪndɪ'skriːt] *adj* indiscreto, imprudente.

indiscretion [ɪndɪ'skrɛʃən] *n* indiscreción *f*, imprudencia.

indiscriminate [ɪndɪ'skrɪmɪnət] *adj* indiscriminado.

indispensable [ɪndɪ'spɛnsəbl] *adj* indispensable, imprescindible.

indisposed [ɪndɪ'spəʊzd] *adj* (*unwell*) indispuesto.

indisposition [ɪndɪspə'zɪʃən] *n* indisposición *f*.

indisputable [ɪndɪ'spjuːtəbl] *adj* incontestable.

indistinct [ɪndɪ'stɪŋkt] *adj* indistinto.

indistinguishable [ɪndɪ'stɪŋgwɪʃəbl] *adj* indistinguible.

individual [ɪndɪ'vɪdjuəl] *n* individuo ♦ *adj* individual; (*personal*) personal; (*for/of one only*) particular.

individualist [ɪndɪ'vɪdjuəlɪst] *n* individualista *m/f*.

individuality [ɪndɪvɪdju'ælɪtɪ] *n* individualidad *f*.

individually [ɪndɪ'vɪdjuəlɪ] *adv* individualmente; particularmente.

indivisible [ɪndɪ'vɪzəbl] *adj* indivisible.

Indo-China ['ɪndəʊ'tʃaɪnə] *n* Indochina.

indoctrinate [ɪn'dɒktrɪneɪt] *vt* adoctrinar.

indoctrination [ɪndɒktrɪ'neɪʃən] *n* adoctrinamiento.

indolence ['ɪndələns] *n* indolencia.

indolent ['ɪndələnt] *adj* indolente, perezoso.

Indonesia [ɪndə'niːzɪə] *n* Indonesia.

Indonesian [ɪndə'niːzɪən] *adj* indonesio ♦ *n* indonesio/a; (*LING*) indonesio.

indoor ['ɪndɔː*] *adj* (*swimming pool*) cubierto; (*plant*) de interior; (*sport*) bajo cubierta.

indoors [ɪn'dɔːz] *adv* dentro; (*at home*) en casa.

indubitable [ɪn'djuːbɪtəbl] *adj* indudable.

indubitably [ɪn'djuːbɪtəblɪ] *adv* indudablemente.

induce [ɪn'djuːs] *vt* inducir, persuadir; (*bring about*) producir; **to ~ sb to do sth** persuadir a algn a que haga algo.

inducement [ɪn'djuːsmənt] *n* (*incentive*) incentivo, aliciente *m*.

induct [ɪn'dʌkt] *vt* iniciar; (*in job, rank, position*) instalar.

induction [ɪn'dʌkʃən] *n* (*MED: of birth*) inducción *f*.

induction course *n* (*BRIT*) cursillo introductorio *or* de iniciación.

indulge [ɪn'dʌldʒ] *vt* (*whim*) satisfacer; (*person*) complacer; (*child*) mimar ♦ *vi*: **to ~ in** darse el gusto de.

indulgence [ɪn'dʌldʒəns] *n* vicio.

indulgent [ɪn'dʌldʒənt] *adj* indulgente.

industrial [ɪn'dʌstrɪəl] *adj* industrial.

industrial action *n* huelga.

industrial estate *n* (*BRIT*) polígono *or* zona (*LAM*) industrial.

industrial goods *npl* bienes *mpl* de producción.

industrialist [ɪn'dʌstrɪəlɪst] *n* industrial *m/f*.

industrialize [ɪn'dʌstrɪəlaɪz] *vt* industrializar.

industrial park *n* (*US*) = **industrial estate**.

industrial relations *npl* relaciones *fpl* empresariales.

industrial tribunal *n* magistratura de trabajo, tribunal *m* laboral.

industrial unrest *n* (*BRIT*) agitación *f* obrera.

industrious [ɪn'dʌstrɪəs] *adj* (*gen*) trabajador(a); (*student*) aplicado.

industry ['ɪndəstrɪ] *n* industria; (*diligence*) aplicación *f*.

inebriated [ɪ'niːbrɪeɪtɪd] *adj* borracho.

inedible [ɪn'ɛdɪbl] *adj* incomible; (*plant etc*) no comestible.

ineffective [ɪnɪ'fɛktɪv], **ineffectual**

[ɪnɪ'fɛktʃuəl] *adj* ineficaz, inútil.
inefficiency [ɪnɪ'fɪʃənsɪ] *n* ineficacia.
inefficient [ɪnɪ'fɪʃənt] *adj* ineficaz, ineficiente.
inelegant [ɪn'ɛlɪgənt] *adj* poco elegante.
ineligible [ɪn'ɛlɪdʒɪbl] *adj* inelegible.
inept [ɪ'nɛpt] *adj* incompetente, incapaz.
ineptitude [ɪ'nɛptɪtjuːd] *n* incapacidad *f*, ineptitud *f*.
inequality [ɪnɪ'kwɔlɪtɪ] *n* desigualdad *f*.
inequitable [ɪn'ɛkwɪtəbl] *adj* injusto.
ineradicable [ɪnɪ'rædɪkəbl] *adj* inextirpable.
inert [ɪ'nɜːt] *adj* inerte, inactivo; (*immobile*) inmóvil.
inertia [ɪ'nɜːʃə] *n* inercia; (*laziness*) pereza.
inertia-reel seat-belt [ɪ'nɜːʃə'riːl-] *n* cinturón *m* de seguridad retráctil.
inescapable [ɪnɪ'skeɪpəbl] *adj* ineludible, inevitable.
inessential [ɪnɪ'sɛnʃl] *adj* no esencial.
inestimable [ɪn'ɛstɪməbl] *adj* inestimable.
inevitability [ɪnɛvɪtə'bɪlɪtɪ] *n* inevitabilidad *f*.
inevitable [ɪn'ɛvɪtəbl] *adj* inevitable; (*necessary*) forzoso.
inevitably [ɪn'ɛvɪtəblɪ] *adv* inevitablemente; **as ~ happens ...** como siempre pasa ....
inexact [ɪnɪg'zaekt] *adj* inexacto.
inexcusable [ɪnɪks'kjuːzəbl] *adj* imperdonable.
inexhaustible [ɪnɪg'zɔːstɪbl] *adj* inagotable.
inexorable [ɪn'ɛksərəbl] *adj* inexorable, implacable.
inexpensive [ɪnɪk'spɛnsɪv] *adj* económico.
inexperience [ɪnɪk'spɪərɪəns] *n* falta de experiencia.
inexperienced [ɪnɪk'spɪərɪənst] *adj* inexperto; **to be ~ in sth** no tener experiencia en algo.
inexplicable [ɪnɪk'splɪkəbl] *adj* inexplicable.
inexpressible [ɪnɪk'sprɛsəbl] *adj* inexpresable.
inextricable [ɪnɪks'trɪkəbl] *adj* inseparable.
inextricably [ɪnɪks'trɪkəblɪ] *adv* indisolublemente.
infallibility [ɪnfælə'bɪlɪtɪ] *n* infalibilidad *f*.
infallible [ɪn'fælɪbl] *adj* infalible.
infamous ['ɪnfəməs] *adj* infame.
infamy ['ɪnfəmɪ] *n* infamia.
infancy ['ɪnfənsɪ] *n* infancia.
infant ['ɪnfənt] *n* niño/a.
infantile ['ɪnfəntaɪl] *adj* infantil; (*pej*) aniñado.
infant mortality *n* mortalidad *f* infantil.
infantry ['ɪnfəntrɪ] *n* infantería.
infantryman ['ɪnfəntrɪmən] *n* soldado de

infantería.
infant school *n* (*BRIT*) escuela de párvulos; *see also* **primary school**.
infatuated [ɪn'fætjueɪtɪd] *adj*: **~ with** (*in love*) loco por; **to become ~ (with sb)** enamoriscarse (de algn), encapricharse (con algn).
infatuation [ɪnfætju'eɪʃən] *n* enamoramiento.
infect [ɪn'fɛkt] *vt* (*wound*) infectar; (*person*) contagiar; (*fig: pej*) corromper; **~ed with** (*illness*) contagiado de; **to become ~ed** (*wound*) infectarse.
infection [ɪn'fɛkʃən] *n* infección *f*; (*fig*) contagio.
infectious [ɪn'fɛkʃəs] *adj* contagioso; (*also fig*) infeccioso.
infer [ɪn'fɜː*] *vt* deducir, inferir; **to ~ (from)** inferir (de), deducir (de).
inference ['ɪnfərəns] *n* deducción *f*, inferencia.
inferior [ɪn'fɪərɪə*] *adj*, *n* inferior *m/f*; **to feel ~** sentirse inferior.
inferiority [ɪnfɪərɪ'ɔrətɪ] *n* inferioridad *f*.
inferiority complex *n* complejo de inferioridad.
infernal [ɪn'fɜːnl] *adj* infernal.
inferno [ɪn'fɜːnəu] *n* infierno; (*fig*) hoguera.
infertile [ɪn'fɜːtaɪl] *adj* estéril; (*person*) infecundo.
infertility [ɪnfəː'tɪlɪtɪ] *n* esterilidad *f*; infecundidad *f*.
infest [ɪn'fɛst] *vt* infestar.
infested [ɪn'fɛstɪd] *adj*: **~ (with)** plagado (de).
infidel ['ɪnfɪdəl] *n* infiel *m/f*.
infidelity [ɪnfɪ'dɛlɪtɪ] *n* infidelidad *f*.
in-fighting ['ɪnfaɪtɪŋ] *n* (*fig*) lucha(s) *f(pl)* interna(s).
infiltrate ['ɪnfɪltreɪt] *vt* (*troops etc*) infiltrarse en ♦ *vi* infiltrarse.
infinite ['ɪnfɪnɪt] *adj* infinito; **an ~ amount of money/time** un sinfín de dinero/tiempo.
infinitely ['ɪnfɪnɪtlɪ] *adv* infinitamente.
infinitesimal [ɪnfɪnɪ'tɛsɪməl] *adj* infinitésimo.
infinitive [ɪn'fɪnɪtɪv] *n* infinitivo.
infinity [ɪn'fɪnɪtɪ] *n* (*also MATH*) infinito; (*an ~*) infinidad *f*.
infirm [ɪn'fɜːm] *adj* enfermizo, débil.
infirmary [ɪn'fɜːmərɪ] *n* hospital *m*.
infirmity [ɪn'fɜːmɪtɪ] *n* debilidad *f*; (*illness*) enfermedad *f*, achaque *m*.
inflame [ɪn'fleɪm] inflamar.
inflamed [ɪn'fleɪmd] *adj*: **to become ~** inflamarse.
inflammable [ɪn'flæməbl] *adj* (*BRIT*)

inflamable; (*situation etc*) explosivo.

inflammation [ɪnflə'meɪʃən] *n* inflamación *f.*

inflammatory [ɪn'flæmətərɪ] *adj* (*speech*) incendiario.

inflatable [ɪn'fleɪtəbl] *adj* inflable.

inflate [ɪn'fleɪt] *vt* (*tyre, balloon*) inflar; (*fig*) hinchar.

inflated [ɪn'fleɪtɪd] *adj* (*tyre etc*) inflado; (*price, self-esteem etc*) exagerado.

inflation [ɪn'fleɪʃən] *n* (*ECON*) inflación *f.*

inflationary [ɪn'fleɪʃnərɪ] *adj* inflacionario.

inflationary spiral *n* espiral *f* inflacionista.

inflexible [ɪn'flɛksɪbl] *adj* inflexible.

inflict [ɪn'flɪkt] *vt*: **to ~ on** infligir en; (*tax etc*) imponer a.

infliction [ɪn'flɪkʃən] *n* imposición *f.*

in-flight ['ɪnflaɪt] *adj* durante el vuelo.

inflow ['ɪnfləu] *n* afluencia.

influence ['ɪnfluəns] *n* influencia ♦ *vt* influir en, influenciar; **under the ~ of alcohol** en estado de embriaguez.

influential [ɪnflu'ɛnʃl] *adj* influyente.

influenza [ɪnflu'ɛnzə] *n* gripe *f.*

influx ['ɪnflʌks] *n* afluencia.

inform [ɪn'fɔːm] *vt*: **to ~ sb of sth** informar a algn sobre *or* de algo; (*warn*) avisar a algn de algo; (*communicate*) comunicar algo a algn ♦ *vi*: **to ~ on sb** delatar a algn.

informal [ɪn'fɔːml] *adj* (*manner, tone*) desenfadado; (*dress, interview, occasion*) informal.

informality [ɪnfɔː'mælɪtɪ] *n* falta de ceremonia; (*intimacy*) intimidad *f*; (*familiarity*) familiaridad *f*; (*ease*) afabilidad *f.*

informally [ɪn'fɔːmalɪ] *adv* sin ceremonia; (*invite*) informalmente.

informant [ɪn'fɔːmənt] *n* informante *m/f.*

informatics [ɪnfɔː'mætɪks] *n* informática.

information [ɪnfə'meɪʃən] *n* información *f*; (*news*) noticias *fpl*; (*knowledge*) conocimientos *mpl*; (*LAW*) delación *f*; **a piece of ~** un dato; **for your ~** para su información.

information bureau *n* oficina de información.

information processing *n* procesamiento de datos.

information retrieval *n* recuperación *f* de información.

information science *n* gestión *f* de la información.

information technology (IT) *n* informática.

informative [ɪn'fɔːmətɪv] *adj* informativo.

informed [ɪn'fɔːmd] *adj* (*observer*) informado, al corriente; **an ~ guess** una opinión bien fundamentada.

informer [ɪn'fɔːmə*] *n* delator(a) *m/f*; (*also:* **police ~**) soplón/ona *m/f.*

infra dig ['ɪnfrə'dɪg] *adj abbr* (*col:* = *infra dignitatem*) denigrante.

·infra-red [ɪnfrə'rɛd] *adj* infrarrojo.

infrastructure ['ɪnfrəstrʌktʃə*] *n* (*of system etc, ECON*) infraestructura.

infrequent [ɪn'friːkwənt] *adj* infrecuente.

infringe [ɪn'frɪndʒ] *vt* infringir, violar ♦ *vi*: **to ~ on** invadir.

infringement [ɪn'frɪndʒmənt] *n* infracción *f*; (*of rights*) usurpación *f*; (*SPORT*) falta.

infuriate [ɪn'fjuərɪeɪt] *vt*: **to become ~d** ponerse furioso.

infuriating [ɪn'fjuərɪeɪtɪŋ] *adj*: **I find it ~** me saca de quicio.

infuse [ɪn'fjuːz] *vt* (*with courage, enthusiasm*): **to ~ sb with sth** infundir algo a algn.

infusion [ɪn'fjuːʒən] *n* (*tea etc*) infusión *f.*

ingenious [ɪn'dʒiːnjəs] *adj* ingenioso.

ingenuity [ɪndʒɪ'njuːɪtɪ] *n* ingeniosidad *f.*

ingenuous [ɪn'dʒɛnjuəs] *adj* ingenuo.

ingot ['ɪŋgət] *n* lingote *m*, barra.

ingrained [ɪn'greɪnd] *adj* arraigado.

ingratiate [ɪn'greɪʃɪeɪt] *vt*: **to ~ o.s. with** congraciarse con.

ingratiating [ɪn'greɪʃɪeɪtɪŋ] *adj* (*smile, speech*) insinuante; (*person*) zalamero, congraciador(a).

ingratitude [ɪn'grætɪtjuːd] *n* ingratitud *f.*

ingredient [ɪn'griːdɪənt] *n* ingrediente *m.*

ingrowing ['ɪngrəuɪŋ] *adj*: **~ (toe)nail** uña encarnada.

inhabit [ɪn'hæbɪt] *vt* vivir en; (*occupy*) ocupar.

inhabitable [ɪn'hæbɪtəbl] *adj* habitable.

inhabitant [ɪn'hæbɪtənt] *n* habitante *m/f.*

inhale [ɪn'heɪl] *vt* inhalar ♦ *vi* (*in smoking*) tragar.

inhaler [ɪn'heɪlə*] *n* inhalador *m.*

inherent [ɪn'hɪərənt] *adj*: **~ in** *or* **to** inherente a.

inherently [ɪn'hɪərəntlɪ] *adv* intrínsecamente.

inherit [ɪn'hɛrɪt] *vt* heredar.

inheritance [ɪn'hɛrɪtəns] *n* herencia; (*fig*) patrimonio.

inhibit [ɪn'hɪbɪt] *vt* inhibir, impedir; **to ~ sb from doing sth** impedir a algn hacer algo.

inhibited [ɪn'hɪbɪtɪd] *adj* (*person*) cohibido.

inhibition [ɪnhɪ'bɪʃən] *n* cohibición *f.*

inhospitable [ɪnhɔs'pɪtəbl] *adj* (*person*) inhospitalario; (*place*) inhóspito.

in-house ['ɪnhaus] *adj* dentro de la empresa.

inhuman [ɪn'hjuːmən] *adj* inhumano.

inhumane [ɪnhjuː'meɪn] *adj* inhumano.
inimitable [ɪ'nɪmɪtəbl] *adj* inimitable.
iniquity [ɪ'nɪkwɪtɪ] *n* iniquidad *f*; (*injustice*) injusticia.
initial [ɪ'nɪʃl] *adj* inicial; (*first*) primero ♦ *n* inicial *f* ♦ *vt* firmar con las iniciales; **~s** *npl* iniciales *fpl*; (*abbreviation*) siglas *fpl*.
initialize [ɪ'nɪʃəlaɪz] *vt* (*COMPUT*) inicializar.
initially [ɪ'nɪʃəlɪ] *adv* en un principio.
initiate [ɪ'nɪʃɪeɪt] *vt* (*start*) iniciar; **to ~ sb into a secret** iniciar a algn en un secreto; **to ~ proceedings against sb** (*LAW*) poner una demanda contra algn.
initiation [ɪnɪʃɪ'eɪʃən] *n* (*into secret etc*) iniciación *f*; (*beginning*) comienzo.
initiative [ɪ'nɪʃətɪv] *n* iniciativa; **to take the ~** tomar la iniciativa.
inject [ɪn'dʒɛkt] *vt* inyectar; (*money, enthusiasm*) aportar.
injection [ɪn'dʒɛkʃən] *n* inyección *f*; **to have an ~** ponerse una inyección.
injudicious [ɪndʒu'dɪʃəs] *adj* imprudente, indiscreto.
injunction [ɪn'dʒʌŋkʃən] *n* entredicho, interdicto.
injure ['ɪndʒə*] *vt* herir; (*hurt*) lastimar; (*fig: reputation etc*) perjudicar; (*feelings*) herir; **to ~ o.s** hacerse daño, lastimarse.
injured ['ɪndʒəd] *adj* (*also fig*) herido; **~ party** (*LAW*) parte *f* perjudicada.
injurious [ɪn'dʒuərɪəs] *adj:* **~ (to)** perjudicial (para).
injury ['ɪndʒərɪ] *n* herida, lesión *f*; (*wrong*) perjuicio, daño; **to escape without ~** salir ileso.
injury time *n* (*SPORT*) descuento.
injustice [ɪn'dʒʌstɪs] *n* injusticia; **you do me an ~** usted es injusto conmigo.
ink [ɪŋk] *n* tinta.
ink-jet printer ['ɪŋkdʒɛt-] *n* impresora de chorro de tinta.
inkling ['ɪŋklɪŋ] *n* sospecha; (*idea*) idea.
inkpad ['ɪŋkpæd] *n* almohadilla.
inlaid ['ɪnleɪd] *adj* (*wood*) taraceado; (*tiles*) entarimado.
inland *adj* ['ɪnlənd] interior; (*town*) del interior ♦ *adv* [ɪn'lænd] tierra adentro.
Inland Revenue *n* (*BRIT*) Hacienda.
in-laws ['ɪnlɔːz] *npl* suegros *mpl*.
inlet ['ɪnlet] *n* (*GEO*) ensenada, cala; (*TECH*) admisión *f*, entrada.
inmate ['ɪnmeɪt] *n* (*in prison*) preso/a, presidiario/a; (*in asylum*) internado/a.
inmost ['ɪnməust] *adj* más íntimo, más secreto.
inn [ɪn] *n* posada, mesón *m*; **the I~s of Court** *see* **barrister.**
innards ['ɪnədz] *npl* (*col*) tripas *fpl*.

innate [ɪ'neɪt] *adj* innato.
inner ['ɪnə*] *adj* interior, interno.
inner city *n* barrios deprimidos del centro de una ciudad.
innermost ['ɪnəməust] *adj* más íntimo, más secreto.
inner tube *n* (*of tyre*) cámara, llanta (*LAM*).
innings ['ɪnɪŋz] *n* (*CRICKET*) entrada, turno.
innocence ['ɪnəsns] *n* inocencia.
innocent ['ɪnəsnt] *adj* inocente.
innocuous [ɪ'nɔkjuəs] *adj* inocuo.
innovation [ɪnəu'veɪʃən] *n* novedad *f*.
innuendo, ~es [ɪnju'ɛndəu] *n* indirecta.
innumerable [ɪ'njuːmrəbl] *adj* innumerable.
inoculate [ɪ'nɔkjuleɪt] *vt:* **to ~ sb with sth/ against sth** inocular *or* vacunar a algn con algo/contra algo.
inoculation [ɪnɔkju'leɪʃən] *n* inoculación *f*.
inoffensive [ɪnə'fɛnsɪv] *adj* inofensivo.
inopportune [ɪn'ɔpətjuːn] *adj* inoportuno.
inordinate [ɪ'nɔːdɪnət] *adj* excesivo, desmesurado.
inordinately [ɪ'nɔːdɪnətlɪ] *adv* excesivamente, desmesuradamente.
inorganic [ɪnɔː'gaenɪk] *adj* inorgánico.
in-patient ['ɪnpeɪʃənt] *n* (*paciente m/f*) interno/a.
input ['ɪnput] *n* (*ELEC*) entrada; (*COMPUT*) entrada de datos ♦ *vt* (*COMPUT*) introducir, entrar.
inquest ['ɪnkwɛst] *n* (*coroner's*) investigación *f* post-mortem.
inquire [ɪn'kwaɪə*] *vi* preguntar ♦ *vt:* **to ~ when/where/whether** preguntar cuándo/dónde/si; **to ~ about** (*person*) preguntar por; (*fact*) informarse de.
▶**inquire into** *vt fus:* **to ~ into sth** investigar *or* indagar algo.
inquiring [ɪn'kwaɪərɪŋ] *adj* (*mind*) inquieto; (*look*) interrogante.
inquiry [ɪn'kwaɪərɪ] *n* pregunta; (*LAW*) investigación *f*, pesquisa; (*commission*) comisión *f* investigadora; **to hold an ~ into sth** emprender una investigación sobre algo.
inquiry desk *n* mesa de información.
inquiry office *n* (*BRIT*) oficina de información.
inquisition [ɪnkwɪ'zɪʃən] *n* inquisición *f*.
inquisitive [ɪn'kwɪzɪtɪv] *adj* (*mind*) inquisitivo; (*person*) fisgón/ona.
inroad ['ɪnrəud] *n* incursión *f*; (*fig*) invasión *f*; **to make ~s into** (*time*) ocupar parte de; (*savings, supplies*) agotar parte de.
insane [ɪn'seɪn] *adj* loco; (*MED*) demente.
insanitary [ɪn'sænɪtərɪ] *adj* insalubre.
insanity [ɪn'sænɪtɪ] *n* demencia, locura.

insatiable [ɪn'seɪʃəbl] *adj* insaciable.
inscribe [ɪn'skraɪb] *vt* inscribir; (*book etc*): **to ~ (to sb)** dedicar (a algn).
inscription [ɪn'skrɪpʃən] *n* (*gen*) inscripción *f*; (*in book*) dedicatoria.
inscrutable [ɪn'skru:təbl] *adj* inescrutable, insondable.
inseam measurement ['ɪnsi:m-] *n* (*US*) = **inside leg measurement**.
insect ['ɪnsɛkt] *n* insecto.
insect bite *n* picadura.
insecticide [ɪn'sɛktɪsaɪd] *n* insecticida *m*.
insect repellent *n* loción *f* contra los insectos.
insecure [ɪnsɪ'kjuə*] *adj* inseguro.
insecurity [ɪnsɪ'kjuərɪtɪ] *n* inseguridad *f*.
insemination [ɪnsɛmɪ'neɪʃn] *n*: **artificial ~** inseminación *f* artificial.
insensible [ɪn'sɛnsɪbl] *adj* inconsciente; (*unconscious*) sin conocimiento.
insensitive [ɪn'sɛnsɪtɪv] *adj* insensible.
insensitivity [ɪnsɛnsɪ'tɪvɪtɪ] *n* insensibilidad *f*.
inseparable [ɪn'sɛprəbl] *adj* inseparable; **they were ~ friends** los unía una estrecha amistad.
insert *vt* [ɪn'sə:t] (*into sth*) introducir; (*COMPUT*) insertar ♦ *n* ['ɪnsə:t] encarte *m*.
insertion [ɪn'sə:ʃən] *n* inserción *f*.
in-service [ɪn'sə:vɪs] *adj* (*training, course*) en el trabajo, a cargo de la empresa.
inshore [ɪn'ʃɔ:*] *adj*: **~ fishing** pesca *f* costera ♦ *adv* (*fish*) a lo largo de la costa; (*move*) hacia la orilla.
inside ['ɪn'saɪd] *n* interior *m*; (*lining*) forro; (*of road: BRIT*) izquierdo; (: *US, Europe etc*) derecho ♦ *adj* interior, interno; (*information*) confidencial ♦ *adv* (*within*) (por) dentro, adentro (*esp LAM*); (*with movement*) hacia dentro; (*fam: in prison*) en chirona ♦ *prep* dentro de; (*of time*): **~ 10 minutes** en menos de 10 minutos; **~s** *npl* (*col*) tripas *fpl*; **~ out** *adv* (*turn*) al revés; (*know*) a fondo.
inside forward *n* (*SPORT*) interior *m*.
inside information *n* información *f* confidencial.
inside lane *n* (*AUT: in Britain*) carril *m* izquierdo; (: *in US, Europe*) carril *m* derecho.
inside leg measurement *n* medida de pernera.
insider [ɪn'saɪdə*] *n* enterado/a.
insider dealing, insider trading *n* (*STOCK EXCHANGE*) abuso de información privilegiada.
inside story *n* historia íntima.
insidious [ɪn'sɪdɪəs] *adj* insidioso.

insight ['ɪnsaɪt] *n* perspicacia, percepción *f*; **to gain** *or* **get an ~ into sth** comprender algo mejor.
insignia [ɪn'sɪgnɪə] *npl* insignias *fpl*.
insignificant [ɪnsɪg'nɪfɪknt] *adj* insignificante.
insincere [ɪnsɪn'sɪə*] *adj* poco sincero.
insincerity [ɪnsɪn'sɛrɪtɪ] *n* falta de sinceridad, doblez *f*.
insinuate [ɪn'sɪnjueɪt] *vt* insinuar.
insinuation [ɪnsɪnju'eɪʃən] *n* insinuación *f*.
insipid [ɪn'sɪpɪd] *adj* soso, insulso.
insist [ɪn'sɪst] *vi* insistir; **to ~ on doing** empeñarse en hacer; **to ~ that** insistir en que; (*claim*) exigir que.
insistence [ɪn'sɪstəns] *n* insistencia; (*stubbornness*) empeño.
insistent [ɪn'sɪstənt] *adj* insistente; empeñado.
insofar as [ɪnsəu'fɑ:-] *conj* en la medida en que, en tanto que.
insole ['ɪnsəul] *n* plantilla.
insolence ['ɪnsələns] *n* insolencia, descaro.
insolent ['ɪnsələnt] *adj* insolente, descarado.
insoluble [ɪn'sɔljubl] *adj* insoluble.
insolvency [ɪn'sɔlvənsɪ] *n* insolvencia.
insolvent [ɪn'sɔlvənt] *adj* insolvente.
insomnia [ɪn'sɔmnɪə] *n* insomnio.
insomniac [ɪn'sɔmnɪæk] *n* insomne *m/f*.
inspect [ɪn'spɛkt] *vt* inspeccionar, examinar; (*troops*) pasar revista a.
inspection [ɪn'spɛkʃən] *n* inspección *f*, examen *m*.
inspector [ɪn'spɛktə*] *n* inspector(a) *m/f*; (*BRIT: on buses, trains*) revisor(a) *m/f*.
inspiration [ɪnspə'reɪʃən] *n* inspiración *f*.
inspire [ɪn'spaɪə*] *vt* inspirar; **to ~ sb (to do sth)** alentar a algn (a hacer algo).
inspired [ɪn'spaɪəd] *adj* (*writer, book etc*) inspirado, genial, iluminado; **in an ~ moment** en un momento de inspiración.
inspiring [ɪn'spaɪərɪŋ] *adj* inspirador(a).
inst. *abbr* (*BRIT COMM: = instant, of the present month*) cte.
instability [ɪnstə'bɪlɪtɪ] *n* inestabilidad *f*.
install [ɪn'stɔ:l] *vt* instalar.
installation [ɪnstə'leɪʃən] *n* instalación *f*.
installment plan *n* (*US*) compra a plazos.
instalment, (US) installment
[ɪn'stɔ:lmənt] *n* plazo; (*of story*) entrega; (*of TV serial etc*) capítulo; **in ~s** (*pay, receive*) a plazos; **to pay in ~s** pagar a plazos *or* por abonos.
instance ['ɪnstəns] *n* ejemplo, caso; **for ~** por ejemplo; **in the first ~** en primer lugar; **in that ~** en ese caso.
instant ['ɪnstənt] *n* instante *m*, momento

♦ *adj* inmediato; (*coffee*) instantáneo.
instantaneous [ɪnstən'teɪnɪəs] *adj*
instantáneo.
instantly ['ɪnstəntlɪ] *adv* en seguida, al
instante.
instant replay *n* (*US TV*) repetición *f* de la
jugada.
instead [ɪn'stɛd] *adv* en cambio; ~ **of** en
lugar de, en vez de.
instep ['ɪnstɛp] *n* empeine *m*.
instigate ['ɪnstɪɡeɪt] *vt* (*rebellion, strike,
crime*) instigar; (*new ideas etc*) fomentar.
instigation [ɪnstɪ'ɡeɪʃən] *n* instigación *f*; **at
sb's** ~ a instigación de algn.
instil [ɪn'stɪl] *vt:* **to** ~ **into** inculcar a.
instinct ['ɪnstɪŋkt] *n* instinto.
instinctive [ɪn'stɪŋktɪv] *adj* instintivo.
instinctively [ɪn'stɪŋktɪvlɪ] *adv* por instinto.
institute ['ɪnstɪtjuːt] *n* instituto;
(*professional body*) colegio ♦ *vt* (*begin*)
iniciar, empezar; (*proceedings*) entablar.
institution [ɪnstɪ'tjuːʃən] *n* institución *f*;
(*beginning*) iniciación *f*; (*MED: home*) asilo;
(*asylum*) manicomio; (*custom*) costumbre
f arraigada.
institutional [ɪnstɪ'tjuːʃnl] *adj*
institucional.
instruct [ɪn'strʌkt] *vt:* **to** ~ **sb in sth**
instruir a algn en *or* sobre algo; **to** ~ **sb
to do sth** dar instrucciones a algn de *or*
mandar a algn hacer algo.
instruction [ɪn'strʌkʃən] *n* (*teaching*)
instrucción *f*; ~**s** *npl* órdenes *fpl*; ~**s (for
use)** modo *sg* de empleo.
instruction book *n* manual *m*.
instructive [ɪn'strʌktɪv] *adj* instructivo.
instructor [ɪn'strʌktə*] *n* instructor(a) *m/f*.
instrument ['ɪnstrəmənt] *n* instrumento.
instrumental [ɪnstrə'mɛntl] *adj* (*MUS*)
instrumental; **to be** ~ **in** ser el artífice de;
to be ~ **in sth/in doing sth** ser
responsable de algo/de hacer algo.
instrumentalist [ɪnstrə'mɛntəlɪst] *n*
instrumentista *m/f*.
instrument panel *n* tablero (de
instrumentos).
insubordinate [ɪnsə'bɔːdənɪt] *adj*
insubordinado.
insubordination [ɪnsəbɔːdə'neɪʃən] *n*
insubordinación *f*.
insufferable [ɪn'sʌfrəbl] *adj* insoportable.
insufficient [ɪnsə'fɪʃənt] *adj* insuficiente.
insufficiently [ɪnsə'fɪʃəntlɪ] *adv*
insuficientemente.
insular ['ɪnsjulə*] *adj* insular; (*outlook*)
estrecho de miras.
insularity [ɪnsju'lærɪtɪ] *n* insularidad *f*.
insulate ['ɪnsjuleɪt] *vt* aislar.

insulating tape ['ɪnsjuleɪtɪŋ-] *n* cinta
aislante.
insulation [ɪnsju'leɪʃən] *n* aislamiento.
insulator ['ɪnsjuleɪtə*] *n* aislante *m*.
insulin ['ɪnsjulɪn] *n* insulina.
insult *n* ['ɪnsʌlt] insulto; (*offence*) ofensa
♦ *vt* [ɪn'sʌlt] insultar; ofender.
insulting [ɪn'sʌltɪŋ] *adj* insultante;
ofensivo.
insuperable [ɪn'sjuːprəbl] *adj* insuperable.
insurance [ɪn'ʃuərəns] *n* seguro; **fire/life** ~
seguro de incendios/vida; **to take out** ~
(against) hacerse un seguro (contra).
insurance agent *n* agente *m/f* de seguros.
insurance broker *n* corredor(a) *m/f or*
agente *m/f* de seguros.
insurance policy *n* póliza (de seguros).
insurance premium *n* prima de seguros.
insure [ɪn'ʃuə*] *vt* asegurar; **to** ~ **sb** *or* **sb's
life** hacer un seguro de vida a algn; **to** ~
(against) asegurar (contra); **to be** ~**d for
£5000** tener un seguro de 5000 libras.
insured [ɪn'ʃuəd] *n:* **the** ~ el/la asegurado/a.
insurer [ɪn'ʃuərə*] *n* asegurador(a).
insurgent [ɪn'sə:dʒənt] *adj, n* insurgente *m/f*,
insurrecto/a *m/f*.
insurmountable [ɪnsə'mauntəbl] *adj*
insuperable.
insurrection [ɪnsə'rɛkʃən] *n* insurrección *f*.
intact [ɪn'tækt] *adj* íntegro; (*untouched*)
intacto.
intake ['ɪnteɪk] *n* (*TECH*) entrada, toma;
(: *pipe*) tubo de admisión; (*of food*)
ingestión *f*; (*BRIT SCOL*) **an** ~ **of 200 a year**
200 matriculados al año.
intangible [ɪn'tændʒɪbl] *adj* intangible.
integer ['ɪntɪdʒə*] *n* (número) entero.
integral ['ɪntɪɡrəl] *adj* (*whole*) íntegro; (*part*)
integrante.
integrate ['ɪntɪɡreɪt] *vt* integrar ♦ *vi*
integrarse.
integrated circuit ['ɪntɪɡreɪtɪd-] *n*
(*COMPUT*) circuito integrado.
integration [ɪntɪ'ɡreɪʃən] *n* integración *f*;
racial ~ integración de razas.
integrity [ɪn'tɛɡrɪtɪ] *n* honradez *f*, rectitud *f*;
(*COMPUT*) integridad *f*.
intellect ['ɪntəlɛkt] *n* intelecto.
intellectual [ɪntə'lɛktjuəl] *adj, n* intelectual
m/f.
intelligence [ɪn'tɛlɪdʒəns] *n* inteligencia.
intelligence quotient (IQ) *n* coeficiente *m*
intelectual.
Intelligence Service *n* Servicio de
Inteligencia.
intelligence test *n* prueba de inteligencia.
intelligent [ɪn'tɛlɪdʒənt] *adj* inteligente.
intelligently [ɪn'tɛlɪdʒəntlɪ] *adv*

inteligentemente.
intelligentsia [ıntɛlı'dʒɛntsıə] *n*
intelectualidad *f*.
intelligible [ın'tɛlıdʒıbl] *adj* inteligible,
comprensible.
intemperate [ın'tɛmpərət] *adj* inmoderado.
intend [ın'tɛnd] *vt* (*gift etc*): **to ~ sth for**
destinar algo a; **to ~ to do sth** tener
intención de *or* pensar hacer algo.
intended [ın'tɛndıd] *adj* (*effect*) deseado.
intense [ın'tɛns] *adj* intenso; **to be ~**
(*person*) tomárselo todo muy en serio.
intensely [ın'tɛnslı] *adv* intensamente;
(*very*) sumamente.
intensify [ın'tɛnsıfaı] *vt* intensificar;
(*increase*) aumentar.
intensity [ın'tɛnsıtı] *n* (*gen*) intensidad *f*.
intensive [ın'tɛnsıv] *adj* intensivo.
intensive care *n*: **to be in ~** estar bajo
cuidados intensivos; **~ unit** *n* unidad *f* de
vigilancia intensiva.
intensively [ın'tɛnsıvlı] *adv*
intensivamente.
intent [ın'tɛnt] *n* propósito ♦ *adj* (*absorbed*)
absorto; (*attentive*) atento; **to all ~s and
purposes** a efectos prácticos; **to be ~ on
doing sth** estar resuelto *or* decidido a
hacer algo.
intention [ın'tɛnʃən] *n* intención *f*,
propósito.
intentional [ın'tɛnʃənl] *adj* deliberado.
intentionally [ın'tɛnʃnəlı] *adv* a propósito.
intently [ın'tɛntlı] *adv* atentamente,
fijamente.
inter [ın'tɔː*] *vt* enterrar, sepultar.
inter- ['ıntə*] *pref* inter-.
interact [ıntər'ækt] *vi* (*substances*) influirse
mutuamente; (*people*) relacionarse.
interaction [ıntər'ækʃən] *n* interacción *f*,
acción *f* recíproca.
interactive [ıntər'æktıv] *adj* (*also COMPUT*)
interactivo.
intercede [ıntə'siːd] *vi*: **to ~ (with)**
interceder (con); **to ~ with sb/on behalf
of sb** interceder con algn/en nombre de
algn.
intercept [ıntə'sɛpt] *vt* interceptar; (*stop*)
detener.
interception [ıntə'sɛpʃən] *n* interceptación
f; detención *f*.
interchange *n* ['ıntətʃeındʒ] intercambio;
(*on motorway*) intersección *f* ♦ *vt*
[ıntə'tʃeındʒ] intercambiar.
interchangeable [ıntə'tʃeındʒəbl] *adj*
intercambiable.
intercity [ıntə'sıtı] *adj*: **~ (train)** (tren *m*)
intercity *m*.
intercom ['ıntəkɔm] *n* interfono.

interconnect [ıntəkə'nɛkt] *vi* (*rooms*)
comunicar(se).
intercontinental ['ıntəkɔntı'nɛntl] *adj*
intercontinental.
intercourse ['ıntəkɔːs] *n* (*sexual ~*)
relaciones *fpl* sexuales, contacto sexual;
(*social*) trato.
interdependence [ıntədı'pɛndəns] *n*
interdependencia.
interdependent [ıntədı'pɛndənt] *adj*
interdependiente.
interest ['ıntrıst] *n* (*also COMM*) interés *m*
♦ *vt* interesar; **compound/simple ~** interés
compuesto/simple; **business ~s** negocios
mpl; **British ~s in the Middle East** los
intereses británicos en el Medio Oriente.
interested ['ıntrıstıd] *adj* interesado; **to be
~ in** interesarse por.
interest-free ['ıntrıst'friː] *adj* libre de
interés.
interesting ['ıntrıstıŋ] *adj* interesante.
interest rate *n* tipo de interés.
interface ['ıntəfeıs] *n* (*COMPUT*) junción *f*,
interface *m*.
interfere [ıntə'fıə*] *vi*: **to ~ in** (*quarrel, other
people's business*) entrometerse en; **to ~
with** (*hinder*) estorbar; (*damage*)
estropear; (*radio*) interferir con.
interference [ıntə'fıərəns] *n* (*gen*)
intromisión *f*; (*RADIO, TV*) interferencia.
interfering [ıntə'fıərıŋ] *adj* entrometido.
interim ['ıntərım] *adj*: **~ dividend** dividendo
parcial ♦ *n*: **in the ~** en el ínterin.
interior [ın'tıərıə*] *n* interior *m* ♦ *adj*
interior.
interior decorator, interior designer *n*
interiorista *m/f*, diseñador(a) *m/f* de
interiores.
interjection [ıntə'dʒɛkʃən] *n* interrupción *f*.
interlock [ıntə'lɔk] *vi* entrelazarse; (*wheels
etc*) endentarse.
interloper ['ıntələupə*] *n* intruso/a.
interlude ['ıntəluːd] *n* intervalo; (*rest*)
descanso; (*THEAT*) intermedio.
intermarriage [ıntə'mærıdʒ] *n* endogamia.
intermarry [ıntə'mærı] *vi* casarse (entre
parientes).
intermediary [ıntə'miːdıərı] *n*
intermediario/a.
intermediate [ıntə'miːdıət] *adj* intermedio.
interminable [ın'təːmınəbl] *adj* inacabable.
intermission [ıntə'mıʃən] *n* (*THEAT*)
descanso.
intermittent [ıntə'mıtnt] *adj* intermitente.
intermittently [ıntə'mıtntlı] *adv*
intermitentemente.
intern *vt* [ın'təːn] internar; (*enclose*)
encerrar ♦ *n* ['ıntəːn] (*US*) médico/a *m/f*

interno/a.
internal [ɪn'təːnl] *adj* interno, interior; ~
  injuries heridas *fpl or* lesiones *fpl* internas.
internally [ɪn'təːnəlɪ] *adv* interiormente;
  "not to be taken ~" "uso externo".
Internal Revenue Service (IRS) *n* (*US*)
  Hacienda.
international [ɪntə'næʃənl] *adj*
  internacional; ~ **(game)** partido
  internacional; ~ **(player)** jugador(a) *m/f*
  internacional.
**International Atomic Energy Agency
  (IAEA)** *n* Organismo Internacional de
  Energía Atómica.
**International Chamber of Commerce
  (ICC)** *n* Cámara de Comercio
  Internacional (CCI *f*).
International Court of Justice (ICJ) *n*
  Corte *f* Internacional de Justicia (CIJ *f*).
international date line *n* línea de cambio
  de fecha.
internationally [ɪntə'næʃnəlɪ] *adv*
  internacionalmente.
International Monetary Fund (IMF) *n*
  Fondo Monetario Internacional (FMI *m*).
internee [ɪntəː'niː] *n* interno/a, recluso/a.
Internet ['ɪntənet] *n*: **the** ~ (el *or* la) Internet.
Internet café *n* cibercafé *m*.
Internet Service Provider *n* proveedor *m*
  de (acceso a) Internet.
internment [ɪn'təːnmənt] *n* internamiento.
interplanetary [ɪntə'plænɪtərɪ] *adj*
  interplanetario.
interplay ['ɪntəpleɪ] *n* interacción *f*.
Interpol ['ɪntəpɔl] *n* Interpol *f*.
interpret [ɪn'təːprɪt] *vt* interpretar;
  (*translate*) traducir; (*understand*) entender
  ♦ *vi* hacer de intérprete.
interpretation [ɪntəːprɪ'teɪʃən] *n*
  interpretación *f*; traducción *f*.
interpreter [ɪn'təːprɪtə*] *n* intérprete *m/f*.
interrelated [ɪntərɪ'leɪtɪd] *adj*
  interrelacionado.
interrogate [ɪn'terəugeɪt] *vt* interrogar.
interrogation [ɪnterəu'geɪʃən] *n*
  interrogatorio.
interrogative [ɪntə'rɔɡətɪv] *adj*
  interrogativo.
interrupt [ɪntə'rʌpt] *vt*, *vi* interrumpir.
interruption [ɪntə'rʌpʃən] *n* interrupción *f*.
intersect [ɪntə'sekt] *vt* cruzar ♦ *vi* (*roads*)
  cruzarse.
intersection [ɪntə'sekʃən] *n* intersección *f*;
  (*of roads*) cruce *m*.
intersperse [ɪntə'spəːs] *vt*: **to** ~ **with**
  salpicar de.
intertwine [ɪntə'twaɪn] *vt* entrelazar ♦ *vi*
  entrelazarse.

interval ['ɪntəvl] *n* intervalo; (*BRIT*: *THEAT*,
  SPORT) descanso; **at** ~**s** a ratos, de vez en
  cuando; **sunny** ~**s** (*in weather*) claros *mpl*.
intervene [ɪntə'viːn] *vi* intervenir; (*take
  part*) participar; (*occur*) sobrevenir.
intervening [ɪntə'viːnɪŋ] *adj* intermedio.
intervention [ɪntə'venʃən] *n* intervención *f*.
interview ['ɪntəvjuː] *n* (*RADIO, TV etc*)
  entrevista ♦ *vt* entrevistar a.
interviewee [ɪntəvjuː'iː] *n* entrevistado/a.
interviewer ['ɪntəvjuːə*] *n*
  entrevistador(a) *m/f*.
intestate [ɪn'testeɪt] *adj* intestado.
intestinal [ɪn'testɪnl] *adj* intestinal.
intestine [ɪn'testɪn] *n*: **large/small** ~
  intestino grueso/delgado.
intimacy ['ɪntɪməsɪ] *n* intimidad *f*;
  (*relations*) relaciones *fpl* íntimas.
intimate *adj* ['ɪntɪmət] íntimo; (*friendship*)
  estrecho; (*knowledge*) profundo ♦ *vt*
  ['ɪntɪmeɪt] (*announce*) dar a entender.
intimately ['ɪntɪmətlɪ] *adv* íntimamente.
intimidate [ɪn'tɪmɪdeɪt] *vt* intimidar.
intimidation [ɪntɪmɪ'deɪʃən] *n* intimidación
  f.
into ['ɪntuː] *prep* (*gen*) en; (*towards*) a;
  (*inside*) hacia el interior de; ~ **3 pieces/
  French** en 3 pedazos/al francés; **to change
  pounds** ~ **dollars** cambiar libras por
  dólares.
intolerable [ɪn'tɔlərəbl] *adj* intolerable,
  insoportable.
intolerance [ɪn'tɔlərəns] *n* intolerancia.
intolerant [ɪn'tɔlərənt] *adj*: ~ **(of)**
  intolerante (con).
intonation [ɪntəu'neɪʃən] *n* entonación *f*.
intoxicate [ɪn'tɔksɪkeɪt] *vt* embriagar.
intoxicated [ɪn'tɔksɪkeɪtɪd] *adj* embriagado.
intoxication [ɪntɔksɪ'keɪʃən] *n* embriaguez *f*.
intractable [ɪn'træktəbl] *adj* (*person*)
  intratable; (*problem*) irresoluble; (*illness*)
  incurable.
intranet ['ɪntrənet] *n* intranet *f*.
intransigence [ɪn'trænsɪdʒəns] *n*
  intransigencia.
intransigent [ɪn'trænsɪdʒənt] *adj*
  intransigente.
intransitive [ɪn'trænsɪtɪv] *adj* intransitivo.
intravenous [ɪntrə'viːnəs] *adj* intravenoso.
in-tray ['ɪntreɪ] *n* bandeja de entrada.
intrepid [ɪn'trepɪd] *adj* intrépido.
intricacy ['ɪntrɪkəsɪ] *n* complejidad *f*.
intricate ['ɪntrɪkət] *adj* intrincado; (*plot,
  problem*) complejo.
intrigue [ɪn'triːg] *n* intriga ♦ *vt* fascinar ♦ *vi*
  andar en intrigas.
intriguing [ɪn'triːgɪŋ] *adj* fascinante.
intrinsic [ɪn'trɪnsɪk] *adj* intrínseco.

introduce [ɪntrə'djuːs] vt introducir, meter; **to ~ sb (to sb)** presentar algn (a otro); **to ~ sb to** (*pastime, technique*) introducir a algn a; **may I ~ ...?** permítame presentarle a ....

introduction [ɪntrə'dʌkʃən] n introducción f; (*of person*) presentación f; **a letter of ~** una carta de recomendación.

introductory [ɪntrə'dʌktərɪ] adj introductorio; **an ~ offer** una oferta introductoria; **~ remarks** comentarios mpl preliminares.

introspection [ɪntrəu'spɛkʃən] n introspección f.

introspective [ɪntrəu'spɛktɪv] adj introspectivo.

introvert ['ɪntrəuvɜːt] adj, n introvertido/a m/f.

intrude [ɪn'truːd] vi (*person*) entrometerse; **to ~ on** estorbar.

intruder [ɪn'truːdə*] n intruso/a.

intrusion [ɪn'truːʒən] n invasión f.

intrusive [ɪn'truːsɪv] adj intruso.

intuition [ɪntjuː'ɪʃən] n intuición f.

intuitive [ɪn'tjuːɪtɪv] adj intuitivo.

intuitively [ɪn'tjuːɪtɪvlɪ] adv por intuición, intuitivamente.

inundate ['ɪnʌndeɪt] vt: **to ~ with** inundar de.

inure [ɪn'juə*] vt: **to ~ (to)** acostumbrar or habituar (a).

invade [ɪn'veɪd] vt invadir.

invader [ɪn'veɪdə*] n invasor(a) m/f.

invalid n ['ɪnvəlɪd] minusválido/a ◆ adj [ɪn'vælɪd] (*not valid*) inválido, nulo.

invalidate [ɪn'vælɪdeɪt] vt invalidar, anular.

invalid chair n silla de ruedas.

invaluable [ɪn'væljuəbl] adj inestimable.

invariable [ɪn'vɛərɪəbl] adj invariable.

invariably [ɪn'vɛərɪəblɪ] adv sin excepción, siempre; **she is ~ late** siempre llega tarde.

invasion [ɪn'veɪʒən] n invasión f.

invective [ɪn'vɛktɪv] n invectiva.

inveigle [ɪn'viːgl] vt: **to ~ sb into (doing) sth** embaucar or engatusar a algn para (que haga) algo.

invent [ɪn'vɛnt] vt inventar.

invention [ɪn'vɛnʃən] n invento; (*inventiveness*) inventiva; (*lie*) invención f.

inventive [ɪn'vɛntɪv] adj inventivo.

inventiveness [ɪn'vɛntɪvnɪs] n ingenio, inventiva.

inventor [ɪn'vɛntə*] n inventor(a) m/f.

inventory ['ɪnvəntrɪ] n inventario.

inventory control n control m de existencias.

inverse [ɪn'vɜːs] adj, n inverso; **in ~ proportion (to)** en proporción inversa (a).

inversely [ɪn'vɜːslɪ] adv a la inversa.

invert [ɪn'vɜːt] vt invertir.

invertebrate [ɪn'vɜːtɪbrət] n invertebrado.

inverted commas [ɪn'vɜːtɪd] npl (*BRIT*) comillas fpl.

invest [ɪn'vɛst] vt invertir; (*fig: time, effort*) dedicar ◆ vi invertir; **to ~ sb with sth** conferir algo a algn.

investigate [ɪn'vɛstɪgeɪt] vt investigar; (*study*) estudiar, examinar.

investigation [ɪnvɛstɪ'geɪʃən] n investigación f, pesquisa; examen m.

investigative journalism [ɪn'vɛstɪgətɪv-] n periodismo de investigación.

investigator [ɪn'vɛstɪgeɪtə*] n investigador(a) m/f; **private ~** investigador(a) m/f privado/a.

investiture [ɪn'vɛstɪtʃə*] n investidura.

investment [ɪn'vɛstmənt] n inversión f.

investment grant n subvención f para la inversión.

investment income n ingresos mpl procedentes de inversiones.

investment portfolio n cartera de inversiones.

investment trust n compañía inversionista, sociedad f de cartera.

investor [ɪn'vɛstə*] n inversor(a) m/f.

inveterate [ɪn'vɛtərət] adj empedernido.

invidious [ɪn'vɪdɪəs] adj odioso.

invigilate [ɪn'vɪdʒɪleɪt] vt, vi (*in exam*) vigilar.

invigilator [ɪn'vɪdʒɪleɪtə*] n celador(a) m/f.

invigorating [ɪn'vɪgəreɪtɪŋ] adj vigorizante.

invincible [ɪn'vɪnsɪbl] adj invencible.

inviolate [ɪn'vaɪələt] adj inviolado.

invisible [ɪn'vɪzɪbl] adj invisible.

invisible assets npl activo invisible.

invisible ink n tinta simpática.

invisible mending n puntada invisible.

invitation [ɪnvɪ'teɪʃən] n invitación f; **at sb's ~** a invitación de algn; **by ~ only** solamente por invitación.

invite [ɪn'vaɪt] vt invitar; (*opinions etc*) solicitar, pedir; (*trouble*) buscarse; **to ~ sb (to do)** invitar a algn (a hacer); **to ~ sb to dinner** invitar a algn a cenar.
▶**invite out** vt invitar a salir.
▶**invite over** vt invitar a casa.

inviting [ɪn'vaɪtɪŋ] adj atractivo; (*look*) provocativo; (*food*) apetitoso.

invoice ['ɪnvɔɪs] n factura ◆ vt facturar; **to ~ sb for goods** facturar a algn las mercancías.

invoicing ['ɪnvɔɪsɪŋ] n facturación f.

invoke [ɪn'vəuk] vt invocar; (*aid*) pedir; (*law*) recurrir a.

involuntary [ɪn'vɔləntrɪ] *adj* involuntario.

involve [ɪn'vɔlv] *vt* (*entail*) suponer, implicar; **to ~ sb (in)** involucrar a algn (en).

involved [ɪn'vɔlvd] *adj* complicado; **to be/ become ~ in sth** estar involucrado/ involucrarse en algo.

involvement [ɪn'vɔlvmənt] *n* (*gen*) enredo; (*obligation*) compromiso; (*difficulty*) apuro.

invulnerable [ɪn'vʌlnərəbl] *adj* invulnerable.

inward ['ɪnwəd] *adj* (*movement*) interior, interno; (*thought, feeling*) íntimo.

inwardly ['ɪnwədlɪ] *adv* (*feel, think etc*) para sí, para dentro.

inward(s) ['ɪnwəd(z)] *adv* hacia dentro.

I/O *abbr* (*COMPUT* = *input/output*) E/S; **~ error** error *m* de E/S.

IOC *n abbr* (= *International Olympic Committee*) COI *m*.

iodine ['aɪəudiːn] *n* yodo.

ion ['aɪən] *n* ion *m*.

Ionian Sea [aɪ'əunɪən-] *n*: **the ~** el Mar Jónico.

ioniser ['aɪənaɪzə*] *n* ionizador *m*.

iota [aɪ'əutə] *n* (*fig*) jota, ápice *m*.

IOU *n abbr* (= *I owe you*) pagaré *m*.

IOW *abbr* (*BRIT*) = *Isle of Wight*.

IPA *n abbr* (= *International Phonetic Alphabet*) AFI *m*.

IQ *n abbr* (= *intelligence quotient*) C.I. *m*.

IRA *n abbr* (= *Irish Republican Army*) IRA *m*; (*US*) = *individual retirement account*.

Iran [ɪ'rɑːn] *n* Irán *m*.

Iranian [ɪ'reɪnɪən] *adj* iraní ♦ *n* iraní *m/f*; (*LING*) iraní *m*.

Iraq [ɪ'rɑːk] *n* Irak *m*.

Iraqi [ɪ'rɑːkɪ] *adj, n* irakí *m/f*.

irascible [ɪ'ræsɪbl] *adj* irascible.

irate [aɪ'reɪt] *adj* enojado, airado.

Ireland ['aɪələnd] *n* Irlanda; **Republic of ~** República de Irlanda.

iris, ~es ['aɪrɪs, -ɪz] *n* (*ANAT*) iris *m*; (*BOT*) lirio.

Irish ['aɪrɪʃ] *adj* irlandés/esa ♦ *n* (*LING*) irlandés *m*; **the ~** *npl* los irlandeses.

Irishman ['aɪrɪʃmən] *n* irlandés *m*.

Irish Sea *n*: **the ~** el Mar de Irlanda.

Irishwoman ['aɪrɪʃwumən] *n* irlandesa.

irk [əːk] *vt* fastidiar.

irksome ['əːksəm] *adj* fastidioso.

IRN *n abbr* (= *Independent Radio News*) servicio de noticias en las cadenas de radio privadas.

IRO *n abbr* (*US*) = *International Refugee Organization*.

iron ['aɪən] *n* hierro; (*for clothes*) plancha ♦ *adj* de hierro ♦ *vt* (*clothes*) planchar; **~s** *npl* (*chains*) grilletes *mpl*.

▶**iron out** *vt* (*crease*) quitar; (*fig*) allanar, resolver.

Iron Curtain *n*: **the ~** el Telón de Acero.

iron foundry *n* fundición *f*, fundidora.

ironic(al) [aɪ'rɔnɪk(l)] *adj* irónico.

ironically [aɪ'rɔnɪklɪ] *adv* irónicamente.

ironing ['aɪənɪŋ] *n* (*act*) planchado; (*ironed clothes*) ropa planchada; (*to be ironed*) ropa por planchar.

ironing board *n* tabla de planchar.

iron lung *n* (*MED*) pulmón *m* de acero.

ironmonger ['aɪənmʌŋgə*] *n* (*BRIT*) ferretero/a; **~'s (shop)** ferretería.

iron ore *n* mineral *m* de hierro.

ironworks ['aɪənwəːks] *n* fundición *f*.

irony ['aɪrənɪ] *n* ironía; **the ~ of it is that ...** lo irónico del caso es que ....

irrational [ɪ'ræʃənl] *adj* irracional.

irreconcilable [ɪrɛkən'saɪləbl] *adj* inconciliable; (*enemies*) irreconciliable.

irredeemable [ɪrɪ'diːməbl] *adj* irredimible.

irrefutable [ɪrɪ'fjuːtəbl] *adj* irrefutable.

irregular [ɪ'rɛgjulə*] *adj* irregular; (*surface*) desigual.

irregularity [ɪrɛgju'lærɪtɪ] *n* irregularidad *f*; desigualdad *f*.

irrelevance [ɪ'rɛləvəns] *n* irrelevancia.

irrelevant [ɪ'rɛləvənt] *adj* irrelevante; **to be ~** estar fuera de lugar, no venir al caso.

irreligious [ɪrɪ'lɪdʒəs] *adj* irreligioso.

irreparable [ɪ'rɛprəbl] *adj* irreparable.

irreplaceable [ɪrɪ'pleɪsəbl] *adj* irremplazable.

irrepressible [ɪrɪ'prɛsəbl] *adj* incontenible.

irreproachable [ɪrɪ'prəutʃəbl] *adj* irreprochable.

irresistible [ɪrɪ'zɪstɪbl] *adj* irresistible.

irresolute [ɪ'rɛzəluːt] *adj* indeciso.

irrespective [ɪrɪ'spɛktɪv]: **~ of** *prep* sin tener en cuenta, no importa.

irresponsibility [ɪrɪspɔnsɪ'bɪlɪtɪ] *n* irresponsabilidad *f*.

irresponsible [ɪrɪ'spɔnsɪbl] *adj* (*act*) irresponsable; (*person*) poco serio.

irretrievable [ɪrɪ'triːvəbl] *adj* (*object*) irrecuperable; (*loss, damage*) irremediable, irreparable.

irretrievably [ɪrɪ'triːvəblɪ] *adv* irremisiblemente.

irreverence [ɪ'rɛvərns] *n* irreverencia.

irreverent [ɪ'rɛvərnt] *adj* irreverente, irrespetuoso.

irrevocable [ɪ'rɛvəkəbl] *adj* irrevocable.

irrigate ['ɪrɪgeɪt] *vt* regar.

irrigation [ɪrɪ'geɪʃən] *n* riego.

irritability [ɪrɪtə'bɪlɪtɪ] *n* irritabilidad *f*.

irritable ['ɪrɪtəbl] *adj* (*person: temperament*) irritable; (: *mood*) de mal humor.

irritant ['ırıtənt] n agente m irritante.
irritate ['ırıteıt] vt fastidiar; (MED) picar.
irritating ['ırıteıtıŋ] adj fastidioso.
irritation [ırı'teıʃən] n fastidio; picazón f.
IRS n abbr (US) see **Internal Revenue Service**.
is [ız] vb see **be**.
ISA ['aısə] n abbr (BRIT COMM = Individual Savings Account) plan de ahorro personal para pequeños inversores con fiscalidad cero.
ISBN n abbr (= International Standard Book Number) ISBN m.
ISDN n abbr (= Integrated Services Digital Network) RDSI f.
Islam ['ızlɑːm] n Islam m.
island ['aılənd] n isla; (also: **traffic** ~) isleta.
islander ['aıləndə*] n isleño/a.
isle [aıl] n isla.
isn't ['ıznt] = **is not**.
isobar ['aısəubɑː*] n isobara.
isolate ['aısəleıt] vt aislar.
isolated ['aısəleıtıd] adj aislado.
isolation [aısə'leıʃən] n aislamiento.
isolation ward n pabellón m de aislamiento.
isotope ['aısəutəup] n isótopo.
Israel ['ızreıl] n Israel m.
Israeli [ız'reılı] adj, n israelí m/f.
issue ['ısjuː] n cuestión f, asunto; (outcome) resultado; (of banknotes etc) emisión f; (of newspaper etc) número; (offspring) sucesión f, descendencia ♦ vt (rations, equipment) distribuir, repartir; (orders) dar; (certificate, passport) expedir; (decree) promulgar; (magazine) publicar; (cheques) extender; (banknotes, stamps) emitir ♦ vi: **to** ~ **(from)** derivar (de), brotar (de); **at** ~ en cuestión; **to take** ~ **with sb (over)** disentir con algn (en); **to avoid the** ~ andarse con rodeos; **to make an** ~ **of sth** dar a algo más importancia de lo necesario; **to** ~ **sth to sb,** ~ **sb with sth** entregar algo a algn.
Istanbul [ıstæn'buːl] n Estambul m.
isthmus ['ısməs] n istmo.
IT n abbr = **information technology**.

================= KEYWORD

it [ıt] pron **1** (specific: subject: not generally translated) él/ella; (: direct object) lo, la; (: indirect object) le; (after prep) él/ella; (abstract concept) ello; ~'**s on the table** está en la mesa; **I can't find** ~ no lo (or la) encuentro; **give** ~ **to me** dámelo (or dámela); **I spoke to him about** ~ le hablé del asunto; **what did you learn from** ~? ¿qué aprendiste de él (or ella)?; **did you go to** ~? (party, concert) ¿fuiste?

2 (impersonal): ~'**s raining** llueve, está lloviendo; ~'**s 6 o'clock/the 10th of August** son las 6/es el 10 de agosto; **how far is** ~? — ~'**s 10 miles/2 hours on the train** ¿a qué distancia está? — a 10 millas/2 horas en tren; **who is** ~? — ~'**s me** ¿quién es? — soy yo.

Italian [ı'tæljən] adj italiano ♦ n italiano/a; (LING) italiano.
italic [ı'tælık] adj cursivo; ~**s** npl cursiva sg.
Italy ['ıtəlı] n Italia.
itch [ıtʃ] n picazón f; (fig) prurito ♦ vi (person) sentir or tener comezón; (part of body) picar; **to be** ~**ing to do sth** rabiar por or morirse de ganas de hacer algo.
itching ['ıtʃıŋ] n picazón f, comezón f.
itchy ['ıtʃı] adj: **to be** ~ picar.
item ['aıtəm] n artículo; (on agenda) asunto (a tratar); (in programme) número; (also: **news** ~) noticia; ~**s of clothing** prendas fpl de vestir.
itemize ['aıtəmaız] vt detallar.
itemized bill ['aıtəmaızd-] n recibo detallado.
itinerant [ı'tınərənt] adj ambulante.
itinerary [aı'tınərərı] n itinerario.
it'll ['ıtl] = **it will, it shall**.
ITN n abbr see **ITV**.
its [ıts] adj su.
it's [ıts] = **it is; it has**.
itself [ıt'self] pron (reflexive) sí mismo/a; (emphatic) él mismo/ella misma.
ITV n abbr (BRIT: = Independent Television) ver recuadro.

ITV

En el Reino Unido la **ITV** ("Independent Television) es una cadena de emisoras comerciales regionales con licencia exclusiva para emitir en su región. Suelen producir sus propios programas, se financian con publicidad y están bajo el control del organismo oficial independiente "Independent Broadcasting Authority" ("IBA"). El servicio de noticias nacionales e internacionales, "ITN" ("Independent Television News"), funciona como una compañía productora para toda la cadena.

IUD n abbr (= intra-uterine device) DIU m.
I've [aıv] = **I have**.
ivory ['aıvərı] n marfil m.
Ivory Coast n: **the** ~ la Costa de Marfil.
ivory tower n (fig) torre f de marfil.
ivy ['aıví] n hiedra.

Ivy League n (US) ver recuadro.

IVY LEAGUE

Las ocho universidades más prestigiosas
del nordeste de los Estados Unidos reciben
el nombre colectivo de **Ivy League**, por sus
muros cubiertos de hiedra. Son: Brown,
Columbia, Cornell, Dartmouth College,
Harvard, Princeton, la universidad de
Pennsylvania y Yale. También se llaman así
las competiciones deportivas que celebran
entre ellas.

J j

J, j [dʒeɪ] n (letter) J, j f; **J for Jack**, (US) **J for Jig** J de José.
JA n abbr = **judge advocate**.
J/A abbr = **joint account**.
jab [dʒæb] vt (elbow) dar un codazo a; (punch) dar un golpe rápido a ♦ vi: **to ~ at** intentar golpear a; **to ~ sth into sth** clavar algo en algo ♦ n codazo; golpe m (rápido); (MED col) pinchazo.
jabber ['dʒæbə*] vt, vi farfullar.
jack [dʒæk] n (AUT) gato; (BOWLS) boliche m; (CARDS) sota.
► **jack in** vt (col) dejar.
► **jack up** vt (AUT) levantar con el gato.
jackal ['dʒækl] n (ZOOL) chacal m.
jackass ['dʒækæs] n (also fig) asno, burro.
jackdaw ['dʒækdɔ:] n grajo/a, chova.
jacket ['dʒækɪt] n chaqueta, americana, saco (LAM); (of boiler etc) camisa; (of book) sobrecubierta.
jacket potato n patata asada (con piel).
jack-in-the-box ['dʒækɪnðəbɔks] n caja sorpresa, caja de resorte.
jack-knife ['dʒæknaɪf] vi colear.
jack-of-all-trades ['dʒækəv'ɔ:ltreɪdz] n aprendiz m de todo.
jack plug n (ELEC) enchufe m de clavija.
jackpot ['dʒækpɔt] n premio gordo.
Jacuzzi ® [dʒə'ku:zɪ] n jacuzzi ® m.
jade [dʒeɪd] n (stone) jade m.
jaded ['dʒeɪdɪd] adj (tired) cansado; (fed up) hastiado.
jagged ['dʒægɪd] adj dentado.
jaguar ['dʒægjuə*] n jaguar m.

jail [dʒeɪl] n cárcel f ♦ vt encarcelar.
jailbird ['dʒeɪlbəɪd] n preso/a reincidente.
jailbreak ['dʒeɪlbreɪk] n fuga or evasión f (de la cárcel).
jailer ['dʒeɪlə*] n carcelero/a.
jam [dʒæm] n mermelada; (also: **traffic ~**) atasco, embotellamiento; (difficulty) apuro ♦ vt (passage etc) obstruir; (mechanism, drawer etc) atascar; (RADIO) interferir ♦ vi atascarse, trabarse; **to get sb out of a ~** sacar a algn del paso or de un apuro; **to ~ sth into sth** meter algo a la fuerza en algo; **the telephone lines are ~med** las líneas están saturadas.
Jamaica [dʒə'meɪkə] n Jamaica.
Jamaican [dʒə'meɪkən] adj, n jamaicano/a m/f.
jamb [dʒæm] n jamba.
jamboree [dʒæmbə'ri:] n congreso de niños exploradores.
jam-packed [dʒæm'pækt] adj: **~ (with)** atestado (de).
jam session n concierto improvisado de jazz/rock etc.
Jan. abbr (= January) ene.
jangle ['dʒæŋgl] vi sonar (de manera) discordante.
janitor ['dʒænɪtə*] n (caretaker) portero, conserje m.
January ['dʒænjuərɪ] n enero.
Japan [dʒə'pæn] n (el) Japón.
Japanese [dʒæpə'ni:z] adj japonés/esa ♦ n (pl inv) japonés/esa m/f; (LING) japonés m.
jar [dʒɑ:*] n (glass: large) jarra; (: small) tarro ♦ vi (sound) chirriar; (colours) desentonar.
jargon ['dʒɑ:gən] n jerga.
jarring ['dʒɑ:rɪŋ] adj (sound) discordante, desafinado; (colour) chocante.
Jas. abbr = **James**.
jasmin(e) ['dʒæzmɪn] n jazmín m.
jaundice ['dʒɔ:ndɪs] n ictericia.
jaundiced ['dʒɔ:ndɪst] adj (fig: embittered) amargado; (: disillusioned) desilusionado.
jaunt [dʒɔ:nt] n excursión f.
jaunty ['dʒɔ:ntɪ] adj alegre; (relaxed) desenvuelto.
javelin ['dʒævlɪn] n jabalina.
jaw [dʒɔ:] n mandíbula; **~s** npl (TECH: of vice etc) mordaza sg.
jawbone ['dʒɔ:bəun] n mandíbula, quijada.
jay [dʒeɪ] n (ZOOL) arrendajo.
jaywalker ['dʒeɪwɔ:kə*] n peatón/ona m/f imprudente.
jazz [dʒæz] n jazz m.
► **jazz up** vt (liven up) animar.
jazz band n orquesta de jazz.
jazzy ['dʒæzɪ] adj de colores llamativos.

JCB ® *n abbr* excavadora.
JCS *n abbr* (*US*) = Joint Chiefs of Staff.
JD *n abbr* (*US*: = Doctor of Laws) título universitario; (: = Justice Department) Ministerio de Justicia.
jealous ['dʒɛləs] *adj* (*gen*) celoso; (*envious*) envidioso; **to be** ~ tener celos.
jealously ['dʒɛləslɪ] *adv* (*enviously*) envidiosamente; (*watchfully*) celosamente.
jealousy ['dʒɛləsɪ] *n* celos *mpl*; envidia.
jeans [dʒiːnz] *npl* (pantalones *mpl*) vaqueros *mpl or* tejanos *mpl*, bluejean *m inv* (*LAM*).
Jeep ® [dʒiːp] *n* jeep *m*.
jeer [dʒɪə*] *vi*: **to** ~ **(at)** (*boo*) abuchear; (*mock*) mofarse (de).
jeering ['dʒɪərɪŋ] *adj* (*crowd*) insolente, ofensivo ♦ *n* protestas *fpl*; (*mockery*) burlas *fpl*.
jelly ['dʒɛlɪ] *n* gelatina, jalea.
jellyfish ['dʒɛlɪfɪʃ] *n* medusa.
jemmy ['dʒɛmɪ] *n* palanqueta.
jeopardize ['dʒɛpədaɪz] *vt* arriesgar, poner en peligro.
jeopardy ['dʒɛpədɪ] *n*. **to be in** ~ estar en peligro.
jerk [dʒəːk] *n* (*jolt*) sacudida; (*wrench*) tirón *m*; (*US col*) imbécil *m/f*, pendejo/a (*LAM*) ♦ *vt* dar una sacudida a; tirar bruscamente de ♦ *vi* (*vehicle*) dar una sacudida.
jerkin ['dʒəːkɪn] *n* chaleco.
jerky ['dʒəːkɪ] *adj* espasmódico.
jerry-built ['dʒɛrɪbɪlt] *adj* mal construido.
jerry can ['dʒɛrɪ-] *n* bidón *m*.
Jersey ['dʒəːzɪ] *n* Jersey *m*.
jersey ['dʒəːzɪ] *n* jersey *m*; (*fabric*) tejido de punto.
Jerusalem [dʒəˈruːsləm] *n* Jerusalén *m*.
jest [dʒɛst] *n* broma.
jester ['dʒɛstə*] *n* bufón *m*.
Jesus ['dʒiːzəs] *n* Jesús *m*; ~ **Christ** Jesucristo.
jet [dʒɛt] *n* (*of gas, liquid*) chorro; (*AVIAT*) avión *m* a reacción.
jet-black ['dʒɛt'blæk] *adj* negro como el azabache.
jet engine *n* motor *m* a reacción.
jet lag *n* desorientación *f* por desfase horario.
jetsam ['dʒɛtsəm] *n* echazón *f*.
jet-setter ['dʒɛtsɛtə*] *n* personaje *m* de la jet.
jettison ['dʒɛtɪsn] *vt* desechar.
jetty ['dʒɛtɪ] *n* muelle *m*, embarcadero.
Jew [dʒuː] *n* judío.
jewel ['dʒuːəl] *n* joya; (*in watch*) rubí *m*.
jeweller, (*US*) **jeweler** ['dʒuːələ*] *n* joyero/a; ~'**s (shop)** joyería.

jewellery, (*US*) **jewelry** ['dʒuːəlrɪ] *n* joyas *fpl*, alhajas *fpl*.
Jewess ['dʒuːɪs] *n* judía.
Jewish ['dʒuːɪʃ] *adj* judío.
JFK *n abbr* (*US*) = John Fitzgerald Kennedy International Airport.
jib [dʒɪb] *vi* (*horse*) plantarse; **to** ~ **at doing sth** resistirse a hacer algo.
jibe [dʒaɪb] *n* mofa.
jiffy ['dʒɪfɪ] *n* (*col*): **in a** ~ en un santiamén.
jig [dʒɪg] *n* (*dance, tune*) giga.
jigsaw ['dʒɪgsɔː] *n* (*also:* ~ **puzzle**) rompecabezas *m inv*; (*tool*) sierra de vaivén.
jilt [dʒɪlt] *vt* dejar plantado a.
jingle ['dʒɪŋgl] *n* (*advert*) musiquilla ♦ *vi* tintinear.
jingoism ['dʒɪŋgəʊɪzəm] *n* patriotería, jingoísmo.
jinx [dʒɪŋks] *n*: **there's a** ~ **on it** está gafado.
jitters ['dʒɪtəz] *npl* (*col*): **to get the** ~ ponerse nervioso.
jittery ['dʒɪtərɪ] *adj* (*col*) agitado.
jiujitsu [dʒuːˈdʒɪtsuː] *n* ju-jitsu *m*.
job [dʒɔb] *n* trabajo; (*task*) tarea; (*duty*) deber *m*; (*post*) empleo; (*fam: difficulty*) dificultad *f*; **it's a good** ~ **that...** menos mal que...; **just the** ~! ¡justo lo que necesito!; **a part-time/full-time** ~ un trabajo a tiempo parcial/tiempo completo; **that's not my** ~ eso no me incumbe *or* toca a mí; **he's only doing his** ~ está cumpliendo nada más.
job centre *n* (*BRIT*) oficina de empleo.
job creation scheme *n* plan *m* de creación de puestos de trabajo.
job description *n* descripción *f* del puesto de trabajo.
jobless ['dʒɔblɪs] *adj* sin trabajo ♦ *n*: **the** ~ los parados.
job lot *n* lote *m* de mercancías, saldo.
job satisfaction *n* satisfacción *f* en el trabajo.
job security *n* garantía de trabajo.
job specification *n* especificación *f* del trabajo, profesiograma *m*.
Jock *n* (*col: Scotsman*) escocés *m*.
jockey ['dʒɔkɪ] *n* jockey *m/f* ♦ *vi*: **to** ~ **for position** maniobrar para sacar delantera.
jockey box *n* (*US AUT*) guantera.
jockstrap ['dʒɔkstræp] *n* suspensorio.
jocular ['dʒɔkjulə*] *adj* (*humorous*) gracioso; (*merry*) alegre.
jodhpurs ['dʒɔdpəz] *npl* pantalón *msg* de montar.
jog [dʒɔg] *vt* empujar (ligeramente) ♦ *vi* (*run*) hacer footing; **to** ~ **along** (*fig*) ir tirando; **to** ~ **sb's memory** refrescar la

memoria a algn.

jogger ['dʒɔgə*] *n* corredor(a) *m/f.*

jogging ['dʒɔgɪŋ] *n* footing *m.*

john [dʒɔn] *n* (*US col*) wáter *m.*

join [dʒɔɪn] *vt* (*things*) unir, juntar; (*become member of: club*) hacerse socio de; (*POL: party*) afiliarse a; (*meet: people*) reunirse con; (*fig*) unirse a ♦ *vi* (*roads*) empalmar; (*rivers*) confluir ♦ *n* juntura; **will you ~ us for dinner?** ¿quieres cenar con nosotros?; **I'll ~ you later** me reuniré contigo luego; **to ~ forces (with)** aliarse (con).

▶**join in** *vi* tomar parte, participar ♦ *vt fus* tomar parte *or* participar en.

▶**join up** *vi* unirse; (*MIL*) alistarse.

joiner ['dʒɔɪnə*] *n* carpintero/a.

joinery ['dʒɔɪnərɪ] *n* carpintería.

joint [dʒɔɪnt] *n* (*TECH*) juntura, unión *f*; (*ANAT*) articulación *f*; (*BRIT CULIN*) pieza de carne (para asar); (*col: place*) garito ♦ *adj* (*common*) común; (*combined*) conjunto; (*responsibility*) compartido; (*committee*) mixto.

joint account (J/A) *n* (*with bank etc*) cuenta común.

jointly ['dʒɔɪntlɪ] *adv* (*gen*) en común; (*together*) conjuntamente.

joint owners *npl* copropietarios *mpl.*

joint ownership *n* copropiedad *f*, propiedad *f* común.

joint-stock bank ['dʒɔɪntstɔk-] *n* banco por acciones.

joint-stock company ['dʒɔɪntstɔk-] *n* sociedad *f* anónima.

joint venture *n* empresa conjunta.

joist [dʒɔɪst] *n* viga.

joke [dʒəuk] *n* chiste *m*; (*also:* **practical ~**) broma ♦ *vi* bromear; **to play a ~ on** gastar una broma a.

joker ['dʒəukə*] *n* chistoso/a, bromista *m/f*; (*CARDS*) comodín *m.*

joking ['dʒəukɪŋ] *n* bromas *fpl.*

jokingly ['dʒəukɪŋlɪ] *adv* en broma.

jollity ['dʒɔlɪtɪ] *n* alegría.

jolly ['dʒɔlɪ] *adj* (*merry*) alegre; (*enjoyable*) divertido ♦ *adv* (*col*) muy, la mar de ♦ *vt*: **to ~ sb along** animar *or* darle ánimos a algn; **~ good!** ¡estupendo!

jolt [dʒəult] *n* (*shake*) sacudida; (*blow*) golpe *m*; (*shock*) susto ♦ *vt* sacudir.

Jordan ['dʒɔːdən] *n* (*country*) Jordania; (*river*) Jordán *m.*

joss stick [dʒɔs-] *n* barrita de incienso, pebete *m.*

jostle ['dʒɔsl] *vt* dar empujones *or* empellones a.

jot [dʒɔt] *n*: **not one ~** ni pizca, ni un ápice.

▶**jot down** *vt* apuntar.

jotter ['dʒɔtə*] *n* (*BRIT*) bloc *m.*

journal ['dʒəːnl] *n* (*paper*) periódico; (*magazine*) revista; (*diary*) diario.

journalese [dʒəːnə'liːz] *n* (*pej*) lenguaje *m* periodístico.

journalism ['dʒəːnəlɪzəm] *n* periodismo.

journalist ['dʒəːnəlɪst] *n* periodista *m/f.*

journey ['dʒəːnɪ] *n* viaje *m*; (*distance covered*) trayecto ♦ *vi* viajar; **return ~** viaje de regreso; **a 5-hour ~** un viaje de 5 horas.

jovial ['dʒəuvɪəl] *adj* risueño, alegre.

jowl [dʒaul] *n* quijada.

joy [dʒɔɪ] *n* alegría.

joyful ['dʒɔɪful] *adj* alegre.

joyfully ['dʒɔɪfulɪ] *adv* alegremente.

joyous ['dʒɔɪəs] *adj* alegre.

joyride ['dʒɔɪraɪd] *n*: **to go for a ~** darse una vuelta en un coche robado.

joyrider ['dʒɔɪraɪdə*] *n persona que se da una vuelta en un coche robado.*

joystick ['dʒɔɪstɪk] *n* (*AVIAT*) palanca de mando; (*COMPUT*) palanca de control.

JP *n abbr see* **Justice of the Peace.**

Jr. *abbr* = **junior.**

JTPA *n abbr* (*US:* = *Job Training Partnership Act*) *programa gubernamental de formación profesional.*

jubilant ['dʒuːbɪlnt] *adj* jubiloso.

jubilation [dʒuːbɪ'leɪʃən] *n* júbilo.

jubilee ['dʒuːbɪliː] *n* aniversario; **silver ~** vigésimo quinto aniversario.

judge [dʒʌdʒ] *n* juez *m/f* ♦ *vt* juzgar; (*competition*) actuar de *or* ser juez en; (*estimate*) considerar; (*: weight, size etc*) calcular ♦ *vi*: **judging** *or* **to ~ by his expression** a juzgar por su expresión; **as far as I can ~** por lo que puedo entender, a mi entender; **I ~d it necessary to inform him** consideré necesario informarle.

judge advocate *n* (*MIL*) auditor *m* de guerra.

judg(e)ment ['dʒʌdʒmənt] *n* juicio; (*punishment*) sentencia, fallo; **to pass ~ (on)** (*LAW*) pronunciar *or* dictar sentencia (sobre); (*fig*) emitir un juicio crítico *or* dictaminar (sobre); **in my ~** a mi juicio.

judicial [dʒuː'dɪʃl] *adj* judicial.

judiciary [dʒuː'dɪʃɪərɪ] *n* poder *m* judicial, magistratura.

judicious [dʒuː'dɪʃəs] *adj* juicioso.

judo ['dʒuːdəu] *n* judo.

jug [dʒʌg] *n* jarro.

jugged hare [dʒʌgd-] *n* (*BRIT*) estofado de liebre.

juggernaut ['dʒʌgənɔːt] *n* (*BRIT: huge truck*) camión *m* de carga pesada.

juggle ['dʒʌgl] *vi* hacer juegos malabares.

juggler ['dʒʌglə*] n malabarista m/f.
Jugoslav ['juːgəuslɑːv] etc = **Yugoslav** etc.
jugular ['dʒʌgjulə*] adj: ~ **vein** (vena)
   yugular f.
juice [dʒuːs] n jugo, zumo (SP); (of meat)
   jugo; (col: petrol): **we've run out of** ~ se
   nos acabó la gasolina.
juicy ['dʒuːsɪ] adj jugoso.
jujitsu [dʒuː'dʒɪtsuː] n = **juijitsu**.
jukebox ['dʒuːkbɔks] n máquina de discos.
Jul. abbr (= July) jul.
July [dʒuː'laɪ] n julio; **the first of** ~ el uno or
   primero de julio; **during** ~ en el mes de
   julio; **in** ~ **of next year** en julio del año
   que viene.
jumble ['dʒʌmbl] n revoltijo ♦ vt (also: ~
   together, ~ **up:** mix up) revolver;
   (: disarrange) mezclar.
jumble sale n (BRIT) mercadillo; ver
   recuadro.

JUMBLE SALE

En cada **jumble sale** pueden comprarse
todo tipo de objetos baratos de segunda
mano, especialmente ropa, juguetes, libros,
vajillas y muebles. Suelen organizarse en
los locales de un colegio, iglesia,
ayuntamiento o similar, con fines
benéficos, bien en ayuda de una
organización benéfica conocida o para
solucionar problemas más concretos de la
comunidad.

---

jumbo (jet) ['dʒʌmbəu-] n jumbo.
jump [dʒʌmp] vi saltar, dar saltos; (start)
   sobresaltarse; (increase) aumentar ♦ vt
   saltar ♦ n salto; (fence) obstáculo;
   (increase) aumento; **to** ~ **the queue** (BRIT)
   colarse.
▶**jump about** vi dar saltos, brincar.
▶**jump at** vt fus (fig) apresurarse a
   aprovechar; **he ~ed at the offer** se
   apresuró a aceptar la oferta.
▶**jump down** vi bajar de un salto, saltar a
   tierra.
▶**jump up** vi levantarse de un salto.
jumped-up ['dʒʌmptʌp] adj (pej) engreído.
jumper ['dʒʌmpə*] n (BRIT: pullover)
   jersey m, suéter m; (US: pinafore dress)
   pichi m; (SPORT) saltador(a) m/f.
jump leads, (US) **jumper cables** npl
   cables mpl puente de batería.
jump-start ['dʒʌmpstɑːt] vt (car) arrancar
   con ayuda de otra batería or empujando;
   (fig: economy) reactivar.
jump suit n mono.
jumpy ['dʒʌmpɪ] adj nervioso.

Jun. abbr = **junior**; (= June) jun.
junction ['dʒʌŋkʃən] n (BRIT: of roads) cruce
   m; (RAIL) empalme m.
juncture ['dʒʌŋktʃə*] n: **at this** ~ en este
   momento, en esta coyuntura.
June [dʒuːn] n junio.
jungle ['dʒʌŋgl] n selva, jungla.
junior ['dʒuːnɪə*] adj (in age) menor, más
   joven; (competition) juvenil; (position)
   subalterno ♦ n menor m/f, joven m/f; **he's** ~
   to me es menor que yo.
junior high school n (US) centro de educación secundaria; see also **high school**.
junior school n (BRIT) escuela primaria;
   see also **primary school**.
junk [dʒʌŋk] n (cheap goods) baratijas fpl;
   (lumber) trastos mpl viejos, (rubbish)
   basura; (ship) junco ♦ vt (esp US)
   deshacerse de.
junk bond n (COMM) obligación f basura
   inv.
junk dealer n vendedor(a) m/f de objetos
   usados.
junket ['dʒʌŋkɪt] n (CULIN) dulce de leche
   cuajada; (BRIT col): **to go on a** ~, **go** ~**ing**
   viajar a costa ajena or del erario público.
junk food n comida basura or de plástico.
junkie ['dʒʌŋkɪ] n (col) yonqui m/f,
   heroinómano/a.
junk mail n propaganda (buzoneada).
junk room n trastero.
junk shop n tienda de objetos usados.
junta ['dʒʌntə] n junta militar.
Jupiter ['dʒuːpɪtə*] n (MYTHOLOGY, ASTRO)
   Júpiter m.
jurisdiction [dʒuərɪs'dɪkʃən] n jurisdicción
   f; **it falls** or **comes within/outside our** ~
   es/no es de nuestra competencia.
jurisprudence [dʒuərɪs'pruːdəns] n
   jurisprudencia.
juror ['dʒuərə*] n jurado.
jury ['dʒuərɪ] n jurado.
jury box n tribuna del jurado.
juryman ['dʒuərɪmən] n miembro del
   jurado.
just [dʒʌst] adj justo ♦ adv (exactly)
   exactamente; (only) sólo, solamente, no
   más (LAM); **he's** ~ **done it/left** acaba de
   hacerlo/irse; **I've** ~ **seen him** acabo de
   verle; ~ **right** perfecto; ~ **two o'clock** las
   dos en punto; **she's** ~ **as clever as you** es
   tan lista como tú; ~ **as well that...** menos
   mal que...; **it's** ~ **as well you didn't go**
   menos mal que no fuiste; **it's** ~ **as good**
   (as) es igual (que), es tan bueno (como);
   ~ **as he was leaving** en el momento en
   que se marchaba; **we were** ~ **going** ya
   nos íbamos; **I was** ~ **about to phone**

estaba a punto de llamar; ~ **before/ enough** justo antes/lo suficiente; ~ **here** aquí mismo; **he** ~ **missed** falló por poco; ~ **listen to this** escucha esto un momento; ~ **ask someone the way** simplemente pregúntale a algn por dónde se va; **not** ~ **now** ahora no.

justice ['dʒʌstɪs] *n* justicia; **this photo doesn't do you** ~ esta foto no te favorece.

Justice of the Peace (JP) *n* juez *m/f* de paz; *see also* **Crown Court**.

justifiable [dʒʌstɪ'faɪəbl] *adj* justificable, justificado.

justifiably [dʒʌstɪ'faɪəblɪ] *adv* justificadamente, con razón.

justification [dʒʌstɪfɪ'keɪʃən] *n* justificación *f*.

justify ['dʒʌstɪfaɪ] *vt* justificar; (*text*) alinear, justificar; **to be justified in doing sth** tener motivo para *or* razón al hacer algo.

justly ['dʒʌstlɪ] *adv* (*gen*) justamente; (*with reason*) con razón.

justness ['dʒʌstnɪs] *n* justicia.

jut [dʒʌt] *vi* (*also:* ~ **out**) sobresalir.

jute [dʒuːt] *n* yute *m*.

juvenile ['dʒuːvənaɪl] *adj* juvenil; (*court*) de menores ♦ *n* joven *m/f*, menor *m/f* de edad.

juvenile delinquency *n* delincuencia juvenil.

juvenile delinquent *n* delincuente *m/f* juvenil.

juxtapose ['dʒʌkstəpəʊz] *vt* yuxtaponer.

juxtaposition ['dʒʌkstəpə'zɪʃən] *n* yuxtaposición *f*.

Kk

K, k [keɪ] *n* (*letter*) K, k *f*; **K for King** K de Kilo.

K *abbr* (= *one thousand*) K; = *kilobyte*; (*BRIT*: = *Knight*) *caballero de una orden*.

kaftan ['kæftæn] *n* caftán *m*.

Kalahari Desert [kælə'hɑːrɪ-] *n* desierto de Kalahari.

kale [keɪl] *n* col *f* rizada.

kaleidoscope [kə'laɪdəskəʊp] *n* calidoscopio.

kamikaze [kæmɪ'kɑːzɪ] *adj* kamikaze.

Kampala [kæm'pɑːlə] *n* Kampala.

Kampuchea [kæmpu'tʃɪə] *n* Kampuchea.

kangaroo [kæŋgə'ruː] *n* canguro.

Kans. *abbr* (*US*) = *Kansas*.

kaput [kə'put] *adj* (*col*) roto, estropeado.

karaoke [kɑːrə'əʊkɪ] *n* karaoke.

karate [kə'rɑːtɪ] *n* karate *m*.

Kashmir [kæʃ'mɪə*] *n* Cachemira.

kayak ['kaɪæk] *n* kayak *m*.

Kazakhstan [kɑːzɑːk'stæn] *n* Kazajstán *m*.

KC *n abbr* (*BRIT LAW*: = *King's Counsel*) título concedido a determinados abogados.

kd *abbr* (*US*: = *knocked down*) desmontado.

kebab [kə'bæb] *n* pincho moruno, brocheta.

keel [kiːl] *n* quilla; **on an even** ~ (*fig*) en equilibrio.

▶**keel over** *vi* (*NAUT*) zozobrar, volcarse; (*person*) desplomarse.

keen [kiːn] *adj* (*interest, desire*) grande, vivo; (*eye, intelligence*) agudo; (*competition*) intenso; (*edge*) afilado; (*BRIT: eager*) entusiasta; **to be** ~ **to do** *or* **on doing sth** tener muchas ganas de hacer algo; **to be** ~ **on sth/sb** interesarse por algo/uno; **I'm not** ~ **on going** no tengo ganas de ir.

keenly ['kiːnlɪ] *adv* (*enthusiastically*) con entusiasmo; (*acutely*) vivamente; (*intensely*) intensamente.

keenness ['kiːnnɪs] *n* (*eagerness*) entusiasmo, interés *m*.

keep [kiːp] *vb* (*pt, pp* **kept** [kɛpt]) *vt* (*retain, preserve*) guardar; (*hold back*) quedarse con; (*shop*) ser propietario de; (*feed: family etc*) mantener; (*promise*) cumplir; (*chickens, bees etc*) criar ♦ *vi* (*food*) conservarse; (*remain*) seguir, continuar ♦ *n* (*of castle*) torreón *m*; (*food etc*) comida, sustento; **to** ~ **doing sth** seguir haciendo algo; **to** ~ **sb from doing sth** impedir a algn hacer algo; **to** ~ **sth from happening** impedir que algo ocurra; **to** ~ **sb happy** tener a algn contento; **to** ~ **sb waiting** hacer esperar a algn; **to** ~ **a place tidy** mantener un lugar limpio; **to** ~ **sth to o.s.** no decirle algo a nadie; **to** ~ **time** (*clock*) mantener la hora exacta; ~ **the change** quédese con la vuelta; **to** ~ **an appointment** acudir a una cita; **to** ~ **a record** *or* **note of sth** tomar nota de *or* apuntar algo; *see also* **keeps**.

▶**keep away** *vt*: **to** ~ **sth/sb away from sb** mantener algo/a algn apartado de algn ♦ *vi*: **to** ~ **away (from)** mantenerse apartado (de).

▶**keep back** *vt* (*crowd, tears*) contener; (*money*) quedarse con; (*conceal: information*): **to** ~ **sth back from sb** ocultar algo a algn ♦ *vi* hacerse a un lado.

▶**keep down** *vt* (*control: prices, spending*)

controlar; (*retain: food*) retener ♦ *vi* seguir agachado, no levantar la cabeza.

▶**keep in** *vt* (*invalid, child*) impedir que salga, no dejar salir; (*SCOL*) castigar (a quedarse en el colegio) ♦ *vi* (*col*): **to ~ in with sb** mantener la relación con algn.

▶**keep off** *vt* (*dog, person*) mantener a distancia ♦ *vi* evitar; **~ your hands off!** ¡no toques!; "**~ off the grass**" "prohibido pisar el césped".

▶**keep on** *vi* seguir, continuar.

▶**keep out** *vi* (*stay out*) permanecer fuera; "**~ out**" "prohibida la entrada".

▶**keep up** *vt* mantener, conservar ♦ *vi* no rezagarse; (*fig: in comprehension*) seguir (el hilo); **to ~ up with** (*pace*) ir al paso de; (*level*) mantenerse a la altura de; **to ~ up with sb** seguir el ritmo a algn; (*fig*) seguir a algn.

keeper ['ki:pə*] *n* guarda *m/f*.

keep-fit [ki:p'fɪt] *n* gimnasia (de mantenimiento).

keeping ['ki:pɪŋ] *n* (*care*) cuidado; **in ~ with** de acuerdo con.

keeps [ki:ps] *n*: **for ~** (*col*) para siempre.

keepsake ['ki:pseɪk] *n* recuerdo.

keg [kɛg] *n* barrilete *m*, barril *m*.

Ken. *abbr* (*US*) = *Kentucky*.

kennel ['kɛnl] *n* perrera; **~s** *npl* perrera.

Kenya ['ki:njə] *n* Kenia.

Kenyan ['ki:njən] *adj*, *n* keniata *m/f*, keniano/a *m/f*.

kept [kɛpt] *pt, pp of* **keep**.

kerb [kə:b] *n* (*BRIT*) bordillo.

kerb crawler [-krɔ:lə*] *n conductor en busca de prostitutas desde su coche.*

kernel ['kə:nl] *n* (*nut*) fruta; (*fig*) meollo.

kerosene ['kɛrəsi:n] *n* keroseno.

kestrel ['kɛstrəl] *n* cernícalo.

ketchup ['kɛtʃəp] *n* salsa de tomate, ketchup *m*.

kettle ['kɛtl] *n* hervidor *m*.

kettle drum *n* (*MUS*) timbal *m*.

key [ki:] *n* (*gen*) llave *f*; (*MUS*) tono; (*of piano, typewriter*) tecla; (*on map*) clave *f* ♦ *cpd* (*vital: position, industry etc*) clave ♦ *vt* (*also*: **~ in**) teclear.

keyboard ['ki:bɔ:d] *n* teclado ♦ *vt* (*text*) teclear.

keyboarder ['ki:bɔ:də*] *n* teclista *m/f*.

keyed up [ki:d-] *adj* (*person*) nervioso; **to be (all) ~** estar nervioso *or* emocionado.

keyhole ['ki:həul] *n* ojo (de la cerradura).

keyhole surgery *n* cirugía cerrada *or* no invasiva.

key man *n* hombre *m* clave.

keynote ['ki:nəut] *n* (*MUS*) tónica; (*fig*) idea fundamental.

keynote speech *n* discurso de apertura.

keypad ['ki:pæd] *n* teclado numérico.

keyring ['ki:rɪŋ] *n* llavero.

keystone ['ki:stəun] *n* piedra clave.

keystroke ['ki:strəuk] *n* pulsación *f* (de una tecla).

kg *abbr* (= *kilogram*) kg.

KGB *n abbr* KGB *m*.

khaki ['kɑ:kɪ] *n* caqui.

kibbutz, ~im [kɪ'buts, -ɪm] *n* kibutz *m*.

kick [kɪk] *vt* (*person*) dar una patada a; (*ball*) dar un puntapié a ♦ *vi* (*horse*) dar coces ♦ *n* patada; puntapié *m*, tiro; (*of rifle*) culetazo; (*col: thrill*): **he does it for ~s** lo hace por pura diversión.

▶**kick around** *vt* (*idea*) dar vueltas a; (*person*) tratar a patadas a.

▶**kick off** *vi* (*SPORT*) hacer el saque inicial.

kick-start ['kɪkstɑ:t] *n* (*also*: **~er**) (pedal *m* de) arranque *m*.

kid [kɪd] *n* (*col: child*) niño/a, chiquillo/a; (*animal*) cabrito; (*leather*) cabritilla ♦ *vi* (*col*) bromear.

kid gloves *npl*: **to treat sb with ~** andarse con pies de plomo con algn.

kidnap ['kɪdnæp] *vt* secuestrar.

kidnapper ['kɪdnæpə*] *n* secuestrador(a) *m/f*.

kidnapping ['kɪdnæpɪŋ] *n* secuestro.

kidney ['kɪdnɪ] *n* riñón *m*.

kidney bean *n* judía, alubia.

kidney machine *n* riñón *m* artificial.

Kilimanjaro [kɪlɪmæn'dʒɑ:rəu] *n* Kilimanjaro.

kill [kɪl] *vt* matar; (*murder*) asesinar; (*fig: rumour, conversation*) acabar con ♦ *n* matanza; **to ~ time** matar el tiempo.

▶**kill off** *vt* exterminar, terminar con; (*fig*) echar por tierra.

killer ['kɪlə*] *n* asesino/a.

killer instinct *n*: **to have the ~** ir a por todas.

killing ['kɪlɪŋ] *n* (*one*) asesinato; (*several*) matanza; (*COMM*): **to make a ~** tener un gran éxito financiero.

killjoy ['kɪldʒɔɪ] *n* (*BRIT*) aguafiestas *m/f inv*.

kiln [kɪln] *n* horno.

kilo ['ki:ləu] *n* (*abbr.* = *kilogram(me)*) kilo.

kilobyte ['kɪləubaɪt] *n* (*COMPUT*) kilobyte *m*, kilocteto.

kilogram(me) ['kɪləugræm] *n* kilogramo.

kilometre, (*US*) **kilometer** ['kɪləmi:tə*] *n* kilómetro.

kilowatt ['kɪləuwɔt] *n* kilovatio.

kilt [kɪlt] *n* falda escocesa.

kilter ['kɪltə*] *n*: **out of ~** desbaratado.

kimono [kɪ'məunəu] *n* quimono.

kin [kɪn] *n* parientes *mpl*.

kind [kaɪnd] adj (treatment) bueno, cariñoso; (person, act, word) amable, atento ♦ n clase f, especie f; (species) género; **in ~** (COMM) en especie; **a ~ of** una especie de; **to be two of a ~** ser tal para cual; **would you be ~ enough to ...?, would you be so ~ as to ...?** ¿me hace el favor de ...?; **it's very ~ of you (to do)** le agradezco mucho (el que haya hecho).

kindergarten ['kɪndəgɑːtn] n jardín m de infancia.

kind-hearted [kaɪnd'hɑːtɪd] adj bondadoso, de buen corazón.

kindle ['kɪndl] vt encender.

kindliness ['kaɪndlɪnəs] n bondad f, amabilidad f.

kindling ['kɪndlɪŋ] n leña (menuda).

kindly ['kaɪndlɪ] adj bondadoso; (gentle) cariñoso ♦ adv bondadosamente, amablemente; **will you ~ ...** sería usted tan amable de ....

kindness ['kaɪndnɪs] n bondad f, amabilidad f.

kindred ['kɪndrɪd] n familia, parientes mpl ♦ adj: **~ spirits** almas fpl gemelas.

kinetic [kɪ'nɛtɪk] adj cinético.

king [kɪŋ] n rey m.

kingdom ['kɪŋdəm] n reino.

kingfisher ['kɪŋfɪʃə*] n martín m pescador.

kingpin ['kɪŋpɪn] n (TECH) perno real or pinzote; (fig) persona clave.

king-size(d) ['kɪŋsaɪz(d)] adj de tamaño gigante; (cigarette) extra largo.

kink [kɪŋk] n (in rope etc) enroscadura; (in hair) rizo; (fig: emotional, psychological) manía.

kinky ['kɪŋkɪ] adj (pej) perverso.

kinship ['kɪnʃɪp] n parentesco; (fig) afinidad f.

kinsman ['kɪnzmən] n pariente m.

kinswoman ['kɪnzwumən] n parienta.

kiosk ['kiːɔsk] n quiosco; (BRIT TEL) cabina; **newspaper ~** quiosco, kiosco.

kipper ['kɪpə*] n arenque m ahumado.

Kirghizia [kəː'gɪzɪə] n Kirguizistán m.

kiss [kɪs] n beso ♦ vt besar; **~ of life** (artificial respiration) respiración f artificial; **to ~ sb goodbye** dar un beso de despedida a algn; **to ~ (each other)** besarse.

kissogram ['kɪsəgræm] n servicio de felicitaciones mediante el que se envía a una persona vestida de manera sugerente para besar a algn.

kit [kɪt] n equipo; (set of tools etc) (caja de) herramientas fpl; (assembly ~) juego de armar; **tool ~** juego or estuche m de herramientas.

►**kit out** vt equipar.

kitbag ['kɪtbæg] n (MIL) macuto.

kitchen ['kɪtʃɪn] n cocina.

kitchen garden n huerto.

kitchen sink n fregadero.

kitchen unit n módulo de cocina.

kitchenware ['kɪtʃɪnwɛə*] n batería de cocina.

kite [kaɪt] n (toy) cometa.

kith [kɪθ] n: **~ and kin** parientes mpl y allegados.

kitten ['kɪtn] n gatito/a.

kitty ['kɪtɪ] n (pool of money) fondo común; (CARDS) bote m.

kiwi ['kiːwiː] n (col: New Zealander) neozelandés/esa m/f; (also: **~ fruit**) kiwi m.

KKK n abbr (US) = Ku Klux Klan.

kleptomaniac [klɛptəu'meɪnɪæk] n cleptómano/a.

km abbr (= kilometre) km.

km/h abbr (= kilometres per hour) km/h.

knack [næk] n: **to have the ~ of doing sth** tener facilidad para hacer algo.

knackered ['nækəd] adj (col) hecho polvo.

knapsack ['næpsæk] n mochila.

knead [niːd] vt amasar.

knee [niː] n rodilla.

kneecap ['niːkæp] vt destrozar a tiros la rótula de ♦ n rótula.

knee-deep ['niː'diːp] adj: **the water was ~** el agua llegaba hasta la rodilla.

kneel [niːl], pt, pp **knelt** [niːl, nɛlt] vi (also: **~ down**) arrodillarse.

kneepad ['niːpæd] n rodillera.

knell [nɛl] n toque m de difuntos.

knelt [nɛlt] pt, pp of **kneel**.

knew [njuː] pt of **know**.

knickers ['nɪkəz] npl (BRIT) bragas fpl, calzones mpl (LAM).

knick-knack ['nɪknæk] n chuchería, baratija.

knife [naɪf] (pl **knives**) n cuchillo ♦ vt acuchillar; **~, fork and spoon** cubiertos mpl.

knife edge n: **to be on a ~** estar en la cuerda floja.

knight [naɪt] n caballero; (CHESS) caballo.

knighthood ['naɪthud] n (title): **to get a ~** recibir el título de Sir.

knit [nɪt] vt tejer, tricotar; (brows) fruncir; (fig): **to ~ together** unir, juntar ♦ vi hacer punto, tejer, tricotar; (bones) soldarse.

knitted ['nɪtɪd] adj de punto.

knitting ['nɪtɪŋ] n labor f de punto.

knitting machine n máquina de tricotar.

knitting needle n, (US) **knit pin** n aguja de hacer punto or tejer.

knitting pattern n patrón m para tricotar.

knitwear ['nɪtwɛə*] n prendas fpl de punto.

knives [naɪvz] *pl of* **knife.**
knob [nɔb] *n* (*of door*) pomo; (*of stick*) puño; (*lump*) bulto; (*fig*): **a ~ of butter** (*BRIT*) un pedazo de mantequilla.
knobbly ['nɔblɪ], (*US*) **knobby** ['nɔbɪ] *adj* (*wood, surface*) nudoso; (*knee*) huesudo.
knock [nɔk] *vt* (*strike*) golpear; (*bump into*) chocar contra; (*fig: col*) criticar ♦ *vi* (*at door etc*): **to ~ at/on** llamar a ♦ *n* golpe *m*; (*on door*) llamada; **he ~ed at the door** llamó a la puerta.
▶**knock down** *vt* (*pedestrian*) atropellar; (*price*) rebajar.
▶**knock off** *vi* (*col: finish*) salir del trabajo ♦ *vt* (*col: steal*) birlar; (*strike off*) quitar; (*fig: from price, record*): **to ~ off £10** rebajar en £10.
▶**knock out** *vt* dejar sin sentido; (*BOXING*) poner fuera de combate, dejar K.O.; (*stop*) estropear, dejar fuera de servicio.
▶**knock over** *vt* (*object*) derribar, tirar; (*pedestrian*) atropellar.
knockdown ['nɔkdaun] *adj* (*price*) de saldo.
knocker ['nɔkə*] *n* (*on door*) aldaba.
knocking ['nɔkɪŋ] *n* golpes *mpl*, golpeteo.
knock-kneed [nɔk'niːd] *adj* patizambo.
knockout ['nɔkaut] *n* (*BOXING*) K.O. *m*, knockout *m*.
knock-up ['nɔkʌp] *n* (*TENNIS*) peloteo.
knot [nɔt] *n* (*gen*) nudo ♦ *vt* anudar; **to tie a ~** hacer un nudo.
knotted ['nɔtɪd] *adj* anudado.
knotty ['nɔtɪ] *adj* (*fig*) complicado.
know [nəu] *vb* (*pt* **knew**, *pp* **known** [nju:, nəun]) *vt* (*gen*) saber; (*person, author, place*) conocer ♦ *vi*: **as far as I ~** ... que yo sepa ...; **yes, I ~** sí, ya lo sé; **I don't ~** no lo sé; **to ~ how to do** saber hacer; **to ~ how to swim** saber nadar; **to ~ about** *or* **of sb/sth** saber de algn/algo; **to get to ~ sth** enterarse de algo; **I ~ nothing about it** no sé nada de eso; **I don't ~ him** no lo *or* le conozco; **to ~ right from wrong** saber distinguir el bien del mal.
know-all ['nəuɔːl] *n* (*BRIT pej*) sabelotodo *m/f inv*, sabihondo/a.
know-how ['nəuhau] *n* conocimientos *mpl*.
knowing ['nəuɪŋ] *adj* (*look*) de complicidad.
knowingly ['nəuɪŋlɪ] *adv* (*purposely*) a sabiendas; (*smile, look*) con complicidad.
know-it-all ['nəuɪtɔːl] *n* (*US*) = **know-all.**
knowledge ['nɔlɪdʒ] *n* (*gen*) conocimiento; (*learning*) saber *m*, conocimientos *mpl*; **to have no ~ of** no saber nada de; **with my ~** con mis conocimientos, sabiéndolo; **to (the best of) my ~** a mi entender, que yo sepa; **not to my ~** que yo sepa, no; **it is common ~ that** ... es del dominio público

que ...; **it has come to my ~ that** ... me he enterado de que ...; **to have a working ~ of Spanish** defenderse con el español.
knowledgeable ['nɔlɪdʒəbl] *adj* entendido.
known [nəun] *pp of* **know** ♦ *adj* (*thief, facts*) conocido; (*expert*) reconocido.
knuckle ['nʌkl] *n* nudillo.
▶**knuckle down** *vi* (*col*) ponerse a trabajar en serio.
▶**knuckle under** *vi* someterse.
knuckleduster ['nʌkldʌstə*] *n* puño de hierro.
KO *abbr n* (= *knockout*) K.O. *m* ♦ *vt* (= *knock out*) dejar K.O.
kook [kuːk] *n* (*US col*) chiflado/a *m/f*, majareta *m/f*.
Koran [kɔ'raɪn] *n* Corán *m*.
Korea [kə'rɪə] *n* Corea; **North/South ~** Corea del Norte/Sur.
Korean [kə'rɪən] *adj*, *n* coreano/a *m/f*.
kosher ['kəuʃə*] *adj* autorizado por la ley judía.
Kosovan ['kɒsəvən], **Kosovar** ['kɒsəvɑː*] *adj* Kosovar.
Kosovo ['kɒsəvəu] *n* Kosovo *m*.
kowtow ['kau'tau] *vi*: **to ~ to sb** humillarse ante algn.
KS *abbr* (*US*) = *Kansas.*
Kt *abbr* (*BRIT*: = *Knight*) *caballero de una orden.*
Kuala Lumpur ['kwɑːlə'lumpuə*] *n* Kuala Lumpur *m*.
kudos ['kjuːdɒs] *n* gloria, prestigio.
Kurd [kəːd] *n* kurdo/a.
Kuwait [ku'weɪt] *n* Kuwait *m*.
Kuwaiti [ku'weɪtɪ] *adj*, *n* Kuwaití *m/f*.
kW *abbr* (= *kilowatt*) Kv.
KY, Ky. *abbr* (*US*) = *Kentucky.*

L l

L, l [εl] *n* (*letter*) L, l *f*; **L for Lucy**, (*US*) **L for Love** L de Lorenzo.
L *abbr* (*on maps etc*) = **lake**; **large**; (= *left*) izq.; (*BRIT AUT*: = *learner*) L.
l. *abbr* = **litre.**
LA *n abbr* (*US*) = *Los Angeles* ♦ *abbr* (*US*) = *Louisiana.*
La. *abbr* (*US*) = *Louisiana.*
lab [læb] *n abbr* = **laboratory.**
Lab. *abbr* (*Canada*) = *Labrador.*

label ['leɪbl] n etiqueta; (*brand: of record*) sello (discográfico) ♦ vt poner una etiqueta a, etiquetar.

labor *etc* ['leɪbə*] (*US*) = **labour**.

laboratory [ləˈbɔrətərɪ] n laboratorio.

Labor Day n (*US*) día m de los trabajadores (*primer lunes de septiembre*).

laborious [ləˈbɔːrɪəs] adj penoso.

laboriously [ləˈbɔːrɪəslɪ] adv penosamente.

labor union n (*US*) sindicato.

labor unrest n (*US*) conflictividad f laboral.

Labour ['leɪbə*] n (*BRIT POL: also:* **the ~ Party**) el partido laborista, los laboristas.

labour, (*US*) **labor** ['leɪbə*] n (*task*) trabajo; (*~ force*) mano f de obra; (*workers*) trabajadores mpl; (*MED*) (dolores mpl de) parto ♦ vi: **to ~ (at)** trabajar (en) ♦ vt insistir en; **hard ~** trabajos mpl forzados; **to be in ~** estar de parto.

labo(u)r cost n costo de la mano de obra.

labo(u)r dispute n conflicto laboral.

labo(u)red ['leɪbəd] adj (*breathing*) fatigoso; (*style*) forzado, pesado.

labo(u)rer ['leɪbərə*] n peón m; (*on farm*) peón m, obrero; (*day ~*) jornalero.

labo(u)r force n mano f de obra.

labo(u)r-intensive [leɪbərɪnˈtɛnsɪv] adj que necesita mucha mano de obra.

labo(u)r relations npl relaciones fpl laborales.

labo(u)r-saving ['leɪbəseɪvɪŋ] adj que ahorra trabajo.

laburnum [ləˈbəːnəm] n codeso.

labyrinth ['læbɪrɪnθ] n laberinto.

lace [leɪs] n encaje m; (*of shoe etc*) cordón m ♦ vt (*shoes: also:* **~ up**) atarse; (*drink: fortify with spirits*) echar licor a.

lacemaking ['leɪsmeɪkɪŋ] n obra de encaje.

lacerate ['læsəreɪt] vt lacerar.

laceration [læsəˈreɪʃən] n laceración f.

lace-up ['leɪsʌp] adj (*shoes etc*) con cordones.

lack [læk] n (*absence*) falta, carencia; (*scarcity*) escasez f ♦ vt faltarle a algn, carecer de; **through** *or* **for ~ of** por falta de; **to be ~ing** faltar, no haber.

lackadaisical [lækəˈdeɪzɪkl] adj (*careless*) descuidado; (*indifferent*) indiferente.

lackey ['lækɪ] n (*also fig*) lacayo.

lacklustre, (*US*) **lackluster** ['læklʌstə*] adj (*surface*) deslustrado, deslucido; (*style*) inexpresivo; (*eyes*) apagado.

laconic [ləˈkɔnɪk] adj lacónico.

lacquer ['lækə*] n laca; **hair ~** laca para el pelo.

lacrosse [ləˈkrɔs] n lacrosse f.

lacy ['leɪsɪ] adj (*like lace*) parecido al encaje.

lad [læd] n muchacho, chico; (*in stable etc*) mozo.

ladder ['lædə*] n escalera (de mano); (*BRIT: in tights*) carrera ♦ vt (*BRIT: tights*) hacer una carrera en.

laden ['leɪdn] adj: **~ (with)** cargado (de); **fully ~** (*truck, ship*) cargado hasta el tope.

ladle ['leɪdl] n cucharón m.

lady ['leɪdɪ] n señora; (*distinguished, noble*) dama; **young ~** señorita; **the ladies' (room)** los servicios de señoras.

ladybird ['leɪdɪbəːd], (*US*) **ladybug** ['leɪdɪbʌg] n mariquita.

lady doctor n médica, doctora.

lady-in-waiting ['leɪdɪɪnˈweɪtɪŋ] n dama de honor.

ladykiller ['leɪdɪkɪlə*] n robacorazones m inv.

ladylike ['leɪdɪlaɪk] adj fino.

Ladyship ['leɪdɪʃɪp] n: **your ~** su Señoría.

LAFTA n abbr (= *Latin American Free Trade Association*) ALALC f.

lag [læg] vi (*also:* **~ behind**) retrasarse, quedarse atrás ♦ vt (*pipes*) revestir.

lager ['lɑːgə*] n cerveza (rubia).

lager lout n (*BRIT col*) gamberro borracho.

lagging ['lægɪŋ] n revestimiento.

lagoon [ləˈguːn] n laguna.

Lagos ['leɪgɔs] n Lagos m.

laid [leɪd] pt, pp of **lay**.

laid-back [leɪdˈbæk] adj (*col*) tranquilo, relajado.

laid up adj: **to be ~** (*person*) tener que guardar cama.

lain [leɪn] pp of **lie**.

lair [lɛə*] n guarida.

laissez-faire [lɛseɪˈfɛə*] n laissez-faire m.

laity ['leɪtɪ] n laicado.

lake [leɪk] n lago.

Lake District n (*BRIT*): **the ~** la Región de los Lagos.

lamb [læm] n cordero; (*meat*) carne f de cordero.

lamb chop n chuleta de cordero.

lambswool ['læmzwul] n lana de cordero.

lame [leɪm] adj cojo, rengo (*LAM*); (*weak*) débil, poco convincente; **~ duck** (*fig: person*) inútil m/f; (: *firm*) empresa en quiebra.

lamely ['leɪmlɪ] adv (*fig*) sin convicción.

lament [ləˈmɛnt] n lamento ♦ vt lamentarse de.

lamentable ['læməntəbl] adj lamentable.

lamentation [læmənˈteɪʃən] n lamento.

laminated ['læmɪneɪtɪd] adj laminado.

lamp [læmp] n lámpara.

lamplight ['læmplaɪt] n: **by ~** a la luz de la lámpara.

lampoon [læm'pu:n] *vt* satirizar.
lamppost ['læmppəʊst] *n* (*BRIT*) farola.
lampshade ['læmpʃeɪd] *n* pantalla.
lance [lɑ:ns] *n* lanza ♦ *vt* (*MED*) abrir con lanceta.
lance corporal *n* (*BRIT*) soldado de primera clase.
lancet ['lɑ:nsɪt] *n* (*MED*) lanceta.
Lancs [læŋks] *abbr* (*BRIT*) = *Lancashire*.
land [lænd] *n* tierra; (*country*) país *m*; (*piece of* ~) terreno; (*estate*) tierras *fpl*, finca; (*AGR*) campo ♦ *vi* (*from ship*) desembarcar; (*AVIAT*) aterrizar; (*fig: fall*) caer ♦ *vt* (*obtain*) conseguir; (*passengers, goods*) desembarcar; **to go/travel by** ~ ir/viajar por tierra; **to own** ~ ser dueño de tierras; **to** ~ **on one's feet** caer de pie; (*fig: to be lucky*) salir bien parado.
►**land up** *vi*: **to** ~ **up in/at** ir a parar a/en.
landed ['lændɪd] *adj*: ~ **gentry** terratenientes *mpl*.
landfill site ['lændfɪl-] *n* vertedero.
landing ['lændɪŋ] *n* desembarco; aterrizaje *m*; (*of staircase*) rellano.
landing card *n* tarjeta de desembarque.
landing craft *n* lancha de desembarco.
landing gear *n* (*AVIAT*) tren *m* de aterrizaje.
landing stage *n* (*BRIT*) desembarcadero.
landing strip *n* pista de aterrizaje.
landlady ['lændleɪdɪ] *n* (*of boarding house*) patrona; (*owner*) dueña.
landlocked ['lændlɔkt] *adj* cercado de tierra.
landlord ['lændlɔ:d] *n* propietario; (*of pub etc*) patrón *m*.
landlubber ['lændlʌbə*] *n* marinero de agua dulce.
landmark ['lændmɑ:k] *n* lugar *m* conocido; **to be a** ~ (*fig*) hacer época.
landowner ['lændəʊnə*] *n* terrateniente *m/f*.
landscape ['lænskeɪp] *n* paisaje *m*.
landscape architecture *n* arquitectura paisajista.
landscaped ['lænskeɪpt] *adj* reformado artísticamente.
landscape gardener *n* diseñador(a) *m/f* de paisajes.
landscape gardening *n* jardinería paisajista.
landscape painting *n* (*ART*) paisaje *m*.
landslide ['lændslaɪd] *n* (*GEO*) corrimiento de tierras; (*fig: POL*) victoria arrolladora.
lane [leɪn] *n* (*in country*) camino *m*; (*in town*) callejón *m*; (*AUT*) carril *m*; (*in race*) calle *f*; (*tor air or sea traffic*) ruta; **shipping** ~ ruta marina.

language ['læŋgwɪdʒ] *n* lenguaje *m*; (*national tongue*) idioma *m*, lengua; **bad** ~ palabrotas *fpl*.
language laboratory *n* laboratorio de idiomas.
language studies *npl* estudios *mpl* filológicos.
languid ['læŋgwɪd] *adj* lánguido.
languish ['læŋgwɪʃ] *vi* languidecer.
languor ['læŋgə*] *n* languidez *f*.
languorous ['læŋgərəs] *adj* lánguido.
lank [læŋk] *adj* (*hair*) lacio.
lanky ['læŋkɪ] *adj* larguirucho.
lanolin(e) ['lænəlɪn] *n* lanolina.
lantern ['læntn] *n* linterna, farol *m*.
lanyard ['lænjed] *n* acollador *m*.
Laos [laʊs] *n* Laos *m*.
lap [læp] *n* (*of track*) vuelta; (*of body*): **to sit on sb's** ~ sentarse en las rodillas de algn ♦ *vt* (*also*: ~ **up**) beber a lengüetadas *or* con la lengua ♦ *vi* (*waves*) chapotear.
►**lap up** *vt* beber a lengüetadas *or* con la lengua; (*fig: compliments, attention*) disfrutar; (*lies etc*) tragarse.
La Paz [læ'pæz] *n* La Paz.
lapdog ['læpdɔg] *n* perro faldero.
lapel [lə'pɛl] *n* solapa.
Lapland ['læplænd] *n* Laponia.
Laplander ['læplændə*] *n* lapón/ona *m/f*.
lapse [læps] *n* (*fault*) error *m*, fallo; (*moral*) desliz *m* ♦ *vi* (*expire*) caducar; (*morally*) cometer un desliz; (*time*) pasar, transcurrir; **to** ~ **into bad habits** volver a las andadas; ~ **of time** lapso, período; **a** ~ **of memory** un lapsus de memoria.
laptop ['læptɔp] *n* (*also*: ~ **computer**) (ordenador *m*) portátil *m*.
larceny ['lɑ:sənɪ] *n* latrocinio.
lard [lɑ:d] *n* manteca (de cerdo).
larder ['lɑ:də*] *n* despensa.
large [lɑ:dʒ] *adj* grande ♦ *adv*: **by and** ~ en general, en términos generales; **at** ~ (*free*) en libertad; (*generally*) en general; **to make** ~(**r**) hacer mayor *or* más extenso; **a** ~ **number of people** una gran cantidad de personas; **on a** ~ **scale** a gran escala.
largely ['lɑ:dʒlɪ] *adv* en gran parte.
large-scale ['lɑ:dʒ'skeɪl] *adj* (*map, drawing*) a gran escala; (*reforms, business activities*) importante.
largesse [lɑ:'ʒɛs] *n* generosidad *f*.
lark [lɑ:k] *n* (*bird*) alondra; (*joke*) broma.
►**lark about** *vi* bromear, hacer el tonto.
larva, *pl* **larvae** ['lɑ:və, -i:] *n* larva.
laryngitis [lærɪn'dʒaɪtɪs] *n* laringitis *f*.
larynx ['lærɪŋks] *n* laringe *f*.
lasagne [lə'zænjə] *n* lasaña.

lascivious [lə'sɪvɪəs] *adj* lascivo.
laser ['leɪzə*] *n* láser *m*.
laser beam *n* rayo láser.
laser printer *n* impresora láser.
lash [læʃ] *n* latigazo; (*punishment*) azote *m*;
 (*also*: **eye~**) pestaña ♦ *vt* azotar; (*tie*) atar.
►**lash down** *vt* sujetar con cuerdas ♦ *vi*
 (*rain*) caer a trombas.
►**lash out** *vi* (*col*: *spend*) gastar a la loca; **to**
 ~ out at *or* **against sb** lanzar invectivas
 contra algn.
lashing ['læʃɪŋ] *n* (*beating*) azotaina,
 flagelación *f*; **~s of** (*col*) montones *mpl* de.
lass [læs] *n* chica.
lassitude ['læsɪtjuːd] *n* lasitud *f*.
lasso [læ'suː] *n* lazo ♦ *vt* coger con lazo.
last [lɑːst] *adj* (*gen*) último; (*final*) último,
 final ♦ *adv* por último ♦ *vi* (*endure*) durar;
 (*continue*) continuar, seguir; **~ night**
 anoche; **~ week** la semana pasada; **at ~**
 por fin; **~ but one** penúltimo; **~ time** la
 última vez; **it ~s (for) 2 hours** dura dos
 horas.
last-ditch ['lɑːst'dɪtʃ] *adj* (*attempt*) de
 último recurso, último, desesperado.
lasting ['lɑːstɪŋ] *adj* duradero.
lastly ['lɑːstlɪ] *adv* por último, finalmente.
last-minute ['lɑːstmɪnɪt] *adj* de última
 hora.
latch [lætʃ] *n* picaporte *m*, pestillo.
►**latch on to** *vt fus* (*cling to*: *person*)
 pegarse a; (: *idea*) agarrarse de.
latchkey ['lætʃkiː] *n* llavín *m*.
latchkey child *n* niño cuyos padres
 trabajan.
late [leɪt] *adj* (*not on time*) tarde, atrasado;
 (*towards end of period*, *life*) tardío; (*hour*)
 avanzado; (*dead*) fallecido ♦ *adv* tarde;
 (*behind time*, *schedule*) con retraso; **to be**
 (10 minutes) ~ llegar con (diez minutos
 de) retraso; **to be ~ with** estar atrasado
 con; **~ delivery** entrega tardía; **~ in life** a
 una edad avanzada; **of ~** últimamente; **in**
 ~ May hacia fines de mayo; **the ~ Mr X** el
 difunto Sr X; **to work ~** trabajar hasta
 tarde.
latecomer ['leɪtkʌmə*] *n* recién llegado/a.
lately ['leɪtlɪ] *adv* últimamente.
lateness ['leɪtnɪs] *n* (*of person*) demora; (*of*
 event) tardanza.
latent ['leɪtnt] *adj* latente; **~ defect** defecto
 latente.
later ['leɪtə*] *adj* (*date etc*) posterior;
 (*version etc*) más reciente ♦ *adv* más tarde,
 después; **~ on today** hoy más tarde.
lateral ['lætərl] *adj* lateral.
latest ['leɪtɪst] *adj* último; **at the ~** a más
 tardar.

latex ['leɪtɛks] *n* látex *m*.
lathe [leɪð] *n* torno.
lather ['lɑːðə*] *n* espuma (de jabón) ♦ *vt*
 enjabonar.
Latin ['lætɪn] *n* latín *m* ♦ *adj* latino.
Latin America *n* América Latina,
 Latinoamérica.
Latin American *adj*, *n* latinoamericano/a
 m/f.
Latino [læ'tiːnəu] *adj*, *n* latino/a *m/f*.
latitude ['lætɪtjuːd] *n* latitud *f*; (*fig*: *freedom*)
 libertad *f*.
latrine [lə'triːn] *n* letrina.
latter ['lætə*] *adj* último; (*of two*) segundo
 ♦ *n*: **the ~** el último, éste.
latter-day ['lætədeɪ] *adj* moderno.
latterly ['lætəlɪ] *adv* últimamente.
lattice ['lætɪs] *n* enrejado.
lattice window *n* ventana enrejada *or* de
 celosía.
lattice work *n* enrejado.
Latvia ['lætvɪə] *n* Letonia.
Latvian ['lætvɪən] *adj* letón/ona ♦ *n*
 letón/ona *m/f*; (*LING*) letón *m*.
laudable ['lɔːdəbl] *adj* loable.
laugh [lɑːf] *n* risa; (*loud*) carcajada ♦ *vi*
 reírse, reír; reírse a carcajadas.
►**laugh at** *vt fus* reírse de.
►**laugh off** *vt* tomar a risa.
laughable ['lɑːfəbl] *adj* ridículo.
laughing ['lɑːfɪŋ] *adj* risueño ♦ *n*: **it's no ~**
 matter no es cosa de risa.
laughing gas *n* gas *m* hilarante.
laughing stock *n*: **to be the ~ of the town**
 ser el hazmerreír de la ciudad.
laughter ['lɑːftə*] *n* risa.
launch [lɔːntʃ] *n* (*boat*) lancha; *see also*
 launching ♦ *vt* (*ship*) botar; (*rocket*, *plan*)
 lanzar.
►**launch forth** *vi*: **to ~ forth (into)** lanzarse
 a *or* en, emprender.
►**launch out** *vi* = **launch forth**.
launching ['lɔːntʃɪŋ] *n* (*of rocket etc*)
 lanzamiento; (*inauguration*) estreno.
launch(ing) pad *n* plataforma de
 lanzamiento.
launder ['lɔːndə*] *vt* lavar.
Launderette ® [lɔːn'drɛt], (*US*)
 Laundromat ® ['lɔːndrəmæt] *n*
 lavandería (automática).
laundry ['lɔːndrɪ] *n* lavandería; (*clothes*)
 ropa sucia; **to do the ~** hacer la colada.
laureate ['lɔːrɪət] *adj see* **poet**.
laurel ['lɔrl] *n* laurel *m*; **to rest on one's ~s**
 dormirse en *or* sobre los laureles.
lava ['lɑːvə] *n* lava.
lavatory ['lævətərɪ] *n* wáter *m*; **lavatories** *npl*
 servicios *mpl*, aseos *mpl*, sanitarios *mpl*

(*LAM*).
lavatory paper *n* papel *m* higiénico.
lavender ['lævəndə*] *n* lavanda.
lavish ['lævɪʃ] *adj* abundante; (*giving freely*):
~ **with** pródigo en ♦ *vt*: **to** ~ **sth on sb**
colmar a algn de algo.
lavishly ['lævɪʃlɪ] *adv* (*give, spend*)
generosamente; (*furnished*) lujosamente.
law [lɔ:] *n* ley *f*; (*study*) derecho; (*of game*)
regla; **against the** ~ contra la ley; **to**
study ~ estudiar derecho; **to go to** ~
recurrir a la justicia.
law-abiding ['lɔ:əbaɪdɪŋ] *adj* respetuoso
con la ley.
law and order *n* orden *m* público.
lawbreaker ['lɔ:breɪkə*] *n* infractor(a) *m/f*
de la ley.
law court *n* tribunal *m* (de justicia).
lawful ['lɔ:ful] *adj* legítimo, lícito.
lawfully ['lɔ:fulɪ] *adv* legalmente.
lawless ['lɔ:lɪs] *adj* (*act*) ilegal; (*person*)
rebelde; (*country*) ingobernable.
Law Lord *n* (*BRIT*) *miembro de la Cámara*
de los Lores y del más alto tribunal de
apelación.
lawmaker ['lɔ:meɪkə*] *n* legislador(a) *m/f*.
lawn [lɔ:n] *n* césped *m*.
lawnmower ['lɔ:nməuə*] *n* cortacésped *m*.
lawn tennis *n* tenis *m* sobre hierba.
law school *n* (*US*) facultad *f* de derecho.
law student *n* estudiante *m/f* de derecho.
lawsuit ['lɔ:su:t] *n* pleito; **to bring a** ~
against entablar un pleito contra.
lawyer ['lɔ:jə*] *n* abogado/a; (*for sales, wills*
etc) notario/a.
lax [læks] *adj* (*discipline*) relajado; (*person*)
negligente.
laxative ['læksətɪv] *n* laxante *m*.
laxity ['læksɪtɪ] *n* flojedad *f*; (*moral*)
relajamiento; (*negligence*) negligencia.
lay [leɪ] *pt of* **lie** ♦ *adj* laico; (*not expert*) lego
♦ *vt* (*pt, pp* **laid** [leɪd]) (*place*) colocar; (*eggs,*
table) poner; (*trap*) tender; **to** ~ **the facts/**
one's proposals before sb presentar los
hechos/sus propuestas a algn.
►**lay aside, lay by** *vt* dejar a un lado.
►**lay down** *vt* (*pen etc*) dejar; (*arms*)
rendir; (*policy*) trazar; **to** ~ **down the law**
imponer las normas.
►**lay in** *vt* abastecerse de.
►**lay into** *vt fus* (*col: attack, scold*) arremeter
contra.
►**lay off** *vt* (*workers*) despedir.
►**lay on** *vt* (*water, gas*) instalar; (*meal,*
facilities) proveer.
►**lay out** *vt* (*plan*) trazar; (*display*) exponer;
(*spend*) gastar.
►**lay up** *vt* (*store*) guardar; (*ship*)

desarmar; (*subj: illness*) obligar a guardar
cama.
layabout ['leɪəbaut] *n* vago/a.
lay-by ['leɪbaɪ] *n* (*BRIT AUT*) apartadero.
lay days *npl* días *mpl* de inactividad.
layer ['leɪə*] *n* capa.
layette [leɪ'et] *n* ajuar *m* (de niño).
layman ['leɪmən] *n* lego.
lay-off ['leɪɔf] *n* despido, paro forzoso.
layout ['leɪaut] *n* (*design*) plan *m*, trazado;
(*disposition*) disposición *f*; (*PRESS*)
composición *f*.
laze [leɪz] *vi* no hacer nada; (*pej*)
holgazanear.
lazily ['leɪzɪlɪ] *adv* perezosamente.
laziness ['leɪzɪnɪs] *n* pereza.
lazy ['leɪzɪ] *adj* perezoso, vago, flojo (*LAM*).
LB *abbr* (*Canada*) = Labrador.
lb. *abbr* = **pound** (*weight*).
lbw *abr* (*CRICKET*) = *leg before wicket*.
LC *n abbr* (*US*) = *Library of Congress.*
lc *abbr* (*TYP*: = *lower case*) min.
L/C *abbr* = **letter of credit**.
LCD *n abbr see* **liquid crystal display**.
Ld *abbr* (= *Lord*) título de nobleza.
LDS *n abbr* (= *Licentiate in Dental Surgery*)
diploma universitario; (= *Latter-day*
Saints) Iglesia de Jesucristo de los Santos
del último día.
LEA *n abbr* (*BRIT*: = *local education authority*)
organismos locales encargados de la
enseñanza.
lead [li:d] *n* (*front position*) delantera;
(*distance, time ahead*) ventaja; (*clue*) pista;
(*ELEC*) cable *m*; (*for dog*) correa; (*THEAT*)
papel *m* principal; [led] (*metal*) plomo; (*in*
pencil) mina ♦ *vb* (*pt, pp* **led** [led]) *vt*
conducir; (*life*) llevar; (*be leader of*)
dirigir; (*SPORT*) ir en cabeza de;
(*orchestra: BRIT*) ser el primer violín en;
(: *US*) dirigir ♦ *vi* ir primero; **to be in the**
~ (*SPORT*) llevar la delantera; (*fig*) ir a la
cabeza; **to take the** ~ (*SPORT*) tomar la
delantera; (*fig*) tomar la iniciativa; **to** ~
sb to believe that ... hacer creer a algn
que ...; **to** ~ **sb to do sth** llevar a algn a
hacer algo.
►**lead astray** *vt* llevar por mal camino.
►**lead away** *vt* llevar.
►**lead back** *vt* hacer volver.
►**lead off** *vt* llevar ♦ *vi* (*in game*) abrir.
►**lead on** *vt* (*tease*) engañar; **to** ~ **sb on to**
(*induce*) incitar a algn a.
►**lead to** *vt fus* producir, provocar.
►**lead up to** *vt fus* conducir a.
leaded ['ledɪd] *adj*: ~ **windows** ventanas *fpl*
emplomadas.
leaden ['ledn] *adj* (*sky, sea*) plomizo; (*heavy:*

footsteps) pesado.

leader ['liːdə*] *n* jefe/a *m/f*, líder *m*; (*of union etc*) dirigente *m/f*; (*guide*) guía *m/f*; (*of newspaper*) editorial *m*; **they are ~s in their field** (*fig*) llevan la delantera en su especialidad.

leadership ['liːdəʃɪp] *n* dirección *f*; **qualities of ~** iniciativa *sg*; **under the ~ of ...** bajo la dirección de ..., al mando de ....

lead-free ['lɛdfriː] *adj* sin plomo.

leading ['liːdɪŋ] *adj* (*main*) principal; (*outstanding*) destacado; (*first*) primero; (*front*) delantero; **a ~ question** una pregunta tendenciosa.

leading lady *n* (*THEAT*) primera actriz *f*.

leading light *n* (*fig: person*) figura principal.

leading man *n* (*THEAT*) primer actor *m*.

leading role *n* papel *m* principal.

lead pencil *n* lápiz *m*.

lead poisoning *n* envenenamiento plúmbico.

lead time *n* (*COMM*) plazo de entrega.

lead-up ['liːdʌp] *n*: **in the ~ to the election** cuando falta *etc* poco para las elecciones.

lead weight *n* peso de plomo.

leaf, *pl* **leaves** [liːf, liːvz] *n* hoja; **to turn over a new ~** (*fig*) volver la hoja, hacer borrón y cuenta nueva; **to take a ~ out of sb's book** (*fig*) seguir el ejemplo de algn.

►**leaf through** *vt fus* (*book*) hojear.

leaflet ['liːflɪt] *n* folleto.

leafy ['liːfɪ] *adj* frondoso.

league [liːg] *n* sociedad *f*; (*FOOTBALL*) liga; **to be in ~ with** estar confabulado con.

league table *n* clasificación *f*.

leak [liːk] *n* (*of liquid, gas*) escape *m*, fuga; (*in pipe*) agujero; (*in roof*) gotera; (*fig: of information, in security*) filtración *f* ♦ *vi* (*ship*) hacer agua; (*shoes*) tener un agujero; (*pipe*) tener un escape; (*roof*) tener goteras; (*also: ~ out: liquid, gas*) escaparse, salirse; (*fig: news*) trascender, divulgarse ♦ *vt* (*gen*) dejar escapar; (*fig: information*) filtrar.

leakage ['liːkɪdʒ] *n* (*of water, gas etc*) escape *m*, fuga.

leaky ['liːkɪ] *adj* (*roof*) con goteras; (*bucket, shoe*) con agujeros; (*pipe*) con un escape; (*boat*) que hace agua.

lean [liːn] *adj* (*thin*) flaco; (*meat*) magro ♦ *vb* (*pt, pp* **leaned** *or* **leant** [lɛnt]) *vt*: **to ~ sth on sth** apoyar algo en algo ♦ *vi* (*slope*) inclinarse; (*rest*): **to ~ against** apoyarse contra; **to ~ on** apoyarse en.

►**lean back** *vi* inclinarse hacia atrás.

►**lean forward** *vi* inclinarse hacia

adelante.

►**lean out** *vi*: **to ~ out (of)** asomarse (a).

►**lean over** *vi* inclinarse.

leaning ['liːnɪŋ] *adj* inclinado ♦ *n*: **~ (towards)** inclinación *f* (hacia); **the L~ Tower of Pisa** la Torre Inclinada de Pisa.

leant [lɛnt] *pt, pp of* **lean**.

lean-to ['liːntuː] *n* (*roof*) tejado de una sola agua; (*building*) cobertizo.

leap [liːp] *n* salto ♦ *vi* (*pt, pp* **leaped** *or* **leapt** [lɛpt]) saltar; **to ~ at an offer** apresurarse a aceptar una oferta.

►**leap up** *vi* (*person*) saltar.

leapfrog ['liːpfrɔg] *n* pídola ♦ *vi*: **to ~ over sb/sth** saltar por encima de algn/algo.

leapt [lɛpt] *pt, pp of* **leap**.

leap year *n* año bisiesto.

learn, *pt, pp* **learned** *or* **learnt** [ləːn, -t] *vt* (*gen*) aprender; (*come to know of*) enterarse de ♦ *vi* aprender; **to ~ how to do sth** aprender a hacer algo; **to ~ that ...** enterarse *or* informarse de que ...; **to ~ about sth** (*SCOL*) aprender algo; (*hear*) enterarse *or* informarse de algo; **we were sorry to ~ that ...** nos dio tristeza saber que ....

learned ['ləːnɪd] *adj* erudito.

learner ['ləːnə*] *n* principiante *m/f*; (*BRIT also*: **~ driver**) conductor(a) *m/f* en prácticas; *see also* **L-plates**.

learning ['ləːnɪŋ] *n* saber *m*, conocimientos *mpl*.

learnt [ləːnt] *pp of* **learn**.

lease [liːs] *n* arriendo ♦ *vt* arrendar; **on ~** en arriendo.

►**lease back** *vt* subarrendar.

leaseback ['liːsbæk] *n* subarriendo.

leasehold ['liːshəuld] *n* (*contract*) derechos *mpl* de arrendamiento ♦ *adj* arrendado.

leash [liːʃ] *n* correa.

least [liːst] *adj* (*slightest*) menor, más pequeño; (*smallest amount of*) mínimo ♦ *adv* menos ♦ *n*: **the ~** lo menos; **the ~ expensive car** el coche menos caro; **at ~** por lo menos, al menos; **not in the ~** en absoluto.

leather ['lɛðə*] *n* cuero ♦ *cpd*: **~ goods** artículos *mpl* de cuero *or* piel.

leathery ['lɛðərɪ] *adj* (*skin*) curtido.

leave [liːv] *vb* (*pt, pp* **left** [lɛft]) *vt* dejar; (*go away from*) abandonar ♦ *vi* irse; (*train*) salir ♦ *n* permiso; **to ~ school** dejar la escuela *or* el colegio; **~ it to me!** ¡yo me encargo!; **he's already left for the airport** ya se ha marchado al aeropuerto; **to be left** quedar, sobrar; **there's some milk left over** sobra *or* queda algo de leche; **on ~**

de permiso; **to take one's ~ of** despedirse de.

▶**leave behind** *vt* (*on purpose*) dejar (atrás); (*accidentally*) olvidar.

▶**leave off** *vt* (*lid*) no poner; (*switch*) no encender; (*col: stop*): **to ~ off doing sth** dejar de hacer algo.

▶**leave on** *vt* (*lid*) dejar puesto; (*light, fire, cooker*) dejar encendido.

▶**leave out** *vt* omitir.

▶**leave over** *vt* (*postpone*) dejar, aplazar.

leave of absence *n* excedencia.

leaves [li:vz] *pl of* **leaf**.

leavetaking ['li:vteɪkɪŋ] *n* despedida.

Lebanon ['lɛbənən] *n*: **the ~** el Líbano.

lecherous ['lɛtʃərəs] *adj* lascivo.

lectern ['lɛktə:n] *n* atril *m*.

lecture ['lɛktʃə*] *n* conferencia; (*SCOL*) clase *f* ♦ *vi* dar clase(s) ♦ *vt* (*scold*) sermonear; (*reprove*) echar una reprimenda a; **to give a ~ on** dar una conferencia sobre.

lecture hall *n* sala de conferencias; (*UNIV*) aula.

lecturer ['lɛktʃərə*] *n* conferenciante *m/f*; (*BRIT: at university*) profesor(a) *m/f*.

lecture theatre *n* = **lecture hall**.

LED *n abbr* (= *light-emitting diode*) LED *m*.

led [lɛd] *pt, pp of* **lead**.

ledge [lɛdʒ] *n* (*of window, on wall*) repisa, reborde *m*; (*of mountain*) saliente *m*.

ledger ['lɛdʒə*] *n* libro mayor.

lee [li:] *n* sotavento; **in the ~ of** al abrigo de.

leech [li:tʃ] *n* sanguijuela.

leek [li:k] *n* puerro.

leer [lɪə*] *vi*: **to ~ at sb** mirar de manera lasciva a algn.

leeward ['li:wəd] *adj* (*NAUT*) de sotavento ♦ *n* (*NAUT*) sotavento; **to ~** a sotavento.

leeway ['li:weɪ] *n* (*fig*): **to have some ~** tener cierta libertad de acción.

left [lɛft] *pt, pp of* **leave** ♦ *adj* izquierdo ♦ *n* izquierda ♦ *adv* a la izquierda; **on** *or* **to the ~** a la izquierda; **the L~** (*POL*) la izquierda.

left-hand drive ['lɛfthænd-] *n* conducción *f* por la izquierda.

left-handed [lɛft'hændɪd] *adj* zurdo; **~ scissors** tijeras *fpl* zurdas *or* para zurdos.

left-hand side ['lɛfthænd-] *n* izquierda.

leftie ['lɛftɪ] *n* = **lefty**.

leftist ['lɛftɪst] *adj* (*POL*) izquierdista.

left-luggage (office) [lɛft'lʌgɪdʒ(-)] *n* (*BRIT*) consigna.

left-overs ['lɛftəuvəz] *npl* sobras *fpl*.

left-wing [lɛft'wɪŋ] *adj* (*POL*) de izquierda(s), izquierdista.

left-winger ['lɛft'wɪŋə*] *n* (*POL*) izquierdista *m/f*.

lefty ['lɛftɪ] *n* (*col: POL*) rojillo/a.

leg [lɛg] *n* pierna; (*of animal, chair*) pata; (*CULIN: of meat*) pierna; (*of journey*) etapa; **1st/2nd ~** (*SPORT*) partido de ida/de vuelta; **to pull sb's ~** tomar el pelo a algn; **to stretch one's ~s** dar una vuelta.

legacy ['lɛgəsɪ] *n* herencia; (*fig*) herencia, legado.

legal ['li:gl] *adj* (*permitted by law*) lícito; (*of law*) legal; (*inquiry etc*) jurídico; **to take ~ action** *or* **proceedings against sb** entablar *or* levantar un pleito contra algn.

legal adviser *n* asesor(a) *m/f* jurídico/a.

legal holiday *n* (*US*) fiesta oficial.

legality [lɪ'gælɪtɪ] *n* legalidad *f*.

legalize ['li:gəlaɪz] *vt* legalizar.

legally ['li:gəlɪ] *adv* legalmente; **~ binding** con fuerza legal.

legal tender *n* moneda de curso legal.

legatee [lɛgə'ti:] *n* legatario/a.

legation [lɪ'geɪʃən] *n* legación *f*.

legend ['lɛdʒənd] *n* leyenda.

legendary ['lɛdʒəndərɪ] *adj* legendario.

-legged ['lɛgɪd] *suff*: **two-~** (*table etc*) de dos patas.

leggings ['lɛgɪŋz] *npl* mallas *fpl*, leggins *mpl*.

leggy ['lɛgɪ] *adj* de piernas largas.

legibility [lɛdʒɪ'bɪlɪtɪ] *n* legibilidad *f*.

legible ['lɛdʒəbl] *adj* legible.

legibly ['lɛdʒəblɪ] *adv* legiblemente.

legion ['li:dʒən] *n* legión *f*.

legionnaire [li:dʒə'nɛə*] *n* legionario.

legionnaire's disease *n* enfermedad *f* del legionario.

legislation [lɛdʒɪs'leɪʃən] *n* legislación *f*; **a piece of ~** (*bill*) un proyecto de ley; (*act*) una ley.

legislative ['lɛdʒɪslətɪv] *adj* legislativo.

legislator ['lɛdʒɪsleɪtə*] *n* legislador(a) *m/f*.

legislature ['lɛdʒɪslətʃə*] *n* cuerpo legislativo.

legitimacy [lɪ'dʒɪtɪməsɪ] *n* legitimidad *f*.

legitimate [lɪ'dʒɪtɪmət] *adj* legítimo.

legitimize [lɪ'dʒɪtɪmaɪz] *vt* legitimar.

legless ['lɛglɪs] *adj* (*BRIT col*) mamado.

leg-room ['lɛgru:m] *n* espacio para las piernas.

Leics *abbr* (*BRIT*) = *Leicestershire*.

leisure ['lɛʒə*] *n* ocio, tiempo libre; **at ~** con tranquilidad.

leisure centre *n* centro recreativo.

leisurely ['lɛʒəlɪ] *adj* sin prisa; lento.

leisure suit *n* conjunto tipo chandal.

lemon ['lɛmən] *n* limón *m*.

lemonade [lɛmə'neɪd] *n* (*fruit juice*) limonada; (*fizzy*) gaseosa.

lemon cheese, lemon curd *n* queso de limón.
lemon juice *n* zumo de limón.
lemon tea *n* té *m* con limón.
lend, *pt, pp* **lent** [lɛnd, lɛnt] *vt*: **to ~ sth to sb** prestar algo a algn.
lender ['lɛndə*] *n* prestamista *m/f*.
lending library ['lɛndɪŋ-] *n* biblioteca de préstamo.
length [lɛŋθ] *n* (*size*) largo, longitud *f*; (*section: of road, pipe*) tramo; (: *of rope etc*) largo; **at ~** (*at last*) por fin, finalmente; (*lengthily*) largamente; **it is 2 metres in ~** tiene dos metros de largo; **what ~ is it?** ¿cuánto tiene de largo?; **to fall full ~** caer de bruces; **to go to any ~(s) to do sth** ser capaz de hacer cualquier cosa para hacer algo.
lengthen ['lɛŋθn] *vt* alargar ♦ *vi* alargarse.
lengthways ['lɛŋθweɪz] *adv* a lo largo.
lengthy ['lɛŋθɪ] *adj* largo, extenso; (*meeting*) prolongado.
lenient ['liːnɪənt] *adj* indulgente.
lens [lɛnz] *n* (*of spectacles*) lente *f*; (*of camera*) objetivo.
Lent [lɛnt] *n* Cuaresma.
lent [lɛnt] *pt, pp of* **lend**.
lentil ['lɛntl] *n* lenteja.
Leo ['liːəu] *n* Leo.
leopard ['lɛpəd] *n* leopardo.
leotard ['liːətɑːd] *n* leotardo.
leper ['lɛpə*] *n* leproso/a.
leper colony *n* colonia de leprosos.
leprosy ['lɛprəsɪ] *n* lepra.
lesbian ['lɛzbɪən] *adj* lesbiano ♦ *n* lesbiana.
lesion ['liːʒən] *n* (*MED*) lesión *f*.
Lesotho [lɪ'suːtuː] *n* Lesotho.
less [lɛs] *adj* (*in size, degree etc*) menor; (*in quantity*) menos ♦ *pron, adv* menos; **~ than half** menos de la mitad; **~ than £1/a kilo/3 metres** menos de una libra/un kilo/tres metros; **~ than ever** menos que nunca; **~ 5%** menos el cinco por ciento; **~ and ~** cada vez menos; **the ~ he works...** cuanto menos trabaja ....
lessee [lɛ'siː] *n* inquilino/a, arrendatario/a.
lessen ['lɛsn] *vi* disminuir, reducirse ♦ *vt* disminuir, reducir.
lesser ['lɛsə*] *adj* menor; **to a ~ extent** *or* **degree** en menor grado.
lesson ['lɛsn] *n* clase *f*; **a maths ~** una clase de matemáticas; **to give ~s in** dar clases de; **it taught him a ~** (*fig*) le sirvió de lección.
lessor ['lɛsɔː* *or* lɛ'sɔː*] *n* arrendador(a) *m/f*.
lest [lɛst] *conj*: **~ it happen** para que no pase.
let, *pt, pp* **let** [lɛt] *vt* (*allow*) dejar, permitir;

(*BRIT: lease*) alquilar; **to ~ sb do sth** dejar que algn haga algo; **to ~ sb have sth** dar algo a algn; **to ~ sb know sth** comunicar algo a algn; **~'s go** ¡vamos!; **~ him come** que venga; **"to ~"** "se alquila".
►**let down** *vt* (*lower*) bajar; (*dress*) alargar; (*tyre*) desinflar; (*hair*) soltar; (*disappoint*) defraudar.
►**let go** *vi* soltar; (*fig*) dejarse ir ♦ *vt* soltar.
►**let in** *vt* dejar entrar; (*visitor etc*) hacer pasar; **what have you ~ yourself in for?** ¿en qué te has metido?
►**let off** *vt* dejar escapar; (*firework etc*) disparar; (*bomb*) accionar; (*passenger*) dejar, bajar; **to ~ off steam** (*fig, col*) desahogarse, desfogarse.
►**let on** *vi*: **to ~ on that ...** revelar que ...
►**let out** *vt* dejar salir; (*dress*) ensanchar; (*rent out*) alquilar.
►**let up** *vi* disminuir; (*rain etc*) amainar.
let-down ['lɛtdaun] *n* (*disappointment*) decepción *f*.
lethal ['liːθl] *adj* (*weapon*) mortífero; (*poison, wound*) mortal.
lethargic [lɛ'θɑːdʒɪk] *adj* aletargado.
lethargy ['lɛθədʒɪ] *n* letargo.
letter ['lɛtə*] *n* (*of alphabet*) letra; (*correspondence*) carta; **~s** *npl* (*literature, learning*) letras *fpl*; **small/capital ~** minúscula/mayúscula; **covering ~** carta adjunta.
letter bomb *n* carta-bomba.
letterbox ['lɛtəbɔks] *n* (*BRIT*) buzón *m*.
letterhead ['lɛtəhɛd] *n* membrete *m*, encabezamiento.
lettering ['lɛtərɪŋ] *n* letras *fpl*.
letter of credit *n* carta de crédito; **documentary ~** carta de crédito documentaria; **irrevocable ~** carta de crédito irrevocable.
letter-opener ['lɛtərəupnə*] *n* abrecartas *m inv*.
letterpress ['lɛtəprɛs] *n* (*method*) prensa de copiar; (*printed page*) impresión *f* tipográfica.
letter quality *n* calidad *f* de correspondencia.
letters patent *npl* letra *sg* de patente.
lettuce ['lɛtɪs] *n* lechuga.
let-up ['lɛtʌp] *n* descanso, tregua.
leukaemia, (*US*) **leukemia** [luː'kiːmɪə] *n* leucemia.
level ['lɛvl] *adj* (*flat*) llano; (*flattened*) nivelado; (*uniform*) igual ♦ *adv* a nivel ♦ *n* nivel *m* ♦ *vt* nivelar, allanar; (*gun*) apuntar; (*accusation*) to ~ (*against*) levantar (contra) ♦ *vi* (*col*): **to ~ with sb** ser franco con algn; **to be ~ with** estar a

nivel de; **a** ~ **spoonful** (*CULIN*) una cucharada rasa; **to draw** ~ **with** (*team*) igualar; (*runner, car*) alcanzar a; **"A"** ~**s** *npl* (*BRIT*) ≈ Bachillerato Superior *sg*, B.U.P. *msg*; **"O"** ~**s** *npl* (*BRIT*) ≈ bachillerato *sg* elemental, octavo *sg* de Básica; **on the** ~ (*fig: honest*) en serio; **talks at ministerial** ~ charlas *fpl* a nivel ministerial.

▶**level off** *or* **out** *vi* (*prices etc*) estabilizarse; (*ground*) nivelarse; (*aircraft*) ponerse en una trayectoria horizontal.

level crossing *n* (*BRIT*) paso a nivel.

level-headed [lɛvl'hɛdɪd] *adj* sensato.

levelling, (*US*) **leveling** ['lɛvlɪŋ] *adj* (*process, effect*) de nivelación ♦ *n* igualación *f*, allanamiento.

level playing field *n* situación *f* de igualdad; **to compete on a** ~ competir en igualdad de condiciones.

lever ['liːvə*] *n* palanca ♦ *vt*: **to** ~ **up** levantar con palanca.

leverage ['liːvərɪdʒ] *n* (*fig: influence*) influencia.

levity ['lɛvɪtɪ] *n* frivolidad *f*, informalidad *f*.

levy ['lɛvɪ] *n* impuesto ♦ *vt* exigir, recaudar.

lewd [luːd] *adj* lascivo; obsceno, colorado (*LAM*).

lexicographer [lɛksɪ'kɔgrəfə*] *n* lexicógrafo/a *m/f*.

lexicography [lɛksɪ'kɔgrəfɪ] *n* lexicografía.

LGV *n abbr* (= *Large Goods Vehicle*) vehículo pesado.

LI *abbr* (*US*) = *Long Island*.

liabilities [laɪə'bɪlətɪz] *npl* obligaciones *fpl*; pasivo *sg*.

liability [laɪə'bɪlətɪ] *n* responsabilidad *f*; (*handicap*) desventaja.

liable ['laɪəbl] *adj* (*subject*): ~ **to** sujeto a; (*responsible*): ~ **for** responsable de; (*likely*): ~ **to do** propenso a hacer; **to be** ~ **to a fine** exponerse a una multa.

liaise [liː'eɪz] *vi*: **to** ~ **(with)** colaborar (con); **to** ~ **with sb** mantener informado · a algn.

liaison [liː'eɪzɔn] *n* (*coordination*) enlace *m*; (*affair*) relación *f*.

liar ['laɪə*] *n* mentiroso/a.

libel ['laɪbl] *n* calumnia ♦ *vt* calumniar.

libellous ['laɪbləs] *adj* difamatorio, calumnioso.

liberal ['lɪbərl] *adj* (*gen*) liberal; (*generous*): ~ **with** generoso con ♦ *n*: **L**~ (*POL*) liberal *m/f*.

Liberal Democrat *n* (*BRIT*) demócrata *m/f* liberal.

liberality [lɪbə'rælɪtɪ] *n* (*generosity*) liberalidad *f*, generosidad *f*.

liberalize ['lɪbərəlaɪz] *vt* liberalizar.

liberally ['lɪbərəlɪ] *adv* liberalmente.

liberal-minded ['lɪbərl'maɪndɪd] *adj* de miras anchas, liberal.

liberate ['lɪbəreɪt] *vt* liberar.

liberation [lɪbə'reɪʃən] *n* liberación *f*.

liberation theology *n* teología de la liberación.

Liberia [laɪ'bɪərɪə] *n* Liberia.

Liberian [laɪ'bɪərɪən] *adj*, *n* liberiano/a *m/f*.

liberty ['lɪbətɪ] *n* libertad *f*; **to be at** ~ **to do** estar libre para hacer; **to take the** ~ **of doing sth** tomarse la libertad de hacer algo.

libido [lɪ'biːdəu] *n* libido.

Libra ['liːbrə] *n* Libra.

librarian [laɪ'brɛərɪən] *n* bibliotecario/a *m/f*.

library ['laɪbrərɪ] *n* biblioteca.

library book *n* libro de la biblioteca.

libretto [lɪ'brɛtəu] *n* libreto.

Libya ['lɪbɪə] *n* Libia.

Libyan ['lɪbɪən] *adj*, *n* libio/a *m/f*.

lice [laɪs] *pl of* **louse**.

licence, (*US*) **license** ['laɪsns] *n* licencia; (*permit*) permiso; (*also*: **driving licence**, (*US*) **driver's license**) carnet *m* de conducir; (*excessive freedom*) libertad *f*; **import** ~ licencia *or* permiso de importación; **produced under** ~ elaborado bajo licencia.

licence number *n* (número de) matrícula.

licence plate *n* (placa de) matrícula.

license ['laɪsns] (*US*) = **licence** ♦ *vt* autorizar, dar permiso a; (*car*) sacar la matrícula de *or* la patente (*LAM*) de.

licensed ['laɪsnst] *adj* (*for alcohol*) autorizado para vender bebidas alcohólicas.

licensed trade *n* comercio *or* negocio autorizado.

licensee [laɪsən'siː] *n* (*in a pub*) concesionario/a, dueño/a de un bar.

licentious [laɪ'sɛnʃəs] *adj* licencioso.

lichen ['laɪkən] *n* liquen *m*.

lick [lɪk] *vt* lamer; (*col: defeat*) dar una paliza a ♦ *n* lamedura; **a** ~ **of paint** una mano de pintura.

licorice ['lɪkərɪs] *n* = **liquorice**.

lid [lɪd] *n* (*of box, case*) tapa; (*of pan*) cobertera; **to take the** ~ **off sth** (*fig*) exponer algo a la luz pública.

lido ['laɪdəu] *n* (*BRIT*) piscina, alberca (*LAM*).

lie [laɪ] *n* mentira ♦ *vi* mentir; (*pt* **lay**, *pp* **lain** [leɪ, leɪn]) (*rest*) estar echado, estar acostado; (*of object: be situated*) estar, encontrarse; **to tell** ~**s** mentir; **to** ~ **low** (*fig*) mantenerse a escondidas.

▶**lie about**, **lie around** *vi* (*things*) estar

tirado; (*BRIT: people*) estar acostado *or* tumbado.

▶**lie back** *vi* recostarse.

▶**lie down** *vi* echarse, tumbarse.

▶**lie up** *vi* (*hide*) esconderse.

Liechtenstein ['lıktənstaın] *n* Liechtenstein *m*.

lie detector *n* detector *m* de mentiras.

lie-down ['laıdaun] *n* (*BRIT*): **to have a ~** echarse (una siesta).

lie-in ['laıın] *n* (*BRIT*): **to have a ~** quedarse en la cama.

lieu [luː]: **in ~ of** *prep* en lugar de.

Lieut *abbr* = **lieutenant**.

lieutenant [lɛf'tɛnənt, (*US*) luː'tɛnənt] *n* (*MIL*) teniente *m*.

lieutenant colonel *n* teniente *m* coronel.

life, *pl* **lives** [laıf, laıvz] *n* vida; (*of licence etc*) vigencia; **to be sent to prison for ~** ser condenado a cadena perpetua; **country/city ~** la vida en el campo/en la ciudad; **true to ~** fiel a la realidad; **to paint from ~** pintar del natural; **to put** *or* **breathe new ~ into** (*person*) reanimar; (*project, area etc*) infundir nueva vida a.

life annuity *n* pensión *f* anual vitalicia.

life assurance *n* (*BRIT*) seguro de vida.

lifebelt ['laıfbɛlt] *n* (*BRIT*) salvavidas *m inv*.

lifeblood ['laıfblʌd] *n* (*fig*) alma, nervio.

lifeboat ['laıfbəut] *n* lancha de socorro.

life-buoy ['laıfbɔı] *n* boya *or* guindola salvavidas.

life expectancy *n* esperanza de vida.

lifeguard ['laıfgɑːd] *n* vigilante *m/f*.

life imprisonment *n* cadena perpetua.

life insurance *n* = **life assurance**.

life jacket *n* chaleco salvavidas.

lifeless ['laıflıs] *adj* sin vida; (*dull*) soso.

lifelike ['laıflaık] *adj* natural.

lifeline ['laıflaın] *n* (*fig*) cordón *m* umbilical.

lifelong ['laıflɔŋ] *adj* de toda la vida.

life preserver *n* (*US*) = **lifebelt**.

lifer ['laıfə*] *n* (*col*) condenado/a *m/f* a cadena perpetua.

life-saver ['laıfseıvə*] *n* socorrista *m/f*.

life sentence *n* cadena perpetua.

life-sized ['laıfsaızd] *adj* de tamaño natural.

life span *n* vida.

lifestyle ['laıfstaıl] *n* estilo de vida.

life support system *n* (*MED*) sistema *m* de respiración asistida.

lifetime ['laıftaım] *n*: **in his ~** durante su vida; **once in a ~** una vez en la vida; **the chance of a ~** una oportunidad única.

lift [lıft] *vt* levantar; (*copy*) plagiar ♦ *vi* (*fog*) disiparse ♦ *n* (*BRIT: elevator*) ascensor *m*, elevador *m* (*LAM*); **to give sb a ~** (*BRIT*)

llevar a algn en coche.

▶**lift off** *vt* levantar, quitar ♦ *vi* (*rocket, helicopter*) despegar.

▶**lift out** *vt* sacar; (*troops, evacuees etc*) evacuar.

▶**lift up** *vt* levantar.

lift-off ['lıftɔf] *n* despegue *m*.

ligament ['lıgəmənt] *n* ligamento.

light [laıt] *n* luz *f*; (*flame*) lumbre *f*; (*lamp*) luz *f*, lámpara; (*daylight*) luz *f* del día; (*headlight*) faro; (*rear ~*) luz *f* trasera; (*for cigarette etc*): **have you got a ~?** ¿tienes fuego? ♦ *vt* (*pt, pp* **lighted** *or* **lit** [lıt]) (*candle, cigarette, fire*) encender; (*room*) alumbrar ♦ *adj* (*colour*) claro; (*not heavy, also fig*) ligero, liviano (*esp LAM*); (*room*) alumbrado ♦ *adv* (*travel*) con poco equipaje; **to turn the ~ on/off** encender/apagar la luz; **in the ~ of** a la luz de; **to come to ~** salir a la luz; **to cast** *or* **shed** *or* **throw ~ on** arrojar luz sobre; **to make ~ of sth** (*fig*) no dar importancia a algo.

▶**light up** *vi* (*smoke*) encender un cigarrillo; (*face*) iluminarse ♦ *vt* (*illuminate*) iluminar, alumbrar.

light bulb *n* bombilla, bombillo (*LAM*), foco (*LAM*).

lighten ['laıtn] *vi* (*grow light*) clarear ♦ *vt* (*give light to*) iluminar; (*make lighter*) aclarar; (*make less heavy*) aligerar.

lighter ['laıtə*] *n* (*also:* **cigarette ~**) encendedor *m* (*esp LAM*), mechero.

light-fingered [laıt'fıŋgəd] *adj* de manos largas.

light-headed [laıt'hɛdıd] *adj* (*dizzy*) mareado; (*excited*) exaltado; (*by nature*) atolondrado.

light-hearted [laıt'hɑːtıd] *adj* alegre.

lighthouse ['laıthaus] *n* faro.

lighting ['laıtıŋ] *n* (*act*) iluminación *f*; (*system*) alumbrado.

lighting-up time [laıtıŋ'ʌp-] *n* (*BRIT*) hora de encendido del alumbrado.

lightly ['laıtlı] *adv* ligeramente; (*not seriously*) con poca seriedad; **to get off ~** ser castigado con poca severidad.

light meter *n* (*PHOT*) fotómetro.

lightness ['laıtnıs] *n* claridad *f*; (*in weight*) ligereza.

lightning ['laıtnıŋ] *n* relámpago, rayo.

lightning conductor, (*US*) **lightning rod** *n* pararrayos *m inv*.

lightning strike *n* huelga relámpago.

light pen *n* lápiz *m* óptico.

lightweight ['laıtweıt] *adj* (*suit*) ligero ♦ *n* (*BOXING*) peso ligero.

light year *n* año luz.

like [laık] *vt* (*person*) querer a; (*thing*): **I ~**

swimming/apples me gusta nadar/me gustan las manzanas ♦ *prep* como ♦ *adj* parecido, semejante ♦ *n*: **did you ever see the ~ (of it)?** ¿has visto cosa igual?; **his ~s and dislikes** sus gustos y aversiones; **the ~s of him** personas como él; **I would ~, I'd ~** me gustaría; (*for purchase*) quisiera; **would you ~ a coffee?** ¿te apetece un café?; **to be** *or* **look ~ sb/sth** parecerse a algn/algo; **that's just ~ him** es muy de él, es típico de él; **do it ~ this** hazlo así; **it is nothing ~**... no tiene parecido alguno con...; **what's he ~?** ¿cómo es (él)?; **what's the weather ~?** ¿qué tiempo hace?; **something ~ that** algo así *or* por el estilo; **I feel ~ a drink** me apetece algo de beber; **if you ~** si quieres.

likeable ['laɪkəbl] *adj* simpático, agradable.

likelihood ['laɪklɪhud] *n* probabilidad *f*; **in all ~** todas las probabilidades.

likely ['laɪklɪ] *adj* probable, capaz (*LAM*); **he's ~ to leave** es probable *or* capaz (*LAM*) que se vaya; **not ~!** ¡ni hablar!

like-minded [laɪk'maɪndɪd] *adj* de la misma opinión.

liken ['laɪkən] *vt*: **to ~ to** comparar con.

likeness ['laɪknɪs] *n* (*similarity*) semejanza, parecido.

likewise ['laɪkwaɪz] *adv* igualmente.

liking ['laɪkɪŋ] *n*: **~ (for)** (*person*) cariño (a); (*thing*) afición (a); **to take a ~ to sb** tomar cariño a algn; **to be to sb's ~** ser del gusto de algn.

lilac ['laɪlək] *n* lila ♦ *adj* (*colour*) de color lila.

Lilo ® ['laɪləu] *n* colchoneta inflable.

lilt [lɪlt] *n* deje *m*.

lilting ['lɪltɪŋ] *adj* melodioso.

lily ['lɪlɪ] *n* lirio, azucena.

lily of the valley *n* lirio de los valles.

Lima ['liːmə] *n* Lima.

limb [lɪm] *n* miembro; (*of tree*) rama; **to be out on a ~** (*fig*) estar aislado.

limber up ['lɪmbə*-*] *vi* (*fig*) entrenarse; (*SPORT*) hacer (ejercicios de) precalentamiento.

limbo ['lɪmbəu] *n*: **to be in ~** (*fig*) quedar a la expectativa.

lime [laɪm] *n* (*tree*) limero; (*fruit*) lima; (*GEO*) cal *f*.

lime juice *n* zumo (*SP*) *or* jugo de lima.

limelight ['laɪmlaɪt] *n*: **to be in the ~** (*fig*) ser el centro de atención.

limerick ['lɪmərɪk] *n* quintilla humorística.

limestone ['laɪmstəun] *n* piedra caliza.

limit ['lɪmɪt] *n* límite *m* ♦ *vt* limitar; **weight/speed ~** peso máximo/velocidad *f* máxima; **within ~s** entre límites.

limitation [lɪmɪ'teɪʃən] *n* limitación *f*.

limited ['lɪmɪtɪd] *adj* limitado; **to be ~ to** limitarse a; **~ edition** edición limitada.

limited (liability) company (Ltd) *n* (*BRIT*) sociedad *f* anónima (SA).

limitless ['lɪmɪtlɪs] *adj* sin límites.

limousine ['lɪməziːn] *n* limusina.

limp [lɪmp] *n*: **to have a ~** tener cojera ♦ *vi* cojear, renguear (*LAM*) ♦ *adj* flojo.

limpet ['lɪmpɪt] *n* lapa.

limpid ['lɪmpɪd] *adj* (*poetic*) límpido, cristalino.

limply ['lɪmplɪ] *adv* desmayadamente; **to say ~** decir débilmente.

linchpin ['lɪntʃpɪn] *n* pezonera; (*fig*) eje *m*.

Lincs [lɪŋks] *abbr* (*BRIT*) = **Lincolnshire**.

line [laɪn] *n* (*also COMM*) línea; (*straight ~*) raya; (*rope*) cuerda; (*for fishing*) sedal *m*; (*wire*) hilo; (*row, series*) fila, hilera; (*of writing*) renglón *m*; (*on face*) arruga; (*speciality*) rama ♦ *vt* (*SEWING*): **to ~ (with)** forrar (de); **to ~ the streets** ocupar las aceras; **in ~ with** de acuerdo con; **she's in ~ for promotion** (*fig*) tiene muchas posibilidades de que la asciendan; **to bring sth into ~ with sth** poner algo de acuerdo con algo; **~ of research/business** campo de investigación/comercio; **to take the ~ that ...** ser de la opinión que ...; **hold the ~ please** (*TEL*) no cuelgue usted, por favor; **to draw the ~ at doing sth** negarse a hacer algo; no permitir que se haga algo; **on the right ~s** por buen camino; **a new ~ in cosmetics** una nueva línea en cosméticos; *see also* **lines**.

▶ **line up** *vi* hacer cola ♦ *vt* alinear, poner en fila; **to have sth ~d up** tener algo arreglado.

linear ['lɪnɪə*] *adj* lineal.

lined [laɪnd] *adj* (*face*) arrugado; (*paper*) rayado; (*clothes*) forrado.

line editing *n* (*COMPUT*) corrección *f* por líneas.

line feed *n* (*COMPUT*) avance *m* de línea.

lineman ['laɪnmən] *n* (*US*) técnico de las líneas; (*FOOTBALL*) delantero.

linen ['lɪnɪn] *n* ropa blanca; (*cloth*) lino.

line printer *n* impresora de línea.

liner ['laɪnə*] *n* vapor *m* de línea, transatlántico; **dustbin ~** bolsa de la basura.

lines [laɪnz] *npl* (*RAIL*) vía *sg*, raíles *mpl*.

linesman ['laɪnzmən] *n* (*SPORT*) juez *m* de línea.

line-up ['laɪnʌp] *n* alineación *f*.

linger ['lɪŋgə*] *vi* retrasarse, tardar en marcharse; (*smell, tradition*) persistir.

lingerie ['lænʒəriː] *n* ropa interior *or* íntima

(de mujer).

lingering ['lɪŋgərɪŋ] *adj* persistente; (*death*) lento.

lingo, ~**es** ['lɪŋgəu] *n* (*pej*) jerga.

linguist ['lɪŋgwɪst] *n* lingüista *m/f*.

linguistic [lɪŋ'gwɪstɪk] *adj* lingüístico.

linguistics [lɪŋ'gwɪstɪks] *n* lingüística.

liniment ['lɪnɪmənt] *n* linimento.

lining ['laɪnɪŋ] *n* forro; (*TECH*) revestimiento; (*of brake*) guarnición *f*.

link [lɪŋk] *n* (*of a chain*) eslabón *m*; (*connection*) conexión *f*; (*bond*) vínculo, lazo ♦ *vt* vincular, unir; **rail** ~ línea de ferrocarril, servicio de trenes.

▶**link up** *vt* acoplar ♦ *vi* unirse.

links [lɪŋks] *npl* (*GOLF*) campo *sg* de golf.

link-up ['lɪŋkʌp] *n* (*gen*) unión *f*; (*meeting*) encuentro, reunión *f*; (*of roads*) empalme *m*; (*of spaceships*) acoplamiento; (*RADIO, TV*) enlace *m*.

lino ['laɪnəu] (*BRIT*), **linoleum** [lɪ'nəuliəm] *n* linóleo.

linseed oil ['lɪnsiːd-] *n* aceite *m* de linaza.

lint [lɪnt] *n* gasa.

lintel ['lɪntl] *n* dintel *m*.

lion ['laɪən] *n* león *m*.

lioness ['laɪənɪs] *n* leona.

lip [lɪp] *n* labio; (*of jug*) pico; (*of cup etc*) borde *m*.

liposuction ['lɪpəusʌkʃən] *n* liposucción *f*.

lipread ['lɪpriːd] *vi* leer los labios.

lip salve *n* crema protectora para labios.

lip service *n*: **to pay** ~ **to sth** alabar algo pero sin hacer nada.

lipstick ['lɪpstɪk] *n* lápiz *m or* barra de labios, carmín *m*.

liquefy ['lɪkwɪfaɪ] *vt* licuar ♦ *vi* licuarse.

liqueur [lɪ'kjuə*] *n* licor *m*.

liquid ['lɪkwɪd] *adj*, *n* líquido.

liquidate ['lɪkwɪdeɪt] *vt* liquidar.

liquidation [lɪkwɪ'deɪʃən] *n* liquidación *f*; **to go into** ~ entrar en liquidación.

liquid crystal display (LCD) *n* pantalla de cristal líquido.

liquidity [lɪ'kwɪdɪtɪ] *n* (*COMM*) liquidez *f*.

liquidize ['lɪkwɪdaɪz] *vt* (*CULIN*) licuar.

liquidizer ['lɪkwɪdaɪzə*] *n* (*CULIN*) licuadora.

liquor ['lɪkə*] *n* licor *m*, bebidas *fpl* alcohólicas.

liquorice ['lɪkərɪs] *n* regaliz *m*.

liquor store *n* (*US*) bodega, *tienda de vinos y bebidas alcohólicas*.

Lisbon ['lɪzbən] *n* Lisboa.

lisp [lɪsp] *n* ceceo.

lissom ['lɪsəm] *adj* ágil.

list [lɪst] *n* lista; (*of ship*) inclinación *f* ♦ *vt* (*write down*) hacer una lista de; (*enumerate*) catalogar; (*COMPUT*) hacer un

listado de ♦ *vi* (*ship*) inclinarse; **shopping** ~ lista de las compras; *see also* **lists**.

listed building ['lɪstɪd-] *n* (*ARCHIT*) edificio de interés histórico-artístico.

listed company ['lɪstɪd-] *n* compañía cotizable.

listen ['lɪsn] *vi* escuchar, oír; (*pay attention*) atender.

listener ['lɪsnə*] *n* oyente *m/f*.

listeria [lɪs'tɪərɪə] *n* listeria.

listing ['lɪstɪŋ] *n* (*COMPUT*) listado.

listless ['lɪstlɪs] *adj* apático, indiferente.

listlessly ['lɪstlɪslɪ] *adv* con indiferencia.

listlessness ['lɪstlɪsnɪs] *n* indiferencia, apatía.

list price *n* precio de catálogo.

lists [lɪsts] *npl* (*HISTORY*) liza *sg*; **to enter the** ~ (**against sb/sth**) salir a la palestra (contra algn/algo).

lit [lɪt] *pt, pp of* **light**.

litany ['lɪtənɪ] *n* letanía.

liter ['liːtə*] *n* (*US*) = **litre**.

literacy ['lɪtərəsɪ] *n* capacidad *f* de leer y escribir; ~ **campaign** campaña de alfabetización.

literal ['lɪtərl] *adj* literal.

literally ['lɪtrəlɪ] *adv* literalmente.

literary ['lɪtərərɪ] *adj* literario.

literate ['lɪtərət] *adj* que sabe leer y escribir; (*fig*) culto.

literature ['lɪtərɪtʃə*] *n* literatura; (*brochures etc*) folletos *mpl*.

lithe [laɪð] *adj* ágil.

litho(graph) ['lɪθəu(grɑːf)] *n* litografía.

lithography [lɪ'θɔgrəfɪ] *n* litografía.

Lithuania [lɪθju'eɪnɪə] *n* Lituania.

Lithuanian [lɪθju'eɪnɪən] *adj* lituano ♦ *n* lituano/a; (*LING*) lituano.

litigate ['lɪtɪgeɪt] *vi* litigar.

litigation [lɪtɪ'geɪʃən] *n* litigio.

litmus paper ['lɪtməs-] *n* papel *m* de tornasol.

litre, (*US*) **liter** ['liːtə*] *n* litro.

litter ['lɪtə*] *n* (*rubbish*) basura; (*paper*) papeles *mpl* (tirados); (*young animals*) camada, cría.

litter bin *n* (*BRIT*) papelera.

littered ['lɪtəd] *adj*: ~ **with** lleno de.

litter lout, (*US*) **litterbug** ['lɪtəbʌg] *n* persona que tira papeles usados en la vía pública.

little ['lɪtl] *adj* (*small*) pequeño, chico (*esp LAM*); (*not much*) poco; (*often translated by suffix, eg*): ~ **house** casita ♦ *adv* poco; **a** ~ un poco (de); ~ **by** ~ poco a poco; ~ **finger** (dedo) meñique *m*; **for a** ~ **while** (durante) un rato; **with** ~ **difficulty** sin problema *or* dificultad; **as** ~ **as possible**

lo menos posible.

little-known ['lɪtl'nəun] *adj* poco conocido.

liturgy ['lɪtədʒɪ] *n* liturgia.

live *vb* [lɪv] *vi* vivir ♦ *vt* (*a life*) llevar; (*experience*) vivir ♦ *adj* [laɪv] (*animal*) vivo; (*wire*) conectado; (*broadcast*) en directo; (*issue*) de actualidad; (*unexploded*) sin explotar; **to ~ in London** vivir en Londres; **to ~ together** vivir juntos.

▶**live down** *vt* hacer olvidar.

▶**live off** *vt fus* (*land, fish etc*) vivir de; (*pej: parents etc*) vivir a costa de.

▶**live on** *vt fus* (*food*) vivir de, alimentarse de; **to ~ on £50 a week** vivir con 50 libras semanales *or* a la semana.

▶**live out** *vi* (*students*) ser externo ♦ *vt*: **to ~ out one's days** *or* **life** pasar el resto de la vida.

▶**live up** *vt*: **to ~ it up** (*col*) tirarse la gran vida.

▶**live up to** *vt fus* (*fulfil*) cumplir con; (*justify*) justificar.

live-in ['lɪvɪn] *adj*: **~ partner** pareja, compañero/a sentimental; **~ maid** asistenta interna.

livelihood ['laɪvlɪhud] *n* sustento.

liveliness ['laɪvlɪnɪs] *n* viveza.

lively ['laɪvlɪ] *adj* (*gen*) vivo; (*talk*) animado; (*pace*) rápido; (*party, tune*) alegre.

liven up ['laɪvn-] *vt* (*discussion, evening*) animar.

liver ['lɪvə*] *n* hígado.

liverish ['lɪvərɪʃ] *adj*: **to feel ~** sentirse *or* encontrarse mal, no estar muy católico.

Liverpudlian [lɪvə'pʌdlɪən] *adj* de Liverpool ♦ *n* nativo/a (*or* habitante *m/f*) de Liverpool.

livery ['lɪvərɪ] *n* librea.

lives [laɪvz] *npl of* **life**.

livestock ['laɪvstɔk] *n* ganado.

live wire [laɪv-] *n* (*fig, col*): **he's a real ~!** ¡tiene una marcha!

livid ['lɪvɪd] *adj* lívido; (*furious*) furioso.

living ['lɪvɪŋ] *adj* (*alive*) vivo ♦ *n*: **to earn** *or* **make a ~** ganarse la vida; **cost of ~** coste *m* de la vida; **in ~ memory** que se recuerde *or* recuerda.

living conditions *npl* condiciones *fpl* de vida.

living expenses *npl* gastos *mpl* de mantenimiento.

living room *n* sala (de estar), living *m* (*LAM*).

living standards *npl* nivel *msg* de vida.

living wage *n* sueldo suficiente para vivir.

lizard ['lɪzəd] *n* lagartija.

llama ['lɑːmə] *n* llama.

LLB *n abbr* (= *Bachelor of Laws*) Ldo./a. en

Dcho; *see also* **Bachelor's Degree**.

LLD *n abbr* (= *Doctor of Laws*) Dr(a). en Dcho.

LMT *n abbr* (*US*: = *Local Mean Time*) hora local.

load [ləud] *n* (*gen*) carga; (*weight*) peso ♦ *vt* (*COMPUT*) cargar; (*also*: **~ up**): **to ~ (with)** cargar (con *or* de); **a ~ of**, **~s of** (*fig*) (*gran*) cantidad de, montones de.

loaded ['ləudɪd] *adj* (*dice*) cargado; (*question*) intencionado; (*col: rich*) forrado (de dinero).

loading ['ləudɪŋ] *n* (*COMM*) sobreprima.

loading bay *n* área de carga y descarga.

loaf, *pl* **loaves** [ləuf, ləuvz] *n* (barra de) pan *m* ♦ *vi* (*also*: **~ about**, **~ around**) holgazanear.

loam [ləum] *n* marga.

loan [ləun] *n* préstamo; (*COMM*) empréstito ♦ *vt* prestar; **on ~** (*book, painting*) prestado; **to raise a ~** (*money*) procurar un empréstito.

loan account *n* cuenta de crédito.

loan capital *n* empréstito.

loan shark *n* (*col: pej*) prestamista *m/f* sin escrúpulos.

loath [ləuθ] *adj*: **to be ~ to do sth** ser reacio a hacer algo.

loathe [ləuð] *vt* aborrecer; (*person*) odiar.

loathing ['ləuðɪŋ] *n* aversión *f*; odio.

loathsome ['ləuðsəm] *adj* asqueroso, repugnante; (*person*) odioso.

loaves [ləuvz] *pl of* **loaf**.

lob [lɔb] *vt* (*ball*) volear por alto.

lobby ['lɔbɪ] *n* vestíbulo, sala de espera; (*POL: pressure group*) grupo de presión ♦ *vt* presionar.

lobbyist ['lɔbɪɪst] *n* cabildero/a.

lobe [ləub] *n* lóbulo.

lobster ['lɔbstə*] *n* langosta.

lobster pot *n* nasa, langostera.

local ['ləukl] *adj* local ♦ *n* (*pub*) bar *m*; **the ~s** *npl* los vecinos, los del lugar.

local anaesthetic *n* (*MED*) anestesia local.

local authority *n* municipio, ayuntamiento (*SP*).

local call *n* (*TEL*) llamada local.

local government *n* gobierno municipal.

locality [ləu'kælɪtɪ] *n* localidad *f*.

localize ['ləukəlaɪz] *vt* localizar.

locally ['ləukəlɪ] *adv* en la vecindad.

locate [ləu'keɪt] *vt* (*find*) localizar; (*situate*) situar, ubicar (*LAM*).

location [ləu'keɪʃən] *n* situación *f*; **on ~** (*CINE*) en exteriores, fuera del estudio.

loch [lɔx] *n* lago.

lock [lɔk] *n* (*of door, box*) cerradura, chapa (*LAM*); (*of canal*) esclusa; (*of hair*) mechón

m ♦ *vt* (*with key*) cerrar con llave;
(*immobilize*) inmovilizar ♦ *vi* (*door etc*)
cerrarse con llave; (*wheels*) trabarse; ~
stock and barrel (*fig*) por completo *or*
entero; **on full** ~ (*AUT*) con el volante
girado al máximo.

▶**lock away** *vt* (*valuables*) guardar bajo
llave; (*criminal*) encerrar.

▶**lock out** *vt*: **the workers were** ~**ed out** los
trabajadores tuvieron que enfrentarse
con un cierre patronal.

▶**lock up** *vi* echar la llave.

locker ['lɔkə*] *n* casillero.

locker-room ['lɔkərum] *n* (*US SPORT*)
vestuario.

locket ['lɔkɪt] *n* medallón *m*.

lockout ['lɔkaut] *n* (*INDUSTRY*) paro *or*
cierre *m* patronal, lockout *m*.

locksmith ['lɔksmɪθ] *n* cerrajero/a.

lock-up ['lɔkʌp] *n* (*prison*) cárcel *f*; (*cell*)
jaula; (~ *garage*) jaula, cochera.

locomotive [lɔukə'məutɪv] *n* locomotora.

locum ['ləukəm] *n* (*MED*) (médico/a)
suplente *m/f*.

locust ['ləukəst] *n* langosta.

lodge [lɔdʒ] *n* casa del guarda; (*porter's*)
portería; (*FREEMASONRY*) logia ♦ *vi*
(*person*): **to** ~ (**with**) alojarse (en casa de)
♦ *vt* (*complaint*) presentar.

lodger ['lɔdʒə*] *n* huésped(a) *m/f*.

lodgings ['lɔdʒɪŋz] *npl* alojamiento *sg*;
(*house*) casa *sg* de huéspedes.

loft [lɔft] *n* desván *m*.

lofty ['lɔftɪ] *adj* alto; (*haughty*) altivo,
arrogante; (*sentiments, aims*) elevado,
noble.

log [lɔg] *n* (*of wood*) leño, tronco; (*book*)
= **logbook** ♦ *n abbr* (= *logarithm*) log. ♦ *vt*
anotar, registrar.

▶**log in, log on** *vi* (*COMPUT*) iniciar la (*or*
una) sesión.

▶**log off, log out** *vi* (*COMPUT*) finalizar la
sesión.

logarithm ['lɔgərɪðəm] *n* logaritmo.

logbook ['lɔgbuk] *n* (*NAUT*) diario de a
bordo; (*AVIAT*) libro de vuelo; (*of car*)
documentación *f* (del coche).

log cabin *n* cabaña de troncos.

log fire *n* fuego de leña.

logger ['lɔgə*] *n* leñador(a) *m/f*.

loggerheads ['lɔgəhɛdz] *npl*: **at** ~ (**with**) de
pique (con).

logic ['lɔdʒɪk] *n* lógica.

logical ['lɔdʒɪkl] *adj* lógico.

logically ['lɔdʒɪkəlɪ] *adv* lógicamente.

logistics [lɔ'dʒɪstɪks] *n* logística.

log jam *n*: **to break the** ~ poner fin al
estancamiento.

logo ['ləugəu] *n* logotipo.

loin [lɔɪn] *n* (*CULIN*) lomo, solomillo; ~**s** *npl*
lomos *mpl*.

loin cloth *n* taparrabos *m inv*.

loiter ['lɔɪtə*] *vi* vagar; (*pej*) merodear.

loll [lɔl] *vi* (*also*: ~ **about**) repantigarse.

lollipop ['lɔlɪpɔp] *n* pirulí *m*; (*iced*)
polo.

lollipop lady *n* (*BRIT*) *ver recuadro*.

lollipop man *n* (*BRIT*) *ver recuadro*.

LOLLIPOP LADY, LOLLIPOP MAN

Se llama **lollipop lady** *o* **lollipop man** *a la
persona encargada de parar el tráfico en las
carreteras cercanas a los colegios
británicos para que los niños las crucen sin
peligro. Suelen ser personas ya jubiladas,
vestidas con un abrigo de color luminoso y
llevando una señal de stop en un poste
portátil, la cual recuerda por su forma a un
pirulí, de ahí su nombre.*

---

lolly ['lɔlɪ] *n* (*col: ice cream*) polo; (: *lollipop*)
piruleta; (: *money*) guita.

Lombardy ['lɔmbədɪ] *n* Lombardía.

London ['lʌndən] *n* Londres *m*.

Londoner ['lʌndənə*] *n* londinense *m/f*.

lone [ləun] *adj* solitario.

loneliness ['ləunlɪnɪs] *n* soledad *f*,
aislamiento.

lonely ['ləunlɪ] *adj* solitario, solo.

lonely hearts *adj*: ~ **ad** anuncio de la
sección de contactos; ~ **column** sección *f*
de contactos.

lone parent family *n* familia
monoparental.

loner ['ləunə*] *n* solitario/a.

lonesome ['ləunsəm] *adj* (*esp US*) = **lonely**.

long [lɔŋ] *adj* largo ♦ *adv* mucho tiempo,
largamente ♦ *vi*: **to** ~ **for sth** anhelar algo
♦ *n*: **the** ~ **and the short of it is that** ...
(*fig*) en resumidas cuentas ...; **in the** ~
run a la larga; **so** *or* **as** ~ **as** mientras, con
tal de que; **don't be** ~**!** ¡no tardes!,
¡vuelve pronto!; **how** ~ **is the street?**
¿cuánto tiene la calle de largo?; **how** ~ **is
the lesson?** ¿cuánto dura la clase?; **6
metres** ~ que mide 6 metros, de 6 metros
de largo; **6 months** ~ que dura 6 meses,
de 6 meses de duración; **all night** ~ toda
la noche; ~ **ago** hace mucho (tiempo); **he
no** ~**er comes** ya no viene; ~ **before**
mucho antes; **before** ~ (+ *future*) dentro
de poco; (+ *past*) poco tiempo después; **at**
~ **last** al fin, por fin; **I shan't be** ~ termino
pronto.

long-distance [lɔŋ'dɪstəns] *adj* (*race*) de

larga distancia; (*call*) interurbano.
longevity [lɔn'dʒɛvɪtɪ] *n* longevidad *f*.
long-haired ['lɔŋ'hɛəd] *adj* de pelo largo.
longhand ['lɔŋhænd] *n* escritura
(corriente).
longing ['lɔŋɪŋ] *n* anhelo, ansia; (*nostalgia*)
nostalgia ♦ *adj* anhelante.
longingly ['lɔŋɪŋlɪ] *adv* con ansia.
longitude ['lɔŋɡɪtjuːd] *n* longitud *f*.
long jump *n* salto de longitud.
long-lost ['lɔŋlɔst] *adj* desaparecido hace
mucho tiempo.
long-playing record (LP) ['lɔŋpleɪɪŋ-] *n*
elepé *m*, disco de larga duración.
long-range ['lɔŋ'reɪndʒ] *adj* de gran
alcance; (*weather forecast*) a largo plazo.
longshoreman ['lɔŋʃɔːmən] *n* (*US*)
estibador *m*.
long-sighted ['lɔŋ'saɪtɪd] *adj* (*BRIT*)
présbita.
long-standing ['lɔŋ'stændɪŋ] *adj* de mucho
tiempo.
long-suffering [lɔŋ'sʌfərɪŋ] *adj* sufrido.
long-term ['lɔŋtəːm] *adj* a largo plazo.
long wave *n* onda larga.
long-winded [lɔŋ'wɪndɪd] *adj* prolijo.
loo [luː] *n* (*BRIT*: *col*) wáter *m*.
loofah ['luːfə] *n* esponja de lufa.
look [luk] *vi* mirar; (*seem*) parecer;
(*building etc*): **to ~ south/on to the sea**
dar al sur/al mar ♦ *n* mirada; (*glance*)
vistazo; (*appearance*) aire *m*, aspecto; **~s**
npl físico *sg*, belleza *sg*; **to ~ ahead** mirar
hacia delante; **it ~s about 4 metres long**
yo calculo que tiene unos 4 metros de
largo; **it ~s all right to me** a mí me
parece que está bien; **to have a ~ at sth**
echar un vistazo a algo; **to have a ~ for**
sth buscar algo.
▶**look after** *vt fus* cuidar.
▶**look around** *vi* echar una mirada
alrededor.
▶**look at** *vt fus* mirar; (*consider*) considerar.
▶**look back** *vi* mirar hacia atrás; **to ~ back**
at sb/sth mirar hacia atrás algo/a algn;
to ~ back on (*event, period*) recordar.
▶**look down on** *vt fus* (*fig*) despreciar,
mirar con desprecio.
▶**look for** *vt fus* buscar.
▶**look forward to** *vt fus* esperar con
ilusión; (*in letters*): **we ~ forward to**
hearing from you quedamos a la espera
de su respuesta *or* contestación; **I'm not**
~ing forward to it no tengo ganas de eso,
no me hace ilusión.
▶**look in** *vi*: **to ~ in on sb** (*visit*) pasar por
casa de algn.
▶**look into** *vt fus* investigar.

▶**look on** *vi* mirar (como espectador).
▶**look out** *vi* (*beware*): **to ~ out (for)** tener
cuidado (de).
▶**look out for** *vt fus* (*seek*) buscar; (*await*)
esperar.
▶**look over** *vt* (*essay*) revisar; (*town,*
building) inspeccionar, registrar; (*person*)
examinar.
▶**look round** *vi* (*turn*) volver la cabeza; **to**
~ round for sth buscar algo.
▶**look through** *vt fus* (*papers, book*) hojear;
(*briefly*) echar un vistazo a; (*telescope*)
mirar por.
▶**look to** *vt fus* ocuparse de; (*rely on*) contar
con.
▶**look up** *vi* mirar hacia arriba; (*improve*)
mejorar ♦ *vt* (*word*) buscar; (*friend*)
visitar.
▶**look up to** *vt fus* admirar.
look-out ['lukaut] *n* (*tower etc*) puesto de
observación; (*person*) vigía *m/f*; **to be on**
the ~ for sth estar al acecho de algo.
look-up table ['lukʌp-] *n* (*COMPUT*) tabla de
consulta.
LOOM *n abbr* (*US*: = *Loyal Order of Moose*)
asociación benéfica.
loom [luːm] *n* telar *m* ♦ *vi* (*threaten*)
amenazar.
loony ['luːnɪ] *adj*, *n* (*col*) loco/a *m/f*.
loop [luːp] *n* lazo; (*bend*) vuelta, recodo;
(*COMPUT*) bucle *m*.
loophole ['luːphəul] *n* laguna.
loose [luːs] *adj* (*gen*) suelto; (*not tight*) flojo;
(*wobbly etc*) movedizo; (*clothes*) ancho;
(*morals, discipline*) relajado ♦ *vt* (*free*)
soltar; (*slacken*) aflojar; (*also*: **~ off**: *arrow*)
disparar, soltar; **~ connection** (*ELEC*) hilo
desempalmado; **to be at a ~ end** *or* (*US*)
at ~ ends no saber qué hacer; **to tie up ~**
ends (*fig*) no dejar ningún cabo suelto,
atar cabos.
loose change *n* cambio.
loose chippings [-'tʃɪpɪŋz] *npl* (*on road*)
gravilla *sg* suelta.
loose-fitting ['luːsfɪtɪŋ] *adj* suelto.
loose-leaf ['luːsliːf] *adj*: **~ binder** *or* folder
carpeta de anillas.
loose-limbed ['luːslɪmd] *adj* ágil, suelto.
loosely ['luːslɪ] *adv* libremente,
aproximadamente.
loosely-knit [-nɪt] *adj* de estructura
abierta.
loosen ['luːsn] *vt* (*free*) soltar; (*untie*)
desatar; (*slacken*) aflojar.
▶**loosen up** *vi* (*before game*) hacer
(ejercicios de) precalentamiento; (*col*:
relax) soltarse, relajarse.
looseness ['luːsnɪs] *n* soltura; flojedad *f*.

loot [luːt] *n* botín *m* ♦ *vt* saquear.
looter ['luːtə*] *n* saqueador(a) *m/f.*
looting ['luːtɪŋ] *n* pillaje *m.*
lop [lɔp]: **to ~ off** *vt* cortar; (*branches*) podar.
lop-sided ['lɔp'saɪdɪd] *adj* desequilibrado.
lord [lɔːd] *n* señor *m*; **L~ Smith** Lord Smith; **the L~** el Señor; **the (House of) L~s** (*BRIT*) la Cámara de los Lores.
lordly ['lɔːdlɪ] *adj* señorial.
Lordship ['lɔːdʃɪp] *n*: **your ~** su Señoría.
lore [lɔː*] *n* saber *m* popular, tradiciones *fpl.*
lorry ['lɔrɪ] *n* (*BRIT*) camión *m.*
lorry driver *n* camionero/a.
lorry load *n* carga.
lose, *pt, pp* **lost** [luːz, lɔst] *vt* perder ♦ *vi* perder, ser vencido; **to ~ (time)** (*clock*) atrasarse; **to ~ no time (in doing sth)** no tardar (en hacer algo); **to get lost** (*object*) extraviarse; (*person*) perderse.
▶**lose out** *vi* salir perdiendo.
loser ['luːzə*] *n* perdedor(a) *m/f*; **to be a bad ~** no saber perder.
losing ['luːzɪŋ] *adj* (*team etc*) vencido, perdedor(a).
loss [lɔs] *n* pérdida; **heavy ~es** (*MIL*) grandes pérdidas *fpl*; **to be at a ~** no saber qué hacer; **to be a dead ~** ser completamente inútil; **to cut one's ~es** reducir las pérdidas; **to sell sth at a ~** vender algo perdiendo dinero.
loss adjuster *n* (*INSURANCE*) perito/a *m/f or* tasador(a) *m/f* de pérdidas.
loss leader *n* (*COMM*) artículo de promoción.
lost [lɔst] *pt, pp of* **lose** ♦ *adj* perdido; **~ in thought** absorto, ensimismado.
lost and found *n* (*US*) = **lost property, lost property office** *or* **department.**
lost cause *n* causa perdida.
lost property *n* (*BRIT*) objetos *mpl* perdidos.
lost property office *or* **department** *n* (*BRIT*) departamento de objetos perdidos.
lot [lɔt] *n* (*at auctions*) lote *m*; (*destiny*) suerte *f*; **the ~** el todo, todos *mpl*, todas *fpl*; **a ~** mucho, bastante; **a ~ of, ~s of** mucho(s)/a(s) (*pl*); **I read a ~** leo bastante; **to draw ~s (for sth)** echar suertes (para decidir algo).
lotion ['ləuʃən] *n* loción *f.*
lottery ['lɔtərɪ] *n* lotería.
loud [laud] *adj* (*voice, sound*) fuerte; (*laugh, shout*) estrepitoso; (*gaudy*) chillón/ona ♦ *adv* (*speak etc*) fuerte; **out ~** en voz alta.
loudhailer [laud'heɪlə*] *n* (*BRIT*) megáfono.
loudly ['laudlɪ] *adv* (*noisily*) fuerte; (*aloud*) en alta voz.

loudness ['laudnɪs] *n* (*of sound etc*) fuerza.
loudspeaker [laud'spiːkə*] *n* altavoz *m.*
lounge [laundʒ] *n* salón *m*, sala de estar; (*of hotel*) salón *m*; (*of airport*) sala de embarque ♦ *vi* (*also*: **~ about, ~ around**) holgazanear, no hacer nada; *see also* **pub.**
lounge bar *n* salón *m.*
lounge suit *n* (*BRIT*) traje *m* de calle.
louse, *pl* **lice** [laus, laɪs] *n* piojo.
▶**louse up** *vt* (*col*) echar a perder.
lousy ['lauzɪ] *adj* (*fig*) vil, asqueroso.
lout [laut] *n* gamberro/a.
louvre, (*US*) **louver** ['luːvə*] *adj*: **~ door** puerta de rejilla; **~ window** ventana de libro.
lovable ['lʌvəbl] *adj* amable, simpático.
love [lʌv] *n* amor *m* ♦ *vt* amar, querer; **to send one's ~ to sb** dar sus recuerdos a algn; **~ from Anne** (*in letter*) con cariño de Anne; **I ~ to read** me encanta leer; **to be in ~ with** estar enamorado de; **to make ~** hacer el amor; **for the ~ of** por amor a; **"15 ~"** (*TENNIS*) "15 a cero"; **I ~ paella** me encanta la paella; **I'd ~ to come** me gustaría muchísimo venir.
love affair *n* aventura sentimental *or* amorosa.
love child *n* hijo/a natural.
loved ones ['lʌvdwʌnz] *npl* seres *mpl* queridos.
love-hate relationship ['lʌvheɪt-] *n* relación *f* de amor y odio.
love letter *n* carta de amor.
love life *n* vida sentimental.
lovely ['lʌvlɪ] *adj* (*delightful*) precioso, encantador(a), lindo (*esp LAM*); (*beautiful*) hermoso, lindo (*esp LAM*); **we had a ~ time** lo pasamos estupendo.
lovemaking ['lʌvmeɪkɪŋ] *n* relaciones *fpl* sexuales.
lover ['lʌvə*] *n* amante *m/f*; (*amateur*): **a ~ of** un(a) aficionado/a *or* un(a) amante de.
lovesick ['lʌvsɪk] *adj* enfermo de amor, amartelado.
lovesong ['lʌvsɔŋ] *n* canción *f* de amor.
loving ['lʌvɪŋ] *adj* amoroso, cariñoso.
lovingly ['lʌvɪŋlɪ] *adv* amorosamente, cariñosamente.
low [ləu] *adj, adv* bajo ♦ *n* (*METEOROLOGY*) área de baja presión ♦ *vi* (*cow*) mugir; **to feel ~** sentirse deprimido; **to turn (down) ~** bajar; **to reach a new** *or* **an all-time ~** llegar a su punto más bajo.
low-alcohol [ləu'ælkəhɔl] *adj* bajo en alcohol.
lowbrow ['ləubrau] *adj* (*person*) de poca cultura.
low-calorie ['ləu'kælərɪ] *adj* bajo en

calorías.

low-cut ['ləukʌt] adj (dress) escotado.

low-down ['ləudaun] n (col): **he gave me the ~ on it** me puso al corriente ♦ adj (mean) vil, bajo.

lower ['ləuə*] vt bajar; (reduce: price) reducir, rebajar; (: resistance) debilitar: **to ~ o.s. to** (fig) rebajarse a ♦ vi ['lauə*]: **to ~ (at sb)** fulminar (a algn) con la mirada.

lower case n (TYP) minúscula.

Lower House n (POL): **the ~** la Cámara baja.

lowering ['lauərɪŋ] adj (sky) amenazador(a).

low-fat ['ləu'fæt] adj (milk, yoghurt) desnatado; (diet) bajo en calorías.

low-key ['ləu'kiː] adj de mínima intensidad; (operation) de poco perfil.

lowland ['ləulənd] n tierra baja.

low-level ['ləulɛvl] adj de bajo nivel; (flying) a poca altura.

low-loader ['ləuləudə*] n camión m de caja a bajo nivel.

lowly ['ləulɪ] adj humilde.

low-lying [ləu'laɪɪŋ] adj bajo.

low-rise ['ləuraɪz] adj bajo.

low-tech ['ləutɛk] adj de baja tecnología.

loyal ['lɔɪəl] adj leal.

loyalist ['lɔɪəlɪst] n legitimista m/f.

loyally ['lɔɪəlɪ] adv lealmente.

loyalty ['lɔɪəltɪ] n lealtad f.

loyalty card n (BRIT) tarjeta cliente.

lozenge ['lɔzɪndʒ] n (MED) pastilla.

LP n abbr see **long-playing record**.

L-plates ['ɛlpleɪts] npl (BRIT) (placas fpl de) la L; ver recuadro.

L-PLATES

En el Reino Unido las personas que están aprendiendo a conducir han de llevar indicativos blancos con una L en rojo llamados normalmente **L-plates** (de "learner") en la parte delantera y trasera de los automóviles que conducen. No tienen que ir a clases teóricas, sino que desde el principio se les entrega un carnet de conducir provisional ("provisional driving licence") para que realicen sus prácticas, que han de estar supervisadas por un conductor con carnet definitivo ("full driving licence"). Tampoco se les permite hacer prácticas en autopistas aunque vayan acompañados.

LPN n abbr (US: = Licensed Practical Nurse) enfermero/a practicante.

LRAM n abbr (BRIT) = Licentiate of the Royal Academy of Music.

LSD n abbr (= lysergic acid diethylamide) LSD m; (BRIT: = pounds, shillings and pence) sistema monetario usado en Gran Bretaña hasta 1971.

LSE n abbr = London School of Economics.

Ltd abbr (= limited company) S.A.

lubricant ['luːbrɪkənt] n lubricante m.

lubricate ['luːbrɪkeɪt] vt lubricar, engrasar.

lubrication [luːbrɪ'keɪʃən] n lubricación f.

lucid ['luːsɪd] adj lúcido.

lucidity [luː'sɪdɪtɪ] n lucidez f.

lucidly ['luːsɪdlɪ] adv lúcidamente.

luck [lʌk] n suerte f; **good/bad ~** buena/ mala suerte; **good ~!** ¡(que tengas) suerte!; **to be in ~** estar de suerte; **to be out of ~** tener mala suerte.

luckily ['lʌkɪlɪ] adv afortunadamente.

lucky ['lʌkɪ] adj afortunado.

lucrative ['luːkrətɪv] adj lucrativo.

ludicrous ['luːdɪkrəs] adj absurdo.

ludo ['luːdəu] n parchís m.

lug [lʌg] vt (drag) arrastrar.

luggage ['lʌgɪdʒ] n equipaje m.

luggage rack n (in train) rejilla, redecilla; (on car) baca, portaequipajes m inv.

luggage van n furgón m or vagón m de equipaje.

lugubrious [lu'guːbrɪəs] adj lúgubre.

lukewarm ['luːkwɔːm] adj tibio, templado.

lull [lʌl] n tregua ♦ vt (child) acunar; (person, fear) calmar.

lullaby ['lʌləbaɪ] n nana.

lumbago [lʌm'beɪgəu] n lumbago.

lumber ['lʌmbə*] n (junk) trastos mpl viejos; (wood) maderos mpl ♦ vt (BRIT col): **to ~ sb with sth/sb** hacer que algn cargue con algo/algn ♦ vi (also: ~ **about**, ~ **along**) moverse pesadamente.

lumberjack ['lʌmbədʒæk] n maderero.

lumber room n (BRIT) cuarto trastero.

lumber yard n (US) almacén m de madera.

luminous ['luːmɪnəs] adj luminoso.

lump [lʌmp] n terrón m; (fragment) trozo; (in sauce) grumo; (in throat) nudo; (swelling) bulto ♦ vt (also: ~ **together**) juntar; (persons) poner juntos.

lump sum n suma global.

lumpy ['lʌmpɪ] adj (sauce) lleno de grumos.

lunacy ['luːnəsɪ] n locura.

lunar ['luːnə*] adj lunar.

lunatic ['luːnətɪk] adj, n loco/a m/f.

lunatic asylum n manicomio.

lunch [lʌntʃ] n almuerzo, comida ♦ vi almorzar; **to invite sb to** or **for ~** invitar a algn a almorzar.

lunch break, lunch hour n hora del almuerzo.

luncheon ['lʌntʃən] n almuerzo.
luncheon meat n tipo de fiambre.
luncheon voucher n vale m de comida.
lunchtime ['lʌntʃtaɪm] n hora del almuerzo
or de comer.
lung [lʌŋ] n pulmón m.
lung cancer n cáncer m del pulmón.
lunge [lʌndʒ] vi (also: ~ **forward**)
abalanzarse; **to ~ at** arremeter contra.
lupin ['lu:pɪn] n altramuz m.
lurch [ləːtʃ] vi dar sacudidas ♦ n sacudida;
to leave sb in the ~ dejar a algn
plantado.
lure [luə*] n (bait) cebo; (decoy) señuelo ♦ vt
convencer con engaños.
lurid ['luərɪd] adj (colour) chillón/ona;
(account) sensacional; (detail)
horripilante.
lurk [ləːk] vi (hide) esconderse; (wait) estar
al acecho.
luscious ['lʌʃəs] adj delicioso.
lush [lʌʃ] adj exuberante.
lust [lʌst] n lujuria; (greed) codicia.
►**lust after** vt fus codiciar.
lustful ['lʌstful] adj lascivo, lujurioso.
lustre, (US) **luster** ['lʌstə*] n lustre m,
brillo.
lustrous ['lʌstrəs] adj brillante.
lusty ['lʌstɪ] adj robusto, fuerte.
lute [lu:t] n laúd m.
Luxembourg ['lʌksəmbəːg] n Luxemburgo.
luxuriant [lʌg'zjuərɪənt] adj exuberante.
luxurious [lʌg'zjuərɪəs] adj lujoso.
luxury ['lʌkʃərɪ] n lujo ♦ cpd de lujo.
luxury tax n impuesto de lujo.
LV n abbr (BRIT) = **luncheon voucher**.
LW abbr (RADIO) = **long wave**.
Lycra ® ['laɪkrə] n licra ®.
lying ['laɪɪŋ] n mentiras fpl ♦ adj (statement,
story) falso; (person) mentiroso.
lynch [lɪntʃ] vt linchar.
lynx [lɪŋks] n lince m.
Lyons ['laɪənz] n Lyón m.
lyre ['laɪə*] n lira.
lyric ['lɪrɪk] adj lírico; ~**s** npl (of song)
letra sg.
lyrical ['lɪrɪkl] adj lírico.

M m

M, m [ɛm] n (letter) M, m f; **M for Mary**, (US)
M for Mike M de Madrid.
M n abbr = **million(s)**; (= medium) M; (BRIT:
= motorway): **the M8** ≈ la A8.
m abbr (= metre) m.; = **mile(s)**.
MA n abbr (US) = Military Academy; see
Master of Arts ♦ abbr (US) =
Massachusetts.
mac [mæk] n (BRIT) impermeable m.
macabre [mə'kɑːbrə] adj macabro.
macaroni [mækə'rəunɪ] n macarrones mpl.
macaroon [mækə'ruːn] n macarrón m,
mostachón m.
mace [meɪs] n (weapon, ceremonial) maza;
(spice) macis f.
Macedonia [mæsɪ'dəunɪə] n Macedonia.
Macedonian [mæsɪ'dəunɪən] adj macedonio
♦ n macedonio/a; (LING) macedonio.
machinations [mæʃɪ'neɪʃənz] npl intrigas
fpl, maquinaciones fpl.
machine [mə'ʃiːn] n máquina ♦ vt (dress etc)
coser a máquina; (TECH) trabajar a
máquina.
machine code n (COMPUT) código
máquina.
machine gun n ametralladora.
machine language n (COMPUT) lenguaje
m máquina.
machine readable adj (COMPUT) legible
por máquina.
machinery [mə'ʃiːnərɪ] n maquinaria; (fig)
mecanismo.
machine shop n taller m de máquinas.
machine tool n máquina herramienta.
machine translation n traducción f
automática.
machine washable adj lavable a
máquina.
machinist [mə'ʃiːnɪst] n operario/a m/f (de
máquina).
macho ['mætʃəu] adj macho.
mackerel ['mækrl] n, pl inv caballa.
mackintosh ['mækɪntɔʃ] n (BRIT)
impermeable m.
macro ... ['mækrəu] pref macro....
macro-economics ['mækrəuiːkə'nɔmɪks] n
macroeconomía.
mad [mæd] adj loco; (idea) disparatado;

(*angry*) furioso, enojado (*LAM*); ~ (**at** *or* **with sb**) furioso con algn; **to be ~ (keen) about** *or* **on sth** estar loco por algo; **to go ~** volverse loco, enloquecer(se).

madam ['mædəm] *n* señora; **can I help you ~?** ¿le puedo ayudar, señora?; **M~ Chairman** señora presidenta.

madcap ['mædkæp] *adj* (*col*) alocado, disparatado.

mad cow disease *n* encefalopatía espongiforme bovina.

madden ['mædn] *vt* volver loco.

maddening ['mædnɪŋ] *adj* enloquecedor(a).

made [meɪd] *pt, pp of* **make**.

Madeira [mə'dɪərə] *n* (*GEO*) Madeira; (*wine*) madeira *m*.

made-to-measure ['meɪdtəmɛʒə*] *adj* (*BRIT*) hecho a la medida.

made-up ['meɪdʌp] *adj* (*story*) ficticio.

madhouse ['mædhaus] *n* (*also fig*) manicomio.

madly ['mædlɪ] *adv* locamente.

madman ['mædmən] *n* loco.

madness ['mædnɪs] *n* locura.

Madonna [mə'dɒnə] *n* Virgen *f*.

Madrid [mə'drɪd] *n* Madrid *m*.

madrigal ['mædrɪgəl] *n* madrigal *m*.

Mafia ['mæfɪə] *n* Mafia.

mag [mæg] *n abbr* (*BRIT col*) = **magazine**.

magazine [mægə'ziːn] *n* revista; (*MIL: store*) almacén *m*; (*of firearm*) recámara.

maggot ['mægət] *n* gusano.

magic ['mædʒɪk] *n* magia ♦ *adj* mágico.

magical ['mædʒɪkəl] *adj* mágico.

magician [mə'dʒɪʃən] *n* mago/a.

magistrate ['mædʒɪstreɪt] *n* juez *m/f* (municipal); **M~s' Courts** *see* **crown court**.

magnanimity [mægnə'nɪmɪtɪ] *n* magnanimidad *f*.

magnanimous [mæg'nænɪməs] *adj* magnánimo.

magnate ['mægneɪt] *n* magnate *m/f*.

magnesium [mæg'niːzɪəm] *n* magnesio.

magnet ['mægnɪt] *n* imán *m*.

magnetic [mæg'nɛtɪk] *adj* magnético.

magnetic disk *n* (*COMPUT*) disco magnético.

magnetic tape *n* cinta magnética.

magnetism ['mægnɪtɪzəm] *n* magnetismo.

magnification [mægnɪfɪ'keɪʃən] *n* aumento.

magnificence [mæg'nɪfɪsns] *n* magnificencia.

magnificent [mæg'nɪfɪsnt] *adj* magnífico.

magnificently [mæg'nɪfɪsntlɪ] *adv* magníficamente.

magnify ['mægnɪfaɪ] *vt* aumentar; (*fig*) exagerar.

magnifying glass ['mægnɪfaɪɪŋ-] *n* lupa.

magnitude ['mægnɪtjuːd] *n* magnitud *f*.

magnolia [mæg'nəulɪə] *n* magnolia.

magpie ['mægpaɪ] *n* urraca.

maharajah [mɑːhə'rɑːdʒə] *n* maharajá *m*.

mahogany [mə'hɒgənɪ] *n* caoba ♦ *cpd* de caoba.

maid [meɪd] *n* criada; **old ~** (*pej*) solterona.

maiden ['meɪdn] *n* doncella ♦ *adj* (*aunt etc*) solterona; (*speech, voyage*) inaugural.

maiden name *n* apellido de soltera.

mail [meɪl] *n* correo; (*letters*) cartas *fpl* ♦ *vt* (*post*) echar al correo; (*send*) mandar por correo; **by ~** por correo.

mailbox ['meɪlbɒks] *n* (*US: for letters etc*; *COMPUT*) buzón *m*.

mailing list ['meɪlɪŋ-] *n* lista de direcciones.

mailman ['meɪlmæn] *n* (*US*) cartero.

mail-order ['meɪlɔːdə*] *n* pedido postal; (*business*) venta por correo ♦ *adj*: ~ **firm** *or* **house** casa de venta por correo.

mailshot ['meɪlʃɒt] *n* mailing *m inv*.

mailtrain ['meɪltreɪn] *n* tren *m* correo.

mail van, (*US*) **mail truck** *n* (*AUT*) camioneta de correos *or* de reparto.

maim [meɪm] *vt* mutilar, lisiar.

main [meɪn] *adj* principal, mayor ♦ *n* (*pipe*) cañería principal *or* maestra; (*US*) red *f* eléctrica; **the ~s** (*BRIT ELEC*) la red eléctrica; **in the ~** en general.

main course *n* (*CULIN*) plato principal.

mainframe ['meɪnfreɪm] *n* (*also*: ~ **computer**) ordenador *m or* computadora central.

mainland ['meɪnlənd] *n* continente *m*.

main line *n* línea principal.

mainly ['meɪnlɪ] *adv* principalmente, en su mayoría.

main road *n* carretera principal.

mainstay ['meɪnsteɪ] *n* (*fig*) pilar *m*.

mainstream ['meɪnstriːm] *n* (*fig*) corriente *f* principal.

main street *n* calle *f* mayor.

maintain [meɪn'teɪn] *vt* mantener; (*affirm*) sostener; **to ~ that** ... mantener *or* sostener que ... .

maintenance ['meɪntənəns] *n* mantenimiento; (*alimony*) pensión *f* alimenticia.

maintenance contract *n* contrato de mantenimiento.

maintenance order *n* (*LAW*) obligación *f* de pagar una pensión alimenticia al cónyuge.

maisonette [meɪzə'nɛt] *n* dúplex *m*.

maize [meɪz] *n* (*BRIT*) maíz *m*, choclo (*LAM*).

Maj. *abbr* (*MIL*) = **major**.

majestic [mə'dʒɛstɪk] *adj* majestuoso.

majesty ['mædʒɪstɪ] n majestad f.
major ['meɪdʒə*] n (MIL) comandante m
♦ adj principal; (MUS) mayor ♦ vi (US
UNIV): **to ~ (in)** especializarse en; **a ~
operation** una operación or intervención
de gran importancia.
Majorca [mə'jɔːkə] n Mallorca.
major general n (MIL) general m de
división.
majority [mə'dʒɔrɪtɪ] n mayoría ♦ cpd
(verdict) mayoritario.
majority holding n (COMM): **to have a ~**
tener un interés mayoritario.
make [meɪk] vt (pt, pp made [meɪd]) hacer;
(manufacture) hacer, fabricar; (cause to
be): **to ~ sb sad** poner triste or
entristecer a algn; (force): **to ~ sb do sth**
obligar a algn a hacer algo; (equal): **2 and
2 ~ 4** 2 y 2 son 4 ♦ n marca; **to ~ a fool of
sb** poner a algn en ridículo; **to ~ a
profit/loss** obtener ganancias/sufrir
pérdidas; **to ~ a profit of £500** sacar una
ganancia de 500 libras; **to ~ it** (arrive)
llegar; (achieve sth) tener éxito; **what
time do you ~ it?** ¿qué hora tienes?; **to ~
do with** contentarse con.
►**make for** vt fus (place) dirigirse a.
►**make off** vi largarse.
►**make out** vt (decipher) descifrar;
(understand) entender; (see) distinguir;
(write: cheque) extender; **to ~ out (that)**
(claim, imply) dar a entender (que); **to ~
out a case for sth** dar buenas razones en
favor de algo.
►**make over** vt (assign): **to ~ over (to)**
ceder or traspasar (a).
►**make up** vt (invent) inventar; (parcel)
hacer ♦ vi reconciliarse; (with cosmetics)
maquillarse; **to be made up of** estar
compuesto de.
►**make up for** vt fus compensar.
make-believe ['meɪkbɪliːv] n ficción f,
fantasía.
maker ['meɪkə*] n fabricante m/f.
makeshift ['meɪkʃɪft] adj improvisado.
make-up ['meɪkʌp] n maquillaje m.
make-up bag n bolsita del maquillaje or
de los cosméticos.
make-up remover n desmaquillador m.
making ['meɪkɪŋ] n (fig): **in the ~** en vías de
formación; **to have the ~s of** (person)
tener madera de.
maladjusted [mælə'dʒʌstɪd] adj
inadaptado.
maladroit [mælə'drɔɪt] adj torpe.
malaise [mæ'leɪz] n malestar m.
malaria [mə'lɛərɪə] n malaria.
Malawi [mə'lɑːwɪ] n Malawi m.

Malay [mə'leɪ] adj malayo ♦ n
malayo/a; (LING) malayo.
Malaya [mə'leɪə] n Malaya, Malaca.
Malayan [mə'leɪən] adj, n = **Malay**.
Malaysia [mə'leɪzɪə] n Malaisia, Malaysia.
Malaysian [mə'leɪzɪən] adj, n malaisio/a m/f,
malaysio/a m/f.
Maldive Islands ['mɔːldaɪv-], **Maldives**
['mɔːldaɪvz] npl: **the ~** las Maldivas.
male [meɪl] n (BIOL, ELEC) macho ♦ adj (sex,
attitude) masculino; (child etc) varón.
male chauvinist (pig) n machista m.
male nurse n enfermero.
malevolence [mə'lɛvələns] n malevolencia.
malevolent [mə'lɛvələnt] adj malévolo.
malfunction [mæl'fʌŋkʃən] n mal
funcionamiento.
malice ['mælɪs] n (ill will) malicia; (rancour)
rencor m.
malicious [mə'lɪʃəs] adj malicioso;
rencoroso.
maliciously [mə'lɪʃəslɪ] adv con
malevolencia, con malicia;
rencorosamente.
malign [mə'laɪn] vt difamar, calumniar
♦ adj maligno.
malignant [mə'lɪgnənt] adj (MED) maligno.
malinger [mə'lɪŋgə*] vi fingirse enfermo.
malingerer [mə'lɪŋgərə*] n enfermo/a
fingido/a.
mall [mɔːl] n (US: also: **shopping ~**) centro
comercial.
malleable ['mælɪəbl] adj maleable.
mallet ['mælɪt] n mazo.
malnutrition [mælnjuː'trɪʃən] n
desnutrición f.
malpractice [mæl'præktɪs] n negligencia
profesional.
malt [mɔːlt] n malta.
Malta ['mɔːltə] n Malta.
Maltese [mɔːl'tiːz] adj maltés/esa ♦ n, pl inv
maltés/esa m/f; (LING) maltés m.
maltreat [mæl'triːt] vt maltratar.
mammal ['mæml] n mamífero.
mammoth ['mæməθ] n mamut m ♦ adj
gigantesco.
man, pl **men** [mæn, mɛn] n hombre m;
(CHESS) pieza ♦ vt (NAUT) tripular; (MIL)
defender; **an old ~** un viejo; **~ and wife**
marido y mujer.
Man. abbr (Canada) = Manitoba.
manacle ['mænəkl] n esposa, manilla; **~s**
npl grillos mpl.
manage ['mænɪdʒ] vi arreglárselas ♦ vt (be
in charge of) dirigir; (person etc) manejar;
to ~ to do sth conseguir hacer algo; **to ~
without sth/sb** poder prescindir de algo/
algn.

manageable ['mænɪdʒəbl] adj manejable.

management ['mænɪdʒmənt] n dirección f, administración f; **"under new ~"** "bajo nueva dirección".

management accounting n contabilidad f de gestión.

management consultant n consultor(a) m/f en dirección de empresas.

manager ['mænɪdʒə*] n director m; (SPORT) entrenador m; **sales ~** jefe/a m/f de ventas.

manageress ['mænɪdʒərɛs] n directora; (SPORT) entrenadora.

managerial [mænə'dʒɪərɪəl] adj directivo.

managing director (MD) ['mænɪdʒɪŋ-] n director(a) m/f general.

Mancunian [mæŋ'kjuːnɪən] adj de Manchester ♦ n nativo/a (or habitante m/f) de Manchester.

mandarin ['mændərɪn] n (also: ~ **orange**) mandarina; (person) mandarín m.

mandate ['mændeɪt] n mandato.

mandatory ['mændətərɪ] adj obligatorio.

mandolin(e) ['mændəlɪn] n mandolina.

mane [meɪn] n (of horse) crin f; (of lion) melena.

maneuver [mə'nuːvə*] (US) = **manoeuvre**.

manful ['mænful] adj resuelto.

manfully ['mænfəlɪ] adv resueltamente.

mangetout [mɒnʒ'tuː] n tirabeque m.

mangle ['mæŋgl] vt mutilar, destrozar ♦ n escurridor m.

mango, ~es ['mæŋgəu] n mango.

mangrove ['mæŋgrəuv] n mangle m.

mangy ['meɪndʒɪ] adj roñoso; (MED) sarnoso.

manhandle ['mænhændl] vt maltratar; (move by hand: goods) manipular.

manhole ['mænhəul] n boca de acceso.

manhood ['mænhud] n edad f viril; (manliness) virilidad f.

man-hour ['mæn'auə*] n hora-hombre f.

manhunt ['mænhʌnt] n caza de hombre.

mania ['meɪnɪə] n manía.

maniac ['meɪnɪæk] n maníaco/a; (fig) maniático.

manic ['mænɪk] adj (behaviour, activity) frenético.

manic-depressive ['mænɪkdɪ'prɛsɪv] adj, n maniacodepresivo/a m/f.

manicure ['mænɪkjuə*] n manicura.

manicure set n estuche m de manicura.

manifest ['mænɪfɛst] vt manifestar, mostrar ♦ adj manifiesto ♦ n manifiesto.

manifestation [mænɪfɛs'teɪʃən] n manifestación f.

manifestly ['mænɪfɛstlɪ] adv evidentemente.

manifesto [mænɪ'fɛstəu] n manifiesto.

manifold ['mænɪfəuld] adj múltiples ♦ n (AUT etc): **exhaust ~** colector m de escape.

Manila [mə'nɪlə] n Manila.

manil(l)a [mə'nɪlə] n (paper, envelope) manila.

manipulate [mə'nɪpjuleɪt] vt manipular.

manipulation [mənɪpju'leɪʃən] n manipulación f, manejo.

mankind [mæn'kaɪnd] n humanidad f, género humano.

manliness ['mænlɪnɪs] n virilidad f, hombría.

manly ['mænlɪ] adj varonil.

man-made ['mæn'meɪd] adj artificial.

manna ['mænə] n maná m.

mannequin ['mænɪkɪn] n (dummy) maniquí m; (fashion model) maniquí m/f.

manner ['mænə*] n manera, modo; (behaviour) conducta, manera de ser; (type) clase f; **~s** npl modales mpl, educación fsg; **(good) ~s** (buena) educación fsg, (buenos) modales mpl; **bad ~s** falta sg de educación, pocos modales mpl; **all ~ of** toda clase or suerte de.

mannerism ['mænərɪzəm] n gesto típico.

mannerly ['mænəlɪ] adj bien educado, formal.

man(o)euvrable [mə'nuːvrəbl] adj (car etc) manejable.

manoeuvre, (US) maneuver [mə'nuːvə*] vt, vi maniobrar ♦ n maniobra; **to ~ sb into doing sth** manipular a algn para que haga algo.

manor ['mænə*] n (also: ~ **house**) casa solariega.

manpower ['mænpauə*] n mano f de obra.

Manpower Services Commission (MSC) n (BRIT) comisión para el aprovechamiento de los recursos humanos.

manservant ['mænsəvənt] n criado.

mansion ['mænʃən] n mansión f.

manslaughter ['mænslɔːtə*] n homicidio involuntario.

mantelpiece ['mæntlpiːs] n repisa de la chimenea.

mantle ['mæntl] n manto.

man-to-man ['mæntə'mæn] adj de hombre a hombre.

manual ['mænjuəl] adj manual ♦ n manual m; **~ worker** obrero, trabajador m manual.

manufacture [mænju'fæktʃə*] vt fabricar ♦ n fabricación f.

manufactured goods [mænju'fæktʃəd-] npl manufacturas fpl, bienes mpl manufacturados.

manufacturer [mænju'fæktʃərə*] *n*
fabricante *m/f*.
manufacturing industries [mænju'fæk
tʃərɪŋ-] *npl* industrias *fpl* manufactureras.
manure [mə'njuə*] *n* estiércol *m*, abono.
manuscript ['mænjuskrɪpt] *n* manuscrito.
Manx [mæŋks] *adj* de la Isla de Man.
many ['mɛnɪ] *adj* muchos/as ◆ *pron* muchos/
as; **a great ~** muchísimos, un buen
número de; **~ a time** muchas veces; **too
~ difficulties** demasiadas dificultades;
twice as ~ el doble; **how ~?** ¿cuántos?
Maori ['maurɪ] *adj*, *n* maorí *m/f*.
map [mæp] *n* mapa *m* ◆ *vt* trazar el mapa
de.
▶**map out** *vt* (*fig: career, holiday, essay*)
proyectar, planear.
maple ['meɪpl] *n* arce *m*, maple *m* (*LAM*).
mar [ma:*] *vt* estropear.
Mar. *abbr* (= *March*) mar.
marathon ['mærəθən] *n* maratón *m* ◆ *adj*: **a
~ session** una sesión maratoniana.
marathon runner *n* corredor(a) *m/f* de
maratones.
marauder [mə'rɔ:də*] *n* merodeador(a) *m/f*.
marble ['ma:bl] *n* mármol *m*; (*toy*) canica.
March [ma:tʃ] *n* marzo.
march [ma:tʃ] *vi* (*MIL*) marchar; (*fig*)
caminar con resolución ◆ *n* marcha;
(*demonstration*) manifestación *f*.
marcher ['ma:tʃə*] *n* manifestante *m/f*.
marching ['ma:tʃɪŋ] *n*: **to give sb his ~
orders** (*fig*) mandar a paseo a algn;
(*employee*) poner de patitas en la calle a
algn.
march-past ['ma:tʃpa:st] *n* desfile *m*.
mare [mɛə*] *n* yegua.
margarine [ma:dʒə'ri:n] *n* margarina.
marg(e) [ma:dʒ] *n abbr* = **margarine**.
margin ['ma:dʒɪn] *n* margen *m*.
marginal ['ma:dʒɪnl] *adj* marginal.
marginally ['ma:dʒɪnəlɪ] *adv* ligeramente.
marginal seat *n* (*POL*) circunscripción *f*
políticamente no definida.
marigold ['mærɪgəuld] *n* caléndula.
marijuana [mærɪ'wa:nə] *n* marihuana.
marina [mə'ri:nə] *n* marina.
marinade [mærɪ'neɪd] *n* adobo.
marinate ['mærɪneɪt] *vt* adobar.
marine [mə'ri:n] *adj* marino ◆ *n* soldado de
infantería de marina.
marine insurance *n* seguro marítimo.
mariner ['mærɪnə*] *n* marinero, marino.
marionette [mærɪə'nɛt] *n* marioneta, títere
m.
marital ['mærɪtl] *adj* matrimonial; **~ status**
estado civil.
maritime ['mærɪtaɪm] *adj* marítimo.

marjoram ['ma:dʒərəm] *n* mejorana.
mark [ma:k] *n* marca, señal *f*; (*imprint*)
huella; (*stain*) mancha; (*BRIT SCOL*) nota;
(*currency*) marco ◆ *vt* (*also SPORT: player*)
marcar; (*stain*) manchar; (*BRIT SCOL*)
calificar, corregir; **punctuation ~s** signos
mpl de puntuación; **to be quick off the ~**
(*fig*) ser listo; **up to the ~** (*in efficiency*) a
la altura de las circunstancias; **to ~ time**
marcar el paso.
▶**mark down** *vt* (*reduce: prices, goods*)
rebajar.
▶**mark off** *vt* (*tick*) indicar, señalar.
▶**mark out** *vt* trazar.
▶**mark up** *vt* (*price*) aumentar.
marked [ma:kt] *adj* marcado, acusado.
markedly ['ma:kɪdlɪ] *adv* marcadamente,
apreciablemente.
marker ['ma:kə*] *n* (*sign*) marcador *m*;
(*bookmark*) registro.
market ['ma:kɪt] *n* mercado ◆ *vt* (*COMM*)
comercializar; (*promote*) publicitar; **open
~** mercado libre; **to be on the ~** estar en
venta; **to play the ~** jugar a la bolsa.
marketable ['ma:kɪtəbl] *adj* comerciable.
market analysis *n* análisis *m* del mercado.
market day *n* día *m* de mercado.
market demand *n* demanda de mercado.
market economy *n* economía de
mercado.
market forces *npl* tendencias *fpl* del
mercado.
market garden *n* (*BRIT*) huerto.
marketing ['ma:kɪtɪŋ] *n* marketing *m*,
mercadotecnia.
marketing manager *n* director *m* de
marketing.
market leader *n* líder *m* de ventas.
marketplace ['ma:kɪtpleɪs] *n* mercado.
market price *n* precio de mercado.
market research *n* (*COMM*) estudios *mpl* de
mercado.
market value *n* valor *m* en el mercado.
marking ['ma:kɪŋ] *n* (*on animal*) pinta; (*on
road*) señal *f*.
marking ink *n* tinta indeleble *or* de
marcar.
marksman ['ma:ksmən] *n* tirador *m*.
marksmanship ['ma:ksmənʃɪp] *n* puntería.
mark-up ['ma:kʌp] *n* (*COMM: margin*)
margen *m* de beneficio; (: *increase*)
aumento.
marmalade ['ma:məleɪd] *n* mermelada de
naranja.
maroon [mə'ru:n] *vt*: **to be ~ed**
(*shipwrecked*) naufragar; (*fig*) quedar
abandonado ◆ *adj* granate *inv*.
marquee [ma:'ki:] *n* carpa, entoldado.

marquess, marquis ['mɑːkwɪs] n marqués m.

Marrakech, Marrakesh [mærə'keʃ] n Marrakech m.

marriage ['mærɪdʒ] n (state) matrimonio; (wedding) boda; (act) casamiento.

marriage bureau n agencia matrimonial.

marriage certificate n partida de casamiento.

marriage guidance, (US) **marriage counseling** n orientación f matrimonial.

marriage of convenience n matrimonio de conveniencia.

married ['mærɪd] adj casado; (life, love) conyugal.

marrow ['mærəu] n médula; (vegetable) calabacín m.

marry ['mærɪ] vt casarse con; (subj: father, priest etc) casar ♦ vi (also: get married) casarse.

Mars [mɑːz] n Marte m.

Marseilles [mɑː'seɪ] n Marsella.

marsh [mɑːʃ] n pantano; (salt ~) marisma.

marshal ['mɑːʃl] n (MIL) mariscal m; (at sports meeting, demonstration etc) oficial m; (US: of police, fire department) jefe/a m/f ♦ vt (facts) ordenar; (soldiers) formar.

marshalling yard ['mɑːʃəlɪŋ-] n (RAIL) estación f clasificadora.

marshmallow ['mɑːʃmæləu] n (BOT) malvavisco; (sweet) esponja, dulce m de merengue blando.

marshy ['mɑːʃɪ] adj pantanoso.

marsupial [mɑː'suːpɪəl] adj, n marsupial m.

martial ['mɑːʃl] adj marcial.

martial arts npl artes fpl marciales.

martial law n ley f marcial.

martin ['mɑːtɪn] n (also: house ~) avión m.

martyr ['mɑːtə*] n mártir m/f ♦ vt martirizar.

martyrdom ['mɑːtədəm] n martirio.

marvel ['mɑːvl] n maravilla, prodigio ♦ vi. **to ~ (at)** maravillarse (de).

marvellous, (US) **marvelous** ['mɑːvləs] adj maravilloso.

marvel(l)ously ['mɑːvləslɪ] adv maravillosamente.

Marxism ['mɑːksɪzəm] n marxismo.

Marxist ['mɑːksɪst] adj, n marxista m/f.

marzipan ['mɑːzɪpæn] n mazapán m.

mascara [mæs'kɑːrə] n rimel m.

mascot ['mæskət] n mascota.

masculine ['mæskjulɪn] adj masculino.

masculinity [mæskju'lɪnɪtɪ] n masculinidad f.

MASH [mæʃ] n abbr (US) = mobile army surgical hospital.

mash [mæʃ] n (mix) mezcla; (CULIN) puré m; (pulp) amasijo.

mashed potatoes [mæʃt-] npl puré m de patatas or papas (LAM).

mask [mɑːsk] n (also ELEC) máscara ♦ vt enmascarar.

masochism ['mæsəkɪzəm] n masoquismo.

masochist ['mæsəukɪst] n masoquista m/f.

mason ['meɪsn] n (also: stone~) albañil m; (also: free~) masón m.

masonic [mə'sɒnɪk] adj masónico.

masonry ['meɪsnrɪ] n masonería; (building) mampostería.

masquerade [mæskə'reɪd] n baile m de máscaras; (fig) mascarada ♦ vi: **to ~ as** disfrazarse de, hacerse pasar por.

mass [mæs] n (people) muchedumbre f; (PHYSICS) masa; (REL) misa; (great quantity) montón m ♦ vi reunirse; (MIL) concentrarse; **the ~es** las masas; **to go to ~** ir a or oír misa.

Mass. abbr (US) = Massachusetts.

massacre ['mæsəkə*] n masacre f ♦ vt masacrar.

massage ['mæsɑːʒ] n masaje m ♦ vt dar masajes or un masaje a.

masseur [mæ'sɜː*] n masajista m.

masseuse [mæ'sɜːz] n masajista f.

massive ['mæsɪv] adj enorme; (support, intervention) masivo.

mass media npl medios mpl de comunicación de masas.

mass meeting n (of everyone concerned) reunión f en masa; (huge) mitin m.

mass-produce ['mæsprə'djuːs] vt fabricar en serie.

mass-production ['mæsprə'dʌkʃən] n fabricación f or producción f en serie.

mast [mɑːst] n (NAUT) mástil m; (RADIO etc) torre f, antena.

mastectomy [mæs'tektəmɪ] n mastectomía.

master ['mɑːstə*] n (of servant, animal) amo; (fig: of situation) dueño; (ART, MUS) maestro; (in secondary school) profesor m; (title for boys): **M~ X** Señorito X ♦ vt dominar.

master disk n (COMPUT) disco maestro.

masterful ['mɑːstəful] adj magistral, dominante.

master key n llave f maestra.

masterly ['mɑːstəlɪ] adj magistral.

mastermind ['mɑːstəmaɪnd] n inteligencia superior ♦ vt dirigir, planear.

Master of Arts (MA) n licenciatura superior en Letras; see also **master's degree**.

Master of Ceremonies n encargado de protocolo.

Master of Science (MSc) *n* licenciatura superior en Ciencias; *see also* **master's degree**.

masterpiece ['mɑːstəpiːs] *n* obra maestra.

master plan *n* plan *m* rector.

master's degree *n* máster *m*; *ver recuadro*.

MASTER'S DEGREE

Los estudios de postgrado británicos que llevan a la obtención de un **master's degree** *consisten generalmente en una combinación de curso(s) académico(s) y tesina ("dissertation") sobre un tema original, o bien únicamente la redacción de una tesina. El primer caso es el más frecuente para los títulos de "MA" ("Master of Arts") y "MSc" ("Master of Science"), mientras que los de "MLitt" ("Master of Letters") o "MPhil" ("Master of Philosophy") se obtienen normalmente mediante tesina. En algunas universidades, como las escocesas, el título de* **master's degree** *no es de postgrado, sino que corresponde a la licenciatura.*

---

master stroke *n* golpe *m* maestro.

mastiff ['mæstɪf] *n* mastín *m*.

masturbate ['mæstəbeɪt] *vi* masturbarse.

masturbation [mæstə'beɪʃən] *n* masturbación *f*.

mat [mæt] *n* alfombrilla; (*also:* **door~**) felpudo ♦ *adj* = **matt**.

MAT *n abbr* (= *machine-assisted translation*) TAO.

match [mætʃ] *n* cerilla, fósforo; (*game*) partido; (*fig*) igual *m/f* ♦ *vt* emparejar; (*go well with*) hacer juego con; (*equal*) igualar ♦ *vi* hacer juego; **to be a good ~** hacer buena pareja.

matchbox ['mætʃbɒks] *n* caja de cerillas.

matching ['mætʃɪŋ] *adj* que hace juego.

matchless ['mætʃlɪs] *adj* sin par.

matchmaker ['mætʃmeɪkə*] *n* casamentero.

mate [meɪt] *n* (*work~*) compañero/a, colega *m/f*; (*col: friend*) amigo/a, compadre *m/f* (*LAM*); (*animal*) macho/hembra; (*in merchant navy*) primer oficial *m* ♦ *vi* acoplarse, parearse ♦ *vt* acoplar, parear.

material [mə'tɪərɪəl] *n* (*substance*) materia; (*equipment*) material *m*; (*cloth*) tela, tejido ♦ *adj* material; (*important*) esencial; **~s** *npl* materiales *mpl*; (*equipment etc*) artículos *mpl*.

materialistic [mətɪərɪə'lɪstɪk] *adj* materialista.

materialize [mə'tɪərɪəlaɪz] *vi*

materializarse.

materially [mə'tɪərɪəlɪ] *adv* materialmente.

maternal [mə'tɜːnl] *adj* maternal; **~ grandmother** abuela materna.

maternity [mə'tɜːnɪtɪ] *n* maternidad *f*.

maternity benefit *n* subsidio por maternidad.

maternity dress *n* vestido premamá.

maternity hospital *n* hospital *m* de maternidad.

maternity leave *n* baja por maternidad.

math [mæθ] *n abbr* (*US*: = *mathematics*) matemáticas *fpl*.

mathematical [mæθə'mætɪkl] *adj* matemático.

mathematically [mæθɪ'mætɪklɪ] *adv* matemáticamente.

mathematician [mæθəmə'tɪʃən] *n* matemático.

mathematics [mæθə'mætɪks] *n* matemáticas *fpl*.

maths [mæθs] *n abbr* (*BRIT*: = *mathematics*) matemáticas *fpl*.

matinée ['mætɪneɪ] *n* función *f* de la tarde, vermú(t) *m* (*LAM*).

mating ['meɪtɪŋ] *n* apareamiento.

mating call *n* llamada del macho.

mating season *n* época de celo.

matins ['mætɪnz] *n* maitines *mpl*.

matriarchal [meɪtrɪ'ɑːkl] *adj* matriarcal.

matrices ['meɪtrɪsiːz] *pl of* **matrix**.

matriculation [mətrɪkju'leɪʃən] *n* matriculación *f*, matrícula.

matrimonial [mætrɪ'məunɪəl] *adj* matrimonial.

matrimony ['mætrɪmənɪ] *n* matrimonio.

matrix, *pl* **matrices** ['meɪtrɪks, 'meɪtrɪsiːz] *n* matriz *f*.

matron ['meɪtrən] *n* (*in hospital*) enfermera jefe; (*in school*) ama de llaves.

matronly ['meɪtrənlɪ] *adj* de matrona; (*fig: figure*) corpulento.

matt [mæt] *adj* mate.

matted ['mætɪd] *adj* enmarañado.

matter ['mætə*] *n* cuestión *f*, asunto; (*PHYSICS*) sustancia, materia; (*content*) contenido; (*MED: pus*) pus *m* ♦ *vi* importar; **it doesn't ~** no importa; **what's the ~?** ¿qué pasa?; **no ~ what** pase lo que pase; **as a ~ of course** por rutina; **as a ~ of fact** en realidad; **printed ~** impresos *mpl*; **reading ~** material *m* de lectura, lecturas *fpl*.

matter-of-fact ['mætərəv'fækt] *adj* (*style*) prosaico; (*person*) práctico; (*voice*) neutro.

mattress ['mætrɪs] *n* colchón *m*.

mature [mə'tjuə*] adj maduro ♦ vi madurar.
mature student n estudiante de más de 21 años.
maturity [mə'tjuərɪtɪ] n madurez f.
maudlin ['mɔːdlɪn] adj llorón/ona.
maul [mɔːl] vt magullar.
Mauritania [mɔːrɪ'teɪnɪə] n Mauritania.
Mauritius [mə'rɪʃəs] n Mauricio.
mausoleum [mɔːsə'lɪəm] n mausoleo.
mauve [məuv] adj de color malva.
maverick ['mævrɪk] n (fig) inconformista m/f, persona independiente.
mawkish ['mɔːkɪʃ] adj sensiblero, empalagoso.
max. abbr = maximum.
maxim ['mæksɪm] n máxima.
maxima ['mæksɪmə] pl of **maximum**.
maximize ['mæksɪmaɪz] vt (profits etc) llevar al máximo; (chances) maximizar.
maximum ['mæksɪməm] adj máximo ♦ n (pl **maxima** ['mæksɪmə]) máximo.
May [meɪ] n mayo.
may [meɪ] vi (conditional: **might**) (indicating possibility): **he ~ come** puede que venga; (be allowed to): **~ I smoke?** ¿puedo fumar?; (wishes): **~ God bless you!** ¡que Dios le bendiga!; **~ I sit here?** ¿me puedo sentar aquí?
maybe ['meɪbiː] adv quizá(s); **~ not** quizá(s) no.
May Day n el primero de Mayo.
mayday ['meɪdeɪ] n señal f de socorro.
mayhem ['meɪhem] n caos m total.
mayonnaise [meɪə'neɪz] n mayonesa.
mayor [mɛə*] n alcalde m.
mayoress ['mɛərɛs] n alcaldesa.
maypole ['meɪpəul] n mayo.
maze [meɪz] n laberinto.
MB abbr (COMPUT) = **megabyte**; (Canada) = Manitoba.
MBA n abbr (= Master of Business Administration) título universitario.
MBBS, MBChB n abbr (BRIT: = Bachelor of Medicine and Surgery) título universitario.
MBE n abbr (BRIT: = Member of the Order of the British Empire) título ceremonial.
MC n abbr (= master of ceremonies) e.p.; (US: = Member of Congress) diputado del Congreso de los Estados Unidos.
MCAT n abbr (US) = Medical College Admissions Test.
MCP n abbr (BRIT col) = **male chauvinist pig**.
MD n abbr (= Doctor of Medicine) título universitario; (COMM) = **managing director** ♦ abbr (US) = Maryland.
Md. abbr (US) = Maryland.
MDT n abbr (US: = mountain daylight time) hora de verano de las Montañas

Rocosas.
ME abbr (US POST) = Maine ♦ n abbr (US MED) = medical examiner; (MED = myalgic encephalomyelitis) encefalomielitis f miálgica.
me [miː] pron (direct) me; (stressed, after pronoun) mí; **can you hear ~?** ¿me oyes?; **he heard ME!** me oyó a mí; **it's ~** soy yo; **give them to ~** dámelos; **with/without ~** conmigo/sin mí; **it's for ~** es para mí.
meadow ['mɛdəu] n prado, pradera.
meagre, (US) **meager** ['miːgə*] adj escaso, pobre.
meal [miːl] n comida; (flour) harina; **to go out for a ~** salir a comer.
meals on wheels nsg (BRIT) servicio de alimentación a domicilio para necesitados y tercera edad.
mealtime ['miːltaɪm] n hora de comer.
mealy-mouthed ['miːlɪmauðd] adj: **to be ~** no decir nunca las cosas claras.
mean [miːn] adj (with money) tacaño; (unkind) mezquino, malo; (average) medio; (US: vicious: animal) resabiado; (: person) malicioso ♦ vt (pt, pp **meant** [mɛnt]) (signify) querer decir, significar; (intend): **to ~ to do sth** tener la intención de or pensar hacer algo ♦ n medio, término medio; **do you ~ it?** ¿lo dices en serio?; **what do you ~?** ¿qué quiere decir?; **to be meant for sb/sth** ser para algn/algo; see also **means**.
meander [mɪ'ændə*] vi (river) serpentear; (person) vagar.
meaning ['miːnɪŋ] n significado, sentido.
meaningful ['miːnɪŋful] adj significativo.
meaningless ['miːnɪŋlɪs] adj sin sentido.
meanness ['miːnnɪs] n (with money) tacañería; (unkindness) maldad f, mezquindad f.
means [miːnz] npl medio sg, manera sg; (resource) recursos mpl, medios mpl; **by ~ of** mediante, por medio de; **by all ~!** ¡naturalmente!, ¡claro que sí!
means test n control m de los recursos económicos.
meant [mɛnt] pt, pp of **mean**.
meantime ['miːntaɪm], **meanwhile** ['miːnwaɪl] adv (also: **in the meantime**) mientras tanto.
measles ['miːzlz] n sarampión m.
measly ['miːzlɪ] adj (col) miserable.
measurable ['mɛʒərəbl] adj mensurable, que se puede medir.
measure ['mɛʒə*] vt medir; (for clothes etc) tomar las medidas a ♦ vi medir ♦ n medida; (ruler) cinta métrica, metro; **a litre ~** una medida de un litro; **some ~ of**

success cierto éxito; **to take ~s to do sth** tomar medidas para hacer algo.

▶**measure up** *vi*: **to ~ up (to)** estar a la altura (de).

measured ['mɛʒəd] *adj* moderado; (*tone*) mesurado.

measurement ['mɛʒəmənt] *n* (*measure*) medida; (*act*) medición *f*; **to take sb's ~s** tomar las medidas a algn.

meat [miːt] *n* carne *f*; **cold ~s** fiambres *mpl*; **crab ~** carne *f* de cangrejo.

meatball ['miːtbɔːl] *n* albóndiga.

meat pie *n* pastel *m* de carne.

meaty ['miːtɪ] *adj* (*person*) fuerte, corpulento; (*role*) sustancioso; **a ~ meal** una comida con bastante carne.

Mecca ['mɛkə] *n* (*city*) la Meca; (*fig*) meca.

mechanic [mɪ'kænɪk] *n* mecánico/a.

mechanical [mɪ'kænɪkl] *adj* mecánico.

mechanical engineering *n* (*science*) ingeniería mecánica; (*industry*) construcción *f* mecánica.

mechanics [mə'kænɪks] *n* mecánica ♦ *npl* mecanismo *sg*.

mechanism ['mɛkənɪzəm] *n* mecanismo.

mechanization [mɛkənaɪ'zeɪʃən] *n* mecanización *f*.

mechanize ['mɛkənaɪz] *vt* mecanizar; (*factory etc*) automatizar.

MEd *n abbr* (= *Master of Education*) título universitario.

medal ['mɛdl] *n* medalla.

medallion [mɪ'dælɪən] *n* medallón *m*.

medallist, (*US*) **medalist** ['mɛdlɪst] *n* (*SPORT*) medallista *m/f*.

meddle ['mɛdl] *vi*: **to ~ in** entrometerse en; **to ~ with sth** manosear algo.

meddlesome ['mɛdlsəm], **meddling** ['mɛdlɪŋ] *adj* (*interfering*) entrometido; (*touching things*) curioso.

media ['miːdɪə] *npl* medios *mpl* de comunicación.

media circus *n* excesivo despliegue informativo.

mediaeval [mɛdɪ'iːvl] *adj* = **medieval.**

median ['miːdɪən] *n* (*US*: *also*: **~ strip**) mediana.

media research *n* estudio de los medios de publicidad.

mediate ['miːdɪeɪt] *vi* mediar.

mediation [miːdɪ'eɪʃən] *n* mediación *f*.

mediator ['miːdɪeɪtə*] *n* mediador(a) *m/f*.

Medicaid ['mɛdɪkeɪd] *n* (*US*) *programa de ayuda médica.*

medical ['mɛdɪkl] *adj* médico ♦ *n* (*also*: **~ examination**) reconocimiento médico.

medical certificate *n* certificado *m* médico.

Medicare ['mɛdɪkɛə*] *n* (*US*) *seguro médico del Estado.*

medicated ['mɛdɪkeɪtɪd] *adj* medicinal.

medication [mɛdɪ'keɪʃən] *n* (*drugs etc*) medicación *f*.

medicinal [mɛ'dɪsɪnl] *adj* medicinal.

medicine ['mɛdsɪn] *n* medicina; (*drug*) medicamento.

medicine chest *n* botiquín *m*.

medicine man *n* hechicero.

medieval, mediaeval [mɛdɪ'iːvl] *adj* medieval.

mediocre [miːdɪ'əukə*] *adj* mediocre.

mediocrity [miːdɪ'ɔkrɪtɪ] *n* mediocridad *f*.

meditate ['mɛdɪteɪt] *vi* meditar.

meditation [mɛdɪ'teɪʃən] *n* meditación *f*.

Mediterranean [mɛdɪtə'reɪnɪən] *adj* mediterráneo; **the ~ (Sea)** el (Mar *m*) Mediterráneo.

medium ['miːdɪəm] *adj* mediano; (*level, height*) medio ♦ *n* (*pl* **media**: *means*) medio; (*pl* **mediums**: *person*) médium *m/f*; **happy ~** punto justo.

medium-dry ['miːdɪəm'draɪ] *adj* semiseco.

medium-sized ['miːdɪəm'saɪzd] *adj* de tamaño mediano; (*clothes*) de (la) talla mediana.

medium wave *n* onda media.

medley ['mɛdlɪ] *n* mezcla; (*MUS*) popurrí *m*.

meek [miːk] *adj* manso, sumiso.

meekly ['miːklɪ] *adv* mansamente, dócilmente.

meet [miːt] *vb* (*pt, pp* **met** [mɛt]) *vt* encontrar; (*accidentally*) encontrarse con; (*by arrangement*) reunirse con; (*for the first time*) conocer; (*go and fetch*) ir a buscar; (*opponent*) enfrentarse con; (*obligations*) cumplir; (*bill, expenses*) pagar, costear ♦ *vi* encontrarse; (*in session*) reunirse; (*join*: *objects*) unirse; (*get to know*) conocerse ♦ *n* (*BRIT*: *HUNTING*) cacería; (*US*: *SPORT*) encuentro; **pleased to ~ you!** ¡encantado (de conocerle)!, ¡mucho gusto!

▶**meet up** *vi*: **to ~ up with sb** reunirse con algn.

▶**meet with** *vt fus* reunirse con; (*difficulty*) tropezar con.

meeting ['miːtɪŋ] *n* (*also SPORT*: *rally*) encuentro; (*arranged*) cita, compromiso (*LAM*); (*formal session, business meet*) reunión *f*; (*POL*) mitin *m*; **to call a ~** convocar una reunión.

meeting place *n* lugar *m* de reunión *or* encuentro.

megabyte ['mɛgəbaɪt] *n* (*COMPUT*) megabyte *m*, megaocteto.

megalomaniac [mɛgələu'meɪnɪæk] *adj, n* megalómano/a *m/f*.

megaphone ['mɛgəfəun] n megáfono.
megawatt ['mɛgəwɔt] n megavatio.
melancholy ['mɛlənkəlɪ] n melancolía ♦ adj melancólico.
melee ['mɛleɪ] n refriega.
mellow ['mɛləu] adj (wine) añejo; (sound, colour) suave; (fruit) maduro ♦ vi (person) madurar.
melodious [mɪ'ləudɪəs] adj melodioso.
melodrama ['mɛləudrɑːmə] n melodrama m.
melodramatic [mɛləudrə'mætɪk] adj melodramático.
melody ['mɛlədɪ] n melodía.
melon ['mɛlən] n melón m.
melt [mɛlt] vi (metal) fundirse; (snow) derretirse; (fig) ablandarse ♦ vt (also: ~ down) fundir; ~ed butter mantequilla derretida.
►**melt away** vi desvanecerse.
meltdown ['mɛltdaun] n (in nuclear reactor) fusión f (de un reactor nuclear).
melting point ['mɛltɪŋ-] n punto de fusión.
melting pot ['mɛltɪŋ-] n (fig) crisol m; to be in the ~ estar sobre el tapete.
member ['mɛmbə*] n (of political party) miembro; (of club) socio/a; M~ of Parliament (MP) (BRIT) diputado/a; M~ of the European Parliament (MEP) (BRIT) eurodiputado/a; M~ of the House of Representatives (MHR) (US) diputado/a del Congreso de los Estados Unidos; M~ of the Scottish Parliament (MSP) (BRIT) diputado/a del Parlamento escocés.
membership ['mɛmbəʃɪp] n (members) miembros mpl; socios mpl; (numbers) número de miembros or socios; to seek ~ of pedir el ingreso a.
membership card n carnet m de socio.
membrane ['mɛmbreɪn] n membrana.
memento [mə'mɛntəu] n recuerdo.
memo ['mɛməu] n nota (de servicio).
memoirs ['mɛmwɑːz] npl memorias fpl.
memo pad n bloc m de notas.
memorable ['mɛmərəbl] adj memorable.
memorandum, pl **memoranda** [mɛmə'rændəm, -də] n nota (de servicio); (POL) memorándum m.
memorial [mɪ'mɔːrɪəl] n monumento conmemorativo ♦ adj conmemorativo.
Memorial Day n (US) día de conmemoración de los caídos en la guerra.
memorize ['mɛməraɪz] vt aprender de memoria.
memory ['mɛmərɪ] n memoria; (recollection) recuerdo; to have a good/ bad ~ tener buena/mala memoria; loss of

~ pérdida de memoria.
men [mɛn] pl of **man**.
menace ['mɛnəs] n amenaza; (col: nuisance) lata ♦ vt amenazar; a public ~ un peligro público.
menacing ['mɛnɪsɪŋ] adj amenazador(a).
menacingly ['mɛnɪsɪŋlɪ] adv amenazadoramente.
menagerie [mɪ'nædʒərɪ] n casa de fieras.
mend [mɛnd] vt reparar, arreglar; (darn) zurcir ♦ vi reponerse ♦ n (gen) remiendo; (darn) zurcido; to be on the ~ ir mejorando.
mending ['mɛndɪŋ] n arreglo, reparación f; (clothes) ropa por remendar.
menial ['miːnɪəl] adj (pej) bajo, servil.
meningitis [mɛnɪn'dʒaɪtɪs] n meningitis f.
menopause ['mɛnəupɔːz] n menopausia.
men's room n (US): the ~ el servicio de caballeros.
menstrual ['mɛnstruəl] adj menstrual.
menstruate ['mɛnstrueɪt] vi menstruar.
menstruation [mɛnstru'eɪʃən] n menstruación f.
menswear ['mɛnzwɛə*] n confección f de caballero.
mental ['mɛntl] adj mental; ~ illness enfermedad f mental.
mental hospital n (hospital m) psiquiátrico.
mentality [mɛn'tælɪtɪ] n mentalidad f.
mentally ['mɛntlɪ] adv: to be ~ handicapped ser un disminuido mental.
menthol ['mɛnθɔl] n mentol m.
mention ['mɛnʃən] n mención f ♦ vt mencionar; (speak of) hablar de; don't ~ it! ¡de nada!; I need hardly ~ that ... huelga decir que ...; not to ~, without ~ing sin contar.
mentor ['mɛntɔː*] n mentor m.
menu ['mɛnjuː] n (set ~) menú m; (printed) carta; (COMPUT) menú m.
menu-driven ['mɛnjuːdrɪvn] adj (COMPUT) guiado por menú.
MEP n abbr see **Member of the European Parliament**.
mercantile ['məːkəntaɪl] adj mercantil.
mercenary ['məːsɪnərɪ] adj, n mercenario.
merchandise ['məːtʃəndaɪz] n mercancías fpl.
merchandiser ['məːtʃəndaɪzə*] n comerciante m/f, tratante m.
merchant ['məːtʃənt] n comerciante m/f.
merchant bank n (BRIT) banco comercial.
merchantman ['məːtʃəntmən] n buque m mercante.
merchant navy, (US) **merchant marine** n marina mercante.

merciful ['mɔːsɪful] *adj* compasivo.
mercifully ['mɔːsɪfulɪ] *adv* con compasión;
(*fortunately*) afortunadamente.
merciless ['mɔːsɪlɪs] *adj* despiadado.
mercilessly ['mɔːsɪlɪslɪ] *adv*
despiadadamente, sin piedad.
mercurial [mɔː'kjuərɪəl] *adj* veleidoso,
voluble.
mercury ['mɔːkjurɪ] *n* mercurio.
mercy ['mɔːsɪ] *n* compasión *f*; (*REL*)
misericordia; **at the ~ of** a la merced de.
mercy killing *n* eutanasia.
mere [mɪə*] *adj* simple, mero.
merely ['mɪəlɪ] *adv* simplemente, sólo.
merge [mɔːdʒ] *vt* (*join*) unir; (*mix*) mezclar;
(*fuse*) fundir; (*COMPUT: files, text*)
intercalar ♦ *vi* unirse; (*COMM*) fusionarse.
merger ['mɔːdʒə*] *n* (*COMM*) fusión *f*.
meridian [mə'rɪdɪən] *n* meridiano.
meringue [mə'ræŋ] *n* merengue *m*.
merit ['mɛrɪt] *n* mérito ♦ *vt* merecer.
meritocracy [mɛrɪ'tɔkrəsɪ] *n* meritocracia.
mermaid ['mɔːmeɪd] *n* sirena.
merrily ['mɛrɪlɪ] *adv* alegremente.
merriment ['mɛrɪmənt] *n* alegría.
merry ['mɛrɪ] *adj* alegre; **M~ Christmas!**
¡Felices Pascuas!
merry-go-round ['mɛrɪɡəuraund] *n* tiovivo.
mesh [mɛʃ] *n* malla; (*TECH*) engranaje *m* ♦
vi (*gears*) engranar; **wire ~** tela metálica.
mesmerize ['mɛzməraɪz] *vt* hipnotizar.
mess [mɛs] *n* confusión *f*; (*of objects*)
revoltijo; (*tangle*) lío; (*MIL*) comedor *m*; **to
be (in) a ~** (*room*) estar revuelto; **to be/
get o.s. in a ~** estar/meterse en un lío.
▶**mess about**, **mess around** *vi* (*col*)
perder el tiempo; (*pass the time*) pasar el
rato.
▶**mess about** *or* **around with** *vt fus* (*col:
play with*) divertirse con; (: *handle*)
manosear.
▶**mess up** *vt* (*disarrange*) desordenar;
(*spoil*) estropear; (*dirty*) ensuciar.
message ['mɛsɪdʒ] *n* recado, mensaje *m*; **to
get the ~** (*fig, col*) enterarse.
message switching *n* (*COMPUT*)
conmutación *f* de mensajes.
messenger ['mɛsɪndʒə*] *n* mensajero/a.
Messiah [mɪ'saɪə] *n* Mesías *m*.
Messrs *abbr* (*on letters:* = *Messieurs*) Sres.
messy ['mɛsɪ] *adj* (*dirty*) sucio; (*untidy*)
desordenado; (*confused: situation etc*)
confuso.
Met [mɛt] *n abbr* (*US*) = *Metropolitan Opera*.
met [mɛt] *pt, pp of* **meet** ♦ *adj abbr*
= **meteorological**.
metabolism [mɛ'tæbəlɪzəm] *n*
metabolismo.

metal ['mɛtl] *n* metal *m*.
metallic [mɛ'tælɪk] *adj* metálico.
metallurgy [mɛ'tælədʒɪ] *n* metalurgia.
metalwork ['mɛtlwɔːk] *n* (*craft*)
metalistería.
metamorphosis, *pl* **metamorphoses**
[mɛtə'mɔːfəsɪs, -siːz] *n* metamorfosis *f inv*.
metaphor ['mɛtəfə*] *n* metáfora.
metaphorical [mɛtə'fɔrɪkl] *adj* metafórico.
metaphysics [mɛtə'fɪzɪks] *n* metafísica.
mete [miːt]: **to ~ out** *vt fus* (*punishment*)
imponer.
meteor ['miːtɪə*] *n* meteoro.
meteoric [miːtɪ'ɔrɪk] *adj* (*fig*) meteórico.
meteorite ['miːtɪəraɪt] *n* meteorito.
meteorological [miːtɪərə'lɔdʒɪkl] *adj*
meteorológico.
meteorology [miːtɪə'rɔlədʒɪ] *n*
meteorología.
meter ['miːtə*] *n* (*instrument*) contador *m*;
(*US: unit*) = **metre** ♦ *vt* (*US POST*)
franquear; **parking ~** parquímetro.
methane ['miːθeɪn] *n* metano.
method ['mɛθəd] *n* método; **~ of payment**
método de pago.
methodical [mɪ'θɔdɪkl] *adj* metódico.
Methodist ['mɛθədɪst] *adj, n* metodista *m/f*.
methodology [mɛθə'dɔlədʒɪ] *n*
metodología.
meths [mɛθs], **methylated spirit(s)**
['mɛθɪleɪtɪd-] *n* (*BRIT*) alcohol *m* metilado *or*
desnaturalizado.
meticulous [mɛ'tɪkjuləs] *adj* meticuloso.
metre, (*US*) **meter** ['miːtə*] *n* metro.
metric ['mɛtrɪk] *adj* métrico; **to go ~** pasar
al sistema métrico.
metrication [mɛtrɪ'keɪʃən] *n* conversión *f* al
sistema métrico.
metric system *n* sistema *m* métrico.
metric ton *n* tonelada métrica.
metronome ['mɛtrənəum] *n* metrónomo.
metropolis [mɪ'trɔpəlɪs] *n* metrópoli(s) *f*.
metropolitan [mɛtrə'pɔlɪtən] *adj*
metropolitano.
Metropolitan Police *n* (*BRIT*): **the ~** la
policía londinense.
mettle ['mɛtl] *n* valor *m*, ánimo.
mew [mjuː] *vi* (*cat*) maullar.
mews [mjuːz] (*BRIT*) *n*: **~ cottage** *casa
acondicionada en antiguos establos o
cocheras*; **~ flat** *piso en antiguos establos
o cocheras*.
Mexican ['mɛksɪkən] *adj, n* mejicano/a *m/f*,
mexicano/a *m/f* (*LAM*).
Mexico ['mɛksɪkəu] *n* Méjico, México
(*LAM*).
Mexico City *n* Ciudad *f* de Méjico *or*
México (*LAM*).

mezzanine ['mɛtsəniːn] n entresuelo.
MFA n abbr (US: = Master of Fine Arts) título universitario.
mfr abbr (= manufacturer) fab.
mg abbr (= milligram) mg.
Mgr abbr (= Monseigneur, Monsignor) Mons.
mgr abbr = manager.
MHR n abbr (US) see **Member of the House of Representatives.**
MHz abbr (= megahertz) MHz.
MI abbr (US) = Michigan.
MI5 n abbr (BRIT: = Military Intelligence 5) servicio de contraespionaje del gobierno británico.
MI6 n abbr (BRIT: = Military Intelligence 6) servicio de inteligencia del gobierno británico.
MIA abbr (= missing in action) desaparecido.
miaow [miːˈau] vi maullar.
mice [maɪs] pl of **mouse.**
Mich. abbr (US) = Michigan.
mickey ['mɪkɪ] n: **to take the ~ out of sb** tomar el pelo a algn.
micro... [maɪkrəu] pref micro....
microbe ['maɪkrəub] n microbio.
microbiology [maɪkrəubaɪˈɔlədʒɪ] n microbiología.
microchip ['maɪkrəutʃɪp] n microchip m, microplaqueta.
micro(computer) ['maɪkrəu(kəmˈpjuːtə*)] n microordenador m, microcomputador m.
microcosm ['maɪkrəukɔzəm] n microcosmo.
microeconomics ['maɪkrəuiːkəˈnɔmɪks] n microeconomía.
microfiche ['maɪkrəufiːʃ] n microficha.
microfilm ['maɪkrəufɪlm] n microfilm m.
microlight ['maɪkrəulaɪt] n ultraligero.
micrometer [maɪˈkrɔmɪtə*] n micrómetro.
microphone ['maɪkrəfəun] n micrófono.
microprocessor ['maɪkrəuˈprəusɛsə*] n microprocesador m.
microscope ['maɪkrəskəup] n microscopio; **under the ~** al microscopio.
microscopic [maɪkrəˈskɔpɪk] adj microscópico.
microwave ['maɪkrəuweɪv] n (also: ~ **oven**) horno microondas.
mid [mɪd] adj: **in ~ May** a mediados de mayo; **in ~ afternoon** a media tarde; **in ~ air** en el aire; **he's in his ~ thirties** tiene unos treinta y cinco años.
midday [mɪdˈdeɪ] n mediodía m.
middle ['mɪdl] n medio, centro; (waist) cintura ♦ adj de en medio; **in the ~ of the night** en plena noche; **I'm in the ~ of reading it** lo estoy leyendo ahora mismo.
middle-aged [mɪdlˈeɪdʒd] adj de mediana

edad.
Middle Ages npl: **the ~** la Edad sg Media.
middle class n: **the ~(es)** la clase media ♦ adj (also: **middle-class**) de clase media.
Middle East n Oriente m Medio.
middleman ['mɪdlmæn] n intermediario.
middle management n dirección f de nivel medio.
middle name n segundo nombre m.
middle-of-the-road ['mɪdləvðəˈrəud] adj moderado.
middleweight ['mɪdlweɪt] n (BOXING) peso medio.
middling ['mɪdlɪŋ] adj mediano.
Middx abbr (BRIT) = Middlesex.
midge [mɪdʒ] n mosquito.
midget ['mɪdʒɪt] n enano/a.
midi system n cadena midi.
Midlands ['mɪdləndz] npl región central de Inglaterra.
midnight ['mɪdnaɪt] n medianoche f; **at ~** a medianoche.
midriff ['mɪdrɪf] n diafragma m.
midst [mɪdst] n: **in the ~ of** entre, en medio de.
midsummer [mɪdˈsʌmə*] n: **a ~ day** un día de pleno verano.
Midsummer's Day n Día m de San Juan.
midway [mɪdˈweɪ] adj, adv: ~ **(between)** a mitad de camino or a medio camino (entre).
midweek [mɪdˈwiːk] adv entre semana.
midwife, pl **midwives** ['mɪdwaɪf, -waɪvz] n comadrona.
midwifery ['mɪdwɪfərɪ] n tocología.
midwinter [mɪdˈwɪntə*] n: **in ~** en pleno invierno.
miffed [mɪft] adj (col) mosqueado.
might [maɪt] vb see **may** ♦ n fuerza, poder m; **he ~ be there** puede que esté allí, a lo mejor está allí; **I ~ as well go** más vale que vaya, **you ~ like to try** podría intentar.
mightily ['maɪtɪlɪ] adv fuertemente, poderosamente; **I was ~ surprised** me sorprendí enormemente.
mightn't ['maɪtnt] = might not.
mighty ['maɪtɪ] adj fuerte, poderoso.
migraine ['miːgreɪn] n jaqueca.
migrant ['maɪgrənt] adj migratorio ♦ n (bird) ave f migratoria; (worker) emigrante m/f.
migrate [maɪˈgreɪt] vi emigrar.
migration [maɪˈgreɪʃən] n emigración f.
mike [maɪk] n abbr (= microphone) micro.
Milan [mɪˈlæn] n Milán m.
mild [maɪld] adj (person) apacible; (climate) templado; (slight) ligero; (taste) suave;

(*illness*) leve.
mildew ['mɪldjuː] *n* moho.
mildly ['maɪldlɪ] *adv* ligeramente;
suavemente; **to put it** ~ por no decir algo
peor.
mildness ['maɪldnɪs] *n* suavidad *f*; (*of
illness*) levedad *f*.
mile [maɪl] *n* milla; **to do 20** ~**s per gallon**
hacer 20 millas por galón.
mileage ['maɪlɪdʒ] *n* número de millas;
(*AUT*) kilometraje *m*.
mileage allowance *n* ≈ asignación *f* por
kilometraje.
mileometer [maɪ'lɔmɪtə*] *n* (*BRIT*) =
milometer.
milestone ['maɪlstəun] *n* mojón *m*; (*fig*)
hito.
milieu ['miːljəː] *n* (medio) ambiente *m*,
entorno.
militant ['mɪlɪtnt] *adj, n* militante *m/f*.
militarism ['mɪlɪtərɪzəm] *n* militarismo.
militaristic [mɪlɪtə'rɪstɪk] *adj* militarista.
military ['mɪlɪtərɪ] *adj* militar.
military service *n* servicio militar.
militate ['mɪlɪteɪt] *vi*: **to** ~ **against** militar
en contra de.
militia [mɪ'lɪʃə] *n* milicia.
milk [mɪlk] *n* leche *f* ♦ *vt* (*cow*) ordeñar; (*fig*)
chupar.
milk chocolate *n* chocolate *m* con leche.
milk float *n* (*BRIT*) furgoneta de la leche.
milking ['mɪlkɪŋ] *n* ordeño.
milkman ['mɪlkmən] *n* lechero.
milk shake *n* batido, malteada (*LAM*).
milk tooth *n* diente *m* de leche.
milk truck *n* (*US*) = **milk float**.
milky ['mɪlkɪ] *adj* lechoso.
Milky Way *n* Vía Láctea.
mill [mɪl] *n* (*windmill etc*) molino; (*coffee* ~)
molinillo; (*factory*) fábrica; (*spinning* ~)
hilandería ♦ *vt* moler ♦ *vi* (*also:* ~ **about**)
arremolinarse.
milled [mɪld] (*grain*) molido; (*coin, edge*)
acordonado.
millennium, *pl* ~**s** *or* **millennia**
[mɪ'lɛnɪəm, 'lɛnɪə] *n* milenio, milenario.
millennium bug *n* (*COMPUT*): **the** ~ el
(problema del) efecto 2000.
miller ['mɪlə*] *n* molinero.
millet ['mɪlɪt] *n* mijo.
milli... ['mɪlɪ] *pref* mili....
milligram(me) ['mɪlɪgraem] *n* miligramo.
millilitre, (*US*) **milliliter** ['mɪlɪliːtə*] *n*
mililitro.
millimetre, (*US*) **millimeter** ['mɪlɪmiːtə*] *n*
milímetro.
milliner ['mɪlɪnə*] *n* sombrerero/a.
millinery ['mɪlɪnərɪ] *n* sombrerería.

million ['mɪljən] *n* millón *m*; **a** ~ **times** un
millón de veces.
millionaire [mɪljə'nɛə*] *n* millonario/a.
millipede ['mɪlɪpiːd] *n* milpiés *m inv*.
millstone ['mɪlstəun] *n* piedra de molino.
millwheel ['mɪlwiːl] *n* rueda de molino.
milometer [maɪ'lɔmɪtə*] *n* (*BRIT*)
cuentakilómetros *m inv*.
mime [maɪm] *n* mímica; (*actor*) mimo/a ♦ *vt*
remedar ♦ *vi* actuar de mimo.
mimic ['mɪmɪk] *n* imitador(a) *m/f* ♦ *adj*
mímico ♦ *vt* remedar, imitar.
mimicry ['mɪmɪkrɪ] *n* imitación *f*.
Min. *abbr* (*BRIT POL*: = *Ministry*) Min.
min. *abbr* (= *minute(s)*) m.; = **minimum**.
minaret [mɪnə'rɛt] *n* alminar *m*.
mince [mɪns] *vt* picar ♦ *vi* (*in walking*) andar
con pasos menudos ♦ *n* (*BRIT CULIN*) carne
f picada, picadillo.
mincemeat ['mɪnsmiːt] *n conserva de fruta
picada*.
mince pie *n pastelillo relleno de fruta
picada*.
mincer ['mɪnsə*] *n* picadora de carne.
mincing ['mɪnsɪŋ] *adj* afectado.
mind [maɪnd] *n* (*gen*) mente *f*; (*contrasted
with matter*) espíritu *m* ♦ *vt* (*attend to, look
after*) ocuparse de, cuidar; (*be careful of*)
tener cuidado con; (*object to*): **I don't** ~
the noise no me molesta el ruido; **it is on
my** ~ me preocupa; **to my** ~ a mi
parecer *or* juicio; **to change one's** ~
cambiar de idea *or* de parecer; **to bring**
or **call sth to** ~ recordar algo; **to have
sth/sb in** ~ tener algo/a algn en mente; **to
be out of one's** ~ haber perdido el juicio;
to bear sth in ~ tomar *or* tener algo en
cuenta; **to make up one's** ~ decidirse; **it
went right out of my** ~ se me fue por
completo (de la cabeza); **to be in two** ~**s
about sth** estar indeciso *or* dudar ante
algo; **I don't** ~ me es igual; ~ **you, ...** te
advierto que ...; **never** ~! ¡es igual!, ¡no
importa!; (*don't worry*) ¡no te preocupes!;
'~ **the step**' 'cuidado con el escalón'.
mind-boggling ['maɪndbɔglɪŋ] *adj* (*col*)
alucinante, increíble.
-minded [-maɪndɪd] *adj*: **fair**~ imparcial; **an
industrially**~ **nation** una nación orientada
a la industria.
minder ['maɪndə*] *n* guardaespaldas *m inv*.
mindful ['maɪndful] *adj*: ~ **of** consciente de.
mindless ['maɪndlɪs] *adj* (*violence, crime*) sin
sentido; (*work*) de autómata.
mine [maɪn] *pron* (el) mío/(la) mía *etc*; **a
friend of** ~ un(a) amigo/a mío/mía ♦ *adj*:
this book is ~ este libro es mío ♦ *n* mina
♦ *vt* (*coal*) extraer; (*ship, beach*) minar.

mine detector n detector m de minas.
minefield ['maɪnfiːld] n campo de minas.
miner ['maɪnə*] n minero/a.
mineral ['mɪnərəl] adj mineral ♦ n mineral m; **~s** npl (BRIT: soft drinks) refrescos mpl con gas.
mineral water n agua mineral.
minesweeper ['maɪnswiːpə*] n dragaminas m inv.
mingle ['mɪŋgl] vi: **to ~ with** mezclarse con.
mingy ['mɪndʒɪ] adj (col) tacaño.
mini ... [mɪnɪ] pref mini..., micro....
miniature ['mɪnətʃə*] adj (en) miniatura ♦ n miniatura.
minibus ['mɪnɪbʌs] n microbús m.
minicab ['mɪnɪkæb] n taxi m (que sólo puede pedirse por teléfono).
minicomputer ['mɪnɪkəm'pjuːtə*] n miniordenador m.
MiniDisc® ['mɪnɪdɪsk] n MiniDisc® m.
minim ['mɪnɪm] n (BRIT MUS) blanca.
minimal ['mɪnɪml] adj mínimo.
minimalist ['mɪnɪməlɪst] adj, n minimalista m/f.
minimize ['mɪnɪmaɪz] vt minimizar.
minimum ['mɪnɪməm] n (pl **minima** ['mɪnɪmə]) mínimo ♦ adj mínimo; **to reduce to a ~** reducir algo al mínimo; **~ wage** salario mínimo.
minimum lending rate (MLR) n tipo de interés mínimo.
mining ['maɪnɪŋ] n minería ♦ adj minero.
minion ['mɪnjən] n secuaz m.
mini-series ['mɪnɪsɪəriːz] n serie f de pocos capítulos, miniserie f.
miniskirt ['mɪnɪskəːt] n minifalda.
minister ['mɪnɪstə*] n (BRIT POL) ministro/a; (REL) pastor m ♦ vi: **to ~ to** atender a.
ministerial [mɪnɪs'tɪərɪəl] adj (BRIT POL) ministerial.
ministry ['mɪnɪstrɪ] n (BRIT POL) ministerio; (REL) sacerdocio; **M~ of Defence** Ministerio de Defensa.
mink [mɪŋk] n visón m.
mink coat n abrigo de visón.
Minn. abbr (US) = Minnesota.
minnow ['mɪnəu] n pececillo (de agua dulce).
minor ['maɪnə*] adj (unimportant) secundario; (MUS) menor ♦ n (LAW) menor m/f de edad.
Minorca [mɪ'nɔːkə] n Menorca.
minority [maɪ'nɔrɪtɪ] n minoría; **to be in a ~** estar en or ser minoría.
minority interest n participación f minoritaria.
minster ['mɪnstə*] n catedral f.

minstrel ['mɪnstrəl] n juglar m.
mint [mɪnt] n (plant) menta, hierbabuena; (sweet) caramelo de menta ♦ vt (coins) acuñar; **the (Royal) M~**, (US) **the (US) M~** la Casa de la Moneda; **in ~ condition** en perfecto estado.
mint sauce n salsa de menta.
minuet [mɪnjuˈet] n minué m.
minus ['maɪnəs] n (also: **~ sign**) signo menos ♦ prep menos.
minuscule ['mɪnəskjuːl] adj minúsculo.
minute n ['mɪnɪt] minuto; (fig) momento; **~s** npl actas fpl ♦ adj [maɪ'njuːt] diminuto; (search) minucioso; **it is 5 ~s past 3** son las 3 y 5 (minutos); **at the last ~** a última hora; **wait a ~!** ¡espera un momento!; **up to the ~** de última hora; **in ~ detail** con todo detalle.
minute book n libro de actas.
minute hand n minutero.
minutely [maɪ'njuːtlɪ] adv (by a small amount) por muy poco; (in detail) detalladamente, minuciosamente.
minutiae [mɪ'njuːʃiː] npl minucias fpl.
miracle ['mɪrəkl] n milagro.
miracle play n auto, milagro.
miraculous [mɪ'rækjuləs] adj milagroso.
miraculously [mɪ'rækjuləslɪ] adv milagrosamente.
mirage ['mɪrɑːʒ] n espejismo.
mire [maɪə*] n fango, lodo.
mirror ['mɪrə*] n espejo; (in car) retrovisor m ♦ vt reflejar.
mirror image n reflejo inverso.
mirth [məːθ] n alegría; (laughter) risa, risas.
misadventure [mɪsəd'vɛntʃə*] n desventura; **death by ~** muerte f accidental.
misanthropist [mɪ'zænθrəpɪst] n misántropo/a.
misapply [mɪsə'plaɪ] vt emplear mal.
misapprehension ['mɪsæprɪ'henʃən] n equivocación f.
misappropriate [mɪsə'prəuprɪeɪt] vt (funds) malversar.
misappropriation ['mɪsəprəuprɪ'eɪʃən] n malversación f, desfalco.
misbehave [mɪsbɪ'heɪv] vi portarse mal.
misbehaviour, (US) **misbehavior** [mɪsbɪ'heɪvjə*] n mala conducta.
misc. abbr = miscellaneous.
miscalculate [mɪs'kælkjuleɪt] vt calcular mal.
miscalculation [mɪskælkju'leɪʃən] n error m (de cálculo).
miscarriage ['mɪskærɪdʒ] n (MED) aborto (no provocado); **~ of justice** error m judicial.

miscarry [mɪs'kærɪ] *vi* (*MED*) abortar (de forma natural); (*fail: plans*) fracasar, malograrse.

miscellaneous [mɪsɪ'leɪnɪəs] *adj* varios/as, diversos/as; ~ **expenses** gastos diversos.

miscellany [mɪ'sɛlənɪ] *n* miscelánea.

mischance [mɪs'tʃɑːns] *n* desgracia, mala suerte *f*; **by (some)** ~ por (alguna) desgracia.

mischief ['mɪstʃɪf] *n* (*naughtiness*) travesura; (*harm*) mal *m*, daño; (*maliciousness*) malicia.

mischievous ['mɪstʃɪvəs] *adj* travieso; dañino; (*playful*) malicioso.

mischievously ['mɪstʃɪvəslɪ] *adv* por travesura; maliciosamente.

misconception ['mɪskən'sɛpʃən] *n* concepto erróneo; equivocación *f*.

misconduct [mɪs'kɒndʌkt] *n* mala conducta; **professional** ~ falta profesional.

miscount [mɪs'kaunt] *vt, vi* contar mal.

misconstrue [mɪskən'struː] *vt* interpretar mal.

misdeed [mɪs'diːd] *n* (*old*) fechoría, delito.

misdemeanour, (*US*) **misdemeanor** [mɪsdɪ'miːnə*] *n* delito, ofensa.

misdirect [mɪsdɪ'rɛkt] *vt* (*person*) informar mal; (*letter*) poner señas incorrectas en.

miser ['maɪzə*] *n* avaro/a.

miserable ['mɪzərəbl] *adj* (*unhappy*) triste, desgraciado; (*wretched*) miserable; **to feel** ~ sentirse triste.

miserably ['mɪzərəblɪ] *adv* (*smile, answer*) tristemente; (*fail*) rotundamente; **to pay** ~ pagar una miseria.

miserly ['maɪzəlɪ] *adj* avariento, tacaño.

misery ['mɪzərɪ] *n* (*unhappiness*) tristeza; (*wretchedness*) miseria, desdicha.

misfire [mɪs'faɪə*] *vi* fallar.

misfit ['mɪsfɪt] *n* (*person*) inadaptado/a.

misfortune [mɪs'fɔːtʃən] *n* desgracia.

misgiving(s) [mɪs'ɡɪvɪŋ(z)] *n(pl)* (*mistrust*) recelo; (*apprehension*) presentimiento; **to have** ~**s about sth** tener dudas sobre algo.

misguided [mɪs'ɡaɪdɪd] *adj* equivocado.

mishandle [mɪs'hændl] *vt* (*treat roughly*) maltratar; (*mismanage*) manejar mal.

mishap ['mɪshæp] *n* desgracia, contratiempo.

mishear [mɪs'hɪə*] *vt, vi* (*irreg: like* **hear**) oír mal.

mishmash ['mɪʃmæʃ] *n* (*col*) revoltijo.

misinform [mɪsɪn'fɔːm] *vt* informar mal.

misinterpret [mɪsɪn'təːprɪt] *vt* interpretar mal.

misinterpretation ['mɪsɪntə:prɪ'teɪʃən] *n*

mala interpretación *f*.

misjudge [mɪs'dʒʌdʒ] *vt* juzgar mal.

mislay [mɪs'leɪ] *vt* (*irreg: like* **lay**) extraviar, perder.

mislead [mɪs'liːd] *vt* (*irreg: like* **lead**) llevar a conclusiones erróneas; (*deliberately*) engañar.

misleading [mɪs'liːdɪŋ] *adj* engañoso.

misled [mɪs'lɛd] *pt, pp of* **mislead**.

mismanage [mɪs'mænɪdʒ] *vt* administrar mal.

mismanagement [mɪs'mænɪdʒmənt] *n* mala administración *f*.

misnomer [mɪs'nəumə*] *n* término inapropiado *or* equivocado.

misogynist [mɪ'sɒdʒɪnɪst] *n* misógino.

misplace [mɪs'pleɪs] *vt* (*lose*) extraviar; ~**d** (*trust etc*) inmerecido.

misprint ['mɪsprɪnt] *n* errata, error *m* de imprenta.

mispronounce [mɪsprə'nauns] *vt* pronunciar mal.

misquote ['mɪs'kwəut] *vt* citar incorrectamente.

misread [mɪs'riːd] *vt* (*irreg: like* **read**) leer mal.

misrepresent [mɪsrɛprɪ'zɛnt] *vt* falsificar.

misrepresentation [mɪsrɛprɪzɛn'teɪʃən] *n* (*LAW*) falsa declaración *f*.

Miss [mɪs] *n* Señorita; **Dear** ~ **Smith** Estimada Señorita Smith.

miss [mɪs] *vt* (*train etc*) perder; (*shot*) errar, fallar; (*appointment, class*) faltar a; (*escape, avoid*) evitar; (*notice loss of: money etc*) notar la falta de, echar en falta; (*regret the absence of*): **I** ~ **him** le echo de menos ♦ *vi* fallar ♦ *n* (*shot*) tiro fallido; **the bus just** ~**ed the wall** faltó poco para que el autobús se estrella contra el muro; **you're** ~**ing the point** no has entendido la idea.

▶**miss out** *vt* (*BRIT*) omitir.

▶**miss out on** *vt fus* (*fun, party, opportunity*) perderse.

Miss. *abbr* (*US*) = **Mississippi**.

missal ['mɪsl] *n* misal *m*.

misshapen [mɪs'ʃeɪpən] *adj* deforme.

missile ['mɪsaɪl] *n* (*AVIAT*) misil *m*; (*object thrown*) proyectil *m*.

missile base *n* base *f* de misiles.

missile launcher *n* lanzamisiles *m inv*.

missing ['mɪsɪŋ] *adj* (*pupil*) ausente, que falta; (*thing*) perdido; (*MIL*) desaparecido; **to be** ~ faltar; ~ **person** desaparecido/a.

mission ['mɪʃən] *n* misión *f*; **on a** ~ **for sb** en una misión para algn.

missionary ['mɪʃənrɪ] *n* misionero/a.

misspell [mɪs'spɛl] *vt* (*irreg: like* **spell**)

escribir mal.

misspent ['mɪs'spɛnt] *adj*: **his ~ youth** su juventud disipada.

mist [mɪst] *n* (*light*) neblina; (*heavy*) niebla; (*at sea*) bruma ♦ *vi* (*also*: **~ over**, **~ up**: *weather*) nublarse; (: *BRIT*: *windows*) empañarse.

mistake [mɪs'teɪk] *n* error *m* ♦ *vt* (*irreg*: *like* **take**) entender mal; **by ~** por equivocación; **to make a ~** (*about sb/sth*) equivocarse; (*in writing, calculating etc*) cometer un error; **to ~ A for B** confundir A con B.

mistaken [mɪs'teɪkən] *pp of* **mistake** ♦ *adj* (*idea etc*) equivocado; **to be ~** equivocarse, engañarse; **~ identity** identificación f errónea

mistakenly [mɪs'teɪkənlɪ] *adv* erróneamente.

mister ['mɪstə*] *n* (*col*) señor *m*; *see* **Mr.**

mistletoe ['mɪsltəu] *n* muérdago.

mistook [mɪs'tuk] *pt of* **mistake**.

mistranslation [mɪstræns'leɪʃən] *n* mala traducción *f*.

mistreat [mɪs'triːt] *vt* maltratar, tratar mal.

mistress ['mɪstrɪs] *n* (*lover*) amante *f*; (*of house*) señora (de la casa); (*BRIT*: *in primary school*) maestra; (*in secondary school*) profesora; *see* **Mrs.**

mistrust [mɪs'trʌst] *vt* desconfiar de ♦ *n*: **~ (of)** desconfianza (de).

mistrustful [mɪs'trʌstful] *adj*: **~ (of)** desconfiado (de), receloso (de).

misty ['mɪstɪ] *adj* nebuloso, brumoso; (*day*) de niebla; (*glasses*) empañado.

misty-eyed ['mɪstɪ'aɪd] *adj* sentimental.

misunderstand [mɪsʌndə'stænd] *vt, vi* (*irreg*: *like* **understand**) entender mal.

misunderstanding [mɪsʌndə'stændɪŋ] *n* malentendido.

misunderstood [mɪsʌndə'stud] *pt, pp of* **misunderstand** ♦ *adj* (*person*) incomprendido.

misuse *n* [mɪs'juːs] mal uso; (*of power*) abuso ♦ *vt* [mɪs'juːz] abusar de; (*funds*) malversar.

MIT *n abbr* (*US*) = *Massachusetts Institute of Technology*.

mite [maɪt] *n* (*small quantity*) pizca; **poor ~!** ¡pobrecito!

mitigate ['mɪtɪgeɪt] *vt* mitigar; **mitigating circumstances** circunstancias *fpl* atenuantes.

mitigation [mɪtɪ'geɪʃən] *n* mitigación *f*, alivio.

mitre, (*US*) **miter** ['maɪtə*] *n* mitra.

mitt(en) ['mɪt(n)] *n* manopla.

mix [mɪks] *vt* (*gen*) mezclar; (*combine*) unir ♦ *vi* mezclarse; (*people*) llevarse bien ♦ *n* mezcla; **to ~ sth with sth** mezclar algo con algo; **to ~ business with pleasure** combinar los negocios con el placer; **cake ~** preparado para pastel.

►**mix in** *vt* (*eggs etc*) añadir.

►**mix up** *vt* mezclar; (*confuse*) confundir; **to be ~ed up in sth** estar metido en algo.

mixed [mɪkst] *adj* (*assorted*) variado, surtido; (*school, marriage etc*) mixto.

mixed-ability ['mɪkstə'bɪlɪtɪ] *adj* (*class etc*) de alumnos de distintas capacidades.

mixed bag *n*: **these results are a bit of a ~** en estos resultados hay un poco de todo.

mixed blessing *n*: **it's a ~** tiene su lado bueno y su lado malo

mixed doubles *n* (*SPORT*) mixtos *mpl*.

mixed economy *n* economía mixta.

mixed grill *n* (*BRIT*) parrillada mixta.

mixed-up [mɪkst'ʌp] *adj* (*confused*) confuso, revuelto.

mixer ['mɪksə*] *n* (*for food*) batidora; (*person*): **he's a good ~** tiene don de gentes.

mixer tap *n* (grifo) monomando.

mixture ['mɪkstʃə*] *n* mezcla.

mix-up ['mɪksʌp] *n* confusión *f*.

Mk *abbr* (*BRIT TECH*: = *mark*) Mk.

mk *abbr* = **mark** (*currency*).

mkt *abbr* = **market**.

MLitt *n abbr* (= *Master of Literature, Master of Letters*) título universitario de postgrado; *see also* **master's degree.**

MLR *n abbr* (*BRIT*) = **minimum lending rate**.

mm *abbr* (= *millimetre*) mm.

MN *abbr* (*BRIT*) = **Merchant Navy**; (*US*) = *Minnesota*.

MO *n abbr* (*MED*) = *medical officer*; (*US col*) = **modus operandi** ♦ *abbr* (*US*) = *Missouri*.

Mo. *abbr* (*US*) = *Missouri*.

m.o. *abbr* (= *money order*) g/.

moan [məun] *n* gemido ♦ *vi* gemir; (*col*: *complain*): **to ~ (about)** quejarse (de).

moaning ['məunɪŋ] *n* gemidos *mpl*; quejas *fpl*.

moat [məut] *n* foso.

mob [mɔb] *n* multitud *f*; (*pej*): **the ~** el populacho ♦ *vt* acosar.

mobile ['məubaɪl] *adj* móvil ♦ *n* móvil *m*.

mobile home *n* caravana.

mobile phone *n* teléfono móvil.

mobility [məu'bɪlɪtɪ] *n* movilidad *f*; **~ of labour** *or* (*US*) **labor** movilidad *f* de la mano de obra.

mobilize ['məubɪlaɪz] *vt* movilizar.

moccasin ['mɔkəsɪn] *n* mocasín *m*.

mock [mɔk] *vt* (*make ridiculous*) ridiculizar;

(*laugh at*) burlarse de ♦ *adj* fingido.
mockery ['mɔkərɪ] *n* burla; **to make a ~ of** desprestigiar.
mocking ['mɔkɪŋ] *adj* (*tone*) burlón/ona.
mockingbird ['mɔkɪŋbɔːd] *n* sinsonte *m* (*LAM*), zenzontle (*LAM*).
mock-up ['mɔkʌp] *n* maqueta.
mod cons ['mɔd'kɔnz] *npl abbr* (= *modern conveniences*) *see* **convenience**.
mode [məud] *n* modo; (*of transport*) medio; (*COMPUT*) modo, modalidad *f*.
model ['mɔdl] *n* (*gen*) modelo; (*ARCH*) maqueta; (*person: for fashion, ART*) modelo *m/f* ♦ *adj* modelo *inv* ♦ *vt* modelar ♦ *vi* ser modelo; **~ railway** ferrocarril *m* de juguete; **to ~ clothes** pasar modelos, ser modelo; **to ~ on** crear a imitación de.
modelling, (*US*) **modeling** ['mɔdlɪŋ] *n* (*modelmaking*) modelado.
modem ['məudəm] *n* módem *m*.
moderate *adj, n* ['mɔdərət] moderado/a *m/f* ♦ (*vb*: ['mɔdəreɪt]) *vi* moderarse, calmarse ♦ *vt* moderar.
moderately ['mɔdərətlɪ] *adv* (*act*) con moderación; (*expensive, difficult*) medianamente; (*pleased, happy*) bastante.
moderation [mɔdə'reɪʃən] *n* moderación *f*; **in ~** con moderación.
moderator ['mɔdəreɪtə*] *n* (*mediator*) moderador(a) *m/f*.
modern ['mɔdən] *adj* moderno; **~ languages** lenguas *fpl* modernas.
modernity [mə'dɔːnɪtɪ] *n* modernidad *f*.
modernization [mɔdənaɪ'zeɪʃən] *n* modernización *f*.
modernize ['mɔdənaɪz] *vt* modernizar.
modest ['mɔdɪst] *adj* modesto.
modestly ['mɔdɪstlɪ] *adv* modestamente.
modesty ['mɔdɪstɪ] *n* modestia.
modicum ['mɔdɪkəm] *n*: **a ~ of** un mínimo de.
modification [mɔdɪfɪ'keɪʃən] *n* modificación *f*; **to make ~s** hacer cambios *or* modificaciones.
modify ['mɔdɪfaɪ] *vt* modificar.
modish ['məudɪʃ] *adj* de moda.
Mods [mɔdz] *n abbr* (*BRIT*: = (*Honour*) *Moderations*) *examen de licenciatura de la universidad de Oxford*.
modular ['mɔdjulə*] *adj* (*filing, unit*) modular.
modulate ['mɔdjuleɪt] *vt* modular.
modulation [mɔdju'leɪʃən] *n* modulación *f*.
module ['mɔdjuːl] *n* (*unit, component, SPACE*) módulo.
modus operandi ['məudəsɔpə'rændiː] *n* manera de actuar.
Mogadishu [mɔgə'dɪʃuː] *n* Mogadiscio.

mogul ['məugəl] *n* (*fig*) magnate *m*.
MOH *n abbr* (*BRIT*) = *Medical Officer of Health*.
mohair ['məuhɛə*] *n* mohair *m*.
Mohammed [mə'hæmɛd] *n* Mahoma *m*.
moist [mɔɪst] *adj* húmedo.
moisten ['mɔɪsn] *vt* humedecer.
moisture ['mɔɪstʃə*] *n* humedad *f*.
moisturize ['mɔɪstʃəraɪz] *vt* (*skin*) hidratar.
moisturizer ['mɔɪstʃəraɪzə*] *n* crema hidratante.
molar ['məulə*] *n* muela.
molasses [məu'læsɪz] *n* melaza.
mold [məuld] *n, vt* (*US*) = **mould**.
Moldavia [mɔl'deɪvɪə], **Moldova** [mɔl'dəuvə] *n* Moldavia, Moldova.
Moldavian [mɔl'deɪvɪən], **Moldovan** [mɔl'dəuvən] *adj, n* moldavo/a *m/f*.
mole [məul] *n* (*animal*) topo; (*spot*) lunar *m*.
molecular [mə'lɛkjulə*] *adj* molecular.
molecule ['mɔlɪkjuːl] *n* molécula.
molest [məu'lɛst] *vt* importunar; (*sexually*) abordar con propósitos deshonestos.
moll [mɔl] *n* (*slang*) amiga.
mollusc, (*US*) **mollusk** ['mɔləsk] *n* molusco.
mollycoddle ['mɔlɪkɔdl] *vt* mimar.
Molotov cocktail ['mɔlətɔf-] *n* cóctel *m* Molotov.
molt [məult] *vi* (*US*) = **moult**.
molten ['məultən] *adj* fundido; (*lava*) líquido.
mom [mɔm] *n* (*US*) = **mum**.
moment ['məumənt] *n* momento; **at** *or* **for the ~** de momento, por el momento, por ahora; **in a ~** dentro de un momento.
momentarily ['məuməntrɪlɪ] *adv* momentáneamente; (*US: very soon*) de un momento a otro.
momentary ['məuməntərɪ] *adj* momentáneo.
momentous [məu'mɛntəs] *adj* trascendental, importante.
momentum [məu'mɛntəm] *n* momento; (*fig*) ímpetu *m*; **to gather ~** cobrar velocidad; (*fig*) cobrar fuerza.
mommy ['mɔmɪ] *n* (*US*) = **mummy**.
Mon. *abbr* (= *Monday*) lun.
Monaco ['mɔnəkəu] *n* Mónaco.
monarch ['mɔnək] *n* monarca *m/f*.
monarchist ['mɔnəkɪst] *n* monárquico/a.
monarchy ['mɔnəkɪ] *n* monarquía.
monastery ['mɔnəstərɪ] *n* monasterio.
monastic [mə'næstɪk] *adj* monástico.
Monday ['mʌndɪ] *n* lunes *m inv*.
Monegasque [mɔnɪ'gæsk] *adj, n* monegasco/a *m/f*.
monetarist ['mʌnɪtərɪst] *n* monetarista *m*.

monetary ['mʌnɪtərɪ] *adj* monetario.
monetary policy *n* política monetaria.
money ['mʌnɪ] *n* dinero, plata (*LAM*); **to make ~** ganar dinero; **I've got no ~ left** no me queda dinero.
moneyed ['mʌnɪd] *adj* adinerado.
moneylender ['mʌnɪlendə*] *n* prestamista *m/f*.
moneymaker ['mʌnɪmeɪkə*] *n* (*BRIT col*: *business*) filón *m*.
moneymaking ['mʌnɪmeɪkɪŋ] *adj* rentable.
money market *n* mercado monetario.
money order *n* giro.
money-spinner ['mʌnɪspɪnə*] *n* (*col*: *person, idea, business*) filón *m*.
money supply *n* oferta monetaria, medio circulante, volumen *m* monetario.
Mongol ['mɔŋgəl] *n* mongol(a) *m/f*; (*LING*) mongol *m*.
mongol ['mɔŋgəl] *adj, n* (*MED*) mongólico.
Mongolia [mɔŋ'gəulɪə] *n* Mongolia.
Mongolian [mɔŋ'gəulɪən] *adj* mongol(a) ♦ *n* mongol(a) *m/f*; (*LING*) mongol *m*.
mongoose ['mɔŋguːs] *n* mangosta.
mongrel ['mʌŋgrəl] *n* (*dog*) perro cruzado.
monitor ['mɔnɪtə*] *n* monitor *m* ♦ *vt* controlar; (*foreign station*) escuchar.
monk [mʌŋk] *n* monje *m*.
monkey ['mʌŋkɪ] *n* mono.
monkey business *n*, **monkey tricks** *npl* tejemanejes *mpl*.
monkey nut *n* (*BRIT*) cacahuete *m*, maní (*LAM*).
monkey wrench *n* llave *f* inglesa.
mono ['mɔnəu] *adj* (*broadcast etc*) mono *inv*.
mono... [mɔnəu] *pref* mono ... .
monochrome ['mɔnəukrəum] *adj* monocromo.
monocle ['mɔnəkl] *n* monóculo.
monogamous [mə'nɔgəməs] *adj* monógamo.
monogram ['mɔnəgræm] *n* monograma *m*.
monolith ['mɔnəlɪθ] *n* monolito.
monolithic [mɔnə'lɪθɪk] *adj* monolítico.
monologue ['mɔnəlɔg] *n* monólogo.
monoplane ['mɔnəpleɪn] *n* monoplano.
monopolist [mə'nɔpəlɪst] *n* monopolista *m/f*.
monopolize [mə'nɔpəlaɪz] *vt* monopolizar.
monopoly [mə'nɔpəlɪ] *n* monopolio;
Monopolies and Mergers Commission (*BRIT*) *comisión reguladora de monopolios y fusiones*.
monorail ['mɔnəureɪl] *n* monocarril *m*, monorraíl *m*.
monosodium glutamate [mɔnə'səudɪəm 'gluːtəmeɪt] *n* glutamato monosódico.
monosyllabic [mɔnəsɪ'læbɪk] *adj* monosílabo.

monosyllable ['mɔnəsɪləbl] *n* monosílabo.
monotone ['mɔnətəun] *n* voz *f* (*or* tono) monocorde.
monotonous [mə'nɔtənəs] *adj* monótono.
monotony [mə'nɔtənɪ] *n* monotonía.
monoxide [mə'nɔksaɪd] *n*: **carbon ~** monóxido de carbono.
monseigneur [mɔnsɛn'jɜː*], **monsignor** [mɔn'siːnjə*] *n* monseñor *m*.
monsoon [mɔn'suːn] *n* monzón *m*.
monster ['mɔnstə*] *n* monstruo.
monstrosity [mɔns'trɔsɪtɪ] *n* monstruosidad *f*.
monstrous ['mɔnstrəs] *adj* (*huge*) enorme; (*atrocious*) monstruoso.
Mont. *abbr* (*US*) = Montana.
montage [mɔn'tɑːʒ] *n* montaje *m*.
Mont Blanc [mɔ̃'blɑ̃] *n* Mont Blanc *m*.
month [mʌnθ] *n* mes *m*; **300 dollars a ~** 300 dólares al mes; **every ~** cada mes.
monthly ['mʌnθlɪ] *adj* mensual ♦ *adv* mensualmente ♦ *n* (*magazine*) revista mensual; **twice ~** dos veces al mes; **~ instalment** mensualidad *f*.
monument ['mɔnjumənt] *n* monumento.
monumental [mɔnju'mentl] *adj* monumental.
moo [muː] *vi* mugir.
mood [muːd] *n* humor *m*; **to be in a good/ bad ~** estar de buen/mal humor.
moodily ['muːdɪlɪ] *adv* malhumoradamente.
moodiness ['muːdɪnɪs] *n* humor *m* cambiante; (*bad mood*) mal humor *m*.
moody ['muːdɪ] *adj* (*variable*) de humor variable; (*sullen*) malhumorado.
moon [muːn] *n* luna.
moonbeam ['muːnbiːm] *n* rayo de luna.
moon landing *n* alunizaje *m*.
moonless ['muːnlɪs] *adj* sin luna.
moonlight ['muːnlaɪt] *n* luz *f* de la luna ♦ *vi* hacer pluriempleo.
moonlighting ['muːnlaɪtɪŋ] *n* pluriempleo.
moonlit ['muːnlɪt] *adj*: **a ~ night** una noche de luna.
moonshot ['muːnʃɔt] *n* lanzamiento de una astronave a la luna.
moonstruck ['muːnstrʌk] *adj* chiflado.
moony ['muːnɪ] *adj*: **to have ~ eyes** estar soñando despierto, estar pensando en las musarañas.
Moor [muə*] *n* moro/a.
moor [muə*] *n* páramo ♦ *vt* (*ship*) amarrar ♦ *vi* echar las amarras.
moorings ['muərɪŋz] *npl* (*chains*) amarras *fpl*; (*place*) amarradero *sg*.
Moorish ['muərɪʃ] *adj* moro; (*architecture*) árabe.
moorland ['muələnd] *n* páramo, brezal *m*.

moose [muːs] *n*, *pl inv* alce *m*.
moot [muːt] *vt* proponer para la discusión, sugerir ♦ *adj*: ~ **point** punto discutible.
mop [mɔp] *n* fregona; (*of hair*) greñas *fpl* ♦ *vt* fregar.
▸**mop up** *vt* limpiar.
mope [məʊp] *vi* estar deprimido.
▸**mope about, mope around** *vi* andar abatido.
moped ['məʊpɛd] *n* ciclomotor *m*.
moquette [mɔ'kɛt] *n* moqueta.
MOR *adj abbr* (*MUS*: = *middle-of-the-road*) para el gran público.
moral ['mɔrl] *adj* moral ♦ *n* moraleja; ~**s** *npl* moralidad *f*, moral *f*.
morale [mɔ'rɑːl] *n* moral *f*.
morality [mə'rælıtı] *n* moralidad *f*.
moralize ['mɔrəlaız] *vi*: **to** ~ (**about**) moralizar (sobre).
morally ['mɔrəlı] *adv* moralmente.
moral victory *n* victoria moral.
morass [mə'ræs] *n* pantano.
moratorium [mɔrə'tɔːrıəm] *n* moratoria.
morbid ['mɔːbıd] *adj* (*interest*) morboso; (*MED*) mórbido.

================= *KEYWORD*

more [mɔː*] *adj* **1** (*greater in number etc*) más; ~ **people/work than before** más gente/trabajo que antes
2 (*additional*) más; **do you want (some)** ~ **tea?** ¿quieres más té?; **is there any** ~ **wine?** ¿queda vino?; **it'll take a few** ~ **weeks** tardará unas semanas más; **it's 2 kms** ~ **to the house** faltan 2 kms para la casa; ~ **time/letters than we expected** más tiempo del que/más cartas de las que esperábamos; **I have no** ~ **money, I don't have any** ~ **money** (ya) no tengo más dinero
♦ *pron* (*greater amount, additional amount*) más; ~ **than 10** más de 10; **it cost** ~ **than the other one/than we expected** costó más que el otro/más de lo que esperábamos; **is there any** ~**?** ¿hay más?; **I want** ~ quiero más; **and what's** ~ ... y además ...; **many/much** ~ muchos(as)/mucho(a) más
♦ *adv* más; ~ **dangerous/easily (than)** más peligroso/fácilmente (que); ~ **and** ~ **expensive** cada vez más caro; ~ **or less** más o menos; ~ **than ever** más que nunca; **she doesn't live here any** ~ ya no vive aquí.

moreover [mɔː'rəʊvə*] *adv* además, por otra parte.
morgue [mɔːg] *n* depósito de cadáveres.

MORI ['mɔːrı] *n abbr* (*BRIT*) = Market and Opinion Research Institute.
moribund ['mɔrıbʌnd] *adj* moribundo.
Mormon ['mɔːmən] *n* mormón/ona *m/f*.
morning ['mɔːnıŋ] *n* (*gen*) mañana; (*early* ~) madrugada; **in the** ~ por la mañana; **7 o'clock in the** ~ las 7 de la mañana; **this** ~ esta mañana.
morning-after pill ['mɔːnıŋ'ɑːftə-] *n* píldora del día después.
morning sickness *n* (*MED*) náuseas *fpl* del embarazo.
Moroccan [mə'rɔkən] *adj*, *n* marroquí *m/f*.
Morocco [mə'rɔkəʊ] *n* Marruecos *m*.
moron ['mɔːrɔn] *n* imbécil *m/f*.
morose [mə'rəʊs] *adj* hosco, malhumorado.
morphine ['mɔːfiːn] *n* morfina.
morris dancing ['mɔrıs] *n* (*BRIT*) *baile tradicional inglés en el que se llevan cascabeles en la ropa.*
Morse [mɔːs] *n* (*also*: ~ **code**) (alfabeto) morse *m*.
morsel ['mɔːsl] *n* (*of food*) bocado.
mortal ['mɔːtl] *adj*, *n* mortal *m*.
mortality [mɔː'tælıtı] *n* mortalidad *f*.
mortality rate *n* tasa de mortalidad.
mortally ['mɔːtəlı] *adv* mortalmente.
mortar ['mɔːtə*] *n* argamasa; (*implement*) mortero.
mortgage ['mɔːgıdʒ] *n* hipoteca ♦ *vt* hipotecar; **to take out a** ~ sacar una hipoteca.
mortgage company *n* (*US*) ≈ banco hipotecario.
mortgagee [mɔːgə'dʒiː] *n* acreedor(a) *m/f* hipotecario/a.
mortgager ['mɔːgədʒə*] *n* deudor(a) *m/f* hipotecario/a.
mortice ['mɔːtıs] = **mortise**.
mortician [mɔː'tıʃən] *n* (*US*) director(a) *m/f* de pompas fúnebres.
mortification ['mɔːtıfı'keıʃən] *n* mortificación *f*, humillación *f*.
mortified ['mɔːtıfaıd] *adj*: **I was** ~ me dio muchísima vergüenza.
mortise (lock) ['mɔːtıs-] *n* cerradura de muesca.
mortuary ['mɔːtjuərı] *n* depósito de cadáveres.
mosaic [məʊ'zeıık] *n* mosaico.
Moscow ['mɔskəʊ] *n* Moscú *m*.
Moslem ['mɔzləm] *adj*, *n* = **Muslim**.
mosque [mɔsk] *n* mezquita.
mosquito, ~**es** [mɔs'kiːtəʊ] *n* mosquito.
moss [mɔs] *n* musgo.
mossy ['mɔsı] *adj* musgoso, cubierto de musgo.
most [məʊst] *adj* la mayor parte de, la

mayoría de ♦ *pron* la mayor parte, la mayoría ♦ *adv* el más; (*very*) muy; **the ~** (*also*: + *adjective*) el más; **~ of them** la mayor parte de ellos; **I saw the ~** yo fui el que más vi; **at the (very) ~** a lo sumo, todo lo más; **to make the ~ of** aprovechar (al máximo); **a ~ interesting book** un libro interesantísimo.

mostly ['məustlɪ] *adv* en su mayor parte, principalmente.

MOT *n abbr* (*BRIT* = *Ministry of Transport*): **the ~ (test)** ≈ la ITV.

motel [məu'tɛl] *n* motel *m*.

moth [mɔθ] *n* mariposa nocturna; (*clothes* ~) polilla.

mothball ['mɔθbɔːl] *n* bola de naftalina.

moth-eaten ['mɔθiːtn] *adj* apolillado.

mother ['mʌðə*] *n* madre *f* ♦ *adj* materno ♦ *vt* (*care for*) cuidar (como una madre).

mother board *n* (*COMPUT*) placa madre.

motherhood ['mʌðəhud] *n* maternidad *f*.

mother-in-law ['mʌðərinlɔː] *n* suegra.

motherly ['mʌðəlɪ] *adj* maternal.

mother-of-pearl ['mʌðərəv'pɔːl] *n* nácar *m*.

mother's help *n* niñera.

mother-to-be ['mʌðətə'biː] *n* futura madre.

mother tongue *n* lengua materna.

mothproof ['mɔθpruːf] *adj* a prueba de polillas.

motif [məu'tiːf] *n* motivo; (*theme*) tema *m*.

motion ['məuʃən] *n* movimiento; (*gesture*) ademán *m*, señal *f*; (*at meeting*) moción *f*; (*BRIT*: *also*: **bowel ~**) evacuación *f* intestinal ♦ *vt*, *vi*: **to ~ (to) sb to do sth** hacer señas a algn para que haga algo; **to be in ~** (*vehicle*) estar en movimiento; **to set in ~** poner en marcha; **to go through the ~s of doing sth** (*fig*) hacer algo mecánicamente *or* sin convicción.

motionless ['məuʃənlɪs] *adj* inmóvil.

motion picture *n* película.

motivate ['məutɪveɪt] *vt* motivar.

motivated ['məutɪveɪtɪd] *adj* motivado.

motivation [məutɪ'veɪʃən] *n* motivación *f*.

motivational research [məutɪ'veɪʃənl-] *n* estudios *mpl* de motivación.

motive ['məutɪv] *n* motivo; **from the best ~s** con las mejores intenciones.

motley ['mɔtlɪ] *adj* variopinto.

motor ['məutə*] *n* motor *m*; (*BRIT*: *col*: *vehicle*) coche *m*, carro (*LAM*), automóvil *m*, auto *m* (*esp LAM*) ♦ *adj* motor (*f*: motora, motriz).

motorbike ['məutəbaɪk] *n* moto *f*.

motorboat ['məutəbəut] *n* lancha motora.

motorcade ['məutəkeɪd] *n* desfile *m* de automóviles.

motorcar ['məutəkɑː*] *n* (*BRIT*) coche *m*, carro (*LAM*), automóvil *m*, auto *m* (*esp LAM*).

motorcoach ['məutəkəutʃ] *n* autocar *m*, autobús *m*, camión *m* (*LAM*).

motorcycle ['məutəsaɪkl] *n* motocicleta.

motorcycle racing *n* motociclismo.

motorcyclist ['məutəsaɪklɪst] *n* motociclista *m/f*.

motoring ['məutərɪŋ] *n* (*BRIT*) automovilismo ♦ *adj* (*accident, offence*) de tráfico *or* tránsito.

motorist ['məutərɪst] *n* conductor(a) *m/f*, automovilista *m/f*.

motorize ['məutəraɪz] *vt* motorizar.

motor oil *n* aceite *m* para motores.

motor racing *n* (*BRIT*) carreras *fpl* de coches, automovilismo.

motor scooter *n* vespa ®.

motor vehicle *n* automóvil *m*.

motorway ['məutəweɪ] *n* (*BRIT*) autopista.

mottled ['mɔtld] *adj* moteado.

motto, ~es ['mɔtəu] *n* lema *m*; (*watchword*) consigna.

mould, (*US*) mold [məuld] *n* molde *m*; (*mildew*) moho ♦ *vt* moldear; (*fig*) formar.

mo(u)lder ['məuldə*] *vi* (*decay*) decaer.

mo(u)lding ['məuldɪŋ] *n* (*ARCH*) moldura.

mo(u)ldy ['məuldɪ] *adj* enmohecido.

moult, (*US*) molt [məult] *vi* mudar la piel; (*bird*) mudar las plumas.

mound [maund] *n* montón *m*, montículo.

mount [maunt] *n* monte *m*; (*horse*) montura; (*for jewel etc*) engarce *m*; (*for picture*) marco ♦ *vt* montar en, subir a; (*stairs*) subir; (*exhibition*) montar; (*attack*) lanzar; (*stamp*) pegar, fijar; (*picture*) enmarcar ♦ *vi* (*also*: **~ up**) subirse, montarse.

mountain ['mauntɪn] *n* montaña ♦ *cpd* de montaña; **to make a ~ out of a molehill** hacer una montaña de un grano de arena.

mountain bike *n* bicicleta de montaña.

mountaineer [mauntɪ'nɪə*] *n* montañero/a, alpinista *m/f*, andinista *m/f* (*LAM*).

mountaineering [mauntɪ'nɪərɪŋ] *n* montañismo, alpinismo, andinismo (*LAM*).

mountainous ['mauntɪnəs] *adj* montañoso.

mountain range *n* sierra.

mountain rescue team *n* equipo de rescate de montaña.

mountainside ['mauntɪnsaɪd] *n* ladera de la montaña.

mounted ['mauntɪd] *adj* montado.

Mount Everest *n* Monte *m* Everest.

mourn [mɔːn] *vt* llorar, lamentar ♦ *vi*: **to ~**

for llorar la muerte de, lamentarse por.

mourner ['mɔːnə*] n doliente m/f.

mournful ['mɔːnful] adj triste, lúgubre.

mourning ['mɔːnɪŋ] n luto ♦ cpd (dress) de luto; **in ~** de luto.

mouse, pl **mice** [maus, maɪs] n (also COMPUT) ratón m.

mouse mat, mouse pad n (COMPUT) alfombrilla, almohadilla.

mousetrap ['maustræp] n ratonera.

moussaka [mu'sɑːkə] n moussaka.

mousse [muːs] n (CULIN) mousse f; (for hair) espuma (moldeadora).

moustache [məs'tɑːʃ], (US) **mustache** ['mʌstæʃ] n bigote m.

mousy ['mausɪ] adj (person) tímido; (hair) pardusco.

mouth, pl **mouths** [mauθ, -ðz] n boca; (of river) desembocadura.

mouthful ['mauθful] n bocado.

mouth organ n armónica.

mouthpiece ['mauθpiːs] n (MUS) boquilla; (TEL) micrófono; (person) portavoz m/f.

mouth-to-mouth ['mauθtə'mauθ] adj: **~ resuscitation** boca a boca m.

mouthwash ['mauθwɔʃ] n enjuague m bucal.

mouth-watering ['mauθwɔːtərɪŋ] adj apetitoso.

movable ['muːvəbl] adj movible.

move [muːv] n (movement) movimiento; (in game) jugada; (: turn to play) turno; (change of house) mudanza ♦ vt mover; (emotionally) conmover; (POL: resolution etc) proponer ♦ vi (gen) moverse; (traffic) circular; (also: BRIT: ~ house) trasladarse, mudarse; **to ~ sb to do sth** mover a algn a hacer algo; **to be ~d** estar conmovido; **to get a ~ on** darse prisa.

▶**move about** or **around** vi moverse; (travel) viajar.

▶**move along** vi (stop loitering) circular; (along seat etc) correrse.

▶**move away** vi (leave) marcharse.

▶**move back** vi (return) volver.

▶**move down** vt (demote) degradar.

▶**move forward** vi avanzar ♦ vt adelantar.

▶**move in** vi (to a house) instalarse.

▶**move off** vi ponerse en camino.

▶**move on** vi seguir viaje ♦ vt (onlookers) hacer circular.

▶**move out** vi (of house) mudarse.

▶**move over** vi hacerse a un lado.

▶**move up** vi subir; (employee) ascender.

movement ['muːvmənt] n movimiento; (TECH) mecanismo; **~ (of the bowels)** (MED) evacuación f.

mover ['muːvə*] n proponente m/f.

movie ['muːvɪ] n película; **the ~s** el cine.

movie camera n cámara cinematográfica.

moviegoer ['muːvɪgəuə*] n (US) aficionado/a al cine.

moving ['muːvɪŋ] adj (emotional) conmovedor(a); (that moves) móvil; (instigating) motor(a).

mow, pt **mowed,** pp **mowed** or **mown** [məu, -n] vt (grass) cortar; (corn: also: **~ down**) segar; (shoot) acribillar.

mower ['məuə*] n (also: **lawn~**) cortacésped m.

Mozambique [məuzæm'biːk] n Mozambique m.

MP n abbr (= Military Police) PM; BRIT: = **Member of Parliament;** (Canada) = Mounted Police.

mpg n abbr (= miles per gallon) millas por galón.

mph abbr = miles per hour.

MPhil n abbr (= Master of Philosophy) título universitario de postgrado; see also **master's degree.**

MPS n abbr (BRIT) = Member of the Pharmaceutical Society.

Mr, Mr. ['mɪstə*] n: **~ Smith** (el) Sr. Smith.

MRC n abbr (BRIT: = Medical Research Council) departamento estatal que controla la investigación médica.

MRCP n abbr (BRIT) = Member of the Royal College of Physicians.

MRCS n abbr (BRIT) = Member of the Royal College of Surgeons.

MRCVS n abbr (BRIT) = Member of the Royal College of Veterinary Surgeons.

Mrs, Mrs. ['mɪsɪz] n: **~ Smith** (la) Sra. de Smith.

MS n abbr (= manuscript) MS; = **multiple sclerosis;** (US: = Master of Science) título universitario ♦ abbr (US) = Mississippi.

Ms, Ms. [mɪz] n (= Miss or Mrs) abreviatura con la que se evita hacer expreso el estado civil de una mujer.

MSA n abbr (US: = Master of Science in Agriculture) título universitario.

MSc abbr see **Master of Science.**

MSG n abbr = monosodium glutamate.

MSP n abbr (BRIT) = **Member of the Scottish Parliament.**

MSS n abbr (= manuscripts) MSS.

MST abbr (US: = Mountain Standard Time) hora de invierno de las Montañas Rocosas.

MSW n abbr (US: = Master of Social Work) título universitario.

MT abbr (US) = Montana.

Mt abbr (GEO: = mount) m.

MTV n abbr = music television.

mth *abbr* (= *month*) m.
much [mʌtʃ] *adj* mucho ♦ *adv, n, pron* mucho; (*before pp*) muy; **how** ~ **is it?** ¿cuánto es?, ¿cuánto cuesta?; **too** ~ demasiado; **so** ~ tanto; **it's not** ~ no es mucho; **as** ~ **as** tanto como; **however** ~ **he tries** por mucho que se esfuerce; **I like it very/so** ~ me gusta mucho/tanto; **thank you very** ~ muchas gracias, muy agradecido.
muck [mʌk] *n* (*dirt*) suciedad *f*; (*fig*) porquería.
▶**muck about** *or* **around** *vi* (*col*) perder el tiempo; (*enjoy o.s.*) entretenerse; (*tinker*) manosear.
▶**muck in** *vi* (*col*) arrimar el hombro.
▶**muck out** *vt* (*stable*) limpiar.
▶**muck up** *vt* (*col: dirty*) ensuciar; (: *spoil*) echar a perder; (: *ruin*) estropear.
muckraking ['mʌkreɪkɪŋ] (*fig col*) *n* amarillismo ♦ *adj* especializado en escándalos.
mucky ['mʌkɪ] *adj* (*dirty*) sucio.
mucus ['mjuːkəs] *n* mucosidad *f*, moco.
mud [mʌd] *n* barro, lodo.
muddle ['mʌdl] *n* desorden *m*, confusión *f*, (*mix-up*) embrollo, lío ♦ *vt* (*also:* ~ **up**) embrollar, confundir.
▶**muddle along, muddle on** *vi* arreglárselas de alguna manera.
▶**muddle through** *vi* salir del paso.
muddle-headed [mʌdl'hedɪd] *adj* (*person*) despistado, confuso.
muddy ['mʌdɪ] *adj* fangoso, cubierto de lodo.
mudguard ['mʌdɡɑːd] *n* guardabarros *m inv*.
mudpack ['mʌdpæk] *n* mascarilla.
mud-slinging ['mʌdslɪŋɪŋ] *n* injurias *fpl*, difamación *f*.
muesli ['mjuːzlɪ] *n* muesli *m*.
muff [mʌf] *n* manguito ♦ *vt* (*chance*) desperdiciar; (*lines*) estropear; (*shot, catch etc*) fallar; **to** ~ **it** fracasar.
muffin ['mʌfɪn] *n* bollo.
muffle ['mʌfl] *vt* (*sound*) amortiguar; (*against cold*) abrigar.
muffled ['mʌfld] *adj* sordo, apagado.
muffler ['mʌflə*] *n* (*scarf*) bufanda; (*US AUT*) silenciador *m*; (*on motorbike*) silenciador *m*, mofle *m*.
mufti ['mʌftɪ] *n*: **in** ~ (vestido) de paisano.
mug [mʌɡ] *n* (*cup*) taza alta; (*for beer*) jarra; (*col: face*) jeta; (: *fool*) bobo ♦ *vt* (*assault*) atracar; **it's a** ~**'s game** es cosa de bobos.
▶**mug up** *vt* (*col: also:* ~ **up on**) empollar.
mugger ['mʌɡə*] *n* atracador(a) *m/f*.
mugging ['mʌɡɪŋ] *n* atraco callejero.
muggins ['mʌɡɪnz] *nsg* (*col*) tonto/a el bote.

muggy ['mʌɡɪ] *adj* bochornoso.
mug shot *n* (*col*) foto *f* (para la ficha policial).
mulatto, ~**es** [mjuː'lætəu] *n* mulato/a.
mulberry ['mʌlbrɪ] *n* (*fruit*) mora; (*tree*) morera, moral *m*.
mule [mjuːl] *n* mula.
mull [mʌl]: **to** ~ **over** *vt* meditar sobre.
mulled [mʌld] *adj*: ~ **wine** vino caliente (*con especias*).
mullioned ['mʌliənd] *adj* (*windows*) dividido por parteluces.
multi... [mʌltɪ] *pref* multi....
multi-access ['mʌltɪ'æksɛs] *adj* (*COMPUT*) multiacceso, de acceso múltiple.
multicoloured, (*US*) **multicolored** ['mʌltɪkʌləd] *adj* multicolor.
multifarious [mʌltɪ'fɛərɪəs] *adj* múltiple, vario.
multilateral [mʌltɪ'lætərl] *adj* (*POL*) multilateral.
multi-level [mʌltɪ'lɛvl] *adj* (*US*) = **multi-storey**.
multimillionaire [mʌltɪmɪljə'nɛə*] *n* multimillonario/a.
multinational [mʌltɪ'næʃənl] *n* multinacional *f* ♦ *adj* multinacional.
multiple ['mʌltɪpl] *adj* múltiple ♦ *n* múltiplo; (*BRIT: also:* ~ **store**) (cadena de) grandes almacenes *mpl*.
multiple choice *n* examen *m* de tipo test.
multiple crash *n* colisión *f* en cadena.
multiple sclerosis [-sklɪ'rəusɪs] *n* esclerosis *f* múltiple.
multiplex ['mʌltɪplɛks] *n* (*also:* ~ **cinema**) multicines *m inv*.
multiplication [mʌltɪplɪ'keɪʃən] *n* multiplicación *f*.
multiplication table *n* tabla de multiplicar.
multiplicity [mʌltɪ'plɪsɪtɪ] *n* multiplicidad *f*.
multiply ['mʌltɪplaɪ] *vt* multiplicar ♦ *vi* multiplicarse.
multiracial [mʌltɪ'reɪʃl] *adj* multirracial.
multistorey [mʌltɪ'stɔːrɪ] *adj* (*BRIT: building, car park*) de muchos pisos.
multistrike ribbon ['mʌltɪstraɪk-] *n* (*COMPUT: on printer*) cinta de múltiples impactos.
multi-tasking ['mʌltɪtɑːskɪŋ] *n* (*COMPUT*) ejecución *f* de tareas múltiples, multitarea.
multitude ['mʌltɪtjuːd] *n* multitud *f*.
mum [mʌm] *n* (*BRIT*) mamá ♦ *adj*: **to keep** ~ (**about sth**) no decir ni mu (de algo).
mumble ['mʌmbl] *vt* decir entre dientes ♦ *vi* hablar entre dientes, musitar.
mumbo jumbo ['mʌmbəu-] *n* (*col*)

galimatías *m inv.*
mummify ['mʌmɪfaɪ] *vt* momificar.
mummy ['mʌmɪ] *n* (*BRIT*: *mother*) mamá; (*embalmed*) momia.
mumps [mʌmps] *n* paperas *fpl.*
munch [mʌntʃ] *vt, vi* mascar.
mundane [mʌn'deɪn] *adj* mundano.
municipal [mju:'nɪsɪpl] *adj* municipal.
municipality [mju:nɪsɪ'pælɪtɪ] *n* municipio.
munificence [mu:'nɪfɪsns] *n* munificencia.
munitions [mju:'nɪʃənz] *npl* municiones *fpl.*
mural ['mjuərl] *n* (*pintura*) mural *m.*
murder ['mə:də*] *n* asesinato; (*in law*) homicidio ♦ *vt* asesinar, matar; **to commit** ~ cometer un asesinato *or* homicidio.
murderer ['mə:dərə*] *n* asesino.
murderess ['mə:dərɪs] *n* asesina.
murderous ['mə:dərəs] *adj* homicida.
murk [mə:k] *n* oscuridad *f*, tinieblas *fpl.*
murky ['mə:kɪ] *adj* (*water, past*) turbio; (*room*) sombrío.
murmur ['mə:mə*] *n* murmullo ♦ *vt, vi* murmurar; **heart** ~ soplo cardíaco.
MusB(ac) *n abbr* (= *Bachelor of Music*) título universitario.
muscle ['mʌsl] *n* músculo.
►**muscle in** *vi* entrometerse.
muscular ['mʌskjulə*] *adj* muscular; (*person*) musculoso.
muscular dystrophy *n* distrofia muscular.
MusD(oc) *n abbr* (= *Doctor of Music*) título universitario.
muse [mju:z] *vi* meditar ♦ *n* musa.
museum [mju:'zɪəm] *n* museo.
mush [mʌʃ] *n* gachas *fpl.*
mushroom ['mʌʃrum] *n* (*gen*) seta, hongo; (*small*) champiñón *m* ♦ *vi* (*fig*) crecer de la noche a la mañana.
mushy ['mʌʃɪ] *adj* (*vegetables*) casi hecho puré; (*story*) sentimentaloide.
music ['mju:zɪk] *n* música.
musical ['mju:zɪkl] *adj* melodioso; (*person*) musical ♦ *n* (*show*) (comedia) musical *m.*
music(al) box *n* caja de música.
musical chairs *n* juego de las sillas; (*fig*) **to play** ~ cambiar de puesto continuamente.
musical instrument *n* instrumento musical.
musically ['mju:zɪklɪ] *adv* melodiosamente, armoniosamente.
music centre *n* equipo de música.
music hall *n* teatro de variedades.
musician [mju:'zɪʃən] *n* músico/a.
music stand *n* atril *m.*
musk [mʌsk] *n* (*perfume m de*) almizcle *m.*
musket ['mʌskɪt] *n* mosquete *m.*

musk rat *n* ratón *m* almizclero.
musk rose *n* (*BOT*) rosa almizcleña.
Muslim ['mʌzlɪm] *adj, n* musulmán/ana *m/f.*
muslin ['mʌzlɪn] *n* muselina.
musquash ['mʌskwɔʃ] *n* (*fur*) piel *f* del ratón almizclero.
muss [mʌs] *vt* (*col: hair*) despeinar; (: *dress*) arrugar.
mussel ['mʌsl] *n* mejillón *m.*
must [mʌst] *aux vb* (*obligation*): **I** ~ **do it** debo hacerlo, tengo que hacerlo; (*probability*): **he** ~ **be there by now** ya debe (de) estar allí ♦ *n*: **it's a** ~ es imprescindible.
mustache ['mʌstæʃ] *n* (*US*) = **moustache**.
mustard ['mʌstəd] *n* mostaza.
mustard gas *n* gas *m* mostaza.
muster ['mʌstə*] *vt* juntar, reunir; (*also:* ~ **up**) reunir; (: *courage*) armarse de.
mustiness ['mʌstɪnɪs] *n* olor *m* a cerrado.
mustn't ['mʌsnt] = **must not**.
musty ['mʌstɪ] *adj* mohoso, que huele a humedad.
mutant ['mju:tənt] *adj, n* mutante *m.*
mutate [mju:'teɪt] *vi* sufrir mutación, transformarse.
mutation [mju:'teɪʃən] *n* mutación *f.*
mute [mju:t] *adj, n* mudo/a *m/f.*
muted ['mju:tɪd] *adj* (*noise*) sordo; (*criticism*) callado.
mutilate ['mju:tɪleɪt] *vt* mutilar.
mutilation [mju:tɪ'leɪʃən] *n* mutilación *f.*
mutinous ['mju:tɪnəs] *adj* (*troops*) amotinado; (*attitude*) rebelde.
mutiny ['mju:tɪnɪ] *n* motín *m* ♦ *vi* amotinarse.
mutter ['mʌtə*] *vt, vi* murmurar.
mutton ['mʌtn] *n* (*carne f de*) cordero.
mutual ['mju:tʃuəl] *adj* mutuo; (*friend*) común.
mutually ['mju:tʃuəlɪ] *adv* mutuamente.
Muzak ® ['mju:zæk] *n* hilo musical.
muzzle ['mʌzl] *n* hocico; (*protective device*) bozal *m*; (*of gun*) boca ♦ *vt* amordazar; (*dog*) poner un bozal a.
MVP *n abbr* (*US SPORT*) = *most valuable player.*
MW *abbr* (= *medium wave*) onda media.
my [maɪ] *adj* mi(s); ~ **house/brother/sisters** mi casa/hermano/mis hermanas; **I've washed** ~ **hair/cut** ~ **finger** me he lavado el pelo/cortado un dedo; **is this** ~ **pen or yours?** ¿este bolígrafo es mío o tuyo?
Myanmar ['maɪænmɑ:*] *n* Myanmar.
myopic [maɪ'ɔpɪk] *adj* miope.
myriad ['mɪrɪəd] *n* (*of people, things*) miríada.
myrrh [mə:*] *n* mirra.

myself [maɪ'sɛlf] *pron* (*reflexive*) me; (*emphatic*) yo mismo; (*after prep*) mí (mismo); *see also* **oneself**.
mysterious [mɪs'tɪərɪəs] *adj* misterioso.
mysteriously [mɪs'tɪərɪəslɪ] *adv* misteriosamente.
mystery ['mɪstərɪ] *n* misterio.
mystery play *n* auto, misterio.
mystic ['mɪstɪk] *adj*, *n* místico/a *m/f*.
mystical ['mɪstɪkl] *adj* místico.
mysticism ['mɪstɪsɪzəm] *n* misticismo.
mystification [mɪstɪfɪ'keɪʃən] *n* perplejidad *f*; desconcierto.
mystify ['mɪstɪfaɪ] *vt* (*perplex*) dejar perplejo; (*disconcert*) desconcertar.
mystique [mɪs'tiːk] *n* misterio.
myth [mɪθ] *n* mito.
mythical ['mɪθɪkl] *adj* mítico.
mythological [mɪθə'lɔdʒɪkl] *adj* mitológico.
mythology [mɪ'θɔlədʒɪ] *n* mitología.

N n

N, n [ɛn] *n* (*letter*) N, n *f*; **N for Nellie**, (*US*) **N for Nan** N de Navarra.
N *abbr* (= *North*) N.
NA *n abbr* (*US*: = *Narcotics Anonymous*) *organización de ayuda a los drogadictos*; (*US*) = *National Academy*.
n/a *abbr* (= *not applicable*) no interesa; (*COMM etc*) = *no account*.
NAACP *n abbr* (*US*) = *National Association for the Advancement of Colored People*.
NAAFI ['næfɪ] *n abbr* (*BRIT*: = *Navy, Army & Air Force Institute*) *servicio de cantinas etc para las fuerzas armadas*.
nab [næb] *vt* (*col: grab*) coger (*SP*); (*LAM*); (: *catch out*) pillar.
NACU *n abbr* (*US*) = *National Association of Colleges and Universities*.
nadir ['neɪdɪə*] *n* (*ASTRO*) nadir *m*; (*fig*) punto más bajo.
NAFTA ['næftə] *n abbr* (= *North Atlantic Free Trade Agreement*) TLC *m*.
nag [næg] *n* (*pej: horse*) rocín *m* ♦ *vt* (*scold*) regañar; (*annoy*) fastidiar.
nagging ['nægɪŋ] *adj* (*doubt*) persistente; (*pain*) continuo ♦ *n* quejas *fpl*.
nail [neɪl] *n* (*human*) uña; (*metal*) clavo ♦ *vt* clavar; (*fig: catch*) coger (*SP*), pillar; **to pay cash on the** ~ pagar a tocateja; **to** ~

sb down to a date/price hacer que algn se comprometa a una fecha/un precio.
nailbrush ['neɪlbrʌʃ] *n* cepillo para las uñas.
nailfile ['neɪlfaɪl] *n* lima para las uñas.
nail polish *n* esmalte *m or* laca para las uñas.
nail polish remover *n* quitaesmalte *m*.
nail scissors *npl* tijeras *fpl* para las uñas.
nail varnish *n* (*BRIT*) = **nail polish**.
Nairobi [naɪ'rəubɪ] *n* Nairobi *m*.
naïve [naɪ'iːv] *adj* ingenuo.
naïvely [naɪ'iːvlɪ] *adv* ingenuamente.
naïveté [naːi'iːvteɪ], **naivety** [naɪ'iːvɪtɪ] *n* ingenuidad *f*, candidez *f*.
naked ['neɪkɪd] *adj* (*nude*) desnudo; (*flame*) expuesto al aire; **with the** ~ **eye** a simple vista.
NAM *n abbr* (*US*) = *National Association of Manufacturers*.
name [neɪm] *n* (*gen*) nombre *m*; (*surname*) apellido; (*reputation*) fama, renombre *m* ♦ *vt* (*child*) poner nombre a; (*appoint*) nombrar; **by** ~ de nombre; **in the** ~ **of** en nombre de; **what's your** ~? ¿cómo se llama usted?; **my** ~ **is Peter** me llamo Pedro; **to give one's** ~ **and address** dar sus señas; **to take sb's** ~ **and address** apuntar las señas de algn; **to make a** ~ **for o.s.** hacerse famoso; **to get (o.s.) a bad** ~ forjarse una mala reputación.
name-drop ['neɪmdrɔp] *vi*: **he's always** ~**ping** siempre está presumiendo de la gente que conoce.
nameless ['neɪmlɪs] *adj* anónimo, sin nombre.
namely ['neɪmlɪ] *adv* a saber.
nameplate ['neɪmpleɪt] *n* (*on door etc*) placa.
namesake ['neɪmseɪk] *n* tocayo/a.
nan bread [naːn-] *n pan indio sin apenas levadura*.
nanny ['nænɪ] *n* niñera.
nap [næp] *n* (*sleep*) sueñecito, siesta; **they were caught** ~**ping** les pilló desprevenidos.
NAPA *n abbr* (*US*: = *National Association of Performing Artists*) *sindicato de trabajadores del espectáculo*.
napalm ['neɪpaːm] *n* napalm *m*.
nape [neɪp] *n*: ~ **of the neck** nuca, cogote *m*.
napkin ['næpkɪn] *n* (*also*: **table** ~) servilleta.
Naples ['neɪplz] *n* Nápoles.
nappy ['næpɪ] *n* (*BRIT*) pañal *m*.
nappy liner *n* gasa.
nappy rash *n* prurito.
narcissism [naː'sɪsɪzəm] *n* narcisismo.

narcissus, _pl_ **narcissi** [nɑːˈsɪsəs, -saɪ] _n_
narciso.
narcotic [nɑːˈkɔtɪk] _adj, n_ narcótico.
narrate [nəˈreɪt] _vt_ narrar, contar.
narration [nəˈreɪʃən] _n_ narración _f_, relato.
narrative [ˈnærətɪv] _n_ narrativa ♦ _adj_
narrativo.
narrator [nəˈreɪtə*] _n_ narrador(a) _m/f_.
narrow [ˈnærəu] _adj_ estrecho; (_resources,
means_) escaso ♦ _vi_ estrecharse; (_diminish_)
reducirse; **to have a ~ escape** escaparse
por los pelos; **to ~ sth down** reducir
algo.
narrow gauge _adj_ (_RAIL_) de vía estrecha.
narrowly [ˈnærəlɪ] _adv_ (_miss_) por poco.
narrow-minded [nærəuˈmaɪndɪd] _adj_ de
miras estrechas.
narrow-mindedness [ˈnærəuˈmaɪndɪdnɪs] _n_
estrechez _f_ de miras.
NAS _n abbr_ (_US_) = _National Academy of
Sciences_.
NASA _n abbr_ (_US_: = _National Aeronautics and
Space Administration_) NASA _f_.
nasal [ˈneɪzl] _adj_ nasal.
Nassau [ˈnæsɔː] _n_ (_in Bahamas_) Nassau _m_.
nastily [ˈnɑːstɪlɪ] _adv_ (_unpleasantly_) de mala
manera; (_spitefully_) con rencor.
nastiness [ˈnɑːstɪnɪs] _n_ (_malice_)
malevolencia; (_rudeness_) grosería; (_of
person, remark_) maldad _f_; (_spitefulness_)
rencor _m_.
nasturtium [nəsˈtəːʃəm] _n_ capuchina.
nasty [ˈnɑːstɪ] _adj_ (_remark_) feo; (_person_)
antipático; (_revolting: taste, smell_)
asqueroso; (_wound, disease etc_) peligroso,
grave; **to turn ~** (_situation_) ponerse feo;
(_weather_) empeorar; (_person_) ponerse
negro.
NAS/UWT _n abbr_ (_BRIT_: = _National
Association of Schoolmasters/Union of
Women Teachers_) sindicato de profesores.
nation [ˈneɪʃən] _n_ nación _f_.
national [ˈnæʃənl] _adj_ nacional ♦ _n_ súbdito/
a.
national anthem _n_ himno nacional.
National Curriculum _n_ (_BRIT_) plan _m_
general de estudios (_en Inglaterra y Gales_).
national debt _n_ deuda pública.
national dress _n_ traje _m_ típico del país.
National Guard _n_ (_US_) Guardia Nacional.
National Health Service (NHS) _n_ (_BRIT_)
servicio nacional de sanidad, ≈
INSALUD _m_ (_SP_).
National Insurance _n_ (_BRIT_) seguro social
nacional, ≈ Seguridad _f_ Social.
nationalism [ˈnæʃnəlɪzəm] _n_ nacionalismo.
nationalist [ˈnæʃnəlɪst] _adj, n_ nacionalista
_m/f_.

nationality [næʃəˈnælɪtɪ] _n_ nacionalidad _f_.
nationalization [næʃnəlaɪˈzeɪʃən] _n_
nacionalización _f_.
nationalize [ˈnæʃnəlaɪz] _vt_ nacionalizar; **~d
industry** industria nacionalizada.
nationally [ˈnæʃnəlɪ] _adv_ (_nationwide_) a
escala nacional; (_as a nation_) como
nación.
national press _n_ prensa nacional.
national service _n_ (_MIL_) servicio militar.
National Trust _n_ (_BRIT_) _organización
encargada de preservar el patrimonio
histórico británico_.
nationwide [ˈneɪʃənwaɪd] _adj_ a escala
nacional.
native [ˈneɪtɪv] _n_ (_local inhabitant_) natural
_m/f_; (_in colonies_) indígena _m/f_, nativo/a ♦ _adj_
(_indigenous_) indígena; (_country_) natal;
(_innate_) natural, innato; **a ~ of Russia**
un(a) natural de Rusia; **~ language**
lengua materna; **a ~ speaker of French** un
hablante nativo de francés.
Native American _adj, n_ americano/a
indígena _m/f_, amerindio/a _m/f_.
Nativity [nəˈtɪvɪtɪ] _n_: **the ~** Navidad _f_.
nativity play _n_ auto del nacimiento.
NATO [ˈneɪtəu] _n abbr_ (= _North Atlantic
Treaty Organization_) OTAN _f_.
natter [ˈnætə*] _vi_ (_BRIT_) charlar ♦ _n_: **to have
a ~** charlar.
natural [ˈnætʃrəl] _adj_ natural; **death from ~
causes** (_LAW_) muerte _f_ por causas
naturales.
natural childbirth _n_ parto natural.
natural gas _n_ gas _m_ natural.
natural history _n_ historia natural.
naturalist [ˈnætʃrəlɪst] _n_ naturalista _m/f_.
naturalization [nætʃrəlaɪˈzeɪʃən] _n_
naturalización _f_.
naturalize [ˈnætʃrəlaɪz] _vt_: **to become ~d**
(_person_) naturalizarse; (_plant_)
aclimatarse.
naturally [ˈnætʃrəlɪ] _adv_ (_speak etc_)
naturalmente; (_of course_) desde luego,
por supuesto, ¡cómo no! (_esp LAM_);
(_instinctively_) por naturaleza.
naturalness [ˈnætʃrəlnɪs] _n_ naturalidad _f_.
natural resources _npl_ recursos _mpl_
naturales.
natural selection _n_ selección _f_ natural.
natural wastage _n_ (_INDUSTRY_) desgaste _m_
natural.
nature [ˈneɪtʃə*] _n_ naturaleza; (_group, sort_)
género, clase _f_; (_character_) modo de ser,
carácter _m_; **by ~** por naturaleza;
documents of a confidential ~
documentos _mpl_ de tipo confidencial.
-natured [ˈneɪtʃəd] _suff_: **ill~** malhumorado.

nature reserve *n* reserva natural.
nature trail *n* camino forestal educativo.
naturist ['neɪtʃərɪst] *n* naturista *m/f.*
naught [nɔːt] = **nought.**
naughtily ['nɔːtɪlɪ] *adv* (*behave*) mal; (*say*) con malicia.
naughtiness ['nɔːtɪnɪs] *n* travesuras *fpl.*
naughty ['nɔːtɪ] *adj* (*child*) travieso; (*story, film*) picante, escabroso, colorado (*LAM*).
nausea ['nɔːsɪə] *n* náusea.
nauseate ['nɔːsɪeɪt] *vt* dar náuseas a; (*fig*) dar asco a.
nauseating ['nɔːsɪeɪtɪŋ] *adj* nauseabundo; (*fig*) asqueroso, repugnante.
nauseous ['nɔːsɪəs] *adj* nauseabundo; **to feel** ~ sentir náuseas.
nautical ['nɔːtɪkl] *adj* náutico, marítimo; ~ **mile** milla marina.
naval ['neɪvl] *adj* naval, de marina.
naval officer *n* oficial *m/f* de marina.
nave [neɪv] *n* nave *f.*
navel ['neɪvl] *n* ombligo.
navigable ['nævɪgəbl] *adj* navegable.
navigate ['nævɪgeɪt] *vt* (*ship*) gobernar; (*river etc*) navegar por ♦ *vi* navegar; (*AUT*) hacer de copiloto.
navigation [nævɪ'geɪʃən] *n* (*action*) navegación *f*; (*science*) náutica.
navigator ['nævɪgeɪtə*] *n* navegante *m/f.*
navvy ['nævɪ] *n* (*BRIT*) peón *m* caminero.
navy ['neɪvɪ] *n* marina de guerra; (*ships*) armada, flota.
navy(-blue) ['neɪvɪ('bluː)] *adj* azul marino.
Nazareth ['næzərɪθ] *n* Nazaret *m.*
Nazi ['nɑːtsɪ] *adj*, *n* nazi *m/f.*
NB *abbr* (= *nota bene*) nótese; (*Canada*) = *New Brunswick.*
NBA *n abbr* (*US*) = *National Basketball Association, National Boxing Association.*
NBC *n abbr* (*US*: = *National Broadcasting Company*) *cadena de televisión.*
NBS *n abbr* (*US*: = *National Bureau of Standards*) ~ Oficina Nacional de Normalización.
NC *abbr* (*COMM etc*) = *no charge*; (*US*) = *North Carolina.*
NCC *n abbr* (*BRIT*: = *Nature Conservancy Council*) ≈ ICONA *m*; (*US*) = *National Council of Churches.*
NCCL *n abbr* (*BRIT*: = *National Council for Civil Liberties*) *asociación para la defensa de las libertades públicas.*
NCO *n abbr* = **non-commissioned officer.**
ND *abbr* (*US*) = *North Dakota.*
N. Dak. *abbr* (*US*) = *North Dakota.*
NE *abbr* (*US*) = *Nebraska, New England.*
NEA *n abbr* (*US*) = *National Education Association.*

Neapolitan [nɪə'pɒlɪtən] *adj, n* napolitano/a *m/f.*
neap tide [niːp-] *n* marea muerta.
near [nɪə*] *adj* (*place, relation*) cercano; (*time*) próximo ♦ *adv* cerca ♦ *prep* (*also*: ~ **to**: *space*) cerca de, junto a; (: *time*) cerca de ♦ *vt* acercarse a, aproximarse a; ~ **here/there** cerca de aquí/de allí; **£25,000 or** ~**est offer** 25,000 libras o precio a discutir; **in the** ~ **future** en fecha próxima; **the building is** ~**ing completion** el edificio está casi terminado.
nearby [nɪə'baɪ] *adj* cercano, próximo ♦ *adv* cerca.
nearly ['nɪəlɪ] *adv* casi, por poco; **I** ~ **fell** por poco me caigo; **not** ~ ni mucho menos, ni con mucho.
near miss *n* (*shot*) tiro casi en el blanco; (*AVIAT*) *accidente evitado por muy poco.*
nearness ['nɪənɪs] *n* cercanía, proximidad *f.*
nearside ['nɪəsaɪd] *n* (*AUT*: *right-hand drive*) lado izquierdo (: *left-hand drive*) lado derecho.
near-sighted [nɪə'saɪtɪd] *adj* miope, corto de vista.
neat [niːt] *adj* (*place*) ordenado, bien cuidado; (*person*) pulcro; (*plan*) ingenioso; (*spirits*) solo.
neatly ['niːtlɪ] *adv* (*tidily*) con esmero; (*skilfully*) ingeniosamente.
neatness ['niːtnɪs] *n* (*tidiness*) orden *m*; (*skilfulness*) destreza, habilidad *f.*
Nebr. *abbr* (*US*) = *Nebraska.*
nebulous ['nɛbjuləs] *adj* (*fig*) vago, confuso.
necessarily ['nɛsɪsrɪlɪ] *adv* necesariamente; **not** ~ no necesariamente.
necessary ['nɛsɪsrɪ] *adj* necesario, preciso; **he did all that was** ~ hizo todo lo necesario; **if** ~ si es necesario.
necessitate [nɪ'sɛsɪteɪt] *vt* necesitar, precisar.
necessity [nɪ'sɛsɪtɪ] *n* necesidad *f*; **necessities** *npl* artículos *mpl* de primera necesidad; **in case of** ~ en caso de urgencia.
neck [nɛk] *n* (*ANAT*) cuello; (*of animal*) pescuezo ♦ *vi* besuquearse; ~ **and** ~ parejos; **to stick one's** ~ **out** (*col*) arriesgarse.
necklace ['nɛklɪs] *n* collar *m.*
neckline ['nɛklaɪn] *n* escote *m.*
necktie ['nɛktaɪ] *n* (*US*) corbata *f.*
nectar ['nɛktə*] *n* néctar *m.*
nectarine ['nɛktərɪn] *n* nectarina.
NEDC *n abbr* (*BRIT*: = *National Economic Development Council*) ~ Consejo Económico y Social.

Neddy ['nɛdɪ] *n abbr* (*BRIT col*) = **NEDC**.
née [neɪ] *adj*: ~ **Scott** de soltera Scott.
need [niːd] *n* (*lack*) escasez *f*, falta;
(*necessity*) necesidad *f* ♦ *vt* (*require*)
necesitar; **in case of** ~ en caso de
necesidad; **there's no** ~ **for ...** no hace(n)
falta ...; **to be in** ~ **of, have** ~ **of**
necesitar; **10 will meet my immediate** ~**s**
10 satisfacerán mis necesidades más
apremiantes; **the** ~**s of industry** las
necesidades de la industria; **I** ~ **it** lo
necesito; **a signature is** ~**ed** se requiere
una firma; **I** ~ **to do it** tengo que hacerlo;
you don't ~ **to go** no hace falta que
vayas.
needle ['niːdl] *n* aguja ♦ *vt* (*fig: col*) picar,
fastidiar.
needless ['niːdlɪs] *adj* innecesario, inútil; ~
to say huelga decir que.
needlessly ['niːdlɪslɪ] *adv*
innecesariamente, inútilmente.
needlework ['niːdlwəːk] *n* (*activity*) costura,
labor *f* de aguja.
needn't ['niːdnt] = **need not**.
needy ['niːdɪ] *adj* necesitado.
negation [nɪ'geɪʃən] *n* negación *f*.
negative ['nɛɡətɪv] *n* (*PHOT*) negativo;
(*answer*) negativa; (*LING*) negación *f* ♦ *adj*
negativo.
negative cash flow *n* flujo negativo de
efectivo.
negative equity *n situación en la que el*
valor de la vivienda es menor que el de
la hipoteca que pesa sobre ella.
neglect [nɪ'ɡlɛkt] *vt* (*one's duty*) faltar a, no
cumplir con; (*child*) descuidar,
desatender ♦ *n* (*state*) abandono;
(*personal*) dejadez *f*; (*of duty*)
incumplimiento; **to** ~ **to do sth** olvidarse
de hacer algo.
neglected [nɪ'ɡlɛktɪd] *adj* abandonado.
neglectful [nɪ'ɡlɛktful] *adj* negligente; **to be**
~ **of sth/sb** desatender algo/a algn.
negligee ['nɛɡlɪʒeɪ] *n* (*nightdress*) salto de
cama.
negligence ['nɛɡlɪdʒəns] *n* negligencia.
negligent ['nɛɡlɪdʒənt] *adj* negligente;
(*casual*) descuidado.
negligently ['nɛɡlɪdʒəntlɪ] *adv*
negligentemente; (*casually*) con descuido.
negligible ['nɛɡlɪdʒɪbl] *adj* insignificante,
despreciable.
negotiable [nɪ'ɡəuʃɪəbl] *adj* (*cheque*)
negociable; **not** ~ (*cheque*) no trasferible.
negotiate [nɪ'ɡəuʃɪeɪt] *vt* (*treaty, loan*)
negociar; (*obstacle*) franquear; (*bend in
road*) tomar ♦ *vi*: **to** ~ **(with)** negociar
(con); **to** ~ **with sb for sth** tratar *or*

negociar con algn por algo.
negotiating table [nɪ'ɡəuʃɪeɪtɪŋ-] *n* mesa
de negociaciones.
negotiation [nɪɡəuʃɪ'eɪʃən] *n* negociación *f*,
gestión *f*; **to enter into** ~**s with sb** entrar
en negociaciones con algn.
negotiator [nɪ'ɡəuʃɪeɪtə*] *n* negociador(a)
m/f.
Negress ['niːɡrɪs] *n* negra.
Negro ['niːɡrəu] *adj*, *n* negro.
neigh [neɪ] *n* relincho ♦ *vi* relinchar.
neighbour, (*US*) **neighbor** ['neɪbə*] *n*
vecino/a.
neighbo(u)rhood ['neɪbəhud] *n* (*place*)
vecindad *f*, barrio; (*people*) vecindario.
neighbourhood watch *n* (*BRIT: also*: ~
scheme) *vigilancia del barrio por los*
propios vecinos.
neighbo(u)ring ['neɪbərɪŋ] *adj* vecino.
neighbo(u)rly ['neɪbəlɪ] *adj* amigable,
sociable.
neither ['naɪðə*] *adj* ni ♦ *conj*: **I didn't move**
and ~ **did John** no me he movido, ni Juan
tampoco ♦ *pron* ninguno; ~ **is true**
ninguno/a de los/las dos es cierto/a ♦ *adv*:
~ **good nor bad** ni bueno ni malo.
neo ... [niːəu] *pref* neo....
neolithic [niːəu'lɪθɪk] *adj* neolítico.
neologism [nɪ'ɔlədʒɪzəm] *n* neologismo.
neon ['niːɔn] *n* neón *m*.
neon light *n* lámpara de neón.
Nepal [nɪ'pɔːl] *n* Nepal *m*.
nephew ['nɛvjuː] *n* sobrino.
nepotism ['nɛpətɪzəm] *n* nepotismo.
nerd [nəːd] *n* (*col*) primo/a.
nerve [nəːv] *n* (*ANAT*) nervio; (*courage*)
valor *m*; (*impudence*) descaro, frescura; **a**
fit of ~**s** un ataque de nervios; **to lose**
one's ~ (*self-confidence*) perder el valor.
nerve centre *n* (*ANAT*) centro nervioso;
(*fig*) punto neurálgico.
nerve gas *n* gas *m* nervioso.
nerve-racking ['nəːvrækɪŋ] *adj* angustioso.
nervous ['nəːvəs] *adj* (*anxious, ANAT*)
nervioso; (*timid*) tímido, miedoso.
nervous breakdown *n* crisis *f* nerviosa.
nervously ['nəːvəslɪ] *adv* nerviosamente;
tímidamente.
nervousness ['nəːvəsnɪs] *n* nerviosismo;
timidez *f*.
nervous wreck *n* (*col*): **to be a** ~ estar de
los nervios.
nervy ['nəːvɪ] *adj*: **to be** ~ estar nervioso.
nest [nɛst] *n* (*of bird*) nido ♦ *vi* anidar.
nest egg *n* (*fig*) ahorros *mpl*.
nestle ['nɛsl] *vi*: **to** ~ **down** acurrucarse.
nestling ['nɛstlɪŋ] *n* pajarito.
net [nɛt] *n* (*gen*) red *f*; (*fabric*) tul *m* ♦ *adj*

(*COMM*) neto, líquido; (*weight, price, salary*) neto ♦ *vt* coger (*SP*) *or* agarrar (*LAM*) con red; (*money: subj: person*) cobrar; (: *deal, sale*) conseguir; (*SPORT*) marcar; ~ **of tax** neto; **he earns £10,000 ~ per year** gana 10,000 libras netas por año; **the N~** (*Internet*) la Red.

netball ['nɛtbɔ:l] *n* básquet *m*.

net curtain *n* visillo.

Netherlands ['nɛðələndz] *npl*: **the ~** los Países Bajos.

net income *n* renta neta.

net loss *n* pérdida neta.

net profit *n* beneficio neto.

nett [nɛt] *adj* = **net.**

netting ['nɛtɪŋ] *n* red *f*, redes *fpl*.

nettle ['nɛtl] *n* ortiga

network ['nɛtwə:k] *n* red *f* ♦ *vt* (*RADIO, TV*) difundir por la red de emisores; **local area ~** red local.

neuralgia [njuə'rældʒə] *n* neuralgia.

neurological [njuərə'lɔdʒɪkl] *adj* neurológico.

neurosis, *pl* **-ses** [njuə'rəusɪs, -si:z] *n* neurosis *f inv*.

neurotic [njuə'rɔtɪk] *adj, n* neurótico/a *m/f*.

neuter ['nju:tə*] *adj* (*LING*) neutro ♦ *vt* castrar, capar.

neutral ['nju:trəl] *adj* (*person*) neutral; (*colour etc, ELEC*) neutro ♦ *n* (*AUT*) punto muerto.

neutrality [nju:'trælɪtɪ] *n* neutralidad *f*.

neutralize ['nju:trəlaɪz] *vt* neutralizar.

neutron ['nju:trɔn] *n* neutrón *m*.

neutron bomb *n* bomba de neutrones.

Nev. *abbr* (*US*) = *Nevada*.

never ['nɛvə*] *adv* nunca, jamás; **I ~ went** no fui nunca; **~ in my life** jamás en la vida; *see also* **mind.**

never-ending [nɛvər'ɛndɪŋ] *adj* interminable, sin fin.

nevertheless [nɛvəðə'lɛs] *adv* sin embargo, no obstante.

new [nju:] *adj* nuevo; (*recent*) reciente; **as good as ~** como nuevo.

New Age *n* Nueva era.

newborn ['nju:bɔ:n] *adj* recién nacido.

newcomer ['nju:kʌmə*] *n* recién venido *or* llegado.

new-fangled ['nju:fæŋgld] *adj* (*pej*) modernísimo.

new-found ['nju:faund] *adj* (*friend*) nuevo; (*enthusiasm*) recién adquirido.

New Guinea *n* Nueva Guinea.

newly ['nju:lɪ] *adv* recién.

newly-weds ['nju:lɪwɛdz] *npl* recién casados.

new moon *n* luna nueva.

newness ['nju:nɪs] *n* novedad *f*.

news [nju:z] *n* noticias *fpl*; **a piece of ~** una noticia; **the ~** (*RADIO, TV*) las noticias *fpl*, el telediario; **good/bad ~** buenas/malas noticias *fpl*; **financial ~** noticias *fpl* financieras.

news agency *n* agencia de noticias.

newsagent ['nju:zeɪdʒənt] *n* (*BRIT*) vendedor(a) *m/f* de periódicos.

news bulletin *n* (*RADIO, TV*) noticiario.

newscaster ['nju:zkɑ:stə*] *n* presentador(a) *m/f*, locutor(a) *m/f*.

news dealer *n* (*US*) = **newsagent.**

news flash *n* noticia de última hora.

newsletter ['nju:zlɛtə*] *n* hoja informativa, boletín *m*.

newspaper ['nju:zpeɪpə*] *n* periódico, diario; **daily ~** diario; **weekly ~** periódico semanal.

newsprint ['nju:zprɪnt] *n* papel *m* de periódico.

newsreader ['nju:zri:də*] *n* = **newscaster.**

newsreel ['nju:zri:l] *n* noticiario.

newsroom ['nju:zru:m] *n* (*PRESS, RADIO, TV*) sala de redacción.

news stand *n* quiosco *or* puesto de periódicos.

newsworthy ['nju:zwə:ðɪ] *adj*: **to be ~** ser de interés periodístico.

newt [nju:t] *n* tritón *m*.

new town *n* (*BRIT*) ciudad *f* nueva (*construida con subsidios estatales*).

New Year *n* Año Nuevo; **Happy ~!** ¡Feliz Año Nuevo!; **to wish sb a happy ~** desear a algn un feliz año nuevo.

New Year's Day *n* Día *m* de Año Nuevo.

New Year's Eve *n* Nochevieja.

New York [-'jɔ:k] *n* Nueva York.

New Zealand [-'zi:lənd] *n* Nueva Zelanda (*SP*), Nueva Zelandia (*LAM*) ♦ *adj* neozelandés/esa.

New Zealander [-'zi:ləndə*] *n* neozelandés/esa *m/f*.

next [nɛkst] *adj* (*house, room*) vecino, de al lado; (*meeting*) próximo; (*page*) siguiente ♦ *adv* después; **the ~ day** el día siguiente; **~ time** la próxima vez; **~ year** el año próximo *or* que viene; **~ month** el mes que viene *or* entrante; **the week after ~** no la semana que viene sino la otra; **"turn to the ~ page"** "vuelva a la página siguiente"; **you're ~** le toca; **~ to** *prep* junto a, al lado de; **~ to nothing** casi nada.

next door *adv* en la casa de al lado ♦ *adj* vecino, de al lado.

next-of-kin ['nɛkstəv'kɪn] *n* pariente(s) *m(pl)* más cercano(s).

NF *n abbr* (*BRIT POL*: = *National Front*) *partido político de la extrema derecha* ♦ *abbr* (*Canada*) = *Newfoundland*.

NFL *n abbr* (*US*) = *National Football League*.

Nfld. *abbr* (*Canada*) = *Newfoundland*.

NG *abbr* (*US*) = **National Guard**.

NGO *n abbr* (= *non-governmental organization*) ONG *f*.

NH *abbr* (*US*) = *New Hampshire*.

NHL *n abbr* (*US*) = *National Hockey League*.

NHS *n abbr see* **National Health Service**.

NI *abbr* = **Northern Ireland**; (*BRIT*) = **National Insurance**.

nib [nɪb] *n* plumilla.

nibble ['nɪbl] *vt* mordisquear.

Nicaragua [nɪkə'ræɡjuə] *n* Nicaragua.

Nicaraguan [nɪkə'ræɡjuən] *adj, n* nicaragüense *m/f*, nicaragüeño/a *m/f*.

Nice [niːs] *n* Niza.

nice [naɪs] *adj* (*likeable*) simpático, majo; (*kind*) amable; (*pleasant*) agradable; (*attractive*) bonito, mono; (*distinction*) fino; (*taste, smell, meal*) rico.

nice-looking ['naɪslʊkɪŋ] *adj* guapo.

nicely ['naɪslɪ] *adv* amablemente; (*of health etc*) bien; **that will do ~** perfecto.

niceties ['naɪsɪtɪz] *npl* detalles *mpl*.

niche [niːʃ] *n* (*ARCH*) nicho, hornacina.

nick [nɪk] *n* (*wound*) rasguño; (*cut, indentation*) mella, muesca ♦ *vt* (*cut*) cortar; (*col*) birlar, mangar; (: *arrest*) pillar; **in the ~ of time** justo a tiempo; **in good ~** en buen estado; **to ~ o.s.** cortarse.

nickel ['nɪkl] *n* níquel *m*; (*US*) *moneda de 5 centavos*.

nickname ['nɪkneɪm] *n* apodo, mote *m* ♦ *vt* apodar.

Nicosia [nɪkə'siːə] *n* Nicosia.

nicotine ['nɪkətiːn] *n* nicotina.

nicotine patch *n* parche *m* de nicotina.

niece [niːs] *n* sobrina.

nifty ['nɪftɪ] *adj* (*col*: *car, jacket*) elegante, chulo; (: *gadget, tool*) ingenioso.

Niger ['naɪdʒə*] *n* (*country, river*) Níger *m*.

Nigeria [naɪ'dʒɪərɪə] *n* Nigeria.

Nigerian [naɪ'dʒɪərɪən] *adj, n* nigeriano/a *m/f*.

niggardly ['nɪɡədlɪ] *adj* (*person*) avaro, tacaño, avariento; (*allowance, amount*) miserable.

nigger ['nɪɡə*] *n* (*col!*: *highly offensive*) negro/a.

niggle ['nɪɡl] *vt* preocupar ♦ *vi* (*complain*) quejarse; (*fuss*) preocuparse por minucias.

niggling ['nɪɡlɪŋ] *adj* (*detail*: *trifling*) nimio, insignificante; (*annoying*) molesto; (*doubt, pain*) constante.

night [naɪt] *n* (*gen*) noche *f*; (*evening*) tarde *f*; **last ~** anoche; **the ~ before last** anteanoche, antes de ayer por la noche; **at ~, by ~** de noche, por la noche; **in the ~, during the ~** durante la noche, por la noche.

night-bird ['naɪtbəːd] *n* pájaro nocturno; (*fig*) trasnochador(a) *m/f*, madrugador(a) *m/f* (*LAM*).

nightcap ['naɪtkæp] *n* (*drink*) *bebida que se toma antes de acostarse*.

night club *n* club nocturno, discoteca.

nightdress ['naɪtdrɛs] *n* (*BRIT*) camisón *m*.

nightfall ['naɪtfɔːl] *n* anochecer *m*.

nightgown ['naɪtɡaun], **nightie** ['naɪtɪ] (*BRIT*) *n* = **nightdress**.

nightingale ['naɪtɪŋɡeɪl] *n* ruiseñor *m*.

night life *n* vida nocturna.

nightly ['naɪtlɪ] *adj* de todas las noches ♦ *adv* todas las noches, cada noche.

nightmare ['naɪtmɛə*] *n* pesadilla.

night porter *n* guardián *m* nocturno.

night safe *n* caja fuerte.

night school *n* clase(s) *f*(*pl*) nocturna(s).

nightshade ['naɪtʃeɪd] *n*: **deadly ~** (*BOT*) belladona.

night shift *n* turno nocturno *or* de noche.

night-time ['naɪttaɪm] *n* noche *f*.

night watchman *n* vigilante *m* nocturno, sereno.

nihilism ['naɪɪlɪzəm] *n* nihilismo.

nil [nɪl] *n* (*BRIT SPORT*) cero, nada.

Nile [naɪl] *n*: **the ~** el Nilo.

nimble ['nɪmbl] *adj* (*agile*) ágil, ligero; (*skilful*) diestro.

nimbly ['nɪmblɪ] *adv* ágilmente; con destreza.

nine [naɪn] *num* nueve.

nineteen [naɪn'tiːn] *num* diecinueve.

nineteenth [naɪn'tiːnθ] *num* decimonoveno, decimonono.

ninety ['naɪntɪ] *num* noventa.

ninth [naɪnθ] *num* noveno.

nip [nɪp] *vt* (*pinch*) pellizcar; (*bite*) morder ♦ *vi* (*BRIT col*): **to ~ out/down/up** salir/ bajar/subir un momento ♦ *n* (*drink*) trago.

nipple ['nɪpl] *n* (*ANAT*) pezón *m*; (*of bottle*) tetilla; (*TECH*) boquilla, manguito.

nippy ['nɪpɪ] *adj* (*BRIT*: *person*) rápido; (*taste*) picante; **it's a very ~ car** es un coche muy potente para el tamaño que tiene.

nit [nɪt] *n* (*of louse*) liendre *f*; (*col*: *idiot*) imbécil *m/f*.

nit-pick ['nɪtpɪk] *vi* (*col*) sacar punta a todo.

nitrogen ['naɪtrədʒən] *n* nitrógeno.

nitroglycerin(e) ['naɪtrəu'ɡlɪsəriːn] *n* nitroglicerina.

nitty-gritty [nɪtɪ'ɡrɪtɪ] *n* (*col*): **to get down**

to the ~ ir al grano.
nitwit ['nɪtwɪt] n cretino/a.
NJ abbr (US) = New Jersey.
NLF n abbr (= National Liberation Front) FLN m.
NLQ abbr (= near letter quality) calidad f casi de correspondencia.
NLRB n abbr (US: = National Labor Relations Board) organismo de protección al trabajador.
NM, N. Mex. abbr (US) = New Mexico.

═══════════════════════════════ KEYWORD

no [nəu] (pl ~es) adv (opposite of "yes") no; **are you coming? —** ~ **(I'm not)** ¿vienes? — no; **would you like some more? —** ~ **thank you** ¿quieres más? — no gracias
♦ adj (not any): **I have** ~ **money/time/ books** no tengo dinero/tiempo/libros; ~ **other man would have done it** ningún otro lo hubiera hecho; **"~ entry"** "prohibido el paso"; **"~ smoking"** "prohibido fumar"
♦ n no m.

no. abbr (= number) nº., núm.
nobble ['nɔbl] vt (BRIT col: bribe) sobornar; (: catch) pescar; (: RACING) drogar.
Nobel prize [nəu'bɛl-] n premio Nobel.
nobility [nəu'bɪlɪtɪ] n nobleza.
noble ['nəubl] adj (person) noble; (title) de nobleza.
nobleman ['nəublmən] n noble m.
nobly ['nəublɪ] adv (selflessly) noblemente.
nobody ['nəubədɪ] pron nadie.
no-claims bonus ['nəukleɪmz-] n bonificación f por carencia de reclamaciones.
nocturnal [nɔk'tɜːnl] adj nocturno.
nod [nɔd] vi saludar con la cabeza; (in agreement) asentir con la cabeza ♦ vt: **to** ~ **one's head** inclinar la cabeza ♦ n inclinación f de cabeza; **they ~ded their agreement** asintieron con la cabeza.
►**nod off** vi cabecear.
no-fly zone [nəu'flaɪ-] n zona de exclusión aérea.
noise [nɔɪz] n ruido; (din) escándalo, estrépito.
noisily ['nɔɪzɪlɪ] adv ruidosamente, estrepitosamente.
noisy ['nɔɪzɪ] adj (gen) ruidoso; (child) escandaloso.
nomad ['nəumæd] n nómada m/f.
nomadic [nəu'mædɪk] adj nómada.
no man's land n tierra de nadie.
nominal ['nɔmɪnl] adj nominal.
nominate ['nɔmɪneɪt] vt (propose)

proponer; (appoint) nombrar.
nomination [nɔmɪ'neɪʃən] n propuesta; nombramiento.
nominee [nɔmɪ'niː] n candidato/a.
non... [nɔn] pref no, des..., in....
nonalcoholic [nɔnælkə'hɔlɪk] adj sin alcohol.
nonaligned [nɔnə'laɪnd] adj no alineado.
nonarrival [nɔnə'raɪvl] n falta de llegada.
nonce word [nɔns-] n hápax m.
nonchalant ['nɔnʃələnt] adj indiferente.
noncommissioned [nɔnkə'mɪʃənd] adj: ~ **officer** suboficial m/f.
noncommittal ['nɔnkə'mɪtl] adj (reserved) reservado; (uncommitted) evasivo.
nonconformist [nɔnkən'fɔːmɪst] adj inconformista ♦ n inconformista m/f; (BRIT REL) no conformista m/f.
noncontributory [nɔnkən'trɪbjutərɪ] adj: ~ **pension scheme** or (US) **plan** fondo de pensiones no contributivo.
noncooperation ['nɔnkəuɔpə'reɪʃən] n no cooperación f.
nondescript ['nɔndɪskrɪpt] adj anodino, soso.
none [nʌn] pron ninguno/a ♦ adv de ninguna manera; ~ **of you** ninguno de vosotros; **I've** ~ **left** no me queda ninguno/a; **he's** ~ **the worse for it** no le ha perjudicado; **I have** ~ no tengo ninguno; ~ **at all** (not one) ni uno.
nonentity [nɔ'nɛntɪtɪ] n cero a la izquierda, nulidad f.
nonessential [nɔnɪ'sɛnʃl] adj no esencial ♦ n: ~**s** cosas fpl secundarias or sin importancia.
nonetheless [nʌnðə'lɛs] adv sin embargo, no obstante, aún así.
non-event [nɔnɪ'vɛnt] n acontecimiento sin importancia; **it was a** ~ no pasó absolutamente nada.
nonexecutive [nɔnɪg'zɛkjutɪv] adj: ~ **director** director m no ejecutivo.
nonexistent [nɔnɪg'zɪstənt] adj inexistente.
nonfiction [nɔn'fɪkʃən] n no ficción f.
nonintervention [nɔnɪntə'vɛnʃən] n no intervención f.
no-no ['nəunəu] n (col): **it's a** ~ de eso ni hablar.
non obst. abbr (= non obstante: notwithstanding) no obstante.
no-nonsense [nəu'nɔnsəns] adj sensato.
nonpayment [nɔn'peɪmənt] n falta de pago.
nonplussed [nɔn'plʌst] adj perplejo.
non-profit-making [nɔn'prɔfɪtmeɪkɪŋ] adj no lucrativo.
nonsense ['nɔnsəns] n tonterías fpl,

disparates *fpl*; ~! ¡qué tonterías!; **it is ~ to say that ...** es absurdo decir que ....

nonsensical [nɔn'sɛnsɪkl] *adj* disparatado, absurdo.

nonshrink [nɔn'ʃrɪŋk] *adj* que no encoge.

nonskid [nɔn'skɪd] *adj* antideslizante.

nonsmoker ['nɔn'sməukə*] *n* no fumador(a) *m/f*.

nonstarter [nɔn'stɑːtə*] *n*: **it's a ~** no tiene futuro.

nonstick ['nɔn'stɪk] *adj* (*pan, surface*) antiadherente.

nonstop ['nɔn'stɔp] *adj* continuo; (*RAIL*) directo ♦ *adv* sin parar.

nontaxable [nɔn'tæksəbl] *adj*: **~ income** renta no imponible.

non-U ['nɔnjuː] *adj abbr* (*BRIT col*: = *non-upper class*) *que no pertenece a la clase alta.*

nonvolatile [nɔn'vɔlətaɪl] *adj*: **~ memory** (*COMPUT*) memoria permanente.

nonvoting [nɔn'vəutɪŋ] *adj*: **~ shares** acciones *fpl* sin derecho a voto.

nonwhite ['nɔn'waɪt] *adj* de color ♦ *n* (*person*) persona de color.

noodles ['nuːdlz] *npl* tallarines *mpl*.

nook [nuk] *n* rincón *m*; **~s and crannies** escondrijos *mpl*.

noon [nuːn] *n* mediodía *m*.

no-one ['nəuwʌn] *pron* = **nobody**.

noose [nuːs] *n* lazo corredizo.

nor [nɔː*] *conj* = **neither** ♦ *adv see* **neither**.

Norf *abbr* (*BRIT*) = **Norfolk**.

norm [nɔːm] *n* norma.

normal ['nɔːml] *adj* normal; **to return to ~** volver a la normalidad.

normality [nɔː'mælɪtɪ] *n* normalidad *f*.

normally ['nɔːməlɪ] *adv* normalmente.

Normandy ['nɔːməndɪ] *n* Normandía.

north [nɔːθ] *n* norte *m* ♦ *adj* del norte ♦ *adv* al *or* hacia el norte.

North Africa *n* África del Norte.

North African *adj*, *n* norteafricano/a *m/f*.

North America *n* América del Norte.

North American *adj*, *n* norteamericano/a *m/f*.

Northants *abbr* (*BRIT*) = **Northamptonshire**.

northbound ['nɔːθbaund] *adj* (*traffic*) que se dirige al norte; (*carriageway*) de dirección norte.

Northd *abbr* (*BRIT*) = **Northumberland**.

north-east [nɔːθ'iːst] *n* nor(d)este *m*.

northerly ['nɔːðəlɪ] *adj* (*point, direction*) hacia el norte, septentrional; (*wind*) del norte.

northern ['nɔːðən] *adj* norteño, del norte.

Northern Ireland *n* Irlanda del Norte.

North Korea *n* Corea del Norte.

North Pole *n*: **the ~** el Polo Norte.

North Sea *n*: **the ~** el Mar del Norte.

North Sea oil *n* petróleo del Mar del Norte.

northward(s) ['nɔːθwəd(z)] *adv* hacia el norte.

north-west [nɔːθ'wɛst] *n* noroeste *m*.

Norway ['nɔːweɪ] *n* Noruega.

Norwegian [nɔː'wiːdʒən] *adj* noruego ♦ *n* noruego/a; (*LING*) noruego.

nos. *abbr* (= *numbers*) núms.

nose [nəuz] *n* (*ANAT*) nariz *f*; (*ZOOL*) hocico; (*sense of smell*) olfato ♦ *vi* (*also*: **~ one's way**) avanzar con cautela; **to pay through the ~** (**for sth**) (*col*) pagar un dineral (por algo).

▸**nose about, nose around** *vi* curiosear.

nosebleed ['nəuzbliːd] *n* hemorragia nasal.

nose-dive ['nəuzdaɪv] *n* picado vertical.

nose drops *npl* gotas *fpl* para la nariz.

nosey ['nəuzɪ] *adj* curioso, fisgón(ona).

nostalgia [nɔs'tældʒɪə] *n* nostalgia.

nostalgic [nɔs'tældʒɪk] *adj* nostálgico.

nostril ['nɔstrɪl] *n* ventana *or* orificio de la nariz.

nosy ['nəuzɪ] *adj* = **nosey**.

not [nɔt] *adv* no; **~ at all** no ... en absoluto; **~ that...** no es que...; **it's too late, isn't it?** es demasiado tarde, ¿verdad?; **~ yet** todavía no; **~ now** ahora no; **why ~?** ¿por qué no?; **I hope ~** espero que no; **~ at all** no ... nada; (*after thanks*) de nada.

notable ['nəutəbl] *adj* notable.

notably ['nəutəblɪ] *adv* especialmente; (*in particular*) sobre todo.

notary ['nəutərɪ] *n* (*also*: **~ public**) notario/a.

notation [nəu'teɪʃən] *n* notación *f*.

notch [nɔtʃ] *n* muesca, corte *m*.

▸**notch up** *vt* (*score, victory*) apuntarse.

note [nəut] *n* (*MUS, record, letter*) nota; (*banknote*) billete *m*; (*tone*) tono ♦ *vt* (*observe*) notar, observar; (*write down*) apuntar, anotar; **delivery ~** nota de entrega; **to compare ~s** (*fig*) cambiar impresiones; **of ~** conocido, destacado; **to take ~** prestar atención a; **just a quick ~ to let you know that ...** sólo unas líneas para informarte que ....

notebook ['nəutbuk] *n* libreta, cuaderno; (*for shorthand*) libreta.

notecase ['nəutkeɪs] *n* (*BRIT*) cartera, billetero.

noted ['nəutɪd] *adj* célebre, conocido.

notepad ['nəutpæd] *n* bloc *m*.

notepaper ['nəutpeɪpə*] *n* papel *m* para cartas.

noteworthy ['nəutwəːðı] adj notable, digno de atención.

nothing ['nʌθıŋ] n nada; (zero) cero; **he does** ~ no hace nada; ~ **new** nada nuevo; **for** ~ (free) gratis; (in vain) en balde; ~ **at all** nada en absoluto.

notice ['nəutıs] n (announcement) anuncio; (dismissal) despido; (resignation) dimisión f; (review: of play etc) reseña ♦ vt (observe) notar, observar; **to take** ~ **of** hacer caso de, prestar atención a; **at short** ~ con poca antelación; **without** ~ sin previo aviso; **advance** ~ previo aviso; **until further** ~ hasta nuevo aviso; **to give sb** ~ **of sth** avisar a algn de algo; **to give** ~, **hand in one's** ~ dimitir, renunciar; **it has come to my** ~ **that** ... he llegado a saber que ...; **to escape** or **avoid** ~ pasar inadvertido.

noticeable ['nəutısəbl] adj evidente, obvio.

notice board n (BRIT) tablón m de anuncios.

notification [nəutıfı'keıʃən] n aviso; (announcement) anuncio.

notify ['nəutıfaı] vt: **to** ~ **sb** (**of sth**) comunicar (algo) a algn.

notion ['nəuʃən] n noción f, concepto; (opinion) opinión f.

notions ['nəuʃənz] npl (US) mercería.

notoriety [nəutə'raıətı] n notoriedad f, mala fama.

notorious [nəu'tɔːrıəs] adj notorio, tristemente célebre.

notoriously [nəu'tɔːrıəslı] adv notoriamente.

Notts abbr (BRIT) = Nottinghamshire.

notwithstanding [nɔtwıθ'stændıŋ] adv no obstante, sin embargo; ~ **this** a pesar de esto.

nougat ['nuːgaː] n turrón m.

nought [nɔːt] n cero.

noun [naun] n nombre m, sustantivo.

nourish ['nʌrıʃ] vt nutrir, alimentar; (fig) fomentar, nutrir.

nourishing ['nʌrıʃıŋ] adj nutritivo, rico.

nourishment ['nʌrıʃmənt] n alimento, sustento.

Nov. abbr (= November) nov.

novel ['nɔvl] n novela ♦ adj (new) nuevo, original; (unexpected) insólito.

novelist ['nɔvəlıst] n novelista m/f.

novelty ['nɔvəltı] n novedad f.

November [nəu'vɛmbə*] n noviembre m.

novice ['nɔvıs] n principiante m/f, novato/a; (REL) novicio/a.

NOW [nau] n abbr (US) = National Organization for Women.

now [nau] adv (at the present time) ahora; (these days) actualmente, hoy día ♦ conj: ~ (that) ya que, ahora que; **right** ~ ahora mismo; **by** ~ ya; **just** ~: **I'll do it just** ~ ahora mismo lo hago; ~ **and then,** ~ **and again** de vez en cuando; **from** ~ **on** de ahora en adelante; **between** ~ **and Monday** entre hoy y el lunes; **In 3 days from** ~ de hoy en 3 días; **that's all for** ~ eso es todo por ahora.

nowadays ['nauədeız] adv hoy (en) día, actualmente.

nowhere ['nəuwɛə*] adv (direction) a ninguna parte; (location) en ninguna parte; ~ **else** en or a ninguna otra parte.

no-win situation [nəu'wın-] n: **I'm in a** ~ haga lo que haga, llevo las de perder.

noxious ['nɔkʃəs] adj nocivo.

nozzle ['nɔzl] n boquilla.

NP n abbr = **notary public.**

NS abbr (Canada) = Nova Scotia.

NSC n abbr (US) = National Security Council.

NSF n abbr (US) = National Science Foundation.

NSPCC n abbr (BRIT) = National Society for the Prevention of Cruelty to Children.

NSW abbr (Australia) = New South Wales.

NT n abbr = New Testament ♦ abbr (Canada) = Northwest Territories.

nth [ɛnθ] adj: **for the** ~ **time** (col) por enésima vez.

nuance ['njuːɑːns] n matiz m.

nubile ['njuːbaıl] adj núbil.

nuclear ['njuːklıə*] adj nuclear.

nuclear disarmament n desarme m nuclear.

nuclear family n familia nuclear.

nuclear-free zone ['njuːklıə'friː-] n zona desnuclearizada.

nucleus, pl **nuclei** ['njuːklıəs, 'njuːklıaı] n núcleo.

NUCPS n abbr (BRIT = National Union of Civil and Public Servants) sindicato de funcionarios.

nude [njuːd] adj, n desnudo/a m/f; **in the** ~ desnudo.

nudge [nʌdʒ] vt dar un codazo a.

nudist ['njuːdıst] n nudista m/f.

nudist colony n colonia de desnudistas.

nudity ['njuːdıtı] n desnudez f.

nugget ['nʌgıt] n pepita.

nuisance ['njuːsns] n molestia, fastidio; (person) pesado, latoso; **what a** ~! ¡qué lata!

NUJ n abbr (BRIT: = National Union of Journalists) sindicato de periodistas.

nuke [njuːk] (col) n bomba atómica ♦ vt atacar con arma nuclear.

null [nʌl] adj: ~ **and void** nulo y sin efecto.

nullify ['nʌlɪfaɪ] *vt* anular, invalidar.
NUM *n abbr (BRIT:* = *National Union of Mineworkers) sindicato de mineros.*
numb [nʌm] *adj* entumecido; *(fig)* insensible ♦ *vt* quitar la sensación a, entumecer, entorpecer; **to be ~ with cold** estar entumecido de frío; **~ with fear** paralizado de miedo; **~ with grief** paralizado de dolor.
number ['nʌmbə*] *n* número; *(numeral)* número, cifra ♦ *vt (pages etc)* numerar, poner número a; *(amount to)* sumar, ascender a; **reference ~** número de referencia; **telephone ~** número de teléfono; **wrong ~** *(TEL)* número equivocado; **opposite ~** *(person)* homólogo/a; **to be ~ed among** figurar entre; **a ~ of** varios, algunos; **they were ten in ~** eran diez.
numbered account *n (in bank)* cuenta numerada.
number plate *n (BRIT)* matrícula, placa.
Number Ten *n (BRIT: 10 Downing Street) residencia del primer ministro.*
numbness ['nʌmnɪs] *n* insensibilidad *f*, parálisis *f inv*; *(due to cold)* entumecimiento.
numbskull ['nʌmskʌl] *n (col)* papanatas *m/f inv.*
numeral ['nju:mərəl] *n* número, cifra.
numerate ['nju:mərɪt] *adj* competente en aritmética.
numerical [nju:'merɪkl] *adj* numérico.
numerous ['nju:mərəs] *adj* numeroso, muchos.
nun [nʌn] *n* monja, religiosa.
nunnery ['nʌnərɪ] *n* convento de monjas.
nuptial ['nʌpʃəl] *adj* nupcial.
nurse [nə:s] *n* enfermero/a; *(nanny)* niñera ♦ *vt (patient)* cuidar, atender; *(baby: Brit)* mecer; *(: US)* criar, amamantar; **male ~** enfermero.
nursery ['nə:sərɪ] *n (institution)* guardería infantil; *(room)* cuarto de los niños; *(for plants)* criadero, semillero.
nursery rhyme *n* canción *f* infantil.
nursery school *n* escuela de preescolar.
nursery slope *n (BRIT SKI)* cuesta para principiantes.
nursing ['nə:sɪŋ] *n (profession)* profesión *f* de enfermera; *(care)* asistencia, cuidado ♦ *adj (mother)* lactante.
nursing home *n* clínica de reposo.
nurture ['nə:tʃə*] *vt (child, plant)* alimentar, nutrir.
NUS *n abbr (BRIT:* = *National Union of Students) sindicato de estudiantes.*
NUT *n abbr (BRIT:* = *National Union of Teachers) sindicato de profesores.*
nut [nʌt] *n (TECH)* tuerca; *(BOT)* nuez *f* ♦ *adj (chocolate etc)* con nueces; **~s** *(CULIN)* frutos secos.
nutcrackers ['nʌtkrækəz] *npl* cascanueces *m inv.*
nutmeg ['nʌtmeg] *n* nuez *f* moscada.
nutrient ['nju:trɪənt] *adj* nutritivo ♦ *n* elemento nutritivo.
nutrition [nju:'trɪʃən] *n* nutrición *f*, alimentación *f.*
nutritionist [nju:'trɪʃənɪst] *n* dietista *m/f.*
nutritious [nju:'trɪʃəs] *adj* nutritivo.
nuts [nʌts] *adj (col)* chiflado.
nutshell ['nʌtʃel] *n* cáscara de nuez; **in a ~** en resumidas cuentas.
nutty ['nʌtɪ] *adj (flavour)* a frutos secos; *(col: foolish)* chalado.
nuzzle ['nʌzl] *vi:* **to ~ up to** arrimarse a.
NV *abbr (US)* = *Nevada.*
NWT *abbr (Canada)* = *Northwest Territories.*
NY *abbr (US)* = *New York.*
NYC *abbr (US)* = *New York City.*
nylon ['naɪlɔn] *n* nylon *m*, nilón *m* ♦ *adj* de nylon *or* nilón.
nymph [nɪmf] *n* ninfa.
nymphomaniac ['nɪmfəu'meɪnɪæk] *adj, n* ninfómana.
NYSE *n abbr (US)* = *New York Stock Exchange.*

O o

O, o [əu] *(letter)* O, o *f*; **O for Oliver,** *(US)* **O for Oboe** O de Oviedo.
oaf [əuf] *n* zoquete *m/f.*
oak [əuk] *n* roble *m* ♦ *adj* de roble.
OAP *abbr see* **old-age pensioner**.
oar [ɔ:*] *n* remo; **to put** *or* **shove one's ~ in** *(fig: col)* entrometerse.
oarsman ['ɔ:zmən] *n* remero.
OAS *n abbr (*= *Organization of American States)* OEA *f.*
oasis, *pl* **oases** [əu'eɪsɪs, əu'eɪsi:z] *n* oasis *m inv.*
oath [əuθ] *n* juramento; *(swear word)* palabrota; **on** *(BRIT) or* **under ~** bajo juramento.
oatmeal ['əutmi:l] *n* harina de avena.
oats [əuts] *n* avena.
OAU *n abbr (*= *Organization of African Unity)*

OUA *f.*

obdurate ['ɔbdjurɪt] *adj* (*stubborn*) terco, obstinado; (*sinner*) empedernido; (*unyielding*) inflexible, firme.

OBE *n abbr* (*BRIT:* = *Order of the British Empire*) título ceremonial.

obedience [ə'biːdɪəns] *n* obediencia; **in ~ to** de acuerdo con.

obedient [ə'biːdɪənt] *adj* obediente.

obelisk ['ɔbɪlɪsk] *n* obelisco.

obese [əu'biːs] *adj* obeso.

obesity [əu'biːsɪtɪ] *n* obesidad *f.*

obey [ə'beɪ] *vt* obedecer; (*instructions, regulations*) cumplir.

obituary [ə'bɪtjuərɪ] *n* necrología.

object ['ɔbdʒɪkt] *n* (*gen*) objeto; (*purpose*) objeto, propósito; (*LING*) objeto, complemento ♦ *vi* [əb'dʒɛkt]: **to ~ to** (*attitude*) protestar contra; (*proposal*) oponerse a; **expense is no ~** no importan los gastos; **I ~!** ¡protesto!; **to ~ that** objetar que.

objection [əb'dʒɛkʃən] *n* objeción *f*; **I have no ~ to ...** no tengo inconveniente en que ....

objectionable [əb'dʒɛkʃənəbl] *adj* (*gen*) desagradable; (*conduct*) censurable.

objective [əb'dʒɛktɪv] *adj, n* objetivo.

objectively [əb'dʒɛktɪvlɪ] *adv* objetivamente.

objectivity [ɔbdʒɪk'tɪvɪtɪ] *n* objetividad *f.*

object lesson *n* (*fig*) (buen) ejemplo.

objector [əb'dʒɛktə*] *n* objetor(a) *m/f.*

obligation [ɔblɪ'geɪʃən] *n* obligación *f*; (*debt*) deber *m*; "**without ~**" "sin compromiso"; **to be under an ~ to sb/to do sth** estar comprometido con algn/a hacer algo.

obligatory [ə'blɪgətərɪ] *adj* obligatorio.

oblige [ə'blaɪdʒ] *vt* (*do a favour for*) complacer, hacer un favor a; **to ~ sb to do sth** obligar a algn a hacer algo; **to be ~d to sb for sth** estarle agradecido a algn por algo; **anything to ~!** (*col*) todo sea por complacerte.

obliging [ə'blaɪdʒɪŋ] *adj* servicial, atento.

oblique [ə'bliːk] *adj* oblicuo; (*allusion*) indirecto ♦ *n* (*TYP*) barra.

obliterate [ə'blɪtəreɪt] *vt* arrasar; (*memory*) borrar.

oblivion [ə'blɪvɪən] *n* olvido.

oblivious [ə'blɪvɪəs] *adj*: **~ of** inconsciente de.

oblong ['ɔblɔŋ] *adj* rectangular ♦ *n* rectángulo.

obnoxious [əb'nɔkʃəs] *adj* odioso, detestable; (*smell*) nauseabundo.

o.b.o. *abbr* (*US:* = *or best offer: in classified*

ads) abierto ofertas.

oboe ['əubəu] *n* oboe *m.*

obscene [əb'siːn] *adj* obsceno.

obscenity [əb'sɛnɪtɪ] *n* obscenidad *f.*

obscure [əb'skjuə*] *adj* oscuro ♦ *vt* oscurecer; (*hide: sun*) ocultar.

obscurity [əb'skjuərɪtɪ] *n* oscuridad *f*; (*obscure point*) punto oscuro; **to rise from ~** salir de la nada.

obsequious [əb'siːkwɪəs] *adj* servil.

observable [əb'zə:vəbl] *adj* observable, perceptible.

observance [əb'zə:vns] *n* observancia, cumplimiento; (*ritual*) práctica; **religious ~s** prácticas *fpl* religiosas.

observant [əb'zə:vnt] *adj* observador(a).

observation [ɔbzə'veɪʃən] *n* (*also MED*) observación *f*; (*by police etc*) vigilancia.

observation post *n* (*MIL*) puesto de observación.

observatory [əb'zə:vətrɪ] *n* observatorio.

observe [əb'zə:v] *vt* (*gen*) observar; (*rule*) cumplir.

observer [əb'zə:və*] *n* observador(a) *m/f.*

obsess [əb'sɛs] *vt* obsesionar; **to be ~ed by** *or* **with sb/sth** estar obsesionado con algn/algo.

obsession [əb'sɛʃən] *n* obsesión *f.*

obsessive [əb'sɛsɪv] *adj* obsesivo.

obsolescence [ɔbsə'lɛsns] *n* obsolescencia.

obsolescent [ɔbsə'lɛsnt] *adj* que está cayendo en desuso.

obsolete ['ɔbsəliːt] *adj* obsoleto.

obstacle ['ɔbstəkl] *n* obstáculo; (*nuisance*) estorbo.

obstacle race *n* carrera de obstáculos.

obstetrician [ɔbstə'trɪʃən] *n* obstetra *m/f.*

obstetrics [ɔb'stɛtrɪks] *n* obstetricia.

obstinacy ['ɔbstɪnəsɪ] *n* terquedad *f*, obstinación *f*; tenacidad *f.*

obstinate ['ɔbstɪnɪt] *adj* terco, obstinado; (*determined*) tenaz.

obstinately ['ɔbstɪnɪtlɪ] *adv* tercamente, obstinadamente.

obstreperous [əb'strɛpərəs] *adj* ruidoso; (*unruly*) revoltoso.

obstruct [əb'strʌkt] *vt* (*block*) obstruir; (*hinder*) estorbar, obstaculizar.

obstruction [əb'strʌkʃən] *n* obstrucción *f*; estorbo, obstáculo.

obstructive [əb'strʌktɪv] *adj* obstruccionista; **stop being ~!** ¡deja de poner peros!

obtain [əb'teɪn] *vt* (*get*) obtener; (*achieve*) conseguir; **to ~ sth (for o.s.)** conseguir *or* adquirir algo.

obtainable [əb'teɪnəbl] *adj* asequible.

obtrusive [əb'truːsɪv] *adj* (*person*)

importuno; (: *interfering*) entrometido; (*building etc*) demasiado visible.

obtuse [əb'tjuːs] *adj* obtuso.

obverse ['ɔbvəːs] *n* (*of medal*) anverso; (*fig*) complemento.

obviate ['ɔbvɪeɪt] *vt* obviar, evitar.

obvious ['ɔbvɪəs] *adj* (*clear*) obvio, evidente; (*unsubtle*) poco sutil; **it's ~ that** ... está claro que ..., **is evidente que** ....

obviously ['ɔbvɪəslɪ] *adv* obviamente, evidentemente; **~ not!** ¡por supuesto que no!; **he was ~ not drunk** era evidente que no estaba borracho; **he was not ~ drunk** no se le notaba que estaba borracho.

OCAS *n abbr* (= *Organization of Central American States*) ODECA *f*.

occasion [ə'keɪʒən] *n* oportunidad *f*, ocasión *f*; (*event*) acontecimiento ♦ *vt* ocasionar, causar; **on that ~** esa vez, en aquella ocasión; **to rise to the ~** ponerse a la altura de las circunstancias.

occasional [ə'keɪʒənl] *adj* poco frecuente, ocasional.

occasionally [ə'keɪʒənlɪ] *adv* de vez en cuando; **very ~** muy de tarde en tarde, en muy contadas ocasiones.

occasional table *n* mesita.

occult [ɔ'kʌlt] *adj* (*gen*) oculto.

occupancy ['ɔkjupənsɪ] *n* ocupación *f*.

occupant ['ɔkjupənt] *n* (*of house*) inquilino/a; (*of boat, car*) ocupante *m/f*.

occupation [ɔkju'peɪʃən] *n* (*of house*) tenencia; (*job*) trabajo; (: *calling*) oficio.

occupational accident [ɔkju'peɪʃənl] *n* accidente *m* laboral.

occupational guidance *n* orientación *f* profesional.

occupational hazard *n* gajes *mpl* del oficio.

occupational pension scheme *n* plan *m* profesional de jubilación.

occupational therapy *n* terapia ocupacional.

occupier ['ɔkjupaɪə*] *n* inquilino/a.

occupy ['ɔkjupaɪ] *vt* (*seat, post, time*) ocupar; (*house*) habitar; **to ~ o.s. with** *or* **by doing** (*as job*) dedicarse a hacer; (*to pass time*) entretenerse haciendo; **to be occupied with sth/in doing sth** estar ocupado con algo/haciendo algo.

occur [ə'kəː*] *vi* ocurrir, suceder; **to ~ to sb** ocurrírsele a algn.

occurrence [ə'kʌrəns] *n* suceso.

ocean ['əuʃən] *n* océano; **~s of** (*col*) la mar de.

ocean bed *n* fondo del océano.

ocean-going ['əuʃəngəuɪŋ] *adj* de alta mar.

Oceania [əuʃɪ'eɪnɪə] *n* Oceanía.

ocean liner *n* buque *m* transoceánico.

ochre, (*US*) **ocher** ['əukə*] *n* ocre *m*.

o'clock [ə'klɔk] *adv*: **it is 5 ~** son las 5.

OCR *n abbr see* **optical character recognition/reader**.

Oct. *abbr* (= *October*) oct.

octagonal [ɔk'tægənl] *adj* octagonal.

octane ['ɔkteɪn] *n* octano; **high ~ petrol** *or* (*US*) **gas** gasolina de alto octanaje.

octave ['ɔktɪv] *n* octava.

October [ɔk'təubə*] *n* octubre *m*.

octogenarian ['ɔktəudʒɪ'nɛərɪən] *n* octogenario/a.

octopus ['ɔktəpəs] *n* pulpo.

oculist ['ɔkjulɪst] *n* oculista *m/f*.

odd [ɔd] *adj* (*strange*) extraño, raro; (*number*) impar; (*left over*) sobrante, suelto; **60-~** 60 y pico; **at ~ times** de vez en cuando; **to be the ~ one out** estar de más; **if you have the ~ minute** si tienes unos minutos libres; *see also* **odds**.

oddball ['ɔdbɔːl] *n* (*col*) bicho raro.

oddity ['ɔdɪtɪ] *n* rareza; (*person*) excéntrico/a.

odd-job man [ɔd'dʒɔb-] *n* hombre *m* que hace chapuzas.

odd jobs *npl* chapuzas *fpl*.

oddly ['ɔdlɪ] *adv* extrañamente.

oddments ['ɔdmənts] *npl* (*BRIT COMM*) restos *mpl*.

odds [ɔdz] *npl* (*in betting*) puntos *mpl* de ventaja; **it makes no ~** da lo mismo; **at ~** reñidos/as; **to succeed against all the ~** tener éxito contra todo pronóstico; **~ and ends** cachivaches *mpl*.

odds-on [ɔdz'ɔn] *adj* (*col*): **the ~ favourite** el máximo favorito; **it's ~ he'll come** seguro que viene.

ode [əud] *n* oda.

odious ['əudɪəs] *adj* odioso.

odometer [ɔ'dɔmɪtə*] *n* (*US*) cuentakilómetros *m inv*.

odour, (*US*) **odor** ['əudə*] *n* olor *m*; (*perfume*) perfume *m*.

odo(u)rless ['əudəlɪs] *adj* sin olor.

OECD *n abbr* (= *Organization for Economic Co-operation and Development*) OCDE *f*.

oesophagus, (*US*) **esophagus** [iː'sɔfəgəs] *n* esófago.

oestrogen, (*US*) **estrogen** ['iːstrədʒən] *n* estrógeno.

─────────────── *KEYWORD*

of [ɔv, əv] *prep* **1** (*gen*) de; **a friend ~ ours** un amigo nuestro; **a boy ~ 10** un chico de 10 años; **that was kind ~ you** eso fue muy amable de tu parte

2 (expressing quantity, amount, dates etc) de; **a kilo ~ flour** un kilo de harina; **there were 3 ~ them** había tres; **3 ~ us went** tres de nosotros fuimos; **the 5th ~ July** el 5 de julio; **a quarter ~ 4** (US) las 4 menos cuarto
3 (from, out of) de; **made ~ wood** (hecho) de madera.

off [ɔf] adj, adv (engine, light) apagado; (tap) cerrado; (BRIT: food: bad) pasado, malo; (: milk) cortado; (cancelled) suspendido; (removed): **the lid was ~** no estaba puesta la tapadera ♦ prep de; **to be ~** (to leave) irse, marcharse; **to be ~ sick** estar enfermo or de baja; **a day ~** un día libre; **to have an ~ day** tener un mal día; **he had his coat ~** se había quitado el abrigo; **10% ~** (COMM) (con el) 10% de descuento; **it's a long way ~** está muy lejos; **5 km ~ (the road)** a 5 km (de la carretera); **~ the coast** frente a la costa; **I'm ~ meat** (no longer eat/like it) paso de la carne; **on the ~ chance** por si acaso; **~ and on, on and ~** de vez en cuando; **I must be ~** tengo que irme; **to be well/ badly ~** andar bien/mal de dinero; **I'm afraid the chicken is ~** desgraciadamente ya no queda pollo; **that's a bit ~, isn't it!** (fig, col) ¡eso no se hace!

offal ['ɔfl] n (BRIT CULIN) menudillos mpl, asaduras fpl.
off-centre, (US) **off-center** [ɔf'sɛntə*] adj descentrado, ladeado.
off-colour ['ɔf'kʌlə*] adj (BRIT: ill) indispuesto; **to feel ~** sentirse or estar mal.
offence, (US) **offense** [ə'fɛns] n (crime) delito; (insult) ofensa; **to take ~ at** ofenderse por; **to commit an ~** cometer un delito.
offend [ə'fɛnd] vt (person) ofender ♦ vi: **to ~ against** (law, rule) infringir.
offender [ə'fɛndə*] n delincuente m/f; (against regulations) infractor(a) m/f.
offending [ə'fɛndɪŋ] adj culpable; (object) molesto; (word) problemático.
offense [ə'fɛns] n (US) = **offence**.
offensive [ə'fɛnsɪv] adj ofensivo; (smell etc) repugnante ♦ n (MIL) ofensiva.
offer ['ɔfə*] n (gen) oferta, ofrecimiento; (proposal) propuesta ♦ vt ofrecer; **"on ~"** (COMM) "en oferta"; **to make an ~ for sth** hacer una oferta por algo; **to ~ sth to sb, ~ sb sth** ofrecer algo a algn; **to ~ to do sth** ofrecerse a hacer algo.
offering ['ɔfərɪŋ] n (REL) ofrenda.
offer price n precio de oferta.
offertory ['ɔfətrɪ] n (REL) ofertorio.

offhand [ɔf'hænd] adj informal; (brusque) desconsiderado ♦ adv de improviso, sin pensarlo; **I can't tell you ~** no te lo puedo decir así de improviso or así nomás (LAM).
office ['ɔfɪs] n (place) oficina; (room) despacho; (position) cargo, oficio; **doctor's ~** (US) consultorio; **to take ~** entrar en funciones; **through his good ~s** gracias a sus buenos oficios; **O~ of Fair Trading** (BRIT) oficina que regula normas comerciales.
office automation n ofimática, buromática.
office bearer n (of club etc) titular m/f (de una cartera).
office block, (US) **office building** n bloque m de oficinas.
office boy n ordenanza m.
office hours npl horas fpl de oficina; (US MED) horas fpl de consulta.
office manager n jefe/a m/f de oficina.
officer ['ɔfɪsə*] n (MIL etc) oficial m/f; (of organization) director(a) m/f; (also: **police ~**) agente m/f de policía.
office work n trabajo de oficina.
office worker n oficinista m/f.
official [ə'fɪʃl] adj (authorized) oficial, autorizado; (strike) oficial ♦ n funcionario/a.
officialdom [ə'fɪʃldəm] n burocracia.
officially [ə'fɪʃəlɪ] adv oficialmente.
official receiver n síndico.
officiate [ə'fɪʃɪeɪt] vi (also REL) oficiar; **to ~ as Mayor** ejercer las funciones de alcalde; **to ~ at a marriage** celebrar una boda.
officious [ə'fɪʃəs] adj oficioso.
offing ['ɔfɪŋ] n: **in the ~** (fig) en perspectiva.
off-key [ɔf'kiː] adj desafinado ♦ adv desafinadamente.
off-licence ['ɔflaɪsns] n (BRIT: shop) tienda de bebidas alcohólicas; ver recuadro.

OFF-LICENCE

En el Reino Unido una **off-licence** es una tienda especializada en la venta de bebidas alcohólicas para el consumo fuera del establecimiento. De ahí su nombre, pues se necesita un permiso especial para tal venta, que está estrictamente regulada. Suelen vender además bebidas sin alcohol, tabaco, chocolate, patatas fritas etc y a menudo son parte de grandes cadenas nacionales.

---

off-limits [ɔf'lɪmɪts] adj (US MIL) prohibido al personal militar.

off line adj, adv (COMPUT) fuera de línea; (switched off) desconectado.

off-load ['ɔfləud] vt descargar, desembarcar.

off-peak ['ɔf'piːk] adj (holiday) de temporada baja; (electricity) de banda económica.

off-putting ['ɔfputɪŋ] adj (BRIT: person) poco amable, difícil; (behaviour) chocante.

off-season ['ɔf'siːzn] adj, adv fuera de temporada.

offset ['ɔfsɛt] vt (irreg: like set) (counteract) contrarrestar, compensar ♦ n (also: ~ printing) offset m.

offshoot ['ɔfʃuːt] n (BOT) vástago; (fig) ramificación f.

offshore [ɔf'ʃɔː*] adj (breeze, island) costero; (fishing) de bajura; ~ oilfield campo petrolífero submarino.

offside ['ɔf'saɪd] n (AUT: with right-hand drive) lado derecho; (: with left-hand drive) lado izquierdo ♦ adj (SPORT) fuera de juego; (AUT) del lado derecho; del lado izquierdo.

offspring ['ɔfsprɪŋ] n descendencia.

offstage [ɔf'steɪdʒ] adv entre bastidores.

off-the-cuff [ɔfðə'kʌf] adj espontáneo.

off-the-job [ɔfðə'dʒɔb] adj: ~ **training** formación f fuera del trabajo.

off-the-peg [ɔfðə'pɛg], (US) **off-the-rack** [ɔfðə'ræk] adv confeccionado.

off-the-record ['ɔfðə'rɛkɔːd] adj extraoficial, confidencial ♦ adv extraoficialmente, confidencialmente.

off-white ['ɔfwaɪt] adj blanco grisáceo.

Ofgas ['ɔfgæs] n (BRIT: = Office of Gas Supply) organismo que controla a las empresas del gas en Gran Bretaña.

Oftel ['ɔftɛl] n (BRIT: = Office of Telecommunications) organismo que controla las telecomunicaciones británicas.

often ['ɔfn] adv a menudo, con frecuencia, seguido (LAM); **how** ~ **do you go?** ¿cada cuánto vas?

Ofwat ['ɔfwɔt] n (BRIT: = Office of Water Services) organismo que controla a las empresas suministradoras del agua en Inglaterra y Gales.

ogle ['əugl] vt comerse con los ojos a.

ogre ['əugə*] n ogro.

OH abbr (US) = Ohio.

oh [əu] excl ¡ah!

OHMS abbr (BRIT) On His (or Her) Majesty's Service.

oil [ɔɪl] n aceite m; (petroleum) petróleo ♦ vt (machine) engrasar; **fried in** ~ frito en aceite.

oilcan ['ɔɪlkæn] n lata de aceite.

oilfield ['ɔɪlfiːld] n campo petrolífero.

oil filter n (AUT) filtro de aceite.

oil-fired ['ɔɪlfaɪəd] adj de fuel-oil.

oil gauge n indicador m del aceite.

oil industry n industria petrolífera.

oil level n nivel m del aceite.

oil painting n pintura al óleo.

oil refinery n refinería de petróleo.

oil rig n torre f de perforación.

oilskins ['ɔɪlskɪnz] npl impermeable msg, chubasquero sg.

oil tanker n petrolero.

oil well n pozo (de petróleo).

oily ['ɔɪlɪ] adj aceitoso; (food) grasiento.

ointment ['ɔɪntmənt] n ungüento.

OK abbr (US) = Oklahoma.

O.K., okay ['əu'keɪ] excl O.K., ¡está bien!, ¡vale! ♦ adj bien ♦ n: **to give sth one's** ~ dar el visto bueno a or aprobar algo ♦ vt dar el visto bueno a; **it's** ~ **with** or **by me** estoy de acuerdo, me parece bien; **are you** ~ **for money?** ¿andas or vas bien de dinero?

Okla. abbr (US) = Oklahoma.

old [əuld] adj viejo; (former) antiguo; **how** ~ **are you?** ¿cuántos años tienes?, ¿qué edad tienes?; **he's 10 years** ~ tiene 10 años; ~**er brother** hermano mayor; **any** ~ **thing will do** sirve cualquier cosa.

old age n vejez f.

old-age pension ['əuldeɪdʒ-] n (BRIT) jubilación f, pensión f.

old-age pensioner (OAP) ['əuldeɪdʒ-] n (BRIT) jubilado/a.

olden ['əuldən] adj antiguo.

old-fashioned ['əuld'fæʃənd] adj anticuado, pasado de moda.

old maid n solterona.

old-style ['əuldstaɪl] adj tradicional, chapado a la antigua.

old-time ['əuld'taɪm] adj antiguo, de antaño.

old-timer ['əuld'taɪmə*] n veterano/a; (old person) anciano/a.

old wives' tale n cuento de viejas, patraña.

olive ['ɔlɪv] n (fruit) aceituna; (tree) olivo ♦ adj (also: ~-**green**) verde oliva inv.

olive branch n (fig): **to offer an** ~ **to sb** ofrecer hacer las paces con algn.

olive oil n aceite m de oliva.

Olympic [əu'lɪmpɪk] adj olímpico; **the** ~ **Games, the** ~**s** npl las Olimpíadas.

OM n abbr (BRIT: = Order of Merit) título ceremonial.

O & M n abbr = organization and method.

Oman [əu'maːn] n Omán m.

OMB n abbr (US: = Office of Management and

Budget) *servicio que asesora al presidente en materia presupuestaria.*
omelet(te) ['ɔmlɪt] *n* tortilla, tortilla de huevo (*LAM*).
omen ['əumən] *n* presagio.
ominous ['ɔmɪnəs] *adj* de mal agüero, amenazador(a).
omission [əu'mɪʃən] *n* omisión *f*; (*error*) descuido.
omit [əu'mɪt] *vt* omitir; (*by mistake*) olvidar, descuidar; **to ~ to do sth** olvidarse *or* dejar de hacer algo.
omnivorous [ɔm'nɪvərəs] *adj* omnívoro.
ON *abbr* (*Canada*) = Ontario.

========================= *KEYWORD*

on [ɔn] *prep* **1** (*indicating position*) en; sobre; **~ the wall** en la pared; **it's ~ the table** está sobre *or* en la mesa; **~ the left** a la izquierda; **I haven't got any money ~ me** no llevo dinero encima
2 (*indicating means, method, condition etc*): **~ foot** a pie; **~ the train/plane** (*go*) en tren/avión; (*be*) en el tren/el avión; **~ the radio/television** por *or* en la radio/ televisión; **~ the telephone** al teléfono; **to be ~ drugs** drogarse; (*MED*) estar a tratamiento; **to be ~ holiday/business** estar de vacaciones/en viaje de negocios; **we're ~ irregular verbs** estamos con los verbos irregulares
3 (*referring to time*): **~ Friday** el viernes; **~ Fridays** los viernes; **~ June 20th** el 20 de junio; **a week ~ Friday** del viernes en una semana; **~ arrival** al llegar; **~ seeing this** al ver esto
4 (*about, concerning*) sobre, acerca de; **a book ~ physics** un libro de *or* sobre física
5 (*at the expense of*): **this round's ~ me** esta ronda la pago yo, invito yo (a esta ronda); (*earning*): **he's ~ £16,000 a year** gana dieciséis mil libras al año
♦ *adv* **1** (*referring to dress*): **to have one's coat ~** tener *or* llevar el abrigo puesto; **she put her gloves ~** se puso los guantes
2 (*referring to covering*): **"screw the lid ~ tightly"** "cerrar bien la tapa"
3 (*further, continuously*): **to walk/run** *etc* **~** seguir caminando/corriendo *etc*; **from that day ~** desde aquel día; **it was well ~ in the evening** estaba ya entrada la tarde
4 (*in phrases*): **I'm ~ to sth** creo haber encontrado algo; **my father's always ~ at me to get a job** (*col*) mi padre siempre me está dando la lata para que me ponga a trabajar
♦ *adj* **1** (*functioning, in operation: machine,*

radio, TV, light) encendido/a (*SP*), prendido/a (*LAM*); (: *tap*) abierto/a; (: *brakes*) echado/a, puesto/a; **is the meeting still ~?** (*in progress*) ¿todavía continúa la reunión?; (*not cancelled*) ¿va a haber reunión al fin?; **there's a good film ~ at the cinema** ponen una buena película en el cine
2: **that's not ~!** (*inf: not possible*) ¡eso ni hablar!; (: *not acceptable*) ¡eso no se hace!

ONC *n abbr* (*BRIT*: = Ordinary National Certificate*) título escolar.
once [wʌns] *adv* una vez; (*formerly*) antiguamente ♦ *conj* una vez que; **~ he had left/it was done** una vez que se había marchado/se hizo; **at ~** en seguida, inmediatamente; (*simultaneously*) a la vez; **~ a week** una vez a la semana; **~ more** otra vez; **~ and for all** de una vez por todas; **~ upon a time** érase una vez; **I knew him ~** le conocía hace tiempo.
oncoming ['ɔnkʌmɪŋ] *adj* (*traffic*) que viene de frente.
OND *n abbr* (*BRIT.* = Ordinary National Diploma*) título escolar.

========================= *KEYWORD*

one [wʌn] *num* un(o)/una; **~ hundred and fifty** ciento cincuenta; **~ by ~** uno a uno; **it's ~ (o'clock)** es la una
♦ *adj* **1** (*sole*) único; **the ~ book which** el único libro que; **the ~ man who** el único que
2 (*same*) mismo/a; **they came in the ~ car** vinieron en un solo coche
♦ *pron* **1**: **this ~** éste/ésta; **that ~** ése/ésa; (*more remote*) aquél/aquélla; **I've already got (a red) ~** ya tengo uno/a (rojo/a); **~ by ~** uno/a por uno/a; **to be ~ up on sb** llevar ventaja a algn; **to be at ~ (with sb)** estar completamente de acuerdo (con algn)
2: **~ another** (*US*) nos; (*you*) os (*SP*); (*you: polite, them*) se; **do you two ever see ~ another?** ¿os veis alguna vez? (*SP*), ¿se ven alguna vez?; **the two boys didn't dare look at ~ another** los dos chicos no se atrevieron a mirarse (el uno al otro); **they all kissed ~ another** se besaron unos a otros
3 (*impers*): **~ never knows** nunca se sabe; **to cut ~'s finger** cortarse el dedo; **~ needs to eat** hay que comer.

one-armed bandit ['wʌnɑːmd-] *n* máquina tragaperras.
one-day excursion ['wʌndeɪ-] *n* (*US*)

billete *m* de ida y vuelta en un día.
One-hundred share index ['wʌnhʌndrəd-] *n* índice *m* bursátil (*del Financial Times*).
one-man ['wʌn'mæn] *adj* (*business*) individual.
one-man band *n* hombre-orquesta *m*.
one-off [wʌn'ɔf] *n* (*BRIT col: object*) artículo único; (: *event*) caso especial.
one-parent family ['wʌnpɛərənt-] *n* familia monoparental.
one-piece ['wʌnpiːs] *adj* (*bathing suit*) de una pieza.
onerous ['ɔnərəs] *adj* (*task, duty*) pesado; (*responsibility*) oneroso.
oneself [wʌn'sɛlf] *pron* uno mismo; (*after prep, also emphatic*) sí (mismo/a); **to do sth by** ~ hacer algo solo *or* por sí solo.
one-shot [wʌn'ʃɔt] *n* (*US*) = **one-off**.
one-sided [wʌn'saɪdɪd] *adj* (*argument*) parcial; (*decision, view*) unilateral; (*game, contest*) desigual.
one-time ['wʌntaɪm] *adj* antiguo, ex-.
one-to-one ['wʌntəwʌn] *adj* (*relationship*) individualizado.
one-upmanship [wʌn'ʌpmənʃɪp] *n*: **the art of** ~ el arte de quedar siempre por encima.
one-way ['wʌnweɪ] *adj* (*street, traffic*) de dirección única; (*ticket*) sencillo.
ongoing ['ɔngəuɪŋ] *adj* continuo.
onion ['ʌnjən] *n* cebolla.
on line *adj, adv* (*COMPUT*) en línea; (*switched on*) conectado.
onlooker ['ɔnlukə*] *n* espectador(a) *m/f*.
only ['əunlɪ] *adv* solamente, sólo, nomás (*LAM*) ♦ *adj* único, solo ♦ *conj* solamente que, pero; **an** ~ **child** un hijo único; **not** ~ ... **but also**... no sólo ... sino también...; **I'd be** ~ **too pleased to help** encantado de ayudarles; **I saw her** ~ **yesterday** le vi ayer mismo; **I would come,** ~ **I'm very busy** iría, sólo que estoy muy atareado.
ono *abbr* (= *or nearest offer: in classified ads*) abierto ofertas.
onset ['ɔnsɛt] *n* comienzo.
onshore ['ɔnʃɔː*] *adj* (*wind*) que sopla del mar hacia la tierra.
onslaught ['ɔnslɔːt] *n* ataque *m*, embestida.
Ont. *abbr* (*Canada*) = Ontario.
on-the-job ['ɔnðə'dʒɔb] *adj*: ~ **training** formación *f* en el trabajo *or* sobre la práctica.
onto ['ɔntu] *prep* = **on to**.
onus ['əunəs] *n* responsabilidad *f*; **the** ~ **is upon him to prove it** le incumbe a él demostrarlo.
onward(s) ['ɔnwəd(z)] *adv* (*move*) (hacia) adelante.

onyx ['ɔnɪks] *n* ónice *m*, onyx *m*.
oops [ups] *excl* (*also*: ~-**a-daisy!**) ¡huy!
ooze [uːz] *vi* rezumar.
opal ['əupl] *n* ópalo.
opaque [əu'peɪk] *adj* opaco.
OPEC ['əupɛk] *n abbr* (= *Organization of Petroleum-Exporting Countries*) OPEP *f*.
open ['əupn] *adj* abierto; (*car*) descubierto; (*road, view*) despejado; (*meeting*) público; (*admiration*) manifiesto ♦ *vt* abrir ♦ *vi* (*flower, eyes, door, debate*) abrirse; (*book etc: commence*) comenzar; **in the** ~ **(air)** al aire libre; ~ **verdict** veredicto inconcluso; ~ **ticket** billete *m* sin fecha; ~ **ground** (*among trees*) claro; (*waste ground*) solar *m*; **to have an** ~ **mind (on sth)** estar sin decidirse aún (sobre algo); **to** ~ **a bank account** abrir una cuenta en el banco.
▶**open on to** *vt fus* (*subj: room, door*) dar a.
▶**open out** *vt* abrir ♦ *vi* (*person*) abrirse.
▶**open up** *vt* abrir; (*blocked road*) despejar ♦ *vi* abrirse.
open-and-shut ['əupənən'ʃʌt] *adj*: ~ **case** caso claro *or* evidente.
open day *n* (*BRIT*) jornada de puertas abiertas *or* acceso público.
open-ended [əupn'ɛndɪd] *adj* (*fig*) indefinido, sin definir.
opener ['əupnə*] *n* (*also*: **can** ~, **tin** ~) abrelatas *m inv*.
open-heart surgery [əupn'haːt-] *n* cirugía a corazón abierto.
opening ['əupnɪŋ] *n* abertura; (*beginning*) comienzo; (*opportunity*) oportunidad *f*; (*job*) puesto vacante, vacante *f*.
opening night *n* estreno.
open learning *n* enseñanza flexible a tiempo parcial.
openly ['əupnlɪ] *adv* abiertamente.
open-minded [əupn'maɪndɪd] *adj* de amplias miras, sin prejuicios.
open-necked ['əupnnɛkt] *adj* sin corbata.
openness ['əupnnɪs] *n* (*frankness*) franqueza.
open-plan ['əupn'plæn] *adj* sin tabiques, de plan abierto.
open prison *n* centro penitenciario de régimen abierto.
open return *n* vuelta con fecha abierta.
open shop *n empresa que contrata a mano de obra no afiliada a ningún sindicato*.
Open University *n* (*BRIT*) ≈ Universidad *f* Nacional de Enseñanza a Distancia, UNED *f*; *ver recuadro*.

opera ['ɔpərə] n ópera.
opera glasses npl gemelos mpl.
opera house n teatro de la ópera.
opera singer n cantante m/f de ópera.
operate ['ɔpəreɪt] vt (machine) hacer
funcionar; (company) dirigir ♦ vi
funcionar; (drug) hacer efecto; **to ~ on sb**
(MED) operar a algn.
operatic [ɔpə'rætɪk] adj de ópera.
operating costs ['ɔpəreɪtɪŋ-] npl gastos mpl
operacionales.
operating profit n beneficio de
explotación.
operating room n (US) quirófano, sala de
operaciones.
operating table n mesa de operaciones.
operating theatre n quirófano, sala de
operaciones.
operation [ɔpə'reɪʃən] n (gen) operación f;
(of machine) funcionamiento; **to be in ~**
estar funcionando or en funcionamiento;
to have an ~ (MED) ser operado; **to have
an ~ for** operarse de; **the company's ~s
during the year** las actividades de la
compañía durante el año.
operational [ɔpə'reɪʃənl] adj operacional,
en buen estado; (COMM) en condiciones
de servicio; (ready for use or action) en
condiciones de funcionar.
operative ['ɔpərətɪv] adj (measure) en
vigor; **the ~ word** la palabra clave.
operator ['ɔpəreɪtə*] n (of machine)
operario/a; (TEL) operador(a) m/f,
telefonista m/f.
operetta [ɔpə'retə] n opereta.
ophthalmic [ɔf'θælmɪk] adj oftálmico.
ophthalmologist [ɔfθæl'mɔlədʒɪst] n
oftalmólogo/a.
opinion [ə'pɪnjən] n (gen) opinión f; **in my ~**
en mi opinión, a mi juicio; **to seek a
second ~** pedir una segunda opinión.
opinionated [ə'pɪnjəneɪtɪd] adj testarudo.
opinion poll n encuesta, sondeo.

opium ['əupɪəm] n opio.
opponent [ə'pəunənt] n adversario/a,
contrincante m/f.
opportune ['ɔpətjuːn] adj oportuno.
opportunism [ɔpə'tjuːnɪzm] n
oportunismo.
opportunist [ɔpə'tjuːnɪst] n oportunista m/f.
opportunity [ɔpə'tjuːnɪtɪ] n oportunidad f,
chance m or f (LAM); **to take the ~ to do or
of doing** aprovechar la ocasión para
hacer.
oppose [ə'pəuz] vt oponerse a; **to be ~d to
sth** oponerse a algo; **as ~d to** en vez de;
(unlike) a diferencia de.
opposing [ə'pəuzɪŋ] adj (side) opuesto,
contrario.
opposite ['ɔpəzɪt] adj opuesto, contrario;
(house etc) de enfrente ♦ adv en frente
♦ prep en frente de, frente a
♦ n lo contrario; **the ~ sex** el otro sexo, el
sexo opuesto.
opposite number n (BRIT) homólogo/a.
opposition [ɔpə'zɪʃən] n oposición f.
oppress [ə'pres] vt oprimir.
oppression [ə'preʃən] n opresión f.
oppressive [ə'presɪv] adj opresivo.
opprobrium [ə'prəubrɪəm] n (formal)
oprobio.
opt [ɔpt] vi: **to ~ for** optar por; **to ~ to do**
optar por hacer; **to ~ out** (of NHS etc)
salirse.
optical ['ɔptɪkl] adj óptico.
**optical character recognition/reader
(OCR)** n reconocimiento/lector m óptico
de caracteres.
optical fibre n fibra óptica.
optician [ɔp'tɪʃən] n óptico m/f.
optics ['ɔptɪks] n óptica.
optimism ['ɔptɪmɪzəm] n optimismo.
optimist ['ɔptɪmɪst] n optimista m/f.
optimistic [ɔptɪ'mɪstɪk] adj optimista.
optimum ['ɔptɪməm] adj óptimo.
option ['ɔpʃən] n opción f; **to keep one's ~s
open** (fig) mantener las opciones
abiertas; **I have no ~** no tengo más or
otro remedio.
optional ['ɔpʃənl] adj opcional; (course)
optativo; **~ extras** opciones fpl extras.
opulence ['ɔpjuləns] n opulencia.
opulent ['ɔpjulənt] adj opulento.
OR abbr (US) = Oregon.
or [ɔː*] conj o; (before o, ho) u; (with
negative): **he hasn't seen ~ heard
anything** no ha visto ni oído nada; **~ else**
si no; **let me go ~ I'll scream!** ¡suélteme,
o me pongo a gritar!
oracle ['ɔrəkl] n oráculo.
oral ['ɔːrəl] adj oral ♦ n examen m oral.

orange ['ɔrɪndʒ] n (*fruit*) naranja ♦ adj (de color) naranja.
orangeade [ɔrɪndʒ'eɪd] n naranjada, refresco de naranja.
orange squash n zumo (*SP*) or jugo de naranja.
orang-outang, orang-utan [ɔ'ræŋuː'tæn] n orangután m.
oration [ɔː'reɪʃən] n discurso solemne; **funeral** ~ oración f fúnebre.
orator ['ɔrətə*] n orador(a) m/f.
orbit ['ɔːbɪt] n órbita ♦ vt, vi orbitar; **to be in/go into** ~ **(round)** estar en/entrar en órbita (alrededor de).
orbital ['ɔːbɪtl] n (*also:* ~ **motorway**) autopista de circunvalación.
orchard ['ɔːtʃəd] n huerto; **apple** ~ manzanar m, manzanal m.
orchestra ['ɔːkɪstrə] n orquesta; (*US: seating*) platea.
orchestral [ɔː'kestrəl] adj de orquesta.
orchestrate ['ɔːkɪstreɪt] vt (*MUS, fig*) orquestar.
orchid ['ɔːkɪd] n orquídea.
ordain [ɔː'deɪn] vt (*also REL*) ordenar.
ordeal [ɔː'diːl] n experiencia terrible.
order ['ɔːdə*] n orden m; (*command*) orden f; (*type, kind*) clase f; (*state*) estado; (*COMM*) pedido, encargo ♦ vt (*also:* **put in** ~) ordenar, poner en orden; (*COMM*) encargar, pedir; (*command*) mandar, ordenar; **in** ~ (*gen*) en orden; (*of document*) en regla; **in (working)** ~ en funcionamiento; **to be out of** ~ (*machine, toilets*) estar estropeado or descompuesto (*LAM*); **in** ~ **to do** para hacer; **in** ~ **that** para que + subj; **on** ~ (*COMM*) pedido; **to be on** ~ estar pedido; **we are under** ~s **to do it** tenemos orden de hacerlo; **a point of** ~ una cuestión de procedimiento; **to place an** ~ **for sth with sb** hacer un pedido de algo a algn; **made to** ~ hecho a la medida; **his income is of the** ~ **of £24,000 per year** sus ingresos son del orden de 24 mil libras al año; **to the** ~ **of** (*BANKING*) a la orden de; **to** ~ **sb to do sth** mandar a algn hacer algo.
order book n cartera de pedidos.
order form n hoja de pedido.
orderly ['ɔːdəlɪ] n (*MIL*) ordenanza m; (*MED*) auxiliar m/f (de hospital) ♦ adj ordenado.
orderly officer m (*MIL*) oficial m del día.
order number n número de pedido.
ordinal ['ɔːdɪnl] adj ordinal.
ordinarily ['ɔːdnrɪlɪ] adv por lo común.
ordinary ['ɔːdnrɪ] adj corriente, normal; (*pej*) común y corriente; **out of the** ~ fuera de lo común, extraordinario.

ordinary degree n (*BRIT*) diploma m; *ver recuadro.*

ordinary shares npl acciones fpl ordinarias.
ordination [ɔːdɪ'neɪʃən] n ordenación f.
ordnance ['ɔːdnəns] n (*MIL: unit*) artillería.
ordnance factory n fábrica de artillería.
Ordnance Survey n (*BRIT*) *servicio oficial de topografía y cartografía.*
ore [ɔː*] n mineral m.
Ore(g). abbr (*US*) = *Oregon.*
organ ['ɔːgən] n órgano.
organic [ɔː'gænɪk] adj orgánico; (*vegetables, produce*) biológico.
organism ['ɔːgənɪzəm] n organismo.
organist ['ɔːgənɪst] n organista m/f.
organization [ɔːgənaɪ'zeɪʃən] n organización f.
organize ['ɔːgənaɪz] vt organizar; **to get** ~d organizarse.
organized crime n crimen organizado.
organizer ['ɔːgənaɪzə*] n organizador(a) m/f.
orgasm ['ɔːgæzəm] n orgasmo.
orgy ['ɔːdʒɪ] n orgía.
Orient ['ɔːrɪənt] n Oriente m.
oriental [ɔːrɪ'entl] adj oriental.
orientate ['ɔːrɪənteɪt] vt orientar.
origin ['ɔrɪdʒɪn] n origen m; (*point of departure*) procedencia.
original [ə'rɪdʒɪnl] adj original; (*first*) primero; (*earlier*) primitivo ♦ n original m.
originality [ərɪdʒɪ'nælɪtɪ] n originalidad f.
originally [ə'rɪdʒɪnəlɪ] adv (*at first*) al principio; (*with originality*) con originalidad.
originate [ə'rɪdʒɪneɪt] vi: **to** ~ **from**, **to** ~ **in** surgir de, tener su origen en.
originator [ə'rɪdʒɪneɪtə*] n inventor(a) m/f, autor(a) m/f.
Orkneys ['ɔːknɪz] npl: **the** ~ (*also:* **the Orkney Islands**) las Orcadas.

ornament ['ɔ:nəmənt] n adorno.
ornamental [ɔ:nə'mɛntl] adj decorativo, de adorno.
ornamentation [ɔ:nəmɛn'teɪʃən] n ornamentación f.
ornate [ɔ:'neɪt] adj recargado.
ornithologist [ɔ:nɪ'θɒlədʒɪst] n ornitólogo/a.
ornithology [ɔ:nɪ'θɒlədʒɪ] n ornitología.
orphan ['ɔ:fn] n huérfano/a ♦ vt: **to be ~ed** quedar huérfano/a.
orphanage ['ɔ:fənɪdʒ] n orfanato.
orthodox ['ɔ:θədɒks] adj ortodoxo.
orthodoxy ['ɔ:θədɒksɪ] n ortodoxia.
orthopaedic, (US) **orthopedic** [ɔ:θə'pi:dɪk] adj ortopédico.
orthop(a)edics [ɔ:θə'pi:dɪks] n ortopedia.
OS abbr (BRIT: = Ordnance Survey) servicio oficial de topografía y cartografía; (: NAUT) = **ordinary seaman**; (: DRESS) = **outsize**.
O/S abbr = **out of stock**.
Oscar ['ɒskə*] n óscar m.
oscillate ['ɒsɪleɪt] vi oscilar; (person) vacilar.
oscillation [ɒsɪ'leɪʃən] n oscilación f; (of prices) fluctuación f.
OSHA n abbr (US: = Occupational Safety and Health Administration) oficina de la higiene y la seguridad en el trabajo.
Oslo ['ɒzləu] n Oslo.
ostensible [ɒs'tɛnsɪbl] adj aparente.
ostensibly [ɒs'tɛnsɪblɪ] adv aparentemente.
ostentatious [ɒstɛn'teɪʃəs] adj pretencioso, aparatoso; (person) ostentativo.
osteopath ['ɒstɪəpæθ] n osteópata m/f.
ostracize ['ɒstrəsaɪz] vt hacer el vacio a.
ostrich ['ɒstrɪtʃ] n avestruz m.
OT n abbr (= Old Testament) A.T. m.
OTB n abbr (US: = off-track betting) apuestas hechas fuera del hipódromo.
O.T.E. abbr (= on-target earnings) beneficios según objetivos.
other ['ʌðə*] adj otro ♦ pron: **the ~** (one) el/la otro/a; **~s** (~ people) otros; **~ than** (apart from) aparte de; **the ~ day** el otro día; **some ~ people have still to arrive** quedan por llegar otros; **some actor or ~** un actor cualquiera; **somebody or ~** alguien, alguno; **it was no ~ than the bishop** no era otro que el obispo.
otherwise ['ʌðəwaɪz] adv, conj de otra manera; (if not) si no; **an ~ good piece of work** un trabajo que, quitando eso, es bueno.
OTT abbr (col) = **over the top**; see **top**.
otter ['ɒtə*] n nutria.
OU n abbr (BRIT) = **Open University**.

ouch [autʃ] excl ¡ay!
ought, pt **ought** [ɔ:t] aux vb: **I ~ to do it** debería hacerlo; **this ~ to have been corrected** esto debiera de haberse corregido; **he ~ to win** (probability) debiera ganar; **you ~ to go and see it** vale la pena ir a verlo.
ounce [auns] n onza (28.35g; 16 in a pound).
our ['auə*] adj nuestro; see also **my**.
ours ['auəz] pron (el) nuestro/(la) nuestra etc; see also **mine**.
ourselves [auə'sɛlvz] pron pl (reflexive, after prep) nosotros; (emphatic) nosotros mismos; **we did it (all) by ~** lo hicimos nosotros solos; see also **oneself**.
oust [aust] vt desalojar.
out [aut] adv fuera, afuera; (not at home) fuera (de casa); (light, fire) apagado; (on strike) en huelga ♦ vt: **to ~ sb** revelar públicamente la homosexualidad de algn; **~ there** allí (fuera); **he's ~** (absent) no está, ha salido; **to be ~ in one's calculations** equivocarse (en sus cálculos); **to run ~** salir corriendo; **~ loud** en alta voz; **~ of** prep (outside) fuera de; (because of: anger etc) por; **to look ~ of the window** mirar por la ventana; **to drink ~ of a cup** beber de una taza; **made ~ of wood** de madera; **~ of petrol** sin gasolina; **"~ of order"** "no funciona"; **it's ~ of stock** (COMM) está agotado; **to be ~ and about again** estar repuesto y levantado; **the journey ~** el viaje de ida; **the boat was 10 km ~** el barco estaba a diez kilómetros de la costa; **before the week was ~** antes del fin de la semana; **he's ~ for all he can get** busca sus propios fines, anda detrás de lo suyo.
out-and-out ['autəndaut] adj (liar, thief etc) redomado, empedernido.
outback ['autbæk] n interior m.
outbid [aut'bɪd] vt pujar más alto que, sobrepujar.
outboard ['autbɔ:d] adj: **~ motor** (motor m) fuera borda m.
outbound ['autbaund] adj: **~ from/for** con salida de/hacia.
outbreak ['autbreɪk] n (of war) comienzo; (of disease) epidemia; (of violence etc) ola.
outbuilding ['autbɪldɪŋ] n dependencia; (shed) cobertizo.
outburst ['autbə:st] n explosión f, arranque m.
outcast ['autkɑ:st] n paria m/f.
outclass [aut'klɑ:s] vt aventajar, superar.
outcome ['autkʌm] n resultado.
outcrop ['autkrɒp] n (of rock) afloramiento.
outcry ['autkraɪ] n protestas fpl.

outdated [aut'deɪtɪd] *adj* anticuado.
outdistance [aut'dɪstəns] *vt* dejar atrás.
outdo [aut'duː] *vt* (*irreg: like* **do**) superar.
outdoor [aut'dɔː*] *adj* al aire libre.
outdoors [aut'dɔːz] *adv* al aire libre.
outer ['autə*] *adj* exterior, externo.
outer space *n* espacio exterior.
outfit ['autfɪt] *n* equipo; (*clothes*) traje *m*;
  (*col: organization*) grupo, organización *f*.
outfitter's ['autfɪtəz] *n* (*BRIT*) sastrería.
outgoing ['autgəuɪŋ] *adj* (*president, tenant*)
  saliente; (*means of transport*) que sale;
  (*character*) extrovertido.
outgoings ['autgəuɪŋz] *npl* (*BRIT*) gastos *mpl*.
outgrow [aut'grəu] *vt*: (*irreg: like* **grow**) **he
  has ~n his clothes** su ropa le queda
  pequeña ya.
outhouse ['authaus] *n* dependencia.
outing ['autɪŋ] *n* excursión *f*, paseo.
outlandish [aut'lændɪʃ] *adj* estrafalario.
outlast [aut'lɑːst] *vt* durar más tiempo que,
  sobrevivir a.
outlaw ['autlɔː] *n* proscrito/a ♦ *vt* (*person*)
  declarar fuera de la ley; (*practice*)
  declarar ilegal.
outlay ['autleɪ] *n* inversión *f*.
outlet ['autlɛt] *n* salida; (*of pipe*) desagüe *m*;
  (*US ELEC*) toma de corriente; (*for emotion*)
  desahogo; (*also*: **retail ~**) punto de venta.
outline ['autlaɪn] *n* (*shape*) contorno, perfil
  m; **in ~** (*fig*) a grandes rasgos.
outlive [aut'lɪv] *vt* sobrevivir a.
outlook ['autluk] *n* perspectiva; (*opinion*)
  punto de vista.
outlying ['autlaɪŋ] *adj* remoto, aislado.
outmanoeuvre, (*US*) **outmaneuver**
  [autmə'nuːvə*] *vt* (*MIL, fig*) superar en la
  estrategia.
outmoded [aut'məudɪd] *adj* anticuado,
  pasado de moda.
outnumber [aut'nʌmbə*] *vt* exceder *or*
  superar en número.
out of bounds [autəv'baundz] *adj*: **it's ~**
  está prohibido el paso.
out-of-court [autəv'kɔːt] *adj, adv* sin ir a
  juicio.
out-of-date [autəv'deɪt] *adj* (*passport*)
  caducado, vencido; (*theory, idea*)
  anticuado; (*clothes, customs*) pasado de
  moda.
out-of-doors [autəv'dɔːz] *adv* al aire libre.
out-of-the-way [autəvðə'weɪ] *adj* (*remote*)
  apartado; (*unusual*) poco común *or*
  corriente.
out-of-touch [autəv'tʌtʃ] *adj*: **to be ~** estar
  desconectado.
outpatient ['autpeɪʃənt] *n* paciente *m/f*
  externo/a.

outpost ['autpəust] *n* puesto avanzado.
outpouring ['autpɔːrɪŋ] *n* (*fig*) efusión *f*.
output ['autput] *n* (*volumen m de*)
  producción *f*, rendimiento; (*COMPUT*)
  salida ♦ *vt* (*COMPUT: to power*)
  imprimir.
outrage ['autreɪdʒ] *n* (*scandal*) escándalo;
  (*atrocity*) atrocidad *f* ♦ *vt* ultrajar.
outrageous [aut'reɪdʒəs] *adj* (*clothes*)
  extravagante; (*behaviour*) escandaloso.
outright [aut'raɪt] *adv* (*win*) de manera
  absoluta; (*be killed*) en el acto; (*ask*)
  abiertamente; (*completely*)
  completamente ♦ *adj* ['autraɪt] completo;
  (*winner*) absoluto; (*refusal*) rotundo.
outrun [aut'rʌn] *vt* (*irreg: like* **run**) correr
  más que, dejar atrás.
outset ['autset] *n* principio.
outshine [aut'ʃaɪn] *vt* (irreg: *like* **shine**) (*fig*)
  eclipsar, brillar más que.
outside [aut'saɪd] *n* exterior *m* ♦ *adj*
  exterior, externo ♦ *adv* fuera, afuera (*esp
  LAM*) ♦ *prep* fuera de; (*beyond*) más allá
  de; **at the ~** (*fig*) a lo sumo; **an ~ chance**
  una posibilidad remota; **~ left/right**
  (*FOOTBALL*) extremo izquierdo/derecho.
outside broadcast *n* (*RADIO, TV*) emisión *f*
  exterior.
outside contractor *n* contratista *m/f*
  independiente.
outside lane *n* (*AUT*) carril *m* de
  adelantamiento.
outside line *n* (*TEL*) línea (exterior).
outsider [aut'saɪdə*] *n* (*stranger*) forastero.
outsize ['autsaɪz] *adj* (*clothes*) de talla
  grande.
outskirts ['autskəːts] *npl* alrededores *mpl*,
  afueras *fpl*.
outsmart [aut'smɑːt] *vt* ser más listo que.
outspoken [aut'spəukən] *adj* muy franco.
outspread [aut'spred] *adj* extendido;
  (*wings*) desplegado.
outstanding [aut'stændɪŋ] *adj* excepcional,
  destacado; (*unfinished*) pendiente.
outstay [aut'steɪ] *vt*: **to ~ one's welcome**
  quedarse más de la cuenta.
outstretched [aut'stretʃt] *adj* (*arm*)
  extendido.
outstrip [aut'strɪp] *vt* (*competitors, demand,
  also fig*) dejar atrás, aventajar.
out-tray ['auttreɪ] *n* bandeja de salida.
outvote [aut'vəut] *vt*: **it was ~d (by ...)** fue
  rechazado en el voto (por ...).
outward ['autwəd] *adj* (*sign, appearances*)
  externo; (*journey*) de ida.
outwardly ['autwədlɪ] *adv* por fuera.
outweigh [aut'weɪ] *vt* pesar más que.
outwit [aut'wɪt] *vt* ser más listo que.

outworn [aut'wɔːn] adj (expression) cansado.

oval ['əuvl] adj ovalado ♦ n óvalo.

ovarian [əu'vɛərɪən] adj ovárico; (cancer) de ovario.

ovary ['əuvərɪ] n ovario.

ovation [əu'veɪʃən] n ovación f.

oven ['ʌvn] n horno.

ovenproof ['ʌvnpruːf] adj refractario, resistente al horno.

oven-ready ['ʌvnrɛdɪ] adj listo para el horno.

ovenware ['ʌvnwɛə*] n artículos mpl para el horno.

over ['əuvə*] adv encima, por encima ♦ adj (or adv) (finished) terminado; (surplus) de sobra; (excessively) demasiado ♦ prep (por) encima de; (above) sobre; (on the other side of) al otro lado de; (more than) más de; (during) durante; (about, concerning): **they fell out ~ money** riñeron por una cuestión de dinero; **~ here** (por) aquí; **~ there** (por) allí or allá; **all ~** (everywhere) por todas partes; **~ and ~ (again)** una y otra vez; **~ and above** además de; **to ask sb ~** invitar a algn a casa; **to bend ~** inclinarse; **now ~ to our Paris correspondent** damos la palabra a nuestro corresponsal de París; **the world ~** en todo el mundo, en el mundo entero; **she's not ~ intelligent** no es muy lista que digamos.

over ... [əuvə*] pref sobre..., super....

overact [əuvər'ækt] vi (THEAT) exagerar el papel.

overall ['əuvərɔːl] adj (length) total; (study) de conjunto ♦ adv [əuvər'ɔːl] en conjunto ♦ n (BRIT) guardapolvo; **~s** npl mono sg, overol msg (LAM).

overall majority n mayoría absoluta.

overanxious [əuvər'æŋkʃəs] adj demasiado preocupado or ansioso.

overawe [əuvər'ɔː] vt intimidar.

overbalance [əuvə'bæləns] vi perder el equilibrio.

overbearing [əuvə'bɛərɪŋ] adj autoritario, imperioso.

overboard ['əuvəbɔːd] adv (NAUT) por la borda; **to go ~ for sth** (fig) enloquecer por algo.

overbook [əuvə'buk] vt sobrereservar, reservar con exceso.

overcapitalize [əuvə'kæpɪtəlaɪz] vi sobrecapitalizar.

overcast ['əuvəkɑːst] adj encapotado.

overcharge [əuvə'tʃɑːdʒ] vt: **to ~ sb** cobrar un precio excesivo a algn.

overcoat ['əuvəkəut] n abrigo.

overcome [əuvə'kʌm] vt (irreg: like **come**) (gen) vencer; (difficulty) superar; **she was quite ~ by the occasion** la ocasión le conmovió mucho.

overconfident [əuvə'kɒnfɪdənt] adj demasiado confiado.

overcrowded [əuvə'kraudɪd] adj atestado de gente; (city, country) superpoblado.

overcrowding [əuvə'kraudɪŋ] n (in town, country) superpoblación f; (in bus etc) hacinamiento, apiñamiento.

overdo [əuvə'duː] vt (irreg: like **do**) exagerar; (overcook) cocer demasiado; **to ~ it, to ~ things** (work too hard) trabajar demasiado.

overdose ['əuvədəus] n sobredosis f inv.

overdraft ['əuvədrɑːft] n saldo deudor.

overdrawn [əuvə'drɔːn] adj (account) en descubierto.

overdrive ['əuvədraɪv] n (AUT) sobremarcha, superdirecta.

overdue [əuvə'djuː] adj retrasado; (recognition) tardío; (bill) vencido y no pagado; **that change was long ~** ese cambio tenía que haberse hecho hace tiempo.

overemphasis [əuvər'ɛmfəsɪs] n: **to put an ~ on** poner énfasis excesivo en.

overenthusiastic ['əuvərənθuːzɪ'æstɪk] adj demasiado entusiasta.

overestimate [əuvər'ɛstɪmeɪt] vt sobreestimar.

overexcited [əuvərɪk'saɪtɪd] adj sobreexcitado.

overexertion [əuvərɪg'zə:ʃən] n agotamiento, fatiga.

overexpose [əuvərɪk'spəuz] vt (PHOT) sobreexponer.

overflow [əuvə'fləu] vi desbordarse ♦ n ['əuvəfləu] (excess) exceso; (of river) desbordamiento; (also: ~ pipe) (cañería de) desagüe m.

overfly [əuvə'flaɪ] vt (irreg: like **fly**) sobrevolar.

overgenerous [əuvə'dʒenərəs] adj demasiado generoso.

overgrown [əuvə'grəun] adj (garden) cubierto de hierba; **he's just an ~ schoolboy** es un niño en grande.

overhang [əuvə'hæŋ] (irreg: like **hang**) vt sobresalir por encima de ♦ vi sobresalir.

overhaul vt [əuvə'hɔːl] revisar, repasar ♦ n ['əuvəhɔːl] revisión f.

overhead adv [əuvə'hɛd] por arriba or encima ♦ adj ['əuvəhɛd] (cable) aéreo; (railway) elevado, aéreo ♦ n ['əuvəhɛd] (US) = **overheads**.

overheads ['əuvəhɛdz] *npl* (*BRIT*) gastos *mpl* generales.

overhear [əuvə'hɪə*] *vt* (*irreg: like* **hear**) oír por casualidad.

overheat [əuvə'hiːt] *vi* (*engine*) recalentarse.

overjoyed [əuvə'dʒɔɪd] *adj* encantado, lleno de alegría.

overkill ['əuvəkɪl] *n* (*MIL*) capacidad *f* excesiva de destrucción; (*fig*) exceso.

overland ['əuvəlænd] *adj, adv* por tierra.

overlap *vi* [əuvə'læp] superponerse ♦ *n* ['əuvəlæp] superposición *f*.

overleaf [əuvə'liːf] *adv* al dorso.

overload [əuvə'ləud] *vt* sobrecargar.

overlook [əuvə'luk] *vt* (*have view of*) dar a, tener vistas a; (*miss*) pasar por alto; (*forgive*) hacer la vista gorda a.

overlord ['əuvəlɔːd] *n* señor *m*.

overmanning [əuvə'mænɪŋ] *n* exceso de mano de obra; (*in organization*) exceso de personal.

overnight [əuvə'naɪt] *adv* durante la noche; (*fig*) de la noche a la mañana ♦ *adj* de noche; **to stay** ~ pasar la noche.

overnight bag *n* fin *m* de semana, neceser *m* de viaje.

overnight stay *n* estancia de una noche.

overpass ['əuvəpɑːs] *n* (*US*) paso elevado *or* a desnivel.

overpay [əuvə'peɪ] *vt*: **to** ~ **sb by £50** pagar 50 libras de más a algn.

overplay [əuvə'pleɪ] *vt* exagerar; **to** ~ **one's hand** desmedirse.

overpower [əuvə'pauə*] *vt* dominar; (*fig*) embargar.

overpowering [əuvə'pauərɪŋ] *adj* (*heat*) agobiante; (*smell*) penetrante.

overproduction [əuvəprə'dʌkʃən] *n* superproducción *f*.

overrate [əuvə'reɪt] *vt* sobrevalorar.

overreach [əuvə'riːtʃ] *vt*: **to** ~ **o.s.** ir demasiado lejos, pasarse.

override [əuvə'raɪd] *vt* (*irreg: like* **ride**) (*order, objection*) no hacer caso de.

overriding [əuvə'raɪdɪŋ] *adj* predominante.

overrule [əuvə'ruːl] *vt* (*decision*) anular; (*claim*) denegar.

overrun [əuvə'rʌn] *vt* (*irreg: like* **run**) (*MIL: country*) invadir; (*time limit*) rebasar, exceder ♦ *vi* rebasar el límite previsto; **the town is** ~ **with tourists** el pueblo está inundado de turistas.

overseas [əuvə'siːz] *adv* en ultramar; (*abroad*) en el extranjero ♦ *adj* (*trade*) exterior; (*visitor*) extranjero.

oversee [əuvə'siː] *vt* supervisar.

overseer ['əuvəsɪə*] *n* (*in factory*)

supervisor(a) *m/f*; (*foreman*) capataz *m*.

overshadow [əuvə'ʃædəu] *vt* (*fig*) eclipsar.

overshoot [əuvə'ʃuːt] *vt* (*irreg: like* **shoot**) excederse.

oversight ['əuvəsaɪt] *n* descuido; **due to an** ~ a causa de un descuido *or* una equivocación.

oversimplify [əuvə'sɪmplɪfaɪ] *vt* simplificar demasiado.

oversleep [əuvə'sliːp] *vi* (*irreg: like* **sleep**) dormir más de la cuenta, no despertarse a tiempo.

overspend [əuvə'spɛnd] *vi* gastar más de la cuenta; **we have overspent by 5 dollars** hemos excedido el presupuesto en 5 dólares.

overspill ['əuvəspɪl] *n* exceso de población.

overstaffed [əuvə'stɑːft] *adj*: **to be** ~ tener exceso de plantilla.

overstate [əuvə'steɪt] *vt* exagerar.

overstatement ['əuvəsteɪtmənt] *n* exageración *f*.

overstay [əuvə'steɪ] *vt*: **to** ~ **one's time** *or* **welcome** quedarse más de lo conveniente.

overstep [əuvə'stɛp] *vt*: **to** ~ **the mark** *or* **the limits** pasarse de la raya.

overstock [əuvə'stɔk] *vt* abarrotar.

overstretched [əuvə'strɛtʃt] *adj* utilizado por encima de su capacidad.

overstrike *n* ['əuvəstraɪk] (*on printer*) superposición *f* ♦ *vt* (*irreg: like* **strike**) [əuvə'straɪk] superponer.

oversubscribed [əuvəsəb'skraɪbd] *adj* suscrito en exceso.

overt [əu'vəːt] *adj* abierto.

overtake [əuvə'teɪk] *vt* (*irreg: like* **take**) sobrepasar; (*BRIT AUT*) adelantar.

overtax [əuvə'tæks] *vt* (*ECON*) exigir contribuciones *fpl* excesivas *or* impuestos *mpl* excesivos a; (*fig: strength, patience*) agotar, abusar de; **to** ~ **o.s.** fatigarse demasiado.

overthrow [əuvə'θrəu] *vt* (*irreg: like* **throw**) (*government*) derrocar.

overtime ['əuvətaɪm] *n* horas *fpl* extraordinarias; **to do** *or* **work** ~ hacer *or* trabajar horas extraordinarias *or* extras.

overtime ban *n* prohibición *f* de (hacer) horas extraordinarias.

overtone ['əuvətəun] *n* (*fig*) tono.

overture ['əuvətʃuə*] *n* (*MUS*) obertura; (*fig*) propuesta.

overturn [əuvə'təːn] *vt, vi* volcar.

overview ['əuvəvjuː] *n* visión *f* de conjunto.

overweight [əuvə'weɪt] *adj* demasiado

gordo or pesado.

overwhelm [əuvə'wɛlm] vt aplastar.

overwhelming [əuvə'wɛlmɪŋ] adj (victory, defeat) arrollador(a); (desire) irresistible; one's ~ **impression is of heat** lo que más impresiona es el calor.

overwhelmingly [əuvə'wɛlmɪŋlɪ] adv abrumadoramente.

overwork [əuvə'wəːk] n trabajo excesivo ♦ vt hacer trabajar demasiado ♦ vi trabajar demasiado.

overwrite [əuvə'raɪt] vt (irreg: like **write**) (COMPUT) sobreescribir.

ovulation [ɔvju'leɪʃən] n ovulación f.

owe [əu] vt deber; **to ~ sb sth, to ~ sth to sb** deber algo a algn.

owing to ['əuɪŋtuː] prep debido a, por causa de.

owl [aul] n (long-eared ~) búho; (barn ~) lechuza.

own [əun] vt tener, poseer ♦ vi: **to ~ to sth/ to having done sth** confesar or reconocer algo/haber hecho algo ♦ adj propio; **a room of my ~** mi propia habitación; **to get one's ~ back** tomarse la revancha; **on one's ~** solo, a solas; **can I have it for my (very) ~?** ¿puedo quedarme con él?; **to come into one's ~** llegar a realizarse.
▶**own up** vi confesar.

own brand n (COMM) marca propia.

owner ['əunə*] n dueño/a.

owner-occupier ['əunər'ɔkjupaɪə*] n ocupante propietario/a m/f.

ownership ['əunəʃɪp] n posesión f; **it's under new ~** está bajo nueva dirección.

own goal n (SPORT) autogol m; **to score an ~** marcar un gol en propia puerta, marcar un autogol.

ox, pl **oxen** [ɔks, 'ɔksn] n buey m.

Oxbridge ['ɔksbrɪdʒ] n (BRIT) universidades de Oxford y Cambridge; ver recuadro.

OXBRIDGE

El término **Oxbridge** es una fusión de Ox(ford) y (Cam)bridge, las dos universidades británicas más antiguas y con mayor prestigio académico y social. Muchos miembros destacados de la clase dirigente del país son antiguos alumnos de una de las dos. El mismo término suele aplicarse a todo lo que ambas representan en cuestión de prestigio y privilegios sociales.

Oxfam ['ɔksfæm] n abbr (BRIT: = Oxford Committee for Famine Relief) OXFAM.

oxide ['ɔksaɪd] n óxido.

Oxon. ['ɔksn] abbr (BRIT: =Oxoniensis) = of Oxford.

oxtail ['ɔksteɪl] n: ~ **soup** sopa de rabo de buey.

oxygen ['ɔksɪdʒən] n oxígeno.

oxygen mask n máscara de oxígeno.

oxygen tent n tienda de oxígeno.

oyster ['ɔɪstə*] n ostra.

oz. abbr = **ounce(s)**.

ozone ['əuzəun] n ozono; ~ **layer** capa de ozono.

Pp

P, p [piː] n (letter) P, p f; **P for Peter** P de París.

P abbr = **president, prince**.

p abbr (= page) pág.; (BRIT) = **penny, pence**.

PA n abbr see **personal assistant, public address system** ♦ abbr (US) = Pennsylvania.

pa [pɑː] n (col) papá m.

p.a. abbr = **per annum**.

PAC n abbr (US) = political action committee.

pace [peɪs] n paso; (rhythm) ritmo ♦ vi: **to ~ up and down** pasearse de un lado a otro; **to keep ~ with** llevar el mismo paso que; (events) mantenerse a la altura de or al corriente de; **to set the ~** (running) marcar el paso; (fig) marcar la pauta; **to put sb through his ~s** (fig) poner a algn a prueba.

pacemaker ['peɪsmeɪkə*] n (MED) marcapasos m inv.

pacific [pə'sɪfɪk] adj pacífico ♦ n: **the P~ (Ocean)** el (Océano) Pacífico.

pacification [pæsɪfɪ'keɪʃən] n pacificación f.

pacifier ['pæsɪfaɪə*] n (US: dummy) chupete m.

pacifism ['pæsɪfɪzəm] n pacifismo.

pacifist ['pæsɪfɪst] n pacifista m/f.

pacify ['pæsɪfaɪ] vt (soothe) apaciguar; (country) pacificar.

pack [pæk] n (packet) paquete m; (COMM) embalaje m; (of hounds) jauría; (of wolves) manada; (of thieves etc) banda; (of cards) baraja; (bundle) fardo; (US: of cigarettes) paquete m, cajetilla ♦ vt (wrap) empaquetar; (fill) llenar; (in suitcase etc) meter, poner; (cram) llenar, atestar; (fig: meeting etc) llenar de partidarios; (COMPUT) comprimir; **to ~ (one's bags)**

hacer las maletas; **to ~ sb off** despachar a algn; **the place was ~ed** el local estaba (lleno) hasta los topes; **to send sb ~ing** (*col*) echar a algn con cajas destempladas.

▶**pack in** *vi* (*break down: watch, car*) estropearse ♦ *vt* (*col*) dejar; **~ it in!** ¡para!, ¡basta ya!

▶**pack up** *vi* (*col: machine*) estropearse; (*person*) irse ♦ *vt* (*belongings, clothes*) recoger; (*goods, presents*) empaquetar, envolver.

package ['pækɪdʒ] *n* paquete *m*; (*bulky*) bulto; (*also:* ~ **deal**) acuerdo global ♦ *vt* (*COMM: goods*) envasar, embalar.

package holiday *n* viaje *m* organizado (con todo incluido).

package tour *n* viaje *m* organizado.

packaging ['pækɪdʒɪŋ] *n* envase *m*.

packed lunch [pækt-] *n* almuerzo frío.

packer ['pækə*] *n* (*person*) empacador(a) *m/f*.

packet ['pækɪt] *n* paquete *m*.

packet switching [-'swɪtʃɪŋ] *n* (*COMPUT*) conmutación *f* por paquetes.

packhorse ['pækhɔːs] *n* caballo de carga.

pack ice *n* banco de hielo.

packing ['pækɪŋ] *n* embalaje *m*.

packing case *n* cajón *m* de embalaje.

pact [pækt] *n* pacto.

pad [pæd] *n* (*of paper*) bloc *m*; (*cushion*) cojinete *m*; (*launching ~*) plataforma (de lanzamiento); (*col: flat*) casa ♦ *vt* rellenar.

padded cell ['pædɪd-] *n* celda acolchada.

padding ['pædɪŋ] *n* relleno; (*fig*) paja.

paddle ['pædl] *n* (*oar*) canalete *m*, pala; (*US: for table tennis*) pala ♦ *vt* remar ♦ *vi* (*with feet*) chapotear.

paddle steamer *n* vapor *m* de ruedas.

paddling pool ['pædlɪŋ-] *n* (*BRIT*) piscina para niños.

paddock ['pædək] *n* (*field*) potrero.

paddy field ['pædɪ-] *n* arrozal *m*.

padlock ['pædlɔk] *n* candado ♦ *vt* cerrar con candado.

padre ['pɑːdrɪ] *n* capellán *m*.

paediatrician, (*US*) **pediatrician** [piːdɪə'trɪʃən] *n* pediatra *m/f*.

paediatrics, (*US*) **pediatrics** [piːdɪ'ætrɪks] *n* pediatría.

paedophile, (*US*) **pedophile** ['piːdəufaɪl] *adj* de pedófilos ♦ *n* pedófilo/a.

pagan ['peɪgən] *adj, n* pagano/a *m/f*.

page [peɪdʒ] *n* página; (*also:* ~ **boy**) paje *m* ♦ *vt* (*in hotel etc*) llamar por altavoz a.

pageant ['pædʒənt] *n* (*procession*) desfile *m*; (*show*) espectáculo.

pageantry ['pædʒəntrɪ] *n* pompa.

page break *n* límite *m* de la página.

pager ['peɪdʒə*] *n* busca *m*.

paginate ['pædʒɪneɪt] *vt* paginar.

pagination [pædʒɪ'neɪʃən] *n* paginación *f*.

pagoda [pə'gəudə] *n* pagoda.

paid [peɪd] *pt, pp of* **pay** ♦ *adj* (*work*) remunerado; (*official*) asalariado; **to put ~ to** (*BRIT*) acabar con.

paid-up ['peɪdʌp], (*US*) **paid-in** ['peɪdɪn] *adj* (*member*) con sus cuotas pagadas or al día; (*share*) liberado; **~ capital** capital *m* desembolsado.

pail [peɪl] *n* cubo, balde *m*.

pain [peɪn] *n* dolor *m*; **to be in ~** sufrir; **on ~ of death** so or bajo pena de muerte; *see also* **pains**.

pained [peɪnd] *adj* (*expression*) afligido.

painful ['peɪnful] *adj* doloroso; (*difficult*) penoso; (*disagreeable*) desagradable.

painfully ['peɪnfəlɪ] *adv* (*fig: very*) terriblemente.

painkiller ['peɪnkɪlə*] *n* analgésico.

painless ['peɪnlɪs] *adj* sin dolor; (*method*) fácil.

pains [peɪnz] *npl* (*efforts*) esfuerzos *mpl*; **to take ~ to do sth** tomarse trabajo en hacer algo.

painstaking ['peɪnzteɪkɪŋ] *adj* (*person*) concienzudo, esmerado.

paint [peɪnt] *n* pintura ♦ *vt* pintar; **a tin of ~** un bote de pintura; **to ~ the door blue** pintar la puerta de azul.

paintbox ['peɪntbɔks] *n* caja de pinturas.

paintbrush ['peɪntbrʌʃ] *n* (*artist's*) pincel *m*; (*decorator's*) brocha.

painter ['peɪntə*] *n* pintor(a) *m/f*.

painting ['peɪntɪŋ] *n* pintura.

paintwork ['peɪntwəːk] *n* pintura.

pair [pɛə*] *n* (*of shoes, gloves etc*) par *m*; (*of people*) pareja; **a ~ of scissors** unas tijeras; **a ~ of trousers** unos pantalones, un pantalón.

▶**pair off** *vi*: **to ~ off (with sb)** hacer pareja (con algn).

pajamas [pɪ'dʒɑːməz] *npl* (*US*) pijama *msg*, piyama *msg* (*LAM*).

Pakistan [pɑːkɪ'stɑːn] *n* Paquistán *m*.

Pakistani [pɑːkɪ'stɑːnɪ] *adj, n* paquistaní *m/f*.

PAL [pæl] *n abbr* (*TV*) = *phase alternation line*.

pal [pæl] *n* (*col*) amiguete/a *m/f*, colega *m/f*.

palace ['pæləs] *n* palacio.

palatable ['pælɪtəbl] *adj* sabroso; (*acceptable*) aceptable.

palate ['pælɪt] *n* paladar *m*.

palatial [pə'leɪʃəl] *adj* (*surroundings, residence*) suntuoso, espléndido.

palaver [pə'lɑːvə*] *n* (*fuss*) lío.

pale [peɪl] *adj* (*gen*) pálido; (*colour*) claro

◆ n: **to be beyond the** ~ pasarse de la raya ◆ vi palidecer; **to grow** or **turn** ~ palidecer; **to** ~ **into insignificance (beside)** no poderse comparar (con).
paleness ['peɪlnɪs] n palidez f.
Palestine ['pælɪstaɪn] n Palestina.
Palestinian [pælɪs'tɪnɪən] adj, n palestino/a m/f.
palette ['pælɪt] n paleta.
paling ['peɪlɪŋ] n (stake) estaca; (fence) valla.
palisade [pælɪ'seɪd] n palizada.
pall [pɔːl] n (of smoke) cortina ◆ vi cansar.
pallbearer ['pɔːlbɛərə*] n portador m del féretro.
pallet ['pælɪt] n (for goods) pallet m.
palliative ['pælɪətɪv] n paliativo.
pallid ['pælɪd] adj pálido.
pallor ['pælə*] n palidez f.
pally ['pælɪ] adj (col): **to be very** ~ **with sb** ser muy amiguete de algn.
palm [pɑːm] n (ANAT) palma; (also: ~ **tree**) palmera, palma ◆ vt: **to** ~ **sth off on sb** (BRIT col) endosarle algo a algn.
palmist ['pɑːmɪst] n quiromántico/a, palmista m/f.
Palm Sunday n Domingo de Ramos.
palpable ['pælpəbl] adj palpable.
palpably ['pælpəblɪ] adv obviamente.
palpitation [pælpɪ'teɪʃən] n palpitación f; **to have** ~**s** tener palpitaciones.
paltry ['pɔːltrɪ] adj (amount etc) miserable; (insignificant: person) insignificante.
pamper ['pæmpə*] vt mimar.
pamphlet ['pæmflət] n folleto; (political: handed out in street) panfleto.
pan [pæn] n (also: **sauce**~) cacerola, cazuela, olla; (also: **frying** ~) sartén m; (of lavatory) taza ◆ vi (CINE) tomar panorámicas; **to** ~ **for gold** cribar oro.
pan- [pæn] pref pan-.
panacea [pænə'sɪə] n panacea.
panache [pə'næʃ] n gracia, garbo.
Panama ['pænəmɑː] n Panamá m.
Panama Canal n el Canal de Panamá.
pancake ['pænkeɪk] n crepe f, panqueque m (LAM).
Pancake Day n martes m de carnaval.
pancake roll n rollito de primavera.
pancreas ['pæŋkrɪəs] n páncreas m.
panda ['pændə] n panda m.
panda car n (BRIT) coche m de la policía.
pandemonium [pændɪ'məʊnɪəm] n (noise): **there was** ~ se armó un tremendo jaleo; (mess) caos m.
pander ['pændə*] vi: **to** ~ **to** complacer a.
p&h abbr (US: = postage and handling) gastos de envío.

P&L abbr = profit and loss.
p & p abbr (BRIT: = postage and packing) gastos de envío.
pane [peɪn] n cristal m.
panel ['pænl] n (of wood) panel m; (of cloth) paño; (RADIO, TV) panel m de invitados.
panel game n (TV) programa m concurso para equipos.
panelling, (US) **paneling** ['pænəlɪŋ] n paneles mpl.
panellist, (US) **panelist** ['pænəlɪst] n miembro del jurado.
pang [pæŋ] n: ~**s of conscience** remordimientos mpl; ~**s of hunger** dolores mpl del hambre.
panhandler ['pænhændlə*] n (US col) mendigo/a.
panic ['pænɪk] n pánico ◆ vi dejarse llevar por el pánico.
panic buying [-baɪɪŋ] n compras masivas por miedo a futura escasez.
panic-stricken ['pænɪkstrɪkən] adj preso del pánico.
pannier ['pænɪə*] n (on bicycle) cartera; (on mule etc) alforja.
panorama [pænə'rɑːmə] n panorama m.
panoramic [pænə'ræmɪk] adj panorámico.
pansy ['pænzɪ] n (BOT) pensamiento; (col: pej) maricón m.
pant [pænt] vi jadear.
panther ['pænθə*] n pantera.
panties ['pæntɪz] npl bragas fpl.
pantihose ['pæntɪhəʊz] n (US) medias fpl, panties mpl.
panto ['pæntəʊ] n (BRIT col) = **pantomime**.
pantomime ['pæntəmaɪm] n (BRIT) representación f musical navideña; ver recuadro.

PANTOMIME

En época navideña los teatros británicos ponen en escena representaciones llamadas **pantomimes**, versiones libres de cuentos tradicionales como Aladino o El gato con botas. En ella nunca faltan personajes como la dama ("dame"), papel que siempre interpreta un actor; el protagonista joven ("principal boy"), normalmente interpretado por una actriz, y el malvado ("villain"). Es un espectáculo familiar dirigido a los niños pero con grandes dosis de humor para adultos en el que se alienta la participación del público.

---

pantry ['pæntrɪ] n despensa.
pants [pænts] n (BRIT: underwear: woman's) bragas fpl; (: man's) calzoncillos mpl; (US:

trousers) pantalones *mpl*.
pantsuit ['pæntsjuːt] *n* (*US*) traje *m* de chaqueta y pantalón.
papal ['peɪpəl] *adj* papal.
paparazzi [pæpə'rætsɪ] *npl* paparazzi *mpl*.
paper ['peɪpə*] *n* papel *m*; (*also*: news~) periódico, diario; (*study, article*) artículo; (*exam*) examen *m* ◊ *adj* de papel ◊ *vt* empapelar; (**identity**) ~**s** *npl* papeles *mpl*, documentos *mpl*; **a piece of** ~ un papel; **to put sth down on** ~ poner algo por escrito.
paper advance *n* (*on printer*) avance *m* de papel.
paperback ['peɪpəbæk] *n* libro de bolsillo.
paper bag *n* bolsa de papel.
paperboy ['peɪpəbɔɪ] *n* (*selling*) vendedor *m* de periódicos; (*delivering*) repartidor *m* de periódicos.
paper clip *n* clip *m*.
paper hankie *n* pañuelo de papel.
paper money *n* papel *m* moneda.
paper profit *n* beneficio no realizado.
paper shop *n* (*BRIT*) tienda de periódicos.
paperweight ['peɪpəweɪt] *n* pisapapeles *m inv*.
paperwork ['peɪpəwɜːk] *n* trabajo administrativo; (*pej*) papeleo.
papier-mâché ['pæpɪeɪ'mæʃeɪ] *n* cartón *m* piedra.
paprika ['pæprɪkə] *n* pimentón *m*.
Pap test ['pæp-] *n* (*MED*) frotis *m* (cervical).
papyrus [pə'paɪərəs] *n* papiro.
par [paː*] *n* par *f*; (*GOLF*) par *m* ◊ *adj* a la par; **to be on a** ~ **with** estar a la par con; **at** ~ a la par; **to be above/below** ~ estar sobre/bajo par; **to feel under** ~ sentirse en baja forma.
parable ['pærəbl] *n* parábola.
parachute ['pærəʃuːt] *n* paracaídas *m inv* ◊ *vi* lanzarse en paracaídas.
parachutist ['pærəʃuːtɪst] *n* paracaidista *m/f*.
parade [pə'reɪd] *n* desfile *m* ◊ *vt* (*gen*) recorrer, desfilar por; (*show off*) hacer alarde de ◊ *vi* desfilar; (*MIL*) pasar revista; **a fashion** ~ un desfile de modelos.
parade ground *n* plaza de armas.
paradise ['pærədaɪs] *n* paraíso.
paradox ['pærədɔks] *n* paradoja.
paradoxical [pærə'dɔksɪkl] *adj* paradójico.
paradoxically [pærə'dɔksɪklɪ] *adv* paradójicamente.
paraffin ['pærəfɪn] *n* (*BRIT*): ~ (**oil**) parafina.
paraffin heater *n* estufa de parafina.
paraffin lamp *n* quinqué *m*.
paragon ['pærəgən] *n* modelo.

paragraph ['pærəgrɑːf] *n* párrafo, acápite *m* (*LAM*); **new** ~ punto y aparte, punto acápite (*LAM*).
Paraguay ['pærəgwaɪ] *n* Paraguay *m*.
Paraguayan [pærə'gwaɪən] *adj, n* paraguayo/a *m/f*, paraguayano/a *m/f*.
parallel ['pærəlɛl] *adj*: ~ (**with/to**) en paralelo (con/a); (*fig*) semejante (a) ◊ *n* (*line*) paralela; (*fig, GEO*) paralelo.
paralysis [pə'rælɪsɪs] *n* parálisis *f inv*.
paralytic [pærə'lɪtɪk] *adj* paralítico.
paralyze ['pærəlaɪz] *vt* paralizar.
paramedic [pærə'mɛdɪk] *n* auxiliar *m/f* sanitario/a.
parameter [pə'ræmɪtə*] *n* parámetro.
paramilitary [pærə'mɪlɪtərɪ] *adj* (*organization, operations*) paramilitar.
paramount ['pærəmaunt] *adj*: **of** ~ **importance** de suma importancia.
paranoia [pærə'nɔɪə] *n* paranoia.
paranoid ['pærənɔɪd] *adj* (*person, feeling*) paranoico.
paranormal [pærə'nɔːml] *adj* paranormal.
parapet ['pærəpɪt] *n* parapeto.
paraphernalia [pærəfə'neɪlɪə] *n* parafernalia.
paraphrase ['pærəfreɪz] *vt* parafrasear.
paraplegic [pærə'pliːdʒɪk] *n* parapléjico/a.
parapsychology [pærəsaɪ'kɔlədʒɪ] *n* parasicología.
parasite ['pærəsaɪt] *n* parásito/a.
parasol ['pærəsɔl] *n* sombrilla, quitasol *m*.
paratrooper ['pærətruːpə*] *n* paracaidista *m/f*.
parcel ['pɑːsl] *n* paquete *m* ◊ *vt* (*also*: ~ **up**) empaquetar, embalar; **to be part and** ~ **of** ser parte integrante de.
▶**parcel out** *vt* parcelar, repartir.
parcel bomb *n* paquete *m* bomba.
parcel post *n* servicio de paquetes postales.
parch [pɑːtʃ] *vt* secar, resecar.
parched [pɑːtʃt] *adj* (*person*) muerto de sed.
parchment ['pɑːtʃmənt] *n* pergamino.
pardon ['pɑːdn] *n* perdón *m*; (*LAW*) indulto ◊ *vt* perdonar; indultar; ~ **me!, I beg your** ~! ¡perdone usted!; (**I beg your**) ~?, (*US*) ~ **me?** ¿cómo (dice)?
pare [pɛə*] *vt* (*nails*) cortar; (*fruit etc*) pelar.
parent ['pɛərənt] *n*: ~**s** *npl* padres *mpl*.
parentage ['pɛərəntɪdʒ] *n* familia, linaje *m*; **of unknown** ~ de padres desconocidos.
parental [pə'rɛntl] *adj* paternal/maternal.
parent company *n* casa matriz.
parenthesis, pl parentheses [pə'rɛnθɪsɪs, -θɪsiːz] *n* paréntesis *m inv*; **in parentheses** entre paréntesis.

parenthood – particular

parenthood ['pɛərənthud] n el ser padres.
parent ship n buque m nodriza.
Paris ['pærɪs] n París m.
parish ['pærɪʃ] n parroquia.
parish council n consejo parroquial.
parishioner [pə'rɪʃənə*] n feligrés/esa m/f.
Parisian [pə'rɪzɪən] adj, n parisino/a m/f,
parisiense m/f.
parity ['pærɪtɪ] n paridad f, igualdad f.
park [pɑːk] n parque m, jardín m público
♦ vt aparcar, estacionar ♦ vi aparcar,
estacionar.
parka ['pɑːkə] n parka.
parking ['pɑːkɪŋ] n aparcamiento,
estacionamiento; **"no ~"** "prohibido
aparcar or estacionarse".
parking lights npl luces fpl de
estacionamiento.
parking lot n (US) parking m, aparcamiento, playa f de estacionamiento (LAM).
parking meter n parquímetro.
parking offence, (US) **parking violation**
n ofensa por aparcamiento indebido.
parking place n sitio para aparcar,
aparcamiento.
parking ticket n multa de aparcamiento.
Parkinson's n (also: ~ **disease**)
(enfermedad f de) Parkinson m.
parkway ['pɑːkweɪ] n (US) alameda.
parlance ['pɑːləns] n lenguaje m; **in
common/modern** ~ en lenguaje
corriente/moderno.
parliament ['pɑːləmənt] n parlamento;
(Spanish) las Cortes fpl; ver recuadro.

PARLIAMENT

El Parlamento británico (**Parliament**) tiene
como sede el palacio de Westminster,
también llamado "Houses of Parliament".
Consta de dos cámaras: la Cámara de los
Comunes ("House of Commons") está
formada por 650 diputados ("Members of
Parliament") que acceden a ella tras ser
elegidos por sufragio universal en su
respectiva área o circunscripción electoral
("constituency"). Se reúne 175 días al año y
sus sesiones son presididas y moderadas
por el Presidente de la Cámara ("Speaker").
La cámara alta es la Cámara de los Lores
("House of Lords") y sus miembros son
nombrados por el monarca o bien han
heredado su escaño. Su poder es limitado,
aunque actúa como tribunal supremo de
apelación, excepto en Escocia.

---

parliamentary [pɑːlə'mɛntərɪ] adj
parlamentario.

parlour, (US) **parlor** ['pɑːlə*] n salón m,
living m (LAM).
parlous ['pɑːləs] adj peligroso, alarmante.
Parmesan [pɑːmɪ'zæn] n (also: ~ **cheese**)
queso parmesano.
parochial [pə'rəukɪəl] adj parroquial; (pej)
de miras estrechas.
parody ['pærədɪ] n parodia ♦ vt parodiar.
parole [pə'rəul] n: **on** ~ en libertad
condicional.
paroxysm ['pærəksɪzəm] n (MED)
paroxismo, ataque m; (of anger, laughter,
coughing) ataque m; (of grief) crisis f.
parquet ['pɑːkeɪ] n: ~ **floor(ing)** parquet m.
parrot ['pærət] n loro, papagayo.
parrot fashion adv como un loro.
parsimonious [pɑːsɪ'məunɪəs] adj tacaño.
parsley ['pɑːslɪ] n perejil m.
parsnip ['pɑːsnɪp] n chirivía.
parson ['pɑːsn] n cura m.
part [pɑːt] n (gen, MUS) parte f; (bit) trozo;
(of machine) pieza; (THEAT etc) papel m; (of
serial) entrega; (US: in hair) raya ♦ adv
= **partly** ♦ vt separar; (break) partir ♦ vi
(people) separarse; (roads) bifurcarse;
(crowd) apartarse; (break) romperse; **to
take** ~ **in** participar or tomar parte en; **to
take sb's** ~ tomar partido por algn; **for
my** ~ por mi parte; **for the most** ~ en su
mayor parte; (people) en su mayoría; **for
the better** ~ **of the day** durante la mayor
parte del día; ~ **of speech** (LING)
categoría gramatical, parte f de la
oración; **to take sth in good/bad** ~
aceptar algo bien/tomarse algo a mal.
▶**part with** vt fus ceder, entregar; (money)
pagar; (get rid of) deshacerse de.
partake [pɑː'teɪk] vi (irreg: like **take**)
(formal): **to** ~ **of sth** (food) comer algo;
(drink) tomar or beber algo.
part exchange n (BRIT): **in** ~ como parte
del pago.
partial ['pɑːʃl] adj parcial; **to be** ~ **to** (like)
ser aficionado a.
partially ['pɑːʃəlɪ] adv en parte,
parcialmente.
participant [pɑː'tɪsɪpənt] n (in competition)
concursante m/f.
participate [pɑː'tɪsɪpeɪt] vi: **to** ~ **in**
participar en.
participation [pɑːtɪsɪ'peɪʃən] n
participación f.
participle ['pɑːtɪsɪpl] n participio.
particle ['pɑːtɪkl] n partícula; (of dust)
mota; (fig) pizca.
particular [pə'tɪkjulə*] adj (special)
particular; (concrete) concreto; (given)
determinado; (detailed) detallado,

minucioso; (*fussy*) quisquilloso, exigente; ~**s** *npl* (*information*) datos *mpl*, detalles *mpl*; (*details*) pormenores *mpl*; **in** ~ en particular; **to be very** ~ **about** ser muy exigente en cuanto a; **I'm not** ~ me es *or* da igual.

particularly [pə'tɪkjʊləlɪ] *adv* especialmente, en particular.

parting ['pɑːtɪŋ] *n* (*act of*) separación *f*; (*farewell*) despedida; (*BRIT: in hair*) raya ♦ *adj* de despedida; ~ **shot** (*fig*) golpe *m* final.

partisan [pɑːtɪ'zæn] *adj* partidista ♦ *n* partidario/a; (*fighter*) partisano/a.

partition [pɑː'tɪʃən] *n* (*POL*) división *f*; (*wall*) tabique *m* ♦ *vt* dividir; dividir con tabique.

partly ['pɑːtlɪ] *adv* en parte.

partner ['pɑːtnə*] *n* (*COMM*) socio/a; (*SPORT, at dance*) pareja; (*spouse*) cónyuge *m/f*; (*friend etc*) compañero/a ♦ *vt* acompañar.

partnership ['pɑːtnəʃɪp] *n* (*gen*) asociación *f*; (*COMM*) sociedad *f*; **to go into** ~ (**with**), **form a** ~ (**with**) asociarse (con).

part payment *n* pago parcial.

partridge ['pɑːtrɪdʒ] *n* perdiz *f*.

part-time ['pɑːt'taɪm] *adj, adv* a tiempo parcial.

part-timer [pɑːt'taɪmə*] *n* trabajador(a) *m/f* a tiempo parcial.

party ['pɑːtɪ] *n* (*POL*) partido; (*celebration*) fiesta; (*group*) grupo; (*LAW*) parte *f*, interesado ♦ *adj* (*POL*) de partido; (*dress etc*) de fiesta, de gala; **to have** *or* **give** *or* **throw a** ~ organizar una fiesta; **dinner** ~ cena; **to be a** ~ **to a crime** ser cómplice *m/f* de un crimen.

party line *n* (*POL*) línea política del partido; (*TEL*) línea compartida.

party piece *n*: **to do one's** ~ hacer su numerito (de fiesta).

party political broadcast *n* ≈ espacio electoral.

pass [pɑːs] *vt* (*time, object*) pasar; (*place*) pasar por; (*exam, law*) aprobar; (*overtake, surpass*) rebasar; (*approve*) aprobar ♦ *vi* pasar; (*SCOL*) aprobar ♦ *n* (*permit*) permiso, pase *m*; (*membership card*) carnet *m*; (*in mountains*) puerto; (*SPORT*) pase *m*; (*SCOL: also:* ~ **mark**) aprobado; **to** ~ **sth through sth** pasar algo por algo; **to** ~ **the time of day with sb** pasar el rato con algn; **things have come to a pretty** ~! ¡hasta dónde hemos llegado!; **to make a** ~ **at sb** (*col*) insinuársele a algn.

▶**pass away** *vi* fallecer.

▶**pass by** *vi* pasar ♦ *vt* (*ignore*) pasar por alto.

▶**pass down** *vt* (*customs, inheritance*) pasar, transmitir.

▶**pass for** *vt fus* pasar por; **she could** ~ **for twenty-five** se podría creer que sólo tiene 25 años.

▶**pass on** *vi* (*die*) fallecer, morir ♦ *vt* (*hand on*): **to** ~ **on (to)** transmitir (a); (*cold, illness*) pegar (a); (*benefits*) dar (a); (*price rises*) pasar (a).

▶**pass out** *vi* desmayarse; (*MIL*) graduarse.

▶**pass over** *vi* (*die*) fallecer ♦ *vt* omitir, pasar por alto.

▶**pass up** *vt* (*opportunity*) dejar pasar, no aprovechar.

passable ['pɑːsəbl] *adj* (*road*) transitable; (*tolerable*) pasable.

passably ['pɑːsəblɪ] *adv* pasablemente.

passage ['pæsɪdʒ] *n* pasillo; (*act of passing*) tránsito; (*fare, in book*) pasaje *m*; (*by boat*) travesía.

passageway ['pæsɪdʒweɪ] *n* (*in house*) pasillo, corredor *m*; (*between buildings etc*) pasaje *m*, pasadizo.

passenger ['pæsɪndʒə*] *n* pasajero/a, viajero/a.

passer-by [pɑːsə'baɪ] *n* transeúnte *m/f*.

passing ['pɑːsɪŋ] *adj* (*fleeting*) pasajero; **in** ~ de paso.

passing place *n* (*AUT*) apartadero.

passion ['pæʃən] *n* pasión *f*.

passionate ['pæʃənɪt] *adj* apasionado.

passionately ['pæʃənɪtlɪ] *adv* apasionadamente, con pasión.

passion fruit *n* fruta de la pasión, granadilla.

passion play *n* drama *m* de la Pasión.

passive ['pæsɪv] *adj* (*also LING*) pasivo.

passive smoking *n* efectos del tabaco en fumadores pasivos.

passkey ['pɑːskiː] *n* llave *f* maestra.

Passover ['pɑːsəʊvə*] *n* Pascua (de los judíos).

passport ['pɑːspɔːt] *n* pasaporte *m*.

passport control *n* control *m* de pasaporte.

password ['pɑːswɔːd] *n* (*also COMPUT*) contraseña.

past [pɑːst] *prep* (*further than*) más allá de; (*later than*) después de ♦ *adj* pasado; (*president etc*) antiguo ♦ *n* (*time*) pasado; (*of person*) antecedentes *mpl*; **quarter/half** ~ **four** las cuatro y cuarto/media; **he's** ~ **forty** tiene más de cuarenta años; **I'm** ~ **caring** ya no me importa; **to be** ~ **it** (*col: person*) estar acabado; **for the** ~ **few/3 days** durante los últimos días/últimos 3 días; **to run** ~ pasar corriendo por; **in the** ~ en el pasado, antes.

pasta ['pæstə] n pasta.
paste [peɪst] n (gen) pasta; (glue) engrudo ♦ vt (stick) pegar; (glue) engomar; **tomato** ~ tomate concentrado.
pastel ['pæstl] adj pastel; (painting) al pastel.
pasteurized ['pæstəraɪzd] adj pasteurizado.
pastille ['pæstl] n pastilla.
pastime ['pɑːstaɪm] n pasatiempo.
past master n: **to be a** ~ **at** ser un maestro en.
pastor ['pɑːstə*] n pastor m.
pastoral ['pɑːstərl] adj pastoral.
pastry ['peɪstrɪ] n (dough) pasta; (cake) pastel m.
pasture ['pɑːstʃə*] n (grass) pasto.
pasty n ['pæstɪ] empanada ♦ adj ['peɪstɪ] pastoso; (complexion) pálido.
pat [pæt] vt dar una palmadita a; (dog etc) acariciar ♦ n (of butter) porción f ♦ adj: **he knows it (off)** ~ se lo sabe de memoria or al dedillo; **to give sb/o.s. a** ~ **on the back** (fig) felicitar a algn/felicitarse.
patch [pætʃ] n (of material) parche m; (mended part) remiendo; (of land) terreno; (COMPUT) ajuste m ♦ vt (clothes) remendar; **(to go through) a bad** ~ (pasar por) una mala racha.
▶**patch up** vt (mend temporarily) reparar; **to** ~ **up a quarrel** hacer las paces.
patchwork ['pætʃwəːk] n labor f de retales.
patchy ['pætʃɪ] adj desigual.
pate [peɪt] n: **bald** ~ calva.
pâté ['pæteɪ] n paté m.
patent ['peɪtnt] n patente f ♦ vt patentar ♦ adj patente, evidente.
patent leather n charol m.
patently ['peɪtntlɪ] adv evidentemente.
patent medicine n específico.
patent office n oficina de patentes y marcas.
patent rights npl derechos mpl de patente.
paternal [pə'təːnl] adj paternal; (relation) paterno.
paternalistic [pətəːnə'lɪstɪk] adj paternalista.
paternity [pə'təːnɪtɪ] n paternidad f.
paternity suit n (LAW) caso de paternidad.
path [pɑːθ] n camino, sendero; (trail, track) pista; (of missile) trayectoria.
pathetic [pə'θɛtɪk] adj (pitiful) penoso, patético; (very bad) malísimo; (moving) conmovedor(a).
pathetically [pə'θɛtɪklɪ] adv penosamente, patéticamente; (very badly) malísimamente mal, de pena.
pathological [pæθə'lɔdʒɪkəl] adj patológico.
pathologist [pə'θɔlədʒɪst] n patólogo/a.

pathology [pə'θɔlədʒɪ] n patología.
pathos ['peɪθɔs] n patetismo.
pathway ['pɑːθweɪ] n sendero, vereda.
patience ['peɪʃns] n paciencia; (BRIT CARDS) solitario; **to lose one's** ~ perder la paciencia.
patient ['peɪʃnt] n paciente m/f ♦ adj paciente, sufrido; **to be** ~ **with sb** tener paciencia con algn.
patiently ['peɪʃəntlɪ] adv pacientemente, con paciencia.
patio ['pætɪəu] n patio.
patriot ['peɪtrɪət] n patriota m/f.
patriotic [pætrɪ'ɔtɪk] adj patriótico.
patriotism ['pætrɪətɪzəm] n patriotismo.
patrol [pə'trəul] n patrulla ♦ vt patrullar por; **to be on** ~ patrullar, estar de patrulla.
patrol boat n patrullero, patrullera.
patrol car n coche m patrulla.
patrolman [pə'trəulmən] n (US) policía m.
patron ['peɪtrən] n (in shop) cliente m/f; (of charity) patrocinador(a) m/f; ~ **of the arts** mecenas m.
patronage ['pætrənɪdʒ] n patrocinio, protección f.
patronize ['pætrənaɪz] vt (shop) ser cliente de; (look down on) tratar con condescendencia a.
patronizing ['pætrənaɪzɪŋ] adj condescendiente.
patron saint n santo/a patrón/ona.
patter ['pætə*] n golpeteo; (sales talk) labia ♦ vi (rain) tamborilear.
pattern ['pætən] n (SEWING) patrón m; (design) dibujo; (behaviour, events) esquema m; ~ **of events** curso de los hechos; **behaviour** ~**s** modelos mpl de comportamiento.
patterned ['pætənd] adj (material) estampado.
paucity ['pɔːsɪtɪ] n escasez f.
paunch [pɔːntʃ] n panza, barriga.
pauper ['pɔːpə*] n pobre m/f.
pause [pɔːz] n pausa; (interval) intervalo ♦ vi hacer una pausa; **to** ~ **for breath** detenerse para tomar aliento.
pave [peɪv] vt pavimentar; **to** ~ **the way for** preparar el terreno para.
pavement ['peɪvmənt] n (BRIT) acera, vereda (LAM), andén m (LAM), banqueta (LAM); (US) calzada, pavimento.
pavilion [pə'vɪlɪən] n pabellón m; (SPORT) vestuarios mpl.
paving ['peɪvɪŋ] n pavimento.
paving stone n losa.
paw [pɔː] n pata; (claw) garra ♦ vt (animal) tocar con la pata; (pej: touch) tocar,

manosear.

pawn [pɔːn] *n* (*CHESS*) peón *m*; (*fig*) instrumento ♦ *vt* empeñar.

pawnbroker ['pɔːnbrəukə*] *n* prestamista *m/f*.

pawnshop ['pɔːnʃɔp] *n* casa de empeños.

pay [peɪ] *n* paga; (*wage etc*) sueldo, salario ♦ (*vb: pt, pp* **paid**) *vt* pagar; (*visit*) hacer; (*respect*) ofrecer ♦ *vi* pagar; (*be profitable*) rendir, compensar, ser rentable; **to be in sb's** ~ estar al servicio de algn; **to ~ attention (to)** prestar atención (a); **I paid £5 for that record** pagué 5 libras por ese disco; **how much did you ~ for it?** ¿cuánto pagaste por él?; **to ~ one's way** (*contribute one's share*) pagar su parte; (*remain solvent: company*) ser solvente; **to ~ dividends** (*COMM*) pagar dividendos; (*fig*) compensar; **it won't ~ you to do that** no te merece la pena hacer eso; **to put paid to** (*plan, person*) acabar con.

▶**pay back** *vt* (*money*) devolver, reembolsar; (*person*) pagar.

▶**pay for** *vt fus* pagar.

▶**pay in** *vt* ingresar.

▶**pay off** *vt* liquidar; (*person*) pagar; (*debts*) liquidar, saldar; (*creditor*) cancelar, redimir; (*workers*) despedir; (*mortgage*) cancelar, redimir ♦ *vi* (*scheme, decision*) dar resultado; **to ~ sth off in instalments** pagar algo a plazos.

▶**pay out** *vt* (*rope*) ir dando; (*money*) gastar, desembolsar.

▶**pay up** *vt* pagar.

payable ['peɪəbl] *adj* pagadero; **to make a cheque ~ to sb** extender un cheque a favor de algn.

pay award *n* aumento de sueldo.

pay day *n* día *m* de paga.

PAYE *n abbr* (*BRIT*: = *pay as you earn*) *sistema de retención fiscal en la fuente de ingresos*.

payee [peɪ'iː] *n* portador(a) *m/f*.

pay envelope *n* (*US*) = **pay packet**.

paying ['peɪɪŋ] *adj*: ~ **guest** huésped(a) *m/f* que la paga.

payload ['peɪləud] *n* carga útil.

payment ['peɪmənt] *n* pago; **advance** ~ (*part sum*) anticipo, adelanto; (*total sum*) saldo; **monthly** ~ mensualidad *f*; **deferred** ~, ~ **by instalments** pago a plazos *or* diferido; **on** ~ **of £5** mediante pago de *or* pagando £5; **in** ~ **for** (*goods, sum owed*) en pago de.

pay packet *n* (*BRIT*) sobre *m* (de la paga).

pay-phone ['peɪfəun] *n* teléfono público.

payroll ['peɪrəul] *n* nómina; **to be on a firm's** ~ estar en la nómina de una

compañía.

pay slip *n* hoja del sueldo.

pay station *n* (*US*) teléfono público.

PBS *n abbr* (*US*: = *Public Broadcasting Service*) *agrupación de ayuda a la realización de emisiones para la TV pública*.

PC *n abbr see* **personal computer;** (*BRIT*) = **police constable** ♦ *abbr* (*BRIT*) = *Privy Councillor* ♦ *adj abbr* = **politically correct.**

pc *abbr* = **per cent, postcard.**

p/c *abbr* = **petty cash.**

PCB *n abbr see* **printed circuit board.**

PD *n abbr* (*US*) = **police department.**

pd *abbr* = **paid.**

PDSA *n abbr* (*BRIT*) = *People's Dispensary for Sick Animals*.

PDT *n abbr* (*US*: = *Pacific Daylight Time*) *hora de verano del Pacífico*.

PE *n abbr* (= *physical education*) ed. física ♦ *abbr* (*Canada*) = *Prince Edward Island*.

pea [piː] *n* guisante *m*, chícharo (*LAM*), arveja (*LAM*).

peace [piːs] *n* paz *f*; (*calm*) paz *f*, tranquilidad *f*; **to be at** ~ **with sb/sth** estar en paz con algn/algo; **to keep the** ~ (*policeman*) mantener el orden; (*citizen*) guardar el orden.

peaceable ['piːsəbl] *adj* pacífico.

peaceably [piːsəblɪ] *adv* pacíficamente.

peaceful ['piːsful] *adj* (*gentle*) pacífico; (*calm*) tranquilo, sosegado.

peacekeeping ['piːskiːpɪŋ] *adj* de pacificación ♦ *n* pacificación *f*.

peacekeeping force *n* fuerza de pacificación.

peace offering *n* (*fig*) prenda de paz.

peacetime ['piːstaɪm] *n*: **in** ~ en tiempo de paz.

peach [piːtʃ] *n* melocotón *m*, durazno (*LAM*).

peacock ['piːkɔk] *n* pavo real.

peak [piːk] *n* (*of mountain: top*) cumbre *f*, cima; (: *point*) pico; (*of cap*) visera; (*fig*) cumbre *f*.

peak-hour ['piːkauə*] *adj* (*traffic etc*) de horas punta.

peak hours *npl*, **peak period** *n* horas *fpl* punta.

peak rate *n* tarifa máxima.

peaky ['piːkɪ] *adj* (*BRIT col*) pálido, paliducho; **I'm feeling a bit** ~ estoy malucho, no me encuentro bien.

peal [piːl] *n* (*of bells*) repique *m*; ~ **of laughter** carcajada.

peanut ['piːnʌt] *n* cacahuete *m*, maní *m* (*LAM*).

peanut butter *n* mantequilla de cacahuete.

pear [pɛə*] n pera.
pearl [pə:l] n perla.
peasant ['pɛznt] n campesino/a.
peat [pi:t] n turba.
pebble ['pɛbl] n guijarro.
peck [pɛk] vt (also: ~ **at**) picotear; (food) comer sin ganas ♦ n picotazo; (kiss) besito.
pecking order ['pɛkɪŋ-] n orden m de jerarquía.
peckish ['pɛkɪʃ] adj (BRIT col): **I feel** ~ tengo ganas de picar algo.
peculiar [pɪ'kju:lɪə*] adj (odd) extraño, raro; (typical) propio, característico; (particular: importance, qualities) particular; ~ **to** propio de.
peculiarity [pɪkju:lɪ'ærɪtɪ] n peculiaridad f, característica.
peculiarly [pɪ'kju:lɪəlɪ] adv extrañamente; particularmente.
pedal ['pɛdl] n pedal m ♦ vi pedalear.
pedal bin n cubo de la basura con pedal.
pedant ['pɛdənt] n pedante m/f.
pedantic [pɪ'dæntɪk] adj pedante.
pedantry ['pɛdəntrɪ] n pedantería.
peddle ['pɛdl] vt (goods) ir vendiendo or vender de puerta en puerta; (drugs) traficar con; (gossip) divulgar.
peddler ['pɛdlə*] n vendedor(a) m/f ambulante.
pedestal ['pɛdəstl] n pedestal m.
pedestrian [pɪ'dɛstrɪən] n peatón m ♦ adj pedestre.
pedestrian crossing n (BRIT) paso de peatones.
pedestrian precinct n zona reservada para peatones.
pediatrics [pi:dɪ'ætrɪks] n (US) = **paediatrics**.
pedigree ['pɛdɪgri:] n genealogía; (of animal) pedigrí m ♦ cpd (animal) de raza, de casta.
pedlar ['pɛdlə*] n (BRIT) = **peddler**.
pee [pi:] vi (col) mear.
peek [pi:k] vi mirar a hurtadillas; (COMPUT) inspeccionar.
peel [pi:l] n piel f; (of orange, lemon) cáscara; (: removed) peladuras fpl ♦ vt pelar ♦ vi (paint etc) desconcharse; (wallpaper) despegarse, desprenderse.
►**peel back** vt pelar.
peeler ['pi:lə*] n: **potato** ~ mondador m or pelador m de patatas, pelapatatas m inv.
peep [pi:p] n (BRIT: look) mirada furtiva; (sound) pío ♦ vi (BRIT) piar.
►**peep out** vi asomar la cabeza.
peephole ['pi:phəul] n mirilla.
peer [pɪə*] vi: **to** ~ **at** escudriñar ♦ n (noble)

par m; (equal) igual m.
peerage ['pɪərɪdʒ] n nobleza.
peerless ['pɪəlɪs] adj sin par, incomparable, sin igual.
peeved [pi:vd] adj enojado.
peevish ['pi:vɪʃ] adj malhumorado.
peevishness ['pi:vɪʃnɪs] n mal humor m.
peg [pɛg] n clavija; (for coat etc) gancho, colgador m; (BRIT: also: **clothes** ~) pinza; (tent ~) estaca ♦ vt (clothes) tender; (groundsheet) fijar con estacas; (fig: wages, prices) fijar.
pejorative [pɪ'dʒɔrətɪv] adj peyorativo.
Pekin [pi:'kɪn], **Peking** [pi:'kɪŋ] n Pekín m.
pekinese [pi:kɪ'ni:z] n pequinés/esa m/f.
pelican ['pɛlɪkən] n pelícano.
pelican crossing n (BRIT AUT) paso de peatones señalizado.
pellet ['pɛlɪt] n bolita; (bullet) perdigón m.
pell-mell ['pɛl'mɛl] adv en tropel.
pelmet ['pɛlmɪt] n galería.
pelt [pɛlt] vt: **to** ~ **sb with sth** arrojarle algo a algn ♦ vi (rain: also: ~ **down**) llover a cántaros ♦ n pellejo.
pelvis ['pɛlvɪs] n pelvis f.
pen [pɛn] n (ballpoint ~) bolígrafo; (fountain ~) pluma; (for sheep) redil m; (US col: prison) cárcel f, chirona; **to put** ~ **to paper** tomar la pluma.
penal ['pi:nl] adj penal; ~ **servitude** trabajos mpl forzados.
penalize ['pi:nəlaɪz] vt (punish) castigar; (SPORT) sancionar, penalizar.
penalty ['pɛnltɪ] n (gen) pena; (fine) multa; (SPORT) sanción f; ~ **(kick)** (FOOTBALL) penalty m.
penalty area n (BRIT SPORT) área de castigo.
penalty clause n cláusula de penalización.
penalty shoot-out [-'ʃu:taut] n (FOOTBALL) tanda de penaltis.
penance ['pɛnəns] n penitencia.
pence [pɛns] pl of **penny**.
penchant ['pã:ʃã:ŋ] n predilección f, inclinación f.
pencil ['pɛnsl] n lápiz m, lapicero (esp LAM) ♦ vt (also: ~ **in**) escribir con lápiz.
pencil case n estuche m.
pencil sharpener n sacapuntas m inv.
pendant ['pɛndnt] n pendiente m.
pending ['pɛndɪŋ] prep antes de ♦ adj pendiente; ~ **the arrival of** ... hasta que llegue ..., hasta llegar ... .
pendulum ['pɛndjuləm] n péndulo.
penetrate ['pɛnɪtreɪt] vt penetrar.
penetrating ['pɛnɪtreɪtɪŋ] adj penetrante.
penetration [pɛnɪ'treɪʃən] n penetración f.
penfriend ['pɛnfrɛnd] n (BRIT) amigo/a por

correspondencia.
penguin ['pɛŋgwɪn] *n* pingüino.
penicillin [pɛnɪ'sɪlɪn] *n* penicilina.
peninsula [pə'nɪnsjulə] *n* península.
penis ['piːnɪs] *n* pene *m*.
penitence ['pɛnɪtns] *n* penitencia.
penitent ['pɛnɪtnt] *adj* arrepentido; (*REL*)
penitente.
penitentiary [pɛnɪ'tɛnʃərɪ] *n* (*US*) cárcel *f*,
presidio.
penknife ['pɛnnaɪf] *n* navaja.
Penn(a). *abbr* (*US*) = Pennsylvania.
pen name *n* seudónimo.
pennant ['pɛnənt] *n* banderola; banderín *m*.
penniless ['pɛnɪlɪs] *adj* sin dinero.
Pennines ['pɛnaɪnz] *npl* (Montes *mpl*)
Peninos *mpl*.
penny, *pl* **pennies** *or* (*BRIT*) **pence** ['pɛnɪ,
'pɛnɪz, pɛns] *n* penique *m*; (*US*) centavo.
penpal ['pɛnpæl] *n* amigo/a por
correspondencia.
penpusher ['pɛnpuʃə*] *n* (*pej*) chupatintas
m/f inv.
pension ['pɛnʃən] *n* (*allowance, state
payment*) pensión *f*; (*old-age*) jubilación *f.*
▶**pension off** *vt* jubilar.
pensioner ['pɛnʃənə*] *n* (*BRIT*) jubilado/a.
pension fund *n* fondo de pensiones.
pensive ['pɛnsɪv] *adj* pensativo; (*withdrawn*)
preocupado.
pentagon ['pɛntəgən] *n* pentágono; **the P**~
(*US POL*) el Pentágono; *ver recuadro.*

PENTAGON

Se conoce como el Pentágono (**the
Pentagon**) *al edificio de planta pentagonal
que acoge las dependencias del Ministerio
de Defensa estadounidense ("Department
of Defense") en Arlington, Virginia. En
lenguaje periodístico se aplica también a la
dirección militar del país.*

Pentecost ['pɛntɪkɔst] *n* Pentecostés *m*.
penthouse ['pɛnthaus] *n* ático (de lujo).
pent-up ['pɛntʌp] *adj* (*feelings*) reprimido.
penultimate [pɛ'nʌltɪmət] *adj* penúltimo.
people ['piːpl] *npl* gente *f*; (*citizens*) pueblo
sg, ciudadanos *mpl* ♦ *n* (*nation, race*) pueblo,
nación *f* ♦ *vt* poblar; **several** ~ **came**
vinieron varias personas; ~ **say that** ...
dice la gente que ...; **old/young** ~ los
ancianos/jóvenes; ~ **at large** la gente en
general; **a man of the** ~ un hombre del
pueblo.
PEP *n abbr* (= *Personal Equity Plan*) plan
*personal de inversión con desgravación
fiscal.*

pep [pɛp] *n* (*col*) energía.
▶**pep up** *vt* animar.
pepper ['pɛpə*] *n* (*spice*) pimienta;
(*vegetable*) pimiento, ají *m* (*LAM*), chile *m*
(*LAM*) ♦ *vt* (*fig*) salpicar.
peppermint ['pɛpəmɪnt] *n* menta; (*sweet*)
pastilla de menta.
pepperoni [pɛpə'rəunɪ] *n* ≈ salchichón *m*
picante.
pepperpot ['pɛpəpɔt] *n* pimentero.
peptalk ['pɛptɔːk] *n* (*col*): **to give sb a** ~
darle a algn una inyección de ánimo.
per [pəː*] *prep* por; ~ **day/person** por día/
persona; **as** ~ **your instructions** de
acuerdo con sus instrucciones.
per annum *adv* al año.
per capita *adj*, *adv* per cápita.
perceive [pə'siːv] *vt* percibir; (*realize*) darse
cuenta de.
per cent, (*US*) **percent** [pə'sɛnt] *n* por
ciento; **a 20** ~ **discount** un descuento del
20 por ciento.
percentage [pə'sɛntɪdʒ] *n* porcentaje *m*; **to
get a** ~ **on all sales** percibir un tanto por
ciento sobre todas las ventas; **on a** ~
basis a porcentaje.
percentage point *n* punto (porcentual).
perceptible [pə'sɛptəbl] *adj* perceptible;
(*notable*) sensible.
perception [pə'sɛpʃən] *n* percepción *f*;
(*insight*) perspicacia.
perceptive [pə'sɛptɪv] *adj* perspicaz.
perch [pəːtʃ] *n* (*fish*) perca; (*for bird*) percha
♦ *vi* posarse.
percolate ['pəːkəleɪt] *vt* (*coffee*) filtrar ♦ *vi*
(*coffee, fig*) filtrarse.
percolator ['pəːkəleɪtə*] *n* cafetera de
filtro.
percussion [pə'kʌʃən] *n* percusión *f*.
percussionist [pə'kʌʃənɪst] *n* percusionista
m/f.
peremptory [pə'rɛmptərɪ] *adj* perentorio.
perennial [pə'rɛnɪəl] *adj* perenne.
perfect *adj* ['pəːfɪkt] perfecto ♦ *n* (*also*: ~
tense) perfecto ♦ *vt* [pə'fɛkt]
perfeccionar; **he's a** ~ **stranger to me** no
le conozco de nada, me es
completamente desconocido.
perfection [pə'fɛkʃən] *n* perfección *f.*
perfectionist [pə'fɛkʃənɪst] *n*
perfeccionista *m/f.*
perfectly ['pəːfɪktlɪ] *adv* perfectamente; **I'm**
~ **happy with the situation** estoy muy
contento con la situación; **you know** ~
well lo sabes muy bien *or* perfectamente.
perforate ['pəːfəreɪt] *vt* perforar.
perforation [pəːfə'reɪʃən] *n* perforación *f.*
perform [pə'fɔːm] *vt* (*carry out*) realizar,

llevar a cabo; (*THEAT*) representar; (*piece of music*) interpretar ♦ *vi* (*THEAT*) actuar; (*TECH*) funcionar.

performance [pə'fɔːməns] *n* (*of task*) realización *f*; (*of a play*) representación *f*; (*of player etc*) actuación *f*; (*of engine*) rendimiento; (*of car*) prestaciones *fpl*; (*of function*) desempeño; **the team put up a good** ~ el equipo se defendió bien.

performer [pə'fɔːmə*] *n* (*actor*) actor *m*, actriz *f*; (*MUS*) intérprete *m/f*.

performing [pə'fɔːmɪŋ] *adj* (*animal*) amaestrado.

performing arts *npl*: **the** ~ las artes teatrales.

perfume ['pəːfjuːm] *n* perfume *m*.

perfunctory [pə'fʌŋktərɪ] *adj* superficial.

perhaps [pə'hæps] *adv* quizá(s), tal vez; ~ **so/not** puede que sí/no.

peril ['pɛrɪl] *n* peligro, riesgo.

perilous ['pɛrɪləs] *adj* peligroso.

perilously ['pɛrɪləslɪ] *adv*: **they came** ~ **close to being caught** por poco les cogen *or* agarran.

perimeter [pə'rɪmɪtə*] *n* perímetro.

period ['pɪərɪəd] *n* período, periodo; (*HISTORY*) época; (*SCOL*) clase *f*; (*full stop*) punto; (*MED*) regla, periodo; (*US SPORT*) tiempo ♦ *adj* (*costume, furniture*) de época; **for a** ~ **of three weeks** durante (un período de) tres semanas; **the holiday** ~ el período de vacaciones.

periodic [pɪərɪ'ɔdɪk] *adj* periódico.

periodical [pɪərɪ'ɔdɪkl] *adj* periódico ♦ *n* revista, publicación *f* periódica.

periodically [pɪərɪ'ɔdɪklɪ] *adv* de vez en cuando, cada cierto tiempo.

period pains *npl* dolores *mpl* de la regla *or* de la menstruación.

peripatetic [pɛrɪpə'tɛtɪk] *adj* (*salesman*) ambulante; (*teacher*) con trabajo en varios colegios.

peripheral [pə'rɪfərəl] *adj* periférico ♦ *n* (*COMPUT*) periférico, unidad *f* periférica.

periphery [pə'rɪfərɪ] *n* periferia.

periscope ['pɛrɪskəup] *n* periscopio.

perish ['pɛrɪʃ] *vi* perecer; (*decay*) echarse a perder.

perishable ['pɛrɪʃəbl] *adj* perecedero.

perishables ['pɛrɪʃəblz] *npl* productos *mpl* perecederos.

peritonitis [pɛrɪtə'naɪtɪs] *n* peritonitis *f*.

perjure ['pəːdʒə*] *vt*: **to** ~ **o.s.** perjurar.

perjury ['pəːdʒərɪ] *n* (*LAW*) perjurio.

perk [pəːk] *n* beneficio, extra *m*.

▶**perk up** *vi* (*cheer up*) animarse.

perky ['pəːkɪ] *adj* alegre, animado.

perm [pəːm] *n* permanente *f* ♦ *vt*: **to have**

one's hair ~**ed** hacerse una permanente.

permanence ['pəːmənəns] *n* permanencia.

permanent ['pəːmənənt] *adj* permanente; (*job, position*) fijo; (*dye, ink*) indeleble; ~ **address** domicilio permanente; **I'm not** ~ **here** no estoy fijo aquí.

permanently ['pəːmənəntlɪ] *adv* (*lastingly*) para siempre, de modo definitivo; (*all the time*) permanentemente.

permeate ['pəːmɪeɪt] *vi* penetrar, trascender ♦ *vt* penetrar, trascender a.

permissible [pə'mɪsɪbl] *adj* permisible, lícito.

permission [pə'mɪʃən] *n* permiso; **to give sb** ~ **to do sth** autorizar a algn para que haga algo; **with your** ~ con su permiso.

permissive [pə'mɪsɪv] *adj* permisivo.

permit *n* ['pəːmɪt] permiso, licencia; (*entrance pass*) pase *m* ♦ *vt* [pə'mɪt] permitir; (*accept*) tolerar ♦ *vi* [pə'mɪt]: **weather** ~**ting** si el tiempo lo permite; **fishing** ~ permiso de pesca; **building/export** ~ licencia *or* permiso de construcción/exportación.

permutation [pəːmjuˈteɪʃən] *n* permutación *f*.

pernicious [pəːˈnɪʃəs] *adj* nocivo; (*MED*) pernicioso.

pernickety [pə'nɪkɪtɪ] *adj* (*col: person*) quisquilloso; (: *task*) delicado.

perpendicular [pəːpən'dɪkjulə*] *adj* perpendicular.

perpetrate ['pəːpɪtreɪt] *vt* cometer.

perpetual [pə'pɛtjuəl] *adj* perpetuo.

perpetually [pə'pɛtjuəlɪ] *adv* (*eternally*) perpetuamente; (*continuously*) constantemente, continuamente.

perpetuate [pə'pɛtjueɪt] *vt* perpetuar.

perpetuity [pəːpɪ'tjuːɪtɪ] *n*: **in** ~ a perpetuidad.

perplex [pə'plɛks] *vt* dejar perplejo.

perplexed [pə'plɛkst] *adj* perplejo, confuso.

perplexing [pə'plɛksɪŋ] *adj* que causa perplejidad.

perplexity [pə'plɛksɪtɪ] *n* perplejidad *f*, confusión *f*.

perquisites ['pəːkwɪzɪts] *npl* (*also*: **perks**) beneficios *mpl*.

persecute ['pəːsɪkjuːt] *vt* (*pursue*) perseguir; (*harass*) acosar.

persecution [pəːsɪ'kjuːʃən] *n* persecución *f*.

perseverance [pəːsɪ'vɪərəns] *n* perseverancia.

persevere [pəːsɪ'vɪə*] *vi* perseverar.

Persia ['pəːʃə] *n* Persia.

Persian ['pəːʃən] *adj, n* persa *m/f* ♦ *n* (*LING*) persa *m*; **the** ~ **Gulf** el Golfo Pérsico.

Persian cat *n* gato persa.

persist [pə'sɪst] *vi* persistir; **to ~ in doing sth** empeñarse en hacer algo.
persistence [pə'sɪstəns] *n* empeño.
persistent [pə'sɪstənt] *adj* (*lateness, rain*) persistente; (*determined*) porfiado; (*continuing*) constante; **~ offender** (*LAW*) multirreincidente *m/f*.
persistently [pə'sɪstəntlɪ] *adv* persistentemente; (*continually*) constantemente.
persnickety [pə'snɪkətɪ] *adj* (*US col*) = **pernickety**.
person ['pɜːsn] *n* persona; **in ~** en persona; **on** *or* **about one's ~** (*weapon, money*) encima; **a ~ to ~ call** (*TEL*) una llamada (de) persona a persona.
personable ['pɜːsnəbl] *adj* atractivo.
personal ['pɜːsnl] *adj* personal, individual; (*visit*) en persona; (*BRIT TEL*) persona a persona.
personal allowance *n* desgravación *f* personal.
personal assistant (PA) *n* ayudante *m/f* personal.
personal belongings *npl* efectos *mpl* personales.
personal column *n* anuncios *mpl* personales.
personal computer (PC) *n* ordenador *m* personal.
personal effects *npl* efectos *mpl* personales.
personal identification number (PIN) *n* (*COMPUT, BANKING*) número personal de identificación.
personality [pɜːsə'nælɪtɪ] *n* personalidad *f*.
personal loan *n* préstamo personal.
personally ['pɜːsnəlɪ] *adv* personalmente.
personal organizer *n* agenda (*profesional*); (*electronic*) organizador *m* personal.
personal property *n* bienes *mpl* muebles.
personal stereo *n* walkman ® *m*.
personification [pɜːsɔnɪfɪ'keɪʃən] *n* personificación *f*.
personify [pɜː'sɔnɪfaɪ] *vt* encarnar, personificar.
personnel [pɜːsə'nel] *n* personal *m*.
personnel department *n* departamento de personal.
personnel management *n* gestión *f* de personal.
personnel manager *n* jefe *m* de personal.
perspective [pə'spektɪv] *n* perspectiva; **to get sth into ~** ver algo en perspectiva *or* como es.
Perspex ® ['pɜːspeks] *n* (*BRIT*) vidrio acrílico, plexiglás *m* ®.

perspiration [pɜːspɪ'reɪʃən] *n* transpiración *f*, sudor *m*.
perspire [pə'spaɪə*] *vi* transpirar, sudar.
persuade [pə'sweɪd] *vt*: **to ~ sb to do sth** persuadir a algn para que haga algo; **to ~ sb of sth/that** persuadir *or* convencer a algn de algo/de que; **I am ~d that ...** estoy convencido de que ....
persuasion [pə'sweɪʒən] *n* persuasión *f*; (*persuasiveness*) persuasiva; (*creed*) creencia.
persuasive [pə'sweɪsɪv] *adj* persuasivo.
persuasively [pə'sweɪsɪvlɪ] *adv* de modo persuasivo.
pert [pɜːt] *adj* impertinente, fresco, atrevido.
pertaining [pɜː'teɪnɪŋ]: **~ to** *prep* relacionado con.
pertinent ['pɜːtɪnənt] *adj* pertinente, a propósito.
perturb [pə'tɜːb] *vt* perturbar.
perturbing [pə'tɜːbɪŋ] *adj* inquietante, perturbador(a).
Peru [pə'ruː] *n* el Perú.
perusal [pə'ruːzəl] *n* (*quick*) lectura somera; (*careful*) examen *m*.
peruse [pə'ruːz] *vt* (*examine*) leer con detención, examinar; (*glance at*) mirar por encima.
Peruvian [pə'ruːvɪən] *adj, n* peruano/a *m/f*.
pervade [pə'veɪd] *vt* impregnar; (*influence, ideas*) extenderse por.
pervasive [pə'veɪsɪv] *adj* (*smell*) penetrante; (*influence*) muy extendido; (*gloom, feelings, ideas*) reinante.
perverse [pə'vɜːs] *adj* perverso; (*stubborn*) terco; (*wayward*) travieso.
perversely [pə'vɜːslɪ] *adv* perversamente; tercamente; traviesamente.
perverseness [pə'vɜːsnɪs] *n* perversidad *f*, terquedad *f*, travesura.
perversion [pə'vɜːʃən] *n* perversión *f*.
pervert *n* ['pɜːvɜːt] pervertido/a ♦ *vt* [pə'vɜːt] pervertir.
pessary ['pesərɪ] *n* pesario.
pessimism ['pesɪmɪzəm] *n* pesimismo.
pessimist ['pesɪmɪst] *n* pesimista *m/f*.
pessimistic [pesɪ'mɪstɪk] *adj* pesimista.
pest [pest] *n* (*insect*) insecto nocivo; (*fig*) lata, molestia; **~s** *npl* plaga.
pest control *n* control *m* de plagas.
pester ['pestə*] *vt* molestar, acosar.
pesticide ['pestɪsaɪd] *n* pesticida *m*.
pestilence ['pestɪləns] *n* pestilencia.
pestle ['pesl] *n* mano *f* de mortero *or* de almirez.
pet [pet] *n* animal *m* doméstico; (*favourite*) favorito/a ♦ *vt* acariciar ♦ *vi* (*col*)

besuquearse ♦ *cpd*: **my ~ aversion** mi
manía.
petal ['pɛtl] *n* pétalo.
peter ['piːtə*]: **to ~ out** *vi* agotarse,
acabarse.
petite [pə'tiːt] *adj* menuda, chiquita.
petition [pə'tɪʃən] *n* petición *f* ♦ *vt*
presentar una petición a ♦ *vi*: **to ~ for**
divorce pedir el divorcio.
pet name *n* nombre *m* cariñoso, apodo.
petrified ['pɛtrɪfaɪd] *adj* (*fig*) pasmado,
horrorizado.
petrochemical [pɛtrə'kɛmɪkl] *adj*
petroquímico.
petrodollars ['pɛtrəudɔləz] *npl*
petrodólares *mpl*.
petrol ['pɛtrəl] (*BRIT*) *n* gasolina; (*for lighter*)
bencina; **two/four-star ~** gasolina
normal/súper.
petrol bomb *n* cóctel *m* Molotov.
petrol can *n* bidón *m* de gasolina.
petrol engine *n* (*BRIT*) motor *m* de
gasolina.
petroleum [pə'trəuliəm] *n* petróleo.
petroleum jelly *n* vaselina.
petrol pump *n* (*BRIT*) (*in car*) bomba de
gasolina; (*in garage*) surtidor *m* de
gasolina.
petrol station *n* (*BRIT*) gasolinera.
petrol tank *n* (*BRIT*) depósito (de gasolina).
petticoat ['pɛtɪkəut] *n* combinación *f*,
enagua(s) *f(pl)* (*LAM*).
pettifogging ['pɛtɪfɔgɪŋ] *adj* quisquilloso.
pettiness ['pɛtɪnɪs] *n* mezquindad *f*.
petty ['pɛtɪ] *adj* (*mean*) mezquino;
(*unimportant*) insignificante.
petty cash *n* dinero para gastos
menores.
petty cash book *n* libro de caja auxiliar.
petty officer *n* contramaestre *m*.
petulant ['pɛtjulənt] *adj* malhumorado.
pew [pjuː] *n* banco.
pewter ['pjuːtə*] *n* peltre *m*.
Pfc *abbr* (*US MIL*) = *private first class*.
PG *n abbr* (*CINE*) = *parental guidance*.
PGA *n abbr* = *Professional Golfers'*
Association.
PH *n abbr* (*US MIL*: = *Purple Heart*) decoración
otorgada a los heridos de guerra.
pH *n abbr* (= *pH value*) pH.
PHA *n abbr* (*US*) = *Public Housing*
Administration.
phallic ['fælɪk] *adj* fálico.
phantom ['fæntəm] *n* fantasma *m*.
Pharaoh ['fɛərəu] *n* faraón *m*.
pharmaceutical [faːmə'sjuːtɪkl] *adj*
farmacéutico.
pharmacist ['faːməsɪst] *n* farmacéutico/a.

pharmacy ['faːməsɪ] *n* (*US*) farmacia.
phase [feɪz] *n* fase *f* ♦ *vt*: **to ~ sth in/out**
introducir/retirar algo por etapas; **~d**
withdrawal retirada progresiva.
PhD *abbr* = **Doctor of Philosophy**.
pheasant ['fɛznt] *n* faisán *m*.
phenomenal [fɪ'nɔmɪnl] *adj* fenomenal,
extraordinario.
phenomenally [fɪ'nɔmɪnlɪ] *adv*
extraordinariamente.
phenomenon, pl phenomena
[fə'nɔmɪnən, -nə] *n* fenómeno.
phial ['faɪəl] *n* ampolla.
philanderer [fɪ'lændərə*] *n* donjuán *m*, don
Juan *m*.
philanthropic [fɪlən'θrɔpɪk] *adj* filantrópico.
philanthropist [fɪ'lænθrəpɪst] *n* filántropo/a.
philatelist [fɪ'lætəlɪst] *n* filatelista *m/f*.
philately [fɪ'lætəlɪ] *n* filatelia.
Philippines ['fɪlɪpiːnz] *npl*: **the ~** (las Islas)
Filipinas.
philosopher [fɪ'lɔsəfə*] *n* filósofo/a.
philosophical [fɪlə'sɔfɪkl] *adj* filosófico.
philosophy [fɪ'lɔsəfɪ] *n* filosofía.
phlegm [flɛm] *n* flema.
phlegmatic [flɛg'mætɪk] *adj* flemático.
phobia ['fəubjə] *n* fobia.
phone [fəun] *n* teléfono ♦ *vt* telefonear,
llamar por teléfono; **to be on the ~** tener
teléfono; (*be calling*) estar hablando por
teléfono.
▶**phone back** *vt, vi* volver a llamar.
▶**phone up** *vt, vi* llamar por teléfono.
phone book *n* guía telefónica.
phone box, phone booth *n* cabina
telefónica.
phone call *n* llamada (telefónica).
phonecard ['fəunkɑːd] *n* tarjeta telefónica.
phone-in ['fəunɪn] *n* (*BRIT RADIO, TV*)
programa de radio o televisión con las
líneas abiertas al público.
phone tapping [-tæpɪŋ] *n* escuchas
telefónicas.
phonetics [fə'nɛtɪks] *n* fonética.
phon(e)y ['fəunɪ] *adj* falso ♦ *n* (*person*)
farsante *m/f*.
phonograph ['fəunəgræf] *n* (*US*) fonógrafo,
tocadiscos *m inv*.
phonology [fəu'nɔlədʒɪ] *n* fonología.
phosphate ['fɔsfeɪt] *n* fosfato.
phosphorus ['fɔsfərəs] *n* fósforo.
photo ['fəutəu] *n* foto *f*.
photo... ['fəutəu] *pref* foto....
photocall ['fəutəukɔːl] *n* sesión *f*
fotográfica para la prensa.
photocopier ['fəutəukɔpɪə*] *n*
fotocopiadora.
photocopy ['fəutəukɔpɪ] *n* fotocopia ♦ *vt*

fotocopiar.

photoelectric [fəutəui'lɛktrɪk] _adj:_ ~ **cell** célula fotoeléctrica.

photo finish _n_ resultado comprobado por fotocontrol.

Photofit ® ['fəutəufɪt] _n (also:_ ~ **picture)** retrato robot.

photogenic [fəutəu'dʒɛnɪk] _adj_ fotogénico.

photograph ['fəutəgræf] _n_ fotografía ♦ _vt_ fotografiar; **to take a** ~ **of sb** sacar una foto de algn.

photographer [fə'tɔgrəfə*] _n_ fotógrafo.

photographic [fəutə'græfɪk] _adj_ fotográfico.

photography [fə'tɔgrəfɪ] _n_ fotografía.

photo opportunity _n oportunidad de salir en la foto._

Photostat ® ['fəutəustæt] _n_ fotóstato.

photosynthesis [fəutəu'sɪnθəsɪs] _n_ fotosíntesis _f._

phrase [freɪz] _n_ frase _f_ ♦ _vt (letter)_ expresar, redactar.

phrase book _n_ libro de frases.

physical ['fɪzɪkl] _adj_ físico; ~ **examination** reconocimiento médico; ~ **exercises** ejercicios _mpl_ físicos.

physical education _n_ educación _f_ física.

physically ['fɪsɪklɪ] _adv_ físicamente.

physical training _n_ gimnasia.

physician [fɪ'zɪʃən] _n_ médico/a.

physicist ['fɪzɪsɪst] _n_ físico/a.

physics ['fɪzɪks] _n_ física.

physiological [fɪzɪə'lɔdʒɪkl] _adj_ fisiológico.

physiology [fɪzɪ'ɔlədʒɪ] _n_ fisiología.

physiotherapy [fɪzɪəu'θɛrəpɪ] _n_ fisioterapia.

physique [fɪ'zi:k] _n_ físico.

pianist ['pɪənɪst] _n_ pianista _m/f._

piano [pɪ'ænəu] _n_ piano.

piano accordion _n (BRIT)_ acordeón-piano _m._

piccolo ['pɪkələu] _n (MUS)_ flautín _m._

pick [pɪk] _n (tool: also:_ ~**-axe)** pico, piqueta ♦ _vt (select)_ elegir, escoger; _(gather)_ coger _(SP)_, recoger _(LAM); (lock)_ abrir con ganzúa; _(scab, spot)_ rascar ♦ _vi:_ **to** ~ **and choose** ser muy exigente; **take your** ~ escoja lo que quiera; **the** ~ **of** lo mejor de; **to** ~ **one's nose/teeth** hurgarse las narices/escarbarse los dientes; **to** ~ **pockets** ratear, ser carterista; **to** ~ **one's way through** andar a tientas, abrirse camino; **to** ~ **a fight/quarrel with sb** buscar pelea/camorra con algn; **to** ~ **sb's brains** aprovecharse de los conocimientos de algn.

▸**pick at** _vt fus:_ **to** ~ **at one's food** comer con poco apetito.

▸**pick off** _vt (kill)_ matar de un tiro.

▸**pick on** _vt fus (person)_ meterse con.

▸**pick out** _vt_ escoger; _(distinguish)_ identificar.

▸**pick up** _vi (improve: sales)_ ir mejor; _(: patient)_ reponerse; _(: FINANCE)_ recobrarse ♦ _vt (from floor)_ recoger; _(buy)_ comprar; _(find)_ encontrar; _(learn)_ aprender; _(RADIO, TV, TEL)_ captar; **to** ~ **up speed** acelerarse; **to** ~ **o.s. up** levantarse; **to** ~ **up where one left off** reempezar algo donde lo había dejado.

pickaxe, _(US)_ **pickax** ['pɪkæks] _n_ pico, zapapico.

picket ['pɪkɪt] _n (in strike)_ piquete _m_ ♦ _vt_ hacer un piquete en, piquetear; **to be on** ~ **duty** estar de piquete.

picketing ['pɪkɪtɪŋ] _n_ organización _f_ de piquetes.

picket line _n_ piquete _m._

pickings ['pɪkɪŋz] _npl (pilferings):_ **there are good** ~ **to be had here** se pueden sacar buenas ganancias de aquí.

pickle ['pɪkl] _n (also:_ ~**s:** _as condiment)_ escabeche _m; (fig: mess)_ apuro ♦ _vt_ conservar en escabeche; _(in vinegar)_ conservar en vinagre; **in a** ~ en un lío, en apuros.

pick-me-up ['pɪkmɪʌp] _n_ reconstituyente _m._

pickpocket ['pɪkpɔkɪt] _n_ carterista _m/f._

pickup ['pɪkʌp] _n (BRIT: on record player)_ brazo; _(small truck: also:_ ~ **truck,** ~ **van)** furgoneta.

picnic ['pɪknɪk] _n_ picnic _m,_ merienda ♦ _vi_ merendar en el campo.

pictorial [pɪk'tɔːrɪəl] _adj_ pictórico; _(magazine etc)_ ilustrado.

picture ['pɪktʃə*] _n_ cuadro; _(painting)_ pintura; _(photograph)_ fotografía; _(film)_ película; _(TV)_ imagen _f_ ♦ _vt_ pintar; **the** ~**s** _(BRIT)_ el cine; **we get a good** ~ **here** captamos bien la imagen aquí; **to take a** ~ **of sb/sth** hacer _or_ sacar una foto a algn/de algo; **the garden is a** ~ **in June** el jardín es una preciosidad en junio; **the overall** ~ la impresión general; **to put sb in the** ~ poner a algn al corriente _or_ al tanto.

picture book _n_ libro de dibujos.

picturesque [pɪktʃə'rɛsk] _adj_ pintoresco.

piddling ['pɪdlɪŋ] _adj_ insignificante.

pidgin ['pɪdʒɪn] _adj:_ ~ **English** _lengua franca basada en el inglés._

pie [paɪ] _n (of meat etc: large)_ pastel _m; (: small)_ empanada; _(sweet)_ tarta.

piebald ['paɪbɔːld] _adj_ pío.

piece [pi:s] _n_ pedazo, trozo; _(of cake)_ trozo;

(*DRAUGHTS etc*) ficha; (*CHESS, part of a set*) pieza; (*item*): **a ~ of furniture/advice** un mueble/un consejo ♦ *vt*: **to ~ together** juntar; (*TECH*) armar; **to take to ~s** desmontar; **a ~ of news** una noticia; **a 10p ~** una moneda de 10 peniques; **a six-~ band** un conjunto de seis (músicos); **in one ~** (*object*) de una sola pieza; **~ by ~** pieza por *or* a pieza; **to say one's ~** decir su parecer.

piecemeal ['piːsmiːl] *adv* poco a poco.

piece rate *n* tarifa a destajo.

piecework ['piːswəːk] *n* trabajo a destajo.

pie chart *n* gráfico de sectores *or* de tarta.

pier [pɪə*] *n* muelle *m*, embarcadero.

pierce [pɪəs] *vt* penetrar en, perforar; **to have one's ears ~d** hacerse los agujeros de las orejas.

piercing ['pɪəsɪŋ] *adj* (*cry*) penetrante.

piety ['paɪətɪ] *n* piedad *f*.

pig [pɪg] *n* cerdo, puerco, chancho (*LAM*); (*person: greedy*) tragón/ona *m/f*, comilón/ona *m/f*; (: *nasty*) cerdo/a.

pigeon ['pɪdʒən] *n* paloma; (*as food*) pichón *m*.

pigeonhole ['pɪdʒənhəul] *n* casilla.

piggy bank ['pɪgɪbæŋk] *n* hucha (*en forma de cerdito*).

pigheaded ['pɪg'hɛdɪd] *adj* terco, testarudo.

piglet ['pɪglɪt] *n* cerdito, cochinillo.

pigment ['pɪgmənt] *n* pigmento.

pigmentation [pɪgmən'teɪʃən] *n* pigmentación *f*.

pigmy ['pɪgmɪ] *n* = **pygmy**.

pigskin ['pɪgskɪn] *n* piel *f* de cerdo.

pigsty ['pɪgstaɪ] *n* pocilga.

pigtail ['pɪgteɪl] *n* (*girl's*) trenza; (*Chinese, TAUR*) coleta.

pike [paɪk] *n* (*spear*) pica; (*fish*) lucio.

pilchard ['pɪltʃəd] *n* sardina.

pile [paɪl] *n* (*heap*) montón *m*; (*of carpet*) pelo ♦ (*vb: also: ~ up*) *vt* amontonar; (*fig*) acumular ♦ *vi* amontonarse; **in a ~** en un montón; **to ~ into** (*car*) meterse en.

▶**pile on** *vt*: **to ~ it on** (*col*) exagerar.

piles [paɪlz] *npl* (*MED*) almorranas *fpl*, hemorroides *mpl*.

pile-up ['paɪlʌp] *n* (*AUT*) accidente *m* múltiple.

pilfer ['pɪlfə*] *vt, vi* ratear, robar, sisar.

pilfering ['pɪlfərɪŋ] *n* ratería.

pilgrim ['pɪlgrɪm] *n* peregrino/a; **the Pilgrim Fathers** *or* **Pilgrims** *los primeros colonos norteamericanos*; *see also* **Thanksgiving (Day)**.

pilgrimage ['pɪlgrɪmɪdʒ] *n* peregrinación *f*, romería.

pill [pɪl] *n* píldora; **the ~** la píldora; **to be on**

the **~** tomar la píldora (anticonceptiva).

pillage ['pɪlɪdʒ] *vt* pillar, saquear.

pillar ['pɪlə*] *n* pilar *m*, columna.

pillar box *n* (*BRIT*) buzón *m*.

pillion ['pɪljən] *n* (*of motorcycle*) asiento trasero; **to ride ~** ir en el asiento trasero.

pillion passenger *n* pasajero que va detrás.

pillory ['pɪlərɪ] *vt* poner en ridículo.

pillow ['pɪləu] *n* almohada.

pillowcase ['pɪləukeɪs], **pillowslip** ['pɪləuslɪp] *n* funda (de almohada).

pilot ['paɪlət] *n* piloto *inv* ♦ *adj* (*scheme etc*) piloto ♦ *vt* pilotar; (*fig*) guiar, conducir.

pilot light *n* piloto.

pimento [pɪ'mɛntəu] *n* pimiento morrón.

pimp [pɪmp] *n* chulo, cafiche *m* (*LAM*).

pimple ['pɪmpl] *n* grano.

pimply ['pɪmplɪ] *adj* lleno de granos.

PIN *n abbr see* **personal identification number**.

pin [pɪn] *n* alfiler *m*; (*ELEC: of plug*) clavija; (*TECH*) perno; (: *wooden*) clavija; (*drawing ~*) chincheta; (*in grenade*) percutor *m* ♦ *vt* prender (con alfiler); sujetar con perno; **~s and needles** hormigueo *sg*; **to ~ sth on sb** (*fig*) cargar a algn con la culpa de algo.

▶**pin down** *vt* (*fig*): **there's something strange here, but I can't quite ~ it down** aquí hay algo raro pero no puedo precisar qué es; **to ~ sb down** hacer que algn concrete.

pinafore ['pɪnəfɔː*] *n* delantal *m*.

pinafore dress *n* (*BRIT*) pichi *m*.

pinball ['pɪnbɔːl] *n* (*also: ~ machine*) millón *m*, fliper *m*.

pincers ['pɪnsəz] *npl* pinzas *fpl*, tenazas *fpl*.

pinch [pɪntʃ] *n* pellizco; (*of salt etc*) pizca ♦ *vt* pellizcar; (*col: steal*) birlar ♦ *vi* (*shoe*) apretar; **at a ~** en caso de apuro; **to feel the ~** (*fig*) pasar apuros *or* estrecheces.

pinched [pɪntʃt] *adj* (*drawn*) cansado; **~ with cold** transido de frío; **~ for money/space** mal *or* falto de dinero/espacio *or* sitio.

pincushion ['pɪnkuʃən] *n* acerico.

pine [paɪn] *n* (*also: ~ tree*) pino ♦ *vi*: **to ~ for** suspirar por.

▶**pine away** *vi* morirse de pena.

pineapple ['paɪnæpl] *n* piña, ananá(s) (*LAM*) *m*.

pine cone *n* piña.

pine needle *n* aguja de pino.

ping [pɪŋ] *n* (*noise*) sonido agudo.

Ping-Pong ® ['pɪŋpɔŋ] *n* pingpong *m*.

pink [pɪŋk] *adj* (*de color*) rosa ♦ *n* (*colour*) rosa; (*BOT*) clavel *m*.

pinking shears ['pɪŋkɪŋ-] *npl* tijeras *fpl* dentadas.

pin money *n* dinero para gastos extra.

pinnacle ['pɪnəkl] *n* cumbre *f*.

pinpoint ['pɪnpɔɪnt] *vt* precisar.

pinstripe ['pɪnstraɪp] *adj*: ~ **suit** traje *m* a rayas.

pint [paɪnt] *n* pinta (*BRIT* = 0.57 *l*; *US* = 0.47 *l*); (*BRIT col*: *of beer*) pinta de cerveza, ≈ jarra (*SP*).

pin-up ['pɪnʌp] *n* (*picture*) *fotografía de mujer u hombre medio desnudos*; ~ **(girl)** ≈ chica de calendario.

pioneer [paɪə'nɪə*] *n* pionero/a ♦ *vt* promover.

pious ['paɪəs] *adj* piadoso, devoto.

pip [pɪp] *n* (*seed*) pepita; **the ~s** (*BRIT TEL*) la señal.

pipe [paɪp] *n* tubería, cañería; (*for smoking*) pipa, cachimba (*LAM*), cachimbo (*LAM*) ♦ *vt* conducir en cañerías; **(bag)~s** *npl* gaita *sg*.

▶**pipe down** *vi* (*col*) callarse.

pipe cleaner *n* limpiapipas *m inv*.

piped music [paɪpt-] *n* música ambiental.

pipe dream *n* sueño imposible.

pipeline ['paɪplaɪn] *n* tubería, cañería; (*for oil*) oleoducto; (*for natural gas*) gaseoducto; **it is in the** ~ (*fig*) está en trámite.

piper ['paɪpə*] *n* (*gen*) flautista *m/f*; (*with bagpipes*) gaitero/a.

pipe tobacco *n* tabaco de pipa.

piping ['paɪpɪŋ] *adv*: **to be** ~ **hot** estar calentito.

piquant ['piːkənt] *adj* picante.

pique [piːk] *n* pique *m*, resentimiento.

pirate ['paɪərət] *n* pirata *m/f* ♦ *vt* (*record, video, book*) hacer una copia pirata de.

pirated ['paɪərətɪd] *adj* (*book, record etc*) pirata *inv*.

pirate radio *n* (*BRIT*) emisora pirata.

pirouette [pɪru'ɛt] *n* pirueta ♦ *vi* piruetear.

Pisces ['paɪsiːz] *n* Piscis *m*.

piss [pɪs] *vi* (*col!*) mear.

pissed [pɪst] *adj* (*col!*: *drunk*) mamado.

pistol ['pɪstl] *n* pistola.

piston ['pɪstən] *n* pistón *m*, émbolo.

pit [pɪt] *n* hoyo; (*also*: **coal** ~) mina; (*in garage*) foso de inspección; (*also*: **orchestra** ~) foso de la orquesta; (*quarry*) cantera ♦ *vt* (*subj*: *chickenpox*) picar; (*: rust*) comer; **to** ~ **A against B** oponer A a B; **~s** *npl* (*AUT*) box *msg*; **~ted with** (*chickenpox*) picado de.

pitapat ['pɪtə'pæt] *adv*: **to go** ~ (*heart*) latir rápidamente; (*rain*) golpetear.

pitch [pɪtʃ] *n* (*throw*) lanzamiento; (*MUS*)

tono; (*BRIT SPORT*) campo, terreno; (*tar*) brea; (*in market etc*) puesto; (*fig*: *degree*) nivel *m*, grado ♦ *vt* (*throw*) arrojar, lanzar ♦ *vi* (*fall*) caer(se); (*NAUT*) cabecear; **I can't keep working at this** ~ no puedo seguir trabajando a este ritmo; **at its (highest)** ~ en su punto máximo; **his anger reached such a** ~ **that** ... su ira *or* cólera llegó a tal extremo que ...; **to** ~ **a tent** montar una tienda (de campaña); **to** ~ **one's aspirations too high** tener ambiciones desmesuradas.

pitch-black ['pɪtʃ'blæk] *adj* negro como boca de lobo.

pitched battle [pɪtʃt-] *n* batalla campal.

pitcher ['pɪtʃə*] *n* cántaro, jarro.

pitchfork ['pɪtʃfɔːk] *n* horca.

piteous ['pɪtɪəs] *adj* lastimoso.

pitfall ['pɪtfɔːl] *n* riesgo.

pith [pɪθ] *n* (*of orange*) piel *f* blanca; (*fig*) meollo.

pithead ['pɪthɛd] *n* (*BRIT*) bocamina.

pithy ['pɪθɪ] *adj* jugoso.

pitiful ['pɪtɪful] *adj* (*touching*) lastimoso, conmovedor(a); (*contemptible*) lamentable.

pitifully ['pɪtɪfəlɪ] *adv*: **it's** ~ **obvious** es tan evidente que da pena.

pitiless ['pɪtɪlɪs] *adj* despiadado, implacable.

pitilessly ['pɪtɪlɪslɪ] *adv* despiadadamente, implacablemente.

pittance ['pɪtns] *n* miseria.

pity ['pɪtɪ] *n* (*compassion*) compasión *f*, piedad *f*; (*shame*) lástima ♦ *vt* compadecer(se de); **to have** *or* **take** ~ **on sb** compadecerse de algn; **what a** ~! ¡qué pena!; **it is a** ~ **that you can't come** ¡qué pena que no puedas venir!

pitying ['pɪtɪɪŋ] *adj* compasivo, de lástima.

pivot ['pɪvət] *n* eje *m* ♦ *vi*: **to** ~ **on** girar sobre; (*fig*) depender de.

pixel ['pɪksl] *n* (*COMPUT*) pixel *m*, punto.

pixie ['pɪksɪ] *n* duendecillo.

pizza ['piːtsə] *n* pizza.

placard ['plækɑːd] *n* (*in march etc*) pancarta.

placate [plə'keɪt] *vt* apaciguar.

place [pleɪs] *n* lugar *m*, sitio; (*rank*) rango; (*seat*) plaza, asiento; (*post*) puesto; (*in street names*) plaza; (*home*): **at/to his** ~ en/a su casa ♦ *vt* (*object*) poner, colocar; (*identify*) reconocer; (*find a post for*) dar un puesto a, colocar; (*goods*) vender; **to take** ~ tener lugar; **to be** ~**d** (*in race, exam*) colocarse; **out of** ~ (*not suitable*) fuera de lugar; **in the first** ~ (*first of all*) en primer lugar; **to change** ~**s with sb** cambiarse de sitio con algn; **from** ~ **to** ~

de un sitio a *or* para otro; **all over the** ~
por todas partes; **he's going** ~**s** (*fig, col*)
llegará lejos; **I feel rather out of** ~ **here**
me encuentro algo desplazado; **to put sb
in his** ~ (*fig*) poner a algn en su lugar; **it
is not my** ~ **to do it** no me incumbe a mí
hacerlo; **to** ~ **an order with sb (for)** hacer
un pedido a algn (de); **we are better** ~**d
than a month ago** estamos en mejor
posición que hace un mes.

placebo [plə'si:bəu] *n* placebo.

place mat *n* (*wooden etc*) salvamanteles *m
inv*; (*in linen etc*) mantel *m* individual.

placement ['pleɪsmənt] *n* colocación *f*.

place name *n* topónimo.

placenta [plə'sentə] *n* placenta.

placid ['plæsɪd] *adj* apacible, plácido.

placidity [plæ'sɪdɪtɪ] *n* placidez *f*.

plagiarism ['pleɪdʒjərɪzm] *n* plagio.

plagiarist ['pleɪdʒjərɪst] *n* plagiario/a.

plagiarize ['pleɪdʒjəraɪz] *vt* plagiar.

plague [pleɪg] *n* plaga; (*MED*) peste *f* ♦ *vt*
(*fig*) acosar, atormentar; **to** ~ **sb with
questions** acribillar a algn a preguntas.

plaice [pleɪs] *n*, *pl inv* platija.

plaid [plæd] *n* (*material*) tela de cuadros.

plain [pleɪn] *adj* (*clear*) claro, evidente;
(*simple*) sencillo; (*frank*) franco, abierto;
(*not handsome*) poco atractivo; (*pure*)
natural, puro ♦ *adv* claramente ♦ *n* llano,
llanura; **in** ~ **clothes** (*police*) vestido de
paisano; **to make sth** ~ **to sb** dejar algo
en claro a algn.

plain chocolate *n* chocolate *m* oscuro *or*
amargo.

plainly ['pleɪnlɪ] *adv* claramente,
evidentemente; (*frankly*) francamente.

plainness ['pleɪnnɪs] *n* (*clarity*) claridad *f*;
(*simplicity*) sencillez *f*; (*of face*) falta de
atractivo.

plain speaking *n*: **there has been some** ~
se ha hablado claro.

plaintiff ['pleɪntɪf] *n* demandante *m/f*.

plaintive ['pleɪntɪv] *adj* (*cry, voice*)
lastimero, quejumbroso; (*look*) que da
lástima.

plait [plæt] *n* trenza ♦ *vt* trenzar.

plan [plæn] *n* (*drawing*) plano; (*scheme*) plan
m, proyecto ♦ *vt* (*think*) pensar; (*prepare*)
proyectar, planear; (*intend*) pensar, tener
la intención de ♦ *vi* hacer proyectos; **have
you any** ~**s for today?** ¿piensas hacer
algo hoy?; **to** ~ **to do** pensar hacer; **how
long do you** ~ **to stay?** ¿cuánto tiempo
piensas quedarte?; **to** ~ **(for)** planear,
proyectar.

►**plan out** *vt* planear detalladamente.

plane [pleɪn] *n* (*AVIAT*) avión *m*; (*tree*)

plátano; (*tool*) cepillo; (*MATH*) plano.

planet ['plænɪt] *n* planeta *m*.

planetarium [plænɪ'tɛərɪəm] *n* planetario.

planetary ['plænɪtərɪ] *adj* planetario.

plank [plæŋk] *n* tabla.

plankton ['plæŋktən] *n* plancton *m*.

planned economy [plænd-] *n* economía
planificada.

planner ['plænə*] *n* planificador(a) *m/f*;
(*chart*) diagrama *m* de planificación; **town**
~ urbanista *m/f*.

planning ['plænɪŋ] *n* (*POL, ECON*)
planificación *f*; **family** ~ planificación
familiar.

planning committee *n* (*in local
government*) comité *m* de planificación.

planning permission *n* licencia de obras.

plant [plɑ:nt] *n* planta; (*machinery*)
maquinaria; (*factory*) fábrica ♦ *vt* plantar;
(*field*) sembrar; (*bomb*) colocar.

plantain ['plæntein] *n* llantén *m*.

plantation [plæn'teɪʃən] *n* plantación *f*;
(*estate*) hacienda.

planter ['plɑ:ntə*] *n* hacendado.

plant pot *n* maceta, tiesto.

plaque [plæk] *n* placa.

plasma ['plæzmə] *n* plasma *m*.

plaster ['plɑ:stə*] *n* (*for walls*) yeso; (*also*: ~
of Paris) yeso mate; (*MED: for broken leg
etc*) escayola; (*BRIT: also*: **sticking** ~)
tirita, esparadrapo ♦ *vt* enyesar; (*cover*):
to ~ **with** llenar *or* cubrir de; **to be** ~**ed
with mud** estar cubierto de barro.

plasterboard ['plɑ:stəbɔ:d] *n* cartón *m*
yeso.

plaster cast *n* (*MED*) escayola; (*model,
statue*) vaciado de yeso.

plastered ['plɑ:stəd] *adj* (*col*) borracho.

plasterer ['plɑ:stərə*] *n* yesero.

plastic ['plæstɪk] *n* plástico ♦ *adj* de
plástico.

plastic bag *n* bolsa de plástico.

plastic bullet *n* bala de goma.

plastic explosive *n* goma 2 ®.

plasticine ® ['plæstɪsi:n] *n* (*BRIT*) plastilina
®.

plastic surgery *n* cirugía plástica.

plate [pleɪt] *n* (*dish*) plato; (*metal, in book*)
lámina; (*PHOT, on door*) placa; (*AUT:
number* ~) matrícula.

plateau, ~**s** *or* ~**x** ['plætəu, -z] *n* meseta,
altiplanicie *f*.

plateful ['pleɪtful] *n* plato.

plate glass *n* vidrio *or* cristal *m*
cilindrado.

platen ['plætən] *n* (*on typewriter, printer*)
rodillo.

plate rack *n* escurreplatos *m inv*.

platform ['plætfɔːm] *n* (*RAIL*) andén *m*; (*stage*) plataforma; (*at meeting*) tribuna; (*POL*) programa *m* (electoral); **the train leaves from** ~ **7** el tren sale del andén número 7.

platform ticket *n* (*BRIT*) billete *m* de andén.

platinum ['plætɪnəm] *n* platino.

platitude ['plætɪtjuːd] *n* tópico, lugar *m* común.

platonic [plə'tɔnɪk] *adj* platónico.

platoon [plə'tuːn] *n* pelotón *m*.

platter ['plætə*] *n* fuente *f*.

plaudits ['plɔːdɪts] *npl* aplausos *mpl*.

plausibility [plɔːzɪ'bɪlɪtɪ] *n* verosimilitud *f*, credibilidad *f*.

plausible ['plɔːzɪbl] *adj* verosímil; (*person*) convincente.

play [pleɪ] *n* (*gen*) juego; (*THEAT*) obra ♦ *vt* (*game*) jugar; (*instrument*) tocar; (*THEAT*) representar; (: *part*) hacer el papel de; (*fig*) desempeñar ♦ *vi* jugar; (*frolic*) juguetear; **to** ~ **safe** ir a lo seguro; **to bring** *or* **call into** ~ poner en juego; **to** ~ **a trick on sb** gastar una broma a algn; **they're** ~**ing at soldiers** están jugando a (los) soldados; **to** ~ **for time** (*fig*) tratar de ganar tiempo; **to** ~ **into sb's hands** (*fig*) hacerle el juego a algn; **a smile** ~**ed on his lips** una sonrisa le bailaba en los labios.

►**play about, play around** *vi* (*person*) hacer el tonto; **to** ~ **about** *or* **around with** (*fiddle with*) juguetear con; (*idea*) darle vueltas a.

►**play along** *vi*: **to** ~ **along with** seguirle el juego a ♦ *vt*: **to** ~ **sb along** (*fig*) jugar con algn.

►**play back** *vt* poner.

►**play down** *vt* quitar importancia a.

►**play on** *vt fus* (*sb's feelings, credulity*) aprovecharse de; **to** ~ **on sb's nerves** atacarle los nervios a algn.

►**play up** *vi* (*cause trouble*) dar guerra.

playact ['pleɪækt] *vi* (*fig*) hacer comedia *or* teatro.

play-acting ['pleɪæktɪŋ] *n* teatro.

playboy ['pleɪbɔɪ] *n* playboy *m*.

player ['pleɪə*] *n* jugador(a) *m/f*; (*THEAT*) actor *m*, actriz *f*; (*MUS*) músico/a.

playful ['pleɪful] *adj* juguetón/ona.

playground ['pleɪgraund] *n* (*in school*) patio de recreo.

playgroup ['pleɪgruːp] *n* jardín *m* de infancia.

playing card ['pleɪɪŋ-] *n* naipe *m*, carta.

playing field *n* campo de deportes.

playmaker ['pleɪmeɪkə*] *n* (*SPORT*) jugador

encargado de facilitar buenas jugadas a sus compañeros.

playmate ['pleɪmeɪt] *n* compañero/a de juego.

play-off ['pleɪɔf] *n* (*SPORT*) (partido de) desempate *m*.

playpen ['pleɪpɛn] *n* corral *m*.

playroom ['pleɪruːm] *n* cuarto de juego.

playschool ['pleɪskuːl] *n* = **playgroup**.

plaything ['pleɪθɪŋ] *n* juguete *m*.

playtime ['pleɪtaɪm] *n* (*SCOL*) (hora de) recreo.

playwright ['pleɪraɪt] *n* dramaturgo/a.

plc *abbr* (= *public limited company*) S.A.

plea [pliː] *n* (*request*) súplica, petición *f*; (*excuse*) pretexto, disculpa; (*LAW*) alegato, defensa.

plea bargaining *n* (*LAW*) acuerdo entre fiscal y defensor para agilizar los trámites judiciales.

plead [pliːd] *vt* (*LAW*): **to** ~ **sb's case** defender a alguien; (*give as excuse*) poner como pretexto ♦ *vi* (*LAW*) declararse; (*beg*): **to** ~ **with sb** suplicar *or* rogar a algn; **to** ~ **guilty/not guilty** (*defendant*) declararse culpable/inocente; **to** ~ **for sth** (*beg for*) suplicar algo.

pleasant ['plɛznt] *adj* agradable.

pleasantly ['plɛzntlɪ] *adv* agradablemente.

pleasantries ['plɛzntrɪz] *npl* (*polite remarks*) cortesías *fpl*; **to exchange** ~ conversar amablemente.

please [pliːz] *vt* (*give pleasure to*) dar gusto a, agradar ♦ *vi* (*think fit*): **do as you** ~ haz lo que quieras *or* lo que te dé la gana; **to** ~ **o.s.** hacer lo que le parezca; ~**!** ¡por favor!; ~ **yourself!** ¡haz lo que quieras!, ¡como quieras!; ~ **don't cry!** ¡no llores! te lo ruego.

pleased [pliːzd] *adj* (*happy*) alegre, contento; (*satisfied*): ~ **(with)** satisfecho (de); ~ **to meet you** (*col*) ¡encantado!, ¡tanto *or* mucho gusto!; **to be** ~ **(about sth)** alegrarse (de algo); **we are** ~ **to inform you that** ... tenemos el gusto de comunicarle que ....

pleasing ['pliːzɪŋ] *adj* agradable, grato.

pleasurable ['plɛʒərəbl] *adj* agradable, grato.

pleasurably ['plɛʒərəblɪ] *adv* agradablemente, gratamente.

pleasure ['plɛʒə*] *n* placer *m*, gusto; (*will*) voluntad *f* ♦ *cpd* de recreo; "**it's a** ~" "el gusto es mío"; **it's a** ~ **to see him** da gusto verle; **I have much** ~ **in informing you that** ... tengo el gran placer de comunicarles que ...; **with** ~ con mucho *or* todo gusto; **is this trip for business or**

~? ¿este viaje es de negocios o de placer?

pleasure cruise n crucero de placer.

pleasure ground n parque m de atracciones.

pleasure-seeking ['plɛʒəsiːkɪŋ] adj hedonista.

pleat [pliːt] n pliegue m.

pleb [plɛb] n: **the ~s** la gente baja, la plebe.

plebeian [plɪ'biːən] n plebeyo/a ♦ adj plebeyo; (pej) ordinario.

plebiscite ['plɛbɪsɪt] n plebiscito.

plectrum ['plɛktrəm] n plectro.

pledge [plɛdʒ] n (object) prenda; (promise) promesa, voto ♦ vt (pawn) empeñar; (promise) prometer; **to ~ support for sb** prometer su apoyo a algn; **to ~ sb to secrecy** hacer jurar a algn que guardará el secreto.

plenary ['pliːnəri] adj: **in ~ session** en sesión plenaria.

plentiful ['plɛntɪful] adj copioso, abundante.

plenty ['plɛntɪ] n abundancia; **~ of** mucho(s)/a(s); **we've got ~ of time to get there** tenemos tiempo de sobra para llegar.

plethora ['plɛθərə] n plétora.

pleurisy ['pluərɪsɪ] n pleuresía.

pliability [plaɪə'bɪlɪtɪ] n flexibilidad f.

pliable ['plaɪəbl] adj flexible.

pliers ['plaɪəz] npl alicates mpl, tenazas fpl.

plight [plaɪt] n condición f or situación f difícil.

plimsolls ['plɪmsəlz] npl (BRIT) zapatillas fpl de tenis.

plinth [plɪnθ] n plinto.

PLO n abbr (= Palestine Liberation Organization) OLP f.

plod [plɒd] vi caminar con paso pesado; (fig) trabajar laboriosamente.

plodder ['plɒdə*] n trabajador(a) diligente pero lento/a.

plodding ['plɒdɪŋ] adj (student) empollón(ona); (worker) más aplicado que brillante.

plonk [plɒŋk] (col) n (BRIT: wine) vino peleón ♦ vt: **to ~ sth down** dejar caer algo.

plot [plɒt] n (scheme) complot m, conjura; (of story, play) argumento; (of land) terreno, parcela ♦ vt (mark out) trazar; (conspire) tramar, urdir ♦ vi conspirar; **a vegetable ~** un cuadro de hortalizas.

plotter ['plɒtə*] n (instrument) trazador m (de gráficos); (COMPUT) trazador m.

plotting ['plɒtɪŋ] n conspiración f, intrigas fpl.

plough, (US) **plow** [plau] n arado ♦ vt (earth) arar.

►**plough back** vt (COMM) reinvertir.

►**plough through** vt fus (crowd) abrirse paso a la fuerza por.

ploughing ['plauɪŋ] n labranza.

ploughman ['plaumən] n: **~'s lunch** pan m con queso y cebolla.

plow [plau] (US) = **plough**.

ploy [plɔɪ] n truco, estratagema.

pluck [plʌk] vt (fruit) coger (SP), recoger (LAM); (musical instrument) puntear; (bird) desplumar ♦ n valor m, ánimo; **to ~ up courage** hacer de tripas corazón; **to ~ one's eyebrows** depilarse las cejas.

plucky ['plʌkɪ] adj valiente.

plug [plʌg] n tapón m; (ELEC) enchufe m, clavija; (AUT: also: **spark(ing) ~**) bujía ♦ vt (hole) tapar; (col: advertise) dar publicidad a; **to give sb/sth a ~** dar publicidad a algn/algo; **to ~ a lead into a socket** enchufar un hilo en una toma.

►**plug in** vt, vi (ELEC) enchufar.

plughole ['plʌghəul] n desagüe m.

plum [plʌm] n (fruit) ciruela; (also ~ **job**) chollo.

plumage ['pluːmɪdʒ] n plumaje m.

plumb [plʌm] adj vertical ♦ n plomo ♦ adv (exactly) exactamente, en punto ♦ vt sondar; (fig) sondear.

►**plumb in** vt (washing machine) conectar.

plumber ['plʌmə*] n fontanero/a, plomero/a (LAM).

plumbing ['plʌmɪŋ] n (trade) fontanería, plomería (LAM); (piping) cañerías.

plume [pluːm] n (gen) pluma; (on helmet) penacho.

plummet ['plʌmɪt] vi: **to ~ (down)** caer a plomo.

plump [plʌmp] adj rechoncho, rollizo ♦ vt: **to ~ sth (down) on** dejar caer algo en.

►**plump for** vt fus (col: choose) optar por.

►**plump up** vt ahuecar.

plumpness ['plʌmpnɪs] n gordura.

plunder ['plʌndə*] n pillaje m; (loot) botín m ♦ vt saquear, pillar.

plunge [plʌndʒ] n zambullida ♦ vt sumergir, hundir ♦ vi (fall) caer; (dive) saltar; (person) arrojarse; (sink) hundirse; **to take the ~** lanzarse; **to ~ a room into darkness** sumir una habitación en la oscuridad.

plunger ['plʌndʒə*] n émbolo; (for drain) desatascador m.

plunging ['plʌndʒɪŋ] adj (neckline) escotado.

pluperfect [pluː'pəːfɪkt] n pluscuamperfecto.

plural ['pluərl] n plural m.

plus [plʌs] n (also: **~ sign**) signo más; (fig) punto a favor ♦ adj: **a ~ factor** (fig) un factor *m* a favor ♦ *prep* más, y, además de; **ten/twenty** ~ más de diez/veinte.

plush [plʌʃ] *adj* de felpa.

plutonium [pluːˈtəʊnɪəm] *n* plutonio.

ply [plaɪ] *vt* (*a trade*) ejercer ♦ *vi* (*ship*) ir y venir; (*for hire*) ofrecerse (para alquilar); **three** ~ (*wool*) de tres cabos; **to** ~ **sb with drink** no dejar de ofrecer copas a algn.

plywood [ˈplaɪwʊd] *n* madera contrachapada.

PM *abbr* (*BRIT*) *see* **Prime Minister**.

p.m. *adv abbr* (= *post meridiem*) de la tarde *or* noche.

PMS *n abbr* (= *premenstrual syndrome*) SPM *m*.

PMT *n abbr* (= *premenstrual tension*) SPM *m*.

pneumatic [njuːˈmætɪk] *adj* neumático.

pneumatic drill *n* taladradora neumática.

pneumonia [njuːˈməʊnɪə] *n* pulmonía, neumonía.

PO *n abbr* (= *Post Office*) Correos *mpl*; (*NAUT*) = **petty officer**.

po *abbr* = **postal order**.

POA *n abbr* (*BRIT*) = *Prison Officers' Association*.

poach [pəʊtʃ] *vt* (*cook*) escalfar; (*steal*) cazar/pescar en vedado ♦ *vi* cazar/pescar en vedado.

poached [pəʊtʃt] *adj* (*egg*) escalfado.

poacher [ˈpəʊtʃə*] *n* cazador(a) *m/f* furtivo/a.

poaching [ˈpəʊtʃɪŋ] *n* caza/pesca furtiva.

PO Box *n abbr see* **Post Office Box**.

pocket [ˈpɒkɪt] *n* bolsillo; (*of air, GEO, fig*) bolsa; (*BILLIARDS*) tronera ♦ *vt* meter en el bolsillo; (*steal*) embolsarse; (*BILLIARDS*) entronerar; **breast** ~ bolsillo de pecho; ~ **of resistance** foco de resistencia; ~ **of warm air** bolsa de aire caliente; **to be out of** ~ salir perdiendo; **to be £5 in/out of** ~ salir ganando/perdiendo 5 libras.

pocketbook [ˈpɒkɪtbʊk] *n* (*US: wallet*) cartera; (: *handbag*) bolso.

pocketful [ˈpɒkɪtfʊl] *n* bolsillo lleno.

pocket knife *n* navaja.

pocket money *n* asignación *f*.

pockmarked [ˈpɒkmɑːkt] *adj* (*face*) picado de viruelas.

pod [pɒd] *n* vaina.

podgy [ˈpɒdʒɪ] *adj* gordinflón/ona.

podiatrist [pəˈdiːətrɪst] *n* (*US*) podólogo/a.

podiatry [pəˈdiːətrɪ] *n* (*US*) podología.

podium [ˈpəʊdɪəm] *n* podio.

POE *n abbr* = *port of embarkation, port of entry*.

poem [ˈpəʊɪm] *n* poema *m*.

poet [ˈpəʊɪt] *n* poeta *m/f*.

poetic [pəʊˈetɪk] *adj* poético.

poet laureate [-ˈlɔːrɪɪt] *n* poeta *m* laureado; *ver recuadro*.

POET LAUREATE

El poeta de la corte, denominado **Poet Laureate**, *ocupa como tal un puesto vitalicio al servicio de la Casa Real británica. Era tradición que escribiera poemas conmemorativos para ocasiones oficiales, aunque hoy día esto es poco frecuente. El primer poeta así distinguido fue Ben Jonson, en 1616.*

---

poetry [ˈpəʊɪtrɪ] *n* poesía.

poignant [ˈpɔɪnjənt] *adj* conmovedor(a).

poignantly [ˈpɔɪnjəntlɪ] *adv* de modo conmovedor.

point [pɔɪnt] *n* punto; (*tip*) punta; (*purpose*) fin *m*, propósito; (*BRIT ELEC: also:* **power** ~) toma de corriente, enchufe *m*; (*use*) utilidad *f*; (*significant part*) lo esencial; (*place*) punto, lugar *m*; (*also:* **decimal** ~): **2** ~ **3 (2.3)** dos coma tres (2,3) ♦ *vt* (*gun etc*): **to** ~ **sth at sb** apuntar con algo a algn ♦ *vi* señalar con el dedo; ~**s** *npl* (*AUT*) contactos *mpl*; (*RAIL*) agujas *fpl*; **to be on the** ~ **of doing sth** estar a punto de hacer algo; **to make a** ~ **of doing sth** poner empeño en hacer algo; **to get the** ~ comprender; **to come to the** ~ ir al meollo; **there's no** ~ **(in doing)** no tiene sentido (hacer); ~ **of departure** (*also fig*) punto de partida; ~ **of order** cuestión *f* de procedimiento; ~ **of sale** (*COMM*) punto de venta; ~**-of-sale advertising** publicidad *f* en el punto de venta; **the train stops at Carlisle and all** ~**s south** el tren para en Carlisle, y en todas las estaciones al sur; **when it comes to the** ~ a la hora de la verdad; **in** ~ **of fact** en realidad; **that's the whole** ~! ¡de eso se trata!; **to be beside the** ~ no venir al caso; **you've got a** ~ **there!** ¡tienes razón!

▶**point out** *vt* señalar.

▶**point to** *vt fus* indicar con el dedo; (*fig*) indicar, señalar.

point-blank [ˈpɔɪntˈblæŋk] *adv* (*also:* **at** ~ **range**) a quemarropa.

pointed [ˈpɔɪntɪd] *adj* (*shape*) puntiagudo, afilado; (*remark*) intencionado.

pointedly [ˈpɔɪntɪdlɪ] *adv* intencionadamente.

pointer [ˈpɔɪntə*] *n* (*stick*) puntero; (*needle*) aguja, indicador *m*; (*clue*) indicación *f*, pista; (*advice*) consejo.

pointless [ˈpɔɪntlɪs] *adj* sin sentido.

pointlessly [ˈpɔɪntlɪslɪ] *adv* inútilmente, sin

motivo.

point of view n punto de vista.

poise [pɔɪz] n (of head, body) porte m; (calmness) aplomo.

poised [pɔɪzd] adj (in temperament) sereno.

poison ['pɔɪzn] n veneno ♦ vt envenenar.

poisoning ['pɔɪznɪŋ] n envenenamiento.

poisonous ['pɔɪznəs] adj venenoso; (fumes etc) tóxico; (fig: ideas, literature) pernicioso; (: rumours, individual) nefasto.

poke [pəuk] vt (fire) hurgar, atizar; (jab with finger, stick etc) dar; (COMPUT) almacenar; (put): **to ~ sth in(to)** introducir algo en ♦ n (jab) empujoncito; (with elbow) codazo; **to ~ one's head out of the window** asomar la cabeza por la ventana; **to ~ fun at sb** ridiculizar a algn; **to give the fire a ~** atizar el fuego.

►**poke about** vi fisgonear.

poker ['pəukə*] n atizador m; (CARDS) póker m.

poker-faced ['pəukə'feɪst] adj de cara impasible.

poky ['pəukɪ] adj estrecho.

Poland ['pəulənd] n Polonia.

polar ['pəulə*] adj polar.

polar bear n oso polar.

polarization [pəulərai'zeɪʃən] n polarización f.

polarize ['pəuləraiz] vt polarizar.

Pole [pəul] n polaco/a.

pole [pəul] n palo; (GEO) polo; (TEL) poste m; (flag ~) asta; (tent ~) mástil m.

poleaxe ['pəulæks] vt (fig) desnucar.

pole bean n (US) judía trepadora.

polecat ['pəulkæt] n (BRIT) turón m; (US) mofeta.

Pol. Econ. ['pɔlɪkən] n abbr = political economy.

polemic [pɔ'lɛmɪk] n polémica.

polemicist [pɔ'lɛmɪsɪst] n polemista m/f.

pole star n estrella polar.

pole vault n salto con pértiga.

police [pə'liːs] n policía ♦ vt (streets, city, frontier) vigilar.

police car n coche-patrulla m.

police constable n (BRIT) guardia m, policía m.

police department n (US) policía.

police force n cuerpo de policía.

policeman [pə'liːsmən] n guardia m, policía m, agente m (LAM).

police officer n guardia m, policía m.

police record n: **to have a ~** tener antecedentes penales.

police state n estado policial.

police station n comisaría.

policewoman [pə'liːswumən] n mujer f policía.

policy ['pɔlɪsɪ] n política; (also: **insurance ~**) póliza; (of newspaper, company) política; **it is our ~ to do that** tenemos por norma hacer eso; **to take out a ~** sacar una póliza, hacerse un seguro.

policy holder n asegurado/a.

policy-making ['pɔlɪsɪmeɪkɪŋ] n elaboración f de directrices generales; **~ body** organismo encargado de elaborar las directrices generales.

polio ['pəuliəu] n polio f.

Polish ['pəulɪʃ] adj polaco ♦ n (LING) polaco.

polish ['pɔlɪʃ] n (for shoes) betún m; (for floor) cera (de lustrar); (for nails) esmalte m; (shine) brillo, lustre m; (fig: refinement) refinamiento ♦ vt (shoes) limpiar; (make shiny) pulir, sacar brillo a; (fig: improve) perfeccionar, refinar.

►**polish off** vt (work) terminar; (food) despachar.

►**polish up** vt (shoes, furniture etc) limpiar, sacar brillo a; (fig: language) perfeccionar.

polished ['pɔlɪʃt] adj (fig: person) refinado.

polite [pə'laɪt] adj cortés, atento; (formal) correcto; **it's not ~ to do that** es de mala educación hacer eso.

politely [pə'laɪtlɪ] adv cortésmente.

politeness [pə'laɪtnɪs] n cortesía.

politic ['pɔlɪtɪk] adj prudente.

political [pə'lɪtɪkl] adj político.

political asylum n asilo político.

politically [pə'lɪtɪkəlɪ] adv políticamente.

politically correct adj políticamente correcto.

politician [pɔlɪ'tɪʃən] n político/a.

politics ['pɔlɪtɪks] n política.

polka ['pɔlkə] n polca.

polka dot n lunar m.

poll [pəul] n (votes) votación f, votos mpl; (also: **opinion ~**) sondeo, encuesta ♦ vt (votes) obtener; (in opinion ~) encuestar; **to go to the ~s** (voters) votar; (government) acudir a las urnas.

pollen ['pɔlən] n polen m.

pollen count n índice m de polen.

pollination [pɔlɪ'neɪʃən] n polinización f.

polling ['pəulɪŋ] n (BRIT POL) votación f; (TEL) interrogación f.

polling booth n cabina de votar.

polling day n día m de elecciones.

polling station n centro electoral.

pollster ['pəulstə*] n (person) encuestador(a) m/f; (organization) empresa de encuestas or sondeos.

poll tax n (BRIT, formerly) contribución f municipal (no progresiva).

pollutant [pə'luːtənt] *n* (agente *m*) contaminante *m*.
pollute [pə'luːt] *vt* contaminar.
pollution [pə'luːʃən] *n* contaminación *f*, polución *f*.
polo ['pəuləu] *n* (*sport*) polo.
polo-neck ['pəuləunɛk] *adj* de cuello vuelto ♦ *n* (*sweater*) suéter *m* de cuello vuelto.
poly ['pɔlɪ] *n abbr* (*BRIT*) = **polytechnic**.
poly... [pɔlɪ] *pref* poli....
poly bag *n* (*BRIT col*) bolsa de plástico.
polyester [pɔlɪ'ɛstə*] *n* poliéster *m*.
polyethylene [pɔlɪ'ɛθɪliːn] *n* (*US*) polietileno.
polygamy [pə'lɪgəmɪ] *n* poligamia.
polygraph ['pɔlɪgrɑːf] *n* polígrafo.
polymath ['pɔlɪmæθ] *n* erudito/a.
Polynesia [pɔlɪ'niːzɪə] *n* Polinesia.
Polynesian [pɔlɪ'niːzɪən] *adj*, *n* polinesio/a *m/f*.
polyp ['pɔlɪp] *n* (*MED*) pólipo.
polystyrene [pɔlɪ'staɪriːn] *n* poliestireno.
polytechnic [pɔlɪ'tɛknɪk] *n* escuela politécnica.
polythene ['pɔlɪθiːn] *n* (*BRIT*) polietileno.
polythene bag *n* bolsa de plástico.
polyurethane [pɔlɪ'juərɪθeɪn] *n* poliuretano.
pomegranate ['pɔmɪgrænɪt] *n* granada.
pommel ['pɔml] *n* pomo ♦ *vt* = **pummel**.
pomp [pɔmp] *n* pompa.
pompom ['pɔmpɔm] *n* borla.
pompous ['pɔmpəs] *adj* pomposo; (*person*) presumido.
pond [pɔnd] *n* (*natural*) charca; (*artificial*) estanque *m*.
ponder ['pɔndə*] *vt* meditar.
ponderous ['pɔndərəs] *adj* pesado.
pong [pɔŋ] *n* (*BRIT col*) peste *f* ♦ *vi* (*BRIT col*) apestar.
pontiff ['pɔntɪf] *n* pontífice *m*.
pontificate [pɔn'tɪfɪkeɪt] *vi* (*fig*): **to ~ (about)** pontificar (sobre).
pontoon [pɔn'tuːn] *n* pontón *m*; (*BRIT: card game*) veintiuna.
pony ['pəunɪ] *n* poney *m*, potro.
ponytail ['pəunɪteɪl] *n* coleta, cola de caballo.
pony trekking *n* (*BRIT*) excursión *f* a caballo.
poodle ['puːdl] *n* caniche *m*.
pooh-pooh [puː'puː] *vt* desdeñar.
pool [puːl] *n* (*natural*) charca; (*pond*) estanque *m*; (*also*: **swimming ~**) piscina, alberca (*LAM*); (*billiards*) billar *m* americano; (*COMM: consortium*) consorcio; (: *US: monopoly trust*) trust *m* ♦ *vt* juntar; **typing ~** servicio de

mecanografía; (**football**) ~**s** *npl* quinielas *fpl*.
poor [puə*] *adj* pobre; (*bad*) malo ♦ *npl*: **the ~** los pobres.
poorly ['puəlɪ] *adj* mal, enfermo.
pop [pɔp] *n* ¡pum!; (*sound*) ruido seco; (*MUS*) (música) pop *m*; (*US col: father*) papá *m*; (*col: drink*) gaseosa ♦ *vt* (*burst*) hacer reventar ♦ *vi* reventar; (*cork*) saltar; **she ~ped her head out (of the window)** sacó de repente la cabeza (por la ventana).
►**pop in** *vi* entrar un momento.
►**pop out** *vi* salir un momento.
►**pop up** *vi* aparecer inesperadamente.
pop concert *n* concierto pop.
popcorn ['pɔpkɔːn] *n* palomitas *fpl* (de maíz).
pope [pəup] *n* papa *m*.
poplar ['pɔplə*] *n* álamo.
poplin ['pɔplɪn] *n* popelina.
popper ['pɔpə*] *n* corchete *m*, botón *m* automático.
poppy ['pɔpɪ] *n* amapola; *see also* **Remembrance Sunday**.
poppycock ['pɔpɪkɔk] *n* (*col*) tonterías *fpl*.
Popsicle ® ['pɔpsɪkl] *n* (*US*) polo.
populace ['pɔpjuləs] *n* pueblo.
popular ['pɔpjulə*] *adj* popular; **a ~ song** una canción popular; **to be ~ (with)** (*person*) caer bien (a); (*decision*) ser popular (entre).
popularity [pɔpju'lærɪtɪ] *n* popularidad *f*.
popularize ['pɔpjuləraɪz] *vt* popularizar; (*disseminate*) vulgarizar.
populate ['pɔpjuleɪt] *vt* poblar.
population [pɔpju'leɪʃən] *n* población *f*.
population explosion *n* explosión *f* demográfica.
populous ['pɔpjuləs] *adj* populoso.
porcelain ['pɔːslɪn] *n* porcelana.
porch [pɔːtʃ] *n* pórtico, entrada.
porcupine ['pɔːkjupaɪn] *n* puerco *m* espín.
pore [pɔː*] *n* poro ♦ *vi*: **to ~ over** enfrascarse en.
pork [pɔːk] *n* (carne *f* de) cerdo *or* chancho (*LAM*).
pork chop *n* chuleta de cerdo.
porn [pɔːn] *adj* (*col*) porno *inv* ♦ *n* porno.
pornographic [pɔːnə'græfɪk] *adj* pornográfico.
pornography [pɔː'nɔgrəfɪ] *n* pornografía.
porous ['pɔːrəs] *adj* poroso.
porpoise ['pɔːpəs] *n* marsopa.
porridge ['pɔrɪdʒ] *n* gachas *fpl* de avena.
port [pɔːt] *n* (*harbour*) puerto; (*NAUT: left side*) babor *m*; (*wine*) oporto; (*COMPUT*) puerta, puerto, port *m*; ~ **of call** puerto de

escala.
portable ['pɔːtəbl] *adj* portátil.
portal ['pɔːtl] *n* puerta (grande), portalón *m*.
port authorities *npl* autoridades *fpl* portuarias.
portcullis [pɔːt'kʌlɪs] *n* rastrillo.
portend [pɔː'tend] *vt* presagiar, anunciar.
portent ['pɔːtent] *n* presagio, augurio.
porter ['pɔːtə*] *n* (*for luggage*) maletero; (*doorkeeper*) portero/a, conserje *m/f*; (*US RAIL*) mozo de los coches-cama.
portfolio [pɔːt'fəulɪəu] *n* (*case, of artist*) cartera, carpeta; (*POL, FINANCE*) cartera.
porthole ['pɔːthəul] *n* portilla.
portico ['pɔːtɪkəu] *n* pórtico.
portion ['pɔːʃən] *n* porción *f*; (*helping*) ración *f*.
portly ['pɔːtlɪ] *adj* corpulento.
portrait ['pɔːtreɪt] *n* retrato.
portray [pɔː'treɪ] *vt* retratar; (*in writing*) representar.
portrayal [pɔː'treɪəl] *n* representación *f*.
Portugal ['pɔːtjugl] *n* Portugal *m*.
Portuguese [pɔːtjuˈyiːz] *adj* portugués/esa ♦ *n, pl inv* portugués/esa *m/f*; (*LING*) portugués *m*.
Portuguese man-of-war [-mænəu'wɔː*] *n* (*jellyfish*) *especie de medusa*.
pose [pəuz] *n* postura, actitud *f*; (*pej*) afectación *f*, pose *f* ♦ *vi* posar; (*pretend*): to ~ as hacerse pasar por ♦ *vt* (*question*) plantear; to strike a ~ tomar *or* adoptar una pose *or* actitud.
poser ['pəuzə*] *n* problema *m*/pregunta difícil; (*person*) = poseur.
poseur [pəu'zɜː*] *n* presumido/a, persona afectada.
posh [pɔʃ] *adj* (*col*) elegante, de lujo ♦ *adv* (*col*): to talk ~ hablar con acento afectado.
position [pə'zɪʃən] *n* posición *f*; (*job*) puesto ♦ *vt* colocar; to be in a ~ to do sth estar en condiciones de hacer algo.
positive ['pɔzɪtɪv] *adj* positivo; (*certain*) seguro; (*definite*) definitivo; we look forward to a ~ reply (*COMM*) esperamos que pueda darnos una respuesta en firme; he's a ~ nuisance es un auténtico pelmazo; ~ cash flow (*COMM*) flujo positivo de efectivo.
positively ['pɔzɪtɪvlɪ] *adv* (*affirmatively, enthusiastically*) de forma positiva; (*col: really*) absolutamente.
posse ['pɔsɪ] *n* (*US*) pelotón *m*.
possess [pə'zes] *vt* poseer; like one ~ed como un poseído; whatever can have · ed you? ¿cómo se te ocurrió?

possessed [pə'zest] *adj* poseso, poseído.
possession [pə'zeʃən] *n* posesión *f*; to take ~ of sth tomar posesión de algo.
possessive [pə'zesɪv] *adj* posesivo.
possessiveness [pə'zesɪvnɪs] *n* posesividad *f*.
possessor [pə'zesə*] *n* poseedor(a) *m/f*, dueño/a.
possibility [pɔsɪ'bɪlɪtɪ] *n* posibilidad *f*; he's a ~ for the part es uno de los posibles para el papel.
possible ['pɔsɪbl] *adj* posible; as big as ~ lo más grande posible; it is ~ to do it es posible hacerlo; as far as ~ en la medida de lo posible; a ~ candidate un(a) posible candidato/a.
possibly ['pɔsɪblɪ] *adv* (*perhaps*) posiblemente, tal vez; I cannot ~ come me es imposible venir; could you ~ ...? ¿podrías ...?
post [pəust] *n* (*BRIT: letters, delivery*) correo; (*job, situation*) puesto; (*trading* ~) factoría; (*pole*) poste *m* ♦ *vt* (*BRIT: send by* ~) mandar por correo; (: *put in mailbox*) echar al correo, (*MIL*) apostar; (*bills*) fijar, pegar; (*BRIT: appoint*): to ~ to destinar a; by ~ por correo; by return of ~ a vuelta de correo; to keep sb ~ed tener a algn al corriente.
post ... [pəust] *pref* post..., pos...; ~ 1950 pos(t) 1950.
postage ['pəustɪdʒ] *n* porte *m*, franqueo.
postage stamp *n* sello (de correo).
postal ['pəustl] *adj* postal, de correos.
postal order *n* giro postal.
postbag ['pəustbæg] *n* (*BRIT*) correspondencia, cartas *fpl*.
postbox ['pəustbɔks] *n* (*BRIT*) buzón *m*.
postcard ['pəustkɑːd] *nf* (tarjeta) postal *f*.
postcode ['pəustkəud] *n* (*BRIT*) código postal.
postdate [pəust'deɪt] *vt* (*cheque*) poner fecha adelantada a.
poster ['pəustə*] *n* cartel *m*, afiche *m* (*LAM*).
poste restante [pəust'restɔnt] *n* (*BRIT*) lista de correos.
posterior [pɔs'tɪərɪə*] *n* (*col*) trasero.
posterity [pɔs'terɪtɪ] *n* posteridad *f*.
poster paint *n* pintura al agua.
post-free [pəust'friː] *adj* (con) porte pagado.
postgraduate ['pəust'grædjuɪt] *n* posgraduado/a.
posthumous ['pɔstjuməs] *adj* póstumo.
posthumously ['pɔstjuməslɪ] *adv* póstumamente, con carácter póstumo.
posting ['pəustɪŋ] *n* destino.
postman ['pəustmən] *n* cartero.

postmark ['pəustmɑːk] *n* matasellos *m inv.*

postmaster ['pəustmɑːstə*] *n* administrador *m* de correos.

Postmaster General *n* director *m* general de correos.

postmistress ['pəustmɪstrɪs] *n* administradora de correos.

post-mortem [pəust'mɔːtəm] *n* autopsia.

postnatal ['pəust'neɪtl] *adj* postnatal, postparto.

post office *n* (*building*) (oficina de) correos *m*; (*organization*): **the P~ O~** Administración *f* General de Correos.

Post Office Box (PO Box) *n* apartado postal, casilla de correos (*LAM*).

post-paid ['pəust'peɪd] *adj* porte pagado.

postpone [pəs'pəun] *vt* aplazar, postergar (*LAM*).

postponement [pəs'pəunmənt] *n* aplazamiento.

postscript ['pəustskrɪpt] *n* posdata.

postulate ['pɔstjuleɪt] *vt* postular.

posture ['pɔstʃə*] *n* postura, actitud *f.*

postwar [pəust'wɔː*] *adj* de la posguerra.

posy ['pəuzɪ] *n* ramillete *m* (de flores).

pot [pɔt] *n* (*for cooking*) olla; (*for flowers*) maceta; (*for jam*) tarro, pote *m* (*LAM*); (*piece of pottery*) cacharro; (*col: marijuana*) costo ♦ *vt* (*plant*) poner en tiesto; (*conserve*) conservar (en tarros); **~s of** (*col*) montones de; **to go to ~** (*col: work, performance*) irse al traste.

potash ['pɔtæʃ] *n* potasa.

potassium [pə'tæsɪəm] *n* potasio.

potato, ~es [pə'teɪtəu] *n* patata, papa (*LAM*).

potato crisps, (*US*) **potato chips** *npl* patatas *fpl or* papas *fpl* (*LAM*) fritas.

potato peeler *n* pelapatatas *m inv.*

potbellied ['pɔtbelɪd] *adj* (*from overeating*) barrigón/ona; (*from malnutrition*) con el vientre hinchado.

potency ['pəutnsɪ] *n* potencia.

potent ['pəutnt] *adj* potente, poderoso; (*drink*) fuerte.

potentate ['pəutnteɪt] potentado.

potential [pə'tenʃl] *adj* potencial, posible ♦ *n* potencial *m*; **to have ~** prometer.

potentially [pə'tenʃəlɪ] *adv* en potencia.

pothole ['pɔthəul] *n* (*in road*) bache *m*; (*BRIT: underground*) gruta.

potholer ['pɔthəulə*] *n* (*BRIT*) espeleólogo/a.

potholing ['pɔthəulɪŋ] *n* (*BRIT*): **to go ~** dedicarse a la espeleología.

potion ['pəuʃən] *n* poción *f*, pócima.

potluck [pɔt'lʌk] *n*: **to take ~** conformarse con lo que haya.

pot roast *n* carne *f* asada.

potshot ['pɔtʃɔt] *n*: **to take a ~ at sth** tirar a algo sin apuntar.

potted ['pɔtɪd] *adj* (*food*) en conserva; (*plant*) en tiesto *or* maceta; (*fig: shortened*) resumido.

potter ['pɔtə*] *n* alfarero/a ♦ *vi*: **to ~ around, ~ about** entretenerse haciendo cosillas; **to ~ round the house** estar en casa haciendo cosillas; **~'s wheel** torno de alfarero.

pottery ['pɔtərɪ] *n* cerámica, alfarería; **a piece of ~** un objeto de cerámica.

potty ['pɔtɪ] *adj* (*col: mad*) chiflado ♦ *n* orinal *m* de niño.

potty-trained ['pɔtɪtreɪnd] *adj* que ya no necesita pañales.

pouch [pautʃ] *n* (*ZOOL*) bolsa; (*for tobacco*) petaca.

pouf(fe) [puːf] *n* (*stool*) pouf *m.*

poultry ['pəultrɪ] *n* aves *fpl* de corral; (*dead*) pollos *mpl.*

poultry farm *n* granja avícola.

poultry farmer *n* avicultor(a) *m/f.*

pounce [pauns] *vi*: **to ~ on** precipitarse sobre ♦ *n* salto, ataque *m.*

pound [paund] *n* libra; (*for dogs*) perrera; (*for cars*) depósito ♦ *vt* (*beat*) golpear; (*crush*) machacar ♦ *vi* (*beat*) dar golpes; **half a ~** media libra; **a one ~ note** un billete de una libra.

pounding ['paundɪŋ] *n*: **to take a ~** (*team*) recibir una paliza.

pound sterling *n* libra esterlina.

pour [pɔː*] *vt* echar; (*tea*) servir ♦ *vi* correr, fluir; (*rain*) llover a cántaros.

▶**pour away, pour off** *vt* vaciar, verter.

▶**pour in** *vi* (*people*) entrar en tropel; **to come ~ing in** (*water*) entrar a raudales; (*letters*) llegar a montones; (*cars, people*) llegar en tropel.

▶**pour out** *vi* (*people*) salir en tropel ♦ *vt* (*drink*) echar, servir.

pouring ['pɔːrɪŋ] *adj*: **~ rain** lluvia torrencial.

pout [paut] *vi* hacer pucheros.

poverty ['pɔvtɪ] *n* pobreza, miseria; (*fig*) falta, escasez *f.*

poverty line *n*: **below the ~** por debajo del umbral de pobreza.

poverty-stricken ['pɔvətɪstrɪkn] *adj* necesitado.

poverty trap *n* trampa de la pobreza.

POW *n abbr* = **prisoner of war.**

powder ['paudə*] *n* polvo; (*face ~*) polvos *mpl*; (*gun~*) pólvora ♦ *vt* empolvar; **to ~ one's face** ponerse polvos; **to ~ one's nose** empolvarse la nariz, ponerse

polvos; (*euphemism*) ir al baño.
powder compact *n* polvera.
powdered milk ['paudəd-] *n* leche *f* en polvo.
powder keg *n* (*fig*) polvorín *m*.
powder puff *n* borla (para empolvarse).
powder room *n* aseos *mpl*.
powdery ['paudərı] *adj* polvoriento.
power ['pauə*] *n* poder *m*; (*strength*) fuerza; (*nation*) potencia; (*drive*) empuje *m*; (*TECH*) potencia; (*ELEC*) energía ♦ *vt* impulsar; **to be in** ~ (*POL*) estar en el poder; **to do all in one's** ~ **to help sb** hacer todo lo posible por ayudar a algn; **the world** ~**s** las potencias mundiales.
powerboat ['pauəbəut] *n* lancha a motor.
power cut *n* (*BRIT*) apagón *m*.
powered ['pauəd] *adj*: ~ **by** impulsado por; **nuclear-**~ **submarine** submarino nuclear.
power failure *n* = **power cut**.
powerful ['pauəful] *adj* poderoso; (*engine*) potente; (*strong*) fuerte; (*play, speech*) conmovedor(a).
powerhouse ['pauəhaus] *n* (*fig: person*) fuerza motriz; **a** ~ **of ideas** una cantera de ideas.
powerless ['pauəlıs] *adj* impotente, ineficaz.
power line *n* línea de conducción eléctrica.
power of attorney *n* poder *m*, procuración *f*.
power point *n* (*BRIT*) enchufe *m*.
power station *n* central *f* eléctrica.
power steering *n* (*AUT*) dirección *f* asistida.
powwow ['pauwau] *n* conferencia ♦ *vi* conferenciar.
pp *abbr* (= *per procurationem: by proxy*) p.p.
PPE *n abbr* (*BRIT SCOL*) = *philosophy, politics and economics*.
PPS *abbr* (= *post postscriptum*) *posdata adicional*; (*BRIT*: = *Parliamentary Private Secretary*) *ayudante de un ministro*.
PQ *abbr* (*Canada*) = *Province of Quebec*.
PR *n abbr see* **proportional representation**; (= *public relations*) relaciones *fpl* públicas ♦ *abbr* (*US*) = *Puerto Rico*.
Pr. *abbr* (= *prince*) P.
practicability [præktıkə'bılıtı] *n* factibilidad *f*.
practicable ['præktıkəbl] *adj* (*scheme*) factible.
practical ['præktıkl] *adj* práctico.
practicality [præktı'kælıtı] *n* (*of situation etc*) aspecto práctico.
practical joke *n* broma pesada.
practically ['præktıklı] *adv* (*almost*) casi,

prácticamente.
practice ['præktıs] *n* (*habit*) costumbre *f*; (*exercise*) práctica; (*training*) adiestramiento; (*MED*) clientela ♦ *vt, vi* (*US*) = **practise**; **in** ~ (*in reality*) en la práctica; **out of** ~ desentrenado; **to put sth into** ~ poner algo en práctica; **it's common** ~ es bastante corriente; **target** ~ práctica de tiro; **he has a small** ~ (*doctor*) tiene pocos pacientes; **to set up in** ~ **as** establecerse como.
practise, (*US*) **practice** ['præktıs] *vt* (*carry out*) practicar; (*profession*) ejercer; (*train at*) practicar ♦ *vi* ejercer; (*train*) practicar.
practised, (*US*) **practiced** ['præktıst] *adj* (*person*) experto; (*performance*) ensayado; (*liar*) consumado; **with a** ~ **eye** con ojo experto.
practising, (*US*) **practicing** ['præktısıŋ] *adj* (*Christian etc*) practicante; (*lawyer*) que ejerce; (*homosexual*) activo.
practitioner [præk'tıʃənə*] *n* practicante *m/f*; (*MED*) médico/a.
pragmatic [præg'mætık] *adj* pragmático.
pragmatism ['prægmətızəm] *n* pragmatismo.
pragmatist ['prægmətıst] *n* pragmatista *m/f*.
Prague [prɑːg] *n* Praga.
prairie ['prɛərı] *n* (*US*) pampa.
praise [preız] *n* alabanza(s) *f(pl)*, elogio(s) *m(pl)*.
praiseworthy ['preızwəːðı] *adj* loable.
pram [præm] *n* (*BRIT*) cochecito de niño.
prance [prɑːns] *vi* (*horse*) hacer cabriolas.
prank [præŋk] *n* travesura.
prat [præt] *n* (*BRIT col*) imbécil *m/f*.
prattle ['prætl] *vi* parlotear; (*child*) balbucear.
prawn [prɔːn] *n* gamba.
pray [preı] *vi* rezar; **to** ~ **for forgiveness** pedir perdón.
prayer [prɛə*] *n* oración *f*, rezo; (*entreaty*) ruego, súplica.
prayer book *n* devocionario, misal *m*.
pre- ['priː] *pref* pre..., ante-; ~**1970** pre 1970.
preach [priːtʃ] *vi* predicar.
preacher ['priːtʃə*] *n* predicador(a) *m/f*; (*US: minister*) pastor(a) *m/f*.
preamble [prı'æmbl] *n* preámbulo.
prearrange [priːə'reındʒ] *vt* organizar *or* acordar de antemano.
prearrangement [priːə'reındʒmənt] *n*: **by** ~ por previo acuerdo.
precarious [prı'kɛərıəs] *adj* precario.
precariously [prı'kɛərıəslı] *adv* precariamente.
precaution [prı'kɔːʃən] *n* precaución *f*.

precautionary [prɪˈkɔːʃənrɪ] *adj* (*measure*) de precaución.
precede [prɪˈsiːd] *vt, vi* preceder.
precedence [ˈprɛsɪdəns] *n* precedencia; (*priority*) preferencia.
precedent [ˈprɛsɪdənt] *n* precedente *m*; **to establish** *or* **set a** ~ sentar un precedente.
preceding [prɪˈsiːdɪŋ] *adj* precedente.
precept [ˈpriːsɛpt] *n* precepto.
precinct [ˈpriːsɪŋkt] *n* recinto; (*US: district*) distrito, barrio; ~**s** *npl* recinto; **pedestrian** ~ (*BRIT*) zona peatonal; **shopping** ~ (*BRIT*) centro comercial.
precious [ˈprɛʃəs] *adj* precioso; (*treasured*) querido; (*stylized*) afectado ♦ *adv* (*col*): ~ **little/few** muy poco/pocos; **your** ~ **dog** (*ironic*) tu querido perro.
precipice [ˈprɛsɪpɪs] *n* precipicio.
precipitate *adj* [prɪˈsɪpɪtɪt] (*hasty*) precipitado ♦ *vt* [prɪˈsɪpɪteɪt] precipitar.
precipitation [prɪsɪpɪˈteɪʃən] *n* precipitación *f*.
precipitous [prɪˈsɪpɪtəs] *adj* (*steep*) escarpado; (*hasty*) precipitado.
précis [ˈpreɪsiː] *n* resumen *m*.
precise [prɪˈsaɪs] *adj* preciso, exacto; (*person*) escrupuloso.
precisely [prɪˈsaɪslɪ] *adv* exactamente, precisamente.
precision [prɪˈsɪʒən] *n* precisión *f*.
preclude [prɪˈkluːd] *vt* excluir.
precocious [prɪˈkəʊʃəs] *adj* precoz.
preconceived [priːkənˈsiːvd] *adj* (*idea*) preconcebido.
preconception [priːkənˈsɛpʃən] *n* (*idea*) idea preconcebida.
precondition [priːkənˈdɪʃən] *n* condición *f* previa.
precursor [priːˈkəːsə*] *n* precursor(a) *m/f*.
predate [ˈpriːˈdeɪt] *vt* (*precede*) preceder.
predator [ˈprɛdətə*] *n* depredador *m*.
predatory [ˈprɛdətərɪ] *adj* depredador(a).
predecessor [ˈpriːdɪsɛsə*] *n* antecesor(a) *m/f*.
predestination [priːdɛstɪˈneɪʃən] *n* predestinación *f*.
predestine [priːˈdɛstɪn] *vt* predestinar.
predetermine [priːdɪˈtəːmɪn] *vt* predeterminar.
predicament [prɪˈdɪkəmənt] *n* apuro.
predicate [ˈprɛdɪkɪt] *n* predicado.
predict [prɪˈdɪkt] *vt* predecir, pronosticar.
predictable [prɪˈdɪktəbl] *adj* previsible.
predictably [prɪˈdɪktəblɪ] *adv* (*behave, react*) de forma previsible; ~ **she didn't arrive** como era de prever, no llegó.
prediction [prɪˈdɪkʃən] *n* pronóstico,

predicción *f*.
predispose [ˈpriːdɪsˈpəuz] *vt* predisponer.
predominance [prɪˈdɒmɪnəns] *n* predominio.
predominant [prɪˈdɒmɪnənt] *adj* predominante.
predominantly [prɪˈdɒmɪnəntlɪ] *adv* en su mayoría.
predominate [prɪˈdɒmɪneɪt] *vi* predominar.
pre-eminent [priːˈɛmɪnənt] *adj* preeminente.
pre-empt [priːˈɛmt] *vt* (*BRIT*) adelantarse a.
pre-emptive [priːˈɛmtɪv] *adj*: ~ **strike** ataque *m* preventivo.
preen [priːn] *vt*: **to** ~ **itself** (*bird*) limpiarse las plumas; **to** ~ **o.s.** pavonearse.
prefab [ˈpriːfæb] *n* casa prefabricada.
prefabricated [priːˈfæbrɪkeɪtɪd] *adj* prefabricado.
preface [ˈprɛfəs] *n* prefacio.
prefect [ˈpriːfɛkt] *n* (*BRIT: in school*) monitor(a) *m/f*.
prefer [prɪˈfəː*] *vt* preferir; (*LAW: charges, complaint*) presentar; (: *action*) entablar; **to** ~ **coffee to tea** preferir el café al té.
preferable [ˈprɛfrəbl] *adj* preferible.
preferably [ˈprɛfrəblɪ] *adv* preferentemente, más bien.
preference [ˈprɛfrəns] *n* preferencia; **in** ~ **to sth** antes que algo.
preference shares *npl* acciones *fpl* privilegiadas.
preferential [prɛfəˈrɛnʃəl] *adj* preferente.
prefix [ˈpriːfɪks] *n* prefijo.
pregnancy [ˈprɛgnənsɪ] *n* embarazo.
pregnancy test *n* prueba del embarazo.
pregnant [ˈprɛgnənt] *adj* embarazada; **3 months** ~ embarazada de tres meses; ~ **with meaning** cargado de significado.
prehistoric [ˈpriːhɪsˈtɒrɪk] *adj* prehistórico.
prehistory [priːˈhɪstərɪ] *n* prehistoria.
prejudge [priːˈdʒʌdʒ] *vt* prejuzgar.
prejudice [ˈprɛdʒudɪs] *n* (*bias*) prejuicio; (*harm*) perjuicio ♦ *vt* (*bias*) predisponer; (*harm*) perjudicar; **to** ~ **sb in favour of/ against** (*bias*) predisponer a algn a favor de/en contra de.
prejudiced [ˈprɛdʒudɪst] *adj* (*person*) predispuesto; (*view*) parcial, interesado; **to be** ~ **against sb/sth** estar predispuesto en contra de algn/algo.
prelate [ˈprɛlət] *n* prelado.
preliminaries [prɪˈlɪmɪnərɪz] *npl* preliminares *mpl*, preparativos *mpl*.
preliminary [prɪˈlɪmɪnərɪ] *adj* preliminar.
prelude [ˈprɛljuːd] *n* preludio.
premarital [ˈpriːˈmærɪtl] *adj* prematrimonial, premarital.

premature ['prɛmətʃuə*] adj (arrival etc)
prematuro; **you are being a little** ~ te has
adelantado.
prematurely [prɛmə'tʃuəlɪ] adv
prematuramente, antes de tiempo.
premeditate [priː'mɛdɪteɪt] vt
premeditar.
premeditated [priː'mɛdɪteɪtɪd] adj
premeditado.
premeditation [priːmɛdɪ'teɪʃən] n
premeditación f.
premenstrual [priː'mɛnstruəl] adj
premenstrual.
premenstrual tension n (MED) tensión f
premenstrual.
premier ['prɛmɪə*] adj primero, principal
♦ n (POL) primer(a) ministro/a.
première ['prɛmɪɛə*] n estreno.
premise ['prɛmɪs] n premisa.
premises ['prɛmɪsɪs] npl local msg; **on the** ~
en el lugar mismo; **business** ~ locales mpl
comerciales.
premium ['priːmɪəm] n prima; **to be at a** ~
estar muy solicitado; **to sell at a** ~
(shares) vender caro.
premium bond n (BRIT) bono del estado
que participa en una lotería
nacional.
premium deal n (COMM) oferta
extraordinaria.
premium gasoline n (US) (gasolina)
súper m.
premonition [prɛmə'nɪʃən] n
presentimiento.
preoccupation [priːɔkjuˈpeɪʃən] n
preocupación f.
preoccupied [priːˈɔkjupaɪd] adj
(worried) preocupado; (absorbed)
ensimismado.
prep [prɛp] adj abbr: ~ **school** = **preparatory
school** ♦ n abbr (SCOL: = preparation)
deberes mpl.
prepaid [priːˈpeɪd] adj porte pagado; ~
envelope sobre m de porte pagado.
preparation [prɛpəˈreɪʃən] n preparación f;
~**s** npl preparativos mpl; **in** ~ **for sth** en
preparación para algo.
preparatory [prɪ'pærətərɪ] adj
preparatorio, preliminar; ~ **to sth/to
doing sth** como preparación para algo/
para hacer algo.
preparatory school n (BRIT) colegio
privado de enseñanza primaria; (US)
colegio privado de enseñanza
secundaria; see also **public school**.
prepare [prɪ'pɛə*] vt preparar, disponer
♦ vi: **to** ~ **for** prepararse or disponerse
para, (make preparations) hacer

preparativos para.
prepared [prɪ'pɛəd] adj (willing): **to be** ~
to help sb estar dispuesto a ayudar a
algn.
preponderance [prɪ'pɔndərns] n
preponderancia, predominio.
preposition [prɛpə'zɪʃən] n preposición
f.
prepossessing [priːpə'zɛsɪŋ] adj agradable,
atractivo.
preposterous [prɪ'pɔstərəs] adj absurdo,
ridículo.
prerecorded ['priːrɪ'kɔːdɪd] adj: ~
broadcast programa m grabado de
antemano; ~ **cassette** cassette f
pregrabada.
prerequisite [priː'rɛkwɪzɪt] n requisito
previo.
prerogative [prɪ'rɔgətɪv] n
prerrogativa.
Presbyterian [prɛzbɪ'tɪərɪən] adj, n
presbiteriano/a m/f.
presbytery ['prɛzbɪtərɪ] n casa
parroquial.
preschool ['priː'skuːl] adj (child, age)
preescolar.
prescribe [prɪ'skraɪb] vt prescribir; (MED)
recetar; ~**d books** (BRIT SCOL) libros mpl
del curso.
prescription [prɪ'skrɪpʃən] n (MED) receta;
to make up or (US) **fill a** ~ preparar una
receta; **only available on** ~ se vende
solamente con receta (médica).
prescription charges npl (BRIT) precio sg
de las recetas.
prescriptive [prɪ'skrɪptɪv] adj
normativo.
presence ['prɛzns] n presencia;
(attendance) asistencia.
presence of mind n aplomo.
present adj ['prɛznt] (in attendance)
presente; (current) actual ♦ n (gift) regalo;
(actuality) actualidad f, presente m ♦ vt
[prɪ'zɛnt] (introduce) presentar; (expound)
exponer; (give) presentar, dar, ofrecer;
(THEAT) representar; **to be** ~ **at** asistir a,
estar presente en; **those** ~ los presentes;
to give sb a ~, **make sb a** ~ **of sth** regalar
algo a algn; **at** ~ actualmente; **to** ~ o.s.
for an interview presentarse a una
entrevista; **may I** ~ **Miss Clark**
permítame presentarle or le presento a
la Srta Clark.
presentable [prɪ'zɛntəbl] adj: **to make o.s.**
~ arreglarse.
presentation [prɛzn'teɪʃən] n presentación
f; (gift) obsequio; (of case) exposición f;
(THEAT) representación f; **on** ~ **of the**

voucher al presentar el vale.

present-day ['prezntdeɪ] *adj* actual.

presenter [prɪ'zɛntə*] *n* (*RADIO, TV*) locutor(a) *m/f*.

presently ['prezntlɪ] *adv* (*soon*) dentro de poco; (*US: now*) ahora.

present participle *n* participio (de) presente.

present tense *n* (tiempo) presente *m*.

preservation [prezə'veɪʃən] *n* conservación *f*.

preservative [prɪ'zɜːvətɪv] *n* conservante *m*.

preserve [prɪ'zɜːv] *vt* (*keep safe*) preservar, proteger; (*maintain*) mantener; (*food*) conservar; (*in salt*) salar ♦ *n* (*for game*) coto, vedado; (*often pl: jam*) confitura.

preshrunk [priː'ʃrʌŋk] *adj* inencogible.

preside [prɪ'zaɪd] *vi* presidir.

presidency ['prezɪdənsɪ] *n* presidencia.

president ['prezɪdənt] *n* presidente *m/f*; (*US: of company*) director(a) *m/f*.

presidential [prezɪ'denʃl] *adj* presidencial.

press [pres] *n* (*tool, machine, newspapers*) prensa; (*printer's*) imprenta; (*of hand*) apretón *m* ♦ *vt* (*push*) empujar; (*squeeze*) apretar; (*grapes*) pisar; (*clothes: iron*) planchar; (*pressure*) presionar; (*doorbell*) apretar, pulsar, tocar; (*insist*): **to ~ sth on sb** insistir en que algn acepte algo ♦ *vi* (*squeeze*) apretar; (*pressurize*) ejercer presión; **to go to ~** (*newspaper*) entrar en prensa; **to be in the ~** (*being printed*) estar en prensa; (*in the newspapers*) aparecer en la prensa; **we are ~ed for time** tenemos poco tiempo; **to ~ sb to do** *or* **into doing sth** (*urge, entreat*) presionar a algn para que haga algo; **to ~ sb for an answer** insistir a algn para que conteste; **to ~ charges against sb** (*LAW*) demandar a algn.

▶**press ahead** *vi* seguir adelante.

▶**press on** *vi* avanzar; (*hurry*) apretar el paso.

press agency *n* agencia de prensa.

press clipping *n* = **press cutting**.

press conference *n* rueda de prensa.

press cutting *n* recorte *m* (de periódico).

pressing ['presɪŋ] *adj* apremiante.

pressman ['presmæn] *n* periodista *m*.

press officer *n* jefe/a *m/f* de prensa.

press release *n* comunicado de prensa.

press stud *n* (*BRIT*) botón *m* de presión.

press-up ['presʌp] *n* (*BRIT*) flexión *f*.

pressure ['preʃə*] *n* presión *f*; (*urgency*) apremio, urgencia; (*influence*) influencia; **high/low ~** alta/baja presión; **to put ~ on sb** presionar a algn, hacer presión sobre

algn.

pressure cooker *n* olla a presión.

pressure gauge *n* manómetro.

pressure group *n* grupo de presión.

pressurize ['preʃəraɪz] *vt* presurizar; **to ~ sb (into doing sth)** presionar a algn (para que haga algo).

pressurized ['preʃəraɪzd] *adj* (*container*) a presión.

Prestel ® ['prestel] *n* videotex *m*.

prestige [pres'tiːʒ] *n* prestigio.

prestigious [pres'tɪdʒəs] *adj* prestigioso.

presumably [prɪ'zjuːməblɪ] *adv* es de suponer que, cabe presumir que; **~ he did it** es de suponer que lo hizo él.

presume [prɪ'zjuːm] *vt* suponer, presumir; **to ~ to do** (*dare*) atreverse a hacer.

presumption [prɪ'zʌmpʃən] *n* suposición *f*; (*pretension*) presunción *f*.

presumptuous [prɪ'zʌmptjuəs] *adj* presumido.

presuppose [priːsə'pəuz] *vt* presuponer.

presupposition [priːsʌpə'zɪʃən] *n* presuposición *f*.

pre-tax [priː'tæks] *adj* anterior al impuesto.

pretence, (*US*) **pretense** [prɪ'tens] *n* (*claim*) pretensión *f*; (*pretext*) pretexto; (*make-believe*) fingimiento; **on** *or* **under the ~ of doing sth** bajo *or* con el pretexto de hacer algo; **she is devoid of all ~** no es pretenciosa.

pretend [prɪ'tend] *vt* (*feign*) fingir ♦ *vi* (*feign*) fingir; (*claim*): **to ~ to sth** pretender a algo.

pretense [prɪ'tens] *n* (*US*) = **pretence**.

pretension [prɪ'tenʃən] *n* (*claim*) pretensión *f*; **to have no ~s to sth/to being sth** no engañarse en cuanto a algo/a ser algo.

pretentious [prɪ'tenʃəs] *adj* pretencioso.

pretext ['priːtekst] *n* pretexto; **on** *or* **under the ~ of doing sth** con el pretexto de hacer algo.

prettily ['prɪtɪlɪ] *adv* encantadoramente, con gracia.

pretty ['prɪtɪ] *adj* (*gen*) bonito, lindo (*LAM*) ♦ *adv* bastante.

prevail [prɪ'veɪl] *vi* (*gain mastery*) prevalecer; (*be current*) predominar; (*persuade*): **to ~ (up)on sb to do sth** persuadir a algn para que haga algo.

prevailing [prɪ'veɪlɪŋ] *adj* (*dominant*) predominante.

prevalent ['prevələnt] *adj* (*dominant*) dominante; (*widespread*) extendido; (*fashionable*) de moda.

prevarication [prɪværɪ'keɪʃən] *n* evasivas *fpl*.

prevent [prɪ'vent] *vt*: **to ~ (sb) from doing**

sth impedir (a algn) hacer algo.
preventable [prɪ'ventəbl] *adj* evitable.
preventative [prɪ'ventətɪv] *adj* preventivo.
prevention [prɪ'venʃən] *n* prevención *f*.
preventive [prɪ'ventɪv] *adj* preventivo.
preview ['priːvjuː] *n* (*of film*) preestreno.
previous ['priːvɪəs] *adj* previo, anterior; **he has no ~ experience in that field** no tiene experiencia previa en ese campo; **I have a ~ engagement** tengo un compromiso anterior.
previously ['priːvɪəslɪ] *adv* antes.
prewar [priː'wɔː*] *adj* antes de la guerra.
prey [preɪ] *n* presa ♦ *vi*: **to ~ on** vivir a costa de; (*feed on*) alimentarse de; **it was ~ing on his mind** le obsesionaba.
price [praɪs] *n* precio; (*BETTING: odds*) puntos *mpl* de ventaja ♦ *vt* (*goods*) fijar el precio de; **to go up** *or* **rise in ~** subir de precio; **what is the ~ of ...?** ¿qué precio tiene ...?; **to put a ~ on sth** poner precio a algo; **what ~ his promises now?** ¿para qué sirven ahora sus promesas?; **he regained his freedom, but at a ~** recobró su libertad, pero le había costado caro; **to be ~d out of the market** (*article*) no encontrar comprador por ese precio; (*nation*) no ser competitivo.
price control *n* control *m* de precios.
price-cutting ['praɪskʌtɪŋ] *n* reducción *f* de precios.
priceless ['praɪslɪs] *adj* que no tiene precio; (*col: amusing*) divertidísimo.
price list *n* tarifa.
price tag *n* etiqueta.
price war *n* guerra de precios.
pricey ['praɪsɪ] *adj* (*BRIT col*) caro.
prick [prɪk] *n* pinchazo; (*with pin*) alfilerazo; (*sting*) picadura ♦ *vt* pinchar; picar; **to ~ up one's ears** aguzar el oído.
prickle ['prɪkl] *n* (*sensation*) picor *m*; (*BOT*) espina; (*ZOOL*) púa.
prickly ['prɪklɪ] *adj* espinoso; (*fig: person*) enojadizo.
prickly heat *n* sarpullido causado por exceso de calor.
pride [praɪd] *n* orgullo; (*pej*) soberbia ♦ *vt*: **to ~ o.s. on** enorgullecerse de; **to take (a) ~ in** enorgullecerse de; **her ~ and joy** su orgullo; **to have ~ of place** tener prioridad.
priest [priːst] *n* sacerdote *m*.
priestess ['priːstɪs] *n* sacerdotisa.
priesthood ['priːsthud] *n* (*practice*) sacerdocio; (*priests*) clero.
prim [prɪm] *adj* (*demure*) remilgado; (*prudish*) gazmoño.
primacy ['praɪməsɪ] *n* primacía.

prima donna ['priːmə'dɒnə] *n* primadonna.
primal ['praɪməl] *adj* original; (*important*) principal.
primarily ['praɪmərɪlɪ] *adv* (*above all*) ante todo, primordialmente.
primary ['praɪmərɪ] *adj* primario; (*first in importance*) principal ♦ *n* (*US: also: ~ election*) (elección *f*) primaria; *ver recuadro*.

PRIMARY

*Las elecciones primarias (**primaries**) sirven para preseleccionar a los candidatos de los partidos Demócrata (**"Democratic"**) y Republicano (**"Republican"**) durante la campaña que precede a las elecciones a presidente de los Estados Unidos. Se inician en New Hampshire y tienen lugar en 35 estados de febrero a junio. El número de votos obtenidos por cada candidato determina el número de delegados que votarán en el congreso general (**"National Convention"**) de julio y agosto, cuando se decide el candidato definitivo de cada partido.*

---

primary colour, (*US*) **primary color** *n* color *m* primario.
primary education *n* enseñanza primaria.
primary school *n* (*BRIT*) escuela primaria; *ver recuadro*.

PRIMARY SCHOOL

*En el Reino Unido la escuela a la que van los niños entre cinco y once años se llama **primary school**, a menudo dividida en "infant school" (entre cinco y siete años de edad) y "junior school" (entre siete y once).*

---

primate *n* ['praɪmɪt] (*REL*) primado ♦ *n* ['praɪmeɪt] (*ZOOL*) primate *m*.
prime [praɪm] *adj* primero, principal; (*basic*) fundamental; (*excellent*) selecto, de primera clase ♦ *n*: **in the ~ of life** en la flor de la vida ♦ *vt* (*gun, pump*) cebar; (*fig*) preparar.
Prime Minister (PM) *n* primer(a) ministro/a; *see also* **Downing Street**.
primer ['praɪmə*] *n* (*book*) texto elemental; (*paint*) capa preparatoria.
prime time *n* (*RADIO, TV*) horas *fpl* de mayor audiencia.
primeval [praɪ'miːvəl] *adj* primitivo.
primitive ['prɪmɪtɪv] *adj* primitivo; (*crude*) rudimentario; (*uncivilized*) inculto.
primly ['prɪmlɪ] *adv* remilgadamente; con

gazmoñería.

primrose ['prɪmrəuz] n primavera, prímula.

primus (stove) ® ['praɪməs-] n (BRIT) hornillo de camping.

prince [prɪns] n príncipe m.

prince charming n príncipe m azul.

princess [prɪn'sɛs] n princesa.

principal ['prɪnsɪpl] adj principal ♦ n director(a) m/f; (in play) protagonista principal m/f; (COMM) capital m, principal m; see also **pantomime**.

principality [prɪnsɪ'pælɪtɪ] n principado.

principle ['prɪnsɪpl] n principio; **in** ~ en principio; **on** ~ por principio.

print [prɪnt] n (impression) marca, impresión f; huella; (letters) letra de molde; (fabric) estampado; (ART) grabado; (PHOT) impresión f ♦ vt (gen) imprimir; (on mind) grabar; (write in capitals) escribir en letras de molde; **out of** ~ agotado.

▶**print out** vt (COMPUT) imprimir.

printed circuit ['prɪntɪd-] n circuito impreso.

printed circuit board (PCB) n tarjeta de circuito impreso (TCI).

printed matter n impresos mpl.

printer ['prɪntə*] n (person) impresor(a) m/f; (machine) impresora.

printhead ['prɪnthɛd] n cabeza impresora.

printing ['prɪntɪŋ] n (art) imprenta; (act) impresión f; (quantity) tirada.

printing press n prensa.

printout ['prɪntaut] n (COMPUT) printout m.

print wheel n rueda impresora.

prior ['praɪə*] adj anterior, previo ♦ n prior m; ~ **to doing** antes de or hasta hacer; **without** ~ **notice** sin previo aviso; **to have a** ~ **claim to sth** tener prioridad en algo.

prioress [praɪə'rɛs] n priora.

priority [praɪ'ɔrɪtɪ] n prioridad f; **to have** or **take** ~ **over sth** tener prioridad sobre algo.

priory ['praɪərɪ] n priorato.

prise, (US) **prize** [praɪz] vt: **to** ~ **open** abrir con palanca.

prism ['prɪzəm] n prisma m.

prison ['prɪzn] n cárcel f, prisión f ♦ cpd carcelario.

prison camp n campamento para prisioneros.

prisoner ['prɪznə*] n (in prison) preso/a; (under arrest) detenido/a; (in dock) acusado/a; **the** ~ **at the bar** el/la acusado/a; **to take sb** ~ hacer or tomar prisionero a algn.

prisoner of war n prisionero/a or preso/a de guerra.

prissy ['prɪsɪ] adj remilgado.

pristine ['prɪstiːn] adj pristino.

privacy ['prɪvəsɪ] n (seclusion) soledad f; (intimacy) intimidad f; **in the strictest** ~ con el mayor secreto.

private ['praɪvɪt] adj (personal) particular; (confidential) secreto, confidencial; (intimate) privado, íntimo; (sitting etc) a puerta cerrada ♦ n soldado raso; "~" (on envelope) "confidencial"; (on door) "privado"; **in** ~ en privado; **in (his)** ~ **life** en su vida privada; **to be in** ~ **practice** tener consulta particular.

private enterprise n la empresa privada.

private eye n detective m/f privado/a.

private hearing n (LAW) vista a puerta cerrada.

private limited company n (BRIT) sociedad f de responsabilidad limitada.

privately ['praɪvɪtlɪ] adv en privado; (in o.s.) en secreto.

private parts npl partes fpl pudendas.

private property n propiedad f privada.

private school n colegio privado.

privation [praɪ'veɪʃən] n (state) privación f; (hardship) privaciones fpl, estrecheces fpl.

privatize ['praɪvɪtaɪz] vt privatizar.

privet ['prɪvɪt] n alheña.

privilege ['prɪvɪlɪdʒ] n privilegio; (prerogative) prerrogativa.

privileged ['prɪvɪlɪdʒd] adj privilegiado; **to be** ~ **to do sth** gozar del privilegio de hacer algo.

privy ['prɪvɪ] adj: **to be** ~ **to** estar enterado de.

Privy Council n consejo privado (de la Corona); ver recuadro.

PRIVY COUNCIL

El consejo de asesores de la Corona conocido como **Privy Council** tuvo su origen en la época de los normandos, y fue adquiriendo mayor importancia hasta ser substituido en 1688 por el actual Consejo de Ministros ("Cabinet"). Hoy día sigue existiendo con un carácter fundamentalmente honorífico y los ministros del gobierno y otras personalidades políticas, eclesiásticas y jurídicas adquieren el rango de "privy councillors" de manera automática.

---

prize [praɪz] n premio ♦ adj (first class) de primera clase ♦ vt apreciar, estimar; (US) = **prise**.

prize fighter n boxeador m profesional.

prize fighting n boxeo m profesional.

prize-giving ['praɪzgɪvɪŋ] n distribución f de premios.

prize money n (SPORT) bolsa.

prizewinner ['praɪzwɪnə*] n premiado/a.

prizewinning ['praɪzwɪnɪŋ] adj (novel, essay) premiado.

PRO n abbr = **public relations officer.**

pro [prəu] n (SPORT) profesional m/f; **the ~s and cons** los pros y los contras.

pro- [prəu] pref (in favour of) pro, en pro de; **~Soviet** pro-soviético.

proactive [prəu'æktɪv] adj: **to be ~** impulsar la actividad.

probability [prɔbə'bɪlɪtɪ] n probabilidad f; **in all ~** lo más probable.

probable ['prɔbəbl] adj probable; **it is ~/ hardly ~ that** es probable/poco probable que.

probably ['prɔbəblɪ] adv probablemente.

probate ['prəubeɪt] n (LAW) legalización f de un testamento.

probation [prə'beɪʃən] n: **on ~** (employee) a prueba; (LAW) en libertad condicional.

probationary [prə'beɪʃənrɪ] adj: **~ period** período de prueba.

probationer [prə'beɪʃənə*] n (LAW) persona en libertad condicional; (nurse) ≈ ATS m/f (SP) or enfermero/a en prácticas.

probation officer n persona a cargo de los presos en libertad condicional.

probe [prəub] n (MED, SPACE) sonda; (enquiry) investigación f ♦ vt sondar; (investigate) investigar.

probity ['prəubɪtɪ] n probidad f.

problem ['prɔbləm] n problema m; **what's the ~?** ¿cuál es el problema?, ¿qué pasa?; **no ~!** ¡por supuesto!; **to have ~s with the car** tener problemas con el coche.

problematic(al) [prɔblə'mætɪk(l)] adj problemático.

problem-solving [prɔbləm'sɔlvɪŋ] n resolución f de problemas; **~ skills** tecnicas de resolución de problemas.

procedural [prəu'si:dʒərəl] adj de procedimiento; (LAW) procesal.

procedure [prə'si:dʒə*] n procedimiento; (bureaucratic) trámites mpl; **cashing a cheque is a simple ~** cobrar un cheque es un trámite sencillo.

proceed [prə'si:d] vi proceder; (continue): **to ~ (with)** continuar (con); **to ~ against sb** (LAW) proceder contra algn; **I am not sure how to ~** no sé cómo proceder; see also **proceeds.**

proceedings [prə'si:dɪŋz] npl acto sg, actos mpl; (LAW) proceso sg; (meeting) función fsg; (records) actas fpl.

proceeds ['prəusi:dz] npl ganancias fpl,

ingresos mpl.

process ['prəuses] n proceso; (method) método, sistema m; (proceeding) procedimiento ♦ vt tratar, elaborar ♦ vi [prə'ses] (BRIT formal: go in procession) desfilar; **in ~** en curso; **we are in the ~ of moving to ...** estamos en vías de mudarnos a ....

processed cheese ['prəusest-], (US) **process cheese** n queso fundido.

processing ['prəusesɪŋ] n elaboración f.

procession [prə'seʃən] n desfile m; **funeral ~** cortejo fúnebre.

pro-choice [prəu'tʃɔɪs] adj en favor del derecho de elegir de la madre.

proclaim [prə'kleɪm] vt proclamar; (announce) anunciar.

proclamation [prɔklə'meɪʃən] n proclamación f; (written) proclama.

proclivity [prə'klɪvɪtɪ] n propensión f, inclinación f.

procrastinate [prəu'kræstɪneɪt] vi demorarse.

procrastination [prəukræstɪ'neɪʃən] n dilación f.

procreation [prəukrɪ'eɪʃən] n procreación f.

Procurator Fiscal ['prɔkjureɪtə-] n (Scottish) fiscal m/f.

procure [prə'kjuə*] vt conseguir, obtener.

procurement [prə'kjuəmənt] n obtención f.

prod [prɔd] vt (push) empujar; (with elbow) dar un codazo a ♦ n empujoncito; codazo.

prodigal ['prɔdɪgl] adj pródigo.

prodigious [prə'dɪdʒəs] adj prodigioso.

prodigy ['prɔdɪdʒɪ] n prodigio.

produce n ['prɔdjuːs] (AGR) productos mpl agrícolas ♦ vt [prə'djuːs] producir; (yield) rendir; (bring) sacar; (show) presentar, mostrar; (proof of identity) enseñar, presentar; (THEAT) presentar, poner en escena; (offspring) dar a luz.

produce dealer n (US) verdulero/a.

producer [prə'djuːsə*] n (THEAT) director(a) m/f; (AGR, CINE) productor(a) m/f.

product ['prɔdʌkt] n producto.

production [prə'dʌkʃən] n (act) producción f; (THEAT) representación f, montaje m; **to put into ~** lanzar a la producción.

production agreement n (US) acuerdo de productividad.

production line n línea de producción.

production manager n jefe/jefa m/f de producción.

productive [prə'dʌktɪv] adj productivo.

productivity [prɔdʌk'tɪvɪtɪ] n productividad f.

productivity agreement n (BRIT) acuerdo

de productividad.
productivity bonus n bono de
productividad.
Prof. [prɔf] abbr (= professor) Prof.
profane [prə'feɪn] adj profano.
profess [prə'fɛs] vt profesar; **I do not ~ to
be an expert** no pretendo ser experto.
professed [prə'fɛst] adj (self-declared)
declarado.
profession [prə'fɛʃən] n profesión f.
professional [prə'fɛʃnl] n profesional m/f
♦ adj profesional; (by profession) de
profesión; **to take ~ advice** buscar un
consejo profesional.
professionalism [prə'fɛʃnəlɪzm] n
profesionalismo.
professionally [prə'fɛʃnəlɪ] adv: **I only
know him ~** sólo le conozco por nuestra
relación de trabajo.
professor [prə'fɛsə*] n (BRIT) catedrático/a;
(US: teacher) profesor(a) m/f.
professorship [prə'fɛsəʃɪp] n cátedra.
proffer ['prɔfə*] vt ofrecer.
proficiency [prə'fɪʃənsɪ] n capacidad f,
habilidad f.
proficiency test n prueba de
capacitación.
proficient [prə'fɪʃənt] adj experto, hábil.
profile ['prəufaɪl] n perfil m; **to keep a high/
low ~** tratar de llamar la atención/pasar
inadvertido.
profit ['prɔfɪt] n (COMM) ganancia; (fig)
provecho ♦ vi: **to ~ by** or **from**
aprovechar or sacar provecho de; **~ and
loss account** cuenta de ganancias y
pérdidas; **with ~s endowment assurance**
seguro dotal con beneficios; **to sell sth at
a ~** vender algo con ganancia.
profitability [prɔfɪtə'bɪlɪtɪ] n rentabilidad f.
profitable ['prɔfɪtəbl] adj (ECON) rentable;
(beneficial) provechoso, útil.
profitably ['prɔfɪtəblɪ] adv rentablemente;
provechosamente.
profit centre, (US) **profit center** n centro
de beneficios.
profiteering [prɔfɪ'tɪərɪŋ] n (pej)
explotación f.
profit-making ['prɔfɪtmeɪkɪŋ] adj rentable.
profit margin n margen m de ganancia.
profit-sharing ['prɔfɪtʃɛərɪŋ] n
participación f de empleados en los
beneficios.
profits tax n impuesto sobre los
beneficios.
profligate ['prɔflɪgɪt] adj (dissolute:
behaviour, act) disoluto; (: person)
libertino; (extravagant): **he's very ~ with
his money** es muy derrochador.

pro forma ['prəu'fɔːmə] adj: **~ invoice**
factura pro-forma.
profound [prə'faund] adj profundo.
profoundly [prə'faundlɪ] adv
profundamente.
profusely [prə'fjuːslɪ] adv profusamente.
profusion [prə'fjuːʒən] n profusión f,
abundancia.
progeny ['prɔdʒɪnɪ] n progenie f.
programme, (US) **program** ['prəugræm] n
programa m ♦ vt programar.
program(m)er ['prəugræmə*] n
programador(a) m/f.
program(m)ing ['prəugræmɪŋ] n
programación f.
program(m)ing language n lenguaje m
de programación.
progress n ['prəugrɛs] progreso;
(development) desarrollo ♦ vi [prə'grɛs]
progresar, avanzar; desarrollarse; **in ~**
(meeting, work etc) en curso; **as the match
~ed** a medida que avanzaba el partido.
progression [prə'grɛʃən] n progresión f.
progressive [prə'grɛsɪv] adj progresivo;
(person) progresista.
progressively [prə'grɛsɪvlɪ] adv
progresivamente, poco a poco.
progress report n (MED) informe m sobre
el estado del paciente; (ADMIN) informe m
sobre la marcha del trabajo.
prohibit [prə'hɪbɪt] vt prohibir; **to ~ sb
from doing sth** prohibir a algn hacer
algo; **"smoking ~ed"** "prohibido fumar".
prohibition [prəuɪ'bɪʃən] n (US)
prohibicionismo.
prohibitive [prə'hɪbɪtɪv] adj (price etc)
prohibitivo.
project n ['prɔdʒɛkt] proyecto; (SCOL, UNIV:
research) trabajo, proyecto ♦ (vb:
[prə'dʒɛkt]) vt proyectar ♦ vi (stick out)
salir, sobresalir.
projectile [prə'dʒɛktaɪl] n proyectil m.
projection [prə'dʒɛkʃən] n proyección f;
(overhang) saliente m.
projectionist [prə'dʒɛkʃənɪst] n (CINE)
operador(a) m/f de cine.
projection room n (CINE) cabina de
proyección.
projector [prə'dʒɛktə*] n proyector m.
proletarian [prəulɪ'tɛərɪən] adj proletario.
proletariat [prəulɪ'tɛərɪət] n proletariado.
pro-life [prəu'laɪf] adj pro-vida.
proliferate [prə'lɪfəreɪt] vi proliferar,
multiplicarse.
proliferation [prəlɪfə'reɪʃən] n
proliferación f.
prolific [prə'lɪfɪk] adj prolífico.
prologue, (US) **prolog** ['prəulɔg] n prólogo.

prolong [prə'lɔŋ] *vt* prolongar, extender.
prom [prɔm] *n abbr* (*BRIT*) = **promenade,
promenade concert** ♦ *n* (*US: ball*) baile *m*
de gala; *ver recuadro.*

PROM

*Los conciertos de música clásica más
conocidos en Inglaterra son los llamados
Proms (o **promenade concerts**), que tienen
lugar en el "Royal Albert Hall" de Londres,
aunque también se llama así a cualquier
concierto de esas características. Su
nombre se debe al hecho de que en un
principio el público paseaba durante las
actuaciones; en la actualidad parte de la
gente que acude a ellos permanece de pie.
En Estados Unidos se llama **prom** a un
baile de gala en un colegio o universidad.*

---

promenade [prɔmə'nɑːd] *n* (*by sea*) paseo
marítimo ♦ *vi* (*stroll*) pasearse.
promenade concert *n* concierto (*en que
parte del público permanece de pie*).
promenade deck *n* cubierta de paseo.
prominence ['prɔminəns] *n* (*fig*)
importancia.
prominent ['prɔminənt] *adj* (*standing out*)
saliente; (*important*) eminente,
importante; **he is ~ in the field of ...**
destaca en el campo de ....
prominently ['prɔminəntli] *adv* (*display, set*)
muy a la vista; **he figured ~ in the case**
desempeñó un papel destacado en el
juicio.
promiscuity [prɔmis'kjuːiti] *n*
promiscuidad *f*.
promiscuous [prə'miskjuəs] *adj* (*sexually*)
promiscuo.
promise ['prɔmis] *n* promesa ♦ *vt, vi*
prometer; **to make sb a ~** prometer algo
a algn; **a young man of ~** un joven con
futuro; **to ~ (sb) to do sth** prometer (a
algn) hacer algo; **to ~ well** ser muy
prometedor.
promising ['prɔmisiŋ] *adj* prometedor(a).
promissory note ['prɔmisəri-] *n* pagaré *m*.
promontory ['prɔməntri] *n* promontorio.
promote [prə'məut] *vt* promover; (*new
product*) dar publicidad a, lanzar; (*MIL*)
ascender; **the team was ~d to the second
division** (*BRIT FOOTBALL*) el equipo
ascendió a la segunda división.
promoter [prə'məutə*] *n* (*of sporting event*)
promotor(a) *m/f*; (*of company, business*)
patrocinador(a) *m/f*.
promotion [prə'məuʃən] *n* (*gen*) promoción
f; (*MIL*) ascenso.

prompt [prɔmpt] *adj* pronto ♦ *adv*: **at 6
o'clock ~** a las seis en punto ♦ *n* (*COMPUT*)
aviso, guía ♦ *vt* (*urge*) mover, incitar;
(*THEAT*) apuntar; **to ~ sb to do sth** instar
a algn a hacer algo; **to be ~ to do sth** no
tardar en hacer algo; **they're very ~
(*punctual*) son muy puntuales.
prompter ['prɔmptə*] *n* (*THEAT*)
apuntador(a) *m/f*.
promptly ['prɔmptli] *adv* (*punctually*)
puntualmente; (*rapidly*) rápidamente.
promptness ['prɔmptnis] *n* puntualidad *f*;
rapidez *f*.
promulgate ['prɔmʌlgeit] *vt* promulgar.
prone [prəun] *adj* (*lying*) postrado; **~ to**
propenso a.
prong [prɔŋ] *n* diente *m*, punta.
pronoun ['prəunaun] *n* pronombre *m*.
pronounce [prə'nauns] *vt* pronunciar;
(*declare*) declarar ♦ *vi*: **to ~ (up)on**
pronunciarse sobre; **they ~d him unfit to
plead** le declararon incapaz de
defenderse.
pronounced [prə'naunst] *adj* (*marked*)
marcado.
pronouncement [prə'naunsmənt] *n*
declaración *f*.
pronunciation [prənʌnsi'eiʃən] *n*
pronunciación *f*.
proof [pruːf] *n* prueba; **70° ~** graduación *f*
del 70 por 100 ♦ *adj*: **~ against** a prueba
de ♦ *vt* (*tent, anorak*) impermeabilizar.
proofreader ['pruːfriːdə*] *n* corrector(a) *m/f*
de pruebas.
prop [prɔp] *n* apoyo; (*fig*) sostén *m* ♦ *vt* (*also:
~ up*) apoyar; (*lean*): **to ~ sth against**
apoyar algo contra.
Prop. *abbr* (*COMM*) = **proprietor**.
propaganda [prɔpə'gændə] *n* propaganda.
propagate ['prɔpəgeit] *vt* propagar.
propel [prə'pel] *vt* impulsar, propulsar.
propeller [prə'pelə*] *n* hélice *f*.
propelling pencil [prə'peliŋ-] *n* (*BRIT*)
lapicero.
propensity [prə'pensiti] *n* propensión *f*.
proper ['prɔpə*] *adj* (*suited, right*) propio;
(*exact*) justo; (*apt*) apropiado,
conveniente; (*timely*) oportuno; (*seemly*)
correcto, decente; (*authentic*) verdadero;
(*col: real*) auténtico; **to go through the ~
channels** (*ADMIN*) ir por la vía oficial.
properly ['prɔpəli] *adv* (*adequately*)
correctamente; (*decently*) decentemente.
proper noun *n* nombre *m* propio.
properties ['prɔpətiz] *npl* (*THEAT*)
accesorios *mpl*, atrezzo *msg*.
property ['prɔpəti] *n* propiedad *f*; (*estate*)
finca; **lost ~** objetos *mpl* perdidos;

personal ~ bienes *mpl* muebles.
property developer *n* promotor(a) *m/f* de construcciones.
property owner *n* dueño/a de propiedades.
property tax *n* impuesto sobre la propiedad.
prophecy ['prɔfɪsɪ] *n* profecía.
prophesy ['prɔfɪsaɪ] *vt* profetizar; (*fig*) predecir.
prophet ['prɔfɪt] *n* profeta *m/f*.
prophetic [prə'fɛtɪk] *adj* profético.
proportion [prə'pɔːʃən] *n* proporción *f*; (*share*) parte *f*; **to be in/out of** ~ **to** *or* **with sth** estar en/no guardar proporción con algo; **to see sth in** ~ (*fig*) ver algo en su justa medida.
proportional [prə'pɔːʃənl] *adj* proporcional.
proportionally [prəpɔːʃnəlɪ] *adv* proporcionalmente, en proporción.
proportional representation (PR) *n* (*POL*) representación *f* proporcional.
proportional spacing *n* (*on printer*) espaciado proporcional.
proportionate [prə'pɔːʃənɪt] *adj* proporcionado.
proportionately [prə'pɔːʃnɪtlɪ] *adv* proporcionadamente, en proporción.
proportioned [prə'pɔːʃənd] *adj* proporcionado.
proposal [prə'pəuzl] *n* propuesta; (*offer of marriage*) oferta de matrimonio; (*plan*) proyecto; (*suggestion*) sugerencia.
propose [prə'pəuz] *vt* proponer; (*have in mind*): **to** ~ **sth/to do** *or* **doing sth** proponer algo/proponerse hacer algo ♦ *vi* declararse.
proposer [prə'pəuzə*] *n* (*of motion*) proponente *m/f*.
proposition [prɔpə'zɪʃən] *n* propuesta, proposición *f*; **to make sb a** ~ proponer algo a algn.
propound [prə'paund] *vt* (*theory*) exponer.
proprietary [prə'praɪətərɪ] *adj* (*COMM*): ~ **article** artículo de marca; ~ **brand** marca comercial.
proprietor [prə'praɪətə*] *n* propietario/a, dueño/a.
propriety [prə'praɪətɪ] *n* decoro.
propulsion [prə'pʌlʃən] *n* propulsión *f*.
pro rata [prəu'rɑːtə] *adv* a prorrata.
prosaic [prəu'zeɪɪk] *adj* prosaico.
Pros. Atty. *abbr* (*US*) = *prosecuting attorney*.
proscribe [prə'skraɪb] *vt* proscribir.
prose [prəuz] *n* prosa; (*SCOL*) traducción *f* inversa.
prosecute ['prɔsɪkjuːt] *vt* (*LAW*) procesar; "**trespassers will be ~d**" (*LAW*) "se

procesará a los intrusos".
prosecution [prɔsɪ'kjuːʃən] *n* proceso, causa; (*accusing side*) acusación *f*.
prosecutor ['prɔsɪkjuːtə*] *n* acusador(a) *m/f*; (*also*: **public** ~) fiscal *m/f*.
prospect *n* ['prɔspɛkt] (*chance*) posibilidad *f*; (*outlook*) perspectiva; (*hope*) esperanza ♦ (*vb*: [prə'spɛkt]) *vt* explorar ♦ *vi* buscar; ~**s** *npl* (*for work etc*) perspectivas *fpl*; **to be faced with the** ~ **of** tener que enfrentarse a la posibilidad de que ...; **we were faced with the** ~ **of leaving early** se nos planteó la posibilidad de marcharnos pronto; **there is every** ~ **of an early victory** hay buenas perspectivas de una pronta victoria.
prospecting [prə'spɛktɪŋ] *n* prospección *f*.
prospective [prə'spɛktɪv] *adj* (*possible*) probable, eventual; (*certain*) futuro; (*buyer*) presunto; (*legislation, son-in-law*) futuro.
prospector [prə'spɛktə*] *n* explorador(a) *m/f*; **gold** ~ buscador *m* de oro.
prospectus [prə'spɛktəs] *n* prospecto.
prosper ['prɔspə*] *vi* prosperar.
prosperity [prɔ'spɛrɪtɪ] *n* prosperidad *f*.
prosperous ['prɔspərəs] *adj* próspero.
prostate ['prɔsteɪt] *n* (*also*: ~ **gland**) próstata.
prostitute ['prɔstɪtjuːt] *n* prostituta; **male** ~ prostituto.
prostitution [prɔstɪ'tjuːʃən] *n* prostitución *f*.
prostrate ['prɔstreɪt] *adj* postrado; (*fig*) abatido ♦ *vt*: **to** ~ **o.s.** postrarse.
protagonist [prə'tægənɪst] *n* protagonista *m/f*.
protect [prə'tɛkt] *vt* proteger.
protection [prə'tɛkʃən] *n* protección *f*; **to be under sb's** ~ estar amparado por algn.
protectionism [prə'tɛkʃənɪzəm] *n* proteccionismo.
protection racket *n* chantaje *m*.
protective [prə'tɛktɪv] *adj* protector(a); ~ **custody** (*LAW*) detención *f* preventiva.
protector [prə'tɛktə*] *n* protector(a) *m/f*.
protégé ['prəuteʒeɪ] *n* protegido/a.
protein ['prəutiːn] *n* proteína.
pro tem [prəu'tɛm] *adv abbr* (= *pro tempore*: *for the time being*) provisionalmente.
protest *n* ['prəutɛst] protesta ♦ (*vb*: [prə'tɛst]) *vi* protestar ♦ *vt* (*affirm*) afirmar, declarar; **to do sth under** ~ hacer algo bajo protesta; **to** ~ **against/about** protestar en contra de/por.
Protestant ['prɔtɪstənt] *adj, n* protestante *m/f*.
protester, protestor [prə'tɛstə*] *n* (*in

demonstration) manifestante *m/f.*
protest march *n* manifestación *f* or marcha (de protesta).
protocol ['prəutəkɔl] *n* protocolo.
prototype ['prəutətaip] *n* prototipo.
protracted [prə'træktid] *adj* prolongado.
protractor [prə'træktə*] *n* (GEOM) transportador *m.*
protrude [prə'tru:d] *vi* salir, sobresalir.
protuberance [prə'tju:bərəns] *n* protuberancia.
proud [praud] *adj* orgulloso; *(pej)* soberbio, altanero ♦ *adv*: **to do sb ~** tratar a algn a cuerpo de rey; **to do o.s. ~** no privarse de nada; **to be ~ to do sth** estar orgulloso de hacer algo.
proudly ['praudli] *adv* orgullosamente, con orgullo; *(pej)* con soberbia, con altanería.
prove [pru:v] *vt* probar; *(verify)* comprobar; *(show)* demostrar ♦ *vi*: **to ~ correct** resultar correcto; **to ~ o.s.** ponerse a prueba; **he was ~d right in the end** al final se vio que tenía razón.
proverb ['prɔvə:b] *n* refrán *m.*
proverbial [prə'və:biəl] *adj* proverbial.
proverbially [prə'və:biəli] *adv* proverbialmente.
provide [prə'vaid] *vt* proporcionar, dar; **to ~ sb with sth** proveer a algn de algo; **to be ~d with** ser provisto de.
▶**provide for** *vt fus (person)* mantener a; *(problem etc)* tener en cuenta.
provided [prə'vaidid] *conj*: **~ (that)** con tal de que, a condición de que.
Providence ['prɔvidəns] *n* Divina Providencia.
providing [prə'vaidiŋ] *conj* a condición de que, con tal de que.
province ['prɔvins] *n* provincia; *(fig)* esfera.
provincial [prə'vinʃəl] *adj* provincial; *(pej)* provinciano.
provision [prə'viʒən] *n* provisión *f*; *(supply)* suministro, abastecimiento; **~s** *npl* provisiones *fpl*, víveres *mpl*; **to make ~ for** *(one's family, future)* atender las necesidades de.
provisional [prə'viʒənl] *adj* provisional, provisorio (LAM); *(temporary)* interino ♦ *n*: **P~** *(Irish POL)* Provisional *m (miembro de la tendencia activista del IRA).*
provisional driving licence *n (BRIT AUT)* carnet *m* de conducir provisional; *see also* **L-plates.**
proviso [prə'vaizəu] *n* condición *f*, estipulación *f*; **with the ~ that** a condición de que.

Provo ['prɔvəu] *n abbr (col)* = **Provisional.**
provocation [prɔvə'keiʃən] *n* provocación *f.*
provocative [prə'vɔkətiv] *adj* provocativo.
provoke [prə'vəuk] *vt (arouse)* provocar, incitar; *(cause)* causar, producir; *(anger)* enojar; **to ~ sb to sth/to do sth** provocar a algn a algo/a hacer algo.
provoking [prə'vəukiŋ] *adj* provocador(a).
provost ['prɔvəst] *n (BRIT: of university)* rector(a) *m/f*; *(Scottish)* alcalde(sa) *m/f.*
prow [prau] *n* proa.
prowess ['prauis] *n (skill)* destreza, habilidad *f*; *(courage)* valor *m*; **his ~ as a footballer** *(skill)* su habilidad como futbolista.
prowl [praul] *vi (also: ~ about, ~ around)* merodear ♦ *n*: **on the ~** de merodeo, merodeando.
prowler ['praulə*] *n* merodeador(a) *m/f.*
proximity [prɔk'simiti] *n* proximidad *f.*
proxy ['prɔksi] *n* poder *m*; *(person)* apoderado/a; **by ~** por poderes.
PRP *n abbr (= performance related pay)* retribución en función del rendimiento en el trabajo.
prude [pru:d] *n* gazmono/a, mojigato/a.
prudence ['pru:dns] *n* prudencia.
prudent ['pru:dnt] *adj* prudente.
prudently ['pru:dntli] *adv* prudentemente, con prudencia.
prudish ['pru:diʃ] *adj* gazmoño.
prudishness [pru:diʃnis] *n* gazmoñería, ñoñería.
prune [pru:n] *n* ciruela pasa ♦ *vt* podar.
pry [prai] *vi*: **to ~ into** entrometerse en.
PS *abbr (= postscript)* P.D.
psalm [sɑ:m] *n* salmo.
PSAT *n abbr (US)* = *Preliminary Scholastic Aptitude Test.*
PSBR *n abbr (BRIT: = public sector borrowing requirement)* endeudamiento público.
pseud [sju:d] *n (BRIT col: intellectually)* farsante *m/f*; *(: socially)* pretencioso/a.
pseudo ... [sju:dəu] *pref* seudo....
pseudonym ['sju:dənim] *n* seudónimo.
PST *n abbr (US: = Pacific Standard Time)* hora de invierno del Pacífico.
PSV *n abbr (BRIT) see* **public service vehicle.**
psyche ['saiki] *n* psique *f.*
psychiatric [saiki'ætrik] *adj* psiquiátrico.
psychiatrist [sai'kaiətrist] *n* psiquiatra *m/f.*
psychiatry [sai'kaiətri] *n* psiquiatría.
psychic ['saikik] *adj (also: ~al)* psíquico.
psycho ['saikəu] *n (col)* psicópata *m/f*, pirado/a.
psychoanalyse, psychoanalyze [saikəu-'ænəlaiz] *vt* psicoanalizar.
psychoanalysis, *pl* **psychoanalyses**

[saɪkəuə'nælɪsɪs, -siːz] n psicoanálisis m inv.
psychoanalyst [saɪkəu'ænəlɪst] n
psicoanalista m/f.
psychological [saɪkə'lɒdʒɪkl] adj
psicológico.
psychologically [saɪkə'lɒdʒɪklɪ] adv
psicológicamente.
psychologist [saɪ'kɒlədʒɪst] n psicólogo/a.
psychology [saɪ'kɒlədʒɪ] n psicología.
psychopath ['saɪkəupæθ] n psicópata m/f.
psychosis, pl **psychoses** [saɪ'kəusɪs, -siːz]
n psicosis f inv.
psychotherapy [saɪkəu'θɛrəpɪ] n
psicoterapia.
psychotic [saɪ'kɒtɪk] adj, n psicótico/a.
PT n abbr (BRIT: = Physical Training) Ed. Fís.
pt abbr = pint(s), point(s).
Pt. abbr (GEO: = Point) Pta.
PTA n abbr (BRIT: = Parent-Teacher
Association) ≈ Asociación f de Padres de
Alumnos.
Pte. abbr (BRIT MIL) = private.
PTO abbr (= please turn over) sigue.
PTV n abbr (US) = pay television, public
television.
pub [pʌb] n abbr (= public house) pub m, bar
m; ver recuadro.

PUB

En un **pub** (o **public house**) se pueden
consumir fundamentalmente bebidas
alcohólicas, aunque en la actualidad
también se sirven platos ligeros durante el
almuerzo. Es, además, un lugar de
encuentro donde se juega a los dardos o al
billar, entre otras actividades. La estricta
regulación sobre la venta de alcohol
controla las horas de apertura, aunque
éstas son más flexibles desde hace unos
años. No se puede servir alcohol a los
menores de 18 años.

---

pub crawl n (col): **to go on a ~** ir a
recorrer bares.
puberty ['pjuːbətɪ] n pubertad f.
pubic ['pjuːbɪk] adj púbico.
public ['pʌblɪk] adj, n público; **in ~** en
público; **to make sth ~** revelar or hacer
público algo; **to be ~ knowledge** ser del
dominio público; **to go ~** (COMM)
proceder a la venta pública de acciones.
public address system (PA) n
megafonía, sistema m de altavoces.
publican ['pʌblɪkən] n dueño/a or
encargado/a de un bar.
publication [pʌblɪ'keɪʃən] n publicación f.
public company n sociedad f anónima.

public convenience n (BRIT) aseos mpl
públicos, sanitarios mpl (LAM).
public holiday n día m de fiesta, (día)
feriado (LAM).
public house n (BRIT) bar m, pub m.
publicity [pʌb'lɪsɪtɪ] n publicidad f.
publicize ['pʌblɪsaɪz] vt publicitar;
(advertise) hacer propaganda para.
public limited company (plc) n sociedad
f anónima (S.A.).
publicly ['pʌblɪklɪ] adv públicamente, en
público.
public opinion n opinión f pública.
public ownership n propiedad f pública;
to be taken into ~ ser nacionalizado.
Public Prosecutor n Fiscal m/f del Estado.
public relations (PR) n relaciones fpl
públicas.
public relations officer n encargado/a de
relaciones públicas.
public school n (BRIT) colegio privado;
(US) instituto; ver recuadro.

PUBLIC SCHOOL

En Inglaterra el término **public school** se
usa para referirse a un colegio privado de
pago, generalmente de alto prestigio social
y en régimen de internado. Algunos de los
más conocidos son Eton o Harrow. Muchos
de sus alumnos estudian previamente
hasta los 13 años en un centro privado de
pago llamado "prep(aratory) school" y al
terminar el bachiller pasan a estudiar en las
universidades de Oxford y Cambridge.
En otros lugares como Estados Unidos el
mismo término se refiere a una escuela
pública de enseñanza gratuita administrada
por el Estado.

---

public sector n sector m público.
public-spirited [pʌblɪk'spɪrɪtɪd] adj cívico.
**public transport, (US) public
transportation** n transporte m público.
public works npl obras fpl públicas.
publish ['pʌblɪʃ] vt publicar.
publisher ['pʌblɪʃə*] n (person) editor(a)
m/f; (firm) editorial f.
publishing ['pʌblɪʃɪŋ] n (industry) industria
del libro.
publishing company n (casa) editorial f.
puce [pjuːs] adj de color pardo rojizo.
puck [pʌk] n (ICE HOCKEY) puck m.
pucker ['pʌkə*] vt (pleat) arrugar; (brow
etc) fruncir.
pudding ['pudɪŋ] n pudín m; (BRIT: sweet)
postre m; **black ~** morcilla; **rice ~** arroz m
con leche.

puddle ['pʌdl] n charco.
puerile ['pjuəraɪl] adj pueril.
Puerto Rican ['pwəːtəu'riːkən] adj, n puertorriqueño/a m/f.
Puerto Rico [-'riːkəu] n Puerto Rico.
puff [pʌf] n soplo; (of smoke) bocanada; (of breathing, engine) resoplido; (powder ~) borla ♦ vt: to ~ one's pipe dar chupadas a la pipa; (also: ~ out: sails, cheeks) hinchar, inflar ♦ vi (gen) soplar; (pant) jadear; to ~ out smoke echar humo.
puffed [pʌft] adj (col: out of breath) sin aliento.
puffin ['pʌfɪn] n frailecillo.
puff pastry, (US) **puff paste** n hojaldre m.
puffy ['pʌfɪ] adj hinchado.
pull [pul] n (tug): **to give sth a ~** dar un tirón a algo; (fig: advantage) ventaja; (: influence) influencia ♦ vt tirar de, jalar (LAM); (haul) tirar, jalar (LAM), arrastrar; (strain): **to ~ a muscle** sufrir un tirón ♦ vi tirar, jalar (LAM); **to ~ to pieces** hacer pedazos; **to ~ one's punches** andarse con bromas; **to ~ one's weight** hacer su parte; **to ~ o.s. together** tranquilizarse; **to ~ sb's leg** tomar el pelo a algn; **to ~ strings (for sb)** enchufar (a algn).
▶**pull about** vt (handle roughly: object) manosear; (: person) maltratar.
▶**pull apart** vt (take apart) desmontar.
▶**pull down** vt (house) derribar.
▶**pull in** vi (AUT: at the kerb) parar (junto a la acera); (RAIL) llegar.
▶**pull off** vt (deal etc) cerrar.
▶**pull out** vi irse, marcharse; (AUT: from kerb) salir ♦ vt sacar, arrancar.
▶**pull over** vi (AUT) hacerse a un lado.
▶**pull round, pull through** vi salvarse; (MED) recobrar la salud.
▶**pull up** vi (stop) parar ♦ vt (uproot) arrancar, desarraigar; (stop) parar.
pulley ['pulɪ] n polea.
pull-out ['pulaut] n suplemento ♦ cpd (pages, magazine) separable.
pullover ['puləuvə*] n jersey m, suéter m.
pulp [pʌlp] n (of fruit) pulpa; (for paper) pasta; (pej: also: ~ **magazines** etc) prensa amarilla; **to reduce sth to ~** hacer algo papilla.
pulpit ['pulpɪt] n púlpito.
pulsate [pʌl'seɪt] vi pulsar, latir.
pulse [pʌls] n (ANAT) pulso; (of music, engine) pulsación f; (BOT) legumbre f; **to feel** or **take sb's ~** tomar el pulso a algn.
pulverize ['pʌlvəraɪz] vt pulverizar; (fig) hacer polvo.
puma ['pjuːmə] n puma m.
pumice (stone) ['pʌmɪs-] n piedra pómez.

pummel ['pʌml] vt aporrear.
pump [pʌmp] n bomba; (shoe) zapatilla de tenis ♦ vt sacar con una bomba; (fig: col) (son)sacar; **to ~ sb for information** (son)sacarle información a algn.
▶**pump up** vt inflar.
pumpkin ['pʌmpkɪn] n calabaza.
pun [pʌn] n juego de palabras.
punch [pʌntʃ] n (blow) golpe m, puñetazo; (tool) punzón m; (for paper) perforadora; (for tickets) taladro; (drink) ponche m ♦ vt (hit): **to ~ sb/sth** dar un puñetazo or golpear a algn/algo; (make a hole in) punzar; perforar.
punch-drunk ['pʌntʃdrʌŋk] adj (BRIT) grogui, sonado.
punch(ed) card [pʌntʃ(t)-] n tarjeta perforada.
punch line n (of joke) remate m.
punch-up ['pʌntʃʌp] n (BRIT col) riña.
punctual ['pʌŋktjuəl] adj puntual.
punctuality [pʌŋktju'ælɪtɪ] n puntualidad f.
punctually ['pʌŋktjuəlɪ] adv: **it will start ~ at 6** empezará a las 6 en punto.
punctuate ['pʌŋktjueɪt] vt puntuar; (fig) interrumpir.
punctuation [pʌŋktju'eɪʃən] n puntuación f.
punctuation mark n signo de puntuación.
puncture ['pʌŋktʃə*] (BRIT) n pinchazo ♦ vt pinchar; **to have a ~** tener un pinchazo.
pundit ['pʌndɪt] n experto/a.
pungent ['pʌndʒənt] adj acre.
punish ['pʌnɪʃ] vt castigar; **to ~ sb for sth/ for doing sth** castigar a algn por algo/por haber hecho algo.
punishable ['pʌnɪʃəbl] adj punible, castigable.
punishing ['pʌnɪʃɪŋ] adj (fig: exhausting) agotador(a).
punishment ['pʌnɪʃmənt] n castigo; (fig, col): **to take a lot of ~** (boxer) recibir una paliza; (car) ser maltratado.
punitive ['pjuːnɪtɪv] adj punitivo.
punk [pʌŋk] n (also: ~ **rocker**) punki m/f; (also: ~ **rock**) música punk; (US col: hoodlum) matón m.
punt [pʌnt] n (boat) batea; (IRELAND) libra irlandesa ♦ vi (bet) apostar.
punter ['pʌntə*] n (gambler) jugador(a) m/f.
puny ['pjuːnɪ] adj enclenque.
pup [pʌp] n cachorro.
pupil ['pjuːpl] n alumno/a; (of eye) pupila.
puppet ['pʌpɪt] n títere m.
puppet government n gobierno títere.
puppy ['pʌpɪ] n cachorro, perrito.
purchase ['pəːtʃɪs] n compra; (grip) agarre m, asidero ♦ vt comprar.
purchase order n orden f de compra.

purchase price *n* precio de compra.
purchaser ['pɔːtʃɪsə*] *n* comprador(a) *m/f*.
purchase tax *n* (*BRIT*) impuesto sobre la venta.
purchasing power ['pɔːtʃɪsɪŋ-] *n* poder *m* adquisitivo.
pure [pjuə*] *adj* puro; **a ~ wool jumper** un jersey de pura lana; **it's laziness, ~ and simple** es pura vagancia.
purebred ['pjuəbrɛd] *adj* de pura sangre.
purée ['pjuəreɪ] *n* puré *m*.
purely ['pjuəlɪ] *adv* puramente.
purgatory ['pɔːgətərɪ] *n* purgatorio.
purge [pɔːdʒ] *n* (*MED, POL*) purga ♦ *vt* purgar.
purification [pjuərɪfɪ'keɪʃən] *n* purificación *f*, depuración *f*.
purify ['pjuərɪfaɪ] *vt* purificar, depurar.
purist ['pjuərɪst] *n* purista *m/f*.
puritan ['pjuərɪtən] *n* puritano/a.
puritanical [pjuərɪ'tænɪkl] *adj* puritano.
purity ['pjuərɪtɪ] *n* pureza.
purl [pɔːl] *n* punto del revés.
purloin [pɔː'lɔɪn] *vt* hurtar, robar.
purple ['pɔːpl] *adj* morado.
purport [pɔː'pɔːt] *vi*: **to ~ to be/do** dar a entender que es/hace.
purpose ['pɔːpəs] *n* propósito; **on ~** a propósito, adrede; **to no ~** para nada, en vano; **for teaching ~s** con fines pedagógicos; **for the ~s of this meeting** para los fines de esta reunión.
purpose-built ['pɔːpəs'bɪlt] *adj* (*BRIT*) construido especialmente.
purposeful ['pɔːpəsful] *adj* resuelto, determinado.
purposely ['pɔːpəslɪ] *adv* a propósito, adrede.
purr [pɔː*] *n* ronroneo ♦ *vi* ronronear.
purse [pɔːs] *n* monedero; (*US: handbag*) bolso ♦ *vt* fruncir.
purser ['pɔːsə*] *n* (*NAUT*) comisario/a.
purse snatcher [-snætʃə*] *n* (*US*) persona que roba por el procedimiento del tirón.
pursue [pə'sjuː] *vt* seguir; (*harass*) perseguir; (*profession*) ejercer; (*pleasures*) buscar; (*inquiry, matter*) seguir.
pursuer [pə'sjuːə*] *n* perseguidor(a) *m/f*.
pursuit [pə'sjuːt] *n* (*chase*) caza; (*of pleasure etc*) busca; (*occupation*) actividad *f*; **in (the) ~ of sth** en busca de algo.
purveyor [pə'veɪə*] *n* proveedor(a) *m/f*.
pus [pʌs] *n* pus *m*.
push [puʃ] *n* empujón *m*; (*MIL*) ataque *m*; (*drive*) empuje *m* ♦ *vt* empujar; (*button*) apretar; (*promote*) promover; (*fig: press, advance: views*) fomentar; (*thrust*): **to ~ sth (into)** meter algo a la fuerza (en) ♦ *vi*

empujar; (*fig*) hacer esfuerzos; **at a ~** (*col*) a duras penas; **she is ~ing 50** (*col*) raya en los 50; **to be ~ed for time/money** andar justo de tiempo/escaso de dinero; **to ~ a door open/shut** abrir/cerrar una puerta empujándola; **to ~ for** (*better pay, conditions*) reivindicar; "~" (*on door*) "empujar"; (*on bell*) "pulse".
▶**push aside** *vt* apartar con la mano.
▶**push in** *vi* colarse.
▶**push off** *vi* (*col*) largarse.
▶**push on** *vi* (*continue*) seguir adelante.
▶**push through** *vt* (*measure*) despachar.
▶**push up** *vt* (*total, prices*) hacer subir.
push-bike ['puʃbaɪk] *n* (*BRIT*) bicicleta.
push-button ['puʃbʌtn] *adj* con botón de mando.
pushchair ['puʃtʃeə*] *n* (*BRIT*) silla de niño.
pusher ['puʃə*] *n* (*drug ~*) traficante *m/f* de drogas.
pushover ['puʃəuvə*] *n* (*col*): **it's a ~** está tirado.
push-up ['puʃʌp] *n* (*US*) flexión *f*.
pushy ['puʃɪ] *adj* (*pej*) agresivo.
puss [pus], **pussy(-cat)** ['pusɪ(kæt)] *n* minino.
put [put], *pt, pp* **put** *vt* (*place*) poner, colocar; (*~ into*) meter; (*express, say*) expresar; (*a question*) hacer; (*estimate*) calcular; (*cause to be*): **to ~ sb in a good/bad mood** poner a algn de buen/mal humor; **to ~ a lot of time into sth** dedicar mucho tiempo a algo; **to ~ money on a horse** apostar dinero en un caballo; **to ~ money into a company** invertir dinero en una compañía; **to ~ sb to a lot of trouble** causar mucha molestia a algn; **we ~ the children to bed** acostamos a los niños; **how shall I ~ it?** ¿cómo puedo explicarlo *or* decirlo?; **I ~ it to you that ...** le sugiero que ...; **to stay ~** no moverse.
▶**put about** *vi* (*NAUT*) virar ♦ *vt* (*rumour*) hacer correr.
▶**put across** *vt* (*ideas etc*) comunicar.
▶**put aside** *vt* (*lay down: book etc*) dejar *or* poner a un lado; (*save*) ahorrar; (*in shop*) guardar.
▶**put away** *vt* (*store*) guardar.
▶**put back** *vt* (*replace*) devolver a su lugar; (*postpone*) posponer; (*set back: watch, clock*) retrasar; **this will ~ us back 10 years** esto nos retrasará 10 años.
▶**put by** *vt* (*money*) guardar.
▶**put down** *vt* (*on ground*) poner en el suelo; (*animal*) sacrificar; (*in writing*) apuntar; (*suppress: revolt etc*) sofocar; (*attribute*) atribuir; **~ me down for £15** apúntame por 15 libras; **~ it down on my**

account (*COMM*) póngalo en mi cuenta.
►**put forward** *vt* (*ideas*) presentar,
proponer; (*date*) adelantar.
►**put in** *vt* (*application, complaint*)
presentar.
►**put in for** *vt fus* (*job*) solicitar; (*promotion*)
pedir.
►**put off** *vt* (*postpone*) aplazar; (*discourage*)
desanimar, quitar las ganas a.
►**put on** *vt* (*clothes, lipstick etc*) ponerse;
(*light etc*) encender; (*play etc*) presentar;
(*brake*) echar; (*assume: accent, manner*)
afectar, fingir; (*airs*) adoptar, darse;
(*concert, exhibition etc*) montar; (*extra bus,
train etc*) poner; (*col: kid, have on: esp US*)
tomar el pelo a; (*inform, indicate*): **to ~ sb
on to sb/sth** informar a algn de algn/
algo; **to ~ on weight** engordar.
►**put out** *vt* (*fire, light*) apagar; (*one's hand*)
alargar; (*news, rumour*) hacer circular;
(*tongue etc*) sacar; (*person: inconvenience*)
molestar, fastidiar; (*dislocate: shoulder,
vertebra, knee*) dislocar(se) ♦ *vi* (*NAUT*): **to
~ out to sea** hacerse a la mar; **to ~ out
from Plymouth** salir de Plymouth.
►**put through** *vt* (*call*) poner; **~ me
through to Miss Blair** póngame *or*
comuníqueme (*LAM*) con la Señorita
Blair.
►**put together** *vt* unir, reunir; (*assemble:
furniture*) armar, montar; (*meal*) preparar.
►**put up** *vt* (*raise*) levantar, alzar; (*hang*)
colgar; (*build*) construir; (*increase*)
aumentar; (*accommodate*) alojar; (*incite*):
to ~ sb up to doing sth instar *or* incitar a
algn a hacer algo; **to ~ sth up for sale**
poner algo a la venta.
►**put upon** *vt fus*: **to be ~ upon** (*imposed
upon*) dejarse explotar.
►**put up with** *vt fus* aguantar.
putrid ['pjuːtrɪd] *adj* podrido.
putsch [putʃ] *n* golpe *m* de estado.
putt [pʌt] *vt* hacer un putt ♦ *n* putt *m*, golpe
m corto.
putter ['pʌtə*] *n* putter *m*.
putting green ['pʌtɪŋ-] *n* green *m*, minigolf
m.
putty ['pʌtɪ] *n* masilla.
put-up ['putʌp] *adj*: **~ job** (*BRIT*) estafa.
puzzle ['pʌzl] *n* (*riddle*) acertijo; (*jigsaw*)
rompecabezas *m inv*; (*also*: **crossword ~**)
crucigrama *m*; (*mystery*) misterio ♦ *vt*
dejar perplejo, confundir ♦ *vi*: **to ~ about**
quebrar la cabeza por; **to ~ over** (*sb's
actions*) quebrarse la cabeza por;
(*mystery, problem*) devanarse los sesos
sobre; **to be ~d about sth** no llegar a
entender algo.

puzzling ['pʌzlɪŋ] *adj* (*question*) misterioso,
extraño; (*attitude, set of instructions*)
extraño.
PVC *n abbr* (= *polyvinyl chloride*) P.V.C. *m*.
Pvt. *abbr* (*US MIL*) = **private**.
PW *n abbr* (*US*) = **prisoner of war**.
pw *abbr* (= *per week*) por semana.
PX *n abbr* (*US*: = *post exchange*) *economato
militar*.
pygmy ['pɪgmɪ] *n* pigmeo/a.
pyjamas, (*US*) **pajamas** [pɪ'dʒɑːməz] *npl*
(*BRIT*) pijama *m*, piyama *m* (*LAM*); **a pair of
~** un pijama.
pylon ['paɪlən] *n* torre *f* de conducción
eléctrica.
pyramid ['pɪrəmɪd] *n* pirámide *f*.
Pyrenean [pɪrə'niːən] *adj* pirenaico.
Pyrenees [pɪrə'niːz] *npl*: **the ~** los Pirineos.
Pyrex ® ['paɪreks] *n* pírex *m* ♦ *cpd*: **~
casserole** cazuela de pírex.
python ['paɪθən] *n* pitón *m*.

Qq

Q, q [kjuː] *n* (*letter*) Q, q *f*; **Q for Queen** Q de
Quebec.
Qatar [kæ'tɑː] *n* Qatar *m*.
QC *n abbr* (*BRIT*: = *Queen's Council*) *título
concedido a determinados abogados.*
QED *abbr* (= *quod erat demonstrandum*)
Q.E.D.
QM *n abbr* = **quartermaster**.
q.t. *n abbr* (*col*: = *quiet*): **on the ~** a
hurtadillas.
qty *abbr* (= *quantity*) ctdad.
quack [kwæk] *n* (*of duck*) graznido; (*pej:
doctor*) curandero/a, matasanos *m inv* ♦ *vi*
graznar.
quad [kwɔd] *abbr* = **quadrangle, quadruple,
quadruplet**.
quadrangle ['kwɔdræŋgl] *n* (*BRIT: courtyard:
abbr*: **quad**) patio.
quadruple [kwɔ'druːpl] *vt, vi* cuadruplicar.
quadruplet [kwɔ'druːplɪt] *n* cuatrillizo.
quagmire ['kwægmaɪə*] *n* lodazal *m*,
cenegal *m*.
quail [kweɪl] *n* (*bird*) codorniz *f* ♦ *vi*
amedrentarse.
quaint [kweɪnt] *adj* extraño; (*picturesque*)
pintoresco.
quaintly ['kweɪntlɪ] *adv* extrañamente;

pintorescamente.

quake [kweɪk] *vi* temblar ♦ *n abbr*
= **earthquake**.

Quaker ['kweɪkə*] *n* cuáquero/a.

qualification [kwɔlɪfɪ'keɪʃən] *n* (*reservation*)
reserva; (*modification*) modificación *f*;
(*act*) calificación *f*; (*paper* ~) título; **what
are your ~s?** ¿qué títulos tienes?

qualified ['kwɔlɪfaɪd] *adj* (*trained*)
cualificado; (*fit*) capacitado; (*limited*)
limitado; (*professionally*) titulado; ~ **for/to
do sth** capacitado para/para hacer algo;
he's not ~ **for the job** no está capacitado
para ese trabajo; **it was a** ~ **success** fue
un éxito relativo.

qualify ['kwɔlɪfaɪ] *vt* (*LING*) calificar a;
(*capacitate*) capacitar; (*modify*) matizar;
(*limit*) moderar ♦ *vi* (*SPORT*) clasificarse;
to ~ **(as)** calificarse (de), graduarse (en),
recibirse (de) (*LAM*); **to** ~ **(for)** reunir los
requisitos (para); **to** ~ **as an engineer**
sacar el título de ingeniero.

qualifying ['kwɔlɪfaɪɪŋ] *adj* (*exam, round*)
eliminatorio.

qualitative ['kwɔlɪtətɪv] *adj* cualitativo.

quality ['kwɔlɪtɪ] *n* calidad *f*; (*moral*)
cualidad *f*; **of good/poor** ~ de buena *or*
alta/poca calidad.

quality control *n* control *m* de calidad.

quality of life *n* calidad *f* de vida.

quality press *n* prensa seria; *ver recuadro*.

> **QUALITY PRESS**
>
> *La expresión* **quality press** *se refiere los
> periódicos que dan un tratamiento serio de
> las noticias, ofreciendo información
> detallada sobre un amplio espectro de
> temas y análisis en profundidad de la
> actualidad. Por su tamaño, considera-
> blemente mayor que el de los periódicos
> sensacionalistas, se les llama también
> "broadsheets".*

qualm [kwɑːm] *n* escrúpulo; **to have ~s
about sth** sentir escrúpulos por algo.

quandary ['kwɔndrɪ] *n*: **to be in a** ~ **verse**
en un dilema.

quango ['kwæŋɡəu] *n abbr* (*BRIT*: = *quasi-
autonomous non-governmental organization*)
*organismo semi-autónomo de subvención
estatal.*

quantifiable [kwɔntɪ'faɪəbl] *adj*
cuantificable.

quantitative ['kwɔntɪtətɪv] *adj*
cuantitativo.

quantity ['kwɔntɪtɪ] *n* cantidad *f*; **in** ~ en
grandes cantidades.

quantity surveyor *n* aparejador(a) *m/f*.

quantum leap ['kwɔntəm-] *n* (*fig*) avance *m*
espectacular.

quarantine ['kwɔrntiːn] *n* cuarentena.

quark [kwɑːk] *n* cuark *m*.

quarrel ['kwɔrl] *n* riña, pelea ♦ *vi* reñir,
pelearse; **to have a** ~ **with sb** reñir *or*
pelearse con algn; **I can't** ~ **with that** no
le veo pegas.

quarrelsome ['kwɔrəlsəm] *adj* pendenciero.

quarry ['kwɔrɪ] *n* (*for stone*) cantera;
(*animal*) presa.

quart [kwɔːt] *n cuarto de galón = 1.136 l.*

quarter ['kwɔːtə*] *n* cuarto, cuarta parte *f*;
(*of year*) trimestre *m*; (*district*) barrio; (*US,
Canada: 25 cents*) cuarto de dólar ♦ *vt*
dividir en cuartos; (*MIL: lodge*) alojar; ~**s**
npl (*barracks*) cuartel *m*; (*living* ~s) alojamiento *sg*; **a** ~ **of an hour** un cuarto de
hora; **to pay by the** ~ pagar trimestralmente *or* cada 3 meses; **it's a** ~ **to** *or* (*US*)
of 3 son las 3 menos cuarto; **it's a** ~ **past**
or (*US*) **after 3** son las 3 y cuarto; **from all
~s** de todas partes; **at close ~s** de cerca.

quarterback ['kwɔːtəbæk] *n* (*US: football*)
mariscal *m* de campo.

quarter-deck ['kwɔːtədɛk] *n* (*NAUT*) alcázar
m.

quarter final *n* cuarto de final.

quarterly ['kwɔːtəlɪ] *adj* trimestral ♦ *adv*
cada 3 meses, trimestralmente.

quartermaster ['kwɔːtəmɑːstə*] *n* (*MIL*)
comisario, intendente *m* militar.

quartet(te) [kwɔː'tɛt] *n* cuarteto.

quarto ['kwɔːtəu] *n* tamaño holandés ♦ *adj*
de tamaño holandés.

quartz [kwɔːts] *n* cuarzo.

quash [kwɔʃ] *vt* (*verdict*) anular, invalidar.

quasi- ['kweɪzaɪ] *pref* cuasi.

quaver ['kweɪvə*] *n* (*BRIT MUS*) corchea ♦ *vi*
temblar.

quay [kiː] *n* (*also:* ~**side**) muelle *m*.

Que. *abbr* (*Canada*) = *Quebec*.

queasiness ['kwiːzɪnɪs] *n* malestar *m*,
náuseas *fpl*.

queasy ['kwiːzɪ] *adj*: **to feel** ~ tener
náuseas.

Quebec [kwɪ'bɛk] *n* Quebec *m*.

queen [kwiːn] *n* reina; (*CARDS etc*)
dama.

queen mother *n* reina madre.

Queen's Speech *n ver recuadro*.

> **QUEEN'S SPEECH**
>
> *Se llama* **Queen's Speech** (*o "King's
> Speech"*) *al discurso que pronuncia el
> monarca durante la sesión de apertura del*

Parlamento británico, en el que se expresan las líneas generales de la política del gobierno para la nueva legislatura. El Primer Ministro se encarga de redactarlo con la ayuda del Consejo de Ministros y es leído en la Cámara de los Lores ("House of Lords") ante los miembros de ambas cámaras.

queer [kwɪə*] *adj* (*odd*) raro, extraño ♦ *n* (*pej: col*) marica *m*.

quell [kwɛl] *vt* calmar; (*put down*) sofocar.

quench [kwɛntʃ] *vt* (*flames*) apagar; **to ~ one's thirst** apagar la sed.

querulous ['kwerʊləs] *adj* (*person, voice*) quejumbroso.

query ['kwɪərɪ] *n* (*question*) pregunta; (*doubt*) duda ♦ *vt* preguntar; (*disagree with, dispute*) no estar conforme con, dudar de.

quest [kwɛst] *n* busca, búsqueda.

question ['kwɛstʃən] *n* pregunta; (*matter*) asunto, cuestión *f* ♦ *vt* (*doubt*) dudar de; (*interrogate*) interrogar, hacer preguntas a; **to ask sb a ~, put a ~ to sb** hacerle una pregunta a algn; **the ~ is ...** el asunto es ...; **to bring** *or* **call sth into ~** poner algo en (tela de) duda; **beyond ~** fuera de toda duda; **it's out of the ~** imposible, ni hablar.

questionable ['kwɛstʃənəbl] *adj* discutible; (*doubtful*) dudoso.

questioner ['kwɛstʃənə*] *n* interrogador(a) *m/f*.

questioning ['kwɛstʃənɪŋ] *adj* inquisitivo ♦ *n* preguntas *fpl*; (*by police etc*) interrogatorio.

question mark *n* punto de interrogación.

questionnaire [kwɛstʃə'nɛə*] *n* cuestionario.

queue [kjuː] (*BRIT*) *n* cola ♦ *vi* hacer cola; **to jump the ~** colarse.

quibble ['kwɪbl] *vi* andarse con sutilezas.

quick [kwɪk] *adj* rápido; (*temper*) vivo; (*agile*) ágil; (*mind*) listo; (*eye*) agudo; (*ear*) fino ♦ *n*: **cut to the ~** (*fig*) herido en lo más vivo; **be ~!** ¡date prisa!; **to act** obrar con prontitud; **she was ~ to see that** se dio cuenta de eso en seguida.

quicken ['kwɪkən] *vt* apresurar ♦ *vi* apresurarse, darse prisa.

quick-fire ['kwɪkfaɪə*] *adj* (*questions etc*) rápido, (hecho) a quemarropa.

quick fix *n* (*pej*) parche *m*.

quickly ['kwɪklɪ] *adv* rápidamente, de prisa; **we must act ~** tenemos que actuar cuanto antes.

quickness ['kwɪknɪs] *n* rapidez *f*, (*of*

temper) viveza; (*agility*) agilidad *f*; (*of mind, eye etc*) agudeza.

quicksand ['kwɪksænd] *n* arenas *fpl* movedizas.

quickstep ['kwɪkstɛp] *n baile de ritmo rápido.*

quick-tempered [kwɪk'tɛmpəd] *adj* de genio vivo.

quick-witted [kwɪk'wɪtɪd] *adj* listo, despabilado.

quid [kwɪd] *n*, *pl inv* (*BRIT col*) libra.

quid pro quo ['kwɪdprəu'kwəu] *n* quid pro quo *m*, compensación *f*.

quiet ['kwaɪət] *adj* (*not busy: day*) tranquilo; (*silent*) callado; (*reserved*) reservado; (*discreet*) discreto; (*not noisy: engine*) silencioso ♦ *n* tranquilidad *f* ♦ *vt*, *vi* (*US*) **= quieten; keep ~!** ¡cállate!, ¡silencio!; **business is ~ at this time of year** hay poco movimiento en esta época.

quieten ['kwaɪətn] (*also*: **~ down**) *vi* (*grow calm*) calmarse; (*grow silent*) callarse ♦ *vt* calmar; hacer callar.

quietly ['kwaɪətlɪ] *adv* tranquilamente; (*silently*) silenciosamente.

quietness ['kwaɪətnɪs] *n* (*silence*) silencio; (*calm*) tranquilidad *f*

quill [kwɪl] *n* (*of porcupine*) púa; (*pen*) pluma.

quilt [kwɪlt] *n* (*BRIT*) edredón *m*.

quin [kwɪn] *n abbr* = **quintuplet**.

quince [kwɪns] *n* membrillo.

quinine [kwɪ'niːn] *n* quinina.

quintet(te) [kwɪn'tɛt] *n* quinteto.

quintuplet [kwɪn'tjuːplɪt] *n* quintillizo.

quip [kwɪp] *n* ocurrencia ♦ *vi* decir con ironía.

quirk [kwəːk] *n* peculiaridad *f*; **by some ~ of fate** por algún capricho del destino.

quit *pt*, *pp* **quit** *or* **quitted** [kwɪt] *vt* dejar, abandonar; (*premises*) desocupar; (*COMPUT*) abandonar ♦ *vi* (*give up*) renunciar; (*go away*) irse; (*resign*) dimitir; **~ stalling!** (*US col*) ¡déjate de evasivas!

quite [kwaɪt] *adv* (*rather*) bastante; (*entirely*) completamente; **~ a few of them** un buen número de ellos; **~ (so)!** ¡así es!, ¡exactamente!; **~ new** bastante nuevo; **that's not ~ right** eso no está del todo bien; **not ~ as many as last time** no tantos como la última vez; **she's ~ pretty** es bastante guapa.

Quito ['kiːtəu] *n* Quito.

quits [kwɪts] *adj*: **~ (with)** en paz (con); **let's call it ~** quedamos en paz.

quiver ['kwɪvə*] *vi* estremecerse ♦ *n* (*for arrows*) carcaj *m*.

quiz [kwɪz] *n* (*game*) concurso; (: *TV, RADIO*)

programa-concurso; (*questioning*)
interrogatorio ♦ *vt* interrogar.
quizzical ['kwɪzɪkl] *adj* burlón(ona).
quoits [kwɔɪts] *npl* juego de aros.
quorum ['kwɔːrəm] *n* quórum *m*.
quota ['kwəʊtə] *n* cuota.
quotation [kwəʊ'teɪʃən] *n* cita; (*estimate*)
presupuesto.
quotation marks *npl* comillas *fpl*.
quote [kwəʊt] *n* cita ♦ *vt* (*sentence*) citar;
(*COMM: sum, figure*) cotizar ♦ *vi*: **to ~ from**
citar de; **~s** *npl* (*inverted commas*)
comillas *fpl*; **in ~s** entre comillas; **the
figure ~d** for the repairs el presupuesto
dado para las reparaciones; **~ ... unquote**
(*in dictation*) comillas iniciales ... finales.
quotient ['kwəʊʃənt] *n* cociente *m*.
qv *n abbr* (= *quod vide: which see*) q.v.
qwerty keyboard ['kwɜːtɪ-] *n* teclado
QWERTY.

Rr

R, r [ɑː*] *n* (*letter*) R, r *f*; **R for Robert,** (*US*) **R
for Roger** R de Ramón.
R *abbr* (= *right*) dcha.; (= *river*) R.;
(= *Réaumur (scale)*) R; (*US CINE:* =
restricted) *sólo mayores*; (*US POL*) =
republican; (*BRIT*: = *Rex, Regina*) R.
RA *abbr* = *rear admiral* ♦ *n abbr* (*BRIT*) = **Royal
Academy,** *Royal Academician*.
RAAF *n abbr* = *Royal Australian Air Force*.
Rabat [rə'bɑːt] *n* Rabat *m*.
rabbi ['ræbaɪ] *n* rabino.
rabbit ['ræbɪt] *n* conejo ♦ *vi*: **to ~ (on)** (*BRIT
col*) hablar sin ton ni son.
rabbit hutch *n* conejera.
rabble ['ræbl] *n* (*pej*) chusma, populacho.
rabies ['reɪbiːz] *n* rabia.
RAC *n abbr* (*BRIT*: = *Royal Automobile Club*)
≈ RACE *m* (*SP*).
raccoon [rə'kuːn] *n* mapache *m*.
race [reɪs] *n* carrera; (*species*) raza ♦ *vt*
(*horse*) hacer correr; (*person*) competir
contra; (*engine*) acelerar ♦ *vi* (*compete*)
competir; (*run*) correr; (*pulse*) latir a
ritmo acelerado; **the arms ~** la carrera
armamentista; **the human ~** el género
humano; **he ~d across the road** cruzó
corriendo la carretera; **to ~ in/out**
entrar/salir corriendo.

race car *n* (*US*) = **racing car**.
race car driver *n* (*US*) = **racing driver**.
racecourse ['reɪskɔːs] *n* hipódromo.
racehorse ['reɪshɔːs] *n* caballo de carreras.
race meeting *n* concurso hípico.
race relations *npl* relaciones *fpl* raciales.
racetrack ['reɪstræk] *n* hipódromo; (*for cars*)
circuito de carreras.
racial ['reɪʃl] *adj* racial.
racial discrimination *n* discriminación *f*
racial.
racial integration *n* integración *f* racial.
racialism ['reɪʃəlɪzəm] *n* racismo.
racialist ['reɪʃəlɪst] *adj, n* racista *m/f*.
racing ['reɪsɪŋ] *n* carreras *fpl*.
racing car *n* (*BRIT*) coche *m* de carreras.
racing driver *n* (*BRIT*) corredor(a) *m/f* de
coches.
racism ['reɪsɪzəm] *n* racismo.
racist ['reɪsɪst] *adj, n* racista *m/f*.
rack [ræk] *n* (*also*: **luggage ~**) rejilla
(portaequipajes); (*shelf*) estante *m*; (*also*:
roof ~) baca; (*clothes ~*) perchero ♦ *vt*
(*cause pain to*) atormentar; **to go to ~ and
ruin** venirse abajo; **to ~ one's brains**
devanarse los sesos.
▶**rack up** *vt* conseguir, ganar.
racket ['rækɪt] *n* (*for tennis*) raqueta; (*noise*)
ruido, estrépito; (*swindle*) estafa, timo.
racketeer [rækɪ'tɪə*] *n* (*esp US*)
estafador(a) *m/f*.
racoon [rə'kuːn] *n* = **raccoon**.
racquet ['rækɪt] *n* raqueta.
racy ['reɪsɪ] *adj* picante, subido.
RADA ['rɑːdə] *n abbr* (*BRIT*) = *Royal Academy
of Dramatic Art*.
radar ['reɪdɑː*] *n* radar *m*.
radar trap *n* trampa radar.
radial ['reɪdɪəl] *adj* (*tyre: also*: **~-ply**) radial.
radiance ['reɪdɪəns] *n* brillantez *f*,
resplandor *m*.
radiant ['reɪdɪənt] *adj* brillante,
resplandeciente.
radiate ['reɪdɪeɪt] *vt* (*heat*) radiar, irradiar
♦ *vi* (*lines*) extenderse.
radiation [reɪdɪ'eɪʃən] *n* radiación *f*.
radiation sickness *n* enfermedad *f* de
radiación.
radiator ['reɪdɪeɪtə*] *n* (*AUT*) radiador *m*.
radiator cap *n* tapón *m* de radiador.
radiator grill *n* (*AUT*) rejilla del radiador.
radical ['rædɪkl] *adj* radical.
radically ['rædɪkəlɪ] *adv* radicalmente.
radii ['reɪdɪaɪ] *npl of* **radius**.
radio ['reɪdɪəʊ] *n* radio *f* or *m* (*LAM*) ♦ *vi*: **to ~
to sb** mandar un mensaje por radio a
algn ♦ *vt* (*information*) radiar, transmitir
por radio; (*one's position*) indicar por

radio; (*person*) llamar por radio; **on the ~** en *or* por la radio.
radioactive [reɪdɪəʊ'æktɪv] *adj* radi(o)activo.
radioactivity [reɪdɪəʊæk'tɪvɪtɪ] *n* radi(o)actividad *f*.
radio announcer *n* locutor(a) *m/f* de radio.
radio-controlled [reɪdɪəʊkən'trəʊld] *adj* teledirigido.
radiographer [reɪdɪ'ɒgrəfə*] *n* radiógrafo/a.
radiography [reɪdɪ'ɒgrəfɪ] *n* radiografía.
radiology [reɪdɪ'ɒlədʒɪ] *n* radiología.
radio station *n* emisora.
radio taxi *n* radio taxi *m*.
radiotelephone [reɪdɪəʊ'telɪfəʊn] *n* radioteléfono.
radiotelescope [reɪdɪəʊ'telɪskəʊp] *n* radiotelescopio.
radiotherapist [reɪdɪəʊ'θerəpɪst] *n* radioterapeuta *m/f*.
radiotherapy ['reɪdɪəʊθerəpɪ] *n* radioterapia.
radish ['rædɪʃ] *n* rábano.
radium ['reɪdɪəm] *n* radio.
radius, *pl* **radii** ['reɪdɪəs, -ɪaɪ] *n* radio; **within a ~ of 50 miles** en un radio de 50 millas.
RAF *n abbr see* **Royal Air Force.**
raffia ['ræfɪə] *n* rafia.
raffle ['ræfl] *n* rifa, sorteo ♦ *vt* (*object*) rifar.
raft [rɑːft] *n* (*craft*) balsa; (*also*: **life ~**) balsa salvavidas.
rafter ['rɑːftə*] *n* viga.
rag [ræg] *n* (*piece of cloth*) trapo; (*torn cloth*) harapo; (*pej: newspaper*) periodicucho; (*for charity*) actividades estudiantiles benéficas ♦ *vt* (*BRIT*) tomar el pelo a; **~s** *npl* harapos *mpl*; **in ~s** en harapos, hecho jirones.
rag-and-bone man [rægən'bəʊnmæn] *n* (*BRIT*) trapero.
rag doll *n* muñeca de trapo.
rage [reɪdʒ] *n* (*fury*) rabia, furor *m* ♦ *vi* (*person*) rabiar, estar furioso; (*storm*) bramar; **to fly into a ~** montar en cólera; **it's all the ~** es lo último.
ragged ['rægɪd] *adj* (*edge*) desigual, mellado; (*cuff*) roto; (*appearance*) andrajoso, harapiento; **~ left/right** (*text*) margen *m* izquierdo/derecho irregular.
raging ['reɪdʒɪŋ] *adj* furioso; **in a ~ temper** de un humor de mil demonios.
rag week *n ver recuadro.*

RAG WEEK

En la universidad los estudiantes suelen organizar cada año lo que llaman **rag week**

Consiste en una serie de actos festivos y de participación general como teatro en la calle, marchas patrocinadas etc, para hacer colectas con fines benéficos. En ocasiones hacen también una revista ("rag mag"), que consiste básicamente en chistes más bien picantes para vender a los transeúntes, e incluso un baile de gala ("rag ball").

raid [reɪd] *n* (*MIL*) incursión *f*; (*criminal*) asalto; (*by police*) redada, allanamiento (*LAM*) ♦ *vt* invadir, atacar; asaltar.
raider ['reɪdə*] *n* invasor(a) *m/f*.
rail [reɪl] *n* (*on stair*) barandilla, pasamanos *m inv*; (*on bridge*) pretil *m*; (*of balcony, ship*) barandilla; (*for train*) riel *m*, carril *m*; **~s** *npl* vía *sg*; **by ~** por ferrocarril, en tren.
railcard ['reɪlkɑːd] *n* (*BRIT*) tarjeta para obtener descuentos en el tren; **Young Person's ~** ≈ Tarjeta joven (*ESP*).
railing(s) ['reɪlɪŋz] *n(pl)* verja *sg*.
railway ['reɪlweɪ], (*US*) **railroad** ['reɪlrəʊd] *n* ferrocarril *m*, vía férrea.
railway engine *n* (máquina) locomotora.
railway line *n* (*BRIT*) línea (de ferrocarril).
railwayman ['reɪlweɪmən] *n* (*BRIT*) ferroviario.
railway station *n* (*BRIT*) estación *f* de ferrocarril.
rain [reɪn] *n* lluvia ♦ *vi* llover; **in the ~** bajo la lluvia; **it's ~ing** llueve, está lloviendo; **it's ~ing cats and dogs** está lloviendo a cántaros *or* a mares.
rainbow ['reɪnbəʊ] *n* arco iris.
raincoat ['reɪnkəʊt] *n* impermeable *m*.
raindrop ['reɪndrɒp] *n* gota de lluvia.
rainfall ['reɪnfɔːl] *n* lluvia.
rainforest ['reɪnfɒrɪst] *n* selva tropical.
rainproof ['reɪnpruːf] *adj* impermeable, a prueba de lluvia.
rainstorm ['reɪnstɔːm] *n* temporal *m* (de lluvia).
rainwater ['reɪnwɔːtə*] *n* agua de lluvia.
rainy ['reɪnɪ] *adj* lluvioso.
raise [reɪz] *n* aumento ♦ *vt* (*lift*) levantar; (*build*) erigir, edificar; (*increase*) aumentar; (*doubts*) suscitar; (*a question*) plantear; (*cattle, family*) criar; (*crop*) cultivar; (*army*) reclutar; (*funds*) reunir; (*loan*) obtener; (*end: embargo*) levantar; **to ~ one's voice** alzar la voz; **to ~ one's glass to sb/sth** brindar por algn/algo; **to ~ a laugh/a smile** provocar risa/una sonrisa; **to ~ sb's hopes** dar esperanzas a algn.
raisin ['reɪzn] *n* pasa de Corinto.

rake [reɪk] *n* (*tool*) rastrillo; (*person*) libertino ♦ *vt* (*garden*) rastrillar; (*fire*) hurgar; (*with machine gun*) barrer.
▶**rake in, rake together** *vt* sacar.
rake-off ['reɪkɔf] *n* (*col*) comisión *f*, tajada.
rakish ['reɪkɪʃ] *adj* (*dissolute*) libertino; **at a ~ angle** (*hat*) echado a un lado, de lado.
rally ['rælɪ] *n* reunión *f*; (*POL*) mitin *m*; (*AUT*) rallye *m*; (*TENNIS*) peloteo ♦ *vt* reunir ♦ *vi* reunirse; (*sick person, STOCK EXCHANGE*) recuperarse.
▶**rally round** *vt fus* (*fig*) dar apoyo a.
rallying point ['rælɪɪŋ-] *n* (*POL, MIL*) punto de reunión.
RAM [ræm] *n abbr* (= *random access memory*) RAM *f*.
ram [ræm] *n* carnero; (*TECH*) pisón *m* ♦ *vt* (*crash into*) dar contra, chocar con; (*tread down*) apisonar.
ramble ['ræmbl] *n* caminata, excursión *f* en el campo ♦ *vi* (*pej: also: ~* **on**) divagar.
rambler ['ræmblə*] *n* excursionista *m/f*; (*BOT*) trepadora.
rambling ['ræmblɪŋ] *adj* (*speech*) inconexo; (*BOT*) trepador(a); (*house*) laberíntico.
rambunctious [ræm'bʌŋkʃəs] *adj* (*US*) = **rumbustious**.
RAMC *n abbr* (*BRIT*) = *Royal Army Medical Corps*.
ramification [ræmɪfɪ'keɪʃən] *n* ramificación *f*.
ramp [ræmp] *n* rampa; **on/off ~** *n* (*US AUT*) vía de acceso/salida; "**~**" (*AUT*) "rampa".
rampage [ræm'peɪdʒ] *n*: **to be on the ~** desmandarse.
rampant ['ræmpənt] *adj* (*disease etc*): **to be ~** estar muy extendido.
rampart ['ræmpɑːt] *n* terraplén *m*; (*wall*) muralla.
ram raid *vt* atracar (*rompiendo el escaparate con un coche*).
ramshackle ['ræmʃækl] *adj* destartalado.
RAN *n abbr* = *Royal Australian Navy*.
ran [ræn] *pt of* **run**.
ranch [rɑːntʃ] *n* (*US*) hacienda, estancia.
rancher ['rɑːntʃə*] *n* ganadero.
rancid ['rænsɪd] *adj* rancio.
rancour, (*US*) **rancor** ['ræŋkə*] *n* rencor *m*.
random ['rændəm] *adj* fortuito, sin orden; (*COMPUT, MATH*) aleatorio ♦ *n*: **at ~** al azar.
random access *n* (*COMPUT*) acceso aleatorio.
randy ['rændɪ] *adj* (*BRIT col*) cachondo, caliente.
rang [ræŋ] *pt of* **ring**.
range [reɪndʒ] *n* (*of mountains*) cadena de montañas, cordillera; (*of missile*) alcance

m; (*of voice*) registro; (*series*) serie *f*; (*of products*) surtido; (*MIL: also:* **shooting ~**) campo de tiro; (*also:* **kitchen ~**) fogón *m* ♦ *vt* (*place*) colocar; (*arrange*) arreglar ♦ *vi*: **to ~ over** (*wander*) recorrer; (*extend*) extenderse por; **within (firing) ~** a tiro; **do you have anything else in this price ~?** ¿tiene algo más de esta gama de precios?; **intermediate-/short-~ missile** proyectil *m* de medio/corto alcance; **to ~ from ... to...** oscilar entre ... y...; **~d left/ right** (*text*) alineado a la izquierda/ derecha.
ranger [reɪndʒə*] *n* guardabosques *m inv*.
Rangoon [ræŋ'guːn] *n* Rangún *m*.
rangy ['reɪndʒɪ] *adj* alto y delgado.
rank [ræŋk] *n* (*row*) fila; (*MIL*) rango; (*status*) categoría; (*BRIT: also:* **taxi ~**) parada ♦ *vi*: **to ~ among** figurar entre ♦ *adj* (*stinking*) fétido, rancio; (*hypocrisy, injustice etc*) manifiesto; **the ~ and file** (*fig*) las bases; **to close ~s** (*MIL*) cerrar filas; (*fig*) hacer un frente común; **~ outsider** participante *m/f* sin probabilidades de vencer; **I ~ him 6th** yo le pongo en sexto lugar.
rankle ['ræŋkl] *vi* (*insult*) doler.
ransack ['rænsæk] *vt* (*search*) registrar; (*plunder*) saquear.
ransom ['rænsəm] *n* rescate *m*; **to hold sb to ~** (*fig*) poner a algn entre la espada y la pared.
rant [rænt] *vi* despotricar.
ranting ['ræntɪŋ] *n* desvaríos *mpl*.
rap [ræp] *vt* golpear, dar un golpecito en.
rape [reɪp] *n* violación *f*; (*BOT*) colza ♦ *vt* violar.
rape(seed) oil ['reɪp(siːd)-] *n* aceite *m* de colza.
rapid ['ræpɪd] *adj* rápido.
rapidity [rə'pɪdɪtɪ] *n* rapidez *f*.
rapidly ['ræpɪdlɪ] *adv* rápidamente.
rapids ['ræpɪdz] *npl* (*GEO*) rápidos *mpl*.
rapier ['reɪpɪə*] *n* estoque *m*.
rapist ['reɪpɪst] *n* violador *m*.
rapport [ræ'pɔː*] *n* entendimiento.
rapprochement [ræ'prɔʃmɑ̃ːŋ] *n* acercamiento.
rapt [ræpt] *adj* (*attention*) profundo; **to be ~ in contemplation** estar ensimismado.
rapture ['ræptʃə*] *n* éxtasis *m*.
rapturous ['ræptʃərəs] *adj* extático; (*applause*) entusiasta; **a ~ (party)** *macrofiesta con música máquina*; **~ music** música máquina.
rare [reə*] *adj* raro, poco común; (*CULIN: steak*) poco hecho; **it is ~ to find that ...** es raro descubrir que ....
rarefied ['reərɪʃaɪd] *adj* (*air, atmosphere*)

enrarecido.

rarely ['rɛəlɪ] *adv* rara vez, pocas veces.

raring ['rɛərɪŋ] *adj*: **to be ~ to go** (*col*) tener muchas ganas de empezar.

rarity ['rɛərɪtɪ] *n* rareza.

rascal ['rɑːskl] *n* pillo/a, pícaro/a.

rash [ræʃ] *adj* imprudente, precipitado ♦ *n* (*MED*) salpullido, erupción *f* (cutánea); **to come out in a ~** salir salpullidos.

rasher ['ræʃə*] *n* loncha.

rashly ['ræʃlɪ] *adv* imprudentemente, precipitadamente.

rashness ['ræʃnɪs] *n* imprudencia, precipitación *f*.

rasp [rɑːsp] *n* (*tool*) escofina ♦ *vt* (*speak: also:* **~ out**) decir con voz áspera.

raspberry ['rɑːzbərɪ] *n* frambuesa.

rasping ['rɑːspɪŋ] *adj*: **a ~ noise** un ruido áspero.

Rastafarian [ræstə'fɛərɪən] *adj, n* rastafari *m/f*.

rat [ræt] *n* rata.

ratchet ['rætʃɪt] *n* (*TECH*) trinquete *m*.

rate [reɪt] *n* (*ratio*) razón *f*; (*percentage*) tanto por ciento; (*price*) precio; (: *of hotel*) tarifa; (*of interest*) tipo; (*speed*) velocidad *f* ♦ *vt* (*value*) tasar; (*estimate*) estimar; **to ~ as** ser considerado como; **~s** *npl* (*BRIT*) impuesto *sg* municipal; (*fees*) tarifa *sg*; **failure ~** porcentaje *m* de fallos; **pulse ~** pulsaciones *fpl* por minuto; **~ of pay** tipos *mpl* de sueldo; **at a ~ of 60 kph** a una velocidad de 60 kph; **~ of growth** ritmo de crecimiento; **~ of return** (*COMM*) tasa de rendimiento; **bank ~** tipo *or* tasa de interés bancario; **at any ~** en todo caso; **to ~ sb/sth highly** tener a algn/algo en alta estima; **the house is ~d at £84 per annum** (*BRIT*) la casa está tasada en 84 libras al año.

rateable value ['reɪtəbl-] *n* (*BRIT*) valor *m* impuesto.

rate-capping ['reɪtkæpɪŋ] *n* (*BRIT*) fijación *f* de las contribuciones.

ratepayer ['reɪtpeɪə*] *n* (*BRIT*) contribuyente *m/f*.

rather ['rɑːðə*] *adv* antes, más bien; (*somewhat*) algo, un poco; (*quite*) bastante; **it's ~ expensive** es algo caro; (*too much*) es demasiado caro; **there's ~ a lot** hay bastante; **I would** *or* **I'd ~ go** preferiría ir; **I'd ~ not** prefiero que no; **I ~ think he won't come** me inclino a creer que no vendrá; **or ~** (*more accurately*) o mejor dicho.

ratification [rætɪfɪ'keɪʃən] *n* ratificación *f*.

ratify ['rætɪfaɪ] *vt* ratificar.

rating ['reɪtɪŋ] *n* (*valuation*) tasación *f*;

(*standing*) posición *f*; (*BRIT NAUT*: *sailor*) marinero; **~s** *npl* (*RADIO*, *TV*) clasificación *f*.

ratio ['reɪʃɪəu] *n* razón *f*; **in the ~ of 100 to 1** a razón de *or* en la proporción de 100 a 1.

ration ['ræʃən] *n* ración *f*; **~s** *npl* víveres *mpl* ♦ *vt* racionar.

rational ['ræʃənl] *adj* racional; (*solution, reasoning*) lógico, razonable; (*person*) cuerdo, sensato.

rationale [ræʃə'nɑːl] *n* razón *f* fundamental.

rationalism ['ræʃnəlɪzəm] *n* racionalismo.

rationalization [ræʃnəlaɪ'zeɪʃən] *n* racionalización *f*.

rationalize ['ræʃnəlaɪz] *vt* (*reorganize: industry*) racionalizar.

rationally ['ræʃnəlɪ] *adv* racionalmente; (*logically*) lógicamente.

rationing ['ræʃnɪŋ] *n* racionamiento.

ratpack ['rætpæk] *n* (*BRIT col*) periodistas *que persiguen a los famosos.*

rat race *n* lucha incesante por la supervivencia.

rattan [ræ'tæn] *n* rota, caña de Indias.

rattle ['rætl] *n* golpeteo; (*of train etc*) traqueteo; (*object: of baby*) sonaja, sonajero; (: *of sports fan*) matraca ♦ *vi* sonar, golpear; traquetear; (*small objects*) castañetear ♦ *vt* hacer sonar agitando; (*col: disconcert*) poner nervioso a.

rattlesnake ['rætlsneɪk] *n* serpiente *f* de cascabel.

ratty ['rætɪ] *adj* (*col*) furioso; **to get ~** mosquearse.

raucous ['rɔːkəs] *adj* estridente, ronco.

raucously ['rɔːkəslɪ] *adv* de modo estridente, roncamente.

raunchy ['rɔːntʃɪ] *adj* (*col*) lascivo.

ravage ['rævɪdʒ] *vt* hacer estragos en, destrozar; **~s** *npl* estragos *mpl*.

rave [reɪv] *vi* (*in anger*) encolerizarse; (*with enthusiasm*) entusiasmarse; (*MED*) delirar, desvariar ♦ *cpd*: **a ~** (*party*) macrofiesta con música máquina; **~ music** música máquina.

raven ['reɪvən] *n* cuervo.

ravenous ['rævənəs] *adj*: **to be ~** tener un hambre canina.

ravine [rə'viːn] *n* barranco.

raving ['reɪvɪŋ] *adj*: **~ lunatic** loco de atar.

ravings ['reɪvɪŋz] *npl* desvaríos *mpl*.

ravioli [rævɪ'əulɪ] *n* ravioles *mpl*, ravioli *mpl*.

ravish ['rævɪʃ] *vt* (*charm*) encantar, embelesar; (*rape*) violar.

ravishing ['rævɪʃɪŋ] *adj* encantador(a).

raw [rɔː] *adj* (*uncooked*) crudo; (*not processed*) bruto; (*sore*) vivo;

(_inexperienced_) novato, inexperto.
Rawalpindi [rɔːl'pɪndɪ] _n_ Rawalpindi _m_.

raw data _n_ (_COMPUT_) datos _mpl_ en bruto.
raw deal _n_ (_col: bad deal_) mala pasada _or_ jugada; (: _harsh treatment_) injusticia.
raw material _n_ materia prima.
ray [reɪ] _n_ rayo; ~ **of hope** (rayo de) esperanza.
rayon ['reɪɔn] _n_ rayón _m_.
raze [reɪz] _vt_ (_also_: ~ **to the ground**) arrasar, asolar.
razor ['reɪzə*] _n_ (_open_) navaja; (_safety_ ~) máquina de afeitar.
razor blade _n_ hoja de afeitar.
razzle(-dazzle) ['ræzl('dæzl)] _n_ (_BRIT col_): **to be/go on the** ~ estar/irse de juerga.
razzmatazz ['ræzmə'tæz] _n_ (_col_) animación _f_, bullicio.
R & B _n abbr_ = _rhythm and blues_.
RC _abbr_ = **Roman Catholic**.
RCAF _n abbr_ = _Royal Canadian Air Force_.
RCMP _n abbr_ = _Royal Canadian Mounted Police_.
RCN _n abbr_ = _Royal Canadian Navy_.
RD _abbr_ (_US POST_) = _rural delivery_.
Rd _abbr_ = **road**.
R & D _n abbr_ (= _research and development_) I + D.
RDC _n abbr_ (_BRIT_) = _rural district council_.
RE _n abbr_ (_BRIT_) = _religious education_; (_BRIT MIL_) = _Royal Engineers_.
re [riː] _prep_ con referencia a.
re ... [riː] _pref_ re....
reach [riːtʃ] _n_ alcance _m_; (_BOXING_) envergadura; (_of river etc_) extensión _f_ entre dos recodos ♦ _vt_ alcanzar, llegar a; (_achieve_) lograr ♦ _vi_ extenderse; (_stretch out hand_: _also_: ~ **down**, ~ **over**, ~ **across** _etc_) tender la mano; **within** ~ al alcance (de la mano); **out of** ~ fuera del alcance; **to** ~ **out for sth** alargar _or_ tender la mano para tomar algo; **can I** ~ **you at your hotel?** ¿puedo localizarte en tu hotel?; **to** ~ **sb by phone** comunicarse con algn por teléfono.
react [riː'ækt] _vi_ reaccionar.
reaction [riː'ækʃən] _n_ reacción _f_.
reactionary [riː'ækʃənrɪ] _adj_, _n_ reaccionario/a _m/f_.
reactor [riː'æktə*] _n_ reactor _m_.
read, _pt_, _pp_ **read** [riːd, rɛd] _vi_ leer ♦ _vt_ leer; (_understand_) entender; (_study_) estudiar; **to take sth as read** (_fig_) dar algo por sentado; **do you** ~ **me?** (_TEL_) ¿me escucha?; **to** ~ **between the lines** leer entre líneas.
►**read out** _vt_ leer en alta voz.
►**read over** _vt_ repasar.

►**read through** _vt_ (_quickly_) leer rápidamente, echar un vistazo a; (_thoroughly_) leer con cuidado _or_ detenidamente.
►**read up** _vt_, **read up on** _vt fus_ documentarse sobre.
readable ['riːdəbl] _adj_ (_writing_) legible; (_book_) que merece la pena leer.
reader ['riːdə*] _n_ lector(a) _m/f_; (_book_) libro de lecturas; (_BRIT_: _at university_) profesor(a) _m/f_.
readership ['riːdəʃɪp] _n_ (_of paper etc_) número de lectores.
readily ['rɛdɪlɪ] _adv_ (_willingly_) de buena gana; (_easily_) fácilmente; (_quickly_) en seguida.
readiness ['rɛdɪnɪs] _n_ buena voluntad; (_preparedness_) preparación _f_; **in** ~ (_prepared_) listo, preparado.
reading ['riːdɪŋ] _n_ lectura; (_understanding_) comprensión _f_; (_on instrument_) indicación _f_.
reading lamp _n_ lámpara portátil.
reading matter _n_ lectura.
reading room _n_ sala de lectura.
readjust [riːə'dʒʌst] _vt_ reajustar ♦ _vi_ (_person_): **to** ~ **to** reajustarse a.
readjustment [riːə'dʒʌstmənt] _n_ reajuste _m_.
ready ['rɛdɪ] _adj_ listo, preparado; (_willing_) dispuesto; (_available_) disponible ♦ _n_: **at the** ~ (_MIL_) listo para tirar; ~ **for use** listo para usar; **to be** ~ **to do sth** estar listo para hacer algo; **to get** ~ _vi_ prepararse ♦ _vt_ preparar.
ready cash _n_ efectivo.
ready-made ['rɛdɪ'meɪd] _adj_ confeccionado.
ready money _n_ dinero contante.
ready reckoner _n_ tabla de cálculos hechos.
ready-to-wear ['rɛdɪtə'wɛə*] _adj_ confeccionado.
reaffirm [riːə'fəːm] _vt_ reafirmar.
reagent [riː'eɪdʒənt] _n_ reactivo.
real [rɪəl] _adj_ verdadero, auténtico; **in** ~ **terms** en términos reales; **in** ~ **life** en la vida real, en la realidad.
real ale _n_ cerveza elaborada tradicionalmente.
real estate _n_ bienes _mpl_ raíces.
real estate agency _n_ = **estate agency**.
realism ['rɪəlɪzəm] _n_ (_also ART_) realismo.
realist ['rɪəlɪst] _n_ realista _m/f_.
realistic [rɪə'lɪstɪk] _adj_ realista.
realistically [rɪə'lɪstɪklɪ] _adv_ de modo realista.
reality [riː'ælɪtɪ] _n_ realidad _f_; **in** ~ en

realidad.

realization [rɪəlaɪ'zeɪʃən] n comprensión f; (of a project; COMM: of assets) realización f.

realize ['rɪəlaɪz] vt (understand) darse cuenta de; (a project; COMM: asset) realizar; I ~ that ... comprendo or entiendo que ....

really ['rɪəlɪ] adv realmente; ~? ¿de veras?

realm [rɛlm] n reino; (fig) esfera.

real time n (COMPUT) tiempo real.

Realtor ® ['rɪəltɔ:*] n (US) corredor(a) m/f de bienes raíces.

ream [ri:m] n resma; ~s (fig, col) montones mpl.

reap [ri:p] vt segar; (fig) cosechar, recoger.

reaper ['ri:pə*] n segador(a) m/f.

reappear [ri:ə'pɪə*] vi reaparecer.

reappearance [ri:ə'pɪərəns] n reaparición f.

reapply [ri:ə'plaɪ] vi volver a presentarse, hacer or presentar una nueva solicitud.

reappoint [ri:ə'pɔɪnt] vt volver a nombrar.

reappraisal [ri:ə'preɪzl] n revaluación f.

rear [rɪə*] adj trasero ♦ n parte f trasera ♦ vt (cattle, family) criar ♦ vi (also: ~ up) (animal) encabritarse.

rear-engined ['rɪər'endʒɪnd] adj (AUT) con motor trasero.

rearguard ['rɪəgɑ:d] n retaguardia.

rearm [ri:'ɑ:m] vt rearmar ♦ vi rearmarse.

rearmament [ri:'ɑ:məmənt] n rearme m.

rearrange [ri:ə'reɪndʒ] vt ordenar or arreglar de nuevo.

rear-view ['rɪəvju:]: ~ **mirror** n (AUT) espejo retrovisor.

reason ['ri:zn] n razón f ♦ vi: **to ~ with sb** tratar de que algn entre en razón; **it stands to ~ that** es lógico que; **the ~ for/ why** la causa de/la razón por la cual; **she claims with good ~ that she's underpaid** dice con razón que está mal pagada; **all the more ~ why you should not sell it** razón de más para que no lo vendas.

reasonable ['ri:znəbl] adj razonable; (sensible) sensato.

reasonably ['ri:znəblɪ] adv razonablemente; **a ~ accurate report** un informe bastante exacto.

reasoned ['ri:znd] adj (argument) razonado.

reasoning ['ri:znɪŋ] n razonamiento, argumentos mpl.

reassemble [ri:ə'sembl] vt volver a reunir; (machine) montar de nuevo ♦ vi volver a reunirse.

reassert [ri:ə'sə:t] vt reafirmar, reiterar.

reassurance [ri:ə'ʃuərəns] n consuelo.

reassure [ri:ə'ʃuə*] vt tranquilizar; **to ~ sb that** tranquilizar a algn asegurándole que.

reassuring [ri:ə'ʃuərɪŋ] adj tranquilizador(a).

reawakening [ri:ə'weɪknɪŋ] n despertar m.

rebate ['ri:beɪt] n (on product) rebaja; (on tax etc) desgravación f; (repayment) reembolso.

rebel ['rɛbl] n rebelde m/f ♦ vi [rɪ'bɛl] rebelarse, sublevarse.

rebellion [rɪ'bɛljən] n rebelión f, sublevación f.

rebellious [rɪ'bɛljəs] adj rebelde; (child) revoltoso.

rebirth [ri:'bə:θ] n renacimiento.

rebound [rɪ'baund] vi (ball) rebotar ♦ n ['ri:baund] rebote m.

rebuff [rɪ'bʌf] n desaire m, rechazo ♦ vt rechazar.

rebuild [ri:'bɪld] vt (irreg: like build) reconstruir.

rebuilding [ri:'bɪldɪŋ] n reconstrucción f.

rebuke [rɪ'bju:k] n reprimenda ♦ vt reprender.

rebut [rɪ'bʌt] vt rebatir.

recalcitrant [rɪ'kælsɪtrənt] adj reacio.

recall [rɪ'kɔ:l] vt (remember) recordar; (ambassador etc) retirar; (COMPUT) volver a llamar ♦ n recuerdo.

recant [rɪ'kænt] vi retractarse.

recap ['ri:kæp] vt, vi recapitular.

recapitulate [ri:kə'pɪtjuleɪt] vt, vi = recap.

recapture [ri:'kæptʃə*] vt (town) reconquistar; (atmosphere) hacer revivir.

recd., rec'd abbr (= received) rbdo.

recede [rɪ'si:d] vi retroceder.

receding [rɪ'si:dɪŋ] adj (forehead, chin) hundido; ~ **hairline** entradas fpl.

receipt [rɪ'si:t] n (document) recibo; (act of receiving) recepción f; ~s npl (COMM) ingresos mpl; **to acknowledge ~ of** acusar recibo de; **we are in ~ of ...** obra en nuestro poder ....

receivable [rɪ'si:vəbl] adj (COMM) a cobrar.

receive [rɪ'si:v] vt recibir; (guest) acoger; (wound) sufrir; "~ed with thanks" (COMM) "recibí".

Received Pronunciation [rɪ'si:vd-] n see RP.

receiver [rɪ'si:və*] n (TEL) auricular m; (RADIO) receptor m; (of stolen goods) perista m/f; (LAW) administrador m jurídico.

receivership [rɪ'si:vəʃɪp] n: **to go into ~** entrar en liquidación.

recent ['ri:snt] adj reciente; **in ~ years** en los últimos años.

recently ['ri:sntlɪ] adv recientemente, recién (LAM); ~ **arrived** recién llegado; **until ~** hasta hace poco.

receptacle [rɪ'sɛptɪkl] _n_ receptáculo.
reception [rɪ'sɛpʃən] _n_ (_in building, office etc_) recepción _f_; (_welcome_) acogida.
reception centre _n_ (_BRIT_) centro de recepción.
reception desk _n_ recepción _f_.
receptionist [rɪ'sɛpʃənɪst] _n_ recepcionista _m/f_.
receptive [rɪ'sɛptɪv] _adj_ receptivo.
recess [rɪ'sɛs] _n_ (_in room_) hueco; (_for bed_) nicho; (_secret place_) escondrijo; (_POL etc_: _holiday_) período vacacional; (_US LAW_: _short break_) descanso; (_SCOL_: _esp US_) recreo.
recession [rɪ'sɛʃən] _n_ recesión _f_, depresión _f_.
recharge [riː'tʃɑːdʒ] _vt_ (_battery_) recargar.
rechargeable [riː'tʃɑːdʒəbl] _adj_ recargable.
recipe ['rɛsɪpɪ] _n_ receta.
recipient [rɪ'sɪpɪənt] _n_ recibidor(a) _m/f_; (_of letter_) destinatario/a.
reciprocal [rɪ'sɪprəkl] _adj_ recíproco.
reciprocate [rɪ'sɪprəkeɪt] _vt_ devolver, corresponder a ♦ _vi_ corresponder.
recital [rɪ'saɪtl] _n_ (_MUS_) recital _m_.
recitation [rɛsɪ'teɪʃən] _n_ (_of poetry_) recitado; (_of complaints etc_) enumeración _f_, relación _f_.
recite [rɪ'saɪt] _vt_ (_poem_) recitar; (_complaints etc_) enumerar.
reckless ['rɛkləs] _adj_ temerario, imprudente; (_speed_) peligroso.
recklessly ['rɛkləslɪ] _adv_ imprudentemente; de modo peligroso.
recklessness ['rɛkləsnɪs] _n_ temeridad _f_, imprudencia.
reckon ['rɛkən] _vt_ (_count_) contar; (_consider_) considerar ♦ _vi_: **to ~ without sb/sth** dejar de contar con algn/algo; **he is somebody to be ~ed with** no se le puede descartar; **I ~ that ...** me parece que ..., creo que ....
▶**reckon on** _vt fus_ contar con.
reckoning ['rɛkənɪŋ] _n_ (_calculation_) cálculo.
reclaim [rɪ'kleɪm] _vt_ (_land_) recuperar; (: _from sea_) rescatar; (_demand back_) reclamar.
reclamation [rɛklə'meɪʃən] _n_ recuperación _f_; rescate _m_.
recline [rɪ'klaɪn] _vi_ reclinarse.
reclining [rɪ'klaɪnɪŋ] _adj_ (_seat_) reclinable.
recluse [rɪ'kluːs] _n_ recluso/a.
recognition [rɛkəg'nɪʃən] _n_ reconocimiento; **transformed beyond ~** irreconocible; **in ~ of** en reconocimiento de.
recognizable ['rɛkəgnaɪzəbl] _adj_: ~ **(by)** reconocible (por).
recognize ['rɛkəgnaɪz] _vt_ reconocer,

conocer; **to ~ (by/as)** reconocer (por/como).
recoil [rɪ'kɔɪl] _vi_ (_person_): **to ~ from doing sth** retraerse de hacer algo ♦ _n_ (_of gun_) retroceso.
recollect [rɛkə'lɛkt] _vt_ recordar, acordarse de.
recollection [rɛkə'lɛkʃən] _n_ recuerdo; **to the best of my ~** que yo recuerde.
recommend [rɛkə'mɛnd] _vt_ recomendar; **she has a lot to ~ her** tiene mucho a su favor.
recommendation [rɛkəmɛn'deɪʃən] _n_ recomendación _f_.
recommended retail price (RRP) _n_ (_BRIT_) precio (recomendado) de venta al público.
recompense ['rɛkəmpɛns] _vt_ recompensar ♦ _n_ recompensa.
reconcilable ['rɛkənsaɪləbl] _adj_ (re)conciliable.
reconcile ['rɛkənsaɪl] _vt_ (_two people_) reconciliar; (_two facts_) conciliar; **to ~ o.s. to sth** resignarse _or_ conformarse a algo.
reconciliation [rɛkənsɪlɪ'eɪʃən] _n_ reconciliación _f_.
recondite [rɪ'kɒndaɪt] _adj_ recóndito.
recondition [riːkən'dɪʃən] _vt_ (_machine_) reparar, reponer.
reconditioned [riːkən'dɪʃənd] _adj_ renovado, reparado.
reconnaissance [rɪ'kɒnɪsns] _n_ (_MIL_) reconocimiento.
reconnoitre, (_US_) **reconnoiter** [rɛkə'nɔɪtə*] _vt_, _vi_ (_MIL_) reconocer.
reconsider [riːkən'sɪdə*] _vt_ repensar.
reconstitute [riː'kɒnstɪtjuːt] _vt_ reconstituir.
reconstruct [riːkən'strʌkt] _vt_ reconstruir.
reconstruction [riːkən'strʌkʃən] _n_ reconstrucción _f_.
reconvene [riːkən'viːn] _vt_ volver a convocar ♦ _vi_ volver a reunirse.
record _n_ ['rɛkɔːd] (_MUS_) disco; (_of meeting etc_) relación _f_; (_register_) registro, partida; (_file_) archivo; (_also_: **police** _or_ **criminal ~**) antecedentes _mpl_ penales; (_written_) expediente _m_; (_SPORT_) récord _m_; (_COMPUT_) registro ♦ _vt_ [rɪ'kɔːd] (_set down, also COMPUT_) registrar; (_relate_) hacer constar; (_MUS: song etc_) grabar; **in ~ time** en un tiempo récord; **public ~s** archivos _mpl_ nacionales; **he is on ~ as saying that ...** hay pruebas de que ha dicho públicamente que ...; **Spain's excellent ~** el excelente historial de España; **off the ~** _adj_ no oficial ♦ _adv_ confidencialmente.
record card _n_ (_in file_) ficha.

recorded delivery letter [rɪ'kɔːdɪd-] *n*
(*BRIT POST*) carta de entrega con acuse de
recibo.
recorded music *n* música grabada.
recorder [rɪ'kɔːdə*] *n* (*MUS*) flauta de pico;
(*TECH*) contador *m*.
record holder *n* (*SPORT*) actual
poseedor(a) *m/f* del récord.
recording [rɪ'kɔːdɪŋ] *n* (*MUS*) grabación *f*.
recording studio *n* estudio de grabación.
record library *n* discoteca.
record player *n* tocadiscos *m inv.*
recount *vt* [rɪ'kaunt] contar.
re-count ['riːkaunt] *n* (*POL: of votes*)
segundo escrutinio, recuento ♦ *vt*
[riː'kaunt] volver a contar.
recoup [rɪ'kuːp] *vt*: **to ~ one's losses**
recuperar las pérdidas.
recourse [rɪ'kɔːs] *n* recurso; **to have ~ to**
recurrir a.
recover [rɪ'kʌvə*] *vt* recuperar; (*rescue*)
rescatar ♦ *vi* recuperarse.
recovery [rɪ'kʌvərɪ] *n* recuperación *f*;
rescate *m*; (*MED*): **to make a ~**
restablecerse.
recreate [riːkrɪ'eɪt] *vt* recrear.
recreation [rɛkrɪ'eɪʃən] *n* recreación *f*;
(*amusement*) recreo.
recreational [rɛkrɪ'eɪʃənl] *adj* de
recreo.
recreational drug *n* droga recreativa.
recreational vehicle *n* (*US*) caravana *or*
roulotte *f* pequeña.
recrimination [rɪkrɪmɪ'neɪʃən] *n*
recriminación *f*.
recruit [rɪ'kruːt] *n* recluta *m/f* ♦ *vt* reclutar;
(*staff*) contratar.
recruitment [rɪ'kruːtmənt] *n*
reclutamiento.
rectangle ['rɛktæŋgl] *n* rectángulo.
rectangular [rɛk'tæŋgjulə*] *adj*
rectangular.
rectify ['rɛktɪfaɪ] *vt* rectificar.
rector ['rɛktə*] *n* (*REL*) párroco; (*SCOL*)
rector(a) *m/f*.
rectory ['rɛktərɪ] *n* casa del párroco.
rectum ['rɛktəm] *n* (*ANAT*) recto.
recuperate [rɪ'kuːpəreɪt] *vi* reponerse,
restablecerse.
recur [rɪ'kəː*] *vi* repetirse; (*pain, illness*)
producirse de nuevo.
recurrence [rɪ'kəːrns] *n* repetición *f*.
recurrent [rɪ'kəːrnt] *adj* repetido.
recycle [riː'saɪkl] *vt* reciclar.
red [rɛd] *n* rojo ♦ *adj* rojo; **to be in the ~**
(*account*) estar en números rojos;
(*business*) tener un saldo negativo; **to
give sb the ~ carpet treatment** recibir a

algn con todos los honores.
red alert *n* alerta roja.
red-blooded ['rɛd'blʌdɪd] *adj* (*col*) viril.
redbrick university ['rɛdbrɪk-] *n ver*
recuadro.

REDBRICK UNIVERSITY

El término **redbrick university** *se aplica a
las universidades construidas en los
grandes centros urbanos industriales como
Birmingham, Liverpool o Manchester a
finales del siglo XIX o principios del XX.
Deben su nombre a que sus edificios son
normalmente de ladrillo, a diferencia de las
universidades tradicionales de Oxford y
Cambridge, cuyos edificios suelen ser de
piedra.*

Red Cross *n* Cruz *f* Roja.
redcurrant ['rɛdkʌrənt] *n* grosella.
redden ['rɛdn] *vt* enrojecer ♦ *vi*
enrojecerse.
reddish ['rɛdɪʃ] *adj* (*hair*) rojizo.
redecorate [riː'dɛkəreɪt] pintar de nuevo;
volver a decorar.
redecoration [riːdɛkə'reɪʃən] *n* renovación *f*.
redeem [rɪ'diːm] *vt* (*sth in pawn*)
desempeñar; (*fig, also REL*) rescatar.
redeemable [rɪ'diːməbl] *adj* canjeable.
redeeming [rɪ'diːmɪŋ] *adj*: **~ feature** punto
bueno *or* favorable.
redefine [riːdɪ'faɪn] *vt* redefinir.
redemption [rɪ'dɛmpʃən] *n* (*REL*) redención
f; **to be past *or* beyond ~** no tener
remedio.
redeploy [riːdɪ'plɔɪ] *vt* (*resources*) disponer
de nuevo.
redevelop [riːdɪ'vɛləp] *vt* reorganizar.
redevelopment [riːdɪ'vɛləpmənt] *n*
reorganización *f*.
red-handed [rɛd'hændɪd] *adj*: **he was
caught ~** le pillaron con las manos en la
masa.
redhead ['rɛdhɛd] *n* pelirrojo/a.
red herring *n* (*fig*) pista falsa.
red-hot [rɛd'hɔt] *adj* candente.
redirect [riːdaɪ'rɛkt] *vt* (*mail*) reexpedir.
rediscover [riːdɪs'kʌvə*] *vt* redescubrir.
rediscovery [riːdɪs'kʌvərɪ] *n*
redescubrimiento.
redistribute [riːdɪs'trɪbjuːt] *vt* redistribuir,
hacer una nueva distribución de.
red-letter day [rɛd'lɛtə-] *n* día *m* señalado,
día *m* especial.
red light *n*: **to go through *or* jump a ~**
(*AUT*) saltarse un semáforo.
red-light district *n* barrio chino, zona de

tolerancia.

red meat *n* carne *f* roja.

redness ['rɛdnɪs] *n* rojez *f*.

redo [riː'duː] *vt* (*irreg: like* **do**) rehacer.

redolent ['rɛdələnt] *adj*: ~ **of** (*smell*) con fragancia a; **to be** ~ **of** (*fig*) evocar.

redouble [riː'dʌbl] *vt*: **to** ~ **one's efforts** redoblar los esfuerzos.

redraft [riː'drɑːft] *vt* volver a redactar.

redress [rɪ'drɛs] *n* reparación *f* ♦ *vt* reparar, corregir; **to** ~ **the balance** restablecer el equilibrio.

Red Sea *n*: **the** ~ el mar Rojo.

redskin ['rɛdskɪn] *n* piel roja *m/f*.

red tape *n* (*fig*) trámites *mpl*, papeleo (*col*).

reduce [rɪ'djuːs] *vt* reducir; (*lower*) rebajar; **to** ~ **sth by/to** reducir algo en/a; **to** ~ **sb to silence/despair/tears** hacer callar/ desesperarse/llorar a algn; "~ **speed now**" (*AUT*) "reduzca la velocidad".

reduced [rɪ'djuːst] *adj* (*decreased*) reducido, rebajado; **at a** ~ **price** con rebaja *or* descuento; "**greatly** ~ **prices**" "grandes rebajas".

reduction [rɪ'dʌkʃən] *n* reducción *f*; (*of price*) rebaja; (*discount*) descuento.

redundancy [rɪ'dʌndənsɪ] *n* despido; (*unemployment*) desempleo; **voluntary** ~ baja voluntaria.

redundancy payment *n* indemnización *f* por desempleo.

redundant [rɪ'dʌndənt] *adj* (*BRIT: worker*) parado, sin trabajo; (*detail, object*) superfluo; **to be made** ~ quedar(se) sin trabajo, perder el empleo.

reed [riːd] *n* (*BOT*) junco, caña; (*MUS: of clarinet etc*) lengüeta.

re-educate [riː'ɛdjukeɪt] *vt* reeducar.

reedy ['riːdɪ] *adj* (*voice, instrument*) aflautado.

reef [riːf] *n* (*at sea*) arrecife *m*.

reek [riːk] *vi*: **to** ~ (**of**) oler *or* apestar (a).

reel [riːl] *n* carrete *m*, bobina; (*of film*) rollo ♦ *vt* (*TECH*) devanar; (*also*: ~ **in**) sacar ♦ *vi* (*sway*) tambalear(se); **my head is** ~**ing** me da vueltas la cabeza.

▶**reel off** *vt* recitar de memoria.

re-election [riː'ɪlɛkʃən] *n* reelección *f*.

re-engage [riːɪn'geɪdʒ] *vt* contratar de nuevo.

re-enter [riː'ɛntə*] *vt* reingresar en, volver a entrar en.

re-entry [riː'ɛntrɪ] *n* reingreso, reentrada.

re-examine [riːɪg'zæmɪn] *vt* reexaminar.

re-export *vt* ['riːɪks'pɔːt] reexportar ♦ *n* [riː'ɛkspɔːt] reexportación *f*.

ref [rɛf] *n abbr* (*col*) = **referee**.

ref. *abbr* (*COMM*: = *with reference to*) Ref.

refectory [rɪ'fɛktərɪ] *n* comedor *m*.

refer [rɪ'fəː*] *vt* (*send*) remitir; (*ascribe*) referir a, relacionar con ♦ *vi*: **to** ~ **to** (*allude to*) referirse a, aludir a; (*apply to*) relacionarse con; (*consult*) remitirse a; **he** ~**red me to the manager** me envió al gerente.

referee [rɛfə'riː] *n* árbitro; (*BRIT: for job application*) persona que da referencias de otro ♦ *vt* (*match*) arbitrar en.

reference ['rɛfrəns] *n* (*mention, in book*) referencia; (*sending*) remisión *f*; (*relevance*) relación *f*; (*for job application: letter*) carta de recomendación; **with** ~ **to** con referencia a; (*COMM: in letter*) me remito a.

reference book *n* libro de consulta.

reference library *n* biblioteca de consulta.

reference number *n* número de referencia.

referendum, *pl* **referenda** [rɛfə'rɛndəm, -də] *n* referéndum *m*.

referral [rɪ'fəːrəl] *n* remisión *f*.

refill *vt* [riː'fɪl] rellenar ♦ *n* ['riːfɪl] repuesto, recambio.

refine [rɪ'faɪn] *vt* (*sugar, oil*) refinar.

refined [rɪ'faɪnd] *adj* (*person, taste*) refinado, culto.

refinement [rɪ'faɪnmənt] *n* (*of person*) cultura, educación *f*.

refinery [rɪ'faɪnərɪ] *n* refinería.

refit (*NAUT*) *n* ['riːfɪt] reparación *f* ♦ *vt* [riː'fɪt] reparar.

reflate [riː'fleɪt] *vt* (*economy*) reflacionar.

reflation [riː'fleɪʃən] *n* reflación *f*.

reflationary [riː'fleɪʃənrɪ] *adj* reflacionario.

reflect [rɪ'flɛkt] *vt* (*light, image*) reflejar ♦ *vi* (*think*) reflexionar, pensar; **it** ~**s badly/ well on him** le perjudica/le hace honor.

reflection [rɪ'flɛkʃən] *n* (*act*) reflexión *f*; (*image*) reflejo; (*discredit*) crítica; **on** ~ pensándolo bien.

reflector [rɪ'flɛktə*] *n* (*AUT*) catafaros *m inv*; (*telescope*) reflector *m*.

reflex ['riːflɛks] *adj, n* reflejo.

reflexive [rɪ'flɛksɪv] *adj* (*LING*) reflexivo.

reform [rɪ'fɔːm] *n* reforma ♦ *vt* reformar.

reformat [riː'fɔːmæt] *vt* (*COMPUT*) recomponer.

Reformation [rɛfə'meɪʃən] *n*: **the** ~ la Reforma.

reformatory [rɪ'fɔːmətərɪ] *n* (*US*) reformatorio.

reformer [rɪ'fɔːmə*] *n* reformador(a) *m/f*.

refrain [rɪ'freɪn] *vi*: **to** ~ **from doing** abstenerse de hacer ♦ *n* (*MUS etc*) estribillo.

refresh [rɪ'frɛʃ] *vt* refrescar.

refresher course [rɪ'frɛʃə-] n (BRIT) curso de repaso.

refreshing [rɪ'frɛʃɪŋ] adj (drink) refrescante; (sleep) reparador; (change etc) estimulante; (idea, point of view) estimulante, interesante.

refreshments [rɪ'frɛʃmənts] npl (drinks) refrescos mpl.

refrigeration [rɪfrɪdʒə'reɪʃən] n refrigeración f.

refrigerator [rɪ'frɪdʒəreɪtə*] n frigorífico, refrigeradora (LAM), heladera (LAM).

refuel [riː'fjuəl] vi repostar (combustible).

refuelling, (US) **refueling** [riː'fjuəlɪŋ] n reabastecimiento de combustible.

refuge ['rɛfjuːdʒ] n refugio, asilo; **to take ~ in** refugiarse en.

refugee [rɛfju'dʒiː] n refugiado/a.

refugee camp n campamento para refugiados.

refund n ['riːfʌnd] reembolso ♦ vt [rɪ'fʌnd] devolver, reembolsar.

refurbish [riː'fəːbɪʃ] vt restaurar, renovar.

refurnish [riː'fəːnɪʃ] vt amueblar de nuevo.

refusal [rɪ'fjuːzəl] n negativa; **first ~** primera opción; **to have first ~ on sth** tener la primera opción a algo.

refuse n ['rɛfjuːs] basura ♦ (vb: [rɪ'fjuːz]) vt (reject) rehusar; (say no to) negarse a ♦ vi negarse; (horse) rehusar; **to ~ to do sth** negarse a or rehusar hacer algo.

refuse bin n cubo or bote m (LAM) or balde m (LAM) de la basura.

refuse collection n recogida de basuras.

refuse disposal n eliminación f de basuras.

refusenik [rɪ'fjuːznɪk] n judío/a que tenía prohibido emigrar de la ex-URSS.

refuse tip n vertedero.

refute [rɪ'fjuːt] vt refutar, rebatir.

regain [rɪ'geɪn] vt recobrar, recuperar.

regal ['riːgl] adj regio, real.

regale [rɪ'geɪl] vt agasajar, entretener.

regalia [rɪ'geɪlɪə] n galas fpl.

regard [rɪ'gaːd] n (gaze) mirada; (aspect) respecto; (esteem) respeto, consideración f ♦ vt (consider) considerar; (look at) mirar; **to give one's ~s to** saludar de su parte a; **"(kind) ~s"** "muy atentamente"; **"with kindest ~s"** "con muchos recuerdos"; **~s to María, please give my ~s to María** recuerdos a María, dele recuerdos a María de mi parte; **as ~s, with ~ to** con respecto a, en cuanto a.

regarding [rɪ'gaːdɪŋ] prep con respecto a, en cuanto a.

regardless [rɪ'gaːdlɪs] adv a pesar de todo; **~ of** sin reparar en.

regatta [rɪ'gætə] n regata.

regency ['riːdʒənsɪ] n regencia.

regenerate [rɪ'dʒɛnəreɪt] vt regenerar.

regent ['riːdʒənt] n regente m/f.

reggae ['regeɪ] n reggae m.

régime [reɪ'ʒiːm] n régimen m.

regiment n ['rɛdʒɪmənt] regimiento ♦ vt ['rɛdʒɪmɛnt] reglamentar.

regimental [rɛdʒɪ'mɛntl] adj militar.

regimentation [rɛdʒɪmɛn'teɪʃən] n regimentación f.

region ['riːdʒən] n región f; **in the ~ of** (fig) alrededor de.

regional ['riːdʒənl] adj regional.

regional development n desarrollo regional.

register ['rɛdʒɪstə*] n registro ♦ vt registrar; (birth) declarar; (letter) certificar; (subj: instrument) marcar, indicar ♦ vi (at hotel) registrarse; (sign on) inscribirse; (make impression) producir impresión; **to ~ a protest** presentar una queja; **to ~ for a course** matricularse or inscribirse en un curso.

registered ['rɛdʒɪstəd] adj (design) registrado; (BRIT: letter) certificado; (student) matriculado; (voter) registrado.

registered company n sociedad f legalmente constituida.

registered nurse n (US) enfermero/a titulado/a.

registered office n domicilio social.

registered trademark n marca registrada.

registrar ['rɛdʒɪstraː*] n secretario/a (del registro civil).

registration [rɛdʒɪs'treɪʃən] n (act) declaración f; (AUT: also: ~ **number**) matrícula.

registry ['rɛdʒɪstrɪ] n registro.

registry office n (BRIT) registro civil; **to get married in a ~** casarse por lo civil.

regret [rɪ'grɛt] n sentimiento, pesar m; (remorse) remordimiento ♦ vt sentir, lamentar; (repent of) arrepentirse de; **we ~ to inform you that ...** sentimos informarle que ....

regretful [rɪ'grɛtful] adj pesaroso, arrepentido.

regretfully [rɪ'grɛtfəlɪ] adv con pesar, sentidamente.

regrettable [rɪ'grɛtəbl] adj lamentable; (loss) sensible.

regrettably [rɪ'grɛtəblɪ] adv desgraciadamente.

regroup [riː'gruːp] vt reagrupar ♦ vi reagruparse.

regt abbr = **regiment**.

regular ['rɛgjulə*] *adj* regular; (*soldier*) profesional; (*col: intensive*) verdadero; (*listener, reader*) asiduo, habitual ♦ *n* (*client etc*) cliente/a *m/f* habitual.

regularity [rɛgju'lærɪtɪ] *n* regularidad *f*.

regularly ['rɛgjulǝlɪ] *adv* con regularidad.

regulate ['rɛgjuleɪt] *vt* (*gen*) controlar; (*TECH*) regular, ajustar.

regulation [rɛgju'leɪʃǝn] *n* (*rule*) regla, reglamento; (*adjustment*) regulación *f*.

rehabilitate [riːǝ'bɪlɪteɪt] *vt* rehabilitar.

rehabilitation ['riːǝbɪlɪ'teɪʃǝn] *n* rehabilitación *f*.

rehash [riː'hæʃ] *vt* (*col*) hacer un refrito de.

rehearsal [rɪ'hǝːsǝl] *n* ensayo; **dress** ~ ensayo general *or* final.

rehearse [rɪ'hǝːs] *vt* ensayar.

rehouse [riː'hauz] *vt* dar nueva vivienda a.

reign [reɪn] *n* reinado; (*fig*) predominio ♦ *vi* reinar; (*fig*) imperar.

reigning ['reɪnɪŋ] *adj* (*monarch*) reinante, actual; (*predominant*) imperante.

reimburse [riːɪm'bǝːs] *vt* reembolsar.

rein [reɪn] *n* (*for horse*) rienda; **to give sb free** ~ dar rienda suelta a algn.

reincarnation [riːɪnkɑː'neɪʃǝn] *n* reencarnación *f*.

reindeer ['reɪndɪǝ*] *n* (*pl inv*) reno.

reinforce [riːɪn'fɔːs] *vt* reforzar.

reinforced concrete [riːɪn'fɔːst-] *n* hormigón armado.

reinforcement [riːɪn'fɔːsmǝnt] *n* (*action*) refuerzo; ~**s** *npl* (*MIL*) refuerzos *mpl*.

reinstate [riːɪn'steɪt] *vt* (*worker*) reintegrar (a su puesto).

reinstatement [riːɪn'steɪtmǝnt] *n* reintegración *f*.

reissue [riː'ɪʃuː] *vt* (*record, book*) reeditar.

reiterate [riː'ɪtǝreɪt] *vt* reiterar, repetir.

reject *n* ['riːdʒɛkt] (*thing*) desecho ♦ *vt* [rɪ'dʒɛkt] rechazar; (*proposition, offer etc*) descartar.

rejection [rɪ'dʒɛkʃǝn] *n* rechazo.

rejoice [rɪ'dʒɔɪs] *vi*: **to** ~ **at** *or* **over** regocijarse *or* alegrarse de.

rejoinder [rɪ'dʒɔɪndǝ*] *n* (*retort*) réplica.

rejuvenate [rɪ'dʒuːvǝneɪt] *vt* rejuvenecer.

rekindle [riː'kɪndl] *vt* volver a encender; (*fig*) despertar.

relapse [rɪ'læps] *n* (*MED*) recaída; (*into crime*) reincidencia.

relate [rɪ'leɪt] *vt* (*tell*) contar, relatar; (*connect*) relacionar ♦ *vi* relacionarse; **to** ~ **to** (*connect*) relacionarse *or* tener que ver con.

related [rɪ'leɪtɪd] *adj* afín; (*person*) emparentado; ~ **to** con referencia a, relacionado con.

relating [rɪ'leɪtɪŋ]: ~ **to** *prep* referente a.

relation [rɪ'leɪʃǝn] *n* (*person*) pariente *m/f*; (*link*) relación *f*; **in** ~ **to** en relación con, en lo que se refiere a; ~ **to** guardar relación con; **diplomatic/ international** ~**s** relaciones *fpl* diplomáticas/internacionales.

relationship [rɪ'leɪʃǝnʃɪp] *n* relación *f*; (*personal*) relaciones *fpl*; (*also: family* ~) parentesco.

relative ['rɛlǝtɪv] *n* pariente *m/f*, familiar *m/f* ♦ *adj* relativo.

relatively ['rɛlǝtɪvlɪ] *adv* (*fairly, rather*) relativamente.

relative pronoun *n* pronombre *m* relativo.

relax [rɪ'læks] *vi* descansar; (*quieten down*) relajarse ♦ *vt* relajar; (*grip*) aflojar; ~! (*calm down*) ¡tranquilo!

relaxation [riːlæk'seɪʃǝn] *n* (*rest*) descanso; (*easing*) relajación *f*, relajamiento *m*; (*amusement*) recreo; (*entertainment*) diversión *f*.

relaxed [rɪ'lækst] *adj* relajado; (*tranquil*) tranquilo.

relaxing [rɪ'læksɪŋ] *adj* relajante.

relay *n* ['riːleɪ] (*race*) carrera de relevos ♦ *vt* [rɪ'leɪ] (*RADIO, TV, pass on*) retransmitir.

release [rɪ'liːs] *n* (*liberation*) liberación *f*; (*discharge*) puesta en libertad *f*; (*of gas etc*) escape *m*; (*of film etc*) estreno ♦ *vt* (*prisoner*) poner en libertad; (*film*) estrenar; (*book*) publicar; (*piece of news*) difundir; (*gas etc*) despedir, arrojar; (*free: from wreckage etc*) liberar; (*TECH: catch, spring etc*) desenganchar; (*let go*) soltar, aflojar.

relegate ['rɛlǝgeɪt] *vt* relegar; (*SPORT*): **to be** ~**d** bajar a.

relent [rɪ'lɛnt] *vi* ceder, ablandarse; (*let up*) descansar.

relentless [rɪ'lɛntlɪs] *adj* implacable.

relentlessly [rɪ'lɛntlɪslɪ] *adv* implacablemente.

relevance ['rɛlǝvǝns] *n* relación *f*.

relevant ['rɛlǝvǝnt] *adj* (*fact*) pertinente; ~ **to** relacionado con.

reliability [rɪlaɪǝ'bɪlɪtɪ] *n* fiabilidad *f*; seguridad *f*; veracidad *f*.

reliable [rɪ'laɪǝbl] *adj* (*person, firm*) de confianza, de fiar; (*method, machine*) seguro; (*source*) fidedigno.

reliably [rɪ'laɪǝblɪ] *adv*: **to be** ~ **informed that** ... saber de fuente fidedigna que ....

reliance [rɪ'laɪǝns] *n*: ~ **(on)** dependencia (de).

reliant [rɪ'laɪǝnt] *adj*: **to be** ~ **on sth/sb**

dcpender de algo/algn.

relic ['rɛlɪk] n (REL) reliquia; (of the past) vestigio.

relief [rɪ'liːf] n (from pain, anxiety) alivio, desahogo; (help, supplies) socorro, ayuda; (ART, GEO) relieve m; **by way of light ~ a** modo de diversión.

relief road n carretera de descongestionamiento.

relieve [rɪ'liːv] vt (pain, patient) aliviar; (bring help to) ayudar, socorrer; (burden) aligerar; (take over from: gen) sustituir a; (: guard) relevar; **to ~ sb of sth** quitar algo a algn; **to ~ sb of his command** (MIL) relevar a algn de su mando; **to ~ o.s.** hacer sus necesidades; **I am ~d to hear you are better** me alivia saber que estás or te encuentras mejor.

religion [rɪ'lɪdʒən] n religión f.

religious [rɪ'lɪdʒəs] adj religioso.

religious education n educación f religiosa.

religiously [rɪ'lɪdʒəslɪ] adv religiosamente.

relinquish [rɪ'lɪŋkwɪʃ] vt abandonar; (plan, habit) renunciar a.

relish ['rɛlɪʃ] n (CULIN) salsa; (enjoyment) entusiasmo; (flavour) sabor m, gusto ♦ vt (food, challenge etc) saborear; **to ~ doing** gozar haciendo.

relive [riː'lɪv] vt vivir de nuevo, volver a vivir.

relocate [riːləʊ'keɪt] vt trasladar ♦ vi trasladarse.

reluctance [rɪ'lʌktəns] n desgana, renuencia.

reluctant [rɪ'lʌktənt] adj reacio; **to be ~ to do sth** resistirse a hacer algo.

reluctantly [rɪ'lʌktəntlɪ] adv de mala gana.

rely [rɪ'laɪ]: **to ~ on** vt fus confiar en, fiarse de; (be dependent on) depender de; **you can ~ on my discretion** puedes contar con mi discreción.

remain [rɪ'meɪn] vi (survive) quedar; (be left) sobrar; (continue) quedar(se), permanecer; **to ~ silent** permanecer callado.

remainder [rɪ'meɪndə*] n resto.

remaining [rɪ'meɪnɪŋ] adj sobrante.

remains [rɪ'meɪnz] npl restos mpl.

remand [rɪ'mɑːnd] n: **on ~** detenido (bajo custodia) ♦ vt: **to ~ in custody** mantener bajo custodia.

remand home n (BRIT) reformatorio.

remark [rɪ'mɑːk] n comentario ♦ vt comentar; **to ~ on sth** hacer observaciones sobre algo.

remarkable [rɪ'mɑːkəbl] adj notable; (outstanding) extraordinario.

remarkably [rɪ'mɑːkəblɪ] adv extraordinariamente.

remarry [riː'mærɪ] vi casarse por segunda vez, volver a casarse.

remedial [rɪ'miːdɪəl] adj: **~ education** educación f de los niños atrasados.

remedy ['rɛmədɪ] n remedio ♦ vt remediar, curar.

remember [rɪ'mɛmbə*] vt recordar, acordarse de; (bear in mind) tener presente; **I ~ seeing it, I ~ having seen it** recuerdo haberlo visto; **she ~ed doing it** se acordó de hacerlo; **~ me to your wife and children!** ¡déle recuerdos a su familia!

remembrance [rɪ'mɛmbrəns] n (memory, souvenir) recuerdo; **in ~ of** en conmemoración de.

Remembrance Day, Remembrance Sunday n (BRIT) ver recuadro.

remind [rɪ'maɪnd] vt: **to ~ sb to do sth** recordar a algn que haga algo; **to ~ sb of sth** recordar algo a algn; **she ~s me of her mother** me recuerda a su madre; **that ~s me!** ¡a propósito!

reminder [rɪ'maɪndə*] n notificación f; (memento) recuerdo.

reminisce [rɛmɪ'nɪs] vi recordar (viejas historias).

reminiscent [rɛmɪ'nɪsnt] adj: **to be ~ of sth** recordar algo.

remiss [rɪ'mɪs] adj descuidado; **it was ~ of me** fue un descuido de mi parte.

remission [rɪ'mɪʃən] n remisión f; (of sentence) reducción f de la pena.

remit [rɪ'mɪt] vt (send: money) remitir, enviar.

remittance [rɪ'mɪtns] n remesa, envío.

remnant ['rɛmnənt] n resto; (of cloth) retal m, retazo; **~s** npl (COMM) restos de serie.

remonstrate ['rɛmənstreɪt] *vi* protestar.
remorse [rɪ'mɔːs] *n* remordimientos *mpl*.
remorseful [rɪ'mɔːsful] *adj* arrepentido.
remorseless [rɪ'mɔːslɪs] *adj* (*fig*)
implacable, inexorable.
remorselessly [rɪ'mɔːslɪslɪ] *adv*
implacablemente, inexorablemente.
remote [rɪ'məut] *adj* remoto; (*distant*)
lejano; (*person*) distante; **there is a** ~
possibility that ... hay una posibilidad
remota de que ....
remote control *n* mando a distancia.
remote-controlled [rɪ'məutkən'trəuld] *adj*
teledirigido, con mando a distancia.
remotely [rɪ'məutlɪ] *adv* remotamente;
(*slightly*) levemente.
remoteness [rɪ'məutnɪs] *n* alejamiento;
distancia.
remould ['riːməuld] *n* (*BRIT: tyre*) neumático
or llanta (*LAM*) recauchutado/a.
removable [rɪ'muːvəbl] *adj* (*detachable*)
separable.
removal [rɪ'muːvəl] *n* (*taking away*) (el)
quitar; (*BRIT: from house*) mudanza; (*from
office: dismissal*) destitución *f*; (*MED*)
extirpación *f*.
removal van *n* (*BRIT*) camión *m* de
mudanzas.
remove [rɪ'muːv] *vt* quitar; (*employee*)
destituir; (*name: from list*) tachar, borrar;
(*doubt*) disipar; (*TECH*) retirar, separar;
(*MED*) extirpar; **first cousin once** ~**d**
(*parent's cousin*) tío/a segundo/a; (*cousin's
child*) sobrino/a segundo/a.
remover [rɪ'muːvə*] *n*: **make-up** ~
desmaquilladora.
remunerate [rɪ'mjuːnəreɪt] *vt* remunerar.
remuneration [rɪmjuːnə'reɪʃən] *n*
remuneración *f*.
Renaissance [rɪ'neɪsɔ̃s] *n*: **the** ~ el
Renacimiento.
rename [riː'neɪm] *vt* poner nuevo nombre
a.
render ['rɛndə*] *vt* (*thanks*) dar; (*aid*)
proporcionar; (*honour*) dar, conceder;
(*assistance*) dar, prestar; **to** ~ **sth** + *adj*
volver algo + *adj*.
rendering ['rɛndərɪŋ] *n* (*MUS etc*)
interpretación *f*.
rendez-vous ['rɔndɪvuː] *n* cita ♦ *vi*
reunirse, encontrarse; (*spaceship*)
efectuar una reunión espacial.
rendition [rɛn'dɪʃən] *n* (*MUS*)
interpretación *f*.
renegade ['rɛnɪgeɪd] *n* renegado/a.
renew [rɪ'njuː] *vt* renovar; (*resume*)
reanudar; (*extend date*) prorrogar;
(*negotiations*) volver a.

renewable [rɪ'njuːəbl] *adj* renovable; ~
energy, ~**s** energías renovables.
renewal [rɪ'njuːəl] *n* renovación *f*;
reanudación *f*; prórroga.
renounce [rɪ'nauns] *vt* renunciar a; (*right,
inheritance*) renunciar.
renovate ['rɛnəveɪt] *vt* renovar.
renovation [rɛnə'veɪʃən] *n* renovación *f*.
renown [rɪ'naun] *n* renombre *m*.
renowned [rɪ'naund] *adj* renombrado.
rent [rɛnt] *n* alquiler *m*; (*for house*)
arriendo, renta ♦ *vt* (*also*: ~ **out**) alquilar.
rental ['rɛntl] *n* (*for television, car*) alquiler
m.
rent boy *n* (*BRIT col*) chapero.
renunciation [rɪnʌnsɪ'eɪʃən] *n* renuncia.
reopen [riː'əupən] *vt* volver a abrir,
reabrir.
reorder [riː'ɔːdə*] *vt* volver a pedir, repetir
el pedido de; (*rearrange*) volver a ordenar
or arreglar.
reorganization [riːɔːgənaɪ'zeɪʃən] *n*
reorganización *f*.
reorganize [riː'ɔːgənaɪz] *vt* reorganizar.
rep [rɛp] *n abbr* (*COMM*) = **representative;**
(*THEAT*) = **repertory**.
Rep. *abbr* (*US POL*) = **representative,
republican**.
repair [rɪ'pɛə*] *n* reparación *f*, arreglo;
(*patch*) remiendo ♦ *vt* reparar, arreglar;
in good/bad ~ en buen/mal estado; **under**
~ en obras.
repair kit *n* caja de herramientas.
repair man *n* mecánico.
repair shop *n* taller *m* de reparaciones.
repartee [rɛpɑː'tiː] *n* réplicas *fpl* agudas.
repast [rɪ'pɑːst] *n* (*formal*) comida.
repatriate [riː'pætrɪeɪt] *vt* repatriar.
repay [riː'peɪ] *vt* (*irreg: like* **pay**) (*money*)
devolver, reembolsar; (*person*) pagar;
(*debt*) liquidar; (*sb's efforts*) devolver,
corresponder a.
repayment [riː'peɪmənt] *n* reembolso,
devolución *f*; (*sum of money*) recompensa.
repeal [rɪ'piːl] *n* revocación *f* ♦ *vt* revocar.
repeat [rɪ'piːt] *n* (*RADIO, TV*) reposición *f* ♦ *vt*
repetir ♦ *vi* repetirse.
repeatedly [rɪ'piːtɪdlɪ] *adv* repetidas veces.
repeat order *n* (*COMM*): **to place a** ~ **for**
renovar un pedido de.
repel [rɪ'pɛl] *vt* repugnar.
repellent [rɪ'pɛlənt] *adj* repugnante ♦ *n*:
insect ~ crema/loción *f* anti-insectos.
repent [rɪ'pɛnt] *vi*: **to** ~ (**of**) arrepentirse
(de).
repentance [rɪ'pɛntəns] *n* arrepentimiento.
repercussion [riːpə'kʌʃən] *n* (*consequence*)
repercusión *f*; **to have** ~**s** repercutir.

repertoire ['rɛpətwɑː*] n repertorio.
repertory ['rɛpətərɪ] n (also: ~ **theatre**) teatro de repertorio.
repertory company n compañía de repertorio.
repetition [rɛpɪ'tɪʃən] n repetición f.
repetitious [rɛpɪ'tɪʃəs] adj repetidor(a), que se repite.
repetitive [rɪ'pɛtɪtɪv] adj (movement, work) repetitivo, reiterativo; (speech) lleno de repeticiones.
rephrase [riː'freɪz] vt decir or formular de otro modo.
replace [rɪ'pleɪs] vt (put back) devolver a su sitio; (take the place of) reemplazar, sustituir.
replacement [rɪ'pleɪsmənt] n reemplazo; (act) reposición f; (thing) recambio; (person) suplente m/f.
replacement cost n costo de sustitución.
replacement part n repuesto.
replacement value n valor m de sustitución.
replay ['riːpleɪ] n (SPORT) partido de desempate; (TV: playback) repetición f.
replenish [rɪ'plɛnɪʃ] vt (tank etc) rellenar; (stock etc) reponer; (with fuel) repostar.
replete [rɪ'pliːt] adj repleto, lleno.
replica ['rɛplɪkə] n réplica, reproducción f.
reply [rɪ'plaɪ] n respuesta, contestación f ♦ vi contestar, responder; **in** ~ en respuesta; **there's no** ~ (TEL) no contestan.
reply coupon n cupón-respuesta m.
reply-paid [rɪ'plaɪ'peɪd] adj: ~ **postcard** tarjeta postal con respuesta pagada.
report [rɪ'pɔːt] n informe m; (PRESS etc) reportaje m; (BRIT: also: **school** ~) informe m escolar; (of gun) detonación f ♦ vt informar sobre; (PRESS etc) hacer un reportaje sobre; (notify: accident, culprit) denunciar ♦ vi (make a ~) presentar un informe; (present o.s.): **to** · (**to sb**): presentarse (ante algn); **annual** ~ (COMM) informe m anual; **to** ~ (**on**) hacer un informe (sobre); **it is** ~**ed from Berlin that** ... se informa desde Berlín que ....
report card n (US, Scottish) cartilla escolar.
reportedly [rɪ'pɔːtɪdlɪ] adv según se dice, según se informa.
reporter [rɪ'pɔːtə*] n (PRESS) periodista m/f, reportero/a; (RADIO, TV) locutor(a) m/f.
repose [rɪ'pəuz] n: **in** ~ (face, mouth) en reposo.
repossess [riːpə'zɛs] vt recuperar.
repossession order [riːpə'zɛʃən-] n orden de devolución de la vivienda por el impago de la hipoteca.
reprehensible [rɛprɪ'hɛnsɪbl] adj reprensible, censurable.
represent [rɛprɪ'zɛnt] vt representar; (COMM) ser agente de.
representation [rɛprɪzɛn'teɪʃən] n representación f; (petition) petición f; ~**s** npl (protest) quejas fpl.
representative [rɛprɪ'zɛntətɪv] n (US POL) representante m/f, diputado/a; (COMM) representante m/f ♦ adj: ~ (**of**) representativo (de).
repress [rɪ'prɛs] vt reprimir.
repression [rɪ'prɛʃən] n represión f.
repressive [rɪ'prɛsɪv] adj represivo.
reprieve [rɪ'priːv] n (LAW) indulto; (fig) alivio ♦ vt indultar; (fig) salvar.
reprimand ['rɛprɪmɑːnd] n reprimenda ♦ vt reprender.
reprint ['riːprɪnt] n reimpresión f ♦ vt [riː'prɪnt] reimprimir.
reprisal [rɪ'praɪzl] n represalia; **to take** ~**s** tomar represalias.
reproach [rɪ'prəutʃ] n reproche m ♦ vt: **to** ~ **sb with sth** reprochar algo a algn; **beyond** ~ intachable.
reproachful [rɪ'prəutʃful] adj de reproche, de acusación.
reproduce [riːprə'djuːs] vt reproducir ♦ vi reproducirse.
reproduction [riːprə'dʌkʃən] n reproducción f.
reproductive [riːprə'dʌktɪv] adj reproductor(a).
reproof [rɪ'pruːf] n reproche m.
reprove [rɪ'pruːv] vt: **to** ~ **sb for sth** reprochar algo a algn.
reptile ['rɛptaɪl] n reptil m.
republic [rɪ'pʌblɪk] n república.
republican [rɪ'pʌblɪkən] adj, n republicano/a m/f.
repudiate [rɪ'pjuːdɪeɪt] vt (accusation) rechazar; (obligation) negarse a reconocer.
repudiation [rɪpjuːdɪ'eɪʃən] n incumplimiento.
repugnance [rɪ'pʌgnəns] n repugnancia.
repugnant [rɪ'pʌgnənt] adj repugnante.
repulse [rɪ'pʌls] vt rechazar.
repulsion [rɪ'pʌlʃən] n repulsión f, repugnancia.
repulsive [rɪ'pʌlsɪv] adj repulsivo.
repurchase [riː'pɜːtʃəs] vt volver a comprar, readquirir.
reputable ['rɛpjutəbl] adj (make etc) de renombre.
reputation [rɛpju'teɪʃən] n reputación f; **he has a** · **for being awkward** tiene fama de

difícil.

repute [rɪ'pjuːt] _n_ reputación _f_, fama.

reputed [rɪ'pjuːtɪd] _adj_ supuesto; **to be ~ to be rich/intelligent** _etc_ tener fama de rico/inteligente _etc_.

reputedly [rɪ'pjuːtɪdlɪ] _adv_ según dicen _or_ se dice.

request [rɪ'kwɛst] _n_ solicitud _f_, petición _f_ ♦ _vt_: **to ~ sth of** _or_ **from sb** solicitar algo a algn; **at the ~ of** a petición de; **"you are ~ed not to smoke"** "se ruega no fumar".

request stop _n_ (_BRIT_) parada discrecional.

requiem ['rɛkwɪəm] _n_ réquiem _m_.

require [rɪ'kwaɪə*] _vt_ (_need: subj: person_) necesitar, tener necesidad de; (: _thing, situation_) exigir, requerir; (_want_) pedir; (_demand_) insistir en que; **to ~ sb to do sth/sth of sb** exigir que algn haga algo; **what qualifications are ~d?** ¿qué títulos se requieren?; **~d by law** requerido por la ley.

requirement [rɪ'kwaɪəmənt] _n_ requisito; (_need_) necesidad _f_.

requisite ['rɛkwɪzɪt] _n_ requisito ♦ _adj_ necesario, requerido.

requisition [rɛkwɪ'zɪʃən] _n_ solicitud _f_; (_MIL_) requisa ♦ _vt_ (_MIL_) requisar.

reroute [riː'ruːt] _vt_ desviar.

resale ['riːseɪl] _n_ reventa.

resale price maintenance _n_ mantenimiento del precio de venta.

rescind [rɪ'sɪnd] _vt_ (_LAW_) abrogar; (_contract_) rescindir; (_order etc_) anular.

rescue ['rɛskjuː] _n_ rescate _m_ ♦ _vt_ rescatar; **to come/go to sb's ~** ir en auxilio de uno, socorrer a algn; **to ~ from** librar de.

rescue party _n_ equipo de salvamento.

rescuer ['rɛskjuə*] _n_ salvador(a) _m/f_.

research [rɪ'səːtʃ] _n_ investigaciones _fpl_ ♦ _vt_ investigar; **a piece of ~** un trabajo de investigación; **to ~ (into sth)** investigar (algo).

research and development (R & D) _n_ investigación _f_ y desarrollo.

researcher [rɪ'səːtʃə*] _n_ investigador(a) _m/f_.

research work _n_ investigación _f_.

resell [riː'sɛl] _vt_ revender.

resemblance [rɪ'zɛmbləns] _n_ parecido; **to bear a strong ~ to** parecerse mucho a.

resemble [rɪ'zɛmbl] _vt_ parecerse a.

resent [rɪ'zɛnt] _vt_ resentirse por, ofenderse por; **he ~s my being here** le molesta que esté aquí.

resentful [rɪ'zɛntful] _adj_ resentido.

resentment [rɪ'zɛntmənt] _n_ resentimiento.

reservation [rɛzə'veɪʃən] _n_ reserva; (_BRIT: also: **central ~**_) mediana; **with ~s** con reservas.

reservation desk _n_ (_US: in hotel_) recepción _f_.

reserve [rɪ'zəːv] _n_ reserva; (_SPORT_) suplente _m/f_ ♦ _vt_ (_seats etc_) reservar; **~s** _npl_ (_MIL_) reserva _sg_; **in ~** en reserva.

reserve currency _n_ divisa de reserva.

reserved [rɪ'zəːvd] _adj_ reservado.

reserve price _n_ (_BRIT_) precio mínimo.

reserve team _n_ (_SPORT_) equipo de reserva.

reservist [rɪ'zəːvɪst] _n_ (_MIL_) reservista _m_.

reservoir ['rɛzəvwɑː*] _n_ (_artificial lake_) embalse _m_, represa; (_small_) depósito.

reset [riː'sɛt] _vt_ (_COMPUT_) reinicializar.

reshape [riː'ʃeɪp] _vt_ (_policy_) reformar, rehacer.

reshuffle [riː'ʃʌfl] _n_: **Cabinet ~** (_POL_) remodelación _f_ del gabinete.

reside [rɪ'zaɪd] _vi_ residir.

residence ['rɛzɪdəns] _n_ residencia; (_formal: home_) domicilio; (_length of stay_) permanencia; **in ~** (_doctor_) residente; **to take up ~** instalarse.

residence permit _n_ (_BRIT_) permiso de residencia.

resident ['rɛzɪdənt] _n_ vecino/a; (_in hotel_) huésped/a _m/f_ ♦ _adj_ residente; (_population_) permanente.

residential [rɛzɪ'dɛnʃəl] _adj_ residencial.

residue ['rɛzɪdjuː] _n_ resto, residuo.

resign [rɪ'zaɪn] _vt_ (_gen_) renunciar a ♦ _vi_: **to ~ (from)** dimitir (de), renunciar (a); **to ~ o.s. to** (_endure_) resignarse a.

resignation [rɛzɪg'neɪʃən] _n_ dimisión _f_; (_state of mind_) resignación _f_; **to tender one's ~** presentar la dimisión.

resigned [rɪ'zaɪnd] _adj_ resignado.

resilience [rɪ'zɪlɪəns] _n_ (_of material_) elasticidad _f_; (_of person_) resistencia.

resilient [rɪ'zɪlɪənt] _adj_ (_person_) resistente.

resin ['rɛzɪn] _n_ resina.

resist [rɪ'zɪst] _vt_ resistirse a; (_temptation, damage_) resistir.

resistance [rɪ'zɪstəns] _n_ resistencia.

resistant [rɪ'zɪstənt] _adj_: **~ (to)** resistente (a).

resolute ['rɛzəluːt] _adj_ resuelto.

resolutely ['rɛzəluːtlɪ] _adv_ resueltamente.

resolution [rɛzə'luːʃən] _n_ (_gen_) resolución _f_; (_purpose_) propósito; (_COMPUT_) definición _f_; **to make a ~** tomar una resolución.

resolve [rɪ'zɔlv] _n_ (_determination_) resolución _f_; (_purpose_) propósito ♦ _vt_ resolver ♦ _vi_ resolverse; **to ~ to do** resolver hacer.

resolved [rɪ'zɔlvd] _adj_ resuelto.

resonance ['rɛzənəns] _n_ resonancia.

resonant ['rɛzənənt] *adj* resonante.

resort [rɪ'zɔːt] *n* (*town*) centro turístico; (*recourse*) recurso ♦ *vi*: **to ~ to** recurrir a; **in the last ~** como último recurso; **seaside/winter sports ~** playa, estación *f* balnearia/centro de deportes de invierno.

resound [rɪ'zaund] *vi*: **to ~ (with)** resonar (con).

resounding [rɪ'zaundɪŋ] *adj* sonoro; (*fig*) clamoroso.

resource [rɪ'sɔːs] *n* recurso; **~s** *npl* recursos *mpl*; **natural ~s** recursos *mpl* naturales; **to leave sb to his/her own ~s** (*fig*) abandonar a algn/a a sus propios recursos.

resourceful [rɪ'sɔːsful] *adj* ingenioso.

resourcefulness [rɪ'sɔːsfulnɪs] *n* inventiva, iniciativa.

respect [rɪs'pɛkt] *n* (*consideration*) respeto; (*relation*) respecto; **~s** *npl* recuerdos *mpl*, saludos *mpl* ♦ *vt* respetar; **with ~ to** con respecto a; **in this ~** en cuanto a eso; **to have** *or* **show ~ for** tener *or* mostrar respeto a; **out of ~ for** por respeto a; **in some ~s** en algunos aspectos; **with due ~ I still think you're wrong** con el respeto debido, sigo creyendo que está equivocado.

respectability [rɪspɛktə'bɪlɪtɪ] *n* respetabilidad *f*.

respectable [rɪs'pɛktəbl] *adj* respetable; (*quite big: amount etc*) apreciable; (*passable*) tolerable; (*quite good: player, result etc*) bastante bueno.

respected [rɪs'pɛktɪd] *adj* respetado, estimado.

respectful [rɪs'pɛktful] *adj* respetuoso.

respectfully [rɪs'pɛktfulɪ] *adv* respetuosamente; **Yours ~** Le saluda atentamente.

respecting [rɪs'pɛktɪŋ] *prep* (con) respecto a, en cuanto a.

respective [rɪs'pɛktɪv] *adj* respectivo.

respectively [rɪs'pɛktɪvlɪ] *adv* respectivamente.

respiration [rɛspɪ'reɪʃən] *n* respiración *f*.

respiratory [rɛs'pɪrətərɪ] *adj* respiratorio.

respite ['rɛspaɪt] *n* respiro; (*LAW*) prórroga.

resplendent [rɪs'plɛndənt] *adj* resplandeciente.

respond [rɪs'pɒnd] *vi* responder; (*react*) reaccionar.

respondent [rɪs'pɒndənt] *n* (*LAW*) demandado/a.

response [rɪs'pɒns] *n* respuesta; (*reaction*) reacción *f*; **in ~ to** como respuesta a.

responsibility [rɪspɒnsɪ'bɪlɪtɪ] *n* responsabilidad *f*; **to take ~ for sth/sb** admitir responsabilidad por algo/uno.

responsible [rɪs'pɒnsɪbl] *adj* (*liable*): **~ (for)** responsable (de); (*character*) serio, formal; (*job*) de responsabilidad; **to be ~ to sb (for sth)** ser responsable ante algn (de algo).

responsibly [rɪs'pɒnsɪblɪ] *adv* con seriedad.

responsive [rɪs'pɒnsɪv] *adj* sensible.

rest [rɛst] *n* descanso, reposo; (*MUS*) pausa, silencio; (*support*) apoyo; (*remainder*) resto ♦ *vi* descansar; (*be supported*): **to ~ on** apoyarse en ♦ *vt* (*lean*): **to ~ sth on/against** apoyar algo en *or* sobre/contra; **the ~ of them** (*people, objects*) los demás; **to set sb's mind at ~** tranquilizar a algn; **to ~ one's eyes** *or* **gaze on** fijar la mirada en; **it ~s with him** depende de él; **~ assured that ...** tenga por seguro que ....

restaurant ['rɛstərɒŋ] *n* restaurante *m*.

restaurant car *n* (*BRIT*) coche-comedor *m*.

restaurant owner *n* dueño/a *or* propietario/a de un restaurante.

rest cure *n* cura de reposo.

restful ['rɛstful] *adj* descansado, tranquilo.

rest home *n* residencia de ancianos.

restitution [rɛstɪ'tjuːʃən] *n*: **to make ~ to sb for sth** restituir algo a algn; (*paying*) indemnizar a algn por algo.

restive ['rɛstɪv] *adj* inquieto; (*horse*) rebelón/ona.

restless ['rɛstlɪs] *adj* inquieto; **to get ~** impacientarse.

restlessly ['rɛstlɪslɪ] *adv* inquietamente, con inquietud *f*.

restlessness ['rɛstlɪsnɪs] *n* inquietud *f*.

restock [riː'stɔk] *vt* reaprovisionar.

restoration [rɛstə'reɪʃən] *n* restauración *f*; (*giving back*) devolución *f*, restitución *f*.

restorative [rɪ'stɔːrətɪv] *adj* reconstituyente, fortalecedor(a) ♦ *n* reconstituyente *m*.

restore [rɪ'stɔː*] *vt* (*building*) restaurar; (*sth stolen*) devolver, restituir; (*health*) restablecer.

restorer [rɪ'stɔːrə*] *n* (*ART etc*) restaurador(a) *m/f*.

restrain [rɪs'treɪn] *vt* (*feeling*) contener, refrenar; (*person*): **to ~ (from doing)** disuadir (de hacer).

restrained [rɪs'treɪnd] *adj* (*style*) reservado.

restraint [rɪs'treɪnt] *n* (*restriction*) freno, control *m*; (*of style*) reserva; **wage ~** control *m* de los salarios.

restrict [rɪs'trɪkt] *vt* restringir, limitar.

restricted [rɪs'trɪktɪd] *adj* restringido, limitado.

restriction [rɪs'trɪkʃən] *n* restricción *f*,

limitación *f*.
restrictive [rɪsˈtrɪktɪv] *adj* restrictivo.
restrictive practices *npl* (*INDUSTRY*)
prácticas *fpl* restrictivas.
rest room *n* (*US*) aseos *mpl*.
restructure [riːˈstrʌktʃə*] *vt* reestructurar.
result [rɪˈzʌlt] *n* resultado ◆ *vi*: **to ~ in**
terminar en, tener por resultado; **as a ~**
of a *or* como consecuencia de; **to ~ (from)**
resultar (de).
resultant [rɪˈzʌltənt] *adj* resultante.
resume [rɪˈzjuːm] *vt* (*work, journey*)
reanudar; (*sum up*) resumir ◆ *vi* (*meeting*)
continuar.
résumé [ˈreɪzjuːmeɪ] *n* resumen *m*.
resumption [rɪˈzʌmpʃən] *n* reanudación *f*.
resurgence [rɪˈsɜːdʒəns] *n* resurgimiento.
resurrection [rezəˈrekʃən] *n* resurrección *f*.
resuscitate [rɪˈsʌsɪteɪt] *vt* (*MED*) resucitar.
resuscitation [rɪsʌsɪˈteɪʃn] *n* resucitación *f*.
retail [ˈriːteɪl] *n* venta al por menor ◆ *cpd* al
por menor ◆ *vt* vender al por menor *or* al
detalle ◆ *vi*: **to ~ at** (*COMM*) tener precio
de venta al público de.
retailer [ˈriːteɪlə*] *n* minorista *m/f*, detallista
m/f.
retail outlet *n* punto de venta.
retail price *n* precio de venta al público,
precio al detalle *or* al por menor.
retail price index *n* índice *m* de precios al
por menor.
retain [rɪˈteɪn] *vt* (*keep*) retener, conservar;
(*employ*) contratar.
retainer [rɪˈteɪnə*] *n* (*servant*) criado; (*fee*)
anticipo.
retaliate [rɪˈtælɪeɪt] *vi*: **to ~ (against)** tomar
represalias (contra).
retaliation [rɪtælɪˈeɪʃən] *n* represalias *fpl*; **in**
~ for como represalia por.
retaliatory [rɪˈtælɪətərɪ] *adj* de represalia.
retarded [rɪˈtɑːdɪd] *adj* retrasado.
retch [retʃ] *vi* darle a algn arcadas.
retentive [rɪˈtentɪv] *adj* (*memory*) retentivo.
rethink [riːˈθɪŋk] *vt* repensar.
reticence [ˈretɪsns] *n* reticencia, reserva.
reticent [ˈretɪsnt] *adj* reticente, reservado.
retina [ˈretɪnə] *n* retina.
retinue [ˈretɪnjuː] *n* séquito, comitiva.
retire [rɪˈtaɪə*] *vi* (*give up work*) jubilarse;
(*withdraw*) retirarse; (*go to bed*)
acostarse.
retired [rɪˈtaɪəd] *adj* (*person*) jubilado.
retirement [rɪˈtaɪəmənt] *n* jubilación *f*;
early ~ jubilación *f* anticipada.
retiring [rɪˈtaɪərɪŋ] *adj* (*departing: chairman*)
saliente; (*shy*) retraído.
retort [rɪˈtɔːt] *n* (*reply*) réplica ◆ *vi* replicar.
retrace [riːˈtreɪs] *vt*: **to ~ one's steps** volver

sobre sus pasos, desandar lo andado.
retract [rɪˈtrækt] *vt* (*statement*) retirar;
(*claws*) retraer; (*undercarriage, aerial*)
replegar ◆ *vi* retractarse.
retractable [rɪˈtræktəbl] *adj* replegable.
retrain [riːˈtreɪn] *vt* reciclar.
retraining [riːˈtreɪnɪŋ] *n* reciclaje *m*,
readaptación *f* profesional.
retread [ˈriːtred] *n* neumático *or* llanta
(*LAM*) recauchutado/a.
retreat [rɪˈtriːt] *n* (*place*) retiro; (*MIL*)
retirada ◆ *vi* retirarse; (*flood*) bajar; **to**
beat a hasty ~ (*fig*) retirarse en
desbandada.
retrial [ˈriːtraɪəl] *n* nuevo proceso.
retribution [retrɪˈbjuːʃən] *n* desquite *m*.
retrieval [rɪˈtriːvəl] *n* recuperación *f*;
information ~ recuperación *f* de datos.
retrieve [rɪˈtriːv] *vt* recobrar; (*situation,*
honour) salvar; (*COMPUT*) recuperar;
(*error*) reparar.
retriever [rɪˈtriːvə*] *n* perro cobrador.
retroactive [retrəuˈæktɪv] *adj* retroactivo.
retrograde [ˈretrəgreɪd] *adj* retrógrado.
retrospect [ˈretrəspekt] *n*: **in ~**
retrospectivamente.
retrospective [retrəˈspektɪv] *adj*
retrospectivo; (*law*) retroactivo ◆ *n*
exposición *f* retrospectiva.
return [rɪˈtɜːn] *n* (*going or coming back*)
vuelta, regreso; (*of sth stolen etc*)
devolución *f*; (*recompense*) recompensa;
(*FINANCE: from land, shares*) ganancia,
ingresos *mpl*; (*COMM: of merchandise*)
devolución *f* ◆ *cpd* (*journey*) de regreso;
(*BRIT: ticket*) de ida y vuelta; (*match*) de
vuelta ◆ *vi* (*person etc: come or go back*)
volver, regresar; (*symptoms etc*)
reaparecer ◆ *vt* devolver; (*favour, love etc*)
corresponder a; (*verdict*) pronunciar;
(*POL: candidate*) elegir; **~s** *npl* (*COMM*)
ingresos *mpl*; **tax ~** declaración *f* de la
renta; **in ~ (for)** a cambio (de); **by ~ of**
post a vuelta de correo; **many happy ~s**
(of the day)! ¡feliz cumpleaños!
returnable [rɪˈtɜːnəbl] *adj*: **~ bottle** envase
m retornable.
returner [rɪˈtɜːnə*] *n* *mujer que vuelve a*
trabajar tras un tiempo dedicada a la
familia.
returning officer [rɪˈtɜːnɪŋ-] *n* (*BRIT POL*)
escrutador(a) *m/f*.
return key *n* (*COMPUT*) tecla de retorno.
reunion [riːˈjuːnɪən] *n* reencuentro.
reunite [riːjuːˈnaɪt] *vt* reunir; (*reconcile*)
reconciliar.
rev [rev] *n* *abbr* (*AUT*: = *revolution*)
revolución *f* ◆ (*vb: also*: **~ up**) *vt* acelerar.

revaluation [riːvæljuːˈeɪʃən] n revalorización f.

revamp [riːˈvæmp] vt renovar.

Rev(d). abbr (= reverend) R., Rvdo.

reveal [rɪˈviːl] vt (make known) revelar.

revealing [rɪˈviːlɪŋ] adj revelador(a).

reveille [rɪˈvælɪ] n (MIL) diana.

revel [ˈrɛvl] vi: **to ~ in sth/in doing sth** gozar de algo/haciendo algo.

revelation [rɛvəˈleɪʃən] n revelación f.

reveller, (US) **reveler** [ˈrɛvlə*] n jaranero, juerguista m/f.

revelry [ˈrɛvlrɪ] n jarana, juerga.

revenge [rɪˈvɛndʒ] n venganza; (in sport) revancha; **to take ~ on** vengarse de; **to get one's ~ (for sth)** vengarse (de algo).

revengeful [rɪˈvɛndʒful] adj vengativo.

revenue [ˈrɛvənjuː] n ingresos mpl, rentas fpl.

revenue account n cuenta de ingresos presupuestarios.

revenue expenditure n gasto corriente.

reverberate [rɪˈvəːbəreɪt] vi (sound) resonar, retumbar.

reverberation [rɪvəːbəˈreɪʃən] n resonancia.

revere [rɪˈvɪə*] vt reverenciar, venerar.

reverence [ˈrɛvərəns] n reverencia.

Reverend [ˈrɛvərənd] adj (in titles): **the ~ John Smith** (Anglican) el Reverendo John Smith; (Catholic) el Padre John Smith; (Protestant) el Pastor John Smith.

reverent [ˈrɛvərənt] adj reverente.

reverie [ˈrɛvərɪ] n ensueño.

reversal [rɪˈvəːsl] n (of order) inversión f; (of policy) cambio de rumbo; (of decision) revocación f.

reverse [rɪˈvəːs] n (opposite) contrario; (back: of cloth) revés m; (: of coin) reverso; (: of paper) dorso; (AUT: also: ~ **gear**) marcha atrás ♦ adj (order) inverso; (direction) contrario ♦ vt (decision, AUT) dar marcha atrás a; (position, function) invertir ♦ vi (BRIT AUT) poner en marcha atrás; **in ~ order** en orden inverso; **the ~** lo contrario; **to go into ~** dar marcha atrás.

reverse-charge call [rɪˈvəːstʃɑːdʒ-] n (BRIT) llamada a cobro revertido.

reverse video n vídeo inverso.

reversible [rɪˈvəːsəbl] adj (garment, procedure) reversible.

reversing lights [rɪˈvəːsɪŋ-] npl (BRIT AUT) luces fpl de marcha atrás.

revert [rɪˈvəːt] vi: **to ~ to** volver or revertir a.

review [rɪˈvjuː] n (magazine, MIL) revista; (of book, film) reseña; (US: examination) repaso, examen m ♦ vt repasar, examinar; (MIL) pasar revista a; (book, film) reseñar; **to come under ~** ser examinado.

reviewer [rɪˈvjuːə*] n crítico/a.

revile [rɪˈvaɪl] vt injuriar, vilipendiar.

revise [rɪˈvaɪz] vt (manuscript) corregir; (opinion) modificar; (BRIT: study: subject) repasar; (look over) revisar; **~d edition** edición f corregida.

revision [rɪˈvɪʒən] n corrección f; modificación f; (of subject) repaso; (revised version) revisión f.

revisit [riːˈvɪzɪt] vt volver a visitar.

revitalize [riːˈvaɪtəlaɪz] vt revivificar.

revival [rɪˈvaɪvəl] n (recovery) reanimación f; (POL) resurgimiento; (of interest) renacimiento; (THEAT) reestreno; (of faith) despertar m

revive [rɪˈvaɪv] vt resucitar; (custom) restablecer; (hope, courage) reanimar; (play) reestrenar ♦ vi (person) volver en sí; (from tiredness) reponerse; (business) reactivarse.

revoke [rɪˈvəuk] vt revocar.

revolt [rɪˈvəult] n rebelión f ♦ vi rebelarse, sublevarse ♦ vt dar asco a, repugnar; **to ~ (against sb/sth)** rebelarse (contra algn/algo).

revolting [rɪˈvəultɪŋ] adj asqueroso, repugnante.

revolution [rɛvəˈluːʃən] n revolución f.

revolutionary [rɛvəˈluːʃənrɪ] adj, n revolucionario/a m/f.

revolutionize [rɛvəˈluːʃənaɪz] vt revolucionar.

revolve [rɪˈvɔlv] vi dar vueltas, girar.

revolver [rɪˈvɔlvə*] n revólver m.

revolving [rɪˈvɔlvɪŋ] adj (chair, door etc) giratorio.

revue [rɪˈvjuː] n (THEAT) revista.

revulsion [rɪˈvʌlʃən] n asco, repugnancia.

reward [rɪˈwɔːd] n premio, recompensa ♦ vt: **to ~ (for)** recompensar or premiar (por).

rewarding [rɪˈwɔːdɪŋ] adj (fig) gratificante; **financially ~** económicamente provechoso.

rewind [riːˈwaɪnd] vt (watch) dar cuerda a; (wool etc) devanar.

rewire [riːˈwaɪə*] vt (house) renovar la instalación eléctrica de.

reword [riːˈwəːd] vt expresar en otras palabras.

rewrite [riːˈraɪt] vt (irreg: like **write**) reescribir.

Reykjavik [ˈreɪkjəviːk] n Reykjavik m.

RFD abbr (US POST)= rural free delivery.

Rh abbr (= rhesus) Rh m.

rhapsody ['ræpsədɪ] n (MUS) rapsodia; (fig):
to go into rhapsodies over extasiarse por.
rhesus negative ['riːsəs-] adj (MED) Rh
negativo.
rhesus positive adj (MED) Rh positivo.
rhetoric ['rɛtərɪk] n retórica.
rhetorical [rɪ'tɔrɪkl] adj retórico.
rheumatic [ruː'mætɪk] adj reumático.
rheumatism ['ruːmətɪzəm] n reumatismo,
reúma.
rheumatoid arthritis ['ruːmətɔɪd-] n
reúma m articular.
Rhine [raɪn] n: the ~ el (río) Rin.
rhinestone ['raɪnstəun] n diamante m de
imitación.
rhinoceros [raɪ'nɔsərəs] n rinoceronte m.
Rhodes [rəudz] n Rodas f.
rhododendron [rəudə'dɛndrn] n
rododendro.
Rhone [rəun] n: the ~ el (río) Ródano.
rhubarb ['ruːbɑːb] n ruibarbo.
rhyme [raɪm] n rima; (verse) poesía ♦ vi: to
~ (with) rimar (con); without ~ or reason
sin ton ni son.
rhythm ['rɪðm] n ritmo.
rhythmic(al) ['rɪðmɪk(l)] adj rítmico.
rhythmically ['rɪðmɪklɪ] adv rítmicamente.
rhythm method n método (de) Ogino.
RI n abbr (BRIT: = religious instruction) ed.
religiosa ♦ abbr (US) = Rhode Island.
rib [rɪb] n (ANAT) costilla ♦ vt (mock) tomar
el pelo a.
ribald ['rɪbəld] adj escabroso.
ribbon ['rɪbən] n cinta; in ~s (torn) hecho
trizas.
rice [raɪs] n arroz m.
ricefield ['raɪsfiːld] n arrozal m.
rice pudding n arroz m con leche.
rich [rɪtʃ] adj rico; (soil) fértil; (food)
pesado; (: sweet) empalagoso; the ~ npl
los ricos; ~es npl riqueza sg; to be ~ in sth
abundar en algo.
richly ['rɪtʃlɪ] adv ricamente.
richness ['rɪtʃnɪs] n riqueza; (of soil)
fertilidad f.
rickets ['rɪkɪts] n raquitismo.
rickety ['rɪkɪtɪ] adj (old) desvencijado;
(shaky) tambaleante.
rickshaw ['rɪkʃɔː] n carro de culí.
ricochet ['rɪkəʃeɪ] n rebote m ♦ vi rebotar.
rid, pt, pp **rid** [rɪd] vt: to ~ sb of sth librar a
algn de algo; to get ~ of deshacerse or
desembarazarse de.
riddance ['rɪdns] n: good ~! ¡y adiós muy
buenas!
ridden ['rɪdn] pp of ride.
-ridden ['rɪdn] suff: disease~ plagado de
enfermedades; inflation~ minado por la

inflación.
riddle ['rɪdl] n (conundrum) acertijo;
(mystery) enigma m, misterio ♦ vt: to be
~d with ser lleno or plagado de.
ride [raɪd] n paseo; (distance covered) viaje
m, recorrido ♦ vb (pt rode, pp ridden) vi
(horse: as sport) montar; (go somewhere:
on horse, bicycle) dar un paseo, pasearse;
(journey: on bicycle, motor cycle, bus)
viajar ♦ vt (a horse) montar a; (distance)
viajar; to ~ a bicycle andar en bicicleta;
to ~ at anchor (NAUT) estar fondeado;
can you ~ a bike? ¿sabes montar en
bici(cleta)?; to go for a ~ dar un paseo;
to take sb for a ~ (fig) tomar el pelo a
algn.
▶**ride out** vt: to ~ out the storm (fig)
capear el temporal.
rider ['raɪdə*] n (on horse) jinete m; (on
bicycle) ciclista m/f; (on motorcycle)
motociclista m/f.
ridge [rɪdʒ] n (of hill) cresta; (of roof)
caballete m; (wrinkle) arruga.
ridicule ['rɪdɪkjuːl] n irrisión f, burla ♦ vt
poner en ridículo a, burlarse de; to hold
sth/sb up to ~ poner algo/a algn en
ridículo.
ridiculous [rɪ'dɪkjuləs] adj ridículo.
ridiculously [rɪ'dɪkjuləslɪ] adv
ridículamente, de modo ridículo.
riding ['raɪdɪŋ] n equitación f; I like ~ me
gusta montar a caballo.
riding habit n traje m de montar.
riding school n escuela de equitación.
rife [raɪf] adj: to be ~ ser muy común; to be
~ with abundar en.
riffraff ['rɪfræf] n chusma, gentuza.
rifle ['raɪfl] n rifle m, fusil m ♦ vt saquear.
▶**rifle through** vt fus saquear.
rifle range n campo de tiro; (at fair) tiro al
blanco.
rift [rɪft] n (fig: between friends)
desavenencia; (: in party) escisión f.
rig [rɪg] n (also: oil ~: on land) torre f de
perforación; (: at sea) plataforma
petrolera ♦ vt (election etc) amañar los
resultados de.
▶**rig out** vt (BRIT) ataviar.
▶**rig up** vt improvisar.
rigging ['rɪgɪŋ] n (NAUT) aparejo.
right [raɪt] adj (true, correct) correcto,
exacto; (suitable) indicado, debido;
(proper) apropiado, propio; (just) justo;
(morally good) bueno; (not left) derecho
♦ n (title, claim) derecho; (not left) derecha
♦ adv (correctly) bien, correctamente;
(straight) derecho, directamente; (not on
the left) a la derecha; (to the ~) hacia la

derecha ♦ vt (put straight) enderezar ♦ excl ¡bueno!, ¡está bien!; **to be** ~ (person) tener razón; **to get sth** ~ acertar en algo; **you did the** ~ **thing** hiciste bien; **let's get it** ~ **this time!** ¡a ver si esta vez nos sale bien!; **to put a mistake** ~ corregir un error; **the** ~ **time** la hora exacta; (fig) el momento oportuno; **by** ~**s** en justicia; ~ **and wrong** el bien y el mal; **film** ~**s** derechos mpl de la película; **on the** ~ a la derecha; **to be in the** ~ tener razón; ~ **now** ahora mismo; ~ **before/after** inmediatamente antes/después; ~ **in the middle** exactamente en el centro; ~ **away** en seguida; **to go** ~ **to the end of sth** llegar hasta el final de algo; ~**, who's next?** bueno, ¿quién sigue?; **all** ~! ¡vale!; **I'm/I feel all** ~ **now** ya estoy bien.

right angle n ángulo recto.

righteous ['raɪtʃəs] adj justo, honrado; (anger) justificado.

righteousness ['raɪtʃəsnɪs] n justicia.

rightful ['raɪtful] adj (heir) legítimo.

right-hand ['raɪthænd] adj (drive, turn) por la derecha.

right-handed [raɪt'hændɪd] adj (person) que usa la mano derecha.

right-hand man n brazo derecho.

right-hand side n derecha.

rightly ['raɪtlɪ] adv correctamente, debidamente; (with reason) con razón; **if I remember** ~ si recuerdo bien.

right-minded ['raɪt'maɪndɪd] adj (sensible) sensato; (decent) honrado.

right of way n (on path etc) derecho de paso; (AUT) prioridad f de paso.

rights issue n (STOCK EXCHANGE) emisión f gratuita de acciones.

right-wing [raɪt'wɪŋ] adj (POL) de derechas, derechista.

right-winger [raɪt'wɪŋə*] n (POL) persona de derechas, derechista m/f; (SPORT) extremo derecha.

rigid ['rɪdʒɪd] adj rígido; (person, ideas) inflexible.

rigidity [rɪ'dʒɪdɪtɪ] n rigidez f; inflexibilidad f.

rigidly ['rɪdʒɪdlɪ] adv rígidamente; (inflexibly) inflexiblemente.

rigmarole ['rɪgmərəul] n galimatías m inv.

rigor mortis ['rɪgə'mɔːtɪs] n rigidez f cadavérica.

rigorous ['rɪgərəs] adj riguroso.

rigorously ['rɪgərəslɪ] adv rigurosamente.

rigour, (US) rigor ['rɪgə*] n rigor m, severidad f.

rig-out ['rɪgaut] n (BRIT col) atuendo.

rile [raɪl] vt irritar.

rim [rɪm] n borde m; (of spectacles) montura, aro; (of wheel) llanta.

rimless ['rɪmlɪs] adj (spectacles) sin aros.

rimmed [rɪmd] adj: ~ **with** con un borde de, bordeado de.

rind [raɪnd] n (of bacon, cheese) corteza; (of lemon etc) cáscara.

ring [rɪŋ] n (of metal) aro; (on finger) anillo; (of people) corro; (of objects) círculo; (gang) banda; (for boxing) cuadrilátero; (of circus) pista; (bull ~) ruedo, plaza; (sound of bell) toque m; (telephone call) llamada ♦ vb (pt **rang**, pp **rung** [ræŋ, rʌŋ]) vi (on telephone) llamar por teléfono; (large bell) repicar; (also: ~ **out**: voice, words) sonar; (ears) zumbar ♦ vt (BRIT TEL: also: ~ **up**) llamar; (bell etc) hacer sonar; (doorbell) tocar; **that has the** ~ **of truth about it** eso suena a verdad; **to give sb a** ~ (BRIT TEL) llamar por teléfono a algn, dar un telefonazo a algn; **the name doesn't** ~ **a bell (with me)** el nombre no me suena; **to** ~ **sb (up)** llamar a algn.

▶**ring back** vt, vi (TEL) devolver la llamada.

▶**ring off** vi (BRIT TEL) colgar, cortar la comunicación.

ring binder n carpeta de anillas.

ring finger n (dedo) anular m.

ringing ['rɪŋɪŋ] n (of bell) toque m, tañido; (louder: of large bell) repique m; (in ears) zumbido.

ringing tone n (TEL) tono de llamada.

ringleader ['rɪŋliːdə*] n (of gang) cabecilla m/f.

ringlets ['rɪŋlɪts] npl tirabuzones mpl, bucles mpl.

ring road n (BRIT) carretera periférica or de circunvalación.

rink [rɪŋk] n (also: **ice** ~) pista de hielo; (for roller-skating) pista de patinaje.

rinse [rɪns] n (of dishes) enjuague m; (of clothes) aclarado; (of hair) reflejo ♦ vt enjuagar; aclarar; dar reflejos a.

Rio (de Janeiro) ['riːəu(dədʒə'nɪərəu)] n Río de Janeiro.

riot ['raɪət] n motín m, disturbio ♦ vi amotinarse; **to run** ~ desmandarse.

rioter ['raɪətə*] n amotinado/a.

riot gear n uniforme m antidisturbios inv.

riotous ['raɪətəs] adj alborotado; (party) bullicioso; (uncontrolled) desenfrenado.

riotously ['raɪətəslɪ] adv bulliciosamente.

riot police n policía antidisturbios.

RIP abbr (= rest in peace) q.e.p.d.

rip [rɪp] n rasgón m, desgarrón m ♦ vt rasgar, desgarrar ♦ vi rasgarse.

▶**rip up** vt hacer pedazos.

ripcord ['rɪpkɔːd] n cabo de desgarre.

ripe [raɪp] *adj* (*fruit*) maduro.
ripen ['raɪpən] *vt, vi* madurar.
ripeness ['raɪpnɪs] *n* madurez *f*.
rip-off ['rɪpɔf] *n* (*col*): **it's a ~!** ¡es una estafa!, ¡es un timo!
riposte [rɪ'pɔst] *n* respuesta aguda, réplica.
ripple ['rɪpl] *n* onda, rizo; (*sound*) murmullo ♦ *vi* rizarse ♦ *vt* rizar.
rise [raɪz] *n* (*slope*) cuesta, pendiente *f*; (*hill*) altura; (*increase: in wages: Brit*) aumento; (: *in prices, temperature*) subida, alza; (*fig: to power etc*) ascenso; (: *ascendancy*) auge *m* ♦ *vi* (*pt* **rose**, *pp* **risen** [rəuz, 'rɪzn]) (*gen*) elevarse; (*prices*) subir; (*waters*) crecer; (*river*) nacer; (*sun*) salir; (*person: from bed etc*) levantarse; (*also:* ~ **up**: *rebel*) sublevarse; (*in rank*) ascender; ~ **to power** ascenso al poder; **to give ~ to** dar lugar *or* origen a; **to ~ to the occasion** ponerse a la altura de las circunstancias.
rising ['raɪzɪŋ] *adj* (*increasing: number*) creciente; (: *prices*) en aumento *or* alza; (*tide*) creciente; (*sun, moon*) naciente ♦ *n* (*uprising*) sublevación *f*.
rising damp *n* humedad *f* de paredes.
rising star *n* (*fig*) figura en alza.
risk [rɪsk] *n* riesgo, peligro ♦ *vt* (*gen*) arriesgar; (*dare*) atreverse a; **to take** *or* **run the ~ of doing** correr el riesgo de hacer; **at ~** en peligro; **at one's own ~** bajo su propia responsabilidad; **fire/health/security ~** peligro de incendio/para la salud/para la seguridad.
risk capital *n* capital *m* de riesgo.
risky ['rɪskɪ] *adj* arriesgado, peligroso.
risqué ['riːskeɪ] *adj* (*joke*) subido de color.
rissole ['rɪsəul] *n* croqueta.
rite [raɪt] *n* rito; **last ~s** últimos sacramentos *mpl*.
ritual ['rɪtjuəl] *adj* ritual ♦ *n* ritual *m*, rito.
rival ['raɪvl] *n* rival *m/f*; (*in business*) competidor(a) *m/f* ♦ *adj* rival, opuesto ♦ *vt* competir con.
rivalry ['raɪvlrɪ] *n* rivalidad *f*, competencia.
river ['rɪvə*] *n* río ♦ *cpd* (*port, traffic*) de río, del río; **up/down ~** río arriba/abajo.
riverbank ['rɪvəbæŋk] *n* orilla (del río).
riverbed ['rɪvəbed] *n* lecho, cauce *m*.
rivet ['rɪvɪt] *n* roblón *m*, remache *m* ♦ *vt* remachar; (*fig*) fascinar.
riveting ['rɪvɪtɪŋ] *adj* (*fig*) fascinante.
Riviera [rɪvɪ'eərə] *n*: **the (French) ~** la Costa Azul; **the Italian ~** la Riviera italiana.
Riyadh [rɪ'jɑːd] *n* Riyadh *m*.
RMT *n abbr* (=*Rail, Maritime and Transport*) *sindicato de transportes*.
RN *n abbr* (*BRIT*) *see* **Royal Navy**; (*US*)

= **registered nurse**.
RNA *n abbr* (= *ribonucleic acid*) ARN *m*, RNA *m*.
RNLI *n abbr* (*BRIT*: = *Royal National Lifeboat Institution*) *servicio de lanchas de socorro*.
RNZAF *n abbr* = *Royal New Zealand Air Force*.
RNZN *n abbr* = *Royal New Zealand Navy*.
road [rəud] *n* (*gen*) camino; (*motorway etc*) carretera; (*in town*) calle *f*; **major/minor ~** carretera general/secundaria; **main ~** carretera; **it takes 4 hours by ~** se tarda 4 horas por carretera; **on the ~ to success** camino del éxito.
roadblock ['rəudblɔk] *n* barricada, control *m*, retén *m* (*LAM*).
road haulage *n* transporte *m* por carretera.
roadhog ['rəudhɔg] *n* loco/a del volante.
road map *n* mapa *m* de carreteras.
road rage *n conducta agresiva de los conductores*.
road safety *n* seguridad *f* vial.
roadside ['rəudsaɪd] *n* borde *m* (del camino) ♦ *cpd* al lado de la carretera; **by the ~** al borde del camino.
roadsign ['rəudsaɪn] *n* señal *f* de tráfico.
roadsweeper ['rəudswiːpə*] *n* (*BRIT: person*) barrendero/a.
road user *n* usuario/a de la vía pública.
roadway ['rəudweɪ] *n* calzada.
roadworks ['rəudwɔːks] *npl* obras *fpl*.
roadworthy ['rəudwɔːðɪ] *adj* (*car*) en buen estado para circular.
roam [rəum] *vi* vagar ♦ *vt* vagar por.
roar [rɔː*] *n* (*of animal*) rugido, bramido; (*of crowd*) clamor *m*, rugido; (*of vehicle, storm*) estruendo; (*of laughter*) carcajada ♦ *vi* rugir, bramar; hacer estruendo; **to ~ with laughter** reírse a carcajadas.
roaring ['rɔːrɪŋ] *adj*: **a ~ success** un tremendo éxito; **to do a ~ trade** hacer buen negocio.
roast [rəust] *n* carne *f* asada, asado ♦ *vt* (*meat*) asar; (*coffee*) tostar.
roast beef *n* rosbif *m*.
roasting ['rəustɪŋ] *n*: **to give sb a ~** (*col*) echar una buena bronca a algn.
rob [rɔb] *vt* robar; **to ~ sb of sth** robar algo a algn; (*fig: deprive*) quitar algo a algn.
robber ['rɔbə*] *n* ladrón/ona *m/f*.
robbery ['rɔbərɪ] *n* robo.
robe [rəub] *n* (*for ceremony etc*) toga; (*also: bath ~*) bata.
robin ['rɔbɪn] *n* petirrojo.
robot ['rəubɔt] *n* robot *m*.
robotics [rəu'bɔtɪks] *n* robótica.
robust [rəu'bʌst] *adj* robusto, fuerte.
rock [rɔk] *n* (*gen*) roca; (*boulder*) peña,

peñasco; (*BRIT: sweet*) ≈ pirulí *m* ♦ *vt*
(*swing gently*) mecer; (*shake*) sacudir ♦ *vi*
mecerse, balancearse; sacudirse; **on the**
~**s** (*drink*) con hielo; **their marriage is on
the** ~**s** su matrimonio se está yendo a
pique; **to** ~ **the boat** (*fig*) crear
problemas.

rock and roll *n* rock and roll *m*, rocanrol *m*.

rock-bottom ['rɔk'bɔtəm] *adj* (*fig*) por los
suelos; **to reach** *or* **touch rock bottom**
(*price*) estar por los suelos; (*person*) tocar
fondo.

rock cake *n* (*BRIT*) bollito *de pasas con
superficie rugosa*.

rock climber *n* escalador(a) *m/f*.

rock climbing *n* (*SPORT*) escalada.

rockery ['rɔkərɪ] *n* cuadro alpino.

rocket ['rɔkɪt] *n* cohete *m* ♦ *vi* (*prices*)
disparaise, ponerse por las nubes.

rocket launcher *n* lanzacohetes *m inv*.

rock face *n* pared *f* de roca.

rocking chair ['rɔkɪŋ-] *n* mecedora.

rocking horse *n* caballo de balancín.

rocky ['rɔkɪ] *adj* (*gen*) rocoso; (*unsteady:
table*) inestable.

Rocky Mountains *npl*: **the** ~ las Montañas
Rocosas.

rococo [rə'kəukəu] *adj* rococó *inv* ♦ *n* rococó.

rod [rɔd] *n* vara, varilla; (*TECH*) barra; (*also:
fishing* ~) caña.

rode [rəud] *pt of* **ride**.

rodent ['rəudnt] *n* roedor *m*.

rodeo ['rəudɪəu] *n* rodeo.

roe [rəu] *n* (*species: also:* ~ **deer**) corzo; (*of
fish*): **hard/soft** ~ hueva/lecha.

rogue [rəug] *n* picaro, pillo.

roguish ['rəugɪʃ] *adj* (*child*) travieso; (*smile
etc*) pícaro.

role [rəul] *n* papel *m*, rol *m*.

role-model ['rəulmɔdl] *n* modelo a imitar.

role play *n* (*also:* ~**ing**) juego de papeles *or*
roles.

roll [rəul] *n* rollo; (*of bank notes*) fajo; (*also:
bread* ~) panecillo; (*register*) lista,
nómina; (*sound: of drums etc*) redoble *m*;
(*movement: of ship*) balanceo ♦ *vt* hacer
rodar; (*also:* ~ **up**: *string*) enrollar;
(: *sleeves*) arremangar; (*cigarettes*) liar;
(*also:* ~ **out**: *pastry*) aplanar ♦ *vi* (*gen*)
rodar; (*drum*) redoblar; (*in walking*)
bambolearse; (*ship*) balancearse; **cheese**
~ panecillo de queso.

►**roll about, roll around** *vi* (*person*)
revolcarse.

►**roll by** *vi* (*time*) pasar.

►**roll in** *vi* (*mail, cash*) entrar a raudales.

►**roll over** *vi* dar una vuelta.

►**roll up** *vi* (*col: arrive*) presentarse,

aparecer ♦ *vt* (*carpet, cloth, map*) arrollar;
(*sleeves*) arremangar; **to** ~ **o.s. up into a
ball** acurrucarse, hacerse un ovillo.

roll call *n*: **to take a** ~ pasar lista.

rolled [rəuld] *adj* (*umbrella*) plegado.

roller ['rəulə*] *n* rodillo; (*wheel*) rueda.

roller blind *n* (*BRIT*) persiana (enrollable).

roller coaster *n* montaña rusa.

roller skates *npl* patines *mpl* de rueda.

rollicking ['rɔlɪkɪŋ] *adj*: **we had a** ~ **time**
nos divertimos una barbaridad.

rolling ['rəulɪŋ] *adj* (*landscape*) ondulado.

rolling mill *n* taller *m* de laminación.

rolling pin *n* rodillo (de cocina).

rolling stock *n* (*RAIL*) material *m* rodante.

ROM [rɔm] *n abbr* (= *read only memory*)
(memoria) ROM *f*.

Roman ['rəumən] *adj*, *n* romano/a *m/f*.

Roman Catholic *adj*, *n* católico/a *m/f*
(romano/a).

romance [rə'mæns] *n* (*love affair*) amor *m*,
idilio; (*charm*) lo romántico; (*novel*)
novela de amor.

romanesque [rəumə'nɛsk] *adj* románico.

Romania [ruː'meɪnɪə] *n* = **Rumania**.

Romanian [ruː'meɪnɪən] *adj*, *n* = **Rumanian**.

Roman numeral *n* número romano.

romantic [rə'mæntɪk] *adj* romántico.

romanticism [rə'mæntɪsɪzəm] *n*
romanticismo.

Romany ['rəumənɪ] *adj* gitano ♦ *n* (*person*)
gitano/a; (*LING*) lengua gitana, caló (*SP*).

Rome [rəum] *n* Roma.

romp [rɔmp] *n* retozo, jugueteo ♦ *vi* (*also:* ~
about) juguetear; **to** · **home** (*horse*)
ganar fácilmente.

rompers ['rɔmpəz] *npl* pelele *m*.

roof [ruːf] *n* (*gen*) techo; (*of house*) tejado
♦ *vt* techar, poner techo a; ~ **of the
mouth** paladar *m*.

roofing ['ruːfɪŋ] *n* techumbre *f*.

roof rack *n* (*AUT*) baca.

rook [ruk] *n* (*bird*) graja; (*CHESS*) torre *f*.

rookie ['rukɪ] *n* (*col*) novato/a; (*MIL*) chivo.

room [ruːm] *n* (*in house*) cuarto, habitación
f, pieza (*esp LAm*); (*also:* **bed**~)
dormitorio; (*in school etc*) sala; (*space*)
sitio; ~**s** *npl* (*lodging*) alojamiento *sg*; "~**s
to let**", (*US*) "~**s for rent**" "se alquilan
pisos *or* cuartos"; **single/double** ~
habitación individual/doble *or* para dos
personas; **is there** ~ **for this?** ¿cabe esto?;
to make ~ **for sb** hacer sitio para algn;
there is ~ **for improvement** podría
mejorarse.

roominess ['ruːmɪnɪs] *n* amplitud *f*,
espaciosidad *f*.

rooming house ['ruːmɪŋ-] *n* (*US*) pensión *f*.

roommate ['ru:mmeɪt] *n* compañero/a de cuarto.
room service *n* servicio de habitaciones.
room temperature *n* temperatura ambiente.
roomy ['ru:mɪ] *adj* espacioso.
roost [ru:st] *n* percha ♦ *vi* pasar la noche.
rooster ['ru:stə*] *n* gallo.
root [ru:t] *n* (*BOT, MATH*) raíz *f* ♦ *vi* (*plant, belief*) arraigar(se); **to take** ~ (*plant*) echar raíces; (*idea*) arraigar(se); **the** ~ **of the problem is that ...** la raíz del problema es que ....
►**root about** *vi* (*fig*) rebuscar.
►**root for** *vt fus* apoyar a.
►**root out** *vt* desarraigar.
root beer *n* (*US*) *refresco sin alcohol de extractos de hierbas.*
rooted ['ru:tɪd] *adj* enraizado; (*opinions etc*) arraigado.
rope [rəup] *n* cuerda; (*NAUT*) cable *m* ♦ *vt* (*box*) atar *or* amarrar con (una) cuerda; (*climbers: also:* ~ **together**) encordarse; **to** ~ **sb in** (*fig*) persuadir a algn a tomar parte; **to know the** ~**s** (*fig*) conocer los trucos (del oficio).
rope ladder *n* escala de cuerda.
ropey ['rəupɪ] *adj* (*col*) chungo.
rosary ['rəuzərɪ] *n* rosario.
rose [rəuz] *pt of* **rise** ♦ *n* rosa; (*also:* ~**bush**) rosal *m*; (*on watering can*) roseta ♦ *adj* color de rosa.
rosé ['rəuzeɪ] *n* vino rosado, clarete *m*.
rosebed ['rəuzbɛd] *n* rosaleda.
rosebud ['rəuzbʌd] *n* capullo de rosa.
rosebush ['rəuzbuʃ] *n* rosal *m*.
rosemary ['rəuzmərɪ] *n* romero.
rosette [rəu'zɛt] *n* rosetón *m*.
ROSPA ['rɔspə] *n abbr* (*BRIT*) = *Royal Society for the Prevention of Accidents*.
roster ['rɔstə*] *n*: **duty** ~ lista de tareas.
rostrum ['rɔstrəm] *n* tribuna.
rosy ['rəuzɪ] *adj* rosado, sonrosado; **the future looks** ~ el futuro parece prometedor.
rot [rɔt] *n* (*decay*) putrefacción *f*, podredumbre *f*; (*fig: pej*) tonterías *fpl* ♦ *vt* pudrir, corromper ♦ *vi* pudrirse, corromperse; **it has** ~**ted** está podrido; **to stop the** ~ (*fig*) poner fin a las pérdidas.
rota ['rəutə] *n* lista (de tareas).
rotary ['rəutərɪ] *adj* rotativo.
rotate [rəu'teɪt] *vt* (*revolve*) hacer girar, dar vueltas a; (*change round: crops*) cultivar en rotación; (: *jobs*) alternar ♦ *vi* (*revolve*) girar, dar vueltas.
rotating [rəu'teɪtɪŋ] *adj* (*movement*) rotativo.

rotation [rəu'teɪʃən] *n* rotación *f*; **in** ~ por turno.
rote [rəut] *n*: **by** ~ de memoria.
rotor ['rəutə*] *n* rotor *m*.
rotten ['rɔtn] *adj* (*decayed*) podrido; (: *wood*) carcomido; (*fig*) corrompido; (*col: bad*) pésimo; **to feel** ~ (*ill*) sentirse fatal; ~ **to the core** completamente podrido.
rotund [rəu'tʌnd] *adj* rotundo.
rouble, (*US*) **ruble** ['ru:bl] *n* rublo.
rouge [ru:ʒ] *n* colorete *m*.
rough [rʌf] *adj* (*skin, surface*) áspero; (*terrain*) accidentado; (*road*) desigual; (*voice*) bronco; (*person, manner: coarse*) tosco, grosero; (*weather*) borrascoso; (*treatment*) brutal; (*sea*) embravecido; (*cloth*) basto; (*plan*) preliminar; (*guess*) aproximado; (*violent*) violento ♦ *n* (*GOLF*): **in the** ~ en las hierbas altas; **to** ~ **it** vivir sin comodidades; **to sleep** ~ (*BRIT*) pasar la noche al raso; **the sea is** ~ **today** el mar está agitado hoy; **to have a** ~ **time (of it)** pasar una mala racha; ~ **estimate** cálculo aproximado.
roughage ['rʌfɪdʒ] *n* fibra(s) *f(pl)*, forraje *m*.
rough-and-ready ['rʌfən'rɛdɪ] *adj* improvisado, tosco.
rough-and-tumble ['rʌfən'tʌmbl] *n* pelea.
roughcast ['rʌfkɑ:st] *n* mezcla gruesa.
rough copy, rough draft *n* borrador *m*.
roughen ['rʌfn] *vt* (*a surface*) poner áspero.
roughly ['rʌflɪ] *adv* (*handle*) torpemente; (*make*) toscamente; (*approximately*) aproximadamente; ~ **speaking** más o menos.
roughness ['rʌfnɪs] *n* aspereza; tosquedad *f*; brutalidad *f*.
roughshod ['rʌfʃɔd] *adv*: **to ride** ~ **over** (*person*) pisotear a; (*objections*) hacer caso omiso de.
rough work *n* (*SCOL etc*) borrador *m*.
roulette [ru:'lɛt] *n* ruleta.
Roumania [ru:'meɪnɪə] *n* = **Rumania**.
round [raund] *adj* redondo ♦ *n* círculo; (*of policeman*) ronda; (*of milkman*) recorrido; (*of doctor*) visitas *fpl*; (*game: of cards, in competition*) partida; (*of ammunition*) cartucho; (*BOXING*) asalto; (*of talks*) ronda ♦ *vt* (*corner*) doblar ♦ *prep* alrededor de ♦ *adv*: **all** ~ por todos lados; **the long way** ~ por el camino menos directo; **all the year** ~ durante todo el año; **it's just** ~ **the corner** (*fig*) está a la vuelta de la esquina; **to ask sb** ~ invitar a algn a casa; **I'll be** ~ **at 6 o'clock** llegaré a eso de las 6; **she arrived** ~ (**about**) **noon** llegó alrededor del mediodía; ~ **the clock** *adv* las 24

horas; **to go ~ to sb's (house)** ir a casa de
algn; **to go ~ the back** pasar por atrás; **to
go ~ a house** visitar una casa; **enough to
go ~** bastante (para todos); **in ~ figures**
en números redondos; **to go the ~s**
(*story*) divulgarse; **a ~ of applause** una
salva de aplausos; **a ~ of drinks/
sandwiches** una ronda de bebidas/
bocadillos; **a ~ of toast** (*BRIT*) una
tostada; **the daily ~** la rutina cotidiana.
►**round off** *vt* (*speech etc*) acabar, poner
término a.
►**round up** *vt* (*cattle*) acorralar; (*people*)
reunir; (*prices*) redondear.
roundabout ['raundəbaut] *n* (*BRIT: AUT*)
glorieta, rotonda; (: *at fair*) tiovivo ♦ *adj*
(*route, means*) indirecto.
rounded ['raundɪd] *adj* redondeado,
redondo.
rounders ['raundəz] *n* (*BRIT: game*) *juego
similar al béisbol.*
roundly ['raundlɪ] *adv* (*fig*) rotundamente.
round-robin ['raundrɔbɪn] *n* (*SPORT: also:* ~
tournament) liguilla.
round trip *n* viaje *m* de ida y vuelta.
roundup ['raundʌp] *n* rodeo; (*of criminals*)
redada; **a ~ of the latest news** un
resumen de las últimas noticias.
rouse [rauz] *vt* (*wake up*) despertar; (*stir up*)
suscitar.
rousing ['rauzɪŋ] *adj* (*applause*) caluroso;
(*speech*) conmovedor(a).
rout [raut] *n* (*MIL*) derrota; (*flight*)
desbandada ♦ *vt* derrotar.
route [ru:t] *n* ruta, camino; (*of bus*)
recorrido; (*of shipping*) rumbo, derrota;
the best ~ to London el mejor camino *or*
la mejor ruta para ir a Londres; **en ~
from ... to** en el viaje de ... a; **en ~ for**
rumbo a, con destino en.
route map *n* (*BRIT: for journey*) mapa *m* de
carreteras.
routine [ruː'tiːn] *adj* (*work*) rutinario ♦ *n*
rutina; (*THEAT*) número; (*COMPUT*) rutina.
roving ['rəuvɪŋ] *adj* (*wandering*) errante;
(*salesman*) ambulante; (*reporter*) volante.
row [rəu] *n* (*line*) fila, hilera; (*KNITTING*)
vuelta; [rau] (*noise*) escándalo; (*dispute*)
bronca, pelea; (*fuss*) jaleo; (*scolding*)
reprimenda ♦ *vi* (*in boat*) remar; [rau]
reñir(se) ♦ *vt* (*boat*) conducir remando; **4
days in a ~** 4 días seguidos; **to make a ~**
armar un lío; **to have a ~** pelearse, reñir.
rowboat ['rəubəut] *n* (*US*) bote *m* de remos.
rowdy ['raudɪ] *adj* (*person: noisy*) ruidoso;
(: *quarrelsome*) pendenciero; (*occasion*)
alborotado ♦ *n* pendenciero.
row houses *npl* (*US*) casas *fpl* adosadas.

rowing ['rəuɪŋ] *n* remo.
rowing boat *n* (*BRIT*) bote *m or* barco de
remos.
royal ['rɔɪəl] *adj* real.
Royal Academy (of Arts) *n* (*BRIT*) la Real
Academia (de Bellas Artes); *ver recuadro.*

ROYAL ACADEMY (OF ARTS)

La **Royal Academy (of Arts)**, *fundada en
1768 durante el reinado de Jorge III, es una
institución dedicada al fomento de la
pintura, escultura y arquitectura en el Reino
Unido. Además de dar cursos de arte,
presenta una exposición anual de artistas
contemporáneos en su sede de Burlington
House, en el centro de Londres. No existe
una institución equivalente a la Real
Academia de la Lengua.*

Royal Air Force (RAF) *n* Fuerzas Aéreas
Británicas *fpl.*
royal blue *n* azul *m* marino.
royalist ['rɔɪəlɪst] *adj, n* monárquico/a *m/f.*
Royal Navy (RN) *n* (*BRIT*) Marina
Británica.
royalty ['rɔɪəltɪ] *n* (*royal persons*) (miembros *mpl* de la) familia real; (*payment to
author*) derechos *mpl* de autor.
RP *n abbr* (= *Received Pronunciation*) *ver
recuadro.*

RP

*El acento con el que suelen hablar las
clases medias y altas de Inglaterra se
denomina* **RP** *(o* **Received Pronunciation***).
Es el acento estándar, sin variaciones
regionales, que aún usan los locutores en
los informativos nacionales de la "BBC".
También suele tomarse como norma en la
enseñanza del inglés británico como lengua
extranjera. Todavía conserva un gran
prestigio, aunque la gran mayoría de la
población habla con el acento de su región,
que puede ser más o menos fuerte según
su educación o clase social.*

---

rpm *abbr* (= *revs per minute*) r.p.m.
RR *abbr* (*US*) = **railroad**.
RSA *n abbr* (*BRIT*) = *Royal Society of Arts,
Royal Scottish Academy.*
RSI *n abbr* (*MED*: = *repetitive strain injury*)
*traumatismo producido por un esfuerzo
continuado* (*como el de las mecanógrafas*).
RSPB *n abbr* (*BRIT*) = *Royal Society for the
Protection of Birds.*
RSPCA *n abbr* (*BRIT*) = *Royal Society for the*

Prevention of Cruelty to Animals.

R.S.V.P. *abbr* (= *répondez s'il vous plaît*) SRC.

RTA *n abbr* (= *road traffic accident*) accidente *m* de carretera.

Rt. Hon. *abbr* (*BRIT*: = *Right Honourable*) *tratamiento honorífico de diputado.*

Rt. Rev. *abbr* (= *Right Reverend*) Rvdo.

rub [rʌb] *vt* (*gen*) frotar; (*hard*) restregar ♦ *n* (*gen*) frotamiento; (*touch*) roce *m; **to ~ sb up** *or* (*US*) **~ sb the wrong way** sacar de quicio a algn.

▶**rub down** *vt* (*body*) secar frotando; (*horse*) almohazar.

▶**rub in** *vt* (*ointment*) frotar.

▶**rub off** *vt* borrarse ♦ *vi* quitarse (frotando); **to ~ off on sb** influir en algn, pegársele a algn.

▶**rub out** *vt* borrar ♦ *vi* borrarse.

rubber ['rʌbə*] *n* caucho, goma; (*BRIT*: *eraser*) goma de borrar.

rubber band *n* goma, gomita.

rubber bullet *n* bala de goma.

rubber plant *n* ficus *m*.

rubber ring *n* (*for swimming*) flotador *m*.

rubber stamp *n* sello (de caucho) ♦ *vt*: **rubber-stamp** (*fig*) aprobar maquinalmente.

rubbery ['rʌbəri] *adj* (como) de goma.

rubbish ['rʌbɪʃ] (*BRIT*) *n* (*from household*) basura; (*waste*) desperdicios *mpl*; (*fig: pej*) tonterías *fpl*; (*trash*) basura, porquería ♦ *vt* (*col*) poner por los suelos; **what you've just said is ~** lo que acabas de decir es una tontería.

rubbish bin *n* cubo *or* bote *m* (*LAM*) de la basura.

rubbish dump *n* (*in town*) vertedero, basurero.

rubbishy ['rʌbɪʃɪ] *adj* de mala calidad, de pacotilla.

rubble ['rʌbl] *n* escombros *mpl.*

ruby ['ruːbɪ] *n* rubí *m*.

RUC *n abbr* (= *Royal Ulster Constabulary*) *fuerza de policía en Irlanda del Norte.*

rucksack ['rʌksæk] *n* mochila.

ructions ['rʌkʃənz] *npl*: **there will be ~** se va a armar la gorda.

ruddy ['rʌdɪ] *adj* (*face*) rubicundo; (*col*: *damned*) condenado.

rude [ruːd] *adj* (*impolite*: *person*) grosero, maleducado; (: *word, manners*) rudo, grosero; (*indecent*) indecente; **to be ~ to sb** ser grosero con algn.

rudeness ['ruːdnɪs] *n* grosería, tosquedad *f*.

rudiment ['ruːdɪmənt] *n* rudimento.

rudimentary [ruːdɪ'mɛntərɪ] *adj*

rudimentario.

rue [ruː] *vt* arrepentirse de.

rueful ['ruːful] *adj* arrepentido.

ruffian ['rʌfɪən] *n* matón *m*, criminal *m*.

ruffle ['rʌfl] *vt* (*hair*) despeinar; (*clothes*) arrugar; (*fig: person*) agitar.

rug [rʌg] *n* alfombra; (*BRIT*: *for knees*) manta.

rugby ['rʌgbɪ] *n* (*also*: ~ **football**) rugby *m*.

rugged ['rʌgɪd] *adj* (*landscape*) accidentado; (*features*) robusto.

rugger ['rʌgə*] *n* (*BRIT col*) rugby *m*.

ruin ['ruːɪn] *n* ruina ♦ *vt* arruinar; (*spoil*) estropear; **~s** *npl* ruinas *fpl*, restos *mpl*; **in ~s** en ruinas.

ruinous ['ruːɪnəs] *adj* ruinoso.

rule [ruːl] *n* (*norm*) norma, costumbre *f*; (*regulation, ruler*) regla; (*government*) dominio; (*dominion etc*): **under British ~** bajo el dominio británico ♦ *vt* (*country, person*) gobernar; (*decide*) disponer; (*draw lines*) trazar ♦ *vi* gobernar; (*LAW*) fallar; **to ~ against/in favour of/on** fallar en contra de/a favor de/sobre; **to ~ that** ... (*umpire, judge*) fallar que ...; **it's against the ~s** está prohibido; **as a ~** por regla general, generalmente; **by ~ of thumb** por experiencia; **majority ~** (*POL*) gobierno mayoritario.

▶**rule out** *vt* excluir.

ruled [ruːld] *adj* (*paper*) rayado.

ruler ['ruːlə*] *n* (*sovereign*) soberano; (*for measuring*) regla.

ruling ['ruːlɪŋ] *adj* (*party*) gobernante; (*class*) dirigente ♦ *n* (*LAW*) fallo, decisión *f*.

rum [rʌm] *n* ron *m*.

Rumania [ruː'meɪnɪə] *n* Rumanía.

Rumanian [ruː'meɪnɪən] *adj, n* rumano/a *m/f*.

rumble ['rʌmbl] *n* ruido sordo; (*of thunder*) redoble *m* ♦ *vi* retumbar, hacer un ruido sordo; (*stomach, pipe*) sonar.

rumbustious [rʌm'bʌstʃəs] *adj* (*person*) bullicioso.

rummage ['rʌmɪdʒ] *vi* revolverlo todo.

rumour, (US) rumor ['ruːmə*] *n* rumor *m* ♦ *vt*: **it is ~ed that** ... se rumorea que ...; **~ has it that** ... corre la voz de que ....

rump [rʌmp] *n* (*of animal*) ancas *fpl*, grupa.

rumple ['rʌmpl] *vt* (*clothes*) arrugar; (*hair*) despeinar.

rump steak *n* filete *m* de lomo.

rumpus ['rʌmpəs] *n* (*col*) lío, jaleo; (*quarrel*) pelea, riña; **to kick up a ~** armar un follón *or* armar bronca.

run [rʌn] *n* (*SPORT*) carrera; (*outing*) paseo, excursión *f*; (*distance travelled*) trayecto; (*series*) serie *f*; (*THEAT*) temporada; (*SKI*) pista; (*in tights, stockings*) carrera; ♦ *vb* (*pt*

ran, pp **run** [ræn, rʌn]) vt (operate: business) dirigir; (: competition, course) organizar; (: hotel, house) administrar, llevar; (COMPUT: program) ejecutar; (to pass: hand) pasar; (bath): **to ~ a bath** llenar la bañera ♦ vi (gen) correr; (work: machine) funcionar, marchar; (bus, train: operate) circular, ir; (: travel) ir; (: continue: play) seguir en cartel; (: contract) ser válido; (flow: river, bath) fluir; (colours, washing) desteñirse; (in election) ser candidato; **to go for a ~** ir a correr; **to make a ~ for it** echar(se) a correr, escapar(se), huir; **to have the ~ of sb's house** tener el libre uso de la casa de algn; **a ~ of luck** una racha de suerte; **there was a ~ on** (meat, tickets) hubo mucha demanda de; **in the long ~** a la larga; **on the ~** en fuga; **I'll ~ you to the station** te llevaré a la estación en coche; **to ~ a risk** correr un riesgo; **to ~ errands** hacer recados; **it's very cheap to ~** es muy económico; **to be ~ off one's feet** estar ocupadísimo; **to ~ for the bus** correr tras el autobús; **we shall have to ~ for it** tendremos que escapar; **the train ~s between Gatwick and Victoria** el tren circula entre Gatwick y Victoria; **the bus ~s every 20 minutes** el autobús pasa cada 20 minutos; **to ~ on petrol/on diesel/off batteries** funcionar con gasolina/gasoil/ baterías; **my salary won't ~ to a car** mi sueldo no me da para comprarme un coche; **the car ran into the lamppost** el coche chocó contra el farol.
► **run about, run around** vi (children) correr por todos lados.
► **run across** vt fus (find) dar or topar con.
► **run away** vi huir.
► **run down** vi (clock) pararse ♦ vt (reduce: production) ir reduciendo; (factory) restringir la producción de; (AUT) atropellar; (criticize) criticar; **to be ~ down** (person: tired) encontrarse agotado.
► **run in** vt (BRIT: car) rodar.
► **run into** vt fus (meet: person, trouble) tropezar con; (collide with) chocar con; **to ~ into debt** contraer deudas, endeudarse.
► **run off** vt (water) dejar correr ♦ vi huir corriendo.
► **run out** vi (person) salir corriendo; (liquid) irse; (lease) caducar, vencer; (money) acabarse.
► **run out of** vt fus quedar sin; **I've ~ out of petrol** se me acabó la gasolina.
► **run over** vt (AUT) atropellar ♦ vt fus (revise) repasar.
► **run through** vt fus (instructions) repasar.

► **run up** vt (debt) incurrir en; **to ~ up against** (difficulties) tropezar con.
run-around ['rʌnəraund] n: **to give sb the ~** traer a algn al retortero.
runaway ['rʌnəweɪ] adj (horse) desbocado; (truck) sin frenos; (person) fugitivo.
rundown ['rʌndaun] n (BRIT: of industry etc) cierre m gradual.
rung [rʌŋ] pp of **ring** ♦ n (of ladder) escalón m, peldaño.
run-in ['rʌnɪn] n (col) altercado.
runner ['rʌnə*] n (in race: person) corredor(a) m/f; (: horse) caballo; (on sledge) patín m; (wheel) ruedecilla.
runner bean n (BRIT) judía escarlata.
runner-up [rʌnər'ʌp] n subcampeón/ona m/f.
running ['rʌnɪŋ] n (sport) atletismo; (race) carrera ♦ adj (costs, water) corriente; (commentary) en directo; **to be in/out of the ~ for sth** tener/no tener posibilidades de ganar algo; **6 days ~** 6 días seguidos.
running costs npl (of business) gastos mpl corrientes; (of car) gastos mpl de mantenimiento.
running head n (TYP, WORD PROCESSING) encabezamiento normal.
running mate n (US POL) candidato/a a la vice-presidencia.
runny ['rʌnɪ] adj derretido.
run-off ['rʌnɔf] n (in contest, election) desempate m; (extra race) carrera de desempate.
run-of-the-mill ['rʌnəvðə'mɪl] adj común y corriente.
runt [rʌnt] n (also pej) enano.
run-up ['rʌnʌp] n: **~ to** (election etc) período previo a.
runway ['rʌnweɪ] n (AVIAT) pista (de aterrizaje).
rupee [ruː'piː] n rupia.
rupture ['rʌptʃə*] n (MED) hernia ♦ vt: **to ~ o.s.** causarse una hernia.
rural ['ruərl] adj rural.
ruse [ruːz] n ardid m.
rush [rʌʃ] n ímpetu m; (hurry) prisa, apuro (LAM); (COMM) demanda repentina; (BOT) junco; (current) corriente f fuerte, ráfaga ♦ vt apresurar; (work) hacer de prisa; (attack: town etc) asaltar ♦ vi correr, precipitarse; **gold ~** fiebre f del oro; **we've had a ~ of orders** ha habido una gran demanda; **I'm in a ~ (to do)** tengo prisa or apuro (LAM) (por hacer); **is there any ~ for this?** ¿te corre prisa esto?; **to ~ sth off** hacer algo de prisa y corriendo.
► **rush through** vt fus (meal) comer de prisa; (book) leer de prisa; (work) hacer de prisa; (town) atravesar a toda

velocidad; (*COMM: order*) despachar
rápidamente.
rush hour *n* horas *fpl* punta.
rush job *n* (*urgent*) trabajo urgente.
rusk [rʌsk] *n* bizcocho tostado.
Russia ['rʌʃə] *n* Rusia.
Russian ['rʌʃən] *adj* ruso ♦ *n* ruso/a; (*LING*)
ruso.
rust [rʌst] *n* herrumbre *f*, moho ♦ *vi*
oxidarse.
rustic ['rʌstɪk] *adj* rústico.
rustle ['rʌsl] *vi* susurrar ♦ *vt* (*paper*) hacer
crujir; (*US: cattle*) hurtar, robar.
rustproof ['rʌstpru:f] *adj* inoxidable.
rusty ['rʌstɪ] *adj* oxidado.
rut [rʌt] *n* surco; (*ZOOL*) celo; **to be in a ~**
ser esclavo de la rutina.
ruthless ['ru:θlɪs] *adj* despiadado.
RV *abbr* (= *revised version*) *traducción*
inglesa de la Biblia de 1855 ♦ *n abbr* (*US*)
= **recreational vehicle**.
rye [raɪ] *n* centeno.
rye bread *n* pan de centeno.

S s

S, s [ɛs] *n* (*letter*) S, s *f*; **S for Sugar** S de
sábado.
S *abbr* (= *Saint*) Sto./a.; (*US SCOL: mark*:
= *satisfactory*) suficiente; (= *south*) S;
= **small**.
SA *n abbr* = **South Africa, South America.**
sabbath ['sæbəθ] *n* domingo; (*Jewish*)
sábado.
sabbatical [sə'bætɪkl] *adj*: ~ **year** año
sabático.
sabotage ['sæbətɑ:ʒ] *n* sabotaje *m* ♦ *vt*
sabotear.
sabre, (*US*) **saber** ['seɪbə*] *n* sable *m*.
saccharin(e) ['sækərɪn] *n* sacarina.
sachet ['sæʃeɪ] *n* sobrecito.
sack [sæk] *n* (*bag*) saco, costal *m* ♦ *vt*
(*dismiss*) despedir, echar; (*plunder*)
saquear; **to get the** ~ ser despedido; **to**
give sb the ~ despedir *or* echar a algn.
sackful ['sækful] *n* saco.
sacking ['sækɪŋ] *n* (*material*) arpillera.
sacrament ['sækrəmənt] *n* sacramento.
sacred ['seɪkrɪd] *adj* sagrado, santo.
sacred cow *n* (*fig*) vaca sagrada.
sacrifice ['sækrɪfaɪs] *n* sacrificio ♦ *vt*

sacrificar; **to make ~s (for sb)**
sacrificarse (por algn).
sacrilege ['sækrɪlɪdʒ] *n* sacrilegio.
sacrosanct ['sækrəusæŋkt] *adj* sacrosanto.
sad [sæd] *adj* (*unhappy*) triste; (*deplorable*)
lamentable.
sadden ['sædn] *vt* entristecer.
saddle ['sædl] *n* silla (de montar); (*of cycle*)
sillín *m* ♦ *vt* (*horse*) ensillar; **to ~ sb with**
sth (*col: task, bill, name*) cargar a algn con
algo; (: *responsibility*) gravar a algn con
algo; **to be ~d with sth** (*col*) quedar
cargado con algo.
saddlebag ['sædlbæg] *n* alforja.
sadism ['seɪdɪzm] *n* sadismo.
sadist ['seɪdɪst] *n* sádico/a.
sadistic [sə'dɪstɪk] *adj* sádico.
sadly ['sædlɪ] *adv* tristemente; (*regrettably*)
desgraciadamente; ~ **lacking (in)** muy
deficiente (en).
sadness ['sædnɪs] *n* tristeza.
sado-masochism [seɪdəu'mæsəkɪzɪm] *n*
sadomasoquismo.
sae *abbr* (*BRIT*: = *stamped addressed*
envelope) *sobre con las propias señas de*
uno y con sello.
safari [sə'fɑ:rɪ] *n* safari *m*.
safari park *n* safari *m*.
safe [seɪf] *adj* (*out of danger*) fuera de
peligro; (*not dangerous, sure*) seguro;
(*unharmed*) ileso; (*trustworthy*) digno de
confianza ♦ *n* caja de caudales, caja
fuerte; ~ **and sound** sano y salvo; **(just)**
to be on the ~ **side** para mayor
seguridad; ~ **journey!** ¡buen viaje!; **it is** ~
to say that ... se puede decir con
confianza que ....
safe bet *n* apuesta segura; **it's a** ~ **she'll**
turn up seguro que viene.
safe-breaker ['seɪfbreɪkə*] *n* (*BRIT*) ladrón/
ona *m/f* de cajas fuertes.
safe-conduct [seɪf'kɔndʌkt] *n*
salvoconducto.
safe-cracker ['seɪfkrækə*] *n* (*US*) = **safe-**
breaker.
safe-deposit ['seɪfdɪpɔzɪt] *n* (*vault*) cámara
acorazada; (*box*) caja de seguridad *or* de
caudales.
safeguard ['seɪfgɑ:d] *n* protección *f*,
garantía ♦ *vt* proteger, defender.
safe haven *n* refugio.
safekeeping ['seɪf'ki:pɪŋ] *n* custodia.
safely ['seɪflɪ] *adv* seguramente, con
seguridad; (*without mishap*) sin peligro; **I**
can ~ say puedo decir *or* afirmar con
toda seguridad.
safeness ['seɪfnɪs] *n* seguridad *f*.
safe passage *n* garantías *fpl* para

marcharse en libertad.

safe sex *n* sexo seguro *or* sin riesgo.

safety ['seɪftɪ] *n* seguridad *f* ♦ *cpd* de seguridad; **road** ~ seguridad *f* en carretera; ~ **first!** ¡precaución!

safety belt *n* cinturón *m* (de seguridad).

safety catch *n* seguro.

safety net *n* red *f* (de seguridad).

safety pin *n* imperdible *m*, seguro (*LAM*).

safety valve *n* válvula de seguridad *or* de escape.

saffron ['sæfrən] *n* azafrán *m*.

sag [sæg] *vi* aflojarse.

saga ['sɑːgə] *n* (*HISTORY*) saga; (*fig*) epopeya.

sage [seɪdʒ] *n* (*herb*) salvia; (*man*) sabio.

Sagittarius [sædʒɪ'tɛərɪəs] *n* Sagitario.

sago ['seɪɡəu] *n* sagú *m*.

Sahara [sə'hɑːrə] *n*: **the** ~ **(Desert)** el Sáhara.

Sahel [sæ'hɛl] *n* Sahel *m*.

said [sɛd] *pt, pp of* **say**.

Saigon [saɪ'ɡɔn] *n* Saigón *m*.

sail [seɪl] *n* (*on boat*) vela ♦ *vt* (*boat*) gobernar ♦ *vi* (*travel: ship*) navegar; (: *passenger*) pasear en barco; (*set off: also*: **to set** ~) zarpar; **to go for a** ~ dar un paseo en barco; **they** ~**ed into Copenhagen** arribaron a Copenhague.

▶**sail through** *vt fus* (*exam*) aprobar fácilmente.

sailboat ['seɪlbəut] *n* (*US*) velero, barco de vela.

sailing ['seɪlɪŋ] *n* (*SPORT*) balandrismo; **to go** ~ salir en balandro.

sailing ship *n* barco de vela.

sailor ['seɪlə*] *n* marinero, marino.

saint [seɪnt] *n* santo; **S**~ **John** San Juan.

saintliness ['seɪntlɪnɪs] *n* santidad *f*.

saintly ['seɪntlɪ] *adj* santo.

sake [seɪk] *n*: **for the** ~ **of** por; **for the** ~ **of argument** digamos, es un decir; **art for art's** ~ el arte por el arte.

salad ['sæləd] *n* ensalada; **tomato** ~ ensalada de tomate.

salad bowl *n* ensaladera.

salad cream *n* (*BRIT*) mayonesa.

salad dressing *n* aliño.

salad oil *n* aceite *m* para ensalada.

salami [sə'lɑːmɪ] *n* salami *m*, salchichón *m*.

salaried ['sælərɪd] *adj* asalariado.

salary ['sælərɪ] *n* sueldo.

salary earner *n* asalariado/a.

salary scale *n* escala salarial.

sale [seɪl] *n* venta; (*at reduced prices*) liquidación *f*, saldo; **"for** ~**"** "se vende"; **on** ~ en venta; **on** ~ **or return** (*goods*) venta por reposición; **closing-down** *or*

(*US*) **liquidation** ~ liquidación *f*; ~ **and lease back** venta y arrendamiento al vendedor.

saleroom ['seɪlruːm] *n* sala de subastas.

sales assistant *n* (*BRIT*) dependiente/a *m/f*.

sales campaign *n* campaña de venta.

sales clerk *n* (*US*) dependiente/a *m/f*.

sales conference *n* conferencia de ventas.

sales drive *n* promoción *f* de ventas.

sales figures *npl* cifras *fpl* de ventas.

sales force *n* personal *m* de ventas.

salesman ['seɪlzmən] *n* vendedor *m*; (*in shop*) dependiente *m*; (*representative*) viajante *m*.

sales manager *n* gerente *m/f* de ventas.

salesmanship ['seɪlzmənʃɪp] *n* arte *m* de vender.

sales meeting *n* reunión *f* de ventas.

sales tax *n* (*US*) = **purchase tax.**

saleswoman ['seɪlzwumən] *n* vendedora; (*in shop*) dependienta; (*representative*) viajante *f*.

salient ['seɪlɪənt] *adj* (*features, points*) sobresaliente.

saline ['seɪlaɪn] *adj* salino.

saliva [sə'laɪvə] *n* saliva.

sallow ['sæləu] *adj* cetrino.

sally forth, sally out *vi* salir, ponerse en marcha.

salmon ['sæmən] *n* (*pl inv*) salmón *m*.

salon ['sælɔn] *n* (*hairdressing* ~, *beauty* ~) salón *m*.

saloon [sə'luːn] *n* (*US*) bar *m*, taberna; (*BRIT AUT*) (coche *m* de) turismo; (*ship's lounge*) cámara, salón *m*.

SALT [sɔːlt] *n abbr* (= *Strategic Arms Limitation Treaty*) tratado SALT.

salt [sɔːlt] *n* sal *f* ♦ *vt* salar; (*put* ~ *on*) poner sal en; **an old** ~ un lobo de mar.

▶**salt away** *vt* (*col: money*) ahorrar.

salt cellar *n* salero.

salt mine *n* mina de sal.

saltwater ['sɔːlt'wɔːtə*] *adj* (*fish etc*) de agua salada, de mar.

salty ['sɔːltɪ] *adj* salado.

salubrious [sə'luːbrɪəs] *adj* sano; (*fig: district etc*) atractivo.

salutary ['sæljutərɪ] *adj* saludable.

salute [sə'luːt] *n* saludo; (*of guns*) salva ♦ *vt* saludar.

salvage ['sælvɪdʒ] *n* (*saving*) salvamento, recuperación *f*; (*things saved*) objetos *mpl* salvados ♦ *vt* salvar.

salvage vessel *n* buque *m* de salvamento.

salvation [sæl'veɪʃən] *n* salvación *f*.

Salvation Army *n* Ejército de Salvación.

salve [sælv] *n* (*cream etc*) ungüento,

bálsamo.
salver ['sælvə*] *n* bandeja.
salvo ['sælvəu] *n* (*MIL*) salva.
Samaritan [sə'mærɪtən] *n*: **to call the ~s** llamar al teléfono de la esperanza.
same [seɪm] *adj* mismo ♦ *pron*: **the ~** el mismo/la misma; **the ~ book as** el mismo libro que; **on the ~ day** el mismo día; **at the ~ time** (*at the ~ moment*) al mismo tiempo; (*yet*) sin embargo; **all** *or* **just the ~** sin embargo, aun así; **they're one and the ~** (*person*) son la misma persona; (*thing*) son iguales; **to do the ~** (**as sb**) hacer lo mismo (que otro); **and the ~ to you!** ¡igualmente!; **~ here!** ¡yo también!; **the ~ again** (*in bar etc*) otro igual.
sampan ['sæmpæn] *n* sampán *m*.
sample ['sɑːmpl] *n* muestra ♦ *vt* (*food, wine*) probar; **to take a ~** tomar una muestra; **free ~** muestra gratuita.
sanatorium, *pl* **-ria** [sænə'tɔːrɪəm, -rɪə] *n* (*BRIT*) sanatorio.
sanctify ['sæŋktɪfaɪ] *vt* santificar.
sanctimonious [sæŋktɪ'məunɪəs] *adj* santurrón/ona.
sanction ['sæŋkʃən] *n* sanción *f* ♦ *vt* sancionar; **to impose economic ~s on** *or* **against** imponer sanciones económicas a *or* contra.
sanctity ['sæŋktɪtɪ] *n* (*gen*) santidad *f*; (*inviolability*) inviolabilidad *f*.
sanctuary ['sæŋktjuərɪ] *n* (*gen*) santuario; (*refuge*) asilo, refugio.
sand [sænd] *n* arena; (*beach*) playa ♦ *vt* (*also:* **~ down**: *wood etc*) lijar.
sandal ['sændl] *n* sandalia.
sandalwood ['sændlwud] *n* sándalo.
sandbag ['sændbæg] *n* saco de arena.
sandblast ['sændblɑːst] *vt* limpiar con chorro de arena.
sandbox ['sændbɔks] *n* (*US*) = **sandpit**.
sandcastle ['sændkɑːsl] *n* castillo de arena.
sand dune *n* duna.
sander ['sændə*] *n* pulidora.
S & M *n abbr* (= *sadomasochism*) sadomasoquismo.
sandpaper ['sændpeɪpə*] *n* papel *m* de lija.
sandpit ['sændpɪt] *n* (*for children*) cajón *m* de arena.
sands [sændz] *npl* playa *sg* de arena.
sandstone ['sændstəun] *n* piedra arenisca.
sandstorm ['sændstɔːm] *n* tormenta de arena.
sandwich ['sændwɪtʃ] *n* bocadillo (*SP*), sandwich *m* (*LAM*) ♦ *vt* (*also:* **~ in**) intercalar; **to be ~ed between** estar apretujado entre; **cheese/ham ~** sandwich de queso/jamón.

sandwich board *n* cartelón *m*.
sandwich course *n* (*BRIT*) *programa que intercala períodos de estudio con prácticas profesionales.*
sandy ['sændɪ] *adj* arenoso; (*colour*) rojizo.
sane [seɪn] *adj* cuerdo, sensato.
sang [sæŋ] *pt of* **sing**.
sanitarium [sænɪ'tɛərɪəm] *n* (*US*) = **sanatorium**.
sanitary ['sænɪtərɪ] *adj* (*system, arrangements*) sanitario; (*clean*) higiénico.
sanitary towel, (*US*) **sanitary napkin** *n* paño higiénico, compresa.
sanitation [sænɪ'teɪʃən] *n* (*in house*) servicios *mpl* higiénicos; (*in town*) servicio de desinfección.
sanitation department *n* (*US*) departamento de limpieza y recogida de basuras.
sanity ['sænɪtɪ] *n* cordura; (*of judgment*) sensatez *f*.
sank [sæŋk] *pt of* **sink**.
San Marino ['sænmə'riːnəu] *n* San Marino.
Santa Claus [sæntə'klɔːz] *n* San Nicolás *m*, Papá Noel *m*.
Santiago [sæntɪ'ɑːgəu] *n* (*also:* **~ de Chile**) Santiago (de Chile).
sap [sæp] *n* (*of plants*) savia ♦ *vt* (*strength*) minar, agotar.
sapling ['sæplɪŋ] *n* árbol nuevo *or* joven.
sapphire ['sæfaɪə*] *n* zafiro.
Saragossa [særə'gɔsə] *n* Zaragoza.
sarcasm ['sɑːkæzm] *n* sarcasmo.
sarcastic [sɑː'kæstɪk] *adj* sarcástico; **to be ~** ser sarcástico.
sarcophagus, *pl* **sarcophagi** [sɑː'kɔfəgəs, -gaɪ] *n* sarcófago.
sardine [sɑː'diːn] *n* sardina.
Sardinia [sɑː'dɪnɪə] *n* Cerdeña.
Sardinian [sɑː'dɪnɪən] *adj, n* sardo/a *m/f*.
sardonic [sɑː'dɔnɪk] *adj* sardónico.
sari ['sɑːrɪ] *n* sari *m*.
SAS *n abbr* (*BRIT MIL*: = *Special Air Service*) *cuerpo del ejército británico encargado de misiones clandestinas.*
SASE *n abbr* (*US*: = *self-addressed stamped envelope*) *sobre con las propias señas de uno y con sello.*
sash [sæʃ] *n* faja.
Sask. *abbr* (*Canada*) = *Saskatchewan*.
SAT *n abbr* (*US*) = *Scholastic Aptitude Test*.
sat [sæt] *pt, pp of* **sit**.
Sat. *abbr* (= *Saturday*) sáb.
Satan ['seɪtn] *n* Satanás *m*.
satanic [sə'tænɪk] *adj* satánico.
satchel ['sætʃl] *n* bolsa; (*child's*) cartera, mochila (*LAM*).
sated ['seɪtɪd] *adj* (*appetite, person*) saciado.

satellite ['sætəlaɪt] n satélite m.
satellite television n televisión f por satélite.
satiate ['seɪʃɪeɪt] vt saciar, hartar.
satin ['sætɪn] n raso ♦ adj de raso; **with a ~ finish** satinado.
satire ['sætaɪə*] n sátira.
satirical [sə'tɪrɪkl] adj satírico.
satirist ['sætɪrɪst] n (writer etc) escritor(a) m/f satírico/a; (cartoonist) caricaturista m/f.
satirize ['sætɪraɪz] vt satirizar.
satisfaction [sætɪs'fækʃən] n satisfacción f; **it gives me great ~** es para mí una gran satisfacción; **has it been done to your ~?** ¿se ha hecho a su satisfacción?
satisfactorily [sætɪs'fæktərɪlɪ] adv satisfactoriamente, de modo satisfactorio.
satisfactory [sætɪs'fæktərɪ] adj satisfactorio.
satisfied ['sætɪsfaɪd] adj satisfecho; **to be ~ (with sth)** estar satisfecho (de algo).
satisfy ['sætɪsfaɪ] vt satisfacer; (pay) liquidar; (convince) convencer; **to ~ the requirements** llenar los requisitos; **to ~ sb that** convencer a algn de que; **to ~ o.s. of sth** convencerse de algo.
satisfying ['sætɪsfaɪɪŋ] adj satisfactorio.
satsuma [sæt'suːmə] n satsuma.
saturate ['sætʃəreɪt] vt: **to ~ (with)** empapar or saturar (de).
saturated fat [sætʃəreɪtɪd-] n grasa saturada.
saturation [sætʃə'reɪʃən] n saturación f.
Saturday ['sætədɪ] n sábado.
sauce [sɔːs] n salsa; (sweet) crema; (fig: cheek) frescura.
saucepan ['sɔːspən] n cacerola, olla.
saucer ['sɔːsə*] n platillo.
saucily ['sɔːsɪlɪ] adv con frescura, descaradamente.
sauciness ['sɔːsɪnɪs] n frescura, descaro.
saucy ['sɔːsɪ] adj fresco, descarado.
Saudi Arabia ['saʊdɪ-] n Arabia Saudí or Saudita.
Saudi (Arabian) ['saʊdɪ-] adj, n saudí m/f, saudita m/f.
sauna ['sɔːnə] n sauna.
saunter ['sɔːntə*] vi deambular.
sausage ['sɔsɪdʒ] n salchicha; (salami etc) salchichón m.
sausage roll n empanadilla.
sauté ['səʊteɪ] adj (CULIN: potatoes) salteado; (: onions) dorado, rehogado ♦ vt saltear; dorar.
savage ['sævɪdʒ] adj (cruel, fierce) feroz, furioso; (primitive) salvaje ♦ n salvaje m/f ♦ vt (attack) embestir.

savagely ['sævɪdʒlɪ] adv con ferocidad, furiosamente; de modo salvaje.
savagery ['sævɪdʒrɪ] n ferocidad f; salvajismo.
save [seɪv] vt (rescue) salvar, rescatar; (money, time) ahorrar; (put by) guardar; (COMPUT) salvar (y guardar); (avoid: trouble) evitar ♦ vi (also: ~ up) ahorrar ♦ n (SPORT) parada ♦ prep salvo, excepto; **to ~ face** salvar las apariencias; **God ~ the Queen!** ¡Dios guarde a la Reina!, ¡Viva la Reina!; **I ~d you a piece of cake** te he guardado un trozo de tarta; **it will ~ me an hour** con ello ganaré una hora.
saving ['seɪvɪŋ] n (on price etc) economía ♦ adj: **the ~ grace of** el único mérito de; **~s** npl ahorros mpl; **to make ~s** economizar.
savings account n cuenta de ahorros.
savings bank n caja de ahorros.
saviour, (US) **savior** ['seɪvjə*] n salvador(a) m/f.
savoir-faire ['sævwɑː'feə*] n don m de gentes.
savour, (US) **savor** ['seɪvə*] n sabor m, gusto ♦ vt saborear.
savo(u)ry ['seɪvərɪ] adj sabroso; (dish: not sweet) salado.
savvy ['sævɪ] n (col) conocimiento, experiencia.
saw [sɔː] pt of **see** ♦ n (tool) sierra ♦ vt (pt sawed or sawn [sɔːn]) serrar; **to ~ sth up** (a)serrar algo.
sawdust ['sɔːdʌst] n (a)serrín m.
sawmill ['sɔːmɪl] n aserradero.
sawn [sɔːn] pp of **saw.**
sawn-off ['sɔːnɔf], (US) **sawed-off** ['sɔːdɔf] adj: **~ shotgun** escopeta de cañones recortados.
saxophone ['sæksəfəʊn] n saxófono.
say [seɪ] n: **to have one's ~** expresar su opinión; **to have a or some ~ in sth** tener voz y voto en algo ♦ vt, vi (pt, pp said [sɛd]) decir; **to ~ yes/no** decir que sí/no; **my watch ~s 3 o'clock** mi reloj marca las tres; **that is to ~** es decir; **that goes without ~ing** ni que decir tiene; **she said (that) I was to give you this** me pidió que te diera esto; **I should ~ ~ it's worth about £100** yo diría que vale unas 100 libras; **~ after me** repite lo que yo diga; **shall we ~ Tuesday?** ¿quedamos, por ejemplo, el martes?; **that doesn't ~ much for him** eso no dice nada a su favor; **when all is said and done** al fin y al cabo, a fin de cuentas; **there is something or a lot to be said for it** hay algo or mucho que decir a su favor.
saying ['seɪɪŋ] n dicho, refrán m.
say-so ['seɪsəʊ] n (col) autorización f.

SBA *n abbr* (*US*) = Small Business Administration.

SC *n abbr* (*US*) = **Supreme Court** ♦ *abbr* (*US*) = South Carolina.

s/c *abbr* = **self-contained**.

scab [skæb] *n* costra; (*pej*) esquirol(a) *m/f*.

scaffold ['skæfəld] *n* (*for execution*) cadalso.

scaffolding ['skæfəldɪŋ] *n* andamio, andamiaje *m*.

scald [skɔːld] *n* escaldadura ♦ *vt* escaldar.

scalding ['skɔːldɪŋ] *adj* (*also*: ~ **hot**) hirviendo, que arde.

scale [skeɪl] *n* (*gen*, *MUS*) escala; (*of fish*) escama; (*of salaries, fees etc*) escalafón *m* ♦ *vt* (*mountain*) escalar; (*tree*) trepar; ~**s** *npl* (*small*) balanza *sg*; (*large*) báscula *sg*; **on a large** ~ a gran escala; ~ **of charges** tarifa, lista de precios; **pay** ~ escala salarial; **to draw sth to** ~ dibujar algo a escala.

▶**scale down** *vt* reducir.

scaled-down [skeɪld'daun] *adj* reducido proporcionalmente.

scale model *n* modelo a escala.

scallop ['skɔləp] *n* (*ZOOL*) venera; (*SEWING*) festón *m*.

scalp [skælp] *n* cabellera ♦ *vt* escalpar.

scalpel ['skælpl] *n* bisturí *m*.

scam [skæm] *n* (*col*) estafa, timo.

scamper ['skæmpə*] *vi*: **to** ~ **away**, ~ **off** escabullirse.

scampi ['skæmpɪ] *npl* gambas *fpl*.

scan [skæn] *vt* (*examine*) escudriñar; (*glance at quickly*) dar un vistazo a; (*TV, RADAR*) explorar, registrar ♦ *n* (*MED*) examen *m* ultrasónico.

scandal ['skændl] *n* escándalo; (*gossip*) chismes *mpl*.

scandalize ['skændəlaɪz] *vt* escandalizar.

scandalous ['skændələs] *adj* escandaloso.

Scandinavia [skændɪ'neɪvɪə] *n* Escandinavia.

Scandinavian [skændɪ'neɪvɪən] *adj*, *n* escandinavo/a *m/f*.

scanner ['skænə*] *n* (*RADAR, MED*) escáner *m*.

scant [skænt] *adj* escaso.

scantily ['skæntɪlɪ] *adv*: ~ **clad** *or* **dressed** ligero de ropa.

scantiness ['skæntɪnɪs] *n* escasez *f*, insuficiencia.

scanty ['skæntɪ] *adj* (*meal*) insuficiente; (*clothes*) ligero.

scapegoat ['skeɪpgəut] *n* cabeza de turco, chivo expiatorio.

scar [skɑː] *n* cicatriz *f* ♦ *vt* marcar con una cicatriz ♦ *vi* cicatrizarse.

scarce [skɛəs] *adj* escaso.

scarcely ['skɛəslɪ] *adv* apenas; ~ **anybody** casi nadie; **I can** ~ **believe it** casi no puedo creerlo.

scarceness ['skɛəsnɪs], **scarcity** ['skɛəsɪtɪ] *n* escasez *f*.

scarcity value *n* valor *m* de escasez.

scare [skɛə*] *n* susto, sobresalto; (*panic*) pánico ♦ *vt* asustar, espantar; **to** ~ **sb stiff** dar a algn un susto de muerte; **bomb** ~ amenaza de bomba.

▶**scare away, scare off** *vt* espantar, ahuyentar.

scarecrow ['skɛəkrəu] *n* espantapájaros *m inv*.

scared [skɛəd] *adj*: **to be** ~ asustarse, estar asustado.

scaremonger ['skɛəmʌŋgə*] *n* alarmista *m/f*.

scarf, *pl* **scarves** [skɑːf, skɑːvz] *n* (*long*) bufanda; (*square*) pañuelo.

scarlet ['skɑːlɪt] *adj* escarlata.

scarlet fever *n* escarlatina.

scarper ['skɑːpə*] *vi* (*BRIT col*) largarse.

scarred [skɑːd] *adj* lleno de cicatrices.

scarves [skɑːvz] *npl* of **scarf**.

scary ['skɛərɪ] *adj* (*col*) de miedo; **it's** ~ da miedo.

scathing ['skeɪðɪŋ] *adj* mordaz; **to be** ~ **about sth** criticar algo duramente.

scatter ['skætə*] *vt* (*spread*) esparcir, desparramar; (*put to flight*) dispersar ♦ *vi* desparramarse; dispersarse.

scatterbrained ['skætəbreɪnd] *adj* ligero de cascos.

scavenge ['skævɪndʒ] *vi*: **to** ~ (**for**) (*person*) revolver entre la basura (para encontrar); **to** ~ **for food** (*hyenas etc*) nutrirse de carroña.

scavenger ['skævɪndʒə*] *n* (*person*) mendigo/a que rebusca en la basura; (*ZOOL: animal*) animal *m* de carroña; (: *bird*) ave *f* de carroña.

SCE *n abbr* = Scottish Certificate of Education.

scenario [sɪ'nɑːrɪəu] *n* (*THEAT*) argumento; (*CINE*) guión *m*; (*fig*) escenario.

scene [siːn] *n* (*THEAT, fig etc*) escena; (*of crime, accident*) escenario; (*sight, view*) vista, perspectiva; (*fuss*) escándalo; **the political** ~ **in Spain** el panorama político español; **behind the** ~**s** (*also fig*) entre bastidores; **to appear** *or* **come on the** ~ (*also fig*) aparecer, presentarse; **to make a** ~ (*col: fuss*) armar un escándalo.

scenery ['siːnərɪ] *n* (*THEAT*) decorado; (*landscape*) paisaje *m*.

scenic ['siːnɪk] *adj* (*picturesque*) pintoresco.

scent [sɛnt] *n* perfume *m*, olor *m*; (*fig: track*) rastro, pista; (*sense of smell*) olfato ♦ *vt* perfumar; (*suspect*) presentir; **to put** *or* **throw sb off the** ~ (*fig*) despistar a algn.

sceptic, (*US*) **skeptic** ['skɛptɪk] *n* escéptico/a.

sceptical, (*US*) **skeptical** ['skɛptɪkl] *adj* escéptico.

scepticism, (*US*) **skepticism** ['skɛptɪsɪzm] *n* escepticismo.

sceptre, (*US*) **scepter** ['sɛptə*] *n* cetro.

schedule ['ʃɛdjuːl, (*US*) 'skɛdjuːl] *n* (*of trains*) horario; (*of events*) programa *m*; (*list*) lista ♦ *vt* (*timetable*) establecer el horario de; (*list*) catalogar; (*visit*) fijar la hora de; **on** ~ a la hora, sin retraso; **to be ahead of/behind** ~ estar adelantado/ retrasado; **we are working to a very tight** ~ tenemos un programa de trabajo muy apretado; **everything went according to** ~ todo salió según lo previsto; **the meeting is** ~**d for 7** *or* **to begin at 7** la reunión está fijada para las 7.

scheduled ['ʃɛdjuːld, (*US*) 'skɛdjuːld] *adj* (*date, time*) fijado; (*visit, event, bus, train*) programado; (*stop*) previsto; ~ **flight** vuelo regular.

schematic [skɪ'mætɪk] *adj* (*diagram etc*) esquemático.

scheme [skiːm] *n* (*plan*) plan *m*, proyecto; (*method*) esquema *m*; (*plot*) intriga; (*trick*) ardid *m*; (*arrangement*) disposición *f*; (*pension* ~ *etc*) sistema *m* ♦ *vt* proyectar ♦ *vi* (*plan*) hacer proyectos; (*intrigue*) intrigar; **colour** ~ combinación *f* de colores.

scheming ['skiːmɪŋ] *adj* intrigante.

schism ['skɪzəm] *n* cisma *m*.

schizophrenia [skɪtsə'friːnɪə] *n* esquizofrenia.

schizophrenic [skɪtsə'frɛnɪk] *adj* esquizofrénico.

scholar ['skɔlə*] *n* (*pupil*) alumno/a, estudiante *m/f*; (*learned person*) sabio/a, erudito/a.

scholarly ['skɔləlɪ] *adj* erudito.

scholarship ['skɔləʃɪp] *n* erudición *f*; (*grant*) beca.

school [skuːl] *n* (*gen*) escuela, colegio; (*in university*) facultad *f*; (*of fish*) banco ♦ *vt* (*animal*) amaestrar; **to be at** *or* **go to** ~ ir al colegio *or* a la escuela.

school age *n* edad *f* escolar.

schoolbook ['skuːlbuk] *n* libro de texto.

schoolboy ['skuːlbɔɪ] *n* alumno.

schoolchild, *pl* **-children** ['skuːltʃaɪld, -tʃɪldrən] *n* alumno/a.

schooldays ['skuːldeɪz] *npl* años *mpl* del colegio.

schoolgirl ['skuːlgɜːl] *n* alumna.

schooling ['skuːlɪŋ] *n* enseñanza.

school-leaver ['skuːlliːvə*] *n* (*BRIT*) joven *que ha terminado la educación secundaria.*

schoolmaster ['skuːlmɑːstə*] *n* (*primary*) maestro; (*secondary*) profesor *m*.

schoolmistress ['skuːlmɪstrɪs] *n* (*primary*) maestra; (*secondary*) profesora.

schoolroom ['skuːlrum] *n* clase *f*.

schoolteacher ['skuːltiːtʃə*] *n* (*primary*) maestro/a; (*secondary*) profesor(a) *m/f*.

schoolyard ['skuːljɑːd] *n* (*US*) patio del colegio.

schooner ['skuːnə*] *n* (*ship*) goleta.

sciatica [saɪ'ætɪkə] *n* ciática.

science ['saɪəns] *n* ciencia; **the** ~**s** las ciencias.

science fiction *n* ciencia ficción *f*.

scientific [saɪən'tɪfɪk] *adj* científico.

scientist ['saɪəntɪst] *n* científico/a.

sci-fi ['saɪfaɪ] *n abbr* (*col*) = **science fiction.**

Scilly Isles ['sɪlɪ-], **Scillies** ['sɪlɪz] *npl*: **the** ~ las Islas Sorlingas.

scintillating ['sɪntɪleɪtɪŋ] *adj* (*wit, conversation, company*) brillante, chispeante, ingenioso.

scissors ['sɪzəz] *npl* tijeras *fpl*; **a pair of** ~ unas tijeras.

scoff [skɔf] *vt* (*BRIT col: eat*) engullir ♦ *vi*: **to** ~ **(at)** (*mock*) mofarse (de).

scold [skəuld] *vt* regañar.

scolding ['skəuldɪŋ] *n* riña, reprimenda.

scone [skɔn] *n pastel de pan.*

scoop [skuːp] *n* cucharón *m*; (*for flour etc*) pala; (*PRESS*) exclusiva ♦ *vt* (*COMM: market*) adelantarse a; (: *profit*) sacar; (*COMM, PRESS: competitors*) adelantarse a.

▶**scoop out** *vt* excavar.

▶**scoop up** *vt* recoger.

scooter ['skuːtə*] *n* (*motor cycle*) Vespa ®; (*toy*) patinete *m*.

scope [skəup] *n* (*of plan, undertaking*) ámbito; (*reach*) alcance *m*; (*of person*) competencia; (*opportunity*) libertad *f* (de acción); **there is plenty of** ~ **for improvement** hay bastante campo para efectuar mejoras.

scorch [skɔːtʃ] *vt* (*clothes*) chamuscar; (*earth, grass*) quemar, secar.

scorcher ['skɔːtʃə*] *n* (*col: hot day*) día *m* abrasador.

scorching ['skɔːtʃɪŋ] *adj* abrasador(a).

score [skɔː*] *n* (*points etc*) puntuación *f*; (*MUS*) partitura; (*reckoning*) cuenta; (*twenty*) veintena ♦ *vt* (*goal, point*) ganar; (*mark, cut*) rayar ♦ *vi* marcar un tanto; (*FOOTBALL*) marcar un gol; (*keep score*) llevar el tanteo; **to keep (the)** ~ llevar la

cuenta; **to have an old ~ to settle with sb**
(*fig*) tener cuentas pendientes con algn;
on that ~ en lo que se refiere a eso; **~s of**
people (*fig*) muchísima gente, cantidad
de gente; **to ~ 6 out of 10** obtener una
puntuación de 6 sobre 10.

▶**score out** *vt* tachar.

scoreboard ['skɔːbɔːd] *n* marcador *m*.

scoreline ['skɔːlaɪn] *n* (*SPORT*) resultado
final.

scorer ['skɔːrə*] *n* marcador *m*; (*keeping
score*) encargado/a del marcador.

scorn [skɔːn] *n* desprecio ♦ *vt* despreciar.

scornful ['skɔːnful] *adj* desdeñoso,
despreciativo.

scornfully ['skɔːnfulɪ] *adv* desdeñosamente,
con desprecio.

Scorpio ['skɔːpɪəu] *n* Escorpión *m*.

scorpion ['skɔːpɪən] *n* alacrán *m*, escorpión
m.

Scot [skɔt] *n* escocés/esa *m/f*.

Scotch [skɔtʃ] *n* whisky *m* escocés.

scotch [skɔtʃ] *vt* (*rumour*) desmentir; (*plan*)
frustrar.

Scotch tape ® *n* (*US*) cinta adhesiva, celo,
scotch ® *m*.

scot-free [skɔt'friː] *adv*: **to get off ~**
(*unpunished*) salir impune; (*unhurt*) salir
ileso.

Scotland ['skɔtlənd] *n* Escocia.

Scots [skɔts] *adj* escocés/esa.

Scotsman ['skɔtsmən] *n* escocés *m*.

Scotswoman ['skɔtswumən] *n* escocesa.

Scottish ['skɔtɪʃ] *adj* escocés/esa; **the ~**
National Party *partido político*
independista escocés; **the ~ Parliament**
el Parlamento escocés.

scoundrel ['skaundrəl] *n* canalla *m/f*,
sinvergüenza *m/f*.

scour ['skauə*] *vt* (*clean*) fregar, estregar;
(*search*) recorrer, registrar.

scourer ['skauərə*] *n* (*pad*) estropajo;
(*powder*) limpiador *m*.

scourge [skəːdʒ] *n* azote *m*.

scout [skaut] *n* (*MIL*, *also*: **boy ~**)
explorador *m*.

▶**scout around** *vi* reconocer el terreno.

scowl [skaul] *vi* fruncir el ceño; **to ~ at sb**
mirar con ceño a algn.

scrabble ['skræbl] *vi* (*claw*): **to ~ (at)** arañar
♦ *n*: **S~** ® Intelect *m* ®; **to ~ about** or
around for sth revolver todo buscando
algo.

scraggy ['skrægɪ] *adj* flaco, delgaducho.

scram [skræm] *vi* (*col*) largarse.

scramble ['skræmbl] *n* (*climb*) subida
(difícil); (*struggle*) pelea ♦ *vi*: **to ~ out/**
through salir/abrirse paso con dificultad;

to ~ for pelear por; **to go scrambling**
(*SPORT*) hacer motocrós.

scrambled eggs ['skræmbld-] *npl* huevos
mpl revueltos.

scrap [skræp] *n* (*bit*) pedacito; (*fig*) pizca;
(*fight*) riña, bronca; (*also*: **~ iron**)
chatarra, hierro viejo ♦ *vt* (*discard*)
desechar, descartar ♦ *vi* reñir, armar
(una) bronca; **~s** *npl* (*waste*) sobras *fpl*,
desperdicios *mpl*; **to sell sth for ~** vender
algo como chatarra.

scrapbook ['skræpbuk] *n* álbum *m* de
recortes.

scrap dealer *n* chatarrero/a.

scrape [skreɪp] *n* (*fig*) lío, apuro ♦ *vt* raspar;
(*skin etc*) rasguñar; (**~ against**) rozar.

▶**scrape through** *vi* (*succeed*) salvarse por
los pelos; (*exam*) aprobar por los pelos.

scraper ['skreɪpə*] *n* raspador *m*.

scrap heap *n* (*fig*): **on the ~** desperdiciado;
to throw sth on the ~ desechar or
descartar algo.

scrap iron *n* chatarra.

scrap merchant *n* (*BRIT*) chatarrero/a.

scrap metal *n* chatarra, desecho de metal.

scrap paper *n* pedazos *mpl* de papel.

scrappy ['skræpɪ] *adj* (*essay etc*)
deshilvanado; (*education*) incompleto.

scrap yard *n* depósito de chatarra; (*for
cars*) cementerio de coches.

scratch [skrætʃ] *n* rasguño; (*from claw*)
arañazo ♦ *adj*: **~ team** equipo
improvisado ♦ *vt* (*record*) rayar; (*with
claw, nail*) rasguñar, arañar; (*COMPUT*)
borrar ♦ *vi* rascarse; **to start from ~**
partir de cero; **to be up to ~** cumplir con
los requisitos.

scratchpad ['skrætʃpæd] *n* (*US*) bloc *m* de
notas.

scrawl [skrɔːl] *n* garabatos *mpl* ♦ *vi* hacer
garabatos.

scrawny ['skrɔːnɪ] *adj* (*person, neck*) flaco.

scream [skriːm] *n* chillido ♦ *vi* chillar; **it**
was a ~ (*fig, col*) fue para morirse de
risa; **he's a ~** (*fig, col*) es muy divertido
or de lo más gracioso; **to ~ at sb (to do**
sth) gritarle a algn (para que haga algo).

scree [skriː] *n* cono de desmoronamiento.

screech [skriːtʃ] *vi* chirriar.

screen [skriːn] *n* (*CINE*, *TV*) pantalla;
(*movable*) biombo; (*wall*) tabique *m*; (*also*:
wind~) parabrisas *m inv* ♦ *vt* (*conceal*)
tapar; (*from the wind etc*) proteger; (*film*)
proyectar; (*fig*: *person*: *for security*)
investigar; (: *for illness*) hacer una
exploración a.

screen editing *n* (*COMPUT*) corrección *f* en
pantalla.

screening ['skri:nɪŋ] n (of film) proyección f; (for security) investigación f; (MED) exploración f.

screen memory n (COMPUT) memoria de la pantalla.

screenplay ['skri:npleɪ] n guión m.

screen saver [-seɪvə*] n salvapantallas m inv.

screen test n prueba de pantalla.

screw [skru:] n tornillo; (propeller) hélice f ♦ vt atornillar; **to ~ sth to the wall** fijar algo a la pared con tornillos.

▶**screw up** vt (paper, material etc) arrugar; (col: ruin) fastidiar; **to ~ up one's eyes** arrugar el entrecejo; **to ~ up one's face** torcer or arrugar la cara.

screwdriver ['skru:draɪvə*] n destornillador m.

screwed-up ['skru:d'ʌp] adj (col): **she's totally ~** está trastornada.

screwy ['skru:ɪ] adj (col) chiflado.

scribble ['skrɪbl] n garabatos mpl ♦ vt escribir con prisa; **to ~ sth down** garabatear algo.

script [skrɪpt] n (CINE etc) guión m; (writing) escritura, letra.

scripted ['skrɪptɪd] adj (RADIO, TV) escrito.

Scripture ['skrɪptʃə*] n Sagrada Escritura.

scriptwriter ['skrɪptraɪtə*] n guionista m/f.

scroll [skrəul] n rollo ♦ vt (COMPUT) desplazar.

scrotum ['skrəutəm] n escroto.

scrounge [skraundʒ] (col) vt: **to ~ sth off** or **from sb** gorronear algo a algn ♦ vi: **to ~ on sb** vivir a costa de algn.

scrounger ['skraundʒə*] n gorrón/ona m/f.

scrub [skrʌb] n (clean) fregado; (land) maleza ♦ vt fregar, restregar; (reject) cancelar, anular.

scrubbing brush ['skrʌbɪŋ-] n cepillo de fregar.

scruff [skrʌf] n: **by the ~ of the neck** por el pescuezo.

scruffy ['skrʌfɪ] adj desaliñado, desaseado.

scrum(mage) ['skrʌm(mɪdʒ)] n (RUGBY) melée f.

scruple ['skru:pl] n escrúpulo; **to have no ~s about doing sth** no tener reparos en or escrúpulos para hacer algo.

scrupulous ['skru:pjuləs] adj escrupuloso.

scrupulously ['skru:pjuləslɪ] adv escrupulosamente; **to be ~ fair/honest** ser sumamente justo/honesto.

scrutinize ['skru:tɪnaɪz] vt escudriñar; (votes) escrutar.

scrutiny ['skru:tɪnɪ] n escrutinio, examen m; **under the ~ of sb** bajo la mirada or el escrutinio de algn.

scuba ['sku:bə] n escafandra autónoma.

scuba diving n submarinismo.

scuff [skʌf] vt (shoes, floor) rayar.

scuffle ['skʌfl] n refriega.

scullery ['skʌlərɪ] n trascocina.

sculptor ['skʌlptə*] n escultor(a) m/f.

sculpture ['skʌlptʃə*] n escultura.

scum [skʌm] n (on liquid) espuma; (pej: people) escoria.

scupper ['skʌpə*] vt (BRIT: boat) hundir; (: fig: plans etc) acabar con.

scurrilous ['skʌrɪləs] adj difamatorio, calumnioso.

scurry ['skʌrɪ] vi: **to ~ off** escabullirse.

scurvy ['skə:vɪ] n escorbuto.

scuttle ['skʌtl] n (also: **coal ~**) cubo, carbonera ♦ vt (ship) barrenar ♦ vi (scamper): **to ~ away**, **~ off** escabullirse.

scythe [saɪð] n guadaña.

SD, S. Dak. abbr (US) = South Dakota.

SDI n abbr (= Strategic Defense Initiative) IDE f.

SDLP n abbr (BRIT POL) = Social Democratic and Labour Party.

SDP n abbr (BRIT POL) = Social Democratic Party.

sea [si:] n mar m/f; **by ~** (travel) en barco; **on the ~** (boat) en el mar; (town) junto al mar; **to be all at ~** (fig) estar despistado; **out to sea** or **at ~** en alta mar; **to go by ~** ir en barco; **heavy** or **rough ~s** marejada; **by** or **beside the ~** (holiday) en la playa; (village) a orillas del mar; **a ~ of faces** una multitud de caras.

sea bed n fondo del mar.

sea bird n ave f marina.

seaboard ['si:bɔ:d] n litoral m.

sea breeze n brisa de mar.

seadog ['si:dɔg] n lobo de mar.

seafarer ['si:fɛərə*] n marinero.

seafaring ['si:fɛərɪŋ] adj (community) marinero; (life) de marinero.

seafood ['si:fu:d] n mariscos mpl.

sea front n paseo marítimo.

seagoing ['si:gəuɪŋ] adj (ship) de alta mar.

seagull ['si:gʌl] n gaviota.

seal [si:l] n (animal) foca; (stamp) sello ♦ vt (close) cerrar; (: with ~) sellar; (decide: sb's fate) decidir; (: bargain) cerrar; **~ of approval** sello de aprobación.

▶**seal off** vt obturar.

seal cull n matanza de crías de foca.

sea level n nivel m del mar.

sealing wax ['si:lɪŋ-] n lacre m.

sea lion n león m marino.

sealskin ['si:lskɪn] n piel f de foca.

seam [si:m] n costura; (of metal) juntura; (of coal) veta, filón m; **the hall was**

bursting at the ~s la sala rebosaba de gente.
seaman ['siːmən] *n* marinero.
seamanship ['siːmənʃɪp] *n* náutica.
seamless ['siːmlɪs] *adj* sin costura(s).
seance ['seɪɒns] *n* sesión *f* de espiritismo.
seaplane ['siːpleɪn] *n* hidroavión *m*.
seaport ['siːpɔːt] *n* puerto de mar.
search [səːtʃ] *n* (*for person, thing*) busca, búsqueda; (*of drawer, pockets*) registro; (*inspection*) reconocimiento ♦ *vt* (*look in*) buscar en; (*examine*) examinar; (*person, place*) registrar; (*COMPUT*) buscar ♦ *vi*: to ~ for buscar; in ~ of en busca de; "~ and replace" (*COMPUT*) "buscar y reemplazar".
►**search through** *vt fus* registrar.
searcher ['səːtʃə*] *n* buscador(a) *m/f*.
searching ['səːtʃɪŋ] *adj* (*question*) penetrante.
searchlight ['səːtʃlaɪt] *n* reflector *m*.
search party *n* equipo de salvamento.
search warrant *n* mandamiento judicial.
searing ['sɪərɪŋ] *adj* (*heat*) abrasador(a); (*pain*) agudo.
seashore ['siːʃɔː*] *n* playa, orilla del mar; on the ~ a la orilla del mar.
seasick ['siːsɪk] *adj* mareado; to be ~ marearse.
seaside ['siːsaɪd] *n* playa, orilla del mar; to go to the ~ ir a la playa.
seaside resort *n* playa.
season ['siːzn] *n* (*of year*) estación *f*; (*sporting etc*) temporada; (*gen*) época, período ♦ *vt* (*food*) sazonar; to be in/out of ~ estar en sazón/fuera de temporada; the busy ~ (*for shops, hotels etc*) la temporada alta; the open ~ (*HUNTING*) la temporada de caza *or* de pesca.
seasonal ['siːznl] *adj* estacional.
seasoned ['siːznd] *adj* (*wood*) curado; (*fig: worker, actor*) experimentado; (*troops*) curtido; ~ **campaigner** veterano/a.
seasoning ['siːznɪŋ] *n* condimento.
season ticket *n* abono.
seat [siːt] *n* (*in bus, train: place*) asiento; (*chair*) silla; (*PARLIAMENT*) escaño; (*buttocks*) trasero; (*centre: of government etc*) sede *f* ♦ *vt* sentar; (*have room for*) tener cabida para; are there any ~s left? ¿quedan plazas?; to take one's ~ sentarse, tomar asiento; to be ~ed estar sentado, sentarse.
seat belt *n* cinturón *m* de seguridad.
seating ['siːtɪŋ] *n* asientos *mpl*.
seating arrangements *npl* distribución *fsg* de los asientos.
seating capacity *n* número de asientos,

aforo.
SEATO ['siːtəu] *n abbr* (= *Southeast Asia Treaty Organization*) OTASE *f*.
sea water *n* agua *m* del mar.
seaweed ['siːwiːd] *n* alga marina.
seaworthy ['siːwəːðɪ] *adj* en condiciones de navegar.
SEC *n abbr* (*US*: = *Securities and Exchange Commission*) comisión de operaciones bursátiles.
sec. *abbr* = **second(s)**.
secateurs [sɛkə'təːz] *npl* podadera *sg*.
secluded [sɪ'kluːdɪd] *adj* retirado.
seclusion [sɪ'kluːʒən] *n* retiro.
second ['sɛkənd] *adj* segundo ♦ *adv* (*in race etc*) en segundo lugar ♦ *n* (*gen*) segundo; (*AUT: also*: ~ **gear**) segunda; (*COMM*) artículo con algún desperfecto; (*BRIT SCOL: degree*) título universitario de segunda clase ♦ *vt* (*motion*) apoyar; [sɪ'kɒnd] (*employee*) trasladar temporalmente; ~ **floor** (*BRIT*) segundo piso; (*US*) primer piso; **Charles the S**~ Carlos Segundo; to ask for a ~ opinion (*MED*) pedir una segunda opinión; just a ~! ¡un momento!; to have ~ thoughts cambiar de opinión; on ~ thoughts *or* (*US*) thought pensándolo bien; ~ mortgage segunda hipoteca.
secondary ['sɛkəndərɪ] *adj* secundario.
secondary education *n* enseñanza secundaria.
secondary school *n* escuela secundaria; *ver recuadro*.

SECONDARY SCHOOL

En el Reino Unido se llama **secondary school** *a un centro educativo para alumnos de 11 a 18 años, si bien muchos estudiantes acaban a los 16, edad mínima de escolarización obligatoria. La mayor parte de estos centros funcionan como "comprehensive schools", aunque aún existen algunos de tipo selectivo.*

---

second-best [sɛkənd'bɛst] *n* segundo.
second-class ['sɛkənd'klɑːs] *adj* de segunda clase ♦ *adv*: to send sth ~ enviar algo por correo de segunda clase; to travel ~ viajar en segunda; ~ citizen ciudadano/a de segunda (clase).
second cousin *n* primo/a segundo/a.
seconder ['sɛkəndə*] *n* el/la que apoya una moción.
second-guess ['sɛkənd'gɛs] *vt* (*evaluate*) juzgar (a posteriori); (*anticipate*): to ~ sth/sb (intentar) adivinar algo/lo que va

a hacer algn.

secondhand ['sɛkənd'hænd] *adj* de segunda mano, usado ♦ *adv*: **to buy sth** ~ comprar algo de segunda mano; **to hear sth** ~ oír algo indirectamente.

second hand *n* (*on clock*) segundero.

second-in-command ['sɛkəndınkə'maːnd] *n* (*MIL*) segundo en el mando; (*ADMIN*) segundo/a, ayudante *m/f*.

secondly ['sɛkəndlı] *adv* en segundo lugar.

secondment [sı'kɔndmənt] *n* (*BRIT*) traslado temporal.

second-rate ['sɛkənd'reıt] *adj* de segunda categoría.

secrecy ['siːkrəsı] *n* secreto.

secret ['siːkrıt] *adj*, *n* secreto; **in** ~ *adv* en secreto; **to keep sth** ~ **(from sb)** ocultarle algo (a algn); **to make no** ~ **of sth** no ocultar algo.

secret agent *n* agente *m/f* secreto/a, espía *m/f*.

secretarial [sɛkrı'tɛərıəl] *adj* (*course*) de secretariado; (*staff*) de secretaría; (*work, duties*) de secretaria.

secretariat [sɛkrı'tɛərıət] *n* secretaría.

secretary ['sɛkrətərı] *n* secretario/a; **S~ of State** (*BRIT POL*) Ministro (con cartera).

secretary-general ['sɛkrətərı'dʒɛnərl] *n* secretario/a general.

secretary pool *n* (*US*) = **typing pool**.

secrete [sı'kriːt] *vt* (*MED, ANAT, BIO*) secretar; (*hide*) ocultar, esconder.

secretion [sı'kriːʃən] *n* secreción *f*.

secretive ['siːkrətıv] *adj* reservado, sigiloso.

secretly ['siːkrıtlı] *adv* en secreto.

secret police *n* policía secreta.

secret service *n* servicio secreto.

sect [sɛkt] *n* secta.

sectarian [sɛk'tɛərıən] *adj* sectario.

section ['sɛkʃən] *n* sección *f*; (*part*) parte *f*; (*of document*) artículo; (*of opinion*) sector *m*; **business** ~ (*PRESS*) sección *f* de economía.

sectional ['sɛkʃənl] *adj* (*regional*) regional, local.

sector ['sɛktə*] *n* (*gen, COMPUT*) sector *m*.

secular ['sɛkjulə*] *adj* secular, seglar.

secure [sı'kjuə*] *adj* (*free from anxiety*) seguro; (*firmly fixed*) firme, fijo ♦ *vt* (*fix*) asegurar, afianzar; (*get*) conseguir; (*COMM: loan*) garantizar; **to make sth** ~ afianzar algo; **to** ~ **sth for sb** conseguir algo para algn.

secured creditor [sı'kjuəd-] *n* acreedor(a) *m/f* con garantía.

securely [sı'kjuəlı] *adv* firmemente; **it is** ~ **fastened** está bien sujeto.

security [sı'kjuərıtı] *n* seguridad *f*; (*for loan*) fianza; (: *object*) prenda; **securities** *npl* (*COMM*) valores *mpl*, títulos *mpl*; ~ **of tenure** tenencia asegurada; **to increase/ tighten** ~ aumentar/estrechar las medidas de seguridad; **job** ~ seguridad *f* en el empleo.

Security Council *n*: **the** ~ el Consejo de Seguridad.

security forces *npl* fuerzas *fpl* de seguridad.

security guard *n* guardia *m/f* de seguridad.

security risk *n* riesgo para la seguridad.

secy. *abbr* (= *secretary*) Srio/a.

sedan [sı'dæn] *n* (*US AUT*) sedán *m*.

sedate [sı'deıt] *adj* tranquilo ♦ *vt* administrar sedantes a, sedar.

sedation [sı'deıʃən] *n* (*MED*) sedación *f*; **to be under** ~ estar bajo sedación.

sedative ['sɛdıtıv] *n* sedante *m*, calmante *m*.

sedentary ['sɛdntrı] *adj* sedentario.

sediment ['sɛdımənt] *n* sedimento.

sedimentary [sɛdı'mɛntərı] *adj* (*GEO*) sedimentario.

sedition [sı'dıʃən] *n* sedición *f*.

seduce [sı'djuːs] *vt* (*gen*) seducir.

seduction [sı'dʌkʃən] *n* seducción *f*.

seductive [sı'dʌktıv] *adj* seductor(a).

see [siː] *vb* (*pt* **saw**, *pp* **seen** [sɔː, siːn]) *vt* (*gen*) ver; (*understand*) ver, comprender; (*look at*) mirar ♦ *vi* ver ♦ *n* sede *f*; **to** ~ **sb to the door** acompañar a algn a la puerta; **to** ~ **that** (*ensure*) asegurarse de que; ~ **you soon/later/tomorrow!** ¡hasta pronto/ luego/mañana!; **as far as I can** ~ por lo visto *or* por lo que veo; **there was nobody to be** ~**n** no se veía a nadie; **let me** ~ (*show me*) a ver; (*let me think*) vamos a ver; **to go and** ~ **sb** ir a ver a algn; ~ **for yourself** compruébalo tú mismo; **I don't know what she** ~**s in him** no sé qué le encuentra.

▶**see about** *vt fus* atender a, encargarse de.

▶**see off** *vt* despedir.

▶**see through** *vt fus* calar ♦ *vt* llevar a cabo.

▶**see to** *vt fus* atender a, encargarse de.

seed [siːd] *n* semilla; (*in fruit*) pepita; (*fig*) germen *m*; (*TENNIS*) preseleccionado/a; **to go to** ~ (*plant*) granar; (*fig*) descuidarse.

seedless ['siːdlıs] *adj* sin semillas *or* pepitas.

seedling ['siːdlıŋ] *n* planta de semillero.

seedy ['siːdı] *adj* (*person*) desaseado; (*place*) sórdido.

seeing ['siːıŋ] *conj*: ~ **(that)** visto que, en vista de que.

seek, *pt, pp* **sought** [si:k, sɔ:t] *vt* (*gen*)
buscar; (*post*) solicitar; **to ~ advice/help
from sb** pedir consejos/solicitar ayuda a
algn.
▶**seek out** *vt* (*person*) buscar.
seem [si:m] *vi* parecer; **there ~s to be...**
parece que hay ...; **it ~s (that)** ... parece
que ...; **what ~s to be the trouble?** ¿qué
pasa?; **I did what ~ed best** hice lo que
parecía mejor.
seemingly ['si:mɪŋlɪ] *adv* aparentemente,
según parece.
seen [si:n] *pp of* **see**.
seep [si:p] *vi* filtrarse.
seer [sɪə*] *n* vidente *m/f*, profeta *m/f*.
seersucker [sɪə'sʌkə*] *n* sirsaca.
seesaw ['si:sɔ:] *n* balancín *m*, subibaja *m*.
seethe [si:ð] *vi* hervir; **to ~ with anger**
enfurecerse.
see-through ['si:θru:] *adj* transparente.
segment ['sɛgmənt] *n* segmento.
segregate ['sɛgrɪgeɪt] *vt* segregar.
segregation [sɛgrɪ'geɪʃən] *n* segregación *f*.
Seine [seɪn] *n* Sena *m*.
seismic ['saɪzmɪk] *adj* sísmico.
seize [si:z] *vt* (*grasp*) agarrar, asir; (*take
possession of*) secuestrar; (: *territory*)
apoderarse de; (*opportunity*)
aprovecharse de.
▶**seize up** *vi* (*TECH*) agarrotarse.
▶**seize (up)on** *vt fus* valerse de.
seizure ['si:ʒə*] *n* (*MED*) ataque *m*; (*LAW*)
incautación *f*.
seldom ['sɛldəm] *adv* rara vez.
select [sɪ'lɛkt] *adj* selecto, escogido; (*hotel,
restaurant, clubs*) exclusivo ♦ *vt* escoger,
elegir; (*SPORT*) seleccionar; **a ~ few** una
minoría selecta.
selection [sɪ'lɛkʃən] *n* selección *f*, elección
f; (*COMM*) surtido.
selection committee *n* comisión *f* de
nombramiento.
selective [sɪ'lɛktɪv] *adj* selectivo.
self [sɛlf] *n* (*pl* **selves** [sɛlvz]) uno mismo
♦ *pref* auto ...; **the ~** el yo.
self-addressed ['sɛlfə'drɛst] *adj*: **~
envelope** sobre *m* con la dirección propia.
self-adhesive [sɛlfəd'hi:zɪv] *adj*
autoadhesivo, autoadherente.
self-appointed [sɛlfə'pɔɪntɪd] *adj*
autonombrado.
self-assurance [sɛlfə'ʃuərəns] *n* confianza
en sí mismo.
self-assured [sɛlfə'ʃuəd] *adj* seguro de sí
mismo.
self-catering [sɛlf'keɪtərɪŋ] *adj* (*BRIT*) sin
pensión *or* servicio de comida; **~
apartment** apartamento con cocina

propia.
self-centred, (*US*) **self-centered**
[sɛlf'sɛntəd] *adj* egocéntrico.
self-cleaning [sɛlf'kli:nɪŋ] *adj*
autolimpiador.
self-confessed [sɛlfkən'fɛst] *adj* (*alcoholic
etc*) confeso.
self-confidence [sɛlf'kɔnfɪdns] *n* confianza
en sí mismo.
self-confident [sɛlf'kɔnfɪdnt] *adj* seguro de
sí (mismo), lleno de confianza en sí
mismo.
self-conscious [sɛlf'kɔnʃəs] *adj* cohibido.
self-contained [sɛlfkən'teɪnd] *adj* (*gen*)
independiente; (*BRIT: flat*) con entrada
particular.
self-control [sɛlfkən'trəul] *n* autodominio.
self-defeating [sɛlfdɪ'fi:tɪŋ] *adj*
contraproducente.
self-defence, (*US*) **self-defense**
[sɛlfdɪ'fɛns] *n* defensa propia.
self-discipline [sɛlf'dɪsɪplɪn] *n*
autodisciplina.
self-employed [sɛlfɪm'plɔɪd] *adj* que
trabaja por cuenta propia, autónomo.
self-esteem [sɛlfɪ'sti:m] *n* amor *m* propio.
self-evident [sɛlf'ɛvɪdnt] *adj* patente.
self-explanatory [sɛlfɪks'plænətərɪ] *adj* que
no necesita explicación.
self-financing [sɛlffaɪ'nænsɪŋ] *adj*
autofinanciado.
self-governing [sɛlf'gʌvənɪŋ] *adj*
autónomo.
self-help ['sɛlf'hɛlp] *n* autosuficiencia,
ayuda propia.
self-importance [sɛlfɪm'pɔ:tns] *n*
presunción *f*, vanidad *f*.
self-important [sɛlfɪm'pɔ:tnt] *adj* vanidoso.
self-indulgent [sɛlfɪn'dʌldʒənt] *adj*
indulgente consigo mismo.
self-inflicted [sɛlfɪn'flɪktɪd] *adj* infligido a sí
mismo.
self-interest [sɛlf'ɪntrɪst] *n* egoísmo.
selfish ['sɛlfɪʃ] *adj* egoísta.
selfishly ['sɛlfɪʃlɪ] *adv* con egoísmo, de
modo egoísta.
selfishness ['sɛlfɪʃnɪs] *n* egoísmo.
selflessly ['sɛlflɪslɪ] *adv*
desinteresadamente.
selfless ['sɛlflɪs] *adj* desinteresado.
self-made man ['sɛlfmeɪd-] *n hombre que
ha triunfado por su propio esfuerzo*.
self-pity [sɛlf'pɪtɪ] *n* lástima de sí mismo.
self-portrait [sɛlf'pɔ:treɪt] *n* autorretrato.
self-possessed [sɛlfpə'zɛst] *adj* sereno,
dueño de sí mismo.
self-preservation ['sɛlfprɛzə'veɪʃən] *n*
propia conservación *f*.

self-propelled [sɛlfprə'pɛld] *adj*
autopropulsado, automotor/triz.

self-raising [sɛlf'reızıŋ], (*US*) **self-rising**
[sɛlf'raızıŋ] *adj*: ~ **flour** harina con
levadura.

self-reliant [sɛlfrɪ'laıənt] *adj* independiente,
autosuficiente.

self-respect [sɛlfrɪ'spɛkt] *n* amor *m* propio.

self-respecting [sɛlfrɪ'spɛktıŋ] *adj* que
tiene amor propio.

self-righteous [sɛlf'raıtʃəs] *adj* santurrón/
ona.

self-rising [sɛlf'raızıŋ] *adj* (*US*) = **self-
raising**.

self-sacrifice [sɛlf'sækrıfaıs] *n* abnegación *f*.

self-same [sɛlfseɪm] *adj* mismo,
mismísimo.

self-satisfied [sɛlf'sætısfaıd] *adj* satisfecho
de sí mismo.

self-service [sɛlf'sə:vıs] *adj* de
autoservicio.

self-styled ['sɛlfstaıld] *adj* supuesto,
sedicente.

self-sufficient [sɛlfsə'fıʃənt] *adj*
autosuficiente.

self-supporting [sɛlfsə'pɔ:tıŋ] *adj*
económicamente independiente.

self-tanning [sɛlf'tænıŋ] *adj*
autobronceador.

self-taught [sɛlf'tɔ:t] *adj* autodidacta.

self-test ['sɛlftɛst] *n* (*COMPUT*)
autocomprobación *f*.

sell, *pt*, *pp* **sold** [sɛl, səuld] *vt* vender ♦ *vi*
venderse; **to ~ at** *or* **for £10** venderse a
10 libras; **to ~ sb an idea** (*fig*) convencer
a algn de una idea.

►**sell off** *vt* liquidar.

►**sell out** *vi* transigir, transar (*LAM*); **to ~
out (to sb/sth)** (*COMM*) vender su negocio
(a algn/algo) ♦ *vt* agotar las existencias
de, venderlo todo; **the tickets are all sold
out** las entradas están agotadas.

►**sell up** *vi* (*COMM*) liquidarse.

sell-by date ['sɛlbaı-] *n* fecha de
caducidad.

seller ['sɛlə*] *n* vendedor(a) *m/f*; ~**'s market**
mercado de demanda.

selling price ['sɛlıŋ-] *n* precio de venta.

Sellotape ® ['sɛləuteɪp] *n* (*BRIT*) cinta
adhesiva, celo, scotch ® *m*.

sellout ['sɛlaut] *n* traición *f*; **it was a ~**
(*THEAT etc*) fue un éxito de taquilla.

selves [sɛlvz] *npl of* **self**.

semantic [sı'mæntık] *adj* semántico.

semaphore ['sɛməfɔ:*] *n* semáforo.

semblance ['sɛmbləns] *n* apariencia.

semen ['si:mən] *n* semen *m*

semester [sı'mɛstə*] *n* (*US*) semestre *m*.

semi ['sɛmı] *n* = **semidetached house**.

semi... [sɛmı] *pref* semi..., medio....

semicircle ['sɛmısə:kl] *n* semicírculo.

semicircular ['sɛmı'sə:kjulə*] *adj*
semicircular.

semicolon [sɛmı'kəulən] *n* punto y coma.

semiconductor [sɛmıkən'dʌktə*] *n*
semiconductor *m*.

semiconscious [sɛmı'kɔnʃəs] *adj*
semiconsciente.

semidetached (house) [sɛmıdı'tætʃt-] *n*
casa adosada.

semi-final [sɛmı'faınl] *n* semi-final *f*.

seminar ['sɛmınɑ:*] *n* seminario.

seminary ['sɛmınərı] *n* (*REL*) seminario.

semiprecious stone [sɛmı'prɛʃəs-] *n*
piedra semipreciosa.

semiquaver ['sɛmıkweıvə*] *n* (*BRIT*)
semicorchea.

semiskilled ['sɛmıskıld] *adj* (*work, worker*)
semicualificado.

semi-skimmed *adj* semidesnatado.

semitone ['sɛmıtəun] *n* semitono.

semolina [sɛmə'li:nə] *n* sémola.

SEN *n abbr* (*BRIT*) = *State Enrolled Nurse*.

Sen., sen. *abbr* = **senator, senior**.

senate ['sɛnıt] *n* senado; *see also* **Congress**.

senator ['sɛnıtə*] *n* senador(a) *m/f*.

send, *pt*, *pp* **sent** [sɛnd, sɛnt] *vt* mandar,
enviar; **to ~ by post** mandar por correo;
to ~ sb for sth mandar a algn a buscar
algo; **to ~ word that ...** avisar *or* mandar
aviso de que ...; **she ~s (you) her love** te
manda *or* envía cariñosos recuerdos; **to
~ sb to sleep/into fits of laughter**
dormir/hacer reír a algn; **to ~ sb flying**
echar a algn; **to ~ sth flying** tirar algo.

►**send away** *vt* (*letter, goods*) despachar.

►**send away for** *vt fus* pedir.

►**send back** *vt* devolver.

►**send for** *vt fus* mandar traer; (*by post*)
escribir pidiendo algo.

►**send in** *vt* (*report, application*) mandar.

►**send off** *vt* (*goods*) despachar; (*BRIT
SPORT: player*) expulsar.

►**send on** *vt* (*letter*) mandar, expedir;
(*luggage etc: in advance*) facturar.

►**send out** *vt* (*invitation*) mandar; (*emit:
light, heat*) emitir, difundir; (: *signal*)
emitir.

►**send round** *vt* (*letter, document etc*) hacer
circular.

►**send up** *vt* (*person, price*) hacer subir;
(*BRIT: parody*) parodiar.

sender ['sɛndə*] *n* remitente *m/f*.

send-off ['sɛndɔf] *n*: **a good ~** una buena
despedida

send-up ['sɛndʌp] *n* (*col*) parodia, sátira.

Senegal [senɪ'gɔːl] *n* Senegal *m*.
Senegalese [senɪgə'liːz] *adj, n* senegalés/
esa *m/f*.
senile ['siːnaɪl] *adj* senil.
senility [sɪ'nɪlɪtɪ] *n* senilidad *f*.
senior ['siːnɪə*] *adj* (*older*) mayor, más
viejo; (: *on staff*) más antiguo; (*of higher
rank*) superior ♦ *n* mayor *m*; **P.** Jones ~ P.
Jones padre.
senior citizen *n* persona de la tercera
edad.
senior high school *n* (*US*) ≈ instituto de
enseñanza media; *see also* **high school**.
seniority [siːnɪ'ɔrɪtɪ] *n* antigüedad *f*; (*in
rank*) rango superior.
sensation [sen'seɪʃən] *n* (*physical feeling,
impression*) sensación *f*.
sensational [sen'seɪʃənl] *adj* sensacional.
sense [sens] *n* (*faculty, meaning*) sentido;
(*feeling*) sensación *f*; (*good ~*) sentido
común, juicio ♦ *vt* sentir, percibir; ~ **of
humour** sentido del humor; **it makes ~**
tiene sentido; **there is no ~ in (doing) that**
no tiene sentido (hacer) eso; **to come to
one's ~s** (*regain consciousness*) volver en
sí, recobrar el sentido; **to take leave of
one's ~s** perder el juicio.
senseless ['senslɪs] *adj* estúpido, insensato;
(*unconscious*) sin conocimiento.
senselessly ['senslɪslɪ] *adv* estúpidamente,
insensatamente.
sensibility [sensɪ'bɪlɪtɪ] *n* sensibilidad *f*;
sensibilities *npl* delicadeza *sg*.
sensible ['sensɪbl] *adj* sensato; (*reasonable*)
razonable, lógico.
sensibly ['sensɪblɪ] *adv* sensatamente;
razonablemente, de modo lógico.
sensitive ['sensɪtɪv] *adj* sensible; (*touchy*)
susceptible; **he is very ~ about it** es muy
susceptible acerca de eso.
sensitivity [sensɪ'tɪvɪtɪ] *n* sensibilidad *f*;
susceptibilidad *f*.
sensual ['sensjʊəl] *adj* sensual.
sensuous ['sensjʊəs] *adj* sensual.
sent [sent] *pt, pp of* **send**.
sentence ['sentəns] *n* (*LING*) frase *f*, oración
f; (*LAW*) sentencia, fallo ♦ *vt*: **to ~ sb to
death/to 5 years** condenar a algn a
muerte/a 5 años de cárcel; **to pass ~ on
sb** (*also fig*) sentenciar *or* condenar a
algn.
sentiment ['sentɪmənt] *n* sentimiento;
(*opinion*) opinión *f*.
sentimental [sentɪ'mentl] *adj* sentimental.
sentimentality [sentɪmen'tælɪtɪ] *n*
sentimentalismo, sensiblería.
sentinel ['sentɪnl] *n* centinela *m*.
sentry ['sentrɪ] *n* centinela *m*.

sentry duty *n*: **to be on ~** estar de
guardia, hacer guardia.
Seoul [səul] *n* Seúl *m*.
separable ['sepərəbl] *adj* separable.
separate *adj* ['seprɪt] separado; (*distinct*)
distinto ♦ (*vb*: ['sepəreɪt]) *vt* separar; (*part*)
dividir ♦ *vi* separarse; ~ **from** separado
or distinto de; **under ~ cover** (*COMM*) por
separado; **to ~ into** dividir *or* separar en;
he is ~d from his wife, but not divorced
está separado de su mujer, pero no (está)
divorciado.
separately ['sepritlɪ] *adv* por separado.
separates ['seprɪts] *npl* (*clothes*)
coordinados *mpl*.
separation [sepə'reɪʃən] *n* separación *f*.
sepia ['siːpɪə] *adj* color sepia *inv*.
Sept. *abbr* (= *September*) sep.
September [sep'tembə*] *n* se(p)tiembre *m*.
septic ['septɪk] *adj* séptico; **to go ~** ponerse
séptico.
septicaemia, (*US*) **septicemia**
[septɪ'siːmɪə] *n* septicemia.
septic tank *n* fosa séptica.
sequel ['siːkwl] *n* consecuencia, resultado;
(*of story*) continuación *f*.
sequence ['siːkwəns] *n* sucesión *f*, serie *f*;
(*CINE*) secuencia; **in ~** en orden *or* serie.
sequential [sɪ'kwenʃəl] *adj*: ~ **access**
(*COMPUT*) acceso en serie.
sequin ['siːkwɪn] *n* lentejuela.
Serb [səːb] *adj, n* = **Serbian**.
Serbia ['səːbɪə] *n* Serbia.
Serbian ['səːbɪən] *adj* serbio ♦ *n* serbio/a;
(*LING*) serbio.
Serbo-Croat ['səːbəu'krəuæt] *n* (*LING*)
serbocroata *m*.
serenade [serə'neɪd] *n* serenata ♦ *vt* dar
serenata a.
serene [sɪ'riːn] *adj* sereno, tranquilo.
serenely [sɪ'riːnlɪ] *adv* serenamente,
tranquilamente.
serenity [sə'renɪtɪ] *n* serenidad *f*,
tranquilidad *f*.
sergeant ['saːdʒənt] *n* sargento.
sergeant major *n* sargento mayor.
serial ['sɪərɪəl] *n* novela por entregas; (*TV*)
telenovela.
serial access *n* (*COMPUT*) acceso en serie.
serial interface *n* (*COMPUT*) interface *m* en
serie.
serialize ['sɪərɪəlaɪz] *vt* publicar/televisar
por entregas.
serial killer *n* asesino/a múltiple.
serial number *n* número de serie.
serial printer *n* (*COMPUT*) impresora en
serie.
series ['sɪərɪːz] *n, pl inv* serie *f*.

serious ['sɪərɪəs] *adj* serio; (*grave*) grave; **are you ~ (about it)?** ¿lo dices en serio?

seriously ['sɪərɪəslɪ] *adv* en serio; (*ill, wounded etc*) gravemente; (*col: extremely*) de verdad; **to take sth/sb ~** tomar algo/a algn en serio; **he's ~ rich** es una pasada de rico.

seriousness ['sɪərɪəsnɪs] *n* seriedad *f*; gravedad *f*.

sermon ['sə:mən] *n* sermón *m*.

serpent ['sə:pənt] *n* serpiente *f*.

serrated [sɪ'reɪtɪd] *adj* serrado, dentellado.

serum ['sɪərəm] *n* suero.

servant ['sə:vənt] *n* (*gen*) servidor(a) *m/f*; (*house ~*) criado/a.

serve [sə:v] *vt* servir; (*customer*) atender; (*subj: train*) tener parada en; (*apprenticeship*) hacer; (*prison term*) cumplir ♦ *vi* (*servant, soldier etc*) servir; (*TENNIS*) sacar ♦ *n* (*TENNIS*) saque *m*; **it ~s him right** se lo merece, se lo tiene merecido; **to ~ a summons on sb** entregar una citación a algn; **it ~s my purpose** me sirve para lo que quiero; **are you being ~d?** ¿le atienden?; **the power station ~s the entire region** la central eléctrica abastece a toda la región; **to ~ as/for/to do** servir de/para/para hacer; **to ~ on a committee/a jury** ser miembro de una comisión/un jurado.

▶**serve out, serve up** *vt* (*food*) servir.

service ['sə:vɪs] *n* (*gen*) servicio; (*REL: Catholic*) misa; (*: other*) oficio (religioso); (*AUT*) mantenimiento; (*of dishes*) juego ♦ *vt* (*car, washing machine*) mantener; (*: repair*) reparar; **the S~s** las fuerzas armadas; **funeral ~** exequias *fpl*; **to hold a ~** celebrar un oficio religioso; **the essential ~s** los servicios esenciales; **medical/social ~s** servicios *mpl* médicos/ sociales; **the train ~ to London** los trenes a Londres; **to be of ~ to sb** ser útil a algn.

serviceable ['sə:vɪsəbl] *adj* servible, utilizable.

service area *n* (*on motorway*) área de servicios.

service charge *n* (*BRIT*) servicio.

service industries *npl* industrias *fpl* del servicio.

serviceman ['sə:vɪsmən] *n* militar *m*.

service station *n* estación *f* de servicio.

servicing ['sə:vɪsɪŋ] *n* (*of car*) revisión *f*; (*of washing machine etc*) servicio de reparaciones.

serviette [sə:vɪ'ɛt] *n* (*BRIT*) servilleta.

servile ['sə:vaɪl] *adj* servil.

session ['sɛʃən] *n* (*sitting*) sesión *f*; **to be in ~** estar en sesión.

session musician *n* músico *m/f* de estudio.

set [sɛt] *n* juego; (*RADIO*) aparato; (*TV*) televisor *m*; (*of utensils*) batería; (*of cutlery*) cubierto; (*of books*) colección *f*; (*TENNIS*) set *m*; (*group of people*) grupo; (*CINE*) plató *m*; (*THEAT*) decorado; (*HAIRDRESSING*) marcado ♦ *adj* (*fixed*) fijo; (*ready*) listo; (*resolved*) resuelto, decidido ♦ (*vb: pt, pp set*) *vt* (*place*) poner, colocar; (*fix*) fijar; (*adjust*) ajustar, arreglar; (*decide: rules etc*) establecer, decidir; (*assign: task*) asignar; (*: homework*) poner ♦ *vi* (*sun*) ponerse; (*jam, jelly*) cuajarse; (*concrete*) fraguar; **a ~ of false teeth** una dentadura postiza; **a ~ of dining-room furniture** muebles *mpl* de comedor; **~ in one's ways** con costumbres arraigadas; **a ~ phrase** una frase hecha; **to be all ~ to do sth** estar listo para hacer algo; **to be ~ on doing sth** estar empeñado en hacer algo; **a novel ~ in Valencia** una novela ambientada en Valencia; **to ~ to music** poner música a; **to ~ on fire** incendiar, prender fuego a; **to ~ free** poner en libertad; **to ~ sth going** poner algo en marcha; **to ~ sail** zarpar, hacerse a la mar.

▶**set about** *vt fus*: **to ~ about doing sth** ponerse a hacer algo.

▶**set aside** *vt* poner aparte, dejar de lado.

▶**set back** *vt* (*progress*): **to ~ back (by)** retrasar (por); **a house ~ back from the road** una casa apartada de la carretera.

▶**set down** *vt* (*subj: bus, train*) dejar; (*record*) poner por escrito.

▶**set in** *vi* (*infection*) declararse; (*complications*) comenzar; **the rain has ~ in for the day** parece que va a llover todo el día.

▶**set off** *vi* partir ♦ *vt* (*bomb*) hacer estallar; (*cause to start*) poner en marcha; (*show up well*) hacer resaltar.

▶**set out** *vi*: **to ~ out to do sth** proponerse hacer algo ♦ *vt* (*arrange*) disponer; (*state*) exponer; **to ~ out (from)** salir (de).

▶**set up** *vt* (*organization*) establecer.

setback ['sɛtbæk] *n* (*hitch*) revés *m*, contratiempo; (*in health*) recaída.

set menu *n* menú *m*.

set phrase *n* frase *f* hecha.

set square *n* cartabón *m*.

settee [sɛ'ti:] *n* sofá *m*.

setting ['sɛtɪŋ] *n* (*scenery*) marco; (*of jewel*) engaste *m*, montadura.

setting lotion *n* fijador *m* (para el pelo).

settle ['sɛtl] *vt* (*argument, matter*) resolver; (*pay: bill, accounts*) pagar, liquidar; (*colonize: land*) colonizar; (*MED: calm*)

calmar, sosegar ♦ *vi* (*dust etc*)
depositarse; (*weather*) estabilizarse; (*also*:
~ **down**) instalarse; (*calm down*)
tranquilizarse; **to ~ for sth** convenir en
aceptar algo; **to ~ on sth** decidirse por
algo; **that's ~d then** bueno, está
arreglado; **to ~ one's stomach** asentar el
estómago.
►**settle in** *vi* instalarse.
►**settle up** *vi*: **to ~ up with sb** ajustar
cuentas con algn.
settlement ['sɛtlmənt] *n* (*payment*)
liquidación *f*; (*agreement*) acuerdo,
convenio; (*village etc*) poblado; **in ~ of our
account** (*COMM*) en pago *or* liquidación
de nuestra cuenta.
settler ['sɛtlə*] *n* colono/a, colonizador(a)
m/f.
setup ['sɛtʌp] *n* sistema *m*.
seven ['sɛvn] *num* siete.
seventeen [sɛvn'tiːn] *num* diez y siete,
diecisiete.
seventh ['sɛvnθ] *adj* séptimo.
seventy ['sɛvntɪ] *num* setenta.
sever ['sɛvə*] *vt* cortar; (*relations*) romper.
several ['sɛvərl] *adj*, *pron* varios/as *m/fpl*,
algunos/as *m/fpl*; **~ of us** varios de
nosotros; **~ times** varias veces.
severance ['sɛvərəns] *n* (*of relations*)
ruptura.
severance pay *n* indemnización *f* por
despido.
severe [sɪ'vɪə*] *adj* severo; (*serious*) grave;
(*hard*) duro; (*pain*) intenso.
severely [sɪ'vɪəlɪ] *adv* severamente;
(*wounded, ill*) de gravedad, gravemente.
severity [sɪ'vɛrɪtɪ] *n* severidad *f*; gravedad
f; intensidad *f*.
Seville [sə'vɪl] *n* Sevilla.
sew, *pt* **sewed**, *pp* **sewn** [səu, səud, səun] *vt*,
vi coser.
►**sew up** *vt* coser.
sewage ['suːɪdʒ] *n* (*effluence*) aguas *fpl*
residuales; (*system*) alcantarillado.
sewage works *n* estación *f* depuradora
(de aguas residuales).
sewer ['suːə*] *n* alcantarilla, cloaca.
sewing ['səuɪŋ] *n* costura.
sewing machine *n* máquina de coser.
sewn [səun] *pp of* **sew.**
sex [sɛks] *n* sexo; **the opposite ~** el sexo
opuesto; **to have ~ with sb** tener
relaciones (sexuales) con algn.
sex act *n* acto sexual, coito.
sex appeal *n* sex-appeal *m*, gancho.
sex education *n* educación *f* sexual.
sexism ['sɛksɪzəm] *n* sexismo.
sexist ['sɛksɪst] *adj*, *n* sexista *m/f*.

sex life *n* vida sexual.
sex object *n* objeto sexual.
sextant ['sɛkstənt] *n* sextante *m*.
sextet [sɛks'tɛt] *n* sexteto.
sexual ['sɛksjuəl] *adj* sexual; **~ assault**
atentado contra el pudor; **~ harassment**
acoso sexual; **~ intercourse** relaciones *fpl*
sexuales.
sexually ['sɛksjuəlɪ] *adv* sexualmente.
sexy ['sɛksɪ] *adj* sexy.
Seychelles [seɪ'ʃɛlz] *npl*: **the ~** las
Seychelles.
SF *n abbr* = **science fiction.**
SG *n abbr* (*US*: = *Surgeon General*) *jefe del
servicio federal de sanidad*.
Sgt *abbr* (= *sergeant*) sgto.
shabbily ['ʃæbɪlɪ] *adv* (*treat*) injustamente;
(*dressed*) pobremente.
shabbiness ['ʃæbɪnɪs] *n* (*of dress, person*)
aspecto desharrapado; (*of building*) mal
estado.
shabby ['ʃæbɪ] *adj* (*person*) desharrapado;
(*clothes*) raído, gastado.
shack [ʃæk] *n* choza, chabola.
shackle ['ʃækl] *vt* encadenar; (*fig*): **to be ~d
by sth** verse obstaculizado por algo.
shackles ['ʃæklz] *npl* grillos *mpl*, grilletes
mpl.
shade [ʃeɪd] *n* sombra; (*for lamp*) pantalla;
(*for eyes*) visera; (*of colour*) tono *m*,
tonalidad *f*; (*US*: *window* ~) persiana ♦ *vt*
dar sombra a; **~s** *npl* (*US*: *sunglasses*)
gafas *fpl* de sol; **in the ~** a la sombra;
(*small quantity*): **a ~ of** un poquito de; **a ~
smaller** un poquito más pequeño.
shadow ['ʃædəu] *n* sombra ♦ *vt* (*follow*)
seguir y vigilar; **without** *or* **beyond a ~
of doubt** sin lugar a dudas.
shadow cabinet *n* (*BRIT POL*) gobierno en
la oposición.
shadowy ['ʃædəuɪ] *adj* oscuro; (*dim*)
indistinto.
shady ['ʃeɪdɪ] *adj* sombreado; (*fig*:
dishonest) sospechoso; (: *deal*) turbio.
shaft [ʃɑːft] *n* (*of arrow, spear*) astil *m*; (*AUT,
TECH*) eje *m*, árbol *m*; (*of mine*) pozo; (*of
lift*) hueco, caja; (*of light*) rayo; **ventilator
~** chimenea de ventilación.
shaggy ['ʃægɪ] *adj* peludo.
shake [ʃeɪk] *vb* (*pt* **shook**, *pp* **shaken** [ʃuk,
'ʃeɪkn]) *vt* sacudir; (*building*) hacer
temblar; (*perturb*) inquietar, perturbar;
(*weaken*) debilitar; (*alarm*) trastornar ♦ *vi*
estremecerse; (*tremble*) temblar ♦ *n*
(*movement*) sacudida; **to ~ one's head** (*in
refusal*) negar con la cabeza; (*in dismay*)
mover *or* menear la cabeza, incrédulo; **to
~ hands with sb** estrechar la mano a

algn; **to ~ in one's shoes** (*fig*) temblar de miedo.

▶**shake off** *vt* sacudirse; (*fig*) deshacerse de.

▶**shake up** *vt* agitar.

shake-up ['ʃeɪkʌp] *n* reorganización *f*.

shakily ['ʃeɪkɪlɪ] *adv* (*reply*) con voz temblorosa *or* trémula; (*walk*) con paso vacilante; (*write*) con mano temblorosa.

shaky ['ʃeɪkɪ] *adj* (*unstable*) inestable, poco firme; (*trembling*) tembloroso; (*health*) delicado; (*memory*) defectuoso; (*person: from illness*) temblando; (*premise etc*) incierto.

shale [ʃeɪl] *n* esquisto.

shall [ʃæl] *aux vb*: **I ~ go** iré.

shallot [ʃə'lɒt] *n* (*BRIT*) cebollita, chalote *m*.

shallow ['ʃæləu] *adj* poco profundo; (*fig*) superficial.

shallows ['ʃæləuz] *npl* bajío *sg*, bajos *mpl*.

sham [ʃæm] *n* fraude *m*, engaño ♦ *adj* falso, fingido ♦ *vt* fingir, simular.

shambles ['ʃæmblz] *n* desorden *m*, confusión *f*; **the economy is (in) a complete ~** la economía está en un estado desastroso.

shambolic [ʃæm'bɒlɪk] *adj* (*col*) caótico.

shame [ʃeɪm] *n* vergüenza; (*pity*) lástima, pena ♦ *vt* avergonzar; **it is a ~ that/to do** es una lástima *or* pena que/hacer; **what a ~!** ¡qué lástima *or* pena!; **to put sth/sb to ~** (*fig*) ridiculizar algo/a algn.

shamefaced ['ʃeɪmfeɪst] *adj* avergonzado.

shameful ['ʃeɪmful] *adj* vergonzoso.

shamefully ['ʃeɪmfulɪ] *adv* vergonzosamente.

shameless ['ʃeɪmlɪs] *adj* descarado.

shampoo [ʃæm'puː] *n* champú *m* ♦ *vt* lavar con champú.

shampoo and set *n* lavado y marcado.

shamrock ['ʃæmrɒk] *n* trébol *m*.

shandy ['ʃændɪ], (*US*) **shandygaff** ['ʃændɪgæf] *n* clara, cerveza con gaseosa.

shan't [ʃɑːnt] = **shall not**.

shantytown ['ʃæntɪtaun] *n* barrio de chabolas.

SHAPE [ʃeɪp] *n abbr* (= *Supreme Headquarters Allied Powers, Europe*) cuartel general de las fuerzas aliadas en Europa.

shape [ʃeɪp] *n* forma ♦ *vt* formar, dar forma a; (*clay*) modelar; (*stone*) labrar; (*sb's ideas*) formar; (*sb's life*) determinar ♦ *vi* (*also: ~ up*) (*events*) desarrollarse; (*person*) formarse; **to take ~** tomar forma; **to get o.s. into ~** ponerse en forma *or* en condiciones; **in the ~ of a heart** en forma de corazón; **I can't bear gardening in any ~ or form** no aguanto la

jardinería de ningún modo.

-shaped *suff*: **heart~** en forma de corazón.

shapeless ['ʃeɪplɪs] *adj* informe, sin forma definida.

shapely ['ʃeɪplɪ] *adj* bien formado *or* proporcionado.

share [ʃɛə*] *n* (*part*) parte *f*, porción *f*; (*contribution*) cuota; (*COMM*) acción *f* ♦ *vt* dividir; (*fig: have in common*) compartir; **to have a ~ in the profits** tener una proporción de las ganancias; **he has a 50% ~ in a new business venture** tiene una participación del 50% en un nuevo negocio; **to ~ in** participar en; **to ~ out (among *or* between)** repartir (entre).

share capital *n* (*COMM*) capital *m* social en acciones.

share certificate *n* certificado *or* título de una acción.

shareholder ['ʃɛəhəuldə*] *n* (*BRIT*) accionista *m/f*.

share index *n* (*COMM*) índice *m* de la bolsa.

share issue *n* emisión *f* de acciones.

share price *n* (*COMM*) cotización *f*.

shark [ʃɑːk] *n* tiburón *m*.

sharp [ʃɑːp] *adj* (*razor, knife*) afilado, (*point*) puntiagudo; (*outline*) definido; (*pain*) intenso; (*MUS*) desafinado; (*contrast*) marcado; (*voice*) agudo; (*curve, bend*) cerrado; (*person: quick-witted*) avispado; (: *dishonest*) poco escrupuloso ♦ *n* (*MUS*) sostenido ♦ *adv*: **at 2 o'clock ~** a las 2 en punto; **to be ~ with sb** hablar a algn de forma brusca y tajante; **turn ~ left** tuerce del todo a la izquierda.

sharpen ['ʃɑːpn] *vt* afilar; (*pencil*) sacar punta a; (*fig*) agudizar.

sharpener ['ʃɑːpnə*] *n* (*gen*) afilador *m*; (*pencil ~*) sacapuntas *m inv*.

sharp-eyed [ʃɑːp'aɪd] *adj* de vista aguda.

sharpish ['ʃɑːpɪʃ] *adv* (*BRIT col: quickly*) prontito, bien pronto.

sharply ['ʃɑːplɪ] *adv* (*abruptly*) bruscamente; (*clearly*) claramente; (*harshly*) severamente.

sharp-tempered [ʃɑːp'tempəd] *adj* de genio arisco.

sharp-witted [ʃɑːp'wɪtɪd] *adj* listo, despabilado.

shatter ['ʃætə*] *vt* hacer añicos *or* pedazos; (*fig: ruin*) destruir, acabar con ♦ *vi* hacerse añicos.

shattered ['ʃætəd] *adj* (*grief-stricken*) destrozado, deshecho; (*exhausted*) agotado, hecho polvo.

shattering ['ʃætərɪŋ] *adj* (*experience*) devastador(a), anonadante.

shatterproof ['ʃætəpruːf] *adj* inastillable.

shave [ʃeɪv] _vt_ afeitar, rasurar ♦ _vi_ afeitarse ♦ _n_: **to have a ~** afeitarse.
shaven [ʃeɪvn] _adj_ (_head_) rapado.
shaver [ˈʃeɪvə*] _n_ (_also_: **electric ~**) máquina de afeitar (eléctrica).
shaving [ˈʃeɪvɪŋ] _n_ (_action_) afeitado, **~s** _npl_ (_of wood etc_) virutas _fpl_.
shaving brush _n_ brocha (de afeitar).
shaving cream _n_ crema (de afeitar).
shaving point _n_ enchufe _m_ para máquinas de afeitar.
shaving soap _n_ jabón _m_ de afeitar.
shawl [ʃɔːl] _n_ chal _m_.
she [ʃiː] _pron_ ella; **there ~ is** allí está; **~-cat** gata; _NB: for ships, countries follow the gender of your translation._
sheaf, _pl_ sheaves [ʃiːf, ʃiːvz] _n_ (_of corn_) gavilla; (_of arrows_) haz _m_; (_of papers_) fajo.
shear [ʃɪə*] _vt_ (_pt_ **~ed**, _pp_ **~ed** _or_ **shorn** [ʃɔːn]) (_sheep_) esquilar, trasquilar.
▶**shear off** _vi_ romperse.
shears [ˈʃɪəz] _npl_ (_for hedge_) tijeras _fpl_ de jardín.
sheath [ʃiːθ] _n_ vaina; (_contraceptive_) preservativo.
sheath knife _n_ cuchillo de monte.
sheaves [ʃiːvz] _npl of_ **sheaf**.
shed [ʃed] _n_ cobertizo; (_INDUSTRY, RAIL_) nave _f_ ♦ _vt_ (_pt, pp_ **shed**) (_skin_) mudar; (_tears_) derramar; **to ~ light on** (_problem, mystery_) aclarar, arrojar luz sobre.
she'd [ʃiːd] = **she had, she would.**
sheen [ʃiːn] _n_ brillo, lustre _m_.
sheep [ʃiːp] _n_ (_pl inv_) oveja.
sheepdog [ˈʃiːpdɔg] _n_ perro pastor.
sheep farmer _n_ ganadero (de ovejas).
sheepish [ˈʃiːpɪʃ] _adj_ tímido, vergonzoso.
sheepskin [ˈʃiːpskɪn] _n_ piel _f_ de carnero.
sheepskin jacket _n_ zamarra.
sheer [ʃɪə*] _adj_ (_utter_) puro, completo; (_steep_) escarpado; (_material_) diáfano ♦ _adv_ verticalmente; **by ~ chance** de pura casualidad.
sheet [ʃiːt] _n_ (_on bed_) sábana; (_of paper_) hoja; (_of glass, metal_) lámina.
sheet feed _n_ (_on printer_) alimentador _m_ de papel.
sheet lightning _n_ relámpago (difuso).
sheet metal _n_ metal _m_ en lámina.
sheet music _n_ hojas _fpl_ de partitura.
sheik(h) [ʃeɪk] _n_ jeque _m_.
shelf, _pl_ shelves [ʃelf, ʃelvz] _n_ estante _m_.
shelf life _n_ (_COMM_) periodo de conservación antes de la venta.
shell [ʃel] _n_ (_on beach_) concha, caracol (_LAM_); (_of egg, nut etc_) cáscara; (_explosive_) proyectil _m_, obús _m_; (_of building_) armazón _m_ ♦ _vt_ (_peas_) desenvainar; (_MIL_) bombardear.
▶**shell out** _vi_ (_col_): **to ~ out (for)** soltar el dinero (para), desembolsar (para).
she'll [ʃiːl] = **she will, she shall.**
shellfish [ˈʃelfɪʃ] _n_ (_pl inv_) crustáceo; (_pl: as food_) mariscos _mpl_.
shellsuit [ˈʃelsuːt] _n_ chándal _m_ (de tactel ®).
shelter [ˈʃeltə*] _n_ abrigo, refugio ♦ _vt_ (_aid_) amparar, proteger; (_give lodging to_) abrigar; (_hide_) esconder ♦ _vi_ abrigarse, refugiarse; **to take ~ (from)** refugiarse _or_ asilarse (de); **bus ~** parada de autobús cubierta.
sheltered [ˈʃeltəd] _adj_ (_life_) protegido; (_spot_) abrigado.
shelve [ʃelv] _vt_ (_fig_) dar carpetazo a.
shelves [ʃelvz] _npl of_ **shelf**.
shelving [ˈʃelvɪŋ] _n_ estantería.
shepherd [ˈʃepəd] _n_ pastor _m_ ♦ _vt_ (_guide_) guiar, conducir.
shepherdess [ˈʃepədɪs] _n_ pastora.
shepherd's pie _n_ pastel de carne y puré de patatas.
sherbert [ˈʃɔːbət] _n_ (_BRIT: powder_) polvos _mpl_ azucarados; (_US: water ice_) sorbete _m_.
sheriff [ˈʃerɪf] _n_ (_US_) sheriff _m_.
sherry [ˈʃerɪ] _n_ jerez _m_.
she's [ʃiːz] = **she is, she has.**
Shetland [ˈʃetlənd] _n_ (_also_: **the ~s, the ~ Isles**) las Islas _fpl_ Shetland.
Shetland pony _n_ pony _m_ de Shetland.
shield [ʃiːld] _n_ escudo; (_TECH_) blindaje _m_ ♦ _vt_: **to ~ (from)** proteger (de).
shift [ʃɪft] _n_ (_change_) cambio; (_at work_) turno ♦ _vt_ trasladar; (_remove_) quitar ♦ _vi_ moverse; (_change place_) cambiar de sitio; **the wind has ~ed to the south** el viento ha virado al sur; **a ~ in demand** (_COMM_) un desplazamiento de la demanda.
shift key _n_ (_on typewriter_) tecla de mayúsculas.
shiftless [ˈʃɪftlɪs] _adj_ (_person_) vago.
shift work _n_ (_BRIT_) trabajo por turnos; **to do ~** trabajar por turnos.
shifty [ˈʃɪftɪ] _adj_ tramposo; (_eyes_) furtivo.
Shiite [ˈʃiːaɪt] _adj, n_ shiíta _m/f_.
shilling [ˈʃɪlɪŋ] _n_ (_BRIT_) chelín _m_ (= _12 old pence; 20 in a pound_).
shilly-shally [ˈʃɪlɪʃælɪ] _vi_ titubear, vacilar.
shimmer [ˈʃɪmə*] _n_ reflejo trémulo ♦ _vi_ relucir.
shimmering [ˈʃɪmərɪŋ] _adj_ reluciente; (_haze_) trémulo; (_satin etc_) lustroso.
shin [ʃɪn] _n_ espinilla ♦ _vi_: **to ~ down/up a tree** bajar de/trepar un árbol.
shindig [ˈʃɪndɪg] _n_ (_col_) fiesta, juerga.
shine [ʃaɪn] _n_ brillo, lustre _m_ ♦ (_vb: pt, pp_

shone [ʃɔn]) vi brillar, relucir ♦ vt (shoes) lustrar, sacar brillo a; **to ~ a torch on sth** dirigir una linterna hacia algo.

shingle ['ʃɪŋgl] n (on beach) guijarras fpl.

shingles ['ʃɪŋglz] n (MED) herpes msg.

shining ['ʃaɪnɪŋ] adj (surface, hair) lustroso; (light) brillante.

shiny ['ʃaɪnɪ] adj brillante, lustroso.

ship [ʃɪp] n buque m, barco ♦ vt (goods) embarcar; (oars) desarmar; (send) transportar or enviar por vía marítima; **~'s manifest** manifiesto del buque; **on board ~** a bordo.

shipbuilder ['ʃɪpbɪldə*] n constructor(a) m/f naval.

shipbuilding ['ʃɪpbɪldɪŋ] n construcción f naval.

ship canal n canal m de navegación.

ship chandler [-'tʃɑːndlə*] n proveedor m de efectos navales.

shipment ['ʃɪpmənt] n (act) embarque m; (goods) envío.

shipowner ['ʃɪpəʊnə*] n naviero, armador m.

shipper ['ʃɪpə*] n compañía naviera.

shipping ['ʃɪpɪŋ] n (act) embarque m; (traffic) buques mpl.

shipping agent n agente m/f marítimo/a.

shipping company n compañía naviera.

shipping lane n ruta de navegación.

shipping line n = **shipping company**.

shipshape ['ʃɪpʃeɪp] adj en buen orden.

shipwreck ['ʃɪprɛk] n naufragio ♦ vt: **to be ~ed** naufragar.

shipyard ['ʃɪpjɑːd] n astillero.

shire ['ʃaɪə*] n (BRIT) condado.

shirk [ʃəːk] vt eludir, esquivar; (obligations) faltar a.

shirt [ʃəːt] n camisa; **in ~ sleeves** en mangas de camisa.

shirty ['ʃəːtɪ] adj (BRIT col): **to be ~** estar de malas pulgas.

shit [ʃɪt] (col!) n mierda; (nonsense) chorradas fpl; **to be a ~** ser un cabrón ♦ excl ¡mierda!; **tough ~!** ¡te jodes!

shiver ['ʃɪvə*] vi temblar, estremecerse; (with cold) tiritar.

shoal [ʃəʊl] n (of fish) banco.

shock [ʃɔk] n (impact) choque m; (ELEC) descarga (eléctrica); (emotional) conmoción f; (start) sobresalto, susto; (MED) postración f nerviosa ♦ vt dar un susto a; (offend) escandalizar; **to get a ~** (ELEC) sentir una sacudida eléctrica; **to give sb a ~** dar un susto a algn; **to be suffering from ~** padecer una postración nerviosa; **it came as a ~ to hear that ...**

me (etc) asombró descubrir que ....

shock absorber [-əbsɔːbə*] n amortiguador m.

shocker ['ʃɔkə*] n (col): **it was a real ~** fue muy fuerte.

shocking ['ʃɔkɪŋ] adj (awful: weather, handwriting) espantoso, horrible; (improper) escandaloso; (result) inesperado.

shock therapy, shock treatment n (MED) terapia de choque.

shock wave n onda expansiva or de choque.

shod [ʃɔd] pt, pp of **shoe** ♦ adj calzado.

shoddiness ['ʃɔdɪnɪs] n baja calidad f.

shoddy ['ʃɔdɪ] adj de pacotilla.

shoe [ʃuː] n zapato; (for horse) herradura; (brake ~) zapata ♦ vt (pt, pp **shod** [ʃɔd]) (horse) herrar.

shoebrush ['ʃuːbrʌʃ] n cepillo para zapatos.

shoehorn ['ʃuːhɔːn] n calzador m.

shoelace ['ʃuːleɪs] n cordón m.

shoemaker ['ʃuːmeɪkə*] n zapatero/a.

shoe polish n betún m.

shoeshop ['ʃuːʃɔp] n zapatería.

shoestring ['ʃuːstrɪŋ] n (shoelace) cordón m; (fig): **on a ~** con muy poco dinero, a lo barato.

shone [ʃɔn] pt, pp of **shine**.

shoo [ʃuː] excl ¡fuera!; (to animals) ¡zape! ♦ vt (also: **~ away, ~ off**) ahuyentar.

shook [ʃuk] pt of **shake**.

shoot [ʃuːt] n (on branch, seedling) retoño, vástago; (shooting party) cacería; (competition) concurso de tiro; (preserve) coto de caza ♦ (vb: pt, pp **shot** [ʃɔt]) vt disparar; (kill) matar a tiros; (execute) fusilar; (CINE: film, scene) rodar, filmar ♦ vi (FOOTBALL) chutar; **to ~ (at)** tirar (a); **to ~ past** pasar como un rayo; **to ~ in/out** vi entrar corriendo/salir disparado.

► **shoot down** vt (plane) derribar.

► **shoot up** vi (prices) dispararse.

shooting ['ʃuːtɪŋ] n (shots) tiros mpl, tiroteo; (HUNTING) caza con escopeta; (act: murder) asesinato (a tiros); (CINE) rodaje m.

shooting star n estrella fugaz.

shop [ʃɔp] n tienda; (workshop) taller m ♦ vi (also: **go ~ping**) ir de compras; **to talk ~** (fig) hablar del trabajo; **repair ~** taller m de reparaciones.

► **shop around** vi comparar precios.

shopaholic ['ʃɔpə'hɔlɪk] n (col) adicto/a a las compras.

shop assistant n (BRIT) dependiente/a m/f.

shop floor n (BRIT fig) taller m, fábrica.

shopkeeper ['ʃɒpkiːpə*] n (BRIT) tendero/a.
shoplift ['ʃɒplɪft] vi robar en las tiendas.
shoplifter ['ʃɒplɪftə*] n ratero/a.
shoplifting ['ʃɒplɪftɪŋ] n ratería, robo (en las tiendas).
shopper ['ʃɒpə*] n comprador(a) m/f.
shopping ['ʃɒpɪŋ] n (goods) compras fpl.
shopping bag n bolsa (de compras).
shopping centre, (US) shopping center n centro comercial.
shopping mall n centro comercial.
shop-soiled ['ʃɒpsɔɪld] adj (BRIT) deteriorado.
shop steward n (BRIT INDUSTRY) enlace m/f sindical.
shop window n escaparate m, vidriera (LAM).
shopworn ['ʃɒpwɔːn] adj (US) usado.
shore [ʃɔː*] n (of sea, lake) orilla ♦ vt: to ~ (up) reforzar; on ~ en tierra.
shore leave n (NAUT) permiso para bajar a tierra.
shorn [ʃɔːn] pp of shear.
short [ʃɔːt] adj (not long) corto; (in time) breve, de corta duración; (person) bajo; (curt) brusco, seco ♦ vi (ELEC) ponerse en cortocircuito ♦ n (also: ~ film) cortometraje m; (a pair of) ~s (unos) pantalones mpl cortos; to be ~ of sth estar falto de algo; in ~ en pocas palabras; a ~ time ago hace poco (tiempo); in the ~ term a corto plazo; to be in ~ supply escasear, haber escasez de; I'm ~ of time me falta tiempo; ~ of doing... a menos que hagamos etc...; everything ~ of... todo menos...; it is ~ for es la forma abreviada de; to cut ~ (speech, visit) interrumpir, terminar inesperadamente; to fall ~ of no alcanzar; to run ~ of sth acabársele algo; to stop ~ parar en seco; to stop ~ of detenerse antes de.
shortage ['ʃɔːtɪdʒ] n escasez f, falta.
shortbread ['ʃɔːtbrɛd] n pasta de mantequilla.
short-change [ʃɔːt'tʃeɪndʒ] vt: to ~ sb no dar el cambio completo a algn.
short-circuit [ʃɔːt'sɜːkɪt] n cortocircuito ♦ vt poner en cortocircuito ♦ vi ponerse en cortocircuito.
shortcoming ['ʃɔːtkʌmɪŋ] n defecto, deficiencia.
short(crust) pastry ['ʃɔːt(krʌst)-] n (BRIT) pasta quebradiza.
shortcut ['ʃɔːtkʌt] n atajo.
shorten ['ʃɔːtn] vt acortar; (visit) interrumpir.
shortfall ['ʃɔːtfɔːl] n déficit m, deficiencia.

shorthand ['ʃɔːthænd] n (BRIT) taquigrafía; to take sth down in ~ taquigrafiar algo.
shorthand notebook n cuaderno de taquigrafía.
shorthand typist n (BRIT) taquimecanógrafo/a.
short list n (BRIT: for job) lista de candidatos pre-seleccionados.
short-lived ['ʃɔːt'lɪvd] adj efímero.
shortly ['ʃɔːtlɪ] adv en breve, dentro de poco.
shortness ['ʃɔːtnɪs] n (of distance) cortedad f; (of time) brevedad f; (manner) brusquedad f.
short-sighted [ʃɔːt'saɪtɪd] adj (BRIT) miope, corto de vista; (fig) imprudente.
short-sightedness [ʃɔːt'saɪtɪdnɪs] n miopía; (fig) falta de previsión, imprudencia.
short-staffed [ʃɔːt'stɑːft] adj falto de personal.
short story n cuento.
short-tempered [ʃɔːt'tɛmpəd] adj enojadizo.
short-term ['ʃɔːttɜːm] adj (effect) a corto plazo.
short time n: to work ~, be on ~ (INDUSTRY) trabajar con sistema de horario reducido.
short-time working ['ʃɔːttaɪm-] n trabajo de horario reducido.
short wave n (RADIO) onda corta.
shot [ʃɒt] pt, pp of shoot ♦ n (sound) tiro, disparo; (person) tirador(a) m/f; (try) tentativa; (injection) inyección f; (PHOT) toma, fotografía; (shotgun pellets) perdigones mpl; to fire a ~ at sb/sth tirar or disparar contra algn/algo; to have a ~ at (doing) sth probar suerte con algo; like a ~ (without any delay) como un rayo; a big ~ (col) un pez gordo; to get ~ of sth/sb (col) deshacerse de algo/algn, quitarse algo/a algn de encima.
shotgun ['ʃɒtgʌn] n escopeta.
should [ʃʊd] aux vb: I ~ go now debo irme ahora; he ~ be there now debe de haber llegado (ya); I ~ go if I were you yo en tu lugar me iría; I ~ like to me gustaría; ~ he phone ... si llamara ..., en caso de que llamase ....
shoulder ['ʃəʊldə*] n hombro; (BRIT: of road): hard ~ arcén m ♦ vt (fig) cargar con; to look over one's ~ mirar hacia atrás; to rub ~s with sb (fig) codearse con algn; to give sb the cold ~ (fig) dar de lado a algn.
shoulder blade n omóplato.
shoulder bag n bolso de bandolera.
shoulder strap n tirante m.
shouldn't ['ʃʊdnt] = should not.

shout [ʃaut] n grito ♦ vt gritar ♦ vi gritar, dar voces.
▶**shout down** vt hundir a gritos.
shouting [ʃautɪŋ] n griterío.
shouting match n (col) discusión f a voz en grito.
shove [ʃʌv] n empujón m ♦ vt empujar; (col: put): **to ~ sth in** meter algo a empellones; **he ~d me out of the way** me quitó de en medio de un empujón.
▶**shove off** vi (NAUT) alejarse del muelle; (fig: col) largarse.
shovel [ʃʌvl] n pala; (mechanical) excavadora ♦ vt mover con pala.
show [ʃəu] n (of emotion) demostración f; (semblance) apariencia; (COMM, TECH: exhibition) exhibición f, exposición f; (THEAT) función f, espectáculo; (organization) negocio, empresa ♦ vb (pt **showed**, pp **shown** [ʃəun]) vt mostrar, enseñar; (courage etc) mostrar, manifestar; (exhibit) exponer; (film) proyectar ♦ vi mostrarse; (appear) aparecer; **on ~** (exhibits etc) expuesto; **to be on ~** estar expuesto; **it's just for ~** es sólo para impresionar; **to ask for a ~ of hands** pedir una votación a mano alzada; **who's running the ~ here?** ¿quién manda aquí?; **to ~ a profit/loss** (COMM) arrojar un saldo positivo/negativo; **I have nothing to ~ for it** no saqué ningún provecho (de ello); **to ~ sb to his seat/to the door** acompañar a algn a su asiento/a la puerta; **as ~n in the illustration** como se ve en el grabado; **it just goes to ~ that ...** queda demostrado que ...; **it doesn't ~** no se ve or nota.
▶**show in** vt (person) hacer pasar.
▶**show off** vi (pej) presumir ♦ vt (display) lucir; (pej) hacer alarde de.
▶**show out** vt: **to ~ sb out** acompañar a algn a la puerta.
▶**show up** vi (stand out) destacar; (col: turn up) presentarse ♦ vt descubrir; (unmask) desenmascarar.
showbiz [ʃəubɪz] n (col) = **show business**.
show business n el mundo del espectáculo.
showcase [ʃəukeɪs] n vitrina; (fig) escaparate m.
showdown [ʃəudaun] n enfrentamiento m.
shower [ʃauə*] n (rain) chaparrón m, chubasco; (of stones etc) lluvia; (also: ~ **bath**) ducha ♦ vi llover ♦ vt: **to ~ sb with sth** colmar a algn de algo; **to have or take a ~** ducharse.
shower cap n gorro de baño.
showerproof [ʃauəpruːf] adj impermeable.

showery [ʃauərɪ] adj (weather) lluvioso.
showground [ʃəugraund] n ferial m, real m (de la feria).
showing [ʃəuɪŋ] n (of film) proyección f.
show jumping n hípica.
showman [ʃəumən] n (at fair, circus) empresario (de espectáculos); (fig) actor m consumado.
showmanship [ʃəumənʃɪp] n dotes fpl teatrales.
shown [ʃəun] pp of **show**.
show-off [ʃəuɔf] n (col: person) fantasmón/ona m/f.
showpiece [ʃəupiːs] n (of exhibition etc) objeto más valioso, joya; **that hospital is a ~** ese hospital es un modelo del género.
showroom [ʃəuruːm] n sala de muestras.
show trial n juicio propagandístico.
showy [ʃəuɪ] adj ostentoso.
shrank [ʃræŋk] pt of **shrink**.
shrapnel [ʃræpnl] n metralla.
shred [ʃrɛd] n (gen pl) triza, jirón m; (fig: of truth, evidence) pizca, chispa ♦ vt hacer trizas; (documents) triturar; (CULIN) desmenuzar.
shredder [ʃrɛdə*] n (vegetable ~) picadora; (document ~) trituradora (de papel).
shrewd [ʃruːd] adj astuto.
shrewdly [ʃruːdlɪ] adv astutamente.
shrewdness [ʃruːdnɪs] n astucia.
shriek [ʃriːk] n chillido ♦ vt, vi chillar.
shrill [ʃrɪl] adj agudo, estridente.
shrimp [ʃrɪmp] n camarón m.
shrine [ʃraɪn] n santuario, sepulcro.
shrink, pt **shrank,** pp **shrunk** [ʃrɪŋk, ʃræŋk, ʃrʌŋk] vi encogerse; (be reduced) reducirse ♦ vt encoger; **to ~ from (doing) sth** no atreverse a hacer algo.
▶**shrink away** vi retroceder, retirarse.
shrinkage [ʃrɪŋkɪdʒ] n encogimiento; reducción f; (COMM: in shops) pérdidas fpl.
shrink-wrap [ʃrɪŋkræp] vt empaquetar en envase termorretráctil.
shrivel [ʃrɪvl] (also: ~ **up**) vt (dry) secar; (crease) arrugar ♦ vi secarse; arrugarse.
shroud [ʃraud] n sudario ♦ vt: ~**ed in mystery** envuelto en el misterio.
Shrove Tuesday [ʃrəuv-] n martes m de carnaval.
shrub [ʃrʌb] n arbusto.
shrubbery [ʃrʌbərɪ] n arbustos mpl.
shrug [ʃrʌg] n encogimiento de hombros ♦ vt, vi: **to ~ (one's shoulders)** encogerse de hombros.
▶**shrug off** vt negar importancia a; (cold, illness) deshacerse de.

shrunk [ʃrʌŋk] *pp of* **shrink.**
shrunken ['ʃrʌŋkn] *adj* encogido.
shudder ['ʃʌdə*] *n* estremecimiento, escalofrío ♦ *vi* estremecerse.
shuffle ['ʃʌfl] *vt* (*cards*) barajar; **to ~ (one's feet)** arrastrar los pies.
shun [ʃʌn] *vt* rehuir, esquivar.
shunt [ʃʌnt] *vt* (*RAIL*) maniobrar.
shunting yard ['ʃʌntɪŋ-] *n* estación *f* de maniobras.
shut, *pt, pp* **shut** [ʃʌt] *vt* cerrar ♦ *vi* cerrarse.
►**shut down** *vt, vi* cerrar; (*machine*) parar.
►**shut off** *vt* (*stop: power, water supply etc*) interrumpir, cortar; (: *engine*) parar.
►**shut out** *vt* (*person*) excluir, dejar fuera; (*noise, cold*) no dejar entrar; (*block: view*) tapar; (: *memory*) tratar de olvidar.
►**shut up** *vi* (*col: keep quiet*) callarse ♦ *vt* (*close*) cerrar; (*silence*) callar.
shutdown ['ʃʌtdaun] *n* cierre *m*.
shutter ['ʃʌtə*] *n* contraventana; (*PHOT*) obturador *m*.
shuttle ['ʃʌtl] *n* lanzadera; (*also*: ~ **service**: *AVIAT*) puente *m* aéreo ♦ *vi* (*subj: vehicle, person*) ir y venir ♦ *vt* (*passengers*) transportar, trasladar.
shuttlecock ['ʃʌtlkɔk] *n* volante *m*.
shuttle diplomacy *n* viajes *mpl* diplomáticos.
shy [ʃai] *adj* tímido ♦ *vi*: **to ~ away from doing sth** (*fig*) rehusar hacer algo; **to be ~ of doing sth** esquivar hacer algo.
shyly ['ʃaili] *adv* tímidamente.
shyness ['ʃainis] *n* timidez *f*.
Siam [sai'æm] *n* Siam *m*.
Siamese [saiə'miːz] *adj* siamés/esa ♦ *n* (*person*) siamés/esa *m/f*; (*LING*) siamés *m*; ~ **cat** gato siamés; ~ **twins** gemelos/as *m/fpl* siameses/as.
Siberia [sai'biəriə] *n* Siberia.
sibling ['siblɪŋ] *n* (*formal*) hermano/a.
Sicilian [si'siliən] *adj, n* siciliano/a *m/f*.
Sicily ['sisili] *n* Sicilia.
sick [sik] *adj* (*ill*) enfermo; (*nauseated*) mareado; (*humour*) morboso; **to be ~** (*BRIT*) vomitar; **to feel ~** estar mareado; **to be ~ of** (*fig*) estar harto de; **a ~ person** un(a) enfermo/a; **to be (off) ~** estar ausente por enfermedad; **to fall** *or* **take ~** ponerse enfermo.
sickbag ['sikbæg] *n* bolsa para el mareo.
sick bay *n* enfermería.
sickbed ['sikbed] *n* lecho de enfermo.
sick building syndrome *n* enfermedad causada por falta de ventilación y luz natural en un edificio.
sicken ['sikn] *vt* dar asco a ♦ *vi* enfermar; **to be ~ing for** (*cold, flu etc*) mostrar

síntomas de.
sickening ['sikniŋ] *adj* (*fig*) asqueroso.
sickle ['sikl] *n* hoz *f*.
sick leave *n* baja por enfermedad.
sickle-cell anaemia ['sikls εl-] *n* anemia de células falciformes, drepanocitosis *f*.
sick list *n*: **to be on the ~** estar de baja.
sickly ['sikli] *adj* enfermizo; (*taste*) empalagoso.
sickness ['siknis] *n* enfermedad *f*, mal *m*; (*vomiting*) náuseas *fpl*.
sickness benefit *n* subsidio de enfermedad.
sick pay *n* prestación por enfermedad pagada por la empresa.
sickroom ['sikruːm] *n* cuarto del enfermo.
side [said] *n* (*gen*) lado; (*face, surface*) cara; (*of paper*) cara; (*slice of bread*) rebanada; (*of body*) costado; (*of animal*) ijar *m*, ijada; (*of lake*) orilla; (*part*) lado; (*aspect*) aspecto; (*team: SPORT*) equipo; (: *POL etc*) partido; (*of hill*) ladera ♦ *adj* (*door, entrance*) lateral ♦ *vi*: **to ~ with sb** ponerse de parte de algn; **by the ~ of** al lado de; ~ **by** ~ juntos/as; **from all ~s** de todos lados; **to take ~s (with)** tomar partido (por); ~ **of beef** flanco de vaca; **the right/wrong ~** el derecho/revés; **from ~ to ~** de un lado a otro.
sideboard ['saidbɔːd] *n* aparador *m*.
sideboards ['saidbɔːdz] (*BRIT*), **sideburns** ['saidbəːnz] *npl* patillas *fpl*.
sidecar ['saidkɑː*] *n* sidecar *m*.
side dish *n* entremés *m*.
side drum *n* (*MUS*) tamboril *m*.
side effect *n* efecto secundario.
sidekick ['saidkik] *n* compinche *m*.
sidelight ['saidlait] *n* (*AUT*) luz *f* lateral.
sideline ['saidlain] *n* (*SPORT*) línea lateral; (*fig*) empleo suplementario.
sidelong ['saidlɔŋ] *adj* de soslayo; **to give a ~ glance at sth** mirar algo de reojo.
side plate *n* platito.
side road *n* (*BRIT*) calle *f* lateral.
sidesaddle ['saidsædl] *adv* a la amazona.
side show *n* (*stall*) caseta; (*fig*) atracción *f* secundaria.
sidestep ['saidstep] *vt* (*question*) eludir; (*problem*) esquivar ♦ *vi* (*BOXING etc*) dar un quiebro.
side street *n* calle *f* lateral.
sidetrack ['saidtræk] *vt* (*fig*) desviar (de su propósito).
sidewalk ['saidwɔːk] *n* (*US*) acera, vereda (*LAM*), andén *m* (*LAM*), banqueta (*LAM*).
sideways ['saidweiz] *adv* de lado.
siding ['saidɪŋ] *n* (*RAIL*) apartadero, vía muerta.

sidle ['saɪdl] *vi*: **to ~ up (to)** acercarse furtivamente (a).

SIDS [sɪdz] *n abbr* (= *sudden infant death syndrome*) (síndrome *m* de la) muerte *f* súbita.

siege [siːdʒ] *n* cerco, sitio; **to lay ~ to** cercar, sitiar.

siege economy *n* economía de sitio *or* de asedio.

Sierra Leone [sɪ'ɛrəlɪ'əun] *n* Sierra Leona.

siesta [sɪ'ɛstə] *n* siesta.

sieve [sɪv] *n* colador *m* ♦ *vt* cribar.

sift [sɪft] *vt* cribar ♦ *vi*: **to ~ through** pasar por una criba; (*information*) analizar cuidadosamente.

sigh [saɪ] *n* suspiro ♦ *vi* suspirar.

sight [saɪt] *n* (*faculty*) vista; (*spectacle*) espectáculo; (*on gun*) mira, alza ♦ *vt* ver, divisar; **in ~** a la vista; **out of ~** fuera de (la) vista; **at ~** a la vista; **at first ~** a primera vista; **to lose ~ of sth/sb** perder algo/a algn de vista; **to catch ~ of sth/sb** divisar algo/a algn; **I know her by ~** la conozco de vista; **to set one's ~s on (doing) sth** aspirar a *or* ambicionar (hacer) algo.

sighted ['saɪtɪd] *adj* vidente, de vista normal; **partially ~** de vista limitada.

sightseer ['saɪtsiːə*] *n* excursionista *m/f*, turista *m/f*.

sightseeing ['saɪtsiːɪŋ] *n* excursionismo, turismo; **to go ~** visitar monumentos.

sign [saɪn] *n* (*with hand*) señal *f*, seña; (*trace*) huella, rastro; (*notice*) letrero; (*written*) signo; (*road ~*) indicador *m*; (: *with instructions*) señal *f* de tráfico ♦ *vt* firmar; **as a ~ of** en señal de; **it's a good/bad ~** es buena/mala señal; **plus/minus ~** signo de más/de menos; **to ~ one's name** firmar.

▶**sign away** *vt* (*rights etc*) ceder.

▶**sign off** *vi* (*RADIO, TV*) cerrar el programa.

▶**sign on** *vi* (*MIL*) alistarse; (*as unemployed*) apuntarse al paro; (*employee*) firmar un contrato ♦ *vt* (*MIL*) alistar; (*employee*) contratar; **to ~ on for a course** matricularse en un curso.

▶**sign out** *vi* firmar el registro (al salir).

▶**sign over** *vt*: **to ~ sth over to sb** traspasar algo a algn.

▶**sign up** *vi* (*MIL*) alistarse ♦ *vt* (*contract*) contratar.

signal ['sɪgnl] *n* señal *f* ♦ *vi* (*AUT*) señalizar ♦ *vt* (*person*) hacer señas a; (*message*) transmitir; **the engaged ~** (*TEL*) la señal de comunicando; **the ~ is very weak** (*TV*) no captamos bien el canal; **to ~ a left/**

right turn (*AUT*) indicar que se va a doblar a la izquierda/derecha; **to ~ to sb (to do sth)** hacer señas a algn (para que haga algo).

signal box *n* (*RAIL*) garita de señales.

signalman ['sɪgnlmən] *n* (*RAIL*) guardavía *m*.

signatory ['sɪgnətərɪ] *n* firmante *m/f*.

signature ['sɪgnətʃə*] *n* firma.

signature tune *n* sintonía.

signet ring ['sɪgnət-] *n* (anillo de) sello.

significance [sɪg'nɪfɪkəns] *n* significado; (*importance*) trascendencia; **that is of no ~** eso no tiene importancia.

significant [sɪg'nɪfɪkənt] *adj* significativo; trascendente; **it is ~ that** ... es significativo que ....

significantly [sɪg'nɪfɪkəntlɪ] *adv* (*smile*) expresivamente; (*improve, increase*) sensiblemente; **and, ~** ... y debe notarse que ....

signify ['sɪgnɪfaɪ] *vt* significar.

sign language *n* mímica, lenguaje *m* por *or* de señas.

signpost ['saɪnpəust] *n* indicador *m*.

silage ['saɪlɪdʒ] *n* ensilaje *m*.

silence ['saɪlns] *n* silencio ♦ *vt* hacer callar; (*guns*) reducir al silencio.

silencer ['saɪlnsə*] *n* (*on gun, BRIT AUT*) silenciador *m*.

silent ['saɪlnt] *adj* (*gen*) silencioso; (*not speaking*) callado; (*film*) mudo; **to keep** *or* **remain ~** guardar silencio.

silently ['saɪlntlɪ] *adv* silenciosamente, en silencio.

silent partner *n* (*COMM*) socio/a comanditario/a.

silhouette [sɪluː'ɛt] *n* silueta; **~d against** destacado sobre *or* contra.

silicon ['sɪlɪkən] *n* silicio.

silicon chip *n* chip *m*, plaqueta de silicio.

silicone ['sɪlɪkəun] *n* silicona.

silk [sɪlk] *n* seda ♦ *cpd* de seda.

silky ['sɪlkɪ] *adj* sedoso.

sill [sɪl] *n* (*also*: **window~**) alféizar *m*; (*AUT*) umbral *m*.

silliness ['sɪlɪnɪs] *n* (*of person*) necedad *f*; (*of idea*) lo absurdo.

silly ['sɪlɪ] *adj* (*person*) tonto; (*idea*) absurdo; **to do sth ~** hacer una tontería.

silo ['saɪləu] *n* silo.

silt [sɪlt] *n* sedimento.

silver ['sɪlvə*] *n* plata; (*money*) moneda suelta ♦ *adj* de plata.

silver paper (*BRIT*), **silver foil** *n* papel *m* de plata.

silver plate *n* vajilla de plata.

silver-plated [sɪlvə'pleɪtɪd] *adj* plateado.

silversmith ['sɪlvəsmɪθ] *n* platero/a.
silverware ['sɪlvəwɛə*] *n* plata.
silver wedding (anniversary) *n* (*BRIT*)
   bodas *fpl* de plata.
silvery ['sɪlvrɪ] *adj* plateado.
similar ['sɪmɪlə*] *adj*: ~ **to** parecido *or*
   semejante a.
similarity [sɪmɪ'lærɪtɪ] *n* parecido,
   semejanza.
similarly ['sɪmɪləlɪ] *adv* del mismo modo; (*in
   a similar way*) de manera parecida;
   (*equally*) igualmente.
simile ['sɪmɪlɪ] *n* símil *m*.
simmer ['sɪmə*] *vi* hervir a fuego lento.
▶**simmer down** *vi* (*fig, col*) calmarse,
   tranquilizarse.
simpering ['sɪmpərɪŋ] *adj* afectado; (*foolish*)
   bobo.
simple ['sɪmpl] *adj* (*easy*) sencillo; (*foolish,
   COMM*) simple; **the** ~ **truth** la pura
   verdad.
simple interest *n* (*COMM*) interés *m*
   simple.
simple-minded [sɪmpl'maɪndɪd] *adj* simple,
   ingenuo.
simpleton ['sɪmpltən] *n* inocentón/ona *m/f*.
simplicity [sɪm'plɪsɪtɪ] *n* sencillez *f*;
   (*foolishness*) ingenuidad *f*.
simplification [sɪmplɪfɪ'keɪʃən] *n*
   simplificación *f*.
simplify ['sɪmplɪfaɪ] *vt* simplificar.
simply ['sɪmplɪ] *adv* (*in a simple way: live,
   talk*) sencillamente; (*just, merely*) sólo.
simulate ['sɪmjuleɪt] *vt* simular.
simulation [sɪmju'leɪʃən] *n* simulación *f*.
simultaneous [sɪməl'teɪnɪəs] *adj*
   simultáneo.
simultaneously [sɪməl'teɪnɪəslɪ] *adv*
   simultáneamente, a la vez.
sin [sɪn] *n* pecado ♦ *vi* pecar.
since [sɪns] *adv* desde entonces ♦ *prep* desde
   ♦ *conj* (*time*) desde que; (*because*) ya que,
   puesto que; ~ **then** desde entonces; ~
   Monday desde el lunes; (*ever*) ~ **I arrived**
   desde que llegué.
sincere [sɪn'sɪə*] *adj* sincero.
sincerely [sɪn'sɪəlɪ] *adv* sinceramente;
   yours ~ (*in letters*) le saluda
   (afectuosamente); ~ **yours** (*US: in letters*)
   le saluda atentamente.
sincerity [sɪn'sɛrɪtɪ] *n* sinceridad *f*.
sinecure ['saɪnɪkjuə*] *n* chollo.
sinew ['sɪnjuː] *n* tendón *m*.
sinful ['sɪnful] *adj* (*thought*) pecaminoso;
   (*person*) pecador(a).
sing, *pt* **sang**, *pp* **sung** [sɪŋ, sæŋ, sʌŋ] *vt*
   cantar ♦ *vi* (*gen*) cantar; (*bird*) trinar;
   (*ears*) zumbar.

Singapore [sɪŋə'pɔː*] *n* Singapur *m*.
singe [sɪndʒ] *vt* chamuscar.
singer ['sɪŋə*] *n* cantante *m/f*.
Singhalese [sɪŋə'liːz] *adj* = **Sinhalese**.
singing ['sɪŋɪŋ] *n* (*of person, bird*) canto;
   (*songs*) canciones *fpl*; (*in the ears*)
   zumbido; (*of kettle*) silbido.
single ['sɪŋgl] *adj* único, solo; (*unmarried*)
   soltero; (*not double*) individual, sencillo
   ♦ *n* (*BRIT: also:* ~ **ticket**) billete *m* sencillo;
   (*record*) sencillo, single *m*; ~**s** *npl* (*TENNIS*)
   individual *msg*; **not a** ~ **one was left** no
   quedaba ni uno; **every** ~ **day** todos los
   días (sin excepción).
▶**single out** *vt* (*choose*) escoger; (*point out*)
   singularizar.
single bed *n* cama individual.
single-breasted [sɪŋgl'brɛstɪd] *adj* (*jacket,
   suit*) recto, sin cruzar.
single-density ['sɪŋgldɛnsɪtɪ] *adj* (*COMPUT:
   disk*) de densidad sencilla.
single-entry book-keeping ['sɪŋglɛntrɪ-] *n*
   contabilidad *f* por partida simple.
Single European Market *n*: **the** ~ el
   Mercado Único Europeo.
single file *n*: **in** ~ en fila de uno.
single-handed [sɪŋgl'hændɪd] *adv* sin
   ayuda.
single-minded [sɪŋgl'maɪndɪd] *adj* resuelto,
   firme.
single parent *n* (*mother*) madre *f* soltera;
   (*father*) padre *m* soltero.
single-parent family ['sɪŋglpɛərənt-] *n*
   familia monoparental.
single room *n* habitación *f* individual.
singles bar *n* (*esp US*) bar *m* para solteros.
single-sex school ['sɪŋglsɛks-] *n* escuela
   no mixta.
single-sided [sɪŋgl'saɪdɪd] *adj* (*COMPUT:
   disk*) de una cara.
single spacing *n* (*TYP*): **in** ~ a un espacio.
singlet ['sɪŋglɪt] *n* camiseta.
singly ['sɪŋglɪ] *adv* uno por uno.
singsong ['sɪŋsɔŋ] *adj* (*tone*) cantarín/ina
   ♦ *n* (*songs*): **to have a** ~ tener un
   concierto improvisado.
singular ['sɪŋgjulə*] *adj* singular,
   extraordinario; (*odd*) extraño; (*LING*)
   singular ♦ *n* (*LING*) singular *m*; **in the
   feminine** ~ en femenino singular.
singularly ['sɪŋgjuləlɪ] *adv* singularmente,
   extraordinariamente.
Sinhalese [sɪnhə'liːz] *adj* singhalese.
sinister ['sɪnɪstə*] *adj* siniestro.
sink [sɪŋk] *n* fregadero ♦ *vb* (*pt* **sank**, *pp* **sunk**
   [sæŋk, sʌŋk]) *vt* (*ship*) hundir, echar a
   pique; (*foundations*) excavar; (*piles etc*): **to**
   ~ **sth into** hundir algo en ♦ *vi* (*gen*)

hundirse; **he sank into a chair/the mud** se dejó caer en una silla/se hundió en el barro; **the shares** *or* **share prices have sunk to 3 dollars** las acciones han bajado a 3 dólares.

▶**sink in** *vi* (*fig*) penetrar, calar; **the news took a long time to** ~ **in** la noticia tardó mucho en hacer mella en él (*or* mí *etc*).

sinking ['sɪŋkɪŋ] *adj*: **that** ~ **feeling** la sensación esa de desmoralización.

sinking fund *n* fondo de amortización.

sink unit *n* fregadero.

sinner ['sɪnə*] *n* pecador(a) *m/f*.

Sinn Féin [ʃɪn'feɪn] *n partido político republicano de Irlanda del Norte.*

sinuous ['sɪnjuəs] *adj* sinuoso.

sinus ['saɪnəs] *n* (*ANAT*) seno.

sip [sɪp] *n* sorbo ♦ *vt* sorber, beber a sorbitos.

siphon ['saɪfən] *n* sifón *m* ♦ *vt* (*also*: ~ **off**) (*funds*) desviar.

sir [sə:*] *n* señor *m*; **S**~ **John Smith** el Señor John Smith; **yes** ~ sí, señor; **Dear S**~ (*in letter*) Muy señor mío, Estimado Señor; **Dear S**~**s** Muy señores nuestros, Estimados Señores.

siren ['saɪərn] *n* sirena.

sirloin ['sə:lɔɪn] *n* solomillo; ~ **steak** filete *m* de solomillo.

sisal ['saɪsəl] *n* pita, henequén *m* (*LAM*).

sissy ['sɪsɪ] *n* (*col*) marica *m*.

sister ['sɪstə*] *n* hermana; (*BRIT: nurse*) enfermera jefe.

sister-in-law ['sɪstərɪnlɔ:] *n* cuñada.

sister organization *n* organización *f* hermana.

sister ship *n* barco gemelo.

sit [sɪt], *pt, pp* **sat** [sɪt, sæt] *vi* sentarse; (*be sitting*) estar sentado; (*assembly*) reunirse; (*dress etc*) caer, sentar ♦ *vt* (*exam*) presentarse a; **that jacket** ~**s well** esa chaqueta sienta bien; **to** ~ **on a committee** ser miembro de una comisión *or* un comité.

▶**sit about, sit around** *vi* holgazanear.

▶**sit back** *vi* (*in seat*) recostarse.

▶**sit down** *vi* sentarse; **to be** ~**ting down** estar sentado.

▶**sit in on** *vt fus*: **to** ~ **in on a discussion** asistir a una discusión.

▶**sit up** *vi* incorporarse; (*not go to bed*) no acostarse.

sitcom ['sɪtkɔm] *n abbr* (= *situation comedy*) telecomedia.

sit-down ['sɪtdaun] *adj*: ~ **strike** huelga de brazos caídos; **a** ~ **meal** una comida sentada.

site [saɪt] *n* sitio; (*also*: **building** ~) solar *m* ♦ *vt* situar.

sit-in ['sɪtɪn] *n* (*demonstration*) sentada *f*.

siting ['saɪtɪŋ] *n* (*location*) situación *f*, emplazamiento.

sitter ['sɪtə*] *n* (*ART*) modelo *m/f*; (*baby*~) canguro *m/f*.

sitting ['sɪtɪŋ] *n* (*of assembly etc*) sesión *f*; (*in canteen*) turno.

sitting member *n* (*POL*) titular *m/f* de un escaño.

sitting room *n* sala de estar.

sitting tenant *n* inquilino con derechos de estancia en una vivienda.

situate ['sɪtjueɪt] *vt* situar, ubicar (*LAM*).

situated ['sɪtjueɪtɪd] *adj* situado, ubicado (*LAM*).

situation [sɪtju'eɪʃən] *n* situación *f*; "~**s vacant**" (*BRIT*) "ofertas de trabajo".

situation comedy *n* (*TV, RADIO*) serie *f* cómica, comedia de situación.

six [sɪks] *num* seis.

six-pack ['sɪkspæk] *n* (*esp US*) paquete *m* de seis cervezas.

sixteen [sɪks'ti:n] *num* dieciséis.

sixth [sɪksθ] *adj* sexto; **the upper/lower** ~ (*SCOL*) el séptimo/sexto año.

sixty ['sɪkstɪ] *num* sesenta.

size [saɪz] *n* (*gen*) tamaño; (*extent*) extensión *f*; (*of clothing*) talla; (*of shoes*) número; **I take** ~ **5 shoes** calzo el número cinco; **I take** ~ **14** mi talla es la 42; **I'd like the small/large** ~ (*of soap powder etc*) quisiera el tamaño pequeño/grande.

▶**size up** *vt* formarse una idea de.

sizeable ['saɪzəbl] *adj* importante, considerable.

sizzle ['sɪzl] *vi* crepitar.

SK *abbr* (*Canada*) = *Saskatchewan*.

skate [skeɪt] *n* patín *m*; (*fish: pl inv*) raya ♦ *vi* patinar.

▶**skate over, skate round** *vt fus* (*problem, issue*) pasar por alto.

skateboard ['skeɪtbɔ:d] *n* monopatín *m*.

skater ['skeɪtə*] *n* patinador(a) *m/f*.

skating ['skeɪtɪŋ] *n* patinaje *m*; **figure** ~ patinaje *m* artístico.

skating rink *n* pista de patinaje.

skeleton ['skelɪtn] *n* esqueleto; (*TECH*) armazón *m*; (*outline*) esquema *m*.

skeleton key *n* llave *f* maestra.

skeleton staff *n* personal *m* reducido.

skeptic ['skeptɪk] *etc* (*US*) = **sceptic**.

sketch [sketʃ] *n* (*drawing*) dibujo; (*outline*) esbozo, bosquejo; (*THEAT*) pieza corta ♦ *vt* dibujar; esbozar.

sketch book *n* bloc *m* de dibujo.

sketching ['sketʃɪŋ] *n* dibujo.

sketch pad *n* bloc *m* de dibujo.

sketchy ['sketʃɪ] *adj* incompleto.

skewer ['skjuːə*] n broqueta.
ski [skiː] n esquí m ♦ vi esquiar.
ski boot n bota de esquí.
skid [skɪd] n patinazo ♦ vi patinar; **to go into a** ~ comenzar a patinar.
skid mark n señal f de patinazo.
skier ['skiːə*] n esquiador(a) m/f.
skiing ['skiːɪŋ] n esquí m; **to go** ~ practicar el esquí, (ir a) esquiar.
ski instructor n instructor(a) m/f de esquí.
ski jump n pista para salto de esquí.
skilful, (US) **skillful** ['skɪlful] adj diestro, experto.
ski lift n telesilla m, telesquí m.
skill [skɪl] n destreza, pericia; (technique) arte m, técnica; **there's a certain** ~ **to doing it** se necesita cierta habilidad para hacerlo.
skilled [skɪld] adj hábil, diestro; (worker) cualificado.
skillet ['skɪlɪt] n sartén f pequeña.
skillful ['skɪlful] etc (US) = **skilful** etc.
skil(l)fully ['skɪlfulɪ] adv hábilmente, con destreza.
skim [skɪm] vt (milk) desnatar; (glide over) rozar, rasar ♦ vi: **to** ~ **through** (book) hojear.
skimmed milk [skɪmd-] n leche f desnatada or descremada.
skimp [skɪmp] vt (work) chapucear; (cloth etc) escatimar; **to** ~ **on** (material etc) economizar; (work) escatimar.
skimpy ['skɪmpɪ] adj (meagre) escaso; (skirt) muy corto.
skin [skɪn] n (gen) piel f; (complexion) cutis m; (of fruit, vegetable) piel f, cáscara; (crust: on pudding, paint) nata ♦ vt (fruit etc) pelar; (animal) despellejar; **wet** or **soaked to the** ~ calado hasta los huesos.
skin cancer n cáncer m de piel.
skin-deep ['skɪn'diːp] adj superficial.
skin diver n buceador(a) m/f.
skin diving n buceo.
skinflint ['skɪnflɪnt] n tacaño/a, roñoso/a.
skinhead ['skɪnhɛd] n cabeza m/f rapada, skin(head) m/f.
skinny ['skɪnɪ] adj flaco, magro.
skintight ['skɪntaɪt] adj (dress etc) muy ajustado.
skip [skɪp] n brinco, salto; (container) contenedor m ♦ vi brincar; (with rope) saltar a la comba ♦ vt (pass over) omitir, saltar.
ski pants npl pantalones mpl de esquí.
ski pole n bastón m de esquiar.
skipper ['skɪpə*] n (NAUT, SPORT) capitán m.
skipping rope ['skɪpɪŋ-] n (BRIT) comba, cuerda (de saltar).

ski resort n estación f de esquí.
skirmish ['skəːmɪʃ] n escaramuza.
skirt [skəːt] n falda, pollera (LAM) ♦ vt (surround) ceñir, rodear; (go round) ladear.
skirting board ['skəːtɪŋ-] n (BRIT) rodapié m.
ski run n pista de esquí.
ski suit n traje m de esquiar.
skit [skɪt] n sátira, parodia.
ski tow n arrastre m (de esquí).
skittle ['skɪtl] n bolo; ~**s** (game) boliche m.
skive [skaɪv] vi (BRIT col) gandulear.
skulk [skʌlk] vi esconderse.
skull [skʌl] n calavera; (ANAT) cráneo.
skullcap ['skʌlkæp] n (worn by Jews) casquete m; (worn by Pope) solideo.
skunk [skʌŋk] n mofeta.
sky [skaɪ] n cielo; **to praise sb to the skies** poner a algn por las nubes.
sky-blue [skaɪ'bluː] adj (azul) celeste.
skydiving ['skaɪdaɪvɪŋ] n paracaidismo acrobático.
sky-high ['skaɪ'haɪ] adj (col) por las nubes ♦ adv (throw) muy alto; **prices have gone** ~ (col) los precios están por las nubes.
skylark ['skaɪlɑːk] n (bird) alondra.
skylight ['skaɪlaɪt] n tragaluz m, claraboya.
skyline ['skaɪlaɪn] n (horizon) horizonte m; (of city) perfil m.
skyscraper ['skaɪskreɪpə*] n rascacielos m inv.
slab [slæb] n (stone) bloque m; (of wood) tabla, plancha; (flat) losa; (of cake) trozo; (of meat, cheese) tajada, trozo.
slack [slæk] adj (loose) flojo; (slow) de poca actividad; (careless) descuidado; (COMM: market) poco activo; (: demand) débil; (period) bajo; **business is** ~ hay poco movimiento en el negocio.
slacken ['slækn] (also: ~ **off**) vi aflojarse ♦ vt aflojar; (speed) disminuir.
slackness ['slæknɪs] n flojedad f; negligencia.
slacks [slæks] npl pantalones mpl.
slag [slæg] n escoria, escombros mpl.
slag heap n escorial m, escombrera.
slain [sleɪn] pp of **slay**.
slake [sleɪk] vt (one's thirst) apagar.
slalom ['slɑːləm] n eslálom m.
slam [slæm] vt (door) cerrar de golpe; (throw) arrojar (violentamente); (criticize) vapulear, vituperar ♦ vi cerrarse de golpe.
slammer [slæmə*] n (col): **the** ~ la trena, el talego.
slander ['slɑːndə*] n calumnia, difamación f ♦ vt calumniar, difamar.

slanderous ['slɑ:ndərəs] *adj* calumnioso, difamatorio.

slang [slæŋ] *n* argot *m*; (*jargon*) jerga.

slanging match ['slæŋɪŋ-] *n* (*BRIT col*) bronca gorda.

slant [slɑ:nt] *n* sesgo, inclinación *f*; (*fig*) punto de vista; **to get a new ~ on sth** obtener un nuevo punto de vista sobre algo.

slanted ['slɑ:ntɪd], **slanting** ['slɑ:ntɪŋ] *adj* inclinado.

slap [slæp] *n* palmada; (*in face*) bofetada ♦ *vt* dar una palmada/bofetada a ♦ *adv* (*directly*) de lleno.

slapdash ['slæpdæʃ] *adj* chapucero.

slaphead ['slæphɛd] *n* (*BRIT col*) colgado/a.

slapstick ['slæpstɪk] *n*: **~ comedy** comedia de payasadas.

slap-up ['slæpʌp] *adj*: **a ~ meal** (*BRIT*) un banquetazo, una comilona.

slash [slæʃ] *vt* acuchillar; (*fig: prices*) quemar.

slat [slæt] *n* (*of wood, plastic*) tablilla, listón *m*.

slate [sleɪt] *n* pizarra ♦ *vt* (*BRIT: fig: criticize*) vapulear.

slaughter ['slɔ:tə*] *n* (*of animals*) matanza; (*of people*) carnicería ♦ *vt* matar.

slaughterhouse ['slɔ:təhaus] *n* matadero.

Slav [slɑ:v] *adj* eslavo.

slave [sleɪv] *n* esclavo/a ♦ *vi* (*also:* **~ away**) trabajar como un negro; **to ~ (away) at sth** trabajar como un negro en algo.

slave driver *n* (*col, pej*) tirano/a.

slave labour, (*US*) **slave labor** *n* trabajo de esclavos.

slaver ['slævə*] *vi* (*dribble*) babear.

slavery ['sleɪvərɪ] *n* esclavitud *f*.

slavish ['sleɪvɪʃ] *adj* (*devotion*) de esclavo; (*imitation*) servil.

slay, *pt* **slew,** *pp* **slain** [sleɪ, slu:, sleɪn] *vt* (*literary*) matar.

SLD *n abbr* (*BRIT POL*) = *Social and Liberal Democrats.*

sleazy ['sli:zɪ] *adj* (*fig: place*) sórdido.

sledge [slɛdʒ], (*US*) **sled** [slɛd] *n* trineo.

sledgehammer ['slɛdʒhæmə*] *n* mazo.

sleek [sli:k] *adj* (*shiny*) lustroso.

sleep [sli:p] *n* sueño ♦ *vb* (*pt, pp* **slept** [slɛpt]) *vi* dormir ♦ *vt*: **we can ~ 4** podemos alojar a 4, tenemos cabida para 4; **to go to ~** dormirse; **to have a good night's ~** dormir toda la noche; **to put to ~** (*patient*) dormir; (*animal: euphemism: kill*) sacrificar; **to ~ lightly** tener el sueño ligero; **to ~ with sb** (*euphemism*) acostarse con algn.

▶ **sleep in** *vi* (*oversleep*) quedarse dormido.

sleeper ['sli:pə*] *n* (*person*) durmiente *m/f*; (*BRIT RAIL: on track*) traviesa; (*: train*) coche-cama *m*.

sleepiness ['sli:pɪnɪs] *n* somnolencia.

sleeping bag ['sli:pɪŋ-] *n* saco de dormir.

sleeping car *n* coche-cama *m*.

sleeping partner *n* (*COMM*) socio/a comanditario/a.

sleeping pill *n* somnífero.

sleeping sickness *n* enfermedad *f* del sueño.

sleepless ['sli:plɪs] *adj*: **a ~ night** una noche en blanco.

sleeplessness ['sli:plɪsnɪs] *n* insomnio.

sleepwalk ['sli:pwɔ:k] *vi* caminar dormido; (*habitually*) ser sonámbulo.

sleepwalker ['sli:pwɔ:kə*] *n* sonámbulo/a.

sleepy ['sli:pɪ] *adj* soñoliento; **to be** *or* **feel ~** tener sueño.

sleet [sli:t] *n* aguanieve *f*.

sleeve [sli:v] *n* manga; (*TECH*) manguito; (*of record*) funda.

sleeveless ['sli:vlɪs] *adj* (*garment*) sin mangas.

sleigh [sleɪ] *n* trineo.

sleight [slaɪt] *n*: **~ of hand** prestidigitación *f*.

slender ['slɛndə*] *adj* delgado; (*means*) escaso.

slept [slɛpt] *pt, pp of* **sleep**.

sleuth [slu:θ] *n* (*col*) detective *m/f*.

slew [slu:] *vi* (*veer*) torcerse ♦ *pt of* **slay**.

slice [slaɪs] *n* (*of meat*) tajada; (*of bread*) rebanada; (*of lemon*) rodaja; (*utensil*) paleta ♦ *vt* cortar, tajar; rebanar; **~d bread** pan *m* de molde.

slick [slɪk] *adj* (*skilful*) hábil, diestro ♦ *n* (*also:* **oil ~**) capa de aceite.

slid [slɪd] *pt, pp of* **slide**.

slide [slaɪd] *n* (*in playground*) tobogán *m*; (*PHOT*) diapositiva; (*microscope ~*) portaobjetos *m inv*, plaquilla de vidrio; (*BRIT: also:* **hair ~**) pasador *m* ♦ *vb* (*pt, pp* **slid** [slɪd]) *vt* correr, deslizar ♦ *vi* (*slip*) resbalarse; (*glide*) deslizarse; **to let things ~** (*fig*) dejar que ruede la bola.

slide projector *n* (*PHOT*) proyector *m* de diapositivas.

slide rule *n* regla de cálculo.

sliding ['slaɪdɪŋ] *adj* (*door*) corredizo; **~ roof** (*AUT*) techo de corredera.

sliding scale *n* escala móvil.

slight [slaɪt] *adj* (*slim*) delgado; (*frail*) delicado; (*pain etc*) leve; (*trifling*) insignificante; (*small*) pequeño ♦ *n* desaire *m* ♦ *vt* (*offend*) ofender, desairar; **a ~ improvement** una ligera mejora; **not in the ~-est** en absoluto; **there's not the**

~**est possibility** no hay la menor *or* más mínima posibilidad.

slightly ['slaɪtlɪ] *adv* ligeramente, un poco; ~ **built** delgado.

slim [slɪm] *adj* delgado, esbelto ♦ *vi* adelgazar.

slime [slaɪm] *n* limo, cieno.

slimming ['slɪmɪŋ] *n* adelgazamiento ♦ *adj* (*diet, pills*) adelgazante.

slimness ['slɪmnɪs] *n* delgadez *f*.

slimy ['slaɪmɪ] *adj* limoso; (*covered with mud*) fangoso; (*also fig: person*) adulón, zalamero.

sling [slɪŋ] *n* (*MED*) cabestrillo; (*weapon*) honda ♦ *vt* (*pt, pp* **slung** [slʌŋ]) tirar, arrojar; **to have one's arm in a** ~ llevar el brazo en cabestrillo.

slink, *pt, pp* **slunk** [slɪŋk, slʌŋk] *vi*: **to** ~ **away,** ~ **off** escabullirse.

slinky ['slɪŋkɪ] *adj* (*clothing*) pegado al cuerpo, superajustado.

slip [slɪp] *n* (*slide*) resbalón *m*; (*mistake*) descuido; (*underskirt*) combinación *f*; (*of paper*) papelito ♦ *vt* (*slide*) deslizar ♦ *vi* (*slide*) deslizarse; (*stumble*) resbalar(se); (*decline*) decaer; (*move smoothly*): **to** ~ **into/out of** (*room etc*) colarse en/salirse de; **to let a chance** ~ **by** dejar escapar la oportunidad; **to** ~ **sth on/off** ponerse/ quitarse algo; **to** ~ **on a jumper** ponerse un jersey *or* un suéter; **it** ~**ped from her hand** se la cayó de la mano; **to give sb the** ~ dar esquinazo a algn; **wages** ~ (*BRIT*) hoja del sueldo; **a** ~ **of the tongue** un lapsus.

▸**slip away** *vi* escabullirse.

▸**slip in** *vt* meter ♦ *vi* meterse, colarse.

▸**slip out** *vi* (*go out*) salir (un momento).

slip-on ['slɪpɔn] *adj* de quita y pon; (*shoes*) sin cordones.

slipped disc [slɪpt-] *n* vértebra dislocada.

slipper ['slɪpə*] *n* zapatilla, pantufla.

slippery ['slɪpərɪ] *adj* resbaladizo.

slip road *n* (*BRIT*) carretera de acceso.

slipshod ['slɪpʃɔd] *adj* descuidado, chapucero.

slipstream ['slɪpstriːm] *n* viento de la hélice.

slip-up ['slɪpʌp] *n* (*error*) desliz *m*.

slipway ['slɪpweɪ] *n* grada, gradas *fpl*.

slit [slɪt] *n* raja; (*cut*) corte *m* ♦ *vt* (*pt, pp* **slit**) rajar, cortar; **to** ~ **sb's throat** cortarle el pescuezo a algn.

slither ['slɪðə*] *vi* deslizarse.

sliver ['slɪvə*] *n* (*of glass, wood*) astilla; (*of cheese, sausage*) lonja, loncha.

slob [slɔb] *n* (*col*) patán/ana *m/f*, palurdo/a.

slog [slɔg] (*BRIT*) *vi* sudar tinta ♦ *n*: **it was a**

~ costó trabajo (hacerlo).

slogan ['sləʊgən] *n* eslogan *m*, lema *m*.

slop [slɔp] *vi* (*also:* ~ **over**) derramarse, desbordarse ♦ *vt* derramar, verter.

slope [sləʊp] *n* (*up*) cuesta, pendiente *f*; (*down*) declive *m*; (*side of mountain*) falda, vertiente *f* ♦ *vi*: **to** ~ **down** estar en declive; **to** ~ **up** subir (en pendiente).

sloping ['sləʊpɪŋ] *adj* en pendiente; en declive.

sloppily ['slɔpɪlɪ] *adv* descuidadamente; con descuido *or* desaliño.

sloppiness ['slɔpɪnɪs] *n* descuido; desaliño.

sloppy ['slɔpɪ] *adj* (*work*) descuidado; (*appearance*) desaliñado.

slosh [slɔʃ] *vi*: **to** ~ **about** *or* **around** chapotear.

sloshed [slɔʃt] *adj* (*col: drunk*): **to get** ~ agarrar una trompa.

slot [slɔt] *n* ranura; (*fig: in timetable*) hueco; (*RADIO, TV*) espacio ♦ *vt*: **to** ~ **into** encajar en.

sloth [sləʊθ] *n* (*vice*) pereza; (*ZOOL*) oso perezoso.

slot machine *n* (*BRIT: vending machine*) máquina expendedora, (*for gambling*) máquina tragaperras.

slot meter *n* contador *m*.

slouch [slaʊtʃ] *vi*: **to** ~ **about,** ~ **around** (*laze*) gandulear.

Slovak ['sləʊvæk] *adj* eslovaco ♦ *n* eslovaco/a; (*LING*) eslovaco; **the** ~ **Republic** Eslovaquia.

Slovakia [sləʊˈvækɪə] *n* Eslovaquia.

Slovakian [sləʊˈvækɪən] *adj, n* = **Slovak**.

Slovene [sləʊˈviːn] *adj* esloveno ♦ *n* esloveno/a; (*LING*) esloveno.

Slovenia [sləʊˈviːnɪə] *n* Eslovenia.

Slovenian [sləʊˈviːnɪən] *adj, n* = **Slovene**.

slovenly ['slʌvənlɪ] *adj* (*dirty*) desaliñado, desaseado; (*careless*) descuidado.

slow [sləʊ] *adj* lento; (*watch*): **to be** ~ estar atrasado ♦ *adv* lentamente, despacio ♦ *vt* (*also:* ~ **down,** ~ **up**) retardar; (*engine, machine*) reducir la marcha de ♦ *vi* (*also:* ~ **down,** ~ **up**) ir más despacio; "~" (*road sign*) "disminuir la velocidad"; **at a** ~ **speed** a una velocidad lenta; **the** ~ **lane** el carril derecho; **business is** ~ (*COMM*) hay poca actividad; **my watch is 20 minutes** ~ mi reloj lleva 20 minutos de retraso; **bake for two hours in a** ~ **oven** cocer *or* asar 2 horas en el horno a fuego lento; **to be** ~ **to act/decide** tardar en obrar/decidir; **to go** ~ (*driver*) conducir despacio; (*in industrial dispute*) trabajar a ritmo lento.

slow-acting [sləʊˈæktɪŋ] *adj* de efecto

retardado.

slowcoach ['slǝʊkǝʊtʃ] *n* (*BRIT col*) tortuga.

slowdown ['slǝʊdaʊn] *n* (*US*) huelga de celo.

slowly ['slǝʊlɪ] *adv* lentamente, despacio; **to drive ~** conducir despacio; **~ but surely** lento pero seguro.

slow motion *n*: **in ~** a cámara lenta.

slow-moving ['slǝʊ'muːvɪŋ] *adj* lento.

slowpoke ['slǝʊpǝʊk] *n* (*US col*) = **slowcoach**.

sludge [slʌdʒ] *n* lodo, fango.

slug [slʌg] *n* babosa; (*bullet*) posta.

sluggish ['slʌgɪʃ] *adj* (*slow*) lento; (*lazy*) perezoso; (*business, market, sales*) inactivo.

sluggishly ['slʌgɪʃlɪ] *adv* lentamente.

sluggishness ['slʌgɪʃnɪs] *n* lentitud *f*.

sluice [sluːs] *n* (*gate*) esclusa; (*channel*) canal *m* ♦ *vt*: **to ~ down** *or* **out** regar.

slum [slʌm] *n* (*area*) barrios *mpl* bajos; (*house*) casucha.

slumber ['slʌmbǝ*] *n* sueño.

slum clearance (programme) *n* (programa *m* de) deschabolización *f*.

slump [slʌmp] *n* (*economic*) depresión *f* ♦ *vi* hundirse; **the ~ in the price of copper** la baja repentina del precio del cobre; **he was ~ed over the wheel** se había desplomado encima del volante.

slung [slʌŋ] *pt, pp of* **sling**.

slunk [slʌŋk] *pt, pp of* **slink**.

slur [slǝː*] *n* calumnia ♦ *vt* calumniar, difamar; (*word*) pronunciar mal; **to cast a ~ on sb** manchar la reputación de algn, difamar a algn.

slurp [slǝːp] *vt, vi* sorber ruidosamente.

slurred [slǝːd] *adj* (*pronunciation*) poco claro.

slush [slʌʃ] *n* nieve *f* a medio derretir.

slush fund *n* fondos *mpl* para sobornar.

slushy ['slʌʃɪ] *adj* (*col: poetry etc*) sentimentaloide.

slut [slʌt] *n* marrana.

sly [slaɪ] *adj* (*clever*) astuto; (*nasty*) malicioso.

slyly ['slaɪlɪ] *adv* astutamente; taimadamente.

slyness ['slaɪnɪs] *n* astucia.

smack [smæk] *n* (*slap*) manotada; (*blow*) golpe *m* ♦ *vt* dar una manotada a; golpear con la mano ♦ *vi*: **to ~ of** saber a, oler a ♦ *adv*: **it fell ~ in the middle** (*col*) cayó justo en medio.

smacker ['smækǝ*] *n* (*col: kiss*) besazo; (: *BRIT: pound note*) billete *m* de una libra; (: *US: dollar bill*) billete *m* de un dólar.

small [smɔːl] *adj* pequeño, chico (*esp LAM*);

(*in height*) bajo, chaparro (*LAM*); (*letter*) en minúscula ♦ *n*: **~ of the back** región *f* lumbar; **~ shopkeeper** pequeño/a comerciante *m/f*; **to get** *or* **grow ~er** (*stain, town*) empequeñecer; (*debt, organization, numbers*) reducir, disminuir; **to make ~er** (*amount, income*) reducir; (*garden, object, garment*) achicar.

small ads *npl* (*BRIT*) anuncios *mpl* por palabras.

small arms *npl* armas *fpl* cortas.

small business *n* pequeño negocio; **~es** la pequeña empresa.

small change *n* suelto, cambio.

smallholder ['smɔːlhǝʊldǝ*] *n* (*BRIT*) granjero/a, parcelero/a.

smallholding ['smɔːlhǝʊldɪŋ] *n* parcela, minifundio.

small hours *npl*: **in the ~** a altas horas de la noche.

smallish ['smɔːlɪʃ] *adj* más bien pequeño.

small-minded [smɔːl'maɪndɪd] *adj* mezquino, de miras estrechas.

smallness ['smɔːlnɪs] *n* pequeñez *f*.

smallpox ['smɔːlpɒks] *n* viruela.

small print *n* letra pequeña *or* menuda.

small-scale ['smɔːlskeɪl] *adj* (*map, model*) a escala reducida; (*business, farming*) en pequeña escala.

small talk *n* cháchara.

small-time ['smɔːltaɪm] *adj* (*col*) de poca categoría *or* monta; **a ~ thief** un(a) ratero/a.

small-town ['smɔːltǝʊn] *adj* de provincias.

smarmy ['smɑːmɪ] *adj* (*BRIT pej*) pelotillero (*fam*).

smart [smɑːt] *adj* elegante; (*clever*) listo, inteligente; (*quick*) rápido, vivo; (*weapon*) inteligente ♦ *vi* escocer, picar; **the ~ set** la gente de buen tono; **to look ~** estar elegante; **my eyes are ~ing** me pican los ojos.

smartcard ['smɑːtkɑːd] *n* tarjeta inteligente.

smarten up ['smɑːtn-] *vi* arreglarse ♦ *vt* arreglar.

smartness ['smɑːtnɪs] *n* elegancia; (*cleverness*) inteligencia.

smash [smæʃ] *n* (*also*: **~-up**) choque *m*; (*sound*) estrépito ♦ *vt* (*break*) hacer pedazos; (*car etc*) estrellar; (*SPORT: record*) batir ♦ *vi* hacerse pedazos; (*against wall etc*) estrellarse.

▶**smash up** *vt* (*car*) hacer pedazos; (*room*) destrozar.

smash hit *n* exitazo.

smashing ['smæʃɪŋ] *adj* (*col*) cojonudo.

smattering ['smætǝrɪŋ] *n*: **a ~ of Spanish**

algo de español.

smear [smɪə*] n mancha; (*MED*) frotis m inv (cervical); (*insult*) calumnia ♦ vt untar; (*fig*) calumniar, difamar; **his hands were ~ed with oil/ink** tenía las manos manchadas de aceite/tinta.

smear campaign n campaña de calumnias.

smear test n (*MED*) citología, frotis m inv (cervical).

smell [smɛl] n olor m; (*sense*) olfato ♦ (*vb: pt, pp* **smelt** *or* **~ed** [smɛlt, smɛld]) vt, vi oler; **it ~s good/of garlic** huele bien/a ajo.

smelly ['smɛlɪ] adj maloliente.

smelt [smɛlt] vt (*ore*) fundir ♦ pt, pp of **smell**.

smile [smaɪl] n sonrisa ♦ vi sonreír.

smiling ['smaɪlɪŋ] adj sonriente, risueño.

smirk [smə:k] n sonrisa falsa or afectada.

smith [smɪθ] n herrero.

smithy ['smɪðɪ] n herrería.

smitten ['smɪtn] adj: **he's really ~ with her** está totalmente loco por ella.

smock [smɔk] n blusón; (*children's*) babi m; (*US: overall*) guardapolvo, bata.

smog [smɔg] n smog m.

smoke [sməuk] n humo ♦ vi fumar; (*chimney*) echar humo ♦ vt (*cigarettes*) fumar; **to go up in ~** (*house etc*) quemarse; (*fig*) quedar en agua de borrajas; **do you ~?** ¿fumas?

smoked [sməukt] adj (*bacon, glass*) ahumado.

smokeless fuel ['sməuklɪs-] n combustible m sin humo.

smokeless zone ['sməuklɪs-] n zona libre de humo.

smoker ['sməukə*] n (*person*) fumador(a) m/f; (*RAIL*) coche m de fumadores.

smoke screen n cortina de humo.

smoke shop n (*US*) estanco, tabaquería.

smoking ['sməukɪŋ] n: **"no ~"** "prohibido fumar"; **he's given up ~** ha dejado de fumar.

smoking compartment, (*US*) **smoking car** n departamento de fumadores.

smoky ['sməukɪ] adj (*room*) lleno de humo.

smolder ['sməuldə*] vi (*US*) = **smoulder**.

smoochy ['smu:tʃɪ] adj (*col*) blandengue.

smooth [smu:ð] adj liso; (*sea*) tranquilo; (*flavour, movement*) suave; (*person: pej*) meloso ♦ vt alisar; (*also: ~ out*) (*creases*) alisar; (*difficulties*) allanar.

▶**smooth over** vt: **to ~ things over** (*fig*) limar las asperezas.

smoothly ['smu:ðlɪ] adv (*easily*) fácilmente; **everything went ~** todo fue sobre ruedas.

smoothness ['smu:ðnɪs] n (*of skin, cloth*) tersura; (*of surface, flavour, movement*) suavidad f.

smother ['smʌðə*] vt sofocar; (*repress*) contener.

smoulder, (*US*) **smolder** ['sməuldə*] vi arder sin llama.

smudge [smʌdʒ] n mancha ♦ vt manchar.

smug [smʌg] adj engreído.

smuggle ['smʌgl] vt pasar de contrabando; **to ~ in/out** (*goods etc*) meter/sacar de contrabando.

smuggler ['smʌglə*] n contrabandista m/f.

smuggling ['smʌglɪŋ] n contrabando.

smugly ['smʌglɪ] adv con suficiencia.

smugness ['smʌgnɪs] n suficiencia.

smut [smʌt] n (*grain of soot*) carbonilla, hollín m; (*mark*) tizne m; (*in conversation etc*) obscenidades fpl.

smutty ['smʌtɪ] adj (*fig*) verde, obsceno.

snack [snæk] n bocado, tentempié m; **to have a ~** tomar un bocado.

snack bar n cafetería.

snag [snæg] n problema m; **to run into** or **hit a ~** encontrar inconvenientes, dar con un obstáculo.

snail [sneɪl] n caracol m.

snake [sneɪk] n (*gen*) serpiente f; (*harmless*) culebra; (*poisonous*) víbora.

snap [snæp] n (*sound*) chasquido; golpe m seco; (*photograph*) foto f ♦ adj (*decision*) instantáneo ♦ vt (*fingers etc*) castañetear; (*break*) partir, quebrar; (*photograph*) tomar una foto de ♦ vi (*break*) partirse, quebrarse; (*fig: person*) contestar bruscamente; **to ~ (at sb)** (*subj: person*) hablar con brusquedad (a algn); (: *dog*) intentar morder (a algn); **to ~ shut** cerrarse de golpe; **to ~ one's fingers at sth/sb** (*fig*) burlarse de algo/uno; **a cold ~** (*of weather*) una ola de frío.

▶**snap off** vi (*break*) partirse.

▶**snap up** vt agarrar.

snap fastener n (*US*) botón m de presión.

snappy ['snæpɪ] adj (*col: answer*) instantáneo; (*slogan*) conciso; **make it ~!** (*hurry up*) ¡date prisa!

snapshot ['snæpʃɔt] n foto f (instantánea).

snare [snɛə*] n trampa ♦ vt cazar con trampa; (*fig*) engañar.

snarl [snɑ:l] n gruñido ♦ vi gruñir; **to get ~ed up** (*wool, plans*) enmarañarse, enredarse; (*traffic*) quedar atascado.

snatch [snætʃ] n (*fig*) robo; **~es of** trocitos mpl de ♦ vt (*~ away*) arrebatar; (*grasp*) coger (*SP*), agarrar; **~es of conversation** fragmentos mpl de conversación; **to ~ a sandwich** comer un bocadillo a prisa; **to ~ some sleep** buscar tiempo para dormir; **don't ~!** ¡no me lo quites!

▶**snatch up** *vt* agarrar.

snazzy ['snæzɪ] *adj* (*col*) guapo.

sneak [sniːk] *vi*: **to ~ in/out** entrar/salir a hurtadillas ♦ *vt*: **to ~ a look at sth** mirar algo de reojo ♦ *n* (*fam*) soplón/ona *m/f*.

sneakers ['sniːkəz] *npl* (*US*) zapatos *mpl* de lona, zapatillas *fpl*.

sneaking ['sniːkɪŋ] *adj*: **to have a ~ feeling/ suspicion that ...** tener la sensación/ sospecha de que ....

sneaky ['sniːkɪ] *adj* furtivo.

sneer [snɪə*] *n* sonrisa de desprecio ♦ *vi* sonreír con desprecio; **to ~ at sth/sb** burlarse *or* mofarse de algo/uno.

sneeze [sniːz] *n* estornudo ♦ *vi* estornudar.

snide [snaɪd] *adj* (*col*: *sarcastic*) sarcástico.

sniff [snɪf] *vi* sorber (por la nariz) ♦ *vt* husmear, oler; (*glue, drug*) esnifar.

▶**sniff at** *vt fus*: **it's not to be ~ed at** no es de despreciar.

sniffer dog ['snɪfə-] *n* (*for drugs*) perro antidroga; (*for explosives*) perro antiexplosivos.

snigger ['snɪgə*] *n* risa disimulada ♦ *vi* reírse con disimulo.

snip [snɪp] *n* (*piece*) recorte *m*; (*bargain*) ganga ♦ *vt* tijeretear.

sniper ['snaɪpə*] *n* francotirador(a) *m/f*.

snippet ['snɪpɪt] *n* retazo.

snivelling, (*US*) **sniveling** ['snɪvlɪŋ] *adj* llorón/ona.

snob [snɔb] *n* (e)snob *m/f*.

snobbery ['snɔbərɪ] *n* (e)snobismo.

snobbish ['snɔbɪʃ] *adj* (e)snob.

snobbishness ['snɔbɪʃnɪs] *n* (e)snobismo.

snog [snɔg] *vi* (*BRIT col*) besuquearse, morrear; **to ~ sb** besuquear a algn.

snooker ['snuːkə*] *n* snooker *m*.

snoop [snuːp] *vi*: **to ~ about** fisgonear.

snooper ['snuːpə*] *n* fisgón/ona *m/f*.

snooty ['snuːtɪ] *adj* (e)snob.

snooze [snuːz] *n* siesta ♦ *vi* echar una siesta.

snore [snɔː*] *vi* roncar ♦ *n* ronquido.

snoring ['snɔːrɪŋ] *n* ronquidos *mpl*.

snorkel ['snɔːkl] *n* tubo de respiración.

snort [snɔːt] *n* bufido ♦ *vi* bufar ♦ *vt* (*col*: *drugs*) esnifar.

snotty ['snɔtɪ] *adj* (*col*) creído.

snout [snaut] *n* hocico, morro.

snow [snəu] *n* nieve *f* ♦ *vi* nevar ♦ *vt*: **to be ~ed under with work** estar agobiado de trabajo.

snowball ['snəubɔːl] *n* bola de nieve ♦ *vi* ir aumentándose.

snow-blind ['snəublaɪnd] *adj* cegado por la nieve.

snowbound ['snəubaund] *adj* bloqueado por la nieve.

snow-capped ['snəukæpt] *adj* (*peak*) cubierto de nieve, nevado.

snowdrift ['snəudrɪft] *n* ventisquero.

snowdrop ['snəudrɔp] *n* campanilla.

snowfall ['snəufɔːl] *n* nevada.

snowflake ['snəufleɪk] *n* copo de nieve.

snowline ['snəulaɪn] *n* límite *m* de las nieves perpetuas.

snowman ['snəumæn] *n* figura de nieve.

snowplough, (*US*) **snowplow** ['snəuplau] *n* quitanieves *m inv*.

snowshoe ['snəuʃuː] *n* raqueta (de nieve).

snowstorm ['snəustɔːm] *n* tormenta de nieve, nevasca.

Snow White *n* Blancanieves *f*.

snowy ['snəuɪ] *adj* de (mucha) nieve.

SNP *n abbr* (*BRIT POL*) = Scottish National Party.

snub [snʌb] *vt*: **to ~ sb** desairar a algn ♦ *n* desaire *m*, repulsa.

snub-nosed [snʌb'nəuzd] *adj* chato.

snuff [snʌf] *n* rapé *m* ♦ *vt* (*also*: **~ out**: *candle*) apagar.

snuffbox ['snʌfbɔks] *n* caja de rapé.

snuff movie *n* (*col*) película porno (*que acaba con un asesinato real*).

snug [snʌg] *adj* (*cosy*) cómodo; (*fitted*) ajustado.

snuggle ['snʌgl] *vi*: **to ~ down in bed** hacerse un ovillo *or* acurrucarse en la cama; **to ~ up to sb** acurrucarse junto a algn.

snugly ['snʌglɪ] *adv* cómodamente; **it fits ~** (*object in pocket etc*) cabe perfectamente; (*garment*) ajusta perfectamente.

SO *abbr* (*BANKING*) = standing order.

═══════════════════════════ *KEYWORD*

so [səu] *adv* **1** (*thus, likewise*) así, de este modo; **if ~** de ser así; **I like swimming — ~ do I** a mí me gusta nadar — a mí también; **I've got work to do — ~ has Paul** tengo trabajo que hacer — Paul también; **it's 5 o'clock — ~ it is!** son las cinco — ¡pues es verdad!; **I hope/think ~** espero/creo que sí; **~ far** hasta ahora; (*in past*) hasta este momento; **~ to speak** por decirlo así

2 (*in comparisons etc: to such a degree*) tan; **~ quickly (that)** tan rápido (que); **~ big (that)** tan grande (que); **she's not ~ clever as her brother** no es tan lista como su hermano; **we were ~ worried** estábamos preocupadísimos

3: **~ much** *adj* tanto/a ♦ *adv* tanto; **~ many** tantos/as

4 (*phrases*): **10 or ~** unos 10, 10 o así; **~**

long! (*inf: goodbye*) ¡hasta luego!; **she didn't ~ much as send me a birthday card** no me mandó ni una tarjeta siquiera por mi cumpleaños; **~ (what)?** (*col*) ¿y (qué)? ♦ *conj* **1** (*expressing purpose*): **~ as to do** para hacer; **~ (that)** para que +*sub*; **we hurried ~ (that) we wouldn't be late** nos dimos prisa para no llegar tarde **2** (*expressing result*) así que; **~ you see, I could have gone** así que ya ves, (yo) podría haber ido; **~ that's the reason!** ¡así que es por eso *or* por eso es!

soak [səuk] *vt* (*drench*) empapar; (*put in water*) remojar ♦ *vi* remojarse, estar a remojo.
► **soak in** *vi* penetrar.
► **soak up** *vt* absorber.
soaking ['səukɪŋ] *adj* (*also*: **~ wet**) calado *or* empapado (hasta los huesos *or* el tuétano).
so-and-so ['səuənsəu] *n* (*somebody*) fulano/a de tal.
soap [səup] *n* jabón *m*.
soapbox ['səupbɔks] *n* tribuna improvisada.
soapflakes ['səupfleɪks] *npl* jabón *msg* en escamas.
soap opera *n* (*TV*) telenovela; (*RADIO*) radionovela.
soap powder *n* jabón *m* en polvo.
soapsuds ['səupsʌdz] *npl* espuma *sg*.
soapy ['səupɪ] *adj* jabonoso.
soar [sɔː*] *vi* (*on wings*) remontarse; (*building etc*) elevarse; (*price*) subir vertiginosamente; (*morale*) elevarse.
soaring ['sɔːrɪŋ] *adj* (*flight*) por lo alto; (*prices*) en alza *or* aumento; **~ inflation** inflación *f* altísima *or* en aumento.
sob [sɔb] *n* sollozo ♦ *vi* sollozar.
s.o.b. *n abbr* (*US col! = son of a bitch*) hijo de puta (*!*).
sober ['səubə*] *adj* (*moderate*) moderado; (*serious*) serio; (*not drunk*) sobrio; (*colour, style*) discreto.
► **sober up** *vi* pasársele a algn la borrachera.
soberly ['səubəlɪ] *adv* sobriamente.
sobriety [sə'braɪətɪ] *n* (*not being drunk*) sobriedad *f*; (*seriousness, sedateness*) seriedad *f*, sensatez *f*.
sob story *n* (*col, pej*) dramón *m*.
Soc. *abbr* (= *society*) S.
so-called ['səu'kɔːld] *adj* presunto, supuesto.
soccer ['sɔkə*] *n* fútbol *m*.
soccer pitch *n* campo *or* cancha (*LAM*) de fútbol.

soccer player *n* jugador(a) *m/f* de fútbol.
sociability [səuʃə'bɪlɪtɪ] *n* sociabilidad *f*.
sociable ['səuʃəbl] *adj* sociable.
social ['səuʃl] *adj* social ♦ *n* velada, fiesta.
social class *n* clase *f* social.
social climber *n* arribista *m/f*.
social club *n* club *m*.
Social Democrat *n* socialdemócrata *m/f*.
social insurance *n* (*US*) seguro social.
socialism ['səuʃəlɪzəm] *n* socialismo.
socialist ['səuʃəlɪst] *adj, n* socialista *m/f*.
socialite ['səuʃəlaɪt] *n persona que alterna con la buena sociedad*.
socialize ['səuʃəlaɪz] *vi* hacer vida social; **to ~ with** (*colleagues*) salir con.
social life *n* vida social
socially ['səuʃəlɪ] *adv* socialmente.
social science(s) *n(pl)* ciencias *fpl* sociales.
social security *n* seguridad *f* social.
social services *npl* servicios *mpl* sociales.
social welfare *n* asistencia social.
social work *n* asistencia social.
social worker *n* asistente/a *m/f* social.
society [sə'saɪətɪ] *n* sociedad *f*; (*club*) asociación *f*; (*also*: **high ~**) buena sociedad ♦ *cpd* (*party, column*) social, de sociedad.
socio-economic ['səusɪəuiːkə'nɔmɪk] *adj* socioeconómico.
sociological [səusɪə'lɔdʒɪkəl] *adj* sociológico.
sociologist [səusɪ'ɔlədʒɪst] *n* sociólogo/a.
sociology [səusɪ'ɔlədʒɪ] *n* sociología.
sock [sɔk] *n* calcetín *m*, media (*LAM*); **to pull one's ~s up** (*fig*) hacer esfuerzos, despabilarse.
socket ['sɔkɪt] *n* (*ELEC*) enchufe *m*.
sod [sɔd] *n* (*of earth*) césped *m*; (*col!*) cabrón/ona *m/f* (*!*) ♦ *excl*: **~ off!** (*col!*) ¡vete a la porra!
soda ['səudə] *n* (*CHEM*) sosa; (*also*: **~ water**) soda; (*US: also*: **~ pop**) gaseosa.
sodden ['sɔdn] *adj* empapado.
sodium ['səudɪəm] *n* sodio.
sodium chloride *n* cloruro sódico *or* de sodio.
sofa ['səufə] *n* sofá *m*.
Sofia ['səufɪə] *n* Sofía.
soft [sɔft] *adj* (*teacher, parent*) blando; (*gentle, not loud*) suave; (*stupid*) bobo; **~ currency** divisa blanda *or* débil.
soft-boiled ['sɔftbɔɪld] *adj* (*egg*) pasado por agua.
soft copy *n* (*COMPUT*) copia transitoria.
soft drink *n* bebida no alcohólica.
soft drugs *npl* drogas *fpl* blandas.
soften ['sɔfn] *vt* ablandar; suavizar ♦ *vi*

ablandarse; suavizarse.
softener ['sɔfnə*] n suavizante m.
soft fruit n bayas fpl.
soft furnishings npl tejidos mpl para el hogar.
soft-hearted [sɔft'hɑːtɪd] adj bondadoso.
softly ['sɔftlɪ] adv suavemente; (gently) delicadamente, con delicadeza.
softness ['sɔftnɪs] n blandura; suavidad f.
soft option n alternativa fácil.
soft sell n venta persuasiva.
soft target n blanco or objetivo fácil.
soft toy n juguete m de peluche.
software ['sɔftwɛə*] n (COMPUT) software m.
soft water n agua blanda.
soggy ['sɔgɪ] adj empapado.
soil [sɔɪl] n (earth) tierra, suelo ♦ vt ensuciar.
soiled [sɔɪld] adj sucio, manchado.
sojourn ['sɔdʒɜːn] n (formal) estancia.
solace ['sɔlɪs] n consuelo.
solar ['səʊlə*] adj solar.
solarium, pl **solaria** [sə'lɛərɪəm, -rɪə] n solario.
solar panel n panel m solar.
solar plexus [-'plɛksəs] n (ANAT) plexo solar.
solar power n energía solar.
solar system n sistema m solar.
sold [səʊld] pt, pp of **sell**.
solder ['səʊldə*] vt soldar ♦ n soldadura.
soldier ['səʊldʒə*] n (gen) soldado; (army man) militar m ♦ vi: **to ~ on** seguir adelante; **toy ~** soldadito de plomo.
sold out adj (COMM) agotado.
sole [səʊl] n (of foot) planta; (of shoe) suela; (fish: pl inv) lenguado ♦ adj único; **the ~ reason** la única razón.
solely ['səʊllɪ] adv únicamente, sólo, solamente; **I will hold you ~ responsible** le consideraré el único responsable.
solemn ['sɔləm] adj solemne.
sole trader n (COMM) comerciante m/f exclusivo/a.
solicit [sə'lɪsɪt] vt (request) solicitar ♦ vi (prostitute) abordar clientes.
solicitor [sə'lɪsɪtə*] n abogado/a; see also **barrister**.
solid ['sɔlɪd] adj sólido; (gold etc) macizo; (line) continuo; (vote) unánime ♦ n sólido; **we waited 2 ~ hours** esperamos 2 horas enteras; **to be on ~ ground** estar en tierra firme; (fig) estar seguro.
solidarity [sɔlɪ'dærɪtɪ] n solidaridad f.
solid fuel n combustible m sólido.
solidify [sə'lɪdɪfaɪ] vi solidificarse.
solidity [sə'lɪdɪtɪ] n solidez f.

solidly ['sɔlɪdlɪ] adv sólidamente; (fig) unánimemente.
solid-state ['sɔlɪdsteɪt] adj (ELEC) estado sólido.
soliloquy [sə'lɪləkwɪ] n soliloquio.
solitaire [sɔlɪ'tɛə*] n (game, gem) solitario.
solitary ['sɔlɪtərɪ] adj solitario, solo; (isolated) apartado, aislado; (only) único.
solitary confinement n incomunicación f; **to be in ~** estar incomunicado.
solitude ['sɔlɪtjuːd] n soledad f.
solo ['səʊləʊ] n solo.
soloist ['səʊləʊɪst] n solista m/f.
Solomon Islands ['sɔləmən-] npl: **the ~** las Islas Salomón.
solstice ['sɔlstɪs] n solsticio.
soluble ['sɔljubl] adj soluble.
solution [sə'luːʃən] n solución f.
solve [sɔlv] vt resolver, solucionar.
solvency ['sɔlvənsɪ] n (COMM) solvencia.
solvent ['sɔlvənt] adj (COMM) solvente ♦ n (CHEM) solvente m.
solvent abuse n uso indebido de disolventes.
Som. abbr (BRIT) = **Somerset**.
Somali [sə'mɑːlɪ] adj, n somalí m/f.
Somalia [sə'mɑːlɪə] n Somalia.
Somaliland [sə'mɑːlɪlænd] n Somaliland f.
sombre, (US) **somber** ['sɔmbə*] adj sombrío.

—————————————————— KEYWORD

some [sʌm] adj **1** (a certain amount or number of): ~ **tea/water/biscuits** té/agua/ (unas) galletas; **have** ~ **tea** tómese un té; **there's** ~ **milk in the fridge** hay leche en el frigo; **there were** ~ **people outside** había algunas personas fuera; **I've got** ~ **money, but not much** tengo algo de dinero, pero no mucho
2 (certain: in contrasts) algunos/as; ~ **people say that ...** hay quien dice que ...; ~ **films were excellent, but most were mediocre** hubo películas excelentes, pero la mayoría fueron mediocres
3 (unspecified): ~ **woman was asking for you** una mujer estuvo preguntando por ti; ~ **day** algún día; ~ **day next week** un día de la semana que viene; **he was asking for** ~ **book (or other)** pedía no sé qué libro; **in** ~ **way or other** de alguna que otra manera
4 (considerable amount of) bastante; ~ **days ago** hace unos cuantos días; **after** ~ **time** pasado algún tiempo; **at** ~ **length** con mucho detalle
5 (col: intensive): **that was** ~ **party!** ¡menuda fiesta!

♦ *pron* **1** (*a certain number*): **I've got ~** (*books etc*) tengo algunos/as **2** (*a certain amount*) algo; **I've got ~** (*money, milk*) tengo algo; **would you like ~?** (*coffee etc*) ¿quiere un poco?; (*books etc*) ¿quiere alguno?; **could I have ~ of that cheese?** ¿me puede dar un poco de ese queso?; **I've read ~ of the book** he leído parte del libro ♦ *adv*: **~ 10 people** unas 10 personas, una decena de personas.

somebody ['sʌmbədɪ] *pron* alguien; **~ or other** alguien.

someday ['sʌmdeɪ] *adv* algún día.

somehow ['sʌmhau] *adv* de alguna manera; (*for some reason*) por una u otra razón.

someone ['sʌmwʌn] *pron* = **somebody**.

someplace ['sʌmpleɪs] *adv* (*US*) = **somewhere**.

somersault ['sʌməsɔːlt] *n* (*deliberate*) salto mortal; (*accidental*) vuelco ♦ *vi* dar un salto mortal; dar vuelcos.

something ['sʌmθɪŋ] *pron* algo ♦ *adv*: **he's ~ like me** es un poco como yo; **~ to do** algo que hacer; **it's ~ of a problem** es bastante problemático.

sometime ['sʌmtaɪm] *adv* (*in future*) algún día, en algún momento; **~ last month** durante el mes pasado; **I'll finish it ~** lo terminaré un día de éstos.

sometimes ['sʌmtaɪmz] *adv* a veces.

somewhat ['sʌmwɔt] *adv* algo.

somewhere ['sʌmwɛə*] *adv* (*be*) en alguna parte; (*go*) a alguna parte; **~ else** (*be*) en otra parte; (*go*) a otra parte.

son [sʌn] *n* hijo.

sonar ['səunɑː*] *n* sonar *m*.

sonata [sə'nɑːtə] *n* sonata.

song [sɔŋ] *n* canción *f*.

songwriter ['sɔŋraɪtə*] *n* compositor(a) *m/f* de canciones.

sonic ['sɔnɪk] *adj* (*boom*) sónico.

son-in-law ['sʌnɪnlɔː] *n* yerno.

sonnet ['sɔnɪt] *n* soneto.

sonny ['sʌnɪ] *n* (*col*) hijo.

soon [suːn] *adv* pronto, dentro de poco; **~ afterwards** poco después; **very/quite ~** muy/bastante pronto; **how ~ can you be ready?** ¿cuánto tardas en prepararte?; **it's too ~ to tell** es demasiado pronto para saber; **see you ~!** ¡hasta pronto!; *see also* **as**.

sooner ['suːnə*] *adv* (*time*) antes, más temprano; **I would ~ do that** preferiría hacer eso; **~ or later** tarde o temprano; **no ~ said than done** dicho y hecho; **the ~ the better** cuanto antes mejor; **no ~ had**

we left than ... apenas nos habíamos marchado cuando ....

soot [sut] *n* hollín *m*.

soothe [suːð] *vt* tranquilizar; (*pain*) aliviar.

soothing ['suːðɪŋ] *adj* (*ointment etc*) sedante; (*tone, words etc*) calmante, tranquilizante.

SOP *n abbr* = *standard operating procedure*.

sophisticated [sə'fɪstɪkeɪtɪd] *adj* sofisticado.

sophistication [səfɪstɪ'keɪʃən] *n* sofisticación *f*.

sophomore ['sɔfəmɔː*] *n* (*US*) estudiante *m/f* de segundo año.

soporific [sɔpə'rɪfɪk] *adj* soporífero.

sopping ['sɔpɪŋ] *adj*: **~ (wet)** empapado.

soppy ['sɔpɪ] *adj* (*pej*) bobo, tonto.

soprano [sə'prɑːnəu] *n* soprano *f*.

sorbet ['sɔːbeɪ] *n* sorbete *m*.

sorcerer ['sɔːsərə*] *n* hechicero.

sordid ['sɔːdɪd] *adj* (*place etc*) sórdido; (*motive etc*) mezquino.

sore [sɔː*] *adj* (*painful*) doloroso, que duele; (*offended*) resentido ♦ *n* llaga; **~ throat** dolor *m* de garganta; **my eyes are ~, I have ~ eyes** me duelen los ojos; **it's a ~ point** es un asunto delicado *or* espinoso.

sorely *adv*: **I am ~ tempted to (do it)** estoy muy tentado a (hacerlo).

soreness ['sɔːnɪs] *n* dolor *m*.

sorrel ['sɔrəl] *n* (*BOT*) acedera.

sorrow ['sɔrəu] *n* pena, dolor *m*.

sorrowful ['sɔrəuful] *adj* afligido, triste.

sorrowfully ['sɔrəufulɪ] *adv* tristemente.

sorry ['sɔrɪ] *adj* (*regretful*) arrepentido; (*condition, excuse*) lastimoso; (*sight, failure*) triste; **~!** ¡perdón!, ¡perdone!; **I am ~** lo siento; **I feel ~ for him** me da lástima *or* pena; **I'm ~ to hear that ...** siento saber que ...; **to be ~ about sth** lamentar algo.

sort [sɔːt] *n* clase *f*, género, tipo; (*make: of coffee, car etc*) marca ♦ *vt* (*also*: **~ out**: *papers*) clasificar; (: *problems*) arreglar, solucionar; (*COMPUT*) clasificar; **what ~ do you want?** (*make*) ¿qué marca quieres?; **what ~ of car?** ¿qué tipo de coche?; **I shall do nothing of the ~** no pienso hacer nada parecido; **it's ~ of awkward** (*col*) es bastante difícil.

sortie ['sɔːtɪ] *n* salida.

sorting office ['sɔːtɪŋ-] *n* oficina de clasificación del correo.

SOS *n* SOS *m*.

so-so ['səusəu] *adv* regular, así así.

soufflé ['suːfleɪ] *n* suflé *m*.

sought [sɔːt] *pt, pp* of **seek**.

sought-after ['sɔːtɑːftə*] *adj* solicitado,

codiciado.
soul [səul] *n* alma *f*; **God rest his** ~ Dios le reciba en su seno *or* en su gloria; **I didn't see a** ~ no vi a nadie; **the poor** ~ **had nowhere to sleep** el pobre no tenía dónde dormir.
soul-destroying ['səuldɪstrɔɪɪŋ] *adj* (*work*) deprimente.
soulful ['səulful] *adj* lleno de sentimiento.
soulmate ['səulmeɪt] *n* compañero/a del alma.
soul-searching ['səulsəːtʃɪŋ] *n*: **after much** ~ después de pensarlo mucho, después de darle muchas vueltas.
sound [saund] *adj* (*healthy*) sano; (*safe, not damaged*) en buen estado; (*valid*: *argument, policy, claim*) válido; (: *move*) acertado; (*dependable*: *person*) de fiar; (*sensible*) sensato, razonable ♦ *adv*: ~ **asleep** profundamente dormido ♦ *n* (*noise*) sonido, ruido; (*GEO*) estrecho ♦ *vt* (*alarm*) sonar; (*also*: ~ **out**: *opinions*) consultar, sondear ♦ *vi* sonar, resonar; (*fig: seem*) parecer; **to** ~ **like** sonar a; **to be of** ~ **mind** estar en su sano juicio; **I don't like the** ~ **of it** no me gusta nada; **it** ~**s as if ...** parece que ....
▸**sound off** *vi* (*col*): **to** ~ **off (about)** (*give one's opinions*) despotricar (contra).
sound barrier *n* barrera del sonido.
sound bite *n* cita jugosa.
sound effects *npl* efectos *mpl* sonoros.
sound engineer *n* ingeniero/a del sonido.
sounding ['saundɪŋ] *n* (*NAUT etc*) sondeo.
sounding board *n* caja de resonancia.
soundly ['saundlɪ] *adv* (*sleep*) profundamente; (*beat*) completamente.
soundproof ['saundpruːf] *adj* insonorizado.
sound system *n* equipo de sonido.
soundtrack ['saundtræk] *n* (*of film*) banda sonora.
sound wave *n* (*PHYSICS*) onda sonora.
soup [suːp] *n* (*thick*) sopa; (*thin*) caldo; **in the** ~ (*fig*) en apuros.
soup kitchen *n* comedor *m* de beneficencia.
soup plate *n* plato sopero.
soupspoon ['suːpspuːn] *n* cuchara sopera.
sour ['sauə*] *adj* agrio; (*milk*) cortado; **it's just** ~ **grapes!** (*fig*) ¡pura envidia!, ¡están verdes!; **to go** *or* **turn** ~ (*milk*) cortarse; (*wine*) agriarse; (*fig: relationship*) agriarse; (: *plans*) irse a pique.
source [sɔːs] *n* fuente *f*; **I have it from a reliable** ~ **that ...** sé de fuente fidedigna que ....
source language *n* (*COMPUT*) lenguaje *m*

fuente *or* de origen.
south [sauθ] *n* sur *m* ♦ *adj* del sur ♦ *adv* al sur, hacia el sur; (**to the**) ~ **of** al sur de; **the S~ of France** el Sur de Francia; **to travel** ~ viajar hacia el sur.
South Africa *n* Sudáfrica.
South African *adj*, *n* sudafricano/a *m/f*.
South America *n* América del Sur, Sudamérica.
South American *adj*, *n* sudamericano/a *m/f*.
southbound ['sauθbaund] *adj* (con) rumbo al sur.
south-east [sauθ'iːst] *n* sudeste *m* ♦ *adj* (*counties etc*) (del) sudeste.
Southeast Asia *n* Sudeste *m* asiático.
southerly ['sʌðəlɪ] *adj* sur; (*from the south*) del sur.
southern ['sʌðən] *adj* del sur, meridional; **the** ~ **hemisphere** el hemisferio sur.
South Korea *n* Corea del Sur.
South Pole *n* Polo Sur.
South Sea Islands *npl*: **the** ~ Oceanía.
South Seas *npl*: **the** ~ los Mares del Sur.
South Vietnam *n* Vietnam *m* del Sur.
southward(s) ['sauθwəd(z)] *adv* hacia el sur.
south-west [sauθ'wɛst] *n* suroeste *m*.
souvenir [suːvə'nɪə*] *n* recuerdo.
sovereign ['sɔvrɪn] *adj*, *n* soberano/a *m/f*.
sovereignty ['sɔvrɪntɪ] *n* soberanía.
soviet ['səuvɪət] *adj* soviético.
Soviet Union *n*: **the** ~ la Unión Soviética.
sow [sau] *n* cerda, puerca ♦ *vt* [səu] (*pt* ~**ed**, *pp* ~**n** [səun]) (*gen*) sembrar; (*spread*) esparcir.
soya ['sɔɪə], (*US*) **soy** [sɔɪ] *n* soja.
soy(a) bean *n* semilla de soja.
soy(a) sauce *n* salsa de soja.
sozzled ['sɔzld] *adj* (*BRIT col*) mamado.
spa [spɑː] *n* balneario.
space [speɪs] *n* espacio; (*room*) sitio ♦ *vt* (*also*: ~ **out**) espaciar; **to clear a** ~ **for sth** hacer sitio para algo; **in a confined** ~ en un espacio restringido; **in a short** ~ **of time** en poco *or* un corto espacio de tiempo; (**with**)**in the** ~ **of an hour/three generations** en el espacio de una hora/tres generaciones.
space bar *n* (*on typewriter*) barra espaciadora.
spacecraft ['speɪskrɑːft] *n* nave *f* espacial, astronave *f*.
spaceman ['speɪsmæn] *n* astronauta *m*, cosmonauta *m*.
spaceship ['speɪsʃɪp] *n* = **spacecraft**.
space shuttle *n* transportador *m* espacial.
spacesuit ['speɪssuːt] *n* traje *m* espacial.

spacewoman ['speɪswumən] *n* astronauta, cosmonauta.

spacing ['speɪsɪŋ] *n* espacio.

spacious ['speɪʃəs] *adj* amplio.

spade [speɪd] *n* (*tool*) pala; ~**s** *npl* (*CARDS: British*) picas *fpl*; (: *Spanish*) espadas *fpl*.

spadework ['speɪdwəːk] *n* (*fig*) trabajo preliminar.

spaghetti [spə'gɛtɪ] *n* espaguetis *mpl*.

Spain [speɪn] *n* España.

span [spæn] *n* (*of bird, plane*) envergadura; (*of hand*) palmo; (*of arch*) luz *f*; (*in time*) lapso ♦ *vt* extenderse sobre, cruzar; (*fig*) abarcar.

Spaniard ['spænjəd] *n* español(a) *m/f*.

spaniel ['spænjəl] *n* perro de aguas.

Spanish ['spænɪʃ] *adj* español(a) ♦ *n* (*LING*) español *m*, castellano; **the** ~ *npl* (*people*) los españoles; ~ **omelette** tortilla española *or* de patata.

spank [spæŋk] *vt* zurrar, dar unos azotes a.

spanner ['spænə*] *n* (*BRIT*) llave *f* inglesa.

spar [spaː*] *n* palo, verga ♦ *vi* (*BOXING*) entrenarse (en el boxeo).

spare [spɛə*] *adj* de reserva; (*surplus*) sobrante, de más ♦ *n* (*part*) pieza de repuesto ♦ *vt* (*do without*) pasarse sin; (*afford to give*) tener de sobra; (*refrain from hurting*) perdonar; (*details etc*) ahorrar; **to** ~ (*surplus*) sobrante, de sobra; **there are 2 going** ~ sobran *or* quedan 2; **to** ~ **no expense** no escatimar gastos; **can you** ~ **(me) £10?** ¿puedes prestarme *or* darme 10 libras?; **can you** ~ **the time?** ¿tienes tiempo?; **I've a few minutes to** ~ tengo unos minutos libres; **there is no time to** ~ no hay tiempo que perder.

spare part *n* pieza de repuesto.

spare room *n* cuarto de los invitados.

spare time *n* ratos *mpl* de ocio, tiempo libre.

spare tyre, (*US*) **spare tire** *n* (*AUT*) neumático *or* llanta (*LAM*) de recambio.

spare wheel *n* (*AUT*) rueda de recambio.

sparing ['spɛərɪŋ] *adj*: **to be** ~ **with** ser parco en.

sparingly ['spɛərɪŋlɪ] *adv* escasamente.

spark [spaːk] *n* chispa; (*fig*) chispazo.

spark(ing) plug ['spaːk(ɪŋ)-] *n* bujía.

sparkle ['spaːkl] *n* centelleo, destello ♦ *vi* centellear; (*shine*) relucir, brillar.

sparkler ['spaːklə*] *n* bengala.

sparkling ['spaːklɪŋ] *adj* centelleante; (*wine*) espumoso.

sparring partner ['spaːrɪŋ-] *n* sparring *m*; (*fig*) contrincante *m/f*.

sparrow ['spærəu] *n* gorrión *m*.

sparse [spaːs] *adj* esparcido, escaso.

sparsely ['spaːslɪ] *adv* escasamente; **a** ~ **furnished room** un cuarto con pocos muebles.

spartan ['spaːtən] *adj* (*fig*) espartano.

spasm ['spæzəm] *n* (*MED*) espasmo; (*fig*) arranque *m*, ataque *m*.

spasmodic [spæz'mɔdɪk] *adj* espasmódico.

spastic ['spæstɪk] *n* espástico/a.

spat [spæt] *pt, pp of* **spit** ♦ *n* (*US*) riña.

spate [speɪt] *n* (*fig*): ~ **of** torrente *m* de; **in** ~ (*river*) crecido.

spatial ['speɪʃl] *adj* espacial.

spatter ['spætə*] *vt*: **to** ~ **with** salpicar de.

spatula ['spætjulə] *n* espátula.

spawn [spɔːn] *vt* (*pej*) engendrar ♦ *vi* desovar, frezar ♦ *n* huevas *fpl*.

SPCA *n abbr* (*US*) = *Society for the Prevention of Cruelty to Animals.*

SPCC *n abbr* (*US*) = *Society for the Prevention of Cruelty to Children.*

speak, *pt* **spoke,** *pp* **spoken** [spiːk, spəuk, 'spəukn] *vt* (*language*) hablar; (*truth*) decir ♦ *vi* hablar; (*make a speech*) intervenir; **to** ~ **one's mind** hablar claro *or* con franqueza; **to** ~ **to sb/of** *or* **about sth** hablar con algn/de *or* sobre algo; **to** ~ **at a conference/in a debate** hablar en un congreso/un debate; **he has no money to** ~ **of** no tiene mucho dinero que digamos; ~**ing!** ¡al habla!; ~ **up!** ¡habla más alto!

▶**speak for** *vt fus*: **to** ~ **for sb** hablar por *or* en nombre de algn; **that picture is already spoken for** (*in shop*) ese cuadro está reservado.

speaker ['spiːkə*] *n* (*in public*) orador(a) *m/f*; (*also:* **loud**~) altavoz *m*; (*for stereo etc*) bafle *m*; (*POL*): **the S**~ (*BRIT*) el Presidente de la Cámara de los Comunes; (*US*) el Presidente del Congreso; **are you a Welsh** ~? ¿habla Ud galés?

speaking ['spiːkɪŋ] *adj* hablante.

-speaking ['spiːkɪŋ] *suff* -hablante; **Spanish**~ **people** los hispanohablantes.

spear [spɪə*] *n* lanza; (*for fishing*) arpón *m* ♦ *vt* alancear; arponear.

spearhead ['spɪəhɛd] *vt* (*attack etc*) encabezar ♦ *n* punta de lanza, vanguardia.

spearmint ['spɪəmɪnt] *n* (*BOT etc*) menta verde.

spec [spɛk] *n* (*col*): **on** ~ por si acaso; **to buy on** ~ arriesgarse a comprar.

special ['spɛʃl] *adj* especial; (*edition etc*) extraordinario; (*delivery*) urgente ♦ *n* (*train*) tren *m* especial; **nothing** ~ nada de particular, nada extraordinario.

special agent *n* agente *m/f* especial.

special correspondent n corresponsal m/f especial.

special delivery n (POST): **by** ~ por entrega urgente.

special effects npl (CINE) efectos mpl especiales.

specialist ['spɛʃəlɪst] n especialista m/f; **a heart** ~ (MED) un(a) especialista del corazón.

speciality [spɛʃɪ'ælɪtɪ], (US) **specialty** ['spɛʃəltɪ] n especialidad f.

specialize ['spɛʃəlaɪz] vi: **to** ~ **(in)** especializarse (en).

specially ['spɛʃlɪ] adv especialmente.

special offer n (COMM) oferta especial.

special train n tren m especial.

specialty ['spɛʃəltɪ] n (US) = **speciality**.

species ['spi:ʃi:z] n especie f.

specific [spə'sɪfɪk] adj específico.

specifically [spə'sɪfɪklɪ] adv (explicitly: state, warn) específicamente, expresamente; (especially: design, intend) especialmente.

specification [spɛsɪfɪ'keɪʃən] n especificación f; ~**s** npl (plan) presupuesto sg; (of car, machine) descripción f técnica; (for building) plan msg detallado.

specify ['spɛsɪfaɪ] vt, vi especificar, precisar; **unless otherwise specified** salvo indicaciones contrarias.

specimen ['spɛsɪmən] n ejemplar m; (MED: of urine) espécimen m; (: of blood) muestra.

specimen copy n ejemplar m de muestra.

specimen signature n muestra de firma.

speck [spɛk] n grano, mota.

speckled ['spɛkld] adj moteado.

specs [spɛks] npl (col) gafas fpl (SP), anteojos mpl.

spectacle ['spɛktəkl] n espectáculo.

spectacle case n estuche m or funda (de gafas).

spectacles ['spɛktəklz] npl (BRIT) gafas fpl (SP), anteojos mpl.

spectacular [spɛk'tækjulə*] adj espectacular; (success) impresionante.

spectator [spɛk'teɪtə*] n espectador(a) m/f.

spectator sport n deporte m espectáculo.

spectra ['spɛktrə] npl of **spectrum**.

spectre, (US) **specter** ['spɛktə*] n espectro, fantasma m.

spectrum, pl **spectra** ['spɛktrəm, -trə] n espectro.

speculate ['spɛkjuleɪt] vi especular; (try to guess): **to** ~ **about** especular sobre.

speculation [spɛkju'leɪʃən] n especulación f.

speculative ['spɛkjulətɪv] adj especulativo.

speculator ['spɛkjuleɪtə*] n especulador(a)

m/f.

sped [spɛd] pt, pp of **speed**.

speech [spi:tʃ] n (faculty) habla; (formal talk) discurso; (words) palabras fpl; (manner of speaking) forma de hablar; (language) idioma m, lenguaje m.

speech day n (BRIT SCOL) ≈ día de reparto de premios.

speech impediment n defecto del habla.

speechless ['spi:tʃlɪs] adj mudo, estupefacto.

speech therapy n logopedia.

speed [spi:d] n (also: AUT, TECH: gear) velocidad f; (haste) prisa; (promptness) rapidez f ♦ vi (pt, pp **sped** [spɛd]) (AUT: exceed ~ limit) conducir con exceso de velocidad; **at full** or **top** ~ a máxima velocidad; **at a** ~ **of 70 km/h** a una velocidad de 70 km por hora; **at** ~ a gran velocidad; **a five-**~ **gearbox** una caja de cambios de 5 velocidades; **shorthand/ typing** ~ rapidez f en taquigrafía/ mecanografía; **the years sped by** los años pasaron volando.

▶**speed up** vi acelerarse ♦ vt acelerar.

speedboat ['spi:dbəut] n lancha motora.

speedily ['spi:dɪlɪ] adv rápido, rápidamente.

speeding ['spi:dɪŋ] n (AUT) exceso de velocidad.

speed limit n límite m de velocidad, velocidad f máxima.

speedometer [spɪ'dɒmɪtə*] n velocímetro.

speed trap n (AUT) control m de velocidades.

speedway ['spi:dweɪ] n (SPORT) pista de carrera.

speedy ['spi:dɪ] adj (fast) veloz, rápido; (prompt) pronto.

spell [spɛl] n (also: magic ~) encanto, hechizo; (period of time) rato, período; (turn) turno ♦ vt (pt, pp **spelt** or ~**ed** [spɛlt, spɛld]) (also: ~ **out**) deletrear; (fig) anunciar, presagiar; **to cast a** ~ **on sb** hechizar a algn; **he can't** ~ no sabe escribir bien, comete faltas de ortografía; **can you** ~ **it for me?** ¿cómo se deletrea or se escribe?; **how do you** ~ **your name?** ¿cómo se escribe tu nombre?

spellbound ['spɛlbaund] adj embelesado, hechizado.

spelling ['spɛlɪŋ] n ortografía.

spelling mistake n falta de ortografía.

spelt [spɛlt] pt, pp of **spell**.

spend, pt, pp **spent** [spɛnd, spɛnt] vt (money) gastar; (time) pasar; (life) dedicar; **to** ~ **time/money/effort on sth** gastar tiempo/ dinero/energías en algo.

spending ['spɛndɪŋ] _n_: **government** ~ gastos _mpl_ del gobierno.
spending money _n_ dinero para gastos.
spending power _n_ poder _m_ adquisitivo.
spendthrift ['spɛndθrɪft] _n_ derrochador(a) _m/f_, manirroto/a.
spent [spɛnt] _pt, pp of_ **spend** ♦ _adj_ (_cartridge, bullets, match_) usado.
sperm [spɔːm] _n_ esperma.
sperm bank _n_ banco de esperma.
sperm whale _n_ cachalote _m._
spew [spjuː] _vt_ vomitar, arrojar.
sphere [sfɪə*] _n_ esfera.
spherical ['sfɛrɪkl] _adj_ esférico.
sphinx [sfɪŋks] _n_ esfinge _f._
spice [spaɪs] _n_ especia ♦ _vt_ especiar.
spiciness ['spaɪsɪnɪs] _n_ lo picante.
spicy ['spaɪsɪ] _adj_ picante.
spick-and-span ['spɪkən'spæn] _adj_ impecable.
spider ['spaɪdə*] _n_ araña.
spider's web _n_ telaraña.
spiel [ʃpiːl] _n_ (_col_) rollo.
spike [spaɪk] _n_ (_point_) punta; (_ZOOL_) pincho, púa; (_BOT_) espiga; (_ELEC_) pico parásito ♦ _vt_: **to ~ a quote** cancelar una cita; ~**s** _npl_ (_SPORT_) zapatillas _fpl_ con clavos.
spiky ['spaɪkɪ] _adj_ (_bush, branch_) cubierto de púas; (_animal_) erizado.
spill, _pt, pp_ **spilt** _or_ ~**ed** [spɪl, spɪlt, spɪld] _vt_ derramar, verter; (_blood_) derramar ♦ _vi_ derramarse; **to ~ the beans** (_col_) descubrir el pastel.
▶**spill out** _vi_ derramarse, desparramarse.
▶**spill over** _vi_ desbordarse.
spillage ['spɪlɪdʒ] _n_ (_event_) derrame _m_; (_substance_) vertidos.
spin [spɪn] _n_ (_revolution of wheel_) vuelta, revolución _f_; (_AVIAT_) barrena; (_trip in car_) paseo (en coche) ♦ _vb_ (_pt, pp_ **spun** [spʌn]) _vt_ (_wool etc_) hilar; (_wheel_) girar ♦ _vi_ girar, dar vueltas; **the car spun out of control** el coche se descontroló y empezó a dar vueltas.
▶**spin out** _vt_ alargar, prolongar.
spina bifida ['spaɪnə'bɪfɪdə] _n_ espina _f_ bífida.
spinach ['spɪnɪtʃ] _n_ espinacas _fpl._
spinal ['spaɪnl] _adj_ espinal.
spinal column _n_ columna vertebral.
spinal cord _n_ médula espinal.
spindly ['spɪndlɪ] _adj_ (_leg_) zanquivano.
spin doctor _n_ (_col_) informador(a) parcial al servicio de un partido político.
spin-dry ['spɪn'draɪ] _vt_ centrifugar.
spin-dryer [spɪn'draɪə*] _n_ (_BRIT_) secadora centrífuga.
spine [spaɪn] _n_ espinazo, columna

vertebral; (_thorn_) espina.
spine-chilling ['spaɪntʃɪlɪŋ] _adj_ terrorífico.
spineless ['spaɪnlɪs] _adj_ (_fig_) débil, flojo.
spinet [spɪ'nɛt] _n_ espineta.
spinning ['spɪnɪŋ] _n_ (_of thread_) hilado; (_art_) hilandería.
spinning top _n_ peonza.
spinning wheel _n_ rueca, torno de hilar.
spin-off ['spɪnɔf] _n_ derivado, producto secundario.
spinster ['spɪnstə*] _n_ soltera; (_pej_) solterona.
spiral ['spaɪərl] _n_ espiral _f_ ♦ _adj_ en espiral ♦ _vi_ (_prices_) dispararse; **the inflationary** ~ la espiral inflacionista.
spiral staircase _n_ escalera de caracol.
spire ['spaɪə*] _n_ aguja, chapitel _m._
spirit ['spɪrɪt] _n_ (_soul_) alma _f_; (_ghost_) fantasma _m_; (_attitude_) espíritu _m_; (_courage_) valor _m_, ánimo; ~**s** _npl_ (_drink_) alcohol _msg_, bebidas _fpl_ alcohólicas; **in good** ~ alegre, de buen ánimo; **Holy S**~ Espíritu _m_ Santo; **community** ~, **public** ~ civismo.
spirit duplicator _n_ copiadora al alcohol.
spirited ['spɪrɪtɪd] _adj_ enérgico, vigoroso.
spirit level _n_ nivel _m_ de aire.
spiritual ['spɪrɪtjuəl] _adj_ espiritual ♦ _n_ (_also_: **Negro** ~) canción _f_ religiosa, espiritual _m._
spiritualism ['spɪrɪtjuəlɪzəm] _n_ espiritualismo.
spit [spɪt] _n_ (_for roasting_) asador _m_, espetón _m_; (_spittle_) esputo, escupitajo; (_saliva_) saliva ♦ _vi_ (_pt, pp_ **spat** [spæt]) escupir; (_sound_) chisporrotear.
spite [spaɪt] _n_ rencor _m_, ojeriza ♦ _vt_ fastidiar; **in** ~ **of** a pesar de, pese a.
spiteful ['spaɪtful] _adj_ rencoroso, malévolo.
spitting ['spɪtɪŋ] _n_: "~ **prohibited**" "se prohíbe escupir" ♦ _adj_: **to be the** ~ **image of sb** ser la viva imagen de algn.
spittle ['spɪtl] _n_ saliva, baba.
splash [splæʃ] _n_ (_sound_) chapoteo; (_of colour_) mancha ♦ _vt_ salpicar de ♦ _vi_ (_also_: ~ **about**) chapotear; **to** ~ **paint on the floor** manchar el suelo de pintura.
splashdown ['splæʃdaun] _n_ amaraje _m_, amerizaje _m._
spleen [spliːn] _n_ (_ANAT_) bazo.
splendid ['splɛndɪd] _adj_ espléndido.
splendidly ['splɛndɪdlɪ] _adv_ espléndidamente; **everything went** ~ todo fue a las mil maravillas.
splendour, (_US_) **splendor** ['splɛndə*] _n_ esplendor _m_; (_of achievement_) brillo, gloria.
splice [splaɪs] _vt_ empalmar.
splint [splɪnt] _n_ tablilla.

splinter ['splɪntə*] n astilla ♦ vi astillarse, hacer astillas.

splinter group n grupo disidente, facción f.

split [splɪt] n hendedura, raja; (fig) división f; (POL) escisión f ♦ (vb: pt, pp **split**) vt partir, rajar; (party) dividir; (work, profits) repartir ♦ vi (divide) dividirse, escindirse; **to ~ the difference** partir la diferencia; **to do the ~s** hacer el espagat; **to ~ sth down the middle** (also fig) dividir algo en dos.

▶**split up** vi (couple) separarse, romper; (meeting) acabarse.

split-level ['splɪtlɛvl] adj (house) dúplex.

split peas npl guisantes mpl secos.

split personality n doble personalidad f.

split second n fracción f de segundo.

splitting ['splɪtɪŋ] adj (headache) horrible.

splutter ['splʌtə*] vi chisporrotear; (person) balbucear.

spoil, pt, pp **spoilt** or **~ed** [spɔɪl, spɔɪlt, spɔɪld] vt (damage) dañar; (ruin) estropear, echar a perder; (child) mimar, consentir; (ballot paper) invalidar ♦ vi: **to be ~ing for a fight** estar con ganas de lucha, andar con ganas de pelea.

spoiled [spɔɪld] adj (US: food: bad) pasado, malo; (: milk) cortado.

spoils [spɔɪlz] npl despojo sg, botín msg.

spoilsport ['spɔɪlspɔːt] n aguafiestas m inv.

spoilt [spɔɪlt] pt, pp of **spoil** ♦ adj (child) mimado, consentido; (ballot paper) invalidado.

spoke [spəuk] pt of **speak** ♦ n rayo, radio.

spoken ['spəukn] pp of **speak**.

spokesman ['spəuksmən] n portavoz m, vocero (LAM).

spokesperson ['spəukspə:sn] n portavoz m/f, vocero/a (LAM).

spokeswoman ['spəukswumən] n portavoz f, vocera (LAM).

sponge [spʌndʒ] n esponja; (CULIN: also: ~ **cake**) bizcocho ♦ vt (wash) lavar con esponja ♦ vi: **to ~ on** or (US) **off sb** vivir a costa de algn.

sponge bag n (BRIT) neceser m.

sponge cake n bizcocho, pastel m.

sponger ['spʌndʒə*] n gorrón/ona m/f.

spongy ['spʌndʒɪ] adj esponjoso.

sponsor ['spɔnsə*] n (RADIO, TV) patrocinador(a) m/f; (for membership) padrino/madrina; (COMM) fiador(a) m/f, avalador(a) m/f ♦ vt patrocinar; apadrinar; (parliamentary bill) apoyar, respaldar; (idea etc) presentar, promover; **I ~ed him at 3p a mile** (in fund-raising race) me apunté para darle 3 peniques la milla.

sponsorship ['spɔnsəʃɪp] n patrocinio.

spontaneity [spɔntə'neɪɪtɪ] n espontaneidad f.

spontaneous [spɔn'teɪnɪəs] adj espontáneo.

spontaneously [spɔn'teɪnɪəslɪ] adv espontáneamente.

spooky ['spuːkɪ] adj (col: place, atmosphere) espeluznante, horripilante.

spool [spuːl] n carrete m; (of sewing machine) canilla.

spoon [spuːn] n cuchara.

spoon-feed ['spuːnfiːd] vt dar de comer con cuchara a; (fig) dárselo todo mascado a.

spoonful ['spuːnful] n cucharada.

sporadic [spə'rædɪk] adj esporádico.

sport [spɔːt] n deporte m; (person) buen(a) perdedor(a) m/f; (amusement) juego, diversión f; **indoor/outdoor ~s** deportes mpl en sala cubierta/al aire libre; **to say sth in ~** decir algo en broma.

sport coat n (US) = **sports jacket**.

sporting ['spɔːtɪŋ] adj deportivo; **to give sb a ~ chance** darle a algn su oportunidad.

sports car n coche m sport.

sports coat n (US) = **sports jacket**.

sports ground n campo de deportes, centro deportivo.

sports jacket, (US) **sport jacket** n chaqueta deportiva.

sportsman ['spɔːtsmən] n deportista m.

sportsmanship ['spɔːtsmənʃɪp] n deportividad f.

sports pages npl páginas fpl deportivas.

sportswear ['spɔːtswɛə*] n ropa de deporte.

sportswoman ['spɔːtswumən] n deportista.

sporty ['spɔːtɪ] adj deportivo.

spot [spɔt] n sitio, lugar m; (dot: on pattern) punto, mancha; (pimple) grano; (also: advertising ~) spot m; (small amount): **a ~ of** un poquito de ♦ vt (notice) notar, observar ♦ adj (COMM) inmediatamente efectivo; **on the ~** en el acto, acto seguido; (in difficulty) en un aprieto; **to do sth on the ~** hacer algo en el acto; **to put sb on the ~** poner a algn en un apuro.

spot check n reconocimiento rápido.

spotless ['spɔtlɪs] adj (clean) inmaculado; (reputation) intachable.

spotlessly ['spɔtlɪslɪ] adv: **~ clean** limpísimo.

spotlight ['spɔtlaɪt] n foco, reflector m; (AUT) faro auxiliar.

spot-on [spɔt'ɔn] adj (BRIT col) exacto.

spot price n precio de entrega inmediata.

spotted ['spɔtɪd] adj (pattern) de puntos.

spotty ['spɔtɪ] adj (face) con granos.

spouse [spauz] *n* cónyuge *m/f.*
spout [spaut] *n* (*of jug*) pico; (*pipe*) caño ♦ *vi* chorrear.
sprain [spreɪn] *n* torcedura, esguince *m* ♦ *vt*: **to ~ one's ankle** torcerse el tobillo.
sprang [spræŋ] *pt of* **spring**.
sprawl [sprɔːl] *vi* tumbarse ♦ *n*: **urban ~** crecimiento urbano descontrolado; **to send sb ~ing** tirar a algn al suelo.
sprawling ['sprɔːlɪŋ] *adj* (*town*) desparramado.
spray [spreɪ] *n* rociada; (*of sea*) espuma; (*container*) atomizador *m*; (*of paint*) pistola rociadora; (*of flowers*) ramita ♦ *vt* rociar; (*crops*) regar ♦ *cpd* (*deodorant*) en atomizador.
spread [sprɛd] *n* extensión *f*; (*of idea*) diseminación *f*; (*col: food*) comilona; (*PRESS, TYP: two pages*) plana ♦ *vb* (*pt, pp* **spread**) *vt* extender; diseminar; (*butter*) untar; (*wings, sails*) desplegar; (*scatter*) esparcir ♦ *vi* extenderse; diseminarse; untarse; desplegarse; esparcirse; **middle-age ~** gordura de la mediana edad; **repayments will be ~ over 18 months** los pagos se harán a lo largo de 18 meses.
spread-eagled ['sprɛdiːgld] *adj*: **to be ~** estar despatarrado.
spreadsheet ['sprɛdʃiːt] *n* (*COMPUT*) hoja de cálculo.
spree [spriː] *n*: **to go on a ~** ir de juerga *or* farra (*LAM*).
sprightly ['spraɪtlɪ] *adj* vivo, enérgico.
spring [sprɪŋ] *n* (*season*) primavera; (*leap*) salto, brinco; (*coiled metal*) resorte *m*; (*of water*) fuente *f*, manantial *m*; (*bounciness*) elasticidad *f* ♦ *vb* (*pt* **sprang**, *pp* **sprung** [spræŋ, sprʌŋ]) *vi* (*arise*) brotar, nacer; (*leap*) saltar, brincar ♦ *vt*: **to ~ a leak** (*pipe etc*) empezar a hacer agua; **he sprang the news on me** de repente me soltó la noticia; **in (the) ~** en (la) primavera; **to walk with a ~ in one's step** andar dando saltos *or* brincos; **to ~ into action** lanzarse a la acción.
▶**spring up** *vi* (*problem*) surgir.
springboard ['sprɪŋbɔːd] *n* trampolín *m*.
spring-clean [sprɪŋ'kliːn] *n* (*also: ~ing*) limpieza general.
spring onion *n* cebolleta.
spring roll *n* rollito de primavera.
springtime ['sprɪŋtaɪm] *n* primavera.
springy ['sprɪŋɪ] *adj* elástico; (*grass*) mullido.
sprinkle ['sprɪŋkl] *vt* (*pour*) rociar; **to ~ water on, ~ with water** rociar *or* salpicar de agua.

sprinkler ['sprɪŋklə*] *n* (*for lawn*) aspersor *m*; (*to put out fire*) aparato de rociadura automática.
sprinkling ['sprɪŋklɪŋ] *n* (*of water*) rociada; (*of salt, sugar*) un poco de.
sprint [sprɪnt] *n* (e)sprint *m* ♦ *vi* (*gen*) correr a toda velocidad; (*SPORT*) esprintar; **the 200 metres ~** el (e)sprint de 200 metros.
sprinter ['sprɪntə*] *n* velocista *m/f.*
spritzer ['sprɪtsə*] *n* vino blanco con soda.
sprocket ['sprɒkɪt] *n* (*on printer etc*) rueda dentada.
sprocket feed *n* avance *m* por rueda dentada.
sprout [spraut] *vi* brotar, retoñar ♦ *n*: **(Brussels) ~s** *npl* coles *fpl* de Bruselas.
spruce [spruːs] *n* (*BOT*) pícea ♦ *adj* aseado, pulcro.
▶**spruce up** *vt* (*tidy*) arreglar, acicalar; (*smarten up: room etc*) ordenar; **to ~ o.s. up** arreglarse.
sprung [sprʌŋ] *pp of* **spring**.
spry [spraɪ] *adj* ágil, activo.
SPUC *n abbr* (= *Society for the Protection of Unborn Children*) ≈ Federación *f* Española de Asociaciones Pro-vida.
spun [spʌn] *pt, pp of* **spin**.
spur [spə:*] *n* espuela; (*fig*) estímulo, aguijón *m* ♦ *vt* (*also: ~ on*) estimular, incitar; **on the ~ of the moment** de improviso.
spurious ['spjuərɪəs] *adj* falso.
spurn [spə:n] *vt* desdeñar, rechazar.
spurt [spə:t] *n* chorro; (*of energy*) arrebato ♦ *vi* chorrear; **to put in** *or* **on a ~** (*runner*) acelerar; (*fig: in work etc*) hacer un gran esfuerzo.
sputter ['spʌtə*] *vi* = **splutter**.
spy [spaɪ] *n* espía *m/f* ♦ *vi*: **to ~ on** espiar a ♦ *vt* (*see*) divisar, lograr ver ♦ *cpd* (*film, story*) de espionaje.
spying ['spaɪɪŋ] *n* espionaje *m*.
Sq. *abbr* (*in address*: = *Square*) Plza.
sq. *abbr* (*MATH etc*) = **square**.
squabble ['skwɒbl] *n* riña, pelea ♦ *vi* reñir, pelear.
squad [skwɒd] *n* (*MIL*) pelotón *m*; (*POLICE*) brigada; (*SPORT*) equipo; **flying ~** (*POLICE*) brigada móvil.
squad car *n* (*POLICE*) coche-patrulla *m*.
squaddie ['skwɒdɪ] *n* (*MIL: col*) chivo.
squadron ['skwɒdrn] *n* (*MIL*) escuadrón *m*; (*AVIAT, NAUT*) escuadra.
squalid ['skwɒlɪd] *adj* miserable.
squall [skwɔːl] *n* (*storm*) chubasco; (*wind*) ráfaga.
squalor ['skwɒlə*] *n* miseria.
squander ['skwɒndə*] *vt* (*money*)

derrochar, despilfarrar; (*chances*) desperdiciar.

square [skwɛə*] n cuadro; (*in town*) plaza; (*US: block of houses*) manzana, cuadra (*LAM*) ♦ adj cuadrado ♦ vt (*arrange*) arreglar; (*MATH*) cuadrar; (*reconcile*): **can you ~ it with your conscience?** ¿cómo se justifica ante sí mismo? ♦ vi cuadrar, conformarse; **all ~** igual(es); **a ~ meal** una comida decente; **2 metres ~** 2 metros por 2; **1 ~ metre** un metro cuadrado; **to get one's accounts ~** dejar las cuentas claras; **I'll ~ it with him** (*col*) yo lo arreglo con él; **we're back to ~ one** (*fig*) hemos vuelto al punto de partida.

▶**square up** vi (*settle*): **to ~ up (with sb)** ajustar cuentas (con algn).

square bracket n (*TYP*) corchete m.

squarely ['skwɛəlɪ] adv (*fully*) de lleno; (*honestly, fairly*) honradamente, justamente.

square root n raíz f cuadrada.

squash [skwɔʃ] n (*vegetable*) calabaza; (*SPORT*) squash m; (*BRIT: drink*): **lemon/ orange ~** zumo (*SP*) or jugo (*LAM*) de limón/naranja ♦ vt aplastar.

squat [skwɔt] adj achaparrado ♦ vi agacharse, sentarse en cuclillas; (*on property*) ocupar ilegalmente.

squatter ['skwɔtə*] n ocupante m/f ilegal, okupa m/f.

squawk [skwɔːk] vi graznar.

squeak [skwiːk] vi (*hinge, wheel*) chirriar, rechinar; (*shoe, wood*) crujir ♦ n (*of hinge, wheel etc*) chirrido, rechinamiento; (*of shoes*) crujir m; (*of mouse etc*) chillido.

squeaky ['skwiːkɪ] adj que cruje; **to be ~ clean** (*fig*) ser superhonrado.

squeal [skwiːl] vi chillar, dar gritos agudos.

squeamish ['skwiːmɪʃ] adj delicado, remilgado.

squeeze [skwiːz] n presión f, (*of hand*) apretón m; (*COMM: credit ~*) restricción f ♦ vt (*lemon etc*) exprimir; (*hand, arm*) apretar; **a ~ of lemon** unas gotas de limón; **to ~ past/under sth** colarse al lado de/por debajo de algo.

▶**squeeze out** vt exprimir; (*fig*) excluir.

▶**squeeze through** vi abrirse paso con esfuerzos.

squelch [skwɛltʃ] vi chapotear.

squid [skwɪd] n calamar m.

squiggle ['skwɪgl] n garabato.

squint [skwɪnt] vi entrecerrar los ojos ♦ n (*MED*) estrabismo; **to ~ at sth** mirar algo entornando los ojos.

squire ['skwaɪə*] n (*BRIT*) terrateniente m

squirm [skwəːm] vi retorcerse, revolverse.

squirrel ['skwɪrəl] n ardilla.

squirt [skwəːt] vi salir a chorros.

Sr abbr = **senior, sister** (*REL*).

SRC n abbr (*BRIT:* = *Students' Representative Council*) consejo de estudiantes.

Sri Lanka [srɪ'læŋkə] n Sri Lanka m.

SRN n abbr (*BRIT*) = *State Registered Nurse*.

SRO abbr (*US*) = *standing room only*.

SS abbr (= *steamship*) M.V.

SSA n abbr (*US:* = *Social Security Administration*) ≈ Seguro Social.

SST n abbr (*US*) = *supersonic transport*.

ST abbr (*US:* = *Standard Time*) hora oficial.

St abbr (= *saint*) Sto./a.; (= *street*) c/.

stab [stæb] n (*with knife etc*) puñalada; (*of pain*) pinchazo; **to have a ~ at (doing) sth** (*col*) probar (a hacer) algo ♦ vt apuñalar; **to ~ sb to death** matar a algn a puñaladas.

stabbing ['stæbɪŋ] n: **there's been a ~** han apuñalado a alguien ♦ adj (*pain*) punzante.

stability [stə'bɪlɪtɪ] n estabilidad f.

stabilization [steɪbəlaɪ'zeɪʃən] n estabilización f.

stabilize ['steɪbəlaɪz] vt estabilizar ♦ vi estabilizarse.

stabilizer ['steɪbəlaɪzə*] n (*AVIAT, NAUT*) estabilizador m.

stable ['steɪbl] adj estable ♦ n cuadra, caballeriza; **riding ~s** escuela hípica.

staccato [stə'kɑːtəu] adj, adv staccato.

stack [stæk] n montón m, pila; (*col*) mar f ♦ vt amontonar, apilar; **there's ~s of time to finish it** hay cantidad de tiempo para acabarlo.

stacker ['stækə*] n (*for printer*) apiladora.

stadium ['steɪdɪəm] n estadio.

staff [stɑːf] n (*work force*) personal m, plantilla; (*BRIT SCOL: also:* **teaching ~**) cuerpo docente; (*stick*) bastón m ♦ vt proveer de personal; **to be ~ed by Asians/women** tener una plantilla asiática/femenina.

staffroom ['stɑːfruːm] n sala de profesores.

Staffs abbr (*BRIT*) = *Staffordshire*.

stag [stæg] n ciervo, venado; (*BRIT STOCK EXCHANGE*) especulador m con nuevas emisiones.

stage [steɪdʒ] n escena; (*point*) etapa; (*platform*) plataforma; **the ~** el escenario, el teatro ♦ vt (*play*) poner en escena, representar; (*organize*) montar, organizar; (*fig: perform: recovery etc*) efectuar; **in ~s** por etapas; **in the early/ final ~s** en las primeras/últimas etapas; **to go through a difficult ~** pasar una fase or etapa mala.

stagecoach ['steɪdʒkəutʃ] n diligencia.

stage door n entrada de artistas.

stagehand ['steɪdʒhænd] n tramoyista m/f.

stage-manage ['steɪdʒmænɪdʒ] vt (fig) manipular.

stage manager n director(a) m/f de escena.

stagger ['stægə*] vi tambalear ♦ vt (amaze) asombrar; (hours, holidays) escalonar.

staggering ['stægərɪŋ] adj (amazing) asombroso, pasmoso.

staging post ['steɪdʒɪŋ-] n escala.

stagnant ['stægnənt] adj estancado.

stagnate [stæg'neɪt] vi estancarse; (fig: economy, mind) quedarse estancado.

stagnation [stæg'neɪʃən] n estancamiento.

stag night, stag party n despedida de soltero.

staid [steɪd] adj (clothes) serio, formal.

stain [steɪn] n mancha; (colouring) tintura ♦ vt manchar; (wood) teñir.

stained glass window [steɪnd-] n vidriera de colores.

stainless ['steɪnlɪs] adj (steel) inoxidable.

stain remover n quitamanchas m inv.

stair [stɛə*] n (step) peldaño, escalón m; ~s npl escaleras fpl.

staircase ['stɛəkeɪs], **stairway** ['stɛəweɪ] n escalera.

stairwell ['stɛəwɛl] n hueco or caja de la escalera.

stake [steɪk] n estaca, poste m; (BETTING) apuesta ♦ vt (bet) apostar; (also: ~ out: area) cercar con estacas; **to be at** ~ estar en juego; **to have a** ~ **in sth** tener interés en algo; **to** ~ **a claim to (sth)** presentar reclamación por or reclamar (algo).

stake-out ['steɪkaut] n vigilancia; **to be on a** ~ estar de vigilancia.

stalactite ['stæləktaɪt] n estalactita.

stalagmite ['stæləgmaɪt] n estalagmita.

stale [steɪl] adj (bread) duro; (food) pasado.

stalemate ['steɪlmeɪt] n tablas fpl; **to reach** ~ (fig) estancarse, alcanzar un punto muerto.

stalk [stɔ:k] n tallo, caña ♦ vt acechar, cazar al acecho; **to** ~ **off** irse airado.

stall [stɔ:l] n (in market) puesto; (in stable) casilla (de establo) ♦ vt (AUT) parar, calar ♦ vi (AUT) pararse, calarse; (fig) buscar evasivas; ~s npl (BRIT: in cinema, theatre) butacas fpl; **a newspaper** ~ un quiosco (de periódicos); **a flower** ~ un puesto de flores.

stallholder ['stɔ:lhəuldə*] n dueño/a de un puesto.

stallion ['stælɪən] n semental m, garañón m.

stalwart ['stɔ:lwət] n partidario/a incondicional.

stamen ['steɪmən] n estambre m.

stamina ['stæmɪnə] n resistencia.

stammer ['stæmə*] n tartamudeo, balbuceo ♦ vi tartamudear, balbucir.

stamp [stæmp] n sello, estampilla (LAM); (mark, also fig) marca, huella; (on document) timbre m ♦ vi (also: ~ one's foot) patear ♦ vt patear, golpear con el pie; (letter) poner sellos en; (with rubber ~) marcar con sello; ~ed addressed envelope (sae) sobre m sellado con las señas propias.

▶**stamp out** vt (fire) apagar con el pie; (crime, opposition) acabar con.

stamp album n álbum m para sellos.

stamp collecting n filatelia.

stamp duty n (BRIT) derecho de timbre.

stampede [stæm'pi:d] n (of cattle) estampida.

stamp machine n máquina (expendedora) de sellos.

stance [stæns] n postura.

stand [stænd] n (attitude) posición f, postura; (for taxis) parada; (music ~) atril m; (SPORT) tribuna; (at exhibition) stand m ♦ vb (pt, pp **stood** [stud]) vi (be) estar, encontrarse; (be on foot) estar de pie; (rise) levantarse; (remain) quedar en pie ♦ vt (place) poner, colocar; (tolerate, withstand) aguantar, soportar; **to make a** ~ resistir; (fig) mantener una postura firme; **to take a** ~ **on an issue** adoptar una actitud hacia una cuestión; **to** ~ **for parliament** (BRIT) presentarse (como candidato) a las elecciones; **nothing** ~**s in our way** nada nos lo impide; **to** ~ **still** quedarse inmóvil; **to let sth** ~ **as it is** dejar algo como está; **as things** ~ tal como están las cosas; **to** ~ **sb a drink/meal** invitar a algn a una copa/a comer; **the company will have to** ~ **the loss** la empresa tendrá que hacer frente a las pérdidas; **I can't** ~ **him** no le aguanto, no le puedo ver; **to** ~ **guard** or **watch** (MIL) hacer guardia.

▶**stand aside** vi apartarse, mantenerse aparte.

▶**stand by** vi (be ready) estar listo ♦ vt fus (opinion) mantener.

▶**stand down** vi (withdraw) ceder el puesto; (MIL, LAW) retirarse.

▶**stand for** vt fus (signify) significar; (tolerate) aguantar, permitir.

▶**stand in for** vt fus suplir a.

▶**stand out** vi (be prominent) destacarse.

▶**stand up** vi (rise) levantarse, ponerse de

pie.
▶**stand up for** *vt fus* defender.
▶**stand up to** *vt fus* hacer frente a.
stand-alone ['stændələun] *adj* (*COMPUT*)
autónomo.
standard ['stændəd] *n* patrón *m*, norma;
(*flag*) estandarte *m* ♦ *adj* (*size etc*) normal,
corriente, estándar; ~**s** *npl* (*morals*)
valores *mpl* morales; **the gold** ~ (*COMM*)
el patrón oro; **high/low** ~ de alto/bajo
nivel; **below** *or* **not up to** ~ (*work*) de
calidad inferior; **to be** *or* **come up to** ~
satisfacer los requisitos; **to apply a
double** ~ aplicar un doble criterio.
standardization [stændədaɪˈzeɪʃən] *n*
normalización *f*.
standardize ['stændədaɪz] *vt* estandarizar.
standard lamp *n* (*BRIT*) lámpara de pie.
standard model *n* modelo standard.
standard of living *n* nivel *m* de vida.
standard practice *n* norma, práctica
común.
standard rate *n* tasa de imposición.
standard time *n* hora oficial.
stand-by ['stændbaɪ] *n* (*alert*) alerta, aviso;
(*also*: ~ **ticket**: *THEAT*) entrada reducida
de última hora; (: *AVIAT*) billete *m*
standby; **to be on** ~ estar preparado;
(*doctor*) estar listo para acudir; (*AVIAT*)
estar en la lista de espera.
stand-by generator *n* generador *m* de
reserva.
stand-by passenger *n* (*AVIAT*) pasajero/a
en lista de espera.
stand-by ticket *n* (*AVIAT*) (billete *m*)
standby *m*.
stand-in ['stændɪn] *n* suplente *m/f*; (*CINE*)
doble *m/f*.
standing ['stændɪŋ] *adj* (*upright*) derecho;
(*on foot*) de pie, en pie; (*permanent*:
committee) permanente; (: *rule*) fijo;
(: *army*) permanente, regular; (*grievance*)
constante, viejo ♦ *n* reputación *f*,
(*duration*): **of 6 months'** ~ que lleva 6
meses; **of many years'** ~ que lleva
muchos años; **he was given a** ~ **ovation** le
dieron una calurosa ovación de pie; ~
joke motivo constante de broma; **a man
of some** ~ un hombre de cierta posición
or categoría.
standing order *n* (*BRIT*: *at bank*) giro
bancario; **standing orders** *npl* (*MIL*)
reglamento *sg* general.
standing room *n* sitio para estar de pie.
stand-off ['stændɔf] *n* (*esp US*: *stalemate*)
punto muerto.
stand-offish [stændˈɔfɪʃ] *adj* distante.
standpat ['stændpæt] *adj* (*US*) inmovilista.

standpipe ['stændpaɪp] *n* tubo vertical.
standpoint ['stændpɔɪnt] *n* punto de vista.
standstill ['stændstɪl] *n*: **at a** ~ paralizado,
en un punto muerto; **to come to a** ~
pararse, quedar paralizado.
stank [stæŋk] *pt of* **stink**.
staple ['steɪpl] *n* (*for papers*) grapa;
(*product*) producto *or* artículo de primera
necesidad ♦ *adj* (*crop, industry, food etc*)
básico ♦ *vt* grapar.
stapler ['steɪplə*] *n* grapadora.
star [stɑ:*] *n* estrella; (*celebrity*) estrella,
astro ♦ *vi*: **to** ~ **in** ser la estrella de; **four-**
~ **hotel** hotel *m* de cuatro estrellas; **4-**~
petrol gasolina extra.
star attraction *n* atracción *f* principal.
starboard ['stɑ:bəd] *n* estribor *m*.
starch [stɑ:tʃ] *n* almidón *m*.
starchy ['stɑ:tʃɪ] *adj* (*food*) feculento.
stardom ['stɑ:dəm] *n* estrellato.
stare [steə*] *n* mirada fija ♦ *vi*: **to** ~ **at**
mirar fijo.
starfish ['stɑ:fɪʃ] *n* estrella de mar.
stark [stɑ:k] *adj* (*bleak*) severo, escueto;
(*simplicity, colour*) austero; (*reality, truth*)
puro; (*poverty*) absoluto ♦ *adv*: ~ **naked** en
cueros.
starkers ['stɑ:kəz] *adj* (*BRIT col*): **to be** ~
estar en cueros.
starlet ['stɑ:lɪt] *n* (*CINE*) actriz *f*
principiante.
starling ['stɑ:lɪŋ] *n* estornino.
starry ['stɑ:rɪ] *adj* estrellado.
starry-eyed [stɑ:rɪˈaɪd] *adj* (*gullible,
innocent*) inocentón/ona, ingenuo;
(*idealistic*) idealista; (*from wonder*)
asombrado; (*from love*) enamoradísimo.
Stars and Stripes *npl*: **the** ~ las barras y
las estrellas, la bandera de EEUU.
star sign *n* signo del zodíaco.
star-studded ['stɑ:stʌdɪd] *adj*: **a** ~ **cast** un
elenco estelar.
start [stɑ:t] *n* (*beginning*) principio,
comienzo; (*departure*) salida; (*sudden
movement*) sobresalto; (*advantage*)
ventaja ♦ *vt* empezar, comenzar; (*cause*)
causar; (*found*: *business, newspaper*)
establecer, fundar; (*engine*) poner en
marcha ♦ *vi* (*begin*) comenzar, empezar;
(*with fright*) asustarse, sobresaltarse;
(*train etc*) salir; **to give sb a** ~ dar un
susto a algn; **at the** ~ al principio; **for a** ~
en primer lugar; **to make an early** ~
ponerse en camino temprano; **the thieves
had 3 hours'** ~ los ladrones llevaban 3
horas de ventaja; **to** ~ **a fire** provocar un
incendio; **to** ~ **doing** *or* **to do sth**
empezar a hacer algo; **to** ~ **(off) with** ...

(*firstly*) para empezar; (*at the beginning*) al principio.
▶**start off** *vi* empezar, comenzar; (*leave*) salir, ponerse en camino.
▶**start over** *vi* (*US*) volver a empezar.
▶**start up** *vi* comenzar; (*car*) ponerse en marcha ♦ *vt* comenzar; (*car*) poner en marcha.
starter ['stɑːtə*] *n* (*AUT*) botón *m* de arranque; (*SPORT: official*) juez *m/f* de salida; (: *runner*) corredor(a) *m/f*; (*BRIT CULIN*) entrada.
starting point ['stɑːtɪŋ-] *n* punto de partida.
starting price *n* (*COMM*) precio inicial.
startle ['stɑːtl] *vt* asustar, sobresaltar.
startling ['stɑːtlɪŋ] *adj* alarmante.
star turn *n* (*BRIT*) atracción *f* principal.
starvation [stɑː'veɪʃən] *n* hambre *f*, hambruna (*LAM*); (*MED*) inanición *f*.
starvation wages *npl* sueldo *sg* de hambre.
starve [stɑːv] *vi* pasar hambre; (*to death*) morir de hambre ♦ *vt* hacer pasar hambre; (*fig*) privar; **I'm starving** estoy muerto de hambre.
stash [stæʃ] *vt*: **to ~ sth away** (*col*) poner algo a buen recaudo.
state [steɪt] *n* estado; (*pomp*): **in ~** con mucha ceremonia ♦ *vt* (*say, declare*) afirmar; (*a case*) presentar, exponer; **~ of emergency** estado de excepción *or* emergencia; **~ of mind** estado de ánimo; **to lie in ~** (*corpse*) estar de cuerpo presente; **to be in a ~** estar agitado.
State Department *n* (*US*) Ministerio de Asuntos Exteriores.
state education *n* (*BRIT*) enseñanza pública.
stateless ['steɪtlɪs] *adj* desnacionalizado.
stately ['steɪtlɪ] *adj* majestuoso, imponente.
statement ['steɪtmənt] *n* afirmación *f*; (*LAW*) declaración *f*; (*COMM*) estado; **official ~** informe *m* oficial; **~ of account, bank ~** estado de cuenta.
state-of-the-art ['steɪtəvðɪ'ɑːt] *adj* (*technology etc*) puntero.
state-owned ['steɪtəund] *adj* estatal, del estado.
States [steɪts] *npl*: **the ~** los Estados Unidos.
state school *n* escuela *or* colegio estatal.
statesman ['steɪtsmən] *n* estadista *m*.
statesmanship ['steɪtsmənʃɪp] *n* habilidad *f* política, arte *m* de gobernar.
static ['stætɪk] *n* (*RADIO*) parásitos *mpl* ♦ *adj* estático.
static electricity *n* electricidad *f* estática.

station ['steɪʃən] *n* (*gen*) estación *f*; (*place*) puesto, sitio; (*RADIO*) emisora; (*rank*) posición *f* social ♦ *vt* colocar, situar; (*MIL*) apostar; **action ~s!** ¡a los puestos de combate!; **to be ~ed in** (*MIL*) estar estacionado en.
stationary ['steɪʃnərɪ] *adj* estacionario, fijo.
stationer ['steɪʃənə*] *n* papelero/a.
stationer's (shop) *n* (*BRIT*) papelería.
stationery ['steɪʃənərɪ] *n* (*writing paper*) papel *m* de escribir; (*writing materials*) artículos *mpl* de escritorio.
station master *n* (*RAIL*) jefe *m* de estación.
station wagon *n* (*US*) coche *m* familiar con ranchera.
statistic [stə'tɪstɪk] *n* estadística.
statistical [stə'tɪstɪkl] *adj* estadístico.
statistics [stə'tɪstɪks] *n* (*science*) estadística.
statue ['stætjuː] *n* estatua.
statuette [stætju'et] *n* figurilla.
stature ['stætʃə*] *n* estatura; (*fig*) talla.
status ['steɪtəs] *n* condición *f*, estado; (*reputation*) reputación *f*, estatus *m*; **the ~ quo** el statu quo.
status line *n* (*COMPUT*) línea de situación *or* de estado.
status symbol *n* símbolo de prestigio.
statute ['stætjuːt] *n* estatuto, ley *f*.
statute book *n* código de leyes.
statutory ['stætjutrɪ] *adj* estatutario; **~ meeting** junta ordinaria.
staunch [stɔːntʃ] *adj* leal, incondicional ♦ *vt* (*flow, blood*) restañar.
stave [steɪv] *vt*: **to ~ off** (*attack*) rechazar; (*threat*) evitar.
stay [steɪ] *n* (*period of time*) estancia; (*LAW*): **~ of execution** aplazamiento de una sentencia ♦ *vi* (*remain*) quedar(se); (*as guest*) hospedarse; **to ~ put** seguir en el mismo sitio; **to ~ the night/5 days** pasar la noche/estar *or* quedarse 5 días.
▶**stay behind** *vi* quedar atrás.
▶**stay in** *vi* (*at home*) quedarse en casa.
▶**stay on** *vi* quedarse.
▶**stay out** *vi* (*of house*) no volver a casa; (*strikers*) no volver al trabajo.
▶**stay up** *vi* (*at night*) velar, no acostarse.
staying power ['steɪŋ-] *n* resistencia, aguante *m*.
STD *n abbr* (*BRIT*: = *subscriber trunk dialling*) servicio de conferencias automáticas; (= *sexually transmitted disease*) ETS *f*.
stead [sted] *n*: **in sb's ~** en lugar de algn; **to stand sb in good ~** ser muy útil a algn.
steadfast ['stedfɑːst] *adj* firme, resuelto.
steadily ['stedɪlɪ] *adv* (*firmly*) firmemente; (*unceasingly*) sin parar; (*fixedly*)

fijamente; (*walk*) normalmente; (*drive*) a velocidad constante.

steady ['stɛdɪ] *adj* (*fixed*) firme, fijo; (*regular*) regular; (*boyfriend etc*) formal, fijo; (*person, character*) sensato, juicioso ♦ *vt* (*hold*) mantener firme; (*stabilize*) estabilizar; (*nerves*) calmar; **to ~ o.s. on** *or* **against sth** afirmarse en algo.

steak [steɪk] *n* (*gen*) filete *m*; (*beef*) bistec *m*.

steal, *pt* **stole,** *pp* **stolen** [stiːl, stɔul, 'stɔuln] *vt, vi* robar.

▶**steal away, steal off** *vi* marcharse furtivamente, escabullirse.

stealth [stɛlθ] *n*: **by ~** a escondidas, sigilosamente.

stealthy ['stɛlθɪ] *adj* cauteloso, sigiloso.

steam [stiːm] *n* vapor *m*; (*mist*) vaho, humo ♦ *vt* (*CULIN*) cocer al vapor ♦ *vi* echar vapor; (*ship*): **to ~ along** avanzar, ir avanzando; **under one's own ~** (*fig*) por sus propios medios *or* propias fuerzas; **to run out of ~** (*fig: person*) quedar(se) agotado, quemarse; **to let off ~** (*fig*) desahogarse.

▶**steam up** *vi* (*window*) empañarse; **to get ~ed up about sth** (*fig*) ponerse negro por algo.

steam engine *n* máquina de vapor.

steamer ['stiːmə*] *n* (buque *m* de) vapor *m*; (*CULIN*) *recipiente para cocinar al vapor.*

steam iron *n* plancha de vapor.

steamroller ['stiːmrəulə*] *n* apisonadora.

steamship ['stiːmʃɪp] *n* = **steamer**.

steamy ['stiːmɪ] *adj* (*room*) lleno de vapor; (*window*) empañado.

steel [stiːl] *n* acero ♦ *adj* de acero.

steel band *n* banda de percusión del Caribe.

steel industry *n* industria siderúrgica.

steel mill *n* fábrica de acero.

steelworks ['stiːlwəːks] *n* acería, fundición *f* de acero.

steely ['stiːlɪ] *adj* (*determination*) inflexible; (*gaze*) duro; (*eyes*) penetrante; **~ grey** gris *m* metálico.

steelyard ['stiːljɑːd] *n* romana.

steep [stiːp] *adj* escarpado, abrupto; (*stair*) empinado; (*price*) exorbitante, excesivo ♦ *vt* empapar, remojar.

steeple ['stiːpl] *n* aguja, campanario.

steeplechase ['stiːpltʃeɪs] *n* carrera de obstáculos.

steeplejack ['stiːpldʒæk] *n* reparador(a) *m/f* de chimeneas *or* de campanarios.

steer [stɪə*] *vt* (*car*) conducir (*SP*), manejar (*LAM*); (*person*) dirigir, guiar ♦ *vi* conducir; **to ~ clear of sb/sth** (*fig*) esquivar a algn/evadir algo.

steering ['stɪərɪŋ] *n* (*AUT*) dirección *f*.

steering committee *n* comisión *f* directiva.

steering wheel *n* volante *m*.

stellar ['stɛlə*] *adj* estelar.

stem [stɛm] *n* (*of plant*) tallo; (*of glass*) pie *m*; (*of pipe*) cañón *m* ♦ *vt* detener; (*blood*) restañar.

▶**stem from** *vt fus* ser consecuencia de.

stench [stɛntʃ] *n* hedor *m*.

stencil ['stɛnsl] *n* (*typed*) cliché *m*, clisé *m*; (*lettering*) plantilla ♦ *vt* hacer un cliché de.

stenographer [stɛ'nɔɡrəfə*] *n* (*US*) taquígrafo/a.

step [stɛp] *n* paso; (*sound*) paso, pisada; (*stair*) peldaño, escalón *m* ♦ *vi*: **to ~ forward** dar un paso adelante; **~s** *npl* (*BRIT*) = **~ladder**; **~ by ~** paso a paso; (*fig*) poco a poco; **to keep in ~ (with)** llevar el paso de; (*fig*) llevar el paso de, estar de acuerdo con; **to be in/out of ~ with** estar acorde con/estar en disonancia con; **to take ~s to solve a problem** tomar medidas para resolver un problema.

▶**step down** *vi* (*fig*) retirarse.

▶**step in** *vi* entrar; (*fig*) intervenir.

▶**step off** *vt fus* bajar de.

▶**step on** *vt fus* pisar.

▶**step over** *vt fus* pasar por encima de.

▶**step up** *vt* (*increase*) aumentar.

step aerobics *npl* step *m*.

stepbrother ['stɛpbrʌðə*] *n* hermanastro.

stepdaughter ['stɛpdɔːtə*] *n* hijastra.

stepfather ['stɛpfɑːðə*] *n* padrastro.

stepladder ['stɛplædə*] *n* escalera doble *or* de tijera.

stepmother ['stɛpmʌðə*] *n* madrastra.

stepping stone ['stɛpɪŋ-] *n* pasadera.

step Reebok ® [-'riːbɔk] *n* step *m*.

stepsister ['stɛpsɪstə*] *n* hermanastra.

stepson ['stɛpsʌn] *n* hijastro.

stereo ['stɛrɪəu] *n* estéreo ♦ *adj* (*also*: **~phonic**) estéreo, estereofónico; **in ~** en estéreo.

stereotype ['stɪərɪətaɪp] *n* estereotipo ♦ *vt* estereotipar.

sterile ['stɛraɪl] *adj* estéril.

sterilization [stɛrɪlaɪ'zeɪʃən] *n* esterilización *f*.

sterilize ['stɛrɪlaɪz] *vt* esterilizar.

sterling ['stəːlɪŋ] *adj* (*silver*) de ley ♦ *n* (*ECON*) libras *fpl* esterlinas; **a pound ~** una libra esterlina; **he is of ~ character** tiene un carácter excelente.

stern [stəːn] *adj* severo, austero ♦ *n* (*NAUT*) popa.

sternum ['stəːnəm] *n* esternón *m*.

steroid ['stɪərɔɪd] *n* esteroide *m*.
stethoscope ['stɛθəskəup] *n* estetoscopio.
stevedore ['stiːvədɔː*] *n* estibador *m*.
stew [stjuː] *n* cocido, estofado, guisado (*LAM*) ♦ *vt, vi* estofar, guisar; (*fruit*) cocer; ~**ed fruit** compota de fruta.
steward ['stjuːəd] *n* (*BRIT: gen*) camarero; (*shop* ~) enlace *m/f* sindical.
stewardess ['stjuːədəs] *n* azafata.
stewardship ['stjuədʃɪp] *n* tutela.
stewing steak ['stjuːɪŋ-], (*US*) **stew meat** *n* carne *f* de vaca.
St. Ex. *abbr* = **stock exchange.**
stg *abbr* (= *sterling*) ester.
stick [stɪk] *n* palo; (*as weapon*) porra; (*walking* ~) bastón *m* ♦ *vb* (*pt, pp* **stuck** [stʌk]) *vt* (*glue*) pegar; (*col: put*) meter; (: *tolerate*) aguantar, soportar ♦ *vi* pegarse; (*come to a stop*) quedarse parado; (*get jammed: door, lift*) atascarse; **to get hold of the wrong end of the** ~ entender al revés; **to** ~ **to** (*word, principles*) atenerse a, ser fiel a; (*promise*) cumplir; **it stuck in my mind** se me quedó grabado; **to** ~ **sth into** clavar *or* hincar algo en.
▶**stick around** *vi* (*col*) quedarse.
▶**stick out** *vi* sobresalir ♦ *vt*: **to** ~ **it out** (*col*) aguantar.
▶**stick up** *vi* sobresalir.
▶**stick up for** *vt fus* defender.
sticker ['stɪkə*] *n* (*label*) etiqueta adhesiva; (*with slogan*) pegatina.
sticking plaster ['stɪkɪŋ-] *n* (*BRIT*) esparadrapo.
sticking point *n* (*fig*) punto de fricción.
stickler ['stɪklə*] *n*: **to be a** ~ **for** insistir mucho en.
stick shift *n* (*US AUT*) palanca de cambios.
stick-up ['stɪkʌp] *n* asalto, atraco.
sticky ['stɪkɪ] *adj* pegajoso; (*label*) adhesivo; (*fig*) difícil.
stiff [stɪf] *adj* rígido, tieso; (*hard*) duro; (*difficult*) difícil; (*person*) inflexible; (*price*) exorbitante; **to have a** ~ **neck/back** tener tortícolis/dolor de espalda; **the door's** ~ la puerta está atrancada.
stiffen ['stɪfn] *vt* hacer más rígido; (*limb*) entumecer ♦ *vi* endurecerse; (*grow stronger*) fortalecerse.
stiffness ['stɪfnɪs] *n* rigidez *f*.
stifle ['staɪfl] *vt* ahogar, sofocar.
stifling ['staɪflɪŋ] *adj* (*heat*) sofocante, bochornoso.
stigma, *pl* (*BOT, MED, REL*) ~**ta**, (*fig*) ~**s** ['stɪgmə, stɪg'maːtə] *n* estigma *m*.
stile [staɪl] *n* escalera (*para pasar una cerca*).
stiletto [stɪ'lɛtəu] *n* (*BRIT: also*: ~ **heel**) tacón *m* de aguja.

still [stɪl] *adj* inmóvil, quieto; (*orange juice etc*) sin gas ♦ *adv* (*up to this time*) todavía; (*even*) aún; (*nonetheless*) sin embargo, aun así ♦ *n* (*CINE*) foto *f* fija; **keep** ~! ¡estate quieto!, ¡no te muevas!; **he** ~ **hasn't arrived** todavía no ha llegado.
stillborn ['stɪlbɔːn] *adj* nacido muerto.
still life *n* naturaleza muerta.
stilt [stɪlt] *n* zanco; (*pile*) pilar *m*, soporte *m*.
stilted ['stɪltɪd] *adj* afectado, artificial.
stimulant ['stɪmjulənt] *n* estimulante *m*.
stimulate ['stɪmjuleɪt] *vt* estimular.
stimulating ['stɪmjuleɪtɪŋ] *adj* estimulante.
stimulation [stɪmju'leɪʃən] *n* estímulo.
stimulus, *pl* **-li** ['stɪmjuləs, -laɪ] *n* estímulo, incentivo.
sting [stɪŋ] *n* (*wound*) picadura; (*pain*) escozor *m*, picazón *m*; (*organ*) aguijón *m*; (*col: confidence trick*) timo ♦ *vb* (*pt, pp* **stung** [stʌŋ]) *vt* picar ♦ *vi* picar, escocer; **my eyes are** ~**ing** me pican *or* escuecen los ojos.
stingy ['stɪndʒɪ] *adj* tacaño.
stink [stɪŋk] *n* hedor *m*, tufo ♦ *vi* (*pt* **stank**, *pp* **stunk** [stæŋk, stʌŋk]) heder, apestar.
stinking ['stɪŋkɪŋ] *adj* hediondo, fétido; (*fig: col*) horrible.
stint [stɪnt] *n* tarea, destajo; **to do one's** ~ **at sth** hacer su parte (de algo), hacer lo que corresponde (de algo) ♦ *vi*: **to** ~ **on** escatimar.
stipend ['staɪpɛnd] *n* salario, remuneración *f*.
stipendiary [staɪ'pɛndɪərɪ] *adj*: ~ **magistrate** magistrado/a estipendiario/a.
stipulate ['stɪpjuleɪt] *vt* estipular.
stipulation [stɪpju'leɪʃən] *n* estipulación *f*.
stir [stəː*] *n* (*fig: agitation*) conmoción *f* ♦ *vt* (*tea etc*) remover; (*fire*) atizar; (*move*) agitar; (*fig: emotions*) conmover ♦ *vi* moverse; **to give sth a** ~ remover algo; **to cause a** ~ causar conmoción *or* sensación.
▶**stir up** *vt* excitar; (*trouble*) fomentar.
stir-fry ['stəːfraɪ] *vt* sofreír removiendo ♦ *n* plato preparado sofriendo y removiendo los ingredientes.
stirrup ['stɪrəp] *n* estribo.
stitch [stɪtʃ] *n* (*SEWING*) puntada; (*KNITTING*) punto; (*MED*) punto (de sutura); (*pain*) punzada ♦ *vt* coser; (*MED*) suturar.
stoat [stəut] *n* armiño.
stock [stɔk] *n* (*COMM: reserves*) existencias *fpl*, stock *m*; (: *selection*) surtido; (*AGR*) ganado, ganadería; (*CULIN*) caldo; (*fig: lineage*) estirpe *f*, cepa; (*FINANCE*) capital *m*; (: *shares*) acciones *fpl*; (*RAIL: rolling* ~) material *m* rodante ♦ *adj* (*COMM: goods,*

size) normal, de serie; (*fig: reply etc*) clásico, trillado; (: *greeting*) acostumbrado ♦ *vt* (*have in* ~) tener existencias de; (*supply*) proveer, abastecer; **in** ~ en existencia *or* almacén; **to have sth in** ~ tener existencias de algo; **out of** ~ agotado; **to take** ~ **of** (*fig*) considerar, examinar; ~**s** *npl* (*HISTORY: punishment*) cepo *sg*; ~**s and shares** acciones y valores; **government** ~ papel *m* del Estado.

▶**stock up with** *vt fus* abastecerse de.

stockbroker ['stɔkbrəukə*] *n* agente *m/f or* corredor(a) *m/f* de bolsa.

stock control *n* (*COMM*) control *m* de existencias.

stock cube *n* pastilla *or* cubito de caldo.

stock exchange *n* bolsa.

stockholder ['stɔkhəuldə*] *n* (*US*) accionista *m/f*.

Stockholm ['stɔkhəum] *n* Estocolmo.

stocking ['stɔkɪŋ] *n* media.

stock-in-trade ['stɔkɪn'treɪd] *n* (*tools etc*) herramientas *fpl*; (*stock*) existencia de mercancías; (*fig*): **it's his** ~ es su especialidad.

stockist ['stɔkɪst] *n* (*BRIT*) distribuidor(a) *m/f*.

stock market *n* bolsa (de valores).

stock phrase *n* vieja frase *f*.

stockpile ['stɔkpaɪl] *n* reserva ♦ *vt* acumular, almacenar.

stockroom ['stɔkruːm] *n* almacén *m*, depósito.

stocktaking ['stɔkteɪkɪŋ] *n* (*BRIT COMM*) inventario, balance *m*.

stocky ['stɔkɪ] *adj* (*strong*) robusto; (*short*) achaparrado.

stodgy ['stɔdʒɪ] *adj* indigesto, pesado.

stoical ['stəuɪkəl] *adj* estoico.

stoke [stəuk] *vt* atizar.

stole [stəul] *pt of* **steal** ♦ *n* estola.

stolen ['stəuln] *pp of* **steal**.

stolid ['stɔlɪd] *adj* (*person*) imperturbable, impasible.

stomach ['stʌmək] *n* (*ANAT*) estómago; (*belly*) vientre *m* ♦ *vt* tragar, aguantar.

stomach ache *n* dolor *m* de estómago.

stomach pump *n* bomba gástrica.

stomach ulcer *n* úlcera de estómago.

stomp [stɔmp] *vi*: **to** ~ **in/out** entrar/salir con pasos ruidosos.

stone [stəun] *n* piedra; (*in fruit*) hueso; (*BRIT: weight*) = 6.348 *kg*; 14 *pounds* ♦ *adj* de piedra ♦ *vt* apedrear; **within a** ~**'s throw of the station** a tiro de piedra *or* a dos pasos de la estación.

Stone Age *n*: **the** ~ la Edad de Piedra.

stone-cold ['stəun'kəuld] *adj* helado.

stoned [stəund] *adj* (*col: drunk*) trompa, borracho, colocado.

stone-deaf ['stəun'dɛf] *adj* sordo como una tapia.

stonemason ['stəunmeɪsən] *n* albañil *m*.

stonewall [stəun'wɔːl] *vi* alargar la cosa innecesariamente ♦ *vt* dar largas a.

stonework ['stəunwəːk] *n* (*art*) cantería.

stony ['stəunɪ] *adj* pedregoso; (*glance*) glacial.

stood [stud] *pt*, *pp of* **stand**.

stooge [stuːdʒ] *n* (*col*) hombre *m* de paja.

stool [stuːl] *n* taburete *m*.

stoop [stuːp] *vi* (*also*: **have a** ~) ser cargado de espaldas; (*bend*) inclinarse, encorvarse; **to** ~ **to (doing) sth** rebajarse a (hacer) algo.

stop [stɔp] *n* parada, alto; (*in punctuation*) punto ♦ *vt* parar, detener; (*break off*) suspender; (*block*) tapar, cerrar; (*prevent*) impedir; (*also*: **put a** ~ **to**) poner término a ♦ *vi* pararse, detenerse; (*end*) acabarse; **to** ~ **doing sth** dejar de hacer algo; **to** ~ **sb (from) doing sth** impedir a algn hacer algo; **to** ~ **dead** pararse en seco; ~ **it!** ¡basta ya!, ¡párate!

▶**stop by** *vi* pasar por.

▶**stop off** *vi* interrumpir el viaje.

▶**stop up** *vt* (*hole*) tapar.

stopcock ['stɔpkɔk] *n* llave *f* de paso.

stopgap ['stɔpgæp] *n* interino; (*person*) sustituto/a; (*measure*) medida provisional ♦ *cpd* (*situation*) provisional.

stoplights ['stɔplaɪts] *npl* (*AUT*) luces *fpl* de detención.

stopover ['stɔpəuvə*] *n* parada intermedia; (*AVIAT*) escala.

stoppage ['stɔpɪdʒ] *n* (*strike*) paro; (*temporary stop*) interrupción *f*; (*of pay*) suspensión *f*; (*blockage*) obstrucción *f*.

stopper ['stɔpə*] *n* tapón *m*.

stop press *n* noticias *fpl* de última hora.

stopwatch ['stɔpwɔtʃ] *n* cronómetro.

storage ['stɔːrɪdʒ] *n* almacenaje *m*; (*COMPUT*) almacenamiento.

storage capacity *n* espacio de almacenaje.

storage heater *n* acumulador *m* de calor.

store [stɔː*] *n* (*stock*) provisión *f*; (*depot; BRIT: large shop*) almacén *m*; (*US*) tienda; (*reserve*) reserva, repuesto ♦ *vt* (*gen, COMPUT*) almacenar; (*keep*) guardar; (*in filing system*) archivar; ~**s** *npl* víveres *mpl*; **who knows what is in** ~ **for us** quién sabe lo que nos espera; **to set great/little** ~ **by sth** dar mucha/poca importancia a algo, valorar mucho/poco algo.

▶**store up** *vt* acumular.
storehouse ['stɔːhaus] *n* almacén *m*, depósito.
storekeeper ['stɔːkiːpə*] *n* (*US*) tendero/a.
storeroom ['stɔːruːm] *n* despensa.
storey, (*US*) **story** ['stɔːrɪ] *n* piso.
stork [stɔːk] *n* cigüeña.
storm [stɔːm] *n* tormenta; (*wind*) vendaval *m*; (*fig*) tempestad *f* ♦ *vi* (*fig*) rabiar ♦ *vt* tomar por asalto, asaltar; **to take a town by** ~ (*MIL*) tomar una ciudad por asalto.
storm cloud *n* nubarrón *m*.
storm door *n* contrapuerta.
stormy ['stɔːmɪ] *adj* tempestuoso.
story ['stɔːrɪ] *n* historia; (*PRESS*) artículo; (*joke*) cuento, chiste *m*; (*plot*) argumento; (*lie*) cuento; (*US*) = **storey**.
storybook ['stɔːrɪbuk] *n* libro de cuentos.
storyteller ['stɔːrɪtelə*] *n* cuentista *m/f*.
stout [staut] *adj* (*strong*) sólido; (*fat*) gordo, corpulento ♦ *n* cerveza negra.
stove [stəuv] *n* (*for cooking*) cocina; (*for heating*) estufa; **gas/electric** ~ cocina de gas/eléctrica.
stow [stəu] *vt* meter, poner; (*NAUT*) estibar.
stowaway ['stəuəweɪ] *n* polizón/ona *m/f*.
straddle ['strædl] *vt* montar a horcajadas.
straggle ['strægl] *vi* (*wander*) vagar en desorden; (*lag behind*) rezagarse.
straggler ['stræglə*] *n* rezagado/a.
straggling ['stræglɪŋ], **straggly** ['stræglɪ] *adj* (*hair*) desordenado.
straight [streɪt] *adj* (*direct*) recto, derecho; (*plain, uncomplicated*) sencillo; (*frank*) franco, directo; (*in order*) en orden; (*continuous*) continuo; (*THEAT: part, play*) serio; (*person: conventional*) recto, convencional; (: *heterosexual*) heterosexual ♦ *adv* derecho, directamente; (*drink*) solo; **to put** *or* **get sth** ~ dejar algo en claro; **10** ~ **wins** 10 victorias seguidas; **to be (all)** ~ (*tidy*) estar en orden; (*clarified*) estar claro; **I went** ~ **home** (me) fui directamente a casa; ~ **away**, ~ **off** (*at once*) en seguida.
straighten ['streɪtn] *vt* (*also*: ~ **out**) enderezar, poner derecho; **to** ~ **things out** poner las cosas en orden.
straight-faced [streɪt'feɪst] *adj* serio ♦ *adv* sin mostrar emoción, impávido.
straightforward [streɪt'fɔːwəd] *adj* (*simple*) sencillo; (*honest*) sincero.
strain [streɪn] *n* (*gen*) tensión *f*; (*TECH*) esfuerzo; (*MED*) distensión *f*, torcedura; (*breed*) raza; (*lineage*) linaje *m*; (*of virus*) variedad *f* ♦ *vt* (*back etc*) distender, torcerse; (*tire*) cansar; (*stretch*) estirar; (*filter*) filtrar; (*meaning*) tergiversar ♦ *vi*

esforzarse; ~**s** *npl* (*MUS*) son *m*; **she's under a lot of** ~ está bajo mucha tensión.
strained [streɪnd] *adj* (*muscle*) torcido; (*laugh*) forzado; (*relations*) tenso.
strainer ['streɪnə*] *n* colador *m*.
strait [streɪt] *n* (*GEO*) estrecho; **to be in dire** ~**s** (*fig*) estar en un gran aprieto.
straitjacket ['streɪtdʒækɪt] *n* camisa de fuerza.
strait-laced [streɪt'leɪst] *adj* mojigato, gazmoño.
strand [strænd] *n* (*of thread*) hebra; (*of rope*) ramal *m*; **a** ~ **of hair** un pelo.
stranded ['strændɪd] *adj* (*person*) colgado.
strange [streɪndʒ] *adj* (*not known*) desconocido; (*odd*) extraño, raro.
stranger ['streɪndʒə*] *n* desconocido/a; (*from another area*) forastero/a; **I'm a** ~ **here** no soy de aquí.
strangle ['stræŋgl] *vt* estrangular.
stranglehold ['stræŋglhəuld] *n* (*fig*) dominio completo.
strangulation [stræŋgju'leɪʃən] *n* estrangulación *f*.
strap [stræp] *n* correa; (*of slip, dress*) tirante *m* ♦ *vt* atar con correa.
straphanging ['stræphæŋɪŋ] *n* viajar *m* de pie *or* parado (*LAM*).
strapless ['stræplɪs] *adj* (*bra, dress*) sin tirantes.
strapped [stræpt] *adj*: **to be** ~ **for cash** (*col*) andar mal de dinero.
strapping ['stræpɪŋ] *adj* robusto, fornido.
Strasbourg ['stræzbə:g] *n* Estrasburgo.
strata ['strɑːtə] *npl of* **stratum**.
stratagem ['strætɪdʒəm] *n* estratagema.
strategic [strə'tiːdʒɪk] *adj* estratégico.
strategy ['strætɪdʒɪ] *n* estrategia.
stratum, *pl* **strata** ['strɑːtəm, 'strɑːtə] *n* estrato.
straw [strɔː] *n* paja; (*drinking* ~) caña, pajita; **that's the last** ~! ¡eso es el colmo!
strawberry ['strɔːbərɪ] *n* fresa, frutilla (*LAM*).
stray [streɪ] *adj* (*animal*) extraviado; (*bullet*) perdido; (*scattered*) disperso ♦ *vi* extraviarse, perderse; (*wander: walker*) vagar, ir sin rumbo fijo; (: *speaker*) desvariar.
streak [striːk] *n* raya; (*fig: of madness etc*) vena ♦ *vt* rayar ♦ *vi*: **to** ~ **past** pasar como un rayo; **to have** ~**s in one's hair** tener vetas en el pelo; **a winning/losing** ~ una racha de buena/mala suerte.
streaker ['striːkə*] *n* corredor(a) *m/f* desnudo/a.
streaky ['striːkɪ] *adj* rayado.
stream [striːm] *n* riachuelo, arroyo; (*jet*)

chorro; (*flow*) corriente *f*; (*of people*) oleada ♦ *vt* (*SCOL*) dividir en grupos por habilidad ♦ *vi* correr, fluir; **to ~ in/out** (*people*) entrar/salir en tropel; **against the ~** a contracorriente; **on ~** (*new power plant etc*) en funcionamiento.

streamer ['stri:mə*] *n* serpentina.

stream feed *n* (*on photocopier etc*) alimentación *f* continua.

streamline ['stri:mlaɪn] *vt* aerodinamizar; (*fig*) racionalizar.

streamlined ['stri:mlaɪnd] *adj* aerodinámico.

street [stri:t] *n* calle *f* ♦ *adj* callejero; **the back ~s** las callejuelas; **to be on the ~s** (*homeless*) estar sin vivienda; (*as prostitute*) hacer la calle.

streetcar ['stri:tka:] *n* (*US*) tranvía *m*.

street cred [-krɛd] *n* (*col*) imagen *de estar en la onda*.

street lamp *n* farol *m*.

street lighting *n* alumbrado público.

street market *n* mercado callejero.

street plan *n* plano callejero.

streetwise ['stri:twaɪz] *adj* (*col*) pícaro.

strength [strɛŋθ] *n* fuerza; (*of girdor, knot etc*) resistencia; (*of chemical solution*) potencia; (*of wine*) graduación *f* de alcohol; **on the ~ of** a base de, en base a; **to be at full/below ~** tener/no tener completo el cupo.

strengthen ['strɛŋθn] *vt* fortalecer, reforzar.

strenuous ['strɛnjuəs] *adj* (*tough*) arduo; (*energetic*) enérgico; (*opposition*) firme, tenaz; (*efforts*) intensivo.

stress [strɛs] *n* (*force, pressure*) presión *f*; (*mental strain*) estrés *m*, tensión *f*; (*accent, emphasis*) énfasis *m*, acento; (*LING, POETRY*) acento; (*TECH*) tensión *f*, carga ♦ *vt* subrayar, recalcar; **to be under ~** estar estresado; **to lay great ~ on sth** hacer hincapié en algo.

stressful ['strɛsful] *adj* (*job*) estresante.

stretch [strɛtʃ] *n* (*of sand etc*) trecho; (*of road*) tramo; (*of time*) período, tiempo ♦ *vi* estirarse; (*extend*): **to ~ to** *or* **as far as** extenderse hasta; (*be enough: money, food*): **to ~ to** alcanzar para, dar de sí para ♦ *vt* extender, estirar; (*make demands of*) exigir el máximo esfuerzo a; **to ~ one's legs** estirar las piernas.

▶**stretch out** *vi* tenderse ♦ *vt* (*arm etc*) extender; (*spread*) estirar.

stretcher ['strɛtʃə*] *n* camilla.

stretcher-bearer ['strɛtʃəbɛərə*] *n* camillero/a.

stretch marks *npl* estrías *fpl*.

strewn [stru:n] *adj*: **~ with** cubierto *or* sembrado de.

stricken ['strɪkən] *adj* (*person*) herido; (*city, industry etc*) condenado; **~ with** (*arthritis, disease*) afligido por; **grief-~** destrozado por el dolor.

strict [strɪkt] *adj* (*order, rule etc*) estricto; (*discipline, ban*) severo; **in ~ confidence** en la más absoluta confianza.

strictly ['strɪktlɪ] *adv* estrictamente; (*totally*) terminantemente; **~ confidential** estrictamente confidencial; **~ speaking** en (el) sentido estricto (de la palabra); **~ between ourselves** ... entre nosotros ....

stridden ['strɪdn] *pp of* **stride**.

stride [straɪd] *n* zancada, tranco ♦ *vi* (*pt* **strode**, *pp* **stridden** [strəud, 'strɪdn]) dar zancadas, andar a trancos; **to take in one's ~** (*fig: changes etc*) tomar con calma.

strident ['straɪdnt] *adj* estridente; (*colour*) chillón/ona.

strife [straɪf] *n* lucha.

strike [straɪk] *n* huelga; (*of oil etc*) descubrimiento; (*attack*) ataque *m*; (*SPORT*) golpe *m* ♦ *vb* (*pt, pp* **struck** [strʌk]) *vt* golpear, pegar; (*oil etc*) descubrir; (*obstacle*) topar con; (*produce: coin, medal*) acuñar; (: *agreement, deal*) concertar ♦ *vi* declarar la huelga; (*attack*: *MIL etc*) atacar; (*clock*) dar la hora; **on ~** (*workers*) en huelga; **to call a ~** declarar una huelga; **to go on** *or* **come out on ~** ponerse *or* declararse en huelga; **to ~ a match** encender una cerilla; **to ~ a balance** (*fig*) encontrar un equilibrio; **to ~ a bargain** cerrar un trato; **the clock struck 9 o'clock** el reloj dio las nueve.

▶**strike back** *vi* (*MIL*) contraatacar; (*fig*) devolver el golpe.

▶**strike down** *vt* derribar.

▶**strike off** *vt* (*from list*) tachar; (*doctor etc*) suspender.

▶**strike out** *vt* borrar, tachar.

▶**strike up** *vt* (*MUS*) empezar a tocar; (*conversation*) entablar; (*friendship*) trabar.

strikebreaker ['straɪkbreɪkə*] *n* rompehuelgas *m/f inv*.

striker ['straɪkə*] *n* huelguista *m/f*; (*SPORT*) delantero.

striking ['straɪkɪŋ] *adj* (*colour*) llamativo; (*obvious*) notorio.

Strimmer ® ['strɪmə*] *n* cortacéspedes *m inv* (*especial para los bordes*).

string [strɪŋ] *n* (*gen*) cuerda; (*row*) hilera; (*COMPUT*) cadena ♦ *vt* (*pt, pp* **strung** [strʌŋ]): **to ~ together** ensartar; **to ~ out**

extenderse; **the** ~**s** *npl* (*MUS*) los instrumentos de cuerda; **to pull** ~**s** (*fig*) mover palancas; **to get a job by pulling** ~**s** conseguir un trabajo por enchufe; **with no** ~**s attached** (*fig*) sin compromiso.

string bean *n* judía verde, habichuela.

string(ed) instrument [strɪŋ(d)-] *n* (*MUS*) instrumento de cuerda.

stringent ['strɪndʒənt] *adj* riguroso, severo.

string quartet *n* cuarteto de cuerdas.

strip [strɪp] *n* tira; (*of land*) franja; (*of metal*) cinta, lámina ♦ *vt* desnudar; (*also:* ~ **down:** *machine*) desmontar ♦ *vi* desnudarse.

strip cartoon *n* tira cómica, historieta (*LAM*).

stripe [straɪp] *n* raya; (*MIL*) galón *m*; **white with green** ~**s** blanco con rayas verdes.

striped [straɪpt] *adj* a rayas, rayado.

strip lighting *n* alumbrado fluorescente.

stripper ['strɪpə*] *n* artista *m/f* de striptease.

strip-search ['strɪpsəːtʃ] *vt:* **to** ~ **sb** desnudar y registrar a algn.

striptease ['strɪptiːz] *n* striptease *m*.

strive, *pt* **strove,** *pp* **striven** [straɪv, strəuv, 'strɪvn] *vi:* **to** ~ **to do sth** esforzarse *or* luchar por hacer algo.

strobe [strəub] *n* (*also:* ~ **light**) luz *f* estroboscópica.

strode [strəud] *pt of* **stride**.

stroke [strəuk] *n* (*blow*) golpe *m*; (*MED*) apoplejía; (*caress*) caricia; (*of pen*) trazo; (*SWIMMING: style*) estilo; (*of piston*) carrera ♦ *vt* acariciar; **at a** ~ de golpe; **a** ~ **of luck** un golpe de suerte; **two-**~ **engine** motor *m* de dos tiempos.

stroll [strəul] *n* paseo, vuelta ♦ *vi* dar un paseo *or* una vuelta; **to go for a** ~, **have** *or* **take a** ~ dar un paseo.

stroller ['strəulə*] *n* (*US: pushchair*) cochecito.

strong [strɒŋ] *adj* fuerte; (*bleach, acid*) concentrado ♦ *adv:* **to be going** ~ (*company*) marchar bien; (*person*) conservarse bien; **they are 50** ~ son 50.

strong-arm ['strɒŋɑːm] *adj* (*tactics, methods*) represivo.

strongbox ['strɒŋbɒks] *n* caja fuerte.

strong drink *n* bebida cargada *or* fuerte.

stronghold ['strɒŋhəuld] *n* fortaleza; (*fig*) baluarte *m*.

strong language *n* lenguaje *m* fuerte.

strongly ['strɒŋlɪ] *adv* fuertemente, con fuerza; (*believe*) firmemente; **to feel** ~ **about sth** tener una opinión firme sobre algo.

strongman ['strɒŋmæn] *n* forzudo; (*fig*) hombre *m* robusto.

strongroom ['strɒŋruːm] *n* cámara acorazada.

stroppy ['strɒpɪ] *adj* (*BRIT col*) borde; **to get** ~ ponerse borde.

strove [strəuv] *pt of* **strive**.

struck [strʌk] *pt, pp of* **strike**.

structural ['strʌktʃərəl] *adj* estructural.

structure ['strʌktʃə*] *n* estructura; (*building*) construcción *f*.

struggle ['strʌgl] *n* lucha ♦ *vi* luchar; **to have a** ~ **to do sth** esforzarse por hacer algo.

strum [strʌm] *vt* (*guitar*) rasguear.

strung [strʌŋ] *pt, pp of* **string**.

strut [strʌt] *n* puntal *m* ♦ *vi* pavonearse.

strychnine ['strɪkniːn] *n* estricnina.

stub [stʌb] *n* (*of ticket etc*) matriz *f*; (*of cigarette*) colilla ♦ *vt:* **to** ~ **one's toe on sth** dar con el dedo del pie contra algo.

▶**stub out** *vt* (*cigarette*) apagar.

stubble ['stʌbl] *n* rastrojo; (*on chin*) barba (incipiente).

stubborn ['stʌbən] *adj* terco, testarudo.

stucco ['stʌkəu] *n* estuco.

stuck [stʌk] *pt, pp of* **stick** ♦ *adj* (*jammed*) atascado.

stuck-up [stʌk'ʌp] *adj* engreído, presumido.

stud [stʌd] *n* (*shirt* ~) corchete *m*; (*of boot*) taco; (*of horses*) caballeriza; (*also:* ~ **horse**) caballo semental ♦ *vt* (*fig*): ~**ded with** salpicado de.

student ['stjuːdənt] *n* estudiante *m/f* ♦ *adj* estudiantil; **a law/medical** ~ un(a) estudiante de derecho/medicina.

student driver *n* (*US AUT*) aprendiz(a) *m/f* de conductor.

students' union *n* (*BRIT: association*) sindicato de estudiantes; (: *building*) centro de estudiantes.

studio ['stjuːdɪəu] *n* estudio; (*artist's*) taller *m*.

studio flat, (*US*) **studio apartment** *n* estudio.

studious ['stjuːdɪəs] *adj* estudioso; (*studied*) calculado.

studiously ['stjuːdɪəslɪ] *adv* (*carefully*) con esmero.

study ['stʌdɪ] *n* estudio ♦ *vt* estudiar; (*examine*) examinar, investigar ♦ *vi* estudiar; **to make a** ~ **of sth** realizar una investigación de algo; **to** ~ **for an exam** preparar un examen.

stuff [stʌf] *n* materia; (*cloth*) tela; (*substance*) material *m*, sustancia; (*things, belongings*) cosas *fpl* ♦ *vt* llenar; (*CULIN*)

rellenar; (*animal: for exhibition*) disecar;
my nose is ~**ed up** tengo la nariz tapada;
~**ed toy** juguete *m or* muñeco de trapo.
stuffing ['stʌfɪŋ] *n* relleno.
stuffy ['stʌfɪ] *adj* (*room*) mal ventilado;
(*person*) de miras estrechas.
stumble ['stʌmbl] *vi* tropezar, dar un
traspié.
▶**stumble across** *vt fus* (*fig*) tropezar con.
stumbling block ['stʌmblɪŋ-] *n* tropiezo,
obstáculo.
stump [stʌmp] *n* (*of tree*) tocón *m*; (*of limb*)
muñón *m* ♦ *vt:* **to be** ~**ed** quedarse
perplejo; **to be** ~**ed for an answer**
quedarse sin saber qué contestar.
stun [stʌn] *vt* aturdir.
stung [stʌŋ] *pt, pp of* **sting**.
stunk [stʌŋk] *pp of* **stink**.
stunning ['stʌnɪŋ] *adj* (*fig*) pasmoso.
stunt [stʌnt] *n* (*AVIAT*) vuelo acrobático;
(*publicity* ~) truco publicitario.
stunted ['stʌntɪd] *adj* enano, achaparrado.
stuntman ['stʌntmæn] *n* especialista *m*.
stupefaction [stjuːpɪ'fækʃən] *n*
estupefacción *f*.
stupefy ['stjuːpɪfaɪ] *vt* dejar estupefacto.
stupendous [stjuː'pɛndəs] *adj* estupendo,
asombroso.
stupid ['stjuːpɪd] *adj* estúpido, tonto.
stupidity [stjuː'pɪdɪtɪ] *n* estupidez *f*.
stupor ['stjuːpə*] *n* estupor *m*.
sturdy ['stɜːdɪ] *adj* robusto, fuerte.
stutter ['stʌtə*] *n* tartamudeo ♦ *vi*
tartamudear.
sty [staɪ] *n* (*for pigs*) pocilga.
stye [staɪ] *n* (*MED*) orzuelo.
style [staɪl] *n* estilo; (*fashion*) moda; (*of
dress etc*) hechura; (*hair* ~) corte *m*; **in the
latest** ~ en el último modelo.
stylish ['staɪlɪʃ] *adj* elegante, a la moda.
stylist ['staɪlɪst] *n* (*hair* ~) peluquero/a
stylus, *pl* **styli** *or* **styluses** ['staɪləs, -laɪ] *n*
(*of record player*) aguja.
Styrofoam ® ['staɪrəfəum] *n* (*US*)
poliestireno ♦ *adj* (*cup*) de poliestireno.
suave [swɑːv] *adj* cortés, fino.
sub [sʌb] *n abbr* = **submarine, subscription.**
sub... [sʌb] *pref* sub....
subcommittee ['sʌbkəmɪtɪ] *n* subcomisión
f.
subconscious [sʌb'kɔnʃəs] *adj*
subconsciente ♦ *n* subconsciente *m*.
subcontinent [sʌb'kɔntɪnənt] *n:* **the Indian**
~ el subcontinente (de la India).
subcontract *n* ['sʌb'kɔntrækt] subcontrato
♦ *vt* ['sʌbkən'trækt] subcontratar.
subcontractor ['sʌbkən'træktə*] *n*
subcontratista *m/f*.

subdivide [sʌbdɪ'vaɪd] *vt* subdividir.
subdue [səb'djuː] *vt* sojuzgar; (*passions*)
dominar.
subdued [səb'djuːd] *adj* (*light*) tenue;
(*person*) sumiso, manso.
sub-editor ['sʌb'ɛdɪtə*] *n* (*BRIT*) redactor(a)
m/f.
subject *n* ['sʌbdʒɪkt] súbdito; (*SCOL*) tema
m, materia ♦ *vt* [səb'dʒɛkt]: **to** ~ **sb to sth**
someter a algn a algo ♦ *adj* ['sʌbdʒɪkt]: **to
be** ~ **to** (*law*) estar sujeto a; ~ **to
confirmation in writing** sujeto a
confirmación por escrito; **to change the**
~ cambiar de tema.
subjective [səb'dʒɛktɪv] *adj* subjetivo.
subject matter *n* materia; (*content*)
contenido.
sub judice [sʌb'djuːdɪsɪ] *adj* (*LAW*)
pendiente de resolución.
subjugate ['sʌbdʒugeɪt] *vt* subyugar,
sojuzgar.
subjunctive [səb'dʒʌŋktɪv] *adj, n*
subjuntivo.
sublet [sʌb'lɛt] *vt, vi* subarrendar,
realquilar.
sublime [sə'blaɪm] *adj* sublime.
subliminal [sʌb'lɪmɪnl] *adj* subliminal.
submachine gun ['sʌbmə'ʃiːn-] *n*
metralleta.
submarine [sʌbmə'riːn] *n* submarino.
submerge [səb'mɜːdʒ] *vt* sumergir; (*flood*)
inundar ♦ *vi* sumergirse.
submersion [səb'mɜːʃən] *n* submersión *f*.
submission [səb'mɪʃən] *n* sumisión *f*; (*to
committee* etc) ponencia.
submissive [səb'mɪsɪv] *adj* sumiso.
submit [səb'mɪt] *vt* someter; (*proposal,
claim*) presentar ♦ *vi* someterse; **I** ~ **that**
... me permito sugerir que ....
subnormal [sʌb'nɔːməl] *adj* subnormal.
subordinate [sə'bɔːdɪnət] *adj, n*
subordinado/a *m/f*.
subpoena [səb'piːnə] (*LAW*) *n* citación *f* ♦ *vt*
citar.
subroutine [sʌbruː'tiːn] *n* (*COMPUT*)
subrutina.
subscribe [səb'skraɪb] *vi* suscribir; **to**
~ **to** (*fund*) suscribir, aprobar; (*opinion*)
estar de acuerdo con; (*newspaper*)
suscribirse a.
subscribed capital [səb'skraɪbd-] *n* capital
m suscrito.
subscriber [səb'skraɪbə*] *n* (*to periodical*)
suscriptor(a) *m/f*; (*to telephone*)
abonado/a.
subscript ['sʌbskrɪpt] *n* (*TYP*) subíndice *m*.
subscription [səb'skrɪpʃən] *n* (*to club*)
abono, (*to magazine*) suscripción *f*; **to take**

out a ~ **to** suscribirse a.
subsequent ['sʌbsɪkwənt] *adj* subsiguiente, posterior; ~ **to** posterior a.
subsequently ['sʌbsɪkwəntlɪ] *adv* posteriormente, más tarde.
subservient [səb'sə:vɪənt] *adj*: ~ **(to)** servil (a).
subside [səb'saɪd] *vi* hundirse; (*flood*) bajar; (*wind*) amainar.
subsidence [səb'saɪdns] *n* hundimiento; (*in road*) socavón *m*.
subsidiarity [səbsɪdɪ'ærɪtɪ] *n* (*POL*) subsidiariedad *f*.
subsidiary [səb'sɪdɪərɪ] *n* sucursal *f*, filial *f* ♦ *adj* (*UNIV*: *subject*) secundario.
subsidize ['sʌbsɪdaɪz] *vt* subvencionar.
subsidy ['sʌbsɪdɪ] *n* subvención *f*.
subsist [səb'sɪst] *vi*: **to** ~ **on sth** subsistir a base de algo, sustentarse con algo.
subsistence [səb'sɪstəns] *n* subsistencia.
subsistence allowance *n* dietas *fpl*.
subsistence level *n* nivel *m* de subsistencia.
subsistence wage *n* sueldo de subsistencia.
substance ['sʌbstəns] *n* sustancia; (*fig*) esencia; **to lack** ~ (*argument*) ser poco convincente; (*accusation*) no tener fundamento; (*film, book*) tener poca profundidad.
substance abuse *n* uso indebido de sustancias tóxicas.
substandard [sʌb'stændəd] *adj* (*goods*) inferior; (*housing*) deficiente.
substantial [səb'stænʃl] *adj* sustancial, sustancioso; (*fig*) importante.
substantially [səb'stænʃəlɪ] *adv* sustancialmente; ~ **bigger** bastante más grande.
substantiate [səb'stænʃɪeɪt] *vt* comprobar.
substitute ['sʌbstɪtjuːt] *n* (*person*) suplente *m/f*; (*thing*) sustituto ♦ *vt*: **to** ~ **A for B** sustituir B por A, reemplazar A por B.
substitution [sʌbstɪ'tjuːʃən] *n* sustitución *f*.
subterfuge ['sʌbtəfjuːdʒ] *n* subterfugio.
subterranean [sʌbtə'reɪnɪən] *adj* subterráneo.
subtitle ['sʌbtaɪtl] *n* subtítulo.
subtle ['sʌtl] *adj* sutil.
subtlety ['sʌtltɪ] *n* sutileza.
subtly ['sʌtlɪ] *adv* sutilmente.
subtotal [sʌb'təʊtl] *n* subtotal *m*.
subtract [səb'trækt] *vt* restar; sustraer.
subtraction [səb'trækʃən] *n* resta; sustracción *f*.
suburb ['sʌbə:b] *n* barrio residencial; **the** ~**s** las afueras (de la ciudad).
suburban [sə'bə:bən] *adj* suburbano; (*train*

etc) de cercanías.
suburbia [sə'bə:bɪə] *n* barrios *mpl* residenciales.
subversion [səb'və:ʃən] *n* subversión *f*.
subversive [səb'və:sɪv] *adj* subversivo.
subway ['sʌbweɪ] *n* (*BRIT*) paso subterráneo *or* inferior; (*US*) metro.
sub-zero [sʌb'zɪərəʊ] *adj*: ~ **temperatures** temperaturas *fpl* por debajo del cero.
succeed [sək'siːd] *vi* (*person*) tener éxito; (*plan*) salir bien ♦ *vt* suceder a; **to** ~ **in doing** lograr hacer.
succeeding [sək'siːdɪŋ] *adj* (*following*) sucesivo; ~ **generations** generaciones *fpl* futuras.
success [sək'sɛs] *n* éxito; (*gain*) triunfo.
successful [sək'sɛsful] *adj* (*venture*) de éxito, exitoso (*esp LAM*); **to be** ~ **(in doing)** lograr (hacer).
successfully [sək'sɛsfulɪ] *adv* con éxito.
succession [sək'sɛʃən] *n* (*series*) sucesión *f*, serie *f*; (*descendants*) descendencia; **in** ~ sucesivamente.
successive [sək'sɛsɪv] *adj* sucesivo, consecutivo; **on 3** ~ **days** tres días seguidos.
successor [sək'sɛsə*] *n* sucesor(a) *m/f*.
succinct [sək'sɪŋkt] *adj* sucinto.
succulent ['sʌkjulənt] *adj* suculento ♦ *n* (*BOT*): ~**s** plantas *fpl* carnosas.
succumb [sə'kʌm] *vi* sucumbir.
such [sʌtʃ] *adj* tal, semejante; (*of that kind*): ~ **a book** tal libro; ~ **books** tales libros; (*so much*): ~ **courage** tanto valor ♦ *adv* tan; ~ **a long trip** un viaje tan largo; ~ **a lot of** tanto; ~ **as** (*like*) tal como; **a noise** ~ **as to** un ruido tal que; ~ **books as I have** cuantos libros tengo; **I said no** ~ **thing** no dije tal cosa; **it's** ~ **a long time since we saw each other** hace tanto tiempo que no nos vemos; ~ **a long time ago** hace tantísimo tiempo; **as** ~ *adv* como tal.
such-and-such ['sʌtʃənsʌtʃ] *adj* tal o cual.
suchlike ['sʌtʃlaɪk] *pron* (*col*): **and** ~ y cosas por el estilo.
suck [sʌk] *vt* chupar; (*bottle*) sorber; (*breast*) mamar; (*subj: pump, machine*) aspirar.
sucker ['sʌkə*] *n* (*BOT*) serpollo; (*ZOOL*) ventosa; (*col*) bobo, primo.
sucrose ['suːkrəʊz] *n* sacarosa.
suction ['sʌkʃən] *n* succión *f*.
suction pump *n* bomba aspirante *or* de succión.
Sudan [su'dæn] *n* Sudán *m*.
Sudanese [suːdə'niːz] *adj*, *n* sudanés/esa *m/f*.
sudden ['sʌdn] *adj* (*rapid*) repentino, súbito; (*unexpected*) imprevisto; **all of a** ~ de

repente.

sudden-death [sʌdn'dɛθ] n (also: ~ **play off**) desempate m instantáneo, muerte f súbita.

suddenly ['sʌdnlɪ] adv de repente.

suds [sʌdz] npl espuma sg de jabón.

sue [suː] vt demandar; **to ~ (for)** demandar (por); **to ~ for divorce** solicitar or pedir el divorcio; **to ~ for damages** demandar por daños y perjuicios.

suede [sweɪd] n ante m, gamuza (LAM).

suet ['suɪt] n sebo.

Suez Canal ['suːɪz-] n Canal m de Suez.

Suff. abbr (BRIT) = Suffolk.

suffer ['sʌfə*] vt sufrir, padecer; (tolerate) aguantar, soportar; (undergo: loss, setback) experimentar ♦ vi sufrir, padecer; **to ~ from** sufrir, tener; **to ~ from the effects of alcohol/a fall** sufrir los efectos del alcohol/resentirse de una caída.

sufferance ['sʌfərns] n: **he was only there on ~** estuvo allí sólo porque se lo toleraron.

sufferer ['sʌfərə*] n víctima f; (MED) ~ **from** enfermo/a de.

suffering ['sʌfərɪŋ] n (hardship, deprivation) sufrimiento; (pain) dolor m.

suffice [sə'faɪs] vi bastar, ser suficiente.

sufficient [sə'fɪʃənt] adj suficiente, bastante.

sufficiently [sə'fɪʃəntlɪ] adv suficientemente, bastante.

suffix ['sʌfɪks] n sufijo.

suffocate ['sʌfəkeɪt] vi ahogarse, asfixiarse.

suffocation [sʌfə'keɪʃən] n sofocación f, asfixia.

suffrage ['sʌfrɪdʒ] n sufragio.

suffuse [sə'fjuːz] vt: **to ~ (with)** (colour) bañar (de); **her face was ~d with joy** su cara estaba llena de alegría.

sugar ['ʃugə*] n azúcar m ♦ vt echar azúcar a, azucarar.

sugar basin n (BRIT) = **sugar bowl**.

sugar beet n remolacha.

sugar bowl n azucarero.

sugar cane n caña de azúcar.

sugar-coated [ʃugə'kəutɪd] adj azucarado.

sugar lump n terrón m de azúcar.

sugar refinery n refinería de azúcar.

sugary ['ʃugərɪ] adj azucarado.

suggest [sə'dʒɛst] vt sugerir; (recommend) aconsejar; **what do you ~ I do?** ¿qué sugieres que haga?; **this ~s that ...** esto hace pensar que ....

suggestion [sə'dʒɛstʃən] n sugerencia; **there's no ~ of ...** no hay indicación or

evidencia de ....

suggestive [sə'dʒɛstɪv] adj sugestivo; (pej: indecent) indecente.

suicidal ['suɪsaɪdl] adj suicida; (fig) suicida, peligroso.

suicide ['suɪsaɪd] n suicidio; (person) suicida m/f; **to commit ~** suicidarse.

suicide attempt, suicide bid n intento de suicidio.

suit [suːt] n (man's) traje m; (woman's) traje de chaqueta; (LAW) pleito; (CARDS) palo ♦ vt convenir; (clothes) sentar bien a, ir bien a; (adapt): **to ~ sth to** adaptar or ajustar algo a; **to be ~ed to sth** (suitable for) ser apto para algo; **well ~ed** (couple) hechos el uno para el otro; **to bring a ~ against sb** entablar demanda contra algn; **to follow ~** (CARDS) seguir el palo; (fig) seguir el ejemplo (de algn); **that ~s me** me va bien.

suitable ['suːtəbl] adj conveniente; (apt) indicado.

suitably ['suːtəblɪ] adv convenientemente; (appropriately) en forma debida.

suitcase ['suːtkeɪs] n maleta, valija (LAM).

suite [swiːt] n (of rooms, MUS) suite f; (furniture): **bedroom/dining room ~** (juego de) dormitorio/comedor m; **a three-piece ~** un tresillo.

suitor ['suːtə*] n pretendiente m.

sulfate ['sʌlfeɪt] n (US) = **sulphate**.

sulfur ['sʌlfə*] n (US) = **sulphur**.

sulk [sʌlk] vi estar de mal humor.

sulky ['sʌlkɪ] adj malhumorado.

sullen ['sʌlən] adj hosco, malhumorado.

sulphate, (US) sulfate ['sʌlfeɪt] n sulfato; **copper ~** sulfato de cobre.

sulphur, (US) sulfur ['sʌlfə*] n azufre m.

sulphur dioxide n dióxido de azufre.

sultan ['sʌltən] n sultán m.

sultana [sʌl'tɑːnə] n (fruit) pasa de Esmirna.

sultry ['sʌltrɪ] adj (weather) bochornoso; (seductive) seductor(a).

sum [sʌm] n suma; (total) total m.
▶**sum up** vt resumir; (evaluate rapidly) evaluar ♦ vi hacer un resumen.

Sumatra [su'mɑːtrə] n Sumatra.

summarize ['sʌməraɪz] vt resumir.

summary ['sʌmərɪ] n resumen m ♦ adj (justice) sumario.

summer ['sʌmə*] n verano ♦ adj de verano; **in (the) ~** en (el) verano.

summerhouse ['sʌməhaus] n (in garden) cenador m, glorieta.

summertime ['sʌmətaɪm] n (season) verano.

summer time n (by clock) hora de verano.

summery ['sʌmərɪ] *adj* veraniego.
summing-up [sʌmɪŋ'ʌp] *n (LAW)* resumen *m*.
summit ['sʌmɪt] *n* cima, cumbre *f*.
summit (conference) *n* (conferencia) cumbre *f*.
summon ['sʌmən] *vt (person)* llamar; *(meeting)* convocar; **to ~ a witness** citar a un testigo.
▶**summon up** *vt (courage)* armarse de.
summons ['sʌmənz] *n* llamamiento, llamada ♦ *vt* citar, emplazar; **to serve a ~ on sb** citar a algn ante el juicio.
sumo ['su:məu] *n (also: ~ wrestling)* sumo.
sump [sʌmp] *n (BRIT AUT)* cárter *m*.
sumptuous ['sʌmptjuəs] *adj* suntuoso.
sun [sʌn] *n* sol *m*; **they have everything under the ~** no les falta nada, tienen de todo.
Sun. *abbr* (= *Sunday*) dom.
sunbathe ['sʌnbeɪð] *vi* tomar el sol.
sunbeam ['sʌnbi:m] *n* rayo de sol.
sunbed ['sʌnbed] *n* cama solar.
sunburn ['sʌnbə:n] *n (painful)* quemadura del sol; *(tan)* bronceado.
sunburnt ['sʌnbə:nt], **sunburned** ['sʌnbə:nd] *adj (tanned)* bronceado; *(painfully)* quemado por el sol.
sundae ['sʌndeɪ] *n helado con frutas y nueces*.
Sunday ['sʌndɪ] *n* domingo.
Sunday paper *n* (periódico) dominical *m*.
Sunday school *n* catequesis *f*.
sundial ['sʌndaɪəl] *n* reloj *m* de sol.
sundown ['sʌndaun] *n* anochecer *m*, puesta de sol.
sundries ['sʌndrɪz] *npl* géneros *mpl* diversos.
sundry ['sʌndrɪ] *adj* varios, diversos; **all and ~** todos sin excepción.
sunflower ['sʌnflauə*] *n* girasol *m*.
sung [sʌŋ] *pp of* **sing**.
sunglasses ['sʌngla:sɪz] *npl* gafas *fpl* de sol.
sunk [sʌŋk] *pp of* **sink**.
sunken ['sʌŋkn] *adj (bath)* hundido.
sunlamp ['sʌnlæmp] *n* lámpara solar ultravioleta.
sunlight ['sʌnlaɪt] *n* luz *f* del sol.
sunlit ['sʌnlɪt] *adj* iluminado por el sol.
sunny ['sʌnɪ] *adj* soleado; *(day)* de sol; *(fig)* alegre; **it is ~** hace sol.
sunrise ['sʌnraɪz] *n* salida del sol.
sun roof *n (AUT)* techo corredizo *or* solar; *(on building)* azotea, terraza.
sunscreen ['sʌnskri:n] *n* protector *m* solar.
sunset ['sʌnset] *n* puesta del sol.
sunshade ['sʌnʃeɪd] *n (over table)* sombrilla.

sunshine ['sʌnʃaɪn] *n* sol *m*.
sunstroke ['sʌnstrəuk] *n* insolación *f*.
suntan ['sʌntæn] *n* bronceado.
suntanned ['sʌntænd] *adj* bronceado.
suntan oil *n* aceite *m* bronceador.
super ['su:pə*] *adj (col)* bárbaro.
superannuation [su:pərænju'eɪʃən] *n* jubilación *f*, pensión *f*.
superb [su:'pə:b] *adj* magnífico, espléndido.
Super Bowl *n (US SPORT) super copa de fútbol americano*.
supercilious [su:pə'sɪlɪəs] *adj (disdainful)* desdeñoso; *(haughty)* altanero.
superconductor [su:pəkən'dʌktə*] *n* superconductor *m*.
superficial [su:pə'fɪʃəl] *adj* superficial.
superfluous [su'pə:fluəs] *adj* superfluo, de sobra.
superglue ['su:pəglu:] *n* cola de contacto, supercola.
superhighway ['su:pəhaɪweɪ] *n (US)* superautopista; **the information ~** la superautopista de la información.
superhuman [su:pə'hju:mən] *adj* sobrehumano.
superimpose ['su:pərɪm'pəuz] *vt* sobreponer.
superintend [su:pərɪn'tend] *vt* supervisar.
superintendent [su:pərɪn'tendənt] *n* director(a) *m/f*; *(police ~)* subjefe/a *m/f*.
superior [su'pɪərɪə*] *adj* superior; *(smug: person)* altivo, desdeñoso; *(: smile, air)* de suficiencia; *(: remark)* desdeñoso ♦ *n* superior *m*; **Mother S~** *(REL)* madre *f* superiora.
superiority [supɪərɪ'ɔrɪtɪ] *n* superioridad *f*, desdén *m*.
superlative [su'pə:lətɪv] *adj, n* superlativo.
superman ['su:pəmæn] *n* superhombre *m*.
supermarket ['su:pəma:kɪt] *n* supermercado.
supermodel ['su:pəmɔdl] *n* top model *f*, supermodelo *f*.
supernatural [su:pə'nætʃərəl] *adj* sobrenatural.
supernova [su:pə'nəuvə] *n* supernova.
superpower ['su:pəpauə*] *n (POL)* superpotencia.
supersede [su:pə'si:d] *vt* suplantar.
supersonic ['su:pə'sɔnɪk] *adj* supersónico.
superstar ['su:pəsta:*] *n* superestrella ♦ *adj* de superestrella.
superstition [su:pə'stɪʃən] *n* superstición *f*.
superstitious [su:pə'stɪʃəs] *adj* supersticioso.
superstore ['su:pəstɔ:*] *n (BRIT)* hipermercado.
supertanker ['su:pətæŋkə*] *n*

superpetrolero.

supertax ['su:pətæks] n sobretasa, sobreimpuesto.

supervise ['su:pəvaɪz] vt supervisar.

supervision [su:pə'vɪʒən] n supervisión f.

supervisor ['su:pəvaɪzə*] n (gen, UNIV) supervisor(a) m/f.

supervisory ['su:pəvaɪzərɪ] adj de supervisión.

supine ['su:paɪn] adj supino.

supper ['sʌpə*] n cena; **to have ~** cenar.

supplant [sə'plɑ:nt] vt suplantar, reemplazar.

supple ['sʌpl] adj flexible.

supplement n ['sʌplɪmənt] suplemento ♦ vt [sʌplɪ'mɛnt] suplir.

supplementary [sʌplɪ'mɛntərɪ] adj suplementario.

supplementary benefit n (BRIT) subsidio adicional de la seguridad social.

supplier [sə'plaɪə*] n suministrador(a) m/f; (COMM) distribuidor(a) m/f.

supply [sə'plaɪ] vt (provide) suministrar; (information) facilitar; (fill: need, want) suplir, satisfacer; (equip): **to ~ (with)** proveer (de) ♦ n provisión f; (of gas, water etc) suministro ♦ adj (BRIT: teacher etc) suplente; **supplies** npl (food) víveres mpl; (MIL) pertrechos mpl; **office supplies** materiales mpl para oficina; **to be in short ~** escasear, haber escasez de; **the electricity/water/gas ~** el suministro de electricidad/agua/gas; **~ and demand** la oferta y la demanda.

support [sə'pɔ:t] n (moral, financial etc) apoyo; (TECH) soporte m ♦ vt apoyar; (financially) mantener; (uphold) sostener; (SPORT: team) seguir, ser hincha de; **they stopped work in ~ (of)** pararon de trabajar en apoyo (de); **to ~ o.s.** (financially) ganarse la vida.

support buying [-'baɪɪŋ] n compra proteccionista.

supporter [sə'pɔ:tə*] n (POL etc) partidario/a; (SPORT) aficionado/a; (FOOTBALL) hincha m/f.

supporting [sə'pɔ:tɪŋ] adj (wall) de apoyo; **~ role** papel m secundario; **~ actor/ actress** actor/actriz m/f secundario/a.

supportive [sə'pɔ:tɪv] adj de apoyo; **I have a ~ family/wife** mi familia/mujer me apoya.

suppose [sə'pəuz] vt, vi suponer; (imagine) imaginarse; **to be ~d to do sth** deber hacer algo; **I don't ~ she'll come** no creo que venga; **he's ~d to be an expert** se le supone un experto.

supposedly [sə'pəuzɪdlɪ] adv según cabe

suponer.

supposing [sə'pəuzɪŋ] conj en caso de que; **always ~ (that) he comes** suponiendo que venga.

supposition [sʌpə'zɪʃən] n suposición f.

suppository [sə'pɔzɪtrɪ] n supositorio.

suppress [sə'prɛs] vt suprimir; (yawn) ahogar.

suppression [sə'prɛʃən] n represión f.

supremacy [su'prɛməsɪ] n supremacía.

supreme [su'pri:m] adj supremo.

Supreme Court n (US) Tribunal m Supremo, Corte f Suprema.

supremo [su'pri:məu] n autoridad f máxima.

Supt. abbr (POLICE) = **superintendent**.

surcharge ['sə:tʃɑ:dʒ] n sobretasa, recargo.

sure [ʃuə*] adj seguro; (definite, convinced) cierto; (aim) certero ♦ adv: **that ~ is pretty, that's ~ pretty** (US) ¡qué bonito es!; **to be ~ of sth** estar seguro de algo; **to be ~ of o.s.** estar seguro de sí mismo; **to make ~ of sth/that** asegurarse de algo/asegurar que; **I'm not ~ how/why/ when** no estoy seguro de cómo/por qué/ cuándo; **~!** (of course) ¡claro!, ¡por supuesto!; **~ enough** efectivamente.

sure-fire ['ʃuəfaɪə*] adj (col) infalible.

sure-footed [ʃuə'futɪd] adj de pie firme.

surely ['ʃuəlɪ] adv (certainly) seguramente; **~ you don't mean that!** ¡no lo dices en serio!

surety ['ʃuərətɪ] n fianza; (person) fiador(a) m/f; **to go** or **stand ~ for sb** ser fiador de algn, salir garante por algn.

surf [sə:f] n olas fpl.

surface ['sə:fɪs] n superficie f ♦ vt (road) revestir ♦ vi salir a la superficie ♦ cpd (MIL, NAUT) de (la) superficie; **on the ~ it seems that ...** (fig) a primera vista parece que ....

surface area n área de la superficie.

surface mail n vía terrestre.

surface-to-air ['sə:fɪstə'ɛə*] adj (MIL) tierra-aire.

surface-to-surface ['sə:fɪstə'sə:fɪs] adj (MIL) tierra-tierra.

surfboard ['sə:fbɔ:d] n plancha (de surf).

surfeit ['sə:fɪt] n: **a ~ of** un exceso de.

surfer ['sə:fə*] n súrfer m/f.

surfing ['sə:fɪŋ] n surf m.

surge [sə:dʒ] n oleada, oleaje m; (ELEC) sobretensión f transitoria ♦ vi avanzar a tropel; **to ~ forward** avanzar rápidamente.

surgeon ['sə:dʒən] n cirujano/a.

surgery ['sə:dʒərɪ] n cirugía; (BRIT: room)

consultorio; (: *POL*) *horas en las que los electores pueden reunirse personalmente con su diputado*; **to undergo** ~ operarse; *see also* **constituency.**

surgery hours *npl* (*BRIT*) horas *fpl* de consulta.

surgical ['sə:dʒɪkl] *adj* quirúrgico.

surgical spirit *n* (*BRIT*) alcohol *m*.

surly ['sə:lɪ] *adj* hosco, malhumorado.

surmount [sə:'maunt] *vt* superar, vencer.

surname ['sə:neɪm] *n* apellido.

surpass [sə:'pɑːs] *vt* superar, exceder.

surplus ['sə:pləs] *n* excedente *m*; (*COMM*) superávit *m* ♦ *adj* (*COMM*) excedente, sobrante; **to have a** ~ **of sth** tener un excedente de algo; **it is** ~ **to our requirements** nos sobra; ~ **stock** saldos *mpl*.

surprise [sə'praɪz] *n* sorpresa ♦ *vt* sorprender; **to take by** ~ (*person*) coger a algn desprevenido *or* por sorpresa, sorprender a algn; (*MIL*: *town, fort*) atacar por sorpresa.

surprising [sə'praɪzɪŋ] *adj* sorprendente.

surprisingly [sə'praɪzɪŋlɪ] *adv* (*easy, helpful*) de modo sorprendente; (**somewhat**) ~, **he agreed** para sorpresa de todos, aceptó.

surrealism [sə'rɪəlɪzəm] *n* surrealismo.

surrealist [sə'rɪəlɪst] *adj, n* surrealista *m/f*.

surrender [sə'rɛndə*] *n* rendición *f*, entrega ♦ *vi* rendirse, entregarse ♦ *vt* (*claim, right*) renunciar.

surrender value *n* valor *m* de rescate.

surreptitious [sʌrəp'tɪʃəs] *adj* subrepticio.

surrogate ['sʌrəgɪt] *n* (*BRIT*: *substitute*) sustituto/a ♦ *adj*: ~ **coffee** sucedáneo de café.

surrogate mother *n* madre *f* de alquiler.

surround [sə'raund] *vt* rodear, circundar; (*MIL etc*) cercar.

surrounding [sə'raundɪŋ] *adj* circundante.

surroundings [sə'raundɪŋz] *npl* alrededores *mpl*, cercanías *fpl*.

surtax ['sə:tæks] *n* sobretasa, sobreimpuesto.

surveillance [sə:'veɪləns] *n* vigilancia.

survey *n* ['sə:veɪ] inspección *f*, reconocimiento; (*inquiry*) encuesta; (*comprehensive view: of situation etc*) vista de conjunto ♦ *vt* [sə:'veɪ] examinar, inspeccionar; (*SURVEYING: building*) inspeccionar; (: *land*) hacer un reconocimiento de, reconocer; (*look at*) mirar, contemplar; (*make inquiries about*) hacer una encuesta de; **to carry out a** ~ **of** inspeccionar, examinar.

surveyor [sə'veɪə*] *n* (*BRIT*) (*of building*) perito *m/f*; (*of land*) agrimensor(a) *m/f*.

survival [sə'vaɪvl] *n* supervivencia.

survival course *n* curso de supervivencia.

survival kit *n* equipo de emergencia.

survive [sə'vaɪv] *vi* sobrevivir; (*custom etc*) perdurar ♦ *vt* sobrevivir a.

survivor [sə'vaɪvə*] *n* superviviente *m/f*.

susceptibility [səsɛptə'bɪlɪtɪ] *n* (*to illness*) propensión *f*.

susceptible [sə'sɛptəbl] *adj* (*easily influenced*) influenciable; (*to disease, illness*): ~ **to** propenso a.

suspect *adj, n* ['sʌspɛkt] sospechoso/a *m/f* ♦ *vt* [səs'pɛkt] sospechar.

suspected [səs'pɛktɪd] *adj* presunto; **to have a** ~ **fracture** tener una posible fractura.

suspend [səs'pɛnd] *vt* suspender.

suspended animation [səs'pɛndəd-] *n*: **in a state of** ~ en (estado de) hibernación.

suspended sentence *n* (*LAW*) libertad *f* condicional.

suspender belt [səs'pɛndə*-] *n* (*BRIT*) liguero, portaligas *m inv* (*AM*).

suspenders [səs'pɛndəz] *npl* (*BRIT*) ligas *fpl*; (*US*) tirantes *mpl*.

suspense [səs'pɛns] *n* incertidumbre *f*, duda; (*in film etc*) suspense *m*.

suspension [səs'pɛnʃən] *n* (*gen, AUT*) suspensión *f*; (*of driving licence*) privación *f*.

suspension bridge *n* puente *m* colgante.

suspension file *n* archivador *m* colgante.

suspicion [səs'pɪʃən] *n* sospecha; (*distrust*) recelo; (*trace*) traza; **to be under** ~ estar bajo sospecha; **arrested on** ~ **of murder** detenido bajo sospecha de asesinato.

suspicious [səs'pɪʃəs] *adj* (*suspecting*) receloso; (*causing suspicion*) sospechoso; **to be** ~ **of** *or* **about sb/sth** tener sospechas de algn/algo.

suss out [sʌs-] *vt* (*BRIT col*) calar.

sustain [səs'teɪn] *vt* sostener, apoyar; (*suffer*) sufrir, padecer.

sustainable [səs'teɪnəbl] *adj* sostenible.

sustained [səs'teɪnd] *adj* (*effort*) sostenido.

sustenance ['sʌstɪnəns] *n* sustento.

suture ['suːtʃə*] *n* sutura.

SW *abbr* = **short wave.**

swab [swɔb] *n* (*MED*) algodón *m*, frotis *m inv* ♦ *vt* (*NAUT*: *also*: ~ **down**) limpiar, fregar.

swagger ['swægə*] *vi* pavonearse.

swallow ['swɔləu] *n* (*bird*) golondrina; (*of food*) bocado; (*of drink*) trago ♦ *vt* tragar.

►**swallow up** *vt* (*savings etc*) consumir.

swam [swæm] *pt of* **swim.**

swamp [swɔmp] *n* pantano, ciénaga ♦ *vt* abrumar, agobiar.

swampy ['swɔmpɪ] *adj* pantanoso.

swan [swɔn] n cisne m.
swank [swæŋk] (col) n (vanity, boastfulness) fanfarronada ♦ vi fanfarronear, presumir.
swan song n (fig) canto del cisne.
swap [swɔp] n canje m, trueque m ♦ vt: **to ~ (for)** canjear (por).
SWAPO ['swɑːpəu] n abbr (= South-West Africa People's Organization) SWAPO f.
swarm [swɔːm] n (of bees) enjambre m; (fig) multitud f ♦ vi (fig) hormiguear, pulular.
swarthy ['swɔːðɪ] adj moreno.
swashbuckling ['swɔʃbʌklɪŋ] adj (person) aventurero; (film) de capa y espada.
swastika ['swɔstɪkə] n esvástika, cruz f gamada.
swat [swɔt] vt aplastar ♦ n (also: **fly ~**) matamoscas m inv.
SWAT [swɔt] n abbr (US: = Special Weapons and Tactics) unidad especial de la policía.
swathe [sweɪð] vt: **to ~ in** (blankets) envolver en; (bandages) vendar en.
sway [sweɪ] vi mecerse, balancearse ♦ vt (influence) mover, influir en ♦ n (rule, power): · **(over)** dominio (sobre), **to hold ~ over sb** dominar a algn, mantener el dominio sobre algn.
Swaziland ['swɑːzɪlænd] n Swazilandia.
swear, pt **swore**, pp **sworn** [sweə*, swɔː*, swɔːn] vi jurar; (with swearwords) decir tacos ♦ vt: **to ~ an oath** prestar juramento, jurar; **to ~ to sth** declarar algo bajo juramento.
▶**swear in** vt tomar juramento (a).
swearword ['sweəwɔːd] n taco, palabrota.
sweat [swɛt] n sudor m ♦ vi sudar.
sweatband ['swɛtbænd] n (SPORT: on head) banda; (: on wrist) muñequera.
sweater ['swɛtə*] n suéter m.
sweatshirt ['swɛtʃɔːt] n sudadera.
sweatshop ['swɛtʃɔp] n fábrica donde se explota al obrero.
sweaty ['swɛtɪ] adj sudoroso.
Swede [swiːd] n sueco/a.
swede [swiːd] n (BRIT) nabo.
Sweden ['swiːdn] n Suecia.
Swedish ['swiːdɪʃ] adj, n (LING) sueco.
sweep [swiːp] n (act) barrida; (of arm) manotazo m; (curve) curva, alcance m; (also: **chimney ~**) deshollinador(a) m/f ♦ vb (pt, pp **swept** [swɛpt]) vt barrer; (disease, fashion) recorrer ♦ vi barrer.
▶**sweep away** vt barrer; (rub out) borrar.
▶**sweep past** vi pasar rápidamente; (brush by) rozar.
▶**sweep up** vi barrer.
sweeper ['swiːpə*] n (person) barrendero/
a; (machine) barredora; (FOOTBALL) líbero, libre m.
sweeping ['swiːpɪŋ] adj (gesture) dramático; (generalized) generalizado; (changes, reforms) radical.
sweepstake ['swiːpsteɪk] n lotería.
sweet [swiːt] n (candy) dulce m, caramelo; (BRIT: pudding) postre m ♦ adj dulce; (sugary) azucarado; (charming: person) encantador(a); (: smile, character) dulce, amable, agradable ♦ adv: **to smell/taste ~** oler/saber dulce.
sweet and sour adj agridulce.
sweetcorn ['swiːtkɔːn] n maíz m (dulce).
sweeten ['swiːtn] vt (person) endulzar; (add sugar to) poner azúcar a.
sweetener ['swiːtnə*] n (CULIN) edulcorante m.
sweetheart ['swiːthɑːt] n amor m, novio/a; (in speech) amor, cariño.
sweetness ['swiːtnɪs] n (gen) dulzura.
sweet pea n guisante m de olor.
sweet potato n batata, camote m (LAM).
sweetshop ['swiːtʃɔp] n (BRIT) confitería, bombonería.
swell [swɛl] n (of sea) marejada, oleaje m ♦ adj (US: col: excellent) estupendo, fenomenal ♦ vb (pt ~**ed**, pp **swollen** or ~**ed** ['swəulən]) vt hinchar, inflar ♦ vi hincharse, inflarse.
swelling ['swɛlɪŋ] n (MED) hinchazón f.
sweltering ['swɛltərɪŋ] adj sofocante, de mucho calor.
swept [swɛpt] pt, pp of **sweep**.
swerve [swɔːv] n regate m; (in car) desvío brusco ♦ vi desviarse bruscamente.
swift [swɪft] n (bird) vencejo ♦ adj rápido, veloz.
swiftly ['swɪftlɪ] adv rápidamente.
swiftness ['swɪftnɪs] n rapidez f, velocidad f.
swig [swɪg] n (col: drink) trago.
swill [swɪl] n bazofia ♦ vt (also: ~ **out**, ~ **down**) lavar, limpiar con agua.
swim [swɪm] n: **to go for a ~** ir a nadar or a bañarse ♦ vb (pt **swam**, pp **swum** [swæm, swʌm]) vi nadar; (head, room) dar vueltas ♦ vt pasar a nado; **to go ~ming** ir a nadar; **to ~ a length** nadar or hacer un largo.
swimmer ['swɪmə*] n nadador(a) m/f.
swimming ['swɪmɪŋ] n natación f.
swimming cap n gorro de baño.
swimming costume n bañador m, traje m de baño.
swimmingly ['swɪmɪŋlɪ] adv: **to go ~** (wonderfully) ir como una seda or sobre ruedas.
swimming pool n piscina, alberca (LAM).

swimming trunks *npl* bañador *msg.*
swimsuit ['swɪmsuːt] *n* = **swimming costume**.
swindle ['swɪndl] *n* estafa ♦ *vt* estafar.
swine [swaɪn] *n, pl inv* cerdo, puerco; (*col!*) canalla *m* (*!*).
swing [swɪŋ] *n* (*in playground*) columpio; (*movement*) balanceo, vaivén *m*; (*change of direction*) viraje *m*; (*rhythm*) ritmo; (*POL: in votes etc*): **there has been a ~ towards/away from Labour** ha habido un viraje en favor/en contra del Partido Laborista ♦ *vb* (*pt, pp* **swung** [swʌŋ]) *vt* balancear; (*on a ~*) columpiar; (*also: ~* **round**) voltear, girar ♦ *vi* balancearse, columpiarse; (*also: ~* **round**) dar media vuelta; **a ~ to the left** un movimiento hacia la izquierda; **to be in full ~** estar en plena marcha; **to get into the ~ of things** meterse en situación; **the road ~s south** la carretera gira hacia el sur.
swing bridge *n* puente *m* giratorio.
swing door, (*US*) **swinging door** ['swɪŋɪŋ-] *n* puerta giratoria.
swingeing ['swɪndʒɪŋ] *adj* (*BRIT*) abrumador(a).
swipe [swaɪp] *n* golpe *m* fuerte ♦ *vt* (*hit*) golpear fuerte; (*col: steal*) guindar; (*credit card etc*) pasar.
swirl [swəːl] *vi* arremolinarse.
swish [swɪʃ] *n* (*sound: of whip*) chasquido; (*: of skirts*) frufrú *m*; (*: of grass*) crujido ♦ *adj* (*col: smart*) elegante ♦ *vi* chasquear.
Swiss [swɪs] *adj, n* (*pl inv*) suizo/a *m/f.*
switch [swɪtʃ] *n* (*for light, radio etc*) interruptor *m*; (*change*) cambio ♦ *vt* (*change*) cambiar de; (*invert: also: ~* **round, ~ over**) intercambiar.
▶**switch off** *vt* apagar; (*engine*) parar.
▶**switch on** *vt* (*AUT: ignition*) encender, prender (*LAM*); (*engine, machine*) arrancar; (*water supply*) conectar.
switchboard ['swɪtʃbɔːd] *n* (*TEL*) centralita (de teléfonos), conmutador *m* (*LAM*).
Switzerland ['swɪtsələnd] *n* Suiza.
swivel ['swɪvl] *vi* (*also: ~* **round**) girar.
swollen ['swəʊlən] *pp of* **swell**.
swoon [swuːn] *vi* desmayarse.
swoop [swuːp] *n* (*by police etc*) redada; (*of bird etc*) descenso en picado, calada ♦ *vi* (*also: ~* **down**) caer en picado.
swop [swɔp] = **swap**.
sword [sɔːd] *n* espada.
swordfish ['sɔːdfɪʃ] *n* pez *m* espada.
swore [swɔː*] *pt of* **swear**.
sworn [swɔːn] *pp of* **swear**.
swot [swɔt] (*BRIT*) *vt, vi* empollar ♦ *n* empollón/ona *m/f.*

swum [swʌm] *pp of* **swim**.
swung [swʌŋ] *pt, pp of* **swing**.
sycamore ['sɪkəmɔː*] *n* sicomoro.
sycophant ['sɪkəfænt] *n* adulador(a) *m/f,* pelotillero/a.
Sydney ['sɪdnɪ] *n* Sidney *m.*
syllable ['sɪləbl] *n* sílaba.
syllabus ['sɪləbəs] *n* programa *m* de estudios; **on the ~** en el programa de estudios.
symbol ['sɪmbl] *n* símbolo.
symbolic(al) [sɪm'bɔlɪk(l)] *adj* simbólico; **to be ~ of sth** simbolizar algo.
symbolism ['sɪmbəlɪzəm] *n* simbolismo.
symbolize ['sɪmbəlaɪz] *vt* simbolizar.
symmetrical [sɪ'mɛtrɪkl] *adj* simétrico.
symmetry ['sɪmɪtrɪ] *n* simetría.
sympathetic [sɪmpə'θɛtɪk] *adj* compasivo; (*understanding*) comprensivo; **to be ~ to a cause** (*well-disposed*) apoyar una causa; **to be ~ towards** (*person*) ser comprensivo con.
sympathize ['sɪmpəθaɪz] *vi*: **to ~ with sb** compadecerse de algn; (*understand*) comprender a algn.
sympathizer ['sɪmpəθaɪzə*] *n* (*POL*) simpatizante *m/f.*
sympathy ['sɪmpəθɪ] *n* (*pity*) compasión *f*; (*understanding*) comprensión *f*; **a letter of ~** un pésame; **with our deepest ~** nuestro más sentido pésame.
symphony ['sɪmfənɪ] *n* sinfonía.
symposium [sɪm'pəʊzɪəm] *n* simposio.
symptom ['sɪmptəm] *n* síntoma *m*, indicio.
symptomatic [sɪmptə'mætɪk] *adj*: **~ (of)** sintomático (de).
synagogue ['sɪnəgɔg] *n* sinagoga.
sync [sɪŋk] *n* (*col*): **to be in/out of ~ (with)** ir/no ir al mismo ritmo (que); (*fig: people*) conectar/no conectar con.
synchromesh ['sɪŋkrəʊmɛʃ] *n* cambio sincronizado de velocidades.
synchronize ['sɪŋkrənaɪz] *vt* sincronizar ♦ *vi*: **to ~ with** sincronizarse con.
synchronized swimming ['sɪŋkrənaɪzd-] *n* natación *f* sincronizada.
syncopated ['sɪŋkəpeɪtɪd] *adj* sincopado.
syndicate ['sɪndɪkɪt] *n* (*gen*) sindicato; (*PRESS*) agencia (de noticias).
syndrome ['sɪndrəʊm] *n* síndrome *m.*
synonym ['sɪnənɪm] *n* sinónimo.
synonymous [sɪ'nɒnɪməs] *adj*: **~ (with)** sinónimo (con).
synopsis, *pl* **synopses** [sɪ'nɒpsɪs, -siːz] *n* sinopsis *f inv.*
syntax ['sɪntæks] *n* sintaxis *f.*
syntax error *n* (*COMPUT*) error *m* sintáctico.

synthesis, *pl* **syntheses** ['sɪnθəsɪs, -siːz] *n* síntesis *f inv.*
synthesizer ['sɪnθəsaɪzə*] *n* sintetizador *m.*
synthetic [sɪn'θetɪk] *adj* sintético ♦ *n* sintético.
syphilis ['sɪfɪlɪs] *n* sífilis *f.*
syphon ['saɪfən] = **siphon.**
Syria ['sɪrɪə] *n* Siria.
Syrian ['sɪrɪən] *adj, n* sirio/a *m/f.*
syringe [sɪ'rɪndʒ] *n* jeringa.
syrup ['sɪrəp] *n* jarabe *m,* almíbar *m.*
system ['sɪstəm] *n* sistema *m;* (*ANAT*) organismo; **it was quite a shock to his ~** fue un golpe para él.
systematic [sɪstə'mætɪk] *adj* sistemático; metódico.
system disk *n* (*COMPUT*) disco del sistema.
systems analyst *n* analista *m/f* de sistemas.

Tt

T, t [tiː] *n* (*letter*) T, t *f;* **T for Tommy** T de Tarragona.
TA *n abbr* (*BRIT*) = *Territorial Army.*
ta [taː] *excl* (*BRIT col*) ¡gracias!
tab [tæb] *n abbr* = **tabulator** ♦ *n* lengüeta; (*label*) etiqueta; **to keep ~s on** (*fig*) vigilar.
tabby ['tæbɪ] *n* (*also:* ~ **cat**) gato atigrado.
tabernacle ['tæbənækl] *n* tabernáculo.
table ['teɪbl] *n* mesa; (*chart: of statistics etc*) cuadro, tabla ♦ *vt* (*BRIT: motion etc*) presentar; **to lay** *or* **set the ~** poner la mesa; **to clear the ~** quitar *or* levantar la mesa; **league ~** (*FOOTBALL, RUGBY*) clasificación *f* del campeonato; **~ of contents** índice *m* de materias.
tablecloth ['teɪblklɒθ] *n* mantel *m.*
table d'hôte [taːbl'dəut] *n* menú *m.*
table lamp *n* lámpara de mesa.
tablemat ['teɪblmæt] *n* salvamanteles *m inv,* posaplatos *m inv.*
tablespoon ['teɪblspuːn] *n* cuchara grande; (*also:* ~**ful:** *as measurement*) cucharada.
tablet ['tæblɪt] *n* (*MED*) pastilla, comprimido; (*for writing*) bloc *m;* (*of stone*) lápida; **~ of soap** pastilla de jabón.
table talk *n* conversación *f* de sobremesa.
table tennis *n* ping-pong *m,* tenis *m* de mesa.

table wine *n* vino de mesa.
tabloid ['tæblɔɪd] *n* (*newspaper*) periódico popular sensacionalista.
tabloid press *n ver recuadro.*

taboo [tə'buː] *adj, n* tabú *m.*
tabulate ['tæbjuleɪt] *vt* disponer en tablas.
tabulator ['tæbjuleɪtə*] *n* tabulador *m.*
tachograph ['tækəgrɑːf] *n* tacógrafo.
tacit ['tæsɪt] *adj* tácito.
tacitly ['tæsɪtlɪ] *adv* tácitamente.
taciturn ['tæsɪtɜːn] *adj* taciturno.
tack [tæk] *n* (*nail*) tachuela; (*stitch*) hilván *m;* (*NAUT*) bordada ♦ *vt* (*nail*) clavar con tachuelas; (*stitch*) hilvanar ♦ *vi* virar; **to ~ sth on to (the end of) sth** (*of letter, book*) añadir algo a(l final de) algo.
tackle ['tækl] *n* (*gear*) equipo; (*fishing ~, for lifting*) aparejo; (*FOOTBALL*) entrada, tackle *m;* (*RUGBY*) placaje *m* ♦ *vt* (*difficulty*) enfrentarse a; (*grapple with*) agarrar; (*FOOTBALL*) entrar a; (*RUGBY*) placar.
tacky ['tækɪ] *adj* pegajoso; (*fam*) hortera *inv.*
tact [tækt] *n* tacto, discreción *f.*
tactful ['tæktful] *adj* discreto, diplomático; **to be ~** tener tacto.
tactfully ['tæktfulɪ] *adv* diplomáticamente, con tacto.
tactical ['tæktɪkl] *adj* táctico.
tactical voting *n* voto útil.
tactician [tæk'tɪʃən] *n* táctico/a.
tactics ['tæktɪks] *n, npl* táctica *sg.*
tactless ['tæktlɪs] *adj* indiscreto.
tactlessly ['tæktlɪslɪ] *adv* indiscretamente, sin tacto.
tadpole ['tædpəul] *n* renacuajo.
taffy ['tæfɪ] *n* (*US*) melcocha.
tag [tæg] *n* (*label*) etiqueta; **price/name ~** etiqueta del precio/con el nombre.
►**tag along** *vi:* **to ~ along with sb** engancharse a algn.
Tahiti [taː'hiːtɪ] *n* Tahití *m.*
tail [teɪl] *n* cola; (*ZOOL*) rabo; (*of shirt, coat*)

faldón *m* ♦ *vt* (*follow*) vigilar a; **heads or** ~**s** cara o cruz; **to turn** ~ volver la espalda.

►**tail away, tail off** *vi* (*in size, quality etc*) ir disminuyendo.

tailback ['teɪlbæk] *n* (*BRIT AUT*) cola.

tail coat *n* frac *m*.

tail end *n* cola, parte *f* final.

tailgate ['teɪlgeɪt] *n* (*AUT*) puerta trasera.

tail light *n* (*AUT*) luz *f* trasera.

tailor ['teɪlə*] *n* sastre *m* ♦ *vt*: **to** ~ **sth** (**to**) confeccionar algo a medida (para); ~**'s** (**shop**) sastrería.

tailoring ['teɪlərɪŋ] *n* (*cut*) corte *m*; (*craft*) sastrería.

tailor-made ['teɪlə'meɪd] *adj* (*also fig*) hecho a (la) medida.

tailwind ['teɪlwɪnd] *n* viento de cola.

taint [teɪnt] *vt* (*meat, food*) contaminar; (*fig: reputation*) manchar, tachar (*LAM*).

tainted ['teɪntɪd] *adj* (*water, air*) contaminado; (*fig*) manchado.

Taiwan [taɪ'wɑːn] *n* Taiwán *m*.

Tajikistan [tɑːdʒɪkɪ'stɑːn] *n* Tayikistán *m*.

take [teɪk] *vb* (*pt* **took**, *pp* **taken** [tuk, 'teɪkn]) *vt* tomar; (*grab*) coger (*SP*), agarrar (*LAM*); (*gain: prize*) ganar; (*require: effort, courage*) exigir; (*support weight of*) aguantar; (*hold: passengers etc*) tener cabida para; (*accompany, bring, carry*) llevar; (*exam*) presentarse a; (*conduct: meeting*) presidir ♦ *vi* (*fire*) prender; (*dye*) coger (*SP*), agarrar, tomar ♦ *n* (*CINE*) toma; **to** ~ **sth from** (*drawer etc*) sacar algo de; (*person*) coger (*SP*) algo a; **to** ~ **sb's hand** tomar de la mano a algn; **to** ~ **notes** tomar apuntes; **to be** ~**n ill** ponerse enfermo; ~ **the first on the left** toma la primera a la izquierda; **I only took Russian for one year** sólo estudié ruso un año; **I took him for a doctor** le tenía por médico; **it won't** ~ **long** durará poco; **it will** ~ **at least 5 litres** tiene cabida por lo menos para 5 litros; **to be** ~**n with sb/sth** (*attracted*) tomarle cariño a algn/tomarle gusto a algo; **I** ~ **it that** ... supongo que ....

►**take after** *vt fus* parecerse a.

►**take apart** *vt* desmontar.

►**take away** *vt* (*remove*) quitar; (*carry off*) llevar ♦ *vi*: **to** ~ **away from** quitar mérito a.

►**take back** *vt* (*return*) devolver; (*one's words*) retractar.

►**take down** *vt* (*building*) derribar; (*dismantle: scaffolding*) desmantelar; (*message etc*) apuntar, tomar nota de.

►**take in** *vt* (*BRIT: deceive*) engañar; (*understand*) entender; (*include*) abarcar;

(*lodger*) acoger, recibir; (*orphan, stray dog*) recoger; (*SEWING*) achicar.

►**take off** *vi* (*AVIAT*) despegar, decolar (*LAM*) ♦ *vt* (*remove*) quitar; (*imitate*) imitar, remedar.

►**take on** *vt* (*work*) emprender; (*employee*) contratar; (*opponent*) desafiar.

►**take out** *vt* sacar; (*remove*) quitar; **don't** ~ **it out on me!** ¡no te desquites conmigo!

►**take over** *vt* (*business*) tomar posesión de ♦ *vi*: **to** ~ **over from sb** reemplazar a algn.

►**take to** *vt fus* (*person*) coger cariño a (*SP*), encariñarse con (*LAM*); (*activity*) aficionarse a; **to** ~ **to doing sth** aficionarse a (hacer) algo.

►**take up** *vt* (*a dress*) acortar; (*occupy: time, space*) ocupar; (*engage in: hobby etc*) dedicarse a; (*absorb: liquids*) absorber; (*accept: offer, challenge*) aceptar ♦ *vi*: **to** ~ **up with sb** hacerse amigo de algn.

►**take upon** *vt*: **to** ~ **it upon o.s. to do sth** encargarse de hacer algo.

takeaway ['teɪkəweɪ] *adj* (*BRIT: food*) para llevar.

take-home pay ['teɪkhəum-] *n* salario neto.

taken ['teɪkən] *pp of* **take**.

takeoff ['teɪkɔf] *n* (*AVIAT*) despegue *m*, decolaje *m* (*LAM*).

takeover ['teɪkəuvə*] *n* (*COMM*) absorción *f*.

takeover bid *n* oferta pública de adquisición.

takings ['teɪkɪŋz] *npl* (*COMM*) ingresos *mpl*.

talc [tælk] *n* (*also*: ~**um powder**) talco.

tale [teɪl] *n* (*story*) cuento; (*account*) relación *f*; **to tell** ~**s** (*fig*) contar chismes.

talent ['tælnt] *n* talento.

talented ['tæləntɪd] *adj* talentoso, de talento.

talisman ['tælɪzmən] *n* talismán *m*.

talk [tɔːk] *n* charla; (*gossip*) habladurías *fpl*, chismes *mpl*; (*conversation*) conversación *f* ♦ *vi* (*speak*) hablar; (*chatter*) charlar; ~**s** *npl* (*POL etc*) conversaciones *fpl*; **to give a** ~ dar una charla *or* conferencia; **to** ~ **about** hablar de; **to** ~ **sb into doing sth** convencer a algn para que haga algo; **to** ~ **sb out of doing sth** disuadir a algn de que haga algo; **to** ~ **shop** hablar del trabajo; ~**ing of films, have you seen** ...? hablando de películas, ¿has visto ...?

►**talk over** *vt* discutir.

talkative ['tɔːkətɪv] *adj* hablador(a).

talker ['tɔːkə*] *n* hablador(a) *m/f*.

talking point ['tɔːkɪŋ-] *n* tema *m* de conversación.

talking-to ['tɔːkɪŋtuː] *n*: **to give sb a good** ~ echar una buena bronca a algn.

talk show *n* programa *m* magazine.
tall [tɔːl] *adj* alto; (*tree*) grande; **to be 6 feet**
~ ≈ medir 1 metro 80, tener 1 metro 80
de alto; **how ~ are you?** ¿cuánto mides?
tallboy ['tɔːlbɔɪ] *n* (*BRIT*) cómoda alta.
tallness ['tɔːlnɪs] *n* altura.
tall story *n* cuento chino.
tally ['tælɪ] *n* cuenta ♦ *vi:* **to ~ (with)**
concordar (con), cuadrar (con); **to keep a**
~ of sth llevar la cuenta de algo.
talon ['tælən] *n* garra.
tambourine [tæmbə'riːn] *n* pandereta.
tame [teɪm] *adj* (*mild*) manso; (*tamed*)
domesticado; (*fig: story, style, person*)
soso, anodino.
tameness ['teɪmnɪs] *n* mansedumbre *f.*
Tamil ['tæmɪl] *adj* tamil ♦ *n* tamil *m/f;* (*LING*)
tamil *m,*
tamper ['tæmpə*] *vi:* **to ~ with** (*lock etc*)
intentar forzar; (*papers*) falsificar.
tampon ['tæmpən] *n* tampón *m.*
tan [tæn] *n* (*also:* **sun~**) bronceado ♦ *vt*
broncear ♦ *vi* ponerse moreno ♦ *adj*
(*colour*) marrón; **to get a ~** broncearse,
ponerse moreno.
tandem ['tændəm] *n* tándem *m.*
tandoori [tæn'dʊərɪ] *adj,n* tandoori *m* (*asado*
a la manera hindú, en horno de barro).
tang [tæŋ] *n* sabor *m* fuerte.
tangent ['tændʒənt] *n* (*MATH*) tangente *f;* **to**
go off at a ~ (*fig*) salirse por la tangente.
tangerine [tændʒə'riːn] *n* mandarina.
tangible ['tændʒəbl] *adj* tangible; **~ assets**
bienes *mpl* tangibles.
Tangier [tæn'dʒɪə*] *n* Tánger *m.*
tangle ['tæŋgl] *n* enredo; **to get in(to) a ~**
enredarse.
tango ['tæŋgəu] *n* tango.
tank [tæŋk] *n* (*water ~*) depósito, tanque *m;*
(*for fish*) acuario; (*MIL*) tanque *m.*
tankard ['tæŋkəd] *n* bock *m.*
tanker ['tæŋkə*] *n* (*ship*) petrolero; (*truck*)
camión *m* cisterna.
tankful ['tæŋkful] *n:* **to get a ~ of petrol**
llenar el depósito de gasolina.
tanned [tænd] *adj* (*skin*) moreno,
bronceado.
tannin ['tænɪn] *n* tanino.
tanning ['tænɪŋ] *n* (*of leather*) curtido.
tannoy ® ['tænɔɪ] *n:* **over the ~** por el
altavoz.
tantalizing ['tæntəlaɪzɪŋ] *adj* tentador(a).
tantamount ['tæntəmaunt] *adj:* **~ to**
equivalente a.
tantrum ['tæntrəm] *n* rabieta; **to throw a ~**
coger una rabieta.
Tanzania [tænzə'nɪə] *n* Tanzania.
Tanzanian [tænzə'nɪən] *adj, n* tanzano/a *m/f.*

tap [tæp] *n* (*BRIT: on sink etc*) grifo, canilla
(*LAM*); (*gentle blow*) golpecito; (*gas ~*)
llave *f* ♦ *vt* (*table etc*) tamborilear;
(*shoulder etc*) dar palmaditas en;
(*resources*) utilizar, explotar; (*telephone*
conversation) intervenir, pinchar; **on ~**
(*fig: resources*) a mano; **beer on ~** cerveza
de barril.
tap-dancing ['tæpdɑːnsɪŋ] *n* claqué *m.*
tape [teɪp] *n* cinta; (*also:* **magnetic ~**) cinta
magnética; (*sticky ~*) cinta adhesiva ♦ *vt*
(*record*) grabar (en cinta); **on ~** (*song etc*)
grabado (en cinta).
tape deck *n* pletina.
tape measure *n* cinta métrica, metro.
taper ['teɪpə*] *n* cirio ♦ *vi* afilarse.
tape-record ['teɪprɪkɔːd] *vt* grabar (en
cinta).
tape recorder *n* grabadora.
tape recording *n* grabación *f.*
tapered ['teɪpəd], **tapering** ['teɪpərɪŋ] *adj*
terminado en punta.
tapestry ['tæpɪstrɪ] *n* (*object*) tapiz *m;* (*art*)
tapicería.
tape-worm ['teɪpwɔːm] *n* solitaria, tenia.
tapioca [tæpɪ'əukə] *n* tapioca.
tappet ['tæpɪt] *n* excéntrica.
tar [tɑː*] *n* alquitrán *m,* brea; **low/middle ~**
cigarettes cigarrillos con contenido
bajo/medio de alquitrán.
tarantula [tə'ræntjulə] *n* tarántula.
tardy ['tɑːdɪ] *adj* (*late*) tardío; (*slow*) lento.
tare [tɛə*] *n* (*COMM*) tara.
target ['tɑːgɪt] *n* (*gen*) blanco; **to be on ~**
(*project*) seguir el curso previsto.
target audience *n* público al que va
destinado un programa etc.
target market *n* (*COMM*) mercado al que
va destinado un producto etc.
target practice *n* tiro al blanco.
tariff ['tærɪf] *n* tarifa.
tariff barrier *n* (*COMM*) barrera
arancelaria.
tarmac ['tɑːmæk] *n* (*BRIT: on road*)
alquitranado; (*AVIAT*) pista (de
aterrizaje).
tarn [tɑːn] *n* lago pequeño de montaña.
tarnish ['tɑːnɪʃ] *vt* deslustrar.
tarot ['tærəu] *n* tarot *m.*
tarpaulin [tɑː'pɔːlɪn] *n* alquitranado.
tarragon ['tærəgən] *n* estragón *m.*
tarry ['tærɪ] *vi* entretenerse, quedarse
atrás.
tart [tɑːt] *n* (*CULIN*) tarta; (*BRIT col. pej:*
woman) fulana ♦ *adj* (*flavour*) agrio, ácido.
►**tart up** *vt* (*room, building*) dar tono a.
tartan ['tɑːtn] *n* tartán *m* ♦ *adj* de tartán.
tartar ['tɑːtə*] *n* (*on teeth*) sarro.

tartar sauce *n* salsa tártara.
tartly ['tɑːtlɪ] *adv* (*answer*) ásperamente.
task [tɑːsk] *n* tarea; **to take to** ~ reprender.
task force *n* (*MIL, POLICE*) grupo de operaciones.
taskmaster ['tɑːskmɑːstə*] *n*: **he's a hard** ~ es muy exigente.
Tasmania [tæz'meɪnɪə] *n* Tasmania.
tassel ['tæsl] *n* borla.
taste [teɪst] *n* sabor *m*, gusto; (*also*: **after**~) dejo; (*sip*) sorbo; (*fig*: *glimpse, idea*) muestra, idea ♦ *vt* probar ♦ *vi*: **to** ~ **of** *or* **like** (*fish etc*) saber a; **you can** ~ **the garlic** (**in it**) se nota el sabor a ajo; **can I have a** ~ **of this wine?** ¿puedo probar este vino?; **to have a** ~ **for sth** ser aficionado a algo; **in good/bad** ~ de buen/mal gusto; **to be in bad** *or* **poor** ~ ser de mal gusto.
taste bud *n* papila gustativa *or* del gusto.
tasteful ['teɪstful] *adj* de buen gusto.
tastefully ['teɪstfulɪ] *adv* elegantemente, con buen gusto.
tasteless ['teɪstlɪs] *adj* (*food*) soso; (*remark*) de mal gusto.
tastelessly ['teɪstlɪslɪ] *adv* con mal gusto.
tastily ['teɪstɪlɪ] *adv* sabrosamente.
tastiness ['teɪstɪnɪs] *n* (buen) sabor *m*, lo sabroso.
tasty ['teɪstɪ] *adj* sabroso, rico.
ta-ta ['tæ'tɑː] *interj* (*BRIT col*) hasta luego, adiós.
tatters ['tætəz] *npl*: **in** ~ (*also*: **tattered**) hecho jirones.
tattoo [tə'tuː] *n* tatuaje *m*; (*spectacle*) espectáculo militar ♦ *vt* tatuar.
tatty ['tætɪ] *adj* (*BRIT col*) cochambroso.
taught [tɔːt] *pt, pp* **of teach**.
taunt [tɔːnt] *n* pulla ♦ *vt* lanzar pullas a.
Taurus ['tɔːrəs] *n* Tauro.
taut [tɔːt] *adj* tirante, tenso.
tavern ['tævən] *n* (*old*) posada, fonda.
tawdry ['tɔːdrɪ] *adj* de mal gusto.
tawny ['tɔːnɪ] *adj* leonado.
tax [tæks] *n* impuesto ♦ *vt* gravar (con un impuesto); (*fig*: *test*) poner a prueba; (: *patience*) agotar; **before/after** ~ impuestos excluidos/incluidos; **free of** ~ libre de impuestos.
taxable ['tæksəbl] *adj* (*income*) imponible, sujeto a impuestos.
tax allowance *n* desgravación *f* fiscal.
taxation [tæk'seɪʃən] *n* impuestos *mpl*; **system of** ~ sistema *m* tributario.
tax avoidance *n* evasión *f* de impuestos.
tax collector *n* recaudador(a) *m/f*.
tax disc *n* (*BRIT AUT*) pegatina del impuesto de circulación.
tax evasion *n* evasión *f* fiscal.

tax exemption *n* exención *f* de impuestos.
tax-free ['tæksfriː] *adj* libre de impuestos.
tax haven *n* paraíso fiscal.
taxi ['tæksɪ] *n* taxi *m* ♦ *vi* (*AVIAT*) rodar por la pista.
taxidermist ['tæksɪdəːmɪst] *n* taxidermista *m/f*.
taxi driver *n* taxista *m/f*.
tax inspector *n* inspector(a) *m/f* de Hacienda.
taxi rank (*BRIT*), **taxi stand** *n* parada de taxis.
tax payer *n* contribuyente *m/f*.
tax rebate *n* devolución *f* de impuestos, reembolso fiscal.
tax relief *n* desgravación *f* fiscal.
tax return *n* declaración *f* de la renta.
tax shelter *n* protección *f* fiscal.
tax year *n* año fiscal.
TB *n abbr* = **tuberculosis**.
TD *n abbr* (*US*) = **Treasury Department**; (: *FOOTBALL*) = **touchdown**.
tea [tiː] *n* té *m*; (*BRIT*: *snack*) ≈ merienda; **high** ~ (*BRIT*) ≈ merienda-cena.
tea bag *n* bolsita de té.
tea break *n* (*BRIT*) descanso para el té.
teacake ['tiːkeɪk] *n* bollito, queque *m* (*LAM*).
teach, *pt, pp* **taught** [tiːtʃ, tɔːt] *vt*: **to** ~ **sb sth,** ~ **sth to sb** enseñar algo a algn ♦ *vi* enseñar; (*be a teacher*) ser profesor(a); **it taught him a lesson** (eso) le sirvió de escarmiento.
teacher ['tiːtʃə*] *n* (*in secondary school*) profesor(a) *m/f*; (*in primary school*) maestro/a; **Spanish** ~ profesor(a) *m/f* de español.
teacher training college *n* (*for primary schools*) escuela normal; (*for secondary schools*) centro de formación del profesorado.
teach-in ['tiːtʃɪn] *n* seminario.
teaching ['tiːtʃɪŋ] *n* enseñanza.
teaching aids *npl* materiales *mpl* pedagógicos.
teaching hospital *n* hospital universitario.
tea cosy *n* cubretetera *m*.
teacup ['tiːkʌp] *n* taza de té.
teak [tiːk] *n* (madera de) teca.
tea leaves *npl* hojas *fpl* de té.
team [tiːm] *n* equipo; (*of animals*) pareja.
▶**team up** *vi* asociarse.
team spirit *n* espíritu *m* de equipo.
teamwork ['tiːmwəːk] *n* trabajo en equipo.
tea party *n* té *m*.
teapot ['tiːpɔt] *n* tetera.
tear [tɛə*] *n* rasgón *m*, desgarrón *m*; [tɪə*] lágrima ♦ *vb* [tɛə*] (*pt* **tore,** *pp* **torn** [tɔː*,

tɔːn]) *vt* romper, rasgar ♦ *vi* rasgarse; **in ~s** llorando; **to burst into ~s** deshacerse en lágrimas; **to ~ to pieces** *or* **to bits** *or* **to shreds** (*also fig*) hacer pedazos, destrozar.
►**tear along** *vi* (*rush*) precipitarse.
►**tear apart** *vt* (*also fig*) hacer pedazos.
►**tear away** *vt*: **to ~ o.s. away (from sth)** alejarse (de algo).
►**tear out** *vt* (*sheet, cheque*) arrancar.
►**tear up** *vt* (*sheet of paper etc*) romper.
tearaway ['tɛərəweɪ] *n* (*col*) gamberro/a.
teardrop ['tɪədrɔp] *n* lágrima.
tearful ['tɪəful] *adj* lloroso.
tear gas *n* gas *m* lacrimógeno.
tearing ['tɛərɪŋ] *adj*: **to be in a ~ hurry** tener muchísima prisa.
tearoom ['tiːruːm] *n* salón *m* de té.
tease [tiːz] *n* bromista *m/f* ♦ *vt* tomar el pelo a.
tea set *n* servicio de té.
teashop ['tiːʃɔp] *n* café *m*, cafetería.
Teasmaid ® ['tiːzmeɪd] *n* tetera automática.
teaspoon ['tiːspuːn] *n* cucharita; (*also: ~ful: as measurement*) cucharadita.
tea strainer *n* colador *m* de té.
teat [tiːt] *n* (*of bottle*) boquilla, tetilla.
teatime ['tiːtaɪm] *n* hora del té.
tea towel *n* (*BRIT*) paño de cocina.
tea urn *n* tetera grande.
tech [tɛk] *n abbr* (*col*) = **technology; technical college**.
technical ['tɛknɪkl] *adj* técnico.
technical college *n* centro de formación profesional.
technicality [tɛknɪˈkælɪtɪ] *n* detalle *m* técnico; **on a legal ~** por una cuestión formal.
technically ['tɛknɪklɪ] *adv* técnicamente.
technician [tɛkˈnɪʃn] *n* técnico/a.
technique [tɛkˈniːk] *n* técnica.
techno ['tɛknəʊ] *n* (*MUS*) (música) tecno.
technocrat ['tɛknəkræt] *n* tecnócrata *m/f*.
technological [tɛknəˈlɔdʒɪkl] *adj* tecnológico.
technologist [tɛkˈnɔlədʒɪst] *n* tecnólogo/a.
technology [tɛkˈnɔlədʒɪ] *n* tecnología.
teddy (bear) ['tɛdɪ-] *n* osito de peluche.
tedious ['tiːdɪəs] *adj* pesado, aburrido.
tedium ['tiːdɪəm] *n* tedio.
tee [tiː] *n* (*GOLF*) tee *m*.
teem [tiːm] *vi*: **to ~ with** rebosar de; **it is ~ing (with rain)** llueve a mares.
teenage ['tiːneɪdʒ] *adj* (*fashions etc*) juvenil.
teenager ['tiːneɪdʒə*] *n* adolescente *m/f*.
teens [tiːnz] *npl*: **to be in one's ~** ser adolescente.

tee-shirt ['tiːʃəːt] *n* = **T-shirt**.
teeter ['tiːtə*] *vi* balancearse.
teeth [tiːθ] *npl of* **tooth**.
teethe [tiːð] *vi* echar los dientes.
teething ring ['tiːðɪŋ-] *n* mordedor *m*.
teething troubles ['tiːðɪŋ-] *npl* (*fig*) dificultades *fpl* iniciales.
teetotal ['tiːˈtəʊtl] *adj* (*person*) abstemio.
teetotaller, (*US*) **teetotaler** ['tiːˈtəʊtlə*] *n* (*person*) abstemio/a.
TEFL ['tɛfl] *n abbr* = *Teaching of English as a Foreign Language*; **~ qualification** título para la enseñanza del inglés como lengua extranjera.
Teflon ® ['tɛflɔn] *n* tefflón *m* ®.
Teheran [tɛəˈrɑːn] *n* Teherán *m*.
tel. *abbr* (= *telephone*) tel.
Tel Aviv ['tɛləˈviːv] *n* Tel Aviv *m*.
telecast ['tɛlɪkɑːst] *vt, vi* transmitir por televisión.
telecommunications ['tɛlɪkəmjuːnɪˈkeɪʃənz] *n* telecomunicaciones *fpl*.
teleconferencing [tɛlɪˈkɔnfərənsɪŋ] *n* teleconferencias *fpl*.
telefax ['tɛlɪfæks] *n* telefax *m*.
telegram ['tɛlɪɡræm] *n* telegrama *m*.
telegraph ['tɛlɪɡrɑːf] *n* telégrafo.
telegraphic [tɛlɪˈɡræfɪk] *adj* telegráfico.
telegraph pole *n* poste *m* telegráfico.
telegraph wire *n* hilo telegráfico.
telepathic [tɛlɪˈpæθɪk] *adj* telepático.
telepathy [təˈlɛpəθɪ] *n* telepatía.
telephone ['tɛlɪfəʊn] *n* teléfono ♦ *vt* llamar por teléfono, telefonear; **to be on the ~** (*subscriber*) tener teléfono; (*be speaking*) estar hablando por teléfono.
telephone booth, (*BRIT*) **telephone box** *n* cabina telefónica.
telephone call *n* llamada telefónica.
telephone directory *n* guía telefónica.
telephone exchange *n* central *f* telefónica.
telephone number *n* número de teléfono.
telephonist [təˈlɛfənɪst] *n* (*BRIT*) telefonista *m/f*.
telephoto ['tɛlɪˈfəʊtəʊ] *adj*: **~ lens** teleobjetivo.
teleprinter ['tɛlɪprɪntə*] *n* teletipo, teleimpresora.
teleprompter ® ['tɛlɪprɔmptə*] *n* teleapuntador *m*.
telesales ['tɛlɪseɪlz] *npl* televentas *fpl*.
telescope ['tɛlɪskəʊp] *n* telescopio.
telescopic [tɛlɪˈskɔpɪk] *adj* telescópico; (*umbrella*) plegable.
Teletext ® ['tɛlɪtɛkst] *n* teletexto *m*.
telethon ['tɛlɪθɔn] *n* telemaratón *m*,

maratón *m* televisivo (*con fines benéficos*).
televise ['tɛlɪvaɪz] *vt* televisar.
television ['tɛlɪvɪʒən] *n* televisión *f*; **to watch ~** mirar *or* ver la televisión.
television licence *n* impuesto por uso de televisor.
television set *n* televisor *m*.
teleworking ['tɛlɪ,wɜːkɪŋ] *n* teletrabajo.
telex ['tɛlɛks] *n* télex *m* ♦ *vt* (*message*) enviar por télex; (*person*) enviar un télex a ♦ *vi* enviar un télex.
tell *pt, pp* **told** [tɛl, təʊld] *vt* decir; (*relate*: *story*) contar; (*distinguish*): **to ~ sth from** distinguir algo de ♦ *vi* (*talk*): **to ~ (of)** contar; (*have effect*) tener efecto; **to ~ sb to do sth** decir a algn que haga algo; **to ~ sb about sth** contar algo a algn; **to ~ the time** dar *or* decir la hora; **can you ~ me the time?** ¿me puedes decir la hora?; (**I) ~ you what ...** fíjate ...; **I couldn't ~ them apart** no podía distinguirlos.
►**tell off** *vt*: **to ~ sb off** regañar a algn.
►**tell on** *vt fus*: **to ~ on sb** chivarse de algn.
teller ['tɛlə*] *n* (*in bank*) cajero/a.
telling ['tɛlɪŋ] *adj* (*remark, detail*) revelador(a).
telltale ['tɛlteɪl] *adj* (*sign*) indicador(a).
telly ['tɛlɪ] *n* (*BRIT col*) tele *f*.
temerity [tə'mɛrɪtɪ] *n* temeridad *f*.
temp [tɛmp] *n abbr* (*BRIT*: = *temporary office worker*) empleado/a eventual ♦ *vi* trabajar como empleado/a eventual.
temper ['tɛmpə*] *n* (*mood*) humor *m*; (*bad ~*) (*mal*) genio; (*fit of anger*) ira; (*of child*) rabieta ♦ *vt* (*moderate*) moderar; **to be in a ~** estar furioso; **to lose one's ~** enfadarse, enojarse (*LAM*); **to keep one's ~** contenerse, no alterarse.
temperament ['tɛmprəmənt] *n* (*nature*) temperamento.
temperamental [tɛmprə'mɛntl] *adj* temperamental.
temperance ['tɛmpərns] *n* moderación *f*; (*in drinking*) sobriedad *f*.
temperate ['tɛmprət] *adj* moderado; (*climate*) templado.
temperature ['tɛmprətʃə*] *n* temperatura; **to have** *or* **run a ~** tener fiebre.
tempered ['tɛmpəd] *adj* (*steel*) templado.
tempest ['tɛmpɪst] *n* tempestad *f*.
tempestuous [tɛm'pɛstjʊəs] *adj* (*relationship, meeting*) tempestuoso.
tempi ['tɛmpiː] *npl of* **tempo**.
template ['tɛmplɪt] *n* plantilla.
temple ['tɛmpl] *n* (*REL*) templo; (*ANAT*) sien *f*.
templet ['tɛmplɪt] *n* = **template**.
tempo, *pl* **~s** *or* **tempi** ['tɛmpəʊ, 'tɛmpiː] *n* tempo; (*fig: of life etc*) ritmo.

temporal ['tɛmpərl] *adj* temporal.
temporarily ['tɛmpərərɪlɪ] *adv* temporalmente.
temporary ['tɛmpərərɪ] *adj* provisional, temporal; (*passing*) transitorio; (*worker*) eventual; **~ teacher** maestro/a interino/a.
tempt [tɛmpt] *vt* tentar; **to ~ sb into doing sth** tentar *or* inducir a algn a hacer algo; **to be ~ed to do sth** (*person*) sentirse tentado de hacer algo.
temptation [tɛmp'teɪʃən] *n* tentación *f*.
tempting ['tɛmptɪŋ] *adj* tentador(a).
ten [tɛn] *num* diez; **~s of thousands** decenas *fpl* de miles.
tenable ['tɛnəbl] *adj* sostenible.
tenacious [tə'neɪʃəs] *adj* tenaz.
tenaciously [tə'neɪʃəslɪ] *adv* tenazmente.
tenacity [tə'næsɪtɪ] *n* tenacidad *f*.
tenancy ['tɛnənsɪ] *n* alquiler *m*.
tenant ['tɛnənt] *n* (*rent-payer*) inquilino/a; (*occupant*) habitante *m/f*.
tend [tɛnd] *vt* (*sick etc*) cuidar, atender; (*cattle, machine*) vigilar, cuidar ♦ *vi*: **to ~ to do sth** tener tendencia a hacer algo.
tendency ['tɛndənsɪ] *n* tendencia.
tender ['tɛndə*] *adj* tierno, blando; (*delicate*) delicado; (*sore*) sensible; (*affectionate*) tierno, cariñoso ♦ *n* (*COMM*: *offer*) oferta; (*money*): **legal ~** moneda de curso legal ♦ *vt* ofrecer; **to put in a ~ (for)** hacer una oferta (para); **to put work out to ~** ofrecer un trabajo a contrata; **to ~ one's resignation** presentar la dimisión.
tenderize ['tɛndəraɪz] *vt* (*CULIN*) ablandar.
tenderly ['tɛndəlɪ] *adv* tiernamente.
tenderness ['tɛndənɪs] *n* ternura; (*of meat*) blandura.
tendon ['tɛndən] *n* tendón *m*.
tendril ['tɛndrɪl] *n* zarcillo.
tenement ['tɛnəmənt] *n* casa *or* bloque *m* de pisos *or* vecinos (*LAM*).
Tenerife [tɛnə'riːf] *n* Tenerife *m*.
tenet ['tɛnət] *n* principio.
Tenn. *abbr* (*US*) = *Tennessee*.
tenner ['tɛnə*] *n* (billete *m* de) diez libras *fpl*.
tennis ['tɛnɪs] *n* tenis *m*.
tennis ball *n* pelota de tenis.
tennis club *n* club *m* de tenis.
tennis court *n* cancha de tenis.
tennis elbow *n* (*MED*) sinovitis *f* del codo.
tennis match *n* partido de tenis.
tennis player *n* tenista *m/f*.
tennis racket *n* raqueta de tenis.
tennis shoes *npl* zapatillas *fpl* de tenis.
tenor ['tɛnə*] *n* (*MUS*) tenor *m*.
tenpin bowling ['tɛnpɪn-] *n* bolos *mpl*.
tense [tɛns] *adj* tenso; (*stretched*) tirante;

(*stiff*) rígido, tieso; (*person*) nervioso ♦ *n*
(*LING*) tiempo ♦ *vt* (*tighten: muscles*)
tensar.
tensely ['tɛnslɪ] *adv*: **they waited** ~
esperaban tensos.
tenseness ['tɛnsnɪs] *n* tirantez *f*, tensión *f*.
tension ['tɛnʃən] *n* tensión *f*.
tent [tɛnt] *n* tienda (de campaña), carpa
(*LAM*).
tentacle ['tɛntəkl] *n* tentáculo.
tentative ['tɛntətɪv] *adj* (*person*) indeciso;
(*provisional*) provisional.
tentatively ['tɛntətɪvlɪ] *adv* con indecisión;
(*provisionally*) provisionalmente.
tenterhooks ['tɛntəhuks] *npl*: **on** ~ sobre
ascuas.
tenth [tɛnθ] *adj* décimo.
tent peg *n* clavija, estaca.
tent pole *n* mástil *m*.
tenuous ['tɛnjuəs] *adj* tenue.
tenure ['tɛnjuə*] *n* posesión *f*, tenencia; **to**
have ~ tener posesión *or* título de
propiedad.
tepid ['tɛpɪd] *adj* tibio.
term [təːm] *n* (*limit*) límite *m*; (*COMM*) plazo;
(*word*) término; (*period*) período; (*SCOL*)
trimestre *m* ♦ *vt* llamar, calificar de; ~**s**
npl (*conditions*) condiciones *fpl*; (*COMM*)
precio, tarifa; **in the short/long** ~ a
corto/largo plazo; **during his** ~ **of office**
bajo su mandato; **to be on good** ~**s with**
sb llevarse bien con algn; **to come to** ~**s**
with (*problem*) aceptar; **in** ~**s of** ... en
cuanto a ..., en términos de ....
terminal ['təːmɪnl] *adj* terminal ♦ *n* (*ELEC*)
borne *m*; (*COMPUT*) terminal *m*; (*also*: **air**
~) terminal *f*; (*BRIT: also*: **coach** ~)
(estación *f*) terminal *f*.
terminate ['təːmɪneɪt] *vt* poner término a;
(*pregnancy*) interrumpir ♦ *vi*: **to** ~ **in**
acabar en.
termination [təːmɪ'neɪʃən] *n* fin *m*; (*of*
contract) terminación *f*; ~ **of pregnancy**
interrupción *f* del embarazo.
termini ['təːmɪnaɪ] *npl of* **terminus**.
terminology [təːmɪ'nɔlədʒɪ] *n*
terminología.
terminus, *pl* **termini** ['təːmɪnəs, 'təːmɪnaɪ] *n*
término, (estación *f*) terminal *f*.
termite ['təːmaɪt] *n* termita, comején *m*.
term paper *n* (*US UNIV*) trabajo escrito
trimestral *or* semestral.
Ter(r). *abbr* = **terrace.**
terrace ['tɛrəs] *n* terraza; (*BRIT: row of*
houses) hilera de casas adosadas; **the** ~**s**
(*BRIT SPORT*) las gradas *fpl*.
terraced ['tɛrəst] *adj* (*garden*) escalonado;
(*house*) adosado.

terracotta ['tɛrə'kɔtə] *n* terracota.
terrain [tɛ'reɪn] *n* terreno.
terrible ['tɛrɪbl] *adj* terrible, horrible; (*fam*)
malísimo.
terribly ['tɛrɪblɪ] *adv* terriblemente; (*very*
badly) malísimamente.
terrier ['tɛrɪə*] *n* terrier *m*.
terrific [tə'rɪfɪk] *adj* fantástico, fenomenal,
macanudo (*LAM*); (*wonderful*) maravilloso.
terrify ['tɛrɪfaɪ] *vt* aterrorizar; **to be**
terrified estar aterrado *or* aterrorizado.
terrifying ['tɛrɪfaɪɪŋ] *adj* aterrador(a).
territorial [tɛrɪ'tɔːrɪəl] *adj* territorial.
territorial waters *npl* aguas *fpl*
jurisdiccionales.
territory ['tɛrɪtərɪ] *n* territorio.
terror ['tɛrə*] *n* terror *m*.
terrorism ['tɛrərɪzəm] *n* terrorismo.
terrorist ['tɛrərɪst] *n* terrorista *m/f*.
terrorize ['tɛrəraɪz] *vt* aterrorizar.
terse [təːs] *adj* (*style*) conciso; (*reply*)
brusco.
tertiary ['təːʃərɪ] *adj* terciario; ~ **education**
enseñanza superior.
Terylene ® ['tɛrəliːn] *n* (*BRIT*) terylene *m* ®.
TESL [tɛsl] *n abbr* – *Teaching of English as a*
Second Language.
TESSA ['tɛsə] *n abbr* (*BRIT*: = *Tax Exempt*
Special Savings Account) plan de ahorro
por el que se invierte a largo plazo a
cambio de intereses libres de impuestos.
test [tɛst] *n* (*trial, check*) prueba, ensayo; (:
of goods in factory) control *m*; (*of courage*
etc, CHEM, MED) prueba; (*of blood, urine*)
análisis *m inv*; (*exam*) examen *m*, test *m*;
(*also*: **driving** ~) examen *m* de conducir
♦ *vt* probar, poner a prueba; (*MED*)
examinar; (: *blood*) analizar; **to put sth to**
the ~ someter algo a prueba; **to** ~ **sth for**
sth analizar algo en busca de algo.
testament ['tɛstəmənt] *n* testamento; **the**
Old/New T~ el Antiguo/Nuevo
Testamento.
test ban *n* (*also*: **nuclear** ~) suspensión *f* de
pruebas nucleares.
test card *n* (*TV*) carta de ajuste.
test case *n* (*JUR*) juicio que sienta
precedente.
testes ['tɛstiːz] *npl* testes *mpl*.
test flight *n* vuelo de ensayo.
testicle ['tɛstɪkl] *n* testículo.
testify ['tɛstɪfaɪ] *vi* (*LAW*) prestar
declaración; **to** ~ **to sth** atestiguar algo.
testimonial [tɛstɪ'məunɪəl] *n* (*of character*)
(carta de) recomendación *f*.
testimony ['tɛstɪmənɪ] *n* (*LAW*) testimonio,
declaración *f*.
testing ['tɛstɪŋ] *adj* (*difficult: time*) duro.

test match n (*CRICKET, RUGBY*) partido internacional.
testosterone [tɛs'tɔstərəun] n testosterona.
test paper n examen m, test m.
test pilot n piloto m/f de pruebas.
test tube n probeta.
test-tube baby n bebé m probeta inv.
tetanus ['tɛtənəs] n tétano.
tetchy ['tɛtʃɪ] adj irritable.
tether ['tɛðə*] vt atar (con una cuerda) ♦ n: **to be at the end of one's** ~ no aguantar más.
Tex. abbr (*US*) = *Texas*.
text [tɛkst] n texto.
textbook ['tɛkstbuk] n libro de texto.
textiles ['tɛkstaɪlz] npl tejidos mpl.
textual ['tɛkstjuəl] adj del texto, textual.
texture ['tɛkstʃə*] n textura.
TGWU n abbr (*BRIT*: = *Transport and General Workers' Union*) sindicato de transportistas.
Thai [taɪ] adj, n tailandés/esa m/f.
Thailand ['taɪlænd] n Tailandia.
Thames [tɛmz] n: **the** ~ el (río) Támesis.
than [ðæn, ðən] conj que; (*with numerals*): **more** ~ **10/once** más de 10/una vez; **I have more/less** ~ **you** tengo más/menos que tú; **it is better to phone** ~ **to write** es mejor llamar por teléfono que escribir; **no sooner did he leave** ~ **the phone rang** en cuanto se marchó, sonó el teléfono.
thank [θæŋk] vt dar las gracias a, agradecer; ~ **you (very much)** muchas gracias; ~ **heavens,** ~ **God!** ¡gracias a Dios!, ¡menos mal!
thankful ['θæŋkful] adj: ~ **for** agradecido (por).
thankfully ['θæŋkfəlɪ] adv (*gratefully*) con agradecimiento; (*with relief*) por suerte; ~ **there were few victims** afortunadamente hubo pocas víctimas.
thankless ['θæŋklɪs] adj ingrato.
thanks [θæŋks] npl gracias fpl ♦ excl ¡gracias!; ~ **to** prep gracias a.
Thanksgiving (Day) ['θæŋksgɪvɪŋ-] n día m de Acción de Gracias; ver recuadro.

┌─────────────────────────────┐
│ **THANKSGIVING DAY** │
└─────────────────────────────┘

En Estados Unidos el cuarto jueves de noviembre es **Thanksgiving Day**, *fiesta oficial en la que se conmemora la celebración que tuvieron los primeros colonos norteamericanos ("Pilgrims" o "Pilgrim Fathers") tras la estupenda cosecha de 1621, por la que se dan gracias a Dios. En Canadá se celebra una fiesta semejante el segundo lunes de octubre, aunque no está relacionada con dicha fecha histórica.*

═══════════════════════ *KEYWORD*

that [ðæt](*pl* **those**) adj (*demonstrative*) ese/a, pl esos/as; (*more remote*) aquel/aquella, pl aquellos/as; **leave those books on the table** deja esos libros sobre la mesa; ~ **one** ése/ésa; (*more remote*) aquél/aquélla; ~ **one over there** ése/ésa de ahí; aquél/aquélla de allí
♦ pron **1** (*demonstrative*) ése/a, pl ésos/as; (*neuter*) eso; (*more remote*) aquél/aquélla, pl aquéllos/as; (*neuter*) aquello; **what's** ~? ¿qué es eso (*or* aquello)?; **who's** ~? ¿quién es?; (*when pointing etc*) ¿quién es ése/a?; **is** ~ **you?** ¿eres tú?; **will you eat all** ~? ¿vas a comer todo eso?; ~'**s my house** ésa es mi casa; ~'**s what he said** eso es lo que dijo; ~ **is (to say)** es decir; **at** *or* **with** ~ **she ...** en eso, ella ...; **do it like** ~ hazlo así
2 (*relative: subject, object*) que; (*with preposition*) (el/la) que, el/la cual; **the book (**~**) I read** el libro que leí; **the books** ~ **are in the library** los libros que están en la biblioteca; **all (**~**) I have** todo lo que tengo; **the box (**~**) I put it in** la caja en la que *or* donde lo puse; **the people (**~**) I spoke to** la gente con la que hablé; **not** ~ **I know of** que yo sepa, no
3 (*relative: of time*) que; **the day (**~**) he came** el día (en) que vino
♦ conj que; **he thought** ~ **I was ill** creyó que yo estaba enfermo
♦ adv (*demonstrative*): **I can't work** ~ **much** no puedo trabajar tanto; **I didn't realise it was** ~ **bad** no creí que fuera tan malo; ~ **high** así de alto.

thatched [θætʃt] adj (*roof*) de paja; ~ **cottage** casita con tejado de paja.
Thatcherism ['θætʃərɪzəm] n thatcherismo.
thaw [θɔ:] n deshielo ♦ vi (*ice*) derretirse; (*food*) descongelarse ♦ vt (*food*) descongelar.

═══════════════════════ *KEYWORD*

the [ðiː, ðə] def art **1** (*gen*) el, f la, pl los, fpl las (*NB* = *el immediately before feminine noun beginning with stressed (h)a; a+el* = *al; de+el* = *del*); ~ **boy/girl** el chico/la chica; ~ **books/flowers** los libros/las flores; **to** ~ **postman/from** ~ **drawer** al cartero/del cajón; **I haven't** ~ **time/money** no tengo tiempo/dinero; **100 pesetas to** ~ **dollar**

100 pesetas por dólar; **paid by** ~ **hour**
pagado por hora
2 (+*adj to form noun*) los; lo; ~ **rich**
and ~ **poor** los ricos y los pobres; **to**
attempt ~ **impossible** intentar lo
imposible
3 (*in titles, surnames*): **Elizabeth** ~ **First**
Isabel Primera; **Peter** ~ **Great** Pedro el
Grande; **do you know** ~ **Smiths?** ¿conoce
a los Smith?
4 (*in comparisons*): ~ **more he works** ~
more he earns cuanto más trabaja más
gana.

theatre, (*US*) **theater** ['θɪətə*] *n*
teatro.
theatre-goer, (*US*) **theater-goer**
['θɪətəgəʊə*] *n* aficionado/a al teatro.
theatrical [θɪ'ætrɪkl] *adj* teatral.
theft [θɛft] *n* robo.
their [ðɛə*] *adj* su.
theirs [ðɛəz] *pron* (el) suyo/(la) suya *etc*; *see*
also **my, mine.**
them [ðɛm, ðəm] *pron* (*direct*) los/las;
(*indirect*) les; (*stressed, after prep*) ellos/
ellas; **I see** ~ los veo; **both of** ~ ambos/as,
los/las dos; **give me a few of** ~ dame
algunos/as; *see also* **me.**
theme [θiːm] *n* tema *m*.
theme park *n* parque *m* temático.
theme song *n* tema *m* (musical).
themselves [ðəm'sɛlvz] *pl pron* (*subject*)
ellos mismos/ellas mismas; (*complement*)
se; (*after prep*) sí (mismos/as); *see also*
oneself.
then [ðɛn] *adv* (*at that time*) entonces; (*next*)
pues; (*later*) luego, después; (*and also*)
además ♦ *conj* (*therefore*) en ese caso,
entonces ♦ *adj*: **the** ~ **president** el
entonces presidente; **from** ~ **on** desde
entonces; **until** ~ hasta entonces; **and** ~
what? y luego, ¿qué?; **what do you want**
me to do, ~**?** ¿entonces, qué quiere que
haga?
theologian [θɪə'ləʊdʒən] *n* teólogo/a.
theological [θɪə'lɒdʒɪkl] *adj* teológico.
theology [θɪ'ɒlədʒɪ] *n* teología.
theorem ['θɪərəm] *n* teorema *m*.
theoretical [θɪə'rɛtɪkl] *adj* teórico.
theoretically [θɪə'rɛtɪklɪ] *adv* teóricamente,
en teoría.
theorize ['θɪəraɪz] *vi* teorizar.
theory ['θɪərɪ] *n* teoría.
therapeutic(al) [θɛrə'pjuːtɪk(l)] *adj*
terapéutico.
therapist ['θɛrəpɪst] *n* terapeuta
m/f.
therapy ['θɛrəpɪ] *n* terapia.

═══════════════════════ KEYWORD

there ['ðɛə*] *adv* **1**: ~ **is,** ~ **are** hay; ~ **is no-**
one here no hay nadie aquí; ~ **is no bread**
left no queda pan; ~ **has been an accident**
ha habido un accidente
2 (*referring to place*) ahí; (*distant*) allí; **it's**
~ está ahí; **put it in/on/up/down** ~ ponlo
ahí dentro/encima/arriba/abajo; **I want**
that book ~ quiero ese libro de ahí; ~ **he**
is! ¡ahí está!; ~**'s the bus** ahí *or* ya viene
el autobús; **back/down** ~ allí atrás/abajo;
over ~, **through** ~ por allí
3: ~, ~ (*esp to child*) ¡venga, venga!

thereabouts ['ðɛərə'baʊts] *adv* por ahí.
thereafter [ðɛər'ɑːftə*] *adv* después.
thereby ['ðɛəbaɪ] *adv* así, de ese modo.
therefore ['ðɛəfɔː*] *adv* por lo tanto.
there's [ðɛəz] = **there is; there has.**
thereupon [ðɛərə'pɒn] *adv* (*at that point*) en
eso, en seguida.
thermal ['θəːml] *adj* termal.
thermal paper *n* papel *m* térmico.
thermal printer *n* termoimpresora.
thermodynamics ['θəːmədaɪnæmɪks] *n*
termodinámica.
thermometer [θə'mɒmɪtə*] *n* termómetro.
thermonuclear [θəːməʊ'njuːklɪə*] *adj*
termonuclear.
Thermos ® ['θəːməs] *n* (*also*: ~ **flask**)
termo.
thermostat ['θəːməʊstæt] *n* termostato.
thesaurus [θɪ'sɔːrəs] *n* tesoro, diccionario
de sinónimos.
these [ðiːz] *pl adj* estos/as ♦ *pl pron* éstos/as.
thesis, *pl* **theses** ['θiːsɪs, -siːz] *n* tesis *f inv*;
see also **doctorate.**
they [ðeɪ] *pl pron* ellos/ellas; ~ **say that ...** (*it*
is said that) se dice que ....
they'd [ðeɪd] = **they had; they would.**
they'll [ðeɪl] = **they shall, they will.**
they're [ðɛə*] = **they are.**
they've [ðeɪv] = **they have.**
thick [θɪk] *adj* (*wall, slice*) grueso; (*dense:*
liquid, smoke etc) espeso; (*vegetation,*
beard) tupido; (*stupid*) torpe ♦ *n*: **in the** ~
of the battle en lo más reñido de la
batalla; **it's 20 cm** ~ tiene 20 cm de
espesor.
thicken ['θɪkn] *vi* espesarse ♦ *vt* (*sauce etc*)
espesar.
thicket ['θɪkɪt] *n* espesura.
thickly ['θɪklɪ] *adv* (*spread*) en capa espesa;
(*cut*) en rebanada gruesa; (*populated*)
densamente.
thickness ['θɪknɪs] *n* espesor *m*, grueso.
thickset [θɪk'sɛt] *adj* fornido.

thickskinned [θɪk'skɪnd] *adj* (*fig*) insensible.
thief, *pl* **thieves** [θiːf, θiːvz] *n* ladrón/ona *m/f*.
thieving ['θiːvɪŋ] *n* tobo, hurto ♦ *adj* ladrón/ona.
thigh [θaɪ] *n* muslo.
thighbone ['θaɪbəʊn] *n* fémur *m*.
thimble ['θɪmbl] *n* dedal *m*.
thin [θɪn] *adj* delgado; (*wall, layer*) fino; (*watery*) aguado; (*light*) tenue; (*hair*) escaso; (*fog*) ligero; (*crowd*) disperso ♦ *vt*: **to ~ (down)** (*sauce, paint*) diluir ♦ *vi* (*fog*) aclararse; (*also*: **~ out:** *crowd*) dispersarse; **his hair is ~ning** se está quedando calvo.
thing [θɪŋ] *n* cosa; (*object*) objeto, artículo; (*contraption*) chisme *m*; (*mania*) manía; **~s** *npl* (*belongings*) cosas *fpl*; **the best ~ would be to...** lo mejor sería...; **the main ~ is ...** lo principal es ...; **first ~ (in the morning)** a primera hora (de la mañana); **last ~ (at night)** a última hora (de la noche); **the ~ is ...** lo que pasa es que ...; **how are ~s?** ¿qué tal van las cosas?; **she's got a ~ about mice** le dan no sé qué los ratones; **poor ~!** ¡pobre! *m/f*, ¡pobrecito/a!
think, *pt, pp* **thought** [θɪŋk, θɔːt] *vi* pensar ♦ *vt* pensar, creer; (*imagine*) imaginar; **what did you ~ of it?** ¿qué te parece?; **what did you ~ of them?** ¿qué te parecieron?; **to ~ about sth/sb** pensar en algo/uno; **I'll ~ about it** lo pensaré; **to ~ of doing sth** pensar en hacer algo; **I ~ so/ not** creo que sí/no; **~ again!** ¡piénsalo bien!; **to ~ aloud** pensar en voz alta; **to ~ well of sb** tener buen concepto de algn.
▶**think out** *vt* (*plan*) elaborar, tramar; (*solution*) encontrar.
▶**think over** *vt* reflexionar sobre, meditar; **I'd like to ~ things over** me gustaría pensármelo.
▶**think through** *vt* pensar bien.
▶**think up** *vt* imaginar.
thinking ['θɪŋkɪŋ] *n*: **to my (way of) ~** a mi parecer.
think tank *n* grupo de expertos.
thinly ['θɪnlɪ] *adv* (*cut*) en lonchas finas; (*spread*) en una capa fina.
thinness ['θɪnnɪs] *n* delgadez *f*.
third [θɜːd] *adj* (*before nmsg*: **tercer**) tercero ♦ *n* tercero/a; (*fraction*) tercio; (*BRIT SCOL: degree*) título universitario de tercera clase.
third degree *adj* (*burns*) de tercer grado.
thirdly ['θɜːdlɪ] *adv* en tercer lugar.
third party insurance *n* (*BRIT*) seguro a terceros.
third-rate ['θɜːd'reɪt] *adj* de poca calidad.
Third World *n*: **the ~** el Tercer Mundo ♦ *cpd* tercermundista.
thirst [θɜːst] *n* sed *f*.
thirsty ['θɜːstɪ] *adj* (*person*) sediento; **to be ~** tener sed.
thirteen [θɜː'tiːn] *num* trece.
thirteenth [θɜː'tiːnθ] *adj* decimotercero ♦ *n* (*in series*) decimotercero/a; (*fraction*) decimotercio.
thirtieth ['θɜːtɪəθ] *adj* trigésimo ♦ *n* (*in series*) trigésimo/a; (*fraction*) treintavo.
thirty ['θɜːtɪ] *num* treinta.

═══════════════════════ *KEYWORD*

this [ðɪs] (*pl* **these**) *adj* (*demonstrative*) este/a; *pl* estos/as; (*neuter*) esto; **~ man/ woman** este hombre/esta mujer; **these children/flowers** estos chicos/estas flores; **~ way** por aquí; **~ time last year** hoy hace un año; **~ one (here)** éste/a, esto (de aquí)
♦ *pron* (*demonstrative*) éste/a; *pl* éstos/as; (*neuter*) esto; **who is ~?** ¿quién es éste/ ésta?; **what is ~?** ¿qué es esto?; **~ is where I live** aquí vivo; **~ is what he said** esto es lo que dijo; **~ is Mr Brown** (*in introductions*) le presento al Sr. Brown; (*photo*) éste es el Sr. Brown; (*on telephone*) habla el Sr. Brown; **they were talking of ~ and that** hablaban de esto y lo otro
♦ *adv* (*demonstrative*): **~ high/long** así de alto/largo; **~ far** hasta aquí.

thistle ['θɪsl] *n* cardo.
thong [θɒŋ] *n* correa.
thorn [θɔːn] *n* espina.
thorny ['θɔːnɪ] *adj* espinoso.
thorough ['θʌrə] *adj* (*search*) minucioso; (*knowledge*) profundo; (*research*) a fondo.
thoroughbred ['θʌrəbrɛd] *adj* (*horse*) de pura sangre.
thoroughfare ['θʌrəfɛə*] *n* calle *f*; **"no ~"** "prohibido el paso".
thoroughgoing ['θʌrəgəʊɪŋ] *adj* a fondo.
thoroughly ['θʌrəlɪ] *adv* minuciosamente; a fondo.
thoroughness ['θʌrənɪs] *n* minuciosidad *f*.
those [ðəʊz] *pl pron* ésos/ésas; (*more remote*) aquéllos/as ♦ *pl adj* esos/esas; aquellos/as.
though [ðəʊ] *conj* aunque ♦ *adv* sin embargo, aún así; **even ~** aunque; **it's not so easy, ~** sin embargo no es tan fácil.
thought [θɔːt] *pt, pp of* **think** ♦ *n* pensamiento; (*opinion*) opinión *f*; (*intention*) intención *f*; **to give sth some ~**

pensar algo detenidamente; **after much ~** después de pensarlo bien; **I've just had a ~** se me acaba de ocurrir una idea.

thoughtful ['θɔːtful] adj pensativo; (considerate) atento.

thoughtfully ['θɔːtfəlɪ] adv pensativamente; atentamente.

thoughtless ['θɔːtlɪs] adj desconsiderado.

thoughtlessly ['θɔːtlɪslɪ] adv insensatamente.

thought-provoking ['θɔːtprəvəukɪŋ] adj estimulante.

thousand ['θauzənd] num mil; **two ~** dos mil; **~s of** miles de.

thousandth ['θauzəntθ] num milésimo.

thrash [θræʃ] vt dar una paliza a.

►**thrash about** vi revolverse.

►**thrash out** vt discutir a fondo.

thrashing ['θræʃɪŋ] n: **to give sb a ~** dar una paliza a algn.

thread [θrɛd] n hilo; (of screw) rosca ♦ vt (needle) enhebrar.

threadbare ['θrɛdbɛə*] adj raído.

threat [θrɛt] n amenaza; **to be under ~ of** estar amenazado de.

threaten ['θrɛtn] vi amenazar ♦ vt: **to ~ sb with sth/to do** amenazar a algn con algo/con hacer.

threatening ['θrɛtnɪŋ] adj amenazador(a), amenazante.

three [θriː] num tres.

three-dimensional [θriːdɪ'mɛnʃənl] adj tridimensional.

threefold ['θriːfəuld] adv: **to increase ~** triplicar.

three-piece ['θriːpiːs]: **~ suit** n traje m de tres piezas; **~ suite** n tresillo.

three-ply [θriː'plaɪ] adj (wood) de tres capas; (wool) triple.

three-quarter [θriː'kwɔːtə*] adj: **~ length sleeves** mangas fpl tres cuartos.

three-quarters [θriː'kwɔːtəz] npl tres cuartas partes; **~ full** tres cuartas partes lleno.

three-wheeler [θriː'wiːlə*] n (car) coche m cabina.

thresh [θrɛʃ] vt (AGR) trillar.

threshing machine ['θrɛʃɪŋ-] n trilladora.

threshold ['θrɛʃhəuld] n umbral m; **to be on the ~ of** (fig) estar al borde de.

threshold agreement n convenio de nivel crítico.

threw [θruː] pt of **throw**.

thrift [θrɪft] n economía.

thrifty ['θrɪftɪ] adj económico.

thrill [θrɪl] n (excitement) emoción f ♦ vt emocionar; **to be ~ed** (with gift etc) estar encantado.

thriller ['θrɪlə*] n película/novela de suspense.

thrilling ['θrɪlɪŋ] adj emocionante.

thrive, pt thrived, throve, pp thrived, thriven [θraɪv, θrəuv, 'θrɪvn] vi (grow) crecer; (do well) prosperar.

thriving ['θraɪvɪŋ] adj próspero.

throat [θrəut] n garganta; **I have a sore ~** me duele la garganta.

throb [θrɔb] n (of heart) latido; (of engine) vibración f ♦ vi latir; vibrar; (with pain) dar punzadas; **my head is ~bing** la cabeza me da punzadas.

throes [θrəuz] npl: **in the ~ of** en medio de.

thrombosis [θrɔm'bəusɪs] n trombosis f.

throne [θrəun] n trono.

throng [θrɔŋ] n multitud f, muchedumbre f ♦ vt, vi apiñarse, agolparse.

throttle ['θrɔtl] n (AUT) acelerador m ♦ vt estrangular.

through [θruː] prep por, a través de; (time) durante; (by means of) por medio de, mediante; (owing to) gracias a ♦ adj (ticket, train) directo ♦ adv completamente, de parte a parte; de principio a fin; **(from) Monday ~ Friday** (US) de lunes a viernes; **to go ~ sb's papers** mirar entre los papeles de algn; **I am halfway ~ the book** voy por la mitad del libro; **the soldiers didn't let us ~** los soldados no nos dejaron pasar; **to put sb ~ to sb** (TEL) poner or pasar a algn con algn; **to be ~** (TEL) tener comunicación; (have finished) haber terminado; **"no ~ road"** (BRIT) "calle sin salida".

throughout [θruː'aut] prep (place) por todas partes de, por todo; (time) durante todo ♦ adv por or en todas partes.

throughput ['θruːput] n (of goods, materials) producción f; (COMPUT) capacidad f de procesamiento.

throve [θrəuv] pt of **thrive**.

throw [θrəu] n tiro; (SPORT) lanzamiento ♦ vt (pt threw, pp thrown [θruː, θrəun]) tirar, echar, botar (LAM); (SPORT) lanzar; (rider) derribar; (fig) desconcertar; **to ~ a party** dar una fiesta.

►**throw about, throw around** vt (litter etc) tirar, esparcir.

►**throw away** vt tirar.

►**throw off** vt deshacerse de.

►**throw open** vt (doors, windows) abrir de par en par; (house, gardens etc) abrir al público; (competition, race) abrir a todos.

►**throw out** vt tirar, botar (LAM).

►**throw together** vt (clothes) amontonar; (meal) preparar a la carrera; (essay) hacer sin cuidado.

▸**throw up** *vi* vomitar, devolver.
throwaway ['θrəuəweɪ] *adj* para tirar, desechable.
throwback ['θrəubæk] *n*: **it's a ~ to** (*fig*) eso nos lleva de nuevo a.
throw-in ['θrəuɪn] *n* (*SPORT*) saque *m* de banda.
thrown [θrəun] *pp of* **throw**.
thru [θruː] (*US*) = **through**.
thrush [θrʌʃ] *n* zorzal *m*, tordo; (*MED*) candiasis *f*.
thrust [θrʌst] *n* (*TECH*) empuje *m* ♦ *vt* (*pt, pp* **thrust**) empujar; (*push in*) introducir.
thrusting ['θrʌstɪŋ] *adj* (*person*) dinámico, con empuje.
thud [θʌd] *n* golpe *m* sordo.
thug [θʌg] *n* gamberro/a.
thumb [θʌm] *n* (*ANAT*) pulgar *m* ♦ *vt*: **to ~ a lift** hacer dedo; **to give sth/sb the ~s up/down** aprobar/desaprobar algo/a algn.
▸**thumb through** *vt fus* (*book*) hojear.
thumb index *n* uñero, índice *m* recortado.
thumbnail ['θʌmneɪl] *n* uña del pulgar.
thumbnail sketch *n* esbozo.
thumbtack ['θʌmtæk] *n* (*US*) chincheta, chinche *f*.
thump [θʌmp] *n* golpe *m*; (*sound*) ruido seco *or* sordo ♦ *vt, vi* golpear.
thumping ['θʌmpɪŋ] *adj* (*col*: *huge*) descomunal.
thunder ['θʌndə*] *n* trueno; (*of applause etc*) estruendo ♦ *vi* tronar; (*train etc*): **to ~ past** pasar como un trueno.
thunderbolt ['θʌndəbəult] *n* rayo.
thunderclap ['θʌndəklæp] *n* trueno.
thunderous ['θʌndərəs] *adj* ensordecedor(a), estruendoso.
thunderstorm ['θʌndəstɔːm] *n* tormenta.
thunderstruck ['θʌndəstrʌk] *adj* pasmado.
thundery ['θʌndərɪ] *adj* tormentoso.
Thur(s). *abbr* (= *Thursday*) juev.
Thursday ['θɔːzdɪ] *n* jueves *m inv*.
thus [ðʌs] *adv* así, de este modo.
thwart [θwɔːt] *vt* frustrar.
thyme [taɪm] *n* tomillo.
thyroid ['θaɪrɔɪd] *n* tiroides *m inv*.
tiara [tɪ'ɑːrə] *n* tiara, diadema.
Tiber ['taɪbə*] *n* Tíber *m*.
Tibet [tɪ'bɛt] *n* el Tibet.
Tibetan [tɪ'bɛtən] *adj* tibetano ♦ *n* tibetano/a; (*LING*) tibetano.
tibia ['tɪbɪə] *n* tibia.
tic [tɪk] *n* tic *m*.
tick [tɪk] *n* (*sound*: *of clock*) tictac *m*; (*mark*) señal *f* (de visto bueno), palomita (*LAM*); (*ZOOL*) garrapata; (*BRIT col*): **in a ~** en un instante; (*BRIT col*: *credit*): **to buy sth on ~** comprar algo a crédito ♦ *vi* hacer tictac

♦ *vt* marcar, señalar; **to put a ~ against sth** poner una señal en algo.
▸**tick off** *vt* marcar; (*person*) reñir.
▸**tick over** *vi* (*BRIT*: *engine*) girar en marcha lenta; (: *fig*) ir tirando.
ticker tape ['tɪkə-] *n* cinta perforada.
ticket ['tɪkɪt] *n* billete *m*, tíquet *m*, boleto (*LAM*); (*for cinema etc*) entrada, boleto (*LAM*); (*in shop*: *on goods*) etiqueta; (*for library*) tarjeta; (*US POL*) lista (de candidatos); **to get a parking ~** (*AUT*) ser multado por estacionamiento ilegal.
ticket agency *n* (*THEAT*) agencia de venta de entradas.
ticket collector *n* revisor(a) *m/f*.
ticket holder *n* poseedor(a) *m/f* de billete *or* entrada.
ticket inspector *n* revisor(a) *m/f*, inspector(a) *m/f* de boletos (*LAM*).
ticket office *n* (*THEAT*) taquilla, boletería (*LAM*); (*RAIL*) despacho de billetes *or* boletos (*LAM*).
ticking-off ['tɪkɪŋ'ɔf] *n* (*col*): **to give sb a ~** echarle una bronca a algn.
tickle ['tɪkl] *n*: **to give sb a ~** hacer cosquillas a algn ♦ *vt* hacer cosquillas a.
ticklish ['tɪklɪʃ] *adj* (*which tickles*: *blanket*) que pica; (: *cough*) irritante; **to be ~** tener cosquillas.
tidal ['taɪdl] *adj* de marea.
tidal wave *n* maremoto.
tidbit ['tɪdbɪt] (*US*) = **titbit**.
tiddlywinks ['tɪdlɪwɪŋks] *n* juego de la pulga.
tide [taɪd] *n* marea; (*fig*: *of events*) curso, marcha ♦ *vt*: **to ~ sb over** *or* **through** (**until**) sacar a algn del apuro (hasta); **high/low ~** marea alta/baja; **the ~ of public opinion** la tendencia de la opinión pública.
tidily ['taɪdɪlɪ] *adv* bien, ordenadamente; **to arrange ~** ordenar; **to dress ~** vestir bien.
tidiness ['taɪdɪnɪs] *n* (*order*) orden *m*; (*cleanliness*) aseo.
tidy ['taɪdɪ] *adj* (*room*) ordenado; (*drawing, work*) limpio; (*person*) (bien) arreglado; (: *in character*) metódico; (*mind*) claro, metódico ♦ *vt* (*also*: **~ up**) ordenar, poner en orden.
tie [taɪ] *n* (*string etc*) atadura; (*BRIT*: *neck~*) corbata; (*fig*: *link*) vínculo, lazo; (*SPORT*: *draw*) empate *m* ♦ *vt* atar ♦ *vi* (*SPORT*) empatar; **family ~s** obligaciones *fpl* familiares; **cup ~** (*SPORT*: *match*) partido de copa; **to ~ in a bow** hacer un lazo; **to ~ a knot in sth** hacer un nudo en algo.
▸**tie down** *vt* atar; (*fig*): **to ~ sb down to**

obligar a algn a.

▶**tie in** *vi*: **to ~ in (with)** (*correspond*) concordar (con).

▶**tie on** *vt* (*BRIT*: *label etc*) atar.

▶**tie up** *vt* (*parcel*) envolver; (*dog*) atar; (*boat*) amarrar; (*arrangements*) concluir; **to be ~d up** (*busy*) estar ocupado.

tie-break(er) ['taɪbreɪk(ə*)] *n* (*TENNIS*) tiebreak *m*, muerte *f* súbita; (*in quiz*) punto decisivo.

tie-on ['taɪɔn] *adj* (*BRIT*: *label*) para atar.

tie-pin ['taɪpɪn] *n* (*BRIT*) alfiler *m* de corbata.

tier [tɪə*] *n* grada; (*of cake*) piso.

tie tack *n* (*US*) alfiler *m* de corbata.

tiff [tɪf] *n* (*col*) pelea, riña.

tiger ['taɪgə*] *n* tigre *m*.

tight [taɪt] *adj* (*rope*) tirante; (*money*) escaso; (*clothes, budget*) ajustado; (*programme*) apretado; (*col*: *drunk*) borracho ♦ *adv* (*squeeze*) muy fuerte; (*shut*) herméticamente; **to be packed ~** (*suitcase*) estar completamente lleno; (*people*) estar apretados; **everybody hold ~!** ¡agárense bien!

tighten ['taɪtn] *vt* (*rope*) tensar, estirar; (*screw*) apretar ♦ *vi* estirarse; apretarse.

tight-fisted [taɪt'fɪstɪd] *adj* tacaño.

tight-lipped ['taɪt'lɪpt] *adj*: **to be ~** (*silent*) rehusar hablar; (*angry*) apretar los labios.

tightly ['taɪtlɪ] *adv* (*grasp*) muy fuerte.

tightness ['taɪtnɪs] *n* (*of rope*) tirantez *f*; (*of clothes*) estrechez *f*; (*of budget*) lo ajustado.

tightrope ['taɪtrəup] *n* cuerda floja.

tightrope walker *n* equilibrista *m/f*, funambulista *m/f*.

tights [taɪts] *npl* (*BRIT*) medias *fpl*, panties *mpl*.

tigress ['taɪgrɪs] *n* tigresa.

tilde ['tɪldə] *n* tilde *f*.

tile [taɪl] *n* (*on roof*) teja; (*on floor*) baldosa; (*on wall*) azulejo ♦ *vt* (*floor*) poner baldosas en; (*wall*) alicatar.

tiled [taɪld] *adj* (*floor*) embaldosado; (*wall, bathroom*) alicatado; (*roof*) con tejas.

till [tɪl] *n* caja (registradora) ♦ *vt* (*land*) cultivar ♦ *prep, conj* = **until.**

tiller ['tɪlə*] *n* (*NAUT*) caña del timón.

tilt [tɪlt] *vt* inclinar ♦ *vi* inclinarse ♦ *n* (*slope*) inclinación *f*; **to wear one's hat at a ~** llevar el sombrero echado a un lado *or* terciado; (**at**) **full ~** a toda velocidad *or* carrera.

timber ['tɪmbə*] *n* (*material*) madera; (*trees*) árboles *mpl*.

time [taɪm] *n* tiempo; (*epoch*: *often pl*) época; (*by clock*) hora; (*moment*)

momento; (*occasion*) vez *f*; (*MUS*) compás *m* ♦ *vt* calcular *or* medir el tiempo de; (*race*) cronometrar; (*remark etc*) elegir el momento para; **a long ~** mucho tiempo; **4 at a ~** 4 a la vez; **for the ~ being** de momento, por ahora; **at ~s** a veces, a ratos; **~ after ~, ~ and again** repetidas veces, una y otra vez; **from ~ to ~** de vez en cuando; **in ~** (*soon enough*) a tiempo; (*after some time*) con el tiempo; (*MUS*) al compás; **in a week's ~** dentro de una semana; **in no ~** en un abrir y cerrar de ojos; **any ~** cuando sea; **on ~** a la hora; **to be 30 minutes behind/ahead of ~** llevar media hora de retraso/adelanto; **to take one's ~** tomárselo con calma; **he'll do it in his own ~** (*without being hurried*) lo hará sin prisa; (*out of working hours*) lo hará en su tiempo libre; **by the ~ he arrived** cuando llegó; **5 ~s 5** 5 por 5; **what ~ is it?** ¿qué hora es?; **what ~ do you make it?** ¿qué hora es *or* tiene?; **to be behind the ~s** estar atrasado; **to carry 3 boxes at a ~** llevar 3 cajas a la vez; **to keep ~** llevar el ritmo *or* el compás; **to have a good ~** pasarlo bien, divertirse; **to ~ sth well/badly** elegir un buen/mal momento para algo; **the bomb was ~d to explode 5 minutes later** la bomba estaba programada para explotar 5 minutos más tarde.

time-and-motion expert ['taɪmənd'məuʃən-] *n* experto/a en la ciencia de la producción.

time-and-motion study ['taɪmənd'məuʃən-] *n* estudio de desplazamientos y tiempos.

time bomb *n* bomba de relojería.

time card *n* tarjeta de registro horario.

time clock *n* reloj *m* registrador.

time-consuming ['taɪmkənsju:mɪŋ] *adj* que requiere mucho tiempo.

time frame *n* plazo.

time-honoured, (*US*) **time-honored** ['taɪmɔnəd] *adj* consagrado.

timekeeper ['taɪmki:pə*] *n* (*SPORT*) cronómetro.

time lag *n* desfase *m*.

timeless ['taɪmlɪs] *adj* eterno.

time limit *n* (*gen*) límite *m* de tiempo; (*COMM*) plazo.

timely ['taɪmlɪ] *adj* oportuno.

time off *n* tiempo libre.

timer ['taɪmə*] *n* (*~ switch*) interruptor *m*; (*in kitchen, TECH*) temporizador *m*.

time-saving ['taɪmseɪvɪŋ] *adj* que ahorra tiempo.

time scale *n* escala de tiempo.

time sharing *n* (*COMPUT*) tiempo compartido.

time sheet *n* = **time card**.

time signal *n* señal *f* horaria.

time switch *n* (*BRIT*) interruptor *m* (horario).

timetable ['taɪmteɪbl] *n* horario; (*programme of events etc*) programa *m*.

time zone *n* huso horario.

timid ['tɪmɪd] *adj* tímido.

timidity [tɪ'mɪdɪtɪ] *n* timidez *f*.

timidly ['tɪmɪdlɪ] *adv* tímidamente.

timing ['taɪmɪŋ] *n* (*SPORT*) cronometraje *m*; **the ~ of his resignation** el momento que eligió para dimitir.

timpani ['tɪmpənɪ] *npl* tímpanos *mpl*.

tin [tɪn] *n* estaño; (*also*: **~ plate**) hojalata; (*BRIT*: *can*) lata.

tinfoil ['tɪnfɔɪl] *n* papel *m* de estaño.

tinge [tɪndʒ] *n* matiz *m* ♦ *vt*: **~d with** teñido de.

tingle ['tɪŋgl] *n* hormigueo ♦ *vi* (*cheeks, skin*: *from cold*) sentir comezón; (: *from bad circulation*) sentir hormigueo.

tinker ['tɪŋkə*] *n* calderero/a; (*gipsy*) gitano/a.

▶**tinker with** *vt fus* jugar con, tocar.

tinkle ['tɪŋkl] *vi* tintinear.

tin mine *n* mina de estaño.

tinned [tɪnd] *adj* (*BRIT*: *food*) en lata, en conserva.

tinnitus ['tɪnɪtəs] *n* (*MED*) acufeno.

tinny ['tɪnɪ] *adj* (*sound, taste*) metálico; (*pej*: *car*) poco sólido, de pacotilla.

tin opener [-əupnə*] *n* (*BRIT*) abrelatas *m inv*.

tinsel ['tɪnsl] *n* oropel *m*.

tint [tɪnt] *n* matiz *m*; (*for hair*) tinte *m* ♦ *vt* (*hair*) teñir.

tinted ['tɪntɪd] *adj* (*hair*) teñido; (*glass, spectacles*) ahumado.

tiny ['taɪnɪ] *adj* minúsculo, pequeñito.

tip [tɪp] *n* (*end*) punta; (*gratuity*) propina; (*BRIT*: *for rubbish*) vertedero; (*advice*) consejo ♦ *vt* (*waiter*) dar una propina a; (*tilt*) inclinar; (*empty*: *also* **~ out**) vaciar, echar; (*predict*: *winner*) pronosticar; (: *horse*) recomendar; **he ~ped out the contents of the box** volcó el contenido de la caja.

▶**tip off** *vt* avisar, poner sobreaviso a.

▶**tip over** *vt* volcar ♦ *vi* volcarse.

tip-off ['tɪpɔf] *n* (*hint*) advertencia.

tipped [tɪpt] *adj* (*BRIT*: *cigarette*) con filtro.

Tipp-Ex ® ['tɪpɛks] *n* Tipp-Ex ® *m*.

tipple ['tɪpl] *n* (*BRIT*): **his ~ is Cointreau** bebe Cointreau.

tipster ['tɪpstə*] *n* (*RACING*) pronosticador(a) *m/f*.

tipsy ['tɪpsɪ] *adj* alegre, achispado.

tiptoe ['tɪptəu] *n* (*BRIT*): **on ~** de puntillas.

tiptop ['tɪptɔp] *adj*: **in ~ condition** en perfectas condiciones.

tirade [taɪ'reɪd] *n* diatriba.

tire ['taɪə*] *n* (*US*) = **tyre** ♦ *vt* cansar ♦ *vi* (*gen*) cansarse; (*become bored*) aburrirse.

▶**tire out** *vt* agotar, rendir.

tired ['taɪəd] *adj* cansado; **to be ~ of sth** estar harto de algo; **to be/feel/look ~** estar/sentirse/parecer cansado.

tiredness ['taɪədnɪs] *n* cansancio.

tireless ['taɪəlɪs] *adj* incansable.

tirelessly ['taɪəlɪslɪ] *adv* incansablemente.

tiresome ['taɪəsəm] *adj* aburrido.

tiring ['taɪrɪŋ] *adj* cansado.

tissue ['tɪʃuː] *n* tejido; (*paper handkerchief*) pañuelo de papel, kleenex *m* ®.

tissue paper *n* papel *m* de seda.

tit [tɪt] *n* (*bird*) herrerillo común; **to give ~ for tat** dar ojo por ojo.

titbit ['tɪtbɪt], (*US*) **tidbit** ['tɪdbɪt] *n* (*food*) golosina; (*news*) pedazo.

titillate ['tɪtɪleɪt] *vt* estimular, excitar.

titillation [tɪtɪ'leɪʃən] *n* estimulación *f*, excitación *f*.

titivate ['tɪtɪveɪt] *vt* emperejilar.

title ['taɪtl] *n* título; (*LAW*: *right*): **~ (to)** derecho (a).

title deed *n* (*LAW*) título de propiedad.

title page *n* portada.

title role *n* papel *m* principal.

titter ['tɪtə*] *vi* reírse entre dientes.

tittle-tattle ['tɪtltætl] *n* chismes *mpl*.

titular ['tɪtjulə*] *adj* (*in name only*) nominal.

T-junction ['tiːdʒʌŋkʃən] *n* cruce *m* en T.

TM *abbr* (= *trademark*) marca de fábrica; = **transcendental meditation**.

TN *abbr* (*US*) = *Tennessee*.

TNT *n abbr* (= *trinitrotoluene*) TNT *m*.

━━━━━━━━━━━━━━━━━━━━━━━ *KEYWORD*

to [tuː, tə] *prep* **1** (*direction*) a; **to go ~ France/London/school/the station** ir a Francia/Londres/al colegio/a la estación; **to go ~ Claude's/the doctor's** ir a casa de Claude/al médico; **the road ~ Edinburgh** la carretera de Edimburgo; **~ the left/right** a la izquierda/derecha

2 (*as far as*) hasta, a; **from here ~ London** de aquí a *or* hasta Londres; **to count ~ 10** contar hasta 10; **from 40 ~ 50 people** entre 40 y 50 personas

3 (*with expressions of time*): **a quarter/twenty ~ 5** las 5 menos cuarto/veinte

4 (*for, of*): **the key ~ the front door** la llave de la puerta principal; **she is**

secretary ~ **the director** es la secretaria del director; **a letter** ~ **his wife** una carta a *or* para su mujer
5 (*expressing indirect object*) a; **to give sth** ~ **sb** darle algo a algn; **give it** ~ **me** dámelo; **to talk** ~ **sb** hablar con algn; **to be a danger** ~ **sb** ser un peligro para algn; **to carry out repairs** ~ **sth** hacer reparaciones en algo
6 (*in relation to*): **3 goals** ~ **2** 3 goles a 2; **30 miles** ~ **the gallon** ≈ 9,4 litros a los cien (kilómetros); **8 apples** ~ **the kilo** 8 manzanas por kilo
7 (*purpose, result*): **to come** ~ **sb's aid** venir en auxilio *or* ayuda de algn; **to sentence sb** ~ **death** condenar a algn a muerte; ~ **my great surprise** con gran sorpresa mía
♦ *with vb* **1** (*simple infin*): ~ **go/eat** ir/comer
2 (*following another vb*): **to want/try/start** ~ **do** querer/intentar/empezar a hacer; *see also relevant vb*
3 (*with vb omitted*): **I don't want** ~ no quiero
4 (*purpose, result*) para; **I did it** ~ **help you** lo hice para ayudarte; **he came** ~ **see you** vino a verte
5 (*equivalent to relative clause*): **I have things** ~ **do** tengo cosas que hacer; **the main thing is** ~ **try** lo principal es intentarlo
6 (*after adj etc*): **ready** ~ **go** listo para irse; **too old** ~ ... demasiado viejo (como) para ...
♦ *adv*: **pull/push the door** ~ tirar de/empujar la puerta; **to go** ~ **and fro** ir y venir.

toad [təud] *n* sapo.
toadstool ['təudstu:l] *n* seta venenosa.
toady ['təudɪ] *n* pelota *m/f* ♦ *vi*: **to** ~ **to sb** hacer la pelota *or* dar coba a algn.
toast [təust] *n* (*CULIN: also:* **piece of** ~) tostada; (*drink, speech*) brindis *m inv* ♦ *vt* (*CULIN*) tostar; (*drink to*) brindar.
toaster ['təustə*] *n* tostador *m*.
toastmaster ['təustmɑːstə*] *n persona que propone brindis y anuncia a los oradores en un banquete*.
toast rack *n* rejilla para tostadas.
tobacco [tə'bækəu] *n* tabaco; **pipe** ~ tabaco de pipa.
tobacconist [tə'bækənɪst] *n* estanquero/a, tabaquero/a (*LAM*); ~**'s (shop)** (*BRIT*) estanco, tabaquería (*LAM*).
tobacco plantation *n* plantación *f* de tabaco, tabacal *m*.
Tobago [tə'beɪgəu] *n see* **Trinidad and Tobago**.
toboggan [tə'bɔgən] *n* tobogán *m*.
today [tə'deɪ] *adv, n* (*also fig*) hoy *m*; **what day is it** ~? ¿qué día es hoy?; **what date is it** ~? ¿a qué fecha estamos hoy?; ~ **is the 4th of March** hoy es el 4 de marzo; ~**'s paper** el periódico de hoy; **a fortnight** ~ de hoy en 15 días, dentro de 15 días.
toddle ['tɔdl] *vi* empezar a andar, dar los primeros pasos.
toddler ['tɔdlə*] *n* niño/a (que empieza a andar).
toddy ['tɔdɪ] *n* ponche *m*.
to-do [tə'du:] *n* (*fuss*) lío.
toe [təu] *n* dedo (del pie); (*of shoe*) punta
♦ *vt*: **to** ~ **the line** (*fig*) acatar las normas; **big/little** ~ dedo gordo/pequeño del pie.
TOEFL *n abbr* = *Test(ing) of English as a Foreign Language*.
toehold ['təuhəuld] *n* punto de apoyo (para el pie).
toenail ['təuneɪl] *n* uña del pie.
toffee ['tɔfɪ] *n* caramelo.
toffee apple *n* (*BRIT*) manzana de caramelo.
tofu ['təufuː] *n* tofu *m*.
toga ['təugə] *n* toga.
together [tə'gɛðə*] *adv* juntos; (*at same time*) al mismo tiempo, a la vez; ~ **with** *prep* junto con.
togetherness [tə'gɛðənɪs] *n* compañerismo.
toggle switch ['tɔgl-] *n* (*COMPUT*) conmutador *m* de palanca.
Togo ['təugəu] *n* Togo.
togs [tɔgz] *npl* (*col: clothes*) atuendo, ropa.
toil [tɔɪl] *n* trabajo duro, labor *f* ♦ *vi* esforzarse.
toilet ['tɔɪlət] *n* (*BRIT: lavatory*) servicios *mpl*, wáter *m* ♦ *cpd* (*bag, soap etc*) de aseo; **to go to the** ~ ir al baño; *see also* **toilets**.
toilet bag *n* neceser *m*, bolsa de aseo.
toilet bowl *n* taza (de retrete).
toilet paper *n* papel *m* higiénico.
toiletries ['tɔɪlətrɪz] *npl* artículos *mpl* de aseo; (*make-up etc*) artículos *mpl* de tocador.
toilet roll *n* rollo de papel higiénico.
toilets ['tɔɪləts] *npl* (*BRIT*) servicios *mpl*.
toilet soap *n* jabón *m* de tocador.
toilet water *n* (agua de) colonia.
to-ing and fro-ing ['tuɪŋən'frəuɪŋ] *n* vaivén *m*.
token ['təukən] *n* (*sign*) señal *f*, muestra; (*souvenir*) recuerdo; (*voucher*) vale *m*; (*disc*) ficha ♦ *cpd* (*fee, strike*) nominal, simbólico; **book/record** ~ (*BRIT*) vale *m* para comprar libros/discos; **by the same**

~ (*fig*) por la misma razón.
tokenism ['təukənızəm] *n* (*POL*) política
simbólica *or* de fachada.
Tokyo ['təukjəu] *n* Tokio, Tokío.
told [təuld] *pt, pp of* **tell.**
tolerable ['tɔlərəbl] *adj* (*bearable*)
soportable; (*fairly good*) pasable.
tolerably ['tɔlərəblı] *adv* (*good, comfortable*)
medianamente.
tolerance ['tɔlərns] *n* (*also*: *TECH*)
tolerancia.
tolerant ['tɔlərnt] *adj*: ~ **of** tolerante con.
tolerantly ['tɔlərntlı] *adv* con tolerancia.
tolerate ['tɔləreɪt] *vt* tolerar.
toleration [tɔlə'reɪʃən] *n* tolerancia.
toll [təul] *n* (*of casualties*) número de
víctimas; (*tax, charge*) peaje *m* ♦ *vi* (*bell*)
doblar.
toll bridge *n* puente *m* de peaje.
toll call *n* (*US TELEC*) conferencia, llamada
interurbana.
toll-free *adj, adv* (*US*) gratis.
toll road *n* carretera de peaje.
tomato, ~**es** [tə'mɑːtəu] *n* tomate *m*.
tomato puree *n* puré *m* de tomate.
tomb [tuːm] *n* tumba.
tombola [tɔm'bəulə] *n* tómbola.
tomboy ['tɔmbɔɪ] *n* marimacho.
tombstone ['tuːmstəun] *n* lápida.
tomcat ['tɔmkæt] *n* gato.
tomorrow [tə'mɔrəu] *adv, n* (*also fig*)
mañana; **the day after** ~ pasado mañana;
~ **morning** mañana por la mañana; **a
week** ~ de mañana en ocho (días).
ton [tʌn] *n* (*BRIT* = 1016 kg; *US*: *also* **short** ~
= 907,18 kg) tonelada; ~**s of** (*col*)
montones de.
tonal ['təunl] *adj* tonal.
tone [təun] *n* tono ♦ *vi* armonizar; **dialling** ~
(*TEL*) señal *f* para marcar.
►**tone down** *vt* (*criticism*) suavizar;
(*colour*) atenuar.
►**tone up** *vt* (*muscles*) tonificar.
tone-deaf [təun'dɛf] *adj* sin oído musical.
toner ['təunə*] *n* (*for photocopier*) virador *m*.
Tonga ['tɔŋə] *n* Islas *fpl* Tonga.
tongs [tɔŋz] *npl* (*for coal*) tenazas *fpl*; (*for
hair*) tenacillas *fpl*.
tongue [tʌŋ] *n* lengua; ~ **in cheek** *adv* en
plan de broma.
tongue-tied ['tʌŋtaɪd] *adj* (*fig*) mudo.
tongue-twister ['tʌŋtwɪstə*] *n*
trabalenguas *m inv*.
tonic ['tɔnɪk] *n* (*MED*) tónico; (*MUS*) tónica;
(*also*: ~ **water**) (agua) tónica.
tonight [tə'naɪt] *adv, n* esta noche; **I'll see
you** ~ nos vemos esta noche.
tonnage ['tʌnɪdʒ] *n* (*NAUT*) tonelaje *m*.

tonsil ['tɔnsl] *n* amígdala; **to have one's** ~**s
out** sacarse las amígdalas *or* anginas.
tonsillitis [tɔnsɪ'laɪtɪs] *n* amigdalitis *f*; **to
have** ~ tener amigdalitis.
too [tuː] *adv* (*excessively*) demasiado; (*very*)
muy; (*also*) también; **it's** ~ **sweet** está
demasiado dulce; **I'm not** ~ **sure about
that** no estoy muy seguro de eso; **I went**
~ yo también fui; ~ **much** *adv, adj*
demasiado; ~ **many** *adj* demasiados/as; ~
bad! ¡mala suerte!
took [tuk] *pt of* **take.**
tool [tuːl] *n* herramienta; (*fig*: *person*)
instrumento.
tool box *n* caja de herramientas.
tool kit *n* juego de herramientas.
tool shed *n* cobertizo (para
herramientas).
toot [tuːt] *n* (*of horn*) bocinazo; (*of whistle*)
silbido ♦ *vi* (*with car horn*) tocar la bocina.
tooth, *pl* **teeth** [tuːθ, tiːθ] *n* (*ANAT, TECH*)
diente *m*; (*molar*) muela; **to clean one's
teeth** lavarse los dientes; **to have a** ~ **out**
sacarse una muela; **by the skin of one's
teeth** por un pelo.
toothache ['tuːθeɪk] *n* dolor *m* de muelas.
toothbrush ['tuːθbrʌʃ] *n* cepillo de dientes.
toothpaste ['tuːθpeɪst] *n* pasta de dientes.
toothpick ['tuːθpɪk] *n* palillo.
tooth powder *n* polvos *mpl* dentífricos.
top [tɔp] *n* (*of mountain*) cumbre *f*, cima; (*of
head*) coronilla; (*of ladder*) (lo) alto; (*of
cupboard, table*) superficie *f*; (*of bottle, jar*) tapa; (*: of bottle*) tapón *m*; (*of list, table,
queue, page*) cabeza; (*toy*) peonza; (*DRESS*:
blouse) blusa; (*: T-shirt*) camiseta; (*: of
pyjamas*) chaqueta ♦ *adj* de arriba; (*in
rank*) principal, primero; (*best*) mejor ♦ *vt*
(*exceed*) exceder; (*be first in*) encabezar;
on ~ **of** sobre, encima de; **from** ~ **to
bottom** de pies a cabeza; **the** ~ **of the
milk** la nata; **at the** ~ **of the stairs** en lo
alto de la escalera; **at the** ~ **of the street**
al final de la calle; **at the** ~ **of one's voice**
(*fig*) a voz en grito; **at** ~ **speed** a máxima
velocidad; **a** ~ **surgeon** un cirujano
eminente; **over the** ~ (*col*) excesivo,
desmesurado; **to go over the** ~ pasarse.
►**top up**, (*US*) **top off** *vt* volver a llenar.
topaz ['təupæz] *n* topacio.
top-class ['tɔp'klɑːs] *adj* de primera clase.
topcoat ['tɔpkəut] *n* sobretodo, abrigo.
topflight ['tɔpflaɪt] *adj* de primera
(categoría *or* clase).
top floor *n* último piso.
top hat *n* sombrero de copa.
top-heavy [tɔp'hɛvɪ] *adj* (*object*) con más
peso en la parte superior.

topic ['tɔpɪk] n tema m.

topical ['tɔpɪkl] adj actual.

topless ['tɔplɪs] adj (bather etc) topless.

top-level ['tɔplɛvl] adj (talks) al más alto nivel.

topmost ['tɔpməust] adj más alto.

top-notch ['tɔp'nɔtʃ] adj (col) de primerísima categoría.

topography [tə'pɔgrəfɪ] n topografía.

topping ['tɔpɪŋ] n (CULIN): **with a ~ of cream** con nata por encima.

topple ['tɔpl] vt volcar, derribar ♦ vi caerse.

top-ranking ['tɔpræŋkɪŋ] adj de alto rango.

top-secret [tɔp'siːkrɪt] adj de alto secreto.

top-security ['tɔpsɪ'kjuərɪtɪ] adj (BRIT) de máxima seguridad.

topsy-turvy ['tɔpsɪ'təːvɪ] adj, adv patas arriba.

top-up ['tɔpʌp] n: **would you like a ~?** ¿quiere que se lo vuelva a llenar?

top-up loan n (BRIT) préstamo complementario.

torch [tɔːtʃ] n antorcha; (BRIT: electric) linterna.

torc [tɔː*] pt of **tear**.

torment n ['tɔːmɛnt] tormento ♦ vt [tɔː'mɛnt] atormentar; (fig: annoy) fastidiar.

torn [tɔːn] pp of **tear**.

tornado, ~es [tɔː'neɪdəu] n tornado.

torpedo, ~es [tɔː'piːdəu] n torpedo.

torpedo boat n torpedero, lancha torpedera.

torpor ['tɔːpə*] n letargo.

torrent ['tɔrnt] n torrente m.

torrential [tɔ'rɛnʃl] adj torrencial.

torrid ['tɔrɪd] adj tórrido; (fig) apasionado.

torso ['tɔːsəu] n torso.

tortoise ['tɔːtəs] n tortuga.

tortoiseshell ['tɔːtəʃel] adj de carey.

tortuous ['tɔːtjuəs] adj tortuoso.

torture ['tɔːtʃə*] n tortura ♦ vt torturar; (fig) atormentar.

torturer ['tɔːtʃərə*] n torturador(a) m/f.

Tory ['tɔːrɪ] adj, n (BRIT POL) conservador(a) m/f.

toss [tɔs] vt tirar, echar; (head) sacudir ♦ n (movement: of head etc) sacudida; (of coin) tirada, echada (LAM); **to ~ a coin** echar a cara o cruz; **to ~ up for sth** jugar algo a cara o cruz; **to ~ and turn** (in bed) dar vueltas (en la cama); **to win/lose the ~** (also SPORT) ganar/perder (a cara o cruz).

tot [tɔt] n (BRIT: drink) copita; (child) nene/a m/f.

▶**tot up** vt sumar.

total ['təutl] adj total, entero ♦ n total m,

suma ♦ vt (add up) sumar; (amount to) ascender a; **grand ~** cantidad f total; (cost) importe m total; **in ~** en total, en suma.

totalitarian [təutælɪ'tɛərɪən] adj totalitario.

totality [təu'tælɪtɪ] n totalidad f.

total loss n siniestra total.

totally ['təutəlɪ] adv totalmente.

tote [təut] vt (col) acarrear, cargar con.

tote bag n bolsa.

totem pole ['təutəm-] n poste m totémico.

totter ['tɔtə*] vi tambalearse.

touch [tʌtʃ] n (sense) tacto; (contact) contacto; (FOOTBALL) fuera de juego ♦ vt tocar; (emotionally) conmover; **a ~ of** (fig) una pizca or un poquito de; **to get in ~ with sb** ponerse en contacto con algn; **I'll be in ~** le llamaré/escribiré; **to lose ~** (friends) perder contacto; **to be out of ~ with events** no estar al corriente (de los acontecimientos); **the personal ~** el toque personal; **to put the finishing ~es to sth** dar el último toque a algo; **no artist in the country can ~ him** no hay artista en todo el país que le iguale.

▶**touch on** vt fus (topic) aludir (brevemente) a.

▶**touch up** vt (paint) retocar.

touch-and-go ['tʌtʃən'gəu] adj arriesgado.

touchdown ['tʌtʃdaun] n aterrizaje m; (US FOOTBALL) ensayo.

touched [tʌtʃt] adj conmovido; (col) chiflado.

touchiness ['tʌtʃɪnɪs] n susceptibilidad f.

touching ['tʌtʃɪŋ] adj conmovedor(a).

touchline ['tʌtʃlaɪn] n (SPORT) línea de banda.

touch-sensitive ['tʌtʃ'sɛnsɪtɪv] adj sensible al tacto.

touch-type ['tʌtʃtaɪp] vi mecanografiar al tacto.

touchy ['tʌtʃɪ] adj (person) quisquilloso.

tough [tʌf] adj (meat) duro; (journey) penoso; (task, problem, situation) difícil; (resistant) resistente; (person) fuerte; (: pej) bruto ♦ n (gangster etc) gorila m; **they got ~ with the workers** se pusieron muy duros con los trabajadores.

toughen ['tʌfn] vt endurecer.

toughness ['tʌfnɪs] n dureza; (resistance) resistencia; (strictness) inflexibilidad f.

toupée ['tuːpeɪ] n peluquín m.

tour ['tuə*] n viaje m; (also: **package ~**) viaje m con todo incluido; (of town, museum) visita ♦ vt viajar por; **to go on a ~ of** (region, country) ir de viaje por; (museum, castle) visitar; **to go on ~** partir or ir de gira.

touring ['tuərɪŋ] n viajes mpl turísticos, turismo.

tourism ['tuərɪzm] n turismo.

tourist ['tuərɪst] n turista m/f ♦ cpd turístico; **the ~ trade** el turismo.

tourist class n (AVIAT) clase f turista.

tourist office n oficina de turismo.

tournament ['tuənəmənt] n torneo.

tourniquet ['tuənɪkeɪ] n (MED) torniquete m.

tour operator n touroperador(a) m/f, operador(a) m/f turístico/a.

tousled ['tauzld] adj (hair) despeinado.

tout [taut] vi: **to ~ for business** solicitar clientes ♦ n: **ticket ~** revendedor(a) m/f.

tow [təu] n: **to give sb a ~** (AUT) remolcar a algn ♦ vt remolcar; "**on** or (US) **in ~**" (AUT) "a remolque".

toward(s) [tə'wɔ:d(z)] prep hacia; (of attitude) respecto a, con; (of purpose) para; **~ noon** alrededor de mediodía; **~ the end of the year** hacia finales de año; **to feel friendly ~ sb** sentir amistad hacia algn.

towel ['tauəl] n toalla; **to throw in the ~** (fig) darse por vencido, renunciar.

towelling ['tauəlɪŋ] n (fabric) felpa.

towel rail, (US) **towel rack** n toallero.

tower ['tauə*] n torre f ♦ vi (building, mountain) elevarse; **to ~ above** or **over sth/sb** dominar algo/destacarse sobre algn.

tower block n (BRIT) bloque m de pisos.

towering ['tauərɪŋ] adj muy alto, imponente.

town [taun] n ciudad f; **to go to ~** ir a la ciudad; (fig) tirar la casa por la ventana; **in the ~** en la ciudad; **to be out of ~** estar fuera de la ciudad.

town centre n centro de la ciudad.

town clerk n secretario/a del Ayuntamiento.

town council n Ayuntamiento, consejo municipal.

town crier [-kraɪə*] n (BRIT) pregonero.

town hall n ayuntamiento.

townie ['taunɪ] n (BRIT col) persona de la ciudad.

town plan n plano de la ciudad.

town planner n urbanista m/f.

town planning n urbanismo.

township ['taunʃɪp] n municipio habitado sólo por negros en Sudáfrica.

townspeople ['taunzpi:pl] npl gente f de ciudad.

towpath ['təupɑ:θ] n camino de sirga.

towrope ['təurəup] n cable m de remolque.

tow truck n (US) camión m grúa.

toxic ['tɔksɪk] adj tóxico.

toxin ['tɔksɪn] n toxina.

toy [tɔɪ] n juguete m.

▶**toy with** vt fus jugar con; (idea) acariciar.

toyshop ['tɔɪʃɔp] n juguetería.

toy train n tren m de juguete.

trace [treɪs] n rastro ♦ vt (draw) trazar, delinear; (locate) encontrar; **there was no ~ of it** no había ningún indicio de ello.

trace element n oligoelemento.

trachea [trə'kɪə] n (ANAT) tráquea.

tracing paper ['treɪsɪŋ-] n papel m de calco.

track [træk] n (mark) huella, pista; (path: gen) camino, senda; (: of bullet etc) trayectoria; (: of suspect, animal) pista, rastro; (RAIL) vía; (COMPUT, SPORT) pista; (on record) canción f ♦ vt seguir la pista de; **to keep ~ of** mantenerse al tanto de, seguir; **a 4-~ tape** una cinta de 4 pistas; **the first ~ on the record/tape** la primera canción en el disco/la cinta; **to be on the right ~** (fig) ir por buen camino.

▶**track down** vt (person) localizar; (sth lost) encontrar.

tracker dog ['trækə*-] n (BRIT) perro rastreador.

track events npl (SPORT) pruebas fpl en pista.

tracking station ['trækɪŋ-] n (SPACE) estación f de seguimiento.

track meet n (US) concurso de carreras y saltos.

track record n: **to have a good ~** (fig) tener un buen historial.

tracksuit ['træksu:t] n chandal m.

tract [trækt] n (GEO) región f; (pamphlet) folleto.

traction ['trækʃən] n (AUT, power) tracción f; **in ~** (MED) en tracción.

traction engine n locomotora de tracción.

tractor ['træktə*] n tractor m.

trade [treɪd] n comercio, negocio; (skill, job) oficio, empleo; (industry) industria ♦ vi negociar, comerciar; **foreign ~** comercio exterior.

▶**trade in** vt (old car etc) ofrecer como parte del pago.

trade barrier n barrera comercial.

trade deficit n déficit m comercial.

Trade Descriptions Act n (BRIT) ley sobre descripciones comerciales.

trade discount n descuento comercial.

trade fair n feria de muestras.

trade-in ['treɪdɪn] adj: **~ price/value** precio/ valor de un artículo usado que se descuenta del precio de otro nuevo.

trademark ['treɪdmɑ:k] n marca de fábrica.

trade mission n misión f comercial.

trade name n marca registrada.
trade-off n: **a ~ (between)** un equilibrio (entre).
trade price n precio al detallista.
trader ['treɪdə*] n comerciante m/f.
trade reference n referencia comercial.
trade secret n secreto profesional.
tradesman ['treɪdzmən] n (shopkeeper) comerciante m/f.
trade union n sindicato.
trade unionist [-'juːnjənɪst] n sindicalista m/f.
trade wind n viento alisio.
trading ['treɪdɪŋ] n comercio.
trading account n cuenta de compraventa.
trading estate n (BRIT) polígono industrial.
trading stamp n cupón m, sello de prima.
tradition [trə'dɪʃən] n tradición f.
traditional [trə'dɪʃənl] adj tradicional.
traditionally [trə'dɪʃənlɪ] adv tradicionalmente.
traffic ['træfɪk] n (gen, AUT) tráfico, circulación f, tránsito ♦ vi: **to ~ in** (pej: liquor, drugs) traficar en; **air ~** tráfico aéreo.
traffic calming [-'kɑːmɪŋ] n reducción f de la velocidad de la circulación.
traffic circle n (US) glorieta de tráfico.
traffic island n refugio, isleta.
traffic jam n embotellamiento, atasco.
trafficker ['træfɪkə*] n traficante m/f.
traffic lights npl semáforo sg.
traffic offence, (US) **traffic violation** n infracción f de tráfico.
traffic warden n guardia m/f de tráfico.
tragedy ['trædʒədɪ] n tragedia.
tragic ['trædʒɪk] adj trágico.
tragically ['trædʒɪkəlɪ] adv trágicamente.
trail [treɪl] n (tracks) rastro, pista; (path) camino, sendero; (dust, smoke) estela ♦ vt (drag) arrastrar; (follow) seguir la pista de; (follow closely) vigilar ♦ vi arrastrarse; **to be on sb's ~** seguir la pista de algn.
▶**trail away, trail off** vi (sound) desvanecerse; (interest, voice) desaparecer.
▶**trail behind** vi quedar a la zaga.
trailer ['treɪlə*] n (AUT) remolque m; (caravan) caravana; (CINE) trailer m, avance m.
trail truck n (US) trailer m.
train [treɪn] n tren m; (of dress) cola; (series): **~ of events** curso de los acontecimientos ♦ vt (educate) formar; (teach skills to) adiestrar; (sportsman) entrenar; (dog) amaestrar; (point: gun

etc): **to ~ on** apuntar a ♦ vi (SPORT) entrenarse; (be educated, learn a skill) formarse; **to go by ~** ir en tren; **one's ~ of thought** el razonamiento de algn; **to ~ sb to do sth** enseñar a algn a hacer algo.
train attendant n (US RAIL) empleado/a de coches-cama.
trained [treɪnd] adj (worker) cualificado; (animal) amaestrado.
trainee [treɪ'niː] n trabajador(a) m/f en prácticas ♦ cpd: **he's a ~ teacher** (primary) es estudiante de magisterio; (secondary) está haciendo las prácticas del I.C.E.
trainer ['treɪnə*] n (SPORT) entrenador(a) m/f; (of animals) domador(a) m/f; **~s** npl (shoes) zapatillas fpl (de deporte).
training ['treɪnɪŋ] n formación f; entrenamiento; **to be in ~** (SPORT) estar entrenando; (: fit) estar en forma.
training college n (gen) colegio de formación profesional; (for teachers) escuela normal.
training course n curso de formación.
traipse [treɪps] vi andar penosamente.
trait [treɪt] n rasgo.
traitor ['treɪtə*] n traidor(a) m/f.
trajectory [trə'dʒɛktərɪ] n trayectoria, curso.
tram [træm] n (BRIT: also: **~car**) tranvía m.
tramline ['træmlaɪn] n carril m de tranvía.
tramp [træmp] n (person) vagabundo/a; (col: offensive: woman) puta ♦ vi andar con pasos pesados.
trample ['træmpl] vt: **to ~ (underfoot)** pisotear.
trampoline ['træmpəliːn] n trampolín m.
trance [trɑːns] n trance m; **to go into a ~** entrar en trance.
tranquil ['træŋkwɪl] adj tranquilo.
tranquillity, (US) **tranquility** [træŋ'kwɪlɪtɪ] n tranquilidad f.
tranquillizer, (US) **tranquilizer** ['træŋkwɪlaɪzə*] n (MED) tranquilizante m.
trans- [trænz] pref trans-, tras-.
transact [træn'zækt] vt (business) tramitar.
transaction [træn'zækʃən] n transacción f, operación f; **cash ~s** transacciones al contado.
transatlantic ['trænzət'læntɪk] adj transatlántico.
transcend [træn'sɛnd] vt rebasar.
transcendent [træn'sɛndənt] adj trascendente.
transcendental [trænsɛn'dɛntl] adj: **~ meditation** meditación f transcendental.
transcribe [træn'skraɪb] vt transcribir, copiar.
transcript ['trænskrɪpt] n copia.

transcription [træn'skrıpʃən] n transcripción f.

transept ['trænsɛpt] n crucero.

transfer n ['trænsfə*] transferencia; (*SPORT*) traspaso; (*picture, design*) calcomanía ♦ vt [træns'fə:*] trasladar, pasar; **to ~ the charges** (*BRIT TEL*) llamar a cobro revertido; **by bank ~** por transferencia bancaria *or* giro bancario; **to ~ money from one account to another** transferir dinero de una cuenta a otra; **to ~ sth to sb's name** transferir algo al nombre de algn.

transferable [træns'fə:rəbl] adj: **not ~** intransferible.

transfix [træns'fıks] vt traspasar; (*fig*): **~ed with fear** paralizado por el miedo.

transform [træns'fɔ:m] vt transformar.

transformation [trænsfə'meıʃən] n transformación f.

transformer [træns'fɔ:mə*] n (*ELEC*) transformador m.

transfusion [træns'fju:ʒən] n transfusión f.

transgress [træns'grɛs] vt (*go beyond*) traspasar; (*violate*) violar, infringir.

tranship [træn'ʃıp] vt trasbordar.

transient ['trænzıənt] adj transitorio.

transistor [træn'zıstə*] n (*ELEC*) transistor m.

transistorized [træn'zıstəraızd] adj (*circuit*) transistorizado.

transistor radio n transistor m.

transit ['trænzıt] n: **in ~** en tránsito.

transit camp n campamento de tránsito.

transition [træn'zıʃən] n transición f.

transitional [træn'zıʃənl] adj transitorio.

transition period n período de transición.

transitive ['trænzıtıv] adj (*LING*) transitivo.

transitively ['trænzıtıvlı] adv transitivamente.

transitory ['trænzıtərı] adj transitorio.

transit visa n visado de tránsito.

translate [trænz'leıt] vt: **to ~ (from/into)** traducir (de/a).

translation [trænz'leıʃən] n traducción f.

translator [trænz'leıtə*] n traductor(a) m/f.

translucent [trænz'lu:snt] adj traslúcido.

transmission [trænz'mıʃən] n transmisión f.

transmit [trænz'mıt] vt transmitir.

transmitter [trænz'mıtə*] n transmisor m; (*station*) emisora.

transparency [træns'pɛərnsı] n (*BRIT PHOT*) diapositiva.

transparent [træns'pærnt] adj transparente.

transpire [træns'paıə*] vi (*turn out*) resultar (ser); (*happen*) ocurrir, suceder; (*become known*): **it finally ~d that ...** por fin se supo que ....

transplant vt [træns'plɑ:nt] transplantar ♦ n ['trænsplɑ:nt] (*MED*) transplante m; **to have a heart ~** hacerse un transplante de corazón.

transport n ['trænspɔ:t] transporte m ♦ vt [træns'pɔ:t] transportar; **public ~** transporte m público.

transportable [træns'pɔ:təbl] adj transportable.

transportation [trænspɔ:'teıʃən] n transporte m; (*of prisoners*) deportación f.

transport café n (*BRIT*) bar-restaurante m de carretera.

transpose [træns'pəuz] vt transponer.

transsexual [trænz'sɛksjuəl] adj, n transexual m/f.

transverse ['trænzvə:s] adj transverso, transversal.

transvestite [trænz'vɛstaıt] n travesti m/f.

trap [træp] n (*snare, trick*) trampa; (*carriage*) cabriolé m ♦ vt coger (*SP*) *or* agarrar (*LAM*) en una trampa; (*immobilize*) bloquear; (*jam*) atascar; **to set** *or* **lay a ~ (for sb)** poner(le) una trampa (a algn); **to ~ one's finger in the door** pillarse el dedo en la puerta.

trap door n escotilla.

trapeze [trə'pi:z] n trapecio.

trapper ['træpə*] n trampero, cazador m.

trappings ['træpıŋz] npl adornos mpl.

trash [træʃ] n basura; (*nonsense*) tonterías fpl.

trash can n (*US*) cubo, balde m (*LAM*) *or* bote m (*LAM*) de la basura.

trash can liner n (*US*) bolsa de basura.

trashy ['træʃı] adj (*col*) chungo.

trauma ['trɔ:mə] n trauma m.

traumatic [trɔ:'mætık] adj (*PSYCH, fig*) traumático.

travel ['trævl] n viaje m ♦ vi viajar ♦ vt (*distance*) recorrer; **this wine doesn't ~ well** este vino pierde con los viajes.

travel agency n agencia de viajes.

travel agent n agente m/f de viajes.

travel brochure n folleto turístico.

traveller, (*US*) **traveler** ['trævlə*] n viajero/a; (*COMM*) viajante m/f.

traveller's cheque, (*US*) **traveler's check** n cheque m de viaje.

travelling, (*US*) **traveling** ['trævlıŋ] n los viajes, el viajar ♦ adj (*circus, exhibition*) ambulante ♦ cpd (*bag, clock*) de viaje.

travel(l)ing expenses npl dietas fpl.

travel(l)ing salesman n viajante m.

travelogue ['trævələg] n (*book*) relación f de viajes; (*film*) documental m de viajes;

(*talk*) recuento de viajes.
travel sickness *n* mareo.
traverse ['trævəs] *vt* atravesar.
travesty ['trævəstɪ] *n* parodia.
trawler ['trɔːlə*] *n* pesquero de arrastre.
tray [treɪ] *n* (*for carrying*) bandeja; (*on desk*) cajón *m*.
treacherous ['trɛtʃərəs] *adj* traidor(a); **road conditions are** ~ el estado de las carreteras es peligroso.
treachery ['trɛtʃərɪ] *n* traición *f*.
treacle ['triːkl] *n* (*BRIT*) melaza.
tread [trɛd] *n* paso, pisada; (*of tyre*) banda de rodadura ♦ *vi* (*pt* **trod**, *pp* **trodden** [trɔd, 'trɔdn]) pisar.
▶**tread on** *vt fus* pisar.
treas. *abbr* = **treasurer**.
treason ['triːzn] *n* traición *f*.
treasure ['trɛʒə*] *n* tesoro ♦ *vt* (*value*) apreciar, valorar.
treasure hunt *n* caza del tesoro.
treasurer ['trɛʒərə*] *n* tesorero/a.
treasury ['trɛʒərɪ] *n*: **the T**~, (*US*) **the T**~ **Department** ≈ el Ministerio de Economía y de Hacienda.
treasury bill *n* bono del Tesoro.
treat [triːt] *n* (*present*) regalo; (*pleasure*) placer *m* ♦ *vt* tratar; (*consider*) considerar; **to give sb a** ~ hacer un regalo a algn; **to** ~ **sb to sth** invitar a algn a algo; **to** ~ **sth as a joke** tomar algo a broma.
treatise ['triːtɪz] *n* tratado.
treatment ['triːtmənt] *n* tratamiento; **to have** ~ **for sth** recibir tratamiento por algo.
treaty ['triːtɪ] *n* tratado.
treble ['trɛbl] *adj* triple ♦ *vt* triplicar ♦ *vi* triplicarse.
treble clef *n* (*MUS*) clave *f* de sol.
tree [triː] *n* árbol *m*.
tree-lined ['triːlaɪnd] *adj* bordeado de árboles.
tree trunk *n* tronco de árbol.
trek [trɛk] *n* (*long journey*) expedición *f*; (*tiring walk*) caminata.
trellis ['trɛlɪs] *n* enrejado.
tremble ['trɛmbl] *vi* temblar.
trembling ['trɛmblɪŋ] *n* temblor *m* ♦ *adj* tembloroso.
tremendous [trɪ'mɛndəs] *adj* tremendo; (*enormous*) enorme; (*excellent*) estupendo.
tremendously [trɪ'mɛndəslɪ] *adv* enormemente, sobremanera; **he enjoyed it** ~ lo disfrutó de lo lindo.
tremor ['trɛmə*] *n* temblor *m*; (*also:* **earth** ~) temblor *m* de tierra.
trench [trɛntʃ] *n* zanja; (*MIL*) trinchera.
trench coat *n* trinchera.

trench warfare *n* guerra de trincheras.
trend [trɛnd] *n* (*tendency*) tendencia; (*of events*) curso; (*fashion*) moda; ~ **towards/away from sth** tendencia hacia/ en contra de algo; **to set the** ~ marcar la pauta.
trendy ['trɛndɪ] *adj* de moda.
trepidation [trɛpɪ'deɪʃən] *n* inquietud *f*.
trespass ['trɛspəs] *vi*: **to** ~ **on** entrar sin permiso en; **"no** ~**ing"** "prohibido el paso".
trespasser ['trɛspəsə*] *n* intruso/a *m/f*; **"**~**s will be prosecuted"** "se procesará a los intrusos".
tress [trɛs] *n* guedeja.
trestle ['trɛsl] *n* caballete *m*.
trestle table *n* mesa de caballete.
tri- [traɪ] *pref* tri-.
trial ['traɪəl] *n* (*LAW*) juicio, proceso; (*test: of machine etc*) prueba; (*hardship*) desgracia; ~**s** *npl* (*ATHLETICS, of horses*) pruebas *fpl*; **to bring sb to** ~ (**for a crime**) llevar a algn a juicio (por un delito); ~ **by jury** juicio ante jurado; **to be sent for** ~ ser remitido al tribunal; **by** ~ **and error** a fuerza de probar.
trial balance *n* balance *m* de comprobación.
trial basis *n*: **on a** ~ a modo de prueba.
trial offer *n* oferta de prueba.
trial run *n* prueba.
triangle ['traɪæŋgl] *n* (*MATH, MUS*) triángulo.
triangular [traɪ'æŋgjulə*] *adj* triangular.
triathlon [traɪ'æθlɔn] *n* triatlón *m*.
tribal ['traɪbəl] *adj* tribal.
tribe [traɪb] *n* tribu *f*.
tribesman ['traɪbzmən] *n* miembro de una tribu.
tribulation [trɪbju'leɪʃən] *n* tribulación *f*.
tribunal [traɪ'bjuːnl] *n* tribunal *m*.
tributary ['trɪbjuːtərɪ] *n* (*river*) afluente *m*.
tribute ['trɪbjuːt] *n* homenaje *m*, tributo; **to pay** ~ **to** rendir homenaje a.
trice [traɪs] *n*: **in a** ~ en un santiamén.
trick [trɪk] *n* trampa; (*conjuring* ~, *deceit*) truco; (*joke*) broma; (*CARDS*) baza ♦ *vt* engañar; **it's a** ~ **of the light** es una ilusión óptica; **to play a** ~ **on sb** gastar una broma a algn; **that should do the** ~ eso servirá; **to** ~ **sb out of sth** quitarle algo a algn con engaños; **to** ~ **sb into doing sth** hacer que algn haga algo con engaños.
trickery ['trɪkərɪ] *n* engaño.
trickle ['trɪkl] *n* (*of water etc*) hilo ♦ *vi* gotear.
trick question *n* pregunta capciosa.

trickster ['trɪkstə*] *n* estafador(a) *m/f.*
tricky ['trɪkɪ] *adj* difícil; (*problem*) delicado.
tricycle ['traɪsɪkl] *n* triciclo.
tried [traɪd] *adj* probado.
trifle ['traɪfl] *n* bagatela; (*CULIN*) *dulce de bizcocho, gelatina, fruta y natillas* ♦ *adv*: **a ~ long** un pelín largo ♦ *vi*: **to ~ with** jugar con.
trifling ['traɪflɪŋ] *adj* insignificante.
trigger ['trɪgə*] *n* (*of gun*) gatillo.
▶**trigger off** *vt* desencadenar.
trigonometry [trɪgə'nɔmətrɪ] *n* trigonometría.
trilby ['trɪlbɪ] *n* (*also*: **~ hat**) sombrero flexible *or* tirolés.
trill [trɪl] *n* (*of bird*) gorjeo; (*MUS*) trino.
trilogy ['trɪlədʒɪ] *n* trilogía.
trim [trɪm] *adj* (*elegant*) aseado; (*house, garden*) en buen estado; (*figure*): **to be ~** tener buen talle ♦ *n* (*haircut etc*) recorte *m* ♦ *vt* (*neaten*) arreglar; (*cut*) recortar; (*decorate*) adornar; (*NAUT: a sail*) orientar; **to keep in (good) ~** mantener en buen estado.
trimmings ['trɪmɪŋz] *npl* (*extras*) accesorios *mpl*; (*cuttings*) recortes *mpl.*
Trinidad and Tobago ['trɪnɪdæd-] *n* Trinidad *f* y Tobago.
Trinity ['trɪnɪtɪ] *n*: **the ~** la Trinidad.
trinket ['trɪŋkɪt] *n* chuchería, baratija.
trio ['triːəu] *n* trío.
trip [trɪp] *n* viaje *m*; (*excursion*) excursión *f*; (*stumble*) traspié *m* ♦ *vi* (*stumble*) tropezar; (*go lightly*) andar a paso ligero; **on a ~** de viaje.
▶**trip over** *vt fus* tropezar con.
▶**trip up** *vi* tropezar, caerse ♦ *vt* hacer tropezar *or* caer.
tripartite [traɪ'pɑːtaɪt] *adj* (*agreement, talks*) tripartito.
tripe [traɪp] *n* (*CULIN*) callos *mpl*; (*pej*: *rubbish*) bobadas *fpl.*
triple ['trɪpl] *adj* triple ♦ *adv*: **~ the distance/the speed** 3 veces la distancia/la velocidad.
triple jump *n* triple salto.
triplets ['trɪplɪts] *npl* trillizos/as *m/fpl.*
triplicate ['trɪplɪkət] *n*: **in ~** por triplicado.
tripod ['traɪpɔd] *n* trípode *m.*
Tripoli ['trɪpəlɪ] *n* Trípoli *m.*
tripper ['trɪpə*] *n* turista *m/f*, excursionista *m/f.*
tripwire ['trɪpwaɪə*] *n* cable *m* de trampa.
trite [traɪt] *adj* trillado.
triumph ['traɪʌmf] *n* triunfo ♦ *vi*: **to ~ (over)** vencer.
triumphal [traɪ'ʌmfl] *adj* triunfal.
triumphant [traɪ'ʌmfənt] *adj* triunfante.

triumphantly [traɪ'ʌmfəntlɪ] *adv* triunfalmente, en tono triunfal.
trivia ['trɪvɪə] *npl* trivialidades *fpl.*
trivial ['trɪvɪəl] *adj* insignificante, trivial.
triviality [trɪvɪ'ælɪtɪ] *n* insignificancia, trivialidad *f.*
trivialize ['trɪvɪəlaɪz] *vt* trivializar.
trod [trɔd] *pt of* **tread.**
trodden ['trɔdn] *pp of* **tread.**
trolley ['trɔlɪ] *n* carrito; (*in hospital*) camilla.
trolley bus *n* trolebús *m.*
trombone [trɔm'bəun] *n* trombón *m.*
troop [truːp] *n* grupo, banda; *see also* **troops.**
▶**troop in** *vi* entrar en tropel.
▶**troop out** *vi* salir en tropel.
troop carrier *n* (*plane*) transporte *m* (militar); (*NAUT: also*: **troopship**) (buque *m* de) transporte *m.*
trooper ['truːpə*] *n* (*MIL*) soldado (de caballería); (*US: policeman*) policía *m/f* montado/a.
trooping the colour ['truːpɪŋ-] *n* (*ceremony*) presentación *f* de la bandera.
troopship ['truːpʃɪp] *n* (buque *m* de) transporte *m.*
trophy ['trəufɪ] *n* trofeo.
tropic ['trɔpɪk] *n* trópico; **the ~s** los trópicos, la zona tropical; **T~ of Cancer/ Capricorn** trópico de Cáncer/Capricornio.
tropical ['trɔpɪkl] *adj* tropical.
trot [trɔt] *n* trote *m* ♦ *vi* trotar; **on the ~** (*BRIT fig*) seguidos/as.
▶**trot out** *vt* (*excuse, reason*) volver a usar; (*names, facts*) sacar a relucir.
trouble ['trʌbl] *n* problema *m*, dificultad *f*; (*worry*) preocupación *f*; (*bother, effort*) molestia, esfuerzo; (*unrest*) inquietud *f*; (*with machine etc*) fallo, avería; (*MED*): **stomach ~** problemas *mpl* gástricos ♦ *vt* molestar; (*worry*) preocupar, inquietar ♦ *vi*: **to ~ to do sth** molestarse en hacer algo; **~s** *npl* (*POL etc*) conflictos *mpl*; **to be in ~** estar en un apuro; (*for doing wrong*) tener problemas; **to have ~ doing sth** tener dificultad en *or* para hacer algo; **to go to the ~ of doing sth** tomarse la molestia de hacer algo; **what's the ~?** ¿qué pasa?; **the ~ is ...** el problema es ..., lo que pasa es ...; **please don't ~ yourself** por favor no se moleste.
troubled ['trʌbld] *adj* (*person*) preocupado; (*epoch, life*) agitado.
trouble-free ['trʌblfriː] *adj* sin problemas *or* dificultades.
troublemaker ['trʌblmeɪkə*] *n* agitador(a) *m/f.*
troubleshooter ['trʌblʃuːtə*] *n* (*in conflict*)

mediador(a) *m/f*.
troublesome ['trʌblsəm] *adj* molesto,
inoportuno.
trouble spot *n* centro de fricción, punto
caliente.
troubling ['trʌblɪŋ] *adj* (*thought*)
preocupante; **these are ~ times** son
malos tiempos.
trough [trɔf] *n* (*also:* **drinking ~**)
abrevadero; (*also:* **feeding ~**) comedero;
(*channel*) canal *m*.
trounce [trauns] *vt* dar una paliza a.
troupe [tru:p] *n* grupo.
trouser press *n* prensa para pantalones.
trousers ['trauzəz] *npl* pantalones *mpl*; **short
~** pantalones *mpl* cortos.
trouser suit *n* traje *m* de chaqueta y
pantalón.
trousseau, *pl* **~x** *or* **~s** ['tru:səu, -z] *n*
ajuar *m*.
trout [traut] *n* (*pl inv*) trucha.
trowel ['trauəl] *n* paleta.
truant ['truənt] *n*: **to play ~** (*BRIT*) hacer
novillos.
truce [tru:s] *n* tregua.
truck [trʌk] *n* (*US*) camión *m*; (*RAIL*) vagón
m.
truck driver *n* camionero/a.
trucker ['trʌkə*] *n* (*esp US*) camionero/a.
truck farm *n* (*US*) huerto de hortalizas.
trucking ['trʌkɪŋ] *n* (*esp US*) transporte *m*
en camión.
trucking company *n* (*US*) compañía de
transporte por carretera.
truckload ['trʌkləud] *n* camión *m* lleno.
truculent ['trʌkjulənt] *adj* agresivo.
trudge [trʌdʒ] *vi* caminar penosamente.
true [tru:] *adj* verdadero; (*accurate*) exacto;
(*genuine*) auténtico; (*faithful*) fiel; (*wheel*)
centrado; (*wall*) a plomo; (*beam*) alineado;
~ to life verídico; **to come ~** realizarse,
cumplirse.
truffle ['trʌfl] *n* trufa.
truly ['tru:lɪ] *adv* realmente; (*faithfully*)
fielmente; **yours ~** (*in letter-writing*)
atentamente.
trump [trʌmp] *n* (*CARDS*) triunfo; **to turn up
~s** (*fig*) salir *or* resultar bien.
trump card *n* triunfo; (*fig*) baza.
trumped-up ['trʌmptʌp] *adj* inventado.
trumpet ['trʌmpɪt] *n* trompeta.
truncated [trʌŋ'keɪtɪd] *adj* truncado.
truncheon ['trʌntʃən] *n* (*BRIT*) porra.
trundle ['trʌndl] *vt, vi*: **to ~ along** rodar
haciendo ruido.
trunk [trʌŋk] *n* (*of tree, person*) tronco; (*of
elephant*) trompa; (*case*) baúl *m*; (*US AUT*)
maletero, baúl *m* (*LAM*); *see also* **trunks**.

trunk call *n* (*BRIT TEL*) llamada
interurbana.
trunk road *n* carretera principal.
trunks [trʌŋks] *npl* (*also:* **swimming ~**)
bañador *m*.
truss [trʌs] *n* (*MED*) braguero ♦ *vt*: **to ~ (up)**
atar.
trust [trʌst] *n* confianza; (*COMM*) trust *m*;
(*LAW*) fideicomiso ♦ *vt* (*rely on*) tener
confianza en; (*entrust*): **to ~ sth to sb**
confiar algo a algn; (*hope*): **to ~ (that)**
esperar (que); **in ~** en fideicomiso; **you'll
have to take it on ~** tienes que aceptarlo
a ojos cerrados.
trust company *n* banco fideicomisario.
trusted ['trʌstɪd] *adj* de confianza, fiable, de
fiar.
trustee [trʌs'ti:] *n* (*LAW*) fideicomisario.
trustful ['trʌstful] *adj* confiado.
trust fund *n* fondo fiduciario *or* de
fideicomiso.
trusting ['trʌstɪŋ] *adj* confiado.
trustworthy ['trʌstwə:ðɪ] *adj* digno de
confianza, fiable, de fiar.
trusty ['trʌstɪ] *adj* fiel.
truth, ~s [tru:θ, tru:ðz] *n* verdad *f*.
truthful ['tru:θfəl] *adj* (*person*) sincero;
(*account*) fidedigno.
truthfully ['tru:θfulɪ] *adv* (*answer*) con
sinceridad.
truthfulness ['tru:θfulnɪs] *n* (*of account*)
verdad *f*; (*of person*) sinceridad *f*.
try [traɪ] *n* tentativa, intento; (*RUGBY*)
ensayo ♦ *vt* (*LAW*) juzgar, procesar; (*test:
sth new*) probar, someter a prueba;
(*attempt*) intentar; (*strain: patience*) hacer
perder ♦ *vi* probar; **to give sth a ~**
intentar hacer algo; **to ~ one's (very)
best** *or* **hardest** poner todo su empeño,
esmerarse; **to ~ to do sth** intentar hacer
algo.
▶**try on** *vt* (*clothes*) probarse.
▶**try out** *vt* probar, poner a prueba.
trying ['traɪɪŋ] *adj* cansado; (*person*) pesado.
tsar [zɑ:*] *n* zar *m*.
T-shirt ['ti:ʃə:t] *n* camiseta.
T-square ['ti:skwɛə*] *n* regla en T.
TT *adj abbr* (*BRIT col*) = **teetotal** ♦ *abbr* (*US*)
= *Trust Territory*.
tub [tʌb] *n* cubo (*SP*), balde *m* (*LAM*); (*bath*)
bañera, tina (*esp LAM*).
tuba ['tju:bə] *n* tuba.
tubby ['tʌbɪ] *adj* regordete.
tube [tju:b] *n* tubo; (*BRIT: underground*)
metro; (*US col: television*) tele *f*.
tubeless ['tju:blɪs] *adj* (*tyre*) sin cámara.
tuber ['tju:bə*] *n* (*BOT*) tubérculo.
tuberculosis [tjubəːkju'ləusɪs] *n*

tuberculosis *f inv.*
tube station *n* (*BRIT*) estación *f* de metro.
tubing ['tjuːbɪŋ] *n* tubería (*SP*), cañería; **a piece of** ~ un trozo de tubo.
tubular ['tjuːbjulə*] *adj* tubular.
TUC *n abbr* (*BRIT*: = *Trades Union Congress*) *federación nacional de sindicatos.*
tuck [tʌk] *n* (*SEWING*) pliegue *m* ♦ *vt* (*put*) poner.
▶**tuck away** *vt* esconder.
▶**tuck in** *vt* meter; (*child*) arropar ♦ *vi* (*eat*) comer con apetito.
▶**tuck up** *vt* (*child*) arropar.
tuck shop *n* (*SCOL*) tienda de golosinas.
Tue(s). *abbr* (= *Tuesday*) mart.
Tuesday ['tjuːzdɪ] *n* martes *m inv*; **on** ~ el martes; **on** ~**s** los martes; **every** ~ todos los martes; **every other** ~ cada dos martes, un martes sí y otro no; **last/next** ~ el martes pasado/próximo; **a week/ fortnight on** ~, ~ **week/fortnight** del martes en 8/15 días, del martes en una semana/dos semanas.
tuft [tʌft] *n* mechón *m*; (*of grass etc*) manojo.
tug [tʌg] *n* (*ship*) remolcador *m* ♦ *vt* remolcar.
tug-of-love [tʌgəv'lʌv] *n*: ~ **children** *hijos envueltos en el litigio de los padres por su custodia.*
tug-of-war [tʌgəv'wɔː*] *n* juego de la cuerda.
tuition [tjuː'ɪʃən] *n* (*BRIT*) enseñanza; (: *private* ~) clases *fpl* particulares; (*US*: *school fees*) matrícula.
tulip ['tjuːlɪp] *n* tulipán *m*.
tumble ['tʌmbl] *n* (*fall*) caída ♦ *vi* caerse, tropezar; **to** ~ **to sth** (*col*) caer en la cuenta de algo.
tumbledown ['tʌmbldaun] *adj* ruinoso.
tumble dryer *n* (*BRIT*) secadora.
tumbler ['tʌmblə*] *n* vaso.
tummy ['tʌmɪ] *n* (*col*) barriga, vientre *m*.
tumour, (*US*) **tumor** ['tjuːmə*] *n* tumor *m*.
tumult ['tjuːmʌlt] *n* tumulto.
tumultuous [tjuː'mʌltjuəs] *adj* tumultuoso.
tuna ['tjuːnə] *n* (*pl inv*) (*also*: ~ **fish**) atún *m*.
tundra ['tʌndrə] *n* tundra.
tune [tjuːn] *n* (*melody*) melodía ♦ *vt* (*MUS*) afinar; (*RADIO, TV, AUT*) sintonizar; **to be in/out of** ~ (*instrument*) estar afinado/ desafinado; (*singer*) afinar/desafinar; **to be in/out of** ~ **with** (*fig*) armonizar/ desentonar con; **to the** ~ **of** (*fig: amount*) por (la) cantidad de.
▶**tune in** *vi* (*RADIO, TV*): **to** ~ **in** (**to**) sintonizar (con).
▶**tune up** *vi* (*musician*) afinar (su instrumento).

tuneful ['tjuːnful] *adj* melodioso.
tuner ['tjuːnə*] *n* (*radio set*) sintonizador *m*; **piano** ~ afinador(a) *m/f* de pianos.
tungsten ['tʌŋstn] *n* tungsteno.
tunic ['tjuːnɪk] *n* túnica.
tuning ['tjuːnɪŋ] *n* sintonización *f*; (*MUS*) afinación *f*.
tuning fork *n* diapasón *m*.
Tunis ['tjuːnɪs] *n* Túnez *m*.
Tunisia [tjuː'nɪzɪə] *n* Túnez *m*.
Tunisian [tjuː'nɪzɪən] *adj*, *n* tunecino/a *m/f*.
tunnel ['tʌnl] *n* túnel *m*; (*in mine*) galería ♦ *vi* construir un túnel/una galería.
tunnel vision *n* (*MED*) visión *f* periférica restringida; (*fig*) estrechez *f* de miras.
tunny ['tʌnɪ] *n* atún *m*.
turban ['təːbən] *n* turbante *m*.
turbid ['təːbɪd] *adj* turbio.
turbine ['təːbaɪn] *n* turbina.
turbo ['təːbəu] *n* turbo.
turboprop ['təːbəuprɔp] *n* turbohélice *m*.
turbot ['təːbət] *n* (*pl inv*) rodaballo.
turbulence ['təːbjuləns] *n* (*AVIAT*) turbulencia.
turbulent ['təːbjulənt] *adj* turbulento.
tureen [tə'riːn] *n* sopera.
turf [təːf] *n* césped *m*; (*clod*) tepe *m* ♦ *vt* cubrir con césped.
▶**turf out** *vt* (*col*) echar a la calle.
turf accountant *n* corredor(a) *m/f* de apuestas.
turgid ['təːdʒɪd] *adj* (*prose*) pesado.
Turin [tjuə'rɪn] *n* Turín *m*.
Turk [təːk] *n* turco/a.
Turkey ['təːkɪ] *n* Turquía.
turkey ['təːkɪ] *n* pavo.
Turkish ['təːkɪʃ] *adj* turco ♦ *n* (*LING*) turco.
Turkish bath *n* baño turco.
turmeric ['təːmərɪk] *n* cúrcuma.
turmoil ['təːmɔɪl] *n* desorden *m*, alboroto.
turn [təːn] *n* turno; (*in road*) curva; (*THEAT*) número; (*MED*) ataque *m* ♦ *vt* girar, volver, voltear (*LAM*); (*collar, steak*) dar la vuelta a; (*shape: wood, metal*) tornear; (*change*): **to** ~ **sth into** convertir algo en ♦ *vi* volver, voltearse (*LAM*); (*person: look back*) volverse; (*reverse direction*) dar la vuelta, voltear (*LAM*); (*milk*) cortarse; (*change*) cambiar; (*become*): **to** ~ **into sth** convertirse *or* transformarse en algo; **a good** ~ un favor; **it gave me quite a** ~ me dio un susto; **"no left** ~**"** (*AUT*) "prohibido girar a la izquierda"; **it's your** ~ te toca a ti; **in** ~ por turnos; **to take** ~**s** turnarse; **at the** ~ **of the year/century** a fin de año/a finales de siglo; **to take a** ~ **for the worse** (*situation, patient*) empeorar; **they** ~**ed him against us** le pusieron en contra

nuestra; **the car ~ed the corner** el coche dobló la esquina; **to ~ left** (*AUT*) torcer *or* girar a la izquierda; **she has no-one to ~** to no tiene a quién recurrir.
►**turn away** *vi* apartar la vista ♦ *vt* (*reject: person, business*) rechazar.
►**turn back** *vi* volverse atrás.
►**turn down** *vt* (*refuse*) rechazar; (*reduce*) bajar; (*fold*) doblar.
►**turn in** *vi* (*col: go to bed*) acostarse ♦ *vt* (*fold*) doblar hacia dentro.
►**turn off** *vi* (*from road*) desviarse ♦ *vt* (*light, radio etc*) apagar; (*engine*) parar.
►**turn on** *vt* (*light, radio etc*) encender, prender (*LAM*); (*engine*) poner en marcha.
►**turn out** *vt* (*light, gas*) apagar; (*produce: goods, novel etc*) producir ♦ *vi* (*attend: troops*) presentarse; (*: doctor*) atender; **to ~ out to be ... resultar ser ....
►**turn over** *vi* (*person*) volverse ♦ *vt* (*mattress, card*) dar la vuelta a; (*page*) volver.
►**turn round** *vi* volverse; (*rotate*) girar.
►**turn to** *vt fus:* **to ~ to sb** acudir a algn.
►**turn up** *vi* (*person*) llegar, presentarse; (*lost object*) aparecer ♦ *vt* (*radio*) subir, poner más alto; (*heat, gas*) poner más fuerte.
turnabout ['tɜːnəbaut], **turnaround** ['tɜːnəraund] *n* (*fig*) giro total.
turncoat ['tɜːnkəut] *n* renegado/a.
turned-up ['tɜːndʌp] *adj* (*nose*) respingón/ona.
turning ['tɜːnɪŋ] *n* (*side road*) bocacalle *f*; (*bend*) curva; **the first ~ on the right** la primera bocacalle a la derecha.
turning point *n* (*fig*) momento decisivo.
turnip ['tɜːnɪp] *n* nabo.
turnkey system ['tɜːnkiː-] *n* (*COMPUT*) sistema *m* de seguridad.
turnout ['tɜːnaut] *n* asistencia, número de asistentes, público.
turnover ['tɜːnəuvə*] *n* (*COMM: amount of money*) facturación *f*; (*: of goods*) movimiento; **there is a rapid ~ in staff** hay mucho movimiento de personal.
turnpike ['tɜːnpaɪk] *n* (*US*) autopista de peaje.
turnstile ['tɜːnstaɪl] *n* torniquete *m*.
turntable ['tɜːnteɪbl] *n* plato.
turn-up ['tɜːnʌp] *n* (*BRIT: on trousers*) vuelta.
turpentine ['tɜːpəntaɪn] *n* (*also:* **turps**) trementina.
turquoise ['tɜːkwɔɪz] *n* (*stone*) turquesa ♦ *adj* color turquesa.
turret ['tʌrɪt] *n* torreón *m*.
turtle ['tɜːtl] *n* tortuga (marina).

turtleneck (sweater) ['tɜːtlnɛk-] *n* (jersey *m* de) cuello cisne.
Tuscany ['tʌskənɪ] *n* Toscana.
tusk [tʌsk] *n* colmillo.
tussle ['tʌsl] *n* lucha, pelea.
tutor ['tjuːtə*] *n* profesor(a) *m/f*.
tutorial [tjuː'tɔːrɪəl] *n* (*SCOL*) seminario.
tuxedo [tʌk'siːdəu] *n* (*US*) smóking *m*, esmoquin *m*.
TV [tiː'viː] *n abbr* (= *television*) televisión *f*.
TV dinner *n* cena precocinada.
TV licence *n licencia que se paga por el uso del televisor, destinada a financiar la BBC.*
twaddle ['twɔdl] *n* (*col*) tonterías *fpl*.
twang [twæŋ] *n* (*of instrument*) tañido; (*of voice*) timbre *m* nasal.
tweak [twiːk] *vt* (*nose, ear*) pellizcar; (*hair*) tirar.
tweed [twiːd] *n* tweed *m*.
tweezers ['twiːzəz] *npl* pinzas *fpl* (de depilar).
twelfth [twelfθ] *num* duodécimo.
Twelfth Night *n* (Día *m* de) Reyes *mpl*.
twelve [twelv] *num* doce; **at ~ o'clock** (*midday*) a mediodía; (*midnight*) a medianoche.
twentieth ['twentɪθ] *num* vigésimo.
twenty ['twentɪ] *num* veinte.
twerp [twɜːp] *n* (*col*) idiota *m/f*.
twice [twaɪs] *adv* dos veces; **~ as much** dos veces más, el doble; **she is ~ your age** ella te dobla edad; **~ a week** dos veces a la *or* por semana.
twiddle ['twɪdl] *vt, vi:* **to ~ (with) sth** dar vueltas a algo; **to ~ one's thumbs** (*fig*) estar de brazos cruzados.
twig [twɪg] *n* ramita ♦ *vi* (*col*) caer en la cuenta.
twilight ['twaɪlaɪt] *n* crepúsculo; (*morning*) madrugada; **in the ~** en la media luz.
twill [twɪl] *n* sarga, estameña.
twin [twɪn] *adj, n* gemelo/a *m/f* ♦ *vt* hermanar.
twin(-bedded) room ['twɪn('bɛdɪd)-] *n* habitación *f* con dos camas.
twin beds *npl* camas *fpl* gemelas.
twin-carburettor ['twɪnkɑːbju'rɛtə*] *adj* de dos carburadores.
twine [twaɪn] *n* bramante *m* ♦ *vi* (*plant*) enroscarse.
twin-engined [twɪn'ɛndʒɪnd] *adj* bimotor; **~ aircraft** avión *m* bimotor.
twinge [twɪndʒ] *n* (*of pain*) punzada; (*of conscience*) remordimiento.
twinkle ['twɪŋkl] *n* centelleo ♦ *vi* centellear; (*eyes*) parpadear.
twin town *n* ciudad *f* hermanada *or*

gemela.
twirl [twɜ:l] *n* giro ♦ *vt* dar vueltas a ♦ *vi* piruetear.
twist [twɪst] *n (action)* torsión *f*; *(in road, coil)* vuelta; *(in wire, flex)* doblez *f*; *(in story)* giro ♦ *vt* torcer, retorcer; *(roll around)* enrollar; *(fig)* deformar ♦ *vi* serpentear; **to ~ one's ankle/wrist** *(MED)* torcerse el tobillo/la muñeca.
twisted ['twɪstɪd] *adj (wire, rope)* trenzado, enroscado; *(ankle, wrist)* torcido; *(fig: logic, mind)* retorcido.
twit [twɪt] *n (col)* tonto.
twitch [twɪtʃ] *n* sacudida; *(nervous)* tic *m* nervioso ♦ *vi* moverse nerviosamente.
two [tu:] *num* dos; **~ by ~, in ~s** de dos en dos; **to put ~ and ~ together** *(fig)* atar cabos.
two-bit [tu:'bɪt] *adj (esp US col, pej)* de poca monta, de tres al cuarto.
two-door [tu:'dɔ:*] *adj (AUT)* de dos puertas.
two-faced [tu:'feɪst] *adj (pej: person)* falso, hipócrita.
twofold ['tu:fəʊld] *adv:* **to increase ~** duplicarse ♦ *adj (increase)* doble; *(reply)* en dos partes.
two-piece [tu:'pi:s] *n (also: ~ suit)* traje *m* de dos piezas; *(also: ~ swimsuit)* dos piezas *m inv*, bikini *m*.
two-seater [tu:'si:tə*] *n (plane, car)* avión *m*/coche *m* de dos plazas, biplaza *m*.
twosome ['tu:səm] *n (people)* pareja.
two-stroke ['tu:strəʊk] *n (also: ~ engine)* motor *m* de dos tiempos ♦ *adj* de dos tiempos.
two-tone ['tu:'təʊn] *adj (colour)* bicolor, de dos tonos.
two-way ['tu:weɪ] *adj:* **~ traffic** circulación *f* de dos sentidos; **~ radio** radio *f* emisora y receptora.
TX *abbr (US)* = Texas.
tycoon [taɪ'ku:n] *n:* **(business) ~** magnate *m/f*.
type [taɪp] *n (category)* tipo, género; *(model)* modelo; *(TYP)* tipo, letra ♦ *vt (letter etc)* escribir a máquina; **what ~ do you want?** ¿qué tipo quieres?; **in bold/italic ~** en negrita/cursiva.
type-cast ['taɪpkɑ:st] *adj (actor)* encasillado.
typeface ['taɪpfeɪs] *n* tipo de letra.
typescript ['taɪpskrɪpt] *n* texto mecanografiado.
typeset ['taɪpsɛt] *vt (irreg: like* set*)* componer.
typesetter ['taɪpsɛtə*] *n* cajista *m/f*.
typewriter ['taɪpraɪtə*] *n* máquina de

escribir.
typewritten ['taɪprɪtn] *adj* mecanografiado.
typhoid ['taɪfɔɪd] *n* (fiebre *f*) tifoidea.
typhoon [taɪ'fu:n] *n* tifón *m*.
typhus ['taɪfəs] *n* tifus *m*.
typical ['tɪpɪkl] *adj* típico.
typically ['tɪpɪklɪ] *adv* típicamente.
typify ['tɪpɪfaɪ] *vt* tipificar.
typing ['taɪpɪŋ] *n* mecanografía.
typing pool *n (BRIT)* servicio de mecanógrafos.
typist ['taɪpɪst] *n* mecanógrafo/a.
typography [taɪ'pɒgrəfɪ] *n* tipografía.
tyranny ['tɪrənɪ] *n* tiranía.
tyrant ['taɪərənt] *n* tirano/a.
tyre, (*US*) **tire** ['taɪə*] *n* neumático, llanta (*LAM*).
tyre pressure *n* presión *f* de los neumáticos.
Tyrol [tɪ'rəʊl] *n* Tirol *m*.
Tyrolean [tɪrə'lɪən], **Tyrolese** [tɪrə'li:z] *adj* tirolés/esa.
Tyrrhenian Sea [tɪ'ri:nɪən-] *n* Mar *m* Tirreno.
tzar [zɑ:*] *n* = **tsar**.

U u

U, u [ju:] *n (letter)* U, u *f*; **U for Uncle** U de Uruguay.
U *n abbr (BRIT CINE: = universal)* todos los públicos.
UB40 *n abbr (BRIT: = unemployment benefit form 40)* número de referencia en la solicitud de inscripción en la lista de parados; por extensión, la tarjeta del paro o su beneficiario.
U-bend ['ju:bɛnd] *n (AUT, in pipe)* recodo.
ubiquitous [ju:'bɪkwɪtəs] *adj* omnipresente, ubicuo.
UCAS ['ju:kæs] *n abbr BRIT: = Universities and Colleges Admissions Service.*
UDA *n abbr (BRIT: = Ulster Defence Association)* organización paramilitar protestante de Irlanda del Norte.
UDC *n abbr (BRIT) = Urban District Council.*
udder ['ʌdə*] *n* ubre *f*.
UDI *n abbr (BRIT POL) = unilateral declaration of independence.*
UDR *n abbr (BRIT: = Ulster Defence Regiment)* fuerza de seguridad de Irlanda del Norte.

UEFA [ju:'eɪfə] *n abbr* (= *Union of European Football Associations*) U.E.F.A. *f.*

UFO ['ju:fəu] *n abbr* = (*unidentified flying object*) OVNI *m.*

Uganda [ju:'gændə] *n* Uganda.

Ugandan [ju:'gændən] *adj* de Uganda.

UGC *n abbr* (*BRIT:* = *University Grants Committee*) entidad gubernamental que controla las finanzas de las universidades.

ugh [ə:h] *excl* ¡uf!

ugliness ['ʌglɪnɪs] *n* fealdad *f.*

ugly ['ʌglɪ] *adj* feo; (*dangerous*) peligroso.

UHF *abbr* (= *ultra-high frequency*) UHF *f.*

UHT *adj abbr* (= *ultra heat treated*): ~ **milk** leche *f* uperizada.

UK *n abbr* (= *United Kingdom*) Reino Unido, R.U.

Ukraine [ju:'kreɪn] *n* Ucrania.

Ukrainian [ju:'kreɪnɪən] *adj* ucraniano ♦ *n* ucraniano/a; (*LING*) ucraniano.

ulcer ['ʌlsə*] *n* úlcera; **mouth** ~ úlcera bucal.

Ulster ['ʌlstə*] *n* Ulster *m.*

ulterior [ʌl'tɪərɪə*] *adj* ulterior; ~ **motive** segundas intenciones *fpl.*

ultimate ['ʌltɪmət] *adj* último, final; (*greatest*) mayor ♦ *n*: **the** ~ **in luxury** el colmo del lujo.

ultimately ['ʌltɪmətlɪ] *adv* (*in the end*) por último, al final; (*fundamentally*) a fin de cuentas.

ultimatum, *pl* ~**s or ultimata** [ʌltɪ'meɪtəm, -tə] *n* ultimátum *m.*

ultra- ['ʌltrə] *pref* ultra-.

ultrasonic [ʌltrə'sɔnɪk] *adj* ultrasónico.

ultrasound ['ʌltrəsaund] *n* (*MED*) ultrasonido.

ultraviolet ['ʌltrə'vaɪəlɪt] *adj* ultravioleta.

um [ʌm] *interj*; (*col: in hesitation*) esto, este (*LAM*).

umbilical cord [ʌmbɪ'laɪkl-] *n* cordón *m* umbilical.

umbrage ['ʌmbrɪdʒ] *n*: **to take** ~ **(at)** ofenderse (por).

umbrella [ʌm'brɛlə] *n* paraguas *m inv*; **under the** ~ **of** (*fig*) bajo la protección de.

umlaut ['umlaut] *n* diéresis *f inv.*

umpire ['ʌmpaɪə*] *n* árbitro ♦ *vt* arbitrar.

umpteen [ʌmp'ti:n] *num* enésimos/as; **for the** ~**th time** por enésima vez.

UMW *n abbr* (= *United Mineworkers of America*) sindicato de mineros.

UN *n abbr* (= *United Nations*) ONU *f.*

un- [ʌn] *pref* in-; des-; no ...; poco ...; nada ....

unabashed [ʌnə'bæʃt] *adj* nada avergonzado.

unabated [ʌnə'beɪtɪd] *adj*: **to continue** ~

seguir con la misma intensidad.

unable [ʌn'eɪbl] *adj*: **to be** ~ **to do sth** no poder hacer algo; (*not know how to*) ser incapaz de hacer algo, no saber hacer algo.

unabridged [ʌnə'brɪdʒd] *adj* íntegro.

unacceptable [ʌnək'sɛptəbl] *adj* (*proposal, behaviour, price*) inaceptable; **it's** ~ **that** no se puede aceptar que.

unaccompanied [ʌnə'kʌmpənɪd] *adj* no acompañado; (*singing, song*) sin acompañamiento.

unaccountably [ʌnə'kauntəblɪ] *adv* inexplicablemente.

unaccounted [ʌnə'kauntɪd] *adj*: **two passengers are** ~ **for** faltan dos pasajeros.

unaccustomed [ʌnə'kʌstəmd] *adj*: **to be** ~ **to** no estar acostumbrado a.

unacquainted [ʌnə'kweɪntɪd] *adj*: **to be** ~ **with** (*facts*) desconocer, ignorar.

unadulterated [ʌnə'dʌltəreɪtɪd] *adj* (*gen*) puro; (*wine*) sin mezcla.

unaffected [ʌnə'fɛktɪd] *adj* (*person, behaviour*) sin afectación, sencillo; (*emotionally*): **to be** ~ **by** no estar afectado por.

unafraid [ʌnə'freɪd] *adj*: **to be** ~ no tener miedo.

unaided [ʌn'eɪdɪd] *adj* sin ayuda, por sí solo.

unanimity [ju:nə'nɪmɪtɪ] *n* unanimidad *f.*

unanimous [ju:'nænɪməs] *adj* unánime.

unanimously [ju:'nænɪməslɪ] *adv* unánimemente.

unanswered [ʌn'ɑ:nsəd] *adj* (*question, letter*) sin contestar; (*criticism*) incontestado.

unappetizing [ʌn'æpɪtaɪzɪŋ] *adj* poco apetitoso.

unappreciative [ʌnə'pri:ʃɪətɪv] *adj* desagradecido.

unarmed [ʌn'ɑ:md] *adj* (*person*) desarmado; (*combat*) sin armas.

unashamed [ʌnə'ʃeɪmd] *adj* desvergonzado.

unassisted [ʌnə'sɪstɪd] *adj, adv* sin ayuda.

unassuming [ʌnə'sju:mɪŋ] *adj* modesto, sin pretensiones.

unattached [ʌnə'tætʃt] *adj* (*person*) soltero; (*part etc*) suelto.

unattended [ʌnə'tɛndɪd] *adj* (*car, luggage*) sin atender.

unattractive [ʌnə'træktɪv] *adj* poco atractivo.

unauthorized [ʌn'ɔ:θəraɪzd] *adj* no autorizado.

unavailable [ʌnə'veɪləbl] *adj* (*article, room,*

book) no disponible; (*person*) ocupado.
unavoidable [ʌnə'vɔɪdəbl] *adj* inevitable.
unavoidably [ʌnə'vɔɪdəblɪ] *adv* (*detained*)
por causas ajenas a su voluntad.
unaware [ʌnə'wɛə*] *adj*: **to be ~ of** ignorar.
unawares [ʌnə'wɛəz] *adv* de improviso.
unbalanced [ʌn'bælənst] *adj*
desequilibrado; (*mentally*) trastornado.
unbearable [ʌn'bɛərəbl] *adj* insoportable.
unbeatable [ʌn'biːtəbl] *adj* (*gen*)
invencible; (*price*) inmejorable.
unbeaten [ʌn'biːtn] *adj* (*team*) imbatido;
(*army*) invicto; (*record*) no batido.
unbecoming [ʌnbɪ'kʌmɪŋ] *adj* (*unseemly*:
language, behaviour) indecoroso,
impropio; (*unflattering*: *garment*) poco
favorecedor(a).
unbeknown(st) [ʌnbɪ'nəun(st)] *adv*: **~ to
me** sin saberlo yo.
unbelief [ʌnbɪ'liːf] *n* incredulidad *f*.
unbelievable [ʌnbɪ'liːvəbl] *adj* increíble.
unbelievingly [ʌnbɪ'liːvɪŋlɪ] *adv* sin creer.
unbend [ʌn'bɛnd] (*irreg*: *like* **bend**) *vi* (*fig*:
person) relajarse ♦ *vt* (*wire*) enderezar.
unbending [ʌn'bɛndɪŋ] *adj* (*fig*) inflexible.
unbias(s)ed [ʌn'baɪəst] *adj* imparcial.
unblemished [ʌn'blɛmɪʃt] *adj* sin mancha.
unblock [ʌn'blɔk] *vt* (*pipe*) desatascar;
(*road*) despejar.
unborn [ʌn'bɔːn] *adj* que va a nacer.
unbounded [ʌn'baundɪd] *adj* ilimitado, sin
límite.
unbreakable [ʌn'breɪkəbl] *adj* irrompible.
unbridled [ʌn'braɪdld] *adj* (*fig*)
desenfrenado.
unbroken [ʌn'brəukən] *adj* (*seal*) intacto;
(*series*) continuo, ininterrumpido; (*record*)
no batido; (*spirit*) indómito.
unbuckle [ʌn'bʌkl] *vt* desabrochar.
unburden [ʌn'bəːdn] *vt*: **to ~ o.s.**
desahogarse.
unbusinesslike [ʌn'bɪznɪslaɪk] *adj* (*trader*)
poco profesional; (*transaction*) incorrecto;
(*fig*: *person*) poco práctico; (: *without
method*) desorganizado.
unbutton [ʌn'bʌtn] *vt* desabrochar.
uncalled-for [ʌn'kɔːldfɔː*] *adj* gratuito,
inmerecido.
uncanny [ʌn'kænɪ] *adj* extraño,
extraordinario.
unceasing [ʌn'siːsɪŋ] *adj* incesante.
unceremonious [ʌnsɛrɪ'məunɪəs] *adj*
(*abrupt, rude*) brusco, hosco.
uncertain [ʌn'səːtn] *adj* incierto; (*indecisive*)
indeciso; **it's ~ whether** no se sabe si; **in
no ~ terms** sin dejar lugar a dudas.
uncertainty [ʌn'səːtntɪ] *n* incertidumbre *f*.
unchallenged [ʌn'tʃælɪndʒd] *adj* (*LAW etc*)

incontestado; **to go ~** no encontrar
respuesta.
unchanged [ʌn'tʃeɪndʒd] *adj* sin cambiar
or alterar.
uncharitable [ʌn'tʃærɪtəbl] *adj* (*remark,
behaviour*) demasiado duro.
uncharted [ʌn'tʃɑːtɪd] *adj* inexplorado.
unchecked [ʌn'tʃɛkt] *adj* desenfrenado.
uncivil [ʌn'sɪvɪl] *adj* descortés, grosero.
uncivilized [ʌn'sɪvɪlaɪzd] *adj* (*gen*) inculto,
poco civilizado; (*fig*: *behaviour etc*)
bárbaro.
uncle ['ʌŋkl] *n* tío.
unclear [ʌn'klɪə*] *adj* poco claro; **I'm still ~
about what I'm supposed to do** todavía
no tengo muy claro lo que tengo que
hacer.
uncoil [ʌn'kɔɪl] *vt* desenrollar ♦ *vi*
desenrollarse.
uncomfortable [ʌn'kʌmfətəbl] *adj*
incómodo; (*uneasy*) inquieto.
uncomfortably [ʌn'kʌmfətəblɪ] *adv*
(*uneasily*: *say*) con inquietud; (: *think*) con
remordimiento *or* nerviosismo.
uncommitted [ʌnkə'mɪtɪd] *adj* (*attitude,
country*) no comprometido; **to remain ~ to**
(*policy, party*) no comprometerse a.
uncommon [ʌn'kɔmən] *adj* poco común,
raro.
uncommunicative [ʌnkə'mjuːnɪkətɪv] *adj*
poco comunicativo, reservado.
uncomplicated [ʌn'kɔmplɪkeɪtɪd] *adj* sin
complicaciones.
uncompromising [ʌn'kɔmprəmaɪzɪŋ] *adj*
intransigente.
unconcerned [ʌnkən'səːnd] *adj* indiferente;
to be ~ about ser indiferente a, no
preocuparse de.
unconditional [ʌnkən'dɪʃənl] *adj*
incondicional.
uncongenial [ʌnkən'dʒiːnɪəl] *adj*
desagradable.
unconnected [ʌnkə'nɛktɪd] *adj* (*unrelated*):
to be ~ with no estar relacionado con.
unconscious [ʌn'kɔnʃəs] *adj* sin sentido;
(*unaware*) inconsciente ♦ *n*: **the ~** el
inconsciente; **to knock sb ~** dejar a algn
sin sentido.
unconsciously [ʌn'kɔnʃəslɪ] *adv*
inconscientemente.
unconsciousness [ʌn'kɔnʃəsnɪs] *n*
inconsciencia.
unconstitutional [ʌnkɔnstɪ'tjuːʃənl] *adj*
anti-constitucional.
uncontested [ʌnkən'tɛstɪd] *adj* (*champion*)
incontestado; (*PARLIAMENT*: *seat*) ganado
sin oposición.
uncontrollable [ʌnkən'trəuləbl] *adj* (*temper*)

indomable; (*laughter*) incontenible.
uncontrolled [ʌnkən'trəuld] *adj* (*child, dog, emotion*) incontrolado; (*inflation, price rises*) desenfrenado.
unconventional [ʌnkən'vɛnʃənl] *adj* poco convencional.
unconvinced [ʌnkən'vɪnst] *adj*: **to be** *or* **remain** ~ seguir sin convencerse.
unconvincing [ʌnkən'vɪnsɪŋ] *adj* poco convincente.
uncork [ʌn'kɔːk] *vt* descorchar.
uncorroborated [ʌnkə'rɔbəreɪtɪd] *adj* no confirmado.
uncouth [ʌn'kuːθ] *adj* grosero, inculto.
uncover [ʌn'kʌvə*] *vt* (*gen*) descubrir; (*take lid off*) destapar.
undamaged [ʌn'dæmɪdʒd] *adj* (*goods*) en buen estado; (*fig: reputation*) intacto.
undaunted [ʌn'dɔːntɪd] *adj*: ~ **by** sin dejarse desanimar por.
undecided [ʌndɪ'saɪdɪd] *adj* (*character*) indeciso; (*question*) no resuelto, pendiente.
undelivered [ʌndɪ'lɪvəd] *adj* no entregado al destinatario; **if** ~ **return to sender** en caso de no llegar a su destino devolver al remitente.
undeniable [ʌndɪ'naɪəbl] *adj* innegable.
undeniably [ʌndɪ'naɪəblɪ] *adv* innegablemente.
under ['ʌndə*] *prep* debajo de; (*less than*) menos de; (*according to*) según, de acuerdo con ♦ *adv* debajo, abajo; ~ **there** ahí debajo; ~ **construction** en construcción; en obras; ~ **the circumstances** dadas las circunstancias; **in** ~ **2 hours** en menos de dos horas; ~ **anaesthetic** bajo los efectos de la anestesia; ~ **discussion** en discusión, sobre el tapete.
under... [ʌndə*] *pref* sub....
under-age [ʌndər'eɪdʒ] *adj* menor de edad.
underarm ['ʌndərɑːm] *n* axila, sobaco ♦ *cpd*: ~ **deodorant** desodorante *m* corporal.
undercapitalised [ʌndə'kæpɪtəlaɪzd] *adj* descapitalizado.
undercarriage ['ʌndəkærɪdʒ] *n* (*BRIT AVIAT*) tren *m* de aterrizaje.
undercharge [ʌndə'tʃɑːdʒ] *vt* cobrar de menos.
underclass ['ʌndəklɑːs] *n* clase *f* marginada.
underclothes ['ʌndəkləuðz] *npl* ropa *sg* interior *or* íntima (*LAM*).
undercoat ['ʌndəkəut] *n* (*paint*) primera mano.
undercover [ʌndə'kʌvə*] *adj* clandestino.
undercurrent ['ʌndəkʌrnt] *n* corriente *f*

submarina; (*fig*) tendencia oculta.
undercut ['ʌndəkʌt] *vt* (*irreg: like* cut) vender más barato que; fijar un precio más barato que.
underdeveloped [ʌndədɪ'vɛləpt] *adj* subdesarrollado.
underdog ['ʌndədɔg] *n* desvalido/a.
underdone [ʌndə'dʌn] *adj* (*CULIN*) poco hecho.
underemployment [ʌndərɪm'plɔɪmənt] *n* subempleo.
underestimate [ʌndər'ɛstɪmeɪt] *vt* subestimar.
underexposed [ʌndərɪks'pəuzd] *adj* (*PHOT*) subexpuesto.
underfed [ʌndə'fɛd] *adj* subalimentado.
underfoot [ʌndə'fut] *adv*: **it's wet** ~ el suelo está mojado.
underfunded [ʌndə'fʌndɪd] *adj* infradotado (económicamente).
undergo [ʌndə'gəu] *vt* (*irreg: like* go) sufrir; (*treatment*) recibir, someterse a; **the car is** ~**ing repairs** están reparando el coche.
undergraduate ['ʌndə'grædjuət] *n* estudiante *m/f* ♦ *cpd*: ~ **courses** cursos *mpl* de licenciatura.
underground ['ʌndəgraund] *n* (*BRIT: railway*) metro; (*POL*) movimiento clandestino ♦ *adj* subterráneo.
undergrowth ['ʌndəgrəuθ] *n* maleza.
underhand(ed) [ʌndə'hænd(ɪd)] *adj* (*fig*) poco limpio.
underinsured [ʌndərɪn'ʃuəd] *adj* insuficientemente asegurado.
underlie [ʌndə'laɪ] *vt* (*irreg: like* lie) (*fig*) ser la razón fundamental de; **the underlying cause** la causa fundamental.
underline [ʌndə'laɪn] *vt* subrayar.
underling ['ʌndəlɪŋ] *n* (*pej*) subalterno/a.
undermanning [ʌndə'mænɪŋ] *n* falta de personal.
undermentioned [ʌndə'mɛnʃənd] *adj* abajo citado.
undermine [ʌndə'maɪn] *vt* socavar, minar.
underneath [ʌndə'niːθ] *adv* debajo ♦ *prep* debajo de, bajo.
undernourished [ʌndə'nʌrɪʃt] *adj* desnutrido.
underpaid [ʌndə'peɪd] *adj* mal pagado.
underpants ['ʌndəpænts] *npl* calzoncillos *mpl*.
underpass ['ʌndəpɑːs] *n* (*BRIT*) paso subterráneo.
underpin [ʌndə'pɪn] *vt* (*argument, case*) secundar, sostener.
underplay [ʌndə'pleɪ] *vt* (*BRIT*) minimizar.
underpopulated [ʌndə'pɔpjuleɪtɪd] *adj* poco poblado.

underprice [ʌndə'praɪs] *vt* vender demasiado barato.

underpriced [ʌndə'praɪst] *adj* con precio demasiado bajo.

underprivileged [ʌndə'prɪvɪlɪdʒd] *adj* desvalido.

underrate [ʌndə'reɪt] *vt* infravalorar, subestimar.

underscore ['ʌndəskɔː*] *vt* subrayar, sostener.

underseal [ʌndə'siːl] *vt* (*AUT*) proteger contra la corrosión.

undersecretary [ʌndə'sɛkrətrɪ] *n* subsecretario/a.

undersell [ʌndə'sɛl] *vt* (*competitors*) vender más barato que.

undershirt ['ʌndəʃəːt] *n* (*US*) camiseta.

undershorts ['ʌndəʃɔːts] *npl* (*US*) calzoncillos *mpl*.

underside ['ʌndəsaɪd] *n* parte *f* inferior, revés *m*.

undersigned ['ʌndəsaɪnd] *adj*, *n*: **the ~** el/la *etc* abajo firmante.

underskirt ['ʌndəskəːt] *n* (*BRIT*) enaguas *fpl*.

understaffed [ʌndə'stɑːft] *adj* falto de personal.

understand [ʌndə'stænd] (*irreg: like* **stand**) *vt*, *vi* entender, comprender; (*assume*) tener entendido; **to make o.s. understood** hacerse entender; **I ~ you have been absent** tengo entendido que (usted) ha estado ausente.

understandable [ʌndə'stændəbl] *adj* comprensible.

understanding [ʌndə'stændɪŋ] *adj* comprensivo ♦ *n* comprensión *f*, entendimiento; (*agreement*) acuerdo; **to come to an ~ with sb** llegar a un acuerdo con algn; **on the ~ that** a condición de que (+ *subjun*).

understate [ʌndə'steɪt] *vt* minimizar.

understatement [ʌndə'steɪtmənt] *n* subestimación *f*; (*modesty*) modestia (excesiva); **to say it was good is quite an ~** decir que estuvo bien es quedarse corto.

understood [ʌndə'stud] *pt*, *pp of* **understand** ♦ *adj* entendido; (*implied*): **it is ~ that** se sobreentiende que.

understudy ['ʌndəstʌdɪ] *n* suplente *m/f*.

undertake [ʌndə'teɪk] (*irreg: like* **take**) *vt* emprender; **to ~ to do sth** comprometerse a hacer algo.

undertaker ['ʌndəteɪkə*] *n* director(a) *m/f* de pompas fúnebres.

undertaking ['ʌndəteɪkɪŋ] *n* empresa; (*promise*) promesa.

undertone ['ʌndətəun] *n* (*of criticism*) connotación *f*; (*low voice*): **in an ~** en voz baja.

undervalue [ʌndə'væljuː] *vt* (*fig*) subestimar, infravalorar; (*COMM etc*) valorizar por debajo de su precio.

underwater [ʌndə'wɔːtə*] *adv* bajo el agua ♦ *adj* submarino.

underwear ['ʌndəwɛə*] *n* ropa interior *or* íntima (*LAM*).

underweight [ʌndə'weɪt] *adj* de peso insuficiente; (*person*) demasiado delgado.

underworld ['ʌndəwəːld] *n* (*of crime*) hampa, inframundo.

underwrite [ʌndə'raɪt] (*irreg: like* **write**) *vt* (*COMM*) suscribir; (*INSURANCE*) asegurar (*contra riesgos*).

underwriter ['ʌndəraɪtə*] *n* (*INSURANCE*) asegurador/a *m/f*.

undeserving [ʌndɪ'zəːvɪŋ] *adj*: **to be ~ of** no ser digno de.

undesirable [ʌndɪ'zaɪərəbl] *adj* indeseable.

undeveloped [ʌndɪ'vɛləpt] *adj* (*land, resources*) sin explotar.

undies ['ʌndɪz] *npl* (*col*) paños *mpl* menores.

undiluted [ʌndaɪ'luːtɪd] *adj* (*concentrate*) concentrado.

undiplomatic [ʌndɪplə'mætɪk] *adj* poco diplomático.

undischarged [ʌndɪs'tʃɑːdʒd] *adj*: **~ bankrupt** quebrado/a no rehabilitado/a.

undisciplined [ʌn'dɪsɪplɪnd] *adj* indisciplinado.

undiscovered [ʌndɪs'kʌvəd] *adj* no descubierto; (*unknown*) desconocido.

undisguised [ʌndɪs'gaɪzd] *adj* franco, abierto.

undisputed [ʌndɪ'spjuːtɪd] *adj* incontestable.

undistinguished [ʌndɪs'tɪŋgwɪʃt] *adj* mediocre.

undisturbed [ʌndɪs'təːbd] *adj* (*sleep*) ininterrumpido; **to leave sth ~** dejar algo tranquilo *or* como está.

undivided [ʌndɪ'vaɪdɪd] *adj*: **I want your ~ attention** quiero su completa atención.

undo [ʌn'duː] *vt* (*irreg: like* **do**) deshacer.

undoing [ʌn'duːɪŋ] *n* ruina, perdición *f*.

undone [ʌn'dʌn] *pp of* **undo** ♦ *adj*: **to come ~** (*clothes*) desabrocharse; (*parcel*) desatarse.

undoubted [ʌn'dautɪd] *adj* indudable.

undoubtedly [ʌn'dautɪdlɪ] *adv* indudablemente, sin duda.

undress [ʌn'drɛs] *vi* desnudarse, desvestirse (*esp LAM*).

undrinkable [ʌn'drɪŋkəbl] *adj* (*unpalatable*) imbebible; (*poisonous*) no potable.

undue [ʌn'djuː] *adj* indebido, excesivo.

undulating ['ʌndjuleɪtɪŋ] adj ondulante.
unduly [ʌn'dju:lɪ] adv excesivamente, demasiado.
undying [ʌn'daɪɪŋ] adj eterno.
unearned [ʌn'ɔːnd] adj (praise, respect) inmerecido; ~ **income** ingresos mpl no ganados, renta no ganada or salarial.
unearth [ʌn'ɔːθ] vt desenterrar.
unearthly [ʌn'ɔːθlɪ] adj: ~ **hour** (col) hora intempestiva.
unease [ʌn'iːz] n malestar m.
uneasy [ʌn'iːzɪ] adj intranquilo; (worried) preocupado; **to feel** ~ **about doing sth** sentirse incómodo con la idea de hacer algo.
uneconomic(al) ['ʌniːkə'nɒmɪk(l)] adj no económico.
uneducated [ʌn'ɛdjukeɪtɪd] adj ignorante, inculto.
unemployed [ʌnɪm'plɔɪd] adj parado, sin trabajo ♦ n: **the** ~ los parados.
unemployment [ʌnɪm'plɔɪmənt] n paro, desempleo, cesantía (LAM).
unemployment benefit n (BRIT) subsidio de desempleo or paro.
unending [ʌn'ɛndɪŋ] adj interminable.
unenviable [ʌn'ɛnvɪəbl] adj poco envidiable.
unequal [ʌn'iːkwəl] adj (length, objects etc) desigual; (amounts) distinto; (division of labour) poco justo.
unequalled, (US) **unequaled** [ʌn'iːkwəld] adj inigualado, sin par.
unequivocal [ʌnɪ'kwɪvəkəl] adj (answer) inequívoco, claro; (person) claro.
unerring [ʌn'ɔːrɪŋ] adj infalible.
UNESCO [ju:'nɛskəu] n abbr (= United Nations Educational, Scientific and Cultural Organization) UNESCO f.
unethical [ʌn'ɛθɪkəl] adj (methods) inmoral; (doctor's behaviour) que infringe la ética profesional.
uneven [ʌn'iːvn] adj desigual, (road etc) con baches.
uneventful [ʌnɪ'vɛntful] adj sin incidentes.
unexceptional [ʌnɪk'sɛpʃənl] adj sin nada de extraordinario, corriente.
unexciting [ʌnɪk'saɪtɪŋ] adj (news) sin interés; (film, evening) aburrido.
unexpected [ʌnɪk'spɛktɪd] adj inesperado.
unexpectedly [ʌnɪk'spɛktɪdlɪ] adv inesperadamente.
unexplained [ʌnɪks'pleɪnd] adj inexplicado.
unexploded [ʌnɪks'pləudɪd] adj sin explotar.
unfailing [ʌn'feɪlɪŋ] adj (support) indefectible; (energy) inagotable.
unfair [ʌn'fɛə*] adj: ~ **(to sb)** injusto (con

algn); **it's** ~ **that** ... es injusto que ..., no es justo que ....
unfair dismissal n despido improcedente.
unfairly [ʌn'fɛəlɪ] adv injustamente.
unfaithful [ʌn'feɪθful] adj infiel.
unfamiliar [ʌnfə'mɪlɪə*] adj extraño, desconocido; **to be** ~ **with sth** desconocer or ignorar algo.
unfashionable [ʌn'fæʃnəbl] adj (clothes) pasado or fuera de moda; (district) poco elegante.
unfasten [ʌn'fɑːsn] vt desatar.
unfathomable [ʌn'fæðəməbl] adj insondable.
unfavourable, (US) **unfavorable** [ʌn'feɪvərəbl] adj desfavorable.
unfavo(u)rably [ʌn'feɪvrəblɪ] adv: **to look** ~ **upon** ser adverso a.
unfeeling [ʌn'fiːlɪŋ] adj insensible.
unfinished [ʌn'fɪnɪʃt] adj inacabado, sin terminar.
unfit [ʌn'fɪt] adj en baja forma; (incompetent) incapaz; ~ **for work** no apto para trabajar.
unflagging [ʌn'flægɪŋ] adj incansable.
unflappable [ʌn'flæpəbl] adj imperturbable.
unflattering [ʌn'flætərɪŋ] adj (dress, hairstyle) poco favorecedor.
unflinching [ʌn'flɪntʃɪŋ] adj impávido.
unfold [ʌn'fəuld] vt desdoblar; (fig) revelar ♦ vi abrirse; revelarse.
unforeseeable [ʌnfɔː'siːəbl] adj imprevisible.
unforeseen ['ʌnfɔː'siːn] adj imprevisto.
unforgettable [ʌnfə'gɛtəbl] adj inolvidable.
unforgivable [ʌnfə'gɪvəbl] adj imperdonable.
unformatted [ʌn'fɔːmætɪd] adj (disk, text) sin formatear.
unfortunate [ʌn'fɔːtʃnət] adj desgraciado; (event, remark) inoportuno.
unfortunately [ʌn'fɔːtʃnətlɪ] adv desgraciadamente, por desgracia.
unfounded [ʌn'faundɪd] adj infundado.
unfriendly [ʌn'frɛndlɪ] adj antipático.
unfulfilled [ʌnful'fɪld] adj (ambition) sin realizar; (prophecy, promise, terms of contract) incumplido; (desire, person) insatisfecho.
unfurl [ʌn'fɔːl] vt desplegar.
unfurnished [ʌn'fɔːnɪʃt] adj sin amueblar.
ungainly [ʌn'geɪnlɪ] adj (walk) desgarbado.
ungodly [ʌn'gɒdlɪ] adj: **at an** ~ **hour** a una hora intempestiva.
ungrateful [ʌn'greɪtful] adj ingrato.
unguarded [ʌn'gɑːdɪd] adj (moment) de descuido.

unhappily [ʌn'hæpɪlɪ] *adv* (*unfortunately*) desgraciadamente.

unhappiness [ʌn'hæpɪnɪs] *n* tristeza.

unhappy [ʌn'hæpɪ] *adj* (*sad*) triste; (*unfortunate*) desgraciado; (*childhood*) infeliz; ~ **with** (*arrangements etc*) poco contento con, descontento de.

unharmed [ʌn'hɑːmd] *adj* (*person*) ileso.

UNHCR *n abbr* (= *United Nations High Commission for Refugees*) ACNUR *m*.

unhealthy [ʌn'hɛlθɪ] *adj* (*gen*) malsano, insalubre; (*person*) enfermizo; (*interest*) morboso.

unheard-of [ʌn'hɔːdɔv] *adj* inaudito, sin precedente.

unhelpful [ʌn'hɛlpful] *adj* (*person*) poco servicial; (*advice*) inútil.

unhesitating [ʌn'hɛzɪteɪtɪŋ] *adj* (*loyalty*) automático; (*reply, offer*) inmediato; (*person*) resuelto.

unholy [ʌn'həulɪ] *adj*: **an** ~ **alliance** una alianza nefasta; **he returned at an** ~ **hour** volvió a una hora intempestiva.

unhook [ʌn'huk] *vt* desenganchar; (*from wall*) descolgar; (*undo*) desabrochar.

unhurt [ʌn'hɔːt] *adj* ileso.

unhygienic [ʌnhaɪ'dʒiːnɪk] *adj* antihigiénico.

UNICEF ['juːnɪsɛf] *n abbr* (= *United Nations International Children's Emergency Fund*) UNICEF *f*.

unidentified [ʌnaɪ'dɛntɪfaɪd] *adj* no identificado; ~ **flying object (UFO)** objeto volante no identificado.

unification [juːnɪfɪ'keɪʃən] *n* unificación *f*.

uniform ['juːnɪfɔːm] *n* uniforme *m* ♦ *adj* uniforme.

uniformity [juːnɪ'fɔːmɪtɪ] *n* uniformidad *f*.

unify ['juːnɪfaɪ] *vt* unificar, unir.

unilateral [juːnɪ'lætərəl] *adj* unilateral.

unimaginable [ʌnɪ'mædʒɪnəbl] *adj* inconcebible, inimaginable.

unimaginative [ʌnɪ'mædʒɪnətɪv] *adj* falto de imaginación.

unimpaired [ʌnɪm'pɛəd] *adj* (*unharmed*) intacto; (*not lessened*) no disminuido; (*unaltered*) inalterado.

unimportant [ʌnɪm'pɔːtənt] *adj* sin importancia.

unimpressed [ʌnɪm'prɛst] *adj* poco impresionado.

uninhabited [ʌnɪn'hæbɪtɪd] *adj* desierto; (*country*) despoblado; (*house*) deshabitado, desocupado.

uninhibited [ʌnɪn'hɪbɪtɪd] *adj* nada cohibido, desinhibido.

uninjured [ʌn'ɪndʒəd] *adj* (*person*) ileso.

uninspiring [ʌnɪn'spaɪərɪŋ] *adj* anodino.

unintelligent [ʌnɪn'tɛlɪdʒənt] *adj* poco inteligente.

unintentional [ʌnɪn'tɛnʃənəl] *adj* involuntario.

unintentionally [ʌnɪn'tɛnʃnəlɪ] *adv* sin querer.

uninvited [ʌnɪn'vaɪtɪd] *adj* (*guest*) sin invitación.

uninviting [ʌnɪn'vaɪtɪŋ] *adj* (*place, offer*) poco atractivo; (*food*) poco apetecible.

union ['juːnjən] *n* unión *f*; (*also:* **trade** ~) sindicato ♦ *cpd* sindical; **the U**~ (*US*) la Unión.

union card *n* carnet *m* de sindicato.

unionize ['juːnjənaɪz] *vt* sindicalizar.

Union Jack *n* bandera del Reino Unido.

Union of Soviet Socialist Republics (USSR) *n* Unión *f* de Repúblicas Socialistas Soviéticas.

union shop *n* (*US*) empresa de afiliación sindical obligatoria.

unique [juː'niːk] *adj* único.

unisex ['juːnɪsɛks] *adj* unisex.

Unison ['juːnɪsn] *n* (*trade union*) gran sindicato de funcionarios.

unison ['juːnɪsn] *n*: **in** ~ en armonía.

unissued capital [ʌn'ɪʃuːd-] *n* capital *m* no emitido.

unit ['juːnɪt] *n* unidad *f*; (*team, squad*) grupo; **kitchen** ~ módulo de cocina; **production** ~ taller *m* de fabricación; **sink** ~ fregadero.

unit cost *n* costo unitario.

unite [juː'naɪt] *vt* unir ♦ *vi* unirse.

united [juː'naɪtɪd] *adj* unido.

United Arab Emirates *npl* Emiratos *mpl* Árabes Unidos.

United Kingdom (UK) *n* Reino Unido.

United Nations (Organization) (UN, UNO) *n* Naciones Unidas *fpl* (ONU *f*).

United States (of America) (US, USA) *n* Estados Unidos *mpl* (de América) (EE.UU. *mpl*).

unit price *n* precio unitario.

unit trust *n* (*BRIT*) bono fiduciario.

unity ['juːnɪtɪ] *n* unidad *f*.

Univ. *abbr* = **university**.

universal [juːnɪ'vɔːsl] *adj* universal.

universally [juːnɪ'vɔːsəlɪ] *adv* universalmente.

universe ['juːnɪvɔːs] *n* universo.

university [juːnɪ'vɔːsɪtɪ] *n* universidad *f* ♦ *cpd* (*student, professor, education, degree*) universitario; (*year*) académico; **to be at/ go to** ~ estudiar en/ir a la universidad.

unjust [ʌn'dʒʌst] *adj* injusto.

unjustifiable [ʌndʒʌstɪ'faɪəbl] *adj* injustificable.

unjustified [ʌn'dʒʌstɪfaɪd] adj (text) no alineado or justificado.

unkempt [ʌn'kɛmpt] adj descuidado; (hair) despeinado.

unkind [ʌn'kaɪnd] adj poco amable; (comment etc) cruel.

unkindly [ʌn'kaɪndlɪ] adv (speak) severamente; (treat) cruelmente, mal.

unknown [ʌn'nəun] adj desconocido ♦ adv: ~ **to me** sin saberlo yo; ~ **quantity** (MATH, fig) incógnita.

unladen [ʌn'leɪdən] adj (weight) vacío, sin cargamento.

unlawful [ʌn'lɔːful] adj ilegal, ilícito.

unleaded [ʌn'lɛdɪd] n (also: ~ **petrol**) gasolina sin plomo.

unleash [ʌn'liːʃ] vt desatar.

unleavened [ʌn'lɛvənd] adj ácimo, sin levadura.

unless [ʌn'lɛs] conj a menos que; ~ **he comes** a menos que venga; ~ **otherwise stated** salvo indicación contraria; ~ **I am mistaken** si no mi equivoco.

unlicensed [ʌn'laɪsənst] adj (BRIT: to sell alcohol) no autorizado.

unlike [ʌn'laɪk] adj distinto ♦ prep a diferencia de.

unlikelihood [ʌn'laɪklɪhud] n improbabilidad f.

unlikely [ʌn'laɪklɪ] adj improbable.

unlimited [ʌn'lɪmɪtɪd] adj ilimitado; ~ **liability** responsabilidad f ilimitada.

unlisted [ʌn'lɪstɪd] adj (US TEL) que no figura en la guía; ~ **company** empresa sin cotización en bolsa.

unlit [ʌn'lɪt] adj (room) oscuro, sin luz.

unload [ʌn'ləud] vt descargar.

unlock [ʌn'lɔk] vt abrir (con llave).

unlucky [ʌn'lʌkɪ] adj desgraciado; (object, number) que da mala suerte; **to be** ~ (person) tener mala suerte.

unmanageable [ʌn'mænɪdʒəbl] adj (unwieldy: tool, vehicle) difícil de manejar; (: situation) incontrolable.

unmanned [ʌn'mænd] adj (spacecraft) sin tripulación.

unmannerly [ʌn'mænəlɪ] adj mal educado, descortés.

unmarked [ʌn'mɑːkt] adj (unstained) sin mancha; ~ **police car** vehículo policial camuflado.

unmarried [ʌn'mærɪd] adj soltero.

unmask [ʌn'mɑːsk] vt desenmascarar.

unmatched [ʌn'mætʃt] adj incomparable.

unmentionable [ʌn'mɛnʃnəbl] adj (topic, vice) indecible; (word) que no se debe decir.

unmerciful [ʌn'mɑːsɪful] adj despiadado.

unmistakable [ʌnmɪs'teɪkəbl] adj inconfundible.

unmistakably [ʌnmɪs'teɪkəblɪ] adv de modo inconfundible.

unmitigated [ʌn'mɪtɪgeɪtɪd] adj rematado, absoluto.

unnamed [ʌn'neɪmd] adj (nameless) sin nombre; (anonymous) anónimo.

unnatural [ʌn'nætʃrəl] adj (gen) antinatural; (manner) afectado; (habit) perverso.

unnecessary [ʌn'nɛsəsərɪ] adj innecesario, inútil.

unnerve [ʌn'nɔːv] vt (subj: accident) poner nervioso; (: hostile attitude) acobardar; (: long wait, interview) intimidar.

unnoticed [ʌn'nəutɪst] adj: **to go** or **pass** ~ pasar desapercibido.

UNO ['juːnəu] n abbr = (United Nations Organization) ONU f.

unobservant [ʌnəb'zɔːvnt] adj: **to be** ~ ser poco observador, ser distraído.

unobtainable [ʌnəb'teɪnəbl] adj inasequible; (TEL) inexistente.

unobtrusive [ʌnəb'truːsɪv] adj discreto.

unoccupied [ʌn'ɔkjupaɪd] adj (house etc) libre, desocupado.

unofficial [ʌnə'fɪʃl] adj no oficial; ~ **strike** huelga no oficial.

unopened [ʌn'əupənd] adj (letter, present) sin abrir.

unopposed [ʌnə'pəuzd] adj (enter, be elected) sin oposición.

unorthodox [ʌn'ɔːθədɔks] adj poco ortodoxo.

unpack [ʌn'pæk] vi deshacer las maletas, desempacar (LAM).

unpaid [ʌn'peɪd] adj (bill, debt) sin pagar, impagado; (COMM) pendiente; (holiday) sin sueldo; (work) sin pago, voluntario.

unpalatable [ʌn'pælətəbl] adj (truth) desagradable.

unparalleled [ʌn'pærəlɛld] adj (unequalled) sin par; (unique) sin precedentes.

unpatriotic [ʌnpætrɪ'ɔtɪk] adj (person) poco patriota; (speech, attitude) antipatriótico.

unplanned [ʌn'plænd] adj (visit) imprevisto; (baby) no planeado.

unpleasant [ʌn'plɛznt] adj (disagreeable) desagradable; (person, manner) antipático.

unplug [ʌn'plʌg] vt desenchufar, desconectar.

unpolluted [ʌnpə'luːtɪd] adj impoluto, no contaminado.

unpopular [ʌn'pɔpjulə*] adj poco popular; **to be** ~ **with sb** (person, law) no ser popular con algn; **to make o.s.** ~ **(with)**

hacerse impopular (con).
unprecedented [ʌn'prɛsɪdəntɪd] *adj* sin precedentes.
unpredictable [ʌnprɪ'dɪktəbl] *adj* imprevisible.
unprejudiced [ʌn'prɛdʒudɪst] *adj* (*not biased*) imparcial; (*having no prejudices*) sin prejuicio.
unprepared [ʌnprɪ'pɛəd] *adj* (*person*) desprevenido; (*speech*) improvisado.
unprepossessing [ʌnpriːpə'zɛsɪŋ] *adj* poco atractivo.
unprincipled [ʌn'prɪnsɪpld] *adj* sin escrúpulos.
unproductive [ʌnprə'dʌktɪv] *adj* improductivo; (*discussion*) infructuoso.
unprofessional [ʌnprə'fɛʃənl] *adj* poco profesional; ~ **conduct** negligencia.
unprofitable [ʌn'prɒfɪtəbl] *adj* poco provechoso, no rentable.
UNPROFOR *n abbr* (= *United Nations Protection Force*) FORPRONU *f*, Unprofor *f*.
unprotected ['ʌnprə'tɛktɪd] *adj* (*sex*) sin protección.
unprovoked [ʌnprə'vəukt] *adj* no provocado.
unpunished [ʌn'pʌnɪʃt] *adj*: **to go** ~ quedar sin castigo, salir impune.
unqualified [ʌn'kwɒlɪfaɪd] *adj* sin título, no cualificado; (*success*) total, incondicional.
unquestionably [ʌn'kwɛstʃənəblɪ] *adv* indiscutiblemente.
unquestioning [ʌn'kwɛstʃənɪŋ] *adj* (*obedience, acceptance*) incondicional.
unravel [ʌn'rævl] *vt* desenmarañar.
unreal [ʌn'rɪəl] *adj* irreal.
unrealistic [ʌnrɪə'lɪstɪk] *adj* poco realista.
unreasonable [ʌn'riːznəbl] *adj* irrazonable; **to make** ~ **demands on sb** hacer demandas excesivas a algn.
unrecognizable [ʌn'rɛkəgnaɪzəbl] *adj* irreconocible.
unrecognized [ʌn'rɛkəgnaɪzd] *adj* (*talent, genius*) ignorado; (*POL: regime*) no reconocido.
unrecorded [ʌnrɪ'kɔːdɪd] *adj* no registrado.
unrefined [ʌnrɪ'faɪnd] *adj* (*sugar, petroleum*) sin refinar.
unrehearsed [ʌnrɪ'həːst] *adj* (*THEAT etc*) improvisado; (*spontaneous*) espontáneo.
unrelated [ʌnrɪ'leɪtɪd] *adj* sin relación; (*family*) no emparentado.
unrelenting [ʌnrɪ'lɛntɪŋ] *adj* implacable.
unreliable [ʌnrɪ'laɪəbl] *adj* (*person*) informal; (*machine*) poco fiable.
unrelieved [ʌnrɪ'liːvd] *adj* (*monotony*) constante.

unremitting [ʌnrɪ'mɪtɪŋ] *adj* incesante.
unrepeatable [ʌnrɪ'piːtəbl] *adj* irrepetible.
unrepentant [ʌnrɪ'pɛntənt] *adj* (*smoker, sinner*) impenitente; **to be** ~ **about sth** no arrepentirse de algo.
unrepresentative [ʌnrɛprɪ'zɛntətɪv] *adj* (*untypical*) poco representativo.
unreserved [ʌnrɪ'zəːvd] *adj* (*seat*) no reservado; (*approval, admiration*) total.
unreservedly [ʌnrɪ'zəːvɪdlɪ] *adv* sin reserva.
unresponsive [ʌnrɪ'spɒnsɪv] *adj* insensible.
unrest [ʌn'rɛst] *n* inquietud *f*, malestar *m*; (*POL*) disturbios *mpl*.
unrestricted [ʌnrɪ'strɪktɪd] *adj* (*power, time*) sin restricción; (*access*) libre.
unrewarded [ʌnrɪ'wɔːdɪd] *adj* sin recompensa.
unripe [ʌn'raɪp] *adj* verde, inmaduro.
unrivalled, (US**) unrivaled** [ʌn'raɪvəld] *adj* incomparable, sin par.
unroll [ʌn'rəul] *vt* desenrollar.
unruffled [ʌn'rʌfld] *adj* (*person*) imperturbable; (*hair*) liso.
unruly [ʌn'ruːlɪ] *adj* indisciplinado.
unsafe [ʌn'seɪf] *adj* (*journey*) peligroso; (*car etc*) inseguro; (*method*) arriesgado; ~ **to drink/eat** no apto para el consumo humano.
unsaid [ʌn'sɛd] *adj*: **to leave sth** ~ dejar algo sin decir.
unsaleable, (US**) unsalable** [ʌn'seɪləbl] *adj* invendible.
unsatisfactory ['ʌnsætɪs'fæktərɪ] *adj* poco satisfactorio.
unsatisfied [ʌn'sætɪsfaɪd] *adj* (*desire, need etc*) insatisfecho.
unsavoury, (US**) unsavory** [ʌn'seɪvərɪ] *adj* (*fig*) repugnante.
unscathed [ʌn'skeɪðd] *adj* ileso.
unscientific [ʌnsaɪən'tɪfɪk] *adj* poco científico.
unscrew [ʌn'skruː] *vt* destornillar.
unscrupulous [ʌn'skruːpjuləs] *adj* sin escrúpulos.
unseat [ʌn'siːt] *vt* (*rider*) hacer caerse de la silla a; (*fig: official*) hacer perder su escaño a.
unsecured [ʌnsɪ'kjuəd] *adj*: ~ **creditor** acreedor(a) *m/f* común.
unseeded [ʌn'siːdɪd] *adj* (*SPORT*) no preseleccionado.
unseen [ʌn'siːn] *adj* (*person, danger*) oculto.
unselfish [ʌn'sɛlfɪʃ] *adj* generoso, poco egoísta; (*act*) desinteresado.
unsettled [ʌn'sɛtld] *adj* inquieto; (*situation*) inestable; (*weather*) variable.
unsettling [ʌn'sɛtlɪŋ] *adj* perturbador(a),

inquietante.
unshak(e)able [ʌn'ʃeɪkəbl] adj
inquebrantable.
unshaven [ʌn'ʃeɪvn] adj sin afeitar.
unsightly [ʌn'saɪtlɪ] adj desagradable.
unskilled [ʌn'skɪld] adj: ~ **workers** mano f
de obra no cualificada.
unsociable [ʌn'səʊʃəbl] adj insociable.
unsocial [ʌn'səʊʃl] adj: ~ **hours** horario
nocturno.
unsold [ʌn'səʊld] adj sin vender.
unsolicited [ʌnsə'lɪsɪtɪd] adj no solicitado.
unsophisticated [ʌnsə'fɪstɪkeɪtɪd] adj
(person) sencillo, ingenuo; (method) poco
sofisticado.
unsound [ʌn'saʊnd] adj (health) malo; (in
construction: floor, foundations) defectuoso;
(policy, advice, judgment) erróneo;
(investment) poco seguro.
unspeakable [ʌn'spiːkəbl] adj indecible;
(awful) incalificable.
unspoken [ʌn'spəʊkn] adj (words)
sobreententido; (agreement, approval)
tácito.
unstable [ʌn'steɪbl] adj inestable.
unsteady [ʌn'stedɪ] adj inestable.
unstinting [ʌn'stɪntɪŋ] adj (support etc)
pródigo.
unstuck [ʌn'stʌk] adj: **to come** ~
despegarse; (fig) fracasar.
unsubstantiated [ʌnsəb'stænʃɪeɪtɪd] adj
(rumour, accusation) no comprobado.
unsuccessful [ʌnsək'sesful] adj (attempt)
infructuoso; (writer, proposal) sin éxito; **to
be** ~ (in attempting sth) no tener éxito,
fracasar.
unsuccessfully [ʌnsək'sesfulɪ] adv en vano,
sin éxito.
unsuitable [ʌn'suːtəbl] adj inconveniente,
inapropiado; (time) inoportuno.
unsuited [ʌn'suːtɪd] adj: **to be** ~ **for** or **to** no
ser apropiado para.
unsung ['ʌnsʌŋ] adj: **an** ~ **hero** un héroe
desconocido.
unsupported [ʌnsə'pɔːtɪd] adj (claim) sin
fundamento; (theory) sin base firme.
unsure [ʌn'ʃʊə*] adj inseguro, poco seguro;
to be ~ **of o.s.** estar poco seguro de sí
mismo.
unsuspecting [ʌnsə'spektɪŋ] adj confiado.
unsweetened [ʌn'swiːtnd] adj sin azúcar.
unsympathetic [ʌnsɪmpə'θetɪk] adj
(attitude) poco comprensivo; (person) sin
compasión; ~ **(to)** indiferente (a).
untangle [ʌn'tæŋgl] vt desenredar.
untapped [ʌn'tæpt] adj (resources) sin
explotar.
untaxed [ʌn'tækst] adj (goods) libre de

impuestos; (income) antes de impuestos.
unthinkable [ʌn'θɪŋkəbl] adj inconcebible,
impensable.
unthinkingly [ʌn'θɪŋkɪŋlɪ] adv
irreflexivamente.
untidy [ʌn'taɪdɪ] adj (room) desordenado,
en desorden; (appearance) desaliñado.
untie [ʌn'taɪ] vt desatar.
until [ən'tɪl] prep hasta ♦ conj hasta que; ~
he comes hasta que venga; ~ **now** hasta
ahora; ~ **then** hasta entonces; **from
morning** ~ **night** de la mañana a la noche.
untimely [ʌn'taɪmlɪ] adj inoportuno; (death)
prematuro.
untold [ʌn'təʊld] adj (story) nunca contado;
(suffering) indecible; (wealth)
incalculable.
untouched [ʌn'tʌtʃt] adj (not used etc)
intacto, sin tocar; (safe: person) indemne,
ileso; (unaffected): ~ **by** insensible a.
untoward [ʌntə'wɔːd] adj (behaviour)
impropio; (event) adverso.
untrained [ʌn'treɪnd] adj (worker) sin
formación; (troops) no entrenado; **to the**
~ **eye** para los no entendidos.
untrammelled, (US) **untrammeled**
[ʌn'træməld] adj ilimitado.
untranslatable [ʌntrænz'leɪtəbl] adj
intraducible.
untried [ʌn'traɪd] adj (plan) no probado.
untrue [ʌn'truː] adj (statement) falso.
untrustworthy [ʌn'trʌstwəːðɪ] adj (person)
poco fiable.
unusable [ʌn'juːzəbl] adj inservible.
unused [ʌn'juːzd] adj sin usar, nuevo; **to be**
~ **to (doing) sth** no estar acostumbrado a
(hacer) algo.
unusual [ʌn'juːʒuəl] adj insólito, poco
común.
unusually [ʌn'juːʒuəlɪ] adv: **he arrived** ~
early llegó más temprano que de
costumbre.
unveil [ʌn'veɪl] vt (statue) descubrir.
unwanted [ʌn'wɒntɪd] adj (person, effect) no
deseado.
unwarranted [ʌn'wɒrəntɪd] adj
injustificado.
unwary [ʌn'wɛərɪ] adj imprudente, incauto.
unwavering [ʌn'weɪvərɪŋ] adj
inquebrantable.
unwelcome [ʌn'welkəm] adj (at a bad time)
inoportuno, molesto; **to feel** ~ sentirse
incómodo.
unwell [ʌn'wel] adj: **to feel** ~ estar
indispuesto, sentirse mal.
unwieldy [ʌn'wiːldɪ] adj difícil de manejar.
unwilling [ʌn'wɪlɪŋ] adj: **to be** ~ **to do sth**
estar poco dispuesto a hacer algo.

unwillingly [ʌn'wɪlɪŋlɪ] *adv* de mala gana.
unwind [ʌn'waɪnd] (*irreg: like* **wind**) *vt* desenvolver ♦ *vi* (*relax*) relajarse.
unwise [ʌn'waɪz] *adj* imprudente.
unwitting [ʌn'wɪtɪŋ] *adj* inconsciente.
unworkable [ʌn'wə:kəbl] *adj* (*plan*) impracticable.
unworthy [ʌn'wə:ðɪ] *adj* indigno; **to be ~ of sth/to do sth** ser indigno de algo/de hacer algo.
unwrap [ʌn'ræp] *vt* deshacer.
unwritten [ʌn'rɪtn] *adj* (*agreement*) tácito; (*rules, law*) no escrito.
unzip [ʌn'zɪp] *vt* abrir la cremallera de.

============================ *KEYWORD*

up [ʌp] *prep:* **to go/be ~ sth** subir/estar subido en algo; **he went ~ the stairs/the hill** subió las escaleras/la colina; **we walked/climbed ~ the hill** subimos la colina; **they live further ~ the street** viven más arriba en la calle; **go ~ that road and turn left** sigue por esa calle y gira a la izquierda
♦ *adv* **1** (*upwards, higher*) más arriba; **~ in the mountains** en lo alto (de la montaña); **put it a bit higher ~** ponlo un poco más arriba *or* alto; **to stop halfway ~** pararse a la mitad del camino *or* de la subida; **~ there** ahí *or* allí arriba; **~ above** en lo alto, por encima, arriba; **"this side ~"** "este lado hacia arriba"; **to live/go ~ North** vivir en el norte/ir al norte
2: **to be ~** (*out of bed*) estar levantado; (*prices, level*) haber subido; (*building*) estar construido; (*tent*) estar montado; (*curtains, paper etc*) estar puesto; **time's ~** se acabó el tiempo; **when the year was ~** al terminarse el año; **he's well ~ in** *or* **on politics** (*BRIT: knowledgeable*) está muy al día en política; **what's up?** (*wrong*) ¿qué pasa?; **what's ~ with him?** ¿qué le pasa?; **prices are ~ on last year** los precios han subido desde el año pasado
3: **~ to** (*as far as*) hasta; **~ to now** hasta ahora *or* la fecha
4: **to be ~ to** (*depending on*): **it's ~ to you** depende de ti; **he's not ~ to it** (*job, task etc*) no es capaz de hacerlo; **I don't feel ~ to it** no me encuentro con ánimos para ello; **his work is not ~ to the required standard** su trabajo no da la talla; (*inf: be doing*): **what is he ~ to?** ¿qué estará tramando?
♦ *vi* (*col*): **she ~ped and left** se levantó y se marchó
♦ *vt* (*col: price*) subir

♦ *n:* **~s and downs** altibajos *mpl*.

up-and-coming [ʌpənd'kʌmɪŋ] *adj* prometedor(a).
upbeat ['ʌpbi:t] *n* (*MUS*) tiempo no acentuado; (*in economy, prosperity*) aumento ♦ *adj* (*col*) optimista, animado.
upbraid [ʌp'breɪd] *vt* censurar, reprender.
upbringing ['ʌpbrɪŋɪŋ] *n* educación *f*.
upcoming ['ʌpkʌmɪŋ] *adj* próximo.
update [ʌp'deɪt] *vt* poner al día.
upend [ʌp'ɛnd] *vt* poner vertical.
upfront [ʌp'frʌnt] *adj* claro, directo ♦ *adv* a las claras; (*pay*) por adelantado; **to be ~ about sth** admitir algo claramente.
upgrade [ʌp'greɪd] *vt* ascender; (*COMPUT*) modernizar.
upheaval [ʌp'hi:vl] *n* trastornos *mpl*; (*POL*) agitación *f*.
uphill [ʌp'hɪl] *adj* cuesta arriba; (*fig: task*) penoso, difícil ♦ *adv:* **to go ~** ir cuesta arriba.
uphold [ʌp'həuld] (*irreg: like* **hold**) *vt* sostener.
upholstery [ʌp'həulstərɪ] *n* tapicería.
upkeep ['ʌpki:p] *n* mantenimiento.
upmarket [ʌp'ma:kɪt] *adj* (*product*) de categoría.
upon [ə'pɔn] *prep* sobre.
upper ['ʌpə*] *adj* superior, de arriba ♦ *n* (*of shoe: also:* **~s**) pala.
upper case *n* (*TYP*) mayúsculas *fpl*.
upper-class [ʌpə'kla:s] *adj* (*district, people, accent*) de clase alta; (*attitude*) altivo.
uppercut ['ʌpəkʌt] *n* uppercut *m*, gancho a la cara.
upper hand *n:* **to have the ~** tener la sartén por el mango.
Upper House *n* (*POL*): **the ~** la Cámara alta.
uppermost ['ʌpəməust] *adj* el más alto; **what was ~ in my mind** lo que me preocupaba más.
Upper Volta [-'vɔultə] *n* Alto Volta *m*.
upright ['ʌpraɪt] *adj* vertical; (*fig*) honrado.
uprising ['ʌpraɪzɪŋ] *n* sublevación *f*.
uproar ['ʌprɔ:*] *n* tumulto, escándalo.
uproarious [ʌp'rɔ:rɪəs] *adj* escandaloso; (*hilarious*) graciosísimo; (*exceptional*) espectacular.
uproot [ʌp'ru:t] *vt* desarraigar.
upset *n* ['ʌpsɛt] (*to plan etc*) revés *m*, contratiempo; (*MED*) trastorno ♦ *vt* [ʌp'sɛt] (*irreg: like* **set**) (*glass etc*) volcar; (*spill*) derramar; (*plan*) alterar; (*person*) molestar, perturbar ♦ *adj* [ʌp'sɛt] preocupado, perturbado; (*stomach*) revuelto; **to have a stomach ~** (*BRIT*) tener el estómago revuelto; **to get ~**

molestarse, llevarse un disgusto.
upset price *n* (*US, Scottish*) precio mínimo
or de reserva.
upsetting [ʌp'sɛtɪŋ] *adj* (*worrying*)
inquietante; (*offending*) ofensivo;
(*annoying*) molesto.
upshot ['ʌpʃɒt] *n* resultado.
upside-down ['ʌpsaɪd'daun] *adv* al revés.
upstage ['ʌp'steɪdʒ] *vt* robar protagonismo
a.
upstairs [ʌp'stɛəz] *adv* arriba ♦ *adj* (*room*)
de arriba ♦ *n* el piso superior.
upstart ['ʌpstɑːt] *n* advenedizo.
upstream [ʌp'striːm] *adv* río arriba.
upsurge ['ʌpsɔːdʒ] *n* (*of enthusiasm etc*)
arrebato.
uptake ['ʌpteɪk] *n*: **he is quick/slow on the**
~ **es muy listo/torpe.**
uptight [ʌp'taɪt] *adj* tenso, nervioso.
up-to-date ['ʌptə'deɪt] *adj* moderno, actual;
to bring sb ~ **(on sth)** poner a algn al
corriente/tanto (de algo).
upturn ['ʌptəːn] *n* (*in luck*) mejora; (*COMM*:
in market) resurgimiento económico; (: *in
value of currency*) aumento.
upturned ['ʌptəːnd] *adj*: ~ **nose** nariz *f*
respingona.
upward ['ʌpwəd] *adj* ascendente.
upwardly-mobile ['ʌpwədlɪ'məubaɪl] *adj*: **to
be** ~ mejorar socialmente.
upward(s) ['ʌpwəd(z)] *adv* hacia arriba.
URA *n abbr* (*US*) = **Urban Renewal
Administration.**
Ural Mountains ['juərəl-] *npl*: **the** ~ (*also*:
the Urals) los Montes Urales.
uranium [juə'reɪnɪəm] *n* uranio.
Uranus [juə'reɪnəs] *n* (*ASTRO*) Urano.
urban ['əːbən] *adj* urbano.
urbane [əː'beɪn] *adj* cortés, urbano.
urbanization ['əːbənaɪ'zeɪʃən] *n*
urbanización *f*.
urchin ['əːtʃɪn] *n* pilluelo, golfillo.
Urdu ['uəduː] *n* urdu *m*.
urge [əːdʒ] *n* (*force*) impulso; (*desire*) deseo
♦ *vt*: **to** ~ **sb to do sth** animar a algn a
hacer algo.
▶**urge on** *vt* animar.
urgency ['əːdʒənsɪ] *n* urgencia.
urgent ['əːdʒənt] *adj* (*earnest, persistent*:
plea) insistente; (: *tone*) urgente.
urgently ['əːdʒəntlɪ] *adv* con urgencia,
urgentemente.
urinal ['juərɪnl] *n* (*building*) urinario;
(*vessel*) orinal *m*.
urinate ['juərɪneɪt] *vi* orinar.
urine ['juərɪn] *n* orina.
urn [əːn] *n* urna; (*also*: **tea** ~) tetera
(grande).

Uruguay ['juərəgwaɪ] *n* el Uruguay.
Uruguayan [juərə'gwaɪən] *adj, n*
uruguayo/a *m/f*.
US *n abbr* (= *United States*) EE.UU.
us [ʌs] *pron* nos; (*after prep*) nosotros/as;
(*col*: *me*): **give** ~ **a kiss** dame un beso; *see
also* **me.**
USA *n abbr see* **United States of America;**
(*MIL*) = *United States Army.*
usable ['juːzəbl] *adj* utilizable.
USAF *n abbr* = *United States Air Force.*
usage ['juːzɪdʒ] *n* (*LING*) uso; (*utilization*)
utilización *f*.
USCG *n abbr* = *United States Coast
Guard.*
USDA *n abbr* = *United States Department of
Agriculture.*
USDAW ['ʌzdɔ] *n abbr* (*BRIT*: – *Union
of Shop, Distributive and Allied Workers*)
sindicato de empleados de
comercio.
USDI *n abbr* = *United States Department of
the Interior.*
use *n* [juːs] uso, empleo; (*usefulness*)
utilidad *f* ♦ *vt* [juːz] usar, emplear; **in** ~ en
uso; **out of** ~ en desuso; **to be of** ~ servir;
ready for ~ listo (para usar); **to make** ~
of sth aprovecharse *or* servirse de algo;
it's no ~ (*pointless*) es inútil; (*not useful*)
no sirve; **what's this** ~**d for?** ¿para qué
sirve esto?; **to be** ~**d to** estar
acostumbrado a (*SP*), acostumbrar; **to
get** ~**d to** acostumbrarse a; **she** ~**d to do
it** (ella) solía *or* acostumbraba hacerlo.
▶**use up** *vt* agotar.
used [juːzd] *adj* (*car*) usado.
useful ['juːsful] *adj* útil; **to come in** ~ ser
útil.
usefulness ['juːsfəlnɪs] *n* utilidad.
useless ['juːslɪs] *adj* inútil; (*unusable*: *object*)
inservible.
uselessly ['juːslɪslɪ] *adv* inútilmente, en
vano.
uselessness ['juːslɪsnɪs] *n* inutilidad *f*.
user ['juːzə*] *n* usuario/a; (*of petrol, gas etc*)
consumidor(a) *m/f*.
user-friendly ['juːzə'frɛndlɪ] *adj* (*COMPUT*)
fácil de utilizar.
USES *n abbr* = *United States Employment
Service.*
usher ['ʌʃə*] *n* (*at wedding*) ujier *m*; (*in
cinema etc*) acomodador *m* ♦ *vt*: **to** ~ **sb in**
(*into room*) hacer pasar a algn; **it** ~**ed in a
new era** (*fig*) inició una nueva era.
usherette [ʌʃə'rɛt] *n* (*in cinema*)
acomodadora.
USIA *n abbr* = *United States Information
Agency.*

USM *n abbr* = *United States Mail; United States Mint.*
USN *n abbr* = *United States Navy.*
USPHS *n abbr* = *United States Public Health Service.*
USPO *n abbr* = *United States Post Office.*
USS *abbr* = *United States Ship (or Steamer).*
USSR *n abbr*: **the ~** la U.R.S.S.
usu. *abbr* = **usually.**
usual ['juːʒuəl] *adj* normal, corriente; **as ~** como de costumbre, como siempre.
usually ['juːʒuəlɪ] *adv* normalmente.
usurer ['juːʒərə*] *n* usurero.
usurp [juːˈzəːp] *vt* usurpar.
usury ['juːʒərɪ] *n* usura.
UT *abbr* (*US*) = *Utah.*
utensil [juːˈtɛnsl] *n* utensilio; **kitchen ~s** batería de cocina.
uterus ['juːtərəs] *n* útero.
utilitarian [juːtɪlɪˈtɛərɪən] *adj* utilitario.
utility [juːˈtɪlɪtɪ] *n* utilidad *f.*
utility room *n* trascocina.
utilization [juːtɪlaɪˈzeɪʃən] *n* utilización *f.*
utilize ['juːtɪlaɪz] *vt* utilizar.
utmost ['ʌtməust] *adj* mayor ♦ *n*: **to do one's ~** hacer todo lo posible; **it is of the ~ importance that ...** es de la mayor importancia que ....
utter ['ʌtə*] *adj* total, completo ♦ *vt* pronunciar, proferir.
utterance ['ʌtərns] *n* palabras *fpl,* declaración *f.*
utterly ['ʌtəlɪ] *adv* completamente, totalmente.
U-turn ['juːˈtəːn] *n* cambio de sentido; (*fig*) giro de 180 grados.
Uzbekistan [ʌzbɛkɪˈstɑːn] *n* Uzbekistán *m.*

V v

V, v [viː] (*letter*) V, v *f;* **V for Victor** V de Valencia.
v. *abbr* (= *verse*) vers.º (= *vide: see*) V, vid., vide; (= *versus*) vs.; = **volt.**
VA, Va. *abbr* (*US*) = *Virginia.*
vac [væk] *n abbr* (*BRIT col*) = **vacation.**
vacancy ['veɪkənsɪ] *n* (*BRIT: job*) vacante *f;* (*room*) cuarto libro; **have you any vacancies?** ¿tiene *or* hay alguna habitación *or* algún cuarto libre?

vacant ['veɪkənt] *adj* desocupado, libre; (*expression*) distraído.
vacant lot *n* (*US*) solar *m.*
vacate [vəˈkeɪt] *vt* (*house*) desocupar; (*job*) dejar (vacante).
vacation [vəˈkeɪʃən] *n* vacaciones *fpl;* **on ~** de vacaciones; **to take a ~** (*esp US*) tomarse unas vacaciones.
vacation course *n* curso de vacaciones.
vacationer [vəˈkeɪʃənə*], **vacationist** [vəˈkeɪʃənɪst] *n* (*US*) turista *m/f.*
vaccinate ['væksɪneɪt] *vt* vacunar.
vaccination [væksɪˈneɪʃən] *n* vacunación *f.*
vaccine ['væksiːn] *n* vacuna.
vacuum ['vækjum] *n* vacío.
vacuum bottle *n* (*US*) = **vacuum flask.**
vacuum cleaner *n* aspiradora.
vacuum flask *n* (*BRIT*) termo.
vacuum-packed ['vækjum'pækt] *adj* envasado al vacío.
vagabond ['vægəbɔnd] *n* vagabundo/a.
vagary ['veɪgərɪ] *n* capricho.
vagina [vəˈdʒaɪnə] *n* vagina.
vagrancy ['veɪgrənsɪ] *n* vagabundeo.
vagrant ['veɪgrənt] *n* vagabundo/a.
vague [veɪg] *adj* vago; (*blurred: memory*) borroso; (*uncertain*) incierto, impreciso; (*person*) distraído; **I haven't the ~st idea** no tengo la más remota idea.
vaguely ['veɪglɪ] *adv* vagamente.
vagueness ['veɪgnɪs] *n* vaguedad *f;* imprecisión *f;* (*absent-mindedness*) despiste *m.*
vain [veɪn] *adj* (*conceited*) presumido; (*useless*) vano, inútil; **in ~** en vano.
vainly ['veɪnlɪ] *adv* (*to no effect*) en vano; (*conceitedly*) vanidosamente.
valance ['væləns] *n* (*for bed*) *volante alrededor de la colcha o sábana que cuelga hasta el suelo.*
valedictory [vælɪˈdɪktərɪ] *adj* de despedida.
valentine ['vælntaɪn] *n* (*also:* **~ card**) tarjeta del Día de los Enamorados.
valet ['væleɪ] *n* ayuda *m* de cámara.
valet service *n* (*for clothes*) planchado.
valiant ['væljənt] *adj* valiente.
valiantly ['væljəntlɪ] *adv* valientemente, con valor.
valid ['vælɪd] *adj* válido; (*ticket*) valedero; (*law*) vigente.
validate ['vælɪdeɪt] *vt* (*contract, document*) convalidar; (*argument, claim*) dar validez a.
validity [vəˈlɪdɪtɪ] *n* validez *f;* vigencia.
valise [vəˈliːz] *n* maletín *m.*
valley ['vælɪ] *n* valle *m.*
valour, (*US*) valor ['vælə*] *n* valor *m,* valentía.

valuable ['væijuəbl] adj (jewel) de valor;
(time) valioso; ~s npl objetos mpl de valor.
valuation [vælju'eɪʃən] n tasación f,
valuación f.
value ['vælju:] n valor m; (importance)
importancia ♦ vt (fix price of) tasar,
valorar; (esteem) apreciar; ~s npl (moral)
valores mpl morales; **to lose (in)** ~
(currency) bajar; (property)
desvalorizarse; **to gain (in)** ~ (currency)
subir; (property) valorizarse; **you get
good** ~ **(for money) in that shop** la
relación calidad-precio es muy buena en
esa tienda; **to be of great** ~ **to sb** ser de
gran valor para algn; **it is** ~**d at £8** está
valorado en ocho libras.
value added tax (VAT) n (BRIT) impuesto
sobre el valor añadido or agregado (LAM)
(IVA m).
valued ['vælju:d] adj (appreciated)
apreciado.
valueless ['vælju:lɪs] adj sin valor.
valuer ['vælju:ə*] n tasador(a) m/f.
valve [vælv] n (ANAT, TECH) válvula.
vampire ['væmpaɪə*] n vampiro.
van [væn] n (AUT) furgoneta, camioneta
(LAM); (BRIT RAIL) furgón m (de equipajes).
V and A n abbr (BRIT) = Victoria and Albert
Museum.
vandal ['vændl] n vándalo/a.
vandalism ['vændəlɪzəm] n vandalismo.
vandalize ['vændəlaɪz] vt dañar, destruir,
destrozar.
vanguard ['vænga:d] n vanguardia.
vanilla [və'nɪlə] n vainilla.
vanish ['vænɪʃ] vi desaparecer, esfumarse.
vanity ['vænɪtɪ] n vanidad f.
vanity case n neceser m.
vantage point ['va:ntɪdʒ-] n posición f
ventajosa.
vaporize ['veɪpəraɪz] vt vaporizar ♦ vi
vaporizarse.
vapour, (US) **vapor** ['veɪpə*] n vapor m; (on
breath, window) vaho.
vapo(u)r trail n (AVIAT) estela.
variable ['vɛərɪəbl] adj variable ♦ n variable
f.
variance ['vɛərɪəns] n: **to be at** ~ **(with)**
estar en desacuerdo (con), no cuadrar
(con).
variant ['vɛərɪənt] n variante f.
variation [vɛərɪ'eɪʃən] n variación f.
varicose ['værɪkəus] adj: ~ **veins** varices fpl.
varied ['vɛərɪd] adj variado.
variety [və'raɪətɪ] n variedad f, diversidad f;
(quantity) surtido; **for a** ~ **of reasons** por
varias or diversas razones.
variety show n espectáculo de

variedades.
various ['vɛərɪəs] adj varios/as, diversos/as;
at ~ **times** (different) en distintos
momentos; (several) varias veces.
varnish ['va:nɪʃ] n (gen) barniz m; (nail ~)
esmalte m ♦ vt (gen) barnizar; (nails)
pintar (con esmalte).
vary ['vɛərɪ] vt variar; (change) cambiar ♦ vi
variar; (disagree) discrepar; **to** ~ **with** or
according to variar según or de acuerdo
con.
varying ['vɛərɪɪŋ] adj diversos/as.
vase [va:z] n florero.
vasectomy [və'sɛktəmɪ] n vasectomía.
Vaseline ® ['væsɪli:n] n vaselina ®.
vast [va:st] adj enorme; (success)
abrumador(a), arrollador(a).
vastly ['va:stlɪ] adv enormemente.
vastness ['va:stnɪs] n inmensidad f.
VAT [væt] n abbr (BRIT: = value added tax)
IVA m.
vat [væt] n tina, tinaja.
Vatican ['vætɪkən] n: **the** ~ el Vaticano.
vatman ['vætmæn] n (BRIT col) inspector m
or recaudador m del IVA; **"how to avoid
the** ~**"** "cómo evitar pagar el IVA".
vaudeville ['vɔːdəvɪl] n (US) vodevil m.
vault [vɔːlt] n (of roof) bóveda; (tomb)
tumba; (in bank) cámara acorazada ♦ vt
(also: ~ **over**) saltar (por encima de).
vaunted ['vɔːntɪd] adj: **much** ~ cacareado.
VC n abbr = **vice-chairman, vice-chancellor;**
(BRIT: = Victoria Cross) condecoración
militar.
VCR n abbr = **video cassette recorder.**
VD n abbr see **venereal disease.**
VDU n abbr see **visual display unit.**
veal [vi:l] n ternera.
veer [vɪə*] vi (ship) virar.
veg. [vɛdʒ] n abbr (BRIT col) = **vegetable(s).**
vegan ['vi:gən] n vegetariano/a estricto/a.
vegeburger, veggieburger ['vɛdʒɪbə:gə*]
n hamburguesa vegetal.
vegetable ['vɛdʒtəbl] n (BOT) vegetal m;
(edible plant) legumbre f, hortaliza ♦ adj
vegetal; ~s npl (cooked) verduras fpl.
vegetable garden n huerta, huerto.
vegetarian [vɛdʒɪ'tɛərɪən] adj, n
vegetariano/a m/f.
vegetate ['vɛdʒɪteɪt] vi vegetar.
vegetation [vɛdʒɪ'teɪʃən] n vegetación f.
vegetative ['vɛdʒɪtətɪv] adj vegetativo;
(BOT) vegetal.
vehemence ['vi:ɪməns] n vehemencia;
violencia.
vehement ['vi:ɪmənt] adj vehemente,
apasionado; (dislike, hatred) violento.
vehicle ['vi:ɪkl] n vehículo; (fig) vehículo,

medio.
vehicular [vɪ'hɪkjʊlə*] *adj*: ~ **traffic**
circulación *f* rodada.
veil [veɪl] *n* velo ♦ *vt* velar; **under a ~ of
secrecy** (*fig*) en el mayor secreto.
veiled [veɪld] *adj* (*also fig*) disimulado,
velado.
vein [veɪn] *n* vena; (*of ore etc*) veta.
Velcro ® ['vɛlkrəʊ] *n* velcro *m* ®.
vellum ['vɛləm] *n* (*writing paper*) papel *m*
vitela.
velocity [vɪ'lɒsɪtɪ] *n* velocidad *f*.
velour [və'luə*] *n* terciopelo.
velvet ['vɛlvɪt] *n* terciopelo ♦ *adj*
aterciopelado.
vendetta [vɛn'dɛtə] *n* vendetta.
vending machine ['vɛndɪŋ-] *n* máquina
expendedora, expendedor *m*.
vendor ['vɛndə*] *n* vendedor(a) *m/f*; **street**
~ vendedor(a) *m/f* callejero/a.
veneer [və'nɪə*] *n* chapa, enchapado; (*fig*)
barniz *m*.
venereal [vɪ'nɪərɪəl] *adj*: ~ **disease (VD)**
enfermedad *f* venérea.
Venetian blind [vɪ'niːʃən-] *n* persiana.
Venezuela [vɛnɛ'zweɪlə] *n* Venezuela.
Venezuelan [vɛnɛ'zweɪlən] *adj*, *n*
venezolano/a *m/f*.
vengeance ['vɛndʒəns] *n* venganza; **with a**
~ (*fig*) con creces.
vengeful ['vɛndʒful] *adj* vengativo.
Venice ['vɛnɪs] *n* Venecia.
venison ['vɛnɪsn] *n* carne *f* de venado.
venom ['vɛnəm] *n* veneno.
venomous ['vɛnəməs] *adj* venenoso.
venomously ['vɛnəməslɪ] *adv* con odio.
vent [vɛnt] *n* (*opening*) abertura; (*air-hole*)
respiradero; (*in wall*) rejilla (de
ventilación) ♦ *vt* (*fig: feelings*) desahogar.
ventilate ['vɛntɪleɪt] *vt* ventilar.
ventilation [vɛntɪ'leɪʃən] *n* ventilación *f*.
ventilation shaft *n* pozo de ventilación.
ventilator ['vɛntɪleɪtə*] *n* ventilador *m*.
ventriloquist [vɛn'trɪləkwɪst] *n*
ventrílocuo/a.
venture ['vɛntʃə*] *n* empresa ♦ *vt*
arriesgar; (*opinion*) ofrecer ♦ *vi*
arriesgarse, lanzarse; **a business** ~ una
empresa comercial; **to** ~ **to do sth**
aventurarse a hacer algo.
venture capital *n* capital *m* arriesgado.
venue ['vɛnjuː] *n* (*meeting place*) lugar *m* de
reunión; (*for concert*) local *m*.
Venus ['viːnəs] *n* (*ASTRO*) Venus *m*.
veracity [və'ræsɪtɪ] *n* veracidad *f*.
veranda(h) [və'rændə] *n* terraza; (*with
glass*) galería.
verb [vɜːb] *n* verbo.

verbal ['vɜːbl] *adj* verbal.
verbally ['vɜːbəlɪ] *adv* verbalmente, de
palabra.
verbatim [vɜː'beɪtɪm] *adj*, *adv* al pie de la
letra, palabra por palabra.
verbose [vɜː'bəʊs] *adj* prolijo.
verdict ['vɜːdɪkt] *n* veredicto, fallo; (*fig:
opinion*) opinión *f*, juicio; ~ **of guilty/not
guilty** veredicto de culpabilidad/
inocencia.
verge [vɜːdʒ] *n* (*BRIT*) borde *m*; **to be on the**
~ **of doing sth** estar a punto de hacer
algo.
▶**verge on** *vt fus* rayar en.
verger ['vɜːdʒə*] *n* sacristán *m*.
verification [vɛrɪfɪ'keɪʃən] *n* comprobación
f, verificación *f*.
verify ['vɛrɪfaɪ] *vt* comprobar, verificar;
(*COMPUT*) verificar; (*prove the truth of*)
confirmar.
veritable ['vɛrɪtəbl] *adj* verdadero,
auténtico.
vermin ['vɜːmɪn] *npl* (*animals*) bichos *mpl*;
(*insects, fig*) sabandijas *fpl*.
vermouth ['vɜːməθ] *n* vermut *m*.
vernacular [və'nækjʊlə*] *n* lengua
vernácula.
versatile ['vɜːsətaɪl] *adj* (*person*)
polifacético; (*machine, tool etc*) versátil.
versatility [vɜːsə'tɪlɪtɪ] *n* versatilidad *f*.
verse [vɜːs] *n* versos *mpl*, poesía; (*stanza*)
estrofa; (*in bible*) versículo; **in** ~ en
verso.
versed [vɜːst] *adj*: **(well-)**~ **in** versado en.
version ['vɜːʃən] *n* versión *f*.
versus ['vɜːsəs] *prep* contra.
vertebra, *pl* ~**e** ['vɜːtɪbrə, briː] *n* vértebra.
vertebrate ['vɜːtɪbrɪt] *n* vertebrado.
vertical ['vɜːtɪkl] *adj* vertical.
vertically ['vɜːtɪkəlɪ] *adv* verticalmente.
vertigo ['vɜːtɪgəʊ] *n* vértigo; **to suffer from**
~ tener vértigo.
verve [vɜːv] *n* brío.
very ['vɛrɪ] *adv* muy ♦ *adj*: **the** ~ **book which**
el mismo libro que; **the** ~ **last** el último
(de todos); **at the** ~ **least** al menos; ~
much muchísimo; ~ **well/little** muy bien/
poco; ~ **high frequency** (*RADIO*)
frecuencia muy alta; **it's** ~ **cold** hace
mucho frío; **the** ~ **thought (of it) alarms
me** con sólo pensarlo me entra miedo.
vespers ['vɛspəz] *npl* vísperas *fpl*.
vessel ['vɛsl] *n* (*ANAT*) vaso; (*ship*) barco;
(*container*) vasija.
vest [vɛst] *n* (*BRIT*) camiseta; (*US: waistcoat*)
chaleco.
vested interests ['vɛstɪd-] *npl* (*COMM*)
intereses *mpl* creados.

vestibule ['vɛstɪbjuːl] n vestíbulo.
vestige ['vɛstɪdʒ] n vestigio, rastro.
vestry ['vɛstrɪ] n sacristía.
Vesuvius [vɪ'suːvɪəs] n Vesubio.
vet [vɛt] n abbr = veterinary surgeon ♦ vt revisar; **to ~ sb for a job** someter a investigación a algn para un trabajo.
veteran ['vɛtərn] n veterano/a ♦ adj: **she is a ~ campaigner for** ... es una veterana de la campaña de ... .
veteran car n coche m antiguo.
veterinarian [vɛtrɪ'nɛərɪən] n (US) = veterinary surgeon.
veterinary ['vɛtrɪnərɪ] adj veterinario.
veterinary surgeon n (BRIT) veterinario/a.
veto ['viːtəu] n (pl ~es) veto ♦ vt prohibir, vedar; **to put a ~ on** vetar.
vetting ['vɛtɪŋ] n: **positive ~** investigación gubernamental de los futuros altos cargos de la Administración.
vex [vɛks] vt (irritate) fastidiar; (make impatient) impacientar.
vexed [vɛkst] adj (question) controvertido.
vexing ['vɛksɪŋ] adj molesto, engorroso.
VFD n abbr (US) = voluntary fire department.
VG n abbr (BRIT SCOL etc: = very good) S (= sobresaliente).
VHF abbr (= very high frequency) VHF f.
VI abbr (US) = Virgin Islands.
via ['vaɪə] prep por, por vía de.
viability [vaɪə'bɪlɪtɪ] n viabilidad f.
viable ['vaɪəbl] adj viable.
viaduct ['vaɪədʌkt] n viaducto.
vial ['vaɪəl] n frasco pequeño.
vibes [vaɪbz] npl (col): **I got good/bad ~** me dio buen/mal rollo.
vibrant ['vaɪbrənt] adj (lively, bright) vivo; (full of emotion: voice) vibrante; (colour) fuerte.
vibraphone ['vaɪbrəfəun] n vibráfono.
vibrate [vaɪ'breɪt] vi vibrar.
vibration [vaɪ'breɪʃən] n vibración f.
vibrator [vaɪ'breɪtə*] n vibrador m.
vicar ['vɪkə*] n párroco.
vicarage ['vɪkərɪdʒ] n parroquia.
vicarious [vɪ'kɛərɪəs] adj indirecto; (responsibility) delegado.
vice [vaɪs] n (evil) vicio; (TECH) torno de banco.
vice- [vaɪs] pref vice....
vice-chairman ['vaɪs'tʃɛəmən] n vicepresidente m.
vice-chancellor [vaɪs'tʃɑːnsələ*] n (BRIT UNIV) rector(a) m/f.
vice-president [vaɪs'prɛzɪdənt] n vicepresidente/a m/f.
viceroy ['vaɪsrɔɪ] n virrey m.
vice versa ['vaɪsɪ'vəːsə] adv viceversa.

vicinity [vɪ'sɪnɪtɪ] n (area) vecindad f; (nearness) proximidad f; **in the ~ (of)** cercano (a).
vicious ['vɪʃəs] adj (remark) malicioso; (blow) brutal; **a ~ circle** un círculo vicioso.
viciousness ['vɪʃəsnɪs] n brutalidad f.
vicissitudes [vɪ'sɪsɪtjuːdz] npl vicisitudes fpl, peripecias fpl.
victim ['vɪktɪm] n víctima; **to be the ~ of** ser víctima de.
victimization [vɪktɪmaɪ'zeɪʃən] n persecución f; (of striker etc) represalias fpl.
victimize ['vɪktɪmaɪz] vt (strikers etc) tomar represalias contra.
victor ['vɪktə*] n vencedor(a) m/f.
Victorian [vɪk'tɔːrɪən] adj victoriano.
victorious [vɪk'tɔːrɪəs] adj vencedor(a).
victory ['vɪktərɪ] n victoria; **to win a ~ over sb** obtener una victoria sobre algn.
video ['vɪdɪəu] cpd de vídeo ♦ n vídeo ♦ vt grabar (en vídeo).
video camera n videocámara, cámara de vídeo.
video cassette n videocassette f.
video (cassette) recorder n vídeo, videocassette f.
videodisk ['vɪdɪəudɪsk] n videodisco.
video game n videojuego.
video nasty n vídeo de violencia y/o porno duro.
videophone ['vɪdɪəufəun] n videoteléfono, videófono.
video recording n videograbación f.
video tape n cinta de vídeo.
vie [vaɪ] vi: **to ~ with** competir con.
Vienna [vɪ'ɛnə] n Viena.
Viennese [vɪə'niːz] adj, n vienés/esa m/f.
Vietnam, Viet Nam [vjɛt'næm] n Vietnam m.
Vietnamese [vjɛtnə'miːz] adj vietnamita ♦ n (pl inv) vietnamita m/f; (LING) vietnamita m.
view [vjuː] n vista; (landscape) paisaje m; (opinion) opinión f, criterio ♦ vt (look at) mirar; (examine) examinar; **on ~** (in museum etc) expuesto; **in full ~ of sb** a la vista de algn; **to be within ~ (of sth)** estar a la vista (de algo); **an overall ~ of the situation** una visión de conjunto de la situación; **in ~ of the fact that** en vista de que; **to take** or **hold the ~ that** ... opinar or pensar que ...; **with a ~ to doing sth** con miras or vistas a hacer algo.
viewdata ['vjuːdeɪtə] n (BRIT) videodatos mpl.
viewer ['vjuːə*] n (small projector) visionadora; (TV) televidente m/f,

telespectador(a) *m/f.*
viewfinder ['vju:faɪndə*] *n* visor *m* de imagen.
viewpoint ['vju:pɔɪnt] *n* punto de vista.
vigil ['vɪdʒɪl] *n* vigilia; **to keep** ~ velar.
vigilance ['vɪdʒɪləns] *n* vigilancia.
vigilance committee *n* (*US*) comité *m* de autodefensa.
vigilant ['vɪdʒɪlənt] *adj* vigilante.
vigilante [vɪdʒɪ'læntɪ] *n* vecino/a que se toma la justicia por su mano.
vigorous ['vɪgərəs] *adj* enérgico, vigoroso.
vigorously ['vɪgərəslɪ] *adv* enérgicamente, vigorosamente.
vigour, (US**) vigor** ['vɪgə*] *n* energía, vigor *m*.
vile [vaɪl] *adj* (*action*) vil, infame; (*smell*) repugnante.
vilify ['vɪlɪfaɪ] *vt* denigrar, vilipendiar.
villa ['vɪlə] *n* (*country house*) casa de campo; (*suburban house*) chalet *m*.
village ['vɪlɪdʒ] *n* aldea.
villager ['vɪlɪdʒə*] *n* aldeano/a.
villain ['vɪlən] *n* (*scoundrel*) malvado/a; (*criminal*) maleante *m/f*; *see also* **pantomime.**
VIN *n abbr* (*US*) = *vehicle identification number.*
vinaigrette [vɪneɪ'grɛt] *n* vinagreta.
vindicate ['vɪndɪkeɪt] *vt* vindicar, justificar.
vindication [vɪndɪ'keɪʃən] *n*: **in** ~ **of** en justificación de.
vindictive [vɪn'dɪktɪv] *adj* vengativo.
vine [vaɪn] *n* vid *f.*
vinegar ['vɪnɪgə*] *n* vinagre *m.*
vine-growing ['vaɪngrəʊɪŋ] *adj* (*region*) viticultor(a).
vineyard ['vɪnjɑːd] *n* viña, viñedo.
vintage ['vɪntɪdʒ] *n* (*year*) vendimia, cosecha; **the 1970** ~ la cosecha de 1970.
vintage car *n* coche *m* antiguo *or* de época.
vintage wine *n* vino añejo.
vintage year *n*: **it's been a** ~ **for plays** ha sido un año destacado en lo que a teatro se refiere.
vinyl ['vaɪnl] *n* vinilo.
viola [vɪ'əʊlə] *n* (*MUS*) viola.
violate ['vaɪəleɪt] *vt* violar.
violation [vaɪə'leɪʃən] *n* violación *f*; **in** ~ **of sth** en violación de algo.
violence ['vaɪələns] *n* violencia; **acts of** ~ actos *mpl* de violencia.
violent ['vaɪələnt] *adj* (*gen*) violento; (*pain*) intenso; **a** ~ **dislike of sb/sth** una profunda antipatía *or* manía a algn/algo.
violently ['vaɪələntlɪ] *adv* (*severely: ill, angry*) muy.
violet ['vaɪələt] *adj* violado, violeta ♦ *n*

(*plant*) violeta.
violin [vaɪə'lɪn] *n* violín *m.*
violinist [vaɪə'lɪnɪst] *n* violinista *m/f.*
VIP *n abbr* (= *very important person*) VIP *m.*
viper ['vaɪpə*] *n* víbora.
viral ['vaɪərəl] *adj* vírico.
virgin ['vɜːdʒɪn] *n* virgen *m/f* ♦ *adj* virgen; **the Blessed V**~ la Santísima Virgen.
virginity [vɜː'dʒɪnɪtɪ] *n* virginidad *f.*
Virgo ['vɜːgəʊ] *n* Virgo.
virile ['vɪraɪl] *adj* viril.
virility [vɪ'rɪlɪtɪ] *n* virilidad *f.*
virtual ['vɜːtjuəl] *adj* virtual.
virtually ['vɜːtjuəlɪ] *adv* (*almost*) prácticamente, virtualmente; **it is** ~ **impossible** es prácticamente imposible.
virtual reality *n* realidad *f* virtual.
virtue ['vɜːtjuː] *n* virtud *f*; **by** ~ **of** en virtud de.
virtuosity [vɜːtju'ɔsɪtɪ] *n* virtuosismo.
virtuoso [vɜːtju'əʊsəu] *n* virtuoso.
virtuous ['vɜːtjuəs] *adj* virtuoso.
virulence ['vɪruləns] *n* virulencia.
virulent ['vɪrulənt] *adj* virulento, violento.
virus ['vaɪərəs] *n* virus *m.*
visa ['viːzə] *n* visado, visa (*LAM*).
vis-à-vis [viːzə'viː] *prep* con respecto a.
viscount ['vaɪkaunt] *n* vizconde *m.*
viscous ['vɪskəs] *adj* viscoso.
vise [vaɪs] *n* (*US TECH*) = **vice.**
visibility [vɪzɪ'bɪlɪtɪ] *n* visibilidad *f.*
visible ['vɪzəbl] *adj* visible; ~ **exports/ imports** exportaciones *fpl*/importaciones *fpl* visibles.
visibly ['vɪzɪblɪ] *adv* visiblemente.
vision ['vɪʒən] *n* (*sight*) vista; (*foresight, in dream*) visión *f.*
visionary ['vɪʒənrɪ] *n* visionario/a.
visit ['vɪzɪt] *n* visita ♦ *vt* (*person*) visitar, hacer una visita a; (*place*) ir a, (ir a) conocer; **to pay a** ~ **to** (*person*) visitar a; **on a private/official** ~ en visita privada/ oficial.
visiting ['vɪzɪtɪŋ] *adj* (*speaker, professor*) invitado; (*team*) visitante.
visiting card *n* tarjeta de visita.
visiting hours *npl* (*in hospital etc*) horas *fpl* de visita.
visitor *n* (*gen*) visitante *m/f*; (*to one's house*) visita; (*tourist*) turista *m/f*; (*tripper*) excursionista *m/f*; **to have** ~**s** (*at home*) tener visita.
visitors' book *n* libro de visitas.
visor ['vaɪzə*] *n* visera.
VISTA ['vɪstə] *n abbr* (= *Volunteers In Service to America*) programa de ayuda voluntaria a los necesitados.
vista ['vɪstə] *n* vista, panorama.

visual ['vɪzjuəl] *adj* visual.
visual aid *n* medio visual.
visual arts *npl* artes *fpl* plásticas.
visual display unit (VDU) *n* unidad *f* de despliegue visual, monitor *m*.
visualize ['vɪzjuəlaɪz] *vt* imaginarse; (*foresee*) prever.
visually ['vɪzjuəlɪ] *adv*: ~ **handicapped** con visión deficiente.
vital ['vaɪtl] *adj* (*essential*) esencial, imprescindible; (*crucial*) crítico; (*person*) enérgico, vivo; (*of life*) vital; **of ~ importance (to sb/sth)** de suma importancia (para algn/algo).
vitality [vaɪ'tælɪtɪ] *n* energía, vitalidad *f*.
vitally ['vaɪtəlɪ] *adv*: ~ **important** de suma importancia.
vital statistics *npl* (*of population*) estadísticas *fpl* demográficas; (*col*: *woman's*) medidas *fpl* (corporales).
vitamin ['vɪtəmɪn] *n* vitamina.
vitamin pill *n* pastilla de vitaminas.
vitreous ['vɪtrɪəs] *adj* (*china, enamel*) vítreo.
vitriolic [vɪtrɪ'ɒlɪk] *adj* mordaz.
viva ['vaɪvə] *n* (*also*: ~ **voce**) examen *m* oral.
vivacious [vɪ'veɪʃəs] *adj* vivaz, alegre.
vivacity [vɪ'væsɪtɪ] *n* vivacidad *f*.
vivid ['vɪvɪd] *adj* (*account*) gráfico; (*light*) intenso; (*imagination*) vivo.
vividly ['vɪvɪdlɪ] *adv* (*describe*) gráficamente; (*remember*) como si fuera hoy.
vivisection [vɪvɪ'sɛkʃən] *n* vivisección *f*.
vixen ['vɪksn] *n* (*ZOOL*) zorra, raposa; (*pej*: *woman*) arpía, bruja.
viz *abbr* (= *videlicet*: *namely*) v.gr.
VLF *abbr* = *very low frequency*.
V-neck ['viːnɛk] *n* cuello de pico.
VOA *n abbr* (= *Voice of America*) Voz *f* de América.
vocabulary [vəu'kæbjulərɪ] *n* vocabulario.
vocal ['vəukl] *adj* vocal; (*articulate*) elocuente.
vocal cords *npl* cuerdas *fpl* vocales.
vocalist ['vəukəlɪst] *n* cantante *m/f*.
vocation [vəu'keɪʃən] *n* vocación *f*.
vocational [vəu'keɪʃənl] *adj* vocacional; ~ **guidance** orientación *f* profesional; ~ **training** formación *f* profesional.
vociferous [və'sɪfərəs] *adj* vociferante.
vociferously [və'sɪfərəslɪ] *adv* a gritos.
vodka ['vɒdkə] *n* vodka *m*.
vogue [vəug] *n* boga, moda; **to be in ~, be the ~** estar de moda or en boga.
voice [vɔɪs] *n* voz *f* ♦ *vt* (*opinion*) expresar; **in a loud/soft ~** en voz alta/baja; **to give ~ to** expresar.
voice mail *n* fonobuzón *m*.
voice-over ['vɔɪsəuvə*] *n* voz *f* en off.

void [vɔɪd] *n* vacío; (*hole*) hueco ♦ *adj* (*invalid*) nulo, inválido; (*empty*): ~ **of** carente or desprovisto de.
voile [vɔɪl] *n* gasa.
vol. *abbr* (= *volume*) t.
volatile ['vɒlətaɪl] *adj* volátil; (*COMPUT*: *memory*) no permanente.
volcanic [vɒl'kænɪk] *adj* volcánico.
volcano, ~**es** [vɒl'keɪnəu] *n* volcán *m*.
volition [və'lɪʃən] *n*: **of one's own ~** por su propia voluntad.
volley ['vɒlɪ] *n* (*of gunfire*) descarga; (*of stones etc*) lluvia; (*TENNIS etc*) volea.
volleyball *n* voleibol *m*, balonvolea *m*.
volt [vəult] *n* voltio.
voltage ['vəultɪdʒ] *n* voltaje *m*; **high/low ~** alto/bajo voltaje, alta/baja tensión.
volte-face ['vɒlt'fɑːs] *n* viraje *m*.
voluble ['vɒljubl] *adj* locuaz, hablador(a).
volume ['vɒljuːm] *n* (*of tank*) volumen *m*; (*book*) tomo; ~ **one/two** (*of book*) tomo primero/segundo; ~**s** *npl* (*great quantities*) cantidad *fsg*; **his expression spoke ~s** su expresión (lo) decía todo.
volume control *n* (*RADIO, TV*) (botón *m* del) volumen *m*.
volume discount *n* (*COMM*) descuento por volumen de compras.
voluminous [və'luːmɪnəs] *adj* (*large*) voluminoso; (*prolific*) prolífico.
voluntarily ['vɒləntrɪlɪ] *adv* libremente, voluntariamente.
voluntary ['vɒləntərɪ] *adj* voluntario, espontáneo.
voluntary liquidation *n* (*COMM*) liquidación *f* voluntaria.
voluntary redundancy *n* (*BRIT*) despido voluntario.
volunteer [vɒlən'tɪə*] *n* voluntario/a ♦ *vi* ofrecerse (de voluntario); **to ~ to do** ofrecerse a hacer.
voluptuous [və'lʌptjuəs] *adj* voluptuoso.
vomit ['vɒmɪt] *n* vómito ♦ *vt, vi* vomitar.
voracious [və'reɪʃəs] *adj* voraz; (*reader*) ávido.
vote [vəut] *n* voto; (*votes cast*) votación *f*; (*right to* ~) derecho a votar; (*franchise*) sufragio ♦ *vt* (*chairman*) elegir ♦ *vi* votar, ir a votar; ~ **of thanks** voto de gracias; **to put sth to the ~, to take a ~ on sth** someter algo a votación; ~ **for** *or* **in favour of/against** voto a favor de/en contra de; **to ~ to do sth** votar por hacer algo; **he was ~d secretary** fue elegido secretario por votación; **to pass a ~ of confidence/no confidence** aprobar un voto de confianza/de censura.
voter ['vəutə*] *n* votante *m/f*.

voting ['vəʊtɪŋ] n votación f.
voting paper n (BRIT) papeleta de votación.
voting right n derecho a voto.
vouch [vautʃ]: **to ~ for** vt fus garantizar, responder de.
voucher ['vautʃə*] n (for meal, petrol) vale m; **luncheon/travel ~** vale m de comida/de viaje.
vow [vau] n voto ♦ vi hacer voto; **to take** or **make a ~ to do sth** jurar hacer algo, comprometerse a hacer algo.
vowel ['vauəl] n vocal f.
voyage ['vɔɪɪdʒ] n (journey) viaje m; (crossing) travesía.
voyeur [vwɑː'jəː*] n voyeur m/f, mirón/ona m/f.
VP n abbr (= vice-president) V.P.
vs abbr (= versus) vs.
VSO n abbr (BRIT: = Voluntary Service Overseas) organización que envía jóvenes voluntarios a trabajar y enseñar en los países del Tercer Mundo.
VT, Vt. abbr (US) = Vermont.
vulgar ['vʌlgə*] adj (rude) ordinario, grosero; (in bad taste) de mal gusto.
vulgarity [vʌl'gærɪtɪ] n grosería; mal gusto.
vulnerability [vʌlnərə'bɪlɪtɪ] n vulnerabilidad f.
vulnerable ['vʌlnərəbl] adj vulnerable.
vulture ['vʌltʃə*] n buitre m, gallinazo (LAM).

W w

W, w ['dʌblju:] n (letter) W, w f; **W for William** W de Washington.
W abbr (= west) O; (ELEC: = watt) v.
WA abbr (US) = Washington.
wad [wɔd] n (of cotton wool, paper) bolita; (of banknotes etc) fajo.
wadding ['wɔdɪŋ] n relleno.
waddle ['wɔdl] vi andar como un pato.
wade [weɪd] vi: **to ~ through** caminar por el agua; (fig: a book) leer con dificultad.
wading pool ['weɪdɪŋ-] n (US) piscina para niños.
wafer ['weɪfə*] n (biscuit) barquillo; (REL) oblea; (: consecrated) hostia; (COMPUT) oblea, microplaqueta.
wafer-thin ['weɪfə'θɪn] adj finísimo.

waffle ['wɔfl] n (CULIN) gofre m ♦ vi meter el rollo.
waffle iron n molde m para hacer gofres.
waft [wɔft] vt llevar por el aire ♦ vi flotar.
wag [wæg] vt menear, agitar ♦ vi moverse, menearse; **the dog ~ged its tail** el perro meneó la cola.
wage [weɪdʒ] n (also: ~s) sueldo, salario ♦ vt: **to ~ war** hacer la guerra; **a day's ~** el sueldo de un día.
wage claim n reivindicación f salarial.
wage differential n diferencia salarial.
wage earner n asalariado/a.
wage freeze n congelación f de salarios.
wage packet n sobre m de la paga.
wager ['weɪdʒə*] n apuesta ♦ vt apostar.
waggle ['wægl] vt menear, mover.
wag(g)on ['wægən] n (horse-drawn) carro; (BRIT RAIL) vagón m.
wail [weɪl] n gemido ♦ vi gemir.
waist [weɪst] n cintura, talle m.
waistcoat ['weɪstkəut] n (BRIT) chaleco.
waistline ['weɪstlaɪn] n talle m.
wait [weɪt] n espera; (interval) pausa ♦ vi esperar; **to lie in ~ for** acechar a; **I can't ~ to** (fig) estoy deseando; **to ~ for** esperar (a); **to keep sb ~ing** hacer esperar a algn; **~ a moment!** ¡un momento!, ¡un momentito!; **"repairs while you ~"** "reparaciones en el acto".
▶**wait behind** vi quedarse.
▶**wait on** vt fus servir a.
▶**wait up** vi esperar levantado.
waiter ['weɪtə*] n camarero.
waiting ['weɪtɪŋ] n: **"no ~"** (BRIT AUT) "prohibido estacionarse".
waiting list n lista de espera.
waiting room n sala de espera.
waitress ['weɪtrɪs] n camarera.
waive [weɪv] vt suspender.
waiver ['weɪvə*] n renuncia.
wake [weɪk] vb (pt woke or waked, pp woken or waked ['wəuk, 'wəukn]) vt (also: ~ up) despertar ♦ vi (also: ~ up) despertarse ♦ n (for dead person) velatorio; (NAUT) estela; **to ~ up to sth** (fig) darse cuenta de algo; **in the ~ of** tras, después de; **to follow in sb's ~** (fig) seguir las huellas de algn.
waken ['weɪkn] vt, vi = wake.
Wales [weɪlz] n País m de Gales.
walk [wɔːk] n (stroll) paseo; (hike) excursión f a pie, caminata; (gait) paso, andar m; (in park etc) paseo ♦ vi andar, caminar; (for pleasure, exercise) pasearse ♦ vt (distance) recorrer a pie, andar; (dog) (sacar a) pasear; **to go for a ~** ir a dar un paseo; **10 minutes' ~ from here** a 10

minutos de aquí andando; **people from all ~s of life** gente de todas las esferas; **to ~ in one's sleep** ser sonámbulo/a; **I'll ~ you home** te acompañaré a casa.

▶**walk out** *vi* (*go out*) salir; (*as protest*) marcharse, salirse; (*strike*) declararse en huelga; **to ~ out on sb** abandonar a algn.

walkabout ['wɔːkəbaut] *n*: **to go (on a) ~** darse un baño de multitudes.

walker ['wɔːkə*] *n* (*person*) paseante *m/f*, caminante *m/f*.

walkie-talkie ['wɔːkɪ'tɔːkɪ] *n* walkie-talkie *m*.

walking ['wɔːkɪŋ] *n* (el) andar; **it's within ~ distance** se puede ir andando *or* a pie.

walking shoes *npl* zapatos *mpl* para andar.

walking stick *n* bastón *m*.

Walkman ® *n* walkman *m* ®.

walk-on ['wɔːkɔn] *adj* (*THEAT: part*) de comparsa.

walkout ['wɔːkaut] *n* (*of workers*) huelga.

walkover ['wɔːkəuvə*] *n* (*col*) pan *m* comido.

walkway ['wɔːkweɪ] *n* paseo.

wall [wɔːl] *n* pared *f*; (*exterior*) muro; (*city ~ etc*) muralla; **to go to the ~** (*fig. firm etc*) quebrar, ir a la bancarrota.

▶**wall in** *vt* (*garden etc*) cercar con una tapia.

walled [wɔːld] *adj* (*city*) amurallado; (*garden*) con tapia.

wallet ['wɔlɪt] *n* cartera, billetera (*esp LAM*).

wallflower ['wɔːlflauə*] *n* alhelí *m*; **to be a ~** (*fig*) comer pavo.

wall hanging *n* tapiz *m*.

wallop ['wɔləp] *vt* (*col*) zurrar.

wallow ['wɔləu] *vi* revolcarse; **to ~ in one's grief** sumirse en su pena.

wallpaper ['wɔːlpeɪpə*] *n* papel *m* pintado.

wall-to-wall ['wɔːltə'wɔːl] *adj*: **~ carpeting** moqueta.

wally ['wɔlɪ] *n* (*col*) majadero/a.

walnut ['wɔːlnʌt] *n* nuez *f*; (*tree*) nogal *m*.

walrus, *pl* **~** *or* **~es** ['wɔːlrəs] *n* morsa.

waltz [wɔːlts] *n* vals *m* ♦ *vi* bailar el vals.

wan [wɔn] *adj* pálido.

wand [wɔnd] *n* (*also*: **magic ~**) varita (mágica).

wander ['wɔndə*] *vi* (*person*) vagar; deambular; (*thoughts*) divagar; (*get lost*) extraviarse ♦ *vt* recorrer, vagar por.

wanderer ['wɔndərə*] *n* vagabundo/a.

wandering ['wɔndərɪŋ] *adj* (*tribe*) nómada; (*minstrel, actor*) ambulante; (*path, river*) sinuoso; (*glance, mind*) distraído.

wane [weɪn] *vi* menguar.

wangle ['wæŋgl] (*BRIT col*) *vt*: **to ~ sth** agenciarse *or* conseguir algo ♦ *n* chanchullo.

wanker ['wæŋkə*] *n* (*col!*) pajero/a (*!*); (*as insult*) mamón/ona (*!*) *m/f*.

want [wɔnt] *vt* (*wish for*) querer, desear; (*need*) necesitar; (*lack*) carecer de ♦ *n* (*poverty*) pobreza; **for ~ of** por falta de; **~s** *npl* (*needs*) necesidades *fpl*; **to ~ to do** querer hacer; **to ~ sb to do sth** querer que algn haga algo; **you're ~ed on the phone** te llaman al teléfono; **to be in ~** estar necesitado; **"cook ~ed"** "se necesita cocinero/a".

want ads *npl* (*US*) anuncios *mpl* por palabras.

wanting ['wɔntɪŋ] *adj*: **to be ~ (in)** estar falto (de); **to be found ~** no estar a la altura de las circunstancias.

wanton ['wɔntn] *adj* (*playful*) juguetón/ona; (*licentious*) lascivo.

war [wɔː*] *n* guerra; **to make ~** hacer la guerra; **the First/Second World W~** la primera/segunda guerra mundial.

warble ['wɔːbl] *n* (*of bird*) trino, gorjeo ♦ *vi* (*bird*) trinar.

war cry *n* grito de guerra.

ward [wɔːd] *n* (*in hospital*) sala; (*POL*) distrito electoral; (*LAW: child*) pupilo/a.

▶**ward off** *vt* desviar, parar; (*attack*) rechazar.

warden ['wɔːdn] *n* (*BRIT: of institution*) director(a) *m/f*; (*of park, game reserve*) guardián/ana *m/f*; (*BRIT: also*: **traffic ~**) guardia *m/f*.

warder ['wɔːdə*] *n* (*BRIT*) guardián/ana *m/f*, carcelero/a.

wardrobe ['wɔːdrəub] *n* armario, guardarropa, ropero, clóset/closet *m* (*LAM*).

warehouse ['wɛəhaus] *n* almacén *m*, depósito.

wares [wɛəz] *npl* mercancías *fpl*.

warfare ['wɔːfɛə*] *n* guerra.

war game *n* juego de estrategia militar.

warhead ['wɔːhɛd] *n* cabeza armada; **nuclear ~s** cabezas *fpl* nucleares.

warily ['wɛərɪlɪ] *adv* con cautela, cautelosamente.

warlike ['wɔːlaɪk] *adj* guerrero.

warm [wɔːm] *adj* caliente; (*person, greeting, heart*) afectuoso, cariñoso; (*supporter*) entusiasta; (*thanks, congratulations, apologies*) efusivo; (*clothes etc*) que abriga; (*welcome, day*) caluroso; **it's ~** hace calor; **I'm ~** tengo calor; **to keep sth ~** mantener algo caliente.

▶**warm up** *vi* (*room*) calentarse; (*person*) entrar en calor; (*athlete*) hacer ejercicios

de calentamiento; (*discussion*) acalorarse
♦ *vt* calentar.
warm-blooded ['wɔːm'blʌdɪd] *adj* de
sangre caliente.
war memorial *n* monumento a los caídos.
warm-hearted [wɔːm'hɑːtɪd] *adj* afectuoso.
warmly ['wɔːmlɪ] *adv* afectuosamente.
warmonger ['wɔːmʌŋgə*] *n* belicista *m/f.*
warmongering ['wɔːmʌŋgrɪŋ] *n* belicismo.
warmth [wɔːmθ] *n* calor *m.*
warm-up ['wɔːmʌp] *n* (*SPORT*) ejercicios
mpl de calentamiento.
warn [wɔːn] *vt* avisar, advertir; **to ~ sb not
to do sth** *or* **against doing sth** aconsejar a
algn que no haga algo.
warning ['wɔːnɪŋ] *n* aviso, advertencia;
gale ~ (*METEOROLOGY*) aviso de vendaval;
without (any) ~ sin aviso *or* avisar.
warning light *n* luz *f* de advertencia.
warning triangle *n* (*AUT*) triángulo
señalizador.
warp [wɔːp] *vi* (*wood*) combarse.
warpath ['wɔːpɑːθ] *n*: **to be on the ~** (*fig*)
estar en pie de guerra.
warped [wɔːpt] *adj* (*wood*) alabeado; (*fig:
character, sense of humour etc*) pervertido.
warrant ['wɔrnt] *n* (*LAW: to arrest*) orden *f*
de detención; (: *to search*) mandamiento
de registro ♦ *vt* (*justify, merit*) merecer.
warrant officer *n* (*MIL*) brigada *m*; (*NAUT*)
contramaestre *m.*
warranty ['wɔrəntɪ] *n* garantía; **under ~**
(*COMM*) bajo garantía.
warren ['wɔrən] *n* (*of rabbits*) madriguera;
(*fig*) laberinto.
warring ['wɔːrɪŋ] *adj* (*interests etc*) opuesto;
(*nations*) en guerra.
warrior ['wɔrɪə*] *n* guerrero/a.
Warsaw ['wɔːsɔː] *n* Varsovia.
warship ['wɔːʃɪp] *n* buque *m or* barco de
guerra.
wart [wɔːt] *n* verruga.
wartime ['wɔːtaɪm] *n*: **in ~** en tiempos de
guerra, en la guerra.
wary ['wɛərɪ] *adj* cauteloso; **to be ~ about**
or **of doing sth** tener cuidado con hacer
algo.
was [wɔz] *pt of* be.
wash [wɔʃ] *vt* lavar; (*sweep, carry: sea etc*)
llevar ♦ *vi* lavarse ♦ *n* (*clothes etc*) lavado;
(*bath*) baño; (*of ship*) estela; **he was ~ed
overboard** fue arrastrado del barco por
las olas; **to have a ~** lavarse.
▶**wash away** *vt* (*stain*) quitar lavando;
(*subj: river etc*) llevarse; (*fig*) limpiar.
▶**wash down** *vt* lavar.
▶**wash off** *vt* quitar lavando.
▶**wash up** *vi* (*BRIT*) fregar los platos; (*US*:

have a wash) lavarse.
Wash. *abbr* (*US*) = Washington.
washable ['wɔʃəbl] *adj* lavable.
washbasin ['wɔʃbeɪsn], (*US*) **washbowl**
['wɔʃbəul] *n* lavabo.
washcloth ['wɔʃklɔθ] *n* (*US*) manopla.
washer ['wɔʃə*] *n* (*TECH*) arandela.
washing ['wɔʃɪŋ] *n* (*dirty*) ropa sucia;
(*clean*) colada.
washing line *n* cuerda de (colgar) la ropa.
washing machine *n* lavadora.
washing powder *n* (*BRIT*) detergente *m*
(en polvo).
Washington ['wɔʃɪŋtən] *n* (*city, state*)
Washington *m.*
washing-up [wɔʃɪŋ'ʌp] *n* fregado; (*dishes*)
platos *mpl* (para fregar); **to do the ~**
fregar los platos.
washing-up liquid *n* lavavajillas *m inv.*
wash leather *n* gamuza.
wash-out ['wɔʃaut] *n* (*col*) fracaso.
washroom ['wɔʃrum] *n* servicios *mpl.*
wasn't ['wɔznt] = was not.
Wasp, WASP [wɔsp] *n abbr* (*US col*: = *White
Anglo-Saxon Protestant*) sobrenombre, *en
general peyorativo, que se da a los
americanos de origen anglosajón,
acomodados y de tendencia
conservadora.*
wasp [wɔsp] *n* avispa.
waspish ['wɔspɪʃ] *adj* (*character*) irascible;
(*comment*) mordaz, punzante.
wastage ['weɪstɪdʒ] *n* desgaste *m*; (*loss*)
pérdida; **natural ~** desgaste natural.
waste [weɪst] *n* derroche *m*, despilfarro;
(*misuse*) desgaste *m*; (*of time*) pérdida;
(*food*) sobras *fpl*; (*rubbish*) basura,
desperdicios *mpl* ♦ *adj* (*material*) de
desecho; (*left over*) sobrante; (*energy,
heat*) desperdiciado; (*land, ground: in city*)
sin construir; (: *in country*) baldío ♦ *vt*
(*squander*) malgastar, derrochar; (*time*)
perder; (*opportunity*) desperdiciar; **~s** *npl*
(*area of land*) tierras *fpl* baldías; **to lay ~**
devastar, arrasar; **it's a ~ of money** es
tirar el dinero; **to go to ~**
desperdiciarse.
▶**waste away** *vi* consumirse.
wastebasket ['weɪstbɑːskɪt] *n* (*esp US*)
= **wastepaper basket**.
waste disposal (unit) *n* (*BRIT*) triturador
m de basura.
wasteful ['weɪstful] *adj* derrochador(a);
(*process*) antieconómico.
wastefully ['weɪstfulɪ] *adv*: **to spend money
~** derrochar dinero.
waste ground *n* (*BRIT*) terreno baldío.
wasteland ['weɪstlənd] *n* (*urban*)

descampados *mpl.*
wastepaper basket ['weɪstpeɪpə-] *n* papelera.
waste pipe *n* tubo de desagüe.
waste products *npl* (*INDUSTRY*) residuos *mpl.*
waster ['weɪstə*] *n* (*col*) gandul *m/f.*
watch [wɔtʃ] *n* reloj *m*; (*vigil*) vigilia; (*vigilance*) vigilancia; (*MIL: guard*) centinela *m*; (*NAUT: spell of duty*) guardia ♦ *vt* (*look at*) mirar, observar; (: *match, programme*) ver; (*spy on, guard*) vigilar; (*be careful of*) cuidar, tener cuidado de ♦ *vi* ver, mirar; (*keep guard*) montar guardia; **to keep a close ~ on sth/sb** vigilar algo/a algn de cerca; **~ how you drive/what you're doing** ten cuidado al conducir/con lo que haces.
▶**watch out** *vi* cuidarse, tener cuidado.
watch band *n* (*US*) pulsera (de reloj).
watchdog ['wɔtʃdɔg] *n* perro guardián; (*fig*) organismo de control.
watchful ['wɔtʃful] *adj* vigilante, sobre aviso.
watchfully ['wɔtʃfulɪ] *adv:* **to stand ~** permanecer vigilante.
watchmaker ['wɔtʃmeɪkə*] *n* relojero/a.
watchman *n* guardián *m*; (*also:* **night ~**) sereno, vigilante *m*; (*in factory*) vigilante *m* nocturno.
watch stem *n* (*US*) cuerda.
watch strap *n* pulsera (de reloj).
watchword ['wɔtʃwəːd] *n* consigna, contraseña.
water ['wɔːtə*] *n* agua ♦ *vt* (*plant*) regar ♦ *vi* (*eyes*) llorar; **I'd like a drink of ~** quisiera un vaso de agua; **in British ~s** en aguas británicas; **to pass ~** orinar; **his mouth ~ed** se le hizo la boca agua.
▶**water down** *vt* (*milk etc*) aguar.
water closet *n* wáter *m.*
watercolour, (*US*) **watercolor** ['wɔːtəkʌlə*] *n* acuarcla.
water-cooled ['wɔːtəkuːld] *adj* refrigerado (por agua).
watercress ['wɔːtəkrɛs] *n* berro.
waterfall ['wɔːtəfɔːl] *n* cascada, salto de agua.
waterfront ['wɔːtəfrʌnt] *n* (*seafront*) parte *f* que da al mar; (*at docks*) muelles *mpl.*
water heater *n* calentador *m* de agua.
water hole *n* abrevadero.
watering can ['wɔːtərɪŋ-] *n* regadera.
water level *n* nivel *m* del agua.
water lily *n* nenúfar *m.*
waterline ['wɔːtəlaɪn] *n* (*NAUT*) línea de flotación.
waterlogged ['wɔːtəlɔgd] *adj* (*boat*)

anegado; (*ground*) inundado.
water main *n* cañería del agua.
watermark ['wɔːtəmɑːk] *n* (*on paper*) filigrana.
watermelon ['wɔːtəmɛlən] *n* sandía.
water polo *n* waterpolo, polo acuático.
waterproof ['wɔːtəpruːf] *adj* impermeable.
water-repellent ['wɔːtərɪ'pɛlənt] *adj* hidrófugo.
watershed ['wɔːtəʃɛd] *n* (*GEO*) cuenca; (*fig*) momento crítico.
water-skiing ['wɔːtəskiːɪŋ] *n* esquí *m* acuático.
water softener *n* ablandador *m* de agua.
water tank *n* depósito de agua.
watertight ['wɔːtətaɪt] *adj* hermético.
water vapour, (*US*) **water vapor** *n* vapor *m* de agua.
waterway ['wɔːtəweɪ] *n* vía fluvial *or* navegable.
waterworks ['wɔːtəwəːks] *npl* central *fsg* depuradora.
watery ['wɔːtərɪ] *adj* (*colour*) desvaído; (*coffee*) aguado; (*eyes*) lloroso.
watt [wɔt] *n* vatio.
wattage ['wɔtɪdʒ] *n* potencia en vatios.
wattle ['wɔtl] *n* zarzo.
wave [weɪv] *n* ola; (*of hand*) señal *f* con la mano; (*RADIO, in hair*) onda; (*fig: of enthusiasm, strikes*) oleada ♦ *vi* agitar la mano; (*flag*) ondear ♦ *vt* (*handkerchief, gun*) agitar; **short/medium/long ~** (*RADIO*) onda corta/media/larga; **the new ~** (*CINE, MUS*) la nueva ola; **to ~ goodbye to sb** decir adiós a algn con la mano; **he ~d us over to his table** nos hizo señas (con la mano) para que nos acercásemos a su mesa.
▶**wave aside, wave away** *vt* (*person*): **to ~ sb aside** apartar a algn con la mano; (*fig: suggestion, objection*) rechazar; (*doubts*) desechar.
waveband ['weɪvbænd] *n* banda de ondas.
wavelength ['weɪvlɛŋθ] *n* longitud *f* de onda.
waver ['weɪvə*] *vi* oscilar; (*confidence*) disminuir; (*faith*) flaquear.
wavy ['weɪvɪ] *adj* ondulado.
wax [wæks] *n* cera ♦ *vt* encerar ♦ *vi* (*moon*) crecer.
waxen ['wæksn] *adj* (*fig: pale*) blanco como la cera.
waxworks ['wækswəːks] *npl* museo *sg* de cera.
way [weɪ] *n* camino; (*distance*) trayecto, recorrido; (*direction*) dirección *f*, sentido; (*manner*) modo, manera; (*habit*) costumbre *f*; **which ~?** — **this ~** ¿por

dónde? *or* ¿en qué dirección? — por aquí; **on the** ~ (*en route*) en (el) camino; (*expected*) en camino; **to be on one's** ~ estar en camino; **you pass it on your** ~ **home** está de camino a tu casa; **to be in the** ~ bloquear el camino; (*fig*) estorbar; **to keep out of sb's** ~ esquivar a algn; **to make** ~ (**for sb/sth**) dejar paso (a algn/algo); (*fig*) abrir camino (a algn/algo); **to go out of one's** ~ **to do sth** desvivirse por hacer algo; **to lose one's** ~ perderse, extraviarse; **to be the wrong** ~ **round** estar del *or* al revés; **in a** ~ en cierto modo *or* sentido; **by the** ~ a propósito; **by** ~ **of** (*via*) pasando por; (*as a sort of*) como, a modo de; "~ **in**" (*BRIT*) "entrada"; "~ **out**" (*BRIT*) "salida"; **the** ~ **back** el camino de vuelta; **the village is rather out of the** ~ el pueblo está un poco apartado *or* retirado; **it's a long** ~ **away** está muy lejos; **to get one's own** ~ salirse con la suya; "**give** ~"! (*BRIT AUT*) "ceda el paso"; **no** ~! (*col*) ¡ni pensarlo!; **put it the right** ~ **up** ponlo boca arriba; **he's in a bad** ~ está grave; **to be under** ~ (*work, project*) estar en marcha.

waybill ['weɪbɪl] *n* (*COMM*) hoja de ruta, carta de porte.

waylay [weɪ'leɪ] *vt* (*irreg: like* lay) atacar.

wayside ['weɪsaɪd] *n* borde *m* del camino; **to fall by the** ~ (*fig*) fracasar.

way station *n* (*US RAIL*) apeadero; (*fig*) paso intermedio.

wayward ['weɪwəd] *adj* díscolo, caprichoso.

WC ['dʌblju'si:] *n abbr* (*BRIT*: = *water closet*) wáter *m*.

WCC *n abbr* = *World Council of Churches*.

we [wi:] *pl pron* nosotros/as; ~ **understand** (nosotros) entendemos; **here** ~ **are** aquí estamos.

weak [wi:k] *adj* débil, flojo; (*tea, coffee*) flojo, aguado; **to grow** ~(**er**) debilitarse.

weaken ['wi:kən] *vi* debilitarse; (*give way*) ceder ♦ *vt* debilitar.

weak-kneed [wi:k'ni:d] *adj* (*fig*) sin voluntad *or* carácter.

weakling ['wi:klɪŋ] *n* debilucho/a.

weakly ['wi:klɪ] *adj* enfermizo, débil ♦ *adv* débilmente.

weakness ['wi:knɪs] *n* debilidad *f*; (*fault*) punto débil.

wealth [wɛlθ] *n* (*money, resources*) riqueza; (*of details*) abundancia.

wealth tax *n* impuesto sobre el patrimonio.

wealthy ['wɛlθɪ] *adj* rico.

wean [wi:n] *vt* destetar.

weapon ['wɛpən] *n* arma.

wear [wɛə*] *n* (*use*) uso; (*deterioration*) desgaste *m*; (*clothing*): **sports/baby**~ ropa de deportes/de niños ♦ *vb* (*pt* **wore**, *pp* **worn** [wɔ:*, wɔ:n]) *vt* (*clothes, beard*) llevar; (*shoes*) calzar; (*look, smile*) tener; (*damage*) gastar, usar ♦ *vi* (*last*) durar; (*rub through etc*) desgastarse; **evening** ~ (*man's*) traje *m* de etiqueta; (*woman's*) traje *m* de noche; **to** ~ **a hole in sth** hacer un agujero en algo.

▶**wear away** *vt* gastar ♦ *vi* desgastarse.

▶**wear down** *vt* gastar; (*strength*) agotar.

▶**wear off** *vi* (*pain, excitement etc*) pasar.

▶**wear out** *vt* desgastar; (*person, strength*) agotar.

wearable ['wɛərəbl] *adj* que se puede llevar, ponible.

wear and tear *n* desgaste *m*.

wearer ['wɛərə*] *n*: **the** ~ **of this jacket** el/la que lleva puesta esta chaqueta.

wearily ['wɪərɪlɪ] *adv* con cansancio.

weariness ['wɪərɪnɪs] *n* cansancio; abatimiento.

wearisome ['wɪərɪsəm] *adj* (*tiring*) cansado, pesado; (*boring*) aburrido.

weary ['wɪərɪ] *adj* (*tired*) cansado; (*dispirited*) abatido ♦ *vt* cansar ♦ *vi*: **to** ~ **of** cansarse de, aburrirse de.

weasel ['wi:zl] *n* (*ZOOL*) comadreja.

weather ['wɛðə*] *n* tiempo ♦ *vt* (*storm, crisis*) hacer frente a; **under the** ~ (*fig: ill*) mal, pachucho; **what's the** ~ **like?** ¿qué tiempo hace?, ¿cómo hace?

weather-beaten ['wɛðəbi:tn] *adj* curtido.

weathercock ['wɛðəkɔk] *n* veleta.

weather forecast *n* boletín *m* meteorológico.

weatherman ['wɛðəmæn] *n* hombre *m* del tiempo.

weatherproof ['wɛðəpru:f] *adj* (*garment*) impermeable.

weather report *n* parte *m* meteorológico.

weather vane *n* = **weathercock**.

weave, *pt* **wove,** *pp* **woven** [wi:v, wəuv, 'wəuvn] *vt* (*cloth*) tejer; (*fig*) entretejer ♦ *vi* (*fig:pt,pp* ~**d**: *move in and out*) zigzaguear.

weaver ['wi:və*] *n* tejedor(a) *m/f*.

weaving ['wi:vɪŋ] *n* tejeduría.

web [wɛb] *n* (*of spider*) telaraña; (*on foot*) membrana; (*network*) red *f*; **the (World Wide) W**~ el *or* la Web.

webbed [wɛbd] *adj* (*foot*) palmeado.

webbing ['wɛbɪŋ] *n* (*on chair*) cinchas *fpl*.

website ['wɛbsaɪt] *n* sitio web.

wed [wɛd] *vt* (*pt, pp* **wedded**) casar ♦ *n*: **the newly-**~**s** los recién casados.

Wed. *abbr* (= *Wednesday*) miérc.

we'd [wi:d] = **we had; we would.**
wedded ['wɛdɪd] *pt, pp of* **wed.**
wedding ['wɛdɪŋ] *n* boda, casamiento.
wedding anniversary *adj* aniversario de boda; **silver/golden** ~ bodas *fpl* de plata/de oro.
wedding day *n* día *m* de la boda.
wedding dress *n* traje *m* de novia.
wedding present *n* regalo de boda.
wedding ring *n* alianza.
wedge [wɛdʒ] *n* (*of wood etc*) cuña; (*of cake*) trozo ♦ *vt* acuñar; (*push*) apretar.
wedge-heeled ['wɛdʒ'hi:ld] *adj* con suela de cuña.
wedlock ['wɛdlɔk] *n* matrimonio.
Wednesday ['wɛdnzdɪ] *n* miércoles *m inv.*
wee [wi:] *adj* (*Scottish*) pequeñito.
weed [wi:d] *n* mala hierba, maleza ♦ *vt* escardar, deshierbar.
▶**weed out** *vt* eliminar.
weedkiller ['wi:dkɪlə*] *n* herbicida *m.*
weedy ['wi:dɪ] *adj* (*person*) debilucho.
week [wi:k] *n* semana; **a** ~ **today** de hoy en ocho días; **Tuesday** ~, **a** ~ **on Tuesday** del martes en una semana; **once/twice a** ~ una vez/dos veces a la semana; **this** ~ esta semana; **in 2** ~**s' time** dentro de 2 semanas; **every other** ~ cada 2 semanas.
weekday ['wi:kdeɪ] *n* día *m* laborable; **on** ~**s** entre semana, en días laborables.
weekend [wi:k'ɛnd] *n* fin *m* de semana.
weekend case *n* neceser *m.*
weekly ['wi:klɪ] *adv* semanalmente, cada semana ♦ *adj* semanal ♦ *n* semanario; ~ **newspaper** semanario.
weep, *pt, pp* **wept** [wi:p, wɛpt] *vi, vt* llorar; (*MED: wound etc*) supurar.
weeping willow ['wi:pɪŋ-] *n* sauce *m* llorón.
weepy ['wi:pɪ] *n* (*col: film*) película lacrimógena; (: *story*) historia lacrimógena.
weft [wɛft] *n* (*TEXTILES*) trama.
weigh [weɪ] *vt, vi* pesar; **to** ~ **anchor** levar anclas; **to** ~ **the pros and cons** pesar los pros y los contras.
▶**weigh down** *vt* sobrecargar; (*fig: with worry*) agobiar.
▶**weigh out** *vt* (*goods*) pesar.
▶**weigh up** *vt* pesar.
weighbridge ['weɪbrɪdʒ] *n* báscula para camiones.
weighing machine ['weɪɪŋ-] *n* báscula, peso.
weight [weɪt] *n* peso; (*on scale*) pesa; **to lose/put on** ~ adelgazar/engordar; ~**s and measures** pesas y medidas.
weighting ['weɪtɪŋ] *n* (*allowance*): **(London)**

~ *dietas fpl* (*por residir en Londres*).
weightlessness ['weɪtlɪsnɪs] *n* ingravidez *f.*
weight lifter *n* levantador(a) *m/f* de pesas.
weight limit *n* límite *m* de peso.
weight training *n* musculación *f* (con pesas).
weighty ['weɪtɪ] *adj* pesado.
weir [wɪə*] *n* presa.
weird [wɪəd] *adj* raro, extraño.
weirdo ['wɪədəu] *n* (*col*) tío/a raro/a.
welcome ['wɛlkəm] *adj* bienvenido ♦ *n* bienvenida ♦ *vt* dar la bienvenida a; (*be glad of*) alegrarse de; **to make sb** ~ recibir *or* acoger bien a algn; **thank you** — **you're** ~ gracias — de nada; **you're** ~ **to try** puede intentar cuando quiera; **we** ~ **this step** celebramos esta medida.
weld [wɛld] *n* soldadura ♦ *vt* soldar.
welding ['wɛldɪŋ] *n* soldadura.
welfare ['wɛlfɛə*] *n* bienestar *m*; (*social aid*) asistencia social; **W**~ (*US*) subsidio de paro; **to look after sb's** ~ cuidar del bienestar de algn.
welfare state *n* estado del bienestar.
welfare work *n* asistencia social.
well [wɛl] *n* pozo ♦ *adv* bien ♦ *adj*: **to be** ~ estar bien (de salud) ♦ *excl* ¡vaya!, ¡bueno!; **as** ~ (*in addition*) además, también; **as** ~ **as** además de; **you might as** ~ **tell me** más vale que me lo digas; **it would be as** ~ **to ask** más valdría preguntar; ~ **done!** ¡bien hecho!; **get** ~ **soon!** ¡que te mejores pronto!; **to do** ~ (*business*) ir bien; **I did** ~ **in my exams** me han salido bien los exámenes; **they are doing** ~ **now** les va bien ahora; **to think** ~ **of sb** pensar bien de algn; **I don't feel** ~ no me encuentro *or* siento bien; ~, **as I was saying** ... bueno, como decía ....
▶**well up** *vi* brotar.
we'll [wi:l] = **we will, we shall.**
well-behaved ['wɛlbɪ'heɪvd] *adj*: **to be** ~ portarse bien.
well-being ['wɛl'bi:ɪŋ] *n* bienestar *m.*
well-bred ['wɛl'brɛd] *adj* bien educado.
well-built ['wɛl'bɪlt] *adj* (*person*) fornido.
well-chosen ['wɛl'tʃəuzn] *adj* (*remarks, words*) acertado.
well-deserved ['wɛldɪ'zɜ:vd] *adj* merecido.
well-developed ['wɛldɪ'vɛləpt] *adj* (*arm, muscle etc*) bien desarrollado; (*sense*) agudo, fino.
well-disposed ['wɛldɪs'pəuzd] *adj*: ~ **to(wards)** bien dispuesto a.
well-dressed ['wɛl'drɛst] *adj* bien vestido.
well-earned ['wɛl'ɜ:nd] *adj* (*rest*) merecido.
well-groomed ['wɛl'gru:md] *adj* de apariencia cuidada.

well-heeled ['wɛl'hiːld] *adj* (*col: wealthy*) rico.
well-informed ['wɛlɪn'fɔːmd] *adj* (*having knowledge of sth*) enterado, al corriente.
Wellington ['wɛlɪŋtən] *n* Wellington *m*.
wellingtons ['wɛlɪŋtənz] *npl* (*also:* **Wellington boots**) botas *fpl* de goma.
well-kept ['wɛl'kɛpt] *adj* (*secret*) bien guardado; (*hair, house*) bien cuidado.
well-known ['wɛl'nəun] *adj* (*person*) conocido.
well-mannered ['wɛl'mænəd] *adj* educado.
well-meaning ['wɛl'miːnɪŋ] *adj* bienintencionado.
well-nigh ['wɛl'naɪ] *adv:* ~ **impossible** casi imposible.
well-off ['wɛl'ɔf] *adj* acomodado.
well-read ['wɛl'rɛd] *adj* culto.
well-spoken ['wɛl'spəukən] *adj* bienhablado.
well-stocked ['wɛl'stɔkt] *adj* (*shop, larder*) bien surtido.
well-timed ['wɛl'taɪmd] *adj* oportuno.
well-to-do ['wɛltə'duː] *adj* acomodado.
well-wisher ['wɛlwɪʃə*] *n* admirador(a) *m/f*.
well-woman clinic ['wɛlwumən-] *n centro de prevención médica para mujeres*.
Welsh [wɛlʃ] *adj* galés/esa ♦ *n* (*LING*) galés *m*; **the** ~ *npl* los galeses; **the** ~ **Assembly** el Parlamento galés.
Welshman ['wɛlʃmən] *n* galés *m*.
Welsh rarebit [-'rɛəbɪt] *n* pan *m* con queso tostado.
Welshwoman ['wɛlʃwumən] *n* galesa.
welter ['wɛltə*] *n* mescolanza, revoltijo.
went [wɛnt] *pt of* **go**.
wept [wɛpt] *pt, pp of* **weep**.
were [wəː*] *pt of* **be**.
we're [wɪə*] = **we are**.
weren't [wəːnt] = **were not**.
werewolf, *pl* **-wolves** ['wɪəwulf, -wulvz] *n* hombre *m* lobo.
west [wɛst] *n* oeste *m* ♦ *adj* occidental, del oeste ♦ *adv* al *or* hacia el oeste; **the W**~ Occidente *m*.
westbound ['wɛstbaund] *adj* (*traffic, carriageway*) con rumbo al oeste.
West Country *n:* **the** ~ el suroeste de Inglaterra.
westerly ['wɛstəlɪ] *adj* (*wind*) del oeste.
western ['wɛstən] *adj* occidental ♦ *n* (*CINE*) película del oeste.
westerner ['wɛstənə*] *n* (*POL*) occidental *m/f*.
westernized ['wɛstənaɪzd] *adj* occidentalizado.
West German (*formerly*) *adj* de Alemania Occidental ♦ *n* alemán/ana *m/f* (de Alemania Occidental).
West Germany *n* (*formerly*) Alemania Occidental.
West Indian *adj, n* antillano/a *m/f*.
West Indies [-'ɪndɪz] *npl:* **the** ~ las Antillas.
Westminster ['wɛstmɪnstə*] *n el parlamento británico*, Westminster *m*.
westward(s) ['wɛstwəd(z)] *adv* hacia el oeste.
wet [wɛt] *adj* (*damp*) húmedo; (~ *through*) mojado; (*rainy*) lluvioso ♦ *vt:* **to** ~ **one's pants** *or* **o.s.** mearse; **to get** ~ mojarse; **"~ paint"** 'recién pintado'.
wet blanket *n:* **to be a** ~ (*fig*) ser un/una aguafiestas.
wetness ['wɛtnɪs] *n* humedad *f*.
wet rot *n* putrefacción *f* por humedad.
wet suit *n* traje *m* de buzo.
we've [wiːv] = **we have**.
whack [wæk] *vt* dar un buen golpe a.
whale [weɪl] *n* (*ZOOL*) ballena.
whaler ['weɪlə*] *n* (*ship*) ballenero.
whaling ['weɪlɪŋ] *n* pesca de ballenas.
wharf, *pl* **wharves** [wɔːf, wɔːvz] *n* muelle *m*.

━━━━━━━━━━━━━━━━━━ *KEYWORD*

what [wɔt] *adj* **1** (*in direct/indirect questions*) qué; ~ **size is he?** ¿qué talla usa?; ~ **colour/shape is it?** ¿de qué color/forma es?; ~ **books do you need?** ¿qué libros necesitas?
2 (*in exclamations*): ~ **a mess!** ¡qué desastre!; ~ **a fool I am!** ¡qué tonto soy!
♦ *pron* **1** (*interrogative*) qué; ~ **are you doing?** ¿qué haces *or* estás haciendo?; ~ **is happening?** ¿qué pasa *or* está pasando?; ~ **is it called?** ¿cómo se llama?; ~ **about me?** ¿y yo qué?; ~ **about doing ...?** ¿qué tal si hacemos ...?; ~ **is his address?** ¿cuáles son sus señas?; ~ **will it cost?** ¿cuánto costará?
2 (*relative*) lo que; **I saw** ~ **you did/was on the table** vi lo que hiciste/había en la mesa; ~ **I want is a cup of tea** lo que quiero es una taza de té; **I don't know** ~ **to do** no sé qué hacer; **tell me** ~ **you're thinking about** dime en qué estás pensando
3 (*reported questions*): **she asked me** ~ **I wanted** me preguntó qué quería
♦ *excl* (*disbelieving*) ¡cómo!; ~**, no coffee!** ¡que no hay café!

━━━━━━━━━━━━━━━━━━

whatever [wɔt'ɛvə*] *adj:* ~ **book you choose** cualquier libro que elijas ♦ *pron:* **do** ~ **is necessary** haga lo que sea necesario; **no reason** ~ ninguna razón en absoluto; **nothing** ~ nada en absoluto; ~ **it costs** cueste lo que cueste.

wheat [wiːt] *n* trigo.

wheatgerm ['wiːtdʒəːm] *n* germen *m* de trigo.

wheatmeal ['wiːtmiːl] *n* harina de trigo.

wheedle ['wiːdl] *vt*: **to** ~ **sb into doing sth** engatusar a algn para que haga algo; **to** ~ **sth out of sb** sonsacar algo a algn.

wheel [wiːl] *n* rueda; (*AUT*: *also*: **steering** ~) volante *m*; (*NAUT*) timón *m* ♦ *vt* (*pram etc*) empujar ♦ *vi* (*also*: ~ **round**) dar la vuelta, girar; **four-**~ **drive** tracción *f* en las cuatro ruedas; **front-/rear-**~ **drive** tracción *f* delantera/trasera.

wheelbarrow ['wiːlbærəu] *n* carretilla.

wheelbase ['wiːlbeɪs] *n* batalla.

wheelchair ['wiːltʃɛə*] *n* silla de ruedas.

wheel clamp *n* (*AUT*) cepo.

wheeler-dealer ['wiːlə'diːlə*] *n* chanchullero/a.

wheelie-bin ['wiːlɪbɪn] *n* (*BRIT*) contenedor *m* de basura.

wheeling ['wiːlɪŋ] *n*: ~ **and dealing** (*col*) chanchullos *mpl*.

wheeze [wiːz] *vi* resollar.

wheezy ['wiːzɪ] *adj* silbante.

=========================== *KEYWORD*

when [wɛn] *adv* cuando; ~ **did it happen?** ¿cuándo ocurrió?; **I know** ~ **it happened** sé cuándo ocurrió

♦ *conj* **1** (*at, during, after the time that*) cuando; **be careful** ~ **you cross the road** ten cuidado al cruzar la calle; **that was** ~ **I needed you** entonces era cuando te necesitaba; **I'll buy you a car** ~ **you're 18** te compraré un coche cuando cumplas 18 años

2 (*on, at which*): **on the day** ~ **I met him** el día en qué le conocí

3 (*whereas*) cuando; **you said I was wrong** ~ **in fact I was right** dijiste que no tenía razón, cuando en realidad sí la tenía.

━━━━━━━━━━━━━━━━━━━━━━━━━━━

whenever [wɛn'ɛvə*] *conj* cuando; (*every time*) cada vez que; **I go** ~ **I can** voy siempre *or* todas las veces que puedo.

where [wɛə*] *adv* dónde ♦ *conj* donde; **this is** ~ aquí es donde; ~ **possible** donde sea posible; ~ **are you from?** ¿de dónde es usted?

whereabouts ['wɛərəbauts] *adv* dónde ♦ *n*: **nobody knows his** ~ nadie conoce su paradero.

whereas [wɛər'æz] *conj* mientras.

whereby [wɛə'baɪ] *adv* mediante el/la cual *etc*.

whereupon [wɛərə'pɔn] *conj* con lo cual, después de lo cual.

wherever [wɛər'ɛvə*] *adv* dondequiera que; (*interrogative*) dónde; **sit** ~ **you like** siéntese donde quiera.

wherewithal ['wɛəwɪðɔːl] *n* recursos *mpl*; **the** ~ **(to do sth)** los medios económicos (para hacer algo).

whet [wɛt] *vt* estimular; (*appetite*) abrir.

whether ['wɛðə*] *conj* si; **I don't know** ~ **to accept or not** no sé si aceptar o no; ~ **you go or not** vayas o no vayas.

whey [weɪ] *n* suero.

=========================== *KEYWORD*

which [wɪtʃ] *adj* **1** (*interrogative: direct, indirect*) qué; ~ **picture(s) do you want?** ¿qué cuadro(s) quieres?; ~ **one?** ¿cuál?; ~ **one of you?** ¿cuál de vosotros?; **tell me** ~ **one you want** dime cuál (es el que) quieres

2: **in** ~ **case** en cuyo caso; **we got there at 8 pm, by** ~ **time the cinema was full** llegamos allí a las 8, cuando el cine estaba lleno

♦ *pron* **1** (*interrogative*) cual; **I don't mind** ~ el/la que sea; ~ **do you want?** ¿cuál quieres?

2 (*relative: replacing noun*) que; (: *replacing clause*) lo que; (: *after preposition*) (el/la) que, el/la cual; **the apple** ~ **you ate/**~ **is on the table** la manzana que comiste/que está en la mesa; **the chair on** ~ **you are sitting** la silla en la que estás sentado; **he didn't believe it,** ~ **upset me** no se lo creyó, lo cual *or* lo que me disgustó; **after** ~ **después de lo cual.**

━━━━━━━━━━━━━━━━━━━━━━━━━━━

whichever [wɪtʃ'ɛvə*] *adj*: **take** ~ **book you prefer** coja el libro que prefiera; ~ **book you take** cualquier libro que coja.

whiff [wɪf] *n* bocanada; **to catch a** ~ **of sth** oler algo.

while [waɪl] *n* rato, momento ♦ *conj* durante; (*whereas*) mientras; (*although*) aunque ♦ *vt*: **to** ~ **away the time** pasar el rato; **for a** ~ durante algún tiempo; **in a** ~ dentro de poco; **all the** ~ todo el tiempo; **we'll make it worth your** ~ te compensaremos generosamente.

whilst [waɪlst] *conj* = **while**.

whim [wɪm] *n* capricho.

whimper ['wɪmpə*] *n* (*weeping*) lloriqueo; (*moan*) quejido ♦ *vi* lloriquear; quejarse.

whimsical ['wɪmzɪkl] *adj* (*person*) caprichoso.

whine [waɪn] *n* (*of pain*) gemido; (*of engine*)

zumbido ♦ *vi* gemir; zumbar.

whip [wɪp] *n* látigo; (*BRIT POL*) diputado encargado de la disciplina del partido en el parlamento ♦ *vt* azotar; (*snatch*) arrebatar; (*US CULIN*) batir; *ver recuadro*.

▶**whip up** *vt* (*cream etc*) batir (rápidamente); (*col: meal*) preparar rápidamente; (: *stir up: support, feeling*) avivar.

WHIP

En el Parlamento británico la disciplina de partido (en concreto de voto y de asistencia a la Cámara de los Comunes) está a cargo de un grupo de parlamentarios llamados **whips**, encabezados por el "Chief Whip". Por lo general todos ellos tienen también altos cargos en la Administración del Estado si pertenecen al partido en el poder.

---

whiplash ['wɪplæʃ] *n* (*MED: also:* ~ **injury**) latigazo.

whipped cream [wɪpt-] *n* nata montada.

whipping boy ['wɪpɪŋ-] *n* (*fig*) cabeza de turco.

whip-round ['wɪpraund] *n* (*BRIT*) colecta.

whirl [wə:l] *n* remolino ♦ *vt* hacer girar, dar vueltas a ♦ *vi* (*dancers*) girar, dar vueltas; (*leaves, dust, water etc*) arremolinarse.

whirlpool ['wə:lpu:l] *n* remolino.

whirlwind ['wə:lwɪnd] *n* torbellino.

whirr [wə:*] *vi* zumbar.

whisk [wɪsk] *n* (*BRIT CULIN*) batidor *m* ♦ *vt* (*BRIT CULIN*) batir; **to** ~ **sb away** *or* **off** llevarse volando a algn.

whiskers ['wɪskəz] *npl* (*of animal*) bigotes *mpl*; (*of man*) patillas *fpl*.

whisky, (*US, Ireland*) **whiskey** ['wɪskɪ] *n* whisky *m*.

whisper ['wɪspə*] *n* cuchicheo; (*rumour*) rumor *m*; (*fig*) susurro, murmullo ♦ *vi* cuchichear, hablar bajo; (*fig*) susurrar ♦ *vt* decir en voz muy baja; **to** ~ **sth to sb** decirle algo al oído a algn.

whispering ['wɪspərɪŋ] *n* cuchicheo.

whist [wɪst] *n* (*BRIT*) whist *m*.

whistle ['wɪsl] *n* (*sound*) silbido; (*object*) silbato ♦ *vi* silbar; **to** ~ **a tune** silbar una melodía.

whistle-stop ['wɪslstɔp] *adj*: ~ **tour** (*US POL*) gira electoral rápida; (*fig*) recorrido rápido.

Whit [wɪt] *n* Pentecostés *m*.

white [waɪt] *adj* blanco; (*pale*) pálido ♦ *n* blanco; (*of egg*) clara; **to turn** *or* **go** ~ (*person*) palidecer, ponerse blanco; (*hair*) encanecer; **the** ~**s** (*washing*) la ropa blanca; **tennis** ~**s** ropa *f* de tenis.

whitebait ['waɪtbeɪt] *n* chanquetes *mpl*.

white coffee *n* (*BRIT*) café *m* con leche.

white-collar worker ['waɪtkɔlə-] *n* oficinista *m/f*.

white elephant *n* (*fig*) maula.

white goods *npl* (*appliances*) electrodomésticos *mpl* de línea blanca; (*linen etc*) ropa blanca.

white-hot [waɪt'hɔt] *adj* (*metal*) candente, calentado al (rojo) blanco.

white lie *n* mentirijilla.

whiteness ['waɪtnɪs] *n* blancura.

white noise *n* sonido blanco.

white paper *n* (*POL*) libro blanco.

whitewash ['waɪtwɔʃ] *n* (*paint*) cal *f*, jalbegue *m* ♦ *vt* encalar, blanquear; (*fig*) encubrir.

whiting ['waɪtɪŋ] *n* (*pl inv*) (*fish*) pescadilla.

Whit Monday *n* lunes *m* de Pentecostés.

Whitsun ['wɪtsn] *n* (*BRIT*) Pentecostés *m*.

whittle ['wɪtl] *vt*: **to** ~ **away**, ~ **down** ir reduciendo.

whizz [wɪz] *vi*: **to** ~ **past** *or* **by** pasar a toda velocidad.

whizz kid *n* (*col*) prodigio/a.

WHO *n abbr* (= World Health Organization) OMS *f*.

================ KEYWORD

who [hu:] *pron* **1** (*interrogative*) quién; ~ **is it?**, ~**'s there?** ¿quién es?; ~ **are you looking for?** ¿a quién buscas?; **I told her** ~ **I was** le dije quién era yo

2 (*relative*) que; **the man/woman** ~ **spoke to me** el hombre/la mujer que habló conmigo; **those** ~ **can swim** los que saben *or* sepan nadar.

---

whodun(n)it [hu:'dʌnɪt] *n* (*col*) novela policíaca.

whoever [hu:'ɛvə*] *pron*: ~ **finds it** cualquiera *or* quienquiera que lo encuentre; **ask** ~ **you like** pregunta a quien quieras; ~ **he marries** se case con quien se case.

whole [həul] *adj* (*complete*) todo, entero; (*not broken*) intacto ♦ *n* (*total*) total *m*; (*sum*) conjunto; ~ **villages were destroyed** pueblos enteros fueron destruidos; **the** ~ **of the town** toda la ciudad, la ciudad entera; **on the** ~, **as a** ~ en general.

wholehearted [həul'hɑ:tɪd] *adj* (*support, approval*) total; (*sympathy*) todo.

wholeheartedly [həul'hɑ:tɪdlɪ] *adv* con entusiasmo.

wholemeal ['həulmi:l] *adj* (*BRIT: flour, bread*) integral.

wholesale ['həulseɪl] n venta al por mayor
♦ adj al por mayor; (destruction)
sistemático.
wholesaler ['həulseɪlə*] n mayorista
m/f.
wholesome ['həulsəm] adj sano.
wholewheat ['həulwiːt] adj
= **wholemeal**.
wholly ['həulɪ] adv totalmente,
enteramente.

================================ KEYWORD

whom [huːm] pron 1 (interrogative): ~ did
you see? ¿a quién viste?; to ~ did you
give it? ¿a quién se lo diste?; tell me from
~ you received it dígame de quién lo
recibiste
2 (relative) que; to ~ a quien(es); of ~
de quien(es), del/de la que; the man ~ I
saw el hombre que vi; the man to ~ I
wrote el hombre a quien escribí; the lady
about ~ I was talking la señora de (la)
que hablaba; the lady with ~ I was
talking la señora con quien or (la) que
hablaba.

whooping cough ['huːpɪŋ-] n tos f
ferina.
whoops [wuːps] excl (also: ~-a-daisy!)
¡huy!
whoosh [wuʃ] n: it came out with a ~
(sauce etc) salió todo de repente; (air)
salió con mucho ruido.
whopper ['wɔpə*] n (col: lie) embuste m;
(: large thing): a ~ uno/a enorme.
whopping ['wɔpɪŋ] adj (col) enorme.
whore [hɔː*] n (col: pej) puta.

================================ KEYWORD

whose [huːz] adj 1 (possessive: interrogative)
de quién; ~ book is this?, ~ is this book?
¿de quién es este libro?; ~ pencil have
you taken? ¿de quién es el lápiz que has
cogido?; ~ daughter are you? ¿de quién
eres hija?
2 (possessive: relative) cuyo/a, pl cuyos/as;
the man ~ son they rescued el hombre
cuyo hijo rescataron; the girl ~ sister he
was speaking to la chica con cuya
hermana estaba hablando; those ~
passports I have aquellas personas cuyos
pasaportes tengo; the woman ~ car was
stolen la mujer a quien le robaron el
coche
♦ pron de quién; ~ is this? ¿de quién
es esto?; I know ~ it is sé de quién
es.

================================ KEYWORD

why [waɪ] adv por qué; ~ not? ¿por qué
no?; ~ not do it now? ¿por qué no lo
haces (or hacemos) ahora?
♦ conj: I wonder ~ he said that me
pregunto por qué dijo eso; that's not ~
I'm here no es por eso (por lo) que estoy
aquí; the reason ~ la razón por la que
♦ excl (expressing surprise, shock,
annoyance) ¡hombre!, ¡vaya!; (explaining):
~, it's you! ¡hombre, eres tú!; ~, that's
impossible ¡pero si eso es imposible!

whyever [waɪ'ɛvə*] adv por qué.
WI n abbr (BRIT: = Women's Institute)
asociación de amas de casa ♦ abbr (GEO)
= **West Indies**; (US) = Wisconsin.
wick [wɪk] n mecha.
wicked ['wɪkɪd] adj malvado, cruel.
wickedness ['wɪkɪdnɪs] n maldad f,
crueldad f.
wicker ['wɪkə*] n mimbre m.
wickerwork ['wɪkəwɜːk] n artículos mpl de
mimbre.
wicket ['wɪkɪt] n (CRICKET) palos mpl.
wicket keeper n guardameta m.
wide [waɪd] adj ancho; (area, knowledge)
vasto, grande; (choice) grande ♦ adv: to
open ~ abrir de par en par; to shoot ~
errar el tiro; it is 3 metres ~ tiene 3
metros de ancho.
wide-angle lens ['waɪdæŋgl-] n (objetivo)
gran angular m.
wide-awake [waɪdə'weɪk] adj bien
despierto.
wide-eyed [waɪd'aɪd] adj con los ojos muy
abiertos; (fig) ingenuo.
widely ['waɪdlɪ] adv (differing) muy; it is ~
believed that ... existe la creencia
generalizada de que ...; to be ~ read
(author) ser muy leído; (reader) haber
leído mucho.
widen ['waɪdn] vt ensanchar.
wideness ['waɪdnɪs] n anchura; amplitud f.
wide open adj abierto de par en par.
wide-ranging [waɪd'reɪndʒɪŋ] adj (survey,
report) de gran alcance; (interests) muy
diversos.
widespread ['waɪdspred] adj (belief etc)
extendido, general.
widow ['wɪdəu] n viuda.
widowed ['wɪdəud] adj viudo.
widower ['wɪdəuə*] n viudo.
width [wɪdθ] n anchura; (of cloth) ancho;
it's 7 metres in ~ tiene 7 metros de
ancho.
widthways ['wɪdθweɪz] adv a lo ancho.

wield [wi:ld] *vt* (*sword*) manejar; (*power*) ejercer.

wife, *pl* **wives** [waif, waivz] *n* mujer *f*, esposa.

wig [wig] *n* peluca.

wigging ['wigiŋ] *n* (*BRIT col*) rapapolvo, bronca.

wiggle ['wigl] *vt* menear ♦ *vi* menearse.

wiggly ['wigli] *adj* (*line*) ondulado.

wigwam ['wigwæm] *n* tipi *m*, tienda india.

wild [waild] *adj* (*animal*) salvaje; (*plant*) silvestre; (*rough*) furioso, violento; (*idea*) descabellado; (*col: angry*) furioso ♦ *n*: **the ~ la naturaleza; ~s** *npl* regiones *fpl* salvajes, tierras *fpl* vírgenes; **to be ~ about** (*enthusiastic*) estar *or* andar loco por; **in its ~ state** en estado salvaje.

wild card *n* (*COMPUT*) comodín *m*.

wildcat ['waildkæt] *n* gato montés.

wildcat strike *n* huelga salvaje.

wilderness ['wildənis] *n* desierto; (*jungle*) jungla.

wildfire ['waildfaiə*] *n*: **to spread like ~** correr como un reguero de pólvora.

wild-goose chase [waild'gu:s-] *n* (*fig*) búsqueda inútil.

wildlife ['waildlaif] *n* fauna.

wildly ['waildli] *adv* (*roughly*) violentamente; (*foolishly*) locamente; (*rashly*) descabelladamente.

wiles [wailz] *npl* artimañas *fpl*, ardides *mpl*.

wilful, (*US*) **willful** ['wilful] *adj* (*action*) deliberado; (*obstinate*) testarudo.

======================= *KEYWORD*

will [wil] *aux vb* **1** (*forming future tense*): **I ~ finish it tomorrow** lo terminaré *or* voy a terminar mañana; **I ~ have finished it by tomorrow** lo habré terminado para mañana; **~ you do it? — yes I ~/no I won't** ¿lo harás? — sí/no; **you won't lose it, ~ you?** no lo vayas a perder *or* no lo perderás ¿verdad?

2 (*in conjectures, predictions*): **he ~** *or* **he'll be there by now** ya habrá llegado, ya debe (de) haber llegado; **that ~ be the postman** será el cartero, debe ser el cartero

3 (*in commands, requests, offers*): **~ you be quiet!** ¿quieres callarte?; **~ you help me?** ¿quieres ayudarme?; **~ you have a cup of tea?** ¿te apetece un té?; **I won't put up with it!** ¡no lo soporto!

4 (*habits, persistence*): **the car won't start** el coche no arranca; **accidents ~ happen** son cosas que pasan

♦ *vt* (*pt, pp* **willed**): **to ~ sb to do sth** desear que algn haga algo; **he ~ed himself to go**

on con gran fuerza de voluntad, continuó ♦ *n* **1** (*desire*) voluntad *f*; **against sb's ~** contra la voluntad de algn; **he did it of his own free ~** lo hizo por su propia voluntad **2** (*LAW*) testamento; **to make a** *or* **one's ~** hacer su testamento.

willful ['wilful] *adj* (*US*) = **wilful**.

willing ['wiliŋ] *adj* (*with goodwill*) de buena voluntad; complaciente; **he's ~ to do it** está dispuesto a hacerlo; **to show ~** mostrarse dispuesto.

willingly ['wiliŋli] *adv* con mucho gusto.

willingness ['wiliŋnis] *n* buena voluntad.

will-o'-the-wisp ['wiləðə'wisp] *n* fuego fatuo; (*fig*) quimera.

willow ['wiləu] *n* sauce *m*.

willpower ['wilpauə*] *n* fuerza de voluntad.

willy-nilly [wili'nili] *adv* quiérase o no.

wilt [wilt] *vi* marchitarse.

Wilts *abbr* (*BRIT*) = *Wiltshire*.

wily ['waili] *adj* astuto.

wimp [wimp] *n* (*col*) enclenque *m/f*; (*character*) calzonazos *m inv*.

win [win] *n* (*in sports etc*) victoria, triunfo ♦ *vb* (*pt, pp* **won** [wʌn]) *vt* ganar; (*obtain: contract etc*) conseguir, lograr ♦ *vi* ganar.

►**win over,** (*BRIT*) **win round** *vt* convencer a.

wince [wins] *vi* encogerse.

winch [wintʃ] *n* torno.

Winchester disk ® ['wintʃistə-] *n* (*COMPUT*) disco Winchester ®.

wind *n* [wind] viento; (*MED*) gases *mpl*; (*breath*) aliento ♦ *vb* [waind] (*pt, pp* **wound** [waund]) *vt* enrollar; (*wrap*) envolver; (*clock, toy*) dar cuerda a; [wind] (*take breath away from*) dejar sin aliento a ♦ *vi* (*road, river*) serpentear; **into** *or* **against the ~** contra el viento; **to get ~ of sth** enterarse de algo; **to break ~** ventosear.

►**wind down** *vt* (*car window*) bajar; (*fig: production, business*) disminuir.

►**wind up** *vt* (*clock*) dar cuerda a; (*debate*) concluir, terminar.

windbreak ['windbreik] *n* barrera contra el viento.

windcheater ['windtʃi:tə*], (*US*) **windbreaker** ['windbreikə*] *n* cazadora.

winder ['waində*] *n* (*on watch*) cuerda.

wind erosion *n* erosión *f* del viento.

windfall ['windfɔ:l] *n* golpe *m* de suerte.

winding ['waindiŋ] *adj* (*road*) tortuoso.

wind instrument *n* (*MUS*) instrumento de viento.

windmill ['windmil] *n* molino de viento.

window ['windəu] *n* ventana; (*in car, train*)

ventana; (*in shop etc*) escaparate *m*,
vitrina (*LAM*), vidriera (*LAM*); (*COMPUT*)
ventana.
window box *n* jardinera (de ventana).
window cleaner *n* (*person*)
limpiacristales *m inv*.
window dressing *n* decoración *f* de
escaparates.
window envelope *n* sobre *m* de
ventanilla.
window frame *n* marco de ventana.
window ledge *n* alféizar *m*, repisa.
window pane *n* cristal *m*.
window-shopping [ˈwɪndəuˈʃɔpɪŋ] *n*: **to go**
~ **ir a ver** *or* mirar escaparates.
windowsill [ˈwɪndəusɪl] *n* alféizar *m*,
repisa.
windpipe [ˈwɪndpaɪp] *n* tráquea.
wind power *n* energía eólica.
windscreen [ˈwɪndskriːn], (*US*)
windshield [ˈwɪndʃiːld] *n* parabrisas
m inv.
windscreen washer, (*US*) **windshield
washer** *n* lavaparabrisas *m inv*.
windscreen wiper, (*US*) **windshield
wiper** *n* limpiaparabrisas *m inv*.
windsurfing [ˈwɪndsəːfɪŋ] *n* windsurf *m*.
windswept [ˈwɪndswept] *adj* azotado por el
viento.
wind tunnel *n* túnel *m* aerodinámico.
windy [ˈwɪndɪ] *adj* de mucho viento; **it's** ~
hace viento.
wine [waɪn] *n* vino ♦ *vt*: **to** ~ **and dine sb**
agasajar *or* festejar a algn.
wine bar *n bar especializado en vinos*.
wine cellar *n* bodega.
wine glass *n* copa (de *or* para vino).
wine-growing [ˈwaɪngrəuɪŋ] *adj*
viticultor(a).
wine list *n* lista de vinos.
wine merchant *n* vinatero.
wine tasting *n* degustación *f* de vinos.
wine waiter *n* escanciador *m*.
wing [wɪŋ] *n* ala; (*BRIT AUT*) aleta; ~**s** *npl*
(*THEAT*) bastidores *mpl*.
winger [ˈwɪŋə*] *n* (*SPORT*) extremo.
wing mirror *n* (espejo) retrovisor *m*.
wing nut *n* tuerca (de) mariposa.
wingspan [ˈwɪŋspaen], **wingspread**
[ˈwɪŋspred] *n* envergadura.
wink [wɪŋk] *n* guiño; (*blink*) pestañeo ♦ *vi*
guiñar; (*blink*) pestañear; (*light etc*)
parpadear.
winkle [ˈwɪŋkl] *n* bígaro, bigarro.
winner [ˈwɪnə*] *n* ganador(a) *m/f*.
winning [ˈwɪnɪŋ] *adj* (*team*) ganador(a);
(*goal*) decisivo; (*charming*) encantador(a).
winning post *n* meta.

winnings [ˈwɪnɪŋz] *npl* ganancias *fpl*.
winsome [ˈwɪnsəm] *adj* atractivo.
winter [ˈwɪntə*] *n* invierno ♦ *vi* invernar.
winter sports *npl* deportes *mpl* de
invierno.
wintry [ˈwɪntrɪ] *adj* invernal.
wipe [waɪp] *n*: **to give sth a** ~ pasar un
trapo sobre algo ♦ *vt* limpiar; **to** ~ **one's
nose** limpiarse la nariz.
►**wipe off** *vt* limpiar con un trapo.
►**wipe out** *vt* (*debt*) liquidar; (*memory*)
borrar; (*destroy*) destruir.
►**wipe up** *vt* limpiar.
wire [ˈwaɪə*] *n* alambre *m*; (*ELEC*) cable *m*
(eléctrico); (*TEL*) telegrama *m* ♦ *vt* (*house*)
poner la instalación eléctrica en; (*also:* ~
up) conectar.
wire cutters *npl* cortaalambres *msg inv*.
wireless [ˈwaɪəlɪs] *n* (*BRIT*) radio *f*.
wire mesh, wire netting *n* tela metálica.
wire service *n* (*US*) agencia de noticias.
wire-tapping [ˈwaɪəˈtæpɪŋ] *n* intervención *f*
telefónica.
wiring [ˈwaɪərɪŋ] *n* instalación *f* eléctrica.
wiry [ˈwaɪərɪ] *adj* enjuto y fuerte.
Wis(c). *abbr* (*US*) = *Wisconsin*.
wisdom [ˈwɪzdəm] *n* sabiduría, saber *m*;
(*good sense*) cordura.
wisdom tooth *n* muela del juicio.
wise [waɪz] *adj* sabio; (*sensible*) juicioso;
I'm none the ~**r** sigo sin entender.
►**wise up** *vi* (*col*): **to** ~ **up (to sth)**
enterarse (de algo).
...wise [waɪz] *suff*: **time**~ en cuanto a *or*
respecto al tiempo.
wisecrack [ˈwaɪzkræk] *n* broma.
wish [wɪʃ] *n* (*desire*) deseo ♦ *vt* desear;
(*want*) querer; **best** ~**es** (*on birthday etc*)
felicidades *fpl*; **with best** ~**es** (*in letter*)
saludos *mpl*, recuerdos *mpl*; **to** ~ **sb
goodbye** despedirse de algn; **he** ~**ed me
well** me deseó mucha suerte; **to** ~ **sth on
sb** imponer algo a algn; **to** ~ **to do/sb to
do sth** querer hacer/que algn haga algo;
to ~ **for** desear.
wishbone [ˈwɪʃbəun] *n* espoleta (*de la que
tiran dos personas; quien se quede con el
hueso más largo pide un deseo*).
wishful [ˈwɪʃful] *n*: **it's** ~ **thinking** eso es
hacerse ilusiones.
wishy-washy [ˈwɪʃɪwɔʃɪ] *adj* (*col: colour*)
desvaído; (*: ideas, thinking*) flojo.
wisp [wɪsp] *n* mechón *m*; (*of smoke*) voluta.
wistful [ˈwɪstful] *adj* pensativo; (*nostalgic*)
nostálgico.
wit [wɪt] *n* (*wittiness*) ingenio, gracia;
(*intelligence: also:* ~**s**) inteligencia;
(*person*) chistoso/a; **to have** *or* **keep one's**

~**s about one** no perder la cabeza.
witch [wɪtʃ] n bruja.
witchcraft ['wɪtʃkrɑːft] n brujería.
witch doctor n hechicero.
witch-hunt ['wɪtʃhʌnt] n (POL) caza de
  brujas.

================================ **KEYWORD**

with [wɪð, wɪθ] prep 1 (accompanying, in the
  company of) con (con+ mí, ti, sí = conmigo,
  contigo, consigo); **I was** ~ **him** estaba con
  él; **we stayed** ~ **friends** nos quedamos en
  casa de unos amigos
  2 (descriptive, indicating manner etc) con;
  de; **a room** ~ **a view** una habitación con
  vistas; **the man** ~ **the grey hat/blue eyes**
  el hombre del sombrero gris/de los ojos
  azules; **red** ~ **anger** rojo de ira; **to shake**
  ~ **fear** temblar de miedo; **to fill sth** ~
  water llenar algo de agua
  3: **I'm** ~ **you/I'm not** ~ **you** (understand)
  ya te entiendo/no te entiendo; **I'm not**
  really ~ **it today** no doy pie con bola hoy.

withdraw [wɪθ'drɔː] vb (irreg: like draw) vt
  retirar ♦ vi retirarse; (go back on promise)
  retractarse; **to** ~ **money (from the bank)**
  retirar fondos (del banco); **to** ~ **into o.s.**
  ensimismarse.
withdrawal [wɪθ'drɔːəl] n retirada.
withdrawal symptoms npl síndrome m
  de abstinencia.
withdrawn [wɪθ'drɔːn] adj (person)
  reservado, introvertido ♦ pp of **withdraw**.
wither ['wɪðə*] vi marchitarse.
withered ['wɪðəd] adj marchito, seco.
withhold [wɪθ'həuld] vt (irreg: like hold)
  (money) retener; (decision) aplazar;
  (permission) negar; (information) ocultar.
within [wɪð'ɪn] prep dentro de ♦ adv dentro;
  ~ **reach** al alcance de la mano; ~ **sight of**
  a la vista de; ~ **the week** antes de que
  acabe la semana; **to be** ~ **the law**
  atenerse a la legalidad; ~ **an hour from**
  now dentro de una hora.
without [wɪð'aut] prep sin; **to go** or **do** ~
  sth prescindir de algo; ~ **anybody**
  knowing sin saberlo nadie.
withstand [wɪθ'stænd] vt (irreg: like stand)
  resistir a.
witness ['wɪtnɪs] n (person) testigo m/f;
  (evidence) testimonio ♦ vt (event)
  presenciar, ser testigo de; (document)
  atestiguar la veracidad de; ~ **for the**
  prosecution/defence testigo de cargo/
  descargo; **to** ~ **to (having seen) sth** dar
  testimonio de (haber visto) algo.
witness box, (US) **witness stand** n

tribuna de los testigos.
witticism ['wɪtɪsɪzm] n dicho ingenioso.
wittily ['wɪtɪlɪ] adv ingeniosamente.
witty ['wɪtɪ] adj ingenioso.
wives [waɪvz] npl of **wife**.
wizard ['wɪzəd] n hechicero.
wizened ['wɪznd] adj arrugado, marchito.
wk abbr = **week**.
Wm. abbr = **William**.
WO n abbr = **warrant officer**.
wobble ['wɔbl] vi tambalearse.
wobbly ['wɔblɪ] adj (hand, voice)
  tembloroso; (table, chair) tambaleante,
  cojo.
woe [wəu] n desgracia.
woeful ['wəuful] adj (bad) lamentable; (sad)
  apesadumbrado.
wok [wɔk] n wok m.
woke [wəuk] pt of **wake**.
woken ['wəukn] pp of **wake**.
wolf, pl **wolves** [wulf, wulvz] n lobo.
woman, pl **women** ['wumən, 'wɪmɪn] n
  mujer f; **young** ~ (mujer f) joven f;
  women's page (PRESS) sección f de la
  mujer.
woman doctor n doctora.
woman friend n amiga.
womanize ['wumənaɪz] vi ser un
  mujeriego.
womanly ['wumənlɪ] adj femenino.
womb [wuːm] n (ANAT) matriz f, útero.
women ['wɪmɪn] npl of **woman**.
Women's (Liberation) Movement n
  (also: **women's lib**) Movimiento de
  liberación de la mujer.
won [wʌn] pt, pp of **win**.
wonder ['wʌndə*] n maravilla, prodigio;
  (feeling) asombro ♦ vi: **to** ~ **whether**
  preguntarse si; **to** ~ **at** asombrarse de; **to**
  ~ **about** pensar sobre or en; **it's no** ~ **that**
  no es de extrañar que.
wonderful ['wʌndəful] adj maravilloso.
wonderfully ['wʌndəfəlɪ] adv
  maravillosamente, estupendamente.
wonky ['wɔŋkɪ] adj (BRIT col: unsteady) poco
  seguro, cojo; (: broken down) estropeado.
wont [wɔnt] n: **as is his/her** ~ como tiene
  por costumbre.
won't [wəunt] = **will not**.
woo [wuː] vt (woman) cortejar.
wood [wud] n (timber) madera; (forest)
  bosque m ♦ cpd de madera.
wood alcohol n (US) alcohol m
  desnaturalizado.
wood carving n tallado en madera.
wooded ['wudɪd] adj arbolado.
wooden ['wudn] adj de madera; (fig)
  inexpresivo.

woodland ['wudlənd] *n* bosque *m*.
woodpecker ['wudpɛkə*] *n* pájaro carpintero.
wood pigeon *n* paloma torcaz.
woodwind ['wudwɪnd] *n* (*MUS*) instrumentos *mpl* de viento de madera.
woodwork ['wudwə:k] *n* carpintería.
woodworm ['wudwə:m] *n* carcoma.
woof [wuf] *n* (*of dog*) ladrido ♦ *vi* ladrar; ~, ~! ¡guau, guau!
wool [wul] *n* lana; **knitting** ~ lana (de hacer punto); **to pull the** ~ **over sb's eyes** (*fig*) dar a algn gato por liebre.
woollen, (*US*) **woolen** ['wulən] *adj* de lana ♦ *n*: ~s géneros *mpl* de lana.
woolly, (*US*) **wooly** ['wulɪ] *adj* de lana; (*fig: ideas*) confuso.
woozy ['wu:zɪ] *adj* (*col*) mareado.
word [wə:d] *n* palabra; (*news*) noticia; (*promise*) palabra (de honor) ♦ *vt* redactar; ~ **for** ~ palabra por palabra; **what's the** ~ **for "pen" in Spanish?** ¿cómo se dice "pen" en español?; **to put sth into** ~s expresar algo en palabras; **to have a** ~ **with sb** hablar (dos palabras) con algn; **in other** ~s en otras palabras; **to break/ keep one's** ~ faltar a la palabra/cumplir la promesa; **to leave** ~ **(with/for sb) that** ... dejar recado (con/para algn) de que ...; **to have** ~s **with sb** (*quarrel with*) discutir *or* reñir con algn.
wording ['wə:dɪŋ] *n* redacción *f*.
word-of-mouth [wə:dəv'mauθ] *n*: **by** *or* **through** ~ de palabra, por el boca a boca.
word-perfect ['wə:d'pə:fɪkt] *adj* (*speech etc*) sin faltas de expresión.
word processing *n* procesamiento *or* tratamiento de textos.
word processor [-'prəusɛsə*] *n* procesador *m* de textos.
wordwrap ['wə:dræp] *n* (*COMPUT*) salto de línea automático.
wordy ['wə:dɪ] *adj* verboso, prolijo.
wore [wɔ:*] *pt of* **wear**.
work [wə:k] *n* trabajo; (*job*) empleo, trabajo; (*ART, LIT*) obra ♦ *vi* trabajar; (*mechanism*) funcionar, marchar; (*medicine*) ser eficaz, surtir efecto ♦ *vt* (*shape*) trabajar; (*stone etc*) tallar; (*mine etc*) explotar; (*machine*) manejar, hacer funcionar; (*cause*) producir; **to go to** ~ ir a trabajar *or* al trabajo; **to be at** ~ **(on sth)** estar trabajando (en algo); **to set to** ~, **start** ~ ponerse a trabajar; **to be out of** ~ estar parado, no tener trabajo; **his life's** ~ el trabajo de su vida; **to** ~ **hard** trabajar mucho *or* duro; **to** ~ **to rule** (*INDUSTRY*) hacer una huelga de celo; **to**

~ **loose** (*part*) desprenderse; (*knot*) aflojarse; *see also* **works**.
►**work off** *vt*: **to** ~ **off one's feelings** desahogarse.
►**work on** *vt fus* trabajar en, dedicarse a; (*principle*) basarse en; **he's** ~**ing on the car** está reparando el coche.
►**work out** *vi* (*plans etc*) salir bien, funcionar; (*SPORT*) hacer ejercicios ♦ *vt* (*problem*) resolver; (*plan*) elaborar; **it** ~**s out at £100** asciende a 100 libras.
►**work up** *vt*: **he** ~**ed his way up in the company** ascendió en la compañía mediante sus propios esfuerzos.
workable ['wə:kəbl] *adj* (*solution*) práctico, factible.
workaholic [wə:kə'hɒlɪk] *n* adicto/a al trabajo.
workbench ['wə:kbɛntʃ] *n* banco *or* mesa de trabajo.
worked up [wə:kt-] *adj*: **to get** ~ excitarse.
worker ['wə:kə*] *n* trabajador(a) *m/f*, obrero/a; **office** ~ oficinista *m/f*.
work force *n* mano *f* de obra.
work-in ['wə:kɪn] *n* (*BRIT*) ocupación *f* (de la empresa) sin interrupción del trabajo.
working ['wə:kɪŋ] *adj* (*day, week*) laborable; (*tools, conditions, clothes*) de trabajo; (*wife*) que trabaja; (*partner*) activo.
working capital *n* (*COMM*) capital *m* circulante.
working class *n* clase *f* obrera ♦ *adj*: **working-class** obrero.
working knowledge *n* conocimientos *mpl* básicos.
working man *n* obrero.
working order *n*: **in** ~ en funcionamiento.
working party *n* comisión *f* de investigación, grupo de trabajo.
working week *n* semana laboral.
work-in-progress ['wə:kɪn'prəugrɛs] *n* (*COMM*) trabajo en curso.
workload ['wə:kləud] *n* cantidad *f* de trabajo.
workman ['wə:kmən] *n* obrero.
workmanship ['wə:kmənʃɪp] *n* (*art*) hechura; (*skill*) habilidad *f*.
workmate ['wə:kmeɪt] *n* compañero/a de trabajo.
workout ['wə:kaut] *n* (*SPORT*) sesión *f* de ejercicios.
work permit *n* permiso de trabajo.
works [wə:ks] *nsg* (*BRIT: factory*) fábrica ♦ *npl* (*of clock, machine*) mecanismo; **road** ~ obras *fpl*.
works council *n* comité *m* de empresa.
worksheet ['wə:kʃi:t] *n* (*COMPUT*) hoja de trabajo; (*SCOL*) hoja de ejercicios.

workshop ['wə:kʃɔp] n taller m.
work station n estación f de trabajo.
work study n estudio del trabajo.
worktop ['wə:ktɔp] n encimera.
work-to-rule ['wə:ktə'ru:l] n (BRIT) huelga de celo.
world [wə:ld] n mundo ♦ cpd (champion) del mundo; (power, war) mundial; **all over the** ~ por todo el mundo, en el mundo entero; **the business** ~ el mundo de los negocios; **what in the** ~ **is he doing?** ¿qué diablos está haciendo?; **to think the** ~ **of sb** (fig) tener un concepto muy alto de algn; **to do sb a** ~ **of good** sentar muy bien a algn; **W**~ **War One/Two** la primera/segunda Guerra Mundial.
World Cup n (FOOTBALL): **the** ~ el Mundial, los Mundiales.
world-famous [wə:ld'feɪməs] adj de fama mundial, mundialmente famoso.
worldly ['wə:ldlɪ] adj mundano.
world music n música étnica.
World Series n: **the** ~ (US BASEBALL) el campeonato nacional de béisbol de EEUU.
World Service n see BBC.
world-wide ['wə:ldwaɪd] adj mundial, universal.
worm [wə:m] n gusano; (earth~) lombriz f.
worn [wɔ:n] pp of **wear** ♦ adj usado.
worn-out ['wɔ:naut] adj (object) gastado; (person) rendido, agotado.
worried ['wʌrɪd] adj preocupado; **to be** ~ **about sth** estar preocupado por algo.
worrisome ['wʌrɪsəm] adj preocupante, inquietante.
worry ['wʌrɪ] n preocupación f ♦ vt preocupar, inquietar ♦ vi preocuparse; **to** ~ **about** or **over sth/sb** preocuparse por algo/algn.
worrying ['wʌrɪɪŋ] adj inquietante.
worse [wə:s] adj, adv peor ♦ n el peor, lo peor; **a change for the** ~ un empeoramiento; **so much the** ~ **for you** tanto peor para ti; **he is none the** ~ **for it** se ha quedado tan fresco or tan tranquilo; **to get** ~, **to grow** ~ empeorar.
worsen ['wə:sn] vt, vi empeorar.
worse off adj (fig): **you'll be** ~ **this way** de esta forma estarás peor que antes.
worship ['wə:ʃɪp] n (organized ~) culto; (act) adoración f ♦ vt adorar; **Your W**~ (BRIT: to mayor) su Ilustrísima; (: to judge) su señoría.
worshipper, (US) **worshiper** ['wə:ʃɪpə*] n devoto/a.
worst [wə:st] adj (el/la) peor ♦ adv peor ♦ n lo peor; **at** ~ en el peor de los casos; **to**

come off ~ llevar la peor parte; **if the** ~ **comes to the** ~ en el peor de los casos.
worst-case ['wə:stkeɪs] adj: **the** ~ **scenario** el peor de los casos.
worsted ['wustɪd] n: **(wool)** ~ estambre m.
worth [wə:θ] n valor m ♦ adj: **to be** ~ valer; **how much is it** ~? ¿cuánto vale?; **it's** ~ **it** vale or merece la pena; **to be** ~ **one's while (to do)** merecer la pena (hacer); **it's not** ~ **the trouble** no vale or merece la pena.
worthless ['wə:θlɪs] adj sin valor; (useless) inútil.
worthwhile ['wə:θwaɪl] adj (activity) que merece la pena; (cause) loable.
worthy ['wə:ðɪ] adj (person) respetable; (motive) honesto; ~ **of** digno de.

═══════════════════════ *KEYWORD*

would [wud] aux vb **1** (conditional tense): **if you asked him he** ~ **do it** si se lo pidieras, lo haría; **if you had asked him he** ~ **have done it** si se lo hubieras pedido, lo habría or hubiera hecho
2 (in offers, invitations, requests): ~ **you like a biscuit?** ¿quieres una galleta?; (formal) ¿querría una galleta?; ~ **you ask him to come in?** ¿quiere hacerle pasar?; ~ **you open the window please?** ¿quiere or podría abrir la ventana, por favor?
3 (in indirect speech): **I said I** ~ **do it** dije que lo haría
4 (emphatic): **it WOULD have to snow today!** ¡tenía que nevar precisamente hoy!
5 (insistence): **she** ~**n't behave** no quiso comportarse bien
6 (conjecture): **it** ~ **have been midnight** sería medianoche; **it** ~ **seem so** parece ser que sí
7 (indicating habit): **he** ~ **go there on Mondays** iba allí los lunes.

would-be ['wudbi:] adj (pej) presunto.
wouldn't ['wudnt] = **would not**.
wound vb [waund] pt, pp of **wind** ♦ n, vt [wu:nd] n herida ♦ vt herir.
wove [wəuv] pt of **weave**.
woven ['wəuvən] pp of **weave**.
WP n abbr = **word processing; word processor** ♦ abbr (BRIT col: = weather permitting) si lo permite el tiempo.
WPC n abbr (BRIT) = woman police constable.
wpm abbr (= words per minute) p.p.m.
WRAC n abbr (BRIT: = Women's Royal Army Corps) cuerpo auxiliar femenino del ejército de tierra.
WRAF n abbr (BRIT: = Women's Royal Air

Force) cuerpo *auxiliar femenino del ejército del aire.*

wrangle ['ræŋgl] *n* riña ♦ *vi* reñir.

wrap [ræp] *n* (*stole*) chal *m* ♦ *vt* (*also*: ~ **up**) envolver; **under** ~**s** (*fig: plan, scheme*) oculto, tapado.

wrapper ['ræpə*] *n* (*BRIT: of book*) sobrecubierta; (*on chocolate etc*) envoltura.

wrapping paper ['ræpɪŋ-] *n* papel *m* de envolver.

wrath [rɔθ] *n* cólera.

wreak [ri:k] *vt* (*destruction*) causar; **to** ~ **havoc (on)** hacer *or* causar estragos (en); **to** ~ **vengeance (on)** vengarse (en).

wreath, ~**s** [ri:θ, ri:ðz] *n* (*funeral* ~) corona; (*of flowers*) guirnalda.

wreck [rɛk] *n* (*ship: destruction*) naufragio; (: *remains*) restos *mpl* del barco, (*pej. person*) ruina ♦ *vt* destrozar; **to be** ~**ed** (*NAUT*) naufragar.

wreckage ['rɛkɪdʒ] *n* (*remains*) restos *mpl*; (*of building*) escombros *mpl.*

wrecker ['rɛkə*] *n* (*US: breakdown van*) camión-grúa *m.*

WREN [rɛn] *n abbr* (*BRIT*) *miembro del WRNS.*

wren [rɛn] *n* (*ZOOL*) reyezuelo.

wrench [rɛntʃ] *n* (*TECH*) llave *f* inglesa; (*tug*) tirón *m* ♦ *vt* arrancar; **to** ~ **sth from sb** arrebatar algo violentamente a algn.

wrest [rɛst] *vt*: **to** ~ **sth from sb** arrebatar *or* arrancar algo a algn.

wrestle ['rɛsl] *vi*: **to** ~ **(with sb)** luchar (con *or* contra algn).

wrestler ['rɛslə*] *n* luchador(a) *m/f* (de lucha libre).

wrestling ['rɛslɪŋ] *n* lucha libre.

wrestling match *n* combate *m* de lucha libre.

wretch [rɛtʃ] *n* desgraciado/a, miserable *m/f*, **little** ~! (*often humorous*) ¡granuja!

wretched ['rɛtʃɪd] *adj* miserable.

wriggle ['rɪgl] *vi* serpentear.

wring *pt, pp* **wrung** [rɪŋ, rʌŋ] *vt* torcer, retorcer; (*wet clothes*) escurrir; (*fig*): **to** ~ **sth out of sb** sacar algo por la fuerza a algn.

wringer ['rɪŋə*] *n* escurridor *m.*

wringing ['rɪŋɪŋ] *adj* (*also*: ~ **wet**) empapado.

wrinkle ['rɪŋkl] *n* arruga ♦ *vt* arrugar ♦ *vi* arrugarse.

wrinkled ['rɪŋkld], **wrinkly** ['rɪŋklɪ] *adj* (*fabric, paper, etc*) arrugado.

wrist [rɪst] *n* muñeca.

wristband ['rɪstbænd] *n* (*BRIT: of shirt*) puño; (: *of watch*) correa.

wrist watch *n* reloj *m* de pulsera.

writ [rɪt] *n* mandato judicial; **to serve a** ~ **on sb** notificar un mandato judicial a algn.

write, *pt* **wrote,** *pp* **written** [raɪt, rəut, 'rɪtn] *vt, vi* escribir; **to** ~ **sb a letter** escribir una carta a algn.

▶**write away** *vi*: **to** ~ **away for** (*information, goods*) pedir por escrito *or* carta.

▶**write down** *vt* escribir; (*note*) apuntar.

▶**write off** *vt* (*debt*) borrar (como incobrable); (*fig*) desechar por inútil; (*smash up: car*) destrozar.

▶**write out** *vt* escribir.

▶**write up** *vt* redactar.

write-off ['raɪtɔf] *n* siniestro total; **the car is a** ~ el coche es pura chatarra.

write-protect ['raɪtprə'tɛkt] *vt* (*COMPUT*) proteger contra escritura.

writer ['raɪtə*] *n* escritor(a) *m/f.*

write-up ['raɪtʌp] *n* (*review*) crítica, reseña.

writhe [raɪð] *vi* retorcerse.

writing ['raɪtɪŋ] *n* escritura; (*hand*~) letra; (*of author*) obras; **in** ~ por escrito; **to put sth in** ~ poner algo por escrito; **in my own** ~ escrito por mí; *see also* **writings.**

writing case *n* estuche *m* de papel de escribir.

writing desk *n* escritorio.

writing paper *n* papel *m* de escribir.

writings *npl* obras *fpl.*

written ['rɪtn] *pp of* **write.**

WRNS *n abbr* (*BRIT*: = *Women's Royal Naval Service*) *cuerpo auxiliar femenino de la armada.*

wrong [rɔŋ] *adj* (*wicked*) malo; (*unfair*) injusto; (*incorrect*) equivocado, incorrecto; (*not suitable*) inoportuno, inconveniente ♦ *adv* mal ♦ *n* mal *m*; (*injustice*) injusticia ♦ *vt* ser injusto con; (*hurt*) agraviar; **to be** ~ (*answer*) estar equivocado; (*in doing, saying*) equivocarse; **it's** ~ **to steal, stealing is** ~ es mal robar; **you are** ~ **to do it** haces mal en hacerlo; **you are** ~ **about that, you've got it** ~ en eso estás equivocado; **to be in the** ~ no tener razón; (*guilty*) tener la culpa; **what's** ~? ¿qué pasa?; **what's** ~ **with the car?** ¿qué le pasa al coche?; **there's nothing** ~ no pasa nada; **you have the** ~ **number** (*TEL*) se ha equivocado de número; **to go** ~ (*person*) equivocarse; (*plan*) salir mal; (*machine*) estropearse.

wrongdoer ['rɔŋduə*] *n* malhechor(a) *m/f.*

wrong-foot [rɔŋ'fut] *vt* (*SPORT*) hacer perder el equilibrio a; (*fig*) poner en un aprieto a.

wrongful ['rɔŋful] *adj* injusto; ~ **dismissal** (*INDUSTRY*) despido improcedente.

wrongly ['rɔŋlɪ] *adv* (*answer, do, count*) incorrectamente; (*treat*) injustamente.

wrote [rəut] *pt of* **write**.

wrought [rɔːt] *adj*: ~ **iron** hierro forjado.

wrung [rʌŋ] *pt, pp of* **wring**.

WRVS *n abbr* (*BRIT*: = *Women's Royal Voluntary Service*) cuerpo de voluntarias al servicio de la comunidad.

wry [raɪ] *adj* irónico.

wt. *abbr* = **weight**.

WV, W. Va. *abbr* (*US*) = *West Virginia*.

WWW *n abbr* (= *World Wide Web*) WWW *m* or *f*.

WY, Wyo. *abbr* (*US*) = *Wyoming*.

WYSIWYG ['wɪzɪwɪg] *abbr* (*COMPUT*: = *what you see is what you get*) tipo de presentación en un procesador de textos.

X x

X, x [eks] *n* (*letter*) X, x *f*: (*BRIT CINE: formerly*) no apto para menores de 18 años; **X for Xmas** X de Xiquena; **if you earn X dollars a year** si ganas X dólares al año.

X-certificate ['ɛksəˈtɪfɪkɪt] *adj* (*BRIT: film: formerly*) no apto para menores de 18 años.

Xerox ® ['zɪərɔks] *n* (*also*: ~ **machine**) fotocopiadora; (*photocopy*) fotocopia ♦ *vt* fotocopiar.

XL *abbr* = *extra large*.

Xmas ['ɛksməs] *n abbr* = **Christmas**.

X-rated ['eks'reɪtɪd] *adj* (*US: film*) no apto para menores de 18 años.

X-ray [ɛks'reɪ] *n* radiografía; ~**s** *npl* rayos *mpl* X ♦ *vt* radiografiar.

xylophone ['zaɪləfəun] *n* xilófono.

Y y

Y, y [waɪ] *n* (*letter*) Y, y *f*; **Y for Yellow**, (*US*) **Y for Yoke** Y de Yegua.

Y2K [ˌwaɪtuːˈkeɪ] *abbr* (= *Year 2000*): **the** ~ **problem** (*COMPUT*) el efecto 2000.

yacht [jɔt] *n* yate *m*.

yachting ['jɔtɪŋ] *n* (*sport*) balandrismo.

yachtsman ['jɔtsmən] *n* balandrista *m*.

yachtswoman ['jɔtswumən] balandrista.

yam [jæm] *n* ñame *m*; (*sweet potato*) batata, camote *m* (*LAM*).

Yank [jæŋk], **Yankee** ['jæŋkɪ] *n* (*pej*) yanqui *m/f*.

yank [jæŋk] *vt* tirar de, jalar de (*LAM*) ♦ *n* tirón *m*.

yap [jæp] *vi* (*dog*) aullar.

yard [jɑːd] *n* patio; (*US: garden*) jardín *m*; (*measure*) yarda; **builder's** ~ almacén *m*.

yardstick ['jɑːdstɪk] *n* (*fig*) criterio, norma.

yarn [jɑːn] *n* hilo; (*tale*) cuento (chino).

yawn [jɔːn] *n* bostezo ♦ *vi* bostezar.

yawning ['jɔːnɪŋ] *adj* (*gap*) muy abierto.

yd. *abbr* (= *yard*) yda.

yeah [jɛə] *adv* (*col*) sí.

year [jɪə*] *n* año; (*SCOL, UNIV*) curso; **this** ~ este año; ~ **in,** ~ **out** año tras año; **a** *or* **per** ~ al año; **to be 8** ~**s old** tener 8 años; **she's three** ~**s old** tiene tres años; **an eight-**~**-old child** un niño de ocho años (de edad).

yearbook ['jɪəbuk] *n* anuario.

yearling ['jɪəlɪŋ] *n* (*horse*) potro de un año.

yearly ['jɪəlɪ] *adj* anual ♦ *adv* anualmente, cada año; **twice** ~ dos veces al año.

yearn [jəːn] *vi*: **to** ~ **for sth** añorar algo, suspirar por algo.

yearning ['jəːnɪŋ] *n* ansia; (*longing*) añoranza.

yeast [jiːst] *n* levadura.

yell [jɛl] *n* grito, alarido ♦ *vi* gritar.

yellow ['jɛləu] *adj, n* amarillo.

yellow fever *n* fiebre *f* amarilla.

yellowish ['jɛləuɪʃ] *adj* amarillento.

Yellow Pages ® *npl* páginas *fpl* amarillas.

Yellow Sea *n*: **the** ~ el Mar Amarillo.

yelp [jɛlp] *n* aullido ♦ *vi* aullar.

Yemen ['jɛmən] *n* Yemen *m*.

Yemeni ['jɛmənɪ] *adj, n* yemení *m/f*, yemenita *m/f*.

yen [jɛn] n (*currency*) yen m.
yeoman ['jəumən] n: Y~ **of the Guard** *alabardero de la Casa Real*.
yes [jɛs] adv, n sí m; **to say/answer** ~ decir/contestar que sí; **to say** ~ **(to)** decir que sí (a), conformarse (con).
yes man n pelotillero.
yesterday ['jɛstədɪ] adv, n ayer m; ~ **morning/evening** ayer por la mañana/tarde; **all day** ~ todo el día de ayer; **the day before** ~ antes de ayer, anteayer.
yet [jɛt] adv todavía ♦ conj sin embargo, a pesar de todo; ~ **again** de nuevo; **it is not finished** ~ todavía no está acabado; **the best** ~ el/la mejor hasta ahora; **as** ~ hasta ahora, todavía.
yew [ju:] n tejo.
Y-fronts ® ['waɪfrʌnts] npl (*BRIT*) calzoncillos mpl, eslip msg tradicional.
YHA n abbr (*BRIT* = *Youth Hostel Association*) ≈ Red f Española de Albergues Juveniles.
Yiddish ['jɪdɪʃ] n yiddish m.
yield [ji:ld] n producción f; (*AGR*) cosecha; (*COMM*) rendimiento ♦ vt producir, dar; (*profit*) rendir ♦ vi rendirse, ceder; (*US AUT*) ceder el paso; **a** ~ **of 5%** un rédito del 5 por ciento.
YMCA n abbr (= *Young Men's Christian Association*) Asociación f de Jóvenes Cristianos.
yob(bo) ['jɔb(bəu)] n (*BRIT col*) gamberro.
yodel ['jəudl] vi cantar a la tirolesa.
yoga ['jəugə] n yoga m.
yog(h)ourt, yog(h)urt ['jəugət] n yogur m.
yoke [jəuk] n (*of oxen*) yunta; (*on shoulders*) balancín m; (*fig*) yugo ♦ vt (*also*: ~ **together**: *oxen*) uncir.
yolk [jəuk] n yema (de huevo).
yonder ['jɔndə*] adv allá (a lo lejos).
yonks [jɔŋks] npl (*col*): **I haven't seen him for** ~ hace siglos que no lo veo.
Yorks abbr (*BRIT*) = *Yorkshire*.

═══════════════════════ KEYWORD

you [ju:] pron **1** (*subject*: *familiar*) tú, pl vosotros/as (*SP*), ustedes (*LAM*); (*polite*) usted, pl ustedes; ~ **are very kind** eres/es etc muy amable; ~ **French enjoy your food** a vosotros (*or* ustedes) los franceses os (*or* les) gusta la comida; ~ **and I will go** iremos tú y yo
2 (*object*: *direct*: *familiar*) te, pl os (*SP*), les (*LAM*); (*polite*) lo *or* le, pl los *or* les, f la, pl las; **I know** ~ te/le etc conozco
3 (*object*: *indirect*: *familiar*) te, pl os (*SP*), les (*LAM*); (*polite*) le, pl les; **I gave the letter to** ~ **yesterday** te/os etc di la carta ayer
4 (*stressed*): **I told YOU to do it** te dije a ti que lo hicieras, es a ti a quien dije que lo hicieras; *see also* **3, 5**
5 (*after prep*: NB: con+ti = contigo: *familiar*) ti, pl vosotros/as (*SP*), ustedes (*LAM*); (: *polite*) usted, pl ustedes; **it's for** ~ es para ti/vosotros etc
6 (*comparisons*: *familiar*) tú, pl vosotros/as (*SP*), ustedes (*LAM*); (: *polite*) usted, pl ustedes; **she's younger than** ~ es más joven que tú/vosotros etc
7 (*impersonal*: *one*): **fresh air does** ~ **good** el aire puro (te) hace bien; ~ **never know** nunca se sabe; ~ **can't do that!** ¡eso no se hace!

you'd [ju:d] = **you had**; **you would**.
you'll [ju:l] = **you will**, **you shall**.
young [jʌŋ] adj joven ♦ npl (*of animal*) cría; (*people*): **the** ~ los jóvenes, la juventud; **a** ~ **man/lady** un(a) joven; **my** ~**er brother** mi hermano menor *or* pequeño; **the** ~**er generation** la nueva generación.
youngster ['jʌŋstə*] n joven m/f.
your [jɔ:*] adj tu; (pl) vuestro; (*formal*) su; ~ **house** tu etc casa; *see also* **my**.
you're [juə*] = **you are**.
yours [jɔ:z] pron tuyo; (: pl) vuestro; (*formal*) suyo; **a friend of** ~ un amigo tuyo etc; *see also* **faithfully, mine, sincerely**.
yourself [jɔ:'sɛlf] pron (*reflexive*) tú mismo; (*complement*) te; (*after prep*) tí (mismo); (*formal*) usted mismo; (: *complement*) se; (: *after prep*) sí (mismo); **you** ~ **told me** me lo dijiste tú mismo; **(all) by** ~ sin ayuda de nadie, solo; *see also* **oneself**.
yourselves [jɔ:'sɛlvz] pl pron vosotros mismos; (*after prep*) vosotros (mismos); (*formal*) ustedes (mismos); (: *complement*) se; (: *after prep*) sí mismos.
youth [ju:θ] n juventud f; (*young man*) (pl ~**s** [ju:ðz]) joven m; **in my** ~ en mi juventud.
youth club n club m juvenil.
youthful ['ju:θful] adj juvenil.
youthfulness ['ju:θfəlnɪs] n juventud f.
youth hostel n albergue m juvenil.
youth movement n movimiento juvenil.
you've [ju:v] = **you have**.
yowl [jaul] n (*of animal, person*) aullido ♦ vi aullar.
yr. abbr (= *year*) a.
YT abbr (*Canada*) = *Yukon Territory*.
Yugoslav ['ju:gəuslɑ:v] adj, n yugoslavo/a m/f.
Yugoslavia [ju:gəu'slɑ:vɪə] n Yugoslavia.
Yugoslavian [ju:gəu'slɑ:vɪən] adj yugoslavo/a.

yuppie ['jʌpɪ] (*col*) *adj, n* yuppie *m/f*.
YWCA *n abbr* (= *Young Women's Christian Association*) Asociación *f* de Jóvenes Cristianas.

Z z

Z, z [zɛd, (*US*) ziː] *n* (*letter*) Z, z *f*; **Z for Zebra** Z de Zaragoza.
Zaire [zɑːˈiːə*] *n* Zaire *m*.
Zambia ['zæmbɪə] *n* Zambia.
Zambian ['zæmbɪən] *adj, n* zambiano/a *m/f*.
zany ['zeɪnɪ] *adj* estrafalario.
zap [zæp] *vt* (*COMPUT*) borrar.
zeal [ziːl] *n* celo, entusiasmo.
zealot ['zɛlət] *n* fanático/a.
zealous ['zɛləs] *adj* celoso, entusiasta.
zebra ['ziːbrə] *n* cebra.
zebra crossing *n* (*BRIT*) paso de peatones.
zenith ['zɛnɪθ] *n* (*ASTRO*) cénit *m*; (*fig*) apogeo.
zero ['zɪərəu] *n* cero; **5 degrees below** ~ 5 grados bajo cero.
zero hour *n* hora cero.
zero option *n* (*POL*) opción *f* cero.

zero-rated ['zɪərəureɪtɪd] *adj* (*BRIT*) de tasa cero.
zest [zɛst] *n* entusiasmo; ~ **for living** brío.
zigzag ['zɪgzæg] *n* zigzag *m* ♦ *vi* zigzaguear.
Zimbabwe [zɪmˈbɑːbwɪ] *n* Zimbabwe *m*.
Zimbabwean [zɪmˈbɑːbwɪən] *adj, n* zimbabuo/a *m/f*.
Zimmer ® ['zɪmə*] *n* (*also*: ~ **frame**) andador *m*, andaderas *fpl*.
zinc [zɪŋk] *n* cinc *m*, zinc *m*.
Zionism ['zaɪənɪzm] *n* sionismo.
Zionist ['zaɪənɪst] *adj, n* sionista *m/f*.
zip [zɪp] *n* (*also*: ~ **fastener**, (*US*) ~**per**) cremallera, cierre *m* relámpago (*LAM*); (*energy*) energía, vigor *m* ♦ *vt* (*also*: ~ **up**) cerrar la cremallera de ♦ *vi*: **to** ~ **along to the shops** ir de compras volando.
zip code *n* (*US*) código postal.
zither ['zɪðə*] *n* cítara.
zodiac ['zəudɪæk] *n* zodíaco.
zombie ['zɔmbɪ] *n* zombi *m*.
zone [zəun] *n* zona.
zonked [zɔŋkt] *adj* (*col*) hecho polvo.
zoo [zuː] *n* zoo, (parque *m*) zoológico.
zoological [zuːəˈlɔdʒɪkəl] *adj* zoológico.
zoologist [zuːˈɔlədʒɪst] *n* zoólogo/a.
zoology [zuːˈɔlədʒɪ] *n* zoología.
zoom [zuːm] *vi*: **to** ~ **past** pasar zumbando; **to** ~ **in (on sth/sb)** (*PHOT, CINE*) enfocar (algo/a algn) con el zoom.
zoom lens *n* zoom *m*.
zucchini [zuːˈkiːnɪ] *n(pl)* (*US*) calabacín(ines) *m(pl)*.

Grammar
Gramática

USING THE GRAMMAR

The Grammar section deals systematically and comprehensively with all the information you will need in order to communicate accurately in Spanish. The user-friendly layout explains the grammar point on a left hand page, leaving the facing page free for illustrative examples. The boxed numbers, (→ ⬚1) etc, direct you to the relevant example in every case. Another strong point of the Grammar section is its comprehensive treatment of verbs. Regular verbs are fully explained, and 80 major irregular verbs are conjugated in their simple tenses. The irregular verbs are given in alphabetical order and laid out in tables, making them easy and efficient to consult. In addition, a verb index lists over 2,800 Spanish verbs, each cross-referred to the appropriate conjugation model.

The Grammar section also provides invaluable guidance on the danger of translating English structures by identical structures in Spanish. Use of Numbers and Punctuation are important areas covered towards the end of the section. Finally, the index lists the main words and grammatical terms in both English and Spanish.

ABBREVIATIONS

algn	alguien	**masc**	masculine	**sing**	singular
cond	conditional	**p(p)**	page(s)	**sth**	something
fem	feminine	**plur**	plural	**subj**	subjunctive
ff	and following pages	**sb**	somebody		

CONTENTS 4

CONTENTS

5

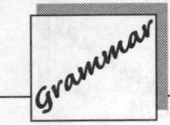

☐ Simple Tenses: Formation

In Spanish the simple tenses are:

Present	→ 1
Imperfect	→ 2
Future	→ 3
Conditional	→ 4
Preterite	→ 5
Present Subjunctive	→ 6
Imperfect Subjunctive	→ 7

They are formed by adding endings to a verb stem. The endings show the number and person of the subject of the verb → 8

The stem and endings of regular verbs are totally predictable. The following sections show all the patterns for regular verbs. For irregular verbs see pp 80 ff.

Regular Verbs

There are three regular verb patterns (called conjugations), each identifiable by the ending of the infinitive:

- First conjugation verbs end in **-ar** e.g. **hablar** to speak.
- Second conjugation verbs end in **-er** e.g. **comer** to eat.
- Third conjugation verbs end in **-ir** e.g. **vivir** to live.

These three conjugations are treated in order on the following pages. The subject pronouns will appear in brackets because they are not always necessary in Spanish (see p 226).

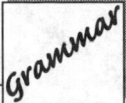

☐1	**(yo) hablo**	I speak I am speaking I do speak
☐2	**(yo) hablaba**	I spoke I was speaking I used to speak
☐3	**(yo) hablaré**	I shall speak I shall be speaking
☐4	**(yo) hablaría**	I should/would speak I should/would be speaking
☐5	**(yo) hablé**	I spoke
☐6	**(que) (yo) hable**	(that) I speak
☐7	**(que) (yo) hablara** *or* **hablase**	(that) I speak
☐8	**(yo) hablo** **(nosotros) hablamos** **(yo) hablaría** **(nosotros) hablaríamos**	I speak we speak I would speak we would speak

❐ Simple Tenses: First Conjugation

◆ The stem is formed as follows:

TENSE	FORMATION	EXAMPLE
Present Imperfect Preterite Present Subjunctive Imperfect Subjunctive*	infinitive minus -**ar** * For irregular verbs see p 80	**habl-**
Future Conditional	infinitive	**hablar-**

◆ To the appropriate stem add the following endings:

		PRESENT → ①	IMPERFECT → ②	PRETERITE → ③
sing	1st person 2nd person 3rd person	**-o** **-as** **-a**	**-aba** **-abas** **-aba**	**-é** **-aste** **-ó**
plur	1st person 2nd person 3rd person	**-amos** **-áis** **-an**	**-ábamos** **-abais** **-aban**	**-amos** **-asteis** **-aron**

		PRESENT SUBJUNCTIVE → ④	IMPERFECT SUBJUNCTIVE → ⑤
sing	1st person 2nd person 3rd person	**-e** **-es** **-e**	**-ara** or **-ase** **-aras** or **-ases** **-ara** or **-ase**
plur	1st person 2nd person 3rd person	**-emos** **-éis** **-en**	**-áramos** or **-ásemos** **-arais** or **-aseis** **-aran** or **-asen**

		FUTURE → ⑥	CONDITIONAL → ⑦
sing	1st person 2nd person 3rd person	**-é** **-ás** **-á**	**-ía** **-ías** **-ía**
plur	1st person 2nd person 3rd person	**-emos** **-éis** **-án**	**-íamos** **-íais** **-ían**

Examples

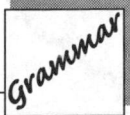

Grammar

---

1 PRESENT   **2 IMPERFECT**   **3 PRETERITE**

	PRESENT	IMPERFECT	PRETERITE
(yo)	hablo	hablaba	hablé
(tú)	hablas	hablabas	hablaste
(él/ella/Vd)	habla	hablaba	habló
(nosotros/as)	hablamos	hablábamos	hablamos
(vosotros/as)	habláis	hablabais	hablasteis
(ellos/as/Vds)	hablan	hablaban	hablaron

---

4 PRESENT SUBJUNCTIVE   **5 IMPERFECT SUBJUNCTIVE**

	PRESENT SUBJUNCTIVE	IMPERFECT SUBJUNCTIVE
(yo)	hable	hablara or hablase
(tú)	hables	hablaras or hablases
(él/ella/Vd)	hable	hablara or hablase
(nosotros/as)	hablemos	habláramos or hablásemos
(vosotros/as)	habléis	hablarais or hablaseis
(ellos/as/Vds)	hablen	hablaran or hablasen

---

6 FUTURE   **7 CONDITIONAL**

	FUTURE	CONDITIONAL
(yo)	hablaré	hablaría
(tú)	hablarás	hablarías
(él/ella/Vd)	hablará	hablaría
(nosotros/as)	hablaremos	hablaríamos
(vosotros/as)	hablaréis	hablaríais
(ellos/as/Vds)	hablarán	hablarían

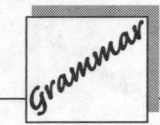

❐ Simple Tenses: Second Conjugation

◆ The stem is formed as follows:

TENSE	FORMATION	EXAMPLE
Present Imperfect Preterite Present Subjunctive Imperfect Subjunctive*	infinitive minus **-er** * For irregular verbs see p 80	**com-**
Future Conditional	infinitive	**comer-**

◆ To the appropriate stem add the following endings:

		PRESENT → 1	IMPERFECT → 2	PRETERITE → 3
sing	1st person 2nd person 3rd person	**-o** **-es** **-e**	**-ía** **-ías** **-ía**	**-í** **-iste** **-ió**
plur	1st person 2nd person 3rd person	**-emos** **-éis** **-en**	**-íamos** **-íais** **-ían**	**-imos** **-isteis** **-ieron**

		PRESENT SUBJUNCTIVE → 4	IMPERFECT SUBJUNCTIVE → 5
sing	1st person 2nd person 3rd person	**-a** **-as** **-a**	**-iera** or **-iese** **-ieras** or **-ieses** **-iera** or **-iese**
plur	1st person 2nd person 3rd person	**-amos** **-áis** **-an**	**-iéramos** or **-iésemos** **-ierais** or **-ieseis** **-ieran** or **-iesen**

		FUTURE → 6	CONDITIONAL → 7
sing	1st person 2nd person 3rd person	**-é** **-ás** **-á**	**-ía** **-ías** **-ía**
plur	1st person 2nd person 3rd person	**-emos** **-éis** **-án**	**-íamos** **-íais** **-ían**

Examples

1 PRESENT		2 IMPERFECT	3 PRETERITE
(yo)	como	comía	comí
(tú)	comes	comías	comiste
(él/ella/Vd)	come	comía	comió
(nosotros/as)	comemos	comíamos	comimos
(vosotros/as)	coméis	comíais	comisteis
(ellos/as/Vds)	comen	comían	comieron

4 PRESENT SUBJUNCTIVE		5 IMPERFECT SUBJUNCTIVE
(yo)	coma	comiera *or* comiese
(tú)	comas	comieras *or* comieses
(él/ella/Vd)	coma	comiera *or* comiese
(nosotros/as)	comamos	comiéramos *or* comiésemos
(vosotros/as)	comáis	comierais *or* comieseis
(ellos/as/Vds)	coman	comieran *or* comiesen

6 FUTURE		7 CONDITIONAL
(yo)	comeré	comería
(tú)	comerás	comerías
(él/ella/Vd)	comerá	comería
(nosotros/as)	comeremos	comeríamos
(vosotros/as)	comeréis	comeríais
(ellos/as/Vds)	comerán	comerían

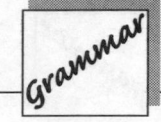

☐ Simple Tenses: Third Conjugation

◆ The stem is formed as follows:

TENSE	FORMATION	EXAMPLE
Present		
Imperfect		
Preterite	infinitive minus -**ir**	**viv-**
Present Subjunctive		
Imperfect Subjunctive*	* For irregular verbs see p 80	
Future		
Conditional	infinitive	**vivir-**

◆ To the appropriate stem add the following endings:

		PRESENT → ①	IMPERFECT → ②	PRETERITE → ③
	1st person	-**o**	-**ía**	-**í**
sing	2nd person	-**es**	-**ías**	-**iste**
	3rd person	-**e**	-**ía**	-**ió**
	1st person	-**imos**	-**íamos**	-**imos**
plur	2nd person	-**ís**	-**íais**	-**isteis**
	3rd person	-**en**	-**ían**	-**ieron**

		PRESENT SUBJUNCTIVE → ④	IMPERFECT SUBJUNCTIVE → ⑤
	1st person	-**a**	-**iera** or -**iese**
sing	2nd person	-**as**	-**ieras** or -**ieses**
	3rd person	-**a**	-**iera** or -**iese**
	1st person	-**amos**	-**iéramos** or -**iésemos**
plur	2nd person	-**áis**	-**ierais** or -**ieseis**
	3rd person	-**an**	-**ieran** or -**iesen**

		FUTURE → ⑥	CONDITIONAL → ⑦
	1st person	-**é**	-**ía**
sing	2nd person	-**ás**	-**ías**
	3rd person	-**á**	-**ía**
	1st person	-**emos**	-**íamos**
plur	2nd person	-**éis**	-**íais**
	3rd person	-**án**	-**ían**

Examples

---

1 PRESENT **2 IMPERFECT** **3 PRETERITE**

(yo)	viv**o**	viv**ía**	viv**í**
(tú)	viv**es**	viv**ías**	viv**iste**
(él/ella/Vd)	viv**e**	viv**ía**	viv**ió**
(nosotros/as)	viv**imos**	viv**íamos**	viv**imos**
(vosotros/as)	viv**ís**	viv**íais**	viv**isteis**
(ellos/as/Vds)	viv**en**	viv**ían**	viv**ieron**

---

4 PRESENT SUBJUNCTIVE **5 IMPERFECT SUBJUNCTIVE**

(yo)	viv**a**	viv**iera** or viv**iese**
(tú)	viv**as**	viv**ieras** or viv**ieses**
(él/ella/Vd)	viv**a**	viv**iera** or viv**iese**
(nosotros/as)	viv**amos**	viv**iéramos** or viv**iésemos**
(vosotros/as)	viv**áis**	viv**ierais** or viv**ieseis**
(ellos/as/Vds)	viv**an**	viv**ieran** or viv**iesen**

---

6 FUTURE **7 CONDITIONAL**

(yo)	vivir**é**	vivir**ía**
(tú)	vivir**ás**	vivir**ías**
(él/ella/Vd)	vivir**á**	vivir**ía**
(nosotros/as)	vivir**emos**	vivir**íamos**
(vosotros/as)	vivir**éis**	vivir**íais**
(ellos/as/Vds)	vivir**án**	vivir**ían**

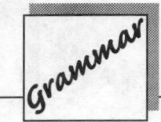

☐ The Imperative

The imperative is the form of the verb used to give commands or orders. It can be used politely, as in English 'Shut the door, please'.

In POSITIVE commands, the imperative forms for **Vd, Vds** and **nosotros** are the same as the subjunctive. The other forms are as follows:

> **tú** (same as 3rd person singular present indicative)
> **vosotros** (final **-r** of infinitive changes to **-d**) → ①

(tú)	**habla**	**come**	**vive**
	speak	*eat*	*live*
(Vd)	**hable**	**coma**	**viva**
	speak	*eat*	*live*
(nosotros)	**hablemos**	**comamos**	**vivamos**
	let's speak	*let's eat*	*let's live*
(vosotros)	**hablad**	**comed**	**vivid**
	speak	*eat*	*live*
(Vds)	**hablen**	**coman**	**vivan**
	speak	*eat*	*live*

In NEGATIVE commands, all the imperative forms are exactly the same as the present subjunctive.

♦ The imperative of irregular verbs is given in the verb tables, pp 82 ff.

Position of object pronouns with the imperative

In POSITIVE commands: they follow the verb and are attached to it. An accent is needed to show the correct position for stress (see p 292) → ②

In NEGATIVE commands: they precede the verb and are not attached to it → ③

♦ For the order of object pronouns, see page 232.

Examples

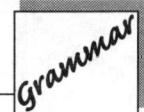

☐ 1	**cantar**	**cantad**
	to sing	sing

☐ 2	**Perdóneme**	**Enviémoselos**
	Excuse me	Let's send them to him/her/them
	Elíjanos	**Explíquemelo**
	Choose us	Explain it to me
	Esperémosla	**Devuélvaselo**
	Let's wait for her/it	Give it back to him/her/them

☐ 3	**No me molestes**	**No se la devolvamos**
	Don't disturb me	Let's not give it back to him/her/them
	No les castiguemos	**No me lo mandes**
	Let's not punish them	Don't send it to me
	No las conteste	**No nos lo hagan**
	Don't answer them	Don't do it to us

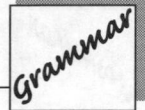

☐ **The Imperative** (Continued)

◆ For reflexive verbs – e.g. **levantarse** *to get up* – the object pronoun is the reflexive pronoun. It should be noted that the imperative forms need an accent to show the correct position for stress (see p 292). The forms **nosotros** and **vosotros** also drop the final **-s** and **-d** respectively before the pronoun → ①

BUT: **idos (vosotros)** *go*

⚠ NOTE: For general instructions, the infinitive is used instead of the imperative →②, but when it is preceded by **vamos a** it often translates *let's …* → ③

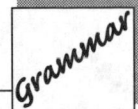

1.
Levántate
Get up
No te levantes
Don't get up
Levántese (Vd)
Get up
No se levante (Vd)
Don't get up
Levantémonos
Let's get up
No nos levantemos
Let's not get up
Levantaos
Get up
No os levantéis
Don't get up
Levántense (Vds)
Get up
No se levanten (Vds)
Don't get up

2.
Ver pág ...
See page
No pasar
Do not pass ...

3.
Vamos a ver
Let's see
Vamos a empezar
Let's start

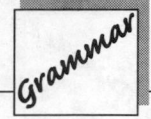

❐ Compound Tenses: Formation

In Spanish the compound tenses are:

Perfect   → 1
Pluperfect   → 2
Future Perfect   → 3
Conditional Perfect   → 4
Past Anterior   → 5
Perfect Subjunctive   → 6
Pluperfect Subjunctive   → 7

They consist of the past participle of the verb together with the auxiliary verb **haber**.

Compound tenses are formed in exactly the same way for both regular and irregular verbs, the only difference being that irregular verbs may have an irregular past participle.

The Past Participle

For all compound tenses you need to know how to form the past participle of the verb. For regular verbs this is as follows:

◆ 1st conjugation: replace the **-ar** of the infinitive by **-ado** → 8

◆ 2nd conjugation: replace the **-er** of the infinitive by **-ido** → 9

◆ 3rd conjugation: replace the **-ir** of the infinitive by **-ido** → 10

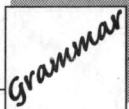

Grammar

1	**(yo) he hablado** I have spoken	
2	**(yo) había hablado** I had spoken	
3	**(yo) habré hablado** I shall have spoken	
4	**(yo) habría hablado** I should/would have spoken	
5	**(yo) hube hablado** I had spoken	
6	**(que) (yo) haya hablado** (that) I spoke, have spoken	
7	**(que) (yo) hubiera/hubiese hablado** (that) I had spoken	
8	**cantar** →	**cantado**
	to sing	sung
9	**comer** →	**comido**
	to eat	eaten
10	**vivir** →	**vivido**
	to live	lived

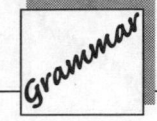

☐ **Compound Tenses: Formation** (Continued)

Perfect tense: the present tense of **haber** plus the past participle → 1

Pluperfect tense: the imperfect tense of **haber** plus the past participle → 2

Future Perfect: the future tense of **haber** plus the past participle → 3

Conditional Perfect: the conditional of **haber** plus the past participle → 4

Examples

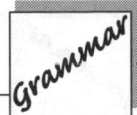

---

1 PERFECT	(yo)	**he** habl**ado**
	(tú)	**has** habl**ado**
	(él/ella/Vd)	**ha** habl**ado**
	(nosotros/as)	**hemos** habl**ado**
	(vosotros/as)	**habéis** habl**ado**
	(ellos/as/Vds)	**han** habl**ado**

---

2 PLUPERFECT	(yo)	**había** habl**ado**
	(tú)	**habías** habl**ado**
	(él/ella/Vd)	**había** habl**ado**
	(nosotros/as)	**habíamos** habl**ado**
	(vosotros/as)	**habíais** habl**ado**
	(ellos/as/Vds)	**habían** habl**ado**

---

3 FUTURE PERFECT	(yo)	**habré** habl**ado**
	(tú)	**habrás** habl**ado**
	(él/ella/Vd)	**habrá** habl**ado**
	(nosotros/as)	**habremos** habl**ado**
	(vosotros/as)	**habréis** habl**ado**
	(ellos/as/Vds)	**habrán** habl**ado**

---

4 CONDITIONAL PERFECT	(yo)	**habría** habl**ado**
	(tú)	**habrías** habl**ado**
	(él/ella/Vd)	**habría** habl**ado**
	(nosotros/as)	**habríamos** habl**ado**
	(vosotros/as)	**habríais** habl**ado**
	(ellos/as/Vds)	**habrían** habl**ado**

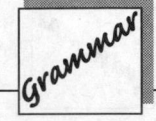

☐ **Compound Tenses: Formation** (Continued)

Past Anterior: the preterite of **haber** plus the past
participle → ①

Perfect Subjunctive: the present subjunctive of **haber** plus
the past participle → ②

Pluperfect Subjunctive: the imperfect subjunctive of **haber** plus
the past participle → ③

♦ For how to form the past participle of regular verbs see p 18. The past
participle of irregular verbs is given for each verb in the verb tables, pp
82 to 161.

Examples

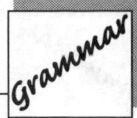

---

①	PAST ANTERIOR	(yo) **hube** hablado
		(tú) **hubiste** hablado
		(él/ella/Vd) **hubo** hablado
		(nosotros/as) **hubimos** hablado
		(vosotros/as) **hubisteis** hablado
		(ellos/as/Vds) **hubieron** hablado

---

②	PRESENT SUBJUNCTIVE	(yo) **haya** hablado
		(tú) **hayas** hablado
		(él/ella/Vd) **haya** hablado
		(nosotros/as) **hayamos** hablado
		(vosotros/as) **hayáis** hablado
		(ellos/as/Vds) **hayan** hablado

---

③	PLUPERFECT SUBJUNCTIVE	(yo) **hubiera** or **hubiese** hablado
		(tú) **hubieras** or **hubieses** hablado
		(él/ella/Vd) **hubiera** or **hubiese** hablado
		(nosotros/as) **hubiéramos** or **hubiésemos** hablado
		(vosotros/as) **hubierais** or **hubieseis** hablado
		(ellos/as/Vds) **hubieran** or **hubiesen** hablado

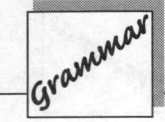

❐ **Reflexive Verbs**

A reflexive verb is one accompanied by a reflexive pronoun. The infinitive of a reflexive verb ends with the pronoun **se**, which is added to the verb form e.g.

levantarse *to get up*; **lavarse** *to wash (oneself)*

The reflexive pronouns are:

PERSON	SINGULAR	PLURAL
1st	**me**	**nos**
2nd	**te**	**os**
3rd	**se**	**se**

◆　The reflexive pronoun 'reflects back' to the subject, but it is not always translated in English → ①

　　The plural pronouns are sometimes translated as *one another*, *each other* (the 'reciprocal' meaning) → ②

　　The reciprocal meaning may be emphasized by **el uno al otro/la una a la otra (los unos a los otros/las unas a las otras)** → ③

◆　Both simple and compound tenses of reflexive verbs are conjugated in exactly the same way as those of non-reflexive verbs, except that the reflexive pronoun is always used.

　　The only irregularity is in the 1st and 2nd person plural of the affirmative imperative (see p 16). A sample reflexive verb is conjugated in full on pp 28 to 31.

Position of reflexive pronouns

◆　Except with the infinitive, gerund and positive commands, the pronoun comes before the verb → ④

◆　In the infinitive, gerund and positive commands, the pronoun follows the verb and is attached to it (but see also p 228) → ⑤

Examples

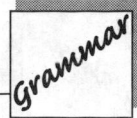

---

1. **Me visto**
   I'm dressing (myself)

   Nos lavamos
   We're washing (ourselves)

   Se levanta
   He gets up

2. **Nos queremos**   **Se parecen**
   We love each other   They resemble one another

3. **Se miraban el uno al otro**
   They were looking at each other

4. **Me acuesto temprano**   **¿Cómo se llama Vd?**
   I go to bed early   What is your name?

   No se ha despertado   **No te levantes**
   He hasn't woken up   Don't get up

5. **Quiero irme**   **Estoy levantándome**
   I want to go away   I am getting up

   Siéntense   **Vámonos**
   Sit down   Let's go

☐ **Reflexive Verbs** (Continued)

Some verbs have both a reflexive and non-reflexive form. When used reflexively, they have a different but closely related meaning, as shown in the following examples.

NON-REFLEXIVE	REFLEXIVE
acostar *to put to bed*	**acostarse** *to go to bed*
casar *to marry (off)*	**casarse** *to get married*
detener *to stop*	**detenerse** *to come to a halt*
dormir *to sleep*	**dormirse** *to go to sleep*
enfadar *to annoy*	**enfadarse** *to get annoyed*
hacer *to make*	**hacerse** *to become*
ir *to go*	**irse** *to leave, go away*
lavar *to wash*	**lavarse** *to get washed*
levantar *to raise*	**levantarse** *to get up*
llamar *to call*	**llamarse** *to be called*
poner *to put*	**ponerse** *to put on (clothing), to become*
sentir *to feel (something)*	**sentirse** *to feel (sick, tired, etc)*
vestir *to dress (someone)*	**vestirse** *to get dressed*
volver *to return*	**volverse** *to turn round*

♦ Some other verbs exist only in the reflexive:

arrepentirse *to repent*	**jactarse** *to boast*
atreverse *to dare*	**quejarse** *to complain*

♦ Some verbs acquire a different nuance when used reflexively:

caer *to fall* → ☐1

caerse *to fall down (by accident)* → ☐2

morir *to die, be killed (by accident or on purpose)* → ☐3

morirse *to die (from natural causes)* → ☐4

♦ Often a reflexive verb can be used:

— to avoid the passive (see p 34) → ☐5

— in impersonal expressions (see p 40) → ☐6

1. **El agua caía desde las rocas**
   Water fell from the rocks

2. **Me caí y me rompí el brazo**
   I fell and broke my arm

3. **Tres personas han muerto en un accidente/atentado terrorista**
   Three people were killed in an accident/a terrorist attack

4. **Mi abuelo se murió a los ochenta años**
   My grandfather died at the age of eighty

5. **Se perdió la batalla**
   The battle was lost

   No se veían las casas
   The houses could not be seen

6. **Se dice que ...**
   (It is said that) People say that ...

   No se puede entrar
   You/One can't go in

   No se permite
   It is not allowed

☐ **Reflexive Verbs** (Continued)

Conjugation of: **lavarse** *to wash oneself*

I SIMPLE TENSES

PRESENT	
(yo)	**me** lav**o**
(tú)	**te** lav**as**
(él/ella/Vd)	**se** lav**a**
(nosotros/as)	**nos** lav**amos**
(vosotros/as)	**os** lav**áis**
(ellos/as/Vds)	**se** lav**an**

IMPERFECT	
(yo)	**me** lav**aba**
(tú)	**te** lav**abas**
(él/ella/Vd)	**se** lav**aba**
(nosotros/as)	**nos** lav**ábamos**
(vosotros/as)	**os** lav**abais**
(ellos/as/Vds)	**se** lav**aban**

FUTURE	
(yo)	**me** lavar**é**
(tú)	**te** lavar**ás**
(él/ella/Vd)	**se** lavar**á**
(nosotros/as)	**nos** lavar**emos**
(vosotros/as)	**os** lavar**éis**
(ellos/as/Vds)	**se** lavar**án**

CONDITIONAL	
(yo)	**me** lavar**ía**
(tú)	**te** lavar**ías**
(él/ella/Vd)	**se** lavar**ía**
(nosotros/as)	**nos** lavar**íamos**
(vosotros/as)	**os** lavar**íais**
(ellos/as/Vds)	**se** lavar**ían**

☐ **Reflexive Verbs** (Continued)

Conjugation of: **lavarse** *to wash oneself*

I SIMPLE TENSES

PRETERITE	
(yo)	**me** lav**é**
(tú)	**te** lav**aste**
(él/ella/Vd)	**se** lav**ó**
(nosotros/as)	**nos** lav**amos**
(vosotros/as)	**os** lav**asteis**
(ellos/as/Vds)	**se** lav**aron**
PRESENT SUBJUNCTIVE	
(yo)	**me** lav**e**
(tú)	**te** lav**es**
(él/ella/Vd)	**se** lav**e**
(nosotros/as)	**nos** lav**emos**
(vosotros/as)	**os** lav**éis**
(ellos/as/Vds)	**se** lav**en**
IMPERFECT SUBJUNCTIVE	
(yo)	**me** lav**ara** *or* lav**ase**
(tú)	**te** lav**aras** *or* lav**ases**
(él/ella/Vd)	**se** lav**ara** *or* lav**ase**
(nosotros/as)	**nos** lav**áramos** *or* lav**ásemos**
(vosotros/as)	**os** lav**arais** *or* lav**aseis**
(ellos/as/Vds)	**se** lav**aran** *or* lav**asen**

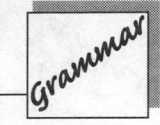

❑ **Reflexive Verbs** (Continued)

Conjugation of: **lavarse** *to wash oneself*

II COMPOUND TENSES

PERFECT

(yo)	**me he** lav**ado**
(tú)	**te has** lav**ado**
(él/ella/Vd)	**se ha** lav**ado**
(nosotros/as)	**nos hemos** lav**ado**
(vosotros/as)	**os habéis** lav**ado**
(ellos/as/Vds)	**se han** lav**ado**

PLUPERFECT

(yo)	**me había** lav**ado**
(tú)	**te habías** lav**ado**
(él/ella/Vd)	**se había** lav**ado**
(nosotros/as)	**nos habíamos** lav**ado**
(vosotros/as)	**os habíais** lav**ado**
(ellos/as/Vds)	**se habían** lav**ado**

FUTURE PERFECT

(yo)	**me habré** lav**ado**
(tú)	**te habrás** lav**ado**
(él/ella/Vd)	**se habrá** lav**ado**
(nosotros/as)	**nos habremos** lav**ado**
(vosotros/as)	**os habréis** lav**ado**
(ellos/as/Vds)	**se habrán** lav**ado**

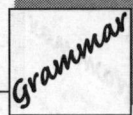

❏ **Reflexive Verbs** (Continued)

Conjugation of: **lavarse** *to wash oneself*

II COMPOUND TENSES

PAST ANTERIOR

(yo)	**me hube** lav**ado**
(tú)	**te hubiste** lav**ado**
(él/ella/Vd)	**se hubo** lav**ado**
(nosotros/as)	**nos hubimos** lav**ado**
(vosotros/as)	**os hubisteis** lav**ado**
(ellos/as/Vds)	**se hubieron** lav**ado**

PERFECT SUBJUNCTIVE

(yo)	**me haya** lav**ado**
(tú)	**te hayas** lav**ado**
(él/ella/Vd)	**se haya** lav**ado**
(nosotros/as)	**nos hayamos** lav**ado**
(vosotros/as)	**os hayáis** lav**ado**
(ellos/as/Vds)	**se hayan** lav**ado**

PLUPERFECT SUBJUNCTIVE

(yo)	**me hubiera** *or* **hubiese** lav**ado**
(tú)	**te hubieras** *or* **hubieses** lav**ado**
(él/ella/Vd)	**se hubiera** *or* **hubiese** lav**ado**
(nosotros/as)	**nos hubiéramos** *or* **hubiésemos** lav**ado**
(vosotros/as)	**os hubierais** *or* **hubieseis** lav**ado**
(ellos/as/Vds)	**se hubieran** *or* **hubiesen** lav**ado**

☐ **The Passive**

In active sentences, the subject of a verb carries out the action of that verb, but in passive sentences the subject receives the action. Compare the following:

> *The car hit Jane* (subject: *the car*)
> *Jane was hit by the car* (subject: *Jane*)

◆ English uses the verb *'to be'* with the past participle to form passive sentences. Spanish forms them in the same way, i.e.:

a tense of **ser** + past participle

The past participle agrees in number and gender with the subject → ①

A sample verb is conjugated in the passive voice on pp 36 to 39.

◆ In English, the word *'by'* usually introduces the agent through which the action of a passive sentence is performed. In Spanish this agent is preceded by **por** → ②

◆ The Passive voice is used much less frequently in Spanish than English. It is, however, often used in expressions where the identity of the agent is unknown or unimportant → ③

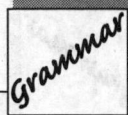

1   **Pablo ha sido despedido**
Paul has been sacked
Su madre era muy admirada
His mother was greatly admired
El palacio será vendido
The palace will be sold
Las puertas habían sido cerradas
The doors had been closed

2   **La casa fue diseñada por mi hermano**
The house was designed by my brother

3   **La ciudad fue conquistada tras un largo asedio**
The city was conquered after a long siege
Ha sido declarado el estado de excepción
A state of emergency has been declared

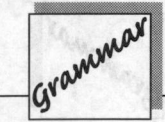

❏ **The Passive** (Continued)

In English the indirect object in an active sentence can become the subject of the related passive sentence, e.g.

> *His mother gave him the book* (indirect object: *him*)
> He was given the book by his mother

This is not possible in Spanish. The indirect object remains as such, while the object of the active sentence becomes the subject of the passive sentence → ①

Other ways to express a passive meaning

Since modern Spanish tends to avoid the passive, it uses various other constructions to replace it:

- ◆ If the agent (person or object performing the action) is known, the active is often preferred where English might prefer the passive → ②

- ◆ The 3rd person plural of the active voice can be used. The meaning is equivalent to *they* + verb → ③

- ◆ When the action of the sentence is performed on a person, the reflexive form of the verb can be used in the 3rd person singular, and the person becomes the object → ④

- ◆ When the action is performed on a thing, this becomes the subject of the sentence and the verb is made reflexive, agreeing in number with the subject → ⑤

Examples

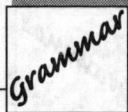

---

1. **Su madre le regaló el libro**
   His mother gave him the book

   becomes

   El libro le fue regalado por su madre
   The book was given to him by his mother

2. **La policía interrogó al sospechoso**
   The police questioned the suspect

   rather than

   El sospechoso fue interrogado por la policía

3. **Usan demasiada publicidad en la televisión**
   Too much advertising is used on television

4. **Últimamente no se le/les ha visto mucho en público**
   He has/they have not been seen much in public recently

5. **Esta palabra ya no se usa**
   This word is no longer used
   Todos los libros se han vendido
   All the books have been sold

☐ **The Passive** (Continued)

Conjugation of: **ser amado** *to be loved*

PRESENT	
(yo)	**soy** am**ado(a)**
(tú)	**eres** am**ado(a)**
(él/ella/Vd)	**es** am**ado(a)**
(nosotros/as)	**somos** am**ado(a)s**
(vosotros/as)	**sois** am**ado(a)s**
(ellos/as/Vds)	**son** am**ado(a)s**

IMPERFECT	
(yo)	**era** am**ado(a)**
(tú)	**eras** am**ado(a)**
(él/ella/Vd)	**era** am**ado(a)**
(nosotros/as)	**éramos** am**ado(a)s**
(vosotros/as)	**erais** am**ado(a)s**
(ellos/as/Vds)	**eran** am**ado(a)s**

FUTURE	
(yo)	**seré** am**ado(a)**
(tú)	**serás** am**ado(a)**
(él/ella/Vd)	**será** am**ado(a)**
(nosotros/as)	**seremos** am**ado(a)s**
(vosotros/as)	**seréis** am**ado(a)s**
(ellos/as/Vds)	**serán** am**ado(a)s**

CONDITIONAL	
(yo)	**sería** am**ado(a)**
(tú)	**serías** am**ado(a)**
(él/ella/Vd)	**sería** am**ado(a)**
(nosotros/as)	**seríamos** am**ado(a)s**
(vosotros/as)	**seríais** am**ado(a)s**
(ellos/as/Vds)	**serían** am**ado(a)s**

Examples

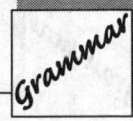
Grammar

☐ **The Passive** (Continued)

Conjugation of: **ser amado** *to be loved*

PRETERITE	
(yo)	**fui** am**ado(a)**
(tú)	**fuiste** am**ado(a)**
(él/ella/Vd)	**fue** am**ado(a)**
(nosotros/as)	**fuimos** am**ado(a)s**
(vosotros/as)	**fuisteis** am**ado(a)s**
(ellos/as/Vds)	**fueron** am**ado(a)s**

PRESENT SUBJUNCTIVE	
(yo)	**sea** am**ado(a)**
(tú)	**seas** am**ado(a)**
(él/ella/Vd)	**sea** am**ado(a)**
(nosotros/as)	**seamos** am**ado(a)s**
(vosotros/as)	**seáis** am**ado(a)s**
(ellos/as/Vds)	**sean** am**ado(a)s**

IMPERFECT SUBJUNCTIVE	
(yo)	**fuera** *or* **fuese** am**ado(a)**
(tú)	**fueras** *or* **fueses** am**ado(a)**
(él/ella/Vd)	**fuera** *or* **fuese** am**ado(a)**
(nosotros/as)	**fuéramos** *or* **fuésemos** am**ado(a)s**
(vosotros/as)	**fuerais** *or* **fueseis** am**ado(a)s**
(ellos/as/Vds)	**fueran** *or* **fuesen** am**ado(a)s**

❑ **The Passive** (Continued)

Conjugation of: **ser amado** *to be loved*

PERFECT	
(yo)	**he sido** am**ado(a)**
(tú)	**has sido** am**ado(a)**
(él/ella/Vd)	**ha sido** am**ado(a)**
(nosotros/as)	**hemos sido** am**ado(a)s**
(vosotros/as)	**habéis sido** am**ado(a)s**
(ellos/as/Vds)	**han sido** am**ado(a)s**

PLUPERFECT	
(yo)	**había sido** am**ado(a)**
(tú)	**habías sido** am**ado(a)**
(él/ella/Vd)	**había sido** am**ado(a)**
(nosotros/as)	**habíamos sido** am**ado(a)s**
(vosotros/as)	**habíais sido** am**ado(a)s**
(ellos/as/Vds)	**habían sido** am**ado(a)s**

FUTURE PERFECT	
(yo)	**habré sido** am**ado(a)**
(tú)	**habrás sido** am**ado(a)**
(él/ella/Vd)	**habrá sido** am**ado(a)**
(nosotros/as)	**habremos sido** am**ado(a)s**
(vosotros/as)	**habréis sido** am**ado(a)s**
(ellos/as/Vds)	**habrán sido** am**ado(a)s**

CONDITIONAL PERFECT	
(yo)	**habría sido** am**ado(a)**
(tú)	**habrías sido** am**ado(a)**
(él/ella/Vd)	**habría sido** am**ado(a)**
(nosotros/as)	**habríamos sido** am**ado(a)s**
(vosotros/as)	**habríais sido** am**ado(a)s**
(ellos/as/Vds)	**habrían sido** am**ado(a)s**

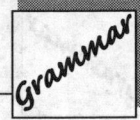

❏ **The Passive** (Continued)

Conjugation of: **ser amado** *to be loved*

PAST ANTERIOR

(yo)	**hube sido** amado(a)
(tú)	**hubiste sido** amado(a)
(él/ella/Vd)	**hubo sido** amado(a)
(nosotros/as)	**hubimos sido** amado(a)s
(vosotros/as)	**hubisteis sido** amado(a)s
(ellos/as/Vds)	**hubieron sido** amado(a)s

PERFECT SUBJUNCTIVE

(yo)	**haya sido** amado(a)
(tú)	**hayas sido** amado(a)
(él/ella/Vd)	**haya sido** amado(a)
(nosotros/as)	**hayamos sido** amado(a)s
(vosotros/as)	**hayáis sido** amado(a)s
(ellos/as/Vds)	**hayan sido** amado(a)s

PLUPERFECT SUBJUNCTIVE

(yo)	**hubiera/-se sido** amado(a)
(tú)	**hubieras/-ses sido** amado(a)
(él/ella/Vd)	**hubiera/-se sido** amado(a)
(nosotros/as)	**hubiéramos/-semos sido** amado(a)s
(vosotros/as)	**hubierais/-seis sido** amado(a)s
(ellos/as/Vds)	**hubieran/-sen sido** amado(a)s

☐ Impersonal Verbs

Impersonal verbs are used only in the infinitive, the gerund, and in the 3rd person (usually singular); unlike English, Spanish does not use the subject pronoun with impersonal verbs, e.g.

> **llueve**
> *it's raining*
>
> **es fácil decir que ...**
> *it's easy to say that ...*

The most common impersonal verbs are:

INFINITIVE	CONSTRUCTION
amanecer	**amanece/está amaneciendo**
	it's daybreak
anochecer	**anochece/está anocheciendo**
	it's getting dark
granizar	**graniza/está granizando**
	it's hailing
llover	**llueve/está lloviendo**
	it's raining → 1
lloviznar	**llovizna/está lloviznando**
	it's drizzling
nevar	**nieva/está nevando**
	it's snowing
tronar	**truena/está tronando**
	it's thundering

Some reflexive verbs are also used impersonally.
The most common are:

INFINITIVE	CONSTRUCTION
creerse	**se cree que*** + indicative → 2
	it is thought that; people think that
decirse	**se dice que*** + indicative → 3
	it is said that; people say that

Examples

☐1   **Llovía a cántaros**
It was raining cats and dogs
Estaba nevando cuando salieron
It was snowing when they left

☐2   **Se cree que llegarán mañana**
It is thought they will arrive tomorrow

☐3   **Se dice que ha sido el peor invierno en 50 años**
People say it's been the worst winter in 50 years

❏ **Impersonal Verbs** (Continued)

INFINITIVE	CONSTRUCTION
poderse	**se puede** + infinitive → ①
	one/people can, it is possible to
tratarse de	**se trata de** + noun → ②
	it's a question/matter of something
	it's about something
	se trata de + infinitive → ③
	it's a question/matter of doing;
	somebody must do
venderse	**se vende*** + noun → ④
	to be sold; for sale

* This impersonal construction conveys the same meaning as the 3rd person plural of these verbs; **creen que, dicen que, venden**

The following verbs are also commonly used in impersonal constructions:

INFINITIVE	CONSTRUCTION
bastar	**basta con** + infinitive → ⑤
	it is enough to do
	basta con + noun → ⑥
	something is enough, it only takes something
faltar	**falta** + infinitive → ⑦
	we still have to/one still has to
haber	**hay** + noun → ⑧
	there is/are
	hay que + infinitive → ⑨
	one has to/we have to
hacer	**hace** + noun/adjective depicting weather/ dark/light etc → ⑩
	it is
	hace + time expression + **que** + indicative → ⑪
	somebody has done OR *been doing something since …*
	hace + time expression + **que** + negative indicative → ⑫
	it is … since

1. **Aquí se puede aparcar**
   One can park here

2. **No se trata de dinero**
   It isn't a question/matter of money

3. **Se trata de poner fin al asunto**
   We must put an end to the matter

4. **Se vende coche**
   Car for sale

5. **Basta con telefonear para reservar un asiento**
   You need only phone to reserve a seat

6. **Basta con un error para que todo se estropee**
   One single error is enough to ruin everything

7. **Aún falta cerrar las maletas**
   We/One still have/has to close the suitcases

8. **Hay una habitación libre**
   There is one spare room

   No había cartas esta mañana
   There were no letters this morning

9. **Hay que cerrar las puertas**
   We have/One has to shut the doors

10. **Hace calor/viento/sol**
    It is hot/windy/sunny

    Mañana hará bueno
    It'll be nice (weather) tomorrow

11. **Hace seis meses que vivo/vivimos aquí**
    I/We have lived or been living here for six months

12. **Hace tres años que no le veo**
    It is three years since I last saw him

❐ Impersonal Verbs (Continued)

INFINITIVE	CONSTRUCTION
hacer falta	**hace falta** + noun object (+ indirect object) → ① *(somebody) needs something, something is necessary (to somebody)* **hace falta** + infinitive (+ indirect object) → ② *it is necessary to do* **hace falta que** + subjunctive → ③ *it is necessary to do, somebody must do*
parecer	**parece que** (+ indirect object) + indicative → ④ *it seems/appears that*
ser	**es/son** + time expression → ⑤ *it is* **es** + de día/noche → ⑥ *it is* **es** + adjective + infinitive → ⑦ *it is*
ser mejor	**es mejor** + infinitive → ⑧ *it's better to do* **es mejor que** + subjunctive → ⑨ *it's better if/that*
valer más	**más vale** + infinitive → ⑩ *it's better to do* **más vale que** + subjunctive → ⑪ *it's better to do/that somebody does*

1	**Hace falta valor para hacer eso** One needs courage to do that, Courage is needed to do that
	Me hace falta otro vaso más I need an extra glass
2	**Hace falta volver** It is necessary to return, We/I/You must return*
	Me hacía falta volver I had to return
3	**Hace falta que Vd se vaya** You have to/must leave
4	**(Me) parece que estás equivocado** It seems (to me) you are wrong
5	**Son las tres y media** It is half past three **Ya es primavera** It is spring now
6	**Era de noche cuando llegamos** It was night when we arrived
7	**Era inútil protestar** It was useless to complain
8	**Es mejor no decir nada** It's better to keep quiet
9	**Es mejor que lo pongas aquí** It's better if/that you put it here
10	**Más vale prevenir que curar** Prevention is better than cure
11	**Más valdría que no fuéramos** It would be better if we didn't go/We'd better not go

* The translation here obviously depends on context

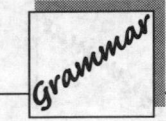

◻ **The Infinitive**

The infinitive is the form of the verb found in dictionary entries meaning *'to ...'*, e.g. **hablar** *to speak*, **vivir** *to live*.

The infinitive is used in the following ways:

◆ After a preposition → ①

◆ As a verbal noun → ②
  In this use the article may precede the infinitive, especially when the infinitive is the subject and begins the sentence → ③

◆ As a dependent infinitive, in the following verbal constructions:

  — with no linking preposition → ④

  — with the linking preposition **a** → ⑤
    (see also p 66)

  — with the linking preposition **de** → ⑥
    (see also p 66)

  — with the linking preposition **en** → ⑦
    (see also p 66)

  — with the linking preposition **con** → ⑧
    (see also p 66)

  — with the linking preposition **por** → ⑨
    (see also p 66)

◆ The following construction should also be noted: indefinite pronoun + **que** + infinitive → ⑩

◆ The object pronouns generally follow the infinitive and are attached to it. For exceptions see p 228.

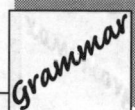

1   **Después de acabar el desayuno, salió de casa**
After finishing her breakfast she went out

Al enterarse de lo ocurrido se puso furiosa
When she found out what had happened she was furious

Me hizo daño sin saberlo
She hurt me without her knowing

2   **Su deporte preferido es montar a caballo**
Her favourite sport is horse riding

Ver es creer
Seeing is believing

3   **El viajar tanto me resulta cansado**
I find so much travelling tiring

4   **¿Quiere Vd esperar?**
Would you like to wait?

5   **Aprenderán pronto a nadar**
They will soon learn to swim

6   **Pronto dejará de llover**
It'll stop raining soon

7   **La comida tarda en hacerse**
The meal is taking a long time to cook

8   **Amenazó con denunciarles**
He threatened to report them (to the police)

9   **Comience Vd por decirme su nombre**
Please start by giving me your name

10   **Tengo algo que decirte**
I have something to tell you

❒ **The Infinitive** (Continued)

The verbs set out below are followed by the infinitive with no linking preposition.

- ◆ **deber, poder, saber, querer** and **tener que** (**hay que** in impersonal constructions) → ①

- ◆ **valer más, hacer falta:** see Impersonal Verbs, p 44.

- ◆ verbs of seeing or hearing, e.g. **ver** to see, **oír** to hear → ②

- ◆ **hacer** → ③

- ◆ **dejar** to let, allow → ③

- ◆ The following common verbs:

aconsejar	to advise → ④	
conseguir	to manage to → ⑤	
decidir	to decide	
desear	to wish, want → ⑥	
esperar	to hope → ⑦	
evitar	to avoid → ⑧	
impedir	to prevent → ⑨	
intentar	to try → ⑩	
lograr	to manage to → ⑤	
necesitar	to need → ⑪	
odiar	to hate	
olvidar	to forget → ⑫	
pensar	to think → ⑬	
preferir	to prefer → ⑭	
procurar	to try → ⑩	
prohibir	to forbid → ⑮	
prometer	to promise → ⑯	
proponer	to propose → ⑰	

Grammar

1	**¿Quiere Vd esperar?**	
	Would you like to wait?	
	No puede venir	
	She can't come	
2	**Nos ha visto llegar**	**Se les oye cantar**
	She saw us arriving	You can hear them singing
3	**No me hagas reír**	**Déjeme pasar**
	Don't make me laugh	Let me past
4	**Le aconsejamos dejarlo para mañana**	
	We advise you to leave it until tomorrow	
5	**Aún no he conseguido/logrado entenderlo**	
	I still haven't managed to understand it	
6	**No desea tener más hijos**	
	She doesn't want to have any more children	
7	**Esperamos ir de vacaciones este verano**	
	We are hoping to go on holiday this summer	
8	**Evite beber cuando conduzca**	
	Avoid drinking and driving	
9	**No pudo impedirle hablar**	
	He couldn't prevent him from speaking	
10	**Intentamos/procuramos pasar desapercibidos**	
	We tried not to be noticed	
11	**Necesitaba salir a la calle**	
	I/he/she needed to go out	
12	**Olvidó dejar su dirección**	
	He/she forgot to leave his/her address	
13	**¿Piensan venir por Navidad?**	
	Are you thinking of coming for Christmas?	
14	**Preferiría elegirlo yo mismo**	
	I'd rather choose it myself	
15	**Prohibió fumar a los alumnos**	
	He forbade the pupils to smoke	
16	**Prometieron volver pronto**	
	They promised to come back soon	
17	**Propongo salir cuanto antes**	
	I propose to leave as soon as possible	

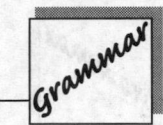

☐ The Infinitive: Set Expressions

The following are set in Spanish with the meaning shown:

dejar caer	*to drop* →	1
hacer entrar	*to show in* →	2
hacer saber	*to let know, make known* →	3
hacer salir	*to let out* →	4
hacer venir	*to send for* →	5
ir(se) a buscar	*to go for, go and get* →	6
mandar hacer	*to order* →	7
mandar llamar	*to send for* →	8
oír decir que	*to hear it said that* →	9
oír hablar de	*to hear of/about* →	10
querer decir	*to mean* →	11

The Perfect Infinitive

- The perfect infinitive is formed using the auxiliary verb **haber** with the past participle of the verb → 12

- The perfect infinitive is found:
  — following certain prepositions, especially **después de** *after* → 13
  — following certain verbal constructions → 14

Examples

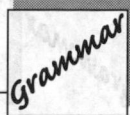

1	**Al verlo, dejó caer lo que llevaba en las manos**
	When he saw him he dropped what he was carrying
2	**Haz entrar a nuestros invitados**
	Show our guests in
3	**Quiero hacerles saber que no serán bien recibidos**
	I want to let them know that they won't be welcome
4	**Hágale salir, por favor**
	Please let him out
5	**Le he hecho venir a Vd porque ...**
	I sent for you because ...
6	**Vete a buscar los guantes**
	Go and get your gloves
7	**Me he mandado hacer un traje**
	I have ordered a suit
8	**Mandaron llamar al médico**
	They sent for the doctor
9	**He oído decir que está enfermo**
	I've heard it said that he's ill
10	**No he oído hablar más de él**
	I haven't heard anything more (said) of him
11	**¿Qué quiere decir eso?**
	What does that mean?
12	**haber terminado** **haberse vestido**
	to have finished to have got dressed
13	**Después de haber comprado el regalo, volvió a casa**
	After buying/having bought the present, he went back home
	Después de haber madrugado tanto, el taxi se retrasó
	After she got up so early, the taxi arrived late
14	**perdonar a alguien por haber hecho**
	to forgive somebody for doing/having done
	dar las gracias a alguien por haber hecho
	to thank somebody for doing/having done
	pedir perdón por haber hecho
	to be sorry for doing/having done

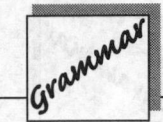

☐ The Gerund

Formation

- ◆ 1st conjugation
  Replace the **-ar** of the infinitive by **-ando** → ①
- ◆ 2nd conjugation
  Replace the **-er** of the infinitive by **-iendo** → ②
- ◆ 3rd conjugation
  Replace the **-ir** of the infinitive by **-iendo** → ③
- ◆ For irregular gerunds, see irregular verbs, p 80 ff.

Uses

- ◆ After the verb **estar**, to form the continuous tenses → ④
- ◆ After the verbs **seguir** and **continuar** *to continue*, and **ir** when meaning *to happen gradually* → ⑤
- ◆ In time constructions, after **llevar** → ⑥
- ◆ When the action in the main clause needs to be complemented by another action → ⑦
- ◆ The position of object pronouns is the same as for the infinitive (see p 46).
- ◆ The gerund is invariable and strictly verbal in sense.

☐ The Present Participle

- ◆ It is formed by replacing the **-ar** of the infinitive of 1st conjugation verbs by **-ante**, and the **-er** and **-ir** of the 2nd and 3rd conjugations by **-iente** → ⑧
- ◆ A very limited number of verbs have a present participle, which is either used as an adjective or a noun → ⑨/⑩

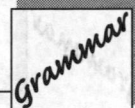

1   **cantar** → **cantando**
    to sing   singing

2   **temer** → **temiendo**
    to fear   fearing

3   **partir** → **partiendo**
    to leave   leaving

4   **Estoy escribiendo una carta**
    I am writing a letter
    Estaban esperándonos
    They were waiting for us

5   **Sigue viniendo todos los días**
    He/she is still coming every day
    Continuarán subiendo los precios
    Prices will continue to go up
    El ejército iba avanzando poco a poco
    The army was gradually advancing

6   **Lleva dos años estudiando inglés**
    He/she has been studying English for two years

7   **Pasamos el día tomando el sol en la playa**
    We spent the day sunbathing on the beach
    Iba cojeando
    He/she/I was limping
    Salieron corriendo
    They ran out

8   **cantar** → **cantante**
    to sing   singing/singer

    pender → **pendiente**
    to hang   hanging

    seguir → **siguiente**
    to follow   following

9   **agua corriente**
    running water

10 **un estudiante**
    a student

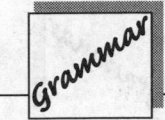

❑ Use of Tenses

The Present

- Unlike English, Spanish often uses the same verb form for the simple present (e.g. *I smoke, he reads, we live*) and the continuous present (e.g. *I am smoking, he is reading, we are living*) → ①

- Normally, however, the continuous present is used to translate the English:

    to be doing   **estar haciendo** → ②

- Spanish uses the present tense where English uses the perfect in the following cases:

    — with certain prepositions of time – notably **desde** *for/since* – when an action begun in the past is continued in the present → ③

    ⚠ NOTE: The perfect can be used as in English when the verb is negative → ④

    — in the construction **acabar de hacer** *to have just done* → ⑤

- Like English, Spanish often uses the present where a future action is implied → ⑥

The Future

The future is generally used as in English → 7, but note the following:

- Immediate future time is often expressed by means of the present tense of **ir** + **a** + infinitive → ⑧

- When '*will*' or '*shall*' mean '*wish to*', '*are willing to*', **querer** is used → ⑨

The Future Perfect

- Used as in English *shall/will have done* → ⑩

- It can also express conjecture, usually about things in the recent past → ⑪

☐1	**Fumo** I smoke OR: I am smoking
	Lee He reads OR: He is reading
	Vivimos We live OR: We are living
☐2	**Está fumando**
	He is smoking
☐3	**Linda estudia español desde hace seis meses**
	Linda's been learning Spanish for six months (*and still is*)
	Estoy de pie desde las siete
	I've been up since seven
	¿Hace mucho que esperan?
	Have you been waiting long?
	Ya hace dos semanas que estamos aquí
	That's two weeks we've been here (now)
☐4	**No se han visto desde hace meses**
	They haven't seen each other for months
☐5	**Isabel acaba de salir**
	Isabel has just left
☐6	**Mañana voy a Madrid**
	I am going to Madrid tomorrow
☐7	**Lo haré mañana**
	I'll do it tomorrow
☐8	**Te vas a caer si no tienes cuidado**
	You'll fall if you're not careful
	Va a perder el tren
	He's going to miss the train
	Va a llevar una media hora
	It'll take about half an hour
☐9	**¿Me quieres esperar un momento, por favor?**
	Will you wait for me a second, please?
☐10	**Lo habré acabado para mañana**
	I will have finished it for tomorrow
☐11	**Ya habrán llegado a casa**
	They must have arrived home by now

❏ **Use of Tenses** (Continued)

The Imperfect

- The imperfect describes:
  - an action or state in the past without definite limits in time → ①
  - habitual action(s) in the past (often expressed in English by means of *would* or *used to*) → ②

- Spanish uses the imperfect tense where English uses the pluperfect in the following cases:
  - with certain prepositions of time – notably **desde** *for/since* – when an action begun in the remoter past was continued in the more recent past → ③

  ⚠ NOTE: The pluperfect is used as in English when the verb is negative or the action has been completed → ④
  - in the construction **acabar de hacer** *to have just done* → ⑤

- Both the continuous and simple forms in English can be translated by the Spanish simple imperfect, but the continuous imperfect is used when the emphasis is on the fact that an action was going on at a precise moment in the past → ⑥

The Perfect

- The perfect is generally used as in English → ⑦

The Preterite

- The preterite generally corresponds to the English simple past in both written and spoken Spanish → ⑧

  However, while English can use the simple past to describe habitual actions or settings, Spanish uses the imperfect (see above) → ⑨

The Past Anterior

- This tense is only ever used in written, literary Spanish, to replace the pluperfect in time clauses where the verb in the main clause is in the preterite → ⑩

Examples

1	**Todos mirábamos en silencio** We were all watching in silence **Nuestras habitaciones daban a la playa** Our rooms overlooked the beach
2	**En su juventud se levantaba de madrugada** In his youth he got up at dawn **Hablábamos sin parar durante horas** We would talk non-stop for hours on end **Mi hermano siempre me tomaba el pelo** My brother always used to tease me
3	**Hacía dos años que vivíamos en Irlanda** We had been living in Ireland for two years **Estaba enfermo desde 1990** He had been ill since 1990 **Hacía mucho tiempo que salían juntos** They had been going out together for a long time
4	**Hacía un año que no le había visto** I hadn't seen him for a year **Hacía una hora que había llegado** She had arrived an hour before
5	**Acababa de encontrármelos** I had just met them
6	**Cuando llegué, todos estaban fumando** When I arrived, they were all smoking
7	**Todavía no han salido** They haven't come out yet
8	**Me desperté y salté de la cama** I woke up and jumped out of bed
9	**Siempre iban en coche al trabajo** They always travelled to work by car
10	**Apenas hubo acabado, se oyeron unos golpes en la puerta** She had scarcely finished when there was a knock at the door

❏ The Subjunctive: when to use it

(For how to form the subjunctive see pp 6 ff.)

◆ After verbs of:

— 'wishing'

querer que } to wish that, want → ①
desear que

— 'emotion' (e.g. regret, surprise, shame, pleasure, etc)
sentir que to be sorry that → ②
sorprender que to be surprised that → ③
alegrarse de que to be pleased that → ④

— 'asking' and 'advising'
pedir que to ask that → ⑤
aconsejar que to advise that → ⑥

In all the above constructions, when the subject of the verbs in the main and subordinate clause is the same, the infinitive is used, and the conjunction **que** omitted → ⑦

— 'ordering', 'forbidding', 'allowing'

mandar que* } to order that → ⑧
ordenar que

permitir que* } to allow that → ⑨
dejar que*

prohibir que* to forbid that → ⑩
impedir que* to prevent that → ⑪

* With these verbs either the subjunctive or the infinitive is used when the object of the main verb is the subject of the subordinate verb → ⑫

◆ Always after verbs expressing doubt or uncertainty, and verbs of opinion used negatively

dudar que to doubt that → ⑬
no creer que } not to think that → ⑭
no pensar que

Examples

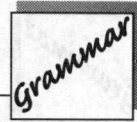

1. **Queremos que esté contenta**
We want her to be happy (literally: We want that she is happy)
¿Desea Vd que lo haga yo?
Do you want me to do it?

2. **Sentí mucho que no vinieran**
I was very sorry that they didn't come

3. **Nos sorprendió que no les vieran Vds**
We were surprised you didn't see them

4. **Me alegro de que te gusten**
I'm pleased that you like them

5. **Solo les pedimos que tengan cuidado**
We're only asking you to take care

6. **Le aconsejé que no llegara tarde**
I advised him not to be late

7. **Quiero que lo termines pronto**
I want you to finish it soon
⚠ BUT: **Quiero terminarlo pronto**
I want to finish it soon

8. **Ha mandado que vuelvan**
He has ordered them to come back
Ordenó que fueran castigados
He ordered them to be punished

9. **No permitas que te tomen el pelo**
Don't let them pull your leg
No me dejó que la llevara a casa
She didn't allow me to take her home

10. **Te prohíbo que digas eso**
I forbid you to say that

11. **No les impido que vengan**
I am not preventing them from coming

12. **Les ordenó que salieran** OR: **Les ordenó salir**
She ordered them to go out

13. **Dudo que lo sepan hacer**
I doubt they can do it

14. **No creo que sean tan listos**
I don't think they are as clever as that

☐ The Subjunctive: when to use it (Continued)

- In impersonal constructions which express necessity, possibility, etc:

  hace falta que } *it is necessary that* → ☐1
  es necesario que

  es posible que *it is possible that* → ☐2

  más vale que *it is better that* → ☐3

  es una lástima que *it is a pity that* → ☐4

  ⚠ NOTE: In impersonal constructions which state a fact or express certainty the indicative is used when the impersonal verb is affirmative. When it is negative, the subjunctive is used → ☐5

- After certain conjunctions

  para que } *so that* → ☐6
  a fin de que*

  como si *as if* → ☐7

  sin que* *without* → ☐8

  a condición de que* }
  con tal (de) que* *provided that,*
  siempre que *on condition that* → ☐9

  a menos que }
  a no ser que *unless* → ☐10

  antes (de) que* *before* → ☐11

  no sea que *lest/in case* → ☐12

  mientras (que) }
  siempre que *as long as* → ☐13

  (el) que *the fact that* → ☐14

* When the subject of both verbs is the same, the infinitive is used, and the final **que** is omitted → ☐8

1	**¿Hace falta que vaya Jaime?**
	Does James have to go?
2	**Es posible que tengan razón**
	It's possible that they are right
3	**Más vale que se quede Vd en su casa**
	It's better that you stay at home
4	**Es una lástima que haya perdido su perrito**
	It's a shame/pity that she has lost her puppy
5	**Es verdad que va a venir**
	It's true that he's coming
	⚠ BUT: **No es verdad que vayan a hacerlo**
	It's not true that they are going to do it
6	**Átalas bien para que no se caigan**
	Tie them up tightly so that they won't fall
7	**Hablaba como si no creyera en sus propias palabras**
	He talked as if he didn't believe in his own words
8	**Salimos sin que nos vieran**
	We left without them seeing us
	⚠ BUT: **Me fui sin esperarla**
	I went without waiting for her
9	**Lo haré con tal de que me cuentes todo lo que pasó**
	I'll do it provided you tell me all that happened
10	**Saldremos de paseo a menos que esté lloviendo**
	We'll go for a walk unless it's raining
11	**Avísale antes de que sea demasiado tarde**
	Warn him before it's too late
12	**Habla en voz baja, no sea que alguien nos oiga**
	Speak softly in case anyone hears us
13	**Eso no pasará mientras yo sea el jefe aquí**
	That won't happen as long as I am the boss here
14	**El que no me escribiera no me importaba demasiado**
	The fact that he didn't write didn't matter to me too much

☐ **The Subjunctive: when to use it** (Continued)

◆ After the conjunctions

> **de modo que**
> **de forma que** ⎫ *so that* (indicating a purpose) → ①
> **de manera que** ⎭

⚠ NOTE: When these conjunctions introduce a result and not a purpose the subjunctive is not used → ②

◆ In relative clauses with an antecedent which is:

— negative → ③

— indefinite → ④

— non-specific → ⑤

◆ In main clauses, to express a wish or exhortation. The verb may be preceded by expressions like **ojalá** or **que** → ⑥

◆ In the **si** clause of conditions where the English sentence contains a conditional tense → ⑦

◆ In set expressions → ⑧

◆ In the following constructions which translate *however*:

— **por** + adjective + subjunctive → ⑨

— **por** + adverb + subjunctive → ⑩

— **por** + **mucho** + subjunctive → ⑪

1	**Vuélvanse de manera que les vea bien**
	Turn round so that I can see you properly
2	**No quieren hacerlo, de manera que tendré que hacerlo yo**
	They won't do it, so I'll have to do it myself
3	**No he encontrado a nadie que la conociera**
	I haven't met anyone who knows her
	No dijo nada que no supiéramos ya
	He/she didn't say anything we didn't already know
4	**Necesito alguien que sepa conducir**
	I need someone who can drive
	Busco algo que me distraiga
	I'm looking for something to take my mind off it
5	**Busca una casa que tenga calefacción central**
	He/she's looking for a house which has central heating
	(*subjunctive used since such a house may or may not exist*)
	El que lo haya visto tiene que decírmelo
	Anyone who has seen it must tell me
	(*subjunctive used since it is not known who has seen it*)
6	**¡Ojalá haga buen tiempo!**
	Let's hope the weather will be good!
	¡Que te diviertas!
	Have a good time!
7	**Si fuéramos en coche llegaríamos a tiempo**
	If we went by car we'd be there in time
8	**Diga lo que diga ...** **Sea lo que sea ...**
	Whatever he may say ... Be that as it may ...
	Pase lo que pase ... **Sea como sea ...**
	Come what may ... One way or another ...
9	**Por cansado que esté, seguirá trabajando**
	No matter how/however tired he may be, he'll go on working
10	**Por lejos que viva, iremos a buscarle**
	No matter how/however far away he lives, we'll go and look for him
11	**Por mucho que lo intente, nunca lo conseguirá**
	No matter how/however hard he tries, he'll never succeed

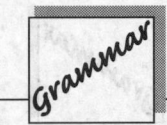

❑ **The Subjunctive: when to use it** (Continued)

Clauses taking either a subjunctive or an indicative

In certain constructions, a subjunctive is needed when the action refers to future events or hypothetical situations, whereas an indicative is used when stating a fact or experience → 1

The commonest of these are:

- The conjunctions

cuando	*when* → 1
en cuanto **tan pronto como** }	*as soon as* → 2
después (de) que*	*after* → 3
hasta que	*until* → 4
mientras	*while* → 5
siempre que	*whenever* → 6
aunque	*even though* → 7

  All conjunctions and pronouns ending in **-quiera** (*-ever*) → 8

  * ⚠ NOTE: If the subject of both verbs is the same, the subjunctive introduced by **después (de) que** may be replaced by **después de** + infinitive → 9

Sequence of tenses in Subordinate Clauses

- If the verb in the main clause is in the present, future or imperative, the verb in the dependent clause will be in the present or perfect subjunctive → 10

- If the verb in the main clause is in the conditional or any past tense, the verb in the dependent clause will be in the imperfect or pluperfect subjunctive → 11

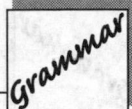

1. **Le aconsejé que oyera música cuando estuviera nervioso**
   I advised him to listen to music when he felt nervous
   Me gusta nadar cuando hace calor
   I like to swim when it is warm

2. **Te devolveré el libro tan pronto como lo haya leído**
   I'll give you back the book as soon as I have read it

3. **Te lo diré después de que te hayas sentado**
   I'll tell you after you've sat down

4. **Quédate aquí hasta que volvamos**
   Stay here until we come back

5. **No hablen en voz alta mientras estén ellos aquí**
   Don't speak loudly while they are here

6. **Vuelvan por aquí siempre que quieran**
   Come back whenever you wish to

7. **No le creeré aunque diga la verdad**
   I won't believe him even if he tells the truth

8. **La encontraré dondequiera que esté**
   I will find her wherever she might be

9. **Después de cenar nos fuimos al cine**
   After dinner we went to the cinema

10. **Quiero que lo hagas** (*pres + pres subj*)
    I want you to do it
    Temo que no haya venido (*pres + perf subj*)
    I fear he hasn't come (might not have come)
    Iremos por aquí para que no nos vean
    (*future + pres subj*)
    We'll go this way so that they won't see us

11. **Me gustaría que llegaras temprano**
    (*cond + imperf subj*)
    I'd like you to arrive early
    Les pedí que me esperaran (*preterite + imperf subj*)
    I asked them to wait for me
    Sentiría mucho que hubiese muerto
    (*cond + pluperf subj*)
    I would be very sorry if he were dead

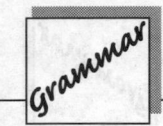

❐ Verbs governing a, de, con, en, por and para

The following lists (pp 66 to 73) contain common verbal constructions using the prepositions **a, de, con, en, por** and **para**.

Note the following abbreviations:

infin	infinitive
perf infin	perfect infinitive*
algn	alguien
sb	somebody
sth	something

* For formation see p 50

aburrirse de + infin	*to get bored with doing* → ①
acabar con algo/algn	*to put an end to sth/finish with sb* → ②
acabar de* + infin	*to have just done* → ③
acabar por + infin	*to end up doing* → ④
acercarse a algo/algn	*to approach sth/sb*
acordarse de algo/algn/de + infin	*to remember sth/sb/doing* → ⑤
acostumbrarse a algo/algn/a + infin	*to get used to sth/sb/to doing* → ⑥
acusar a algn de algo/de + perf infin	*to accuse sb of sth/of doing, having done* → ⑦
advertir a algn de algo	*to notify, warn sb about sth* → ⑧
aficionarse a algo/a + infin	*to grow fond of sth/of doing* → ⑨
alegrarse de algo/de + perf infin	*to be glad about sth/of doing, having done* → ⑩
alejarse de algn/algo	*to move away from sb/sth*
amenazar a algn con algo/ con + infin	*to threaten sb with sth/to do* → ⑪
animar a algn a + infin	*to encourage sb to do*
apresurarse a + infin	*to hurry to do* → ⑫

* See also Use of Tenses, pp 54 and 56

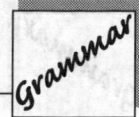

1   **Me aburría de no poder salir de casa**
I used to get bored with not being able to leave the house

2   **Quiso acabar con su vida**
He wanted to put an end to his life

3   **Acababan de llegar cuando ...**
They had just arrived when ...

4   **El acusado acabó por confesarlo todo**
The accused ended up by confessing everything

5   **Nos acordamos muy bien de aquellas vacaciones**
We remember that holiday very well

6   **Me he acostumbrado a levantarme temprano**
I've got used to getting up early

7   **Le acusó de haber mentido**
She accused him of lying

8   **Advertí a mi amigo del peligro que corría**
I warned my friend about the danger he was in

9   **Nos hemos aficionado a la música clásica**
We've grown fond of classical music

10   **Me alegro de haberle conocido**
I'm glad I met him

11   **Amenazó con denunciarles**
He threatened to report them

12   **Se apresuraron a coger sitio**
They hurried to find a seat

❐ Verbs governing a, de, con, en, por and para
(Continued)

aprender a + infin	*to learn to do* → 1
aprovecharse de algo/algn	*to take advantage of sth/sb*
aproximarse a algn/algo	*to approach sb/sth*
asistir a algo	*to attend sth, be at sth*
asomarse a/por	*to lean out of* → 2
asombrarse de + infin	*to be surprised at doing* → 3
atreverse a + infin	*to dare to do*
avergonzarse de algo/algn/de + perf infin	*to be ashamed of sth/sb/of doing, having done* → 4
ayudar a algn a + infin	*to help sb to do* → 5
bajarse de (+ place/vehicle)	*to get off/out of* → 6
burlarse de algn	*to make fun of sb*
cansarse de algo/algn/de + infin	*to tire of sth/sb/of doing*
carecer de algo	*to lack sth* → 7
cargar de algo	*to load with sth* → 8
casarse con algn	*to get married to sb* → 9
cesar de + infin	*to stop doing*
chocar con algo	*to crash/bump into sth* → 10
comenzar a + infin	*to begin to do*
comparar con algn/algo	*to compare with sb/sth*
consentir en + infin	*to agree to do*
consistir en + infin	*to consist of doing* → 11
constar de algo	*to consist of sth* → 12
contar con algn/algo	*to rely on sb/sth* → 13
convenir en + infin	*to agree to do* → 14
darse cuenta de algo	*to realize sth*
dejar de + infin	*to stop doing* → 15
depender de algo/algn	*to depend on sth/sb* → 16
despedirse de algn	*to say goodbye to sb*
dirigirse a + place/**a algn**	*to head for/address sb*
disponerse a + infin	*to get ready to do*
empezar a + infin	*to begin to do*
empezar por + infin	*to begin by doing* → 17

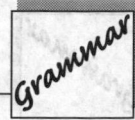
①	**Me gustaría aprender a nadar**	
	I'd like to learn to swim	
②	**No te asomes a la ventana**	
	Don't lean out of the window	
③	**Nos asombramos mucho de verles ahí**	
	We were very surprised at seeing them there	
④	**No me avergüenzo de haberlo hecho**	
	I'm not ashamed of having done it	
⑤	**Ayúdeme a llevar estas maletas**	
	Help me to carry these cases	
⑥	**Se bajó del coche**	
	He got out of the car	
⑦	**La casa carecía de jardín**	
	The house lacked (did not have) a garden	
⑧	**El carro iba cargado de paja**	
	The cart was loaded with straw	
⑨	**Se casó con Andrés**	
	She married Andrew	
⑩	**Enciende la luz, o chocarás con la puerta**	
	Turn the light on, or you'll bump into the door	
⑪	**Mi plan consistía en vigilarles de cerca**	
	My plan consisted of keeping a close eye on them	
⑫	**El examen consta de tres partes**	
	The exam consists of three parts	
⑬	**Cuento contigo para que me ayudes a hacerlo**	
	I rely on you to help me do it	
⑭	**Convinieron en reunirse al día siguiente**	
	They agreed to meet the following day	
⑮	**¿Quieres dejar de hablar?**	
	Will you stop talking?	
⑯	**No depende de mí**	
	It doesn't depend on me	
⑰	**Empieza por enterarte de lo que se trata**	
	Begin by finding out what it is about	

❐ Verbs governing a, de, con, en, por and para
(Continued)

encontrarse con algn	*to meet sb (by chance)* → 1
enfadarse con algn	*to get annoyed with sb*
enseñar a algn a + infin	*to teach sb to* → 2
enterarse de algo	*to find out about sth* → 3
entrar en (+ place)	*to enter, go into*
esperar a + infin	*to wait until* → 4
estar de acuerdo con algn/algo	*to agree with sb/sth*
fiarse de algn/algo	*to trust sb/sth*
fijarse en algo/algn	*to notice sth/sb* → 5
hablar con algn	*to talk to sb* → 6
hacer caso a algn	*to pay attention to sb*
hartarse de algo/algn/de + infin	*to get fed up with sth/sb/with doing* → 7
interesarse por algo/algn	*to be interested in sth/sb* → 8
invitar a algn a + infin	*to invite sb to do*
jugar a (+ sports, games)	*to play*
luchar por algo/por + infin	*to fight, strive for/to do* → 9
llegar a (+ place)/**a** + infin	*to reach/to manage to do* → 10
llenar de algo	*to fill with sth*
negarse a + infin	*to refuse to do* → 11
obligar a algn a + infin	*to make sb do* → 12
ocuparse de algn/algo	*to take care of sb/attend to sth*
oler a algo	*to smell of sth* → 13
olvidarse de algo/algn/de + infin	*to forget sth/sb/to do* → 14
oponerse a algo/a + infin	*to be opposed to sth/to doing*
parecerse a algn/algo	*to resemble sb/sth*
pensar en algo/algn/en + infin	*to think about sth/sb/about doing* → 15
preguntar por algn	*to ask for/about sb*
preocuparse de *or* **por algo/algn**	*to worry about sth/sb* → 16

Examples

1	**Me encontré con ella al entrar en el banco** I met her as I was entering the bank
2	**Le estoy enseñando a nadar** I am teaching him to swim
3	**¿Te has enterado del sitio adonde hay que ir?** Have you found out where we have to go?
4	**Espera a saber lo que quiere antes de comprar el regalo** Wait until you know what he wants before buying the present
5	**Me fijé en él cuando subía a su coche** I noticed him when he was getting into his car
6	**¿Puedo hablar con Vd un momento?** May I talk to you for a moment?
7	**Me he hartado de escribirle** I've got fed up with writing to him
8	**Me interesaba mucho por la arqueología** I was very interested in archaeology
9	**Hay que luchar por mantener la paz** One must strive to preserve peace
10	**Lo intenté sin llegar a conseguirlo** I tried without managing to do it
11	**Se negó a hacerlo** He refused to do it
12	**Le obligó a sentarse** He made him sit down
13	**Este perfume huele a jazmín** This perfume smells of jasmine
14	**Siempre me olvido de cerrar la puerta** I always forget to shut the door
15	**No quiero pensar en eso** I don't want to think about that
16	**Se preocupa mucho de/por su apariencia** He worries a lot about his appearance

❏ Verbs governing a, de, con, en, por and para
(Continued)

prepararse a + infin	*to prepare to do*
probar a + infin	*to try to do*
quedar en + infin	*to agree to do* → ①
quedar por + infin	*to remain to be done* → ②
quejarse de algo	*to complain of sth*
referirse a algo	*to refer to sth*
reírse de algo/algn	*to laugh at sth/sb*
rodear de	*to surround with* → ③
romper a + infin	*to (suddenly) start to do* → ④
salir de (+ place)	*to leave*
sentarse a (+ table etc)	*to sit down at*
subir(se) a (+ vehicle/place)	*to get on, into/to climb* → ⑤
servir de algo a algn	*to be useful to/serve sb as sth* → ⑥
servir para algo/para + infin	*to be good as sth/for doing* → ⑦
servirse de algo	*to use sth* → ⑧
soñar con algn/algo/con + infin	*to dream about/of sb/sth/of doing*
sorprenderse de algo	*to be surprised at sth*
tardar en + infin	*to take time to do* → ⑨
tener ganas de algo/de + infin	*to want sth/to do* → ⑩
tener miedo de algo	*to be afraid of sth* → ⑪
tener miedo a algn	*to be afraid of sb* → ⑫
terminar por + infin	*to end by doing*
tirar de algo/algn	*to pull sth/sb*
trabajar de (+ occupation)	*to work as* → ⑬
trabajar en (+ place of work)	*to work at/in* → ⑭
traducir a (+ language)	*to translate into*
tratar de + infin	*to try to do* → ⑮
tratarse de algo/algn/de + infin	*to be a question of sth/about sb/about doing* → ⑯
vacilar en + infin	*to hesitate to do* → ⑰
volver a + infin	*to do again* → ⑱

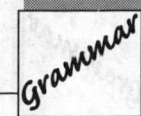
1	**Habíamos quedado en encontrarnos a las 8** We had agreed to meet at 8
2	**Queda por averiguar dónde se ocultan** It remains to be discovered where they are hiding
3	**Habían rodeado el jardín de un seto de cipreses** They had surrounded the garden with a hedge of cypress trees
4	**Al apagarse la luz, el niño rompió a llorar** When the lights went out, the little boy suddenly started to cry
5	**¡De prisa, sube al coche!** Get into the car, quick!
6	**Esto me servirá de bastón** This will serve me as a walking stick
7	**No sirvo para (ser) jardinero** I'm no good as a gardener
8	**Se sirvió de un destornillador para abrirlo** She used a screwdriver to open it
9	**Tardaron mucho en salir** They took a long time to come out
10	**Tengo ganas de volver a España** I want to go back to Spain
11	**Mi hija tiene miedo de la oscuridad** My daughter is afraid of the dark
12	**Nunca tuvieron miedo a su padre** They were never afraid of their father
13	**Pedro trabaja de camarero en Londres** Peter works as a waiter in London
14	**Trabajaba en una oficina** I used to work in an office
15	**No trates de engañarme** Don't try to fool me
16	**Se trata de nuestro nuevo vecino** It's about our new neighbour
17	**Nunca vacilaban en pedir dinero** They never hesitated to borrow money
18	**No vuelvas a hacerlo nunca más** Don't ever do it again

❐ Ser and Estar

Spanish has two verbs – **ser** and **estar** – for *to be*.

They are not interchangeable and each one is used in defined contexts.

ser is used:

- ◆ With an adjective, to express a permanent or inherent quality → ①
- ◆ To express occupation or nationality → ②
- ◆ To express possession → ③
- ◆ To express origin or the material from which something is made → ④
- ◆ With a noun, pronoun or infinitive following the verb → ⑤
- ◆ To express the time and date → ⑥
- ◆ To form the passive, with the past participle (see p 32).

⚠ NOTE: This use emphasizes the action of the verb. If, however, the resultant state or condition needs to be emphasized, **estar** is used. The past participle then functions as an adjective (see p 204) and has to agree in gender and in number with the noun → ⑦

estar is used:

- ◆ Always, to indicate place or location → ⑧
- ◆ With an adjective or adjectival phrase, to express a quality or state seen by the speaker as subject to change or different from expected → ⑨
- ◆ When speaking of a person's state of health → ⑩
- ◆ To form the continuous tenses, used with the gerund (see p 52) → ⑪
- ◆ With **de** + noun, to indicate a temporary occupation → ⑫

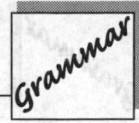

①	**Mi hermano es alto**	**María es inteligente**
	My brother is tall	Mary is intelligent
②	**Javier es aviador**	**Sus padres son italianos**
	Javier is an airman	His parents are Italian
③	**La casa es de Miguel**	
	The house belongs to Michael	
④	**Mi hermana es de Granada**	**Las paredes son de ladrillo**
	My sister is from Granada	The walls are made of brick
⑤	**Andrés es un niño travieso**	
	Andrew is a naughty boy	
	Soy yo, Enrique	
	It's me, Henry	
	Todo es proponérselo	
	It's all a question of putting your mind to it	
⑥	**Son las tres y media**	**Mañana es sábado**
	It's half past three	Tomorrow is Saturday
⑦	**Las puertas eran cerradas sigilosamente**	
	The doors were being silently closed	
	Las puertas estaban cerradas	
	The doors were closed (*resultant action*)	
⑧	**La comida está en la mesa**	
	The meal is on the table	
⑨	**Su amigo está enfermo**	**El lavabo está ocupado**
	Her friend is ill	The toilet is engaged
	Hoy estoy de mal humor	**Las tiendas están cerradas**
	I'm in a bad mood today	The shops are closed
⑩	**¿Cómo están Vds?**	**Estamos todos bien**
	How are you?	We are all well
⑪	**Estamos aprendiendo mucho**	
	We are learning a great deal	
⑫	**Mi primo está de médico en un pueblo**	
	My cousin works as a doctor in a village	

❏ **Ser and Estar** (Continued)

With certain adjectives, both **ser** and **estar** can be used, although they are not interchangeable when used in this way:

— **ser** will express a permanent or inherent quality → ①

— **estar** will express a temporary state or quality → ②

Both **ser** and **estar** may also be used in set expressions.

The commonest of these are:

◆ With **ser**

Sea como sea	*Be that as it may*
Es igual/Es lo mismo	*It's all the same*
llegar a ser	*to become*
¿Cómo fue eso?	*How did that happen?*
¿Qué ha sido de él?	*What has become of him?*
ser para (with the idea of purpose)	*to be for* → ③

◆ With **estar**

estar de pie/de rodillas	*to be standing/kneeling*
estar de viaje	*to be travelling*
estar de vacaciones	*to be on holiday*
estar de vuelta	*to be back*
estar de moda	*to be in fashion*
Está bien	*It's all right*
estar para	*to be about to do sth/to be in a mood for* → ④
estar por	*to be inclined to/to be (all) for* → ⑤
estar a punto de	*to be just about to do sth* → ⑥

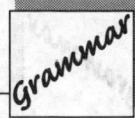

1   **Su hermana es muy joven/vieja**
His sister is very young/old
Son muy ricos/pobres
They are very rich/poor
Su amigo era un enfermo
His friend was an invalid
Es un borracho
He is a drunkard
Mi hijo es bueno/malo
My son is good/naughty
Viajar es cansado
Travelling is tiring

2   **Está muy joven/vieja con ese vestido**
She looks very young/old in that dress
Ahora están muy ricos/pobres
They have become very rich/poor lately
Estaba enfermo
He was ill
Está borracho
He is drunk
Está bueno/malo
He is well/ill
Hoy estoy cansada
I am tired today

3   **Este paquete es para Vd**
This parcel is for you
Esta caja es para guardar semillas
This box is for keeping seeds in

4   **Están para llegar**
They're about to arrive

5   **Estoy por irme a vivir a España**
I'm inclined to go and live in Spain

6   **Las rosas están a punto de salir**
The roses are about to come out

☐ Verbal Idioms

Special Intransitive Verbs

With the following verbs the Spanish construction is the opposite of the English. The subject in English becomes the indirect object of the Spanish verb, while the object in English becomes the subject of the Spanish verb.

Compare the following:

> *I like that house* (subject: *I*, object: *that house*)
> **Esa casa me gusta** (subject: **esa casa**, indirect object: **me**)

The commonest of these verbs are:

gustar	*to like* → ①
gustar más	*to prefer* → ②
encantar	(colloquial) *to love* → ③
faltar	*to need/to be short of/to have missing* → ④
quedar	*to be/have left* → ⑤
doler	*to have a pain in/to hurt, ache* → ⑥
interesar	*to be interested in* → ⑦
importar	*to mind* → ⑧

Examples

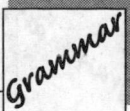

1. **Me gusta este vestido**
   I like this dress (This dress pleases me)

2. **Me gustan más éstas**
   I prefer these

3. **Nos encanta hacer deporte**
   We love sport

4. **Me faltaban 100 pesetas**
   I was short of 100 pesetas

   Sólo le falta el toque final
   It just needs the finishing touch

   Le faltaban tres dientes
   He/she had three teeth missing

5. **Sólo nos quedan dos kilómetros**
   We only have two kilometres (left) to go

6. **Me duele la cabeza**
   I have a headache

7. **Nos interesa mucho la política**
   We are very interested in politics

8. **No me importa la lluvia**
   I don't mind the rain

☐ **Irregular Verbs**

The verbs listed opposite and conjugated on pp 82 to 161 provide the main patterns for irregular verbs. The verbs are grouped opposite according to their infinitive ending and are shown in the following tables in alphabetical order.

In the tables, the most important irregular verbs are given in their most common simple tenses, together with the imperative and the gerund.

The past participle is also shown for each verb, to enable you to form all the compound tenses, as on pp 18 to 23.

The pronouns **ella** and **Vd** take the same verb endings as **él**, while **ellas** and **Vds** take the same endings as **ellos**.

◆   All the verbs included in the tables differ from the three conjugations set out on pp 8 to 13. Many – e.g. **contar** – serve as models for groups of verbs, while others – e.g. **ir** – are unique. On pp 162 to 186 you will find over 2,800 commonly used verbs listed alphabetically and cross-referred either to the relevant basic conjugation or to the appropriate model in the verb tables.

Imperfect Subjunctive of Irregular Verbs

For verbs with an irregular root form in the preterite tense – e.g. **andar** → **anduvieron** – the imperfect subjunctive is formed by using the root form of the 3rd person plural of the preterite tense, and adding the imperfect subjunctive endings **-iera/-iese** etc where the verb has an 'i' in the preterite ending – e.g. anduv**ieron** → anduv**iera/iese**. Where the verb has no 'i' in the preterite ending, add **-era/-ese** etc – e.g. produj**eron** → produj**era/ese**.

Grammar

'-ar':	'-er':	'-ir':
actuar	entender	adquirir
almorzar	haber	bendecir
andar	hacer	conducir
aunar	hay	construir
avergonzar	leer	cubrir
averiguar	llover	decir
contar	mover	dirigir
cruzar	nacer	distinguir
dar	oler	dormir
empezar	poder	elegir
enviar	poner	erguir
errar	querer	escribir
estar	resolver	freír
jugar	romper	gruñir
negar	saber	ir
pagar	satisfacer	lucir
pensar	ser	morir
rehusar	tener	oír
rogar	torcer	pedir
sacar	traer	prohibir
volcar	valer	reír
	vencer	reñir
'-er':	ver	reunir
	volver	salir
caber		seguir
caer	'-ir':	sentir
cocer		venir
coger	abolir	zurcir
crecer	abrir	

abolir *to abolish*

PAST PARTICIPLE	IMPERATIVE
abol**ido**	abol**id**

GERUND

abol**iendo**

PRESENT*	PRESENT SUBJUNCTIVE
nosotros abol**imos** vosotros abol**ís**	*not used*
* Present tense only used in persons shown	

FUTURE		CONDITIONAL	
yo	abolir**é**	yo	abolir**ía**
tú	abolir**ás**	tú	abolir**ías**
él	abolir**á**	él	abolir**ía**
nosotros	abolir**emos**	nosotros	abolir**íamos**
vosotros	abolir**éis**	vosotros	abolir**íais**
ellos	abolir**án**	ellos	abolir**ían**

IMPERFECT		PRETERITE	
yo	abol**ía**	yo	abol**í**
tú	abol**ías**	tú	abol**iste**
él	abol**ía**	él	abol**ió**
nosotros	abol**íamos**	nosotros	abol**imos**
vosotros	abol**íais**	vosotros	abol**isteis**
ellos	abol**ían**	ellos	abol**ieron**

---

abrir *to open*

PAST PARTICIPLE   IMPERATIVE

abierto   abre

           abrid

GERUND

abriendo

PRESENT		PRESENT SUBJUNCTIVE	
yo	abro	**yo**	abra
tú	abres	**tú**	abras
él	abre	**él**	abra
nosotros	abrimos	**nosotros**	abramos
vosotros	abrís	**vosotros**	abráis
ellos	abren	**ellos**	abran

FUTURE		CONDITIONAL	
yo	abriré	**yo**	abriría
tú	abrirás	**tú**	abrirías
él	abrirá	**él**	abriría
nosotros	abriremos	**nosotros**	abriríamos
vosotros	abriréis	**vosotros**	abriríais
ellos	abrirán	**ellos**	abrirían

IMPERFECT		PRETERITE	
yo	abría	**yo**	abrí
tú	abrías	**tú**	abriste
él	abría	**él**	abrió
nosotros	abríamos	**nosotros**	abrimos
vosotros	abríais	**vosotros**	abristeis
ellos	abrían	**ellos**	abrieron

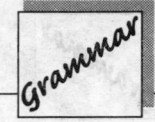
---

actuar *to act*

PAST PARTICIPLE

actu**ado**

GERUND

actu**ando**

IMPERATIVE

actúa
actua**d**

PRESENT		PRESENT SUBJUNCTIVE	
yo	**actúo**	yo	**actúe**
tú	**actúas**	tú	**actúes**
él	**actúa**	él	**actúe**
nosotros	actu**amos**	nosotros	actu**emos**
vosotros	actu**áis**	vosotros	actu**éis**
ellos	**actúan**	ellos	**actúen**

FUTURE		CONDITIONAL	
yo	actuar**é**	yo	actuar**ía**
tú	actuar**ás**	tú	actuar**ías**
él	actuar**á**	él	actuar**ía**
nosotros	actuar**emos**	nosotros	actuar**íamos**
vosotros	actuar**éis**	vosotros	actuar**íais**
ellos	actuar**án**	ellos	actuar**ían**

IMPERFECT		PRETERITE	
yo	actu**aba**	yo	actu**é**
tú	actu**abas**	tú	actu**aste**
él	actu**aba**	él	actu**ó**
nosotros	actu**ábamos**	nosotros	actu**amos**
vosotros	actu**abais**	vosotros	actu**asteis**
ellos	actu**aban**	ellos	actu**aron**

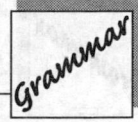

---

adquirir *to acquire*

PAST PARTICIPLE	IMPERATIVE
adquir**ido**	**adquiere**
	adquiri**d**
GERUND	
adquir**iendo**	

PRESENT		PRESENT SUBJUNCTIVE	
yo	**adquiero**	yo	**adquiera**
tú	**adquieres**	tú	**adquieras**
él	**adquiere**	él	**adquiera**
nosotros	adquir**imos**	nosotros	adquir**amos**
vosotros	adquir**ís**	vosotros	adquir**áis**
ellos	**adquieren**	ellos	**adquieran**

FUTURE		CONDITIONAL	
yo	adquirir**é**	yo	adquirir**ía**
tú	adquirir**ás**	tú	adquirir**ías**
él	adquirir**á**	él	adquirir**ía**
nosotros	adquirir**emos**	nosotros	adquirir**íamos**
vosotros	adquirir**éis**	vosotros	adquirir**íais**
ellos	adquirir**án**	ellos	adquirir**ían**

IMPERFECT		PRETERITE	
yo	adquir**ía**	yo	adquir**í**
tú	adquir**ías**	tú	adquir**iste**
él	adquir**ía**	él	adquir**ió**
nosotros	adquir**íamos**	nosotros	adquir**imos**
vosotros	adquir**íais**	vosotros	adquir**isteis**
ellos	adquir**ían**	ellos	adquir**ieron**

almorzar *to have lunch*

PAST PARTICIPLE	IMPERATIVE
almorz**ado**	**almuerza**
	almorza**d**
GERUND	
almorz**ando**	

PRESENT

yo	**almuerzo**
tú	**almuerzas**
él	**almuerza**
nosotros	almorz**amos**
vosotros	almorz**áis**
ellos	**almuerzan**

PRESENT SUBJUNCTIVE

yo	**almuerce**
tú	**almuerces**
él	**almuerce**
nosotros	**almorcemos**
vosotros	**almorcéis**
ellos	**almuercen**

FUTURE

yo	almorzar**é**
tú	almorzar**ás**
él	almorzar**á**
nosotros	almorzar**emos**
vosotros	almorzar**éis**
ellos	almorzar**án**

CONDITIONAL

yo	almorzar**ía**
tú	almorzar**ías**
él	almorzar**ía**
nosotros	almorzar**íamos**
vosotros	almorzar**íais**
ellos	almorzar**ían**

IMPERFECT

yo	almorz**aba**
tú	almorz**abas**
él	almorz**aba**
nosotros	almorz**ábamos**
vosotros	almorz**abais**
ellos	almorz**aban**

PRETERITE

yo	**almorcé**
tú	almorz**aste**
él	almorz**ó**
nosotros	almorz**amos**
vosotros	almorz**asteis**
ellos	almorz**aron**

andar *to walk*	

PAST PARTICIPLE	IMPERATIVE
and**ado**	and**a**
	and**ad**
GERUND	
and**ando**	

PRESENT		PRESENT SUBJUNCTIVE	
yo	and**o**	yo	and**e**
tú	and**as**	tú	and**es**
él	and**a**	él	and**e**
nosotros	and**amos**	nosotros	and**emos**
vosotros	and**áis**	vosotros	and**éis**
ellos	and**an**	ellos	and**en**

FUTURE		CONDITIONAL	
yo	andar**é**	yo	andar**ía**
tú	andar**ás**	tú	andar**ías**
él	andar**á**	él	andar**ía**
nosotros	andar**emos**	nosotros	andar**íamos**
vosotros	andar**éis**	vosotros	andar**íais**
ellos	andar**án**	ellos	andar**ían**

IMPERFECT		PRETERITE	
yo	and**aba**	yo	**anduve**
tú	and**abas**	tú	**anduviste**
él	and**aba**	él	**anduvo**
nosotros	and**ábamos**	nosotros	**anduvimos**
vosotros	and**abais**	vosotros	**anduvisteis**
ellos	and**aban**	ellos	**anduvieron**

aunar *to join together*

PAST PARTICIPLE	IMPERATIVE
aun**ado**	**aúna**
	auna**d**
GERUND	
aun**ando**	

PRESENT		PRESENT SUBJUNCTIVE	
yo	aúno	yo	aúne
tú	aúnas	tú	aúnes
él	aúna	él	aúne
nosotros	aunamos	nosotros	aunemos
vosotros	aunáis	vosotros	aunéis
ellos	aúnan	ellos	aúnen

FUTURE		CONDITIONAL	
yo	aunaré	yo	aunaría
tú	aunarás	tú	aunarías
él	aunará	él	aunaría
nosotros	aunaremos	nosotros	aunaríamos
vosotros	aunaréis	vosotros	aunaríais
ellos	aunarán	ellos	aunarían

IMPERFECT		PRETERITE	
yo	aunaba	yo	auné
tú	aunabas	tú	aunaste
él	aunaba	él	aunó
nosotros	aunábamos	nosotros	aunamos
vosotros	aunabais	vosotros	aunasteis
ellos	aunaban	ellos	aunaron

---

avergonzar *to shame*

PAST PARTICIPLE	IMPERATIVE
avergonz**ado**	**avergüenza**
	avergonza**d**
GERUND	
avergonz**ando**	

PRESENT

yo	avergüenzo
tú	avergüenzas
él	avergüenza
nosotros	avergonzamos
vosotros	avergonzáis
ellos	avergüenzan

PRESENT SUBJUNCTIVE

yo	avergüence
tú	avergüences
él	avergüence
nosotros	avergoncemos
vosotros	avergoncéis
ellos	avergüencen

FUTURE

yo	avergonzaré
tú	avergonzarás
él	avergonzará
nosotros	avergonzaremos
vosotros	avergonzaréis
ellos	avergonzarán

CONDITIONAL

yo	avergonzaría
tú	avergonzarías
él	avergonzaría
nosotros	avergonzaríamos
vosotros	avergonzaríais
ellos	avergonzarían

IMPERFECT

yo	avergonzaba
tú	avergonzabas
él	avergonzaba
nosotros	avergonzábamos
vosotros	avergonzabais
ellos	avergonzaban

PRETERITE

yo	avergoncé
tú	avergonzaste
él	avergonzó
nosotros	avergonzamos
vosotros	avergonzasteis
ellos	avergonzaron

averiguar *to find out*

PAST PARTICIPLE	IMPERATIVE
averigu**ado**	averigu**a**
	averigu**ad**
GERUND	
averigu**ando**	

PRESENT		PRESENT SUBJUNCTIVE	
yo	averigu**o**	yo	**averigüe**
tú	averigu**as**	tú	**averigües**
él	averigu**a**	él	**averigüe**
nosotros	averigu**amos**	nosotros	**averigüemos**
vosotros	averigu**áis**	vosotros	**averigüéis**
ellos	averigu**an**	ellos	**averigüen**

FUTURE		CONDITIONAL	
yo	averiguar**é**	yo	averiguar**ía**
tú	averiguar**ás**	tú	averiguar**ías**
él	averiguar**á**	él	averiguar**ía**
nosotros	averiguar**emos**	nosotros	averiguar**íamos**
vosotros	averiguar**éis**	vosotros	averiguar**íais**
ellos	averiguar**án**	ellos	averiguar**ían**

IMPERFECT		PRETERITE	
yo	averigu**aba**	yo	**averigüé**
tú	averigu**abas**	tú	averigu**aste**
él	averigu**aba**	él	averigu**ó**
nosotros	averigu**ábamos**	nosotros	averigu**amos**
vosotros	averigu**abais**	vosotros	averigu**asteis**
ellos	averigu**aban**	ellos	averigu**aron**

VERB TABLE

---

bendecir *to bless*

PAST PARTICIPLE

bendec**ido**

GERUND

bendiciendo

IMPERATIVE

bendice
bendeci**d**

PRESENT		PRESENT SUBJUNCTIVE	
yo	**bendigo**	yo	**bendiga**
tú	**bendices**	tú	**bendigas**
él	**bendice**	él	**bendiga**
nosotros	bendec**imos**	nosotros	**bendigamos**
vosotros	bendec**ís**	vosotros	**bendigáis**
ellos	**bendicen**	ellos	**bendigan**

FUTURE		CONDITIONAL	
yo	bendecir**é**	yo	bendecir**ía**
tú	bendecir**ás**	tú	bendecir**ías**
él	bendecir**á**	él	bendecir**ía**
nosotros	bendecir**emos**	nosotros	bendecir**íamos**
vosotros	bendecir**éis**	vosotros	bendecir**íais**
ellos	bendecir**án**	ellos	bendecir**ían**

IMPERFECT		PRETERITE	
yo	bendec**ía**	yo	**bendije**
tú	bendec**ías**	tú	**bendijiste**
él	bendec**ía**	él	**bendijo**
nosotros	bendec**íamos**	nosotros	**bendijimos**
vosotros	bendec**íais**	vosotros	**bendijisteis**
ellos	bendec**ían**	ellos	**bendijeron**

caber *to fit*

PAST PARTICIPLE	IMPERATIVE
cab**ido**	cab**e**
	cab**ed**
GERUND	
cab**iendo**	

PRESENT		PRESENT SUBJUNCTIVE	
yo	quepo	yo	quepa
tú	cabes	tú	quepas
él	cabe	él	quepa
nosotros	cabemos	nosotros	quepamos
vosotros	cabéis	vosotros	quepáis
ellos	caben	ellos	quepan

FUTURE		CONDITIONAL	
yo	cabré	yo	cabría
tú	cabrás	tú	cabrías
él	cabrá	él	cabría
nosotros	cabremos	nosotros	cabríamos
vosotros	cabréis	vosotros	cabríais
ellos	cabrán	ellos	cabrían

IMPERFECT		PRETERITE	
yo	cabía	yo	cupe
tú	cabías	tú	cupiste
él	cabía	él	cupo
nosotros	cabíamos	nosotros	cupimos
vosotros	cabíais	vosotros	cupisteis
ellos	cabían	ellos	cupieron

VERB TABLE

---

caer *to fall*

PAST PARTICIPLE

caído

IMPERATIVE

ca**e**
cae**d**

GERUND

cayendo

PRESENT		PRESENT SUBJUNCTIVE	
yo	caigo	yo	caiga
tú	caes	tú	caigas
él	cae	él	caiga
nosotros	caemos	nosotros	caigamos
vosotros	caéis	vosotros	caigáis
ellos	caen	ellos	caigan

FUTURE		CONDITIONAL	
yo	caeré	yo	caería
tú	caerás	tú	caerías
él	caerá	él	caería
nosotros	caeremos	nosotros	caeríamos
vosotros	caeréis	vosotros	caeríais
ellos	caerán	ellos	caerían

IMPERFECT		PRETERITE	
yo	caía	yo	caí
tú	caías	tú	caíste
él	caía	él	cayó
nosotros	caíamos	nosotros	caímos
vosotros	caíais	vosotros	caísteis
ellos	caían	ellos	cayeron

cocer *to boil*

PAST PARTICIPLE	IMPERATIVE
coc**ido**	**cuece**
	coc**ed**
GERUND	
coc**iendo**	

PRESENT		PRESENT SUBJUNCTIVE	
yo	**cuezo**	yo	**cueza**
tú	**cueces**	tú	**cuezas**
él	**cuece**	él	**cueza**
nosotros	cocemos	nosotros	cozamos
vosotros	cocéis	vosotros	cozáis
ellos	**cuecen**	ellos	**cuezan**

FUTURE		CONDITIONAL	
yo	coceré	yo	cocería
tú	cocerás	tú	cocerías
él	cocerá	él	cocería
nosotros	coceremos	nosotros	coceríamos
vosotros	coceréis	vosotros	coceríais
ellos	cocerán	ellos	cocerían

IMPERFECT		PRETERITE	
yo	cocía	yo	cocí
tú	cocías	tú	cociste
él	cocía	él	coció
nosotros	cocíamos	nosotros	cocimos
vosotros	cocíais	vosotros	cocisteis
ellos	cocían	ellos	cocieron

VERB TABLE

Grammar

coger *to catch*

PAST PARTICIPLE	IMPERATIVE
cog**ido**	cog**e**
	cog**ed**
GERUND	
cog**iendo**	

PRESENT		PRESENT SUBJUNCTIVE	
yo	co**jo**	yo	co**ja**
tú	cog**es**	tú	co**jas**
él	cog**e**	él	co**ja**
nosotros	cog**emos**	nosotros	co**jamos**
vosotros	cog**éis**	vosotros	co**jáis**
ellos	cog**en**	ellos	co**jan**

FUTURE		CONDITIONAL	
yo	coger**é**	yo	coger**ía**
tú	coger**ás**	tú	coger**ías**
él	coger**á**	él	coger**ía**
nosotros	coger**emos**	nosotros	coger**íamos**
vosotros	coger**éis**	vosotros	coger**íais**
ellos	coger**án**	ellos	coger**ían**

IMPERFECT		PRETERITE	
yo	cog**ía**	yo	cog**í**
tú	cog**ías**	tú	cog**iste**
él	cog**ía**	él	cog**ió**
nosotros	cog**íamos**	nosotros	cog**imos**
vosotros	cog**íais**	vosotros	cog**isteis**
ellos	cog**ían**	ellos	cog**ieron**

conducir _to drive, to lead_	
PAST PARTICIPLE	IMPERATIVE
conducido	conduce
	conducid
GERUND	
conduciendo	

PRESENT		PRESENT SUBJUNCTIVE	
yo	conduzco	yo	conduzca
tú	conduces	tú	conduzcas
él	conduce	él	conduzca
nosotros	conducimos	nosotros	conduzcamos
vosotros	conducís	vosotros	conduzcáis
ellos	conducen	ellos	conduzcan

FUTURE		CONDITIONAL	
yo	conduciré	yo	conduciría
tú	conducirás	tú	conducirías
él	conducirá	él	conduciría
nosotros	conduciremos	nosotros	conduciríamos
vosotros	conduciréis	vosotros	conduciríais
ellos	conducirán	ellos	conducirían

IMPERFECT		PRETERITE	
yo	conducía	yo	conduje
tú	conducías	tú	condujiste
él	conducía	él	condujo
nosotros	conducíamos	nosotros	condujimos
vosotros	conducíais	vosotros	condujisteis
ellos	conducían	ellos	condujeron

VERB TABLE

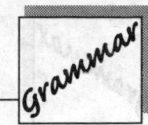

construir *to build*

PAST PARTICIPLE	IMPERATIVE
construí**do**	**construye**
	construi**d**
GERUND	
construyendo	

PRESENT		PRESENT SUBJUNCTIVE	
yo	**construyo**	yo	**construya**
tú	**construyes**	tú	**construyas**
él	**construye**	él	**construya**
nosotros	construí**mos**	nosotros	**construyamos**
vosotros	construí**s**	vosotros	**construyáis**
ellos	**construyen**	ellos	**construyan**

FUTURE		CONDITIONAL	
yo	construir**é**	yo	construir**ía**
tú	construir**ás**	tú	construir**ías**
él	construir**á**	él	construir**ía**
nosotros	construir**emos**	nosotros	construir**íamos**
vosotros	construir**éis**	vosotros	construir**íais**
ellos	construir**án**	ellos	construir**ían**

IMPERFECT		PRETERITE	
yo	construí**a**	yo	construí
tú	construí**as**	tú	construi**ste**
él	construí**a**	él	**construyó**
nosotros	construí**amos**	nosotros	construi**mos**
vosotros	construí**ais**	vosotros	construi**steis**
ellos	construí**an**	ellos	**construyeron**

contar *to tell, to count*

PAST PARTICIPLE	IMPERATIVE
contado	cuenta
	contad
GERUND	
contando	

PRESENT	PRESENT SUBJUNCTIVE
yo cuento	yo cuente
tú cuentas	tú cuentes
él cuenta	él cuente
nosotros contamos	nosotros contemos
vosotros contáis	vosotros contéis
ellos cuentan	ellos cuenten

FUTURE	CONDITIONAL
yo contaré	yo contaría
tú contarás	tú contarías
él contará	él contaría
nosotros contaremos	nosotros contaríamos
vosotros contaréis	vosotros contaríais
ellos contarán	ellos contarían

IMPERFECT	PRETERITE
yo contaba	yo conté
tú contabas	tú contaste
él contaba	él contó
nosotros contábamos	nosotros contamos
vosotros contabais	vosotros contasteis
ellos contaban	ellos contaron

VERB TABLE

---

crecer *to grow*

PAST PARTICIPLE

crec**ido**

GERUND

crec**iendo**

IMPERATIVE

crec**e**
crec**ed**

PRESENT		PRESENT SUBJUNCTIVE	
yo	crez**co**	yo	crez**ca**
tú	crec**es**	tú	crez**cas**
él	crec**e**	él	crez**ca**
nosotros	crec**emos**	nosotros	crez**camos**
vosotros	crec**éis**	vosotros	crez**cáis**
ellos	crec**en**	ellos	crez**can**

FUTURE		CONDITIONAL	
yo	crecer**é**	yo	crecer**ía**
tú	crecer**ás**	tú	crecer**ías**
él	crecer**á**	él	crecer**ía**
nosotros	crecer**emos**	nosotros	crecer**íamos**
vosotros	crecer**éis**	vosotros	crecer**íais**
ellos	crecer**án**	ellos	crecer**ían**

IMPERFECT		PRETERITE	
yo	crec**ía**	yo	crec**í**
tú	crec**ías**	tú	crec**iste**
él	crec**ía**	él	crec**ió**
nosotros	crec**íamos**	nosotros	crec**imos**
vosotros	crec**íais**	vosotros	crec**isteis**
ellos	crec**ían**	ellos	crec**ieron**

cruzar *to cross*

PAST PARTICIPLE	IMPERATIVE
cruz**ado**	cruz**a**
	cruza**d**
GERUND	
cruz**ando**	

PRESENT	PRESENT SUBJUNCTIVE
yo cruz**o**	yo **cruce**
tú cruz**as**	tú **cruces**
él cruz**a**	él **cruce**
nosotros cruz**amos**	nosotros **crucemos**
vosotros cruz**áis**	vosotros **crucéis**
ellos cruz**an**	ellos **crucen**

FUTURE	CONDITIONAL
yo cruzar**é**	yo cruzar**ía**
tú cruzar**ás**	tú cruzar**ías**
él cruzar**á**	él cruzar**ía**
nosotros cruzar**emos**	nosotros cruzar**íamos**
vosotros cruzar**éis**	vosotros cruzar**íais**
ellos cruzar**án**	ellos cruzar**ían**

IMPERFECT	PRETERITE
yo cruz**aba**	yo cruz**é**
tú cruz**abas**	tú cruz**aste**
él cruz**aba**	él cruz**ó**
nosotros cruz**ábamos**	nosotros cruz**amos**
vosotros cruz**abais**	vosotros cruz**asteis**
ellos cruz**aban**	ellos cruz**aron**

cubrir *to cover*

PAST PARTICIPLE	IMPERATIVE
cubierto	cub**re**
	cubri**d**
GERUND	
cubr**iendo**	

PRESENT		PRESENT SUBJUNCTIVE	
yo	cubr**o**	**yo**	cubr**a**
tú	cubr**es**	**tú**	cubr**as**
él	cubr**e**	**él**	cubr**a**
nosotros	cubr**imos**	**nosotros**	cubr**amos**
vosotros	cubr**ís**	**vosotros**	cubr**áis**
ellos	cubr**en**	**ellos**	cubr**an**

FUTURE		CONDITIONAL	
yo	cubrir**é**	**yo**	cubrir**ía**
tú	cubrir**ás**	**tú**	cubrir**ías**
él	cubrir**á**	**él**	cubrir**ía**
nosotros	cubrir**emos**	**nosotros**	cubrir**íamos**
vosotros	cubrir**éis**	**vosotros**	cubrir**íais**
ellos	cubrir**án**	**ellos**	cubrir**ían**

IMPERFECT		PRETERITE	
yo	cubr**ía**	**yo**	cubr**í**
tú	cubr**ías**	**tú**	cubr**iste**
él	cubr**ía**	**él**	cubr**ió**
nosotros	cubr**íamos**	**nosotros**	cubr**imos**
vosotros	cubr**íais**	**vosotros**	cubr**isteis**
ellos	cubr**ían**	**ellos**	cubr**ieron**

dar *to give*

PAST PARTICIPLE	IMPERATIVE
d**ado**	d**a**
	da**d**
GERUND	
d**ando**	

PRESENT		PRESENT SUBJUNCTIVE	
yo	doy	yo	dé
tú	das	tú	des
él	da	él	dé
nosotros	damos	nosotros	demos
vosotros	dais	vosotros	deis
ellos	dan	ellos	den

FUTURE		CONDITIONAL	
yo	daré	yo	daría
tú	darás	tú	darías
él	dará	él	daría
nosotros	daremos	nosotros	daríamos
vosotros	daréis	vosotros	daríais
ellos	darán	ellos	darían

IMPERFECT		PRETERITE	
yo	daba	yo	di
tú	dabas	tú	diste
él	daba	él	dio
nosotros	dábamos	nosotros	dimos
vosotros	dabais	vosotros	disteis
ellos	daban	ellos	dieron

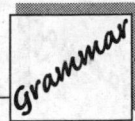

decir *to say*

PAST PARTICIPLE	IMPERATIVE
dicho	**di**
	dec**id**
GERUND	
diciendo	

PRESENT		PRESENT SUBJUNCTIVE	
yo	**digo**	yo	**diga**
tú	**dices**	tú	**digas**
él	**dice**	él	**diga**
nosotros	dec**imos**	nosotros	**digamos**
vosotros	dec**ís**	vosotros	**digáis**
ellos	**dicen**	ellos	**digan**

FUTURE		CONDITIONAL	
yo	**diré**	yo	**diría**
tú	**dirás**	tú	**dirías**
él	**dirá**	él	**diría**
nosotros	**diremos**	nosotros	**diríamos**
vosotros	**diréis**	vosotros	**diríais**
ellos	**dirán**	ellos	**dirían**

IMPERFECT		PRETERITE	
yo	dec**ía**	yo	**dije**
tú	dec**ías**	tú	**dijiste**
él	dec**ía**	él	**dijo**
nosotros	dec**íamos**	nosotros	**dijimos**
vosotros	dec**íais**	vosotros	**dijisteis**
ellos	dec**ían**	ellos	**dijeron**

dirigir *to direct*

PAST PARTICIPLE	IMPERATIVE
dirig**ido**	dirig**e**
	dirig**id**
GERUND	
dirig**iendo**	

PRESENT		PRESENT SUBJUNCTIVE	
yo	**dirijo**	yo	**dirija**
tú	dirig**es**	tú	**dirijas**
él	dirig**e**	él	**dirija**
nosotros	dirig**imos**	nosotros	**dirijamos**
vosotros	dirig**ís**	vosotros	**dirijáis**
ellos	dirig**en**	ellos	**dirijan**

FUTURE		CONDITIONAL	
yo	dirigir**é**	yo	dirigir**ía**
tú	dirigir**ás**	tú	dirigir**ías**
él	dirigir**á**	él	dirigir**ía**
nosotros	dirigir**emos**	nosotros	dirigir**íamos**
vosotros	dirigir**éis**	vosotros	dirigir**íais**
ellos	dirigir**án**	ellos	dirigir**ían**

IMPERFECT		PRETERITE	
yo	dirig**ía**	yo	dirig**í**
tú	dirig**ías**	tú	dirig**iste**
él	dirig**ía**	él	dirig**ió**
nosotros	dirig**íamos**	nosotros	dirig**imos**
vosotros	dirig**íais**	vosotros	dirig**isteis**
ellos	dirig**ían**	ellos	dirig**ieron**

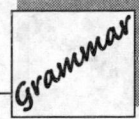

---

distinguir *to distinguish*

PAST PARTICIPLE	IMPERATIVE
distingu**ido**	distingu**e**
	distingu**id**
GERUND	
distingu**iendo**	

PRESENT		PRESENT SUBJUNCTIVE	
yo	distingo	yo	distinga
tú	distingues	tú	distingas
él	distingue	él	distinga
nosotros	distinguimos	nosotros	distingamos
vosotros	distinguís	vosotros	distingáis
ellos	distinguen	ellos	distingan

FUTURE		CONDITIONAL	
yo	distinguiré	yo	distinguiría
tú	distinguirás	tú	distinguirías
él	distinguirá	él	distinguiría
nosotros	distinguiremos	nosotros	distinguiríamos
vosotros	distinguiréis	vosotros	distinguiríais
ellos	distinguirán	ellos	distinguirían

IMPERFECT		PRETERITE	
yo	distinguía	yo	distinguí
tú	distinguías	tú	distinguiste
él	distinguía	él	distinguió
nosotros	distinguíamos	nosotros	distinguimos
vosotros	distinguíais	vosotros	distinguisteis
ellos	distinguían	ellos	distinguieron

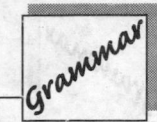

dormir to sleep

PAST PARTICIPLE

dorm**ido**

GERUND

durmiendo

IMPERATIVE

duerme
dorm**id**

PRESENT		PRESENT SUBJUNCTIVE	
yo	**duermo**	yo	**duerma**
tú	**duermes**	tú	**duermas**
él	**duerme**	él	**duerma**
nosotros	dorm**imos**	nosotros	**durmamos**
vosotros	dorm**ís**	vosotros	**durmáis**
ellos	**duermen**	ellos	**duerman**

FUTURE		CONDITIONAL	
yo	dormir**é**	yo	dormir**ía**
tú	dormir**ás**	tú	dormir**ías**
él	dormir**á**	él	dormir**ía**
nosotros	dormir**emos**	nosotros	dormir**íamos**
vosotros	dormir**éis**	vosotros	dormir**íais**
ellos	dormir**án**	ellos	dormir**ían**

IMPERFECT		PRETERITE	
yo	dorm**ía**	yo	dorm**í**
tú	dorm**ías**	tú	dorm**iste**
él	dorm**ía**	él	**durmió**
nosotros	dorm**íamos**	nosotros	dorm**imos**
vosotros	dorm**íais**	vosotros	dorm**isteis**
ellos	dorm**ían**	ellos	**durmieron**

VERB TABLE

---

elegir *to choose*

PAST PARTICIPLE	IMPERATIVE
eleg**ido**	**elige**
	elegi**d**
GERUND	
eligiendo	

PRESENT	PRESENT SUBJUNCTIVE
yo eli**jo**	yo eli**ja**
tú eli**ges**	tú eli**jas**
él eli**ge**	él eli**ja**
nosotros eleg**imos**	nosotros eli**jamos**
vosotros eleg**ís**	vosotros eli**jáis**
ellos eli**gen**	ellos eli**jan**

FUTURE	CONDITIONAL
yo elegir**é**	yo elegir**ía**
tú elegir**ás**	tú elegir**ías**
él elegir**á**	él elegir**ía**
nosotros elegir**emos**	nosotros elegir**íamos**
vosotros elegir**éis**	vosotros elegir**íais**
ellos elegir**án**	ellos elegir**ían**

IMPERFECT	PRETERITE
yo eleg**ía**	yo eleg**í**
tú eleg**ías**	tú eleg**iste**
él eleg**ía**	él eli**gió**
nosotros eleg**íamos**	nosotros eleg**imos**
vosotros eleg**íais**	vosotros eleg**isteis**
ellos eleg**ían**	ellos eli**gieron**

empezar *to begin*

PAST PARTICIPLE	IMPERATIVE
empez**ado**	**empieza**
	empeza**d**
GERUND	
empez**ando**	

PRESENT		PRESENT SUBJUNCTIVE	
yo	**empiezo**	yo	**empiece**
tú	**empiezas**	tú	**empieces**
él	**empieza**	él	**empiece**
nosotros	empez**amos**	nosotros	**empecemos**
vosotros	empez**áis**	vosotros	**empecéis**
ellos	**empiezan**	ellos	**empiecen**

FUTURE		CONDITIONAL	
yo	empezar**é**	yo	empezar**ía**
tú	empezar**ás**	tú	empezar**ías**
él	empezar**á**	él	empezar**ía**
nosotros	empezar**emos**	nosotros	empezar**íamos**
vosotros	empezar**éis**	vosotros	empezar**íais**
ellos	empezar**án**	ellos	empezar**ían**

IMPERFECT		PRETERITE	
yo	empez**aba**	yo	**empecé**
tú	empez**abas**	tú	empez**aste**
él	empez**aba**	él	empez**ó**
nosotros	empez**ábamos**	nosotros	empez**amos**
vosotros	empez**abais**	vosotros	empez**asteis**
ellos	empez**aban**	ellos	empez**aron**

VERB TABLE

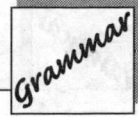

---

entender *to understand*

PAST PARTICIPLE

entend**ido**

GERUND

entend**iendo**

IMPERATIVE

entiende
entend**ed**

PRESENT		PRESENT SUBJUNCTIVE	
yo	**entiendo**	yo	**entienda**
tú	**entiendes**	tú	**entiendas**
él	**entiende**	él	**entienda**
nosotros	entend**emos**	nosotros	entend**amos**
vosotros	entend**éis**	vosotros	entend**áis**
ellos	**entienden**	ellos	**entiendan**

FUTURE		CONDITIONAL	
yo	entender**é**	yo	entender**ía**
tú	entender**ás**	tú	entender**ías**
él	entender**á**	él	entender**ía**
nosotros	entender**emos**	nosotros	entender**íamos**
vosotros	entender**éis**	vosotros	entender**íais**
ellos	entender**án**	ellos	entender**ían**

IMPERFECT		PRETERITE	
yo	entend**ía**	yo	entend**í**
tú	entend**ías**	tú	entend**iste**
él	entend**ía**	él	entend**ió**
nosotros	entend**íamos**	nosotros	entend**imos**
vosotros	entend**íais**	vosotros	entend**isteis**
ellos	entend**ían**	ellos	entend**ieron**

enviar *to send*

PAST PARTICIPLE	IMPERATIVE
enviado	**envía**
	enviad
GERUND	
enviando	

PRESENT		PRESENT SUBJUNCTIVE	
yo	envío	yo	envíe
tú	envías	tú	envíes
él	envía	él	envíe
nosotros	enviamos	nosotros	enviemos
vosotros	enviáis	vosotros	enviéis
ellos	envían	ellos	envíen

FUTURE		CONDITIONAL	
yo	enviaré	yo	enviaría
tú	enviarás	tú	enviarías
él	enviará	él	enviaría
nosotros	enviaremos	nosotros	enviaríamos
vosotros	enviaréis	vosotros	enviaríais
ellos	enviarán	ellos	enviarían

IMPERFECT		PRETERITE	
yo	enviaba	yo	envié
tú	enviabas	tú	enviaste
él	enviaba	él	envió
nosotros	enviábamos	nosotros	enviamos
vosotros	enviabais	vosotros	enviasteis
ellos	enviaban	ellos	enviaron

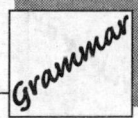
Grammar

erguir *to erect*	

PAST PARTICIPLE	IMPERATIVE
ergu**ido**	**yergue**
	ergui**d**
GERUND	
irguiendo	

PRESENT		PRESENT SUBJUNCTIVE	
yo	**yergo**	yo	**yerga**
tú	**yergues**	tú	**yergas**
él	**yergue**	él	**yerga**
nosotros	erguimos	nosotros	**irgamos**
vosotros	erguís	vosotros	**irgáis**
ellos	**yerguen**	ellos	**yergan**

FUTURE		CONDITIONAL	
yo	erguiré	yo	erguiría
tú	erguirás	tú	erguirías
él	erguirá	él	erguiría
nosotros	erguiremos	nosotros	erguiríamos
vosotros	erguiréis	vosotros	erguiríals
ellos	erguirán	ellos	erguirían

IMPERFECT		PRETERITE	
yo	erguía	yo	erguí
tú	erguías	tú	erguiste
él	erguía	él	**irguió**
nosotros	erguíamos	nosotros	erguimos
vosotros	erguíais	vosotros	erguisteis
ellos	erguían	ellos	**irguieron**

errar *to err*

PAST PARTICIPLE	IMPERATIVE
err**ado**	**yerra** erra**d**
GERUND	
err**ando**	

PRESENT		PRESENT SUBJUNCTIVE	
yo	**yerro**	yo	**yerre**
tú	**yerras**	tú	**yerres**
él	**yerra**	él	**yerre**
nosotros	err**amos**	nosotros	err**emos**
vosotros	err**áis**	vosotros	err**éis**
ellos	**yerran**	ellos	**yerren**

FUTURE		CONDITIONAL	
yo	errar**é**	yo	errar**ía**
tú	errar**ás**	tú	errar**ías**
él	errar**á**	él	errar**ía**
nosotros	errar**emos**	nosotros	errar**íamos**
vosotros	errar**éis**	vosotros	errar**íais**
ellos	errar**án**	ellos	errar**ían**

IMPERFECT		PRETERITE	
yo	err**aba**	yo	err**é**
tú	err**abas**	tú	err**aste**
él	err**aba**	él	err**ó**
nosotros	err**ábamos**	nosotros	err**amos**
vosotros	err**abais**	vosotros	err**asteis**
ellos	err**aban**	ellos	err**aron**

VERB TABLE

Grammar

---

escribir *to write*

PAST PARTICIPLE

escrito

GERUND

escrib**iendo**

IMPERATIVE

escrib**e**
escrib**id**

PRESENT		PRESENT SUBJUNCTIVE	
yo	escrib**o**	**yo**	escrib**a**
tú	escrib**es**	**tú**	escrib**as**
él	escrib**e**	**él**	escrib**a**
nosotros	escrib**imos**	**nosotros**	escrib**amos**
vosotros	escrib**ís**	**vosotros**	escrib**áis**
ellos	escrib**en**	**ellos**	escrib**an**

FUTURE		CONDITIONAL	
yo	escribir**é**	**yo**	escribir**ía**
tú	escribir**ás**	**tú**	escribir**ías**
él	escribir**á**	**él**	escribir**ía**
nosotros	escribir**emos**	**nosotros**	escribir**íamos**
vosotros	escribir**éis**	**vosotros**	escribir**íais**
ellos	escribir**án**	**ellos**	escribir**ían**

IMPERFECT		PRETERITE	
yo	escrib**ía**	**yo**	escrib**í**
tú	escrib**ías**	**tú**	escrib**iste**
él	escrib**ía**	**él**	escrib**ió**
nosotros	escrib**íamos**	**nosotros**	escrib**imos**
vosotros	escrib**íais**	**vosotros**	escrib**isteis**
ellos	escrib**ían**	**ellos**	escrib**ieron**

estar *to be*

PAST PARTICIPLE	IMPERATIVE
estado	está
	estad
GERUND	
estando	

PRESENT		PRESENT SUBJUNCTIVE	
yo	estoy	yo	esté
tú	estás	tú	estés
él	está	él	esté
nosotros	estamos	nosotros	estemos
vosotros	estáis	vosotros	estéis
ellos	están	ellos	estén

FUTURE		CONDITIONAL	
yo	estaré	yo	estaría
tú	estarás	tú	estarías
él	estará	él	estaría
nosotros	estaremos	nosotros	estaríamos
vosotros	estaréis	vosotros	estaríais
ellos	estarán	ellos	estarían

IMPERFECT		PRETERITE	
yo	estaba	yo	estuve
tú	estabas	tú	estuviste
él	estaba	él	estuvo
nosotros	estábamos	nosotros	estuvimos
vosotros	estabais	vosotros	estuvisteis
ellos	estaban	ellos	estuvieron

VERB TABLE

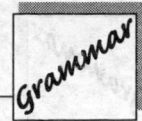

---

freír *to fry*

PAST PARTICIPLE	IMPERATIVE
frito	**fríe**
	freíd
GERUND	
friendo	

PRESENT		PRESENT SUBJUNCTIVE	
yo	**frío**	yo	**fría**
tú	**fríes**	tú	**frías**
él	**fríe**	él	**fría**
nosotros	fre**ímos**	nosotros	fri**amos**
vosotros	fre**ís**	vosotros	fri**áis**
ellos	**fríen**	ellos	**frían**

FUTURE		CONDITIONAL	
yo	freir**é**	yo	freir**ía**
tú	freir**ás**	tú	freir**ías**
él	freir**á**	él	freir**ía**
nosotros	freir**emos**	nosotros	freir**íamos**
vosotros	freir**éis**	vosotros	freir**íais**
ellos	freir**án**	ellos	freir**ían**

IMPERFECT		PRETERITE	
yo	fre**ía**	yo	fre**í**
tú	fre**ías**	tú	fre**íste**
él	fre**ía**	él	**frió**
nosotros	fre**íamos**	nosotros	fre**ímos**
vosotros	fre**íais**	vosotros	fre**ísteis**
ellos	fre**ían**	ellos	**frieron**

gruñir *to grunt*

PAST PARTICIPLE	IMPERATIVE
gruñ**ido**	gruñ**e**
	gruñ**id**
GERUND	
gruñendo	

PRESENT		PRESENT SUBJUNCTIVE	
yo	gruñ**o**	yo	gruñ**a**
tú	gruñ**es**	tú	gruñ**as**
él	gruñ**e**	él	gruñ**a**
nosotros	gruñ**imos**	nosotros	gruñ**amos**
vosotros	gruñ**ís**	vosotros	gruñ**áis**
ellos	gruñ**en**	ellos	gruñ**an**

FUTURE		CONDITIONAL	
yo	gruñir**é**	yo	gruñir**ía**
tú	gruñir**ás**	tú	gruñir**ías**
él	gruñir**á**	él	gruñir**ía**
nosotros	gruñir**emos**	nosotros	gruñir**íamos**
vosotros	gruñir**éis**	vosotros	gruñir**íais**
ellos	gruñir**án**	ellos	gruñir**ían**

IMPERFECT		PRETERITE	
yo	gruñ**ía**	yo	gruñ**í**
tú	gruñ**ías**	tú	gruñ**iste**
él	gruñ**ía**	él	**gruñó**
nosotros	gruñ**íamos**	nosotros	gruñ**imos**
vosotros	gruñ**íais**	vosotros	gruñ**isteis**
ellos	gruñ**ían**	ellos	**gruñeron**

---

haber to have (auxiliary)

PAST PARTICIPLE	IMPERATIVE
hab**ido**	not used
GERUND	
hab**iendo**	

PRESENT		PRESENT SUBJUNCTIVE	
yo	he	yo	haya
tú	has	tú	hayas
él	ha	él	haya
nosotros	hemos	nosotros	hayamos
vosotros	hab**éis**	vosotros	hayáis
ellos	han	ellos	hayan

FUTURE		CONDITIONAL	
yo	habré	yo	habría
tú	habrás	tú	habrías
él	habrá	él	habría
nosotros	habremos	nosotros	habríamos
vosotros	habréis	vosotros	habríais
ellos	habrán	ellos	habrían

IMPERFECT		PRETERITE	
yo	había	yo	hube
tú	habías	tú	hubiste
él	había	él	hubo
nosotros	habíamos	nosotros	hubimos
vosotros	habíais	vosotros	hubisteis
ellos	habían	ellos	hubieron

hacer *to do, to make*

PAST PARTICIPLE	IMPERATIVE
hecho	**haz**
	hace**d**
GERUND	
hac**iendo**	

PRESENT		PRESENT SUBJUNCTIVE	
yo	**hago**	yo	**haga**
tú	haces	tú	**hagas**
él	hace	él	**haga**
nosotros	hacemos	nosotros	**hagamos**
vosotros	hacéis	vosotros	**hagáis**
ellos	hacen	ellos	**hagan**

FUTURE		CONDITIONAL	
yo	**haré**	yo	**haría**
tú	**harás**	tú	**harías**
él	**hará**	él	**haría**
nosotros	**haremos**	nosotros	**haríamos**
vosotros	**haréis**	vosotros	**haríais**
ellos	**harán**	ellos	**harían**

IMPERFECT		PRETERITE	
yo	hac**ía**	yo	**hice**
tú	hac**ías**	tú	**hiciste**
él	hac**ía**	él	**hizo**
nosotros	hac**íamos**	nosotros	**hicimos**
vosotros	hac**íais**	vosotros	**hicisteis**
ellos	hac**ían**	ellos	**hicieron**

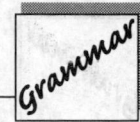

Grammar

hay *there is, there are*

PAST PARTICIPLE	IMPERATIVE
hab**ido**	*not used*
GERUND	
hab**iendo**	

PRESENT	PRESENT SUBJUNCTIVE
hay	**haya**

FUTURE	CONDITIONAL
habrá	**habría**

IMPERFECT	PRETERITE
hab**ía**	**hubo**

ir *to go*

PAST PARTICIPLE	IMPERATIVE
ido	**ve**
	id
GERUND	
yendo	

PRESENT		PRESENT SUBJUNCTIVE	
yo	**voy**	yo	**vaya**
tú	**vas**	tú	**vayas**
él	**va**	él	**vaya**
nosotros	**vamos**	nosotros	**vayamos**
vosotros	**vais**	vosotros	**vayáis**
ellos	**van**	ellos	**vayan**

FUTURE		CONDITIONAL	
yo	**iré**	yo	**iría**
tú	**irás**	tú	**irías**
él	**irá**	él	**iría**
nosotros	**iremos**	nosotros	**iríamos**
vosotros	**iréis**	vosotros	**iríais**
ellos	**irán**	ellos	**irían**

IMPERFECT		PRETERITE	
yo	**iba**	yo	**fui**
tú	**ibas**	tú	**fuiste**
él	**iba**	él	**fue**
nosotros	**íbamos**	nosotros	**fuimos**
vosotros	**ibais**	vosotros	**fuisteis**
ellos	**iban**	ellos	**fueron**

jugar *to play*

PAST PARTICIPLE	IMPERATIVE
jug**ado**	**juega**
	juga**d**
GERUND	
jug**ando**	

PRESENT		PRESENT SUBJUNCTIVE	
yo	**juego**	yo	**juegue**
tú	**juegas**	tú	**juegues**
él	**juega**	él	**juegue**
nosotros	jug**amos**	nosotros	**juguemos**
vosotros	jug**áis**	vosotros	**juguéis**
ellos	**juegan**	ellos	**jueguen**

FUTURE		CONDITIONAL	
yo	jugar**é**	yo	jugar**ía**
tú	jugar**ás**	tú	jugar**ías**
él	jugar**á**	él	jugar**ía**
nosotros	jugar**emos**	nosotros	jugar**íamos**
vosotros	jugar**éis**	vosotros	jugar**íais**
ellos	jugar**án**	ellos	jugar**ían**

IMPERFECT		PRETERITE	
yo	jug**aba**	yo	**jugué**
tú	jug**abas**	tú	jug**aste**
él	jug**aba**	él	jug**ó**
nosotros	jug**ábamos**	nosotros	jug**amos**
vosotros	jug**abais**	vosotros	jug**asteis**
ellos	jug**aban**	ellos	jug**aron**

leer *to read*

PAST PARTICIPLE	IMPERATIVE
le**í**do	le**e**
	lee**d**
GERUND	
leyendo	

PRESENT		PRESENT SUBJUNCTIVE	
yo	leo	yo	lea
tú	lees	tú	leas
él	lee	él	lea
nosotros	leemos	nosotros	leamos
vosotros	leéis	vosotros	leáis
ellos	leen	ellos	lean

FUTURE		CONDITIONAL	
yo	leeré	yo	leería
tú	leerás	tú	leerías
él	leerá	él	leería
nosotros	leeremos	nosotros	leeríamos
vosotros	leeréis	vosotros	leeríais
ellos	leerán	ellos	leerían

IMPERFECT		PRETERITE	
yo	leía	yo	leí
tú	leías	tú	leíste
él	leía	él	leyó
nosotros	leíamos	nosotros	leímos
vosotros	leíais	vosotros	leísteis
ellos	leían	ellos	leyeron

lucir *to shine*

PAST PARTICIPLE	IMPERATIVE
lucido	luce
	lucid
GERUND	
luciendo	

PRESENT		PRESENT SUBJUNCTIVE	
yo	luzco	yo	luzca
tú	luces	tú	luzcas
él	luce	él	luzca
nosotros	lucimos	nosotros	luzcamos
vosotros	lucís	vosotros	luzcáis
ellos	lucen	ellos	luzcan

FUTURE		CONDITIONAL	
yo	luciré	yo	luciría
tú	lucirás	tú	lucirías
él	lucirá	él	luciría
nosotros	luciremos	nosotros	luciríamos
vosotros	luciréis	vosotros	luciríais
ellos	lucirán	ellos	lucirían

IMPERFECT		PRETERITE	
yo	lucía	yo	lucí
tú	lucías	tú	luciste
él	lucía	él	lució
nosotros	lucíamos	nosotros	lucimos
vosotros	lucíais	vosotros	lucisteis
ellos	lucían	ellos	lucieron

llover *to rain*

PAST PARTICIPLE	IMPERATIVE
llov**ido**	*not used*

GERUND

llov**iendo**

PRESENT	PRESENT SUBJUNCTIVE
llueve	**llueva**

FUTURE	CONDITIONAL
llover**á**	llover**ía**

IMPERFECT	PRETERITE
llov**ía**	llov**ió**

morir *to die*

PAST PARTICIPLE	IMPERATIVE
muerto	**muere**
	morid
GERUND	
muriendo	

PRESENT		PRESENT SUBJUNCTIVE	
yo	**muero**	yo	**muera**
tú	**mueres**	tú	**mueras**
él	**muere**	él	**muera**
nosotros	mor**imos**	nosotros	**muramos**
vosotros	mor**ís**	vosotros	**muráis**
ellos	**mueren**	ellos	**mueran**

FUTURE		CONDITIONAL	
yo	morir**é**	yo	morir**ía**
tú	morir**ás**	tú	morir**ías**
él	morir**á**	él	morir**ía**
nosotros	morir**emos**	nosotros	morir**íamos**
vosotros	morir**éis**	vosotros	morir**íais**
ellos	morir**án**	ellos	morir**ían**

IMPERFECT		PRETERITE	
yo	mor**ía**	yo	mor**í**
tú	mor**ías**	tú	mor**iste**
él	mor**ía**	él	**murió**
nosotros	mor**íamos**	nosotros	mor**imos**
vosotros	mor**íais**	vosotros	mor**isteis**
ellos	mor**ían**	ellos	**murieron**

mover *to move*

PAST PARTICIPLE	IMPERATIVE
movido	mueve
	moved
GERUND	
moviendo	

PRESENT		PRESENT SUBJUNCTIVE	
yo	muevo	yo	mueva
tú	mueves	tú	muevas
él	mueve	él	mueva
nosotros	movemos	nosotros	movamos
vosotros	movéis	vosotros	mováis
ellos	mueven	ellos	muevan

FUTURE		CONDITIONAL	
yo	moveré	yo	movería
tú	moverás	tú	moverías
él	moverá	él	movería
nosotros	moveremos	nosotros	moveríamos
vosotros	moveréis	vosotros	moveríais
ellos	moverán	ellos	moverían

IMPERFECT		PRETERITE	
yo	movía	yo	moví
tú	movías	tú	moviste
él	movía	él	movió
nosotros	movíamos	nosotros	movimos
vosotros	movíais	vosotros	movisteis
ellos	movían	ellos	movieron

---

nacer *to be born*

PAST PARTICIPLE

nac**ido**

GERUND

nac**iendo**

IMPERATIVE

nac**e**

nac**ed**

PRESENT		PRESENT SUBJUNCTIVE	
yo	nazco	yo	nazca
tú	naces	tú	nazcas
él	nace	él	nazca
nosotros	nacemos	nosotros	nazcamos
vosotros	nacéis	vosotros	nazcáis
ellos	nacen	ellos	nazcan

FUTURE		CONDITIONAL	
yo	naceré	yo	nacería
tú	nacerás	tú	nacerías
él	nacerá	él	nacería
nosotros	naceremos	nosotros	naceríamos
vosotros	naceréis	vosotros	naceríais
ellos	nacerán	ellos	nacerían

IMPERFECT		PRETERITE	
yo	nacía	yo	nací
tú	nacías	tú	naciste
él	nacía	él	nació
nosotros	nacíamos	nosotros	nacimos
vosotros	nacíais	vosotros	nacisteis
ellos	nacían	ellos	nacieron

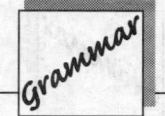

negar *to deny*

PAST PARTICIPLE	IMPERATIVE
negado	**niega**
	negad
GERUND	
negando	

PRESENT		PRESENT SUBJUNCTIVE	
yo	**niego**	yo	**niegue**
tú	**niegas**	tú	**niegues**
él	**niega**	él	**niegue**
nosotros	neg**amos**	nosotros	neg**uemos**
vosotros	neg**áis**	vosotros	neg**uéis**
ellos	**niegan**	ellos	**nieguen**

FUTURE		CONDITIONAL	
yo	negar**é**	yo	negar**ía**
tú	negar**ás**	tú	negar**ías**
él	negar**á**	él	negar**ía**
nosotros	negar**emos**	nosotros	negar**íamos**
vosotros	negar**éis**	vosotros	negar**íais**
ellos	negar**án**	ellos	negar**ían**

IMPERFECT		PRETERITE	
yo	neg**aba**	yo	**negué**
tú	neg**abas**	tú	neg**aste**
él	neg**aba**	él	neg**ó**
nosotros	neg**ábamos**	nosotros	neg**amos**
vosotros	neg**abais**	vosotros	neg**asteis**
ellos	neg**aban**	ellos	neg**aron**

VERB TABLE

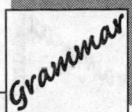

---

oír *to hear*

PAST PARTICIPLE

oído

GERUND

oyendo

IMPERATIVE

oye
oíd

PRESENT		PRESENT SUBJUNCTIVE	
yo	**oigo**	yo	**oiga**
tú	**oyes**	tú	**oigas**
él	**oye**	él	**oiga**
nosotros	**oímos**	nosotros	**oigamos**
vosotros	**oís**	vosotros	**oigáis**
ellos	**oyen**	ellos	**oigan**

FUTURE		CONDITIONAL	
yo	**oiré**	yo	**oiría**
tú	**oirás**	tú	**oirías**
él	**oirá**	él	**oiría**
nosotros	**oiremos**	nosotros	**oiríamos**
vosotros	**oiréis**	vosotros	**oiríais**
ellos	**oirán**	ellos	**oirían**

IMPERFECT		PRETERITE	
yo	**oía**	yo	**oí**
tú	**oías**	tú	**oíste**
él	**oía**	él	**oyó**
nosotros	**oíamos**	nosotros	**oímos**
vosotros	**oíais**	vosotros	**oísteis**
ellos	**oían**	ellos	**oyeron**

oler *to smell*

PAST PARTICIPLE	IMPERATIVE
ol**ido**	**huele**
	ol**ed**
GERUND	
ol**iendo**	

PRESENT		PRESENT SUBJUNCTIVE	
yo	**huelo**	yo	**huela**
tú	**hueles**	tú	**huelas**
él	**huele**	él	**huela**
nosotros	ol**emos**	nosotros	ol**amos**
vosotros	ol**éis**	vosotros	ol**áis**
ellos	**huelen**	ellos	**huelan**

FUTURE		CONDITIONAL	
yo	oler**é**	yo	oler**ía**
tú	oler**ás**	tú	oler**ías**
él	oler**á**	él	oler**ía**
nosotros	oler**emos**	nosotros	oler**íamos**
vosotros	oler**éis**	vosotros	oler**íais**
ellos	oler**án**	ellos	oler**ían**

IMPERFECT		PRETERITE	
yo	ol**ía**	yo	ol**í**
tú	ol**ías**	tú	ol**iste**
él	ol**ía**	él	ol**ió**
nosotros	ol**íamos**	nosotros	ol**imos**
vosotros	ol**íais**	vosotros	ol**isteis**
ellos	ol**ían**	ellos	ol**ieron**

VERB TABLE

pagar *to pay*

PAST PARTICIPLE	IMPERATIVE
pagado	paga
	pagad
GERUND	
pagando	

PRESENT		PRESENT SUBJUNCTIVE	
yo	pago	yo	pague
tú	pagas	tú	pagues
él	paga	él	pague
nosotros	pagamos	nosotros	paguemos
vosotros	pagáis	vosotros	paguéis
ellos	pagan	ellos	paguen

FUTURE		CONDITIONAL	
yo	pagaré	yo	pagaría
tú	pagarás	tú	pagarías
él	pagará	él	pagaría
nosotros	pagaremos	nosotros	pagaríamos
vosotros	pagaréis	vosotros	pagaríais
ellos	pagarán	ellos	pagarían

IMPERFECT		PRETERITE	
yo	pagaba	yo	pagué
tú	pagabas	tú	pagaste
él	pagaba	él	pagó
nosotros	pagábamos	nosotros	pagamos
vosotros	pagabais	vosotros	pagasteis
ellos	pagaban	ellos	pagaron

pedir *to ask for*

PAST PARTICIPLE	IMPERATIVE
ped**ido**	**pide**
	ped**id**
GERUND	
pidiendo	

PRESENT		PRESENT SUBJUNCTIVE	
yo	**pido**	yo	**pida**
tú	**pides**	tú	**pidas**
él	**pide**	él	**pida**
nosotros	ped**imos**	nosotros	**pidamos**
vosotros	ped**ís**	vosotros	**pidáis**
ellos	**piden**	ellos	**pidan**

FUTURE		CONDITIONAL	
yo	pedir**é**	yo	pedir**ía**
tú	pedir**ás**	tú	pedir**ías**
él	pedir**á**	él	pedir**ía**
nosotros	pedir**emos**	nosotros	pedir**íamos**
vosotros	pedir**éis**	vosotros	pedir**íais**
ellos	pedir**án**	ellos	pedir**ían**

IMPERFECT		PRETERITE	
yo	ped**ía**	yo	ped**í**
tú	ped**ías**	tú	ped**iste**
él	ped**ía**	él	**pidió**
nosotros	ped**íamos**	nosotros	ped**imos**
vosotros	ped**íais**	vosotros	ped**isteis**
ellos	ped**ían**	ellos	**pidieron**

pensar *to think*

PAST PARTICIPLE	IMPERATIVE
pensado	piensa
	pensad
GERUND	
pensando	

PRESENT		PRESENT SUBJUNCTIVE	
yo	pienso	yo	piense
tú	piensas	tú	pienses
él	piensa	él	piense
nosotros	pensamos	nosotros	pensemos
vosotros	pensáis	vosotros	penséis
ellos	piensan	ellos	piensen

FUTURE		CONDITIONAL	
yo	pensaré	yo	pensaría
tú	pensarás	tú	pensarías
él	pensará	él	pensaría
nosotros	pensaremos	nosotros	pensaríamos
vosotros	pensaréis	vosotros	pensaríais
ellos	pensarán	ellos	pensarían

IMPERFECT		PRETERITE	
yo	pensaba	yo	pensé
tú	pensabas	tú	pensaste
él	pensaba	él	pensó
nosotros	pensábamos	nosotros	pensamos
vosotros	pensabais	vosotros	pensasteis
ellos	pensaban	ellos	pensaron

poder *to be able*

PAST PARTICIPLE	IMPERATIVE
podido	**puede**
	poded
GERUND	
pudiendo	

PRESENT		PRESENT SUBJUNCTIVE	
yo	**puedo**	yo	**pueda**
tú	**puedes**	tú	**puedas**
él	**puede**	él	**pueda**
nosotros	pod**emos**	nosotros	pod**amos**
vosotros	pod**éis**	vosotros	pod**áis**
ellos	**pueden**	ellos	**puedan**

FUTURE		CONDITIONAL	
yo	**podré**	yo	**podría**
tú	**podrás**	tú	**podrías**
él	**podrá**	él	**podría**
nosotros	**podremos**	nosotros	**podríamos**
vosotros	**podréis**	vosotros	**podríais**
ellos	**podrán**	ellos	**podrían**

IMPERFECT		PRETERITE	
yo	pod**ía**	yo	**pude**
tú	pod**ías**	tú	**pudiste**
él	pod**ía**	él	**pudo**
nosotros	pod**íamos**	nosotros	**pudimos**
vosotros	pod**íais**	vosotros	**pudisteis**
ellos	pod**ían**	ellos	**pudieron**

---

poner *to put*

PAST PARTICIPLE   IMPERATIVE

puesto   **pon**

                                           pon**ed**

GERUND

pon**iendo**

PRESENT		PRESENT SUBJUNCTIVE	
yo	**pongo**	yo	**ponga**
tú	pon**es**	tú	**pongas**
él	pon**e**	él	**ponga**
nosotros	pon**emos**	nosotros	**pongamos**
vosotros	pon**éis**	vosotros	**pongáis**
ellos	pon**en**	ellos	**pongan**

FUTURE		CONDITIONAL	
yo	**pondré**	yo	**pondría**
tú	**pondrás**	tú	**pondrías**
él	**pondrá**	él	**pondría**
nosotros	**pondremos**	nosotros	**pondríamos**
vosotros	**pondréis**	vosotros	**pondríais**
ellos	**pondrán**	ellos	**pondrían**

IMPERFECT		PRETERITE	
yo	pon**ía**	yo	**puse**
tú	pon**ías**	tú	**pusiste**
él	pon**ía**	él	**puso**
nosotros	pon**íamos**	nosotros	**pusimos**
vosotros	pon**íais**	vosotros	**pusisteis**
ellos	pon**ían**	ellos	**pusieron**

prohibir *to forbid*

PAST PARTICIPLE	IMPERATIVE
prohib**ido**	proh**íbe**
	prohib**id**
GERUND	
prohib**iendo**	

PRESENT

yo	proh**íbo**
tú	proh**íbes**
él	proh**íbe**
nosotros	prohib**imos**
vosotros	prohib**ís**
ellos	proh**íben**

PRESENT SUBJUNCTIVE

yo	proh**íba**
tú	proh**íbas**
él	proh**íba**
nosotros	prohib**amos**
vosotros	prohib**áis**
ellos	proh**íban**

FUTURE

yo	prohibir**é**
tú	prohibir**ás**
él	prohibir**á**
nosotros	prohibir**emos**
vosotros	prohibir**éis**
ellos	prohibir**án**

CONDITIONAL

yo	prohibir**ía**
tú	prohibir**ías**
él	prohibir**ía**
nosotros	prohibir**íamos**
vosotros	prohibir**íais**
ellos	prohibir**ían**

IMPERFECT

yo	prohib**ía**
tú	prohib**ías**
él	prohib**ía**
nosotros	prohib**íamos**
vosotros	prohib**íais**
ellos	prohib**ían**

PRETERITE

yo	prohib**í**
tú	prohib**iste**
él	prohib**ió**
nosotros	prohib**imos**
vosotros	prohib**isteis**
ellos	prohib**ieron**

VERB TABLE

querer *to want*

PAST PARTICIPLE	IMPERATIVE
quer**ido**	**quiere**
	quer**ed**
GERUND	
quer**iendo**	

PRESENT		PRESENT SUBJUNCTIVE	
yo	**quiero**	yo	**quiera**
tú	**quieres**	tú	**quieras**
él	**quiere**	él	**quiera**
nosotros	quer**emos**	nosotros	quer**amos**
vosotros	quer**éis**	vosotros	quer**áis**
ellos	**quieren**	ellos	**quieran**

FUTURE		CONDITIONAL	
yo	**querré**	yo	**querría**
tú	**querrás**	tú	**querrías**
él	**querrá**	él	**querría**
nosotros	**querremos**	nosotros	**querríamos**
vosotros	**querréis**	vosotros	**querríais**
ellos	**querrán**	ellos	**querrían**

IMPERFECT		PRETERITE	
yo	quer**ía**	yo	**quise**
tú	quer**ías**	tú	**quisiste**
él	quer**ía**	él	**quiso**
nosotros	quer**íamos**	nosotros	**quisimos**
vosotros	quer**íais**	vosotros	**quisisteis**
ellos	quer**ían**	ellos	**quisieron**

---

rehusar *to refuse*

PAST PARTICIPLE

rehus**ado**

GERUND

rehus**ando**

IMPERATIVE

rehús**a**
rehusa**d**

PRESENT		PRESENT SUBJUNCTIVE	
yo	rehús**o**	yo	rehús**e**
tú	rehús**as**	tú	rehús**es**
él	rehús**a**	él	rehús**e**
nosotros	rehus**amos**	nosotros	rehus**emos**
vosotros	rehus**áis**	vosotros	rehus**éis**
ellos	rehús**an**	ellos	rehús**en**

FUTURE		CONDITIONAL	
yo	rehusar**é**	yo	rehusar**ía**
tú	rehusar**ás**	tú	rehusar**ías**
él	rehusar**á**	él	rehusar**ía**
nosotros	rehusar**emos**	nosotros	rehusar**íamos**
vosotros	rehusar**éis**	vosotros	rehusar**íais**
ellos	rehusar**án**	ellos	rehusar**ían**

IMPERFECT		PRETERITE	
yo	rehus**aba**	yo	rehus**é**
tú	rehus**abas**	tú	rehus**aste**
él	rehus**aba**	él	rehus**ó**
nosotros	rehus**ábamos**	nosotros	rehus**amos**
vosotros	rehus**abais**	vosotros	rehus**asteis**
ellos	rehus**aban**	ellos	rehus**aron**

reír *to laugh*

PAST PARTICIPLE	IMPERATIVE
reí**do**	rí**e**
	reí**d**
GERUND	
r**iendo**	

PRESENT		PRESENT SUBJUNCTIVE	
yo	río	yo	ría
tú	ríes	tú	rías
él	ríe	él	ría
nosotros	reímos	nosotros	riamos
vosotros	reís	vosotros	riáis
ellos	ríen	ellos	rían

FUTURE		CONDITIONAL	
yo	reiré	yo	reiría
tú	reirás	tú	reirías
él	reirá	él	reiría
nosotros	reiremos	nosotros	reiríamos
vosotros	reiréis	vosotros	reiríais
ellos	reirán	ellos	reirían

IMPERFECT		PRETERITE	
yo	reía	yo	reí
tú	reías	tú	reíste
él	reía	él	rió
nosotros	reíamos	nosotros	reímos
vosotros	reíais	vosotros	reísteis
ellos	reían	ellos	rieron

reñir *to scold*

PAST PARTICIPLE	IMPERATIVE
reñ**ido**	**riñe**
	reñ**id**
GERUND	
riñendo	

PRESENT		PRESENT SUBJUNCTIVE	
yo	ri**ño**	yo	ri**ña**
tú	ri**ñes**	tú	ri**ñas**
él	ri**ñe**	él	ri**ña**
nosotros	reñ**imos**	nosotros	ri**ñamos**
vosotros	reñ**ís**	vosotros	ri**ñáis**
ellos	ri**ñen**	ellos	ri**ñan**

FUTURE		CONDITIONAL	
yo	reñir**é**	yo	reñir**ía**
tú	reñir**ás**	tú	reñir**ías**
él	reñir**á**	él	reñir**ía**
nosotros	reñir**emos**	nosotros	reñir**íamos**
vosotros	reñir**éis**	vosotros	reñir**íais**
ellos	reñir**án**	ellos	reñir**ían**

IMPERFECT		PRETERITE	
yo	reñ**ía**	yo	reñ**í**
tú	reñ**ías**	tú	reñ**iste**
él	reñ**ía**	él	ri**ñó**
nosotros	reñ**íamos**	nosotros	reñ**imos**
vosotros	reñ**íais**	vosotros	reñ**isteis**
ellos	reñ**ían**	ellos	ri**ñeron**

VERB TABLE

---

resolver *to solve*

PAST PARTICIPLE	IMPERATIVE
resuelto	**resuelve**
	resolve**d**
GERUND	
resolv**iendo**	

PRESENT		PRESENT SUBJUNCTIVE	
yo	**resuelvo**	yo	**resuelva**
tú	**resuelves**	tú	**resuelvas**
él	**resuelve**	él	**resuelva**
nosotros	resolv**emos**	nosotros	resolv**amos**
vosotros	resolv**éis**	vosotros	resolv**áis**
ellos	**resuelven**	ellos	**resuelvan**

FUTURE		CONDITIONAL	
yo	resolver**é**	yo	resolver**ía**
tú	resolver**ás**	tú	resolver**ías**
él	resolver**á**	él	resolver**ía**
nosotros	resolver**emos**	nosotros	resolver**íamos**
vosotros	resolver**éis**	vosotros	resolver**íais**
ellos	resolver**án**	ellos	resolver**ían**

IMPERFECT		PRETERITE	
yo	resolv**ía**	yo	resolv**í**
tú	resolv**ías**	tú	resolv**iste**
él	resolv**ía**	él	resolv**ió**
nosotros	resolv**íamos**	nosotros	resolv**imos**
vosotros	resolv**íais**	vosotros	resolv**isteis**
ellos	resolv**ían**	ellos	resolv**ieron**

reunir *to put together, to gather*

PAST PARTICIPLE	IMPERATIVE
reun**ido**	**reúne**
	reun**id**
GERUND	
reun**iendo**	

PRESENT		PRESENT SUBJUNCTIVE	
yo	**reúno**	yo	**reúna**
tú	**reúnes**	tú	**reúnas**
él	**reúne**	él	**reúna**
nosotros	reun**imos**	**nosotros**	reun**amos**
vosotros	reun**ís**	**vosotros**	reun**áis**
ellos	**reúnen**	**ellos**	**reúnan**

FUTURE		CONDITIONAL	
yo	reunir**é**	yo	reunir**ía**
tú	reunir**ás**	tú	reunir**ías**
él	reunir**á**	él	reunir**ía**
nosotros	reunir**emos**	**nosotros**	reunir**íamos**
vosotros	reunir**éis**	**vosotros**	reunir**íais**
ellos	reunir**án**	**ellos**	reunir**ían**

IMPERFECT		PRETERITE	
yo	reun**ía**	yo	reun**í**
tú	reun**ías**	tú	reun**iste**
él	reun**ía**	él	reun**ió**
nosotros	reun**íamos**	**nosotros**	reun**imos**
vosotros	reun**íais**	**vosotros**	reun**isteis**
ellos	reun**ían**	**ellos**	reun**ieron**

VERB TABLE

rogar *to beg*	

PAST PARTICIPLE	IMPERATIVE
rog**ado**	**ruega**
	roga**d**
GERUND	
rog**ando**	

PRESENT		PRESENT SUBJUNCTIVE	
yo	**ruego**	yo	**ruegue**
tú	**ruegas**	tú	**ruegues**
él	**ruega**	él	**ruegue**
nosotros	rog**amos**	nosotros	**roguemos**
vosotros	rog**áis**	vosotros	**roguéis**
ellos	**ruegan**	ellos	**rueguen**

FUTURE		CONDITIONAL	
yo	rogar**é**	yo	rogar**ía**
tú	rogar**ás**	tú	rogar**ías**
él	rogar**á**	él	rogar**ía**
nosotros	rogar**emos**	nosotros	rogar**íamos**
vosotros	rogar**éis**	vosotros	rogar**íais**
ellos	rogar**án**	ellos	rogar**ían**

IMPERFECT		PRETERITE	
yo	rog**aba**	yo	**rogué**
tú	rog**abas**	tú	rog**aste**
él	rog**aba**	él	rog**ó**
nosotros	rog**ábamos**	nosotros	rog**amos**
vosotros	rog**abais**	vosotros	rog**asteis**
ellos	rog**aban**	ellos	rog**aron**

romper *to break*

PAST PARTICIPLE	IMPERATIVE
roto	rompe
	romped
GERUND	
rompiendo	

PRESENT		PRESENT SUBJUNCTIVE	
yo	rompo	yo	rompa
tú	rompes	tú	rompas
él	rompe	él	rompa
nosotros	rompemos	nosotros	rompamos
vosotros	rompéis	vosotros	rompáis
ellos	rompen	ellos	rompan

FUTURE		CONDITIONAL	
yo	romperé	yo	rompería
tú	romperás	tú	romperías
él	romperá	él	rompería
nosotros	romperemos	nosotros	romperíamos
vosotros	romperéis	vosotros	romperíais
ellos	romperán	ellos	romperían

IMPERFECT		PRETERITE	
yo	rompía	yo	rompí
tú	rompías	tú	rompiste
él	rompía	él	rompió
nosotros	rompíamos	nosotros	rompimos
vosotros	rompíais	vosotros	rompisteis
ellos	rompían	ellos	rompieron

VERB TABLE

saber *to know*

PAST PARTICIPLE	IMPERATIVE
sab**ido**	sab**e**
	sab**ed**
GERUND	
sab**iendo**	

PRESENT

yo	sé
tú	sabes
él	sabe
nosotros	sabemos
vosotros	sabéis
ellos	saben

PRESENT SUBJUNCTIVE

yo	sepa
tú	sepas
él	sepa
nosotros	sepamos
vosotros	sepáis
ellos	sepan

FUTURE

yo	sabré
tú	sabrás
él	sabrá
nosotros	sabremos
vosotros	sabréis
ellos	sabrán

CONDITIONAL

yo	sabría
tú	sabrías
él	sabría
nosotros	sabríamos
vosotros	sabríais
ellos	sabrían

IMPERFECT

yo	sabía
tú	sabías
él	sabía
nosotros	sabíamos
vosotros	sabíais
ellos	sabían

PRETERITE

yo	supe
tú	supiste
él	supo
nosotros	supimos
vosotros	supisteis
ellos	supieron

sacar *to take out*

PAST PARTICIPLE	IMPERATIVE
sac**ado**	sac**a**
	sac**ad**
GERUND	
sac**ando**	

PRESENT		PRESENT SUBJUNCTIVE	
yo	sac**o**	yo	saque
tú	sac**as**	tú	saques
él	sac**a**	él	saque
nosotros	sac**amos**	nosotros	saquemos
vosotros	sac**áis**	vosotros	saqueís
ellos	sac**an**	ellos	saquen

FUTURE		CONDITIONAL	
yo	sacar**é**	yo	sacar**ía**
tú	sacar**ás**	tú	sacar**ías**
él	sacar**á**	él	sacar**ía**
nosotros	sacar**emos**	nosotros	sacar**íamos**
vosotros	sacar**éis**	vosotros	sacar**íais**
ellos	sacar**án**	ellos	sacar**ían**

IMPERFECT		PRETERITE	
yo	sac**aba**	yo	saqué
tú	sac**abas**	tú	sac**aste**
él	sac**aba**	él	sac**ó**
nosotros	sac**ábamos**	nosotros	sac**amos**
vosotros	sac**abais**	vosotros	sac**asteis**
ellos	sac**aban**	ellos	sac**aron**

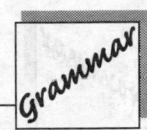

---

salir *to go out*

PAST PARTICIPLE	IMPERATIVE
salido	sal
	salid
GERUND	
saliendo	

PRESENT		PRESENT SUBJUNCTIVE	
yo	salgo	yo	salga
tú	sales	tú	salgas
él	sale	él	salga
nosotros	salimos	nosotros	salgamos
vosotros	salís	vosotros	salgáis
ellos	salen	ellos	salgan

FUTURE		CONDITIONAL	
yo	saldré	yo	saldría
tú	saldrás	tú	saldrías
él	saldrá	él	saldría
nosotros	saldremos	nosotros	saldríamos
vosotros	saldréis	vosotros	saldríais
ellos	saldrán	ellos	saldrían

IMPERFECT		PRETERITE	
yo	salía	yo	salí
tú	salías	tú	saliste
él	salía	él	salió
nosotros	salíamos	nosotros	salimos
vosotros	salíais	vosotros	salisteis
ellos	salían	ellos	salieron

satisfacer *to satisfy*

PAST PARTICIPLE	IMPERATIVE
satisfecho	**satisfaz**/satisfac**e**
	satisfac**d**
GERUND	
satisfac**iendo**	

PRESENT		PRESENT SUBJUNCTIVE	
yo	**satisfago**	yo	**satisfaga**
tú	satisfac**es**	tú	**satisfagas**
él	satisfac**e**	él	**satisfaga**
nosotros	satisfac**emos**	nosotros	**satisfagamos**
vosotros	satisfac**éis**	vosotros	**satisfagáis**
ellos	satisfac**en**	ellos	**satisfagan**

FUTURE		CONDITIONAL	
yo	**satisfaré**	yo	**satisfaría**
tú	**satisfarás**	tú	**satisfarías**
él	**satisfará**	él	**satisfaría**
nosotros	**satisfaremos**	nosotros	**satisfaríamos**
vosotros	**satisfaréis**	vosotros	**satisfaríais**
ellos	**satisfarán**	ellos	**satisfarían**

IMPERFECT		PRETERITE	
yo	satisfac**ía**	yo	**satisfice**
tú	satisfac**ías**	tú	**satisficiste**
él	satisfac**ía**	él	**satisfizo**
nosotros	satisfac**íamos**	nosotros	**satisficimos**
vosotros	satisfac**íais**	vosotros	**satisficisteis**
ellos	satisfac**ían**	ellos	**satisficieron**

VERB TABLE

seguir *to follow*

PAST PARTICIPLE	IMPERATIVE
seguido	sigue
	seguid
GERUND	
siguiendo	

PRESENT

yo	sigo
tú	sigues
él	sigue
nosotros	seguimos
vosotros	seguís
ellos	siguen

PRESENT SUBJUNCTIVE

yo	siga
tú	sigas
él	siga
nosotros	sigamos
vosotros	sigáis
ellos	sigan

FUTURE

yo	seguiré
tú	seguirás
él	seguirá
nosotros	seguiremos
vosotros	seguiréis
ellos	seguirán

CONDITIONAL

yo	seguiría
tú	seguirías
él	seguiría
nosotros	seguiríamos
vosotros	seguiríais
ellos	seguirían

IMPERFECT

yo	seguía
tú	seguías
él	seguía
nosotros	seguíamos
vosotros	seguíais
ellos	seguían

PRETERITE

yo	seguí
tú	seguiste
él	siguió
nosotros	seguimos
vosotros	seguisteis
ellos	siguieron

sentir *to feel*

PAST PARTICIPLE	IMPERATIVE
sent**ido**	**siente**
	sent**id**
GERUND	
sintiendo	

PRESENT

yo	**siento**
tú	**sientes**
él	**siente**
nosotros	sent**imos**
vosotros	sent**ís**
ellos	**sienten**

PRESENT SUBJUNCTIVE

yo	**sienta**
tú	**sientas**
él	**sienta**
nosotros	**sintamos**
vosotros	**sintáis**
ellos	**sientan**

FUTURE

yo	sentir**é**
tú	sentir**ás**
él	sentir**á**
nosotros	sentir**emos**
vosotros	sentir**éis**
ellos	sentir**án**

CONDITIONAL

yo	sentir**ía**
tú	sentir**ías**
él	sentir**ía**
nosotros	sentir**íamos**
vosotros	sentir**íais**
ellos	sentir**ían**

IMPERFECT

yo	sent**ía**
tú	sent**ías**
él	sent**ía**
nosotros	sent**íamos**
vosotros	sent**íais**
ellos	sent**ían**

PRETERITE

yo	sent**í**
tú	sent**iste**
él	**sintió**
nosotros	sent**imos**
vosotros	sent**isteis**
ellos	**sintieron**

VERB TABLE

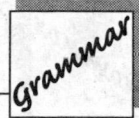

ser *to be*

PAST PARTICIPLE	IMPERATIVE
sido	**sé**
	sed
GERUND	
siendo	

PRESENT

yo	**soy**
tú	**eres**
él	**es**
nosotros	**somos**
vosotros	**sois**
ellos	**son**

PRESENT SUBJUNCTIVE

yo	**sea**
tú	**seas**
él	**sea**
nosotros	**seamos**
vosotros	**seáis**
ellos	**sean**

FUTURE

yo	**seré**
tú	**serás**
él	**será**
nosotros	**seremos**
vosotros	**seréis**
ellos	**serán**

CONDITIONAL

yo	**sería**
tú	**serías**
él	**sería**
nosotros	**seríamos**
vosotros	**seríais**
ellos	**serían**

IMPERFECT

yo	**era**
tú	**eras**
él	**era**
nosotros	**éramos**
vosotros	**erais**
ellos	**eran**

PRETERITE

yo	**fui**
tú	**fuiste**
él	**fue**
nosotros	**fuimos**
vosotros	**fuisteis**
ellos	**fueron**

tener *to have*

PAST PARTICIPLE	IMPERATIVE
ten**ido**	**ten**
	tene**d**
GERUND	
ten**iendo**	

PRESENT		PRESENT SUBJUNCTIVE	
yo	**tengo**	yo	**tenga**
tú	**tienes**	tú	**tengas**
él	**tiene**	él	**tenga**
nosotros	ten**emos**	nosotros	**tengamos**
vosotros	ten**éis**	vosotros	**tengáis**
ellos	**tienen**	ellos	**tengan**

FUTURE		CONDITIONAL	
yo	**tendré**	yo	**tendría**
tú	**tendrás**	tú	**tendrías**
él	**tendrá**	él	**tendría**
nosotros	**tendremos**	nosotros	**tendríamos**
vosotros	**tendréis**	vosotros	**tendríais**
ellos	**tendrán**	ellos	**tendrían**

IMPERFECT		PRETERITE	
yo	ten**ía**	yo	**tuve**
tú	ten**ías**	tú	**tuviste**
él	ten**ía**	él	**tuvo**
nosotros	ten**íamos**	nosotros	**tuvimos**
vosotros	ten**íais**	vosotros	**tuvisteis**
ellos	ten**ían**	ellos	**tuvieron**

---

torcer *to twist*

PAST PARTICIPLE	IMPERATIVE
torc**ido**	**tuerce**
	torc**ed**
GERUND	
torc**iendo**	

PRESENT		PRESENT SUBJUNCTIVE	
yo	**tuerzo**	yo	**tuerza**
tú	**tuerces**	tú	**tuerzas**
él	**tuerce**	él	**tuerza**
nosotros	torcemos	nosotros	torzamos
vosotros	torcéis	vosotros	torzáis
ellos	**tuercen**	ellos	**tuerzan**

FUTURE		CONDITIONAL	
yo	torceré	yo	torcería
tú	torcerás	tú	torcerías
él	torcerá	él	torcería
nosotros	torceremos	nosotros	torceríamos
vosotros	torceréis	vosotros	torceríais
ellos	torcerán	ellos	torcerían

IMPERFECT		PRETERITE	
yo	torcía	yo	torcí
tú	torcías	tú	torciste
él	torcía	él	torció
nosotros	torcíamos	nosotros	torcimos
vosotros	torcíais	vosotros	torcisteis
ellos	torcían	ellos	torcieron

traer *to bring*

PAST PARTICIPLE	IMPERATIVE
traído	tra**e**
	tra**ed**
GERUND	
trayendo	

PRESENT		PRESENT SUBJUNCTIVE	
yo	**traigo**	yo	**traiga**
tú	traes	tú	**traigas**
él	trae	él	**traiga**
nosotros	tra**emos**	nosotros	**traigamos**
vosotros	tra**éis**	vosotros	**traigáis**
ellos	traen	ellos	**traigan**

FUTURE		CONDITIONAL	
yo	traer**é**	yo	traer**ía**
tú	traer**ás**	tú	traer**ías**
él	traer**á**	él	traer**ía**
nosotros	traer**emos**	nosotros	traer**íamos**
vosotros	traer**éis**	vosotros	traer**íais**
ellos	traer**án**	ellos	traer**ían**

IMPERFECT		PRETERITE	
yo	tra**ía**	yo	**traje**
tú	tra**ías**	tú	**trajiste**
él	tra**ía**	él	**trajo**
nosotros	tra**íamos**	nosotros	**trajimos**
vosotros	tra**íais**	vosotros	**trajisteis**
ellos	tra**ían**	ellos	**trajeron**

valer *to be worth*	

PAST PARTICIPLE	IMPERATIVE
val**ido**	val**e**
	val**ed**
GERUND	
val**iendo**	

PRESENT		PRESENT SUBJUNCTIVE	
yo	**valgo**	yo	**valga**
tú	vales	tú	**valgas**
él	vale	él	**valga**
nosotros	valemos	nosotros	**valgamos**
vosotros	valéis	vosotros	**valgáis**
ellos	valen	ellos	**valgan**

FUTURE		CONDITIONAL	
yo	**valdré**	yo	**valdría**
tú	**valdrás**	tú	**valdrías**
él	**valdrá**	él	**valdría**
nosotros	**valdremos**	nosotros	**valdríamos**
vosotros	**valdréis**	vosotros	**valdríais**
ellos	**valdrán**	ellos	**valdrían**

IMPERFECT		PRETERITE	
yo	val**ía**	yo	val**í**
tú	val**ías**	tú	val**iste**
él	val**ía**	él	val**ió**
nosotros	val**íamos**	nosotros	val**imos**
vosotros	val**íais**	vosotros	val**isteis**
ellos	val**ían**	ellos	val**ieron**

vencer *to win*

PAST PARTICIPLE	IMPERATIVE
vencido	vence
	venced
GERUND	
venciendo	

PRESENT		PRESENT SUBJUNCTIVE	
yo	venzo	yo	venza
tú	vences	tú	venzas
él	vence	él	venza
nosotros	vencemos	nosotros	venzamos
vosotros	vencéis	vosotros	venzáis
ellos	vencen	ellos	venzan

FUTURE		CONDITIONAL	
yo	venceré	yo	vencería
tú	vencerás	tú	vencerías
él	vencerá	él	vencería
nosotros	venceremos	nosotros	venceríamos
vosotros	venceréis	vosotros	venceríais
ellos	vencerán	ellos	vencerían

IMPERFECT		PRETERITE	
yo	vencía	yo	vencí
tú	vencías	tú	venciste
él	vencía	él	venció
nosotros	vencíamos	nosotros	vencimos
vosotros	vencíais	vosotros	vencisteis
ellos	vencían	ellos	vencieron

VERB TABLE

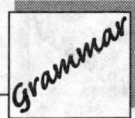

---

venir *to come*

PAST PARTICIPLE	IMPERATIVE
ven**ido**	**ven**
	veni**d**
GERUND	
viniendo	

PRESENT		PRESENT SUBJUNCTIVE	
yo	vengo	yo	venga
tú	vienes	tú	vengas
él	viene	él	venga
nosotros	venimos	nosotros	vengamos
vosotros	venís	vosotros	vengáis
ellos	vienen	ellos	vengan

FUTURE		CONDITIONAL	
yo	vendré	yo	vendría
tú	vendrás	tú	vendrías
él	vendrá	él	vendría
nosotros	vendremos	nosotros	vendríamos
vosotros	vendréis	vosotros	vendríais
ellos	vendrán	ellos	vendrían

IMPERFECT		PRETERITE	
yo	venía	yo	vine
tú	venías	tú	viniste
él	venía	él	vino
nosotros	veníamos	nosotros	vinimos
vosotros	veníais	vosotros	vinisteis
ellos	venían	ellos	vinieron

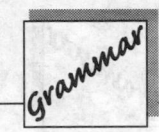

ver *to see*

PAST PARTICIPLE	IMPERATIVE
visto	**ve**
	ved
GERUND	
v**iendo**	

PRESENT		PRESENT SUBJUNCTIVE	
yo	veo	yo	vea
tú	ves	tú	veas
él	ve	él	vea
nosotros	vemos	nosotros	veamos
vosotros	veis	vosotros	veáis
ellos	ven	ellos	vean

FUTURE		CONDITIONAL	
yo	veré	yo	vería
tú	verás	tú	verías
él	verá	él	vería
nosotros	veremos	nosotros	veríamos
vosotros	veréis	vosotros	veríais
ellos	verán	ellos	verían

IMPERFECT		PRETERITE	
yo	veía	yo	vi
tú	veías	tú	viste
él	veía	él	vio
nosotros	veíamos	nosotros	vimos
vosotros	veíais	vosotros	visteis
ellos	veían	ellos	vieron

VERB TABLE

---

volcar *to overturn*

PAST PARTICIPLE

volc**ado**

GERUND

volc**ando**

IMPERATIVE

vuelca

volca**d**

PRESENT		PRESENT SUBJUNCTIVE	
yo	**vuelco**	yo	**vuelque**
tú	**vuelcas**	tú	**vuelques**
él	**vuelca**	él	**vuelque**
nosotros	volc**amos**	nosotros	**volquemos**
vosotros	volc**áis**	vosotros	**volquéis**
ellos	**vuelcan**	ellos	**vuelquen**

FUTURE		CONDITIONAL	
yo	volcar**é**	yo	volcar**ía**
tú	volcar**ás**	tú	volcar**ías**
él	volcar**á**	él	volcar**ía**
nosotros	volcar**emos**	nosotros	volcar**íamos**
vosotros	volcar**éis**	vosotros	volcar**íais**
ellos	volcar**án**	ellos	volcar**ían**

IMPERFECT		PRETERITE	
yo	volc**aba**	yo	**volqué**
tú	volc**abas**	tú	volc**aste**
él	volc**aba**	él	volc**ó**
nosotros	volc**ábamos**	nosotros	volc**amos**
vosotros	volc**abais**	vosotros	volc**asteis**
ellos	volc**aban**	ellos	volc**aron**

volver *to return*

PAST PARTICIPLE	IMPERATIVE
vuelto	**vuelve**
	volve**d**
GERUND	
volv**iendo**	

PRESENT		PRESENT SUBJUNCTIVE	
yo	**vuelvo**	yo	**vuelva**
tú	**vuelves**	tú	**vuelvas**
él	**vuelve**	él	**vuelva**
nosotros	volv**emos**	nosotros	volv**amos**
vosotros	volv**éis**	vosotros	volv**áis**
ellos	**vuelven**	ellos	**vuelvan**

FUTURE		CONDITIONAL	
yo	volver**é**	yo	volver**ía**
tú	volver**ás**	tú	volver**ías**
él	volver**á**	él	volver**ía**
nosotros	volver**emos**	nosotros	volver**íamos**
vosotros	volver**éis**	vosotros	volver**íais**
ellos	volver**án**	ellos	volver**ían**

IMPERFECT		PRETERITE	
yo	volv**ía**	yo	volv**í**
tú	volv**ías**	tú	volv**iste**
él	volv**ía**	él	volv**ió**
nosotros	volv**íamos**	nosotros	volv**imos**
vosotros	volv**íais**	vosotros	volv**isteis**
ellos	volv**ían**	ellos	volv**ieron**

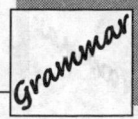

zurcir *to darn*

PAST PARTICIPLE	IMPERATIVE
zurc**ido**	zurc**e**
	zurc**id**
GERUND	
zurc**iendo**	

PRESENT		PRESENT SUBJUNCTIVE	
yo	zur**zo**	yo	zur**za**
tú	zur**ces**	tú	zur**zas**
él	zur**ce**	él	zur**za**
nosotros	zurc**imos**	nosotros	zur**zamos**
vosotros	zurc**ís**	vosotros	zur**záis**
ellos	zur**cen**	ellos	zur**zan**

FUTURE		CONDITIONAL	
yo	zurcir**é**	yo	zurcir**ía**
tú	zurcir**ás**	tú	zurcir**ías**
él	zurcir**á**	él	zurcir**ía**
nosotros	zurcir**emos**	nosotros	zurcir**íamos**
vosotros	zurcir**éis**	vosotros	zurcir**íais**
ellos	zurcir**án**	ellos	zurcir**ían**

IMPERFECT		PRETERITE	
yo	zurc**ía**	yo	zurc**í**
tú	zurc**ías**	tú	zurc**iste**
él	zurc**ía**	él	zurc**ió**
nosotros	zurc**íamos**	nosotros	zurc**imos**
vosotros	zurc**íais**	vosotros	zurc**isteis**
ellos	zurc**ían**	ellos	zurc**ieron**

The following pages, 163 to 186, contain an index of over 2,800 commonly used verbs cross-referred to the appropriate conjugation model.

- Regular verbs belonging to the first, second and third conjugation are numbered 1, 2 and 3 respectively. For the regular conjugations see pp 6 to 13.

- Irregular verbs are numerically cross-referred to the appropriate model as conjugated on pp 82 to 161. Thus, **alzar** is cross-referred to p 100 where **cruzar**, the model for this verb group, is conjugated.

- Verbs which are most commonly used in the reflexive form – e.g. **amodorrarse** – have been cross-referred to the appropriate non-reflexive model. For the full conjugation of a reflexive verb, see pp 28 to 31.

- Verbs printed in **bold** – e.g. **abrir** – are themselves models.

- Superior numbers refer you to notes on p 187 which indicate how the verb differs from its model.

VERBS INDEX

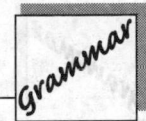

☐ Notes

The notes below indicate special peculiarities of individual verbs. When only some forms of a given tense are affected, all these are shown. When all forms of the tense are affected, only the 1st and 2nd persons are shown, followed by *etc*.

1 Gerund *2* Past Participle *3* Present *4* Preterite *5* Present Subjunctive *6* Imperfect Subjunctive

1) **acaecer, acontecer, amanecer, anochecer, competer, deshelar, escampar, granizar, helar, nevar, nublarse, relampaguear, tronar, verdear, verdecer:** used almost exclusively in infinitive and 3rd person singular

2) **asir** *3* asgo *5* asga, asgas *etc*

3) **atañer** *1* atañendo *4* atañó: see also 1) above

4) **balbucir** *3* balbuceo *5* balbucee, balbucees *etc*

5) **concernir** *3* concierne, conciernen *5* concierna, conciernan: only used in 3rd person

6) **degollar** *3* degüello, degüellas, degüella, degüellan *5* degüelle, degüelles, degüellen

7) **delinquir** *3* delinco *5* delinca, delincas *etc*

8) **desasir** *3* desasgo *5* desasga, desasgas *etc*

9) **discernir** *3* discierno, disciernes, discierne, disciernen *5* discierna, disciernas, disciernan

10) **enraizar** *3* enraízo, enraízas, enraíza, enraízan *5* enraíce, enraíces, enraícen

11) **pudrir** *2* podrido

12) **rehuir** *3* rehúyo, rehúyes, rehúye, rehúyen *5* rehúya, rehúyas, rehúyan

13) **roer** *4* royó, royeron *6* royera, royeras *etc*

14) **soler:** used only in present and imperfect indicative

15) **yacer** *3* yazgo *or* yazco *or* yago *5* yazga *etc or* yazca *etc or* yaga *etc*

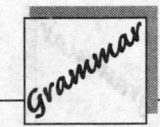

❏ The Gender of Nouns

In Spanish, all nouns are either masculine or feminine, whether denoting people, animals or things. Gender is largely unpredictable and has to be learnt for each noun. However, the following guidelines will help you determine the gender for certain types of nouns.

◆ Nouns denoting male people and animals are usually – but not always – masculine, e.g.

un hombre	**un toro**
a man	*a bull*
un enfermero	**un semental**
a (male) nurse	*a stallion*

◆ Nouns denoting female people and animals are usually – but not always – feminine, e.g.

una niña	**una vaca**
a girl	*a cow*
una enfermera	**una yegua**
a nurse	*a mare*

◆ Some nouns are masculine *or* feminine depending on the sex of the person to whom they refer, e.g.

un camarada	**una camarada**
a (male) comrade	*a (female) comrade*
un belga	**una belga**
a Belgian (man)	*a Belgian (woman)*
un marroquí	**una marroquí**
a Moroccan (man)	*a Moroccan (woman)*

◆ Other nouns referring to either men or women have only one gender which applies to both, e.g.

una persona	**una visita**
a person	*a visitor*
una víctima	**una estrella**
a victim	*a star*

◆ Often the ending of a noun indicates its gender. Shown below are some of the most important to guide you.

NOUNS

Masculine endings

-o	**un clavo** *a nail*, **un plátano** *a banana* EXCEPTIONS: **mano** *hand*, **foto** *photograph*, **moto(cicleta)** *motorbike.*
-l	**un tonel** *a barrel*, **un hotel** *a hotel* EXCEPTIONS: **cal** *lime*, **cárcel** *prison*, **catedral** *cathedral*, **col** *cabbage*, **miel** *honey*, **piel** *skin*, **sal** *salt*, **señal** *sign*
-r	**un tractor** *a tractor*, **el altar** *the altar* EXCEPTIONS: **coliflor** *cauliflower*, **flor** *flower*, **labor** *task*
-y	**el rey** *the king*, **un buey** *an ox* EXCEPTION: **ley** *law*

Feminine endings

-a	**una casa** *a house*, **la cara** *the face* EXCEPTIONS: **día** *day*, **mapa** *map*, **planeta** *planet*, **tranvía** *tram*, and most words ending in -**ma** (**tema** *subject*, **problema** *problem*, etc)
-ión	**una canción** *a song*, **una procesión** *a procession* EXCEPTIONS: most nouns not ending in -**ción** or -**sión**, e.g. **avión** *aeroplane*, **camión** *lorry*, **gorrión** *sparrow*
-dad, -tad, **-tud**	**una ciudad** *a town*, **la libertad** *freedom*, **una multitud** *a crowd*
-ed	**una pared** *a wall*, **la sed** *thirst* EXCEPTION: **césped** *lawn*
-itis	**una faringitis** *pharyngitis*, **la celulitis** *cellulitis*
-iz	**una perdiz** *a partridge*, **una matriz** *a matrix* EXCEPTIONS: **lápiz** *pencil*, **maíz** *corn*, **tapiz** *tapestry*
-sis	**una tesis** *a thesis*, **una dosis** *a dose* EXCEPTIONS: **análisis** *analysis*, **énfasis** *emphasis*, **paréntesis** *parenthesis*
-umbre	**la podredumbre** *rot*, **la muchedumbre** *crowd*

☐ Gender of nouns (Continued)

Some nouns change meaning according to gender. The most common are
set out below:

	MASCULINE	FEMININE
capital	capital (money)	capital (city) → ☐1
clave	harpsichord	clue
cólera	cholera	anger → ☐2
cometa	comet	kite
corriente	current month	current
corte	cut	court (royal) → ☐3
coma	coma	comma → ☐4
cura	priest	cure → ☐5
frente	front (in war)	forehead → ☐6
guardia	guard(sman)	guard → ☐7
guía	guide (person)	guide(book) → ☐8
moral	mulberry tree	morals
orden	order (arrangement)	order (command) → ☐9
ordenanza	office boy	ordinance
papa	Pope	potato
parte	dispatch	part → ☐10
pendiente	earring	slope
pez	fish	pitch
policía	policeman	police
radio	radius, radium	radio

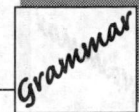

1	**Invirtieron mucho capital** They invested a lot of capital **La capital es muy fea** The capital city is very ugly	
2	**Es difícil luchar contra el cólera** Cholera is difficult to combat	**Montó en cólera** He got angry
3	**Me encanta tu corte de pelo** I love your haircut **Se trasladó la corte a Madrid** The court was moved to Madrid	
4	**Entró en un coma profundo** He went into a deep coma **Aquí hace falta una coma** You need to put a comma here	
5	**¿Quién es? – El cura** Who is It? – The priest	**No tiene cura** It's hopeless
6	**Han mandado a su hijo al frente** Her son has been sent to the front **Tiene la frente muy ancha** She has a very broad forehead	
7	**Vino un guardia de tráfico** A traffic policeman came **Están relevando la guardia ahora** They're changing the guard now	
8	**Nuestro guía nos hizo reír a carcajadas** Our guide had us falling about laughing **Busco una guía turística** I'm looking for a guidebook	
9	**Están en orden alfabético** They're in alphabetical order **No hemos recibido la orden de pago** We haven't had the payment order	
10	**Le mandó un parte al general** He sent a dispatch to the general **En alguna parte debe estar** It must be somewhere or other	

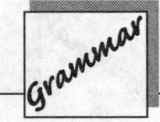

☐ Gender: the formation of feminines

As in English, male and female are sometimes differentiated by the use of two quite separate words, e.g.

mi marido	**mi mujer**
my husband	*my wife*
un toro	**una vaca**
a bull	*a cow*

There are, however, some words in Spanish which show this distinction by the form of their ending:

◆ Nouns ending in **-o** change to **-a** to form the feminine → ①

◆ If the masculine singular form already ends in **-a**, no further **-a** is added to the feminine → ②

◆ If the last letter of the masculine singular form is a consonant, an **-a** is normally added in the feminine* → ③

Feminine forms to note

MASCULINE	FEMININE	
el abad	**la abadesa**	abbot/abbess
un actor	**una actriz**	actor/actress
el alcalde	**la alcaldesa**	mayor/mayoress
el conde	**la condesa**	count/countess
el duque	**la duquesa**	duke/duchess
el emperador	**la emperatriz**	emperor/empress
un poeta	**una poetisa**	poet/poetess
el príncipe	**la princesa**	prince/princess
el rey	**la reina**	king/queen
un sacerdote	**una sacerdotisa**	priest/priestess
un tigre	**una tigresa**	tiger/tigress
el zar	**la zarina**	tzar/tzarina

* If the last syllable has an accent, it disappears in the feminine (see p 292) → ④

Examples

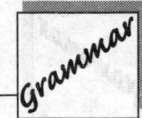

①	**un amigo** a (male) friend	**una amiga** a (female) friend
	un empleado a (male) employee	**una empleada** a (female) employee
	un gato a cat	**una gata** a (female) cat
②	**un deportista** a sportsman	**una deportista** a sportswoman
	un colega a (male) colleague	**una colega** a (female) colleague
	un camarada a (male) comrade	**una camarada** a (female) comrade
③	**un español** a Spaniard, a Spanish man	**una española** a Spanish woman
	un vendedor a salesman	**una vendedora** a saleswoman
	un jugador a (male) player	**una jugadora** a (female) player
④	**un lapón** a Laplander (man)	**una lapona** a Laplander (woman)
	un león a lion	**una leona** a lioness
	un neocelandés a New Zealander (man)	**una neocelandesa** a New Zealander (woman)

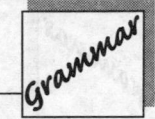

◻ The formation of plurals

◆ Nouns ending in an unstressed vowel add -**s** to the singular form → ①

◆ Nouns ending in a consonant or a stressed vowel add -**es** to the singular form → ②

⚠ BUT:

café	*coffee shop*	(plur: **cafés**)
mamá	*mummy*	(plur: **mamás**)
papá	*daddy*	(plur: **papás**)
pie	*foot*	(plur: **pies**)
sofá	*sofa*	(plur: **sofás**)
té	*tea*	(plur: **tes**)

and words of foreign origin ending in a consonant, e.g.:

coñac	*brandy*	(plur: **coñacs**)
jersey	*jumper*	(plur: **jerseys**)

⚠ NOTE:

— nouns ending in -**n** or -**s** with an accent on the last syllable drop this accent in the plural (see p 292) → ③

— nouns ending in -**n** with the stress on the second-last syllable in the singular add an accent to that syllable in the plural in order to show the correct position for stress (see p 292) → ④

— nouns ending in -**z** change this to **c** in the plural → ⑤

◆ Nouns with an unstressed final syllable ending in -**s** do not change in the plural → ⑥

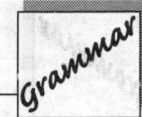
Grammar

1	**la casa** the house **el libro** the book	**las casas** the houses **los libros** the books
2	**un rumor** a rumour **un jabalí** a boar	**unos rumores** (some) rumours **unos jabalíes** (some) boars
3	**la canción** the song **el autobús** the bus	**las canciones** the songs **los autobuses** the buses
4	**un examen** an exam **un crimen** a crime	**unos exámenes** (some) exams **unos crímenes** (some) crimes
5	**la luz** the light	**las luces** the lights
6	**un paraguas** an umbrella **la dosis** the dose **el lunes** Monday	**unos paraguas** (some) umbrellas **las dosis** the doses **los lunes** Mondays

❑ The Definite Article

	WITH MASC NOUN	WITH FEM NOUN	
SING	**el**	**la**	*the*
PLUR	**los**	**las**	*the*

- The gender and number of the noun determine the form of the article → ①

  ⚠ NOTE: However, if the article comes directly before a feminine singular noun which starts with a stressed **a**- or **ha**-, the masculine form **el** is used instead of the feminine **la** → ②

- For uses of the definite article see p 199.

- **a** + **el** becomes **al** → ③

- **de** + **el** becomes **del** → ④

1 **el tren** the train	**la estación** the station
el actor the actor	**la actriz** the actress
los hoteles the hotels	**las escuelas** the schools
los profesores the teachers	**las mujeres** the women

2 **el agua** ⚠ BUT: **la misma agua**
the water   the same water

el hacha ⚠ BUT: **la mejor hacha**
the axe   the best axe

3 **al cine**
to the cinema
al empleado
to the employee
al hospital
to the hospital

4 **del departamento**
from/of the department
del autor
from/of the author
del presidente
from/of the president

❐ Uses of the definite article

While the definite article is used in much the same way in Spanish as it is in English, its use is more widespread in Spanish. Unlike English the definite article is also used:

- ◆ with abstract nouns, except when following certain prepositions → ①

- ◆ in generalizations, especially with plural or uncountable* nouns → ②

- ◆ with parts of the body → ③
  'Ownership' is often indicated by an indirect object pronoun or a reflexive pronoun → ④

- ◆ with titles/ranks/professions followed by a proper name → ⑤

  ⚠ EXCEPTIONS: with **Don/Doña, San/Santo(a)** → ⑥

- ◆ before nouns of official, academic and religious buildings, and names of meals and games → ⑦

- ◆ The definite article is NOT used with nouns in apposition unless those nouns are individualized → ⑧

* An uncountable noun is one which cannot be used in the plural or with an indefinite article, e.g. **el acero** *steel*, **la leche** milk.

Examples

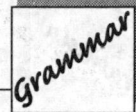

☐1 **Los precios suben**
Prices are rising
El tiempo es oro
Time is money

⚠ BUT:

con pasión   **sin esperanza**
with passion   without hope

☐2 **No me gusta el café**
I don't like coffee
Los niños necesitan ser queridos
Children need to be loved

☐3 **Vuelva la cabeza hacia la izquierda**
Turn your head to the left
No puedo mover las piernas
I can't move my legs

☐4 **La cabeza me da vueltas**
My head is spinning
Lávate las manos
Wash your hands

☐5 **El rey Jorge III**   **el capitán Menéndez**
King George III   Captain Menéndez
el doctor Ochoa   **el señor Ramírez**
Doctor Ochoa   Mr Ramírez

☐6 **Don Arturo Ruiz**   **Santa Teresa**
Mr Arturo Ruiz   Saint Teresa

☐7 **en la cárcel**   **en la universidad**
in prison   at university
en la iglesia   **la cena**
at church   dinner
el tenis   **el ajedrez**
tennis   chess

☐8 **Madrid, capital de España, es la ciudad que ...**
Madrid, the capital of Spain, is the city which ...

⚠ BUT:

Maria Callas, la famosa cantante de ópera ...
Maria Callas, the famous opera singer ...

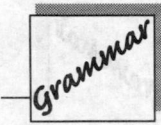

☐ The Indefinite Article

	WITH MASC NOUN	WITH FEM NOUN	
SING	**un**	**una**	*a*
PLUR	**unos**	**unas**	*some*

The indefinite article is used in Spanish largely as it is in English.

⚠ BUT:

◆ There is no article when a person's profession is being stated → ①
  The article is used, however, when the profession is qualified by an adjective → ②

◆ The article is not used with the following words:

otro	*another*	→ ③
cierto	*certain*	→ ④
semejante	*such (a)*	→ ⑤
tal	*such (a)*	→ ⑥
cien	*a hundred*	→ ⑦
mil	*a thousand*	→ ⑧
sin	*without*	→ ⑨
qué	*what a*	→ ⑩

◆ There is no article with a noun in apposition → ⑪. When an abstract noun is qualified by an adjective, the indefinite article is used, but is not translated in English → ⑫

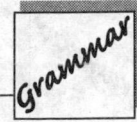

1	**Es profesor**	**Mi madre es enfermera**

1   **Es profesor**   **Mi madre es enfermera**
He's a teacher   My mother is a nurse

2   **Es un buen médico**
He's a good doctor
Se hizo una escritora célebre
She became a famous writer

3   **otro libro**
another book

4   **cierta calle**
a certain street

5   **semejante ruido**
such a noise

6   **tal mentira**
such a lie

7   **cien soldados**
a hundred soldiers

8   **mil años**
a thousand years

9   **sin casa**
without a house

10   **¡Qué sorpresa!**
What a surprise!

11   **Baroja, gran escritor de la Generación del 98**
Baroja, a great writer of the 'Generación del 98'

12   **con una gran sabiduría/un valor admirable**
with great wisdom/admirable courage

Dieron pruebas de una sangre fría increíble
They showed incredible coolness

una película de un mal gusto espantoso
a film in appallingly bad taste

☐ The Article 'lo'

This is never used with a noun. Instead, it is used in the following ways:

♦ As an intensifier before an adjective or adverb in the construction

lo + adjective/adverb + **que** → ①

⚠ NOTE: The adjective agrees with the noun it refers to → ②

♦ With an adjective or participle to form an abstract noun → ③

♦ In the phrase **lo de** to refer to a subject of which speaker and listener are already aware. It can often be translated as *the business/affair of/about ...* → ④

♦ In set expressions, the commonest of which are:

a lo mejor	*maybe, perhaps*	→ ⑤
a lo lejos	*in the distance*	→ ⑥
a lo largo de	*along, through*	→ ⑦
por lo menos	*at least*	→ ⑧
por lo tanto	*therefore, so*	→ ⑨
por lo visto	*apparently*	→ ⑩

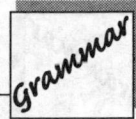
Grammar

1	**No sabíamos lo pequeña que era la casa** We didn't know how small the house was **Sé lo mucho que te gusta la música** I know how much you like music
2	**No te imaginas lo simpáticos que son** You can't imagine how nice they are **Ya sabes lo buenas que son estas manzanas** You already know how good these apples are
3	**Lo bueno de eso es que ...** The good thing about it is that ... **Sentimos mucho lo ocurrido** We are very sorry about what happened
4	**Lo de ayer es mejor que lo olvides** It's better if you forget what happened yesterday **Lo de tu hermano me preocupa mucho** The business about your brother worries me very much
5	**A lo mejor ha salido** Perhaps he's gone out
6	**A lo lejos se veían unas casas** Some houses could be seen in the distance
7	**A lo largo de su vida** Throughout his life **A lo largo de la carretera** Along the road
8	**Hubo por lo menos cincuenta heridos** At least fifty people were injured
9	**No hemos recibido ninguna instrucción al respecto, y por lo tanto no podemos ...** We have not received any instructions about it, therefore we cannot ...
10	**Por lo visto, no viene** Apparently he's not coming OR: He's not coming, it seems

❑ Adjectives

Most adjectives agree in number and in gender with the noun or pronoun.

⚠️ NOTE that:

— if the adjective refers to two or more singular nouns of the same gender, a plural ending of that gender is required → ①
— if the adjective refers to two or more singular nouns of different genders, a masculine plural ending is required → ②

The formation of feminines

◆ Adjectives ending in **-o** change to **-a** → ③
◆ Some groups of adjectives add **-a**:
  – adjectives of nationality or geographical origin → ④
  – adjectives ending in **-or** (except irregular comparatives: see p 210), **-án, -ón, -ín** → ⑤

  ⚠️ NOTE: When there is an accent on the last syllable, it disappears in the feminine (see p 292).

◆ Other adjectives do not change → ⑥

The formation of plurals

◆ Adjectives ending in an unstressed vowel add **-s** → ⑦
◆ Adjectives ending in a stressed vowel or a consonant add **-es** → ⑧

  ⚠️ NOTE:

  – if there is an accent on the last syllable of a word ending in a consonant, it will disappear in the plural (see p 292) → ⑨
  – if the last letter is a **z** it will become a **c** in the plural → ⑩

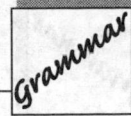

№		
①	**la lengua y la literatura españolas** (the) Spanish language and literature	
②	**Nunca había visto árboles y flores tan raros** I had never seen such strange trees and flowers	
③	**mi hermano pequeño** my little brother	**mi hermana pequeña** my little sister
④	**un chico español** a Spanish boy	**una chica española** a Spanish girl
	el equipo barcelonés the team from Barcelona	**la vida barcelonesa** the Barcelona way of life
⑤	**un niño encantador** a charming little boy	**una niña encantadora** a charming little girl
	un hombre holgazán an idle man	**una mujer holgazana** an idle woman
	un gesto burlón a mocking gesture	**una sonrisa burlona** a mocking smile
	un chico cantarín a boy fond of singing	**una chica cantarina** a girl fond of singing
⑥	**un final feliz** a happy ending	**una infancia feliz** a happy childhood
	mi amigo belga my Belgian (male) friend	**mi amiga belga** my Belgian (female) friend
	el vestido verde the green dress	**la blusa verde** the green blouse
⑦	**el último tren** the last train	**los últimos trenes** the last trains
	una casa vieja an old house	**unas casas viejas** (some) old houses
⑧	**un médico iraní** an Iranian doctor	**unos médicos iraníes** (some) Iranian doctors
	un examen fácil an easy exam	**unos exámenes fáciles** (some) easy exams
⑨	**un río francés** a French river	**unos ríos franceses** (some) French rivers
⑩	**un día feliz** a happy day	**unos días felices** (some) happy days

☐ Invariable Adjectives

Some adjectives and other parts of speech when used adjectivally never change in the feminine or plural.

The commonest of these are:

— nouns denoting colour → ☐1
— compound adjectives → ☐2
— nouns used as adjectives → ☐3

Shortening of Adjectives

◆ The following drop the final **-o** before a masculine singular noun:

bueno *good* → ☐4

malo *bad*

alguno* *some* → ☐5

ninguno* *none*

uno *one* → ☐6

primero *first* → ☐7

tercero *third*

postrero *last* → ☐8

   * ⚠ NOTE: An accent is required to show the correct position for stress.

◆ **Grande** *big, great* is usually shortened to **gran** before a masculine *or* feminine singular noun → ☐9

◆ **Santo** *Saint* changes to **San** except with saints' names beginning with **Do-** or **To-** → ☐10

◆ **Ciento** *a hundred* is shortened to **cien** before a masculine *or* feminine plural noun → ☐11

◆ **Cualquiera** drops the final **-a** before a masculine *or* feminine singular noun → ☐12

Grammar

1	**los vestidos naranja** the orange dresses	
2	**las chaquetas azul marino** the navy blue jackets	
3	**bebés probeta** test-tube babies	**mujeres soldado** women soldiers
4	**un buen libro** a good book	
5	**algún libro** some book	
6	**cuarenta y un años** forty-one years	
7	**el primer hijo** the first child	
8	**un postrer deseo** a last wish	
9	**un gran actor** a great actor	**una gran decepción** a great disappointment
10	**San Antonio** Saint Anthony	**Santo Tomás** Saint Thomas
11	**cien años** a hundred years **cien millones** a hundred million	
12	**cualquier día** any day	**a cualquier hora** any time

☐ Comparatives and Superlatives

Comparatives

These are formed using the following constructions:

más ... (que)	*more ... (than)*	→ 1
menos ... (que)	*less ... (than)*	→ 2
tanto ... como	*as ... as*	→ 3
tan ... como	*as ... as*	→ 4
tan ... que	*so ... that*	→ 5
demasiado ...	*too ...*	
bastante ... } **para**	*enough ...* } *to*	→ 6
suficiente ...	*enough ...*	

♦ *'Than'* followed by a clause is translated by **de lo que** → 7

Superlatives

These are formed using the following constructions:

el/la/los/las más ... (que)	*the most ... (that)*	→ 8
el/la/los/las menos ... (que)	*the least ... (that)*	→ 9

♦ After a superlative the preposition **de** is often translated as *in* → 10

♦ The absolute superlative (*very, most, extremely + adjective*) is expressed in Spanish by **muy** + adjective, or by adding **-ísimo/a/os/as** to the adjective when it ends in a consonant, or to its stem (adjective minus final vowel) when it ends in a vowel → 11

⚠ NOTE: It is sometimes necessary to change the spelling of the adjective when **-ísimo** is added, in order to maintain the same sound (see p 296) → 12

1	**una razón más seria**	
	a more serious reason	
	Es más alto que mi hermano	
	He's taller than my brother	
2	**una película menos conocida**	
	a less well known film	
	Luis es menos tímido que tú	
	Luis is less shy than you	
3	**Pablo tenía tanto miedo como yo**	
	Paul was as frightened as I was	
4	**No es tan grande como creía**	
	It isn't as big as I thought	
5	**El examen era tan difícil que nadie aprobó**	
	The exam was so difficult that nobody passed	
6	**No tengo suficiente dinero para comprarlo**	
	I haven't got enough money to buy it	
7	**Está más cansada de lo que parece**	
	She is more tired than she seems	

8	**el caballo más veloz**	**la casa más pequeña**
	the fastest horse	the smallest house
	los días más lluviosos	**las manzanas más maduras**
	the wettest days	the ripest apples
9	**el hombre menos simpático**	**la niña menos habladora**
	the least likeable man	the least talkative girl
	los cuadros menos bonitos	**las camisas menos viejas**
	the least attractive paintings	the least old shirts
10	**la estación más ruidosa de Londres**	
	the noisiest station in London	
11	**Este libro es muy interesante**	**Tienen un coche rapidísimo**
	This book is very interesting	They have an extremely fast car
	Era facilísimo de hacer	
	It was very easy to make	
12	**Mi tío era muy rico**	**Se hizo riquísimo**
	My uncle was very rich	He became extremely rich
	un león muy feroz	**un tigre ferocísimo**
	a very ferocious lion	an extremely ferocious tiger

ADJECTIVES

❑ Comparatives and Superlatives (Continued)

Adjectives with irregular comparatives/superlatives

ADJECTIVE	COMPARATIVE	SUPERLATIVE
bueno *good*	**mejor** *better*	**el mejor** *the best*
malo *bad*	**peor** *worse*	**el peor** *the worst*
grande *big*	**mayor** OR: **más grande** *bigger; older*	**el mayor** OR: **el más grande** *the biggest; the oldest*
pequeño *small*	**menor** OR: **más pequeño** *smaller; younger; lesser*	**el menor** OR: **el más pequeño** *the smallest; the youngest; the least*

◆ The irregular comparative and superlative forms of **grande** and **pequeño** are used mainly to express:
— age, in which case they come after the noun → ①
— abstract size and degrees of importance, in which case they come before the noun → ②
The regular forms are used mainly to express physical size → ③

◆ Irregular comparatives and superlatives have one form for both masculine and feminine, but always agree in number with the noun → ①

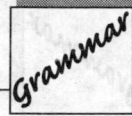

[1] **mis hermanos mayores**
my older brothers
la hija menor
the youngest daughter

[2] **el menor ruido**
the slightest sound
las mayores dificultades
the biggest difficulties

[3] **Este plato es más grande que aquél**
This plate is bigger than that one
Mi casa es más pequeña que la tuya
My house is smaller than yours

❒ Demonstrative Adjectives

	MASCULINE	FEMININE	
SING	este	esta	*this*
	ese	esa	*that*
	aquel	aquella	
PLUR	estos	estas	*these*
	esos	esas	*those*
	aquellos	aquellas	

♦ Demonstrative adjectives normally precede the noun and always agree in number and in gender → ①

♦ The forms **ese/a/os/as** are used:
  — to indicate distance from the speaker but proximity to the person addressed → ②
  — to indicate a not too remote distance → ③

♦ The forms **aquel/la/los/las** are used to indicate distance, in space or time → ④

Examples

---

① **Este bolígrafo no escribe**
This pen is not working
Esa revista es muy mala
That is a very bad magazine
Aquella montaña es muy alta
That mountain (over there) is very high
¿Conoces a esos señores?
Do you know those gentlemen?
Siga Vd hasta aquellos edificios
Carry on until you come to those buildings
¿Ves aquellas personas?
Can you see those people (over there)?

② **Ese papel en donde escribes ...**
That paper you are writing on ...

③ **No me gustan esos cuadros**
I don't like those pictures

④ **Aquella calle parece muy ancha**
That street (over there) looks very wide
Aquellos años sí que fueron felices
Those were really happy years

☐ Interrogative Adjectives

	MASCULINE	FEMININE	
SING {	¿qué?	¿qué?	what?, which?
	¿cuánto?	¿cuánta?	how much?; how many?
PLUR {	¿qué?	¿qué?	what?, which?
	¿cuántos?	¿cuántas?	how much?; how many?

◆ Interrogative adjectives, when not invariable, agree in number and gender with the noun → ☐1

◆ The forms shown above are also used in indirect questions → ☐2

☐ Exclamatory Adjectives

	MASCULINE	FEMININE	
SING {	¡qué!	¡qué!	what (a)
	¡cuánto!	¡cuánta!	what (a lot of)
PLUR {	¡qué!	¡qué!	what
	¡cuántos!	¡cuántas!	what (a lot of)

◆ Exclamatory adjectives, when not invariable, agree in number and gender with the noun → ☐3

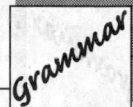

---

[1]   **¿Qué libro te gustó más?**
       Which book did you like most?
       ¿Qué clase de hombre es?
       What type of man is he?
       ¿Qué instrumentos toca Vd?
       What instruments do you play?
       ¿Qué ofertas ha recibido Vd?
       What offers have you received?
       ¿Cuánto dinero te queda?
       How much money have you got left?
       ¿Cuánta lluvia ha caído?
       How much rain have we had?
       ¿Cuántos vestidos quieres comprar?
       How many dresses do you want to buy?
       ¿Cuántas personas van a venir?
       How many people are coming?

[2]   **No sé a qué hora llegó**
       I don't know at what time she arrived
       Dígame cuántas postales quiere
       Tell me how many postcards you'd like

[3]   **¡Qué pena!**
       What a pity!
       ¡Qué tiempo tan/más malo!
       What lousy weather!
       ¡Cuánto tiempo!
       What a long time!
       ¡Cuánta pobreza!
       What poverty!
       ¡Cuántos autobuses!
       What a lot of buses!
       ¡Cuántas mentiras!
       What a lot of lies!

☐ Possessive Adjectives

Weak forms

WITH SING NOUN		WITH PLUR NOUN		
MASC	*FEM*	*MASC*	*FEM*	
mi	**mi**	**mis**	**mis**	*my*
tu	**tu**	**tus**	**tus**	*your*
su	**su**	**sus**	**sus**	*his; her; its; your*
				(of **Vd**)
nuestro	**nuestra**	**nuestros**	**nuestras**	*our*
vuestro	**vuestra**	**vuestros**	**vuestras**	*your*
su	**su**	**sus**	**sus**	*their; your*
				(of **Vds**)

- All possessive adjectives agree in number and (when applicable) in gender with the noun, NOT WITH THE OWNER → ①

- The weak forms always precede the noun → ①

- Since the form **su(s)** can mean *his, her, your* (of **Vd, Vds**) or *their*, clarification is often needed. This is done by adding **de él, de ella, de Vds** etc to the noun, and usually (but not always) changing the possessive to a definite article → ②

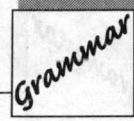

1. **Pilar no ha traído nuestros libros**
Pilar hasn't brought our books
Antonio irá a vuestra casa
Anthony will go to your house
¿Han vendido su coche tus vecinos?
Have your neighbours sold their car?
Mi hermano y tu primo no se llevan bien
My brother and your cousin don't get on

2. **su casa → la casa de él**
his house
sus amigos → los amigos de Vd
your friends
sus coches → los coches de ellos
their cars
su abrigo → el abrigo de ella
her coat

◻ **Possessive Adjectives** (Continued)

Strong forms

WITH SING NOUN		WITH PLUR NOUN		
MASC	*FEM*	*MASC*	*FEM*	
mío	**mía**	**míos**	**mías**	*my*
tuyo	**tuya**	**tuyos**	**tuyas**	*your*
suyo	**suya**	**suyos**	**suyas**	*his; her; its; your (of* **Vd***)*
nuestro	**nuestra**	**nuestros**	**nuestras**	*our*
vuestro	**vuestra**	**vuestros**	**vuestras**	*your*
suyo	**suya**	**suyos**	**suyas**	*their; your (of* **Vds***)*

◆ The strong forms agree in the same way as the weak forms (see p 216).

◆ The strong forms always follow the noun, and they are used:
— to translate the English *of mine, of yours,* etc → ⏹ 1
— to address people → ⏹ 2

1 **Es un capricho suyo**
It's a whim of hers
un amigo nuestro
a friend of ours
una revista tuya
a magazine of yours

2 **Muy señor mío** (in letters)
Dear Sir
hija mía
my daughter
¡Dios mío!
My God!
Amor mío
Darling/My love

☐ Indefinite Adjectives

alguno(a)s	*some*
ambos(as)	*both*
cada	*each; every*
cierto(a)s	*certain; definite*
cualquiera, plur **cualesquiera**	*some; any*
los (las) demás	*the others; the remainder*
mismo(a)s	*same; -self*
mucho(a)s	*many; much*
ningún, ninguna	*any; no*
plur **ningunos, ningunas**	
otro(a)s	*other; another*
poco(a)s	*few; little*
tal(es)	*such (a)*
tanto(a)s	*so much; so many*
todo(a)s	*all; every*
varios(as)	*several; various*

Unless invariable, all indefinite adjectives agree in number and gender with the noun → ①

◆ **alguno**

Before a masculine singular noun it drops the final **-o** and adds an accent to show the correct position for stress → ② (see also p 292)

◆ **ambos**

Usually it is only used in written Spanish. The spoken language prefers the form **los dos/las dos** → ③

◆ **cierto** and **mismo**

They change their meaning according to their position in relation to the noun (see also **Position of Adjectives**, p 224) → ④

◆ **cualquiera**

It drops the final **-a** before a masculine *or* feminine noun → ⑤

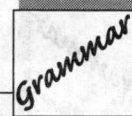

1	**el mismo día** the same day	**las mismas películas** the same films
	mucha/poca gente many/few people	**mucho/poco dinero** much/little money
2	**algún día** some day	**alguna razón** some reason
3	**Me gustan los dos cuadros** I like both pictures	
	¿Conoces a las dos enfermeras? Do you know both nurses?	
4	**cierto tiempo** ⚠ BUT: a certain time	**éxito cierto** sure success
	el mismo color ⚠ BUT: the same colour	**en la iglesia misma** in the church itself
5	**cualquier casa** ⚠ BUT: any house	**una revista cualquiera** any magazine

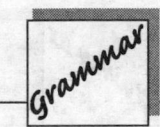
☐ **Indefinite Adjectives** (Continued)

◆ **ningún** is only used in negative sentences or phrases → ①

◆ **otro**
It is never preceded by an indefinite article → ②

◆ **tal**
It is never followed by an indefinite article → ③

◆ **todo**
It can be followed by a definite article, a demonstrative or possessive adjective or a place name → ④

⚠ EXCEPTIONS:

— when **todo** in the singular means *any*, *every*, or *each* → ⑤

— in some set expressions → ⑥

1. **No es ninguna tonta**
   She's no fool
   ¿No tienes parientes? – No, ninguno
   Haven't you any relatives? – No, none

2. **¿Me das otra manzana?**
   Will you give me another apple?
   Prefiero estos otros zapatos
   I prefer these other shoes

3. **Nunca dije tal cosa**
   I never said such a thing

4. **Estudian durante toda la noche**
   They study all night
   Ha llovido toda esta semana
   It has rained all this week
   Pondré en orden todos mis libros
   I'll sort out all my books
   Lo sabe todo Madrid
   All Madrid knows it

5. **Podrá entrar toda persona que lo desee**
   Any person who wishes to enter may do so

   ⚠ BUT:

   Vienen todos los días
   They come every day

6. | **de todos modos** | **a toda velocidad** |
   |---|---|
   | anyway | at full/top speed |
   | **por todas partes** | |
   | **por todos lados** | |
   | **a/en todas partes** | everywhere |
   | **a/en todos lados** | |

❒ **Position of Adjectives**

◆ Spanish adjectives usually follow the noun → ①, ②

◆ Note that when used figuratively or to express a quality already inherent in the noun, adjectives can precede the noun → ③

◆ As in English, demonstrative, possessive (weak forms), numerical, interrogative and exclamatory adjectives precede the noun → ④

◆ Indefinite adjectives also usually precede the noun → ⑤

⚠ NOTE: **alguno** *some* in negative expressions follows the noun → ⑥

◆ Some adjectives can precede or follow the noun, but their meaning varies according to their position:

	BEFORE NOUN	AFTER NOUN	
antiguo	*former*	*old, ancient*	→ ⑦
diferente	*various*	*different*	→ ⑧
grande	*great*	*big*	→ ⑨
medio	*half*	*average*	→ ⑩
mismo	*same*	*-self, very/precisely*	→ ⑪
nuevo	*new, another, fresh*	*brand new*	→ ⑫
pobre	*poor (wretched)*	*poor (not rich)*	→ ⑬
puro	*sheer, mere*	*pure (clear)*	→ ⑭
varios	*several*	*various, different*	→ ⑮
viejo	*old (long known, etc)*	*old (aged)*	→ ⑯

◆ Adjectives following the noun are linked by **y** → ⑰

1	**la página siguiente** the following page	**la hora exacta** the right time	
2	**una corbata azul** a blue tie	**una palabra española** a Spanish word	
3	**un dulce sueño** a sweet dream		
	un terrible desastre (all disasters are terrible) a terrible disaster		
4	**este sombrero** this hat	**mi padre** my father	**¿qué hombre?** what man?
5	**cada día** every day	**otra vez** another time	**poco dinero** little money
6	**sin duda alguna** without any doubt		
7	**un antiguo colega** a former colleague	**la historia antigua** ancient history	
8	**diferentes capítulos** various chapters	**personas diferentes** different people	
9	**un gran pintor** a great painter	**una casa grande** a big house	
10	**medio melón** half a melon	**velocidad media** average speed	
11	**la misma respuesta** the same answer	**yo mismo** myself	**eso mismo** precisely that
12	**mi nuevo coche** my new car	**unos zapatos nuevos** (some) brand new shoes	
13	**esa pobre mujer** that poor woman	**un país pobre** a poor country	
14	**la pura verdad** the plain truth	**aire puro** fresh air	
15	**varios caminos** several ways/paths	**artículos varios** various items	
16	**un viejo amigo** an old friend	**esas toallas viejas** those old towels	
17	**una acción cobarde y falsa** a cowardly, deceitful act		

❐ Personal Pronouns

SUBJECT PRONOUNS

PERSON	SINGULAR	PLURAL
1st	**yo**	**nosotros**
	I	*we* (masc/masc + fem)
		nosotras
		we (all fem)
2nd	**tú**	**vosotros**
	you	*you* (masc/masc + fem)
		vosotras
		you (all fem)
3rd	**él**	**ellos**
	he; it	*they* (masc/masc + fem)
	ella	**ellas**
	she; it	*they* (all fem)
	usted (Vd)	**ustedes (Vds)**
	you	*you*

◆ Subject pronouns have a limited usage in Spanish. Normally they are only used:

— for emphasis → ①

— for clarity → ②

⚠️ BUT: **Vd** and **Vds** should always be used for politeness, whether they are otherwise needed or not → ③

◆ *It* as subject and *they*, referring to things, are never translated into Spanish → ④

◆ **tú/usted**

As a general rule, you should use **tú** (or **vosotros,** if plural) when addressing a friend, a child, a relative, someone you know well, or when invited to do so. In all other cases, use **usted** (or **ustedes**)

◆ **nosotros/as; vosotros/as; él/ella; ellos/ellas**

All these forms reflect the number and gender of the noun(s) they replace. **Nosotros, vosotros** and **ellos** also replace a combination of masculine and feminine nouns.

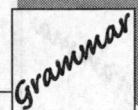

1. **Ellos sí que llegaron tarde**
   They really did arrive late
   Tú no tienes por qué venir
   There is no reason for you to come
   Ella jamás creería eso
   She would never believe that

2. **Yo estudio español pero él estudia francés**
   I study Spanish but he studies French
   Ella era muy deportista pero él prefería jugar a las cartas
   She was a sporty type but he preferred to play cards
   Vosotros saldréis primero y nosotros os seguiremos
   You leave first and we will follow you

3. **Pase Vd por aquí**
   Please come this way
   ¿Habían estado Vds antes en esta ciudad?
   Had you been to this town before?

4. **¿Qué es? – Es una sorpresa**
   What is it? – It's a surprise
   ¿Qué son? – Son abrelatas
   What are they? – They are tin-openers

☐ **Personal Pronouns** (Continued)

DIRECT OBJECT PRONOUNS

PERSON	SINGULAR	PLURAL
1st	**me** *me*	**nos** *us*
2nd	**te** *you*	**os** *you*
3rd (masculine)	**lo** *him; it; you* (of **Vd**)	**los** *them; you* (of **Vds**)
(feminine)	**la** *her; it; you* (of **Vd**)	**las** *them; you* (of **Vds**)

◆ **lo** sometimes functions as a 'neuter' pronoun, referring to an idea or information contained in a previous statement or question. It is often not translated → ①

Position of direct object pronouns

◆ In constructions other than the imperative affirmative, infinitive or gerund, the pronoun always comes before the verb → ②

In the imperative affirmative, infinitive and gerund, the pronoun follows the verb and is attached to it. An accent is needed in certain cases to show the correct position for stress (see also p 292) → ③

◆ Where an infinitive or gerund depends on a previous verb, the pronoun may be used either after the infinitive or gerund, or before the main verb → ④

⚠ NOTE: see how this applies to reflexive verbs → ④

◆ For further information, see **Order of Object Pronouns**, p 232.

Reflexive Pronouns

These are dealt with under reflexive verbs, p 24.

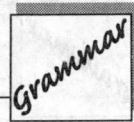

1.   **¿Va a venir María? – No lo sé**
   Is Maria coming? – I don't know
   Hay que regar las plantas – Yo lo haré
   The plants need watering → I'll do it
   Habían comido ya pero no nos lo dijeron
   They had already eaten, but they didn't tell us
   Yo conduzco de prisa pero él lo hace despacio
   I drive fast but he drives slowly

2.   **Te quiero**
   I love you
   ¿Las ve Vd?
   Can you see them?
   ¿No me oyen Vds?
   Can't you hear me?
   Tu hija no nos conoce
   Your daughter doesn't know us
   No los toques
   Don't touch them

3.   **Ayúdame**   **Acompáñenos**
   Help me   Come with us
   Quiero decirte algo
   I want to tell you something
   Estaban persiguiéndonos
   They were coming after us

4.   **Lo está comiendo** OR: **Está comiéndolo**
   She is eating it
   Nos vienen a ver OR: **Vienen a vernos**
   They are coming to see us
   No quería levantarse OR: **No se quería levantar**
   He didn't want to get up
   Estoy afeitándome OR: **Me estoy afeitando**
   I'm shaving

☐ **Personal Pronouns** (Continued)

	INDIRECT OBJECT PRONOUNS	
PERSON	SINGULAR	PLURAL
1st	**me**	**nos**
2nd	**te**	**os**
3rd	**le**	**les**

◆ The pronouns shown in the above table replace the preposition **a** + noun → ①

Position of indirect object pronouns

◆ In constructions other than the imperative affirmative, the infinitive or the gerund, the pronoun comes before the verb → ②

In the imperative affirmative, infinitive and gerund, the pronoun follows the verb and is attached to it. An accent is needed in certain cases to show the correct position for stress (see also p 292) → ③

◆ Where an infinitive or gerund depends on a previous verb, the pronoun may be used either after the infinitive or gerund, or before the main verb → ④

◆ For further information, see **Order of Object Pronouns**, p 232.

Reflexive Pronouns

These are dealt with under reflexive verbs, p 24.

1   **Estoy escribiendo a Teresa** → **Le estoy escribiendo**
       I am writing to Teresa   I am writing to her
       Da de comer al gato   → **Dale de comer**
       Give the cat some food   Give it some food

2   **Sofía os ha escrito**   **¿Os ha escrito Sofía?**
       Sophie has written to you   Has Sophie written to you?
       Carlos no nos habla
       Charles doesn't speak to us
       ¿Qué te pedían?
       What were they asking you for?
       No les haga caso Vd
       Don't take any notice of them

3   **Respóndame Vd**   **Díganos Vd la respuesta**
       Answer me   Tell us the answer
       No quería darte la noticia todavía
       I didn't want to tell you the news yet
       Llegaron diciéndome que ...
       They came telling me that ...

4   **Estoy escribiéndole** OR: **Le estoy escribiendo**
       I am writing to him/her
       Les voy a hablar OR: **Voy a hablarles**
       I'm going to talk to them

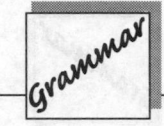

☐ **Personal Pronouns** (Continued)

Order of object pronouns

◆ When two object pronouns of different persons are combined, the order is: indirect before direct, i.e.

$$
\left.\begin{array}{l}
\textbf{me} \\
\textbf{te} \\
\textbf{nos} \\
\textbf{os}
\end{array}\right\} \text{before} \left\{\begin{array}{l}
\textbf{lo} \\
\textbf{la} \\
\textbf{los} \\
\textbf{las}
\end{array}\right. \rightarrow \boxed{1}
$$

⚠ NOTE: When two 3rd person object pronouns are combined, the first (i.e. the indirect object pronoun) becomes **se** → 2

Points to note on object pronouns

◆ As **le/les** can refer to either gender, and **se** to either gender, singular or plural, sometimes clarification is needed. This is done by adding **a él** *to him*, **a ella** *to her*, **a Vd** *to you* etc to the phrase, usually after the verb → 3

◆ When a noun object precedes the verb, the corresponding object pronoun must be used too → 4

◆ Indirect object pronouns are often used instead of possessive adjectives with parts of the body or clothing to indicate 'ownership', and also in certain common constructions involving reflexive verbs (see also **The Indefinite Article**, p 198) → 5

◆ **Le** and **les** are often used in Spanish instead of **lo** and **los** when referring to people. Equally **la** is sometimes used instead of **le** when referring to a feminine person or animal, although this usage is considered incorrect by some speakers of Spanish → 6

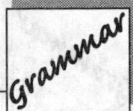

1	**Paloma os lo mandará mañana**
	Paloma is sending it to you tomorrow
	¿Te los ha enseñado mi hermana?
	Has my sister shown them to you?
	No me lo digas
	Don't tell me (that)
	Todos estaban pidiéndotelo
	They were all asking you for it
	No quiere prestárnosla
	He won't lend it to us
2	**Se lo di ayer**
	I gave it to him/her/them yesterday
3	**Le escriben mucho a ella**
	They write to her often
	Se lo van a mandar pronto a ellos
	They will be sending it to them soon
4	**A tu hermano lo conozco bien**
	I know your brother well
	A María la vemos algunas veces
	We sometimes see Maria
5	**La chaqueta le estaba ancha**
	His jacket was too loose
	Me duele el tobillo
	My ankle is aching
	Se me ha perdido el bolígrafo
	I have lost my pen
6	**Le/lo encontraron en el cine**
	They met him at the cinema
	Les/los oímos llegar
	We heard them coming
	Le/la escribimos una carta
	We wrote a letter to her

☐ **Personal Pronouns** (Continued)

Pronouns after prepositions

- These are the same as the subject pronouns, except for the forms **mí** *me*, **ti** *you* (sing), and the reflexive **sí** *himself, herself, themselves, yourselves* → ①

- **Con** *with* combines with **mí, ti** and **sí** to form

  conmigo *with me* → ②
  contigo *with you*
  consigo *with himself/herself etc*

- The following prepositions always take a subject pronoun:

entre	*between, among* → ③
hasta **incluso** }	*even, including* → ④
salvo **menos** }	*except* → ⑤
según	*according to* → ⑥

- These pronouns are used for emphasis, especially where contrast is involved → ⑦

- **Ello** *it, that* is used after a preposition when referring to an idea already mentioned, but never to a concrete noun → ⑧

- **A él, de él** NEVER contract → ⑨

Examples

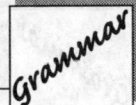

1. **Pienso en ti**
   I think about you

   ¿Son para mí?
   Are they for me?

   Es para ella
   This is for her

   Iban hacia ellos
   They were going towards them

   Volveréis sin nosotros
   You'll come back without us

   Volaban sobre vosotros
   They were flying above you

   Hablaba para si
   He was talking to himself

2. **Venid conmigo**
   Come with me

   Lo trajeron consigo ⚠ BUT: **¿Hablaron con vosotros?**
   They brought it/him with them   Did they talk to you?

3. **entre tú y ella**
   between you and her

4. **Hasta yo puedo hacerlo**
   Even I can do it

5. **todos menos yo**
   everybody except me

6. **según tú**
   according to you

7. **¿A ti no te escriben?**
   Don't they write to you?

   Me lo manda a mí, no a ti
   She is sending it to me, not to you

8. **Nunca pensaba en ello**
   He never thought about it

   Por todo ello me parece que ...
   For all those reasons it seems to me that ...

9. **A él no lo conozco**
   I don't know him

   No he sabido nada de él
   I haven't heard from him

☐ Indefinite Pronouns

algo	*something, anything*	→ 1
alguien	*somebody, anybody*	→ 2
alguno/a/os/as	*some, a few*	→ 3
cada uno/a	*each (one)*	→ 4
	everybody	
cualquiera	*anybody; any*	→ 5
los/las demás	*the others*	
	the rest	→ 6
mucho/a/os/as	*many; much*	→ 7
nada	*nothing*	→ 8
nadie	*nobody*	→ 9
ninguno/a	*none, not any*	→ 10
poco/a/os/as	*few; little*	→ 11
tanto/a/os/as	*so much; so many*	→ 12
todo/a/os/as	*all; everything*	→ 13
uno ... (el) otro	*(the) one ... the other*	
una ... (la) otra		→ 14
unos ... (los) otros	*some ... (the) others*	
unas ... (las) otras		
varios/as	*several*	→ 15

- **algo, alguien, alguno**

  They can never be used after a negative. The appropriate negative pronouns are used instead: **nada, nadie, ninguno** (see also negatives, p 272) → 16

Examples

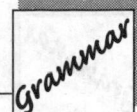

1	**Tengo algo para ti**	**¿Viste algo?**
	I have something for you	Did you see anything?
2	**Alguien me lo ha dicho**	**¿Has visto a alguien?**
	Somebody said it to me	Have you seen anybody?
3	**Algunos de los niños ya sabían leer**	
	Some of the children could read already	
4	**Le dió una manzana a cada uno**	**¡Cada uno a su casa!**
	She gave each of them an apple	Everybody go home!
5	**Cualquiera puede hacerlo**	
	Anybody can do it	
	Cualquiera de las explicaciones vale	
	Any of the explanations is a valid one	
6	**Yo me fui, los demás se quedaron**	
	I went, the others stayed	
7	**Muchas de las casas no tenían jardín**	
	Many of the houses didn't have a garden	
8	**¿Qué tienes en la mano? – Nada**	
	What have you got in your hand? – Nothing	
9	**¡A quién ves? – A nadie**	
	Who can you see? – Nobody	
10	**¿Cuántas tienes? – Ninguna**	
	How many have you got? – None	
11	**Había muchos cuadros, pero vi pocos que me gustaran**	
	There were many pictures, but I saw few I liked	
12	**¿Se oía mucho ruido? – No tanto**	
	Was it very noisy? – Not so very	
13	**Lo ha estropeado todo**	**Todo va bien**
	He has spoiled everything	All is going well
14	**Unos cuestan 300 pesetas, los otros 400 pesetas**	
	Some cost 300 pesetas, the others 400 pesetas	
15	**Varios de ellos me gustaron mucho**	
	I liked several of them very much	
16	**Veo a alguien**	**No veo a nadie**
	I can see somebody	I can't see anybody
	Tengo algo que hacer	**No tengo nada que hacer**
	I have something to do	I don't have anything to do

☐ Relative Pronouns

PEOPLE

SINGULAR	PLURAL	
que	que	who, that (subject) → ①
que	que	
a quien	a quienes	} who(m), that (direct object) → ②
a quien	a quienes	to whom, that → ③
de que	de que	
de quien	de quienes	} of whom, that → ④
cuyo/a	cuyos/as	whose → ⑤

THINGS

SINGULAR AND PLURAL		
que	which, that (subject)	→ ⑥
que	which, that (direct object)	→ ⑦
a que	to which, that	→ ⑧
de que	of which, that	→ ⑨
cuyo	whose	→ ⑩

⚠ NOTE: These forms can also refer to people.

- **cuyo** agrees with the noun it accompanies, NOT WITH THE OWNER → ⑤/⑩

- You cannot omit the relative pronoun in Spanish as you can in English → ②/⑦

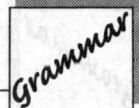

1.   **Mi hermano, que tiene veinte años, es el más joven**
My brother, who is twenty, is the youngest

2.   **Los amigos que más quiero son ...**
The friends (that) I like best are ...

     María, a quien Daniel admira tanto, es ...
Maria, whom Daniel admires so much, is ...

3.   **Mis abogados, a quienes he escrito hace poco, están ...**
My lawyers, to whom I wrote recently, are ...

4.   **La chica de que te hablé llega mañana**
The girl (that) I told you about is coming tomorrow

     los niños de quienes se ocupa Vd
the children (that) you look after

5.   **Vendrá la mujer cuyo hijo está enfermo**
The woman whose son is ill will be coming

6.   **Hay una escalera que lleva a la buhardilla**
There's a staircase which leads to the loft

7.   **La casa que hemos comprado tiene ...**
The house (which) we've bought has ...

     Este es el regalo que me ha mandado mi amiga
This is the present (that) my friend has sent to me

8.   **la tienda a que siempre va**
the shop (which) she always goes to

9.   **las injusticias de que se quejan**
the injustices (that) they're complaining about

10.   **la ventana cuyas cortinas están corridas**
the window whose curtains are drawn

☐ **Relative Pronouns** (Continued)

el cual, el que

◆ These are used when the relative is separated from the word it refers to, or when it would otherwise be unclear which word it referred to. The pronouns always agree in number and gender with the noun → ①

El cual may also be used when the verb in the relative clause is separated from the relative pronoun → ②

lo que, lo cual

◆ The neuter form **lo** is normally used when referring to an idea, statement or abstract noun. In certain expressions, the form **lo cual** may also be used as the subject of the relative clause → ③

Relative pronouns after prepositions

◆ **Que** and **quienes** are generally used after the prepositions:

a	to	→	④
con	with	→	⑤
de	from, about, of	→	⑥
en	in, on, into	→	⑦

It should be noted that **en que** can sometimes be translated by:

— *where*. In this case it can also be replaced by **en donde** or **donde** → ⑧

— *when*. Sometimes here it can be replaced by **cuando** → ⑨

◆ **El que** or **el cual** are used after other prepositions, and they always agree → ⑩

Examples

① **El padre de Elena, el cual tiene mucho dinero, es ...**
Elena's father, who has a lot of money, is ...
(**el cual** is *used here since* **que** *or* **quien** *might equally refer to Elena*)
Su hermana, a la cual/la que hacía mucho que no veía, estaba también allí
His sister, whom I hadn't seen for a long time, was also there

② **Vieron a su tío, el cual, después de levantarse, salió**
They saw their uncle, who, after having got up, went out

③ **No sabe lo que hace**
He doesn't know what he is doing
Lo que dijiste fue una tontería
What you said was foolish
Todo estaba en silencio, lo que (*or* **lo cual**) **me pareció muy raro**
All was silent, which I thought most odd

④ **las tiendas a (las) que íbamos**
the shops we used to go to

⑤ **la chica con quien** (*or* **la que**) **sale**
the girl he's going out with

⑥ **el libro de(l) que te hablé**
the book I told you about

⑦ **el lío en (el) que te has metido**
the trouble you've got yourself into

⑧ **el sitio en que (en donde/donde) se escondía**
the place where he/she was hiding

⑨ **el año en que naciste**
the year (when) you were born

⑩ **el puente debajo del que/cual pasa el río**
the bridge under which the river flows
las obras por las cuales/que es famosa
the plays for which she is famous

❐ **Relative Pronouns** (Continued)

el que, la que; los que, las que
These mean *the one(s) who/which, those who* → 1

⚠ NOTE: **quien(es)** can replace **el que** *etc* when used in a general sense
→ 2

todos los que, todas las que
These mean *all who, all those/the ones which* → 3

todo lo que
This translates *all that, everything that* → 4

el de, la de; los de, las de
These can mean:
— *the one(s) of, that/those of* → 5
— *the one(s) with* → 6

Examples

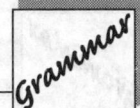

1. **Esa película es la que quiero ver**
   That film is the one I want to see
   ¿Te acuerdas de ese amigo? El que te presenté ayer
   Do you remember that friend? The one I introduced you to
   yesterday
   Los que quieran entrar tendrán que pagar
   Those who want to go in will have to pay

2. **Quien (*or* el que) llegue antes ganará el premio**
   He who arrives first will win the prize

3. **Todos los que salían iban de negro**
   All those who were coming out were dressed in black
   **¿Qué autobuses puedo tomar? – Todos los que pasen
   por aquí**
   Which buses can I take? – Any (All those) that come this
   way

4. **Quiero saber todo lo que ha pasado**
   I want to know all that has happened

5. **Trae la foto de tu novio y la de tu hermano**
   Bring the photo of your boyfriend and the one of your
   brother
   Viajamos en mi coche y en el de María
   We travelled in my car and Maria's
   Te doy estos libros y también los de mi hermana
   I'll give you these books and my sister's too

6. **Tu amigo, el de las gafas, me lo contó**
   Your friend, the one with glasses, told me

☐ Interrogative Pronouns

¿qué?	what?; which?
¿cuál(es)?	which?; what?
¿quién(es)?	who?

qué

It always translates *what* → ①

⚠ NOTE: **por** + **qué** is normally translated by *why* → ②

cuál

It normally implies a choice, and translates *which* → ③

⚠ EXCEPT when no choice is implied or more specific information is required → ④

⚠ NOTE: Whilst the pronoun **qué** can also work as an adjective, **cuál** only works as a pronoun → ⑤

quién

— **quién(es)** (subject or after preposition)	who	→ ⑥
— **a quién(es)** (object)	whom	→ ⑦
— **de quién(es)**	whose	→ ⑧

◆ All the forms shown above are also used in indirect questions → ⑨

1. **¿Qué estan haciendo?**   **¿Qué dices?**
   What are they doing?   What are you saying?
   ¿Para qué lo quieres?
   What do you want it for?

2. **¿Por qué no llegaron Vds antes?**
   Why didn't you arrive earlier?

3. **¿Cuál de estos vestidos te gusta más?**
   Which of these dresses do you like best?
   ¿Cuáles viste?
   Which ones did you see?

4. **¿Cuál es la capital de España?**
   What is the capital of Spain?
   ¿Cuál es tu consejo?
   What is your advice?
   ¿Cuál es su fecha de nacimiento?
   What is your date of birth?

5. **¿Qué libro es más interesante?**
   Which book is more interesting?
   ¿Cuál (de estos libros) es más interesante?
   Which (of these books) is more interesting?

6. **¿Quién ganó la carrera?**
   Who won the race?
   ¿Con quiénes los viste?
   Who did you see them with?

7. **¿A quiénes ayudaste?**   **¿A quién se lo diste?**
   Who(m) did you help?   Who did you give it to?

8. **¿De quién es este libro?**
   Whose is this book?

9. **Le pregunté para qué lo quería**
   I asked him/her what he/she wanted it for
   No me dijeron cuáles preferían
   They didn't tell me which ones they preferred
   No sabía a quién acudir
   I didn't know who to turn to

☐ **Possessive Pronouns**

These are the same as the strong forms of the possessive adjectives, but they are always accompanied by the definite article.

SINGULAR		
MASCULINE	FEMININE	
el mío	**la mía**	*mine*
el tuyo	**la tuya**	*yours* (of **tú**)
el suyo	**la suya**	*his; hers; its; yours* (of **Vd**)
el nuestro	**la nuestra**	*ours*
el vuestro	**la vuestra**	*yours* (of **vosotros**)
el suyo	**la suya**	*theirs; yours* (of **Vds**)

PLURAL		
MASCULINE	FEMININE	
los míos	**las mías**	*mine*
los tuyos	**las tuyas**	*yours* (of **tú**)
los suyos	**las suyas**	*his; hers; its; yours* (of **Vd**)
los nuestros	**las nuestras**	*ours*
los vuestros	**las vuestras**	*yours* (of **vosotros**)
los suyos	**las suyas**	*theirs; yours* (of **Vds**)

◆ The pronoun agrees in number and gender with the noun it replaces, NOT WITH THE OWNER → ①

◆ Alternative translations are *my own, your own*, etc → ②

◆ After the prepositions **a** and **de** the article **el** is contracted in the normal way (see p 196)

> **a + el mío → al mío** → ③
> **de + el mío → del mío** → ④

① **Pregunta a Cristina si este bolígrafo es el suyo**
Ask Christine if this pen is hers
¿Qué equipo ha ganado, el suyo o el nuestro?
Which team won – theirs or ours?
Mi perro es más joven que el tuyo
My dog is younger than yours
Daniel pensó que esos libros eran los suyos
Daniel thought those books were his
Si no tienes discos, te prestaré los míos
If you don't have any records, I'll lend you mine
Las habitaciones son menos amplias que las vuestras
The rooms are smaller than yours

② **¿Es su familia tan grande como la tuya?**
Is his/her/their family as big as your own?
Sus precios son más bajos que los nuestros
Their prices are lower than our own

③ **¿Por qué prefieres este sombrero al mío?**
Why do you prefer this hat to mine?
Su coche se parece al vuestro
His/her/their car looks like yours

④ **Mi libro está encima del tuyo**
My book is on top of yours
Su padre vive cerca del nuestro
His/her/their father lives near ours

☐ Demonstrative Pronouns

	MASCULINE	FEMININE	NEUTER	
SING	éste	ésta	esto	*this*
	ése	ésa	eso	*that*
	aquél	aquélla	aquello	
PLUR	éstos	éstas		*these*
	ésos	ésas		*those*
	aquéllos	aquéllas		

◆ The pronoun agrees in number and gender with the noun it replaces
→ ①

◆ The difference in meaning between the forms **ése** and **aquél** is the same as between the corresponding adjectives (see p 212)

◆ The masculine and feminine forms have an accent, which is the only thing that differentiates them from the corresponding adjectives.

◆ The neuter forms always refer to an idea or a statement or to an object when we want to identify it, etc, but never to specified nouns
→ ②

◆ An additional meaning of **aquél** is *the former*, and of **éste** *the latter*
→ ③

☐1 **¿Qué abrigo te gusta más? – Este de aquí**
Which coat do you like best? – This one here

Aquella casa era más grande que ésta
That house was bigger than this one

estos libros y aquéllos
these books and those (over there)

Quiero estas sandalias y ésas
I'd like these sandals and those ones

☐2 **No puedo creer que esto me esté pasando a mí**
I can't believe this is really happening to me

Eso de madrugar es algo que no le gusta
(This business of) getting up early is something she doesn't like

Aquello sí que me gustó
I really did like that

Esto es una bicicleta
This is a bicycle

☐3 **Hablaban Jaime y Andrés, éste a voces y aquél casi en un susurro**
James and Andrew were talking, the latter in a loud voice and the former almost in a whisper

❐ Adverbs

Formation

♦ Most adverbs are formed by adding **-mente** to the feminine form of the adjective. Accents on the adjective are not affected since the suffix **-mente** is stressed independently → ①

⚠ NOTE: **-mente** is omitted:

— in the first of two or more of these adverbs when joined by a conjunction → ②

— in **recientemente** *recently* when immediately preceding a past participle → ③

An accent is then needed on the last syllable (see p 292)

♦ The following adverbs are formed in an irregular way:

bueno → bien	
good	*well*
malo → mal	
bad	*badly*

Adjectives used as adverbs

Certain adjectives are used adverbially. These include:
alto, bajo, barato, caro, claro, derecho, fuerte and **rápido** → ④

⚠ NOTE: Other adjectives used as adverbs agree with the subject, and can normally be replaced by the adverb ending in **-mente** or an adverbial phrase → ⑤

Position of Adverbs

♦ When the adverb accompanies a verb, it may either immediately follow it or precede it for emphasis → ⑥

⚠ NOTE: The adverb can never be placed between **haber** and the past participle in compound tenses → ⑦

♦ When the adverb accompanies an adjective or another adverb, it generally precedes the adjective or adverb → ⑧

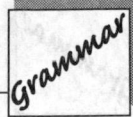

1　FEM ADJECTIVE　　　　　ADVERB
　　lenta slow　　　　　　　**lentamente** slowly
　　franca frank　　　　　　**francamente** frankly
　　feliz happy　　　　　　　**felizmente** happily
　　fácil easy　　　　　　　　**fácilmente** easily

2　**Lo hicieron lenta pero eficazmente**
　　They did it slowly but efficiently

3　**El pan estaba recién hecho**
　　The bread had just been baked

4　**hablar alto/bajo**　　　　**cortar derecho**
　　to speak loudly/softly　　　to cut (in a) straight (line)
　　costar barato/caro　　　**Habla muy fuerte**
　　to be cheap/expensive　　　He talks very loudly
　　ver claro　　　　　　　　**correr rápido**
　　to see clearly　　　　　　　to run fast

5　**Esperaban impacientes** (*or* **impacientemente/con impaciencia**)
　　They were waiting impatiently
　　Vivieron muy felices (*or* **muy felizmente**)
　　They lived very happily

6　**No conocemos aún al nuevo médico**
　　We still haven't met the new doctor
　　Aún estoy esperando
　　I'm still waiting
　　Han hablado muy bien
　　They have spoken very well
　　Siempre le regalaban flores
　　They always gave her flowers

7　**Lo he hecho ya**
　　I've already done it
　　No ha estado nunca en Italia
　　She's never been to Italy

8　**un sombrero muy bonito**　　**hablar demasiado alto**
　　a very nice hat　　　　　　　to talk too loud
　　mañana temprano　　　　**hoy mismo**
　　early tomorrow　　　　　　　today

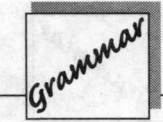

❒ Comparatives and Superlatives

Comparatives

These are formed using the following constructions:

más ... (que)	more ... (than)	→	1
menos ... (que)	less ... (than)	→	2
tanto como	as much as	→	3
tan ... como	as ... as	→	4
tan ... que	so ... that	→	5
demasiado ... para	too ... to	→	6
(lo) bastante ... **(lo) suficientemente ...** } **para**	enough to	→	7
cada vez más/menos	more and more/ less and less	→	8

Superlatives

♦ These are formed by placing **más/menos** *the most/the least* before the adverb → 9

♦ **lo** is added before a superlative which is qualified → 10

♦ The absolute superlative (*very, most, extremely* + adverb) is formed by placing **muy** before the adverb. The form **-ísimo** (see also p 292) is also occasionally found → 11

Adverbs with irregular comparatives/superlatives

ADVERB	COMPARATIVE	SUPERLATIVE
bien	**mejor***	**(lo) mejor**
well	*better*	*(the) best*
mal	**peor**	**(lo) peor**
badly	*worse*	*(the) worst*
mucho	**más**	**(lo) más**
a lot	*more*	*(the) most*
poco	**menos**	**(lo) menos**
little	*less*	*(the) least*

* **más bien** also exists, meaning *rather* → 12

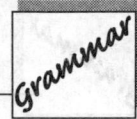

1	**más de prisa** more quickly	**más abiertamente** more openly
	Mi hermana canta más fuerte que yo My sister sings louder than me	
2	**menos fácilmente** less easily	**menos a menudo** less often
	Nos vemos menos frecuentemente que antes We see each other less frequently than before	
3	**Daniel no lee tanto como Andrés** Daniel doesn't read as much as Andrew	
4	**Hágalo tan rápido como le sea posible** Do it as quickly as you can	
	Ganan tan poco como nosotros They earn as little as we do	
5	**Llegaron tan pronto que tuvieron que esperarnos** They arrived so early that they had to wait for us	
6	**Es demasiado tarde para ir al cine** It's too late to go to the cinema	
7	**Eres (lo) bastante grande para hacerlo solo** You're old enough to do it by yourself	
8	**Me gusta el campo cada vez más** I like the countryside more and more	
9	**María es la que corre más rápido** Maria is the one who runs fastest	
	El que llegó menos tarde fue Miguel Miguel was the one to arrive the least late	
10	**Lo hice lo más de prisa que pude** I did it as quickly as I could	
11	**muy lentamente** very slowly	**tempranísimo** **muchísimo** extremely early very much
12	**Era un hombre más bien bajito** He was a rather short man	
	Estaba más bien inquieta que impaciente I was restless rather than impatient	

◻ Common Adverbs and their usage

bastante	*enough; quite*	→ 1
bien	*well*	→ 2
cómo	*how*	→ 3
cuánto	*how much*	→ 4
demasiado	*too much; too*	→ 5
más	*more*	→ 6
menos	*less*	→ 7
mucho	*a lot; much*	→ 8
poco	*little, not much; not very*	→ 9
siempre	*always*	→ 10
también	*also, too*	→ 11
tan	*as*	→ 12
tanto	*as much*	→ 13
todavía/aún	*still; yet; even*	→ 14
ya	*already*	→ 15

◆ **bastante, cuánto, demasiado, mucho, poco** and **tanto** are also used as adjectives that agree with the noun they qualify (see indefinite adjectives, p 220 and interrogative adjectives, p 214)

1	**Es bastante tarde** It's quite late	
2	**¡Bien hecho!** Well done!	
3	**¡Cómo me ha gustado!** How I liked it!	
4	**¿Cuánto cuesta este libro?** How much is this book?	
5	**He comido demasiado** I've eaten too much	**Es demasiado caro** It's too expensive
6	**Mi hermano trabaja más ahora** My brother works more now	**Es más tímida que Sofía** She is shyer than Sophie
7	**Se debe beber menos** One must drink less	**Estoy menos sorprendida que tú** I'm less surprised than you are
8	**¿Lees mucho?** Do you read a lot?	**¿Está mucho más lejos?** Is it much further?
9	**Comen poco** They don't eat (very) much	**María es poco decidida** Maria is not very daring
10	**Siempre dicen lo mismo** They always say the same (thing)	
11	**A mí también me gusta** I like it too	
12	**Ana es tan alta como yo** Ana is as tall as I am	
13	**Nos aburrimos tanto como vosotros** We got as bored as you did	
14	**Todavía/aún tengo dos** I've still got two **Mejor aún/todavía** Even better	**Todavía/aún no han llegado** They haven't arrived yet
15	**Ya lo he hecho** I've done it already	

On the following pages you will find some of the most frequent uses of prepositions in Spanish. Particular attention is paid to cases where usage differs markedly from English. It is often difficult to give an English equivalent for Spanish prepositions, since usage *does* vary so much between the two languages. In the list below, the broad meaning of the preposition is given on the left, with examples of usage following. Prepositions are dealt with in alphabetical order, except **a**, **de**, **en** and **por** which are shown first.

a

at	**echar algo a algn**	*to throw sth at sb*
	a 50 pesetas el kilo	*(at) 50 pesetas a kilo*
	a 100 km por hora	*at 100 km per hour*
	sentarse a la mesa	*to sit down at the table*
in	**al sol**	*in the sun*
	a la sombra	*in the shade*
onto	**cayeron al suelo**	*they fell onto the floor*
	pegar una foto al álbum	*to stick a photo into the album*
to	**ir al cine**	*to go to the cinema*
	dar algo a algn	*to give sth to sb*
	venir a hacer	*to come to do*
from	**quitarle algo a algn**	*to take sth from sb*
	robarle algo a algn	*to steal sth from sb*
	arrebatarle algo a algn	*to snatch sth from sb*
	comprarle algo a algn	*to buy sth from/for sb**
	esconderle algo a algn	*to hide sth from sb*
means	**a mano**	*by hand*
	a caballo	*on horseback (but note other forms of transport used with **en** and **por**)*
	a pie	*on foot*

* The translation here obviously depends on the context.

manner	**a la inglesa**	*in the English manner*
	a pasos lentos	*with slow steps*
	poco a poco	*little by little*
	a ciegas	*blindly*
time, date:	**a medianoche**	*at midnight*
at, on	**a las dos y cuarto**	*at quarter past two*
	a tiempo	*on time*
	a final/fines de mes	*at the end of the month*
	a veces	*at times*
distance	**a 8 km de aquí**	*(at a distance of) 8 kms from here*
	a dos pasos de mi casa	*just a step from my house*
	a lo lejos	*in the distance*
with **el** + infin	**al levantarse**	*on getting up*
	al abrir la puerta	*on opening the door*
after certain	**dispuesto a todo**	*ready for anything*
adjectives	**parecido a esto**	*similar to this*
	obligado a ello	*obliged to (do) that*
after certain verbs	see p 66	

Personal a

When the direct object of a verb is a person or pet animal, **a** must always be placed immediately before it.

EXAMPLES: **querían mucho a sus hijos**
they loved their children dearly
el niño miraba a su perro con asombro
the boy kept looking at his dog in astonishment

⚠ EXCEPTION: **tener**   **tienen dos hijos**
to have   *they have two children*

de

from	**venir de Londres**	*to come from London*
	un médico de Valencia	*a doctor from Valencia*
	de la mañana a la noche	*from morning till night*
	de 10 a 15	*from 10 to 15*
belonging to, of	**el sombrero de mi padre**	*my father's hat*
	las lluvias de abril	*April showers*
contents, composition, material	**una caja de cerillas**	*a box of matches*
	una taza de té	*a cup of tea; a tea-cup*
	un vestido de seda	*a silk dress*
destined for	**una silla de cocina**	*a kitchen chair*
	un traje de noche	*an evening dress*
descriptive	**la mujer del sombrero verde**	*the woman with the green hat*
	el vecino de al lad/lado	*the next door neighbour*
manner	**de manera irregular**	*in an irregular way*
	de una puñalada	*by stabbing*
quality	**una mujer de edad**	*an aged lady*
	objetos de valor	*valuable items*
comparative + number	**había más/menos de 100 personas**	*there were more/fewer than 100 people*
after superlatives: in	**la ciudad más/menos bonita del mundo**	*the most/least beautiful city in the world*
after certain adjectives	**contento de ver**	*pleased to see*
	fácil/difícil de entender	*easy/difficult to understand*
	capaz de hacer	*capable of doing*
after certain verbs	see p 66	

en

in, at	**en el campo**	*in the country*
	en Londres	*in London*
	en la cama	*in bed*
	con un libro en la mano	*with a book in his hand*
	en voz baja	*in a low voice*
	en la escuela	*in/at school*
into	**entra en la casa**	*go into the house*
	metió la mano en su bolso	*she put her hand into her handbag*
on	**un cuadro en la pared**	*a picture on the wall*
	sentado en una silla	*sitting on a chair*
	en la planta baja	*on the ground floor*
time, dates, months: *at, in*	**en este momento**	*at this moment*
	en 1994	*in 1994*
	en enero	*in January*
transport: *by*	**en coche**	*by car*
	en avión	*by plane*
	en tren	*by train* (but see also **por**)
language	**en español**	*in Spanish*
duration	**lo haré en una semana**	*I'll do it in one week*
after certain adjectives	**es muy buena/mala en geografía**	*she is very good/bad at geography*
	fueron los primeros/ últimos/únicos en + infin	*they were the first/ last/only ones + infin*
after certain verbs	see p 66	

por

motion: along, through, around	**vaya por ese camino** **por el túnel** **pasear por el campo**	go along that path through the tunnel to walk around the countryside
vague location	**tiene que estar por** **aquí** **le busqué por todas** **partes**	it's got to be somewhere around here I looked for him everywhere
vague time	**por la tarde** **por aquellos días**	in the afternoon in those days
rate	**90 km por hora** **un cinco por ciento** **ganaron por 3 a 0**	90 km per hour five per cent they won by 3 to 0
agent of passive: by	**descubierto por unos** **niños** **odiado por sus** **enemigos**	discovered by some children hated by his enemies
by (means of)	**por barco** **por tren** **por correo aéreo** **llamar por teléfono**	by boat by train (freight) by airmail to telephone
cause, reason: for, because	**¿por qué?** **por todo eso** **por lo que he oído**	why?, for what reason? because of all that judging by what I've heard
+ infinitive: to	**libros por leer** **cuentas por pagar**	books to be read bills to be paid
equivalence	**¿me tienes por tonto?**	do you think I'm stupid?

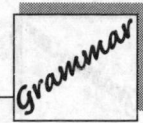

+ adjective/ + adverb + **que**: however	**por buenos que sean** **por mucho que lo quieras**	*however good they are* *however much you want it*
for	**¿cuanto me darán por este libro?** **te lo cambio por éste**	*how much will they give me for this book?* *I'll swap you this one for it*
	no siento nada por ti **si no fuera por ti** **¡Por Dios!**	*I feel nothing for you* *if it weren't for you* *For God's sake!*
for the benefit of	**lo hago por ellos**	*I do it for their benefit*
on behalf of	**firma por mí**	*sign on my behalf*

por also combines with other prepositions to form double prepositions usually conveying the idea of movement. The commonest of these are:

over	**saltó por encima de la mesa**	*she jumped over the table*
under	**nadamos por debajo del puente**	*we swam under the bridge*
past	**pasaron por delante de Correos**	*they went past the post office*
behind	**por detrás de la puerta**	*behind the door*
through	**la luz entraba por entre las cortinas**	*light was coming in through the curtains*
+ donde	**¿por dónde has venido?**	*which way did you come?*

ante

faced with, before	**lo hicieron ante mis propios ojos**	*they did it before my very eyes*
	ante eso no se puede hacer nada	*one can't do anything when faced with that*
preference	**la salud ante todo**	*health above all things*

antes de

before (time)	**antes de las 5**	*before 5 o'clock*

bajo/debajo de

These are usually equivalent, although **bajo** is used more frequently in a figurative sense and with temperatures.

under	**bajo/debajo de la cama**	*under the bed*
	bajo el dominio romano	*under Roman rule*
below	**un grado bajo cero**	*one degree below zero*

con

with	**vino con su amigo**	*she came with her friend*
after certain	**enfadado con ellos**	*angry with them*
adjectives	**magnánimo con sus súbditos**	*magnanimous with his subjects*

contra

against	**no tengo nada contra ti**	*I've nothing against you*
	apoyado contra la pared	*leaning against the wall*

delante de

in front of	**iba delante de mí**	*she was walking in front of me*

desde

from	**desde aquí se puede ver**	*you can see it from here*
	llamaban desde España	*they were phoning from Spain*
	desde otro punto de vista	*from a different point of view*
	desde la 1 hasta las 6	*from 1 till 6*
	desde entonces	*from then onwards*
since	**desde que volvieron**	*since they returned*
for	**viven en esa casa desde hace 3 años**	*they've been living in that house for 3 years*

⚠ (NOTE TENSE)

detrás de

behind	**están detrás de la puerta**	*they are behind the door*

durante

during	**durante la guerra**	*during the war*
for	**anduvieron durante 3 días**	*they walked for 3 days*

entre

between	**entre 8 y 10**	*between 8 and 10*
among	**María y Elena, entre otras**	*Maria and Elena, among others*
reciprocal	**ayudarse entre sí**	*to help each other*

excepto

except (for)	**todos excepto tú**	*everybody except you*

hacia

towards	**van hacia ese edificio**	*they're going towards that building*
around (time)	**hacia las 3**	*at around 3 (o'clock)*
	hacia fines de enero	*around the end of January*

Hacia can also combine with some adverbs to convey a sense of motion in a particular direction:

hacia arriba	*upwards*
hacia abajo	*downwards*
hacia adelante	*forwards*
hacia atrás	*backwards*
hacia adentro	*inwards*
hacia afuera	*outwards*

hasta

until	**hasta la noche**	*until night*
as far as	**viajaron hasta Sevilla**	*they travelled as far as Seville*
up to	**conté hasta 300 ovejas**	*I counted up to 300 lambs*
	hasta ahora no los había visto	*up to now I hadn't seen them*
even	**hasta un tonto lo entendería**	*even an imbecile would understand that*

para

for	**es para ti**	*it's for you*
	es para mañana	*it's for tomorrow*
	una habitación para dos noches	*a room for two nights*
	para ser un niño, lo hace muy bien	*for a child he is very good at it*
	salen para Cádiz	*they are leaving for Cádiz*
	se conserva muy bien para sus años	*he keeps very well for his age*
+ infin: *(in order) to*	**es demasiado torpe para comprenderlo**	*he's too stupid to understand*
+ sí: *to oneself*	**hablar para sí**	*to talk to oneself*
	reír para sí	*to laugh to oneself*
with time	**todavía tengo para 1 hora**	*I'll be another hour (at it) yet*

salvo

except (for)	**todos salvo él**	*all except him*
	salvo cuando llueve	*except when it's raining*
barring	**salvo imprevistos**	*barring the unexpected*
	salvo contraorden	*unless you hear to the contrary*

según

| according to | **según su consejo** | according to her advice |
| | **según lo que me dijiste** | according to what you told me |

sin

without	**sin agua/dinero**	without water/money
	sin mi marido	without my husband
+ infinitive	**sin contar a los otros**	without counting the others

sobre

on	**sobre la cama**	on the bed
	sobre el armario	on (top of) the wardrobe
on (to)	**póngalo sobre la mesa**	put it on the table
about, on	**un libro sobre Eva Perón**	a book about Eva Perón
above, over	**volábamos sobre el mar**	we were flying over the sea
	la nube sobre aquella montaña	the cloud above that mountain
approximately	**vendré sobre las 4**	I'll come about 4 o'clock
about	**Madrid tiene sobre 4 millones de habitantes**	Madrid has about 4 million inhabitants

tras

behind	**está tras el asiento**	it's behind the seat
after	**uno tras otro**	one after another
	día tras día	day after day
	corrieron tras el ladrón	they ran after the thief

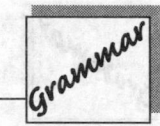

❑ Conjunctions

There are conjunctions which introduce a main clause, such as **y** *and*, **pero** *but*, **si** *if*, **o** *or* etc, and those which introduce subordinate clauses like **porque** *because*, **mientras que** *while*, **después de que** *after* etc. They are used in much the same way as in English, but the following points are of note:

◆ Some conjunctions in Spanish require a following subjunctive, see pp 60 to 63.

◆ Some conjunctions are 'split' in Spanish like *both ... and, either ... or* in English:

tanto ... como	*both ... and*	→ 1
ni ... ni	*neither ... nor*	→ 2
o (bien) ... o (bien)	*either ... or (else)*	→ 3
sea ... sea	*either ... or,*	→ 4
	whether ... or	

◆ **y**
— Before words beginning with **i-** or **hi-** + consonant it becomes **e** → 5

◆ **o**
— Before words beginning with **o-** or **ho-** it becomes **u** → 6
— Between numerals it becomes **ó** → 7

◆ **que**
— meaning *that* → 8
— in comparisons, meaning *than* → 9
— followed by the subjunctive, see p 58.

◆ **porque** (Not to be confused with **por qué** *why*)
— **como** should be used instead at the beginning of a sentence → 10

◆ **pero, sino**
— **pero** normally translates *but* → 11
— **sino** is used when there is a direct contrast after a negative → 12

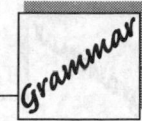

1	**Estas flores crecen tanto en verano como en invierno** These flowers grow in both summer and winter
2	**Ni él ni ella vinieron** Neither he nor she came **No tengo ni dinero ni comida** I have neither money nor food
3	**Debe de ser o ingenua o tonta** She must be either naïve or stupid **O bien me huyen o bien no me reconocen** Either they're avoiding me or else they don't recognize me
4	**Sea en verano, sea en invierno, siempre me gusta andar** I always like walking, whether in summer or in winter
5	**Diana e Isabel** Diana and Isabel **madre e hija** BUT: **árboles y hierba** mother and daughter trees and grass
6	**diez u once** **minutos u horas** ten or eleven minutes or hours
7	**37 ó 38** 37 or 38
8	**Dicen que te han visto** They say (that) they've seen you **¿Sabías que estábamos allí?** Did you know that we were there?
9	**Le gustan más que nunca** He likes them more than ever **María es menos guapa que su hermana** Maria is less attractive than her sister
10	**Como estaba lloviendo no pudimos salir** Because/As it was raining we couldn't go out (Compare with: **No pudimos salir porque estaba lloviendo**)
11	**Me gustaría ir, pero estoy muy cansada** I'd like to go, but I am very tired
12	**No es escocesa sino irlandesa** She is not Scottish but Irish

☐ Augmentative, diminutive and pejorative suffixes

These can be used after nouns, adjectives and some adverbs. They are attached to the end of the word after any final vowel has been removed

e.g. **puerta → puertita**
doctor → doctorcito

⚠ NOTE: Further changes sometimes take place (see p 296).

Augmentatives

These are used mainly to imply largeness, but they can also suggest clumsiness, ugliness or grotesqueness. The commonest augmentatives are:

ón/ona	→ ①
azo/a	→ ②
ote/a	→ ③

Diminutives

These are used mainly to suggest smallness or to express a feeling of affection. Occasionally they can be used to express ridicule or contempt. The commonest diminutives are:

ito/a	→ ④
(e)cito/a	→ ⑤
(ec)illo/a	→ ⑥
(z)uelo/a	→ ⑦

Pejoratives

These are used to convey the idea that something is unpleasant or to express contempt. The commonest suffixes are:

ucho/a	→ ⑧
acho/a	→ ⑨
uzo/a	→ ⑩
uco/a	→ ⑪
astro/a	→ ⑫

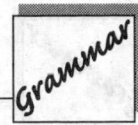

ORIGINAL WORD	DERIVED FORM
1 **un hombre** a man	**un hombrón** a big man
2 **bueno** good	**buenazo** (person) easily imposed on
un perro a dog	**un perrazo** a really big dog
gripe flu	**un gripazo** a really bad bout of flu
3 **grande** big	**grandote** huge
palabra word	**palabrota** swear word
amigo friend	**amigote** old pal
4 **una casa** a house	**una casita** a cottage
un poco a little	**un poquito** a little bit
un rato a while	**un ratito** a little while
mi hija my daughter	**mi hijita** my dear sweet daughter
despacio slowly	**despacito** nice and slowly
5 **un viejo** an old man	**un viejecito** a little old man
un pueblo a village	**un pueblecito** a small village
una voz a voice	**una vocecita** a sweet little voice
6 **una ventana** a window	**una ventanilla** a small window (car, train etc)
un chico a boy	**un chiquillo** a small boy
una campana a bell	**una campanilla** a small bell
un palo a stick	**un palillo** a toothpick
un médico a doctor	**un mediquillo** a quack (doctor)
7 **los pollos** the chickens	**los polluelos** the little chicks
hoyos hollows	**hoyuelos** dimples
un ladrón a thief	**un ladronzuelo** a petty thief
una mujer a woman	**una mujerzuela** a whore
8 **un animal** an animal	**un animalucho** a wretched animal
un cuarto a room	**un cuartucho** a poky little room
una casa a house	**una casucha** a shack
9 **rico** rich	**ricacho** nouveau riche
10 **gente** people	**gentuza** scum
11 **una ventana** a window	**un ventanuco** a miserable little window
12 **un político** a politician	**un politicastro** a third-rate politician

❒ Word order

Word order in Spanish is much more flexible than in English. You can often find the subject placed after the verb or the object before the verb, either for emphasis or for stylistic reasons → ①

There are some cases, however, where the order is always different from English. Most of these have already been dealt with under the appropriate part of speech, but are summarized here along with other instances not covered elsewhere.

◆ Object pronouns nearly always come before the verb → ②
For details, see pp 228 to 231.

◆ Qualifying adjectives nearly always come after the noun → ③
For details, see p 224.

◆ Following direct speech the subject always follows the verb → ④

For word order in negative sentences, see p 272.

For word order in interrogative sentences, see p 276.

Examples

1. **Ese libro te lo di yo**
   I gave you that book
   No nos vio nadie
   Nobody saw us

2. **Ya los veo**   **Me lo dieron ayer**
   I can see them now   They gave it to me yesterday

3. **una ciudad española**   **vino tinto**
   a Spanish town   red wine

4. **– Pienso que sí – dijo María**
   'I think so,' said Maria
   – No importa – replicó Daniel
   'It doesn't matter,' Daniel replied

☐ Negatives

A sentence is made negative by adding **no** between the subject and the verb (and any preceding object pronouns) → ①

There are, however, some points to note:

— in phrases like *not her, not now,* etc the Spanish **no** usually comes after the word it qualifies → ②

— with verbs of saying, hoping, thinking etc *not* is translated by **que no** → ③

Double negatives

no ... nada	*nothing*	*(not ... anything)*
no ... nadie	*nobody*	*(not ... anybody)*
no ... más	*no longer*	*(not ... any more)*
no ... nunca	*never*	*(not ... ever)*
no ... jamás	*never* (stronger)	*(not ... ever)*
no ... más que	*only*	*(not ... more than)*
no ... ningún(o)(a)	*no*	*(not any)*
no ... tampoco	*not ... either*	
no ... ni ... ni	*neither ... nor*	
no ... ni siquiera	*not even*	

Word order

♦ **No** precedes the verb (and any object pronouns) in both simple and compound tenses, and the second element follows the **verb** → ④

♦ Sometimes the above negatives are placed before the verb (with the exception of **más** and **más que**), and **no** is then dropped → ⑤

♦ For use of **nada, nadie** and **ninguno** as pronouns, see p 236.

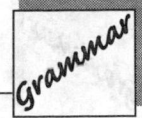

|1| AFFIRMATIVE | NEGATIVE
El coche es suyo → **El coche no es suyo**
The car is his — The car is not his
Yo me lo pondré → **Yo no me lo pondré**
I will put it on — I will not put it on

|2| **¿Quién lo ha hecho? – Ella no**
Who did it? – Not her
¿Quieres un cigarrillo? – Ahora no
Do you want a cigarette? – Not now
Dame ese libro, el que está a tu lado no, el otro
Give me that book, not the one near you, the other one

|3| **Opino que no** | **Dijeron que no**
I think not — They said not

|4| **No dicen nada**
They don't say anything
No han visto a nadie
They haven't seen anybody
No me veréis más
You won't see me any more
No te olvidaré nunca/jamás
I'll never forget you
No habían recorrido más que 40 kms cuando ...
They hadn't travelled more than 40 kms when ...
No se me ha ocurrido ninguna idea
I haven't had any ideas
No les estaban esperando ni mi hijo ni mi hija
Neither my son nor my daughter were waiting for them
No ha venido ni siquiera Juan
Even John hasn't come

|5| **Nadie ha venido hoy**
Nobody came today
Nunca me han gustado
I've never liked them
Ni mi hermano ni mi hermana fuman
Neither my brother nor my sister smokes

☐ **Negatives** (Continued)

Negatives in short replies

♦ **No**, *no* is the usual negative response to a question → ①

⚠ NOTE: It is often translated as *not* → ②
(see also p 272).

♦ Nearly all the other negatives listed on p 272 may be used without a verb in a short reply → ③

Combinations of negatives

These are the most common combinations of negative particles:

no ... nunca más	→ ④
no ... nunca a nadie	→ ⑤
no ... nunca nada/nada nunca	→ ⑥
no ... nunca más que	→ ⑦
no ... ni ... nunca	→ ⑧

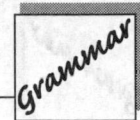

1. **¿Quieres venir con nosotros? – No**
   Do you want to come with us? – No

2. **¿Vienes o no?**
   Are you coming or not?

3. **¿Ha venido alguien? – ¡Nadie!**
   Has anyone come? – Nobody!
   ¿Has ido al Japón alguna vez? – Nunca
   Have you ever been to Japan? – Never

4. **No lo haré nunca más**
   I'll never do it again

5. **No se ve nunca a nadie por allí**
   i You never see anybody around there

6. **No cambiaron nada nunca**
   They never changed anything

7. **No he hablado nunca más que con su mujer**
   I've only ever spoken to his wife

8. **No me ha escrito ni llamado por teléfono nunca**
   He/she has never written to me or phoned me

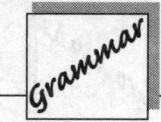

◻ Question forms

Direct

There are two ways of forming direct questions in Spanish:

- ◆ by inverting the normal word order so that
  subject + verb → *verb + subject* → ①

- ◆ by maintaining the word order *subject + verb,* but by using a rising intonation at the end of the sentence → ②

⚠ NOTE: In compound tenses the auxiliary may never be separated from the past participle, as happens in English → ③

Indirect

An indirect question is one that is 'reported', e.g. he asked me *what the time was,* tell me *which way to go.* Word order in indirect questions can adopt one of the two following patterns:

- ◆ interrogative word + subject + verb → ④

- ◆ interrogative word + verb + subject → ⑤

¿verdad?, ¿no?

These are used wherever English would use *isn't it?, don't they?, weren't we?, is it?* etc tagged on to the end of a sentence → ⑥

sí

Sí is the word for *yes* in answer to a question put either in the affirmative or in the negative → ⑦

Examples

1. **¿Vendrá tu madre?**
   Will your mother come?
   ¿Es posible eso?
   Is it possible?
   ¿Lo trajo Vd?
   Did you bring it?
   ¿Cuándo volverán Vds?
   When will you come back?

2. **El gato, ¿se bebió toda la leche?**
   Did the cat drink up all his milk?
   Andrés, ¿va a venir?
   Is Andrew coming?

3. **¿Lo ha terminado Vd?**
   Have you finished it?
   ¿Había llegado tu amigo?
   Had your friend arrived?

4. **Dime qué autobuses pasan por aquí**
   Tell me which buses come this way
   No sé cuántas personas vendrán
   I don't know how many people will turn up

5. **Me preguntó dónde trabajaba mi hermano**
   He asked me where my brother worked
   No sabemos a qué hora empieza la película
   We don't know what time the film starts

6. **Hace calor, ¿verdad?**
   It's warm, isn't it?
   No se olvidará Vd, ¿verdad?
   You won't forget, will you?
   Estaréis cansados, ¿no?
   You will be tired, won't you?
   Te lo dijo María, ¿no?
   Maria told you, didn't she?

7. **¿Lo has hecho? – Sí**
   Have you done it? – Yes (I have)
   ¿No lo has hecho? – Sí
   Haven't you done it? – Yes (I have)

Beware of translating word by word. While on occasions this is quite possible, quite often it is not. The need for caution is illustrated by the following:

♦ English phrasal verbs (i.e. verbs followed by a preposition), e.g. *to run away, to fall down*, are often translated by one word in Spanish → 1

♦ English verbal constructions often contain a preposition where none exists in Spanish, or vice versa → 2

♦ Two or more prepositions in English may have a single rendering in Spanish → 3

♦ A word which is singular in English may be plural in Spanish, or vice versa → 4

♦ Spanish has no equivalent of the possessive construction denoted by ...'s/...s' → 5

☐ Specific problems

-ing

This is translated in a variety of ways in Spanish:

♦ *to be ... -ing* can sometimes be translated by a simple tense (see also pp 54 to 56) → 6

But, when a physical position is denoted, a past participle is used → 7

♦ in the construction *to see/hear sb ... -ing*, use an infinitive → 8 *-ing* can also be translated by:
— an infinitive → 9
(see p 46)
— a perfect infinitive → 10
(see p 50)
— a gerund → 11
(see p 52)
— a noun → 12

Grammar

---

1. **huir** | **caerse** | **ceder**
   to run away | to fall down | to give in

2. **pagar** | **mirar** | **escuchar**
   to pay for | to look at | to listen to
   encontrarse con | **fijarse en** | **servirse de**
   to meet | to notice | to use

3. **extrañarse de** | **harto de**
   to be surprised at | fed up with
   soñar con | **contar con**
   to dream of | to count on

4. **unas vacaciones** | **sus cabellos**
   a holiday | his/her hair
   la gente | **mi pantalón**
   people | my trousers

5. **el coche de mi hermano** | **el cuarto de las niñas**
   my brother's car | the children's bedroom
   (literally: ... of my brother) | *(literally: ... of the children)*

6. **Se va mañana** | **¿Qué haces?**
   He/she is leaving tomorrow | What are you doing?

7. **Está sentado ahí** | **Estaba tendida en el suelo**
   He is sitting over there | She was lying on the ground

8. **Les veo venir** | **La he oído cantar**
   I can see them coming | I've heard her singing

9. **Me gusta ir al cine** | **¡Deja de hablar!**
   I like going to the cinema | Stop talking!
   En vez de contestar | **Antes de salir**
   Instead of answering | Before leaving

10. **Después de haber abierto la caja, María ...**
    After opening the box, Maria ...

11. **Pasamos la tarde fumando y charlando**
    We spent the afternoon smoking and chatting

12. **El esquí me mantiene en forma**
    Skiing keeps me fit

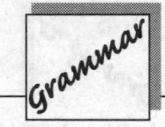

to be

(See also **Verbal Idioms**, pp 74 to 76)

- In set expressions, describing physical and emotional conditions, **tener** is used:

tener calor/frío	to be warm/cold
tener hambre/sed	to be hungry/thirsty
tener miedo	to be afraid
tener razón	to be right

- Describing the weather, e.g. *what's the weather like?, it's windy/sunny,* use **hacer** → ①

- For ages, e.g. *he is 6,* use **tener** (see also p 306) → ②

there is/there are

- Both are translated by **hay** → ③

can, be able

- Physical ability is expressed by **poder** → ④

- If the meaning is *to know how to,* use **saber** → ⑤

- *Can* + a 'verb of hearing or seeing etc' in English is not translated in Spanish → ⑥

to

- Generally translated by **a** → ⑦

- In time expressions, e.g. *10 to 6,* use **menos** → ⑧

- When the meaning is *in order to,* use **para** → ⑨

- Following a verb, as in *to try to do, to like to do,* see pp 46 and 48.

- *easy/difficult/impossible* etc *to do* are translated by **fácil/difícil/ imposible** etc **de hacer** → ⑩

1. **¿Qué tiempo hace?** **Hace bueno/malo/viento**
What's the weather like? It's lovely/miserable/windy

2. **¿Cuántos años tienes?** **Tengo quince (años)**
How old are you? I'm fifteen

3. **Hay un señor en la puerta**
There's a gentleman at the door
Hay cinco libros en la mesa
There are five books on the table

4. **No puedo salir contigo**
I can't go out with you

5. **¿Sabes nadar?**
Can you swim?

6. **No veo nada** **¿Es que no me oyes?**
I can't see anything Can't you hear me?

7. **Dale el libro a Isabel**
Give the book to Isabel

8. **las diez menos cinco** **a las siete menos cuarto**
five to ten at a quarter to seven

9. **Lo hice para ayudaros**
I did it to help you
Se inclinó para atarse el cordón de zapato
He bent down to tie his shoe-lace

10. **Este libro es fácil/difícil de leer**
This book is easy/difficult to read

must

♦ When *must* expresses an assumption, **deber de** is often used → 1

⚠ NOTE: This meaning is also often expressed by **deber** directly followed by the infinitive → 2

♦ When it expresses obligation, there are three possible translations:
  — **tener que**   → 3
  — **deber**   → 4
  — **hay que** (impersonal) → 5

may

♦ If *may* expresses possibility, it can be translated by:
  — **poder**
  — **puede (ser) que** + subjunctive } → 6

♦ To express permission, use **poder** → 7

will

♦ If *will* expresses willingness or desire rather than the future, the present tense of **querer** is used → 8

would

♦ If *would* expresses willingness, use the preterite or imperfect of **querer** → 9

♦ When a repeated or habitual action in the past is referred to, use
  — the imperfect → 10
  — the imperfect of **soler** + infinitive → 11

Examples

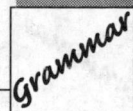

1. **Ha debido de mentir**
   He must have lied
   Debe de gustarle
   She must like it
2. **Debe estar por aquí cerca**
   It must be near here
   Debo haberlo dejado en el tren
   I must have left it on the train
3. **Tenemos que salir temprano mañana**
   We must leave early tomorrow
   Tengo que irme
   I must go
4. **Debo visitarles**
   I must visit them
   Debéis escuchar lo que se os dice
   You must listen to what is said to you
5. **Hay que entrar por ese lado**
   One (We *etc*) must get in that way
6. **Todavía puede cambiar de opinión**
   He may still change his mind
   Creo que puede llover esta tarde
   I think it may rain this afternoon
   Puede (ser) que no lo sepa
   She may not know
7. **¿Puedo irme?**   **Puede sentarse**
   May I go?   You may sit down
8. **Quiere Vd esperar un momento, por favor?**
   Will you wait a moment, please?
   No quiere ayudarme
   He won't help me
9. **No quisieron venir**
   They wouldn't come
10. **Las miraba hora tras hora**
    She would watch them for hours on end
11. **Últimamente solía comer muy poco**
    Latterly he would eat very little

☐ Pronunciation of Vowels

Spanish vowels are always clearly pronounced and not relaxed in unstressed syllables as happens in English.

	EXAMPLES	HINTS ON PRONUNCIATION
[a]	casa	Between English *a* as in *hat* and *u* as in *hut*
[e]	pensar	Similar to English *e* in *pet*
[i]	filo	Between English *i* as in *pin* and *ee* as in *been*
[o]	loco	Similar to English *o* in *hot*
[u]	luna	Between English *ew* as in *few* and *u* as in *put*

☐ Pronunciation of Diphthongs

All these diphthongs are shorter than similar English diphthongs.

[ai]	baile, hay	Like *i* in *side*
[au]	causa	Like *ou* in *sound*
[ei]	peine, rey	Like *ey* in *grey*
[eu]	deuda	Like the vowel sounds in English *may you*, but without the sound of the *y*
[oi]	boina, voy	Like *oy* in *boy*

☐ Semi-consonants

[j]	hacia, ya tiene, yeso labio, yo	**i** following a consonant and preceding a vowel, and **y** preceding a vowel are pronounced as *y* in English *yet*
[w]	agua, bueno arduo, ruido	**u** following a consonant and preceding a vowel is pronounced as *w* in English *walk*

⚠ EXCEPTIONS: **gue, gui** (see p 286)

PRONUNCIATION

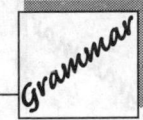

❏ Pronunciation of Consonants

Some consonants are pronounced almost exactly as in English: [l, m, n, f, k, and in some cases g].

Others, listed below, are similar to English, but differences should be noted.

EXAMPLES

[p]	**p**adre	They are not aspirated, unlike
[k]	**c**o**c**o	English *pot*, *cook* and *ten*.
[t]	**t**an	
[t]	**t**odo, **t**ú	Pronounced with the tip of the
[d]	**d**oy, bal**d**e	tongue touching the upper front teeth and not the roof of the mouth as in English.

The following consonants are not heard in English:

EXAMPLES

[β]	la**b**io	This is pronounced between upper and lower lips, which do not touch, unlike English *b* as in *bend*.
[ɣo]	ha**g**a	Similar to English *g* as in *gate*, but tongue does not touch the soft palate.
[ɲ]	a**ñ**o	Similar to *ni* in o*ni*on
[x]	**j**ota	Like the guttural *ch* in lo*ch*
[ɾ]	pe**r**a	A single trill with the tip of the tongue against the teeth ridge.
[rr]	**r**ojo, pe**rr**o	A multiple trill with the tip of the tongue against the teeth ridge.

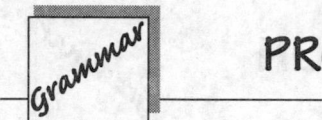

☐ From spelling to sounds

Note the pronunciation of the following (groups of) letters.

LETTER PRONOUNCED

b, v	[b]	These letters have the same value. At the start of a breath group, and after written **m** and **n**, the sound is similar to English *boy* → ①
	[β]	in all other positions, the sound is unknown in English (see p 285) → ②
c	[k]	Before **a, o, u** or a consonant, like English *keep*, but not aspirated → ③
	[θ/s]	Before **e, i** like English *thin*, or, in Latin America and parts of Spain, like English *same* → ④
ch	[tʃ]	Like English *church* → ⑤
d	[d]	At the start of the breath group and after **l** or **n**, it is pronounced similar to English *deep* (see p 285) → ⑥
	[ð]	Between vowels and after consonants (except **l** or **n**), it is pronounced very like English *though* → ⑦
	[(ð)]	At the end of words, and in the verb ending -**ado**, it is often not pronounced → ⑧
g	[x]	Before **e, i**, pronounced gutturally, similar to English lo*ch* → ⑨
	[g]	At the start of the breath group and after **n**, it is pronounced like English *get* → ⑩
	[ɣ]	In other positions the sound is unknown in English → ⑪
gue	[ge/ɣe]	The **u** is silent → ⑫
gui	[gi/ɣi]	
güe	[gwe/ɣwe]	The **u** is pronounced like English
güi	[gwi/ɣwi]	*walk* → ⑬

Examples

1	**bomba** ['bomba]	**voy** [boi]	**vicio** ['biθjo]
2	**hubo** ['uβo]	**de veras** [de 'βeras]	**lavar** [la'βar]
3	**casa** ['kasa]	**coco** ['koko]	**cumbre** ['kumbre]
4	**cero** ['θero/'sero]	**cinco** ['θiŋko/'siŋko]	
5	**mucho** ['mutʃo]	**chuchería** [tʃutʃe'ria]	
6	**doy** [doi]	**balde** ['balde]	**bondad** [bon'daδ]
7	**modo** ['moδo]	**ideal** [iδe'al]	
8	**Madrid** [ma'δri(δ)]	**comprado** [kom'pra(δ)o]	
9	**gente** ['xente]	**giro** ['xiro]	**general** [xene'ral]
10	**ganar** [ga'nar]	**pongo** ['poŋgo]	
11	**agua** ['aɣwa]	**agrícola** [a'ɣrikola]	
12	**guija** ['gixa]	**guerra** ['gerra]	**pague** ['paɣe]
13	**agüero** [a 'ɣwero]	**argüir** [ar'ɣwir]	

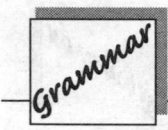
☐ **From spelling to sounds** (Continued)

h	[-]	This is always silent → ①
j	[x]	Like the guttural sound in English lo*ch*, but often aspirated at the end of a word → ②
ll	[ʎ]	Similar to English -*ll*- in mi*ll*ion → ③
	[j/ʒ]	In some parts of Spain and in Latin America, like English *y*et or plea*s*ure → ④
-nv-	[mb]	This combination of letters is pronounced as in English i*mb*ibe → ⑤
ñ	[ɲ]	As in English o*ni*on → ⑥
q	[k]	Always followed by silent letter **u**, and pronounced as in English *k*eep, but not aspirated → ⑦
s	[s]	Except where mentioned below, like English *s*ing → ⑧
	[z]	When followed by **b, d, g, l, m, n** like English *z*oo → ⑨
w	[w]	Like English *v*, *w* → ⑩
x	[ks]	Between vowels, often like English e*x*it → ⑪
	[s]	Before a consonant, and, increasingly, even between vowels, like English *s*end → ⑫
y	[j]	Like English *y*es → ⑬
	[ʒ]	In some parts of Latin America, like English lei*s*ure → ⑭
z	[θ]	Like English *th*in → ⑮
	[s]	In some parts of Spain and in Latin America, like English *s*end → ⑯

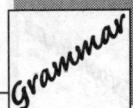

№			
1	**hombre** ['ombre]	**hoja** ['oxa]	**ahorrar** [ao'rrar]
2	**jota** ['xota]	**tejer** [te'xer]	**reloj** [re'lo(h)]
3	**calle** ['kaʎe]	**llamar** [ʎa'mar]	
4	**pillar** [pi'jar/pi'ʒar]	**olla** ['oja/'oʒa]	
5	**enviar** [em'bjar]	**sin valor** ['sim ba'lor]	
6	**uña** ['uɲa]	**bañar** [ba'ɲar]	
7	**aquel** [a'kel]	**querer** [ke'rer]	
8	**está** [es'ta]	**serio** ['serjo]	
9	**desde** ['dezðe]	**mismo** ['mizmo]	**asno** ['azno]
10	**wáter** ['bater]	**Walkman**® [wak'man]	
11	**éxito** ['eksito]	**máximo** ['maksimo]	
12	**extra** ['estra]	**sexto** ['sesto]	
13	**yo** [jo]	**yedra** ['jeðra]	
14	**yeso** ['ʒeso]	**yerno** ['ʒerno]	
15	**zapato** [θa'pato]	**zona** ['θona]	**luz** [luθ]
16	**zaguán** [sa'ɣwan]	**zueco** ['sweko]	**pez** [pes]

❐ Normal Word Stress

There are simple rules to establish which syllable in a Spanish word is stressed. When an exception to these rules occurs an acute accent (stress-mark) is needed (see p 292). These rules are as follows:

— words ending in a vowel or combination of vowels, or with the consonants **-s** or **-n** are stressed on the next to last syllable. The great majority of Spanish words fall into this category → 1

— words ending in a consonant other than **-s** or **-n** bear the stress on the last syllable → 2

— a minority of words bear the stress on the second to last syllable, and these always need an accent → 3

— some nouns change their stress from singular to plural → 4

❐ Stress in diphthongs

In the case of diphthongs there are rules to establish which of the vowels is stressed (see p 284 for pronunciation). These rules are as follows:

— diphthongs formed by the combination of a 'weak' vowel (**i, u**) and a 'strong' vowel (**a, e** or **o**) bear the stress on the strong vowel → 5

— diphthongs formed by the combination of two 'weak' vowels bear the stress on the second vowel → 6

⚠ NOTE: Two 'strong' vowels don't form a diphthong but are pronounced as two separate vowels. In these cases stress follows the normal rules → 7

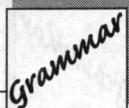

① **ca**sa **ca**sas
house houses

corre **co**rren
he runs they run

pa**la**bra pa**la**bras
word words

crisis **cri**sis
crisis crises

② re**loj**
watch

ver**dad**
truth

bati**dor**
beater

③ mur**cié**lago
bat

pájaro
bird

④ ca**rác**ter ca**rac**te**res**
character characters

régimen re**gí**menes
regime regimes

⑤ **ba**ile
dance

boina **pe**ine
beret comb

causa **re**ina
cause queen

⑥ fu**i** vi**u**do
I went widower

⑦ me ma**re**o ca**er**
I feel dizzy to fall

caos co**rre**a
chaos leash

☐ The acute accent (´)

This is used in writing to show that a word is stressed contrary to the normal rules for stress (see p 290) → ①

The following points should be noted:

◆ The same syllable is stressed in the plural form of adjectives and nouns as in the singular. To show this, it is necessary to

— add an accent in the case of unaccented nouns and adjectives ending in -**n** → ②

— drop the accent from nouns and adjectives ending in -**n** or -**s** which have an accent on the last syllable → ③

◆ The feminine form of accented nouns or adjectives does not have an accent → ④

◆ When object pronouns are added to certain verb forms an accent is required to show that the syllable stressed in the verb form does not change. These verb forms are:

— the gerund → ⑤
— the infinitive, when followed by two pronouns → ⑥
— imperative forms, except for the 2nd person plural → ⑦

◆ The absolute superlative forms of adjectives are always accented → ⑧

◆ Accents on adjectives are not affected by the addition of the adverbial suffix -**mente** → ⑨

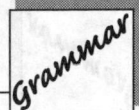

1	**autobús** bus		**revolución** revolution
	relámpago lightning		**árboles** trees
2	**orden** order	→	**órdenes** orders
	examen examination	→	**exámenes** examinations
	joven young	→	**jóvenes** young
3	**revolución** revolution	→	**revoluciones** revolutions
	autobús bus	→	**autobuses** buses
	parlanchín chatty	→	**parlanchines** chatty
4	**marqués** marquis	→	**marquesa** marchioness
	francés French *(masc)*	→	**francesa** French *(fem)*
5	**comprando** buying	→	**comprándo(se)lo** buying it (for him/her/them)
6	**vender** to sell	→	**vendérselas** to sell them to him/her/them
7	**compra** buy	→	**cómpralo** buy it
	hagan do	→	**háganselo** do it for him/her/them
8	**viejo** old	→	**viejísimo** ancient
	caro expensive	→	**carísimo** very expensive
9	**fácil** easy	→	**fácilmente** easily

☐ The acute accent (Continued)

It is also used to distinguish between the written forms of words which are pronounced the same but have a different meaning or function. These are as follows:

◆ Possessive adjectives/personal pronouns → ①

◆ Demonstrative adjectives/demonstrative pronouns → ②

◆ Interrogative and exclamatory forms of adverbs, pronouns and adjectives → ③

⚠ NOTE: The accent is used in indirect as well as direct questions and exclamations → ④

◆ The pronoun **él** and the article **el** → ⑤

◆ A small group of words which could otherwise be confused.
These are:

de	of, from	**dé**	give (pres subj)
mas	but	**más**	more
si	if	**sí**	yes; himself etc → ⑥
solo/a	alone	**sólo**	only → ⑦
te	you	**té**	tea

☐ The dieresis (¨)

This is used only in the combinations **güi** or **güe** to show that the **u** is pronounced as a semi-consonant (see p 284) → ⑧

1. **Han robado mi coche**
They've stolen my car
¿Te gusta tu trabajo?
Do you like your job?

   A mí no me vio
He didn't see me
Tú, ¿que opinas?
What do you think?

2. **Me gusta esta casa**
I like this house
¿Ves aquellos edificios?
Can you see those buildings?

   Me quedo con ésta
I'll take this one
Aquéllos son más bonitos
Those are prettier

3. **El chico con quien viajé**
The boy I travelled with
Donde quieras
Wherever you want

   ¿Con quién viajaste?
Who did you travel with?
¿Dónde encontraste eso?
Where did you find that?

4. **¿Cómo se abre?**
How does it open?

   No sé cómo se abre
I don't know how it opens

5. **El puerto queda cerca**
The harbour's nearby

   Él no quiso hacerlo
HE refused to do it

6. **si no viene**
if he doesn't come

   Sí que lo sabe
Yes he DOES know

7. **Vino solo**
He came by himself

   Sólo lo sabe él
Only he knows

8. **¡Qué vergüenza!**
How shocking!
En seguida averigüé dónde estaba
I found out straight away where it was

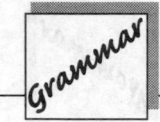

❐ Regular spelling changes

The consonants **c**, **g** and **z** are modified by the addition of certain verb or plural endings and by some suffixes. Most of the cases where this occurs have already been dealt with under the appropriate part of speech, but are summarized here along with other instances not covered elsewhere.

Verbs

The changes set out below occur so that the consonant of the verb stem is always pronounced the same as in the infinitive. For verbs affected by these changes see the list of verbs on p 81.

INFINITIVE	CHANGE			TENSES AFFECTED
-car	c + e	→	**-que**	Present subj, pret → 1
-cer, -cir	c + a, o	→	**-za, -zo**	Present, pres subj → 2
-gar	g + e, i	→	**-gue**	Present subj, pret → 3
-guar	gu + e	→	**-güe**	Present subj, pret → 4
-ger, -gir	g + a, o	→	**-ja, -jo**	Present, pres subi → 5
-guir	gu + a, o	→	**-ga, -go**	Present, pres subj → 6
-zar	z + e	→	**-ce**	Present subj, pret → 7

Noun and adjective plurals

SINGULAR	PLURAL
vowel + **z**	→ **-ces** → 8

Nouns and adjectives + suffixes

ENDING	SUFFIX	NEW ENDING
vowel + **z** +	**-cito**	**-cecito** → 9
-go, -ga +	**-ito, -illo**	**-guito/a, -guillo/a** → 10
-co, -ca +	**-ito, -illo**	**-quito/a, -quillo/a** → 11

Adjective absolute superlatives

ENDING	SUPERLATIVE
-co	**-quísimo** → 12
-go	**-guísimo** → 13
vowel + **z**	**-císimo** → 14

Examples

1. **Es inútil que lo busques aquí**
   It's no good looking for it here
   Saqué dos entradas
   I got two tickets

2. **Hace falta que venzas tu miedo**
   You must overcome your fear

3. **No creo que lleguemos antes**
   I don't think we'll be there any sooner
   Ya le pagué
   I've already paid her

4. **Averigüé dónde estaba la casa**
   I found out where the house was

5. **Cojo el autobús, es más barato**
   I take the bus, it's cheaper

6. **¿Sigo?**
   Shall I go on?

7. **No permiten que se cruce la frontera**
   They don't allow people to cross the border
   Nunca simpaticé mucho con él
   I never got on very well with him

8. **voz → voces**   **luz → luces**
   voice   voices   light   lights
   veloz → veloces   **capaz → capaces**
   quick   capable

9. **luz →**   **lucecita**
   light   little light

10. **amigo →**   **amiguito**
    friend   chum

11. **chico →**   **chiquillo**
    boy   little boy

12. **rico →**   **riquísimo**
    rich   extremely rich

13. **largo →**   **larguísimo**
    long   very, very long

14. **feroz →**   **ferocísimo**
    fierce   extremely fierce

A, a	[a]	**J, j**	['xota]	**R, r**	['erre]
B, b	[be]	**K, k**	[ka]	**S, s**	['ese]
C, c	[θe]	**L, l**	['ele]	**T, t**	[te]
Ch, ch	[tʃe]	**Ll, ll**	['eʎe]	**U, u**	[u]
D, d	[de]	**M, m**	['eme]	**V, v**	['uβe]
E, e	[e]	**N, n**	['ene]	**W, w**	['uβe'doble]
F, f	['efe]	**Ñ, ñ**	['eɲe]	**X, x**	['ekis]
G, g	[xe]	**O, o**	[o]	**Y, y**	[i'ɣrjeɣa]
H, h	['atʃe]	**P, p**	[pe]	**Z, z**	['θeta]
I, i	[i]	**Q, q**	[ku]		

◆ The letters are feminine and you therefore talk of **una a**, or **la a**.

◆ Capital letters are used as in English except for the following:
  — adjectives of nationality:

  e.g. **una ciudad alemana**   **un autor español**
     a German town   a Spanish author

  — languages:

  e.g. **¿Habla Vd inglés?**   **Hablan español e italiano**
     Do you speak English?   They speak Spanish and Italian

  — days of the week:

lunes	Monday
martes	Tuesday
miércoles	Wednesday
jueves	Thursday
viernes	Friday
sábado	Saturday
domingo	Sunday

  — months of the year:

enero	January	**julio**	July
febrero	February	**agosto**	August
marzo	March	**se(p)tiembre**	September
abril	April	**octubre**	October
mayo	May	**noviembre**	November
junio	June	**diciembre**	December

Spanish punctuation differs from English in the following ways:

Question marks

There are inverted question marks and exclamation marks at the beginning of a question or exclamation, as well as upright ones at the end.

Indications of dialogue

Dashes are used to indicate dialogue, and are equivalent to the English inverted commas:

– ¿Vendrás conmigo? – le preguntó María
'Will you come with me?' Maria asked him

⚠ NOTE: When no expression of saying, replying etc follows, only one dash is used at the beginning:
– Sí. 'Yes.'

Letter headings

At the beginning of a letter, a colon is used instead of the English comma:

Querida Cristina: Dear Cristina,   **Muy Sr. mío**: Dear Sir,

Punctuation terms in Spanish

.	punto	!	se cierra admiración
,	coma	" "	comillas (used as '...')
;	punto y coma	"	se abren comillas
:	dos puntos	"	se cierran comillas
...	puntos suspensivos	( )	paréntesis
¿ ?	interrogación	(	se abre paréntesis
¿	se abre interrogación	)	se cierra paréntesis
?	se cierra interrogación	–	guión
¡ !	admiración		
¡	se abre admiración	punto y aparte	new paragraph
		punto final	last full stop

```
4 6 2
8 1 5
9 3 1
```
NUMBERS 300

☐ Cardinal numbers *(one, two, three etc)*

cero	0	setenta	70
uno (un, una)	1	ochenta	80
dos	2	noventa	90
tres	3	cien (ciento)	100
cuatro	4	ciento uno(una)	101
cinco	5	ciento dos	102
seis	6	ciento diez	110
siete	7	ciento cuarenta y dos	142
ocho	8	doscientos(as)	200
nueve	9	doscientos(as) uno(una)	201
diez	10	doscientos(as) dos	202
once	11	trescientos(as)	300
doce	12	cuatrocientos(as)	400
trece	13	quinientos(as)	500
catorce	14	seiscientos(as)	600
quince	15	setecientos(as)	700
dieciséis	16	ochocientos(as)	800
diecisiete	17	novecientos(as)	900
dieciocho	18	mil	1.000
diecinueve	19	mil uno(una)	1.001
veinte	20	mil dos	1.002
veintiuno	21	mil doscientos veinte	1.220
veintidós	22	dos mil	2.000
treinta	30	cien mil	100.000
treinta y uno	31	doscientos(as) mil	200.000
cuarenta	40	un millón	1.000.000
cincuenta	50	dos millones	2.000.000
sesenta	60	un billón	1.000.000.000.000

☐ Fractions

un medio; medio(a)	½
un tercio	⅓
dos tercios	⅔
un cuarto	¼
tres cuartos	¾
un quinto	⅕
cinco y tres cuartos	5¾

Others

cero coma cinco	0,5
uno coma tres	1,3
(el, un) diez por ciento	10%
dos más/y dos	2 + 2
dos menos dos	2 − 2
dos por dos	2 × 2
dos dividido por dos	2 ÷ 2

```
4 6 2
8 1 5
9 3 1
```

☐ Points to note on cardinals

◆ **uno** drops the **o** before masculine nouns, and the same applies when in compound numerals:

> **un libro** *1 book*, **treinta y un niños** *31 children*

◆ 1, 21, 31 etc and 200, 300, 400 etc have feminine forms:

> **cuarenta y una pesetas** *41 pesetas*, **quinientas libras** *£500*

◆ **ciento** is used before numbers smaller than 100, otherwise **cien** is used:

> **ciento cuatro** *104 but* **cien pesetas** *100 pesetas*, **cien mil** *100,000* (see also p 206)

◆ **millón** takes **de** before a noun:

> **un millón de personas** *1,000,000 people*

◆ **mil** is only found in the plural when meaning *thousands of:*

> **miles de solicitantes** *thousands of applicants*

◆ cardinals normally precede ordinals:

> **los tres primeros pisos** *the first three floors*

⚠ NOTE: The full stop is used with numbers over one thousand and the comma with decimals i.e. the opposite of English usage.

```
4 6 2
8 1 5
9 3 1
```
NUMBERS   302

☐ **Ordinal numbers** (first, second, third etc)

primero (primer, primera)	1°,1ª	**undécimo(a)**	11°,11ª
segundo(a)	2°,2ª	**duodécimo(a)**	12°,12ª
tercero (tercer, tercera)	3°,3ª	**decimotercer(o)(a)**	13°,13ª
cuarto(a)	4°,4ª	**decimocuarto(a)**	14°,14ª
quinto(a)	5°,5ª	**decimoquinto(a)**	15°,15ª
sexto(a)	6°,6ª	**decimosexto(a)**	16°,16ª
séptimo(a)	7°,7ª	**decimoséptimo(a)**	17°,17ª
octavo(a)	8°,8ª	**decimoctavo(a)**	18°,18ª
noveno(a)	9°,9ª	**decimonoveno(a)**	19°,19ª
décimo(a)	10°,10ª	**vigésimo(a)**	20°,20ª

Points to note on ordinals

◆ They agree in gender and in number with the noun, which they normally precede, except with royal titles:

la primera vez	**Felipe segundo**
the first time	Philip II

◆ **primero** and **tercero** drop the **o** before a masculine singular noun:

el primer premio	**el tercer día**
the first prize	the third day

◆ Beyond **décimo** ordinal numbers are rarely used, and they are replaced by the cardinal number placed immediately after the noun:

el siglo diecisiete	**Alfonso doce**	**en el piso trece**
the seventeenth century	Alfonso XII	on the 13th floor

⚠ BUT: **vigésimo(a)** 20th
(but not with royal titles or centuries)

centésimo(a) 100th

milésimo(a) 1,000th

millonésimo(a) 1,000,000th

☐ Numbers: Other Uses

◆ collective numbers:

un par	2, a couple
una decena (de personas)	about 10 (people)
una docena (de niños)	(about) a dozen (children)
una quincena (de hombres)	about fifteen (men)
una veintena* (de coches)	about twenty (cars)
un centenar, una centena (de casas)	about a hundred (houses)
cientos/centenares de personas	hundreds of people
un millar (de soldados)	about a thousand (soldiers)
miles/millares de moscas	thousands of flies

* 20, 30, 40, 50 can also be converted in the same way.

◆ measurements:

veinte metros cuadrados	20 square metres
veinte metros cúbicos	20 cubic metres
un puente de cuarenta metros de largo/longitud	a bridge 40 metres long

◆ distance:

De aquí a Madrid hay 400 km	Madrid is 400 km away
a siete km de aquí	7 km from here

☐ Telephone Numbers

Póngame con Madrid, el cuatro, cincuenta y ocho, veintidós, noventa y tres
I would like Madrid 458 22 93
Me da Valencia, el veinte, cincuenta y uno, setenta y tres
Could you get me Valencia 20 51 73
Extensión tres, tres, cinco/trescientos treinta y cinco
Extension number 335

⚠ NOTE: In Spanish telephone numbers may be read out individually, but more frequently they are broken down into groups of two. They are written in groups of two or three numbers (never four).

☐ The Time

¿Qué hora es? *What time is it?*
Es ... *(1 o'clock, midnight, noon)* } *It's ...*
Son las ... *(other times)*
Es la una y cuarto   *It's 1.15*
Son las diez menos cinco   *It's 9.55*

00.00	**medianoche; las doce (de la noche)** *midnight, twelve o'clock*	
00.10	**las doce y diez (de la noche)**	
00.15	**las doce y cuarto**	
00.30	**las doce y media**	
00.45	**la una menos cuarto**	
01.00	**la una (de la madrugada)** *one a.m., one o'clock in the morning*	
01.10	**la una y diez (de la madrugada)**	
02.45	**las tres menos cuarto**	
07.00	**las siete (de la mañana)**	
07.50	**las ocho menos diez**	
12.00	**mediodía; las doce (de la mañana)** *noon, twelve o'clock*	
13.00	**la una (de la tarde)** *one p.m., one o'clock in the afternoon*	
19.00	**las siete (de la tarde)** *seven p.m., seven o'clock in the evening*	
21.00	**las nueve (de la noche)** *nine p.m., nine o'clock at night*	

⚠ NOTE: When referring to a timetable, the 24 hour clock is used:

las dieciséis cuarenta y cinco	16.45
las veintiuna quince	21.15

Examples

¿A qué hora vas a venir? – A las siete
What time are you coming? – At seven o'clock
Las oficinas cierran de dos a cuatro
The offices are closed from two until four
Vendré a eso de/hacia las siete y media
I'll come at around 7.30
a las seis y pico
just after 6 o'clock
a las cinco en punto
at 5 o'clock sharp
entre las ocho y las nueve
between 8 and 9 o'clock
Son más de las tres y media
It's after half past three
Hay que estar allí lo más tarde a las diez
You have to be there by ten o'clock at the latest
Tiene para media hora
He'll be half an hour (at it)
Estuvo sin conocimiento durante un cuarto de hora
She was unconscious for a quarter of an hour
Les estoy esperando desde hace una hora/desde las dos
I've been waiting for them for an hour/since two o'clock
Se fueron hace unos minutos
They left a few minutes ago
Lo hice en veinte minutos
I did it in twenty minutes
El tren llega dentro de una hora
The train arrives in an hour('s time)
¿Cuánto (tiempo) dura la película?
How long does the film last?
por la mañana/tarde/noche
in the morning/afternoon *or* evening/at night

mañana por la mañana	**ayer por la tarde**
tomorrow morning	yesterday afternoon *or* evening
anoche **anteayer**	**pasado mañana**
last night the day before yesterday	the day after tomorrow

❐ Dates

¿Qué día es hoy?	
¿A qué día estamos?	What's the date today?
Es (el) ...	
Estamos a ...	It's the ...
uno/primero de mayo	1st of May
dos de mayo	2nd of May
veintiocho de mayo	28th of May
lunes tres de octubre	Monday the 3rd of October
Vienen el siete de marzo	They're coming on the 7th of March

⚠ NOTE: Use cardinal numbers for dates. Only for the first of the month can the ordinal number sometimes be used.

❐ Years

Nací en 1970
I was born in 1970
el veinte de enero de mil novecientos setenta
(on) 20th January 1970

❐ Other expressions

en los años cincuenta	during the fifties
en el siglo veinte	in the twentieth century
en mayo	in May
lunes (quince)	Monday (the 15th)
el quince de marzo	on March the 15th
el/los lunes	on Monday/Mondays
dentro de diez días	in 10 days' time
hace diez días	10 days ago

❐ Age

¿Qué edad tiene?	
¿Cuántos años tiene?	How old is he/she?
Tiene 23 (años)	He/She is 23
Tiene unos 40 años	He/She is around 40
A los 21 años	At the age of 21

The following index lists comprehensively both grammatical terms and key words in English and Spanish.